Profiles
of
Illinois

Third Edition

Profiles
of
Illinois

A Universal Reference Book

Grey House
Publishing

PUBLISHER: Leslie Mackenzie
EDITORIAL DIRECTOR: Laura Mars
EDITOR: David Garoogian
MARKETING DIRECTOR: Jessica Moody

Grey House Publishing, Inc.
4919 Route 22
Amenia, NY 12501
518.789.8700
FAX 845.373.6390
www.greyhouse.com
e-mail: books @greyhouse.com

While every effort has been made to ensure the reliability of the information presented in this publication, Grey House Publishing neither guarantees the accuracy of the data contained herein nor assumes any responsibility for errors, omissions or discrepancies. Grey House accepts no payment for listing; inclusion in the publication of any organization, agency, institution, publication, service or individual does not imply endorsement of the editors or publisher.

Errors brought to the attention of the publisher and verified to the satisfaction of the publisher will be corrected in future editions.

First edition published 2005
Printed in Canada

ISBN: 978-1-59237-773-2

Table of Contents

Introduction

This is the third edition of *Profiles of Illinois—Facts, Figures & Statistics for 1,436 Populated Places in Illinois*. As with the other titles in our *State Profiles* series, we built this work using content from Grey House Publishing's award-winning *Profiles of America*—a 4-volume compilation of data on more than 42,000 places in the United States. We have updated and included the Illinois chapter from *Profiles of America,* and added entire fresh chapters of demographic information and ranking sections, so that *Profiles of Illinois* is the most comprehensive portrait of the state of Illinois ever published.

This third edition provides data on all populated communities and counties in the state of Illinois for which the US Census provides individual statistics. It includes seven major sections that cover everything from **Education** to **Ethnic Backgrounds** to **Climate**. All sections include **Comparative Statistics** or **Rankings**, and full-color **Maps** at the back of the book provide valuable information in a quickly processed, visual format. Here's an overview of each section:

1. Profiles

This section, organized by county, gives detailed profiles of 1,436 places plus 102 counties. Based on core Census data, these numbers reflect extensive updates from the U.S. Census Bureau's American Community Survey, and Nielsen Claritas, a trusted source for up-to-date demographic information. In addition, we have added current government statistics and original research, so that these profiles pull together statistical and descriptive information on every Census-recognized place in the state. Major fields of information include:

Geography	*Housing*	*Education*	*Religion*
Ancestry	*Transportation*	*Population*	*Climate*
Economy	*Industry*	*Health*	

In addition to place profiles, this section includes an **Alphabetical Place Index** and **Comparative Statistics** that compare Illinois' 100 largest communities by dozens of data points.

2. Education

This section begins with an **Educational State Profile,** summarizing number of schools, students, diplomas granted and educational dollars spent. Following the state profile are **School District Rankings** on 16 topics ranging from *Teacher/Student Ratios* to *High School Drop-Out Rates*. Following these rankings are statewide *National Assessment of Educational Progress (NAEP)* results and data from the *Illinois State Report Card*—an overview of student performance by grade and subject.

3. Ancestry

This section provides a detailed look at the ancestral and racial makeup of Illinois. 217 ethnic categories are ranked three ways: 1) by number, based on all places regardless of population; 2) by percent, based on all places regardless of population; 3) by percent, based on places with populations of 10,000 or more. You will discover, for example, that Moline has the greatest number of *Belgians* in the state (2,686), and that 37.3% of the population of Fulton are of *Dutch* ancestry.

4. Hispanic Population

This section defines Illinois' Hispanic population by 23 Hispanic backgrounds from *Argentinian* to *Venezuelan*. It ranks each of 15 categories, from Median Age to Median Home Value, by each Hispanic background. For example, you'll see that New Lennox has the highest percentage of *Mexicans* who speak English-only at home (76.3%), and that Naperville has the highest percentage of *Puerto Ricans* who are four-year college graduates (46.6%).

5. Asian Population

Similar in format to the section on Hispanic Population, this section defines Illinois' Asian population by 21 Asian backgrounds from *Bangladeshi* to *Vietnamese*. It ranks each of 14 categories, from Median Age to Median Home Value, by each Asian background. You will learn that *Koreans* in Buffalo Grove have a median household income of $83,219 and that 93.6% of *Thais* in Chicago are high-school graduates.

6. Climate

This important topic has been greatly expanded and updated since the last edition. Each state chapter includes a State Summary, two new maps—weather stations and a relief map—and profiles of both National and Cooperative Weather Stations. In addition, you'll find Weather Station Rankings with hundreds of interesting details, such as Fulton L&D #13 and Paw Paw 2 NW reporting the lowest annual extreme minimum temperatures (-33° F).

These sections also include Significant Storm Event data from January 2000 through December 2009. Here you will learn that a 100 mph thunderstorm wind caused $175 million in property damage in Williamson County in May 2009 and that excessive heat was responsible for 24 deaths in Cook County in August 2006.

7. Maps

For a more visual point of view, there are 16 full-color maps of Illinois at the back of the book. They provide information on topics such as *Federal Lands and Indian Reservations, Core-Based Statistical Areas and Counties, Hazard Events, Population Demographics, Median Age, Income, Median Home Values, Educational Attainment, Congressional Districts,* and the *2008 Presidential Election.*

Note: The extensive **User's Guide** that follows this Introduction is segmented into six sections and examines, in some detail, each data field in the individual profiles and comparative sections for all chapters. It provides sources for all data points and statistical definitions as necessary.

User's Guide: Profiles

Places Covered

All 102 counties.

1,299 incorporated municipalities. Municipalities are incorporated as either cities, towns or villages.

25 census designated places (CDP). The U.S. Bureau of the Census defines a CDP as "a statistical entity, defined for each decennial census according to Census Bureau guidelines, comprising a densely settled concentration of population that is not within an incorporated place, but is locally identified by a name. CDPs are delineated cooperatively by state and local officials and the Census Bureau, following Census Bureau guidelines. Beginning with Census 2000 there are no size limits."

112 unincorporated communities. The communities included have both their own zip code and statistics for their ZIP Code Tabulation Area (ZCTA) available from the Census Bureau. They are referred to as "postal areas." A ZCTA is a statistical entity developed by the Census Bureau to approximate the delivery area for a US Postal Service 5-digit or 3-digit ZIP Code in the US and Puerto Rico. A ZCTA is an aggregation of census blocks that have the same predominant ZIP Code associated with the mailing addresses in the Census Bureau's Master Address File. Thus, the Postal Service's delivery areas have been adjusted to encompass whole census blocks so that the Census Bureau can tabulate census data for the ZCTAs. ZCTAs do not include all ZIP Codes used for mail delivery and therefore do not precisely depict the area within which mail deliveries associated with that ZIP Code occur. Additionally, some areas that are known by a unique name, although they are part of a larger incorporated place, are also included as "postal areas."

Important Notes

- *Profiles of Illinois* uses the term "community" to refer to all places except counties. The term "county" is used to refer to counties and county-equivalents. All places are defined as of the 2010 Census.

- In each community profile, only school districts that have schools that are physically located within the community are shown. In addition, statistics for each school district cover the entire district, regardless of the physical location of the schools within the district.

- Special care should be taken when interpreting certain statistics for communities containing large colleges or universities. College students were counted as residents of the area in which they were living while attending college (as they have been since the 1950 census). One effect this may have is skewing the figures for population, income, housing, and educational attainment.

- Some information (e.g. unemployment rates) is available for both counties and individual communities. Other information is available for just counties (e.g. election results), or just individual communities (e.g. local newspapers).

- Some statistical information is available only for larger communities. In addition, the larger places are more apt to have services such as newspapers, airports, school districts, etc.

- For the most complete information on any community, you should also check the entry for the county in which the community is located. In addition, more information and services will be listed under the larger places in the county.

For a more in-depth discussion of geographic areas, please refer to the Census Bureau's Geographic Areas Reference Manual at http://www.census.gov/geo/www/garm.html.

Data Sources

CENSUS 2000

The parts of the data which are from the 2000 Decennial Census are from the following sources: *U.S. Bureau of the Census, Census of Population and Housing, 2000: Summary Files 1 and 3.* Summary File 3 (SF 3) consists of 813 detailed tables of Census 2000 social, economic and housing characteristics compiled from a sample of approximately 19 million housing units (about 1 in 6 households) that received the Census 2000 long-form questionnaire. Summary File 1 (SF 1) contains 286 tables focusing on age, sex, households, families, and housing units. This file presents 100-percent population and housing figures for the total population, for 63 race categories, and for many other race and Hispanic or Latino categories.

Comparing SF 3 Estimates with Corresponding Values in SF 1

As in earlier censuses, the responses from the sample of households reporting on long forms must be weighted to reflect the entire population. Specifically, each responding household represents, on average, six or seven other households who reported using short forms.

One consequence of the weighting procedures is that each estimate based on the long form responses has an associated confidence interval. These confidence intervals are wider (as a percentage of the estimate) for geographic areas with smaller populations and for characteristics that occur less frequently in the area being examined (such as the proportion of people in poverty in a middle-income neighborhood).

In order to release as much useful information as possible, statisticians must balance a number of factors. In particular, for Census 2000, the Bureau of the Census created weighting areas—geographic areas from which about two hundred or more long forms were completed—which are large enough to produce good quality estimates. If smaller weighting areas had been used, the confidence intervals around the estimates would have been significantly wider, rendering many estimates less useful due to their lower reliability.

The disadvantage of using weighting areas this large is that, for smaller geographic areas within them, the estimates of characteristics that are also reported on the short form will not match the counts reported in SF 1. Examples of these characteristics are the total number of people, the number of people reporting specific racial categories, and the number of housing units. The official values for items reported on the short form come from SF 1 and SF 2.

The differences between the long form estimates in SF 3 and values in SF 1 are particularly noticeable for the smallest places, tracts, and block groups. The long form estimates of total population and total housing units in SF 3 will, however, match the SF 1 counts for larger geographic areas such as counties and states, and will be essentially the same for medium and large cities.

SF 1 gives exact numbers even for very small groups and areas, whereas SF 3 gives estimates for small groups and areas such as tracts and small places that are less exact. The goal of SF 3 is to identify large differences among areas or large changes over time. Estimates for small areas and small population groups often do exhibit large changes from one census to the next, so having the capability to measure them is worthwhile.

2010 Estimates and 2015 Projections

Most 2000 Census data has been updated with data provided by Nielsen Claritas. Founded in 1971, Nielsen Claritas is the industry leader in applied demography and the preeminent provider of small-area demographic estimates.

Information for Communities

PHYSICAL CHARACTERISTICS

Place Type: Lists the type of place (city, town, village, borough, special city, CDP, township, plantation, gore, district, grant, location, reservation, or postal area). *Source: U.S. Bureau of the Census, Census of Population and Housing, 2000: Summary File 1 and U.S. Postal Service, City State File.*

Land and Water Area: Land and water area in square miles. *Source: U.S. Bureau of the Census, Census of Population and Housing, 2000: Summary File 1.*

Latitude and Longitude: Latitude and longitude in degrees. *Source: U.S. Bureau of the Census, Census of Population and Housing, 2000: Summary File 1.*

Elevation: Elevation in feet. *Source: U.S. Geological Survey, Geographic Names Information System (GNIS).*

HISTORY

History: Historical information. *Source: Columbia University Press, The Columbia Gazetteer of North America; Original research.*

POPULATION

Population: 1990 and 2000 figures are a 100% count of population. 2010 estimates and 2015 projections were provided by Nielsen Claritas. *Source: Nielsen Claritas; U.S. Bureau of the Census, Census of Population and Housing, 2000: Summary File 1.*

Population by Race: 2010 estimates includes the U.S. Bureau of the Census categories of White alone; Black alone; Asian alone; and Hispanic of any race. Alone refers to the fact that these figures are not in combination with any other race. 2010 data for American Indian/Alaska Native and Native Hawaiian/Other Pacific Islander was not available.

The concept of race, as used by the Census Bureau, reflects self-identification by people according to the race or races with which they most closely identify. These categories are socio-political constructs and should not be interpreted as being scientific or anthropological in nature. Furthermore, the race categories include both racial and national-origin groups.

- **White.** A person having origins in any of the original peoples of Europe, the Middle East, or North Africa. It includes people who indicate their race as White or report entries such as Irish, German, Italian, Lebanese, Near Easterner, Arab, or Polish.
- **Black or African American.** A person having origins in any of the Black racial groups of Africa. It includes people who indicate their race as Black, African American, or Negro, or provide written entries such as African American, Afro-American, Kenyan, Nigerian, or Haitian.
- **Asian.** A person having origins in any of the original peoples of the Far East, Southeast Asia, or the Indian subcontinent including, for example, Cambodia, China, India, Japan, Korea, Malaysia, Pakistan, the Philippine Islands, Thailand, and Vietnam. It includes Asian Indian, Chinese, Filipino, Korean, Japanese, Vietnamese, and Other Asian.
- **Hispanic.** The data on the Hispanic or Latino population, which was asked of all people, were derived from answers to long-form questionnaire Item 5, and short-form questionnaire Item 7. The terms Spanish, Hispanic origin, and Latino are used interchangeably. Some respondents identify with all three terms, while others may identify with only one of these three specific terms. Hispanics or Latinos who identify with the terms Spanish, Hispanic, or Latino are those who classify themselves in one of the specific Hispanic or Latino categories listed on the questionnaire—Mexican, Puerto Rican, or Cuban—as well as those who indicate that they are other Spanish, Hispanic, or Latino. People who do not identify with one of the specific origins listed on the questionnaire but indicate that they are other Spanish, Hispanic, or Latino are those whose origins are from Spain, the Spanish-speaking countries of Central or South America, the Dominican Republic, or people identifying themselves generally as Spanish, Spanish-American, Hispanic, Hispano, Latino, and so on. All write-in responses to the other Spanish/Hispanic/Latino category were coded. Origin can be viewed as the heritage, nationality group, lineage, or country of birth of the person or the person's parents or ancestors before their arrival in the United States. People who identify their origin as Spanish, Hispanic, or Latino may be of any race.

Population Density: 2010 population estimate divided by the land area in square miles. *Source: Nielsen Claritas; U.S. Bureau of the Census, Census of Population and Housing, 2000: Summary File 1.*

Average Household Size: Average household size was calculated by dividing the total population by the total number of households. Figures are 2010 estimates. *Source: Nielsen Claritas.*

Median Age: Figures are 2010 estimates. *Source: Nielsen Claritas.*

Male/Female Ratio: Number of males per 100 females. Figures are 2010 estimates. *Source: Nielsen Claritas.*

Marital Status: Percentage of population never married, now married, widowed, or divorced. *Source: U.S. Census Bureau, American Community Survey, 2005-2009 Five-Year Estimates.*

The marital status classification refers to the status at the time of enumeration. Data on marital status are tabulated only for the population 15 years old and over. Each person was asked whether they were "Now married," "Widowed," "Divorced," or "Never married." Couples who live together (for example, people in common-law marriages) were able to report the marital status they considered to be the most appropriate.

- **Never married.** Never married includes all people who have never been married, including people whose only marriage(s) was annulled.
- **Now married.** All people whose current marriage has not ended by widowhood or divorce. This category includes people defined as "separated."
- **Widowed.** This category includes widows and widowers who have not remarried.
- **Divorced.** This category includes people who are legally divorced and who have not remarried.

Foreign Born: Percentage of population who were not U.S. citizens at birth. Foreign-born people are those who indicated they were either a U.S. citizen by naturalization or they were not a citizen of the United States. *Source: U.S. Census Bureau, American Community Survey, 2005-2009 Five-Year Estimates.*

Ancestry: Largest ancestry groups reported (up to five). Includes multiple ancestries. *Source: U.S. Census Bureau, American Community Survey, 2005-2009 Five-Year Estimates.*

The data represent self-classification by people according to the ancestry group or groups with which they most closely identify. Ancestry refers to a person's ethnic origin or descent, "roots," heritage, or the place of birth of the person, the person's parents, or their ancestors before their arrival in the United States. Some ethnic identities, such as Egyptian or Polish, can be traced to geographic areas outside the United States, while other ethnicities such as Pennsylvania German or Cajun evolved in the United States.

The ancestry question was intended to provide data for groups that were not included in the Hispanic origin and race questions. Therefore, although data on all groups are collected, the ancestry data shown in these tabulations are for non-Hispanic and non-race groups. *See* Population by Race for information on Hispanic and race groups.

The ancestry question allowed respondents to report one or more ancestry groups, although only the first two were coded. If a response was in terms of a dual ancestry, for example, "Irish English," the person was assigned two codes, in this case one for Irish and another for English. However, in certain cases, multiple responses such as "French Canadian," "Greek Cypriote," and "Scotch Irish" were assigned a single code reflecting their status as unique groups. If a person reported one of these unique groups in addition to another group, for example, "Scotch Irish English," resulting in three terms, that person received one code for the unique group (Scotch-Irish) and another one for the remaining group (English). If a person reported "English Irish French," only English and Irish were coded. Certain combinations of ancestries where the ancestry group is a part of another, such as "German-Bavarian," were coded as a single ancestry using the more specific group (Bavarian). Also, responses such as "Polish-American" or "Italian-American" were coded and tabulated as a single entry (Polish or Italian).

The Census Bureau accepted "American" as a unique ethnicity if it was given alone, with an ambiguous response, or with state names. If the respondent listed any other ethnic identity such as "Italian-American," generally the "American" portion of the response was not coded. However, distinct groups such as "American Indian," "Mexican American," and "African American" were coded and identified separately because they represented groups who considered themselves different from those who reported as "Indian," "Mexican," or "African," respectively.

The data is based on the total number of ancestries reported and coded. Thus, the sum of the counts in this type of presentation is not the total population but the total of all responses.

ECONOMY

Unemployment Rate: August 2011. Includes all civilians age 16 or over who were unemployed and looking for work. *Source: U.S. Department of Labor, Bureau of Labor Statistics, Local Area Unemployment Statistics (http://www.bls.gov/lau/home.htm).*

Total Civilian Labor Force: August 2011. Includes all civilians age 16 or over who were either employed, or unemployed and looking for work. *Source: U.S. Department of Labor, Bureau of Labor Statistics, Local Area Unemployment Statistics (http://www.bls.gov/lau/home.htm).*

Single-Family Building Permits Issued: Building permits issued for new single-family housing units in 2010. *Source: U.S. Census Bureau, Manufacturing and Construction Division (http://www.census.gov/const/www/permitsindex.html).*

Multi-Family Building Permits Issued: Building permits issued for new multi-family housing units in 2010. *Source: U.S. Census Bureau, Manufacturing and Construction Division (http://www.census.gov/const/www/permitsindex.html).*

Statistics on housing units authorized by building permits include housing units issued in local permit-issuing jurisdictions by a building or zoning permit. Not all areas of the country require a building or zoning permit. The statistics only represent those areas that do require a permit. Current surveys indicate that construction is undertaken for all but a very small percentage of housing units authorized by building permits. A major portion typically get under way during the month of permit issuance and most of the remainder begin within the three following months. Because of this lag, the housing unit authorization statistics do not represent the number of units actually put into construction for the period shown, and should therefore not be directly interpreted as "housing starts."

Statistics are based upon reports submitted by local building permit officials in response to a mail survey. They are obtained using Form C-404 const/www/c404.pdf, "Report of New Privately-Owned Residential Building or Zoning Permits Issued." When a report is not received, missing data are either (1) obtained from the Survey of Use of Permits (SUP) which is used to collect information on housing starts, or (2) imputed based on the assumption that the ratio of current month authorizations to those of a year ago should be the same for reporting and non-reporting places.

Employment by Occupation: Percentage of the employed civilian population 16 years and over in management, professional, service, sales, farming, construction, and production occupations. *Source: U.S. Census Bureau, American Community Survey, 2005-2009 Five-Year Estimates.*

- **Management** includes management, business, and financial operations occupations:
  Management occupations, except farmers and farm managers
  Farmers and farm managers
  Business and financial operations occupations:
    Business operations specialists
    Financial specialists

- **Professional** includes professional and related occupations:
  Computer and mathematical occupations
  Architecture and engineering occupations:
    Architects, surveyors, cartographers, and engineers
    Drafters, engineering, and mapping technicians
  Life, physical, and social science occupations
  Community and social services occupations
  Legal occupations
  Education, training, and library occupations
  Arts, design, entertainment, sports, and media occupations
  Healthcare practitioners and technical occupations:
    Health diagnosing and treating practitioners and technical occupations
    Health technologists and technicians

- **Service** occupations include:
  Healthcare support occupations
  Protective service occupations:
    Fire fighting, prevention, and law enforcement workers, including supervisors

Other protective service workers, including supervisors
Food preparation and serving related occupations
Building and grounds cleaning and maintenance occupations
Personal care and service occupations

- **Sales** and office occupations include:
  Sales and related occupations
  Office and administrative support occupations

- **Farming,** fishing, and forestry occupations

- **Construction,** extraction, and maintenance occupations include:
  Construction and extraction occupations:
  Supervisors, construction, and extraction workers
  Construction trades workers
  Extraction workers
  Installation, maintenance, and repair occupations

- **Production,** transportation, and material moving occupations include:
  Production occupations
  Transportation and material moving occupations:
  Supervisors, transportation, and material moving workers
  Aircraft and traffic control occupations
  Motor vehicle operators
  Rail, water, and other transportation occupations
  Material moving workers

INCOME

Per Capita Income: Per capita income is the mean income computed for every man, woman, and child in a particular group. It is derived by dividing the total income of a particular group by the total population in that group. Per capita income is rounded to the nearest whole dollar. Figures shown are 2010 estimates. *Source: Nielsen Claritas.*

Median Household Income: Includes the income of the householder and all other individuals 15 years old and over in the household, whether they are related to the householder or not. The median divides the income distribution into two equal parts: one-half of the cases falling below the median income and one-half above the median. For households, the median income is based on the distribution of the total number of households including those with no income. Median income for households is computed on the basis of a standard distribution and is rounded to the nearest whole dollar. Figures shown are 2010 estimates. *Source: Nielsen Claritas.*

Average Household Income: Average household income is obtained by dividing total household income by the total number of households. Figures shown are 2010 estimates. *Source: Nielsen Claritas.*

Percent of Households with Income of $100,000 or more: Figures shown are 2010 estimates. *Source: Nielsen Claritas.*

Poverty Rate: Percentage of population with income below the poverty level. Based on individuals for whom poverty status is determined. Poverty status was determined for all people except institutionalized people, people in military group quarters, people in college dormitories, and unrelated individuals under 15 years old. *Source: U.S. Census Bureau, American Community Survey, 2005-2009 Five-Year Estimates.*

TAXES

Total City Taxes Per Capita: Total city taxes collected divided by the population of the city. *Source: U.S. Bureau of the Census, State and Local Government Finances, 2007 (http://www.census.gov/govs/www/estimate.html).*

Taxes include:
- Property Taxes
- Sales and Gross Receipts Taxes
- Federal Customs Duties
- General Sales and Gross Receipts Taxes

- Selective Sales Taxes (alcoholic beverages; amusements; insurance premiums; motor fuels; pari-mutuels; public utilities; tobacco products; other)
- License Taxes (alcoholic beverages; amusements; corporations in general; hunting and fishing; motor vehicles motor vehicle operators; public utilities; occupation and business, NEC; other)
- Income Taxes (individual income; corporation net income; other)
- Death and Gift
- Documentary & Stock Transfer
- Severance
- Taxes, NEC

Total City Property Taxes Per Capita: Total city property taxes collected divided by the population of the city. *Source: U.S. Bureau of the Census, State and Local Government Finances, 2007 (http://www.census.gov/govs/www/estimate.html).*

Property Taxes include general property taxes, relating to property as a whole, taxed at a single rate or at classified rates according to the class of property. Property refers to real property (e.g. land and structures) as well as personal property; personal property can be either tangible (e.g. automobiles and boats) or intangible (e.g. bank accounts and stocks and bonds). Special property taxes, levied on selected types of property (e.g. oil and gas properties, house trailers, motor vehicles, and intangibles) and subject to rates not directly related to general property tax rates. Taxes based on income produced by property as a measure of its value on the assessment date.

EDUCATION

Educational Attainment: Figures shown are 2010 estimates and show the percent of population age 25 and over with:

- **High school diploma (including GED) or higher:** includes people whose highest degree is a high school diploma or its equivalent, people who attended college but did not receive a degree, and people who received a college, university, or professional degree.
- **Bachelor's degree or higher**
- **Master's degree or higher:** Master's degrees include the traditional MA and MS degrees and field-specific degrees, such as MSW, MEd, MBA, and MLS. *Source: Nielsen Claritas.*

School Districts: Lists the name of each school district, the grade range (PK=pre-kindergarten; KG=kindergarten), the student enrollment, and the district headquarters' phone number. In each community profile, only school districts that have schools that are physically located within the community are shown. In addition, statistics for each school district cover the entire district, regardless of the physical location of the schools within the district. *Source: U.S. Department of Education, National Center for Educational Statistics, Directory of Public Elementary and Secondary Education Agencies, 2009-10.*

Four-year Colleges: Lists the name of each four-year college, the type of institution (private or public; for-profit or non-profit; religious affiliation; historically black), the total student enrollment (Fall 2009), the general telephone number, and the annual tuition and fees for full-time, first-time undergraduate students (in-state and out-of-state). *Source: U.S. Department of Education, National Center for Educational Statistics, IPEDS College Data, 2010-11.*

Two-year Colleges: Lists the name of each two-year college, the type of institution (private or public; for-profit or non-profit; religious affiliation; historically black), the total student enrollment (Fall 2009), the general telephone number, and the annual tuition and fees for full-time, first-time undergraduate students (in-state and out-of-state). *Source: U.S. Department of Education, National Center for Educational Statistics, IPEDS College Data, 2010-11.*

Vocational/Technical Schools: Lists the name of each vocational/technical school, the type of institution (private or public; for-profit or non-profit; religious affiliation; historically black), the total student enrollment (Fall 2009), the general telephone number, and the annual tuition and fees for full-time students. *Source: U.S. Department of Education, National Center for Educational Statistics, IPEDS College Data, 2010-11.*

HOUSING

Homeownership Rate: Percentage of housing units that are owner-occupied. Figures shown are 2010 estimates. *Source: Nielsen Claritas.*

Median Home Value: Median value of all owner-occupied housing units as reported by the owner. Figures shown are 2010 estimates. *Source: Nielsen Claritas.*

Median Rent: Median monthly contract rent on specified renter-occupied and specified vacant-for-rent units. Specified renter-occupied and specified vacant-for-rent units exclude 1-family houses on 10 acres or more. Contract rent is the monthly rent agreed to or contracted for, regardless of any furnishings, utilities, fees, meals, or services that may be included. For vacant units, it is the monthly rent asked for the rental unit at the time of enumeration. *Source: U.S. Census Bureau, American Community Survey, 2005-2009 Five-Year Estimates.*

Median Year Structure Built: Year structure built refers to when the building was first constructed, not when it was remodeled, added to, or converted. For mobile homes, houseboats, RVs, etc, the manufacturer's model year was assumed to be the year built. The data relate to the number of units built during the specified periods that were still in existence at the time of enumeration. *Source: U.S. Census Bureau, American Community Survey, 2005-2009 Five-Year Estimates.*

HOSPITALS

Lists the hospital name and the number of licensed beds. *Source: Grey House Publishing, Directory of Hospital Personnel, 2010.*

SAFETY

Violent Crime Rate: Number of violent crimes reported per 10,000 population. Violent crimes include murder, forcible rape, robbery, and aggravated assault. *Source: Federal Bureau of Investigation, Uniform Crime Reports 2010 (http://www.fbi.gov/ucr/ucr.htm).*

Property Crime Rate: Number of property crimes reported per 10,000 population. Property crimes include burglary, larceny-theft, and motor vehicle theft. *Source: Federal Bureau of Investigation, Uniform Crime Reports 2010 (http://www.fbi.gov/ucr/ucr.htm).*

NEWSPAPERS

Lists the name, circulation and news focus of daily and weekly newspapers. Includes newspapers with offices located in the community profiled. *Source: MediaContactsPro 2009*

TRANSPORTATION

Commute to Work: Percentage of workers 16 years old and over that use the following means of transportation to commute to work: car; public transportation; walk; work from home. *Source: U.S. Census Bureau, American Community Survey, 2005-2009 Five-Year Estimates.*

The means of transportation data for some areas may show workers using modes of public transportation that are not available in those areas (e.g. subway or elevated riders in a metropolitan area where there actually is no subway or elevated service). This result is largely due to people who worked during the reference week at a location that was different from their usual place of work (such as people away from home on business in an area where subway service was available) and people who used more than one means of transportation each day but whose principal means was unavailable where they lived (e.g. residents of non-metropolitan areas who drove to the fringe of a metropolitan area and took the commuter railroad most of the distance to work).

Travel Time to Work: Travel time to work for workers 16 years old and over. Reported for the following intervals: less than 15 minutes; 15 to 30 minutes; 30 to 45 minutes; 45 to 60 minutes; 60 minutes or more. *Source: U.S. Census Bureau, American Community Survey, 2005-2009 Five-Year Estimates.*

Travel time to work refers to the total number of minutes that it usually took the person to get from home to work each day during the reference week. The elapsed time includes time spent waiting for public transportation, picking up passengers in carpools, and time spent in other activities related to getting to work.

Amtrak: Indicates if Amtrak rail or bus service is available. Please note that the cities being served continually change. *Source: National Railroad Passenger Corporation, Amtrak National Timetable, 2011 (www.amtrak.com).*

AIRPORTS

Lists the local airport(s) along with type of service and hub size. *Source: U.S. Department of Transportation, Bureau of Transportation Statistics (http://www.bts.gov).*

ADDITIONAL INFORMATION CONTACTS

The following phone numbers are provided as sources of additional information: Chambers of Commerce; Economic Development Agencies; and Convention & Visitors Bureaus. Efforts have been made to provide the most recent area codes. However, area code changes may have occurred in listed numbers. *Source: Original research.*

Information for Counties

PHYSICAL CHARACTERISTICS

Physical Location: Describes the physical location of the county. *Source: Columbia University Press, The Columbia Gazetteer of North America and original research.*

Land and Water Area: Land and water area in square miles. *Source: U.S. Bureau of the Census, Census of Population and Housing, 2000: Summary File 1.*

Time Zone: Lists the time zone. *Source: Original research.*

Year Organized: Year the county government was organized. *Source: National Association of Counties (www.naco.org).*

County Seat: Lists the county seat. If a county has more than one seat, then both are listed. *Source: National Association of Counties (www.naco.org).*

Metropolitan Area: Indicates the metropolitan area the county is located in. Also lists all the component counties of that metropolitan area. The Office of Management and Budget (OMB) defines metropolitan and micropolitan statistical areas. The most current definitions are as of December 2009. *Source: U.S. Bureau of the Census (http://www.census.gov/population/www/estimates/metrodef.html).*

Climate: Includes all weather stations located within the county. Indicates the station name and elevation as well as the monthly average high and low temperatures, average precipitation, and average snowfall. The period of record is generally 1980-2009, however, certain weather stations contain averages going back as far as 1900. *Source: Grey House Publishing, Weather America: A Thirty-Year Summary of Statistical Weather Data and Rankings, 2010.*

POPULATION

Population: 1990 and 2000 figures are a 100% count of population. 2010 estimates and 2015 projections were provided by Nielsen Claritas. *Source: Nielsen Claritas; U.S. Bureau of the Census, Census of Population and Housing, 2000: Summary File 1.*

Population by Race: 2010 estimates includes the U.S. Bureau of the Census categories of White alone; Black alone; Asian alone; and Hispanic of any race. Alone refers to the fact that these figures are not in combination with any other race. 2010 data for American Indian/Alaska Native and Native Hawaiian/Other Pacific Islander was not available.

The concept of race, as used by the Census Bureau, reflects self-identification by people according to the race or races with which they most closely identify. These categories are socio-political constructs and should not be interpreted as being scientific or anthropological in nature. Furthermore, the race categories include both racial and national-origin groups.

- **White.** A person having origins in any of the original peoples of Europe, the Middle East, or North Africa. It includes people who indicate their race as White or report entries such as Irish, German, Italian, Lebanese, Near Easterner, Arab, or Polish.

- **Black or African American.** A person having origins in any of the Black racial groups of Africa. It includes people who indicate their race as Black, African American, or Negro, or provide written entries such as African American, Afro-American, Kenyan, Nigerian, or Haitian.

- **Asian.** A person having origins in any of the original peoples of the Far East, Southeast Asia, or the Indian subcontinent including, for example, Cambodia, China, India, Japan, Korea, Malaysia, Pakistan, the Philippine Islands, Thailand, and Vietnam. It includes Asian Indian, Chinese, Filipino, Korean, Japanese, Vietnamese, and Other Asian.

- **Hispanic.** The data on the Hispanic or Latino population, which was asked of all people, were derived from answers to long-form questionnaire Item 5, and short-form questionnaire Item 7. The terms Spanish, Hispanic origin, and Latino are used interchangeably. Some respondents identify with all three terms, while others may identify with only one of these three specific terms. Hispanics or Latinos who identify with the terms Spanish, Hispanic, or Latino are those who classify themselves in one of the specific Hispanic or Latino categories listed on the questionnaire—Mexican, Puerto Rican, or Cuban—as well as those who indicate that they are other Spanish, Hispanic, or Latino. People who do not identify with one of the specific origins listed on the questionnaire but indicate that they are other Spanish, Hispanic, or Latino are those whose origins are from Spain, the Spanish-speaking countries of Central or South

America, the Dominican Republic, or people identifying themselves generally as Spanish, Spanish-American, Hispanic, Hispano, Latino, and so on. All write-in responses to the other Spanish/Hispanic/Latino category were coded. Origin can be viewed as the heritage, nationality group, lineage, or country of birth of the person or the person's parents or ancestors before their arrival in the United States. People who identify their origin as Spanish, Hispanic, or Latino may be of any race.

Population Density: 2010 population estimate divided by the land area in square miles. *Source: Nielsen Claritas; U.S. Bureau of the Census, Census of Population and Housing, 2000: Summary File 1.*

Average Household Size: Average household size was calculated by dividing the total population by the total number of households. Figures are 2010 estimates. *Source: Nielsen Claritas.*

Median Age: Figures are 2010 estimates. *Source: Nielsen Claritas.*

Male/Female Ratio: Number of males per 100 females. Figures are 2010 estimates. *Source: Nielsen Claritas.*

RELIGION

Religion: Lists the largest religious groups (up to five) based on the number of adherents divided by the population of the county. Adherents are defined as "all members, including full members, their children and the estimated number of other regular participants who are not considered as communicant, confirmed or full members." The data is based on a study of 149 religious bodies sponsored by the Association of Statisticians of American Religious Bodies. The 149 bodies reported 268,254 congregations and 141,371,963 adherents. *Source: Glenmary Research Center, Religious Congregations & Membership in the United States 2000.*

ECONOMY

Unemployment Rate: August 2011. Includes all civilians age 16 or over who were unemployed and looking for work. *Source: U.S. Department of Labor, Bureau of Labor Statistics, Local Area Unemployment Statistics (http://www.bls.gov/lau/home.htm).*

Total Civilian Labor Force: August 2011. Includes all civilians age 16 or over who were either employed, or unemployed and looking for work. *Source: U.S. Department of Labor, Bureau of Labor Statistics, Local Area Unemployment Statistics (http://www.bls.gov/lau/home.htm).*

Leading Industries: Lists the three largest industries (excluding government) based on the number of employees. *Source: U.S. Bureau of the Census, County Business Patterns 2009 (http://www.census.gov/epcd/cbp/view/cbpview.html).*

Farms: The total number of farms and the total acreage they occupy. *Source: U.S. Department of Agriculture, National Agricultural Statistics Service, 2007 Census of Agriculture (http://www.agcensus.usda.gov).*

Companies that Employ 500 or more persons: The numbers of companies that employ 500 or more persons. Includes private employers only. *Source: U.S. Bureau of the Census, County Business Patterns 2009 (http://www.census.gov/epcd/cbp/view/cbpview.html).*

Companies that Employ 100 - 499 persons: The numbers of companies that employ 100 - 499 persons. Includes private employers only. *Source: U.S. Bureau of the Census, County Business Patterns 2009 (http://www.census.gov/epcd/cbp/view/cbpview.html).*

Companies that Employ 1 - 99 persons: The numbers of companies that employ 1 - 99 persons. Includes private employers only. *Source: U.S. Bureau of the Census, County Business Patterns 2009 (http://www.census.gov/epcd/cbp/view/cbpview.html)*

Black-Owned Businesses: Number of businesses that are majority-owned by a Black or African-American person(s). Majority ownership is defined as having 51 percent or more of the stock or equity in the business. Black or African American is defined as a person having origins in any of the black racial groups of Africa, including those who consider themselves to be "Haitian." *Source: U.S. Bureau of the Census, 2007 Economic Census, Survey of Business Owners: Black-Owned Firms, 2007 (http://www.census.gov/csd/sbo/index.html).*

Asian-Owned Businesses: Number of businesses that are majority-owned by an Asian person(s). Majority ownership is defined as having 51 percent or more of the stock or equity in the business. *Source: U.S. Bureau of the Census, 2007 Economic Census, Survey of Business Owners: Asian-Owned Firms, 2007 (http://www.census.gov/csd/sbo/index.html).*

Hispanic-Owned Businesses: Number of businesses that are majority-owned by a person(s) of Hispanic or Latino origin. Majority ownership is defined as having 51 percent or more of the stock or equity in the business. Hispanic or Latino origin is defined as a person of Cuban, Mexican, Puerto Rican, South or Central American, or other Spanish culture or origin, regardless of race. *Source: U.S. Bureau of the Census, 2007 Economic Census, Survey of Business Owners: Hispanic-Owned Firms, 2007 (http://www.census.gov/csd/sbo/index.html).*

Women-Owned Businesses: Number of businesses that are majority-owned by a woman. Majority ownership is defined as having 51 percent or more of the stock or equity in the business. *Source: U.S. Bureau of the Census, 2007 Economic Census, Survey of Business Owners: Women-Owned Firms, 2007 (http://www.census.gov/csd/sbo/index.html).*

The Survey of Business Owners (SBO) provides statistics that describe the composition of U.S. businesses by gender, Hispanic or Latino origin, and race. Additional statistics include owner's age, education level, veteran status, and primary function in the business; family- and home-based businesses; types of customers and workers; and sources of financing for expansion, capital improvements, or start-up. Economic policymakers in federal, state and local governments use the SBO data to understand conditions of business success and failure by comparing census-to-census changes in business performances and by comparing minority-/nonminority- and women-/men-owned businesses.

Retail Sales per Capita: Total dollar amount of estimated retail sales divided by the population of the county in 2010. *Source: Editor & Publisher Market Guide 2010; U.S. Census Bureau, 2010 Census*

Single-Family Building Permits Issued: Building permits issued for new, single-family housing units in 2010. *Source: U.S. Census Bureau, Manufacturing and Construction Division (http://www.census.gov/const/www/permitsindex.html).*

Multi-Family Building Permits Issued: Building permits issued for new, multi-family housing units in 2010. *Source: U.S. Census Bureau, Manufacturing and Construction Division (http://www.census.gov/const/www/permitsindex.html).*

Statistics on housing units authorized by building permits include housing units issued in local permit-issuing jurisdictions by a building or zoning permit. Not all areas of the country require a building or zoning permit. The statistics only represent those areas that do require a permit. Current surveys indicate that construction is undertaken for all but a very small percentage of housing units authorized by building permits. A major portion typically get under way during the month of permit issuance and most of the remainder begin within the three following months. Because of this lag, the housing unit authorization statistics do not represent the number of units actually put into construction for the period shown, and should therefore not be directly interpreted as "housing starts."

Statistics are based upon reports submitted by local building permit officials in response to a mail survey. They are obtained using Form C-404 const/www/c404.pdf, "Report of New Privately-Owned Residential Building or Zoning Permits Issued." When a report is not received, missing data are either (1) obtained from the Survey of Use of Permits (SUP) which is used to collect information on housing starts, or (2) imputed based on the assumption that the ratio of current month authorizations to those of a year ago should be the same for reporting and non-reporting places.

INCOME

Per Capita Income: Per capita income is the mean income computed for every man, woman, and child in a particular group. It is derived by dividing the total income of a particular group by the total population in that group. Per capita income is rounded to the nearest whole dollar. Figures shown are 2010 estimates. *Source: Nielsen Claritas.*

Median Household Income: Includes the income of the householder and all other individuals 15 years old and over in the household, whether they are related to the householder or not. The median divides the income distribution into two equal parts: one-half of the cases falling below the median income and one-half above the median. For households, the median income is based on the distribution of the total number of households including those with no income. Median income for households is computed on the basis of a standard distribution and is rounded to the nearest whole dollar. Figures shown are 2010 estimates. *Source: Nielsen Claritas.*

Average Household Income: Average household income is obtained by dividing total household income by the total number of households. Figures shown are 2010 estimates. *Source: Nielsen Claritas.*

Percent of Households with Income of $100,000 or more: Figures shown are 2010 estimates. *Source: Nielsen Claritas.*

Poverty Rate: Estimated percentage of population with income in 2009 below the poverty level. *Source: U.S. Bureau of the Census, Small Area Income & Poverty Estimates.*

Bankruptcy Rate: The personal bankruptcy filing rate is the number of bankruptcies per thousand residents in 2010. Personal bankruptcy filings include both Chapter 7 (liquidations) and Chapter 13 (reorganizations) based on the county of residence of the filer. *Source: Federal Deposit Insurance Corporation, Regional Economic Conditions (http://www2.fdic.gov/recon/index.html).*

TAXES

Total County Taxes Per Capita: Total county taxes collected divided by the population of the county. *Source: U.S. Bureau of the Census, State and Local Government Finances, 2007 (http://www.census.gov/govs/www/estimate.html).*

Taxes include:
- Property Taxes
- Sales and Gross Receipts Taxes
- Federal Customs Duties
- General Sales and Gross Receipts Taxes
- Selective Sales Taxes (alcoholic beverages; amusements; insurance premiums; motor fuels; pari-mutuels; public utilities; tobacco products; other)
- License Taxes (alcoholic beverages; amusements; corporations in general; hunting and fishing; motor vehicles motor vehicle operators; public utilities; occupation and business, NEC; other)
- Income Taxes (individual income; corporation net income; other)
- Death and Gift
- Documentary & Stock Transfer
- Severance
- Taxes, NEC

Total County Property Taxes Per Capita: Total county property taxes collected divided by the population of the county. *Source: U.S. Bureau of the Census, State and Local Government Finances, 2007 (http://www.census.gov/govs/www/estimate.html).*

Property Taxes include general property taxes, relating to property as a whole, taxed at a single rate or at classified rates according to the class of property. Property refers to real property (e.g. land and structures) as well as personal property; personal property can be either tangible (e.g. automobiles and boats) or intangible (e.g. bank accounts and stocks and bonds). Special property taxes, levied on selected types of property (e.g. oil and gas properties, house trailers, motor vehicles, and intangibles) and subject to rates not directly related to general property tax rates. Taxes based on income produced by property as a measure of its value on the assessment date.

EDUCATION

Educational Attainment: Figures shown are 2010 estimates and show the percent of population age 25 and over with:

- **High school diploma (including GED) or higher:** includes people whose highest degree was a high school diploma or its equivalent, people who attended college but did not receive a degree, and people who received a college, university, or professional degree.
- **Bachelor's degree or higher**
- **Master's degree or higher:** Master's degrees include the traditional MA and MS degrees and field-specific degrees, such as MSW, MEd, MBA, and MLS. *Source: Nielsen Claritas.*

HOUSING

Homeownership Rate: Percentage of housing units that are owner-occupied. Figures shown are 2010 estimates. *Source: Nielsen Claritas.*

Median Home Value: Median value of all owner-occupied housing units as reported by the owner. Figures shown are 2010 estimates. *Source: Nielsen Claritas.*

Median Rent: Median monthly contract rent on specified renter-occupied and specified vacant-for-rent units. Specified renter-occupied and specified vacant-for-rent units exclude 1-family houses on 10 acres or more. Contract rent is the monthly rent agreed to or contracted for, regardless of any furnishings, utilities, fees, meals, or services that may be included. For vacant units, it is the monthly rent asked for the rental unit at the time of enumeration. *Source: U.S. Census Bureau, American Community Survey, 2005-2009 Five-Year Estimates.*

Median Year Structure Built: Year structure built refers to when the building was first constructed, not when it was remodeled, added to, or converted. For mobile homes, houseboats, RVs, etc, the manufacturer's model year was assumed to be the year built. The data relate to the number of units built during the specified periods that were still in existence at the time of enumeration. *Source: U.S. Census Bureau, American Community Survey, 2005-2009 Five-Year Estimates.*

HEALTH AND VITAL STATISTICS

Birth Rate: Estimated number of births per 10,000 population in 2009. *Source: U.S. Census Bureau, Annual Components of Population Change, July 1, 2008 - July 1, 2009 (http://www.census.gov/popest/births.html).*

Death Rate: Estimated number of deaths per 10,000 population in 2009. *Source: U.S. Census Bureau, Annual Components of Population Change, July 1, 2008 - July 1, 2009 (http://www.census.gov/popest/births.html).*

Age-adjusted Cancer Mortality Rate: Number of age-adjusted deaths from cancer per 100,000 population in 2007. Cancer is defined as International Classification of Disease (ICD) codes C00 - D48.9 Neoplasms. *Source: Centers for Disease Control, CDC Wonder (http://wonder.cdc.gov).*

Age-adjusted death rates are weighted averages of the age-specific death rates, where the weights represent a fixed population by age. They are used because the rates of almost all causes of death vary by age. Age adjustment is a technique for "removing" the effects of age from crude rates, so as to allow meaningful comparisons across populations with different underlying age structures. For example, comparing the crude rate of heart disease in New York to that of California is misleading, because the relatively older population in New York will lead to a higher crude death rate, even if the age-specific rates of heart disease in New York and California are the same. For such a comparison, age-adjusted rates would be preferable. Age-adjusted rates should be viewed as relative indexes rather than as direct or actual measures of mortality risk.

Death rates based on counts of twenty or less (≤ 20) are flagged as "Unreliable". Death rates based on fewer than three years of data for counties with populations of less than 100,000 in the 2000 Census counts, are also flagged as "Unreliable" if the number of deaths is five or less (≤ 5).

Number of Physicians: The number of active, non-federal physicians per 10,000 population in 2008. *Source: Area Resource File (ARF) 2009-2010. U.S. Department of Health and Human Services, Health Resources and Services Administration, Bureau of Health Professions, Rockville, MD.*

Number of Hospital Beds: The number of hospital beds per 10,000 population in 2007. *Source: Area Resource File (ARF) 2009-2010. U.S. Department of Health and Human Services, Health Resources and Services Administration, Bureau of Health Professions, Rockville, MD.*

Number of Hospital Admissions: The number of hospital admissions per 10,000 population in 2007. *Source: Area Resource File (ARF) 2009-2010. U.S. Department of Health and Human Services, Health Resources and Services Administration, Bureau of Health Professions, Rockville, MD.*

ENVIRONMENT

Air Quality Index: The percentage of days in 2008 the AQI fell into the Good (0-50), Moderate (51-100), Unhealthy for Sensitive Groups (101-150), and Unhealthy (151+) ranges. Data covers January 2008 through December 2008. Counties with less than 90 days of air quality data were excluded. *Source: AirData: Access to Air Pollution Data, U.S. Environmental Protection Agency, Office of Air and Radiation (http://www.epa.gov/air/data/index.html).*

The AQI is an index for reporting daily air quality. It tells you how clean or polluted your air is, and what associated health concerns you should be aware of. The AQI focuses on health effects that can happen within a few hours or days after breathing polluted air. EPA uses the AQI for five major air pollutants regulated by the Clean Air Act: ground-level ozone, particulate matter, carbon monoxide, sulfur dioxide, and nitrogen dioxide. For each of these pollutants, EPA has established national air quality standards to protect against harmful health effects.

The AQI runs from 0 to 500. The higher the AQI value, the greater the level of air pollution and the greater the health danger. For example, an AQI value of 50 represents good air quality and little potential to affect public health, while an AQI value over 300 represents hazardous air quality. An AQI value of 100 generally corresponds to the national air quality standard for the pollutant, which is the level EPA has set to protect public health. So, AQI values below 100 are generally thought of as satisfactory. When AQI values are above 100, air quality is considered to be unhealthy—at first for certain sensitive groups of people, then for everyone as AQI values get higher. Each category corresponds to a different level of health concern. For example, when the AQI for a pollutant is between 51 and 100, the health concern is "Moderate." Here are the six levels of health concern and what they mean:

- "Good" The AQI value for your community is between 0 and 50. Air quality is considered satisfactory and air pollution poses little or no risk.

- "Moderate" The AQI for your community is between 51 and 100. Air quality is acceptable; however, for some pollutants there may be a moderate health concern for a very small number of individuals. For example, people who are unusually sensitive to ozone may experience respiratory symptoms.

- "Unhealthy for Sensitive Groups" Certain groups of people are particularly sensitive to the harmful effects of certain air pollutants. This means they are likely to be affected at lower levels than the general public. For example, children and adults who are active outdoors and people with respiratory disease are at greater risk from exposure to ozone, while people with heart disease are at greater risk from carbon monoxide. Some people may be sensitive to more than one pollutant. When AQI values are between 101 and 150, members of sensitive groups may experience health effects. The general public is not likely to be affected when the AQI is in this range.

- "Unhealthy" AQI values are between 151 and 200. Everyone may begin to experience health effects. Members of sensitive groups may experience more serious health effects.

- "Very Unhealthy" AQI values between 201 and 300 trigger a health alert, meaning everyone may experience more serious health effects.

- "Hazardous" AQI values over 300 trigger health warnings of emergency conditions. The entire population is more likely to be affected.

ELECTIONS

Elections: 2008 Presidential election results. *Source: Dave Leip's Atlas of U.S. Presidential Elections (http://www.uselectionatlas.org).*

NATIONAL AND STATE PARKS

Lists National and State parks located in the area. *Source: U.S. Geological Survey, Geographic Names Information System.*

ADDITIONAL INFORMATION CONTACTS

The following phone numbers are provided as sources of additional information: Chambers of Commerce; Economic Development Agencies; and Convention & Visitors Bureaus. Efforts have been made to provide the most recent area codes. However, area code changes may have occurred in listed numbers. *Source: Original research.*

User's Guide: Education

School District Rankings

Number of Schools: Total number of schools in the district. *Source: U.S. Department of Education, National Center for Education Statistics, Common Core of Data, Public Elementary/Secondary School Universe Survey: School Year 2009-2010.*

Number of Teachers: Teachers are defined as individuals who provide instruction to pre-kindergarten, kindergarten, grades 1 through 12, or ungraded classes, or individuals who teach in an environment other than a classroom setting, and who maintain daily student attendance records. Numbers reported are full-time equivalents (FTE). *Source: U.S. Department of Education, National Center for Education Statistics, Common Core of Data, Local Education Agency (School District) Universe Survey: School Year 2009-2010.*

Number of Students: A student is an individual for whom instruction is provided in an elementary or secondary education program that is not an adult education program and is under the jurisdiction of a school, school system, or other education institution. *Sources: U.S. Department of Education, National Center for Education Statistics, Common Core of Data, Local Education Agency (School District) Universe Survey: School Year 2009-2010 and Public Elementary/Secondary School Universe Survey: School Year 2009-2010*

Individual Education Program (IEP) Students: A written instructional plan for students with disabilities designated as special education students under IDEA-Part B. The written instructional plan includes a statement of present levels of educational performance of a child; statement of annual goals, including short-term instructional objectives; statement of specific educational services to be provided and the extent to which the child will be able to participate in regular educational programs; the projected date for initiation and anticipated duration of services; the appropriate objectives, criteria and evaluation procedures; and the schedules for determining, on at least an annual basis, whether instructional objectives are being achieved. *Source: U.S. Department of Education, National Center for Education Statistics, Common Core of Data, Local Education Agency (School District) Universe Survey: School Year 2009-2010*

English Language Learner (ELL) Students: Formerly referred to as Limited English Proficient (LEP). Students being served in appropriate programs of language assistance (e.g., English as a Second Language, High Intensity Language Training, bilingual education). Does not include pupils enrolled in a class to learn a language other than English. Also Limited-English-Proficient students are individuals who were not born in the United States or whose native language is a language other than English; or individuals who come from environments where a language other than English is dominant; or individuals who are American Indians and Alaskan Natives and who come from environments where a language other than English has had a significant impact on their level of English language proficiency; and who, by reason thereof, have sufficient difficulty speaking, reading, writing, or understanding the English language, to deny such individuals the opportunity to learn successfully in classrooms where the language of instruction is English or to participate fully in our society. *Source: U.S. Department of Education, National Center for Education Statistics, Common Core of Data, Local Education Agency (School District) Universe Survey: School Year 2009-2010*

Students Eligible for Free Lunch Program: The free lunch program is defined as a program under the National School Lunch Act that provides cash subsidies for free lunches to students based on family size and income criteria. *Source: U.S. Department of Education, National Center for Education Statistics, Common Core of Data, Public Elementary/Secondary School Universe Survey: School Year 2009-2010*

Students Eligible for Reduced-Price Lunch Program: A student who is eligible to participate in the Reduced-Price Lunch Program under the National School Lunch Act. *Source: U.S. Department of Education, National Center for Education Statistics, Common Core of Data, Public Elementary/Secondary School Universe Survey: School Year 2009-2010*

Student/Teacher Ratio: The number of students divided by the number of teachers. Teachers are defined as individuals who provide instruction to pre-kindergarten, kindergarten, grades 1 through 12, or ungraded classes, or individuals who teach in an environment other than a classroom setting, and who maintain daily student attendance records. Numbers are based on full-time equivalents (FTE). *Source: U.S. Department of Education, National Center for Education Statistics, Common Core of Data, Local Education Agency (School District) Universe Survey: School Year 2009-2010.*

Student/Librarian Ratio: The number of students divided by the number of library and media support staff. Library and media support staff are defined as staff members who render other professional library and media services; also includes library aides and those involved in library/media support. Their duties include selecting, preparing, caring for, and making available to instructional staff, equipment, films, filmstrips, transparencies, tapes, TV programs, and similar materials maintained separately or as part of an instructional materials center. Also included are activities in the audio-visual center, TV studio, related-work-study areas, and services provided by audio-visual personnel. Numbers are based on full-time equivalents (FTE). *Source: U.S. Department of Education, National Center for Education Statistics, Common Core of Data, Local Education Agency (School District) Universe Survey: School Year 2009-2010.*

Student/Counselor Ratio: The number of students divided by the number of guidance counselors. Guidance counselors are professional staff assigned specific duties and school time for any of the following activities in an elementary or secondary setting: counseling with students and parents; consulting with other staff members on learning problems; evaluating student abilities; assisting students in making educational and career choices; assisting students in personal and social development; providing referral assistance; and/or working with other staff members in planning and conducting guidance programs for students. The state applies its own standards in apportioning the aggregate of guidance counselors/directors into the elementary and secondary level components. Numbers reported are full-time equivalents (FTE). *Source: U.S. Department of Education, National Center for Education Statistics, Common Core of Data, Local Education Agency (School District) Universe Survey: School Year 2009-2010.*

Total Current Expenditures:
State Profile. The total current expenditures for public elementary and secondary education as reported in the state finance file. Expenditures for equipment, non-public education, school construction, debt financing and community services are excluded. *Source: U.S. Department of Education, National Center for Education Statistics, Common Core of Data, National Public Education Financial Survey, School Year 2007-08 (Fiscal Year 2008)*

District Rankings. The district's total current expenditures for public elementary and secondary education as reported in the district finance file. *Source: U.S. Department of Education, National Center for Education Statistics, Common Core of Data, School District Finance Survey (F-33), Fiscal Year 2008*

Instruction:
State Profile. The total of instructional expenditures as reported in the state finance file. Instruction expenditures are for services and materials directly related to classroom instruction and the interaction between teachers and students. Teacher salaries and benefits, textbooks, classroom supplies and extra curricular activities are included. *Source: U.S. Department of Education, National Center for Education Statistics, Common Core of Data, National Public Education Financial Survey, School Year 2007-08 (Fiscal Year 2008)*

District Rankings. The total current expenditures for instruction for public prekindergarten and kindergarten through grade 12 programs as reported in the district finance file. The expenditures include teacher salaries and benefits and instructional supplies and purchased services. Tuition payments to other school districts are excluded. *Source: U.S. Department of Education, National Center for Education Statistics, Common Core of Data, School District Finance Survey (F-33), Fiscal Year 2008*

Support Services:
State Profile. The total of support services expenditures as reported in the state finance file. *Source: U.S. Department of Education, National Center for Education Statistics, Common Core of Data, National Public Education Financial Survey, School Year 2007-08 (Fiscal Year 2008)*

District Rankings. The total current expenditures for activities that support instruction as reported in the district finance file. Support services include operation and maintenance of buildings, school adminstration, student support services (e.g., nurses, therapists, and guidance counselors), student transportation, instructional staff support (e.g., librarians, instructional specialists), school district administration, business services, research, and data processing. *Source: U.S. Department of Education, National Center for Education Statistics, Common Core of Data, School District Finance Survey (F-33), Fiscal Year 2008*

Total General Revenue:
State Profile. The sum of revenue contributions emerging from local, state, and federal sources as reported in the state finance file. *Source: U.S. Department of Education, National Center for Education Statistics, Common Core of Data, National Public Education Financial Survey, School Year 2007-08 (Fiscal Year 2008)*

District Rankings. The sum of revenue contributions emerging from local, state, and federal sources as reported in the district finance file. *Source: U.S. Department of Education, National Center for Education Statistics, Common Core of Data, School District Finance Survey (F-33), Fiscal Year 2008*

Federal Revenue:
State Profile. Include direct grants-in-aid to schools or agencies, funds distributed through a state or intermediate

agency, and revenues in lieu of taxes to compensate a school district for nontaxable federal institutions within a district's boundary. *Source: U.S. Department of Education, National Center for Education Statistics, Common Core of Data, National Public Education Financial Survey, School Year 2007-08 (Fiscal Year 2008)*

District Rankings. Includes direct revenue and revenue distributed by state governments. Direct Revenue: Aid from project grants for programs such as Impact Aid (P.L. 81- 815 and P.L. 81-874), Indian Education, Bilingual Education, Head Start, Follow Through, Magnet Schools, Dropout Demonstration Assistance, and Gifted/Talented. Revenue Distributed by State Governments: Aid from formula grants distributed through state government agencies. This includes revenue from programs such as the following: Child Nutrition Act; Children with Disabilities-IDEA; Title I; vocational and technical education; other federal aid distributed by the state; and nonspecified federal aid distributed by the state. *Source: U.S. Department of Education, National Center for Education Statistics, Common Core of Data, School District Finance Survey (F-33), Fiscal Year 2008*

State Revenue:
State Profile. Include both direct funds from state governments and funds in lieu of taxation. Revenues in lieu of taxes are paid to compensate a school district for nontaxable state institutions or facilities within the district's boundary. *Source: U.S. Department of Education, National Center for Education Statistics, Common Core of Data, National Public Education Financial Survey, School Year 2007-08 (Fiscal Year 2008)*

District Rankings. Includes state revenue paid to the school system for any purpose, restricted or unrestricted, including the following: capital outlay/debt service; compensatory and basic skills programs; payments on behalf of LEA; special education programs; staff improvement programs; transportation programs; vocational programs; other programs; and nonspecified. *Source: U.S. Department of Education, National Center for Education Statistics, Common Core of Data, School District Finance Survey (F-33), Fiscal Year 2008*

Local Revenue:
State Profile. Include revenues from such sources as local property and nonproperty taxes, investments, and student activities such as textbook sales, transportation and tuition fees, and food service revenues. *Source: U.S. Department of Education, National Center for Education Statistics, Common Core of Data, National Public Education Financial Survey, School Year 2007-08 (Fiscal Year 2008)*

District Rankings. Includes revenue raised within the boundaries of the LEA. These revenues are primarily raised through property taxes, but also come from other types of taxes and fees. *Source: U.S. Department of Education, National Center for Education Statistics, Common Core of Data, School District Finance Survey (F-33), Fiscal Year 2008*

Long-Term Debt:
State Profile. Includes long-term credit obligations of the school system or its parent government and all interest-bearing short-term (repayable within 1 year) credit obligations. Excludes non-interestbearing short-term obligations, interfund obligations, amounts owed in a trust agency capacity, advances and contingent loans from other governments, and rights of individuals to benefits from school system employee retirement funds. *Source: U.S. Department of Education, National Center for Education Statistics, Common Core of Data, National Public Education Financial Survey, School Year 2007-08 (Fiscal Year 2008)*

District Rankings. Includes long-term credit obligations of the school system or its parent government and all interest-bearing short-term (repayable within 1 year) credit obligations. Excludes non-interestbearing short-term obligations, interfund obligations, amounts owed in a trust agency capacity, advances and contingent loans from other governments, and rights of individuals to benefits from school system employee retirement funds. *Source: U.S. Department of Education, National Center for Education Statistics, Common Core of Data, School District Finance Survey (F-33), Fiscal Year 2008*

Note: All financial values shown are dollars per pupil per year. They were calculated by dividing the total dollar amounts by the fall membership. Fall membership is comprised of the total student enrollment on October 1 (or the closest school day to October 1) for all grade levels (including prekindergarten and kindergarten) and ungraded pupils. Membership includes students both present and absent on the measurement day.

Drop-out Rate: A dropout is a student who was enrolled in school at some time during the previous school year; was not enrolled at the beginning of the current school year; has not graduated from high school or completed a state or district approved educational program; and does not meet any of the following exclusionary conditions: has transferred to another public school district, private school, or state- or district-approved educational program; is temporarily absent due to suspension or school-approved illness; or has died. The values shown cover grades 9 through 12. *Note: Drop-out rates are no longer available to the general public disaggregated by grade, race/ethnicity, and gender at the school district level. Beginning with the 2005–06 school year the CCD is reporting dropout data aggregated from the local education agency (district) level to the state level. This allows data users to compare event* dropout rates across states, regions, and other jurisdictions. *Source: U.S. Department of Education, National Center for Education Statistics, Common Core of Data, Local Education Agency (School District) Universe Survey Dropout and Completion Data, 2008-2009; U.S. Department of Education, National Center for Education Statistics, Common Core of Data, State Dropout and Completion Data File, 2008-2009*

Average Freshman Graduation Rate (AFGR): The AFGR is the number of regular diploma recipients in a given year divided by the average of the membership in grades 8, 9, and 10, reported 5, 4, and 3 years earlier, respectively. For example, the denominator of the 2008–09 AFGR is the average of the 8th-grade membership in 2004–05, 9th-grade membership in 2005–06, and 10th-grade membership in 2006–07. Ungraded students are prorated into these grades. Averaging these three grades provides an estimate of the number of first-time freshmen in the class of 2005–06 freshmen in order to estimate the on-time graduation rate for 2008–09.

Caution in interpreting the AFGR. Although the AFGR was selected as the best of the available alternatives, several factors make it fall short of a true on-time graduation rate. First, the AFGR does not take into account any imbalances in the number of students moving in and out of the nation or individual states over the high school years. As a result, the averaged freshman class is at best an approximation of the actual number of freshmen, where differences in the rates of transfers, retention, and dropping out in the three grades affect the average. Second, by including all graduates in a specific year, the graduates may include students who repeated a grade in high school or completed high school early and thus are not on-time graduates in that year. *Source: U.S. Department of Education, National Center for Education Statistics, Common Core of Data, Local Education Agency (School District) Universe Survey Dropout and Completion Data, 2008-2009; U.S. Department of Education, National Center for Education Statistics, Common Core of Data, State Dropout and Completion Data File, 2008-2009*

Number of Diploma Recipients: A student who has received a diploma during the previous school year or subsequent summer school. This category includes regular diploma recipients and other diploma recipients. A High School Diploma is a formal document certifying the successful completion of a secondary school program prescribed by the state education agency or other appropriate body. *Note: Diploma counts are no longer available to the general public disaggregated by grade, race/ethnicity, and gender at the school district level. Source: U.S. Department of Education, National Center for Education Statistics, Common Core of Data, Local Education Agency (School District) Universe Survey Dropout and Completion Data, 2008-2009; U.S. Department of Education, National Center for Education Statistics, Common Core of Data, State Dropout and Completion Data File, 2008-2009*

Note: n/a indicates data not available.

State Educational Profile

Please refer to the District Rankings section in the front of this User's Guide for an explanation of data for all items except for the following:

Average Salary: The average salary for classroom teachers in 2010-2011. *Source: National Education Association, Rankings & Estimates: Rankings of the States 2010 and Estimates of School Statistics 2011*

College Entrance Exam Scores:

Scholastic Aptitude Test (SAT). Note: The College Board strongly discourages the comparison or ranking of states on the basis of SAT scores alone. *Source: The College Board, SAT Trends: Background on the SAT Takers in the Class of 2011*

American College Testing Program (ACT). *Source: ACT, Inc., 2011 ACT National and State Scores*

National Assessment of Educational Progress (NAEP)

The National Assessment of Educational Progress (NAEP), also known as "the Nation's Report Card," is the only nationally representative and continuing assessment of what America's students know and can do in various subject areas. As a result of the "No Child Left Behind" legislation, all states are required to participate in NAEP.

For more information, visit the U.S. Department of Education, National Center for Education Statistics at http://nces.ed.gov/nationsreportcard.

User's Guide: Ancestry

Places Covered

The ranking tables are based on **1,311 places** in Illinois. Places include 1,285 municipalities and 26 census designated places (CDP). The U.S. Bureau of the Census defines a CDP as "a statistical entity, defined for each decennial census according to Census Bureau guidelines, comprising a densely settled concentration of population that is not within an incorporated place, but is locally identified by a name. CDPs are delineated cooperatively by state and local officials and the Census Bureau, following Census Bureau guidelines. Beginning with Census 2000 there are no size limits."

Source of Data

The ancestries shown in this chapter were compiled from three different sections of the 2000 Census: Race; Hispanic Origin; and Ancestry. While the ancestries are sorted alphabetically for ease-of-use, it's important to note the origin of each piece of data. Data for Race and Hispanic Origin was taken from Summary File 1 (SF1) while Ancestry data was taken from Summary File 3 (SF3). The distinction is important because SF1 contains the 100-percent data, which is the information compiled from the questions asked of all people and about every housing unit. SF3 was compiled from a sample of approximately 19 million housing units (about 1 in 6 households) that received the Census 2000 long-form questionnaire.

Ancestries Based on Race

The data on race were derived from answers to the question on race that was asked of all people. The concept of race, as used by the Census Bureau, reflects self-identification by people according to the race or races with which they most closely identify. These categories are sociopolitical constructs and should not be interpreted as being scientific or anthropological in nature. Furthermore, the race categories include both racial and national-origin groups.

If an individual did not provide a race response, the race or races of the householder or other household members were assigned using specific rules of precedence of household relationship. For example, if race was missing for a natural-born child in the household, then either the race or races of the householder, another natural-born child, or the spouse of the householder were assigned. If race was not reported for anyone in the household, the race or races of a householder in a previously processed household were assigned.

African-American/Black:
  Not Hispanic
  Hispanic
Alaska Native tribes, specified:
  Alaska Athabascan
  Aleut
  Eskimo
  Tlingit-Haida
  All other tribes
Alaska Native tribes, not specified
American Indian or Alaska Native
  tribes, not specified
American Indian tribes, specified:
  Apache
  Blackfeet
  Cherokee
  Cheyenne
  Chickasaw
  Chippewa
  Choctaw
  Colville
  Comanche
  Cree
  Creek
  Crow

Delaware
Houma
Iroquois
Kiowa
Latin American Indians
Lumbee
Menominee
Navajo
Osage
Ottawa
Paiute
Pima
Potawatomi
Pueblo
Puget Sound Salish
Seminole
Shoshone
Sioux
Tohono O'Odham
Ute
Yakama
Yaqui
Yuman
All other tribes

American Indian tribes,
  not specified
Asian:
  Bangladeshi
  Cambodian
  Chinese, except Taiwanese
  Filipino
  Hmong
  Indian
  Indonesian
  Japanese
  Korean
  Laotian
  Malaysian
  Pakistani
  Sri Lankan
  Taiwanese
  Thai
  Vietnamese
  Other Asian, specified
  Other Asian, not specified
Hawaii Native/Pacific Islander:
  Melanesian:
    Fijian
    Other Melanesian

Micronesian:
  Guamanian/Chamorro
  Other Micronesian
Polynesian:
  Native Hawaiian
  Samoan
  Tongan
  Other Polynesian
Other Pacific Islander, specified
Other Pacific Islander,
  not specified
White:
  Not Hispanic
  Hispanic

African American or Black: A person having origins in any of the Black racial groups of Africa. It includes people who indicate their race as "Black, African Am., or Negro," or provide written entries such as African American, Afro American, Kenyan, Nigerian, or Haitian.

American Indian or Alaska Native: A person having origins in any of the original peoples of North and South America (including Central America) and who maintain tribal affiliation or community attachment. It includes people who classified themselves as described below.

American Indian - Includes people who indicated their race as "American Indian," entered the name of an Indian tribe, or reported such entries as Canadian Indian, French American Indian, or Spanish-American Indian.

Respondents who identified themselves as American Indian were asked to report their enrolled or principal tribe. Therefore, tribal data in tabulations reflect the written entries reported on the questionnaires. Some of the entries (for example, Iroquois, Sioux, Colorado River, and Flathead) represent nations or reservations. The information on tribe is based on self identification and therefore does not reflect any designation of federally or state-recognized tribe. Information on American Indian tribes is presented in summary files. The information for Census 2000 is derived from the American Indian Tribal Classification List for the 1990 census that was updated based on a December 1997 Federal Register Notice, entitled "Indian Entities Recognized and Eligible to Receive Service From the United States Bureau of Indian Affairs," Department of the Interior, Bureau of Indian Affairs, issued by the Office of Management and Budget.

Alaska Native - Includes written responses of Eskimos, Aleuts, and Alaska Indians, as well as entries such as Arctic Slope, Inupiat, Yupik, Alutiiq, Egegik, and Pribilovian. The Alaska tribes are the Alaskan Athabascan, Tlingit, and Haida. The information for Census 2000 is based on the American Indian Tribal Classification List for the 1990 census, which was expanded to list the individual Alaska Native Villages when provided as a written response for race.

Asian: A person having origins in any of the original peoples of the Far East, Southeast Asia, or the Indian subcontinent including, for example, Cambodia, China, India, Japan, Korea, Malaysia, Pakistan, the Philippine Islands, Thailand, and Vietnam. It includes "Asian Indian," "Chinese," "Filipino," "Korean," "Japanese," "Vietnamese," and "Other Asian."

Asian Indian - Includes people who indicated their race as "Asian Indian" or identified themselves as Bengalese, Bharat, Dravidian, East Indian, or Goanese.

Chinese - Includes people who indicate their race as "Chinese" or who identify themselves as Cantonese, or Chinese American.

Filipino - Includes people who indicate their race as "Filipino" or who report entries such as Philipino, Philipine, or Filipino American.

Japanese - Includes people who indicate their race as "Japanese" or who report entries such as Nipponese or Japanese American.

Korean - Includes people who indicate their race as "Korean" or who provide a response of Korean American.

Vietnamese - Includes people who indicate their race as "Vietnamese" or who provide a response of Vietnamese American.

Cambodian - Includes people who provide a response such as Cambodian or Cambodia.

Hmong - Includes people who provide a response such as Hmong, Laohmong, or Mong.

Laotian - Includes people who provide a response such as Laotian, Laos, or Lao.

Thai - Includes people who provide a response such as Thai, Thailand, or Siamese.

Other Asian - Includes people who provide a response of Bangladeshi; Bhutanese; Burmese; Indochinese; Indonesian; Iwo Jiman; Madagascar; Malaysian; Maldivian; Nepalese; Okinawan; Pakistani; Singaporean; Sri Lankan; or Other Asian, specified and Other Asian, not specified.

Native Hawaiian or Other Pacific Islander: A person having origins in any of the original peoples of Hawaii, Guam, Samoa, or other Pacific Islands. It includes people who indicate their race as "Native Hawaiian," "Guamanian or Chamorro," "Samoan," and "Other Pacific Islander."

Native Hawaiian - Includes people who indicate their race as "Native Hawaiian" or who identify themselves as "Part Hawaiian" or "Hawaiian."

Guamanian or Chamorro - Includes people who indicate their race as such, including written entries of Chamorro or Guam.

Samoan - Includes people who indicate their race as "Samoan" or who identify themselves as American Samoan or Western Samoan.

Other Pacific Islander - Includes people who provide a write-in response of a Pacific Islander group, such as Carolinian, Chuukese (Trukese), Fijian, Kosraean, Melanesian, Micronesian, Northern Mariana Islander, Palauan, Papua New Guinean, Pohnpeian, Polynesian, Solomon Islander, Tahitian, Tokelauan, Tongan, Yapese, or Pacific Islander, not specified.

White: A person having origins in any of the original peoples of Europe, the Middle East, or North Africa. It includes people who indicate their race as "White" or report entries such as Irish, German, Italian, Lebanese, Near Easterner, Arab, or Polish.

Ancestries Based on Hispanic Origin

Hispanic or Latino:	Salvadoran	Argentinean	Uruguayan
Central American:	Other Central American	Bolivian	Venezuelan
Costa Rican	Cuban	Chilean	Other South American
Guatemalan	Dominican Republic	Colombian	Other Hispanic/Latino
Honduran	Mexican	Ecuadorian	
Nicaraguan	Puerto Rican	Paraguayan	
Panamanian	South American:	Peruvian	

The data on the Hispanic or Latino population were derived from answers to a question that was asked of all people. The terms "Spanish," "Hispanic origin," and "Latino" are used interchangeably. Some respondents identify with all three terms while others may identify with only one of these three specific terms. Hispanics or Latinos who identify with the terms "Spanish," "Hispanic," or "Latino" are those who classify themselves in one of the specific Spanish, Hispanic, or Latino categories listed on the questionnaire ("Mexican," "Puerto Rican," or "Cuban") as well as those who indicate that they are "other Spanish/Hispanic/Latino." People who do not identify with one of the specific origins listed on the questionnaire but indicate that they are "other Spanish, Hispanic, or Latino" are those whose origins are from Spain, the Spanish-speaking countries of Central or South America, the Dominican Republic, or people identifying themselves generally as Spanish, Spanish-American, Hispanic, Hispano, Latino, and so on. All write-in responses to the "other Spanish/Hispanic/Latino" category were coded.

Origin can be viewed as the heritage, nationality group, lineage, or country of birth of the person or the person's parents or ancestors before their arrival in the United States. People who identify their origin as Spanish, Hispanic, or Latino may be of any race.

In all cases where the origin of households, families, or occupied housing units is classified as Spanish, Hispanic, or Latino, the origin of the householder is used. If an individual could not provide a Hispanic origin response, their origin was assigned using specific rules of precedence of household relationship. For example, if origin was missing for a natural-born daughter in the household, then either the origin of the householder, another natural-born child, or spouse of the householder was assigned. If Hispanic origin was not reported for anyone in the household, the Hispanic origin of a householder in a previously processed household with the same race was assigned.

Other Ancestries

Acadian/Cajun	Moroccan	French, except Basque	Scottish
Afghan	Palestinian	French Canadian	Serbian
African, Subsaharan:	Syrian	German	Slavic
African	Other Arab	German Russian	Slovak
Cape Verdean	Armenian	Greek	Slovene
Ethiopian	Assyrian/Chaldean/Syriac	Guyanese	Soviet Union
Ghanian	Australian	Hungarian	Swedish
Kenyan	Austrian	Icelander	Swiss
Liberian	Basque	Iranian	Turkish
Nigerian	Belgian	Irish	Ukrainian
Senegalese	Brazilian	Israeli	United States or American
Sierra Leonean	British	Italian	Welsh
Somalian	Bulgarian	Latvian	West Indian, excluding Hispanic:
South African	Canadian	Lithuanian	Bahamian
Sudanese	Carpatho Rusyn	Luxemburger	Barbadian
Ugandan	Celtic	Macedonian	Belizean
Zairian	Croatian	Maltese	Bermudan
Zimbabwean	Cypriot	New Zealander	British West Indian
Other Subsaharan African	Czech	Northern European	Dutch West Indian
Albanian	Czechoslovakian	Norwegian	Haitian
Alsatian	Danish	Pennsylvania German	Jamaican
Arab:	Dutch	Polish	Trinidadian and
Arab/Arabic	Eastern European	Portuguese	Tobagonian
Egyptian	English	Romanian	U.S. Virgin Islander
Iraqi	Estonian	Russian	West Indian
Jordanian	European	Scandinavian	Other West Indian
Lebanese	Finnish	Scotch-Irish	Yugoslavian

The data on ancestry were derived from answers to long-form questionnaire Item 10, which was asked of a sample of the population. The data represent self-classification by people according to the ancestry group or groups with which they most closely identify. Ancestry refers to a person's ethnic origin or descent, "roots," heritage, or the place of birth of the person, the person's parents, or their ancestors before their arrival in the United States. Some ethnic identities, such as Egyptian or Polish, can be traced to geographic areas outside the United States, while other ethnicities, such as Pennsylvania German or Cajun, evolved in the United States.

The intent of the ancestry question was not to measure the degree of attachment the respondent had to a particular ethnicity. For example, a response of "Irish" might reflect total involvement in an Irish community or only a memory of ancestors several generations removed from the individual. Also, the question was intended to provide data for groups that were not included in the Hispanic origin and race questions. Official Hispanic origin data come from long-form questionnaire Item 5, and official race data come from long-form questionnaire Item 6. Therefore, although data on all groups are collected, the ancestry data shown in these tabulations are for non-Hispanic and non-race groups.

The ancestry question allowed respondents to report one or more ancestry groups, although only the first two were coded. If a response was in terms of a dual ancestry, for example, "Irish English," the person was assigned two codes, in this case one for Irish and another for English. However, in certain cases, multiple responses such as "French Canadian," "Greek Cypriote," and "Scotch Irish" were assigned a single code reflecting their status as unique groups. If a person reported one of these unique groups in addition to another group, for example, "Scotch Irish English," resulting in three terms, that person received one code for the unique group (Scotch-Irish) and another one for the remaining group (English). If a person reported "English Irish French," only English and Irish were coded. Certain combinations of ancestries where the ancestry group is a part of another, such as "German-Bavarian," were coded as a single ancestry using the more specific group (Bavarian). Also, responses such as "Polish-American" or "Italian-American" were coded and tabulated as a single entry (Polish or Italian).

The Census Bureau accepted "American" as a unique ethnicity if it was given alone, with an ambiguous response, or with state names. If the respondent listed any other ethnic identity such as "Italian-American," generally the "American" portion of the response was not coded. However, distinct groups such as "American Indian," "Mexican American," and "African American" were coded and identified separately because they represented groups who considered themselves different from those who reported as "Indian," "Mexican," or "African," respectively.

Census 2000 tabulations on ancestry are presented using two types of data presentations — one using total people as the base, and the other using total responses as the base. This chapter uses total responses as the base and includes the total number of ancestries reported and coded. If a person reported a multiple ancestry such as "French

Danish," that response was counted twice in the tabulations — once in the French category and again in the Danish category. Thus, the sum of the counts in this type of presentation is not the total population but the total of all responses.

An automated coding system was used for coding ancestry in Census 2000. This greatly reduced the potential for error associated with a clerical review. Specialists with knowledge of the subject matter reviewed, edited, coded, and resolved inconsistent or incomplete responses. The code list used in Census 2000, containing over 1,000 categories, reflects the results of the Census Bureau's experience with the 1990 ancestry question, research, and consultation with many ethnic experts. Many decisions were made to determine the classification of responses. These decisions affected the grouping of the tabulated data. For example, the Italian category includes the responses of Sicilian and Tuscan, as well as a number of other responses.

Although some people consider religious affiliation a component of ethnic identity, the ancestry question was not designed to collect any information concerning religion. Thus, if a religion was given as an answer to the ancestry question, it was listed in the "Other groups" category which is not shown in this chapter.

Ancestry should not be confused with a person's place of birth, although a person's place of birth and ancestry may be the same.

Ranking Section

In the ranking section of this chapter, each ancestry has three tables. The first table shows the top 10 places sorted by number (based on all places, regardless of population), the second table shows the top 10 places sorted by percent (based on all places, regardless of population), the third table shows the top 10 places sorted by percent (based on places with populations of 10,000 or more).

Within each table, column one displays the place name, the state, and the county (if a place spans more than one county, the county that holds the majority of the population is shown). Column two displays the number of people reporting each ancestry, and column three is the percent of the total population reporting each ancestry. For tables representing ancestries based on race or Hispanic origin, the 100-percent population figure from SF1 is used to calculate the value in the "%" column. For all other ancestries the sample population figure from SF3 is used to calculate the value in the "%" column.

Alphabetical Ancestry Cross-Reference Guide

Acadian/Cajun
Afghan
African *See African, sub-Saharan: African*
African American/Black
African American/Black: Hispanic
African American/Black: Not Hispanic
African, sub-Saharan
African, sub-Saharan: African
African, sub-Saharan: Cape Verdean
African, sub-Saharan: Ethiopian
African, sub-Saharan: Ghanian
African, sub-Saharan: Kenyan
African, sub-Saharan: Liberian
African, sub-Saharan: Nigerian
African, sub-Saharan: Other
African, sub-Saharan: Senegalese
African, sub-Saharan: Sierra Leonean
African, sub-Saharan: Somalian
African, sub-Saharan: South African
African, sub-Saharan: Sudanese
African, sub-Saharan: Ugandan
African, sub-Saharan: Zairian
African, sub-Saharan: Zimbabwean
Alaska Athabascan *See Alaska Native: Alaska Athabascan*
Alaska Native tribes, not specified
Alaska Native tribes, specified
Alaska Native: Alaska Athabascan
Alaska Native: Aleut
Alaska Native: All other tribes
Alaska Native: Eskimo
Alaska Native: Tlingit-Haida
Albanian
Aleut *See Alaska Native: Aleut*
Alsatian
American *See United States or American*
American Indian or Alaska Native tribes, not specified
American Indian tribes, not specified
American Indian tribes, specified
American Indian: All other tribes
American Indian: Apache
American Indian: Blackfeet
American Indian: Cherokee
American Indian: Cheyenne
American Indian: Chickasaw
American Indian: Chippewa
American Indian: Choctaw
American Indian: Colville
American Indian: Comanche
American Indian: Cree
American Indian: Creek
American Indian: Crow
American Indian: Delaware
American Indian: Houma
American Indian: Iroquois
American Indian: Kiowa
American Indian: Latin American Indians
American Indian: Lumbee
American Indian: Menominee
American Indian: Navajo
American Indian: Osage
American Indian: Ottawa
American Indian: Paiute
American Indian: Pima
American Indian: Potawatomi

American Indian: Pueblo
American Indian: Puget Sound Salish
American Indian: Seminole
American Indian: Shoshone
American Indian: Sioux
American Indian: Tohono O'Odham
American Indian: Ute
American Indian: Yakama
American Indian: Yaqui
American Indian: Yuman
Apache *See American Indian: Apache*
Arab
Arab/Arabic *See Arab: Arab/Arabic*
Arab: Arab/Arabic
Arab: Egyptian
Arab: Iraqi
Arab: Jordanian
Arab: Lebanese
Arab: Moroccan
Arab: Other
Arab: Palestinian
Arab: Syrian
Argentinean *See Hispanic: Argentinean*
Armenian
Asian
Asian: Bangladeshi
Asian: Cambodian
Asian: Chinese, except Taiwanese
Asian: Filipino
Asian: Hmong
Asian: Indian
Asian: Indonesian
Asian: Japanese
Asian: Korean
Asian: Laotian
Asian: Malaysian
Asian: Other Asian, not specified
Asian: Other Asian, specified
Asian: Pakistani
Asian: Sri Lankan
Asian: Taiwanese
Asian: Thai
Asian: Vietnamese
Assyrian/Chaldean/Syriac
Australian
Austrian
Bahamian *See West Indian: Bahamian, excluding Hispanic*
Bangladeshi *See Asian: Bangladeshi*
Barbadian *See West Indian: Barbadian, excluding Hispanic*
Basque
Belgian
Belizean *See West Indian: Belizean, excluding Hispanic*
Bermudan *See West Indian: Bermudan, excluding Hispanic*
Blackfeet *See American Indian: Blackfeet*
Bolivian *See Hispanic: Bolivian*
Brazilian
British
British West Indian *See West Indian: British West Indian, excluding Hispanic*
Bulgarian
Cambodian *See Asian: Cambodian*
Canadian

Cape Verdean *See African, sub-Saharan: Cape Verdean*
Carpatho Rusyn
Celtic
Central American: *See Hispanic: Central American*
Cherokee *See American Indian: Cherokee*
Cheyenne *See American Indian: Cheyenne*
Chickasaw *See American Indian: Chickasaw*
Chilean *See Hispanic: Chilean*
Chinese, except Taiwanese *See Asian: Chinese, except Taiwanese*
Chippewa *See American Indian: Chippewa*
Choctaw *See American Indian: Choctaw*
Colombian *See Hispanic: Colombian*
Colville *See American Indian: Colville*
Comanche *See American Indian: Comanche*
Costa Rican *See Hispanic: Costa Rican*
Cree *See American Indian: Cree*
Creek *See American Indian: Creek*
Croatian
Crow *See American Indian: Crow*
Cuban *See Hispanic: Cuban*
Cypriot
Czech
Czechoslovakian
Danish
Delaware *See American Indian: Delaware*
Dominican Republic *See Hispanic: Dominican Republic*
Dutch
Dutch West Indian *See West Indian: Dutch West Indian, excluding Hispanic*
Eastern European
Ecuadorian *See Hispanic: Ecuadorian*
Egyptian *See Arab: Egyptian*
English
Eskimo *See Alaska Native: Eskimo*
Estonian
Ethiopian *See African, sub-Saharan: Ethiopian*
European
Fijian *See Hawaii Native/Pacific Islander: Fijian*
Filipino *See Asian: Filipino*
Finnish
French Canadian
French, except Basque
German
German Russian
Ghanian *See African, sub-Saharan: Ghanian*
Greek
Guamanian or Chamorro *See Hawaii Native/Pacific Islander: Guamanian or Chamorro*
Guatemalan *See Hispanic: Guatemalan*
Guyanese
Haitian *See West Indian: Haitian, excluding Hispanic*
Hawaii Native/Pacific Islander
Hawaii Native/Pacific Islander: Fijian
Hawaii Native/Pacific Islander: Guamanian or Chamorro
Hawaii Native/Pacific Islander: Melanesian
Hawaii Native/Pacific Islander: Micronesian
Hawaii Native/Pacific Islander: Native Hawaiian

Hawaii Native/Pacific Islander: Other Melanesian
Hawaii Native/Pacific Islander: Other Micronesian
Hawaii Native/Pacific Islander: Other Pacific Islander, not specified
Hawaii Native/Pacific Islander: Other Pacific Islander, specified
Hawaii Native/Pacific Islander: Other Polynesian
Hawaii Native/Pacific Islander: Polynesian
Hawaii Native/Pacific Islander: Samoan
Hawaii Native/Pacific Islander: Tongan
Hispanic or Latino
Hispanic: Argentinean
Hispanic: Bolivian
Hispanic: Central American
Hispanic: Chilean
Hispanic: Colombian
Hispanic: Costa Rican
Hispanic: Cuban
Hispanic: Dominican Republic
Hispanic: Ecuadorian
Hispanic: Guatemalan
Hispanic: Honduran
Hispanic: Mexican
Hispanic: Nicaraguan
Hispanic: Other
Hispanic: Other Central American
Hispanic: Other South American
Hispanic: Panamanian
Hispanic: Paraguayan
Hispanic: Peruvian
Hispanic: Puerto Rican
Hispanic: Salvadoran
Hispanic: South American
Hispanic: Uruguayan
Hispanic: Venezuelan
Hmong *See Asian: Hmong*
Honduran *See Hispanic: Honduran*
Houma *See American Indian: Houma*
Hungarian
Icelander
Indian, American *See American Indian*
Indian, Asian *See Asian: Indian*
Indonesian *See Asian: Indonesian*
Iranian
Iraqi *See Arab: Iraqi*
Irish
Iroquois *See American Indian: Iroquois*
Israeli
Italian
Jamaican *See West Indian: Jamaican, excluding Hispanic*
Japanese *See Asian: Japanese*
Jordanian *See Arab: Jordanian*
Kenyan *See African, sub-Saharan: Kenyan*
Kiowa *See American Indian: Kiowa*
Korean *See Asian: Korean*
Laotian *See Asian: Laotian*
Latin American Indians *See American Indian: Latin American Indians*
Latino *See Hispanic or Latino*
Latvian
Lebanese *See Arab: Lebanese*
Liberian *See African, sub-Saharan: Liberian*
Lithuanian
Lumbee *See American Indian: Lumbee*
Luxemburger
Macedonian
Malaysian *See Asian: Malaysian*
Maltese

Melanesian: *See Hawaii Native/Pacific Islander: Melanesian*
Menominee *See American Indian: Menominee*
Mexican *See Hispanic: Mexican*
Micronesian: *See Hawaii Native/Pacific Islander: Micronesian*
Moroccan *See Arab: Moroccan*
Native Hawaiian *See Hawaii Native/Pacific Islander: Native Hawaiian*
Navajo *See American Indian: Navajo*
New Zealander
Nicaraguan *See Hispanic: Nicaraguan*
Nigerian *See African, sub-Saharan: Nigerian*
Northern European
Norwegian
Osage *See American Indian: Osage*
Ottawa *See American Indian: Ottawa*
Paiute *See American Indian: Paiute*
Pakistani *See Asian: Pakistani*
Palestinian *See Arab: Palestinian*
Panamanian *See Hispanic: Panamanian*
Paraguayan *See Hispanic: Paraguayan*
Pennsylvania German
Peruvian *See Hispanic: Peruvian*
Pima *See American Indian: Pima*
Polish
Polynesian: *See Hawaii Native/Pacific Islander: Polynesian*
Portuguese
Potawatomi *See American Indian: Potawatomi*
Pueblo *See American Indian: Pueblo*
Puerto Rican *See Hispanic: Puerto Rican*
Puget Sound Salish *See American Indian: Puget Sound Salish*
Romanian
Russian
Salvadoran *See Hispanic: Salvadoran*
Samoan *See Hawaii Native/Pacific Islander: Samoan*
Scandinavian
Scotch-Irish
Scottish
Seminole *See American Indian: Seminole*
Senegalese *See African, sub-Saharan: Senegalese*
Serbian
Shoshone *See American Indian: Shoshone*
Sierra Leonean *See African, sub-Saharan: Sierra Leonean*
Sioux *See American Indian: Sioux*
Slavic
Slovak
Slovene
Somalian *See African, sub-Saharan: Somalian*
South African *See African, sub-Saharan: South African*
South American: *See Hispanic: South American*
Soviet Union
Sri Lankan *See Asian: Sri Lankan*
sub-Saharan African *See African, sub-Saharan*
Sudanese *See African, sub-Saharan: Sudanese*
Swedish
Swiss
Syrian *See Arab: Syrian*
Taiwanese *See Asian: Taiwanese*
Thai *See Asian: Thai*
Tlingit-Haida *See Alaska Native: Tlingit-Haida*
Tohono O'Odham *See American Indian: Tohono O'Odham*
Tongan *See Hawaii Native/Pacific Islander: Tongan*

Trinidadian and Tobagonian *See West Indian: Trinidadian and Tobagonian, excluding Hispanic*
Turkish
U.S. Virgin Islander *See West Indian: U.S. Virgin Islander, excluding Hispanic*
Ugandan *See African, sub-Saharan: Ugandan*
Ukrainian
United States or American
Uruguayan *See Hispanic: Uruguayan*
Ute *See American Indian: Ute*
Venezuelan *See Hispanic: Venezuelan*
Vietnamese *See Asian: Vietnamese*
Welsh
West Indian, excluding Hispanic
West Indian: Bahamian, excluding Hispanic
West Indian: Barbadian, excluding Hispanic
West Indian: Belizean, excluding Hispanic
West Indian: Bermudan, excluding Hispanic
West Indian: British West Indian, excluding Hispanic
West Indian: Dutch West Indian, excluding Hispanic
West Indian: Haitian, excluding Hispanic
West Indian: Jamaican, excluding Hispanic
West Indian: Other, excluding Hispanic
West Indian: Trinidadian and Tobagonian, excluding Hispanic
West Indian: U.S. Virgin Islander, excluding Hispanic
West Indian: West Indian, excluding Hispanic
White
White: Hispanic
White: Not Hispanic
Yakama *See American Indian: Yakama*
Yaqui *See American Indian: Yaqui*
Yugoslavian
Yuman *See American Indian: Yuman*
Zairian *See African, sub-Saharan: Zairian*
Zimbabwean *See African, sub-Saharan: Zimbabwean*

User's Guide: Hispanic Population

Places Covered

Ranking tables cover all counties and all places in Illinois with populations of 10,000 or more.

Source of Data

CENSUS 2000

Data for this chapter was derived from following source: *U.S. Bureau of the Census, Census of Population and Housing, 2000: Summary File 4.* Summary File 4 (SF 4) contains sample data, which is the information compiled from the questions asked of a sample (generally 1-in-6) of all people and housing units. Summary File 4 is repeated or iterated for the total population and 335 additional population groups. This chapter focuses on the following 24 population groups:

Hispanic or Latino (of any race)
    Central American
        Costa Rican
        Guatemalan
        Honduran
        Nicaraguan
        Panamanian
        Salvadoran
    Cuban
    Dominican (Dominican Republic)
    Mexican
    Puerto Rican
    South American
        Argentinian
        Bolivian
        Chilean
        Colombian
        Ecuadorian
        Paraguayan
        Peruvian
        Uruguayan
        Venezuelan
    Spaniard
    Other Hispanic or Latino

Please note that the above list only includes Spanish-speaking population groups. Groups such as Brazilian are not classified as Hispanic by the Bureau of the Census because they primarily speak Portugese.

In order for any of the tables for a specific group to be shown in Summary File 4, the data must meet a minimum population threshold. For Summary File 4, all tables are repeated for each race group, American Indian and Alaska Native tribe, and Hispanic or Latino group if the 100-percent count of people of that specific group in a particular geographic area is 100 or more. There also must be 50 or more unweighted people of that specific group in a particular geographic area. For example, if there are 100 or more 100-percent people tabulated as Chilean in County A, and there are 50 or more unweighted people, then all matrices for Chilean are shown in SF 4 for County A.

To maintain confidentiality, the Census Bureau applies statistical procedures that introduce some uncertainty into data for small geographic areas with small population groups. Therefore, tables may contain both sampling and nonsampling error.

In an iterated file such as SF 4, the universes *households, families,* and *occupied housing units* are classified by the race or ethnic group of the householder. In any population table where there is no note, the universe classification is always based on the race or ethnicity of the person. In all housing tables, the universe classification is based on the race or ethnicity of the householder.

Comparing SF 4 Estimates with Corresponding Values in SF 1 and SF 2

As in earlier censuses, the responses from the sample of households reporting on long forms must be weighted to reflect the entire population. Specifically, each responding household represents, on average, six or seven other households who reported using short forms. One consequence of the weighting procedures is that each estimate based on the long form responses has an associated confidence interval. These confidence intervals are wider (as a percentage of the estimate) for geographic areas with smaller populations and for characteristics that occur less frequently in the area being examined (such as the proportion of people in poverty in a middle-income neighborhood). In order to release as much useful information as possible, statisticians must balance a number of factors. In particular, for Census 2000, the Bureau of the Census created weighting areas—geographic areas from which about two hundred or more long forms were completed—which are large enough to produce good quality estimates. If smaller weighting areas had been used, the confidence intervals around the estimates would have been significantly wider, rendering many estimates less useful due to their lower reliability. The disadvantage of using weighting areas this large is that, for smaller geographic areas within them, the estimates of characteristics that are also reported on the short form will not match the counts reported in SF 1 or SF 2. Examples of these characteristics are the total number of people, the number of people reporting specific racial categories, and the number of housing units. The official values for items reported on the short form come from SF 1 and SF 2. The differences between the long form estimates in SF 4 and values in SF 1 or SF 2 are particularly noticeable for the smallest places, tracts, and block groups. The long form estimates of total population and total housing units in SF 4 will, however, match the SF 1 and SF 2 counts for larger geographic areas such as counties and states, and will be essentially the same for medium and large cities. This phenomenon also occurred for the 1990 Census, although in that case, the weighting areas included relatively small places. As a result, the long form estimates matched the short form counts for those places, but the confidence intervals around the estimates of characteristics collected only on the long form were often significantly wider (as a percentage of the estimate). SF 1 gives exact numbers even for very small groups and areas; whereas, SF 4 gives estimates for small groups and areas such as tracts and small places that are less exact. The goal of SF 4 is to identify large differences among areas or large changes over time. Estimates for small areas and small population groups often do exhibit large changes from one census to the next, so having the capability to measure them is worthwhile.

Topics

POPULATION

Total Population: Sample count of total population.

Hispanic Population: The data on the Hispanic or Latino population, which was asked of all people, were derived from answers to long-form questionnaire Item 5, and short-form questionnaire Item 7. The terms "Spanish," "Hispanic origin," and "Latino" are used interchangeably. Some respondents identify with all three terms, while others may identify with only one of these three specific terms. Hispanics or Latinos who identify with the terms "Spanish," "Hispanic," or "Latino" are those who classify themselves in one of the specific Hispanic or Latino categories listed on the questionnaire — "Mexican," "Puerto Rican," or "Cuban" — as well as those who indicate that they are "other Spanish, Hispanic, or Latino." People who do not identify with one of the specific origins listed on the questionnaire but indicate that they are "other Spanish, Hispanic, or Latino" are those whose origins are from Spain, the Spanish-speaking countries of Central or South America, the Dominican Republic, or people identifying themselves generally as Spanish, Spanish-American, Hispanic, Hispano, Latino, and so on. All write-in responses to the "other Spanish/Hispanic/Latino" category were coded. Origin can be viewed as the heritage, nationality group, lineage, or country of birth of the person or the person's parents or ancestors before their arrival in the United States. People who identify their origin as Spanish, Hispanic, or Latino may be of any race.

Population groups whose primary language is not Spanish are not classified as Hispanic by the Bureau of the Census and are not included in this chapter (eg. Brazilian).

AGE

Median Age: Divides the age distribution into two equal parts: one-half of the cases falling below the median age and one-half above the median. Median age is computed on the basis of a single year of age standard distribution.

The data on age, which was asked of all people, were derived from answers to the long-form questionnaire Item 4 and short-form questionnaire Item 6. The age classification is based on the age of the person in complete years as of April 1, 2000. The age of the person usually was derived from their date of birth information. Their reported age was used only when date of birth information was unavailable.

HOUSEHOLD SIZE

Average Household Size: A measure obtained by dividing the number of people in households by the total number of households (or householders). In cases where household members are tabulated by race or Hispanic origin, household members are classified by the race or Hispanic origin of the householder rather than the race or Hispanic origin of each individual. Average household size is rounded to the nearest hundredth.

LANGUAGE SPOKEN AT HOME

English Only: Number and percentage of population 5 years and over who report speaking English-only at home.

Spanish: Number and percentage of population 5 years and over who report speaking Spanish at home.

Language spoken at home data were derived from answers to long-form questionnaire Items 11a and 11b, which were asked of a sample of the population. Data were edited to include in tabulations only the population 5 years old and over. Questions 11a and 11b referred to languages spoken at home in an effort to measure the current use of languages other than English. People who knew languages other than English but did not use them at home or who only used them elsewhere were excluded. Most people who reported speaking a language other than English at home also speak English. The questions did not permit determination of the primary or dominant language of people who spoke both English and another language.

FOREIGN-BORN

Foreign Born: Number and percentage of population who were not U.S. citizens at birth. Foreign-born people are those who indicated they were either a U.S. citizen by naturalization or they were not a citizen of the United States.

Foreign-Born Naturalized Citizens: Number and percentage of population who were not U.S. citizens at birth but became U.S. citizens by naturalization.

The data on place of birth were derived from answers to long-form questionnaire Item 12 which was asked of a sample of the population. Respondents were asked to report the U.S. state, Puerto Rico, U.S. Island Area, or foreign country where they were born. People not reporting a place of birth were assigned the state or country of birth of another family member or their residence 5 years earlier, or were imputed the response of another person with similar characteristics. People born outside the United States were asked to report their place of birth according to current international boundaries. Since numerous changes in boundaries of foreign countries have occurred in the last century, some people may have reported their place of birth in terms of boundaries that existed at the time of their birth or emigration, or in accordance with their own national preference.

EDUCATIONAL ATTAINMENT

High School Graduates: Number and percentage of the population age 25 and over who have a high school diploma or higher. This category includes people whose highest degree was a high school diploma or its equivalent, people who attended college but did not receive a degree, and people who received a college, university, or professional degree. People who reported completing the 12th grade but not receiving a diploma are not high school graduates.

4-Years College Graduates: Number and percentage of the population age 25 and over who have a 4-year college, university, or professional degree.

Data on educational attainment were derived from answers to long-form questionnaire Item 9, which was asked of a sample of the population. Data on attainment are tabulated for the population 25 years old and over.

The order in which degrees were listed on the questionnaire suggested that doctorate degrees were "higher" than professional school degrees, which were "higher" than master's degrees. The question included instructions for people currently enrolled in school to report the level of the previous grade attended or the highest degree received. Respondents who did not report educational attainment or enrollment level were assigned the attainment of a person of the same age, race, Hispanic or Latino origin, occupation and sex, where possible, who resided in the same or a nearby area. Respondents who filled more than one box were edited to the highest level or degree reported.

The question included a response category that allowed respondents to report completing the 12th grade without receiving a high school diploma. It allowed people who received either a high school diploma or the equivalent (Test of General Educational Development—G.E.D.) and did not attend college, to be reported as "high school graduate(s)." The category "Associate degree" included people whose highest degree is an associate degree, which generally requires 2 years of college level work and is either in an occupational program that prepares them for a specific occupation, or an academic program primarily in the arts and sciences. The course work may or may not be transferable to a bachelor's degree. Master's degrees include the traditional MA and MS degrees and field-specific degrees, such as MSW, MEd, MBA, MLS, and MEng. Some examples of professional degrees include medicine, dentistry, chiropractic, optometry, osteopathic medicine, pharmacy, podiatry, veterinary medicine, law, and theology. Vocational and technical training such as barber school training; business, trade, technical, and vocational schools; or other training for a specific trade, are specifically excluded.

INCOME AND POVERTY

Median Household Income (in dollars): Includes the income of the householder and all other individuals 15 years old and over in the household, whether they are related to the householder or not. The median divides the income distribution into two equal parts: one-half of the cases falling below the median income and one-half above the median. For households, the median income is based on the distribution of the total number of households including those with no income. Median income for households is computed on the basis of a standard distribution and is rounded to the nearest whole dollar.

Per Capita Income (in dollars): Per capita income is the mean income computed for every man, woman, and child in a particular group. It is derived by dividing the total income of a particular group by the total population in that group. Per capita income is rounded to the nearest whole dollar.

The data on income in 1999 were derived from answers to long-form questionnaire Items 31 and 32, which were asked of a sample of the population 15 years old and over. "Total income" is the sum of the amounts reported separately for wage or salary income; net self-employment income; interest, dividends, or net rental or royalty income or income from estates and trusts; social security or railroad retirement income; Supplemental Security Income (SSI); public assistance or welfare payments; retirement, survivor, or disability pensions; and all other income.

Receipts from the following sources are not included as income: capital gains, money received from the sale of property (unless the recipient was engaged in the business of selling such property); the value of income "in kind" from food stamps, public housing subsidies, medical care, employer contributions for individuals, etc.; withdrawal of bank deposits; money borrowed; tax refunds; exchange of money between relatives living in the same household; and gifts and lump-sum inheritances, insurance payments, and other types of lump-sum receipts.

The eight types of income reported in the census are defined as follows:

Wage or salary income. Wage or salary income includes total money earnings received for work performed as an employee during the calendar year 1999. It includes wages, salary, armed forces pay, commissions, tips, piece-rate payments, and cash bonuses earned before deductions were made for taxes, bonds, pensions, union dues, etc.

Self-employment income. Self-employment income includes both farm and nonfarm self-employment income. Nonfarm self-employment income includes net money income (gross receipts minus expenses) from one's own business, professional enterprise, or partnership. Gross receipts include the value of all goods sold and services rendered. Expenses include costs of goods purchased, rent, heat, light, power, depreciation charges, wages and salaries paid, business taxes (not personal income taxes), etc. Farm self-employment income includes net money income (gross receipts minus operating expenses) from the operation of a farm by a person on his or her own account, as an owner, renter, or sharecropper. Gross receipts include the value of all products sold, government farm programs, money received from the rental of farm equipment to others, and incidental receipts from the sale of wood, sand, gravel, etc. Operating expenses include cost of feed, fertilizer, seed, and other farming supplies, cash wages paid to farmhands, depreciation charges, cash rent, interest on farm mortgages, farm building repairs, farm taxes (not state and federal personal income taxes), etc. The value of fuel, food, or other farm products used for family living is not included as part of net income.

Interest, dividends, or net rental income. Interest, dividends, or net rental income includes interest on savings or bonds, dividends from stockholdings or membership in associations, net income from rental of property to others and receipts from boarders or lodgers, net royalties, and periodic payments from an estate or trust fund.

Social Security income. Social security income includes social security pensions and survivors benefits, permanent disability insurance payments made by the Social Security Administration prior to deductions for medical insurance, and railroad retirement insurance checks from the U.S. government. Medicare reimbursements are not included.

Supplemental Security Income (SSI). Supplemental Security Income (SSI) is a nationwide U.S. assistance program administered by the Social Security Administration that guarantees a minimum level of income for needy aged, blind, or disabled individuals. The census questionnaire for Puerto Rico asked about the receipt of SSI; however, SSI is not a federally administered program in Puerto Rico. Therefore, it is probably not being interpreted by most respondents as the same as SSI in the United States. The only way a resident of Puerto Rico could have appropriately reported SSI would have been if they lived in the United States at any time during calendar year 1999 and received SSI.

Public assistance income. Public assistance income includes general assistance and Temporary Assistance to Needy Families (TANF). Separate payments received for hospital or other medical care (vendor payments) are excluded. This does not include Supplemental Security Income (SSI).

Retirement income. Retirement income includes: (1) retirement pensions and survivor benefits from a former employer; labor union; or federal, state, or local government; and the U.S. military; (2) income from workers' compensation; disability income from companies or unions; federal, state, or local government; and the U.S. military; (3) periodic receipts from annuities and insurance; and (4) regular income from IRA and KEOGH plans. This does not include social security income.

All other income. All other income includes unemployment compensation, Veterans' Administration (VA) payments, alimony and child support, contributions received periodically from people not living in the household, military family allotments, and other kinds of periodic income other than earnings.

Poverty Status: Number and percentage of population with income in 1999 below the poverty level. Based on individuals for whom poverty status is determined. Poverty status was determined for all people except institutionalized people, people in military group quarters, people in college dormitories, and unrelated individuals under 15 years old.

The poverty status of families and unrelated individuals in 1999 was determined using 48 thresholds (income cutoffs) arranged in a two dimensional matrix. The matrix consists of family size (from 1 person to 9 or more people) cross-classified by presence and number of family members under 18 years old (from no children present to 8 or more children present). Unrelated individuals and 2-person families were further differentiated by the age of the reference person (RP) (under 65 years old and 65 years old and over).

To determine a person's poverty status, one compares the person's total family income with the poverty threshold appropriate for that person's family size and composition. If the total income of that person's family is less than the threshold appropriate for that family, then the person is considered poor, together with every member of his or her family. If a person is not living with anyone related by birth, marriage, or adoption, then the person's own income is compared with his or her poverty threshold.

HOUSING

Homeownership: Number and percentage of housing units that are owner-occupied.

The data on tenure, which was asked at all occupied housing units, were obtained from answers to long-form questionnaire Item 33, and short-form questionnaire Item 2. All occupied housing units are classified as either owner occupied or renter occupied.

A housing unit is owner occupied if the owner or co-owner lives in the unit even if it is mortgaged or not fully paid for. The owner or co-owner must live in the unit and usually is Person 1 on the questionnaire. The unit is "Owned by you or someone in this household with a mortgage or loan" if it is being purchased with a mortgage or some other debt arrangement, such as a deed of trust, trust deed, contract to purchase, land contract, or purchase agreement. The unit is also considered owned with a mortgage if it is built on leased land and there is a mortgage on the unit. Mobile homes occupied by owners with installment loans balances are also included in this category.

Median Gross Rent (in dollars): Median monthly gross rent on specified renter-occupied and specified vacant-for-rent units. Specified renter-occupied and specified vacant-for-rent units exclude 1-family houses on 10 acres or more.

The data on gross rent were obtained from answers to long-form questionnaire Items 45a-d, which were asked on a sample basis. Gross rent is the contract rent plus the estimated average monthly cost of utilities (electricity, gas, water and sewer) and fuels (oil, coal, kerosene, wood, etc.) if these are paid by the renter (or paid for the renter by someone else). Gross rent is intended to eliminate differentials that result from varying practices with respect to the inclusion of utilities and fuels as part of the rental payment. The estimated costs of utilities and fuels are reported on an annual basis but are converted to monthly figures for the tabulations. Renter units occupied without payment of cash rent are shown separately as "No cash rent" in the tabulations.

Housing units that are renter occupied without payment of cash rent are shown separately as "No cash rent" in census data products. The unit may be owned by friends or relatives who live elsewhere and who allow occupancy without charge. Rent-free houses or apartments may be provided to compensate caretakers, ministers, tenant farmers, sharecroppers, or others.

Contract rent is the monthly rent agreed to or contracted for, regardless of any furnishings, utilities, fees, meals, or services that may be included. For vacant units, it is the monthly rent asked for the rental unit at the time of enumeration.

If the contract rent includes rent for a business unit or for living quarters occupied by another household, only that part of the rent estimated to be for the respondent's unit was included. Excluded was any rent paid for additional units or for business premises.

If a renter pays rent to the owner of a condominium or cooperative, and the condominium fee or cooperative carrying charge also is paid by the renter to the owner, the condominium fee or carrying charge was included as rent.

If a renter receives payments from lodgers or roomers who are listed as members of the household, the rent without deduction for any payments received from the lodgers or roomers was to be reported. The respondent was to report the rent agreed to or contracted for even if paid by someone else such as friends or relatives living elsewhere, a church or welfare agency, or the government through subsidies or vouchers.

The median divides the rent distribution into two equal parts: one-half of the cases falling below the median contract rent and one-half above the median. Median contract rents are computed on the basis of a standard distribution and are rounded to the nearest whole dollar. Units reported as "No cash rent" are excluded.

Median Home Value (in dollars): Reported by the owner of specified owner-occupied or specified vacant-for-sale housing units. Specified owner-occupied and specified vacant-for-sale housing units include only 1-family houses on less than 10 acres without a business or medical office on the property. The data for "specified units" exclude mobile homes, houses with a business or medical office, houses on 10 or more acres, and housing units in multi-unit buildings.

The data on value (also referred to as "price asked" for vacant units) were obtained from answers to long-form questionnaire Item 51, which was asked on a sample basis at owner-occupied housing units and units that were being bought, or vacant for sale at the time of enumeration. Value is the respondent's estimate of how much the property (house and lot, mobile home and lot, or condominium unit) would sell for if it were for sale. If the house or mobile home was owned or being bought, but the land on which it sits was not, the respondent was asked to estimate the combined value of the house or mobile home and the land. For vacant units, value was the price asked for the property. Value was tabulated separately for all owner-occupied and vacant-for-sale housing units, owner-occupied and vacant-for-sale mobile homes, and specified owner-occupied and specified vacant-for-sale housing units.

The median divides the value distribution into two equal parts: one-half of the cases falling below the median value of the property (house and lot, mobile home and lot, or condominium unit) and one-half above the median. Median values are computed on the basis of a standard distribution and are rounded to the nearest hundred dollars.

User's Guide: Asian Population

Places Covered

Ranking tables cover all counties and places in Illinois with Asian and/or Native Hawaiian and other Pacific Islander residents.

Source of Data

CENSUS 2000

Data for this chapter was derived from following source: *U.S. Bureau of the Census, Census of Population and Housing, 2000: Summary File 4.* Summary File 4 (SF 4) contains sample data, which is the information compiled from the questions asked of a sample (generally 1-in-6) of all people and housing units. Summary File 4 is repeated or iterated for the total population and 335 additional population groups. This chapter focuses on the following 23 population groups:

Asian
     Asian Indian
     Bangladeshi
     Cambodian
     Chinese (except Taiwanese)
     Filipino
     Hmong
     Indonesian
     Japanese
     Korean
     Laotian
     Malaysian
     Pakistani
     Sri Lankan
     Taiwanese
     Thai
     Vietnamese
Native Hawaiian and Other Pacific Islander
     Fijian
     Guamanian or Chamorro
     Hawaiian, Native
     Samoan
     Tongan

Please note that this chapter only includes people who responded to the question on race by indicating only one race. These people are classified by the Census Bureau as the race *alone* population. For example, respondents reporting a single detailed Asian group, such as Korean or Filipino, would be included in the Asian *alone* population. Respondents reporting more than one detailed Asian group, such as Chinese and Japanese or Asian Indian and Chinese and Vietnamese would also be included in the Asian *alone* population. This is because all of the detailed groups in these example combinations are part of the larger Asian race category. The same criteria apply to the Native Hawaiian and Other Pacific Islander groups.

In order for any of the tables for a specific group to be shown in Summary File 4, the data must meet a minimum population threshold. For Summary File 4, all tables are repeated for each race group, American Indian and Alaska Native tribe, and Hispanic or Latino group if the 100-percent count of people of that specific group in a particular geographic area is 100 or more. There also must be 50 or more unweighted people of that specific group in a particular geographic area. For example, if there are 100 or more 100-percent people tabulated as Korean in County A, and there are 50 or more unweighted people, then all matrices for Korean are shown in SF 4 for County A.

To maintain confidentiality, the Census Bureau applies statistical procedures that introduce some uncertainty into data for small geographic areas with small population groups. Therefore, tables may contain both sampling and nonsampling error.

In an iterated file such as SF 4, the universes *households, families,* and *occupied housing units* are classified by the race or ethnic group of the householder. In any population table where there is no note, the universe classification is always based on the race or ethnicity of the person. In all housing tables, the universe classification is based on the race or ethnicity of the householder.

Comparing SF 4 Estimates with Corresponding Values in SF 1 and SF 2

As in earlier censuses, the responses from the sample of households reporting on long forms must be weighted to reflect the entire population. Specifically, each responding household represents, on average, six or seven other households who reported using short forms. One consequence of the weighting procedures is that each estimate based on the long form responses has an associated confidence interval. These confidence intervals are wider (as a percentage of the estimate) for geographic areas with smaller populations and for characteristics that occur less frequently in the area being examined (such as the proportion of people in poverty in a middle-income neighborhood). In order to release as much useful information as possible, statisticians must balance a number of factors. In particular, for Census 2000, the Bureau of the Census created weighting areas—geographic areas from which about two hundred or more long forms were completed—which are large enough to produce good quality estimates. If smaller weighting areas had been used, the confidence intervals around the estimates would have been significantly wider, rendering many estimates less useful due to their lower reliability. The disadvantage of using weighting areas this large is that, for smaller geographic areas within them, the estimates of characteristics that are also reported on the short form will not match the counts reported in SF 1 or SF 2. Examples of these characteristics are the total number of people, the number of people reporting specific racial categories, and the number of housing units. The official values for items reported on the short form come from SF 1 and SF 2. The differences between the long form estimates in SF 4 and values in SF 1 or SF 2 are particularly noticeable for the smallest places, tracts, and block groups. The long form estimates of total population and total housing units in SF 4 will, however, match the SF 1 and SF 2 counts for larger geographic areas such as counties and states, and will be essentially the same for medium and large cities. This phenomenon also occurred for the 1990 Census, although in that case, the weighting areas included relatively small places. As a result, the long form estimates matched the short form counts for those places, but the confidence intervals around the estimates of characteristics collected only on the long form were often significantly wider (as a percentage of the estimate). SF 1 gives exact numbers even for very small groups and areas; whereas, SF 4 gives estimates for small groups and areas such as tracts and small places that are less exact. The goal of SF 4 is to identify large differences among areas or large changes over time. Estimates for small areas and small population groups often do exhibit large changes from one census to the next, so having the capability to measure them is worthwhile.

Topics

POPULATION

Total Population: Sample count of total population of all races.

Asian Population: A person having origins in any of the original peoples of the Far East, Southeast Asia, or the Indian subcontinent including, for example, Cambodia, China, India, Japan, Korea, Malaysia, Pakistan, the Philippine Islands, Thailand, and Vietnam. It includes Asian Indian, Bangladeshi, Cambodian, Chinese (except Taiwanese), Filipino, Hmong, Indonesian, Japanese, Korean, Laotian, Malaysian, Pakistani, Sri Lankan, Taiwanese, Thai, and Vietnamese.

Native Hawaiian or Other Pacific Islander (NHPI) Population: A person having origins in any of the original peoples of Hawaii, Guam, Samoa, or other Pacific Islands. It includes people who indicate their race as Fijian, Guamanian or Chamorro, Native Hawaiian, Samoan, and Tongan.

The data on race, which was asked of all people, were derived from answers to long-form questionnaire Item 6 and short-form questionnaire Item 8. The concept of race, as used by the Census Bureau, reflects self-identification by people according to the race or races with which they most closely identify. These categories are socio-political constructs and should not be interpreted as being scientific or anthropological in nature. Furthermore, the race categories include both racial and national-origin groups.

If an individual did not provide a race response, the race or races of the householder or other household members were assigned using specific rules of precedence of household relationship. For example, if race was missing for a natural-born child in the household, then either the race or races of the householder, another natural-born child, or the spouse of the householder were assigned. If race was not reported for anyone in the household, the race or races of a householder in a previously processed household were assigned.

AGE

Median Age: Divides the age distribution into two equal parts: one-half of the cases falling below the median age and one-half above the median. Median age is computed on the basis of a single year of age standard distribution.

The data on age, which was asked of all people, were derived from answers to the long-form questionnaire Item 4 and short-form questionnaire Item 6. The age classification is based on the age of the person in complete years as of April 1, 2000. The age of the person usually was derived from their date of birth information. Their reported age was used only when date of birth information was unavailable.

HOUSEHOLD SIZE

Average Household Size: A measure obtained by dividing the number of people in households by the total number of households (or householders). In cases where household members are tabulated by race or Hispanic origin, household members are classified by the race or Hispanic origin of the householder rather than the race or Hispanic origin of each individual. Average household size is rounded to the nearest hundredth.

LANGUAGE SPOKEN AT HOME

English Only: Number and percentage of population 5 years and over who report speaking English-only at home.

Language spoken at home data were derived from answers to long-form questionnaire Items 11a and 11b, which were asked of a sample of the population. Data were edited to include in tabulations only the population 5 years old and over. Questions 11a and 11b referred to languages spoken at home in an effort to measure the current use of languages other than English. People who knew languages other than English but did not use them at home or who only used them elsewhere were excluded. Most people who reported speaking a language other than English at home also speak English. The questions did not permit determination of the primary or dominant language of people who spoke both English and another language.

FOREIGN-BORN

Foreign Born: Number and percentage of population who were not U.S. citizens at birth. Foreign-born people are those who indicated they were either a U.S. citizen by naturalization or they were not a citizen of the United States.

Foreign-Born Naturalized Citizens: Number and percentage of population who were not U.S. citizens at birth but became U.S. citizens by naturalization.

The data on place of birth were derived from answers to long-form questionnaire Item 12 which was asked of a sample of the population. Respondents were asked to report the U.S. state, Puerto Rico, U.S. Island Area, or foreign country where they were born. People not reporting a place of birth were assigned the state or country of birth of another family member or their residence 5 years earlier, or were imputed the response of another person with similar characteristics. People born outside the United States were asked to report their place of birth according to current international boundaries. Since numerous changes in boundaries of foreign countries have occurred in the last century, some people may have reported their place of birth in terms of boundaries that existed at the time of their birth or emigration, or in accordance with their own national preference.

EDUCATIONAL ATTAINMENT

High School Graduates: Number and percentage of the population age 25 and over who have a high school diploma or higher. This category includes people whose highest degree was a high school diploma or its equivalent, people who attended college but did not receive a degree, and people who received a college, university, or professional degree. People who reported completing the 12th grade but not receiving a diploma are not high school graduates.

Four-Year College Graduates: Number and percentage of the population age 25 and over who have a 4-year college, university, or professional degree.

Data on educational attainment were derived from answers to long-form questionnaire Item 9, which was asked of a sample of the population. Data on attainment are tabulated for the population 25 years old and over.

The order in which degrees were listed on the questionnaire suggested that doctorate degrees were "higher" than professional school degrees, which were "higher" than master's degrees. The question included instructions for people currently enrolled in school to report the level of the previous grade attended or the highest degree received.

Respondents who did not report educational attainment or enrollment level were assigned the attainment of a person of the same age, race, Hispanic or Latino origin, occupation and sex, where possible, who resided in the same or a nearby area. Respondents who filled more than one box were edited to the highest level or degree reported.

The question included a response category that allowed respondents to report completing the 12th grade without receiving a high school diploma. It allowed people who received either a high school diploma or the equivalent (Test of General Educational Development—G.E.D.) and did not attend college, to be reported as "high school graduate(s)." The category "Associate degree" included people whose highest degree is an associate degree, which generally requires 2 years of college level work and is either in an occupational program that prepares them for a specific occupation, or an academic program primarily in the arts and sciences. The course work may or may not be transferable to a bachelor's degree. Master's degrees include the traditional MA and MS degrees and field-specific degrees, such as MSW, MEd, MBA, MLS, and MEng. Some examples of professional degrees include medicine, dentistry, chiropractic, optometry, osteopathic medicine, pharmacy, podiatry, veterinary medicine, law, and theology. Vocational and technical training such as barber school training; business, trade, technical, and vocational schools; or other training for a specific trade, are specifically excluded.

INCOME AND POVERTY

Median Household Income (in dollars): Includes the income of the householder and all other individuals 15 years old and over in the household, whether they are related to the householder or not. The median divides the income distribution into two equal parts: one-half of the cases falling below the median income and one-half above the median. For households, the median income is based on the distribution of the total number of households including those with no income. Median income for households is computed on the basis of a standard distribution and is rounded to the nearest whole dollar.

Per Capita Income (in dollars): Per capita income is the mean income computed for every man, woman, and child in a particular group. It is derived by dividing the total income of a particular group by the total population in that group. Per capita income is rounded to the nearest whole dollar.

The data on income in 1999 were derived from answers to long-form questionnaire Items 31 and 32, which were asked of a sample of the population 15 years old and over. "Total income" is the sum of the amounts reported separately for wage or salary income; net self-employment income; interest, dividends, or net rental or royalty income or income from estates and trusts; social security or railroad retirement income; Supplemental Security Income (SSI); public assistance or welfare payments; retirement, survivor, or disability pensions; and all other income.

Receipts from the following sources are not included as income: capital gains, money received from the sale of property (unless the recipient was engaged in the business of selling such property); the value of income "in kind" from food stamps, public housing subsidies, medical care, employer contributions for individuals, etc.; withdrawal of bank deposits; money borrowed; tax refunds; exchange of money between relatives living in the same household; and gifts and lump-sum inheritances, insurance payments, and other types of lump-sum receipts.

The eight types of income reported in the census are defined as follows:

Wage or salary income. Wage or salary income includes total money earnings received for work performed as an employee during the calendar year 1999. It includes wages, salary, armed forces pay, commissions, tips, piece-rate payments, and cash bonuses earned before deductions were made for taxes, bonds, pensions, union dues, etc.

Self-employment income. Self-employment income includes both farm and nonfarm self-employment income. Nonfarm self-employment income includes net money income (gross receipts minus expenses) from one's own business, professional enterprise, or partnership. Gross receipts include the value of all goods sold and services rendered. Expenses include costs of goods purchased, rent, heat, light, power, depreciation charges, wages and salaries paid, business taxes (not personal income taxes), etc. Farm self-employment income includes net money income (gross receipts minus operating expenses) from the operation of a farm by a person on his or her own account, as an owner, renter, or sharecropper. Gross receipts include the value of all products sold, government farm programs, money received from the rental of farm equipment to others, and incidental receipts from the sale of wood, sand, gravel, etc. Operating expenses include cost of feed, fertilizer, seed, and other farming supplies, cash wages paid to farmhands, depreciation charges, cash rent, interest on farm mortgages, farm building repairs, farm taxes (not state and federal personal income taxes), etc. The value of fuel, food, or other farm products used for family living is not included as part of net income.

Interest, dividends, or net rental income. Interest, dividends, or net rental income includes interest on savings or bonds, dividends from stockholdings or membership in associations, net income from rental of property to others and receipts from boarders or lodgers, net royalties, and periodic payments from an estate or trust fund.

Social Security income. Social security income includes social security pensions and survivors benefits, permanent disability insurance payments made by the Social Security Administration prior to deductions for medical insurance, and railroad retirement insurance checks from the U.S. government. Medicare reimbursements are not included.

Supplemental Security Income (SSI). Supplemental Security Income (SSI) is a nationwide U.S. assistance program administered by the Social Security Administration that guarantees a minimum level of income for needy aged, blind, or disabled individuals. The census questionnaire for Puerto Rico asked about the receipt of SSI; however, SSI is not a federally administered program in Puerto Rico. Therefore, it is probably not being interpreted by most respondents as the same as SSI in the United States. The only way a resident of Puerto Rico could have appropriately reported SSI would have been if they lived in the United States at any time during calendar year 1999 and received SSI.

Public assistance income. Public assistance income includes general assistance and Temporary Assistance to Needy Families (TANF). Separate payments received for hospital or other medical care (vendor payments) are excluded. This does not include Supplemental Security Income (SSI).

Retirement income. Retirement income includes: (1) retirement pensions and survivor benefits from a former employer; labor union; or federal, state, or local government; and the U.S. military; (2) income from workers' compensation; disability income from companies or unions; federal, state, or local government; and the U.S. military; (3) periodic receipts from annuities and insurance; and (4) regular income from IRA and KEOGH plans. This does not include social security income.

All other income. All other income includes unemployment compensation, Veterans' Administration (VA) payments, alimony and child support, contributions received periodically from people not living in the household, military family allotments, and other kinds of periodic income other than earnings.

Poverty Status: Number and percentage of population with income in 1999 below the poverty level. Based on individuals for whom poverty status is determined. Poverty status was determined for all people except institutionalized people, people in military group quarters, people in college dormitories, and unrelated individuals under 15 years old.

The poverty status of families and unrelated individuals in 1999 was determined using 48 thresholds (income cutoffs) arranged in a two dimensional matrix. The matrix consists of family size (from 1 person to 9 or more people) cross-classified by presence and number of family members under 18 years old (from no children present to 8 or more children present). Unrelated individuals and 2-person families were further differentiated by the age of the reference person (RP) (under 65 years old and 65 years old and over).

To determine a person's poverty status, one compares the person's total family income with the poverty threshold appropriate for that person's family size and composition. If the total income of that person's family is less than the threshold appropriate for that family, then the person is considered poor, together with every member of his or her family. If a person is not living with anyone related by birth, marriage, or adoption, then the person's own income is compared with his or her poverty threshold.

HOUSING

Homeownership: Number and percentage of housing units that are owner-occupied.

The data on tenure, which was asked at all occupied housing units, were obtained from answers to long-form questionnaire Item 33, and short-form questionnaire Item 2. All occupied housing units are classified as either owner occupied or renter occupied.

A housing unit is owner occupied if the owner or co-owner lives in the unit even if it is mortgaged or not fully paid for. The owner or co-owner must live in the unit and usually is Person 1 on the questionnaire. The unit is "Owned by you or someone in this household with a mortgage or loan" if it is being purchased with a mortgage or some other debt arrangement, such as a deed of trust, trust deed, contract to purchase, land contract, or purchase agreement. The unit is also considered owned with a mortgage if it is built on leased land and there is a mortgage on the unit. Mobile homes occupied by owners with installment loans balances are also included in this category.

Median Gross Rent (in dollars): Median monthly gross rent on specified renter-occupied and specified vacant-for-rent units. Specified renter-occupied and specified vacant-for-rent units exclude 1-family houses on 10 acres or more.

The data on gross rent were obtained from answers to long-form questionnaire Items 45a-d, which were asked on a sample basis. Gross rent is the contract rent plus the estimated average monthly cost of utilities (electricity, gas, water and sewer) and fuels (oil, coal, kerosene, wood, etc.) if these are paid by the renter (or paid for the renter by someone else). Gross rent is intended to eliminate differentials that result from varying practices with respect to the inclusion of utilities and fuels as part of the rental payment. The estimated costs of utilities and fuels are reported on an annual basis but are converted to monthly figures for the tabulations. Renter units occupied without payment of cash rent are shown separately as "No cash rent" in the tabulations.

Housing units that are renter occupied without payment of cash rent are shown separately as "No cash rent" in census data products. The unit may be owned by friends or relatives who live elsewhere and who allow occupancy without charge. Rent-free houses or apartments may be provided to compensate caretakers, ministers, tenant farmers, sharecroppers, or others.

Contract rent is the monthly rent agreed to or contracted for, regardless of any furnishings, utilities, fees, meals, or services that may be included. For vacant units, it is the monthly rent asked for the rental unit at the time of enumeration.

If the contract rent includes rent for a business unit or for living quarters occupied by another household, only that part of the rent estimated to be for the respondent's unit was included. Excluded was any rent paid for additional units or for business premises.

If a renter pays rent to the owner of a condominium or cooperative, and the condominium fee or cooperative carrying charge also is paid by the renter to the owner, the condominium fee or carrying charge was included as rent.

If a renter receives payments from lodgers or roomers who are listed as members of the household, the rent without deduction for any payments received from the lodgers or roomers was to be reported. The respondent was to report the rent agreed to or contracted for even if paid by someone else such as friends or relatives living elsewhere, a church or welfare agency, or the government through subsidies or vouchers.

The median divides the rent distribution into two equal parts: one-half of the cases falling below the median contract rent and one-half above the median. Median contract rents are computed on the basis of a standard distribution and are rounded to the nearest whole dollar. Units reported as "No cash rent" are excluded.

Median Home Value (in dollars): Reported by the owner of specified owner-occupied or specified vacant-for-sale housing units. Specified owner-occupied and specified vacant-for-sale housing units include only 1-family houses on less than 10 acres without a business or medical office on the property. The data for "specified units" exclude mobile homes, houses with a business or medical office, houses on 10 or more acres, and housing units in multi-unit buildings.

The data on value (also referred to as "price asked" for vacant units) were obtained from answers to long-form questionnaire Item 51, which was asked on a sample basis at owner-occupied housing units and units that were being bought, or vacant for sale at the time of enumeration. Value is the respondent's estimate of how much the property (house and lot, mobile home and lot, or condominium unit) would sell for if it were for sale. If the house or mobile home was owned or being bought, but the land on which it sits was not, the respondent was asked to estimate the combined value of the house or mobile home and the land. For vacant units, value was the price asked for the property. Value was tabulated separately for all owner-occupied and vacant-for-sale housing units, owner-occupied and vacant-for-sale mobile homes, and specified owner-occupied and specified vacant-for-sale housing units.

The median divides the value distribution into two equal parts: one-half of the cases falling below the median value of the property (house and lot, mobile home and lot, or condominium unit) and one-half above the median. Median values are computed on the basis of a standard distribution and are rounded to the nearest hundred dollars.

User's Guide: Climate

Sources of the Data

The National Climactic Data Center (NCDC) has two main classes or types of weather stations; first-order stations which are staffed by professional meteorologists and cooperative stations which are staffed by volunteers. All 243 National Weather Service (NWS) stations included in this book are first-order stations.

The data in *Weather America** is compiled from several sources. The majority comes from the original NCDC computer tapes (DSI-3220 Summary of Month Cooperative). This data was used to create the entire table for each cooperative station and part of each National Weather Service station. The remainder of the data for each NWS station comes from the International Station Meteorological Climate Summary, Version 4.0, September 1996, which is also available from the NCDC.

Storm events come from the NCDC Storm Events Database which is accessible over the Internet at http://www4.ncdc.noaa.gov/ cgi-win/wwcgi.dll?wwevent~storms.

Weather Station Tables

The weather station tables are grouped by type (National Weather Service and Cooperative) and then arranged alphabetically within each state section. The station name is almost always a place name, and is shown here just as it appears in NCDC data. The station name is followed by the county in which the station is located (or by county equivalent name), the elevation of the station (at the time beginning of the thirty year period) and the latitude and longitude.

The National Weather Service Station tables contain 32 data elements which were compiled from two different sources, the International Station Meteorological Climate Summary (ISMCS) and NCDC DSI-3220 data tapes. The following 13 elements are from the ISMCS: maximum precipitation, minimum precipitation, maximum snowfall, maximum 24-hour snowfall, thunderstorm days, foggy days, predominant sky cover, relative humidity (morning and afternoon), dewpoint, wind speed and direction, and maximum wind gust. The remaining 19 elements come from the DSI-3220 data tapes. The period of record (POR) for data from the DSI-3220 data tapes is 1980-2009. The POR for ISMCS data varies from station to station and appears in a note below each station.

The Cooperative Station tables contain 19 data elements which were all compiled from the DSI-3220 data tapes with a POR of 1980-2009.

Weather Elements (NWS and Cooperative Stations)

The following elements were compiled by the editor from the NCDC DSI-3220 data tapes using a period of record of 1980-2009.

The average temperatures (maximum, minimum, and mean) are the average (see Methodology below) of those temperatures for all available values for a given month. For example, for a given station the average maximum temperature for July is the arithmetic average of all available maximum July temperatures for that station. (Maximum means the highest recorded temperature, minimum means the lowest recorded temperature, and mean means an arithmetic average temperature.)

The extreme maximum temperature is the highest temperature recorded in each month over the period 1980-2009. The extreme minimum temperature is the lowest temperature recorded in each month over the same time period. The extreme maximum daily precipitation is the largest amount of precipitation recorded over a 24-hour period in each month from 1980-2009. The maximum snow depth is the maximum snow depth recorded in each month over the period 1980-2009.

The days for maximum temperature and minimum temperature are the average number of days those criteria were met for all available instances. The symbol $\geq$ means greater than or equal to, the symbol $\leq$ means less than or equal to. For example, for a given station, the number of days the maximum temperature was greater than or equal to 90°F in July, is just an arithmetic average of the number of days in all the available Julys for that station.

Heating and cooling degree days are based on the median temperature for a given day and its variance from 65°F. For example, for a given station if the day's high temperature was 50°F and the day's low temperature was 30°F, the median (midpoint) temperature was 40°F. 40°F is 25 degrees below 65°F, hence on this day there would be 25 heating degree days. The also applies for cooling degree days. For example, for a given station if the day's high temperature was 80°F and the day's low temperature was 70°F, the median (midpoint) temperature was 75°F. 75°F is 10 degrees above 65°F, hence on this day there would be 10 cooling degree days. All heating and/or cooling degree days in a month are summed for the month giving respective totals for each element for that month. These sums for a given month for a given station over the past thirty years are again summed and then arithmetically averaged. It should be noted that the heating and cooling degree days do not cancel each other out. It is possible to have both for a given station in the same month.

Precipitation data is computed the same as heating and cooling degree days. Mean precipitation and mean snowfall are arithmetic averages of cumulative totals for the month. All available values for the thirty year period for a given month for a given station are summed and then divided by the number of values. The same is true for days of greater than or equal to 0.1", 0.5",and 1.0" of precipitation, and days of greater than or equal to 1.0" of snow depth on the ground. The word trace appears for precipitation and snowfall amounts that are too small to measure.

Finally, remember that all values presented in the tables and the rankings are averages, maximums, or minimums of available data (see Methodology below) for that specific data element for the last thirty years (1980-2009).

Weather Elements (NWS Stations Only)

The following elements were taken directly from the International Station Meteorological Climate Summary. The periods of records vary per station and are noted at the bottom of each table.

Maximum precipitation, minimum precipitation, maximum snowfall, maximum snow depth, maximum 24-hour snowfall, thunderstorm days, foggy days, relative humidity (morning and afternoon), dewpoint, prevailing wind speed and direction, and maximum wind gust are all self-explanatory.

The word trace appears for precipitation and snowfall amounts that are too small to measure.

Predominant sky cover contains four possible entries: CLR (clear); SCT (scattered); BRK (broken); and OVR (overcast).

Inclusion Criteria—How Stations Were Selected

The basic criteria is that a station must have data for temperature, precipitation, heating and cooling degree days of sufficient quantity in order to create a meaningful average. More specifically, the definition of sufficiency here has two parts. First, there must be 22 values for a given data element, and second, ten of the nineteen elements included in the table must pass this sufficiency test. For example, in regard to mean maximum temperature (the first element on every data table), a given station needs to have a value for every month of at least 22 of the last thirty years in order to meet the criteria, and, in addition, every station included must have at least ten of the nineteen elements at least this minimal level of completeness in order to fulfill the criteria. We then removed stations that were geographicaly close together, giving preference to stations with better data quality. By using this procedure, 1,778 cooperative stations met these requirements and are included here. The 243 National Weather Service stations did not have to meet any minimum requirements.

Methodology

The following discussion applies only to data compiled from the NCDC DSI-3220 data tapes and excludes weather elements that are extreme maximums or minimums.

*Weather America** is based on an arithmetic average of all available data for a specific data element at a given station. For example, the average maximum daily high temperature during July for Alma, Michigan, was abstracted from NCDC source tapes for the thirty Julys, starting in July, 1980 and ending in July, 2009. These thirty figures were then summed and divided by thirty to produce an arithmetic average. As might be expected, there were not thirty values for every data element on every table. For a variety of reasons, NCDC data is sometimes incomplete. Thus the following standards were established.

For those data elements where there were 26-30 values, the data was taken to be essentially complete and an average was computed. For data elements where there were 22-25 values, the data was taken as being partly complete but still valid enough to use to compute an average. Such averages are shown in **bold italic** type to indicate that there was less than 26 values. For the few data elements where there were not even 22 values, no average was computed and 'na' appears in the space. If any of the twelve months for a given data element reported a value of 'na', no annual average was computed and the annual average was reported as 'na' as well.

Thus the basic computational methodology of *Weather America** is to provide an arithmetic average. Because of this, such a pure arithmetic average is somewhat different from the special type of average (called a "normal") which NCDC procedures produces and appears in federal publications.

Perhaps the best outline of the contrasting normalization methodology is found in the following paragraph (which appears as part of an NCDC technical document titled, CLIM81 1961-1990 NORMALS TD-9641 prepared by Lewis France of NCDC in May, 1992):

Normals have been defined as the arithmetic mean of a climatological element computed over a long time period. International agreements eventually led to the decision that the appropriate time period would be three consecutive decades (Guttman, 1989). The data record should be consistent (have no changes in location, instruments, observation practices, etc.; these are identified here as "exposure changes") and have no missing values so a normal will reflect the actual average climatic conditions. If any significant exposure changes have occurred, the data record is said to be "inhomogeneous," and the normal may not reflect a true climatic average. Such data need to be adjusted to remove the nonclimatic inhomogeneities. The resulting (adjusted) record is then said to be "homogeneous." If no exposure changes have occurred at a station, the normal is calculated simply by averaging the appropriate 30 values from the 1961-1990 record.

In the main, there are two "inhomogeneities" that NCDC is correcting for with normalization: adjusting for variances in time of day of observation (at the so-called First Order stations data is based on midnight to midnight observation times and this practice is not necessarily followed at cooperative stations which are staffed by volunteers), and second, estimating data that is either missing or incongruent.

A long discussion of the normalization process is not required here but a short note concerning comparative results of the two methodologies is appropriate.

When the editors first started compiling *Weather America* * a concern arose because the normalization process would not be replicated: would our methodology produce strikingly different results than NCDC's? To allay concerns, results of the two processes were compared for the time period normalized results are available (1971-2000). In short, what was found was that the answer to this question is no. Never-the-less, users should be aware that because of both the time period covered (1980-2009) and the methodology used, data in *Weather America* * is not compatible with data from other sources.

Potential cautions in using *Weather America* *

First, as with any statistical reference work of this type, users need to be aware of the source of the data. The information here comes from NOAA, and it is the most comprehensive and reliable core data available. Although it is the best, it is not perfect. Most weather stations are staffed by volunteers, times of observation sometimes vary, stations occasionally are moved (especially over a thirty year period), equipment is changed or upgraded, and all of these factors affect the uniformity of the data. *Weather America* * does not attempt to correct for these factors, and is not intended for either climatologists or atmospheric scientists. Users with concerns about data collection and reporting protocols are both referred to NCDC technical documentation, and also, they are perhaps better served by using the original computer tapes themselves as well.

Second, users need to be aware of the methodology here which is described above. Although this methodology has produced fully satisfactory results, it is not directly compatible with other methodologies, hence variances in the results published here and those which appear in other publications will doubtlessly arise.

Third, is the trap of that informal logical fallacy known as "hasty generalization," and its corollaries. This may involve presuming the future will be like the past (specifically, next year will be an average year), or it may involve misunderstanding the limitations of an arithmetic average, but more interestingly, it may involve those mistakes made most innocently by generalizing informally on too broad a basis. As weather is highly localized, the data should be taken in that context. A weather station collects data about climatic conditions at that spot, and that spot may or may not be an effective paradigm for an entire town or area. For example, the weather station in Burlington, Vermont is located at the airport about 3 miles east of the center of town. Most of Burlington is a lot closer to Lake Champlain, and that should mean to a careful user that there could be a significant difference between the temperature readings gathered at the weather station and readings that might be gathered at City Hall downtown. How much would this difference be? How could it be estimated? There are no answers here for these sorts of questions, but it is important for users of this book to raise them for themselves. (It is interesting to note that similar situations abound across the country. For example, compare different readings for the multiple stations in San Francisco, CA or for those around New York City.)

Our source of data has been consistent, so has our methodology. The data has been computed and reported consistently as well. As a result, the *Weather America* * should prove valuable to the careful and informed reader.

Adams County

Located in western Illinois; bounded on the west by the Mississippi River and the Missouri border. Covers a land area of 856.63 square miles, a water area of 14.64 square miles, and is located in the Central Time Zone at 39.96° N. Lat., 91.26° W. Long. The county was founded in 1825. County seat is Quincy.

Adams County is part of the Quincy, IL-MO Micropolitan Statistical Area. The entire metro area includes: Adams County, IL; Lewis County, MO

Weather Station: Golden   Elevation: 725 feet

	Jan	Feb	Mar	Apr	May	Jun	Jul	Aug	Sep	Oct	Nov	Dec
High	34	38	51	63	74	83	87	85	78	66	50	37
Low	17	20	31	41	52	62	65	63	54	43	32	21
Precip	1.5	1.8	2.5	3.5	5.0	4.5	4.2	4.0	3.1	3.1	3.0	2.1
Snow	5.1	4.2	1.4	0.5	0.0	0.0	0.0	0.0	0.0	tr	0.7	3.8

High and Low temperatures in degrees Fahrenheit; Precipitation and Snow in inches

Weather Station: Quincy Dam 21   Elevation: 482 feet

	Jan	Feb	Mar	Apr	May	Jun	Jul	Aug	Sep	Oct	Nov	Dec
High	35	40	51	64	73	83	87	86	79	66	53	39
Low	18	22	31	42	53	62	67	65	56	44	34	22
Precip	1.4	1.9	2.6	3.6	4.5	3.7	4.0	3.3	2.9	2.7	2.8	2.2
Snow	na	na	1.3	0.3	0.0	0.0	0.0	0.0	0.0	0.0	0.1	2.2

High and Low temperatures in degrees Fahrenheit; Precipitation and Snow in inches

Weather Station: Quincy Muni Baldwin Fld   Elevation: 763 feet

	Jan	Feb	Mar	Apr	May	Jun	Jul	Aug	Sep	Oct	Nov	Dec
High	35	39	51	63	73	82	86	85	77	65	51	38
Low	19	23	32	43	53	62	66	64	56	44	34	22
Precip	1.5	1.9	2.6	3.5	4.6	3.8	3.8	3.7	3.3	3.1	3.0	2.3
Snow	na	na	na	na	na	tr	tr	na	na	na	na	na

High and Low temperatures in degrees Fahrenheit; Precipitation and Snow in inches

Population: 66,090 (1990); 68,277 (2000); 66,841 (2010); 65,903 (2015 projected); Race: 94.2% White, 3.4% Black, 0.5% Asian, 2.0% Other, 0.9% Hispanic of any race (2010); Density: 78.0 persons per square mile (2010); Average household size: 2.39 (2010); Median age: 39.3 (2010); Males per 100 females: 93.4 (2010).

Religion: Five largest groups: 23.3% Catholic Church, 5.4% The United Methodist Church, 4.9% Christian Churches and Churches of Christ, 4.7% United Church of Christ, 4.3% Lutheran Church—Missouri Synod (2000).

Economy: Unemployment rate: 6.7% (August 2011); Total civilian labor force: 37,967 (August 2011); Leading industries: 17.6% health care and social assistance; 16.9% manufacturing; 16.6% retail trade (2009); Farms: 1,295 totaling 374,133 acres (2007); Companies that employ 500 or more persons: 6 (2009); Companies that employ 100 to 499 persons: 40 (2009); Companies that employ less than 100 persons: 1,809 (2009); Black-owned businesses: n/a (2007); Hispanic-owned businesses: n/a (2007); Asian-owned businesses: 84 (2007); Women-owned businesses: 1,367 (2007); Retail sales per capita: $15,194 (2010). Single-family building permits issued: 51 (2010); Multi-family building permits issued: 88 (2010).

Income: Per capita income: $23,084 (2010); Median household income: $44,318 (2010); Average household income: $56,151 (2010); Percent of households with income of $100,000 or more: 10.8% (2010); Poverty rate: 15.7% (2009); Bankruptcy rate: 3.94% (2010).

Taxes: Total county taxes per capita: $96 (2007); County property taxes per capita: $96 (2007).

Education: Percent of population age 25 and over with: High school diploma (including GED) or higher: 89.9% (2010); Bachelor's degree or higher: 21.9% (2010); Master's degree or higher: 7.1% (2010).

Housing: Homeownership rate: 73.9% (2010); Median home value: $90,201 (2010); Median contract rent: $389 per month (2005-2009 5-year est.); Median year structure built: 1959 (2005-2009 5-year est.)

Health: Birth rate: 129.1 per 10,000 population (2009); Death rate: 123.2 per 10,000 population (2009); Age-adjusted cancer mortality rate: 185.7 deaths per 100,000 population (2007); Number of physicians: 27.2 per 10,000 population (2008); Hospital beds: 50.4 per 10,000 population (2007); Hospital admissions: 2,107.3 per 10,000 population (2007).

Environment: Air Quality Index: 96.9% good, 3.1% moderate, 0.0% unhealthy for sensitive individuals, 0.0% unhealthy (percent of days in 2008)

Elections: 2008 Presidential election results: 38.3% Obama, 60.7% McCain, 0.5% Nader

National and State Parks: Sid Simpson State Park; Siloam Springs State Park

Additional Information Contacts

Adams County Government.	(217) 277-2150
http://www.co.adams.il.us	
City of Quincy.	(217) 228-4500
http://www.ci.quincy.il.us	
Quincy Area Chamber of Commerce.	(217) 222-7980
http://www.quincychamber.org	

Adams County Communities

CAMP POINT (village). Covers a land area of 0.948 square miles and a water area of 0 square miles. Located at 40.04° N. Lat; 91.06° W. Long. Elevation is 722 feet.

History: Camp Point was settled about 1870 by people of German ancestry.

Population: 1,230 (1990); 1,244 (2000); 1,239 (2010); 1,229 (2015 projected); Race: 99.0% White, 0.0% Black, 0.1% Asian, 0.9% Other, 0.4% Hispanic of any race (2010); Density: 1,306.8 persons per square mile (2010); Average household size: 2.57 (2010); Median age: 39.7 (2010); Males per 100 females: 89.4 (2010); Marriage status: 20.9% never married, 59.6% now married, 10.3% widowed, 9.3% divorced (2005-2009 5-year est.); Foreign born: 0.2% (2005-2009 5-year est.); Ancestry (includes multiple ancestries): 58.1% German, 16.0% Irish, 9.8% English, 5.8% American, 3.3% French (2005-2009 5-year est.).

Economy: Single-family building permits issued: 1 (2010); Multi-family building permits issued: 0 (2010); Employment by occupation: 3.3% management, 19.4% professional, 13.2% services, 27.1% sales, 0.8% farming, 14.0% construction, 22.2% production (2005-2009 5-year est.).

Income: Per capita income: $21,596 (2010); Median household income: $44,816 (2010); Average household income: $56,734 (2010); Percent of households with income of $100,000 or more: 11.6% (2010); Poverty rate: 9.4% (2005-2009 5-year est.).

Taxes: Total city taxes per capita: $139 (2007); City property taxes per capita: $100 (2007).

Education: Percent of population age 25 and over with: High school diploma (including GED) or higher: 90.6% (2010); Bachelor's degree or higher: 12.5% (2010); Master's degree or higher: 4.2% (2010).

School District(s)
Central CUSD 3 (PK-12)
    2009-10 Enrollment: 946 . . . . (217) 593-7116

Housing: Homeownership rate: 74.2% (2010); Median home value: $73,636 (2010); Median contract rent: $272 per month (2005-2009 5-year est.); Median year structure built: 1958 (2005-2009 5-year est.).

Newspapers: Camp Point Journal (Community news; Circulation 800); The Golden Clayton New Era (Community news; Circulation 300); Golden New Era (Community news; Circulation 600); Mendon Dispatch-Times (Community news; Circulation 875);

Transportation: Commute to work: 88.9% car, 2.3% public transportation, 3.7% walk, 4.7% work from home (2005-2009 5-year est.); Travel time to work: 35.3% less than 15 minutes, 28.3% 15 to 30 minutes, 30.5% 30 to 45 minutes, 2.0% 45 to 60 minutes, 3.9% 60 minutes or more (2005-2009 5-year est.)

CLAYTON (village). Covers a land area of 0.874 square miles and a water area of 0.002 square miles. Located at 40.02° N. Lat; 90.95° W. Long. Elevation is 732 feet.

Population: 726 (1990); 904 (2000); 809 (2010); 775 (2015 projected); Race: 75.9% White, 22.0% Black, 0.0% Asian, 2.1% Other, 2.3% Hispanic of any race (2010); Density: 925.3 persons per square mile (2010); Average household size: 2.38 (2010); Median age: 37.6 (2010); Males per 100 females: 124.1 (2010); Marriage status: 42.9% never married, 33.5% now married, 4.8% widowed, 18.8% divorced (2005-2009 5-year est.); Foreign born: 0.0% (2005-2009 5-year est.); Ancestry (includes multiple ancestries): 22.9% German, 13.8% American, 6.6% Irish, 4.3% English, 3.0% European (2005-2009 5-year est.).

Economy: Single-family building permits issued: 0 (2010); Multi-family building permits issued: 0 (2010); Employment by occupation: 7.2% management, 10.2% professional, 23.0% services, 21.4% sales, 5.3% farming, 13.8% construction, 19.1% production (2005-2009 5-year est.).

Income: Per capita income: $19,607 (2010); Median household income: $35,978 (2010); Average household income: $50,353 (2010); Percent of households with income of $100,000 or more: 11.4% (2010); Poverty rate: 23.3% (2005-2009 5-year est.).

Taxes: Total city taxes per capita: $20 (2007); City property taxes per capita: $20 (2007).

Education: Percent of population age 25 and over with: High school diploma (including GED) or higher: 70.6% (2010); Bachelor's degree or higher: 7.3% (2010); Master's degree or higher: 3.9% (2010).
Housing: Homeownership rate: 79.0% (2010); Median home value: $46,607 (2010); Median contract rent: $250 per month (2005-2009 5-year est.); Median year structure built: before 1940 (2005-2009 5-year est.).
Safety: Violent crime rate: 0.0 per 10,000 population; Property crime rate: 86.0 per 10,000 population (2010).
Transportation: Commute to work: 90.5% car, 4.3% public transportation, 1.3% walk, 3.9% work from home (2005-2009 5-year est.); Travel time to work: 35.3% less than 15 minutes, 15.1% 15 to 30 minutes, 30.8% 30 to 45 minutes, 18.8% 45 to 60 minutes, 0.0% 60 minutes or more (2005-2009 5-year est.)

COATSBURG (village). Covers a land area of 0.122 square miles and a water area of 0 square miles. Located at 40.03° N. Lat; 91.16° W. Long. Elevation is 758 feet.
History: Coatsburg was surveyed by R.P. Coates in 1855, and developed as a shipping center for grain and livestock. Coatsburg was incorporated as a village in 1885.
Population: 201 (1990); 226 (2000); 220 (2010); 215 (2015 projected); Race: 99.1% White, 0.0% Black, 0.0% Asian, 0.9% Other, 0.9% Hispanic of any race (2010); Density: 1,806.4 persons per square mile (2010); Average household size: 2.53 (2010); Median age: 37.1 (2010); Males per 100 females: 98.2 (2010); Marriage status: 26.7% never married, 58.8% now married, 5.5% widowed, 9.1% divorced (2005-2009 5-year est.); Foreign born: 0.0% (2005-2009 5-year est.); Ancestry (includes multiple ancestries): 19.0% Irish, 15.3% German, 9.3% English, 5.6% Polish, 4.6% Italian (2005-2009 5-year est.).
Economy: Employment by occupation: 5.7% management, 16.3% professional, 13.8% services, 22.8% sales, 0.0% farming, 25.2% construction, 16.3% production (2005-2009 5-year est.).
Income: Per capita income: $20,828 (2010); Median household income: $49,423 (2010); Average household income: $52,414 (2010); Percent of households with income of $100,000 or more: 6.9% (2010); Poverty rate: 5.6% (2005-2009 5-year est.).
Taxes: Total city taxes per capita: $9 (2007); City property taxes per capita: $9 (2007).
Education: Percent of population age 25 and over with: High school diploma (including GED) or higher: 89.0% (2010); Bachelor's degree or higher: 13.8% (2010); Master's degree or higher: 2.1% (2010).
Housing: Homeownership rate: 81.6% (2010); Median home value: $89,000 (2010); Median contract rent: n/a per month (2005-2009 5-year est.); Median year structure built: before 1940 (2005-2009 5-year est.).
Transportation: Commute to work: 80.5% car, 16.1% public transportation, 0.0% walk, 3.4% work from home (2005-2009 5-year est.); Travel time to work: 26.3% less than 15 minutes, 53.5% 15 to 30 minutes, 12.3% 30 to 45 minutes, 2.6% 45 to 60 minutes, 5.3% 60 minutes or more (2005-2009 5-year est.)

COLUMBUS (village). Covers a land area of 0.252 square miles and a water area of 0 square miles. Located at 39.98° N. Lat; 91.14° W. Long. Elevation is 722 feet.
History: Vigorously competed with Quincy for seat of Adams county in 19th century.
Population: 88 (1990); 112 (2000); 110 (2010); 110 (2015 projected); Race: 97.3% White, 0.0% Black, 0.0% Asian, 2.7% Other, 0.0% Hispanic of any race (2010); Density: 436.6 persons per square mile (2010); Average household size: 2.75 (2010); Median age: 40.0 (2010); Males per 100 females: 103.7 (2010); Marriage status: 13.9% never married, 62.5% now married, 9.7% widowed, 13.9% divorced (2005-2009 5-year est.); Foreign born: 0.0% (2005-2009 5-year est.); Ancestry (includes multiple ancestries): 26.8% German, 15.9% Irish, 12.2% American, 3.7% Dutch, 3.7% Italian (2005-2009 5-year est.).
Economy: Employment by occupation: 12.0% management, 10.0% professional, 38.0% services, 18.0% sales, 0.0% farming, 6.0% construction, 16.0% production (2005-2009 5-year est.).
Income: Per capita income: $21,647 (2010); Median household income: $55,000 (2010); Average household income: $65,500 (2010); Percent of households with income of $100,000 or more: 12.5% (2010); Poverty rate: 37.8% (2005-2009 5-year est.).
Taxes: Total city taxes per capita: $27 (2007); City property taxes per capita: $18 (2007).

Education: Percent of population age 25 and over with: High school diploma (including GED) or higher: 86.8% (2010); Bachelor's degree or higher: 18.4% (2010); Master's degree or higher: 2.6% (2010).
Housing: Homeownership rate: 90.0% (2010); Median home value: $115,000 (2010); Median contract rent: n/a per month (2005-2009 5-year est.); Median year structure built: 1954 (2005-2009 5-year est.).
Transportation: Commute to work: 92.0% car, 0.0% public transportation, 0.0% walk, 8.0% work from home (2005-2009 5-year est.); Travel time to work: 13.0% less than 15 minutes, 58.7% 15 to 30 minutes, 28.3% 30 to 45 minutes, 0.0% 45 to 60 minutes, 0.0% 60 minutes or more (2005-2009 5-year est.)

FOWLER (unincorporated postal area, zip code 62338). Covers a land area of 26.247 square miles and a water area of 0.076 square miles. Located at 39.98° N. Lat; 91.25° W. Long. Elevation is 732 feet.
Population: 1,364 (2000); Race: 98.8% White, 0.0% Black, 0.0% Asian, 1.2% Other, 0.4% Hispanic of any race (2000); Density: 52.0 persons per square mile (2000); Age: 25.7% under 18, 11.3% over 64 (2000); Marriage status: 19.2% never married, 64.8% now married, 5.9% widowed, 10.1% divorced (2000); Foreign born: 0.1% (2000); Ancestry (includes multiple ancestries): 48.4% German, 17.9% Irish, 5.8% American, 4.8% English (2000).
Economy: Employment by occupation: 10.9% management, 23.0% professional, 14.1% services, 25.8% sales, 0.7% farming, 9.3% construction, 16.2% production (2000).
Income: Per capita income: $18,181 (2000); Median household income: $45,192 (2000); Poverty rate: 3.3% (2000).
Education: Percent of population age 25 and over with: High school diploma (including GED) or higher: 86.9% (2000); Bachelor's degree or higher: 14.6% (2000).
Housing: Homeownership rate: 94.1% (2000); Median home value: $77,500 (2000); Median contract rent: $292 per month (2000); Median year structure built: 1974 (2000).
Transportation: Commute to work: 94.3% car, 0.7% public transportation, 0.0% walk, 5.0% work from home (2000); Travel time to work: 24.4% less than 15 minutes, 62.9% 15 to 30 minutes, 11.4% 30 to 45 minutes, 0.9% 45 to 60 minutes, 0.4% 60 minutes or more (2000)

GOLDEN (village). Covers a land area of 0.628 square miles and a water area of 0 square miles. Located at 40.11° N. Lat; 91.01° W. Long. Elevation is 715 feet.
Population: 578 (1990); 629 (2000); 640 (2010); 648 (2015 projected); Race: 98.9% White, 0.0% Black, 0.2% Asian, 0.9% Other, 0.9% Hispanic of any race (2010); Density: 1,018.4 persons per square mile (2010); Average household size: 2.60 (2010); Median age: 38.4 (2010); Males per 100 females: 91.0 (2010); Marriage status: 13.1% never married, 59.5% now married, 19.1% widowed, 8.4% divorced (2005-2009 5-year est.); Foreign born: 1.2% (2005-2009 5-year est.); Ancestry (includes multiple ancestries): 57.9% German, 18.7% Irish, 5.8% American, 5.3% English, 3.7% French (2005-2009 5-year est.).
Economy: Employment by occupation: 8.8% management, 8.5% professional, 27.3% services, 29.6% sales, 0.9% farming, 5.6% construction, 19.4% production (2005-2009 5-year est.).
Income: Per capita income: $23,022 (2010); Median household income: $50,000 (2010); Average household income: $60,021 (2010); Percent of households with income of $100,000 or more: 13.8% (2010); Poverty rate: 1.8% (2005-2009 5-year est.).
Taxes: Total city taxes per capita: $27 (2007); City property taxes per capita: $27 (2007).
Education: Percent of population age 25 and over with: High school diploma (including GED) or higher: 92.2% (2010); Bachelor's degree or higher: 15.3% (2010); Master's degree or higher: 2.7% (2010).
School District(s)
Central CUSD 3 (PK-12)
    2009-10 Enrollment: 946 . . . . (217) 593-7116
Housing: Homeownership rate: 80.8% (2010); Median home value: $81,600 (2010); Median contract rent: $325 per month (2005-2009 5-year est.); Median year structure built: 1953 (2005-2009 5-year est.).
Transportation: Commute to work: 90.3% car, 0.0% public transportation, 2.9% walk, 6.7% work from home (2005-2009 5-year est.); Travel time to work: 41.5% less than 15 minutes, 10.1% 15 to 30 minutes, 34.6% 30 to 45 minutes, 13.8% 45 to 60 minutes, 0.0% 60 minutes or more (2005-2009 5-year est.)

LA PRAIRIE (town). Covers a land area of 0.224 square miles and a water area of 0 square miles. Located at 40.14° N. Lat; 91.00° W. Long. Elevation is 709 feet.
Population: 68 (1990); 60 (2000); 63 (2010); 63 (2015 projected); Race: 100.0% White, 0.0% Black, 0.0% Asian, 0.0% Other, 0.0% Hispanic of any race (2010); Density: 281.9 persons per square mile (2010); Average household size: 2.63 (2010); Median age: 36.9 (2010); Males per 100 females: 133.3 (2010); Marriage status: 23.1% never married, 19.2% now married, 11.5% widowed, 46.2% divorced (2005-2009 5-year est.); Foreign born: 0.0% (2005-2009 5-year est.); Ancestry (includes multiple ancestries): 78.6% German, 21.4% English, 21.4% Irish, 14.3% French (2005-2009 5-year est.).
Economy: Employment by occupation: 0.0% management, 0.0% professional, 14.3% services, 33.3% sales, 0.0% farming, 0.0% construction, 52.4% production (2005-2009 5-year est.).
Income: Per capita income: $21,745 (2010); Median household income: $57,143 (2010); Average household income: $60,000 (2010); Percent of households with income of $100,000 or more: 12.5% (2010); Poverty rate: 0.0% (2005-2009 5-year est.).
Taxes: Total city taxes per capita: $17 (2007); City property taxes per capita: $17 (2007).
Education: Percent of population age 25 and over with: High school diploma (including GED) or higher: 92.3% (2010); Bachelor's degree or higher: 7.7% (2010); Master's degree or higher: 0.0% (2010).
Housing: Homeownership rate: 79.2% (2010); Median home value: $77,500 (2010); Median contract rent: n/a per month (2005-2009 5-year est.); Median year structure built: before 1940 (2005-2009 5-year est.).
Transportation: Commute to work: 100.0% car, 0.0% public transportation, 0.0% walk, 0.0% work from home (2005-2009 5-year est.); Travel time to work: 14.3% less than 15 minutes, 19.0% 15 to 30 minutes, 33.3% 30 to 45 minutes, 33.3% 45 to 60 minutes, 0.0% 60 minutes or more (2005-2009 5-year est.)

LIBERTY (village). Covers a land area of 0.374 square miles and a water area of 0 square miles. Located at 39.88° N. Lat; 91.10° W. Long. Elevation is 751 feet.
Population: 548 (1990); 519 (2000); 480 (2010); 461 (2015 projected); Race: 99.8% White, 0.0% Black, 0.0% Asian, 0.2% Other, 0.4% Hispanic of any race (2010); Density: 1,282.5 persons per square mile (2010); Average household size: 2.45 (2010); Median age: 38.5 (2010); Males per 100 females: 100.8 (2010); Marriage status: 9.6% never married, 70.6% now married, 6.7% widowed, 13.0% divorced (2005-2009 5-year est.); Foreign born: 0.0% (2005-2009 5-year est.); Ancestry (includes multiple ancestries): 62.9% German, 19.0% Irish, 9.9% English, 8.8% American, 5.4% Dutch (2005-2009 5-year est.).
Economy: Employment by occupation: 9.8% management, 19.1% professional, 20.7% services, 19.9% sales, 0.0% farming, 1.6% construction, 28.9% production (2005-2009 5-year est.).
Income: Per capita income: $24,537 (2010); Median household income: $54,245 (2010); Average household income: $61,684 (2010); Percent of households with income of $100,000 or more: 10.2% (2010); Poverty rate: 14.0% (2005-2009 5-year est.).
Taxes: Total city taxes per capita: $31 (2007); City property taxes per capita: $21 (2007).
Education: Percent of population age 25 and over with: High school diploma (including GED) or higher: 89.7% (2010); Bachelor's degree or higher: 15.9% (2010); Master's degree or higher: 7.1% (2010).
School District(s)
Liberty CUSD 2 (PK-12)
   2009-10 Enrollment: 686 . . . . (217) 645-3433
Housing: Homeownership rate: 79.6% (2010); Median home value: $108,000 (2010); Median contract rent: $261 per month (2005-2009 5-year est.); Median year structure built: 1965 (2005-2009 5-year est.).
Newspapers: Liberty Bee-Times (Community news; Circulation 1,400)
Transportation: Commute to work: 88.2% car, 0.0% public transportation, 6.9% walk, 4.9% work from home (2005-2009 5-year est.); Travel time to work: 20.5% less than 15 minutes, 45.3% 15 to 30 minutes, 30.3% 30 to 45 minutes, 3.8% 45 to 60 minutes, 0.0% 60 minutes or more (2005-2009 5-year est.)

LIMA (village). Covers a land area of 0.214 square miles and a water area of 0 square miles. Located at 40.17° N. Lat; 91.37° W. Long. Elevation is 653 feet.
Population: 120 (1990); 159 (2000); 157 (2010); 156 (2015 projected); Race: 98.7% White, 0.0% Black, 0.0% Asian, 1.3% Other, 1.3% Hispanic of any race (2010); Density: 732.5 persons per square mile (2010); Average household size: 2.57 (2010); Median age: 39.1 (2010); Males per 100 females: 121.1 (2010); Marriage status: 30.4% never married, 51.9% now married, 3.0% widowed, 14.8% divorced (2005-2009 5-year est.); Foreign born: 0.0% (2005-2009 5-year est.); Ancestry (includes multiple ancestries): 53.6% German, 26.8% American, 16.4% Irish, 7.7% English (2005-2009 5-year est.).
Economy: Employment by occupation: 5.1% management, 0.0% professional, 32.1% services, 2.6% sales, 2.6% farming, 14.1% construction, 43.6% production (2005-2009 5-year est.).
Income: Per capita income: $22,207 (2010); Median household income: $50,694 (2010); Average household income: $58,402 (2010); Percent of households with income of $100,000 or more: 9.8% (2010); Poverty rate: 35.0% (2005-2009 5-year est.).
Taxes: Total city taxes per capita: $6 (2007); City property taxes per capita: $6 (2007).
Education: Percent of population age 25 and over with: High school diploma (including GED) or higher: 89.5% (2010); Bachelor's degree or higher: 12.4% (2010); Master's degree or higher: 1.9% (2010).
Housing: Homeownership rate: 80.3% (2010); Median home value: $81,429 (2010); Median contract rent: $305 per month (2005-2009 5-year est.); Median year structure built: before 1940 (2005-2009 5-year est.).
Transportation: Commute to work: 100.0% car, 0.0% public transportation, 0.0% walk, 0.0% work from home (2005-2009 5-year est.); Travel time to work: 11.5% less than 15 minutes, 47.4% 15 to 30 minutes, 30.8% 30 to 45 minutes, 10.3% 45 to 60 minutes, 0.0% 60 minutes or more (2005-2009 5-year est.)

LORAINE (village). Covers a land area of 0.846 square miles and a water area of 0 square miles. Located at 40.15° N. Lat; 91.22° W. Long. Elevation is 643 feet.
Population: 390 (1990); 363 (2000); 351 (2010); 344 (2015 projected); Race: 99.4% White, 0.0% Black, 0.0% Asian, 0.6% Other, 0.0% Hispanic of any race (2010); Density: 414.9 persons per square mile (2010); Average household size: 2.56 (2010); Median age: 38.5 (2010); Males per 100 females: 104.1 (2010); Marriage status: 18.3% never married, 61.5% now married, 7.2% widowed, 13.0% divorced (2005-2009 5-year est.); Foreign born: 0.0% (2005-2009 5-year est.); Ancestry (includes multiple ancestries): 36.2% German, 22.8% Irish, 5.8% American, 3.3% Austrian, 3.3% Scotch-Irish (2005-2009 5-year est.).
Economy: Employment by occupation: 0.7% management, 14.3% professional, 17.0% services, 19.7% sales, 0.0% farming, 10.2% construction, 38.1% production (2005-2009 5-year est.).
Income: Per capita income: $28,852 (2010); Median household income: $62,868 (2010); Average household income: $72,190 (2010); Percent of households with income of $100,000 or more: 16.8% (2010); Poverty rate: 5.9% (2005-2009 5-year est.).
Taxes: Total city taxes per capita: $22 (2007); City property taxes per capita: $17 (2007).
Education: Percent of population age 25 and over with: High school diploma (including GED) or higher: 90.1% (2010); Bachelor's degree or higher: 12.9% (2010); Master's degree or higher: 2.2% (2010).
School District(s)
CUSD 4 (PK-12)
   2009-10 Enrollment: 756 . . . . (217) 936-2111
Housing: Homeownership rate: 82.5% (2010); Median home value: $63,125 (2010); Median contract rent: $298 per month (2005-2009 5-year est.); Median year structure built: 1952 (2005-2009 5-year est.).
Transportation: Commute to work: 100.0% car, 0.0% public transportation, 0.0% walk, 0.0% work from home (2005-2009 5-year est.); Travel time to work: 4.1% less than 15 minutes, 51.0% 15 to 30 minutes, 42.1% 30 to 45 minutes, 2.8% 45 to 60 minutes, 0.0% 60 minutes or more (2005-2009 5-year est.)

MENDON (village). Covers a land area of 0.731 square miles and a water area of 0 square miles. Located at 40.08° N. Lat; 91.28° W. Long. Elevation is 761 feet.
Population: 854 (1990); 883 (2000); 844 (2010); 821 (2015 projected); Race: 99.4% White, 0.2% Black, 0.0% Asian, 0.4% Other, 0.5% Hispanic of any race (2010); Density: 1,154.2 persons per square mile (2010); Average household size: 2.50 (2010); Median age: 39.4 (2010); Males per 100 females: 85.1 (2010); Marriage status: 16.0% never married, 55.1% now married, 20.4% widowed, 8.5% divorced (2005-2009 5-year est.);

Foreign born: 0.0% (2005-2009 5-year est.); Ancestry (includes multiple ancestries): 37.4% German, 16.0% Irish, 8.2% American, 6.6% English, 5.0% French (2005-2009 5-year est.).

Economy: Employment by occupation: 14.3% management, 10.3% professional, 17.9% services, 24.1% sales, 1.1% farming, 3.1% construction, 29.2% production (2005-2009 5-year est.).

Income: Per capita income: $23,010 (2010); Median household income: $49,388 (2010); Average household income: $57,018 (2010); Percent of households with income of $100,000 or more: 10.1% (2010); Poverty rate: 9.7% (2005-2009 5-year est.).

Taxes: Total city taxes per capita: $32 (2007); City property taxes per capita: $30 (2007).

Education: Percent of population age 25 and over with: High school diploma (including GED) or higher: 88.1% (2010); Bachelor's degree or higher: 16.5% (2010); Master's degree or higher: 3.9% (2010).

School District(s)

CUSD 4 (PK-12)

   2009-10 Enrollment: 756 . . . . (217) 936-2111

Housing: Homeownership rate: 78.8% (2010); Median home value: $73,944 (2010); Median contract rent: $400 per month (2005-2009 5-year est.); Median year structure built: 1963 (2005-2009 5-year est.).

Transportation: Commute to work: 98.5% car, 0.0% public transportation, 0.0% walk, 0.0% work from home (2005-2009 5-year est.); Travel time to work: 23.5% less than 15 minutes, 58.0% 15 to 30 minutes, 15.3% 30 to 45 minutes, 3.2% 45 to 60 minutes, 0.0% 60 minutes or more (2005-2009 5-year est.)

PALOMA (unincorporated postal area, zip code 62359). Covers a land area of 10.096 square miles and a water area of 0.003 square miles. Located at 40.02° N. Lat; 91.21° W. Long. Elevation is 732 feet.

Population: 192 (2000); Race: 100.0% White, 0.0% Black, 0.0% Asian, 0.0% Other, 0.0% Hispanic of any race (2000); Density: 19.0 persons per square mile (2000); Age: 17.7% under 18, 14.2% over 64 (2000); Marriage status: 8.9% never married, 85.4% now married, 0.0% widowed, 5.7% divorced (2000); Foreign born: 0.0% (2000); Ancestry (includes multiple ancestries): 39.0% American, 21.3% German, 15.6% English, 14.9% Irish, 4.3% Croatian (2000).

Economy: Employment by occupation: 6.7% management, 16.0% professional, 12.0% services, 28.0% sales, 8.0% farming, 0.0% construction, 29.3% production (2000).

Income: Per capita income: $18,310 (2000); Median household income: $43,295 (2000); Poverty rate: 0.0% (2000).

Education: Percent of population age 25 and over with: High school diploma (including GED) or higher: 85.0% (2000); Bachelor's degree or higher: 7.5% (2000).

Housing: Homeownership rate: 85.7% (2000); Median home value: $95,000 (2000); Median contract rent: $368 per month (2000); Median year structure built: 1984 (2000).

Transportation: Commute to work: 84.0% car, 0.0% public transportation, 0.0% walk, 16.0% work from home (2000); Travel time to work: 12.7% less than 15 minutes, 54.0% 15 to 30 minutes, 25.4% 30 to 45 minutes, 0.0% 45 to 60 minutes, 7.9% 60 minutes or more (2000)

PAYSON (village). Covers a land area of 1.147 square miles and a water area of 0 square miles. Located at 39.81° N. Lat; 91.24° W. Long. Elevation is 761 feet.

Population: 1,114 (1990); 1,066 (2000); 1,020 (2010); 993 (2015 projected); Race: 98.3% White, 0.0% Black, 0.0% Asian, 1.7% Other, 0.4% Hispanic of any race (2010); Density: 889.3 persons per square mile (2010); Average household size: 2.68 (2010); Median age: 35.9 (2010); Males per 100 females: 95.8 (2010); Marriage status: 17.5% never married, 62.6% now married, 6.8% widowed, 13.1% divorced (2005-2009 5-year est.); Foreign born: 0.0% (2005-2009 5-year est.); Ancestry (includes multiple ancestries): 46.7% German, 24.0% American, 8.8% Irish, 4.9% English, 3.1% French (2005-2009 5-year est.).

Economy: Employment by occupation: 7.4% management, 13.4% professional, 16.8% services, 31.8% sales, 0.0% farming, 9.8% construction, 20.8% production (2005-2009 5-year est.).

Income: Per capita income: $20,100 (2010); Median household income: $50,490 (2010); Average household income: $54,158 (2010); Percent of households with income of $100,000 or more: 7.9% (2010); Poverty rate: 9.8% (2005-2009 5-year est.).

Taxes: Total city taxes per capita: $17 (2007); City property taxes per capita: $13 (2007).

Education: Percent of population age 25 and over with: High school diploma (including GED) or higher: 91.3% (2010); Bachelor's degree or higher: 12.9% (2010); Master's degree or higher: 3.9% (2010).

School District(s)

Payson CUSD 1 (PK-12)

   2009-10 Enrollment: 546 . . . . (217) 656-3323

Housing: Homeownership rate: 81.3% (2010); Median home value: $82,027 (2010); Median contract rent: $279 per month (2005-2009 5-year est.); Median year structure built: 1974 (2005-2009 5-year est.).

Transportation: Commute to work: 91.6% car, 0.0% public transportation, 0.0% walk, 7.7% work from home (2005-2009 5-year est.); Travel time to work: 6.4% less than 15 minutes, 64.2% 15 to 30 minutes, 21.0% 30 to 45 minutes, 2.9% 45 to 60 minutes, 5.5% 60 minutes or more (2005-2009 5-year est.)

PLAINVILLE (village). Covers a land area of 0.230 square miles and a water area of 0 square miles. Located at 39.78° N. Lat; 91.18° W. Long. Elevation is 692 feet.

Population: 270 (1990); 248 (2000); 241 (2010); 238 (2015 projected); Race: 97.9% White, 0.0% Black, 0.0% Asian, 2.1% Other, 0.0% Hispanic of any race (2010); Density: 1,048.3 persons per square mile (2010); Average household size: 2.65 (2010); Median age: 38.7 (2010); Males per 100 females: 99.2 (2010); Marriage status: 13.0% never married, 76.9% now married, 2.9% widowed, 7.1% divorced (2005-2009 5-year est.); Foreign born: 0.0% (2005-2009 5-year est.); Ancestry (includes multiple ancestries): 36.6% German, 14.3% American, 11.5% Irish, 8.4% English, 6.3% Polish (2005-2009 5-year est.).

Economy: Employment by occupation: 3.0% management, 16.7% professional, 16.1% services, 21.4% sales, 1.8% farming, 11.3% construction, 29.8% production (2005-2009 5-year est.).

Income: Per capita income: $20,465 (2010); Median household income: $48,125 (2010); Average household income: $53,791 (2010); Percent of households with income of $100,000 or more: 7.7% (2010); Poverty rate: 1.4% (2005-2009 5-year est.).

Taxes: Total city taxes per capita: $16 (2007); City property taxes per capita: $16 (2007).

Education: Percent of population age 25 and over with: High school diploma (including GED) or higher: 90.0% (2010); Bachelor's degree or higher: 8.1% (2010); Master's degree or higher: 1.9% (2010).

Housing: Homeownership rate: 85.7% (2010); Median home value: $102,500 (2010); Median contract rent: n/a per month (2005-2009 5-year est.); Median year structure built: 1947 (2005-2009 5-year est.).

Transportation: Commute to work: 96.4% car, 0.0% public transportation, 2.4% walk, 1.2% work from home (2005-2009 5-year est.); Travel time to work: 7.2% less than 15 minutes, 44.6% 15 to 30 minutes, 47.0% 30 to 45 minutes, 0.0% 45 to 60 minutes, 1.2% 60 minutes or more (2005-2009 5-year est.)

QUINCY (city). County seat. Covers a land area of 14.619 square miles and a water area of 0.027 square miles. Located at 39.93° N. Lat; 91.38° W. Long. Elevation is 568 feet.

History: The first settlement at Quincy was called The Bluffs, and centered around the cabin of John Wood. Wood later served as lieutenant governor and governor of Illinois. When Adams County was created in 1825, Quincy was named as the county seat, and the town was platted. In the mid-1800's Quincy was an active shipping center.

Population: 41,151 (1990); 40,366 (2000); 39,376 (2010); 38,766 (2015 projected); Race: 92.2% White, 4.9% Black, 0.5% Asian, 2.4% Other, 1.1% Hispanic of any race (2010); Density: 2,693.5 persons per square mile (2010); Average household size: 2.26 (2010); Median age: 39.6 (2010); Males per 100 females: 90.5 (2010); Marriage status: 29.9% never married, 48.4% now married, 9.7% widowed, 11.9% divorced (2005-2009 5-year est.); Foreign born: 1.4% (2005-2009 5-year est.); Ancestry (includes multiple ancestries): 41.6% German, 14.0% Irish, 11.3% American, 9.6% English, 2.5% French (2005-2009 5-year est.).

Economy: Unemployment rate: 7.4% (August 2011); Total civilian labor force: 22,124 (August 2011); Single-family building permits issued: 50 (2010); Multi-family building permits issued: 88 (2010); Employment by occupation: 11.2% management, 18.9% professional, 23.0% services, 25.4% sales, 0.1% farming, 5.8% construction, 15.5% production (2005-2009 5-year est.).

Income: Per capita income: $21,522 (2010); Median household income: $38,749 (2010); Average household income: $49,995 (2010); Percent of households with income of $100,000 or more: 8.2% (2010); Poverty rate: 17.1% (2005-2009 5-year est.).

Taxes: Total city taxes per capita: $304 (2007); City property taxes per capita: $83 (2007).

Education: Percent of population age 25 and over with: High school diploma (including GED) or higher: 89.1% (2010); Bachelor's degree or higher: 23.1% (2010); Master's degree or higher: 7.8% (2010).

School District(s)

Adams/Pike Roe (06-12)
    2009-10 Enrollment: n/a . . . . (217) 277-2080
Quincy Area Voc Ctr (11-12)
    2009-10 Enrollment: n/a . . . . (217) 224-3775
Quincy SD 172 (PK-12)
    2009-10 Enrollment: 7,081 . . . . (217) 223-8700

Four-year College(s)

Blessing Rieman College of Nursing (Private, Not-for-profit)
    Fall 2009 Enrollment: 222 . . . . (217) 228-5520
Quincy University (Private, Not-for-profit, Roman Catholic)
    Fall 2009 Enrollment: 1,845 . . . . (217) 222-8020
    2010-11 Tuition: In-state $23,000; Out-of-state $23,000

Two-year College(s)

Blessing Hospital School of Medical Laboratory Technology (Private, Not-for-profit)
    Fall 2009 Enrollment: 5 . . . . (217) 223-8400
Blessing Hospital School of Radiologic Technology (Private, Not-for-profit)
    Fall 2009 Enrollment: 18 . . . . (217) 223-8400
John Wood Community College (Public)
    Fall 2009 Enrollment: 2,757 . . . . (217) 224-6500
    2010-11 Tuition: In-state $7,110; Out-of-state $7,110
Vatterott College (Private, For-profit)
    Fall 2009 Enrollment: 550 . . . . (800) 438-5621
    2010-11 Tuition: In-state $10,991; Out-of-state $10,991

Vocational/Technical School(s)

Gem City College (Private, For-profit)
    Fall 2009 Enrollment: 66 . . . . (217) 222-0391
    2010-11 Tuition: $12,975

Housing: Homeownership rate: 67.3% (2010); Median home value: $82,915 (2010); Median contract rent: $402 per month (2005-2009 5-year est.); Median year structure built: 1953 (2005-2009 5-year est.).

Hospitals: Blessing Hospital (426 beds)

Safety: Violent crime rate: 47.0 per 10,000 population; Property crime rate: 338.3 per 10,000 population (2010).

Newspapers: Quincy Herald-Whig (Local news; Circulation 24,153)

Transportation: Commute to work: 91.2% car, 1.2% public transportation, 3.7% walk, 3.2% work from home (2005-2009 5-year est.); Travel time to work: 66.9% less than 15 minutes, 26.6% 15 to 30 minutes, 3.8% 30 to 45 minutes, 1.2% 45 to 60 minutes, 1.5% 60 minutes or more (2005-2009 5-year est.); Amtrak: train service available.

Airports: Quincy Regional-Baldwin Field (general aviation)

Additional Information Contacts

City of Quincy. . . . . (217) 228-4500
    http://www.ci.quincy.il.us
Quincy Area Chamber of Commerce. . . . . (217) 222-7980
    http://www.quincychamber.org

URSA (village). Covers a land area of 0.682 square miles and a water area of 0 square miles. Located at 40.07° N. Lat; 91.37° W. Long. Elevation is 610 feet.

Population: 578 (1990); 595 (2000); 565 (2010); 549 (2015 projected); Race: 98.6% White, 0.0% Black, 0.4% Asian, 1.1% Other, 1.6% Hispanic of any race (2010); Density: 828.9 persons per square mile (2010); Average household size: 2.48 (2010); Median age: 37.2 (2010); Males per 100 females: 90.2 (2010); Marriage status: 16.8% never married, 61.9% now married, 8.6% widowed, 12.8% divorced (2005-2009 5-year est.); Foreign born: 0.0% (2005-2009 5-year est.); Ancestry (includes multiple ancestries): 37.6% German, 16.7% American, 14.1% Irish, 7.8% French, 7.0% Scotch-Irish (2005-2009 5-year est.).

Economy: Employment by occupation: 12.1% management, 24.2% professional, 12.1% services, 21.2% sales, 0.0% farming, 8.3% construction, 22.1% production (2005-2009 5-year est.).

Income: Per capita income: $22,616 (2010); Median household income: $53,378 (2010); Average household income: $56,787 (2010); Percent of households with income of $100,000 or more: 9.2% (2010); Poverty rate: 2.5% (2005-2009 5-year est.).

Taxes: Total city taxes per capita: $22 (2007); City property taxes per capita: $20 (2007).

Education: Percent of population age 25 and over with: High school diploma (including GED) or higher: 89.8% (2010); Bachelor's degree or higher: 15.6% (2010); Master's degree or higher: 4.0% (2010).

School District(s)

CUSD 4 (PK-12)
    2009-10 Enrollment: 756 . . . . (217) 936-2111

Housing: Homeownership rate: 79.4% (2010); Median home value: $76,765 (2010); Median contract rent: $363 per month (2005-2009 5-year est.); Median year structure built: 1971 (2005-2009 5-year est.).

Transportation: Commute to work: 83.0% car, 0.0% public transportation, 9.1% walk, 6.6% work from home (2005-2009 5-year est.); Travel time to work: 37.5% less than 15 minutes, 45.6% 15 to 30 minutes, 12.8% 30 to 45 minutes, 2.7% 45 to 60 minutes, 1.4% 60 minutes or more (2005-2009 5-year est.)

Alexander County

Located in southern Illinois; bounded on the west and south by the Mississippi River and the Missouri border, and on the southeast by the Ohio River; includes part of Shawnee National Forest. Covers a land area of 236.38 square miles, a water area of 16.16 square miles, and is located in the Central Time Zone at 37.14° N. Lat., 89.28° W. Long. The county was founded in 1819. County seat is Cairo.

Alexander County is part of the Cape Girardeau-Jackson, MO-IL Metropolitan Statistical Area. The entire metro area includes: Alexander County, IL; Bollinger County, MO; Cape Girardeau County, MO

Weather Station: Cairo Wso City									Elevation: 313 feet		
	Jan	Feb	Mar	Apr	May	Jun	Jul	Aug	Sep	Oct	Nov	Dec
High	43	48	58	69	78	86	89	88	82	70	58	45
Low	27	30	38	48	58	66	70	68	60	48	39	29
Precip	3.3	3.9	4.2	4.9	5.4	3.9	4.5	3.2	3.1	4.3	4.2	4.2
Snow	1.9	2.2	0.6	tr	0.0	0.0	0.0	0.0	0.0	0.1	0.1	0.8

High and Low temperatures in degrees Fahrenheit; Precipitation and Snow in inches

Population: 10,626 (1990); 9,590 (2000); 7,928 (2010); 7,517 (2015 projected); Race: 63.3% White, 34.0% Black, 0.5% Asian, 2.3% Other, 1.4% Hispanic of any race (2010); Density: 33.5 persons per square mile (2010); Average household size: 2.31 (2010); Median age: 39.7 (2010); Males per 100 females: 91.6 (2010).

Religion: Five largest groups: 21.4% Southern Baptist Convention, 3.6% American Baptist Churches in the USA, 3.4% Catholic Church, 2.5% The United Methodist Church, 1.5% Assemblies of God (2000).

Economy: Unemployment rate: 14.2% (August 2011); Total civilian labor force: 3,119 (August 2011); Leading industries: 23.0% health care and social assistance; 22.7% transportation & warehousing; 12.2% retail trade (2009); Farms: 143 totaling 47,626 acres (2007); Companies that employ 500 or more persons: 0 (2009); Companies that employ 100 to 499 persons: 2 (2009); Companies that employ less than 100 persons: 116 (2009); Black-owned businesses: n/a (2007); Hispanic-owned businesses: n/a (2007); Asian-owned businesses: n/a (2007); Women-owned businesses: 165 (2007); Retail sales per capita: $4,542 (2010). Single-family building permits issued: 0 (2010); Multi-family building permits issued: 0 (2010).

Income: Per capita income: $18,559 (2010); Median household income: $31,330 (2010); Average household income: $43,045 (2010); Percent of households with income of $100,000 or more: 6.3% (2010); Poverty rate: 29.4% (2009); Bankruptcy rate: 5.04% (2010).

Taxes: Total county taxes per capita: $135 (2007); County property taxes per capita: $134 (2007).

Education: Percent of population age 25 and over with: High school diploma (including GED) or higher: 74.5% (2010); Bachelor's degree or higher: 8.7% (2010); Master's degree or higher: 3.1% (2010).

Housing: Homeownership rate: 70.5% (2010); Median home value: $46,068 (2010); Median contract rent: $267 per month (2005-2009 5-year est.); Median year structure built: 1954 (2005-2009 5-year est.).

Health: Birth rate: 141.5 per 10,000 population (2009); Death rate: 128.9 per 10,000 population (2009); Age-adjusted cancer mortality rate: 279.8 deaths per 100,000 population (2007); Number of physicians: 3.7 per 10,000 population (2008); Hospital beds: 0.0 per 10,000 population (2007); Hospital admissions: 0.0 per 10,000 population (2007).

Elections: 2008 Presidential election results: 55.6% Obama, 43.0% McCain, 0.6% Nader

National and State Parks: Fort Defiance State Park; Horseshoe Lake State Conservation Area

Additional Information Contacts
Alexander County Government . . . . (618) 734-7000

Cairo Chamber of Commerce . . . . (618) 734-2737
Horseshoe Lake Chamber of Commerce . . . . (618) 776-5198
 http://www.horseshoelakechamber.com

Alexander County Communities

CAIRO (city). County seat. Covers a land area of 7.051 square miles and a water area of 2.081 square miles. Located at 37.01° N. Lat; 89.18° W. Long. Elevation is 322 feet.

History: John G. Comegys, a St. Louis merchant, in 1818 secured the incorporation of the city of Cairo, named because he thought its site resembled Cairo, Egypt. Comegys died before he could carry out his plans, but the name Cairo remained when the Cairo City and Canal Company was formed in 1837 by Darius B. Holbrook. When the Illinois Central Railroad tracks were laid between Cairo and Chicago, Cairo's economy grew. Cairo was a Union headquarters during the Civil War, and received many thousands of Confederate prisoners.

Population: 4,873 (1990); 3,632 (2000); 2,799 (2010); 2,588 (2015 projected); Race: 35.0% White, 61.8% Black, 0.9% Asian, 2.3% Other, 0.8% Hispanic of any race (2010); Density: 396.9 persons per square mile (2010); Average household size: 2.21 (2010); Median age: 35.5 (2010); Males per 100 females: 76.6 (2010); Marriage status: 34.5% never married, 36.5% now married, 15.9% widowed, 13.1% divorced (2005-2009 5-year est.); Foreign born: 3.7% (2005-2009 5-year est.); Ancestry (includes multiple ancestries): 11.4% German, 6.5% American, 4.6% English, 4.0% Swedish, 3.0% Irish (2005-2009 5-year est.).

Economy: Single-family building permits issued: 0 (2010); Multi-family building permits issued: 0 (2010); Employment by occupation: 10.8% management, 17.3% professional, 30.4% services, 27.9% sales, 0.0% farming, 9.1% construction, 4.6% production (2005-2009 5-year est.).

Income: Per capita income: $18,610 (2010); Median household income: $25,954 (2010); Average household income: $41,380 (2010); Percent of households with income of $100,000 or more: 6.3% (2010); Poverty rate: 31.9% (2005-2009 5-year est.).

Taxes: Total city taxes per capita: $366 (2007); City property taxes per capita: $164 (2007).

Education: Percent of population age 25 and over with: High school diploma (including GED) or higher: 74.1% (2010); Bachelor's degree or higher: 9.4% (2010); Master's degree or higher: 3.5% (2010).

School District(s)
Alxndr/John/Masc/Pulski/Union Roe (06-12)
 2009-10 Enrollment: n/a . . . . (618) 634-2292
Cairo USD 1 (PK-12)
 2009-10 Enrollment: 602 . . . . (618) 734-4102
Five County Reg Voc System
 2009-10 Enrollment: n/a . . . . (618) 747-2703
Jamp Spec Educ Services (02-12)
 2009-10 Enrollment: n/a . . . . (618) 634-9800

Housing: Homeownership rate: 52.8% (2010); Median home value: $35,104 (2010); Median contract rent: $273 per month (2005-2009 5-year est.); Median year structure built: 1941 (2005-2009 5-year est.).

Safety: Violent crime rate: 319.7 per 10,000 population; Property crime rate: 728.8 per 10,000 population (2010).

Newspapers: Cairo Citizen (Community news; Circulation 3,500)

Transportation: Commute to work: 80.6% car, 2.2% public transportation, 8.1% walk, 1.3% work from home (2005-2009 5-year est.); Travel time to work: 52.1% less than 15 minutes, 21.7% 15 to 30 minutes, 12.2% 30 to 45 minutes, 2.0% 45 to 60 minutes, 12.0% 60 minutes or more (2005-2009 5-year est.)

Additional Information Contacts
Cairo Chamber of Commerce . . . . (618) 734-2737

EAST CAPE GIRARDEAU (village). Covers a land area of 1.969 square miles and a water area of 0.034 square miles. Located at 37.29° N. Lat; 89.49° W. Long. Elevation is 341 feet.

Population: 451 (1990); 437 (2000); 380 (2010); 364 (2015 projected); Race: 96.6% White, 0.5% Black, 1.1% Asian, 1.8% Other, 1.3% Hispanic of any race (2010); Density: 193.0 persons per square mile (2010); Average household size: 2.30 (2010); Median age: 45.4 (2010); Males per 100 females: 91.0 (2010); Marriage status: 23.1% never married, 58.6% now married, 4.1% widowed, 14.3% divorced (2005-2009 5-year est.); Foreign born: 0.6% (2005-2009 5-year est.); Ancestry (includes multiple ancestries): 21.4% German, 17.3% American, 8.8% Irish, 8.2% English, 3.3% French (2005-2009 5-year est.).

Economy: Single-family building permits issued: 0 (2010); Multi-family building permits issued: 0 (2010); Employment by occupation: 5.5% management, 22.8% professional, 12.4% services, 28.3% sales, 0.0% farming, 7.9% construction, 23.1% production (2005-2009 5-year est.).

Income: Per capita income: $18,244 (2010); Median household income: $30,435 (2010); Average household income: $41,227 (2010); Percent of households with income of $100,000 or more: 6.7% (2010); Poverty rate: 3.9% (2005-2009 5-year est.).

Taxes: Total city taxes per capita: $16 (2007); City property taxes per capita: $13 (2007).

Education: Percent of population age 25 and over with: High school diploma (including GED) or higher: 82.5% (2010); Bachelor's degree or higher: 13.5% (2010); Master's degree or higher: 1.1% (2010).

Housing: Homeownership rate: 80.6% (2010); Median home value: $46,765 (2010); Median contract rent: $425 per month (2005-2009 5-year est.); Median year structure built: 1974 (2005-2009 5-year est.).

Transportation: Commute to work: 95.9% car, 0.0% public transportation, 3.4% walk, 0.0% work from home (2005-2009 5-year est.); Travel time to work: 36.4% less than 15 minutes, 42.5% 15 to 30 minutes, 14.6% 30 to 45 minutes, 1.0% 45 to 60 minutes, 5.4% 60 minutes or more (2005-2009 5-year est.)

MCCLURE (village). Covers a land area of 1.528 square miles and a water area of 0 square miles. Located at 37.30° N. Lat; 89.43° W. Long. Elevation is 341 feet.

History: Incorporated 2004.

Population: n/a (1990); n/a (2000); 402 (2010); n/a (2015 projected); Race: 93.5% White, 1.2% Black, 0.5% Asian, 4.7% Other, 1.7% Hispanic of any race (2010); Density: 263.1 persons per square mile (2010); Average household size: 2.51 (2010); Median age: 37.5 (2010); Males per 100 females: 99.0 (2010); Marriage status: 6.5% never married, 61.2% now married, 19.9% widowed, 12.4% divorced (2005-2009 5-year est.); Foreign born: 0.0% (2005-2009 5-year est.); Ancestry (includes multiple ancestries): 22.0% Irish, 19.0% German, 13.9% English, 8.1% Scotch-Irish, 4.6% French (2005-2009 5-year est.).

Economy: Employment by occupation: 18.6% management, 22.8% professional, 22.1% services, 15.2% sales, 11.0% farming, 6.2% construction, 4.1% production (2005-2009 5-year est.).

Income: Per capita income: n/a (2010); Median household income: n/a (2010); Average household income: n/a (2010); Percent of households with income of $100,000 or more: n/a (2010); Poverty rate: 32.9% (2005-2009 5-year est.).

Taxes: Total city taxes per capita: $123 (2007); City property taxes per capita: $36 (2007).

Education: Percent of population age 25 and over with: High school diploma (including GED) or higher: n/a (2010); Bachelor's degree or higher: n/a (2010); Master's degree or higher: n/a (2010).

School District(s)
Shawnee CUSD 84 (PK-12)
 2009-10 Enrollment: 460 . . . . (618) 833-5709

Housing: Homeownership rate: n/a (2010); Median home value: n/a (2010); Median contract rent: $272 per month (2005-2009 5-year est.); Median year structure built: 1968 (2005-2009 5-year est.).

Transportation: Commute to work: 97.2% car, 0.0% public transportation, 2.8% walk, 0.0% work from home (2005-2009 5-year est.); Travel time to work: 29.7% less than 15 minutes, 42.1% 15 to 30 minutes, 17.9% 30 to 45 minutes, 8.3% 45 to 60 minutes, 2.1% 60 minutes or more (2005-2009 5-year est.)

MILLER CITY (unincorporated postal area, zip code 62962). Covers a land area of 37.441 square miles and a water area of 0.523 square miles. Located at 37.09° N. Lat; 89.33° W. Long. Elevation is 331 feet.

Population: 93 (2000); Race: 100.0% White, 0.0% Black, 0.0% Asian, 0.0% Other, 0.0% Hispanic of any race (2000); Density: 2.5 persons per square mile (2000); Age: 0.0% under 18, 14.5% over 64 (2000); Marriage status: 16.4% never married, 61.8% now married, 21.8% widowed, 0.0% divorced (2000); Foreign born: 0.0% (2000); Ancestry (includes multiple ancestries): 43.6% German, 9.1% American, 9.1% Irish (2000).

Economy: Employment by occupation: 47.4% management, 0.0% professional, 0.0% services, 0.0% sales, 26.3% farming, 0.0% construction, 26.3% production (2000).

Income: Per capita income: $18,242 (2000); Median household income: $26,250 (2000); Poverty rate: 50.9% (2000).

Education: Percent of population age 25 and over with: High school diploma (including GED) or higher: 58.7% (2000); Bachelor's degree or higher: 30.4% (2000).
Housing: Homeownership rate: 36.8% (2000); Median home value: $45,000 (2000); Median contract rent: $150 per month (2000); Median year structure built: 1972 (2000).
Transportation: Commute to work: 100.0% car, 0.0% public transportation, 0.0% walk, 0.0% work from home (2000); Travel time to work: 0.0% less than 15 minutes, 73.7% 15 to 30 minutes, 0.0% 30 to 45 minutes, 0.0% 45 to 60 minutes, 26.3% 60 minutes or more (2000)

OLIVE BRANCH (unincorporated postal area, zip code 62969). Covers a land area of 25.996 square miles and a water area of 2.618 square miles. Located at 37.16° N. Lat; 89.35° W. Long. Elevation is 341 feet.
Population: 879 (2000); Race: 98.4% White, 0.0% Black, 0.0% Asian, 1.6% Other, 0.0% Hispanic of any race (2000); Density: 33.8 persons per square mile (2000); Age: 26.0% under 18, 19.5% over 64 (2000); Marriage status: 13.9% never married, 66.5% now married, 11.0% widowed, 8.6% divorced (2000); Foreign born: 0.7% (2000); Ancestry (includes multiple ancestries): 10.0% German, 9.9% American, 7.5% Irish, 7.0% English (2000).
Economy: Employment by occupation: 15.5% management, 14.7% professional, 16.6% services, 17.7% sales, 0.0% farming, 22.3% construction, 13.3% production (2000).
Income: Per capita income: $23,970 (2000); Median household income: $30,833 (2000); Poverty rate: 13.5% (2000).
Education: Percent of population age 25 and over with: High school diploma (including GED) or higher: 72.6% (2000); Bachelor's degree or higher: 12.4% (2000).
Housing: Homeownership rate: 88.3% (2000); Median home value: $59,600 (2000); Median contract rent: $144 per month (2000); Median year structure built: 1973 (2000).
Transportation: Commute to work: 88.3% car, 1.6% public transportation, 4.3% walk, 5.7% work from home (2000); Travel time to work: 18.7% less than 15 minutes, 48.4% 15 to 30 minutes, 20.7% 30 to 45 minutes, 2.0% 45 to 60 minutes, 10.1% 60 minutes or more (2000)
Additional Information Contacts
Horseshoe Lake Chamber of Commerce . . . . (618) 776-5198
   http://www.horseshoelakechamber.com

TAMMS (village). Covers a land area of 2.340 square miles and a water area of 0 square miles. Located at 37.24° N. Lat; 89.26° W. Long. Elevation is 341 feet.
Population: 731 (1990); 724 (2000); 647 (2010); 625 (2015 projected); Race: 46.1% White, 50.7% Black, 0.0% Asian, 3.2% Other, 6.0% Hispanic of any race (2010); Density: 276.5 persons per square mile (2010); Average household size: 2.44 (2010); Median age: 36.6 (2010); Males per 100 females: 146.0 (2010); Marriage status: 41.5% never married, 40.3% now married, 10.0% widowed, 8.3% divorced (2005-2009 5-year est.); Foreign born: 1.5% (2005-2009 5-year est.); Ancestry (includes multiple ancestries): 9.1% German, 8.6% English, 7.6% Irish, 3.5% American, 2.3% Dutch (2005-2009 5-year est.).
Economy: Employment by occupation: 11.4% management, 4.8% professional, 18.7% services, 13.9% sales, 0.0% farming, 12.7% construction, 38.6% production (2005-2009 5-year est.).
Income: Per capita income: $15,526 (2010); Median household income: $25,000 (2010); Average household income: $36,927 (2010); Percent of households with income of $100,000 or more: 6.8% (2010); Poverty rate: 45.3% (2005-2009 5-year est.).
Taxes: Total city taxes per capita: $7 (2007); City property taxes per capita: $7 (2007).
Education: Percent of population age 25 and over with: High school diploma (including GED) or higher: 54.5% (2010); Bachelor's degree or higher: 1.7% (2010); Master's degree or higher: 0.2% (2010).
School District(s)
Egyptian CUSD 5 (PK-12)
   2009-10 Enrollment: 593 . . . . (618) 776-5306
Five County Reg Voc Center (11-12)
   2009-10 Enrollment: n/a . . . . (618) 747-2703
Housing: Homeownership rate: 81.3% (2010); Median home value: $51,111 (2010); Median contract rent: $289 per month (2005-2009 5-year est.); Median year structure built: before 1940 (2005-2009 5-year est.).
Transportation: Commute to work: 98.0% car, 0.0% public transportation, 2.0% walk, 0.0% work from home (2005-2009 5-year est.); Travel time to

work: 29.6% less than 15 minutes, 46.7% 15 to 30 minutes, 23.7% 30 to 45 minutes, 0.0% 45 to 60 minutes, 0.0% 60 minutes or more (2005-2009 5-year est.)

THEBES (village). Covers a land area of 1.800 square miles and a water area of 0.513 square miles. Located at 37.21° N. Lat; 89.45° W. Long. Elevation is 351 feet.
History: Thebes was laid out in 1844, and once served as the seat of Alexander County. The site was earlier known as Sparhawk's Landing.
Population: 461 (1990); 478 (2000); 439 (2010); 429 (2015 projected); Race: 92.3% White, 5.5% Black, 0.0% Asian, 2.3% Other, 0.2% Hispanic of any race (2010); Density: 243.9 persons per square mile (2010); Average household size: 2.61 (2010); Median age: 36.0 (2010); Males per 100 females: 94.2 (2010); Marriage status: 22.4% never married, 61.2% now married, 7.8% widowed, 8.6% divorced (2005-2009 5-year est.); Foreign born: 0.0% (2005-2009 5-year est.); Ancestry (includes multiple ancestries): 16.6% Irish, 13.6% German, 9.4% English, 8.4% American, 3.5% Italian (2005-2009 5-year est.).
Economy: Single-family building permits issued: 0 (2010); Multi-family building permits issued: 0 (2010); Employment by occupation: 8.8% management, 17.6% professional, 27.5% services, 15.7% sales, 0.0% farming, 9.8% construction, 20.6% production (2005-2009 5-year est.).
Income: Per capita income: $16,406 (2010); Median household income: $31,667 (2010); Average household income: $45,789 (2010); Percent of households with income of $100,000 or more: 8.3% (2010); Poverty rate: 49.6% (2005-2009 5-year est.).
Taxes: Total city taxes per capita: $10 (2007); City property taxes per capita: $10 (2007).
Education: Percent of population age 25 and over with: High school diploma (including GED) or higher: 76.5% (2010); Bachelor's degree or higher: 6.7% (2010); Master's degree or higher: 1.9% (2010).
Housing: Homeownership rate: 74.4% (2010); Median home value: $54,167 (2010); Median contract rent: $155 per month (2005-2009 5-year est.); Median year structure built: 1968 (2005-2009 5-year est.).
Transportation: Commute to work: 93.8% car, 0.0% public transportation, 6.3% walk, 0.0% work from home (2005-2009 5-year est.); Travel time to work: 16.7% less than 15 minutes, 49.0% 15 to 30 minutes, 25.0% 30 to 45 minutes, 5.2% 45 to 60 minutes, 4.2% 60 minutes or more (2005-2009 5-year est.)

Bond County

Located in southwest central Illinois; drained by the Kaskaskia River. Covers a land area of 380.20 square miles, a water area of 2.46 square miles, and is located in the Central Time Zone at 38.88° N. Lat., 89.43° W. Long. The county was founded in 1817. County seat is Greenville.

Bond County is part of the St. Louis, MO-IL Metropolitan Statistical Area. The entire metro area includes: Bond County, IL; Calhoun County, IL; Clinton County, IL; Jersey County, IL; Macoupin County, IL; Madison County, IL; Monroe County, IL; St. Clair County, IL; Crawford County, MO (pt.); Franklin County, MO; Jefferson County, MO; Lincoln County, MO; St. Charles County, MO; St. Louis County, MO; Warren County, MO; Washington County, MO; St. Louis city, MO

Population: 14,991 (1990); 17,633 (2000); 18,287 (2010); 18,425 (2015 projected); Race: 90.6% White, 7.3% Black, 0.3% Asian, 1.9% Other, 1.6% Hispanic of any race (2010); Density: 48.1 persons per square mile (2010); Average household size: 2.44 (2010); Median age: 36.1 (2010); Males per 100 females: 117.0 (2010).
Religion: Five largest groups: 10.6% Christian Churches and Churches of Christ, 10.0% Southern Baptist Convention, 8.2% Catholic Church, 5.1% The United Methodist Church, 3.6% Free Methodist Church of North America (2000).
Economy: Unemployment rate: 8.7% (August 2011); Total civilian labor force: 8,585 (August 2011); Leading industries: 20.7% manufacturing; 14.8% health care and social assistance; 9.6% retail trade (2009); Farms: 673 totaling 224,760 acres (2007); Companies that employ 500 or more persons: 1 (2009); Companies that employ 100 to 499 persons: 3 (2009); Companies that employ less than 100 persons: 319 (2009); Black-owned businesses: n/a (2007); Hispanic-owned businesses: n/a (2007); Asian-owned businesses: n/a (2007); Women-owned businesses: 363 (2007); Retail sales per capita: $9,666 (2010). Single-family building permits issued: 28 (2010); Multi-family building permits issued: 0 (2010).
Income: Per capita income: $21,490 (2010); Median household income: $46,293 (2010); Average household income: $55,982 (2010); Percent of

households with income of $100,000 or more: 12.4% (2010); Poverty rate: 13.7% (2009); Bankruptcy rate: 2.97% (2010).
Taxes: Total county taxes per capita: $124 (2007); County property taxes per capita: $122 (2007).
Education: Percent of population age 25 and over with: High school diploma (including GED) or higher: 79.7% (2010); Bachelor's degree or higher: 18.7% (2010); Master's degree or higher: 6.1% (2010).
Housing: Homeownership rate: 78.6% (2010); Median home value: $98,675 (2010); Median contract rent: $429 per month (2005-2009 5-year est.); Median year structure built: 1962 (2005-2009 5-year est.)
Health: Birth rate: 122.6 per 10,000 population (2009); Death rate: 100.0 per 10,000 population (2009); Age-adjusted cancer mortality rate: 308.7 deaths per 100,000 population (2007); Number of physicians: 8.2 per 10,000 population (2008); Hospital beds: 81.9 per 10,000 population (2007); Hospital admissions: 1,070.3 per 10,000 population (2007).
Elections: 2008 Presidential election results: 48.5% Obama, 49.8% McCain, 0.7% Nader
Additional Information Contacts
Bond County Government . . . . (618) 664-0449
  http://bondcountyil.com
Greenville Chamber of Commerce . . . . (618) 664-9272
  http://www.greenvilleusa.org

Bond County Communities

GREENVILLE (city). County seat. Covers a land area of 5.202 square miles and a water area of 0 square miles. Located at 38.89° N. Lat; 89.40° W. Long. Elevation is 617 feet.
History: Greenville was settled in 1815, and developed as the seat of Bond County. Early industries were an evaporated milk plant, a glove plant, and a manufacturer of costumes and uniforms.
Population: 5,168 (1990); 6,955 (2000); 7,347 (2010); 7,502 (2015 projected); Race: 81.5% White, 16.2% Black, 0.5% Asian, 1.9% Other, 2.7% Hispanic of any race (2010); Density: 1,412.3 persons per square mile (2010); Average household size: 2.26 (2010); Median age: 33.6 (2010); Males per 100 females: 149.6 (2010); Marriage status: 33.3% never married, 46.5% now married, 8.1% widowed, 12.2% divorced (2005-2009 5-year est.); Foreign born: 3.0% (2005-2009 5-year est.); Ancestry (includes multiple ancestries): 21.3% German, 11.5% English, 9.9% American, 9.0% Irish, 5.2% Dutch (2005-2009 5-year est.).
Economy: Single-family building permits issued: 10 (2010); Multi-family building permits issued: 0 (2010); Employment by occupation: 9.6% management, 23.4% professional, 24.1% services, 23.4% sales, 0.0% farming, 5.5% construction, 14.0% production (2005-2009 5-year est.).
Income: Per capita income: $19,891 (2010); Median household income: $43,613 (2010); Average household income: $53,863 (2010); Percent of households with income of $100,000 or more: 12.4% (2010); Poverty rate: 13.3% (2005-2009 5-year est.).
Taxes: Total city taxes per capita: $103 (2007); City property taxes per capita: $69 (2007).
Education: Percent of population age 25 and over with: High school diploma (including GED) or higher: 70.9% (2010); Bachelor's degree or higher: 22.6% (2010); Master's degree or higher: 8.5% (2010).
School District(s)
Bond County CUSD 2 (PK-12)
  2009-10 Enrollment: 2,044 . . . . (618) 664-0170
Four-year College(s)
Greenville College (Private, Not-for-profit, Free Methodist)
  Fall 2009 Enrollment: 1,576 . . . . (618) 664-2800
  2010-11 Tuition: In-state $20,924; Out-of-state $20,924
Housing: Homeownership rate: 68.3% (2010); Median home value: $93,309 (2010); Median contract rent: $443 per month (2005-2009 5-year est.); Median year structure built: 1949 (2005-2009 5-year est.).
Hospitals: Greenville Regional Hospital (50 beds)
Safety: Violent crime rate: 2.8 per 10,000 population; Property crime rate: 174.2 per 10,000 population (2010).
Newspapers: Greenville Advocate (Regional news; Circulation 5,100)
Transportation: Commute to work: 89.2% car, 0.5% public transportation, 8.2% walk, 2.1% work from home (2005-2009 5-year est.); Travel time to work: 57.6% less than 15 minutes, 18.9% 15 to 30 minutes, 7.3% 30 to 45 minutes, 10.8% 45 to 60 minutes, 5.4% 60 minutes or more (2005-2009 5-year est.)
Additional Information Contacts
Greenville Chamber of Commerce . . . . (618) 664-9272
  http://www.greenvilleusa.org

MULBERRY GROVE (village). Covers a land area of 0.986 square miles and a water area of 0.009 square miles. Located at 38.92° N. Lat; 89.26° W. Long. Elevation is 561 feet.
Population: 660 (1990); 671 (2000); 647 (2010); 631 (2015 projected); Race: 91.0% White, 7.3% Black, 0.0% Asian, 1.7% Other, 0.3% Hispanic of any race (2010); Density: 656.3 persons per square mile (2010); Average household size: 2.36 (2010); Median age: 37.0 (2010); Males per 100 females: 92.0 (2010); Marriage status: 29.0% never married, 50.4% now married, 6.6% widowed, 13.9% divorced (2005-2009 5-year est.); Foreign born: 0.0% (2005-2009 5-year est.); Ancestry (includes multiple ancestries): 16.5% Irish, 15.3% English, 15.3% German, 11.9% American, 1.9% Dutch (2005-2009 5-year est.).
Economy: Single-family building permits issued: 0 (2010); Multi-family building permits issued: 0 (2010); Employment by occupation: 24.5% management, 13.0% professional, 8.6% services, 16.0% sales, 0.0% farming, 1.1% construction, 36.8% production (2005-2009 5-year est.).
Income: Per capita income: $18,719 (2010); Median household income: $39,909 (2010); Average household income: $44,179 (2010); Percent of households with income of $100,000 or more: 4.7% (2010); Poverty rate: 23.4% (2005-2009 5-year est.).
Taxes: Total city taxes per capita: $81 (2007); City property taxes per capita: $54 (2007).
Education: Percent of population age 25 and over with: High school diploma (including GED) or higher: 82.2% (2010); Bachelor's degree or higher: 9.4% (2010); Master's degree or higher: 2.7% (2010).
School District(s)
Mulberry Grove CUSD 1 (PK-12)
  2009-10 Enrollment: 470 . . . . (618) 326-8812
Housing: Homeownership rate: 76.6% (2010); Median home value: $68,500 (2010); Median contract rent: $318 per month (2005-2009 5-year est.); Median year structure built: 1958 (2005-2009 5-year est.).
Transportation: Commute to work: 91.4% car, 0.0% public transportation, 4.5% walk, 2.6% work from home (2005-2009 5-year est.); Travel time to work: 36.2% less than 15 minutes, 35.0% 15 to 30 minutes, 14.6% 30 to 45 minutes, 2.7% 45 to 60 minutes, 11.5% 60 minutes or more (2005-2009 5-year est.)

OLD RIPLEY (village). Covers a land area of 0.149 square miles and a water area of 0 square miles. Located at 38.89° N. Lat; 89.57° W. Long. Elevation is 561 feet.
Population: 95 (1990); 127 (2000); 117 (2010); 118 (2015 projected); Race: 99.1% White, 0.0% Black, 0.0% Asian, 0.9% Other, 0.0% Hispanic of any race (2010); Density: 784.2 persons per square mile (2010); Average household size: 2.44 (2010); Median age: 42.1 (2010); Males per 100 females: 108.9 (2010); Marriage status: 21.8% never married, 56.3% now married, 4.6% widowed, 17.2% divorced (2005-2009 5-year est.); Foreign born: 0.0% (2005-2009 5-year est.); Ancestry (includes multiple ancestries): 25.7% German, 13.3% American, 10.5% English, 4.8% Swiss, 2.9% French (2005-2009 5-year est.).
Economy: Employment by occupation: 2.4% management, 4.8% professional, 19.0% services, 26.2% sales, 14.3% farming, 9.5% construction, 23.8% production (2005-2009 5-year est.).
Income: Per capita income: $23,365 (2010); Median household income: $55,357 (2010); Average household income: $59,583 (2010); Percent of households with income of $100,000 or more: 12.5% (2010); Poverty rate: 13.3% (2005-2009 5-year est.).
Taxes: Total city taxes per capita: $24 (2007); City property taxes per capita: $16 (2007).
Education: Percent of population age 25 and over with: High school diploma (including GED) or higher: 83.5% (2010); Bachelor's degree or higher: 16.5% (2010); Master's degree or higher: 10.6% (2010).
Housing: Homeownership rate: 87.5% (2010); Median home value: $119,231 (2010); Median contract rent: n/a per month (2005-2009 5-year est.); Median year structure built: 1953 (2005-2009 5-year est.).
Transportation: Commute to work: 100.0% car, 0.0% public transportation, 0.0% walk, 0.0% work from home (2005-2009 5-year est.); Travel time to work: 0.0% less than 15 minutes, 55.0% 15 to 30 minutes, 7.5% 30 to 45 minutes, 27.5% 45 to 60 minutes, 10.0% 60 minutes or more (2005-2009 5-year est.)

PIERRON (village). Covers a land area of 0.851 square miles and a water area of 0 square miles. Located at 38.77° N. Lat; 89.55° W. Long. Elevation is 522 feet.

Population: 554 (1990); 653 (2000); 631 (2010); 629 (2015 projected); Race: 96.7% White, 0.2% Black, 0.3% Asian, 2.9% Other, 1.4% Hispanic of any race (2010); Density: 741.7 persons per square mile (2010); Average household size: 2.69 (2010); Median age: 34.8 (2010); Males per 100 females: 104.2 (2010); Marriage status: 19.8% never married, 56.3% now married, 12.3% widowed, 11.6% divorced (2005-2009 5-year est.); Foreign born: 0.8% (2005-2009 5-year est.); Ancestry (includes multiple ancestries): 38.3% German, 5.1% French, 4.7% Dutch, 4.1% American, 3.4% Irish (2005-2009 5-year est.).
Economy: Single-family building permits issued: 0 (2010); Multi-family building permits issued: 0 (2010); Employment by occupation: 4.0% management, 14.5% professional, 16.7% services, 16.3% sales, 2.6% farming, 26.4% construction, 19.4% production (2005-2009 5-year est.).
Income: Per capita income: $21,178 (2010); Median household income: $47,384 (2010); Average household income: $57,926 (2010); Percent of households with income of $100,000 or more: 10.6% (2010); Poverty rate: 15.2% (2005-2009 5-year est.).
Taxes: Total city taxes per capita: $23 (2007); City property taxes per capita: $21 (2007).
Education: Percent of population age 25 and over with: High school diploma (including GED) or higher: 87.0% (2010); Bachelor's degree or higher: 10.6% (2010); Master's degree or higher: 1.2% (2010).
Housing: Homeownership rate: 89.4% (2010); Median home value: $99,375 (2010); Median contract rent: $359 per month (2005-2009 5-year est.); Median year structure built: 1970 (2005-2009 5-year est.).
Transportation: Commute to work: 85.5% car, 0.0% public transportation, 5.7% walk, 8.8% work from home (2005-2009 5-year est.); Travel time to work: 12.1% less than 15 minutes, 36.7% 15 to 30 minutes, 15.0% 30 to 45 minutes, 11.6% 45 to 60 minutes, 24.6% 60 minutes or more (2005-2009 5-year est.)

POCAHONTAS (village).
Covers a land area of 0.751 square miles and a water area of 0.021 square miles. Located at 38.82° N. Lat; 89.54° W. Long. Elevation is 561 feet.
History: Pocahontas, named for the legendary Indian princess, began as a stagecoach stop on the Cumberland Road.
Population: 837 (1990); 727 (2000); 651 (2010); 613 (2015 projected); Race: 97.2% White, 0.6% Black, 0.3% Asian, 1.8% Other, 0.6% Hispanic of any race (2010); Density: 867.1 persons per square mile (2010); Average household size: 2.33 (2010); Median age: 38.7 (2010); Males per 100 females: 97.9 (2010); Marriage status: 22.2% never married, 60.5% now married, 8.0% widowed, 9.3% divorced (2005-2009 5-year est.); Foreign born: 0.9% (2005-2009 5-year est.); Ancestry (includes multiple ancestries): 17.6% German, 9.7% Irish, 7.6% American, 2.7% Italian, 2.2% Dutch (2005-2009 5-year est.).
Economy: Single-family building permits issued: 1 (2010); Multi-family building permits issued: 0 (2010); Employment by occupation: 11.8% management, 12.3% professional, 18.1% services, 23.7% sales, 0.0% farming, 15.4% construction, 18.6% production (2005-2009 5-year est.).
Income: Per capita income: $18,503 (2010); Median household income: $33,900 (2010); Average household income: $43,297 (2010); Percent of households with income of $100,000 or more: 5.7% (2010); Poverty rate: 25.5% (2005-2009 5-year est.).
Taxes: Total city taxes per capita: $87 (2007); City property taxes per capita: $80 (2007).
Education: Percent of population age 25 and over with: High school diploma (including GED) or higher: 86.7% (2010); Bachelor's degree or higher: 8.7% (2010); Master's degree or higher: 1.3% (2010).
School District(s)
Bond County CUSD 2 (PK-12)
    2009-10 Enrollment: 2,044 . . . . (618) 664-0170
Housing: Homeownership rate: 79.2% (2010); Median home value: $74,324 (2010); Median contract rent: $438 per month (2005-2009 5-year est.); Median year structure built: 1952 (2005-2009 5-year est.).
Transportation: Commute to work: 96.7% car, 0.0% public transportation, 0.0% walk, 3.3% work from home (2005-2009 5-year est.); Travel time to work: 28.2% less than 15 minutes, 49.7% 15 to 30 minutes, 7.4% 30 to 45 minutes, 8.7% 45 to 60 minutes, 6.1% 60 minutes or more (2005-2009 5-year est.)

SMITHBORO (village).
Covers a land area of 1.182 square miles and a water area of 0 square miles. Located at 38.89° N. Lat; 89.34° W. Long. Elevation is 558 feet.
Population: 202 (1990); 200 (2000); 202 (2010); 201 (2015 projected); Race: 97.5% White, 1.5% Black, 0.0% Asian, 1.0% Other, 0.5% Hispanic

of any race (2010); Density: 170.8 persons per square mile (2010); Average household size: 2.62 (2010); Median age: 39.0 (2010); Males per 100 females: 98.0 (2010); Marriage status: 45.8% never married, 35.3% now married, 8.5% widowed, 10.5% divorced (2005-2009 5-year est.); Foreign born: 0.6% (2005-2009 5-year est.); Ancestry (includes multiple ancestries): 21.8% German, 12.4% Irish, 10.0% Italian, 8.8% English, 6.5% American (2005-2009 5-year est.).
Economy: Single-family building permits issued: 0 (2010); Multi-family building permits issued: 0 (2010); Employment by occupation: 4.1% management, 5.5% professional, 30.1% services, 41.1% sales, 0.0% farming, 0.0% construction, 19.2% production (2005-2009 5-year est.).
Income: Per capita income: $32,085 (2010); Median household income: $63,971 (2010); Average household income: $79,935 (2010); Percent of households with income of $100,000 or more: 31.2% (2010); Poverty rate: 30.6% (2005-2009 5-year est.).
Taxes: Total city taxes per capita: $34 (2007); City property taxes per capita: $26 (2007).
Education: Percent of population age 25 and over with: High school diploma (including GED) or higher: 90.3% (2010); Bachelor's degree or higher: 40.3% (2010); Master's degree or higher: 10.4% (2010).
Housing: Homeownership rate: 81.8% (2010); Median home value: $158,333 (2010); Median contract rent: $306 per month (2005-2009 5-year est.); Median year structure built: 1952 (2005-2009 5-year est.).
Transportation: Commute to work: 95.7% car, 1.4% public transportation, 2.9% walk, 0.0% work from home (2005-2009 5-year est.); Travel time to work: 23.2% less than 15 minutes, 37.7% 15 to 30 minutes, 18.8% 30 to 45 minutes, 4.3% 45 to 60 minutes, 15.9% 60 minutes or more (2005-2009 5-year est.)

SORENTO (village).
Covers a land area of 0.541 square miles and a water area of 0 square miles. Located at 38.99° N. Lat; 89.57° W. Long. Elevation is 584 feet.
Population: 596 (1990); 601 (2000); 585 (2010); 567 (2015 projected); Race: 97.6% White, 0.0% Black, 0.0% Asian, 2.4% Other, 0.7% Hispanic of any race (2010); Density: 1,081.0 persons per square mile (2010); Average household size: 2.53 (2010); Median age: 38.5 (2010); Males per 100 females: 95.0 (2010); Marriage status: 24.3% never married, 52.1% now married, 6.0% widowed, 17.7% divorced (2005-2009 5-year est.); Foreign born: 3.8% (2005-2009 5-year est.); Ancestry (includes multiple ancestries): 18.9% German, 10.4% English, 9.3% Irish, 4.7% American, 2.9% Jamaican (2005-2009 5-year est.).
Economy: Single-family building permits issued: 0 (2010); Multi-family building permits issued: 0 (2010); Employment by occupation: 4.8% management, 2.6% professional, 21.1% services, 24.1% sales, 0.0% farming, 29.8% construction, 17.5% production (2005-2009 5-year est.).
Income: Per capita income: $20,809 (2010); Median household income: $43,971 (2010); Average household income: $52,305 (2010); Percent of households with income of $100,000 or more: 10.0% (2010); Poverty rate: 18.0% (2005-2009 5-year est.).
Taxes: Total city taxes per capita: $46 (2007); City property taxes per capita: $43 (2007).
Education: Percent of population age 25 and over with: High school diploma (including GED) or higher: 83.5% (2010); Bachelor's degree or higher: 10.5% (2010); Master's degree or higher: 3.8% (2010).
School District(s)
Bond County CUSD 2 (PK-12)
    2009-10 Enrollment: 2,044 . . . . (618) 664-0170
Housing: Homeownership rate: 87.0% (2010); Median home value: $65,200 (2010); Median contract rent: $241 per month (2005-2009 5-year est.); Median year structure built: 1952 (2005-2009 5-year est.).
Transportation: Commute to work: 95.9% car, 0.0% public transportation, 0.9% walk, 3.2% work from home (2005-2009 5-year est.); Travel time to work: 0.9% less than 15 minutes, 23.7% 15 to 30 minutes, 39.1% 30 to 45 minutes, 20.0% 45 to 60 minutes, 16.3% 60 minutes or more (2005-2009 5-year est.)

Boone County

Located in northern Illinois; bounded on the north by Wisconsin. Covers a land area of 281.27 square miles, a water area of 0.68 square miles, and is located in the Central Time Zone at 42.29° N. Lat., 88.83° W. Long. The county was founded in 1837. County seat is Belvidere.

Boone County is part of the Rockford, IL Metropolitan Statistical Area. The entire metro area includes: Boone County, IL; Winnebago County, IL

Population: 30,806 (1990); 41,786 (2000); 56,091 (2010); 62,400 (2015 projected); Race: 82.2% White, 2.5% Black, 1.4% Asian, 13.9% Other, 21.1% Hispanic of any race (2010); Density: 199.4 persons per square mile (2010); Average household size: 2.87 (2010); Median age: 33.9 (2010); Males per 100 females: 101.4 (2010).

Religion: Five largest groups: 19.1% Catholic Church, 6.0% Lutheran Church—Missouri Synod, 5.2% The United Methodist Church, 2.7% Evangelical Lutheran Church in America, 2.4% Presbyterian Church (U.S.A.) (2000).

Economy: Unemployment rate: 13.6% (August 2011); Total civilian labor force: 25,899 (August 2011); Leading industries: 39.2% manufacturing; 13.9% retail trade; 7.7% health care and social assistance (2009); Farms: 540 totaling 137,162 acres (2007); Companies that employ 500 or more persons: 2 (2009); Companies that employ 100 to 499 persons: 12 (2009); Companies that employ less than 100 persons: 827 (2009); Black-owned businesses: 45 (2007); Hispanic-owned businesses: n/a (2007); Asian-owned businesses: n/a (2007); Women-owned businesses: 953 (2007); Retail sales per capita: $5,590 (2010). Single-family building permits issued: 42 (2010); Multi-family building permits issued: 0 (2010).

Income: Per capita income: $25,092 (2010); Median household income: $59,702 (2010); Average household income: $72,154 (2010); Percent of households with income of $100,000 or more: 19.8% (2010); Poverty rate: 8.9% (2009); Bankruptcy rate: 7.53% (2010).

Taxes: Total county taxes per capita: $188 (2007); County property taxes per capita: $151 (2007).

Education: Percent of population age 25 and over with: High school diploma (including GED) or higher: 86.0% (2010); Bachelor's degree or higher: 19.2% (2010); Master's degree or higher: 6.3% (2010).

Housing: Homeownership rate: 81.5% (2010); Median home value: $159,726 (2010); Median contract rent: $579 per month (2005-2009 5-year est.); Median year structure built: 1978 (2005-2009 5-year est.)

Health: Birth rate: 153.3 per 10,000 population (2009); Death rate: 64.1 per 10,000 population (2009); Age-adjusted cancer mortality rate: 191.5 deaths per 100,000 population (2007); Number of physicians: 13.0 per 10,000 population (2008); Hospital beds: 13.0 per 10,000 population (2007); Hospital admissions: 256.4 per 10,000 population (2007).

Elections: 2008 Presidential election results: 51.1% Obama, 47.0% McCain, 0.8% Nader

Additional Information Contacts

Boone County Government . . . . (815) 547-4770
   http://www.boonecountyil.org
Belvidere Area Chamber of Commerce . . . . (815) 544-4357
   http://www.belviderechamber.com
City of Belvidere . . . . (815) 544-2612
   http://www.ci.belvidere.il.us

Boone County Communities

BELVIDERE (city). County seat. Covers a land area of 9.071 square miles and a water area of 0.053 square miles. Located at 42.25° N. Lat; 88.84° W. Long. Elevation is 781 feet.

History: Belvidere was founded in 1836 as a stop on the Chicago-Galena stagecoach route. The National Sewing Machine Plant was founded here in 1879.

Population: 16,801 (1990); 20,820 (2000); 25,273 (2010); 27,582 (2015 projected); Race: 72.0% White, 2.8% Black, 1.2% Asian, 24.0% Other, 34.3% Hispanic of any race (2010); Density: 2,786.2 persons per square mile (2010); Average household size: 2.77 (2010); Median age: 33.2 (2010); Males per 100 females: 100.0 (2010); Marriage status: 30.1% never married, 53.6% now married, 6.4% widowed, 9.9% divorced (2005-2009 5-year est.); Foreign born: 14.6% (2005-2009 5-year est.); Ancestry (includes multiple ancestries): 20.2% German, 12.2% Irish, 9.3% American, 8.0% English, 5.5% Italian (2005-2009 5-year est.).

Economy: Unemployment rate: 15.8% (August 2011); Total civilian labor force: 12,761 (August 2011); Single-family building permits issued: 8 (2010); Multi-family building permits issued: 0 (2010); Employment by occupation: 7.0% management, 12.1% professional, 12.9% services, 25.0% sales, 0.3% farming, 10.6% construction, 32.1% production (2005-2009 5-year est.).

Income: Per capita income: $19,241 (2010); Median household income: $46,332 (2010); Average household income: $53,215 (2010); Percent of households with income of $100,000 or more: 9.0% (2010); Poverty rate: 14.1% (2005-2009 5-year est.).

Taxes: Total city taxes per capita: $204 (2007); City property taxes per capita: $173 (2007).

Education: Percent of population age 25 and over with: High school diploma (including GED) or higher: 80.4% (2010); Bachelor's degree or higher: 11.9% (2010); Master's degree or higher: 2.5% (2010).

School District(s)

Belvidere CUSD 100 (PK-12)
   2009-10 Enrollment: 9,068 . . . . (815) 544-0301
Boone County Spec Educ Coop (PK-PK)
   2009-10 Enrollment: n/a . . . . (815) 544-9851
Boone/Winnebago Roe (06-12)
   2009-10 Enrollment: n/a . . . . (815) 636-3060

Housing: Homeownership rate: 70.1% (2010); Median home value: $126,453 (2010); Median contract rent: $554 per month (2005-2009 5-year est.); Median year structure built: 1969 (2005-2009 5-year est.).

Hospitals: Northwest Suburban Community Hospital (69 beds)

Safety: Violent crime rate: 25.1 per 10,000 population; Property crime rate: 192.8 per 10,000 population (2010).

Newspapers: Belvidere Daily Republican (Local news; Circulation 5,000); Boone County Shopper (Regional news; Circulation 18,364)

Transportation: Commute to work: 92.4% car, 0.4% public transportation, 1.9% walk, 1.9% work from home (2005-2009 5-year est.); Travel time to work: 31.3% less than 15 minutes, 25.7% 15 to 30 minutes, 19.3% 30 to 45 minutes, 10.6% 45 to 60 minutes, 13.2% 60 minutes or more (2005-2009 5-year est.)

Additional Information Contacts

Belvidere Area Chamber of Commerce . . . . (815) 544-4357
   http://www.belviderechamber.com
City of Belvidere . . . . (815) 544-2612
   http://www.ci.belvidere.il.us

CALEDONIA (village). Aka North Caledonia. Covers a land area of 0.533 square miles and a water area of 0 square miles. Located at 42.36° N. Lat; 88.89° W. Long. Elevation is 928 feet.

Population: 67 (1990); 199 (2000); 291 (2010); 332 (2015 projected); Race: 86.9% White, 5.2% Black, 1.7% Asian, 6.2% Other, 12.4% Hispanic of any race (2010); Density: 545.5 persons per square mile (2010); Average household size: 3.20 (2010); Median age: 30.6 (2010); Males per 100 females: 106.4 (2010); Marriage status: 19.8% never married, 65.5% now married, 6.0% widowed, 8.6% divorced (2005-2009 5-year est.); Foreign born: 0.0% (2005-2009 5-year est.); Ancestry (includes multiple ancestries): 35.4% German, 22.2% Irish, 16.5% Swedish, 12.7% Italian, 10.8% Polish (2005-2009 5-year est.).

Economy: Single-family building permits issued: 0 (2010); Multi-family building permits issued: 0 (2010); Employment by occupation: 15.7% management, 5.6% professional, 11.2% services, 37.1% sales, 0.0% farming, 9.0% construction, 21.3% production (2005-2009 5-year est.).

Income: Per capita income: $23,950 (2010); Median household income: $68,500 (2010); Average household income: $74,038 (2010); Percent of households with income of $100,000 or more: 22.0% (2010); Poverty rate: 1.3% (2005-2009 5-year est.).

Taxes: Total city taxes per capita: $98 (2007); City property taxes per capita: $89 (2007).

Education: Percent of population age 25 and over with: High school diploma (including GED) or higher: 89.3% (2010); Bachelor's degree or higher: 17.2% (2010); Master's degree or higher: 5.9% (2010).

School District(s)

Belvidere CUSD 100 (PK-12)
   2009-10 Enrollment: 9,068 . . . . (815) 544-0301

Housing: Homeownership rate: 95.6% (2010); Median home value: $169,286 (2010); Median contract rent: n/a per month (2005-2009 5-year est.); Median year structure built: before 1940 (2005-2009 5-year est.).

Transportation: Commute to work: 97.6% car, 0.0% public transportation, 0.0% walk, 2.4% work from home (2005-2009 5-year est.); Travel time to work: 18.1% less than 15 minutes, 42.2% 15 to 30 minutes, 22.9% 30 to 45 minutes, 7.2% 45 to 60 minutes, 9.6% 60 minutes or more (2005-2009 5-year est.)

CAPRON (village). Covers a land area of 0.728 square miles and a water area of 0 square miles. Located at 42.39° N. Lat; 88.74° W. Long. Elevation is 909 feet.

Population: 862 (1990); 961 (2000); 1,242 (2010); 1,384 (2015 projected); Race: 77.7% White, 2.3% Black, 0.6% Asian, 19.3% Other, 38.3% Hispanic of any race (2010); Density: 1,705.3 persons per square mile (2010); Average household size: 2.87 (2010); Median age: 33.4 (2010); Males per 100 females: 105.3 (2010); Marriage status: 33.5% never married, 51.2% now married, 2.1% widowed, 13.2% divorced (2005-2009

5-year est.); Foreign born: 10.7% (2005-2009 5-year est.); Ancestry (includes multiple ancestries): 31.8% German, 13.8% American, 9.6% Italian, 7.1% English, 6.9% Irish (2005-2009 5-year est.).
Economy: Single-family building permits issued: 0 (2010); Multi-family building permits issued: 0 (2010); Employment by occupation: 8.3% management, 10.1% professional, 14.0% services, 21.2% sales, 0.3% farming, 9.5% construction, 36.7% production (2005-2009 5-year est.).
Income: Per capita income: $23,755 (2010); Median household income: $59,623 (2010); Average household income: $67,754 (2010); Percent of households with income of $100,000 or more: 14.5% (2010); Poverty rate: 7.9% (2005-2009 5-year est.).
Taxes: Total city taxes per capita: $45 (2007); City property taxes per capita: $34 (2007).
Education: Percent of population age 25 and over with: High school diploma (including GED) or higher: 80.2% (2010); Bachelor's degree or higher: 10.7% (2010); Master's degree or higher: 2.0% (2010).
School District(s)
North Boone CUSD 200 (PK-12)
    2009-10 Enrollment: 1,766 . . . . (815) 765-3322
Housing: Homeownership rate: 84.5% (2010); Median home value: $147,101 (2010); Median contract rent: $755 per month (2005-2009 5-year est.); Median year structure built: 1975 (2005-2009 5-year est.).
Transportation: Commute to work: 94.3% car, 1.2% public transportation, 0.4% walk, 3.7% work from home (2005-2009 5-year est.); Travel time to work: 28.3% less than 15 minutes, 26.5% 15 to 30 minutes, 23.0% 30 to 45 minutes, 14.7% 45 to 60 minutes, 7.5% 60 minutes or more (2005-2009 5-year est.)

GARDEN PRAIRIE (village). Covers a land area of 0.906 square miles and a water area of 0.008 square miles. Located at 42.25° N. Lat; 88.74° W. Long. Elevation is 781 feet.
History: Garden Prairie began in 1849 when a station for the Galena & Chicago Union Railroad was built here.
Population: n/a (1990); n/a (2000); 352 (2010); n/a (2015 projected); Race: 87.2% White, 0.0% Black, 0.0% Asian, 12.8% Other, 16.8% Hispanic of any race (2010); Density: 388.5 persons per square mile (2010); Average household size: 2.79 (2010); Median age: 39.4 (2010); Males per 100 females: 98.9 (2010); Marriage status: 41.8% never married, 31.5% now married, 9.4% widowed, 17.4% divorced (2005-2009 5-year est.); Foreign born: 0.0% (2005-2009 5-year est.); Ancestry (includes multiple ancestries): 44.7% Irish, 33.3% Swedish, 19.7% German, 18.9% Polish, 13.2% Dutch (2005-2009 5-year est.).
Economy: Employment by occupation: 0.0% management, 8.2% professional, 11.5% services, 69.9% sales, 0.0% farming, 0.0% construction, 10.4% production (2005-2009 5-year est.).
Income: Per capita income: n/a (2010); Median household income: n/a (2010); Average household income: n/a (2010); Percent of households with income of $100,000 or more: n/a (2010); Poverty rate: 11.0% (2005-2009 5-year est.).
Education: Percent of population age 25 and over with: High school diploma (including GED) or higher: n/a (2010); Bachelor's degree or higher: n/a (2010); Master's degree or higher: n/a (2010).
School District(s)
Belvidere CUSD 100 (PK-12)
    2009-10 Enrollment: 9,068 . . . . (815) 544-0301
Housing: Homeownership rate: n/a (2010); Median home value: n/a (2010); Median contract rent: $515 per month (2005-2009 5-year est.); Median year structure built: before 1940 (2005-2009 5-year est.).
Transportation: Commute to work: 56.3% car, 0.0% public transportation, 0.0% walk, 43.7% work from home (2005-2009 5-year est.); Travel time to work: 20.4% less than 15 minutes, 41.7% 15 to 30 minutes, 14.6% 30 to 45 minutes, 11.7% 45 to 60 minutes, 11.7% 60 minutes or more (2005-2009 5-year est.)

POPLAR GROVE (village). Covers a land area of 4.495 square miles and a water area of <.001 square miles. Located at 42.35° N. Lat; 88.83° W. Long. Elevation is 899 feet.
Population: 939 (1990); 1,368 (2000); 2,638 (2010); 3,021 (2015 projected); Race: 96.4% White, 0.3% Black, 1.1% Asian, 2.2% Other, 3.8% Hispanic of any race (2010); Density: 586.9 persons per square mile (2010); Average household size: 2.95 (2010); Median age: 33.1 (2010); Males per 100 females: 101.7 (2010); Marriage status: 21.1% never married, 63.2% now married, 6.7% widowed, 9.0% divorced (2005-2009 5-year est.); Foreign born: 6.1% (2005-2009 5-year est.); Ancestry

(includes multiple ancestries): 28.9% German, 17.3% Irish, 12.2% Italian, 10.1% American, 9.2% English (2005-2009 5-year est.).
Economy: Single-family building permits issued: 18 (2010); Multi-family building permits issued: 0 (2010); Employment by occupation: 12.7% management, 16.1% professional, 11.2% services, 26.9% sales, 0.0% farming, 10.5% construction, 22.5% production (2005-2009 5-year est.).
Income: Per capita income: $23,250 (2010); Median household income: $62,108 (2010); Average household income: $69,006 (2010); Percent of households with income of $100,000 or more: 17.5% (2010); Poverty rate: 6.2% (2005-2009 5-year est.).
Taxes: Total city taxes per capita: $91 (2007); City property taxes per capita: $57 (2007).
Education: Percent of population age 25 and over with: High school diploma (including GED) or higher: 90.8% (2010); Bachelor's degree or higher: 14.5% (2010); Master's degree or higher: 3.3% (2010).
School District(s)
North Boone CUSD 200 (PK-12)
    2009-10 Enrollment: 1,766 . . . . (815) 765-3322
Housing: Homeownership rate: 87.4% (2010); Median home value: $168,326 (2010); Median contract rent: $877 per month (2005-2009 5-year est.); Median year structure built: 2000 (2005-2009 5-year est.).
Transportation: Commute to work: 94.5% car, 1.4% public transportation, 0.0% walk, 2.8% work from home (2005-2009 5-year est.); Travel time to work: 14.3% less than 15 minutes, 35.3% 15 to 30 minutes, 24.0% 30 to 45 minutes, 8.1% 45 to 60 minutes, 18.3% 60 minutes or more (2005-2009 5-year est.)

TIMBERLANE (village). Covers a land area of 1.295 square miles and a water area of 0.016 square miles. Located at 42.33° N. Lat; 88.85° W. Long. Elevation is 840 feet.
Population: 88 (1990); 234 (2000); 345 (2010); 394 (2015 projected); Race: 87.2% White, 4.9% Black, 1.4% Asian, 6.4% Other, 12.8% Hispanic of any race (2010); Density: 266.5 persons per square mile (2010); Average household size: 3.19 (2010); Median age: 31.1 (2010); Males per 100 females: 100.6 (2010); Marriage status: 26.2% never married, 69.4% now married, 3.2% widowed, 1.3% divorced (2005-2009 5-year est.); Foreign born: 4.6% (2005-2009 5-year est.); Ancestry (includes multiple ancestries): 45.2% German, 19.6% Irish, 13.1% American, 13.1% Italian, 9.7% Swedish (2005-2009 5-year est.).
Economy: Single-family building permits issued: 4 (2010); Multi-family building permits issued: 0 (2010); Employment by occupation: 21.8% management, 30.1% professional, 4.8% services, 18.3% sales, 0.0% farming, 12.5% construction, 12.5% production (2005-2009 5-year est.).
Income: Per capita income: $23,949 (2010); Median household income: $68,966 (2010); Average household income: $75,880 (2010); Percent of households with income of $100,000 or more: 23.1% (2010); Poverty rate: 1.8% (2005-2009 5-year est.).
Taxes: Total city taxes per capita: $230 (2007); City property taxes per capita: $102 (2007).
Education: Percent of population age 25 and over with: High school diploma (including GED) or higher: 89.0% (2010); Bachelor's degree or higher: 18.5% (2010); Master's degree or higher: 7.0% (2010).
Housing: Homeownership rate: 95.4% (2010); Median home value: $167,683 (2010); Median contract rent: n/a per month (2005-2009 5-year est.); Median year structure built: 2001 (2005-2009 5-year est.).
Transportation: Commute to work: 91.0% car, 0.3% public transportation, 0.0% walk, 8.7% work from home (2005-2009 5-year est.); Travel time to work: 14.5% less than 15 minutes, 44.9% 15 to 30 minutes, 15.2% 30 to 45 minutes, 6.4% 45 to 60 minutes, 19.1% 60 minutes or more (2005-2009 5-year est.)

Brown County

Located in western Illinois; bounded on the southeast by the Illinois River, and on the northeast by the La Moine River. Covers a land area of 305.65 square miles, a water area of 1.59 square miles, and is located in the Central Time Zone at 39.95° N. Lat., 90.74° W. Long. The county was founded in 1839. County seat is Mount Sterling.
Population: 5,836 (1990); 6,950 (2000); 6,534 (2010); 6,319 (2015 projected); Race: 78.8% White, 19.5% Black, 0.1% Asian, 1.6% Other, 4.3% Hispanic of any race (2010); Density: 21.4 persons per square mile (2010); Average household size: 2.31 (2010); Median age: 35.2 (2010); Males per 100 females: 191.2 (2010).
Religion: Five largest groups: 11.9% Catholic Church, 9.0% American Baptist Churches in the USA, 5.0% Christian Churches and Churches of

Christ, 4.3% Christian Church (Disciples of Christ), 4.2% The United Methodist Church (2000).

Economy: Unemployment rate: 4.5% (August 2011); Total civilian labor force: 3,638 (August 2011); Leading industries: Farms: 422 totaling 151,058 acres (2007); Companies that employ 500 or more persons: 1 (2009); Companies that employ 100 to 499 persons: 2 (2009); Companies that employ less than 100 persons: 121 (2009); Black-owned businesses: n/a (2007); Hispanic-owned businesses: n/a (2007); Asian-owned businesses: n/a (2007); Women-owned businesses: n/a (2007); Retail sales per capita: $3,845 (2010). Single-family building permits issued: 0 (2010); Multi-family building permits issued: 0 (2010).

Income: Per capita income: $19,254 (2010); Median household income: $47,846 (2010); Average household income: $54,910 (2010); Percent of households with income of $100,000 or more: 10.1% (2010); Poverty rate: 15.9% (2009); Bankruptcy rate: 2.15% (2010).

Taxes: Total county taxes per capita: $125 (2007); County property taxes per capita: $125 (2007).

Education: Percent of population age 25 and over with: High school diploma (including GED) or higher: 71.3% (2010); Bachelor's degree or higher: 11.7% (2010); Master's degree or higher: 3.3% (2010).

Housing: Homeownership rate: 72.8% (2010); Median home value: $69,167 (2010); Median contract rent: $261 per month (2005-2009 5-year est.); Median year structure built: 1954 (2005-2009 5-year est.)

Health: Birth rate: 100.1 per 10,000 population (2009); Death rate: 69.8 per 10,000 population (2009); Age-adjusted cancer mortality rate: 217.1 (Unreliable) deaths per 100,000 population (2007); Number of physicians: 1.5 per 10,000 population (2008); Hospital beds: 0.0 per 10,000 population (2007); Hospital admissions: 0.0 per 10,000 population (2007).

Elections: 2008 Presidential election results: 38.4% Obama, 60.1% McCain, 0.7% Nader

Additional Information Contacts

Brown County Government . . . . (217) 773-3013
http://www.browncountyil.com

Brown County Communities

MOUND STATION (village). Aka Timewell. Covers a land area of 0.518 square miles and a water area of 0 square miles. Located at 40.00° N. Lat; 90.87° W. Long.

History: Also called Timewell.

Population: 147 (1990); 127 (2000); 107 (2010); 100 (2015 projected); Race: 98.1% White, 0.0% Black, 0.0% Asian, 1.9% Other, 1.9% Hispanic of any race (2010); Density: 206.7 persons per square mile (2010); Average household size: 2.55 (2010); Median age: 39.2 (2010); Males per 100 females: 109.8 (2010); Marriage status: 14.7% never married, 80.2% now married, 1.7% widowed, 3.4% divorced (2005-2009 5-year est.); Foreign born: 2.0% (2005-2009 5-year est.); Ancestry (includes multiple ancestries): 34.0% German, 26.1% English, 12.4% Irish, 9.2% French, 3.9% American (2005-2009 5-year est.).

Economy: Employment by occupation: 9.4% management, 20.0% professional, 2.4% services, 34.1% sales, 2.4% farming, 4.7% construction, 27.1% production (2005-2009 5-year est.).

Income: Per capita income: $23,495 (2010); Median household income: $55,357 (2010); Average household income: $59,464 (2010); Percent of households with income of $100,000 or more: 11.9% (2010); Poverty rate: 0.0% (2005-2009 5-year est.).

Taxes: Total city taxes per capita: $41 (2007); City property taxes per capita: $41 (2007).

Education: Percent of population age 25 and over with: High school diploma (including GED) or higher: 93.1% (2010); Bachelor's degree or higher: 13.9% (2010); Master's degree or higher: 2.8% (2010).

Housing: Homeownership rate: 73.8% (2010); Median home value: $75,714 (2010); Median contract rent: n/a per month (2005-2009 5-year est.); Median year structure built: before 1940 (2005-2009 5-year est.).

Transportation: Commute to work: 97.5% car, 0.0% public transportation, 0.0% walk, 1.3% work from home (2005-2009 5-year est.); Travel time to work: 57.0% less than 15 minutes, 15.2% 15 to 30 minutes, 7.6% 30 to 45 minutes, 16.5% 45 to 60 minutes, 3.8% 60 minutes or more (2005-2009 5-year est.)

MOUNT STERLING (city). County seat. Covers a land area of 1.076 square miles and a water area of 0 square miles. Located at 39.98° N. Lat; 90.76° W. Long. Elevation is 725 feet.

History: Mount Sterling was settled in 1830 by Robert Curry, who named the village for the "sterling" quality of the soil. Mount Sterling developed as the seat of Brown County.

Population: 1,996 (1990); 2,070 (2000); 1,935 (2010); 1,866 (2015 projected); Race: 88.6% White, 10.0% Black, 0.4% Asian, 1.0% Other, 2.2% Hispanic of any race (2010); Density: 1,798.0 persons per square mile (2010); Average household size: 2.21 (2010); Median age: 36.5 (2010); Males per 100 females: 131.5 (2010); Marriage status: 22.0% never married, 57.1% now married, 8.6% widowed, 12.3% divorced (2005-2009 5-year est.); Foreign born: 0.0% (2005-2009 5-year est.); Ancestry (includes multiple ancestries): 27.8% American, 24.9% German, 13.2% Irish, 5.2% English, 4.5% Scottish (2005-2009 5-year est.).

Economy: Single-family building permits issued: 0 (2010); Multi-family building permits issued: 0 (2010); Employment by occupation: 11.9% management, 9.0% professional, 26.4% services, 15.8% sales, 0.0% farming, 19.0% construction, 17.9% production (2005-2009 5-year est.).

Income: Per capita income: $19,111 (2010); Median household income: $41,000 (2010); Average household income: $46,511 (2010); Percent of households with income of $100,000 or more: 5.2% (2010); Poverty rate: 17.9% (2005-2009 5-year est.).

Taxes: Total city taxes per capita: $211 (2007); City property taxes per capita: $143 (2007).

Education: Percent of population age 25 and over with: High school diploma (including GED) or higher: 78.4% (2010); Bachelor's degree or higher: 14.3% (2010); Master's degree or higher: 5.8% (2010).

School District(s)

Brown County CUSD 1 (PK-12)

    2009-10 Enrollment: 806 . . . . (217) 773-3359

Housing: Homeownership rate: 69.6% (2010); Median home value: $66,273 (2010); Median contract rent: $220 per month (2005-2009 5-year est.); Median year structure built: 1956 (2005-2009 5-year est.).

Newspapers: Democrat Message (Community news; Circulation 2,800); Pennypincher (Community news; Circulation 10,000)

Transportation: Commute to work: 86.8% car, 0.0% public transportation, 5.3% walk, 6.9% work from home (2005-2009 5-year est.); Travel time to work: 59.2% less than 15 minutes, 23.1% 15 to 30 minutes, 8.9% 30 to 45 minutes, 7.4% 45 to 60 minutes, 1.4% 60 minutes or more (2005-2009 5-year est.)

RIPLEY (village). Covers a land area of 0.376 square miles and a water area of 0 square miles. Located at 40.02° N. Lat; 90.63° W. Long. Elevation is 548 feet.

History: Ripley experienced prosperity in the 1830's and 1840's when its pottery kilns were producing.

Population: 103 (1990); 103 (2000); 84 (2010); 78 (2015 projected); Race: 97.6% White, 0.0% Black, 0.0% Asian, 2.4% Other, 0.0% Hispanic of any race (2010); Density: 223.5 persons per square mile (2010); Average household size: 2.40 (2010); Median age: 45.8 (2010); Males per 100 females: 110.0 (2010); Marriage status: 6.7% never married, 60.0% now married, 28.9% widowed, 4.4% divorced (2005-2009 5-year est.); Foreign born: 0.0% (2005-2009 5-year est.); Ancestry (includes multiple ancestries): 34.8% German, 21.7% Irish, 19.6% American, 10.9% Dutch, 6.5% Swedish (2005-2009 5-year est.).

Economy: Single-family building permits issued: 0 (2010); Multi-family building permits issued: 0 (2010); Employment by occupation: 0.0% management, 6.7% professional, 26.7% services, 0.0% sales, 0.0% farming, 53.3% construction, 13.3% production (2005-2009 5-year est.).

Income: Per capita income: $28,467 (2010); Median household income: $56,250 (2010); Average household income: $68,500 (2010); Percent of households with income of $100,000 or more: 20.0% (2010); Poverty rate: 15.2% (2005-2009 5-year est.).

Taxes: Total city taxes per capita: $21 (2007); City property taxes per capita: $21 (2007).

Education: Percent of population age 25 and over with: High school diploma (including GED) or higher: 89.1% (2010); Bachelor's degree or higher: 25.0% (2010); Master's degree or higher: 3.1% (2010).

Housing: Homeownership rate: 80.0% (2010); Median home value: $100,000 (2010); Median contract rent: $550 per month (2005-2009 5-year est.); Median year structure built: 1967 (2005-2009 5-year est.).

Transportation: Commute to work: 100.0% car, 0.0% public transportation, 0.0% walk, 0.0% work from home (2005-2009 5-year est.); Travel time to work: 0.0% less than 15 minutes, 33.3% 15 to 30 minutes, 66.7% 30 to 45 minutes, 0.0% 45 to 60 minutes, 0.0% 60 minutes or more (2005-2009 5-year est.)

TIMEWELL (unincorporated postal area, zip code 62375). Aka Mound Station. Covers a land area of 40.583 square miles and a water area of 0.018 square miles. Located at 40.00° N. Lat; 90.87° W. Long. Elevation is 755 feet.
Population: 381 (2000); Race: 97.9% White, 0.0% Black, 0.3% Asian, 1.8% Other, 0.0% Hispanic of any race (2000); Density: 9.4 persons per square mile (2000); Age: 32.5% under 18, 6.9% over 64 (2000); Marriage status: 20.2% never married, 66.4% now married, 6.3% widowed, 7.1% divorced (2000); Foreign born: 2.1% (2000); Ancestry (includes multiple ancestries): 26.0% German, 17.3% American, 14.3% English, 14.0% Irish, 6.6% Scotch-Irish (2000).
Economy: Employment by occupation: 15.1% management, 5.2% professional, 17.4% services, 29.7% sales, 0.0% farming, 10.5% construction, 22.1% production (2000).
Income: Per capita income: $15,507 (2000); Median household income: $42,679 (2000); Poverty rate: 8.3% (2000).
Education: Percent of population age 25 and over with: High school diploma (including GED) or higher: 97.0% (2000); Bachelor's degree or higher: 3.0% (2000).
Housing: Homeownership rate: 78.8% (2000); Median home value: $36,800 (2000); Median contract rent: $263 per month (2000); Median year structure built: before 1940 (2000).
Transportation: Commute to work: 94.5% car, 0.0% public transportation, 3.0% walk, 0.0% work from home (2000); Travel time to work: 47.3% less than 15 minutes, 39.4% 15 to 30 minutes, 0.0% 30 to 45 minutes, 5.5% 45 to 60 minutes, 7.9% 60 minutes or more (2000)

VERSAILLES (village). Covers a land area of 0.922 square miles and a water area of 0.005 square miles. Located at 39.88° N. Lat; 90.65° W. Long. Elevation is 633 feet.
Population: 480 (1990); 567 (2000); 500 (2010); 468 (2015 projected); Race: 99.6% White, 0.0% Black, 0.0% Asian, 0.4% Other, 0.0% Hispanic of any race (2010); Density: 542.0 persons per square mile (2010); Average household size: 2.36 (2010); Median age: 40.7 (2010); Males per 100 females: 102.4 (2010); Marriage status: 14.0% never married, 64.0% now married, 11.7% widowed, 10.4% divorced (2005-2009 5-year est.); Foreign born: 0.0% (2005-2009 5-year est.); Ancestry (includes multiple ancestries): 33.4% German, 20.7% Irish, 16.8% English, 8.4% American, 4.6% Dutch (2005-2009 5-year est.).
Economy: Employment by occupation: 5.4% management, 8.0% professional, 21.4% services, 38.4% sales, 0.0% farming, 14.3% construction, 12.5% production (2005-2009 5-year est.).
Income: Per capita income: $26,227 (2010); Median household income: $56,716 (2010); Average household income: $60,979 (2010); Percent of households with income of $100,000 or more: 13.2% (2010); Poverty rate: 19.0% (2005-2009 5-year est.).
Taxes: Total city taxes per capita: $98 (2007); City property taxes per capita: $66 (2007).
Education: Percent of population age 25 and over with: High school diploma (including GED) or higher: 86.3% (2010); Bachelor's degree or higher: 12.3% (2010); Master's degree or higher: 2.8% (2010).
Housing: Homeownership rate: 80.7% (2010); Median home value: $59,737 (2010); Median contract rent: $131 per month (2005-2009 5-year est.); Median year structure built: before 1940 (2005-2009 5-year est.).
Transportation: Commute to work: 96.9% car, 0.0% public transportation, 0.0% walk, 3.1% work from home (2005-2009 5-year est.); Travel time to work: 18.1% less than 15 minutes, 53.2% 15 to 30 minutes, 22.3% 30 to 45 minutes, 0.0% 45 to 60 minutes, 6.4% 60 minutes or more (2005-2009 5-year est.)

Bureau County

Located in northern Illinois; bounded on the southeast by the Illinois River; includes Lake Depue. Covers a land area of 868.56 square miles, a water area of 4.74 square miles, and is located in the Central Time Zone at 41.38° N. Lat., 89.47° W. Long. The county was founded in 1837. County seat is Princeton.

Bureau County is part of the Ottawa-Streator, IL Micropolitan Statistical Area. The entire metro area includes: Bureau County, IL; La Salle County, IL; Putnam County, IL

Weather Station: Princeton   Elevation: 694 feet

	Jan	Feb	Mar	Apr	May	Jun	Jul	Aug	Sep	Oct	Nov	Dec
High	31	35	48	61	73	82	85	82	76	63	48	34
Low	17	20	30	40	51	61	65	63	55	43	32	20
Precip	2.0	1.9	2.4	3.7	4.5	4.3	na	4.6	3.6	3.0	2.8	2.3
Snow	8.6	6.1	3.3	0.5	tr	0.0	0.0	0.0	0.0	0.1	0.9	7.4

High and Low temperatures in degrees Fahrenheit; Precipitation and Snow in inches

Weather Station: Walnut   Elevation: 689 feet

	Jan	Feb	Mar	Apr	May	Jun	Jul	Aug	Sep	Oct	Nov	Dec
High	30	34	47	61	72	81	84	82	76	64	48	34
Low	13	17	27	38	50	59	63	61	52	40	30	17
Precip	1.3	1.3	2.2	3.2	4.2	4.4	3.8	4.6	3.1	2.8	2.5	1.9
Snow	9.3	7.0	3.3	0.8	tr	0.0	0.0	0.0	0.0	0.1	1.1	9.3

High and Low temperatures in degrees Fahrenheit; Precipitation and Snow in inches

Population: 35,688 (1990); 35,503 (2000); 34,919 (2010); 34,496 (2015 projected); Race: 95.3% White, 0.7% Black, 0.7% Asian, 3.3% Other, 7.0% Hispanic of any race (2010); Density: 40.2 persons per square mile (2010); Average household size: 2.42 (2010); Median age: 40.7 (2010); Males per 100 females: 95.8 (2010).
Religion: Five largest groups: 21.0% Catholic Church, 8.6% The United Methodist Church, 8.4% Evangelical Lutheran Church in America, 2.9% United Church of Christ, 2.5% American Baptist Churches in the USA (2000).
Economy: Unemployment rate: 9.8% (August 2011); Total civilian labor force: 19,255 (August 2011); Leading industries: 22.8% health care and social assistance; 17.8% manufacturing; 12.1% retail trade (2009); Farms: 1,189 totaling 478,389 acres (2007); Companies that employ 500 or more persons: 2 (2009); Companies that employ 100 to 499 persons: 14 (2009); Companies that employ less than 100 persons: 760 (2009); Black-owned businesses: n/a (2007); Hispanic-owned businesses: n/a (2007); Asian-owned businesses: n/a (2007); Women-owned businesses: 837 (2007); Retail sales per capita: $17,513 (2010). Single-family building permits issued: 24 (2010); Multi-family building permits issued: 3 (2010).
Income: Per capita income: $23,997 (2010); Median household income: $47,543 (2010); Average household income: $58,335 (2010); Percent of households with income of $100,000 or more: 12.3% (2010); Poverty rate: 12.8% (2009); Bankruptcy rate: 4.71% (2010).
Taxes: Total county taxes per capita: $115 (2007); County property taxes per capita: $115 (2007).
Education: Percent of population age 25 and over with: High school diploma (including GED) or higher: 87.7% (2010); Bachelor's degree or higher: 15.0% (2010); Master's degree or higher: 4.9% (2010).
Housing: Homeownership rate: 73.8% (2010); Median home value: $99,966 (2010); Median contract rent: $382 per month (2005-2009 5-year est.); Median year structure built: 1949 (2005-2009 5-year est.)
Health: Birth rate: 128.5 per 10,000 population (2009); Death rate: 111.0 per 10,000 population (2009); Age-adjusted cancer mortality rate: 177.5 deaths per 100,000 population (2007); Number of physicians: 12.9 per 10,000 population (2008); Hospital beds: 31.9 per 10,000 population (2007); Hospital admissions: 1,417.8 per 10,000 population (2007).
Elections: 2008 Presidential election results: 51.9% Obama, 46.2% McCain, 0.9% Nader
National and State Parks: Hennepin Canal Parkway State Park; Lake Depue State Fish and Wildlife Area; Miller-Anderson Woods State Nature Preserve
Additional Information Contacts
Bureau County Government . . . . (815) 875-2014
  http://www.bureaucounty.us
City of Princeton. . . . . (815) 875-2631
  http://www.princeton-il.com
City of Spring Valley. . . . . (815) 664-4221
  http://www.spring-valley.il.us
Princeton Area Chamber of Commerce. . . . . (815) 875-2616
  http://www.princetonchamber-il.com
Walnut Chamber of Commerce . . . . (815) 379-2141
  http://www.villageofwalnut.com/chamber.htm

Bureau County Communities

ARLINGTON (village). Covers a land area of 0.428 square miles and a water area of 0 square miles. Located at 41.47° N. Lat; 89.24° W. Long. Elevation is 751 feet.
Population: 200 (1990); 211 (2000); 209 (2010); 208 (2015 projected); Race: 92.3% White, 0.0% Black, 1.0% Asian, 6.7% Other, 8.1% Hispanic

of any race (2010); Density: 488.7 persons per square mile (2010); Average household size: 2.82 (2010); Median age: 37.0 (2010); Males per 100 females: 104.9 (2010); Marriage status: 20.4% never married, 65.5% now married, 4.2% widowed, 9.9% divorced (2005-2009 5-year est.); Foreign born: 3.0% (2005-2009 5-year est.); Ancestry (includes multiple ancestries): 32.9% German, 19.2% Italian, 18.6% Irish, 7.8% Norwegian, 7.2% American (2005-2009 5-year est.).

Economy: Employment by occupation: 7.1% management, 6.0% professional, 20.2% services, 21.4% sales, 0.0% farming, 21.4% construction, 23.8% production (2005-2009 5-year est.).

Income: Per capita income: $20,449 (2010); Median household income: $53,750 (2010); Average household income: $60,034 (2010); Percent of households with income of $100,000 or more: 12.2% (2010); Poverty rate: 8.4% (2005-2009 5-year est.).

Taxes: Total city taxes per capita: $223 (2007); City property taxes per capita: $155 (2007).

Education: Percent of population age 25 and over with: High school diploma (including GED) or higher: 89.6% (2010); Bachelor's degree or higher: 8.2% (2010); Master's degree or higher: 3.0% (2010).

Housing: Homeownership rate: 75.7% (2010); Median home value: $96,000 (2010); Median contract rent: $388 per month (2005-2009 5-year est.); Median year structure built: before 1940 (2005-2009 5-year est.).

Transportation: Commute to work: 92.9% car, 0.0% public transportation, 2.4% walk, 4.8% work from home (2005-2009 5-year est.); Travel time to work: 32.5% less than 15 minutes, 46.3% 15 to 30 minutes, 12.5% 30 to 45 minutes, 0.0% 45 to 60 minutes, 8.8% 60 minutes or more (2005-2009 5-year est.)

BUDA (village). Covers a land area of 1.008 square miles and a water area of 0 square miles. Located at 41.32° N. Lat; 89.68° W. Long. Elevation is 768 feet.

Population: 563 (1990); 592 (2000); 607 (2010); 610 (2015 projected); Race: 98.5% White, 0.0% Black, 0.8% Asian, 0.7% Other, 0.8% Hispanic of any race (2010); Density: 602.2 persons per square mile (2010); Average household size: 2.53 (2010); Median age: 37.6 (2010); Males per 100 females: 90.3 (2010); Marriage status: 19.6% never married, 63.7% now married, 6.5% widowed, 10.2% divorced (2005-2009 5-year est.); Foreign born: 0.0% (2005-2009 5-year est.); Ancestry (includes multiple ancestries): 28.2% German, 23.1% English, 21.0% American, 12.0% Irish, 7.1% Swedish (2005-2009 5-year est.).

Economy: Employment by occupation: 5.6% management, 12.1% professional, 26.4% services, 10.0% sales, 1.7% farming, 14.3% construction, 29.9% production (2005-2009 5-year est.).

Income: Per capita income: $20,787 (2010); Median household income: $44,412 (2010); Average household income: $51,740 (2010); Percent of households with income of $100,000 or more: 8.8% (2010); Poverty rate: 18.0% (2005-2009 5-year est.).

Taxes: Total city taxes per capita: $87 (2007); City property taxes per capita: $87 (2007).

Education: Percent of population age 25 and over with: High school diploma (including GED) or higher: 89.3% (2010); Bachelor's degree or higher: 7.6% (2010); Master's degree or higher: 2.8% (2010).

School District(s)

Bureau Valley CUSD 340 (PK-12)

  2009-10 Enrollment: 1,232 . . . . (815) 445-3101

Housing: Homeownership rate: 79.6% (2010); Median home value: $79,000 (2010); Median contract rent: $325 per month (2005-2009 5-year est.); Median year structure built: before 1940 (2005-2009 5-year est.).

Safety: Violent crime rate: 0.0 per 10,000 population; Property crime rate: 18.1 per 10,000 population (2010).

Transportation: Commute to work: 93.0% car, 0.0% public transportation, 5.7% walk, 1.3% work from home (2005-2009 5-year est.); Travel time to work: 46.0% less than 15 minutes, 34.8% 15 to 30 minutes, 16.1% 30 to 45 minutes, 0.9% 45 to 60 minutes, 2.2% 60 minutes or more (2005-2009 5-year est.)

BUREAU JUNCTION (village). Aka Bureau. Covers a land area of 1.437 square miles and a water area of 0.066 square miles. Located at 41.28° N. Lat; 89.36° W. Long. Elevation is 489 feet.

Population: 350 (1990); 368 (2000); 379 (2010); 379 (2015 projected); Race: 92.1% White, 0.0% Black, 2.6% Asian, 5.3% Other, 22.2% Hispanic of any race (2010); Density: 263.8 persons per square mile (2010); Average household size: 2.67 (2010); Median age: 35.9 (2010); Males per 100 females: 101.6 (2010); Marriage status: 17.6% never married, 58.3% now married, 1.1% widowed, 23.0% divorced (2005-2009 5-year est.);

Foreign born: 4.9% (2005-2009 5-year est.); Ancestry (includes multiple ancestries): 30.9% Irish, 29.4% German, 12.7% Swedish, 10.3% American, 9.3% Polish (2005-2009 5-year est.).

Economy: Employment by occupation: 2.6% management, 8.7% professional, 37.4% services, 11.3% sales, 0.0% farming, 13.0% construction, 27.0% production (2005-2009 5-year est.).

Income: Per capita income: $23,908 (2010); Median household income: $55,357 (2010); Average household income: $63,363 (2010); Percent of households with income of $100,000 or more: 14.8% (2010); Poverty rate: 17.6% (2005-2009 5-year est.).

Taxes: Total city taxes per capita: $53 (2007); City property taxes per capita: $47 (2007).

Education: Percent of population age 25 and over with: High school diploma (including GED) or higher: 83.3% (2010); Bachelor's degree or higher: 9.5% (2010); Master's degree or higher: 4.0% (2010).

School District(s)

Leepertown CCSD 175 (PK-08)

  2009-10 Enrollment: 54 . . . . (815) 659-3191

Housing: Homeownership rate: 76.1% (2010); Median home value: $74,545 (2010); Median contract rent: $220 per month (2005-2009 5-year est.); Median year structure built: before 1940 (2005-2009 5-year est.).

Transportation: Commute to work: 94.3% car, 0.0% public transportation, 2.9% walk, 2.9% work from home (2005-2009 5-year est.); Travel time to work: 18.6% less than 15 minutes, 53.9% 15 to 30 minutes, 11.8% 30 to 45 minutes, 7.8% 45 to 60 minutes, 7.8% 60 minutes or more (2005-2009 5-year est.)

CHERRY (village). Covers a land area of 0.538 square miles and a water area of 0 square miles. Located at 41.42° N. Lat; 89.21° W. Long. Elevation is 679 feet.

History: Cherry was the scene of a mine fire in 1909 that killed 270 miners.

Population: 513 (1990); 509 (2000); 497 (2010); 489 (2015 projected); Race: 97.8% White, 0.4% Black, 0.0% Asian, 1.8% Other, 1.2% Hispanic of any race (2010); Density: 923.7 persons per square mile (2010); Average household size: 2.42 (2010); Median age: 41.4 (2010); Males per 100 females: 91.2 (2010); Marriage status: 17.4% never married, 54.6% now married, 13.5% widowed, 14.5% divorced (2005-2009 5-year est.); Foreign born: 0.0% (2005-2009 5-year est.); Ancestry (includes multiple ancestries): 37.5% German, 17.0% Irish, 16.7% American, 15.6% Polish, 9.9% English (2005-2009 5-year est.).

Economy: Employment by occupation: 3.9% management, 8.9% professional, 13.3% services, 38.3% sales, 0.0% farming, 14.4% construction, 21.1% production (2005-2009 5-year est.).

Income: Per capita income: $24,091 (2010); Median household income: $50,605 (2010); Average household income: $57,915 (2010); Percent of households with income of $100,000 or more: 9.3% (2010); Poverty rate: 3.6% (2005-2009 5-year est.).

Taxes: Total city taxes per capita: $105 (2007); City property taxes per capita: $58 (2007).

Education: Percent of population age 25 and over with: High school diploma (including GED) or higher: 85.4% (2010); Bachelor's degree or higher: 8.8% (2010); Master's degree or higher: 1.8% (2010).

School District(s)

Cherry SD 92 (KG-08)

  2009-10 Enrollment: 58 . . . . (815) 894-2777

Housing: Homeownership rate: 82.9% (2010); Median home value: $104,545 (2010); Median contract rent: $433 per month (2005-2009 5-year est.); Median year structure built: before 1940 (2005-2009 5-year est.).

Transportation: Commute to work: 97.8% car, 0.0% public transportation, 0.0% walk, 2.2% work from home (2005-2009 5-year est.); Travel time to work: 35.8% less than 15 minutes, 54.0% 15 to 30 minutes, 3.4% 30 to 45 minutes, 1.1% 45 to 60 minutes, 5.7% 60 minutes or more (2005-2009 5-year est.)

DALZELL (village). Covers a land area of 1.270 square miles and a water area of 0.010 square miles. Located at 41.35° N. Lat; 89.17° W. Long. Elevation is 633 feet.

Population: 709 (1990); 717 (2000); 760 (2010); 780 (2015 projected); Race: 96.6% White, 0.8% Black, 0.1% Asian, 2.5% Other, 4.9% Hispanic of any race (2010); Density: 598.4 persons per square mile (2010); Average household size: 2.42 (2010); Median age: 40.5 (2010); Males per 100 females: 95.4 (2010); Marriage status: 17.7% never married, 65.4% now married, 5.9% widowed, 11.0% divorced (2005-2009 5-year est.); Foreign born: 1.0% (2005-2009 5-year est.); Ancestry (includes multiple

ancestries): 33.1% Italian, 24.9% German, 13.0% Irish, 12.1% Polish, 10.7% English (2005-2009 5-year est.).
Economy: Single-family building permits issued: 0 (2010); Multi-family building permits issued: 0 (2010); Employment by occupation: 6.1% management, 19.4% professional, 16.5% services, 29.1% sales, 1.7% farming, 7.3% construction, 19.9% production (2005-2009 5-year est.).
Income: Per capita income: $27,659 (2010); Median household income: $58,036 (2010); Average household income: $66,431 (2010); Percent of households with income of $100,000 or more: 16.1% (2010); Poverty rate: 5.7% (2005-2009 5-year est.).
Taxes: Total city taxes per capita: $328 (2007); City property taxes per capita: $70 (2007).
Education: Percent of population age 25 and over with: High school diploma (including GED) or higher: 88.2% (2010); Bachelor's degree or higher: 13.5% (2010); Master's degree or higher: 4.2% (2010).

School District(s)

Dalzell SD 98 (KG-08)
    2009-10 Enrollment: 67 . . . . (815) 663-8821
Housing: Homeownership rate: 81.0% (2010); Median home value: $122,892 (2010); Median contract rent: $554 per month (2005-2009 5-year est.); Median year structure built: 1960 (2005-2009 5-year est.).
Transportation: Commute to work: 98.0% car, 0.0% public transportation, 0.0% walk, 2.0% work from home (2005-2009 5-year est.); Travel time to work: 57.0% less than 15 minutes, 27.9% 15 to 30 minutes, 6.5% 30 to 45 minutes, 1.5% 45 to 60 minutes, 7.0% 60 minutes or more (2005-2009 5-year est.)

DE PUE (village). Aka Depue. Covers a land area of 2.711 square miles and a water area of 0.259 square miles. Located at 41.32° N. Lat; 89.30° W. Long.
Population: 1,774 (1990); 1,842 (2000); 1,762 (2010); 1,719 (2015 projected); Race: 79.7% White, 0.2% Black, 0.4% Asian, 19.8% Other, 59.3% Hispanic of any race (2010); Density: 649.9 persons per square mile (2010); Average household size: 2.72 (2010); Median age: 33.6 (2010); Males per 100 females: 110.8 (2010); Marriage status: 28.9% never married, 53.5% now married, 7.4% widowed, 10.3% divorced (2005-2009 5-year est.); Foreign born: 25.7% (2005-2009 5-year est.); Ancestry (includes multiple ancestries): 14.6% German, 7.6% Polish, 6.1% American, 5.3% Italian, 4.5% English (2005-2009 5-year est.).
Economy: Single-family building permits issued: 0 (2010); Multi-family building permits issued: 0 (2010); Employment by occupation: 2.2% management, 6.1% professional, 13.2% services, 18.1% sales, 17.0% farming, 11.6% construction, 31.7% production (2005-2009 5-year est.).
Income: Per capita income: $19,003 (2010); Median household income: $37,375 (2010); Average household income: $50,413 (2010); Percent of households with income of $100,000 or more: 8.6% (2010); Poverty rate: 20.6% (2005-2009 5-year est.).
Taxes: Total city taxes per capita: $153 (2007); City property taxes per capita: $108 (2007).
Education: Percent of population age 25 and over with: High school diploma (including GED) or higher: 72.2% (2010); Bachelor's degree or higher: 7.3% (2010); Master's degree or higher: 2.3% (2010).

School District(s)

Depue USD 103 (PK-12)
    2009-10 Enrollment: 511 . . . . (815) 447-2121
Housing: Homeownership rate: 72.6% (2010); Median home value: $61,237 (2010); Median contract rent: $362 per month (2005-2009 5-year est.); Median year structure built: before 1940 (2005-2009 5-year est.).
Safety: Violent crime rate: 11.7 per 10,000 population; Property crime rate: 210.9 per 10,000 population (2010).
Transportation: Commute to work: 96.9% car, 0.0% public transportation, 1.5% walk, 1.3% work from home (2005-2009 5-year est.); Travel time to work: 46.1% less than 15 minutes, 36.0% 15 to 30 minutes, 8.2% 30 to 45 minutes, 3.7% 45 to 60 minutes, 6.1% 60 minutes or more (2005-2009 5-year est.)

DOVER (village). Covers a land area of 0.268 square miles and a water area of 0 square miles. Located at 41.43° N. Lat; 89.39° W. Long. Elevation is 741 feet.
Population: 163 (1990); 172 (2000); 150 (2010); 145 (2015 projected); Race: 96.7% White, 0.7% Black, 0.7% Asian, 2.0% Other, 0.0% Hispanic of any race (2010); Density: 559.6 persons per square mile (2010); Average household size: 2.73 (2010); Median age: 37.7 (2010); Males per 100 females: 94.8 (2010); Marriage status: 37.0% never married, 53.1% now married, 3.7% widowed, 6.2% divorced (2005-2009 5-year est.);

Foreign born: 2.0% (2005-2009 5-year est.); Ancestry (includes multiple ancestries): 41.4% German, 25.3% Irish, 10.1% American, 8.1% Italian, 5.1% English (2005-2009 5-year est.).
Economy: Employment by occupation: 11.5% management, 13.5% professional, 15.4% services, 15.4% sales, 0.0% farming, 0.0% construction, 44.2% production (2005-2009 5-year est.).
Income: Per capita income: $25,840 (2010); Median household income: $66,912 (2010); Average household income: $69,955 (2010); Percent of households with income of $100,000 or more: 16.4% (2010); Poverty rate: 32.3% (2005-2009 5-year est.).
Taxes: Total city taxes per capita: $71 (2007); City property taxes per capita: $71 (2007).
Education: Percent of population age 25 and over with: High school diploma (including GED) or higher: 94.9% (2010); Bachelor's degree or higher: 18.2% (2010); Master's degree or higher: 4.0% (2010).
Housing: Homeownership rate: 81.8% (2010); Median home value: $91,250 (2010); Median contract rent: $608 per month (2005-2009 5-year est.); Median year structure built: 1941 (2005-2009 5-year est.).
Transportation: Commute to work: 100.0% car, 0.0% public transportation, 0.0% walk, 0.0% work from home (2005-2009 5-year est.); Travel time to work: 78.4% less than 15 minutes, 17.6% 15 to 30 minutes, 0.0% 30 to 45 minutes, 0.0% 45 to 60 minutes, 3.9% 60 minutes or more (2005-2009 5-year est.)

HOLLOWAYVILLE (village). Covers a land area of 0.049 square miles and a water area of 0 square miles. Located at 41.36° N. Lat; 89.29° W. Long. Elevation is 659 feet.
Population: 37 (1990); 90 (2000); 90 (2010); 89 (2015 projected); Race: 93.3% White, 0.0% Black, 0.0% Asian, 6.7% Other, 8.9% Hispanic of any race (2010); Density: 1,836.6 persons per square mile (2010); Average household size: 2.81 (2010); Median age: 35.0 (2010); Males per 100 females: 136.8 (2010); Marriage status: 13.6% never married, 83.3% now married, 0.0% widowed, 3.0% divorced (2005-2009 5-year est.); Foreign born: 0.0% (2005-2009 5-year est.); Ancestry (includes multiple ancestries): 55.3% American, 22.4% German, 20.0% Italian, 11.8% Polish, 7.1% Swedish (2005-2009 5-year est.).
Economy: Employment by occupation: 17.9% management, 10.3% professional, 5.1% services, 20.5% sales, 0.0% farming, 15.4% construction, 30.8% production (2005-2009 5-year est.).
Income: Per capita income: $20,449 (2010); Median household income: $53,125 (2010); Average household income: $59,766 (2010); Percent of households with income of $100,000 or more: 15.6% (2010); Poverty rate: 0.0% (2005-2009 5-year est.).
Taxes: Total city taxes per capita: $0 (2007); City property taxes per capita: $0 (2007).
Education: Percent of population age 25 and over with: High school diploma (including GED) or higher: 87.9% (2010); Bachelor's degree or higher: 8.6% (2010); Master's degree or higher: 3.4% (2010).
Housing: Homeownership rate: 75.0% (2010); Median home value: $93,333 (2010); Median contract rent: n/a per month (2005-2009 5-year est.); Median year structure built: before 1940 (2005-2009 5-year est.).
Transportation: Commute to work: 100.0% car, 0.0% public transportation, 0.0% walk, 0.0% work from home (2005-2009 5-year est.); Travel time to work: 33.3% less than 15 minutes, 41.0% 15 to 30 minutes, 25.6% 30 to 45 minutes, 0.0% 45 to 60 minutes, 0.0% 60 minutes or more (2005-2009 5-year est.)

LA MOILLE (village). Covers a land area of 1.205 square miles and a water area of 0 square miles. Located at 41.52° N. Lat; 89.28° W. Long. Elevation is 794 feet.
Population: 717 (1990); 773 (2000); 749 (2010); 733 (2015 projected); Race: 96.8% White, 0.4% Black, 0.0% Asian, 2.8% Other, 5.7% Hispanic of any race (2010); Density: 621.5 persons per square mile (2010); Average household size: 2.58 (2010); Median age: 37.4 (2010); Males per 100 females: 99.7 (2010); Marriage status: 20.4% never married, 56.9% now married, 5.9% widowed, 16.8% divorced (2005-2009 5-year est.); Foreign born: 0.0% (2005-2009 5-year est.); Ancestry (includes multiple ancestries): 40.4% German, 14.9% English, 13.4% Irish, 9.1% American, 7.0% Italian (2005-2009 5-year est.).
Economy: Employment by occupation: 9.4% management, 9.4% professional, 22.1% services, 19.9% sales, 0.0% farming, 15.0% construction, 24.3% production (2005-2009 5-year est.).
Income: Per capita income: $21,320 (2010); Median household income: $45,682 (2010); Average household income: $55,914 (2010); Percent of

households with income of $100,000 or more: 9.3% (2010); Poverty rate: 20.1% (2005-2009 5-year est.).

Taxes: Total city taxes per capita: $67 (2007); City property taxes per capita: $65 (2007).

Education: Percent of population age 25 and over with: High school diploma (including GED) or higher: 88.9% (2010); Bachelor's degree or higher: 8.2% (2010); Master's degree or higher: 3.3% (2010).

School District(s)

La Moille CUSD 303 (PK-12)

   2009-10 Enrollment: 278 . . . . (815) 638-2018

Housing: Homeownership rate: 71.4% (2010); Median home value: $119,068 (2010); Median contract rent: $426 per month (2005-2009 5-year est.); Median year structure built: 1951 (2005-2009 5-year est.).

Transportation: Commute to work: 93.6% car, 0.0% public transportation, 2.2% walk, 2.2% work from home (2005-2009 5-year est.); Travel time to work: 38.7% less than 15 minutes, 44.8% 15 to 30 minutes, 10.4% 30 to 45 minutes, 2.5% 45 to 60 minutes, 3.6% 60 minutes or more (2005-2009 5-year est.)

LADD (village). Covers a land area of 1.193 square miles and a water area of 0 square miles. Located at 41.38° N. Lat; 89.21° W. Long. Elevation is 650 feet.

History: Incorporated 1890.

Population: 1,339 (1990); 1,313 (2000); 1,312 (2010); 1,309 (2015 projected); Race: 96.6% White, 0.4% Black, 0.0% Asian, 3.0% Other, 4.4% Hispanic of any race (2010); Density: 1,099.4 persons per square mile (2010); Average household size: 2.27 (2010); Median age: 40.0 (2010); Males per 100 females: 94.4 (2010); Marriage status: 21.0% never married, 61.0% now married, 8.6% widowed, 9.5% divorced (2005-2009 5-year est.); Foreign born: 3.1% (2005-2009 5-year est.); Ancestry (includes multiple ancestries): 33.0% German, 22.5% Italian, 15.9% Irish, 14.4% English, 10.0% American (2005-2009 5-year est.).

Economy: Single-family building permits issued: 0 (2010); Multi-family building permits issued: 0 (2010); Employment by occupation: 9.6% management, 18.7% professional, 22.3% services, 18.0% sales, 2.5% farming, 8.9% construction, 20.0% production (2005-2009 5-year est.).

Income: Per capita income: $26,572 (2010); Median household income: $49,523 (2010); Average household income: $59,822 (2010); Percent of households with income of $100,000 or more: 12.7% (2010); Poverty rate: 13.3% (2005-2009 5-year est.).

Taxes: Total city taxes per capita: $146 (2007); City property taxes per capita: $143 (2007).

Education: Percent of population age 25 and over with: High school diploma (including GED) or higher: 86.5% (2010); Bachelor's degree or higher: 12.9% (2010); Master's degree or higher: 3.9% (2010).

School District(s)

Ladd CCSD 94 (KG-08)

   2009-10 Enrollment: 184 . . . . (815) 894-2363

Housing: Homeownership rate: 76.9% (2010); Median home value: $108,333 (2010); Median contract rent: $518 per month (2005-2009 5-year est.); Median year structure built: 1950 (2005-2009 5-year est.).

Transportation: Commute to work: 95.2% car, 0.0% public transportation, 1.6% walk, 1.2% work from home (2005-2009 5-year est.); Travel time to work: 54.3% less than 15 minutes, 33.0% 15 to 30 minutes, 2.9% 30 to 45 minutes, 1.7% 45 to 60 minutes, 8.1% 60 minutes or more (2005-2009 5-year est.)

MALDEN (village). Covers a land area of 0.274 square miles and a water area of 0 square miles. Located at 41.42° N. Lat; 89.36° W. Long. Elevation is 705 feet.

Population: 381 (1990); 343 (2000); 334 (2010); 323 (2015 projected); Race: 97.0% White, 0.6% Black, 0.3% Asian, 2.1% Other, 0.6% Hispanic of any race (2010); Density: 1,220.8 persons per square mile (2010); Average household size: 2.71 (2010); Median age: 38.1 (2010); Males per 100 females: 108.7 (2010); Marriage status: 25.8% never married, 59.7% now married, 3.8% widowed, 10.6% divorced (2005-2009 5-year est.); Foreign born: 2.5% (2005-2009 5-year est.); Ancestry (includes multiple ancestries): 32.5% German, 28.9% English, 12.6% Irish, 9.0% Italian, 8.7% American (2005-2009 5-year est.).

Economy: Employment by occupation: 4.8% management, 10.9% professional, 25.2% services, 19.0% sales, 0.0% farming, 14.3% construction, 25.9% production (2005-2009 5-year est.).

Income: Per capita income: $25,840 (2010); Median household income: $66,554 (2010); Average household income: $69,573 (2010); Percent of

---

households with income of $100,000 or more: 16.3% (2010); Poverty rate: 11.2% (2005-2009 5-year est.).

Taxes: Total city taxes per capita: $59 (2007); City property taxes per capita: $53 (2007).

Education: Percent of population age 25 and over with: High school diploma (including GED) or higher: 94.1% (2010); Bachelor's degree or higher: 19.2% (2010); Master's degree or higher: 4.6% (2010).

School District(s)

Malden CCSD 84 (PK-08)

   2009-10 Enrollment: 75 . . . . (815) 643-2436

Housing: Homeownership rate: 82.1% (2010); Median home value: $97,059 (2010); Median contract rent: $454 per month (2005-2009 5-year est.); Median year structure built: 1973 (2005-2009 5-year est.).

Transportation: Commute to work: 96.5% car, 0.0% public transportation, 2.1% walk, 0.0% work from home (2005-2009 5-year est.); Travel time to work: 43.4% less than 15 minutes, 38.5% 15 to 30 minutes, 9.1% 30 to 45 minutes, 0.7% 45 to 60 minutes, 8.4% 60 minutes or more (2005-2009 5-year est.)

MANLIUS (village). Covers a land area of 0.306 square miles and a water area of 0 square miles. Located at 41.45° N. Lat; 89.67° W. Long. Elevation is 702 feet.

Population: 365 (1990); 355 (2000); 343 (2010); 341 (2015 projected); Race: 97.7% White, 0.6% Black, 0.0% Asian, 1.7% Other, 4.7% Hispanic of any race (2010); Density: 1,119.5 persons per square mile (2010); Average household size: 2.45 (2010); Median age: 39.4 (2010); Males per 100 females: 96.0 (2010); Marriage status: 19.8% never married, 54.2% now married, 7.1% widowed, 18.9% divorced (2005-2009 5-year est.); Foreign born: 0.0% (2005-2009 5-year est.); Ancestry (includes multiple ancestries): 44.1% German, 21.5% American, 12.9% English, 11.7% Irish, 11.3% Polish (2005-2009 5-year est.).

Economy: Employment by occupation: 3.2% management, 20.2% professional, 12.8% services, 18.1% sales, 2.1% farming, 12.8% construction, 30.9% production (2005-2009 5-year est.).

Income: Per capita income: $23,834 (2010); Median household income: $48,784 (2010); Average household income: $59,054 (2010); Percent of households with income of $100,000 or more: 16.4% (2010); Poverty rate: 29.5% (2005-2009 5-year est.).

Taxes: Total city taxes per capita: $332 (2007); City property taxes per capita: $315 (2007).

Education: Percent of population age 25 and over with: High school diploma (including GED) or higher: 93.1% (2010); Bachelor's degree or higher: 9.1% (2010); Master's degree or higher: 3.4% (2010).

School District(s)

Bureau Valley CUSD 340 (PK-12)

   2009-10 Enrollment: 1,232 . . . . (815) 445-3101

Bureau/Henry/Stark Roe (06-12)

   2009-10 Enrollment: n/a . . . . (309) 936-7890

Housing: Homeownership rate: 72.1% (2010); Median home value: $90,556 (2010); Median contract rent: $272 per month (2005-2009 5-year est.); Median year structure built: 1941 (2005-2009 5-year est.).

Transportation: Commute to work: 97.7% car, 0.0% public transportation, 2.3% walk, 0.0% work from home (2005-2009 5-year est.); Travel time to work: 27.3% less than 15 minutes, 50.0% 15 to 30 minutes, 18.2% 30 to 45 minutes, 2.3% 45 to 60 minutes, 2.3% 60 minutes or more (2005-2009 5-year est.)

MINERAL (village). Covers a land area of 0.308 square miles and a water area of 0 square miles. Located at 41.38° N. Lat; 89.83° W. Long. Elevation is 640 feet.

Population: 250 (1990); 272 (2000); 266 (2010); 259 (2015 projected); Race: 96.2% White, 1.1% Black, 0.0% Asian, 2.6% Other, 1.9% Hispanic of any race (2010); Density: 863.9 persons per square mile (2010); Average household size: 2.33 (2010); Median age: 42.9 (2010); Males per 100 females: 104.6 (2010); Marriage status: 21.4% never married, 55.9% now married, 14.5% widowed, 8.2% divorced (2005-2009 5-year est.); Foreign born: 0.0% (2005-2009 5-year est.); Ancestry (includes multiple ancestries): 21.9% German, 18.2% Irish, 17.1% Belgian, 12.3% English, 10.8% Dutch (2005-2009 5-year est.).

Economy: Employment by occupation: 4.6% management, 9.2% professional, 16.9% services, 20.8% sales, 3.8% farming, 8.5% construction, 36.2% production (2005-2009 5-year est.).

Income: Per capita income: $28,689 (2010); Median household income: $50,000 (2010); Average household income: $64,189 (2010); Percent of

households with income of $100,000 or more: 15.8% (2010); Poverty rate: 2.2% (2005-2009 5-year est.).
Taxes: Total city taxes per capita: $71 (2007); City property taxes per capita: $68 (2007).
Education: Percent of population age 25 and over with: High school diploma (including GED) or higher: 86.7% (2010); Bachelor's degree or higher: 12.2% (2010); Master's degree or higher: 3.1% (2010).
Housing: Homeownership rate: 73.7% (2010); Median home value: $96,000 (2010); Median contract rent: $355 per month (2005-2009 5-year est.); Median year structure built: before 1940 (2005-2009 5-year est.).
Transportation: Commute to work: 92.3% car, 0.0% public transportation, 7.7% walk, 0.0% work from home (2005-2009 5-year est.); Travel time to work: 30.0% less than 15 minutes, 45.4% 15 to 30 minutes, 8.5% 30 to 45 minutes, 14.6% 45 to 60 minutes, 1.5% 60 minutes or more (2005-2009 5-year est.)

NEPONSET (village). Covers a land area of 1.042 square miles and a water area of 0 square miles. Located at 41.29° N. Lat; 89.79° W. Long. Elevation is 830 feet.
Population: 529 (1990); 519 (2000); 493 (2010); 480 (2015 projected); Race: 97.4% White, 0.8% Black, 0.8% Asian, 1.0% Other, 3.4% Hispanic of any race (2010); Density: 473.0 persons per square mile (2010); Average household size: 2.48 (2010); Median age: 46.3 (2010); Males per 100 females: 104.6 (2010); Marriage status: 18.3% never married, 64.6% now married, 5.1% widowed, 11.9% divorced (2005-2009 5-year est.); Foreign born: 2.3% (2005-2009 5-year est.); Ancestry (includes multiple ancestries): 29.5% German, 19.1% English, 14.4% American, 11.6% Polish, 8.4% Swedish (2005-2009 5-year est.).
Economy: Single-family building permits issued: 0 (2010); Multi-family building permits issued: 0 (2010); Employment by occupation: 15.6% management, 16.3% professional, 7.3% services, 28.0% sales, 1.4% farming, 7.6% construction, 23.9% production (2005-2009 5-year est.).
Income: Per capita income: $24,732 (2010); Median household income: $50,852 (2010); Average household income: $62,525 (2010); Percent of households with income of $100,000 or more: 17.1% (2010); Poverty rate: 12.2% (2005-2009 5-year est.).
Taxes: Total city taxes per capita: $120 (2007); City property taxes per capita: $114 (2007).
Education: Percent of population age 25 and over with: High school diploma (including GED) or higher: 85.0% (2010); Bachelor's degree or higher: 12.9% (2010); Master's degree or higher: 3.6% (2010).
School District(s)
Neponset CCSD 307 (PK-08)
    2009-10 Enrollment: 85 . . . . (309) 594-2306
Housing: Homeownership rate: 80.9% (2010); Median home value: $80,357 (2010); Median contract rent: $354 per month (2005-2009 5-year est.); Median year structure built: before 1940 (2005-2009 5-year est.).
Transportation: Commute to work: 88.8% car, 0.0% public transportation, 5.0% walk, 4.7% work from home (2005-2009 5-year est.); Travel time to work: 28.3% less than 15 minutes, 32.5% 15 to 30 minutes, 19.2% 30 to 45 minutes, 7.5% 45 to 60 minutes, 12.5% 60 minutes or more (2005-2009 5-year est.)

NEW BEDFORD (village). Covers a land area of 0.175 square miles and a water area of 0 square miles. Located at 41.51° N. Lat; 89.71° W. Long. Elevation is 643 feet.
Population: 65 (1990); 95 (2000); 89 (2010); 86 (2015 projected); Race: 97.8% White, 1.1% Black, 0.0% Asian, 1.1% Other, 2.2% Hispanic of any race (2010); Density: 509.5 persons per square mile (2010); Average household size: 2.58 (2010); Median age: 41.5 (2010); Males per 100 females: 117.1 (2010); Marriage status: 28.0% never married, 60.0% now married, 12.0% widowed, 0.0% divorced (2005-2009 5-year est.); Foreign born: 0.0% (2005-2009 5-year est.); Ancestry (includes multiple ancestries): 33.3% German, 19.3% French, 14.0% Irish, 10.5% Swedish, 8.8% Scottish (2005-2009 5-year est.).
Economy: Employment by occupation: 6.1% management, 6.1% professional, 33.3% services, 18.2% sales, 0.0% farming, 15.2% construction, 21.2% production (2005-2009 5-year est.).
Income: Per capita income: $25,575 (2010); Median household income: $45,500 (2010); Average household income: $56,136 (2010); Percent of households with income of $100,000 or more: 9.1% (2010); Poverty rate: 24.6% (2005-2009 5-year est.).
Taxes: Total city taxes per capita: $22 (2007); City property taxes per capita: $22 (2007).

Education: Percent of population age 25 and over with: High school diploma (including GED) or higher: 86.7% (2010); Bachelor's degree or higher: 11.7% (2010); Master's degree or higher: 3.3% (2010).
Housing: Homeownership rate: 72.7% (2010); Median home value: $93,333 (2010); Median contract rent: n/a per month (2005-2009 5-year est.); Median year structure built: before 1940 (2005-2009 5-year est.).
Transportation: Commute to work: 93.5% car, 0.0% public transportation, 0.0% walk, 0.0% work from home (2005-2009 5-year est.); Travel time to work: 0.0% less than 15 minutes, 38.7% 15 to 30 minutes, 29.0% 30 to 45 minutes, 22.6% 45 to 60 minutes, 9.7% 60 minutes or more (2005-2009 5-year est.)

OHIO (village). Covers a land area of 0.753 square miles and a water area of 0 square miles. Located at 41.55° N. Lat; 89.46° W. Long. Elevation is 902 feet.
Population: 449 (1990); 540 (2000); 513 (2010); 501 (2015 projected); Race: 98.4% White, 0.4% Black, 0.0% Asian, 1.2% Other, 3.1% Hispanic of any race (2010); Density: 681.4 persons per square mile (2010); Average household size: 2.47 (2010); Median age: 39.6 (2010); Males per 100 females: 91.4 (2010); Marriage status: 27.3% never married, 59.5% now married, 8.5% widowed, 4.8% divorced (2005-2009 5-year est.); Foreign born: 0.4% (2005-2009 5-year est.); Ancestry (includes multiple ancestries): 41.4% German, 20.6% Irish, 10.8% Polish, 7.1% Norwegian, 7.1% Swedish (2005-2009 5-year est.).
Economy: Employment by occupation: 5.0% management, 19.8% professional, 14.0% services, 27.9% sales, 0.0% farming, 13.6% construction, 19.8% production (2005-2009 5-year est.).
Income: Per capita income: $23,661 (2010); Median household income: $51,364 (2010); Average household income: $59,099 (2010); Percent of households with income of $100,000 or more: 12.0% (2010); Poverty rate: 24.1% (2005-2009 5-year est.).
Taxes: Total city taxes per capita: $397 (2007); City property taxes per capita: $393 (2007).
Education: Percent of population age 25 and over with: High school diploma (including GED) or higher: 93.6% (2010); Bachelor's degree or higher: 12.2% (2010); Master's degree or higher: 5.2% (2010).
School District(s)
Ohio CCSD 17 (KG-08)
    2009-10 Enrollment: 85 . . . . (815) 376-4414
Ohio CHSD 505 (09-12)
    2009-10 Enrollment: 41 . . . . (815) 376-2934
Housing: Homeownership rate: 73.6% (2010); Median home value: $97,200 (2010); Median contract rent: $344 per month (2005-2009 5-year est.); Median year structure built: 1954 (2005-2009 5-year est.).
Transportation: Commute to work: 90.4% car, 2.0% public transportation, 3.2% walk, 3.2% work from home (2005-2009 5-year est.); Travel time to work: 25.1% less than 15 minutes, 42.0% 15 to 30 minutes, 22.2% 30 to 45 minutes, 6.2% 45 to 60 minutes, 4.5% 60 minutes or more (2005-2009 5-year est.)

PRINCETON (city). County seat. Covers a land area of 6.730 square miles and a water area of 0 square miles. Located at 41.37° N. Lat; 89.46° W. Long. Elevation is 719 feet.
History: Princeton was laid out in 1833 by settlers from Massachusetts. The town grew as an orchard and farming center, and as the seat of Bureau County.
Population: 7,581 (1990); 7,501 (2000); 7,417 (2010); 7,335 (2015 projected); Race: 96.5% White, 0.8% Black, 1.0% Asian, 1.6% Other, 1.5% Hispanic of any race (2010); Density: 1,102.1 persons per square mile (2010); Average household size: 2.20 (2010); Median age: 44.3 (2010); Males per 100 females: 88.1 (2010); Marriage status: 24.4% never married, 52.4% now married, 10.4% widowed, 12.9% divorced (2005-2009 5-year est.); Foreign born: 1.4% (2005-2009 5-year est.); Ancestry (includes multiple ancestries): 37.0% German, 16.1% Irish, 15.5% Swedish, 10.7% English, 9.9% American (2005-2009 5-year est.).
Economy: Single-family building permits issued: 5 (2010); Multi-family building permits issued: 0 (2010); Employment by occupation: 10.3% management, 16.0% professional, 17.2% services, 25.9% sales, 1.0% farming, 11.4% construction, 18.3% production (2005-2009 5-year est.).
Income: Per capita income: $25,773 (2010); Median household income: $46,081 (2010); Average household income: $57,582 (2010); Percent of households with income of $100,000 or more: 12.3% (2010); Poverty rate: 14.4% (2005-2009 5-year est.).
Taxes: Total city taxes per capita: $205 (2007); City property taxes per capita: $148 (2007).

Education: Percent of population age 25 and over with: High school diploma (including GED) or higher: 91.9% (2010); Bachelor's degree or higher: 20.4% (2010); Master's degree or higher: 7.1% (2010).
School District(s)
Princeton ESD 115 (PK-08)
    2009-10 Enrollment: 1,311 . . . . (815) 875-3162
Princeton HSD 500 (09-12)
    2009-10 Enrollment: 653 . . . . (815) 875-3308
Housing: Homeownership rate: 67.0% (2010); Median home value: $111,850 (2010); Median contract rent: $358 per month (2005-2009 5-year est.); Median year structure built: 1955 (2005-2009 5-year est.).
Hospitals: Perry Memorial Hospital (98 beds)
Newspapers: Bureau County Republican (Community news); Illinois Valley Shopping News (Regional news; Circulation 13,298)
Transportation: Commute to work: 87.3% car, 0.2% public transportation, 5.8% walk, 5.5% work from home (2005-2009 5-year est.); Travel time to work: 63.2% less than 15 minutes, 22.8% 15 to 30 minutes, 6.3% 30 to 45 minutes, 2.1% 45 to 60 minutes, 5.7% 60 minutes or more (2005-2009 5-year est.); Amtrak: train service available.
Additional Information Contacts
City of Princeton. . . . . (815) 875-2631
    http://www.princeton-il.com
Princeton Area Chamber of Commerce. . . . . (815) 875-2616
    http://www.princetonchamber-il.com

SEATONVILLE (village).
Covers a land area of 0.486 square miles and a water area of 0.015 square miles. Located at 41.36° N. Lat; 89.27° W. Long. Elevation is 620 feet.
Population: 259 (1990); 303 (2000); 299 (2010); 298 (2015 projected); Race: 94.3% White, 0.0% Black, 1.3% Asian, 4.3% Other, 5.7% Hispanic of any race (2010); Density: 615.2 persons per square mile (2010); Average household size: 2.45 (2010); Median age: 45.1 (2010); Males per 100 females: 99.3 (2010); Marriage status: 18.8% never married, 69.8% now married, 5.7% widowed, 5.7% divorced (2005-2009 5-year est.); Foreign born: 3.2% (2005-2009 5-year est.); Ancestry (includes multiple ancestries): 47.2% German, 15.9% Irish, 15.1% Italian, 13.9% Polish, 6.7% English (2005-2009 5-year est.).
Economy: Single-family building permits issued: 1 (2010); Multi-family building permits issued: 0 (2010); Employment by occupation: 7.4% management, 0.0% professional, 12.9% services, 43.6% sales, 0.0% farming, 2.5% construction, 33.7% production (2005-2009 5-year est.).
Income: Per capita income: $21,714 (2010); Median household income: $42,800 (2010); Average household income: $51,025 (2010); Percent of households with income of $100,000 or more: 9.0% (2010); Poverty rate: 12.8% (2005-2009 5-year est.).
Taxes: Total city taxes per capita: $65 (2007); City property taxes per capita: $45 (2007).
Education: Percent of population age 25 and over with: High school diploma (including GED) or higher: 83.6% (2010); Bachelor's degree or higher: 11.1% (2010); Master's degree or higher: 2.7% (2010).
Housing: Homeownership rate: 88.5% (2010); Median home value: $95,556 (2010); Median contract rent: $425 per month (2005-2009 5-year est.); Median year structure built: 1949 (2005-2009 5-year est.).
Transportation: Commute to work: 98.7% car, 0.0% public transportation, 1.3% walk, 0.0% work from home (2005-2009 5-year est.); Travel time to work: 31.8% less than 15 minutes, 58.0% 15 to 30 minutes, 7.0% 30 to 45 minutes, 0.0% 45 to 60 minutes, 3.2% 60 minutes or more (2005-2009 5-year est.)

SHEFFIELD (village).
Covers a land area of 0.749 square miles and a water area of 0 square miles. Located at 41.35° N. Lat; 89.73° W. Long. Elevation is 689 feet.
Population: 956 (1990); 946 (2000); 930 (2010); 919 (2015 projected); Race: 97.6% White, 0.2% Black, 0.2% Asian, 1.9% Other, 1.0% Hispanic of any race (2010); Density: 1,242.1 persons per square mile (2010); Average household size: 2.40 (2010); Median age: 42.4 (2010); Males per 100 females: 94.2 (2010); Marriage status: 29.4% never married, 42.6% now married, 9.8% widowed, 18.2% divorced (2005-2009 5-year est.); Foreign born: 0.0% (2005-2009 5-year est.); Ancestry (includes multiple ancestries): 27.6% German, 12.3% English, 11.2% Irish, 10.9% American, 7.4% Belgian (2005-2009 5-year est.).
Economy: Employment by occupation: 7.1% management, 12.4% professional, 13.3% services, 27.7% sales, 0.0% farming, 11.0% construction, 28.6% production (2005-2009 5-year est.).

Income: Per capita income: $23,223 (2010); Median household income: $46,438 (2010); Average household income: $55,266 (2010); Percent of households with income of $100,000 or more: 10.4% (2010); Poverty rate: 13.4% (2005-2009 5-year est.).
Taxes: Total city taxes per capita: $132 (2007); City property taxes per capita: $129 (2007).
Education: Percent of population age 25 and over with: High school diploma (including GED) or higher: 87.9% (2010); Bachelor's degree or higher: 15.2% (2010); Master's degree or higher: 4.2% (2010).
Housing: Homeownership rate: 80.1% (2010); Median home value: $75,915 (2010); Median contract rent: $378 per month (2005-2009 5-year est.); Median year structure built: before 1940 (2005-2009 5-year est.).
Transportation: Commute to work: 92.1% car, 0.5% public transportation, 2.6% walk, 3.7% work from home (2005-2009 5-year est.); Travel time to work: 23.5% less than 15 minutes, 59.1% 15 to 30 minutes, 10.4% 30 to 45 minutes, 5.8% 45 to 60 minutes, 1.2% 60 minutes or more (2005-2009 5-year est.)

SPRING VALLEY (city).
Covers a land area of 3.886 square miles and a water area of 0.019 square miles. Located at 41.32° N. Lat; 89.20° W. Long. Elevation is 597 feet.
History: Spring Valley began as a mining operation, but later the economy was based on manufacturing.
Population: 5,246 (1990); 5,398 (2000); 5,344 (2010); 5,300 (2015 projected); Race: 93.6% White, 1.6% Black, 0.5% Asian, 4.3% Other, 10.3% Hispanic of any race (2010); Density: 1,375.4 persons per square mile (2010); Average household size: 2.40 (2010); Median age: 40.3 (2010); Males per 100 females: 93.7 (2010); Marriage status: 21.0% never married, 51.7% now married, 10.8% widowed, 16.5% divorced (2005-2009 5-year est.); Foreign born: 3.5% (2005-2009 5-year est.); Ancestry (includes multiple ancestries): 27.6% German, 22.6% Italian, 15.2% Irish, 8.9% English, 8.2% American (2005-2009 5-year est.).
Economy: Single-family building permits issued: 2 (2010); Multi-family building permits issued: 0 (2010); Employment by occupation: 7.0% management, 12.9% professional, 19.9% services, 24.6% sales, 0.4% farming, 7.9% construction, 27.2% production (2005-2009 5-year est.).
Income: Per capita income: $24,172 (2010); Median household income: $47,472 (2010); Average household income: $58,442 (2010); Percent of households with income of $100,000 or more: 14.0% (2010); Poverty rate: 9.1% (2005-2009 5-year est.).
Taxes: Total city taxes per capita: $261 (2007); City property taxes per capita: $158 (2007).
Education: Percent of population age 25 and over with: High school diploma (including GED) or higher: 83.6% (2010); Bachelor's degree or higher: 16.4% (2010); Master's degree or higher: 5.7% (2010).
School District(s)
Hall HSD 502 (09-12)
    2009-10 Enrollment: 401 . . . . (815) 664-4500
Spring Valley CCSD 99 (PK-08)
    2009-10 Enrollment: 779 . . . . (815) 664-4242
Housing: Homeownership rate: 70.9% (2010); Median home value: $102,326 (2010); Median contract rent: $375 per month (2005-2009 5-year est.); Median year structure built: 1955 (2005-2009 5-year est.).
Hospitals: St. Margaret's Hospital (155 beds)
Transportation: Commute to work: 89.4% car, 0.0% public transportation, 6.1% walk, 3.5% work from home (2005-2009 5-year est.); Travel time to work: 59.3% less than 15 minutes, 30.9% 15 to 30 minutes, 5.4% 30 to 45 minutes, 0.7% 45 to 60 minutes, 3.7% 60 minutes or more (2005-2009 5-year est.)
Additional Information Contacts
City of Spring Valley. . . . . (815) 664-4221
    http://www.spring-valley.il.us

TISKILWA (village).
Covers a land area of 0.479 square miles and a water area of 0 square miles. Located at 41.29° N. Lat; 89.50° W. Long. Elevation is 522 feet.
Population: 833 (1990); 787 (2000); 752 (2010); 731 (2015 projected); Race: 97.5% White, 0.3% Black, 0.3% Asian, 2.0% Other, 1.3% Hispanic of any race (2010); Density: 1,569.7 persons per square mile (2010); Average household size: 2.42 (2010); Median age: 39.5 (2010); Males per 100 females: 92.8 (2010); Marriage status: 10.0% never married, 73.5% now married, 5.5% widowed, 11.0% divorced (2005-2009 5-year est.); Foreign born: 2.1% (2005-2009 5-year est.); Ancestry (includes multiple ancestries): 33.5% German, 27.3% Irish, 15.4% English, 5.4% American, 4.4% Scotch-Irish (2005-2009 5-year est.).

Economy: Single-family building permits issued: 0 (2010); Multi-family building permits issued: 0 (2010); Employment by occupation: 4.9% management, 6.7% professional, 19.1% services, 20.3% sales, 3.2% farming, 12.8% construction, 33.0% production (2005-2009 5-year est.).
Income: Per capita income: $19,878 (2010); Median household income: $40,875 (2010); Average household income: $48,658 (2010); Percent of households with income of $100,000 or more: 6.1% (2010); Poverty rate: 8.3% (2005-2009 5-year est.).
Taxes: Total city taxes per capita: $97 (2007); City property taxes per capita: $88 (2007).
Education: Percent of population age 25 and over with: High school diploma (including GED) or higher: 89.4% (2010); Bachelor's degree or higher: 9.2% (2010); Master's degree or higher: 2.2% (2010).

School District(s)

Princeton ESD 115 (PK-08)
    2009-10 Enrollment: 1,311 . . . . (815) 875-3162
Housing: Homeownership rate: 78.8% (2010); Median home value: $96,122 (2010); Median contract rent: $433 per month (2005-2009 5-year est.); Median year structure built: before 1940 (2005-2009 5-year est.).
Newspapers: Bureau Valley Chief (Community news; Circulation 2,800)
Transportation: Commute to work: 99.1% car, 0.0% public transportation, 0.9% walk, 0.0% work from home (2005-2009 5-year est.); Travel time to work: 30.4% less than 15 minutes, 48.7% 15 to 30 minutes, 8.9% 30 to 45 minutes, 3.5% 45 to 60 minutes, 8.5% 60 minutes or more (2005-2009 5-year est.)

WALNUT (village). Covers a land area of 0.833 square miles and a water area of 0 square miles. Located at 41.55° N. Lat; 89.59° W. Long. Elevation is 705 feet.
Population: 1,522 (1990); 1,461 (2000); 1,405 (2010); 1,370 (2015 projected); Race: 98.1% White, 0.6% Black, 0.2% Asian, 1.1% Other, 1.6% Hispanic of any race (2010); Density: 1,687.0 persons per square mile (2010); Average household size: 2.45 (2010); Median age: 40.4 (2010); Males per 100 females: 93.0 (2010); Marriage status: 20.1% never married, 56.5% now married, 15.1% widowed, 8.2% divorced (2005-2009 5-year est.); Foreign born: 3.3% (2005-2009 5-year est.); Ancestry (includes multiple ancestries): 45.8% German, 11.5% Irish, 7.3% American, 7.2% English, 5.4% French (2005-2009 5-year est.).
Economy: Single-family building permits issued: 1 (2010); Multi-family building permits issued: 0 (2010); Employment by occupation: 11.4% management, 16.8% professional, 20.3% services, 22.2% sales, 0.0% farming, 10.9% construction, 18.5% production (2005-2009 5-year est.).
Income: Per capita income: $24,444 (2010); Median household income: $46,500 (2010); Average household income: $59,924 (2010); Percent of households with income of $100,000 or more: 14.0% (2010); Poverty rate: 4.5% (2005-2009 5-year est.).
Taxes: Total city taxes per capita: $143 (2007); City property taxes per capita: $126 (2007).
Education: Percent of population age 25 and over with: High school diploma (including GED) or higher: 89.3% (2010); Bachelor's degree or higher: 13.0% (2010); Master's degree or higher: 4.8% (2010).

School District(s)

Bureau Valley CUSD 340 (PK-12)
    2009-10 Enrollment: 1,232 . . . . (815) 445-3101
Housing: Homeownership rate: 76.0% (2010); Median home value: $85,281 (2010); Median contract rent: $422 per month (2005-2009 5-year est.); Median year structure built: 1952 (2005-2009 5-year est.).
Newspapers: Walnut Leader (Local news; Circulation 2,000)
Transportation: Commute to work: 95.1% car, 0.0% public transportation, 1.8% walk, 3.1% work from home (2005-2009 5-year est.); Travel time to work: 43.7% less than 15 minutes, 24.6% 15 to 30 minutes, 23.5% 30 to 45 minutes, 2.0% 45 to 60 minutes, 6.2% 60 minutes or more (2005-2009 5-year est.)
Additional Information Contacts
Walnut Chamber of Commerce . . . . (815) 379-2141
    http://www.villageofwalnut.com/chamber.htm

WYANET (village). Covers a land area of 1.000 square miles and a water area of 0 square miles. Located at 41.36° N. Lat; 89.58° W. Long. Elevation is 659 feet.
Population: 1,016 (1990); 1,028 (2000); 964 (2010); 932 (2015 projected); Race: 99.1% White, 0.0% Black, 0.3% Asian, 0.6% Other, 1.0% Hispanic of any race (2010); Density: 964.0 persons per square mile (2010); Average household size: 2.45 (2010); Median age: 36.4 (2010); Males per 100 females: 97.9 (2010); Marriage status: 21.9% never married, 57.8%

now married, 5.0% widowed, 15.3% divorced (2005-2009 5-year est.); Foreign born: 2.7% (2005-2009 5-year est.); Ancestry (includes multiple ancestries): 24.3% German, 12.8% American, 12.0% Swedish, 10.6% Irish, 9.7% English (2005-2009 5-year est.).
Economy: Employment by occupation: 5.6% management, 9.6% professional, 24.0% services, 21.9% sales, 0.6% farming, 10.8% construction, 27.5% production (2005-2009 5-year est.).
Income: Per capita income: $19,781 (2010); Median household income: $43,693 (2010); Average household income: $48,420 (2010); Percent of households with income of $100,000 or more: 4.1% (2010); Poverty rate: 11.8% (2005-2009 5-year est.).
Taxes: Total city taxes per capita: $110 (2007); City property taxes per capita: $102 (2007).
Education: Percent of population age 25 and over with: High school diploma (including GED) or higher: 87.0% (2010); Bachelor's degree or higher: 6.7% (2010); Master's degree or higher: 1.1% (2010).

School District(s)

Bureau Valley CUSD 340 (PK-12)
    2009-10 Enrollment: 1,232 . . . . (815) 445-3101
Housing: Homeownership rate: 76.4% (2010); Median home value: $89,028 (2010); Median contract rent: $529 per month (2005-2009 5-year est.); Median year structure built: 1951 (2005-2009 5-year est.).
Transportation: Commute to work: 91.8% car, 0.0% public transportation, 4.2% walk, 3.4% work from home (2005-2009 5-year est.); Travel time to work: 39.1% less than 15 minutes, 42.4% 15 to 30 minutes, 9.3% 30 to 45 minutes, 4.7% 45 to 60 minutes, 4.5% 60 minutes or more (2005-2009 5-year est.)

Calhoun County

Located in western Illinois; bounded on the west and south by the Mississippi River and the Missouri border, and on the east by the Illinois River, which joins the Mississippi River at the southeastern tip of the county. Covers a land area of 253.82 square miles, a water area of 29.87 square miles, and is located in the Central Time Zone at 39.16° N. Lat., 90.65° W. Long. The county was founded in 1825. County seat is Hardin.

Calhoun County is part of the St. Louis, MO-IL Metropolitan Statistical Area. The entire metro area includes: Bond County, IL; Calhoun County, IL; Clinton County, IL; Jersey County, IL; Macoupin County, IL; Madison County, IL; Monroe County, IL; St. Clair County, IL; Crawford County, MO (pt.); Franklin County, MO; Jefferson County, MO; Lincoln County, MO; St. Charles County, MO; St. Louis County, MO; Warren County, MO; Washington County, MO; St. Louis city, MO

Population: 5,322 (1990); 5,084 (2000); 5,089 (2010); 5,048 (2015 projected); Race: 98.9% White, 0.0% Black, 0.1% Asian, 1.0% Other, 0.7% Hispanic of any race (2010); Density: 20.0 persons per square mile (2010); Average household size: 2.40 (2010); Median age: 43.1 (2010); Males per 100 females: 101.5 (2010).
Religion: Five largest groups: 41.0% Catholic Church, 7.5% Lutheran Church—Missouri Synod, 5.3% New Testament Association of Independent Baptist Churches and other Fundamental Baptist Associations, 3.6% Presbyterian Church (U.S.A.), 3.6% Churches
Economy: Unemployment rate: 9.0% (August 2011); Total civilian labor force: 2,497 (August 2011); Leading industries: 20.7% accommodation & food services; 17.4% retail trade; 16.9% health care and social assistance (2009); Farms: 464 totaling 87,938 acres (2007); Companies that employ 500 or more persons: 0 (2009); Companies that employ 100 to 499 persons: 0 (2009); Companies that employ less than 100 persons: 95 (2009); Black-owned businesses: n/a (2007); Hispanic-owned businesses: n/a (2007); Asian-owned businesses: n/a (2007); Women-owned businesses: 82 (2007); Retail sales per capita: $7,633 (2010). Single-family building permits issued: 3 (2010); Multi-family building permits issued: 0 (2010).
Income: Per capita income: $21,697 (2010); Median household income: $44,229 (2010); Average household income: $52,533 (2010); Percent of households with income of $100,000 or more: 9.3% (2010); Poverty rate: 11.3% (2009); Bankruptcy rate: 1.57% (2010).
Taxes: Total county taxes per capita: $146 (2007); County property taxes per capita: $144 (2007).
Education: Percent of population age 25 and over with: High school diploma (including GED) or higher: 85.5% (2010); Bachelor's degree or higher: 11.8% (2010); Master's degree or higher: 4.0% (2010).

Housing: Homeownership rate: 79.5% (2010); Median home value: $100,000 (2010); Median contract rent: $313 per month (2005-2009 5-year est.); Median year structure built: 1970 (2005-2009 5-year est.)

Health: Birth rate: 115.6 per 10,000 population (2009); Death rate: 117.6 per 10,000 population (2009); Age-adjusted cancer mortality rate: 213.8 (Unreliable) deaths per 100,000 population (2007); Number of physicians: 8.0 per 10,000 population (2008); Hospital beds: 0.0 per 10,000 population (2007); Hospital admissions: 0.0 per 10,000 population (2007).

Elections: 2008 Presidential election results: 52.7% Obama, 45.2% McCain, 1.2% Nader

National and State Parks: Batchtown State Fish and Waterfowl Management Area; Diamond-Hurricane Island State Fish and Waterfowl; Fuller Lake State Fish and Waterfowl Management Area; Mark Twain National Wildlife Refuge; Mortland Island State Fish And Waterfowl Man; Reds Landing State Fish And Waterfowl Manage; Rip Rap Landing State Fish and Waterfowl Management Area

Additional Information Contacts

Calhoun County Government . . . . (618) 576-2351

Calhoun County Communities

BATCHTOWN (village). Covers a land area of 1.881 square miles and a water area of 0 square miles. Located at 39.03° N. Lat; 90.65° W. Long. Elevation is 581 feet.

Population: 225 (1990); 218 (2000); 217 (2010); 217 (2015 projected); Race: 98.6% White, 0.0% Black, 0.0% Asian, 1.4% Other, 0.5% Hispanic of any race (2010); Density: 115.4 persons per square mile (2010); Average household size: 2.61 (2010); Median age: 38.1 (2010); Males per 100 females: 114.9 (2010); Marriage status: 36.1% never married, 49.0% now married, 5.8% widowed, 9.1% divorced (2005-2009 5-year est.); Foreign born: 1.6% (2005-2009 5-year est.); Ancestry (includes multiple ancestries): 57.8% German, 23.1% Irish, 12.0% Dutch, 12.0% American, 3.6% English (2005-2009 5-year est.).

Economy: Employment by occupation: 17.9% management, 11.3% professional, 22.6% services, 13.2% sales, 0.0% farming, 16.0% construction, 18.9% production (2005-2009 5-year est.).

Income: Per capita income: $22,321 (2010); Median household income: $52,604 (2010); Average household income: $57,440 (2010); Percent of households with income of $100,000 or more: 14.5% (2010); Poverty rate: 13.9% (2005-2009 5-year est.).

Taxes: Total city taxes per capita: $46 (2007); City property taxes per capita: $41 (2007).

Education: Percent of population age 25 and over with: High school diploma (including GED) or higher: 89.4% (2010); Bachelor's degree or higher: 10.6% (2010); Master's degree or higher: 4.2% (2010).

Housing: Homeownership rate: 86.7% (2010); Median home value: $121,154 (2010); Median contract rent: $192 per month (2005-2009 5-year est.); Median year structure built: before 1940 (2005-2009 5-year est.).

Transportation: Commute to work: 90.6% car, 0.0% public transportation, 7.5% walk, 1.9% work from home (2005-2009 5-year est.); Travel time to work: 36.5% less than 15 minutes, 16.3% 15 to 30 minutes, 5.8% 30 to 45 minutes, 7.7% 45 to 60 minutes, 33.7% 60 minutes or more (2005-2009 5-year est.)

BRUSSELS (village). Covers a land area of 0.607 square miles and a water area of 0 square miles. Located at 38.94° N. Lat; 90.58° W. Long. Elevation is 522 feet.

Population: 136 (1990); 141 (2000); 145 (2010); 144 (2015 projected); Race: 99.3% White, 0.0% Black, 0.0% Asian, 0.7% Other, 0.7% Hispanic of any race (2010); Density: 239.0 persons per square mile (2010); Average household size: 2.42 (2010); Median age: 45.2 (2010); Males per 100 females: 93.3 (2010); Marriage status: 22.6% never married, 70.5% now married, 4.1% widowed, 2.7% divorced (2005-2009 5-year est.); Foreign born: 1.1% (2005-2009 5-year est.); Ancestry (includes multiple ancestries): 57.6% German, 23.9% American, 11.4% Irish, 2.2% French, 1.6% Scottish (2005-2009 5-year est.).

Economy: Employment by occupation: 6.5% management, 2.6% professional, 49.4% services, 11.7% sales, 0.0% farming, 14.3% construction, 15.6% production (2005-2009 5-year est.).

Income: Per capita income: $22,763 (2010); Median household income: $48,500 (2010); Average household income: $54,333 (2010); Percent of households with income of $100,000 or more: 11.7% (2010); Poverty rate: 7.6% (2005-2009 5-year est.).

Taxes: Total city taxes per capita: $14 (2007); City property taxes per capita: $14 (2007).

Education: Percent of population age 25 and over with: High school diploma (including GED) or higher: 83.8% (2010); Bachelor's degree or higher: 8.1% (2010); Master's degree or higher: 2.7% (2010).

School District(s)

Brussels CUSD 42 (PK-12)

   2009-10 Enrollment: 147 . . . . (618) 883-2131

Housing: Homeownership rate: 80.0% (2010); Median home value: $112,500 (2010); Median contract rent: $333 per month (2005-2009 5-year est.); Median year structure built: before 1940 (2005-2009 5-year est.).

Transportation: Commute to work: 96.8% car, 0.0% public transportation, 0.0% walk, 3.2% work from home (2005-2009 5-year est.); Travel time to work: 38.3% less than 15 minutes, 11.7% 15 to 30 minutes, 8.3% 30 to 45 minutes, 8.3% 45 to 60 minutes, 33.3% 60 minutes or more (2005-2009 5-year est.)

GOLDEN EAGLE (unincorporated postal area, zip code 62036). Covers a land area of 27.943 square miles and a water area of 0.008 square miles. Located at 38.91° N. Lat; 90.57° W. Long. Elevation is 673 feet.

Population: 601 (2000); Race: 98.7% White, 0.0% Black, 0.9% Asian, 0.4% Other, 0.5% Hispanic of any race (2000); Density: 21.5 persons per square mile (2000); Age: 20.3% under 18, 19.9% over 64 (2000); Marriage status: 20.8% never married, 66.6% now married, 7.1% widowed, 5.5% divorced (2000); Foreign born: 2.0% (2000); Ancestry (includes multiple ancestries): 59.1% German, 9.9% Irish, 5.4% Dutch, 4.5% American (2000).

Economy: Employment by occupation: 11.5% management, 14.3% professional, 15.5% services, 16.3% sales, 0.0% farming, 27.4% construction, 15.1% production (2000).

Income: Per capita income: $17,641 (2000); Median household income: $36,429 (2000); Poverty rate: 6.1% (2000).

Education: Percent of population age 25 and over with: High school diploma (including GED) or higher: 80.1% (2000); Bachelor's degree or higher: 7.8% (2000).

Housing: Homeownership rate: 83.9% (2000); Median home value: $83,800 (2000); Median contract rent: $220 per month (2000); Median year structure built: 1953 (2000).

Transportation: Commute to work: 89.8% car, 0.8% public transportation, 2.0% walk, 6.6% work from home (2000); Travel time to work: 24.1% less than 15 minutes, 10.5% 15 to 30 minutes, 14.5% 30 to 45 minutes, 15.8% 45 to 60 minutes, 35.1% 60 minutes or more (2000)

HAMBURG (village). Covers a land area of 0.522 square miles and a water area of 0.134 square miles. Located at 39.23° N. Lat; 90.71° W. Long. Elevation is 443 feet.

Population: 150 (1990); 126 (2000); 126 (2010); 124 (2015 projected); Race: 98.4% White, 0.0% Black, 0.0% Asian, 1.6% Other, 0.8% Hispanic of any race (2010); Density: 241.5 persons per square mile (2010); Average household size: 2.29 (2010); Median age: 48.5 (2010); Males per 100 females: 117.2 (2010); Marriage status: 10.9% never married, 47.3% now married, 31.0% widowed, 10.9% divorced (2005-2009 5-year est.); Foreign born: 0.0% (2005-2009 5-year est.); Ancestry (includes multiple ancestries): 45.6% German, 30.6% American, 6.8% Scotch-Irish, 6.8% Italian, 5.4% French (2005-2009 5-year est.).

Economy: Employment by occupation: 20.0% management, 22.9% professional, 20.0% services, 14.3% sales, 0.0% farming, 22.9% construction, 0.0% production (2005-2009 5-year est.).

Income: Per capita income: $21,552 (2010); Median household income: $43,250 (2010); Average household income: $51,045 (2010); Percent of households with income of $100,000 or more: 5.5% (2010); Poverty rate: 17.0% (2005-2009 5-year est.).

Taxes: Total city taxes per capita: $56 (2007); City property taxes per capita: $56 (2007).

Education: Percent of population age 25 and over with: High school diploma (including GED) or higher: 85.1% (2010); Bachelor's degree or higher: 12.8% (2010); Master's degree or higher: 4.3% (2010).

Housing: Homeownership rate: 85.5% (2010); Median home value: $98,000 (2010); Median contract rent: $275 per month (2005-2009 5-year est.); Median year structure built: 1955 (2005-2009 5-year est.).

Transportation: Commute to work: 100.0% car, 0.0% public transportation, 0.0% walk, 0.0% work from home (2005-2009 5-year est.); Travel time to work: 11.1% less than 15 minutes, 70.4% 15 to 30 minutes,

0.0% 30 to 45 minutes, 18.5% 45 to 60 minutes, 0.0% 60 minutes or more (2005-2009 5-year est.)

HARDIN (village). County seat. Covers a land area of 2.097 square miles and a water area of 0.182 square miles. Located at 39.15° N. Lat; 90.61° W. Long. Elevation is 443 feet.
History: Hardin developed as a distribution center for the surrounding apple-growing region, and as the seat of Calhoun County.
Population: 1,080 (1990); 959 (2000); 958 (2010); 949 (2015 projected); Race: 99.6% White, 0.0% Black, 0.1% Asian, 0.3% Other, 0.6% Hispanic of any race (2010); Density: 456.7 persons per square mile (2010); Average household size: 2.32 (2010); Median age: 41.7 (2010); Males per 100 females: 93.9 (2010); Marriage status: 13.4% never married, 55.7% now married, 9.0% widowed, 21.9% divorced (2005-2009 5-year est.); Foreign born: 4.0% (2005-2009 5-year est.); Ancestry (includes multiple ancestries): 42.7% German, 13.4% Irish, 10.0% American, 8.7% English, 7.0% Scotch-Irish (2005-2009 5-year est.).
Economy: Employment by occupation: 6.2% management, 17.6% professional, 28.4% services, 19.2% sales, 1.4% farming, 15.4% construction, 11.9% production (2005-2009 5-year est.).
Income: Per capita income: $20,846 (2010); Median household income: $40,704 (2010); Average household income: $50,797 (2010); Percent of households with income of $100,000 or more: 8.7% (2010); Poverty rate: 14.5% (2005-2009 5-year est.).
Taxes: Total city taxes per capita: $54 (2007); City property taxes per capita: $44 (2007).
Education: Percent of population age 25 and over with: High school diploma (including GED) or higher: 84.9% (2010); Bachelor's degree or higher: 13.9% (2010); Master's degree or higher: 3.4% (2010).
School District(s)
Calhoun CUSD 40 (PK-12)
    2009-10 Enrollment: 563 . . . . (618) 576-2722
Housing: Homeownership rate: 70.2% (2010); Median home value: $81,087 (2010); Median contract rent: $241 per month (2005-2009 5-year est.); Median year structure built: 1971 (2005-2009 5-year est.).
Newspapers: Calhoun News-Herald (Community news; Circulation 4,000)
Transportation: Commute to work: 93.2% car, 0.0% public transportation, 3.3% walk, 0.0% work from home (2005-2009 5-year est.); Travel time to work: 47.7% less than 15 minutes, 11.4% 15 to 30 minutes, 8.7% 30 to 45 minutes, 14.7% 45 to 60 minutes, 17.4% 60 minutes or more (2005-2009 5-year est.)

KAMPSVILLE (village). Covers a land area of 1.020 square miles and a water area of 0.220 square miles. Located at 39.29° N. Lat; 90.61° W. Long. Elevation is 433 feet.
Population: 380 (1990); 302 (2000); 296 (2010); 293 (2015 projected); Race: 97.6% White, 0.0% Black, 0.3% Asian, 2.0% Other, 1.0% Hispanic of any race (2010); Density: 290.3 persons per square mile (2010); Average household size: 2.31 (2010); Median age: 41.5 (2010); Males per 100 females: 96.0 (2010); Marriage status: 26.5% never married, 52.1% now married, 14.4% widowed, 7.0% divorced (2005-2009 5-year est.); Foreign born: 1.0% (2005-2009 5-year est.); Ancestry (includes multiple ancestries): 47.1% German, 20.0% Irish, 14.2% English, 9.2% American, 3.4% Norwegian (2005-2009 5-year est.).
Economy: Employment by occupation: 0.0% management, 17.1% professional, 27.9% services, 22.1% sales, 0.0% farming, 24.3% construction, 8.6% production (2005-2009 5-year est.).
Income: Per capita income: $20,441 (2010); Median household income: $38,261 (2010); Average household income: $48,652 (2010); Percent of households with income of $100,000 or more: 6.3% (2010); Poverty rate: 15.9% (2005-2009 5-year est.).
Taxes: Total city taxes per capita: $70 (2007); City property taxes per capita: $37 (2007).
Education: Percent of population age 25 and over with: High school diploma (including GED) or higher: 85.6% (2010); Bachelor's degree or higher: 11.9% (2010); Master's degree or higher: 3.0% (2010).
Housing: Homeownership rate: 75.8% (2010); Median home value: $85,789 (2010); Median contract rent: $229 per month (2005-2009 5-year est.); Median year structure built: 1957 (2005-2009 5-year est.).
Transportation: Commute to work: 85.7% car, 0.0% public transportation, 10.5% walk, 0.0% work from home (2005-2009 5-year est.); Travel time to work: 28.6% less than 15 minutes, 18.8% 15 to 30 minutes, 21.8% 30 to 45 minutes, 3.0% 45 to 60 minutes, 27.8% 60 minutes or more (2005-2009 5-year est.)

MICHAEL (unincorporated postal area, zip code 62065). Covers a land area of 8.873 square miles and a water area of 0.306 square miles. Located at 39.23° N. Lat; 90.62° W. Long. Elevation is 446 feet.
Population: 114 (2000); Race: 96.9% White, 0.0% Black, 0.0% Asian, 3.1% Other, 0.0% Hispanic of any race (2000); Density: 12.8 persons per square mile (2000); Age: 29.8% under 18, 20.6% over 64 (2000); Marriage status: 19.4% never married, 69.4% now married, 6.1% widowed, 5.1% divorced (2000); Foreign born: 6.9% (2000); Ancestry (includes multiple ancestries): 30.5% German, 10.7% American, 6.1% Norwegian, 4.6% French, 3.8% English (2000).
Economy: Employment by occupation: 7.4% management, 14.8% professional, 14.8% services, 40.7% sales, 0.0% farming, 7.4% construction, 14.8% production (2000).
Income: Per capita income: $10,806 (2000); Median household income: $24,583 (2000); Poverty rate: 2.3% (2000).
Education: Percent of population age 25 and over with: High school diploma (including GED) or higher: 71.1% (2000); Bachelor's degree or higher: 4.8% (2000).
Housing: Homeownership rate: 87.7% (2000); Median home value: $53,700 (2000); Median contract rent: $325 per month (2000); Median year structure built: 1964 (2000).
Transportation: Commute to work: 100.0% car, 0.0% public transportation, 0.0% walk, 0.0% work from home (2000); Travel time to work: 44.4% less than 15 minutes, 14.8% 15 to 30 minutes, 11.1% 30 to 45 minutes, 0.0% 45 to 60 minutes, 29.6% 60 minutes or more (2000)

MOZIER (unincorporated postal area, zip code 62070). Aka Baytown. Covers a land area of 10.423 square miles and a water area of 0.258 square miles. Located at 39.32° N. Lat; 90.76° W. Long. Elevation is 446 feet.
Population: 63 (2000); Race: 100.0% White, 0.0% Black, 0.0% Asian, 0.0% Other, 0.0% Hispanic of any race (2000); Density: 6.0 persons per square mile (2000); Age: 21.9% under 18, 35.9% over 64 (2000); Marriage status: 4.0% never married, 72.0% now married, 20.0% widowed, 4.0% divorced (2000); Foreign born: 0.0% (2000); Ancestry (includes multiple ancestries): 39.1% American, 10.9% German, 7.8% English (2000).
Economy: Employment by occupation: 8.3% management, 8.3% professional, 16.7% services, 12.5% sales, 0.0% farming, 16.7% construction, 37.5% production (2000).
Income: Per capita income: $14,966 (2000); Median household income: $33,750 (2000); Poverty rate: 7.8% (2000).
Education: Percent of population age 25 and over with: High school diploma (including GED) or higher: 62.0% (2000); Bachelor's degree or higher: 8.0% (2000).
Housing: Homeownership rate: 96.7% (2000); Median home value: $51,700 (2000); Median contract rent: n/a per month (2000); Median year structure built: 1958 (2000).
Transportation: Commute to work: 100.0% car, 0.0% public transportation, 0.0% walk, 0.0% work from home (2000); Travel time to work: 20.8% less than 15 minutes, 37.5% 15 to 30 minutes, 8.3% 30 to 45 minutes, 16.7% 45 to 60 minutes, 16.7% 60 minutes or more (2000)

Carroll County

Located in northwestern Illinois; bounded on the west by the Mississippi River and the Iowa border; drained by the Plum River and Elkhorn Creek. Covers a land area of 444.21 square miles, a water area of 21.56 square miles, and is located in the Central Time Zone at 42.07° N. Lat., 89.95° W. Long. The county was founded in 1839. County seat is Mount Carroll.

Weather Station: Mount Carroll   Elevation: 640 feet

	Jan	Feb	Mar	Apr	May	Jun	Jul	Aug	Sep	Oct	Nov	Dec
High	30	35	47	60	72	81	84	83	76	63	48	34
Low	10	14	25	35	46	55	59	57	48	36	27	15
Precip	1.4	1.7	2.6	3.7	4.4	4.8	4.3	4.5	3.6	3.1	2.9	2.2
Snow	9.4	7.2	3.5	1.3	tr	0.0	0.0	0.0	tr	0.1	1.3	8.6

High and Low temperatures in degrees Fahrenheit; Precipitation and Snow in inches

Population: 16,805 (1990); 16,674 (2000); 15,731 (2010); 15,210 (2015 projected); Race: 95.9% White, 1.1% Black, 0.6% Asian, 2.4% Other, 2.5% Hispanic of any race (2010); Density: 35.4 persons per square mile (2010); Average household size: 2.38 (2010); Median age: 43.7 (2010); Males per 100 females: 98.5 (2010).
Religion: Five largest groups: 17.2% The United Methodist Church, 14.8% Catholic Church, 8.3% Evangelical Lutheran Church in America, 3.3%

Church of the Brethren, 3.0% Churches of God, General Conference (2000).
Economy: Unemployment rate: 9.4% (August 2011); Total civilian labor force: 8,319 (August 2011); Leading industries: 28.7% manufacturing; 15.1% health care and social assistance; 12.2% retail trade (2009); Farms: 676 totaling 265,153 acres (2007); Companies that employ 500 or more persons: 0 (2009); Companies that employ 100 to 499 persons: 4 (2009); Companies that employ less than 100 persons: 417 (2009); Black-owned businesses: n/a (2007); Hispanic-owned businesses: n/a (2007); Asian-owned businesses: n/a (2007); Women-owned businesses: n/a (2007); Retail sales per capita: $7,289 (2010). Single-family building permits issued: 18 (2010); Multi-family building permits issued: 0 (2010).
Income: Per capita income: $22,320 (2010); Median household income: $43,217 (2010); Average household income: $53,466 (2010); Percent of households with income of $100,000 or more: 9.4% (2010); Poverty rate: 13.2% (2009); Bankruptcy rate: 5.22% (2010).
Taxes: Total county taxes per capita: $183 (2007); County property taxes per capita: $141 (2007).
Education: Percent of population age 25 and over with: High school diploma (including GED) or higher: 87.9% (2010); Bachelor's degree or higher: 16.1% (2010); Master's degree or higher: 4.4% (2010).
Housing: Homeownership rate: 75.4% (2010); Median home value: $106,184 (2010); Median contract rent: $368 per month (2005-2009 5-year est.); Median year structure built: 1952 (2005-2009 5-year est.)
Health: Birth rate: 113.0 per 10,000 population (2009); Death rate: 127.0 per 10,000 population (2009); Age-adjusted cancer mortality rate: 176.1 deaths per 100,000 population (2007); Number of physicians: 4.4 per 10,000 population (2008); Hospital beds: 0.0 per 10,000 population (2007); Hospital admissions: 0.0 per 10,000 population (2007).
Elections: 2008 Presidential election results: 51.7% Obama, 46.9% McCain, 0.6% Nader
National and State Parks: Ayers Sand Prairie State Nature Preserve; Mississippi Palisades State Park
Additional Information Contacts
Carroll County Government. . . . . (815) 244-0221
  http://carroll-county.net
Mount Carroll Chamber of Commerce. . . . . (800) 244-9594
  http://www.mtcarrollil.org
Savanna Chamber of Commerce . . . . (815) 273-2722
  http://www.savanna-il.com
Shannon Chamber of Commerce . . . . (815) 864-2111
  http://www.shannonillinois.com/Chamber_of_commerce.htm

Carroll County Communities

CHADWICK (village). Covers a land area of 0.317 square miles and a water area of 0 square miles. Located at 42.01° N. Lat; 89.88° W. Long. Elevation is 801 feet.
Population: 566 (1990); 505 (2000); 475 (2010); 456 (2015 projected); Race: 98.3% White, 0.0% Black, 0.4% Asian, 1.3% Other, 1.1% Hispanic of any race (2010); Density: 1,500.7 persons per square mile (2010); Average household size: 2.50 (2010); Median age: 40.5 (2010); Males per 100 females: 106.5 (2010); Marriage status: 8.4% never married, 69.5% now married, 10.4% widowed, 11.7% divorced (2005-2009 5-year est.); Foreign born: 0.0% (2005-2009 5-year est.); Ancestry (includes multiple ancestries): 45.3% German, 24.9% Irish, 18.0% English, 9.0% French, 7.7% American (2005-2009 5-year est.).
Economy: Employment by occupation: 18.1% management, 14.1% professional, 12.8% services, 26.9% sales, 0.9% farming, 7.9% construction, 19.4% production (2005-2009 5-year est.).
Income: Per capita income: $23,101 (2010); Median household income: $54,167 (2010); Average household income: $57,329 (2010); Percent of households with income of $100,000 or more: 10.5% (2010); Poverty rate: 3.2% (2005-2009 5-year est.).
Taxes: Total city taxes per capita: $156 (2007); City property taxes per capita: $146 (2007).
Education: Percent of population age 25 and over with: High school diploma (including GED) or higher: 91.5% (2010); Bachelor's degree or higher: 16.0% (2010); Master's degree or higher: 3.6% (2010).
School District(s)
Chadwick-Milledgeville CUSD 399 (PK-12)
  2009-10 Enrollment: 526 . . . . (815) 684-5191
Housing: Homeownership rate: 70.5% (2010); Median home value: $97,692 (2010); Median contract rent: $463 per month (2005-2009 5-year est.); Median year structure built: 1940 (2005-2009 5-year est.).

Transportation: Commute to work: 91.6% car, 0.0% public transportation, 5.7% walk, 0.9% work from home (2005-2009 5-year est.); Travel time to work: 31.6% less than 15 minutes, 24.0% 15 to 30 minutes, 28.0% 30 to 45 minutes, 6.2% 45 to 60 minutes, 10.2% 60 minutes or more (2005-2009 5-year est.)

LANARK (city). Covers a land area of 1.038 square miles and a water area of 0 square miles. Located at 42.10° N. Lat; 89.83° W. Long. Elevation is 879 feet.
History: Lanark developed as a trading center and cannery operation for the surrounding farming community.
Population: 1,404 (1990); 1,584 (2000); 1,448 (2010); 1,377 (2015 projected); Race: 96.1% White, 0.1% Black, 1.7% Asian, 2.1% Other, 0.2% Hispanic of any race (2010); Density: 1,394.7 persons per square mile (2010); Average household size: 2.40 (2010); Median age: 43.4 (2010); Males per 100 females: 95.7 (2010); Marriage status: 20.8% never married, 60.9% now married, 9.2% widowed, 9.0% divorced (2005-2009 5-year est.); Foreign born: 1.8% (2005-2009 5-year est.); Ancestry (includes multiple ancestries): 50.6% German, 14.0% Irish, 12.0% English, 8.3% Dutch, 5.8% American (2005-2009 5-year est.).
Economy: Single-family building permits issued: 0 (2010); Multi-family building permits issued: 0 (2010); Employment by occupation: 13.9% management, 18.0% professional, 12.8% services, 18.7% sales, 2.1% farming, 11.5% construction, 23.0% production (2005-2009 5-year est.).
Income: Per capita income: $20,812 (2010); Median household income: $42,752 (2010); Average household income: $49,812 (2010); Percent of households with income of $100,000 or more: 7.7% (2010); Poverty rate: 9.6% (2005-2009 5-year est.).
Taxes: Total city taxes per capita: $199 (2007); City property taxes per capita: $189 (2007).
Education: Percent of population age 25 and over with: High school diploma (including GED) or higher: 89.5% (2010); Bachelor's degree or higher: 14.0% (2010); Master's degree or higher: 4.5% (2010).
School District(s)
Eastland CUSD 308 (PK-12)
  2009-10 Enrollment: 732 . . . . (815) 493-6301
Housing: Homeownership rate: 80.6% (2010); Median home value: $93,063 (2010); Median contract rent: $441 per month (2005-2009 5-year est.); Median year structure built: 1940 (2005-2009 5-year est.).
Newspapers: Prairie Advocate (Regional news; Circulation 12,500)
Transportation: Commute to work: 93.1% car, 0.0% public transportation, 4.2% walk, 2.6% work from home (2005-2009 5-year est.); Travel time to work: 39.1% less than 15 minutes, 19.8% 15 to 30 minutes, 24.9% 30 to 45 minutes, 9.6% 45 to 60 minutes, 6.7% 60 minutes or more (2005-2009 5-year est.)

MILLEDGEVILLE (village). Covers a land area of 0.708 square miles and a water area of 0 square miles. Located at 41.96° N. Lat; 89.77° W. Long. Elevation is 761 feet.
Population: 1,102 (1990); 1,016 (2000); 967 (2010); 937 (2015 projected); Race: 97.0% White, 0.3% Black, 0.4% Asian, 2.3% Other, 2.5% Hispanic of any race (2010); Density: 1,365.1 persons per square mile (2010); Average household size: 2.41 (2010); Median age: 40.8 (2010); Males per 100 females: 93.8 (2010); Marriage status: 16.7% never married, 64.6% now married, 5.9% widowed, 12.9% divorced (2005-2009 5-year est.); Foreign born: 1.4% (2005-2009 5-year est.); Ancestry (includes multiple ancestries): 37.2% German, 17.2% Irish, 17.1% American, 8.6% English, 5.1% Dutch (2005-2009 5-year est.).
Economy: Single-family building permits issued: 0 (2010); Multi-family building permits issued: 0 (2010); Employment by occupation: 6.9% management, 15.3% professional, 19.1% services, 24.2% sales, 2.0% farming, 11.5% construction, 21.1% production (2005-2009 5-year est.).
Income: Per capita income: $22,818 (2010); Median household income: $43,719 (2010); Average household income: $55,081 (2010); Percent of households with income of $100,000 or more: 7.7% (2010); Poverty rate: 6.3% (2005-2009 5-year est.).
Taxes: Total city taxes per capita: $441 (2007); City property taxes per capita: $373 (2007).
Education: Percent of population age 25 and over with: High school diploma (including GED) or higher: 92.4% (2010); Bachelor's degree or higher: 14.6% (2010); Master's degree or higher: 5.4% (2010).
School District(s)
Chadwick-Milledgeville CUSD 399 (PK-12)
  2009-10 Enrollment: 526 . . . . (815) 684-5191

Housing: Homeownership rate: 78.1% (2010); Median home value: $112,076 (2010); Median contract rent: $364 per month (2005-2009 5-year est.); Median year structure built: 1947 (2005-2009 5-year est.).
Safety: Violent crime rate: 11.1 per 10,000 population; Property crime rate: 321.2 per 10,000 population (2010).
Transportation: Commute to work: 93.0% car, 0.0% public transportation, 3.4% walk, 1.1% work from home (2005-2009 5-year est.); Travel time to work: 29.9% less than 15 minutes, 38.9% 15 to 30 minutes, 17.1% 30 to 45 minutes, 5.5% 45 to 60 minutes, 8.6% 60 minutes or more (2005-2009 5-year est.)

MOUNT CARROLL (city). County seat. Covers a land area of 1.901 square miles and a water area of 0 square miles. Located at 42.09° N. Lat; 89.97° W. Long. Elevation is 810 feet.
History: Founded 1843, incorporated 1867.
Population: 1,737 (1990); 1,832 (2000); 1,667 (2010); 1,583 (2015 projected); Race: 97.7% White, 0.2% Black, 0.3% Asian, 1.8% Other, 1.6% Hispanic of any race (2010); Density: 876.7 persons per square mile (2010); Average household size: 2.43 (2010); Median age: 41.7 (2010); Males per 100 females: 94.7 (2010); Marriage status: 25.8% never married, 56.0% now married, 7.3% widowed, 10.9% divorced (2005-2009 5-year est.); Foreign born: 1.2% (2005-2009 5-year est.); Ancestry (includes multiple ancestries): 52.7% German, 15.7% Irish, 10.0% American, 6.3% English, 5.2% Swedish (2005-2009 5-year est.).
Economy: Single-family building permits issued: 0 (2010); Multi-family building permits issued: 0 (2010); Employment by occupation: 10.0% management, 15.7% professional, 17.6% services, 20.2% sales, 0.2% farming, 13.2% construction, 23.1% production (2005-2009 5-year est.).
Income: Per capita income: $18,639 (2010); Median household income: $38,848 (2010); Average household income: $46,721 (2010); Percent of households with income of $100,000 or more: 6.4% (2010); Poverty rate: 12.9% (2005-2009 5-year est.).
Taxes: Total city taxes per capita: $131 (2007); City property taxes per capita: $106 (2007).
Education: Percent of population age 25 and over with: High school diploma (including GED) or higher: 87.7% (2010); Bachelor's degree or higher: 14.0% (2010); Master's degree or higher: 4.4% (2010).
School District(s)
West Carroll CUSD 314 (PK-12)
    2009-10 Enrollment: 1,388 . . . . (815) 259-2735
Housing: Homeownership rate: 73.0% (2010); Median home value: $114,557 (2010); Median contract rent: $363 per month (2005-2009 5-year est.); Median year structure built: before 1940 (2005-2009 5-year est.).
Safety: Violent crime rate: 6.2 per 10,000 population; Property crime rate: 272.4 per 10,000 population (2010).
Newspapers: Mirror-Democrat (Community news; Circulation 2,100); Northwestern Illinois Dispatch (Community news; Circulation 10,000)
Transportation: Commute to work: 87.1% car, 3.0% public transportation, 2.3% walk, 4.8% work from home (2005-2009 5-year est.); Travel time to work: 38.9% less than 15 minutes, 21.5% 15 to 30 minutes, 17.4% 30 to 45 minutes, 13.4% 45 to 60 minutes, 8.8% 60 minutes or more (2005-2009 5-year est.)
Additional Information Contacts
Mount Carroll Chamber of Commerce . . . . (800) 244-9594
    http://www.mtcarrollil.org

SAVANNA (city). Covers a land area of 2.609 square miles and a water area of 0.094 square miles. Located at 42.09° N. Lat; 90.14° W. Long. Elevation is 600 feet.
History: Savanna was settled in 1828 as a farming center and river port. The coming of the railroad in 1850 made Savanna a trading town and shipping point for livestock and farm produce.
Population: 3,877 (1990); 3,542 (2000); 3,046 (2010); 2,819 (2015 projected); Race: 92.1% White, 2.9% Black, 0.2% Asian, 4.8% Other, 5.7% Hispanic of any race (2010); Density: 1,167.5 persons per square mile (2010); Average household size: 2.16 (2010); Median age: 42.3 (2010); Males per 100 females: 92.7 (2010); Marriage status: 20.7% never married, 52.1% now married, 15.5% widowed, 11.7% divorced (2005-2009 5-year est.); Foreign born: 1.8% (2005-2009 5-year est.); Ancestry (includes multiple ancestries): 36.9% German, 14.3% English, 13.8% Irish, 9.2% American, 6.2% Scottish (2005-2009 5-year est.).
Economy: Single-family building permits issued: 0 (2010); Multi-family building permits issued: 0 (2010); Employment by occupation: 11.1% management, 10.9% professional, 23.8% services, 22.6% sales, 0.7% farming, 6.6% construction, 24.4% production (2005-2009 5-year est.).

Income: Per capita income: $18,202 (2010); Median household income: $31,651 (2010); Average household income: $39,408 (2010); Percent of households with income of $100,000 or more: 4.6% (2010); Poverty rate: 16.1% (2005-2009 5-year est.).
Taxes: Total city taxes per capita: $170 (2007); City property taxes per capita: $144 (2007).
Education: Percent of population age 25 and over with: High school diploma (including GED) or higher: 85.4% (2010); Bachelor's degree or higher: 14.7% (2010); Master's degree or higher: 3.8% (2010).
School District(s)
West Carroll CUSD 314 (PK-12)
    2009-10 Enrollment: 1,388 . . . . (815) 259-2735
Housing: Homeownership rate: 66.3% (2010); Median home value: $69,774 (2010); Median contract rent: $341 per month (2005-2009 5-year est.); Median year structure built: 1940 (2005-2009 5-year est.).
Newspapers: Savanna Times Journal (Community news; Circulation 2,500)
Transportation: Commute to work: 89.2% car, 0.0% public transportation, 6.2% walk, 3.6% work from home (2005-2009 5-year est.); Travel time to work: 61.2% less than 15 minutes, 21.0% 15 to 30 minutes, 7.0% 30 to 45 minutes, 3.6% 45 to 60 minutes, 7.2% 60 minutes or more (2005-2009 5-year est.)
Additional Information Contacts
Savanna Chamber of Commerce . . . . (815) 273-2722
    http://www.savanna-il.com

SHANNON (village). Covers a land area of 0.479 square miles and a water area of 0 square miles. Located at 42.15° N. Lat; 89.74° W. Long. Elevation is 915 feet.
Population: 887 (1990); 854 (2000); 763 (2010); 723 (2015 projected); Race: 95.5% White, 0.7% Black, 2.1% Asian, 1.7% Other, 1.4% Hispanic of any race (2010); Density: 1,593.3 persons per square mile (2010); Average household size: 2.44 (2010); Median age: 46.0 (2010); Males per 100 females: 95.1 (2010); Marriage status: 19.5% never married, 59.9% now married, 7.3% widowed, 13.3% divorced (2005-2009 5-year est.); Foreign born: 2.3% (2005-2009 5-year est.); Ancestry (includes multiple ancestries): 43.6% German, 11.0% English, 9.5% Irish, 9.4% American, 5.1% Polish (2005-2009 5-year est.).
Economy: Single-family building permits issued: 0 (2010); Multi-family building permits issued: 0 (2010); Employment by occupation: 9.6% management, 13.0% professional, 11.3% services, 29.2% sales, 1.5% farming, 13.0% construction, 22.5% production (2005-2009 5-year est.).
Income: Per capita income: $24,506 (2010); Median household income: $53,423 (2010); Average household income: $60,997 (2010); Percent of households with income of $100,000 or more: 12.3% (2010); Poverty rate: 14.3% (2005-2009 5-year est.).
Taxes: Total city taxes per capita: $235 (2007); City property taxes per capita: $170 (2007).
Education: Percent of population age 25 and over with: High school diploma (including GED) or higher: 91.4% (2010); Bachelor's degree or higher: 22.0% (2010); Master's degree or higher: 4.8% (2010).
School District(s)
Eastland CUSD 308 (PK-12)
    2009-10 Enrollment: 732 . . . . (815) 493-6301
Housing: Homeownership rate: 79.1% (2010); Median home value: $99,608 (2010); Median contract rent: $467 per month (2005-2009 5-year est.); Median year structure built: 1954 (2005-2009 5-year est.).
Transportation: Commute to work: 97.0% car, 0.7% public transportation, 2.2% walk, 0.0% work from home (2005-2009 5-year est.); Travel time to work: 24.7% less than 15 minutes, 37.9% 15 to 30 minutes, 21.2% 30 to 45 minutes, 5.2% 45 to 60 minutes, 11.0% 60 minutes or more (2005-2009 5-year est.)
Additional Information Contacts
Shannon Chamber of Commerce . . . . (815) 864-2111
    http://www.shannonillinois.com/Chamber_of_commerce.htm

THOMSON (village). Covers a land area of 2.208 square miles and a water area of 0 square miles. Located at 41.96° N. Lat; 90.10° W. Long. Elevation is 597 feet.
Population: 567 (1990); 559 (2000); 522 (2010); 503 (2015 projected); Race: 96.4% White, 0.4% Black, 1.0% Asian, 2.3% Other, 1.3% Hispanic of any race (2010); Density: 236.4 persons per square mile (2010); Average household size: 2.39 (2010); Median age: 41.8 (2010); Males per 100 females: 91.2 (2010); Marriage status: 30.3% never married, 57.1% now married, 2.9% widowed, 9.7% divorced (2005-2009 5-year est.);

Foreign born: 2.4% (2005-2009 5-year est.); Ancestry (includes multiple ancestries): 31.4% German, 20.9% Irish, 6.8% Dutch, 6.1% English, 5.8% French (2005-2009 5-year est.).

Economy: Single-family building permits issued: 1 (2010); Multi-family building permits issued: 0 (2010); Employment by occupation: 5.4% management, 16.2% professional, 23.7% services, 19.4% sales, 0.0% farming, 12.6% construction, 22.7% production (2005-2009 5-year est.).

Income: Per capita income: $22,997 (2010); Median household income: $44,167 (2010); Average household income: $55,115 (2010); Percent of households with income of $100,000 or more: 11.0% (2010); Poverty rate: 12.7% (2005-2009 5-year est.).

Taxes: Total city taxes per capita: $107 (2007); City property taxes per capita: $84 (2007).

Education: Percent of population age 25 and over with: High school diploma (including GED) or higher: 86.9% (2010); Bachelor's degree or higher: 13.6% (2010); Master's degree or higher: 3.8% (2010).

School District(s)

West Carroll CUSD 314 (PK-12)
    2009-10 Enrollment: 1,388 . . . . (815) 259-2735

Housing: Homeownership rate: 68.3% (2010); Median home value: $110,795 (2010); Median contract rent: $465 per month (2005-2009 5-year est.); Median year structure built: 1949 (2005-2009 5-year est.).

Newspapers: Carroll County Review (Regional news; Circulation 1,993)

Transportation: Commute to work: 85.7% car, 0.0% public transportation, 3.2% walk, 8.9% work from home (2005-2009 5-year est.); Travel time to work: 43.9% less than 15 minutes, 32.5% 15 to 30 minutes, 19.6% 30 to 45 minutes, 0.8% 45 to 60 minutes, 3.1% 60 minutes or more (2005-2009 5-year est.)

Cass County

Located in west central Illinois; bounded on the north by the Sangamon River, and on the west by the Illinois River. Covers a land area of 375.90 square miles, a water area of 7.83 square miles, and is located in the Central Time Zone at 39.97° N. Lat., 90.27° W. Long. The county was founded in 1837. County seat is Virginia.

Population: 13,437 (1990); 13,695 (2000); 13,565 (2010); 13,429 (2015 projected); Race: 89.3% White, 1.5% Black, 0.5% Asian, 8.7% Other, 18.5% Hispanic of any race (2010); Density: 36.1 persons per square mile (2010); Average household size: 2.52 (2010); Median age: 37.5 (2010); Males per 100 females: 102.2 (2010).

Religion: Five largest groups: 27.6% Catholic Church, 10.8% The United Methodist Church, 9.4% Lutheran Church—Missouri Synod, 8.7% Evangelical Lutheran Church in America, 5.1% Christian Churches and Churches of Christ (2000).

Economy: Unemployment rate: 7.2% (August 2011); Total civilian labor force: 7,801 (August 2011); Leading industries: 11.8% retail trade; 8.7% health care and social assistance; 4.3% accommodation & food services (2009); Farms: 433 totaling 173,543 acres (2007); Companies that employ 500 or more persons: 1 (2009); Companies that employ 100 to 499 persons: 2 (2009); Companies that employ less than 100 persons: 255 (2009); Black-owned businesses: n/a (2007); Hispanic-owned businesses: n/a (2007); Asian-owned businesses: n/a (2007); Women-owned businesses: n/a (2007); Retail sales per capita: $8,776 (2010). Single-family building permits issued: 3 (2010); Multi-family building permits issued: 0 (2010).

Income: Per capita income: $19,826 (2010); Median household income: $42,211 (2010); Average household income: $50,000 (2010); Percent of households with income of $100,000 or more: 8.1% (2010); Poverty rate: 12.5% (2009); Bankruptcy rate: 2.86% (2010).

Taxes: Total county taxes per capita: $127 (2007); County property taxes per capita: $127 (2007).

Education: Percent of population age 25 and over with: High school diploma (including GED) or higher: 85.0% (2010); Bachelor's degree or higher: 15.6% (2010); Master's degree or higher: 3.8% (2010).

Housing: Homeownership rate: 73.7% (2010); Median home value: $77,346 (2010); Median contract rent: $381 per month (2005-2009 5-year est.); Median year structure built: 1953 (2005-2009 5-year est.)

Health: Birth rate: 145.3 per 10,000 population (2009); Death rate: 103.3 per 10,000 population (2009); Age-adjusted cancer mortality rate: 226.7 deaths per 100,000 population (2007); Number of physicians: 1.5 per 10,000 population (2008); Hospital beds: 0.0 per 10,000 population (2007); Hospital admissions: 0.0 per 10,000 population (2007).

Elections: 2008 Presidential election results: 49.7% Obama, 48.4% McCain, 0.8% Nader

National and State Parks: Meredosia National Wildlife Refuge; Panther Creek State Conservation Area; Sanganois State Conservation Area; Toppers Hole State Conservation Area

Additional Information Contacts

Cass County Government . . . . (217) 452-2277

Beardstown Chamber of Commerce . . . . (217) 323-3271
    http://www.beardstownil.org

Cass County Communities

ARENZVILLE (village). Covers a land area of 0.785 square miles and a water area of 0 square miles. Located at 39.87° N. Lat; 90.37° W. Long. Elevation is 505 feet.

Population: 432 (1990); 419 (2000); 362 (2010); 336 (2015 projected); Race: 98.9% White, 0.8% Black, 0.0% Asian, 0.3% Other, 0.0% Hispanic of any race (2010); Density: 461.3 persons per square mile (2010); Average household size: 2.45 (2010); Median age: 40.0 (2010); Males per 100 females: 98.9 (2010); Marriage status: 21.0% never married, 56.4% now married, 6.5% widowed, 16.1% divorced (2005-2009 5-year est.); Foreign born: 0.0% (2005-2009 5-year est.); Ancestry (includes multiple ancestries): 54.2% German, 16.6% Irish, 16.6% American, 11.5% English, 2.8% Scotch-Irish (2005-2009 5-year est.).

Economy: Employment by occupation: 12.2% management, 7.6% professional, 12.7% services, 29.5% sales, 8.9% farming, 5.1% construction, 24.1% production (2005-2009 5-year est.).

Income: Per capita income: $26,192 (2010); Median household income: $55,769 (2010); Average household income: $64,713 (2010); Percent of households with income of $100,000 or more: 11.5% (2010); Poverty rate: 4.1% (2005-2009 5-year est.).

Taxes: Total city taxes per capita: $105 (2007); City property taxes per capita: $100 (2007).

Education: Percent of population age 25 and over with: High school diploma (including GED) or higher: 92.9% (2010); Bachelor's degree or higher: 27.4% (2010); Master's degree or higher: 11.2% (2010).

Housing: Homeownership rate: 79.1% (2010); Median home value: $94,000 (2010); Median contract rent: $316 per month (2005-2009 5-year est.); Median year structure built: 1944 (2005-2009 5-year est.).

Transportation: Commute to work: 93.2% car, 0.0% public transportation, 3.4% walk, 0.0% work from home (2005-2009 5-year est.); Travel time to work: 40.0% less than 15 minutes, 32.8% 15 to 30 minutes, 20.0% 30 to 45 minutes, 3.8% 45 to 60 minutes, 3.4% 60 minutes or more (2005-2009 5-year est.)

ASHLAND (village). Covers a land area of 0.743 square miles and a water area of 0 square miles. Located at 39.88° N. Lat; 90.00° W. Long. Elevation is 623 feet.

History: Incorporated 1869.

Population: 1,259 (1990); 1,361 (2000); 1,301 (2010); 1,265 (2015 projected); Race: 97.9% White, 0.3% Black, 0.4% Asian, 1.4% Other, 0.3% Hispanic of any race (2010); Density: 1,751.6 persons per square mile (2010); Average household size: 2.45 (2010); Median age: 38.5 (2010); Males per 100 females: 100.2 (2010); Marriage status: 29.4% never married, 58.6% now married, 4.4% widowed, 7.6% divorced (2005-2009 5-year est.); Foreign born: 0.4% (2005-2009 5-year est.); Ancestry (includes multiple ancestries): 30.4% German, 19.7% American, 14.3% Irish, 7.2% English, 3.9% Swedish (2005-2009 5-year est.).

Economy: Single-family building permits issued: 0 (2010); Multi-family building permits issued: 0 (2010); Employment by occupation: 13.7% management, 13.1% professional, 11.7% services, 31.4% sales, 0.0% farming, 11.3% construction, 18.8% production (2005-2009 5-year est.).

Income: Per capita income: $25,796 (2010); Median household income: $53,734 (2010); Average household income: $63,863 (2010); Percent of households with income of $100,000 or more: 11.7% (2010); Poverty rate: 8.8% (2005-2009 5-year est.).

Taxes: Total city taxes per capita: $71 (2007); City property taxes per capita: $61 (2007).

Education: Percent of population age 25 and over with: High school diploma (including GED) or higher: 89.2% (2010); Bachelor's degree or higher: 22.1% (2010); Master's degree or higher: 4.6% (2010).

School District(s)

A-C Central CUSD 262 (KG-12)
    2009-10 Enrollment: 436 . . . . (217) 476-8112

Housing: Homeownership rate: 77.6% (2010); Median home value: $102,778 (2010); Median contract rent: $382 per month (2005-2009 5-year est.); Median year structure built: 1963 (2005-2009 5-year est.).
Safety: Violent crime rate: 0.0 per 10,000 population; Property crime rate: 46.2 per 10,000 population (2010).
Newspapers: Ashland Sentinel (Community news; Circulation 800)
Transportation: Commute to work: 92.2% car, 2.1% public transportation, 0.8% walk, 3.9% work from home (2005-2009 5-year est.); Travel time to work: 23.3% less than 15 minutes, 21.5% 15 to 30 minutes, 41.8% 30 to 45 minutes, 5.7% 45 to 60 minutes, 7.7% 60 minutes or more (2005-2009 5-year est.)

BEARDSTOWN (city). Covers a land area of 3.408 square miles and a water area of 0.055 square miles. Located at 40.01° N. Lat; 90.42° W. Long. Elevation is 449 feet.
History: Beardstown, first called Beard's Ferry, was settled in 1819 by Thomas Beard, who operated a ferry across the Illinois River. An early commercial fishing and clam industry gave way to farming and shipping. A 1922 flood covered Beardstown with a lake 18 miles wide, prompting the building of a cement sea wall when the waters receded.
Population: 5,379 (1990); 5,766 (2000); 5,725 (2010); 5,755 (2015 projected); Race: 80.6% White, 2.9% Black, 0.6% Asian, 15.9% Other, 37.0% Hispanic of any race (2010); Density: 1,680.1 persons per square mile (2010); Average household size: 2.64 (2010); Median age: 34.9 (2010); Males per 100 females: 104.5 (2010); Marriage status: 27.4% never married, 44.9% now married, 13.4% widowed, 14.4% divorced (2005-2009 5-year est.); Foreign born: 17.3% (2005-2009 5-year est.); Ancestry (includes multiple ancestries): 22.5% American, 14.0% German, 8.0% English, 6.5% Irish, 2.4% Polish (2005-2009 5-year est.).
Economy: Single-family building permits issued: 0 (2010); Multi-family building permits issued: 0 (2010); Employment by occupation: 7.1% management, 9.7% professional, 17.9% services, 13.3% sales, 3.9% farming, 5.8% construction, 42.1% production (2005-2009 5-year est.).
Income: Per capita income: $14,816 (2010); Median household income: $32,678 (2010); Average household income: $38,757 (2010); Percent of households with income of $100,000 or more: 3.4% (2010); Poverty rate: 20.1% (2005-2009 5-year est.).
Taxes: Total city taxes per capita: $329 (2007); City property taxes per capita: $200 (2007).
Education: Percent of population age 25 and over with: High school diploma (including GED) or higher: 80.2% (2010); Bachelor's degree or higher: 11.1% (2010); Master's degree or higher: 2.4% (2010).

School District(s)
Beardstown CUSD 15 (PK-12)
    2009-10 Enrollment: 1,590 . . . . (217) 323-3099
Housing: Homeownership rate: 68.6% (2010); Median home value: $60,603 (2010); Median contract rent: $401 per month (2005-2009 5-year est.); Median year structure built: 1948 (2005-2009 5-year est.).
Newspapers: Cass County Star-Gazette (Community news; Circulation 3,300); Star-Gazette Shopper (Community news; Circulation 9,600)
Transportation: Commute to work: 96.1% car, 0.0% public transportation, 1.0% walk, 2.7% work from home (2005-2009 5-year est.); Travel time to work: 64.3% less than 15 minutes, 11.4% 15 to 30 minutes, 5.8% 30 to 45 minutes, 3.1% 45 to 60 minutes, 15.4% 60 minutes or more (2005-2009 5-year est.)
Additional Information Contacts
Beardstown Chamber of Commerce . . . . (217) 323-3271
   http://www.beardstownil.org

CHANDLERVILLE (village). Covers a land area of 0.861 square miles and a water area of 0 square miles. Located at 40.04° N. Lat; 90.15° W. Long. Elevation is 463 feet.
History: Chandlerville was named for its founder, Dr. Charles Chandler.
Population: 708 (1990); 704 (2000); 674 (2010); 650 (2015 projected); Race: 94.2% White, 1.3% Black, 1.2% Asian, 3.3% Other, 2.8% Hispanic of any race (2010); Density: 783.1 persons per square mile (2010); Average household size: 2.45 (2010); Median age: 37.9 (2010); Males per 100 females: 99.4 (2010); Marriage status: 21.2% never married, 62.9% now married, 6.4% widowed, 9.5% divorced (2005-2009 5-year est.); Foreign born: 0.0% (2005-2009 5-year est.); Ancestry (includes multiple ancestries): 32.9% American, 21.0% German, 13.4% English, 6.2% Irish, 2.2% French (2005-2009 5-year est.).
Economy: Single-family building permits issued: 0 (2010); Multi-family building permits issued: 0 (2010); Employment by occupation: 8.1%

management, 16.6% professional, 21.3% services, 12.2% sales, 0.0% farming, 14.2% construction, 27.7% production (2005-2009 5-year est.).
Income: Per capita income: $19,786 (2010); Median household income: $42,500 (2010); Average household income: $48,818 (2010); Percent of households with income of $100,000 or more: 10.2% (2010); Poverty rate: 11.5% (2005-2009 5-year est.).
Taxes: Total city taxes per capita: $66 (2007); City property taxes per capita: $63 (2007).
Education: Percent of population age 25 and over with: High school diploma (including GED) or higher: 87.0% (2010); Bachelor's degree or higher: 14.3% (2010); Master's degree or higher: 1.3% (2010).

School District(s)
A-C Central CUSD 262 (KG-12)
    2009-10 Enrollment: 436 . . . . (217) 476-8112
Housing: Homeownership rate: 81.5% (2010); Median home value: $68,571 (2010); Median contract rent: $361 per month (2005-2009 5-year est.); Median year structure built: before 1940 (2005-2009 5-year est.).
Transportation: Commute to work: 95.6% car, 0.0% public transportation, 3.7% walk, 0.0% work from home (2005-2009 5-year est.); Travel time to work: 28.4% less than 15 minutes, 24.3% 15 to 30 minutes, 14.2% 30 to 45 minutes, 23.6% 45 to 60 minutes, 9.5% 60 minutes or more (2005-2009 5-year est.)

VIRGINIA (city). County seat. Covers a land area of 1.085 square miles and a water area of 0.012 square miles. Located at 39.94° N. Lat; 90.21° W. Long. Elevation is 610 feet.
History: Virginia was platted in 1836 by Dr. Henry A. Hall, a former surgeon in the British Navy, and was incorporated as a village in 1842. It developed as a city after 1872.
Population: 1,863 (1990); 1,728 (2000); 1,640 (2010); 1,586 (2015 projected); Race: 97.5% White, 0.7% Black, 0.3% Asian, 1.5% Other, 1.2% Hispanic of any race (2010); Density: 1,512.0 persons per square mile (2010); Average household size: 2.30 (2010); Median age: 42.8 (2010); Males per 100 females: 95.5 (2010); Marriage status: 29.0% never married, 48.8% now married, 8.1% widowed, 14.1% divorced (2005-2009 5-year est.); Foreign born: 1.1% (2005-2009 5-year est.); Ancestry (includes multiple ancestries): 26.5% German, 18.9% American, 12.5% English, 12.1% Irish, 3.6% Polish (2005-2009 5-year est.).
Economy: Single-family building permits issued: 0 (2010); Multi-family building permits issued: 0 (2010); Employment by occupation: 12.2% management, 7.7% professional, 21.3% services, 29.6% sales, 0.7% farming, 10.8% construction, 17.7% production (2005-2009 5-year est.).
Income: Per capita income: $23,157 (2010); Median household income: $45,487 (2010); Average household income: $54,055 (2010); Percent of households with income of $100,000 or more: 10.0% (2010); Poverty rate: 11.8% (2005-2009 5-year est.).
Taxes: Total city taxes per capita: $118 (2007); City property taxes per capita: $113 (2007).
Education: Percent of population age 25 and over with: High school diploma (including GED) or higher: 85.7% (2010); Bachelor's degree or higher: 18.0% (2010); Master's degree or higher: 7.2% (2010).

School District(s)
Virginia CUSD 64 (PK-12)
    2009-10 Enrollment: 406 . . . . (217) 452-3085
Housing: Homeownership rate: 72.2% (2010); Median home value: $78,902 (2010); Median contract rent: $355 per month (2005-2009 5-year est.); Median year structure built: 1956 (2005-2009 5-year est.).
Transportation: Commute to work: 93.7% car, 0.0% public transportation, 3.0% walk, 2.5% work from home (2005-2009 5-year est.); Travel time to work: 32.1% less than 15 minutes, 31.0% 15 to 30 minutes, 16.3% 30 to 45 minutes, 14.2% 45 to 60 minutes, 6.5% 60 minutes or more (2005-2009 5-year est.)

Champaign County

Located in eastern Illinois; prairie region, drained by the Sangamon, Kaskaskia, and Embarrass Rivers, and by the South Fork of the Vermilion River. Covers a land area of 996.81 square miles, a water area of 0.73 square miles, and is located in the Central Time Zone at 40.13° N. Lat., 88.21° W. Long. The county was founded in 1833. County seat is Urbana.

Champaign County is part of the Champaign-Urbana, IL Metropolitan Statistical Area. The entire metro area includes: Champaign County, IL; Ford County, IL; Piatt County, IL

Weather Station: Rantoul Chanute AFB   Elevation: 754 feet

	Jan	Feb	Mar	Apr	May	Jun	Jul	Aug	Sep	Oct	Nov	Dec
High	34	38	50	63	74	84	87	85	79	66	51	38
Low	15	19	29	39	50	60	63	61	53	41	31	20
Precip	1.9	2.1	2.9	3.8	4.3	4.0	4.6	4.2	3.1	3.4	3.4	2.6
Snow	3.1	3.5	1.2	0.4	tr	0.0	0.0	0.0	0.0	tr	0.1	1.6

High and Low temperatures in degrees Fahrenheit; Precipitation and Snow in inches

Weather Station: Urbana   Elevation: 743 feet

	Jan	Feb	Mar	Apr	May	Jun	Jul	Aug	Sep	Oct	Nov	Dec
High	34	38	50	63	74	83	85	84	78	65	51	37
Low	18	22	31	41	52	61	65	63	55	43	33	22
Precip	2.0	2.1	2.9	3.7	4.9	4.2	4.6	4.0	3.2	3.1	3.6	2.7
Snow	6.8	5.9	2.5	0.5	tr	0.0	0.0	0.0	0.0	0.1	1.2	5.8

High and Low temperatures in degrees Fahrenheit; Precipitation and Snow in inches

Population: 173,025 (1990); 179,669 (2000); 195,668 (2010); 201,741 (2015 projected); Race: 75.5% White, 11.4% Black, 8.2% Asian, 4.9% Other, 4.5% Hispanic of any race (2010); Density: 196.3 persons per square mile (2010); Average household size: 2.28 (2010); Median age: 28.6 (2010); Males per 100 females: 104.0 (2010).
Religion: Five largest groups: 10.9% Catholic Church, 4.9% The United Methodist Church, 4.4% Evangelical Lutheran Church in America, 2.3% Assemblies of God, 2.1% Christian Churches and Churches of Christ (2000).
Economy: Unemployment rate: 9.0% (August 2011); Total civilian labor force: 98,886 (August 2011); Leading industries: 17.8% health care and social assistance; 15.6% retail trade; 14.1% accommodation & food services (2009); Farms: 1,389 totaling 550,481 acres (2007); Companies that employ 500 or more persons: 6 (2009); Companies that employ 100 to 499 persons: 94 (2009); Companies that employ less than 100 persons: 4,076 (2009); Black-owned businesses: 1,187 (2007); Hispanic-owned businesses: 255 (2007); Asian-owned businesses: n/a (2007); Women-owned businesses: 3,807 (2007); Retail sales per capita: $12,400 (2010). Single-family building permits issued: 210 (2010); Multi-family building permits issued: 268 (2010).
Income: Per capita income: $24,146 (2010); Median household income: $45,210 (2010); Average household income: $59,803 (2010); Percent of households with income of $100,000 or more: 14.6% (2010); Poverty rate: 19.9% (2009); Bankruptcy rate: 3.05% (2010).
Taxes: Total county taxes per capita: $179 (2007); County property taxes per capita: $145 (2007).
Education: Percent of population age 25 and over with: High school diploma (including GED) or higher: 92.2% (2010); Bachelor's degree or higher: 42.6% (2010); Master's degree or higher: 21.7% (2010).
Housing: Homeownership rate: 55.3% (2010); Median home value: $132,711 (2010); Median contract rent: $592 per month (2005-2009 5-year est.); Median year structure built: 1974 (2005-2009 5-year est.)
Health: Birth rate: 127.8 per 10,000 population (2009); Death rate: 62.6 per 10,000 population (2009); Age-adjusted cancer mortality rate: 175.4 deaths per 100,000 population (2007); Number of physicians: 32.3 per 10,000 population (2008); Hospital beds: 27.2 per 10,000 population (2007); Hospital admissions: 1,453.6 per 10,000 population (2007).
Environment: Air Quality Index: 95.5% good, 4.5% moderate, 0.0% unhealthy for sensitive individuals, 0.0% unhealthy (percent of days in 2008)
Elections: 2008 Presidential election results: 57.8% Obama, 40.3% McCain, 0.7% Nader
Additional Information Contacts

Champaign County Government . . . . (217) 384-3720
    http://www.co.champaign.il.us
Champaign County Chamber of Commerce . . . . (217) 359-1791
    http://champaigncounty.org
Champaign County Convention & Visitors Bureau . . . . (217) 351-4133
    http://www.visitchampaigncounty.org
City of Champaign . . . . (217) 403-8700
    http://ci.champaign.il.us
City of Urbana . . . . (217) 384-2366
    http://urbanaillinois.us
Mahomet Area Chamber of Commerce . . . . (217) 586-3165
    http://www.mahometchamberofcommerce.com
Rantoul Area Chamber of Commerce . . . . (217) 893-3323
    http://www.rantoulchamber.com
Village of Rantoul. . . . . (217) 893-1661
    http://www.village.rantoul.il.us

Champaign County Communities

BONDVILLE (village). Covers a land area of 0.254 square miles and a water area of 0 square miles. Located at 40.11° N. Lat; 88.36° W. Long. Elevation is 719 feet.
Population: 366 (1990); 455 (2000); 447 (2010); 446 (2015 projected); Race: 95.5% White, 0.2% Black, 0.2% Asian, 4.0% Other, 1.8% Hispanic of any race (2010); Density: 1,761.7 persons per square mile (2010); Average household size: 2.57 (2010); Median age: 31.8 (2010); Males per 100 females: 101.4 (2010); Marriage status: 39.7% never married, 40.6% now married, 7.3% widowed, 12.4% divorced (2005-2009 5-year est.); Foreign born: 0.0% (2005-2009 5-year est.); Ancestry (includes multiple ancestries): 22.5% American, 15.4% German, 7.6% English, 7.5% Irish, 3.4% European (2005-2009 5-year est.).
Economy: Single-family building permits issued: 1 (2010); Multi-family building permits issued: 0 (2010); Employment by occupation: 6.6% management, 8.5% professional, 9.4% services, 35.8% sales, 0.0% farming, 29.9% construction, 9.7% production (2005-2009 5-year est.).
Income: Per capita income: $25,073 (2010); Median household income: $63,182 (2010); Average household income: $64,598 (2010); Percent of households with income of $100,000 or more: 12.6% (2010); Poverty rate: 6.2% (2005-2009 5-year est.).
Taxes: Total city taxes per capita: $50 (2007); City property taxes per capita: $32 (2007).
Education: Percent of population age 25 and over with: High school diploma (including GED) or higher: 95.0% (2010); Bachelor's degree or higher: 23.5% (2010); Master's degree or higher: 13.1% (2010).
Housing: Homeownership rate: 70.1% (2010); Median home value: $113,265 (2010); Median contract rent: $482 per month (2005-2009 5-year est.); Median year structure built: 1973 (2005-2009 5-year est.).
Transportation: Commute to work: 96.5% car, 0.0% public transportation, 0.0% walk, 1.3% work from home (2005-2009 5-year est.); Travel time to work: 15.0% less than 15 minutes, 70.4% 15 to 30 minutes, 11.8% 30 to 45 minutes, 2.2% 45 to 60 minutes, 0.6% 60 minutes or more (2005-2009 5-year est.)

BROADLANDS (village). Covers a land area of 0.271 square miles and a water area of 0 square miles. Located at 39.90° N. Lat; 87.99° W. Long. Elevation is 679 feet.
Population: 340 (1990); 312 (2000); 295 (2010); 290 (2015 projected); Race: 98.0% White, 0.0% Black, 0.0% Asian, 2.0% Other, 0.0% Hispanic of any race (2010); Density: 1,089.9 persons per square mile (2010); Average household size: 2.54 (2010); Median age: 36.0 (2010); Males per 100 females: 96.7 (2010); Marriage status: 27.2% never married, 57.4% now married, 5.1% widowed, 10.3% divorced (2005-2009 5-year est.); Foreign born: 0.3% (2005-2009 5-year est.); Ancestry (includes multiple ancestries): 45.9% German, 30.5% Irish, 19.0% English, 12.7% American, 5.4% French (2005-2009 5-year est.).
Economy: Single-family building permits issued: 1 (2010); Multi-family building permits issued: 0 (2010); Employment by occupation: 15.3% management, 14.9% professional, 23.8% services, 11.4% sales, 2.0% farming, 7.4% construction, 25.2% production (2005-2009 5-year est.).
Income: Per capita income: $19,948 (2010); Median household income: $41,818 (2010); Average household income: $50,560 (2010); Percent of households with income of $100,000 or more: 7.8% (2010); Poverty rate: 1.5% (2005-2009 5-year est.).
Taxes: Total city taxes per capita: $52 (2007); City property taxes per capita: $49 (2007).
Education: Percent of population age 25 and over with: High school diploma (including GED) or higher: 88.7% (2010); Bachelor's degree or higher: 21.5% (2010); Master's degree or higher: 9.7% (2010).
School District(s)
Heritage CUSD 8 (KG-12)
    2009-10 Enrollment: 560 . . . . (217) 834-3392
Housing: Homeownership rate: 81.9% (2010); Median home value: $96,875 (2010); Median contract rent: $228 per month (2005-2009 5-year est.); Median year structure built: 1945 (2005-2009 5-year est.).
Transportation: Commute to work: 83.3% car, 3.1% public transportation, 3.1% walk, 10.4% work from home (2005-2009 5-year est.); Travel time to work: 19.8% less than 15 minutes, 22.1% 15 to 30 minutes, 27.3% 30 to 45 minutes, 28.5% 45 to 60 minutes, 2.3% 60 minutes or more (2005-2009 5-year est.)

CHAMPAIGN (city). Covers a land area of 16.987 square miles and a water area of 0.023 square miles. Located at 40.11° N. Lat; 88.26° W. Long. Elevation is 738 feet.

History: Champaign came into existence as West Urbana in 1854, built around the railroad station when the Illinois Central Railroad chose a route several miles west of the town of Urbana. Resisting a move to be annexed to Urbana, residents of West Urbana incorporated under the name of Champaign in 1860. Rivalry between the two cities was laid aside when they jointly founded a seminary, later to become the University of Illinois, between them.

Population: 65,449 (1990); 67,518 (2000); 76,962 (2010); 80,417 (2015 projected); Race: 69.4% White, 15.3% Black, 9.2% Asian, 6.1% Other, 6.4% Hispanic of any race (2010); Density: 4,530.6 persons per square mile (2010); Average household size: 2.18 (2010); Median age: 26.4 (2010); Males per 100 females: 105.8 (2010); Marriage status: 55.9% never married, 34.5% now married, 3.2% widowed, 6.4% divorced (2005-2009 5-year est.); Foreign born: 9.6% (2005-2009 5-year est.); Ancestry (includes multiple ancestries): 22.9% German, 13.9% Irish, 9.2% English, 8.7% American, 5.2% Polish (2005-2009 5-year est.).

Economy: Unemployment rate: 9.3% (August 2011); Total civilian labor force: 40,723 (August 2011); Single-family building permits issued: 63 (2010); Multi-family building permits issued: 266 (2010); Employment by occupation: 10.7% management, 33.9% professional, 19.8% services, 23.3% sales, 0.2% farming, 3.9% construction, 8.1% production (2005-2009 5-year est.).

Income: Per capita income: $22,287 (2010); Median household income: $39,158 (2010); Average household income: $53,786 (2010); Percent of households with income of $100,000 or more: 12.3% (2010); Poverty rate: 27.2% (2005-2009 5-year est.).

Taxes: Total city taxes per capita: $592 (2007); City property taxes per capita: $247 (2007).

Education: Percent of population age 25 and over with: High school diploma (including GED) or higher: 92.5% (2010); Bachelor's degree or higher: 47.8% (2010); Master's degree or higher: 24.3% (2010).

School District(s)
Champaign CUSD 4 (PK-12)
2009-10 Enrollment: 9,458 . . . . (217) 351-3838
Champaign/Ford Roe (05-12)
2009-10 Enrollment: n/a . . . . (217) 893-3219
Educ for Employment Sys 330
2009-10 Enrollment: n/a . . . . (217) 355-1382

Four-year College(s)
University of Illinois at Urbana-Champaign (Public)
Fall 2009 Enrollment: 43,881. . . . . (217) 333-1000
2010-11 Tuition: In-state $13,096; Out-of-state $27,238
Urbana Theological Seminary (Private, Not-for-profit)
Fall 2009 Enrollment: 47 . . . . (217) 365-9005

Two-year College(s)
Parkland College (Public)
Fall 2009 Enrollment: 9,633. (217) 351-2200
2010-11 Tuition: In-state $7,830; Out-of-state $12,090

Vocational/Technical School(s)
Regency Beauty Institute-Champaign (Private, For-profit)
Fall 2009 Enrollment: 135 . . . . (800) 787-6456
2010-11 Tuition: $16,075

Housing: Homeownership rate: 46.5% (2010); Median home value: $128,319 (2010); Median contract rent: $629 per month (2005-2009 5-year est.); Median year structure built: 1974 (2005-2009 5-year est.).

Hospitals: Pavilion Foundation Hospital (46 beds)

Newspapers: News-Gazette (Local news; Circulation 46,048); Travel - The News-Gazette

Transportation: Commute to work: 73.3% car, 6.6% public transportation, 12.6% walk, 3.7% work from home (2005-2009 5-year est.); Travel time to work: 53.3% less than 15 minutes, 38.7% 15 to 30 minutes, 4.7% 30 to 45 minutes, 1.9% 45 to 60 minutes, 1.5% 60 minutes or more (2005-2009 5-year est.); Amtrak: train service available.

Additional Information Contacts
Champaign County Chamber of Commerce . . . . (217) 359-1791
http://champaigncounty.org
Champaign County Convention & Visitors Bureau . . . . (217) 351-4133
http://www.visitchampaigncounty.org
City of Champaign . . . . (217) 403-8700
http://ci.champaign.il.us

DEWEY (unincorporated postal area, zip code 61840). Covers a land area of 33.901 square miles and a water area of 0.039 square miles. Located at 40.31° N. Lat; 88.30° W. Long. Elevation is 732 feet.
Population: 709 (2000); Race: 97.6% White, 0.0% Black, 1.5% Asian, 0.9% Other, 2.0% Hispanic of any race (2000); Density: 20.9 persons per square mile (2000); Age: 25.9% under 18, 15.1% over 64 (2000); Marriage status: 16.8% never married, 66.4% now married, 5.6% widowed, 11.2% divorced (2000); Foreign born: 2.1% (2000); Ancestry (includes multiple ancestries): 32.7% German, 14.9% English, 9.8% American, 9.8% Irish, 9.4% Italian (2000).
Economy: Employment by occupation: 21.5% management, 19.6% professional, 12.4% services, 24.0% sales, 1.4% farming, 6.4% construction, 14.6% production (2000).
Income: Per capita income: $24,557 (2000); Median household income: $52,381 (2000); Poverty rate: 1.8% (2000).
Education: Percent of population age 25 and over with: High school diploma (including GED) or higher: 96.3% (2000); Bachelor's degree or higher: 27.7% (2000).
Housing: Homeownership rate: 92.7% (2000); Median home value: $113,900 (2000); Median contract rent: $400 per month (2000); Median year structure built: 1972 (2000).
Transportation: Commute to work: 93.6% car, 0.0% public transportation, 0.0% walk, 6.4% work from home (2000); Travel time to work: 22.7% less than 15 minutes, 52.2% 15 to 30 minutes, 17.4% 30 to 45 minutes, 3.2% 45 to 60 minutes, 4.4% 60 minutes or more (2000)

FISHER (village). Covers a land area of 0.992 square miles and a water area of 0 square miles. Located at 40.31° N. Lat; 88.34° W. Long. Elevation is 712 feet.
Population: 1,578 (1990); 1,647 (2000); 1,683 (2010); 1,773 (2015 projected); Race: 81.9% White, 8.3% Black, 5.5% Asian, 4.3% Other, 3.7% Hispanic of any race (2010); Density: 1,696.6 persons per square mile (2010); Average household size: 2.54 (2010); Median age: 23.7 (2010); Males per 100 females: 78.7 (2010); Marriage status: 24.4% never married, 61.7% now married, 6.7% widowed, 7.2% divorced (2005-2009 5-year est.); Foreign born: 1.1% (2005-2009 5-year est.); Ancestry (includes multiple ancestries): 36.0% German, 17.9% American, 17.5% Irish, 6.3% English, 3.9% French (2005-2009 5-year est.).
Economy: Single-family building permits issued: 6 (2010); Multi-family building permits issued: 0 (2010); Employment by occupation: 9.9% management, 16.5% professional, 12.2% services, 31.3% sales, 1.9% farming, 11.1% construction, 17.0% production (2005-2009 5-year est.).
Income: Per capita income: $18,564 (2010); Median household income: $59,119 (2010); Average household income: $69,380 (2010); Percent of households with income of $100,000 or more: 16.3% (2010); Poverty rate: 8.3% (2005-2009 5-year est.).
Taxes: Total city taxes per capita: $235 (2007); City property taxes per capita: $185 (2007).
Education: Percent of population age 25 and over with: High school diploma (including GED) or higher: 86.1% (2010); Bachelor's degree or higher: 19.8% (2010); Master's degree or higher: 6.1% (2010).
School District(s)
Fisher CUSD 1 (KG-12)
2009-10 Enrollment: 604 . . . . (217) 897-6125
Housing: Homeownership rate: 79.1% (2010); Median home value: $135,817 (2010); Median contract rent: $527 per month (2005-2009 5-year est.); Median year structure built: 1972 (2005-2009 5-year est.).
Newspapers: Fisher Reporter (Community news; Circulation 1,150)
Transportation: Commute to work: 94.9% car, 0.0% public transportation, 4.0% walk, 0.8% work from home (2005-2009 5-year est.); Travel time to work: 26.3% less than 15 minutes, 37.6% 15 to 30 minutes, 28.0% 30 to 45 minutes, 4.3% 45 to 60 minutes, 3.9% 60 minutes or more (2005-2009 5-year est.)

FOOSLAND (village). Covers a land area of 0.072 square miles and a water area of 0 square miles. Located at 40.36° N. Lat; 88.42° W. Long. Elevation is 735 feet.
Population: 132 (1990); 90 (2000); 103 (2010); 111 (2015 projected); Race: 75.7% White, 10.7% Black, 7.8% Asian, 5.8% Other, 4.9% Hispanic of any race (2010); Density: 1,426.7 persons per square mile (2010); Average household size: 2.47 (2010); Median age: 21.0 (2010); Males per 100 females: 71.7 (2010); Marriage status: 23.9% never married, 71.6% now married, 4.5% widowed, 0.0% divorced (2005-2009 5-year est.); Foreign born: 0.0% (2005-2009 5-year est.); Ancestry (includes multiple

ancestries): 37.9% American, 34.5% German, 22.8% English, 15.9% Irish, 1.4% Polish (2005-2009 5-year est.).
Economy: Employment by occupation: 4.3% management, 0.0% professional, 28.6% services, 20.0% sales, 0.0% farming, 28.6% construction, 18.6% production (2005-2009 5-year est.).
Income: Per capita income: $13,414 (2010); Median household income: $48,500 (2010); Average household income: $56,579 (2010); Percent of households with income of $100,000 or more: 10.5% (2010); Poverty rate: 1.4% (2005-2009 5-year est.).
Taxes: Total city taxes per capita: $70 (2007); City property taxes per capita: $23 (2007).
Education: Percent of population age 25 and over with: High school diploma (including GED) or higher: 81.4% (2010); Bachelor's degree or higher: 16.3% (2010); Master's degree or higher: 2.3% (2010).
Housing: Homeownership rate: 78.9% (2010); Median home value: $115,000 (2010); Median contract rent: n/a per month (2005-2009 5-year est.); Median year structure built: 1941 (2005-2009 5-year est.).
Transportation: Commute to work: 100.0% car, 0.0% public transportation, 0.0% walk, 0.0% work from home (2005-2009 5-year est.); Travel time to work: 16.4% less than 15 minutes, 62.7% 15 to 30 minutes, 11.9% 30 to 45 minutes, 9.0% 45 to 60 minutes, 0.0% 60 minutes or more (2005-2009 5-year est.)

GIFFORD (village).
Covers a land area of 0.633 square miles and a water area of 0 square miles. Located at 40.30° N. Lat; 88.02° W. Long. Elevation is 797 feet.
Population: 852 (1990); 815 (2000); 939 (2010); 998 (2015 projected); Race: 97.7% White, 1.2% Black, 0.3% Asian, 0.9% Other, 0.5% Hispanic of any race (2010); Density: 1,484.2 persons per square mile (2010); Average household size: 2.42 (2010); Median age: 40.7 (2010); Males per 100 females: 89.7 (2010); Marriage status: 19.4% never married, 61.9% now married, 9.3% widowed, 9.3% divorced (2005-2009 5-year est.); Foreign born: 2.4% (2005-2009 5-year est.); Ancestry (includes multiple ancestries): 41.1% German, 15.3% Irish, 8.6% English, 6.4% American, 4.2% Swedish (2005-2009 5-year est.).
Economy: Single-family building permits issued: 0 (2010); Multi-family building permits issued: 0 (2010); Employment by occupation: 8.5% management, 12.3% professional, 13.2% services, 27.9% sales, 0.8% farming, 15.3% construction, 21.9% production (2005-2009 5-year est.).
Income: Per capita income: $27,383 (2010); Median household income: $57,143 (2010); Average household income: $64,143 (2010); Percent of households with income of $100,000 or more: 10.9% (2010); Poverty rate: 7.7% (2005-2009 5-year est.).
Taxes: Total city taxes per capita: $80 (2007); City property taxes per capita: $75 (2007).
Education: Percent of population age 25 and over with: High school diploma (including GED) or higher: 83.0% (2010); Bachelor's degree or higher: 17.7% (2010); Master's degree or higher: 4.8% (2010).
School District(s)
Gifford CCSD 188 (KG-08)
   2009-10 Enrollment: 203 . . . . (217) 568-7733
Housing: Homeownership rate: 84.6% (2010); Median home value: $118,493 (2010); Median contract rent: $372 per month (2005-2009 5-year est.); Median year structure built: 1969 (2005-2009 5-year est.).
Safety: Violent crime rate: 10.0 per 10,000 population; Property crime rate: 30.1 per 10,000 population (2010).
Transportation: Commute to work: 92.7% car, 0.0% public transportation, 5.3% walk, 1.4% work from home (2005-2009 5-year est.); Travel time to work: 24.9% less than 15 minutes, 24.4% 15 to 30 minutes, 39.4% 30 to 45 minutes, 9.9% 45 to 60 minutes, 1.4% 60 minutes or more (2005-2009 5-year est.)

HOMER (village).
Covers a land area of 1.026 square miles and a water area of 0 square miles. Located at 40.03° N. Lat; 87.95° W. Long. Elevation is 676 feet.
History: Village formerly on Salt Creek to North but moved in 19th century to be on railroad.
Population: 1,265 (1990); 1,200 (2000); 1,011 (2010); 969 (2015 projected); Race: 98.6% White, 0.1% Black, 0.5% Asian, 0.8% Other, 0.3% Hispanic of any race (2010); Density: 985.2 persons per square mile (2010); Average household size: 2.36 (2010); Median age: 36.1 (2010); Males per 100 females: 103.4 (2010); Marriage status: 14.1% never married, 66.7% now married, 9.5% widowed, 9.6% divorced (2005-2009 5-year est.); Foreign born: 0.2% (2005-2009 5-year est.); Ancestry

(includes multiple ancestries): 26.1% German, 20.1% American, 13.8% English, 9.1% Irish, 3.3% Russian (2005-2009 5-year est.).
Economy: Single-family building permits issued: 1 (2010); Multi-family building permits issued: 0 (2010); Employment by occupation: 10.4% management, 19.6% professional, 13.6% services, 31.1% sales, 0.0% farming, 8.6% construction, 16.8% production (2005-2009 5-year est.).
Income: Per capita income: $22,801 (2010); Median household income: $43,914 (2010); Average household income: $54,563 (2010); Percent of households with income of $100,000 or more: 7.5% (2010); Poverty rate: 6.6% (2005-2009 5-year est.).
Taxes: Total city taxes per capita: $184 (2007); City property taxes per capita: $154 (2007).
Education: Percent of population age 25 and over with: High school diploma (including GED) or higher: 89.3% (2010); Bachelor's degree or higher: 16.7% (2010); Master's degree or higher: 5.5% (2010).
School District(s)
Heritage CUSD 8 (KG-12)
   2009-10 Enrollment: 560 . . . . (217) 834-3392
Housing: Homeownership rate: 86.7% (2010); Median home value: $93,243 (2010); Median contract rent: $408 per month (2005-2009 5-year est.); Median year structure built: 1951 (2005-2009 5-year est.).
Safety: Violent crime rate: 54.0 per 10,000 population; Property crime rate: 54.0 per 10,000 population (2010).
Transportation: Commute to work: 88.4% car, 0.0% public transportation, 2.9% walk, 7.7% work from home (2005-2009 5-year est.); Travel time to work: 23.5% less than 15 minutes, 30.0% 15 to 30 minutes, 39.7% 30 to 45 minutes, 5.2% 45 to 60 minutes, 1.6% 60 minutes or more (2005-2009 5-year est.)

IVESDALE (village).
Covers a land area of 0.749 square miles and a water area of 0 square miles. Located at 39.94° N. Lat; 88.45° W. Long. Elevation is 682 feet.
Population: 339 (1990); 288 (2000); 265 (2010); 258 (2015 projected); Race: 96.2% White, 0.0% Black, 0.0% Asian, 3.8% Other, 0.0% Hispanic of any race (2010); Density: 353.7 persons per square mile (2010); Average household size: 2.50 (2010); Median age: 37.8 (2010); Males per 100 females: 112.0 (2010); Marriage status: 12.3% never married, 68.1% now married, 11.8% widowed, 7.8% divorced (2005-2009 5-year est.); Foreign born: 0.0% (2005-2009 5-year est.); Ancestry (includes multiple ancestries): 45.0% German, 30.0% Irish, 15.8% American, 7.5% English, 4.6% French (2005-2009 5-year est.).
Economy: Single-family building permits issued: 0 (2010); Multi-family building permits issued: 0 (2010); Employment by occupation: 8.0% management, 19.6% professional, 19.6% services, 24.6% sales, 2.9% farming, 13.8% construction, 11.6% production (2005-2009 5-year est.).
Income: Per capita income: $27,046 (2010); Median household income: $60,484 (2010); Average household income: $66,934 (2010); Percent of households with income of $100,000 or more: 16.0% (2010); Poverty rate: 2.5% (2005-2009 5-year est.).
Taxes: Total city taxes per capita: $98 (2007); City property taxes per capita: $87 (2007).
Education: Percent of population age 25 and over with: High school diploma (including GED) or higher: 91.2% (2010); Bachelor's degree or higher: 14.0% (2010); Master's degree or higher: 7.0% (2010).
Housing: Homeownership rate: 84.9% (2010); Median home value: $105,000 (2010); Median contract rent: $275 per month (2005-2009 5-year est.); Median year structure built: before 1940 (2005-2009 5-year est.).
Transportation: Commute to work: 97.8% car, 0.0% public transportation, 0.7% walk, 1.5% work from home (2005-2009 5-year est.); Travel time to work: 31.3% less than 15 minutes, 27.6% 15 to 30 minutes, 33.6% 30 to 45 minutes, 1.5% 45 to 60 minutes, 6.0% 60 minutes or more (2005-2009 5-year est.)

LAKE OF THE WOODS (CDP).
Covers a land area of 2.101 square miles and a water area of 0.014 square miles. Located at 40.20° N. Lat; 88.36° W. Long. Elevation is 748 feet.
History: Covered bridge.
Population: 2,718 (1990); 3,026 (2000); 3,276 (2010); 3,443 (2015 projected); Race: 96.5% White, 0.7% Black, 0.2% Asian, 2.6% Other, 1.4% Hispanic of any race (2010); Density: 1,559.0 persons per square mile (2010); Average household size: 2.65 (2010); Median age: 31.4 (2010); Males per 100 females: 100.7 (2010); Marriage status: 22.9% never married, 62.5% now married, 1.5% widowed, 13.0% divorced (2005-2009 5-year est.); Foreign born: 3.8% (2005-2009 5-year est.); Ancestry

(includes multiple ancestries): 26.7% German, 22.2% American, 9.8% Irish, 7.8% English, 5.3% Italian (2005-2009 5-year est.).
Economy: Employment by occupation: 9.8% management, 8.3% professional, 21.8% services, 35.2% sales, 1.6% farming, 16.5% construction, 6.7% production (2005-2009 5-year est.).
Income: Per capita income: $26,449 (2010); Median household income: $53,557 (2010); Average household income: $69,871 (2010); Percent of households with income of $100,000 or more: 18.8% (2010); Poverty rate: 10.7% (2005-2009 5-year est.).
Education: Percent of population age 25 and over with: High school diploma (including GED) or higher: 93.8% (2010); Bachelor's degree or higher: 33.1% (2010); Master's degree or higher: 12.3% (2010).
Housing: Homeownership rate: 84.4% (2010); Median home value: $112,429 (2010); Median contract rent: $589 per month (2005-2009 5-year est.); Median year structure built: 1990 (2005-2009 5-year est.).
Transportation: Commute to work: 97.4% car, 0.0% public transportation, 0.8% walk, 1.0% work from home (2005-2009 5-year est.); Travel time to work: 33.4% less than 15 minutes, 53.8% 15 to 30 minutes, 10.8% 30 to 45 minutes, 0.0% 45 to 60 minutes, 2.1% 60 minutes or more (2005-2009 5-year est.)

LONGVIEW (village). Aka Long View. Covers a land area of 0.251 square miles and a water area of 0 square miles. Located at 39.88° N. Lat; 88.06° W. Long. Elevation is 679 feet.
Population: 180 (1990); 153 (2000); 154 (2010); 157 (2015 projected); Race: 97.4% White, 0.0% Black, 0.0% Asian, 2.6% Other, 1.9% Hispanic of any race (2010); Density: 614.6 persons per square mile (2010); Average household size: 2.66 (2010); Median age: 31.7 (2010); Males per 100 females: 111.0 (2010); Marriage status: 17.7% never married, 46.8% now married, 17.7% widowed, 17.7% divorced (2005-2009 5-year est.); Foreign born: 0.0% (2005-2009 5-year est.); Ancestry (includes multiple ancestries): 40.8% German, 18.4% American, 14.5% English, 6.6% Irish, 5.3% Dutch (2005-2009 5-year est.).
Economy: Employment by occupation: 6.3% management, 18.8% professional, 15.6% services, 37.5% sales, 0.0% farming, 6.3% construction, 15.6% production (2005-2009 5-year est.).
Income: Per capita income: $24,115 (2010); Median household income: $59,375 (2010); Average household income: $65,172 (2010); Percent of households with income of $100,000 or more: 10.3% (2010); Poverty rate: 11.8% (2005-2009 5-year est.).
Taxes: Total city taxes per capita: $48 (2007); City property taxes per capita: $48 (2007).
Education: Percent of population age 25 and over with: High school diploma (including GED) or higher: 88.8% (2010); Bachelor's degree or higher: 24.7% (2010); Master's degree or higher: 5.6% (2010).
School District(s)
Rural Champaign Co Spec Ed Coop (PK-12)
    2009-10 Enrollment: n/a . . . . (217) 892-8877
Housing: Homeownership rate: 81.0% (2010); Median home value: $146,875 (2010); Median contract rent: $425 per month (2005-2009 5-year est.); Median year structure built: before 1940 (2005-2009 5-year est.).
Transportation: Commute to work: 100.0% car, 0.0% public transportation, 0.0% walk, 0.0% work from home (2005-2009 5-year est.); Travel time to work: 0.0% less than 15 minutes, 12.5% 15 to 30 minutes, 75.0% 30 to 45 minutes, 12.5% 45 to 60 minutes, 0.0% 60 minutes or more (2005-2009 5-year est.)

LUDLOW (village). Covers a land area of 0.348 square miles and a water area of 0 square miles. Located at 40.38° N. Lat; 88.12° W. Long. Elevation is 774 feet.
Population: 323 (1990); 324 (2000); 291 (2010); 277 (2015 projected); Race: 91.8% White, 1.4% Black, 0.3% Asian, 6.5% Other, 7.2% Hispanic of any race (2010); Density: 837.2 persons per square mile (2010); Average household size: 2.39 (2010); Median age: 31.7 (2010); Males per 100 females: 103.5 (2010); Marriage status: 36.8% never married, 44.1% now married, 6.8% widowed, 12.4% divorced (2005-2009 5-year est.); Foreign born: 2.7% (2005-2009 5-year est.); Ancestry (includes multiple ancestries): 27.6% American, 13.8% German, 10.7% Irish, 5.1% English, 5.1% French (2005-2009 5-year est.).
Economy: Single-family building permits issued: 0 (2010); Multi-family building permits issued: 0 (2010); Employment by occupation: 4.2% management, 3.3% professional, 23.5% services, 18.8% sales, 0.5% farming, 10.8% construction, 39.0% production (2005-2009 5-year est.).
Income: Per capita income: $22,834 (2010); Median household income: $43,654 (2010); Average household income: $56,332 (2010); Percent of

households with income of $100,000 or more: 10.7% (2010); Poverty rate: 13.4% (2005-2009 5-year est.).
Taxes: Total city taxes per capita: $143 (2007); City property taxes per capita: $22 (2007).
Education: Percent of population age 25 and over with: High school diploma (including GED) or higher: 80.3% (2010); Bachelor's degree or higher: 11.6% (2010); Master's degree or higher: 3.5% (2010).
School District(s)
Ludlow CCSD 142 (KG-08)
    2009-10 Enrollment: 87 . . . . (217) 396-5261
Housing: Homeownership rate: 73.0% (2010); Median home value: $70,000 (2010); Median contract rent: $382 per month (2005-2009 5-year est.); Median year structure built: 1962 (2005-2009 5-year est.).
Transportation: Commute to work: 96.7% car, 0.5% public transportation, 2.9% walk, 0.0% work from home (2005-2009 5-year est.); Travel time to work: 37.6% less than 15 minutes, 28.6% 15 to 30 minutes, 31.4% 30 to 45 minutes, 2.4% 45 to 60 minutes, 0.0% 60 minutes or more (2005-2009 5-year est.)

MAHOMET (village). Covers a land area of 6.854 square miles and a water area of 0 square miles. Located at 40.19° N. Lat; 88.40° W. Long. Elevation is 732 feet.
Population: 3,980 (1990); 4,877 (2000); 5,529 (2010); 5,716 (2015 projected); Race: 97.8% White, 0.3% Black, 0.6% Asian, 1.4% Other, 1.4% Hispanic of any race (2010); Density: 806.7 persons per square mile (2010); Average household size: 2.85 (2010); Median age: 30.5 (2010); Males per 100 females: 95.2 (2010); Marriage status: 26.1% never married, 65.3% now married, 4.0% widowed, 4.6% divorced (2005-2009 5-year est.); Foreign born: 3.6% (2005-2009 5-year est.); Ancestry (includes multiple ancestries): 34.3% German, 13.6% Irish, 12.0% American, 11.0% English, 6.1% French (2005-2009 5-year est.).
Economy: Single-family building permits issued: 36 (2010); Multi-family building permits issued: 0 (2010); Employment by occupation: 11.7% management, 27.9% professional, 15.3% services, 27.8% sales, 1.9% farming, 8.6% construction, 6.7% production (2005-2009 5-year est.).
Income: Per capita income: $29,165 (2010); Median household income: $68,579 (2010); Average household income: $83,040 (2010); Percent of households with income of $100,000 or more: 25.5% (2010); Poverty rate: 2.9% (2005-2009 5-year est.).
Taxes: Total city taxes per capita: $345 (2007); City property taxes per capita: $216 (2007).
Education: Percent of population age 25 and over with: High school diploma (including GED) or higher: 97.2% (2010); Bachelor's degree or higher: 40.8% (2010); Master's degree or higher: 14.3% (2010).
School District(s)
Mahomet-Seymour CUSD 3 (PK-12)
    2009-10 Enrollment: 2,836 . . . . (217) 586-4995
Housing: Homeownership rate: 81.9% (2010); Median home value: $168,257 (2010); Median contract rent: $595 per month (2005-2009 5-year est.); Median year structure built: 1986 (2005-2009 5-year est.).
Safety: Violent crime rate: 16.2 per 10,000 population; Property crime rate: 109.1 per 10,000 population (2010).
Newspapers: Mahomet Citizen (Local news; Circulation 3,000)
Transportation: Commute to work: 95.0% car, 0.0% public transportation, 1.2% walk, 3.1% work from home (2005-2009 5-year est.); Travel time to work: 30.7% less than 15 minutes, 51.9% 15 to 30 minutes, 7.6% 30 to 45 minutes, 5.3% 45 to 60 minutes, 4.5% 60 minutes or more (2005-2009 5-year est.)
Additional Information Contacts
Mahomet Area Chamber of Commerce . . . . (217) 586-3165
    http://www.mahometchamberofcommerce.com

OGDEN (village). Covers a land area of 0.567 square miles and a water area of 0 square miles. Located at 40.11° N. Lat; 87.95° W. Long. Elevation is 669 feet.
Population: 708 (1990); 743 (2000); 706 (2010); 693 (2015 projected); Race: 98.2% White, 0.3% Black, 0.0% Asian, 1.6% Other, 1.0% Hispanic of any race (2010); Density: 1,245.9 persons per square mile (2010); Average household size: 2.63 (2010); Median age: 32.2 (2010); Males per 100 females: 101.7 (2010); Marriage status: 20.8% never married, 66.1% now married, 6.9% widowed, 6.2% divorced (2005-2009 5-year est.); Foreign born: 2.2% (2005-2009 5-year est.); Ancestry (includes multiple ancestries): 41.2% German, 15.1% American, 12.9% English, 11.6% Irish, 2.4% European (2005-2009 5-year est.).

Economy: Single-family building permits issued: 0 (2010); Multi-family building permits issued: 0 (2010); Employment by occupation: 8.6% management, 12.7% professional, 19.8% services, 35.7% sales, 0.0% farming, 13.1% construction, 10.2% production (2005-2009 5-year est.).
Income: Per capita income: $26,416 (2010); Median household income: $58,667 (2010); Average household income: $68,302 (2010); Percent of households with income of $100,000 or more: 15.3% (2010); Poverty rate: 3.9% (2005-2009 5-year est.).
Taxes: Total city taxes per capita: $94 (2007); City property taxes per capita: $91 (2007).
Education: Percent of population age 25 and over with: High school diploma (including GED) or higher: 91.4% (2010); Bachelor's degree or higher: 19.4% (2010); Master's degree or higher: 3.1% (2010).

School District(s)
Prairieview-Ogden CCSD 197 (KG-08)
    2009-10 Enrollment: 253 . . . . (217) 583-3300
Housing: Homeownership rate: 89.2% (2010); Median home value: $123,250 (2010); Median contract rent: $517 per month (2005-2009 5-year est.); Median year structure built: 1969 (2005-2009 5-year est.).
Safety: Violent crime rate: 0.0 per 10,000 population; Property crime rate: 0.0 per 10,000 population (2010).
Newspapers: Ogden Leader (Community news; Circulation 8,000)
Transportation: Commute to work: 93.9% car, 0.0% public transportation, 4.4% walk, 1.1% work from home (2005-2009 5-year est.); Travel time to work: 24.8% less than 15 minutes, 53.5% 15 to 30 minutes, 19.1% 30 to 45 minutes, 0.9% 45 to 60 minutes, 1.7% 60 minutes or more (2005-2009 5-year est.)

PENFIELD (unincorporated postal area, zip code 61862). Covers a land area of 36.908 square miles and a water area of 0 square miles. Located at 40.29° N. Lat; 87.95° W. Long. Elevation is 712 feet.
Population: 511 (2000); Race: 96.5% White, 0.7% Black, 0.0% Asian, 2.8% Other, 0.9% Hispanic of any race (2000); Density: 13.8 persons per square mile (2000); Age: 33.2% under 18, 10.4% over 64 (2000); Marriage status: 16.8% never married, 74.6% now married, 2.3% widowed, 6.4% divorced (2000); Foreign born: 0.4% (2000); Ancestry (includes multiple ancestries): 49.8% German, 21.4% Irish, 9.7% English, 5.5% Swedish (2000).
Economy: Employment by occupation: 10.5% management, 13.9% professional, 22.4% services, 18.4% sales, 1.7% farming, 10.9% construction, 22.1% production (2000).
Income: Per capita income: $18,170 (2000); Median household income: $47,000 (2000); Poverty rate: 3.9% (2000).
Education: Percent of population age 25 and over with: High school diploma (including GED) or higher: 92.5% (2000); Bachelor's degree or higher: 14.6% (2000).
Housing: Homeownership rate: 79.6% (2000); Median home value: $75,600 (2000); Median contract rent: $278 per month (2000); Median year structure built: 1944 (2000).
Transportation: Commute to work: 86.7% car, 0.7% public transportation, 1.7% walk, 10.9% work from home (2000); Travel time to work: 18.3% less than 15 minutes, 23.3% 15 to 30 minutes, 43.9% 30 to 45 minutes, 10.3% 45 to 60 minutes, 4.2% 60 minutes or more (2000)

PESOTUM (village). Covers a land area of 0.555 square miles and a water area of 0.005 square miles. Located at 39.91° N. Lat; 88.27° W. Long. Elevation is 715 feet.
History: Pesotum developed as a grain storage and shipping center.
Population: 558 (1990); 521 (2000); 505 (2010); 500 (2015 projected); Race: 99.2% White, 0.0% Black, 0.4% Asian, 0.4% Other, 0.6% Hispanic of any race (2010); Density: 909.2 persons per square mile (2010); Average household size: 2.43 (2010); Median age: 40.9 (2010); Males per 100 females: 110.4 (2010); Marriage status: 14.3% never married, 68.1% now married, 11.1% widowed, 6.6% divorced (2005-2009 5-year est.); Foreign born: 0.0% (2005-2009 5-year est.); Ancestry (includes multiple ancestries): 41.6% German, 15.7% Irish, 15.0% English, 13.3% American, 5.4% Dutch (2005-2009 5-year est.).
Economy: Single-family building permits issued: 0 (2010); Multi-family building permits issued: 0 (2010); Employment by occupation: 7.7% management, 14.2% professional, 10.2% services, 35.0% sales, 3.6% farming, 17.2% construction, 12.0% production (2005-2009 5-year est.).
Income: Per capita income: $27,620 (2010); Median household income: $63,281 (2010); Average household income: $67,188 (2010); Percent of households with income of $100,000 or more: 16.8% (2010); Poverty rate: 2.4% (2005-2009 5-year est.).

Taxes: Total city taxes per capita: $141 (2007); City property taxes per capita: $52 (2007).
Education: Percent of population age 25 and over with: High school diploma (including GED) or higher: 95.8% (2010); Bachelor's degree or higher: 20.3% (2010); Master's degree or higher: 5.1% (2010).
Housing: Homeownership rate: 91.3% (2010); Median home value: $114,458 (2010); Median contract rent: n/a per month (2005-2009 5-year est.); Median year structure built: 1961 (2005-2009 5-year est.).
Transportation: Commute to work: 97.8% car, 0.0% public transportation, 0.0% walk, 1.1% work from home (2005-2009 5-year est.); Travel time to work: 15.9% less than 15 minutes, 58.7% 15 to 30 minutes, 18.1% 30 to 45 minutes, 3.3% 45 to 60 minutes, 4.1% 60 minutes or more (2005-2009 5-year est.)

PHILO (village). Covers a land area of 0.762 square miles and a water area of 0 square miles. Located at 40.00° N. Lat; 88.15° W. Long. Elevation is 735 feet.
Population: 1,073 (1990); 1,314 (2000); 1,473 (2010); 1,545 (2015 projected); Race: 98.8% White, 0.3% Black, 0.0% Asian, 0.9% Other, 0.3% Hispanic of any race (2010); Density: 1,932.0 persons per square mile (2010); Average household size: 2.63 (2010); Median age: 34.6 (2010); Males per 100 females: 104.0 (2010); Marriage status: 23.6% never married, 66.3% now married, 3.4% widowed, 6.7% divorced (2005-2009 5-year est.); Foreign born: 1.3% (2005-2009 5-year est.); Ancestry (includes multiple ancestries): 39.3% German, 18.3% Irish, 12.3% American, 9.9% English, 4.2% French (2005-2009 5-year est.).
Economy: Single-family building permits issued: 0 (2010); Multi-family building permits issued: 0 (2010); Employment by occupation: 13.4% management, 22.9% professional, 11.2% services, 26.1% sales, 0.0% farming, 14.3% construction, 12.1% production (2005-2009 5-year est.).
Income: Per capita income: $29,038 (2010); Median household income: $68,082 (2010); Average household income: $76,353 (2010); Percent of households with income of $100,000 or more: 20.4% (2010); Poverty rate: 5.2% (2005-2009 5-year est.).
Taxes: Total city taxes per capita: $95 (2007); City property taxes per capita: $80 (2007).
Education: Percent of population age 25 and over with: High school diploma (including GED) or higher: 92.9% (2010); Bachelor's degree or higher: 28.3% (2010); Master's degree or higher: 13.4% (2010).

School District(s)
Tolono CUSD 7 (PK-12)
    2009-10 Enrollment: 1,660 . . . . (217) 485-6510
Housing: Homeownership rate: 88.8% (2010); Median home value: $146,514 (2010); Median contract rent: $447 per month (2005-2009 5-year est.); Median year structure built: 1967 (2005-2009 5-year est.).
Transportation: Commute to work: 96.7% car, 0.0% public transportation, 1.4% walk, 1.5% work from home (2005-2009 5-year est.); Travel time to work: 13.8% less than 15 minutes, 62.3% 15 to 30 minutes, 20.3% 30 to 45 minutes, 1.4% 45 to 60 minutes, 2.2% 60 minutes or more (2005-2009 5-year est.)

RANTOUL (village). Covers a land area of 7.237 square miles and a water area of 0.113 square miles. Located at 40.30° N. Lat; 88.15° W. Long. Elevation is 745 feet.
History: Rantoul was named for Robert Rantoul who was a director of the Illinois Central Railroad.
Population: 17,218 (1990); 12,857 (2000); 11,472 (2010); 10,934 (2015 projected); Race: 74.6% White, 18.3% Black, 1.6% Asian, 5.5% Other, 3.3% Hispanic of any race (2010); Density: 1,585.2 persons per square mile (2010); Average household size: 2.33 (2010); Median age: 31.4 (2010); Males per 100 females: 94.6 (2010); Marriage status: 28.3% never married, 51.0% now married, 7.7% widowed, 13.0% divorced (2005-2009 5-year est.); Foreign born: 4.3% (2005-2009 5-year est.); Ancestry (includes multiple ancestries): 26.3% German, 12.2% Irish, 10.6% American, 8.7% English, 3.7% Italian (2005-2009 5-year est.).
Economy: Single-family building permits issued: 1 (2010); Multi-family building permits issued: 0 (2010); Employment by occupation: 6.8% management, 16.2% professional, 18.6% services, 31.6% sales, 0.8% farming, 7.5% construction, 18.3% production (2005-2009 5-year est.).
Income: Per capita income: $21,268 (2010); Median household income: $41,590 (2010); Average household income: $49,602 (2010); Percent of households with income of $100,000 or more: 7.8% (2010); Poverty rate: 19.9% (2005-2009 5-year est.).
Taxes: Total city taxes per capita: $460 (2007); City property taxes per capita: $215 (2007).

Education: Percent of population age 25 and over with: High school diploma (including GED) or higher: 89.4% (2010); Bachelor's degree or higher: 18.2% (2010); Master's degree or higher: 6.4% (2010).

School District(s)

Rantoul City SD 137 (PK-08)
 2009-10 Enrollment: 1,598 . . . . (217) 893-4171
Rantoul Township HSD 193 (09-12)
 2009-10 Enrollment: 772 . . . . (217) 892-2151
Rural Champaign Co Spec Ed Coop (PK-12)
 2009-10 Enrollment: n/a . . . . (217) 892-8877

Housing: Homeownership rate: 50.5% (2010); Median home value: $92,843 (2010); Median contract rent: $453 per month (2005-2009 5-year est.); Median year structure built: 1963 (2005-2009 5-year est.).
Safety: Violent crime rate: 107.0 per 10,000 population; Property crime rate: 263.8 per 10,000 population (2010).
Newspapers: Rantoul Press (Community news; Circulation 11,000)
Transportation: Commute to work: 94.7% car, 0.2% public transportation, 1.4% walk, 1.9% work from home (2005-2009 5-year est.); Travel time to work: 45.1% less than 15 minutes, 33.2% 15 to 30 minutes, 15.9% 30 to 45 minutes, 3.3% 45 to 60 minutes, 2.5% 60 minutes or more (2005-2009 5-year est.); Amtrak: train service available.

Additional Information Contacts
Rantoul Area Chamber of Commerce . . . . (217) 893-3323
 http://www.rantoulchamber.com
Village of Rantoul . . . . (217) 893-1661
 http://www.village.rantoul.il.us

ROYAL (village). Covers a land area of 0.225 square miles and a water area of 0 square miles. Located at 40.19° N. Lat; 87.97° W. Long. Elevation is 682 feet.
Population: 290 (1990); 279 (2000); 267 (2010); 262 (2015 projected); Race: 95.9% White, 0.4% Black, 1.9% Asian, 1.9% Other, 0.0% Hispanic of any race (2010); Density: 1,186.6 persons per square mile (2010); Average household size: 2.36 (2010); Median age: 41.2 (2010); Males per 100 females: 93.5 (2010); Marriage status: 21.4% never married, 62.9% now married, 9.4% widowed, 6.3% divorced (2005-2009 5-year est.); Foreign born: 0.0% (2005-2009 5-year est.); Ancestry (includes multiple ancestries): 45.9% German, 29.3% American, 14.9% English, 12.2% Irish, 5.5% Swedish (2005-2009 5-year est.).
Economy: Single-family building permits issued: 0 (2010); Multi-family building permits issued: 0 (2010); Employment by occupation: 28.0% management, 2.2% professional, 2.2% services, 31.2% sales, 3.2% farming, 4.3% construction, 29.0% production (2005-2009 5-year est.).
Income: Per capita income: $27,547 (2010); Median household income: $53,365 (2010); Average household income: $66,040 (2010); Percent of households with income of $100,000 or more: 12.4% (2010); Poverty rate: 0.0% (2005-2009 5-year est.).
Taxes: Total city taxes per capita: $37 (2007); City property taxes per capita: $29 (2007).
Education: Percent of population age 25 and over with: High school diploma (including GED) or higher: 88.5% (2010); Bachelor's degree or higher: 20.8% (2010); Master's degree or higher: 7.7% (2010).

School District(s)

Prairieview-Ogden CCSD 197 (KG-08)
 2009-10 Enrollment: 253 . . . . (217) 583-3300

Housing: Homeownership rate: 84.1% (2010); Median home value: $137,500 (2010); Median contract rent: $425 per month (2005-2009 5-year est.); Median year structure built: 1958 (2005-2009 5-year est.).
Transportation: Commute to work: 81.7% car, 0.0% public transportation, 0.0% walk, 18.3% work from home (2005-2009 5-year est.); Travel time to work: 36.8% less than 15 minutes, 22.4% 15 to 30 minutes, 40.8% 30 to 45 minutes, 0.0% 45 to 60 minutes, 0.0% 60 minutes or more (2005-2009 5-year est.)

SADORUS (village). Covers a land area of 0.846 square miles and a water area of 0 square miles. Located at 39.96° N. Lat; 88.34° W. Long. Elevation is 692 feet.
Population: 469 (1990); 426 (2000); 408 (2010); 403 (2015 projected); Race: 97.1% White, 0.0% Black, 0.2% Asian, 2.7% Other, 0.2% Hispanic of any race (2010); Density: 482.5 persons per square mile (2010); Average household size: 2.53 (2010); Median age: 37.4 (2010); Males per 100 females: 115.9 (2010); Marriage status: 20.0% never married, 70.0% now married, 4.8% widowed, 5.2% divorced (2005-2009 5-year est.); Foreign born: 0.0% (2005-2009 5-year est.); Ancestry (includes multiple

ancestries): 40.0% American, 31.0% German, 13.9% English, 12.8% Irish, 2.7% Dutch (2005-2009 5-year est.).
Economy: Single-family building permits issued: 0 (2010); Multi-family building permits issued: 0 (2010); Employment by occupation: 4.3% management, 14.7% professional, 25.4% services, 15.1% sales, 1.8% farming, 8.6% construction, 30.1% production (2005-2009 5-year est.).
Income: Per capita income: $30,096 (2010); Median household income: $65,938 (2010); Average household income: $77,360 (2010); Percent of households with income of $100,000 or more: 21.7% (2010); Poverty rate: 8.6% (2005-2009 5-year est.).
Taxes: Total city taxes per capita: $133 (2007); City property taxes per capita: $75 (2007).
Education: Percent of population age 25 and over with: High school diploma (including GED) or higher: 90.8% (2010); Bachelor's degree or higher: 17.7% (2010); Master's degree or higher: 7.4% (2010).
Housing: Homeownership rate: 82.6% (2010); Median home value: $106,548 (2010); Median contract rent: $475 per month (2005-2009 5-year est.); Median year structure built: 1971 (2005-2009 5-year est.).
Transportation: Commute to work: 89.1% car, 0.0% public transportation, 8.2% walk, 1.9% work from home (2005-2009 5-year est.); Travel time to work: 28.6% less than 15 minutes, 46.6% 15 to 30 minutes, 19.5% 30 to 45 minutes, 3.8% 45 to 60 minutes, 1.5% 60 minutes or more (2005-2009 5-year est.)

SAINT JOSEPH (village). Covers a land area of 1.132 square miles and a water area of 0.004 square miles. Located at 40.11° N. Lat; 88.03° W. Long. Elevation is 673 feet.
Population: 2,214 (1990); 2,912 (2000); 3,223 (2010); 3,444 (2015 projected); Race: 98.5% White, 0.2% Black, 0.2% Asian, 1.1% Other, 1.5% Hispanic of any race (2010); Density: 2,847.1 persons per square mile (2010); Average household size: 2.50 (2010); Median age: 33.9 (2010); Males per 100 females: 96.6 (2010); Marriage status: 21.1% never married, 66.4% now married, 5.8% widowed, 6.7% divorced (2005-2009 5-year est.); Foreign born: 3.8% (2005-2009 5-year est.); Ancestry (includes multiple ancestries): 42.6% German, 17.7% Irish, 11.0% English, 9.8% American, 3.9% Dutch (2005-2009 5-year est.).
Economy: Single-family building permits issued: 2 (2010); Multi-family building permits issued: 0 (2010); Employment by occupation: 15.8% management, 18.1% professional, 12.1% services, 24.3% sales, 0.0% farming, 12.4% construction, 17.3% production (2005-2009 5-year est.).
Income: Per capita income: $28,095 (2010); Median household income: $63,998 (2010); Average household income: $69,631 (2010); Percent of households with income of $100,000 or more: 17.1% (2010); Poverty rate: 12.6% (2005-2009 5-year est.).
Taxes: Total city taxes per capita: $113 (2007); City property taxes per capita: $67 (2007).
Education: Percent of population age 25 and over with: High school diploma (including GED) or higher: 93.2% (2010); Bachelor's degree or higher: 30.3% (2010); Master's degree or higher: 12.7% (2010).

School District(s)

St Joseph CCSD 169 (PK-08)
 2009-10 Enrollment: 908 . . . . (217) 469-2291
St Joseph Ogden CHSD 305 (09-12)
 2009-10 Enrollment: 457 . . . . (217) 469-2586

Housing: Homeownership rate: 82.0% (2010); Median home value: $147,500 (2010); Median contract rent: $398 per month (2005-2009 5-year est.); Median year structure built: 1990 (2005-2009 5-year est.).
Transportation: Commute to work: 86.1% car, 7.3% public transportation, 3.4% walk, 1.7% work from home (2005-2009 5-year est.); Travel time to work: 21.2% less than 15 minutes, 54.7% 15 to 30 minutes, 16.7% 30 to 45 minutes, 3.4% 45 to 60 minutes, 4.0% 60 minutes or more (2005-2009 5-year est.)

SAVOY (village). Covers a land area of 1.543 square miles and a water area of 0.016 square miles. Located at 40.06° N. Lat; 88.25° W. Long. Elevation is 735 feet.
Population: 3,097 (1990); 4,476 (2000); 4,965 (2010); 5,239 (2015 projected); Race: 81.2% White, 3.8% Black, 11.2% Asian, 3.9% Other, 2.7% Hispanic of any race (2010); Density: 3,216.7 persons per square mile (2010); Average household size: 2.20 (2010); Median age: 36.0 (2010); Males per 100 females: 88.6 (2010); Marriage status: 34.0% never married, 53.1% now married, 6.6% widowed, 6.2% divorced (2005-2009 5-year est.); Foreign born: 13.0% (2005-2009 5-year est.); Ancestry (includes multiple ancestries): 24.2% German, 12.6% Irish, 8.3% English, 7.3% American, 5.2% European (2005-2009 5-year est.).

Economy: Single-family building permits issued: 41 (2010); Multi-family building permits issued: 0 (2010); Employment by occupation: 15.8% management, 46.3% professional, 11.7% services, 13.9% sales, 0.0% farming, 6.1% construction, 6.2% production (2005-2009 5-year est.).
Income: Per capita income: $40,655 (2010); Median household income: $67,567 (2010); Average household income: $90,985 (2010); Percent of households with income of $100,000 or more: 29.5% (2010); Poverty rate: 13.1% (2005-2009 5-year est.).
Taxes: Total city taxes per capita: $252 (2007); City property taxes per capita: $176 (2007).
Education: Percent of population age 25 and over with: High school diploma (including GED) or higher: 96.6% (2010); Bachelor's degree or higher: 62.7% (2010); Master's degree or higher: 35.4% (2010).
Housing: Homeownership rate: 57.2% (2010); Median home value: $207,474 (2010); Median contract rent: $708 per month (2005-2009 5-year est.); Median year structure built: 1994 (2005-2009 5-year est.).
Transportation: Commute to work: 88.8% car, 3.9% public transportation, 0.8% walk, 4.2% work from home (2005-2009 5-year est.); Travel time to work: 52.5% less than 15 minutes, 39.8% 15 to 30 minutes, 4.7% 30 to 45 minutes, 1.0% 45 to 60 minutes, 1.9% 60 minutes or more (2005-2009 5-year est.).
Airports: University of Illinois-Willard (primary service)

SEYMOUR (unincorporated postal area, zip code 61875). Covers a land area of 30.015 square miles and a water area of 0 square miles. Located at 40.10° N. Lat; 88.42° W. Long. Elevation is 699 feet.
Population: 795 (2000); Race: 100.0% White, 0.0% Black, 0.0% Asian, 0.0% Other, 0.0% Hispanic of any race (2000); Density: 26.5 persons per square mile (2000); Age: 30.3% under 18, 6.7% over 64 (2000); Marriage status: 24.0% never married, 68.7% now married, 1.5% widowed, 5.8% divorced (2000); Foreign born: 1.1% (2000); Ancestry (includes multiple ancestries): 31.6% German, 31.2% Irish, 14.1% English, 6.6% Scottish, 5.2% American (2000).
Economy: Employment by occupation: 20.8% management, 13.7% professional, 16.5% services, 20.6% sales, 0.0% farming, 7.3% construction, 21.1% production (2000).
Income: Per capita income: $29,477 (2000); Median household income: $68,750 (2000); Poverty rate: 1.2% (2000).
Education: Percent of population age 25 and over with: High school diploma (including GED) or higher: 98.9% (2000); Bachelor's degree or higher: 30.0% (2000).
Housing: Homeownership rate: 81.7% (2000); Median home value: $118,800 (2000); Median contract rent: $298 per month (2000); Median year structure built: 1961 (2000).
Transportation: Commute to work: 88.1% car, 3.8% public transportation, 3.1% walk, 5.0% work from home (2000); Travel time to work: 17.8% less than 15 minutes, 50.6% 15 to 30 minutes, 17.8% 30 to 45 minutes, 8.8% 45 to 60 minutes, 5.0% 60 minutes or more (2000)

SIDNEY (village). Covers a land area of 0.532 square miles and a water area of 0 square miles. Located at 40.02° N. Lat; 88.07° W. Long. Elevation is 656 feet.
Population: 1,027 (1990); 1,062 (2000); 1,049 (2010); 1,043 (2015 projected); Race: 96.6% White, 0.4% Black, 0.6% Asian, 2.5% Other, 0.3% Hispanic of any race (2010); Density: 1,971.3 persons per square mile (2010); Average household size: 2.45 (2010); Median age: 34.4 (2010); Males per 100 females: 98.7 (2010); Marriage status: 18.5% never married, 67.4% now married, 5.4% widowed, 8.8% divorced (2005-2009 5-year est.); Foreign born: 2.3% (2005-2009 5-year est.); Ancestry (includes multiple ancestries): 33.8% German, 22.6% American, 19.6% Irish, 13.5% English, 4.6% Dutch (2005-2009 5-year est.).
Economy: Single-family building permits issued: 0 (2010); Multi-family building permits issued: 0 (2010); Employment by occupation: 17.4% management, 13.1% professional, 15.9% services, 32.0% sales, 1.3% farming, 11.2% construction, 9.0% production (2005-2009 5-year est.).
Income: Per capita income: $27,906 (2010); Median household income: $61,250 (2010); Average household income: $68,359 (2010); Percent of households with income of $100,000 or more: 17.3% (2010); Poverty rate: 9.3% (2005-2009 5-year est.).
Taxes: Total city taxes per capita: $72 (2007); City property taxes per capita: $64 (2007).
Education: Percent of population age 25 and over with: High school diploma (including GED) or higher: 88.3% (2010); Bachelor's degree or higher: 22.5% (2010); Master's degree or higher: 9.8% (2010).

Housing: Homeownership rate: 79.7% (2010); Median home value: $129,833 (2010); Median contract rent: $495 per month (2005-2009 5-year est.); Median year structure built: 1964 (2005-2009 5-year est.).
Transportation: Commute to work: 96.6% car, 0.0% public transportation, 1.3% walk, 1.1% work from home (2005-2009 5-year est.); Travel time to work: 19.0% less than 15 minutes, 53.6% 15 to 30 minutes, 17.9% 30 to 45 minutes, 5.8% 45 to 60 minutes, 3.8% 60 minutes or more (2005-2009 5-year est.)

THOMASBORO (village). Covers a land area of 1.035 square miles and a water area of 0 square miles. Located at 40.24° N. Lat; 88.18° W. Long. Elevation is 732 feet.
Population: 1,250 (1990); 1,233 (2000); 1,139 (2010); 1,100 (2015 projected); Race: 95.5% White, 0.7% Black, 0.8% Asian, 3.0% Other, 1.5% Hispanic of any race (2010); Density: 1,100.3 persons per square mile (2010); Average household size: 2.40 (2010); Median age: 33.8 (2010); Males per 100 females: 98.8 (2010); Marriage status: 23.5% never married, 59.8% now married, 6.4% widowed, 10.3% divorced (2005-2009 5-year est.); Foreign born: 1.3% (2005-2009 5-year est.); Ancestry (includes multiple ancestries): 39.0% German, 16.4% American, 12.5% Irish, 8.8% English, 2.6% Italian (2005-2009 5-year est.).
Economy: Single-family building permits issued: 2 (2010); Multi-family building permits issued: 0 (2010); Employment by occupation: 7.4% management, 8.9% professional, 14.6% services, 31.7% sales, 2.1% farming, 9.2% construction, 26.1% production (2005-2009 5-year est.).
Income: Per capita income: $21,020 (2010); Median household income: $46,972 (2010); Average household income: $50,955 (2010); Percent of households with income of $100,000 or more: 6.5% (2010); Poverty rate: 4.1% (2005-2009 5-year est.).
Taxes: Total city taxes per capita: $77 (2007); City property taxes per capita: $63 (2007).
Education: Percent of population age 25 and over with: High school diploma (including GED) or higher: 82.3% (2010); Bachelor's degree or higher: 10.4% (2010); Master's degree or higher: 3.3% (2010).

School District(s)
Prairieview-Ogden CCSD 197 (KG-08)
   2009-10 Enrollment: 253 . . . . (217) 583-3300
Thomasboro CCSD 130 (PK-08)
   2009-10 Enrollment: 206 . . . . (217) 643-3275
Housing: Homeownership rate: 73.2% (2010); Median home value: $97,536 (2010); Median contract rent: $406 per month (2005-2009 5-year est.); Median year structure built: 1974 (2005-2009 5-year est.).
Transportation: Commute to work: 90.4% car, 0.0% public transportation, 3.9% walk, 0.6% work from home (2005-2009 5-year est.); Travel time to work: 27.0% less than 15 minutes, 59.1% 15 to 30 minutes, 8.4% 30 to 45 minutes, 3.6% 45 to 60 minutes, 1.9% 60 minutes or more (2005-2009 5-year est.)

TOLONO (village). Covers a land area of 1.869 square miles and a water area of 0 square miles. Located at 39.98° N. Lat; 88.26° W. Long. Elevation is 735 feet.
History: The name of Tolono was made up by J.B. Calhoun of the Illinois Central Railroad.
Population: 2,619 (1990); 2,700 (2000); 2,824 (2010); 2,887 (2015 projected); Race: 96.0% White, 1.2% Black, 0.5% Asian, 2.4% Other, 1.1% Hispanic of any race (2010); Density: 1,510.8 persons per square mile (2010); Average household size: 2.32 (2010); Median age: 35.5 (2010); Males per 100 females: 104.9 (2010); Marriage status: 21.5% never married, 59.4% now married, 4.8% widowed, 14.3% divorced (2005-2009 5-year est.); Foreign born: 0.5% (2005-2009 5-year est.); Ancestry (includes multiple ancestries): 39.0% German, 16.9% Irish, 14.5% American, 9.8% English, 8.4% European (2005-2009 5-year est.).
Economy: Single-family building permits issued: 3 (2010); Multi-family building permits issued: 0 (2010); Employment by occupation: 10.5% management, 16.7% professional, 22.5% services, 25.9% sales, 0.0% farming, 12.8% construction, 11.6% production (2005-2009 5-year est.).
Income: Per capita income: $27,068 (2010); Median household income: $56,796 (2010); Average household income: $62,698 (2010); Percent of households with income of $100,000 or more: 14.8% (2010); Poverty rate: 6.7% (2005-2009 5-year est.).
Taxes: Total city taxes per capita: $80 (2007); City property taxes per capita: $59 (2007).
Education: Percent of population age 25 and over with: High school diploma (including GED) or higher: 91.5% (2010); Bachelor's degree or higher: 22.4% (2010); Master's degree or higher: 7.0% (2010).

School District(s)

Tolono CUSD 7 (PK-12)
    2009-10 Enrollment: 1,660 . . . . (217) 485-6510
Housing: Homeownership rate: 71.6% (2010); Median home value:
$125,000 (2010); Median contract rent: $481 per month (2005-2009 5-year
est.); Median year structure built: 1980 (2005-2009 5-year est.).
Transportation: Commute to work: 94.9% car, 0.0% public transportation,
2.2% walk, 2.9% work from home (2005-2009 5-year est.); Travel time to
work: 19.9% less than 15 minutes, 63.3% 15 to 30 minutes, 10.4% 30 to 45
minutes, 4.5% 45 to 60 minutes, 2.0% 60 minutes or more (2005-2009
5-year est.)

URBANA (city). County seat. Covers a land area of 10.494 square
miles and a water area of 0.012 square miles. Located at 40.11° N. Lat;
88.20° W. Long. Elevation is 728 feet.
History: Urbana was settled in 1822 by Willard Tompkins. Although
designated as the county seat in 1833, the loss of the railroad to nearby
Champaign in 1854 slowed Urbana's development. When the Illinois
Industrial College, later to become the University of Illinois, was sited
between Urbana and Champaign in 1867, the character of Urbana was
determined.
Population: 37,214 (1990); 36,395 (2000); 39,263 (2010); 40,118 (2015
projected); Race: 64.4% White, 14.2% Black, 15.7% Asian, 5.7% Other,
4.9% Hispanic of any race (2010); Density: 3,741.6 persons per square
mile (2010); Average household size: 2.08 (2010); Median age: 25.3
(2010); Males per 100 females: 117.4 (2010); Marriage status: 62.2%
never married, 28.8% now married, 3.6% widowed, 5.4% divorced
(2005-2009 5-year est.); Foreign born: 15.6% (2005-2009 5-year est.);
Ancestry (includes multiple ancestries): 19.0% German, 10.4% Irish, 8.9%
American, 8.1% English, 4.7% Polish (2005-2009 5-year est.).
Economy: Unemployment rate: 9.9% (August 2011); Total civilian labor
force: 19,501 (August 2011); Single-family building permits issued: 28
(2010); Multi-family building permits issued: 2 (2010); Employment by
occupation: 8.0% management, 40.9% professional, 19.2% services,
22.0% sales, 0.3% farming, 2.7% construction, 6.9% production
(2005-2009 5-year est.).
Income: Per capita income: $19,232 (2010); Median household income:
$33,124 (2010); Average household income: $47,245 (2010); Percent of
households with income of $100,000 or more: 9.3% (2010); Poverty rate:
30.4% (2005-2009 5-year est.).
Taxes: Total city taxes per capita: $394 (2007); City property taxes per
capita: $166 (2007).
Education: Percent of population age 25 and over with: High school
diploma (including GED) or higher: 92.7% (2010); Bachelor's degree or
higher: 56.9% (2010); Master's degree or higher: 34.6% (2010).

School District(s)

Champaign/Ford Roe (05-12)
    2009-10 Enrollment: n/a . . . . (217) 893-3219
Urbana SD 116 (PK-12)
    2009-10 Enrollment: 4,124 . . . . (217) 384-3636

Vocational/Technical School(s)

Concept College of Cosmetology (Private, For-profit)
    Fall 2009 Enrollment: 55 . . . . (217) 344-7550
    2010-11 Tuition: $13,000
Housing: Homeownership rate: 38.6% (2010); Median home value:
$128,807 (2010); Median contract rent: $611 per month (2005-2009 5-year
est.); Median year structure built: 1972 (2005-2009 5-year est.).
Hospitals: Carle Foundation Hospital (305 beds); Provena Covenant
Medical Center (268 beds)
Safety: Violent crime rate: 73.4 per 10,000 population; Property crime rate:
315.0 per 10,000 population (2010).
Transportation: Commute to work: 60.0% car, 12.2% public
transportation, 18.9% walk, 3.4% work from home (2005-2009 5-year est.);
Travel time to work: 55.6% less than 15 minutes, 35.9% 15 to 30 minutes,
5.2% 30 to 45 minutes, 1.1% 45 to 60 minutes, 2.2% 60 minutes or more
(2005-2009 5-year est.); Amtrak: train service available.
Airports: Frasca Field (general aviation)
Additional Information Contacts
City of Urbana . . . . (217) 384-2366
    http://urbanaillinois.us

Christian County

Located in central Illinois; bounded on the north by the Sangamon River;
drained by the South Fork of the Sangamon River. Covers a land area of

709.06 square miles, a water area of 6.65 square miles, and is located in
the Central Time Zone at 39.52° N. Lat., 89.26° W. Long. The county was
founded in 1839. County seat is Taylorville.

Christian County is part of the Taylorville, IL Micropolitan Statistical Area.
The entire metro area includes: Christian County, IL

Weather Station: Morrisonville   Elevation: 629 feet

	Jan	Feb	Mar	Apr	May	Jun	Jul	Aug	Sep	Oct	Nov	Dec
High	35	39	51	64	74	83	86	85	80	67	52	38
Low	18	22	31	42	52	62	65	63	54	42	33	22
Precip	2.0	1.9	2.7	3.4	4.4	3.5	3.5	3.0	3.2	3.0	3.6	2.6
Snow	6.1	5.0	3.0	0.3	0.0	0.0	0.0	0.0	0.0	0.1	0.8	4.9

High and Low temperatures in degrees Fahrenheit; Precipitation and Snow in inches

Weather Station: Pana 3 E   Elevation: 700 feet

	Jan	Feb	Mar	Apr	May	Jun	Jul	Aug	Sep	Oct	Nov	Dec
High	37	42	53	65	75	84	88	86	80	67	54	40
Low	20	24	33	43	53	62	66	63	55	44	35	23
Precip	2.4	2.1	3.1	4.0	4.5	4.2	3.9	3.0	3.3	3.6	4.0	3.0
Snow	5.6	4.4	3.4	0.7	0.0	0.0	0.0	0.0	0.0	0.1	1.2	4.8

High and Low temperatures in degrees Fahrenheit; Precipitation and Snow in inches

Population: 34,418 (1990); 35,372 (2000); 34,367 (2010); 33,686 (2015
projected); Race: 95.0% White, 2.6% Black, 0.8% Asian, 1.5% Other, 1.3%
Hispanic of any race (2010); Density: 48.5 persons per square mile (2010);
Average household size: 2.37 (2010); Median age: 39.9 (2010); Males per
100 females: 101.8 (2010).
Religion: Five largest groups: 16.5% Catholic Church, 9.0% The United
Methodist Church, 5.0% Christian Churches and Churches of Christ, 4.1%
Lutheran Church—Missouri Synod, 2.9% American Baptist Churches in the
USA (2000).
Economy: Unemployment rate: 8.9% (August 2011); Total civilian labor
force: 18,682 (August 2011); Leading industries: 19.6% health care and
social assistance; 16.2% retail trade; 12.5% manufacturing (2009); Farms:
910 totaling 449,512 acres (2007); Companies that employ 500 or more
persons: 1 (2009); Companies that employ 100 to 499 persons: 11 (2009);
Companies that employ less than 100 persons: 753 (2009); Black-owned
businesses: n/a (2007); Hispanic-owned businesses: n/a (2007);
Asian-owned businesses: n/a (2007); Women-owned businesses: 905
(2007); Retail sales per capita: $12,172 (2010). Single-family building
permits issued: 35 (2010); Multi-family building permits issued: 0 (2010).
Income: Per capita income: $21,291 (2010); Median household income:
$41,683 (2010); Average household income: $51,394 (2010); Percent of
households with income of $100,000 or more: 9.0% (2010); Poverty rate:
14.7% (2009); Bankruptcy rate: 4.96% (2010).
Taxes: Total county taxes per capita: $83 (2007); County property taxes
per capita: $82 (2007).
Education: Percent of population age 25 and over with: High school
diploma (including GED) or higher: 82.8% (2010); Bachelor's degree or
higher: 12.1% (2010); Master's degree or higher: 3.5% (2010).
Housing: Homeownership rate: 74.0% (2010); Median home value:
$77,014 (2010); Median contract rent: $379 per month (2005-2009 5-year
est.); Median year structure built: 1957 (2005-2009 5-year est.)
Health: Birth rate: 116.5 per 10,000 population (2009); Death rate: 117.7
per 10,000 population (2009); Age-adjusted cancer mortality rate: 252.4
deaths per 100,000 population (2007); Number of physicians: 7.0 per
10,000 population (2008); Hospital beds: 20.3 per 10,000 population
(2007); Hospital admissions: 773.0 per 10,000 population (2007).
Elections: 2008 Presidential election results: 45.8% Obama, 52.1%
McCain, 0.9% Nader
Additional Information Contacts
Christian County Government . . . . (217) 824-4969
    http://christiancountyil.com/contact.htm
City of Taylorville . . . . (217) 824-2101
    http://www.taylorville.net
Pana Chamber of Commerce . . . . (217) 562-4240
    http://www.panachamber.com
The Greater Taylorville Chamber of Commerce . . . . (217) 824-4919
    http://www.taylorvillechamber.com

Christian County Communities

ASSUMPTION (city). Covers a land area of 0.880 square miles and a
water area of 0 square miles. Located at 39.52° N. Lat; 89.04° W. Long.
Elevation is 646 feet.
History: Incorporated 1902.

Population: 1,244 (1990); 1,261 (2000); 1,222 (2010); 1,192 (2015 projected); Race: 99.1% White, 0.0% Black, 0.7% Asian, 0.2% Other, 0.1% Hispanic of any race (2010); Density: 1,388.8 persons per square mile (2010); Average household size: 2.30 (2010); Median age: 39.6 (2010); Males per 100 females: 87.4 (2010); Marriage status: 17.0% never married, 59.5% now married, 10.1% widowed, 13.4% divorced (2005-2009 5-year est.); Foreign born: 0.7% (2005-2009 5-year est.); Ancestry (includes multiple ancestries): 17.9% German, 15.8% English, 15.1% Irish, 11.1% American, 4.9% French (2005-2009 5-year est.).
Economy: Single-family building permits issued: 0 (2010); Multi-family building permits issued: 0 (2010); Employment by occupation: 5.9% management, 19.0% professional, 17.1% services, 24.6% sales, 1.1% farming, 10.7% construction, 21.6% production (2005-2009 5-year est.).
Income: Per capita income: $21,531 (2010); Median household income: $41,859 (2010); Average household income: $48,828 (2010); Percent of households with income of $100,000 or more: 6.0% (2010); Poverty rate: 13.4% (2005-2009 5-year est.).
Taxes: Total city taxes per capita: $101 (2007); City property taxes per capita: $98 (2007).
Education: Percent of population age 25 and over with: High school diploma (including GED) or higher: 84.1% (2010); Bachelor's degree or higher: 10.6% (2010); Master's degree or higher: 3.1% (2010).

School District(s)
Central a & M CUD 21 (PK-12)
    2009-10 Enrollment: 930 . . . . (217) 226-4042
Housing: Homeownership rate: 71.9% (2010); Median home value: $58,636 (2010); Median contract rent: $289 per month (2005-2009 5-year est.); Median year structure built: 1943 (2005-2009 5-year est.).
Newspapers: Golden Prairie News (Community news; Circulation 2,200)
Transportation: Commute to work: 91.4% car, 0.0% public transportation, 5.3% walk, 1.8% work from home (2005-2009 5-year est.); Travel time to work: 45.4% less than 15 minutes, 21.9% 15 to 30 minutes, 24.2% 30 to 45 minutes, 4.9% 45 to 60 minutes, 3.6% 60 minutes or more (2005-2009 5-year est.)

BULPITT (village). Covers a land area of 0.071 square miles and a water area of 0 square miles. Located at 39.59° N. Lat; 89.42° W. Long. Elevation is 600 feet.
Population: 206 (1990); 206 (2000); 203 (2010); 202 (2015 projected); Race: 99.5% White, 0.5% Black, 0.0% Asian, 0.0% Other, 0.0% Hispanic of any race (2010); Density: 2,866.5 persons per square mile (2010); Average household size: 2.36 (2010); Median age: 37.9 (2010); Males per 100 females: 97.1 (2010); Marriage status: 9.1% never married, 69.5% now married, 13.7% widowed, 7.6% divorced (2005-2009 5-year est.); Foreign born: 0.7% (2005-2009 5-year est.); Ancestry (includes multiple ancestries): 25.0% Irish, 24.0% German, 15.8% American, 9.2% Polish, 7.9% Italian (2005-2009 5-year est.).
Economy: Single-family building permits issued: 0 (2010); Multi-family building permits issued: 0 (2010); Employment by occupation: 8.2% management, 12.4% professional, 26.8% services, 27.8% sales, 0.0% farming, 17.5% construction, 7.2% production (2005-2009 5-year est.).
Income: Per capita income: $19,529 (2010); Median household income: $40,000 (2010); Average household income: $46,657 (2010); Percent of households with income of $100,000 or more: 5.8% (2010); Poverty rate: 30.1% (2005-2009 5-year est.).
Taxes: Total city taxes per capita: $20 (2007); City property taxes per capita: $15 (2007).
Education: Percent of population age 25 and over with: High school diploma (including GED) or higher: 75.8% (2010); Bachelor's degree or higher: 8.3% (2010); Master's degree or higher: 1.5% (2010).
Housing: Homeownership rate: 81.4% (2010); Median home value: $66,667 (2010); Median contract rent: $368 per month (2005-2009 5-year est.); Median year structure built: 1941 (2005-2009 5-year est.).
Transportation: Commute to work: 100.0% car, 0.0% public transportation, 0.0% walk, 0.0% work from home (2005-2009 5-year est.); Travel time to work: 25.8% less than 15 minutes, 37.1% 15 to 30 minutes, 27.8% 30 to 45 minutes, 7.2% 45 to 60 minutes, 2.1% 60 minutes or more (2005-2009 5-year est.)

EDINBURG (village). Covers a land area of 0.581 square miles and a water area of 0 square miles. Located at 39.65° N. Lat; 89.39° W. Long. Elevation is 591 feet.
Population: 1,074 (1990); 1,135 (2000); 1,087 (2010); 1,057 (2015 projected); Race: 98.3% White, 0.2% Black, 0.5% Asian, 1.1% Other, 0.4% Hispanic of any race (2010); Density: 1,869.9 persons per square mile

(2010); Average household size: 2.32 (2010); Median age: 39.9 (2010); Males per 100 females: 92.4 (2010); Marriage status: 18.9% never married, 54.5% now married, 10.1% widowed, 16.5% divorced (2005-2009 5-year est.); Foreign born: 3.9% (2005-2009 5-year est.); Ancestry (includes multiple ancestries): 17.2% German, 13.6% English, 12.6% American, 10.5% Irish, 3.8% Italian (2005-2009 5-year est.).
Economy: Single-family building permits issued: 1 (2010); Multi-family building permits issued: 0 (2010); Employment by occupation: 5.2% management, 17.1% professional, 13.1% services, 37.3% sales, 0.6% farming, 10.4% construction, 16.4% production (2005-2009 5-year est.).
Income: Per capita income: $24,828 (2010); Median household income: $46,807 (2010); Average household income: $57,090 (2010); Percent of households with income of $100,000 or more: 9.4% (2010); Poverty rate: 10.6% (2005-2009 5-year est.).
Taxes: Total city taxes per capita: $65 (2007); City property taxes per capita: $60 (2007).
Education: Percent of population age 25 and over with: High school diploma (including GED) or higher: 89.9% (2010); Bachelor's degree or higher: 13.3% (2010); Master's degree or higher: 2.5% (2010).

School District(s)
Edinburg CUSD 4 (PK-12)
    2009-10 Enrollment: 329 . . . . (217) 623-5603
Housing: Homeownership rate: 75.9% (2010); Median home value: $90,685 (2010); Median contract rent: $510 per month (2005-2009 5-year est.); Median year structure built: 1956 (2005-2009 5-year est.).
Safety: Violent crime rate: 9.2 per 10,000 population; Property crime rate: 82.9 per 10,000 population (2010).
Newspapers: Herald Star (Community news; Circulation 750)
Transportation: Commute to work: 90.8% car, 1.0% public transportation, 4.1% walk, 2.7% work from home (2005-2009 5-year est.); Travel time to work: 19.2% less than 15 minutes, 28.0% 15 to 30 minutes, 44.8% 30 to 45 minutes, 4.9% 45 to 60 minutes, 3.1% 60 minutes or more (2005-2009 5-year est.)

JEISYVILLE (village). Covers a land area of 0.058 square miles and a water area of 0 square miles. Located at 39.57° N. Lat; 89.40° W. Long. Elevation is 581 feet.
Population: 126 (1990); 128 (2000); 130 (2010); 130 (2015 projected); Race: 98.5% White, 0.0% Black, 0.0% Asian, 1.5% Other, 0.8% Hispanic of any race (2010); Density: 2,240.0 persons per square mile (2010); Average household size: 2.55 (2010); Median age: 38.3 (2010); Males per 100 females: 109.7 (2010); Marriage status: 19.3% never married, 57.9% now married, 10.0% widowed, 12.9% divorced (2005-2009 5-year est.); Foreign born: 0.0% (2005-2009 5-year est.); Ancestry (includes multiple ancestries): 17.8% German, 9.4% American, 7.8% Scotch-Irish, 7.2% English, 4.4% Italian (2005-2009 5-year est.).
Economy: Employment by occupation: 4.5% management, 7.6% professional, 33.3% services, 18.2% sales, 0.0% farming, 22.7% construction, 13.6% production (2005-2009 5-year est.).
Income: Per capita income: $22,563 (2010); Median household income: $55,833 (2010); Average household income: $69,608 (2010); Percent of households with income of $100,000 or more: 13.7% (2010); Poverty rate: 31.7% (2005-2009 5-year est.).
Taxes: Total city taxes per capita: $8 (2007); City property taxes per capita: $8 (2007).
Education: Percent of population age 25 and over with: High school diploma (including GED) or higher: 80.0% (2010); Bachelor's degree or higher: 8.9% (2010); Master's degree or higher: 3.3% (2010).
Housing: Homeownership rate: 84.3% (2010); Median home value: $81,111 (2010); Median contract rent: $460 per month (2005-2009 5-year est.); Median year structure built: before 1940 (2005-2009 5-year est.).
Transportation: Commute to work: 100.0% car, 0.0% public transportation, 0.0% walk, 0.0% work from home (2005-2009 5-year est.); Travel time to work: 9.1% less than 15 minutes, 36.4% 15 to 30 minutes, 13.6% 30 to 45 minutes, 13.6% 45 to 60 minutes, 27.3% 60 minutes or more (2005-2009 5-year est.)

KINCAID (village). Covers a land area of 0.624 square miles and a water area of 0 square miles. Located at 39.58° N. Lat; 89.41° W. Long. Elevation is 600 feet.
History: Incorporated 1915.
Population: 1,381 (1990); 1,441 (2000); 1,416 (2010); 1,393 (2015 projected); Race: 98.2% White, 0.1% Black, 0.0% Asian, 1.7% Other, 0.4% Hispanic of any race (2010); Density: 2,269.8 persons per square mile (2010); Average household size: 2.33 (2010); Median age: 39.0 (2010);

Males per 100 females: 100.9 (2010); Marriage status: 25.3% never married, 52.7% now married, 9.0% widowed, 13.1% divorced (2005-2009 5-year est.); Foreign born: 0.0% (2005-2009 5-year est.); Ancestry (includes multiple ancestries): 9.3% German, 9.2% Irish, 8.2% Italian, 6.9% English, 6.3% American (2005-2009 5-year est.).
Economy: Single-family building permits issued: 0 (2010); Multi-family building permits issued: 0 (2010); Employment by occupation: 5.9% management, 10.0% professional, 30.7% services, 28.5% sales, 0.3% farming, 13.6% construction, 11.0% production (2005-2009 5-year est.).
Income: Per capita income: $20,430 (2010); Median household income: $41,214 (2010); Average household income: $47,599 (2010); Percent of households with income of $100,000 or more: 6.7% (2010); Poverty rate: 13.1% (2005-2009 5-year est.).
Taxes: Total city taxes per capita: $67 (2007); City property taxes per capita: $60 (2007).
Education: Percent of population age 25 and over with: High school diploma (including GED) or higher: 79.5% (2010); Bachelor's degree or higher: 6.6% (2010); Master's degree or higher: 2.0% (2010).

School District(s)

South Fork SD 14 (PK-12)
    2009-10 Enrollment: 423 . . . . (217) 237-4333
Housing: Homeownership rate: 80.4% (2010); Median home value: $63,058 (2010); Median contract rent: $323 per month (2005-2009 5-year est.); Median year structure built: 1945 (2005-2009 5-year est.).
Safety: Violent crime rate: 35.0 per 10,000 population; Property crime rate: 76.9 per 10,000 population (2010).
Transportation: Commute to work: 93.5% car, 0.0% public transportation, 0.9% walk, 4.5% work from home (2005-2009 5-year est.); Travel time to work: 16.3% less than 15 minutes, 29.2% 15 to 30 minutes, 21.8% 30 to 45 minutes, 22.8% 45 to 60 minutes, 9.9% 60 minutes or more (2005-2009 5-year est.)

MORRISONVILLE (village). Covers a land area of 1.031 square miles and a water area of 0 square miles. Located at 39.41° N. Lat; 89.45° W. Long. Elevation is 630 feet.
History: Incorporated 1872.
Population: 1,113 (1990); 1,068 (2000); 1,042 (2010); 1,023 (2015 projected); Race: 97.7% White, 0.1% Black, 1.5% Asian, 0.7% Other, 1.3% Hispanic of any race (2010); Density: 1,010.2 persons per square mile (2010); Average household size: 2.45 (2010); Median age: 40.8 (2010); Males per 100 females: 98.5 (2010); Marriage status: 21.2% never married, 63.9% now married, 6.8% widowed, 8.0% divorced (2005-2009 5-year est.); Foreign born: 4.6% (2005-2009 5-year est.); Ancestry (includes multiple ancestries): 23.5% German, 12.6% Irish, 11.1% English, 8.5% American, 6.4% Dutch (2005-2009 5-year est.).
Economy: Employment by occupation: 6.6% management, 15.6% professional, 18.9% services, 27.0% sales, 0.6% farming, 10.3% construction, 21.1% production (2005-2009 5-year est.).
Income: Per capita income: $22,664 (2010); Median household income: $44,896 (2010); Average household income: $55,118 (2010); Percent of households with income of $100,000 or more: 11.3% (2010); Poverty rate: 5.6% (2005-2009 5-year est.).
Taxes: Total city taxes per capita: $148 (2007); City property taxes per capita: $143 (2007).
Education: Percent of population age 25 and over with: High school diploma (including GED) or higher: 86.5% (2010); Bachelor's degree or higher: 13.4% (2010); Master's degree or higher: 4.2% (2010).

School District(s)

Christian/Montgomery Roe (06-10)
    2009-10 Enrollment: n/a . . . . (217) 532-9591
Morrisonville CUSD 1 (PK-12)
    2009-10 Enrollment: 356 . . . . (217) 526-4431
Housing: Homeownership rate: 80.7% (2010); Median home value: $78,451 (2010); Median contract rent: $398 per month (2005-2009 5-year est.); Median year structure built: 1950 (2005-2009 5-year est.).
Newspapers: Morrisonville Times (Community news; Circulation 1,000)
Transportation: Commute to work: 92.2% car, 0.0% public transportation, 2.0% walk, 4.6% work from home (2005-2009 5-year est.); Travel time to work: 24.5% less than 15 minutes, 40.6% 15 to 30 minutes, 10.1% 30 to 45 minutes, 19.6% 45 to 60 minutes, 5.2% 60 minutes or more (2005-2009 5-year est.)

MOUNT AUBURN (village). Covers a land area of 0.991 square miles and a water area of 0.001 square miles. Located at 39.76° N. Lat; 89.26° W. Long. Elevation is 699 feet.

Population: 544 (1990); 515 (2000); 510 (2010); 505 (2015 projected); Race: 98.0% White, 0.0% Black, 0.4% Asian, 1.6% Other, 0.2% Hispanic of any race (2010); Density: 514.6 persons per square mile (2010); Average household size: 2.37 (2010); Median age: 44.1 (2010); Males per 100 females: 93.2 (2010); Marriage status: 15.3% never married, 69.0% now married, 7.4% widowed, 8.2% divorced (2005-2009 5-year est.); Foreign born: 0.0% (2005-2009 5-year est.); Ancestry (includes multiple ancestries): 27.3% German, 10.6% Irish, 8.6% English, 7.9% American, 2.6% Norwegian (2005-2009 5-year est.).
Economy: Single-family building permits issued: 1 (2010); Multi-family building permits issued: 0 (2010); Employment by occupation: 5.7% management, 15.5% professional, 10.9% services, 28.7% sales, 0.0% farming, 9.2% construction, 29.9% production (2005-2009 5-year est.).
Income: Per capita income: $24,261 (2010); Median household income: $51,346 (2010); Average household income: $56,860 (2010); Percent of households with income of $100,000 or more: 8.8% (2010); Poverty rate: 15.6% (2005-2009 5-year est.).
Taxes: Total city taxes per capita: $51 (2007); City property taxes per capita: $51 (2007).
Education: Percent of population age 25 and over with: High school diploma (including GED) or higher: 84.0% (2010); Bachelor's degree or higher: 10.5% (2010); Master's degree or higher: 5.8% (2010).
Housing: Homeownership rate: 81.9% (2010); Median home value: $77,600 (2010); Median contract rent: n/a per month (2005-2009 5-year est.); Median year structure built: 1974 (2005-2009 5-year est.).
Transportation: Commute to work: 96.6% car, 0.0% public transportation, 1.7% walk, 1.7% work from home (2005-2009 5-year est.); Travel time to work: 19.3% less than 15 minutes, 13.5% 15 to 30 minutes, 44.4% 30 to 45 minutes, 14.0% 45 to 60 minutes, 8.8% 60 minutes or more (2005-2009 5-year est.)

OWANECO (village). Covers a land area of 0.458 square miles and a water area of 0 square miles. Located at 39.48° N. Lat; 89.19° W. Long. Elevation is 620 feet.
Population: 260 (1990); 256 (2000); 229 (2010); 226 (2015 projected); Race: 48.9% White, 41.5% Black, 0.9% Asian, 8.7% Other, 11.4% Hispanic of any race (2010); Density: 500.2 persons per square mile (2010); Average household size: 2.64 (2010); Median age: 37.5 (2010); Males per 100 females: 458.5 (2010); Marriage status: 24.3% never married, 58.7% now married, 6.4% widowed, 10.6% divorced (2005-2009 5-year est.); Foreign born: 0.8% (2005-2009 5-year est.); Ancestry (includes multiple ancestries): 21.2% German, 11.6% Irish, 7.3% American, 6.9% Dutch, 3.9% Lithuanian (2005-2009 5-year est.).
Economy: Employment by occupation: 9.2% management, 11.5% professional, 14.5% services, 26.7% sales, 5.3% farming, 9.9% construction, 22.9% production (2005-2009 5-year est.).
Income: Per capita income: $18,422 (2010); Median household income: $60,227 (2010); Average household income: $70,000 (2010); Percent of households with income of $100,000 or more: 18.2% (2010); Poverty rate: 17.8% (2005-2009 5-year est.).
Taxes: Total city taxes per capita: $56 (2007); City property taxes per capita: $52 (2007).
Education: Percent of population age 25 and over with: High school diploma (including GED) or higher: 69.2% (2010); Bachelor's degree or higher: 7.6% (2010); Master's degree or higher: 2.7% (2010).
Housing: Homeownership rate: 81.8% (2010); Median home value: $95,000 (2010); Median contract rent: $225 per month (2005-2009 5-year est.); Median year structure built: before 1940 (2005-2009 5-year est.).
Transportation: Commute to work: 91.1% car, 2.4% public transportation, 0.0% walk, 4.8% work from home (2005-2009 5-year est.); Travel time to work: 14.4% less than 15 minutes, 41.5% 15 to 30 minutes, 6.8% 30 to 45 minutes, 23.7% 45 to 60 minutes, 13.6% 60 minutes or more (2005-2009 5-year est.)

PALMER (village). Covers a land area of 0.998 square miles and a water area of 0 square miles. Located at 39.45° N. Lat; 89.40° W. Long. Elevation is 623 feet.
Population: 275 (1990); 248 (2000); 240 (2010); 232 (2015 projected); Race: 95.8% White, 0.0% Black, 1.7% Asian, 2.5% Other, 0.4% Hispanic of any race (2010); Density: 240.5 persons per square mile (2010); Average household size: 2.73 (2010); Median age: 37.9 (2010); Males per 100 females: 110.5 (2010); Marriage status: 37.2% never married, 32.1% now married, 10.3% widowed, 20.5% divorced (2005-2009 5-year est.); Foreign born: 0.8% (2005-2009 5-year est.); Ancestry (includes multiple

ancestries): 18.4% German, 17.6% American, 5.1% Irish, 4.7% Swiss, 4.7% Dutch (2005-2009 5-year est.).

Economy: Single-family building permits issued: 0 (2010); Multi-family building permits issued: 0 (2010); Employment by occupation: 8.4% management, 9.9% professional, 15.3% services, 27.5% sales, 1.5% farming, 11.5% construction, 26.0% production (2005-2009 5-year est.).

Income: Per capita income: $24,418 (2010); Median household income: $52,500 (2010); Average household income: $68,580 (2010); Percent of households with income of $100,000 or more: 14.8% (2010); Poverty rate: 13.3% (2005-2009 5-year est.).

Taxes: Total city taxes per capita: $84 (2007); City property taxes per capita: $72 (2007).

Education: Percent of population age 25 and over with: High school diploma (including GED) or higher: 83.0% (2010); Bachelor's degree or higher: 7.5% (2010); Master's degree or higher: 2.5% (2010).

Housing: Homeownership rate: 76.1% (2010); Median home value: $83,125 (2010); Median contract rent: $350 per month (2005-2009 5-year est.); Median year structure built: before 1940 (2005-2009 5-year est.).

Transportation: Commute to work: 92.9% car, 7.1% public transportation, 0.0% walk, 0.0% work from home (2005-2009 5-year est.); Travel time to work: 18.1% less than 15 minutes, 55.1% 15 to 30 minutes, 6.3% 30 to 45 minutes, 11.0% 45 to 60 minutes, 9.4% 60 minutes or more (2005-2009 5-year est.)

PANA (city). Covers a land area of 2.671 square miles and a water area of 0 square miles. Located at 39.38° N. Lat; 89.08° W. Long. Elevation is 699 feet.

History: Pana developed as a center for rose cultivation, with acres of greenhouses warmed by steam heat.

Population: 5,903 (1990); 5,614 (2000); 5,332 (2010); 5,152 (2015 projected); Race: 98.7% White, 0.1% Black, 0.4% Asian, 0.8% Other, 0.6% Hispanic of any race (2010); Density: 1,996.1 persons per square mile (2010); Average household size: 2.31 (2010); Median age: 40.2 (2010); Males per 100 females: 89.4 (2010); Marriage status: 18.9% never married, 57.9% now married, 13.1% widowed, 10.2% divorced (2005-2009 5-year est.); Foreign born: 4.0% (2005-2009 5-year est.); Ancestry (includes multiple ancestries): 20.9% German, 10.6% American, 9.8% Irish, 9.4% English, 6.1% Polish (2005-2009 5-year est.).

Economy: Single-family building permits issued: 4 (2010); Multi-family building permits issued: 0 (2010); Employment by occupation: 6.1% management, 20.0% professional, 21.4% services, 20.3% sales, 0.3% farming, 14.8% construction, 17.0% production (2005-2009 5-year est.).

Income: Per capita income: $17,638 (2010); Median household income: $33,773 (2010); Average household income: $41,193 (2010); Percent of households with income of $100,000 or more: 4.5% (2010); Poverty rate: 20.6% (2005-2009 5-year est.).

Taxes: Total city taxes per capita: $207 (2007); City property taxes per capita: $129 (2007).

Education: Percent of population age 25 and over with: High school diploma (including GED) or higher: 80.4% (2010); Bachelor's degree or higher: 8.9% (2010); Master's degree or higher: 2.5% (2010).

School District(s)

Pana CUSD 8 (PK-12)
    2009-10 Enrollment: 1,497 . . . . (217) 562-1500

Housing: Homeownership rate: 70.3% (2010); Median home value: $57,335 (2010); Median contract rent: $341 per month (2005-2009 5-year est.); Median year structure built: 1954 (2005-2009 5-year est.).

Hospitals: Pana Community Hospital (44 beds)

Safety: Violent crime rate: 5.4 per 10,000 population; Property crime rate: 196.4 per 10,000 population (2010).

Newspapers: Pana News Palladium (Local news; Circulation 4,600)

Transportation: Commute to work: 95.4% car, 0.6% public transportation, 1.0% walk, 2.7% work from home (2005-2009 5-year est.); Travel time to work: 44.2% less than 15 minutes, 20.8% 15 to 30 minutes, 10.3% 30 to 45 minutes, 15.8% 45 to 60 minutes, 8.9% 60 minutes or more (2005-2009 5-year est.)

Additional Information Contacts

Pana Chamber of Commerce . . . . (217) 562-4240
    http://www.panachamber.com

ROSAMOND (unincorporated postal area, zip code 62083). Covers a land area of 22.766 square miles and a water area of 0 square miles. Located at 39.35° N. Lat; 89.20° W. Long. Elevation is 709 feet.

Population: 317 (2000); Race: 100.0% White, 0.0% Black, 0.0% Asian, 0.0% Other, 0.0% Hispanic of any race (2000); Density: 13.9 persons per square mile (2000); Age: 32.2% under 18, 12.6% over 64 (2000); Marriage status: 25.7% never married, 37.7% now married, 15.4% widowed, 21.1% divorced (2000); Foreign born: 0.0% (2000); Ancestry (includes multiple ancestries): 54.8% German, 16.7% Irish, 13.0% French, 7.5% American (2000).

Economy: Employment by occupation: 4.3% management, 0.0% professional, 34.0% services, 7.4% sales, 11.7% farming, 19.1% construction, 23.4% production (2000).

Income: Per capita income: $16,027 (2000); Median household income: $27,750 (2000); Poverty rate: 22.5% (2000).

Education: Percent of population age 25 and over with: High school diploma (including GED) or higher: 91.9% (2000); Bachelor's degree or higher: 7.4% (2000).

Housing: Homeownership rate: 93.2% (2000); Median home value: $48,600 (2000); Median contract rent: n/a per month (2000); Median year structure built: 1949 (2000).

Transportation: Commute to work: 95.7% car, 0.0% public transportation, 4.3% walk, 0.0% work from home (2000); Travel time to work: 17.0% less than 15 minutes, 31.9% 15 to 30 minutes, 16.0% 30 to 45 minutes, 12.8% 45 to 60 minutes, 22.3% 60 minutes or more (2000)

STONINGTON (village). Covers a land area of 0.454 square miles and a water area of 0 square miles. Located at 39.63° N. Lat; 89.19° W. Long. Elevation is 610 feet.

History: Incorporated 1885.

Population: 1,010 (1990); 960 (2000); 896 (2010); 862 (2015 projected); Race: 99.4% White, 0.0% Black, 0.0% Asian, 0.6% Other, 0.6% Hispanic of any race (2010); Density: 1,973.4 persons per square mile (2010); Average household size: 2.42 (2010); Median age: 36.7 (2010); Males per 100 females: 96.9 (2010); Marriage status: 29.5% never married, 52.3% now married, 5.4% widowed, 12.7% divorced (2005-2009 5-year est.); Foreign born: 0.0% (2005-2009 5-year est.); Ancestry (includes multiple ancestries): 23.9% German, 14.9% Irish, 10.1% American, 9.0% English, 4.4% French (2005-2009 5-year est.).

Economy: Single-family building permits issued: 0 (2010); Multi-family building permits issued: 0 (2010); Employment by occupation: 6.3% management, 13.3% professional, 23.3% services, 19.1% sales, 3.9% farming, 14.3% construction, 19.8% production (2005-2009 5-year est.).

Income: Per capita income: $20,186 (2010); Median household income: $42,405 (2010); Average household income: $49,088 (2010); Percent of households with income of $100,000 or more: 7.8% (2010); Poverty rate: 16.6% (2005-2009 5-year est.).

Taxes: Total city taxes per capita: $70 (2007); City property taxes per capita: $59 (2007).

Education: Percent of population age 25 and over with: High school diploma (including GED) or higher: 82.9% (2010); Bachelor's degree or higher: 13.5% (2010); Master's degree or higher: 3.3% (2010).

School District(s)

Taylorville CUSD 3 (PK-12)
    2009-10 Enrollment: 2,871 . . . . (217) 824-4951

Housing: Homeownership rate: 78.4% (2010); Median home value: $74,800 (2010); Median contract rent: $379 per month (2005-2009 5-year est.); Median year structure built: 1942 (2005-2009 5-year est.).

Transportation: Commute to work: 93.2% car, 0.0% public transportation, 2.2% walk, 1.5% work from home (2005-2009 5-year est.); Travel time to work: 33.8% less than 15 minutes, 28.2% 15 to 30 minutes, 22.7% 30 to 45 minutes, 11.3% 45 to 60 minutes, 4.0% 60 minutes or more (2005-2009 5-year est.)

TAYLORVILLE (city). County seat. Covers a land area of 8.067 square miles and a water area of 1.952 square miles. Located at 39.54° N. Lat; 89.28° W. Long. Elevation is 627 feet.

History: Incorporated 1881.

Population: 11,332 (1990); 11,427 (2000); 10,847 (2010); 10,528 (2015 projected); Race: 96.3% White, 1.0% Black, 1.1% Asian, 1.6% Other, 1.0% Hispanic of any race (2010); Density: 1,344.7 persons per square mile (2010); Average household size: 2.26 (2010); Median age: 40.4 (2010); Males per 100 females: 92.3 (2010); Marriage status: 24.7% never married, 47.5% now married, 10.3% widowed, 17.4% divorced (2005-2009 5-year est.); Foreign born: 3.8% (2005-2009 5-year est.); Ancestry (includes multiple ancestries): 19.8% German, 14.9% Irish, 11.6% American, 9.9% English, 6.4% Italian (2005-2009 5-year est.).

Economy: Single-family building permits issued: 8 (2010); Multi-family building permits issued: 0 (2010); Employment by occupation: 10.1%

management, 14.9% professional, 18.9% services, 30.1% sales, 0.0% farming, 8.9% construction, 17.0% production (2005-2009 5-year est.).
Income: Per capita income: $20,494 (2010); Median household income: $37,743 (2010); Average household income: $46,800 (2010); Percent of households with income of $100,000 or more: 7.2% (2010); Poverty rate: 16.7% (2005-2009 5-year est.).
Taxes: Total city taxes per capita: $253 (2007); City property taxes per capita: $170 (2007).
Education: Percent of population age 25 and over with: High school diploma (including GED) or higher: 84.2% (2010); Bachelor's degree or higher: 14.4% (2010); Master's degree or higher: 4.2% (2010).

School District(s)

Taylorville CUSD 3 (PK-12)
    2009-10 Enrollment: 2,871 . . . . (217) 824-4951
Housing: Homeownership rate: 66.5% (2010); Median home value: $76,006 (2010); Median contract rent: $397 per month (2005-2009 5-year est.); Median year structure built: 1958 (2005-2009 5-year est.).
Hospitals: Taylorville Memorial Hospital
Newspapers: The Breeze-Courier (Local news; Circulation 6,770)
Transportation: Commute to work: 93.9% car, 0.2% public transportation, 2.1% walk, 1.8% work from home (2005-2009 5-year est.); Travel time to work: 52.3% less than 15 minutes, 15.8% 15 to 30 minutes, 15.1% 30 to 45 minutes, 11.9% 45 to 60 minutes, 4.8% 60 minutes or more (2005-2009 5-year est.)
Additional Information Contacts
City of Taylorville . . . . (217) 824-2101
    http://www.taylorville.net
The Greater Taylorville Chamber of Commerce . . . . (217) 824-4919
    http://www.taylorvillechamber.com

TOVEY (village). Aka Humphrey. Covers a land area of 0.185 square miles and a water area of 0 square miles. Located at 39.58° N. Lat; 89.44° W. Long. Elevation is 600 feet.
History: Also known as Humphrey.
Population: 533 (1990); 516 (2000); 510 (2010); 505 (2015 projected); Race: 96.7% White, 0.6% Black, 0.0% Asian, 2.7% Other, 1.8% Hispanic of any race (2010); Density: 2,758.7 persons per square mile (2010); Average household size: 2.45 (2010); Median age: 42.7 (2010); Males per 100 females: 100.0 (2010); Marriage status: 30.5% never married, 52.2% now married, 6.4% widowed, 10.9% divorced (2005-2009 5-year est.); Foreign born: 1.2% (2005-2009 5-year est.); Ancestry (includes multiple ancestries): 14.1% American, 12.8% Italian, 11.8% Irish, 10.4% German, 9.4% French (2005-2009 5-year est.).
Economy: Single-family building permits issued: 0 (2010); Multi-family building permits issued: 0 (2010); Employment by occupation: 13.3% management, 11.5% professional, 17.7% services, 30.5% sales, 0.0% farming, 11.1% construction, 15.9% production (2005-2009 5-year est.).
Income: Per capita income: $19,192 (2010); Median household income: $36,364 (2010); Average household income: $46,995 (2010); Percent of households with income of $100,000 or more: 6.7% (2010); Poverty rate: 17.1% (2005-2009 5-year est.).
Taxes: Total city taxes per capita: $24 (2007); City property taxes per capita: $16 (2007).
Education: Percent of population age 25 and over with: High school diploma (including GED) or higher: 81.7% (2010); Bachelor's degree or higher: 10.1% (2010); Master's degree or higher: 2.6% (2010).
Housing: Homeownership rate: 80.3% (2010); Median home value: $83,913 (2010); Median contract rent: $369 per month (2005-2009 5-year est.); Median year structure built: 1946 (2005-2009 5-year est.).
Transportation: Commute to work: 98.2% car, 0.9% public transportation, 0.0% walk, 0.9% work from home (2005-2009 5-year est.); Travel time to work: 15.7% less than 15 minutes, 19.8% 15 to 30 minutes, 42.4% 30 to 45 minutes, 16.6% 45 to 60 minutes, 5.5% 60 minutes or more (2005-2009 5-year est.)

Clark County

Located in eastern Illinois; bounded on the southeast by the Wabash River and the Indiana border; drained by the North Fork Embarrass River. Covers a land area of 501.50 square miles, a water area of 3.38 square miles, and is located in the Central Time Zone at 39.34° N. Lat., 87.80° W. Long. The county was founded in 1819. County seat is Marshall.
Population: 15,921 (1990); 17,008 (2000); 16,829 (2010); 16,658 (2015 projected); Race: 97.8% White, 0.6% Black, 0.2% Asian, 1.5% Other, 0.8% Hispanic of any race (2010); Density: 33.6 persons per square mile (2010);

Average household size: 2.38 (2010); Median age: 40.0 (2010); Males per 100 females: 94.6 (2010).
Religion: Five largest groups: 19.8% Southern Baptist Convention, 13.1% The United Methodist Church, 6.3% Christian Churches and Churches of Christ, 4.4% Church of the Nazarene, 3.9% Catholic Church (2000).
Economy: Unemployment rate: 11.1% (August 2011); Total civilian labor force: 7,965 (August 2011); Leading industries: 28.8% manufacturing; 13.5% accommodation & food services; 11.0% retail trade (2009); Farms: 588 totaling 238,706 acres (2007); Companies that employ 500 or more persons: 1 (2009); Companies that employ 100 to 499 persons: 2 (2009); Companies that employ less than 100 persons: 329 (2009); Black-owned businesses: n/a (2007); Hispanic-owned businesses: n/a (2007); Asian-owned businesses: n/a (2007); Women-owned businesses: 311 (2007); Retail sales per capita: $9,965 (2010). Single-family building permits issued: 5 (2010); Multi-family building permits issued: 0 (2010).
Income: Per capita income: $22,508 (2010); Median household income: $44,271 (2010); Average household income: $53,973 (2010); Percent of households with income of $100,000 or more: 9.8% (2010); Poverty rate: 13.4% (2009); Bankruptcy rate: 3.80% (2010).
Taxes: Total county taxes per capita: $119 (2007); County property taxes per capita: $119 (2007).
Education: Percent of population age 25 and over with: High school diploma (including GED) or higher: 86.0% (2010); Bachelor's degree or higher: 16.9% (2010); Master's degree or higher: 5.3% (2010).
Housing: Homeownership rate: 76.3% (2010); Median home value: $95,638 (2010); Median contract rent: $354 per month (2005-2009 5-year est.); Median year structure built: 1961 (2005-2009 5-year est.)
Health: Birth rate: 117.7 per 10,000 population (2009); Death rate: 131.5 per 10,000 population (2009); Age-adjusted cancer mortality rate: 180.5 deaths per 100,000 population (2007); Number of physicians: 4.2 per 10,000 population (2008); Hospital beds: 0.0 per 10,000 population (2007); Hospital admissions: 0.0 per 10,000 population (2007).
Environment: Air Quality Index: 98.1% good, 1.9% moderate, 0.0% unhealthy for sensitive individuals, 0.0% unhealthy (percent of days in 2008)
Elections: 2008 Presidential election results: 45.1% Obama, 53.2% McCain, 1.0% Nader
National and State Parks: Lincoln Trail State Park
Additional Information Contacts
Clark County Government . . . . (217) 826-8311
    http://www.clarkcountyil.org
City of Casey . . . . (217) 932-2700
    http://www.cityofcaseyil.org
Marshall Area Chamber of Commerce . . . . (217) 826-2034
    http://www.marshallilchamber.com
Martinsville Chamber of Commerce. . . . . (217) 251-5505

Clark County Communities

CASEY (city). Covers a land area of 2.124 square miles and a water area of 0 square miles. Located at 39.30° N. Lat; 87.99° W. Long. Elevation is 646 feet.
History: Incorporated 1896. Had oil boom in early 20th cent.
Population: 2,914 (1990); 2,942 (2000); 2,873 (2010); 2,819 (2015 projected); Race: 97.2% White, 1.3% Black, 0.0% Asian, 1.5% Other, 0.5% Hispanic of any race (2010); Density: 1,352.5 persons per square mile (2010); Average household size: 2.24 (2010); Median age: 40.5 (2010); Males per 100 females: 83.9 (2010); Marriage status: 22.5% never married, 49.1% now married, 12.8% widowed, 15.6% divorced (2005-2009 5-year est.); Foreign born: 0.0% (2005-2009 5-year est.); Ancestry (includes multiple ancestries): 17.3% German, 16.0% Irish, 15.5% American, 10.6% English, 3.7% Italian (2005-2009 5-year est.).
Economy: Employment by occupation: 16.3% management, 13.3% professional, 17.1% services, 29.4% sales, 0.0% farming, 5.9% construction, 18.1% production (2005-2009 5-year est.).
Income: Per capita income: $19,953 (2010); Median household income: $37,002 (2010); Average household income: $45,939 (2010); Percent of households with income of $100,000 or more: 8.3% (2010); Poverty rate: 18.1% (2005-2009 5-year est.).
Taxes: Total city taxes per capita: $221 (2007); City property taxes per capita: $118 (2007).
Education: Percent of population age 25 and over with: High school diploma (including GED) or higher: 81.6% (2010); Bachelor's degree or higher: 16.3% (2010); Master's degree or higher: 6.4% (2010).

Casey-Westfield CUSD 4c (PK-12)
    2009-10 Enrollment: 1,024 . . . . (217) 932-2184
Housing: Homeownership rate: 69.3% (2010); Median home value: $69,000 (2010); Median contract rent: $314 per month (2005-2009 5-year est.); Median year structure built: 1958 (2005-2009 5-year est.).
Transportation: Commute to work: 92.4% car, 0.0% public transportation, 1.1% walk, 2.6% work from home (2005-2009 5-year est.); Travel time to work: 51.4% less than 15 minutes, 12.8% 15 to 30 minutes, 23.5% 30 to 45 minutes, 9.0% 45 to 60 minutes, 3.3% 60 minutes or more (2005-2009 5-year est.)
Additional Information Contacts
City of Casey . . . . (217) 932-2700
    http://www.cityofcaseyil.org

DENNISON (unincorporated postal area, zip code 62423). Covers a land area of 26.547 square miles and a water area of 0.016 square miles. Located at 39.45° N. Lat; 87.57° W. Long. Elevation is 581 feet.
Population: 738 (2000); Race: 98.7% White, 0.0% Black, 1.3% Asian, 0.0% Other, 0.0% Hispanic of any race (2000); Density: 27.8 persons per square mile (2000); Age: 24.9% under 18, 12.7% over 64 (2000); Marriage status: 18.5% never married, 69.6% now married, 4.1% widowed, 7.8% divorced (2000); Foreign born: 0.0% (2000); Ancestry (includes multiple ancestries): 14.9% English, 14.5% American, 13.2% Irish, 11.3% German (2000).
Economy: Employment by occupation: 4.7% management, 7.9% professional, 22.9% services, 20.5% sales, 0.0% farming, 14.4% construction, 29.6% production (2000).
Income: Per capita income: $17,058 (2000); Median household income: $34,659 (2000); Poverty rate: 4.5% (2000).
Education: Percent of population age 25 and over with: High school diploma (including GED) or higher: 84.7% (2000); Bachelor's degree or higher: 5.8% (2000).
Housing: Homeownership rate: 85.5% (2000); Median home value: $91,700 (2000); Median contract rent: $353 per month (2000); Median year structure built: 1975 (2000).
Transportation: Commute to work: 100.0% car, 0.0% public transportation, 0.0% walk, 0.0% work from home (2000); Travel time to work: 13.2% less than 15 minutes, 49.9% 15 to 30 minutes, 18.5% 30 to 45 minutes, 8.8% 45 to 60 minutes, 9.7% 60 minutes or more (2000)

MARSHALL (city). County seat. Covers a land area of 3.135 square miles and a water area of 0.010 square miles. Located at 39.39° N. Lat; 87.69° W. Long. Elevation is 640 feet.
History: Marshall was founded by William B. Archer and named by him for Chief Justice John Marshall. The town developed as the seat of Clark County.
Population: 3,693 (1990); 3,771 (2000); 3,429 (2010); 3,285 (2015 projected); Race: 96.7% White, 0.7% Black, 0.3% Asian, 2.3% Other, 1.6% Hispanic of any race (2010); Density: 1,093.7 persons per square mile (2010); Average household size: 2.20 (2010); Median age: 39.8 (2010); Males per 100 females: 86.0 (2010); Marriage status: 23.6% never married, 44.3% now married, 15.5% widowed, 16.6% divorced (2005-2009 5-year est.); Foreign born: 0.7% (2005-2009 5-year est.); Ancestry (includes multiple ancestries): 29.7% German, 16.5% Irish, 14.5% English, 7.4% American, 3.2% French (2005-2009 5-year est.).
Economy: Single-family building permits issued: 5 (2010); Multi-family building permits issued: 0 (2010); Employment by occupation: 11.1% management, 18.0% professional, 16.7% services, 23.7% sales, 1.8% farming, 10.6% construction, 18.1% production (2005-2009 5-year est.).
Income: Per capita income: $27,638 (2010); Median household income: $47,422 (2010); Average household income: $61,416 (2010); Percent of households with income of $100,000 or more: 11.9% (2010); Poverty rate: 13.7% (2005-2009 5-year est.).
Taxes: Total city taxes per capita: $130 (2007); City property taxes per capita: $104 (2007).
Education: Percent of population age 25 and over with: High school diploma (including GED) or higher: 83.3% (2010); Bachelor's degree or higher: 18.5% (2010); Master's degree or higher: 5.9% (2010).
School District(s)
Eastern Il Area of Spec Educ (PK-12)
    2009-10 Enrollment: n/a . . . . (217) 348-7700
Marshall CUSD 2c (PK-12)
    2009-10 Enrollment: 1,411 . . . . (217) 826-5912

Housing: Homeownership rate: 65.7% (2010); Median home value: $106,543 (2010); Median contract rent: $417 per month (2005-2009 5-year est.); Median year structure built: 1962 (2005-2009 5-year est.).
Transportation: Commute to work: 94.5% car, 0.0% public transportation, 1.7% walk, 1.0% work from home (2005-2009 5-year est.); Travel time to work: 41.7% less than 15 minutes, 34.6% 15 to 30 minutes, 12.4% 30 to 45 minutes, 3.9% 45 to 60 minutes, 7.5% 60 minutes or more (2005-2009 5-year est.)
Additional Information Contacts
Marshall Area Chamber of Commerce . . . . (217) 826-2034
    http://www.marshallilchamber.com

MARTINSVILLE (city). Covers a land area of 2.056 square miles and a water area of 0.030 square miles. Located at 39.33° N. Lat; 87.88° W. Long. Elevation is 610 feet.
History: Martinsville was platted in 1833 by Joseph Martin, and operated as a trading post, stagecoach station, and tavern. A period of growth came in 1904 when oil and gas were discovered, but by 1916 the wells were dry.
Population: 1,207 (1990); 1,225 (2000); 1,154 (2010); 1,124 (2015 projected); Race: 99.0% White, 0.1% Black, 0.2% Asian, 0.7% Other, 0.4% Hispanic of any race (2010); Density: 561.4 persons per square mile (2010); Average household size: 2.38 (2010); Median age: 38.4 (2010); Males per 100 females: 94.6 (2010); Marriage status: 17.2% never married, 57.4% now married, 13.0% widowed, 12.5% divorced (2005-2009 5-year est.); Foreign born: 3.1% (2005-2009 5-year est.); Ancestry (includes multiple ancestries): 21.4% German, 14.9% American, 14.1% English, 9.5% Irish, 3.3% Scottish (2005-2009 5-year est.).
Economy: Employment by occupation: 7.5% management, 14.1% professional, 16.0% services, 17.6% sales, 7.5% farming, 9.9% construction, 27.5% production (2005-2009 5-year est.).
Income: Per capita income: $17,437 (2010); Median household income: $34,383 (2010); Average household income: $41,813 (2010); Percent of households with income of $100,000 or more: 5.6% (2010); Poverty rate: 21.4% (2005-2009 5-year est.).
Taxes: Total city taxes per capita: $73 (2007); City property taxes per capita: $67 (2007).
Education: Percent of population age 25 and over with: High school diploma (including GED) or higher: 89.5% (2010); Bachelor's degree or higher: 10.6% (2010); Master's degree or higher: 2.7% (2010).
School District(s)
Martinsville CUSD 3c (PK-12)
    2009-10 Enrollment: 404 . . . . (217) 382-4321
Housing: Homeownership rate: 75.6% (2010); Median home value: $64,638 (2010); Median contract rent: $218 per month (2005-2009 5-year est.); Median year structure built: 1953 (2005-2009 5-year est.).
Safety: Violent crime rate: 17.0 per 10,000 population; Property crime rate: 297.1 per 10,000 population (2010).
Transportation: Commute to work: 91.3% car, 0.0% public transportation, 3.9% walk, 3.1% work from home (2005-2009 5-year est.); Travel time to work: 41.0% less than 15 minutes, 26.6% 15 to 30 minutes, 15.9% 30 to 45 minutes, 9.2% 45 to 60 minutes, 7.2% 60 minutes or more (2005-2009 5-year est.)
Additional Information Contacts
Martinsville Chamber of Commerce. . . . . (217) 251-5505

WEST UNION (unincorporated postal area, zip code 62477). Aka Hatton. Covers a land area of 64.596 square miles and a water area of 0.113 square miles. Located at 39.23° N. Lat; 87.66° W. Long. Elevation is 472 feet.
Population: 1,131 (2000); Race: 99.4% White, 0.0% Black, 0.0% Asian, 0.6% Other, 0.0% Hispanic of any race (2000); Density: 17.5 persons per square mile (2000); Age: 30.0% under 18, 11.6% over 64 (2000); Marriage status: 22.7% never married, 57.1% now married, 6.1% widowed, 14.1% divorced (2000); Foreign born: 0.0% (2000); Ancestry (includes multiple ancestries): 22.8% German, 15.6% American, 13.6% English, 7.9% Irish, 5.2% French (2000).
Economy: Employment by occupation: 13.2% management, 13.0% professional, 9.6% services, 19.3% sales, 1.3% farming, 16.5% construction, 27.0% production (2000).
Income: Per capita income: $14,453 (2000); Median household income: $33,000 (2000); Poverty rate: 14.1% (2000).
Education: Percent of population age 25 and over with: High school diploma (including GED) or higher: 85.1% (2000); Bachelor's degree or higher: 11.8% (2000).

Housing: Homeownership rate: 85.6% (2000); Median home value: $40,800 (2000); Median contract rent: $253 per month (2000); Median year structure built: 1947 (2000).

Transportation: Commute to work: 89.9% car, 0.0% public transportation, 2.9% walk, 3.7% work from home (2000); Travel time to work: 17.2% less than 15 minutes, 47.8% 15 to 30 minutes, 19.4% 30 to 45 minutes, 8.3% 45 to 60 minutes, 7.3% 60 minutes or more (2000)

WESTFIELD (village). Covers a land area of 1.004 square miles and a water area of 0 square miles. Located at 39.45° N. Lat; 87.99° W. Long. Elevation is 755 feet.

Population: 676 (1990); 678 (2000); 633 (2010); 608 (2015 projected); Race: 96.2% White, 1.1% Black, 0.6% Asian, 2.1% Other, 1.3% Hispanic of any race (2010); Density: 630.4 persons per square mile (2010); Average household size: 2.42 (2010); Median age: 38.1 (2010); Males per 100 females: 101.0 (2010); Marriage status: 14.8% never married, 63.0% now married, 14.0% widowed, 8.2% divorced (2005-2009 5-year est.); Foreign born: 0.4% (2005-2009 5-year est.); Ancestry (includes multiple ancestries): 26.6% German, 17.3% American, 13.6% Irish, 8.8% English, 6.5% French (2005-2009 5-year est.).

Economy: Single-family building permits issued: 0 (2010); Multi-family building permits issued: 0 (2010); Employment by occupation: 13.1% management, 2.4% professional, 22.0% services, 24.1% sales, 6.1% farming, 6.1% construction, 26.2% production (2005-2009 5-year est.).

Income: Per capita income: $20,742 (2010); Median household income: $42,857 (2010); Average household income: $50,429 (2010); Percent of households with income of $100,000 or more: 9.2% (2010); Poverty rate: 9.2% (2005-2009 5-year est.).

Taxes: Total city taxes per capita: $149 (2007); City property taxes per capita: $85 (2007).

Education: Percent of population age 25 and over with: High school diploma (including GED) or higher: 89.8% (2010); Bachelor's degree or higher: 10.7% (2010); Master's degree or higher: 2.6% (2010).

Housing: Homeownership rate: 77.9% (2010); Median home value: $77,368 (2010); Median contract rent: $245 per month (2005-2009 5-year est.); Median year structure built: 1941 (2005-2009 5-year est.).

Transportation: Commute to work: 94.0% car, 0.9% public transportation, 0.0% walk, 5.0% work from home (2005-2009 5-year est.); Travel time to work: 19.9% less than 15 minutes, 42.4% 15 to 30 minutes, 21.9% 30 to 45 minutes, 6.6% 45 to 60 minutes, 9.3% 60 minutes or more (2005-2009 5-year est.)

Clay County

Located in south central Illinois; drained by the Little Wabash River. Covers a land area of 469.25 square miles, a water area of 0.59 square miles, and is located in the Central Time Zone at 38.73° N. Lat., 88.47° W. Long. The county was founded in 1824. County seat is Louisville.

Weather Station: Flora 5 NW											Elevation: 500 feet	
	Jan	Feb	Mar	Apr	May	Jun	Jul	Aug	Sep	Oct	Nov	Dec
High	40	45	56	68	77	85	89	88	81	69	56	43
Low	23	26	34	44	54	62	66	64	56	45	36	26
Precip	2.9	2.6	3.8	4.0	5.1	4.2	3.8	3.4	3.1	3.7	4.2	3.3
Snow	2.8	1.9	0.9	tr	tr	0.0	0.0	0.0	0.0	tr	0.4	2.0

High and Low temperatures in degrees Fahrenheit; Precipitation and Snow in inches

Population: 14,460 (1990); 14,560 (2000); 13,700 (2010); 13,310 (2015 projected); Race: 97.3% White, 0.4% Black, 0.9% Asian, 1.4% Other, 1.2% Hispanic of any race (2010); Density: 29.2 persons per square mile (2010); Average household size: 2.38 (2010); Median age: 40.4 (2010); Males per 100 females: 94.4 (2010).

Religion: Five largest groups: 20.6% Christian Churches and Churches of Christ, 16.2% Southern Baptist Convention, 10.5% Catholic Church, 9.3% The United Methodist Church, 2.4% Church of the Nazarene (2000).

Economy: Unemployment rate: 10.6% (August 2011); Total civilian labor force: 6,632 (August 2011); Leading industries: 38.2% manufacturing; 13.5% health care and social assistance; 10.9% retail trade (2009); Farms: 707 totaling 209,834 acres (2007); Companies that employ 500 or more persons: 1 (2009); Companies that employ 100 to 499 persons: 9 (2009); Companies that employ less than 100 persons: 339 (2009); Black-owned businesses: n/a (2007); Hispanic-owned businesses: n/a (2007); Asian-owned businesses: n/a (2007); Women-owned businesses: 306 (2007); Retail sales per capita: $11,234 (2010). Single-family building permits issued: 3 (2010); Multi-family building permits issued: 0 (2010).

Income: Per capita income: $19,779 (2010); Median household income: $37,805 (2010); Average household income: $47,514 (2010); Percent of households with income of $100,000 or more: 7.3% (2010); Poverty rate: 14.7% (2009); Bankruptcy rate: 3.07% (2010).

Taxes: Total county taxes per capita: $116 (2007); County property taxes per capita: $116 (2007).

Education: Percent of population age 25 and over with: High school diploma (including GED) or higher: 82.1% (2010); Bachelor's degree or higher: 12.0% (2010); Master's degree or higher: 4.0% (2010).

Housing: Homeownership rate: 78.7% (2010); Median home value: $70,538 (2010); Median contract rent: $280 per month (2005-2009 5-year est.); Median year structure built: 1963 (2005-2009 5-year est.)

Health: Birth rate: 129.3 per 10,000 population (2009); Death rate: 124.8 per 10,000 population (2009); Age-adjusted cancer mortality rate: 188.0 deaths per 100,000 population (2007); Number of physicians: 6.6 per 10,000 population (2008); Hospital beds: 16.1 per 10,000 population (2007); Hospital admissions: 1,004.7 per 10,000 population (2007).

Elections: 2008 Presidential election results: 37.6% Obama, 60.8% McCain, 0.7% Nader

Additional Information Contacts

Clay County Government. . . . . (618) 665-3626
    http://claycountyillinois.org
City of Flora . . . . (618) 662-8313
    http://florail.govoffice2.com
Flora Chamber of Commerce . . . . (618) 662-5646
    http://www.florachamber.com

Clay County Communities

CLAY CITY (village). Covers a land area of 1.782 square miles and a water area of 0 square miles. Located at 38.68° N. Lat; 88.35° W. Long. Elevation is 433 feet.

History: Clay City developed as a shipping and trading center for the surrounding agricultural area when the railroad arrived here. It was built on the site of the first seat of Clay County, called Maysville. Oil was discovered near Clay City in 1937.

Population: 948 (1990); 1,000 (2000); 953 (2010); 933 (2015 projected); Race: 97.8% White, 0.5% Black, 0.4% Asian, 1.3% Other, 0.8% Hispanic of any race (2010); Density: 534.6 persons per square mile (2010); Average household size: 2.36 (2010); Median age: 40.6 (2010); Males per 100 females: 97.7 (2010); Marriage status: 19.3% never married, 43.2% now married, 13.0% widowed, 24.5% divorced (2005-2009 5-year est.); Foreign born: 0.0% (2005-2009 5-year est.); Ancestry (includes multiple ancestries): 22.8% German, 18.6% English, 14.4% American, 9.5% Irish, 4.6% Scotch-Irish (2005-2009 5-year est.).

Economy: Single-family building permits issued: 0 (2010); Multi-family building permits issued: 0 (2010); Employment by occupation: 7.9% management, 11.5% professional, 16.4% services, 21.0% sales, 0.0% farming, 7.1% construction, 36.1% production (2005-2009 5-year est.).

Income: Per capita income: $18,837 (2010); Median household income: $37,711 (2010); Average household income: $44,790 (2010); Percent of households with income of $100,000 or more: 4.7% (2010); Poverty rate: 18.4% (2005-2009 5-year est.).

Taxes: Total city taxes per capita: $50 (2007); City property taxes per capita: $46 (2007).

Education: Percent of population age 25 and over with: High school diploma (including GED) or higher: 87.0% (2010); Bachelor's degree or higher: 8.8% (2010); Master's degree or higher: 1.3% (2010).

School District(s)

Clay City CUSD 10 (PK-12)
    2009-10 Enrollment: 355 . . . . (618) 676-1431

Housing: Homeownership rate: 78.7% (2010); Median home value: $67,059 (2010); Median contract rent: $245 per month (2005-2009 5-year est.); Median year structure built: 1961 (2005-2009 5-year est.).

Transportation: Commute to work: 90.8% car, 0.0% public transportation, 3.2% walk, 1.2% work from home (2005-2009 5-year est.); Travel time to work: 52.3% less than 15 minutes, 35.4% 15 to 30 minutes, 9.6% 30 to 45 minutes, 0.9% 45 to 60 minutes, 1.8% 60 minutes or more (2005-2009 5-year est.)

FLORA (city). Covers a land area of 4.437 square miles and a water area of <.001 square miles. Located at 38.67° N. Lat; 88.48° W. Long. Elevation is 492 feet.

History: Flora was named for the daughter of one of its founders. It developed as an industrial center with a diversity of manufacturing.

Population: 5,206 (1990); 5,086 (2000); 4,655 (2010); 4,461 (2015 projected); Race: 95.6% White, 0.7% Black, 2.1% Asian, 1.6% Other, 1.2% Hispanic of any race (2010); Density: 1,049.1 persons per square mile (2010); Average household size: 2.24 (2010); Median age: 40.3 (2010); Males per 100 females: 86.7 (2010); Marriage status: 22.2% never married, 51.8% now married, 10.6% widowed, 15.4% divorced (2005-2009 5-year est.); Foreign born: 1.5% (2005-2009 5-year est.); Ancestry (includes multiple ancestries): 22.8% German, 12.7% Irish, 9.9% American, 6.2% English, 5.9% Scotch-Irish (2005-2009 5-year est.).
Economy: Single-family building permits issued: 3 (2010); Multi-family building permits issued: 0 (2010); Employment by occupation: 10.0% management, 20.2% professional, 17.3% services, 15.9% sales, 0.0% farming, 8.8% construction, 27.7% production (2005-2009 5-year est.).
Income: Per capita income: $19,941 (2010); Median household income: $33,743 (2010); Average household income: $45,398 (2010); Percent of households with income of $100,000 or more: 6.9% (2010); Poverty rate: 17.7% (2005-2009 5-year est.).
Taxes: Total city taxes per capita: $267 (2007); City property taxes per capita: $179 (2007).
Education: Percent of population age 25 and over with: High school diploma (including GED) or higher: 82.6% (2010); Bachelor's degree or higher: 13.2% (2010); Master's degree or higher: 5.3% (2010).

School District(s)
Flora CUSD 35 (PK-12)
    2009-10 Enrollment: 1,427 . . . . (618) 662-2412
Housing: Homeownership rate: 70.2% (2010); Median home value: $67,471 (2010); Median contract rent: $283 per month (2005-2009 5-year est.); Median year structure built: 1957 (2005-2009 5-year est.).
Hospitals: Clay County Hospital (18 beds)
Safety: Violent crime rate: 8.7 per 10,000 population; Property crime rate: 298.2 per 10,000 population (2010).
Newspapers: Daily Clay County Advocate-Press (Local news; Circulation 2,850)
Transportation: Commute to work: 87.3% car, 0.3% public transportation, 6.9% walk, 2.9% work from home (2005-2009 5-year est.); Travel time to work: 81.5% less than 15 minutes, 7.1% 15 to 30 minutes, 5.8% 30 to 45 minutes, 3.2% 45 to 60 minutes, 2.4% 60 minutes or more (2005-2009 5-year est.)
Additional Information Contacts
City of Flora . . . . (618) 662-8313
    http://florail.govoffice2.com
Flora Chamber of Commerce . . . . (618) 662-5646
    http://www.florachamber.com

INGRAHAM (unincorporated postal area, zip code 62434). Covers a land area of 30.716 square miles and a water area of 0.043 square miles. Located at 38.83° N. Lat; 88.33° W. Long. Elevation is 486 feet.
Population: 540 (2000); Race: 100.0% White, 0.0% Black, 0.0% Asian, 0.0% Other, 0.0% Hispanic of any race (2000); Density: 17.6 persons per square mile (2000); Age: 10.0% under 18, 45.0% over 64 (2000); Marriage status: 22.0% never married, 36.2% now married, 28.0% widowed, 13.8% divorced (2000); Foreign born: 0.0% (2000); Ancestry (includes multiple ancestries): 40.5% German, 16.2% American, 10.2% English, 4.1% Irish (2000).
Economy: Employment by occupation: 11.0% management, 14.4% professional, 9.9% services, 15.5% sales, 5.5% farming, 10.5% construction, 33.1% production (2000).
Income: Per capita income: $15,245 (2000); Median household income: $30,625 (2000); Poverty rate: 8.2% (2000).
Education: Percent of population age 25 and over with: High school diploma (including GED) or higher: 58.4% (2000); Bachelor's degree or higher: 11.8% (2000).
Housing: Homeownership rate: 89.0% (2000); Median home value: $31,300 (2000); Median contract rent: $375 per month (2000); Median year structure built: 1941 (2000).
Transportation: Commute to work: 97.2% car, 0.0% public transportation, 2.8% walk, 0.0% work from home (2000); Travel time to work: 23.9% less than 15 minutes, 40.3% 15 to 30 minutes, 15.3% 30 to 45 minutes, 15.9% 45 to 60 minutes, 4.5% 60 minutes or more (2000)

IOLA (village). Covers a land area of 0.969 square miles and a water area of 0 square miles. Located at 38.83° N. Lat; 88.62° W. Long. Elevation is 525 feet.
History: Incorporated 1914.

Population: 163 (1990); 171 (2000); 158 (2010); 151 (2015 projected); Race: 98.1% White, 0.0% Black, 0.0% Asian, 1.9% Other, 0.0% Hispanic of any race (2010); Density: 163.1 persons per square mile (2010); Average household size: 2.51 (2010); Median age: 35.0 (2010); Males per 100 females: 95.1 (2010); Marriage status: 26.9% never married, 53.8% now married, 10.8% widowed, 8.6% divorced (2005-2009 5-year est.); Foreign born: 0.0% (2005-2009 5-year est.); Ancestry (includes multiple ancestries): 37.7% German, 17.2% Irish, 4.1% Pennsylvania German, 1.6% Italian, 1.6% English (2005-2009 5-year est.).
Economy: Employment by occupation: 10.5% management, 7.0% professional, 24.6% services, 10.5% sales, 0.0% farming, 19.3% construction, 28.1% production (2005-2009 5-year est.).
Income: Per capita income: $18,725 (2010); Median household income: $43,500 (2010); Average household income: $47,500 (2010); Percent of households with income of $100,000 or more: 6.3% (2010); Poverty rate: 18.9% (2005-2009 5-year est.).
Taxes: Total city taxes per capita: $12 (2007); City property taxes per capita: $12 (2007).
Education: Percent of population age 25 and over with: High school diploma (including GED) or higher: 72.1% (2010); Bachelor's degree or higher: 10.6% (2010); Master's degree or higher: 6.7% (2010).
Housing: Homeownership rate: 88.9% (2010); Median home value: $66,667 (2010); Median contract rent: n/a per month (2005-2009 5-year est.); Median year structure built: before 1940 (2005-2009 5-year est.).
Transportation: Commute to work: 91.2% car, 0.0% public transportation, 7.0% walk, 1.8% work from home (2005-2009 5-year est.); Travel time to work: 10.7% less than 15 minutes, 30.4% 15 to 30 minutes, 48.2% 30 to 45 minutes, 10.7% 45 to 60 minutes, 0.0% 60 minutes or more (2005-2009 5-year est.)

LOUISVILLE (village). Aka Louis. County seat. Covers a land area of 0.692 square miles and a water area of 0 square miles. Located at 38.77° N. Lat; 88.50° W. Long. Elevation is 479 feet.
Population: 1,110 (1990); 1,242 (2000); 1,193 (2010); 1,175 (2015 projected); Race: 98.1% White, 0.9% Black, 0.0% Asian, 1.0% Other, 0.8% Hispanic of any race (2010); Density: 1,723.4 persons per square mile (2010); Average household size: 2.29 (2010); Median age: 39.3 (2010); Males per 100 females: 96.2 (2010); Marriage status: 23.8% never married, 49.1% now married, 8.9% widowed, 18.2% divorced (2005-2009 5-year est.); Foreign born: 0.0% (2005-2009 5-year est.); Ancestry (includes multiple ancestries): 21.2% German, 10.5% English, 10.4% Irish, 7.1% Swedish, 3.0% American (2005-2009 5-year est.).
Economy: Employment by occupation: 6.2% management, 9.4% professional, 14.7% services, 25.4% sales, 4.1% farming, 11.2% construction, 29.1% production (2005-2009 5-year est.).
Income: Per capita income: $17,718 (2010); Median household income: $33,813 (2010); Average household income: $41,183 (2010); Percent of households with income of $100,000 or more: 5.6% (2010); Poverty rate: 29.7% (2005-2009 5-year est.).
Taxes: Total city taxes per capita: $72 (2007); City property taxes per capita: $72 (2007).
Education: Percent of population age 25 and over with: High school diploma (including GED) or higher: 80.0% (2010); Bachelor's degree or higher: 13.2% (2010); Master's degree or higher: 3.5% (2010).

School District(s)
Clay/Cwford/Jsper/Lwrnce/Rhland (PK-12)
    2009-10 Enrollment: n/a . . . . (618) 392-4631
North Clay CUSD 25 (PK-12)
    2009-10 Enrollment: 690 . . . . (618) 665-3358
Housing: Homeownership rate: 75.4% (2010); Median home value: $64,179 (2010); Median contract rent: $264 per month (2005-2009 5-year est.); Median year structure built: 1965 (2005-2009 5-year est.).
Newspapers: Clay County Republican (Community news; Circulation 2,250)
Transportation: Commute to work: 90.7% car, 0.0% public transportation, 3.2% walk, 5.5% work from home (2005-2009 5-year est.); Travel time to work: 53.8% less than 15 minutes, 27.5% 15 to 30 minutes, 8.7% 30 to 45 minutes, 5.5% 45 to 60 minutes, 4.5% 60 minutes or more (2005-2009 5-year est.)

SAILOR SPRINGS (village). Covers a land area of 0.254 square miles and a water area of 0 square miles. Located at 38.76° N. Lat; 88.36° W. Long. Elevation is 440 feet.
Population: 136 (1990); 128 (2000); 119 (2010); 113 (2015 projected); Race: 98.3% White, 0.8% Black, 0.0% Asian, 0.8% Other, 0.0% Hispanic

of any race (2010); Density: 468.6 persons per square mile (2010); Average household size: 2.59 (2010); Median age: 44.0 (2010); Males per 100 females: 116.4 (2010); Marriage status: 35.0% never married, 44.0% now married, 14.0% widowed, 7.0% divorced (2005-2009 5-year est.); Foreign born: 0.0% (2005-2009 5-year est.); Ancestry (includes multiple ancestries): 17.1% German, 13.7% Irish, 8.5% Dutch, 4.3% American, 3.4% English (2005-2009 5-year est.).
Economy: Employment by occupation: 0.0% management, 15.9% professional, 18.2% services, 4.5% sales, 0.0% farming, 4.5% construction, 56.8% production (2005-2009 5-year est.).
Income: Per capita income: $15,630 (2010); Median household income: $32,143 (2010); Average household income: $38,913 (2010); Percent of households with income of $100,000 or more: 4.3% (2010); Poverty rate: 23.9% (2005-2009 5-year est.).
Taxes: Total city taxes per capita: $8 (2007); City property taxes per capita: $8 (2007).
Education: Percent of population age 25 and over with: High school diploma (including GED) or higher: 82.0% (2010); Bachelor's degree or higher: 6.7% (2010); Master's degree or higher: 0.0% (2010).
Housing: Homeownership rate: 87.0% (2010); Median home value: $60,000 (2010); Median contract rent: n/a per month (2005-2009 5-year est.); Median year structure built: 1947 (2005-2009 5-year est.).
Transportation: Commute to work: 100.0% car, 0.0% public transportation, 0.0% walk, 0.0% work from home (2005-2009 5-year est.); Travel time to work: 15.9% less than 15 minutes, 72.7% 15 to 30 minutes, 0.0% 30 to 45 minutes, 0.0% 45 to 60 minutes, 11.4% 60 minutes or more (2005-2009 5-year est.)

XENIA (village). Covers a land area of 0.519 square miles and a water area of 0 square miles. Located at 38.63° N. Lat; 88.63° W. Long. Elevation is 541 feet.
Population: 414 (1990); 407 (2000); 426 (2010); 433 (2015 projected); Race: 97.7% White, 0.0% Black, 0.2% Asian, 2.1% Other, 4.5% Hispanic of any race (2010); Density: 821.4 persons per square mile (2010); Average household size: 2.54 (2010); Median age: 40.4 (2010); Males per 100 females: 100.0 (2010); Marriage status: 22.0% never married, 62.2% now married, 7.9% widowed, 7.9% divorced (2005-2009 5-year est.); Foreign born: 2.5% (2005-2009 5-year est.); Ancestry (includes multiple ancestries): 34.0% German, 23.8% Irish, 8.0% English, 4.2% American, 3.2% Dutch (2005-2009 5-year est.).
Economy: Employment by occupation: 13.5% management, 2.4% professional, 17.1% services, 21.8% sales, 2.4% farming, 4.8% construction, 38.1% production (2005-2009 5-year est.).
Income: Per capita income: $23,249 (2010); Median household income: $42,500 (2010); Average household income: $59,311 (2010); Percent of households with income of $100,000 or more: 10.2% (2010); Poverty rate: 2.3% (2005-2009 5-year est.).
Taxes: Total city taxes per capita: $53 (2007); City property taxes per capita: $53 (2007).
Education: Percent of population age 25 and over with: High school diploma (including GED) or higher: 83.6% (2010); Bachelor's degree or higher: 14.0% (2010); Master's degree or higher: 2.4% (2010).
School District(s)
Flora CUSD 35 (PK-12)
    2009-10 Enrollment: 1,427 . . . . (618) 662-2412
Housing: Homeownership rate: 85.6% (2010); Median home value: $91,333 (2010); Median contract rent: $278 per month (2005-2009 5-year est.); Median year structure built: 1969 (2005-2009 5-year est.).
Transportation: Commute to work: 85.2% car, 0.0% public transportation, 4.4% walk, 4.0% work from home (2005-2009 5-year est.); Travel time to work: 51.7% less than 15 minutes, 29.2% 15 to 30 minutes, 5.0% 30 to 45 minutes, 4.6% 45 to 60 minutes, 9.6% 60 minutes or more (2005-2009 5-year est.)

Clinton County

Located in southern Illinois; bounded on the south by the Kaskaskia River. Covers a land area of 474.23 square miles, a water area of 29.25 square miles, and is located in the Central Time Zone at 38.59° N. Lat., 89.43° W. Long. The county was founded in 1824. County seat is Carlyle.

Clinton County is part of the St. Louis, MO-IL Metropolitan Statistical Area. The entire metro area includes: Bond County, IL; Calhoun County, IL; Clinton County, IL; Jersey County, IL; Macoupin County, IL; Madison County, IL; Monroe County, IL; St. Clair County, IL; Crawford County, MO

(pt.); Franklin County, MO; Jefferson County, MO; Lincoln County, MO; St. Charles County, MO; St. Louis County, MO; Warren County, MO; Washington County, MO; St. Louis city, MO

Population: 33,944 (1990); 35,535 (2000); 36,998 (2010); 37,544 (2015 projected); Race: 93.1% White, 4.2% Black, 0.4% Asian, 2.3% Other, 2.4% Hispanic of any race (2010); Density: 78.0 persons per square mile (2010); Average household size: 2.52 (2010); Median age: 37.9 (2010); Males per 100 females: 106.0 (2010).
Religion: Five largest groups: 56.0% Catholic Church, 5.0% Southern Baptist Convention, 4.0% Lutheran Church—Missouri Synod, 3.6% United Church of Christ, 3.5% The United Methodist Church (2000).
Economy: Unemployment rate: 7.8% (August 2011); Total civilian labor force: 18,817 (August 2011); Leading industries: 20.1% health care and social assistance; 16.8% retail trade; 10.8% construction (2009); Farms: 1,031 totaling 268,441 acres (2007); Companies that employ 500 or more persons: 0 (2009); Companies that employ 100 to 499 persons: 11 (2009); Companies that employ less than 100 persons: 855 (2009); Black-owned businesses: n/a (2007); Hispanic-owned businesses: n/a (2007); Asian-owned businesses: n/a (2007); Women-owned businesses: n/a (2007); Retail sales per capita: $11,917 (2010). Single-family building permits issued: 102 (2010); Multi-family building permits issued: 2 (2010).
Income: Per capita income: $24,475 (2010); Median household income: $54,945 (2010); Average household income: $63,538 (2010); Percent of households with income of $100,000 or more: 16.0% (2010); Poverty rate: 8.4% (2009); Bankruptcy rate: 2.72% (2010).
Taxes: Total county taxes per capita: $129 (2007); County property taxes per capita: $128 (2007).
Education: Percent of population age 25 and over with: High school diploma (including GED) or higher: 83.5% (2010); Bachelor's degree or higher: 17.6% (2010); Master's degree or higher: 6.2% (2010).
Housing: Homeownership rate: 79.5% (2010); Median home value: $111,659 (2010); Median contract rent: $456 per month (2005-2009 5-year est.); Median year structure built: 1972 (2005-2009 5-year est.)
Health: Birth rate: 129.5 per 10,000 population (2009); Death rate: 94.0 per 10,000 population (2009); Age-adjusted cancer mortality rate: 169.4 deaths per 100,000 population (2007); Number of physicians: 7.4 per 10,000 population (2008); Hospital beds: 16.6 per 10,000 population (2007); Hospital admissions: 576.3 per 10,000 population (2007).
Elections: 2008 Presidential election results: 44.2% Obama, 54.0% McCain, 0.8% Nader
National and State Parks: Hazlet State Park; South Shore State Park
Additional Information Contacts
Clinton County Government. . . . . (618) 594-2464
    https://www.clintonco.illinois.gov
City of Carlyle. . . . . (618) 594-2468
    http://www.playandstaycarlyle.com
Trenton Chamber of Commerce
    http://www.trenton-ilchamber.com

Clinton County Communities

ALBERS (village). Covers a land area of 0.725 square miles and a water area of 0 square miles. Located at 38.54° N. Lat; 89.61° W. Long. Elevation is 440 feet.
Population: 722 (1990); 878 (2000); 848 (2010); 833 (2015 projected); Race: 98.2% White, 0.4% Black, 0.0% Asian, 1.4% Other, 0.7% Hispanic of any race (2010); Density: 1,169.7 persons per square mile (2010); Average household size: 2.73 (2010); Median age: 33.5 (2010); Males per 100 females: 100.0 (2010); Marriage status: 21.8% never married, 70.2% now married, 2.3% widowed, 5.6% divorced (2005-2009 5-year est.); Foreign born: 4.4% (2005-2009 5-year est.); Ancestry (includes multiple ancestries): 72.2% German, 4.6% Lithuanian, 4.2% Irish, 3.8% American, 2.9% Finnish (2005-2009 5-year est.).
Economy: Single-family building permits issued: 1 (2010); Multi-family building permits issued: 0 (2010); Employment by occupation: 13.9% management, 18.5% professional, 11.1% services, 27.5% sales, 0.8% farming, 13.9% construction, 14.3% production (2005-2009 5-year est.).
Income: Per capita income: $25,228 (2010); Median household income: $59,961 (2010); Average household income: $69,204 (2010); Percent of households with income of $100,000 or more: 20.6% (2010); Poverty rate: 2.1% (2005-2009 5-year est.).
Taxes: Total city taxes per capita: $76 (2007); City property taxes per capita: $56 (2007).

Education: Percent of population age 25 and over with: High school diploma (including GED) or higher: 86.8% (2010); Bachelor's degree or higher: 17.8% (2010); Master's degree or higher: 4.7% (2010).

School District(s)

Albers SD 63 (PK-08)

2009-10 Enrollment: 203 . . . . (618) 248-5146

Housing: Homeownership rate: 80.1% (2010); Median home value: $133,232 (2010); Median contract rent: $504 per month (2005-2009 5-year est.); Median year structure built: 1977 (2005-2009 5-year est.).

Transportation: Commute to work: 84.7% car, 2.5% public transportation, 5.8% walk, 3.3% work from home (2005-2009 5-year est.); Travel time to work: 24.2% less than 15 minutes, 27.4% 15 to 30 minutes, 27.2% 30 to 45 minutes, 10.1% 45 to 60 minutes, 11.1% 60 minutes or more (2005-2009 5-year est.)

AVISTON (village). Covers a land area of 1.103 square miles and a water area of 0 square miles. Located at 38.60° N. Lat; 89.60° W. Long. Elevation is 469 feet.

Population: 1,164 (1990); 1,231 (2000); 1,358 (2010); 1,413 (2015 projected); Race: 98.4% White, 0.3% Black, 0.2% Asian, 1.1% Other, 1.3% Hispanic of any race (2010); Density: 1,230.9 persons per square mile (2010); Average household size: 2.48 (2010); Median age: 39.2 (2010); Males per 100 females: 97.4 (2010); Marriage status: 19.2% never married, 58.6% now married, 14.6% widowed, 7.6% divorced (2005-2009 5-year est.); Foreign born: 0.2% (2005-2009 5-year est.); Ancestry (includes multiple ancestries): 70.2% German, 7.8% American, 6.0% English, 4.6% Irish, 3.7% French (2005-2009 5-year est.).

Economy: Single-family building permits issued: 19 (2010); Multi-family building permits issued: 0 (2010); Employment by occupation: 13.1% management, 15.7% professional, 19.0% services, 24.9% sales, 0.0% farming, 12.3% construction, 15.0% production (2005-2009 5-year est.).

Income: Per capita income: $25,316 (2010); Median household income: $57,212 (2010); Average household income: $63,201 (2010); Percent of households with income of $100,000 or more: 15.7% (2010); Poverty rate: 3.3% (2005-2009 5-year est.).

Taxes: Total city taxes per capita: $57 (2007); City property taxes per capita: $54 (2007).

Education: Percent of population age 25 and over with: High school diploma (including GED) or higher: 89.3% (2010); Bachelor's degree or higher: 22.7% (2010); Master's degree or higher: 6.9% (2010).

School District(s)

Aviston SD 21 (PK-08)

2009-10 Enrollment: 381 . . . . (618) 228-7245

Housing: Homeownership rate: 77.0% (2010); Median home value: $126,741 (2010); Median contract rent: $502 per month (2005-2009 5-year est.); Median year structure built: 1978 (2005-2009 5-year est.).

Safety: Violent crime rate: 0.0 per 10,000 population; Property crime rate: 17.1 per 10,000 population (2010).

Transportation: Commute to work: 95.1% car, 0.3% public transportation, 2.5% walk, 1.5% work from home (2005-2009 5-year est.); Travel time to work: 37.2% less than 15 minutes, 26.1% 15 to 30 minutes, 14.1% 30 to 45 minutes, 11.9% 45 to 60 minutes, 10.7% 60 minutes or more (2005-2009 5-year est.)

BARTELSO (village). Covers a land area of 0.349 square miles and a water area of 0 square miles. Located at 38.53° N. Lat; 89.46° W. Long. Elevation is 449 feet.

Population: 561 (1990); 593 (2000); 616 (2010); 627 (2015 projected); Race: 98.2% White, 0.2% Black, 0.3% Asian, 1.3% Other, 1.5% Hispanic of any race (2010); Density: 1,765.5 persons per square mile (2010); Average household size: 2.92 (2010); Median age: 34.3 (2010); Males per 100 females: 105.3 (2010); Marriage status: 28.2% never married, 61.9% now married, 7.4% widowed, 2.5% divorced (2005-2009 5-year est.); Foreign born: 0.0% (2005-2009 5-year est.); Ancestry (includes multiple ancestries): 75.3% German, 10.3% American, 6.1% Irish, 4.2% European, 2.8% English (2005-2009 5-year est.).

Economy: Employment by occupation: 13.7% management, 16.8% professional, 11.1% services, 24.4% sales, 2.2% farming, 17.8% construction, 14.0% production (2005-2009 5-year est.).

Income: Per capita income: $26,127 (2010); Median household income: $69,250 (2010); Average household income: $75,758 (2010); Percent of households with income of $100,000 or more: 20.9% (2010); Poverty rate: 0.5% (2005-2009 5-year est.).

Taxes: Total city taxes per capita: $29 (2007); City property taxes per capita: $25 (2007).

Education: Percent of population age 25 and over with: High school diploma (including GED) or higher: 85.8% (2010); Bachelor's degree or higher: 15.3% (2010); Master's degree or higher: 3.9% (2010).

School District(s)

Bartelso SD 57 (PK-08)

2009-10 Enrollment: 143 . . . . (618) 765-2164

Housing: Homeownership rate: 88.6% (2010); Median home value: $135,169 (2010); Median contract rent: n/a per month (2005-2009 5-year est.); Median year structure built: 1966 (2005-2009 5-year est.).

Transportation: Commute to work: 97.1% car, 0.0% public transportation, 2.2% walk, 0.6% work from home (2005-2009 5-year est.); Travel time to work: 30.4% less than 15 minutes, 31.7% 15 to 30 minutes, 18.6% 30 to 45 minutes, 8.7% 45 to 60 minutes, 10.6% 60 minutes or more (2005-2009 5-year est.)

BECKEMEYER (village). Covers a land area of 0.492 square miles and a water area of 0 square miles. Located at 38.60° N. Lat; 89.43° W. Long. Elevation is 459 feet.

Population: 1,085 (1990); 1,043 (2000); 981 (2010); 950 (2015 projected); Race: 98.7% White, 0.0% Black, 0.6% Asian, 0.7% Other, 0.8% Hispanic of any race (2010); Density: 1,995.9 persons per square mile (2010); Average household size: 2.48 (2010); Median age: 34.8 (2010); Males per 100 females: 99.0 (2010); Marriage status: 37.8% never married, 46.1% now married, 8.0% widowed, 8.1% divorced (2005-2009 5-year est.); Foreign born: 1.3% (2005-2009 5-year est.); Ancestry (includes multiple ancestries): 44.3% German, 16.7% American, 9.5% European, 5.7% Irish, 3.6% Polish (2005-2009 5-year est.).

Economy: Single-family building permits issued: 0 (2010); Multi-family building permits issued: 0 (2010); Employment by occupation: 1.5% management, 7.9% professional, 21.9% services, 24.3% sales, 0.0% farming, 7.7% construction, 36.6% production (2005-2009 5-year est.).

Income: Per capita income: $21,216 (2010); Median household income: $43,232 (2010); Average household income: $51,970 (2010); Percent of households with income of $100,000 or more: 9.1% (2010); Poverty rate: 7.3% (2005-2009 5-year est.).

Taxes: Total city taxes per capita: $54 (2007); City property taxes per capita: $51 (2007).

Education: Percent of population age 25 and over with: High school diploma (including GED) or higher: 80.4% (2010); Bachelor's degree or higher: 6.7% (2010); Master's degree or higher: 0.0% (2010).

Housing: Homeownership rate: 84.3% (2010); Median home value: $72,459 (2010); Median contract rent: $425 per month (2005-2009 5-year est.); Median year structure built: 1955 (2005-2009 5-year est.).

Safety: Violent crime rate: 0.0 per 10,000 population; Property crime rate: 76.3 per 10,000 population (2010).

Transportation: Commute to work: 92.7% car, 0.2% public transportation, 4.3% walk, 0.8% work from home (2005-2009 5-year est.); Travel time to work: 41.0% less than 15 minutes, 16.3% 15 to 30 minutes, 20.3% 30 to 45 minutes, 17.8% 45 to 60 minutes, 4.6% 60 minutes or more (2005-2009 5-year est.)

BREESE (city). Covers a land area of 2.275 square miles and a water area of 0.025 square miles. Located at 38.61° N. Lat; 89.52° W. Long. Elevation is 453 feet.

History: Breese was named for Judge Sidney Breese (1800-1876), an Illinois jurist and resident of the city. King Edward VII, then Prince of Wales, visited Breese in 1860.

Population: 3,749 (1990); 4,048 (2000); 4,237 (2010); 4,297 (2015 projected); Race: 98.0% White, 0.0% Black, 0.5% Asian, 1.4% Other, 1.7% Hispanic of any race (2010); Density: 1,862.2 persons per square mile (2010); Average household size: 2.53 (2010); Median age: 37.2 (2010); Males per 100 females: 94.6 (2010); Marriage status: 19.7% never married, 63.4% now married, 9.6% widowed, 7.4% divorced (2005-2009 5-year est.); Foreign born: 0.0% (2005-2009 5-year est.); Ancestry (includes multiple ancestries): 66.2% German, 13.1% Irish, 5.3% Italian, 3.7% English, 2.6% Polish (2005-2009 5-year est.).

Economy: Single-family building permits issued: 21 (2010); Multi-family building permits issued: 2 (2010); Employment by occupation: 11.6% management, 21.8% professional, 16.8% services, 23.3% sales, 0.6% farming, 7.8% construction, 18.0% production (2005-2009 5-year est.).

Income: Per capita income: $26,325 (2010); Median household income: $58,457 (2010); Average household income: $67,515 (2010); Percent of households with income of $100,000 or more: 14.8% (2010); Poverty rate: 1.7% (2005-2009 5-year est.).

Taxes: Total city taxes per capita: $363 (2007); City property taxes per capita: $349 (2007).
Education: Percent of population age 25 and over with: High school diploma (including GED) or higher: 87.8% (2010); Bachelor's degree or higher: 23.9% (2010); Master's degree or higher: 6.5% (2010).

School District(s)

Breese SD 12 (PK-08)
   2009-10 Enrollment: 662 . . . . (618) 526-7128
Central CHSD 71 (09-12)
   2009-10 Enrollment: 589 . . . . (618) 526-4510
St Rose SD 14-15 (PK-08)
   2009-10 Enrollment: 179 . . . . (618) 526-7484
Housing: Homeownership rate: 76.8% (2010); Median home value: $126,278 (2010); Median contract rent: $533 per month (2005-2009 5-year est.); Median year structure built: 1968 (2005-2009 5-year est.).
Hospitals: St. Joseph's Hospital (85 beds)
Newspapers: Breese Journal (Local news; Circulation 6,185)
Transportation: Commute to work: 96.2% car, 0.7% public transportation, 1.1% walk, 1.5% work from home (2005-2009 5-year est.); Travel time to work: 45.4% less than 15 minutes, 17.6% 15 to 30 minutes, 15.7% 30 to 45 minutes, 2.3% 45 to 60 minutes, 19.0% 60 minutes or more (2005-2009 5-year est.)

CARLYLE (city). County seat. Covers a land area of 2.993 square miles and a water area of 0.004 square miles. Located at 38.61° N. Lat; 89.37° W. Long. Elevation is 456 feet.
History: Carlyle was sited on the location of John Hill's Fort, built in the early 1800's. Carlyle developed as the seat of Clinton County.
Population: 3,528 (1990); 3,406 (2000); 3,326 (2010); 3,265 (2015 projected); Race: 95.0% White, 3.3% Black, 0.4% Asian, 1.3% Other, 1.6% Hispanic of any race (2010); Density: 1,111.1 persons per square mile (2010); Average household size: 2.30 (2010); Median age: 42.1 (2010); Males per 100 females: 88.2 (2010); Marriage status: 23.0% never married, 48.5% now married, 10.2% widowed, 18.3% divorced (2005-2009 5-year est.); Foreign born: 2.0% (2005-2009 5-year est.); Ancestry (includes multiple ancestries): 54.1% German, 11.5% Irish, 7.9% English, 6.7% American, 3.1% French (2005-2009 5-year est.).
Economy: Single-family building permits issued: 3 (2010); Multi-family building permits issued: 0 (2010); Employment by occupation: 10.3% management, 13.4% professional, 12.6% services, 32.6% sales, 0.0% farming, 10.0% construction, 21.0% production (2005-2009 5-year est.).
Income: Per capita income: $24,624 (2010); Median household income: $47,319 (2010); Average household income: $57,491 (2010); Percent of households with income of $100,000 or more: 14.8% (2010); Poverty rate: 9.9% (2005-2009 5-year est.).
Taxes: Total city taxes per capita: $243 (2007); City property taxes per capita: $220 (2007).
Education: Percent of population age 25 and over with: High school diploma (including GED) or higher: 82.2% (2010); Bachelor's degree or higher: 15.4% (2010); Master's degree or higher: 3.9% (2010).

School District(s)

Carlyle CUSD 1 (PK-12)
   2009-10 Enrollment: 1,176 . . . . (618) 594-8283
Housing: Homeownership rate: 71.0% (2010); Median home value: $97,702 (2010); Median contract rent: $455 per month (2005-2009 5-year est.); Median year structure built: 1968 (2005-2009 5-year est.).
Safety: Violent crime rate: 24.3 per 10,000 population; Property crime rate: 273.4 per 10,000 population (2010).
Newspapers: Union Banner (Community news; Circulation 6,500)
Transportation: Commute to work: 93.6% car, 0.5% public transportation, 1.9% walk, 4.0% work from home (2005-2009 5-year est.); Travel time to work: 45.2% less than 15 minutes, 25.7% 15 to 30 minutes, 15.9% 30 to 45 minutes, 6.2% 45 to 60 minutes, 7.0% 60 minutes or more (2005-2009 5-year est.)
Additional Information Contacts
City of Carlyle. . . . . (618) 594-2468
   http://www.playandstaycarlyle.com

DAMIANSVILLE (village). Covers a land area of 0.242 square miles and a water area of 0 square miles. Located at 38.51° N. Lat; 89.62° W. Long. Elevation is 430 feet.
Population: 383 (1990); 368 (2000); 381 (2010); 386 (2015 projected); Race: 88.5% White, 0.3% Black, 0.3% Asian, 11.0% Other, 11.3% Hispanic of any race (2010); Density: 1,576.6 persons per square mile (2010); Average household size: 2.76 (2010); Median age: 37.7 (2010);

Males per 100 females: 104.8 (2010); Marriage status: 22.7% never married, 59.5% now married, 4.9% widowed, 12.9% divorced (2005-2009 5-year est.); Foreign born: 0.0% (2005-2009 5-year est.); Ancestry (includes multiple ancestries): 44.5% German, 13.4% American, 8.2% Irish, 6.9% English, 5.4% Italian (2005-2009 5-year est.).
Economy: Single-family building permits issued: 1 (2010); Multi-family building permits issued: 0 (2010); Employment by occupation: 10.2% management, 27.4% professional, 11.4% services, 32.9% sales, 1.2% farming, 8.3% construction, 8.6% production (2005-2009 5-year est.).
Income: Per capita income: $30,218 (2010); Median household income: $74,569 (2010); Average household income: $83,759 (2010); Percent of households with income of $100,000 or more: 30.4% (2010); Poverty rate: 2.6% (2005-2009 5-year est.).
Taxes: Total city taxes per capita: $11 (2007); City property taxes per capita: $8 (2007).
Education: Percent of population age 25 and over with: High school diploma (including GED) or higher: 84.7% (2010); Bachelor's degree or higher: 16.0% (2010); Master's degree or higher: 4.1% (2010).

School District(s)

Damiansville SD 62 (PK-08)
   2009-10 Enrollment: 115 . . . . (618) 248-5188
Housing: Homeownership rate: 80.7% (2010); Median home value: $123,276 (2010); Median contract rent: $608 per month (2005-2009 5-year est.); Median year structure built: 1978 (2005-2009 5-year est.).
Transportation: Commute to work: 96.2% car, 1.3% public transportation, 2.5% walk, 0.0% work from home (2005-2009 5-year est.); Travel time to work: 16.7% less than 15 minutes, 28.1% 15 to 30 minutes, 33.4% 30 to 45 minutes, 12.9% 45 to 60 minutes, 8.8% 60 minutes or more (2005-2009 5-year est.)

GERMANTOWN (village). Covers a land area of 0.794 square miles and a water area of 0 square miles. Located at 38.55° N. Lat; 89.53° W. Long. Elevation is 430 feet.
Population: 1,222 (1990); 1,118 (2000); 1,066 (2010); 1,038 (2015 projected); Race: 98.9% White, 0.1% Black, 0.2% Asian, 0.8% Other, 0.6% Hispanic of any race (2010); Density: 1,343.3 persons per square mile (2010); Average household size: 2.55 (2010); Median age: 39.0 (2010); Males per 100 females: 99.6 (2010); Marriage status: 19.1% never married, 67.5% now married, 8.8% widowed, 4.6% divorced (2005-2009 5-year est.); Foreign born: 1.9% (2005-2009 5-year est.); Ancestry (includes multiple ancestries): 72.6% German, 9.3% American, 4.7% Irish, 2.3% Swedish, 1.9% French (2005-2009 5-year est.).
Economy: Employment by occupation: 15.2% management, 16.6% professional, 19.9% services, 20.8% sales, 0.0% farming, 15.7% construction, 11.8% production (2005-2009 5-year est.).
Income: Per capita income: $28,362 (2010); Median household income: $65,833 (2010); Average household income: $72,735 (2010); Percent of households with income of $100,000 or more: 24.3% (2010); Poverty rate: 5.7% (2005-2009 5-year est.).
Taxes: Total city taxes per capita: $124 (2007); City property taxes per capita: $94 (2007).
Education: Percent of population age 25 and over with: High school diploma (including GED) or higher: 83.9% (2010); Bachelor's degree or higher: 12.0% (2010); Master's degree or higher: 4.3% (2010).

School District(s)

Germantown SD 60 (PK-08)
   2009-10 Enrollment: 267 . . . . (618) 523-4253
Housing: Homeownership rate: 83.6% (2010); Median home value: $116,441 (2010); Median contract rent: $378 per month (2005-2009 5-year est.); Median year structure built: 1963 (2005-2009 5-year est.).
Safety: Violent crime rate: 0.0 per 10,000 population; Property crime rate: 8.9 per 10,000 population (2010).
Transportation: Commute to work: 83.6% car, 0.3% public transportation, 5.8% walk, 9.7% work from home (2005-2009 5-year est.); Travel time to work: 41.3% less than 15 minutes, 16.8% 15 to 30 minutes, 15.4% 30 to 45 minutes, 12.4% 45 to 60 minutes, 14.1% 60 minutes or more (2005-2009 5-year est.)

HOFFMAN (village). Covers a land area of 0.362 square miles and a water area of 0 square miles. Located at 38.54° N. Lat; 89.26° W. Long. Elevation is 456 feet.
Population: 511 (1990); 460 (2000); 466 (2010); 466 (2015 projected); Race: 98.1% White, 0.2% Black, 0.4% Asian, 1.3% Other, 0.9% Hispanic of any race (2010); Density: 1,287.0 persons per square mile (2010); Average household size: 2.66 (2010); Median age: 35.7 (2010); Males per

100 females: 97.5 (2010); Marriage status: 18.7% never married, 69.2% now married, 4.0% widowed, 8.1% divorced (2005-2009 5-year est.); Foreign born: 2.9% (2005-2009 5-year est.); Ancestry (includes multiple ancestries): 60.8% German, 12.9% Irish, 8.3% American, 4.5% French, 4.1% Polish (2005-2009 5-year est.).

Economy: Single-family building permits issued: 0 (2010); Multi-family building permits issued: 0 (2010); Employment by occupation: 14.6% management, 17.9% professional, 22.7% services, 23.4% sales, 0.0% farming, 8.4% construction, 13.0% production (2005-2009 5-year est.).

Income: Per capita income: $22,941 (2010); Median household income: $51,389 (2010); Average household income: $59,343 (2010); Percent of households with income of $100,000 or more: 14.9% (2010); Poverty rate: 6.7% (2005-2009 5-year est.).

Taxes: Total city taxes per capita: $27 (2007); City property taxes per capita: $24 (2007).

Education: Percent of population age 25 and over with: High school diploma (including GED) or higher: 89.5% (2010); Bachelor's degree or higher: 11.2% (2010); Master's degree or higher: 6.5% (2010).

Housing: Homeownership rate: 85.1% (2010); Median home value: $83,600 (2010); Median contract rent: $400 per month (2005-2009 5-year est.); Median year structure built: 1961 (2005-2009 5-year est.).

Transportation: Commute to work: 95.0% car, 0.0% public transportation, 1.7% walk, 3.3% work from home (2005-2009 5-year est.); Travel time to work: 33.8% less than 15 minutes, 35.9% 15 to 30 minutes, 7.9% 30 to 45 minutes, 13.1% 45 to 60 minutes, 9.3% 60 minutes or more (2005-2009 5-year est.)

HUEY

HUEY (village). Covers a land area of 0.165 square miles and a water area of 0 square miles. Located at 38.60° N. Lat; 89.29° W. Long. Elevation is 453 feet.

Population: 210 (1990); 196 (2000); 190 (2010); 189 (2015 projected); Race: 95.3% White, 3.7% Black, 0.0% Asian, 1.1% Other, 1.6% Hispanic of any race (2010); Density: 1,149.0 persons per square mile (2010); Average household size: 2.50 (2010); Median age: 42.4 (2010); Males per 100 females: 106.5 (2010); Marriage status: 22.7% never married, 60.7% now married, 9.2% widowed, 7.4% divorced (2005-2009 5-year est.); Foreign born: 0.0% (2005-2009 5-year est.); Ancestry (includes multiple ancestries): 33.6% German, 24.6% American, 15.5% Irish, 5.6% Polish, 5.2% European (2005-2009 5-year est.).

Economy: Single-family building permits issued: 0 (2010); Multi-family building permits issued: 0 (2010); Employment by occupation: 2.7% management, 19.8% professional, 20.7% services, 28.8% sales, 0.0% farming, 3.6% construction, 24.3% production (2005-2009 5-year est.).

Income: Per capita income: $25,505 (2010); Median household income: $56,944 (2010); Average household income: $67,138 (2010); Percent of households with income of $100,000 or more: 15.8% (2010); Poverty rate: 22.0% (2005-2009 5-year est.).

Taxes: Total city taxes per capita: $27 (2007); City property taxes per capita: $27 (2007).

Education: Percent of population age 25 and over with: High school diploma (including GED) or higher: 82.2% (2010); Bachelor's degree or higher: 8.9% (2010); Master's degree or higher: 1.5% (2010).

Housing: Homeownership rate: 82.9% (2010); Median home value: $75,625 (2010); Median contract rent: $512 per month (2005-2009 5-year est.); Median year structure built: 1966 (2005-2009 5-year est.).

Transportation: Commute to work: 96.5% car, 0.0% public transportation, 0.0% walk, 3.5% work from home (2005-2009 5-year est.); Travel time to work: 33.6% less than 15 minutes, 24.5% 15 to 30 minutes, 25.5% 30 to 45 minutes, 10.0% 45 to 60 minutes, 6.4% 60 minutes or more (2005-2009 5-year est.)

KEYESPORT

KEYESPORT (village). Covers a land area of 0.403 square miles and a water area of 0.017 square miles. Located at 38.74° N. Lat; 89.27° W. Long. Elevation is 453 feet.

Population: 440 (1990); 481 (2000); 483 (2010); 488 (2015 projected); Race: 98.6% White, 0.4% Black, 0.2% Asian, 0.8% Other, 0.8% Hispanic of any race (2010); Density: 1,198.6 persons per square mile (2010); Average household size: 2.34 (2010); Median age: 43.3 (2010); Males per 100 females: 95.5 (2010); Marriage status: 21.1% never married, 61.8% now married, 13.0% widowed, 4.2% divorced (2005-2009 5-year est.); Foreign born: 0.0% (2005-2009 5-year est.); Ancestry (includes multiple ancestries): 16.3% German, 15.7% Irish, 9.8% American, 6.7% English, 5.9% French (2005-2009 5-year est.).

Economy: Employment by occupation: 0.0% management, 15.7% professional, 27.0% services, 9.7% sales, 0.0% farming, 5.4% construction, 42.2% production (2005-2009 5-year est.).

Income: Per capita income: $21,526 (2010); Median household income: $43,710 (2010); Average household income: $50,097 (2010); Percent of households with income of $100,000 or more: 9.7% (2010); Poverty rate: 29.9% (2005-2009 5-year est.).

Taxes: Total city taxes per capita: $44 (2007); City property taxes per capita: $34 (2007).

Education: Percent of population age 25 and over with: High school diploma (including GED) or higher: 81.9% (2010); Bachelor's degree or higher: 12.2% (2010); Master's degree or higher: 4.4% (2010).

Housing: Homeownership rate: 80.6% (2010); Median home value: $83,478 (2010); Median contract rent: $320 per month (2005-2009 5-year est.); Median year structure built: 1974 (2005-2009 5-year est.).

Transportation: Commute to work: 94.8% car, 0.0% public transportation, 0.0% walk, 5.2% work from home (2005-2009 5-year est.); Travel time to work: 8.5% less than 15 minutes, 25.0% 15 to 30 minutes, 34.1% 30 to 45 minutes, 6.1% 45 to 60 minutes, 26.2% 60 minutes or more (2005-2009 5-year est.)

NEW BADEN

NEW BADEN (village). Covers a land area of 1.337 square miles and a water area of 0 square miles. Located at 38.53° N. Lat; 89.70° W. Long. Elevation is 459 feet.

Population: 2,755 (1990); 3,001 (2000); 3,476 (2010); 3,669 (2015 projected); Race: 95.8% White, 1.2% Black, 0.7% Asian, 2.3% Other, 1.9% Hispanic of any race (2010); Density: 2,600.8 persons per square mile (2010); Average household size: 2.51 (2010); Median age: 38.3 (2010); Males per 100 females: 93.9 (2010); Marriage status: 25.9% never married, 60.9% now married, 4.8% widowed, 8.4% divorced (2005-2009 5-year est.); Foreign born: 2.6% (2005-2009 5-year est.); Ancestry (includes multiple ancestries): 51.4% German, 11.7% English, 10.1% Irish, 5.5% Italian, 5.4% American (2005-2009 5-year est.).

Economy: Single-family building permits issued: 7 (2010); Multi-family building permits issued: 0 (2010); Employment by occupation: 11.3% management, 17.9% professional, 20.6% services, 25.2% sales, 0.0% farming, 12.7% construction, 12.3% production (2005-2009 5-year est.).

Income: Per capita income: $23,675 (2010); Median household income: $53,259 (2010); Average household income: $60,177 (2010); Percent of households with income of $100,000 or more: 12.8% (2010); Poverty rate: 9.7% (2005-2009 5-year est.).

Taxes: Total city taxes per capita: $216 (2007); City property taxes per capita: $194 (2007).

Education: Percent of population age 25 and over with: High school diploma (including GED) or higher: 85.9% (2010); Bachelor's degree or higher: 24.1% (2010); Master's degree or higher: 11.4% (2010).

School District(s)

Wesclin CUSD 3 (PK-12)

    2009-10 Enrollment: 1,400 . . . . (618) 224-7583

Housing: Homeownership rate: 74.2% (2010); Median home value: $114,493 (2010); Median contract rent: $482 per month (2005-2009 5-year est.); Median year structure built: 1969 (2005-2009 5-year est.).

Transportation: Commute to work: 88.2% car, 1.6% public transportation, 4.5% walk, 2.8% work from home (2005-2009 5-year est.); Travel time to work: 33.3% less than 15 minutes, 34.6% 15 to 30 minutes, 18.8% 30 to 45 minutes, 6.7% 45 to 60 minutes, 6.7% 60 minutes or more (2005-2009 5-year est.)

SHATTUC

SHATTUC (unincorporated postal area, zip code 62283). Covers a land area of 45.974 square miles and a water area of 0.009 square miles. Located at 38.64° N. Lat; 89.20° W. Long. Elevation is 476 feet.

Population: 721 (2000); Race: 99.0% White, 0.0% Black, 0.0% Asian, 1.0% Other, 0.0% Hispanic of any race (2000); Density: 15.7 persons per square mile (2000); Age: 26.8% under 18, 20.2% over 64 (2000); Marriage status: 18.5% never married, 63.3% now married, 6.9% widowed, 11.2% divorced (2000); Foreign born: 0.0% (2000); Ancestry (includes multiple ancestries): 57.0% German, 18.3% American, 11.7% English, 10.0% Italian, 3.2% Irish (2000).

Economy: Employment by occupation: 6.8% management, 15.3% professional, 9.1% services, 26.8% sales, 1.5% farming, 20.6% construction, 19.8% production (2000).

Income: Per capita income: $15,889 (2000); Median household income: $35,694 (2000); Poverty rate: 13.6% (2000).

Education: Percent of population age 25 and over with: High school diploma (including GED) or higher: 83.1% (2000); Bachelor's degree or higher: 8.5% (2000).
Housing: Homeownership rate: 84.2% (2000); Median home value: $63,800 (2000); Median contract rent: $313 per month (2000); Median year structure built: 1961 (2000).
Transportation: Commute to work: 94.3% car, 0.0% public transportation, 0.0% walk, 5.7% work from home (2000); Travel time to work: 16.4% less than 15 minutes, 36.2% 15 to 30 minutes, 31.9% 30 to 45 minutes, 11.7% 45 to 60 minutes, 3.7% 60 minutes or more (2000)

TRENTON (city). Covers a land area of 0.983 square miles and a water area of 0 square miles. Located at 38.60° N. Lat; 89.68° W. Long. Elevation is 495 feet.
History: Incorporated 1865.
Population: 2,555 (1990); 2,610 (2000); 2,865 (2010); 2,971 (2015 projected); Race: 98.4% White, 0.5% Black, 0.6% Asian, 0.6% Other, 3.1% Hispanic of any race (2010); Density: 2,915.6 persons per square mile (2010); Average household size: 2.40 (2010); Median age: 39.8 (2010); Males per 100 females: 94.4 (2010); Marriage status: 21.3% never married, 60.1% now married, 8.8% widowed, 9.7% divorced (2005-2009 5-year est.); Foreign born: 2.0% (2005-2009 5-year est.); Ancestry (includes multiple ancestries): 52.9% German, 14.8% Irish, 10.4% English, 5.8% American, 3.8% European (2005-2009 5-year est.).
Economy: Single-family building permits issued: 6 (2010); Multi-family building permits issued: 0 (2010); Employment by occupation: 8.5% management, 18.1% professional, 16.8% services, 29.4% sales, 0.3% farming, 16.4% construction, 10.5% production (2005-2009 5-year est.).
Income: Per capita income: $27,256 (2010); Median household income: $58,028 (2010); Average household income: $65,652 (2010); Percent of households with income of $100,000 or more: 17.7% (2010); Poverty rate: 11.7% (2005-2009 5-year est.).
Taxes: Total city taxes per capita: $220 (2007); City property taxes per capita: $171 (2007).
Education: Percent of population age 25 and over with: High school diploma (including GED) or higher: 93.2% (2010); Bachelor's degree or higher: 30.0% (2010); Master's degree or higher: 13.8% (2010).

School District(s)
Wesclin CUSD 3 (PK-12)
    2009-10 Enrollment: 1,400 . . . . (618) 224-7583
Housing: Homeownership rate: 79.4% (2010); Median home value: $121,481 (2010); Median contract rent: $495 per month (2005-2009 5-year est.); Median year structure built: 1965 (2005-2009 5-year est.).
Safety: Violent crime rate: 7.7 per 10,000 population; Property crime rate: 84.6 per 10,000 population (2010).
Newspapers: Trenton Sun (Local news; Circulation 1,400)
Transportation: Commute to work: 91.5% car, 0.9% public transportation, 3.5% walk, 2.4% work from home (2005-2009 5-year est.); Travel time to work: 39.1% less than 15 minutes, 21.4% 15 to 30 minutes, 19.7% 30 to 45 minutes, 10.8% 45 to 60 minutes, 9.0% 60 minutes or more (2005-2009 5-year est.)
Additional Information Contacts
Trenton Chamber of Commerce. . . . .
    http://www.trenton-ilchamber.com

Coles County

Located in east central Illinois; drained by the Kaskaskia, Embarrass, and Little Wabash Rivers; includes Paradise Lake. Covers a land area of 508.29 square miles, a water area of 1.78 square miles, and is located in the Central Time Zone at 39.50° N. Lat., 88.25° W. Long. The county was founded in 1830. County seat is Charleston.

Coles County is part of the Charleston-Mattoon, IL Micropolitan Statistical Area. The entire metro area includes: Coles County, IL; Cumberland County, IL

Weather Station: Charleston   Elevation: 680 feet

	Jan	Feb	Mar	Apr	May	Jun	Jul	Aug	Sep	Oct	Nov	Dec
High	37	41	53	65	75	84	87	85	79	67	53	40
Low	21	24	33	44	53	62	66	64	56	45	36	24
Precip	2.4	2.4	3.0	4.2	4.5	3.9	4.2	3.3	3.2	3.9	4.0	3.1
Snow	8.5	3.8	2.1	0.2	tr	0.0	0.0	0.0	0.0	tr	1.0	5.1

High and Low temperatures in degrees Fahrenheit; Precipitation and Snow in inches

Population: 51,644 (1990); 53,196 (2000); 52,077 (2010); 51,283 (2015 projected); Race: 93.7% White, 3.1% Black, 1.1% Asian, 2.2% Other, 2.0% Hispanic of any race (2010); Density: 102.5 persons per square mile (2010); Average household size: 2.26 (2010); Median age: 30.7 (2010); Males per 100 females: 91.6 (2010).
Religion: Five largest groups: 6.3% Catholic Church, 5.9% Christian Churches and Churches of Christ, 5.0% The United Methodist Church, 3.8% Lutheran Church—Missouri Synod, 3.7% Southern Baptist Convention (2000).
Economy: Unemployment rate: 9.7% (August 2011); Total civilian labor force: 26,328 (August 2011); Leading industries: 21.9% health care and social assistance; 18.0% manufacturing; 13.9% retail trade (2009); Farms: 729 totaling 254,869 acres (2007); Companies that employ 500 or more persons: 2 (2009); Companies that employ 100 to 499 persons: 26 (2009); Companies that employ less than 100 persons: 1,210 (2009); Black-owned businesses: 101 (2007); Hispanic-owned businesses: n/a (2007); Asian-owned businesses: n/a (2007); Women-owned businesses: 992 (2007); Retail sales per capita: $14,377 (2010). Single-family building permits issued: 15 (2010); Multi-family building permits issued: 112 (2010).
Income: Per capita income: $19,974 (2010); Median household income: $36,606 (2010); Average household income: $48,325 (2010); Percent of households with income of $100,000 or more: 9.1% (2010); Poverty rate: 19.1% (2009); Bankruptcy rate: 4.70% (2010).
Taxes: Total county taxes per capita: $130 (2007); County property taxes per capita: $130 (2007).
Education: Percent of population age 25 and over with: High school diploma (including GED) or higher: 89.5% (2010); Bachelor's degree or higher: 22.4% (2010); Master's degree or higher: 9.5% (2010).
Housing: Homeownership rate: 59.0% (2010); Median home value: $84,712 (2010); Median contract rent: $445 per month (2005-2009 5-year est.); Median year structure built: 1969 (2005-2009 5-year est.)
Health: Birth rate: 114.7 per 10,000 population (2009); Death rate: 95.5 per 10,000 population (2009); Age-adjusted cancer mortality rate: 227.9 deaths per 100,000 population (2007); Number of physicians: 18.6 per 10,000 population (2008); Hospital beds: 25.3 per 10,000 population (2007); Hospital admissions: 1,420.3 per 10,000 population (2007).
Elections: 2008 Presidential election results: 50.8% Obama, 47.6% McCain, 0.7% Nader
National and State Parks: Fox Ridge State Park; Lincoln Log Cabin State Historic Site
Additional Information Contacts
Coles County Government. . . . . (217) 348-0501
    http://www.co.coles.il.us
Charleston Area Chamber of Commerce. . . . . (217) 345-7041
    http://www.charlestonchamber.com
City of Charleston . . . . (217) 345-5650
    http://www.charlestonillinois.org
City of Mattoon. . . . . (217) 235-5654
    http://mattoon.illinois.gov
Mattoon Chamber of Commerce . . . . (217) 235-5661
    http://www.mattoonchamber.com

Coles County Communities

ASHMORE (village). Covers a land area of 0.834 square miles and a water area of 0 square miles. Located at 39.53° N. Lat; 88.02° W. Long. Elevation is 699 feet.
Population: 888 (1990); 809 (2000); 712 (2010); 664 (2015 projected); Race: 95.5% White, 0.8% Black, 2.0% Asian, 1.7% Other, 1.0% Hispanic of any race (2010); Density: 854.0 persons per square mile (2010); Average household size: 2.56 (2010); Median age: 34.9 (2010); Males per 100 females: 96.7 (2010); Marriage status: 16.8% never married, 60.0% now married, 4.3% widowed, 18.9% divorced (2005-2009 5-year est.); Foreign born: 0.0% (2005-2009 5-year est.); Ancestry (includes multiple ancestries): 23.8% German, 17.3% Irish, 15.5% American, 6.2% English, 5.1% Dutch (2005-2009 5-year est.).
Economy: Single-family building permits issued: 1 (2010); Multi-family building permits issued: 0 (2010); Employment by occupation: 5.1% management, 8.8% professional, 16.4% services, 29.4% sales, 0.0% farming, 13.8% construction, 26.6% production (2005-2009 5-year est.).
Income: Per capita income: $19,549 (2010); Median household income: $48,085 (2010); Average household income: $49,757 (2010); Percent of households with income of $100,000 or more: 4.3% (2010); Poverty rate: 15.5% (2005-2009 5-year est.).

Taxes: Total city taxes per capita: $26 (2007); City property taxes per capita: $18 (2007).
Education: Percent of population age 25 and over with: High school diploma (including GED) or higher: 89.4% (2010); Bachelor's degree or higher: 17.3% (2010); Master's degree or higher: 6.8% (2010).
School District(s)
Charleston CUSD 1 (PK-12)
  2009-10 Enrollment: 2,892 . . . . (217) 639-1000
Housing: Homeownership rate: 82.0% (2010); Median home value: $75,862 (2010); Median contract rent: $358 per month (2005-2009 5-year est.); Median year structure built: 1968 (2005-2009 5-year est.).
Transportation: Commute to work: 94.4% car, 0.0% public transportation, 0.0% walk, 5.6% work from home (2005-2009 5-year est.); Travel time to work: 30.7% less than 15 minutes, 47.6% 15 to 30 minutes, 16.0% 30 to 45 minutes, 2.8% 45 to 60 minutes, 2.8% 60 minutes or more (2005-2009 5-year est.)

CHARLESTON (city). County seat. Covers a land area of 7.993 square miles and a water area of 0.680 square miles. Located at 39.48° N. Lat; 88.17° W. Long. Elevation is 669 feet.
History: Charleston was the site of the fourth Lincoln-Douglas debate in 1858, when 12,000 people gathered to hear Abraham Lincoln state his views on equality of all people.
Population: 20,625 (1990); 21,039 (2000); 21,190 (2010); 21,305 (2015 projected); Race: 89.6% White, 5.9% Black, 1.8% Asian, 2.7% Other, 2.5% Hispanic of any race (2010); Density: 2,651.1 persons per square mile (2010); Average household size: 2.19 (2010); Median age: 24.1 (2010); Males per 100 females: 87.0 (2010); Marriage status: 67.3% never married, 24.9% now married, 2.5% widowed, 5.3% divorced (2005-2009 5-year est.); Foreign born: 3.2% (2005-2009 5-year est.); Ancestry (includes multiple ancestries): 28.0% German, 17.6% Irish, 6.8% English, 6.1% American, 5.3% Polish (2005-2009 5-year est.).
Economy: Single-family building permits issued: 6 (2010); Multi-family building permits issued: 110 (2010); Employment by occupation: 8.3% management, 21.6% professional, 24.6% services, 26.2% sales, 0.0% farming, 5.5% construction, 13.9% production (2005-2009 5-year est.).
Income: Per capita income: $16,843 (2010); Median household income: $28,584 (2010); Average household income: $43,086 (2010); Percent of households with income of $100,000 or more: 9.2% (2010); Poverty rate: 41.1% (2005-2009 5-year est.).
Taxes: Total city taxes per capita: $265 (2007); City property taxes per capita: $170 (2007).
Education: Percent of population age 25 and over with: High school diploma (including GED) or higher: 90.2% (2010); Bachelor's degree or higher: 34.6% (2010); Master's degree or higher: 17.0% (2010).
School District(s)
Charleston CUSD 1 (PK-12)
  2009-10 Enrollment: 2,892 . . . . (217) 639-1000
Clk Cls Cmbn Dglas Edgr Mltr Shlb (06-12)
  2009-10 Enrollment: n/a . . . . (217) 348-0151
Eastern II Efe System
  2009-10 Enrollment: n/a . . . . (217) 348-0151
Four-year College(s)
Eastern Illinois University (Public)
  Fall 2009 Enrollment: 11,966. . . . . (217) 581-5000
  2010-11 Tuition: In-state $9,987; Out-of-state $25,227
Housing: Homeownership rate: 44.5% (2010); Median home value: $91,353 (2010); Median contract rent: $497 per month (2005-2009 5-year est.); Median year structure built: 1976 (2005-2009 5-year est.).
Safety: Violent crime rate: 27.9 per 10,000 population; Property crime rate: 152.8 per 10,000 population (2010).
Newspapers: Times-Courier (Community news; Circulation 6,897)
Transportation: Commute to work: 76.9% car, 1.4% public transportation, 17.9% walk, 2.6% work from home (2005-2009 5-year est.); Travel time to work: 63.4% less than 15 minutes, 23.2% 15 to 30 minutes, 7.7% 30 to 45 minutes, 2.5% 45 to 60 minutes, 3.2% 60 minutes or more (2005-2009 5-year est.).
Additional Information Contacts
Charleston Area Chamber of Commerce. . . . . (217) 345-7041
  http://www.charlestonchamber.com
City of Charleston . . . . (217) 345-5650
  http://www.charlestonillinois.org

HUMBOLDT (village). Covers a land area of 0.562 square miles and a water area of 0 square miles. Located at 39.60° N. Lat; 88.32° W. Long. Elevation is 663 feet.
Population: 470 (1990); 481 (2000); 412 (2010); 381 (2015 projected); Race: 98.1% White, 0.0% Black, 0.0% Asian, 1.9% Other, 5.8% Hispanic of any race (2010); Density: 733.3 persons per square mile (2010); Average household size: 2.53 (2010); Median age: 35.6 (2010); Males per 100 females: 100.0 (2010); Marriage status: 19.3% never married, 64.9% now married, 5.7% widowed, 10.1% divorced (2005-2009 5-year est.); Foreign born: 10.6% (2005-2009 5-year est.); Ancestry (includes multiple ancestries): 26.4% German, 13.2% Irish, 7.9% American, 6.6% English, 4.2% Scottish (2005-2009 5-year est.).
Economy: Employment by occupation: 3.3% management, 6.7% professional, 18.7% services, 17.7% sales, 0.0% farming, 17.7% construction, 35.9% production (2005-2009 5-year est.).
Income: Per capita income: $24,227 (2010); Median household income: $49,013 (2010); Average household income: $63,635 (2010); Percent of households with income of $100,000 or more: 14.1% (2010); Poverty rate: 8.7% (2005-2009 5-year est.).
Taxes: Total city taxes per capita: $23 (2007); City property taxes per capita: $17 (2007).
Education: Percent of population age 25 and over with: High school diploma (including GED) or higher: 93.2% (2010); Bachelor's degree or higher: 14.3% (2010); Master's degree or higher: 5.2% (2010).
School District(s)
Eastern II Area of Spec Educ (PK-12)
  2009-10 Enrollment: n/a . . . . (217) 348-7700
Housing: Homeownership rate: 76.7% (2010); Median home value: $80,968 (2010); Median contract rent: $411 per month (2005-2009 5-year est.); Median year structure built: 1957 (2005-2009 5-year est.).
Transportation: Commute to work: 95.0% car, 0.0% public transportation, 4.0% walk, 1.0% work from home (2005-2009 5-year est.); Travel time to work: 30.0% less than 15 minutes, 44.5% 15 to 30 minutes, 13.5% 30 to 45 minutes, 7.0% 45 to 60 minutes, 5.0% 60 minutes or more (2005-2009 5-year est.)

LERNA (village). Covers a land area of 0.117 square miles and a water area of 0 square miles. Located at 39.41° N. Lat; 88.28° W. Long. Elevation is 751 feet.
Population: 295 (1990); 322 (2000); 359 (2010); 370 (2015 projected); Race: 96.9% White, 1.1% Black, 0.6% Asian, 1.4% Other, 1.7% Hispanic of any race (2010); Density: 3,078.4 persons per square mile (2010); Average household size: 2.59 (2010); Median age: 34.7 (2010); Males per 100 females: 101.7 (2010); Marriage status: 12.0% never married, 78.9% now married, 3.2% widowed, 5.9% divorced (2005-2009 5-year est.); Foreign born: 0.0% (2005-2009 5-year est.); Ancestry (includes multiple ancestries): 25.2% German, 9.7% Irish, 8.8% American, 7.4% English, 3.9% Scottish (2005-2009 5-year est.).
Economy: Employment by occupation: 14.8% management, 5.2% professional, 18.8% services, 21.4% sales, 0.9% farming, 6.1% construction, 32.8% production (2005-2009 5-year est.).
Income: Per capita income: $28,044 (2010); Median household income: $53,704 (2010); Average household income: $73,913 (2010); Percent of households with income of $100,000 or more: 21.7% (2010); Poverty rate: 8.1% (2005-2009 5-year est.).
Taxes: Total city taxes per capita: $35 (2007); City property taxes per capita: $35 (2007).
Education: Percent of population age 25 and over with: High school diploma (including GED) or higher: 95.6% (2010); Bachelor's degree or higher: 22.9% (2010); Master's degree or higher: 10.1% (2010).
School District(s)
Clk Cls Cmbn Dglas Edgr Mltr Shlb (06-12)
  2009-10 Enrollment: n/a . . . . (217) 348-0151
Housing: Homeownership rate: 91.3% (2010); Median home value: $123,214 (2010); Median contract rent: $402 per month (2005-2009 5-year est.); Median year structure built: 1961 (2005-2009 5-year est.).
Transportation: Commute to work: 100.0% car, 0.0% public transportation, 0.0% walk, 0.0% work from home (2005-2009 5-year est.); Travel time to work: 12.6% less than 15 minutes, 55.4% 15 to 30 minutes, 26.6% 30 to 45 minutes, 3.2% 45 to 60 minutes, 2.3% 60 minutes or more (2005-2009 5-year est.)

MATTOON (city). Covers a land area of 9.309 square miles and a water area of 0.004 square miles. Located at 39.47° N. Lat; 88.37° W. Long. Elevation is 735 feet.

History: Mattoon was named for William Mattoon of the Illinois Central Railroad. The town was established in the early 1850's as a railroad station and shipping center.

Population: 18,783 (1990); 18,291 (2000); 16,439 (2010); 15,569 (2015 projected); Race: 96.4% White, 1.3% Black, 0.5% Asian, 1.9% Other, 1.6% Hispanic of any race (2010); Density: 1,765.9 persons per square mile (2010); Average household size: 2.17 (2010); Median age: 38.5 (2010); Males per 100 females: 91.4 (2010); Marriage status: 26.5% never married, 50.7% now married, 8.1% widowed, 14.7% divorced (2005-2009 5-year est.); Foreign born: 1.2% (2005-2009 5-year est.); Ancestry (includes multiple ancestries): 27.8% German, 16.5% Irish, 12.1% English, 9.8% American, 3.1% French (2005-2009 5-year est.).

Economy: Single-family building permits issued: 8 (2010); Multi-family building permits issued: 2 (2010); Employment by occupation: 8.5% management, 15.9% professional, 14.7% services, 23.8% sales, 0.4% farming, 10.5% construction, 26.3% production (2005-2009 5-year est.).

Income: Per capita income: $21,799 (2010); Median household income: $37,533 (2010); Average household income: $48,022 (2010); Percent of households with income of $100,000 or more: 7.6% (2010); Poverty rate: 17.3% (2005-2009 5-year est.).

Taxes: Total city taxes per capita: $423 (2007); City property taxes per capita: $184 (2007).

Education: Percent of population age 25 and over with: High school diploma (including GED) or higher: 87.8% (2010); Bachelor's degree or higher: 14.5% (2010); Master's degree or higher: 4.9% (2010).

School District(s)
Clk Cls Cmbn Dglas Edgr Mltr Shlb (06-12)
    2009-10 Enrollment: n/a . . . . (217) 348-0151
Eastern Il Area of Spec Educ (PK-12)
    2009-10 Enrollment: n/a . . . . (217) 348-7700
Mattoon CUSD 2 (PK-12)
    2009-10 Enrollment: 3,523 . . . . (217) 238-8850

Two-year College(s)
Lake Land College (Public)
    Fall 2009 Enrollment: 7,945. (217) 234-5253
    2010-11 Tuition: In-state $5,949; Out-of-state $10,814

Housing: Homeownership rate: 60.7% (2010); Median home value: $76,474 (2010); Median contract rent: $395 per month (2005-2009 5-year est.); Median year structure built: 1955 (2005-2009 5-year est.).

Hospitals: Sarah Bush Lincoln Health Center (202 beds)

Safety: Violent crime rate: 54.1 per 10,000 population; Property crime rate: 288.7 per 10,000 population (2010).

Newspapers: Journal Gazette (Local news; Circulation 11,278)

Transportation: Commute to work: 93.5% car, 0.2% public transportation, 1.7% walk, 3.4% work from home (2005-2009 5-year est.); Travel time to work: 64.0% less than 15 minutes, 22.3% 15 to 30 minutes, 7.2% 30 to 45 minutes, 2.9% 45 to 60 minutes, 3.6% 60 minutes or more (2005-2009 5-year est.); Amtrak: train service available.

Airports: Coles County Memorial (general aviation)

Additional Information Contacts
City of Mattoon. . . . . (217) 235-5654
    http://mattoon.illinois.gov
Mattoon Chamber of Commerce . . . . (217) 235-5661
    http://www.mattoonchamber.com

OAKLAND (city). Covers a land area of 0.819 square miles and a water area of 0.043 square miles. Located at 39.65° N. Lat; 88.02° W. Long. Elevation is 659 feet.

History: Incorporated 1855.

Population: 996 (1990); 996 (2000); 880 (2010); 829 (2015 projected); Race: 98.1% White, 0.6% Black, 0.1% Asian, 1.3% Other, 1.0% Hispanic of any race (2010); Density: 1,074.2 persons per square mile (2010); Average household size: 2.41 (2010); Median age: 38.8 (2010); Males per 100 females: 94.7 (2010); Marriage status: 20.6% never married, 59.3% now married, 8.5% widowed, 11.6% divorced (2005-2009 5-year est.); Foreign born: 0.5% (2005-2009 5-year est.); Ancestry (includes multiple ancestries): 17.0% German, 12.2% American, 12.0% English, 11.2% Irish, 5.1% Scotch-Irish (2005-2009 5-year est.).

Economy: Single-family building permits issued: 0 (2010); Multi-family building permits issued: 0 (2010); Employment by occupation: 4.3% management, 11.9% professional, 16.1% services, 18.7% sales, 5.9% farming, 13.0% construction, 30.1% production (2005-2009 5-year est.).

Income: Per capita income: $19,631 (2010); Median household income: $42,750 (2010); Average household income: $48,887 (2010); Percent of households with income of $100,000 or more: 7.0% (2010); Poverty rate: 18.7% (2005-2009 5-year est.).

Taxes: Total city taxes per capita: $125 (2007); City property taxes per capita: $114 (2007).

Education: Percent of population age 25 and over with: High school diploma (including GED) or higher: 88.6% (2010); Bachelor's degree or higher: 15.8% (2010); Master's degree or higher: 4.0% (2010).

School District(s)
Oakland CUSD 5 (KG-12)
    2009-10 Enrollment: 310 . . . . (217) 346-2555

Housing: Homeownership rate: 80.3% (2010); Median home value: $69,559 (2010); Median contract rent: $345 per month (2005-2009 5-year est.); Median year structure built: 1957 (2005-2009 5-year est.).

Transportation: Commute to work: 94.7% car, 0.0% public transportation, 1.3% walk, 3.4% work from home (2005-2009 5-year est.); Travel time to work: 31.0% less than 15 minutes, 33.6% 15 to 30 minutes, 27.7% 30 to 45 minutes, 5.5% 45 to 60 minutes, 2.2% 60 minutes or more (2005-2009 5-year est.)

TRILLA (unincorporated postal area, zip code 62469). Covers a land area of 19.320 square miles and a water area of 0.023 square miles. Located at 39.35° N. Lat; 88.33° W. Long. Elevation is 653 feet.

Population: 322 (2000); Race: 100.0% White, 0.0% Black, 0.0% Asian, 0.0% Other, 0.0% Hispanic of any race (2000); Density: 16.7 persons per square mile (2000); Age: 28.0% under 18, 20.8% over 64 (2000); Marriage status: 19.0% never married, 66.7% now married, 5.0% widowed, 9.3% divorced (2000); Foreign born: 0.0% (2000); Ancestry (includes multiple ancestries): 36.1% German, 19.1% American, 11.6% Irish, 7.3% Slovak (2000).

Economy: Employment by occupation: 9.3% management, 16.7% professional, 5.6% services, 34.6% sales, 0.0% farming, 14.8% construction, 19.1% production (2000).

Income: Per capita income: $13,517 (2000); Median household income: $40,375 (2000); Poverty rate: 3.8% (2000).

Education: Percent of population age 25 and over with: High school diploma (including GED) or higher: 82.6% (2000); Bachelor's degree or higher: 14.0% (2000).

Housing: Homeownership rate: 89.4% (2000); Median home value: $81,300 (2000); Median contract rent: $350 per month (2000); Median year structure built: 1961 (2000).

Transportation: Commute to work: 100.0% car, 0.0% public transportation, 0.0% walk, 0.0% work from home (2000); Travel time to work: 21.0% less than 15 minutes, 69.1% 15 to 30 minutes, 6.2% 30 to 45 minutes, 0.0% 45 to 60 minutes, 3.7% 60 minutes or more (2000)

Cook County

Located in northeastern Illinois; bounded on the east by Lake Michigan and Indiana; crossed by the Chicago and Des Plaines Rivers. Covers a land area of 945.68 square miles, a water area of 689.36 square miles, and is located in the Central Time Zone at 41.83° N. Lat., 87.76° W. Long. The county was founded in 1831. County seat is Chicago.

Cook County is part of the Chicago-Joliet-Naperville, IL-IN-WI Metropolitan Statistical Area. The entire metro area includes: Chicago-Joliet-Naperville, IL Metropolitan Division (Cook County, IL; DeKalb County, IL; DuPage County, IL; Grundy County, IL; Kane County, IL; Kendall County, IL; McHenry County, IL; Will County, IL); Gary, IN Metropolitan Division (Jasper County, IN; Lake County, IN; Newton County, IN; Porter County, IN); Lake County-Kenosha County, IL-WI Metropolitan Division (Lake County, IL; Kenosha County, WI)

Weather Station: Chicago Botanical Garden								Elevation: 629 feet			
	Jan	Feb	Mar	Apr	May	Jun	Jul	Aug	Sep	Oct	Nov	Dec
High	32	36	45	56	67	78	83	81	74	62	49	36
Low	16	19	28	38	47	57	63	62	54	42	33	21
Precip	2.0	1.7	2.5	3.5	4.0	3.6	3.5	4.7	3.5	3.3	3.1	2.4
Snow	10.2	8.1	5.2	0.9	tr	0.0	0.0	0.0	0.0	0.1	1.5	7.8

High and Low temperatures in degrees Fahrenheit; Precipitation and Snow in inches

Weather Station: Chicago Midway Arpt   Elevation: 620 feet

	Jan	Feb	Mar	Apr	May	Jun	Jul	Aug	Sep	Oct	Nov	Dec
High	32	36	47	60	71	81	85	83	76	63	49	36
Low	18	22	31	41	51	61	67	66	57	45	35	23
Precip	2.0	1.9	2.7	3.6	4.1	3.9	3.9	4.1	3.4	3.3	3.4	2.6
Snow	11.6	9.3	5.6	1.1	tr	0.0	tr	0.0	tr	0.1	1.4	8.5

High and Low temperatures in degrees Fahrenheit; Precipitation and Snow in inches

Weather Station: Chicago Ohare Intl Arpt   Elevation: 658 feet

	Jan	Feb	Mar	Apr	May	Jun	Jul	Aug	Sep	Oct	Nov	Dec
High	31	35	46	59	70	80	84	82	75	62	48	35
Low	16	20	29	38	48	58	64	63	54	42	32	21
Precip	1.7	1.8	2.5	3.4	3.6	3.4	3.5	5.1	3.3	3.2	3.1	2.3
Snow	11.4	8.6	5.9	1.4	tr	tr	tr	tr	tr	0.3	1.4	8.3

High and Low temperatures in degrees Fahrenheit; Precipitation and Snow in inches

Weather Station: Park Forest   Elevation: 709 feet

	Jan	Feb	Mar	Apr	May	Jun	Jul	Aug	Sep	Oct	Nov	Dec
High	31	35	46	59	70	80	84	82	75	62	49	35
Low	16	19	29	39	49	59	64	63	54	42	33	20
Precip	2.1	1.8	2.6	3.8	4.4	4.4	4.3	4.1	3.3	3.3	3.5	2.6
Snow	9.4	7.8	4.9	0.8	tr	0.0	0.0	0.0	0.0	0.3	0.9	6.7

High and Low temperatures in degrees Fahrenheit; Precipitation and Snow in inches

Population: 5,105,067 (1990); 5,376,741 (2000); 5,296,700 (2010); 5,239,879 (2015 projected); Race: 54.1% White, 25.1% Black, 5.7% Asian, 15.0% Other, 23.6% Hispanic of any race (2010); Density: 5,600.9 persons per square mile (2010); Average household size: 2.67 (2010); Median age: 36.3 (2010); Males per 100 females: 95.6 (2010).

Religion: Five largest groups: 39.9% Catholic Church, 4.4% Jewish Estimate, 1.8% Muslim Estimate, 1.2% Lutheran Church—Missouri Synod, 1.2% Evangelical Lutheran Church in America (2000).

Economy: Unemployment rate: 10.9% (August 2011); Total civilian labor force: 2,622,803 (August 2011); Leading industries: 15.0% health care and social assistance; 9.7% retail trade; 9.2% professional, scientific & technical services (2009); Farms: 184 totaling 8,198 acres (2007); Companies that employ 500 or more persons: 417 (2009); Companies that employ 100 to 499 persons: 3,144 (2009); Companies that employ less than 100 persons: 124,307 (2009); Black-owned businesses: 83,723 (2007); Hispanic-owned businesses: 36,740 (2007); Asian-owned businesses: 35,105 (2007); Women-owned businesses: 165,249 (2007); Retail sales per capita: $11,837 (2010). Single-family building permits issued: 725 (2010); Multi-family building permits issued: 2,009 (2010).

Income: Per capita income: $27,781 (2010); Median household income: $55,658 (2010); Average household income: $75,065 (2010); Percent of households with income of $100,000 or more: 22.4% (2010); Poverty rate: 16.0% (2009); Bankruptcy rate: 7.43% (2010).

Taxes: Total county taxes per capita: $308 (2007); County property taxes per capita: $160 (2007).

Education: Percent of population age 25 and over with: High school diploma (including GED) or higher: 82.5% (2010); Bachelor's degree or higher: 32.1% (2010); Master's degree or higher: 12.7% (2010).

Housing: Homeownership rate: 61.3% (2010); Median home value: $233,656 (2010); Median contract rent: $766 per month (2005-2009 5-year est.); Median year structure built: 1956 (2005-2009 5-year est.)

Health: Birth rate: 147.0 per 10,000 population (2009); Death rate: 77.4 per 10,000 population (2009); Age-adjusted cancer mortality rate: 188.9 deaths per 100,000 population (2007); Number of physicians: 40.8 per 10,000 population (2008); Hospital beds: 37.1 per 10,000 population (2007); Hospital admissions: 1,635.0 per 10,000 population (2007).

Environment: Air Quality Index: 49.7% good, 50.0% moderate, 0.3% unhealthy for sensitive individuals, 0.0% unhealthy (percent of days in 2008)

Elections: 2008 Presidential election results: 76.2% Obama, 22.8% McCain, 0.4% Nader

National and State Parks: Chicago Portage National Historic Site; Illinois and Michigan Canal State Trail

Additional Information Contacts

Cook County Government . . . . (312) 603-5656
    http://blog.cookcountygov.com
Alsip Chamber of Commerce. (708) 597-2668
    http://www.alsipchamber.org
America - Israel Chamber of Commerce Chicago . . . . (847) 597-7070
    http://www.americaisrael.org
Andersonville Chamber of Commerce. . . . . (773) 728-2995
    http://www.andersonville.org
Argo-Summit Chamber of Commerce . . . . (708) 458-3033

Arlington Heights Chamber of Commerce . . . . (847) 253-1703
    http://www.arlingtonhtschamber.com
Barrington Area Chamber of Commerce . . . . (847) 381-2525
    http://www.barringtonchamber.com
Blue Island Area Chamber of Commerce . . . . (708) 388-1000
    http://www.blueislandchamber.org
Bridgeview Chamber of Commerce. . . . . (708) 598-1700
    http://www.bridgeviewchamber.com
Brookfield Chamber of Commerce. . . . . (708) 268-8080
    http://brookfieldchamber.net
Burbank Chamber of Commerce . . . . (708) 425-4668
    http://burbankilchamber.com
Calumet City Chamber of Commerce . . . . (708) 891-5888
    http://www.calumetcitychamber.com
Chicago Area Gay & Lesbian Chamber of Commerce . . . . (773) 303-0167
    http://www.glchamber.org
Chicago Chinatown Chamber of Commerce . . . . (312) 326-5320
    http://www.chicagochinatown.org
Chicago Convention & Tourism Bureau. . . . . (312) 567-8500
    http://www.choosechicago.com
Chicago Southland Chamber of Commerce . . . . (708) 957-6950
    http://www.chicagosouthland.com
Chicago Southland Convention & Visitors Bureau. . . . . . . (708) 895-8200
    http://www.visitchicagosouthland.com
Chicagoland Chamber of Commerce. . . . . (312) 494-6700
    http://www.chicagolandchamber.org
Cicero Chamber of Commerce . . . . (708) 863-6000
    http://www.cicerochamber.org
City of Berwyn . . . . (708) 788-2660
    http://www.berwyn-il.gov
City of Blue Island . . . . (708) 597-8603
    http://www.blueisland.org
City of Burbank . . . . (708) 599-5500
    http://www.burbankil.gov
City of Calumet City . . . . (708) 891-8105
    http://www.calumetcity.org
City of Chicago. . . . . (312) 744-5000
    http://www.cityofchicago.org
City of Chicago Heights . . . . (708) 756-5300
    http://www.chicagoheights.net
City of Country Club Hills. . . . . (708) 798-2616
    http://www.countryclubhills.org
City of Countryside. . . . . (708) 354-7270
    http://www.countryside-il.org
City of Des Plaines. . . . . (847) 391-5300
    http://www.desplaines.org
City of Evanston. . . . . (847) 448-4311
    http://www.cityofevanston.org
City of Harvey . . . . (708) 210-5301
    http://www.cityofharvey.org
City of Hickory Hills . . . . (708) 598-4800
    http://www.hickoryhillsil.org
City of Markham. . . . . (708) 331-4905
    http://cityofmarkham.net
City of Northlake . . . . (708) 343-8700
    http://www.northlakecity.com
City of Oak Forest . . . . (708) 687-4050
    http://www.oak-forest.org
City of Palos Heights . . . . (708) 361-1800
    http://www.palosheights.org
City of Palos Hills . . . . (708) 598-3400
    http://www.paloshillsweb.org
City of Park Ridge . . . . (847) 318-5200
    http://www.parkridge.us
City of Prospect Heights . . . . (847) 398-6070
    http://www.prospect-heights.il.us
City of Rolling Meadows . . . . (847) 394-8500
    http://www.ci.rolling-meadows.il.us
Des Plaines Chamber of Commerce & Industry . . . . (847) 824-4200
    http://www.dpchamber.com
Evergreen Park Chamber of Commerce . . . . (708) 423-1118
    http://www.evergreenparkchamber.org
Forest Park Chamber of Commerce . . . . (708) 366-2543
    http://www.exploreforestpark.com
Franklin Park/Schiller Park Chamber of Commerce . . . . . (708) 865-9510
    http://www.chamberbyohare.org

German American Chamber of Commerce of the Midwest . (312) 644-2662
  http://www.gaccom.org
Glencoe Chamber of Commerce . . . . (847) 835-3333
Glenview Chamber of Commerce . . . . (847) 724-0900
  http://www.glenviewchamber.com
Hanover Park Chamber of Commerce & Industry . . . . (630) 372-2009
  http://www.hanoverparkchamber.com
Hazel Crest Area Chamber of Commerce
  http://hazelcrestareachamber.org
Hillside Chamber of Commerce & Industry . . . . (708) 449-2449
  http://www.hillsidechamberofcommerce.com
Hoffman Estates Chamber of Commerce & Industry . . . . . . (847) 781-9100
  http://www.hechamber.com
Homewood Area Chamber of Commerce . . . . (708) 206-3384
  http://www.homewoodareachamber.com
Illinois Chamber of Commerce. . . . . (312) 983-7100
  http://www.ilchamber.org
Italian American Chamber of Commerce - Midwest . . . . . . (312) 553-9137
  http://iacc-chicago.com
Lake View East Chamber of Commerce . . . . (773) 348-8608
  http://www.lakevieweast.com
Lansing Chamber of Commerce . . . . (708) 474-4170
  http://chamberoflansing.com
Latin American Chamber of Commerce. . . . . (773) 252-5211
  http://www.latinamericanchamberofcommerce.com
Lemont Area Chamber of Commerce . . . . (630) 257-5997
  http://www.lemontchamber.com
Lincoln Park Chamber of Commerce. . . . . (773) 880-5200
  http://www.lincolnparkchamber.com
Lincolnwood Chamber of Commerce & Industry . . . . (847) 679-5760
  http://www.lincolnwoodchamber.org
Logan Square Chamber of Commerce . . . . (773) 489-3222
  http://www.loganchamber.org
Lynwood Chamber of Commerce . . . . (708) 758-6101
  http://www.ynns.com/lcc/location.php
Matteson Area Chamber of Commerce . . . . (708) 747-6000
  http://www.macclink.com
Maywood Chamber of Commerce . . . . (708) 345-7077
  http://maywoodchamber.com
Melrose Park Chamber of Commerce & Industry . . . . (708) 338-1007
  http://www.melroseparkchamber.org
Midlothian Chamber of Commerce . . . . (708) 389-0020
  http://www.villageprofile.com/illinois/midlothian
Mont Clare-Elmwood Park Chamber of Commerce. . . . . . . (708) 456-8000
  http://www.mcepchamber.org
Morton Grove Chamber of Commerce & Industry . . . . (847) 965-0330
  http://chamber.mgcci.org
Mount Prospect Chamber of Commerce . . . . (847) 398-6616
  http://www.mountprospectchamber.org
Niles Chamber of Commerce. . . . . (847) 268-8180
  http://www.nileschamber.org
Northbrook Chamber of Commerce. . . . . (847) 498-5555
  http://www.northbrookchamber.org
Northlake Chamber of Commerce . . . . (708) 562-4200
  http://www.northlakecity.com/links_chamber.htm
Oak Forest-Crestwood Area Chamber of Commerce . . . . . (708) 687-4600
  http://www.oc-chamber.org
Oak Lawn Chamber of Commerce . . . . (708) 424-8300
  http://www.oaklawnchamber.com
Oak Park-River Forest Chamber of Commerce . . . . (708) 771-5760
  http://www.oprfchamber.org
Old Town Merchants & Residents Association . . . . (312) 951-6106
  http://www.oldtownchicago.org
Orland Park Area Chamber of Commerce. . . . . (708) 349-2972
  http://www.orlandparkchamber.org
Palatine Area Chamber of Commerce. . . . . (847) 359-7200
  http://www.palatinechamber.com
Palos Area Chamber of Commerce . . . . (708) 923-2300
  http://palosareachamber.com
Park Ridge Chamber of Commerce. . . . . (847) 825-3121
  http://parkridgechamber.org
Portage Park Chamber of Commerce . . . . (773) 777-2020
  http://www.portageparkchamber.org
Puerto Rico Convention Bureau . . . . (312) 840-8090
  http://www.meetpuertorico.com

River Grove Area Chamber of Commerce. . . . . (708) 452-8259
  http://www.vorg.us
Riverdale Chamber of Commerce . . . . (708) 841-3311
  http://www.district148.net/rcoc
Riverside Chamber of Commerce . . . . (708) 447-8510
  http://www.riversidechamberofcommerce.com
Rolling Meadows Chamber of Commerce . . . . (847) 398-3730
  http://www.rmchamber.org
Rosemont Chamber of Commerce . . . . (847) 698-1190
  http://www.rosemontchamber.com
Schaumburg Business Association . . . . (847) 413-1010
  http://www.schaumburgbusiness.com
Skokie Chamber of Commerce . . . . (847) 673-0240
  http://www.skokiechamber.org
South Holland Business Association . . . . (708) 596-0065
  http://www.shba.org
South Shore Chamber of Commerce. . . . . (617) 479-1111
  http://southshorechamber.org
Southeast Chicago Chamber of Commerce . . . . (773) 734-0626
  http://southeastchgochamber.org
Streamwood Chamber of Commerce . . . . (630) 837-5200
  http://www.streamwoodchamber.com
Streeterville Chamber of Commerce . . . . (312) 664-2560
  http://www.streetervillechamber.org
Tinley Park Chamber of Commerce. . . . . (708) 532-5700
  http://www.tinleychamber.org
Town of Cicero . . . . (708) 656-3600
  http://www.thetownofcicero.com
Turkish American Chamber of Commerce-Midwest . . . . . . (312) 276-5171
  http://www.tacci-midwest.org
Village of Alsip . . . . (708) 385-6902
  http://villageofalsip.org
Village of Arlington Heights . . . . (847) 368-5540
  http://www.vah.com
Village of Barrington. . . . . (847) 304-3400
  http://www.barrington-il.gov
Village of Bellwood. . . . . (708) 547-3500
  http://www.vil.bellwood.il.us
Village of Berkeley . . . . (708) 449-8840
  http://www.berkeley.il.us
Village of Bridgeview . . . . (708) 594-2525
  http://www.bridgeview-il.gov
Village of Broadview . . . . (708) 681-3600
  http://www.villageofbroadview.com
Village of Brookfield . . . . (708) 485-7344
  http://www.villageofbrookfield.com
Village of Calumet Park . . . . (708) 389-0850
  http://www.calumetparkvillage.org
Village of Chicago Ridge . . . . (708) 425-7700
  http://www.chicagoridge.org
Village of Crestwood . . . . (708) 371-4800
  http://www.villageofcrestwood.com
Village of Dolton. . . . . (708) 849-4000
  http://vodolton.org
Village of Elk Grove Village . . . . (847) 357-4040
  http://elkgrove.com
Village of Elmwood Park . . . . (708) 452-7300
  http://www.elmwoodpark.org
Village of Evergreen Park . . . . (708) 422-1551
  http://www.evergreenpark-ill.com
Village of Flossmoor . . . . (708) 798-2300
  http://www.flossmoor.org
Village of Forest Park. . . . . (708) 366-2323
  http://www.forestpark.net
Village of Franklin Park . . . . (847) 671-4800
  http://www.villageoffranklinpark.com
Village of Glencoe . . . . (847) 835-4111
  http://www.villageofglencoe.org
Village of Glenview . . . . (847) 904-4370
  http://www.glenview.il.us
Village of Glenwood. . . . . (708) 753-2400
  http://www.villageofglenwood.com
Village of Hanover Park . . . . (630) 372-4200
  http://www.hanoverparkillinois.org
Village of Harwood Heights . . . . (708) 867-7200
  http://www.harwoodheights.org

Village of Hazel Crest . . . . (708) 335-9600
   http://www.villageofhazelcrest.com
Village of Hillside . . . . (708) 449-6450
   http://www.hillside-il.org
Village of Hoffman Estates. . . . . (847) 882-9100
   http://www.hoffmanestates.com
Village of Homewood . . . . (708) 798-3000
   http://village.homewood.il.us
Village of Inverness . . . . (847) 358-7740
   http://www.villageofinverness.org
Village of Justice . . . . (708) 458-2520
   http://villageofjustice.org
Village of La Grange . . . . (708) 579-2300
   http://www.villageoflagrange.com
Village of La Grange Park . . . . (708) 354-0225
   http://www.lagrangepark.org
Village of Lansing. . . . . (708) 895-7200
   http://www.villageoflansing.com
Village of Lemont . . . . (630) 257-1550
   http://www.lemont.il.us
Village of Lincolnwood . . . . (847) 673-1540
   http://www.lincolnwoodil.org
Village of Lynwood. . . . . (708) 758-6101
   http://www.lynwoodil.us
Village of Lyons . . . . (708) 442-4500
   http://www.villageoflyons-il.net
Village of Matteson . . . . (708) 283-4900
   http://www.villageofmatteson.org
Village of Maywood . . . . (708) 450-6300
   http://www.maywood-il.org
Village of Melrose Park . . . . (708) 343-4000
   http://www.melrosepark.org
Village of Midlothian . . . . (708) 389-0200
   http://www.villageofmidlothian.net
Village of Morton Grove . . . . (847) 965-4100
   http://www.mortongroveil.org
Village of Mount Prospect . . . . (847) 392-6000
   http://www.mountprospect.org
Village of Niles. . . . . (847) 588-8000
   http://www.vniles.com
Village of Norridge . . . . (708) 453-0800
   http://www.villageofnorridge.com
Village of North Riverside . . . . (708) 447-4211
   http://www.northriverside-il.org
Village of Northbrook . . . . (847) 272-5050
   http://www.northbrook.il.us
Village of Northfield . . . . (847) 446-9200
   http://www.northfieldil.org
Village of Oak Lawn. . . . . (708) 636-4400
   http://www.oaklawn-il.gov
Village of Oak Park . . . . (708) 383-6400
   http://www.oak-park.us
Village of Orland Hills. . . . . (708) 349-6865
   http://www.orlandhills.org
Village of Orland Park . . . . (708) 403-6100
   http://www.orland-park.il.us
Village of Palatine . . . . (847) 358-7500
   http://www.palatine.il.us
Village of Park Forest. . . . . (708) 748-1112
   http://www.villageofparkforest.com
Village of Richton Park. . . . . (708) 481-8950
   http://www.richtonpark.org
Village of River Forest . . . . (708) 366-8500
   http://www.river-forest.us
Village of River Grove . . . . (708) 453-8000
   http://www.vorg.us
Village of Riverdale . . . . (708) 841-2200
   http://www.villageofriverdale.org
Village of Riverside . . . . (708) 447-2700
   http://riverside.il.us
Village of Sauk Village . . . . (708) 758-3330
   http://www.saukvillage.org
Village of Schaumburg. . . . . (847) 895-4500
   http://www.ci.schaumburg.il.us
Village of Schiller Park . . . . (847) 678-2550
   http://www.villageofschillerpark.com

Village of Skokie . . . . (847) 673-0500
   http://www.skokie.com
Village of South Holland. . . . . (708) 210-2900
   http://www.southholland.org
Village of Stickney . . . . (708) 749-4400
   http://www.villageofstickney.com
Village of Streamwood . . . . (630) 736-3800
   http://www.streamwood.org
Village of Summit. . . . . (708) 563-4823
   http://thevillageofsummit.com
Village of Tinley Park . . . . (708) 444-5000
   http://www.tinleypark.org
Village of Westchester . . . . (708) 345-0020
   http://www.westchester-il.org
Village of Western Springs. . . . . (708) 246-1800
   http://www.wsprings.com
Village of Wheeling . . . . (847) 459-2600
   http://vi.wheeling.il.us
Village of Willow Springs . . . . (708) 467-3700
   http://www.willowsprings-il.gov
Village of Wilmette . . . . (847) 251-2700
   http://www.wilmette.com
Village of Winnetka . . . . (847) 501-6000
   http://www.villageofwinnetka.org
Village of Worth . . . . (708) 448-1181
   http://www.villageofworth.com
West Suburban Chamber of Commerce & Industry. . . . . . (708) 387-7550
   http://www.wscci.org
Westchester Chamber of Commerce. . . . . (708) 240-8400
   http://www.westchesterchamber.org
Wheeling/Prospect Heights Area Chamber of Commerce & Industr . . (847) 541-0170
   http://www.wphchamber.com
Wicker Park & Bucktown Chamber of Commerce . . . . . . (773) 384-2672
   http://www.wickerparkbucktown.com
Wilmette Chamber of Commerce. . . . . (847) 251-3800
   http://www.wilmettechamber.org
Winnetka-Northfield Chamber of Commerce . . . . (847) 446-4451
   http://www.northfieldchamber.org
Winnetka-Northfield Chamber of Commerce . . . . (847) 446-4451
   http://www.winnetkachamber.com

Cook County Communities

ALSIP (village). Covers a land area of 6.366 square miles and a water area of 0.159 square miles. Located at 41.67° N. Lat; 87.73° W. Long. Elevation is 623 feet.

Population: 18,215 (1990); 19,725 (2000); 19,577 (2010); 19,378 (2015 projected); Race: 77.1% White, 10.6% Black, 2.5% Asian, 9.8% Other, 13.5% Hispanic of any race (2010); Density: 3,075.2 persons per square mile (2010); Average household size: 2.59 (2010); Median age: 37.2 (2010); Males per 100 females: 95.5 (2010); Marriage status: 30.7% never married, 54.4% now married, 7.3% widowed, 7.6% divorced (2005-2009 5-year est.); Foreign born: 12.4% (2005-2009 5-year est.); Ancestry (includes multiple ancestries): 18.1% German, 18.0% Irish, 17.1% Polish, 7.6% Italian, 4.2% English (2005-2009 5-year est.).

Economy: Single-family building permits issued: 2 (2010); Multi-family building permits issued: 0 (2010); Employment by occupation: 12.6% management, 16.1% professional, 15.3% services, 31.3% sales, 0.0% farming, 9.6% construction, 15.2% production (2005-2009 5-year est.).

Income: Per capita income: $25,664 (2010); Median household income: $57,393 (2010); Average household income: $66,442 (2010); Percent of households with income of $100,000 or more: 18.2% (2010); Poverty rate: 7.5% (2005-2009 5-year est.).

Taxes: Total city taxes per capita: $581 (2007); City property taxes per capita: $345 (2007).

Education: Percent of population age 25 and over with: High school diploma (including GED) or higher: 88.2% (2010); Bachelor's degree or higher: 16.2% (2010); Master's degree or higher: 4.8% (2010).

School District(s)
Alsip-Hazlgrn-Oaklwn SD 126 (PK-08)
   2009-10 Enrollment: 1,569 . . . . (708) 389-1900
Atwood Heights SD 125 (PK-08)
   2009-10 Enrollment: 728 . . . . (708) 371-0080

Cook County SD 130 (PK-08)
 2009-10 Enrollment: 3,937 . . . . (708) 385-6800
Housing: Homeownership rate: 73.2% (2010); Median home value:
$185,179 (2010); Median contract rent: $703 per month (2005-2009 5-year
est.); Median year structure built: 1973 (2005-2009 5-year est.).
Transportation: Commute to work: 86.6% car, 9.3% public transportation,
0.9% walk, 1.6% work from home (2005-2009 5-year est.); Travel time to
work: 18.9% less than 15 minutes, 30.9% 15 to 30 minutes, 18.8% 30 to 45
minutes, 13.5% 45 to 60 minutes, 17.9% 60 minutes or more (2005-2009
5-year est.)
Additional Information Contacts
Alsip Chamber of Commerce. . . . . (708) 597-2668
 http://www.alsipchamber.org
Village of Alsip . . . . (708) 385-6902
 http://villageofalsip.org

ARLINGTON HEIGHTS (village). Covers a land area of 16.410
square miles and a water area of 0.031 square miles. Located at 42.09° N.
Lat; 87.98° W. Long. Elevation is 702 feet.
History: Named for Henry Bennet (1618-1685), 1st Earl of Arlington.
Arlington Heights was settled in the 1830's. The Arlington Park Race Track
opened here in 1929, drawing many visitors from Chicago.
Population: 75,201 (1990); 76,031 (2000); 72,264 (2010); 70,290 (2015
projected); Race: 87.9% White, 1.1% Black, 7.3% Asian, 3.7% Other, 6.3%
Hispanic of any race (2010); Density: 4,403.8 persons per square mile
(2010); Average household size: 2.43 (2010); Median age: 41.9 (2010);
Males per 100 females: 93.8 (2010); Marriage status: 23.4% never married,
61.3% now married, 7.7% widowed, 7.6% divorced (2005-2009 5-year
est.); Foreign born: 17.0% (2005-2009 5-year est.); Ancestry (includes
multiple ancestries): 27.0% German, 19.7% Irish, 17.4% Polish, 12.3%
Italian, 7.4% English (2005-2009 5-year est.).
Economy: Unemployment rate: 7.8% (August 2011); Total civilian labor
force: 40,764 (August 2011); Single-family building permits issued: 13
(2010); Multi-family building permits issued: 0 (2010); Employment by
occupation: 22.9% management, 26.1% professional, 9.6% services,
29.3% sales, 0.0% farming, 5.2% construction, 7.0% production
(2005-2009 5-year est.).
Income: Per capita income: $40,083 (2010); Median household income:
$77,984 (2010); Average household income: $98,137 (2010); Percent of
households with income of $100,000 or more: 37.0% (2010); Poverty rate:
3.6% (2005-2009 5-year est.).
Taxes: Total city taxes per capita: $840 (2007); City property taxes per
capita: $573 (2007).
Education: Percent of population age 25 and over with: High school
diploma (including GED) or higher: 94.4% (2010); Bachelor's degree or
higher: 50.0% (2010); Master's degree or higher: 18.3% (2010).
School District(s)
Arlington Heights SD 25 (PK-08)
 2009-10 Enrollment: 5,137 . . . . (847) 758-4900
Comm Cons SD 59 (PK-08)
 2009-10 Enrollment: 6,255 . . . . (847) 593-4300
Northwest Suburban Ed To Careers
 2009-10 Enrollment: n/a . . . . (847) 718-6800
Nw Suburban Spec Educ Org (PK-12)
 2009-10 Enrollment: n/a . . . . (847) 463-8100
Township HSD 214 (09-12)
 2009-10 Enrollment: 12,241 . . . . (847) 718-7600
Wheeling CCSD 21 (PK-08)
 2009-10 Enrollment: 6,952 . . . . (847) 537-8270
Vocational/Technical School(s)
Empire Beauty School-Arlington Heights (Private, For-profit)
 Fall 2009 Enrollment: 142 . . . . (847) 394-8359
 2010-11 Tuition: $17,595
Housing: Homeownership rate: 78.1% (2010); Median home value:
$316,035 (2010); Median contract rent: $967 per month (2005-2009 5-year
est.); Median year structure built: 1971 (2005-2009 5-year est.).
Hospitals: Northwest Community Hospital (488 beds)
Safety: Violent crime rate: 5.7 per 10,000 population; Property crime rate:
160.1 per 10,000 population (2010).
Newspapers: Arlington Heights Post (Community news; Circulation 6,231);
Barrington Courier-Review (Community news; Circulation 7,604); Beep
(Regional news); Buffalo Grove Countryside (Community news; Circulation
6,020); Daily Herald (Local news; Circulation 148,375); Elk Grove Times
(Community news; Circulation 2,547); Glencoe News (Community news;
Circulation 2,345); Hoffman Estates Review (Community news; Circulation

2,281); Palatine Countryside (Community news; Circulation 6,231); Pioneer
Press - Northwest/Arlington Heights Bureau (Local news); Rolling
Meadows Review (Community news; Circulation 1,756); Schaumburg
Review (Local news; Circulation 5,089)
Transportation: Commute to work: 86.3% car, 6.6% public transportation,
2.0% walk, 3.8% work from home (2005-2009 5-year est.); Travel time to
work: 22.6% less than 15 minutes, 34.1% 15 to 30 minutes, 23.6% 30 to 45
minutes, 9.6% 45 to 60 minutes, 9.9% 60 minutes or more (2005-2009
5-year est.)
Additional Information Contacts
Arlington Heights Chamber of Commerce . . . . (847) 253-1703
 http://www.arlingtonhtschamber.com
Village of Arlington Heights . . . . (847) 368-5540
 http://www.vah.com

BARRINGTON (village). Covers a land area of 4.597 square miles
and a water area of 0.171 square miles. Located at 42.15° N. Lat; 88.13°
W. Long. Elevation is 827 feet.
History: Named for Great Barrington, Massachusetts. Barrington was
founded in the 1850's and developed as an agricultural community.
Population: 9,741 (1990); 10,168 (2000); 10,847 (2010); 11,150 (2015
projected); Race: 94.8% White, 0.7% Black, 2.8% Asian, 1.7% Other, 3.2%
Hispanic of any race (2010); Density: 2,359.4 persons per square mile
(2010); Average household size: 2.74 (2010); Median age: 39.6 (2010);
Males per 100 females: 93.7 (2010); Marriage status: 22.2% never married,
63.4% now married, 4.8% widowed, 9.6% divorced (2005-2009 5-year
est.); Foreign born: 6.0% (2005-2009 5-year est.); Ancestry (includes
multiple ancestries): 28.5% German, 23.0% Irish, 13.6% English, 10.5%
Italian, 9.9% Polish (2005-2009 5-year est.).
Economy: Single-family building permits issued: 1 (2010); Multi-family
building permits issued: 0 (2010); Employment by occupation: 26.4%
management, 32.4% professional, 7.0% services, 26.3% sales, 0.0%
farming, 5.3% construction, 2.7% production (2005-2009 5-year est.).
Income: Per capita income: $51,062 (2010); Median household income:
$98,490 (2010); Average household income: $139,894 (2010); Percent of
households with income of $100,000 or more: 49.4% (2010); Poverty rate:
5.9% (2005-2009 5-year est.).
Taxes: Total city taxes per capita: $591 (2007); City property taxes per
capita: $385 (2007).
Education: Percent of population age 25 and over with: High school
diploma (including GED) or higher: 95.9% (2010); Bachelor's degree or
higher: 61.9% (2010); Master's degree or higher: 26.5% (2010).
School District(s)
Barrington CUSD 220 (PK-12)
 2009-10 Enrollment: 9,283 . . . . (847) 381-6300
Housing: Homeownership rate: 82.9% (2010); Median home value:
$465,709 (2010); Median contract rent: $1,114 per month (2005-2009
5-year est.); Median year structure built: 1969 (2005-2009 5-year est.).
Hospitals: Advocate Good Shephard Hospital (154 beds)
Safety: Violent crime rate: 0.0 per 10,000 population; Property crime rate:
124.0 per 10,000 population (2010).
Transportation: Commute to work: 78.9% car, 10.8% public
transportation, 4.1% walk, 5.3% work from home (2005-2009 5-year est.);
Travel time to work: 27.6% less than 15 minutes, 20.8% 15 to 30 minutes,
20.0% 30 to 45 minutes, 11.5% 45 to 60 minutes, 20.1% 60 minutes or
more (2005-2009 5-year est.)
Additional Information Contacts
Barrington Area Chamber of Commerce . . . . (847) 381-2525
 http://www.barringtonchamber.com
Village of Barrington. . . . . (847) 304-3400
 http://www.barrington-il.gov

BARRINGTON HILLS (village). Covers a land area of 27.879
square miles and a water area of 0.520 square miles. Located at 42.14° N.
Lat; 88.20° W. Long. Elevation is 846 feet.
History: Settlers Jesse Miller and William Van Orsdal arrived in 1834; in
the 1840's other settlers formed a town called Miller's Grove, later named
Barrington Center.
Population: 4,069 (1990); 3,915 (2000); 4,532 (2010); 4,772 (2015
projected); Race: 92.3% White, 0.7% Black, 4.7% Asian, 2.4% Other, 3.5%
Hispanic of any race (2010); Density: 162.6 persons per square mile
(2010); Average household size: 2.83 (2010); Median age: 44.0 (2010);
Males per 100 females: 96.1 (2010); Marriage status: 21.9% never married,
71.0% now married, 2.9% widowed, 4.1% divorced (2005-2009 5-year
est.); Foreign born: 10.5% (2005-2009 5-year est.); Ancestry (includes

multiple ancestries): 33.5% German, 15.1% Irish, 14.4% English, 11.0% Italian, 9.3% Polish (2005-2009 5-year est.).
Economy: Single-family building permits issued: 2 (2010); Multi-family building permits issued: 0 (2010); Employment by occupation: 35.1% management, 21.8% professional, 10.7% services, 19.2% sales, 2.1% farming, 4.6% construction, 6.5% production (2005-2009 5-year est.).
Income: Per capita income: $65,413 (2010); Median household income: $134,144 (2010); Average household income: $185,396 (2010); Percent of households with income of $100,000 or more: 63.4% (2010); Poverty rate: 2.8% (2005-2009 5-year est.).
Taxes: Total city taxes per capita: $1,079 (2007); City property taxes per capita: $819 (2007).
Education: Percent of population age 25 and over with: High school diploma (including GED) or higher: 97.5% (2010); Bachelor's degree or higher: 66.3% (2010); Master's degree or higher: 26.9% (2010).
Housing: Homeownership rate: 92.2% (2010); Median home value: $741,745 (2010); Median contract rent: $2,000+ per month (2005-2009 5-year est.); Median year structure built: 1979 (2005-2009 5-year est.).
Safety: Violent crime rate: 4.6 per 10,000 population; Property crime rate: 105.2 per 10,000 population (2010).
Transportation: Commute to work: 83.0% car, 4.8% public transportation, 0.0% walk, 11.6% work from home (2005-2009 5-year est.); Travel time to work: 12.8% less than 15 minutes, 25.2% 15 to 30 minutes, 31.7% 30 to 45 minutes, 10.4% 45 to 60 minutes, 20.0% 60 minutes or more (2005-2009 5-year est.)

BEDFORD PARK (village). Covers a land area of 5.965 square
miles and a water area of 0.109 square miles. Located at 41.76° N. Lat; 87.78° W. Long. Elevation is 617 feet.
Population: 566 (1990); 574 (2000); 578 (2010); 559 (2015 projected); Race: 96.7% White, 0.2% Black, 0.3% Asian, 2.8% Other, 9.5% Hispanic of any race (2010); Density: 96.9 persons per square mile (2010); Average household size: 2.74 (2010); Median age: 39.6 (2010); Males per 100 females: 90.8 (2010); Marriage status: 26.1% never married, 62.5% now married, 9.2% widowed, 2.2% divorced (2005-2009 5-year est.); Foreign born: 13.4% (2005-2009 5-year est.); Ancestry (includes multiple ancestries): 24.2% German, 15.0% Polish, 13.4% Irish, 5.2% English, 4.8% Italian (2005-2009 5-year est.).
Economy: Single-family building permits issued: 0 (2010); Multi-family building permits issued: 0 (2010); Employment by occupation: 16.3% management, 15.6% professional, 18.7% services, 25.6% sales, 0.0% farming, 7.3% construction, 16.6% production (2005-2009 5-year est.).
Income: Per capita income: $25,100 (2010); Median household income: $59,856 (2010); Average household income: $68,685 (2010); Percent of households with income of $100,000 or more: 17.5% (2010); Poverty rate: 10.8% (2005-2009 5-year est.).
Taxes: Total city taxes per capita: $42,092 (2007); City property taxes per capita: $28,346 (2007).
Education: Percent of population age 25 and over with: High school diploma (including GED) or higher: 88.2% (2010); Bachelor's degree or higher: 16.3% (2010); Master's degree or higher: 5.8% (2010).

School District(s)
Summit SD 104 (PK-08)
   2009-10 Enrollment: 1,737 . . . . (708) 458-0505
Two-year College(s)
Fox College Inc (Private, For-profit)
   Fall 2009 Enrollment: 370 . . . . (708) 444-4500
   2010-11 Tuition: In-state $14,680; Out-of-state $14,680
Housing: Homeownership rate: 92.9% (2010); Median home value: $192,143 (2010); Median contract rent: $535 per month (2005-2009 5-year est.); Median year structure built: 1951 (2005-2009 5-year est.).
Transportation: Commute to work: 95.4% car, 3.5% public transportation, 1.1% walk, 0.0% work from home (2005-2009 5-year est.); Travel time to work: 39.9% less than 15 minutes, 36.4% 15 to 30 minutes, 11.7% 30 to 45 minutes, 3.2% 45 to 60 minutes, 8.8% 60 minutes or more (2005-2009 5-year est.)

BELLWOOD (village). Covers a land area of 2.386 square miles and a
water area of 0 square miles. Located at 41.88° N. Lat; 87.87° W. Long. Elevation is 633 feet.
History: Derived from its original name of Bell's Wood, which was probably named for a landowner. Incorporated 1900.
Population: 20,241 (1990); 20,535 (2000); 19,450 (2010); 18,937 (2015 projected); Race: 12.0% White, 79.7% Black, 1.0% Asian, 7.3% Other, 11.3% Hispanic of any race (2010); Density: 8,153.2 persons per square

mile (2010); Average household size: 3.19 (2010); Median age: 34.0 (2010); Males per 100 females: 89.7 (2010); Marriage status: 44.1% never married, 41.2% now married, 5.0% widowed, 9.7% divorced (2005-2009 5-year est.); Foreign born: 11.1% (2005-2009 5-year est.); Ancestry (includes multiple ancestries): 1.8% African, 1.6% German, 1.5% Italian, 1.2% Irish, 0.6% Polish (2005-2009 5-year est.).
Economy: Single-family building permits issued: 0 (2010); Multi-family building permits issued: 0 (2010); Employment by occupation: 9.2% management, 11.0% professional, 14.9% services, 31.7% sales, 0.0% farming, 4.3% construction, 28.9% production (2005-2009 5-year est.).
Income: Per capita income: $22,061 (2010); Median household income: $61,170 (2010); Average household income: $70,253 (2010); Percent of households with income of $100,000 or more: 19.6% (2010); Poverty rate: 10.7% (2005-2009 5-year est.).
Taxes: Total city taxes per capita: $871 (2007); City property taxes per capita: $633 (2007).
Education: Percent of population age 25 and over with: High school diploma (including GED) or higher: 82.6% (2010); Bachelor's degree or higher: 14.6% (2010); Master's degree or higher: 4.6% (2010).

School District(s)
Bellwood SD 88 (PK-08)
   2009-10 Enrollment: 2,888 . . . . (708) 344-9344
Berkeley SD 87 (PK-08)
   2009-10 Enrollment: 2,905 . . . . (708) 449-3350
Housing: Homeownership rate: 78.6% (2010); Median home value: $168,235 (2010); Median contract rent: $811 per month (2005-2009 5-year est.); Median year structure built: 1955 (2005-2009 5-year est.).
Safety: Violent crime rate: 39.5 per 10,000 population; Property crime rate: 199.5 per 10,000 population (2010).
Transportation: Commute to work: 82.3% car, 12.8% public transportation, 1.5% walk, 1.3% work from home (2005-2009 5-year est.); Travel time to work: 24.3% less than 15 minutes, 30.4% 15 to 30 minutes, 27.5% 30 to 45 minutes, 9.1% 45 to 60 minutes, 8.7% 60 minutes or more (2005-2009 5-year est.)
Additional Information Contacts
Village of Bellwood . . . . (708) 547-3500
   http://www.vil.bellwood.il.us

BERKELEY (village). Covers a land area of 1.393 square miles and a
water area of 0 square miles. Located at 41.88° N. Lat; 87.91° W. Long. Elevation is 650 feet.
Population: 5,137 (1990); 5,245 (2000); 4,895 (2010); 4,771 (2015 projected); Race: 48.3% White, 35.1% Black, 3.0% Asian, 13.7% Other, 22.0% Hispanic of any race (2010); Density: 3,514.1 persons per square mile (2010); Average household size: 2.87 (2010); Median age: 40.5 (2010); Males per 100 females: 95.9 (2010); Marriage status: 32.0% never married, 53.8% now married, 4.8% widowed, 9.5% divorced (2005-2009 5-year est.); Foreign born: 16.0% (2005-2009 5-year est.); Ancestry (includes multiple ancestries): 8.8% Polish, 7.8% German, 7.2% Irish, 5.2% Italian, 3.6% English (2005-2009 5-year est.).
Economy: Single-family building permits issued: 0 (2010); Multi-family building permits issued: 0 (2010); Employment by occupation: 11.9% management, 17.3% professional, 9.3% services, 35.1% sales, 0.0% farming, 6.6% construction, 19.9% production (2005-2009 5-year est.).
Income: Per capita income: $27,626 (2010); Median household income: $70,710 (2010); Average household income: $80,983 (2010); Percent of households with income of $100,000 or more: 28.6% (2010); Poverty rate: 5.3% (2005-2009 5-year est.).
Taxes: Total city taxes per capita: $957 (2007); City property taxes per capita: $770 (2007).
Education: Percent of population age 25 and over with: High school diploma (including GED) or higher: 86.2% (2010); Bachelor's degree or higher: 22.5% (2010); Master's degree or higher: 6.9% (2010).

School District(s)
Berkeley SD 87 (PK-08)
   2009-10 Enrollment: 2,905 . . . . (708) 449-3350
Housing: Homeownership rate: 88.2% (2010); Median home value: $195,789 (2010); Median contract rent: $735 per month (2005-2009 5-year est.); Median year structure built: 1957 (2005-2009 5-year est.).
Safety: Violent crime rate: 33.3 per 10,000 population; Property crime rate: 216.7 per 10,000 population (2010).
Transportation: Commute to work: 92.7% car, 6.0% public transportation, 0.8% walk, 0.4% work from home (2005-2009 5-year est.); Travel time to work: 20.2% less than 15 minutes, 29.0% 15 to 30 minutes, 26.8% 30 to 45

minutes, 11.8% 45 to 60 minutes, 12.2% 60 minutes or more (2005-2009 5-year est.)
Additional Information Contacts
Village of Berkeley . . . . (708) 449-8840
http://www.berkeley.il.us

BERWYN (city).
Covers a land area of 3.893 square miles and a water area of 0 square miles. Located at 41.84° N. Lat; 87.79° W. Long. Elevation is 617 feet.
History: Named for Berwyn, Pennsylvania. Berwyn was organized in 1890 by Charles E. Piper and Wilbur J. Andrews, realtors who felt that a town would be populated if they built it. Berwyn was incorporated as a village in 1891 and chartered as a city in 1908. It grew as a residential suburb, with many of the people employed in neighboring Cicero, where the Western Electric Company had a plant.
Population: 45,426 (1990); 54,016 (2000); 50,481 (2010); 48,959 (2015 projected); Race: 61.3% White, 1.6% Black, 2.7% Asian, 34.4% Other, 55.9% Hispanic of any race (2010); Density: 12,968.1 persons per square mile (2010); Average household size: 2.80 (2010); Median age: 36.0 (2010); Males per 100 females: 97.2 (2010); Marriage status: 38.3% never married, 45.7% now married, 6.2% widowed, 9.8% divorced (2005-2009 5-year est.); Foreign born: 25.0% (2005-2009 5-year est.); Ancestry (includes multiple ancestries): 9.4% Polish, 9.2% German, 9.1% Italian, 8.8% Irish, 3.5% Czech (2005-2009 5-year est.).
Economy: Unemployment rate: 11.6% (August 2011); Total civilian labor force: 25,268 (August 2011); Single-family building permits issued: 0 (2010); Multi-family building permits issued: 0 (2010); Employment by occupation: 10.0% management, 15.6% professional, 20.5% services, 26.6% sales, 0.0% farming, 9.6% construction, 17.7% production (2005-2009 5-year est.).
Income: Per capita income: $22,142 (2010); Median household income: $50,915 (2010); Average household income: $62,151 (2010); Percent of households with income of $100,000 or more: 15.4% (2010); Poverty rate: 11.2% (2005-2009 5-year est.).
Taxes: Total city taxes per capita: $665 (2007); City property taxes per capita: $432 (2007).
Education: Percent of population age 25 and over with: High school diploma (including GED) or higher: 80.4% (2010); Bachelor's degree or higher: 20.8% (2010); Master's degree or higher: 7.5% (2010).
School District(s)
Berwyn North SD 98 (PK-08)
    2009-10 Enrollment: 3,439 . . . . (708) 484-6200
Berwyn South SD 100 (PK-08)
    2009-10 Enrollment: 3,601 . . . . (708) 795-2300
J S Morton HSD 201 (09-12)
    2009-10 Enrollment: 8,489 . . . . (708) 222-5704
Vocational/Technical School(s)
American Career College (Private, For-profit)
    Fall 2009 Enrollment: 90 . . . . (708) 795-1500
    2010-11 Tuition: $10,150
Housing: Homeownership rate: 65.5% (2010); Median home value: $208,765 (2010); Median contract rent: $739 per month (2005-2009 5-year est.); Median year structure built: before 1940 (2005-2009 5-year est.).
Hospitals: MacNeal Hospital (427 beds)
Safety: Violent crime rate: 42.1 per 10,000 population; Property crime rate: 257.9 per 10,000 population (2010).
Newspapers: Chicago Deportivo (Local news; Circulation 75,000)
Transportation: Commute to work: 83.8% car, 11.0% public transportation, 3.2% walk, 1.3% work from home (2005-2009 5-year est.); Travel time to work: 18.3% less than 15 minutes, 28.4% 15 to 30 minutes, 28.4% 30 to 45 minutes, 12.8% 45 to 60 minutes, 12.1% 60 minutes or more (2005-2009 5-year est.)
Additional Information Contacts
City of Berwyn . . . . (708) 788-2660
http://www.berwyn-il.gov

BLUE ISLAND (city).
Covers a land area of 4.030 square miles and a water area of 0.095 square miles. Located at 41.65° N. Lat; 87.67° W. Long. Elevation is 640 feet.
History: Blue Island was named because it looked like an island surrounded by marshes, and a blue haze often hung over its woods. Settlers first came in 1835, and the village was laid out in 1872. Many of the early residents were of German and Italian ancestry.
Population: 21,203 (1990); 23,463 (2000); 21,477 (2010); 20,808 (2015 projected); Race: 43.5% White, 26.9% Black, 0.4% Asian, 29.1% Other,

45.7% Hispanic of any race (2010); Density: 5,329.6 persons per square mile (2010); Average household size: 2.92 (2010); Median age: 32.6 (2010); Males per 100 females: 97.9 (2010); Marriage status: 37.7% never married, 47.1% now married, 4.2% widowed, 11.1% divorced (2005-2009 5-year est.); Foreign born: 20.2% (2005-2009 5-year est.); Ancestry (includes multiple ancestries): 8.1% German, 6.1% Irish, 5.4% Polish, 4.1% Italian, 1.6% English (2005-2009 5-year est.).
Economy: Single-family building permits issued: 10 (2010); Multi-family building permits issued: 0 (2010); Employment by occupation: 9.9% management, 11.0% professional, 22.4% services, 24.5% sales, 0.5% farming, 12.3% construction, 19.4% production (2005-2009 5-year est.).
Income: Per capita income: $16,619 (2010); Median household income: $39,807 (2010); Average household income: $48,576 (2010); Percent of households with income of $100,000 or more: 8.0% (2010); Poverty rate: 18.8% (2005-2009 5-year est.).
Taxes: Total city taxes per capita: $435 (2007); City property taxes per capita: $326 (2007).
Education: Percent of population age 25 and over with: High school diploma (including GED) or higher: 72.9% (2010); Bachelor's degree or higher: 14.4% (2010); Master's degree or higher: 4.1% (2010).
School District(s)
CHSD 218 (09-12)
    2009-10 Enrollment: 5,826 . . . . (708) 424-2000
Cook County SD 130 (PK-08)
    2009-10 Enrollment: 3,937 . . . . (708) 385-6800
Exc Children Have Opportunities (PK-12)
    2009-10 Enrollment: n/a . . . . (708) 333-7880
Vocational/Technical School(s)
Cannella School of Hair Design (Private, For-profit)
    Fall 2009 Enrollment: 98 . . . . (708) 388-4949
    2010-11 Tuition: $12,190
Environmental Technical Institute (Private, For-profit)
    Fall 2009 Enrollment: 202 . . . . (630) 285-9100
    2010-11 Tuition: $13,250
Housing: Homeownership rate: 59.0% (2010); Median home value: $141,959 (2010); Median contract rent: $679 per month (2005-2009 5-year est.); Median year structure built: 1950 (2005-2009 5-year est.).
Hospitals: St. Francis Hospital & Health Center (410 beds)
Transportation: Commute to work: 81.5% car, 11.8% public transportation, 4.3% walk, 1.6% work from home (2005-2009 5-year est.); Travel time to work: 22.5% less than 15 minutes, 29.5% 15 to 30 minutes, 24.2% 30 to 45 minutes, 10.1% 45 to 60 minutes, 13.8% 60 minutes or more (2005-2009 5-year est.)
Additional Information Contacts
Blue Island Area Chamber of Commerce . . . . (708) 388-1000
http://www.blueislandchamber.org
City of Blue Island . . . . (708) 597-8603
http://www.blueisland.org

BRIDGEVIEW (village).
Covers a land area of 4.126 square miles and a water area of 0 square miles. Located at 41.74° N. Lat; 87.80° W. Long. Elevation is 620 feet.
History: Named for the city's many bridges. Incorporated 1947.
Population: 14,346 (1990); 15,335 (2000); 15,808 (2010); 15,880 (2015 projected); Race: 81.6% White, 1.3% Black, 2.9% Asian, 14.2% Other, 13.5% Hispanic of any race (2010); Density: 3,831.1 persons per square mile (2010); Average household size: 2.64 (2010); Median age: 38.4 (2010); Males per 100 females: 98.3 (2010); Marriage status: 33.0% never married, 49.7% now married, 7.9% widowed, 9.4% divorced (2005-2009 5-year est.); Foreign born: 23.6% (2005-2009 5-year est.); Ancestry (includes multiple ancestries): 26.7% Polish, 19.8% Irish, 13.7% German, 7.9% Italian, 3.9% Arab (2005-2009 5-year est.).
Economy: Single-family building permits issued: 2 (2010); Multi-family building permits issued: 0 (2010); Employment by occupation: 7.5% management, 10.2% professional, 19.0% services, 28.0% sales, 0.3% farming, 14.5% construction, 20.5% production (2005-2009 5-year est.).
Income: Per capita income: $22,440 (2010); Median household income: $50,880 (2010); Average household income: $60,372 (2010); Percent of households with income of $100,000 or more: 15.4% (2010); Poverty rate: 13.7% (2005-2009 5-year est.).
Taxes: Total city taxes per capita: $451 (2007); City property taxes per capita: $386 (2007).
Education: Percent of population age 25 and over with: High school diploma (including GED) or higher: 79.3% (2010); Bachelor's degree or higher: 11.8% (2010); Master's degree or higher: 3.2% (2010).

School District(s)
Indian Springs SD 109 (PK-08)
    2009-10 Enrollment: 3,057 . . . . (708) 496-8700
Ridgeland SD 122 (PK-08)
    2009-10 Enrollment: 2,294 . . . . (708) 599-5550
Two-year College(s)
Northwestern College-Southwestern Campus (Private, For-profit)
    Fall 2009 Enrollment: 1,195 . . . . (888) 205-2283
    2010-11 Tuition: In-state $20,900; Out-of-state $20,900
Vocational/Technical School(s)
Tricoci University of Beauty Culture (Private, For-profit)
    Fall 2009 Enrollment: 85 . . . . (630) 528-3336
    2010-11 Tuition: $16,650
Housing: Homeownership rate: 79.3% (2010); Median home value: $190,238 (2010); Median contract rent: $746 per month (2005-2009 5-year est.); Median year structure built: 1970 (2005-2009 5-year est.).
Safety: Violent crime rate: 24.3 per 10,000 population; Property crime rate: 309.8 per 10,000 population (2010).
Transportation: Commute to work: 93.2% car, 3.5% public transportation, 0.9% walk, 1.6% work from home (2005-2009 5-year est.); Travel time to work: 24.6% less than 15 minutes, 31.0% 15 to 30 minutes, 24.0% 30 to 45 minutes, 11.5% 45 to 60 minutes, 9.0% 60 minutes or more (2005-2009 5-year est.)
Additional Information Contacts
Bridgeview Chamber of Commerce . . . . (708) 598-1700
    http://www.bridgeviewchamber.com
Village of Bridgeview . . . . (708) 594-2525
    http://www.bridgeview-il.gov

BROADVIEW (village). Covers a land area of 1.779 square miles and a water area of 0 square miles. Located at 41.85° N. Lat; 87.85° W. Long. Elevation is 630 feet.

History: Broadview was incorporated as a village in 1910, and developed as a residential community.
Population: 8,713 (1990); 8,264 (2000); 8,038 (2010); 7,924 (2015 projected); Race: 20.9% White, 73.0% Black, 1.3% Asian, 4.8% Other, 6.0% Hispanic of any race (2010); Density: 4,517.8 persons per square mile (2010); Average household size: 2.57 (2010); Median age: 39.2 (2010); Males per 100 females: 90.5 (2010); Marriage status: 38.6% never married, 40.5% now married, 5.3% widowed, 15.7% divorced (2005-2009 5-year est.); Foreign born: 5.9% (2005-2009 5-year est.); Ancestry (includes multiple ancestries): 3.1% Polish, 3.0% German, 2.5% Czech, 1.6% Irish, 1.5% Italian (2005-2009 5-year est.).
Economy: Single-family building permits issued: 0 (2010); Multi-family building permits issued: 0 (2010); Employment by occupation: 12.2% management, 13.5% professional, 10.8% services, 39.3% sales, 0.0% farming, 7.1% construction, 17.1% production (2005-2009 5-year est.).
Income: Per capita income: $24,126 (2010); Median household income: $51,289 (2010); Average household income: $62,097 (2010); Percent of households with income of $100,000 or more: 15.6% (2010); Poverty rate: 7.4% (2005-2009 5-year est.).
Taxes: Total city taxes per capita: $1,381 (2007); City property taxes per capita: $1,118 (2007).
Education: Percent of population age 25 and over with: High school diploma (including GED) or higher: 86.2% (2010); Bachelor's degree or higher: 19.3% (2010); Master's degree or higher: 5.9% (2010).
School District(s)
Lindop SD 92 (PK-08)
    2009-10 Enrollment: 482 . . . . (708) 345-8834
Maywood-Melrose Park-Broadview 89 (PK-08)
    2009-10 Enrollment: 5,640 . . . . (708) 450-2460
Housing: Homeownership rate: 71.0% (2010); Median home value: $175,082 (2010); Median contract rent: $689 per month (2005-2009 5-year est.); Median year structure built: 1954 (2005-2009 5-year est.).
Safety: Violent crime rate: 48.4 per 10,000 population; Property crime rate: 487.1 per 10,000 population (2010).
Transportation: Commute to work: 80.9% car, 11.1% public transportation, 6.9% walk, 0.8% work from home (2005-2009 5-year est.); Travel time to work: 21.4% less than 15 minutes, 29.6% 15 to 30 minutes, 29.5% 30 to 45 minutes, 9.2% 45 to 60 minutes, 10.2% 60 minutes or more (2005-2009 5-year est.)
Additional Information Contacts
Village of Broadview . . . . (708) 681-3600
    http://www.villageofbroadview.com

BROOKFIELD (village). Covers a land area of 3.052 square miles and a water area of 0.004 square miles. Located at 41.82° N. Lat; 87.84° W. Long. Elevation is 623 feet.

History: Named for the many local brooks. Incorporated 1893.
Population: 18,861 (1990); 19,085 (2000); 18,216 (2010); 17,780 (2015 projected); Race: 90.3% White, 1.2% Black, 1.5% Asian, 7.0% Other, 12.5% Hispanic of any race (2010); Density: 5,967.7 persons per square mile (2010); Average household size: 2.51 (2010); Median age: 40.7 (2010); Males per 100 females: 92.2 (2010); Marriage status: 31.0% never married, 50.4% now married, 7.2% widowed, 11.4% divorced (2005-2009 5-year est.); Foreign born: 12.8% (2005-2009 5-year est.); Ancestry (includes multiple ancestries): 25.5% German, 22.9% Irish, 17.5% Polish, 10.6% Italian, 8.1% Czech (2005-2009 5-year est.).
Economy: Single-family building permits issued: 0 (2010); Multi-family building permits issued: 0 (2010); Employment by occupation: 14.8% management, 22.5% professional, 13.7% services, 26.6% sales, 0.2% farming, 8.5% construction, 13.6% production (2005-2009 5-year est.).
Income: Per capita income: $30,504 (2010); Median household income: $66,325 (2010); Average household income: $77,440 (2010); Percent of households with income of $100,000 or more: 25.8% (2010); Poverty rate: 5.5% (2005-2009 5-year est.).
Taxes: Total city taxes per capita: $559 (2007); City property taxes per capita: $416 (2007).
Education: Percent of population age 25 and over with: High school diploma (including GED) or higher: 91.2% (2010); Bachelor's degree or higher: 30.0% (2010); Master's degree or higher: 9.6% (2010).
School District(s)
Brookfield Lagrange Park SD 95 (PK-08)
    2009-10 Enrollment: 1,002 . . . . (708) 485-0606
La Grange SD 102 (PK-08)
    2009-10 Enrollment: 3,040 . . . . (708) 482-2400
Lyons SD 103 (PK-08)
    2009-10 Enrollment: 2,452 . . . . (708) 783-4100
Riverside SD 96 (PK-08)
    2009-10 Enrollment: 1,523 . . . . (708) 447-5007
Housing: Homeownership rate: 77.0% (2010); Median home value: $231,914 (2010); Median contract rent: $830 per month (2005-2009 5-year est.); Median year structure built: 1950 (2005-2009 5-year est.).
Transportation: Commute to work: 82.3% car, 11.8% public transportation, 1.4% walk, 3.9% work from home (2005-2009 5-year est.); Travel time to work: 21.1% less than 15 minutes, 32.8% 15 to 30 minutes, 24.1% 30 to 45 minutes, 10.7% 45 to 60 minutes, 11.3% 60 minutes or more (2005-2009 5-year est.)
Additional Information Contacts
Brookfield Chamber of Commerce . . . . (708) 268-8080
    http://brookfieldchamber.net
Village of Brookfield . . . . (708) 485-7344
    http://www.villageofbrookfield.com

BURBANK (city). Aka South Stickney. Covers a land area of 4.173 square miles and a water area of 0 square miles. Located at 41.74° N. Lat; 87.77° W. Long. Elevation is 620 feet.

Population: 27,600 (1990); 27,902 (2000); 26,344 (2010); 25,665 (2015 projected); Race: 86.0% White, 0.4% Black, 2.2% Asian, 11.4% Other, 17.3% Hispanic of any race (2010); Density: 6,313.3 persons per square mile (2010); Average household size: 3.01 (2010); Median age: 38.2 (2010); Males per 100 females: 97.0 (2010); Marriage status: 31.9% never married, 54.3% now married, 6.8% widowed, 7.0% divorced (2005-2009 5-year est.); Foreign born: 30.4% (2005-2009 5-year est.); Ancestry (includes multiple ancestries): 33.1% Polish, 13.6% Irish, 11.9% German, 9.5% Italian, 3.4% Lithuanian (2005-2009 5-year est.).
Economy: Unemployment rate: 10.4% (August 2011); Total civilian labor force: 14,347 (August 2011); Single-family building permits issued: 8 (2010); Multi-family building permits issued: 0 (2010); Employment by occupation: 8.6% management, 10.2% professional, 16.6% services, 26.2% sales, 0.0% farming, 17.0% construction, 21.4% production (2005-2009 5-year est.).
Income: Per capita income: $23,076 (2010); Median household income: $60,382 (2010); Average household income: $69,092 (2010); Percent of households with income of $100,000 or more: 20.5% (2010); Poverty rate: 9.9% (2005-2009 5-year est.).
Taxes: Total city taxes per capita: $464 (2007); City property taxes per capita: $251 (2007).

Education: Percent of population age 25 and over with: High school diploma (including GED) or higher: 80.1% (2010); Bachelor's degree or higher: 11.7% (2010); Master's degree or higher: 3.9% (2010).

School District(s)

A E R O Spec Educ Coop (PK-12)
  2009-10 Enrollment: n/a . . . . (708) 496-3330
Burbank SD 111 (PK-08)
  2009-10 Enrollment: 3,266 . . . . (708) 496-0500
Reavis Twp HSD 220 (09-12)
  2009-10 Enrollment: 1,909 . . . . (708) 599-7200

Housing: Homeownership rate: 85.9% (2010); Median home value: $209,295 (2010); Median contract rent: $849 per month (2005-2009 5-year est.); Median year structure built: 1964 (2005-2009 5-year est.).

Safety: Violent crime rate: 24.7 per 10,000 population; Property crime rate: 225.2 per 10,000 population (2010).

Transportation: Commute to work: 93.3% car, 3.6% public transportation, 1.1% walk, 1.4% work from home (2005-2009 5-year est.); Travel time to work: 21.9% less than 15 minutes, 26.6% 15 to 30 minutes, 25.6% 30 to 45 minutes, 12.9% 45 to 60 minutes, 12.9% 60 minutes or more (2005-2009 5-year est.)

Additional Information Contacts

Burbank Chamber of Commerce . . . . (708) 425-4668
  http://burbankilchamber.com
City of Burbank . . . . (708) 599-5500
  http://www.burbankil.gov

BURNHAM (village). Covers a land area of 1.858 square miles and a water area of 0.093 square miles. Located at 41.63° N. Lat; 87.55° W. Long. Elevation is 584 feet.

Population: 3,916 (1990); 4,170 (2000); 3,905 (2010); 3,787 (2015 projected); Race: 27.7% White, 56.1% Black, 1.2% Asian, 15.0% Other, 19.0% Hispanic of any race (2010); Density: 2,102.1 persons per square mile (2010); Average household size: 2.69 (2010); Median age: 38.6 (2010); Males per 100 females: 93.5 (2010); Marriage status: 46.1% never married, 38.1% now married, 4.9% widowed, 11.0% divorced (2005-2009 5-year est.); Foreign born: 7.2% (2005-2009 5-year est.); Ancestry (includes multiple ancestries): 6.9% Polish, 4.3% German, 3.2% Irish, 3.1% Italian, 1.3% Serbian (2005-2009 5-year est.).

Economy: Single-family building permits issued: 1 (2010); Multi-family building permits issued: 0 (2010); Employment by occupation: 4.2% management, 15.0% professional, 13.9% services, 33.8% sales, 0.0% farming, 15.0% construction, 18.1% production (2005-2009 5-year est.).

Income: Per capita income: $18,613 (2010); Median household income: $43,772 (2010); Average household income: $51,961 (2010); Percent of households with income of $100,000 or more: 9.8% (2010); Poverty rate: 20.8% (2005-2009 5-year est.).

Taxes: Total city taxes per capita: $384 (2007); City property taxes per capita: $338 (2007).

Education: Percent of population age 25 and over with: High school diploma (including GED) or higher: 80.7% (2010); Bachelor's degree or higher: 15.3% (2010); Master's degree or higher: 4.1% (2010).

School District(s)

Burnham SD 154-5 (PK-08)
  2009-10 Enrollment: 205 . . . . (708) 862-8636

Housing: Homeownership rate: 78.1% (2010); Median home value: $120,989 (2010); Median contract rent: $766 per month (2005-2009 5-year est.); Median year structure built: 1965 (2005-2009 5-year est.).

Transportation: Commute to work: 90.1% car, 7.5% public transportation, 0.7% walk, 1.3% work from home (2005-2009 5-year est.); Travel time to work: 19.3% less than 15 minutes, 23.0% 15 to 30 minutes, 27.3% 30 to 45 minutes, 12.7% 45 to 60 minutes, 17.8% 60 minutes or more (2005-2009 5-year est.)

CALUMET CITY (city). Covers a land area of 7.265 square miles and a water area of 0.117 square miles. Located at 41.61° N. Lat; 87.54° W. Long. Elevation is 591 feet.

History: Named for the French translation of "straw". Calumet City was platted in 1833, and developed in the 1920's as a residential outgrowth of Hammond, Indiana. Calumet is the French name for the Indian peace-pipe.

Population: 37,803 (1990); 39,071 (2000); 37,604 (2010); 36,997 (2015 projected); Race: 31.6% White, 56.2% Black, 0.6% Asian, 11.5% Other, 15.3% Hispanic of any race (2010); Density: 5,176.1 persons per square mile (2010); Average household size: 2.64 (2010); Median age: 35.6 (2010); Males per 100 females: 89.1 (2010); Marriage status: 39.4% never married, 41.0% now married, 7.6% widowed, 12.0% divorced (2005-2009

5-year est.); Foreign born: 7.5% (2005-2009 5-year est.); Ancestry (includes multiple ancestries): 6.5% Polish, 4.6% German, 2.9% Irish, 1.9% Italian, 1.4% American (2005-2009 5-year est.).

Economy: Unemployment rate: 14.3% (August 2011); Total civilian labor force: 18,199 (August 2011); Single-family building permits issued: 0 (2010); Multi-family building permits issued: 0 (2010); Employment by occupation: 9.6% management, 14.2% professional, 17.8% services, 29.8% sales, 0.1% farming, 7.3% construction, 21.2% production (2005-2009 5-year est.).

Income: Per capita income: $20,087 (2010); Median household income: $44,426 (2010); Average household income: $53,036 (2010); Percent of households with income of $100,000 or more: 10.6% (2010); Poverty rate: 16.8% (2005-2009 5-year est.).

Taxes: Total city taxes per capita: $723 (2007); City property taxes per capita: $450 (2007).

Education: Percent of population age 25 and over with: High school diploma (including GED) or higher: 85.7% (2010); Bachelor's degree or higher: 16.8% (2010); Master's degree or higher: 4.8% (2010).

School District(s)

Calumet City SD 155 (PK-08)
  2009-10 Enrollment: 1,256 . . . . (708) 862-7665
Dolton SD 149 (PK-08)
  2009-10 Enrollment: 3,397 . . . . (708) 868-7861
Hoover-Schrum Memorial SD 157 (PK-08)
  2009-10 Enrollment: 911 . . . . (708) 868-7500
Lincoln ESD 156 (PK-08)
  2009-10 Enrollment: 1,157 . . . . (708) 862-6625
Thornton Fractional Twp HSD 215 (09-12)
  2009-10 Enrollment: 3,678 . . . . (708) 585-2309

Four-year College(s)

Westwood College-River Oaks (Private, For-profit)
  Fall 2009 Enrollment: 579 . . . . (708) 832-1988
  2010-11 Tuition: In-state $14,227; Out-of-state $14,227

Housing: Homeownership rate: 68.4% (2010); Median home value: $125,187 (2010); Median contract rent: $733 per month (2005-2009 5-year est.); Median year structure built: 1965 (2005-2009 5-year est.).

Safety: Violent crime rate: 68.6 per 10,000 population; Property crime rate: 748.3 per 10,000 population (2010).

Transportation: Commute to work: 84.7% car, 11.1% public transportation, 1.8% walk, 2.0% work from home (2005-2009 5-year est.); Travel time to work: 13.6% less than 15 minutes, 23.1% 15 to 30 minutes, 26.2% 30 to 45 minutes, 15.3% 45 to 60 minutes, 21.9% 60 minutes or more (2005-2009 5-year est.)

Additional Information Contacts

Calumet City Chamber of Commerce . . . . (708) 891-5888
  http://www.calumetcitychamber.com
City of Calumet City . . . . (708) 891-8105
  http://www.calumetcity.org

CALUMET PARK (village). Covers a land area of 1.107 square miles and a water area of 0.039 square miles. Located at 41.66° N. Lat; 87.65° W. Long. Elevation is 604 feet.

History: Incorporated 1912; name changed from Burr Oak in 1925.

Population: 8,418 (1990); 8,516 (2000); 8,051 (2010); 7,823 (2015 projected); Race: 12.4% White, 81.6% Black, 0.1% Asian, 5.9% Other, 9.8% Hispanic of any race (2010); Density: 7,275.2 persons per square mile (2010); Average household size: 2.88 (2010); Median age: 34.3 (2010); Males per 100 females: 89.2 (2010); Marriage status: 39.0% never married, 41.8% now married, 6.2% widowed, 13.1% divorced (2005-2009 5-year est.); Foreign born: 6.0% (2005-2009 5-year est.); Ancestry (includes multiple ancestries): 2.4% German, 2.1% American, 1.4% Italian, 1.3% Irish, 1.3% African (2005-2009 5-year est.).

Economy: Single-family building permits issued: 0 (2010); Multi-family building permits issued: 3 (2010); Employment by occupation: 8.1% management, 14.4% professional, 22.8% services, 31.5% sales, 0.0% farming, 4.3% construction, 18.9% production (2005-2009 5-year est.).

Income: Per capita income: $21,039 (2010); Median household income: $52,310 (2010); Average household income: $60,495 (2010); Percent of households with income of $100,000 or more: 15.9% (2010); Poverty rate: 13.9% (2005-2009 5-year est.).

Taxes: Total city taxes per capita: $980 (2007); City property taxes per capita: $654 (2007).

Education: Percent of population age 25 and over with: High school diploma (including GED) or higher: 85.5% (2010); Bachelor's degree or higher: 16.1% (2010); Master's degree or higher: 5.0% (2010).

School District(s)

Calumet Public SD 132 (PK-08)
  2009-10 Enrollment: 1,193 . . . . (708) 388-8920
Housing: Homeownership rate: 71.8% (2010); Median home value:
$125,189 (2010); Median contract rent: $701 per month (2005-2009 5-year
est.); Median year structure built: 1957 (2005-2009 5-year est.).
Transportation: Commute to work: 85.0% car, 13.5% public
transportation, 0.7% walk, 0.8% work from home (2005-2009 5-year est.);
Travel time to work: 6.7% less than 15 minutes, 25.5% 15 to 30 minutes,
31.7% 30 to 45 minutes, 12.4% 45 to 60 minutes, 23.8% 60 minutes or
more (2005-2009 5-year est.)
Additional Information Contacts

Village of Calumet Park . . . . (708) 389-0850
  http://www.calumetparkvillage.org

CHICAGO (city). County seat. Covers a land area of 227.133 square
miles and a water area of 6.869 square miles. Located at 41.84° N. Lat;
87.67° W. Long. Elevation is 587 feet.

History: The river here was called Checagou by the Indians, meaning
something big, strong, or powerful. In 1803 Captain John Whistler and his
men built Fort Dearborn on the site that was to become Chicago, where a
few cabins occupied by Frenchmen and the Sable trading post already
existed. John Kinzie, a Scotch-Canadian trader who took over the trading
post, was the first English settler in the community that developed around
Fort Dearborn. When Chicago was incorporated as a town in 1833, the
population numbered under 200. The projected Illinois & Michigan Canal
brought speculators; Chicago was incorporated as a city in 1837 and soon
became the world's largest grain market and a major slaughterhouse. The
completion of the Illinois & Michigan Canal in 1848 increased the
commercial importance of Chicago, as did the many railroad lines that soon
radiated from it. The quick ramshackle building of Chicago was halted in
1871 when the fire started in Patrick O'Leary's cow barn destroyed 17,450
buildings in 27 hours. Rebuilding was fast and more permanent.
Population: 2,783,726 (1990); 2,896,016 (2000); 2,848,389 (2010);
2,814,480 (2015 projected); Race: 41.4% White, 34.6% Black, 4.9% Asian,
19.0% Other, 29.5% Hispanic of any race (2010); Density: 12,540.6
persons per square mile (2010); Average household size: 2.66 (2010);
Median age: 34.8 (2010); Males per 100 females: 96.4 (2010); Marriage
status: 46.0% never married, 39.3% now married, 6.0% widowed, 8.8%
divorced (2005-2009 5-year est.); Foreign born: 21.0% (2005-2009 5-year
est.); Ancestry (includes multiple ancestries): 7.8% German, 7.6% Irish,
6.8% Polish, 3.8% Italian, 2.4% English (2005-2009 5-year est.).
Economy: Unemployment rate: 11.7% (August 2011); Total civilian labor
force: 1,333,308 (August 2011); Single-family building permits issued: 164
(2010); Multi-family building permits issued: 1,713 (2010); Employment by
occupation: 14.4% management, 21.1% professional, 19.4% services,
24.6% sales, 0.1% farming, 6.5% construction, 13.8% production
(2005-2009 5-year est.).
Income: Per capita income: $24,664 (2010); Median household income:
$47,233 (2010); Average household income: $66,345 (2010); Percent of
households with income of $100,000 or more: 18.1% (2010); Poverty rate:
20.8% (2005-2009 5-year est.).
Taxes: Total city taxes per capita: $720 (2007); City property taxes per
capita: $128 (2007).
Education: Percent of population age 25 and over with: High school
diploma (including GED) or higher: 77.7% (2010); Bachelor's degree or
higher: 30.0% (2010); Master's degree or higher: 12.1% (2010).

School District(s)

Central Stickney SD 110 (PK-08)
  2009-10 Enrollment: 472 . . . . (708) 458-1152
City of Chicago SD 299 (PK-12)
  2009-10 Enrollment: 407,157 . . . . (773) 553-1000
Intermediate Service Center 3
  2009-10 Enrollment: n/a . . . . (312) 263-7767

Four-year College(s)

Adler School of Professional Psychology (Private, Not-for-profit)
  Fall 2009 Enrollment: 703 . . . . (312) 662-4000
American Academy of Art (Private, For-profit)
  Fall 2009 Enrollment: 400 . . . . (312) 461-0600
  2010-11 Tuition: In-state $25,570; Out-of-state $25,570
American College of Education (Private, For-profit)
  Fall 2009 Enrollment: n/a . . . . (312) 821-6300
Argosy University-Chicago (Private, For-profit)
  Fall 2009 Enrollment: 1,348 . . . . (312) 777-7600
  2010-11 Tuition: In-state $19,812; Out-of-state $19,812

Catholic Theological Union at Chicago (Private, Not-for-profit, Roman
Catholic)
  Fall 2009 Enrollment: 439 . . . . (773) 324-8000
Chicago State University (Public)
  Fall 2009 Enrollment: 7,235. . . . . (773) 995-2000
  2010-11 Tuition: In-state $8,752; Out-of-state $15,160
Chicago Theological Seminary (Private, Not-for-profit, United Church of
Christ)
  Fall 2009 Enrollment: 223 . . . . (773) 752-5757
Columbia College Chicago (Private, Not-for-profit)
  Fall 2009 Enrollment: 12,127. . . . . (312) 663-1600
  2010-11 Tuition: In-state $19,610; Out-of-state $19,610
DePaul University (Private, Not-for-profit, Roman Catholic)
  Fall 2009 Enrollment: 25,072. . . . . (312) 362-8000
  2010-11 Tuition: In-state $28,858; Out-of-state $28,858
DeVry University-Illinois (Private, For-profit)
  Fall 2009 Enrollment: 30,127. . . . . (773) 929-8500
  2010-11 Tuition: In-state $14,826; Out-of-state $14,826
East-West University (Private, Not-for-profit)
  Fall 2009 Enrollment: 1,060. . . . . (312) 939-0111
  2010-11 Tuition: In-state $15,750; Out-of-state $15,750
Ellis University (Private, Not-for-profit)
  Fall 2009 Enrollment: 1,950. . . . . (312) 669-5000
  2010-11 Tuition: In-state $13,560; Out-of-state $13,560
Erikson Institute (Private, Not-for-profit)
  Fall 2009 Enrollment: 284 . . . . (312) 755-2250
Harrington College of Design (Private, For-profit)
  Fall 2009 Enrollment: 1,067. . . . . (312) 939-4975
  2010-11 Tuition: In-state $19,100; Out-of-state $19,100
Illinois College of Optometry (Private, Not-for-profit)
  Fall 2009 Enrollment: 628 . . . . (312) 949-7400
Illinois Institute of Technology (Private, Not-for-profit)
  Fall 2009 Enrollment: 7,707. . . . . (312) 567-3000
  2010-11 Tuition: In-state $32,442; Out-of-state $32,442
Institute for Clinical Social Work (Private, Not-for-profit)
  Fall 2009 Enrollment: 107 . . . . (312) 726-8480
International Academy of Design and Technology (Private, For-profit)
  Fall 2009 Enrollment: 1,832. . . . . (312) 980-9200
  2010-11 Tuition: In-state $19,890; Out-of-state $19,890
Kendall College (Private, For-profit)
  Fall 2009 Enrollment: 2,389. . . . . (312) 752-2000
  2010-11 Tuition: In-state $19,225; Out-of-state $19,225
Lexington College (Private, Not-for-profit)
  Fall 2009 Enrollment: 54 . . . . (312) 226-6294
  2010-11 Tuition: In-state $24,500; Out-of-state $24,500
Loyola University Chicago (Private, Not-for-profit, Roman Catholic)
  Fall 2009 Enrollment: 15,879. . . . . (773) 274-3000
  2010-11 Tuition: In-state $32,114; Out-of-state $32,114
Lutheran School of Theology at Chicago (Private, Not-for-profit,
Evangelical Lutheran Church)
  Fall 2009 Enrollment: 302 . . . . (773) 256-0700
McCormick Theological Seminary (Private, Not-for-profit, Presbyterian
Church (USA))
  Fall 2009 Enrollment: 248 . . . . (773) 947-6300
Meadville Lombard Theological School (Private, Not-for-profit, Unitarian
Universalist)
  Fall 2009 Enrollment: 91 . . . . (773) 256-3000
Midwest College of Oriental Medicine (Private, For-profit)
  Fall 2009 Enrollment: 169 . . . . (800) 593-2320
Moody Bible Institute (Private, Not-for-profit, Interdenominational)
  Fall 2009 Enrollment: 2,991. . . . . (312) 329-4000
  2010-11 Tuition: In-state $9,968; Out-of-state $9,968
National-Louis University (Private, Not-for-profit)
  Fall 2009 Enrollment: 6,385. . . . . (800) 443-5522
  2010-11 Tuition: In-state $18,355; Out-of-state $18,355
North Park University (Private, Not-for-profit, Evangelical Covenant Church
of America)
  Fall 2009 Enrollment: 3,186. . . . . (773) 244-6200
  2010-11 Tuition: In-state $19,960; Out-of-state $19,960
Northeastern Illinois University (Public)
  Fall 2009 Enrollment: 11,631. . . . . (773) 583-4050
  2010-11 Tuition: In-state $7,492; Out-of-state $13,732
Pacific College of Oriental Medicine (Private, For-profit)
  Fall 2009 Enrollment: 214 . . . . (773) 477-4822
  2010-11 Tuition: In-state $11,129; Out-of-state $11,129

Robert Morris University Illinois (Private, Not-for-profit)
  Fall 2009 Enrollment: 4,619 . . . . (312) 935-6800
  2010-11 Tuition: In-state $20,100; Out-of-state $20,100
Roosevelt University (Private, Not-for-profit)
  Fall 2009 Enrollment: 7,306 . . . . (312) 341-3500
  2010-11 Tuition: In-state $23,300; Out-of-state $23,300
Rush University (Private, Not-for-profit)
  Fall 2009 Enrollment: 1,804 . . . . (312) 942-7100
Saint Augustine College (Private, Not-for-profit)
  Fall 2009 Enrollment: 1,430 . . . . (773) 878-8756
  2010-11 Tuition: In-state $8,400; Out-of-state $8,400
Saint Xavier University (Private, Not-for-profit, Roman Catholic)
  Fall 2009 Enrollment: 5,028 . . . . (773) 298-3000
  2010-11 Tuition: In-state $25,520; Out-of-state $25,520
School of the Art Institute of Chicago (Private, Not-for-profit)
  Fall 2009 Enrollment: 3,164 . . . . (312) 629-6100
  2010-11 Tuition: In-state $36,150; Out-of-state $36,150
Shimer College (Private, Not-for-profit)
  Fall 2009 Enrollment: 104 . . . . (312) 235-3500
  2010-11 Tuition: In-state $29,100; Out-of-state $29,100
Spertus College (Private, Not-for-profit)
  Fall 2009 Enrollment: 343 . . . . (312) 922-9012
Telshe Yeshiva-Chicago (Private, Not-for-profit, Jewish)
  Fall 2009 Enrollment: 82 . . . . (773) 463-7738
  2010-11 Tuition: In-state $12,000; Out-of-state $12,000
The Chicago School of Professional Psychology at Chicago (Private, Not-for-profit)
  Fall 2009 Enrollment: 2,245 . . . . (312) 329-6600
The Illinois Institute of Art-Chicago (Private, For-profit)
  Fall 2009 Enrollment: 2,990 . . . . (312) 280-3500
  2010-11 Tuition: In-state $18,066; Out-of-state $18,066
The John Marshall Law School (Private, Not-for-profit)
  Fall 2009 Enrollment: 1,539 . . . . (312) 427-2737
Toyota Technological Institute at Chicago (Private, Not-for-profit)
  Fall 2009 Enrollment: 12 . . . . (773) 834-2500
University of Chicago (Private, Not-for-profit)
  Fall 2009 Enrollment: 15,094 . . . . (773) 702-1234
  2010-11 Tuition: In-state $42,041; Out-of-state $42,041
University of Illinois at Chicago (Public)
  Fall 2009 Enrollment: 26,840 . . . . (312) 996-7000
  2010-11 Tuition: In-state $12,056; Out-of-state $24,446
VanderCook College of Music (Private, Not-for-profit)
  Fall 2009 Enrollment: 403 . . . . (312) 225-6288
  2010-11 Tuition: In-state $23,480; Out-of-state $23,480
Westwood College-Chicago Loop (Private, For-profit)
  Fall 2009 Enrollment: 885 . . . . (312) 578-3898
  2010-11 Tuition: In-state $14,227; Out-of-state $14,227
Westwood College-O'Hare Airport (Private, For-profit)
  Fall 2009 Enrollment: 888 . . . . (773) 380-6800
  2010-11 Tuition: In-state $14,227; Out-of-state $14,227

Two-year College(s)

City Colleges of Chicago-Harold Washington College (Public)
  Fall 2009 Enrollment: 8,464 . . . . (312) 553-5600
  2010-11 Tuition: In-state $6,659; Out-of-state $8,191
City Colleges of Chicago-Harry S Truman College (Public)
  Fall 2009 Enrollment: 13,174 . . . . (773) 907-4000
  2010-11 Tuition: In-state $6,659; Out-of-state $8,191
City Colleges of Chicago-Kennedy-King College (Public)
  Fall 2009 Enrollment: 7,180 . . . . (773) 602-5000
  2010-11 Tuition: In-state $6,659; Out-of-state $8,191
City Colleges of Chicago-Malcolm X College (Public)
  Fall 2009 Enrollment: 8,718 . . . . (312) 850-7000
  2010-11 Tuition: In-state $6,659; Out-of-state $8,191
City Colleges of Chicago-Olive-Harvey College (Public)
  Fall 2009 Enrollment: 4,777 . . . . (773) 291-6100
  2010-11 Tuition: In-state $6,659; Out-of-state $8,191
City Colleges of Chicago-Richard J Daley College (Public)
  Fall 2009 Enrollment: 9,991 . . . . (773) 838-7500
  2010-11 Tuition: In-state $6,659; Out-of-state $8,191
City Colleges of Chicago-Wilbur Wright College (Public)
  Fall 2009 Enrollment: 12,866 . . . . (773) 777-7900
  2010-11 Tuition: In-state $6,659; Out-of-state $8,191
Coyne American Institute Inc (Private, For-profit)
  Fall 2009 Enrollment: 938 . . . . (773) 577-8100

Le Cordon Bleu College of Culinary Arts in Chicago (Private, For-profit)
  Fall 2009 Enrollment: 1,047 . . . . (312) 944-0882
  2010-11 Tuition: In-state $20,375; Out-of-state $20,375
MacCormac College (Private, Not-for-profit)
  Fall 2009 Enrollment: 151 . . . . (312) 922-1884
  2010-11 Tuition: In-state $12,960; Out-of-state $12,960
Northwestern College (Private, For-profit)
  Fall 2009 Enrollment: 935 . . . . (773) 777-4220
  2010-11 Tuition: In-state $20,980; Out-of-state $20,980
Taylor Business Institute (Private, For-profit)
  Fall 2009 Enrollment: 431 . . . . (312) 658-5100
  2010-11 Tuition: In-state $13,500; Out-of-state $13,500
The College of Office Technology (Private, For-profit)
  Fall 2009 Enrollment: 276 . . . . (773) 278-0042

Vocational/Technical School(s)

Aveda Institute-Chicago (Private, For-profit)
  Fall 2009 Enrollment: 110 . . . . (773) 883-1560
  2010-11 Tuition: $16,050
BIR Training Center (Private, For-profit)
  Fall 2009 Enrollment: 397 . . . . (773) 866-0111
  2010-11 Tuition: $5,600
CET-Chicago (Private, Not-for-profit)
  Fall 2009 Enrollment: 585 . . . . (408) 287-7924
  2010-11 Tuition: $8,060
Cain's Barber College Inc (Private, For-profit)
  Fall 2009 Enrollment: 125 . . . . (773) 536-4441
  2010-11 Tuition: $9,285
Cannella School of Hair Design (Private, For-profit)
  Fall 2009 Enrollment: 124 . . . . (773) 278-4477
  2010-11 Tuition: $10,190
Cannella School of Hair Design (Private, For-profit)
  Fall 2009 Enrollment: 91 . . . . (773) 221-4700
  2010-11 Tuition: $12,190
Cannella School of Hair Design (Private, For-profit)
  Fall 2009 Enrollment: 122 . . . . (773) 890-0412
  2010-11 Tuition: $10,190
Capri Garfield Ridge School of Beauty Culture (Private, For-profit)
  Fall 2009 Enrollment: 127 . . . . (773) 778-0882
  2010-11 Tuition: $15,000
Cortiva Institute-Chicago (Private, For-profit)
  Fall 2009 Enrollment: 674 . . . . (312) 753-7900
Everest College-Chicago (Private, For-profit)
  Fall 2009 Enrollment: 1,995 . . . . (312) 913-1616
  2010-11 Tuition: $15,543
Illinois School of Health Careers (Private, For-profit)
  Fall 2009 Enrollment: 252 . . . . (312) 913-1230
  2010-11 Tuition: $15,250
Illinois School of Health Careers-O'Hare Campus (Private, For-profit)
  Fall 2009 Enrollment: 362 . . . . (773) 458-1111
  2010-11 Tuition: $15,250
Mac Daniels Beauty School (Private, For-profit)
  Fall 2009 Enrollment: 81 . . . . (773) 883-5100
  2010-11 Tuition: $13,410
National Latino Education Institute (Private, Not-for-profit)
  Fall 2009 Enrollment: 113 . . . . (773) 247-0707
  2010-11 Tuition: $9,000
Pivot Point Beauty School (Private, For-profit)
  Fall 2009 Enrollment: 108 . . . . (773) 463-3121
  2010-11 Tuition: $18,248
Pyramid Career Institute (Private, For-profit)
  Fall 2009 Enrollment: 14 . . . . (773) 975-9898
  2010-11 Tuition: $4,300
Rosel School of Cosmetology (Private, For-profit)
  Fall 2009 Enrollment: 120 . . . . (773) 508-5600
  2010-11 Tuition: $10,100
Soma Institute-The National School of Clinical Massage Therapy (Private, For-profit)
  Fall 2009 Enrollment: 378 . . . . (312) 939-2723
Tricoci University of Beauty Culture (Private, For-profit)
  Fall 2009 Enrollment: 141 . . . . (630) 528-3336
  2010-11 Tuition: $16,650
University of Aesthetics (Private, For-profit)
  Fall 2009 Enrollment: 12 . . . . (773) 661-0026
  2010-11 Tuition: $10,685

Housing: Homeownership rate: 47.7% (2010); Median home value: $229,010 (2010); Median contract rent: $737 per month (2005-2009 5-year est.); Median year structure built: 1945 (2005-2009 5-year est.).

Hospitals: Advocate Bethany Hospital (240 beds); Advocate Illinois Masonic Medical Center (370 beds); Advocate Trinity Hospital; Chicago Lakeshore Hospital (150 beds); Chicago Read Mental Health Center (26 beds); Children's Memorial Hospital (270 beds); Hartgrove Hospital (119 beds); Hazelden Chicago (22 beds); Holy Cross Hospital (244 beds); Jackson Park Hospital & Medical Center (336 beds); John H Stroger, Jr Hospital of Cook County (464 beds); Kindred Chicago Lakeshore (103 beds); La Rabida Childrens Hospital (49 beds); Lincoln Park Hospital (191 beds); Loretto Hospital (189 beds); Mercy Hospital & Medical Center (507 beds); Methodist Hospital of Chicago (198 beds); Michael Reese Hospital (565 beds); Mount Sinai Hospital (432 beds); Neurologic and Orthopedic Insitute of Chicago (78 beds); Northwestern Memorial Hospital (744 beds); Norwegian-American Hospital (200 beds); Our Lady of the Resurrection Medical Center (264 beds); Provident Hospital (243 beds); Rehabilitation Institute of Chicago (155 beds); Resurrection Medical Center (434 beds); Roseland Community Hospital (162 beds); Rush University Medical Center (618 beds); Sacred Heart Hospital (119 beds); Saint Anthony Hospital (183 beds); Saint Bernard Hospital and Health Care Center (183 beds); Saints Mary & Elizabeth Medical Center (387 beds); Schwab Rehabilitation Hospital (85 beds); Shriners Hospital for Children (60 beds); Sinai Community Institute; South Shore Hospital (170 beds); St. Elizabeth's Hospital (276 beds); St. Joseph Hospital (492 beds); Swedish Covenant Hospital (330 beds); Thorek Hospital and Medical Center (218 beds); University of Chicago Comer Children's Hospital (155 beds); University of Chicago Hospitals (662 beds); University of Illinois at Chicago Medical Center (570 beds); Veterans Affairs Lakeside Medical Center (337 beds); Veterans Affairs West Side Medical Center (435 beds); Weiss Memorial Hospital (357 beds).

Safety: Violent crime rate: n/a per 10,000 population; Property crime rate: 423.6 per 10,000 population (2010).

Newspapers: AHA News (National news; Circulation 23,681); African American Times (Local news); Beverly Review (Community news; Circulation 6,400); The Bond Buyer - Chicago Bureau (Regional news); Bridgeport News (Community news; Circulation 25,300); Brighton Park Life-McKinley Park Life (Local news; Circulation 30,000); Central Newspaper (Local news; Circulation 25,000); Chicago Catolico (Local news; Circulation 20,000); Chicago Chinese News (Local news; Circulation 10,000); Chicago Daily Law Bulletin (Regional news; Circulation 7,000); Chicago Defender (Local news; Circulation 525,000); Chicago Free Press (Community news; Circulation 26,000); Chicago Hospital News (Regional news); Chicago Independent Bulletin (Local news; Circulation 64,000); Chicago Post (Community news; Circulation 38,000); Chicago Sun-Times (Local news; Circulation 487,480); Chicago Tribune (National news; Circulation 579,079); Chicago Woman Newspaper (Local news); Chicago's Northwest Side Press (Community news; Circulation 49,000); China Journal (International news; Circulation 20,000); China Star Weekly (Circulation 5,000); Chinese American News (Local news; Circulation 10,000); Citizen Newspapers (Community news); Clear Ridge Reporter (Local news); DSN Retailing Today - Chicago Bureau (National news; Circulation 25,241); Draugas (International news; Circulation 6,000); El Heraldo De Chicago (Local news; Circulation 20,000); Environment & Climate News (National news); Extra (Local news; Circulation 71,205); Financial Times - Chicago Bureau (Local news); Greek Star (Local news; Circulation 7,800); The Herald Extra (Community news; Circulation 20,967); Hoy - Chicago Edition (Local news; Circulation 86,500); Hyde Park Herald (Community news; Circulation 6,738); India Bulletin (Local news; Circulation 26,000); Inside (Community news; Circulation 50,000); Journal (Local news; Circulation 1,500); Journal News (Community news; Circulation 48,000); Korea Times (Local news; Circulation 40,000); La Raza (Local news; Circulation 190,000); Los Angeles Times - Chicago Bureau (Local news); Metro Extra (Local news; Circulation 72,000); Near West Gazette (Local news; Circulation 17,000); The New York Times - Chicago Bureau (Regional news); Nitty Gritty News (Local news); Nuevo Siglo Newspaper (Local news; Circulation 20,000); Polish Daily News (National news; Circulation 28,400); RedEye (Local news; Circulation 200,000); Sauganash Sounds (Community news; Circulation 6,300); School Reform News (Regional news); Sing Tao Daily - Chicago Bureau (Local news; Circulation 8,000); South End Citizen (Local news; Circulation 28,707); South Suburban Citizen (Local news; Circulation 21,500); Southeast Chicago Observer (Local news; Circulation 15,000); Southeast Extra (Local news; Circulation 71,205); Southwest Extra (Local news; Circulation 5,000); Southwest News Herald (Local news; Circulation 26,996); Southwest News-Herald (Community news; Circulation 25,000);

Southwest Shopper (Community news; Circulation 27,000); Suburban Extra (Local news; Circulation 5,580); UIC Today (Local news); USA Today - Chicago Bureau (National news); Villager (Community news; Circulation 50,000); The Wall Street Journal - Chicago Bureau (Regional news); The Washington Post - Chicago Bureau (Local news); Windy City Times (Local news; Circulation 24,000)

Transportation: Commute to work: 61.6% car, 26.4% public transportation, 5.7% walk, 3.7% work from home (2005-2009 5-year est.); Travel time to work: 13.5% less than 15 minutes, 27.9% 15 to 30 minutes, 29.2% 30 to 45 minutes, 14.1% 45 to 60 minutes, 15.3% 60 minutes or more (2005-2009 5-year est.); Amtrak: train service available.

Airports: Chicago Midway International (primary service/large hub); Chicago O'Hare International (primary service/large hub); John H. Stroger Hospital of Cook County (general aviation); Lansing Municipal (general aviation)

Additional Information Contacts

America - Israel Chamber of Commerce Chicago	(847) 597-7070
http://www.americaisrael.org	
Andersonville Chamber of Commerce	(773) 728-2995
http://www.andersonville.org	
Chicago Area Gay & Lesbian Chamber of Commerce	(773) 303-0167
http://www.glchamber.org	
Chicago Chinatown Chamber of Commerce	(312) 326-5320
http://www.chicagochinatown.org	
Chicago Convention & Tourism Bureau	(312) 567-8500
http://www.choosechicago.com	
Chicagoland Chamber of Commerce	(312) 494-6700
http://www.chicagolandchamber.org	
City of Chicago	(312) 744-5000
http://www.cityofchicago.org	
German American Chamber of Commerce of the Midwest	(312) 644-2662
http://www.gaccom.org	
Illinois Chamber of Commerce	(312) 983-7100
http://www.ilchamber.org	
Italian American Chamber of Commerce - Midwest	(312) 553-9137
http://iacc-chicago.com	
Lake View East Chamber of Commerce	(773) 348-8608
http://www.lakevieweast.com	
Latin American Chamber of Commerce	(773) 252-5211
http://www.latinamericanchamberofcommerce.com	
Lincoln Park Chamber of Commerce	(773) 880-5200
http://www.lincolnparkchamber.org	
Logan Square Chamber of Commerce	(773) 489-3222
http://www.loganchamber.org	
Old Town Merchants & Residents Association	(312) 951-6106
http://www.oldtownchicago.org	
Portage Park Chamber of Commerce	(773) 777-2020
http://www.portageparkchamber.org	
Puerto Rico Convention Bureau	(312) 840-8090
http://www.meetpuertorico.com	
South Shore Chamber of Commerce	(617) 479-1111
http://southshorechamber.org	
Southeast Chicago Chamber of Commerce	(773) 734-0626
http://southeastchgochamber.org	
Streeterville Chamber of Commerce	(312) 664-2560
http://www.streetervillechamber.org	
Turkish American Chamber of Commerce-Midwest	(312) 276-5171
http://www.tacci-midwest.org	
Wicker Park & Bucktown Chamber of Commerce	(773) 384-2672
http://www.wickerparkbucktown.com	

CHICAGO HEIGHTS (city).

Covers a land area of 9.571 square miles and a water area of 0.011 square miles. Located at 41.51° N. Lat; 87.64° W. Long. Elevation is 659 feet.

History: Chicago Heights developed at the point where the Hubbard Trail crossed the Sauk Trail, a heavily traveled junction. The first settlement here in the 1830's was called Thorn Grove, but it was renamed Bloom in 1849 by German settlers. In 1890 the Chicago Heights Land Association began encouraging settlers and industry to come here, and the name of the town was changed.

Population: 33,156 (1990); 32,776 (2000); 30,609 (2010); 29,628 (2015 projected); Race: 41.7% White, 35.7% Black, 0.7% Asian, 21.8% Other, 31.3% Hispanic of any race (2010); Density: 3,198.0 persons per square mile (2010); Average household size: 3.03 (2010); Median age: 32.3 (2010); Males per 100 females: 97.6 (2010); Marriage status: 42.6% never married, 41.7% now married, 7.5% widowed, 8.2% divorced (2005-2009 5-year est.); Foreign born: 12.9% (2005-2009 5-year est.); Ancestry (includes multiple ancestries): 9.8% Italian, 8.0% German, 5.2% Irish, 5.0% Polish, 1.7% English (2005-2009 5-year est.).

Economy: Unemployment rate: 15.7% (August 2011); Total civilian labor force: 13,398 (August 2011); Single-family building permits issued: 0 (2010); Multi-family building permits issued: 0 (2010); Employment by occupation: 7.8% management, 16.5% professional, 21.5% services, 28.1% sales, 0.1% farming, 9.5% construction, 16.5% production (2005-2009 5-year est.).

Income: Per capita income: $17,757 (2010); Median household income: $42,624 (2010); Average household income: $54,410 (2010); Percent of households with income of $100,000 or more: 12.6% (2010); Poverty rate: 23.6% (2005-2009 5-year est.).

Taxes: Total city taxes per capita: $592 (2007); City property taxes per capita: $411 (2007).

Education: Percent of population age 25 and over with: High school diploma (including GED) or higher: 77.1% (2010); Bachelor's degree or higher: 15.4% (2010); Master's degree or higher: 5.4% (2010).

School District(s)

Bloom Twp HSD 206 (09-12)
  2009-10 Enrollment: 3,513 . . . . (708) 755-7010
Career Prep Net @ Prairie State
  2009-10 Enrollment: n/a . . . . (708) 709-7903
Chicago Heights SD 170 (PK-08)
  2009-10 Enrollment: 3,373 . . . . (708) 756-4165
Flossmoor SD 161 (PK-08)
  2009-10 Enrollment: 2,334 . . . . (708) 647-7000
Intermediate Service Center 4 (06-12)
  2009-10 Enrollment: n/a . . . . (708) 754-6600
Park Forest SD 163 (PK-08)
  2009-10 Enrollment: 1,841 . . . . (708) 668-9400
Speed Seja #802 (PK-12)
  2009-10 Enrollment: n/a . . . . (708) 481-6100

Two-year College(s)

Prairie State College (Public)
  Fall 2009 Enrollment: 5,854. . . . . (708) 709-3500
  2010-11 Tuition: In-state $6,116; Out-of-state $8,228

Housing: Homeownership rate: 67.2% (2010); Median home value: $128,182 (2010); Median contract rent: $645 per month (2005-2009 5-year est.); Median year structure built: 1956 (2005-2009 5-year est.).

Hospitals: St. James Hospital and Health Center (587 beds)

Newspapers: Chicago Standard News (Community news; Circulation 15,000); South Suburban Standard (Community news; Circulation 25,000)

Transportation: Commute to work: 88.8% car, 6.9% public transportation, 1.3% walk, 0.6% work from home (2005-2009 5-year est.); Travel time to work: 37.0% less than 15 minutes, 25.0% 15 to 30 minutes, 14.5% 30 to 45 minutes, 9.6% 45 to 60 minutes, 13.9% 60 minutes or more (2005-2009 5-year est.)

Additional Information Contacts
City of Chicago Heights . . . . (708) 756-5300
  http://www.chicagoheights.net

CHICAGO RIDGE (village). Covers a land area of 2.230 square miles and a water area of 0 square miles. Located at 41.70° N. Lat; 87.77° W. Long. Elevation is 594 feet.

Population: 13,556 (1990); 14,127 (2000); 13,480 (2010); 12,972 (2015 projected); Race: 85.3% White, 3.5% Black, 1.9% Asian, 9.4% Other, 8.8% Hispanic of any race (2010); Density: 6,046.1 persons per square mile (2010); Average household size: 2.43 (2010); Median age: 36.4 (2010); Males per 100 females: 96.6 (2010); Marriage status: 32.2% never married, 50.5% now married, 6.8% widowed, 10.5% divorced (2005-2009 5-year est.); Foreign born: 21.0% (2005-2009 5-year est.); Ancestry (includes multiple ancestries): 23.2% Irish, 20.0% German, 17.5% Polish, 9.4% Italian, 5.5% Arab (2005-2009 5-year est.).

Economy: Single-family building permits issued: 0 (2010); Multi-family building permits issued: 12 (2010); Employment by occupation: 11.3% management, 15.5% professional, 21.1% services, 30.7% sales, 0.2% farming, 10.5% construction, 10.7% production (2005-2009 5-year est.).

Income: Per capita income: $26,128 (2010); Median household income: $57,165 (2010); Average household income: $64,725 (2010); Percent of households with income of $100,000 or more: 16.7% (2010); Poverty rate: 15.8% (2005-2009 5-year est.).

Taxes: Total city taxes per capita: $732 (2007); City property taxes per capita: $439 (2007).

Education: Percent of population age 25 and over with: High school diploma (including GED) or higher: 86.4% (2010); Bachelor's degree or higher: 16.5% (2010); Master's degree or higher: 4.9% (2010).

School District(s)

Chicago Ridge SD 127-5 (PK-08)
  2009-10 Enrollment: 1,317 . . . . (708) 636-2000

Housing: Homeownership rate: 57.0% (2010); Median home value: $167,524 (2010); Median contract rent: $778 per month (2005-2009 5-year est.); Median year structure built: 1972 (2005-2009 5-year est.).

Transportation: Commute to work: 89.2% car, 4.5% public transportation, 2.3% walk, 0.2% work from home (2005-2009 5-year est.); Travel time to work: 23.1% less than 15 minutes, 32.9% 15 to 30 minutes, 17.7% 30 to 45 minutes, 13.7% 45 to 60 minutes, 12.7% 60 minutes or more (2005-2009 5-year est.)

Additional Information Contacts
Village of Chicago Ridge . . . . (708) 425-7700
  http://www.chicagoridge.org

CICERO (town). Covers a land area of 5.846 square miles and a water area of 0 square miles. Located at 41.84° N. Lat; 87.76° W. Long. Elevation is 604 feet.

History: Named for Marcus Tullius Cicero, a Roman orator. Cicero was settled in the mid-1800's. The first township election was held in 1857, and Cicero was incorporated as a town in 1867 and as a city in 1869, following an influx of homesteaders during the Civil War. Cicero shrank when parts of it were annexed to Chicago in 1892. During the industrial boom that followed the turn of the century, Al Capone was the proprietor of a row of gambling houses here.

Population: 67,436 (1990); 85,616 (2000); 81,668 (2010); 79,702 (2015 projected); Race: 43.7% White, 1.3% Black, 0.6% Asian, 54.5% Other, 86.1% Hispanic of any race (2010); Density: 13,969.9 persons per square mile (2010); Average household size: 3.79 (2010); Median age: 28.6 (2010); Males per 100 females: 106.1 (2010); Marriage status: 36.3% never married, 53.5% now married, 4.4% widowed, 5.8% divorced (2005-2009 5-year est.); Foreign born: 43.7% (2005-2009 5-year est.); Ancestry (includes multiple ancestries): 3.1% Polish, 2.9% Irish, 2.7% German, 2.1% Italian, 1.2% Czech (2005-2009 5-year est.).

Economy: Unemployment rate: 12.6% (August 2011); Total civilian labor force: 32,046 (August 2011); Single-family building permits issued: 0 (2010); Multi-family building permits issued: 0 (2010); Employment by occupation: 5.2% management, 5.8% professional, 20.8% services, 21.4% sales, 0.3% farming, 12.4% construction, 34.1% production (2005-2009 5-year est.).

Income: Per capita income: $14,097 (2010); Median household income: $45,087 (2010); Average household income: $53,484 (2010); Percent of households with income of $100,000 or more: 9.6% (2010); Poverty rate: 16.1% (2005-2009 5-year est.).

Taxes: Total city taxes per capita: $828 (2007); City property taxes per capita: $502 (2007).

Education: Percent of population age 25 and over with: High school diploma (including GED) or higher: 54.4% (2010); Bachelor's degree or higher: 7.8% (2010); Master's degree or higher: 2.9% (2010).

School District(s)

Cicero SD 99 (PK-08)
  2009-10 Enrollment: 13,732 . . . . (708) 863-4856
Intermediate Service Center 2 (06-12)
  2009-10 Enrollment: n/a . . . . (708) 544-4890
J S Morton HSD 201 (09-12)
  2009-10 Enrollment: 8,489 . . . . (708) 222-5704

Two-year College(s)

Morton College (Public)
  Fall 2009 Enrollment: 5,290. . . . . (708) 656-8000
  2010-11 Tuition: In-state $7,284; Out-of-state $9,332

Vocational/Technical School(s)

Bell Mar Beauty College (Private, For-profit)
  Fall 2009 Enrollment: 61 . . . . (708) 863-6644
  2010-11 Tuition: $11,400

Housing: Homeownership rate: 59.9% (2010); Median home value: $180,540 (2010); Median contract rent: $667 per month (2005-2009 5-year est.); Median year structure built: before 1940 (2005-2009 5-year est.).

Newspapers: Cicero/Berwyn Suburban Edition (Local news; Circulation 200,000); Czechoslovak Herald - Nedelni Hlasatel (Local news; Circulation 10,000); El Dia Newspaper (Local news; Circulation 45,000); El Imparcial (Local news; Circulation 20,000); Lawndale News (Regional news; Circulation 200,000)

Transportation: Commute to work: 84.4% car, 9.7% public transportation, 3.6% walk, 0.9% work from home (2005-2009 5-year est.); Travel time to work: 14.8% less than 15 minutes, 30.9% 15 to 30 minutes, 28.1% 30 to 45 minutes, 13.5% 45 to 60 minutes, 12.7% 60 minutes or more (2005-2009 5-year est.)

Additional Information Contacts

Cicero Chamber of Commerce . . . . (708) 863-6000
   http://www.cicerochamber.org
Town of Cicero . . . . (708) 656-3600
   http://www.thetownofcicero.com

COUNTRY CLUB HILLS (city). Covers a land area of 4.614 square miles and a water area of 0.024 square miles. Located at 41.56° N. Lat; 87.72° W. Long. Elevation is 682 feet.

Population: 15,435 (1990); 16,169 (2000); 17,251 (2010); 17,597 (2015 projected); Race: 15.9% White, 80.6% Black, 0.8% Asian, 2.6% Other, 2.1% Hispanic of any race (2010); Density: 3,738.9 persons per square mile (2010); Average household size: 2.92 (2010); Median age: 36.7 (2010); Males per 100 females: 86.0 (2010); Marriage status: 35.9% never married, 47.5% now married, 5.4% widowed, 11.2% divorced (2005-2009 5-year est.); Foreign born: 3.1% (2005-2009 5-year est.); Ancestry (includes multiple ancestries): 2.2% German, 1.3% Polish, 1.3% Jamaican, 1.2% Irish, 1.2% English (2005-2009 5-year est.).
Economy: Single-family building permits issued: 0 (2010); Multi-family building permits issued: 0 (2010); Employment by occupation: 13.0% management, 26.1% professional, 12.9% services, 30.6% sales, 0.0% farming, 6.7% construction, 10.8% production (2005-2009 5-year est.).
Income: Per capita income: $25,526 (2010); Median household income: $64,913 (2010); Average household income: $75,035 (2010); Percent of households with income of $100,000 or more: 23.6% (2010); Poverty rate: 8.4% (2005-2009 5-year est.).
Taxes: Total city taxes per capita: $648 (2007); City property taxes per capita: $527 (2007).
Education: Percent of population age 25 and over with: High school diploma (including GED) or higher: 92.2% (2010); Bachelor's degree or higher: 26.8% (2010); Master's degree or higher: 9.0% (2010).

School District(s)

Bremen CHSD 228 (09-12)
   2009-10 Enrollment: 5,533 . . . . (708) 389-1175
Country Club Hills SD 160 (PK-08)
   2009-10 Enrollment: 1,463 . . . . (708) 957-6200
Prairie-Hills ESD 144 (PK-08)
   2009-10 Enrollment: 2,931 . . . . (708) 210-2888
Speed Seja #802 (PK-12)
   2009-10 Enrollment: n/a . . . . (708) 481-6100
Housing: Homeownership rate: 92.1% (2010); Median home value: $149,152 (2010); Median contract rent: $1,070 per month (2005-2009 5-year est.); Median year structure built: 1975 (2005-2009 5-year est.).
Safety: Violent crime rate: 38.9 per 10,000 population; Property crime rate: 347.3 per 10,000 population (2010).
Transportation: Commute to work: 87.7% car, 10.0% public transportation, 0.3% walk, 1.8% work from home (2005-2009 5-year est.); Travel time to work: 8.8% less than 15 minutes, 28.5% 15 to 30 minutes, 28.8% 30 to 45 minutes, 14.4% 45 to 60 minutes, 19.5% 60 minutes or more (2005-2009 5-year est.).

Additional Information Contacts

City of Country Club Hills . . . . (708) 798-2616
   http://www.countryclubhills.org

COUNTRYSIDE (city). Covers a land area of 2.690 square miles and a water area of 0 square miles. Located at 41.77° N. Lat; 87.87° W. Long. Elevation is 663 feet.

Population: 6,002 (1990); 5,991 (2000); 5,766 (2010); 5,695 (2015 projected); Race: 90.6% White, 2.3% Black, 1.5% Asian, 5.6% Other, 10.1% Hispanic of any race (2010); Density: 2,143.1 persons per square mile (2010); Average household size: 2.20 (2010); Median age: 45.0 (2010); Males per 100 females: 90.5 (2010); Marriage status: 32.0% never married, 49.5% now married, 7.2% widowed, 11.3% divorced (2005-2009 5-year est.); Foreign born: 17.7% (2005-2009 5-year est.); Ancestry (includes multiple ancestries): 18.2% Irish, 16.6% German, 15.2% Polish, 12.5% Italian, 8.2% English (2005-2009 5-year est.).
Economy: Single-family building permits issued: 3 (2010); Multi-family building permits issued: 0 (2010); Employment by occupation: 16.3% management, 15.6% professional, 15.2% services, 32.0% sales, 0.0% farming, 10.3% construction, 10.6% production (2005-2009 5-year est.).

Income: Per capita income: $30,446 (2010); Median household income: $51,996 (2010); Average household income: $67,362 (2010); Percent of households with income of $100,000 or more: 21.2% (2010); Poverty rate: 7.6% (2005-2009 5-year est.).
Taxes: Total city taxes per capita: $198 (2007); City property taxes per capita: $9 (2007).
Education: Percent of population age 25 and over with: High school diploma (including GED) or higher: 88.2% (2010); Bachelor's degree or higher: 27.6% (2010); Master's degree or higher: 11.4% (2010).

School District(s)

La Grange SD 105 South (PK-08)
   2009-10 Enrollment: 1,314 . . . . (708) 482-2700
Housing: Homeownership rate: 77.6% (2010); Median home value: $242,018 (2010); Median contract rent: $789 per month (2005-2009 5-year est.); Median year structure built: 1968 (2005-2009 5-year est.).
Safety: Violent crime rate: 10.5 per 10,000 population; Property crime rate: 370.3 per 10,000 population (2010).
Transportation: Commute to work: 86.0% car, 8.4% public transportation, 2.8% walk, 2.6% work from home (2005-2009 5-year est.); Travel time to work: 30.1% less than 15 minutes, 28.4% 15 to 30 minutes, 18.5% 30 to 45 minutes, 10.9% 45 to 60 minutes, 12.1% 60 minutes or more (2005-2009 5-year est.).

Additional Information Contacts

City of Countryside . . . . (708) 354-7270
   http://www.countryside-il.org

CRESTWOOD (village). Covers a land area of 3.055 square miles and a water area of 0.053 square miles. Located at 41.64° N. Lat; 87.74° W. Long. Elevation is 597 feet.

Population: 11,073 (1990); 11,251 (2000); 11,412 (2010); 11,498 (2015 projected); Race: 91.5% White, 4.7% Black, 0.8% Asian, 3.0% Other, 4.6% Hispanic of any race (2010); Density: 3,735.0 persons per square mile (2010); Average household size: 2.27 (2010); Median age: 42.6 (2010); Males per 100 females: 86.9 (2010); Marriage status: 24.7% never married, 41.3% now married, 18.4% widowed, 15.6% divorced (2005-2009 5-year est.); Foreign born: 5.4% (2005-2009 5-year est.); Ancestry (includes multiple ancestries): 24.5% Irish, 23.4% German, 20.6% Polish, 15.1% Italian, 4.0% Swedish (2005-2009 5-year est.).
Economy: Single-family building permits issued: 0 (2010); Multi-family building permits issued: 0 (2010); Employment by occupation: 10.4% management, 15.1% professional, 13.7% services, 31.6% sales, 0.0% farming, 13.2% construction, 16.0% production (2005-2009 5-year est.).
Income: Per capita income: $28,046 (2010); Median household income: $57,624 (2010); Average household income: $66,373 (2010); Percent of households with income of $100,000 or more: 17.6% (2010); Poverty rate: 4.6% (2005-2009 5-year est.).
Taxes: Total city taxes per capita: $159 (2007); City property taxes per capita: $116 (2007).
Education: Percent of population age 25 and over with: High school diploma (including GED) or higher: 89.5% (2010); Bachelor's degree or higher: 18.7% (2010); Master's degree or higher: 5.3% (2010).

School District(s)

Cook County SD 130 (PK-08)
   2009-10 Enrollment: 3,937 . . . . (708) 385-6800
Eisenhower Cooperative (PK-08)
   2009-10 Enrollment: n/a . . . . (708) 389-7580
Housing: Homeownership rate: 85.7% (2010); Median home value: $176,128 (2010); Median contract rent: $750 per month (2005-2009 5-year est.); Median year structure built: 1976 (2005-2009 5-year est.).
Safety: Violent crime rate: 13.8 per 10,000 population; Property crime rate: 440.8 per 10,000 population (2010).
Transportation: Commute to work: 86.9% car, 7.8% public transportation, 1.3% walk, 2.2% work from home (2005-2009 5-year est.); Travel time to work: 23.9% less than 15 minutes, 29.1% 15 to 30 minutes, 18.9% 30 to 45 minutes, 11.2% 45 to 60 minutes, 16.9% 60 minutes or more (2005-2009 5-year est.).

Additional Information Contacts

Village of Crestwood . . . . (708) 371-4800
   http://www.villageofcrestwood.com

DES PLAINES (city). Covers a land area of 14.423 square miles and a water area of 0.111 square miles. Located at 42.03° N. Lat; 87.90° W. Long. Elevation is 633 feet.

History: Named for the French translation of "the maples," which are abundant along the nearby river. When Des Plaines was founded in the

1830's it was known as Rand, for its first settler, Socrates Rand. The name was changed in 1869 to that of the river which transverses the town.
Population: 54,783 (1990); 58,720 (2000); 59,116 (2010); 59,197 (2015 projected); Race: 78.6% White, 1.5% Black, 9.8% Asian, 10.1% Other, 20.4% Hispanic of any race (2010); Density: 4,098.6 persons per square mile (2010); Average household size: 2.58 (2010); Median age: 41.7 (2010); Males per 100 females: 95.2 (2010); Marriage status: 25.9% never married, 54.7% now married, 9.5% widowed, 9.9% divorced (2005-2009 5-year est.); Foreign born: 27.4% (2005-2009 5-year est.); Ancestry (includes multiple ancestries): 20.3% German, 17.4% Polish, 13.3% Irish, 10.2% Italian, 3.9% English (2005-2009 5-year est.).
Economy: Unemployment rate: 9.4% (August 2011); Total civilian labor force: 29,981 (August 2011); Single-family building permits issued: 37 (2010); Multi-family building permits issued: 0 (2010); Employment by occupation: 15.3% management, 19.2% professional, 15.7% services, 29.0% sales, 0.0% farming, 8.4% construction, 12.4% production (2005-2009 5-year est.).
Income: Per capita income: $28,695 (2010); Median household income: $63,250 (2010); Average household income: $74,582 (2010); Percent of households with income of $100,000 or more: 22.8% (2010); Poverty rate: 6.6% (2005-2009 5-year est.).
Taxes: Total city taxes per capita: $815 (2007); City property taxes per capita: $487 (2007).
Education: Percent of population age 25 and over with: High school diploma (including GED) or higher: 86.4% (2010); Bachelor's degree or higher: 28.4% (2010); Master's degree or higher: 9.7% (2010).

School District(s)

CCSD 62 (PK-08)
    2009-10 Enrollment: 4,759 . . . . (847) 824-1136
Comm Cons SD 59 (PK-08)
    2009-10 Enrollment: 6,255 . . . . (847) 593-4300
East Maine SD 63 (PK-08)
    2009-10 Enrollment: 3,569 . . . . (847) 299-1900
Intermediate Service Center 1 (07-12)
    2009-10 Enrollment: n/a . . . . (847) 824-8300
Maine Township HSD 207 (06-12)
    2009-10 Enrollment: 6,972 . . . . (847) 696-3600

Two-year College(s)

Oakton Community College (Public)
    Fall 2009 Enrollment: 12,087. . . . . (847) 635-1600
    2010-11 Tuition: In-state $8,163; Out-of-state $9,850
Housing: Homeownership rate: 80.5% (2010); Median home value: $250,068 (2010); Median contract rent: $861 per month (2005-2009 5-year est.); Median year structure built: 1965 (2005-2009 5-year est.).
Hospitals: Holy Family Medical Center (184 beds)
Safety: Violent crime rate: 10.1 per 10,000 population; Property crime rate: 129.7 per 10,000 population (2010).
Newspapers: Arlington Heights Journal & Topics (Local news; Circulation 3,923); Buffalo Grove Journal & Topics (Local news; Circulation 3,217); Des Plaines Journal (Local news; Circulation 12,396); Elk Grove Journal (Local news; Circulation 4,689); Golf Mill Park Ridge Journal (Local news; Circulation 43,724); Mount Prospect Family Journal (Local news; Circulation 5,000); Mount Prospect Journal (Local news; Circulation 6,400); Niles Journal (Local news; Circulation 5,759); Northwest Journal (Local news; Circulation 5,637); Palatine Journal & Topics (Local news; Circulation 3,016); Prospect Heights Journal (Local news; Circulation 1,700); Rolling Meadows Journal & Topics (Local news; Circulation 3,171); Rosemont Journal (Local news; Circulation 604); Suburban Journal (Community news; Circulation 5,721); Wheeling Journal & Topics (Local news; Circulation 3,418)
Transportation: Commute to work: 88.5% car, 6.1% public transportation, 1.4% walk, 3.0% work from home (2005-2009 5-year est.); Travel time to work: 21.0% less than 15 minutes, 36.1% 15 to 30 minutes, 25.4% 30 to 45 minutes, 9.4% 45 to 60 minutes, 8.2% 60 minutes or more (2005-2009 5-year est.)
Additional Information Contacts
City of Des Plaines. . . . . (847) 391-5300
    http://www.desplaines.org
Des Plaines Chamber of Commerce & Industry . . . . (847) 824-4200
    http://www.dpchamber.com

DIXMOOR (village). Covers a land area of 1.243 square miles and a water area of 0 square miles. Located at 41.63° N. Lat; 87.66° W. Long. Elevation is 600 feet.
History: Incorporated 1922.

Population: 3,647 (1990); 3,934 (2000); 3,939 (2010); 3,827 (2015 projected); Race: 35.1% White, 45.4% Black, 0.3% Asian, 19.3% Other, 31.3% Hispanic of any race (2010); Density: 3,168.7 persons per square mile (2010); Average household size: 2.84 (2010); Median age: 32.8 (2010); Males per 100 females: 93.5 (2010); Marriage status: 49.2% never married, 30.0% now married, 9.9% widowed, 10.9% divorced (2005-2009 5-year est.); Foreign born: 9.9% (2005-2009 5-year est.); Ancestry (includes multiple ancestries): 8.1% German, 6.5% Polish, 3.3% Irish, 2.7% French, 2.6% Italian (2005-2009 5-year est.).
Economy: Single-family building permits issued: 0 (2010); Multi-family building permits issued: 0 (2010); Employment by occupation: 9.0% management, 10.0% professional, 32.3% services, 18.8% sales, 0.0% farming, 16.6% construction, 13.2% production (2005-2009 5-year est.).
Income: Per capita income: $13,205 (2010); Median household income: $30,442 (2010); Average household income: $37,855 (2010); Percent of households with income of $100,000 or more: 5.6% (2010); Poverty rate: 36.7% (2005-2009 5-year est.).
Taxes: Total city taxes per capita: $129 (2007); City property taxes per capita: $86 (2007).
Education: Percent of population age 25 and over with: High school diploma (including GED) or higher: 72.0% (2010); Bachelor's degree or higher: 9.2% (2010); Master's degree or higher: 2.2% (2010).

School District(s)

W Harvey-Dixmoor Psd 147 (PK-08)
    2009-10 Enrollment: 1,508 . . . . (708) 339-9500
Housing: Homeownership rate: 78.1% (2010); Median home value: $45,854 (2010); Median contract rent: $565 per month (2005-2009 5-year est.); Median year structure built: 1979 (2005-2009 5-year est.).
Transportation: Commute to work: 89.8% car, 5.4% public transportation, 2.9% walk, 0.9% work from home (2005-2009 5-year est.); Travel time to work: 17.5% less than 15 minutes, 38.4% 15 to 30 minutes, 23.5% 30 to 45 minutes, 9.5% 45 to 60 minutes, 11.1% 60 minutes or more (2005-2009 5-year est.)

DOLTON (village). Covers a land area of 4.551 square miles and a water area of 0.116 square miles. Located at 41.62° N. Lat; 87.59° W. Long. Elevation is 604 feet.
History: Named for Andrew H. Dolton, town founder. Settled 1832. Incorporated 1892.
Population: 24,035 (1990); 25,614 (2000); 23,861 (2010); 23,036 (2015 projected); Race: 13.1% White, 83.4% Black, 0.5% Asian, 2.9% Other, 3.3% Hispanic of any race (2010); Density: 5,242.5 persons per square mile (2010); Average household size: 3.02 (2010); Median age: 34.2 (2010); Males per 100 females: 89.2 (2010); Marriage status: 42.7% never married, 39.0% now married, 5.7% widowed, 12.6% divorced (2005-2009 5-year est.); Foreign born: 2.3% (2005-2009 5-year est.); Ancestry (includes multiple ancestries): 2.1% American, 2.0% German, 1.6% Polish, 1.4% African, 0.9% Irish (2005-2009 5-year est.).
Economy: Unemployment rate: 15.6% (August 2011); Total civilian labor force: 12,453 (August 2011); Single-family building permits issued: 3 (2010); Multi-family building permits issued: 0 (2010); Employment by occupation: 10.4% management, 16.7% professional, 18.1% services, 32.7% sales, 0.0% farming, 6.4% construction, 15.7% production (2005-2009 5-year est.).
Income: Per capita income: $20,171 (2010); Median household income: $53,190 (2010); Average household income: $61,149 (2010); Percent of households with income of $100,000 or more: 13.7% (2010); Poverty rate: 16.1% (2005-2009 5-year est.).
Taxes: Total city taxes per capita: $452 (2007); City property taxes per capita: $263 (2007).
Education: Percent of population age 25 and over with: High school diploma (including GED) or higher: 87.4% (2010); Bachelor's degree or higher: 18.5% (2010); Master's degree or higher: 4.4% (2010).

School District(s)

Dolton SD 148 (PK-08)
    2009-10 Enrollment: 2,635 . . . . (708) 841-2290
Dolton SD 149 (PK-08)
    2009-10 Enrollment: 3,397 . . . . (708) 868-7861
Exc Children Have Opportunities (PK-12)
    2009-10 Enrollment: n/a . . . . (708) 333-7880
Thornton Twp HSD 205 (09-12)
    2009-10 Enrollment: 6,179 . . . . (708) 225-4000
Housing: Homeownership rate: 83.3% (2010); Median home value: $129,370 (2010); Median contract rent: $794 per month (2005-2009 5-year est.); Median year structure built: 1964 (2005-2009 5-year est.).

Transportation: Commute to work: 85.5% car, 11.6% public transportation, 0.3% walk, 2.1% work from home (2005-2009 5-year est.); Travel time to work: 9.8% less than 15 minutes, 23.2% 15 to 30 minutes, 30.6% 30 to 45 minutes, 15.9% 45 to 60 minutes, 20.6% 60 minutes or more (2005-2009 5-year est.)
Additional Information Contacts
Village of Dolton. . . . . (708) 849-4000
   http://vodolton.org

EAST HAZEL CREST (village). Covers a land area of 0.767 square miles and a water area of 0 square miles. Located at 41.57° N. Lat; 87.65° W. Long. Elevation is 620 feet.
Population: 1,570 (1990); 1,607 (2000); 1,496 (2010); 1,450 (2015 projected); Race: 55.7% White, 37.4% Black, 0.7% Asian, 6.1% Other, 7.6% Hispanic of any race (2010); Density: 1,949.9 persons per square mile (2010); Average household size: 2.54 (2010); Median age: 38.1 (2010); Males per 100 females: 91.3 (2010); Marriage status: 33.1% never married, 49.1% now married, 7.0% widowed, 10.7% divorced (2005-2009 5-year est.); Foreign born: 7.6% (2005-2009 5-year est.); Ancestry (includes multiple ancestries): 15.4% German, 13.5% Irish, 9.6% Polish, 2.9% Italian, 2.8% French (2005-2009 5-year est.).
Economy: Single-family building permits issued: 0 (2010); Multi-family building permits issued: 0 (2010); Employment by occupation: 9.3% management, 15.8% professional, 16.1% services, 28.0% sales, 0.3% farming, 13.4% construction, 17.1% production (2005-2009 5-year est.).
Income: Per capita income: $22,820 (2010); Median household income: $50,169 (2010); Average household income: $58,060 (2010); Percent of households with income of $100,000 or more: 9.9% (2010); Poverty rate: 4.4% (2005-2009 5-year est.).
Taxes: Total city taxes per capita: $712 (2007); City property taxes per capita: $338 (2007).
Education: Percent of population age 25 and over with: High school diploma (including GED) or higher: 88.8% (2010); Bachelor's degree or higher: 16.4% (2010); Master's degree or higher: 4.8% (2010).
Housing: Homeownership rate: 71.2% (2010); Median home value: $140,782 (2010); Median contract rent: $819 per month (2005-2009 5-year est.); Median year structure built: 1963 (2005-2009 5-year est.).
Safety: Violent crime rate: 6.7 per 10,000 population; Property crime rate: 519.0 per 10,000 population (2010).
Transportation: Commute to work: 88.1% car, 10.5% public transportation, 0.3% walk, 0.4% work from home (2005-2009 5-year est.); Travel time to work: 24.4% less than 15 minutes, 21.4% 15 to 30 minutes, 24.4% 30 to 45 minutes, 9.5% 45 to 60 minutes, 20.3% 60 minutes or more (2005-2009 5-year est.)

ELK GROVE VILLAGE (village). Aka Elk Grove. Covers a land area of 11.039 square miles and a water area of 0.061 square miles. Located at 42.00° N. Lat; 87.99° W. Long. Elevation is 686 feet.
Population: 33,624 (1990); 34,727 (2000); 32,506 (2010); 31,456 (2015 projected); Race: 82.9% White, 1.6% Black, 9.9% Asian, 5.6% Other, 8.7% Hispanic of any race (2010); Density: 2,944.6 persons per square mile (2010); Average household size: 2.55 (2010); Median age: 40.8 (2010); Males per 100 females: 95.5 (2010); Marriage status: 27.8% never married, 59.1% now married, 5.5% widowed, 7.6% divorced (2005-2009 5-year est.); Foreign born: 19.1% (2005-2009 5-year est.); Ancestry (includes multiple ancestries): 22.7% German, 19.5% Polish, 18.2% Irish, 13.8% Italian, 6.2% English (2005-2009 5-year est.).
Economy: Unemployment rate: 8.2% (August 2011); Total civilian labor force: 19,795 (August 2011); Single-family building permits issued: 1 (2010); Multi-family building permits issued: 0 (2010); Employment by occupation: 17.9% management, 19.3% professional, 13.0% services, 33.4% sales, 0.0% farming, 6.9% construction, 9.5% production (2005-2009 5-year est.).
Income: Per capita income: $34,166 (2010); Median household income: $72,357 (2010); Average household income: $86,828 (2010); Percent of households with income of $100,000 or more: 29.8% (2010); Poverty rate: 3.6% (2005-2009 5-year est.).
Taxes: Total city taxes per capita: $990 (2007); City property taxes per capita: $474 (2007).
Education: Percent of population age 25 and over with: High school diploma (including GED) or higher: 93.1% (2010); Bachelor's degree or higher: 35.5% (2010); Master's degree or higher: 10.4% (2010).
School District(s)
Comm Cons SD 59 (PK-08)
   2009-10 Enrollment: 6,255 . . . . (847) 593-4300

Schaumburg CCSD 54 (PK-08)
   2009-10 Enrollment: 14,313 . . . . (847) 357-5000
Township HSD 214 (09-12)
   2009-10 Enrollment: 12,241 . . . . (847) 718-7600
Housing: Homeownership rate: 78.7% (2010); Median home value: $257,083 (2010); Median contract rent: $887 per month (2005-2009 5-year est.); Median year structure built: 1974 (2005-2009 5-year est.).
Hospitals: Alexian Brothers Medical Center (473 beds)
Safety: Violent crime rate: 11.6 per 10,000 population; Property crime rate: 230.5 per 10,000 population (2010).
Transportation: Commute to work: 93.1% car, 2.7% public transportation, 0.7% walk, 2.6% work from home (2005-2009 5-year est.); Travel time to work: 27.6% less than 15 minutes, 36.8% 15 to 30 minutes, 20.5% 30 to 45 minutes, 7.1% 45 to 60 minutes, 8.0% 60 minutes or more (2005-2009 5-year est.)
Additional Information Contacts
Village of Elk Grove Village . . . . (847) 357-4040
   http://elkgrove.com

ELMWOOD PARK (village). Covers a land area of 1.906 square miles and a water area of 0 square miles. Located at 41.92° N. Lat; 87.81° W. Long. Elevation is 643 feet.
Population: 23,206 (1990); 25,405 (2000); 23,983 (2010); 23,381 (2015 projected); Race: 87.4% White, 0.7% Black, 2.8% Asian, 9.1% Other, 17.0% Hispanic of any race (2010); Density: 12,582.4 persons per square mile (2010); Average household size: 2.60 (2010); Median age: 41.2 (2010); Males per 100 females: 92.6 (2010); Marriage status: 34.5% never married, 47.2% now married, 9.1% widowed, 9.2% divorced (2005-2009 5-year est.); Foreign born: 27.6% (2005-2009 5-year est.); Ancestry (includes multiple ancestries): 23.8% Polish, 23.7% Italian, 13.6% German, 12.8% Irish, 3.2% English (2005-2009 5-year est.).
Economy: Unemployment rate: 10.5% (August 2011); Total civilian labor force: 13,137 (August 2011); Single-family building permits issued: 1 (2010); Multi-family building permits issued: 0 (2010); Employment by occupation: 10.9% management, 16.5% professional, 18.0% services, 29.4% sales, 0.0% farming, 10.5% construction, 14.7% production (2005-2009 5-year est.).
Income: Per capita income: $26,586 (2010); Median household income: $57,068 (2010); Average household income: $69,527 (2010); Percent of households with income of $100,000 or more: 20.3% (2010); Poverty rate: 8.8% (2005-2009 5-year est.).
Taxes: Total city taxes per capita: $629 (2007); City property taxes per capita: $418 (2007).
Education: Percent of population age 25 and over with: High school diploma (including GED) or higher: 84.7% (2010); Bachelor's degree or higher: 22.9% (2010); Master's degree or higher: 7.7% (2010).
School District(s)
Elmwood Park CUSD 401 (PK-12)
   2009-10 Enrollment: 2,946 . . . . (708) 583-5831
Housing: Homeownership rate: 68.7% (2010); Median home value: $258,341 (2010); Median contract rent: $783 per month (2005-2009 5-year est.); Median year structure built: 1954 (2005-2009 5-year est.).
Safety: Violent crime rate: 12.3 per 10,000 population; Property crime rate: 159.8 per 10,000 population (2010).
Transportation: Commute to work: 83.2% car, 11.5% public transportation, 2.1% walk, 2.3% work from home (2005-2009 5-year est.); Travel time to work: 21.2% less than 15 minutes, 24.4% 15 to 30 minutes, 31.3% 30 to 45 minutes, 13.2% 45 to 60 minutes, 9.9% 60 minutes or more (2005-2009 5-year est.)
Additional Information Contacts
Mont Clare-Elmwood Park Chamber of Commerce. . . . . . . (708) 456-8000
   http://www.mcepchamber.org
Village of Elmwood Park . . . . (708) 452-7300
   http://www.elmwoodpark.org

EVANSTON (city). Covers a land area of 7.746 square miles and a water area of 0.023 square miles. Located at 42.04° N. Lat; 87.69° W. Long. Elevation is 614 feet.
History: Named for John Evans, founder of Northwestern University. Settlement at Evanston began around the harbor formed by the Grosse Pointe bluffs. The town was platted in 1854, and in 1855 Northwestern University was founded by the Methodist Episcopal Church. One of the first professors here was Frances E. Willard, who later founded the Women's Christian Temperance Union. In 1892 Evanston annexed the community of

South Evanston and was incorporated as a city. The city was named for John Evans, one of the university founders.

Population: 73,233 (1990); 74,239 (2000); 79,418 (2010); 81,431 (2015 projected); Race: 65.0% White, 19.1% Black, 7.6% Asian, 8.3% Other, 8.8% Hispanic of any race (2010); Density: 10,252.7 persons per square mile (2010); Average household size: 2.26 (2010); Median age: 35.2 (2010); Males per 100 females: 90.8 (2010); Marriage status: 40.0% never married, 45.8% now married, 6.0% widowed, 8.2% divorced (2005-2009 5-year est.); Foreign born: 15.0% (2005-2009 5-year est.); Ancestry (includes multiple ancestries): 17.5% German, 13.2% Irish, 9.0% English, 6.7% Polish, 5.5% Italian (2005-2009 5-year est.).

Economy: Unemployment rate: 8.0% (August 2011); Total civilian labor force: 42,728 (August 2011); Single-family building permits issued: 10 (2010); Multi-family building permits issued: 146 (2010); Employment by occupation: 20.5% management, 41.4% professional, 10.0% services, 20.3% sales, 0.0% farming, 2.9% construction, 4.8% production (2005-2009 5-year est.).

Income: Per capita income: $38,730 (2010); Median household income: $66,038 (2010); Average household income: $96,174 (2010); Percent of households with income of $100,000 or more: 32.3% (2010); Poverty rate: 9.7% (2005-2009 5-year est.).

Taxes: Total city taxes per capita: $991 (2007); City property taxes per capita: $545 (2007).

Education: Percent of population age 25 and over with: High school diploma (including GED) or higher: 93.9% (2010); Bachelor's degree or higher: 66.4% (2010); Master's degree or higher: 36.1% (2010).

School District(s)

Evanston CCSD 65 (PK-08)
    2009-10 Enrollment: 6,812 . . . . (847) 859-8010
Evanston Dists 65/202 Jnt Agr (PK-12)
    2009-10 Enrollment: n/a . . . . (847) 492-5986
Evanston Twp HSD 202 (09-12)
    2009-10 Enrollment: 3,054 . . . . (847) 424-7220

Four-year College(s)

Garrett-Evangelical Theological Seminary (Private, Not-for-profit, United Methodist)
    Fall 2009 Enrollment: 335 . . . . (847) 866-3900
NorthShore University HealthSystems School of Nurse Anesthesia (Private, Not-for-profit)
    Fall 2009 Enrollment: 63 . . . . (847) 570-1959
Northwestern University (Private, Not-for-profit)
    Fall 2009 Enrollment: 19,853. . . . . (847) 491-3741
    2010-11 Tuition: In-state $40,223; Out-of-state $40,223
Seabury-Western Theological Seminary (Private, Not-for-profit, Protestant Episcopal)
    Fall 2009 Enrollment: 51 . . . . (847) 328-9300

Vocational/Technical School(s)

Pivot Point Beauty School (Private, For-profit)
    Fall 2009 Enrollment: 142 . . . . (800) 886-0500
    2010-11 Tuition: $18,256

Housing: Homeownership rate: 55.7% (2010); Median home value: $334,802 (2010); Median contract rent: $972 per month (2005-2009 5-year est.); Median year structure built: 1943 (2005-2009 5-year est.).

Hospitals: Evanston Hospital (635 beds); St. Francis Hospital (445 beds)

Safety: Violent crime rate: 27.5 per 10,000 population; Property crime rate: 271.4 per 10,000 population (2010).

Newspapers: National News Reporter (Local news); Tribune Media Services - Evanston Bureau (Local news)

Transportation: Commute to work: 58.4% car, 19.5% public transportation, 11.2% walk, 7.0% work from home (2005-2009 5-year est.); Travel time to work: 26.9% less than 15 minutes, 24.5% 15 to 30 minutes, 21.2% 30 to 45 minutes, 15.5% 45 to 60 minutes, 11.9% 60 minutes or more (2005-2009 5-year est.)

Additional Information Contacts

City of Evanston. . . . . (847) 448-4311
    http://www.cityofevanston.org

EVERGREEN PARK (village). Covers a land area of 3.174 square miles and a water area of 0 square miles. Located at 41.72° N. Lat; 87.70° W. Long. Elevation is 623 feet.

History: Named for the evergreen trees in the area. Incorporated 1893. St. Xavier College nearby.

Population: 20,874 (1990); 20,821 (2000); 18,530 (2010); 17,552 (2015 projected); Race: 82.7% White, 12.1% Black, 1.4% Asian, 3.8% Other, 5.8% Hispanic of any race (2010); Density: 5,838.2 persons per square

mile (2010); Average household size: 2.76 (2010); Median age: 38.1 (2010); Males per 100 females: 92.5 (2010); Marriage status: 32.6% never married, 47.3% now married, 10.5% widowed, 9.6% divorced (2005-2009 5-year est.); Foreign born: 6.3% (2005-2009 5-year est.); Ancestry (includes multiple ancestries): 32.6% Irish, 21.0% German, 10.5% Polish, 10.3% Italian, 4.7% English (2005-2009 5-year est.).

Economy: Single-family building permits issued: 3 (2010); Multi-family building permits issued: 0 (2010); Employment by occupation: 15.7% management, 23.7% professional, 11.9% services, 29.7% sales, 0.0% farming, 9.1% construction, 9.8% production (2005-2009 5-year est.).

Income: Per capita income: $27,410 (2010); Median household income: $64,804 (2010); Average household income: $77,181 (2010); Percent of households with income of $100,000 or more: 25.3% (2010); Poverty rate: 6.4% (2005-2009 5-year est.).

Taxes: Total city taxes per capita: $570 (2007); City property taxes per capita: $334 (2007).

Education: Percent of population age 25 and over with: High school diploma (including GED) or higher: 91.5% (2010); Bachelor's degree or higher: 31.8% (2010); Master's degree or higher: 10.1% (2010).

School District(s)

Evergreen Park CHSD 231 (09-12)
    2009-10 Enrollment: 925 . . . . (708) 424-7400
Evergreen Park ESD 124 (PK-08)
    2009-10 Enrollment: 1,883 . . . . (708) 423-0950

Housing: Homeownership rate: 87.5% (2010); Median home value: $191,411 (2010); Median contract rent: $730 per month (2005-2009 5-year est.); Median year structure built: 1954 (2005-2009 5-year est.).

Hospitals: Little Company of Mary Hospital & Health Care Centers (487 beds)

Safety: Violent crime rate: 17.5 per 10,000 population; Property crime rate: 364.8 per 10,000 population (2010).

Transportation: Commute to work: 84.0% car, 8.7% public transportation, 2.5% walk, 4.2% work from home (2005-2009 5-year est.); Travel time to work: 24.5% less than 15 minutes, 22.1% 15 to 30 minutes, 21.9% 30 to 45 minutes, 12.4% 45 to 60 minutes, 19.1% 60 minutes or more (2005-2009 5-year est.)

Additional Information Contacts

Evergreen Park Chamber of Commerce . . . . (708) 423-1118
    http://www.evergreenparkchamber.org
Village of Evergreen Park . . . . (708) 422-1551
    http://www.evergreenpark-ill.com

FLOSSMOOR (village). Covers a land area of 3.553 square miles and a water area of 0 square miles. Located at 41.54° N. Lat; 87.68° W. Long. Elevation is 676 feet.

History: Incorporated 1924.

Population: 8,759 (1990); 9,301 (2000); 9,117 (2010); 9,012 (2015 projected); Race: 59.3% White, 34.5% Black, 3.1% Asian, 3.2% Other, 3.4% Hispanic of any race (2010); Density: 2,565.8 persons per square mile (2010); Average household size: 2.74 (2010); Median age: 43.4 (2010); Males per 100 females: 92.6 (2010); Marriage status: 22.5% never married, 61.3% now married, 7.0% widowed, 9.2% divorced (2005-2009 5-year est.); Foreign born: 6.1% (2005-2009 5-year est.); Ancestry (includes multiple ancestries): 12.2% Irish, 11.9% German, 10.3% Polish, 7.3% English, 6.8% Italian (2005-2009 5-year est.).

Economy: Single-family building permits issued: 0 (2010); Multi-family building permits issued: 0 (2010); Employment by occupation: 21.7% management, 35.5% professional, 9.8% services, 23.1% sales, 0.0% farming, 2.9% construction, 7.0% production (2005-2009 5-year est.).

Income: Per capita income: $43,152 (2010); Median household income: $93,972 (2010); Average household income: $118,330 (2010); Percent of households with income of $100,000 or more: 46.3% (2010); Poverty rate: 1.3% (2005-2009 5-year est.).

Taxes: Total city taxes per capita: $708 (2007); City property taxes per capita: $528 (2007).

Education: Percent of population age 25 and over with: High school diploma (including GED) or higher: 97.7% (2010); Bachelor's degree or higher: 61.8% (2010); Master's degree or higher: 31.1% (2010).

School District(s)

Flossmoor SD 161 (PK-08)
    2009-10 Enrollment: 2,334 . . . . (708) 647-7000
Homewood Flossmoor CHSD 233 (09-12)
    2009-10 Enrollment: 2,893 . . . . (708) 799-3000

Housing: Homeownership rate: 95.6% (2010); Median home value: $264,996 (2010); Median contract rent: $1,069 per month (2005-2009 5-year est.); Median year structure built: 1966 (2005-2009 5-year est.).
Safety: Violent crime rate: 7.6 per 10,000 population; Property crime rate: 193.4 per 10,000 population (2010).
Transportation: Commute to work: 81.7% car, 11.5% public transportation, 0.0% walk, 5.4% work from home (2005-2009 5-year est.); Travel time to work: 22.3% less than 15 minutes, 24.5% 15 to 30 minutes, 15.9% 30 to 45 minutes, 11.3% 45 to 60 minutes, 25.9% 60 minutes or more (2005-2009 5-year est.)
Additional Information Contacts
Village of Flossmoor . . . . (708) 798-2300
   http://www.flossmoor.org

FORD HEIGHTS (village). Aka East Chicago Heights. Covers a land area of 1.768 square miles and a water area of 0 square miles. Located at 41.50° N. Lat; 87.58° W. Long. Elevation is 663 feet.

Population: 4,271 (1990); 3,456 (2000); 3,135 (2010); 2,973 (2015 projected); Race: 6.2% White, 87.5% Black, 0.2% Asian, 6.0% Other, 6.4% Hispanic of any race (2010); Density: 1,773.3 persons per square mile (2010); Average household size: 3.52 (2010); Median age: 22.2 (2010); Males per 100 females: 88.4 (2010); Marriage status: 62.5% never married, 19.0% now married, 6.7% widowed, 11.9% divorced (2005-2009 5-year est.); Foreign born: 0.4% (2005-2009 5-year est.); Ancestry (includes multiple ancestries): 0.7% English, 0.7% American, 0.5% African, 0.3% Polish, 0.3% Slovak (2005-2009 5-year est.).
Economy: Single-family building permits issued: 0 (2010); Multi-family building permits issued: 0 (2010); Employment by occupation: 3.1% management, 24.3% professional, 29.8% services, 12.5% sales, 0.0% farming, 1.3% construction, 29.0% production (2005-2009 5-year est.).
Income: Per capita income: $9,140 (2010); Median household income: $20,394 (2010); Average household income: $32,357 (2010); Percent of households with income of $100,000 or more: 3.9% (2010); Poverty rate: 47.7% (2005-2009 5-year est.).
Taxes: Total city taxes per capita: $490 (2007); City property taxes per capita: $173 (2007).
Education: Percent of population age 25 and over with: High school diploma (including GED) or higher: 75.8% (2010); Bachelor's degree or higher: 5.8% (2010); Master's degree or higher: 1.5% (2010).

School District(s)
Ford Heights SD 169 (PK-08)
   2009-10 Enrollment: 575 . . . . (708) 758-1370
Housing: Homeownership rate: 37.5% (2010); Median home value: $63,871 (2010); Median contract rent: $492 per month (2005-2009 5-year est.); Median year structure built: 1964 (2005-2009 5-year est.).
Transportation: Commute to work: 86.6% car, 5.1% public transportation, 0.9% walk, 6.0% work from home (2005-2009 5-year est.); Travel time to work: 15.9% less than 15 minutes, 47.3% 15 to 30 minutes, 16.1% 30 to 45 minutes, 5.6% 45 to 60 minutes, 15.1% 60 minutes or more (2005-2009 5-year est.)

FOREST PARK (village). Covers a land area of 2.421 square miles and a water area of 0 square miles. Located at 41.87° N. Lat; 87.81° W. Long. Elevation is 623 feet.

Population: 14,918 (1990); 15,688 (2000); 15,116 (2010); 14,862 (2015 projected); Race: 46.9% White, 39.5% Black, 5.7% Asian, 7.9% Other, 10.8% Hispanic of any race (2010); Density: 6,244.5 persons per square mile (2010); Average household size: 2.08 (2010); Median age: 39.5 (2010); Males per 100 females: 92.7 (2010); Marriage status: 40.5% never married, 40.9% now married, 5.8% widowed, 12.9% divorced (2005-2009 5-year est.); Foreign born: 12.4% (2005-2009 5-year est.); Ancestry (includes multiple ancestries): 13.6% German, 12.8% Irish, 8.0% Italian, 5.1% Polish, 2.9% English (2005-2009 5-year est.).
Economy: Single-family building permits issued: 0 (2010); Multi-family building permits issued: 0 (2010); Employment by occupation: 15.6% management, 25.0% professional, 14.6% services, 28.4% sales, 0.0% farming, 4.8% construction, 11.6% production (2005-2009 5-year est.).
Income: Per capita income: $31,956 (2010); Median household income: $54,966 (2010); Average household income: $67,041 (2010); Percent of households with income of $100,000 or more: 16.3% (2010); Poverty rate: 8.7% (2005-2009 5-year est.).
Taxes: Total city taxes per capita: $601 (2007); City property taxes per capita: $425 (2007).

Education: Percent of population age 25 and over with: High school diploma (including GED) or higher: 91.7% (2010); Bachelor's degree or higher: 41.0% (2010); Master's degree or higher: 17.0% (2010).

School District(s)
Forest Park SD 91 (PK-08)
   2009-10 Enrollment: 931 . . . . (708) 366-5700
Proviso Twp HSD 209 (09-12)
   2009-10 Enrollment: 5,198 . . . . (708) 338-5912
Housing: Homeownership rate: 49.3% (2010); Median home value: $204,176 (2010); Median contract rent: $804 per month (2005-2009 5-year est.); Median year structure built: 1954 (2005-2009 5-year est.).
Hospitals: Riveredge Hospital (210 beds)
Safety: Violent crime rate: 22.8 per 10,000 population; Property crime rate: 477.7 per 10,000 population (2010).
Transportation: Commute to work: 73.6% car, 17.0% public transportation, 4.4% walk, 3.4% work from home (2005-2009 5-year est.); Travel time to work: 19.1% less than 15 minutes, 30.2% 15 to 30 minutes, 27.6% 30 to 45 minutes, 11.7% 45 to 60 minutes, 11.4% 60 minutes or more (2005-2009 5-year est.)
Additional Information Contacts
Forest Park Chamber of Commerce . . . . (708) 366-2543
   http://www.exploreforestpark.com
Village of Forest Park. . . . . (708) 366-2323
   http://www.forestpark.net

FOREST VIEW (village). Covers a land area of 1.037 square miles and a water area of 0.132 square miles. Located at 41.80° N. Lat; 87.78° W. Long. Elevation is 594 feet.

Population: 743 (1990); 778 (2000); 873 (2010); 897 (2015 projected); Race: 86.6% White, 0.5% Black, 0.1% Asian, 12.8% Other, 22.2% Hispanic of any race (2010); Density: 841.5 persons per square mile (2010); Average household size: 2.67 (2010); Median age: 43.2 (2010); Males per 100 females: 95.7 (2010); Marriage status: 29.1% never married, 56.1% now married, 13.1% widowed, 1.7% divorced (2005-2009 5-year est.); Foreign born: 11.7% (2005-2009 5-year est.); Ancestry (includes multiple ancestries): 27.1% Polish, 23.8% German, 19.0% Irish, 17.4% Czech, 10.0% Italian (2005-2009 5-year est.).
Economy: Single-family building permits issued: 0 (2010); Multi-family building permits issued: 0 (2010); Employment by occupation: 13.8% management, 12.8% professional, 20.2% services, 28.5% sales, 0.0% farming, 9.8% construction, 14.9% production (2005-2009 5-year est.).
Income: Per capita income: $23,315 (2010); Median household income: $53,646 (2010); Average household income: $61,911 (2010); Percent of households with income of $100,000 or more: 15.6% (2010); Poverty rate: 6.4% (2005-2009 5-year est.).
Taxes: Total city taxes per capita: $2,167 (2007); City property taxes per capita: $1,008 (2007).
Education: Percent of population age 25 and over with: High school diploma (including GED) or higher: 86.0% (2010); Bachelor's degree or higher: 10.9% (2010); Master's degree or higher: 4.1% (2010).
Housing: Homeownership rate: 92.7% (2010); Median home value: $226,000 (2010); Median contract rent: $625 per month (2005-2009 5-year est.); Median year structure built: 1954 (2005-2009 5-year est.).
Safety: Violent crime rate: 14.3 per 10,000 population; Property crime rate: 471.4 per 10,000 population (2010).
Transportation: Commute to work: 89.2% car, 5.6% public transportation, 0.8% walk, 3.0% work from home (2005-2009 5-year est.); Travel time to work: 24.1% less than 15 minutes, 32.4% 15 to 30 minutes, 25.2% 30 to 45 minutes, 8.0% 45 to 60 minutes, 10.2% 60 minutes or more (2005-2009 5-year est.)

FRANKLIN PARK (village). Covers a land area of 4.658 square miles and a water area of 0 square miles. Located at 41.93° N. Lat; 87.87° W. Long. Elevation is 643 feet.

Population: 18,473 (1990); 19,434 (2000); 18,340 (2010); 17,864 (2015 projected); Race: 73.9% White, 1.0% Black, 3.1% Asian, 22.0% Other, 51.3% Hispanic of any race (2010); Density: 3,937.3 persons per square mile (2010); Average household size: 3.03 (2010); Median age: 36.7 (2010); Males per 100 females: 101.1 (2010); Marriage status: 32.0% never married, 54.5% now married, 6.2% widowed, 7.3% divorced (2005-2009 5-year est.); Foreign born: 33.1% (2005-2009 5-year est.); Ancestry (includes multiple ancestries): 17.4% Polish, 13.2% Italian, 11.4% German, 9.5% Irish, 2.0% English (2005-2009 5-year est.).
Economy: Single-family building permits issued: 0 (2010); Multi-family building permits issued: 0 (2010); Employment by occupation: 6.8%

management, 10.9% professional, 15.7% services, 26.8% sales, 0.0% farming, 12.7% construction, 27.0% production (2005-2009 5-year est.).
Income: Per capita income: $20,590 (2010); Median household income: $55,062 (2010); Average household income: $62,775 (2010); Percent of households with income of $100,000 or more: 16.1% (2010); Poverty rate: 7.9% (2005-2009 5-year est.).
Taxes: Total city taxes per capita: $1,096 (2007); City property taxes per capita: $685 (2007).
Education: Percent of population age 25 and over with: High school diploma (including GED) or higher: 73.1% (2010); Bachelor's degree or higher: 13.8% (2010); Master's degree or higher: 3.9% (2010).

School District(s)
Franklin Park SD 84 (PK-08)
  2009-10 Enrollment: 1,316 . . . . (847) 455-4230
Leyden CHSD 212 (09-12)
  2009-10 Enrollment: 3,497 . . . . (847) 451-3000
Mannheim SD 83 (PK-09)
  2009-10 Enrollment: 2,705 . . . . (847) 455-4413
Housing: Homeownership rate: 75.2% (2010); Median home value: $219,954 (2010); Median contract rent: $693 per month (2005-2009 5-year est.); Median year structure built: 1956 (2005-2009 5-year est.).
Transportation: Commute to work: 90.2% car, 3.4% public transportation, 2.1% walk, 2.0% work from home (2005-2009 5-year est.); Travel time to work: 26.9% less than 15 minutes, 29.6% 15 to 30 minutes, 28.2% 30 to 45 minutes, 7.1% 45 to 60 minutes, 8.3% 60 minutes or more (2005-2009 5-year est.)
Additional Information Contacts
Franklin Park/Schiller Park Chamber of Commerce . . . . . . (708) 865-9510
  http://www.chamberbyohare.org
Village of Franklin Park . . . . (847) 671-4800
  http://www.villageoffranklinpark.com

GLENCOE (village).
Covers a land area of 3.777 square miles and a water area of 0.071 square miles. Located at 42.13° N. Lat; 87.76° W. Long. Elevation is 673 feet.
History: One of the founders of Glencoe was Walter S. Gurnee, and the "coe" part of the town's name came from his wife's maiden name. Glencoe was incorporated as a village in 1869.
Population: 8,499 (1990); 8,762 (2000); 8,603 (2010); 8,504 (2015 projected); Race: 96.3% White, 1.2% Black, 1.2% Asian, 1.3% Other, 1.2% Hispanic of any race (2010); Density: 2,277.7 persons per square mile (2010); Average household size: 2.92 (2010); Median age: 40.8 (2010); Males per 100 females: 95.6 (2010); Marriage status: 16.5% never married, 75.3% now married, 4.3% widowed, 3.9% divorced (2005-2009 5-year est.); Foreign born: 7.4% (2005-2009 5-year est.); Ancestry (includes multiple ancestries): 19.5% German, 15.9% Russian, 15.0% Irish, 10.1% English, 7.6% Polish (2005-2009 5-year est.).
Economy: Single-family building permits issued: 11 (2010); Multi-family building permits issued: 0 (2010); Employment by occupation: 30.0% management, 41.0% professional, 2.3% services, 23.8% sales, 0.4% farming, 1.6% construction, 0.9% production (2005-2009 5-year est.).
Income: Per capita income: $81,917 (2010); Median household income: $186,585 (2010); Average household income: $239,020 (2010); Percent of households with income of $100,000 or more: 70.6% (2010); Poverty rate: 4.8% (2005-2009 5-year est.).
Taxes: Total city taxes per capita: $1,592 (2007); City property taxes per capita: $1,214 (2007).
Education: Percent of population age 25 and over with: High school diploma (including GED) or higher: 98.4% (2010); Bachelor's degree or higher: 82.2% (2010); Master's degree or higher: 41.7% (2010).

School District(s)
Glencoe SD 35 (KG-08)
  2009-10 Enrollment: 1,344 . . . . (847) 835-7800
Housing: Homeownership rate: 93.8% (2010); Median home value: $866,232 (2010); Median contract rent: $1,228 per month (2005-2009 5-year est.); Median year structure built: 1955 (2005-2009 5-year est.).
Transportation: Commute to work: 57.2% car, 28.4% public transportation, 0.9% walk, 12.2% work from home (2005-2009 5-year est.); Travel time to work: 15.2% less than 15 minutes, 23.5% 15 to 30 minutes, 20.7% 30 to 45 minutes, 16.1% 45 to 60 minutes, 24.5% 60 minutes or more (2005-2009 5-year est.)
Additional Information Contacts
Glencoe Chamber of Commerce . . . . (847) 835-3333
Village of Glencoe . . . . (847) 835-4111
  http://www.villageofglencoe.org

GLENVIEW (village).
Covers a land area of 13.450 square miles and a water area of 0.041 square miles. Located at 42.07° N. Lat; 87.81° W. Long. Elevation is 653 feet.
History: Named to promote the town as a good place to live. Settled 1833. Incorporated 1899.
Population: 40,177 (1990); 41,847 (2000); 44,607 (2010); 44,466 (2015 projected); Race: 77.6% White, 5.4% Black, 12.2% Asian, 4.7% Other, 7.6% Hispanic of any race (2010); Density: 3,316.5 persons per square mile (2010); Average household size: 2.68 (2010); Median age: 39.8 (2010); Males per 100 females: 94.0 (2010); Marriage status: 21.5% never married, 64.9% now married, 7.9% widowed, 5.7% divorced (2005-2009 5-year est.); Foreign born: 21.3% (2005-2009 5-year est.); Ancestry (includes multiple ancestries): 19.1% German, 16.0% Irish, 12.4% Polish, 7.1% Italian, 7.1% English (2005-2009 5-year est.).
Economy: Unemployment rate: 7.3% (August 2011); Total civilian labor force: 23,953 (August 2011); Single-family building permits issued: 14 (2010); Multi-family building permits issued: 0 (2010); Employment by occupation: 24.5% management, 29.9% professional, 9.8% services, 27.3% sales, 0.0% farming, 4.0% construction, 4.5% production (2005-2009 5-year est.).
Income: Per capita income: $46,130 (2010); Median household income: $87,533 (2010); Average household income: $124,698 (2010); Percent of households with income of $100,000 or more: 43.1% (2010); Poverty rate: 3.8% (2005-2009 5-year est.).
Taxes: Total city taxes per capita: $1,066 (2007); City property taxes per capita: $786 (2007).
Education: Percent of population age 25 and over with: High school diploma (including GED) or higher: 95.6% (2010); Bachelor's degree or higher: 56.7% (2010); Master's degree or higher: 24.9% (2010).

School District(s)
Avoca SD 37 (PK-08)
  2009-10 Enrollment: 687 . . . . (847) 251-3587
East Maine SD 63 (PK-08)
  2009-10 Enrollment: 3,569 . . . . (847) 299-1900
Glenview CCSD 34 (PK-08)
  2009-10 Enrollment: 4,621 . . . . (847) 998-5005
Northbrook/Glenview SD 30 (PK-08)
  2009-10 Enrollment: 1,139 . . . . (847) 498-4190
Northern Suburban Spec Ed Dist (PK-12)
  2009-10 Enrollment: n/a . . . . (847) 831-5100
Northfield Twp HSD 225 (09-12)
  2009-10 Enrollment: 4,803 . . . . (847) 486-4700
West Northfield SD 31 (PK-08)
  2009-10 Enrollment: 861 . . . . (847) 272-6880
Housing: Homeownership rate: 79.6% (2010); Median home value: $448,127 (2010); Median contract rent: $1,273 per month (2005-2009 5-year est.); Median year structure built: 1972 (2005-2009 5-year est.).
Hospitals: Glenbrook Hospital (144 beds)
Newspapers: Lincolnwood Review (Community news; Circulation 1,475); Mount Prospect Times (Local news; Circulation 2,294); Northbrook Star (Community news; Circulation 7,807); Pioneer Press - North Shore Bureau (Community news); Pioneer Press Newspapers (Community news; Circulation 3,900); Skokie Review (Community news; Circulation 7,116); Wilmette Life (Community news; Circulation 7,309)
Transportation: Commute to work: 82.0% car, 10.3% public transportation, 1.2% walk, 5.8% work from home (2005-2009 5-year est.); Travel time to work: 22.3% less than 15 minutes, 30.6% 15 to 30 minutes, 26.8% 30 to 45 minutes, 10.6% 45 to 60 minutes, 9.6% 60 minutes or more (2005-2009 5-year est.); Amtrak: train service available.
Additional Information Contacts
Glenview Chamber of Commerce . . . . (847) 724-0900
  http://www.glenviewchamber.com
Village of Glenview . . . . (847) 904-4370
  http://www.glenview.il.us

GLENWOOD (village).
Covers a land area of 2.687 square miles and a water area of 0 square miles. Located at 41.54° N. Lat; 87.61° W. Long. Elevation is 620 feet.
Population: 9,402 (1990); 9,000 (2000); 8,317 (2010); 7,996 (2015 projected); Race: 44.4% White, 49.5% Black, 0.5% Asian, 5.5% Other, 7.4% Hispanic of any race (2010); Density: 3,095.8 persons per square mile (2010); Average household size: 2.69 (2010); Median age: 39.7 (2010); Males per 100 females: 89.2 (2010); Marriage status: 33.2% never married, 50.9% now married, 6.1% widowed, 9.7% divorced (2005-2009

5-year est.); Foreign born: 2.5% (2005-2009 5-year est.); Ancestry (includes multiple ancestries): 11.0% German, 7.1% Irish, 5.0% Italian, 4.7% Polish, 3.8% English (2005-2009 5-year est.).
Economy: Single-family building permits issued: 0 (2010); Multi-family building permits issued: 0 (2010); Employment by occupation: 12.2% management, 17.9% professional, 10.6% services, 32.3% sales, 0.3% farming, 8.1% construction, 18.5% production (2005-2009 5-year est.).
Income: Per capita income: $27,604 (2010); Median household income: $62,332 (2010); Average household income: $74,287 (2010); Percent of households with income of $100,000 or more: 22.2% (2010); Poverty rate: 6.1% (2005-2009 5-year est.).
Taxes: Total city taxes per capita: $890 (2007); City property taxes per capita: $773 (2007).
Education: Percent of population age 25 and over with: High school diploma (including GED) or higher: 93.5% (2010); Bachelor's degree or higher: 30.5% (2010); Master's degree or higher: 10.7% (2010).
School District(s)
Brookwood SD 167 (PK-08)
    2009-10 Enrollment: 1,188 . . . . (708) 758-5190
Housing: Homeownership rate: 87.1% (2010); Median home value: $158,891 (2010); Median contract rent: $794 per month (2005-2009 5-year est.); Median year structure built: 1970 (2005-2009 5-year est.).
Safety: Violent crime rate: 22.9 per 10,000 population; Property crime rate: 245.5 per 10,000 population (2010).
Transportation: Commute to work: 86.4% car, 10.9% public transportation, 1.3% walk, 1.1% work from home (2005-2009 5-year est.); Travel time to work: 19.1% less than 15 minutes, 25.4% 15 to 30 minutes, 22.6% 30 to 45 minutes, 14.2% 45 to 60 minutes, 18.7% 60 minutes or more (2005-2009 5-year est.)
Additional Information Contacts
Village of Glenwood . . . . (708) 753-2400
    http://www.villageofglenwood.com

GOLF (village). Covers a land area of 0.445 square miles and a water area of 0 square miles. Located at 42.05° N. Lat; 87.79° W. Long. Elevation is 636 feet.
Population: 454 (1990); 451 (2000); 408 (2010); 385 (2015 projected); Race: 96.1% White, 0.0% Black, 2.7% Asian, 1.2% Other, 2.0% Hispanic of any race (2010); Density: 917.8 persons per square mile (2010); Average household size: 2.58 (2010); Median age: 43.9 (2010); Males per 100 females: 93.4 (2010); Marriage status: 23.4% never married, 69.8% now married, 4.9% widowed, 1.9% divorced (2005-2009 5-year est.); Foreign born: 13.5% (2005-2009 5-year est.); Ancestry (includes multiple ancestries): 37.9% Irish, 29.5% German, 16.6% Polish, 9.5% English, 8.6% Iranian (2005-2009 5-year est.).
Economy: Single-family building permits issued: 0 (2010); Multi-family building permits issued: 0 (2010); Employment by occupation: 33.0% management, 29.1% professional, 3.9% services, 30.0% sales, 0.0% farming, 2.5% construction, 1.5% production (2005-2009 5-year est.).
Income: Per capita income: $60,124 (2010); Median household income: $107,292 (2010); Average household income: $156,139 (2010); Percent of households with income of $100,000 or more: 54.4% (2010); Poverty rate: 3.7% (2005-2009 5-year est.).
Taxes: Total city taxes per capita: $1,667 (2007); City property taxes per capita: $1,410 (2007).
Education: Percent of population age 25 and over with: High school diploma (including GED) or higher: 98.1% (2010); Bachelor's degree or higher: 69.7% (2010); Master's degree or higher: 29.6% (2010).
Housing: Homeownership rate: 94.9% (2010); Median home value: $480,000 (2010); Median contract rent: n/a per month (2005-2009 5-year est.); Median year structure built: 1953 (2005-2009 5-year est.).
Transportation: Commute to work: 58.8% car, 25.6% public transportation, 0.0% walk, 9.5% work from home (2005-2009 5-year est.); Travel time to work: 10.0% less than 15 minutes, 22.2% 15 to 30 minutes, 43.9% 30 to 45 minutes, 20.6% 45 to 60 minutes, 3.3% 60 minutes or more (2005-2009 5-year est.)

HANOVER PARK (village). Covers a land area of 6.794 square miles and a water area of 0 square miles. Located at 41.97° N. Lat; 88.14° W. Long.
Population: 32,993 (1990); 38,278 (2000); 37,977 (2010); 37,758 (2015 projected); Race: 59.6% White, 7.1% Black, 15.1% Asian, 18.1% Other, 33.6% Hispanic of any race (2010); Density: 5,590.1 persons per square mile (2010); Average household size: 3.34 (2010); Median age: 33.4 (2010); Males per 100 females: 104.5 (2010); Marriage status: 30.6%

never married, 58.6% now married, 2.7% widowed, 8.1% divorced (2005-2009 5-year est.); Foreign born: 37.0% (2005-2009 5-year est.); Ancestry (includes multiple ancestries): 15.0% German, 9.6% Polish, 9.0% Irish, 6.8% Italian, 4.5% English (2005-2009 5-year est.).
Economy: Unemployment rate: 10.4% (August 2011); Total civilian labor force: 20,649 (August 2011); Single-family building permits issued: 20 (2010); Multi-family building permits issued: 0 (2010); Employment by occupation: 12.0% management, 14.0% professional, 18.1% services, 30.1% sales, 0.0% farming, 7.9% construction, 17.9% production (2005-2009 5-year est.).
Income: Per capita income: $26,943 (2010); Median household income: $78,521 (2010); Average household income: $89,972 (2010); Percent of households with income of $100,000 or more: 32.1% (2010); Poverty rate: 10.3% (2005-2009 5-year est.).
Taxes: Total city taxes per capita: $436 (2007); City property taxes per capita: $278 (2007).
Education: Percent of population age 25 and over with: High school diploma (including GED) or higher: 83.8% (2010); Bachelor's degree or higher: 25.8% (2010); Master's degree or higher: 6.3% (2010).
School District(s)
CCSD 93 (PK-08)
    2009-10 Enrollment: 4,002 . . . . (630) 893-9393
Keeneyville SD 20 (PK-08)
    2009-10 Enrollment: 1,623 . . . . (630) 894-2250
SD U-46 (PK-12)
    2009-10 Enrollment: 41,446 . . . . (847) 888-5000
Schaumburg CCSD 54 (PK-08)
    2009-10 Enrollment: 14,313 . . . . (847) 357-5000
Vocational/Technical School(s)
Empire Beauty School-Hanover Park (Private, For-profit)
    Fall 2009 Enrollment: 91 . . . . (800) 223-3271
    2010-11 Tuition: $17,595
Housing: Homeownership rate: 84.9% (2010); Median home value: $204,868 (2010); Median contract rent: $871 per month (2005-2009 5-year est.); Median year structure built: 1976 (2005-2009 5-year est.).
Safety: Violent crime rate: 13.5 per 10,000 population; Property crime rate: 148.2 per 10,000 population (2010).
Transportation: Commute to work: 90.0% car, 3.2% public transportation, 1.2% walk, 3.0% work from home (2005-2009 5-year est.); Travel time to work: 17.2% less than 15 minutes, 40.7% 15 to 30 minutes, 23.1% 30 to 45 minutes, 10.4% 45 to 60 minutes, 8.7% 60 minutes or more (2005-2009 5-year est.)
Additional Information Contacts
Hanover Park Chamber of Commerce & Industry . . . . (630) 372-2009
    http://www.hanoverparkchamber.com
Village of Hanover Park . . . . (630) 372-4200
    http://www.hanoverparkillinois.org

HARVEY (city). Covers a land area of 6.196 square miles and a water area of 0 square miles. Located at 41.61° N. Lat; 87.65° W. Long. Elevation is 604 feet.
History: Named for Turlington W. Harvey, town founder. The site of Harvey was purchased in 1889 by Turlington W. Harvey, a Chicago lumberman, who organized a village that attracted other settlers and industries.
Population: 29,771 (1990); 30,000 (2000); 27,753 (2010); 26,755 (2015 projected); Race: 11.0% White, 73.6% Black, 0.6% Asian, 14.8% Other, 19.5% Hispanic of any race (2010); Density: 4,479.5 persons per square mile (2010); Average household size: 3.30 (2010); Median age: 29.6 (2010); Males per 100 females: 94.0 (2010); Marriage status: 46.8% never married, 35.5% now married, 7.4% widowed, 10.4% divorced (2005-2009 5-year est.); Foreign born: 9.3% (2005-2009 5-year est.); Ancestry (includes multiple ancestries): 1.7% German, 1.1% Irish, 0.8% Jamaican, 0.8% African, 0.8% American (2005-2009 5-year est.).
Economy: Unemployment rate: 17.3% (August 2011); Total civilian labor force: 11,264 (August 2011); Single-family building permits issued: 0 (2010); Multi-family building permits issued: 0 (2010); Employment by occupation: 3.8% management, 12.3% professional, 26.2% services, 28.9% sales, 0.5% farming, 9.8% construction, 18.5% production (2005-2009 5-year est.).
Income: Per capita income: $13,729 (2010); Median household income: $35,782 (2010); Average household income: $45,015 (2010); Percent of households with income of $100,000 or more: 7.3% (2010); Poverty rate: 31.9% (2005-2009 5-year est.).

Taxes: Total city taxes per capita: $435 (2007); City property taxes per capita: $293 (2007).
Education: Percent of population age 25 and over with: High school diploma (including GED) or higher: 75.6% (2010); Bachelor's degree or higher: 10.2% (2010); Master's degree or higher: 3.1% (2010).
School District(s)
Harvey SD 152 (PK-08)
  2009-10 Enrollment: 2,607 . . . . (708) 333-0300
South Holland SD 151 (PK-08)
  2009-10 Enrollment: 1,547 . . . . (708) 339-1516
Thornton Twp HSD 205 (09-12)
  2009-10 Enrollment: 6,179 . . . . (708) 225-4000
W Harvey-Dixmoor Psd 147 (PK-08)
  2009-10 Enrollment: 1,508 . . . . (708) 339-9500
Four-year College(s)
Ingalls Memorial Hospital Dietetic Internship (Private, Not-for-profit)
  Fall 2009 Enrollment: 7 . . . . (708) 915-5723
Housing: Homeownership rate: 61.2% (2010); Median home value: $94,775 (2010); Median contract rent: $676 per month (2005-2009 5-year est.); Median year structure built: 1958 (2005-2009 5-year est.).
Hospitals: Ingalls Memorial Hospital (326 beds)
Safety: Violent crime rate: 146.0 per 10,000 population; Property crime rate: 643.1 per 10,000 population (2010).
Transportation: Commute to work: 83.2% car, 12.7% public transportation, 1.6% walk, 1.5% work from home (2005-2009 5-year est.); Travel time to work: 15.3% less than 15 minutes, 31.5% 15 to 30 minutes, 25.6% 30 to 45 minutes, 13.6% 45 to 60 minutes, 14.0% 60 minutes or more (2005-2009 5-year est.)
Additional Information Contacts
City of Harvey . . . . (708) 210-5301
  http://www.cityofharvey.org

HARWOOD HEIGHTS (village). Covers a land area of 0.822 square miles and a water area of 0 square miles. Located at 41.96° N. Lat; 87.80° W. Long. Elevation is 650 feet.
Population: 7,680 (1990); 8,297 (2000); 8,267 (2010); 8,220 (2015 projected); Race: 89.7% White, 0.4% Black, 5.3% Asian, 4.5% Other, 7.6% Hispanic of any race (2010); Density: 10,057.9 persons per square mile (2010); Average household size: 2.40 (2010); Median age: 45.3 (2010); Males per 100 females: 90.6 (2010); Marriage status: 31.0% never married, 55.6% now married, 8.0% widowed, 5.4% divorced (2005-2009 5-year est.); Foreign born: 36.4% (2005-2009 5-year est.); Ancestry (includes multiple ancestries): 28.0% Polish, 19.3% Italian, 11.2% German, 8.1% Irish, 2.8% Ukrainian (2005-2009 5-year est.).
Economy: Single-family building permits issued: 0 (2010); Multi-family building permits issued: 0 (2010); Employment by occupation: 14.6% management, 12.2% professional, 20.4% services, 31.2% sales, 0.0% farming, 9.3% construction, 12.3% production (2005-2009 5-year est.).
Income: Per capita income: $26,510 (2010); Median household income: $52,383 (2010); Average household income: $63,491 (2010); Percent of households with income of $100,000 or more: 16.5% (2010); Poverty rate: 7.6% (2005-2009 5-year est.).
Taxes: Total city taxes per capita: $575 (2007); City property taxes per capita: $167 (2007).
Education: Percent of population age 25 and over with: High school diploma (including GED) or higher: 82.1% (2010); Bachelor's degree or higher: 20.3% (2010); Master's degree or higher: 5.9% (2010).
School District(s)
Union Ridge SD 86 (PK-08)
  2009-10 Enrollment: 600 . . . . (708) 867-5822
Housing: Homeownership rate: 64.5% (2010); Median home value: $286,676 (2010); Median contract rent: $736 per month (2005-2009 5-year est.); Median year structure built: 1964 (2005-2009 5-year est.).
Safety: Violent crime rate: 1.3 per 10,000 population; Property crime rate: 198.8 per 10,000 population (2010).
Transportation: Commute to work: 90.7% car, 5.8% public transportation, 1.1% walk, 1.6% work from home (2005-2009 5-year est.); Travel time to work: 18.7% less than 15 minutes, 33.6% 15 to 30 minutes, 32.3% 30 to 45 minutes, 11.5% 45 to 60 minutes, 3.9% 60 minutes or more (2005-2009 5-year est.)
Additional Information Contacts
Village of Harwood Heights . . . . (708) 867-7200
  http://www.harwoodheights.org

HAZEL CREST (village). Covers a land area of 3.381 square miles and a water area of 0.023 square miles. Located at 41.57° N. Lat; 87.68° W. Long. Elevation is 646 feet.
Population: 13,438 (1990); 14,816 (2000); 14,579 (2010); 14,401 (2015 projected); Race: 20.9% White, 74.1% Black, 1.0% Asian, 4.0% Other, 4.4% Hispanic of any race (2010); Density: 4,311.4 persons per square mile (2010); Average household size: 2.93 (2010); Median age: 35.2 (2010); Males per 100 females: 86.6 (2010); Marriage status: 40.7% never married, 37.5% now married, 7.6% widowed, 14.2% divorced (2005-2009 5-year est.); Foreign born: 5.9% (2005-2009 5-year est.); Ancestry (includes multiple ancestries): 3.9% German, 1.9% Irish, 1.8% Nigerian, 1.5% Polish, 1.3% African (2005-2009 5-year est.).
Economy: Single-family building permits issued: 0 (2010); Multi-family building permits issued: 0 (2010); Employment by occupation: 10.6% management, 19.3% professional, 21.6% services, 26.8% sales, 0.2% farming, 4.6% construction, 16.8% production (2005-2009 5-year est.).
Income: Per capita income: $22,504 (2010); Median household income: $56,742 (2010); Average household income: $66,206 (2010); Percent of households with income of $100,000 or more: 17.1% (2010); Poverty rate: 10.9% (2005-2009 5-year est.).
Taxes: Total city taxes per capita: $428 (2007); City property taxes per capita: $291 (2007).
Education: Percent of population age 25 and over with: High school diploma (including GED) or higher: 92.3% (2010); Bachelor's degree or higher: 27.2% (2010); Master's degree or higher: 10.1% (2010).
School District(s)
Hazel Crest SD 152-5 (PK-08)
  2009-10 Enrollment: 1,081 . . . . (708) 335-0790
Prairie-Hills ESD 144 (PK-08)
  2009-10 Enrollment: 2,931 . . . . (708) 210-2888
Housing: Homeownership rate: 84.6% (2010); Median home value: $136,441 (2010); Median contract rent: $1,057 per month (2005-2009 5-year est.); Median year structure built: 1968 (2005-2009 5-year est.).
Hospitals: Advocate South Suburban Hospital (291 beds)
Safety: Violent crime rate: 29.0 per 10,000 population; Property crime rate: 384.1 per 10,000 population (2010).
Transportation: Commute to work: 84.5% car, 11.7% public transportation, 0.6% walk, 1.6% work from home (2005-2009 5-year est.); Travel time to work: 15.5% less than 15 minutes, 22.5% 15 to 30 minutes, 30.6% 30 to 45 minutes, 12.9% 45 to 60 minutes, 18.4% 60 minutes or more (2005-2009 5-year est.)
Additional Information Contacts
Hazel Crest Area Chamber of Commerce . . . .
  http://hazelcrestareachamber.org
Village of Hazel Crest . . . . (708) 335-9600
  http://www.villageofhazelcrest.com

HICKORY HILLS (city). Covers a land area of 2.834 square miles and a water area of 0 square miles. Located at 41.72° N. Lat; 87.82° W. Long. Elevation is 679 feet.
Population: 13,021 (1990); 13,926 (2000); 13,917 (2010); 13,941 (2015 projected); Race: 81.8% White, 7.5% Black, 2.7% Asian, 8.0% Other, 11.0% Hispanic of any race (2010); Density: 4,909.9 persons per square mile (2010); Average household size: 2.68 (2010); Median age: 38.2 (2010); Males per 100 females: 98.3 (2010); Marriage status: 27.7% never married, 59.2% now married, 5.1% widowed, 8.1% divorced (2005-2009 5-year est.); Foreign born: 24.4% (2005-2009 5-year est.); Ancestry (includes multiple ancestries): 26.7% Polish, 17.3% Irish, 13.7% German, 8.0% Italian, 5.0% Lithuanian (2005-2009 5-year est.).
Economy: Single-family building permits issued: 1 (2010); Multi-family building permits issued: 0 (2010); Employment by occupation: 10.3% management, 18.4% professional, 14.8% services, 26.5% sales, 0.2% farming, 13.4% construction, 16.4% production (2005-2009 5-year est.).
Income: Per capita income: $28,618 (2010); Median household income: $65,468 (2010); Average household income: $76,757 (2010); Percent of households with income of $100,000 or more: 23.8% (2010); Poverty rate: 8.2% (2005-2009 5-year est.).
Taxes: Total city taxes per capita: $296 (2007); City property taxes per capita: $235 (2007).
Education: Percent of population age 25 and over with: High school diploma (including GED) or higher: 87.2% (2010); Bachelor's degree or higher: 24.0% (2010); Master's degree or higher: 6.8% (2010).

School District(s)

North Palos SD 117 (PK-08)

2009-10 Enrollment: 3,079 . . . . (708) 598-5500

Vocational/Technical School(s)

Star Truck Driving School (Private, For-profit)

Fall 2009 Enrollment: 77 . . . . (630) 236-7200

2010-11 Tuition: $4,595

Housing: Homeownership rate: 72.1% (2010); Median home value: $235,324 (2010); Median contract rent: $757 per month (2005-2009 5-year est.); Median year structure built: 1970 (2005-2009 5-year est.).

Safety: Violent crime rate: 15.3 per 10,000 population; Property crime rate: 227.6 per 10,000 population (2010).

Transportation: Commute to work: 91.8% car, 3.9% public transportation, 0.9% walk, 2.6% work from home (2005-2009 5-year est.); Travel time to work: 18.5% less than 15 minutes, 32.8% 15 to 30 minutes, 26.7% 30 to 45 minutes, 9.0% 45 to 60 minutes, 12.9% 60 minutes or more (2005-2009 5-year est.)

Additional Information Contacts

City of Hickory Hills . . . . (708) 598-4800

http://www.hickoryhillsil.org

HILLSIDE (village). Covers a land area of 2.148 square miles and a water area of 0 square miles. Located at 41.87° N. Lat; 87.90° W. Long. Elevation is 656 feet.

History: Incorporated 1905.

Population: 7,672 (1990); 8,155 (2000); 7,515 (2010); 7,237 (2015 projected); Race: 42.7% White, 40.8% Black, 4.1% Asian, 12.3% Other, 19.0% Hispanic of any race (2010); Density: 3,499.4 persons per square mile (2010); Average household size: 2.71 (2010); Median age: 39.8 (2010); Males per 100 females: 92.9 (2010); Marriage status: 37.0% never married, 45.4% now married, 7.3% widowed, 10.3% divorced (2005-2009 5-year est.); Foreign born: 18.1% (2005-2009 5-year est.); Ancestry (includes multiple ancestries): 8.1% German, 6.3% Irish, 5.5% Yugoslavian, 4.8% Italian, 2.9% Polish (2005-2009 5-year est.).

Economy: Single-family building permits issued: 0 (2010); Multi-family building permits issued: 0 (2010); Employment by occupation: 8.1% management, 19.7% professional, 17.5% services, 31.2% sales, 0.0% farming, 5.6% construction, 18.0% production (2005-2009 5-year est.).

Income: Per capita income: $24,357 (2010); Median household income: $58,904 (2010); Average household income: $67,654 (2010); Percent of households with income of $100,000 or more: 17.0% (2010); Poverty rate: 10.3% (2005-2009 5-year est.).

Taxes: Total city taxes per capita: $1,720 (2007); City property taxes per capita: $1,406 (2007).

Education: Percent of population age 25 and over with: High school diploma (including GED) or higher: 86.0% (2010); Bachelor's degree or higher: 22.7% (2010); Master's degree or higher: 6.9% (2010).

School District(s)

Hillside SD 93 (KG-08)

2009-10 Enrollment: 488 . . . . (708) 449-7280

Proviso Twp HSD 209 (09-12)

2009-10 Enrollment: 5,198 . . . . (708) 338-5912

Housing: Homeownership rate: 77.3% (2010); Median home value: $192,256 (2010); Median contract rent: $739 per month (2005-2009 5-year est.); Median year structure built: 1956 (2005-2009 5-year est.).

Transportation: Commute to work: 88.8% car, 6.7% public transportation, 1.8% walk, 1.8% work from home (2005-2009 5-year est.); Travel time to work: 13.4% less than 15 minutes, 38.8% 15 to 30 minutes, 29.3% 30 to 45 minutes, 10.2% 45 to 60 minutes, 8.3% 60 minutes or more (2005-2009 5-year est.)

Additional Information Contacts

Hillside Chamber of Commerce & Industry . . . . (708) 449-2449

http://www.hillsidechamberofcommerce.com

Village of Hillside . . . . (708) 449-6450

http://www.hillside-il.org

HODGKINS (village). Covers a land area of 2.572 square miles and a water area of 0.065 square miles. Located at 41.76° N. Lat; 87.85° W. Long. Elevation is 604 feet.

Population: 1,963 (1990); 2,134 (2000); 2,270 (2010); 2,350 (2015 projected); Race: 85.8% White, 0.1% Black, 0.2% Asian, 13.9% Other, 51.0% Hispanic of any race (2010); Density: 882.5 persons per square mile (2010); Average household size: 2.65 (2010); Median age: 35.8 (2010); Males per 100 females: 119.3 (2010); Marriage status: 31.8% never married, 47.2% now married, 10.4% widowed, 10.5% divorced (2005-2009

5-year est.); Foreign born: 24.9% (2005-2009 5-year est.); Ancestry (includes multiple ancestries): 15.7% German, 15.4% Irish, 11.6% Polish, 4.9% Italian, 3.1% English (2005-2009 5-year est.).

Economy: Single-family building permits issued: 0 (2010); Multi-family building permits issued: 0 (2010); Employment by occupation: 3.5% management, 9.7% professional, 31.8% services, 20.3% sales, 0.0% farming, 14.9% construction, 19.7% production (2005-2009 5-year est.).

Income: Per capita income: $21,537 (2010); Median household income: $44,578 (2010); Average household income: $56,849 (2010); Percent of households with income of $100,000 or more: 13.9% (2010); Poverty rate: 26.7% (2005-2009 5-year est.).

Taxes: Total city taxes per capita: $3,864 (2007); City property taxes per capita: $3,360 (2007).

Education: Percent of population age 25 and over with: High school diploma (including GED) or higher: 71.1% (2010); Bachelor's degree or higher: 11.4% (2010); Master's degree or higher: 3.7% (2010).

School District(s)

La Grange SD 105 South (PK-08)

2009-10 Enrollment: 1,314 . . . . (708) 482-2700

Housing: Homeownership rate: 66.5% (2010); Median home value: $95,500 (2010); Median contract rent: $700 per month (2005-2009 5-year est.); Median year structure built: 1978 (2005-2009 5-year est.).

Safety: Violent crime rate: 19.9 per 10,000 population; Property crime rate: 1,253.7 per 10,000 population (2010).

Transportation: Commute to work: 73.6% car, 5.3% public transportation, 18.4% walk, 0.0% work from home (2005-2009 5-year est.); Travel time to work: 25.1% less than 15 minutes, 32.9% 15 to 30 minutes, 21.0% 30 to 45 minutes, 11.9% 45 to 60 minutes, 9.1% 60 minutes or more (2005-2009 5-year est.)

Additional Information Contacts

West Suburban Chamber of Commerce & Industry. . . . . . . (708) 387-7550

http://www.wscci.org

HOFFMAN ESTATES (village). Covers a land area of 19.710 square miles and a water area of 0.158 square miles. Located at 42.06° N. Lat; 88.11° W. Long. Elevation is 784 feet.

Population: 46,320 (1990); 49,495 (2000); 49,845 (2010); 49,785 (2015 projected); Race: 67.3% White, 4.8% Black, 18.9% Asian, 9.0% Other, 15.1% Hispanic of any race (2010); Density: 2,528.9 persons per square mile (2010); Average household size: 2.84 (2010); Median age: 36.9 (2010); Males per 100 females: 98.6 (2010); Marriage status: 26.8% never married, 60.5% now married, 5.1% widowed, 7.6% divorced (2005-2009 5-year est.); Foreign born: 26.9% (2005-2009 5-year est.); Ancestry (includes multiple ancestries): 19.8% German, 15.3% Polish, 12.1% Irish, 10.0% Italian, 5.1% English (2005-2009 5-year est.).

Economy: Unemployment rate: 8.3% (August 2011); Total civilian labor force: 30,980 (August 2011); Single-family building permits issued: 10 (2010); Multi-family building permits issued: 0 (2010); Employment by occupation: 21.0% management, 23.7% professional, 11.2% services, 28.2% sales, 0.1% farming, 5.8% construction, 9.9% production (2005-2009 5-year est.).

Income: Per capita income: $31,785 (2010); Median household income: $71,913 (2010); Average household income: $90,469 (2010); Percent of households with income of $100,000 or more: 31.0% (2010); Poverty rate: 5.7% (2005-2009 5-year est.).

Taxes: Total city taxes per capita: $1,063 (2007); City property taxes per capita: $800 (2007).

Education: Percent of population age 25 and over with: High school diploma (including GED) or higher: 92.6% (2010); Bachelor's degree or higher: 40.4% (2010); Master's degree or higher: 13.8% (2010).

School District(s)

Palatine CCSD 15 (PK-08)

2009-10 Enrollment: 12,214 . . . . (847) 963-3000

SD U-46 (PK-12)

2009-10 Enrollment: 41,446 . . . . (847) 888-5000

Schaumburg CCSD 54 (PK-08)

2009-10 Enrollment: 14,313 . . . . (847) 357-5000

Township HSD 211 (09-12)

2009-10 Enrollment: 12,749 . . . . (847) 755-6600

Four-year College(s)

American InterContinental University-Online (Private, For-profit)

Fall 2009 Enrollment: 26,630. (877) 701-3800

2010-11 Tuition: In-state $11,700; Out-of-state $11,700

Housing: Homeownership rate: 78.8% (2010); Median home value: $252,012 (2010); Median contract rent: $953 per month (2005-2009 5-year est.); Median year structure built: 1976 (2005-2009 5-year est.).

Hospitals: St. Alexius Medical Center (331 beds)

Safety: Violent crime rate: 10.8 per 10,000 population; Property crime rate: 140.0 per 10,000 population (2010).

Transportation: Commute to work: 91.8% car, 3.1% public transportation, 1.0% walk, 3.0% work from home (2005-2009 5-year est.); Travel time to work: 19.1% less than 15 minutes, 34.7% 15 to 30 minutes, 25.7% 30 to 45 minutes, 10.8% 45 to 60 minutes, 9.7% 60 minutes or more (2005-2009 5-year est.)

Additional Information Contacts

Hoffman Estates Chamber of Commerce & Industry . . . . . . (847) 781-9100
    http://www.hechamber.com
Village of Hoffman Estates . . . . (847) 882-9100
    http://www.hoffmanestates.com

HOMETOWN (city).
Covers a land area of 0.478 square miles and a water area of 0 square miles. Located at 41.73° N. Lat; 87.73° W. Long. Elevation is 620 feet.

Population: 4,769 (1990); 4,467 (2000); 3,826 (2010); 3,539 (2015 projected); Race: 96.3% White, 0.0% Black, 0.2% Asian, 3.5% Other, 5.6% Hispanic of any race (2010); Density: 8,012.3 persons per square mile (2010); Average household size: 2.33 (2010); Median age: 40.2 (2010); Males per 100 females: 85.9 (2010); Marriage status: 32.9% never married, 45.5% now married, 9.4% widowed, 12.2% divorced (2005-2009 5-year est.); Foreign born: 3.6% (2005-2009 5-year est.); Ancestry (includes multiple ancestries): 29.7% Irish, 25.0% Polish, 24.6% German, 15.0% Italian, 8.0% Croatian (2005-2009 5-year est.).

Economy: Single-family building permits issued: 0 (2010); Multi-family building permits issued: 0 (2010); Employment by occupation: 7.1% management, 11.8% professional, 19.2% services, 38.3% sales, 0.0% farming, 12.0% construction, 11.5% production (2005-2009 5-year est.).

Income: Per capita income: $23,399 (2010); Median household income: $46,591 (2010); Average household income: $54,588 (2010); Percent of households with income of $100,000 or more: 12.4% (2010); Poverty rate: 13.6% (2005-2009 5-year est.).

Taxes: Total city taxes per capita: $174 (2007); City property taxes per capita: $89 (2007).

Education: Percent of population age 25 and over with: High school diploma (including GED) or higher: 86.8% (2010); Bachelor's degree or higher: 10.6% (2010); Master's degree or higher: 2.3% (2010).

School District(s)

Oak Lawn-Hometown SD 123 (PK-08)
    2009-10 Enrollment: 3,128 . . . . (708) 423-0150

Housing: Homeownership rate: 80.1% (2010); Median home value: $132,039 (2010); Median contract rent: $289 per month (2005-2009 5-year est.); Median year structure built: 1954 (2005-2009 5-year est.).

Safety: Violent crime rate: 0.0 per 10,000 population; Property crime rate: 134.9 per 10,000 population (2010).

Transportation: Commute to work: 91.5% car, 6.1% public transportation, 1.9% walk, 0.5% work from home (2005-2009 5-year est.); Travel time to work: 26.6% less than 15 minutes, 29.2% 15 to 30 minutes, 17.8% 30 to 45 minutes, 13.0% 45 to 60 minutes, 13.5% 60 minutes or more (2005-2009 5-year est.)

HOMEWOOD (village).
Covers a land area of 5.204 square miles and a water area of 0.052 square miles. Located at 41.55° N. Lat; 87.66° W. Long. Elevation is 659 feet.

History: Named for Homewood, Pennsylvania. The site of Homewood was laid out in 1852 by James Hart and was first known as Hartford.

Population: 19,278 (1990); 19,543 (2000); 18,794 (2010); 18,418 (2015 projected); Race: 68.8% White, 25.7% Black, 1.6% Asian, 3.9% Other, 4.6% Hispanic of any race (2010); Density: 3,611.6 persons per square mile (2010); Average household size: 2.57 (2010); Median age: 41.6 (2010); Males per 100 females: 87.0 (2010); Marriage status: 29.7% never married, 54.7% now married, 6.3% widowed, 9.3% divorced (2005-2009 5-year est.); Foreign born: 5.3% (2005-2009 5-year est.); Ancestry (includes multiple ancestries): 21.5% German, 19.4% Irish, 7.6% Polish, 7.6% English, 7.2% Italian (2005-2009 5-year est.).

Economy: Single-family building permits issued: 0 (2010); Multi-family building permits issued: 0 (2010); Employment by occupation: 17.2% management, 28.6% professional, 12.0% services, 27.5% sales, 0.0% farming, 7.0% construction, 7.7% production (2005-2009 5-year est.).

Income: Per capita income: $30,218 (2010); Median household income: $66,064 (2010); Average household income: $78,994 (2010); Percent of households with income of $100,000 or more: 25.9% (2010); Poverty rate: 2.9% (2005-2009 5-year est.).

Taxes: Total city taxes per capita: $815 (2007); City property taxes per capita: $701 (2007).

Education: Percent of population age 25 and over with: High school diploma (including GED) or higher: 95.3% (2010); Bachelor's degree or higher: 44.9% (2010); Master's degree or higher: 18.9% (2010).

School District(s)

Homewood SD 153 (PK-08)
    2009-10 Enrollment: 1,966 . . . . (708) 799-5661

Housing: Homeownership rate: 87.7% (2010); Median home value: $169,939 (2010); Median contract rent: $779 per month (2005-2009 5-year est.); Median year structure built: 1960 (2005-2009 5-year est.).

Safety: Violent crime rate: 17.7 per 10,000 population; Property crime rate: 408.6 per 10,000 population (2010).

Transportation: Commute to work: 82.6% car, 11.1% public transportation, 3.4% walk, 2.6% work from home (2005-2009 5-year est.); Travel time to work: 28.6% less than 15 minutes, 24.6% 15 to 30 minutes, 18.9% 30 to 45 minutes, 12.4% 45 to 60 minutes, 15.5% 60 minutes or more (2005-2009 5-year est.); Amtrak: train service available.

Additional Information Contacts

Homewood Area Chamber of Commerce . . . . (708) 206-3384
    http://www.homewoodareachamber.com
Village of Homewood . . . . (708) 798-3000
    http://village.homewood.il.us

INDIAN HEAD PARK (village).
Covers a land area of 0.842 square miles and a water area of 0 square miles. Located at 41.76° N. Lat; 87.89° W. Long. Elevation is 653 feet.

Population: 3,628 (1990); 3,685 (2000); 3,900 (2010); 3,879 (2015 projected); Race: 95.4% White, 0.9% Black, 2.2% Asian, 1.5% Other, 2.7% Hispanic of any race (2010); Density: 4,631.9 persons per square mile (2010); Average household size: 2.16 (2010); Median age: 55.4 (2010); Males per 100 females: 83.4 (2010); Marriage status: 25.4% never married, 43.1% now married, 15.6% widowed, 16.0% divorced (2005-2009 5-year est.); Foreign born: 13.1% (2005-2009 5-year est.); Ancestry (includes multiple ancestries): 21.5% German, 20.0% Italian, 19.2% Irish, 10.5% English, 9.3% Polish (2005-2009 5-year est.).

Economy: Single-family building permits issued: 0 (2010); Multi-family building permits issued: 0 (2010); Employment by occupation: 14.2% management, 29.3% professional, 3.5% services, 42.5% sales, 0.0% farming, 3.2% construction, 7.4% production (2005-2009 5-year est.).

Income: Per capita income: $51,798 (2010); Median household income: $87,073 (2010); Average household income: $116,148 (2010); Percent of households with income of $100,000 or more: 41.1% (2010); Poverty rate: 2.7% (2005-2009 5-year est.).

Taxes: Total city taxes per capita: $411 (2007); City property taxes per capita: $242 (2007).

Education: Percent of population age 25 and over with: High school diploma (including GED) or higher: 96.3% (2010); Bachelor's degree or higher: 45.1% (2010); Master's degree or higher: 20.0% (2010).

Housing: Homeownership rate: 96.6% (2010); Median home value: $298,036 (2010); Median contract rent: $1,461 per month (2005-2009 5-year est.); Median year structure built: 1978 (2005-2009 5-year est.).

Transportation: Commute to work: 93.8% car, 1.8% public transportation, 0.0% walk, 4.4% work from home (2005-2009 5-year est.); Travel time to work: 17.8% less than 15 minutes, 31.2% 15 to 30 minutes, 25.3% 30 to 45 minutes, 16.5% 45 to 60 minutes, 9.3% 60 minutes or more (2005-2009 5-year est.)

INVERNESS (village).
Covers a land area of 6.318 square miles and a water area of 0.151 square miles. Located at 42.11° N. Lat; 88.09° W. Long. Elevation is 843 feet.

History: Incorporated 1962.

Population: 6,541 (1990); 6,749 (2000); 6,798 (2010); 6,824 (2015 projected); Race: 87.2% White, 1.0% Black, 9.6% Asian, 2.2% Other, 2.9% Hispanic of any race (2010); Density: 1,076.0 persons per square mile (2010); Average household size: 2.92 (2010); Median age: 42.8 (2010); Males per 100 females: 97.2 (2010); Marriage status: 21.9% never married, 69.5% now married, 4.5% widowed, 4.0% divorced (2005-2009 5-year est.); Foreign born: 12.6% (2005-2009 5-year est.); Ancestry (includes multiple ancestries): 26.6% Irish, 24.1% German, 12.0% Polish, 9.8% Italian, 7.4% English (2005-2009 5-year est.).

Economy: Single-family building permits issued: 0 (2010); Multi-family building permits issued: 0 (2010); Employment by occupation: 36.6% management, 26.3% professional, 7.4% services, 22.9% sales, 0.0% farming, 3.2% construction, 3.6% production (2005-2009 5-year est.).
Income: Per capita income: $58,645 (2010); Median household income: $123,962 (2010); Average household income: $173,187 (2010); Percent of households with income of $100,000 or more: 62.1% (2010); Poverty rate: 4.6% (2005-2009 5-year est.).
Taxes: Total city taxes per capita: $145 (2007); City property taxes per capita: $86 (2007).
Education: Percent of population age 25 and over with: High school diploma (including GED) or higher: 96.2% (2010); Bachelor's degree or higher: 60.5% (2010); Master's degree or higher: 24.8% (2010).
Housing: Homeownership rate: 94.4% (2010); Median home value: $491,549 (2010); Median contract rent: $1,163 per month (2005-2009 5-year est.); Median year structure built: 1981 (2005-2009 5-year est.).
Transportation: Commute to work: 82.5% car, 6.1% public transportation, 1.0% walk, 9.5% work from home (2005-2009 5-year est.); Travel time to work: 16.8% less than 15 minutes, 29.8% 15 to 30 minutes, 28.3% 30 to 45 minutes, 11.1% 45 to 60 minutes, 14.1% 60 minutes or more (2005-2009 5-year est.)
Additional Information Contacts
Village of Inverness . . . . (847) 358-7740
   http://www.villageofinverness.org

JUSTICE (village). Covers a land area of 2.912 square miles and a water area of 0.042 square miles. Located at 41.74° N. Lat; 87.83° W. Long. Elevation is 617 feet.
Population: 11,201 (1990); 12,193 (2000); 12,278 (2010); 12,337 (2015 projected); Race: 71.9% White, 16.6% Black, 1.9% Asian, 9.6% Other, 10.7% Hispanic of any race (2010); Density: 4,216.7 persons per square mile (2010); Average household size: 2.76 (2010); Median age: 35.3 (2010); Males per 100 females: 98.8 (2010); Marriage status: 36.4% never married, 51.4% now married, 5.7% widowed, 6.5% divorced (2005-2009 5-year est.); Foreign born: 19.8% (2005-2009 5-year est.); Ancestry (includes multiple ancestries): 29.6% Polish, 12.9% Irish, 10.8% German, 6.7% Italian, 4.4% Egyptian (2005-2009 5-year est.).
Economy: Single-family building permits issued: 6 (2010); Multi-family building permits issued: 4 (2010); Employment by occupation: 11.4% management, 11.6% professional, 13.0% services, 30.7% sales, 0.0% farming, 14.6% construction, 18.6% production (2005-2009 5-year est.).
Income: Per capita income: $24,753 (2010); Median household income: $60,505 (2010); Average household income: $68,234 (2010); Percent of households with income of $100,000 or more: 17.6% (2010); Poverty rate: 10.8% (2005-2009 5-year est.).
Taxes: Total city taxes per capita: $367 (2007); City property taxes per capita: $232 (2007).
Education: Percent of population age 25 and over with: High school diploma (including GED) or higher: 85.0% (2010); Bachelor's degree or higher: 15.6% (2010); Master's degree or higher: 3.4% (2010).
School District(s)
Indian Springs SD 109 (PK-08)
   2009-10 Enrollment: 3,057 . . . . (708) 496-8700
Housing: Homeownership rate: 62.6% (2010); Median home value: $197,939 (2010); Median contract rent: $751 per month (2005-2009 5-year est.); Median year structure built: 1974 (2005-2009 5-year est.).
Transportation: Commute to work: 92.8% car, 5.3% public transportation, 0.8% walk, 1.1% work from home (2005-2009 5-year est.); Travel time to work: 19.6% less than 15 minutes, 30.4% 15 to 30 minutes, 22.0% 30 to 45 minutes, 12.0% 45 to 60 minutes, 15.9% 60 minutes or more (2005-2009 5-year est.)
Additional Information Contacts
Village of Justice . . . . (708) 458-2520
   http://villageofjustice.org

KENILWORTH (village). Covers a land area of 0.595 square miles and a water area of 0 square miles. Located at 42.08° N. Lat; 87.71° W. Long. Elevation is 617 feet.
History: Kenilworth was named for the novel by Sir Walter Scott. Many streets in the town are named for places or characters in the book. Kenilworth is the burial place of poet Eugene Field.
Population: 2,402 (1990); 2,494 (2000); 2,463 (2010); 2,436 (2015 projected); Race: 97.2% White, 0.1% Black, 2.2% Asian, 0.4% Other, 1.7% Hispanic of any race (2010); Density: 4,138.7 persons per square mile (2010); Average household size: 3.23 (2010); Median age: 33.8 (2010);

Males per 100 females: 91.4 (2010); Marriage status: 19.2% never married, 73.4% now married, 4.6% widowed, 2.8% divorced (2005-2009 5-year est.); Foreign born: 5.3% (2005-2009 5-year est.); Ancestry (includes multiple ancestries): 30.7% Irish, 26.0% German, 22.2% English, 11.5% Italian, 6.3% Polish (2005-2009 5-year est.).
Economy: Single-family building permits issued: 0 (2010); Multi-family building permits issued: 0 (2010); Employment by occupation: 34.6% management, 30.8% professional, 7.1% services, 24.8% sales, 0.0% farming, 1.4% construction, 1.2% production (2005-2009 5-year est.).
Income: Per capita income: $87,489 (2010); Median household income: $288,007 (2010); Average household income: $282,418 (2010); Percent of households with income of $100,000 or more: 85.6% (2010); Poverty rate: 0.9% (2005-2009 5-year est.).
Taxes: Total city taxes per capita: $1,339 (2007); City property taxes per capita: $1,018 (2007).
Education: Percent of population age 25 and over with: High school diploma (including GED) or higher: 99.7% (2010); Bachelor's degree or higher: 90.6% (2010); Master's degree or higher: 50.9% (2010).
School District(s)
Kenilworth SD 38 (PK-08)
   2009-10 Enrollment: 563 . . . . (847) 256-5006
Housing: Homeownership rate: 96.7% (2010); Median home value: $1 million+ (2010); Median contract rent: $2,000+ per month (2005-2009 5-year est.); Median year structure built: before 1940 (2005-2009 5-year est.).
Safety: Violent crime rate: 0.0 per 10,000 population; Property crime rate: 161.4 per 10,000 population (2010).
Transportation: Commute to work: 58.1% car, 28.0% public transportation, 4.9% walk, 7.6% work from home (2005-2009 5-year est.); Travel time to work: 22.2% less than 15 minutes, 15.8% 15 to 30 minutes, 23.6% 30 to 45 minutes, 24.2% 45 to 60 minutes, 14.1% 60 minutes or more (2005-2009 5-year est.)

LA GRANGE (village). Covers a land area of 2.509 square miles and a water area of 0 square miles. Located at 41.80° N. Lat; 87.87° W. Long. Elevation is 646 feet.
History: La Grange was founded by W.D. Cossitt and named for Marquis de Lafayette's home in France. An early settlement along the Chicago, Burlington & Quincy Railroad, La Grange was incorporated in 1879.
Population: 15,352 (1990); 15,608 (2000); 14,898 (2010); 14,540 (2015 projected); Race: 90.5% White, 5.5% Black, 1.0% Asian, 3.0% Other, 5.7% Hispanic of any race (2010); Density: 5,937.7 persons per square mile (2010); Average household size: 2.67 (2010); Median age: 39.1 (2010); Males per 100 females: 96.5 (2010); Marriage status: 26.0% never married, 58.0% now married, 8.0% widowed, 7.9% divorced (2005-2009 5-year est.); Foreign born: 6.7% (2005-2009 5-year est.); Ancestry (includes multiple ancestries): 29.8% Irish, 24.9% German, 14.7% Polish, 11.6% English, 11.1% Italian (2005-2009 5-year est.).
Economy: Single-family building permits issued: 14 (2010); Multi-family building permits issued: 0 (2010); Employment by occupation: 22.2% management, 29.7% professional, 11.0% services, 24.1% sales, 0.0% farming, 3.8% construction, 9.1% production (2005-2009 5-year est.).
Income: Per capita income: $43,781 (2010); Median household income: $95,200 (2010); Average household income: $120,558 (2010); Percent of households with income of $100,000 or more: 47.7% (2010); Poverty rate: 3.6% (2005-2009 5-year est.).
Taxes: Total city taxes per capita: $769 (2007); City property taxes per capita: $639 (2007).
Education: Percent of population age 25 and over with: High school diploma (including GED) or higher: 94.2% (2010); Bachelor's degree or higher: 57.2% (2010); Master's degree or higher: 22.5% (2010).
School District(s)
La Grange SD 102 (PK-08)
   2009-10 Enrollment: 3,040 . . . . (708) 482-2400
La Grange SD 105 South (PK-08)
   2009-10 Enrollment: 1,314 . . . . (708) 482-2700
Lagrange Highlands SD 106 (PK-08)
   2009-10 Enrollment: 918 . . . . (708) 246-3085
Lyons Twp HSD 204 (09-12)
   2009-10 Enrollment: 3,890 . . . . (708) 579-6451
Pleasantdale SD 107 (PK-08)
   2009-10 Enrollment: 828 . . . . (708) 784-2013
Housing: Homeownership rate: 83.1% (2010); Median home value: $380,035 (2010); Median contract rent: $853 per month (2005-2009 5-year est.); Median year structure built: 1951 (2005-2009 5-year est.).

Hospitals: Adventist LaGrange Memorial Hospital (274 beds)
Safety: Violent crime rate: 7.3 per 10,000 population; Property crime rate: 134.8 per 10,000 population (2010).
Transportation: Commute to work: 71.6% car, 17.4% public transportation, 4.8% walk, 5.1% work from home (2005-2009 5-year est.); Travel time to work: 19.9% less than 15 minutes, 30.0% 15 to 30 minutes, 22.2% 30 to 45 minutes, 15.7% 45 to 60 minutes, 12.2% 60 minutes or more (2005-2009 5-year est.); Amtrak: train service available.
Additional Information Contacts
Village of La Grange . . . . (708) 579-2300
   http://www.villageoflagrange.com
West Suburban Chamber of Commerce & Industry. . . . . . (708) 387-7550
   http://www.wscci.org

LA GRANGE PARK (village).
Covers a land area of 2.253 square miles and a water area of 0 square miles. Located at 41.83° N. Lat; 87.86° W. Long. Elevation is 623 feet.
History: Named for the French translation of "the barn". Incorporated 1892.
Population: 12,861 (1990); 13,295 (2000); 12,992 (2010); 12,858 (2015 projected); Race: 90.8% White, 4.6% Black, 1.7% Asian, 2.8% Other, 5.0% Hispanic of any race (2010); Density: 5,765.3 persons per square mile (2010); Average household size: 2.44 (2010); Median age: 42.4 (2010); Males per 100 females: 87.1 (2010); Marriage status: 27.7% never married, 55.6% now married, 9.4% widowed, 7.3% divorced (2005-2009 5-year est.); Foreign born: 8.1% (2005-2009 5-year est.); Ancestry (includes multiple ancestries): 25.3% Irish, 21.0% German, 16.2% Polish, 10.7% Italian, 8.1% Czech (2005-2009 5-year est.).
Economy: Single-family building permits issued: 2 (2010); Multi-family building permits issued: 0 (2010); Employment by occupation: 23.2% management, 25.2% professional, 7.8% services, 28.5% sales, 0.2% farming, 6.3% construction, 8.8% production (2005-2009 5-year est.).
Income: Per capita income: $35,950 (2010); Median household income: $71,415 (2010); Average household income: $89,947 (2010); Percent of households with income of $100,000 or more: 31.5% (2010); Poverty rate: 3.9% (2005-2009 5-year est.).
Taxes: Total city taxes per capita: $391 (2007); City property taxes per capita: $247 (2007).
Education: Percent of population age 25 and over with: High school diploma (including GED) or higher: 94.6% (2010); Bachelor's degree or higher: 45.7% (2010); Master's degree or higher: 16.0% (2010).
School District(s)
Brookfield Lagrange Park SD 95 (PK-08)
   2009-10 Enrollment: 1,002 . . . . (708) 485-0606
La Grange SD 102 (PK-08)
   2009-10 Enrollment: 3,040 . . . . (708) 482-2400
Housing: Homeownership rate: 75.7% (2010); Median home value: $295,190 (2010); Median contract rent: $888 per month (2005-2009 5-year est.); Median year structure built: 1955 (2005-2009 5-year est.).
Safety: Violent crime rate: 5.8 per 10,000 population; Property crime rate: 98.2 per 10,000 population (2010).
Transportation: Commute to work: 78.2% car, 13.4% public transportation, 3.3% walk, 4.8% work from home (2005-2009 5-year est.); Travel time to work: 24.9% less than 15 minutes, 34.0% 15 to 30 minutes, 17.2% 30 to 45 minutes, 14.1% 45 to 60 minutes, 9.8% 60 minutes or more (2005-2009 5-year est.); Amtrak: train service available.
Additional Information Contacts
Village of La Grange Park . . . . (708) 354-0225
   http://www.lagrangepark.org

LANSING (village).
Covers a land area of 6.764 square miles and a water area of 0.064 square miles. Located at 41.56° N. Lat; 87.54° W. Long. Elevation is 630 feet.
History: Named for John Lansing (1754-1829), hero of the American Revolution. Lansing was settled in the 1860's by Dutch and German farmers.
Population: 28,446 (1990); 28,332 (2000); 26,726 (2010); 25,965 (2015 projected); Race: 79.7% White, 15.4% Black, 0.9% Asian, 4.1% Other, 8.4% Hispanic of any race (2010); Density: 3,951.3 persons per square mile (2010); Average household size: 2.47 (2010); Median age: 39.8 (2010); Males per 100 females: 92.1 (2010); Marriage status: 30.9% never married, 52.2% now married, 7.7% widowed, 9.2% divorced (2005-2009 5-year est.); Foreign born: 5.2% (2005-2009 5-year est.); Ancestry (includes multiple ancestries): 17.8% German, 15.4% Polish, 14.3% Irish, 10.6% Dutch, 6.5% Italian (2005-2009 5-year est.).

Economy: Unemployment rate: 11.0% (August 2011); Total civilian labor force: 14,138 (August 2011); Single-family building permits issued: 0 (2010); Multi-family building permits issued: 0 (2010); Employment by occupation: 10.7% management, 17.9% professional, 15.6% services, 30.5% sales, 0.2% farming, 9.9% construction, 15.2% production (2005-2009 5-year est.).
Income: Per capita income: $26,029 (2010); Median household income: $54,586 (2010); Average household income: $64,426 (2010); Percent of households with income of $100,000 or more: 15.5% (2010); Poverty rate: 10.6% (2005-2009 5-year est.).
Taxes: Total city taxes per capita: $733 (2007); City property taxes per capita: $586 (2007).
Education: Percent of population age 25 and over with: High school diploma (including GED) or higher: 90.6% (2010); Bachelor's degree or higher: 21.8% (2010); Master's degree or higher: 6.5% (2010).
School District(s)
Lansing SD 158 (PK-08)
   2009-10 Enrollment: 2,160 . . . . (708) 474-6700
Sunnybrook SD 171 (PK-08)
   2009-10 Enrollment: 1,082 . . . . (708) 895-0750
Thornton Fractional Twp HSD 215 (09-12)
   2009-10 Enrollment: 3,678 . . . . (708) 585-2309
Housing: Homeownership rate: 78.1% (2010); Median home value: $156,491 (2010); Median contract rent: $764 per month (2005-2009 5-year est.); Median year structure built: 1964 (2005-2009 5-year est.).
Transportation: Commute to work: 90.8% car, 6.0% public transportation, 1.2% walk, 0.9% work from home (2005-2009 5-year est.); Travel time to work: 22.7% less than 15 minutes, 27.9% 15 to 30 minutes, 18.3% 30 to 45 minutes, 12.8% 45 to 60 minutes, 18.3% 60 minutes or more (2005-2009 5-year est.)
Additional Information Contacts
Chicago Southland Convention & Visitors Bureau. . . . . (708) 895-8200
   http://www.visitchicagosouthland.com
Lansing Chamber of Commerce . . . . (708) 474-4170
   http://chamberoflansing.com
Village of Lansing. . . . . (708) 895-7200
   http://www.villageoflansing.com

LEMONT (village).
Covers a land area of 6.453 square miles and a water area of 0.348 square miles. Located at 41.66° N. Lat; 87.98° W. Long. Elevation is 607 feet.
History: Named for the French translation of "the mount". Incorporated 1873.
Population: 8,610 (1990); 13,098 (2000); 14,952 (2010); 15,840 (2015 projected); Race: 96.8% White, 0.3% Black, 0.9% Asian, 2.0% Other, 3.7% Hispanic of any race (2010); Density: 2,317.2 persons per square mile (2010); Average household size: 2.91 (2010); Median age: 39.4 (2010); Males per 100 females: 92.2 (2010); Marriage status: 23.3% never married, 64.2% now married, 7.1% widowed, 5.3% divorced (2005-2009 5-year est.); Foreign born: 9.6% (2005-2009 5-year est.); Ancestry (includes multiple ancestries): 30.8% Polish, 23.4% German, 23.3% Irish, 14.7% Italian, 7.3% Lithuanian (2005-2009 5-year est.).
Economy: Single-family building permits issued: 34 (2010); Multi-family building permits issued: 0 (2010); Employment by occupation: 21.7% management, 21.2% professional, 11.1% services, 28.0% sales, 0.0% farming, 9.9% construction, 8.2% production (2005-2009 5-year est.).
Income: Per capita income: $37,578 (2010); Median household income: $92,558 (2010); Average household income: $112,659 (2010); Percent of households with income of $100,000 or more: 45.1% (2010); Poverty rate: 3.5% (2005-2009 5-year est.).
Taxes: Total city taxes per capita: $366 (2007); City property taxes per capita: $180 (2007).
Education: Percent of population age 25 and over with: High school diploma (including GED) or higher: 90.4% (2010); Bachelor's degree or higher: 35.4% (2010); Master's degree or higher: 13.2% (2010).
School District(s)
Lemont Twp HSD 210 (09-12)
   2009-10 Enrollment: 1,507 . . . . (630) 257-5838
Lemont-Bromberek CSD 113a (PK-08)
   2009-10 Enrollment: 2,593 . . . . (630) 257-2286
Housing: Homeownership rate: 84.9% (2010); Median home value: $326,459 (2010); Median contract rent: $830 per month (2005-2009 5-year est.); Median year structure built: 1989 (2005-2009 5-year est.).
Safety: Violent crime rate: 3.1 per 10,000 population; Property crime rate: 103.8 per 10,000 population (2010).

Newspapers: Oak Forest-Palos Heights Villager (Local news; Circulation 1,000); Palos Hills-Palos Park Villager (Local news; Circulation 900); Tinley Park-Crestwood Villager (Local news; Circulation 1,100)

Transportation: Commute to work: 91.3% car, 3.4% public transportation, 1.7% walk, 2.8% work from home (2005-2009 5-year est.); Travel time to work: 19.8% less than 15 minutes, 30.0% 15 to 30 minutes, 26.0% 30 to 45 minutes, 12.0% 45 to 60 minutes, 12.2% 60 minutes or more (2005-2009 5-year est.)

Additional Information Contacts

Lemont Area Chamber of Commerce . . . . (630) 257-5997
http://www.lemontchamber.com
Village of Lemont. . . . . (630) 257-1550
http://www.lemont.il.us

LINCOLNWOOD (village). Covers a land area of 2.687 square miles and a water area of 0 square miles. Located at 42.00° N. Lat; 87.73° W. Long. Elevation is 604 feet.

History: Named for Abraham Lincoln, 16th President of the U.S. Until 1935 called Tessville.

Population: 11,365 (1990); 12,359 (2000); 12,112 (2010); 11,958 (2015 projected); Race: 69.8% White, 0.5% Black, 24.7% Asian, 5.1% Other, 5.2% Hispanic of any race (2010); Density: 4,507.8 persons per square mile (2010); Average household size: 2.74 (2010); Median age: 46.1 (2010); Males per 100 females: 90.8 (2010); Marriage status: 26.2% never married, 59.7% now married, 8.3% widowed, 5.8% divorced (2005-2009 5-year est.); Foreign born: 36.6% (2005-2009 5-year est.); Ancestry (includes multiple ancestries): 8.0% German, 7.8% Russian, 7.6% Greek, 6.5% Polish, 6.3% Assyrian/Chaldean/Syriac (2005-2009 5-year est.).

Economy: Single-family building permits issued: 0 (2010); Multi-family building permits issued: 0 (2010); Employment by occupation: 20.5% management, 29.1% professional, 9.4% services, 28.5% sales, 0.0% farming, 6.0% construction, 6.4% production (2005-2009 5-year est.).

Income: Per capita income: $41,078 (2010); Median household income: $82,014 (2010); Average household income: $113,172 (2010); Percent of households with income of $100,000 or more: 39.1% (2010); Poverty rate: 5.2% (2005-2009 5-year est.).

Taxes: Total city taxes per capita: $1,167 (2007); City property taxes per capita: $559 (2007).

Education: Percent of population age 25 and over with: High school diploma (including GED) or higher: 92.6% (2010); Bachelor's degree or higher: 53.1% (2010); Master's degree or higher: 23.5% (2010).

School District(s)

Lincolnwood SD 74 (PK-08)
    2009-10 Enrollment: 1,221 . . . . (847) 675-8234

Housing: Homeownership rate: 91.5% (2010); Median home value: $442,737 (2010); Median contract rent: $1,412 per month (2005-2009 5-year est.); Median year structure built: 1958 (2005-2009 5-year est.).

Safety: Violent crime rate: 11.2 per 10,000 population; Property crime rate: 418.7 per 10,000 population (2010).

Newspapers: Elmwood Park/River Grove Times (Community news; Circulation 2,497); Evanston Review (Community news; Circulation 4,500); Glenview Announcements (Community news; Circulation 4,500); Harlem/Foster Times (Community news; Circulation 4,252); Niles Herald-Spectator (Local news; Circulation 4,500); North Center/Lincoln Belmont/Lakeview Booster (Community news; Circulation 4,500); North Town/Rogers Park/Edgewater/Ravenswood News-Star (Community news; Circulation 4,500); Park Ridge Advocate (Local news; Circulation 4,500); Wheeling Countryside (Community news; Circulation 4,500); Winnetka Talk (Community news; Circulation 4,500)

Transportation: Commute to work: 88.8% car, 4.5% public transportation, 0.8% walk, 5.7% work from home (2005-2009 5-year est.); Travel time to work: 21.4% less than 15 minutes, 29.5% 15 to 30 minutes, 28.7% 30 to 45 minutes, 13.0% 45 to 60 minutes, 7.4% 60 minutes or more (2005-2009 5-year est.)

Additional Information Contacts

Lincolnwood Chamber of Commerce & Industry . . . . (847) 679-5760
http://www.lincolnwoodchamber.org
Village of Lincolnwood. . . . . (847) 673-1540
http://www.lincolnwoodil.org

LYNWOOD (village). Covers a land area of 4.925 square miles and a water area of 0.070 square miles. Located at 41.52° N. Lat; 87.54° W. Long. Elevation is 617 feet.

Population: 6,721 (1990); 7,377 (2000); 7,724 (2010); 7,872 (2015 projected); Race: 45.8% White, 48.1% Black, 1.3% Asian, 4.8% Other,

5.4% Hispanic of any race (2010); Density: 1,568.3 persons per square mile (2010); Average household size: 2.76 (2010); Median age: 35.9 (2010); Males per 100 females: 92.0 (2010); Marriage status: 38.8% never married, 45.9% now married, 5.3% widowed, 10.0% divorced (2005-2009 5-year est.); Foreign born: 4.4% (2005-2009 5-year est.); Ancestry (includes multiple ancestries): 10.3% German, 6.2% Polish, 5.2% Irish, 4.5% Italian, 3.1% English (2005-2009 5-year est.).

Economy: Single-family building permits issued: 76 (2010); Multi-family building permits issued: 0 (2010); Employment by occupation: 15.6% management, 21.7% professional, 11.1% services, 25.0% sales, 0.0% farming, 12.8% construction, 13.8% production (2005-2009 5-year est.).

Income: Per capita income: $27,354 (2010); Median household income: $66,519 (2010); Average household income: $75,269 (2010); Percent of households with income of $100,000 or more: 24.2% (2010); Poverty rate: 13.0% (2005-2009 5-year est.).

Taxes: Total city taxes per capita: $296 (2007); City property taxes per capita: $146 (2007).

Education: Percent of population age 25 and over with: High school diploma (including GED) or higher: 91.6% (2010); Bachelor's degree or higher: 23.9% (2010); Master's degree or higher: 8.6% (2010).

School District(s)

Sandridge SD 172 (PK-08)
    2009-10 Enrollment: 447 . . . . (708) 895-8339

Housing: Homeownership rate: 90.6% (2010); Median home value: $170,532 (2010); Median contract rent: $784 per month (2005-2009 5-year est.); Median year structure built: 1985 (2005-2009 5-year est.).

Transportation: Commute to work: 88.9% car, 8.4% public transportation, 0.3% walk, 1.0% work from home (2005-2009 5-year est.); Travel time to work: 13.2% less than 15 minutes, 26.4% 15 to 30 minutes, 18.7% 30 to 45 minutes, 14.7% 45 to 60 minutes, 27.0% 60 minutes or more (2005-2009 5-year est.)

Additional Information Contacts

Lynwood Chamber of Commerce . . . . (708) 758-6101
http://www.ynns.com/lcc/location.php
Village of Lynwood. . . . . (708) 758-6101
http://www.lynwoodil.us

LYONS (village). Covers a land area of 2.207 square miles and a water area of 0.048 square miles. Located at 41.81° N. Lat; 87.82° W. Long. Elevation is 620 feet.

History: Lyons was established near the portage between the Chicago and Des Plaines Rivers, used by Marquette and Jolliet. Lyons developed as a residential community.

Population: 9,828 (1990); 10,255 (2000); 9,956 (2010); 9,791 (2015 projected); Race: 79.9% White, 1.4% Black, 1.7% Asian, 16.9% Other, 25.2% Hispanic of any race (2010); Density: 4,511.3 persons per square mile (2010); Average household size: 2.60 (2010); Median age: 37.9 (2010); Males per 100 females: 100.3 (2010); Marriage status: 32.6% never married, 50.3% now married, 5.3% widowed, 11.8% divorced (2005-2009 5-year est.); Foreign born: 19.0% (2005-2009 5-year est.); Ancestry (includes multiple ancestries): 18.5% Polish, 15.6% German, 14.2% Irish, 6.0% Czech, 5.7% Italian (2005-2009 5-year est.).

Economy: Single-family building permits issued: 0 (2010); Multi-family building permits issued: 0 (2010); Employment by occupation: 12.7% management, 12.1% professional, 15.1% services, 28.9% sales, 0.0% farming, 9.4% construction, 21.8% production (2005-2009 5-year est.).

Income: Per capita income: $23,428 (2010); Median household income: $51,224 (2010); Average household income: $61,065 (2010); Percent of households with income of $100,000 or more: 12.6% (2010); Poverty rate: 7.2% (2005-2009 5-year est.).

Taxes: Total city taxes per capita: $423 (2007); City property taxes per capita: $332 (2007).

Education: Percent of population age 25 and over with: High school diploma (including GED) or higher: 83.9% (2010); Bachelor's degree or higher: 18.8% (2010); Master's degree or higher: 7.4% (2010).

School District(s)

Intermediate Service Center 2 (06-12)
    2009-10 Enrollment: n/a . . . . (708) 544-4890
Lyons SD 103 (PK-08)
    2009-10 Enrollment: 2,452 . . . . (708) 783-4100

Housing: Homeownership rate: 65.6% (2010); Median home value: $189,338 (2010); Median contract rent: $759 per month (2005-2009 5-year est.); Median year structure built: 1957 (2005-2009 5-year est.).

Safety: Violent crime rate: 20.8 per 10,000 population; Property crime rate: 259.1 per 10,000 population (2010).

Transportation: Commute to work: 87.9% car, 7.3% public transportation, 1.3% walk, 3.0% work from home (2005-2009 5-year est.); Travel time to work: 19.5% less than 15 minutes, 31.2% 15 to 30 minutes, 26.0% 30 to 45 minutes, 16.0% 45 to 60 minutes, 7.2% 60 minutes or more (2005-2009 5-year est.)

Additional Information Contacts
Village of Lyons . . . . (708) 442-4500
   http://www.villageoflyons-il.net

MARKHAM (city). Covers a land area of 5.214 square miles and a water area of 0 square miles. Located at 41.59° N. Lat; 87.69° W. Long. Elevation is 620 feet.

History: Named for Charles H. Markham, president of the Illinois Central railroad. Native prairie preserved at Indian Boundaries Prairies. Incorporated 1925.

Population: 13,126 (1990); 12,620 (2000); 12,138 (2010); 11,828 (2015 projected); Race: 16.8% White, 77.4% Black, 0.8% Asian, 5.0% Other, 5.0% Hispanic of any race (2010); Density: 2,328.1 persons per square mile (2010); Average household size: 3.24 (2010); Median age: 32.7 (2010); Males per 100 females: 88.8 (2010); Marriage status: 43.7% never married, 39.2% now married, 6.6% widowed, 10.5% divorced (2005-2009 5-year est.); Foreign born: 4.9% (2005-2009 5-year est.); Ancestry (includes multiple ancestries): 3.1% German, 1.6% Irish, 1.2% Polish, 1.1% English, 0.9% Italian (2005-2009 5-year est.).

Economy: Single-family building permits issued: 11 (2010); Multi-family building permits issued: 0 (2010); Employment by occupation: 6.6% management, 15.1% professional, 21.7% services, 33.2% sales, 0.0% farming, 8.0% construction, 15.4% production (2005-2009 5-year est.).

Income: Per capita income: $16,950 (2010); Median household income: $46,544 (2010); Average household income: $54,424 (2010); Percent of households with income of $100,000 or more: 10.4% (2010); Poverty rate: 22.1% (2005-2009 5-year est.).

Taxes: Total city taxes per capita: $754 (2007); City property taxes per capita: $600 (2007).

Education: Percent of population age 25 and over with: High school diploma (including GED) or higher: 83.1% (2010); Bachelor's degree or higher: 12.6% (2010); Master's degree or higher: 4.0% (2010).

School District(s)
Hazel Crest SD 152-5 (PK-08)
   2009-10 Enrollment: 1,081 . . . . (708) 335-0790
Prairie-Hills ESD 144 (PK-08)
   2009-10 Enrollment: 2,931 . . . . (708) 210-2888

Housing: Homeownership rate: 86.6% (2010); Median home value: $110,079 (2010); Median contract rent: $923 per month (2005-2009 5-year est.); Median year structure built: 1961 (2005-2009 5-year est.).

Newspapers: Westside Journal (Local news; Circulation 37,000)

Transportation: Commute to work: 82.3% car, 13.5% public transportation, 0.8% walk, 1.9% work from home (2005-2009 5-year est.); Travel time to work: 25.2% less than 15 minutes, 29.8% 15 to 30 minutes, 21.3% 30 to 45 minutes, 8.9% 45 to 60 minutes, 14.8% 60 minutes or more (2005-2009 5-year est.)

Additional Information Contacts
City of Markham. . . . . (708) 331-4905
   http://cityofmarkham.net

MATTESON (village). Covers a land area of 7.138 square miles and a water area of 0.069 square miles. Located at 41.51° N. Lat; 87.73° W. Long. Elevation is 692 feet.

Population: 11,920 (1990); 12,928 (2000); 15,571 (2010); 16,173 (2015 projected); Race: 29.1% White, 66.5% Black, 1.3% Asian, 3.2% Other, 3.9% Hispanic of any race (2010); Density: 2,181.5 persons per square mile (2010); Average household size: 2.75 (2010); Median age: 39.7 (2010); Males per 100 females: 86.9 (2010); Marriage status: 28.4% never married, 53.2% now married, 6.2% widowed, 12.2% divorced (2005-2009 5-year est.); Foreign born: 2.9% (2005-2009 5-year est.); Ancestry (includes multiple ancestries): 6.7% German, 6.0% Irish, 3.5% Polish, 2.7% Italian, 1.9% English (2005-2009 5-year est.).

Economy: Single-family building permits issued: 7 (2010); Multi-family building permits issued: 0 (2010); Employment by occupation: 16.3% management, 25.5% professional, 12.1% services, 24.1% sales, 0.0% farming, 8.9% construction, 13.0% production (2005-2009 5-year est.).

Income: Per capita income: $30,493 (2010); Median household income: $69,282 (2010); Average household income: $84,148 (2010); Percent of households with income of $100,000 or more: 29.4% (2010); Poverty rate: 6.7% (2005-2009 5-year est.).

Taxes: Total city taxes per capita: $661 (2007); City property taxes per capita: $544 (2007).

Education: Percent of population age 25 and over with: High school diploma (including GED) or higher: 92.1% (2010); Bachelor's degree or higher: 29.8% (2010); Master's degree or higher: 10.8% (2010).

School District(s)
ESD 159 (PK-08)
   2009-10 Enrollment: 2,104 . . . . (708) 720-1300
Matteson ESD 162 (PK-08)
   2009-10 Enrollment: 3,296 . . . . (708) 748-0100

Housing: Homeownership rate: 85.7% (2010); Median home value: $183,636 (2010); Median contract rent: $853 per month (2005-2009 5-year est.); Median year structure built: 1987 (2005-2009 5-year est.).

Transportation: Commute to work: 84.9% car, 12.3% public transportation, 0.5% walk, 1.4% work from home (2005-2009 5-year est.); Travel time to work: 14.3% less than 15 minutes, 25.8% 15 to 30 minutes, 23.6% 30 to 45 minutes, 15.5% 45 to 60 minutes, 20.9% 60 minutes or more (2005-2009 5-year est.)

Additional Information Contacts
Matteson Area Chamber of Commerce . . . . (708) 747-6000
   http://www.macclink.com
Village of Matteson . . . . (708) 283-4900
   http://www.villageofmatteson.org

MAYWOOD (village). Covers a land area of 2.708 square miles and a water area of 0 square miles. Located at 41.88° N. Lat; 87.84° W. Long. Elevation is 627 feet.

History: Named for May, the daugher of W. T. Nichols, owner of the town site. Maywood developed in the 1880's, when industrial growth in the Chicago area created a need for more residential areas.

Population: 27,139 (1990); 26,987 (2000); 24,114 (2010); 22,882 (2015 projected); Race: 10.4% White, 79.2% Black, 0.3% Asian, 10.1% Other, 14.8% Hispanic of any race (2010); Density: 8,904.7 persons per square mile (2010); Average household size: 3.40 (2010); Median age: 32.4 (2010); Males per 100 females: 89.7 (2010); Marriage status: 44.4% never married, 38.6% now married, 6.8% widowed, 10.2% divorced (2005-2009 5-year est.); Foreign born: 9.6% (2005-2009 5-year est.); Ancestry (includes multiple ancestries): 1.5% African, 1.2% Irish, 1.1% German, 0.7% Italian, 0.4% Barbadian (2005-2009 5-year est.).

Economy: Unemployment rate: 17.3% (August 2011); Total civilian labor force: 11,947 (August 2011); Single-family building permits issued: 0 (2010); Multi-family building permits issued: 0 (2010); Employment by occupation: 6.6% management, 13.5% professional, 20.8% services, 28.7% sales, 0.1% farming, 7.4% construction, 22.9% production (2005-2009 5-year est.).

Income: Per capita income: $17,351 (2010); Median household income: $48,543 (2010); Average household income: $59,076 (2010); Percent of households with income of $100,000 or more: 14.6% (2010); Poverty rate: 15.2% (2005-2009 5-year est.).

Taxes: Total city taxes per capita: $868 (2007); City property taxes per capita: $711 (2007).

Education: Percent of population age 25 and over with: High school diploma (including GED) or higher: 80.5% (2010); Bachelor's degree or higher: 13.1% (2010); Master's degree or higher: 5.0% (2010).

School District(s)
Maywood-Melrose Park-Broadview 89 (PK-08)
   2009-10 Enrollment: 5,640 . . . . (708) 450-2460
Proviso Area Exceptional Child (PK-12)
   2009-10 Enrollment: n/a . . . . (708) 450-2100
Proviso Twp HSD 209 (09-12)
   2009-10 Enrollment: 5,198 . . . . (708) 338-5912

Housing: Homeownership rate: 66.7% (2010); Median home value: $160,144 (2010); Median contract rent: $676 per month (2005-2009 5-year est.); Median year structure built: 1942 (2005-2009 5-year est.).

Hospitals: Loyola University Medical Center (589 beds)

Safety: Violent crime rate: 90.4 per 10,000 population; Property crime rate: 393.5 per 10,000 population (2010).

Transportation: Commute to work: 84.7% car, 8.5% public transportation, 2.9% walk, 3.2% work from home (2005-2009 5-year est.); Travel time to work: 20.9% less than 15 minutes, 31.9% 15 to 30 minutes, 27.8% 30 to 45 minutes, 8.5% 45 to 60 minutes, 10.9% 60 minutes or more (2005-2009 5-year est.)

Additional Information Contacts
Maywood Chamber of Commerce . . . . (708) 345-7077
   http://maywoodchamber.com

Village of Maywood . . . . (708) 450-6300
  http://www.maywood-il.org

MCCOOK (village). Covers a land area of 2.603 square miles and a
water area of 0.018 square miles. Located at 41.79° N. Lat; 87.83° W.
Long. Elevation is 617 feet.
Population: 235 (1990); 254 (2000); 284 (2010); 293 (2015 projected);
Race: 84.9% White, 0.0% Black, 0.0% Asian, 15.1% Other, 57.0%
Hispanic of any race (2010); Density: 109.1 persons per square mile
(2010); Average household size: 2.78 (2010); Median age: 33.5 (2010);
Males per 100 females: 129.0 (2010); Marriage status: 31.2% never
married, 48.9% now married, 10.1% widowed, 9.8% divorced (2005-2009
5-year est.); Foreign born: 9.3% (2005-2009 5-year est.); Ancestry
(includes multiple ancestries): 26.8% German, 26.0% Irish, 17.8%
Croatian, 17.0% Polish, 8.0% Italian (2005-2009 5-year est.).
Economy: Single-family building permits issued: 0 (2010); Multi-family
building permits issued: 0 (2010); Employment by occupation: 9.8%
management, 8.8% professional, 29.4% services, 28.4% sales, 0.0%
farming, 15.7% construction, 7.8% production (2005-2009 5-year est.).
Income: Per capita income: $20,591 (2010); Median household income:
$45,714 (2010); Average household income: $57,892 (2010); Percent of
households with income of $100,000 or more: 14.7% (2010); Poverty rate:
3.2% (2005-2009 5-year est.).
Taxes: Total city taxes per capita: $13,967 (2007); City property taxes per
capita: $8,154 (2007).
Education: Percent of population age 25 and over with: High school
diploma (including GED) or higher: 68.4% (2010); Bachelor's degree or
higher: 8.5% (2010); Master's degree or higher: 2.8% (2010).
Housing: Homeownership rate: 62.7% (2010); Median home value:
$40,000 (2010); Median contract rent: $763 per month (2005-2009 5-year
est.); Median year structure built: 1955 (2005-2009 5-year est.).
Safety: Violent crime rate: 474.1 per 10,000 population; Property crime
rate: 1,379.3 per 10,000 population (2010).
Transportation: Commute to work: 83.2% car, 8.9% public transportation,
5.9% walk, 2.0% work from home (2005-2009 5-year est.); Travel time to
work: 34.8% less than 15 minutes, 28.8% 15 to 30 minutes, 19.7% 30 to 45
minutes, 11.1% 45 to 60 minutes, 5.6% 60 minutes or more (2005-2009
5-year est.)

MELROSE PARK (village). Covers a land area of 4.239 square
miles and a water area of 0 square miles. Located at 41.90° N. Lat; 87.86°
W. Long. Elevation is 633 feet.
History: Named for Melrose in Roxburghshire, Scotland. Incorporated
1893.
Population: 20,859 (1990); 23,171 (2000); 22,077 (2010); 21,845 (2015
projected); Race: 64.6% White, 3.8% Black, 1.8% Asian, 29.8% Other,
65.4% Hispanic of any race (2010); Density: 5,207.6 persons per square
mile (2010); Average household size: 3.10 (2010); Median age: 33.5
(2010); Males per 100 females: 102.1 (2010); Marriage status: 34.3%
never married, 50.2% now married, 7.0% widowed, 8.6% divorced
(2005-2009 5-year est.); Foreign born: 38.8% (2005-2009 5-year est.);
Ancestry (includes multiple ancestries): 12.4% Italian, 6.4% Polish, 4.0%
German, 3.5% Irish, 0.9% American (2005-2009 5-year est.).
Economy: Single-family building permits issued: 3 (2010); Multi-family
building permits issued: 0 (2010); Employment by occupation: 7.4%
management, 9.5% professional, 21.6% services, 24.0% sales, 0.0%
farming, 10.6% construction, 26.8% production (2005-2009 5-year est.).
Income: Per capita income: $18,785 (2010); Median household income:
$47,239 (2010); Average household income: $58,365 (2010); Percent of
households with income of $100,000 or more: 13.3% (2010); Poverty rate:
16.4% (2005-2009 5-year est.).
Taxes: Total city taxes per capita: $862 (2007); City property taxes per
capita: $630 (2007).
Education: Percent of population age 25 and over with: High school
diploma (including GED) or higher: 66.5% (2010); Bachelor's degree or
higher: 11.8% (2010); Master's degree or higher: 5.4% (2010).
School District(s)
Bellwood SD 88 (PK-08)
  2009-10 Enrollment: 2,888 . . . . (708) 344-9344
Mannheim SD 83 (PK-09)
  2009-10 Enrollment: 2,705 . . . . (847) 455-4413
Maywood-Melrose Park-Broadview 89 (PK-08)
  2009-10 Enrollment: 5,640 . . . . (708) 450-2460

Two-year College(s)
Lincoln College of Technology (Private, For-profit)
  Fall 2009 Enrollment: 1,670. . . . . (708) 344-4700
Housing: Homeownership rate: 59.1% (2010); Median home value:
$229,077 (2010); Median contract rent: $706 per month (2005-2009 5-year
est.); Median year structure built: 1958 (2005-2009 5-year est.).
Hospitals: Gottlieb Memorial Hospital (250 beds); Westlake Community
Hospital (326 beds)
Safety: Violent crime rate: 26.6 per 10,000 population; Property crime rate:
293.4 per 10,000 population (2010).
Transportation: Commute to work: 86.6% car, 9.4% public transportation,
2.9% walk, 0.6% work from home (2005-2009 5-year est.); Travel time to
work: 29.8% less than 15 minutes, 30.5% 15 to 30 minutes, 24.5% 30 to 45
minutes, 8.4% 45 to 60 minutes, 6.8% 60 minutes or more (2005-2009
5-year est.)
Additional Information Contacts
Melrose Park Chamber of Commerce & Industry . . . . (708) 338-1007
  http://www.melroseparkchamber.org
Village of Melrose Park . . . . (708) 343-4000
  http://www.melrosepark.org

MERRIONETTE PARK (village). Covers a land area of 0.377
square miles and a water area of 0 square miles. Located at 41.68° N. Lat;
87.69° W. Long. Elevation is 620 feet.
History: Incorporated 1947.
Population: 2,065 (1990); 1,999 (2000); 1,726 (2010); 1,633 (2015
projected); Race: 82.2% White, 13.3% Black, 0.5% Asian, 4.0% Other,
6.6% Hispanic of any race (2010); Density: 4,584.2 persons per square
mile (2010); Average household size: 2.18 (2010); Median age: 39.6
(2010); Males per 100 females: 97.3 (2010); Marriage status: 37.3% never
married, 36.5% now married, 10.4% widowed, 15.8% divorced (2005-2009
5-year est.); Foreign born: 4.8% (2005-2009 5-year est.); Ancestry
(includes multiple ancestries): 43.4% Irish, 26.4% German, 14.8% Italian,
11.0% Polish, 6.3% English (2005-2009 5-year est.).
Economy: Single-family building permits issued: 0 (2010); Multi-family
building permits issued: 0 (2010); Employment by occupation: 6.8%
management, 18.0% professional, 17.1% services, 37.6% sales, 0.0%
farming, 5.7% construction, 14.8% production (2005-2009 5-year est.).
Income: Per capita income: $24,743 (2010); Median household income:
$46,737 (2010); Average household income: $54,125 (2010); Percent of
households with income of $100,000 or more: 9.6% (2010); Poverty rate:
13.7% (2005-2009 5-year est.).
Taxes: Total city taxes per capita: $329 (2007); City property taxes per
capita: $224 (2007).
Education: Percent of population age 25 and over with: High school
diploma (including GED) or higher: 91.3% (2010); Bachelor's degree or
higher: 19.7% (2010); Master's degree or higher: 4.9% (2010).
School District(s)
Atwood Heights SD 125 (PK-08)
  2009-10 Enrollment: 728 . . . . (708) 371-0080
Vocational/Technical School(s)
Everest College-Merrionette Park (Private, For-profit)
  Fall 2009 Enrollment: 1,522. . . . . (708) 239-0055
  2010-11 Tuition: $15,193
Housing: Homeownership rate: 73.8% (2010); Median home value:
$141,827 (2010); Median contract rent: $745 per month (2005-2009 5-year
est.); Median year structure built: 1961 (2005-2009 5-year est.).
Transportation: Commute to work: 88.8% car, 5.0% public transportation,
2.1% walk, 0.0% work from home (2005-2009 5-year est.); Travel time to
work: 18.6% less than 15 minutes, 31.4% 15 to 30 minutes, 20.2% 30 to 45
minutes, 12.1% 45 to 60 minutes, 17.7% 60 minutes or more (2005-2009
5-year est.)

MIDLOTHIAN (village). Covers a land area of 2.829 square miles and
a water area of 0 square miles. Located at 41.62° N. Lat; 87.72° W. Long.
Elevation is 614 feet.
History: Named for the title of a novel by Sir Walter Scott. Incorporated
1927.
Population: 14,413 (1990); 14,315 (2000); 13,897 (2010); 13,704 (2015
projected); Race: 84.2% White, 7.6% Black, 2.0% Asian, 6.1% Other,
10.9% Hispanic of any race (2010); Density: 4,911.8 persons per square
mile (2010); Average household size: 2.71 (2010); Median age: 36.6
(2010); Males per 100 females: 96.5 (2010); Marriage status: 33.3% never
married, 48.1% now married, 6.6% widowed, 12.0% divorced (2005-2009
5-year est.); Foreign born: 8.5% (2005-2009 5-year est.); Ancestry

(includes multiple ancestries): 24.5% Irish, 24.0% German, 16.7% Polish, 9.8% Italian, 4.3% English (2005-2009 5-year est.).

Economy: Single-family building permits issued: 0 (2010); Multi-family building permits issued: 0 (2010); Employment by occupation: 12.6% management, 14.5% professional, 15.0% services, 28.3% sales, 0.2% farming, 13.3% construction, 16.1% production (2005-2009 5-year est.).

Income: Per capita income: $24,510 (2010); Median household income: $59,479 (2010); Average household income: $66,356 (2010); Percent of households with income of $100,000 or more: 18.3% (2010); Poverty rate: 11.0% (2005-2009 5-year est.).

Taxes: Total city taxes per capita: $180 (2007); City property taxes per capita: $73 (2007).

Education: Percent of population age 25 and over with: High school diploma (including GED) or higher: 89.3% (2010); Bachelor's degree or higher: 16.4% (2010); Master's degree or higher: 5.2% (2010).

School District(s)
Bremen CHSD 228 (09-12)
   2009-10 Enrollment: 5,533 . . . . (708) 389-1175
Eisenhower Cooperative (PK-08)
   2009-10 Enrollment: n/a . . . . (708) 389-7580
Midlothian SD 143 (PK-08)
   2009-10 Enrollment: 1,976 . . . . (708) 388-6450

Housing: Homeownership rate: 82.4% (2010); Median home value: $159,667 (2010); Median contract rent: $755 per month (2005-2009 5-year est.); Median year structure built: 1967 (2005-2009 5-year est.).

Safety: Violent crime rate: 31.4 per 10,000 population; Property crime rate: 258.2 per 10,000 population (2010).

Newspapers: Alsip Express (Community news; Circulation 4,460); Beverly News (Community news; Circulation 4,080); Bridgeview Independent (Community news; Circulation 2,740); Burbank/Stickney Independent (Community news; Circulation 6,110); Chicago Ridge Citizen (Community news; Circulation 2,915); Evergreen Park Courier (Community news; Circulation 4,410); Hickory Hills Citizen (Community news; Circulation 3,530); Midlothian/Bremen Messenger (Community news; Circulation 10,200); Mount Greenwood Express (Community news; Circulation 7,471); Oak Lawn Independent (Community news; Circulation 10,880); Orland Township Messenger (Community news; Circulation 3,788); Palos Citizen (Community news; Circulation 4,610); Scottsdale-Ashburn Independent (Community news; Circulation 5,975); Worth Citizen (Community news; Circulation 2,660)

Transportation: Commute to work: 85.7% car, 8.8% public transportation, 1.7% walk, 2.1% work from home (2005-2009 5-year est.); Travel time to work: 24.4% less than 15 minutes, 28.5% 15 to 30 minutes, 20.2% 30 to 45 minutes, 12.5% 45 to 60 minutes, 14.4% 60 minutes or more (2005-2009 5-year est.)

Additional Information Contacts
Midlothian Chamber of Commerce . . . . (708) 389-0020
   http://www.villageprofile.com/illinois/midlothian
Village of Midlothian. . . . . (708) 389-0200
   http://www.villageofmidlothian.net

MORTON GROVE (village). Covers a land area of 5.095 square miles and a water area of 0 square miles. Located at 42.04° N. Lat; 87.78° W. Long. Elevation is 623 feet.

History: Named for Marcus Morton, governor of Massachusetts (1840-1843). Incorporated 1895.

Population: 22,435 (1990); 22,451 (2000); 23,089 (2010); 23,218 (2015 projected); Race: 68.4% White, 0.8% Black, 26.6% Asian, 4.2% Other, 6.1% Hispanic of any race (2010); Density: 4,531.6 persons per square mile (2010); Average household size: 2.68 (2010); Median age: 47.1 (2010); Males per 100 females: 91.4 (2010); Marriage status: 24.2% never married, 60.4% now married, 9.3% widowed, 6.1% divorced (2005-2009 5-year est.); Foreign born: 36.1% (2005-2009 5-year est.); Ancestry (includes multiple ancestries): 16.4% German, 13.7% Polish, 10.0% Irish, 5.0% Italian, 4.4% Greek (2005-2009 5-year est.).

Economy: Single-family building permits issued: 1 (2010); Multi-family building permits issued: 11 (2010); Employment by occupation: 17.0% management, 25.3% professional, 12.5% services, 26.3% sales, 0.1% farming, 7.2% construction, 11.7% production (2005-2009 5-year est.).

Income: Per capita income: $32,928 (2010); Median household income: $74,386 (2010); Average household income: $88,835 (2010); Percent of households with income of $100,000 or more: 33.3% (2010); Poverty rate: 4.5% (2005-2009 5-year est.).

Taxes: Total city taxes per capita: $979 (2007); City property taxes per capita: $612 (2007).

Education: Percent of population age 25 and over with: High school diploma (including GED) or higher: 90.8% (2010); Bachelor's degree or higher: 38.3% (2010); Master's degree or higher: 13.1% (2010).

School District(s)
East Maine SD 63 (PK-08)
   2009-10 Enrollment: 3,569 . . . . (847) 299-1900
Golf ESD 67 (PK-08)
   2009-10 Enrollment: 564 . . . . (847) 966-8200
Morton Grove SD 70 (PK-08)
   2009-10 Enrollment: 833 . . . . (847) 965-6200
Niles Twp District for Spec Educ (PK-12)
   2009-10 Enrollment: n/a . . . . (847) 965-9040
Skokie SD 69 (PK-08)
   2009-10 Enrollment: 1,705 . . . . (847) 675-7666

Housing: Homeownership rate: 93.9% (2010); Median home value: $308,799 (2010); Median contract rent: $747 per month (2005-2009 5-year est.); Median year structure built: 1959 (2005-2009 5-year est.).

Safety: Violent crime rate: 5.0 per 10,000 population; Property crime rate: 178.6 per 10,000 population (2010).

Transportation: Commute to work: 86.1% car, 8.0% public transportation, 0.5% walk, 4.2% work from home (2005-2009 5-year est.); Travel time to work: 19.8% less than 15 minutes, 34.6% 15 to 30 minutes, 27.5% 30 to 45 minutes, 9.4% 45 to 60 minutes, 8.8% 60 minutes or more (2005-2009 5-year est.)

Additional Information Contacts
Morton Grove Chamber of Commerce & Industry . . . . (847) 965-0330
   http://chamber.mgcci.org
Village of Morton Grove. . . . . (847) 965-4100
   http://www.mortongroveil.org

MOUNT PROSPECT (village). Covers a land area of 10.206 square miles and a water area of 0.036 square miles. Located at 42.06° N. Lat; 87.93° W. Long. Elevation is 669 feet.

History: Named for its high location, and for the hope that newcomers would view the town as a good place to settle. Incorporated 1917.

Population: 53,114 (1990); 56,265 (2000); 54,473 (2010); 53,579 (2015 projected); Race: 75.7% White, 1.9% Black, 13.7% Asian, 8.7% Other, 16.7% Hispanic of any race (2010); Density: 5,337.5 persons per square mile (2010); Average household size: 2.62 (2010); Median age: 39.2 (2010); Males per 100 females: 100.1 (2010); Marriage status: 27.6% never married, 58.8% now married, 7.0% widowed, 6.6% divorced (2005-2009 5-year est.); Foreign born: 30.1% (2005-2009 5-year est.); Ancestry (includes multiple ancestries): 24.0% German, 18.1% Polish, 13.6% Irish, 9.4% Italian, 4.2% English (2005-2009 5-year est.).

Economy: Unemployment rate: 7.8% (August 2011); Total civilian labor force: 29,702 (August 2011); Single-family building permits issued: 3 (2010); Multi-family building permits issued: 0 (2010); Employment by occupation: 17.3% management, 22.3% professional, 13.8% services, 26.4% sales, 0.0% farming, 7.1% construction, 13.0% production (2005-2009 5-year est.).

Income: Per capita income: $31,503 (2010); Median household income: $66,829 (2010); Average household income: $82,441 (2010); Percent of households with income of $100,000 or more: 27.7% (2010); Poverty rate: 5.9% (2005-2009 5-year est.).

Taxes: Total city taxes per capita: $701 (2007); City property taxes per capita: $444 (2007).

Education: Percent of population age 25 and over with: High school diploma (including GED) or higher: 88.8% (2010); Bachelor's degree or higher: 39.6% (2010); Master's degree or higher: 13.9% (2010).

School District(s)
Comm Cons SD 59 (PK-08)
   2009-10 Enrollment: 6,255 . . . . (847) 593-4300
Mount Prospect SD 57 (PK-08)
   2009-10 Enrollment: 2,145 . . . . (847) 394-7300
River Trails SD 26 (PK-08)
   2009-10 Enrollment: 1,485 . . . . (847) 297-4120
Township HSD 214 (09-12)
   2009-10 Enrollment: 12,241 . . . . (847) 718-7600
Wheeling CCSD 21 (PK-08)
   2009-10 Enrollment: 6,952 . . . . (847) 537-8270

Four-year College(s)
Christian Life College (Private, Not-for-profit, Other Protestant)
   Fall 2009 Enrollment: 44 . . . . (847) 259-1840
   2010-11 Tuition: In-state $10,590; Out-of-state $10,590

ITT Technical Institute-Mount Prospect (Private, For-profit)
Fall 2009 Enrollment: 549 . . . . (847) 375-8800
2010-11 Tuition: In-state $18,048; Out-of-state $18,048
Housing: Homeownership rate: 73.4% (2010); Median home value:
$282,300 (2010); Median contract rent: $825 per month (2005-2009 5-year
est.); Median year structure built: 1968 (2005-2009 5-year est.).
Safety: Violent crime rate: 6.7 per 10,000 population; Property crime rate:
127.6 per 10,000 population (2010).
Transportation: Commute to work: 85.2% car, 6.8% public transportation,
2.6% walk, 3.2% work from home (2005-2009 5-year est.); Travel time to
work: 23.1% less than 15 minutes, 32.7% 15 to 30 minutes, 25.5% 30 to 45
minutes, 8.3% 45 to 60 minutes, 10.4% 60 minutes or more (2005-2009
5-year est.)
Additional Information Contacts
Mount Prospect Chamber of Commerce . . . . (847) 398-6616
http://www.mountprospectchamber.org
Village of Mount Prospect . . . . (847) 392-6000
http://www.mountprospect.org

NILES (village). Covers a land area of 5.875 square miles and a water area of 0 square miles. Located at 42.03° N. Lat; 87.81° W. Long. Elevation is 636 feet.

History: Named for Niles, New York. Settled 1832. Incorporated 1899. The
village has a half size replica of the leaning tower of Pisa. Niles College of
Loyola University is here.
Population: 28,533 (1990); 30,068 (2000); 29,858 (2010); 29,815 (2015
projected); Race: 76.9% White, 0.6% Black, 17.2% Asian, 5.3% Other,
6.8% Hispanic of any race (2010); Density: 5,082.1 persons per square
mile (2010); Average household size: 2.41 (2010); Median age: 49.7
(2010); Males per 100 females: 87.6 (2010); Marriage status: 26.8% never
married, 54.3% now married, 11.8% widowed, 7.0% divorced (2005-2009
5-year est.); Foreign born: 42.0% (2005-2009 5-year est.); Ancestry
(includes multiple ancestries): 21.1% Polish, 13.4% German, 8.8% Italian,
8.7% Irish, 4.9% Assyrian/Chaldean/Syriac (2005-2009 5-year est.).
Economy: Unemployment rate: 9.1% (August 2011); Total civilian labor
force: 14,039 (August 2011); Single-family building permits issued: 3
(2010); Multi-family building permits issued: 0 (2010); Employment by
occupation: 11.0% management, 20.7% professional, 15.3% services,
30.6% sales, 0.0% farming, 9.3% construction, 13.1% production
(2005-2009 5-year est.).
Income: Per capita income: $28,661 (2010); Median household income:
$59,428 (2010); Average household income: $71,036 (2010); Percent of
households with income of $100,000 or more: 21.1% (2010); Poverty rate:
6.3% (2005-2009 5-year est.).
Taxes: Total city taxes per capita: $786 (2007); City property taxes per
capita: $209 (2007).
Education: Percent of population age 25 and over with: High school
diploma (including GED) or higher: 86.1% (2010); Bachelor's degree or
higher: 29.3% (2010); Master's degree or higher: 10.7% (2010).
School District(s)
East Maine SD 63 (PK-08)
2009-10 Enrollment: 3,569 . . . . (847) 299-1900
Niles ESD 71 (PK-08)
2009-10 Enrollment: 537 . . . . (847) 470-3407
Park Ridge CCSD 64 (PK-08)
2009-10 Enrollment: 4,291 . . . . (847) 318-4300
Vocational/Technical School(s)
Niles School of Cosmetology (Private, For-profit)
Fall 2009 Enrollment: 100 . . . . (847) 965-8061
2010-11 Tuition: $9,095
Housing: Homeownership rate: 79.8% (2010); Median home value:
$286,449 (2010); Median contract rent: $817 per month (2005-2009 5-year
est.); Median year structure built: 1964 (2005-2009 5-year est.).
Newspapers: Niles Bugle (Community news; Circulation 34,000)
Transportation: Commute to work: 87.5% car, 6.7% public transportation,
2.1% walk, 2.2% work from home (2005-2009 5-year est.); Travel time to
work: 24.1% less than 15 minutes, 33.9% 15 to 30 minutes, 24.4% 30 to 45
minutes, 8.6% 45 to 60 minutes, 8.9% 60 minutes or more (2005-2009
5-year est.)
Additional Information Contacts
Niles Chamber of Commerce . . . . (847) 268-8180
http://www.nileschamber.org
Village of Niles . . . . (847) 588-8000
http://www.vniles.com

NORRIDGE (village). Covers a land area of 1.820 square miles and a water area of 0 square miles. Located at 41.96° N. Lat; 87.82° W. Long. Elevation is 640 feet.

History: Named for two nearby residential areas, Norwood and Park
Ridge. Incorporated 1948.
Population: 14,463 (1990); 14,582 (2000); 14,047 (2010); 13,692 (2015
projected); Race: 92.5% White, 0.2% Black, 3.7% Asian, 3.6% Other, 5.5%
Hispanic of any race (2010); Density: 7,719.6 persons per square mile
(2010); Average household size: 2.44 (2010); Median age: 49.4 (2010);
Males per 100 females: 88.3 (2010); Marriage status: 24.4% never married,
49.7% now married, 16.1% widowed, 9.8% divorced (2005-2009 5-year
est.); Foreign born: 35.3% (2005-2009 5-year est.); Ancestry (includes
multiple ancestries): 31.7% Polish, 26.0% Italian, 14.7% German, 8.4%
Irish, 4.9% Greek (2005-2009 5-year est.).
Economy: Single-family building permits issued: 2 (2010); Multi-family
building permits issued: 0 (2010); Employment by occupation: 13.9%
management, 14.4% professional, 15.5% services, 29.0% sales, 0.0%
farming, 13.9% construction, 13.3% production (2005-2009 5-year est.).
Income: Per capita income: $27,529 (2010); Median household income:
$56,180 (2010); Average household income: $68,363 (2010); Percent of
households with income of $100,000 or more: 19.3% (2010); Poverty rate:
4.1% (2005-2009 5-year est.).
Taxes: Total city taxes per capita: $417 (2007); City property taxes per
capita: $0 (2007).
Education: Percent of population age 25 and over with: High school
diploma (including GED) or higher: 80.0% (2010); Bachelor's degree or
higher: 19.0% (2010); Master's degree or higher: 6.2% (2010).
School District(s)
Norridge SD 80 (PK-08)
2009-10 Enrollment: 969 . . . . (708) 583-2068
Pennoyer SD 79 (PK-08)
2009-10 Enrollment: 405 . . . . (708) 456-9094
Ridgewood CHSD 234 (09-12)
2009-10 Enrollment: 879 . . . . (708) 456-4242
Housing: Homeownership rate: 83.6% (2010); Median home value:
$303,462 (2010); Median contract rent: $746 per month (2005-2009 5-year
est.); Median year structure built: 1958 (2005-2009 5-year est.).
Safety: Violent crime rate: 10.2 per 10,000 population; Property crime rate:
394.5 per 10,000 population (2010).
Transportation: Commute to work: 86.9% car, 5.5% public transportation,
2.0% walk, 4.2% work from home (2005-2009 5-year est.); Travel time to
work: 23.5% less than 15 minutes, 32.3% 15 to 30 minutes, 26.3% 30 to 45
minutes, 12.2% 45 to 60 minutes, 5.7% 60 minutes or more (2005-2009
5-year est.)
Additional Information Contacts
Village of Norridge . . . . (708) 453-0800
http://www.villageofnorridge.com

NORTH RIVERSIDE (village). Covers a land area of 1.544 square miles and a water area of 0 square miles. Located at 41.84° N. Lat; 87.83° W. Long. Elevation is 617 feet.

Population: 6,005 (1990); 6,688 (2000); 6,555 (2010); 6,453 (2015
projected); Race: 84.0% White, 5.8% Black, 3.5% Asian, 6.7% Other,
13.5% Hispanic of any race (2010); Density: 4,245.1 persons per square
mile (2010); Average household size: 2.20 (2010); Median age: 48.6
(2010); Males per 100 females: 91.8 (2010); Marriage status: 27.7% never
married, 50.8% now married, 10.3% widowed, 11.2% divorced (2005-2009
5-year est.); Foreign born: 12.1% (2005-2009 5-year est.); Ancestry
(includes multiple ancestries): 21.4% German, 13.1% Italian, 12.4% Polish,
12.0% Czech, 8.9% Irish (2005-2009 5-year est.).
Economy: Single-family building permits issued: 0 (2010); Multi-family
building permits issued: 0 (2010); Employment by occupation: 15.7%
management, 20.0% professional, 14.7% services, 35.0% sales, 0.0%
farming, 4.7% construction, 10.0% production (2005-2009 5-year est.).
Income: Per capita income: $28,213 (2010); Median household income:
$55,371 (2010); Average household income: $65,032 (2010); Percent of
households with income of $100,000 or more: 16.5% (2010); Poverty rate:
6.6% (2005-2009 5-year est.).
Taxes: Total city taxes per capita: $906 (2007); City property taxes per
capita: $116 (2007).
Education: Percent of population age 25 and over with: High school
diploma (including GED) or higher: 85.8% (2010); Bachelor's degree or
higher: 28.0% (2010); Master's degree or higher: 9.9% (2010).

School District(s)

Komarek SD 94 (PK-08)

2009-10 Enrollment: 500 . . . . (708) 447-8030

Housing: Homeownership rate: 76.2% (2010); Median home value: $227,051 (2010); Median contract rent: $745 per month (2005-2009 5-year est.); Median year structure built: 1955 (2005-2009 5-year est.).

Safety: Violent crime rate: 26.3 per 10,000 population; Property crime rate: 888.1 per 10,000 population (2010).

Newspapers: Berwyn-Stickney-Forest View Life (Local news; Circulation 30,000); Cicero Life (Local news; Circulation 30,000)

Transportation: Commute to work: 83.7% car, 11.3% public transportation, 1.7% walk, 1.2% work from home (2005-2009 5-year est.); Travel time to work: 27.0% less than 15 minutes, 29.8% 15 to 30 minutes, 23.6% 30 to 45 minutes, 9.9% 45 to 60 minutes, 9.6% 60 minutes or more (2005-2009 5-year est.)

Additional Information Contacts

Village of North Riverside . . . . (708) 447-4211
http://www.northriverside-il.org

NORTHBROOK (village). Covers a land area of 12.919 square miles and a water area of 0.049 square miles. Located at 42.12° N. Lat; 87.84° W. Long. Elevation is 646 feet.

History: Named for the middle forks of the north branch of the Chicago River. It was incorporated as Shermerville in 1901 and was reincorporated as Northbrook in 1923. Once a farming community, Northbrook developed industry after the coming of a railroad in 1871. Settled 1836.

Population: 33,020 (1990); 33,435 (2000); 32,899 (2010); 32,821 (2015 projected); Race: 87.9% White, 0.6% Black, 9.8% Asian, 1.7% Other, 2.1% Hispanic of any race (2010); Density: 2,546.6 persons per square mile (2010); Average household size: 2.66 (2010); Median age: 46.1 (2010); Males per 100 females: 93.3 (2010); Marriage status: 20.9% never married, 65.5% now married, 6.4% widowed, 7.2% divorced (2005-2009 5-year est.); Foreign born: 16.3% (2005-2009 5-year est.); Ancestry (includes multiple ancestries): 15.7% German, 12.7% Russian, 10.8% Irish, 10.0% Polish, 8.3% English (2005-2009 5-year est.).

Economy: Unemployment rate: 7.7% (August 2011); Total civilian labor force: 17,090 (August 2011); Single-family building permits issued: 24 (2010); Multi-family building permits issued: 0 (2010); Employment by occupation: 28.9% management, 31.7% professional, 5.0% services, 28.7% sales, 0.0% farming, 2.1% construction, 3.5% production (2005-2009 5-year est.).

Income: Per capita income: $51,472 (2010); Median household income: $100,171 (2010); Average household income: $138,996 (2010); Percent of households with income of $100,000 or more: 50.1% (2010); Poverty rate: 2.9% (2005-2009 5-year est.).

Taxes: Total city taxes per capita: $762 (2007); City property taxes per capita: $415 (2007).

Education: Percent of population age 25 and over with: High school diploma (including GED) or higher: 96.9% (2010); Bachelor's degree or higher: 65.6% (2010); Master's degree or higher: 28.8% (2010).

School District(s)

Northbrook ESD 27 (PK-08)

2009-10 Enrollment: 1,222 . . . . (847) 498-2610

Northbrook SD 28 (PK-08)

2009-10 Enrollment: 1,710 . . . . (847) 498-7900

Northbrook/Glenview SD 30 (PK-08)

2009-10 Enrollment: 1,139 . . . . (847) 498-4190

Northern Suburban Spec Ed Dist (PK-12)

2009-10 Enrollment: n/a . . . . (847) 831-5100

Northfield Twp HSD 225 (09-12)

2009-10 Enrollment: 4,803 . . . . (847) 486-4700

West Northfield SD 31 (PK-08)

2009-10 Enrollment: 861 . . . . (847) 272-6880

Housing: Homeownership rate: 92.2% (2010); Median home value: $494,977 (2010); Median contract rent: $1,548 per month (2005-2009 5-year est.); Median year structure built: 1972 (2005-2009 5-year est.).

Safety: Violent crime rate: 2.4 per 10,000 population; Property crime rate: 134.6 per 10,000 population (2010).

Newspapers: Gardner Chronicle (Local news; Circulation 847)

Transportation: Commute to work: 81.8% car, 8.7% public transportation, 1.1% walk, 7.0% work from home (2005-2009 5-year est.); Travel time to work: 25.8% less than 15 minutes, 27.8% 15 to 30 minutes, 21.3% 30 to 45 minutes, 11.0% 45 to 60 minutes, 14.1% 60 minutes or more (2005-2009 5-year est.)

Additional Information Contacts

Northbrook Chamber of Commerce . . . . (847) 498-5555
http://www.northbrookchamber.org
Village of Northbrook . . . . (847) 272-5050
http://www.northbrook.il.us

NORTHFIELD (village). Covers a land area of 2.957 square miles and a water area of 0 square miles. Located at 42.10° N. Lat; 87.77° W. Long. Elevation is 633 feet.

History: The Village of Northfield was first settled in the mid-1800s by Mary Young and her two daughters near present day Bracken Lane. When the settlers first arrived, Northfield was a remote swamp.

Population: 4,913 (1990); 5,389 (2000); 5,541 (2010); 5,539 (2015 projected); Race: 91.5% White, 0.5% Black, 6.5% Asian, 1.5% Other, 2.1% Hispanic of any race (2010); Density: 1,873.8 persons per square mile (2010); Average household size: 2.56 (2010); Median age: 46.6 (2010); Males per 100 females: 93.6 (2010); Marriage status: 22.1% never married, 63.2% now married, 7.1% widowed, 7.7% divorced (2005-2009 5-year est.); Foreign born: 11.8% (2005-2009 5-year est.); Ancestry (includes multiple ancestries): 31.9% Irish, 28.7% German, 14.2% English, 8.6% Polish, 6.0% Russian (2005-2009 5-year est.).

Economy: Single-family building permits issued: 2 (2010); Multi-family building permits issued: 0 (2010); Employment by occupation: 20.7% management, 31.6% professional, 9.2% services, 31.2% sales, 0.0% farming, 4.2% construction, 3.1% production (2005-2009 5-year est.).

Income: Per capita income: $63,112 (2010); Median household income: $114,278 (2010); Average household income: $161,351 (2010); Percent of households with income of $100,000 or more: 55.8% (2010); Poverty rate: 2.0% (2005-2009 5-year est.).

Taxes: Total city taxes per capita: $1,023 (2007); City property taxes per capita: $566 (2007).

Education: Percent of population age 25 and over with: High school diploma (including GED) or higher: 98.0% (2010); Bachelor's degree or higher: 73.6% (2010); Master's degree or higher: 31.1% (2010).

School District(s)

New Trier Twp HSD 203 (09-12)

2009-10 Enrollment: 4,143 . . . . (847) 784-6109

Sunset Ridge SD 29 (PK-08)

2009-10 Enrollment: 512 . . . . (847) 881-9456

Housing: Homeownership rate: 94.4% (2010); Median home value: $637,795 (2010); Median contract rent: $1,264 per month (2005-2009 5-year est.); Median year structure built: 1959 (2005-2009 5-year est.).

Safety: Violent crime rate: 0.0 per 10,000 population; Property crime rate: 207.6 per 10,000 population (2010).

Transportation: Commute to work: 83.9% car, 5.2% public transportation, 4.5% walk, 5.9% work from home (2005-2009 5-year est.); Travel time to work: 34.8% less than 15 minutes, 25.5% 15 to 30 minutes, 23.6% 30 to 45 minutes, 9.8% 45 to 60 minutes, 6.4% 60 minutes or more (2005-2009 5-year est.)

Additional Information Contacts

Village of Northfield . . . . (847) 446-9200
http://www.northfieldil.org
Winnetka-Northfield Chamber of Commerce . . . . (847) 446-4451
http://www.northfieldchamber.org

NORTHLAKE (city). Aka North Lake. Covers a land area of 3.015 square miles and a water area of 0 square miles. Located at 41.91° N. Lat; 87.90° W. Long. Elevation is 646 feet.

History: St. John Vianney Roman Catholic Church, which is shaped like a fish, has the largest mosaic-tile mural in the Western Hemisphere. Incorporated 1949.

Population: 12,583 (1990); 11,878 (2000); 11,157 (2010); 10,875 (2015 projected); Race: 66.8% White, 3.1% Black, 3.5% Asian, 26.6% Other, 49.9% Hispanic of any race (2010); Density: 3,700.1 persons per square mile (2010); Average household size: 2.99 (2010); Median age: 37.6 (2010); Males per 100 females: 97.6 (2010); Marriage status: 27.4% never married, 52.1% now married, 11.6% widowed, 8.9% divorced (2005-2009 5-year est.); Foreign born: 30.4% (2005-2009 5-year est.); Ancestry (includes multiple ancestries): 11.6% Polish, 10.9% Italian, 10.6% German, 10.1% Irish, 3.7% English (2005-2009 5-year est.).

Economy: Single-family building permits issued: 0 (2010); Multi-family building permits issued: 0 (2010); Employment by occupation: 6.3% management, 10.7% professional, 16.5% services, 25.5% sales, 0.4% farming, 11.7% construction, 29.0% production (2005-2009 5-year est.).

Income: Per capita income: $21,714 (2010); Median household income: $59,625 (2010); Average household income: $65,810 (2010); Percent of

households with income of $100,000 or more: 18.1% (2010); Poverty rate: 4.8% (2005-2009 5-year est.).
Taxes: Total city taxes per capita: $930 (2007); City property taxes per capita: $493 (2007).
Education: Percent of population age 25 and over with: High school diploma (including GED) or higher: 73.1% (2010); Bachelor's degree or higher: 9.8% (2010); Master's degree or higher: 3.9% (2010).

School District(s)
Berkeley SD 87 (PK-08)
    2009-10 Enrollment: 2,905 . . . . (708) 449-3350
Leyden CHSD 212 (09-12)
    2009-10 Enrollment: 3,497 . . . . (847) 451-3000
Mannheim SD 83 (PK-09)
    2009-10 Enrollment: 2,705 . . . . (847) 455-4413
Housing: Homeownership rate: 79.5% (2010); Median home value: $204,273 (2010); Median contract rent: $721 per month (2005-2009 5-year est.); Median year structure built: 1957 (2005-2009 5-year est.).
Hospitals: Kindred Hospital-Northlake (94 beds)
Safety: Violent crime rate: 9.8 per 10,000 population; Property crime rate: 352.3 per 10,000 population (2010).
Transportation: Commute to work: 92.8% car, 3.5% public transportation, 0.4% walk, 2.3% work from home (2005-2009 5-year est.); Travel time to work: 24.7% less than 15 minutes, 36.2% 15 to 30 minutes, 23.7% 30 to 45 minutes, 10.0% 45 to 60 minutes, 5.4% 60 minutes or more (2005-2009 5-year est.)

Additional Information Contacts
City of Northlake . . . . (708) 343-8700
    http://www.northlakecity.com
Northlake Chamber of Commerce . . . . (708) 562-4200
    http://www.northlakecity.com/links_chamber.htm

OAK FOREST (city). Covers a land area of 5.649 square miles and a water area of 0.053 square miles. Located at 41.60° N. Lat; 87.75° W. Long. Elevation is 673 feet.
History: Named for the many oak trees in the area. In 1911 the Oak Forest Infirmary and Tuberculosis Hospital was established in the town of Oak Forest.
Population: 26,662 (1990); 28,051 (2000); 27,580 (2010); 27,460 (2015 projected); Race: 86.6% White, 4.7% Black, 3.5% Asian, 5.1% Other, 9.0% Hispanic of any race (2010); Density: 4,882.0 persons per square mile (2010); Average household size: 2.78 (2010); Median age: 38.1 (2010); Males per 100 females: 99.8 (2010); Marriage status: 29.7% never married, 56.2% now married, 5.2% widowed, 8.9% divorced (2005-2009 5-year est.); Foreign born: 7.7% (2005-2009 5-year est.); Ancestry (includes multiple ancestries): 28.6% Irish, 22.9% German, 19.5% Polish, 14.8% Italian, 5.3% Swedish (2005-2009 5-year est.).
Economy: Unemployment rate: 10.3% (August 2011); Total civilian labor force: 15,840 (August 2011); Single-family building permits issued: 4 (2010); Multi-family building permits issued: 0 (2010); Employment by occupation: 11.1% management, 20.2% professional, 16.6% services, 29.3% sales, 0.0% farming, 11.2% construction, 11.7% production (2005-2009 5-year est.).
Income: Per capita income: $28,836 (2010); Median household income: $71,307 (2010); Average household income: $81,669 (2010); Percent of households with income of $100,000 or more: 27.7% (2010); Poverty rate: 6.7% (2005-2009 5-year est.).
Taxes: Total city taxes per capita: $419 (2007); City property taxes per capita: $336 (2007).
Education: Percent of population age 25 and over with: High school diploma (including GED) or higher: 92.0% (2010); Bachelor's degree or higher: 25.6% (2010); Master's degree or higher: 8.0% (2010).

School District(s)
Arbor Park SD 145 (PK-08)
    2009-10 Enrollment: 1,456 . . . . (708) 687-8040
Bremen CHSD 228 (09-12)
    2009-10 Enrollment: 5,533 . . . . (708) 389-1175
Forest Ridge SD 142 (PK-08)
    2009-10 Enrollment: 1,652 . . . . (708) 687-3334
Prairie-Hills ESD 144 (PK-08)
    2009-10 Enrollment: 2,931 . . . . (708) 210-2888
Southwest Cook Coop Spec Ed (PK-12)
    2009-10 Enrollment: n/a . . . . (708) 687-0900
Tinley Park CCSD 146 (PK-08)
    2009-10 Enrollment: 2,343 . . . . (708) 614-4500

Vocational/Technical School(s)
Capri Oak Forest Beauty College (Private, For-profit)
    Fall 2009 Enrollment: 137 . . . . (708) 687-3020
    2010-11 Tuition: $17,450
Housing: Homeownership rate: 83.5% (2010); Median home value: $195,996 (2010); Median contract rent: $803 per month (2005-2009 5-year est.); Median year structure built: 1973 (2005-2009 5-year est.).
Hospitals: Oak Forest Hospital of Cook County (600 beds)
Safety: Violent crime rate: 14.3 per 10,000 population; Property crime rate: 167.9 per 10,000 population (2010).
Transportation: Commute to work: 88.3% car, 9.8% public transportation, 0.3% walk, 1.3% work from home (2005-2009 5-year est.); Travel time to work: 19.5% less than 15 minutes, 30.4% 15 to 30 minutes, 21.4% 30 to 45 minutes, 12.2% 45 to 60 minutes, 16.5% 60 minutes or more (2005-2009 5-year est.)

Additional Information Contacts
City of Oak Forest . . . . (708) 687-4050
    http://www.oak-forest.org
Oak Forest-Crestwood Area Chamber of Commerce . . . . . (708) 687-4600
    http://www.oc-chamber.org

OAK LAWN (village). Covers a land area of 8.595 square miles and a water area of <.001 square miles. Located at 41.71° N. Lat; 87.75° W. Long. Elevation is 597 feet.
History: Named for its many oak trees. Incorporated 1909.
Population: 56,325 (1990); 55,245 (2000); 52,284 (2010); 50,899 (2015 projected); Race: 90.5% White, 1.8% Black, 2.2% Asian, 5.5% Other, 7.9% Hispanic of any race (2010); Density: 6,082.8 persons per square mile (2010); Average household size: 2.43 (2010); Median age: 43.5 (2010); Males per 100 females: 89.9 (2010); Marriage status: 30.3% never married, 51.3% now married, 9.8% widowed, 8.6% divorced (2005-2009 5-year est.); Foreign born: 14.5% (2005-2009 5-year est.); Ancestry (includes multiple ancestries): 26.8% Irish, 21.4% Polish, 18.2% German, 11.4% Italian, 3.9% Lithuanian (2005-2009 5-year est.).
Economy: Unemployment rate: 11.3% (August 2011); Total civilian labor force: 26,535 (August 2011); Single-family building permits issued: 5 (2010); Multi-family building permits issued: 0 (2010); Employment by occupation: 13.0% management, 20.2% professional, 15.3% services, 27.8% sales, 0.1% farming, 11.4% construction, 12.2% production (2005-2009 5-year est.).
Income: Per capita income: $28,644 (2010); Median household income: $56,142 (2010); Average household income: $69,676 (2010); Percent of households with income of $100,000 or more: 20.7% (2010); Poverty rate: 6.6% (2005-2009 5-year est.).
Taxes: Total city taxes per capita: $484 (2007); City property taxes per capita: $333 (2007).
Education: Percent of population age 25 and over with: High school diploma (including GED) or higher: 88.0% (2010); Bachelor's degree or higher: 24.5% (2010); Master's degree or higher: 8.2% (2010).

School District(s)
A E R O Spec Educ Coop (PK-12)
    2009-10 Enrollment: n/a . . . . (708) 496-3330
Atwood Heights SD 125 (PK-08)
    2009-10 Enrollment: 728 . . . . (708) 371-0080
CHSD 218 (09-12)
    2009-10 Enrollment: 5,826 . . . . (708) 424-2000
Oak Lawn CHSD 229 (09-12)
    2009-10 Enrollment: 1,883 . . . . (708) 424-5200
Oak Lawn-Hometown SD 123 (PK-08)
    2009-10 Enrollment: 3,128 . . . . (708) 423-0150
Ridgeland SD 122 (PK-08)
    2009-10 Enrollment: 2,294 . . . . (708) 599-5550

Vocational/Technical School(s)
Cameo Beauty Academy (Private, For-profit)
    Fall 2009 Enrollment: 120 . . . . (708) 636-4660
    2010-11 Tuition: $16,675
Housing: Homeownership rate: 85.0% (2010); Median home value: $210,387 (2010); Median contract rent: $799 per month (2005-2009 5-year est.); Median year structure built: 1965 (2005-2009 5-year est.).
Hospitals: Advocate Christ Medical Center and Hope Children's Hospital (64 beds)
Safety: Violent crime rate: 17.1 per 10,000 population; Property crime rate: 214.1 per 10,000 population (2010).
Transportation: Commute to work: 87.7% car, 7.6% public transportation, 2.1% walk, 1.6% work from home (2005-2009 5-year est.); Travel time to

work: 23.9% less than 15 minutes, 25.6% 15 to 30 minutes, 24.1% 30 to 45 minutes, 12.2% 45 to 60 minutes, 14.2% 60 minutes or more (2005-2009 5-year est.)

Additional Information Contacts
Oak Lawn Chamber of Commerce . . . . (708) 424-8300
    http://www.oaklawnchamber.com
Village of Oak Lawn. . . . . (708) 636-4400
    http://www.oaklawn-il.gov

OAK PARK (village). Covers a land area of 4.701 square miles and a water area of 0 square miles. Located at 41.88° N. Lat; 87.79° W. Long. Elevation is 620 feet.

History: Oak Park was settled in 1833 by Joseph Kettlestrings, who came with his wife from Maryland. They named the village for the oak trees growing there. In the 1890's Oak Park was known as Saints' Rest because of its many churches. This was the site of one of Frank Lloyd Wright's early workshops and examples of his architecture graced the village.
Population: 53,648 (1990); 52,524 (2000); 48,529 (2010); 46,694 (2015 projected); Race: 66.2% White, 23.0% Black, 5.0% Asian, 5.8% Other, 5.8% Hispanic of any race (2010); Density: 10,323.5 persons per square mile (2010); Average household size: 2.23 (2010); Median age: 39.3 (2010); Males per 100 females: 89.0 (2010); Marriage status: 31.2% never married, 53.5% now married, 4.7% widowed, 10.6% divorced (2005-2009 5-year est.); Foreign born: 9.9% (2005-2009 5-year est.); Ancestry (includes multiple ancestries): 20.8% German, 19.2% Irish, 9.5% English, 8.4% Italian, 7.6% Polish (2005-2009 5-year est.).
Economy: Unemployment rate: 8.0% (August 2011); Total civilian labor force: 32,312 (August 2011); Single-family building permits issued: 2 (2010); Multi-family building permits issued: 0 (2010); Employment by occupation: 20.9% management, 40.6% professional, 9.1% services, 22.3% sales, 0.1% farming, 2.5% construction, 4.5% production (2005-2009 5-year est.).
Income: Per capita income: $45,311 (2010); Median household income: $71,401 (2010); Average household income: $101,221 (2010); Percent of households with income of $100,000 or more: 34.2% (2010); Poverty rate: 5.6% (2005-2009 5-year est.).
Taxes: Total city taxes per capita: $909 (2007); City property taxes per capita: $632 (2007).
Education: Percent of population age 25 and over with: High school diploma (including GED) or higher: 96.2% (2010); Bachelor's degree or higher: 66.0% (2010); Master's degree or higher: 33.4% (2010).

School District(s)
Intermediate Service Center 2 (06-12)
    2009-10 Enrollment: n/a . . . . (708) 544-4890
Oak Park - River Forest SD 200 (09-12)
    2009-10 Enrollment: 3,256 . . . . (708) 383-0700
Oak Park ESD 97 (PK-08)
    2009-10 Enrollment: 5,464 . . . . (708) 524-3000

Four-year College(s)
West Suburban College of Nursing (Private, Not-for-profit, Roman Catholic)
    Fall 2009 Enrollment: 252 . . . . (708) 763-6530
Housing: Homeownership rate: 59.8% (2010); Median home value: $313,591 (2010); Median contract rent: $853 per month (2005-2009 5-year est.); Median year structure built: before 1940 (2005-2009 5-year est.).
Hospitals: Rush Oak Park Hospital (296 beds); West Suburban Medical Center (245 beds)
Safety: Violent crime rate: 36.5 per 10,000 population; Property crime rate: 327.8 per 10,000 population (2010).
Newspapers: Austin Weekly News (Community news; Circulation 10,000); Chicago Journal (Local news; Circulation 3,600); Elm Leaves (Community news; Circulation 3,592); Forest Leaves (Community news; Circulation 2,403); Forest Park Review (Community news; Circulation 3,200); Franklin Park Herald-Journal (Local news; Circulation 3,010); Maywood Herald (Community news; Circulation 2,856); Melrose Park Herald (Community news; Circulation 1,775); Northlake Herald-Journal (Community news; Circulation 1,583); Oak Leaves (Community news; Circulation 10,031); River Grove Messenger (Community news; Circulation 1,177); Skyline (Community news; Circulation 28,503); Wednesday Journal (Community news; Circulation 14,500); West Proviso Herald (Community news; Circulation 2,292); Westchester Herald (Community news; Circulation 1,100); Wicker Park Booster (Local news; Circulation 10,064)
Transportation: Commute to work: 66.4% car, 21.4% public transportation, 4.1% walk, 5.6% work from home (2005-2009 5-year est.); Travel time to work: 19.7% less than 15 minutes, 23.2% 15 to 30 minutes,

32.7% 30 to 45 minutes, 14.9% 45 to 60 minutes, 9.5% 60 minutes or more (2005-2009 5-year est.)
Additional Information Contacts
Oak Park-River Forest Chamber of Commerce . . . . (708) 771-5760
    http://www.oprfchamber.org
Village of Oak Park . . . . (708) 383-6400
    http://www.oak-park.us

OLYMPIA FIELDS (village). Covers a land area of 2.842 square miles and a water area of 0.004 square miles. Located at 41.51° N. Lat; 87.69° W. Long. Elevation is 692 feet.

History: Olympia Fields was developed in 1926 as a residential community centered around the Olympia Fields Country Club and Golf Course.
Population: 4,245 (1990); 4,732 (2000); 4,701 (2010); 4,689 (2015 projected); Race: 36.2% White, 59.4% Black, 2.2% Asian, 2.2% Other, 3.0% Hispanic of any race (2010); Density: 1,654.4 persons per square mile (2010); Average household size: 2.72 (2010); Median age: 45.8 (2010); Males per 100 females: 91.0 (2010); Marriage status: 26.9% never married, 60.0% now married, 9.2% widowed, 3.9% divorced (2005-2009 5-year est.); Foreign born: 5.7% (2005-2009 5-year est.); Ancestry (includes multiple ancestries): 7.5% Irish, 7.3% German, 4.9% Italian, 3.4% English, 2.9% Polish (2005-2009 5-year est.).
Economy: Single-family building permits issued: 1 (2010); Multi-family building permits issued: 0 (2010); Employment by occupation: 21.2% management, 35.1% professional, 10.3% services, 20.9% sales, 0.0% farming, 4.8% construction, 7.7% production (2005-2009 5-year est.).
Income: Per capita income: $41,364 (2010); Median household income: $88,703 (2010); Average household income: $112,790 (2010); Percent of households with income of $100,000 or more: 42.3% (2010); Poverty rate: 6.6% (2005-2009 5-year est.).
Taxes: Total city taxes per capita: $356 (2007); City property taxes per capita: $142 (2007).
Education: Percent of population age 25 and over with: High school diploma (including GED) or higher: 95.6% (2010); Bachelor's degree or higher: 56.5% (2010); Master's degree or higher: 25.2% (2010).

School District(s)
Matteson ESD 162 (PK-08)
    2009-10 Enrollment: 3,296 . . . . (708) 748-0100
Rich Twp HSD 227 (09-12)
    2009-10 Enrollment: 4,032 . . . . (708) 679-5800
Housing: Homeownership rate: 90.9% (2010); Median home value: $283,947 (2010); Median contract rent: $2,000+ per month (2005-2009 5-year est.); Median year structure built: 1975 (2005-2009 5-year est.).
Hospitals: St. James Hospital and Health Center (201 beds)
Safety: Violent crime rate: 21.4 per 10,000 population; Property crime rate: 437.3 per 10,000 population (2010).
Transportation: Commute to work: 81.0% car, 10.6% public transportation, 0.0% walk, 8.4% work from home (2005-2009 5-year est.); Travel time to work: 20.1% less than 15 minutes, 27.4% 15 to 30 minutes, 21.1% 30 to 45 minutes, 11.2% 45 to 60 minutes, 20.2% 60 minutes or more (2005-2009 5-year est.)

ORLAND HILLS (village). Aka Westhaven. Covers a land area of 1.090 square miles and a water area of 0.008 square miles. Located at 41.58° N. Lat; 87.84° W. Long. Elevation is 702 feet.

Population: 5,547 (1990); 6,779 (2000); 7,329 (2010); 7,557 (2015 projected); Race: 84.6% White, 4.6% Black, 4.7% Asian, 6.2% Other, 7.1% Hispanic of any race (2010); Density: 6,721.6 persons per square mile (2010); Average household size: 3.06 (2010); Median age: 32.9 (2010); Males per 100 females: 98.4 (2010); Marriage status: 27.4% never married, 58.5% now married, 2.8% widowed, 11.3% divorced (2005-2009 5-year est.); Foreign born: 10.5% (2005-2009 5-year est.); Ancestry (includes multiple ancestries): 25.8% Irish, 21.7% Polish, 19.4% German, 17.0% Italian, 4.4% English (2005-2009 5-year est.).
Economy: Single-family building permits issued: 0 (2010); Multi-family building permits issued: 0 (2010); Employment by occupation: 14.2% management, 14.5% professional, 14.1% services, 32.0% sales, 0.0% farming, 14.5% construction, 10.7% production (2005-2009 5-year est.).
Income: Per capita income: $27,866 (2010); Median household income: $80,102 (2010); Average household income: $84,483 (2010); Percent of households with income of $100,000 or more: 28.7% (2010); Poverty rate: 4.4% (2005-2009 5-year est.).
Taxes: Total city taxes per capita: $318 (2007); City property taxes per capita: $213 (2007).

Education: Percent of population age 25 and over with: High school diploma (including GED) or higher: 92.9% (2010); Bachelor's degree or higher: 20.9% (2010); Master's degree or higher: 4.0% (2010).

School District(s)
Cons HSD 230 (09-12)
    2009-10 Enrollment: 8,671 . . . . (708) 745-5210
Housing: Homeownership rate: 82.2% (2010); Median home value: $236,208 (2010); Median contract rent: $957 per month (2005-2009 5-year est.); Median year structure built: 1983 (2005-2009 5-year est.).
Transportation: Commute to work: 91.4% car, 6.3% public transportation, 0.8% walk, 0.9% work from home (2005-2009 5-year est.); Travel time to work: 15.7% less than 15 minutes, 21.1% 15 to 30 minutes, 21.9% 30 to 45 minutes, 19.0% 45 to 60 minutes, 22.3% 60 minutes or more (2005-2009 5-year est.)
Additional Information Contacts
Village of Orland Hills. . . . . (708) 349-6865
    http://www.orlandhills.org

ORLAND PARK (village).
Covers a land area of 19.141 square miles and a water area of 0.295 square miles. Located at 41.61° N. Lat; 87.85° W. Long. Elevation is 705 feet.
Population: 38,946 (1990); 51,077 (2000); 55,374 (2010); 57,081 (2015 projected); Race: 92.8% White, 0.8% Black, 3.6% Asian, 2.8% Other, 4.7% Hispanic of any race (2010); Density: 2,892.9 persons per square mile (2010); Average household size: 2.71 (2010); Median age: 42.5 (2010); Males per 100 females: 92.8 (2010); Marriage status: 25.1% never married, 58.8% now married, 9.0% widowed, 7.1% divorced (2005-2009 5-year est.); Foreign born: 12.8% (2005-2009 5-year est.); Ancestry (includes multiple ancestries): 27.1% Irish, 20.6% Polish, 20.3% German, 14.0% Italian, 4.2% English (2005-2009 5-year est.).
Economy: Unemployment rate: 8.8% (August 2011); Total civilian labor force: 28,792 (August 2011); Single-family building permits issued: 38 (2010); Multi-family building permits issued: 0 (2010); Employment by occupation: 20.1% management, 21.7% professional, 13.6% services, 29.2% sales, 0.1% farming, 7.3% construction, 8.1% production (2005-2009 5-year est.).
Income: Per capita income: $37,220 (2010); Median household income: $83,513 (2010); Average household income: $101,411 (2010); Percent of households with income of $100,000 or more: 38.8% (2010); Poverty rate: 3.8% (2005-2009 5-year est.).
Taxes: Total city taxes per capita: $635 (2007); City property taxes per capita: $378 (2007).
Education: Percent of population age 25 and over with: High school diploma (including GED) or higher: 93.2% (2010); Bachelor's degree or higher: 35.6% (2010); Master's degree or higher: 13.6% (2010).

School District(s)
Cons HSD 230 (09-12)
    2009-10 Enrollment: 8,671 . . . . (708) 745-5210
Kirby SD 140 (PK-08)
    2009-10 Enrollment: 3,928 . . . . (708) 532-6462
Orland SD 135 (PK-08)
    2009-10 Enrollment: 5,466 . . . . (708) 364-3306
Southwest Cook Coop Spec Ed (PK-12)
    2009-10 Enrollment: n/a . . . . (708) 687-0900
Tinley Park CCSD 146 (PK-08)
    2009-10 Enrollment: 2,343 . . . . (708) 614-4500

Four-year College(s)
ITT Technical Institute-Orland Park (Private, For-profit)
    Fall 2009 Enrollment: 562 . . . . (708) 326-3200
    2010-11 Tuition: In-state $18,048; Out-of-state $18,048
Housing: Homeownership rate: 92.5% (2010); Median home value: $269,771 (2010); Median contract rent: $864 per month (2005-2009 5-year est.); Median year structure built: 1987 (2005-2009 5-year est.).
Safety: Violent crime rate: 4.2 per 10,000 population; Property crime rate: 210.5 per 10,000 population (2010).
Transportation: Commute to work: 88.6% car, 5.9% public transportation, 1.5% walk, 3.6% work from home (2005-2009 5-year est.); Travel time to work: 19.3% less than 15 minutes, 26.6% 15 to 30 minutes, 24.0% 30 to 45 minutes, 12.0% 45 to 60 minutes, 18.1% 60 minutes or more (2005-2009 5-year est.)
Additional Information Contacts
Orland Park Area Chamber of Commerce. . . . . (708) 349-2972
    http://www.orlandparkchamber.org
Village of Orland Park . . . . (708) 403-6100
    http://www.orland-park.il.us

PALATINE (village).
Covers a land area of 12.973 square miles and a water area of 0.134 square miles. Located at 42.11° N. Lat; 88.04° W. Long. Elevation is 741 feet.
History: Named for the Rhenish Palatinate, Germany, as "palatine" designates a high official. William Rainey Harper College is in Palatine. Incorporated 1869.
Population: 58,182 (1990); 65,479 (2000); 66,045 (2010); 65,903 (2015 projected); Race: 80.1% White, 1.9% Black, 9.4% Asian, 8.7% Other, 17.8% Hispanic of any race (2010); Density: 5,090.8 persons per square mile (2010); Average household size: 2.56 (2010); Median age: 37.7 (2010); Males per 100 females: 99.6 (2010); Marriage status: 29.2% never married, 56.6% now married, 5.2% widowed, 9.1% divorced (2005-2009 5-year est.); Foreign born: 23.2% (2005-2009 5-year est.); Ancestry (includes multiple ancestries): 22.9% German, 16.0% Irish, 13.5% Polish, 10.6% Italian, 5.4% English (2005-2009 5-year est.).
Economy: Unemployment rate: 7.7% (August 2011); Total civilian labor force: 39,943 (August 2011); Single-family building permits issued: 16 (2010); Multi-family building permits issued: 0 (2010); Employment by occupation: 19.9% management, 23.2% professional, 12.5% services, 28.2% sales, 0.0% farming, 5.6% construction, 10.6% production (2005-2009 5-year est.).
Income: Per capita income: $38,198 (2010); Median household income: $77,830 (2010); Average household income: $97,994 (2010); Percent of households with income of $100,000 or more: 35.0% (2010); Poverty rate: 7.5% (2005-2009 5-year est.).
Taxes: Total city taxes per capita: $617 (2007); City property taxes per capita: $429 (2007).
Education: Percent of population age 25 and over with: High school diploma (including GED) or higher: 91.8% (2010); Bachelor's degree or higher: 45.5% (2010); Master's degree or higher: 15.9% (2010).

School District(s)
Nw Suburban Spec Educ Org (PK-12)
    2009-10 Enrollment: n/a . . . . (847) 463-8100
Palatine CCSD 15 (PK-08)
    2009-10 Enrollment: 12,214 . . . . (847) 963-3000
Township HSD 211 (09-12)
    2009-10 Enrollment: 12,749 . . . . (847) 755-6600

Two-year College(s)
Harper College (Public)
    Fall 2009 Enrollment: 15,711. . . . . (847) 925-6000
    2010-11 Tuition: In-state $8,982; Out-of-state $10,794
Housing: Homeownership rate: 72.8% (2010); Median home value: $263,579 (2010); Median contract rent: $929 per month (2005-2009 5-year est.); Median year structure built: 1977 (2005-2009 5-year est.).
Safety: Violent crime rate: 5.2 per 10,000 population; Property crime rate: 135.3 per 10,000 population (2010).
Transportation: Commute to work: 88.4% car, 4.8% public transportation, 1.4% walk, 4.5% work from home (2005-2009 5-year est.); Travel time to work: 20.7% less than 15 minutes, 34.6% 15 to 30 minutes, 25.9% 30 to 45 minutes, 9.9% 45 to 60 minutes, 8.9% 60 minutes or more (2005-2009 5-year est.)
Additional Information Contacts
Palatine Area Chamber of Commerce. . . . . (847) 359-7200
    http://www.palatinechamber.com
Village of Palatine . . . . (847) 358-7500
    http://www.palatine.il.us

PALOS HEIGHTS (city).
Covers a land area of 3.780 square miles and a water area of 0.086 square miles. Located at 41.66° N. Lat; 87.79° W. Long. Elevation is 623 feet.
History: Named for Palos, Spain. Trinity Christian College is here.
Population: 11,513 (1990); 11,260 (2000); 11,637 (2010); 11,683 (2015 projected); Race: 96.8% White, 0.5% Black, 1.5% Asian, 1.3% Other, 1.8% Hispanic of any race (2010); Density: 3,078.4 persons per square mile (2010); Average household size: 2.54 (2010); Median age: 48.0 (2010); Males per 100 females: 88.9 (2010); Marriage status: 23.6% never married, 63.1% now married, 8.6% widowed, 4.7% divorced (2005-2009 5-year est.); Foreign born: 8.3% (2005-2009 5-year est.); Ancestry (includes multiple ancestries): 28.0% Irish, 23.0% German, 16.2% Polish, 11.4% Italian, 7.6% Dutch (2005-2009 5-year est.).
Economy: Single-family building permits issued: 2 (2010); Multi-family building permits issued: 0 (2010); Employment by occupation: 24.0% management, 25.8% professional, 10.4% services, 28.4% sales, 0.0% farming, 5.4% construction, 6.0% production (2005-2009 5-year est.).

Income: Per capita income: $38,729 (2010); Median household income: $82,422 (2010); Average household income: $104,042 (2010); Percent of households with income of $100,000 or more: 37.9% (2010); Poverty rate: 3.5% (2005-2009 5-year est.).

Taxes: Total city taxes per capita: $552 (2007); City property taxes per capita: $369 (2007).

Education: Percent of population age 25 and over with: High school diploma (including GED) or higher: 93.9% (2010); Bachelor's degree or higher: 43.1% (2010); Master's degree or higher: 18.6% (2010).

School District(s)

CHSD 218 (09-12)
    2009-10 Enrollment: 5,826 . . . . (708) 424-2000
Palos CCSD 118 (PK-08)
    2009-10 Enrollment: 1,873 . . . . (708) 448-4800
Palos Heights SD 128 (PK-08)
    2009-10 Enrollment: 708 . . . . (708) 597-9040

Four-year College(s)

Trinity Christian College (Private, Not-for-profit, Interdenominational)
    Fall 2009 Enrollment: 1,450 . . . . (708) 597-3000
    2010-11 Tuition: In-state $21,733; Out-of-state $21,733

Housing: Homeownership rate: 97.9% (2010); Median home value: $292,097 (2010); Median contract rent: $979 per month (2005-2009 5-year est.); Median year structure built: 1974 (2005-2009 5-year est.).

Hospitals: Palos Community Hospital (436 beds)

Safety: Violent crime rate: 2.4 per 10,000 population; Property crime rate: 177.9 per 10,000 population (2010).

Newspapers: Oak Lawn/Evergreen Park Reporter (Community news; Circulation 17,424); Palos Hills/Hickory Hills Reporter (Community news; Circulation 18,912); Regional News (Community news; Circulation 18,590)

Transportation: Commute to work: 84.5% car, 6.6% public transportation, 1.9% walk, 5.9% work from home (2005-2009 5-year est.); Travel time to work: 25.6% less than 15 minutes, 33.7% 15 to 30 minutes, 16.8% 30 to 45 minutes, 9.2% 45 to 60 minutes, 14.7% 60 minutes or more (2005-2009 5-year est.)

Additional Information Contacts

City of Palos Heights . . . . (708) 361-1800
    http://www.palosheights.org
Palos Area Chamber of Commerce . . . . (708) 923-2300
    http://palosareachamber.org

PALOS HILLS (city).
Covers a land area of 4.167 square miles and a water area of 0.070 square miles. Located at 41.69° N. Lat; 87.82° W. Long. Elevation is 597 feet.

Population: 17,800 (1990); 17,665 (2000); 16,832 (2010); 16,472 (2015 projected); Race: 83.8% White, 6.4% Black, 3.1% Asian, 6.8% Other, 6.6% Hispanic of any race (2010); Density: 4,039.8 persons per square mile (2010); Average household size: 2.38 (2010); Median age: 43.7 (2010); Males per 100 females: 89.7 (2010); Marriage status: 27.9% never married, 51.3% now married, 10.3% widowed, 10.6% divorced (2005-2009 5-year est.); Foreign born: 23.7% (2005-2009 5-year est.); Ancestry (includes multiple ancestries): 25.4% Polish, 15.2% German, 14.0% Irish, 9.1% Italian, 8.2% Greek (2005-2009 5-year est.).

Economy: Single-family building permits issued: 3 (2010); Multi-family building permits issued: 0 (2010); Employment by occupation: 14.1% management, 17.3% professional, 11.4% services, 31.6% sales, 0.0% farming, 9.7% construction, 15.8% production (2005-2009 5-year est.).

Income: Per capita income: $30,474 (2010); Median household income: $62,561 (2010); Average household income: $73,086 (2010); Percent of households with income of $100,000 or more: 22.2% (2010); Poverty rate: 5.6% (2005-2009 5-year est.).

Taxes: Total city taxes per capita: $215 (2007); City property taxes per capita: $99 (2007).

Education: Percent of population age 25 and over with: High school diploma (including GED) or higher: 89.3% (2010); Bachelor's degree or higher: 27.9% (2010); Master's degree or higher: 9.6% (2010).

School District(s)

Cons HSD 230 (09-12)
    2009-10 Enrollment: 8,671 . . . . (708) 745-5210
North Palos SD 117 (PK-08)
    2009-10 Enrollment: 3,079 . . . . (708) 598-5500

Two-year College(s)

Moraine Valley Community College (Public)
    Fall 2009 Enrollment: 17,774 . . . . (708) 974-4300
    2010-11 Tuition: In-state $7,416; Out-of-state $8,676

Vocational/Technical School(s)

Hair Professionals Career College (Private, For-profit)
    Fall 2009 Enrollment: 181 . . . . (708) 430-1755
    2010-11 Tuition: $16,450

Housing: Homeownership rate: 81.1% (2010); Median home value: $218,228 (2010); Median contract rent: $806 per month (2005-2009 5-year est.); Median year structure built: 1976 (2005-2009 5-year est.).

Safety: Violent crime rate: 2.4 per 10,000 population; Property crime rate: 113.5 per 10,000 population (2010).

Transportation: Commute to work: 88.9% car, 7.5% public transportation, 0.8% walk, 1.7% work from home (2005-2009 5-year est.); Travel time to work: 16.1% less than 15 minutes, 26.9% 15 to 30 minutes, 27.0% 30 to 45 minutes, 14.4% 45 to 60 minutes, 15.5% 60 minutes or more (2005-2009 5-year est.)

Additional Information Contacts

City of Palos Hills . . . . (708) 598-3400
    http://www.paloshillsweb.org

PALOS PARK (village).
Covers a land area of 3.776 square miles and a water area of 0.039 square miles. Located at 41.66° N. Lat; 87.83° W. Long. Elevation is 689 feet.

History: The Village of Palos Park was incorporated in 1914. In the early 1920's, an artist colony emerged and by 1940 the Village had become a center for artists, writers and intellectuals. From early on, the art colony in Palos Park played a pivotal role in the personal and artistic development of our community.

Population: 4,454 (1990); 4,689 (2000); 4,739 (2010); 4,787 (2015 projected); Race: 96.3% White, 0.2% Black, 2.2% Asian, 1.2% Other, 2.9% Hispanic of any race (2010); Density: 1,255.0 persons per square mile (2010); Average household size: 2.57 (2010); Median age: 50.0 (2010); Males per 100 females: 90.2 (2010); Marriage status: 18.5% never married, 61.8% now married, 12.4% widowed, 7.4% divorced (2005-2009 5-year est.); Foreign born: 11.2% (2005-2009 5-year est.); Ancestry (includes multiple ancestries): 24.9% Polish, 24.8% Irish, 20.8% German, 10.4% Italian, 6.6% English (2005-2009 5-year est.).

Economy: Single-family building permits issued: 4 (2010); Multi-family building permits issued: 0 (2010); Employment by occupation: 20.3% management, 26.4% professional, 4.9% services, 32.4% sales, 0.0% farming, 10.7% construction, 5.3% production (2005-2009 5-year est.).

Income: Per capita income: $42,903 (2010); Median household income: $88,995 (2010); Average household income: $113,568 (2010); Percent of households with income of $100,000 or more: 43.1% (2010); Poverty rate: 0.5% (2005-2009 5-year est.).

Taxes: Total city taxes per capita: $519 (2007); City property taxes per capita: $264 (2007).

Education: Percent of population age 25 and over with: High school diploma (including GED) or higher: 94.1% (2010); Bachelor's degree or higher: 46.7% (2010); Master's degree or higher: 20.2% (2010).

School District(s)

Palos CCSD 118 (PK-08)
    2009-10 Enrollment: 1,873 . . . . (708) 448-4800

Housing: Homeownership rate: 96.6% (2010); Median home value: $379,091 (2010); Median contract rent: n/a per month (2005-2009 5-year est.); Median year structure built: 1976 (2005-2009 5-year est.).

Safety: Violent crime rate: 2.0 per 10,000 population; Property crime rate: 63.9 per 10,000 population (2010).

Transportation: Commute to work: 82.0% car, 7.5% public transportation, 0.0% walk, 9.7% work from home (2005-2009 5-year est.); Travel time to work: 15.7% less than 15 minutes, 29.4% 15 to 30 minutes, 24.5% 30 to 45 minutes, 9.9% 45 to 60 minutes, 20.4% 60 minutes or more (2005-2009 5-year est.)

Additional Information Contacts

Palos Area Chamber of Commerce . . . . (708) 923-2300
    http://palosareachamber.org

PARK FOREST (village).
Covers a land area of 4.925 square miles and a water area of 0 square miles. Located at 41.48° N. Lat; 87.68° W. Long. Elevation is 712 feet.

Population: 24,770 (1990); 23,462 (2000); 21,965 (2010); 21,507 (2015 projected); Race: 48.8% White, 44.3% Black, 0.8% Asian, 6.0% Other, 7.7% Hispanic of any race (2010); Density: 4,459.7 persons per square mile (2010); Average household size: 2.50 (2010); Median age: 37.0 (2010); Males per 100 females: 89.8 (2010); Marriage status: 37.0% never married, 39.2% now married, 7.8% widowed, 16.0% divorced (2005-2009 5-year est.); Foreign born: 3.6% (2005-2009 5-year est.); Ancestry

(includes multiple ancestries): 14.2% German, 10.6% Irish, 5.7% English, 5.1% Italian, 4.0% Polish (2005-2009 5-year est.).
Economy: Unemployment rate: 13.2% (August 2011); Total civilian labor force: 12,535 (August 2011); Single-family building permits issued: 0 (2010); Multi-family building permits issued: 0 (2010); Employment by occupation: 9.0% management, 24.4% professional, 19.9% services, 28.1% sales, 0.0% farming, 6.1% construction, 12.5% production (2005-2009 5-year est.).
Income: Per capita income: $24,577 (2010); Median household income: $53,252 (2010); Average household income: $61,439 (2010); Percent of households with income of $100,000 or more: 13.9% (2010); Poverty rate: 10.9% (2005-2009 5-year est.).
Taxes: Total city taxes per capita: $612 (2007); City property taxes per capita: $475 (2007).
Education: Percent of population age 25 and over with: High school diploma (including GED) or higher: 91.7% (2010); Bachelor's degree or higher: 30.5% (2010); Master's degree or higher: 12.3% (2010).

School District(s)
Crete Monee CUSD 201u (PK-12)
   2009-10 Enrollment: 5,245 . . . . (708) 367-8300
Matteson ESD 162 (PK-08)
   2009-10 Enrollment: 3,296 . . . . (708) 748-0100
Park Forest SD 163 (PK-08)
   2009-10 Enrollment: 1,841 . . . . (708) 668-9400
Rich Twp HSD 227 (09-12)
   2009-10 Enrollment: 4,032 . . . . (708) 679-5800
Speed Seja #802 (PK-12)
   2009-10 Enrollment: n/a . . . . (708) 481-6100
Housing: Homeownership rate: 77.3% (2010); Median home value: $113,879 (2010); Median contract rent: $697 per month (2005-2009 5-year est.); Median year structure built: 1956 (2005-2009 5-year est.).
Safety: Violent crime rate: 22.6 per 10,000 population; Property crime rate: 195.7 per 10,000 population (2010).
Transportation: Commute to work: 84.1% car, 11.4% public transportation, 0.5% walk, 3.2% work from home (2005-2009 5-year est.); Travel time to work: 21.5% less than 15 minutes, 30.5% 15 to 30 minutes, 18.1% 30 to 45 minutes, 10.8% 45 to 60 minutes, 19.0% 60 minutes or more (2005-2009 5-year est.)

Additional Information Contacts
Matteson Area Chamber of Commerce . . . . (708) 747-6000
   http://www.macclink.com
Village of Park Forest . . . . (708) 748-1112
   http://www.villageofparkforest.com

PARK RIDGE (city). Covers a land area of 7.028 square miles and a water area of 0.042 square miles. Located at 42.01° N. Lat; 87.84° W. Long. Elevation is 643 feet.
History: Named for its location on a mountain ridge, and the pleasant parklike surroundings. Park Ridge began in 1853 when George Penny started a brickyard and lumberyard. Residents called the town Pennyville, but changed it to Brickton when Penny protested. When the clay from which the bricks were produced was gone and the Chicago & North Western Railway had arrived, Brickton became a commuting suburb and changed its name to Park Ridge.
Population: 37,075 (1990); 37,775 (2000); 35,872 (2010); 34,794 (2015 projected); Race: 93.8% White, 0.3% Black, 3.5% Asian, 2.4% Other, 4.2% Hispanic of any race (2010); Density: 5,103.8 persons per square mile (2010); Average household size: 2.62 (2010); Median age: 44.9 (2010); Males per 100 females: 91.4 (2010); Marriage status: 22.6% never married, 62.8% now married, 7.7% widowed, 6.9% divorced (2005-2009 5-year est.); Foreign born: 15.3% (2005-2009 5-year est.); Ancestry (includes multiple ancestries): 23.7% German, 22.2% Irish, 21.0% Polish, 15.5% Italian, 7.2% English (2005-2009 5-year est.).
Economy: Unemployment rate: 8.1% (August 2011); Total civilian labor force: 19,110 (August 2011); Single-family building permits issued: 8 (2010); Multi-family building permits issued: 0 (2010); Employment by occupation: 24.9% management, 28.0% professional, 10.3% services, 27.3% sales, 0.0% farming, 5.7% construction, 3.9% production (2005-2009 5-year est.).
Income: Per capita income: $41,561 (2010); Median household income: $85,331 (2010); Average household income: $109,621 (2010); Percent of households with income of $100,000 or more: 40.7% (2010); Poverty rate: 2.5% (2005-2009 5-year est.).
Taxes: Total city taxes per capita: $740 (2007); City property taxes per capita: $409 (2007).

Education: Percent of population age 25 and over with: High school diploma (including GED) or higher: 94.5% (2010); Bachelor's degree or higher: 50.1% (2010); Master's degree or higher: 20.6% (2010).

School District(s)
Maine Township HSD 207 (06-12)
   2009-10 Enrollment: 6,972 . . . . (847) 696-3600
Park Ridge CCSD 64 (PK-08)
   2009-10 Enrollment: 4,291 . . . . (847) 318-4300
Housing: Homeownership rate: 89.0% (2010); Median home value: $433,080 (2010); Median contract rent: $1,098 per month (2005-2009 5-year est.); Median year structure built: 1958 (2005-2009 5-year est.).
Hospitals: Advocate Lutheran General Children's Hospital
Safety: Violent crime rate: 4.1 per 10,000 population; Property crime rate: 157.2 per 10,000 population (2010).
Newspapers: Des Plaines Times (Local news; Circulation 3,503); Edgebrook Times Review (Local news; Circulation 1,465); Edison-Norwood Times Review (Local news; Circulation 3,405); Harlem-Irving Times (Community news; Circulation 4,457); Morton Grove Champion (Community news; Circulation 3,070); Norridge-Harwood Heights News (Local news; Circulation 3,813); Portage Park Times (Community news; Circulation 3,016); Rosemont Times (Local news; Circulation 1,370)
Transportation: Commute to work: 79.4% car, 11.2% public transportation, 2.7% walk, 6.0% work from home (2005-2009 5-year est.); Travel time to work: 26.3% less than 15 minutes, 27.6% 15 to 30 minutes, 26.2% 30 to 45 minutes, 11.2% 45 to 60 minutes, 8.8% 60 minutes or more (2005-2009 5-year est.)

Additional Information Contacts
City of Park Ridge . . . . (847) 318-5200
   http://www.parkridge.us
Park Ridge Chamber of Commerce . . . . (847) 825-3121
   http://parkridgechamber.org

PHOENIX (village). Covers a land area of 0.451 square miles and a water area of 0 square miles. Located at 41.61° N. Lat; 87.63° W. Long. Elevation is 600 feet.
History: Phoenix developed as a residential outgrowth of its neighbor, Harvey.
Population: 2,217 (1990); 2,157 (2000); 2,018 (2010); 1,991 (2015 projected); Race: 8.1% White, 83.9% Black, 0.1% Asian, 7.9% Other, 11.2% Hispanic of any race (2010); Density: 4,477.1 persons per square mile (2010); Average household size: 2.94 (2010); Median age: 32.9 (2010); Males per 100 females: 93.1 (2010); Marriage status: 51.1% never married, 31.5% now married, 8.0% widowed, 9.4% divorced (2005-2009 5-year est.); Foreign born: 3.1% (2005-2009 5-year est.); Ancestry (includes multiple ancestries): 2.4% African, 0.9% Jamaican, 0.4% Lithuanian, 0.3% Irish, 0.3% Swedish (2005-2009 5-year est.).
Economy: Single-family building permits issued: 0 (2010); Multi-family building permits issued: 0 (2010); Employment by occupation: 7.1% management, 14.3% professional, 25.4% services, 31.6% sales, 0.0% farming, 4.9% construction, 16.7% production (2005-2009 5-year est.).
Income: Per capita income: $17,416 (2010); Median household income: $39,013 (2010); Average household income: $51,164 (2010); Percent of households with income of $100,000 or more: 10.8% (2010); Poverty rate: 13.6% (2005-2009 5-year est.).
Taxes: Total city taxes per capita: $510 (2007); City property taxes per capita: $399 (2007).
Education: Percent of population age 25 and over with: High school diploma (including GED) or higher: 77.6% (2010); Bachelor's degree or higher: 9.6% (2010); Master's degree or higher: 2.6% (2010).

School District(s)
South Holland SD 151 (PK-08)
   2009-10 Enrollment: 1,547 . . . . (708) 339-1516
Housing: Homeownership rate: 72.2% (2010); Median home value: $95,536 (2010); Median contract rent: $487 per month (2005-2009 5-year est.); Median year structure built: 1960 (2005-2009 5-year est.).
Transportation: Commute to work: 82.6% car, 12.8% public transportation, 2.7% walk, 0.5% work from home (2005-2009 5-year est.); Travel time to work: 28.5% less than 15 minutes, 31.2% 15 to 30 minutes, 24.5% 30 to 45 minutes, 5.4% 45 to 60 minutes, 10.4% 60 minutes or more (2005-2009 5-year est.)

POSEN (village). Covers a land area of 1.179 square miles and a water area of 0 square miles. Located at 41.62° N. Lat; 87.68° W. Long. Elevation is 600 feet.

History: Posen was settled in 1893 when a Chicago realtor sold 12,000 lots, mostly to Polish immigrants. Posen was incorporated in 1901.
Population: 4,246 (1990); 4,730 (2000); 5,002 (2010); 5,134 (2015 projected); Race: 65.0% White, 14.7% Black, 0.1% Asian, 20.2% Other, 36.5% Hispanic of any race (2010); Density: 4,241.1 persons per square mile (2010); Average household size: 3.01 (2010); Median age: 34.7 (2010); Males per 100 females: 101.4 (2010); Marriage status: 40.3% never married, 53.0% now married, 4.1% widowed, 2.6% divorced (2005-2009 5-year est.); Foreign born: 26.6% (2005-2009 5-year est.); Ancestry (includes multiple ancestries): 8.8% German, 7.8% Irish, 6.5% Polish, 3.3% Italian, 1.9% Nigerian (2005-2009 5-year est.).
Economy: Single-family building permits issued: 0 (2010); Multi-family building permits issued: 0 (2010); Employment by occupation: 9.8% management, 6.3% professional, 29.5% services, 20.1% sales, 0.0% farming, 20.6% construction, 13.8% production (2005-2009 5-year est.).
Income: Per capita income: $19,663 (2010); Median household income: $55,325 (2010); Average household income: $59,324 (2010); Percent of households with income of $100,000 or more: 13.2% (2010); Poverty rate: 14.5% (2005-2009 5-year est.).
Taxes: Total city taxes per capita: $464 (2007); City property taxes per capita: $363 (2007).
Education: Percent of population age 25 and over with: High school diploma (including GED) or higher: 76.2% (2010); Bachelor's degree or higher: 10.4% (2010); Master's degree or higher: 2.1% (2010).

School District(s)
Posen-Robbins ESD 143-5 (PK-08)
    2009-10 Enrollment: 1,870 . . . . (708) 388-7200
Housing: Homeownership rate: 83.5% (2010); Median home value: $136,947 (2010); Median contract rent: $779 per month (2005-2009 5-year est.); Median year structure built: 1975 (2005-2009 5-year est.).
Safety: Violent crime rate: 26.9 per 10,000 population; Property crime rate: 496.1 per 10,000 population (2010).
Transportation: Commute to work: 94.2% car, 5.2% public transportation, 0.6% walk, 0.0% work from home (2005-2009 5-year est.); Travel time to work: 11.6% less than 15 minutes, 22.9% 15 to 30 minutes, 31.3% 30 to 45 minutes, 17.2% 45 to 60 minutes, 16.9% 60 minutes or more (2005-2009 5-year est.)

PROSPECT HEIGHTS (city).
Covers a land area of 4.258 square miles and a water area of 0.024 square miles. Located at 42.10° N. Lat; 87.92° W. Long. Elevation is 669 feet.
Population: 15,240 (1990); 17,081 (2000); 16,289 (2010); 15,811 (2015 projected); Race: 71.2% White, 1.7% Black, 6.1% Asian, 21.1% Other, 33.4% Hispanic of any race (2010); Density: 3,825.1 persons per square mile (2010); Average household size: 2.46 (2010); Median age: 39.2 (2010); Males per 100 females: 100.2 (2010); Marriage status: 25.3% never married, 63.4% now married, 4.6% widowed, 6.7% divorced (2005-2009 5-year est.); Foreign born: 42.7% (2005-2009 5-year est.); Ancestry (includes multiple ancestries): 19.6% Polish, 15.0% German, 9.8% Irish, 7.4% Italian, 4.6% English (2005-2009 5-year est.).
Economy: Single-family building permits issued: 1 (2010); Multi-family building permits issued: 0 (2010); Employment by occupation: 15.6% management, 16.0% professional, 21.3% services, 22.8% sales, 0.0% farming, 7.5% construction, 16.9% production (2005-2009 5-year est.).
Income: Per capita income: $32,777 (2010); Median household income: $61,683 (2010); Average household income: $80,288 (2010); Percent of households with income of $100,000 or more: 22.3% (2010); Poverty rate: 6.1% (2005-2009 5-year est.).
Taxes: Total city taxes per capita: $362 (2007); City property taxes per capita: $149 (2007).
Education: Percent of population age 25 and over with: High school diploma (including GED) or higher: 84.8% (2010); Bachelor's degree or higher: 36.4% (2010); Master's degree or higher: 12.2% (2010).

School District(s)
Prospect Heights SD 23 (PK-08)
    2009-10 Enrollment: 1,478 . . . . (847) 870-3850
Housing: Homeownership rate: 72.9% (2010); Median home value: $241,064 (2010); Median contract rent: $876 per month (2005-2009 5-year est.); Median year structure built: 1975 (2005-2009 5-year est.).
Safety: Violent crime rate: 5.1 per 10,000 population; Property crime rate: 103.9 per 10,000 population (2010).
Transportation: Commute to work: 91.3% car, 2.4% public transportation, 2.6% walk, 3.3% work from home (2005-2009 5-year est.); Travel time to work: 22.7% less than 15 minutes, 33.5% 15 to 30 minutes, 26.1% 30 to 45

minutes, 10.0% 45 to 60 minutes, 7.6% 60 minutes or more (2005-2009 5-year est.)
Additional Information Contacts
City of Prospect Heights . . . . (847) 398-6070
    http://www.prospect-heights.il.us

RICHTON PARK (village).
Aka Richton. Covers a land area of 3.374 square miles and a water area of 0.021 square miles. Located at 41.48° N. Lat; 87.72° W. Long. Elevation is 725 feet.
Population: 10,653 (1990); 12,533 (2000); 12,909 (2010); 13,082 (2015 projected); Race: 33.3% White, 60.5% Black, 1.5% Asian, 4.7% Other, 5.2% Hispanic of any race (2010); Density: 3,826.1 persons per square mile (2010); Average household size: 2.69 (2010); Median age: 36.4 (2010); Males per 100 females: 88.1 (2010); Marriage status: 35.3% never married, 47.4% now married, 5.3% widowed, 12.0% divorced (2005-2009 5-year est.); Foreign born: 2.7% (2005-2009 5-year est.); Ancestry (includes multiple ancestries): 6.0% German, 5.3% Irish, 4.5% Polish, 1.8% African, 1.6% English (2005-2009 5-year est.).
Economy: Single-family building permits issued: 0 (2010); Multi-family building permits issued: 0 (2010); Employment by occupation: 17.0% management, 22.4% professional, 14.4% services, 28.5% sales, 0.0% farming, 4.8% construction, 13.0% production (2005-2009 5-year est.).
Income: Per capita income: $24,606 (2010); Median household income: $54,596 (2010); Average household income: $66,864 (2010); Percent of households with income of $100,000 or more: 18.9% (2010); Poverty rate: 8.2% (2005-2009 5-year est.).
Taxes: Total city taxes per capita: $500 (2007); City property taxes per capita: $359 (2007).
Education: Percent of population age 25 and over with: High school diploma (including GED) or higher: 93.6% (2010); Bachelor's degree or higher: 28.8% (2010); Master's degree or higher: 8.7% (2010).

School District(s)
ESD 159 (PK-08)
    2009-10 Enrollment: 2,104 . . . . (708) 720-1300
Matteson ESD 162 (PK-08)
    2009-10 Enrollment: 3,296 . . . . (708) 748-0100
Rich Twp HSD 227 (09-12)
    2009-10 Enrollment: 4,032 . . . . (708) 679-5800
Housing: Homeownership rate: 70.9% (2010); Median home value: $163,786 (2010); Median contract rent: $815 per month (2005-2009 5-year est.); Median year structure built: 1978 (2005-2009 5-year est.).
Safety: Violent crime rate: 27.6 per 10,000 population; Property crime rate: 303.3 per 10,000 population (2010).
Transportation: Commute to work: 76.8% car, 18.4% public transportation, 2.9% walk, 0.6% work from home (2005-2009 5-year est.); Travel time to work: 19.5% less than 15 minutes, 23.9% 15 to 30 minutes, 19.8% 30 to 45 minutes, 12.2% 45 to 60 minutes, 24.6% 60 minutes or more (2005-2009 5-year est.)
Additional Information Contacts
Village of Richton Park. . . . . (708) 481-8950
    http://www.richtonpark.org

RIVER FOREST (village).
Covers a land area of 2.509 square miles and a water area of 0.001 square miles. Located at 41.89° N. Lat; 87.81° W. Long. Elevation is 630 feet.
History: Named for the forest along the Des Plaines River. River Forest was settled in 1836 by the Ashbel Steele family. Another early resident was Daniel Cunningham Thatcher, a Chicago businessman who retired to River Forest in 1854. In 1862 Thatcher persuaded the Chicago & North Western Railway to build a station on his property, which was called Thatcher. For ten years, River Forest was known as Thatcher, but in 1880 the community was organized as the Village of River Forest.
Population: 11,669 (1990); 11,635 (2000); 11,378 (2010); 11,261 (2015 projected); Race: 86.9% White, 6.2% Black, 3.5% Asian, 3.4% Other, 5.4% Hispanic of any race (2010); Density: 4,535.7 persons per square mile (2010); Average household size: 2.65 (2010); Median age: 35.6 (2010); Males per 100 females: 86.3 (2010); Marriage status: 38.5% never married, 49.5% now married, 5.3% widowed, 6.7% divorced (2005-2009 5-year est.); Foreign born: 6.9% (2005-2009 5-year est.); Ancestry (includes multiple ancestries): 27.2% German, 24.1% Irish, 15.1% Italian, 10.2% English, 7.1% Polish (2005-2009 5-year est.).
Economy: Single-family building permits issued: 2 (2010); Multi-family building permits issued: 0 (2010); Employment by occupation: 21.7% management, 41.9% professional, 8.6% services, 23.3% sales, 0.2% farming, 0.9% construction, 3.4% production (2005-2009 5-year est.).

Income: Per capita income: $54,492 (2010); Median household income: $106,126 (2010); Average household income: $155,968 (2010); Percent of households with income of $100,000 or more: 51.9% (2010); Poverty rate: 5.3% (2005-2009 5-year est.).

Taxes: Total city taxes per capita: $1,096 (2007); City property taxes per capita: $882 (2007).

Education: Percent of population age 25 and over with: High school diploma (including GED) or higher: 97.9% (2010); Bachelor's degree or higher: 73.1% (2010); Master's degree or higher: 40.9% (2010).

School District(s)

River Forest SD 90 (PK-08)

    2009-10 Enrollment: 1,375 . . . . (708) 771-8282

Four-year College(s)

Concordia University (Private, Not-for-profit, Lutheran Church - Missouri Synod)

    Fall 2009 Enrollment: 5,049. . . . . (708) 771-8300

    2010-11 Tuition: In-state $24,396; Out-of-state $24,396

Dominican University (Private, Not-for-profit, Roman Catholic)

    Fall 2009 Enrollment: 3,909. . . . . (708) 366-2490

    2010-11 Tuition: In-state $25,710; Out-of-state $25,710

Housing: Homeownership rate: 88.8% (2010); Median home value: $518,906 (2010); Median contract rent: $851 per month (2005-2009 5-year est.); Median year structure built: 1943 (2005-2009 5-year est.).

Safety: Violent crime rate: 15.5 per 10,000 population; Property crime rate: 249.9 per 10,000 population (2010).

Transportation: Commute to work: 64.2% car, 15.0% public transportation, 11.6% walk, 8.4% work from home (2005-2009 5-year est.); Travel time to work: 31.8% less than 15 minutes, 18.8% 15 to 30 minutes, 27.5% 30 to 45 minutes, 14.4% 45 to 60 minutes, 7.4% 60 minutes or more (2005-2009 5-year est.)

Additional Information Contacts

Village of River Forest . . . . (708) 366-8500

    http://www.river-forest.us

RIVER GROVE (village). Covers a land area of 2.386 square miles and a water area of 0 square miles. Located at 41.92° N. Lat; 87.84° W. Long. Elevation is 627 feet.

History: Triton College. Incorporated 1888.

Population: 9,961 (1990); 10,668 (2000); 10,093 (2010); 9,797 (2015 projected); Race: 87.8% White, 0.5% Black, 2.6% Asian, 9.2% Other, 15.5% Hispanic of any race (2010); Density: 4,229.4 persons per square mile (2010); Average household size: 2.48 (2010); Median age: 40.3 (2010); Males per 100 females: 95.8 (2010); Marriage status: 27.9% never married, 52.5% now married, 7.4% widowed, 12.2% divorced (2005-2009 5-year est.); Foreign born: 36.4% (2005-2009 5-year est.); Ancestry (includes multiple ancestries): 33.6% Polish, 12.0% Italian, 10.5% German, 9.9% Irish, 4.6% Ukrainian (2005-2009 5-year est.).

Economy: Single-family building permits issued: 1 (2010); Multi-family building permits issued: 0 (2010); Employment by occupation: 10.3% management, 12.9% professional, 18.5% services, 24.7% sales, 0.0% farming, 11.7% construction, 21.9% production (2005-2009 5-year est.).

Income: Per capita income: $23,774 (2010); Median household income: $46,687 (2010); Average household income: $58,719 (2010); Percent of households with income of $100,000 or more: 12.4% (2010); Poverty rate: 12.1% (2005-2009 5-year est.).

Taxes: Total city taxes per capita: $464 (2007); City property taxes per capita: $314 (2007).

Education: Percent of population age 25 and over with: High school diploma (including GED) or higher: 83.5% (2010); Bachelor's degree or higher: 17.2% (2010); Master's degree or higher: 5.0% (2010).

School District(s)

Rhodes SD 84-5 (PK-08)

    2009-10 Enrollment: 647 . . . . (708) 453-1266

River Grove SD 85-5 (PK-08)

    2009-10 Enrollment: 656 . . . . (708) 453-6172

Two-year College(s)

Triton College (Public)

    Fall 2009 Enrollment: 15,706. . . . . (708) 456-0300

    2010-11 Tuition: In-state $7,210; Out-of-state $8,980

Housing: Homeownership rate: 62.4% (2010); Median home value: $222,494 (2010); Median contract rent: $756 per month (2005-2009 5-year est.); Median year structure built: 1960 (2005-2009 5-year est.).

Safety: Violent crime rate: 11.3 per 10,000 population; Property crime rate: 231.6 per 10,000 population (2010).

Transportation: Commute to work: 85.9% car, 8.1% public transportation, 4.2% walk, 0.2% work from home (2005-2009 5-year est.); Travel time to work: 19.5% less than 15 minutes, 30.1% 15 to 30 minutes, 31.6% 30 to 45 minutes, 7.7% 45 to 60 minutes, 11.1% 60 minutes or more (2005-2009 5-year est.)

Additional Information Contacts

River Grove Area Chamber of Commerce. . . . . (708) 452-8259

    http://www.vorg.us

Village of River Grove . . . . (708) 453-8000

    http://www.vorg.us

RIVERDALE (village). Covers a land area of 3.638 square miles and a water area of 0.148 square miles. Located at 41.64° N. Lat; 87.63° W. Long. Elevation is 600 feet.

History: Named for its location along the Calumet River, by Frederick C. Schmidt. Riverdale began when George Dolton and J.C. Matthews established a ferry across the Little Calumet River in 1836. The town later became a railroad center and a steel manufacturing area.

Population: 13,671 (1990); 15,055 (2000); 14,405 (2010); 14,177 (2015 projected); Race: 9.9% White, 87.2% Black, 0.2% Asian, 2.7% Other, 2.8% Hispanic of any race (2010); Density: 3,959.9 persons per square mile (2010); Average household size: 3.11 (2010); Median age: 28.8 (2010); Males per 100 females: 87.4 (2010); Marriage status: 48.2% never married, 36.9% now married, 5.7% widowed, 9.3% divorced (2005-2009 5-year est.); Foreign born: 1.5% (2005-2009 5-year est.); Ancestry (includes multiple ancestries): 2.4% African, 1.5% Polish, 1.2% German, 1.1% Irish, 1.1% Italian (2005-2009 5-year est.).

Economy: Single-family building permits issued: 0 (2010); Multi-family building permits issued: 0 (2010); Employment by occupation: 7.7% management, 19.4% professional, 17.2% services, 33.9% sales, 0.0% farming, 4.1% construction, 17.8% production (2005-2009 5-year est.).

Income: Per capita income: $15,242 (2010); Median household income: $41,156 (2010); Average household income: $47,376 (2010); Percent of households with income of $100,000 or more: 6.5% (2010); Poverty rate: 24.8% (2005-2009 5-year est.).

Taxes: Total city taxes per capita: $500 (2007); City property taxes per capita: $342 (2007).

Education: Percent of population age 25 and over with: High school diploma (including GED) or higher: 86.9% (2010); Bachelor's degree or higher: 14.2% (2010); Master's degree or higher: 2.9% (2010).

School District(s)

Dolton SD 148 (PK-08)

    2009-10 Enrollment: 2,635 . . . . (708) 841-2290

Exc Children Have Opportunities (PK-12)

    2009-10 Enrollment: n/a . . . . (708) 333-7880

Gen George Patton SD 133 (PK-08)

    2009-10 Enrollment: 426 . . . . (708) 841-3955

Housing: Homeownership rate: 61.5% (2010); Median home value: $114,078 (2010); Median contract rent: $777 per month (2005-2009 5-year est.); Median year structure built: 1957 (2005-2009 5-year est.).

Transportation: Commute to work: 77.6% car, 18.5% public transportation, 2.5% walk, 0.7% work from home (2005-2009 5-year est.); Travel time to work: 7.8% less than 15 minutes, 22.4% 15 to 30 minutes, 28.7% 30 to 45 minutes, 18.6% 45 to 60 minutes, 22.6% 60 minutes or more (2005-2009 5-year est.)

Additional Information Contacts

Riverdale Chamber of Commerce . . . . (708) 841-3311

    http://www.district148.net/rcoc

Village of Riverdale . . . . (708) 841-2200

    http://www.villageofriverdale.org

RIVERSIDE (village). Covers a land area of 1.973 square miles and a water area of 0.015 square miles. Located at 41.83° N. Lat; 87.81° W. Long. Elevation is 617 feet.

History: Riverside originated in 1866 with the plan of the Riverside Improvement Company to create an ideal suburb. They commissioned Olmsted and Vaux, New York landscape architects who had designed Central Park. The site for Riverside was selected for its forested terrain, the railroad facilities, and the Des Plaines River whose winding course determined the layout of the town. Incorporated 1923.

Population: 8,774 (1990); 8,895 (2000); 8,204 (2010); 7,904 (2015 projected); Race: 92.9% White, 0.4% Black, 2.0% Asian, 4.7% Other, 8.5% Hispanic of any race (2010); Density: 4,158.8 persons per square mile (2010); Average household size: 2.50 (2010); Median age: 42.5 (2010); Males per 100 females: 94.3 (2010); Marriage status: 24.1% never married,

61.0% now married, 7.8% widowed, 7.1% divorced (2005-2009 5-year est.); Foreign born: 10.4% (2005-2009 5-year est.); Ancestry (includes multiple ancestries): 23.2% German, 20.1% Polish, 16.3% Irish, 12.8% Italian, 8.4% Czech (2005-2009 5-year est.).

Economy: Single-family building permits issued: 0 (2010); Multi-family building permits issued: 0 (2010); Employment by occupation: 23.1% management, 32.5% professional, 6.0% services, 29.4% sales, 0.0% farming, 2.3% construction, 6.6% production (2005-2009 5-year est.).

Income: Per capita income: $39,950 (2010); Median household income: $74,588 (2010); Average household income: $100,434 (2010); Percent of households with income of $100,000 or more: 34.8% (2010); Poverty rate: 3.6% (2005-2009 5-year est.).

Taxes: Total city taxes per capita: $758 (2007); City property taxes per capita: $576 (2007).

Education: Percent of population age 25 and over with: High school diploma (including GED) or higher: 95.5% (2010); Bachelor's degree or higher: 55.1% (2010); Master's degree or higher: 24.7% (2010).

School District(s)

Riverside SD 96 (PK-08)
    2009-10 Enrollment: 1,523 . . . . (708) 447-5007
Riverside-Brookfield Twp SD 208 (09-12)
    2009-10 Enrollment: 1,466 . . . . (708) 442-7500

Housing: Homeownership rate: 79.6% (2010); Median home value: $371,403 (2010); Median contract rent: $757 per month (2005-2009 5-year est.); Median year structure built: before 1940 (2005-2009 5-year est.).

Safety: Violent crime rate: 9.9 per 10,000 population; Property crime rate: 232.5 per 10,000 population (2010).

Transportation: Commute to work: 68.4% car, 18.2% public transportation, 3.8% walk, 7.6% work from home (2005-2009 5-year est.); Travel time to work: 20.8% less than 15 minutes, 24.2% 15 to 30 minutes, 28.6% 30 to 45 minutes, 12.8% 45 to 60 minutes, 13.5% 60 minutes or more (2005-2009 5-year est.)

Additional Information Contacts
Riverside Chamber of Commerce . . . . (708) 447-8510
    http://www.riversidechamberofcommerce.com
Village of Riverside . . . . (708) 447-2700
    http://riverside.il.us

ROBBINS (village).

Covers a land area of 1.469 square miles and a water area of 0 square miles. Located at 41.64° N. Lat; 87.70° W. Long. Elevation is 600 feet.

History: Robbins, named for realtor and developer Eugene S. Robbins, was organized as a residential area and incorporated in 1917.

Population: 7,498 (1990); 6,635 (2000); 5,996 (2010); 5,718 (2015 projected); Race: 10.9% White, 82.3% Black, 0.2% Asian, 6.5% Other, 11.3% Hispanic of any race (2010); Density: 4,081.1 persons per square mile (2010); Average household size: 3.09 (2010); Median age: 33.5 (2010); Males per 100 females: 93.9 (2010); Marriage status: 50.3% never married, 26.5% now married, 10.6% widowed, 12.7% divorced (2005-2009 5-year est.); Foreign born: 1.3% (2005-2009 5-year est.); Ancestry (includes multiple ancestries): 1.1% American, 0.9% West Indian, 0.7% Irish, 0.4% African, 0.3% German (2005-2009 5-year est.).

Economy: Single-family building permits issued: 12 (2010); Multi-family building permits issued: 0 (2010); Employment by occupation: 2.6% management, 15.6% professional, 24.7% services, 26.4% sales, 0.0% farming, 15.5% construction, 15.2% production (2005-2009 5-year est.).

Income: Per capita income: $12,143 (2010); Median household income: $30,825 (2010); Average household income: $38,462 (2010); Percent of households with income of $100,000 or more: 5.5% (2010); Poverty rate: 38.5% (2005-2009 5-year est.).

Taxes: Total city taxes per capita: $254 (2007); City property taxes per capita: $197 (2007).

Education: Percent of population age 25 and over with: High school diploma (including GED) or higher: 73.4% (2010); Bachelor's degree or higher: 11.2% (2010); Master's degree or higher: 2.9% (2010).

School District(s)

CHSD 218 (09-12)
    2009-10 Enrollment: 5,826 . . . . (708) 424-2000
Posen-Robbins ESD 143-5 (PK-08)
    2009-10 Enrollment: 1,870 . . . . (708) 388-7200

Housing: Homeownership rate: 63.5% (2010); Median home value: $81,990 (2010); Median contract rent: $623 per month (2005-2009 5-year est.); Median year structure built: 1959 (2005-2009 5-year est.).

Transportation: Commute to work: 87.2% car, 10.6% public transportation, 0.0% walk, 1.7% work from home (2005-2009 5-year est.);

Travel time to work: 23.9% less than 15 minutes, 35.3% 15 to 30 minutes, 15.6% 30 to 45 minutes, 16.3% 45 to 60 minutes, 9.0% 60 minutes or more (2005-2009 5-year est.)

ROLLING MEADOWS (city).

Covers a land area of 5.455 square miles and a water area of 0.005 square miles. Located at 42.07° N. Lat; 88.02° W. Long. Elevation is 719 feet.

History: Named to promote the town as a pleasant place to live. Incorporated 1955.

Population: 23,056 (1990); 24,604 (2000); 23,929 (2010); 23,772 (2015 projected); Race: 76.9% White, 2.9% Black, 8.6% Asian, 11.6% Other, 23.5% Hispanic of any race (2010); Density: 4,386.7 persons per square mile (2010); Average household size: 2.69 (2010); Median age: 37.7 (2010); Males per 100 females: 102.3 (2010); Marriage status: 28.5% never married, 56.2% now married, 5.1% widowed, 10.2% divorced (2005-2009 5-year est.); Foreign born: 24.8% (2005-2009 5-year est.); Ancestry (includes multiple ancestries): 24.0% German, 13.0% Polish, 11.2% Irish, 9.0% Italian, 5.9% English (2005-2009 5-year est.).

Economy: Single-family building permits issued: 1 (2010); Multi-family building permits issued: 0 (2010); Employment by occupation: 18.4% management, 16.6% professional, 16.2% services, 27.8% sales, 0.3% farming, 8.9% construction, 11.8% production (2005-2009 5-year est.).

Income: Per capita income: $31,625 (2010); Median household income: $69,384 (2010); Average household income: $85,526 (2010); Percent of households with income of $100,000 or more: 28.2% (2010); Poverty rate: 7.0% (2005-2009 5-year est.).

Taxes: Total city taxes per capita: $787 (2007); City property taxes per capita: $428 (2007).

Education: Percent of population age 25 and over with: High school diploma (including GED) or higher: 86.7% (2010); Bachelor's degree or higher: 34.2% (2010); Master's degree or higher: 10.6% (2010).

School District(s)

Palatine CCSD 15 (PK-08)
    2009-10 Enrollment: 12,214 . . . . (847) 963-3000
Township HSD 214 (09-12)
    2009-10 Enrollment: 12,241 . . . . (847) 718-7600

Housing: Homeownership rate: 80.1% (2010); Median home value: $235,593 (2010); Median contract rent: $930 per month (2005-2009 5-year est.); Median year structure built: 1971 (2005-2009 5-year est.).

Transportation: Commute to work: 87.7% car, 5.1% public transportation, 1.2% walk, 4.2% work from home (2005-2009 5-year est.); Travel time to work: 26.2% less than 15 minutes, 40.6% 15 to 30 minutes, 17.6% 30 to 45 minutes, 7.8% 45 to 60 minutes, 7.9% 60 minutes or more (2005-2009 5-year est.)

Additional Information Contacts
City of Rolling Meadows . . . . (847) 394-8500
    http://www.ci.rolling-meadows.il.us
Rolling Meadows Chamber of Commerce . . . . (847) 398-3730
    http://www.rmchamber.org

ROSEMONT (village).

Covers a land area of 1.743 square miles and a water area of 0 square miles. Located at 41.99° N. Lat; 87.87° W. Long. Elevation is 636 feet.

Population: 3,995 (1990); 4,224 (2000); 4,341 (2010); 4,384 (2015 projected); Race: 81.7% White, 1.4% Black, 4.0% Asian, 12.9% Other, 43.2% Hispanic of any race (2010); Density: 2,490.7 persons per square mile (2010); Average household size: 2.50 (2010); Median age: 37.3 (2010); Males per 100 females: 110.4 (2010); Marriage status: 31.1% never married, 54.9% now married, 7.3% widowed, 6.7% divorced (2005-2009 5-year est.); Foreign born: 39.5% (2005-2009 5-year est.); Ancestry (includes multiple ancestries): 13.7% Italian, 11.1% German, 10.6% Polish, 8.9% Irish, 2.0% Greek (2005-2009 5-year est.).

Economy: Single-family building permits issued: 0 (2010); Multi-family building permits issued: 0 (2010); Employment by occupation: 7.7% management, 11.6% professional, 31.9% services, 15.9% sales, 0.0% farming, 6.7% construction, 26.2% production (2005-2009 5-year est.).

Income: Per capita income: $22,214 (2010); Median household income: $40,807 (2010); Average household income: $55,308 (2010); Percent of households with income of $100,000 or more: 12.2% (2010); Poverty rate: 19.9% (2005-2009 5-year est.).

Taxes: Total city taxes per capita: $15,489 (2007); City property taxes per capita: $10,147 (2007).

Education: Percent of population age 25 and over with: High school diploma (including GED) or higher: 76.4% (2010); Bachelor's degree or higher: 20.3% (2010); Master's degree or higher: 7.0% (2010).

School District(s)

Rosemont ESD 78 (PK-08)

2009-10 Enrollment: 267 . . . . (847) 825-0144

Housing: Homeownership rate: 30.7% (2010); Median home value: $344,056 (2010); Median contract rent: $712 per month (2005-2009 5-year est.); Median year structure built: 1966 (2005-2009 5-year est.).

Safety: Violent crime rate: 10.4 per 10,000 population; Property crime rate: 602.2 per 10,000 population (2010).

Transportation: Commute to work: 82.1% car, 10.5% public transportation, 6.4% walk, 0.0% work from home (2005-2009 5-year est.); Travel time to work: 35.1% less than 15 minutes, 40.1% 15 to 30 minutes, 13.8% 30 to 45 minutes, 6.9% 45 to 60 minutes, 4.2% 60 minutes or more (2005-2009 5-year est.)

Additional Information Contacts

Rosemont Chamber of Commerce . . . . (847) 698-1190
http://www.rosemontchamber.com

SAUK VILLAGE (village). Covers a land area of 3.804 square miles and a water area of 0.044 square miles. Located at 41.48° N. Lat; 87.56° W. Long. Elevation is 653 feet.

Population: 10,770 (1990); 10,411 (2000); 9,737 (2010); 9,427 (2015 projected); Race: 53.9% White, 38.3% Black, 0.6% Asian, 7.1% Other, 14.6% Hispanic of any race (2010); Density: 2,560.0 persons per square mile (2010); Average household size: 3.08 (2010); Median age: 32.0 (2010); Males per 100 females: 98.2 (2010); Marriage status: 37.9% never married, 40.3% now married, 6.3% widowed, 15.5% divorced (2005-2009 5-year est.); Foreign born: 2.6% (2005-2009 5-year est.); Ancestry (includes multiple ancestries): 11.6% Irish, 7.7% German, 5.0% Polish, 2.7% English, 2.2% Italian (2005-2009 5-year est.).

Economy: Single-family building permits issued: 0 (2010); Multi-family building permits issued: 0 (2010); Employment by occupation: 9.2% management, 13.4% professional, 20.3% services, 27.8% sales, 0.2% farming, 9.5% construction, 19.5% production (2005-2009 5-year est.).

Income: Per capita income: $18,116 (2010); Median household income: $50,363 (2010); Average household income: $55,706 (2010); Percent of households with income of $100,000 or more: 8.5% (2010); Poverty rate: 19.1% (2005-2009 5-year est.).

Taxes: Total city taxes per capita: $427 (2007); City property taxes per capita: $368 (2007).

Education: Percent of population age 25 and over with: High school diploma (including GED) or higher: 84.7% (2010); Bachelor's degree or higher: 11.5% (2010); Master's degree or higher: 3.0% (2010).

School District(s)

CCSD 168 (PK-08)

2009-10 Enrollment: 1,676 . . . . (708) 758-1614

Housing: Homeownership rate: 83.7% (2010); Median home value: $112,913 (2010); Median contract rent: $828 per month (2005-2009 5-year est.); Median year structure built: 1972 (2005-2009 5-year est.).

Transportation: Commute to work: 94.5% car, 3.4% public transportation, 0.5% walk, 1.2% work from home (2005-2009 5-year est.); Travel time to work: 14.5% less than 15 minutes, 30.8% 15 to 30 minutes, 26.7% 30 to 45 minutes, 12.9% 45 to 60 minutes, 15.2% 60 minutes or more (2005-2009 5-year est.)

Additional Information Contacts

Village of Sauk Village . . . . (708) 758-3330
http://www.saukvillage.org

SCHAUMBURG (village). Aka Schaumburg Center. Covers a land area of 19.003 square miles and a water area of 0.121 square miles. Located at 42.03° N. Lat; 88.08° W. Long. Elevation is 794 feet.

Population: 68,706 (1990); 75,386 (2000); 74,583 (2010); 73,841 (2015 projected); Race: 71.3% White, 3.6% Black, 19.7% Asian, 5.3% Other, 8.2% Hispanic of any race (2010); Density: 3,924.9 persons per square mile (2010); Average household size: 2.44 (2010); Median age: 39.0 (2010); Males per 100 females: 97.1 (2010); Marriage status: 30.5% never married, 53.2% now married, 6.4% widowed, 9.9% divorced (2005-2009 5-year est.); Foreign born: 23.4% (2005-2009 5-year est.); Ancestry (includes multiple ancestries): 23.4% German, 17.0% Polish, 13.9% Irish, 13.2% Italian, 5.8% English (2005-2009 5-year est.).

Economy: Unemployment rate: 8.7% (August 2011); Total civilian labor force: 44,682 (August 2011); Single-family building permits issued: 0 (2010); Multi-family building permits issued: 0 (2010); Employment by occupation: 21.3% management, 24.5% professional, 10.8% services, 28.9% sales, 0.0% farming, 5.4% construction, 9.1% production (2005-2009 5-year est.).

Income: Per capita income: $36,119 (2010); Median household income: $72,953 (2010); Average household income: $88,134 (2010); Percent of households with income of $100,000 or more: 30.1% (2010); Poverty rate: 4.5% (2005-2009 5-year est.).

Taxes: Total city taxes per capita: $671 (2007); City property taxes per capita: $33 (2007).

Education: Percent of population age 25 and over with: High school diploma (including GED) or higher: 94.5% (2010); Bachelor's degree or higher: 42.8% (2010); Master's degree or higher: 13.8% (2010).

School District(s)

Schaumburg CCSD 54 (PK-08)

2009-10 Enrollment: 14,313 . . . . (847) 357-5000

Township HSD 211 (09-12)

2009-10 Enrollment: 12,749 . . . . (847) 755-6600

Four-year College(s)

Argosy University-Schaumburg (Private, For-profit)

Fall 2009 Enrollment: 773 . . . . (847) 969-4900
2010-11 Tuition: In-state $19,812; Out-of-state $19,812

The Illinois Institute of Art-Schaumburg (Private, For-profit)

Fall 2009 Enrollment: 1,420 . . . . (847) 619-3450
2010-11 Tuition: In-state $17,388; Out-of-state $17,388

University of Phoenix-Chicago Campus (Private, For-profit)

Fall 2009 Enrollment: 1,546 . . . . (847) 413-1922
2010-11 Tuition: In-state $11,040; Out-of-state $11,040

Housing: Homeownership rate: 72.2% (2010); Median home value: $234,089 (2010); Median contract rent: $1,015 per month (2005-2009 5-year est.); Median year structure built: 1977 (2005-2009 5-year est.).

Safety: Violent crime rate: 12.1 per 10,000 population; Property crime rate: 325.2 per 10,000 population (2010).

Newspapers: Chicago Tribune - Schaumburg Bureau (Local news)

Transportation: Commute to work: 92.1% car, 3.6% public transportation, 0.7% walk, 2.6% work from home (2005-2009 5-year est.); Travel time to work: 23.0% less than 15 minutes, 35.3% 15 to 30 minutes, 23.3% 30 to 45 minutes, 9.8% 45 to 60 minutes, 8.7% 60 minutes or more (2005-2009 5-year est.)

Airports: Schaumburg Regional (general aviation)

Additional Information Contacts

Schaumburg Business Association . . . . (847) 413-1010
http://www.schaumburgbusiness.com

Village of Schaumburg . . . . (847) 895-4500
http://www.ci.schaumburg.il.us

SCHILLER PARK (village). Covers a land area of 2.766 square miles and a water area of 0 square miles. Located at 41.95° N. Lat; 87.87° W. Long. Elevation is 640 feet.

History: Named for Johann Christopher Friedrich von Schiller (1759-1805), a German poet. Incorporated 1914.

Population: 11,266 (1990); 11,850 (2000); 11,610 (2010); 11,506 (2015 projected); Race: 75.2% White, 2.3% Black, 6.1% Asian, 16.4% Other, 30.6% Hispanic of any race (2010); Density: 4,196.8 persons per square mile (2010); Average household size: 2.86 (2010); Median age: 37.3 (2010); Males per 100 females: 103.8 (2010); Marriage status: 37.0% never married, 49.1% now married, 7.0% widowed, 6.9% divorced (2005-2009 5-year est.); Foreign born: 44.1% (2005-2009 5-year est.); Ancestry (includes multiple ancestries): 27.7% Polish, 10.7% Italian, 8.4% Irish, 7.9% German, 3.9% Greek (2005-2009 5-year est.).

Economy: Single-family building permits issued: 1 (2010); Multi-family building permits issued: 0 (2010); Employment by occupation: 10.4% management, 11.6% professional, 17.2% services, 21.2% sales, 0.0% farming, 20.3% construction, 19.3% production (2005-2009 5-year est.).

Income: Per capita income: $20,158 (2010); Median household income: $47,328 (2010); Average household income: $57,663 (2010); Percent of households with income of $100,000 or more: 12.6% (2010); Poverty rate: 7.4% (2005-2009 5-year est.).

Taxes: Total city taxes per capita: $1,065 (2007); City property taxes per capita: $599 (2007).

Education: Percent of population age 25 and over with: High school diploma (including GED) or higher: 78.7% (2010); Bachelor's degree or higher: 17.8% (2010); Master's degree or higher: 5.9% (2010).

School District(s)

Schiller Park SD 81 (PK-08)

2009-10 Enrollment: 1,249 . . . . (847) 671-1816

Housing: Homeownership rate: 57.6% (2010); Median home value: $240,181 (2010); Median contract rent: $774 per month (2005-2009 5-year est.); Median year structure built: 1964 (2005-2009 5-year est.).

Safety: Violent crime rate: 18.6 per 10,000 population; Property crime rate: 213.7 per 10,000 population (2010).
Transportation: Commute to work: 87.9% car, 4.5% public transportation, 2.3% walk, 3.0% work from home (2005-2009 5-year est.); Travel time to work: 19.8% less than 15 minutes, 28.5% 15 to 30 minutes, 32.1% 30 to 45 minutes, 10.2% 45 to 60 minutes, 9.4% 60 minutes or more (2005-2009 5-year est.)
Additional Information Contacts
Franklin Park/Schiller Park Chamber of Commerce . . . . . . (708) 865-9510
  http://www.chamberbyohare.org
Village of Schiller Park . . . . (847) 678-2550
  http://www.villageofschillerpark.com

SKOKIE (village). Aka Niles Center. Covers a land area of 10.041 square miles and a water area of 0 square miles. Located at 42.03° N. Lat; 87.74° W. Long. Elevation is 607 feet.

History: Named for the Potawatomi translation of "marsh". Hebrew Theological College (1922) was moved here from Chicago in 1958. National Jewish Theater. Incorporated 1888.
Population: 59,432 (1990); 63,348 (2000); 66,192 (2010); 67,326 (2015 projected); Race: 61.8% White, 5.5% Black, 25.6% Asian, 7.1% Other, 7.4% Hispanic of any race (2010); Density: 6,591.9 persons per square mile (2010); Average household size: 2.73 (2010); Median age: 44.0 (2010); Males per 100 females: 91.3 (2010); Marriage status: 29.0% never married, 56.9% now married, 7.6% widowed, 6.6% divorced (2005-2009 5-year est.); Foreign born: 39.2% (2005-2009 5-year est.); Ancestry (includes multiple ancestries): 10.1% German, 7.8% Russian, 6.6% Polish, 6.3% Assyrian/Chaldean/Syriac, 6.2% Irish (2005-2009 5-year est.).
Economy: Unemployment rate: 8.7% (August 2011); Total civilian labor force: 33,874 (August 2011); Single-family building permits issued: 2 (2010); Multi-family building permits issued: 0 (2010); Employment by occupation: 15.5% management, 29.3% professional, 12.8% services, 26.1% sales, 0.1% farming, 4.9% construction, 11.3% production (2005-2009 5-year est.).
Income: Per capita income: $31,422 (2010); Median household income: $68,367 (2010); Average household income: $87,041 (2010); Percent of households with income of $100,000 or more: 29.7% (2010); Poverty rate: 7.6% (2005-2009 5-year est.).
Taxes: Total city taxes per capita: $700 (2007); City property taxes per capita: $410 (2007).
Education: Percent of population age 25 and over with: High school diploma (including GED) or higher: 91.2% (2010); Bachelor's degree or higher: 47.3% (2010); Master's degree or higher: 19.9% (2010).

School District(s)
East Prairie SD 73 (PK-08)
  2009-10 Enrollment: 536 . . . . (847) 673-1141
Evanston CCSD 65 (PK-08)
  2009-10 Enrollment: 6,812 . . . . (847) 859-8010
Fairview SD 72 (PK-08)
  2009-10 Enrollment: 607 . . . . (847) 929-1050
Niles Twp CHSD 219 (09-12)
  2009-10 Enrollment: 4,798 . . . . (847) 626-3000
Skokie SD 68 (KG-08)
  2009-10 Enrollment: 1,676 . . . . (847) 676-9000
Skokie SD 69 (PK-08)
  2009-10 Enrollment: 1,705 . . . . (847) 675-7666
Skokie SD 73-5 (PK-08)
  2009-10 Enrollment: 1,065 . . . . (847) 324-0509
Four-year College(s)
Hebrew Theological College (Private, Not-for-profit, Jewish)
  Fall 2009 Enrollment: 450 . . . . (847) 982-2500
  2010-11 Tuition: In-state $18,230; Out-of-state $18,230
Knowledge Systems Institute (Private, Not-for-profit)
  Fall 2009 Enrollment: 62 . . . . (847) 679-3135
Two-year College(s)
Zarem Golde ORT Technical Institute (Private, Not-for-profit)
  Fall 2009 Enrollment: 524 . . . . (847) 324-5588
Vocational/Technical School(s)
Computer Systems Institute (Private, For-profit)
  Fall 2009 Enrollment: 1,182. (847) 967-5030
  2010-11 Tuition: $12,950
European Massage Therapy School (Private, For-profit)
  Fall 2009 Enrollment: 49 . . . . (847) 673-7595

Everest College-Skokie (Private, For-profit)
  Fall 2009 Enrollment: 1,176. (847) 470-0277
  2010-11 Tuition: $15,193
Housing: Homeownership rate: 77.9% (2010); Median home value: $307,588 (2010); Median contract rent: $898 per month (2005-2009 5-year est.); Median year structure built: 1957 (2005-2009 5-year est.).
Hospitals: Rush North Shore Medical Center (268 beds)
Safety: Violent crime rate: 23.8 per 10,000 population; Property crime rate: 272.4 per 10,000 population (2010).
Newspapers: Chicago Jewish News (Regional news; Circulation 13,500); India Abroad-Midwestern Edition (Regional news; Circulation 95,000)
Transportation: Commute to work: 84.5% car, 8.1% public transportation, 2.4% walk, 3.6% work from home (2005-2009 5-year est.); Travel time to work: 23.6% less than 15 minutes, 34.2% 15 to 30 minutes, 21.4% 30 to 45 minutes, 10.3% 45 to 60 minutes, 10.6% 60 minutes or more (2005-2009 5-year est.)
Additional Information Contacts
Skokie Chamber of Commerce . . . . (847) 673-0240
  http://www.skokiechamber.org
Village of Skokie . . . . (847) 673-0500
  http://www.skokie.com

SOUTH BARRINGTON (village). Covers a land area of 6.555 square miles and a water area of 0.309 square miles. Located at 42.08° N. Lat; 88.15° W. Long. Elevation is 853 feet.

History: The Village of South Barrington was incorporated in December of 1959 and lies in the southeastern portion of Barrington Township and a small portion of western Palatine Township.
Population: 2,960 (1990); 3,760 (2000); 4,367 (2010); 4,616 (2015 projected); Race: 78.2% White, 0.9% Black, 17.7% Asian, 3.2% Other, 2.5% Hispanic of any race (2010); Density: 666.2 persons per square mile (2010); Average household size: 3.20 (2010); Median age: 40.0 (2010); Males per 100 females: 97.7 (2010); Marriage status: 19.8% never married, 71.1% now married, 4.3% widowed, 4.8% divorced (2005-2009 5-year est.); Foreign born: 19.8% (2005-2009 5-year est.); Ancestry (includes multiple ancestries): 17.9% German, 13.9% Polish, 11.1% Italian, 9.1% Greek, 8.2% English (2005-2009 5-year est.).
Economy: Single-family building permits issued: 9 (2010); Multi-family building permits issued: 0 (2010); Employment by occupation: 33.4% management, 39.0% professional, 2.5% services, 22.7% sales, 0.0% farming, 1.1% construction, 1.3% production (2005-2009 5-year est.).
Income: Per capita income: $71,546 (2010); Median household income: $184,515 (2010); Average household income: $228,918 (2010); Percent of households with income of $100,000 or more: 75.7% (2010); Poverty rate: 3.1% (2005-2009 5-year est.).
Taxes: Total city taxes per capita: $1,118 (2007); City property taxes per capita: $459 (2007).
Education: Percent of population age 25 and over with: High school diploma (including GED) or higher: 98.3% (2010); Bachelor's degree or higher: 64.6% (2010); Master's degree or higher: 30.3% (2010).

School District(s)
Barrington CUSD 220 (PK-12)
  2009-10 Enrollment: 9,283 . . . . (847) 381-6300
Housing: Homeownership rate: 98.5% (2010); Median home value: $827,381 (2010); Median contract rent: n/a per month (2005-2009 5-year est.); Median year structure built: 1988 (2005-2009 5-year est.).
Transportation: Commute to work: 93.2% car, 0.7% public transportation, 0.0% walk, 5.7% work from home (2005-2009 5-year est.); Travel time to work: 15.0% less than 15 minutes, 35.4% 15 to 30 minutes, 28.1% 30 to 45 minutes, 10.4% 45 to 60 minutes, 11.1% 60 minutes or more (2005-2009 5-year est.)

SOUTH CHICAGO HEIGHTS (village). Covers a land area of 1.535 square miles and a water area of 0.016 square miles. Located at 41.48° N. Lat; 87.63° W. Long. Elevation is 591 feet.

History: Incorporated 1907.
Population: 3,544 (1990); 3,970 (2000); 3,782 (2010); 3,679 (2015 projected); Race: 70.7% White, 9.9% Black, 1.7% Asian, 17.7% Other, 23.1% Hispanic of any race (2010); Density: 2,463.6 persons per square mile (2010); Average household size: 2.42 (2010); Median age: 40.6 (2010); Males per 100 females: 98.6 (2010); Marriage status: 34.7% never married, 43.8% now married, 9.4% widowed, 12.0% divorced (2005-2009 5-year est.); Foreign born: 10.3% (2005-2009 5-year est.); Ancestry (includes multiple ancestries): 16.6% German, 13.4% Italian, 10.5% Polish, 8.5% Irish, 4.3% English (2005-2009 5-year est.).

Economy: Single-family building permits issued: 0 (2010); Multi-family building permits issued: 0 (2010); Employment by occupation: 7.3% management, 4.2% professional, 17.8% services, 37.8% sales, 0.0% farming, 16.3% construction, 16.6% production (2005-2009 5-year est.).
Income: Per capita income: $22,737 (2010); Median household income: $46,250 (2010); Average household income: $55,524 (2010); Percent of households with income of $100,000 or more: 11.9% (2010); Poverty rate: 17.3% (2005-2009 5-year est.).
Taxes: Total city taxes per capita: $777 (2007); City property taxes per capita: $455 (2007).
Education: Percent of population age 25 and over with: High school diploma (including GED) or higher: 78.1% (2010); Bachelor's degree or higher: 8.6% (2010); Master's degree or higher: 3.6% (2010).

School District(s)
Chicago Heights SD 170 (PK-08)
   2009-10 Enrollment: 3,373 . . . . (708) 756-4165
Steger SD 194 (PK-08)
   2009-10 Enrollment: 1,609 . . . . (708) 755-0022
Housing: Homeownership rate: 74.1% (2010); Median home value: $130,804 (2010); Median contract rent: $615 per month (2005-2009 5-year est.); Median year structure built: 1956 (2005-2009 5-year est.).
Safety: Violent crime rate: 54.0 per 10,000 population; Property crime rate: 402.6 per 10,000 population (2010).
Transportation: Commute to work: 91.5% car, 4.6% public transportation, 0.5% walk, 2.8% work from home (2005-2009 5-year est.); Travel time to work: 40.4% less than 15 minutes, 30.2% 15 to 30 minutes, 10.3% 30 to 45 minutes, 5.9% 45 to 60 minutes, 13.2% 60 minutes or more (2005-2009 5-year est.)

SOUTH HOLLAND (village).
Covers a land area of 7.280 square miles and a water area of 0.015 square miles. Located at 41.59° N. Lat; 87.59° W. Long. Elevation is 600 feet.
History: Named for the province of South Holland, Netherlands, home of early settlers. South Holland was settled in 1840 by immigrants from the Netherlands. An early industry was the raising of onions.
Population: 22,035 (1990); 22,147 (2000); 21,543 (2010); 21,195 (2015 projected); Race: 36.8% White, 57.1% Black, 0.7% Asian, 5.4% Other, 5.9% Hispanic of any race (2010); Density: 2,959.1 persons per square mile (2010); Average household size: 2.83 (2010); Median age: 41.1 (2010); Males per 100 females: 90.1 (2010); Marriage status: 32.8% never married, 49.3% now married, 9.0% widowed, 9.0% divorced (2005-2009 5-year est.); Foreign born: 5.1% (2005-2009 5-year est.); Ancestry (includes multiple ancestries): 6.2% Dutch, 3.8% German, 3.7% Polish, 2.8% Irish, 2.1% Italian (2005-2009 5-year est.).
Economy: Single-family building permits issued: 0 (2010); Multi-family building permits issued: 0 (2010); Employment by occupation: 13.0% management, 23.7% professional, 12.6% services, 30.5% sales, 0.3% farming, 7.6% construction, 12.3% production (2005-2009 5-year est.).
Income: Per capita income: $27,763 (2010); Median household income: $66,916 (2010); Average household income: $79,175 (2010); Percent of households with income of $100,000 or more: 25.9% (2010); Poverty rate: 8.4% (2005-2009 5-year est.).
Taxes: Total city taxes per capita: $811 (2007); City property taxes per capita: $603 (2007).
Education: Percent of population age 25 and over with: High school diploma (including GED) or higher: 91.0% (2010); Bachelor's degree or higher: 29.5% (2010); Master's degree or higher: 11.3% (2010).

School District(s)
Dolton SD 149 (PK-08)
   2009-10 Enrollment: 3,397 . . . . (708) 868-7861
Exc Children Have Opportunities (PK-12)
   2009-10 Enrollment: n/a . . . . (708) 333-7880
South Holland SD 150 (PK-08)
   2009-10 Enrollment: 1,027 . . . . (708) 339-4240
South Holland SD 151 (PK-08)
   2009-10 Enrollment: 1,547 . . . . (708) 339-1516
Thornton Twp HSD 205 (09-12)
   2009-10 Enrollment: 6,179 . . . . (708) 225-4000

Two-year College(s)
South Suburban College (Public)
   Fall 2009 Enrollment: 7,279. . . . . (708) 596-2000
   2010-11 Tuition: In-state $8,813; Out-of-state $10,373
Housing: Homeownership rate: 92.9% (2010); Median home value: $176,770 (2010); Median contract rent: $1,143 per month (2005-2009 5-year est.); Median year structure built: 1966 (2005-2009 5-year est.).

Safety: Violent crime rate: 24.1 per 10,000 population; Property crime rate: 233.2 per 10,000 population (2010).
Newspapers: Calumet City Shopper (Local news); Lansing Shopper (Local news); Munster Shopper (Local news); Riverdale-Dolton Shopper (Local news); South Holland Shopper (Local news)
Transportation: Commute to work: 85.4% car, 10.9% public transportation, 1.3% walk, 2.0% work from home (2005-2009 5-year est.); Travel time to work: 18.5% less than 15 minutes, 23.6% 15 to 30 minutes, 24.0% 30 to 45 minutes, 13.6% 45 to 60 minutes, 20.2% 60 minutes or more (2005-2009 5-year est.)
Additional Information Contacts
South Holland Business Association . . . . (708) 596-0065
   http://www.shba.org
Village of South Holland. . . . . (708) 210-2900
   http://www.southholland.org

STICKNEY (village).
Covers a land area of 1.928 square miles and a water area of 0.033 square miles. Located at 41.81° N. Lat; 87.78° W. Long. Elevation is 604 feet.
History: Incorporated 1913.
Population: 5,678 (1990); 6,148 (2000); 6,813 (2010); 7,125 (2015 projected); Race: 87.6% White, 0.5% Black, 1.4% Asian, 10.6% Other, 34.1% Hispanic of any race (2010); Density: 3,534.4 persons per square mile (2010); Average household size: 2.54 (2010); Median age: 39.3 (2010); Males per 100 females: 100.8 (2010); Marriage status: 28.7% never married, 54.6% now married, 9.2% widowed, 7.4% divorced (2005-2009 5-year est.); Foreign born: 17.7% (2005-2009 5-year est.); Ancestry (includes multiple ancestries): 16.9% Polish, 13.5% Irish, 12.8% German, 12.5% Italian, 7.7% Czech (2005-2009 5-year est.).
Economy: Single-family building permits issued: 1 (2010); Multi-family building permits issued: 0 (2010); Employment by occupation: 11.5% management, 9.5% professional, 12.6% services, 22.9% sales, 0.0% farming, 11.5% construction, 32.0% production (2005-2009 5-year est.).
Income: Per capita income: $21,459 (2010); Median household income: $50,257 (2010); Average household income: $56,937 (2010); Percent of households with income of $100,000 or more: 11.1% (2010); Poverty rate: 9.5% (2005-2009 5-year est.).
Taxes: Total city taxes per capita: $603 (2007); City property taxes per capita: $408 (2007).
Education: Percent of population age 25 and over with: High school diploma (including GED) or higher: 81.8% (2010); Bachelor's degree or higher: 10.9% (2010); Master's degree or higher: 2.9% (2010).

School District(s)
Lyons SD 103 (PK-08)
   2009-10 Enrollment: 2,452 . . . . (708) 783-4100
Housing: Homeownership rate: 80.6% (2010); Median home value: $198,881 (2010); Median contract rent: $743 per month (2005-2009 5-year est.); Median year structure built: 1956 (2005-2009 5-year est.).
Transportation: Commute to work: 89.8% car, 6.0% public transportation, 3.6% walk, 0.6% work from home (2005-2009 5-year est.); Travel time to work: 27.2% less than 15 minutes, 30.1% 15 to 30 minutes, 22.0% 30 to 45 minutes, 5.6% 45 to 60 minutes, 15.0% 60 minutes or more (2005-2009 5-year est.)
Additional Information Contacts
Village of Stickney . . . . (708) 749-4400
   http://www.villageofstickney.com

STONE PARK (village).
Covers a land area of 0.333 square miles and a water area of 0 square miles. Located at 41.90° N. Lat; 87.88° W. Long. Elevation is 640 feet.
History: Incorporated 1939.
Population: 4,383 (1990); 5,127 (2000); 4,807 (2010); 4,667 (2015 projected); Race: 53.8% White, 2.1% Black, 1.2% Asian, 42.9% Other, 85.1% Hispanic of any race (2010); Density: 14,418.3 persons per square mile (2010); Average household size: 4.12 (2010); Median age: 29.0 (2010); Males per 100 females: 112.7 (2010); Marriage status: 31.7% never married, 58.2% now married, 3.4% widowed, 6.7% divorced (2005-2009 5-year est.); Foreign born: 48.8% (2005-2009 5-year est.); Ancestry (includes multiple ancestries): 4.2% Irish, 1.5% German, 1.2% Italian, 0.4% English, 0.4% American (2005-2009 5-year est.).
Economy: Single-family building permits issued: 0 (2010); Multi-family building permits issued: 0 (2010); Employment by occupation: 8.0% management, 6.5% professional, 22.0% services, 21.5% sales, 0.0% farming, 9.5% construction, 32.4% production (2005-2009 5-year est.).

Income: Per capita income: $12,716 (2010); Median household income: $41,148 (2010); Average household income: $52,341 (2010); Percent of households with income of $100,000 or more: 6.3% (2010); Poverty rate: 15.8% (2005-2009 5-year est.).
Taxes: Total city taxes per capita: $700 (2007); City property taxes per capita: $481 (2007).
Education: Percent of population age 25 and over with: High school diploma (including GED) or higher: 50.3% (2010); Bachelor's degree or higher: 5.4% (2010); Master's degree or higher: 2.6% (2010).

School District(s)
Bellwood SD 88 (PK-08)
    2009-10 Enrollment: 2,888 . . . . (708) 344-9344
Housing: Homeownership rate: 65.4% (2010); Median home value: $187,256 (2010); Median contract rent: $789 per month (2005-2009 5-year est.); Median year structure built: 1963 (2005-2009 5-year est.).
Safety: Violent crime rate: 29.3 per 10,000 population; Property crime rate: 203.2 per 10,000 population (2010).
Transportation: Commute to work: 94.3% car, 3.0% public transportation, 1.0% walk, 0.0% work from home (2005-2009 5-year est.); Travel time to work: 28.5% less than 15 minutes, 40.4% 15 to 30 minutes, 18.4% 30 to 45 minutes, 4.4% 45 to 60 minutes, 8.4% 60 minutes or more (2005-2009 5-year est.)

STREAMWOOD (village). Covers a land area of 7.297 square miles and a water area of 0.027 square miles. Located at 42.02° N. Lat; 88.17° W. Long. Elevation is 807 feet.
Population: 31,724 (1990); 36,407 (2000); 35,561 (2010); 35,205 (2015 projected); Race: 68.6% White, 4.4% Black, 12.0% Asian, 15.0% Other, 24.9% Hispanic of any race (2010); Density: 4,873.1 persons per square mile (2010); Average household size: 2.91 (2010); Median age: 36.2 (2010); Males per 100 females: 100.0 (2010); Marriage status: 27.5% never married, 60.0% now married, 4.7% widowed, 7.8% divorced (2005-2009 5-year est.); Foreign born: 29.2% (2005-2009 5-year est.); Ancestry (includes multiple ancestries): 17.1% German, 12.3% Polish, 10.3% Italian, 10.1% Irish, 2.8% English (2005-2009 5-year est.).
Economy: Unemployment rate: 9.7% (August 2011); Total civilian labor force: 21,838 (August 2011); Single-family building permits issued: 6 (2010); Multi-family building permits issued: 0 (2010); Employment by occupation: 14.2% management, 17.5% professional, 15.3% services, 30.3% sales, 0.2% farming, 8.4% construction, 14.0% production (2005-2009 5-year est.).
Income: Per capita income: $30,673 (2010); Median household income: $77,738 (2010); Average household income: $89,571 (2010); Percent of households with income of $100,000 or more: 30.7% (2010); Poverty rate: 6.1% (2005-2009 5-year est.).
Taxes: Total city taxes per capita: $365 (2007); City property taxes per capita: $188 (2007).
Education: Percent of population age 25 and over with: High school diploma (including GED) or higher: 89.1% (2010); Bachelor's degree or higher: 31.4% (2010); Master's degree or higher: 8.9% (2010).

School District(s)
SD U-46 (PK-12)
    2009-10 Enrollment: 41,446 . . . . (847) 888-5000
Township HSD 211 (09-12)
    2009-10 Enrollment: 12,749 . . . . (847) 755-6600
Housing: Homeownership rate: 90.7% (2010); Median home value: $197,684 (2010); Median contract rent: $1,205 per month (2005-2009 5-year est.); Median year structure built: 1980 (2005-2009 5-year est.).
Safety: Violent crime rate: 9.6 per 10,000 population; Property crime rate: 190.6 per 10,000 population (2010).
Transportation: Commute to work: 93.4% car, 3.2% public transportation, 0.6% walk, 1.8% work from home (2005-2009 5-year est.); Travel time to work: 15.1% less than 15 minutes, 35.2% 15 to 30 minutes, 27.9% 30 to 45 minutes, 9.7% 45 to 60 minutes, 12.0% 60 minutes or more (2005-2009 5-year est.)
Additional Information Contacts
Streamwood Chamber of Commerce . . . . (630) 837-5200
    http://www.streamwoodchamber.com
Village of Streamwood. . . . . (630) 736-3800
    http://www.streamwood.org

SUMMIT (village). Covers a land area of 2.124 square miles and a water area of 0.154 square miles. Located at 41.78° N. Lat; 87.81° W. Long. Elevation is 614 feet.

History: Summit developed around the Corn Products Company Plant, a corn refinery. It was named for its location at the crest of the watershed between the Great Lakes and the Mississippi drainage systems. Rain falling on the east side of town drains into the Atlantic Ocean; that falling on the west side into the Gulf of Mexico.
Population: 9,971 (1990); 10,637 (2000); 10,647 (2010); 10,617 (2015 projected); Race: 63.2% White, 8.4% Black, 1.0% Asian, 27.4% Other, 62.2% Hispanic of any race (2010); Density: 5,013.5 persons per square mile (2010); Average household size: 3.24 (2010); Median age: 32.1 (2010); Males per 100 females: 107.3 (2010); Marriage status: 37.6% never married, 45.8% now married, 6.2% widowed, 10.4% divorced (2005-2009 5-year est.); Foreign born: 39.0% (2005-2009 5-year est.); Ancestry (includes multiple ancestries): 10.2% Polish, 6.6% German, 4.2% Irish, 3.3% Lithuanian, 3.0% Italian (2005-2009 5-year est.).
Economy: Single-family building permits issued: 0 (2010); Multi-family building permits issued: 120 (2010); Employment by occupation: 4.1% management, 8.4% professional, 15.2% services, 19.6% sales, 0.3% farming, 14.5% construction, 37.9% production (2005-2009 5-year est.).
Income: Per capita income: $17,087 (2010); Median household income: $44,144 (2010); Average household income: $54,639 (2010); Percent of households with income of $100,000 or more: 13.0% (2010); Poverty rate: 16.6% (2005-2009 5-year est.).
Taxes: Total city taxes per capita: $569 (2007); City property taxes per capita: $378 (2007).
Education: Percent of population age 25 and over with: High school diploma (including GED) or higher: 66.4% (2010); Bachelor's degree or higher: 9.6% (2010); Master's degree or higher: 2.4% (2010).

School District(s)
Argo CHSD 217 (09-12)
    2009-10 Enrollment: 1,843 . . . . (708) 728-3200
Summit SD 104 (PK-08)
    2009-10 Enrollment: 1,737 . . . . (708) 458-0505
Housing: Homeownership rate: 57.7% (2010); Median home value: $177,039 (2010); Median contract rent: $657 per month (2005-2009 5-year est.); Median year structure built: 1951 (2005-2009 5-year est.).
Safety: Violent crime rate: 71.9 per 10,000 population; Property crime rate: 331.4 per 10,000 population (2010).
Newspapers: Des Plaines Valley News (Regional news; Circulation 8,000)
Transportation: Commute to work: 87.2% car, 7.3% public transportation, 3.7% walk, 1.5% work from home (2005-2009 5-year est.); Travel time to work: 26.1% less than 15 minutes, 33.5% 15 to 30 minutes, 20.0% 30 to 45 minutes, 10.0% 45 to 60 minutes, 10.4% 60 minutes or more (2005-2009 5-year est.); Amtrak: train service available.
Additional Information Contacts
Argo-Summit Chamber of Commerce . . . . (708) 458-3033
Village of Summit. . . . . (708) 563-4823
    http://thevillageofsummit.com

THORNTON (village). Covers a land area of 2.334 square miles and a water area of 0.044 square miles. Located at 41.57° N. Lat; 87.61° W. Long. Elevation is 597 feet.
History: Incorporated 1900.
Population: 2,763 (1990); 2,582 (2000); 2,393 (2010); 2,284 (2015 projected); Race: 90.4% White, 5.7% Black, 0.5% Asian, 3.4% Other, 4.8% Hispanic of any race (2010); Density: 1,025.3 persons per square mile (2010); Average household size: 2.42 (2010); Median age: 44.9 (2010); Males per 100 females: 87.8 (2010); Marriage status: 26.0% never married, 53.0% now married, 7.4% widowed, 13.6% divorced (2005-2009 5-year est.); Foreign born: 6.9% (2005-2009 5-year est.); Ancestry (includes multiple ancestries): 27.1% German, 19.6% Irish, 15.6% Polish, 9.2% Italian, 8.7% Dutch (2005-2009 5-year est.).
Economy: Single-family building permits issued: 0 (2010); Multi-family building permits issued: 0 (2010); Employment by occupation: 11.7% management, 9.6% professional, 22.2% services, 28.8% sales, 0.0% farming, 12.0% construction, 15.6% production (2005-2009 5-year est.).
Income: Per capita income: $27,958 (2010); Median household income: $52,591 (2010); Average household income: $67,632 (2010); Percent of households with income of $100,000 or more: 18.3% (2010); Poverty rate: 11.1% (2005-2009 5-year est.).
Taxes: Total city taxes per capita: $970 (2007); City property taxes per capita: $818 (2007).
Education: Percent of population age 25 and over with: High school diploma (including GED) or higher: 91.0% (2010); Bachelor's degree or higher: 17.9% (2010); Master's degree or higher: 3.3% (2010).

School District(s)
Thornton SD 154 (PK-08)
  2009-10 Enrollment: 234 . . . . (708) 877-5160
Housing: Homeownership rate: 90.0% (2010); Median home value: $135,345 (2010); Median contract rent: $750 per month (2005-2009 5-year est.); Median year structure built: 1955 (2005-2009 5-year est.).
Safety: Violent crime rate: 12.9 per 10,000 population; Property crime rate: 214.5 per 10,000 population (2010).
Transportation: Commute to work: 93.1% car, 1.0% public transportation, 1.1% walk, 4.8% work from home (2005-2009 5-year est.); Travel time to work: 34.2% less than 15 minutes, 25.4% 15 to 30 minutes, 16.4% 30 to 45 minutes, 11.0% 45 to 60 minutes, 12.9% 60 minutes or more (2005-2009 5-year est.).

TINLEY PARK (village). Covers a land area of 14.953 square miles and a water area of 0.036 square miles. Located at 41.57° N. Lat; 87.80° W. Long. Elevation is 699 feet.
Population: 38,640 (1990); 48,401 (2000); 53,896 (2010); 56,003 (2015 projected); Race: 90.5% White, 3.4% Black, 2.9% Asian, 3.3% Other, 5.4% Hispanic of any race (2010); Density: 3,604.3 persons per square mile (2010); Average household size: 2.75 (2010); Median age: 38.1 (2010); Males per 100 females: 95.6 (2010); Marriage status: 28.3% never married, 55.6% now married, 7.5% widowed, 8.6% divorced (2005-2009 5-year est.); Foreign born: 8.3% (2005-2009 5-year est.); Ancestry (includes multiple ancestries): 26.9% Irish, 23.7% German, 18.9% Polish, 12.9% Italian, 6.0% English (2005-2009 5-year est.).
Economy: Unemployment rate: 8.6% (August 2011); Total civilian labor force: 32,740 (August 2011); Single-family building permits issued: 8 (2010); Multi-family building permits issued: 0 (2010); Employment by occupation: 14.7% management, 20.7% professional, 13.5% services, 29.1% sales, 0.1% farming, 9.8% construction, 12.1% production (2005-2009 5-year est.).
Income: Per capita income: $31,992 (2010); Median household income: $77,970 (2010); Average household income: $88,522 (2010); Percent of households with income of $100,000 or more: 32.9% (2010); Poverty rate: 5.7% (2005-2009 5-year est.).
Taxes: Total city taxes per capita: $422 (2007); City property taxes per capita: $350 (2007).
Education: Percent of population age 25 and over with: High school diploma (including GED) or higher: 92.6% (2010); Bachelor's degree or higher: 28.5% (2010); Master's degree or higher: 9.1% (2010).

School District(s)
Arbor Park SD 145 (PK-08)
  2009-10 Enrollment: 1,456 . . . . (708) 687-8040
Bremen CHSD 228 (09-12)
  2009-10 Enrollment: 5,533 . . . . (708) 389-1175
Kirby SD 140 (PK-08)
  2009-10 Enrollment: 3,928 . . . . (708) 532-6462
Summit Hill SD 161 (PK-08)
  2009-10 Enrollment: 3,662 . . . . (815) 469-9103
Tinley Park CCSD 146 (PK-08)
  2009-10 Enrollment: 2,343 . . . . (708) 614-4500

Vocational/Technical School(s)
Regency Beauty Insitute-Tinley Park (Private, For-profit)
  Fall 2009 Enrollment: 111 . . . . (800) 787-6456
  2010-11 Tuition: $16,075
Housing: Homeownership rate: 88.1% (2010); Median home value: $228,742 (2010); Median contract rent: $825 per month (2005-2009 5-year est.); Median year structure built: 1984 (2005-2009 5-year est.).
Hospitals: Tinley Park Mental Health Center (150 beds)
Safety: Violent crime rate: 8.2 per 10,000 population; Property crime rate: 163.6 per 10,000 population (2010).
Newspapers: Alsip/Blue Island Star (Local news; Circulation 2,350); Calumet City Star (Local news; Circulation 2,975); Chicago Heights Star (Local news; Circulation 14,640); Chicago Tribune - Tinley Park Bureau (Local news); Crete/University Park Star (Local news; Circulation 3,840); Daily Southtown (Community news; Circulation 56,305); Frankfort Mokena Star (Local news; Circulation 5,300); Harvey Markham Star (Local news; Circulation 5,150); Hazel Crest/Country Club Hills Star (Local news; Circulation 4,560); Homer Township Star (Local news; Circulation 2,075); Homewood/Flossmoor Star (Local news; Circulation 8,220); Lansing/Lynwood Star (Local news; Circulation 3,200); Matteson/Richton Park Star (Local news; Circulation 5,300); New Lenox/Manhattan Star (Local news; Circulation 5,500); Oak Forest/Crestwood/Midlothian Star (Local news; Circulation 4,950); Oak Lawn Star (Local news; Circulation

2,535); Orland Park Star (Local news; Circulation 4,325); Palos Area Star (Local news; Circulation 3,050); Park Forest Star (Local news; Circulation 7,040); South Holland/Dolton Star (Local news); Tinley Park Star (Local news)
Transportation: Commute to work: 87.1% car, 8.1% public transportation, 1.4% walk, 2.4% work from home (2005-2009 5-year est.); Travel time to work: 22.0% less than 15 minutes, 26.1% 15 to 30 minutes, 20.9% 30 to 45 minutes, 11.4% 45 to 60 minutes, 19.6% 60 minutes or more (2005-2009 5-year est.)
Additional Information Contacts
Tinley Park Chamber of Commerce. . . . . (708) 532-5700
  http://www.tinleychamber.org
Village of Tinley Park . . . . (708) 444-5000
  http://www.tinleypark.org

WESTCHESTER (village). Covers a land area of 3.195 square miles and a water area of 0 square miles. Located at 41.85° N. Lat; 87.88° W. Long. Elevation is 636 feet.
Population: 17,309 (1990); 16,824 (2000); 15,650 (2010); 15,152 (2015 projected); Race: 78.0% White, 11.9% Black, 4.7% Asian, 5.4% Other, 9.6% Hispanic of any race (2010); Density: 4,897.8 persons per square mile (2010); Average household size: 2.36 (2010); Median age: 46.8 (2010); Males per 100 females: 89.6 (2010); Marriage status: 24.2% never married, 58.4% now married, 9.4% widowed, 7.9% divorced (2005-2009 5-year est.); Foreign born: 15.9% (2005-2009 5-year est.); Ancestry (includes multiple ancestries): 16.5% Italian, 14.9% German, 13.4% Polish, 13.3% Irish, 4.6% Czech (2005-2009 5-year est.).
Economy: Single-family building permits issued: 0 (2010); Multi-family building permits issued: 0 (2010); Employment by occupation: 16.8% management, 27.3% professional, 13.2% services, 27.4% sales, 0.0% farming, 5.2% construction, 10.2% production (2005-2009 5-year est.).
Income: Per capita income: $35,491 (2010); Median household income: $69,840 (2010); Average household income: $84,448 (2010); Percent of households with income of $100,000 or more: 30.2% (2010); Poverty rate: 3.4% (2005-2009 5-year est.).
Taxes: Total city taxes per capita: $575 (2007); City property taxes per capita: $355 (2007).
Education: Percent of population age 25 and over with: High school diploma (including GED) or higher: 92.2% (2010); Bachelor's degree or higher: 35.8% (2010); Master's degree or higher: 13.1% (2010).

School District(s)
Westchester SD 92-5 (PK-08)
  2009-10 Enrollment: 1,218 . . . . (708) 450-2700
Housing: Homeownership rate: 92.1% (2010); Median home value: $248,339 (2010); Median contract rent: $904 per month (2005-2009 5-year est.); Median year structure built: 1957 (2005-2009 5-year est.).
Safety: Violent crime rate: 9.8 per 10,000 population; Property crime rate: 183.9 per 10,000 population (2010).
Transportation: Commute to work: 88.6% car, 5.6% public transportation, 1.1% walk, 3.5% work from home (2005-2009 5-year est.); Travel time to work: 24.0% less than 15 minutes, 34.0% 15 to 30 minutes, 22.9% 30 to 45 minutes, 10.5% 45 to 60 minutes, 8.6% 60 minutes or more (2005-2009 5-year est.)
Additional Information Contacts
Village of Westchester . . . . (708) 345-0020
  http://www.westchester-il.org
Westchester Chamber of Commerce. . . . . (708) 240-8400
  http://www.westchesterchamber.org

WESTERN SPRINGS (village). Covers a land area of 2.626 square miles and a water area of 0 square miles. Located at 41.80° N. Lat; 87.90° W. Long. Elevation is 673 feet.
History: Western Springs was named for the mineral springs, believed to be medicinal when the community was settled by the Quakers in 1866.
Population: 11,993 (1990); 12,493 (2000); 12,700 (2010); 12,768 (2015 projected); Race: 98.2% White, 0.2% Black, 0.7% Asian, 0.9% Other, 2.1% Hispanic of any race (2010); Density: 4,835.5 persons per square mile (2010); Average household size: 2.89 (2010); Median age: 38.6 (2010); Males per 100 females: 93.3 (2010); Marriage status: 17.6% never married, 73.9% now married, 5.9% widowed, 2.6% divorced (2005-2009 5-year est.); Foreign born: 4.5% (2005-2009 5-year est.); Ancestry (includes multiple ancestries): 32.4% Irish, 29.4% German, 13.3% English, 13.2% Italian, 10.4% Polish (2005-2009 5-year est.).
Economy: Single-family building permits issued: 14 (2010); Multi-family building permits issued: 0 (2010); Employment by occupation: 27.6%

management, 32.7% professional, 4.6% services, 29.8% sales, 0.1% farming, 2.5% construction, 2.6% production (2005-2009 5-year est.).
Income: Per capita income: $50,875 (2010); Median household income: $112,826 (2010); Average household income: $147,002 (2010); Percent of households with income of $100,000 or more: 56.7% (2010); Poverty rate: 1.3% (2005-2009 5-year est.).
Taxes: Total city taxes per capita: $569 (2007); City property taxes per capita: $378 (2007).
Education: Percent of population age 25 and over with: High school diploma (including GED) or higher: 98.0% (2010); Bachelor's degree or higher: 69.5% (2010); Master's degree or higher: 28.8% (2010).

School District(s)
Western Springs SD 101 (PK-08)
  2009-10 Enrollment: 1,566 . . . . (708) 246-3700
Housing: Homeownership rate: 93.9% (2010); Median home value: $487,172 (2010); Median contract rent: $933 per month (2005-2009 5-year est.); Median year structure built: 1956 (2005-2009 5-year est.).
Safety: Violent crime rate: 0.8 per 10,000 population; Property crime rate: 83.1 per 10,000 population (2010).
Transportation: Commute to work: 72.5% car, 17.1% public transportation, 2.0% walk, 7.8% work from home (2005-2009 5-year est.); Travel time to work: 22.8% less than 15 minutes, 22.8% 15 to 30 minutes, 25.2% 30 to 45 minutes, 17.4% 45 to 60 minutes, 11.8% 60 minutes or more (2005-2009 5-year est.)
Additional Information Contacts
Village of Western Springs. . . . . (708) 246-1800
  http://www.wsprings.com

WHEELING (village). Covers a land area of 8.400 square miles and a water area of 0.036 square miles. Located at 42.13° N. Lat; 87.93° W. Long. Elevation is 650 feet.
History: Named for Wheeling, West Virginia. The first building in Wheeling was a country store established in 1830 on the Chicago-Milwaukee stage route.
Population: 30,008 (1990); 34,496 (2000); 34,369 (2010); 34,062 (2015 projected); Race: 67.5% White, 2.3% Black, 11.1% Asian, 19.1% Other, 32.8% Hispanic of any race (2010); Density: 4,091.4 persons per square mile (2010); Average household size: 2.68 (2010); Median age: 38.2 (2010); Males per 100 females: 98.5 (2010); Marriage status: 30.4% never married, 55.3% now married, 5.8% widowed, 8.5% divorced (2005-2009 5-year est.); Foreign born: 39.0% (2005-2009 5-year est.); Ancestry (includes multiple ancestries): 14.2% German, 10.7% Polish, 8.0% Irish, 7.4% Russian, 4.1% Italian (2005-2009 5-year est.).
Economy: Unemployment rate: 8.5% (August 2011); Total civilian labor force: 21,553 (August 2011); Single-family building permits issued: 9 (2010); Multi-family building permits issued: 0 (2010); Employment by occupation: 13.0% management, 17.4% professional, 17.4% services, 26.5% sales, 0.0% farming, 6.9% construction, 18.8% production (2005-2009 5-year est.).
Income: Per capita income: $30,366 (2010); Median household income: $67,287 (2010); Average household income: $81,902 (2010); Percent of households with income of $100,000 or more: 25.8% (2010); Poverty rate: 8.1% (2005-2009 5-year est.).
Taxes: Total city taxes per capita: $638 (2007); City property taxes per capita: $373 (2007).
Education: Percent of population age 25 and over with: High school diploma (including GED) or higher: 85.9% (2010); Bachelor's degree or higher: 35.8% (2010); Master's degree or higher: 12.3% (2010).

School District(s)
Township HSD 214 (09-12)
  2009-10 Enrollment: 12,241 . . . . (847) 718-7600
Wheeling CCSD 21 (PK-08)
  2009-10 Enrollment: 6,952 . . . . (847) 537-8270
Two-year College(s)
Worsham College of Mortuary Science (Private, For-profit)
  Fall 2009 Enrollment: 107 . . . . (847) 808-8444
Vocational/Technical School(s)
SOLEX Medical Academy (Private, For-profit)
  Fall 2009 Enrollment: 23 . . . . (8.4) 723-E+12
  2010-11 Tuition: $9,995
Housing: Homeownership rate: 72.5% (2010); Median home value: $220,762 (2010); Median contract rent: $882 per month (2005-2009 5-year est.); Median year structure built: 1977 (2005-2009 5-year est.).
Safety: Violent crime rate: 17.5 per 10,000 population; Property crime rate: 179.4 per 10,000 population (2010).

Transportation: Commute to work: 90.7% car, 2.5% public transportation, 1.6% walk, 3.3% work from home (2005-2009 5-year est.); Travel time to work: 25.7% less than 15 minutes, 35.5% 15 to 30 minutes, 27.1% 30 to 45 minutes, 5.4% 45 to 60 minutes, 6.3% 60 minutes or more (2005-2009 5-year est.)
Airports: Chicago Executive (general aviation)
Additional Information Contacts
Village of Wheeling . . . . (847) 459-2600
  http://vi.wheeling.il.us
Wheeling/Prospect Heights Area Chamber of Commerce & Industr . . (847) 541-0170
  http://www.wphchamber.com

WILLOW SPRINGS (village). Covers a land area of 3.868 square miles and a water area of 0.110 square miles. Located at 41.73° N. Lat; 87.87° W. Long. Elevation is 617 feet.
Population: 4,660 (1990); 5,027 (2000); 5,593 (2010); 5,861 (2015 projected); Race: 90.0% White, 3.1% Black, 2.3% Asian, 4.6% Other, 7.5% Hispanic of any race (2010); Density: 1,446.1 persons per square mile (2010); Average household size: 2.73 (2010); Median age: 42.3 (2010); Males per 100 females: 99.3 (2010); Marriage status: 25.9% never married, 57.9% now married, 6.5% widowed, 9.7% divorced (2005-2009 5-year est.); Foreign born: 18.5% (2005-2009 5-year est.); Ancestry (includes multiple ancestries): 26.9% Polish, 19.8% German, 16.6% Irish, 9.3% Italian, 8.8% Lithuanian (2005-2009 5-year est.).
Economy: Single-family building permits issued: 0 (2010); Multi-family building permits issued: 0 (2010); Employment by occupation: 20.3% management, 19.7% professional, 11.9% services, 24.0% sales, 0.0% farming, 8.3% construction, 15.8% production (2005-2009 5-year est.).
Income: Per capita income: $35,083 (2010); Median household income: $74,671 (2010); Average household income: $95,631 (2010); Percent of households with income of $100,000 or more: 31.8% (2010); Poverty rate: 2.9% (2005-2009 5-year est.).
Taxes: Total city taxes per capita: $765 (2007); City property taxes per capita: $532 (2007).
Education: Percent of population age 25 and over with: High school diploma (including GED) or higher: 90.0% (2010); Bachelor's degree or higher: 30.6% (2010); Master's degree or higher: 13.9% (2010).

School District(s)
Willow Springs SD 108 (PK-08)
  2009-10 Enrollment: 322 . . . . (708) 839-6828
Housing: Homeownership rate: 88.3% (2010); Median home value: $325,787 (2010); Median contract rent: $768 per month (2005-2009 5-year est.); Median year structure built: 1977 (2005-2009 5-year est.).
Safety: Violent crime rate: 1.7 per 10,000 population; Property crime rate: 81.7 per 10,000 population (2010).
Transportation: Commute to work: 92.8% car, 4.1% public transportation, 0.8% walk, 2.0% work from home (2005-2009 5-year est.); Travel time to work: 22.3% less than 15 minutes, 28.1% 15 to 30 minutes, 28.5% 30 to 45 minutes, 9.8% 45 to 60 minutes, 11.3% 60 minutes or more (2005-2009 5-year est.)
Additional Information Contacts
Village of Willow Springs . . . . (708) 467-3700
  http://www.willowsprings-il.gov

WILMETTE (village). Covers a land area of 5.384 square miles and a water area of 0.006 square miles. Located at 42.07° N. Lat; 87.72° W. Long. Elevation is 636 feet.
History: Wilmette was named for Antoine Ouilmette, a French-Canadian who settled here when his wife received the land under a government treaty in 1829.
Population: 26,685 (1990); 27,651 (2000); 27,504 (2010); 27,369 (2015 projected); Race: 88.5% White, 0.6% Black, 8.9% Asian, 2.1% Other, 2.5% Hispanic of any race (2010); Density: 5,108.5 persons per square mile (2010); Average household size: 2.76 (2010); Median age: 42.8 (2010); Males per 100 females: 92.7 (2010); Marriage status: 21.3% never married, 66.3% now married, 6.5% widowed, 5.9% divorced (2005-2009 5-year est.); Foreign born: 14.4% (2005-2009 5-year est.); Ancestry (includes multiple ancestries): 22.2% Irish, 21.4% German, 11.2% English, 7.5% Polish, 6.7% Russian (2005-2009 5-year est.).
Economy: Unemployment rate: 7.1% (August 2011); Total civilian labor force: 12,592 (August 2011); Single-family building permits issued: 24 (2010); Multi-family building permits issued: 0 (2010); Employment by occupation: 27.7% management, 38.4% professional, 5.8% services,

23.4% sales, 0.0% farming, 1.8% construction, 2.9% production (2005-2009 5-year est.).

Income: Per capita income: $59,264 (2010); Median household income: $120,375 (2010); Average household income: $165,112 (2010); Percent of households with income of $100,000 or more: 58.4% (2010); Poverty rate: 2.1% (2005-2009 5-year est.).

Taxes: Total city taxes per capita: $743 (2007); City property taxes per capita: $406 (2007).

Education: Percent of population age 25 and over with: High school diploma (including GED) or higher: 97.8% (2010); Bachelor's degree or higher: 75.6% (2010); Master's degree or higher: 40.5% (2010).

School District(s)

Avoca SD 37 (PK-08)

    2009-10 Enrollment: 687 . . . . (847) 251-3587

Wilmette SD 39 (PK-08)

    2009-10 Enrollment: 3,723 . . . . (847) 256-2450

Housing: Homeownership rate: 88.8% (2010); Median home value: $611,440 (2010); Median contract rent: $1,283 per month (2005-2009 5-year est.); Median year structure built: 1954 (2005-2009 5-year est.).

Transportation: Commute to work: 70.8% car, 16.5% public transportation, 2.7% walk, 8.1% work from home (2005-2009 5-year est.); Travel time to work: 21.9% less than 15 minutes, 25.4% 15 to 30 minutes, 21.9% 30 to 45 minutes, 14.4% 45 to 60 minutes, 16.4% 60 minutes or more (2005-2009 5-year est.)

Additional Information Contacts

Village of Wilmette . . . . (847) 251-2700

    http://www.wilmette.com

Wilmette Chamber of Commerce . . . . (847) 251-3800

    http://www.wilmettechamber.org

WINNETKA (village). Covers a land area of 3.830 square miles and a water area of 0.086 square miles. Located at 42.10° N. Lat; 87.73° W. Long. Elevation is 653 feet.

History: Named for a variation of the Algonquian translation of "beautiful". Winnetka was incorporated in 1869. The Winnetka public school system, organized in 1919 with Carleton Washburne as superintendent, gained recognition for innovative eucation.

Population: 12,174 (1990); 12,419 (2000); 12,427 (2010); 12,339 (2015 projected); Race: 96.4% White, 0.2% Black, 2.1% Asian, 1.3% Other, 1.6% Hispanic of any race (2010); Density: 3,244.8 persons per square mile (2010); Average household size: 3.06 (2010); Median age: 32.9 (2010); Males per 100 females: 94.8 (2010); Marriage status: 20.1% never married, 72.2% now married, 4.1% widowed, 3.7% divorced (2005-2009 5-year est.); Foreign born: 5.8% (2005-2009 5-year est.); Ancestry (includes multiple ancestries): 27.0% German, 21.9% Irish, 17.6% English, 7.2% Italian, 7.0% American (2005-2009 5-year est.).

Economy: Single-family building permits issued: 31 (2010); Multi-family building permits issued: 0 (2010); Employment by occupation: 38.2% management, 26.3% professional, 5.0% services, 26.2% sales, 0.6% farming, 1.1% construction, 2.6% production (2005-2009 5-year est.).

Income: Per capita income: $77,938 (2010); Median household income: $192,992 (2010); Average household income: $238,410 (2010); Percent of households with income of $100,000 or more: 74.6% (2010); Poverty rate: 1.4% (2005-2009 5-year est.).

Taxes: Total city taxes per capita: $1,143 (2007); City property taxes per capita: $899 (2007).

Education: Percent of population age 25 and over with: High school diploma (including GED) or higher: 99.2% (2010); Bachelor's degree or higher: 86.4% (2010); Master's degree or higher: 45.9% (2010).

School District(s)

New Trier Twp HSD 203 (09-12)

    2009-10 Enrollment: 4,143 . . . . (847) 784-6109

Winnetka SD 36 (PK-08)

    2009-10 Enrollment: 1,930 . . . . (847) 446-9400

Housing: Homeownership rate: 91.5% (2010); Median home value: $952,506 (2010); Median contract rent: $1,007 per month (2005-2009 5-year est.); Median year structure built: before 1940 (2005-2009 5-year est.).

Safety: Violent crime rate: 5.7 per 10,000 population; Property crime rate: 120.9 per 10,000 population (2010).

Transportation: Commute to work: 66.1% car, 21.4% public transportation, 2.3% walk, 9.5% work from home (2005-2009 5-year est.); Travel time to work: 22.5% less than 15 minutes, 20.4% 15 to 30 minutes, 24.0% 30 to 45 minutes, 19.9% 45 to 60 minutes, 13.1% 60 minutes or more (2005-2009 5-year est.)

Additional Information Contacts

Village of Winnetka . . . . (847) 501-6000

    http://www.villageofwinnetka.org

Winnetka-Northfield Chamber of Commerce . . . . (847) 446-4451

    http://www.winnetkachamber.com

WORTH (village). Covers a land area of 2.384 square miles and a water area of 0.022 square miles. Located at 41.68° N. Lat; 87.79° W. Long. Elevation is 610 feet.

Population: 11,211 (1990); 11,047 (2000); 10,060 (2010); 9,629 (2015 projected); Race: 89.1% White, 2.1% Black, 1.6% Asian, 7.1% Other, 8.8% Hispanic of any race (2010); Density: 4,220.4 persons per square mile (2010); Average household size: 2.45 (2010); Median age: 38.8 (2010); Males per 100 females: 97.9 (2010); Marriage status: 27.7% never married, 53.0% now married, 6.1% widowed, 13.3% divorced (2005-2009 5-year est.); Foreign born: 15.3% (2005-2009 5-year est.); Ancestry (includes multiple ancestries): 24.3% Polish, 23.0% German, 20.7% Irish, 9.8% Italian, 5.1% English (2005-2009 5-year est.).

Economy: Single-family building permits issued: 0 (2010); Multi-family building permits issued: 0 (2010); Employment by occupation: 12.5% management, 10.5% professional, 12.7% services, 27.3% sales, 0.0% farming, 21.8% construction, 15.2% production (2005-2009 5-year est.).

Income: Per capita income: $24,084 (2010); Median household income: $49,487 (2010); Average household income: $59,031 (2010); Percent of households with income of $100,000 or more: 13.6% (2010); Poverty rate: 9.2% (2005-2009 5-year est.).

Taxes: Total city taxes per capita: $368 (2007); City property taxes per capita: $242 (2007).

Education: Percent of population age 25 and over with: High school diploma (including GED) or higher: 86.2% (2010); Bachelor's degree or higher: 13.9% (2010); Master's degree or higher: 4.5% (2010).

School District(s)

Worth SD 127 (PK-08)

    2009-10 Enrollment: 1,039 . . . . (708) 448-2800

Housing: Homeownership rate: 72.4% (2010); Median home value: $178,311 (2010); Median contract rent: $775 per month (2005-2009 5-year est.); Median year structure built: 1963 (2005-2009 5-year est.).

Safety: Violent crime rate: 8.8 per 10,000 population; Property crime rate: 153.8 per 10,000 population (2010).

Transportation: Commute to work: 89.3% car, 6.1% public transportation, 0.6% walk, 3.1% work from home (2005-2009 5-year est.); Travel time to work: 23.2% less than 15 minutes, 23.8% 15 to 30 minutes, 22.6% 30 to 45 minutes, 17.5% 45 to 60 minutes, 12.9% 60 minutes or more (2005-2009 5-year est.)

Additional Information Contacts

Chicago Southland Chamber of Commerce . . . . (708) 957-6950

    http://www.chicagosouthland.com

Village of Worth . . . . (708) 448-1181

    http://www.villageofworth.com

Crawford County

Located in southeastern Illinois; bounded on the east by the Wabash River and the Indiana border; drained by the Embarrass River. Covers a land area of 443.53 square miles, a water area of 2.20 square miles, and is located in the Central Time Zone at 39.00° N. Lat., 87.75° W. Long. The county was founded in 1816. County seat is Robinson.

Weather Station: Palestine 2 W								Elevation: 470 feet			
	Jan	Feb	Mar	Apr	May	Jun	Jul	Aug	Sep	Oct	Nov	Dec
High	39	44	55	67	77	86	88	87	81	69	55	42
Low	23	27	35	45	54	62	66	65	55	45	36	26
Precip	3.0	2.5	3.4	4.3	5.1	4.0	3.8	3.7	3.5	3.5	3.9	3.2
Snow	4.9	3.6	1.5	0.1	0.0	0.0	0.0	0.0	0.0	0.1	0.5	4.1

High and Low temperatures in degrees Fahrenheit; Precipitation and Snow in inches

Population: 19,464 (1990); 20,452 (2000); 19,448 (2010); 18,890 (2015 projected); Race: 92.7% White, 5.0% Black, 0.3% Asian, 2.0% Other, 2.3% Hispanic of any race (2010); Density: 43.8 persons per square mile (2010); Average household size: 2.38 (2010); Median age: 39.9 (2010); Males per 100 females: 110.0 (2010).

Religion: Five largest groups: 10.5% The United Methodist Church, 10.3% Christian Churches and Churches of Christ, 8.9% Southern Baptist Convention, 6.9% Christian Church (Disciples of Christ), 4.2% Catholic Church (2000).

Economy: Unemployment rate: 9.3% (August 2011); Total civilian labor force: 9,722 (August 2011); Leading industries: 31.8% manufacturing; 14.5% health care and social assistance; 12.4% retail trade (2009); Farms: 615 totaling 205,356 acres (2007); Companies that employ 500 or more persons: 2 (2009); Companies that employ 100 to 499 persons: 9 (2009); Companies that employ less than 100 persons: 419 (2009); Black-owned businesses: n/a (2007); Hispanic-owned businesses: n/a (2007); Asian-owned businesses: n/a (2007); Women-owned businesses: 421 (2007); Retail sales per capita: $16,874 (2010). Single-family building permits issued: 7 (2010); Multi-family building permits issued: 0 (2010).
Income: Per capita income: $22,461 (2010); Median household income: $44,191 (2010); Average household income: $54,978 (2010); Percent of households with income of $100,000 or more: 10.9% (2010); Poverty rate: 15.2% (2009); Bankruptcy rate: 4.04% (2010).
Taxes: Total county taxes per capita: $146 (2007); County property taxes per capita: $129 (2007).
Education: Percent of population age 25 and over with: High school diploma (including GED) or higher: 85.1% (2010); Bachelor's degree or higher: 12.6% (2010); Master's degree or higher: 4.3% (2010).
Housing: Homeownership rate: 79.2% (2010); Median home value: $71,807 (2010); Median contract rent: $337 per month (2005-2009 5-year est.); Median year structure built: 1958 (2005-2009 5-year est.).
Health: Birth rate: 99.3 per 10,000 population (2009); Death rate: 118.9 per 10,000 population (2009); Age-adjusted cancer mortality rate: 183.4 deaths per 100,000 population (2007); Number of physicians: 11.8 per 10,000 population (2008); Hospital beds: 33.3 per 10,000 population (2007); Hospital admissions: 657.9 per 10,000 population (2007).
Elections: 2008 Presidential election results: 42.5% Obama, 55.5% McCain, 0.9% Nader
National and State Parks: Crawford County State Fish and Wildlife Area
Additional Information Contacts

Crawford County Government . . . . (618) 546-1212
  http://www.crawfordcountycentral.com
City of Robinson. . . . . (618) 544-7616
  http://www.cityofrobinson.com
Oblong Chamber of Commerce . . . . (618) 592-4355
  http://www.theonlyoblong.com
Palestine Chamber of Commerce . . . . (618) 586-2222
  http://www.pioneercity.com/chamberofcommerce
Robinson Chamber of Commerce . . . . (618) 546-1557
  http://www.robinsonchamber.org

Crawford County Communities

ANNAPOLIS (unincorporated postal area, zip code 62413). Covers a land area of 34.895 square miles and a water area of 0.042 square miles. Located at 39.13° N. Lat; 87.83° W. Long. Elevation is 584 feet.
Population: 441 (2000); Race: 99.3% White, 0.0% Black, 0.0% Asian, 0.7% Other, 2.0% Hispanic of any race (2000); Density: 12.6 persons per square mile (2000); Age: 26.5% under 18, 14.7% over 64 (2000); Marriage status: 25.9% never married, 65.2% now married, 6.3% widowed, 2.6% divorced (2000); Foreign born: 0.0% (2000); Ancestry (includes multiple ancestries): 12.5% German, 12.5% American, 10.3% Irish, 9.6% English (2000).
Economy: Employment by occupation: 9.0% management, 8.5% professional, 22.8% services, 17.5% sales, 1.6% farming, 11.6% construction, 29.1% production (2000).
Income: Per capita income: $17,743 (2000); Median household income: $41,827 (2000); Poverty rate: 14.7% (2000).
Education: Percent of population age 25 and over with: High school diploma (including GED) or higher: 86.2% (2000); Bachelor's degree or higher: 7.4% (2000).
Housing: Homeownership rate: 88.4% (2000); Median home value: $34,800 (2000); Median contract rent: $325 per month (2000); Median year structure built: 1959 (2000).
Transportation: Commute to work: 89.4% car, 0.0% public transportation, 1.6% walk, 9.0% work from home (2000); Travel time to work: 12.2% less than 15 minutes, 63.4% 15 to 30 minutes, 15.1% 30 to 45 minutes, 1.7% 45 to 60 minutes, 7.6% 60 minutes or more (2000)

FLAT ROCK (village). Covers a land area of 0.856 square miles and a water area of 0 square miles. Located at 38.90° N. Lat; 87.67° W. Long. Elevation is 502 feet.
Population: 426 (1990); 415 (2000); 374 (2010); 350 (2015 projected); Race: 97.6% White, 0.8% Black, 0.5% Asian, 1.1% Other, 0.0% Hispanic

of any race (2010); Density: 437.1 persons per square mile (2010); Average household size: 2.60 (2010); Median age: 39.3 (2010); Males per 100 females: 93.8 (2010); Marriage status: 25.6% never married, 50.1% now married, 7.5% widowed, 16.7% divorced (2005-2009 5-year est.); Foreign born: 0.0% (2005-2009 5-year est.); Ancestry (includes multiple ancestries): 18.1% German, 11.6% English, 10.0% Irish, 7.9% American, 6.0% Dutch (2005-2009 5-year est.).
Economy: Employment by occupation: 7.4% management, 12.7% professional, 16.4% services, 24.9% sales, 0.0% farming, 13.8% construction, 24.9% production (2005-2009 5-year est.).
Income: Per capita income: $22,404 (2010); Median household income: $47,778 (2010); Average household income: $57,986 (2010); Percent of households with income of $100,000 or more: 6.9% (2010); Poverty rate: 20.4% (2005-2009 5-year est.).
Taxes: Total city taxes per capita: $27 (2007); City property taxes per capita: $25 (2007).
Education: Percent of population age 25 and over with: High school diploma (including GED) or higher: 79.3% (2010); Bachelor's degree or higher: 8.0% (2010); Master's degree or higher: 3.1% (2010).
Housing: Homeownership rate: 92.4% (2010); Median home value: $58,929 (2010); Median contract rent: $286 per month (2005-2009 5-year est.); Median year structure built: 1945 (2005-2009 5-year est.).
Transportation: Commute to work: 96.3% car, 0.0% public transportation, 1.1% walk, 0.0% work from home (2005-2009 5-year est.); Travel time to work: 26.2% less than 15 minutes, 52.9% 15 to 30 minutes, 16.0% 30 to 45 minutes, 1.6% 45 to 60 minutes, 3.2% 60 minutes or more (2005-2009 5-year est.)

HUTSONVILLE (village). Covers a land area of 0.693 square miles and a water area of 0 square miles. Located at 39.10° N. Lat; 87.65° W. Long. Elevation is 436 feet.
Population: 627 (1990); 568 (2000); 515 (2010); 486 (2015 projected); Race: 98.1% White, 1.0% Black, 0.0% Asian, 1.0% Other, 0.8% Hispanic of any race (2010); Density: 743.2 persons per square mile (2010); Average household size: 2.33 (2010); Median age: 44.8 (2010); Males per 100 females: 109.3 (2010); Marriage status: 36.0% never married, 38.1% now married, 5.7% widowed, 20.2% divorced (2005-2009 5-year est.); Foreign born: 0.0% (2005-2009 5-year est.); Ancestry (includes multiple ancestries): 24.7% German, 21.0% English, 15.3% American, 11.6% Irish, 4.1% Italian (2005-2009 5-year est.).
Economy: Single-family building permits issued: 0 (2010); Multi-family building permits issued: 0 (2010); Employment by occupation: 5.5% management, 20.1% professional, 39.8% services, 16.5% sales, 1.2% farming, 5.5% construction, 11.4% production (2005-2009 5-year est.).
Income: Per capita income: $20,252 (2010); Median household income: $41,951 (2010); Average household income: $48,466 (2010); Percent of households with income of $100,000 or more: 8.2% (2010); Poverty rate: 32.7% (2005-2009 5-year est.).
Taxes: Total city taxes per capita: $30 (2007); City property taxes per capita: $17 (2007).
Education: Percent of population age 25 and over with: High school diploma (including GED) or higher: 82.6% (2010); Bachelor's degree or higher: 7.8% (2010); Master's degree or higher: 2.3% (2010).
School District(s)
Hutsonville CUSD 1 (PK-12)
  2009-10 Enrollment: 380 . . . . (618) 563-4912
Housing: Homeownership rate: 77.8% (2010); Median home value: $63,182 (2010); Median contract rent: $240 per month (2005-2009 5-year est.); Median year structure built: 1943 (2005-2009 5-year est.).
Transportation: Commute to work: 93.7% car, 1.7% public transportation, 1.7% walk, 3.0% work from home (2005-2009 5-year est.); Travel time to work: 50.9% less than 15 minutes, 27.4% 15 to 30 minutes, 3.5% 30 to 45 minutes, 11.7% 45 to 60 minutes, 6.5% 60 minutes or more (2005-2009 5-year est.)

OBLONG (village). Covers a land area of 0.950 square miles and a water area of 0.009 square miles. Located at 39.00° N. Lat; 87.90° W. Long. Elevation is 512 feet.
History: Incorporated 1883.
Population: 1,621 (1990); 1,580 (2000); 1,473 (2010); 1,423 (2015 projected); Race: 98.4% White, 0.4% Black, 0.1% Asian, 1.2% Other, 0.2% Hispanic of any race (2010); Density: 1,550.2 persons per square mile (2010); Average household size: 2.35 (2010); Median age: 42.4 (2010); Males per 100 females: 93.8 (2010); Marriage status: 22.0% never married, 45.1% now married, 14.1% widowed, 18.8% divorced (2005-2009 5-year

est.); Foreign born: 0.0% (2005-2009 5-year est.); Ancestry (includes multiple ancestries): 26.0% German, 17.2% American, 11.2% Irish, 8.4% English, 3.5% French (2005-2009 5-year est.).
Economy: Employment by occupation: 4.9% management, 12.5% professional, 20.9% services, 15.6% sales, 0.9% farming, 6.4% construction, 38.7% production (2005-2009 5-year est.).
Income: Per capita income: $19,357 (2010); Median household income: $39,160 (2010); Average household income: $46,147 (2010); Percent of households with income of $100,000 or more: 4.6% (2010); Poverty rate: 11.1% (2005-2009 5-year est.).
Taxes: Total city taxes per capita: $74 (2007); City property taxes per capita: $58 (2007).
Education: Percent of population age 25 and over with: High school diploma (including GED) or higher: 85.3% (2010); Bachelor's degree or higher: 13.5% (2010); Master's degree or higher: 6.5% (2010).
School District(s)
Oblong CUSD 4 (PK-12)
   2009-10 Enrollment: 662 . . . . (618) 592-3933
Housing: Homeownership rate: 80.5% (2010); Median home value: $65,051 (2010); Median contract rent: $289 per month (2005-2009 5-year est.); Median year structure built: 1954 (2005-2009 5-year est.).
Safety: Violent crime rate: 93.9 per 10,000 population; Property crime rate: 134.1 per 10,000 population (2010).
Newspapers: Oblong Gem (Community news; Circulation 2,000)
Transportation: Commute to work: 95.9% car, 0.6% public transportation, 1.7% walk, 1.9% work from home (2005-2009 5-year est.); Travel time to work: 29.5% less than 15 minutes, 44.0% 15 to 30 minutes, 14.9% 30 to 45 minutes, 4.0% 45 to 60 minutes, 7.6% 60 minutes or more (2005-2009 5-year est.)
Additional Information Contacts
Oblong Chamber of Commerce . . . . (618) 592-4355
   http://www.theonlyoblong.com

PALESTINE (village). Covers a land area of 0.746 square miles and a water area of 0 square miles. Located at 39.00° N. Lat; 87.61° W. Long. Elevation is 449 feet.
History: Palestine was the location in 1830 of one of the six land offices in Illinois, where settlers came to register their land claims.
Population: 1,619 (1990); 1,366 (2000); 1,496 (2010); 1,521 (2015 projected); Race: 98.3% White, 0.8% Black, 0.1% Asian, 0.9% Other, 1.1% Hispanic of any race (2010); Density: 2,006.6 persons per square mile (2010); Average household size: 2.16 (2010); Median age: 41.1 (2010); Males per 100 females: 95.3 (2010); Marriage status: 16.6% never married, 58.9% now married, 11.1% widowed, 13.3% divorced (2005-2009 5-year est.); Foreign born: 0.0% (2005-2009 5-year est.); Ancestry (includes multiple ancestries): 25.3% German, 24.6% American, 13.7% Irish, 11.6% English, 4.3% Scottish (2005-2009 5-year est.).
Economy: Employment by occupation: 7.2% management, 11.5% professional, 19.3% services, 23.6% sales, 3.5% farming, 10.8% construction, 24.1% production (2005-2009 5-year est.).
Income: Per capita income: $20,461 (2010); Median household income: $38,333 (2010); Average household income: $44,106 (2010); Percent of households with income of $100,000 or more: 5.8% (2010); Poverty rate: 15.9% (2005-2009 5-year est.).
Taxes: Total city taxes per capita: $65 (2007); City property taxes per capita: $62 (2007).
Education: Percent of population age 25 and over with: High school diploma (including GED) or higher: 84.9% (2010); Bachelor's degree or higher: 11.1% (2010); Master's degree or higher: 5.3% (2010).
School District(s)
Palestine CUSD 3 (PK-12)
   2009-10 Enrollment: 404 . . . . (618) 586-2713
Housing: Homeownership rate: 77.6% (2010); Median home value: $61,386 (2010); Median contract rent: $295 per month (2005-2009 5-year est.); Median year structure built: 1949 (2005-2009 5-year est.).
Safety: Violent crime rate: 7.7 per 10,000 population; Property crime rate: 69.4 per 10,000 population (2010).
Transportation: Commute to work: 94.8% car, 0.0% public transportation, 2.6% walk, 2.2% work from home (2005-2009 5-year est.); Travel time to work: 36.6% less than 15 minutes, 45.5% 15 to 30 minutes, 11.8% 30 to 45 minutes, 2.4% 45 to 60 minutes, 3.7% 60 minutes or more (2005-2009 5-year est.)
Additional Information Contacts
Palestine Chamber of Commerce . . . . (618) 586-2222
   http://www.pioneercity.com/chamberofcommerce

ROBINSON (city). County seat. Covers a land area of 3.625 square miles and a water area of 0.063 square miles. Located at 39.00° N. Lat; 87.73° W. Long. Elevation is 531 feet.
History: Lincoln Trail College here. Incorporated 1875.
Population: 6,951 (1990); 6,822 (2000); 6,140 (2010); 5,812 (2015 projected); Race: 95.7% White, 0.7% Black, 0.6% Asian, 2.9% Other, 1.9% Hispanic of any race (2010); Density: 1,693.8 persons per square mile (2010); Average household size: 2.26 (2010); Median age: 40.3 (2010); Males per 100 females: 89.9 (2010); Marriage status: 19.3% never married, 56.1% now married, 8.8% widowed, 15.8% divorced (2005-2009 5-year est.); Foreign born: 7.1% (2005-2009 5-year est.); Ancestry (includes multiple ancestries): 24.8% German, 12.5% American, 11.7% Irish, 9.6% English, 5.7% Dutch (2005-2009 5-year est.).
Economy: Single-family building permits issued: 7 (2010); Multi-family building permits issued: 0 (2010); Employment by occupation: 11.1% management, 16.8% professional, 21.4% services, 20.0% sales, 0.6% farming, 5.9% construction, 24.2% production (2005-2009 5-year est.).
Income: Per capita income: $21,652 (2010); Median household income: $40,533 (2010); Average household income: $49,901 (2010); Percent of households with income of $100,000 or more: 8.3% (2010); Poverty rate: 22.9% (2005-2009 5-year est.).
Taxes: Total city taxes per capita: $90 (2007); City property taxes per capita: $85 (2007).
Education: Percent of population age 25 and over with: High school diploma (including GED) or higher: 88.1% (2010); Bachelor's degree or higher: 15.1% (2010); Master's degree or higher: 4.6% (2010).
School District(s)
Clay/Cwford/Jsper/Lwrnce/Rhland (PK-12)
   2009-10 Enrollment: n/a . . . . (618) 392-4631
Robinson CUSD 2 (PK-12)
   2009-10 Enrollment: 1,646 . . . . (618) 544-7511
Twin Rivers Career & Tech Ed Sys
   2009-10 Enrollment: n/a . . . . (618) 544-8664
Two-year College(s)
Illinois Eastern Community Colleges-Lincoln Trail College (Public)
   Fall 2009 Enrollment: 1,231 . . . . (618) 393-2982
   2010-11 Tuition: In-state $6,808; Out-of-state $9,081
Housing: Homeownership rate: 71.0% (2010); Median home value: $67,659 (2010); Median contract rent: $362 per month (2005-2009 5-year est.); Median year structure built: 1955 (2005-2009 5-year est.).
Hospitals: Crawford Memorial Hospital (93 beds)
Newspapers: Robinson Constitution (Community news; Circulation 700); Robinson Daily News (Community news; Circulation 7,059)
Transportation: Commute to work: 90.7% car, 0.0% public transportation, 3.3% walk, 3.2% work from home (2005-2009 5-year est.); Travel time to work: 83.3% less than 15 minutes, 5.6% 15 to 30 minutes, 5.7% 30 to 45 minutes, 2.5% 45 to 60 minutes, 3.0% 60 minutes or more (2005-2009 5-year est.)
Additional Information Contacts
City of Robinson. . . . . (618) 544-7616
   http://www.cityofrobinson.com
Robinson Chamber of Commerce . . . . (618) 546-1557
   http://www.robinsonchamber.org

STOY (village). Covers a land area of 0.889 square miles and a water area of 0 square miles. Located at 38.99° N. Lat; 87.83° W. Long. Elevation is 489 feet.
Population: 135 (1990); 119 (2000); 116 (2010); 114 (2015 projected); Race: 99.1% White, 0.0% Black, 0.0% Asian, 0.9% Other, 0.0% Hispanic of any race (2010); Density: 130.5 persons per square mile (2010); Average household size: 2.52 (2010); Median age: 46.2 (2010); Males per 100 females: 93.3 (2010); Marriage status: 16.7% never married, 45.2% now married, 14.3% widowed, 23.8% divorced (2005-2009 5-year est.); Foreign born: 0.0% (2005-2009 5-year est.); Ancestry (includes multiple ancestries): 33.3% German, 20.4% American, 18.5% Scottish, 13.0% English, 7.4% Irish (2005-2009 5-year est.).
Economy: Employment by occupation: 27.3% management, 9.1% professional, 36.4% services, 0.0% sales, 18.2% farming, 0.0% construction, 9.1% production (2005-2009 5-year est.).
Income: Per capita income: $25,450 (2010); Median household income: $52,778 (2010); Average household income: $62,609 (2010); Percent of households with income of $100,000 or more: 13.0% (2010); Poverty rate: 29.6% (2005-2009 5-year est.).

Taxes: Total city taxes per capita: $17 (2007); City property taxes per capita: $17 (2007).
Education: Percent of population age 25 and over with: High school diploma (including GED) or higher: 91.8% (2010); Bachelor's degree or higher: 14.1% (2010); Master's degree or higher: 2.4% (2010).
Housing: Homeownership rate: 91.3% (2010); Median home value: $93,846 (2010); Median contract rent: n/a per month (2005-2009 5-year est.); Median year structure built: 1973 (2005-2009 5-year est.).
Transportation: Commute to work: 90.9% car, 0.0% public transportation, 0.0% walk, 0.0% work from home (2005-2009 5-year est.); Travel time to work: 81.8% less than 15 minutes, 18.2% 15 to 30 minutes, 0.0% 30 to 45 minutes, 0.0% 45 to 60 minutes, 0.0% 60 minutes or more (2005-2009 5-year est.)

WEST YORK (unincorporated postal area, zip code 62478). Covers a land area of 23.200 square miles and a water area of 0.037 square miles. Located at 39.17° N. Lat; 87.72° W. Long. Elevation is 508 feet.
Population: 414 (2000); Race: 100.0% White, 0.0% Black, 0.0% Asian, 0.0% Other, 4.1% Hispanic of any race (2000); Density: 17.8 persons per square mile (2000); Age: 23.7% under 18, 12.5% over 64 (2000); Marriage status: 8.0% never married, 80.3% now married, 6.3% widowed, 5.3% divorced (2000); Foreign born: 1.0% (2000); Ancestry (includes multiple ancestries): 18.1% American, 13.5% German, 9.9% English, 2.3% Norwegian (2000).
Economy: Employment by occupation: 19.6% management, 9.5% professional, 4.8% services, 21.4% sales, 5.4% farming, 8.3% construction, 31.0% production (2000).
Income: Per capita income: $18,541 (2000); Median household income: $32,125 (2000); Poverty rate: 7.9% (2000).
Education: Percent of population age 25 and over with: High school diploma (including GED) or higher: 91.2% (2000); Bachelor's degree or higher: 9.2% (2000).
Housing: Homeownership rate: 82.9% (2000); Median home value: $37,300 (2000); Median contract rent: $153 per month (2000); Median year structure built: 1956 (2000).
Transportation: Commute to work: 84.4% car, 0.0% public transportation, 3.1% walk, 12.5% work from home (2000); Travel time to work: 21.4% less than 15 minutes, 46.4% 15 to 30 minutes, 10.7% 30 to 45 minutes, 15.7% 45 to 60 minutes, 5.7% 60 minutes or more (2000)

Cumberland County

Located in southeast central Illinois; drained by the Embarrass River. Covers a land area of 346.02 square miles, a water area of 0.98 square miles, and is located in the Central Time Zone at 39.27° N. Lat., 88.26° W. Long. The county was founded in 1843. County seat is Toledo.

Cumberland County is part of the Charleston-Mattoon, IL Micropolitan Statistical Area. The entire metro area includes: Coles County, IL; Cumberland County, IL

Population: 10,670 (1990); 11,253 (2000); 10,820 (2010); 10,585 (2015 projected); Race: 98.2% White, 0.4% Black, 0.1% Asian, 1.2% Other, 0.9% Hispanic of any race (2010); Density: 31.3 persons per square mile (2010); Average household size: 2.50 (2010); Median age: 39.9 (2010); Males per 100 females: 96.6 (2010).
Religion: Five largest groups: 8.5% Christian Churches and Churches of Christ, 8.3% Catholic Church, 7.4% Southern Baptist Convention, 6.9% The United Methodist Church, 2.0% Churches of God, General Conference (2000).
Economy: Unemployment rate: 9.4% (August 2011); Total civilian labor force: 5,234 (August 2011); Leading industries: 25.7% manufacturing; 16.6% health care and social assistance; 11.5% retail trade (2009); Farms: 654 totaling 144,981 acres (2007); Companies that employ 500 or more persons: 0 (2009); Companies that employ 100 to 499 persons: 1 (2009); Companies that employ less than 100 persons: 191 (2009); Black-owned businesses: n/a (2007); Hispanic-owned businesses: n/a (2007); Asian-owned businesses: n/a (2007); Women-owned businesses: n/a (2007); Retail sales per capita: $5,325 (2010). Single-family building permits issued: 2 (2010); Multi-family building permits issued: 0 (2010).
Income: Per capita income: $20,822 (2010); Median household income: $43,691 (2010); Average household income: $51,657 (2010); Percent of households with income of $100,000 or more: 8.0% (2010); Poverty rate: 11.4% (2009); Bankruptcy rate: 3.33% (2010).
Taxes: Total county taxes per capita: $143 (2007); County property taxes per capita: $143 (2007).

Education: Percent of population age 25 and over with: High school diploma (including GED) or higher: 85.9% (2010); Bachelor's degree or higher: 12.6% (2010); Master's degree or higher: 3.8% (2010).
Housing: Homeownership rate: 81.1% (2010); Median home value: $101,900 (2010); Median contract rent: $347 per month (2005-2009 5-year est.); Median year structure built: 1970 (2005-2009 5-year est.)
Health: Birth rate: 126.9 per 10,000 population (2009); Death rate: 118.5 per 10,000 population (2009); Age-adjusted cancer mortality rate: 123.6 (Unreliable) deaths per 100,000 population (2007); Number of physicians: 1.9 per 10,000 population (2008); Hospital beds: 0.0 per 10,000 population (2007); Hospital admissions: 0.0 per 10,000 population (2007).
Elections: 2008 Presidential election results: 38.6% Obama, 59.3% McCain, 1.0% Nader
Additional Information Contacts
Cumberland County Government . . . . (217) 849-2631
    http://cumberlandco.org
Neoga Area Chamber of Commerce . . . . (217) 895-3237

Cumberland County Communities

GREENUP (village). Covers a land area of 1.700 square miles and a water area of 0.002 square miles. Located at 39.24° N. Lat; 88.16° W. Long. Elevation is 591 feet.
History: Greenup was named for William C. Greenup, the first clerk of the Illinois Territorial Legislature, who donated the townsite. The village was incorporated in 1836, and served for a time as the seat of Cumberland County.
Population: 1,637 (1990); 1,532 (2000); 1,460 (2010); 1,424 (2015 projected); Race: 98.4% White, 0.1% Black, 0.2% Asian, 1.2% Other, 0.2% Hispanic of any race (2010); Density: 858.8 persons per square mile (2010); Average household size: 2.20 (2010); Median age: 45.3 (2010); Males per 100 females: 91.9 (2010); Marriage status: 24.0% never married, 45.8% now married, 11.6% widowed, 18.6% divorced (2005-2009 5-year est.); Foreign born: 0.4% (2005-2009 5-year est.); Ancestry (includes multiple ancestries): 31.2% German, 13.0% English, 12.7% American, 10.3% Irish, 2.7% Swedish (2005-2009 5-year est.).
Economy: Employment by occupation: 5.6% management, 14.5% professional, 18.4% services, 27.0% sales, 0.0% farming, 9.3% construction, 25.2% production (2005-2009 5-year est.).
Income: Per capita income: $21,340 (2010); Median household income: $37,869 (2010); Average household income: $46,036 (2010); Percent of households with income of $100,000 or more: 5.7% (2010); Poverty rate: 18.5% (2005-2009 5-year est.).
Taxes: Total city taxes per capita: $148 (2007); City property taxes per capita: $146 (2007).
Education: Percent of population age 25 and over with: High school diploma (including GED) or higher: 82.8% (2010); Bachelor's degree or higher: 10.8% (2010); Master's degree or higher: 3.5% (2010).
Housing: Homeownership rate: 76.8% (2010); Median home value: $84,245 (2010); Median contract rent: $273 per month (2005-2009 5-year est.); Median year structure built: 1948 (2005-2009 5-year est.).
Newspapers: Greenup Press (National news; Circulation 1,700)
Transportation: Commute to work: 92.1% car, 0.0% public transportation, 2.0% walk, 4.2% work from home (2005-2009 5-year est.); Travel time to work: 44.5% less than 15 minutes, 16.2% 15 to 30 minutes, 29.2% 30 to 45 minutes, 3.0% 45 to 60 minutes, 7.1% 60 minutes or more (2005-2009 5-year est.)

JEWETT (village). Covers a land area of 1.006 square miles and a water area of 0 square miles. Located at 39.20° N. Lat; 88.24° W. Long. Elevation is 584 feet.
History: The village of Jewett grew from the town of Pleasantville, which had been a stagecoach stop in the mid-1800's.
Population: 194 (1990); 232 (2000); 220 (2010); 213 (2015 projected); Race: 99.1% White, 0.5% Black, 0.0% Asian, 0.5% Other, 0.5% Hispanic of any race (2010); Density: 218.8 persons per square mile (2010); Average household size: 2.53 (2010); Median age: 40.0 (2010); Males per 100 females: 88.0 (2010); Marriage status: 21.7% never married, 59.6% now married, 7.9% widowed, 10.8% divorced (2005-2009 5-year est.); Foreign born: 0.0% (2005-2009 5-year est.); Ancestry (includes multiple ancestries): 30.0% German, 14.8% Irish, 13.5% American, 11.7% English, 7.2% Scottish (2005-2009 5-year est.).
Economy: Employment by occupation: 5.5% management, 7.1% professional, 11.8% services, 7.9% sales, 0.0% farming, 20.5% construction, 47.2% production (2005-2009 5-year est.).

Income: Per capita income: $18,420 (2010); Median household income: $37,727 (2010); Average household income: $47,820 (2010); Percent of households with income of $100,000 or more: 8.1% (2010); Poverty rate: 15.2% (2005-2009 5-year est.).
Taxes: Total city taxes per capita: $57 (2007); City property taxes per capita: $57 (2007).
Education: Percent of population age 25 and over with: High school diploma (including GED) or higher: 84.0% (2010); Bachelor's degree or higher: 9.0% (2010); Master's degree or higher: 3.2% (2010).
Housing: Homeownership rate: 77.9% (2010); Median home value: $90,000 (2010); Median contract rent: $286 per month (2005-2009 5-year est.); Median year structure built: 1969 (2005-2009 5-year est.).
Transportation: Commute to work: 81.0% car, 0.0% public transportation, 0.0% walk, 2.5% work from home (2005-2009 5-year est.); Travel time to work: 13.6% less than 15 minutes, 42.4% 15 to 30 minutes, 29.7% 30 to 45 minutes, 11.0% 45 to 60 minutes, 3.4% 60 minutes or more (2005-2009 5-year est.)

NEOGA (city). Covers a land area of 1.350 square miles and a water area of 0 square miles. Located at 39.32° N. Lat; 88.45° W. Long. Elevation is 659 feet.
History: The name of Neoga is of Indian origin, meaning "place of the Deity."
Population: 1,674 (1990); 1,854 (2000); 1,752 (2010); 1,700 (2015 projected); Race: 96.2% White, 1.4% Black, 0.2% Asian, 2.3% Other, 1.5% Hispanic of any race (2010); Density: 1,297.4 persons per square mile (2010); Average household size: 2.59 (2010); Median age: 36.5 (2010); Males per 100 females: 95.3 (2010); Marriage status: 20.8% never married, 60.2% now married, 10.2% widowed, 8.8% divorced (2005-2009 5-year est.); Foreign born: 0.0% (2005-2009 5-year est.); Ancestry (includes multiple ancestries): 45.2% German, 14.9% English, 13.5% Irish, 12.6% American, 6.8% Scotch-Irish (2005-2009 5-year est.).
Economy: Single-family building permits issued: 2 (2010); Multi-family building permits issued: 0 (2010); Employment by occupation: 7.7% management, 17.2% professional, 23.3% services, 15.2% sales, 0.0% farming, 7.5% construction, 29.1% production (2005-2009 5-year est.).
Income: Per capita income: $21,210 (2010); Median household income: $48,125 (2010); Average household income: $54,619 (2010); Percent of households with income of $100,000 or more: 9.6% (2010); Poverty rate: 10.6% (2005-2009 5-year est.).
Taxes: Total city taxes per capita: $139 (2007); City property taxes per capita: $91 (2007).
Education: Percent of population age 25 and over with: High school diploma (including GED) or higher: 88.6% (2010); Bachelor's degree or higher: 16.7% (2010); Master's degree or higher: 5.8% (2010).
School District(s)
Neoga CUSD 3 (PK-12)
   2009-10 Enrollment: 813 . . . . (217) 895-2201
Housing: Homeownership rate: 80.3% (2010); Median home value: $115,476 (2010); Median contract rent: $419 per month (2005-2009 5-year est.); Median year structure built: 1967 (2005-2009 5-year est.).
Newspapers: Neoga News (Community news; Circulation 800)
Transportation: Commute to work: 92.7% car, 0.0% public transportation, 5.1% walk, 1.6% work from home (2005-2009 5-year est.); Travel time to work: 26.4% less than 15 minutes, 47.0% 15 to 30 minutes, 17.7% 30 to 45 minutes, 4.4% 45 to 60 minutes, 4.5% 60 minutes or more (2005-2009 5-year est.)
Additional Information Contacts
Neoga Area Chamber of Commerce . . . . (217) 895-3237

TOLEDO (village). County seat. Covers a land area of 0.798 square miles and a water area of 0 square miles. Located at 39.27° N. Lat; 88.24° W. Long. Elevation is 597 feet.
Population: 1,272 (1990); 1,166 (2000); 1,118 (2010); 1,093 (2015 projected); Race: 98.7% White, 0.2% Black, 0.0% Asian, 1.2% Other, 0.6% Hispanic of any race (2010); Density: 1,400.8 persons per square mile (2010); Average household size: 2.45 (2010); Median age: 39.6 (2010); Males per 100 females: 93.4 (2010); Marriage status: 25.2% never married, 44.0% now married, 11.3% widowed, 19.4% divorced (2005-2009 5-year est.); Foreign born: 0.0% (2005-2009 5-year est.); Ancestry (includes multiple ancestries): 33.2% German, 14.6% Irish, 10.1% American, 7.5% English, 4.7% Polish (2005-2009 5-year est.).
Economy: Employment by occupation: 11.5% management, 10.6% professional, 12.5% services, 34.1% sales, 0.0% farming, 6.3% construction, 25.1% production (2005-2009 5-year est.).

Income: Per capita income: $19,718 (2010); Median household income: $41,989 (2010); Average household income: $48,001 (2010); Percent of households with income of $100,000 or more: 5.9% (2010); Poverty rate: 21.2% (2005-2009 5-year est.).
Taxes: Total city taxes per capita: $75 (2007); City property taxes per capita: $68 (2007).
Education: Percent of population age 25 and over with: High school diploma (including GED) or higher: 86.8% (2010); Bachelor's degree or higher: 11.8% (2010); Master's degree or higher: 3.2% (2010).
School District(s)
Cumberland CUSD 77 (PK-12)
   2009-10 Enrollment: 942 . . . . (217) 923-3132
Housing: Homeownership rate: 77.3% (2010); Median home value: $95,870 (2010); Median contract rent: $330 per month (2005-2009 5-year est.); Median year structure built: 1967 (2005-2009 5-year est.).
Newspapers: Toledo Democrat (Community news; Circulation 1,860)
Transportation: Commute to work: 96.4% car, 0.0% public transportation, 1.3% walk, 0.0% work from home (2005-2009 5-year est.); Travel time to work: 37.5% less than 15 minutes, 22.8% 15 to 30 minutes, 34.3% 30 to 45 minutes, 4.7% 45 to 60 minutes, 0.8% 60 minutes or more (2005-2009 5-year est.)

De Witt County

Located in central Illinois; drained by Salt Creek. Covers a land area of 397.58 square miles, a water area of 7.58 square miles, and is located in the Central Time Zone at 40.17° N. Lat., 88.91° W. Long. The county was founded in 1839. County seat is Clinton.
Population: 16,516 (1990); 16,798 (2000); 16,289 (2010); 15,958 (2015 projected); Race: 96.7% White, 1.0% Black, 0.4% Asian, 1.9% Other, 1.8% Hispanic of any race (2010); Density: 41.0 persons per square mile (2010); Average household size: 2.41 (2010); Median age: 39.9 (2010); Males per 100 females: 96.4 (2010).
Religion: Five largest groups: 19.7% Christian Churches and Churches of Christ, 10.2% Catholic Church, 9.2% The United Methodist Church, 2.1% Assemblies of God, 1.6% New Testament Association of Independent Baptist Churches and other Fundamental Ba
Economy: Unemployment rate: 8.3% (August 2011); Total civilian labor force: 8,802 (August 2011); Leading industries: 16.1% retail trade; 11.8% health care and social assistance; 11.0% manufacturing (2009); Farms: 508 totaling 198,680 acres (2007); Companies that employ 500 or more persons: 1 (2009); Companies that employ 100 to 499 persons: 5 (2009); Companies that employ less than 100 persons: 375 (2009); Black-owned businesses: n/a (2007); Hispanic-owned businesses: n/a (2007); Asian-owned businesses: n/a (2007); Women-owned businesses: n/a (2007); Retail sales per capita: $11,985 (2010). Single-family building permits issued: 21 (2010); Multi-family building permits issued: 3 (2010).
Income: Per capita income: $25,111 (2010); Median household income: $48,504 (2010); Average household income: $60,608 (2010); Percent of households with income of $100,000 or more: 14.4% (2010); Poverty rate: 11.1% (2009); Bankruptcy rate: 5.13% (2010).
Taxes: Total county taxes per capita: $160 (2007); County property taxes per capita: $160 (2007).
Education: Percent of population age 25 and over with: High school diploma (including GED) or higher: 88.1% (2010); Bachelor's degree or higher: 16.4% (2010); Master's degree or higher: 3.6% (2010).
Housing: Homeownership rate: 73.7% (2010); Median home value: $108,477 (2010); Median contract rent: $383 per month (2005-2009 5-year est.); Median year structure built: 1956 (2005-2009 5-year est.).
Health: Birth rate: 123.5 per 10,000 population (2009); Death rate: 126.0 per 10,000 population (2009); Age-adjusted cancer mortality rate: 217.2 deaths per 100,000 population (2007); Number of physicians: 6.8 per 10,000 population (2008); Hospital beds: 15.3 per 10,000 population (2007); Hospital admissions: 298.9 per 10,000 population (2007).
Elections: 2008 Presidential election results: 42.4% Obama, 55.7% McCain, 0.9% Nader
National and State Parks: Clinton Lake State Recreational Area; Weldon Springs State Park
Additional Information Contacts
De Witt County Government . . . . (217) 935-7780
   http://www.dewittcountyill.com
City of Clinton. . . . . (217) 935-9438
   http://www.clintonillinois.com
Clinton Area Chamber of Commerce. . . . . (217) 935-3364
   http://www.clintonilchamber.com

De Witt County Communities

CLINTON (city). County seat. Covers a land area of 2.653 square miles and a water area of <.001 square miles. Located at 40.15° N. Lat; 88.95° W. Long. Elevation is 732 feet.

History: Clinton was the site of Abraham's Lincoln speech in which he gave the oft-quoted lines of "you can fool all the people part of the time and part of the people all of the time, but you cannot fool all the people all the time."

Population: 7,437 (1990); 7,485 (2000); 7,129 (2010); 6,920 (2015 projected); Race: 95.1% White, 2.0% Black, 0.3% Asian, 2.6% Other, 3.3% Hispanic of any race (2010); Density: 2,687.0 persons per square mile (2010); Average household size: 2.31 (2010); Median age: 38.7 (2010); Males per 100 females: 92.7 (2010); Marriage status: 25.7% never married, 53.2% now married, 7.7% widowed, 13.4% divorced (2005-2009 5-year est.); Foreign born: 1.9% (2005-2009 5-year est.); Ancestry (includes multiple ancestries): 28.3% American, 21.0% German, 15.6% English, 12.2% Irish, 2.0% Italian (2005-2009 5-year est.).

Economy: Single-family building permits issued: 4 (2010); Multi-family building permits issued: 0 (2010); Employment by occupation: 11.7% management, 12.2% professional, 22.3% services, 24.6% sales, 0.4% farming, 10.7% construction, 18.2% production (2005-2009 5-year est.).

Income: Per capita income: $23,404 (2010); Median household income: $41,980 (2010); Average household income: $54,270 (2010); Percent of households with income of $100,000 or more: 12.3% (2010); Poverty rate: 9.4% (2005-2009 5-year est.).

Taxes: Total city taxes per capita: $251 (2007); City property taxes per capita: $237 (2007).

Education: Percent of population age 25 and over with: High school diploma (including GED) or higher: 86.8% (2010); Bachelor's degree or higher: 15.0% (2010); Master's degree or higher: 3.7% (2010).

School District(s)
Clinton CUSD 15 (PK-12)
    2009-10 Enrollment: 2,084 . . . . (217) 935-8321

Housing: Homeownership rate: 66.5% (2010); Median home value: $99,672 (2010); Median contract rent: $380 per month (2005-2009 5-year est.); Median year structure built: 1953 (2005-2009 5-year est.).

Hospitals: Dr. John Warner Hospital (43 beds)

Newspapers: Clinton Daily Journal (Regional news; Circulation 4,000)

Transportation: Commute to work: 94.0% car, 0.0% public transportation, 3.9% walk, 1.1% work from home (2005-2009 5-year est.); Travel time to work: 48.7% less than 15 minutes, 19.1% 15 to 30 minutes, 24.8% 30 to 45 minutes, 4.4% 45 to 60 minutes, 3.1% 60 minutes or more (2005-2009 5-year est.)

Additional Information Contacts
City of Clinton. . . . . (217) 935-9438
    http://www.clintonillinois.com
Clinton Area Chamber of Commerce. . . . . (217) 935-3364
    http://www.clintonilchamber.com

DE WITT (village). Covers a land area of 0.254 square miles and a water area of 0 square miles. Located at 40.18° N. Lat; 88.78° W. Long. Elevation is 735 feet.

Population: 122 (1990); 188 (2000); 192 (2010); 194 (2015 projected); Race: 96.4% White, 0.5% Black, 0.5% Asian, 2.6% Other, 1.0% Hispanic of any race (2010); Density: 756.4 persons per square mile (2010); Average household size: 2.56 (2010); Median age: 38.6 (2010); Males per 100 females: 104.3 (2010); Marriage status: 8.7% never married, 77.5% now married, 11.6% widowed, 2.2% divorced (2005-2009 5-year est.); Foreign born: 0.0% (2005-2009 5-year est.); Ancestry (includes multiple ancestries): 28.0% American, 15.9% English, 13.4% German, 11.5% Irish, 8.3% Scottish (2005-2009 5-year est.).

Economy: Employment by occupation: 6.0% management, 0.0% professional, 34.3% services, 16.4% sales, 0.0% farming, 6.0% construction, 37.3% production (2005-2009 5-year est.).

Income: Per capita income: $30,481 (2010); Median household income: $67,262 (2010); Average household income: $78,967 (2010); Percent of households with income of $100,000 or more: 25.3% (2010); Poverty rate: 7.0% (2005-2009 5-year est.).

Taxes: Total city taxes per capita: $86 (2007); City property taxes per capita: $76 (2007).

Education: Percent of population age 25 and over with: High school diploma (including GED) or higher: 92.3% (2010); Bachelor's degree or higher: 30.0% (2010); Master's degree or higher: 8.5% (2010).

Housing: Homeownership rate: 82.7% (2010); Median home value: $145,833 (2010); Median contract rent: n/a per month (2005-2009 5-year est.); Median year structure built: 1957 (2005-2009 5-year est.).

Transportation: Commute to work: 100.0% car, 0.0% public transportation, 0.0% walk, 0.0% work from home (2005-2009 5-year est.); Travel time to work: 11.9% less than 15 minutes, 74.6% 15 to 30 minutes, 7.5% 30 to 45 minutes, 6.0% 45 to 60 minutes, 0.0% 60 minutes or more (2005-2009 5-year est.)

DEWITT (unincorporated postal area, zip code 61735). Aka De Witt. Covers a land area of 31.520 square miles and a water area of 0.043 square miles. Located at 40.20° N. Lat; 88.80° W. Long.

Population: 408 (2000); Race: 97.7% White, 0.0% Black, 0.3% Asian, 2.0% Other, 0.0% Hispanic of any race (2000); Density: 12.9 persons per square mile (2000); Age: 22.8% under 18, 14.8% over 64 (2000); Marriage status: 11.7% never married, 75.1% now married, 4.9% widowed, 8.4% divorced (2000); Foreign born: 0.0% (2000); Ancestry (includes multiple ancestries): 14.0% German, 10.9% Irish, 9.8% English, 7.8% American, 7.0% Scottish (2000).

Economy: Employment by occupation: 28.4% management, 17.3% professional, 9.6% services, 8.2% sales, 0.0% farming, 13.0% construction, 23.6% production (2000).

Income: Per capita income: $23,504 (2000); Median household income: $45,972 (2000); Poverty rate: 0.5% (2000).

Education: Percent of population age 25 and over with: High school diploma (including GED) or higher: 81.2% (2000); Bachelor's degree or higher: 17.3% (2000).

Housing: Homeownership rate: 87.7% (2000); Median home value: $67,100 (2000); Median contract rent: $275 per month (2000); Median year structure built: 1953 (2000).

Transportation: Commute to work: 90.9% car, 0.0% public transportation, 1.0% walk, 7.7% work from home (2000); Travel time to work: 26.6% less than 15 minutes, 30.2% 15 to 30 minutes, 29.2% 30 to 45 minutes, 10.4% 45 to 60 minutes, 3.6% 60 minutes or more (2000)

FARMER CITY (city). Covers a land area of 2.302 square miles and a water area of 0.049 square miles. Located at 40.24° N. Lat; 88.64° W. Long. Elevation is 725 feet.

History: Incorporated 1869.

Population: 2,169 (1990); 2,055 (2000); 2,020 (2010); 1,985 (2015 projected); Race: 98.9% White, 0.4% Black, 0.0% Asian, 0.6% Other, 0.4% Hispanic of any race (2010); Density: 877.6 persons per square mile (2010); Average household size: 2.43 (2010); Median age: 42.5 (2010); Males per 100 females: 95.9 (2010); Marriage status: 24.7% never married, 54.1% now married, 8.9% widowed, 12.4% divorced (2005-2009 5-year est.); Foreign born: 1.8% (2005-2009 5-year est.); Ancestry (includes multiple ancestries): 28.3% German, 21.6% American, 16.0% Irish, 13.5% English, 1.7% Scotch-Irish (2005-2009 5-year est.).

Economy: Employment by occupation: 8.0% management, 15.8% professional, 18.4% services, 30.1% sales, 0.6% farming, 14.5% construction, 12.5% production (2005-2009 5-year est.).

Income: Per capita income: $23,359 (2010); Median household income: $46,762 (2010); Average household income: $56,839 (2010); Percent of households with income of $100,000 or more: 12.5% (2010); Poverty rate: 10.8% (2005-2009 5-year est.).

Taxes: Total city taxes per capita: $566 (2007); City property taxes per capita: $429 (2007).

Education: Percent of population age 25 and over with: High school diploma (including GED) or higher: 88.5% (2010); Bachelor's degree or higher: 18.4% (2010); Master's degree or higher: 3.5% (2010).

School District(s)
Blue Ridge CUSD 18 (PK-12)
    2009-10 Enrollment: 859 . . . . (309) 928-9141

Housing: Homeownership rate: 75.2% (2010); Median home value: $109,685 (2010); Median contract rent: $388 per month (2005-2009 5-year est.); Median year structure built: 1953 (2005-2009 5-year est.).

Newspapers: Farmer City Journal (Local news; Circulation 1,900)

Transportation: Commute to work: 90.2% car, 0.6% public transportation, 2.8% walk, 4.9% work from home (2005-2009 5-year est.); Travel time to work: 38.0% less than 15 minutes, 20.5% 15 to 30 minutes, 31.0% 30 to 45 minutes, 8.9% 45 to 60 minutes, 1.5% 60 minutes or more (2005-2009 5-year est.)

KENNEY (village). Covers a land area of 0.301 square miles and a water area of 0 square miles. Located at 40.09° N. Lat; 89.08° W. Long. Elevation is 650 feet.
Population: 390 (1990); 374 (2000); 381 (2010); 379 (2015 projected); Race: 99.0% White, 0.3% Black, 0.3% Asian, 0.5% Other, 1.6% Hispanic of any race (2010); Density: 1,266.0 persons per square mile (2010); Average household size: 2.35 (2010); Median age: 45.1 (2010); Males per 100 females: 105.9 (2010); Marriage status: 23.5% never married, 57.7% now married, 10.1% widowed, 8.7% divorced (2005-2009 5-year est.); Foreign born: 0.0% (2005-2009 5-year est.); Ancestry (includes multiple ancestries): 61.9% American, 10.5% German, 6.6% Irish, 5.5% English, 3.7% French (2005-2009 5-year est.).
Economy: Employment by occupation: 2.2% management, 5.0% professional, 11.0% services, 29.3% sales, 0.0% farming, 22.1% construction, 30.4% production (2005-2009 5-year est.).
Income: Per capita income: $28,907 (2010); Median household income: $49,571 (2010); Average household income: $66,111 (2010); Percent of households with income of $100,000 or more: 13.6% (2010); Poverty rate: 12.4% (2005-2009 5-year est.).
Taxes: Total city taxes per capita: $87 (2007); City property taxes per capita: $76 (2007).
Education: Percent of population age 25 and over with: High school diploma (including GED) or higher: 88.6% (2010); Bachelor's degree or higher: 13.4% (2010); Master's degree or higher: 4.7% (2010).
Housing: Homeownership rate: 78.4% (2010); Median home value: $89,286 (2010); Median contract rent: $400 per month (2005-2009 5-year est.); Median year structure built: before 1940 (2005-2009 5-year est.).
Transportation: Commute to work: 92.8% car, 0.0% public transportation, 0.0% walk, 5.5% work from home (2005-2009 5-year est.); Travel time to work: 35.1% less than 15 minutes, 32.7% 15 to 30 minutes, 22.8% 30 to 45 minutes, 5.8% 45 to 60 minutes, 3.5% 60 minutes or more (2005-2009 5-year est.)

WAPELLA (village). Covers a land area of 0.545 square miles and a water area of 0 square miles. Located at 40.22° N. Lat; 88.96° W. Long. Elevation is 745 feet.
Population: 612 (1990); 651 (2000); 642 (2010); 635 (2015 projected); Race: 97.8% White, 0.0% Black, 0.6% Asian, 1.6% Other, 1.1% Hispanic of any race (2010); Density: 1,177.1 persons per square mile (2010); Average household size: 2.41 (2010); Median age: 39.5 (2010); Males per 100 females: 101.3 (2010); Marriage status: 19.0% never married, 60.3% now married, 6.8% widowed, 13.9% divorced (2005-2009 5-year est.); Foreign born: 0.0% (2005-2009 5-year est.); Ancestry (includes multiple ancestries): 34.4% American, 19.1% German, 11.8% Irish, 7.9% English, 4.4% Italian (2005-2009 5-year est.).
Economy: Single-family building permits issued: 1 (2010); Multi-family building permits issued: 0 (2010); Employment by occupation: 16.9% management, 18.2% professional, 11.7% services, 16.0% sales, 0.0% farming, 17.6% construction, 19.5% production (2005-2009 5-year est.).
Income: Per capita income: $26,679 (2010); Median household income: $50,806 (2010); Average household income: $65,729 (2010); Percent of households with income of $100,000 or more: 14.8% (2010); Poverty rate: 5.2% (2005-2009 5-year est.).
Taxes: Total city taxes per capita: $182 (2007); City property taxes per capita: $83 (2007).
Education: Percent of population age 25 and over with: High school diploma (including GED) or higher: 86.1% (2010); Bachelor's degree or higher: 11.9% (2010); Master's degree or higher: 0.0% (2010).
Housing: Homeownership rate: 82.6% (2010); Median home value: $98,750 (2010); Median contract rent: n/a per month (2005-2009 5-year est.); Median year structure built: 1945 (2005-2009 5-year est.).
Transportation: Commute to work: 95.4% car, 0.0% public transportation, 3.3% walk, 1.3% work from home (2005-2009 5-year est.); Travel time to work: 30.0% less than 15 minutes, 20.1% 15 to 30 minutes, 46.2% 30 to 45 minutes, 2.3% 45 to 60 minutes, 1.3% 60 minutes or more (2005-2009 5-year est.)

WAYNESVILLE (village). Covers a land area of 0.322 square miles and a water area of 0 square miles. Located at 40.24° N. Lat; 89.12° W. Long. Elevation is 735 feet.
Population: 440 (1990); 452 (2000); 440 (2010); 431 (2015 projected); Race: 98.6% White, 0.5% Black, 0.0% Asian, 0.9% Other, 1.1% Hispanic of any race (2010); Density: 1,366.8 persons per square mile (2010); Average household size: 2.47 (2010); Median age: 39.7 (2010); Males per

100 females: 100.9 (2010); Marriage status: 23.8% never married, 66.8% now married, 5.0% widowed, 4.5% divorced (2005-2009 5-year est.); Foreign born: 1.2% (2005-2009 5-year est.); Ancestry (includes multiple ancestries): 33.4% American, 21.5% German, 11.7% Irish, 9.3% English, 4.3% French (2005-2009 5-year est.).
Economy: Employment by occupation: 11.4% management, 3.4% professional, 16.5% services, 24.5% sales, 0.8% farming, 19.4% construction, 24.1% production (2005-2009 5-year est.).
Income: Per capita income: $21,069 (2010); Median household income: $42,800 (2010); Average household income: $51,362 (2010); Percent of households with income of $100,000 or more: 9.0% (2010); Poverty rate: 5.5% (2005-2009 5-year est.).
Taxes: Total city taxes per capita: $50 (2007); City property taxes per capita: $45 (2007).
Education: Percent of population age 25 and over with: High school diploma (including GED) or higher: 87.1% (2010); Bachelor's degree or higher: 8.6% (2010); Master's degree or higher: 4.3% (2010).
Housing: Homeownership rate: 87.6% (2010); Median home value: $90,667 (2010); Median contract rent: $317 per month (2005-2009 5-year est.); Median year structure built: 1951 (2005-2009 5-year est.).
Transportation: Commute to work: 90.6% car, 1.3% public transportation, 4.7% walk, 0.0% work from home (2005-2009 5-year est.); Travel time to work: 19.2% less than 15 minutes, 20.1% 15 to 30 minutes, 54.3% 30 to 45 minutes, 3.8% 45 to 60 minutes, 2.6% 60 minutes or more (2005-2009 5-year est.)

WELDON (village). Covers a land area of 0.269 square miles and a water area of 0 square miles. Located at 40.12° N. Lat; 88.75° W. Long. Elevation is 712 feet.
Population: 366 (1990); 440 (2000); 428 (2010); 420 (2015 projected); Race: 96.5% White, 0.0% Black, 0.9% Asian, 2.6% Other, 0.2% Hispanic of any race (2010); Density: 1,590.9 persons per square mile (2010); Average household size: 2.46 (2010); Median age: 40.3 (2010); Males per 100 females: 101.9 (2010); Marriage status: 19.3% never married, 62.3% now married, 4.4% widowed, 14.0% divorced (2005-2009 5-year est.); Foreign born: 2.4% (2005-2009 5-year est.); Ancestry (includes multiple ancestries): 28.0% German, 26.6% American, 13.4% English, 11.8% Irish, 4.7% Scottish (2005-2009 5-year est.).
Economy: Employment by occupation: 2.4% management, 5.7% professional, 17.7% services, 27.3% sales, 0.0% farming, 21.1% construction, 25.8% production (2005-2009 5-year est.).
Income: Per capita income: $27,530 (2010); Median household income: $54,605 (2010); Average household income: $66,638 (2010); Percent of households with income of $100,000 or more: 16.1% (2010); Poverty rate: 14.1% (2005-2009 5-year est.).
Taxes: Total city taxes per capita: $49 (2007); City property taxes per capita: $49 (2007).
Education: Percent of population age 25 and over with: High school diploma (including GED) or higher: 89.2% (2010); Bachelor's degree or higher: 21.7% (2010); Master's degree or higher: 2.7% (2010).

School District(s)

Deland-Weldon CUSD 57 (PK-12)
   2009-10 Enrollment: 205 . . . . (217) 736-2311
Housing: Homeownership rate: 79.3% (2010); Median home value: $95,714 (2010); Median contract rent: $300 per month (2005-2009 5-year est.); Median year structure built: 1947 (2005-2009 5-year est.).
Transportation: Commute to work: 93.0% car, 0.0% public transportation, 0.0% walk, 2.0% work from home (2005-2009 5-year est.); Travel time to work: 6.2% less than 15 minutes, 27.7% 15 to 30 minutes, 44.6% 30 to 45 minutes, 16.4% 45 to 60 minutes, 5.1% 60 minutes or more (2005-2009 5-year est.)

De Kalb County

Located in northern Illinois; drained by branches of the Kishwaukee River. Covers a land area of 634.16 square miles, a water area of 0.81 square miles, and is located in the Central Time Zone at 41.89° N. Lat., 88.73° W. Long. The county was founded in 1837. County seat is Sycamore.

De Kalb County is part of the Chicago-Joliet-Naperville, IL-IN-WI Metropolitan Statistical Area. The entire metro area includes: Chicago-Joliet-Naperville, IL Metropolitan Division (Cook County, IL; DeKalb County, IL; DuPage County, IL; Grundy County, IL; Kane County, IL; Kendall County, IL; McHenry County, IL; Will County, IL); Gary, IN Metropolitan Division (Jasper County, IN; Lake County, IN; Newton County,

IN; Porter County, IN); Lake County-Kenosha County, IL-WI Metropolitan Division (Lake County, IL; Kenosha County, WI)

Population: 77,932 (1990); 88,969 (2000); 109,084 (2010); 117,786 (2015 projected); Race: 84.6% White, 6.2% Black, 2.7% Asian, 6.5% Other, 9.9% Hispanic of any race (2010); Density: 172.0 persons per square mile (2010); Average household size: 2.58 (2010); Median age: 29.1 (2010); Males per 100 females: 99.8 (2010).
Religion: Five largest groups: 19.2% Catholic Church, 6.5% Evangelical Lutheran Church in America, 5.6% The United Methodist Church, 3.5% United Church of Christ, 3.3% Lutheran Church—Missouri Synod (2000).
Economy: Unemployment rate: 10.1% (August 2011); Total civilian labor force: 60,452 (August 2011); Leading industries: 18.9% health care and social assistance; 17.0% retail trade; 15.7% manufacturing (2009); Farms: 930 totaling 370,772 acres (2007); Companies that employ 500 or more persons: 2 (2009); Companies that employ 100 to 499 persons: 45 (2009); Companies that employ less than 100 persons: 1,967 (2009); Black-owned businesses: 163 (2007); Hispanic-owned businesses: 172 (2007); Asian-owned businesses: 161 (2007); Women-owned businesses: 2,445 (2007); Retail sales per capita: $10,631 (2010). Single-family building permits issued: 51 (2010); Multi-family building permits issued: 0 (2010).
Income: Per capita income: $23,309 (2010); Median household income: $54,920 (2010); Average household income: $64,647 (2010); Percent of households with income of $100,000 or more: 17.9% (2010); Poverty rate: 17.0% (2009); Bankruptcy rate: 5.67% (2009).
Taxes: Total county taxes per capita: $161 (2007); County property taxes per capita: $150 (2007).
Education: Percent of population age 25 and over with: High school diploma (including GED) or higher: 91.1% (2010); Bachelor's degree or higher: 26.9% (2010); Master's degree or higher: 10.3% (2010).
Housing: Homeownership rate: 63.5% (2010); Median home value: $172,314 (2010); Median contract rent: $655 per month (2005-2009 5-year est.); Median year structure built: 1974 (2005-2009 5-year est.)
Health: Birth rate: 132.5 per 10,000 population (2009); Death rate: 59.0 per 10,000 population (2009); Age-adjusted cancer mortality rate: 185.6 deaths per 100,000 population (2007); Number of physicians: 9.8 per 10,000 population (2008); Hospital beds: 18.4 per 10,000 population (2007); Hospital admissions: 725.6 per 10,000 population (2007).
Elections: 2008 Presidential election results: 57.5% Obama, 40.8% McCain, 0.7% Nader
National and State Parks: Shabbona Lake State Recreational Area
Additional Information Contacts
De Kalb County Government . . . . (815) 895-7149
   http://www.dekalbcounty.org
City of De Kalb . . . . (815) 748-2095
   http://www.cityofdekalb.com
City of Sandwich . . . . (815) 786-9321
   http://www.sandwich.il.us
City of Sycamore . . . . (815) 895-4515
   http://www.cityofsycamore.com
De Kalb Chamber of Commerce . . . . (815) 756-6306
   http://www.dekalb.org
Genoa Area Chamber of Commerce . . . . (815) 784-2212
   http://www.genoa-il-chamberofcommerce.com
Sandwich Chamber of Commerce . . . . (815) 312-4963
   http://www.sandwich-il.org
Sycamore Chamber of Commerce . . . . (815) 895-3456
   http://www.sycamorechamber.com
Town of Cortland . . . . (815) 756-9041
   http://www.cortlandil.org

De Kalb County Communities

CLARE (unincorporated postal area, zip code 60111). Covers a land area of 23.578 square miles and a water area of 0 square miles. Located at 41.99° N. Lat; 88.84° W. Long. Elevation is 869 feet.
Population: 305 (2000); Race: 98.9% White, 0.0% Black, 0.0% Asian, 1.1% Other, 0.0% Hispanic of any race (2000); Density: 12.9 persons per square mile (2000); Age: 30.1% under 18, 13.0% over 64 (2000); Marriage status: 22.5% never married, 67.2% now married, 6.4% widowed, 3.9% divorced (2000); Foreign born: 1.5% (2000); Ancestry (includes multiple ancestries): 31.6% German, 20.1% American, 17.1% English, 14.5% Swedish, 7.4% Irish (2000).
Economy: Employment by occupation: 16.9% management, 19.5% professional, 2.6% services, 26.0% sales, 0.0% farming, 18.8% construction, 16.2% production (2000).

Income: Per capita income: $27,141 (2000); Median household income: $58,750 (2000); Poverty rate: 1.9% (2000).
Education: Percent of population age 25 and over with: High school diploma (including GED) or higher: 87.8% (2000); Bachelor's degree or higher: 27.1% (2000).
Housing: Homeownership rate: 70.4% (2000); Median home value: $146,300 (2000); Median contract rent: $438 per month (2000); Median year structure built: before 1940 (2000).
Transportation: Commute to work: 90.3% car, 1.9% public transportation, 3.2% walk, 4.5% work from home (2000); Travel time to work: 36.7% less than 15 minutes, 53.1% 15 to 30 minutes, 0.0% 30 to 45 minutes, 7.5% 45 to 60 minutes, 2.7% 60 minutes or more (2000)

CORTLAND (town). Covers a land area of 1.756 square miles and a water area of 0 square miles. Located at 41.92° N. Lat; 88.69° W. Long. Elevation is 902 feet.
Population: 1,079 (1990); 2,066 (2000); 3,396 (2010); 3,950 (2015 projected); Race: 94.1% White, 1.3% Black, 1.4% Asian, 3.2% Other, 8.2% Hispanic of any race (2010); Density: 1,933.5 persons per square mile (2010); Average household size: 2.86 (2010); Median age: 31.6 (2010); Males per 100 females: 100.9 (2010); Marriage status: 25.4% never married, 66.0% now married, 3.2% widowed, 5.4% divorced (2005-2009 5-year est.); Foreign born: 6.7% (2005-2009 5-year est.); Ancestry (includes multiple ancestries): 46.1% German, 15.9% Irish, 11.6% Swedish, 9.1% Polish, 8.6% Italian (2005-2009 5-year est.).
Economy: Single-family building permits issued: 6 (2010); Multi-family building permits issued: 0 (2010); Employment by occupation: 9.1% management, 18.2% professional, 16.5% services, 25.9% sales, 0.0% farming, 12.2% construction, 18.1% production (2005-2009 5-year est.).
Income: Per capita income: $23,819 (2010); Median household income: $62,343 (2010); Average household income: $68,186 (2010); Percent of households with income of $100,000 or more: 17.7% (2010); Poverty rate: 6.5% (2005-2009 5-year est.).
Taxes: Total city taxes per capita: $361 (2007); City property taxes per capita: $136 (2007).
Education: Percent of population age 25 and over with: High school diploma (including GED) or higher: 89.1% (2010); Bachelor's degree or higher: 18.3% (2010); Master's degree or higher: 5.6% (2010).
School District(s)
Dekalb CUSD 428 (PK-12)
   2009-10 Enrollment: 6,018 . . . . (815) 754-2350
Housing: Homeownership rate: 81.3% (2010); Median home value: $164,824 (2010); Median contract rent: $746 per month (2005-2009 5-year est.); Median year structure built: 1998 (2005-2009 5-year est.).
Safety: Violent crime rate: 11.1 per 10,000 population; Property crime rate: 120.0 per 10,000 population (2010).
Transportation: Commute to work: 90.6% car, 0.5% public transportation, 2.1% walk, 6.9% work from home (2005-2009 5-year est.); Travel time to work: 30.1% less than 15 minutes, 16.3% 15 to 30 minutes, 34.0% 30 to 45 minutes, 8.9% 45 to 60 minutes, 10.7% 60 minutes or more (2005-2009 5-year est.)
Additional Information Contacts
Town of Cortland . . . . (815) 756-9041
   http://www.cortlandil.org

DEKALB (city). Covers a land area of 12.611 square miles and a water area of 0.008 square miles. Located at 41.93° N. Lat; 88.75° W. Long. Elevation is 880 feet.
History: De Kalb was named for Baron Johann De Kalb, a major general in the Revolutionary Army. In 1874 Joseph E. Glidden patented an improved barbed wire, and Jacob Haish patented a barbed wire manufacturing process. The two patents overlapped and caused a long legal battle, but until 1938 De Kalb was known as the barbed wire capital of the world.
Population: 36,443 (1990); 39,018 (2000); 46,971 (2010); 50,210 (2015 projected); Race: 72.2% White, 12.4% Black, 5.4% Asian, 10.0% Other, 13.7% Hispanic of any race (2010); Density: 3,724.6 persons per square mile (2010); Average household size: 2.40 (2010); Median age: 24.4 (2010); Males per 100 females: 99.2 (2010); Marriage status: 61.9% never married, 28.9% now married, 3.2% widowed, 6.0% divorced (2005-2009 5-year est.); Foreign born: 10.6% (2005-2009 5-year est.); Ancestry (includes multiple ancestries): 25.7% German, 15.5% Irish, 7.8% Polish, 7.5% English, 7.1% Italian (2005-2009 5-year est.).
Economy: Unemployment rate: 10.1% (August 2011); Total civilian labor force: 24,905 (August 2011); Single-family building permits issued: 3 (2010); Multi-family building permits issued: 0 (2010); Employment by

occupation: 9.3% management, 25.0% professional, 19.8% services, 28.5% sales, 0.2% farming, 5.8% construction, 11.4% production (2005-2009 5-year est.).

Income: Per capita income: $18,244 (2010); Median household income: $40,164 (2010); Average household income: $51,358 (2010); Percent of households with income of $100,000 or more: 11.7% (2010); Poverty rate: 28.2% (2005-2009 5-year est.).

Taxes: Total city taxes per capita: $528 (2007); City property taxes per capita: $232 (2007).

Education: Percent of population age 25 and over with: High school diploma (including GED) or higher: 91.2% (2010); Bachelor's degree or higher: 37.1% (2010); Master's degree or higher: 16.7% (2010).

School District(s)
Dekalb CUSD 428 (PK-12)
    2009-10 Enrollment: 6,018 . . . . (815) 754-2350
Dekalb Roe (07-12)
    2009-10 Enrollment: n/a . . . . (815) 895-3096
Kec Area Voc Center (08-12)
    2009-10 Enrollment: n/a . . . . (815) 754-2400
Kishwaukee Educ Consortium (11-12)
    2009-10 Enrollment: n/a . . . . (815) 825-2000

Four-year College(s)
Northern Illinois University (Public)
    Fall 2009 Enrollment: 24,424. . . . . (800) 892-3050
    2010-11 Tuition: In-state $11,676; Out-of-state $20,156

Housing: Homeownership rate: 44.2% (2010); Median home value: $158,641 (2010); Median contract rent: $668 per month (2005-2009 5-year est.); Median year structure built: 1975 (2005-2009 5-year est.).

Hospitals: Kishwaukee Community Hospital (172 beds)

Safety: Violent crime rate: 35.2 per 10,000 population; Property crime rate: 271.1 per 10,000 population (2010).

Newspapers: Daily Chronicle (Local news; Circulation 12,300); Midweek (Local news; Circulation 30,000)

Transportation: Commute to work: 81.0% car, 3.5% public transportation, 9.9% walk, 4.1% work from home (2005-2009 5-year est.); Travel time to work: 53.0% less than 15 minutes, 21.5% 15 to 30 minutes, 10.9% 30 to 45 minutes, 7.5% 45 to 60 minutes, 7.2% 60 minutes or more (2005-2009 5-year est.)

Airports: De Kalb Taylor Municipal (general aviation)

Additional Information Contacts
City of De Kalb. . . . . (815) 748-2095
    http://www.cityofdekalb.com
De Kalb Chamber of Commerce . . . . (815) 756-6306
    http://www.dekalb.org

ESMOND (unincorporated postal area, zip code 60129). Covers a land area of 22.108 square miles and a water area of 0 square miles. Located at 42.03° N. Lat; 88.97° W. Long. Elevation is 820 feet.

Population: 291 (2000); Race: 95.3% White, 0.0% Black, 0.0% Asian, 4.7% Other, 5.7% Hispanic of any race (2000); Density: 13.2 persons per square mile (2000); Age: 28.3% under 18, 7.7% over 64 (2000); Marriage status: 21.4% never married, 69.4% now married, 3.1% widowed, 6.1% divorced (2000); Foreign born: 3.4% (2000); Ancestry (includes multiple ancestries): 36.7% German, 10.4% Irish, 9.1% English, 7.4% American, 5.4% Dutch (2000).

Economy: Employment by occupation: 14.0% management, 14.5% professional, 12.2% services, 17.4% sales, 1.2% farming, 17.4% construction, 23.3% production (2000).

Income: Per capita income: $17,101 (2000); Median household income: $43,438 (2000); Poverty rate: 4.8% (2000).

Education: Percent of population age 25 and over with: High school diploma (including GED) or higher: 85.6% (2000); Bachelor's degree or higher: 20.3% (2000).

Housing: Homeownership rate: 62.5% (2000); Median home value: $126,100 (2000); Median contract rent: $392 per month (2000); Median year structure built: before 1940 (2000).

Transportation: Commute to work: 89.5% car, 1.2% public transportation, 0.0% walk, 8.1% work from home (2000); Travel time to work: 9.5% less than 15 minutes, 54.4% 15 to 30 minutes, 20.3% 30 to 45 minutes, 8.9% 45 to 60 minutes, 7.0% 60 minutes or more (2000)

GENOA (city). Covers a land area of 1.913 square miles and a water area of 0 square miles. Located at 42.09° N. Lat; 88.69° W. Long. Elevation is 833 feet.

Population: 3,287 (1990); 4,169 (2000); 4,494 (2010); 4,825 (2015 projected); Race: 93.7% White, 0.1% Black, 0.4% Asian, 5.7% Other, 16.5% Hispanic of any race (2010); Density: 2,348.6 persons per square mile (2010); Average household size: 2.68 (2010); Median age: 32.6 (2010); Males per 100 females: 100.9 (2010); Marriage status: 27.9% never married, 59.2% now married, 5.0% widowed, 7.8% divorced (2005-2009 5-year est.); Foreign born: 3.1% (2005-2009 5-year est.); Ancestry (includes multiple ancestries): 45.0% German, 26.9% Irish, 9.5% Italian, 8.1% Polish, 4.9% Swedish (2005-2009 5-year est.).

Economy: Single-family building permits issued: 9 (2010); Multi-family building permits issued: 0 (2010); Employment by occupation: 12.9% management, 12.1% professional, 21.6% services, 20.6% sales, 0.7% farming, 11.5% construction, 20.6% production (2005-2009 5-year est.).

Income: Per capita income: $25,122 (2010); Median household income: $59,148 (2010); Average household income: $67,469 (2010); Percent of households with income of $100,000 or more: 20.0% (2010); Poverty rate: 5.0% (2005-2009 5-year est.).

Taxes: Total city taxes per capita: $235 (2007); City property taxes per capita: $114 (2007).

Education: Percent of population age 25 and over with: High school diploma (including GED) or higher: 85.3% (2010); Bachelor's degree or higher: 11.2% (2010); Master's degree or higher: 2.2% (2010).

School District(s)
Genoa Kingston CUSD 424 (PK-12)
    2009-10 Enrollment: 2,020 . . . . (815) 784-6222

Housing: Homeownership rate: 75.2% (2010); Median home value: $159,202 (2010); Median contract rent: $491 per month (2005-2009 5-year est.); Median year structure built: 1969 (2005-2009 5-year est.).

Safety: Violent crime rate: 9.6 per 10,000 population; Property crime rate: 82.9 per 10,000 population (2010).

Transportation: Commute to work: 93.1% car, 0.0% public transportation, 3.4% walk, 3.5% work from home (2005-2009 5-year est.); Travel time to work: 22.5% less than 15 minutes, 29.2% 15 to 30 minutes, 17.6% 30 to 45 minutes, 9.7% 45 to 60 minutes, 20.9% 60 minutes or more (2005-2009 5-year est.)

Additional Information Contacts
Genoa Area Chamber of Commerce . . . . (815) 784-2212
    http://www.genoa-il-chamberofcommerce.com

HINCKLEY (village). Covers a land area of 0.949 square miles and a water area of 0.006 square miles. Located at 41.77° N. Lat; 88.64° W. Long. Elevation is 745 feet.

Population: 1,795 (1990); 1,994 (2000); 1,976 (2010); 1,988 (2015 projected); Race: 97.2% White, 0.2% Black, 0.1% Asian, 2.5% Other, 3.4% Hispanic of any race (2010); Density: 2,081.7 persons per square mile (2010); Average household size: 2.72 (2010); Median age: 34.8 (2010); Males per 100 females: 102.3 (2010); Marriage status: 24.6% never married, 63.2% now married, 5.6% widowed, 6.6% divorced (2005-2009 5-year est.); Foreign born: 1.8% (2005-2009 5-year est.); Ancestry (includes multiple ancestries): 34.2% German, 23.7% Irish, 15.3% English, 9.8% Swedish, 7.5% Norwegian (2005-2009 5-year est.).

Economy: Single-family building permits issued: 0 (2010); Multi-family building permits issued: 0 (2010); Employment by occupation: 12.1% management, 17.6% professional, 17.4% services, 25.0% sales, 1.0% farming, 14.7% construction, 12.2% production (2005-2009 5-year est.).

Income: Per capita income: $28,265 (2010); Median household income: $70,026 (2010); Average household income: $77,273 (2010); Percent of households with income of $100,000 or more: 24.4% (2010); Poverty rate: 7.4% (2005-2009 5-year est.).

Taxes: Total city taxes per capita: $211 (2007); City property taxes per capita: $127 (2007).

Education: Percent of population age 25 and over with: High school diploma (including GED) or higher: 93.5% (2010); Bachelor's degree or higher: 20.2% (2010); Master's degree or higher: 5.2% (2010).

School District(s)
Hinckley Big Rock CUSD 429 (PK-12)
    2009-10 Enrollment: 761 . . . . (815) 286-7575

Housing: Homeownership rate: 78.8% (2010); Median home value: $188,444 (2010); Median contract rent: $771 per month (2005-2009 5-year est.); Median year structure built: 1973 (2005-2009 5-year est.).

Safety: Violent crime rate: 14.4 per 10,000 population; Property crime rate: 120.3 per 10,000 population (2010).

Transportation: Commute to work: 91.3% car, 0.0% public transportation, 3.2% walk, 1.0% work from home (2005-2009 5-year est.); Travel time to work: 17.0% less than 15 minutes, 33.1% 15 to 30 minutes, 28.1% 30 to 45

minutes, 13.9% 45 to 60 minutes, 7.9% 60 minutes or more (2005-2009 5-year est.)

KINGSTON (village). Covers a land area of 1.003 square miles and a water area of 0 square miles. Located at 42.10° N. Lat; 88.76° W. Long. Elevation is 794 feet.

Population: 745 (1990); 980 (2000); 1,083 (2010); 1,144 (2015 projected); Race: 96.4% White, 0.6% Black, 0.3% Asian, 2.8% Other, 4.3% Hispanic of any race (2010); Density: 1,079.5 persons per square mile (2010); Average household size: 2.97 (2010); Median age: 31.7 (2010); Males per 100 females: 102.4 (2010); Marriage status: 25.9% never married, 51.5% now married, 6.8% widowed, 15.7% divorced (2005-2009 5-year est.); Foreign born: 5.7% (2005-2009 5-year est.); Ancestry (includes multiple ancestries): 40.9% German, 23.1% Irish, 10.3% English, 7.7% Italian, 7.4% Polish (2005-2009 5-year est.).

Economy: Single-family building permits issued: 2 (2010); Multi-family building permits issued: 0 (2010); Employment by occupation: 12.4% management, 8.5% professional, 19.8% services, 26.7% sales, 0.6% farming, 15.1% construction, 16.8% production (2005-2009 5-year est.).

Income: Per capita income: $29,111 (2010); Median household income: $74,048 (2010); Average household income: $83,979 (2010); Percent of households with income of $100,000 or more: 28.3% (2010); Poverty rate: 6.1% (2005-2009 5-year est.).

Taxes: Total city taxes per capita: $135 (2007); City property taxes per capita: $128 (2007).

Education: Percent of population age 25 and over with: High school diploma (including GED) or higher: 91.8% (2010); Bachelor's degree or higher: 14.6% (2010); Master's degree or higher: 3.8% (2010).

School District(s)
Genoa Kingston CUSD 424 (PK-12)
2009-10 Enrollment: 2,020 . . . . (815) 784-6222

Housing: Homeownership rate: 85.0% (2010); Median home value: $165,000 (2010); Median contract rent: $781 per month (2005-2009 5-year est.); Median year structure built: 1991 (2005-2009 5-year est.).

Safety: Violent crime rate: 0.0 per 10,000 population; Property crime rate: 56.2 per 10,000 population (2010).

Transportation: Commute to work: 94.0% car, 0.4% public transportation, 0.0% walk, 5.2% work from home (2005-2009 5-year est.); Travel time to work: 15.5% less than 15 minutes, 31.0% 15 to 30 minutes, 19.8% 30 to 45 minutes, 6.2% 45 to 60 minutes, 27.6% 60 minutes or more (2005-2009 5-year est.)

KIRKLAND (village). Covers a land area of 1.125 square miles and a water area of 0 square miles. Located at 42.09° N. Lat; 88.85° W. Long. Elevation is 768 feet.

Population: 1,082 (1990); 1,166 (2000); 1,425 (2010); 1,562 (2015 projected); Race: 98.2% White, 0.4% Black, 0.0% Asian, 1.4% Other, 2.1% Hispanic of any race (2010); Density: 1,266.2 persons per square mile (2010); Average household size: 2.69 (2010); Median age: 32.6 (2010); Males per 100 females: 108.0 (2010); Marriage status: 29.7% never married, 56.0% now married, 4.4% widowed, 10.0% divorced (2005-2009 5-year est.); Foreign born: 7.0% (2005-2009 5-year est.); Ancestry (includes multiple ancestries): 41.6% German, 15.1% Irish, 11.1% English, 7.0% Swedish, 6.7% Norwegian (2005-2009 5-year est.).

Economy: Single-family building permits issued: 0 (2010); Multi-family building permits issued: 0 (2010); Employment by occupation: 12.0% management, 14.3% professional, 16.6% services, 16.6% sales, 0.0% farming, 11.5% construction, 29.0% production (2005-2009 5-year est.).

Income: Per capita income: $24,426 (2010); Median household income: $59,494 (2010); Average household income: $65,269 (2010); Percent of households with income of $100,000 or more: 15.3% (2010); Poverty rate: 8.9% (2005-2009 5-year est.).

Taxes: Total city taxes per capita: $306 (2007); City property taxes per capita: $225 (2007).

Education: Percent of population age 25 and over with: High school diploma (including GED) or higher: 87.1% (2010); Bachelor's degree or higher: 17.6% (2010); Master's degree or higher: 3.2% (2010).

School District(s)
Hiawatha CUSD 426 (PK-12)
2009-10 Enrollment: 605 . . . . (815) 522-6676

Housing: Homeownership rate: 80.0% (2010); Median home value: $144,175 (2010); Median contract rent: $596 per month (2005-2009 5-year est.); Median year structure built: 1959 (2005-2009 5-year est.).

Transportation: Commute to work: 94.8% car, 0.0% public transportation, 1.4% walk, 2.5% work from home (2005-2009 5-year est.); Travel time to

work: 19.8% less than 15 minutes, 24.5% 15 to 30 minutes, 35.3% 30 to 45 minutes, 7.6% 45 to 60 minutes, 12.8% 60 minutes or more (2005-2009 5-year est.)

MALTA (village). Covers a land area of 0.375 square miles and a water area of 0 square miles. Located at 41.92° N. Lat; 88.86° W. Long. Elevation is 909 feet.

Population: 877 (1990); 969 (2000); 1,026 (2010); 1,064 (2015 projected); Race: 95.7% White, 0.7% Black, 0.2% Asian, 3.4% Other, 1.9% Hispanic of any race (2010); Density: 2,736.0 persons per square mile (2010); Average household size: 2.53 (2010); Median age: 35.8 (2010); Males per 100 females: 99.6 (2010); Marriage status: 21.9% never married, 58.3% now married, 11.0% widowed, 8.7% divorced (2005-2009 5-year est.); Foreign born: 1.2% (2005-2009 5-year est.); Ancestry (includes multiple ancestries): 37.1% German, 25.9% Irish, 12.9% English, 9.1% Norwegian, 7.1% Swedish (2005-2009 5-year est.).

Economy: Single-family building permits issued: 0 (2010); Multi-family building permits issued: 0 (2010); Employment by occupation: 9.9% management, 13.8% professional, 25.1% services, 26.2% sales, 0.0% farming, 12.2% construction, 12.9% production (2005-2009 5-year est.).

Income: Per capita income: $27,705 (2010); Median household income: $62,231 (2010); Average household income: $70,519 (2010); Percent of households with income of $100,000 or more: 20.7% (2010); Poverty rate: 3.7% (2005-2009 5-year est.).

Taxes: Total city taxes per capita: $184 (2007); City property taxes per capita: $108 (2007).

Education: Percent of population age 25 and over with: High school diploma (including GED) or higher: 92.4% (2010); Bachelor's degree or higher: 21.7% (2010); Master's degree or higher: 8.9% (2010).

School District(s)
Dekalb CUSD 428 (PK-12)
2009-10 Enrollment: 6,018 . . . . (815) 754-2350

Two-year College(s)
Kishwaukee College (Public)
Fall 2009 Enrollment: 4,735. (815) 825-2086
2010-11 Tuition: In-state $8,990; Out-of-state $10,430

Housing: Homeownership rate: 79.0% (2010); Median home value: $167,476 (2010); Median contract rent: $431 per month (2005-2009 5-year est.); Median year structure built: 1963 (2005-2009 5-year est.).

Transportation: Commute to work: 98.4% car, 0.0% public transportation, 0.9% walk, 0.7% work from home (2005-2009 5-year est.); Travel time to work: 43.4% less than 15 minutes, 38.2% 15 to 30 minutes, 10.3% 30 to 45 minutes, 4.0% 45 to 60 minutes, 4.2% 60 minutes or more (2005-2009 5-year est.)

SANDWICH (city). Covers a land area of 3.014 square miles and a water area of 0 square miles. Located at 41.64° N. Lat; 88.62° W. Long. Elevation is 666 feet.

History: Sandwich was named for Sandwich, Massachusetts. Early industries were the manufacture of plows, reapers, windmills, and cornshellers.

Population: 5,662 (1990); 6,509 (2000); 6,934 (2010); 7,315 (2015 projected); Race: 94.2% White, 0.2% Black, 0.3% Asian, 5.2% Other, 12.8% Hispanic of any race (2010); Density: 2,300.5 persons per square mile (2010); Average household size: 2.70 (2010); Median age: 34.4 (2010); Males per 100 females: 99.1 (2010); Marriage status: 18.1% never married, 63.3% now married, 7.8% widowed, 10.9% divorced (2005-2009 5-year est.); Foreign born: 5.4% (2005-2009 5-year est.); Ancestry (includes multiple ancestries): 34.3% German, 13.4% Irish, 12.4% English, 9.8% Norwegian, 5.8% French (2005-2009 5-year est.).

Economy: Single-family building permits issued: 4 (2010); Multi-family building permits issued: 0 (2010); Employment by occupation: 9.7% management, 15.7% professional, 17.8% services, 27.5% sales, 0.5% farming, 9.1% construction, 19.6% production (2005-2009 5-year est.).

Income: Per capita income: $23,699 (2010); Median household income: $57,948 (2010); Average household income: $64,409 (2010); Percent of households with income of $100,000 or more: 18.3% (2010); Poverty rate: 6.0% (2005-2009 5-year est.).

Taxes: Total city taxes per capita: $258 (2007); City property taxes per capita: $157 (2007).

Education: Percent of population age 25 and over with: High school diploma (including GED) or higher: 83.8% (2010); Bachelor's degree or higher: 12.3% (2010); Master's degree or higher: 4.9% (2010).

School District(s)

Indian Valley Area Voc Ctr (11-12)

2009-10 Enrollment: n/a . . . . (815) 786-9873

Sandwich CUSD 430 (PK-12)

2009-10 Enrollment: 2,461 . . . . (815) 786-2187

Housing: Homeownership rate: 73.2% (2010); Median home value: $165,759 (2010); Median contract rent: $545 per month (2005-2009 5-year est.); Median year structure built: 1967 (2005-2009 5-year est.).

Hospitals: Valley West Community Hospital (84 beds)

Transportation: Commute to work: 93.0% car, 1.9% public transportation, 2.6% walk, 1.3% work from home (2005-2009 5-year est.); Travel time to work: 33.6% less than 15 minutes, 18.6% 15 to 30 minutes, 27.6% 30 to 45 minutes, 14.4% 45 to 60 minutes, 5.9% 60 minutes or more (2005-2009 5-year est.)

Additional Information Contacts

City of Sandwich . . . . (815) 786-9321
http://www.sandwich.il.us

Sandwich Chamber of Commerce . . . . (815) 312-4963
http://www.sandwich-il.org

SHABBONA (village). Covers a land area of 0.742 square miles and a water area of 0 square miles. Located at 41.76° N. Lat; 88.87° W. Long. Elevation is 899 feet.

Population: 850 (1990); 929 (2000); 927 (2010); 929 (2015 projected); Race: 98.0% White, 0.1% Black, 0.0% Asian, 1.9% Other, 1.7% Hispanic of any race (2010); Density: 1,250.0 persons per square mile (2010); Average household size: 2.62 (2010); Median age: 38.1 (2010); Males per 100 females: 85.0 (2010); Marriage status: 16.4% never married, 50.4% now married, 19.6% widowed, 13.6% divorced (2005-2009 5-year est.); Foreign born: 1.3% (2005-2009 5-year est.); Ancestry (includes multiple ancestries): 37.8% German, 16.1% English, 12.1% Irish, 9.9% Norwegian, 7.8% Italian (2005-2009 5-year est.).

Economy: Single-family building permits issued: 0 (2010); Multi-family building permits issued: 0 (2010); Employment by occupation: 3.7% management, 16.0% professional, 24.9% services, 27.5% sales, 0.7% farming, 14.2% construction, 13.0% production (2005-2009 5-year est.).

Income: Per capita income: $28,003 (2010); Median household income: $64,696 (2010); Average household income: $75,329 (2010); Percent of households with income of $100,000 or more: 23.9% (2010); Poverty rate: 2.4% (2005-2009 5-year est.).

Taxes: Total city taxes per capita: $173 (2007); City property taxes per capita: $90 (2007).

Education: Percent of population age 25 and over with: High school diploma (including GED) or higher: 89.6% (2010); Bachelor's degree or higher: 13.1% (2010); Master's degree or higher: 3.1% (2010).

School District(s)

Indian Creek CUSD 425 (PK-12)

2009-10 Enrollment: 848 . . . . (815) 824-2197

Housing: Homeownership rate: 77.4% (2010); Median home value: $149,786 (2010); Median contract rent: $663 per month (2005-2009 5-year est.); Median year structure built: 1951 (2005-2009 5-year est.).

Transportation: Commute to work: 88.0% car, 0.0% public transportation, 7.7% walk, 3.5% work from home (2005-2009 5-year est.); Travel time to work: 36.0% less than 15 minutes, 13.9% 15 to 30 minutes, 24.6% 30 to 45 minutes, 15.6% 45 to 60 minutes, 10.0% 60 minutes or more (2005-2009 5-year est.)

SOMONAUK (village). Covers a land area of 0.613 square miles and a water area of 0 square miles. Located at 41.63° N. Lat; 88.68° W. Long. Elevation is 686 feet.

Population: 1,263 (1990); 1,295 (2000); 1,385 (2010); 1,430 (2015 projected); Race: 95.5% White, 0.1% Black, 0.2% Asian, 4.3% Other, 4.2% Hispanic of any race (2010); Density: 2,260.3 persons per square mile (2010); Average household size: 2.67 (2010); Median age: 32.6 (2010); Males per 100 females: 101.0 (2010); Marriage status: 29.8% never married, 54.8% now married, 4.5% widowed, 11.0% divorced (2005-2009 5-year est.); Foreign born: 3.8% (2005-2009 5-year est.); Ancestry (includes multiple ancestries): 33.9% German, 11.0% Irish, 10.7% Norwegian, 9.7% French, 8.8% English (2005-2009 5-year est.).

Economy: Single-family building permits issued: 0 (2010); Multi-family building permits issued: 0 (2010); Employment by occupation: 10.3% management, 11.8% professional, 18.5% services, 30.9% sales, 0.0% farming, 15.3% construction, 13.2% production (2005-2009 5-year est.).

Income: Per capita income: $24,464 (2010); Median household income: $57,275 (2010); Average household income: $65,255 (2010); Percent of

households with income of $100,000 or more: 15.8% (2010); Poverty rate: 7.5% (2005-2009 5-year est.).

Taxes: Total city taxes per capita: $364 (2007); City property taxes per capita: $245 (2007).

Education: Percent of population age 25 and over with: High school diploma (including GED) or higher: 94.0% (2010); Bachelor's degree or higher: 13.2% (2010); Master's degree or higher: 4.0% (2010).

School District(s)

Somonauk CUSD 432 (PK-12)

2009-10 Enrollment: 995 . . . . (815) 498-2314

Housing: Homeownership rate: 77.5% (2010); Median home value: $161,006 (2010); Median contract rent: $669 per month (2005-2009 5-year est.); Median year structure built: 1967 (2005-2009 5-year est.).

Safety: Violent crime rate: 5.4 per 10,000 population; Property crime rate: 162.4 per 10,000 population (2010).

Transportation: Commute to work: 94.2% car, 0.0% public transportation, 3.2% walk, 1.5% work from home (2005-2009 5-year est.); Travel time to work: 29.8% less than 15 minutes, 21.5% 15 to 30 minutes, 23.2% 30 to 45 minutes, 11.1% 45 to 60 minutes, 14.5% 60 minutes or more (2005-2009 5-year est.)

SYCAMORE (city). County seat. Covers a land area of 5.485 square miles and a water area of 0.018 square miles. Located at 41.98° N. Lat; 88.69° W. Long. Elevation is 869 feet.

Population: 10,107 (1990); 12,020 (2000); 15,445 (2010); 17,165 (2015 projected); Race: 92.3% White, 2.6% Black, 1.0% Asian, 4.1% Other, 6.3% Hispanic of any race (2010); Density: 2,816.1 persons per square mile (2010); Average household size: 2.55 (2010); Median age: 34.0 (2010); Males per 100 females: 98.8 (2010); Marriage status: 30.4% never married, 55.0% now married, 4.4% widowed, 10.2% divorced (2005-2009 5-year est.); Foreign born: 4.8% (2005-2009 5-year est.); Ancestry (includes multiple ancestries): 36.1% German, 19.6% Irish, 9.3% English, 7.4% Swedish, 7.4% Italian (2005-2009 5-year est.).

Economy: Single-family building permits issued: 19 (2010); Multi-family building permits issued: 0 (2010); Employment by occupation: 14.2% management, 22.9% professional, 16.8% services, 24.3% sales, 0.0% farming, 9.0% construction, 12.9% production (2005-2009 5-year est.).

Income: Per capita income: $27,294 (2010); Median household income: $60,491 (2010); Average household income: $70,351 (2010); Percent of households with income of $100,000 or more: 18.8% (2010); Poverty rate: 8.0% (2005-2009 5-year est.).

Taxes: Total city taxes per capita: $885 (2007); City property taxes per capita: $233 (2007).

Education: Percent of population age 25 and over with: High school diploma (including GED) or higher: 92.8% (2010); Bachelor's degree or higher: 26.8% (2010); Master's degree or higher: 8.9% (2010).

School District(s)

Sycamore CUSD 427 (PK-12)

2009-10 Enrollment: 3,814 . . . . (815) 899-8103

Vocational/Technical School(s)

Hair Professionals Career College Inc (Private, For-profit)

Fall 2009 Enrollment: 133 . . . . (815) 756-3596
2010-11 Tuition: $16,450

Housing: Homeownership rate: 72.5% (2010); Median home value: $167,891 (2010); Median contract rent: $703 per month (2005-2009 5-year est.); Median year structure built: 1980 (2005-2009 5-year est.).

Hospitals: Kindred Hospital - Sycamore (77 beds)

Safety: Violent crime rate: 3.8 per 10,000 population; Property crime rate: 156.4 per 10,000 population (2010).

Newspapers: Genoa/Kingston/Kirkland News (Local news; Circulation 2,000); Hampshire Register (Community news; Circulation 1,700); Hampshire Register News (Local news; Circulation 1,700); Sycamore News (Local news; Circulation 10,221)

Transportation: Commute to work: 92.1% car, 0.8% public transportation, 3.2% walk, 2.9% work from home (2005-2009 5-year est.); Travel time to work: 35.9% less than 15 minutes, 25.1% 15 to 30 minutes, 16.3% 30 to 45 minutes, 10.7% 45 to 60 minutes, 12.0% 60 minutes or more (2005-2009 5-year est.)

Additional Information Contacts

City of Sycamore . . . . (815) 895-4515
http://www.cityofsycamore.com

Sycamore Chamber of Commerce . . . . (815) 895-3456
http://www.sycamorechamber.com

WATERMAN (village). Covers a land area of 1.002 square miles and a water area of 0 square miles. Located at 41.77° N. Lat; 88.77° W. Long. Elevation is 823 feet.

Population: 1,073 (1990); 1,224 (2000); 1,480 (2010); 1,606 (2015 projected); Race: 97.9% White, 0.4% Black, 0.1% Asian, 1.6% Other, 1.4% Hispanic of any race (2010); Density: 1,476.9 persons per square mile (2010); Average household size: 2.65 (2010); Median age: 32.2 (2010); Males per 100 females: 94.0 (2010); Marriage status: 19.0% never married, 63.2% now married, 5.6% widowed, 12.1% divorced (2005-2009 5-year est.); Foreign born: 0.4% (2005-2009 5-year est.); Ancestry (includes multiple ancestries): 47.4% German, 14.4% Irish, 9.6% Norwegian, 8.2% English, 5.2% French (2005-2009 5-year est.).

Economy: Single-family building permits issued: 0 (2010); Multi-family building permits issued: 0 (2010); Employment by occupation: 14.7% management, 15.6% professional, 23.4% services, 19.7% sales, 0.3% farming, 12.1% construction, 14.2% production (2005-2009 5-year est.).

Income: Per capita income: $28,514 (2010); Median household income: $62,054 (2010); Average household income: $75,152 (2010); Percent of households with income of $100,000 or more: 21.1% (2010); Poverty rate: 12.2% (2005-2009 5-year est.).

Taxes: Total city taxes per capita: $116 (2007); City property taxes per capita: $108 (2007).

Education: Percent of population age 25 and over with: High school diploma (including GED) or higher: 91.9% (2010); Bachelor's degree or higher: 18.2% (2010); Master's degree or higher: 2.8% (2010).

School District(s)
Indian Creek CUSD 425 (PK-12)
    2009-10 Enrollment: 848 . . . . (815) 824-2197

Housing: Homeownership rate: 78.4% (2010); Median home value: $167,097 (2010); Median contract rent: $432 per month (2005-2009 5-year est.); Median year structure built: 1958 (2005-2009 5-year est.).

Transportation: Commute to work: 94.7% car, 0.0% public transportation, 3.4% walk, 1.4% work from home (2005-2009 5-year est.); Travel time to work: 28.4% less than 15 minutes, 23.9% 15 to 30 minutes, 25.1% 30 to 45 minutes, 14.6% 45 to 60 minutes, 8.0% 60 minutes or more (2005-2009 5-year est.)

Douglas County

Located in east central Illinois; drained by the Embarrass and Kaskaskia Rivers. Covers a land area of 416.86 square miles, a water area of 0.56 square miles, and is located in the Central Time Zone at 39.77° N. Lat., 88.23° W. Long. The county was founded in 1859. County seat is Tuscola.

Weather Station: Tuscola   Elevation: 652 feet

	Jan	Feb	Mar	Apr	May	Jun	Jul	Aug	Sep	Oct	Nov	Dec
High	35	40	52	65	76	85	87	86	80	67	53	40
Low	19	22	31	42	53	62	65	63	55	43	34	24
Precip	2.2	2.2	2.8	4.0	4.1	4.1	4.5	3.4	3.2	3.4	3.8	2.9
Snow	6.3	5.1	2.3	0.2	tr	0.0	0.0	0.0	0.0	tr	1.0	4.7

High and Low temperatures in degrees Fahrenheit; Precipitation and Snow in inches

Population: 19,464 (1990); 19,922 (2000); 19,331 (2010); 18,898 (2015 projected); Race: 95.0% White, 0.9% Black, 0.7% Asian, 3.5% Other, 5.8% Hispanic of any race (2010); Density: 46.4 persons per square mile (2010); Average household size: 2.55 (2010); Median age: 37.9 (2010); Males per 100 females: 96.2 (2010).

Religion: Five largest groups: 12.4% The United Methodist Church, 11.3% Catholic Church, 8.1% Christian Churches and Churches of Christ, 7.3% Old Order Amish Church, 5.3% Christian Church (Disciples of Christ) (2000).

Economy: Unemployment rate: 9.3% (August 2011); Total civilian labor force: 10,064 (August 2011); Leading industries: 36.0% manufacturing; 18.4% retail trade; 11.0% accommodation & food services (2009); Farms: 657 totaling 261,513 acres (2007); Companies that employ 500 or more persons: 0 (2009); Companies that employ 100 to 499 persons: 6 (2009); Companies that employ less than 100 persons: 628 (2009); Black-owned businesses: n/a (2007); Hispanic-owned businesses: n/a (2007); Asian-owned businesses: n/a (2007); Women-owned businesses: n/a (2007); Retail sales per capita: $11,346 (2010). Single-family building permits issued: 24 (2010); Multi-family building permits issued: 2 (2010).

Income: Per capita income: $22,914 (2010); Median household income: $48,022 (2010); Average household income: $58,779 (2010); Percent of households with income of $100,000 or more: 12.4% (2010); Poverty rate: 8.7% (2009); Bankruptcy rate: 4.19% (2010).

Taxes: Total county taxes per capita: $110 (2007); County property taxes per capita: $110 (2007).

Education: Percent of population age 25 and over with: High school diploma (including GED) or higher: 85.2% (2010); Bachelor's degree or higher: 17.1% (2010); Master's degree or higher: 5.3% (2010).

Housing: Homeownership rate: 75.7% (2010); Median home value: $98,634 (2010); Median contract rent: $411 per month (2005-2009 5-year est.); Median year structure built: 1962 (2005-2009 5-year est.)

Health: Birth rate: 156.0 per 10,000 population (2009); Death rate: 101.2 per 10,000 population (2009); Age-adjusted cancer mortality rate: 164.9 deaths per 100,000 population (2007); Number of physicians: 4.7 per 10,000 population (2008); Hospital beds: 0.0 per 10,000 population (2007); Hospital admissions: 0.0 per 10,000 population (2007).

Elections: 2008 Presidential election results: 38.6% Obama, 59.9% McCain, 0.7% Nader

National and State Parks: Walnut Point State Park

Additional Information Contacts

Douglas County Government. . . . . (217) 253-2411
    http://www.douglascountyil.com
Arcola Chamber of Commerce . . . . (217) 268-4530
    http://www.arcolachamber.com
City of Arcola . . . . (217) 268-4966
    http://www.arcolaillinois.org
Tuscola Chamber of Commerce . . . . (217) 253-5013
    http://www.tuscola.org

Douglas County Communities

ARCOLA (city). Covers a land area of 1.368 square miles and a water area of 0.017 square miles. Located at 39.68° N. Lat; 88.30° W. Long. Elevation is 679 feet.

History: Arcola was laid out in 1855 and named for a town in Italy. Broom corn was grown here, some for the local manufacture of brooms and some for export.

Population: 2,678 (1990); 2,652 (2000); 2,595 (2010); 2,548 (2015 projected); Race: 83.2% White, 0.6% Black, 1.6% Asian, 14.7% Other, 31.1% Hispanic of any race (2010); Density: 1,897.2 persons per square mile (2010); Average household size: 2.65 (2010); Median age: 37.5 (2010); Males per 100 females: 96.9 (2010); Marriage status: 21.7% never married, 63.0% now married, 7.6% widowed, 7.8% divorced (2005-2009 5-year est.); Foreign born: 18.5% (2005-2009 5-year est.); Ancestry (includes multiple ancestries): 19.5% German, 15.4% English, 15.1% Irish, 13.4% American, 2.6% Dutch (2005-2009 5-year est.).

Economy: Single-family building permits issued: 2 (2010); Multi-family building permits issued: 0 (2010); Employment by occupation: 8.0% management, 8.6% professional, 12.2% services, 29.1% sales, 0.4% farming, 12.5% construction, 29.2% production (2005-2009 5-year est.).

Income: Per capita income: $21,444 (2010); Median household income: $45,184 (2010); Average household income: $56,773 (2010); Percent of households with income of $100,000 or more: 12.3% (2010); Poverty rate: 15.2% (2005-2009 5-year est.).

Taxes: Total city taxes per capita: $582 (2007); City property taxes per capita: $564 (2007).

Education: Percent of population age 25 and over with: High school diploma (including GED) or higher: 82.7% (2010); Bachelor's degree or higher: 18.7% (2010); Master's degree or higher: 7.0% (2010).

School District(s)
Arcola CUSD 306 (PK-12)
    2009-10 Enrollment: 781 . . . . (217) 268-4963
Eastern Il Area of Spec Educ (PK-12)
    2009-10 Enrollment: n/a . . . . (217) 348-7700

Housing: Homeownership rate: 76.0% (2010); Median home value: $97,000 (2010); Median contract rent: $422 per month (2005-2009 5-year est.); Median year structure built: 1969 (2005-2009 5-year est.).

Safety: Violent crime rate: 11.2 per 10,000 population; Property crime rate: 41.0 per 10,000 population (2010).

Newspapers: Arcola Record-Herald (Community news; Circulation 2,200)

Transportation: Commute to work: 91.3% car, 0.0% public transportation, 5.4% walk, 2.9% work from home (2005-2009 5-year est.); Travel time to work: 59.1% less than 15 minutes, 26.6% 15 to 30 minutes, 8.0% 30 to 45 minutes, 4.6% 45 to 60 minutes, 1.7% 60 minutes or more (2005-2009 5-year est.)

Additional Information Contacts

Arcola Chamber of Commerce . . . . (217) 268-4530
    http://www.arcolachamber.com

City of Arcola . . . . (217) 268-4966
http://www.arcolaillinois.org

ARTHUR (village). Covers a land area of 1.276 square miles and a water area of 0 square miles. Located at 39.71° N. Lat; 88.47° W. Long. Elevation is 663 feet.

History: Arthur was settled in 1864 by a group of Amish colonists. The village was platted in 1873 by the Paris & Decatur Railroad Company. An early industry was the production of brooms.

Population: 2,268 (1990); 2,203 (2000); 2,213 (2010); 2,179 (2015 projected); Race: 99.4% White, 0.0% Black, 0.1% Asian, 0.5% Other, 0.9% Hispanic of any race (2010); Density: 1,734.6 persons per square mile (2010); Average household size: 2.54 (2010); Median age: 35.9 (2010); Males per 100 females: 89.6 (2010); Marriage status: 15.7% never married, 61.1% now married, 14.0% widowed, 9.2% divorced (2005-2009 5-year est.); Foreign born: 0.0% (2005-2009 5-year est.); Ancestry (includes multiple ancestries): 30.0% German, 11.3% American, 10.3% English, 9.9% Irish, 3.2% Swedish (2005-2009 5-year est.).

Economy: Single-family building permits issued: 2 (2010); Multi-family building permits issued: 2 (2010); Employment by occupation: 19.9% management, 13.9% professional, 13.1% services, 20.7% sales, 0.0% farming, 12.0% construction, 20.4% production (2005-2009 5-year est.).

Income: Per capita income: $22,637 (2010); Median household income: $47,721 (2010); Average household income: $57,353 (2010); Percent of households with income of $100,000 or more: 11.2% (2010); Poverty rate: 4.4% (2005-2009 5-year est.).

Taxes: Total city taxes per capita: $175 (2007); City property taxes per capita: $165 (2007).

Education: Percent of population age 25 and over with: High school diploma (including GED) or higher: 84.6% (2010); Bachelor's degree or higher: 18.9% (2010); Master's degree or higher: 4.3% (2010).

School District(s)

Arthur CUSD 305 (KG-12)
    2009-10 Enrollment: 467 . . . . (217) 543-2511

Housing: Homeownership rate: 74.1% (2010); Median home value: $103,744 (2010); Median contract rent: $413 per month (2005-2009 5-year est.); Median year structure built: 1966 (2005-2009 5-year est.).

Safety: Violent crime rate: 0.0 per 10,000 population; Property crime rate: 206.3 per 10,000 population (2010).

Newspapers: Arthur Graphic Clarion (Local news; Circulation 3,100)

Transportation: Commute to work: 87.3% car, 0.7% public transportation, 2.6% walk, 4.5% work from home (2005-2009 5-year est.); Travel time to work: 69.2% less than 15 minutes, 14.5% 15 to 30 minutes, 8.1% 30 to 45 minutes, 5.4% 45 to 60 minutes, 2.8% 60 minutes or more (2005-2009 5-year est.)

CAMARGO (village). Covers a land area of 1.263 square miles and a water area of 0.013 square miles. Located at 39.79° N. Lat; 88.16° W. Long. Elevation is 663 feet.

Population: 372 (1990); 469 (2000); 454 (2010); 447 (2015 projected); Race: 98.2% White, 0.7% Black, 0.0% Asian, 1.1% Other, 0.2% Hispanic of any race (2010); Density: 359.4 persons per square mile (2010); Average household size: 2.59 (2010); Median age: 41.9 (2010); Males per 100 females: 99.1 (2010); Marriage status: 21.4% never married, 58.9% now married, 6.5% widowed, 13.3% divorced (2005-2009 5-year est.); Foreign born: 0.0% (2005-2009 5-year est.); Ancestry (includes multiple ancestries): 32.1% German, 15.2% Irish, 9.9% English, 6.8% American, 5.1% Scottish (2005-2009 5-year est.).

Economy: Single-family building permits issued: 3 (2010); Multi-family building permits issued: 0 (2010); Employment by occupation: 10.2% management, 11.3% professional, 25.8% services, 25.3% sales, 3.2% farming, 7.0% construction, 17.2% production (2005-2009 5-year est.).

Income: Per capita income: $29,815 (2010); Median household income: $69,932 (2010); Average household income: $78,229 (2010); Percent of households with income of $100,000 or more: 20.6% (2010); Poverty rate: 3.9% (2005-2009 5-year est.).

Taxes: Total city taxes per capita: $146 (2007); City property taxes per capita: $76 (2007).

Education: Percent of population age 25 and over with: High school diploma (including GED) or higher: 92.7% (2010); Bachelor's degree or higher: 17.4% (2010); Master's degree or higher: 4.1% (2010).

Housing: Homeownership rate: 83.4% (2010); Median home value: $134,884 (2010); Median contract rent: $409 per month (2005-2009 5-year est.); Median year structure built: 1976 (2005-2009 5-year est.).

Transportation: Commute to work: 90.2% car, 0.0% public transportation, 1.1% walk, 8.7% work from home (2005-2009 5-year est.); Travel time to work: 29.8% less than 15 minutes, 20.8% 15 to 30 minutes, 41.1% 30 to 45 minutes, 6.5% 45 to 60 minutes, 1.8% 60 minutes or more (2005-2009 5-year est.)

GARRETT (village). Covers a land area of 0.139 square miles and a water area of 0 square miles. Located at 39.79° N. Lat; 88.42° W. Long. Elevation is 669 feet.

Population: 169 (1990); 198 (2000); 208 (2010); 211 (2015 projected); Race: 99.0% White, 0.5% Black, 0.0% Asian, 0.5% Other, 1.0% Hispanic of any race (2010); Density: 1,494.8 persons per square mile (2010); Average household size: 2.89 (2010); Median age: 31.3 (2010); Males per 100 females: 105.9 (2010); Marriage status: 19.8% never married, 30.6% now married, 9.0% widowed, 40.5% divorced (2005-2009 5-year est.); Foreign born: 0.0% (2005-2009 5-year est.); Ancestry (includes multiple ancestries): 28.8% German, 17.8% Irish, 14.4% American, 8.5% English, 1.7% Scottish (2005-2009 5-year est.).

Economy: Employment by occupation: 0.0% management, 3.5% professional, 29.8% services, 17.5% sales, 0.0% farming, 19.3% construction, 29.8% production (2005-2009 5-year est.).

Income: Per capita income: $20,833 (2010); Median household income: $48,929 (2010); Average household income: $59,722 (2010); Percent of households with income of $100,000 or more: 13.9% (2010); Poverty rate: 19.5% (2005-2009 5-year est.).

Taxes: Total city taxes per capita: $71 (2007); City property taxes per capita: $71 (2007).

Education: Percent of population age 25 and over with: High school diploma (including GED) or higher: 89.1% (2010); Bachelor's degree or higher: 12.6% (2010); Master's degree or higher: 4.2% (2010).

Housing: Homeownership rate: 80.6% (2010); Median home value: $110,000 (2010); Median contract rent: $227 per month (2005-2009 5-year est.); Median year structure built: 1952 (2005-2009 5-year est.).

Transportation: Commute to work: 98.2% car, 0.0% public transportation, 0.0% walk, 0.0% work from home (2005-2009 5-year est.); Travel time to work: 33.3% less than 15 minutes, 50.9% 15 to 30 minutes, 14.0% 30 to 45 minutes, 1.8% 45 to 60 minutes, 0.0% 60 minutes or more (2005-2009 5-year est.)

HINDSBORO (village). Covers a land area of 0.308 square miles and a water area of 0 square miles. Located at 39.68° N. Lat; 88.13° W. Long. Elevation is 650 feet.

Population: 359 (1990); 361 (2000); 311 (2010); 286 (2015 projected); Race: 99.4% White, 0.0% Black, 0.6% Asian, 0.0% Other, 2.9% Hispanic of any race (2010); Density: 1,010.6 persons per square mile (2010); Average household size: 2.43 (2010); Median age: 41.3 (2010); Males per 100 females: 99.4 (2010); Marriage status: 28.8% never married, 53.9% now married, 5.1% widowed, 12.2% divorced (2005-2009 5-year est.); Foreign born: 0.0% (2005-2009 5-year est.); Ancestry (includes multiple ancestries): 25.2% German, 11.2% Irish, 10.0% American, 8.6% English, 4.6% French (2005-2009 5-year est.).

Economy: Single-family building permits issued: 0 (2010); Multi-family building permits issued: 0 (2010); Employment by occupation: 1.1% management, 9.3% professional, 20.3% services, 24.7% sales, 5.5% farming, 7.1% construction, 31.9% production (2005-2009 5-year est.).

Income: Per capita income: $20,893 (2010); Median household income: $41,000 (2010); Average household income: $50,363 (2010); Percent of households with income of $100,000 or more: 12.1% (2010); Poverty rate: 12.3% (2005-2009 5-year est.).

Taxes: Total city taxes per capita: $120 (2007); City property taxes per capita: $58 (2007).

Education: Percent of population age 25 and over with: High school diploma (including GED) or higher: 87.4% (2010); Bachelor's degree or higher: 29.4% (2010); Master's degree or higher: 7.9% (2010).

Housing: Homeownership rate: 83.1% (2010); Median home value: $85,294 (2010); Median contract rent: $321 per month (2005-2009 5-year est.); Median year structure built: before 1940 (2005-2009 5-year est.).

Transportation: Commute to work: 91.8% car, 0.0% public transportation, 4.4% walk, 2.7% work from home (2005-2009 5-year est.); Travel time to work: 24.3% less than 15 minutes, 38.4% 15 to 30 minutes, 26.0% 30 to 45 minutes, 4.5% 45 to 60 minutes, 6.8% 60 minutes or more (2005-2009 5-year est.)

Religion: Five largest groups: 38.6% Catholic Church, 3.0% Lutheran Church—Missouri Synod, 3.0% Evangelical Lutheran Church in America, 2.2% The United Methodist Church, 1.7% Muslim Estimate (2000).
Economy: Unemployment rate: 8.4% (August 2011); Total civilian labor force: 526,351 (August 2011); Leading industries: 10.9% administration, support, waste management, remediation services; 10.4% retail trade; 10.2% health care and social assistance (2009); Farms: 73 totaling 7,948 acres (2007); Companies that employ 500 or more persons: 96 (2009); Companies that employ 100 to 499 persons: 873 (2009); Companies that employ less than 100 persons: 32,361 (2009); Black-owned businesses: 2,379 (2007); Hispanic-owned businesses: 4,079 (2007); Asian-owned businesses: 8,523 (2007); Women-owned businesses: 26,506 (2007); Retail sales per capita: $19,710 (2010). Single-family building permits issued: 430 (2010); Multi-family building permits issued: 188 (2010).
Income: Per capita income: $36,160 (2010); Median household income: $77,185 (2010); Average household income: $99,010 (2010); Percent of households with income of $100,000 or more: 34.9% (2010); Poverty rate: 6.7% (2009); Bankruptcy rate: 5.79% (2010).
Taxes: Total county taxes per capita: $165 (2007); County property taxes per capita: $119 (2007).
Education: Percent of population age 25 and over with: High school diploma (including GED) or higher: 92.0% (2010); Bachelor's degree or higher: 44.7% (2010); Master's degree or higher: 17.4% (2010).
Housing: Homeownership rate: 76.2% (2010); Median home value: $275,233 (2010); Median contract rent: $900 per month (2005-2009 5-year est.); Median year structure built: 1976 (2005-2009 5-year est.)
Health: Birth rate: 125.2 per 10,000 population (2009); Death rate: 61.6 per 10,000 population (2009); Age-adjusted cancer mortality rate: 165.5 deaths per 100,000 population (2007); Number of physicians: 45.1 per 10,000 population (2008); Hospital beds: 24.4 per 10,000 population (2007); Hospital admissions: 1,296.8 per 10,000 population (2007).
Environment: Air Quality Index: 77.0% good, 23.0% moderate, 0.0% unhealthy for sensitive individuals, 0.0% unhealthy (percent of days in 2008)
Elections: 2008 Presidential election results: 54.7% Obama, 43.9% McCain, 0.5% Nader

Additional Information Contacts

Du Page County Government . . . . (630) 407-5500
  http://www.co.dupage.il.us
Bartlett Chamber of Commerce . . . . (630) 830-0324
  http://www.bartlettchamber.com
Bloomingdale Chamber of Commerce . . . . (630) 980-9082
  http://www.bloomingdalechamber.com
Carol Stream Chamber of Commerce . . . . (630) 665-3325
  http://www.carolstreamchamber.com
City of Darien . . . . (630) 852-5000
  http://www.darien.il.us
City of Elmhurst . . . . (630) 530-3000
  http://www.elmhurst.org
City of Naperville . . . . (630) 420-6111
  http://www.naperville.il.us
City of Warrenville . . . . (630) 393-9427
  http://www.warrenville.il.us
City of West Chicago . . . . (630) 293-2200
  http://www.westchicago.org
City of Wheaton . . . . (630) 260-2012
  http://www.wheaton.il.us
City of Wood Dale . . . . (630) 766-4900
  http://www.wooddale.com
Clarendon Hills Chamber of Commerce . . . . (630) 323-8700
  http://clarendonhillschamber.com
Darien Chamber of Commerce . . . . (630) 968-0004
  http://www.darienchamber.com
Downers Grove Area Chamber of Commerce . . . . (630) 968-4050
  http://www.downersgrove.org
Elmhurst Chamber of Commerce . . . . (630) 834-6060
  http://www.elmhurstchamber.org
Glen Ellyn Chamber of Commerce . . . . (630) 469-0907
  http://www.glenellynchamber.com
Glendale Heights Chamber of Commerce . . . . (630) 545-1099
  http://www.glendaleheightschamber.com
Greater Oak Brook Chamber of Commerce . . . . (630) 472-9377
  http://www.obchamber.com
Hinsdale Chamber of Commerce . . . . (630) 323-3952
  http://www.hinsdalechamber.com

Lisle Area Chamber of Commerce . . . . (630) 964-0052
  http://www.lislechamber.com
Lisle Convention & Visitors Bureau . . . . (800) 733-9811
  http://www.lislecvb.com
Lombard Chamber of Commerce . . . . (630) 627-5040
  http://www.lombardchamber.com
Naperville Area Chamber of Commerce . . . . (630) 355-4141
  http://www.naperville.net
Roselle Chamber of Commerce & Industry . . . . (630) 894-3010
  http://www.rosellechamber.com
Villa Park Chamber of Commerce . . . . (630) 941-9133
  http://www.villaparkchamber.org
Village of Addison . . . . (630) 693-7503
  http://www.addisonadvantage.org
Village of Bartlett . . . . (630) 837-0800
  http://www.village.bartlett.il.us
Village of Bensenville . . . . (630) 766-8200
  http://www.bensenville.il.us
Village of Bloomingdale . . . . (630) 893-7000
  http://www.villageofbloomingdale.org
Village of Burr Ridge . . . . (630) 654-8181
  http://www.burr-ridge.gov
Village of Carol Stream . . . . (630) 665-7050
  http://www.carolstream.org
Village of Clarendon Hills . . . . (630) 286-5400
  http://www.clarendonhills.us
Village of Downers Grove . . . . (630) 434-5500
  http://www.downers.us
Village of Glen Ellyn . . . . (630) 469-5000
  http://www.glenellyn.org
Village of Glendale Heights . . . . (630) 260-6000
  http://www.glendaleheights.org
Village of Hinsdale . . . . (630) 789-7011
  http://www.villageofhinsdale.org
Village of Itasca . . . . (630) 773-0835
  http://www.itasca.com
Village of Lisle . . . . (630) 271-4100
  http://www.villageoflisle.org
Village of Lombard . . . . (630) 620-5700
  http://www.villageoflombard.org
Village of Oak Brook . . . . (630) 368-5000
  http://www.oak-brook.org
Village of Roselle . . . . (630) 980-2000
  http://www.roselle.il.us
Village of Villa Park . . . . (630) 834-8500
  http://www.invillapark.com
Village of Westmont . . . . (630) 981-6200
  http://www.westmont.il.gov
Village of Willowbrook . . . . (630) 323-8215
  http://www.willowbrookil.org
Village of Winfield . . . . (630) 933-7100
  http://www.villageofwinfield.com
Village of Woodridge . . . . (630) 852-7000
  http://www.vil.woodridge.il.us
West Chicago Chamber of Commerce & Industry . . . . (630) 231-3003
  http://www.wegochamber.org
Western DuPage Chamber of Commerce . . . . (630) 231-3003
  http://www.westerndupagechamber.com
Westmont Chamber of Commerce & Tourism Bureau . . . . (630) 960-5553
  http://www.westmontchamber.com
Wheaton Chamber of Commerce . . . . (630) 668-6464
  http://wheatonchamber.com
Willowbrook/Burr Ridge Chamber of Commerce . . . . (630) 654-0909
  http://www.wbbrchamber.org
Winfield Chamber of Commerce . . . . (630) 682-3712
  http://www.winfieldchamber.biz
Wood Dale Chamber of Commerce . . . . (630) 595-0505
  http://www.wooddalechamber.com
Woodridge Area Chamber of Commerce . . . . (630) 960-7080
  http://www.woodridgechamber.org

Du Page County Communities

ADDISON (village). Covers a land area of 9.432 square miles and a water area of 0.054 square miles. Located at 41.93° N. Lat; 88.00° W. Long. Elevation is 689 feet.
History: Addison developed as a community of German Lutherans in the 1840's. It was named for the 18th-century essayist, Joseph Addison.
Population: 33,723 (1990); 35,914 (2000); 36,688 (2010); 36,774 (2015 projected); Race: 69.2% White, 3.5% Black, 8.2% Asian, 19.1% Other, 39.0% Hispanic of any race (2010); Density: 3,889.7 persons per square mile (2010); Average household size: 3.03 (2010); Median age: 36.3 (2010); Males per 100 females: 103.5 (2010); Marriage status: 32.2% never married, 56.6% now married, 4.8% widowed, 6.5% divorced (2005-2009 5-year est.); Foreign born: 34.9% (2005-2009 5-year est.); Ancestry (includes multiple ancestries): 15.6% Italian, 13.0% Polish, 10.6% German, 7.4% Irish, 3.8% Greek (2005-2009 5-year est.).
Economy: Unemployment rate: 10.0% (August 2011); Total civilian labor force: 19,685 (August 2011); Single-family building permits issued: 1 (2010); Multi-family building permits issued: 0 (2010); Employment by occupation: 12.9% management, 12.3% professional, 12.9% services, 29.1% sales, 0.0% farming, 11.7% construction, 21.1% production (2005-2009 5-year est.).
Income: Per capita income: $24,394 (2010); Median household income: $59,689 (2010); Average household income: $74,022 (2010); Percent of households with income of $100,000 or more: 21.8% (2010); Poverty rate: 11.3% (2005-2009 5-year est.).
Taxes: Total city taxes per capita: $506 (2007); City property taxes per capita: $252 (2007).
Education: Percent of population age 25 and over with: High school diploma (including GED) or higher: 77.8% (2010); Bachelor's degree or higher: 21.1% (2010); Master's degree or higher: 6.3% (2010).
School District(s)
Addison SD 4 (PK-08)
    2009-10 Enrollment: 4,372 . . . . (630) 458-2425
Dupage HSD 88 (09-12)
    2009-10 Enrollment: 4,110 . . . . (630) 530-3980
Dupage Roe (06-12)
    2009-10 Enrollment: n/a . . . . (630) 407-5800
Technology Center of Dupage (11-12)
    2009-10 Enrollment: n/a . . . . (630) 691-7591
Four-year College(s)
Chamberlain College of Nursingâ "Addison Campus (Private, For-profit)
    Fall 2009 Enrollment: 669 . . . . (630) 953-3680
    2010-11 Tuition: In-state $14,820; Out-of-state $14,820
Housing: Homeownership rate: 70.8% (2010); Median home value: $256,749 (2010); Median contract rent: $801 per month (2005-2009 5-year est.); Median year structure built: 1973 (2005-2009 5-year est.).
Safety: Violent crime rate: 18.3 per 10,000 population; Property crime rate: 226.1 per 10,000 population (2010).
Transportation: Commute to work: 92.9% car, 2.8% public transportation, 0.7% walk, 2.1% work from home (2005-2009 5-year est.); Travel time to work: 25.5% less than 15 minutes, 36.3% 15 to 30 minutes, 24.5% 30 to 45 minutes, 6.6% 45 to 60 minutes, 7.1% 60 minutes or more (2005-2009 5-year est.)
Additional Information Contacts
Village of Addison . . . . (630) 693-7503
    http://www.addisonadvantage.org

BARTLETT (village). Covers a land area of 14.814 square miles and a water area of 0.144 square miles. Located at 41.97° N. Lat; 88.19° W. Long.
Population: 19,814 (1990); 36,706 (2000); 39,652 (2010); 41,374 (2015 projected); Race: 81.4% White, 2.9% Black, 11.1% Asian, 4.6% Other, 8.6% Hispanic of any race (2010); Density: 2,676.7 persons per square mile (2010); Average household size: 3.01 (2010); Median age: 36.3 (2010); Males per 100 females: 98.8 (2010); Marriage status: 23.2% never married, 66.5% now married, 3.6% widowed, 6.8% divorced (2005-2009 5-year est.); Foreign born: 14.6% (2005-2009 5-year est.); Ancestry (includes multiple ancestries): 29.5% German, 17.2% Italian, 16.8% Irish, 14.7% Polish, 6.1% English (2005-2009 5-year est.).
Economy: Unemployment rate: 8.5% (August 2011); Total civilian labor force: 24,328 (August 2011); Single-family building permits issued: 1 (2010); Multi-family building permits issued: 0 (2010); Employment by occupation: 22.4% management, 20.0% professional, 10.8% services,

31.6% sales, 0.0% farming, 6.8% construction, 8.4% production (2005-2009 5-year est.).
Income: Per capita income: $36,972 (2010); Median household income: $94,711 (2010); Average household income: $111,160 (2010); Percent of households with income of $100,000 or more: 45.9% (2010); Poverty rate: 3.2% (2005-2009 5-year est.).
Education: Percent of population age 25 and over with: High school diploma (including GED) or higher: 94.4% (2010); Bachelor's degree or higher: 41.7% (2010); Master's degree or higher: 12.7% (2010).
School District(s)
SD U-46 (PK-12)
    2009-10 Enrollment: 41,446 . . . . (847) 888-5000
Housing: Homeownership rate: 94.2% (2010); Median home value: $269,580 (2010); Median contract rent: $918 per month (2005-2009 5-year est.); Median year structure built: 1991 (2005-2009 5-year est.).
Safety: Violent crime rate: 4.9 per 10,000 population; Property crime rate: 86.8 per 10,000 population (2010).
Newspapers: Bartlett Examiner (Community news; Circulation 10,000); Carol Stream Examiner (Community news; Circulation 7,700); Hanover Park Examiner (Community news; Circulation 5,800); Streamwood Examiner (Community news; Circulation 7,000); Wayne Examiner (Community news; Circulation 9,000)
Transportation: Commute to work: 89.8% car, 3.8% public transportation, 0.7% walk, 4.8% work from home (2005-2009 5-year est.); Travel time to work: 14.5% less than 15 minutes, 30.0% 15 to 30 minutes, 28.8% 30 to 45 minutes, 14.1% 45 to 60 minutes, 12.7% 60 minutes or more (2005-2009 5-year est.)
Additional Information Contacts
Bartlett Chamber of Commerce . . . . (630) 830-0324
    http://www.bartlettchamber.com
Village of Bartlett . . . . (630) 837-0800
    http://www.village.bartlett.il.us

BENSENVILLE (village). Covers a land area of 6.006 square miles and a water area of 0 square miles. Located at 41.95° N. Lat; 87.94° W. Long. Elevation is 679 feet.
Population: 17,957 (1990); 20,703 (2000); 20,381 (2010); 20,160 (2015 projected); Race: 60.4% White, 4.9% Black, 6.1% Asian, 28.6% Other, 50.2% Hispanic of any race (2010); Density: 3,393.6 persons per square mile (2010); Average household size: 2.97 (2010); Median age: 36.3 (2010); Males per 100 females: 107.2 (2010); Marriage status: 33.9% never married, 52.0% now married, 5.6% widowed, 8.4% divorced (2005-2009 5-year est.); Foreign born: 36.2% (2005-2009 5-year est.); Ancestry (includes multiple ancestries): 12.1% German, 10.7% Polish, 7.9% Irish, 7.0% Italian, 2.7% English (2005-2009 5-year est.).
Economy: Single-family building permits issued: 0 (2010); Multi-family building permits issued: 0 (2010); Employment by occupation: 11.0% management, 9.7% professional, 16.0% services, 26.8% sales, 0.0% farming, 11.1% construction, 25.5% production (2005-2009 5-year est.).
Income: Per capita income: $22,868 (2010); Median household income: $59,721 (2010); Average household income: $68,100 (2010); Percent of households with income of $100,000 or more: 17.1% (2010); Poverty rate: 13.3% (2005-2009 5-year est.).
Taxes: Total city taxes per capita: $535 (2007); City property taxes per capita: $307 (2007).
Education: Percent of population age 25 and over with: High school diploma (including GED) or higher: 75.4% (2010); Bachelor's degree or higher: 21.0% (2010); Master's degree or higher: 5.2% (2010).
School District(s)
Bensenville SD 2 (PK-08)
    2009-10 Enrollment: 2,094 . . . . (630) 766-5940
Fenton CHSD 100 (09-12)
    2009-10 Enrollment: 1,526 . . . . (630) 860-6257
Vocational/Technical School(s)
Star Truck Driving School (Private, For-profit)
    Fall 2009 Enrollment: 64 . . . . (630) 236-7200
    2010-11 Tuition: $4,595
Housing: Homeownership rate: 55.0% (2010); Median home value: $238,002 (2010); Median contract rent: $856 per month (2005-2009 5-year est.); Median year structure built: 1970 (2005-2009 5-year est.).
Newspapers: KJT International & Polish News (International news; Circulation 10,000)
Transportation: Commute to work: 87.4% car, 4.2% public transportation, 3.2% walk, 2.9% work from home (2005-2009 5-year est.); Travel time to work: 27.6% less than 15 minutes, 39.6% 15 to 30 minutes, 18.4% 30 to 45

minutes, 7.7% 45 to 60 minutes, 6.7% 60 minutes or more (2005-2009 5-year est.)

Additional Information Contacts
Village of Bensenville. . . . . (630) 766-8200
http://www.bensenville.il.us

BLOOMINGDALE (village). Covers a land area of 6.765 square miles and a water area of 0.042 square miles. Located at 41.95° N. Lat; 88.08° W. Long. Elevation is 764 feet.

Population: 16,990 (1990); 21,675 (2000); 22,001 (2010); 21,981 (2015 projected); Race: 79.4% White, 4.2% Black, 11.6% Asian, 4.9% Other, 7.4% Hispanic of any race (2010); Density: 3,252.3 persons per square mile (2010); Average household size: 2.51 (2010); Median age: 42.2 (2010); Males per 100 females: 95.0 (2010); Marriage status: 28.5% never married, 54.6% now married, 8.5% widowed, 8.4% divorced (2005-2009 5-year est.); Foreign born: 18.1% (2005-2009 5-year est.); Ancestry (includes multiple ancestries): 24.1% Italian, 23.2% German, 16.4% Polish, 14.3% Irish, 4.9% English (2005-2009 5-year est.).
Economy: Single-family building permits issued: 1 (2010); Multi-family building permits issued: 0 (2010); Employment by occupation: 21.6% management, 19.4% professional, 11.9% services, 29.4% sales, 0.0% farming, 8.3% construction, 9.4% production (2005-2009 5-year est.).
Income: Per capita income: $36,138 (2010); Median household income: $76,067 (2010); Average household income: $93,169 (2010); Percent of households with income of $100,000 or more: 32.1% (2010); Poverty rate: 5.1% (2005-2009 5-year est.).
Taxes: Total city taxes per capita: $515 (2007); City property taxes per capita: $222 (2007).
Education: Percent of population age 25 and over with: High school diploma (including GED) or higher: 92.3% (2010); Bachelor's degree or higher: 37.6% (2010); Master's degree or higher: 12.4% (2010).

School District(s)
Bloomingdale SD 13 (PK-08)
    2009-10 Enrollment: 1,225 . . . . (630) 893-9590
CCSD 93 (PK-08)
    2009-10 Enrollment: 4,002 . . . . (630) 893-9393
Marquardt SD 15 (PK-08)
    2009-10 Enrollment: 2,666 . . . . (630) 469-7615
Vocational/Technical School(s)
Pivot Point Beauty School (Private, For-profit)
    Fall 2009 Enrollment: 224 . . . . (847) 985-5900
    2010-11 Tuition: $18,106
Housing: Homeownership rate: 72.4% (2010); Median home value: $288,015 (2010); Median contract rent: $1,093 per month (2005-2009 5-year est.); Median year structure built: 1981 (2005-2009 5-year est.).
Safety: Violent crime rate: 5.1 per 10,000 population; Property crime rate: 392.4 per 10,000 population (2010).
Transportation: Commute to work: 90.1% car, 3.1% public transportation, 1.1% walk, 5.2% work from home (2005-2009 5-year est.); Travel time to work: 22.2% less than 15 minutes, 34.7% 15 to 30 minutes, 21.9% 30 to 45 minutes, 11.8% 45 to 60 minutes, 9.4% 60 minutes or more (2005-2009 5-year est.)

Additional Information Contacts
Bloomingdale Chamber of Commerce. . . . . (630) 980-9082
http://www.bloomingdalechamber.com
Village of Bloomingdale . . . . (630) 893-7000
http://www.villageofbloomingdale.org

BURR RIDGE (village). Covers a land area of 6.424 square miles and a water area of 0.112 square miles. Located at 41.75° N. Lat; 87.92° W. Long. Elevation is 702 feet.

History: The International Harvester Company and the Burr Ridges Estates merged with Harvester, changing the community's name to Burr Ridge. The town name is derived from a group of bur oaks (scientists spell it with one r) on a ridge.
Population: 8,340 (1990); 10,408 (2000); 10,963 (2010); 11,074 (2015 projected); Race: 82.5% White, 1.6% Black, 12.7% Asian, 3.2% Other, 3.9% Hispanic of any race (2010); Density: 1,706.5 persons per square mile (2010); Average household size: 2.70 (2010); Median age: 47.1 (2010); Males per 100 females: 94.4 (2010); Marriage status: 17.5% never married, 66.8% now married, 9.0% widowed, 6.7% divorced (2005-2009 5-year est.); Foreign born: 19.2% (2005-2009 5-year est.); Ancestry (includes multiple ancestries): 19.0% Irish, 16.7% German, 12.7% Italian, 10.1% Polish, 6.9% English (2005-2009 5-year est.).

Economy: Single-family building permits issued: 12 (2010); Multi-family building permits issued: 0 (2010); Employment by occupation: 29.3% management, 38.1% professional, 5.7% services, 21.9% sales, 0.0% farming, 3.8% construction, 1.1% production (2005-2009 5-year est.).
Income: Per capita income: $64,607 (2010); Median household income: $123,692 (2010); Average household income: $177,796 (2010); Percent of households with income of $100,000 or more: 58.3% (2010); Poverty rate: 2.0% (2005-2009 5-year est.).
Taxes: Total city taxes per capita: $379 (2007); City property taxes per capita: $84 (2007).
Education: Percent of population age 25 and over with: High school diploma (including GED) or higher: 95.0% (2010); Bachelor's degree or higher: 55.0% (2010); Master's degree or higher: 25.5% (2010).

School District(s)
CCSD 180 (PK-08)
    2009-10 Enrollment: 712 . . . . (630) 734-6600
Gower SD 62 (PK-08)
    2009-10 Enrollment: 912 . . . . (630) 986-5383
Hinsdale CCSD 181 (PK-08)
    2009-10 Enrollment: 4,048 . . . . (630) 887-1070
Pleasantdale SD 107 (PK-08)
    2009-10 Enrollment: 828 . . . . (708) 784-2013
Vocational/Technical School(s)
Everest College-Burr Ridge (Private, For-profit)
    Fall 2009 Enrollment: 865 . . . . (630) 920-1102
    2010-11 Tuition: $15,193
Housing: Homeownership rate: 94.9% (2010); Median home value: $539,425 (2010); Median contract rent: $824 per month (2005-2009 5-year est.); Median year structure built: 1987 (2005-2009 5-year est.).
Safety: Violent crime rate: 0.9 per 10,000 population; Property crime rate: 137.3 per 10,000 population (2010).
Transportation: Commute to work: 85.9% car, 5.5% public transportation, 1.4% walk, 6.6% work from home (2005-2009 5-year est.); Travel time to work: 18.3% less than 15 minutes, 25.9% 15 to 30 minutes, 28.9% 30 to 45 minutes, 14.5% 45 to 60 minutes, 12.4% 60 minutes or more (2005-2009 5-year est.)

Additional Information Contacts
Village of Burr Ridge . . . . (630) 654-8181
http://www.burr-ridge.gov
Willowbrook/Burr Ridge Chamber of Commerce . . . . (630) 654-0909
http://www.wbbrchamber.org

CAROL STREAM (village). Covers a land area of 8.896 square miles and a water area of 0.028 square miles. Located at 41.92° N. Lat; 88.14° W. Long. Elevation is 758 feet.

Population: 32,079 (1990); 40,438 (2000); 40,534 (2010); 40,817 (2015 projected); Race: 71.2% White, 5.5% Black, 15.3% Asian, 8.1% Other, 13.8% Hispanic of any race (2010); Density: 4,556.6 persons per square mile (2010); Average household size: 2.95 (2010); Median age: 34.8 (2010); Males per 100 females: 99.7 (2010); Marriage status: 31.2% never married, 56.9% now married, 4.6% widowed, 7.3% divorced (2005-2009 5-year est.); Foreign born: 20.1% (2005-2009 5-year est.); Ancestry (includes multiple ancestries): 24.2% German, 16.2% Irish, 12.7% Italian, 11.6% Polish, 6.2% English (2005-2009 5-year est.).
Economy: Unemployment rate: 9.3% (August 2011); Total civilian labor force: 23,086 (August 2011); Single-family building permits issued: 11 (2010); Multi-family building permits issued: 0 (2010); Employment by occupation: 13.8% management, 18.8% professional, 15.0% services, 32.5% sales, 0.2% farming, 8.0% construction, 11.7% production (2005-2009 5-year est.).
Income: Per capita income: $30,147 (2010); Median household income: $77,054 (2010); Average household income: $88,911 (2010); Percent of households with income of $100,000 or more: 33.6% (2010); Poverty rate: 7.4% (2005-2009 5-year est.).
Taxes: Total city taxes per capita: $237 (2007); City property taxes per capita: $13 (2007).
Education: Percent of population age 25 and over with: High school diploma (including GED) or higher: 92.3% (2010); Bachelor's degree or higher: 35.1% (2010); Master's degree or higher: 10.8% (2010).

School District(s)
Benjamin SD 25 (PK-08)
    2009-10 Enrollment: 815 . . . . (630) 876-7800
CCSD 93 (PK-08)
    2009-10 Enrollment: 4,002 . . . . (630) 893-9393

Glenbard Twp HSD 87 (09-12)
2009-10 Enrollment: 8,985 . . . . (630) 469-9100
SD U-46 (PK-12)
2009-10 Enrollment: 41,446 . . . . (847) 888-5000
Housing: Homeownership rate: 72.4% (2010); Median home value:
$234,246 (2010); Median contract rent: $859 per month (2005-2009 5-year
est.); Median year structure built: 1983 (2005-2009 5-year est.).
Safety: Violent crime rate: 11.1 per 10,000 population; Property crime rate:
145.8 per 10,000 population (2010).
Transportation: Commute to work: 92.4% car, 2.8% public transportation,
0.8% walk, 3.2% work from home (2005-2009 5-year est.); Travel time to
work: 22.9% less than 15 minutes, 30.0% 15 to 30 minutes, 27.8% 30 to 45
minutes, 7.7% 45 to 60 minutes, 11.6% 60 minutes or more (2005-2009
5-year est.)
Additional Information Contacts
Carol Stream Chamber of Commerce . . . . (630) 665-3325
http://www.carolstreamchamber.com
Village of Carol Stream . . . . (630) 665-7050
http://www.carolstream.org

CLARENDON HILLS (village). Covers a land area of 1.739 square
miles and a water area of 0.003 square miles. Located at 41.79° N. Lat;
87.95° W. Long. Elevation is 728 feet.
History: Incorporated in 1924. The villag motto is: To honor, commemorate
and celebrate the volunteer community.
Population: 7,174 (1990); 7,610 (2000); 7,983 (2010); 8,102 (2015
projected); Race: 92.3% White, 1.2% Black, 3.9% Asian, 2.6% Other, 3.4%
Hispanic of any race (2010); Density: 4,591.6 persons per square mile
(2010); Average household size: 2.74 (2010); Median age: 37.0 (2010);
Males per 100 females: 95.0 (2010); Marriage status: 21.7% never married,
64.9% now married, 6.6% widowed, 6.8% divorced (2005-2009 5-year
est.); Foreign born: 11.6% (2005-2009 5-year est.); Ancestry (includes
multiple ancestries): 26.1% Irish, 24.3% German, 11.8% Italian, 8.8%
Polish, 7.6% English (2005-2009 5-year est.).
Economy: Single-family building permits issued: 16 (2010); Multi-family
building permits issued: 0 (2010); Employment by occupation: 31.4%
management, 33.5% professional, 10.7% services, 16.6% sales, 0.0%
farming, 1.9% construction, 6.0% production (2005-2009 5-year est.).
Income: Per capita income: $48,731 (2010); Median household income:
$97,461 (2010); Average household income: $135,199 (2010); Percent of
households with income of $100,000 or more: 48.6% (2010); Poverty rate:
0.8% (2005-2009 5-year est.).
Taxes: Total city taxes per capita: $524 (2007); City property taxes per
capita: $371 (2007).
Education: Percent of population age 25 and over with: High school
diploma (including GED) or higher: 96.5% (2010); Bachelor's degree or
higher: 66.2% (2010); Master's degree or higher: 30.2% (2010).
School District(s)
Hinsdale CCSD 181 (PK-08)
2009-10 Enrollment: 4,048 . . . . (630) 887-1070
Maercker SD 60 (PK-08)
2009-10 Enrollment: 1,309 . . . . (630) 323-2086
Housing: Homeownership rate: 83.7% (2010); Median home value:
$486,066 (2010); Median contract rent: $790 per month (2005-2009 5-year
est.); Median year structure built: 1965 (2005-2009 5-year est.).
Safety: Violent crime rate: 0.0 per 10,000 population; Property crime rate:
88.6 per 10,000 population (2010).
Transportation: Commute to work: 74.1% car, 13.9% public
transportation, 1.6% walk, 7.8% work from home (2005-2009 5-year est.);
Travel time to work: 27.2% less than 15 minutes, 32.0% 15 to 30 minutes,
16.7% 30 to 45 minutes, 12.0% 45 to 60 minutes, 12.1% 60 minutes or
more (2005-2009 5-year est.)
Additional Information Contacts
Clarendon Hills Chamber of Commerce . . . . (630) 323-8700
http://clarendonhillschamber.com
Village of Clarendon Hills. . . . . (630) 286-5400
http://www.clarendonhills.us

DARIEN (city). Covers a land area of 6.043 square miles and a water
area of 0.073 square miles. Located at 41.74° N. Lat; 87.98° W. Long.
Elevation is 751 feet.
Population: 21,678 (1990); 22,860 (2000); 23,312 (2010); 23,435 (2015
projected); Race: 80.1% White, 4.0% Black, 12.2% Asian, 3.6% Other,
6.1% Hispanic of any race (2010); Density: 3,857.4 persons per square
mile (2010); Average household size: 2.54 (2010); Median age: 44.3

(2010); Males per 100 females: 96.1 (2010); Marriage status: 24.1% never
married, 61.4% now married, 6.0% widowed, 8.6% divorced (2005-2009
5-year est.); Foreign born: 18.7% (2005-2009 5-year est.); Ancestry
(includes multiple ancestries): 21.2% German, 17.8% Irish, 16.0% Polish,
14.6% Italian, 5.2% Czech (2005-2009 5-year est.).
Economy: Single-family building permits issued: 1 (2010); Multi-family
building permits issued: 0 (2010); Employment by occupation: 20.4%
management, 24.9% professional, 11.4% services, 28.8% sales, 0.1%
farming, 6.2% construction, 8.1% production (2005-2009 5-year est.).
Income: Per capita income: $38,329 (2010); Median household income:
$78,075 (2010); Average household income: $98,153 (2010); Percent of
households with income of $100,000 or more: 35.4% (2010); Poverty rate:
3.3% (2005-2009 5-year est.).
Taxes: Total city taxes per capita: $166 (2007); City property taxes per
capita: $66 (2007).
Education: Percent of population age 25 and over with: High school
diploma (including GED) or higher: 94.2% (2010); Bachelor's degree or
higher: 44.9% (2010); Master's degree or higher: 18.4% (2010).
School District(s)
Cass SD 63 (PK-08)
2009-10 Enrollment: 817 . . . . (630) 985-2000
Center Cass SD 66 (PK-08)
2009-10 Enrollment: 1,160 . . . . (630) 783-5000
Darien SD 61 (PK-08)
2009-10 Enrollment: 1,620 . . . . (630) 968-7505
Hinsdale Twp HSD 86 (09-12)
2009-10 Enrollment: 4,560 . . . . (630) 655-6100
Lagrange Area Dept Spec Ed-Ladse (PK-PK)
2009-10 Enrollment: n/a . . . . (708) 354-5730
Vocational/Technical School(s)
Regency Beauty Institute-Darien (Private, For-profit)
Fall 2009 Enrollment: 102 . . . . (800) 787-6456
2010-11 Tuition: $16,075
Housing: Homeownership rate: 83.1% (2010); Median home value:
$289,056 (2010); Median contract rent: $921 per month (2005-2009 5-year
est.); Median year structure built: 1977 (2005-2009 5-year est.).
Safety: Violent crime rate: 5.4 per 10,000 population; Property crime rate:
125.4 per 10,000 population (2010).
Transportation: Commute to work: 89.8% car, 4.2% public transportation,
1.2% walk, 3.5% work from home (2005-2009 5-year est.); Travel time to
work: 19.1% less than 15 minutes, 31.1% 15 to 30 minutes, 27.5% 30 to 45
minutes, 10.8% 45 to 60 minutes, 11.6% 60 minutes or more (2005-2009
5-year est.)
Additional Information Contacts
City of Darien . . . . (630) 852-5000
http://www.darien.il.us
Darien Chamber of Commerce . . . . (630) 968-0004
http://www.darienchamber.com

DOWNERS GROVE (village). Covers a land area of 14.246 square
miles and a water area of 0.010 square miles. Located at 41.79° N. Lat;
88.01° W. Long. Elevation is 741 feet.
History: Named for Pierce Downer, an eary settler. Downers Grove was
settled in 1832 by Pierce Downer at the intersection of two trails. The town
was incorporated in 1873.
Population: 48,477 (1990); 48,724 (2000); 47,318 (2010); 46,451 (2015
projected); Race: 86.4% White, 2.9% Black, 7.4% Asian, 3.3% Other, 5.4%
Hispanic of any race (2010); Density: 3,321.5 persons per square mile
(2010); Average household size: 2.49 (2010); Median age: 41.7 (2010);
Males per 100 females: 95.1 (2010); Marriage status: 26.9% never married,
56.8% now married, 7.3% widowed, 9.0% divorced (2005-2009 5-year
est.); Foreign born: 9.3% (2005-2009 5-year est.); Ancestry (includes
multiple ancestries): 26.7% German, 20.6% Irish, 16.5% Polish, 14.7%
Italian, 9.7% English (2005-2009 5-year est.).
Economy: Unemployment rate: 7.8% (August 2011); Total civilian labor
force: 27,130 (August 2011); Single-family building permits issued: 24
(2010); Multi-family building permits issued: 0 (2010); Employment by
occupation: 20.6% management, 28.5% professional, 9.6% services,
29.1% sales, 0.1% farming, 5.7% construction, 6.4% production
(2005-2009 5-year est.).
Income: Per capita income: $36,375 (2010); Median household income:
$72,780 (2010); Average household income: $91,201 (2010); Percent of
households with income of $100,000 or more: 32.9% (2010); Poverty rate:
3.8% (2005-2009 5-year est.).

Taxes: Total city taxes per capita: $599 (2007); City property taxes per capita: $309 (2007).
Education: Percent of population age 25 and over with: High school diploma (including GED) or higher: 94.7% (2010); Bachelor's degree or higher: 48.6% (2010); Master's degree or higher: 20.5% (2010).

School District(s)

CHSD 99 (09-12)
  2009-10 Enrollment: 5,254 . . . . (630) 795-7100
Center Cass SD 66 (PK-08)
  2009-10 Enrollment: 1,160 . . . . (630) 783-5000
Downers Grove Gsd 58 (PK-08)
  2009-10 Enrollment: 4,947 . . . . (630) 719-5800
Sch Assoc Sped Educ Dupage Sased (PK-12)
  2009-10 Enrollment: n/a . . . . (630) 778-4500

Four-year College(s)

Midwestern University (Private, Not-for-profit)
  Fall 2009 Enrollment: 2,052 . . . . (630) 969-4400

Vocational/Technical School(s)

University of Aesthetics (Private, For-profit)
  Fall 2009 Enrollment: 14 . . . . (630) 434-9053
  2010-11 Tuition: $10,685
Housing: Homeownership rate: 79.0% (2010); Median home value: $286,650 (2010); Median contract rent: $888 per month (2005-2009 5-year est.); Median year structure built: 1971 (2005-2009 5-year est.).
Hospitals: Advocate Good Samaritan Hospital (327 beds)
Safety: Violent crime rate: 8.4 per 10,000 population; Property crime rate: 194.8 per 10,000 population (2010).
Newspapers: Bolingbrook Metropolitan (Local news; Circulation 5,000); Downers Grove Reporter (Local news; Circulation 24,431); Lemont Metropolitan (Community news; Circulation 4,500); Lemont Reporter (Community news; Circulation 7,448); Liberty Suburban Chicago Newspapers (Regional news); Lisle Reporter (Community news; Circulation 7,174); Mokena-Frankfort Villager (Local news); Reporter Metropolitian (Community news; Circulation 2,500); Romeoville Reporter (Community news; Circulation 5,000); Suburban Life (Community news; Circulation 6,400); Suburban Life - Lombard, Oakbrook Terrace, Villa Park (Regional news); Westmont Progress (Community news; Circulation 8,440); Woodridge Progress (Community news; Circulation 8,987)
Transportation: Commute to work: 79.7% car, 10.5% public transportation, 2.4% walk, 6.3% work from home (2005-2009 5-year est.); Travel time to work: 25.2% less than 15 minutes, 33.3% 15 to 30 minutes, 20.8% 30 to 45 minutes, 10.5% 45 to 60 minutes, 10.2% 60 minutes or more (2005-2009 5-year est.)
Additional Information Contacts
Downers Grove Area Chamber of Commerce . . . . (630) 968-4050
  http://www.downersgrove.org
Village of Downers Grove . . . . (630) 434-5500
  http://www.downers.us

ELMHURST (city).

Covers a land area of 10.265 square miles and a water area of 0.004 square miles. Located at 41.89° N. Lat; 87.94° W. Long. Elevation is 686 feet.
History: Elmhurst was first known as Cottage Hill, named for the home built in 1843 by J.L. Hovey. The later name of Elmhurst referred to a double row of elm trees that grew along Cottage Hill Avenue. Poet Carl Sandburg lived in Elmhurst at one time.
Population: 42,108 (1990); 42,762 (2000); 42,564 (2010); 42,102 (2015 projected); Race: 91.5% White, 1.6% Black, 4.0% Asian, 2.8% Other, 5.4% Hispanic of any race (2010); Density: 4,146.7 persons per square mile (2010); Average household size: 2.61 (2010); Median age: 40.8 (2010); Males per 100 females: 95.2 (2010); Marriage status: 26.1% never married, 59.9% now married, 7.0% widowed, 7.0% divorced (2005-2009 5-year est.); Foreign born: 12.0% (2005-2009 5-year est.); Ancestry (includes multiple ancestries): 28.9% German, 23.5% Irish, 14.5% Italian, 11.4% Polish, 6.4% English (2005-2009 5-year est.).
Economy: Unemployment rate: 7.2% (August 2011); Total civilian labor force: 24,860 (August 2011); Single-family building permits issued: 46 (2010); Multi-family building permits issued: 183 (2010); Employment by occupation: 20.7% management, 26.5% professional, 11.2% services, 27.8% sales, 0.3% farming, 6.6% construction, 7.0% production (2005-2009 5-year est.).
Income: Per capita income: $39,575 (2010); Median household income: $82,709 (2010); Average household income: $106,112 (2010); Percent of households with income of $100,000 or more: 39.1% (2010); Poverty rate: 3.2% (2005-2009 5-year est.).

Taxes: Total city taxes per capita: $590 (2007); City property taxes per capita: $315 (2007).
Education: Percent of population age 25 and over with: High school diploma (including GED) or higher: 93.6% (2010); Bachelor's degree or higher: 48.1% (2010); Master's degree or higher: 20.1% (2010).

School District(s)

Elmhurst SD 205 (PK-12)
  2009-10 Enrollment: 8,221 . . . . (630) 834-4530
Salt Creek SD 48 (PK-08)
  2009-10 Enrollment: 482 . . . . (630) 279-8400

Four-year College(s)

Elmhurst College (Private, Not-for-profit, United Church of Christ)
  Fall 2009 Enrollment: 3,363 . . . . (630) 617-3500
  2010-11 Tuition: In-state $28,660; Out-of-state $28,660
Housing: Homeownership rate: 83.2% (2010); Median home value: $340,584 (2010); Median contract rent: $1,022 per month (2005-2009 5-year est.); Median year structure built: 1958 (2005-2009 5-year est.).
Hospitals: Elmhurst Memorial Hospital (427 beds)
Safety: Violent crime rate: 4.8 per 10,000 population; Property crime rate: 141.9 per 10,000 population (2010).
Newspapers: La Grange Suburban Life (Community news; Circulation 3,000); Roselle Press (Community news; Circulation 1,551)
Transportation: Commute to work: 83.4% car, 8.2% public transportation, 2.9% walk, 4.6% work from home (2005-2009 5-year est.); Travel time to work: 28.3% less than 15 minutes, 30.5% 15 to 30 minutes, 21.7% 30 to 45 minutes, 8.7% 45 to 60 minutes, 10.8% 60 minutes or more (2005-2009 5-year est.)
Additional Information Contacts
City of Elmhurst . . . . (630) 530-3000
  http://www.elmhurst.org
Elmhurst Chamber of Commerce . . . . (630) 834-6060
  http://www.elmhurstchamber.org

GLEN ELLYN (village).

Covers a land area of 6.616 square miles and a water area of 0.021 square miles. Located at 41.87° N. Lat; 88.06° W. Long. Elevation is 741 feet.
History: Glen Ellyn was named when the town was platted by Thomas E. Hill for his wife Ellyn. When the Galena & Chicago Union Railroad was constructed south of town in 1849, the residents transplanted their town to the present site, platted in 1851.
Population: 26,153 (1990); 26,999 (2000); 26,875 (2010); 26,463 (2015 projected); Race: 85.6% White, 3.2% Black, 5.6% Asian, 5.6% Other, 7.5% Hispanic of any race (2010); Density: 4,061.9 persons per square mile (2010); Average household size: 2.62 (2010); Median age: 38.8 (2010); Males per 100 females: 97.1 (2010); Marriage status: 23.3% never married, 61.5% now married, 6.9% widowed, 8.4% divorced (2005-2009 5-year est.); Foreign born: 9.8% (2005-2009 5-year est.); Ancestry (includes multiple ancestries): 30.0% German, 25.2% Irish, 12.2% English, 11.9% Italian, 8.3% Polish (2005-2009 5-year est.).
Economy: Unemployment rate: 7.8% (August 2011); Total civilian labor force: 14,540 (August 2011); Single-family building permits issued: 13 (2010); Multi-family building permits issued: 0 (2010); Employment by occupation: 26.9% management, 28.2% professional, 10.9% services, 25.0% sales, 0.2% farming, 3.7% construction, 5.1% production (2005-2009 5-year est.).
Income: Per capita income: $41,503 (2010); Median household income: $79,896 (2010); Average household income: $108,667 (2010); Percent of households with income of $100,000 or more: 39.2% (2010); Poverty rate: 4.4% (2005-2009 5-year est.).
Taxes: Total city taxes per capita: $454 (2007); City property taxes per capita: $295 (2007).
Education: Percent of population age 25 and over with: High school diploma (including GED) or higher: 95.2% (2010); Bachelor's degree or higher: 60.1% (2010); Master's degree or higher: 24.8% (2010).

School District(s)

CCSD 89 (PK-08)
  2009-10 Enrollment: 2,059 . . . . (630) 469-8900
Glen Ellyn SD 41 (PK-08)
  2009-10 Enrollment: 3,677 . . . . (630) 790-6400
Glenbard Twp HSD 87 (09-12)
  2009-10 Enrollment: 8,985 . . . . (630) 469-9100
Philip J Rock Center and School (03-12)
  2009-10 Enrollment: n/a . . . . (630) 790-2474

Two-year College(s)
College of DuPage (Public)
    Fall 2009 Enrollment: 27,083..................... (630) 942-2800
    2010-11 Tuition: In-state $10,112; Out-of-state $12,352
Housing: Homeownership rate: 76.5% (2010); Median home value: $364,216 (2010); Median contract rent: $749 per month (2005-2009 5-year est.); Median year structure built: 1967 (2005-2009 5-year est.).
Safety: Violent crime rate: 3.7 per 10,000 population; Property crime rate: 144.3 per 10,000 population (2010).
Newspapers: Addison Press (Local news); Elmhurst Press (Community news); Glen Ellyn News (Community news); Itasca Press (Community news); Lombard Spectator (Community news); Villa Park Argus (Community news; Circulation 4,019); Warrenville Post (Community news; Circulation 3,400); Wheaton Leader (Local news; Circulation 480)
Transportation: Commute to work: 74.9% car, 12.5% public transportation, 4.0% walk, 6.5% work from home (2005-2009 5-year est.); Travel time to work: 24.0% less than 15 minutes, 31.0% 15 to 30 minutes, 19.3% 30 to 45 minutes, 10.9% 45 to 60 minutes, 14.7% 60 minutes or more (2005-2009 5-year est.)
Additional Information Contacts
Glen Ellyn Chamber of Commerce .... (630) 469-0907
    http://www.glenellynchamber.com
Village of Glen Ellyn.......................... (630) 469-5000
    http://www.glenellyn.org

GLENDALE HEIGHTS (village). Covers a land area of 5.404
square miles and a water area of 0.003 square miles. Located at 41.92° N. Lat; 88.07° W. Long. Elevation is 761 feet.
Population: 28,241 (1990); 31,765 (2000); 31,512 (2010); 31,155 (2015 projected); Race: 54.2% White, 7.1% Black, 22.5% Asian, 16.2% Other, 26.8% Hispanic of any race (2010); Density: 5,831.0 persons per square mile (2010); Average household size: 2.95 (2010); Median age: 35.3 (2010); Males per 100 females: 104.8 (2010); Marriage status: 32.2% never married, 54.2% now married, 4.7% widowed, 8.9% divorced (2005-2009 5-year est.); Foreign born: 34.3% (2005-2009 5-year est.); Ancestry (includes multiple ancestries): 14.1% German, 9.3% Irish, 8.8% Polish, 7.3% Italian, 3.0% English (2005-2009 5-year est.).
Economy: Unemployment rate: 10.2% (August 2011); Total civilian labor force: 18,944 (August 2011); Single-family building permits issued: 0 (2010); Multi-family building permits issued: 0 (2010); Employment by occupation: 12.0% management, 16.4% professional, 12.8% services, 31.9% sales, 0.0% farming, 7.7% construction, 19.2% production (2005-2009 5-year est.).
Income: Per capita income: $25,111 (2010); Median household income: $64,658 (2010); Average household income: $73,850 (2010); Percent of households with income of $100,000 or more: 20.5% (2010); Poverty rate: 9.1% (2005-2009 5-year est.).
Taxes: Total city taxes per capita: $407 (2007); City property taxes per capita: $231 (2007).
Education: Percent of population age 25 and over with: High school diploma (including GED) or higher: 86.1% (2010); Bachelor's degree or higher: 29.3% (2010); Master's degree or higher: 8.1% (2010).
School District(s)
Coop Assoc for Spec Educ (KG-12)
    2009-10 Enrollment: n/a .... (630) 942-5600
Marquardt SD 15 (PK-08)
    2009-10 Enrollment: 2,666 .... (630) 469-7615
Queen Bee SD 16 (PK-08)
    2009-10 Enrollment: 2,052 .... (630) 260-6105
Two-year College(s)
Universal Technical Institute of Illinois Inc (Private, For-profit)
    Fall 2009 Enrollment: 2,759................. (630) 529-2662
Vocational/Technical School(s)
Tricoci University of Beauty Culture (Private, For-profit)
    Fall 2009 Enrollment: 72................. (630) 528-3336
    2010-11 Tuition: $16,650
Housing: Homeownership rate: 71.0% (2010); Median home value: $209,659 (2010); Median contract rent: $925 per month (2005-2009 5-year est.); Median year structure built: 1977 (2005-2009 5-year est.).
Hospitals: Adventist GlenOaks Hospital (186 beds)
Safety: Violent crime rate: 12.4 per 10,000 population; Property crime rate: 184.6 per 10,000 population (2010).
Transportation: Commute to work: 96.1% car, 1.4% public transportation, 0.9% walk, 1.0% work from home (2005-2009 5-year est.); Travel time to work: 24.2% less than 15 minutes, 35.0% 15 to 30 minutes, 23.1% 30 to 45

minutes, 7.4% 45 to 60 minutes, 10.3% 60 minutes or more (2005-2009 5-year est.)
Additional Information Contacts
Glendale Heights Chamber of Commerce .... (630) 545-1099
    http://www.glendaleheightschamber.com
Village of Glendale Heights .... (630) 260-6000
    http://www.glendaleheights.org

HINSDALE (village). Covers a land area of 4.636 square miles and a
water area of 0.005 square miles. Located at 41.80° N. Lat; 87.92° W. Long. Elevation is 699 feet.
History: Hinsdale developed along the route of the Chicago, Burlington & Quincy Railroad, and was named for railroad director H.W. Hinsdale. In 1923 Hinsdale annexed nearby Fullersburg, which had been settled in 1835 by Jacob Fuller and his family.
Population: 16,054 (1990); 17,349 (2000); 16,709 (2010); 16,325 (2015 projected); Race: 91.8% White, 0.9% Black, 5.3% Asian, 2.1% Other, 3.2% Hispanic of any race (2010); Density: 3,604.3 persons per square mile (2010); Average household size: 2.94 (2010); Median age: 37.6 (2010); Males per 100 females: 94.2 (2010); Marriage status: 20.9% never married, 70.1% now married, 5.2% widowed, 3.8% divorced (2005-2009 5-year est.); Foreign born: 9.6% (2005-2009 5-year est.); Ancestry (includes multiple ancestries): 26.7% German, 20.6% Irish, 12.4% English, 12.4% Polish, 11.0% Italian (2005-2009 5-year est.).
Economy: Single-family building permits issued: 33 (2010); Multi-family building permits issued: 0 (2010); Employment by occupation: 35.8% management, 29.3% professional, 7.7% services, 21.6% sales, 0.0% farming, 2.0% construction, 3.6% production (2005-2009 5-year est.).
Income: Per capita income: $61,676 (2010); Median household income: $124,569 (2010); Average household income: $181,903 (2010); Percent of households with income of $100,000 or more: 58.6% (2010); Poverty rate: 1.9% (2005-2009 5-year est.).
Taxes: Total city taxes per capita: $580 (2007); City property taxes per capita: $372 (2007).
Education: Percent of population age 25 and over with: High school diploma (including GED) or higher: 98.0% (2010); Bachelor's degree or higher: 72.4% (2010); Master's degree or higher: 35.1% (2010).
School District(s)
Hinsdale CCSD 181 (PK-08)
    2009-10 Enrollment: 4,048 .... (630) 887-1070
Hinsdale Twp HSD 86 (09-12)
    2009-10 Enrollment: 4,560 .... (630) 655-6100
Housing: Homeownership rate: 85.8% (2010); Median home value: $739,310 (2010); Median contract rent: $1,004 per month (2005-2009 5-year est.); Median year structure built: 1966 (2005-2009 5-year est.).
Hospitals: Hinsdale Hospital (426 beds)
Safety: Violent crime rate: 1.6 per 10,000 population; Property crime rate: 129.1 per 10,000 population (2010).
Newspapers: Darien Doings (Community news; Circulation 300); Doings (Community news; Circulation 5,443); Doings - Clarendon Hills Edition (Local news; Circulation 1,597); Indian Head Park Doings (Local news; Circulation 200); La Grange Doings (Local news; Circulation 4,068); Oak Brook Doings (Community news; Circulation 1,362); Weekly Doings - Burr Ridge/Willowbrook/Darien Edition (Local news; Circulation 3,442); Western Springs Doings with News of Indian Head Park (Local news; Circulation 2,259); Willowbrook Doings (Local news; Circulation 500)
Transportation: Commute to work: 71.8% car, 16.4% public transportation, 2.2% walk, 8.6% work from home (2005-2009 5-year est.); Travel time to work: 25.7% less than 15 minutes, 20.3% 15 to 30 minutes, 24.1% 30 to 45 minutes, 16.1% 45 to 60 minutes, 13.8% 60 minutes or more (2005-2009 5-year est.)
Additional Information Contacts
Hinsdale Chamber of Commerce..................... (630) 323-3952
    http://www.hinsdalechamber.com
Village of Hinsdale............................... (630) 789-7011
    http://www.villageofhinsdale.org

ITASCA (village). Covers a land area of 4.916 square miles and a water
area of 0.069 square miles. Located at 41.97° N. Lat; 88.01° W. Long. Elevation is 702 feet.
Population: 7,247 (1990); 8,302 (2000); 8,817 (2010); 8,999 (2015 projected); Race: 85.4% White, 1.7% Black, 6.8% Asian, 6.2% Other, 8.0% Hispanic of any race (2010); Density: 1,793.5 persons per square mile (2010); Average household size: 2.56 (2010); Median age: 42.2 (2010); Males per 100 females: 95.0 (2010); Marriage status: 23.9% never married,

61.2% now married, 6.2% widowed, 8.7% divorced (2005-2009 5-year est.); Foreign born: 18.9% (2005-2009 5-year est.); Ancestry (includes multiple ancestries): 26.5% German, 20.9% Italian, 15.9% Polish, 12.2% Irish, 3.5% English (2005-2009 5-year est.).
Economy: Single-family building permits issued: 5 (2010); Multi-family building permits issued: 5 (2010); Employment by occupation: 19.9% management, 19.5% professional, 12.4% services, 32.0% sales, 0.3% farming, 6.8% construction, 9.1% production (2005-2009 5-year est.).
Income: Per capita income: $39,952 (2010); Median household income: $83,455 (2010); Average household income: $102,890 (2010); Percent of households with income of $100,000 or more: 38.0% (2010); Poverty rate: 2.7% (2005-2009 5-year est.).
Taxes: Total city taxes per capita: $759 (2007); City property taxes per capita: $503 (2007).
Education: Percent of population age 25 and over with: High school diploma (including GED) or higher: 90.8% (2010); Bachelor's degree or higher: 35.4% (2010); Master's degree or higher: 13.3% (2010).

School District(s)
Itasca SD 10 (PK-08)
    2009-10 Enrollment: 940 . . . . (630) 773-1232
Vocational/Technical School(s)
Environmental Technical Institute (Private, For-profit)
    Fall 2009 Enrollment: 83 . . . . (630) 285-9100
    2010-11 Tuition: $13,250
Housing: Homeownership rate: 82.5% (2010); Median home value: $303,293 (2010); Median contract rent: $866 per month (2005-2009 5-year est.); Median year structure built: 1976 (2005-2009 5-year est.).
Safety: Violent crime rate: 4.7 per 10,000 population; Property crime rate: 147.0 per 10,000 population (2010).
Transportation: Commute to work: 88.4% car, 3.3% public transportation, 2.8% walk, 4.3% work from home (2005-2009 5-year est.); Travel time to work: 26.4% less than 15 minutes, 38.6% 15 to 30 minutes, 19.6% 30 to 45 minutes, 8.4% 45 to 60 minutes, 7.1% 60 minutes or more (2005-2009 5-year est.)
Additional Information Contacts
Village of Itasca . . . . (630) 773-0835
    http://www.itasca.com

LISLE (village).
Covers a land area of 6.373 square miles and a water area of 0.045 square miles. Located at 41.79° N. Lat; 88.08° W. Long. Elevation is 673 feet.
History: Lisle was permanently settled in 1832 by James and Luther Hatch, after the Blackhawk War. The two brothers settled land near what is now Ogden Avenue and began a small farming community. This early beginning makes Lisle the oldest settlement in DuPage County.
Population: 19,275 (1990); 21,182 (2000); 22,782 (2010); 23,196 (2015 projected); Race: 76.7% White, 5.0% Black, 13.1% Asian, 5.2% Other, 8.3% Hispanic of any race (2010); Density: 3,574.8 persons per square mile (2010); Average household size: 2.38 (2010); Median age: 38.1 (2010); Males per 100 females: 102.7 (2010); Marriage status: 33.4% never married, 52.9% now married, 4.7% widowed, 9.0% divorced (2005-2009 5-year est.); Foreign born: 15.1% (2005-2009 5-year est.); Ancestry (includes multiple ancestries): 23.8% German, 18.7% Irish, 14.3% Polish, 11.4% Italian, 6.8% English (2005-2009 5-year est.).
Economy: Single-family building permits issued: 6 (2010); Multi-family building permits issued: 0 (2010); Employment by occupation: 22.2% management, 25.6% professional, 13.3% services, 28.8% sales, 0.0% farming, 5.1% construction, 5.0% production (2005-2009 5-year est.).
Income: Per capita income: $38,437 (2010); Median household income: $70,078 (2010); Average household income: $92,861 (2010); Percent of households with income of $100,000 or more: 31.2% (2010); Poverty rate: 4.0% (2005-2009 5-year est.).
Taxes: Total city taxes per capita: $360 (2007); City property taxes per capita: $158 (2007).
Education: Percent of population age 25 and over with: High school diploma (including GED) or higher: 95.9% (2010); Bachelor's degree or higher: 52.1% (2010); Master's degree or higher: 22.0% (2010).

School District(s)
Lisle CUSD 202 (PK-12)
    2009-10 Enrollment: 1,589 . . . . (630) 493-8001
Naperville CUSD 203 (PK-12)
    2009-10 Enrollment: 17,977 . . . . (630) 420-6311

Four-year College(s)
Benedictine University (Private, Not-for-profit, Roman Catholic)
    Fall 2009 Enrollment: 5,836 . . . . (630) 829-6000
    2010-11 Tuition: In-state $23,240; Out-of-state $23,240
Vocational/Technical School(s)
Empire Beauty School-Lisle (Private, For-profit)
    Fall 2009 Enrollment: 80 . . . . (570) 429-4321
    2010-11 Tuition: $17,595
Housing: Homeownership rate: 54.8% (2010); Median home value: $279,807 (2010); Median contract rent: $886 per month (2005-2009 5-year est.); Median year structure built: 1979 (2005-2009 5-year est.).
Safety: Violent crime rate: 7.0 per 10,000 population; Property crime rate: 136.7 per 10,000 population (2010).
Transportation: Commute to work: 81.8% car, 9.0% public transportation, 1.4% walk, 6.5% work from home (2005-2009 5-year est.); Travel time to work: 27.2% less than 15 minutes, 29.7% 15 to 30 minutes, 18.4% 30 to 45 minutes, 10.5% 45 to 60 minutes, 14.2% 60 minutes or more (2005-2009 5-year est.)
Additional Information Contacts
Lisle Area Chamber of Commerce . . . . (630) 964-0052
    http://www.lislechamber.com
Lisle Convention & Visitors Bureau . . . . (800) 733-9811
    http://www.lislecvb.com
Village of Lisle . . . . (630) 271-4100
    http://www.villageoflisle.org

LOMBARD (village).
Covers a land area of 9.685 square miles and a water area of 0.014 square miles. Located at 41.87° N. Lat; 88.01° W. Long. Elevation is 719 feet.
History: Lombard was settled in 1834 by Winslow Churchill. The town was platted in 1868 by Joseph Lombard of Chicago, for whom it was named. Lombard has been known for its many varieties of lilacs, displayed in Lilacia Park, the gift of Colonel William Plum who collected lilacs from around the world.
Population: 40,229 (1990); 42,322 (2000); 41,791 (2010); 41,335 (2015 projected); Race: 82.5% White, 4.0% Black, 8.4% Asian, 5.1% Other, 8.2% Hispanic of any race (2010); Density: 4,315.0 persons per square mile (2010); Average household size: 2.47 (2010); Median age: 40.5 (2010); Males per 100 females: 97.2 (2010); Marriage status: 28.6% never married, 54.7% now married, 8.3% widowed, 8.4% divorced (2005-2009 5-year est.); Foreign born: 14.0% (2005-2009 5-year est.); Ancestry (includes multiple ancestries): 26.6% German, 20.4% Irish, 14.1% Italian, 13.0% Polish, 7.8% English (2005-2009 5-year est.).
Economy: Unemployment rate: 9.5% (August 2011); Total civilian labor force: 24,479 (August 2011); Single-family building permits issued: 5 (2010); Multi-family building permits issued: 0 (2010); Employment by occupation: 15.5% management, 25.7% professional, 9.3% services, 32.8% sales, 0.1% farming, 7.3% construction, 9.3% production (2005-2009 5-year est.).
Income: Per capita income: $32,064 (2010); Median household income: $67,669 (2010); Average household income: $81,125 (2010); Percent of households with income of $100,000 or more: 25.7% (2010); Poverty rate: 3.3% (2005-2009 5-year est.).
Taxes: Total city taxes per capita: $486 (2007); City property taxes per capita: $166 (2007).
Education: Percent of population age 25 and over with: High school diploma (including GED) or higher: 92.2% (2010); Bachelor's degree or higher: 38.2% (2010); Master's degree or higher: 13.1% (2010).

School District(s)
Glenbard Twp HSD 87 (09-12)
    2009-10 Enrollment: 8,985 . . . . (630) 469-9100
Lombard SD 44 (PK-08)
    2009-10 Enrollment: 3,095 . . . . (630) 827-4400
SD 45 Dupage County (PK-08)
    2009-10 Enrollment: 3,392 . . . . (630) 516-7700
Sch Assoc Sped Educ Dupage Sased (PK-12)
    2009-10 Enrollment: n/a . . . . (630) 778-4500
Four-year College(s)
National University of Health Sciences (Private, Not-for-profit)
    Fall 2009 Enrollment: 787 . . . . (630) 629-2000
Northern Baptist Theological Seminary (Private, Not-for-profit, American Baptist)
    Fall 2009 Enrollment: 137 . . . . (630) 620-2180

The Illinois Center for Broadcasting (Private, For-profit)
    Fall 2009 Enrollment: 292 . . . . (630) 916-1700
    2010-11 Tuition: $15,816
Housing: Homeownership rate: 76.9% (2010); Median home value: $243,396 (2010); Median contract rent: $997 per month (2005-2009 5-year est.); Median year structure built: 1969 (2005-2009 5-year est.).
Safety: Violent crime rate: 12.5 per 10,000 population; Property crime rate: 280.0 per 10,000 population (2010).
Newspapers: Lombardian (Community news; Circulation 13,500); Villa Park Review (Community news; Circulation 8,000)
Transportation: Commute to work: 88.9% car, 4.7% public transportation, 1.8% walk, 3.1% work from home (2005-2009 5-year est.); Travel time to work: 24.7% less than 15 minutes, 33.1% 15 to 30 minutes, 22.4% 30 to 45 minutes, 9.5% 45 to 60 minutes, 10.3% 60 minutes or more (2005-2009 5-year est.)
Additional Information Contacts
Lombard Chamber of Commerce . . . . (630) 627-5040
    http://www.lombardchamber.com
Village of Lombard . . . . (630) 620-5700
    http://www.villageoflombard.org

MEDINAH (unincorporated postal area, zip code 60157). Covers a land area of 1.467 square miles and a water area of 0.007 square miles. Located at 41.84° N. Lat; 88.08° W. Long. Elevation is 732 feet.
Population: 2,111 (2000); Race: 91.2% White, 0.5% Black, 5.8% Asian, 2.5% Other, 4.5% Hispanic of any race (2000); Density: 1,439.0 persons per square mile (2000); Age: 20.0% under 18, 17.7% over 64 (2000); Marriage status: 16.4% never married, 73.3% now married, 8.0% widowed, 2.3% divorced (2000); Foreign born: 13.8% (2000); Ancestry (includes multiple ancestries): 35.7% German, 19.8% Polish, 18.6% Italian, 12.3% Irish (2000).
Economy: Employment by occupation: 25.6% management, 15.2% professional, 3.1% services, 31.6% sales, 0.0% farming, 13.3% construction, 11.1% production (2000).
Income: Per capita income: $36,250 (2000); Median household income: $81,251 (2000); Poverty rate: 3.6% (2000).
Education: Percent of population age 25 and over with: High school diploma (including GED) or higher: 91.8% (2000); Bachelor's degree or higher: 35.3% (2000).
School District(s)
Medinah SD 11 (KG-08)
    2009-10 Enrollment: 667 . . . . (630) 893-3737
Housing: Homeownership rate: 98.1% (2000); Median home value: $254,100 (2000); Median contract rent: $544 per month (2000); Median year structure built: 1962 (2000).
Transportation: Commute to work: 90.5% car, 8.1% public transportation, 0.0% walk, 0.7% work from home (2000); Travel time to work: 18.4% less than 15 minutes, 39.5% 15 to 30 minutes, 20.3% 30 to 45 minutes, 14.7% 45 to 60 minutes, 7.0% 60 minutes or more (2000)

NAPERVILLE (city). Covers a land area of 35.377 square miles and a water area of 0.145 square miles. Located at 41.75° N. Lat; 88.15° W. Long. Elevation is 709 feet.
History: Named for Captain Joseph Naper, founder. The first settlement at Naperville was Fort Payne, built in 1832. That same year, Joseph Naper built a saw mill and platted the town site. From 1839 to 1868 Naperville was the seat of DuPage County.
Population: 90,506 (1990); 128,358 (2000); 147,227 (2010); 155,212 (2015 projected); Race: 77.1% White, 5.1% Black, 14.0% Asian, 3.7% Other, 6.0% Hispanic of any race (2010); Density: 4,161.7 persons per square mile (2010); Average household size: 2.91 (2010); Median age: 35.5 (2010); Males per 100 females: 97.2 (2010); Marriage status: 26.2% never married, 63.5% now married, 3.9% widowed, 6.4% divorced (2005-2009 5-year est.); Foreign born: 15.4% (2005-2009 5-year est.); Ancestry (includes multiple ancestries): 24.2% German, 17.7% Irish, 11.0% Polish, 10.2% Italian, 8.8% English (2005-2009 5-year est.).
Economy: Unemployment rate: 7.9% (August 2011); Total civilian labor force: 76,727 (August 2011); Single-family building permits issued: 94 (2010); Multi-family building permits issued: 0 (2010); Employment by occupation: 24.7% management, 31.7% professional, 8.8% services, 27.7% sales, 0.1% farming, 3.1% construction, 3.8% production (2005-2009 5-year est.).
Income: Per capita income: $42,321 (2010); Median household income: $101,695 (2010); Average household income: $124,373 (2010); Percent of

households with income of $100,000 or more: 51.0% (2010); Poverty rate: 3.3% (2005-2009 5-year est.).
Taxes: Total city taxes per capita: $499 (2007); City property taxes per capita: $290 (2007).
Education: Percent of population age 25 and over with: High school diploma (including GED) or higher: 97.2% (2010); Bachelor's degree or higher: 62.5% (2010); Master's degree or higher: 25.8% (2010).
School District(s)
Indian Prairie CUSD 204 (PK-12)
    2009-10 Enrollment: 29,733 . . . . (630) 375-3000
Naperville CUSD 203 (PK-12)
    2009-10 Enrollment: 17,977 . . . . (630) 420-6311
Sch Assoc Sped Educ Dupage Sased (PK-12)
    2009-10 Enrollment: n/a . . . . (630) 778-4500
Four-year College(s)
North Central College (Private, Not-for-profit, United Methodist)
    Fall 2009 Enrollment: 2,798. . . . . (630) 637-5100
    2010-11 Tuition: In-state $28,224; Out-of-state $28,224
Housing: Homeownership rate: 82.5% (2010); Median home value: $335,587 (2010); Median contract rent: $979 per month (2005-2009 5-year est.); Median year structure built: 1987 (2005-2009 5-year est.).
Hospitals: Edward Hospital (179 beds)
Newspapers: Bolingbrook Sun (Local news; Circulation 17,000); Bolingbrook/Romeoville Sun (Community news; Circulation 7,300); Hollywood Reporter - New York Bureau; Homer Township Sun (Community news; Circulation 1,750); Lisle Sun (Community news; Circulation 13,000); Newsday - United Nations Bureau (Local news); Rockland Edition (Local news); Victoria Advocate - Cuero Bureau (Local news); Wheaton Sun (Local news; Circulation 5,600)
Transportation: Commute to work: 81.0% car, 9.4% public transportation, 1.6% walk, 6.7% work from home (2005-2009 5-year est.); Travel time to work: 21.5% less than 15 minutes, 28.7% 15 to 30 minutes, 19.9% 30 to 45 minutes, 9.9% 45 to 60 minutes, 19.9% 60 minutes or more (2005-2009 5-year est.); Amtrak: train service available.
Additional Information Contacts
City of Naperville . . . . (630) 420-6111
    http://www.naperville.il.us
Naperville Area Chamber of Commerce . . . . (630) 355-4141
    http://www.naperville.net

OAK BROOK (village). Covers a land area of 8.161 square miles and a water area of 0.097 square miles. Located at 41.84° N. Lat; 87.95° W. Long. Elevation is 663 feet.
History: Oak Brook was incorporated as a Village in 1958, due in large part to the efforts of Paul Butler, a prominent civic leader and landowner whose father had first moved to the vicinity in 1898 and opened a dairy farm shortly thereafter.
Population: 9,178 (1990); 8,702 (2000); 9,154 (2010); 9,306 (2015 projected); Race: 77.2% White, 3.0% Black, 17.1% Asian, 2.6% Other, 3.4% Hispanic of any race (2010); Density: 1,121.7 persons per square mile (2010); Average household size: 2.46 (2010); Median age: 55.5 (2010); Males per 100 females: 85.6 (2010); Marriage status: 21.5% never married, 64.5% now married, 6.8% widowed, 7.3% divorced (2005-2009 5-year est.); Foreign born: 25.9% (2005-2009 5-year est.); Ancestry (includes multiple ancestries): 16.5% German, 16.2% Italian, 12.4% Irish, 7.1% English, 6.6% Polish (2005-2009 5-year est.).
Economy: Single-family building permits issued: 8 (2010); Multi-family building permits issued: 0 (2010); Employment by occupation: 30.3% management, 29.2% professional, 6.5% services, 26.4% sales, 0.0% farming, 3.8% construction, 3.9% production (2005-2009 5-year est.).
Income: Per capita income: $61,672 (2010); Median household income: $104,736 (2010); Average household income: $158,874 (2010); Percent of households with income of $100,000 or more: 51.4% (2010); Poverty rate: 1.6% (2005-2009 5-year est.).
Taxes: Total city taxes per capita: $881 (2007); City property taxes per capita: $4 (2007).
Education: Percent of population age 25 and over with: High school diploma (including GED) or higher: 93.9% (2010); Bachelor's degree or higher: 55.7% (2010); Master's degree or higher: 32.2% (2010).
School District(s)
Butler SD 53 (PK-08)
    2009-10 Enrollment: 427 . . . . (630) 573-2887

Four-year College(s)
ITT Technical Institute-Burr Ridge (Private, For-profit)
Fall 2009 Enrollment: 425 . . . . (630) 472-7000
2010-11 Tuition: In-state $18,048; Out-of-state $18,048
Housing: Homeownership rate: 84.4% (2010); Median home value:
$696,335 (2010); Median contract rent: $426 per month (2005-2009 5-year
est.); Median year structure built: 1977 (2005-2009 5-year est.).
Safety: Violent crime rate: 3.4 per 10,000 population; Property crime rate:
695.8 per 10,000 population (2010).
Newspapers: Bensenville Press (Local news; Circulation 1,142); Chicago
Tribune - Oak Brook Bureau (Local news); La Grange Park Press (Local
news; Circulation 880); Suburban Life - DuPage (Regional news;
Circulation 8,370); Suburban Life - Elmhurst (Community news; Circulation
14,800); Suburban Life Citizen (Regional news; Circulation 31,500)
Transportation: Commute to work: 82.9% car, 4.4% public transportation,
2.6% walk, 9.4% work from home (2005-2009 5-year est.); Travel time to
work: 21.3% less than 15 minutes, 37.2% 15 to 30 minutes, 20.5% 30 to 45
minutes, 9.9% 45 to 60 minutes, 11.1% 60 minutes or more (2005-2009
5-year est.)
Additional Information Contacts
Greater Oak Brook Chamber of Commerce . . . . (630) 472-9377
http://www.obchamber.com
Village of Oak Brook . . . . (630) 368-5000
http://www.oak-brook.org

OAKBROOK TERRACE (city). Covers a land area of 1.393
square miles and a water area of 0 square miles. Located at 41.85° N. Lat;
87.96° W. Long. Elevation is 686 feet.
Population: 2,218 (1990); 2,300 (2000); 2,261 (2010); 2,350 (2015
projected); Race: 76.7% White, 4.7% Black, 14.4% Asian, 4.2% Other,
5.6% Hispanic of any race (2010); Density: 1,623.2 persons per square
mile (2010); Average household size: 2.09 (2010); Median age: 47.0
(2010); Males per 100 females: 89.7 (2010); Marriage status: 33.1% never
married, 52.4% now married, 7.3% widowed, 7.2% divorced (2005-2009
5-year est.); Foreign born: 21.5% (2005-2009 5-year est.); Ancestry
(includes multiple ancestries): 24.6% German, 18.1% Irish, 16.8% Italian,
13.6% Polish, 6.0% English (2005-2009 5-year est.).
Economy: Single-family building permits issued: 0 (2010); Multi-family
building permits issued: 0 (2010); Employment by occupation: 30.0%
management, 22.4% professional, 16.4% services, 24.6% sales, 0.0%
farming, 4.8% construction, 1.9% production (2005-2009 5-year est.).
Income: Per capita income: $42,463 (2010); Median household income:
$65,772 (2010); Average household income: $91,577 (2010); Percent of
households with income of $100,000 or more: 25.2% (2010); Poverty rate:
5.1% (2005-2009 5-year est.).
Taxes: Total city taxes per capita: $2,384 (2007); City property taxes per
capita: $305 (2007).
Education: Percent of population age 25 and over with: High school
diploma (including GED) or higher: 92.3% (2010); Bachelor's degree or
higher: 38.6% (2010); Master's degree or higher: 20.1% (2010).
School District(s)
Salt Creek SD 48 (PK-08)
2009-10 Enrollment: 482 . . . . (630) 279-8400
Housing: Homeownership rate: 60.2% (2010); Median home value:
$264,940 (2010); Median contract rent: $1,120 per month (2005-2009
5-year est.); Median year structure built: 1974 (2005-2009 5-year est.).
Safety: Violent crime rate: 12.7 per 10,000 population; Property crime rate:
510.3 per 10,000 population (2010).
Transportation: Commute to work: 84.2% car, 1.7% public transportation,
7.8% walk, 5.2% work from home (2005-2009 5-year est.); Travel time to
work: 20.3% less than 15 minutes, 41.2% 15 to 30 minutes, 22.6% 30 to 45
minutes, 4.4% 45 to 60 minutes, 11.4% 60 minutes or more (2005-2009
5-year est.)

ROSELLE (village). Covers a land area of 5.374 square miles and a
water area of 0.017 square miles. Located at 41.98° N. Lat; 88.08° W.
Long. Elevation is 771 feet.
Population: 21,424 (1990); 23,115 (2000); 22,956 (2010); 22,755 (2015
projected); Race: 84.0% White, 2.6% Black, 8.1% Asian, 5.4% Other, 8.9%
Hispanic of any race (2010); Density: 4,271.5 persons per square mile
(2010); Average household size: 2.73 (2010); Median age: 38.9 (2010);
Males per 100 females: 97.1 (2010); Marriage status: 28.9% never married,
59.0% now married, 2.8% widowed, 9.3% divorced (2005-2009 5-year
est.); Foreign born: 17.4% (2005-2009 5-year est.); Ancestry (includes

multiple ancestries): 29.1% German, 18.2% Polish, 17.0% Irish, 15.9%
Italian, 7.0% English (2005-2009 5-year est.).
Economy: Single-family building permits issued: 2 (2010); Multi-family
building permits issued: 0 (2010); Employment by occupation: 21.6%
management, 21.4% professional, 10.7% services, 27.9% sales, 0.0%
farming, 9.0% construction, 9.5% production (2005-2009 5-year est.).
Income: Per capita income: $32,342 (2010); Median household income:
$72,681 (2010); Average household income: $88,750 (2010); Percent of
households with income of $100,000 or more: 29.8% (2010); Poverty rate:
2.7% (2005-2009 5-year est.).
Taxes: Total city taxes per capita: $382 (2007); City property taxes per
capita: $220 (2007).
Education: Percent of population age 25 and over with: High school
diploma (including GED) or higher: 92.7% (2010); Bachelor's degree or
higher: 35.6% (2010); Master's degree or higher: 10.5% (2010).
School District(s)
Keeneyville SD 20 (PK-08)
2009-10 Enrollment: 1,623 . . . . (630) 894-2250
Lake Park CHSD 108 (09-12)
2009-10 Enrollment: 2,925 . . . . (630) 529-4500
Medinah SD 11 (KG-08)
2009-10 Enrollment: 667 . . . . (630) 893-3737
North Dupage Sp Ed Cooperative (06-12)
2009-10 Enrollment: n/a . . . . (630) 894-0490
Roselle SD 12 (KG-08)
2009-10 Enrollment: 685 . . . . (630) 529-2091
Schaumburg CCSD 54 (PK-08)
2009-10 Enrollment: 14,313 . . . . (847) 357-5000
Housing: Homeownership rate: 82.6% (2010); Median home value:
$248,394 (2010); Median contract rent: $875 per month (2005-2009 5-year
est.); Median year structure built: 1977 (2005-2009 5-year est.).
Safety: Violent crime rate: 10.5 per 10,000 population; Property crime rate:
116.4 per 10,000 population (2010).
Transportation: Commute to work: 89.0% car, 6.0% public transportation,
0.4% walk, 3.6% work from home (2005-2009 5-year est.); Travel time to
work: 16.9% less than 15 minutes, 34.0% 15 to 30 minutes, 28.6% 30 to 45
minutes, 9.7% 45 to 60 minutes, 10.8% 60 minutes or more (2005-2009
5-year est.)
Additional Information Contacts
Roselle Chamber of Commerce & Industry . . . . (630) 894-3010
http://www.rosellechamber.com
Village of Roselle . . . . (630) 980-2000
http://www.roselle.il.us

VILLA PARK (village). Covers a land area of 4.702 square miles and
a water area of 0.004 square miles. Located at 41.88° N. Lat; 87.97° W.
Long. Elevation is 702 feet.
Population: 22,214 (1990); 22,075 (2000); 22,943 (2010); 23,117 (2015
projected); Race: 85.8% White, 2.9% Black, 4.0% Asian, 7.3% Other,
16.6% Hispanic of any race (2010); Density: 4,879.8 persons per square
mile (2010); Average household size: 2.76 (2010); Median age: 38.2
(2010); Males per 100 females: 101.9 (2010); Marriage status: 30.4%
never married, 54.2% now married, 5.6% widowed, 9.8% divorced
(2005-2009 5-year est.); Foreign born: 14.6% (2005-2009 5-year est.);
Ancestry (includes multiple ancestries): 26.0% German, 21.2% Irish, 13.7%
Italian, 12.9% Polish, 5.8% English (2005-2009 5-year est.).
Economy: Single-family building permits issued: 2 (2010); Multi-family
building permits issued: 0 (2010); Employment by occupation: 13.9%
management, 18.0% professional, 13.4% services, 29.4% sales, 0.0%
farming, 10.5% construction, 14.7% production (2005-2009 5-year est.).
Income: Per capita income: $26,120 (2010); Median household income:
$62,423 (2010); Average household income: $72,066 (2010); Percent of
households with income of $100,000 or more: 20.0% (2010); Poverty rate:
7.3% (2005-2009 5-year est.).
Taxes: Total city taxes per capita: $475 (2007); City property taxes per
capita: $309 (2007).
Education: Percent of population age 25 and over with: High school
diploma (including GED) or higher: 89.6% (2010); Bachelor's degree or
higher: 27.0% (2010); Master's degree or higher: 10.1% (2010).
School District(s)
Dupage HSD 88 (09-12)
2009-10 Enrollment: 4,110 . . . . (630) 530-3980
SD 45 Dupage County (PK-08)
2009-10 Enrollment: 3,392 . . . . (630) 516-7700

Salt Creek SD 48 (PK-08)
    2009-10 Enrollment: 482 . . . . (630) 279-8400
Vocational/Technical School(s)
Cannella School of Hair Design (Private, For-profit)
    Fall 2009 Enrollment: 78 . . . . (630) 833-6118
    2010-11 Tuition: $10,190
Ms Roberts Academy of Beauty Culture-Villa Park (Private, For-profit)
    Fall 2009 Enrollment: 139 . . . . (630) 941-3880
    2010-11 Tuition: $12,900
Housing: Homeownership rate: 77.0% (2010); Median home value: $241,365 (2010); Median contract rent: $838 per month (2005-2009 5-year est.); Median year structure built: 1957 (2005-2009 5-year est.).
Safety: Violent crime rate: 13.6 per 10,000 population; Property crime rate: 223.8 per 10,000 population (2010).
Transportation: Commute to work: 88.5% car, 4.1% public transportation, 1.8% walk, 2.9% work from home (2005-2009 5-year est.); Travel time to work: 26.8% less than 15 minutes, 38.7% 15 to 30 minutes, 20.2% 30 to 45 minutes, 7.8% 45 to 60 minutes, 6.5% 60 minutes or more (2005-2009 5-year est.)
Additional Information Contacts
Villa Park Chamber of Commerce . . . . (630) 941-9133
    http://www.villaparkchamber.org
Village of Villa Park . . . . (630) 834-8500
    http://www.invillapark.com

WARRENVILLE (city).
Covers a land area of 5.498 square miles and a water area of 0.119 square miles. Located at 41.82° N. Lat; 88.18° W. Long. Elevation is 696 feet.
History: Named for Daniel Warren (1780-1866), town founder. Warrenville was settled in the 1830's around a tannery and gristmill.
Population: 11,409 (1990); 13,363 (2000); 14,247 (2010); 14,528 (2015 projected); Race: 84.3% White, 3.5% Black, 3.6% Asian, 8.7% Other, 18.1% Hispanic of any race (2010); Density: 2,591.4 persons per square mile (2010); Average household size: 2.67 (2010); Median age: 37.1 (2010); Males per 100 females: 98.3 (2010); Marriage status: 35.7% never married, 49.7% now married, 3.3% widowed, 11.3% divorced (2005-2009 5-year est.); Foreign born: 13.9% (2005-2009 5-year est.); Ancestry (includes multiple ancestries): 24.6% German, 14.4% Irish, 9.1% Italian, 8.5% Polish, 8.3% English (2005-2009 5-year est.).
Economy: Single-family building permits issued: 0 (2010); Multi-family building permits issued: 0 (2010); Employment by occupation: 16.6% management, 22.2% professional, 12.2% services, 28.3% sales, 0.0% farming, 10.5% construction, 10.2% production (2005-2009 5-year est.).
Income: Per capita income: $32,554 (2010); Median household income: $71,224 (2010); Average household income: $86,669 (2010); Percent of households with income of $100,000 or more: 25.9% (2010); Poverty rate: 8.0% (2005-2009 5-year est.).
Taxes: Total city taxes per capita: $1,153 (2007); City property taxes per capita: $810 (2007).
Education: Percent of population age 25 and over with: High school diploma (including GED) or higher: 94.7% (2010); Bachelor's degree or higher: 44.5% (2010); Master's degree or higher: 14.7% (2010).
School District(s)
CUSD 200 (PK-12)
    2009-10 Enrollment: 13,488 . . . . (630) 682-2002
Housing: Homeownership rate: 81.1% (2010); Median home value: $204,551 (2010); Median contract rent: $1,109 per month (2005-2009 5-year est.); Median year structure built: 1979 (2005-2009 5-year est.).
Safety: Violent crime rate: 10.9 per 10,000 population; Property crime rate: 111.8 per 10,000 population (2010).
Transportation: Commute to work: 91.1% car, 2.6% public transportation, 1.0% walk, 4.1% work from home (2005-2009 5-year est.); Travel time to work: 25.4% less than 15 minutes, 36.4% 15 to 30 minutes, 19.3% 30 to 45 minutes, 8.7% 45 to 60 minutes, 10.2% 60 minutes or more (2005-2009 5-year est.)
Additional Information Contacts
City of Warrenville . . . . (630) 393-9427
    http://www.warrenville.il.us
Western DuPage Chamber of Commerce . . . . (630) 231-3003
    http://www.westerndupagechamber.com

WAYNE (village).
Covers a land area of 5.816 square miles and a water area of 0 square miles. Located at 41.95° N. Lat; 88.25° W. Long. Elevation is 758 feet.

Population: 1,461 (1990); 2,137 (2000); 3,017 (2010); 3,345 (2015 projected); Race: 86.8% White, 2.4% Black, 6.9% Asian, 3.9% Other, 7.5% Hispanic of any race (2010); Density: 518.7 persons per square mile (2010); Average household size: 3.07 (2010); Median age: 38.4 (2010); Males per 100 females: 98.5 (2010); Marriage status: 21.4% never married, 71.3% now married, 2.7% widowed, 4.6% divorced (2005-2009 5-year est.); Foreign born: 6.1% (2005-2009 5-year est.); Ancestry (includes multiple ancestries): 42.7% German, 30.4% Irish, 14.9% English, 11.5% Italian, 10.0% Polish (2005-2009 5-year est.).
Economy: Employment by occupation: 33.7% management, 21.7% professional, 10.2% services, 24.2% sales, 0.0% farming, 6.1% construction, 4.0% production (2005-2009 5-year est.).
Income: Per capita income: $51,760 (2010); Median household income: $118,182 (2010); Average household income: $158,684 (2010); Percent of households with income of $100,000 or more: 60.6% (2010); Poverty rate: 0.7% (2005-2009 5-year est.).
Taxes: Total city taxes per capita: $384 (2007); City property taxes per capita: $210 (2007).
Education: Percent of population age 25 and over with: High school diploma (including GED) or higher: 97.6% (2010); Bachelor's degree or higher: 56.3% (2010); Master's degree or higher: 19.6% (2010).
School District(s)
SD U-46 (PK-12)
    2009-10 Enrollment: 41,446 . . . . (847) 888-5000
Housing: Homeownership rate: 96.5% (2010); Median home value: $401,818 (2010); Median contract rent: $1,100 per month (2005-2009 5-year est.); Median year structure built: 1983 (2005-2009 5-year est.).
Safety: Violent crime rate: 0.0 per 10,000 population; Property crime rate: 49.9 per 10,000 population (2010).
Transportation: Commute to work: 88.1% car, 3.0% public transportation, 0.3% walk, 6.3% work from home (2005-2009 5-year est.); Travel time to work: 27.3% less than 15 minutes, 22.6% 15 to 30 minutes, 26.6% 30 to 45 minutes, 9.4% 45 to 60 minutes, 14.1% 60 minutes or more (2005-2009 5-year est.)

WEST CHICAGO (city).
Covers a land area of 13.839 square miles and a water area of 0.004 square miles. Located at 41.88° N. Lat; 88.21° W. Long. Elevation is 784 feet.
Population: 15,874 (1990); 23,469 (2000); 26,382 (2010); 27,552 (2015 projected); Race: 76.8% White, 1.7% Black, 1.9% Asian, 19.6% Other, 56.5% Hispanic of any race (2010); Density: 1,906.4 persons per square mile (2010); Average household size: 3.53 (2010); Median age: 32.9 (2010); Males per 100 females: 111.3 (2010); Marriage status: 33.0% never married, 58.0% now married, 3.1% widowed, 5.9% divorced (2005-2009 5-year est.); Foreign born: 35.8% (2005-2009 5-year est.); Ancestry (includes multiple ancestries): 15.4% German, 8.1% Irish, 6.1% Polish, 5.0% Italian, 3.9% English (2005-2009 5-year est.).
Economy: Unemployment rate: 10.3% (August 2011); Total civilian labor force: 14,395 (August 2011); Single-family building permits issued: 6 (2010); Multi-family building permits issued: 0 (2010); Employment by occupation: 10.4% management, 14.9% professional, 15.7% services, 22.3% sales, 1.2% farming, 12.3% construction, 23.0% production (2005-2009 5-year est.).
Income: Per capita income: $25,365 (2010); Median household income: $72,819 (2010); Average household income: $89,867 (2010); Percent of households with income of $100,000 or more: 30.8% (2010); Poverty rate: 12.1% (2005-2009 5-year est.).
Taxes: Total city taxes per capita: $303 (2007); City property taxes per capita: $141 (2007).
Education: Percent of population age 25 and over with: High school diploma (including GED) or higher: 74.0% (2010); Bachelor's degree or higher: 24.8% (2010); Master's degree or higher: 7.7% (2010).
School District(s)
Benjamin SD 25 (PK-08)
    2009-10 Enrollment: 815 . . . . (630) 876-7800
CHSD 94 (09-12)
    2009-10 Enrollment: 2,183 . . . . (630) 876-6210
St Charles CUSD 303 (PK-12)
    2009-10 Enrollment: 13,953 . . . . (630) 513-3030
West Chicago ESD 33 (PK-08)
    2009-10 Enrollment: 4,242 . . . . (630) 293-6000
Housing: Homeownership rate: 73.1% (2010); Median home value: $248,716 (2010); Median contract rent: $746 per month (2005-2009 5-year est.); Median year structure built: 1975 (2005-2009 5-year est.).

Safety: Violent crime rate: 11.0 per 10,000 population; Property crime rate: 136.4 per 10,000 population (2010).
Newspapers: Warrenville Press (Local news; Circulation 2,200)
Transportation: Commute to work: 91.6% car, 1.9% public transportation, 3.0% walk, 2.0% work from home (2005-2009 5-year est.); Travel time to work: 30.3% less than 15 minutes, 37.1% 15 to 30 minutes, 17.6% 30 to 45 minutes, 7.1% 45 to 60 minutes, 8.0% 60 minutes or more (2005-2009 5-year est.)
Airports: Dupage (general aviation)
Additional Information Contacts
City of West Chicago . . . . (630) 293-2200
   http://www.westchicago.org
West Chicago Chamber of Commerce & Industry . . . . (630) 231-3003
   http://www.wegochamber.org

WESTMONT (village). Covers a land area of 4.897 square miles and a water area of 0.010 square miles. Located at 41.79° N. Lat; 87.97° W. Long. Elevation is 748 feet.

Population: 22,443 (1990); 24,554 (2000); 24,583 (2010); 24,429 (2015 projected); Race: 72.5% White, 7.0% Black, 14.3% Asian, 6.1% Other, 8.9% Hispanic of any race (2010); Density: 5,020.3 persons per square mile (2010); Average household size: 2.38 (2010); Median age: 40.7 (2010); Males per 100 females: 91.4 (2010); Marriage status: 28.5% never married, 51.6% now married, 10.1% widowed, 9.8% divorced (2005-2009 5-year est.); Foreign born: 21.6% (2005-2009 5-year est.); Ancestry (includes multiple ancestries): 19.7% German, 13.5% Polish, 13.4% Irish, 8.5% Italian, 5.3% Czech (2005-2009 5-year est.).
Economy: Unemployment rate: 8.8% (August 2011); Total civilian labor force: 13,541 (August 2011); Single-family building permits issued: 4 (2010); Multi-family building permits issued: 0 (2010); Employment by occupation: 16.2% management, 27.4% professional, 15.3% services, 24.6% sales, 0.0% farming, 7.6% construction, 8.9% production (2005-2009 5-year est.).
Income: Per capita income: $35,003 (2010); Median household income: $64,497 (2010); Average household income: $85,304 (2010); Percent of households with income of $100,000 or more: 26.2% (2010); Poverty rate: 8.2% (2005-2009 5-year est.).
Taxes: Total city taxes per capita: $418 (2007); City property taxes per capita: $173 (2007).
Education: Percent of population age 25 and over with: High school diploma (including GED) or higher: 91.2% (2010); Bachelor's degree or higher: 42.1% (2010); Master's degree or higher: 16.4% (2010).

School District(s)
CUSD 201 (PK-12)
   2009-10 Enrollment: 1,535 . . . . (630) 468-8004
Maercker SD 60 (PK-08)
   2009-10 Enrollment: 1,309 . . . . (630) 323-2086
Sch Assoc Sped Educ Dupage Sased (PK-12)
   2009-10 Enrollment: n/a . . . . (630) 778-4500
Housing: Homeownership rate: 59.7% (2010); Median home value: $274,599 (2010); Median contract rent: $827 per month (2005-2009 5-year est.); Median year structure built: 1976 (2005-2009 5-year est.).
Safety: Violent crime rate: 11.7 per 10,000 population; Property crime rate: 138.2 per 10,000 population (2010).
Transportation: Commute to work: 82.1% car, 10.5% public transportation, 1.7% walk, 4.0% work from home (2005-2009 5-year est.); Travel time to work: 24.6% less than 15 minutes, 29.5% 15 to 30 minutes, 20.3% 30 to 45 minutes, 11.8% 45 to 60 minutes, 13.8% 60 minutes or more (2005-2009 5-year est.)
Additional Information Contacts
Village of Westmont . . . . (630) 981-6200
   http://www.westmont.il.gov
Westmont Chamber of Commerce & Tourism Bureau . . . . (630) 960-5553
   http://www.westmontchamber.com

WHEATON (city). County seat. Covers a land area of 11.221 square miles and a water area of 0.045 square miles. Located at 41.86° N. Lat; 88.10° W. Long. Elevation is 758 feet.

History: Named for the Wheaton family, early settlers. Wheaton was settled in 1838 by Warren and Jesse Wheaton, who were instrumental in bringing to the town the railroad, a college, and the county courthouse. In 1853, Warren Wheaton donated the land for the Illinois Institute, which seven years later became Wheaton College. In 1867 the seat of DuPage County was moved from Naperville to Wheaton, and the courthouse was built on land donated by Warren Wheaton.

Population: 52,280 (1990); 55,416 (2000); 53,627 (2010); 52,569 (2015 projected); Race: 87.3% White, 3.8% Black, 5.6% Asian, 3.3% Other, 5.2% Hispanic of any race (2010); Density: 4,779.1 persons per square mile (2010); Average household size: 2.61 (2010); Median age: 37.9 (2010); Males per 100 females: 95.9 (2010); Marriage status: 32.9% never married, 54.4% now married, 5.6% widowed, 7.2% divorced (2005-2009 5-year est.); Foreign born: 9.1% (2005-2009 5-year est.); Ancestry (includes multiple ancestries): 30.5% German, 18.6% Irish, 13.0% English, 10.4% Italian, 9.8% Polish (2005-2009 5-year est.).
Economy: Unemployment rate: 8.1% (August 2011); Total civilian labor force: 29,477 (August 2011); Single-family building permits issued: 18 (2010); Multi-family building permits issued: 0 (2010); Employment by occupation: 20.5% management, 31.6% professional, 11.3% services, 27.7% sales, 0.1% farming, 3.6% construction, 5.3% production (2005-2009 5-year est.).
Income: Per capita income: $39,279 (2010); Median household income: $82,561 (2010); Average household income: $109,281 (2010); Percent of households with income of $100,000 or more: 39.1% (2010); Poverty rate: 4.8% (2005-2009 5-year est.).
Taxes: Total city taxes per capita: $469 (2007); City property taxes per capita: $318 (2007).
Education: Percent of population age 25 and over with: High school diploma (including GED) or higher: 95.9% (2010); Bachelor's degree or higher: 60.3% (2010); Master's degree or higher: 25.5% (2010).

School District(s)
CCSD 89 (PK-08)
   2009-10 Enrollment: 2,059 . . . . (630) 469-8900
CUSD 200 (PK-12)
   2009-10 Enrollment: 13,488 . . . . (630) 682-2002
Dupage Roe (06-12)
   2009-10 Enrollment: n/a . . . . (630) 407-5800
Sch Assoc Sped Educ Dupage Sased (PK-12)
   2009-10 Enrollment: n/a . . . . (630) 778-4500

Four-year College(s)
Wheaton College (Private, Not-for-profit, Undenominational)
   Fall 2009 Enrollment: 2,920 . . . . (630) 752-5000
   2010-11 Tuition: In-state $27,580; Out-of-state $27,580

Vocational/Technical School(s)
Hair Professionals Academy of Cosmetology (Private, For-profit)
   Fall 2009 Enrollment: 230 . . . . (630) 653-6630
   2010-11 Tuition: $16,866
Housing: Homeownership rate: 74.2% (2010); Median home value: $302,273 (2010); Median contract rent: $973 per month (2005-2009 5-year est.); Median year structure built: 1974 (2005-2009 5-year est.).
Hospitals: Marianjoy Rehabilitation Hospital (120 beds)
Safety: Violent crime rate: 4.5 per 10,000 population; Property crime rate: 145.8 per 10,000 population (2010).
Transportation: Commute to work: 79.0% car, 8.6% public transportation, 5.2% walk, 6.6% work from home (2005-2009 5-year est.); Travel time to work: 31.7% less than 15 minutes, 29.1% 15 to 30 minutes, 17.0% 30 to 45 minutes, 7.8% 45 to 60 minutes, 14.4% 60 minutes or more (2005-2009 5-year est.)
Additional Information Contacts
City of Wheaton . . . . (630) 260-2012
   http://www.wheaton.il.us
Wheaton Chamber of Commerce . . . . (630) 668-6464
   http://wheatonchamber.com

WILLOWBROOK (village). Covers a land area of 2.601 square miles and a water area of 0.025 square miles. Located at 41.76° N. Lat; 87.94° W. Long. Elevation is 732 feet.

Population: 8,791 (1990); 8,967 (2000); 9,010 (2010); 8,953 (2015 projected); Race: 81.3% White, 3.9% Black, 11.1% Asian, 3.7% Other, 5.2% Hispanic of any race (2010); Density: 3,464.4 persons per square mile (2010); Average household size: 2.07 (2010); Median age: 46.4 (2010); Males per 100 females: 88.6 (2010); Marriage status: 28.3% never married, 49.8% now married, 11.4% widowed, 10.5% divorced (2005-2009 5-year est.); Foreign born: 21.4% (2005-2009 5-year est.); Ancestry (includes multiple ancestries): 19.5% German, 15.6% Irish, 10.8% Polish, 9.5% Italian, 6.6% English (2005-2009 5-year est.).
Economy: Single-family building permits issued: 4 (2010); Multi-family building permits issued: 0 (2010); Employment by occupation: 19.9% management, 27.6% professional, 10.0% services, 30.3% sales, 0.0% farming, 4.8% construction, 7.4% production (2005-2009 5-year est.).

Income: Per capita income: $42,646 (2010); Median household income: $59,782 (2010); Average household income: $88,843 (2010); Percent of households with income of $100,000 or more: 25.0% (2010); Poverty rate: 3.2% (2005-2009 5-year est.).

Taxes: Total city taxes per capita: $280 (2007); City property taxes per capita: $22 (2007).

Education: Percent of population age 25 and over with: High school diploma (including GED) or higher: 95.1% (2010); Bachelor's degree or higher: 48.2% (2010); Master's degree or higher: 20.5% (2010).

School District(s)

CCSD 180 (PK-08)

    2009-10 Enrollment: 712 . . . . (630) 734-6600

Gower SD 62 (PK-08)

    2009-10 Enrollment: 912 . . . . (630) 986-5383

Maercker SD 60 (PK-08)

    2009-10 Enrollment: 1,309 . . . . (630) 323-2086

Housing: Homeownership rate: 73.4% (2010); Median home value: $247,062 (2010); Median contract rent: $1,017 per month (2005-2009 5-year est.); Median year structure built: 1978 (2005-2009 5-year est.).

Safety: Violent crime rate: 10.4 per 10,000 population; Property crime rate: 192.5 per 10,000 population (2010).

Transportation: Commute to work: 87.0% car, 7.4% public transportation, 0.9% walk, 4.2% work from home (2005-2009 5-year est.); Travel time to work: 21.1% less than 15 minutes, 31.3% 15 to 30 minutes, 24.7% 30 to 45 minutes, 11.7% 45 to 60 minutes, 11.1% 60 minutes or more (2005-2009 5-year est.)

Additional Information Contacts

Village of Willowbrook . . . . (630) 323-8215

    http://www.willowbrookil.org

WINFIELD (village). Covers a land area of 2.700 square miles and a water area of 0.006 square miles. Located at 41.87° N. Lat; 88.15° W. Long. Elevation is 771 feet.

Population: 7,629 (1990); 8,718 (2000); 8,749 (2010); 8,770 (2015 projected); Race: 90.7% White, 1.6% Black, 3.9% Asian, 3.7% Other, 5.9% Hispanic of any race (2010); Density: 3,239.8 persons per square mile (2010); Average household size: 2.97 (2010); Median age: 38.3 (2010); Males per 100 females: 99.6 (2010); Marriage status: 24.5% never married, 63.0% now married, 5.5% widowed, 7.0% divorced (2005-2009 5-year est.); Foreign born: 7.9% (2005-2009 5-year est.); Ancestry (includes multiple ancestries): 28.6% German, 22.9% Irish, 13.6% Polish, 9.8% Italian, 9.6% English (2005-2009 5-year est.).

Economy: Single-family building permits issued: 41 (2010); Multi-family building permits issued: 0 (2010); Employment by occupation: 21.1% management, 30.9% professional, 8.2% services, 26.9% sales, 0.0% farming, 5.1% construction, 7.9% production (2005-2009 5-year est.).

Income: Per capita income: $40,758 (2010); Median household income: $97,814 (2010); Average household income: $121,279 (2010); Percent of households with income of $100,000 or more: 48.5% (2010); Poverty rate: 4.6% (2005-2009 5-year est.).

Taxes: Total city taxes per capita: $350 (2007); City property taxes per capita: $142 (2007).

Education: Percent of population age 25 and over with: High school diploma (including GED) or higher: 93.8% (2010); Bachelor's degree or higher: 46.1% (2010); Master's degree or higher: 16.3% (2010).

School District(s)

CUSD 200 (PK-12)

    2009-10 Enrollment: 13,488 . . . . (630) 682-2002

Winfield SD 34 (PK-08)

    2009-10 Enrollment: 373 . . . . (630) 909-4900

Housing: Homeownership rate: 94.5% (2010); Median home value: $280,641 (2010); Median contract rent: $1,097 per month (2005-2009 5-year est.); Median year structure built: 1982 (2005-2009 5-year est.).

Hospitals: Behavioral Health Services of Central DuPage Hospital (32 beds); Central DuPage Hospital Behavioral Health Services (20 beds)

Safety: Violent crime rate: 2.0 per 10,000 population; Property crime rate: 59.0 per 10,000 population (2010).

Transportation: Commute to work: 84.8% car, 11.1% public transportation, 0.5% walk, 3.2% work from home (2005-2009 5-year est.); Travel time to work: 22.6% less than 15 minutes, 34.2% 15 to 30 minutes, 17.4% 30 to 45 minutes, 8.5% 45 to 60 minutes, 17.2% 60 minutes or more (2005-2009 5-year est.)

Additional Information Contacts

Village of Winfield . . . . (630) 933-7100

    http://www.villageofwinfield.com

Winfield Chamber of Commerce . . . . (630) 682-3712

    http://www.winfieldchamber.biz

WOOD DALE (city). Covers a land area of 4.671 square miles and a water area of 0 square miles. Located at 41.96° N. Lat; 87.97° W. Long. Elevation is 692 feet.

Population: 12,974 (1990); 13,535 (2000); 13,789 (2010); 13,859 (2015 projected); Race: 82.2% White, 1.2% Black, 4.2% Asian, 12.4% Other, 22.5% Hispanic of any race (2010); Density: 2,952.2 persons per square mile (2010); Average household size: 2.70 (2010); Median age: 41.7 (2010); Males per 100 females: 101.4 (2010); Marriage status: 27.5% never married, 56.6% now married, 7.8% widowed, 8.1% divorced (2005-2009 5-year est.); Foreign born: 25.7% (2005-2009 5-year est.); Ancestry (includes multiple ancestries): 27.7% Polish, 20.0% German, 14.5% Italian, 9.3% Irish, 5.4% English (2005-2009 5-year est.).

Economy: Single-family building permits issued: 6 (2010); Multi-family building permits issued: 0 (2010); Employment by occupation: 13.7% management, 14.7% professional, 15.5% services, 29.1% sales, 0.0% farming, 8.8% construction, 18.2% production (2005-2009 5-year est.).

Income: Per capita income: $29,620 (2010); Median household income: $66,961 (2010); Average household income: $80,001 (2010); Percent of households with income of $100,000 or more: 25.3% (2010); Poverty rate: 7.8% (2005-2009 5-year est.).

Taxes: Total city taxes per capita: $488 (2007); City property taxes per capita: $182 (2007).

Education: Percent of population age 25 and over with: High school diploma (including GED) or higher: 85.6% (2010); Bachelor's degree or higher: 22.5% (2010); Master's degree or higher: 7.8% (2010).

School District(s)

Wood Dale SD 7 (PK-08)

    2009-10 Enrollment: 1,313 . . . . (630) 595-9510

Housing: Homeownership rate: 83.3% (2010); Median home value: $260,367 (2010); Median contract rent: $924 per month (2005-2009 5-year est.); Median year structure built: 1973 (2005-2009 5-year est.).

Safety: Violent crime rate: 5.8 per 10,000 population; Property crime rate: 148.9 per 10,000 population (2010).

Transportation: Commute to work: 90.0% car, 4.6% public transportation, 1.7% walk, 2.5% work from home (2005-2009 5-year est.); Travel time to work: 24.3% less than 15 minutes, 36.5% 15 to 30 minutes, 20.4% 30 to 45 minutes, 10.0% 45 to 60 minutes, 8.8% 60 minutes or more (2005-2009 5-year est.)

Additional Information Contacts

City of Wood Dale . . . . (630) 766-4900

    http://www.wooddale.com

Wood Dale Chamber of Commerce. . . . . (630) 595-0505

    http://www.wooddalechamber.com

WOODRIDGE (village). Covers a land area of 8.323 square miles and a water area of 0.023 square miles. Located at 41.74° N. Lat; 88.04° W. Long. Elevation is 732 feet.

Population: 27,524 (1990); 30,934 (2000); 34,216 (2010); 34,557 (2015 projected); Race: 67.7% White, 10.5% Black, 14.5% Asian, 7.3% Other, 12.6% Hispanic of any race (2010); Density: 4,111.1 persons per square mile (2010); Average household size: 2.68 (2010); Median age: 37.3 (2010); Males per 100 females: 101.3 (2010); Marriage status: 32.8% never married, 55.2% now married, 3.3% widowed, 8.8% divorced (2005-2009 5-year est.); Foreign born: 20.0% (2005-2009 5-year est.); Ancestry (includes multiple ancestries): 19.6% German, 13.3% Irish, 12.8% Polish, 9.3% Italian, 6.5% English (2005-2009 5-year est.).

Economy: Unemployment rate: 9.0% (August 2011); Total civilian labor force: 20,163 (August 2011); Single-family building permits issued: 5 (2010); Multi-family building permits issued: 0 (2010); Employment by occupation: 16.0% management, 24.1% professional, 13.9% services, 29.3% sales, 0.2% farming, 6.1% construction, 10.3% production (2005-2009 5-year est.).

Income: Per capita income: $33,984 (2010); Median household income: $73,855 (2010); Average household income: $90,986 (2010); Percent of households with income of $100,000 or more: 32.1% (2010); Poverty rate: 6.3% (2005-2009 5-year est.).

Taxes: Total city taxes per capita: $368 (2007); City property taxes per capita: $179 (2007).

Education: Percent of population age 25 and over with: High school diploma (including GED) or higher: 93.0% (2010); Bachelor's degree or higher: 44.2% (2010); Master's degree or higher: 16.3% (2010).

School District(s)

Woodridge SD 68 (PK-08)
2009-10 Enrollment: 3,065 . . . . (630) 985-7925

Four-year College(s)

Westwood College-Dupage (Private, For-profit)
Fall 2009 Enrollment: 582 . . . . (630) 434-8250
2010-11 Tuition: In-state $14,227; Out-of-state $14,227

Housing: Homeownership rate: 69.5% (2010); Median home value: $252,310 (2010); Median contract rent: $888 per month (2005-2009 5-year est.); Median year structure built: 1979 (2005-2009 5-year est.).

Safety: Violent crime rate: 14.1 per 10,000 population; Property crime rate: 125.7 per 10,000 population (2010).

Transportation: Commute to work: 88.6% car, 4.3% public transportation, 0.9% walk, 4.3% work from home (2005-2009 5-year est.); Travel time to work: 18.2% less than 15 minutes, 35.7% 15 to 30 minutes, 20.9% 30 to 45 minutes, 12.8% 45 to 60 minutes, 12.4% 60 minutes or more (2005-2009 5-year est.)

Additional Information Contacts

Village of Woodridge . . . . (630) 852-7000
http://www.vil.woodridge.il.us
Woodridge Area Chamber of Commerce. . . . . (630) 960-7080
http://www.woodridgechamber.org

Edgar County

Located in eastern Illinois; bounded on the east by Indiana; drained by tributaries of the Wabash River. Covers a land area of 623.55 square miles, a water area of 0.63 square miles, and is located in the Central Time Zone at 39.66° N. Lat., 87.74° W. Long. The county was founded in 1823. County seat is Paris.

Weather Station: Paris Waterworks　　　　　　　　　Elevation: 680 feet

	Jan	Feb	Mar	Apr	May	Jun	Jul	Aug	Sep	Oct	Nov	Dec
High	35	40	51	64	74	83	86	85	78	66	52	39
Low	19	23	32	42	53	63	66	64	56	45	35	24
Precip	2.4	2.3	2.9	4.1	4.4	4.4	4.4	4.1	3.2	3.4	3.7	3.0
Snow	8.4	5.7	2.9	0.2	0.0	0.0	0.0	0.0	0.0	0.1	0.8	5.4

High and Low temperatures in degrees Fahrenheit; Precipitation and Snow in inches

Population: 19,595 (1990); 19,704 (2000); 18,529 (2010); 17,865 (2015 projected); Race: 96.2% White, 2.0% Black, 0.5% Asian, 1.2% Other, 1.2% Hispanic of any race (2010); Density: 29.7 persons per square mile (2010); Average household size: 2.37 (2010); Median age: 40.6 (2010); Males per 100 females: 95.7 (2010).

Religion: Five largest groups: 15.0% Christian Churches and Churches of Christ, 10.9% The United Methodist Church, 7.2% Catholic Church, 4.4% Christian Church (Disciples of Christ), 2.8% New Testament Association of Independent Baptist Churches and

Economy: Unemployment rate: 10.0% (August 2011); Total civilian labor force: 10,281 (August 2011); Leading industries: 31.7% manufacturing; 15.3% retail trade; 13.5% health care and social assistance (2009); Farms: 670 totaling 352,535 acres (2007); Companies that employ 500 or more persons: 0 (2009); Companies that employ 100 to 499 persons: 12 (2009); Companies that employ less than 100 persons: 368 (2009); Black-owned businesses: n/a (2007); Hispanic-owned businesses: n/a (2007); Asian-owned businesses: n/a (2007); Women-owned businesses: n/a (2007); Retail sales per capita: $8,935 (2010). Single-family building permits issued: 6 (2010); Multi-family building permits issued: 0 (2010).

Income: Per capita income: $21,915 (2010); Median household income: $42,270 (2010); Average household income: $53,124 (2010); Percent of households with income of $100,000 or more: 9.1% (2010); Poverty rate: 16.0% (2009); Bankruptcy rate: 5.63% (2010).

Taxes: Total county taxes per capita: $140 (2007); County property taxes per capita: $138 (2007).

Education: Percent of population age 25 and over with: High school diploma (including GED) or higher: 86.4% (2010); Bachelor's degree or higher: 16.3% (2010); Master's degree or higher: 4.9% (2010).

Housing: Homeownership rate: 73.3% (2010); Median home value: $79,388 (2010); Median contract rent: $361 per month (2005-2009 5-year est.); Median year structure built: 1957 (2005-2009 5-year est.)

Health: Birth rate: 118.6 per 10,000 population (2009); Death rate: 134.8 per 10,000 population (2009); Age-adjusted cancer mortality rate: 224.5 deaths per 100,000 population (2007); Number of physicians: 6.4 per 10,000 population (2008); Hospital beds: 13.3 per 10,000 population (2007); Hospital admissions: 365.7 per 10,000 population (2007).

Elections: 2008 Presidential election results: 45.3% Obama, 53.3% McCain, 0.8% Nader

Additional Information Contacts

Edgar County Government . . . . (217) 466-7433
http://www.edgarcountyillinois.com
City of Paris . . . . (217) 465-7601
http://parisillinois.org
Paris Area Chamber of Commerce & Tourism . . . . (217) 465-4179
http://www.parisilchamber.com

Edgar County Communities

BROCTON (village). Covers a land area of 0.579 square miles and a water area of 0 square miles. Located at 39.71° N. Lat; 87.93° W. Long. Elevation is 663 feet.

Population: 322 (1990); 322 (2000); 279 (2010); 261 (2015 projected); Race: 98.6% White, 0.0% Black, 0.0% Asian, 1.4% Other, 1.1% Hispanic of any race (2010); Density: 482.2 persons per square mile (2010); Average household size: 2.38 (2010); Median age: 43.0 (2010); Males per 100 females: 102.2 (2010); Marriage status: 21.2% never married, 60.8% now married, 7.2% widowed, 10.8% divorced (2005-2009 5-year est.); Foreign born: 0.0% (2005-2009 5-year est.); Ancestry (includes multiple ancestries): 32.4% Irish, 21.8% German, 8.3% English, 8.0% Italian, 4.3% Scottish (2005-2009 5-year est.).

Economy: Single-family building permits issued: 0 (2010); Multi-family building permits issued: 0 (2010); Employment by occupation: 1.8% management, 3.5% professional, 17.6% services, 41.8% sales, 8.2% farming, 8.8% construction, 18.2% production (2005-2009 5-year est.).

Income: Per capita income: $22,641 (2010); Median household income: $44,457 (2010); Average household income: $53,910 (2010); Percent of households with income of $100,000 or more: 7.7% (2010); Poverty rate: 14.3% (2005-2009 5-year est.).

Taxes: Total city taxes per capita: $20 (2007); City property taxes per capita: $17 (2007).

Education: Percent of population age 25 and over with: High school diploma (including GED) or higher: 85.3% (2010); Bachelor's degree or higher: 13.2% (2010); Master's degree or higher: 1.5% (2010).

Housing: Homeownership rate: 78.6% (2010); Median home value: $65,000 (2010); Median contract rent: $301 per month (2005-2009 5-year est.); Median year structure built: 1943 (2005-2009 5-year est.).

Transportation: Commute to work: 97.0% car, 1.8% public transportation, 0.0% walk, 0.0% work from home (2005-2009 5-year est.); Travel time to work: 32.9% less than 15 minutes, 37.1% 15 to 30 minutes, 15.0% 30 to 45 minutes, 6.6% 45 to 60 minutes, 8.4% 60 minutes or more (2005-2009 5-year est.)

CHRISMAN (city). Covers a land area of 0.732 square miles and a water area of 0 square miles. Located at 39.80° N. Lat; 87.67° W. Long. Elevation is 650 feet.

History: Chrisman was platted in 1872 by Matthias Chrisman, and grew as a trading center and shipping point.

Population: 1,228 (1990); 1,318 (2000); 1,185 (2010); 1,124 (2015 projected); Race: 98.6% White, 0.4% Black, 0.3% Asian, 0.8% Other, 0.3% Hispanic of any race (2010); Density: 1,619.8 persons per square mile (2010); Average household size: 2.23 (2010); Median age: 43.5 (2010); Males per 100 females: 95.2 (2010); Marriage status: 16.8% never married, 50.1% now married, 14.3% widowed, 18.8% divorced (2005-2009 5-year est.); Foreign born: 1.4% (2005-2009 5-year est.); Ancestry (includes multiple ancestries): 16.7% German, 12.4% American, 9.8% English, 9.8% Irish, 4.4% Dutch (2005-2009 5-year est.).

Economy: Single-family building permits issued: 1 (2010); Multi-family building permits issued: 0 (2010); Employment by occupation: 10.7% management, 18.3% professional, 29.6% services, 17.2% sales, 0.0% farming, 4.5% construction, 19.7% production (2005-2009 5-year est.).

Income: Per capita income: $22,311 (2010); Median household income: $41,768 (2010); Average household income: $50,647 (2010); Percent of households with income of $100,000 or more: 8.4% (2010); Poverty rate: 10.6% (2005-2009 5-year est.).

Taxes: Total city taxes per capita: $53 (2007); City property taxes per capita: $48 (2007).

Education: Percent of population age 25 and over with: High school diploma (including GED) or higher: 88.6% (2010); Bachelor's degree or higher: 17.3% (2010); Master's degree or higher: 3.8% (2010).

School District(s)

Edgar County CUD 6 (PK-12)
    2009-10 Enrollment: 389 . . . . (217) 269-2513
Housing: Homeownership rate: 70.8% (2010); Median home value: $76,207 (2010); Median contract rent: $371 per month (2005-2009 5-year est.); Median year structure built: 1958 (2005-2009 5-year est.).
Transportation: Commute to work: 93.4% car, 0.0% public transportation, 2.7% walk, 3.1% work from home (2005-2009 5-year est.); Travel time to work: 30.8% less than 15 minutes, 34.2% 15 to 30 minutes, 26.8% 30 to 45 minutes, 5.9% 45 to 60 minutes, 2.3% 60 minutes or more (2005-2009 5-year est.)

HUME (village). Covers a land area of 0.514 square miles and a water area of 0 square miles. Located at 39.79° N. Lat; 87.86° W. Long. Elevation is 663 feet.
Population: 406 (1990); 382 (2000); 359 (2010); 344 (2015 projected); Race: 99.4% White, 0.0% Black, 0.0% Asian, 0.6% Other, 1.7% Hispanic of any race (2010); Density: 698.4 persons per square mile (2010); Average household size: 2.41 (2010); Median age: 41.9 (2010); Males per 100 females: 98.3 (2010); Marriage status: 23.9% never married, 51.2% now married, 5.7% widowed, 19.2% divorced (2005-2009 5-year est.); Foreign born: 0.8% (2005-2009 5-year est.); Ancestry (includes multiple ancestries): 13.1% Irish, 12.9% German, 8.9% English, 8.7% American, 6.0% French (2005-2009 5-year est.).
Economy: Employment by occupation: 8.2% management, 5.8% professional, 22.2% services, 14.0% sales, 8.2% farming, 13.0% construction, 28.5% production (2005-2009 5-year est.).
Income: Per capita income: $24,131 (2010); Median household income: $43,603 (2010); Average household income: $55,503 (2010); Percent of households with income of $100,000 or more: 13.4% (2010); Poverty rate: 16.5% (2005-2009 5-year est.).
Taxes: Total city taxes per capita: $27 (2007); City property taxes per capita: $27 (2007).
Education: Percent of population age 25 and over with: High school diploma (including GED) or higher: 88.5% (2010); Bachelor's degree or higher: 19.8% (2010); Master's degree or higher: 6.1% (2010).

School District(s)

Shiloh CUSD 1 (PK-12)
    2009-10 Enrollment: 435 . . . . (217) 887-2364
Housing: Homeownership rate: 74.5% (2010); Median home value: $76,154 (2010); Median contract rent: $305 per month (2005-2009 5-year est.); Median year structure built: 1958 (2005-2009 5-year est.).
Transportation: Commute to work: 89.7% car, 0.0% public transportation, 5.9% walk, 2.5% work from home (2005-2009 5-year est.); Travel time to work: 26.8% less than 15 minutes, 31.3% 15 to 30 minutes, 31.8% 30 to 45 minutes, 6.6% 45 to 60 minutes, 3.5% 60 minutes or more (2005-2009 5-year est.)

KANSAS (village). Covers a land area of 1.028 square miles and a water area of 0 square miles. Located at 39.55° N. Lat; 87.93° W. Long. Elevation is 712 feet.
Population: 887 (1990); 842 (2000); 789 (2010); 764 (2015 projected); Race: 98.0% White, 0.3% Black, 0.4% Asian, 1.4% Other, 1.9% Hispanic of any race (2010); Density: 767.4 persons per square mile (2010); Average household size: 2.51 (2010); Median age: 38.9 (2010); Males per 100 females: 96.3 (2010); Marriage status: 16.0% never married, 64.8% now married, 5.2% widowed, 14.0% divorced (2005-2009 5-year est.); Foreign born: 0.7% (2005-2009 5-year est.); Ancestry (includes multiple ancestries): 26.3% German, 16.6% American, 14.4% Irish, 8.9% English, 3.4% Scottish (2005-2009 5-year est.).
Economy: Employment by occupation: 13.7% management, 14.8% professional, 14.6% services, 26.9% sales, 3.4% farming, 4.8% construction, 21.7% production (2005-2009 5-year est.).
Income: Per capita income: $17,530 (2010); Median household income: $34,245 (2010); Average household income: $44,252 (2010); Percent of households with income of $100,000 or more: 4.8% (2010); Poverty rate: 17.9% (2005-2009 5-year est.).
Taxes: Total city taxes per capita: $60 (2007); City property taxes per capita: $29 (2007).
Education: Percent of population age 25 and over with: High school diploma (including GED) or higher: 89.6% (2010); Bachelor's degree or higher: 17.1% (2010); Master's degree or higher: 6.5% (2010).

School District(s)

Eastern II Area of Spec Educ (PK-12)
    2009-10 Enrollment: n/a . . . . (217) 348-7700

Kansas CUSD 3 (PK-12)
    2009-10 Enrollment: 257 . . . . (217) 948-5174
Housing: Homeownership rate: 71.0% (2010); Median home value: $76,977 (2010); Median contract rent: $257 per month (2005-2009 5-year est.); Median year structure built: 1954 (2005-2009 5-year est.).
Transportation: Commute to work: 90.6% car, 0.0% public transportation, 2.1% walk, 6.4% work from home (2005-2009 5-year est.); Travel time to work: 25.9% less than 15 minutes, 52.5% 15 to 30 minutes, 12.1% 30 to 45 minutes, 3.3% 45 to 60 minutes, 6.3% 60 minutes or more (2005-2009 5-year est.)

METCALF (village). Covers a land area of 0.552 square miles and a water area of 0 square miles. Located at 39.80° N. Lat; 87.80° W. Long. Elevation is 689 feet.
Population: 227 (1990); 213 (2000); 194 (2010); 186 (2015 projected); Race: 99.5% White, 0.0% Black, 0.0% Asian, 0.5% Other, 1.5% Hispanic of any race (2010); Density: 351.4 persons per square mile (2010); Average household size: 2.43 (2010); Median age: 41.4 (2010); Males per 100 females: 94.0 (2010); Marriage status: 33.7% never married, 51.7% now married, 4.5% widowed, 10.1% divorced (2005-2009 5-year est.); Foreign born: 2.6% (2005-2009 5-year est.); Ancestry (includes multiple ancestries): 21.2% German, 17.7% American, 7.4% Scotch-Irish, 3.9% Irish, 2.2% Hungarian (2005-2009 5-year est.).
Economy: Employment by occupation: 5.8% management, 8.7% professional, 8.7% services, 7.8% sales, 0.0% farming, 26.2% construction, 42.7% production (2005-2009 5-year est.).
Income: Per capita income: $24,131 (2010); Median household income: $44,706 (2010); Average household income: $55,875 (2010); Percent of households with income of $100,000 or more: 13.8% (2010); Poverty rate: 10.0% (2005-2009 5-year est.).
Taxes: Total city taxes per capita: $19 (2007); City property taxes per capita: $14 (2007).
Education: Percent of population age 25 and over with: High school diploma (including GED) or higher: 88.7% (2010); Bachelor's degree or higher: 18.4% (2010); Master's degree or higher: 5.7% (2010).
Housing: Homeownership rate: 75.0% (2010); Median home value: $71,429 (2010); Median contract rent: $410 per month (2005-2009 5-year est.); Median year structure built: 1950 (2005-2009 5-year est.).
Transportation: Commute to work: 93.5% car, 6.5% public transportation, 0.0% walk, 0.0% work from home (2005-2009 5-year est.); Travel time to work: 22.6% less than 15 minutes, 16.1% 15 to 30 minutes, 18.3% 30 to 45 minutes, 33.3% 45 to 60 minutes, 9.7% 60 minutes or more (2005-2009 5-year est.)

PARIS (city). County seat. Covers a land area of 4.815 square miles and a water area of 0.396 square miles. Located at 39.61° N. Lat; 87.69° W. Long. Elevation is 722 feet.
History: Paris was the site of several speeches by Abraham Lincoln. The town was platted in 1853 and grew as the seat of Edgar County.
Population: 9,195 (1990); 9,077 (2000); 8,522 (2010); 8,203 (2015 projected); Race: 96.5% White, 1.5% Black, 0.5% Asian, 1.5% Other, 1.4% Hispanic of any race (2010); Density: 1,770.0 persons per square mile (2010); Average household size: 2.27 (2010); Median age: 39.7 (2010); Males per 100 females: 90.2 (2010); Marriage status: 26.2% never married, 47.2% now married, 9.9% widowed, 16.7% divorced (2005-2009 5-year est.); Foreign born: 3.1% (2005-2009 5-year est.); Ancestry (includes multiple ancestries): 21.2% German, 12.9% Irish, 12.6% American, 11.2% English, 2.6% Scottish (2005-2009 5-year est.).
Economy: Single-family building permits issued: 5 (2010); Multi-family building permits issued: 0 (2010); Employment by occupation: 10.7% management, 13.3% professional, 17.7% services, 20.2% sales, 0.2% farming, 8.1% construction, 29.7% production (2005-2009 5-year est.).
Income: Per capita income: $21,702 (2010); Median household income: $38,671 (2010); Average household income: $49,942 (2010); Percent of households with income of $100,000 or more: 7.6% (2010); Poverty rate: 18.3% (2005-2009 5-year est.).
Taxes: Total city taxes per capita: $341 (2007); City property taxes per capita: $151 (2007).
Education: Percent of population age 25 and over with: High school diploma (including GED) or higher: 84.5% (2010); Bachelor's degree or higher: 15.1% (2010); Master's degree or higher: 4.9% (2010).

School District(s)

Clk Cls Cmbn Dglas Edgr Mltr Shlb (06-12)
    2009-10 Enrollment: n/a . . . . (217) 348-0151

Paris CUSD 4 (PK-12)

    2009-10 Enrollment: 780 . . . . (217) 465-5391

Paris Cooperative High School (09-12)

    2009-10 Enrollment: n/a . . . . (217) 466-1175

Paris-Union SD 95 (PK-12)

    2009-10 Enrollment: 1,355 . . . . (217) 465-8448

Housing: Homeownership rate: 69.3% (2010); Median home value: $69,131 (2010); Median contract rent: $378 per month (2005-2009 5-year est.); Median year structure built: 1956 (2005-2009 5-year est.).

Hospitals: Paris Community Hospital (49 beds)

Safety: Violent crime rate: 53.3 per 10,000 population; Property crime rate: 127.9 per 10,000 population (2010).

Newspapers: Paris Daily Beacon News (Local news; Circulation 5,600)

Transportation: Commute to work: 90.1% car, 0.0% public transportation, 4.4% walk, 4.5% work from home (2005-2009 5-year est.); Travel time to work: 64.3% less than 15 minutes, 10.4% 15 to 30 minutes, 11.4% 30 to 45 minutes, 5.6% 45 to 60 minutes, 8.3% 60 minutes or more (2005-2009 5-year est.)

Additional Information Contacts

City of Paris . . . . (217) 465-7601

    http://parisillinois.org

Paris Area Chamber of Commerce & Tourism . . . . (217) 465-4179

    http://www.parisilchamber.com

REDMON (village).
Covers a land area of 0.148 square miles and a water area of 0 square miles. Located at 39.64° N. Lat; 87.86° W. Long. Elevation is 689 feet.

Population: 201 (1990); 199 (2000); 165 (2010); 154 (2015 projected); Race: 98.8% White, 0.0% Black, 0.0% Asian, 1.2% Other, 1.2% Hispanic of any race (2010); Density: 1,116.7 persons per square mile (2010); Average household size: 2.39 (2010); Median age: 45.6 (2010); Males per 100 females: 101.2 (2010); Marriage status: 15.7% never married, 38.6% now married, 28.3% widowed, 17.3% divorced (2005-2009 5-year est.); Foreign born: 0.0% (2005-2009 5-year est.); Ancestry (includes multiple ancestries): 22.4% English, 21.8% German, 18.2% American, 13.3% Irish, 3.6% Dutch (2005-2009 5-year est.).

Economy: Employment by occupation: 4.2% management, 12.5% professional, 16.7% services, 34.7% sales, 1.4% farming, 5.6% construction, 25.0% production (2005-2009 5-year est.).

Income: Per capita income: $22,641 (2010); Median household income: $43,654 (2010); Average household income: $52,826 (2010); Percent of households with income of $100,000 or more: 7.2% (2010); Poverty rate: 23.6% (2005-2009 5-year est.).

Taxes: Total city taxes per capita: $10 (2007); City property taxes per capita: $10 (2007).

Education: Percent of population age 25 and over with: High school diploma (including GED) or higher: 86.4% (2010); Bachelor's degree or higher: 14.4% (2010); Master's degree or higher: 1.7% (2010).

Housing: Homeownership rate: 78.3% (2010); Median home value: $66,667 (2010); Median contract rent: $354 per month (2005-2009 5-year est.); Median year structure built: 1971 (2005-2009 5-year est.).

Transportation: Commute to work: 100.0% car, 0.0% public transportation, 0.0% walk, 0.0% work from home (2005-2009 5-year est.); Travel time to work: 20.3% less than 15 minutes, 66.7% 15 to 30 minutes, 11.6% 30 to 45 minutes, 0.0% 45 to 60 minutes, 1.4% 60 minutes or more (2005-2009 5-year est.)

VERMILION (village).
Covers a land area of 0.762 square miles and a water area of 0 square miles. Located at 39.58° N. Lat; 87.58° W. Long. Elevation is 692 feet.

History: Formerly Vermillion.

Population: 283 (1990); 239 (2000); 219 (2010); 208 (2015 projected); Race: 98.2% White, 0.0% Black, 0.9% Asian, 0.9% Other, 0.0% Hispanic of any race (2010); Density: 287.4 persons per square mile (2010); Average household size: 2.55 (2010); Median age: 43.0 (2010); Males per 100 females: 95.5 (2010); Marriage status: 18.5% never married, 61.6% now married, 12.3% widowed, 7.5% divorced (2005-2009 5-year est.); Foreign born: 0.0% (2005-2009 5-year est.); Ancestry (includes multiple ancestries): 21.6% Irish, 13.5% German, 10.3% English, 5.9% Italian, 4.3% Scotch-Irish (2005-2009 5-year est.).

Economy: Single-family building permits issued: 0 (2010); Multi-family building permits issued: 0 (2010); Employment by occupation: 1.3% management, 2.7% professional, 20.0% services, 32.0% sales, 4.0% farming, 9.3% construction, 30.7% production (2005-2009 5-year est.).

Income: Per capita income: $21,868 (2010); Median household income: $53,846 (2010); Average household income: $56,628 (2010); Percent of households with income of $100,000 or more: 11.6% (2010); Poverty rate: 8.6% (2005-2009 5-year est.).

Taxes: Total city taxes per capita: $39 (2007); City property taxes per capita: $39 (2007).

Education: Percent of population age 25 and over with: High school diploma (including GED) or higher: 88.7% (2010); Bachelor's degree or higher: 17.0% (2010); Master's degree or higher: 5.0% (2010).

Housing: Homeownership rate: 82.6% (2010); Median home value: $96,250 (2010); Median contract rent: $350 per month (2005-2009 5-year est.); Median year structure built: before 1940 (2005-2009 5-year est.).

Transportation: Commute to work: 100.0% car, 0.0% public transportation, 0.0% walk, 0.0% work from home (2005-2009 5-year est.); Travel time to work: 20.0% less than 15 minutes, 44.6% 15 to 30 minutes, 30.8% 30 to 45 minutes, 4.6% 45 to 60 minutes, 0.0% 60 minutes or more (2005-2009 5-year est.)

Edwards County

Located in southeastern Illinois; drained by the Little Wabash River. Covers a land area of 222.35 square miles, a water area of 0.31 square miles, and is located in the Central Time Zone at 38.39° N. Lat., 88.04° W. Long. The county was founded in 1814. County seat is Albion.

Weather Station: Albion   Elevation: 529 feet

	Jan	Feb	Mar	Apr	May	Jun	Jul	Aug	Sep	Oct	Nov	Dec
High	39	45	55	67	77	86	90	89	82	71	55	43
Low	24	27	35	46	56	65	68	67	59	47	37	26
Precip	2.6	2.5	4.0	4.9	5.4	3.7	3.6	3.2	2.8	3.7	4.1	3.0
Snow	2.0	2.4	1.0	0.0	0.0	0.0	0.0	0.0	0.0	0.1	tr	2.6

High and Low temperatures in degrees Fahrenheit; Precipitation and Snow in inches

Population: 7,440 (1990); 6,971 (2000); 6,438 (2010); 6,157 (2015 projected); Race: 98.7% White, 0.2% Black, 0.4% Asian, 0.8% Other, 0.6% Hispanic of any race (2010); Density: 29.0 persons per square mile (2010); Average household size: 2.34 (2010); Median age: 42.2 (2010); Males per 100 females: 96.1 (2010).

Religion: Five largest groups: 23.3% Christian Churches and Churches of Christ, 14.4% Southern Baptist Convention, 14.2% The United Methodist Church, 9.7% Independent, Non-Charismatic Churches, 4.4% Christian Church (Disciples of Christ) (2000).

Economy: Unemployment rate: 8.0% (August 2011); Total civilian labor force: 3,182 (August 2011); Leading industries: 9.1% wholesale trade; 8.7% retail trade; 6.2% health care and social assistance (2009); Farms: 365 totaling 116,690 acres (2007); Companies that employ 500 or more persons: 1 (2009); Companies that employ 100 to 499 persons: 0 (2009); Companies that employ less than 100 persons: 162 (2009); Black-owned businesses: n/a (2007); Hispanic-owned businesses: n/a (2007); Asian-owned businesses: n/a (2007); Women-owned businesses: 111 (2007); Retail sales per capita: $8,658 (2010). Single-family building permits issued: n/a (2010); Multi-family building permits issued: n/a (2010).

Income: Per capita income: $21,479 (2010); Median household income: $41,384 (2010); Average household income: $50,404 (2010); Percent of households with income of $100,000 or more: 7.5% (2010); Poverty rate: 11.3% (2009); Bankruptcy rate: 2.24% (2010).

Taxes: Total county taxes per capita: $212 (2007); County property taxes per capita: $212 (2007).

Education: Percent of population age 25 and over with: High school diploma (including GED) or higher: 87.3% (2010); Bachelor's degree or higher: 12.1% (2010); Master's degree or higher: 3.6% (2010).

Housing: Homeownership rate: 80.2% (2010); Median home value: $60,148 (2010); Median contract rent: $295 per month (2005-2009 5-year est.); Median year structure built: 1962 (2005-2009 5-year est.)

Health: Birth rate: 114.8 per 10,000 population (2009); Death rate: 119.5 per 10,000 population (2009); Age-adjusted cancer mortality rate: 239.4 deaths per 100,000 population (2007); Number of physicians: 0.0 per 10,000 population (2008); Hospital beds: 0.0 per 10,000 population (2007); Hospital admissions: 0.0 per 10,000 population (2007).

Elections: 2008 Presidential election results: 34.0% Obama, 63.8% McCain, 0.9% Nader

Additional Information Contacts

Edwards County Government . . . . (618) 445-2115

Albion Area Chamber of Commerce . . . . (618) 445-2303

    http://www.albionchamber.com

Edwards County Communities

ALBION (city). County seat. Covers a land area of 2.139 square miles and a water area of 0.049 square miles. Located at 38.37° N. Lat; 88.06° W. Long. Elevation is 522 feet.

History: In 1818 Morris Birkbeck and George Flower came from England to find a place that would provide a better life for the English working class. They settled on this section of prairie and led many English colonists here, who named the town Albion, remembering their former homeland.

Population: 2,150 (1990); 1,933 (2000); 1,762 (2010); 1,672 (2015 projected); Race: 98.5% White, 0.2% Black, 0.6% Asian, 0.7% Other, 0.5% Hispanic of any race (2010); Density: 823.9 persons per square mile (2010); Average household size: 2.18 (2010); Median age: 43.9 (2010); Males per 100 females: 86.7 (2010); Marriage status: 19.6% never married, 58.9% now married, 12.5% widowed, 9.0% divorced (2005-2009 5-year est.); Foreign born: 0.3% (2005-2009 5-year est.); Ancestry (includes multiple ancestries): 24.7% German, 19.0% English, 16.6% American, 8.3% Irish, 2.6% Dutch (2005-2009 5-year est.).

Economy: Employment by occupation: 5.6% management, 15.8% professional, 13.8% services, 18.5% sales, 0.8% farming, 14.7% construction, 30.6% production (2005-2009 5-year est.).

Income: Per capita income: $19,640 (2010); Median household income: $35,991 (2010); Average household income: $43,143 (2010); Percent of households with income of $100,000 or more: 3.8% (2010); Poverty rate: 10.4% (2005-2009 5-year est.).

Taxes: Total city taxes per capita: $177 (2007); City property taxes per capita: $172 (2007).

Education: Percent of population age 25 and over with: High school diploma (including GED) or higher: 84.2% (2010); Bachelor's degree or higher: 11.4% (2010); Master's degree or higher: 4.1% (2010).

School District(s)

Edwards County CUSD 1 (PK-12)

    2009-10 Enrollment: 990 . . . . (618) 445-2814

Housing: Homeownership rate: 72.9% (2010); Median home value: $57,634 (2010); Median contract rent: $240 per month (2005-2009 5-year est.); Median year structure built: 1957 (2005-2009 5-year est.).

Newspapers: Navigator & Journal-Register (Community news; Circulation 3,600); Prairie Post (Community news; Circulation 12,750)

Transportation: Commute to work: 88.4% car, 0.6% public transportation, 5.1% walk, 4.1% work from home (2005-2009 5-year est.); Travel time to work: 61.7% less than 15 minutes, 17.5% 15 to 30 minutes, 8.1% 30 to 45 minutes, 9.5% 45 to 60 minutes, 3.2% 60 minutes or more (2005-2009 5-year est.)

Additional Information Contacts

Albion Area Chamber of Commerce . . . . (618) 445-2303

    http://www.albionchamber.com

BONE GAP (village). Covers a land area of 0.604 square miles and a water area of 0 square miles. Located at 38.44° N. Lat; 87.99° W. Long. Elevation is 482 feet.

Population: 271 (1990); 272 (2000); 254 (2010); 243 (2015 projected); Race: 99.6% White, 0.0% Black, 0.0% Asian, 0.4% Other, 0.4% Hispanic of any race (2010); Density: 420.7 persons per square mile (2010); Average household size: 2.70 (2010); Median age: 34.3 (2010); Males per 100 females: 108.2 (2010); Marriage status: 14.2% never married, 80.7% now married, 2.5% widowed, 2.5% divorced (2005-2009 5-year est.); Foreign born: 4.3% (2005-2009 5-year est.); Ancestry (includes multiple ancestries): 14.6% German, 12.5% English, 6.8% French, 4.3% Swedish, 2.5% American (2005-2009 5-year est.).

Economy: Employment by occupation: 11.0% management, 14.4% professional, 13.6% services, 23.7% sales, 0.0% farming, 9.3% construction, 28.0% production (2005-2009 5-year est.).

Income: Per capita income: $20,323 (2010); Median household income: $45,500 (2010); Average household income: $57,074 (2010); Percent of households with income of $100,000 or more: 7.4% (2010); Poverty rate: 14.2% (2005-2009 5-year est.).

Taxes: Total city taxes per capita: $35 (2007); City property taxes per capita: $35 (2007).

Education: Percent of population age 25 and over with: High school diploma (including GED) or higher: 90.9% (2010); Bachelor's degree or higher: 18.3% (2010); Master's degree or higher: 4.3% (2010).

Housing: Homeownership rate: 86.2% (2010); Median home value: $61,667 (2010); Median contract rent: $340 per month (2005-2009 5-year est.); Median year structure built: 1966 (2005-2009 5-year est.).

Transportation: Commute to work: 83.6% car, 0.0% public transportation, 5.2% walk, 6.0% work from home (2005-2009 5-year est.); Travel time to work: 25.7% less than 15 minutes, 46.8% 15 to 30 minutes, 21.1% 30 to 45 minutes, 0.0% 45 to 60 minutes, 6.4% 60 minutes or more (2005-2009 5-year est.)

BROWNS (village). Covers a land area of 0.292 square miles and a water area of 0 square miles. Located at 38.37° N. Lat; 87.98° W. Long. Elevation is 407 feet.

Population: 207 (1990); 175 (2000); 166 (2010); 160 (2015 projected); Race: 99.4% White, 0.0% Black, 0.6% Asian, 0.0% Other, 1.2% Hispanic of any race (2010); Density: 568.7 persons per square mile (2010); Average household size: 2.44 (2010); Median age: 43.4 (2010); Males per 100 females: 107.5 (2010); Marriage status: 15.8% never married, 71.6% now married, 0.0% widowed, 12.6% divorced (2005-2009 5-year est.); Foreign born: 0.0% (2005-2009 5-year est.); Ancestry (includes multiple ancestries): 27.4% German, 17.9% English, 14.2% Irish, 13.2% American, 8.5% French (2005-2009 5-year est.).

Economy: Employment by occupation: 0.0% management, 5.5% professional, 12.7% services, 18.2% sales, 9.1% farming, 25.5% construction, 29.1% production (2005-2009 5-year est.).

Income: Per capita income: $25,840 (2010); Median household income: $55,000 (2010); Average household income: $61,066 (2010); Percent of households with income of $100,000 or more: 10.3% (2010); Poverty rate: 6.6% (2005-2009 5-year est.).

Taxes: Total city taxes per capita: $96 (2007); City property taxes per capita: $72 (2007).

Education: Percent of population age 25 and over with: High school diploma (including GED) or higher: 87.1% (2010); Bachelor's degree or higher: 13.7% (2010); Master's degree or higher: 4.0% (2010).

Housing: Homeownership rate: 91.2% (2010); Median home value: $68,333 (2010); Median contract rent: n/a per month (2005-2009 5-year est.); Median year structure built: 1971 (2005-2009 5-year est.).

Transportation: Commute to work: 100.0% car, 0.0% public transportation, 0.0% walk, 0.0% work from home (2005-2009 5-year est.); Travel time to work: 51.0% less than 15 minutes, 37.3% 15 to 30 minutes, 11.8% 30 to 45 minutes, 0.0% 45 to 60 minutes, 0.0% 60 minutes or more (2005-2009 5-year est.)

ELLERY (unincorporated postal area, zip code 62833). Covers a land area of 49.474 square miles and a water area of 0.244 square miles. Located at 38.36° N. Lat; 88.16° W. Long.

Population: 376 (2000); Race: 96.5% White, 0.0% Black, 0.0% Asian, 3.5% Other, 0.0% Hispanic of any race (2000); Density: 7.6 persons per square mile (2000); Age: 22.1% under 18, 17.1% over 64 (2000); Marriage status: 13.7% never married, 76.3% now married, 3.0% widowed, 7.0% divorced (2000); Foreign born: 0.0% (2000); Ancestry (includes multiple ancestries): 32.8% English, 16.8% American, 10.4% German, 8.0% Irish (2000).

Economy: Employment by occupation: 18.1% management, 4.8% professional, 22.9% services, 24.1% sales, 2.4% farming, 4.8% construction, 22.9% production (2000).

Income: Per capita income: $12,419 (2000); Median household income: $32,885 (2000); Poverty rate: 7.5% (2000).

Education: Percent of population age 25 and over with: High school diploma (including GED) or higher: 75.1% (2000); Bachelor's degree or higher: 7.1% (2000).

Housing: Homeownership rate: 91.7% (2000); Median home value: $54,700 (2000); Median contract rent: n/a per month (2000); Median year structure built: 1959 (2000).

Transportation: Commute to work: 92.8% car, 0.0% public transportation, 6.0% walk, 1.2% work from home (2000); Travel time to work: 32.3% less than 15 minutes, 46.3% 15 to 30 minutes, 9.8% 30 to 45 minutes, 5.5% 45 to 60 minutes, 6.1% 60 minutes or more (2000)

WEST SALEM (village). Covers a land area of 1.559 square miles and a water area of <.001 square miles. Located at 38.52° N. Lat; 88.00° W. Long. Elevation is 525 feet.

History: West Salem was settled in 1838 by German Moravians from North Carolina.

Population: 1,042 (1990); 1,001 (2000); 952 (2010); 917 (2015 projected); Race: 98.2% White, 0.2% Black, 0.4% Asian, 1.2% Other, 0.4% Hispanic of any race (2010); Density: 610.7 persons per square mile (2010); Average household size: 2.35 (2010); Median age: 41.9 (2010); Males per 100 females: 98.3 (2010); Marriage status: 14.5% never married, 58.9%

now married, 8.6% widowed, 18.0% divorced (2005-2009 5-year est.); Foreign born: 0.4% (2005-2009 5-year est.); Ancestry (includes multiple ancestries): 35.8% German, 21.6% English, 15.8% Irish, 10.4% American, 3.7% Dutch (2005-2009 5-year est.).

Economy: Employment by occupation: 6.4% management, 13.2% professional, 14.9% services, 14.0% sales, 0.7% farming, 8.8% construction, 42.1% production (2005-2009 5-year est.).

Income: Per capita income: $19,619 (2010); Median household income: $39,828 (2010); Average household income: $46,319 (2010); Percent of households with income of $100,000 or more: 6.5% (2010); Poverty rate: 8.0% (2005-2009 5-year est.).

Taxes: Total city taxes per capita: $129 (2007); City property taxes per capita: $129 (2007).

Education: Percent of population age 25 and over with: High school diploma (including GED) or higher: 89.4% (2010); Bachelor's degree or higher: 11.4% (2010); Master's degree or higher: 2.5% (2010).

School District(s)

Edwards County CUSD 1 (PK-12)
   2009-10 Enrollment: 990 . . . . (618) 445-2814

Housing: Homeownership rate: 83.3% (2010); Median home value: $56,200 (2010); Median contract rent: $332 per month (2005-2009 5-year est.); Median year structure built: 1954 (2005-2009 5-year est.).

Newspapers: Edwards County Times Advocate (Community news; Circulation 1,850); Times Advocate Shopping Messenger (Community news; Circulation 5,000); West Salem Times Advocate (Local news; Circulation 6,500)

Transportation: Commute to work: 91.9% car, 0.0% public transportation, 6.3% walk, 0.9% work from home (2005-2009 5-year est.); Travel time to work: 31.7% less than 15 minutes, 45.1% 15 to 30 minutes, 9.3% 30 to 45 minutes, 2.7% 45 to 60 minutes, 11.1% 60 minutes or more (2005-2009 5-year est.)

Effingham County

Located in southeast central Illinois; drained by the Little Wabash River. Covers a land area of 478.70 square miles, a water area of 1.20 square miles, and is located in the Central Time Zone at 39.07° N. Lat., 88.59° W. Long. The county was founded in 1831. County seat is Effingham.

Effingham County is part of the Effingham, IL Micropolitan Statistical Area. The entire metro area includes: Effingham County, IL

Weather Station: Effingham   Elevation: 606 feet

	Jan	Feb	Mar	Apr	May	Jun	Jul	Aug	Sep	Oct	Nov	Dec
High	36	41	52	64	74	84	87	86	79	67	54	40
Low	20	22	32	42	52	62	66	64	55	43	35	23
Precip	2.4	2.7	3.2	3.9	5.1	4.2	4.3	2.9	3.1	3.7	4.0	3.3
Snow	5.7	5.1	2.1	0.1	0.0	0.0	0.0	0.0	0.0	tr	1.0	3.8

High and Low temperatures in degrees Fahrenheit; Precipitation and Snow in inches

Population: 31,704 (1990); 34,264 (2000); 34,269 (2010); 34,053 (2015 projected); Race: 97.7% White, 0.5% Black, 0.4% Asian, 1.4% Other, 1.5% Hispanic of any race (2010); Density: 71.6 persons per square mile (2010); Average household size: 2.53 (2010); Median age: 37.4 (2010); Males per 100 females: 99.1 (2010).

Religion: Five largest groups: 37.1% Catholic Church, 11.1% Lutheran Church—Missouri Synod, 9.3% Southern Baptist Convention, 6.6% The United Methodist Church, 4.0% Christian Churches and Churches of Christ (2000).

Economy: Unemployment rate: 6.9% (August 2011); Total civilian labor force: 18,481 (August 2011); Leading industries: 18.4% manufacturing; 16.3% retail trade; 14.8% health care and social assistance (2009); Farms: 1,150 totaling 242,009 acres (2007); Companies that employ 500 or more persons: 2 (2009); Companies that employ 100 to 499 persons: 30 (2009); Companies that employ less than 100 persons: 1,143 (2009); Black-owned businesses: n/a (2007); Hispanic-owned businesses: n/a (2007); Asian-owned businesses: n/a (2007); Women-owned businesses: n/a (2007); Retail sales per capita: $26,670 (2010). Single-family building permits issued: 18 (2010); Multi-family building permits issued: 129 (2010).

Income: Per capita income: $22,741 (2010); Median household income: $47,080 (2010); Average household income: $57,873 (2010); Percent of households with income of $100,000 or more: 11.5% (2010); Poverty rate: 10.2% (2009); Bankruptcy rate: 4.19% (2010).

Taxes: Total county taxes per capita: $45 (2007); County property taxes per capita: $44 (2007).

Education: Percent of population age 25 and over with: High school diploma (including GED) or higher: 87.7% (2010); Bachelor's degree or higher: 21.0% (2010); Master's degree or higher: 5.8% (2010).

Housing: Homeownership rate: 78.2% (2010); Median home value: $102,279 (2010); Median contract rent: $404 per month (2005-2009 5-year est.); Median year structure built: 1973 (2005-2009 5-year est.)

Health: Birth rate: 141.5 per 10,000 population (2009); Death rate: 101.4 per 10,000 population (2009); Age-adjusted cancer mortality rate: 198.8 deaths per 100,000 population (2007); Number of physicians: 21.3 per 10,000 population (2008); Hospital beds: 42.6 per 10,000 population (2007); Hospital admissions: 2,157.0 per 10,000 population (2007).

Environment: Air Quality Index: 94.9% good, 5.1% moderate, 0.0% unhealthy for sensitive individuals, 0.0% unhealthy (percent of days in 2008)

Elections: 2008 Presidential election results: 31.3% Obama, 67.3% McCain, 0.8% Nader

Additional Information Contacts

Effingham County Government . . . . (217) 342-6535
   http://www.co.effingham.il.us
Altamont Chamber of Commerce . . . . (618) 483-5714
   http://www.altamontchamber.com
City of Altamont . . . . (618) 483-5212
   http://www.altamontil.net
City of Effingham . . . . (217) 342-5301
   http://www.effinghamil.com
The Greater Effingham Chamber of Commerce . . . . (217) 342-4147
   http://www.effinghamchamber.org

Effingham County Communities

ALTAMONT (city). Covers a land area of 1.303 square miles and a water area of 0 square miles. Located at 39.06° N. Lat; 88.74° W. Long. Elevation is 620 feet.

History: Altamont was organized in 1872 along the Pennsylvania and Baltimore & Ohio Railroads. Named for a nearby hill, Altamont developed as a wheat shipping center.

Population: 2,329 (1990); 2,283 (2000); 2,244 (2010); 2,226 (2015 projected); Race: 99.0% White, 0.1% Black, 0.0% Asian, 0.9% Other, 0.4% Hispanic of any race (2010); Density: 1,721.7 persons per square mile (2010); Average household size: 2.43 (2010); Median age: 38.9 (2010); Males per 100 females: 96.8 (2010); Marriage status: 23.4% never married, 57.8% now married, 7.7% widowed, 11.1% divorced (2005-2009 5-year est.); Foreign born: 0.0% (2005-2009 5-year est.); Ancestry (includes multiple ancestries): 40.6% German, 14.3% American, 12.7% Irish, 7.5% English, 4.1% Scotch-Irish (2005-2009 5-year est.).

Economy: Single-family building permits issued: 5 (2010); Multi-family building permits issued: 0 (2010); Employment by occupation: 10.1% management, 19.3% professional, 16.6% services, 22.4% sales, 0.0% farming, 9.8% construction, 21.8% production (2005-2009 5-year est.).

Income: Per capita income: $20,995 (2010); Median household income: $42,971 (2010); Average household income: $51,384 (2010); Percent of households with income of $100,000 or more: 7.0% (2010); Poverty rate: 11.7% (2005-2009 5-year est.).

Taxes: Total city taxes per capita: $139 (2007); City property taxes per capita: $56 (2007).

Education: Percent of population age 25 and over with: High school diploma (including GED) or higher: 84.6% (2010); Bachelor's degree or higher: 18.5% (2010); Master's degree or higher: 4.1% (2010).

School District(s)

Altamont CUSD 10 (PK-12)
   2009-10 Enrollment: 780 . . . . (618) 483-6195

Housing: Homeownership rate: 78.3% (2010); Median home value: $78,506 (2010); Median contract rent: $345 per month (2005-2009 5-year est.); Median year structure built: 1967 (2005-2009 5-year est.).

Newspapers: Altamont Independent (Local news; Circulation 3,500); Altamont News (Local news; Circulation 1,600)

Transportation: Commute to work: 89.1% car, 0.0% public transportation, 6.0% walk, 2.4% work from home (2005-2009 5-year est.); Travel time to work: 33.2% less than 15 minutes, 53.0% 15 to 30 minutes, 6.0% 30 to 45 minutes, 6.1% 45 to 60 minutes, 1.7% 60 minutes or more (2005-2009 5-year est.)

Additional Information Contacts

Altamont Chamber of Commerce . . . . (618) 483-5714
   http://www.altamontchamber.com

City of Altamont . . . . (618) 483-5212
http://www.altamontil.net

BEECHER CITY (village). Covers a land area of 0.905 square miles and a water area of 0 square miles. Located at 39.18° N. Lat; 88.78° W. Long. Elevation is 610 feet.

Population: 437 (1990); 493 (2000); 477 (2010); 466 (2015 projected); Race: 99.0% White, 0.0% Black, 0.0% Asian, 1.0% Other, 0.6% Hispanic of any race (2010); Density: 527.2 persons per square mile (2010); Average household size: 2.51 (2010); Median age: 36.1 (2010); Males per 100 females: 99.6 (2010); Marriage status: 28.9% never married, 49.3% now married, 6.9% widowed, 14.9% divorced (2005-2009 5-year est.); Foreign born: 0.0% (2005-2009 5-year est.); Ancestry (includes multiple ancestries): 35.9% German, 11.4% Irish, 9.4% English, 7.3% American, 4.8% Scottish (2005-2009 5-year est.).
Economy: Employment by occupation: 0.0% management, 6.5% professional, 20.3% services, 18.4% sales, 0.0% farming, 17.1% construction, 37.8% production (2005-2009 5-year est.).
Income: Per capita income: $16,145 (2010); Median household income: $33,000 (2010); Average household income: $40,895 (2010); Percent of households with income of $100,000 or more: 5.8% (2010); Poverty rate: 13.5% (2005-2009 5-year est.).
Taxes: Total city taxes per capita: $59 (2007); City property taxes per capita: $59 (2007).
Education: Percent of population age 25 and over with: High school diploma (including GED) or higher: 87.6% (2010); Bachelor's degree or higher: 15.7% (2010); Master's degree or higher: 5.6% (2010).

School District(s)
Beecher City CUSD 20 (PK-12)
    2009-10 Enrollment: 422 . . . . (618) 487-5100
Housing: Homeownership rate: 77.4% (2010); Median home value: $70,500 (2010); Median contract rent: $264 per month (2005-2009 5-year est.); Median year structure built: 1946 (2005-2009 5-year est.).
Newspapers: Beecher City Journal (Community news; Circulation 1,600)
Transportation: Commute to work: 96.7% car, 0.0% public transportation, 0.0% walk, 1.9% work from home (2005-2009 5-year est.); Travel time to work: 16.1% less than 15 minutes, 48.3% 15 to 30 minutes, 32.7% 30 to 45 minutes, 2.9% 45 to 60 minutes, 0.0% 60 minutes or more (2005-2009 5-year est.)

DIETERICH (village). Covers a land area of 1.185 square miles and a water area of 0 square miles. Located at 39.06° N. Lat; 88.37° W. Long. Elevation is 587 feet.

Population: 606 (1990); 591 (2000); 607 (2010); 610 (2015 projected); Race: 99.2% White, 0.0% Black, 0.0% Asian, 0.8% Other, 0.8% Hispanic of any race (2010); Density: 512.1 persons per square mile (2010); Average household size: 3.16 (2010); Median age: 30.9 (2010); Males per 100 females: 105.1 (2010); Marriage status: 22.2% never married, 62.0% now married, 6.5% widowed, 9.3% divorced (2005-2009 5-year est.); Foreign born: 1.4% (2005-2009 5-year est.); Ancestry (includes multiple ancestries): 39.5% German, 19.8% Irish, 15.5% American, 9.0% English, 6.0% French (2005-2009 5-year est.).
Economy: Employment by occupation: 6.9% management, 11.4% professional, 21.7% services, 19.3% sales, 0.0% farming, 10.2% construction, 30.4% production (2005-2009 5-year est.).
Income: Per capita income: $19,125 (2010); Median household income: $55,392 (2010); Average household income: $61,055 (2010); Percent of households with income of $100,000 or more: 11.5% (2010); Poverty rate: 5.3% (2005-2009 5-year est.).
Taxes: Total city taxes per capita: $284 (2007); City property taxes per capita: $281 (2007).
Education: Percent of population age 25 and over with: High school diploma (including GED) or higher: 88.9% (2010); Bachelor's degree or higher: 15.6% (2010); Master's degree or higher: 6.0% (2010).

School District(s)
Dieterich CUSD 30 (PK-12)
    2009-10 Enrollment: 474 . . . . (217) 925-5249
Housing: Homeownership rate: 89.1% (2010); Median home value: $95,600 (2010); Median contract rent: $416 per month (2005-2009 5-year est.); Median year structure built: 1964 (2005-2009 5-year est.).
Transportation: Commute to work: 94.8% car, 0.0% public transportation, 1.2% walk, 1.8% work from home (2005-2009 5-year est.); Travel time to work: 31.0% less than 15 minutes, 48.9% 15 to 30 minutes, 7.4% 30 to 45 minutes, 4.0% 45 to 60 minutes, 8.7% 60 minutes or more (2005-2009 5-year est.)

EDGEWOOD (village). Covers a land area of 1.003 square miles and a water area of 0.011 square miles. Located at 38.92° N. Lat; 88.66° W. Long. Elevation is 574 feet.

Population: 502 (1990); 527 (2000); 517 (2010); 508 (2015 projected); Race: 99.0% White, 0.0% Black, 0.2% Asian, 0.8% Other, 1.7% Hispanic of any race (2010); Density: 515.3 persons per square mile (2010); Average household size: 2.59 (2010); Median age: 38.0 (2010); Males per 100 females: 104.3 (2010); Marriage status: 21.0% never married, 62.2% now married, 6.4% widowed, 10.4% divorced (2005-2009 5-year est.); Foreign born: 0.4% (2005-2009 5-year est.); Ancestry (includes multiple ancestries): 21.5% German, 9.1% American, 8.3% Irish, 7.0% English, 3.6% Scotch-Irish (2005-2009 5-year est.).
Economy: Employment by occupation: 1.1% management, 10.0% professional, 18.6% services, 13.6% sales, 0.0% farming, 2.5% construction, 54.3% production (2005-2009 5-year est.).
Income: Per capita income: $18,346 (2010); Median household income: $42,500 (2010); Average household income: $47,650 (2010); Percent of households with income of $100,000 or more: 5.5% (2010); Poverty rate: 5.7% (2005-2009 5-year est.).
Taxes: Total city taxes per capita: $97 (2007); City property taxes per capita: $49 (2007).
Education: Percent of population age 25 and over with: High school diploma (including GED) or higher: 81.2% (2010); Bachelor's degree or higher: 7.8% (2010); Master's degree or higher: 2.9% (2010).

School District(s)
Effingham CUSD 40 (PK-12)
    2009-10 Enrollment: 2,877 . . . . (217) 540-1501
Housing: Homeownership rate: 85.0% (2010); Median home value: $57,143 (2010); Median contract rent: $281 per month (2005-2009 5-year est.); Median year structure built: 1956 (2005-2009 5-year est.).
Transportation: Commute to work: 86.4% car, 0.0% public transportation, 0.0% walk, 7.9% work from home (2005-2009 5-year est.); Travel time to work: 5.8% less than 15 minutes, 58.9% 15 to 30 minutes, 31.8% 30 to 45 minutes, 0.0% 45 to 60 minutes, 3.5% 60 minutes or more (2005-2009 5-year est.)

EFFINGHAM (city). County seat. Covers a land area of 8.667 square miles and a water area of 0.058 square miles. Located at 39.12° N. Lat; 88.54° W. Long. Elevation is 594 feet.

History: Effingham was settled by German immigrants, and was incorporated as a village in 1861.
Population: 12,261 (1990); 12,384 (2000); 12,432 (2010); 12,372 (2015 projected); Race: 96.0% White, 1.1% Black, 0.7% Asian, 2.2% Other, 2.3% Hispanic of any race (2010); Density: 1,434.4 persons per square mile (2010); Average household size: 2.22 (2010); Median age: 39.1 (2010); Males per 100 females: 91.9 (2010); Marriage status: 26.3% never married, 50.2% now married, 11.8% widowed, 11.7% divorced (2005-2009 5-year est.); Foreign born: 2.4% (2005-2009 5-year est.); Ancestry (includes multiple ancestries): 41.4% German, 10.7% English, 10.4% Irish, 6.9% American, 3.4% French (2005-2009 5-year est.).
Economy: Single-family building permits issued: 8 (2010); Multi-family building permits issued: 129 (2010); Employment by occupation: 14.3% management, 16.9% professional, 16.8% services, 27.7% sales, 1.1% farming, 6.3% construction, 16.9% production (2005-2009 5-year est.).
Income: Per capita income: $23,585 (2010); Median household income: $42,310 (2010); Average household income: $53,164 (2010); Percent of households with income of $100,000 or more: 10.3% (2010); Poverty rate: 12.3% (2005-2009 5-year est.).
Taxes: Total city taxes per capita: $510 (2007); City property taxes per capita: $410 (2007).
Education: Percent of population age 25 and over with: High school diploma (including GED) or higher: 86.2% (2010); Bachelor's degree or higher: 23.0% (2010); Master's degree or higher: 6.6% (2010).

School District(s)
Bond/Effingham/Fayette Roe (06-12)
    2009-10 Enrollment: n/a . . . . (618) 283-5011
Eastern Il Area of Spec Educ (PK-12)
    2009-10 Enrollment: n/a . . . . (217) 348-7700
Effingham CUSD 40 (PK-12)
    2009-10 Enrollment: 2,877 . . . . (217) 540-1501
Housing: Homeownership rate: 66.6% (2010); Median home value: $100,109 (2010); Median contract rent: $419 per month (2005-2009 5-year est.); Median year structure built: 1972 (2005-2009 5-year est.).
Hospitals: St. Anthony's Memorial Hospital (146 beds)

Safety: Violent crime rate: 20.1 per 10,000 population; Property crime rate: 289.3 per 10,000 population (2010).
Newspapers: Effingham Daily News (Local news; Circulation 13,266)
Transportation: Commute to work: 93.3% car, 0.3% public transportation, 1.1% walk, 2.6% work from home (2005-2009 5-year est.); Travel time to work: 67.3% less than 15 minutes, 21.0% 15 to 30 minutes, 7.5% 30 to 45 minutes, 2.6% 45 to 60 minutes, 1.7% 60 minutes or more (2005-2009 5-year est.); Amtrak: train service available.
Additional Information Contacts
City of Effingham . . . . (217) 342-5301
    http://www.effinghamil.com
The Greater Effingham Chamber of Commerce . . . . (217) 342-4147
    http://www.effinghamchamber.org

MASON (town). Covers a land area of 1.137 square miles and a water area of 0.005 square miles. Located at 38.95° N. Lat; 88.62° W. Long. Elevation is 581 feet.
Population: 387 (1990); 396 (2000); 391 (2010); 384 (2015 projected); Race: 99.0% White, 0.0% Black, 0.3% Asian, 0.8% Other, 1.8% Hispanic of any race (2010); Density: 343.9 persons per square mile (2010); Average household size: 2.59 (2010); Median age: 36.9 (2010); Males per 100 females: 103.6 (2010); Marriage status: 17.9% never married, 59.6% now married, 8.5% widowed, 14.1% divorced (2005-2009 5-year est.); Foreign born: 0.0% (2005-2009 5-year est.); Ancestry (includes multiple ancestries): 23.0% German, 12.0% American, 8.8% English, 3.9% Irish, 2.3% Dutch (2005-2009 5-year est.).
Economy: Employment by occupation: 0.0% management, 2.1% professional, 19.9% services, 18.8% sales, 2.1% farming, 12.0% construction, 45.0% production (2005-2009 5-year est.).
Income: Per capita income: $18,346 (2010); Median household income: $41,477 (2010); Average household income: $46,606 (2010); Percent of households with income of $100,000 or more: 4.6% (2010); Poverty rate: 27.2% (2005-2009 5-year est.).
Taxes: Total city taxes per capita: $60 (2007); City property taxes per capita: $60 (2007).
Education: Percent of population age 25 and over with: High school diploma (including GED) or higher: 81.7% (2010); Bachelor's degree or higher: 7.8% (2010); Master's degree or higher: 2.7% (2010).
Housing: Homeownership rate: 85.4% (2010); Median home value: $56,818 (2010); Median contract rent: $379 per month (2005-2009 5-year est.); Median year structure built: 1968 (2005-2009 5-year est.).
Transportation: Commute to work: 84.7% car, 0.0% public transportation, 0.0% walk, 12.6% work from home (2005-2009 5-year est.); Travel time to work: 14.4% less than 15 minutes, 61.9% 15 to 30 minutes, 15.0% 30 to 45 minutes, 3.1% 45 to 60 minutes, 5.6% 60 minutes or more (2005-2009 5-year est.)

MONTROSE (village). Covers a land area of 0.710 square miles and a water area of 0 square miles. Located at 39.16° N. Lat; 88.37° W. Long. Elevation is 600 feet.
Population: 306 (1990); 257 (2000); 242 (2010); 234 (2015 projected); Race: 99.6% White, 0.0% Black, 0.0% Asian, 0.4% Other, 0.0% Hispanic of any race (2010); Density: 340.8 persons per square mile (2010); Average household size: 2.92 (2010); Median age: 33.4 (2010); Males per 100 females: 105.1 (2010); Marriage status: 29.4% never married, 41.2% now married, 17.1% widowed, 12.4% divorced (2005-2009 5-year est.); Foreign born: 0.0% (2005-2009 5-year est.); Ancestry (includes multiple ancestries): 28.9% German, 18.1% English, 10.3% Irish, 10.3% American, 9.3% Scotch-Irish (2005-2009 5-year est.).
Economy: Employment by occupation: 1.9% management, 10.7% professional, 20.4% services, 23.3% sales, 0.0% farming, 19.4% construction, 24.3% production (2005-2009 5-year est.).
Income: Per capita income: $18,730 (2010); Median household income: $48,269 (2010); Average household income: $54,006 (2010); Percent of households with income of $100,000 or more: 9.6% (2010); Poverty rate: 24.0% (2005-2009 5-year est.).
Taxes: Total city taxes per capita: $115 (2007); City property taxes per capita: $108 (2007).
Education: Percent of population age 25 and over with: High school diploma (including GED) or higher: 88.5% (2010); Bachelor's degree or higher: 16.9% (2010); Master's degree or higher: 4.1% (2010).
School District(s)
Jasper County CUD 1 (PK-12)
    2009-10 Enrollment: 1,428 . . . . (618) 783-8459

Housing: Homeownership rate: 84.3% (2010); Median home value: $97,778 (2010); Median contract rent: $388 per month (2005-2009 5-year est.); Median year structure built: 1961 (2005-2009 5-year est.).
Transportation: Commute to work: 98.0% car, 0.0% public transportation, 0.0% walk, 2.0% work from home (2005-2009 5-year est.); Travel time to work: 23.5% less than 15 minutes, 57.1% 15 to 30 minutes, 12.2% 30 to 45 minutes, 0.0% 45 to 60 minutes, 7.1% 60 minutes or more (2005-2009 5-year est.)

SHUMWAY (village). Covers a land area of 0.312 square miles and a water area of 0 square miles. Located at 39.18° N. Lat; 88.65° W. Long. Elevation is 656 feet.
Population: 243 (1990); 217 (2000); 218 (2010); 216 (2015 projected); Race: 97.2% White, 0.5% Black, 0.0% Asian, 2.3% Other, 0.5% Hispanic of any race (2010); Density: 699.3 persons per square mile (2010); Average household size: 2.73 (2010); Median age: 36.8 (2010); Males per 100 females: 101.9 (2010); Marriage status: 20.1% never married, 64.0% now married, 6.5% widowed, 9.4% divorced (2005-2009 5-year est.); Foreign born: 0.0% (2005-2009 5-year est.); Ancestry (includes multiple ancestries): 40.1% German, 9.9% American, 6.2% English, 5.6% Irish, 3.1% French (2005-2009 5-year est.).
Economy: Employment by occupation: 10.2% management, 17.0% professional, 17.0% services, 30.7% sales, 0.0% farming, 5.7% construction, 19.3% production (2005-2009 5-year est.).
Income: Per capita income: $20,954 (2010); Median household income: $44,167 (2010); Average household income: $59,938 (2010); Percent of households with income of $100,000 or more: 11.3% (2010); Poverty rate: 19.1% (2005-2009 5-year est.).
Taxes: Total city taxes per capita: $41 (2007); City property taxes per capita: $32 (2007).
Education: Percent of population age 25 and over with: High school diploma (including GED) or higher: 89.9% (2010); Bachelor's degree or higher: 21.7% (2010); Master's degree or higher: 9.4% (2010).
School District(s)
Beecher City CUSD 20 (PK-12)
    2009-10 Enrollment: 422 . . . . (618) 487-5100
Housing: Homeownership rate: 88.8% (2010); Median home value: $116,071 (2010); Median contract rent: $300 per month (2005-2009 5-year est.); Median year structure built: 1948 (2005-2009 5-year est.).
Transportation: Commute to work: 100.0% car, 0.0% public transportation, 0.0% walk, 0.0% work from home (2005-2009 5-year est.); Travel time to work: 19.3% less than 15 minutes, 50.0% 15 to 30 minutes, 18.2% 30 to 45 minutes, 2.3% 45 to 60 minutes, 10.2% 60 minutes or more (2005-2009 5-year est.)

TEUTOPOLIS (village). Covers a land area of 1.580 square miles and a water area of 0 square miles. Located at 39.13° N. Lat; 88.47° W. Long. Elevation is 607 feet.
History: Teutopolis was established in 1839 by a group of German Catholics from Cincinnati, Ohio.
Population: 1,468 (1990); 1,559 (2000); 1,561 (2010); 1,554 (2015 projected); Race: 99.8% White, 0.0% Black, 0.1% Asian, 0.1% Other, 0.2% Hispanic of any race (2010); Density: 988.1 persons per square mile (2010); Average household size: 2.82 (2010); Median age: 35.0 (2010); Males per 100 females: 103.8 (2010); Marriage status: 26.6% never married, 59.9% now married, 8.8% widowed, 4.7% divorced (2005-2009 5-year est.); Foreign born: 0.4% (2005-2009 5-year est.); Ancestry (includes multiple ancestries): 60.6% German, 10.9% American, 5.3% Irish, 3.5% English, 2.7% Italian (2005-2009 5-year est.).
Economy: Single-family building permits issued: 5 (2010); Multi-family building permits issued: 0 (2010); Employment by occupation: 17.5% management, 21.0% professional, 15.5% services, 21.8% sales, 0.0% farming, 8.9% construction, 15.3% production (2005-2009 5-year est.).
Income: Per capita income: $27,749 (2010); Median household income: $57,903 (2010); Average household income: $77,246 (2010); Percent of households with income of $100,000 or more: 17.8% (2010); Poverty rate: 5.5% (2005-2009 5-year est.).
Taxes: Total city taxes per capita: $207 (2007); City property taxes per capita: $133 (2007).
Education: Percent of population age 25 and over with: High school diploma (including GED) or higher: 91.6% (2010); Bachelor's degree or higher: 27.6% (2010); Master's degree or higher: 6.4% (2010).
School District(s)
Teutopolis CUSD 50 (PK-12)
    2009-10 Enrollment: 1,205 . . . . (217) 857-3535

Housing: Homeownership rate: 80.8% (2010); Median home value: $125,000 (2010); Median contract rent: $453 per month (2005-2009 5-year est.); Median year structure built: 1965 (2005-2009 5-year est.).
Newspapers: Teutopolis Press-Dieterich Special Gazette (Local news; Circulation 1,000)
Transportation: Commute to work: 94.5% car, 0.0% public transportation, 0.4% walk, 1.6% work from home (2005-2009 5-year est.); Travel time to work: 60.0% less than 15 minutes, 24.6% 15 to 30 minutes, 10.3% 30 to 45 minutes, 1.3% 45 to 60 minutes, 3.7% 60 minutes or more (2005-2009 5-year est.)

WATSON (village).
Covers a land area of 0.977 square miles and a water area of 0 square miles. Located at 39.02° N. Lat; 88.56° W. Long. Elevation is 561 feet.
Population: 712 (1990); 729 (2000); 708 (2010); 694 (2015 projected); Race: 98.3% White, 0.0% Black, 0.3% Asian, 1.4% Other, 0.7% Hispanic of any race (2010); Density: 724.5 persons per square mile (2010); Average household size: 2.74 (2010); Median age: 36.6 (2010); Males per 100 females: 102.3 (2010); Marriage status: 22.6% never married, 59.7% now married, 3.1% widowed, 14.5% divorced (2005-2009 5-year est.); Foreign born: 1.6% (2005-2009 5-year est.); Ancestry (includes multiple ancestries): 32.5% German, 13.2% English, 12.2% Irish, 9.3% American, 4.1% Dutch (2005-2009 5-year est.).
Economy: Employment by occupation: 4.7% management, 7.6% professional, 17.5% services, 31.8% sales, 0.0% farming, 9.0% construction, 29.4% production (2005-2009 5-year est.).
Income: Per capita income: $21,655 (2010); Median household income: $51,948 (2010); Average household income: $58,169 (2010); Percent of households with income of $100,000 or more: 8.5% (2010); Poverty rate: 8.6% (2005-2009 5-year est.).
Taxes: Total city taxes per capita: $53 (2007); City property taxes per capita: $51 (2007).
Education: Percent of population age 25 and over with: High school diploma (including GED) or higher: 84.4% (2010); Bachelor's degree or higher: 10.3% (2010); Master's degree or higher: 0.0% (2010).
Housing: Homeownership rate: 88.8% (2010); Median home value: $92,927 (2010); Median contract rent: $350 per month (2005-2009 5-year est.); Median year structure built: 1977 (2005-2009 5-year est.).
Transportation: Commute to work: 97.3% car, 0.0% public transportation, 0.0% walk, 2.7% work from home (2005-2009 5-year est.); Travel time to work: 25.6% less than 15 minutes, 60.6% 15 to 30 minutes, 6.1% 30 to 45 minutes, 3.0% 45 to 60 minutes, 4.7% 60 minutes or more (2005-2009 5-year est.)

Fayette County

Located in south central Illinois; drained by the Kaskaskia River. Covers a land area of 716.49 square miles, a water area of 8.87 square miles, and is located in the Central Time Zone at 39.00° N. Lat., 88.99° W. Long. The county was founded in 1821. County seat is Vandalia.

Weather Station: Vandalia											Elevation: 540 feet	
	Jan	Feb	Mar	Apr	May	Jun	Jul	Aug	Sep	Oct	Nov	Dec
High	37	42	52	65	75	84	87	87	80	67	54	41
Low	21	24	33	43	53	63	66	64	55	43	34	24
Precip	2.8	2.6	3.4	3.9	5.1	4.0	3.5	2.8	3.2	3.4	3.6	3.0
Snow	5.1	3.0	1.5	tr	0.0	0.0	0.0	0.0	0.0	tr	0.7	3.2

High and Low temperatures in degrees Fahrenheit; Precipitation and Snow in inches

Population: 20,893 (1990); 21,802 (2000); 20,922 (2010); 20,450 (2015 projected); Race: 94.8% White, 3.7% Black, 0.3% Asian, 1.2% Other, 1.1% Hispanic of any race (2010); Density: 29.2 persons per square mile (2010); Average household size: 2.42 (2010); Median age: 38.5 (2010); Males per 100 females: 101.3 (2010).
Religion: Five largest groups: 19.5% Southern Baptist Convention, 7.9% Lutheran Church—Missouri Synod, 7.6% The United Methodist Church, 4.9% Christian Churches and Churches of Christ, 3.9% Catholic Church (2000).
Economy: Unemployment rate: 9.8% (August 2011); Total civilian labor force: 10,561 (August 2011); Leading industries: 20.5% health care and social assistance; 19.0% retail trade; 13.9% manufacturing (2009); Farms: 1,132 totaling 303,258 acres (2007); Companies that employ 500 or more persons: 0 (2009); Companies that employ 100 to 499 persons: 5 (2009); Companies that employ less than 100 persons: 483 (2009); Black-owned businesses: n/a (2007); Hispanic-owned businesses: n/a (2007); Asian-owned businesses: n/a (2007); Women-owned businesses: n/a

(2007); Retail sales per capita: $12,501 (2010). Single-family building permits issued: 4 (2010); Multi-family building permits issued: 0 (2010).
Income: Per capita income: $19,224 (2010); Median household income: $39,061 (2010); Average household income: $47,483 (2010); Percent of households with income of $100,000 or more: 7.2% (2010); Poverty rate: 20.2% (2009); Bankruptcy rate: 2.79% (2010).
Taxes: Total county taxes per capita: $103 (2007); County property taxes per capita: $64 (2007).
Education: Percent of population age 25 and over with: High school diploma (including GED) or higher: 79.9% (2010); Bachelor's degree or higher: 12.8% (2010); Master's degree or higher: 4.7% (2010).
Housing: Homeownership rate: 78.6% (2010); Median home value: $68,805 (2010); Median contract rent: $349 per month (2005-2009 5-year est.); Median year structure built: 1962 (2005-2009 5-year est.).
Health: Birth rate: 120.4 per 10,000 population (2009); Death rate: 108.0 per 10,000 population (2009); Age-adjusted cancer mortality rate: 190.5 deaths per 100,000 population (2007); Number of physicians: 3.8 per 10,000 population (2008); Hospital beds: 52.5 per 10,000 population (2007); Hospital admissions: 922.3 per 10,000 population (2007).
Elections: 2008 Presidential election results: 41.0% Obama, 56.8% McCain, 1.0% Nader
National and State Parks: Carlyle Lake State Wildlife Management Area; Ramsey Lake State Park; Vandalia State House Historic Site
Additional Information Contacts
Fayette County Government . . . . (618) 283-5000
   http://209.175.254.253
Vandalia Chamber of Commerce. . . . . (618) 283-2728
   http://vandaliachamber.org

Fayette County Communities

BINGHAM (village).
Covers a land area of 0.272 square miles and a water area of 0 square miles. Located at 39.11° N. Lat; 89.21° W. Long. Elevation is 600 feet.
Population: 98 (1990); 117 (2000); 109 (2010); 105 (2015 projected); Race: 98.2% White, 0.0% Black, 0.9% Asian, 0.0% Other, 0.0% Hispanic of any race (2010); Density: 400.2 persons per square mile (2010); Average household size: 2.53 (2010); Median age: 36.4 (2010); Males per 100 females: 94.6 (2010); Marriage status: 6.3% never married, 68.8% now married, 2.5% widowed, 22.5% divorced (2005-2009 5-year est.); Foreign born: 0.0% (2005-2009 5-year est.); Ancestry (includes multiple ancestries): 24.3% German, 6.8% Dutch (2005-2009 5-year est.).
Economy: Employment by occupation: 0.0% management, 0.0% professional, 5.7% services, 11.4% sales, 0.0% farming, 31.4% construction, 51.4% production (2005-2009 5-year est.).
Income: Per capita income: $18,673 (2010); Median household income: $40,833 (2010); Average household income: $45,581 (2010); Percent of households with income of $100,000 or more: 4.7% (2010); Poverty rate: 50.5% (2005-2009 5-year est.).
Taxes: Total city taxes per capita: $34 (2007); City property taxes per capita: $34 (2007).
Education: Percent of population age 25 and over with: High school diploma (including GED) or higher: 84.3% (2010); Bachelor's degree or higher: 21.4% (2010); Master's degree or higher: 8.6% (2010).
Housing: Homeownership rate: 81.4% (2010); Median home value: $96,667 (2010); Median contract rent: n/a per month (2005-2009 5-year est.); Median year structure built: 1955 (2005-2009 5-year est.).
Transportation: Commute to work: 62.9% car, 0.0% public transportation, 0.0% walk, 8.6% work from home (2005-2009 5-year est.); Travel time to work: 31.3% less than 15 minutes, 15.6% 15 to 30 minutes, 15.6% 30 to 45 minutes, 37.5% 45 to 60 minutes, 0.0% 60 minutes or more (2005-2009 5-year est.)

BROWNSTOWN (village).
Covers a land area of 0.628 square miles and a water area of 0 square miles. Located at 38.99° N. Lat; 88.95° W. Long. Elevation is 594 feet.
Population: 733 (1990); 705 (2000); 715 (2010); 710 (2015 projected); Race: 97.9% White, 0.4% Black, 0.0% Asian, 1.7% Other, 0.7% Hispanic of any race (2010); Density: 1,139.0 persons per square mile (2010); Average household size: 2.35 (2010); Median age: 37.9 (2010); Males per 100 females: 77.0 (2010); Marriage status: 24.0% never married, 48.7% now married, 9.0% widowed, 18.4% divorced (2005-2009 5-year est.); Foreign born: 0.0% (2005-2009 5-year est.); Ancestry (includes multiple ancestries): 16.1% German, 13.5% English, 11.7% Irish, 10.9% American, 4.9% Italian (2005-2009 5-year est.).

Economy: Employment by occupation: 2.0% management, 23.6% professional, 18.4% services, 21.3% sales, 0.0% farming, 11.5% construction, 23.3% production (2005-2009 5-year est.).
Income: Per capita income: $19,317 (2010); Median household income: $34,375 (2010); Average household income: $46,337 (2010); Percent of households with income of $100,000 or more: 6.6% (2010); Poverty rate: 29.3% (2005-2009 5-year est.).
Taxes: Total city taxes per capita: $141 (2007); City property taxes per capita: $68 (2007).
Education: Percent of population age 25 and over with: High school diploma (including GED) or higher: 90.4% (2010); Bachelor's degree or higher: 15.1% (2010); Master's degree or higher: 7.3% (2010).

School District(s)
Brownstown CUSD 201 (PK-12)
   2009-10 Enrollment: 413 . . . . (618) 427-3355
Housing: Homeownership rate: 79.5% (2010); Median home value: $57,042 (2010); Median contract rent: $344 per month (2005-2009 5-year est.); Median year structure built: 1962 (2005-2009 5-year est.).
Transportation: Commute to work: 94.2% car, 0.0% public transportation, 1.6% walk, 2.9% work from home (2005-2009 5-year est.); Travel time to work: 32.7% less than 15 minutes, 40.3% 15 to 30 minutes, 10.7% 30 to 45 minutes, 2.7% 45 to 60 minutes, 13.7% 60 minutes or more (2005-2009 5-year est.)

FARINA (village).
Covers a land area of 1.440 square miles and a water area of 0.007 square miles. Located at 38.83° N. Lat; 88.77° W. Long. Elevation is 581 feet.
Population: 575 (1990); 558 (2000); 564 (2010); 561 (2015 projected); Race: 98.8% White, 0.0% Black, 0.0% Asian, 1.2% Other, 0.0% Hispanic of any race (2010); Density: 391.8 persons per square mile (2010); Average household size: 2.33 (2010); Median age: 44.9 (2010); Males per 100 females: 84.3 (2010); Marriage status: 15.3% never married, 64.0% now married, 10.1% widowed, 10.6% divorced (2005-2009 5-year est.); Foreign born: 0.4% (2005-2009 5-year est.); Ancestry (includes multiple ancestries): 21.8% German, 17.0% Irish, 12.0% American, 7.4% English, 5.9% Italian (2005-2009 5-year est.).
Economy: Employment by occupation: 2.7% management, 3.7% professional, 15.1% services, 25.6% sales, 0.9% farming, 12.3% construction, 39.7% production (2005-2009 5-year est.).
Income: Per capita income: $21,121 (2010); Median household income: $40,667 (2010); Average household income: $49,286 (2010); Percent of households with income of $100,000 or more: 10.1% (2010); Poverty rate: 15.3% (2005-2009 5-year est.).
Taxes: Total city taxes per capita: $130 (2007); City property taxes per capita: $130 (2007).
Education: Percent of population age 25 and over with: High school diploma (including GED) or higher: 84.4% (2010); Bachelor's degree or higher: 14.0% (2010); Master's degree or higher: 6.5% (2010).

School District(s)
South Central CUD 401 (PK-12)
   2009-10 Enrollment: 693 . . . . (618) 547-3414
Housing: Homeownership rate: 87.0% (2010); Median home value: $48,974 (2010); Median contract rent: $134 per month (2005-2009 5-year est.); Median year structure built: 1952 (2005-2009 5-year est.).
Newspapers: Farina News (Community news; Circulation 1,250)
Transportation: Commute to work: 96.3% car, 0.0% public transportation, 0.0% walk, 2.3% work from home (2005-2009 5-year est.); Travel time to work: 27.1% less than 15 minutes, 32.2% 15 to 30 minutes, 31.3% 30 to 45 minutes, 4.2% 45 to 60 minutes, 5.1% 60 minutes or more (2005-2009 5-year est.)

RAMSEY (village).
Covers a land area of 1.007 square miles and a water area of 0 square miles. Located at 39.14° N. Lat; 89.11° W. Long. Elevation is 610 feet.
Population: 963 (1990); 1,056 (2000); 1,041 (2010); 1,027 (2015 projected); Race: 98.7% White, 0.2% Black, 0.1% Asian, 1.1% Other, 0.6% Hispanic of any race (2010); Density: 1,033.8 persons per square mile (2010); Average household size: 2.47 (2010); Median age: 35.8 (2010); Males per 100 females: 95.7 (2010); Marriage status: 25.8% never married, 53.6% now married, 10.5% widowed, 10.1% divorced (2005-2009 5-year est.); Foreign born: 0.3% (2005-2009 5-year est.); Ancestry (includes multiple ancestries): 19.5% German, 13.9% Irish, 11.6% American, 7.6% English, 1.6% Swedish (2005-2009 5-year est.).

Economy: Employment by occupation: 3.7% management, 15.2% professional, 14.6% services, 17.8% sales, 8.0% farming, 11.4% construction, 29.3% production (2005-2009 5-year est.).
Income: Per capita income: $17,814 (2010); Median household income: $38,864 (2010); Average household income: $43,605 (2010); Percent of households with income of $100,000 or more: 5.0% (2010); Poverty rate: 22.5% (2005-2009 5-year est.).
Taxes: Total city taxes per capita: $59 (2007); City property taxes per capita: $56 (2007).
Education: Percent of population age 25 and over with: High school diploma (including GED) or higher: 80.3% (2010); Bachelor's degree or higher: 11.9% (2010); Master's degree or higher: 5.0% (2010).

School District(s)
Ramsey CUSD 204 (PK-12)
   2009-10 Enrollment: 522 . . . . (618) 423-2335
Housing: Homeownership rate: 78.6% (2010); Median home value: $55,714 (2010); Median contract rent: $265 per month (2005-2009 5-year est.); Median year structure built: 1960 (2005-2009 5-year est.).
Newspapers: Ramsey News-Journal (National news; Circulation 2,000)
Transportation: Commute to work: 96.2% car, 0.0% public transportation, 1.6% walk, 1.6% work from home (2005-2009 5-year est.); Travel time to work: 24.0% less than 15 minutes, 41.0% 15 to 30 minutes, 15.6% 30 to 45 minutes, 11.2% 45 to 60 minutes, 8.2% 60 minutes or more (2005-2009 5-year est.)

SAINT ELMO (city).
Covers a land area of 0.957 square miles and a water area of 0.024 square miles. Located at 39.02° N. Lat; 88.85° W. Long. Elevation is 620 feet.
History: St. Elmo was settled in 1830 by a group of Kentucky Catholics, and developed as a railroad and brick manufacturing town. Later, oil was discovered and the economy boomed.
Population: 1,494 (1990); 1,456 (2000); 1,449 (2010); 1,436 (2015 projected); Race: 98.8% White, 0.0% Black, 0.0% Asian, 1.2% Other, 0.1% Hispanic of any race (2010); Density: 1,514.3 persons per square mile (2010); Average household size: 2.47 (2010); Median age: 37.4 (2010); Males per 100 females: 88.9 (2010); Marriage status: 25.9% never married, 54.1% now married, 10.5% widowed, 9.5% divorced (2005-2009 5-year est.); Foreign born: 1.5% (2005-2009 5-year est.); Ancestry (includes multiple ancestries): 21.1% German, 13.3% American, 10.5% Irish, 5.0% English, 2.9% British (2005-2009 5-year est.).
Economy: Single-family building permits issued: 1 (2010); Multi-family building permits issued: 0 (2010); Employment by occupation: 6.5% management, 6.7% professional, 27.3% services, 16.0% sales, 0.6% farming, 15.4% construction, 27.5% production (2005-2009 5-year est.).
Income: Per capita income: $18,308 (2010); Median household income: $39,486 (2010); Average household income: $46,007 (2010); Percent of households with income of $100,000 or more: 4.9% (2010); Poverty rate: 22.5% (2005-2009 5-year est.).
Taxes: Total city taxes per capita: $99 (2007); City property taxes per capita: $49 (2007).
Education: Percent of population age 25 and over with: High school diploma (including GED) or higher: 84.2% (2010); Bachelor's degree or higher: 12.3% (2010); Master's degree or higher: 4.9% (2010).

School District(s)
St Elmo CUSD 202 (PK-12)
   2009-10 Enrollment: 515 . . . . (618) 829-3264
Housing: Homeownership rate: 80.0% (2010); Median home value: $53,853 (2010); Median contract rent: $354 per month (2005-2009 5-year est.); Median year structure built: 1962 (2005-2009 5-year est.).
Newspapers: Saint Elmo Banner (Local news; Circulation 900)
Transportation: Commute to work: 95.7% car, 0.0% public transportation, 2.6% walk, 1.6% work from home (2005-2009 5-year est.); Travel time to work: 32.6% less than 15 minutes, 32.2% 15 to 30 minutes, 24.3% 30 to 45 minutes, 7.0% 45 to 60 minutes, 3.9% 60 minutes or more (2005-2009 5-year est.)

SAINT PETER (village).
Covers a land area of 0.535 square miles and a water area of 0 square miles. Located at 38.86° N. Lat; 88.85° W. Long. Elevation is 597 feet.
Population: 353 (1990); 386 (2000); 382 (2010); 376 (2015 projected); Race: 98.7% White, 0.0% Black, 0.5% Asian, 0.8% Other, 0.3% Hispanic of any race (2010); Density: 713.9 persons per square mile (2010); Average household size: 2.37 (2010); Median age: 42.3 (2010); Males per 100 females: 100.0 (2010); Marriage status: 15.5% never married, 68.2% now married, 9.1% widowed, 7.2% divorced (2005-2009 5-year est.);

Foreign born: 0.0% (2005-2009 5-year est.); Ancestry (includes multiple ancestries): 36.4% German, 15.9% American, 7.1% English, 1.9% Irish, 1.6% Swedish (2005-2009 5-year est.).

Economy: Employment by occupation: 17.6% management, 4.2% professional, 13.9% services, 27.9% sales, 1.2% farming, 15.2% construction, 20.0% production (2005-2009 5-year est.).

Income: Per capita income: $18,323 (2010); Median household income: $35,776 (2010); Average household income: $43,649 (2010); Percent of households with income of $100,000 or more: 8.1% (2010); Poverty rate: 7.1% (2005-2009 5-year est.).

Taxes: Total city taxes per capita: $88 (2007); City property taxes per capita: $70 (2007).

Education: Percent of population age 25 and over with: High school diploma (including GED) or higher: 83.3% (2010); Bachelor's degree or higher: 11.3% (2010); Master's degree or higher: 1.1% (2010).

Housing: Homeownership rate: 87.0% (2010); Median home value: $61,176 (2010); Median contract rent: n/a per month (2005-2009 5-year est.); Median year structure built: 1952 (2005-2009 5-year est.).

Transportation: Commute to work: 92.7% car, 0.0% public transportation, 2.4% walk, 2.4% work from home (2005-2009 5-year est.); Travel time to work: 49.1% less than 15 minutes, 25.5% 15 to 30 minutes, 21.1% 30 to 45 minutes, 4.3% 45 to 60 minutes, 0.0% 60 minutes or more (2005-2009 5-year est.)

SHOBONIER (unincorporated postal area, zip code 62885). Covers a land area of 56.052 square miles and a water area of 0.065 square miles. Located at 38.86° N. Lat; 89.05° W. Long. Elevation is 515 feet.

Population: 837 (2000); Race: 100.0% White, 0.0% Black, 0.0% Asian, 0.0% Other, 3.8% Hispanic of any race (2000); Density: 14.9 persons per square mile (2000); Age: 27.5% under 18, 14.8% over 64 (2000); Marriage status: 19.5% never married, 62.4% now married, 8.5% widowed, 9.5% divorced (2000); Foreign born: 0.0% (2000); Ancestry (includes multiple ancestries): 31.1% German, 12.7% American, 5.5% English, 5.3% Scotch-Irish (2000).

Economy: Employment by occupation: 17.4% management, 7.1% professional, 24.0% services, 15.5% sales, 2.5% farming, 10.6% construction, 22.9% production (2000).

Income: Per capita income: $14,896 (2000); Median household income: $32,188 (2000); Poverty rate: 16.7% (2000).

Education: Percent of population age 25 and over with: High school diploma (including GED) or higher: 65.7% (2000); Bachelor's degree or higher: 1.6% (2000).

Housing: Homeownership rate: 80.1% (2000); Median home value: $60,600 (2000); Median contract rent: $225 per month (2000); Median year structure built: 1957 (2000).

Transportation: Commute to work: 89.4% car, 0.0% public transportation, 3.0% walk, 7.6% work from home (2000); Travel time to work: 32.4% less than 15 minutes, 39.5% 15 to 30 minutes, 18.3% 30 to 45 minutes, 3.8% 45 to 60 minutes, 5.9% 60 minutes or more (2000)

VANDALIA (city). County seat. Covers a land area of 5.665 square miles and a water area of 0.016 square miles. Located at 38.96° N. Lat; 89.10° W. Long. Elevation is 518 feet.

History: Vandalia was laid out in 1819 at the direction of the Illinois State Legislature, and served until 1839 as the capital. Three capitol buildings were erected in Vandalia during its 20 years as the state capital.

Population: 6,335 (1990); 6,975 (2000); 6,421 (2010); 6,291 (2015 projected); Race: 86.2% White, 11.7% Black, 0.6% Asian, 1.5% Other, 2.4% Hispanic of any race (2010); Density: 1,133.5 persons per square mile (2010); Average household size: 2.26 (2010); Median age: 36.6 (2010); Males per 100 females: 119.2 (2010); Marriage status: 36.8% never married, 42.0% now married, 6.4% widowed, 14.8% divorced (2005-2009 5-year est.); Foreign born: 2.6% (2005-2009 5-year est.); Ancestry (includes multiple ancestries): 25.0% German, 9.5% English, 8.8% American, 7.6% Irish, 3.4% Scottish (2005-2009 5-year est.).

Economy: Single-family building permits issued: 3 (2010); Multi-family building permits issued: 0 (2010); Employment by occupation: 9.9% management, 15.0% professional, 22.0% services, 18.5% sales, 0.3% farming, 10.8% construction, 23.5% production (2005-2009 5-year est.).

Income: Per capita income: $17,989 (2010); Median household income: $38,049 (2010); Average household income: $43,328 (2010); Percent of households with income of $100,000 or more: 5.7% (2010); Poverty rate: 20.5% (2005-2009 5-year est.).

Taxes: Total city taxes per capita: $193 (2007); City property taxes per capita: $111 (2007).

Education: Percent of population age 25 and over with: High school diploma (including GED) or higher: 72.1% (2010); Bachelor's degree or higher: 14.7% (2010); Master's degree or higher: 4.6% (2010).

School District(s)

Bond/Effingham/Fayette Roe (06-12)
    2009-10 Enrollment: n/a . . . . (618) 283-5011
Okaw Area Vocational Center (10-12)
    2009-10 Enrollment: n/a . . . . (618) 283-5150
Vandalia CUSD 203 (PK-12)
    2009-10 Enrollment: 1,713 . . . . (618) 283-4525

Housing: Homeownership rate: 67.3% (2010); Median home value: $70,428 (2010); Median contract rent: $407 per month (2005-2009 5-year est.); Median year structure built: 1953 (2005-2009 5-year est.).

Hospitals: Fayette County Hospital (160 beds)

Newspapers: Vandalia Leader Union (Local news; Circulation 6,100)

Transportation: Commute to work: 88.4% car, 5.7% public transportation, 1.8% walk, 2.8% work from home (2005-2009 5-year est.); Travel time to work: 70.6% less than 15 minutes, 10.9% 15 to 30 minutes, 7.3% 30 to 45 minutes, 1.3% 45 to 60 minutes, 9.9% 60 minutes or more (2005-2009 5-year est.)

Additional Information Contacts

Vandalia Chamber of Commerce. . . . . (618) 283-2728
    http://vandaliachamber.org

Ford County

Located in east central Illinois; drained by the Mackinaw River. Covers a land area of 485.90 square miles, a water area of 0.52 square miles, and is located in the Central Time Zone at 40.55° N. Lat., 88.22° W. Long. The county was founded in 1859. County seat is Paxton.

Ford County is part of the Champaign-Urbana, IL Metropolitan Statistical Area. The entire metro area includes: Champaign County, IL; Ford County, IL; Piatt County, IL

Weather Station: Gibson City 1 E									Elevation: 750 feet		
	Jan	Feb	Mar	Apr	May	Jun	Jul	Aug	Sep	Oct	Nov	Dec
High	32	36	48	61	73	82	85	83	78	64	50	36
Low	16	19	29	39	50	60	63	61	52	40	31	20
Precip	1.6	1.7	2.6	3.4	4.2	3.9	3.8	3.9	2.7	3.0	3.3	2.4
Snow	5.6	6.0	1.7	0.8	0.0	0.0	0.0	0.0	0.0	0.1	1.1	5.2

High and Low temperatures in degrees Fahrenheit; Precipitation and Snow in inches

Weather Station: Piper City									Elevation: 669 feet		
	Jan	Feb	Mar	Apr	May	Jun	Jul	Aug	Sep	Oct	Nov	Dec
High	33	38	49	63	74	83	86	84	78	65	51	37
Low	16	19	28	38	49	59	63	60	52	41	31	20
Precip	2.5	2.2	2.9	3.6	4.4	3.8	4.7	3.9	2.6	3.3	3.4	2.9
Snow	8.2	6.9	3.2	1.0	tr	0.0	0.0	0.0	0.0	0.2	1.4	6.6

High and Low temperatures in degrees Fahrenheit; Precipitation and Snow in inches

Population: 14,275 (1990); 14,241 (2000); 14,032 (2010); 13,854 (2015 projected); Race: 96.5% White, 0.8% Black, 0.7% Asian, 2.0% Other, 2.3% Hispanic of any race (2010); Density: 28.9 persons per square mile (2010); Average household size: 2.44 (2010); Median age: 40.3 (2010); Males per 100 females: 93.6 (2010).

Religion: Five largest groups: 18.0% The United Methodist Church, 12.8% Evangelical Lutheran Church in America, 11.1% Catholic Church, 3.9% New Testament Association of Independent Baptist Churches and other Fundamental Baptist Associations, 3.6% S

Economy: Unemployment rate: 8.5% (August 2011); Total civilian labor force: 6,512 (August 2011); Leading industries: 24.5% health care and social assistance; 20.2% manufacturing; 12.4% retail trade (2009); Farms: 524 totaling 270,720 acres (2007); Companies that employ 500 or more persons: 0 (2009); Companies that employ 100 to 499 persons: 6 (2009); Companies that employ less than 100 persons: 383 (2009); Black-owned businesses: n/a (2007); Hispanic-owned businesses: n/a (2007); Asian-owned businesses: n/a (2007); Women-owned businesses: 468 (2007); Retail sales per capita: $12,642 (2010). Single-family building permits issued: 10 (2010); Multi-family building permits issued: 0 (2010).

Income: Per capita income: $23,185 (2010); Median household income: $47,149 (2010); Average household income: $56,571 (2010); Percent of households with income of $100,000 or more: 12.7% (2010); Poverty rate: 9.9% (2009); Bankruptcy rate: 4.13% (2010).

Taxes: Total county taxes per capita: $169 (2007); County property taxes per capita: $104 (2007).

Education: Percent of population age 25 and over with: High school diploma (including GED) or higher: 90.1% (2010); Bachelor's degree or higher: 16.4% (2010); Master's degree or higher: 5.0% (2010).
Housing: Homeownership rate: 75.0% (2010); Median home value: $99,722 (2010); Median contract rent: $390 per month (2005-2009 5-year est.); Median year structure built: 1951 (2005-2009 5-year est.)
Health: Birth rate: 131.6 per 10,000 population (2009); Death rate: 145.9 per 10,000 population (2009); Age-adjusted cancer mortality rate: 220.7 deaths per 100,000 population (2007); Number of physicians: 10.8 per 10,000 population (2008); Hospital beds: 47.7 per 10,000 population (2007); Hospital admissions: 665.9 per 10,000 population (2007).
Elections: 2008 Presidential election results: 34.9% Obama, 63.9% McCain, 0.5% Nader
Additional Information Contacts
Ford County Government . . . . (217) 379-9400
   http://www.fordcountycourthouse.com
Gibson Area Chamber of Commerce. . . . . (217) 784-5217
   http://www.gibsoncityillinois.com
Paxton Chamber of Commerce . . . . (217) 379-4655
   http://www.paxtonchamber.org

Ford County Communities

CABERY
(village). Covers a land area of 0.350 square miles and a water area of 0 square miles. Located at 40.99° N. Lat; 88.20° W. Long. Elevation is 699 feet.
Population: 268 (1990); 263 (2000); 265 (2010); 267 (2015 projected); Race: 96.2% White, 0.0% Black, 0.0% Asian, 3.8% Other, 3.8% Hispanic of any race (2010); Density: 756.8 persons per square mile (2010); Average household size: 2.76 (2010); Median age: 34.2 (2010); Males per 100 females: 102.3 (2010); Marriage status: 23.1% never married, 56.7% now married, 10.1% widowed, 10.1% divorced (2005-2009 5-year est.); Foreign born: 0.4% (2005-2009 5-year est.); Ancestry (includes multiple ancestries): 35.2% German, 15.7% Irish, 13.9% French, 12.6% American, 12.6% English (2005-2009 5-year est.).
Economy: Employment by occupation: 5.7% management, 11.4% professional, 10.5% services, 23.8% sales, 6.7% farming, 21.9% construction, 20.0% production (2005-2009 5-year est.).
Income: Per capita income: $25,544 (2010); Median household income: $56,579 (2010); Average household income: $68,307 (2010); Percent of households with income of $100,000 or more: 20.8% (2010); Poverty rate: 9.6% (2005-2009 5-year est.).
Taxes: Total city taxes per capita: $68 (2007); City property taxes per capita: $65 (2007).
Education: Percent of population age 25 and over with: High school diploma (including GED) or higher: 95.1% (2010); Bachelor's degree or higher: 21.6% (2010); Master's degree or higher: 8.6% (2010).
Housing: Homeownership rate: 79.2% (2010); Median home value: $123,214 (2010); Median contract rent: $379 per month (2005-2009 5-year est.); Median year structure built: 1944 (2005-2009 5-year est.).
Transportation: Commute to work: 86.1% car, 0.0% public transportation, 6.9% walk, 6.9% work from home (2005-2009 5-year est.); Travel time to work: 23.4% less than 15 minutes, 4.3% 15 to 30 minutes, 38.3% 30 to 45 minutes, 7.4% 45 to 60 minutes, 26.6% 60 minutes or more (2005-2009 5-year est.)

ELLIOTT
(village). Covers a land area of 0.484 square miles and a water area of 0 square miles. Located at 40.46° N. Lat; 88.27° W. Long. Elevation is 781 feet.
Population: 309 (1990); 341 (2000); 310 (2010); 295 (2015 projected); Race: 98.4% White, 0.0% Black, 0.0% Asian, 1.6% Other, 0.3% Hispanic of any race (2010); Density: 640.2 persons per square mile (2010); Average household size: 2.63 (2010); Median age: 37.2 (2010); Males per 100 females: 89.0 (2010); Marriage status: 9.0% never married, 82.0% now married, 4.5% widowed, 4.5% divorced (2005-2009 5-year est.); Foreign born: 0.7% (2005-2009 5-year est.); Ancestry (includes multiple ancestries): 36.1% German, 20.4% American, 14.7% Irish, 13.4% Swedish, 9.7% Italian (2005-2009 5-year est.).
Economy: Employment by occupation: 8.3% management, 13.6% professional, 10.6% services, 40.2% sales, 0.0% farming, 13.6% construction, 13.6% production (2005-2009 5-year est.).
Income: Per capita income: $22,606 (2010); Median household income: $46,591 (2010); Average household income: $59,788 (2010); Percent of households with income of $100,000 or more: 17.8% (2010); Poverty rate: 0.0% (2005-2009 5-year est.).

Taxes: Total city taxes per capita: $50 (2007); City property taxes per capita: $50 (2007).
Education: Percent of population age 25 and over with: High school diploma (including GED) or higher: 90.4% (2010); Bachelor's degree or higher: 19.6% (2010); Master's degree or higher: 5.3% (2010).
Housing: Homeownership rate: 80.5% (2010); Median home value: $121,552 (2010); Median contract rent: $544 per month (2005-2009 5-year est.); Median year structure built: 1948 (2005-2009 5-year est.).
Transportation: Commute to work: 91.7% car, 0.0% public transportation, 4.5% walk, 3.8% work from home (2005-2009 5-year est.); Travel time to work: 48.0% less than 15 minutes, 24.4% 15 to 30 minutes, 18.9% 30 to 45 minutes, 7.1% 45 to 60 minutes, 1.6% 60 minutes or more (2005-2009 5-year est.)

GIBSON CITY
(city). Aka Gibson. Covers a land area of 2.103 square miles and a water area of 0.021 square miles. Located at 40.46° N. Lat; 88.37° W. Long.
Population: 3,404 (1990); 3,373 (2000); 3,154 (2010); 3,061 (2015 projected); Race: 96.7% White, 1.3% Black, 1.0% Asian, 1.0% Other, 1.0% Hispanic of any race (2010); Density: 1,499.8 persons per square mile (2010); Average household size: 2.20 (2010); Median age: 43.4 (2010); Males per 100 females: 86.5 (2010); Marriage status: 18.3% never married, 59.4% now married, 8.8% widowed, 13.5% divorced (2005-2009 5-year est.); Foreign born: 1.3% (2005-2009 5-year est.); Ancestry (includes multiple ancestries): 37.1% German, 15.0% American, 14.6% Irish, 11.6% English, 5.6% Italian (2005-2009 5-year est.).
Economy: Employment by occupation: 8.6% management, 17.1% professional, 14.2% services, 33.7% sales, 0.6% farming, 15.8% construction, 10.1% production (2005-2009 5-year est.).
Income: Per capita income: $21,766 (2010); Median household income: $39,923 (2010); Average household income: $48,505 (2010); Percent of households with income of $100,000 or more: 8.8% (2010); Poverty rate: 5.3% (2005-2009 5-year est.).
Taxes: Total city taxes per capita: $270 (2007); City property taxes per capita: $186 (2007).
Education: Percent of population age 25 and over with: High school diploma (including GED) or higher: 86.0% (2010); Bachelor's degree or higher: 17.5% (2010); Master's degree or higher: 6.4% (2010).
School District(s)
Gibson City-Melvin-Sibley CUSD 5 (PK-12)
   2009-10 Enrollment: 1,061 . . . . (217) 784-8296
Housing: Homeownership rate: 67.1% (2010); Median home value: $101,456 (2010); Median contract rent: $386 per month (2005-2009 5-year est.); Median year structure built: 1948 (2005-2009 5-year est.).
Hospitals: Gibson Area Hospital & Health Services (82 beds)
Safety: Violent crime rate: 21.7 per 10,000 population; Property crime rate: 189.4 per 10,000 population (2010).
Newspapers: Gibson City Courier (Community news; Circulation 2,000); Target (Community news; Circulation 13,875)
Transportation: Commute to work: 94.2% car, 0.0% public transportation, 2.7% walk, 3.2% work from home (2005-2009 5-year est.); Travel time to work: 54.5% less than 15 minutes, 6.9% 15 to 30 minutes, 21.6% 30 to 45 minutes, 12.4% 45 to 60 minutes, 4.6% 60 minutes or more (2005-2009 5-year est.)
Additional Information Contacts
Gibson Area Chamber of Commerce. . . . . (217) 784-5217
   http://www.gibsoncityillinois.com

KEMPTON
(village). Covers a land area of 0.212 square miles and a water area of 0 square miles. Located at 40.93° N. Lat; 88.23° W. Long. Elevation is 735 feet.
Population: 219 (1990); 235 (2000); 231 (2010); 227 (2015 projected); Race: 96.5% White, 0.0% Black, 0.4% Asian, 3.0% Other, 5.2% Hispanic of any race (2010); Density: 1,092.2 persons per square mile (2010); Average household size: 2.72 (2010); Median age: 34.8 (2010); Males per 100 females: 104.4 (2010); Marriage status: 17.1% never married, 65.7% now married, 4.8% widowed, 12.4% divorced (2005-2009 5-year est.); Foreign born: 0.6% (2005-2009 5-year est.); Ancestry (includes multiple ancestries): 26.8% German, 24.8% Irish, 17.2% American, 12.1% English, 7.0% Italian (2005-2009 5-year est.).
Economy: Employment by occupation: 22.5% management, 13.3% professional, 11.7% services, 32.5% sales, 0.0% farming, 3.3% construction, 16.7% production (2005-2009 5-year est.).
Income: Per capita income: $24,548 (2010); Median household income: $53,472 (2010); Average household income: $70,324 (2010); Percent of

households with income of $100,000 or more: 20.0% (2010); Poverty rate: 33.1% (2005-2009 5-year est.).
Taxes: Total city taxes per capita: $72 (2007); City property taxes per capita: $72 (2007).
Education: Percent of population age 25 and over with: High school diploma (including GED) or higher: 97.1% (2010); Bachelor's degree or higher: 28.6% (2010); Master's degree or higher: 13.6% (2010).

School District(s)
Tri Point CUSD 6-J (PK-12)
    2009-10 Enrollment: 548 . . . . (815) 253-6299
Housing: Homeownership rate: 74.1% (2010); Median home value: $110,227 (2010); Median contract rent: $425 per month (2005-2009 5-year est.); Median year structure built: before 1940 (2005-2009 5-year est.).
Transportation: Commute to work: 85.0% car, 0.0% public transportation, 5.8% walk, 7.5% work from home (2005-2009 5-year est.); Travel time to work: 42.3% less than 15 minutes, 18.0% 15 to 30 minutes, 17.1% 30 to 45 minutes, 6.3% 45 to 60 minutes, 16.2% 60 minutes or more (2005-2009 5-year est.)

MELVIN (village).
Covers a land area of 0.339 square miles and a water area of 0 square miles. Located at 40.56° N. Lat; 88.24° W. Long. Elevation is 814 feet.
Population: 466 (1990); 465 (2000); 460 (2010); 455 (2015 projected); Race: 98.7% White, 0.0% Black, 0.0% Asian, 1.3% Other, 2.2% Hispanic of any race (2010); Density: 1,357.5 persons per square mile (2010); Average household size: 2.50 (2010); Median age: 35.5 (2010); Males per 100 females: 99.1 (2010); Marriage status: 17.5% never married, 53.4% now married, 7.1% widowed, 22.0% divorced (2005-2009 5-year est.); Foreign born: 0.8% (2005-2009 5-year est.); Ancestry (includes multiple ancestries): 49.7% German, 15.0% Irish, 12.8% English, 10.3% American, 6.1% Polish (2005-2009 5-year est.).
Economy: Employment by occupation: 4.7% management, 9.1% professional, 10.5% services, 23.3% sales, 3.0% farming, 14.9% construction, 34.5% production (2005-2009 5-year est.).
Income: Per capita income: $24,094 (2010); Median household income: $53,261 (2010); Average household income: $60,992 (2010); Percent of households with income of $100,000 or more: 12.0% (2010); Poverty rate: 16.3% (2005-2009 5-year est.).
Taxes: Total city taxes per capita: $58 (2007); City property taxes per capita: $52 (2007).
Education: Percent of population age 25 and over with: High school diploma (including GED) or higher: 92.1% (2010); Bachelor's degree or higher: 19.5% (2010); Master's degree or higher: 5.1% (2010).
Housing: Homeownership rate: 79.3% (2010); Median home value: $71,875 (2010); Median contract rent: $300 per month (2005-2009 5-year est.); Median year structure built: 1944 (2005-2009 5-year est.).
Newspapers: Ford County Press (Local news; Circulation 1,000)
Transportation: Commute to work: 89.8% car, 0.0% public transportation, 5.4% walk, 4.8% work from home (2005-2009 5-year est.); Travel time to work: 35.7% less than 15 minutes, 16.4% 15 to 30 minutes, 17.5% 30 to 45 minutes, 16.8% 45 to 60 minutes, 13.6% 60 minutes or more (2005-2009 5-year est.)

PAXTON (city).
County seat. Covers a land area of 2.228 square miles and a water area of 0 square miles. Located at 40.45° N. Lat; 88.09° W. Long. Elevation is 791 feet.
History: Paxton was settled in the 1850's by immigrants from Sweden.
Population: 4,408 (1990); 4,525 (2000); 4,386 (2010); 4,298 (2015 projected); Race: 95.2% White, 1.6% Black, 0.7% Asian, 2.5% Other, 3.2% Hispanic of any race (2010); Density: 1,969.0 persons per square mile (2010); Average household size: 2.42 (2010); Median age: 39.1 (2010); Males per 100 females: 94.2 (2010); Marriage status: 22.8% never married, 51.2% now married, 12.3% widowed, 13.8% divorced (2005-2009 5-year est.); Foreign born: 3.0% (2005-2009 5-year est.); Ancestry (includes multiple ancestries): 30.6% German, 16.3% American, 13.4% Irish, 8.3% English, 5.2% French (2005-2009 5-year est.).
Economy: Single-family building permits issued: 2 (2010); Multi-family building permits issued: 0 (2010); Employment by occupation: 13.2% management, 17.2% professional, 19.5% services, 24.6% sales, 0.5% farming, 12.6% construction, 12.5% production (2005-2009 5-year est.).
Income: Per capita income: $22,282 (2010); Median household income: $46,903 (2010); Average household income: $54,244 (2010); Percent of households with income of $100,000 or more: 11.2% (2010); Poverty rate: 10.9% (2005-2009 5-year est.).

Taxes: Total city taxes per capita: $162 (2007); City property taxes per capita: $138 (2007).
Education: Percent of population age 25 and over with: High school diploma (including GED) or higher: 91.7% (2010); Bachelor's degree or higher: 15.5% (2010); Master's degree or higher: 4.3% (2010).

School District(s)
Paxton-Buckley-Loda CUD 10 (PK-12)
    2009-10 Enrollment: 1,533 . . . . (217) 379-3314
Housing: Homeownership rate: 77.2% (2010); Median home value: $91,211 (2010); Median contract rent: $438 per month (2005-2009 5-year est.); Median year structure built: 1952 (2005-2009 5-year est.).
Newspapers: Loda Times (Community news; Circulation 360); Paxton Corporation (Community news; Circulation 2,180); Paxton Daily Record (Local news; Circulation 4,200)
Transportation: Commute to work: 93.3% car, 0.0% public transportation, 2.1% walk, 3.7% work from home (2005-2009 5-year est.); Travel time to work: 44.8% less than 15 minutes, 24.9% 15 to 30 minutes, 24.3% 30 to 45 minutes, 3.0% 45 to 60 minutes, 3.1% 60 minutes or more (2005-2009 5-year est.)
Additional Information Contacts
Paxton Chamber of Commerce . . . . (217) 379-4655
    http://www.paxtonchamber.org

PIPER CITY (village).
Covers a land area of 0.554 square miles and a water area of 0 square miles. Located at 40.75° N. Lat; 88.19° W. Long. Elevation is 673 feet.
Population: 760 (1990); 781 (2000); 774 (2010); 767 (2015 projected); Race: 94.3% White, 0.3% Black, 2.2% Asian, 3.2% Other, 2.5% Hispanic of any race (2010); Density: 1,396.5 persons per square mile (2010); Average household size: 2.52 (2010); Median age: 44.0 (2010); Males per 100 females: 88.8 (2010); Marriage status: 22.1% never married, 54.8% now married, 11.8% widowed, 11.2% divorced (2005-2009 5-year est.); Foreign born: 0.0% (2005-2009 5-year est.); Ancestry (includes multiple ancestries): 38.7% German, 17.5% Irish, 15.0% American, 13.6% English, 8.1% Swedish (2005-2009 5-year est.).
Economy: Single-family building permits issued: 0 (2010); Multi-family building permits issued: 0 (2010); Employment by occupation: 3.5% management, 17.6% professional, 11.4% services, 15.9% sales, 0.0% farming, 12.8% construction, 38.8% production (2005-2009 5-year est.).
Income: Per capita income: $24,994 (2010); Median household income: $47,250 (2010); Average household income: $59,877 (2010); Percent of households with income of $100,000 or more: 9.9% (2010); Poverty rate: 14.2% (2005-2009 5-year est.).
Taxes: Total city taxes per capita: $155 (2007); City property taxes per capita: $122 (2007).
Education: Percent of population age 25 and over with: High school diploma (including GED) or higher: 86.6% (2010); Bachelor's degree or higher: 16.2% (2010); Master's degree or higher: 7.7% (2010).

School District(s)
Tri Point CUSD 6-J (PK-12)
    2009-10 Enrollment: 548 . . . . (815) 253-6299
Housing: Homeownership rate: 77.1% (2010); Median home value: $100,852 (2010); Median contract rent: $438 per month (2005-2009 5-year est.); Median year structure built: 1951 (2005-2009 5-year est.).
Transportation: Commute to work: 88.1% car, 0.0% public transportation, 2.1% walk, 6.3% work from home (2005-2009 5-year est.); Travel time to work: 36.0% less than 15 minutes, 14.2% 15 to 30 minutes, 21.3% 30 to 45 minutes, 15.0% 45 to 60 minutes, 13.5% 60 minutes or more (2005-2009 5-year est.)

ROBERTS (village).
Covers a land area of 0.518 square miles and a water area of 0 square miles. Located at 40.61° N. Lat; 88.18° W. Long. Elevation is 781 feet.
Population: 413 (1990); 387 (2000); 386 (2010); 385 (2015 projected); Race: 99.0% White, 0.0% Black, 0.0% Asian, 1.0% Other, 1.8% Hispanic of any race (2010); Density: 744.9 persons per square mile (2010); Average household size: 2.41 (2010); Median age: 39.7 (2010); Males per 100 females: 93.0 (2010); Marriage status: 9.8% never married, 61.7% now married, 11.4% widowed, 17.1% divorced (2005-2009 5-year est.); Foreign born: 0.0% (2005-2009 5-year est.); Ancestry (includes multiple ancestries): 51.6% German, 16.0% English, 14.5% French, 10.3% Irish, 8.8% American (2005-2009 5-year est.).
Economy: Employment by occupation: 4.2% management, 16.2% professional, 12.6% services, 28.8% sales, 4.7% farming, 10.5% construction, 23.0% production (2005-2009 5-year est.).

Income: Per capita income: $24,453 (2010); Median household income: $52,326 (2010); Average household income: $58,344 (2010); Percent of households with income of $100,000 or more: 11.9% (2010); Poverty rate: 14.7% (2005-2009 5-year est.).
Taxes: Total city taxes per capita: $28 (2007); City property taxes per capita: $28 (2007).
Education: Percent of population age 25 and over with: High school diploma (including GED) or higher: 92.1% (2010); Bachelor's degree or higher: 15.7% (2010); Master's degree or higher: 2.8% (2010).
Housing: Homeownership rate: 81.9% (2010); Median home value: $103,125 (2010); Median contract rent: $319 per month (2005-2009 5-year est.); Median year structure built: 1952 (2005-2009 5-year est.).
Transportation: Commute to work: 93.2% car, 0.0% public transportation, 0.0% walk, 6.8% work from home (2005-2009 5-year est.); Travel time to work: 39.3% less than 15 minutes, 29.8% 15 to 30 minutes, 19.7% 30 to 45 minutes, 8.4% 45 to 60 minutes, 2.8% 60 minutes or more (2005-2009 5-year est.)

SIBLEY (village). Covers a land area of 0.538 square miles and a water area of 0.013 square miles. Located at 40.58° N. Lat; 88.38° W. Long. Elevation is 827 feet.
Population: 359 (1990); 329 (2000); 329 (2010); 330 (2015 projected); Race: 94.2% White, 0.0% Black, 0.0% Asian, 5.8% Other, 5.2% Hispanic of any race (2010); Density: 611.6 persons per square mile (2010); Average household size: 2.70 (2010); Median age: 37.4 (2010); Males per 100 females: 110.9 (2010); Marriage status: 26.1% never married, 51.4% now married, 5.5% widowed, 17.0% divorced (2005-2009 5-year est.); Foreign born: 0.0% (2005-2009 5-year est.); Ancestry (includes multiple ancestries): 51.3% German, 16.8% Irish, 8.8% American, 7.0% English, 3.6% Swedish (2005-2009 5-year est.).
Economy: Employment by occupation: 5.7% management, 7.8% professional, 12.2% services, 22.6% sales, 0.0% farming, 12.6% construction, 39.1% production (2005-2009 5-year est.).
Income: Per capita income: $26,148 (2010); Median household income: $57,857 (2010); Average household income: $69,467 (2010); Percent of households with income of $100,000 or more: 18.9% (2010); Poverty rate: 11.1% (2005-2009 5-year est.).
Taxes: Total city taxes per capita: $58 (2007); City property taxes per capita: $55 (2007).
Education: Percent of population age 25 and over with: High school diploma (including GED) or higher: 87.7% (2010); Bachelor's degree or higher: 10.5% (2010); Master's degree or higher: 1.8% (2010).
Housing: Homeownership rate: 75.4% (2010); Median home value: $71,667 (2010); Median contract rent: $425 per month (2005-2009 5-year est.); Median year structure built: 1942 (2005-2009 5-year est.).
Transportation: Commute to work: 98.7% car, 0.0% public transportation, 0.0% walk, 1.3% work from home (2005-2009 5-year est.); Travel time to work: 36.0% less than 15 minutes, 26.2% 15 to 30 minutes, 23.6% 30 to 45 minutes, 7.6% 45 to 60 minutes, 6.7% 60 minutes or more (2005-2009 5-year est.)

Franklin County

Located in southern Illinois; bounded on the northwest by the Little Muddy River; drained by the Big Muddy River. Covers a land area of 412.08 square miles, a water area of 19.32 square miles, and is located in the Central Time Zone at 37.97° N. Lat., 88.95° W. Long. The county was founded in 1818. County seat is Benton.
Population: 40,319 (1990); 39,018 (2000); 39,578 (2010); 39,609 (2015 projected); Race: 97.5% White, 0.8% Black, 0.3% Asian, 1.4% Other, 1.0% Hispanic of any race (2010); Density: 96.0 persons per square mile (2010); Average household size: 2.31 (2010); Median age: 40.3 (2010); Males per 100 females: 93.1 (2010).
Religion: Five largest groups: 30.8% Southern Baptist Convention, 5.9% Christian Churches and Churches of Christ, 3.9% Catholic Church, 3.6% Church of God (Cleveland, Tennessee), 3.6% The United Methodist Church (2000).
Economy: Unemployment rate: 12.2% (August 2011); Total civilian labor force: 17,771 (August 2011); Leading industries: 22.7% retail trade; 19.7% health care and social assistance; 12.8% accommodation & food services (2009); Farms: 785 totaling 207,877 acres (2007); Companies that employ 500 or more persons: 0 (2009); Companies that employ 100 to 499 persons: 7 (2009); Companies that employ less than 100 persons: 785 (2009); Black-owned businesses: n/a (2007); Hispanic-owned businesses: n/a (2007); Asian-owned businesses: n/a (2007); Women-owned

businesses: 676 (2007); Retail sales per capita: $11,593 (2010). Single-family building permits issued: 15 (2010); Multi-family building permits issued: 0 (2010).
Income: Per capita income: $19,219 (2010); Median household income: $34,863 (2010); Average household income: $44,728 (2010); Percent of households with income of $100,000 or more: 7.2% (2010); Poverty rate: 18.8% (2009); Bankruptcy rate: 6.61% (2010).
Taxes: Total county taxes per capita: $57 (2007); County property taxes per capita: $57 (2007).
Education: Percent of population age 25 and over with: High school diploma (including GED) or higher: 81.0% (2010); Bachelor's degree or higher: 12.7% (2010); Master's degree or higher: 3.5% (2010).
Housing: Homeownership rate: 77.2% (2010); Median home value: $54,557 (2010); Median contract rent: $344 per month (2005-2009 5-year est.); Median year structure built: 1960 (2005-2009 5-year est.)
Health: Birth rate: 126.2 per 10,000 population (2009); Death rate: 139.9 per 10,000 population (2009); Age-adjusted cancer mortality rate: 234.6 deaths per 100,000 population (2007); Number of physicians: 6.1 per 10,000 population (2008); Hospital beds: 6.4 per 10,000 population (2007); Hospital admissions: 149.7 per 10,000 population (2007).
Elections: 2008 Presidential election results: 47.6% Obama, 50.4% McCain, 0.9% Nader
National and State Parks: Wayne Fitzgerrell State Park
Additional Information Contacts

Franklin County Communities

BENTON (city). County seat. Covers a land area of 5.349 square miles and a water area of 0.141 square miles. Located at 38.00° N. Lat; 88.91° W. Long. Elevation is 472 feet.
History: Incorporated 1841.
Population: 7,264 (1990); 6,880 (2000); 6,882 (2010); 6,871 (2015 projected); Race: 96.7% White, 1.7% Black, 0.5% Asian, 1.0% Other, 0.8% Hispanic of any race (2010); Density: 1,286.6 persons per square mile (2010); Average household size: 2.25 (2010); Median age: 42.1 (2010); Males per 100 females: 90.3 (2010); Marriage status: 20.9% never married, 48.1% now married, 11.9% widowed, 19.1% divorced (2005-2009 5-year est.); Foreign born: 0.1% (2005-2009 5-year est.); Ancestry (includes multiple ancestries): 31.6% German, 18.4% Irish, 16.5% English, 8.1% American, 7.2% Italian (2005-2009 5-year est.).
Economy: Single-family building permits issued: 6 (2010); Multi-family building permits issued: 0 (2010); Employment by occupation: 8.3% management, 15.6% professional, 27.7% services, 24.4% sales, 0.3% farming, 11.7% construction, 11.9% production (2005-2009 5-year est.).
Income: Per capita income: $19,398 (2010); Median household income: $35,643 (2010); Average household income: $44,724 (2010); Percent of households with income of $100,000 or more: 7.2% (2010); Poverty rate: 21.0% (2005-2009 5-year est.).
Taxes: Total city taxes per capita: $237 (2007); City property taxes per capita: $69 (2007).
Education: Percent of population age 25 and over with: High school diploma (including GED) or higher: 80.8% (2010); Bachelor's degree or higher: 15.0% (2010); Master's degree or higher: 4.2% (2010).
School District(s)
Benton CCSD 47 (PK-08)
    2009-10 Enrollment: 1,085 . . . . (618) 439-3136
Benton Cons HSD 103 (09-12)
    2009-10 Enrollment: 564 . . . . (618) 439-6415
Housing: Homeownership rate: 71.7% (2010); Median home value: $56,065 (2010); Median contract rent: $354 per month (2005-2009 5-year est.); Median year structure built: 1957 (2005-2009 5-year est.).
Hospitals: Franklin Hospital (25 beds)
Safety: Violent crime rate: 67.3 per 10,000 population; Property crime rate: 482.7 per 10,000 population (2010).

Newspapers: Benton Evening News (Local news; Circulation 4,000); Benton Standard (Community news; Circulation 300)
Transportation: Commute to work: 93.0% car, 0.0% public transportation, 3.5% walk, 3.5% work from home (2005-2009 5-year est.); Travel time to work: 52.4% less than 15 minutes, 17.9% 15 to 30 minutes, 18.8% 30 to 45 minutes, 7.3% 45 to 60 minutes, 3.8% 60 minutes or more (2005-2009 5-year est.)
Additional Information Contacts
Benton/West City Area Chamber of Commerce . . . . (618) 438-2121
   http://www.bentonwestcity.com/chamber

BUCKNER (village). Covers a land area of 0.887 square miles and a water area of 0.013 square miles. Located at 37.98° N. Lat; 89.01° W. Long. Elevation is 404 feet.
Population: 478 (1990); 479 (2000); 527 (2010); 551 (2015 projected); Race: 98.7% White, 0.0% Black, 0.0% Asian, 1.3% Other, 1.7% Hispanic of any race (2010); Density: 594.5 persons per square mile (2010); Average household size: 2.21 (2010); Median age: 41.7 (2010); Males per 100 females: 101.9 (2010); Marriage status: 18.1% never married, 54.8% now married, 3.8% widowed, 23.3% divorced (2005-2009 5-year est.); Foreign born: 0.7% (2005-2009 5-year est.); Ancestry (includes multiple ancestries): 26.7% Irish, 18.0% German, 15.6% Italian, 14.4% English, 10.2% French (2005-2009 5-year est.).
Economy: Employment by occupation: 13.0% management, 11.2% professional, 25.5% services, 11.8% sales, 0.0% farming, 8.1% construction, 30.4% production (2005-2009 5-year est.).
Income: Per capita income: $16,986 (2010); Median household income: $30,116 (2010); Average household income: $37,626 (2010); Percent of households with income of $100,000 or more: 3.8% (2010); Poverty rate: 16.4% (2005-2009 5-year est.).
Taxes: Total city taxes per capita: $331 (2007); City property taxes per capita: $214 (2007).
Education: Percent of population age 25 and over with: High school diploma (including GED) or higher: 77.4% (2010); Bachelor's degree or higher: 6.6% (2010); Master's degree or higher: 0.5% (2010).
Housing: Homeownership rate: 81.9% (2010); Median home value: $33,562 (2010); Median contract rent: $287 per month (2005-2009 5-year est.); Median year structure built: 1955 (2005-2009 5-year est.).
Transportation: Commute to work: 83.5% car, 0.0% public transportation, 13.3% walk, 3.2% work from home (2005-2009 5-year est.); Travel time to work: 38.6% less than 15 minutes, 31.4% 15 to 30 minutes, 22.2% 30 to 45 minutes, 7.8% 45 to 60 minutes, 0.0% 60 minutes or more (2005-2009 5-year est.)

CHRISTOPHER (city). Covers a land area of 1.410 square miles and a water area of 0 square miles. Located at 37.97° N. Lat; 89.05° W. Long. Elevation is 440 feet.
History: Incorporated 1903.
Population: 2,882 (1990); 2,836 (2000); 2,670 (2010); 2,612 (2015 projected); Race: 97.2% White, 0.5% Black, 0.7% Asian, 1.6% Other, 0.7% Hispanic of any race (2010); Density: 1,893.3 persons per square mile (2010); Average household size: 2.16 (2010); Median age: 41.5 (2010); Males per 100 females: 89.2 (2010); Marriage status: 25.2% never married, 51.0% now married, 7.1% widowed, 16.7% divorced (2005-2009 5-year est.); Foreign born: 0.0% (2005-2009 5-year est.); Ancestry (includes multiple ancestries): 21.7% Irish, 21.6% German, 14.2% English, 10.8% American, 10.2% French (2005-2009 5-year est.).
Economy: Single-family building permits issued: 3 (2010); Multi-family building permits issued: 0 (2010); Employment by occupation: 6.3% management, 12.2% professional, 33.2% services, 25.2% sales, 0.0% farming, 4.2% construction, 18.9% production (2005-2009 5-year est.).
Income: Per capita income: $20,087 (2010); Median household income: $34,506 (2010); Average household income: $43,342 (2010); Percent of households with income of $100,000 or more: 5.9% (2010); Poverty rate: 21.4% (2005-2009 5-year est.).
Taxes: Total city taxes per capita: $147 (2007); City property taxes per capita: $72 (2007).
Education: Percent of population age 25 and over with: High school diploma (including GED) or higher: 79.6% (2010); Bachelor's degree or higher: 13.1% (2010); Master's degree or higher: 2.9% (2010).
School District(s)
Christopher USD 99 (PK-12)
   2009-10 Enrollment: 850 . . . . (618) 724-9461

Housing: Homeownership rate: 74.3% (2010); Median home value: $41,454 (2010); Median contract rent: $281 per month (2005-2009 5-year est.); Median year structure built: 1948 (2005-2009 5-year est.).
Newspapers: Franklin Press Shopper (Local news; Circulation 7,400); Progress (Community news; Circulation 900)
Transportation: Commute to work: 95.6% car, 0.0% public transportation, 2.1% walk, 0.6% work from home (2005-2009 5-year est.); Travel time to work: 20.9% less than 15 minutes, 32.1% 15 to 30 minutes, 30.0% 30 to 45 minutes, 12.7% 45 to 60 minutes, 4.3% 60 minutes or more (2005-2009 5-year est.)

EWING (village). Covers a land area of 1.014 square miles and a water area of 0 square miles. Located at 38.09° N. Lat; 88.85° W. Long. Elevation is 469 feet.
Population: 264 (1990); 310 (2000); 297 (2010); 291 (2015 projected); Race: 99.0% White, 0.0% Black, 0.0% Asian, 1.0% Other, 2.0% Hispanic of any race (2010); Density: 293.0 persons per square mile (2010); Average household size: 2.70 (2010); Median age: 35.1 (2010); Males per 100 females: 102.0 (2010); Marriage status: 19.7% never married, 53.2% now married, 11.2% widowed, 15.9% divorced (2005-2009 5-year est.); Foreign born: 0.0% (2005-2009 5-year est.); Ancestry (includes multiple ancestries): 23.5% German, 12.3% American, 11.3% Irish, 6.1% Italian, 5.8% English (2005-2009 5-year est.).
Economy: Employment by occupation: 14.3% management, 7.6% professional, 28.6% services, 26.1% sales, 0.0% farming, 5.0% construction, 18.5% production (2005-2009 5-year est.).
Income: Per capita income: $17,872 (2010); Median household income: $39,000 (2010); Average household income: $47,045 (2010); Percent of households with income of $100,000 or more: 10.0% (2010); Poverty rate: 20.2% (2005-2009 5-year est.).
Taxes: Total city taxes per capita: $28 (2007); City property taxes per capita: $28 (2007).
Education: Percent of population age 25 and over with: High school diploma (including GED) or higher: 83.3% (2010); Bachelor's degree or higher: 9.7% (2010); Master's degree or higher: 2.7% (2010).
School District(s)
Ewing Northern CCSD 115 (PK-08)
   2009-10 Enrollment: 223 . . . . (618) 629-2181
Housing: Homeownership rate: 84.5% (2010); Median home value: $70,556 (2010); Median contract rent: $400 per month (2005-2009 5-year est.); Median year structure built: 1965 (2005-2009 5-year est.).
Transportation: Commute to work: 92.3% car, 0.0% public transportation, 1.7% walk, 6.0% work from home (2005-2009 5-year est.); Travel time to work: 26.4% less than 15 minutes, 33.6% 15 to 30 minutes, 29.1% 30 to 45 minutes, 5.5% 45 to 60 minutes, 5.5% 60 minutes or more (2005-2009 5-year est.)

FREEMAN SPUR (village). Aka Freemanspur. Covers a land area of 0.404 square miles and a water area of 0 square miles. Located at 37.86° N. Lat; 89.00° W. Long. Elevation is 397 feet.
Population: 290 (1990); 273 (2000); 300 (2010); 309 (2015 projected); Race: 95.3% White, 2.7% Black, 0.0% Asian, 2.0% Other, 1.7% Hispanic of any race (2010); Density: 742.9 persons per square mile (2010); Average household size: 2.53 (2010); Median age: 41.9 (2010); Males per 100 females: 98.7 (2010); Marriage status: 27.7% never married, 47.4% now married, 7.2% widowed, 17.7% divorced (2005-2009 5-year est.); Foreign born: 0.0% (2005-2009 5-year est.); Ancestry (includes multiple ancestries): 28.8% English, 16.3% Italian, 14.7% Irish, 14.4% German, 12.1% French (2005-2009 5-year est.).
Economy: Employment by occupation: 0.0% management, 6.7% professional, 26.9% services, 6.0% sales, 0.0% farming, 17.2% construction, 43.3% production (2005-2009 5-year est.).
Income: Per capita income: $18,055 (2010); Median household income: $36,406 (2010); Average household income: $45,748 (2010); Percent of households with income of $100,000 or more: 4.7% (2010); Poverty rate: 15.7% (2005-2009 5-year est.).
Education: Percent of population age 25 and over with: High school diploma (including GED) or higher: 79.3% (2010); Bachelor's degree or higher: 8.9% (2010); Master's degree or higher: 3.3% (2010).
Housing: Homeownership rate: 85.0% (2010); Median home value: $63,333 (2010); Median contract rent: $308 per month (2005-2009 5-year est.); Median year structure built: 1972 (2005-2009 5-year est.).
Transportation: Commute to work: 100.0% car, 0.0% public transportation, 0.0% walk, 0.0% work from home (2005-2009 5-year est.); Travel time to work: 16.0% less than 15 minutes, 60.8% 15 to 30 minutes,

23.2% 30 to 45 minutes, 0.0% 45 to 60 minutes, 0.0% 60 minutes or more (2005-2009 5-year est.)

HANAFORD (village). Aka Logan. Covers a land area of 1.022 square miles and a water area of 0 square miles. Located at 37.95° N. Lat; 88.83° W. Long. Elevation is 480 feet.

History: Also called Logan.
Population: 380 (1990); 55 (2000); 55 (2010); 54 (2015 projected); Race: 98.2% White, 0.0% Black, 0.0% Asian, 1.8% Other, 1.8% Hispanic of any race (2010); Density: 53.8 persons per square mile (2010); Average household size: 2.75 (2010); Median age: 38.9 (2010); Males per 100 females: 103.7 (2010); Marriage status: 32.5% never married, 43.3% now married, 17.1% widowed, 7.1% divorced (2005-2009 5-year est.); Foreign born: 0.0% (2005-2009 5-year est.); Ancestry (includes multiple ancestries): 24.3% German, 24.3% Irish, 17.1% English, 4.9% Scottish, 4.2% Italian (2005-2009 5-year est.).
Economy: Employment by occupation: 8.5% management, 3.4% professional, 37.3% services, 23.7% sales, 0.0% farming, 6.8% construction, 20.3% production (2005-2009 5-year est.).
Income: Per capita income: $18,367 (2010); Median household income: $46,250 (2010); Average household income: $55,875 (2010); Percent of households with income of $100,000 or more: 15.0% (2010); Poverty rate: 13.5% (2005-2009 5-year est.).
Taxes: Total city taxes per capita: $45 (2007); City property taxes per capita: $9 (2007).
Education: Percent of population age 25 and over with: High school diploma (including GED) or higher: 83.3% (2010); Bachelor's degree or higher: 16.7% (2010); Master's degree or higher: 5.6% (2010).
Housing: Homeownership rate: 90.0% (2010); Median home value: $73,333 (2010); Median contract rent: n/a per month (2005-2009 5-year est.); Median year structure built: 1973 (2005-2009 5-year est.).
Transportation: Commute to work: 100.0% car, 0.0% public transportation, 0.0% walk, 0.0% work from home (2005-2009 5-year est.); Travel time to work: 22.5% less than 15 minutes, 35.1% 15 to 30 minutes, 20.7% 30 to 45 minutes, 0.0% 45 to 60 minutes, 21.6% 60 minutes or more (2005-2009 5-year est.)

MULKEYTOWN (unincorporated postal area, zip code 62865). Covers a land area of 50.295 square miles and a water area of 0.441 square miles. Located at 37.96° N. Lat; 89.06° W. Long. Elevation is 446 feet.

Population: 1,879 (2000); Race: 96.5% White, 0.0% Black, 0.0% Asian, 3.5% Other, 2.5% Hispanic of any race (2000); Density: 37.4 persons per square mile (2000); Age: 25.5% under 18, 13.5% over 64 (2000); Marriage status: 18.5% never married, 67.0% now married, 6.4% widowed, 8.1% divorced (2000); Foreign born: 0.1% (2000); Ancestry (includes multiple ancestries): 16.4% English, 15.0% German, 12.4% Irish, 11.7% American (2000).
Economy: Employment by occupation: 11.0% management, 17.8% professional, 20.6% services, 26.1% sales, 0.0% farming, 12.7% construction, 11.8% production (2000).
Income: Per capita income: $17,037 (2000); Median household income: $38,200 (2000); Poverty rate: 12.7% (2000).
Education: Percent of population age 25 and over with: High school diploma (including GED) or higher: 80.1% (2000); Bachelor's degree or higher: 12.4% (2000).
Housing: Homeownership rate: 91.3% (2000); Median home value: $54,000 (2000); Median contract rent: $181 per month (2000); Median year structure built: 1973 (2000).
Transportation: Commute to work: 95.1% car, 0.7% public transportation, 0.2% walk, 4.0% work from home (2000); Travel time to work: 25.4% less than 15 minutes, 38.8% 15 to 30 minutes, 27.8% 30 to 45 minutes, 5.4% 45 to 60 minutes, 2.6% 60 minutes or more (2000)

NORTH CITY (village). Aka Coello. Covers a land area of 2.193 square miles and a water area of 0.040 square miles. Located at 37.99° N. Lat; 89.06° W. Long. Elevation is 469 feet.

Population: 627 (1990); 630 (2000); 610 (2010); 603 (2015 projected); Race: 95.7% White, 0.5% Black, 0.5% Asian, 3.3% Other, 2.8% Hispanic of any race (2010); Density: 278.2 persons per square mile (2010); Average household size: 2.32 (2010); Median age: 39.9 (2010); Males per 100 females: 103.3 (2010); Marriage status: 14.8% never married, 67.4% now married, 8.1% widowed, 9.6% divorced (2005-2009 5-year est.); Foreign born: 2.6% (2005-2009 5-year est.); Ancestry (includes multiple

ancestries): 18.2% Irish, 16.0% German, 14.7% English, 13.7% Italian, 7.6% French (2005-2009 5-year est.).
Economy: Single-family building permits issued: 0 (2010); Multi-family building permits issued: 0 (2010); Employment by occupation: 6.7% management, 18.9% professional, 24.8% services, 18.9% sales, 0.0% farming, 13.4% construction, 17.2% production (2005-2009 5-year est.).
Income: Per capita income: $18,542 (2010); Median household income: $33,684 (2010); Average household income: $43,081 (2010); Percent of households with income of $100,000 or more: 7.0% (2010); Poverty rate: 17.2% (2005-2009 5-year est.).
Taxes: Total city taxes per capita: $19 (2007); City property taxes per capita: $6 (2007).
Education: Percent of population age 25 and over with: High school diploma (including GED) or higher: 81.6% (2010); Bachelor's degree or higher: 12.5% (2010); Master's degree or higher: 7.1% (2010).
Housing: Homeownership rate: 80.6% (2010); Median home value: $51,111 (2010); Median contract rent: n/a per month (2005-2009 5-year est.); Median year structure built: 1957 (2005-2009 5-year est.).
Transportation: Commute to work: 97.4% car, 0.0% public transportation, 0.0% walk, 2.6% work from home (2005-2009 5-year est.); Travel time to work: 19.7% less than 15 minutes, 34.9% 15 to 30 minutes, 28.8% 30 to 45 minutes, 8.7% 45 to 60 minutes, 7.9% 60 minutes or more (2005-2009 5-year est.)

ORIENT (city). Covers a land area of 0.750 square miles and a water area of 0.006 square miles. Located at 37.91° N. Lat; 88.97° W. Long. Elevation is 482 feet.

Population: 457 (1990); 296 (2000); 280 (2010); 271 (2015 projected); Race: 98.9% White, 1.1% Black, 0.0% Asian, 0.0% Other, 0.0% Hispanic of any race (2010); Density: 373.3 persons per square mile (2010); Average household size: 2.35 (2010); Median age: 41.4 (2010); Males per 100 females: 97.2 (2010); Marriage status: 30.8% never married, 44.9% now married, 3.3% widowed, 21.0% divorced (2005-2009 5-year est.); Foreign born: 0.0% (2005-2009 5-year est.); Ancestry (includes multiple ancestries): 32.5% German, 21.1% Irish, 12.8% Italian, 11.1% English, 8.0% Dutch (2005-2009 5-year est.).
Economy: Employment by occupation: 5.8% management, 14.2% professional, 16.1% services, 12.3% sales, 0.0% farming, 1.3% construction, 50.3% production (2005-2009 5-year est.).
Income: Per capita income: $14,907 (2010); Median household income: $28,571 (2010); Average household income: $35,021 (2010); Percent of households with income of $100,000 or more: 4.2% (2010); Poverty rate: 12.8% (2005-2009 5-year est.).
Taxes: Total city taxes per capita: $35 (2007); City property taxes per capita: $9 (2007).
Education: Percent of population age 25 and over with: High school diploma (including GED) or higher: 75.6% (2010); Bachelor's degree or higher: 9.3% (2010); Master's degree or higher: 3.6% (2010).
Housing: Homeownership rate: 93.3% (2010); Median home value: $38,542 (2010); Median contract rent: n/a per month (2005-2009 5-year est.); Median year structure built: before 1940 (2005-2009 5-year est.).
Transportation: Commute to work: 96.4% car, 0.0% public transportation, 3.6% walk, 0.0% work from home (2005-2009 5-year est.); Travel time to work: 52.6% less than 15 minutes, 32.8% 15 to 30 minutes, 4.4% 30 to 45 minutes, 3.6% 45 to 60 minutes, 6.6% 60 minutes or more (2005-2009 5-year est.)

ROYALTON (village). Covers a land area of 1.131 square miles and a water area of 0.001 square miles. Located at 37.88° N. Lat; 89.11° W. Long. Elevation is 394 feet.

History: Incorporated 1907.
Population: 1,191 (1990); 1,130 (2000); 1,082 (2010); 1,051 (2015 projected); Race: 99.3% White, 0.0% Black, 0.1% Asian, 0.6% Other, 0.4% Hispanic of any race (2010); Density: 956.7 persons per square mile (2010); Average household size: 2.17 (2010); Median age: 39.3 (2010); Males per 100 females: 89.5 (2010); Marriage status: 28.0% never married, 56.2% now married, 6.8% widowed, 9.1% divorced (2005-2009 5-year est.); Foreign born: 0.0% (2005-2009 5-year est.); Ancestry (includes multiple ancestries): 21.1% Irish, 17.6% German, 14.7% English, 9.9% American, 7.7% Italian (2005-2009 5-year est.).
Economy: Employment by occupation: 6.8% management, 12.7% professional, 17.0% services, 16.3% sales, 0.5% farming, 21.0% construction, 25.7% production (2005-2009 5-year est.).
Income: Per capita income: $18,382 (2010); Median household income: $29,545 (2010); Average household income: $39,106 (2010); Percent of

households with income of $100,000 or more: 5.6% (2010); Poverty rate: 19.8% (2005-2009 5-year est.).
Taxes: Total city taxes per capita: $82 (2007); City property taxes per capita: $22 (2007).
Education: Percent of population age 25 and over with: High school diploma (including GED) or higher: 77.6% (2010); Bachelor's degree or higher: 9.0% (2010); Master's degree or higher: 3.3% (2010).
Housing: Homeownership rate: 78.3% (2010); Median home value: $43,636 (2010); Median contract rent: $286 per month (2005-2009 5-year est.); Median year structure built: 1955 (2005-2009 5-year est.).
Safety: Violent crime rate: 34.9 per 10,000 population; Property crime rate: 139.7 per 10,000 population (2010).
Transportation: Commute to work: 94.1% car, 0.0% public transportation, 1.5% walk, 0.7% work from home (2005-2009 5-year est.); Travel time to work: 12.6% less than 15 minutes, 41.6% 15 to 30 minutes, 20.8% 30 to 45 minutes, 9.2% 45 to 60 minutes, 15.8% 60 minutes or more (2005-2009 5-year est.)

SESSER (city). Covers a land area of 1.021 square miles and a water area of 0 square miles. Located at 38.09° N. Lat; 89.05° W. Long. Elevation is 479 feet.
History: Incorporated 1906.
Population: 2,155 (1990); 2,128 (2000); 2,073 (2010); 2,040 (2015 projected); Race: 97.8% White, 0.5% Black, 0.0% Asian, 1.6% Other, 0.8% Hispanic of any race (2010); Density: 2,031.0 persons per square mile (2010); Average household size: 2.30 (2010); Median age: 37.0 (2010); Males per 100 females: 88.8 (2010); Marriage status: 15.4% never married, 51.9% now married, 13.2% widowed, 19.5% divorced (2005-2009 5-year est.); Foreign born: 1.6% (2005-2009 5-year est.); Ancestry (includes multiple ancestries): 27.7% Irish, 23.9% German, 16.1% English, 7.3% American, 6.9% Italian (2005-2009 5-year est.).
Economy: Single-family building permits issued: 1 (2010); Multi-family building permits issued: 0 (2010); Employment by occupation: 3.6% management, 12.3% professional, 23.9% services, 28.7% sales, 0.0% farming, 13.4% construction, 18.0% production (2005-2009 5-year est.).
Income: Per capita income: $19,497 (2010); Median household income: $33,138 (2010); Average household income: $45,403 (2010); Percent of households with income of $100,000 or more: 8.1% (2010); Poverty rate: 33.7% (2005-2009 5-year est.).
Taxes: Total city taxes per capita: $55 (2007); City property taxes per capita: $48 (2007).
Education: Percent of population age 25 and over with: High school diploma (including GED) or higher: 80.1% (2010); Bachelor's degree or higher: 11.0% (2010); Master's degree or higher: 3.2% (2010).
School District(s)
Sesser-Valier CUSD 196 (PK-12)
    2009-10 Enrollment: 781 . . . . (618) 625-5105
Housing: Homeownership rate: 79.8% (2010); Median home value: $52,989 (2010); Median contract rent: $265 per month (2005-2009 5-year est.); Median year structure built: 1952 (2005-2009 5-year est.).
Transportation: Commute to work: 92.2% car, 0.0% public transportation, 0.0% walk, 7.8% work from home (2005-2009 5-year est.); Travel time to work: 24.0% less than 15 minutes, 29.8% 15 to 30 minutes, 37.5% 30 to 45 minutes, 5.4% 45 to 60 minutes, 3.3% 60 minutes or more (2005-2009 5-year est.)
Additional Information Contacts
Sesser Area Chamber of Commerce . . . . (618) 625-3611
    http://www.sesser.org/chamber/chamber.htm

THOMPSONVILLE (village). Covers a land area of 2.050 square miles and a water area of 0.013 square miles. Located at 37.91° N. Lat; 88.76° W. Long. Elevation is 502 feet.
Population: 602 (1990); 571 (2000); 533 (2010); 538 (2015 projected); Race: 97.9% White, 0.0% Black, 0.0% Asian, 2.1% Other, 0.4% Hispanic of any race (2010); Density: 260.0 persons per square mile (2010); Average household size: 2.56 (2010); Median age: 38.0 (2010); Males per 100 females: 94.5 (2010); Marriage status: 12.7% never married, 71.5% now married, 3.6% widowed, 12.2% divorced (2005-2009 5-year est.); Foreign born: 5.3% (2005-2009 5-year est.); Ancestry (includes multiple ancestries): 28.1% German, 14.5% Irish, 6.3% American, 5.3% English, 3.5% French (2005-2009 5-year est.).
Economy: Employment by occupation: 4.1% management, 8.8% professional, 29.0% services, 18.7% sales, 0.0% farming, 17.6% construction, 21.8% production (2005-2009 5-year est.).

Income: Per capita income: $19,935 (2010); Median household income: $42,021 (2010); Average household income: $50,769 (2010); Percent of households with income of $100,000 or more: 7.7% (2010); Poverty rate: 11.2% (2005-2009 5-year est.).
Taxes: Total city taxes per capita: $20 (2007); City property taxes per capita: $20 (2007).
Education: Percent of population age 25 and over with: High school diploma (including GED) or higher: 84.7% (2010); Bachelor's degree or higher: 10.1% (2010); Master's degree or higher: 2.7% (2010).
School District(s)
Thompsonville CUSD 174 (PK-12)
    2009-10 Enrollment: 340 . . . . (618) 627-2446
Housing: Homeownership rate: 77.9% (2010); Median home value: $68,485 (2010); Median contract rent: $297 per month (2005-2009 5-year est.); Median year structure built: 1969 (2005-2009 5-year est.).
Transportation: Commute to work: 100.0% car, 0.0% public transportation, 0.0% walk, 0.0% work from home (2005-2009 5-year est.); Travel time to work: 24.5% less than 15 minutes, 47.9% 15 to 30 minutes, 11.2% 30 to 45 minutes, 14.4% 45 to 60 minutes, 2.1% 60 minutes or more (2005-2009 5-year est.)

VALIER (village). Covers a land area of 1.128 square miles and a water area of 0 square miles. Located at 38.01° N. Lat; 89.04° W. Long. Elevation is 459 feet.
Population: 708 (1990); 662 (2000); 651 (2010); 638 (2015 projected); Race: 96.5% White, 0.0% Black, 0.2% Asian, 3.4% Other, 2.2% Hispanic of any race (2010); Density: 577.2 persons per square mile (2010); Average household size: 2.46 (2010); Median age: 39.6 (2010); Males per 100 females: 102.2 (2010); Marriage status: 20.2% never married, 67.3% now married, 4.5% widowed, 8.0% divorced (2005-2009 5-year est.); Foreign born: 2.6% (2005-2009 5-year est.); Ancestry (includes multiple ancestries): 26.3% Irish, 21.2% German, 11.2% American, 10.4% English, 8.1% French (2005-2009 5-year est.).
Economy: Single-family building permits issued: 1 (2010); Multi-family building permits issued: 0 (2010); Employment by occupation: 5.1% management, 7.7% professional, 29.8% services, 27.9% sales, 0.0% farming, 9.6% construction, 19.9% production (2005-2009 5-year est.).
Income: Per capita income: $17,691 (2010); Median household income: $35,818 (2010); Average household income: $44,223 (2010); Percent of households with income of $100,000 or more: 6.8% (2010); Poverty rate: 8.8% (2005-2009 5-year est.).
Taxes: Total city taxes per capita: $85 (2007); City property taxes per capita: $45 (2007).
Education: Percent of population age 25 and over with: High school diploma (including GED) or higher: 87.6% (2010); Bachelor's degree or higher: 10.8% (2010); Master's degree or higher: 3.1% (2010).
Housing: Homeownership rate: 86.7% (2010); Median home value: $64,146 (2010); Median contract rent: $275 per month (2005-2009 5-year est.); Median year structure built: 1942 (2005-2009 5-year est.).
Transportation: Commute to work: 94.9% car, 0.0% public transportation, 0.0% walk, 3.7% work from home (2005-2009 5-year est.); Travel time to work: 12.6% less than 15 minutes, 27.9% 15 to 30 minutes, 37.4% 30 to 45 minutes, 14.5% 45 to 60 minutes, 7.6% 60 minutes or more (2005-2009 5-year est.)

WEST CITY (village). Covers a land area of 1.614 square miles and a water area of 0 square miles. Located at 37.99° N. Lat; 88.94° W. Long. Elevation is 456 feet.
History: Incorporated 1911.
Population: 747 (1990); 716 (2000); 682 (2010); 665 (2015 projected); Race: 94.1% White, 3.5% Black, 0.3% Asian, 2.1% Other, 0.4% Hispanic of any race (2010); Density: 422.7 persons per square mile (2010); Average household size: 2.21 (2010); Median age: 40.5 (2010); Males per 100 females: 90.5 (2010); Marriage status: 21.5% never married, 42.8% now married, 14.1% widowed, 21.5% divorced (2005-2009 5-year est.); Foreign born: 0.0% (2005-2009 5-year est.); Ancestry (includes multiple ancestries): 22.3% Irish, 17.4% English, 16.7% German, 6.6% American, 6.5% Polish (2005-2009 5-year est.).
Economy: Single-family building permits issued: 1 (2010); Multi-family building permits issued: 0 (2010); Employment by occupation: 7.8% management, 5.1% professional, 31.9% services, 22.7% sales, 0.0% farming, 7.2% construction, 25.4% production (2005-2009 5-year est.).
Income: Per capita income: $14,613 (2010); Median household income: $25,481 (2010); Average household income: $32,639 (2010); Percent of

households with income of $100,000 or more: 3.6% (2010); Poverty rate: 23.0% (2005-2009 5-year est.).

Taxes: Total city taxes per capita: $109 (2007); City property taxes per capita: $97 (2007).

Education: Percent of population age 25 and over with: High school diploma (including GED) or higher: 73.8% (2010); Bachelor's degree or higher: 9.3% (2010); Master's degree or higher: 3.0% (2010).

Housing: Homeownership rate: 68.5% (2010); Median home value: $41,316 (2010); Median contract rent: $336 per month (2005-2009 5-year est.); Median year structure built: 1971 (2005-2009 5-year est.).

Safety: Violent crime rate: 131.4 per 10,000 population; Property crime rate: 604.5 per 10,000 population (2010).

Transportation: Commute to work: 90.7% car, 0.0% public transportation, 9.3% walk, 0.0% work from home (2005-2009 5-year est.); Travel time to work: 70.9% less than 15 minutes, 19.8% 15 to 30 minutes, 5.1% 30 to 45 minutes, 0.9% 45 to 60 minutes, 3.3% 60 minutes or more (2005-2009 5-year est.)

WEST FRANKFORT (city). Covers a land area of 4.746 square miles and a water area of 0.013 square miles. Located at 37.89° N. Lat; 88.92° W. Long. Elevation is 400 feet.

History: Incorporated 1901; annexed Frankfort Heights in 1923.

Population: 8,671 (1990); 8,196 (2000); 7,910 (2010); 7,732 (2015 projected); Race: 97.2% White, 0.8% Black, 0.5% Asian, 1.4% Other, 1.4% Hispanic of any race (2010); Density: 1,666.5 persons per square mile (2010); Average household size: 2.22 (2010); Median age: 40.0 (2010); Males per 100 females: 90.0 (2010); Marriage status: 26.1% never married, 45.0% now married, 11.9% widowed, 17.0% divorced (2005-2009 5-year est.); Foreign born: 0.4% (2005-2009 5-year est.); Ancestry (includes multiple ancestries): 20.4% Irish, 18.4% German, 18.0% English, 12.2% American, 5.9% Scotch-Irish (2005-2009 5-year est.).

Economy: Single-family building permits issued: 3 (2010); Multi-family building permits issued: 0 (2010); Employment by occupation: 6.8% management, 17.1% professional, 22.7% services, 26.3% sales, 0.9% farming, 16.7% construction, 9.6% production (2005-2009 5-year est.).

Income: Per capita income: $17,964 (2010); Median household income: $30,891 (2010); Average household income: $40,374 (2010); Percent of households with income of $100,000 or more: 5.9% (2010); Poverty rate: 21.6% (2005-2009 5-year est.).

Taxes: Total city taxes per capita: $138 (2007); City property taxes per capita: $94 (2007).

Education: Percent of population age 25 and over with: High school diploma (including GED) or higher: 80.5% (2010); Bachelor's degree or higher: 12.9% (2010); Master's degree or higher: 3.6% (2010).

School District(s)

Frankfort CUSD 168 (PK-12)
    2009-10 Enrollment: 1,984 . . . . (618) 937-2421

Housing: Homeownership rate: 68.0% (2010); Median home value: $47,926 (2010); Median contract rent: $380 per month (2005-2009 5-year est.); Median year structure built: 1953 (2005-2009 5-year est.).

Safety: Violent crime rate: 33.6 per 10,000 population; Property crime rate: 220.5 per 10,000 population (2010).

Newspapers: Daily American (Local news; Circulation 4,200)

Transportation: Commute to work: 94.4% car, 0.4% public transportation, 0.8% walk, 3.1% work from home (2005-2009 5-year est.); Travel time to work: 43.9% less than 15 minutes, 36.0% 15 to 30 minutes, 13.5% 30 to 45 minutes, 4.2% 45 to 60 minutes, 2.4% 60 minutes or more (2005-2009 5-year est.)

Additional Information Contacts

City of West Frankfort . . . . (618) 932-3262
    http://www.westfrankfort-il.com
West Frankfort Chamber of Commerce . . . . (618) 932-2181
    http://www.westfrankfort-il.com

WHITTINGTON (unincorporated postal area, zip code 62897). Covers a land area of 14.931 square miles and a water area of 0.050 square miles. Located at 38.08° N. Lat; 88.92° W. Long. Elevation is 443 feet.

Population: 335 (2000); Race: 100.0% White, 0.0% Black, 0.0% Asian, 0.0% Other, 0.0% Hispanic of any race (2000); Density: 22.4 persons per square mile (2000); Age: 26.3% under 18, 12.5% over 64 (2000); Marriage status: 16.5% never married, 62.6% now married, 7.1% widowed, 13.8% divorced (2000); Foreign born: 0.0% (2000); Ancestry (includes multiple ancestries): 19.9% English, 16.5% American, 12.8% German, 9.8% Irish (2000).

Economy: Employment by occupation: 11.4% management, 8.3% professional, 20.5% services, 31.1% sales, 0.0% farming, 6.8% construction, 22.0% production (2000).

Income: Per capita income: $14,399 (2000); Median household income: $27,708 (2000); Poverty rate: 14.3% (2000).

Education: Percent of population age 25 and over with: High school diploma (including GED) or higher: 79.5% (2000); Bachelor's degree or higher: 10.5% (2000).

Housing: Homeownership rate: 88.0% (2000); Median home value: $63,100 (2000); Median contract rent: $325 per month (2000); Median year structure built: 1966 (2000).

Transportation: Commute to work: 80.8% car, 0.0% public transportation, 6.2% walk, 13.1% work from home (2000); Travel time to work: 46.0% less than 15 minutes, 23.9% 15 to 30 minutes, 11.5% 30 to 45 minutes, 15.0% 45 to 60 minutes, 3.5% 60 minutes or more (2000)

ZEIGLER (city). Covers a land area of 0.860 square miles and a water area of 0 square miles. Located at 37.90° N. Lat; 89.05° W. Long. Elevation is 410 feet.

Population: 1,752 (1990); 1,669 (2000); 1,656 (2010); 1,665 (2015 projected); Race: 98.1% White, 0.6% Black, 0.2% Asian, 1.0% Other, 0.8% Hispanic of any race (2010); Density: 1,925.7 persons per square mile (2010); Average household size: 2.26 (2010); Median age: 39.6 (2010); Males per 100 females: 94.6 (2010); Marriage status: 26.7% never married, 51.7% now married, 9.5% widowed, 12.1% divorced (2005-2009 5-year est.); Foreign born: 2.5% (2005-2009 5-year est.); Ancestry (includes multiple ancestries): 23.0% German, 19.0% Irish, 15.5% English, 8.9% American, 5.0% Italian (2005-2009 5-year est.).

Economy: Single-family building permits issued: 0 (2010); Multi-family building permits issued: 0 (2010); Employment by occupation: 7.1% management, 15.5% professional, 30.4% services, 16.6% sales, 0.5% farming, 17.2% construction, 12.7% production (2005-2009 5-year est.).

Income: Per capita income: $17,858 (2010); Median household income: $31,364 (2010); Average household income: $39,462 (2010); Percent of households with income of $100,000 or more: 5.9% (2010); Poverty rate: 20.0% (2005-2009 5-year est.).

Taxes: Total city taxes per capita: $134 (2007); City property taxes per capita: $65 (2007).

Education: Percent of population age 25 and over with: High school diploma (including GED) or higher: 77.9% (2010); Bachelor's degree or higher: 10.5% (2010); Master's degree or higher: 1.2% (2010).

School District(s)

Zeigler-Royalton CUSD 188 (PK-12)
    2009-10 Enrollment: 585 . . . . (618) 596-5841

Housing: Homeownership rate: 78.5% (2010); Median home value: $37,811 (2010); Median contract rent: $303 per month (2005-2009 5-year est.); Median year structure built: 1943 (2005-2009 5-year est.).

Transportation: Commute to work: 91.8% car, 0.5% public transportation, 0.8% walk, 5.8% work from home (2005-2009 5-year est.); Travel time to work: 22.7% less than 15 minutes, 36.5% 15 to 30 minutes, 27.3% 30 to 45 minutes, 7.4% 45 to 60 minutes, 6.0% 60 minutes or more (2005-2009 5-year est.)

Fulton County

Located in west central Illinois; bounded on the southeast by the Illinois River; drained by the Spoon River. Covers a land area of 865.62 square miles, a water area of 16.97 square miles, and is located in the Central Time Zone at 40.49° N. Lat., 90.17° W. Long. The county was founded in 1823. County seat is Lewistown.

Fulton County is part of the Canton, IL Micropolitan Statistical Area. The entire metro area includes: Fulton County, IL

Population: 38,080 (1990); 38,250 (2000); 36,515 (2010); 35,511 (2015 projected); Race: 94.3% White, 4.0% Black, 0.3% Asian, 1.4% Other, 1.5% Hispanic of any race (2010); Density: 42.2 persons per square mile (2010); Average household size: 2.37 (2010); Median age: 40.2 (2010); Males per 100 females: 106.7 (2010).

Religion: Five largest groups: 10.2% The United Methodist Church, 5.2% Catholic Church, 4.4% Christian Church (Disciples of Christ), 2.9% Christian Churches and Churches of Christ, 2.3% Church of the Nazarene (2000).

Economy: Unemployment rate: 9.8% (August 2011); Total civilian labor force: 18,923 (August 2011); Leading industries: 30.3% health care and social assistance; 19.8% retail trade; 11.2% accommodation & food

services (2009); Farms: 1,005 totaling 385,302 acres (2007); Companies that employ 500 or more persons: 1 (2009); Companies that employ 100 to 499 persons: 9 (2009); Companies that employ less than 100 persons: 699 (2009); Black-owned businesses: n/a (2007); Hispanic-owned businesses: n/a (2007); Asian-owned businesses: n/a (2007); Women-owned businesses: 731 (2007); Retail sales per capita: $9,743 (2010). Single-family building permits issued: 32 (2010); Multi-family building permits issued: 0 (2010).
Income: Per capita income: $21,485 (2010); Median household income: $42,503 (2010); Average household income: $52,833 (2010); Percent of households with income of $100,000 or more: 10.2% (2010); Poverty rate: 13.9% (2009); Bankruptcy rate: 5.55% (2010).
Taxes: Total county taxes per capita: $113 (2007); County property taxes per capita: $113 (2007).
Education: Percent of population age 25 and over with: High school diploma (including GED) or higher: 83.8% (2010); Bachelor's degree or higher: 12.8% (2010); Master's degree or higher: 3.9% (2010).
Housing: Homeownership rate: 78.2% (2010); Median home value: $75,054 (2010); Median contract rent: $382 per month (2005-2009 5-year est.); Median year structure built: 1953 (2005-2009 5-year est.)
Health: Birth rate: 112.1 per 10,000 population (2009); Death rate: 121.7 per 10,000 population (2009); Age-adjusted cancer mortality rate: 204.4 deaths per 100,000 population (2007); Number of physicians: 6.5 per 10,000 population (2008); Hospital beds: 28.5 per 10,000 population (2007); Hospital admissions: 922.9 per 10,000 population (2007).
Elections: 2008 Presidential election results: 59.6% Obama, 38.3% McCain, 1.1% Nader
National and State Parks: Anderson Lake State Conservation Area; Dickson Mounds State Park; Rice Lake State Conservation Area
Additional Information Contacts
Fulton County Government . . . . (309) 547-3041
  http://www.fultonco.org
Canton Area Chamber of Commerce . . . . (309) 647-2677
  http://www.cantonillinois.org
City of Canton . . . . (309) 647-0065
  http://www.cantonillinois.org
Lewistown Chamber of Commerce . . . . (309) 547-4306
  http://lewistownchamber.org

Fulton County Communities

ASTORIA (town). Aka formerly Vienna. Covers a land area of 0.590 square miles and a water area of 0 square miles. Located at 40.22° N. Lat; 90.35° W. Long. Elevation is 712 feet.
History: The villages of Washington, laid out in 1836, and Vienna, platted in 1837, were later combined and named Astoria, for John Jacob Astor who owned land in the area. Astoria was a station on the stagecoach line between Peoria and Quincy.
Population: 1,228 (1990); 1,193 (2000); 1,134 (2010); 1,097 (2015 projected); Race: 98.1% White, 0.0% Black, 0.4% Asian, 1.6% Other, 1.0% Hispanic of any race (2010); Density: 1,920.8 persons per square mile (2010); Average household size: 2.31 (2010); Median age: 41.8 (2010); Males per 100 females: 90.9 (2010); Marriage status: 22.6% never married, 51.9% now married, 13.3% widowed, 12.2% divorced (2005-2009 5-year est.); Foreign born: 1.5% (2005-2009 5-year est.); Ancestry (includes multiple ancestries): 31.6% German, 19.6% American, 11.1% English, 10.3% Irish, 8.4% Dutch (2005-2009 5-year est.).
Economy: Single-family building permits issued: 1 (2010); Multi-family building permits issued: 0 (2010); Employment by occupation: 11.1% management, 11.5% professional, 27.8% services, 16.1% sales, 1.0% farming, 8.8% construction, 23.6% production (2005-2009 5-year est.).
Income: Per capita income: $18,744 (2010); Median household income: $36,995 (2010); Average household income: $44,695 (2010); Percent of households with income of $100,000 or more: 5.9% (2010); Poverty rate: 15.2% (2005-2009 5-year est.).
Taxes: Total city taxes per capita: $31 (2007); City property taxes per capita: $31 (2007).
Education: Percent of population age 25 and over with: High school diploma (including GED) or higher: 85.2% (2010); Bachelor's degree or higher: 11.7% (2010); Master's degree or higher: 2.3% (2010).
School District(s)
Astoria CUSD 1 (PK-12)
  2009-10 Enrollment: 396 . . . . (309) 329-2111

Housing: Homeownership rate: 79.6% (2010); Median home value: $48,000 (2010); Median contract rent: $269 per month (2005-2009 5-year est.); Median year structure built: 1942 (2005-2009 5-year est.).
Newspapers: South Fulton Argus (Regional news; Circulation 2,200)
Transportation: Commute to work: 97.2% car, 0.0% public transportation, 0.0% walk, 1.4% work from home (2005-2009 5-year est.); Travel time to work: 38.7% less than 15 minutes, 22.5% 15 to 30 minutes, 18.6% 30 to 45 minutes, 6.9% 45 to 60 minutes, 13.4% 60 minutes or more (2005-2009 5-year est.)

AVON (village). Covers a land area of 0.443 square miles and a water area of 0 square miles. Located at 40.66° N. Lat; 90.43° W. Long. Elevation is 640 feet.
Population: 963 (1990); 915 (2000); 853 (2010); 821 (2015 projected); Race: 98.5% White, 0.0% Black, 0.2% Asian, 1.3% Other, 0.8% Hispanic of any race (2010); Density: 1,925.4 persons per square mile (2010); Average household size: 2.40 (2010); Median age: 40.9 (2010); Males per 100 females: 93.0 (2010); Marriage status: 22.2% never married, 54.3% now married, 9.3% widowed, 14.2% divorced (2005-2009 5-year est.); Foreign born: 1.3% (2005-2009 5-year est.); Ancestry (includes multiple ancestries): 28.6% German, 20.5% English, 19.0% American, 12.5% Irish, 6.4% Dutch (2005-2009 5-year est.).
Economy: Single-family building permits issued: 0 (2010); Multi-family building permits issued: 0 (2010); Employment by occupation: 9.1% management, 21.2% professional, 11.6% services, 21.0% sales, 1.3% farming, 9.3% construction, 26.5% production (2005-2009 5-year est.).
Income: Per capita income: $22,912 (2010); Median household income: $44,167 (2010); Average household income: $55,077 (2010); Percent of households with income of $100,000 or more: 11.5% (2010); Poverty rate: 22.9% (2005-2009 5-year est.).
Taxes: Total city taxes per capita: $63 (2007); City property taxes per capita: $55 (2007).
Education: Percent of population age 25 and over with: High school diploma (including GED) or higher: 85.3% (2010); Bachelor's degree or higher: 12.7% (2010); Master's degree or higher: 3.3% (2010).
School District(s)
Avon CUSD 176 (PK-12)
  2009-10 Enrollment: 244 . . . . (309) 465-3708
Housing: Homeownership rate: 78.3% (2010); Median home value: $61,091 (2010); Median contract rent: $338 per month (2005-2009 5-year est.); Median year structure built: 1947 (2005-2009 5-year est.).
Transportation: Commute to work: 93.4% car, 0.0% public transportation, 3.7% walk, 0.5% work from home (2005-2009 5-year est.); Travel time to work: 32.5% less than 15 minutes, 22.7% 15 to 30 minutes, 30.1% 30 to 45 minutes, 5.3% 45 to 60 minutes, 9.5% 60 minutes or more (2005-2009 5-year est.)

BANNER (village). Covers a land area of 0.336 square miles and a water area of 0 square miles. Located at 40.51° N. Lat; 89.91° W. Long. Elevation is 469 feet.
Population: 160 (1990); 149 (2000); 143 (2010); 138 (2015 projected); Race: 97.9% White, 0.0% Black, 0.7% Asian, 1.4% Other, 0.7% Hispanic of any race (2010); Density: 425.7 persons per square mile (2010); Average household size: 2.47 (2010); Median age: 47.2 (2010); Males per 100 females: 101.4 (2010); Marriage status: 27.6% never married, 58.2% now married, 0.0% widowed, 14.3% divorced (2005-2009 5-year est.); Foreign born: 0.0% (2005-2009 5-year est.); Ancestry (includes multiple ancestries): 37.6% German, 31.2% Irish, 17.4% English, 9.2% Swedish, 8.3% American (2005-2009 5-year est.).
Economy: Employment by occupation: 15.1% management, 17.8% professional, 11.0% services, 19.2% sales, 0.0% farming, 19.2% construction, 17.8% production (2005-2009 5-year est.).
Income: Per capita income: $24,838 (2010); Median household income: $53,333 (2010); Average household income: $65,129 (2010); Percent of households with income of $100,000 or more: 17.2% (2010); Poverty rate: 18.3% (2005-2009 5-year est.).
Taxes: Total city taxes per capita: $14 (2007); City property taxes per capita: $0 (2007).
Education: Percent of population age 25 and over with: High school diploma (including GED) or higher: 87.5% (2010); Bachelor's degree or higher: 6.3% (2010); Master's degree or higher: 0.9% (2010).
Housing: Homeownership rate: 84.5% (2010); Median home value: $68,750 (2010); Median contract rent: n/a per month (2005-2009 5-year est.); Median year structure built: 1964 (2005-2009 5-year est.).

Transportation: Commute to work: 90.3% car, 0.0% public transportation, 0.0% walk, 0.0% work from home (2005-2009 5-year est.); Travel time to work: 34.7% less than 15 minutes, 16.7% 15 to 30 minutes, 26.4% 30 to 45 minutes, 16.7% 45 to 60 minutes, 5.6% 60 minutes or more (2005-2009 5-year est.)

BRYANT (village). Covers a land area of 0.256 square miles and a water area of 0 square miles. Located at 40.46° N. Lat; 90.09° W. Long. Elevation is 607 feet.
Population: 273 (1990); 255 (2000); 246 (2010); 243 (2015 projected); Race: 98.8% White, 0.4% Black, 0.0% Asian, 0.8% Other, 0.8% Hispanic of any race (2010); Density: 959.5 persons per square mile (2010); Average household size: 2.67 (2010); Median age: 39.5 (2010); Males per 100 females: 96.8 (2010); Marriage status: 34.3% never married, 42.6% now married, 4.4% widowed, 18.6% divorced (2005-2009 5-year est.); Foreign born: 1.2% (2005-2009 5-year est.); Ancestry (includes multiple ancestries): 28.2% German, 17.9% Irish, 16.7% American, 13.5% English, 4.8% French (2005-2009 5-year est.).
Economy: Employment by occupation: 8.1% management, 5.6% professional, 13.7% services, 33.9% sales, 5.6% farming, 21.8% construction, 11.3% production (2005-2009 5-year est.).
Income: Per capita income: $19,013 (2010); Median household income: $35,938 (2010); Average household income: $49,891 (2010); Percent of households with income of $100,000 or more: 10.9% (2010); Poverty rate: 26.6% (2005-2009 5-year est.).
Taxes: Total city taxes per capita: $12 (2007); City property taxes per capita: $12 (2007).
Education: Percent of population age 25 and over with: High school diploma (including GED) or higher: 89.8% (2010); Bachelor's degree or higher: 5.6% (2010); Master's degree or higher: 1.1% (2010).
Housing: Homeownership rate: 85.9% (2010); Median home value: $81,000 (2010); Median contract rent: $278 per month (2005-2009 5-year est.); Median year structure built: 1951 (2005-2009 5-year est.).
Transportation: Commute to work: 96.8% car, 0.0% public transportation, 0.0% walk, 3.2% work from home (2005-2009 5-year est.); Travel time to work: 4.2% less than 15 minutes, 59.2% 15 to 30 minutes, 6.7% 30 to 45 minutes, 20.0% 45 to 60 minutes, 10.0% 60 minutes or more (2005-2009 5-year est.)

CANTON (city). Covers a land area of 7.849 square miles and a water area of 0.163 square miles. Located at 40.55° N. Lat; 90.03° W. Long. Elevation is 646 feet.
History: Canton was founded in 1825 by Isaac Swan of New York. He selected the name for the town in the belief that the city of Canton in China was located directly opposite on the globe.
Population: 14,212 (1990); 15,288 (2000); 14,278 (2010); 13,836 (2015 projected); Race: 87.8% White, 10.1% Black, 0.4% Asian, 1.7% Other, 2.9% Hispanic of any race (2010); Density: 1,819.1 persons per square mile (2010); Average household size: 2.26 (2010); Median age: 37.6 (2010); Males per 100 females: 120.3 (2010); Marriage status: 30.7% never married, 45.8% now married, 8.4% widowed, 15.1% divorced (2005-2009 5-year est.); Foreign born: 4.5% (2005-2009 5-year est.); Ancestry (includes multiple ancestries): 19.1% German, 16.9% American, 12.5% English, 11.0% Irish, 3.3% Scottish (2005-2009 5-year est.).
Economy: Single-family building permits issued: 4 (2010); Multi-family building permits issued: 0 (2010); Employment by occupation: 8.4% management, 18.5% professional, 24.4% services, 21.4% sales, 0.0% farming, 9.7% construction, 17.7% production (2005-2009 5-year est.).
Income: Per capita income: $19,774 (2010); Median household income: $37,363 (2010); Average household income: $48,667 (2010); Percent of households with income of $100,000 or more: 8.7% (2010); Poverty rate: 16.9% (2005-2009 5-year est.).
Taxes: Total city taxes per capita: $226 (2007); City property taxes per capita: $110 (2007).
Education: Percent of population age 25 and over with: High school diploma (including GED) or higher: 78.8% (2010); Bachelor's degree or higher: 13.0% (2010); Master's degree or higher: 3.8% (2010).
School District(s)
Canton Union SD 66 (PK-12)
    2009-10 Enrollment: 2,658 . . . . (309) 647-9411
Fulton/Schuyler Roe (06-12)
    2009-10 Enrollment: n/a . . . . (309) 547-3041

Two-year College(s)
Graham Hospital School of Nursing (Private, Not-for-profit)
    Fall 2009 Enrollment: 76 . . . . (309) 647-4086
    2010-11 Tuition: In-state $9,718; Out-of-state $9,718
Spoon River College (Public)
    Fall 2009 Enrollment: 2,118. . . . . (309) 647-4645
    2010-11 Tuition: In-state $6,780; Out-of-state $7,860
Housing: Homeownership rate: 71.0% (2010); Median home value: $76,394 (2010); Median contract rent: $416 per month (2005-2009 5-year est.); Median year structure built: 1954 (2005-2009 5-year est.).
Hospitals: Graham Hospital (124 beds)
Safety: Violent crime rate: 32.9 per 10,000 population; Property crime rate: 257.9 per 10,000 population (2010).
Newspapers: The Daily Ledger (Local news; Circulation 9,200)
Transportation: Commute to work: 93.1% car, 0.0% public transportation, 4.3% walk, 1.2% work from home (2005-2009 5-year est.); Travel time to work: 53.5% less than 15 minutes, 12.2% 15 to 30 minutes, 11.3% 30 to 45 minutes, 14.6% 45 to 60 minutes, 8.4% 60 minutes or more (2005-2009 5-year est.)
Airports: Ingersoll (general aviation)
Additional Information Contacts
Canton Area Chamber of Commerce . . . . (309) 647-2677
    http://www.cantonillinois.org
City of Canton . . . . (309) 647-0065
    http://www.cantonillinois.org

CUBA (city). Covers a land area of 0.542 square miles and a water area of 0 square miles. Located at 40.49° N. Lat; 90.19° W. Long. Elevation is 682 feet.
History: Incorporated 1853.
Population: 1,440 (1990); 1,418 (2000); 1,264 (2010); 1,185 (2015 projected); Race: 98.1% White, 0.1% Black, 0.1% Asian, 1.7% Other, 0.6% Hispanic of any race (2010); Density: 2,332.5 persons per square mile (2010); Average household size: 2.44 (2010); Median age: 39.3 (2010); Males per 100 females: 92.1 (2010); Marriage status: 23.9% never married, 48.6% now married, 9.7% widowed, 17.8% divorced (2005-2009 5-year est.); Foreign born: 1.3% (2005-2009 5-year est.); Ancestry (includes multiple ancestries): 23.3% German, 23.1% American, 17.7% Irish, 13.9% English, 6.8% Italian (2005-2009 5-year est.).
Economy: Single-family building permits issued: 0 (2010); Multi-family building permits issued: 0 (2010); Employment by occupation: 8.0% management, 18.0% professional, 21.3% services, 23.3% sales, 0.5% farming, 17.0% construction, 11.9% production (2005-2009 5-year est.).
Income: Per capita income: $18,081 (2010); Median household income: $36,659 (2010); Average household income: $44,237 (2010); Percent of households with income of $100,000 or more: 6.0% (2010); Poverty rate: 15.0% (2005-2009 5-year est.).
Taxes: Total city taxes per capita: $35 (2007); City property taxes per capita: $34 (2007).
Education: Percent of population age 25 and over with: High school diploma (including GED) or higher: 86.1% (2010); Bachelor's degree or higher: 9.5% (2010); Master's degree or higher: 3.4% (2010).
School District(s)
CUSD 3 Fulton County (PK-12)
    2009-10 Enrollment: 547 . . . . (309) 785-5021
Housing: Homeownership rate: 80.4% (2010); Median home value: $71,519 (2010); Median contract rent: $413 per month (2005-2009 5-year est.); Median year structure built: 1948 (2005-2009 5-year est.).
Transportation: Commute to work: 92.2% car, 0.0% public transportation, 2.9% walk, 2.9% work from home (2005-2009 5-year est.); Travel time to work: 36.1% less than 15 minutes, 23.8% 15 to 30 minutes, 13.0% 30 to 45 minutes, 13.4% 45 to 60 minutes, 13.6% 60 minutes or more (2005-2009 5-year est.)

DUNFERMLINE (village). Covers a land area of 0.131 square miles and a water area of 0 square miles. Located at 40.49° N. Lat; 90.03° W. Long. Elevation is 633 feet.
Population: 259 (1990); 262 (2000); 252 (2010); 243 (2015 projected); Race: 97.6% White, 0.0% Black, 0.0% Asian, 2.4% Other, 0.0% Hispanic of any race (2010); Density: 1,923.6 persons per square mile (2010); Average household size: 2.40 (2010); Median age: 40.1 (2010); Males per 100 females: 104.9 (2010); Marriage status: 16.2% never married, 48.6% now married, 21.8% widowed, 13.4% divorced (2005-2009 5-year est.); Foreign born: 5.6% (2005-2009 5-year est.); Ancestry (includes multiple

ancestries): 26.5% American, 19.1% German, 13.0% Irish, 11.1% Polish, 4.9% Turkish (2005-2009 5-year est.).
Economy: Single-family building permits issued: 0 (2010); Multi-family building permits issued: 0 (2010); Employment by occupation: 6.3% management, 20.3% professional, 22.8% services, 11.4% sales, 0.0% farming, 24.1% construction, 15.2% production (2005-2009 5-year est.).
Income: Per capita income: $21,004 (2010); Median household income: $43,750 (2010); Average household income: $51,262 (2010); Percent of households with income of $100,000 or more: 11.4% (2010); Poverty rate: 13.6% (2005-2009 5-year est.).
Taxes: Total city taxes per capita: $30 (2007); City property taxes per capita: $26 (2007).
Education: Percent of population age 25 and over with: High school diploma (including GED) or higher: 87.5% (2010); Bachelor's degree or higher: 4.5% (2010); Master's degree or higher: 1.1% (2010).
Housing: Homeownership rate: 85.7% (2010); Median home value: $60,000 (2010); Median contract rent: n/a per month (2005-2009 5-year est.); Median year structure built: 1949 (2005-2009 5-year est.).
Transportation: Commute to work: 97.4% car, 0.0% public transportation, 0.0% walk, 0.0% work from home (2005-2009 5-year est.); Travel time to work: 21.8% less than 15 minutes, 39.7% 15 to 30 minutes, 9.0% 30 to 45 minutes, 10.3% 45 to 60 minutes, 19.2% 60 minutes or more (2005-2009 5-year est.)

ELLISVILLE (village). Covers a land area of 0.271 square miles and a water area of 0 square miles. Located at 40.62° N. Lat; 90.30° W. Long. Elevation is 551 feet.
Population: 116 (1990); 87 (2000); 80 (2010); 77 (2015 projected); Race: 100.0% White, 0.0% Black, 0.0% Asian, 0.0% Other, 0.0% Hispanic of any race (2010); Density: 294.8 persons per square mile (2010); Average household size: 2.42 (2010); Median age: 46.8 (2010); Males per 100 females: 105.1 (2010); Marriage status: 19.1% never married, 80.9% now married, 0.0% widowed, 0.0% divorced (2005-2009 5-year est.); Foreign born: 0.0% (2005-2009 5-year est.); Ancestry (includes multiple ancestries): 33.0% American, 22.7% German, 15.9% Dutch, 13.6% Irish, 6.8% English (2005-2009 5-year est.).
Economy: Employment by occupation: 0.0% management, 20.4% professional, 28.6% services, 16.3% sales, 0.0% farming, 18.4% construction, 16.3% production (2005-2009 5-year est.).
Income: Per capita income: $21,262 (2010); Median household income: $46,786 (2010); Average household income: $52,121 (2010); Percent of households with income of $100,000 or more: 9.1% (2010); Poverty rate: 4.5% (2005-2009 5-year est.).
Taxes: Total city taxes per capita: $24 (2007); City property taxes per capita: $24 (2007).
Education: Percent of population age 25 and over with: High school diploma (including GED) or higher: 90.8% (2010); Bachelor's degree or higher: 15.4% (2010); Master's degree or higher: 4.6% (2010).
Housing: Homeownership rate: 81.8% (2010); Median home value: $72,500 (2010); Median contract rent: n/a per month (2005-2009 5-year est.); Median year structure built: before 1940 (2005-2009 5-year est.).
Transportation: Commute to work: 100.0% car, 0.0% public transportation, 0.0% walk, 0.0% work from home (2005-2009 5-year est.); Travel time to work: 10.2% less than 15 minutes, 42.9% 15 to 30 minutes, 22.4% 30 to 45 minutes, 4.1% 45 to 60 minutes, 20.4% 60 minutes or more (2005-2009 5-year est.)

FAIRVIEW (village). Covers a land area of 4.162 square miles and a water area of 0.074 square miles. Located at 40.63° N. Lat; 90.16° W. Long. Elevation is 735 feet.
Population: 510 (1990); 493 (2000); 510 (2010); 512 (2015 projected); Race: 99.4% White, 0.0% Black, 0.0% Asian, 0.6% Other, 0.0% Hispanic of any race (2010); Density: 122.5 persons per square mile (2010); Average household size: 2.50 (2010); Median age: 42.5 (2010); Males per 100 females: 109.9 (2010); Marriage status: 23.1% never married, 54.1% now married, 16.9% widowed, 5.9% divorced (2005-2009 5-year est.); Foreign born: 0.0% (2005-2009 5-year est.); Ancestry (includes multiple ancestries): 39.6% German, 15.7% Irish, 15.0% American, 7.7% English, 6.3% Scottish (2005-2009 5-year est.).
Economy: Single-family building permits issued: 0 (2010); Multi-family building permits issued: 0 (2010); Employment by occupation: 10.6% management, 31.9% professional, 14.9% services, 13.3% sales, 0.0% farming, 19.1% construction, 10.1% production (2005-2009 5-year est.).
Income: Per capita income: $20,673 (2010); Median household income: $42,500 (2010); Average household income: $51,520 (2010); Percent of

households with income of $100,000 or more: 9.8% (2010); Poverty rate: 10.3% (2005-2009 5-year est.).
Taxes: Total city taxes per capita: $124 (2007); City property taxes per capita: $124 (2007).
Education: Percent of population age 25 and over with: High school diploma (including GED) or higher: 85.3% (2010); Bachelor's degree or higher: 16.8% (2010); Master's degree or higher: 6.7% (2010).
Housing: Homeownership rate: 81.9% (2010); Median home value: $80,455 (2010); Median contract rent: $192 per month (2005-2009 5-year est.); Median year structure built: 1941 (2005-2009 5-year est.).
Safety: Violent crime rate: 0.0 per 10,000 population; Property crime rate: 21.2 per 10,000 population (2010).
Transportation: Commute to work: 92.6% car, 1.6% public transportation, 4.8% walk, 1.1% work from home (2005-2009 5-year est.); Travel time to work: 22.6% less than 15 minutes, 24.7% 15 to 30 minutes, 8.6% 30 to 45 minutes, 25.8% 45 to 60 minutes, 18.3% 60 minutes or more (2005-2009 5-year est.)

FARMINGTON (city). Covers a land area of 1.241 square miles and a water area of 0 square miles. Located at 40.69° N. Lat; 90.00° W. Long. Elevation is 745 feet.
History: Farmington was laid out in 1834, and grew as a mining town. In 1856 Farmington was the scene of a "whiskey war" when a group of women marched on the saloons, breaking windows and smashing bottles.
Population: 2,547 (1990); 2,601 (2000); 2,284 (2010); 2,184 (2015 projected); Race: 98.3% White, 0.2% Black, 0.1% Asian, 1.4% Other, 0.7% Hispanic of any race (2010); Density: 1,839.8 persons per square mile (2010); Average household size: 2.46 (2010); Median age: 39.8 (2010); Males per 100 females: 90.7 (2010); Marriage status: 18.4% never married, 60.8% now married, 9.8% widowed, 11.1% divorced (2005-2009 5-year est.); Foreign born: 1.7% (2005-2009 5-year est.); Ancestry (includes multiple ancestries): 29.3% German, 15.9% American, 14.9% Irish, 14.8% English, 8.6% Italian (2005-2009 5-year est.).
Economy: Single-family building permits issued: 0 (2010); Multi-family building permits issued: 0 (2010); Employment by occupation: 9.6% management, 13.7% professional, 17.9% services, 24.2% sales, 0.3% farming, 12.0% construction, 22.4% production (2005-2009 5-year est.).
Income: Per capita income: $24,289 (2010); Median household income: $47,277 (2010); Average household income: $59,188 (2010); Percent of households with income of $100,000 or more: 12.2% (2010); Poverty rate: 14.8% (2005-2009 5-year est.).
Taxes: Total city taxes per capita: $108 (2007); City property taxes per capita: $90 (2007).
Education: Percent of population age 25 and over with: High school diploma (including GED) or higher: 89.8% (2010); Bachelor's degree or higher: 13.7% (2010); Master's degree or higher: 5.2% (2010).
School District(s)
Farmington Central CUSD 265 (PK-12)
   2009-10 Enrollment: 1,469 . . . . (309) 245-1000
Housing: Homeownership rate: 82.2% (2010); Median home value: $80,178 (2010); Median contract rent: $364 per month (2005-2009 5-year est.); Median year structure built: 1942 (2005-2009 5-year est.).
Transportation: Commute to work: 90.1% car, 0.0% public transportation, 1.6% walk, 2.3% work from home (2005-2009 5-year est.); Travel time to work: 32.8% less than 15 minutes, 23.8% 15 to 30 minutes, 29.5% 30 to 45 minutes, 10.4% 45 to 60 minutes, 3.5% 60 minutes or more (2005-2009 5-year est.)

IPAVA (village). Covers a land area of 0.270 square miles and a water area of 0 square miles. Located at 40.35° N. Lat; 90.32° W. Long. Elevation is 659 feet.
History: Vestiges of Camp Ellis, a World War II prisoner-of-war camp, nearby.
Population: 483 (1990); 506 (2000); 478 (2010); 459 (2015 projected); Race: 98.1% White, 0.0% Black, 0.2% Asian, 1.7% Other, 1.3% Hispanic of any race (2010); Density: 1,773.1 persons per square mile (2010); Average household size: 2.27 (2010); Median age: 42.4 (2010); Males per 100 females: 98.3 (2010); Marriage status: 21.4% never married, 60.1% now married, 6.8% widowed, 11.7% divorced (2005-2009 5-year est.); Foreign born: 0.0% (2005-2009 5-year est.); Ancestry (includes multiple ancestries): 32.2% American, 22.3% German, 13.1% Irish, 8.4% English, 3.5% Polish (2005-2009 5-year est.).
Economy: Single-family building permits issued: 1 (2010); Multi-family building permits issued: 0 (2010); Employment by occupation: 14.1%

management, 12.0% professional, 13.2% services, 21.8% sales, 2.1% farming, 21.4% construction, 15.4% production (2005-2009 5-year est.).
Income: Per capita income: $20,763 (2010); Median household income: $40,625 (2010); Average household income: $46,315 (2010); Percent of households with income of $100,000 or more: 4.7% (2010); Poverty rate: 12.2% (2005-2009 5-year est.).
Taxes: Total city taxes per capita: $50 (2007); City property taxes per capita: $25 (2007).
Education: Percent of population age 25 and over with: High school diploma (including GED) or higher: 84.3% (2010); Bachelor's degree or higher: 7.9% (2010); Master's degree or higher: 0.9% (2010).
Housing: Homeownership rate: 86.7% (2010); Median home value: $52,500 (2010); Median contract rent: $376 per month (2005-2009 5-year est.); Median year structure built: 1955 (2005-2009 5-year est.).
Transportation: Commute to work: 97.3% car, 0.0% public transportation, 1.3% walk, 1.3% work from home (2005-2009 5-year est.); Travel time to work: 18.1% less than 15 minutes, 22.2% 15 to 30 minutes, 27.6% 30 to 45 minutes, 5.0% 45 to 60 minutes, 27.1% 60 minutes or more (2005-2009 5-year est.)

LEWISTOWN (city). County seat. Covers a land area of 1.838 square miles and a water area of 0 square miles. Located at 40.39° N. Lat; 90.15° W. Long. Elevation is 591 feet.
History: Lewiston was founded in 1821 by Major Ossian M. Ross, who had received the land for his service in the War of 1812. The town was named for the Major's son, Lewis. In 1823 Ross organized Fulton County and had Lewiston named as the seat, with the courthouse built on land he donated.
Population: 2,592 (1990); 2,522 (2000); 2,294 (2010); 2,202 (2015 projected); Race: 98.7% White, 0.0% Black, 0.0% Asian, 1.2% Other, 1.0% Hispanic of any race (2010); Density: 1,248.2 persons per square mile (2010); Average household size: 2.23 (2010); Median age: 43.1 (2010); Males per 100 females: 90.7 (2010); Marriage status: 20.2% never married, 54.0% now married, 11.0% widowed, 14.8% divorced (2005-2009 5-year est.); Foreign born: 1.5% (2005-2009 5-year est.); Ancestry (includes multiple ancestries): 21.5% German, 13.9% American, 13.5% Irish, 12.2% English, 4.3% Italian (2005-2009 5-year est.).
Economy: Single-family building permits issued: 0 (2010); Multi-family building permits issued: 0 (2010); Employment by occupation: 9.6% management, 16.4% professional, 22.4% services, 22.2% sales, 0.0% farming, 13.8% construction, 15.6% production (2005-2009 5-year est.).
Income: Per capita income: $21,991 (2010); Median household income: $42,771 (2010); Average household income: $50,248 (2010); Percent of households with income of $100,000 or more: 9.1% (2010); Poverty rate: 17.1% (2005-2009 5-year est.).
Taxes: Total city taxes per capita: $96 (2007); City property taxes per capita: $59 (2007).
Education: Percent of population age 25 and over with: High school diploma (including GED) or higher: 85.8% (2010); Bachelor's degree or higher: 13.3% (2010); Master's degree or higher: 4.7% (2010).

School District(s)
Lewistown CUSD 97 (PK-12)
    2009-10 Enrollment: 750 . . . . (309) 547-5826
West Central II Spec Educ Coop (06-12)
    2009-10 Enrollment: n/a . . . . (309) 837-3911
Housing: Homeownership rate: 70.3% (2010); Median home value: $73,510 (2010); Median contract rent: $336 per month (2005-2009 5-year est.); Median year structure built: 1955 (2005-2009 5-year est.).
Newspapers: Fulton Democrat (Local news; Circulation 5,300)
Transportation: Commute to work: 95.5% car, 0.0% public transportation, 2.6% walk, 1.9% work from home (2005-2009 5-year est.); Travel time to work: 42.8% less than 15 minutes, 19.5% 15 to 30 minutes, 11.1% 30 to 45 minutes, 8.0% 45 to 60 minutes, 18.6% 60 minutes or more (2005-2009 5-year est.)
Additional Information Contacts
Lewistown Chamber of Commerce . . . . (309) 547-4306
    http://lewistownchamber.org

LIVERPOOL (village). Covers a land area of 0.081 square miles and a water area of 0.001 square miles. Located at 40.39° N. Lat; 90.00° W. Long. Elevation is 446 feet.
History: Liverpool, named for the town in England, began as a river town and shipping center. Commercial fishing developed later.
Population: 129 (1990); 119 (2000); 114 (2010); 110 (2015 projected); Race: 98.2% White, 0.0% Black, 0.9% Asian, 0.9% Other, 0.0% Hispanic of any race (2010); Density: 1,413.7 persons per square mile (2010);

Average household size: 2.48 (2010); Median age: 43.0 (2010); Males per 100 females: 103.6 (2010); Marriage status: 12.7% never married, 77.8% now married, 0.0% widowed, 9.5% divorced (2005-2009 5-year est.); Foreign born: 0.0% (2005-2009 5-year est.); Ancestry (includes multiple ancestries): 26.0% German, 24.7% English, 23.3% American, 15.1% Dutch, 8.2% Scotch-Irish (2005-2009 5-year est.).
Economy: Employment by occupation: 33.3% management, 4.2% professional, 12.5% services, 41.7% sales, 0.0% farming, 8.3% construction, 0.0% production (2005-2009 5-year est.).
Income: Per capita income: $24,838 (2010); Median household income: $54,167 (2010); Average household income: $66,848 (2010); Percent of households with income of $100,000 or more: 17.4% (2010); Poverty rate: 4.1% (2005-2009 5-year est.).
Taxes: Total city taxes per capita: $52 (2007); City property taxes per capita: $34 (2007).
Education: Percent of population age 25 and over with: High school diploma (including GED) or higher: 85.4% (2010); Bachelor's degree or higher: 7.3% (2010); Master's degree or higher: 1.2% (2010).
Housing: Homeownership rate: 84.8% (2010); Median home value: $71,667 (2010); Median contract rent: n/a per month (2005-2009 5-year est.); Median year structure built: 1969 (2005-2009 5-year est.).
Transportation: Commute to work: 66.7% car, 0.0% public transportation, 20.8% walk, 12.5% work from home (2005-2009 5-year est.); Travel time to work: 52.4% less than 15 minutes, 47.6% 15 to 30 minutes, 0.0% 30 to 45 minutes, 0.0% 45 to 60 minutes, 0.0% 60 minutes or more (2005-2009 5-year est.)

LONDON MILLS (village). Covers a land area of 0.694 square miles and a water area of 0 square miles. Located at 40.71° N. Lat; 90.26° W. Long. Elevation is 541 feet.
Population: 485 (1990); 447 (2000); 406 (2010); 383 (2015 projected); Race: 99.5% White, 0.0% Black, 0.0% Asian, 0.5% Other, 0.2% Hispanic of any race (2010); Density: 585.4 persons per square mile (2010); Average household size: 2.64 (2010); Median age: 38.7 (2010); Males per 100 females: 94.3 (2010); Marriage status: 22.1% never married, 64.0% now married, 2.3% widowed, 11.7% divorced (2005-2009 5-year est.); Foreign born: 0.3% (2005-2009 5-year est.); Ancestry (includes multiple ancestries): 21.8% German, 14.1% Swedish, 13.8% Irish, 13.6% American, 12.3% English (2005-2009 5-year est.).
Economy: Employment by occupation: 6.8% management, 17.4% professional, 15.5% services, 23.0% sales, 2.5% farming, 18.6% construction, 16.1% production (2005-2009 5-year est.).
Income: Per capita income: $24,942 (2010); Median household income: $52,083 (2010); Average household income: $67,013 (2010); Percent of households with income of $100,000 or more: 17.5% (2010); Poverty rate: 27.2% (2005-2009 5-year est.).
Taxes: Total city taxes per capita: $106 (2007); City property taxes per capita: $35 (2007).
Education: Percent of population age 25 and over with: High school diploma (including GED) or higher: 89.7% (2010); Bachelor's degree or higher: 15.6% (2010); Master's degree or higher: 6.1% (2010).

School District(s)
Spoon River Valley CUSD 4 (PK-12)
    2009-10 Enrollment: 445 . . . . (309) 778-2204
Housing: Homeownership rate: 88.3% (2010); Median home value: $73,333 (2010); Median contract rent: $350 per month (2005-2009 5-year est.); Median year structure built: before 1940 (2005-2009 5-year est.).
Transportation: Commute to work: 91.9% car, 2.5% public transportation, 5.6% walk, 0.0% work from home (2005-2009 5-year est.); Travel time to work: 32.9% less than 15 minutes, 11.2% 15 to 30 minutes, 17.4% 30 to 45 minutes, 17.4% 45 to 60 minutes, 21.1% 60 minutes or more (2005-2009 5-year est.)

MARIETTA (village). Covers a land area of 0.269 square miles and a water area of 0 square miles. Located at 40.50° N. Lat; 90.39° W. Long. Elevation is 650 feet.
Population: 142 (1990); 150 (2000); 147 (2010); 144 (2015 projected); Race: 97.3% White, 0.0% Black, 0.0% Asian, 2.7% Other, 0.7% Hispanic of any race (2010); Density: 545.9 persons per square mile (2010); Average household size: 2.49 (2010); Median age: 40.0 (2010); Males per 100 females: 90.9 (2010); Marriage status: 9.8% never married, 62.0% now married, 14.1% widowed, 14.1% divorced (2005-2009 5-year est.); Foreign born: 7.4% (2005-2009 5-year est.); Ancestry (includes multiple ancestries): 23.1% German, 23.1% American, 16.7% Turkish, 6.5% English, 6.5% Polish (2005-2009 5-year est.).

Economy: Employment by occupation: 5.0% management, 5.0% professional, 15.0% services, 20.0% sales, 0.0% farming, 17.5% construction, 37.5% production (2005-2009 5-year est.).
Income: Per capita income: $22,022 (2010); Median household income: $44,265 (2010); Average household income: $53,390 (2010); Percent of households with income of $100,000 or more: 8.5% (2010); Poverty rate: 24.1% (2005-2009 5-year est.).
Taxes: Total city taxes per capita: $27 (2007); City property taxes per capita: $21 (2007).
Education: Percent of population age 25 and over with: High school diploma (including GED) or higher: 89.5% (2010); Bachelor's degree or higher: 11.4% (2010); Master's degree or higher: 2.9% (2010).
Housing: Homeownership rate: 86.4% (2010); Median home value: $81,111 (2010); Median contract rent: n/a per month (2005-2009 5-year est.); Median year structure built: 1945 (2005-2009 5-year est.).
Transportation: Commute to work: 100.0% car, 0.0% public transportation, 0.0% walk, 0.0% work from home (2005-2009 5-year est.); Travel time to work: 10.0% less than 15 minutes, 35.0% 15 to 30 minutes, 17.5% 30 to 45 minutes, 0.0% 45 to 60 minutes, 37.5% 60 minutes or more (2005-2009 5-year est.)

NORRIS (village). Covers a land area of 0.281 square miles and a water area of 0 square miles. Located at 40.62° N. Lat; 90.03° W. Long. Elevation is 728 feet.
Population: 212 (1990); 194 (2000); 204 (2010); 207 (2015 projected); Race: 99.5% White, 0.0% Black, 0.0% Asian, 0.5% Other, 0.5% Hispanic of any race (2010); Density: 725.4 persons per square mile (2010); Average household size: 2.58 (2010); Median age: 38.2 (2010); Males per 100 females: 112.5 (2010); Marriage status: 5.1% never married, 84.1% now married, 8.0% widowed, 2.9% divorced (2005-2009 5-year est.); Foreign born: 5.8% (2005-2009 5-year est.); Ancestry (includes multiple ancestries): 25.4% Irish, 15.9% American, 13.2% German, 8.5% English, 7.9% Italian (2005-2009 5-year est.).
Economy: Employment by occupation: 0.0% management, 14.9% professional, 20.3% services, 20.3% sales, 6.8% farming, 24.3% construction, 13.5% production (2005-2009 5-year est.).
Income: Per capita income: $27,126 (2010); Median household income: $58,523 (2010); Average household income: $66,487 (2010); Percent of households with income of $100,000 or more: 17.7% (2010); Poverty rate: 8.5% (2005-2009 5-year est.).
Taxes: Total city taxes per capita: $43 (2007); City property taxes per capita: $32 (2007).
Education: Percent of population age 25 and over with: High school diploma (including GED) or higher: 86.6% (2010); Bachelor's degree or higher: 14.8% (2010); Master's degree or higher: 0.7% (2010).
Housing: Homeownership rate: 87.3% (2010); Median home value: $104,688 (2010); Median contract rent: $395 per month (2005-2009 5-year est.); Median year structure built: before 1940 (2005-2009 5-year est.).
Transportation: Commute to work: 100.0% car, 0.0% public transportation, 0.0% walk, 0.0% work from home (2005-2009 5-year est.); Travel time to work: 38.7% less than 15 minutes, 29.0% 15 to 30 minutes, 17.7% 30 to 45 minutes, 9.7% 45 to 60 minutes, 4.8% 60 minutes or more (2005-2009 5-year est.)

SAINT DAVID (village). Covers a land area of 0.296 square miles and a water area of 0 square miles. Located at 40.49° N. Lat; 90.05° W. Long. Elevation is 627 feet.
Population: 621 (1990); 587 (2000); 555 (2010); 535 (2015 projected); Race: 97.7% White, 0.2% Black, 0.0% Asian, 2.2% Other, 0.0% Hispanic of any race (2010); Density: 1,874.1 persons per square mile (2010); Average household size: 2.41 (2010); Median age: 40.8 (2010); Males per 100 females: 104.8 (2010); Marriage status: 18.2% never married, 64.5% now married, 5.9% widowed, 11.4% divorced (2005-2009 5-year est.); Foreign born: 2.6% (2005-2009 5-year est.); Ancestry (includes multiple ancestries): 30.1% American, 22.0% Irish, 19.6% German, 16.2% English, 4.6% Croatian (2005-2009 5-year est.).
Economy: Single-family building permits issued: 0 (2010); Multi-family building permits issued: 0 (2010); Employment by occupation: 3.6% management, 20.3% professional, 21.2% services, 23.9% sales, 0.0% farming, 11.7% construction, 19.4% production (2005-2009 5-year est.).
Income: Per capita income: $21,004 (2010); Median household income: $43,571 (2010); Average household income: $50,576 (2010); Percent of households with income of $100,000 or more: 11.3% (2010); Poverty rate: 3.0% (2005-2009 5-year est.).

Taxes: Total city taxes per capita: $18 (2007); City property taxes per capita: $16 (2007).
Education: Percent of population age 25 and over with: High school diploma (including GED) or higher: 86.7% (2010); Bachelor's degree or higher: 3.8% (2010); Master's degree or higher: 0.8% (2010).
Housing: Homeownership rate: 85.7% (2010); Median home value: $59,841 (2010); Median contract rent: n/a per month (2005-2009 5-year est.); Median year structure built: 1946 (2005-2009 5-year est.).
Transportation: Commute to work: 98.0% car, 0.0% public transportation, 0.0% walk, 2.0% work from home (2005-2009 5-year est.); Travel time to work: 43.6% less than 15 minutes, 35.9% 15 to 30 minutes, 4.6% 30 to 45 minutes, 5.1% 45 to 60 minutes, 10.8% 60 minutes or more (2005-2009 5-year est.)

SMITHFIELD (village). Covers a land area of 0.476 square miles and a water area of 0 square miles. Located at 40.47° N. Lat; 90.29° W. Long. Elevation is 646 feet.
Population: 277 (1990); 214 (2000); 213 (2010); 209 (2015 projected); Race: 97.7% White, 0.0% Black, 0.0% Asian, 2.3% Other, 0.5% Hispanic of any race (2010); Density: 447.9 persons per square mile (2010); Average household size: 2.57 (2010); Median age: 39.1 (2010); Males per 100 females: 119.6 (2010); Marriage status: 15.5% never married, 71.1% now married, 6.9% widowed, 6.5% divorced (2005-2009 5-year est.); Foreign born: 12.7% (2005-2009 5-year est.); Ancestry (includes multiple ancestries): 25.3% German, 22.9% Irish, 16.1% Ukrainian, 15.1% English, 12.3% American (2005-2009 5-year est.).
Economy: Employment by occupation: 1.6% management, 2.4% professional, 8.0% services, 19.2% sales, 0.0% farming, 19.2% construction, 49.6% production (2005-2009 5-year est.).
Income: Per capita income: $22,119 (2010); Median household income: $46,912 (2010); Average household income: $57,530 (2010); Percent of households with income of $100,000 or more: 10.8% (2010); Poverty rate: 10.3% (2005-2009 5-year est.).
Taxes: Total city taxes per capita: $34 (2007); City property taxes per capita: $34 (2007).
Education: Percent of population age 25 and over with: High school diploma (including GED) or higher: 90.0% (2010); Bachelor's degree or higher: 11.3% (2010); Master's degree or higher: 2.7% (2010).
Housing: Homeownership rate: 83.1% (2010); Median home value: $90,000 (2010); Median contract rent: $250 per month (2005-2009 5-year est.); Median year structure built: 1951 (2005-2009 5-year est.).
Transportation: Commute to work: 89.6% car, 0.0% public transportation, 0.0% walk, 0.0% work from home (2005-2009 5-year est.); Travel time to work: 16.8% less than 15 minutes, 27.2% 15 to 30 minutes, 10.4% 30 to 45 minutes, 4.0% 45 to 60 minutes, 41.6% 60 minutes or more (2005-2009 5-year est.)

TABLE GROVE (village). Covers a land area of 0.280 square miles and a water area of 0 square miles. Located at 40.36° N. Lat; 90.42° W. Long. Elevation is 725 feet.
Population: 408 (1990); 396 (2000); 401 (2010); 400 (2015 projected); Race: 99.5% White, 0.0% Black, 0.0% Asian, 0.5% Other, 0.0% Hispanic of any race (2010); Density: 1,431.6 persons per square mile (2010); Average household size: 2.43 (2010); Median age: 43.5 (2010); Males per 100 females: 94.7 (2010); Marriage status: 17.6% never married, 67.6% now married, 5.0% widowed, 9.7% divorced (2005-2009 5-year est.); Foreign born: 0.2% (2005-2009 5-year est.); Ancestry (includes multiple ancestries): 30.5% American, 19.3% German, 15.2% English, 9.0% Irish, 5.9% French (2005-2009 5-year est.).
Economy: Employment by occupation: 9.8% management, 14.9% professional, 13.8% services, 15.5% sales, 0.0% farming, 24.1% construction, 21.8% production (2005-2009 5-year est.).
Income: Per capita income: $25,983 (2010); Median household income: $57,267 (2010); Average household income: $61,924 (2010); Percent of households with income of $100,000 or more: 12.7% (2010); Poverty rate: 15.6% (2005-2009 5-year est.).
Taxes: Total city taxes per capita: $193 (2007); City property taxes per capita: $185 (2007).
Education: Percent of population age 25 and over with: High school diploma (including GED) or higher: 87.2% (2010); Bachelor's degree or higher: 14.2% (2010); Master's degree or higher: 3.2% (2010).
School District(s)
V I T CUSD 2 (PK-12)
    2009-10 Enrollment: 398 . . . . (309) 758-5138

Housing: Homeownership rate: 86.7% (2010); Median home value: $55,250 (2010); Median contract rent: $271 per month (2005-2009 5-year est.); Median year structure built: 1942 (2005-2009 5-year est.).
Transportation: Commute to work: 89.1% car, 0.0% public transportation, 7.5% walk, 1.1% work from home (2005-2009 5-year est.); Travel time to work: 25.6% less than 15 minutes, 39.0% 15 to 30 minutes, 15.1% 30 to 45 minutes, 7.0% 45 to 60 minutes, 13.4% 60 minutes or more (2005-2009 5-year est.)

VERMONT (village). Covers a land area of 1.263 square miles and a water area of 0 square miles. Located at 40.29° N. Lat; 90.42° W. Long. Elevation is 692 feet.

Population: 806 (1990); 792 (2000); 720 (2010); 683 (2015 projected); Race: 97.4% White, 0.0% Black, 0.3% Asian, 2.4% Other, 0.7% Hispanic of any race (2010); Density: 570.1 persons per square mile (2010); Average household size: 2.49 (2010); Median age: 36.9 (2010); Males per 100 females: 106.9 (2010); Marriage status: 24.8% never married, 61.3% now married, 5.3% widowed, 8.6% divorced (2005-2009 5-year est.); Foreign born: 0.7% (2005-2009 5-year est.); Ancestry (includes multiple ancestries): 28.6% American, 23.1% German, 15.3% English, 14.8% Irish, 4.6% Dutch (2005-2009 5-year est.).
Economy: Employment by occupation: 9.7% management, 8.6% professional, 13.9% services, 20.8% sales, 0.0% farming, 8.6% construction, 38.3% production (2005-2009 5-year est.).
Income: Per capita income: $17,401 (2010); Median household income: $37,237 (2010); Average household income: $43,512 (2010); Percent of households with income of $100,000 or more: 5.2% (2010); Poverty rate: 14.9% (2005-2009 5-year est.).
Taxes: Total city taxes per capita: $112 (2007); City property taxes per capita: $68 (2007).
Education: Percent of population age 25 and over with: High school diploma (including GED) or higher: 84.8% (2010); Bachelor's degree or higher: 7.1% (2010); Master's degree or higher: 2.4% (2010).
Housing: Homeownership rate: 85.8% (2010); Median home value: $39,506 (2010); Median contract rent: $350 per month (2005-2009 5-year est.); Median year structure built: before 1940 (2005-2009 5-year est.).
Safety: Violent crime rate: 0.0 per 10,000 population; Property crime rate: 0.0 per 10,000 population (2010).
Transportation: Commute to work: 92.2% car, 0.0% public transportation, 6.1% walk, 1.7% work from home (2005-2009 5-year est.); Travel time to work: 31.1% less than 15 minutes, 22.6% 15 to 30 minutes, 37.6% 30 to 45 minutes, 2.8% 45 to 60 minutes, 5.9% 60 minutes or more (2005-2009 5-year est.)

Gallatin County

Located in southeastern Illinois, partly in the Ozarks; bounded on the northeast by the Wabash River and the Indiana border, and on the southeast by the Ohio River and the Kentucky border; includes part of Shawnee National Forest. Covers a land area of 323.73 square miles, a water area of 4.68 square miles, and is located in the Central Time Zone at 37.78° N. Lat., 88.23° W. Long. The county was founded in 1812. County seat is Shawneetown.
Population: 6,909 (1990); 6,445 (2000); 5,921 (2010); 5,648 (2015 projected); Race: 98.0% White, 0.3% Black, 0.0% Asian, 1.7% Other, 1.1% Hispanic of any race (2010); Density: 18.3 persons per square mile (2010); Average household size: 2.29 (2010); Median age: 43.0 (2010); Males per 100 females: 92.5 (2010).
Religion: Five largest groups: 17.7% Catholic Church, 14.1% Southern Baptist Convention, 3.7% The United Methodist Church, 3.1% The Church of Jesus Christ of Latter-day Saints, 2.1% Presbyterian Church (U.S.A.) (2000).
Economy: Unemployment rate: 9.1% (August 2011); Total civilian labor force: 2,766 (August 2011); Leading industries: 37.5% transportation & warehousing; 10.2% retail trade; 6.0% wholesale trade (2009); Farms: 210 totaling 185,753 acres (2007); Companies that employ 500 or more persons: 0 (2009); Companies that employ 100 to 499 persons: 0 (2009); Companies that employ less than 100 persons: 107 (2009); Black-owned businesses: n/a (2007); Hispanic-owned businesses: n/a (2007); Asian-owned businesses: n/a (2007); Women-owned businesses: n/a (2007); Retail sales per capita: $4,182 (2010). Single-family building permits issued: n/a (2010); Multi-family building permits issued: n/a (2010).
Income: Per capita income: $19,449 (2010); Median household income: $32,907 (2010); Average household income: $44,922 (2010); Percent of

households with income of $100,000 or more: 6.9% (2010); Poverty rate: 19.3% (2009); Bankruptcy rate: 3.60% (2010).
Taxes: Total county taxes per capita: $117 (2007); County property taxes per capita: $114 (2007).
Education: Percent of population age 25 and over with: High school diploma (including GED) or higher: 80.0% (2010); Bachelor's degree or higher: 9.8% (2010); Master's degree or higher: 3.5% (2010).
Housing: Homeownership rate: 80.1% (2010); Median home value: $54,907 (2010); Median contract rent: $195 per month (2005-2009 5-year est.); Median year structure built: 1967 (2005-2009 5-year est.)
Health: Birth rate: 110.4 per 10,000 population (2009); Death rate: 143.7 per 10,000 population (2009); Age-adjusted cancer mortality rate: 271.6 deaths per 100,000 population (2007); Number of physicians: 1.7 per 10,000 population (2008); Hospital beds: 0.0 per 10,000 population (2007); Hospital admissions: 0.0 per 10,000 population (2007).
Elections: 2008 Presidential election results: 55.5% Obama, 42.4% McCain, 0.9% Nader
Additional Information Contacts
Gallatin County Government . . . . (618) 269-3025

Gallatin County Communities

EQUALITY (village). Covers a land area of 0.901 square miles and a water area of 0 square miles. Located at 37.73° N. Lat; 88.34° W. Long. Elevation is 410 feet.

History: Formerly county seat and site of salt works.
Population: 748 (1990); 721 (2000); 653 (2010); 620 (2015 projected); Race: 98.8% White, 0.0% Black, 0.0% Asian, 1.2% Other, 1.4% Hispanic of any race (2010); Density: 724.8 persons per square mile (2010); Average household size: 2.36 (2010); Median age: 42.6 (2010); Males per 100 females: 92.1 (2010); Marriage status: 12.8% never married, 54.0% now married, 8.1% widowed, 25.1% divorced (2005-2009 5-year est.); Foreign born: 0.3% (2005-2009 5-year est.); Ancestry (includes multiple ancestries): 19.2% Irish, 16.8% English, 16.4% American, 15.9% German, 8.2% French (2005-2009 5-year est.).
Economy: Employment by occupation: 10.9% management, 15.5% professional, 19.4% services, 22.5% sales, 5.6% farming, 13.4% construction, 12.7% production (2005-2009 5-year est.).
Income: Per capita income: $15,844 (2010); Median household income: $28,977 (2010); Average household income: $37,329 (2010); Percent of households with income of $100,000 or more: 2.9% (2010); Poverty rate: 12.6% (2005-2009 5-year est.).
Taxes: Total city taxes per capita: $41 (2007); City property taxes per capita: $7 (2007).
Education: Percent of population age 25 and over with: High school diploma (including GED) or higher: 82.5% (2010); Bachelor's degree or higher: 6.3% (2010); Master's degree or higher: 1.7% (2010).
Housing: Homeownership rate: 80.9% (2010); Median home value: $57,714 (2010); Median contract rent: $178 per month (2005-2009 5-year est.); Median year structure built: 1960 (2005-2009 5-year est.).
Transportation: Commute to work: 95.4% car, 0.0% public transportation, 0.0% walk, 2.8% work from home (2005-2009 5-year est.); Travel time to work: 47.3% less than 15 minutes, 29.3% 15 to 30 minutes, 11.4% 30 to 45 minutes, 2.9% 45 to 60 minutes, 9.2% 60 minutes or more (2005-2009 5-year est.)

JUNCTION (village). Covers a land area of 0.887 square miles and a water area of 0 square miles. Located at 37.72° N. Lat; 88.23° W. Long. Elevation is 361 feet.

Population: 201 (1990); 139 (2000); 127 (2010); 121 (2015 projected); Race: 92.9% White, 0.8% Black, 0.0% Asian, 6.3% Other, 3.9% Hispanic of any race (2010); Density: 143.2 persons per square mile (2010); Average household size: 2.27 (2010); Median age: 43.8 (2010); Males per 100 females: 86.8 (2010); Marriage status: 21.8% never married, 71.4% now married, 5.3% widowed, 1.5% divorced (2005-2009 5-year est.); Foreign born: 0.0% (2005-2009 5-year est.); Ancestry (includes multiple ancestries): 13.0% Irish, 5.6% American, 5.0% Italian, 5.0% German, 5.0% English (2005-2009 5-year est.).
Economy: Employment by occupation: 3.4% management, 4.5% professional, 22.7% services, 33.0% sales, 4.5% farming, 11.4% construction, 20.5% production (2005-2009 5-year est.).
Income: Per capita income: $17,246 (2010); Median household income: $27,143 (2010); Average household income: $37,818 (2010); Percent of

households with income of $100,000 or more: 3.6% (2010); Poverty rate: 0.6% (2005-2009 5-year est.).

Taxes: Total city taxes per capita: $8 (2007); City property taxes per capita: $8 (2007).

Education: Percent of population age 25 and over with: High school diploma (including GED) or higher: 69.2% (2010); Bachelor's degree or higher: 5.5% (2010); Master's degree or higher: 2.2% (2010).

School District(s)

Gallatin CUSD 7 (PK-12)

    2009-10 Enrollment: 740 . . . . (618) 272-3821

Housing: Homeownership rate: 76.4% (2010); Median home value: $40,000 (2010); Median contract rent: $263 per month (2005-2009 5-year est.); Median year structure built: 1984 (2005-2009 5-year est.).

Transportation: Commute to work: 100.0% car, 0.0% public transportation, 0.0% walk, 0.0% work from home (2005-2009 5-year est.); Travel time to work: 44.7% less than 15 minutes, 15.8% 15 to 30 minutes, 14.5% 30 to 45 minutes, 13.2% 45 to 60 minutes, 11.8% 60 minutes or more (2005-2009 5-year est.)

NEW HAVEN (village). Covers a land area of 1.205 square miles and a water area of 0.028 square miles. Located at 37.90° N. Lat; 88.12° W. Long. Elevation is 367 feet.

Population: 459 (1990); 477 (2000); 433 (2010); 409 (2015 projected); Race: 99.3% White, 0.2% Black, 0.0% Asian, 0.5% Other, 0.9% Hispanic of any race (2010); Density: 359.2 persons per square mile (2010); Average household size: 2.22 (2010); Median age: 43.5 (2010); Males per 100 females: 99.5 (2010); Marriage status: 17.9% never married, 58.5% now married, 14.6% widowed, 9.0% divorced (2005-2009 5-year est.); Foreign born: 0.6% (2005-2009 5-year est.); Ancestry (includes multiple ancestries): 18.1% English, 17.7% German, 16.4% Irish, 11.6% French, 9.6% Polish (2005-2009 5-year est.).

Economy: Employment by occupation: 0.0% management, 5.9% professional, 23.2% services, 40.4% sales, 0.0% farming, 11.3% construction, 19.2% production (2005-2009 5-year est.).

Income: Per capita income: $23,516 (2010); Median household income: $41,328 (2010); Average household income: $53,577 (2010); Percent of households with income of $100,000 or more: 6.2% (2010); Poverty rate: 34.3% (2005-2009 5-year est.).

Taxes: Total city taxes per capita: $53 (2007); City property taxes per capita: $13 (2007).

Education: Percent of population age 25 and over with: High school diploma (including GED) or higher: 83.6% (2010); Bachelor's degree or higher: 10.1% (2010); Master's degree or higher: 2.5% (2010).

Housing: Homeownership rate: 83.1% (2010); Median home value: $54,359 (2010); Median contract rent: $187 per month (2005-2009 5-year est.); Median year structure built: 1974 (2005-2009 5-year est.).

Transportation: Commute to work: 92.5% car, 0.5% public transportation, 2.5% walk, 1.5% work from home (2005-2009 5-year est.); Travel time to work: 10.2% less than 15 minutes, 19.9% 15 to 30 minutes, 13.3% 30 to 45 minutes, 48.0% 45 to 60 minutes, 8.7% 60 minutes or more (2005-2009 5-year est.)

OLD SHAWNEETOWN (village). Covers a land area of 0.523 square miles and a water area of 0 square miles. Located at 37.69° N. Lat; 88.13° W. Long. Elevation is 351 feet.

Population: 356 (1990); 278 (2000); 237 (2010); 218 (2015 projected); Race: 97.9% White, 0.0% Black, 0.0% Asian, 2.1% Other, 0.4% Hispanic of any race (2010); Density: 453.3 persons per square mile (2010); Average household size: 2.51 (2010); Median age: 38.8 (2010); Males per 100 females: 83.7 (2010); Marriage status: 12.4% never married, 52.7% now married, 7.1% widowed, 27.8% divorced (2005-2009 5-year est.); Foreign born: 0.0% (2005-2009 5-year est.); Ancestry (includes multiple ancestries): 13.8% Irish, 13.3% German, 5.4% American, 4.2% English, 2.1% French (2005-2009 5-year est.).

Economy: Employment by occupation: 0.0% management, 2.3% professional, 14.9% services, 6.9% sales, 0.0% farming, 21.8% construction, 54.0% production (2005-2009 5-year est.).

Income: Per capita income: $14,564 (2010); Median household income: $23,261 (2010); Average household income: $39,654 (2010); Percent of households with income of $100,000 or more: 7.4% (2010); Poverty rate: 37.5% (2005-2009 5-year est.).

Taxes: Total city taxes per capita: $90 (2007); City property taxes per capita: $37 (2007).

Education: Percent of population age 25 and over with: High school diploma (including GED) or higher: 66.3% (2010); Bachelor's degree or higher: 5.5% (2010); Master's degree or higher: 1.8% (2010).

Housing: Homeownership rate: 81.9% (2010); Median home value: $31,250 (2010); Median contract rent: $156 per month (2005-2009 5-year est.); Median year structure built: 1972 (2005-2009 5-year est.).

Safety: Violent crime rate: 40.8 per 10,000 population; Property crime rate: 163.3 per 10,000 population (2010).

Transportation: Commute to work: 88.3% car, 7.8% public transportation, 3.9% walk, 0.0% work from home (2005-2009 5-year est.); Travel time to work: 58.4% less than 15 minutes, 28.6% 15 to 30 minutes, 2.6% 30 to 45 minutes, 5.2% 45 to 60 minutes, 5.2% 60 minutes or more (2005-2009 5-year est.)

OMAHA (village). Covers a land area of 0.830 square miles and a water area of 0 square miles. Located at 37.89° N. Lat; 88.30° W. Long. Elevation is 374 feet.

Population: 273 (1990); 263 (2000); 265 (2010); 264 (2015 projected); Race: 99.2% White, 0.0% Black, 0.4% Asian, 0.4% Other, 0.0% Hispanic of any race (2010); Density: 319.1 persons per square mile (2010); Average household size: 2.35 (2010); Median age: 44.2 (2010); Males per 100 females: 90.6 (2010); Marriage status: 22.3% never married, 61.9% now married, 8.8% widowed, 6.9% divorced (2005-2009 5-year est.); Foreign born: 0.0% (2005-2009 5-year est.); Ancestry (includes multiple ancestries): 26.6% Irish, 18.3% German, 18.3% American, 17.3% English, 5.1% Dutch (2005-2009 5-year est.).

Economy: Employment by occupation: 14.0% management, 12.5% professional, 17.6% services, 15.4% sales, 2.2% farming, 6.6% construction, 31.6% production (2005-2009 5-year est.).

Income: Per capita income: $19,477 (2010); Median household income: $34,722 (2010); Average household income: $44,403 (2010); Percent of households with income of $100,000 or more: 8.8% (2010); Poverty rate: 20.2% (2005-2009 5-year est.).

Taxes: Total city taxes per capita: $12 (2007); City property taxes per capita: $12 (2007).

Education: Percent of population age 25 and over with: High school diploma (including GED) or higher: 89.3% (2010); Bachelor's degree or higher: 15.3% (2010); Master's degree or higher: 5.6% (2010).

Housing: Homeownership rate: 83.2% (2010); Median home value: $66,667 (2010); Median contract rent: $200 per month (2005-2009 5-year est.); Median year structure built: 1965 (2005-2009 5-year est.).

Transportation: Commute to work: 92.1% car, 0.0% public transportation, 0.8% walk, 4.8% work from home (2005-2009 5-year est.); Travel time to work: 37.5% less than 15 minutes, 26.7% 15 to 30 minutes, 12.5% 30 to 45 minutes, 15.8% 45 to 60 minutes, 7.5% 60 minutes or more (2005-2009 5-year est.)

RIDGWAY (village). Covers a land area of 0.900 square miles and a water area of 0 square miles. Located at 37.79° N. Lat; 88.26° W. Long. Elevation is 371 feet.

History: Incorporated 1886.

Population: 1,103 (1990); 928 (2000); 824 (2010); 779 (2015 projected); Race: 98.9% White, 0.5% Black, 0.0% Asian, 0.6% Other, 0.7% Hispanic of any race (2010); Density: 915.1 persons per square mile (2010); Average household size: 2.23 (2010); Median age: 45.9 (2010); Males per 100 females: 93.0 (2010); Marriage status: 22.7% never married, 49.7% now married, 13.5% widowed, 14.2% divorced (2005-2009 5-year est.); Foreign born: 0.0% (2005-2009 5-year est.); Ancestry (includes multiple ancestries): 34.6% German, 29.3% Irish, 9.6% English, 6.7% American, 6.0% Dutch (2005-2009 5-year est.).

Economy: Employment by occupation: 9.7% management, 16.3% professional, 19.1% services, 25.5% sales, 1.8% farming, 7.9% construction, 19.6% production (2005-2009 5-year est.).

Income: Per capita income: $22,712 (2010); Median household income: $41,078 (2010); Average household income: $51,838 (2010); Percent of households with income of $100,000 or more: 8.9% (2010); Poverty rate: 18.8% (2005-2009 5-year est.).

Taxes: Total city taxes per capita: $158 (2007); City property taxes per capita: $63 (2007).

Education: Percent of population age 25 and over with: High school diploma (including GED) or higher: 82.7% (2010); Bachelor's degree or higher: 13.4% (2010); Master's degree or higher: 4.2% (2010).

Housing: Homeownership rate: 80.2% (2010); Median home value: $52,381 (2010); Median contract rent: $182 per month (2005-2009 5-year est.); Median year structure built: 1964 (2005-2009 5-year est.).

Transportation: Commute to work: 95.1% car, 0.0% public transportation, 0.0% walk, 2.6% work from home (2005-2009 5-year est.); Travel time to work: 26.5% less than 15 minutes, 31.2% 15 to 30 minutes, 16.1% 30 to 45 minutes, 11.4% 45 to 60 minutes, 14.8% 60 minutes or more (2005-2009 5-year est.)

SHAWNEETOWN (city). Aka New Shawneetown. County seat. Covers a land area of 1.193 square miles and a water area of 0.037 square miles. Located at 37.71° N. Lat; 88.18° W. Long. Elevation is 400 feet.

History: Shawneetown, settled in the early 1800s, developed as a port on the Ohio River and as a financial center when Chicago was still a small village. Salt was an important export for the growing town, through which travelers and merchandise passed on the river. Shawneetown State Historical Site is here. Gallatin County Courthouse and most residents moved to (new) Shawneetown in late 1930s after disastrous Ohio River flood of 1937. The first state chartered bank opened here.

Population: 1,575 (1990); 1,410 (2000); 1,298 (2010); 1,238 (2015 projected); Race: 96.8% White, 0.3% Black, 0.0% Asian, 2.9% Other, 1.5% Hispanic of any race (2010); Density: 1,087.9 persons per square mile (2010); Average household size: 2.27 (2010); Median age: 42.3 (2010); Males per 100 females: 88.7 (2010); Marriage status: 17.8% never married, 53.0% now married, 14.5% widowed, 14.6% divorced (2005-2009 5-year est.); Foreign born: 2.1% (2005-2009 5-year est.); Ancestry (includes multiple ancestries): 26.5% Irish, 25.9% German, 10.3% Dutch, 10.1% English, 2.5% French (2005-2009 5-year est.).

Economy: Employment by occupation: 6.7% management, 12.8% professional, 11.7% services, 18.8% sales, 1.1% farming, 15.7% construction, 33.2% production (2005-2009 5-year est.).

Income: Per capita income: $19,445 (2010); Median household income: $29,315 (2010); Average household income: $44,343 (2010); Percent of households with income of $100,000 or more: 7.2% (2010); Poverty rate: 19.1% (2005-2009 5-year est.).

Taxes: Total city taxes per capita: $97 (2007); City property taxes per capita: $39 (2007).

Education: Percent of population age 25 and over with: High school diploma (including GED) or higher: 75.2% (2010); Bachelor's degree or higher: 6.8% (2010); Master's degree or higher: 3.1% (2010).

Housing: Homeownership rate: 78.3% (2010); Median home value: $57,500 (2010); Median contract rent: $216 per month (2005-2009 5-year est.); Median year structure built: 1962 (2005-2009 5-year est.).

Safety: Violent crime rate: 16.4 per 10,000 population; Property crime rate: 98.4 per 10,000 population (2010).

Newspapers: Gallatin Democrat (Local news; Circulation 1,200); Ridgway News (Local news; Circulation 700)

Transportation: Commute to work: 92.6% car, 0.5% public transportation, 0.0% walk, 6.3% work from home (2005-2009 5-year est.); Travel time to work: 43.3% less than 15 minutes, 20.3% 15 to 30 minutes, 23.0% 30 to 45 minutes, 5.0% 45 to 60 minutes, 8.4% 60 minutes or more (2005-2009 5-year est.)

Greene County

Located in southwest central Illinois; bounded on the west by the Illinois River; drained by Macoupin and Apple Creeks. Covers a land area of 543.09 square miles, a water area of 3.25 square miles, and is located in the Central Time Zone at 39.37° N. Lat., 90.38° W. Long. The county was founded in 1821. County seat is Carrollton.

Weather Station: White Hall 1 E | | | | | | | | | Elevation: 580 feet
|---|---|---|---|---|---|---|---|---|---|---|---|---|
| | Jan | Feb | Mar | Apr | May | Jun | Jul | Aug | Sep | Oct | Nov | Dec |
| High | 36 | 41 | 52 | 64 | 74 | 83 | 86 | 85 | 79 | 67 | 53 | 39 |
| Low | 19 | 22 | 31 | 42 | 52 | 62 | 65 | 64 | 55 | 43 | 33 | 22 |
| Precip | 1.7 | 1.8 | 3.0 | 3.8 | 4.4 | 3.8 | 3.6 | 3.1 | 3.1 | 3.1 | 3.5 | 2.6 |
| Snow | 4.7 | 3.9 | 2.0 | 0.4 | 0.0 | 0.0 | 0.0 | 0.0 | 0.0 | tr | 0.5 | 3.6 |

High and Low temperatures in degrees Fahrenheit; Precipitation and Snow in inches

Population: 15,317 (1990); 14,761 (2000); 13,463 (2010); 12,766 (2015 projected); Race: 97.9% White, 0.5% Black, 0.2% Asian, 1.4% Other, 0.6% Hispanic of any race (2010); Density: 24.8 persons per square mile (2010); Average household size: 2.48 (2010); Median age: 39.8 (2010); Males per 100 females: 94.5 (2010).

Religion: Five largest groups: 20.8% Southern Baptist Convention, 17.6% American Baptist Churches in the USA, 13.7% Catholic Church, 6.0% The United Methodist Church, 1.7% Lutheran Church—Missouri Synod (2000).

Economy: Unemployment rate: 8.5% (August 2011); Total civilian labor force: 7,029 (August 2011); Leading industries: 22.4% retail trade; 20.3%

health care and social assistance; 12.6% accommodation & food services (2009); Farms: 600 totaling 273,088 acres (2007); Companies that employ 500 or more persons: 0 (2009); Companies that employ 100 to 499 persons: 1 (2009); Companies that employ less than 100 persons: 273 (2009); Black-owned businesses: n/a (2007); Hispanic-owned businesses: n/a (2007); Asian-owned businesses: n/a (2007); Women-owned businesses: n/a (2007); Retail sales per capita: $8,986 (2010). Single-family building permits issued: 1 (2010); Multi-family building permits issued: 0 (2010).

Income: Per capita income: $19,628 (2010); Median household income: $40,110 (2010); Average household income: $48,900 (2010); Percent of households with income of $100,000 or more: 7.7% (2010); Poverty rate: 14.3% (2009); Bankruptcy rate: 3.24% (2010).

Taxes: Total county taxes per capita: $119 (2007); County property taxes per capita: $106 (2007).

Education: Percent of population age 25 and over with: High school diploma (including GED) or higher: 84.2% (2010); Bachelor's degree or higher: 12.5% (2010); Master's degree or higher: 4.2% (2010).

Housing: Homeownership rate: 74.9% (2010); Median home value: $71,223 (2010); Median contract rent: $338 per month (2005-2009 5-year est.); Median year structure built: 1956 (2005-2009 5-year est.)

Health: Birth rate: 123.8 per 10,000 population (2009); Death rate: 117.2 per 10,000 population (2009); Age-adjusted cancer mortality rate: 211.0 deaths per 100,000 population (2007); Number of physicians: 7.3 per 10,000 population (2008); Hospital beds: 47.5 per 10,000 population (2007); Hospital admissions: 660.8 per 10,000 population (2007).

Elections: 2008 Presidential election results: 45.1% Obama, 52.6% McCain, 1.1% Nader

Additional Information Contacts

Greene County Government . . . . (217) 942-5443
  http://www.greenecountyil.com

Greene County Communities

CARROLLTON (city). County seat. Covers a land area of 1.669 square miles and a water area of 0.002 square miles. Located at 39.29° N. Lat; 90.40° W. Long. Elevation is 620 feet.

History: Carrollton was settled in 1818 and developed as the seat of Green County.

Population: 2,553 (1990); 2,605 (2000); 2,481 (2010); 2,404 (2015 projected); Race: 98.2% White, 0.0% Black, 0.5% Asian, 1.3% Other, 0.4% Hispanic of any race (2010); Density: 1,486.9 persons per square mile (2010); Average household size: 2.45 (2010); Median age: 40.2 (2010); Males per 100 females: 91.9 (2010); Marriage status: 15.2% never married, 60.3% now married, 14.0% widowed, 10.4% divorced (2005-2009 5-year est.); Foreign born: 0.4% (2005-2009 5-year est.); Ancestry (includes multiple ancestries): 42.7% German, 15.5% Irish, 13.1% English, 7.9% American, 2.9% Dutch (2005-2009 5-year est.).

Economy: Single-family building permits issued: 1 (2010); Multi-family building permits issued: 0 (2010); Employment by occupation: 11.1% management, 23.5% professional, 23.8% services, 18.8% sales, 2.0% farming, 7.9% construction, 13.0% production (2005-2009 5-year est.).

Income: Per capita income: $22,913 (2010); Median household income: $43,762 (2010); Average household income: $56,548 (2010); Percent of households with income of $100,000 or more: 10.8% (2010); Poverty rate: 8.0% (2005-2009 5-year est.).

Taxes: Total city taxes per capita: $189 (2007); City property taxes per capita: $135 (2007).

Education: Percent of population age 25 and over with: High school diploma (including GED) or higher: 86.7% (2010); Bachelor's degree or higher: 19.8% (2010); Master's degree or higher: 7.0% (2010).

School District(s)

Carrollton CUSD 1 (PK-12)
  2009-10 Enrollment: 620 . . . . (217) 942-5314

Housing: Homeownership rate: 75.4% (2010); Median home value: $90,261 (2010); Median contract rent: $321 per month (2005-2009 5-year est.); Median year structure built: 1958 (2005-2009 5-year est.).

Hospitals: Thomas H. Boyd Memorial Hospital (65 beds)

Safety: Violent crime rate: 29.2 per 10,000 population; Property crime rate: 154.5 per 10,000 population (2010).

Newspapers: Gazette Patriot (Regional news; Circulation 1,662)

Transportation: Commute to work: 90.1% car, 0.0% public transportation, 4.0% walk, 5.0% work from home (2005-2009 5-year est.); Travel time to work: 54.0% less than 15 minutes, 12.6% 15 to 30 minutes, 10.4% 30 to 45

minutes, 8.0% 45 to 60 minutes, 15.0% 60 minutes or more (2005-2009 5-year est.)

ELDRED (village). Covers a land area of 0.135 square miles and a water area of 0 square miles. Located at 39.28° N. Lat; 90.55° W. Long. Elevation is 449 feet.
Population: 254 (1990); 211 (2000); 194 (2010); 181 (2015 projected); Race: 97.9% White, 0.0% Black, 0.5% Asian, 1.5% Other, 0.0% Hispanic of any race (2010); Density: 1,441.3 persons per square mile (2010); Average household size: 2.31 (2010); Median age: 47.6 (2010); Males per 100 females: 98.0 (2010); Marriage status: 21.5% never married, 30.1% now married, 21.5% widowed, 26.9% divorced (2005-2009 5-year est.); Foreign born: 0.0% (2005-2009 5-year est.); Ancestry (includes multiple ancestries): 21.2% German, 20.2% American, 15.2% English, 12.1% Irish, 7.1% Portuguese (2005-2009 5-year est.).
Economy: Employment by occupation: 8.7% management, 19.6% professional, 10.9% services, 21.7% sales, 8.7% farming, 19.6% construction, 10.9% production (2005-2009 5-year est.).
Income: Per capita income: $25,818 (2010); Median household income: $44,000 (2010); Average household income: $54,315 (2010); Percent of households with income of $100,000 or more: 11.9% (2010); Poverty rate: 8.1% (2005-2009 5-year est.).
Taxes: Total city taxes per capita: $20 (2007); City property taxes per capita: $10 (2007).
Education: Percent of population age 25 and over with: High school diploma (including GED) or higher: 87.1% (2010); Bachelor's degree or higher: 8.2% (2010); Master's degree or higher: 0.7% (2010).
Housing: Homeownership rate: 76.2% (2010); Median home value: $86,000 (2010); Median contract rent: $175 per month (2005-2009 5-year est.); Median year structure built: before 1940 (2005-2009 5-year est.).
Transportation: Commute to work: 89.1% car, 0.0% public transportation, 4.3% walk, 6.5% work from home (2005-2009 5-year est.); Travel time to work: 25.6% less than 15 minutes, 34.9% 15 to 30 minutes, 16.3% 30 to 45 minutes, 2.3% 45 to 60 minutes, 20.9% 60 minutes or more (2005-2009 5-year est.)

GREENFIELD (city). Covers a land area of 1.716 square miles and a water area of 0.063 square miles. Located at 39.34° N. Lat; 90.21° W. Long. Elevation is 587 feet.
History: Incorporated 1837.
Population: 1,209 (1990); 1,179 (2000); 1,113 (2010); 1,065 (2015 projected); Race: 98.9% White, 0.1% Black, 0.0% Asian, 1.0% Other, 0.4% Hispanic of any race (2010); Density: 648.7 persons per square mile (2010); Average household size: 2.45 (2010); Median age: 39.2 (2010); Males per 100 females: 93.6 (2010); Marriage status: 29.8% never married, 45.9% now married, 11.9% widowed, 12.5% divorced (2005-2009 5-year est.); Foreign born: 0.3% (2005-2009 5-year est.); Ancestry (includes multiple ancestries): 39.0% German, 16.4% Irish, 16.3% English, 5.9% American, 4.3% Scottish (2005-2009 5-year est.).
Economy: Single-family building permits issued: 0 (2010); Multi-family building permits issued: 0 (2010); Employment by occupation: 9.4% management, 11.4% professional, 22.6% services, 23.0% sales, 1.9% farming, 9.5% construction, 22.2% production (2005-2009 5-year est.).
Income: Per capita income: $19,356 (2010); Median household income: $40,495 (2010); Average household income: $46,806 (2010); Percent of households with income of $100,000 or more: 5.5% (2010); Poverty rate: 17.2% (2005-2009 5-year est.).
Taxes: Total city taxes per capita: $83 (2007); City property taxes per capita: $83 (2007).
Education: Percent of population age 25 and over with: High school diploma (including GED) or higher: 88.1% (2010); Bachelor's degree or higher: 8.7% (2010); Master's degree or higher: 2.2% (2010).
School District(s)
Greenfield CUSD 10 (PK-12)
    2009-10 Enrollment: 499 . . . . (217) 368-2447
Housing: Homeownership rate: 73.8% (2010); Median home value: $65,556 (2010); Median contract rent: $318 per month (2005-2009 5-year est.); Median year structure built: 1959 (2005-2009 5-year est.).
Transportation: Commute to work: 92.1% car, 0.0% public transportation, 3.6% walk, 3.4% work from home (2005-2009 5-year est.); Travel time to work: 39.3% less than 15 minutes, 18.7% 15 to 30 minutes, 18.3% 30 to 45 minutes, 11.2% 45 to 60 minutes, 12.5% 60 minutes or more (2005-2009 5-year est.)

HILLVIEW (village). Covers a land area of 0.848 square miles and a water area of 0 square miles. Located at 39.45° N. Lat; 90.53° W. Long. Elevation is 440 feet.
Population: 271 (1990); 179 (2000); 162 (2010); 152 (2015 projected); Race: 97.5% White, 0.0% Black, 0.0% Asian, 2.5% Other, 1.9% Hispanic of any race (2010); Density: 191.1 persons per square mile (2010); Average household size: 2.70 (2010); Median age: 41.4 (2010); Males per 100 females: 102.5 (2010); Marriage status: 14.9% never married, 75.4% now married, 0.0% widowed, 9.6% divorced (2005-2009 5-year est.); Foreign born: 0.0% (2005-2009 5-year est.); Ancestry (includes multiple ancestries): 41.7% German, 11.5% Irish, 7.9% English, 6.5% American, 5.8% Scottish (2005-2009 5-year est.).
Economy: Employment by occupation: 5.3% management, 0.0% professional, 36.8% services, 29.8% sales, 10.5% farming, 7.0% construction, 10.5% production (2005-2009 5-year est.).
Income: Per capita income: $16,870 (2010); Median household income: $39,286 (2010); Average household income: $45,083 (2010); Percent of households with income of $100,000 or more: 5.0% (2010); Poverty rate: 23.7% (2005-2009 5-year est.).
Taxes: Total city taxes per capita: $40 (2007); City property taxes per capita: $40 (2007).
Education: Percent of population age 25 and over with: High school diploma (including GED) or higher: 82.7% (2010); Bachelor's degree or higher: 10.0% (2010); Master's degree or higher: 0.9% (2010).
Housing: Homeownership rate: 81.7% (2010); Median home value: $56,667 (2010); Median contract rent: n/a per month (2005-2009 5-year est.); Median year structure built: before 1940 (2005-2009 5-year est.).
Transportation: Commute to work: 96.5% car, 0.0% public transportation, 0.0% walk, 3.5% work from home (2005-2009 5-year est.); Travel time to work: 0.0% less than 15 minutes, 47.3% 15 to 30 minutes, 40.0% 30 to 45 minutes, 7.3% 45 to 60 minutes, 5.5% 60 minutes or more (2005-2009 5-year est.)

KANE (village). Covers a land area of 0.541 square miles and a water area of 0 square miles. Located at 39.19° N. Lat; 90.35° W. Long. Elevation is 561 feet.
Population: 456 (1990); 459 (2000); 416 (2010); 393 (2015 projected); Race: 98.6% White, 0.0% Black, 0.0% Asian, 1.4% Other, 0.2% Hispanic of any race (2010); Density: 768.4 persons per square mile (2010); Average household size: 2.57 (2010); Median age: 38.6 (2010); Males per 100 females: 105.9 (2010); Marriage status: 24.1% never married, 53.4% now married, 8.9% widowed, 13.6% divorced (2005-2009 5-year est.); Foreign born: 0.0% (2005-2009 5-year est.); Ancestry (includes multiple ancestries): 29.8% German, 20.0% Irish, 13.6% English, 8.3% Italian, 5.6% Dutch (2005-2009 5-year est.).
Economy: Employment by occupation: 8.3% management, 14.4% professional, 24.0% services, 13.1% sales, 0.0% farming, 16.2% construction, 24.0% production (2005-2009 5-year est.).
Income: Per capita income: $18,189 (2010); Median household income: $38,281 (2010); Average household income: $45,802 (2010); Percent of households with income of $100,000 or more: 4.9% (2010); Poverty rate: 18.8% (2005-2009 5-year est.).
Taxes: Total city taxes per capita: $29 (2007); City property taxes per capita: $29 (2007).
Education: Percent of population age 25 and over with: High school diploma (including GED) or higher: 81.5% (2010); Bachelor's degree or higher: 11.6% (2010); Master's degree or higher: 2.2% (2010).
Housing: Homeownership rate: 77.8% (2010); Median home value: $67,826 (2010); Median contract rent: $291 per month (2005-2009 5-year est.); Median year structure built: 1950 (2005-2009 5-year est.).
Transportation: Commute to work: 93.1% car, 0.0% public transportation, 0.0% walk, 0.0% work from home (2005-2009 5-year est.); Travel time to work: 36.6% less than 15 minutes, 19.4% 15 to 30 minutes, 16.7% 30 to 45 minutes, 12.0% 45 to 60 minutes, 15.3% 60 minutes or more (2005-2009 5-year est.)

ROCKBRIDGE (village). Covers a land area of 0.739 square miles and a water area of 0 square miles. Located at 39.27° N. Lat; 90.20° W. Long. Elevation is 541 feet.
Population: 197 (1990); 189 (2000); 175 (2010); 165 (2015 projected); Race: 98.9% White, 0.0% Black, 0.0% Asian, 1.1% Other, 0.6% Hispanic of any race (2010); Density: 236.8 persons per square mile (2010); Average household size: 2.57 (2010); Median age: 40.0 (2010); Males per 100 females: 103.5 (2010); Marriage status: 12.5% never married, 77.9%

now married, 2.2% widowed, 7.4% divorced (2005-2009 5-year est.); Foreign born: 0.0% (2005-2009 5-year est.); Ancestry (includes multiple ancestries): 26.2% Irish, 19.3% German, 9.0% English, 5.5% Polish, 5.5% Dutch (2005-2009 5-year est.).

Economy: Employment by occupation: 0.0% management, 6.0% professional, 13.4% services, 40.3% sales, 0.0% farming, 6.0% construction, 34.3% production (2005-2009 5-year est.).

Income: Per capita income: $18,189 (2010); Median household income: $39,286 (2010); Average household income: $44,743 (2010); Percent of households with income of $100,000 or more: 4.4% (2010); Poverty rate: 7.6% (2005-2009 5-year est.).

Taxes: Total city taxes per capita: $33 (2007); City property taxes per capita: $27 (2007).

Education: Percent of population age 25 and over with: High school diploma (including GED) or higher: 81.2% (2010); Bachelor's degree or higher: 11.1% (2010); Master's degree or higher: 1.7% (2010).

Housing: Homeownership rate: 77.9% (2010); Median home value: $63,333 (2010); Median contract rent: n/a per month (2005-2009 5-year est.); Median year structure built: 1966 (2005-2009 5-year est.).

Transportation: Commute to work: 94.0% car, 0.0% public transportation, 6.0% walk, 0.0% work from home (2005-2009 5-year est.); Travel time to work: 35.8% less than 15 minutes, 14.9% 15 to 30 minutes, 29.9% 30 to 45 minutes, 10.4% 45 to 60 minutes, 9.0% 60 minutes or more (2005-2009 5-year est.)

ROODHOUSE (city).
Covers a land area of 1.132 square miles and a water area of 0 square miles. Located at 39.48° N. Lat; 90.37° W. Long. Elevation is 656 feet.

History: Roodhouse was laid out by an early settler, John Roodhouse, and developed as a railroad center.

Population: 2,139 (1990); 2,214 (2000); 1,925 (2010); 1,797 (2015 projected); Race: 94.3% White, 3.6% Black, 0.1% Asian, 2.0% Other, 0.8% Hispanic of any race (2010); Density: 1,700.4 persons per square mile (2010); Average household size: 2.51 (2010); Median age: 34.7 (2010); Males per 100 females: 98.2 (2010); Marriage status: 35.2% never married, 45.4% now married, 5.4% widowed, 14.1% divorced (2005-2009 5-year est.); Foreign born: 1.5% (2005-2009 5-year est.); Ancestry (includes multiple ancestries): 29.7% German, 20.8% Irish, 14.2% American, 12.2% English, 2.0% Welsh (2005-2009 5-year est.).

Economy: Employment by occupation: 9.3% management, 12.1% professional, 12.1% services, 20.2% sales, 2.5% farming, 12.2% construction, 31.6% production (2005-2009 5-year est.).

Income: Per capita income: $15,812 (2010); Median household income: $35,648 (2010); Average household income: $41,311 (2010); Percent of households with income of $100,000 or more: 4.4% (2010); Poverty rate: 31.6% (2005-2009 5-year est.).

Taxes: Total city taxes per capita: $124 (2007); City property taxes per capita: $87 (2007).

Education: Percent of population age 25 and over with: High school diploma (including GED) or higher: 80.6% (2010); Bachelor's degree or higher: 9.2% (2010); Master's degree or higher: 3.6% (2010).

School District(s)
North Greene CUSD 3 (PK-12)

    2009-10 Enrollment: 1,001 . . . . (217) 374-2842

Housing: Homeownership rate: 73.4% (2010); Median home value: $57,299 (2010); Median contract rent: $374 per month (2005-2009 5-year est.); Median year structure built: 1957 (2005-2009 5-year est.).

Safety: Violent crime rate: 10.6 per 10,000 population; Property crime rate: 95.7 per 10,000 population (2010).

Transportation: Commute to work: 86.7% car, 0.0% public transportation, 7.8% walk, 5.5% work from home (2005-2009 5-year est.); Travel time to work: 36.9% less than 15 minutes, 20.9% 15 to 30 minutes, 27.1% 30 to 45 minutes, 5.4% 45 to 60 minutes, 9.7% 60 minutes or more (2005-2009 5-year est.)

WHITE HALL (city).
Aka Whitehall. Covers a land area of 2.579 square miles and a water area of 0.057 square miles. Located at 39.43° N. Lat; 90.39° W. Long. Elevation is 571 feet.

History: White Hall was founded in 1820 and developed around the manufacture of pottery from local clay.

Population: 2,843 (1990); 2,629 (2000); 2,383 (2010); 2,245 (2015 projected); Race: 98.1% White, 0.1% Black, 0.0% Asian, 1.8% Other, 1.0% Hispanic of any race (2010); Density: 923.9 persons per square mile (2010); Average household size: 2.29 (2010); Median age: 42.2 (2010); Males per 100 females: 86.6 (2010); Marriage status: 21.5% never married,

53.4% now married, 13.4% widowed, 11.7% divorced (2005-2009 5-year est.); Foreign born: 1.4% (2005-2009 5-year est.); Ancestry (includes multiple ancestries): 20.4% American, 14.3% German, 11.8% English, 10.9% Irish, 3.2% Dutch (2005-2009 5-year est.).

Economy: Employment by occupation: 2.1% management, 19.6% professional, 21.9% services, 18.2% sales, 1.9% farming, 6.5% construction, 29.9% production (2005-2009 5-year est.).

Income: Per capita income: $18,430 (2010); Median household income: $31,582 (2010); Average household income: $41,841 (2010); Percent of households with income of $100,000 or more: 6.4% (2010); Poverty rate: 19.2% (2005-2009 5-year est.).

Taxes: Total city taxes per capita: $115 (2007); City property taxes per capita: $65 (2007).

Education: Percent of population age 25 and over with: High school diploma (including GED) or higher: 78.1% (2010); Bachelor's degree or higher: 11.0% (2010); Master's degree or higher: 4.7% (2010).

School District(s)
North Greene CUSD 3 (PK-12)

    2009-10 Enrollment: 1,001 . . . . (217) 374-2842

Housing: Homeownership rate: 72.0% (2010); Median home value: $55,230 (2010); Median contract rent: $294 per month (2005-2009 5-year est.); Median year structure built: 1953 (2005-2009 5-year est.).

Safety: Violent crime rate: 4.2 per 10,000 population; Property crime rate: 121.0 per 10,000 population (2010).

Transportation: Commute to work: 88.0% car, 0.0% public transportation, 7.6% walk, 3.8% work from home (2005-2009 5-year est.); Travel time to work: 41.1% less than 15 minutes, 10.5% 15 to 30 minutes, 31.3% 30 to 45 minutes, 6.5% 45 to 60 minutes, 10.6% 60 minutes or more (2005-2009 5-year est.)

WILMINGTON (village).
Aka Patterson. Covers a land area of 0.792 square miles and a water area of 0 square miles. Located at 39.48° N. Lat; 90.49° W. Long.

Population: 129 (1990); 120 (2000); 105 (2010); 99 (2015 projected); Race: 98.1% White, 0.0% Black, 0.0% Asian, 1.9% Other, 1.9% Hispanic of any race (2010); Density: 132.6 persons per square mile (2010); Average household size: 2.69 (2010); Median age: 42.4 (2010); Males per 100 females: 105.9 (2010); Marriage status: 47.6% never married, 40.8% now married, 5.8% widowed, 5.8% divorced (2005-2009 5-year est.); Foreign born: 0.0% (2005-2009 5-year est.); Ancestry (includes multiple ancestries): 20.0% German, 18.3% Irish, 8.7% English, 7.0% Dutch, 2.6% Polish (2005-2009 5-year est.).

Economy: Employment by occupation: 51.0% management, 8.2% professional, 4.1% services, 10.2% sales, 0.0% farming, 0.0% construction, 26.5% production (2005-2009 5-year est.).

Income: Per capita income: $16,870 (2010); Median household income: $41,750 (2010); Average household income: $48,846 (2010); Percent of households with income of $100,000 or more: 7.7% (2010); Poverty rate: 8.7% (2005-2009 5-year est.).

Taxes: Total city taxes per capita: $68 (2007); City property taxes per capita: $68 (2007).

Education: Percent of population age 25 and over with: High school diploma (including GED) or higher: 86.1% (2010); Bachelor's degree or higher: 8.3% (2010); Master's degree or higher: 0.0% (2010).

Housing: Homeownership rate: 82.1% (2010); Median home value: $50,000 (2010); Median contract rent: n/a per month (2005-2009 5-year est.); Median year structure built: 1950 (2005-2009 5-year est.).

Safety: Violent crime rate: 4.8 per 10,000 population; Property crime rate: 187.1 per 10,000 population (2010).

Transportation: Commute to work: 100.0% car, 0.0% public transportation, 0.0% walk, 0.0% work from home (2005-2009 5-year est.); Travel time to work: 30.6% less than 15 minutes, 14.3% 15 to 30 minutes, 44.9% 30 to 45 minutes, 0.0% 45 to 60 minutes, 10.2% 60 minutes or more (2005-2009 5-year est.)

Grundy County

Located in northeastern Illinois; drained by the Illinois, Des Plaines, and Kankakee Rivers. Covers a land area of 419.90 square miles, a water area of 10.52 square miles, and is located in the Central Time Zone at 41.31° N. Lat., 88.36° W. Long. The county was founded in 1841. County seat is Morris.

Grundy County is part of the Chicago-Joliet-Naperville, IL-IN-WI Metropolitan Statistical Area. The entire metro area includes:

Chicago-Joliet-Naperville, IL Metropolitan Division (Cook County, IL; DeKalb County, IL; DuPage County, IL; Grundy County, IL; Kane County, IL; Kendall County, IL; McHenry County, IL; Will County, IL); Gary, IN Metropolitan Division (Jasper County, IN; Lake County, IN; Newton County, IN; Porter County, IN); Lake County-Kenosha County, IL-WI Metropolitan Division (Lake County, IL; Kenosha County, WI)

Population: 32,337 (1990); 37,535 (2000); 49,877 (2010); 55,565 (2015 projected); Race: 92.6% White, 2.2% Black, 1.0% Asian, 4.3% Other, 8.5% Hispanic of any race (2010); Density: 118.8 persons per square mile (2010); Average household size: 2.56 (2010); Median age: 34.3 (2010); Males per 100 females: 100.3 (2010).
Religion: Five largest groups: 26.6% Catholic Church, 6.6% The United Methodist Church, 4.2% Christian Churches and Churches of Christ, 4.2% Evangelical Lutheran Church in America, 2.4% Presbyterian Church (U.S.A.) (2000).
Economy: Unemployment rate: 11.6% (August 2011); Total civilian labor force: 26,593 (August 2011); Leading industries: 15.6% transportation & warehousing; 13.3% retail trade; 13.0% health care and social assistance (2009); Farms: 450 totaling 215,474 acres (2007); Companies that employ 500 or more persons: 4 (2009); Companies that employ 100 to 499 persons: 17 (2009); Companies that employ less than 100 persons: 1,069 (2009); Black-owned businesses: n/a (2007); Hispanic-owned businesses: 89 (2007); Asian-owned businesses: 46 (2007); Women-owned businesses: 1,223 (2007); Retail sales per capita: $12,438 (2010). Single-family building permits issued: 50 (2010); Multi-family building permits issued: 36 (2010).
Income: Per capita income: $27,863 (2010); Median household income: $62,355 (2010); Average household income: $71,436 (2010); Percent of households with income of $100,000 or more: 21.8% (2010); Poverty rate: 6.8% (2009); Bankruptcy rate: 7.97% (2010).
Taxes: Total county taxes per capita: $223 (2007); County property taxes per capita: $215 (2007).
Education: Percent of population age 25 and over with: High school diploma (including GED) or higher: 90.0% (2010); Bachelor's degree or higher: 17.1% (2010); Master's degree or higher: 5.1% (2010).
Housing: Homeownership rate: 77.0% (2010); Median home value: $170,701 (2010); Median contract rent: $678 per month (2005-2009 5-year est.); Median year structure built: 1978 (2005-2009 5-year est.).
Health: Birth rate: 165.8 per 10,000 population (2009); Death rate: 74.3 per 10,000 population (2009); Age-adjusted cancer mortality rate: 227.0 deaths per 100,000 population (2007); Number of physicians: 11.2 per 10,000 population (2008); Hospital beds: 18.3 per 10,000 population (2007); Hospital admissions: 1,027.5 per 10,000 population (2007).
Elections: 2008 Presidential election results: 49.9% Obama, 48.2% McCain, 0.8% Nader
National and State Parks: Gebhard Woods State Park; Goose Lake Prairie State Park; Heidecke State Fish and Wildlife Area; Mazonia State Fish and Wildlife Area; William Stratton State Access Area
Additional Information Contacts
Grundy County Government . . . . (815) 941-3400
    http://www.grundyco.org
Channahon Minooka Chamber of Commerce . . . . (815) 521-9999
    http://www.grundychamber.com/cm_chamber/index.html
City of Morris . . . . (815) 942-0103
    http://city.mornet.org
Grundy County Chamber of Commerce . . . . (815) 634-8662
    http://www.grundychamber.com
Grundy County Chamber of Commerce . . . . (815) 942-0113
    http://www.grundychamber.com

Grundy County Communities

BRACEVILLE (village). Covers a land area of 1.316 square miles and a water area of 0.011 square miles. Located at 41.22° N. Lat; 88.26° W. Long. Elevation is 577 feet.
History: Braceville boomed as a coal-mining town in the late 1800's, but declined when the mines closed.
Population: 590 (1990); 792 (2000); 944 (2010); 1,056 (2015 projected); Race: 98.5% White, 0.0% Black, 0.0% Asian, 1.5% Other, 1.9% Hispanic of any race (2010); Density: 717.3 persons per square mile (2010); Average household size: 2.72 (2010); Median age: 31.9 (2010); Males per 100 females: 98.7 (2010); Marriage status: 26.9% never married, 55.1% now married, 3.6% widowed, 14.4% divorced (2005-2009 5-year est.); Foreign born: 1.1% (2005-2009 5-year est.); Ancestry (includes multiple

ancestries): 37.3% German, 31.6% Irish, 13.0% English, 11.8% Polish, 7.0% Scottish (2005-2009 5-year est.).
Economy: Single-family building permits issued: 0 (2010); Multi-family building permits issued: 0 (2010); Employment by occupation: 6.7% management, 4.4% professional, 24.8% services, 29.2% sales, 0.0% farming, 16.6% construction, 18.4% production (2005-2009 5-year est.).
Income: Per capita income: $21,506 (2010); Median household income: $55,567 (2010); Average household income: $58,473 (2010); Percent of households with income of $100,000 or more: 8.1% (2010); Poverty rate: 10.4% (2005-2009 5-year est.).
Taxes: Total city taxes per capita: $144 (2007); City property taxes per capita: $80 (2007).
Education: Percent of population age 25 and over with: High school diploma (including GED) or higher: 87.3% (2010); Bachelor's degree or higher: 6.9% (2010); Master's degree or higher: 1.2% (2010).
School District(s)
Braceville SD 75 (KG-08)
    2009-10 Enrollment: 185 . . . . (815) 237-8040
Housing: Homeownership rate: 86.2% (2010); Median home value: $125,629 (2010); Median contract rent: $686 per month (2005-2009 5-year est.); Median year structure built: 1970 (2005-2009 5-year est.).
Transportation: Commute to work: 94.5% car, 0.0% public transportation, 0.0% walk, 2.8% work from home (2005-2009 5-year est.); Travel time to work: 19.2% less than 15 minutes, 22.0% 15 to 30 minutes, 38.1% 30 to 45 minutes, 9.1% 45 to 60 minutes, 11.6% 60 minutes or more (2005-2009 5-year est.)

CARBON HILL (village). Covers a land area of 0.176 square miles and a water area of 0 square miles. Located at 41.29° N. Lat; 88.30° W. Long. Elevation is 561 feet.
Population: 362 (1990); 392 (2000); 460 (2010); 510 (2015 projected); Race: 90.2% White, 6.7% Black, 0.2% Asian, 2.8% Other, 3.7% Hispanic of any race (2010); Density: 2,613.2 persons per square mile (2010); Average household size: 2.60 (2010); Median age: 38.8 (2010); Males per 100 females: 99.1 (2010); Marriage status: 35.1% never married, 45.9% now married, 4.5% widowed, 14.5% divorced (2005-2009 5-year est.); Foreign born: 1.0% (2005-2009 5-year est.); Ancestry (includes multiple ancestries): 20.5% German, 18.8% Irish, 14.4% Italian, 4.0% English, 3.8% Dutch (2005-2009 5-year est.).
Economy: Single-family building permits issued: 1 (2010); Multi-family building permits issued: 0 (2010); Employment by occupation: 5.0% management, 9.0% professional, 24.3% services, 14.4% sales, 0.0% farming, 10.4% construction, 36.9% production (2005-2009 5-year est.).
Income: Per capita income: $34,302 (2010); Median household income: $83,712 (2010); Average household income: $87,867 (2010); Percent of households with income of $100,000 or more: 37.9% (2010); Poverty rate: 13.2% (2005-2009 5-year est.).
Taxes: Total city taxes per capita: $143 (2007); City property taxes per capita: $98 (2007).
Education: Percent of population age 25 and over with: High school diploma (including GED) or higher: 93.4% (2010); Bachelor's degree or higher: 15.8% (2010); Master's degree or higher: 2.4% (2010).
Housing: Homeownership rate: 90.4% (2010); Median home value: $282,500 (2010); Median contract rent: $490 per month (2005-2009 5-year est.); Median year structure built: 1976 (2005-2009 5-year est.).
Transportation: Commute to work: 95.4% car, 0.0% public transportation, 0.0% walk, 1.8% work from home (2005-2009 5-year est.); Travel time to work: 20.0% less than 15 minutes, 34.9% 15 to 30 minutes, 32.1% 30 to 45 minutes, 6.5% 45 to 60 minutes, 6.5% 60 minutes or more (2005-2009 5-year est.)

COAL CITY (village). Covers a land area of 2.423 square miles and a water area of 0 square miles. Located at 41.28° N. Lat; 88.28° W. Long. Elevation is 564 feet.
History: Coal City began when shaft mines were opened here in 1875. The shaft mines were followed by strip mining.
Population: 4,021 (1990); 4,797 (2000); 5,615 (2010); 6,333 (2015 projected); Race: 96.7% White, 1.3% Black, 0.0% Asian, 1.9% Other, 3.7% Hispanic of any race (2010); Density: 2,317.7 persons per square mile (2010); Average household size: 2.56 (2010); Median age: 34.3 (2010); Males per 100 females: 98.4 (2010); Marriage status: 29.3% never married, 52.2% now married, 5.9% widowed, 12.5% divorced (2005-2009 5-year est.); Foreign born: 1.5% (2005-2009 5-year est.); Ancestry (includes multiple ancestries): 28.2% Irish, 27.4% German, 19.6% Italian, 9.0% English, 8.3% Czech (2005-2009 5-year est.).

Economy: Single-family building permits issued: 0 (2010); Multi-family building permits issued: 0 (2010); Employment by occupation: 13.0% management, 12.6% professional, 15.5% services, 28.1% sales, 0.0% farming, 13.2% construction, 17.7% production (2005-2009 5-year est.).
Income: Per capita income: $28,447 (2010); Median household income: $64,150 (2010); Average household income: $72,810 (2010); Percent of households with income of $100,000 or more: 24.1% (2010); Poverty rate: 4.1% (2005-2009 5-year est.).
Taxes: Total city taxes per capita: $255 (2007); City property taxes per capita: $153 (2007).
Education: Percent of population age 25 and over with: High school diploma (including GED) or higher: 93.1% (2010); Bachelor's degree or higher: 16.2% (2010); Master's degree or higher: 5.5% (2010).

School District(s)

Coal City CUSD 1 (PK-12)
  2009-10 Enrollment: 2,152 . . . . (815) 634-2287
Housing: Homeownership rate: 76.8% (2010); Median home value: $150,926 (2010); Median contract rent: $673 per month (2005-2009 5-year est.); Median year structure built: 1972 (2005-2009 5-year est.).
Safety: Violent crime rate: 10.3 per 10,000 population; Property crime rate: 271.6 per 10,000 population (2010).
Newspapers: Coal City Courant (Local news; Circulation 2,400)
Transportation: Commute to work: 94.4% car, 2.0% public transportation, 0.6% walk, 3.0% work from home (2005-2009 5-year est.); Travel time to work: 23.3% less than 15 minutes, 34.5% 15 to 30 minutes, 20.4% 30 to 45 minutes, 7.7% 45 to 60 minutes, 14.1% 60 minutes or more (2005-2009 5-year est.)

Additional Information Contacts
Grundy County Chamber of Commerce . . . . (815) 634-8662
  http://www.grundychamber.com

DIAMOND (village). Covers a land area of 1.582 square miles and a water area of 0 square miles. Located at 41.28° N. Lat; 88.25° W. Long. Elevation is 564 feet.
Population: 1,236 (1990); 1,393 (2000); 2,189 (2010); 2,525 (2015 projected); Race: 95.2% White, 0.7% Black, 0.1% Asian, 3.9% Other, 6.6% Hispanic of any race (2010); Density: 1,383.4 persons per square mile (2010); Average household size: 2.48 (2010); Median age: 33.5 (2010); Males per 100 females: 95.4 (2010); Marriage status: 28.8% never married, 55.4% now married, 3.4% widowed, 12.5% divorced (2005-2009 5-year est.); Foreign born: 2.1% (2005-2009 5-year est.); Ancestry (includes multiple ancestries): 26.7% German, 20.6% Irish, 16.5% Italian, 8.2% Polish, 8.2% English (2005-2009 5-year est.).
Economy: Single-family building permits issued: 3 (2010); Multi-family building permits issued: 0 (2010); Employment by occupation: 5.9% management, 11.4% professional, 20.8% services, 24.3% sales, 0.0% farming, 16.3% construction, 21.3% production (2005-2009 5-year est.).
Income: Per capita income: $26,314 (2010); Median household income: $54,969 (2010); Average household income: $65,213 (2010); Percent of households with income of $100,000 or more: 19.5% (2010); Poverty rate: 10.8% (2005-2009 5-year est.).
Taxes: Total city taxes per capita: $181 (2007); City property taxes per capita: $36 (2007).
Education: Percent of population age 25 and over with: High school diploma (including GED) or higher: 89.3% (2010); Bachelor's degree or higher: 11.0% (2010); Master's degree or higher: 3.4% (2010).
Housing: Homeownership rate: 75.2% (2010); Median home value: $139,740 (2010); Median contract rent: $804 per month (2005-2009 5-year est.); Median year structure built: 1993 (2005-2009 5-year est.).
Transportation: Commute to work: 96.7% car, 1.5% public transportation, 0.5% walk, 0.7% work from home (2005-2009 5-year est.); Travel time to work: 24.3% less than 15 minutes, 32.2% 15 to 30 minutes, 19.1% 30 to 45 minutes, 11.7% 45 to 60 minutes, 12.7% 60 minutes or more (2005-2009 5-year est.)

EAST BROOKLYN (village). Covers a land area of 0.052 square miles and a water area of 0 square miles. Located at 41.17° N. Lat; 88.26° W. Long. Elevation is 584 feet.
Population: 88 (1990); 123 (2000); 121 (2010); 129 (2015 projected); Race: 95.0% White, 0.0% Black, 0.0% Asian, 5.0% Other, 6.6% Hispanic of any race (2010); Density: 2,330.9 persons per square mile (2010); Average household size: 2.37 (2010); Median age: 40.0 (2010); Males per 100 females: 98.4 (2010); Marriage status: 34.4% never married, 56.7% now married, 4.4% widowed, 4.4% divorced (2005-2009 5-year est.); Foreign born: 6.4% (2005-2009 5-year est.); Ancestry (includes multiple

ancestries): 30.3% German, 23.9% Irish, 22.9% Italian, 10.1% English, 7.3% Czech (2005-2009 5-year est.).
Economy: Single-family building permits issued: 0 (2010); Multi-family building permits issued: 0 (2010); Employment by occupation: 5.9% management, 13.7% professional, 5.9% services, 23.5% sales, 0.0% farming, 19.6% construction, 31.4% production (2005-2009 5-year est.).
Income: Per capita income: $24,815 (2010); Median household income: $45,227 (2010); Average household income: $56,765 (2010); Percent of households with income of $100,000 or more: 11.8% (2010); Poverty rate: 11.9% (2005-2009 5-year est.).
Taxes: Total city taxes per capita: $49 (2007); City property taxes per capita: $49 (2007).
Education: Percent of population age 25 and over with: High school diploma (including GED) or higher: 83.9% (2010); Bachelor's degree or higher: 9.2% (2010); Master's degree or higher: 3.4% (2010).
Housing: Homeownership rate: 86.3% (2010); Median home value: $126,190 (2010); Median contract rent: $617 per month (2005-2009 5-year est.); Median year structure built: 1955 (2005-2009 5-year est.).
Transportation: Commute to work: 96.1% car, 0.0% public transportation, 0.0% walk, 3.9% work from home (2005-2009 5-year est.); Travel time to work: 20.4% less than 15 minutes, 22.4% 15 to 30 minutes, 34.7% 30 to 45 minutes, 16.3% 45 to 60 minutes, 6.1% 60 minutes or more (2005-2009 5-year est.)

GARDNER (village). Covers a land area of 1.040 square miles and a water area of 0.014 square miles. Located at 41.18° N. Lat; 88.31° W. Long. Elevation is 587 feet.
Population: 1,237 (1990); 1,406 (2000); 1,553 (2010); 1,689 (2015 projected); Race: 94.1% White, 0.9% Black, 0.8% Asian, 4.2% Other, 8.6% Hispanic of any race (2010); Density: 1,492.7 persons per square mile (2010); Average household size: 2.47 (2010); Median age: 33.6 (2010); Males per 100 females: 100.9 (2010); Marriage status: 24.0% never married, 53.7% now married, 7.6% widowed, 14.7% divorced (2005-2009 5-year est.); Foreign born: 3.4% (2005-2009 5-year est.); Ancestry (includes multiple ancestries): 22.5% German, 15.9% English, 15.7% Irish, 14.4% Italian, 8.2% Norwegian (2005-2009 5-year est.).
Economy: Single-family building permits issued: 1 (2010); Multi-family building permits issued: 0 (2010); Employment by occupation: 9.0% management, 13.4% professional, 13.0% services, 17.3% sales, 0.0% farming, 19.4% construction, 28.0% production (2005-2009 5-year est.).
Income: Per capita income: $22,483 (2010); Median household income: $47,336 (2010); Average household income: $55,452 (2010); Percent of households with income of $100,000 or more: 11.1% (2010); Poverty rate: 11.6% (2005-2009 5-year est.).
Taxes: Total city taxes per capita: $787 (2007); City property taxes per capita: $764 (2007).
Education: Percent of population age 25 and over with: High school diploma (including GED) or higher: 86.9% (2010); Bachelor's degree or higher: 10.8% (2010); Master's degree or higher: 3.8% (2010).

School District(s)

Gardner CCSD 72c (PK-08)
  2009-10 Enrollment: 229 . . . . (815) 237-2313
Gardner S Wilmington Twp HSD 73 (09-12)
  2009-10 Enrollment: 214 . . . . (815) 237-2176
Housing: Homeownership rate: 79.8% (2010); Median home value: $125,517 (2010); Median contract rent: $516 per month (2005-2009 5-year est.); Median year structure built: 1959 (2005-2009 5-year est.).
Transportation: Commute to work: 93.0% car, 0.0% public transportation, 0.8% walk, 2.2% work from home (2005-2009 5-year est.); Travel time to work: 27.8% less than 15 minutes, 27.1% 15 to 30 minutes, 23.4% 30 to 45 minutes, 13.1% 45 to 60 minutes, 8.5% 60 minutes or more (2005-2009 5-year est.)

KINSMAN (village). Covers a land area of 0.067 square miles and a water area of 0 square miles. Located at 41.19° N. Lat; 88.57° W. Long. Elevation is 659 feet.
Population: 112 (1990); 109 (2000); 119 (2010); 131 (2015 projected); Race: 97.5% White, 0.0% Black, 0.0% Asian, 2.5% Other, 10.1% Hispanic of any race (2010); Density: 1,788.3 persons per square mile (2010); Average household size: 2.83 (2010); Median age: 31.8 (2010); Males per 100 females: 105.2 (2010); Marriage status: 12.6% never married, 64.0% now married, 7.2% widowed, 16.2% divorced (2005-2009 5-year est.); Foreign born: 0.0% (2005-2009 5-year est.); Ancestry (includes multiple ancestries): 30.6% German, 22.4% Irish, 14.2% Norwegian, 11.2% English, 10.4% Scotch-Irish (2005-2009 5-year est.).

Economy: Single-family building permits issued: 0 (2010); Multi-family building permits issued: 0 (2010); Employment by occupation: 19.3% management, 0.0% professional, 14.0% services, 36.8% sales, 0.0% farming, 21.1% construction, 8.8% production (2005-2009 5-year est.).
Income: Per capita income: $23,678 (2010); Median household income: $60,417 (2010); Average household income: $70,298 (2010); Percent of households with income of $100,000 or more: 16.7% (2010); Poverty rate: 22.4% (2005-2009 5-year est.).
Taxes: Total city taxes per capita: $101 (2007); City property taxes per capita: $101 (2007).
Education: Percent of population age 25 and over with: High school diploma (including GED) or higher: 94.4% (2010); Bachelor's degree or higher: 26.8% (2010); Master's degree or higher: 7.0% (2010).
Housing: Homeownership rate: 81.0% (2010); Median home value: $185,714 (2010); Median contract rent: $396 per month (2005-2009 5-year est.); Median year structure built: before 1940 (2005-2009 5-year est.).
Transportation: Commute to work: 96.3% car, 0.0% public transportation, 3.7% walk, 0.0% work from home (2005-2009 5-year est.); Travel time to work: 13.0% less than 15 minutes, 38.9% 15 to 30 minutes, 27.8% 30 to 45 minutes, 13.0% 45 to 60 minutes, 7.4% 60 minutes or more (2005-2009 5-year est.)

MAZON (village). Covers a land area of 0.598 square miles and a water area of 0 square miles. Located at 41.24° N. Lat; 88.42° W. Long. Elevation is 587 feet.
History: Near the Mazon River, a classic source of fossils from a middle Pennsylvanian formation.
Population: 818 (1990); 904 (2000); 1,020 (2010); 1,099 (2015 projected); Race: 90.1% White, 3.3% Black, 0.5% Asian, 6.1% Other, 4.9% Hispanic of any race (2010); Density: 1,704.5 persons per square mile (2010); Average household size: 2.63 (2010); Median age: 33.4 (2010); Males per 100 females: 102.0 (2010); Marriage status: 20.5% never married, 57.3% now married, 7.4% widowed, 14.9% divorced (2005-2009 5-year est.); Foreign born: 6.1% (2005-2009 5-year est.); Ancestry (includes multiple ancestries): 19.9% German, 19.7% Irish, 14.4% Italian, 14.1% English, 11.8% Norwegian (2005-2009 5-year est.).
Economy: Single-family building permits issued: 0 (2010); Multi-family building permits issued: 0 (2010); Employment by occupation: 25.9% management, 13.8% professional, 13.8% services, 13.1% sales, 0.0% farming, 9.2% construction, 24.2% production (2005-2009 5-year est.).
Income: Per capita income: $25,579 (2010); Median household income: $62,629 (2010); Average household income: $67,107 (2010); Percent of households with income of $100,000 or more: 19.1% (2010); Poverty rate: 7.3% (2005-2009 5-year est.).
Taxes: Total city taxes per capita: $155 (2007); City property taxes per capita: $152 (2007).
Education: Percent of population age 25 and over with: High school diploma (including GED) or higher: 91.3% (2010); Bachelor's degree or higher: 15.0% (2010); Master's degree or higher: 6.1% (2010).

School District(s)

Mazon-Verona-Kinsman ESD 2c (PK-08)
    2009-10 Enrollment: 338 . . . . (815) 448-2200
Housing: Homeownership rate: 80.4% (2010); Median home value: $135,088 (2010); Median contract rent: $610 per month (2005-2009 5-year est.); Median year structure built: 1970 (2005-2009 5-year est.).
Transportation: Commute to work: 97.5% car, 0.0% public transportation, 0.7% walk, 1.2% work from home (2005-2009 5-year est.); Travel time to work: 20.7% less than 15 minutes, 43.8% 15 to 30 minutes, 13.6% 30 to 45 minutes, 13.6% 45 to 60 minutes, 8.3% 60 minutes or more (2005-2009 5-year est.)

MINOOKA (village). Covers a land area of 4.263 square miles and a water area of 0.071 square miles. Located at 41.45° N. Lat; 88.26° W. Long. Elevation is 610 feet.
Population: 3,024 (1990); 3,971 (2000); 5,775 (2010); 6,357 (2015 projected); Race: 96.0% White, 0.8% Black, 0.7% Asian, 2.4% Other, 6.6% Hispanic of any race (2010); Density: 1,354.7 persons per square mile (2010); Average household size: 2.93 (2010); Median age: 33.0 (2010); Males per 100 females: 102.0 (2010); Marriage status: 28.2% never married, 64.4% now married, 1.5% widowed, 5.9% divorced (2005-2009 5-year est.); Foreign born: 3.3% (2005-2009 5-year est.); Ancestry (includes multiple ancestries): 31.1% German, 20.1% Irish, 15.3% Polish, 13.6% Italian, 7.4% English (2005-2009 5-year est.).
Economy: Single-family building permits issued: 24 (2010); Multi-family building permits issued: 0 (2010); Employment by occupation: 16.7%

management, 25.3% professional, 11.0% services, 25.7% sales, 0.0% farming, 8.8% construction, 12.6% production (2005-2009 5-year est.).
Income: Per capita income: $30,112 (2010); Median household income: $76,655 (2010); Average household income: $88,130 (2010); Percent of households with income of $100,000 or more: 33.2% (2010); Poverty rate: 3.8% (2005-2009 5-year est.).
Taxes: Total city taxes per capita: $243 (2007); City property taxes per capita: $134 (2007).
Education: Percent of population age 25 and over with: High school diploma (including GED) or higher: 92.8% (2010); Bachelor's degree or higher: 23.6% (2010); Master's degree or higher: 8.9% (2010).

School District(s)

Grundy/Kendall Roe (06-12)
    2009-10 Enrollment: n/a . . . . (815) 941-3247
Minooka CCSD 201 (PK-08)
    2009-10 Enrollment: 3,940 . . . . (815) 467-6121
Minooka CHSD 111 (09-12)
    2009-10 Enrollment: 2,459 . . . . (815) 467-2557
Housing: Homeownership rate: 87.8% (2010); Median home value: $205,446 (2010); Median contract rent: $741 per month (2005-2009 5-year est.); Median year structure built: 2000 (2005-2009 5-year est.).
Safety: Violent crime rate: 6.0 per 10,000 population; Property crime rate: 148.5 per 10,000 population (2010).
Transportation: Commute to work: 92.9% car, 0.5% public transportation, 1.0% walk, 4.9% work from home (2005-2009 5-year est.); Travel time to work: 17.2% less than 15 minutes, 36.5% 15 to 30 minutes, 24.9% 30 to 45 minutes, 5.4% 45 to 60 minutes, 16.0% 60 minutes or more (2005-2009 5-year est.)
Additional Information Contacts
Channahon Minooka Chamber of Commerce . . . . (815) 521-9999
    http://www.grundychamber.com/cm_chamber/index.html

MORRIS (city). County seat. Covers a land area of 6.879 square miles and a water area of 0.281 square miles. Located at 41.36° N. Lat; 88.42° W. Long. Elevation is 515 feet.
History: Morris was platted in 1842 and named for Isaac N. Morris, an Illinois & Michigan Canal commissioner, who negotiated to have the village named as the county seat. Morris grew as a shipping and paper manufacturing center.
Population: 10,429 (1990); 11,928 (2000); 14,090 (2010); 15,653 (2015 projected); Race: 86.7% White, 4.3% Black, 1.2% Asian, 7.8% Other, 14.5% Hispanic of any race (2010); Density: 2,048.3 persons per square mile (2010); Average household size: 2.35 (2010); Median age: 34.8 (2010); Males per 100 females: 98.7 (2010); Marriage status: 26.5% never married, 52.2% now married, 7.5% widowed, 13.8% divorced (2005-2009 5-year est.); Foreign born: 3.7% (2005-2009 5-year est.); Ancestry (includes multiple ancestries): 27.6% German, 20.0% Irish, 11.3% Norwegian, 9.3% English, 9.1% Italian (2005-2009 5-year est.).
Economy: Single-family building permits issued: 11 (2010); Multi-family building permits issued: 36 (2010); Employment by occupation: 10.0% management, 13.9% professional, 17.9% services, 29.4% sales, 0.4% farming, 13.2% construction, 15.2% production (2005-2009 5-year est.).
Income: Per capita income: $27,950 (2010); Median household income: $53,827 (2010); Average household income: $66,351 (2010); Percent of households with income of $100,000 or more: 18.2% (2010); Poverty rate: 5.5% (2005-2009 5-year est.).
Taxes: Total city taxes per capita: $412 (2007); City property taxes per capita: $356 (2007).
Education: Percent of population age 25 and over with: High school diploma (including GED) or higher: 88.6% (2010); Bachelor's degree or higher: 22.3% (2010); Master's degree or higher: 6.8% (2010).

School District(s)

Grundy Area Vocational Center
    2009-10 Enrollment: n/a . . . . (815) 942-4390
Grundy/Kendall Roe (06-12)
    2009-10 Enrollment: n/a . . . . (815) 941-3247
Morris CHSD 101 (09-12)
    2009-10 Enrollment: 953 . . . . (815) 941-5326
Morris SD 54 (PK-08)
    2009-10 Enrollment: 1,213 . . . . (815) 942-0056
Nettle Creek CCSD 24c (KG-08)
    2009-10 Enrollment: 107 . . . . (815) 942-0511
Saratoga CCSD 60c (PK-08)
    2009-10 Enrollment: 769 . . . . (815) 942-5970

Housing: Homeownership rate: 61.8% (2010); Median home value: $173,711 (2010); Median contract rent: $677 per month (2005-2009 5-year est.); Median year structure built: 1974 (2005-2009 5-year est.).
Hospitals: Morris Hospital (82 beds)
Safety: Violent crime rate: 23.5 per 10,000 population; Property crime rate: 359.8 per 10,000 population (2010).
Newspapers: Morris Daily Herald (Local news; Circulation 7,500)
Transportation: Commute to work: 95.1% car, 0.0% public transportation, 1.8% walk, 2.0% work from home (2005-2009 5-year est.); Travel time to work: 42.8% less than 15 minutes, 18.1% 15 to 30 minutes, 19.7% 30 to 45 minutes, 7.5% 45 to 60 minutes, 11.9% 60 minutes or more (2005-2009 5-year est.)
Additional Information Contacts
City of Morris . . . . (815) 942-0103
    http://city.mornet.org
Grundy County Chamber of Commerce . . . . (815) 942-0113
    http://www.grundychamber.com

SOUTH WILMINGTON (village). Covers a land area of 0.570 square miles and a water area of 0 square miles. Located at 41.17° N. Lat; 88.27° W. Long. Elevation is 587 feet.
Population: 710 (1990); 621 (2000); 655 (2010); 701 (2015 projected); Race: 95.1% White, 0.0% Black, 0.5% Asian, 4.4% Other, 5.8% Hispanic of any race (2010); Density: 1,149.5 persons per square mile (2010); Average household size: 2.35 (2010); Median age: 38.3 (2010); Males per 100 females: 91.5 (2010); Marriage status: 30.3% never married, 53.4% now married, 6.9% widowed, 9.3% divorced (2005-2009 5-year est.); Foreign born: 0.3% (2005-2009 5-year est.); Ancestry (includes multiple ancestries): 28.2% Italian, 23.3% German, 16.6% English, 13.4% Irish, 8.8% Norwegian (2005-2009 5-year est.).
Economy: Single-family building permits issued: 0 (2010); Multi-family building permits issued: 0 (2010); Employment by occupation: 3.0% management, 11.0% professional, 21.7% services, 23.4% sales, 0.0% farming, 25.2% construction, 15.7% production (2005-2009 5-year est.).
Income: Per capita income: $24,753 (2010); Median household income: $46,311 (2010); Average household income: $57,752 (2010); Percent of households with income of $100,000 or more: 12.6% (2010); Poverty rate: 1.8% (2005-2009 5-year est.).
Taxes: Total city taxes per capita: $65 (2007); City property taxes per capita: $57 (2007).
Education: Percent of population age 25 and over with: High school diploma (including GED) or higher: 83.7% (2010); Bachelor's degree or higher: 7.8% (2010); Master's degree or higher: 1.7% (2010).
School District(s)
South Wilmington CCSD 74 (KG-08)
    2009-10 Enrollment: 101 . . . . (815) 237-2281
Housing: Homeownership rate: 85.6% (2010); Median home value: $126,316 (2010); Median contract rent: $538 per month (2005-2009 5-year est.); Median year structure built: 1951 (2005-2009 5-year est.).
Transportation: Commute to work: 97.6% car, 0.0% public transportation, 2.4% walk, 0.0% work from home (2005-2009 5-year est.); Travel time to work: 17.6% less than 15 minutes, 22.8% 15 to 30 minutes, 41.6% 30 to 45 minutes, 11.2% 45 to 60 minutes, 6.7% 60 minutes or more (2005-2009 5-year est.)

VERONA (village). Covers a land area of 0.146 square miles and a water area of 0 square miles. Located at 41.21° N. Lat; 88.50° W. Long. Elevation is 630 feet.
Population: 242 (1990); 257 (2000); 280 (2010); 300 (2015 projected); Race: 95.7% White, 0.0% Black, 1.4% Asian, 2.9% Other, 10.4% Hispanic of any race (2010); Density: 1,920.5 persons per square mile (2010); Average household size: 2.83 (2010); Median age: 32.9 (2010); Males per 100 females: 98.6 (2010); Marriage status: 15.8% never married, 68.9% now married, 1.1% widowed, 14.1% divorced (2005-2009 5-year est.); Foreign born: 2.1% (2005-2009 5-year est.); Ancestry (includes multiple ancestries): 31.4% German, 18.2% Irish, 13.6% English, 7.4% Norwegian, 6.6% Italian (2005-2009 5-year est.).
Economy: Single-family building permits issued: 0 (2010); Multi-family building permits issued: 0 (2010); Employment by occupation: 9.8% management, 9.8% professional, 11.8% services, 35.3% sales, 0.0% farming, 24.5% construction, 8.8% production (2005-2009 5-year est.).
Income: Per capita income: $20,485 (2010); Median household income: $54,435 (2010); Average household income: $57,197 (2010); Percent of households with income of $100,000 or more: 9.1% (2010); Poverty rate: 24.0% (2005-2009 5-year est.).

Taxes: Total city taxes per capita: $114 (2007); City property taxes per capita: $51 (2007).
Education: Percent of population age 25 and over with: High school diploma (including GED) or higher: 86.5% (2010); Bachelor's degree or higher: 10.1% (2010); Master's degree or higher: 0.0% (2010).
Housing: Homeownership rate: 80.8% (2010); Median home value: $145,652 (2010); Median contract rent: $594 per month (2005-2009 5-year est.); Median year structure built: before 1940 (2005-2009 5-year est.).
Transportation: Commute to work: 97.1% car, 0.0% public transportation, 0.0% walk, 2.9% work from home (2005-2009 5-year est.); Travel time to work: 10.1% less than 15 minutes, 19.2% 15 to 30 minutes, 33.3% 30 to 45 minutes, 14.1% 45 to 60 minutes, 23.2% 60 minutes or more (2005-2009 5-year est.)

Hamilton County

Located in southeastern Illinois; drained by the North Fork of the Saline River. Covers a land area of 435.16 square miles, a water area of 0.67 square miles, and is located in the Central Time Zone at 38.09° N. Lat., 88.53° W. Long. The county was founded in 1821. County seat is McLeansboro.

Hamilton County is part of the Mount Vernon, IL Micropolitan Statistical Area. The entire metro area includes: Hamilton County, IL; Jefferson County, IL

Population: 8,499 (1990); 8,621 (2000); 8,254 (2010); 8,067 (2015 projected); Race: 97.6% White, 0.9% Black, 0.1% Asian, 1.3% Other, 1.2% Hispanic of any race (2010); Density: 19.0 persons per square mile (2010); Average household size: 2.44 (2010); Median age: 42.7 (2010); Males per 100 females: 94.9 (2010).
Religion: Five largest groups: 33.3% Southern Baptist Convention, 11.8% Catholic Church, 4.9% The United Methodist Church, 3.7% Christian Churches and Churches of Christ, 1.3% Church of God (Cleveland, Tennessee) (2000).
Economy: Unemployment rate: 8.1% (August 2011); Total civilian labor force: 3,982 (August 2011); Leading industries: 38.0% health care and social assistance; 13.1% retail trade; 9.3% accommodation & food services (2009); Farms: 685 totaling 219,873 acres (2007); Companies that employ 500 or more persons: 0 (2009); Companies that employ 100 to 499 persons: 1 (2009); Companies that employ less than 100 persons: 192 (2009); Black-owned businesses: n/a (2007); Hispanic-owned businesses: n/a (2007); Asian-owned businesses: n/a (2007); Women-owned businesses: n/a (2007); Retail sales per capita: $6,419 (2010). Single-family building permits issued: 0 (2010); Multi-family building permits issued: 0 (2010).
Income: Per capita income: $20,259 (2010); Median household income: $39,544 (2010); Average household income: $50,030 (2010); Percent of households with income of $100,000 or more: 8.7% (2010); Poverty rate: 14.2% (2009); Bankruptcy rate: 3.57% (2010).
Taxes: Total county taxes per capita: $89 (2007); County property taxes per capita: $87 (2007).
Education: Percent of population age 25 and over with: High school diploma (including GED) or higher: 80.4% (2010); Bachelor's degree or higher: 13.2% (2010); Master's degree or higher: 4.9% (2010).
Housing: Homeownership rate: 80.3% (2010); Median home value: $68,508 (2010); Median contract rent: $250 per month (2005-2009 5-year est.); Median year structure built: 1957 (2005-2009 5-year est.)
Health: Birth rate: 108.7 per 10,000 population (2009); Death rate: 121.0 per 10,000 population (2009); Age-adjusted cancer mortality rate: 157.5 deaths per 100,000 population (2007); Number of physicians: 6.1 per 10,000 population (2008); Hospital beds: 104.3 per 10,000 population (2007); Hospital admissions: 1,358.6 per 10,000 population (2007).
Environment: Air Quality Index: 87.5% good, 12.5% moderate, 0.0% unhealthy for sensitive individuals, 0.0% unhealthy (percent of days in 2008)
Elections: 2008 Presidential election results: 42.1% Obama, 55.2% McCain, 1.2% Nader
National and State Parks: Hamilton County State Conservation Area
Additional Information Contacts
Hamilton County Government . . . . (618) 643-2721

Hamilton County Chamber of Commerce
    http://hamcochamber.com

Hamilton County Communities

BELLE PRAIRIE CITY (town). Aka Belle Prairie. Covers a land area of 0.449 square miles and a water area of 0 square miles. Located at 38.22° N. Lat; 88.55° W. Long. Elevation is 476 feet.
Population: 64 (1990); 60 (2000); 58 (2010); 57 (2015 projected); Race: 100.0% White, 0.0% Black, 0.0% Asian, 0.0% Other, 1.7% Hispanic of any race (2010); Density: 129.2 persons per square mile (2010); Average household size: 2.52 (2010); Median age: 46.4 (2010); Males per 100 females: 132.0 (2010); Marriage status: 21.1% never married, 67.6% now married, 11.3% widowed, 0.0% divorced (2005-2009 5-year est.); Foreign born: 0.0% (2005-2009 5-year est.); Ancestry (includes multiple ancestries): 56.8% German, 18.5% Irish, 18.5% English, 12.3% Italian, 7.4% American (2005-2009 5-year est.).
Economy: Employment by occupation: 31.9% management, 0.0% professional, 10.6% services, 21.3% sales, 0.0% farming, 17.0% construction, 19.1% production (2005-2009 5-year est.).
Income: Per capita income: $24,757 (2010); Median household income: $46,250 (2010); Average household income: $61,630 (2010); Percent of households with income of $100,000 or more: 13.0% (2010); Poverty rate: 2.5% (2005-2009 5-year est.).
Taxes: Total city taxes per capita: $17 (2007); City property taxes per capita: $17 (2007).
Education: Percent of population age 25 and over with: High school diploma (including GED) or higher: 86.4% (2010); Bachelor's degree or higher: 13.6% (2010); Master's degree or higher: 2.3% (2010).
Housing: Homeownership rate: 87.0% (2010); Median home value: $66,667 (2010); Median contract rent: n/a per month (2005-2009 5-year est.); Median year structure built: 1960 (2005-2009 5-year est.).
Transportation: Commute to work: 93.6% car, 0.0% public transportation, 0.0% walk, 6.4% work from home (2005-2009 5-year est.); Travel time to work: 11.4% less than 15 minutes, 27.3% 15 to 30 minutes, 43.2% 30 to 45 minutes, 0.0% 45 to 60 minutes, 18.2% 60 minutes or more (2005-2009 5-year est.)

BROUGHTON (village). Covers a land area of 1.918 square miles and a water area of 0 square miles. Located at 37.93° N. Lat; 88.46° W. Long. Elevation is 377 feet.
Population: 218 (1990); 193 (2000); 184 (2010); 179 (2015 projected); Race: 98.9% White, 0.0% Black, 0.0% Asian, 1.1% Other, 1.1% Hispanic of any race (2010); Density: 95.9 persons per square mile (2010); Average household size: 2.45 (2010); Median age: 43.7 (2010); Males per 100 females: 95.7 (2010); Marriage status: 9.6% never married, 65.3% now married, 10.8% widowed, 14.4% divorced (2005-2009 5-year est.); Foreign born: 0.0% (2005-2009 5-year est.); Ancestry (includes multiple ancestries): 17.8% Irish, 14.4% German, 10.0% English, 8.3% French, 7.2% Dutch (2005-2009 5-year est.).
Economy: Employment by occupation: 16.4% management, 0.0% professional, 23.6% services, 34.5% sales, 0.0% farming, 0.0% construction, 25.5% production (2005-2009 5-year est.).
Income: Per capita income: $13,034 (2010); Median household income: $26,500 (2010); Average household income: $31,400 (2010); Percent of households with income of $100,000 or more: 1.3% (2010); Poverty rate: 14.4% (2005-2009 5-year est.).
Taxes: Total city taxes per capita: $42 (2007); City property taxes per capita: $42 (2007).
Education: Percent of population age 25 and over with: High school diploma (including GED) or higher: 77.3% (2010); Bachelor's degree or higher: 3.0% (2010); Master's degree or higher: 1.5% (2010).
Housing: Homeownership rate: 86.7% (2010); Median home value: $62,308 (2010); Median contract rent: n/a per month (2005-2009 5-year est.); Median year structure built: 1949 (2005-2009 5-year est.).
Transportation: Commute to work: 98.1% car, 0.0% public transportation, 1.9% walk, 0.0% work from home (2005-2009 5-year est.); Travel time to work: 9.4% less than 15 minutes, 50.9% 15 to 30 minutes, 18.9% 30 to 45 minutes, 9.4% 45 to 60 minutes, 11.3% 60 minutes or more (2005-2009 5-year est.)

DAHLGREN (village). Covers a land area of 1.004 square miles and a water area of 0 square miles. Located at 38.19° N. Lat; 88.68° W. Long. Elevation is 515 feet.
Population: 512 (1990); 514 (2000); 498 (2010); 485 (2015 projected); Race: 98.0% White, 0.2% Black, 0.0% Asian, 1.8% Other, 1.6% Hispanic of any race (2010); Density: 496.2 persons per square mile (2010); Average household size: 2.55 (2010); Median age: 42.4 (2010); Males per

100 females: 99.2 (2010); Marriage status: 10.1% never married, 72.4% now married, 9.3% widowed, 8.1% divorced (2005-2009 5-year est.); Foreign born: 0.0% (2005-2009 5-year est.); Ancestry (includes multiple ancestries): 34.2% German, 29.7% Irish, 6.8% Dutch, 6.8% American, 6.5% English (2005-2009 5-year est.).
Economy: Employment by occupation: 2.8% management, 15.9% professional, 9.8% services, 32.9% sales, 0.0% farming, 14.2% construction, 24.4% production (2005-2009 5-year est.).
Income: Per capita income: $22,243 (2010); Median household income: $44,716 (2010); Average household income: $55,782 (2010); Percent of households with income of $100,000 or more: 9.7% (2010); Poverty rate: 17.2% (2005-2009 5-year est.).
Taxes: Total city taxes per capita: $26 (2007); City property taxes per capita: $26 (2007).
Education: Percent of population age 25 and over with: High school diploma (including GED) or higher: 85.8% (2010); Bachelor's degree or higher: 13.4% (2010); Master's degree or higher: 4.5% (2010).
School District(s)
Hamilton Co CUSD 10 (PK-12)
    2009-10 Enrollment: 1,297 . . . . (618) 643-2328
Housing: Homeownership rate: 88.2% (2010); Median home value: $66,087 (2010); Median contract rent: $273 per month (2005-2009 5-year est.); Median year structure built: 1943 (2005-2009 5-year est.).
Transportation: Commute to work: 97.2% car, 0.0% public transportation, 2.8% walk, 0.0% work from home (2005-2009 5-year est.); Travel time to work: 18.7% less than 15 minutes, 48.0% 15 to 30 minutes, 13.8% 30 to 45 minutes, 5.7% 45 to 60 minutes, 13.8% 60 minutes or more (2005-2009 5-year est.)

DALE (unincorporated postal area, zip code 62829). Aka Dales. Covers a land area of 6.561 square miles and a water area of 0 square miles. Located at 38.00° N. Lat; 88.50° W. Long. Elevation is 400 feet.
Population: 157 (2000); Race: 100.0% White, 0.0% Black, 0.0% Asian, 0.0% Other, 3.5% Hispanic of any race (2000); Density: 23.9 persons per square mile (2000); Age: 22.9% under 18, 5.3% over 64 (2000); Marriage status: 15.7% never married, 75.7% now married, 0.0% widowed, 8.6% divorced (2000); Foreign born: 1.8% (2000); Ancestry (includes multiple ancestries): 17.1% German, 11.2% American, 11.2% Irish, 8.2% European, 4.7% Danish (2000).
Economy: Employment by occupation: 0.0% management, 28.0% professional, 22.6% services, 15.1% sales, 9.7% farming, 8.6% construction, 16.1% production (2000).
Income: Per capita income: $16,996 (2000); Median household income: $50,417 (2000); Poverty rate: 0.0% (2000).
Education: Percent of population age 25 and over with: High school diploma (including GED) or higher: 83.9% (2000); Bachelor's degree or higher: 11.9% (2000).
Housing: Homeownership rate: 90.2% (2000); Median home value: $58,600 (2000); Median contract rent: n/a per month (2000); Median year structure built: 1957 (2000).
Transportation: Commute to work: 93.5% car, 0.0% public transportation, 0.0% walk, 6.5% work from home (2000); Travel time to work: 21.8% less than 15 minutes, 40.2% 15 to 30 minutes, 19.5% 30 to 45 minutes, 8.0% 45 to 60 minutes, 10.3% 60 minutes or more (2000)

MACEDONIA (village). Covers a land area of 0.271 square miles and a water area of 0 square miles. Located at 38.05° N. Lat; 88.70° W. Long.
Population: 58 (1990); 51 (2000); 49 (2010); 48 (2015 projected); Race: 93.9% White, 6.1% Black, 0.0% Asian, 0.0% Other, 0.0% Hispanic of any race (2010); Density: 181.0 persons per square mile (2010); Average household size: 2.67 (2010); Median age: 48.5 (2010); Males per 100 females: 75.0 (2010); Marriage status: 22.2% never married, 77.8% now married, 0.0% widowed, 0.0% divorced (2005-2009 5-year est.); Foreign born: 0.0% (2005-2009 5-year est.); Ancestry (includes multiple ancestries): 40.7% German, 25.9% Irish (2005-2009 5-year est.).
Economy: Employment by occupation: 21.4% management, 28.6% professional, 0.0% services, 28.6% sales, 0.0% farming, 0.0% construction, 21.4% production (2005-2009 5-year est.).
Income: Per capita income: $20,493 (2010); Median household income: $46,250 (2010); Average household income: $49,861 (2010); Percent of households with income of $100,000 or more: 5.6% (2010); Poverty rate: 0.0% (2005-2009 5-year est.).
Taxes: Total city taxes per capita: $20 (2007); City property taxes per capita: $20 (2007).

Education: Percent of population age 25 and over with: High school diploma (including GED) or higher: 86.5% (2010); Bachelor's degree or higher: 10.8% (2010); Master's degree or higher: 2.7% (2010).
Housing: Homeownership rate: 88.9% (2010); Median home value: $80,000 (2010); Median contract rent: n/a per month (2005-2009 5-year est.); Median year structure built: before 1940 (2005-2009 5-year est.).
Transportation: Commute to work: 100.0% car, 0.0% public transportation, 0.0% walk, 0.0% work from home (2005-2009 5-year est.); Travel time to work: 0.0% less than 15 minutes, 72.7% 15 to 30 minutes, 27.3% 30 to 45 minutes, 0.0% 45 to 60 minutes, 0.0% 60 minutes or more (2005-2009 5-year est.)

MCLEANSBORO (city). County seat. Covers a land area of 2.290 square miles and a water area of 0 square miles. Located at 38.09° N. Lat; 88.53° W. Long. Elevation is 502 feet.

History: Incorporated 1840.
Population: 2,851 (1990); 2,945 (2000); 2,828 (2010); 2,778 (2015 projected); Race: 97.6% White, 1.0% Black, 0.1% Asian, 1.3% Other, 0.6% Hispanic of any race (2010); Density: 1,235.2 persons per square mile (2010); Average household size: 2.28 (2010); Median age: 44.1 (2010); Males per 100 females: 85.9 (2010); Marriage status: 15.9% never married, 51.7% now married, 15.7% widowed, 16.7% divorced (2005-2009 5-year est.); Foreign born: 2.3% (2005-2009 5-year est.); Ancestry (includes multiple ancestries): 22.6% Irish, 22.3% German, 12.6% English, 8.0% American, 4.0% Dutch (2005-2009 5-year est.).
Economy: Single-family building permits issued: 0 (2010); Multi-family building permits issued: 0 (2010); Employment by occupation: 7.4% management, 19.4% professional, 22.9% services, 19.7% sales, 0.7% farming, 8.1% construction, 21.8% production (2005-2009 5-year est.).
Income: Per capita income: $18,732 (2010); Median household income: $31,392 (2010); Average household income: $44,164 (2010); Percent of households with income of $100,000 or more: 8.5% (2010); Poverty rate: 18.7% (2005-2009 5-year est.).
Taxes: Total city taxes per capita: $98 (2007); City property taxes per capita: $98 (2007).
Education: Percent of population age 25 and over with: High school diploma (including GED) or higher: 75.5% (2010); Bachelor's degree or higher: 15.3% (2010); Master's degree or higher: 6.7% (2010).

School District(s)
Hamilton Co CUSD 10 (PK-12)
    2009-10 Enrollment: 1,297 . . . . (618) 643-2328
Housing: Homeownership rate: 69.7% (2010); Median home value: $58,264 (2010); Median contract rent: $246 per month (2005-2009 5-year est.); Median year structure built: 1955 (2005-2009 5-year est.).
Hospitals: Hamilton Memorial Hospital
Newspapers: Times Leader (Local news; Circulation 3,600)
Transportation: Commute to work: 93.5% car, 0.0% public transportation, 0.6% walk, 3.5% work from home (2005-2009 5-year est.); Travel time to work: 58.5% less than 15 minutes, 3.0% 15 to 30 minutes, 23.5% 30 to 45 minutes, 5.0% 45 to 60 minutes, 9.9% 60 minutes or more (2005-2009 5-year est.)
Additional Information Contacts
Hamilton County Chamber of Commerce. . . . .
    http://hamcochamber.com

Hancock County

Located in western Illinois; bounded on the west by Lake Keokuk (on the Mississippi River) and the Iowa and Missouri borders; drained by the La Moine River and Bear Creek. Covers a land area of 794.62 square miles, a water area of 19.92 square miles, and is located in the Central Time Zone at 40.42° N. Lat., 91.18° W. Long. The county was founded in 1825. County seat is Carthage.

Weather Station: La Harpe   Elevation: 700 feet

	Jan	Feb	Mar	Apr	May	Jun	Jul	Aug	Sep	Oct	Nov	Dec
High	34	39	50	63	74	83	87	85	78	65	51	37
Low	15	18	28	39	50	60	63	61	52	40	30	18
Precip	1.5	1.7	2.7	3.8	4.6	4.7	4.4	3.7	3.9	3.0	2.9	2.4
Snow	6.0	3.7	2.7	0.8	0.0	0.0	0.0	0.0	0.0	tr	0.9	5.0

High and Low temperatures in degrees Fahrenheit; Precipitation and Snow in inches

Population: 21,373 (1990); 20,121 (2000); 18,478 (2010); 17,606 (2015 projected); Race: 97.8% White, 0.6% Black, 0.3% Asian, 1.3% Other, 0.8% Hispanic of any race (2010); Density: 23.3 persons per square mile (2010);

Average household size: 2.42 (2010); Median age: 42.9 (2010); Males per 100 females: 93.9 (2010).
Religion: Five largest groups: 12.9% Catholic Church, 9.9% The United Methodist Church, 6.4% Christian Churches and Churches of Christ, 5.7% Evangelical Lutheran Church in America, 3.4% Presbyterian Church (U.S.A.) (2000).
Economy: Unemployment rate: 9.4% (August 2011); Total civilian labor force: 9,555 (August 2011); Leading industries: 21.0% health care and social assistance; 17.3% retail trade; 10.0% accommodation & food services (2009); Farms: 1,063 totaling 392,898 acres (2007); Companies that employ 500 or more persons: 0 (2009); Companies that employ 100 to 499 persons: 2 (2009); Companies that employ less than 100 persons: 424 (2009); Black-owned businesses: n/a (2007); Hispanic-owned businesses: n/a (2007); Asian-owned businesses: n/a (2007); Women-owned businesses: 640 (2007); Retail sales per capita: $8,030 (2010). Single-family building permits issued: 3 (2010); Multi-family building permits issued: 0 (2010).
Income: Per capita income: $21,365 (2010); Median household income: $44,144 (2010); Average household income: $52,128 (2010); Percent of households with income of $100,000 or more: 8.3% (2010); Poverty rate: 11.6% (2009); Bankruptcy rate: 3.34% (2010).
Taxes: Total county taxes per capita: $125 (2007); County property taxes per capita: $113 (2007).
Education: Percent of population age 25 and over with: High school diploma (including GED) or higher: 89.9% (2010); Bachelor's degree or higher: 18.8% (2010); Master's degree or higher: 5.2% (2010).
Housing: Homeownership rate: 79.3% (2010); Median home value: $84,516 (2010); Median contract rent: $353 per month (2005-2009 5-year est.); Median year structure built: 1952 (2005-2009 5-year est.)
Health: Birth rate: 111.7 per 10,000 population (2009); Death rate: 117.1 per 10,000 population (2009); Age-adjusted cancer mortality rate: 210.8 deaths per 100,000 population (2007); Number of physicians: 7.0 per 10,000 population (2008); Hospital beds: 8.0 per 10,000 population (2007); Hospital admissions: 357.1 per 10,000 population (2007).
Elections: 2008 Presidential election results: 43.7% Obama, 54.5% McCain, 0.6% Nader
National and State Parks: Montebello State Park; Nauvoo State Park
Additional Information Contacts
Hancock County Government . . . . (217) 357-3911
    http://www.hancockcountycourthouse.org
Carthage Area Chamber of Commerce . . . . (217) 357-3024
    http://www.carthage-il.com
City of Carthage . . . . (217) 357-3119
    http://www.carthage-il.com
Nauvoo Chamber of Commerce . . . . (217) 453-6648
    http://www.nauvoochamber.org

Hancock County Communities

AUGUSTA (village). Covers a land area of 0.713 square miles and a water area of 0 square miles. Located at 40.23° N. Lat; 90.95° W. Long. Elevation is 663 feet.

Population: 613 (1990); 657 (2000); 590 (2010); 561 (2015 projected); Race: 99.5% White, 0.0% Black, 0.0% Asian, 0.5% Other, 1.4% Hispanic of any race (2010); Density: 827.2 persons per square mile (2010); Average household size: 2.36 (2010); Median age: 45.1 (2010); Males per 100 females: 86.7 (2010); Marriage status: 22.2% never married, 49.7% now married, 10.1% widowed, 18.0% divorced (2005-2009 5-year est.); Foreign born: 1.0% (2005-2009 5-year est.); Ancestry (includes multiple ancestries): 28.4% American, 23.5% German, 11.6% English, 5.3% Irish, 2.1% Swedish (2005-2009 5-year est.).
Economy: Employment by occupation: 8.8% management, 9.9% professional, 22.9% services, 22.9% sales, 4.0% farming, 11.0% construction, 20.6% production (2005-2009 5-year est.).
Income: Per capita income: $22,190 (2010); Median household income: $41,081 (2010); Average household income: $52,560 (2010); Percent of households with income of $100,000 or more: 8.8% (2010); Poverty rate: 24.6% (2005-2009 5-year est.).
Taxes: Total city taxes per capita: $47 (2007); City property taxes per capita: $47 (2007).
Education: Percent of population age 25 and over with: High school diploma (including GED) or higher: 88.7% (2010); Bachelor's degree or higher: 19.8% (2010); Master's degree or higher: 5.0% (2010).

School District(s)
Southeastern CUSD 337 (PK-12)
   2009-10 Enrollment: 560 . . . . (217) 392-2172
Housing: Homeownership rate: 82.4% (2010); Median home value: $51,064 (2010); Median contract rent: $339 per month (2005-2009 5-year est.); Median year structure built: 1945 (2005-2009 5-year est.).
Newspapers: Eagle-Scribe (Local news; Circulation 1,225)
Transportation: Commute to work: 87.2% car, 2.6% public transportation, 1.4% walk, 6.4% work from home (2005-2009 5-year est.); Travel time to work: 38.1% less than 15 minutes, 14.9% 15 to 30 minutes, 30.0% 30 to 45 minutes, 9.6% 45 to 60 minutes, 7.4% 60 minutes or more (2005-2009 5-year est.)

BASCO (village). Covers a land area of 0.227 square miles and a water area of 0 square miles. Located at 40.32° N. Lat; 91.19° W. Long. Elevation is 630 feet.
Population: 99 (1990); 107 (2000); 99 (2010); 96 (2015 projected); Race: 100.0% White, 0.0% Black, 0.0% Asian, 0.0% Other, 1.0% Hispanic of any race (2010); Density: 436.5 persons per square mile (2010); Average household size: 2.61 (2010); Median age: 43.1 (2010); Males per 100 females: 83.3 (2010); Marriage status: 24.6% never married, 53.1% now married, 10.8% widowed, 11.5% divorced (2005-2009 5-year est.); Foreign born: 0.0% (2005-2009 5-year est.); Ancestry (includes multiple ancestries): 39.9% German, 19.6% American, 14.6% Irish, 8.2% English, 4.4% French (2005-2009 5-year est.).
Economy: Employment by occupation: 0.0% management, 13.2% professional, 21.7% services, 19.8% sales, 0.0% farming, 23.6% construction, 21.7% production (2005-2009 5-year est.).
Income: Per capita income: $21,091 (2010); Median household income: $48,125 (2010); Average household income: $54,934 (2010); Percent of households with income of $100,000 or more: 7.9% (2010); Poverty rate: 25.0% (2005-2009 5-year est.).
Taxes: Total city taxes per capita: $20 (2007); City property taxes per capita: $10 (2007).
Education: Percent of population age 25 and over with: High school diploma (including GED) or higher: 90.0% (2010); Bachelor's degree or higher: 25.7% (2010); Master's degree or higher: 4.3% (2010).
Housing: Homeownership rate: 86.8% (2010); Median home value: $61,667 (2010); Median contract rent: $332 per month (2005-2009 5-year est.); Median year structure built: before 1940 (2005-2009 5-year est.).
Transportation: Commute to work: 96.2% car, 0.0% public transportation, 0.0% walk, 3.8% work from home (2005-2009 5-year est.); Travel time to work: 13.0% less than 15 minutes, 67.0% 15 to 30 minutes, 12.0% 30 to 45 minutes, 8.0% 45 to 60 minutes, 0.0% 60 minutes or more (2005-2009 5-year est.)

BENTLEY (town). Aka Bently. Covers a land area of 0.142 square miles and a water area of 0 square miles. Located at 40.34° N. Lat; 91.11° W. Long. Elevation is 676 feet.
Population: 36 (1990); 43 (2000); 41 (2010); 40 (2015 projected); Race: 100.0% White, 0.0% Black, 0.0% Asian, 0.0% Other, 2.4% Hispanic of any race (2010); Density: 287.8 persons per square mile (2010); Average household size: 2.56 (2010); Median age: 34.6 (2010); Males per 100 females: 115.8 (2010); Marriage status: 0.0% never married, 18.2% now married, 45.5% widowed, 36.4% divorced (2005-2009 5-year est.); Foreign born: 0.0% (2005-2009 5-year est.); Ancestry (includes multiple ancestries): 36.4% German, 18.2% English, 18.2% Irish, 9.1% Italian (2005-2009 5-year est.).
Economy: Employment by occupation: 0.0% management, 0.0% professional, 28.6% services, 14.3% sales, 0.0% farming, 57.1% construction, 0.0% production (2005-2009 5-year est.).
Income: Per capita income: $21,091 (2010); Median household income: $46,250 (2010); Average household income: $52,188 (2010); Percent of households with income of $100,000 or more: 6.3% (2010); Poverty rate: 9.1% (2005-2009 5-year est.).
Taxes: Total city taxes per capita: $24 (2007); City property taxes per capita: $24 (2007).
Education: Percent of population age 25 and over with: High school diploma (including GED) or higher: 93.8% (2010); Bachelor's degree or higher: 28.1% (2010); Master's degree or higher: 6.3% (2010).
Housing: Homeownership rate: 87.5% (2010); Median home value: $70,000 (2010); Median contract rent: n/a per month (2005-2009 5-year est.); Median year structure built: before 1940 (2005-2009 5-year est.).
Transportation: Commute to work: 85.7% car, 0.0% public transportation, 0.0% walk, 14.3% work from home (2005-2009 5-year est.); Travel time to work: 0.0% less than 15 minutes, 0.0% 15 to 30 minutes, 100.0% 30 to 45 minutes, 0.0% 45 to 60 minutes, 0.0% 60 minutes or more (2005-2009 5-year est.)

BOWEN (village). Covers a land area of 0.431 square miles and a water area of 0 square miles. Located at 40.23° N. Lat; 91.06° W. Long. Elevation is 689 feet.
Population: 462 (1990); 535 (2000); 486 (2010); 464 (2015 projected); Race: 97.9% White, 0.4% Black, 0.4% Asian, 1.2% Other, 0.6% Hispanic of any race (2010); Density: 1,127.9 persons per square mile (2010); Average household size: 2.60 (2010); Median age: 38.1 (2010); Males per 100 females: 96.0 (2010); Marriage status: 22.6% never married, 68.7% now married, 4.5% widowed, 4.2% divorced (2005-2009 5-year est.); Foreign born: 0.5% (2005-2009 5-year est.); Ancestry (includes multiple ancestries): 21.6% German, 14.0% American, 13.8% Irish, 11.8% English, 8.2% Swedish (2005-2009 5-year est.).
Economy: Employment by occupation: 3.4% management, 22.6% professional, 22.1% services, 15.3% sales, 6.0% farming, 5.5% construction, 25.1% production (2005-2009 5-year est.).
Income: Per capita income: $16,381 (2010); Median household income: $35,500 (2010); Average household income: $42,649 (2010); Percent of households with income of $100,000 or more: 2.7% (2010); Poverty rate: 33.3% (2005-2009 5-year est.).
Taxes: Total city taxes per capita: $28 (2007); City property taxes per capita: $28 (2007).
Education: Percent of population age 25 and over with: High school diploma (including GED) or higher: 87.3% (2010); Bachelor's degree or higher: 13.0% (2010); Master's degree or higher: 2.5% (2010).
School District(s)
Southeastern CUSD 337 (PK-12)
   2009-10 Enrollment: 560 . . . . (217) 392-2172
Housing: Homeownership rate: 78.8% (2010); Median home value: $55,000 (2010); Median contract rent: $291 per month (2005-2009 5-year est.); Median year structure built: 1943 (2005-2009 5-year est.).
Transportation: Commute to work: 89.8% car, 0.0% public transportation, 9.3% walk, 0.0% work from home (2005-2009 5-year est.); Travel time to work: 33.8% less than 15 minutes, 22.7% 15 to 30 minutes, 10.6% 30 to 45 minutes, 26.4% 45 to 60 minutes, 6.5% 60 minutes or more (2005-2009 5-year est.)

BURNSIDE (unincorporated postal area, zip code 62318). Covers a land area of 40.074 square miles and a water area of 0 square miles. Located at 40.51° N. Lat; 91.12° W. Long. Elevation is 646 feet.
Population: 358 (2000); Race: 100.0% White, 0.0% Black, 0.0% Asian, 0.0% Other, 0.0% Hispanic of any race (2000); Density: 8.9 persons per square mile (2000); Age: 22.6% under 18, 15.8% over 64 (2000); Marriage status: 25.5% never married, 58.2% now married, 5.6% widowed, 10.8% divorced (2000); Foreign born: 0.0% (2000); Ancestry (includes multiple ancestries): 24.2% English, 23.9% German, 13.9% American, 8.4% Irish, 2.4% Scottish (2000).
Economy: Employment by occupation: 17.8% management, 22.3% professional, 8.1% services, 21.3% sales, 3.0% farming, 6.1% construction, 21.3% production (2000).
Income: Per capita income: $17,642 (2000); Median household income: $44,063 (2000); Poverty rate: 12.8% (2000).
Education: Percent of population age 25 and over with: High school diploma (including GED) or higher: 83.1% (2000); Bachelor's degree or higher: 14.1% (2000).
Housing: Homeownership rate: 71.4% (2000); Median home value: $48,500 (2000); Median contract rent: $225 per month (2000); Median year structure built: before 1940 (2000).
Transportation: Commute to work: 91.9% car, 0.0% public transportation, 1.0% walk, 7.1% work from home (2000); Travel time to work: 35.5% less than 15 minutes, 38.3% 15 to 30 minutes, 2.7% 30 to 45 minutes, 18.6% 45 to 60 minutes, 4.9% 60 minutes or more (2000)

CARTHAGE (city). County seat. Covers a land area of 1.605 square miles and a water area of 0 square miles. Located at 40.41° N. Lat; 91.13° W. Long. Elevation is 669 feet.
History: Incorporated 1837. In 1844, Joseph Smith, Mormon leader, and his brother were killed in the city jail by a mob; the old jail is now property of the Mormon Church.
Population: 2,658 (1990); 2,725 (2000); 2,444 (2010); 2,318 (2015 projected); Race: 96.3% White, 1.7% Black, 0.8% Asian, 1.2% Other, 0.4% Hispanic of any race (2010); Density: 1,522.9 persons per square mile (2010); Average household size: 2.24 (2010); Median age: 43.6 (2010);

Males per 100 females: 85.0 (2010); Marriage status: 27.5% never married, 51.7% now married, 7.4% widowed, 13.3% divorced (2005-2009 5-year est.); Foreign born: 2.1% (2005-2009 5-year est.); Ancestry (includes multiple ancestries): 33.3% German, 18.9% American, 15.7% English, 8.1% French, 7.5% Irish (2005-2009 5-year est.).

Economy: Single-family building permits issued: 2 (2010); Multi-family building permits issued: 0 (2010); Employment by occupation: 10.9% management, 12.7% professional, 23.2% services, 26.7% sales, 0.9% farming, 8.1% construction, 17.6% production (2005-2009 5-year est.).

Income: Per capita income: $22,320 (2010); Median household income: $41,788 (2010); Average household income: $51,251 (2010); Percent of households with income of $100,000 or more: 10.3% (2010); Poverty rate: 12.8% (2005-2009 5-year est.).

Taxes: Total city taxes per capita: $115 (2007); City property taxes per capita: $69 (2007).

Education: Percent of population age 25 and over with: High school diploma (including GED) or higher: 90.1% (2010); Bachelor's degree or higher: 24.1% (2010); Master's degree or higher: 10.7% (2010).

School District(s)

Carthage ESD 317 (PK-08)
    2009-10 Enrollment: 461 . . . . (217) 357-3922
Hancock/Mcdonough Roe (07-12)
    2009-10 Enrollment: n/a . . . . (309) 837-4821
Illini West H S Dist 307 (09-12)
    2009-10 Enrollment: 473 . . . . (217) 357-9607

Housing: Homeownership rate: 68.9% (2010); Median home value: $91,622 (2010); Median contract rent: $373 per month (2005-2009 5-year est.); Median year structure built: 1945 (2005-2009 5-year est.).

Hospitals: Memorial Hospital (67 beds)

Safety: Violent crime rate: 16.6 per 10,000 population; Property crime rate: 220.5 per 10,000 population (2010).

Newspapers: Hancock County Journal Pilot (Regional news; Circulation 4,500)

Transportation: Commute to work: 87.3% car, 0.0% public transportation, 2.6% walk, 9.1% work from home (2005-2009 5-year est.); Travel time to work: 57.0% less than 15 minutes, 13.2% 15 to 30 minutes, 18.0% 30 to 45 minutes, 7.6% 45 to 60 minutes, 4.2% 60 minutes or more (2005-2009 5-year est.)

Additional Information Contacts

Carthage Area Chamber of Commerce . . . . (217) 357-3024
    http://www.carthage-il.com
City of Carthage . . . . (217) 357-3119
    http://www.carthage-il.com

DALLAS CITY (city).
Covers a land area of 2.375 square miles and a water area of 0.905 square miles. Located at 40.63° N. Lat; 91.16° W. Long. Elevation is 545 feet.

Population: 1,037 (1990); 1,055 (2000); 955 (2010); 898 (2015 projected); Race: 97.9% White, 0.0% Black, 0.1% Asian, 2.0% Other, 0.8% Hispanic of any race (2010); Density: 402.1 persons per square mile (2010); Average household size: 2.32 (2010); Median age: 45.3 (2010); Males per 100 females: 93.3 (2010); Marriage status: 20.0% never married, 59.9% now married, 8.3% widowed, 11.8% divorced (2005-2009 5-year est.); Foreign born: 0.4% (2005-2009 5-year est.); Ancestry (includes multiple ancestries): 42.6% German, 17.0% Irish, 10.4% English, 6.9% Italian, 6.7% American (2005-2009 5-year est.).

Economy: Employment by occupation: 6.8% management, 19.8% professional, 26.4% services, 20.0% sales, 0.5% farming, 4.8% construction, 21.6% production (2005-2009 5-year est.).

Income: Per capita income: $19,459 (2010); Median household income: $38,117 (2010); Average household income: $45,429 (2010); Percent of households with income of $100,000 or more: 6.4% (2010); Poverty rate: 15.5% (2005-2009 5-year est.).

Taxes: Total city taxes per capita: $58 (2007); City property taxes per capita: $42 (2007).

Education: Percent of population age 25 and over with: High school diploma (including GED) or higher: 87.6% (2010); Bachelor's degree or higher: 14.0% (2010); Master's degree or higher: 3.9% (2010).

School District(s)

Dallas ESD 327 (PK-08)
    2009-10 Enrollment: 242 . . . . (217) 852-3204

Housing: Homeownership rate: 78.2% (2010); Median home value: $71,957 (2010); Median contract rent: $303 per month (2005-2009 5-year est.); Median year structure built: before 1940 (2005-2009 5-year est.).

Transportation: Commute to work: 80.2% car, 1.5% public transportation, 8.1% walk, 9.0% work from home (2005-2009 5-year est.); Travel time to work: 24.5% less than 15 minutes, 42.3% 15 to 30 minutes, 23.1% 30 to 45 minutes, 1.6% 45 to 60 minutes, 8.5% 60 minutes or more (2005-2009 5-year est.)

ELVASTON (village).
Covers a land area of 0.797 square miles and a water area of 0 square miles. Located at 40.39° N. Lat; 91.25° W. Long. Elevation is 659 feet.

Population: 198 (1990); 152 (2000); 149 (2010); 144 (2015 projected); Race: 98.7% White, 0.7% Black, 0.7% Asian, 0.0% Other, 0.7% Hispanic of any race (2010); Density: 187.0 persons per square mile (2010); Average household size: 2.53 (2010); Median age: 43.2 (2010); Males per 100 females: 101.4 (2010); Marriage status: 24.3% never married, 54.7% now married, 8.1% widowed, 12.8% divorced (2005-2009 5-year est.); Foreign born: 0.0% (2005-2009 5-year est.); Ancestry (includes multiple ancestries): 26.3% German, 22.5% Irish, 18.1% English, 6.9% American, 3.8% Swedish (2005-2009 5-year est.).

Economy: Employment by occupation: 2.8% management, 4.2% professional, 16.9% services, 15.5% sales, 0.0% farming, 16.9% construction, 43.7% production (2005-2009 5-year est.).

Income: Per capita income: $24,493 (2010); Median household income: $53,906 (2010); Average household income: $66,525 (2010); Percent of households with income of $100,000 or more: 10.2% (2010); Poverty rate: 8.8% (2005-2009 5-year est.).

Taxes: Total city taxes per capita: $104 (2007); City property taxes per capita: $28 (2007).

Education: Percent of population age 25 and over with: High school diploma (including GED) or higher: 95.3% (2010); Bachelor's degree or higher: 19.6% (2010); Master's degree or higher: 2.8% (2010).

Housing: Homeownership rate: 86.4% (2010); Median home value: $106,250 (2010); Median contract rent: $313 per month (2005-2009 5-year est.); Median year structure built: 1960 (2005-2009 5-year est.).

Transportation: Commute to work: 95.7% car, 0.0% public transportation, 1.4% walk, 2.9% work from home (2005-2009 5-year est.); Travel time to work: 58.2% less than 15 minutes, 20.9% 15 to 30 minutes, 16.4% 30 to 45 minutes, 0.0% 45 to 60 minutes, 4.5% 60 minutes or more (2005-2009 5-year est.)

FERRIS (village).
Covers a land area of 1.957 square miles and a water area of 0 square miles. Located at 40.46° N. Lat; 91.16° W. Long. Elevation is 682 feet.

Population: 177 (1990); 168 (2000); 164 (2010); 162 (2015 projected); Race: 98.8% White, 0.0% Black, 0.0% Asian, 1.2% Other, 1.2% Hispanic of any race (2010); Density: 83.8 persons per square mile (2010); Average household size: 2.48 (2010); Median age: 42.1 (2010); Males per 100 females: 110.3 (2010); Marriage status: 27.7% never married, 52.5% now married, 11.9% widowed, 7.9% divorced (2005-2009 5-year est.); Foreign born: 0.0% (2005-2009 5-year est.); Ancestry (includes multiple ancestries): 51.3% German, 16.8% Scottish, 15.0% Irish, 8.0% American, 7.1% English (2005-2009 5-year est.).

Economy: Employment by occupation: 18.5% management, 0.0% professional, 13.0% services, 22.2% sales, 11.1% farming, 9.3% construction, 25.9% production (2005-2009 5-year est.).

Income: Per capita income: $23,875 (2010); Median household income: $48,846 (2010); Average household income: $59,053 (2010); Percent of households with income of $100,000 or more: 13.6% (2010); Poverty rate: 1.8% (2005-2009 5-year est.).

Taxes: Total city taxes per capita: $50 (2007); City property taxes per capita: $50 (2007).

Education: Percent of population age 25 and over with: High school diploma (including GED) or higher: 91.2% (2010); Bachelor's degree or higher: 18.4% (2010); Master's degree or higher: 0.0% (2010).

Housing: Homeownership rate: 78.8% (2010); Median home value: $67,273 (2010); Median contract rent: n/a per month (2005-2009 5-year est.); Median year structure built: before 1940 (2005-2009 5-year est.).

Transportation: Commute to work: 100.0% car, 0.0% public transportation, 0.0% walk, 0.0% work from home (2005-2009 5-year est.); Travel time to work: 45.3% less than 15 minutes, 26.4% 15 to 30 minutes, 20.8% 30 to 45 minutes, 0.0% 45 to 60 minutes, 7.5% 60 minutes or more (2005-2009 5-year est.)

HAMILTON (city).
Covers a land area of 3.748 square miles and a water area of 1.611 square miles. Located at 40.39° N. Lat; 91.34° W. Long. Elevation is 643 feet.

History: Incorporated 1859.
Population: 3,326 (1990); 3,029 (2000); 2,628 (2010); 2,451 (2015 projected); Race: 97.0% White, 1.7% Black, 0.3% Asian, 1.0% Other, 0.9% Hispanic of any race (2010); Density: 701.3 persons per square mile (2010); Average household size: 2.35 (2010); Median age: 44.0 (2010); Males per 100 females: 90.3 (2010); Marriage status: 21.4% never married, 61.3% now married, 5.2% widowed, 12.2% divorced (2005-2009 5-year est.); Foreign born: 2.1% (2005-2009 5-year est.); Ancestry (includes multiple ancestries): 32.5% German, 13.3% Irish, 13.1% English, 7.8% American, 3.2% French (2005-2009 5-year est.).
Economy: Single-family building permits issued: 1 (2010); Multi-family building permits issued: 0 (2010); Employment by occupation: 9.1% management, 15.3% professional, 13.0% services, 25.9% sales, 0.3% farming, 11.1% construction, 25.2% production (2005-2009 5-year est.).
Income: Per capita income: $22,729 (2010); Median household income: $46,697 (2010); Average household income: $54,146 (2010); Percent of households with income of $100,000 or more: 7.6% (2010); Poverty rate: 8.7% (2005-2009 5-year est.).
Taxes: Total city taxes per capita: $166 (2007); City property taxes per capita: $158 (2007).
Education: Percent of population age 25 and over with: High school diploma (including GED) or higher: 89.9% (2010); Bachelor's degree or higher: 16.0% (2010); Master's degree or higher: 2.3% (2010).

School District(s)
Hamilton CCSD 328 (PK-12)
    2009-10 Enrollment: 654 . . . . (217) 847-3315
Housing: Homeownership rate: 80.9% (2010); Median home value: $87,457 (2010); Median contract rent: $368 per month (2005-2009 5-year est.); Median year structure built: 1965 (2005-2009 5-year est.).
Transportation: Commute to work: 94.7% car, 0.0% public transportation, 1.3% walk, 4.0% work from home (2005-2009 5-year est.); Travel time to work: 40.1% less than 15 minutes, 42.0% 15 to 30 minutes, 7.6% 30 to 45 minutes, 2.5% 45 to 60 minutes, 7.8% 60 minutes or more (2005-2009 5-year est.)

LA HARPE (city). Covers a land area of 1.355 square miles and a water area of 0 square miles. Located at 40.58° N. Lat; 90.96° W. Long. Elevation is 699 feet.
History: Incorporated 1859.
Population: 1,407 (1990); 1,385 (2000); 1,266 (2010); 1,203 (2015 projected); Race: 99.8% White, 0.0% Black, 0.0% Asian, 0.2% Other, 0.0% Hispanic of any race (2010); Density: 934.0 persons per square mile (2010); Average household size: 2.39 (2010); Median age: 44.7 (2010); Males per 100 females: 84.3 (2010); Marriage status: 21.3% never married, 54.2% now married, 16.5% widowed, 8.1% divorced (2005-2009 5-year est.); Foreign born: 0.3% (2005-2009 5-year est.); Ancestry (includes multiple ancestries): 30.0% German, 12.6% American, 12.4% English, 7.9% French, 6.6% Irish (2005-2009 5-year est.).
Economy: Employment by occupation: 5.5% management, 18.5% professional, 18.5% services, 19.3% sales, 0.5% farming, 11.5% construction, 26.2% production (2005-2009 5-year est.).
Income: Per capita income: $19,432 (2010); Median household income: $40,192 (2010); Average household income: $47,583 (2010); Percent of households with income of $100,000 or more: 7.6% (2010); Poverty rate: 12.2% (2005-2009 5-year est.).
Taxes: Total city taxes per capita: $63 (2007); City property taxes per capita: $61 (2007).
Education: Percent of population age 25 and over with: High school diploma (including GED) or higher: 87.7% (2010); Bachelor's degree or higher: 16.0% (2010); Master's degree or higher: 4.2% (2010).

School District(s)
La Harpe CSD 347 (PK-08)
    2009-10 Enrollment: 251 . . . . (217) 659-7739
Housing: Homeownership rate: 82.0% (2010); Median home value: $80,455 (2010); Median contract rent: $200 per month (2005-2009 5-year est.); Median year structure built: 1961 (2005-2009 5-year est.).
Newspapers: Hancock County Quill (Community news; Circulation 1,250)
Transportation: Commute to work: 92.3% car, 0.0% public transportation, 3.8% walk, 3.3% work from home (2005-2009 5-year est.); Travel time to work: 37.6% less than 15 minutes, 14.9% 15 to 30 minutes, 29.1% 30 to 45 minutes, 12.5% 45 to 60 minutes, 5.9% 60 minutes or more (2005-2009 5-year est.)

NAUVOO (city). Covers a land area of 3.382 square miles and a water area of 1.441 square miles. Located at 40.54° N. Lat; 91.38° W. Long. Elevation is 650 feet.
History: Joseph Smith built the city of Nauvoo in 1839 as the headquarters for the Mormon church, on the site of a small settlement called Commerce. The charter for Nauvoo gave it a measure of autonomy such as maintaining its own militia and courts. Internal discord and outside opposition troubled the church, and in 1845 the Nauvoo charter was repealed and Brigham Young soon led the members westward. In 1849 the deserted city became the scene of the Icarian colony attempt at a Utopian communistic society, which crumbled in 1856. The resettlement of Nauvoo, mostly by German immigrants, began in the 1860's. Joseph Smith and his brother Hyrum were buried in Nauvoo.
Population: 1,108 (1990); 1,063 (2000); 1,046 (2010); 1,028 (2015 projected); Race: 95.8% White, 1.1% Black, 0.2% Asian, 3.0% Other, 2.3% Hispanic of any race (2010); Density: 309.3 persons per square mile (2010); Average household size: 2.35 (2010); Median age: 47.0 (2010); Males per 100 females: 89.5 (2010); Marriage status: 21.6% never married, 64.6% now married, 7.2% widowed, 6.6% divorced (2005-2009 5-year est.); Foreign born: 1.5% (2005-2009 5-year est.); Ancestry (includes multiple ancestries): 33.6% German, 23.6% English, 13.2% Irish, 8.2% American, 5.7% French (2005-2009 5-year est.).
Economy: Single-family building permits issued: 0 (2010); Multi-family building permits issued: 0 (2010); Employment by occupation: 17.3% management, 26.9% professional, 17.5% services, 21.1% sales, 0.0% farming, 5.8% construction, 11.4% production (2005-2009 5-year est.).
Income: Per capita income: $24,975 (2010); Median household income: $51,838 (2010); Average household income: $59,133 (2010); Percent of households with income of $100,000 or more: 13.5% (2010); Poverty rate: 8.4% (2005-2009 5-year est.).
Taxes: Total city taxes per capita: $323 (2007); City property taxes per capita: $123 (2007).
Education: Percent of population age 25 and over with: High school diploma (including GED) or higher: 94.0% (2010); Bachelor's degree or higher: 26.6% (2010); Master's degree or higher: 12.1% (2010).

School District(s)
Nauvoo-Colusa CUSD 325 (PK-08)
    2009-10 Enrollment: 286 . . . . (217) 453-6639
Housing: Homeownership rate: 79.6% (2010); Median home value: $116,089 (2010); Median contract rent: $381 per month (2005-2009 5-year est.); Median year structure built: 1964 (2005-2009 5-year est.).
Newspapers: Nauvoo New Independent (Community news; Circulation 500)
Transportation: Commute to work: 78.5% car, 0.0% public transportation, 12.3% walk, 7.9% work from home (2005-2009 5-year est.); Travel time to work: 55.0% less than 15 minutes, 23.0% 15 to 30 minutes, 19.2% 30 to 45 minutes, 1.4% 45 to 60 minutes, 1.4% 60 minutes or more (2005-2009 5-year est.)
Additional Information Contacts
Nauvoo Chamber of Commerce . . . . (217) 453-6648
    http://www.nauvoochamber.org

NIOTA (unincorporated postal area, zip code 62358). Covers a land area of 40.663 square miles and a water area of 0.018 square miles. Located at 40.58° N. Lat; 91.26° W. Long. Elevation is 522 feet.
Population: 646 (2000); Race: 96.6% White, 0.0% Black, 0.6% Asian, 2.8% Other, 0.6% Hispanic of any race (2000); Density: 15.9 persons per square mile (2000); Age: 22.2% under 18, 17.3% over 64 (2000); Marriage status: 21.2% never married, 62.0% now married, 8.2% widowed, 8.6% divorced (2000); Foreign born: 1.0% (2000); Ancestry (includes multiple ancestries): 30.8% German, 18.2% Irish, 8.9% English, 7.7% American (2000).
Economy: Employment by occupation: 16.6% management, 7.5% professional, 19.8% services, 15.8% sales, 2.4% farming, 8.8% construction, 29.1% production (2000).
Income: Per capita income: $16,672 (2000); Median household income: $41,630 (2000); Poverty rate: 5.2% (2000).
Education: Percent of population age 25 and over with: High school diploma (including GED) or higher: 87.2% (2000); Bachelor's degree or higher: 13.1% (2000).
Housing: Homeownership rate: 89.2% (2000); Median home value: $47,300 (2000); Median contract rent: $219 per month (2000); Median year structure built: 1954 (2000).

Transportation: Commute to work: 88.7% car, 1.9% public transportation, 2.5% walk, 5.8% work from home (2000); Travel time to work: 27.2% less than 15 minutes, 42.7% 15 to 30 minutes, 24.0% 30 to 45 minutes, 4.1% 45 to 60 minutes, 2.0% 60 minutes or more (2000)

PLYMOUTH (village). Covers a land area of 0.589 square miles and a water area of 0 square miles. Located at 40.29° N. Lat; 90.91° W. Long. Elevation is 650 feet.
Population: 521 (1990); 562 (2000); 528 (2010); 509 (2015 projected); Race: 96.8% White, 0.2% Black, 0.9% Asian, 2.1% Other, 0.9% Hispanic of any race (2010); Density: 896.1 persons per square mile (2010); Average household size: 2.55 (2010); Median age: 37.5 (2010); Males per 100 females: 96.3 (2010); Marriage status: 13.3% never married, 66.6% now married, 9.0% widowed, 11.1% divorced (2005-2009 5-year est.); Foreign born: 3.1% (2005-2009 5-year est.); Ancestry (includes multiple ancestries): 22.4% American, 22.2% English, 14.5% German, 13.9% Irish, 4.0% Dutch (2005-2009 5-year est.).
Economy: Employment by occupation: 4.4% management, 12.1% professional, 17.6% services, 28.6% sales, 2.2% farming, 2.2% construction, 33.0% production (2005-2009 5-year est.).
Income: Per capita income: $15,829 (2010); Median household income: $33,824 (2010); Average household income: $41,875 (2010); Percent of households with income of $100,000 or more: 3.5% (2010); Poverty rate: 16.8% (2005-2009 5-year est.).
Taxes: Total city taxes per capita: $28 (2007); City property taxes per capita: $26 (2007).
Education: Percent of population age 25 and over with: High school diploma (including GED) or higher: 85.3% (2010); Bachelor's degree or higher: 11.5% (2010); Master's degree or higher: 3.2% (2010).
Housing: Homeownership rate: 75.0% (2010); Median home value: $41,481 (2010); Median contract rent: $225 per month (2005-2009 5-year est.); Median year structure built: 1943 (2005-2009 5-year est.).
Safety: Violent crime rate: 19.9 per 10,000 population; Property crime rate: 179.3 per 10,000 population (2010).
Transportation: Commute to work: 90.3% car, 1.1% public transportation, 5.7% walk, 2.8% work from home (2005-2009 5-year est.); Travel time to work: 25.7% less than 15 minutes, 20.5% 15 to 30 minutes, 33.9% 30 to 45 minutes, 18.1% 45 to 60 minutes, 1.8% 60 minutes or more (2005-2009 5-year est.)

PONTOOSUC (village). Covers a land area of 1.409 square miles and a water area of 0.667 square miles. Located at 40.63° N. Lat; 91.21° W. Long. Elevation is 525 feet.
Population: 264 (1990); 171 (2000); 150 (2010); 141 (2015 projected); Race: 97.3% White, 0.0% Black, 0.7% Asian, 2.0% Other, 0.0% Hispanic of any race (2010); Density: 106.4 persons per square mile (2010); Average household size: 2.29 (2010); Median age: 47.3 (2010); Males per 100 females: 97.4 (2010); Marriage status: 9.0% never married, 78.8% now married, 1.1% widowed, 11.1% divorced (2005-2009 5-year est.); Foreign born: 0.0% (2005-2009 5-year est.); Ancestry (includes multiple ancestries): 32.6% German, 25.1% American, 10.7% Irish, 8.4% English, 6.0% French (2005-2009 5-year est.).
Economy: Employment by occupation: 1.9% management, 0.9% professional, 28.3% services, 22.6% sales, 0.0% farming, 4.7% construction, 41.5% production (2005-2009 5-year est.).
Income: Per capita income: $19,065 (2010); Median household income: $36,731 (2010); Average household income: $41,923 (2010); Percent of households with income of $100,000 or more: 4.6% (2010); Poverty rate: 7.9% (2005-2009 5-year est.).
Taxes: Total city taxes per capita: $0 (2007); City property taxes per capita: $0 (2007).
Education: Percent of population age 25 and over with: High school diploma (including GED) or higher: 87.7% (2010); Bachelor's degree or higher: 15.8% (2010); Master's degree or higher: 4.4% (2010).
Housing: Homeownership rate: 78.5% (2010); Median home value: $70,000 (2010); Median contract rent: $218 per month (2005-2009 5-year est.); Median year structure built: 1965 (2005-2009 5-year est.).
Transportation: Commute to work: 91.5% car, 0.0% public transportation, 0.0% walk, 8.5% work from home (2005-2009 5-year est.); Travel time to work: 18.6% less than 15 minutes, 30.9% 15 to 30 minutes, 40.2% 30 to 45 minutes, 3.1% 45 to 60 minutes, 7.2% 60 minutes or more (2005-2009 5-year est.)

SUTTER (unincorporated postal area, zip code 62373). Covers a land area of 52.216 square miles and a water area of 0.210 square miles. Located at 40.24° N. Lat; 91.35° W. Long. Elevation is 656 feet.
Population: 415 (2000); Race: 100.0% White, 0.0% Black, 0.0% Asian, 0.0% Other, 0.0% Hispanic of any race (2000); Density: 7.9 persons per square mile (2000); Age: 34.4% under 18, 12.4% over 64 (2000); Marriage status: 18.5% never married, 75.5% now married, 2.4% widowed, 3.6% divorced (2000); Foreign born: 0.0% (2000); Ancestry (includes multiple ancestries): 28.5% German, 11.5% Irish, 8.5% American, 4.8% English (2000).
Economy: Employment by occupation: 31.8% management, 18.9% professional, 7.0% services, 14.4% sales, 7.5% farming, 4.0% construction, 16.4% production (2000).
Income: Per capita income: $15,697 (2000); Median household income: $46,250 (2000); Poverty rate: 2.4% (2000).
Education: Percent of population age 25 and over with: High school diploma (including GED) or higher: 88.5% (2000); Bachelor's degree or higher: 24.1% (2000).
Housing: Homeownership rate: 75.9% (2000); Median home value: $91,600 (2000); Median contract rent: $192 per month (2000); Median year structure built: before 1940 (2000).
Transportation: Commute to work: 72.6% car, 0.0% public transportation, 5.5% walk, 21.9% work from home (2000); Travel time to work: 34.4% less than 15 minutes, 22.3% 15 to 30 minutes, 40.8% 30 to 45 minutes, 0.0% 45 to 60 minutes, 2.5% 60 minutes or more (2000)

WARSAW (city). Covers a land area of 6.617 square miles and a water area of 0.871 square miles. Located at 40.35° N. Lat; 91.43° W. Long. Elevation is 577 feet.
History: Laid out 1834, incorporated 1837. Two forts were established here in 1814.
Population: 1,882 (1990); 1,793 (2000); 1,556 (2010); 1,437 (2015 projected); Race: 98.3% White, 0.2% Black, 0.0% Asian, 1.5% Other, 1.5% Hispanic of any race (2010); Density: 235.2 persons per square mile (2010); Average household size: 2.41 (2010); Median age: 41.5 (2010); Males per 100 females: 97.2 (2010); Marriage status: 20.8% never married, 55.9% now married, 6.7% widowed, 16.6% divorced (2005-2009 5-year est.); Foreign born: 0.0% (2005-2009 5-year est.); Ancestry (includes multiple ancestries): 43.6% German, 12.6% American, 10.8% Irish, 9.3% English, 3.0% Polish (2005-2009 5-year est.).
Economy: Single-family building permits issued: 0 (2010); Multi-family building permits issued: 0 (2010); Employment by occupation: 6.8% management, 20.4% professional, 15.4% services, 22.1% sales, 0.0% farming, 10.2% construction, 25.2% production (2005-2009 5-year est.).
Income: Per capita income: $20,290 (2010); Median household income: $38,326 (2010); Average household income: $49,271 (2010); Percent of households with income of $100,000 or more: 6.4% (2010); Poverty rate: 12.8% (2005-2009 5-year est.).
Taxes: Total city taxes per capita: $98 (2007); City property taxes per capita: $94 (2007).
Education: Percent of population age 25 and over with: High school diploma (including GED) or higher: 88.3% (2010); Bachelor's degree or higher: 18.8% (2010); Master's degree or higher: 6.9% (2010).
School District(s)
Warsaw CUSD 316 (PK-12)
    2009-10 Enrollment: 499 . . . . (217) 256-4282
Housing: Homeownership rate: 81.1% (2010); Median home value: $86,979 (2010); Median contract rent: $330 per month (2005-2009 5-year est.); Median year structure built: 1945 (2005-2009 5-year est.).
Transportation: Commute to work: 93.3% car, 0.7% public transportation, 1.2% walk, 3.8% work from home (2005-2009 5-year est.); Travel time to work: 31.2% less than 15 minutes, 43.7% 15 to 30 minutes, 12.0% 30 to 45 minutes, 7.0% 45 to 60 minutes, 6.0% 60 minutes or more (2005-2009 5-year est.)

WEST POINT (village). Covers a land area of 0.168 square miles and a water area of 0 square miles. Located at 40.25° N. Lat; 91.18° W. Long. Elevation is 669 feet.
Population: 214 (1990); 195 (2000); 178 (2010); 168 (2015 projected); Race: 99.4% White, 0.0% Black, 0.0% Asian, 0.6% Other, 0.0% Hispanic of any race (2010); Density: 1,057.1 persons per square mile (2010); Average household size: 2.66 (2010); Median age: 38.6 (2010); Males per 100 females: 93.5 (2010); Marriage status: 23.5% never married, 50.0% now married, 3.9% widowed, 22.5% divorced (2005-2009 5-year est.);

Foreign born: 0.0% (2005-2009 5-year est.); Ancestry (includes multiple ancestries): 26.5% German, 14.5% Irish, 12.8% American, 12.8% English, 6.0% Scotch-Irish (2005-2009 5-year est.).

Economy: Employment by occupation: 3.7% management, 9.3% professional, 27.8% services, 16.7% sales, 0.0% farming, 16.7% construction, 25.9% production (2005-2009 5-year est.).

Income: Per capita income: $16,951 (2010); Median household income: $37,500 (2010); Average household income: $42,799 (2010); Percent of households with income of $100,000 or more: 1.5% (2010); Poverty rate: 30.8% (2005-2009 5-year est.).

Taxes: Total city taxes per capita: $22 (2007); City property taxes per capita: $22 (2007).

Education: Percent of population age 25 and over with: High school diploma (including GED) or higher: 88.2% (2010); Bachelor's degree or higher: 14.3% (2010); Master's degree or higher: 0.8% (2010).

Housing: Homeownership rate: 82.1% (2010); Median home value: $66,364 (2010); Median contract rent: n/a per month (2005-2009 5-year est.); Median year structure built: before 1940 (2005-2009 5-year est.).

Transportation: Commute to work: 85.1% car, 0.0% public transportation, 14.9% walk, 0.0% work from home (2005-2009 5-year est.); Travel time to work: 21.3% less than 15 minutes, 14.9% 15 to 30 minutes, 44.7% 30 to 45 minutes, 4.3% 45 to 60 minutes, 14.9% 60 minutes or more (2005-2009 5-year est.)

Hardin County

Located in southeastern Illinois; bounded on the south and east by the Ohio River and the Kentucky border; drained by Big Creek; includes part of Shawnee National Forest. Covers a land area of 178.33 square miles, a water area of 3.20 square miles, and is located in the Central Time Zone at 37.47° N. Lat., 88.28° W. Long. The county was founded in 1839. County seat is Elizabethtown.

Weather Station: Rosiclare 5 NW									Elevation: 399 feet		
	Jan	Feb	Mar	Apr	May	Jun	Jul	Aug	Sep	Oct	Nov	Dec
High	43	48	58	69	77	84	88	88	81	70	58	46
Low	23	26	34	43	52	61	65	64	55	43	35	26
Precip	3.6	3.8	4.6	4.6	5.5	4.4	4.3	3.2	3.5	3.8	4.2	4.5
Snow	2.4	2.2	0.5	tr	0.0	0.0	0.0	0.0	0.0	0.2	tr	1.2

High and Low temperatures in degrees Fahrenheit; Precipitation and Snow in inches

Population: 5,189 (1990); 4,800 (2000); 4,288 (2010); 3,998 (2015 projected); Race: 94.9% White, 2.9% Black, 0.5% Asian, 1.7% Other, 1.4% Hispanic of any race (2010); Density: 24.0 persons per square mile (2010); Average household size: 2.22 (2010); Median age: 43.5 (2010); Males per 100 females: 99.2 (2010).

Religion: Five largest groups: 15.3% Southern Baptist Convention, 4.4% Christian Churches and Churches of Christ, 3.3% Catholic Church, 2.9% Churches of Christ, 2.6% The United Methodist Church (2000).

Economy: Unemployment rate: 11.5% (August 2011); Total civilian labor force: 1,941 (August 2011); Leading industries: 47.0% health care and social assistance; 10.9% mining; 9.5% transportation & warehousing (2009); Farms: 145 totaling 34,733 acres (2007); Companies that employ 500 or more persons: 0 (2009); Companies that employ 100 to 499 persons: 1 (2009); Companies that employ less than 100 persons: 71 (2009); Black-owned businesses: n/a (2007); Hispanic-owned businesses: n/a (2007); Asian-owned businesses: n/a (2007); Women-owned businesses: n/a (2007); Retail sales per capita: $3,494 (2010). Single-family building permits issued: 0 (2010); Multi-family building permits issued: 0 (2010).

Income: Per capita income: $19,716 (2010); Median household income: $33,364 (2010); Average household income: $43,553 (2010); Percent of households with income of $100,000 or more: 6.9% (2010); Poverty rate: 21.4% (2009); Bankruptcy rate: 3.26% (2010).

Taxes: Total county taxes per capita: $176 (2007); County property taxes per capita: $151 (2007).

Education: Percent of population age 25 and over with: High school diploma (including GED) or higher: 75.7% (2010); Bachelor's degree or higher: 12.4% (2010); Master's degree or higher: 3.7% (2010).

Housing: Homeownership rate: 79.2% (2010); Median home value: $59,479 (2010); Median contract rent: $184 per month (2005-2009 5-year est.); Median year structure built: 1965 (2005-2009 5-year est.)

Health: Birth rate: 94.1 per 10,000 population (2009); Death rate: 140.0 per 10,000 population (2009); Age-adjusted cancer mortality rate: 233.8 (Unreliable) deaths per 100,000 population (2007); Number of physicians: 6.8 per 10,000 population (2008); Hospital beds: 56.0 per 10,000

population (2007); Hospital admissions: 1,889.3 per 10,000 population (2007).

Elections: 2008 Presidential election results: 39.6% Obama, 59.0% McCain, 0.7% Nader

National and State Parks: Cave-In-Rock State Park

Additional Information Contacts

Hardin County Government . . . . (618) 287-2251
    http://www.hardincountyil.org

Hardin County Communities

CAVE-IN-ROCK (village). Covers a land area of 0.396 square miles and a water area of 0.029 square miles. Located at 37.47° N. Lat; 88.16° W. Long. Elevation is 371 feet.

History: Cave-in-Rock was named for a natural cave above the water line in the Ohio River bluff, a landmark for boatmen. The cave served as a pirate's den for a number of thieves beginning with Samuel Mason, who in 1797 lured victims there by promises of liquor and entertainment, and then robbed them.

Population: 460 (1990); 346 (2000); 311 (2010); 285 (2015 projected); Race: 98.7% White, 0.0% Black, 0.0% Asian, 1.3% Other, 1.9% Hispanic of any race (2010); Density: 786.1 persons per square mile (2010); Average household size: 2.16 (2010); Median age: 44.2 (2010); Males per 100 females: 85.1 (2010); Marriage status: 24.0% never married, 50.7% now married, 11.6% widowed, 13.7% divorced (2005-2009 5-year est.); Foreign born: 0.0% (2005-2009 5-year est.); Ancestry (includes multiple ancestries): 27.5% German, 20.4% Irish, 12.5% English, 11.0% American, 4.8% French (2005-2009 5-year est.).

Economy: Single-family building permits issued: 0 (2010); Multi-family building permits issued: 0 (2010); Employment by occupation: 11.0% management, 19.2% professional, 13.7% services, 17.8% sales, 0.0% farming, 20.5% construction, 17.8% production (2005-2009 5-year est.).

Income: Per capita income: $13,895 (2010); Median household income: $23,235 (2010); Average household income: $29,514 (2010); Percent of households with income of $100,000 or more: 0.7% (2010); Poverty rate: 28.3% (2005-2009 5-year est.).

Taxes: Total city taxes per capita: $12 (2007); City property taxes per capita: $12 (2007).

Education: Percent of population age 25 and over with: High school diploma (including GED) or higher: 75.0% (2010); Bachelor's degree or higher: 9.5% (2010); Master's degree or higher: 4.1% (2010).

Housing: Homeownership rate: 72.9% (2010); Median home value: $61,765 (2010); Median contract rent: $241 per month (2005-2009 5-year est.); Median year structure built: 1953 (2005-2009 5-year est.).

Transportation: Commute to work: 90.8% car, 0.0% public transportation, 4.6% walk, 4.6% work from home (2005-2009 5-year est.); Travel time to work: 27.4% less than 15 minutes, 24.2% 15 to 30 minutes, 19.4% 30 to 45 minutes, 22.6% 45 to 60 minutes, 6.5% 60 minutes or more (2005-2009 5-year est.)

ELIZABETHTOWN (village). County seat. Covers a land area of 0.702 square miles and a water area of 0 square miles. Located at 37.44° N. Lat; 88.30° W. Long. Elevation is 364 feet.

Population: 427 (1990); 348 (2000); 312 (2010); 291 (2015 projected); Race: 99.0% White, 0.6% Black, 0.0% Asian, 0.3% Other, 1.0% Hispanic of any race (2010); Density: 444.3 persons per square mile (2010); Average household size: 1.97 (2010); Median age: 48.3 (2010); Males per 100 females: 88.0 (2010); Marriage status: 15.1% never married, 47.9% now married, 8.7% widowed, 28.3% divorced (2005-2009 5-year est.); Foreign born: 0.0% (2005-2009 5-year est.); Ancestry (includes multiple ancestries): 36.5% Irish, 25.5% German, 10.0% English, 4.3% Welsh, 4.0% Scotch-Irish (2005-2009 5-year est.).

Economy: Single-family building permits issued: 0 (2010); Multi-family building permits issued: 0 (2010); Employment by occupation: 1.3% management, 25.7% professional, 21.7% services, 17.8% sales, 0.0% farming, 17.8% construction, 15.8% production (2005-2009 5-year est.).

Income: Per capita income: $19,682 (2010); Median household income: $25,000 (2010); Average household income: $39,858 (2010); Percent of households with income of $100,000 or more: 7.0% (2010); Poverty rate: 24.3% (2005-2009 5-year est.).

Taxes: Total city taxes per capita: $37 (2007); City property taxes per capita: $9 (2007).

Education: Percent of population age 25 and over with: High school diploma (including GED) or higher: 81.9% (2010); Bachelor's degree or higher: 17.2% (2010); Master's degree or higher: 5.9% (2010).

Hardin County CUSD 1 (PK-12)
    2009-10 Enrollment: 620 . . . . (618) 287-2411
Housing: Homeownership rate: 73.4% (2010); Median home value: $54,783 (2010); Median contract rent: $189 per month (2005-2009 5-year est.); Median year structure built: 1967 (2005-2009 5-year est.).
Newspapers: Hardin County Independent (National news; Circulation 2,700)
Transportation: Commute to work: 80.3% car, 6.3% public transportation, 2.8% walk, 7.0% work from home (2005-2009 5-year est.); Travel time to work: 48.5% less than 15 minutes, 15.9% 15 to 30 minutes, 20.5% 30 to 45 minutes, 3.0% 45 to 60 minutes, 12.1% 60 minutes or more (2005-2009 5-year est.)

ROSICLARE (city). Covers a land area of 2.168 square miles and a water area of 0.116 square miles. Located at 37.42° N. Lat; 88.34° W. Long. Elevation is 354 feet.
History: Incorporated as village 1874, as city 1932.
Population: 1,378 (1990); 1,213 (2000); 1,052 (2010); 968 (2015 projected); Race: 97.2% White, 0.9% Black, 0.6% Asian, 1.3% Other, 1.5% Hispanic of any race (2010); Density: 485.3 persons per square mile (2010); Average household size: 2.21 (2010); Median age: 43.0 (2010); Males per 100 females: 90.2 (2010); Marriage status: 22.5% never married, 47.7% now married, 12.2% widowed, 17.6% divorced (2005-2009 5-year est.); Foreign born: 1.6% (2005-2009 5-year est.); Ancestry (includes multiple ancestries): 33.0% Irish, 27.4% German, 7.0% Dutch, 6.5% English, 3.9% Scotch-Irish (2005-2009 5-year est.).
Economy: Single-family building permits issued: 0 (2010); Multi-family building permits issued: 0 (2010); Employment by occupation: 5.1% management, 24.2% professional, 18.6% services, 20.6% sales, 0.0% farming, 10.2% construction, 21.4% production (2005-2009 5-year est.).
Income: Per capita income: $20,132 (2010); Median household income: $33,672 (2010); Average household income: $43,459 (2010); Percent of households with income of $100,000 or more: 5.9% (2010); Poverty rate: 26.5% (2005-2009 5-year est.).
Taxes: Total city taxes per capita: $48 (2007); City property taxes per capita: $48 (2007).
Education: Percent of population age 25 and over with: High school diploma (including GED) or higher: 74.1% (2010); Bachelor's degree or higher: 11.0% (2010); Master's degree or higher: 4.3% (2010).
Housing: Homeownership rate: 77.8% (2010); Median home value: $49,604 (2010); Median contract rent: $132 per month (2005-2009 5-year est.); Median year structure built: 1949 (2005-2009 5-year est.).
Hospitals: Hardin County General Hospital (48 beds)
Transportation: Commute to work: 92.2% car, 0.0% public transportation, 5.3% walk, 1.1% work from home (2005-2009 5-year est.); Travel time to work: 48.3% less than 15 minutes, 20.9% 15 to 30 minutes, 12.4% 30 to 45 minutes, 8.1% 45 to 60 minutes, 10.3% 60 minutes or more (2005-2009 5-year est.)

Henderson County

Located in western Illinois; bounded on the west by the Mississippi River and the Iowa border; drained by Henderson Creek. Covers a land area of 378.81 square miles, a water area of 16.31 square miles, and is located in the Central Time Zone at 40.83° N. Lat., 90.94° W. Long. The county was founded in 1841. County seat is Oquawka.

Henderson County is part of the Burlington, IA-IL Micropolitan Statistical Area. The entire metro area includes: Henderson County, IL; Des Moines County, IA

Population: 8,096 (1990); 8,213 (2000); 7,345 (2010); 6,882 (2015 projected); Race: 97.8% White, 0.5% Black, 0.1% Asian, 1.6% Other, 1.3% Hispanic of any race (2010); Density: 19.4 persons per square mile (2010); Average household size: 2.38 (2010); Median age: 44.5 (2010); Males per 100 females: 95.8 (2010).
Religion: Five largest groups: 11.2% The United Methodist Church, 4.4% Catholic Church, 4.0% Presbyterian Church (U.S.A.), 3.7% Christian Churches and Churches of Christ, 2.7% American Baptist Churches in the USA (2000).
Economy: Unemployment rate: 8.0% (August 2011); Total civilian labor force: 3,612 (August 2011); Leading industries: 16.8% retail trade; 13.5% finance & insurance; 10.8% wholesale trade (2009); Farms: 400 totaling 170,443 acres (2007); Companies that employ 500 or more persons: 0 (2009); Companies that employ 100 to 499 persons: 0 (2009); Companies

that employ less than 100 persons: 117 (2009); Black-owned businesses: n/a (2007); Hispanic-owned businesses: n/a (2007); Asian-owned businesses: n/a (2007); Women-owned businesses: n/a (2007); Retail sales per capita: $4,444 (2010). Single-family building permits issued: 17 (2010); Multi-family building permits issued: 0 (2010).
Income: Per capita income: $21,947 (2010); Median household income: $44,071 (2010); Average household income: $52,519 (2010); Percent of households with income of $100,000 or more: 9.2% (2010); Poverty rate: 12.2% (2009); Bankruptcy rate: 4.38% (2010).
Taxes: Total county taxes per capita: $133 (2007); County property taxes per capita: $133 (2007).
Education: Percent of population age 25 and over with: High school diploma (including GED) or higher: 87.5% (2010); Bachelor's degree or higher: 12.6% (2010); Master's degree or higher: 3.9% (2010).
Housing: Homeownership rate: 77.7% (2010); Median home value: $77,968 (2010); Median contract rent: $336 per month (2005-2009 5-year est.); Median year structure built: 1960 (2005-2009 5-year est.)
Health: Birth rate: 84.3 per 10,000 population (2009); Death rate: 115.6 per 10,000 population (2009); Age-adjusted cancer mortality rate: 194.4 deaths per 100,000 population (2007); Number of physicians: 8.0 per 10,000 population (2008); Hospital beds: 0.0 per 10,000 population (2007); Hospital admissions: 0.0 per 10,000 population (2007).
Elections: 2008 Presidential election results: 58.1% Obama, 40.4% McCain, 0.8% Nader
National and State Parks: Big River State Forest; Delabar State Park; Oquawka State Wildlife Refuge
Additional Information Contacts
Henderson County Government . . . . (309) 867-2911

Henderson County Communities

BIGGSVILLE (village). Covers a land area of 0.332 square miles and a water area of 0 square miles. Located at 40.85° N. Lat; 90.86° W. Long. Elevation is 686 feet.
Population: 349 (1990); 343 (2000); 308 (2010); 290 (2015 projected); Race: 98.1% White, 1.0% Black, 0.0% Asian, 1.0% Other, 1.9% Hispanic of any race (2010); Density: 926.7 persons per square mile (2010); Average household size: 2.33 (2010); Median age: 46.0 (2010); Males per 100 females: 100.0 (2010); Marriage status: 18.6% never married, 51.6% now married, 15.1% widowed, 14.8% divorced (2005-2009 5-year est.); Foreign born: 2.4% (2005-2009 5-year est.); Ancestry (includes multiple ancestries): 15.2% German, 14.9% Irish, 9.8% Swedish, 8.6% English, 6.1% American (2005-2009 5-year est.).
Economy: Single-family building permits issued: 0 (2010); Multi-family building permits issued: 0 (2010); Employment by occupation: 12.6% management, 6.5% professional, 14.9% services, 41.9% sales, 0.0% farming, 13.5% construction, 10.7% production (2005-2009 5-year est.).
Income: Per capita income: $24,910 (2010); Median household income: $48,800 (2010); Average household income: $55,966 (2010); Percent of households with income of $100,000 or more: 8.3% (2010); Poverty rate: 11.5% (2005-2009 5-year est.).
Taxes: Total city taxes per capita: $50 (2007); City property taxes per capita: $25 (2007).
Education: Percent of population age 25 and over with: High school diploma (including GED) or higher: 88.5% (2010); Bachelor's degree or higher: 12.3% (2010); Master's degree or higher: 1.2% (2010).
West Central CUSD 235 (PK-12)
    2009-10 Enrollment: 1,031 . . . . (309) 627-2371
Housing: Homeownership rate: 76.5% (2010); Median home value: $65,385 (2010); Median contract rent: $370 per month (2005-2009 5-year est.); Median year structure built: 1941 (2005-2009 5-year est.).
Transportation: Commute to work: 87.9% car, 0.0% public transportation, 4.7% walk, 6.0% work from home (2005-2009 5-year est.); Travel time to work: 20.8% less than 15 minutes, 60.9% 15 to 30 minutes, 8.9% 30 to 45 minutes, 2.5% 45 to 60 minutes, 6.9% 60 minutes or more (2005-2009 5-year est.)

CARMAN (unincorporated postal area, zip code 61425). Covers a land area of 41.606 square miles and a water area of 1.316 square miles. Located at 40.77° N. Lat; 91.05° W. Long. Elevation is 535 feet.
Population: 743 (2000); Race: 98.7% White, 0.0% Black, 1.0% Asian, 0.3% Other, 0.3% Hispanic of any race (2000); Density: 17.9 persons per square mile (2000); Age: 19.7% under 18, 11.6% over 64 (2000); Marriage

status: 19.9% never married, 64.1% now married, 6.1% widowed, 9.9% divorced (2000); Foreign born: 1.0% (2000); Ancestry (includes multiple ancestries): 18.4% German, 13.0% Irish, 10.6% American, 9.3% English (2000).

Economy: Employment by occupation: 10.2% management, 6.9% professional, 20.6% services, 19.1% sales, 0.0% farming, 12.7% construction, 30.5% production (2000).

Income: Per capita income: $20,071 (2000); Median household income: $42,639 (2000); Poverty rate: 7.2% (2000).

Education: Percent of population age 25 and over with: High school diploma (including GED) or higher: 84.2% (2000); Bachelor's degree or higher: 8.5% (2000).

Housing: Homeownership rate: 86.1% (2000); Median home value: $64,100 (2000); Median contract rent: $305 per month (2000); Median year structure built: 1974 (2000).

Transportation: Commute to work: 95.0% car, 0.0% public transportation, 0.8% walk, 2.6% work from home (2000); Travel time to work: 42.2% less than 15 minutes, 44.9% 15 to 30 minutes, 5.4% 30 to 45 minutes, 5.7% 45 to 60 minutes, 1.9% 60 minutes or more (2000)

GLADSTONE (village). Covers a land area of 0.393 square miles and a water area of 0 square miles. Located at 40.86° N. Lat; 90.95° W. Long. Elevation is 551 feet.

History: Gladstone was platted in 1856 and settled by Irish, Swedish, and German immigrants. The town developed around the quarrying of limestone on nearby Henderson Creek.

Population: 272 (1990); 284 (2000); 259 (2010); 244 (2015 projected); Race: 98.1% White, 0.4% Black, 0.0% Asian, 1.5% Other, 0.8% Hispanic of any race (2010); Density: 658.6 persons per square mile (2010); Average household size: 2.33 (2010); Median age: 46.3 (2010); Males per 100 females: 114.0 (2010); Marriage status: 14.3% never married, 55.9% now married, 7.9% widowed, 21.9% divorced (2005-2009 5-year est.); Foreign born: 0.0% (2005-2009 5-year est.); Ancestry (includes multiple ancestries): 18.8% German, 9.8% Irish, 7.6% American, 4.8% English, 4.2% Swedish (2005-2009 5-year est.).

Economy: Single-family building permits issued: 1 (2010); Multi-family building permits issued: 0 (2010); Employment by occupation: 7.3% management, 0.7% professional, 14.6% services, 33.1% sales, 0.0% farming, 11.9% construction, 32.5% production (2005-2009 5-year est.).

Income: Per capita income: $21,428 (2010); Median household income: $43,365 (2010); Average household income: $50,248 (2010); Percent of households with income of $100,000 or more: 8.1% (2010); Poverty rate: 11.8% (2005-2009 5-year est.).

Taxes: Total city taxes per capita: $45 (2007); City property taxes per capita: $41 (2007).

Education: Percent of population age 25 and over with: High school diploma (including GED) or higher: 91.5% (2010); Bachelor's degree or higher: 11.6% (2010); Master's degree or higher: 3.0% (2010).

Housing: Homeownership rate: 82.0% (2010); Median home value: $84,375 (2010); Median contract rent: $248 per month (2005-2009 5-year est.); Median year structure built: 1963 (2005-2009 5-year est.).

Transportation: Commute to work: 92.7% car, 0.0% public transportation, 1.3% walk, 6.0% work from home (2005-2009 5-year est.); Travel time to work: 17.6% less than 15 minutes, 40.1% 15 to 30 minutes, 14.1% 30 to 45 minutes, 23.9% 45 to 60 minutes, 4.2% 60 minutes or more (2005-2009 5-year est.)

GULF PORT (village). Aka Gulfport. Covers a land area of 1.505 square miles and a water area of 0.921 square miles. Located at 40.80° N. Lat; 91.08° W. Long.

Population: 209 (1990); 207 (2000); 171 (2010); 158 (2015 projected); Race: 96.5% White, 0.0% Black, 0.0% Asian, 3.5% Other, 2.9% Hispanic of any race (2010); Density: 113.6 persons per square mile (2010); Average household size: 2.22 (2010); Median age: 50.5 (2010); Males per 100 females: 103.6 (2010); Marriage status: 4.1% never married, 52.6% now married, 11.3% widowed, 32.0% divorced (2005-2009 5-year est.); Foreign born: 7.1% (2005-2009 5-year est.); Ancestry (includes multiple ancestries): 23.9% German, 15.0% Irish, 3.5% American, 3.5% Polish, 2.7% English (2005-2009 5-year est.).

Economy: Single-family building permits issued: 0 (2010); Multi-family building permits issued: 0 (2010); Employment by occupation: 7.0% management, 0.0% professional, 21.1% services, 22.8% sales, 0.0% farming, 17.5% construction, 31.6% production (2005-2009 5-year est.).

Income: Per capita income: $24,797 (2010); Median household income: $51,630 (2010); Average household income: $56,006 (2010); Percent of

households with income of $100,000 or more: 10.4% (2010); Poverty rate: 10.6% (2005-2009 5-year est.).

Taxes: Total city taxes per capita: $198 (2007); City property taxes per capita: $86 (2007).

Education: Percent of population age 25 and over with: High school diploma (including GED) or higher: 89.4% (2010); Bachelor's degree or higher: 15.6% (2010); Master's degree or higher: 5.0% (2010).

Housing: Homeownership rate: 79.2% (2010); Median home value: $53,077 (2010); Median contract rent: $417 per month (2005-2009 5-year est.); Median year structure built: 1974 (2005-2009 5-year est.).

Transportation: Commute to work: 100.0% car, 0.0% public transportation, 0.0% walk, 0.0% work from home (2005-2009 5-year est.); Travel time to work: 62.3% less than 15 minutes, 17.0% 15 to 30 minutes, 0.0% 30 to 45 minutes, 20.8% 45 to 60 minutes, 0.0% 60 minutes or more (2005-2009 5-year est.)

LOMAX (village). Covers a land area of 1.043 square miles and a water area of 0 square miles. Located at 40.68° N. Lat; 91.07° W. Long. Elevation is 548 feet.

Population: 473 (1990); 477 (2000); 439 (2010); 410 (2015 projected); Race: 98.6% White, 0.0% Black, 0.5% Asian, 0.9% Other, 1.6% Hispanic of any race (2010); Density: 420.9 persons per square mile (2010); Average household size: 2.40 (2010); Median age: 42.2 (2010); Males per 100 females: 90.9 (2010); Marriage status: 9.5% never married, 77.6% now married, 7.8% widowed, 5.1% divorced (2005-2009 5-year est.); Foreign born: 3.9% (2005-2009 5-year est.); Ancestry (includes multiple ancestries): 41.2% German, 20.4% Irish, 11.1% English, 5.2% Polish, 3.9% American (2005-2009 5-year est.).

Economy: Single-family building permits issued: 0 (2010); Multi-family building permits issued: 0 (2010); Employment by occupation: 3.7% management, 9.6% professional, 20.5% services, 18.3% sales, 3.7% farming, 8.7% construction, 35.6% production (2005-2009 5-year est.).

Income: Per capita income: $20,714 (2010); Median household income: $43,710 (2010); Average household income: $51,974 (2010); Percent of households with income of $100,000 or more: 8.5% (2010); Poverty rate: 6.5% (2005-2009 5-year est.).

Taxes: Total city taxes per capita: $25 (2007); City property taxes per capita: $9 (2007).

Education: Percent of population age 25 and over with: High school diploma (including GED) or higher: 88.2% (2010); Bachelor's degree or higher: 15.3% (2010); Master's degree or higher: 6.1% (2010).

Housing: Homeownership rate: 77.3% (2010); Median home value: $73,333 (2010); Median contract rent: $240 per month (2005-2009 5-year est.); Median year structure built: 1951 (2005-2009 5-year est.).

Transportation: Commute to work: 98.9% car, 0.0% public transportation, 1.1% walk, 0.0% work from home (2005-2009 5-year est.); Travel time to work: 20.2% less than 15 minutes, 51.9% 15 to 30 minutes, 23.5% 30 to 45 minutes, 4.4% 45 to 60 minutes, 0.0% 60 minutes or more (2005-2009 5-year est.)

MEDIA (village). Covers a land area of 1.698 square miles and a water area of 0 square miles. Located at 40.77° N. Lat; 90.83° W. Long. Elevation is 709 feet.

Population: 146 (1990); 130 (2000); 121 (2010); 114 (2015 projected); Race: 94.2% White, 2.5% Black, 0.0% Asian, 3.3% Other, 1.7% Hispanic of any race (2010); Density: 71.2 persons per square mile (2010); Average household size: 2.57 (2010); Median age: 39.6 (2010); Males per 100 females: 101.7 (2010); Marriage status: 18.5% never married, 54.8% now married, 16.3% widowed, 10.4% divorced (2005-2009 5-year est.); Foreign born: 0.6% (2005-2009 5-year est.); Ancestry (includes multiple ancestries): 32.1% German, 25.8% Irish, 5.7% English, 5.0% Swedish, 3.1% American (2005-2009 5-year est.).

Economy: Single-family building permits issued: 0 (2010); Multi-family building permits issued: 0 (2010); Employment by occupation: 2.1% management, 3.1% professional, 10.3% services, 45.4% sales, 3.1% farming, 9.3% construction, 26.8% production (2005-2009 5-year est.).

Income: Per capita income: $20,905 (2010); Median household income: $41,750 (2010); Average household income: $51,330 (2010); Percent of households with income of $100,000 or more: 8.5% (2010); Poverty rate: 14.5% (2005-2009 5-year est.).

Taxes: Total city taxes per capita: $8 (2007); City property taxes per capita: $8 (2007).

Education: Percent of population age 25 and over with: High school diploma (including GED) or higher: 94.1% (2010); Bachelor's degree or higher: 15.3% (2010); Master's degree or higher: 4.7% (2010).

School District(s)
West Central CUSD 235 (PK-12)
2009-10 Enrollment: 1,031 . . . . (309) 627-2371
Housing: Homeownership rate: 74.5% (2010); Median home value: $88,333 (2010); Median contract rent: $319 per month (2005-2009 5-year est.); Median year structure built: before 1940 (2005-2009 5-year est.).
Transportation: Commute to work: 96.9% car, 0.0% public transportation, 0.0% walk, 3.1% work from home (2005-2009 5-year est.); Travel time to work: 19.1% less than 15 minutes, 51.1% 15 to 30 minutes, 23.4% 30 to 45 minutes, 1.1% 45 to 60 minutes, 5.3% 60 minutes or more (2005-2009 5-year est.)

OQUAWKA (village). County seat. Covers a land area of 1.463 square miles and a water area of 0.389 square miles. Located at 40.93° N. Lat; 90.94° W. Long. Elevation is 554 feet.
History: Oquawka began as a trading post built in 1827 by the Phelps brothers. The name is of Indian origin, a variation of Ozaukee meaning "yellow banks." An early industry was the manufacture of pearl button blanks from mussel shells.
Population: 1,442 (1990); 1,539 (2000); 1,346 (2010); 1,256 (2015 projected); Race: 97.7% White, 0.1% Black, 0.1% Asian, 2.1% Other, 1.5% Hispanic of any race (2010); Density: 919.9 persons per square mile (2010); Average household size: 2.26 (2010); Median age: 45.1 (2010); Males per 100 females: 95.1 (2010); Marriage status: 21.5% never married, 49.8% now married, 12.3% widowed, 16.4% divorced (2005-2009 5-year est.); Foreign born: 1.3% (2005-2009 5-year est.); Ancestry (includes multiple ancestries): 28.2% German, 14.5% Irish, 7.7% English, 6.6% American, 6.6% Swedish (2005-2009 5-year est.).
Economy: Single-family building permits issued: 4 (2010); Multi-family building permits issued: 0 (2010); Employment by occupation: 7.6% management, 8.4% professional, 17.0% services, 13.6% sales, 0.0% farming, 14.6% construction, 38.9% production (2005-2009 5-year est.).
Income: Per capita income: $21,820 (2010); Median household income: $39,338 (2010); Average household income: $48,868 (2010); Percent of households with income of $100,000 or more: 9.9% (2010); Poverty rate: 15.2% (2005-2009 5-year est.).
Taxes: Total city taxes per capita: $85 (2007); City property taxes per capita: $49 (2007).
Education: Percent of population age 25 and over with: High school diploma (including GED) or higher: 80.9% (2010); Bachelor's degree or higher: 7.9% (2010); Master's degree or higher: 3.3% (2010).
Housing: Homeownership rate: 77.9% (2010); Median home value: $79,487 (2010); Median contract rent: $328 per month (2005-2009 5-year est.); Median year structure built: 1965 (2005-2009 5-year est.).
Newspapers: Oquawka Current (Community news; Circulation 2,000)
Transportation: Commute to work: 91.4% car, 3.1% public transportation, 2.9% walk, 2.3% work from home (2005-2009 5-year est.); Travel time to work: 23.8% less than 15 minutes, 43.8% 15 to 30 minutes, 18.1% 30 to 45 minutes, 2.7% 45 to 60 minutes, 11.6% 60 minutes or more (2005-2009 5-year est.)

RARITAN (village). Covers a land area of 0.099 square miles and a water area of 0 square miles. Located at 40.69° N. Lat; 90.82° W. Long. Elevation is 761 feet.
Population: 146 (1990); 140 (2000); 127 (2010); 120 (2015 projected); Race: 94.5% White, 2.4% Black, 3.1% Other, 1.6% Hispanic of any race (2010); Density: 1,280.6 persons per square mile (2010); Average household size: 2.54 (2010); Median age: 44.6 (2010); Males per 100 females: 101.6 (2010); Marriage status: 26.3% never married, 44.5% now married, 5.1% widowed, 24.1% divorced (2005-2009 5-year est.); Foreign born: 0.0% (2005-2009 5-year est.); Ancestry (includes multiple ancestries): 27.8% German, 16.7% Irish, 11.1% Italian, 9.7% English, 8.3% Scottish (2005-2009 5-year est.).
Economy: Single-family building permits issued: 0 (2010); Multi-family building permits issued: 0 (2010); Employment by occupation: 2.0% management, 3.0% professional, 31.7% services, 27.7% sales, 0.0% farming, 32.7% construction, 3.0% production (2005-2009 5-year est.).
Income: Per capita income: $20,905 (2010); Median household income: $42,500 (2010); Average household income: $56,050 (2010); Percent of households with income of $100,000 or more: 10.0% (2010); Poverty rate: 15.3% (2005-2009 5-year est.).
Taxes: Total city taxes per capita: $47 (2007); City property taxes per capita: $47 (2007).
Education: Percent of population age 25 and over with: High school diploma (including GED) or higher: 94.6% (2010); Bachelor's degree or higher: 14.0% (2010); Master's degree or higher: 3.2% (2010).

Housing: Homeownership rate: 76.0% (2010); Median home value: $90,000 (2010); Median contract rent: n/a per month (2005-2009 5-year est.); Median year structure built: before 1940 (2005-2009 5-year est.).
Transportation: Commute to work: 90.1% car, 0.0% public transportation, 8.9% walk, 0.0% work from home (2005-2009 5-year est.); Travel time to work: 40.6% less than 15 minutes, 24.8% 15 to 30 minutes, 15.8% 30 to 45 minutes, 8.9% 45 to 60 minutes, 9.9% 60 minutes or more (2005-2009 5-year est.)

STRONGHURST (village). Covers a land area of 0.887 square miles and a water area of 0 square miles. Located at 40.74° N. Lat; 90.90° W. Long. Elevation is 676 feet.
Population: 824 (1990); 896 (2000); 803 (2010); 751 (2015 projected); Race: 98.3% White, 0.5% Black, 0.1% Asian, 1.1% Other, 1.4% Hispanic of any race (2010); Density: 905.0 persons per square mile (2010); Average household size: 2.45 (2010); Median age: 43.0 (2010); Males per 100 females: 91.2 (2010); Marriage status: 21.9% never married, 51.7% now married, 12.8% widowed, 13.6% divorced (2005-2009 5-year est.); Foreign born: 0.0% (2005-2009 5-year est.); Ancestry (includes multiple ancestries): 18.6% German, 14.4% English, 9.6% Irish, 5.8% Scotch-Irish, 5.7% Swedish (2005-2009 5-year est.).
Economy: Single-family building permits issued: 0 (2010); Multi-family building permits issued: 0 (2010); Employment by occupation: 5.5% management, 17.7% professional, 22.3% services, 21.9% sales, 8.6% farming, 8.8% construction, 15.3% production (2005-2009 5-year est.).
Income: Per capita income: $20,928 (2010); Median household income: $44,052 (2010); Average household income: $51,531 (2010); Percent of households with income of $100,000 or more: 8.1% (2010); Poverty rate: 11.6% (2005-2009 5-year est.).
Taxes: Total city taxes per capita: $53 (2007); City property taxes per capita: $44 (2007).
Education: Percent of population age 25 and over with: High school diploma (including GED) or higher: 89.6% (2010); Bachelor's degree or higher: 14.4% (2010); Master's degree or higher: 5.4% (2010).

School District(s)
West Central CUSD 235 (PK-12)
2009-10 Enrollment: 1,031 . . . . (309) 627-2371
Housing: Homeownership rate: 77.5% (2010); Median home value: $76,957 (2010); Median contract rent: $332 per month (2005-2009 5-year est.); Median year structure built: before 1940 (2005-2009 5-year est.).
Newspapers: Henderson County Quill (Local news; Circulation 1,800)
Transportation: Commute to work: 95.9% car, 0.0% public transportation, 1.1% walk, 2.7% work from home (2005-2009 5-year est.); Travel time to work: 40.3% less than 15 minutes, 33.5% 15 to 30 minutes, 13.6% 30 to 45 minutes, 4.4% 45 to 60 minutes, 8.3% 60 minutes or more (2005-2009 5-year est.)

Henry County

Located in northwestern Illinois; bounded on the northwest by the Rock River; drained by the Green and Edwards Rivers. Covers a land area of 823.21 square miles, a water area of 2.38 square miles, and is located in the Central Time Zone at 41.35° N. Lat., 90.12° W. Long. The county was founded in 1825. County seat is Cambridge.

Henry County is part of the Davenport-Moline-Rock Island, IA-IL Metropolitan Statistical Area. The entire metro area includes: Henry County, IL; Mercer County, IL; Rock Island County, IL; Scott County, IA

Weather Station: Galva   Elevation: 810 feet

	Jan	Feb	Mar	Apr	May	Jun	Jul	Aug	Sep	Oct	Nov	Dec
High	31	35	47	61	72	81	85	83	76	63	48	34
Low	14	18	28	39	50	60	64	62	52	41	30	18
Precip	1.5	1.6	2.6	3.8	4.0	4.3	3.9	4.4	3.5	2.9	2.8	2.1
Snow	5.6	5.0	2.4	1.2	0.0	0.0	0.0	0.0	0.0	0.0	1.0	5.4

High and Low temperatures in degrees Fahrenheit; Precipitation and Snow in inches

Weather Station: Geneseo   Elevation: 639 feet

	Jan	Feb	Mar	Apr	May	Jun	Jul	Aug	Sep	Oct	Nov	Dec
High	31	35	48	62	73	82	85	83	76	63	48	34
Low	15	19	29	40	51	61	65	63	54	43	31	19
Precip	1.5	1.7	2.6	3.6	4.1	4.0	4.0	4.6	3.3	3.4	2.8	2.2
Snow	7.7	5.5	2.7	1.1	0.0	0.0	0.0	0.0	0.0	0.1	0.9	7.4

High and Low temperatures in degrees Fahrenheit; Precipitation and Snow in inches

Weather Station: Kewanee 1 E   Elevation: 779 feet

	Jan	Feb	Mar	Apr	May	Jun	Jul	Aug	Sep	Oct	Nov	Dec
High	30	34	47	61	71	81	84	82	76	63	48	34
Low	13	16	27	38	49	59	63	61	51	40	30	18
Precip	1.7	1.8	2.5	3.5	4.2	4.3	3.8	4.4	3.3	2.7	2.8	2.2
Snow	7.4	6.4	2.7	1.0	tr	0.0	0.0	0.0	0.0	0.3	0.8	6.8

High and Low temperatures in degrees Fahrenheit; Precipitation and Snow in inches

Population: 51,159 (1990); 51,020 (2000); 49,443 (2010); 48,485 (2015 projected); Race: 94.6% White, 1.4% Black, 0.4% Asian, 3.6% Other, 4.5% Hispanic of any race (2010); Density: 60.1 persons per square mile (2010); Average household size: 2.47 (2010); Median age: 40.9 (2010); Males per 100 females: 97.1 (2010).
Religion: Five largest groups: 19.2% Catholic Church, 11.2% The United Methodist Church, 10.3% Evangelical Lutheran Church in America, 3.9% American Baptist Churches in the USA, 3.0% Lutheran Church—Missouri Synod (2000).
Economy: Unemployment rate: 7.3% (August 2011); Total civilian labor force: 27,028 (August 2011); Leading industries: 28.3% manufacturing; 15.2% retail trade; 11.9% health care and social assistance (2009); Farms: 1,473 totaling 489,903 acres (2007); Companies that employ 500 or more persons: 1 (2009); Companies that employ 100 to 499 persons: 10 (2009); Companies that employ less than 100 persons: 1,114 (2009); Black-owned businesses: n/a (2007); Hispanic-owned businesses: n/a (2007); Asian-owned businesses: n/a (2007); Women-owned businesses: n/a (2007); Retail sales per capita: $10,875 (2010). Single-family building permits issued: 28 (2010); Multi-family building permits issued: 0 (2010).
Income: Per capita income: $23,703 (2010); Median household income: $48,509 (2010); Average household income: $58,969 (2010); Percent of households with income of $100,000 or more: 13.7% (2010); Poverty rate: 9.8% (2009); Bankruptcy rate: 4.03% (2010).
Taxes: Total county taxes per capita: $122 (2007); County property taxes per capita: $117 (2007).
Education: Percent of population age 25 and over with: High school diploma (including GED) or higher: 87.1% (2010); Bachelor's degree or higher: 19.5% (2010); Master's degree or higher: 6.6% (2010).
Housing: Homeownership rate: 75.9% (2010); Median home value: $96,489 (2010); Median contract rent: $413 per month (2005-2009 est.); Median year structure built: 1958 (2005-2009 5-year est.)
Health: Birth rate: 117.8 per 10,000 population (2009); Death rate: 104.2 per 10,000 population (2009); Age-adjusted cancer mortality rate: 225.4 deaths per 100,000 population (2007); Number of physicians: 5.3 per 10,000 population (2008); Hospital beds: 21.2 per 10,000 population (2007); Hospital admissions: 456.8 per 10,000 population (2007).
Elections: 2008 Presidential election results: 53.2% Obama, 45.4% McCain, 0.7% Nader
National and State Parks: Johnson Sauk Trail State Park
Additional Information Contacts

Henry County Government . . . . (309) 937-3578
    http://www.co.henry.il.us
City of Colona . . . . (309) 792-0571
    http://www.colonail.com
City of Geneseo . . . . (309) 944-0908
    http://www.cityofgeneseo.com
City of Kewanee . . . . (309) 852-2611
    http://cityofkewanee.com
Geneseo Chamber of Commerce . . . . (309) 944-2686
    http://www.geneseo.org
Kewanee Chamber of Commerce . . . . (309) 852-2175
    http://www.kewanee-il.com
Village of Cambridge . . . . (309) 937-2570
    http://www.cambridgeil.org

Henry County Communities

ALPHA (village). Covers a land area of 0.322 square miles and a water area of 0 square miles. Located at 41.19° N. Lat; 90.38° W. Long. Elevation is 801 feet.
Population: 809 (1990); 726 (2000); 681 (2010); 654 (2015 projected); Race: 98.1% White, 0.0% Black, 0.1% Asian, 1.8% Other, 2.2% Hispanic of any race (2010); Density: 2,115.0 persons per square mile (2010); Average household size: 2.41 (2010); Median age: 43.1 (2010); Males per 100 females: 101.5 (2010); Marriage status: 15.7% never married, 59.6% now married, 15.3% widowed, 9.3% divorced (2005-2009 5-year est.); Foreign born: 0.3% (2005-2009 5-year est.); Ancestry (includes multiple

ancestries): 28.1% Swedish, 25.5% German, 14.4% Irish, 10.1% English, 5.8% American (2005-2009 5-year est.).
Economy: Single-family building permits issued: 0 (2010); Multi-family building permits issued: 0 (2010); Employment by occupation: 9.9% management, 14.7% professional, 19.0% services, 26.2% sales, 0.0% farming, 17.1% construction, 13.1% production (2005-2009 5-year est.).
Income: Per capita income: $19,744 (2010); Median household income: $41,818 (2010); Average household income: $47,890 (2010); Percent of households with income of $100,000 or more: 4.3% (2010); Poverty rate: 5.2% (2005-2009 5-year est.).
Taxes: Total city taxes per capita: $31 (2007); City property taxes per capita: $27 (2007).
Education: Percent of population age 25 and over with: High school diploma (including GED) or higher: 89.4% (2010); Bachelor's degree or higher: 16.2% (2010); Master's degree or higher: 6.3% (2010).
School District(s)
Alwood CUSD 225 (PK-12)
    2009-10 Enrollment: 444 . . . . (309) 334-2719
Housing: Homeownership rate: 85.1% (2010); Median home value: $82,642 (2010); Median contract rent: $401 per month (2005-2009 5-year est.); Median year structure built: 1960 (2005-2009 5-year est.).
Transportation: Commute to work: 90.7% car, 0.0% public transportation, 6.1% walk, 3.3% work from home (2005-2009 5-year est.); Travel time to work: 33.6% less than 15 minutes, 34.5% 15 to 30 minutes, 19.3% 30 to 45 minutes, 10.5% 45 to 60 minutes, 2.1% 60 minutes or more (2005-2009 5-year est.)

ANDOVER (village). Covers a land area of 0.999 square miles and a water area of 0 square miles. Located at 41.29° N. Lat; 90.29° W. Long. Elevation is 774 feet.
Population: 579 (1990); 594 (2000); 562 (2010); 543 (2015 projected); Race: 97.7% White, 0.0% Black, 1.4% Asian, 0.9% Other, 1.6% Hispanic of any race (2010); Density: 562.7 persons per square mile (2010); Average household size: 2.68 (2010); Median age: 45.1 (2010); Males per 100 females: 99.3 (2010); Marriage status: 15.9% never married, 67.6% now married, 8.1% widowed, 8.4% divorced (2005-2009 5-year est.); Foreign born: 1.1% (2005-2009 5-year est.); Ancestry (includes multiple ancestries): 39.5% German, 19.3% Swedish, 16.9% Irish, 4.5% Scotch-Irish, 4.5% Polish (2005-2009 5-year est.).
Economy: Single-family building permits issued: 1 (2010); Multi-family building permits issued: 0 (2010); Employment by occupation: 8.7% management, 14.7% professional, 12.8% services, 24.3% sales, 1.4% farming, 16.1% construction, 22.0% production (2005-2009 5-year est.).
Income: Per capita income: $24,105 (2010); Median household income: $59,896 (2010); Average household income: $64,440 (2010); Percent of households with income of $100,000 or more: 18.1% (2010); Poverty rate: 10.4% (2005-2009 5-year est.).
Taxes: Total city taxes per capita: $71 (2007); City property taxes per capita: $50 (2007).
Education: Percent of population age 25 and over with: High school diploma (including GED) or higher: 89.6% (2010); Bachelor's degree or higher: 16.4% (2010); Master's degree or higher: 1.0% (2010).
Housing: Homeownership rate: 84.8% (2010); Median home value: $100,806 (2010); Median contract rent: $321 per month (2005-2009 5-year est.); Median year structure built: 1954 (2005-2009 5-year est.).
Transportation: Commute to work: 89.0% car, 0.0% public transportation, 0.0% walk, 7.3% work from home (2005-2009 5-year est.); Travel time to work: 21.8% less than 15 minutes, 24.8% 15 to 30 minutes, 50.5% 30 to 45 minutes, 3.0% 45 to 60 minutes, 0.0% 60 minutes or more (2005-2009 5-year est.)

ANNAWAN (village). Covers a land area of 0.682 square miles and a water area of 0 square miles. Located at 41.39° N. Lat; 89.90° W. Long. Elevation is 630 feet.
History: Annawan developed as the center of a stock farming and coal mining region.
Population: 817 (1990); 868 (2000); 908 (2010); 920 (2015 projected); Race: 99.8% White, 0.0% Black, 0.0% Asian, 0.2% Other, 1.7% Hispanic of any race (2010); Density: 1,332.3 persons per square mile (2010); Average household size: 2.40 (2010); Median age: 37.6 (2010); Males per 100 females: 92.8 (2010); Marriage status: 19.2% never married, 63.0% now married, 8.6% widowed, 9.3% divorced (2005-2009 5-year est.); Foreign born: 2.4% (2005-2009 5-year est.); Ancestry (includes multiple ancestries): 24.9% German, 24.3% Belgian, 13.3% Swedish, 12.1% English, 9.5% Irish (2005-2009 5-year est.).

Economy: Single-family building permits issued: 1 (2010); Multi-family building permits issued: 0 (2010); Employment by occupation: 14.0% management, 20.5% professional, 10.1% services, 29.6% sales, 2.3% farming, 10.8% construction, 12.7% production (2005-2009 5-year est.).
Income: Per capita income: $23,338 (2010); Median household income: $46,885 (2010); Average household income: $55,778 (2010); Percent of households with income of $100,000 or more: 9.5% (2010); Poverty rate: 4.0% (2005-2009 5-year est.).
Taxes: Total city taxes per capita: $156 (2007); City property taxes per capita: $147 (2007).
Education: Percent of population age 25 and over with: High school diploma (including GED) or higher: 90.1% (2010); Bachelor's degree or higher: 18.2% (2010); Master's degree or higher: 6.7% (2010).

School District(s)

Annawan CUSD 226 (PK-12)
    2009-10 Enrollment: 387 . . . . (309) 935-6781
Housing: Homeownership rate: 77.6% (2010); Median home value: $94,400 (2010); Median contract rent: $442 per month (2005-2009 5-year est.); Median year structure built: 1956 (2005-2009 5-year est.).
Transportation: Commute to work: 91.1% car, 0.0% public transportation, 6.3% walk, 2.6% work from home (2005-2009 5-year est.); Travel time to work: 31.0% less than 15 minutes, 35.5% 15 to 30 minutes, 19.6% 30 to 45 minutes, 9.2% 45 to 60 minutes, 4.7% 60 minutes or more (2005-2009 5-year est.)

ATKINSON (town). Covers a land area of 1.509 square miles and a water area of 0.004 square miles. Located at 41.41° N. Lat; 90.01° W. Long. Elevation is 659 feet.
Population: 954 (1990); 1,001 (2000); 921 (2010); 883 (2015 projected); Race: 97.8% White, 0.9% Black, 0.0% Asian, 1.3% Other, 1.4% Hispanic of any race (2010); Density: 610.2 persons per square mile (2010); Average household size: 2.26 (2010); Median age: 41.4 (2010); Males per 100 females: 97.2 (2010); Marriage status: 18.0% never married, 62.8% now married, 7.2% widowed, 12.1% divorced (2005-2009 5-year est.); Foreign born: 0.4% (2005-2009 5-year est.); Ancestry (includes multiple ancestries): 30.6% German, 29.6% Belgian, 11.6% Swedish, 8.2% Irish, 7.3% English (2005-2009 5-year est.).
Economy: Single-family building permits issued: 0 (2010); Multi-family building permits issued: 0 (2010); Employment by occupation: 8.4% management, 5.5% professional, 19.3% services, 25.3% sales, 1.2% farming, 17.9% construction, 22.2% production (2005-2009 5-year est.).
Income: Per capita income: $23,172 (2010); Median household income: $46,680 (2010); Average household income: $53,133 (2010); Percent of households with income of $100,000 or more: 10.1% (2010); Poverty rate: 13.8% (2005-2009 5-year est.).
Taxes: Total city taxes per capita: $103 (2007); City property taxes per capita: $92 (2007).
Education: Percent of population age 25 and over with: High school diploma (including GED) or higher: 84.6% (2010); Bachelor's degree or higher: 17.3% (2010); Master's degree or higher: 4.3% (2010).

School District(s)

Henry-Stark County Spec Ed Dist (03-12)
    2009-10 Enrollment: n/a . . . . (309) 852-5696
Housing: Homeownership rate: 74.0% (2010); Median home value: $89,649 (2010); Median contract rent: $357 per month (2005-2009 5-year est.); Median year structure built: 1953 (2005-2009 5-year est.).
Transportation: Commute to work: 96.9% car, 0.0% public transportation, 2.1% walk, 0.5% work from home (2005-2009 5-year est.); Travel time to work: 46.8% less than 15 minutes, 24.1% 15 to 30 minutes, 20.9% 30 to 45 minutes, 4.2% 45 to 60 minutes, 4.0% 60 minutes or more (2005-2009 5-year est.)

BISHOP HILL (village). Covers a land area of 0.539 square miles and a water area of 0 square miles. Located at 41.20° N. Lat; 90.11° W. Long. Elevation is 784 feet.
History: Bishop Hill was settled in 1846 by a group of Swedish emigrants led by Erik Jansson, who envisioned a communistic society based on religion. Jansson's leadership lasted only a few years, and by 1861 the communal property had been divided among individuals.
Population: 131 (1990); 125 (2000); 118 (2010); 113 (2015 projected); Race: 98.3% White, 0.0% Black, 0.8% Asian, 0.8% Other, 0.0% Hispanic of any race (2010); Density: 219.0 persons per square mile (2010); Average household size: 2.57 (2010); Median age: 46.0 (2010); Males per 100 females: 96.7 (2010); Marriage status: 17.8% never married, 54.8% now married, 4.1% widowed, 23.3% divorced (2005-2009 5-year est.);

Foreign born: 0.0% (2005-2009 5-year est.); Ancestry (includes multiple ancestries): 36.3% Swedish, 15.0% American, 12.5% German, 11.3% English, 6.3% Scottish (2005-2009 5-year est.).
Economy: Single-family building permits issued: 0 (2010); Multi-family building permits issued: 0 (2010); Employment by occupation: 0.0% management, 3.7% professional, 7.4% services, 59.3% sales, 0.0% farming, 11.1% construction, 18.5% production (2005-2009 5-year est.).
Income: Per capita income: $21,220 (2010); Median household income: $45,500 (2010); Average household income: $51,902 (2010); Percent of households with income of $100,000 or more: 8.7% (2010); Poverty rate: 8.8% (2005-2009 5-year est.).
Taxes: Total city taxes per capita: $67 (2007); City property taxes per capita: $42 (2007).
Education: Percent of population age 25 and over with: High school diploma (including GED) or higher: 93.1% (2010); Bachelor's degree or higher: 28.7% (2010); Master's degree or higher: 10.3% (2010).
Housing: Homeownership rate: 71.7% (2010); Median home value: $121,154 (2010); Median contract rent: $232 per month (2005-2009 5-year est.); Median year structure built: before 1940 (2005-2009 5-year est.).
Transportation: Commute to work: 77.8% car, 0.0% public transportation, 18.5% walk, 3.7% work from home (2005-2009 5-year est.); Travel time to work: 50.0% less than 15 minutes, 23.1% 15 to 30 minutes, 11.5% 30 to 45 minutes, 0.0% 45 to 60 minutes, 15.4% 60 minutes or more (2005-2009 5-year est.)

CAMBRIDGE (village). County seat. Covers a land area of 1.415 square miles and a water area of 0.013 square miles. Located at 41.30° N. Lat; 90.19° W. Long. Elevation is 810 feet.
History: Incorporated 1861.
Population: 2,153 (1990); 2,180 (2000); 2,071 (2010); 2,003 (2015 projected); Race: 97.2% White, 1.2% Black, 0.5% Asian, 1.1% Other, 0.8% Hispanic of any race (2010); Density: 1,463.2 persons per square mile (2010); Average household size: 2.40 (2010); Median age: 38.9 (2010); Males per 100 females: 103.2 (2010); Marriage status: 28.7% never married, 56.5% now married, 6.6% widowed, 8.2% divorced (2005-2009 5-year est.); Foreign born: 1.8% (2005-2009 5-year est.); Ancestry (includes multiple ancestries): 22.6% German, 19.7% Swedish, 16.4% Irish, 11.0% English, 7.7% American (2005-2009 5-year est.).
Economy: Single-family building permits issued: 1 (2010); Multi-family building permits issued: 0 (2010); Employment by occupation: 10.7% management, 21.1% professional, 20.5% services, 16.4% sales, 0.0% farming, 11.0% construction, 20.4% production (2005-2009 5-year est.).
Income: Per capita income: $23,743 (2010); Median household income: $49,952 (2010); Average household income: $58,494 (2010); Percent of households with income of $100,000 or more: 11.6% (2010); Poverty rate: 7.1% (2005-2009 5-year est.).
Taxes: Total city taxes per capita: $146 (2007); City property taxes per capita: $103 (2007).
Education: Percent of population age 25 and over with: High school diploma (including GED) or higher: 85.8% (2010); Bachelor's degree or higher: 18.1% (2010); Master's degree or higher: 6.3% (2010).

School District(s)

Cambridge CUSD 227 (PK-12)
    2009-10 Enrollment: 427 . . . . (309) 937-2144
Housing: Homeownership rate: 77.2% (2010); Median home value: $91,333 (2010); Median contract rent: $314 per month (2005-2009 5-year est.); Median year structure built: 1955 (2005-2009 5-year est.).
Safety: Violent crime rate: 0.0 per 10,000 population; Property crime rate: 48.7 per 10,000 population (2010).
Newspapers: Cambridge Chronicle (Local news; Circulation 1,500)
Transportation: Commute to work: 94.5% car, 0.0% public transportation, 3.2% walk, 0.8% work from home (2005-2009 5-year est.); Travel time to work: 42.8% less than 15 minutes, 19.9% 15 to 30 minutes, 30.2% 30 to 45 minutes, 5.4% 45 to 60 minutes, 1.7% 60 minutes or more (2005-2009 5-year est.)
Additional Information Contacts
Village of Cambridge . . . . (309) 937-2570
    http://www.cambridgeil.org

CLEVELAND (village). Covers a land area of 0.361 square miles and a water area of 0.003 square miles. Located at 41.50° N. Lat; 90.31° W. Long. Elevation is 571 feet.
Population: 283 (1990); 253 (2000); 235 (2010); 222 (2015 projected); Race: 95.7% White, 0.4% Black, 0.4% Asian, 3.4% Other, 6.8% Hispanic of any race (2010); Density: 650.3 persons per square mile (2010);

Average household size: 2.61 (2010); Median age: 39.8 (2010); Males per 100 females: 102.6 (2010); Marriage status: 12.9% never married, 74.2% now married, 7.6% widowed, 5.3% divorced (2005-2009 5-year est.); Foreign born: 0.0% (2005-2009 5-year est.); Ancestry (includes multiple ancestries): 31.1% German, 23.2% Irish, 16.4% Swedish, 10.7% American, 8.5% Belgian (2005-2009 5-year est.).

Economy: Single-family building permits issued: 0 (2010); Multi-family building permits issued: 0 (2010); Employment by occupation: 13.8% management, 2.3% professional, 11.5% services, 33.3% sales, 0.0% farming, 26.4% construction, 12.6% production (2005-2009 5-year est.).

Income: Per capita income: $27,817 (2010); Median household income: $58,333 (2010); Average household income: $70,472 (2010); Percent of households with income of $100,000 or more: 24.4% (2010); Poverty rate: 15.8% (2005-2009 5-year est.).

Taxes: Total city taxes per capita: $37 (2007); City property taxes per capita: $29 (2007).

Education: Percent of population age 25 and over with: High school diploma (including GED) or higher: 81.1% (2010); Bachelor's degree or higher: 10.1% (2010); Master's degree or higher: 2.5% (2010).

Housing: Homeownership rate: 83.3% (2010); Median home value: $109,821 (2010); Median contract rent: n/a per month (2005-2009 5-year est.); Median year structure built: 1961 (2005-2009 5-year est.).

Transportation: Commute to work: 96.4% car, 0.0% public transportation, 0.0% walk, 3.6% work from home (2005-2009 5-year est.); Travel time to work: 12.5% less than 15 minutes, 60.0% 15 to 30 minutes, 11.3% 30 to 45 minutes, 13.8% 45 to 60 minutes, 2.5% 60 minutes or more (2005-2009 5-year est.)

COLONA (city).
Covers a land area of 3.497 square miles and a water area of 0.061 square miles. Located at 41.47° N. Lat; 90.34° W. Long. Elevation is 604 feet.

Population: 5,152 (1990); 5,173 (2000); 5,123 (2010); 5,047 (2015 projected); Race: 96.5% White, 0.4% Black, 0.1% Asian, 3.0% Other, 4.7% Hispanic of any race (2010); Density: 1,464.8 persons per square mile (2010); Average household size: 2.57 (2010); Median age: 37.7 (2010); Males per 100 females: 99.1 (2010); Marriage status: 22.3% never married, 64.8% now married, 4.6% widowed, 8.4% divorced (2005-2009 5-year est.); Foreign born: 1.5% (2005-2009 5-year est.); Ancestry (includes multiple ancestries): 27.9% German, 16.5% Irish, 13.3% English, 12.2% Swedish, 12.2% American (2005-2009 5-year est.).

Economy: Single-family building permits issued: 6 (2010); Multi-family building permits issued: 0 (2010); Employment by occupation: 8.1% management, 10.4% professional, 16.0% services, 26.4% sales, 0.7% farming, 14.7% construction, 23.6% production (2005-2009 5-year est.).

Income: Per capita income: $23,577 (2010); Median household income: $52,761 (2010); Average household income: $60,688 (2010); Percent of households with income of $100,000 or more: 14.1% (2010); Poverty rate: 12.2% (2005-2009 5-year est.).

Taxes: Total city taxes per capita: $211 (2007); City property taxes per capita: $132 (2007).

Education: Percent of population age 25 and over with: High school diploma (including GED) or higher: 80.6% (2010); Bachelor's degree or higher: 10.8% (2010); Master's degree or higher: 3.1% (2010).

School District(s)
Colona SD 190 (PK-08)
    2009-10 Enrollment: 485 . . . . (309) 792-1232

Housing: Homeownership rate: 80.5% (2010); Median home value: $90,362 (2010); Median contract rent: $439 per month (2005-2009 5-year est.); Median year structure built: 1968 (2005-2009 5-year est.).

Safety: Violent crime rate: 44.7 per 10,000 population; Property crime rate: 159.2 per 10,000 population (2010).

Transportation: Commute to work: 98.7% car, 0.0% public transportation, 0.4% walk, 1.0% work from home (2005-2009 5-year est.); Travel time to work: 18.5% less than 15 minutes, 59.4% 15 to 30 minutes, 16.7% 30 to 45 minutes, 3.1% 45 to 60 minutes, 2.3% 60 minutes or more (2005-2009 5-year est.)

Additional Information Contacts
City of Colona . . . . (309) 792-0571
    http://www.colonail.com

GALVA (city).
Covers a land area of 1.714 square miles and a water area of 0 square miles. Located at 41.16° N. Lat; 90.04° W. Long. Elevation is 850 feet.

History: Galva was founded in 1854 by a group of Swedish settlers, who named it for their home in Sweden, Gefle. These first residents had been members of the religious colony at Bishop Hill.

Population: 2,761 (1990); 2,758 (2000); 2,626 (2010); 2,565 (2015 projected); Race: 97.6% White, 0.5% Black, 0.2% Asian, 1.6% Other, 2.9% Hispanic of any race (2010); Density: 1,532.5 persons per square mile (2010); Average household size: 2.38 (2010); Median age: 41.1 (2010); Males per 100 females: 91.4 (2010); Marriage status: 24.0% never married, 51.2% now married, 11.9% widowed, 12.9% divorced (2005-2009 5-year est.); Foreign born: 2.6% (2005-2009 5-year est.); Ancestry (includes multiple ancestries): 30.7% German, 19.7% Swedish, 12.9% English, 10.1% Irish, 7.8% American (2005-2009 5-year est.).

Economy: Single-family building permits issued: 0 (2010); Multi-family building permits issued: 0 (2010); Employment by occupation: 12.3% management, 16.8% professional, 16.0% services, 21.4% sales, 0.0% farming, 10.0% construction, 23.6% production (2005-2009 5-year est.).

Income: Per capita income: $21,236 (2010); Median household income: $40,545 (2010); Average household income: $50,347 (2010); Percent of households with income of $100,000 or more: 8.8% (2010); Poverty rate: 11.2% (2005-2009 5-year est.).

Taxes: Total city taxes per capita: $129 (2007); City property taxes per capita: $104 (2007).

Education: Percent of population age 25 and over with: High school diploma (including GED) or higher: 88.6% (2010); Bachelor's degree or higher: 20.9% (2010); Master's degree or higher: 6.5% (2010).

School District(s)
Galva CUSD 224 (PK-12)
    2009-10 Enrollment: 609 . . . . (309) 932-2108

Housing: Homeownership rate: 73.7% (2010); Median home value: $69,500 (2010); Median contract rent: $379 per month (2005-2009 5-year est.); Median year structure built: 1946 (2005-2009 5-year est.).

Newspapers: Galva News (Local news; Circulation 2,314); Wrova Shopper (Local news; Circulation 1,283)

Transportation: Commute to work: 92.3% car, 0.0% public transportation, 2.9% walk, 3.6% work from home (2005-2009 5-year est.); Travel time to work: 49.1% less than 15 minutes, 27.7% 15 to 30 minutes, 10.8% 30 to 45 minutes, 3.5% 45 to 60 minutes, 8.8% 60 minutes or more (2005-2009 5-year est.)

GENESEO (city).
Covers a land area of 4.032 square miles and a water area of 0.008 square miles. Located at 41.45° N. Lat; 90.15° W. Long. Elevation is 650 feet.

History: Geneseo was settled in 1836 by people from New York, and named for Geneseo in that state. Early industries were a corn and pea cannery, and a bandage factory.

Population: 6,091 (1990); 6,480 (2000); 6,235 (2010); 6,144 (2015 projected); Race: 97.8% White, 0.3% Black, 0.6% Asian, 1.3% Other, 1.5% Hispanic of any race (2010); Density: 1,546.2 persons per square mile (2010); Average household size: 2.34 (2010); Median age: 43.3 (2010); Males per 100 females: 92.3 (2010); Marriage status: 18.0% never married, 66.7% now married, 7.3% widowed, 7.9% divorced (2005-2009 5-year est.); Foreign born: 1.8% (2005-2009 5-year est.); Ancestry (includes multiple ancestries): 29.8% German, 16.2% Irish, 13.1% English, 8.7% Belgian, 7.3% Swedish (2005-2009 5-year est.).

Economy: Single-family building permits issued: 4 (2010); Multi-family building permits issued: 0 (2010); Employment by occupation: 15.9% management, 16.7% professional, 18.2% services, 27.1% sales, 0.4% farming, 7.7% construction, 14.1% production (2005-2009 5-year est.).

Income: Per capita income: $25,571 (2010); Median household income: $49,343 (2010); Average household income: $60,317 (2010); Percent of households with income of $100,000 or more: 14.2% (2010); Poverty rate: 7.7% (2005-2009 5-year est.).

Taxes: Total city taxes per capita: $199 (2007); City property taxes per capita: $84 (2007).

Education: Percent of population age 25 and over with: High school diploma (including GED) or higher: 91.1% (2010); Bachelor's degree or higher: 30.0% (2010); Master's degree or higher: 8.6% (2010).

School District(s)
Bureau/Henry/Stark Roe (06-12)
    2009-10 Enrollment: n/a . . . . (309) 936-7890
Geneseo CUSD 228 (PK-12)
    2009-10 Enrollment: 2,719 . . . . (309) 945-0450

Housing: Homeownership rate: 73.2% (2010); Median home value: $125,866 (2010); Median contract rent: $460 per month (2005-2009 5-year est.); Median year structure built: 1959 (2005-2009 5-year est.).

Hospitals: Hammond-Henry Hospital (105 beds)
Safety: Violent crime rate: 11.1 per 10,000 population; Property crime rate: 164.5 per 10,000 population (2010).
Newspapers: Geneseo Republic (Community news; Circulation 4,300)
Transportation: Commute to work: 91.7% car, 0.0% public transportation, 2.7% walk, 4.2% work from home (2005-2009 5-year est.); Travel time to work: 57.9% less than 15 minutes, 14.7% 15 to 30 minutes, 20.7% 30 to 45 minutes, 4.2% 45 to 60 minutes, 2.4% 60 minutes or more (2005-2009 5-year est.)

Additional Information Contacts
City of Geneseo . . . . (309) 944-0908
    http://www.cityofgeneseo.com
Geneseo Chamber of Commerce . . . . (309) 944-2686
    http://www.geneseo.org

HOOPPOLE (village).
Covers a land area of 0.347 square miles and a water area of 0 square miles. Located at 41.52° N. Lat; 89.91° W. Long. Elevation is 623 feet.
History: In a grove of hickory trees near Hooppole, coopers cut bands to use in the crafting of their barrels, and from this the town was named.
Population: 196 (1990); 162 (2000); 155 (2010); 152 (2015 projected); Race: 98.1% White, 0.6% Black, 0.0% Asian, 1.3% Other, 3.9% Hispanic of any race (2010); Density: 446.6 persons per square mile (2010); Average household size: 2.50 (2010); Median age: 43.1 (2010); Males per 100 females: 106.7 (2010); Marriage status: 20.9% never married, 68.7% now married, 3.8% widowed, 6.6% divorced (2005-2009 5-year est.); Foreign born: 0.0% (2005-2009 5-year est.); Ancestry (includes multiple ancestries): 42.0% German, 19.6% Irish, 17.9% English, 12.1% Swedish, 6.3% Belgian (2005-2009 5-year est.).
Economy: Single-family building permits issued: 0 (2010); Multi-family building permits issued: 0 (2010); Employment by occupation: 20.5% management, 7.1% professional, 33.1% services, 15.0% sales, 0.0% farming, 7.1% construction, 17.3% production (2005-2009 5-year est.).
Income: Per capita income: $24,630 (2010); Median household income: $54,412 (2010); Average household income: $62,379 (2010); Percent of households with income of $100,000 or more: 11.3% (2010); Poverty rate: 0.0% (2005-2009 5-year est.).
Taxes: Total city taxes per capita: $45 (2007); City property taxes per capita: $45 (2007).
Education: Percent of population age 25 and over with: High school diploma (including GED) or higher: 87.0% (2010); Bachelor's degree or higher: 16.7% (2010); Master's degree or higher: 3.7% (2010).
Housing: Homeownership rate: 69.4% (2010); Median home value: $111,364 (2010); Median contract rent: n/a per month (2005-2009 5-year est.); Median year structure built: 1951 (2005-2009 5-year est.).
Transportation: Commute to work: 92.9% car, 0.0% public transportation, 0.0% walk, 1.6% work from home (2005-2009 5-year est.); Travel time to work: 8.8% less than 15 minutes, 48.0% 15 to 30 minutes, 22.4% 30 to 45 minutes, 17.6% 45 to 60 minutes, 3.2% 60 minutes or more (2005-2009 5-year est.)

KEWANEE (city).
Covers a land area of 6.277 square miles and a water area of 0.013 square miles. Located at 41.24° N. Lat; 89.92° W. Long. Elevation is 850 feet.
History: Kewanee was established in 1836 by the Connecticut Association to promote Protestantism in Illinois. The town was first called Wethersfield after the town in Connecticut. When the railroad line was laid a mile north, a settlement developed around the depot. By 1857 the new settlement, named Kewanee, had surpassed the older Wethersfield, which was incorporated with Kewanee in 1924.
Population: 13,199 (1990); 12,944 (2000); 12,141 (2010); 11,805 (2015 projected); Race: 85.9% White, 4.2% Black, 0.6% Asian, 9.3% Other, 10.1% Hispanic of any race (2010); Density: 1,934.2 persons per square mile (2010); Average household size: 2.37 (2010); Median age: 38.8 (2010); Males per 100 females: 91.9 (2010); Marriage status: 26.8% never married, 50.1% now married, 9.8% widowed, 13.3% divorced (2005-2009 5-year est.); Foreign born: 3.8% (2005-2009 5-year est.); Ancestry (includes multiple ancestries): 30.5% German, 14.1% Irish, 11.3% English, 8.7% Swedish, 7.7% American (2005-2009 5-year est.).
Economy: Single-family building permits issued: 4 (2010); Multi-family building permits issued: 0 (2010); Employment by occupation: 6.0% management, 13.0% professional, 18.8% services, 28.6% sales, 0.5% farming, 6.7% construction, 26.4% production (2005-2009 5-year est.).
Income: Per capita income: $19,267 (2010); Median household income: $36,216 (2010); Average household income: $45,864 (2010); Percent of

households with income of $100,000 or more: 7.8% (2010); Poverty rate: 21.8% (2005-2009 5-year est.).
Taxes: Total city taxes per capita: $195 (2007); City property taxes per capita: $130 (2007).
Education: Percent of population age 25 and over with: High school diploma (including GED) or higher: 82.0% (2010); Bachelor's degree or higher: 14.0% (2010); Master's degree or higher: 5.4% (2010).

School District(s)
Kewanee CUSD 229 (PK-12)
    2009-10 Enrollment: 1,838 . . . . (309) 853-3341
Wethersfield CUSD 230 (PK-12)
    2009-10 Enrollment: 659 . . . . (309) 853-4860
Housing: Homeownership rate: 70.2% (2010); Median home value: $57,102 (2010); Median contract rent: $381 per month (2005-2009 5-year est.); Median year structure built: 1948 (2005-2009 5-year est.).
Hospitals: Kewanee Hospital (82 beds)
Safety: Violent crime rate: 41.5 per 10,000 population; Property crime rate: 446.8 per 10,000 population (2010).
Newspapers: Kewanee Star-Courier (Local news; Circulation 5,800)
Transportation: Commute to work: 93.7% car, 0.0% public transportation, 1.8% walk, 2.3% work from home (2005-2009 5-year est.); Travel time to work: 60.1% less than 15 minutes, 20.1% 15 to 30 minutes, 7.0% 30 to 45 minutes, 5.9% 45 to 60 minutes, 6.9% 60 minutes or more (2005-2009 5-year est.); Amtrak: train service available.

Additional Information Contacts
City of Kewanee . . . . (309) 852-2611
    http://cityofkewanee.com
Kewanee Chamber of Commerce . . . . (309) 852-2175
    http://www.kewanee-il.com

LYNN CENTER (unincorporated postal area, zip code 61262).
Covers a land area of 44.229 square miles and a water area of 0.029 square miles. Located at 41.28° N. Lat; 90.36° W. Long. Elevation is 758 feet.
Population: 878 (2000); Race: 100.0% White, 0.0% Black, 0.0% Asian, 0.0% Other, 0.0% Hispanic of any race (2000); Density: 19.9 persons per square mile (2000); Age: 22.8% under 18, 13.3% over 64 (2000); Marriage status: 16.1% never married, 72.9% now married, 3.9% widowed, 7.1% divorced (2000); Foreign born: 0.2% (2000); Ancestry (includes multiple ancestries): 25.7% German, 25.0% Swedish, 14.7% English, 10.6% Irish, 8.5% Belgian (2000).
Economy: Employment by occupation: 16.1% management, 14.9% professional, 8.3% services, 20.9% sales, 0.2% farming, 14.9% construction, 24.8% production (2000).
Income: Per capita income: $20,088 (2000); Median household income: $51,518 (2000); Poverty rate: 1.1% (2000).
Education: Percent of population age 25 and over with: High school diploma (including GED) or higher: 90.8% (2000); Bachelor's degree or higher: 9.6% (2000).
Housing: Homeownership rate: 80.8% (2000); Median home value: $93,500 (2000); Median contract rent: $243 per month (2000); Median year structure built: 1961 (2000).
Transportation: Commute to work: 92.7% car, 0.0% public transportation, 3.8% walk, 3.5% work from home (2000); Travel time to work: 12.7% less than 15 minutes, 28.9% 15 to 30 minutes, 52.1% 30 to 45 minutes, 4.6% 45 to 60 minutes, 1.7% 60 minutes or more (2000)

OPHEIM (unincorporated postal area, zip code 61468).
Covers a land area of 7.229 square miles and a water area of 0 square miles. Located at 41.25° N. Lat; 90.40° W. Long.
Population: 143 (2000); Race: 92.5% White, 7.5% Black, 0.0% Asian, 0.0% Other, 0.0% Hispanic of any race (2000); Density: 19.8 persons per square mile (2000); Age: 48.5% under 18, 6.7% over 64 (2000); Marriage status: 31.7% never married, 51.2% now married, 6.1% widowed, 11.0% divorced (2000); Foreign born: 0.0% (2000); Ancestry (includes multiple ancestries): 19.4% Swedish, 14.2% American, 11.9% Irish, 4.5% German (2000).
Economy: Employment by occupation: 3.4% management, 6.8% professional, 16.9% services, 23.7% sales, 0.0% farming, 15.3% construction, 33.9% production (2000).
Income: Per capita income: $10,793 (2000); Median household income: $40,750 (2000); Poverty rate: 5.3% (2000).
Education: Percent of population age 25 and over with: High school diploma (including GED) or higher: 88.1% (2000); Bachelor's degree or higher: 11.9% (2000).

Housing: Homeownership rate: 83.3% (2000); Median home value: $53,300 (2000); Median contract rent: $275 per month (2000); Median year structure built: before 1940 (2000).
Transportation: Commute to work: 100.0% car, 0.0% public transportation, 0.0% walk, 0.0% work from home (2000); Travel time to work: 7.8% less than 15 minutes, 9.8% 15 to 30 minutes, 62.7% 30 to 45 minutes, 19.6% 45 to 60 minutes, 0.0% 60 minutes or more (2000)

ORION (village). Covers a land area of 0.861 square miles and a water area of 0 square miles. Located at 41.35° N. Lat; 90.37° W. Long. Elevation is 774 feet.
Population: 1,885 (1990); 1,713 (2000); 1,586 (2010); 1,517 (2015 projected); Race: 98.8% White, 0.0% Black, 0.3% Asian, 0.9% Other, 2.5% Hispanic of any race (2010); Density: 1,841.6 persons per square mile (2010); Average household size: 2.42 (2010); Median age: 42.0 (2010); Males per 100 females: 98.7 (2010); Marriage status: 24.1% never married, 62.5% now married, 5.3% widowed, 8.2% divorced (2005-2009 5-year est.); Foreign born: 1.9% (2005-2009 5-year est.); Ancestry (includes multiple ancestries): 33.6% German, 23.9% Swedish, 14.7% English, 12.6% Irish, 7.0% Belgian (2005-2009 5-year est.).
Economy: Single-family building permits issued: 0 (2010); Multi-family building permits issued: 0 (2010); Employment by occupation: 14.1% management, 20.4% professional, 11.6% services, 27.5% sales, 0.0% farming, 9.5% construction, 17.0% production (2005-2009 5-year est.).
Income: Per capita income: $27,323 (2010); Median household income: $60,417 (2010); Average household income: $66,368 (2010); Percent of households with income of $100,000 or more: 16.2% (2010); Poverty rate: 2.2% (2005-2009 5-year est.).
Taxes: Total city taxes per capita: $176 (2007); City property taxes per capita: $113 (2007).
Education: Percent of population age 25 and over with: High school diploma (including GED) or higher: 92.7% (2010); Bachelor's degree or higher: 22.6% (2010); Master's degree or higher: 6.9% (2010).
School District(s)
Orion CUSD 223 (PK-12)
    2009-10 Enrollment: 1,088 . . . . (309) 526-3388
Housing: Homeownership rate: 77.3% (2010); Median home value: $119,240 (2010); Median contract rent: $449 per month (2005-2009 5-year est.); Median year structure built: 1966 (2005-2009 5-year est.).
Safety: Violent crime rate: 0.0 per 10,000 population; Property crime rate: 151.1 per 10,000 population (2010).
Newspapers: Orion Gazette (Community news; Circulation 2,500)
Transportation: Commute to work: 97.7% car, 0.0% public transportation, 0.8% walk, 1.5% work from home (2005-2009 5-year est.); Travel time to work: 25.6% less than 15 minutes, 46.3% 15 to 30 minutes, 24.8% 30 to 45 minutes, 1.3% 45 to 60 minutes, 2.0% 60 minutes or more (2005-2009 5-year est.)

OSCO (unincorporated postal area, zip code 61274). Covers a land area of 24.924 square miles and a water area of 0 square miles. Located at 41.37° N. Lat; 90.27° W. Long. Elevation is 771 feet.
Population: 404 (2000); Race: 97.8% White, 0.0% Black, 0.0% Asian, 2.2% Other, 0.0% Hispanic of any race (2000); Density: 16.2 persons per square mile (2000); Age: 27.1% under 18, 10.4% over 64 (2000); Marriage status: 20.4% never married, 72.3% now married, 3.4% widowed, 3.9% divorced (2000); Foreign born: 0.0% (2000); Ancestry (includes multiple ancestries): 29.9% German, 29.3% Swedish, 19.1% English, 9.3% American, 8.0% Belgian (2000).
Economy: Employment by occupation: 28.7% management, 0.0% professional, 15.0% services, 24.3% sales, 2.4% farming, 16.6% construction, 13.0% production (2000).
Income: Per capita income: $16,351 (2000); Median household income: $39,808 (2000); Poverty rate: 5.1% (2000).
Education: Percent of population age 25 and over with: High school diploma (including GED) or higher: 93.6% (2000); Bachelor's degree or higher: 0.0% (2000).
Housing: Homeownership rate: 74.5% (2000); Median home value: $85,800 (2000); Median contract rent: $325 per month (2000); Median year structure built: before 1940 (2000).
Transportation: Commute to work: 63.2% car, 0.0% public transportation, 9.3% walk, 27.5% work from home (2000); Travel time to work: 41.9% less than 15 minutes, 27.4% 15 to 30 minutes, 22.9% 30 to 45 minutes, 4.5% 45 to 60 minutes, 3.4% 60 minutes or more (2000)

WOODHULL (village). Covers a land area of 0.825 square miles and a water area of 0 square miles. Located at 41.17° N. Lat; 90.31° W. Long. Elevation is 810 feet.
Population: 826 (1990); 809 (2000); 799 (2010); 787 (2015 projected); Race: 98.9% White, 0.3% Black, 0.3% Asian, 0.6% Other, 1.5% Hispanic of any race (2010); Density: 968.4 persons per square mile (2010); Average household size: 2.30 (2010); Median age: 42.7 (2010); Males per 100 females: 98.3 (2010); Marriage status: 21.1% never married, 63.9% now married, 6.7% widowed, 8.2% divorced (2005-2009 5-year est.); Foreign born: 0.6% (2005-2009 5-year est.); Ancestry (includes multiple ancestries): 32.1% German, 24.1% Swedish, 15.9% Irish, 12.4% English, 9.7% American (2005-2009 5-year est.).
Economy: Single-family building permits issued: 1 (2010); Multi-family building permits issued: 0 (2010); Employment by occupation: 3.8% management, 19.7% professional, 13.2% services, 23.8% sales, 0.9% farming, 13.5% construction, 25.0% production (2005-2009 5-year est.).
Income: Per capita income: $18,529 (2010); Median household income: $36,500 (2010); Average household income: $42,752 (2010); Percent of households with income of $100,000 or more: 4.3% (2010); Poverty rate: 14.0% (2005-2009 5-year est.).
Taxes: Total city taxes per capita: $105 (2007); City property taxes per capita: $98 (2007).
Education: Percent of population age 25 and over with: High school diploma (including GED) or higher: 88.5% (2010); Bachelor's degree or higher: 12.8% (2010); Master's degree or higher: 3.5% (2010).
School District(s)
Alwood CUSD 225 (PK-12)
    2009-10 Enrollment: 444 . . . . (309) 334-2719
Housing: Homeownership rate: 71.2% (2010); Median home value: $84,143 (2010); Median contract rent: $400 per month (2005-2009 5-year est.); Median year structure built: 1948 (2005-2009 5-year est.).
Transportation: Commute to work: 93.3% car, 0.0% public transportation, 3.4% walk, 0.0% work from home (2005-2009 5-year est.); Travel time to work: 35.1% less than 15 minutes, 19.5% 15 to 30 minutes, 25.6% 30 to 45 minutes, 13.4% 45 to 60 minutes, 6.4% 60 minutes or more (2005-2009 5-year est.)

Iroquois County

Located in eastern Illinois; bounded on the east by Indiana; drained by the Iroquois River and Sugar Creek. Covers a land area of 1,116.43 square miles, a water area of 1.60 square miles, and is located in the Central Time Zone at 40.74° N. Lat., 87.83° W. Long. The county was founded in 1833. County seat is Watseka.

Weather Station: Watseka 2 NW										Elevation: 620 feet	
	Jan	Feb	Mar	Apr	May	Jun	Jul	Aug	Sep	Oct	Nov	Dec
High	32	37	48	61	72	82	84	83	78	64	50	36
Low	16	19	28	38	49	59	63	60	52	40	32	20
Precip	1.8	1.7	2.9	3.8	4.0	4.2	4.4	3.5	3.3	3.3	3.2	2.5
Snow	5.8	5.0	1.9	0.8	0.0	0.0	0.0	0.0	0.0	tr	0.7	5.2

High and Low temperatures in degrees Fahrenheit; Precipitation and Snow in inches

Population: 30,787 (1990); 31,334 (2000); 30,245 (2010); 29,666 (2015 projected); Race: 93.8% White, 1.2% Black, 0.5% Asian, 4.6% Other, 5.9% Hispanic of any race (2010); Density: 27.1 persons per square mile (2010); Average household size: 2.48 (2010); Median age: 41.3 (2010); Males per 100 females: 96.1 (2010).
Religion: Five largest groups: 12.9% Catholic Church, 11.4% Lutheran Church—Missouri Synod, 9.7% The United Methodist Church, 7.0% Evangelical Lutheran Church in America, 5.0% Christian Churches and Churches of Christ (2000).
Economy: Unemployment rate: 8.3% (August 2011); Total civilian labor force: 16,986 (August 2011); Leading industries: 27.2% health care and social assistance; 15.0% manufacturing; 14.7% retail trade (2009); Farms: 1,471 totaling 677,803 acres (2007); Companies that employ 500 or more persons: 0 (2009); Companies that employ 100 to 499 persons: 7 (2009); Companies that employ less than 100 persons: 699 (2009); Black-owned businesses: n/a (2007); Hispanic-owned businesses: n/a (2007); Asian-owned businesses: n/a (2007); Women-owned businesses: 646 (2007); Retail sales per capita: $9,602 (2010). Single-family building permits issued: 33 (2010); Multi-family building permits issued: 11 (2010).
Income: Per capita income: $22,727 (2010); Median household income: $46,545 (2010); Average household income: $56,969 (2010); Percent of

households with income of $100,000 or more: 10.8% (2010); Poverty rate: 12.2% (2009); Bankruptcy rate: 3.69% (2010).

Taxes: Total county taxes per capita: $110 (2007); County property taxes per capita: $105 (2007).

Education: Percent of population age 25 and over with: High school diploma (including GED) or higher: 85.6% (2010); Bachelor's degree or higher: 12.8% (2010); Master's degree or higher: 4.2% (2010).

Housing: Homeownership rate: 76.1% (2010); Median home value: $99,769 (2010); Median contract rent: $432 per month (2005-2009 5-year est.); Median year structure built: 1954 (2005-2009 5-year est.)

Health: Birth rate: 126.3 per 10,000 population (2009); Death rate: 128.3 per 10,000 population (2009); Age-adjusted cancer mortality rate: 245.7 deaths per 100,000 population (2007); Number of physicians: 8.7 per 10,000 population (2008); Hospital beds: 28.0 per 10,000 population (2007); Hospital admissions: 815.8 per 10,000 population (2007).

Elections: 2008 Presidential election results: 34.1% Obama, 64.0% McCain, 0.9% Nader

National and State Parks: Iroquois County State Conservation Area

Additional Information Contacts

Iroquois County Government . . . . (815) 432-6960
http://www.co.iroquois.il.us
City of Watseka . . . . (815) 432-2711
http://www.watsekacity.com
Gilman Chamber of Commerce . . . . (815) 265-4818
Onarga Chamber of Commerce
http://onarga.net/OnargaChamber.html
Watseka Area Chamber of Commerce . . . . (815) 432-2416
http://www.watsekachamber.org

Iroquois County Communities

ASHKUM (village). Covers a land area of 0.820 square miles and a water area of 0 square miles. Located at 40.88° N. Lat; 87.95° W. Long. Elevation is 669 feet.

Population: 681 (1990); 724 (2000); 679 (2010); 655 (2015 projected); Race: 97.1% White, 0.1% Black, 0.0% Asian, 2.8% Other, 1.6% Hispanic of any race (2010); Density: 828.3 persons per square mile (2010); Average household size: 2.40 (2010); Median age: 41.4 (2010); Males per 100 females: 100.9 (2010); Marriage status: 13.7% never married, 73.9% now married, 3.6% widowed, 8.8% divorced (2005-2009 5-year est.); Foreign born: 0.0% (2005-2009 5-year est.); Ancestry (includes multiple ancestries): 45.9% German, 25.2% Irish, 15.2% French, 14.3% English, 13.3% American (2005-2009 5-year est.).

Economy: Single-family building permits issued: 0 (2010); Multi-family building permits issued: 4 (2010); Employment by occupation: 10.0% management, 19.6% professional, 7.7% services, 26.5% sales, 0.0% farming, 21.5% construction, 14.6% production (2005-2009 5-year est.).

Income: Per capita income: $22,838 (2010); Median household income: $42,000 (2010); Average household income: $54,317 (2010); Percent of households with income of $100,000 or more: 10.6% (2010); Poverty rate: 6.2% (2005-2009 5-year est.).

Taxes: Total city taxes per capita: $87 (2007); City property taxes per capita: $77 (2007).

Education: Percent of population age 25 and over with: High school diploma (including GED) or higher: 87.1% (2010); Bachelor's degree or higher: 13.3% (2010); Master's degree or higher: 5.0% (2010).

School District(s)

Central CUSD 4 (PK-12)
2009-10 Enrollment: 1,162 . . . . (815) 694-2231

Housing: Homeownership rate: 78.7% (2010); Median home value: $121,667 (2010); Median contract rent: $482 per month (2005-2009 5-year est.); Median year structure built: 1954 (2005-2009 5-year est.).

Transportation: Commute to work: 88.1% car, 0.0% public transportation, 6.2% walk, 4.2% work from home (2005-2009 5-year est.); Travel time to work: 26.1% less than 15 minutes, 29.7% 15 to 30 minutes, 33.3% 30 to 45 minutes, 0.0% 45 to 60 minutes, 10.8% 60 minutes or more (2005-2009 5-year est.)

BEAVERVILLE (village). Covers a land area of 0.262 square miles and a water area of 0.004 square miles. Located at 40.95° N. Lat; 87.65° W. Long. Elevation is 676 feet.

Population: 287 (1990); 391 (2000); 387 (2010); 387 (2015 projected); Race: 87.6% White, 10.1% Black, 0.0% Asian, 2.3% Other, 1.0% Hispanic of any race (2010); Density: 1,476.2 persons per square mile (2010); Average household size: 2.63 (2010); Median age: 38.4 (2010); Males per

100 females: 98.5 (2010); Marriage status: 26.1% never married, 61.4% now married, 4.9% widowed, 7.5% divorced (2005-2009 5-year est.); Foreign born: 0.0% (2005-2009 5-year est.); Ancestry (includes multiple ancestries): 23.2% American, 22.5% French, 21.8% German, 11.0% Irish, 8.9% French Canadian (2005-2009 5-year est.).

Economy: Single-family building permits issued: 1 (2010); Multi-family building permits issued: 0 (2010); Employment by occupation: 10.3% management, 4.7% professional, 14.0% services, 43.0% sales, 1.4% farming, 10.3% construction, 16.4% production (2005-2009 5-year est.).

Income: Per capita income: $21,499 (2010); Median household income: $48,661 (2010); Average household income: $57,517 (2010); Percent of households with income of $100,000 or more: 14.3% (2010); Poverty rate: 19.5% (2005-2009 5-year est.).

Taxes: Total city taxes per capita: $37 (2007); City property taxes per capita: $34 (2007).

Education: Percent of population age 25 and over with: High school diploma (including GED) or higher: 82.6% (2010); Bachelor's degree or higher: 8.9% (2010); Master's degree or higher: 3.1% (2010).

Housing: Homeownership rate: 80.3% (2010); Median home value: $103,571 (2010); Median contract rent: $427 per month (2005-2009 5-year est.); Median year structure built: before 1940 (2005-2009 5-year est.).

Transportation: Commute to work: 90.0% car, 0.0% public transportation, 5.7% walk, 2.9% work from home (2005-2009 5-year est.); Travel time to work: 15.3% less than 15 minutes, 24.1% 15 to 30 minutes, 49.3% 30 to 45 minutes, 4.9% 45 to 60 minutes, 6.4% 60 minutes or more (2005-2009 5-year est.)

BUCKLEY (village). Covers a land area of 0.345 square miles and a water area of 0.006 square miles. Located at 40.59° N. Lat; 88.03° W. Long. Elevation is 702 feet.

Population: 557 (1990); 593 (2000); 570 (2010); 557 (2015 projected); Race: 96.5% White, 0.2% Black, 0.4% Asian, 3.0% Other, 6.3% Hispanic of any race (2010); Density: 1,654.4 persons per square mile (2010); Average household size: 2.39 (2010); Median age: 41.8 (2010); Males per 100 females: 100.0 (2010); Marriage status: 30.9% never married, 58.2% now married, 6.9% widowed, 4.0% divorced (2005-2009 5-year est.); Foreign born: 2.2% (2005-2009 5-year est.); Ancestry (includes multiple ancestries): 32.9% German, 24.6% American, 14.0% Irish, 5.9% Hungarian, 5.0% English (2005-2009 5-year est.).

Economy: Single-family building permits issued: 0 (2010); Multi-family building permits issued: 0 (2010); Employment by occupation: 13.4% management, 5.6% professional, 11.7% services, 31.3% sales, 2.2% farming, 10.6% construction, 25.1% production (2005-2009 5-year est.).

Income: Per capita income: $26,592 (2010); Median household income: $50,000 (2010); Average household income: $63,582 (2010); Percent of households with income of $100,000 or more: 11.8% (2010); Poverty rate: 12.3% (2005-2009 5-year est.).

Taxes: Total city taxes per capita: $133 (2007); City property taxes per capita: $68 (2007).

Education: Percent of population age 25 and over with: High school diploma (including GED) or higher: 87.7% (2010); Bachelor's degree or higher: 15.3% (2010); Master's degree or higher: 3.3% (2010).

Housing: Homeownership rate: 79.8% (2010); Median home value: $94,286 (2010); Median contract rent: $403 per month (2005-2009 5-year est.); Median year structure built: 1945 (2005-2009 5-year est.).

Transportation: Commute to work: 96.1% car, 0.0% public transportation, 3.9% walk, 0.0% work from home (2005-2009 5-year est.); Travel time to work: 36.9% less than 15 minutes, 21.2% 15 to 30 minutes, 17.3% 30 to 45 minutes, 18.4% 45 to 60 minutes, 6.1% 60 minutes or more (2005-2009 5-year est.)

CHEBANSE (village). Covers a land area of 0.437 square miles and a water area of 0 square miles. Located at 41.00° N. Lat; 87.91° W. Long. Elevation is 666 feet.

History: Chebanse developed as an agricultural community, settled by many people of German descent.

Population: 1,182 (1990); 1,148 (2000); 1,101 (2010); 1,080 (2015 projected); Race: 95.5% White, 1.0% Black, 0.5% Asian, 2.9% Other, 3.0% Hispanic of any race (2010); Density: 2,517.9 persons per square mile (2010); Average household size: 2.63 (2010); Median age: 37.6 (2010); Males per 100 females: 91.1 (2010); Marriage status: 39.3% never married, 44.4% now married, 5.0% widowed, 11.3% divorced (2005-2009 5-year est.); Foreign born: 0.6% (2005-2009 5-year est.); Ancestry (includes multiple ancestries): 33.0% German, 15.7% Irish, 13.4% French, 12.6% Polish, 9.5% American (2005-2009 5-year est.).

Economy: Single-family building permits issued: 0 (2010); Multi-family building permits issued: 0 (2010); Employment by occupation: 9.2% management, 10.3% professional, 14.7% services, 24.5% sales, 0.5% farming, 25.0% construction, 15.8% production (2005-2009 5-year est.).
Income: Per capita income: $22,075 (2010); Median household income: $52,358 (2010); Average household income: $58,146 (2010); Percent of households with income of $100,000 or more: 11.2% (2010); Poverty rate: 4.7% (2005-2009 5-year est.).
Taxes: Total city taxes per capita: $95 (2007); City property taxes per capita: $58 (2007).
Education: Percent of population age 25 and over with: High school diploma (including GED) or higher: 92.0% (2010); Bachelor's degree or higher: 9.7% (2010); Master's degree or higher: 3.1% (2010).

School District(s)
Central CUSD 4 (PK-12)
    2009-10 Enrollment: 1,162 . . . . (815) 694-2231
Housing: Homeownership rate: 80.1% (2010); Median home value: $135,256 (2010); Median contract rent: $594 per month (2005-2009 5-year est.); Median year structure built: before 1940 (2005-2009 5-year est.).
Transportation: Commute to work: 92.3% car, 1.4% public transportation, 1.3% walk, 3.9% work from home (2005-2009 5-year est.); Travel time to work: 23.7% less than 15 minutes, 52.8% 15 to 30 minutes, 10.0% 30 to 45 minutes, 1.6% 45 to 60 minutes, 11.9% 60 minutes or more (2005-2009 5-year est.)

CISSNA PARK (village). Covers a land area of 0.719 square miles and a water area of 0 square miles. Located at 40.56° N. Lat; 87.89° W. Long. Elevation is 666 feet.
History: Cissna Park developed as the center of a community of members of the Apostolic Church, known as New Amish, led by Samuel Frolich of Switzerland.
Population: 805 (1990); 811 (2000); 819 (2010); 819 (2015 projected); Race: 98.2% White, 0.5% Black, 0.6% Asian, 0.7% Other, 1.5% Hispanic of any race (2010); Density: 1,139.6 persons per square mile (2010); Average household size: 2.43 (2010); Median age: 43.0 (2010); Males per 100 females: 90.9 (2010); Marriage status: 22.6% never married, 58.3% now married, 8.7% widowed, 10.4% divorced (2005-2009 5-year est.); Foreign born: 0.5% (2005-2009 5-year est.); Ancestry (includes multiple ancestries): 61.2% German, 13.4% Irish, 8.7% American, 6.7% French, 6.4% Swiss (2005-2009 5-year est.).
Economy: Single-family building permits issued: 0 (2010); Multi-family building permits issued: 0 (2010); Employment by occupation: 6.5% management, 16.0% professional, 16.2% services, 33.3% sales, 3.2% farming, 16.2% construction, 8.6% production (2005-2009 5-year est.).
Income: Per capita income: $22,011 (2010); Median household income: $45,731 (2010); Average household income: $53,138 (2010); Percent of households with income of $100,000 or more: 7.8% (2010); Poverty rate: 7.6% (2005-2009 5-year est.).
Taxes: Total city taxes per capita: $144 (2007); City property taxes per capita: $140 (2007).
Education: Percent of population age 25 and over with: High school diploma (including GED) or higher: 87.7% (2010); Bachelor's degree or higher: 16.1% (2010); Master's degree or higher: 3.9% (2010).

School District(s)
Cissna Park CUSD 6 (KG-12)
    2009-10 Enrollment: 326 . . . . (815) 457-2171
Housing: Homeownership rate: 82.0% (2010); Median home value: $93,265 (2010); Median contract rent: $361 per month (2005-2009 5-year est.); Median year structure built: 1953 (2005-2009 5-year est.).
Newspapers: Cissna Park News (Community news; Circulation 1,554); Rankin Independent (Community news; Circulation 472)
Transportation: Commute to work: 85.4% car, 0.0% public transportation, 4.8% walk, 6.7% work from home (2005-2009 5-year est.); Travel time to work: 53.8% less than 15 minutes, 15.9% 15 to 30 minutes, 19.0% 30 to 45 minutes, 3.3% 45 to 60 minutes, 7.9% 60 minutes or more (2005-2009 5-year est.)

CLIFTON (village). Covers a land area of 0.887 square miles and a water area of 0 square miles. Located at 40.93° N. Lat; 87.93° W. Long. Elevation is 669 feet.
Population: 1,364 (1990); 1,317 (2000); 1,149 (2010); 1,079 (2015 projected); Race: 99.0% White, 0.0% Black, 0.3% Asian, 0.8% Other, 0.9% Hispanic of any race (2010); Density: 1,295.7 persons per square mile (2010); Average household size: 2.46 (2010); Median age: 38.0 (2010); Males per 100 females: 90.9 (2010); Marriage status: 23.7% never married,

66.6% now married, 1.9% widowed, 7.8% divorced (2005-2009 5-year est.); Foreign born: 1.6% (2005-2009 5-year est.); Ancestry (includes multiple ancestries): 36.5% German, 23.5% Irish, 16.0% American, 15.8% French, 10.9% English (2005-2009 5-year est.).
Economy: Single-family building permits issued: 0 (2010); Multi-family building permits issued: 0 (2010); Employment by occupation: 8.4% management, 27.4% professional, 15.7% services, 23.1% sales, 0.0% farming, 10.2% construction, 15.3% production (2005-2009 5-year est.).
Income: Per capita income: $27,292 (2010); Median household income: $60,509 (2010); Average household income: $67,468 (2010); Percent of households with income of $100,000 or more: 18.6% (2010); Poverty rate: 10.1% (2005-2009 5-year est.).
Taxes: Total city taxes per capita: $85 (2007); City property taxes per capita: $79 (2007).
Education: Percent of population age 25 and over with: High school diploma (including GED) or higher: 91.3% (2010); Bachelor's degree or higher: 15.8% (2010); Master's degree or higher: 4.7% (2010).

School District(s)
Central CUSD 4 (PK-12)
    2009-10 Enrollment: 1,162 . . . . (815) 694-2231
Housing: Homeownership rate: 77.5% (2010); Median home value: $131,065 (2010); Median contract rent: $520 per month (2005-2009 5-year est.); Median year structure built: 1951 (2005-2009 5-year est.).
Transportation: Commute to work: 91.1% car, 0.0% public transportation, 5.9% walk, 2.0% work from home (2005-2009 5-year est.); Travel time to work: 28.3% less than 15 minutes, 48.8% 15 to 30 minutes, 15.8% 30 to 45 minutes, 4.2% 45 to 60 minutes, 2.9% 60 minutes or more (2005-2009 5-year est.)

CRESCENT CITY (village). Aka Crescent. Covers a land area of 0.503 square miles and a water area of 0 square miles. Located at 40.77° N. Lat; 87.85° W. Long. Elevation is 640 feet.
Population: 549 (1990); 631 (2000); 587 (2010); 573 (2015 projected); Race: 95.9% White, 0.0% Black, 1.5% Asian, 2.6% Other, 1.9% Hispanic of any race (2010); Density: 1,166.3 persons per square mile (2010); Average household size: 2.47 (2010); Median age: 39.8 (2010); Males per 100 females: 103.8 (2010); Marriage status: 17.5% never married, 64.9% now married, 3.9% widowed, 13.7% divorced (2005-2009 5-year est.); Foreign born: 1.3% (2005-2009 5-year est.); Ancestry (includes multiple ancestries): 50.5% German, 19.1% American, 15.1% Irish, 10.0% English, 7.0% French (2005-2009 5-year est.).
Economy: Single-family building permits issued: 0 (2010); Multi-family building permits issued: 3 (2010); Employment by occupation: 6.6% management, 19.5% professional, 11.4% services, 29.0% sales, 2.2% farming, 17.6% construction, 13.6% production (2005-2009 5-year est.).
Income: Per capita income: $23,847 (2010); Median household income: $51,449 (2010); Average household income: $59,223 (2010); Percent of households with income of $100,000 or more: 10.1% (2010); Poverty rate: 3.2% (2005-2009 5-year est.).
Taxes: Total city taxes per capita: $100 (2007); City property taxes per capita: $95 (2007).
Education: Percent of population age 25 and over with: High school diploma (including GED) or higher: 89.1% (2010); Bachelor's degree or higher: 13.1% (2010); Master's degree or higher: 2.8% (2010).

School District(s)
Crescent Iroquois CUSD 249 (KG-12)
    2009-10 Enrollment: 103 . . . . (815) 683-2141
Housing: Homeownership rate: 80.7% (2010); Median home value: $116,279 (2010); Median contract rent: $361 per month (2005-2009 5-year est.); Median year structure built: 1966 (2005-2009 5-year est.).
Transportation: Commute to work: 96.3% car, 2.2% public transportation, 1.5% walk, 0.0% work from home (2005-2009 5-year est.); Travel time to work: 35.7% less than 15 minutes, 32.7% 15 to 30 minutes, 17.1% 30 to 45 minutes, 13.0% 45 to 60 minutes, 1.5% 60 minutes or more (2005-2009 5-year est.)

DANFORTH (village). Covers a land area of 0.477 square miles and a water area of 0 square miles. Located at 40.82° N. Lat; 87.97° W. Long. Elevation is 653 feet.
History: Danforth was settled by immigrants from the Netherlands, on land purchased in the 1850's by A.H. and George Danforth. The swampy land was ditched and drained by the Dutch, who built windmills and established farms.
Population: 460 (1990); 587 (2000); 556 (2010); 539 (2015 projected); Race: 97.5% White, 0.4% Black, 0.0% Asian, 2.2% Other, 2.0% Hispanic

of any race (2010); Density: 1,165.8 persons per square mile (2010); Average household size: 2.53 (2010); Median age: 45.4 (2010); Males per 100 females: 91.7 (2010); Marriage status: 16.9% never married, 23.4% now married, 58.5% widowed, 1.2% divorced (2005-2009 5-year est.); Foreign born: 0.3% (2005-2009 5-year est.); Ancestry (includes multiple ancestries): 10.1% German, 4.6% American, 3.7% French, 2.9% Irish, 1.7% French Canadian (2005-2009 5-year est.).
Economy: Single-family building permits issued: 0 (2010); Multi-family building permits issued: 0 (2010); Employment by occupation: 4.4% management, 23.3% professional, 16.7% services, 20.3% sales, 0.0% farming, 16.7% construction, 18.5% production (2005-2009 5-year est.).
Income: Per capita income: $19,822 (2010); Median household income: $43,594 (2010); Average household income: $52,313 (2010); Percent of households with income of $100,000 or more: 10.0% (2010); Poverty rate: 8.4% (2005-2009 5-year est.).
Taxes: Total city taxes per capita: $63 (2007); City property taxes per capita: $62 (2007).
Education: Percent of population age 25 and over with: High school diploma (including GED) or higher: 85.9% (2010); Bachelor's degree or higher: 11.9% (2010); Master's degree or higher: 4.2% (2010).

School District(s)
Iroquois West CUSD 10 (PK-12)
    2009-10 Enrollment: 970 . . . . (815) 265-4642
Housing: Homeownership rate: 74.1% (2010); Median home value: $113,500 (2010); Median contract rent: $467 per month (2005-2009 5-year est.); Median year structure built: before 1940 (2005-2009 5-year est.).
Transportation: Commute to work: 91.6% car, 0.0% public transportation, 0.9% walk, 4.7% work from home (2005-2009 5-year est.); Travel time to work: 28.4% less than 15 minutes, 18.1% 15 to 30 minutes, 32.4% 30 to 45 minutes, 10.3% 45 to 60 minutes, 10.8% 60 minutes or more (2005-2009 5-year est.)

DONOVAN (village). Covers a land area of 0.311 square miles and a water area of 0 square miles. Located at 40.88° N. Lat; 87.61° W. Long. Elevation is 673 feet.
History: Donovan was settled by Swedish immigrants after the railroad was built here, and named for the operator of the Buckhorn Tavern.
Population: 361 (1990); 351 (2000); 326 (2010); 319 (2015 projected); Race: 96.3% White, 1.2% Black, 0.0% Asian, 2.5% Other, 2.8% Hispanic of any race (2010); Density: 1,047.1 persons per square mile (2010); Average household size: 2.57 (2010); Median age: 40.7 (2010); Males per 100 females: 94.0 (2010); Marriage status: 15.7% never married, 65.9% now married, 6.9% widowed, 11.5% divorced (2005-2009 5-year est.); Foreign born: 3.4% (2005-2009 5-year est.); Ancestry (includes multiple ancestries): 20.0% American, 19.4% German, 15.2% French, 9.6% Irish, 7.3% Dutch (2005-2009 5-year est.).
Economy: Single-family building permits issued: 1 (2010); Multi-family building permits issued: 0 (2010); Employment by occupation: 18.2% management, 14.4% professional, 24.1% services, 12.8% sales, 0.0% farming, 9.6% construction, 20.9% production (2005-2009 5-year est.).
Income: Per capita income: $24,947 (2010); Median household income: $53,214 (2010); Average household income: $65,335 (2010); Percent of households with income of $100,000 or more: 11.8% (2010); Poverty rate: 7.4% (2005-2009 5-year est.).
Taxes: Total city taxes per capita: $33 (2007); City property taxes per capita: $33 (2007).
Education: Percent of population age 25 and over with: High school diploma (including GED) or higher: 89.5% (2010); Bachelor's degree or higher: 15.5% (2010); Master's degree or higher: 5.0% (2010).

School District(s)
Donovan CUSD 3 (PK-12)
    2009-10 Enrollment: 419 . . . . (815) 486-7397
Housing: Homeownership rate: 76.4% (2010); Median home value: $93,636 (2010); Median contract rent: $465 per month (2005-2009 5-year est.); Median year structure built: 1943 (2005-2009 5-year est.).
Transportation: Commute to work: 90.0% car, 0.0% public transportation, 2.8% walk, 2.2% work from home (2005-2009 5-year est.); Travel time to work: 19.9% less than 15 minutes, 52.3% 15 to 30 minutes, 10.8% 30 to 45 minutes, 9.7% 45 to 60 minutes, 7.4% 60 minutes or more (2005-2009 5-year est.)

GILMAN (city). Covers a land area of 2.114 square miles and a water area of 0.020 square miles. Located at 40.76° N. Lat; 87.99° W. Long. Elevation is 650 feet.
History: Incorporated 1867.

Population: 1,816 (1990); 1,793 (2000); 1,794 (2010); 1,791 (2015 projected); Race: 88.9% White, 0.7% Black, 0.2% Asian, 10.2% Other, 14.0% Hispanic of any race (2010); Density: 848.5 persons per square mile (2010); Average household size: 2.52 (2010); Median age: 41.7 (2010); Males per 100 females: 92.5 (2010); Marriage status: 25.9% never married, 54.4% now married, 6.5% widowed, 13.1% divorced (2005-2009 5-year est.); Foreign born: 9.7% (2005-2009 5-year est.); Ancestry (includes multiple ancestries): 27.9% German, 13.2% Irish, 11.8% American, 7.1% English, 4.8% French (2005-2009 5-year est.).
Economy: Single-family building permits issued: 2 (2010); Multi-family building permits issued: 0 (2010); Employment by occupation: 5.3% management, 23.0% professional, 21.2% services, 10.0% sales, 0.2% farming, 15.2% construction, 25.2% production (2005-2009 5-year est.).
Income: Per capita income: $20,466 (2010); Median household income: $42,909 (2010); Average household income: $52,236 (2010); Percent of households with income of $100,000 or more: 6.9% (2010); Poverty rate: 11.9% (2005-2009 5-year est.).
Taxes: Total city taxes per capita: $260 (2007); City property taxes per capita: $218 (2007).
Education: Percent of population age 25 and over with: High school diploma (including GED) or higher: 81.5% (2010); Bachelor's degree or higher: 10.9% (2010); Master's degree or higher: 3.1% (2010).

School District(s)
Iroquois West CUSD 10 (PK-12)
    2009-10 Enrollment: 970 . . . . (815) 265-4642
Housing: Homeownership rate: 74.9% (2010); Median home value: $102,432 (2010); Median contract rent: $412 per month (2005-2009 5-year est.); Median year structure built: 1956 (2005-2009 5-year est.).
Safety: Violent crime rate: 6.1 per 10,000 population; Property crime rate: 30.3 per 10,000 population (2010).
Newspapers: Gilman Star (Local news; Circulation 2,900)
Transportation: Commute to work: 91.2% car, 0.0% public transportation, 3.8% walk, 3.7% work from home (2005-2009 5-year est.); Travel time to work: 39.8% less than 15 minutes, 25.2% 15 to 30 minutes, 18.3% 30 to 45 minutes, 6.4% 45 to 60 minutes, 10.3% 60 minutes or more (2005-2009 5-year est.); Amtrak: train service available.
Additional Information Contacts
Gilman Chamber of Commerce . . . . (815) 265-4818

IROQUOIS (village). Covers a land area of 0.598 square miles and a water area of 0 square miles. Located at 40.82° N. Lat; 87.58° W. Long. Elevation is 659 feet.
History: Iroquois was the name given by the Big Four Railroad in 1871 to its station on the Iroquois River. In 1875 the town of Concord, on the other side of the river, was incorporated under the Iroquois name.
Population: 199 (1990); 207 (2000); 203 (2010); 198 (2015 projected); Race: 96.1% White, 1.0% Black, 0.0% Asian, 3.0% Other, 2.5% Hispanic of any race (2010); Density: 339.4 persons per square mile (2010); Average household size: 2.57 (2010); Median age: 40.4 (2010); Males per 100 females: 88.0 (2010); Marriage status: 13.7% never married, 70.1% now married, 6.8% widowed, 9.4% divorced (2005-2009 5-year est.); Foreign born: 0.0% (2005-2009 5-year est.); Ancestry (includes multiple ancestries): 48.3% German, 31.7% Irish, 24.1% American, 4.1% French, 2.1% Scotch-Irish (2005-2009 5-year est.).
Economy: Single-family building permits issued: 0 (2010); Multi-family building permits issued: 0 (2010); Employment by occupation: 11.8% management, 0.0% professional, 36.8% services, 17.6% sales, 2.9% farming, 2.9% construction, 27.9% production (2005-2009 5-year est.).
Income: Per capita income: $24,947 (2010); Median household income: $51,786 (2010); Average household income: $61,044 (2010); Percent of households with income of $100,000 or more: 11.4% (2010); Poverty rate: 7.6% (2005-2009 5-year est.).
Taxes: Total city taxes per capita: $70 (2007); City property taxes per capita: $50 (2007).
Education: Percent of population age 25 and over with: High school diploma (including GED) or higher: 89.8% (2010); Bachelor's degree or higher: 16.1% (2010); Master's degree or higher: 5.8% (2010).
Housing: Homeownership rate: 77.2% (2010); Median home value: $91,667 (2010); Median contract rent: $388 per month (2005-2009 5-year est.); Median year structure built: 1947 (2005-2009 5-year est.).
Transportation: Commute to work: 95.6% car, 0.0% public transportation, 4.4% walk, 0.0% work from home (2005-2009 5-year est.); Travel time to work: 19.1% less than 15 minutes, 52.9% 15 to 30 minutes, 10.3% 30 to 45 minutes, 14.7% 45 to 60 minutes, 2.9% 60 minutes or more (2005-2009 5-year est.)

LODA (village). Covers a land area of 1.448 square miles and a water area of 0.008 square miles. Located at 40.51° N. Lat; 88.07° W. Long. Elevation is 778 feet.
Population: 390 (1990); 419 (2000); 355 (2010); 331 (2015 projected); Race: 93.2% White, 1.4% Black, 0.0% Asian, 5.4% Other, 7.3% Hispanic of any race (2010); Density: 245.2 persons per square mile (2010); Average household size: 2.37 (2010); Median age: 45.9 (2010); Males per 100 females: 96.1 (2010); Marriage status: 17.2% never married, 64.0% now married, 3.2% widowed, 15.6% divorced (2005-2009 5-year est.); Foreign born: 1.1% (2005-2009 5-year est.); Ancestry (includes multiple ancestries): 32.6% German, 18.4% American, 13.1% English, 8.8% Irish, 6.7% Polish (2005-2009 5-year est.).
Economy: Single-family building permits issued: 1 (2010); Multi-family building permits issued: 0 (2010); Employment by occupation: 5.7% management, 8.6% professional, 22.0% services, 23.9% sales, 1.9% farming, 7.2% construction, 30.6% production (2005-2009 5-year est.).
Income: Per capita income: $28,934 (2010); Median household income: $50,658 (2010); Average household income: $66,283 (2010); Percent of households with income of $100,000 or more: 12.7% (2010); Poverty rate: 9.9% (2005-2009 5-year est.).
Taxes: Total city taxes per capita: $100 (2007); City property taxes per capita: $49 (2007).
Education: Percent of population age 25 and over with: High school diploma (including GED) or higher: 87.5% (2010); Bachelor's degree or higher: 14.8% (2010); Master's degree or higher: 8.7% (2010).
Housing: Homeownership rate: 78.7% (2010); Median home value: $88,235 (2010); Median contract rent: $346 per month (2005-2009 5-year est.); Median year structure built: before 1940 (2005-2009 5-year est.).
Transportation: Commute to work: 88.2% car, 0.0% public transportation, 6.4% walk, 5.4% work from home (2005-2009 5-year est.); Travel time to work: 42.7% less than 15 minutes, 28.1% 15 to 30 minutes, 15.1% 30 to 45 minutes, 6.3% 45 to 60 minutes, 7.8% 60 minutes or more (2005-2009 5-year est.)

MARTINTON (village). Covers a land area of 0.251 square miles and a water area of 0 square miles. Located at 40.91° N. Lat; 87.72° W. Long. Elevation is 627 feet.
History: Martinton was founded in 1871 as a station on the Chicago & Eastern Illinois Railway, and named for Porter Martin, an early resident.
Population: 299 (1990); 375 (2000); 348 (2010); 340 (2015 projected); Race: 95.1% White, 3.2% Black, 0.0% Asian, 1.7% Other, 2.6% Hispanic of any race (2010); Density: 1,385.3 persons per square mile (2010); Average household size: 2.90 (2010); Median age: 33.1 (2010); Males per 100 females: 98.9 (2010); Marriage status: 12.1% never married, 70.7% now married, 3.5% widowed, 13.7% divorced (2005-2009 5-year est.); Foreign born: 2.3% (2005-2009 5-year est.); Ancestry (includes multiple ancestries): 34.6% German, 24.9% French, 14.4% American, 12.2% Italian, 11.0% Irish (2005-2009 5-year est.).
Economy: Single-family building permits issued: 0 (2010); Multi-family building permits issued: 0 (2010); Employment by occupation: 14.1% management, 11.1% professional, 16.2% services, 15.2% sales, 0.0% farming, 15.7% construction, 27.8% production (2005-2009 5-year est.).
Income: Per capita income: $21,596 (2010); Median household income: $57,258 (2010); Average household income: $63,917 (2010); Percent of households with income of $100,000 or more: 10.8% (2010); Poverty rate: 2.3% (2005-2009 5-year est.).
Taxes: Total city taxes per capita: $82 (2007); City property taxes per capita: $77 (2007).
Education: Percent of population age 25 and over with: High school diploma (including GED) or higher: 89.0% (2010); Bachelor's degree or higher: 8.1% (2010); Master's degree or higher: 1.4% (2010).
Housing: Homeownership rate: 77.5% (2010); Median home value: $108,553 (2010); Median contract rent: $335 per month (2005-2009 5-year est.); Median year structure built: 1971 (2005-2009 5-year est.).
Transportation: Commute to work: 93.7% car, 0.0% public transportation, 5.3% walk, 0.0% work from home (2005-2009 5-year est.); Travel time to work: 8.5% less than 15 minutes, 33.3% 15 to 30 minutes, 47.1% 30 to 45 minutes, 0.0% 45 to 60 minutes, 11.1% 60 minutes or more (2005-2009 5-year est.)

MILFORD (village). Covers a land area of 0.632 square miles and a water area of 0 square miles. Located at 40.62° N. Lat; 87.69° W. Long. Elevation is 669 feet.

History: Milford, incorporated as a village in 1874, was first laid out in 1836 by William Pickerel who operated a mill near a ford on Sugar Creek.
Population: 1,512 (1990); 1,369 (2000); 1,291 (2010); 1,247 (2015 projected); Race: 98.8% White, 0.2% Black, 0.0% Asian, 1.1% Other, 2.6% Hispanic of any race (2010); Density: 2,043.4 persons per square mile (2010); Average household size: 2.25 (2010); Median age: 45.1 (2010); Males per 100 females: 100.5 (2010); Marriage status: 21.7% never married, 62.8% now married, 5.9% widowed, 9.7% divorced (2005-2009 5-year est.); Foreign born: 3.1% (2005-2009 5-year est.); Ancestry (includes multiple ancestries): 40.5% German, 17.9% English, 14.6% Irish, 9.8% American, 4.0% French (2005-2009 5-year est.).
Economy: Single-family building permits issued: 0 (2010); Multi-family building permits issued: 0 (2010); Employment by occupation: 9.1% management, 14.6% professional, 21.1% services, 17.4% sales, 1.9% farming, 6.0% construction, 29.9% production (2005-2009 5-year est.).
Income: Per capita income: $22,400 (2010); Median household income: $39,425 (2010); Average household income: $50,506 (2010); Percent of households with income of $100,000 or more: 8.9% (2010); Poverty rate: 9.7% (2005-2009 5-year est.).
Taxes: Total city taxes per capita: $84 (2007); City property taxes per capita: $84 (2007).
Education: Percent of population age 25 and over with: High school diploma (including GED) or higher: 82.2% (2010); Bachelor's degree or higher: 11.0% (2010); Master's degree or higher: 3.4% (2010).
School District(s)
Iroquois Special Education (KG-12)
   2009-10 Enrollment: n/a . . . . (815) 683-2662
Milford CCSD 280 (PK-08)
   2009-10 Enrollment: 432 . . . . (815) 889-5176
Milford Twp HSD 233 (09-12)
   2009-10 Enrollment: 214 . . . . (815) 889-5176
Housing: Homeownership rate: 75.4% (2010); Median home value: $68,732 (2010); Median contract rent: $377 per month (2005-2009 5-year est.); Median year structure built: 1946 (2005-2009 5-year est.).
Transportation: Commute to work: 90.7% car, 0.0% public transportation, 5.5% walk, 3.3% work from home (2005-2009 5-year est.); Travel time to work: 32.1% less than 15 minutes, 40.0% 15 to 30 minutes, 9.8% 30 to 45 minutes, 7.6% 45 to 60 minutes, 10.4% 60 minutes or more (2005-2009 5-year est.)

ONARGA (village). Covers a land area of 1.310 square miles and a water area of 0 square miles. Located at 40.71° N. Lat; 88.00° W. Long. Elevation is 669 feet.
History: Benjamin Hardy, the composer of the song "Darling Nellie Gray," lived in Onarga.
Population: 1,281 (1990); 1,438 (2000); 1,361 (2010); 1,328 (2015 projected); Race: 59.9% White, 4.6% Black, 0.2% Asian, 35.3% Other, 46.6% Hispanic of any race (2010); Density: 1,039.1 persons per square mile (2010); Average household size: 2.85 (2010); Median age: 33.9 (2010); Males per 100 females: 108.7 (2010); Marriage status: 22.8% never married, 61.4% now married, 3.4% widowed, 12.4% divorced (2005-2009 5-year est.); Foreign born: 19.8% (2005-2009 5-year est.); Ancestry (includes multiple ancestries): 26.1% German, 11.1% English, 9.6% Irish, 6.8% American, 3.9% French (2005-2009 5-year est.).
Economy: Single-family building permits issued: 0 (2010); Multi-family building permits issued: 0 (2010); Employment by occupation: 12.3% management, 14.9% professional, 11.1% services, 24.0% sales, 3.3% farming, 5.8% construction, 28.6% production (2005-2009 5-year est.).
Income: Per capita income: $16,494 (2010); Median household income: $41,375 (2010); Average household income: $50,097 (2010); Percent of households with income of $100,000 or more: 7.8% (2010); Poverty rate: 14.2% (2005-2009 5-year est.).
Taxes: Total city taxes per capita: $125 (2007); City property taxes per capita: $90 (2007).
Education: Percent of population age 25 and over with: High school diploma (including GED) or higher: 69.5% (2010); Bachelor's degree or higher: 6.5% (2010); Master's degree or higher: 2.0% (2010).
School District(s)
Iroquois West CUSD 10 (PK-12)
   2009-10 Enrollment: 970 . . . . (815) 265-4642
Housing: Homeownership rate: 75.7% (2010); Median home value: $83,333 (2010); Median contract rent: $438 per month (2005-2009 5-year est.); Median year structure built: 1949 (2005-2009 5-year est.).
Transportation: Commute to work: 90.9% car, 0.0% public transportation, 3.1% walk, 4.9% work from home (2005-2009 5-year est.); Travel time to

work: 49.3% less than 15 minutes, 17.3% 15 to 30 minutes, 17.1% 30 to 45 minutes, 10.5% 45 to 60 minutes, 5.9% 60 minutes or more (2005-2009 5-year est.)

Additional Information Contacts
Onarga Chamber of Commerce . . . .
    http://onarga.net/OnargaChamber.html

PAPINEAU (village). Covers a land area of 0.226 square miles and a water area of 0 square miles. Located at 40.96° N. Lat; 87.71° W. Long. Elevation is 630 feet.
Population: 147 (1990); 196 (2000); 193 (2010); 189 (2015 projected); Race: 95.3% White, 3.1% Black, 0.0% Asian, 1.6% Other, 3.1% Hispanic of any race (2010); Density: 854.4 persons per square mile (2010); Average household size: 2.88 (2010); Median age: 35.6 (2010); Males per 100 females: 99.0 (2010); Marriage status: 14.4% never married, 85.6% now married, 0.0% widowed, 0.0% divorced (2005-2009 5-year est.); Foreign born: 0.0% (2005-2009 5-year est.); Ancestry (includes multiple ancestries): 39.6% American, 29.9% German, 24.7% French, 14.3% Dutch, 13.0% Irish (2005-2009 5-year est.).
Economy: Single-family building permits issued: 0 (2010); Multi-family building permits issued: 0 (2010); Employment by occupation: 21.1% management, 25.0% professional, 17.1% services, 11.8% sales, 3.9% farming, 11.8% construction, 9.2% production (2005-2009 5-year est.).
Income: Per capita income: $21,596 (2010); Median household income: $56,618 (2010); Average household income: $59,888 (2010); Percent of households with income of $100,000 or more: 10.4% (2010); Poverty rate: 7.8% (2005-2009 5-year est.).
Taxes: Total city taxes per capita: $59 (2007); City property taxes per capita: $59 (2007).
Education: Percent of population age 25 and over with: High school diploma (including GED) or higher: 90.0% (2010); Bachelor's degree or higher: 8.3% (2010); Master's degree or higher: 1.7% (2010).
Housing: Homeownership rate: 77.6% (2010); Median home value: $107,500 (2010); Median contract rent: n/a per month (2005-2009 5-year est.); Median year structure built: 1943 (2005-2009 5-year est.).
Transportation: Commute to work: 92.1% car, 0.0% public transportation, 0.0% walk, 7.9% work from home (2005-2009 5-year est.); Travel time to work: 34.3% less than 15 minutes, 38.6% 15 to 30 minutes, 20.0% 30 to 45 minutes, 0.0% 45 to 60 minutes, 7.1% 60 minutes or more (2005-2009 5-year est.)

SHELDON (village). Covers a land area of 0.753 square miles and a water area of 0 square miles. Located at 40.77° N. Lat; 87.56° W. Long. Elevation is 682 feet.
History: Sheldon was established in 1860 by the Toledo, Peoria & Western Railroad as a switching point, and named for a railroad director. The town was a grain shipping center.
Population: 1,109 (1990); 1,232 (2000); 1,129 (2010); 1,082 (2015 projected); Race: 95.3% White, 1.0% Black, 1.1% Asian, 2.7% Other, 2.5% Hispanic of any race (2010); Density: 1,498.6 persons per square mile (2010); Average household size: 2.52 (2010); Median age: 38.9 (2010); Males per 100 females: 97.0 (2010); Marriage status: 20.4% never married, 64.2% now married, 4.7% widowed, 10.8% divorced (2005-2009 5-year est.); Foreign born: 0.6% (2005-2009 5-year est.); Ancestry (includes multiple ancestries): 22.1% German, 21.1% American, 15.1% English, 13.1% Irish, 4.6% Polish (2005-2009 5-year est.).
Economy: Single-family building permits issued: 0 (2010); Multi-family building permits issued: 0 (2010); Employment by occupation: 7.3% management, 8.3% professional, 19.8% services, 27.5% sales, 0.6% farming, 8.3% construction, 28.1% production (2005-2009 5-year est.).
Income: Per capita income: $20,674 (2010); Median household income: $44,423 (2010); Average household income: $52,466 (2010); Percent of households with income of $100,000 or more: 10.3% (2010); Poverty rate: 18.2% (2005-2009 5-year est.).
Taxes: Total city taxes per capita: $134 (2007); City property taxes per capita: $68 (2007).
Education: Percent of population age 25 and over with: High school diploma (including GED) or higher: 84.1% (2010); Bachelor's degree or higher: 11.9% (2010); Master's degree or higher: 2.3% (2010).

School District(s)
Milford CCSD 280 (PK-08)
    2009-10 Enrollment: 432 . . . . (815) 889-5176
Housing: Homeownership rate: 72.9% (2010); Median home value: $85,263 (2010); Median contract rent: $443 per month (2005-2009 5-year est.); Median year structure built: 1953 (2005-2009 5-year est.).

Transportation: Commute to work: 97.7% car, 0.0% public transportation, 0.6% walk, 1.7% work from home (2005-2009 5-year est.); Travel time to work: 28.1% less than 15 minutes, 43.8% 15 to 30 minutes, 7.7% 30 to 45 minutes, 10.2% 45 to 60 minutes, 10.2% 60 minutes or more (2005-2009 5-year est.)

THAWVILLE (village). Covers a land area of 0.324 square miles and a water area of 0 square miles. Located at 40.67° N. Lat; 88.11° W. Long. Elevation is 689 feet.
Population: 241 (1990); 258 (2000); 249 (2010); 243 (2015 projected); Race: 96.8% White, 0.4% Black, 0.0% Asian, 2.8% Other, 6.4% Hispanic of any race (2010); Density: 769.6 persons per square mile (2010); Average household size: 2.39 (2010); Median age: 42.0 (2010); Males per 100 females: 93.0 (2010); Marriage status: 39.0% never married, 38.4% now married, 4.3% widowed, 18.3% divorced (2005-2009 5-year est.); Foreign born: 11.1% (2005-2009 5-year est.); Ancestry (includes multiple ancestries): 30.4% German, 16.4% American, 8.2% English, 5.8% Irish, 5.3% French (2005-2009 5-year est.).
Economy: Single-family building permits issued: 0 (2010); Multi-family building permits issued: 4 (2010); Employment by occupation: 13.6% management, 7.3% professional, 2.7% services, 27.3% sales, 7.3% farming, 9.1% construction, 32.7% production (2005-2009 5-year est.).
Income: Per capita income: $26,592 (2010); Median household income: $50,962 (2010); Average household income: $64,543 (2010); Percent of households with income of $100,000 or more: 12.5% (2010); Poverty rate: 17.9% (2005-2009 5-year est.).
Taxes: Total city taxes per capita: $63 (2007); City property taxes per capita: $63 (2007).
Education: Percent of population age 25 and over with: High school diploma (including GED) or higher: 87.6% (2010); Bachelor's degree or higher: 15.3% (2010); Master's degree or higher: 2.9% (2010).

School District(s)
Iroquois West CUSD 10 (PK-12)
    2009-10 Enrollment: 970 . . . . (815) 265-4642
Housing: Homeownership rate: 79.8% (2010); Median home value: $93,125 (2010); Median contract rent: $415 per month (2005-2009 5-year est.); Median year structure built: before 1940 (2005-2009 5-year est.).
Transportation: Commute to work: 93.6% car, 0.0% public transportation, 1.8% walk, 3.6% work from home (2005-2009 5-year est.); Travel time to work: 24.5% less than 15 minutes, 50.9% 15 to 30 minutes, 17.0% 30 to 45 minutes, 3.8% 45 to 60 minutes, 3.8% 60 minutes or more (2005-2009 5-year est.)

WATSEKA (city). County seat. Covers a land area of 2.618 square miles and a water area of 0 square miles. Located at 40.77° N. Lat; 87.73° W. Long. Elevation is 633 feet.
History: Watseka was first called South Middleport when it was laid out in 1860. The name was changed in 1865 to honor the Potawatomi wife (Watch-e-kee) of Gurdon Hubbard of the American Fur Company. Watseka developed as the seat of Iroquois County.
Population: 5,453 (1990); 5,670 (2000); 5,443 (2010); 5,326 (2015 projected); Race: 94.6% White, 1.4% Black, 0.7% Asian, 3.2% Other, 4.1% Hispanic of any race (2010); Density: 2,078.7 persons per square mile (2010); Average household size: 2.30 (2010); Median age: 41.8 (2010); Males per 100 females: 89.8 (2010); Marriage status: 24.8% never married, 52.1% now married, 9.4% widowed, 13.7% divorced (2005-2009 5-year est.); Foreign born: 1.8% (2005-2009 5-year est.); Ancestry (includes multiple ancestries): 37.0% German, 14.1% Irish, 12.4% English, 9.9% French, 9.6% American (2005-2009 5-year est.).
Economy: Single-family building permits issued: 2 (2010); Multi-family building permits issued: 0 (2010); Employment by occupation: 9.9% management, 9.8% professional, 21.9% services, 19.6% sales, 1.7% farming, 11.5% construction, 25.7% production (2005-2009 5-year est.).
Income: Per capita income: $21,097 (2010); Median household income: $36,784 (2010); Average household income: $49,389 (2010); Percent of households with income of $100,000 or more: 8.4% (2010); Poverty rate: 17.2% (2005-2009 5-year est.).
Taxes: Total city taxes per capita: $773 (2007); City property taxes per capita: $451 (2007).
Education: Percent of population age 25 and over with: High school diploma (including GED) or higher: 82.1% (2010); Bachelor's degree or higher: 12.4% (2010); Master's degree or higher: 4.8% (2010).

School District(s)
Iroquois Area Reg Del System
    2009-10 Enrollment: n/a . . . . (815) 432-5471

Iroquois County CUSD 9 (PK-12)
  2009-10 Enrollment: 1,230 . . . . (815) 432-4931
Housing: Homeownership rate: 66.2% (2010); Median home value: $83,783 (2010); Median contract rent: $439 per month (2005-2009 5-year est.); Median year structure built: 1957 (2005-2009 5-year est.).
Hospitals: Iroquois Memorial Hospital & Resident Home (94 beds)
Safety: Violent crime rate: 24.6 per 10,000 population; Property crime rate: 313.8 per 10,000 population (2010).
Newspapers: Iroquois County's Times-Republic (Local news; Circulation 2,900)
Transportation: Commute to work: 92.4% car, 0.8% public transportation, 2.5% walk, 3.1% work from home (2005-2009 5-year est.); Travel time to work: 64.0% less than 15 minutes, 11.5% 15 to 30 minutes, 6.6% 30 to 45 minutes, 8.6% 45 to 60 minutes, 9.3% 60 minutes or more (2005-2009 5-year est.)
Additional Information Contacts
City of Watseka . . . . (815) 432-2711
  http://www.watsekacity.com
Watseka Area Chamber of Commerce . . . . (815) 432-2416
  http://www.watsekachamber.org

WELLINGTON (village). Covers a land area of 0.277 square miles and a water area of 0 square miles. Located at 40.54° N. Lat; 87.68° W. Long. Elevation is 699 feet.
Population: 294 (1990); 264 (2000); 220 (2010); 204 (2015 projected); Race: 98.2% White, 0.5% Black, 0.0% Asian, 1.4% Other, 2.3% Hispanic of any race (2010); Density: 795.0 persons per square mile (2010); Average household size: 2.44 (2010); Median age: 40.8 (2010); Males per 100 females: 100.0 (2010); Marriage status: 12.6% never married, 77.8% now married, 3.6% widowed, 6.0% divorced (2005-2009 5-year est.); Foreign born: 0.9% (2005-2009 5-year est.); Ancestry (includes multiple ancestries): 38.6% German, 26.4% English, 8.6% Scottish, 8.6% Irish, 6.8% Italian (2005-2009 5-year est.).
Economy: Single-family building permits issued: 0 (2010); Multi-family building permits issued: 0 (2010); Employment by occupation: 10.3% management, 4.7% professional, 12.1% services, 35.5% sales, 0.0% farming, 17.8% construction, 19.6% production (2005-2009 5-year est.).
Income: Per capita income: $24,895 (2010); Median household income: $41,176 (2010); Average household income: $62,889 (2010); Percent of households with income of $100,000 or more: 13.3% (2010); Poverty rate: 12.0% (2005-2009 5-year est.).
Taxes: Total city taxes per capita: $62 (2007); City property taxes per capita: $62 (2007).
Education: Percent of population age 25 and over with: High school diploma (including GED) or higher: 94.5% (2010); Bachelor's degree or higher: 13.0% (2010); Master's degree or higher: 4.1% (2010).
Housing: Homeownership rate: 77.8% (2010); Median home value: $72,727 (2010); Median contract rent: $435 per month (2005-2009 5-year est.); Median year structure built: 1943 (2005-2009 5-year est.).
Transportation: Commute to work: 85.7% car, 0.0% public transportation, 2.9% walk, 3.8% work from home (2005-2009 5-year est.); Travel time to work: 31.7% less than 15 minutes, 8.9% 15 to 30 minutes, 33.7% 30 to 45 minutes, 15.8% 45 to 60 minutes, 9.9% 60 minutes or more (2005-2009 5-year est.)

WOODLAND (village). Covers a land area of 0.449 square miles and a water area of 0 square miles. Located at 40.71° N. Lat; 87.73° W. Long. Elevation is 633 feet.
Population: 333 (1990); 319 (2000); 301 (2010); 292 (2015 projected); Race: 94.0% White, 2.3% Black, 0.7% Asian, 3.0% Other, 3.3% Hispanic of any race (2010); Density: 669.7 persons per square mile (2010); Average household size: 2.51 (2010); Median age: 44.4 (2010); Males per 100 females: 98.0 (2010); Marriage status: 34.1% never married, 48.4% now married, 3.3% widowed, 14.3% divorced (2005-2009 5-year est.); Foreign born: 0.0% (2005-2009 5-year est.); Ancestry (includes multiple ancestries): 27.2% German, 26.8% Irish, 24.1% American, 8.8% English, 7.0% Dutch (2005-2009 5-year est.).
Economy: Single-family building permits issued: 1 (2010); Multi-family building permits issued: 0 (2010); Employment by occupation: 0.0% management, 6.9% professional, 18.5% services, 16.2% sales, 6.2% farming, 23.1% construction, 29.2% production (2005-2009 5-year est.).
Income: Per capita income: $26,872 (2010); Median household income: $50,862 (2010); Average household income: $70,563 (2010); Percent of households with income of $100,000 or more: 19.2% (2010); Poverty rate: 19.0% (2005-2009 5-year est.).

Taxes: Total city taxes per capita: $55 (2007); City property taxes per capita: $55 (2007).
Education: Percent of population age 25 and over with: High school diploma (including GED) or higher: 90.6% (2010); Bachelor's degree or higher: 13.8% (2010); Master's degree or higher: 3.9% (2010).
School District(s)
Iroquois County CUSD 9 (PK-12)
  2009-10 Enrollment: 1,230 . . . . (815) 432-4931
Housing: Homeownership rate: 86.7% (2010); Median home value: $97,778 (2010); Median contract rent: $341 per month (2005-2009 5-year est.); Median year structure built: 1959 (2005-2009 5-year est.).
Transportation: Commute to work: 98.4% car, 0.0% public transportation, 1.6% walk, 0.0% work from home (2005-2009 5-year est.); Travel time to work: 63.5% less than 15 minutes, 24.6% 15 to 30 minutes, 4.8% 30 to 45 minutes, 4.0% 45 to 60 minutes, 3.2% 60 minutes or more (2005-2009 5-year est.)

Jackson County

Located in southwestern Illinois; bounded on the southwest by the Mississippi River and the Missouri border; drained by the Big Muddy and Little Muddy Rivers; includes part of Shawnee National Forest. Covers a land area of 588.12 square miles, a water area of 14.40 square miles, and is located in the Central Time Zone at 37.76° N. Lat., 89.31° W. Long. The county was founded in 1816. County seat is Murphysboro.

Jackson County is part of the Carbondale, IL Micropolitan Statistical Area. The entire metro area includes: Jackson County, IL

Weather Station: Carbondale Sewage Plant   Elevation: 390 feet

	Jan	Feb	Mar	Apr	May	Jun	Jul	Aug	Sep	Oct	Nov	Dec
High	41	46	56	67	76	85	88	88	81	69	57	45
Low	23	26	34	44	54	63	67	64	55	43	35	26
Precip	3.2	3.1	4.3	4.5	5.5	4.6	3.7	3.1	3.1	3.7	4.4	4.1
Snow	2.9	3.6	1.1	tr	0.0	0.0	0.0	0.0	0.0	0.1	0.3	2.7

High and Low temperatures in degrees Fahrenheit; Precipitation and Snow in inches

Population: 61,067 (1990); 59,612 (2000); 58,030 (2010); 56,905 (2015 projected); Race: 79.3% White, 12.5% Black, 4.2% Asian, 4.0% Other, 3.2% Hispanic of any race (2010); Density: 98.7 persons per square mile (2010); Average household size: 2.15 (2010); Median age: 29.8 (2010); Males per 100 females: 104.3 (2010).
Religion: Five largest groups: 10.9% Southern Baptist Convention, 4.7% Catholic Church, 3.9% The United Methodist Church, 3.8% American Baptist Churches in the USA, 3.7% Lutheran Church—Missouri Synod (2000).
Economy: Unemployment rate: 7.8% (August 2011); Total civilian labor force: 32,209 (August 2011); Leading industries: 22.4% health care and social assistance; 21.9% retail trade; 16.7% accommodation & food services (2009); Farms: 810 totaling 224,414 acres (2007); Companies that employ 500 or more persons: 2 (2009); Companies that employ 100 to 499 persons: 20 (2009); Companies that employ less than 100 persons: 1,313 (2009); Black-owned businesses: n/a (2007); Hispanic-owned businesses: n/a (2007); Asian-owned businesses: 173 (2007); Women-owned businesses: 1,190 (2007); Retail sales per capita: $13,588 (2010). Single-family building permits issued: 11 (2010); Multi-family building permits issued: 54 (2010).
Income: Per capita income: $20,450 (2010); Median household income: $31,744 (2010); Average household income: $46,693 (2010); Percent of households with income of $100,000 or more: 9.7% (2010); Poverty rate: 28.5% (2009); Bankruptcy rate: 3.54% (2010).
Taxes: Total county taxes per capita: $170 (2007); County property taxes per capita: $113 (2007).
Education: Percent of population age 25 and over with: High school diploma (including GED) or higher: 89.4% (2010); Bachelor's degree or higher: 36.2% (2010); Master's degree or higher: 18.7% (2010).
Housing: Homeownership rate: 52.4% (2010); Median home value: $85,843 (2010); Median contract rent: $451 per month (2005-2009 5-year est.); Median year structure built: 1972 (2005-2009 5-year est.)
Health: Birth rate: 121.7 per 10,000 population (2009); Death rate: 74.4 per 10,000 population (2009); Age-adjusted cancer mortality rate: 200.8 deaths per 100,000 population (2007); Number of physicians: 31.1 per 10,000 population (2008); Hospital beds: 28.7 per 10,000 population (2007); Hospital admissions: 1,700.6 per 10,000 population (2007).
Elections: 2008 Presidential election results: 59.7% Obama, 37.9% McCain, 0.7% Nader

National and State Parks: Giant City State Park; Lake Murphysboro State Park
Additional Information Contacts
Jackson County Government . . . . (618) 687-7360
   http://www.jacksoncounty-il.gov
Carbondale Chamber of Commerce . . . . (618) 529-2146
   http://www.carbondalechamber.com
City of Carbondale . . . . (618) 549-5302
   http://www.ci.carbondale.il.us
City of Murphysboro . . . . (618) 684-4961
   http://www.murphysboro.com
Murphysboro Chamber of Commerce . . . . (618) 684-6421
   http://murphysborochamber.com

Jackson County Communities

AVA (city). Covers a land area of 1.064 square miles and a water area of 0.006 square miles. Located at 37.88° N. Lat; 89.49° W. Long. Elevation is 604 feet.
Population: 674 (1990); 662 (2000); 664 (2010); 660 (2015 projected); Race: 99.1% White, 0.0% Black, 0.5% Asian, 0.5% Other, 0.9% Hispanic of any race (2010); Density: 623.9 persons per square mile (2010); Average household size: 2.44 (2010); Median age: 37.3 (2010); Males per 100 females: 95.3 (2010); Marriage status: 16.0% never married, 61.8% now married, 10.4% widowed, 11.7% divorced (2005-2009 5-year est.); Foreign born: 0.0% (2005-2009 5-year est.); Ancestry (includes multiple ancestries): 33.8% German, 23.8% English, 17.9% Irish, 10.5% French, 7.3% American (2005-2009 5-year est.).
Economy: Employment by occupation: 4.2% management, 15.8% professional, 19.6% services, 30.2% sales, 0.0% farming, 3.9% construction, 26.3% production (2005-2009 5-year est.).
Income: Per capita income: $23,939 (2010); Median household income: $44,167 (2010); Average household income: $58,309 (2010); Percent of households with income of $100,000 or more: 14.0% (2010); Poverty rate: 24.7% (2005-2009 5-year est.).
Taxes: Total city taxes per capita: $103 (2007); City property taxes per capita: $49 (2007).
Education: Percent of population age 25 and over with: High school diploma (including GED) or higher: 84.5% (2010); Bachelor's degree or higher: 11.8% (2010); Master's degree or higher: 3.5% (2010).
Housing: Homeownership rate: 84.2% (2010); Median home value: $93,226 (2010); Median contract rent: $288 per month (2005-2009 5-year est.); Median year structure built: 1971 (2005-2009 5-year est.).
Transportation: Commute to work: 87.3% car, 0.0% public transportation, 10.8% walk, 2.0% work from home (2005-2009 5-year est.); Travel time to work: 29.7% less than 15 minutes, 43.1% 15 to 30 minutes, 20.7% 30 to 45 minutes, 4.1% 45 to 60 minutes, 2.4% 60 minutes or more (2005-2009 5-year est.)

CAMPBELL HILL (village). Covers a land area of 0.408 square miles and a water area of 0 square miles. Located at 37.92° N. Lat; 89.55° W. Long. Elevation is 561 feet.
Population: 351 (1990); 333 (2000); 299 (2010); 280 (2015 projected); Race: 97.3% White, 2.3% Black, 0.0% Asian, 0.3% Other, 0.0% Hispanic of any race (2010); Density: 732.1 persons per square mile (2010); Average household size: 2.65 (2010); Median age: 33.4 (2010); Males per 100 females: 103.4 (2010); Marriage status: 25.2% never married, 63.0% now married, 5.6% widowed, 6.2% divorced (2005-2009 5-year est.); Foreign born: 1.1% (2005-2009 5-year est.); Ancestry (includes multiple ancestries): 50.5% German, 25.7% Irish, 14.5% English, 7.1% French, 6.8% American (2005-2009 5-year est.).
Economy: Single-family building permits issued: 0 (2010); Multi-family building permits issued: 0 (2010); Employment by occupation: 2.1% management, 5.0% professional, 10.1% services, 30.7% sales, 3.4% farming, 7.6% construction, 41.2% production (2005-2009 5-year est.).
Income: Per capita income: $20,803 (2010); Median household income: $48,676 (2010); Average household income: $54,358 (2010); Percent of households with income of $100,000 or more: 11.5% (2010); Poverty rate: 2.2% (2005-2009 5-year est.).
Taxes: Total city taxes per capita: $45 (2007); City property taxes per capita: $32 (2007).
Education: Percent of population age 25 and over with: High school diploma (including GED) or higher: 78.4% (2010); Bachelor's degree or higher: 17.5% (2010); Master's degree or higher: 9.3% (2010).

Trico CUSD 176 (PK-12)
   2009-10 Enrollment: 984 . . . . (618) 426-1111
Housing: Homeownership rate: 89.4% (2010); Median home value: $74,000 (2010); Median contract rent: $288 per month (2005-2009 5-year est.); Median year structure built: 1963 (2005-2009 5-year est.).
Transportation: Commute to work: 96.6% car, 0.0% public transportation, 3.4% walk, 0.0% work from home (2005-2009 5-year est.); Travel time to work: 36.7% less than 15 minutes, 23.2% 15 to 30 minutes, 12.6% 30 to 45 minutes, 12.1% 45 to 60 minutes, 15.5% 60 minutes or more (2005-2009 5-year est.)

CARBONDALE (city). Covers a land area of 11.895 square miles and a water area of 0.249 square miles. Located at 37.72° N. Lat; 89.22° W. Long. Elevation is 413 feet.
History: Carbondale developed as a coal mining center and a division point on the Illinois Central Railroad. In 1874 the Southern Illinois State Normal University was founded here.
Population: 27,831 (1990); 20,681 (2000); 20,915 (2010); 20,739 (2015 projected); Race: 64.7% White, 22.3% Black, 7.9% Asian, 5.1% Other, 3.6% Hispanic of any race (2010); Density: 1,758.3 persons per square mile (2010); Average household size: 1.94 (2010); Median age: 27.6 (2010); Males per 100 females: 107.4 (2010); Marriage status: 72.2% never married, 19.9% now married, 2.4% widowed, 5.5% divorced (2005-2009 5-year est.); Foreign born: 8.8% (2005-2009 5-year est.); Ancestry (includes multiple ancestries): 23.4% German, 11.9% Irish, 7.4% English, 4.2% Italian, 3.5% American (2005-2009 5-year est.).
Economy: Unemployment rate: 7.0% (August 2011); Total civilian labor force: 14,551 (August 2011); Single-family building permits issued: 10 (2010); Multi-family building permits issued: 50 (2010); Employment by occupation: 5.9% management, 31.3% professional, 29.2% services, 24.1% sales, 0.5% farming, 2.6% construction, 6.5% production (2005-2009 5-year est.).
Income: Per capita income: $17,377 (2010); Median household income: $21,027 (2010); Average household income: $34,463 (2010); Percent of households with income of $100,000 or more: 5.8% (2010); Poverty rate: 48.2% (2005-2009 5-year est.).
Taxes: Total city taxes per capita: $359 (2007); City property taxes per capita: $29 (2007).
Education: Percent of population age 25 and over with: High school diploma (including GED) or higher: 93.4% (2010); Bachelor's degree or higher: 49.9% (2010); Master's degree or higher: 26.5% (2010).
Carbondale CHSD 165 (09-12)
   2009-10 Enrollment: 1,088 . . . . (618) 457-4722
Carbondale ESD 95 (PK-08)
   2009-10 Enrollment: 1,380 . . . . (618) 457-3591
Giant City CCSD 130 (PK-08)
   2009-10 Enrollment: 304 . . . . (618) 457-5391
Unity Point CCSD 140 (PK-08)
   2009-10 Enrollment: 678 . . . . (618) 529-4151
Southern Illinois University Carbondale (Public)
   Fall 2009 Enrollment: 20,350 . . . . (618) 453-2121
   2010-11 Tuition: In-state $10,468; Out-of-state $21,403
Housing: Homeownership rate: 30.2% (2010); Median home value: $93,148 (2010); Median contract rent: $477 per month (2005-2009 5-year est.); Median year structure built: 1972 (2005-2009 5-year est.).
Hospitals: Memorial Hospital Carbondale (150 beds)
Safety: Violent crime rate: 94.0 per 10,000 population; Property crime rate: 444.9 per 10,000 population (2010).
Newspapers: Southern Illinoisan (Local news; Circulation 32,000)
Transportation: Commute to work: 76.1% car, 1.5% public transportation, 15.1% walk, 2.9% work from home (2005-2009 5-year est.); Travel time to work: 73.1% less than 15 minutes, 18.1% 15 to 30 minutes, 4.8% 30 to 45 minutes, 1.8% 45 to 60 minutes, 2.1% 60 minutes or more (2005-2009 5-year est.); Amtrak: train service available.
Airports: Southern Illinois (general aviation)
Additional Information Contacts
Carbondale Chamber of Commerce . . . . (618) 529-2146
   http://www.carbondalechamber.com
City of Carbondale . . . . (618) 549-5302
   http://www.ci.carbondale.il.us

DE SOTO (village). Covers a land area of 0.943 square miles and a water area of 0 square miles. Located at 37.81° N. Lat; 89.22° W. Long. Elevation is 400 feet.
Population: 1,551 (1990); 1,653 (2000); 1,590 (2010); 1,538 (2015 projected); Race: 97.0% White, 0.9% Black, 0.4% Asian, 1.7% Other, 1.9% Hispanic of any race (2010); Density: 1,685.6 persons per square mile (2010); Average household size: 2.39 (2010); Median age: 34.2 (2010); Males per 100 females: 95.1 (2010); Marriage status: 27.8% never married, 51.9% now married, 6.4% widowed, 13.9% divorced (2005-2009 5-year est.); Foreign born: 0.2% (2005-2009 5-year est.); Ancestry (includes multiple ancestries): 26.2% German, 18.6% Irish, 14.6% English, 6.1% American, 5.2% Italian (2005-2009 5-year est.).
Economy: Single-family building permits issued: 1 (2010); Multi-family building permits issued: 4 (2010); Employment by occupation: 10.8% management, 17.7% professional, 19.1% services, 27.4% sales, 0.0% farming, 7.2% construction, 17.8% production (2005-2009 5-year est.).
Income: Per capita income: $19,878 (2010); Median household income: $41,774 (2010); Average household income: $46,404 (2010); Percent of households with income of $100,000 or more: 4.4% (2010); Poverty rate: 15.6% (2005-2009 5-year est.).
Taxes: Total city taxes per capita: $110 (2007); City property taxes per capita: $34 (2007).
Education: Percent of population age 25 and over with: High school diploma (including GED) or higher: 87.2% (2010); Bachelor's degree or higher: 19.2% (2010); Master's degree or higher: 7.5% (2010).
School District(s)
Desoto Cons SD 86 (PK-08)
    2009-10 Enrollment: 269 . . . . (618) 867-2317
Housing: Homeownership rate: 70.6% (2010); Median home value: $80,737 (2010); Median contract rent: $367 per month (2005-2009 5-year est.); Median year structure built: 1975 (2005-2009 5-year est.).
Safety: Violent crime rate: 26.4 per 10,000 population; Property crime rate: 125.2 per 10,000 population (2010).
Transportation: Commute to work: 96.7% car, 1.5% public transportation, 0.3% walk, 1.2% work from home (2005-2009 5-year est.); Travel time to work: 27.9% less than 15 minutes, 53.6% 15 to 30 minutes, 7.7% 30 to 45 minutes, 5.8% 45 to 60 minutes, 5.1% 60 minutes or more (2005-2009 5-year est.)

DOWELL (village). Covers a land area of 0.371 square miles and a water area of 0 square miles. Located at 37.94° N. Lat; 89.24° W. Long. Elevation is 400 feet.
History: Dowell grew around the Kathleen Coal Company Mine in 1916, and was named for George Dowell, legal advisor for the Progressive Miners of America.
Population: 465 (1990); 441 (2000); 379 (2010); 350 (2015 projected); Race: 96.8% White, 0.8% Black, 0.3% Asian, 2.1% Other, 0.3% Hispanic of any race (2010); Density: 1,021.0 persons per square mile (2010); Average household size: 2.24 (2010); Median age: 41.1 (2010); Males per 100 females: 90.5 (2010); Marriage status: 27.8% never married, 41.9% now married, 23.8% widowed, 6.6% divorced (2005-2009 5-year est.); Foreign born: 0.0% (2005-2009 5-year est.); Ancestry (includes multiple ancestries): 30.1% Irish, 26.6% English, 17.5% German, 4.9% Polish, 4.5% Swedish (2005-2009 5-year est.).
Economy: Single-family building permits issued: 0 (2010); Multi-family building permits issued: 0 (2010); Employment by occupation: 17.8% management, 26.7% professional, 30.7% services, 5.0% sales, 0.0% farming, 2.0% construction, 17.8% production (2005-2009 5-year est.).
Income: Per capita income: $16,513 (2010); Median household income: $31,375 (2010); Average household income: $37,411 (2010); Percent of households with income of $100,000 or more: 1.8% (2010); Poverty rate: 9.8% (2005-2009 5-year est.).
Taxes: Total city taxes per capita: $110 (2007); City property taxes per capita: $42 (2007).
Education: Percent of population age 25 and over with: High school diploma (including GED) or higher: 72.8% (2010); Bachelor's degree or higher: 9.4% (2010); Master's degree or higher: 3.4% (2010).
Housing: Homeownership rate: 84.0% (2010); Median home value: $54,857 (2010); Median contract rent: $309 per month (2005-2009 5-year est.); Median year structure built: before 1940 (2005-2009 5-year est.).
Transportation: Commute to work: 100.0% car, 0.0% public transportation, 0.0% walk, 0.0% work from home (2005-2009 5-year est.); Travel time to work: 12.9% less than 15 minutes, 31.7% 15 to 30 minutes,

37.6% 30 to 45 minutes, 17.8% 45 to 60 minutes, 0.0% 60 minutes or more (2005-2009 5-year est.)

ELKVILLE (village). Covers a land area of 0.767 square miles and a water area of 0 square miles. Located at 37.91° N. Lat; 89.23° W. Long. Elevation is 400 feet.
Population: 958 (1990); 1,001 (2000); 1,001 (2010); 989 (2015 projected); Race: 95.6% White, 1.8% Black, 0.0% Asian, 2.6% Other, 2.4% Hispanic of any race (2010); Density: 1,305.6 persons per square mile (2010); Average household size: 2.46 (2010); Median age: 33.5 (2010); Males per 100 females: 99.4 (2010); Marriage status: 23.3% never married, 59.2% now married, 5.3% widowed, 12.2% divorced (2005-2009 5-year est.); Foreign born: 0.0% (2005-2009 5-year est.); Ancestry (includes multiple ancestries): 25.6% English, 24.1% German, 17.1% Irish, 8.6% American, 4.1% Scottish (2005-2009 5-year est.).
Economy: Single-family building permits issued: 0 (2010); Multi-family building permits issued: 0 (2010); Employment by occupation: 7.8% management, 7.8% professional, 23.1% services, 31.5% sales, 1.2% farming, 9.0% construction, 19.7% production (2005-2009 5-year est.).
Income: Per capita income: $19,372 (2010); Median household income: $38,257 (2010); Average household income: $48,401 (2010); Percent of households with income of $100,000 or more: 7.7% (2010); Poverty rate: 29.8% (2005-2009 5-year est.).
Taxes: Total city taxes per capita: $91 (2007); City property taxes per capita: $49 (2007).
Education: Percent of population age 25 and over with: High school diploma (including GED) or higher: 85.1% (2010); Bachelor's degree or higher: 11.6% (2010); Master's degree or higher: 3.1% (2010).
School District(s)
Elverado CUSD 196 (PK-12)
    2009-10 Enrollment: 492 . . . . (618) 568-1321
Housing: Homeownership rate: 75.1% (2010); Median home value: $66,341 (2010); Median contract rent: $329 per month (2005-2009 5-year est.); Median year structure built: 1952 (2005-2009 5-year est.).
Transportation: Commute to work: 93.2% car, 0.0% public transportation, 1.3% walk, 1.0% work from home (2005-2009 5-year est.); Travel time to work: 26.9% less than 15 minutes, 38.0% 15 to 30 minutes, 30.2% 30 to 45 minutes, 2.3% 45 to 60 minutes, 2.6% 60 minutes or more (2005-2009 5-year est.)

GORHAM (village). Covers a land area of 1.218 square miles and a water area of 0.011 square miles. Located at 37.71° N. Lat; 89.48° W. Long. Elevation is 361 feet.
Population: 290 (1990); 256 (2000); 246 (2010); 238 (2015 projected); Race: 98.0% White, 0.0% Black, 0.0% Asian, 2.0% Other, 0.8% Hispanic of any race (2010); Density: 202.0 persons per square mile (2010); Average household size: 2.40 (2010); Median age: 31.6 (2010); Males per 100 females: 96.8 (2010); Marriage status: 21.3% never married, 62.1% now married, 10.3% widowed, 6.3% divorced (2005-2009 5-year est.); Foreign born: 0.0% (2005-2009 5-year est.); Ancestry (includes multiple ancestries): 18.8% Irish, 10.8% German, 5.4% American, 5.4% French, 3.5% English (2005-2009 5-year est.).
Economy: Employment by occupation: 8.0% management, 0.0% professional, 34.7% services, 24.0% sales, 0.0% farming, 9.3% construction, 24.0% production (2005-2009 5-year est.).
Income: Per capita income: $18,090 (2010); Median household income: $30,714 (2010); Average household income: $41,990 (2010); Percent of households with income of $100,000 or more: 8.2% (2010); Poverty rate: 29.6% (2005-2009 5-year est.).
Taxes: Total city taxes per capita: $77 (2007); City property taxes per capita: $56 (2007).
Education: Percent of population age 25 and over with: High school diploma (including GED) or higher: 78.4% (2010); Bachelor's degree or higher: 13.5% (2010); Master's degree or higher: 4.7% (2010).
Housing: Homeownership rate: 80.6% (2010); Median home value: $47,222 (2010); Median contract rent: $245 per month (2005-2009 5-year est.); Median year structure built: 1946 (2005-2009 5-year est.).
Transportation: Commute to work: 84.8% car, 0.0% public transportation, 0.0% walk, 7.6% work from home (2005-2009 5-year est.); Travel time to work: 16.4% less than 15 minutes, 26.2% 15 to 30 minutes, 42.6% 30 to 45 minutes, 9.8% 45 to 60 minutes, 4.9% 60 minutes or more (2005-2009 5-year est.)

GRAND TOWER (city).
Covers a land area of 1.258 square miles and a water area of 0.002 square miles. Located at 37.63° N. Lat; 89.50° W. Long. Elevation is 361 feet.

History: Grand Tower was named for the 60-foot-high Tower Rock in the middle of the Mississippi River.

Population: 775 (1990); 624 (2000); 607 (2010); 590 (2015 projected); Race: 96.7% White, 0.2% Black, 0.0% Asian, 3.1% Other, 0.5% Hispanic of any race (2010); Density: 482.5 persons per square mile (2010); Average household size: 2.44 (2010); Median age: 34.9 (2010); Males per 100 females: 90.9 (2010); Marriage status: 20.4% never married, 56.3% now married, 9.2% widowed, 14.1% divorced (2005-2009 5-year est.); Foreign born: 0.0% (2005-2009 5-year est.); Ancestry (includes multiple ancestries): 26.2% Irish, 15.7% German, 13.7% English, 12.0% American, 4.6% Dutch (2005-2009 5-year est.).

Economy: Single-family building permits issued: 0 (2010); Multi-family building permits issued: 0 (2010); Employment by occupation: 8.5% management, 7.9% professional, 22.6% services, 17.7% sales, 0.0% farming, 6.7% construction, 36.6% production (2005-2009 5-year est.).

Income: Per capita income: $19,182 (2010); Median household income: $39,227 (2010); Average household income: $47,028 (2010); Percent of households with income of $100,000 or more: 8.0% (2010); Poverty rate: 27.8% (2005-2009 5-year est.).

Taxes: Total city taxes per capita: $74 (2007); City property taxes per capita: $26 (2007).

Education: Percent of population age 25 and over with: High school diploma (including GED) or higher: 76.9% (2010); Bachelor's degree or higher: 8.7% (2010); Master's degree or higher: 3.0% (2010).

School District(s)
Shawnee CUSD 84 (PK-12)
   2009-10 Enrollment: 460 . . . . (618) 833-5709

Housing: Homeownership rate: 79.1% (2010); Median home value: $44,054 (2010); Median contract rent: $242 per month (2005-2009 5-year est.); Median year structure built: 1960 (2005-2009 5-year est.).

Safety: Violent crime rate: 0.0 per 10,000 population; Property crime rate: 159.6 per 10,000 population (2010).

Transportation: Commute to work: 85.4% car, 2.4% public transportation, 0.0% walk, 4.3% work from home (2005-2009 5-year est.); Travel time to work: 15.3% less than 15 minutes, 40.8% 15 to 30 minutes, 33.1% 30 to 45 minutes, 5.7% 45 to 60 minutes, 5.1% 60 minutes or more (2005-2009 5-year est.).

JACOB (unincorporated postal area, zip code 62950).
Covers a land area of 28.982 square miles and a water area of 0.074 square miles. Located at 37.75° N. Lat; 89.56° W. Long. Elevation is 361 feet.

Population: 232 (2000); Race: 100.0% White, 0.0% Black, 0.0% Asian, 0.0% Other, 4.7% Hispanic of any race (2000); Density: 8.0 persons per square mile (2000); Age: 14.1% under 18, 32.3% over 64 (2000); Marriage status: 9.7% never married, 80.6% now married, 9.7% widowed, 0.0% divorced (2000); Foreign born: 4.7% (2000); Ancestry (includes multiple ancestries): 60.4% German, 4.7% Italian, 4.7% Lebanese, 3.1% Dutch (2000).

Economy: Employment by occupation: 26.4% management, 14.5% professional, 22.7% services, 24.5% sales, 0.0% farming, 5.5% construction, 6.4% production (2000).

Income: Per capita income: $20,713 (2000); Median household income: $23,750 (2000); Poverty rate: 14.1% (2000).

Education: Percent of population age 25 and over with: High school diploma (including GED) or higher: 65.5% (2000); Bachelor's degree or higher: 10.3% (2000).

Housing: Homeownership rate: 78.6% (2000); Median home value: $32,900 (2000); Median contract rent: $321 per month (2000); Median year structure built: 1949 (2000).

Transportation: Commute to work: 87.3% car, 0.0% public transportation, 0.0% walk, 6.4% work from home (2000); Travel time to work: 35.9% less than 15 minutes, 23.3% 15 to 30 minutes, 34.0% 30 to 45 minutes, 0.0% 45 to 60 minutes, 6.8% 60 minutes or more (2000)

MAKANDA (village).
Covers a land area of 4.332 square miles and a water area of 0 square miles. Located at 37.61° N. Lat; 89.23° W. Long. Elevation is 446 feet.

Population: 404 (1990); 419 (2000); 410 (2010); 407 (2015 projected); Race: 93.7% White, 2.2% Black, 2.7% Asian, 1.5% Other, 1.2% Hispanic of any race (2010); Density: 94.7 persons per square mile (2010); Average household size: 2.32 (2010); Median age: 41.7 (2010); Males per 100 females: 119.3 (2010); Marriage status: 27.5% never married, 64.0% now married, 0.9% widowed, 7.6% divorced (2005-2009 5-year est.); Foreign born: 1.5% (2005-2009 5-year est.); Ancestry (includes multiple ancestries): 17.8% German, 16.5% English, 15.9% Irish, 8.1% Polish, 6.8% American (2005-2009 5-year est.).

Economy: Employment by occupation: 13.5% management, 26.7% professional, 14.8% services, 24.4% sales, 0.6% farming, 12.2% construction, 7.7% production (2005-2009 5-year est.).

Income: Per capita income: $34,206 (2010); Median household income: $60,197 (2010); Average household income: $82,811 (2010); Percent of households with income of $100,000 or more: 25.4% (2010); Poverty rate: 5.1% (2005-2009 5-year est.).

Taxes: Total city taxes per capita: $109 (2007); City property taxes per capita: $104 (2007).

Education: Percent of population age 25 and over with: High school diploma (including GED) or higher: 93.1% (2010); Bachelor's degree or higher: 49.7% (2010); Master's degree or higher: 25.3% (2010).

Housing: Homeownership rate: 80.2% (2010); Median home value: $121,739 (2010); Median contract rent: $606 per month (2005-2009 5-year est.); Median year structure built: 1985 (2005-2009 5-year est.).

Transportation: Commute to work: 98.0% car, 0.0% public transportation, 0.0% walk, 1.0% work from home (2005-2009 5-year est.); Travel time to work: 30.2% less than 15 minutes, 57.5% 15 to 30 minutes, 4.0% 30 to 45 minutes, 5.0% 45 to 60 minutes, 3.3% 60 minutes or more (2005-2009 5-year est.)

MURPHYSBORO (city).
County seat. Covers a land area of 4.832 square miles and a water area of 0.008 square miles. Located at 37.76° N. Lat; 89.33° W. Long. Elevation is 420 feet.

History: A memorial to John A. Logan is in the city. Incorporated 1867.

Population: 9,325 (1990); 13,295 (2000); 11,393 (2010); 10,771 (2015 projected); Race: 80.6% White, 13.3% Black, 1.8% Asian, 4.3% Other, 3.7% Hispanic of any race (2010); Density: 2,357.7 persons per square mile (2010); Average household size: 2.16 (2010); Median age: 24.6 (2010); Males per 100 females: 105.1 (2010); Marriage status: 39.3% never married, 38.1% now married, 11.3% widowed, 11.2% divorced (2005-2009 5-year est.); Foreign born: 0.8% (2005-2009 5-year est.); Ancestry (includes multiple ancestries): 26.9% German, 16.8% Irish, 8.6% English, 7.8% American, 7.7% Italian (2005-2009 5-year est.).

Economy: Single-family building permits issued: 0 (2010); Multi-family building permits issued: 0 (2010); Employment by occupation: 6.5% management, 25.3% professional, 25.9% services, 23.6% sales, 0.2% farming, 7.0% construction, 11.4% production (2005-2009 5-year est.).

Income: Per capita income: $17,221 (2010); Median household income: $33,490 (2010); Average household income: $49,281 (2010); Percent of households with income of $100,000 or more: 9.6% (2010); Poverty rate: 25.1% (2005-2009 5-year est.).

Taxes: Total city taxes per capita: $192 (2007); City property taxes per capita: $63 (2007).

Education: Percent of population age 25 and over with: High school diploma (including GED) or higher: 82.4% (2010); Bachelor's degree or higher: 20.6% (2010); Master's degree or higher: 8.4% (2010).

School District(s)
Jackson/Perry Roe (06-09)
   2009-10 Enrollment: n/a . . . . (618) 687-7290
Murphysboro CUSD 186 (PK-12)
   2009-10 Enrollment: 2,147 . . . . (618) 684-3781
Tri-County Sp Ed Jnt Agreement (PK-12)
   2009-10 Enrollment: n/a . . . . (618) 684-2109

Housing: Homeownership rate: 59.3% (2010); Median home value: $63,619 (2010); Median contract rent: $366 per month (2005-2009 5-year est.); Median year structure built: 1961 (2005-2009 5-year est.).

Hospitals: St. Joseph Memorial Hospital (59 beds)

Newspapers: Murphysboro American (Regional news; Circulation 10,294)

Transportation: Commute to work: 89.8% car, 0.0% public transportation, 7.0% walk, 1.1% work from home (2005-2009 5-year est.); Travel time to work: 44.0% less than 15 minutes, 39.7% 15 to 30 minutes, 8.7% 30 to 45 minutes, 4.6% 45 to 60 minutes, 3.0% 60 minutes or more (2005-2009 5-year est.)

Additional Information Contacts
City of Murphysboro. . . . . (618) 684-4961
   http://www.murphysboro.com
Murphysboro Chamber of Commerce . . . . (618) 684-6421
   http://murphysborochamber.com

POMONA (unincorporated postal area, zip code 62975). Covers a land area of 20.400 square miles and a water area of 0 square miles. Located at 37.61° N. Lat; 89.36° W. Long. Elevation is 407 feet.

Population: 240 (2000); Race: 100.0% White, 0.0% Black, 0.0% Asian, 0.0% Other, 0.0% Hispanic of any race (2000); Density: 11.8 persons per square mile (2000); Age: 29.6% under 18, 5.2% over 64 (2000); Marriage status: 33.1% never married, 55.8% now married, 7.0% widowed, 4.1% divorced (2000); Foreign born: 0.0% (2000); Ancestry (includes multiple ancestries): 20.4% German, 17.0% Irish, 9.1% American, 7.0% Polish (2000).

Economy: Employment by occupation: 21.1% management, 3.7% professional, 15.6% services, 23.9% sales, 0.0% farming, 22.0% construction, 13.8% production (2000).

Income: Per capita income: $19,845 (2000); Median household income: $41,250 (2000); Poverty rate: 16.1% (2000).

Education: Percent of population age 25 and over with: High school diploma (including GED) or higher: 60.9% (2000); Bachelor's degree or higher: 8.7% (2000).

Housing: Homeownership rate: 83.1% (2000); Median home value: $17,500 (2000); Median contract rent: $275 per month (2000); Median year structure built: 1983 (2000).

Transportation: Commute to work: 94.2% car, 0.0% public transportation, 0.0% walk, 0.0% work from home (2000); Travel time to work: 0.0% less than 15 minutes, 27.2% 15 to 30 minutes, 45.6% 30 to 45 minutes, 8.7% 45 to 60 minutes, 18.4% 60 minutes or more (2000)

VERGENNES (village). Covers a land area of 0.362 square miles and a water area of 0 square miles. Located at 37.90° N. Lat; 89.34° W. Long. Elevation is 397 feet.

Population: 311 (1990); 491 (2000); 429 (2010); 411 (2015 projected); Race: 80.2% White, 15.9% Black, 0.5% Asian, 3.5% Other, 3.3% Hispanic of any race (2010); Density: 1,186.2 persons per square mile (2010); Average household size: 2.53 (2010); Median age: 30.6 (2010); Males per 100 females: 131.9 (2010); Marriage status: 18.4% never married, 58.2% now married, 13.9% widowed, 9.4% divorced (2005-2009 5-year est.); Foreign born: 0.6% (2005-2009 5-year est.); Ancestry (includes multiple ancestries): 25.1% German, 13.3% English, 12.7% Irish, 4.6% Swedish, 3.8% Italian (2005-2009 5-year est.).

Economy: Employment by occupation: 9.9% management, 11.5% professional, 9.2% services, 41.2% sales, 0.0% farming, 16.8% construction, 11.5% production (2005-2009 5-year est.).

Income: Per capita income: $19,044 (2010); Median household income: $46,625 (2010); Average household income: $53,917 (2010); Percent of households with income of $100,000 or more: 8.0% (2010); Poverty rate: 28.9% (2005-2009 5-year est.).

Taxes: Total city taxes per capita: $31 (2007); City property taxes per capita: $31 (2007).

Education: Percent of population age 25 and over with: High school diploma (including GED) or higher: 84.5% (2010); Bachelor's degree or higher: 12.4% (2010); Master's degree or higher: 4.4% (2010).

School District(s)
Elverado CUSD 196 (PK-12)
    2009-10 Enrollment: 492 . . . . (618) 568-1321

Housing: Homeownership rate: 84.7% (2010); Median home value: $71,500 (2010); Median contract rent: $360 per month (2005-2009 5-year est.); Median year structure built: 1975 (2005-2009 5-year est.).

Transportation: Commute to work: 93.0% car, 0.0% public transportation, 0.8% walk, 4.7% work from home (2005-2009 5-year est.); Travel time to work: 23.6% less than 15 minutes, 39.0% 15 to 30 minutes, 29.3% 30 to 45 minutes, 5.7% 45 to 60 minutes, 2.4% 60 minutes or more (2005-2009 5-year est.)

Jasper County

Located in southeast central Illinois; drained by the Embarrass River. Covers a land area of 494.40 square miles, a water area of 3.62 square miles, and is located in the Central Time Zone at 39.01° N. Lat., 88.14° W. Long. The county was founded in 1831. County seat is Newton.

Weather Station: Newton 6 SSE									Elevation: 509 feet			
	Jan	Feb	Mar	Apr	May	Jun	Jul	Aug	Sep	Oct	Nov	Dec
High	36	42	51	63	74	83	87	85	79	67	53	40
Low	20	24	32	42	52	62	66	62	54	43	34	24
Precip	2.3	2.4	3.6	4.0	4.9	4.0	4.2	2.9	3.2	3.2	4.0	3.0
Snow	4.3	3.0	2.0	0.1	tr	0.0	0.0	0.0	0.0	0.2	0.8	3.7

High and Low temperatures in degrees Fahrenheit; Precipitation and Snow in inches

Population: 10,609 (1990); 10,117 (2000); 9,661 (2010); 9,414 (2015 projected); Race: 98.8% White, 0.2% Black, 0.2% Asian, 0.8% Other, 0.7% Hispanic of any race (2010); Density: 19.5 persons per square mile (2010); Average household size: 2.50 (2010); Median age: 40.7 (2010); Males per 100 females: 99.0 (2010).

Religion: Five largest groups: 22.2% Catholic Church, 10.1% Christian Churches and Churches of Christ, 8.2% The United Methodist Church, 5.1% Southern Baptist Convention, 4.9% American Baptist Churches in the USA (2000).

Economy: Unemployment rate: 8.2% (August 2011); Total civilian labor force: 4,842 (August 2011); Leading industries: 13.4% retail trade; 9.3% wholesale trade; 7.7% transportation & warehousing (2009); Farms: 882 totaling 243,451 acres (2007); Companies that employ 500 or more persons: 0 (2009); Companies that employ 100 to 499 persons: 2 (2009); Companies that employ less than 100 persons: 215 (2009); Black-owned businesses: n/a (2007); Hispanic-owned businesses: n/a (2007); Asian-owned businesses: n/a (2007); Women-owned businesses: 224 (2007); Retail sales per capita: $15,438 (2010). Single-family building permits issued: 0 (2010); Multi-family building permits issued: 0 (2010).

Income: Per capita income: $21,888 (2010); Median household income: $45,574 (2010); Average household income: $54,805 (2010); Percent of households with income of $100,000 or more: 9.6% (2010); Poverty rate: 11.3% (2009); Bankruptcy rate: 2.90% (2010).

Taxes: Total county taxes per capita: $314 (2007); County property taxes per capita: $304 (2007).

Education: Percent of population age 25 and over with: High school diploma (including GED) or higher: 87.8% (2010); Bachelor's degree or higher: 13.8% (2010); Master's degree or higher: 3.8% (2010).

Housing: Homeownership rate: 82.3% (2010); Median home value: $92,830 (2010); Median contract rent: $283 per month (2005-2009 5-year est.); Median year structure built: 1966 (2005-2009 5-year est.)

Health: Birth rate: 129.1 per 10,000 population (2009); Death rate: 104.9 per 10,000 population (2009); Age-adjusted cancer mortality rate: 186.6 deaths per 100,000 population (2007); Number of physicians: 2.1 per 10,000 population (2008); Hospital beds: 0.0 per 10,000 population (2007); Hospital admissions: 0.0 per 10,000 population (2007).

Elections: 2008 Presidential election results: 40.2% Obama, 57.8% McCain, 1.2% Nader

National and State Parks: Newton Lake State Fish and Wildlife Area; Sam Parr State Park

Additional Information Contacts
Jasper County Government . . . . (618) 783-3409
    http://jaspercountyillinois.org
Jasper County Chamber of Commerce . . . . (618) 783-3399
    http://www.newtonillinois.com

Jasper County Communities

HIDALGO (village). Covers a land area of 0.343 square miles and a water area of 0 square miles. Located at 39.15° N. Lat; 88.15° W. Long. Elevation is 587 feet.

Population: 122 (1990); 123 (2000); 117 (2010); 114 (2015 projected); Race: 99.1% White, 0.0% Black, 0.0% Asian, 0.9% Other, 0.0% Hispanic of any race (2010); Density: 340.7 persons per square mile (2010); Average household size: 2.37 (2010); Median age: 43.9 (2010); Males per 100 females: 95.0 (2010); Marriage status: 25.7% never married, 53.5% now married, 10.9% widowed, 9.9% divorced (2005-2009 5-year est.); Foreign born: 0.0% (2005-2009 5-year est.); Ancestry (includes multiple ancestries): 21.3% Irish, 18.0% American, 14.7% German, 8.7% Polish, 8.7% Welsh (2005-2009 5-year est.).

Economy: Employment by occupation: 4.1% management, 8.2% professional, 24.5% services, 4.1% sales, 0.0% farming, 34.7% construction, 24.5% production (2005-2009 5-year est.).

Income: Per capita income: $22,324 (2010); Median household income: $43,654 (2010); Average household income: $49,337 (2010); Percent of households with income of $100,000 or more: 4.1% (2010); Poverty rate: 26.0% (2005-2009 5-year est.).

Taxes: Total city taxes per capita: $50 (2007); City property taxes per capita: $50 (2007).
Education: Percent of population age 25 and over with: High school diploma (including GED) or higher: 89.5% (2010); Bachelor's degree or higher: 15.1% (2010); Master's degree or higher: 7.0% (2010).
Housing: Homeownership rate: 85.7% (2010); Median home value: $80,000 (2010); Median contract rent: n/a per month (2005-2009 5-year est.); Median year structure built: 1956 (2005-2009 5-year est.).
Transportation: Commute to work: 100.0% car, 0.0% public transportation, 0.0% walk, 0.0% work from home (2005-2009 5-year est.); Travel time to work: 56.5% less than 15 minutes, 0.0% 15 to 30 minutes, 32.6% 30 to 45 minutes, 10.9% 45 to 60 minutes, 0.0% 60 minutes or more (2005-2009 5-year est.)

NEWTON (city). County seat. Covers a land area of 1.863 square miles and a water area of 0 square miles. Located at 38.98° N. Lat; 88.16° W. Long. Elevation is 535 feet.
History: Settled 1828, incorporated 1831.
Population: 3,234 (1990); 3,069 (2000); 2,762 (2010); 2,612 (2015 projected); Race: 98.6% White, 0.3% Black, 0.2% Asian, 0.9% Other, 0.8% Hispanic of any race (2010); Density: 1,482.5 persons per square mile (2010); Average household size: 2.21 (2010); Median age: 41.6 (2010); Males per 100 females: 88.0 (2010); Marriage status: 20.6% never married, 49.6% now married, 13.1% widowed, 16.8% divorced (2005-2009 5-year est.); Foreign born: 0.0% (2005-2009 5-year est.); Ancestry (includes multiple ancestries): 33.3% German, 12.8% Irish, 9.9% American, 7.7% English, 4.1% Italian (2005-2009 5-year est.).
Economy: Employment by occupation: 9.6% management, 9.2% professional, 16.4% services, 22.2% sales, 0.0% farming, 6.5% construction, 36.2% production (2005-2009 5-year est.).
Income: Per capita income: $21,112 (2010); Median household income: $37,605 (2010); Average household income: $47,107 (2010); Percent of households with income of $100,000 or more: 8.2% (2010); Poverty rate: 18.1% (2005-2009 5-year est.).
Taxes: Total city taxes per capita: $138 (2007); City property taxes per capita: $131 (2007).
Education: Percent of population age 25 and over with: High school diploma (including GED) or higher: 85.8% (2010); Bachelor's degree or higher: 15.0% (2010); Master's degree or higher: 5.0% (2010).

School District(s)
Clay/Cwford/Jsper/Lwrnce/Rhland (PK-12)
    2009-10 Enrollment: n/a .... (618) 392-4631
Jasper County CUD 1 (PK-12)
    2009-10 Enrollment: 1,428 .... (618) 783-8459
Housing: Homeownership rate: 71.1% (2010); Median home value: $76,914 (2010); Median contract rent: $281 per month (2005-2009 5-year est.); Median year structure built: 1960 (2005-2009 5-year est.).
Newspapers: Newton Press-Mentor (Local news)
Transportation: Commute to work: 90.6% car, 0.0% public transportation, 3.1% walk, 4.1% work from home (2005-2009 5-year est.); Travel time to work: 52.8% less than 15 minutes, 13.2% 15 to 30 minutes, 23.2% 30 to 45 minutes, 4.3% 45 to 60 minutes, 6.4% 60 minutes or more (2005-2009 5-year est.)
Additional Information Contacts
Jasper County Chamber of Commerce .... (618) 783-3399
    http://www.newtonillinois.com

ROSE HILL (village). Covers a land area of 0.633 square miles and a water area of 0 square miles. Located at 39.10° N. Lat; 88.14° W. Long. Elevation is 564 feet.
Population: 78 (1990); 79 (2000); 76 (2010); 74 (2015 projected); Race: 98.7% White, 0.0% Black, 0.0% Asian, 1.3% Other, 0.0% Hispanic of any race (2010); Density: 120.1 persons per square mile (2010); Average household size: 2.34 (2010); Median age: 45.0 (2010); Males per 100 females: 90.0 (2010); Marriage status: 12.4% never married, 61.0% now married, 10.5% widowed, 16.2% divorced (2005-2009 5-year est.); Foreign born: 0.0% (2005-2009 5-year est.); Ancestry (includes multiple ancestries): 36.9% German, 31.1% Irish, 20.5% American, 8.2% English, 5.7% Italian (2005-2009 5-year est.).
Economy: Employment by occupation: 8.2% management, 22.4% professional, 4.1% services, 22.4% sales, 8.2% farming, 6.1% construction, 28.6% production (2005-2009 5-year est.).
Income: Per capita income: $22,324 (2010); Median household income: $45,000 (2010); Average household income: $52,344 (2010); Percent of

households with income of $100,000 or more: 6.3% (2010); Poverty rate: 7.4% (2005-2009 5-year est.).
Taxes: Total city taxes per capita: $26 (2007); City property taxes per capita: $26 (2007).
Education: Percent of population age 25 and over with: High school diploma (including GED) or higher: 89.5% (2010); Bachelor's degree or higher: 14.0% (2010); Master's degree or higher: 7.0% (2010).
Housing: Homeownership rate: 87.5% (2010); Median home value: $85,000 (2010); Median contract rent: $225 per month (2005-2009 5-year est.); Median year structure built: 1958 (2005-2009 5-year est.).
Transportation: Commute to work: 95.3% car, 0.0% public transportation, 0.0% walk, 4.7% work from home (2005-2009 5-year est.); Travel time to work: 9.8% less than 15 minutes, 22.0% 15 to 30 minutes, 34.1% 30 to 45 minutes, 29.3% 45 to 60 minutes, 4.9% 60 minutes or more (2005-2009 5-year est.).

SAINTE MARIE (village). Aka Saint Marie. Covers a land area of 1.112 square miles and a water area of 0 square miles. Located at 38.93° N. Lat; 88.02° W. Long. Elevation is 486 feet.
Population: 281 (1990); 261 (2000); 243 (2010); 234 (2015 projected); Race: 100.0% White, 0.0% Black, 0.0% Asian, 0.0% Other, 0.0% Hispanic of any race (2010); Density: 218.5 persons per square mile (2010); Average household size: 2.43 (2010); Median age: 40.2 (2010); Males per 100 females: 92.9 (2010); Marriage status: 16.9% never married, 52.7% now married, 11.4% widowed, 18.9% divorced (2005-2009 5-year est.); Foreign born: 0.4% (2005-2009 5-year est.); Ancestry (includes multiple ancestries): 41.6% German, 10.6% French, 10.2% English, 9.8% American, 9.0% Irish (2005-2009 5-year est.).
Economy: Single-family building permits issued: 0 (2010); Multi-family building permits issued: 0 (2010); Employment by occupation: 8.0% management, 16.8% professional, 8.8% services, 26.5% sales, 0.0% farming, 7.1% construction, 32.7% production (2005-2009 5-year est.).
Income: Per capita income: $20,557 (2010); Median household income: $42,742 (2010); Average household income: $49,100 (2010); Percent of households with income of $100,000 or more: 9.0% (2010); Poverty rate: 12.7% (2005-2009 5-year est.).
Taxes: Total city taxes per capita: $67 (2007); City property taxes per capita: $47 (2007).
Education: Percent of population age 25 and over with: High school diploma (including GED) or higher: 81.4% (2010); Bachelor's degree or higher: 21.0% (2010); Master's degree or higher: 3.0% (2010).
School District(s)
Jasper County CUD 1 (PK-12)
    2009-10 Enrollment: 1,428 .... (618) 783-8459
Housing: Homeownership rate: 87.0% (2010); Median home value: $82,727 (2010); Median contract rent: $181 per month (2005-2009 5-year est.); Median year structure built: 1956 (2005-2009 5-year est.).
Transportation: Commute to work: 86.5% car, 0.0% public transportation, 7.2% walk, 6.3% work from home (2005-2009 5-year est.); Travel time to work: 31.7% less than 15 minutes, 44.2% 15 to 30 minutes, 15.4% 30 to 45 minutes, 1.9% 45 to 60 minutes, 6.7% 60 minutes or more (2005-2009 5-year est.)

WEST LIBERTY (unincorporated postal area, zip code 62475). Covers a land area of 28.531 square miles and a water area of 0.057 square miles. Located at 38.86° N. Lat; 88.05° W. Long. Elevation is 482 feet.
Population: 416 (2000); Race: 100.0% White, 0.0% Black, 0.0% Asian, 0.0% Other, 0.0% Hispanic of any race (2000); Density: 14.6 persons per square mile (2000); Age: 29.1% under 18, 11.9% over 64 (2000); Marriage status: 26.3% never married, 72.5% now married, 1.2% widowed, 0.0% divorced (2000); Foreign born: 0.0% (2000); Ancestry (includes multiple ancestries): 55.5% German, 12.6% English, 8.3% Swiss, 7.6% American (2000).
Economy: Employment by occupation: 24.9% management, 1.9% professional, 15.0% services, 36.6% sales, 4.2% farming, 0.0% construction, 17.4% production (2000).
Income: Per capita income: $14,590 (2000); Median household income: $40,179 (2000); Poverty rate: 8.9% (2000).
Education: Percent of population age 25 and over with: High school diploma (including GED) or higher: 89.2% (2000); Bachelor's degree or higher: 12.2% (2000).
Housing: Homeownership rate: 100.0% (2000); Median home value: $56,900 (2000); Median contract rent: n/a per month (2000); Median year structure built: 1950 (2000).

Transportation: Commute to work: 83.6% car, 0.0% public transportation, 8.5% walk, 5.2% work from home (2000); Travel time to work: 37.1% less than 15 minutes, 52.5% 15 to 30 minutes, 9.4% 30 to 45 minutes, 1.0% 45 to 60 minutes, 0.0% 60 minutes or more (2000)

WHEELER (village). Covers a land area of 0.576 square miles and a water area of 0 square miles. Located at 39.04° N. Lat; 88.31° W. Long. Elevation is 561 feet.
Population: 161 (1990); 119 (2000); 126 (2010); 127 (2015 projected); Race: 99.2% White, 0.0% Black, 0.0% Asian, 0.8% Other, 0.8% Hispanic of any race (2010); Density: 218.7 persons per square mile (2010); Average household size: 2.74 (2010); Median age: 37.7 (2010); Males per 100 females: 96.9 (2010); Marriage status: 26.3% never married, 61.8% now married, 7.9% widowed, 3.9% divorced (2005-2009 5-year est.); Foreign born: 0.0% (2005-2009 5-year est.); Ancestry (includes multiple ancestries): 18.8% German, 11.1% Irish, 5.1% English, 1.7% Swedish, 1.7% Polish (2005-2009 5-year est.).
Economy: Employment by occupation: 0.0% management, 13.3% professional, 31.1% services, 11.1% sales, 0.0% farming, 6.7% construction, 37.8% production (2005-2009 5-year est.).
Income: Per capita income: $22,544 (2010); Median household income: $55,000 (2010); Average household income: $62,120 (2010); Percent of households with income of $100,000 or more: 15.2% (2010); Poverty rate: 47.9% (2005-2009 5-year est.).
Taxes: Total city taxes per capita: $34 (2007); City property taxes per capita: $34 (2007).
Education: Percent of population age 25 and over with: High school diploma (including GED) or higher: 89.3% (2010); Bachelor's degree or higher: 10.7% (2010); Master's degree or higher: 2.4% (2010).
Housing: Homeownership rate: 84.8% (2010); Median home value: $113,889 (2010); Median contract rent: $238 per month (2005-2009 5-year est.); Median year structure built: 1955 (2005-2009 5-year est.).
Transportation: Commute to work: 100.0% car, 0.0% public transportation, 0.0% walk, 0.0% work from home (2005-2009 5-year est.); Travel time to work: 25.6% less than 15 minutes, 37.2% 15 to 30 minutes, 37.2% 30 to 45 minutes, 0.0% 45 to 60 minutes, 0.0% 60 minutes or more (2005-2009 5-year est.)

WILLOW HILL (village). Covers a land area of 1.038 square miles and a water area of 0 square miles. Located at 38.99° N. Lat; 88.02° W. Long. Elevation is 502 feet.
Population: 268 (1990); 250 (2000); 238 (2010); 232 (2015 projected); Race: 97.1% White, 0.0% Black, 1.3% Asian, 1.7% Other, 0.8% Hispanic of any race (2010); Density: 229.3 persons per square mile (2010); Average household size: 2.70 (2010); Median age: 39.4 (2010); Males per 100 females: 107.0 (2010); Marriage status: 29.1% never married, 60.2% now married, 3.6% widowed, 7.1% divorced (2005-2009 5-year est.); Foreign born: 0.7% (2005-2009 5-year est.); Ancestry (includes multiple ancestries): 22.2% German, 12.7% English, 10.5% American, 10.2% Irish, 4.7% Norwegian (2005-2009 5-year est.).
Economy: Single-family building permits issued: 0 (2010); Multi-family building permits issued: 0 (2010); Employment by occupation: 15.2% management, 10.1% professional, 10.1% services, 6.3% sales, 0.0% farming, 12.7% construction, 45.6% production (2005-2009 5-year est.).
Income: Per capita income: $21,432 (2010); Median household income: $43,438 (2010); Average household income: $55,966 (2010); Percent of households with income of $100,000 or more: 5.7% (2010); Poverty rate: 31.4% (2005-2009 5-year est.).
Taxes: Total city taxes per capita: $59 (2007); City property taxes per capita: $59 (2007).
Education: Percent of population age 25 and over with: High school diploma (including GED) or higher: 88.9% (2010); Bachelor's degree or higher: 12.4% (2010); Master's degree or higher: 3.9% (2010).
School District(s)
Jasper County CUD 1 (PK-12)
    2009-10 Enrollment: 1,428 . . . . (618) 783-8459
Housing: Homeownership rate: 86.4% (2010); Median home value: $100,000 (2010); Median contract rent: $188 per month (2005-2009 5-year est.); Median year structure built: 1945 (2005-2009 5-year est.).
Transportation: Commute to work: 90.4% car, 0.0% public transportation, 9.6% walk, 0.0% work from home (2005-2009 5-year est.); Travel time to work: 19.2% less than 15 minutes, 49.3% 15 to 30 minutes, 5.5% 30 to 45 minutes, 20.5% 45 to 60 minutes, 5.5% 60 minutes or more (2005-2009 5-year est.)

YALE (village). Covers a land area of 0.575 square miles and a water area of 0 square miles. Located at 39.12° N. Lat; 88.02° W. Long. Elevation is 558 feet.
Population: 94 (1990); 97 (2000); 91 (2010); 87 (2015 projected); Race: 97.8% White, 0.0% Black, 0.0% Asian, 2.2% Other, 3.3% Hispanic of any race (2010); Density: 158.3 persons per square mile (2010); Average household size: 2.60 (2010); Median age: 43.8 (2010); Males per 100 females: 127.5 (2010); Marriage status: 23.7% never married, 61.0% now married, 13.6% widowed, 1.7% divorced (2005-2009 5-year est.); Foreign born: 0.0% (2005-2009 5-year est.); Ancestry (includes multiple ancestries): 41.1% German, 13.7% Swiss, 13.7% American, 4.1% Irish, 2.7% English (2005-2009 5-year est.).
Economy: Employment by occupation: 26.3% management, 13.2% professional, 15.8% services, 26.3% sales, 0.0% farming, 5.3% construction, 13.2% production (2005-2009 5-year est.).
Income: Per capita income: $21,452 (2010); Median household income: $42,500 (2010); Average household income: $51,000 (2010); Percent of households with income of $100,000 or more: 2.9% (2010); Poverty rate: 6.8% (2005-2009 5-year est.).
Taxes: Total city taxes per capita: $74 (2007); City property taxes per capita: $64 (2007).
Education: Percent of population age 25 and over with: High school diploma (including GED) or higher: 85.2% (2010); Bachelor's degree or higher: 11.5% (2010); Master's degree or higher: 3.3% (2010).
Housing: Homeownership rate: 88.6% (2010); Median home value: $92,500 (2010); Median contract rent: $125 per month (2005-2009 5-year est.); Median year structure built: 1958 (2005-2009 5-year est.).
Transportation: Commute to work: 71.1% car, 0.0% public transportation, 13.2% walk, 0.0% work from home (2005-2009 5-year est.); Travel time to work: 50.0% less than 15 minutes, 31.6% 15 to 30 minutes, 5.3% 30 to 45 minutes, 0.0% 45 to 60 minutes, 13.2% 60 minutes or more (2005-2009 5-year est.)

Jefferson County

Located in southern Illinois; drained by the Big Muddy River. Covers a land area of 570.96 square miles, a water area of 12.76 square miles, and is located in the Central Time Zone at 38.31° N. Lat., 88.91° W. Long. The county was founded in 1819. County seat is Mount Vernon.

Jefferson County is part of the Mount Vernon, IL Micropolitan Statistical Area. The entire metro area includes: Hamilton County, IL; Jefferson County, IL

Weather Station: Mt Vernon Mt Vernon-Outland A   Elevation: 465 feet

	Jan	Feb	Mar	Apr	May	Jun	Jul	Aug	Sep	Oct	Nov	Dec
High	39	43	53	65	74	83	87	86	79	67	54	42
Low	21	24	33	44	53	63	67	64	56	44	35	24
Precip	2.3	2.8	3.9	4.3	5.1	3.8	3.7	3.0	3.2	3.7	4.1	3.2
Snow	3.8	4.7	1.3	0.2	0.0	0.0	0.0	0.0	0.0	0.2	0.3	3.3

High and Low temperatures in degrees Fahrenheit; Precipitation and Snow in inches

Population: 37,020 (1990); 40,045 (2000); 40,066 (2010); 39,805 (2015 projected); Race: 88.5% White, 8.5% Black, 0.6% Asian, 2.3% Other, 1.6% Hispanic of any race (2010); Density: 70.2 persons per square mile (2010); Average household size: 2.40 (2010); Median age: 38.6 (2010); Males per 100 females: 105.2 (2010).
Religion: Five largest groups: 25.9% Southern Baptist Convention, 7.5% Christian Churches and Churches of Christ, 6.0% Catholic Church, 5.1% The United Methodist Church, 1.8% National Association of Free Will Baptists (2000).
Economy: Unemployment rate: 9.2% (August 2011); Total civilian labor force: 20,348 (August 2011); Leading industries: 20.3% health care and social assistance; 17.6% manufacturing; 13.8% retail trade (2009); Farms: 1,156 totaling 232,531 acres (2007); Companies that employ 500 or more persons: 3 (2009); Companies that employ 100 to 499 persons: 12 (2009); Companies that employ less than 100 persons: 991 (2009); Black-owned businesses: 83 (2007); Hispanic-owned businesses: n/a (2007); Asian-owned businesses: n/a (2007); Women-owned businesses: 528 (2007); Retail sales per capita: $12,702 (2010). Single-family building permits issued: 0 (2010); Multi-family building permits issued: 0 (2010).
Income: Per capita income: $20,887 (2010); Median household income: $41,693 (2010); Average household income: $52,383 (2010); Percent of households with income of $100,000 or more: 10.2% (2010); Poverty rate: 18.9% (2009); Bankruptcy rate: 4.20% (2010).

Taxes: Total county taxes per capita: $122 (2007); County property taxes per capita: $52 (2007).
Education: Percent of population age 25 and over with: High school diploma (including GED) or higher: 82.6% (2010); Bachelor's degree or higher: 13.7% (2010); Master's degree or higher: 5.2% (2010).
Housing: Homeownership rate: 76.2% (2010); Median home value: $78,829 (2010); Median contract rent: $356 per month (2005-2009 5-year est.); Median year structure built: 1973 (2005-2009 5-year est.)
Health: Birth rate: 119.9 per 10,000 population (2009); Death rate: 99.9 per 10,000 population (2009); Age-adjusted cancer mortality rate: 194.6 deaths per 100,000 population (2007); Number of physicians: 22.2 per 10,000 population (2008); Hospital beds: 44.9 per 10,000 population (2007); Hospital admissions: 2,442.4 per 10,000 population (2007).
Elections: 2008 Presidential election results: 43.5% Obama, 54.3% McCain, 1.1% Nader
National and State Parks: Mount Vernon State Game Farm; Rend Lake State Waterfowl Management Area
Additional Information Contacts
Jefferson County Government . . . . (618) 244-8020
 http://www.jeffil.us
City of Mount Vernon . . . . (618) 242-5000
 http://www.mtvernon.com
Jefferson County Chamber of Commerce . . . . (618) 242-5725
 http://southernillinois.com

Jefferson County Communities

BELLE RIVE (village). Covers a land area of 1.026 square miles and a water area of 0 square miles. Located at 38.23° N. Lat; 88.74° W. Long. Elevation is 479 feet.
Population: 396 (1990); 371 (2000); 341 (2010); 329 (2015 projected); Race: 96.5% White, 2.1% Black, 0.0% Asian, 1.5% Other, 0.0% Hispanic of any race (2010); Density: 332.3 persons per square mile (2010); Average household size: 2.71 (2010); Median age: 40.5 (2010); Males per 100 females: 105.4 (2010); Marriage status: 21.6% never married, 61.2% now married, 7.2% widowed, 10.0% divorced (2005-2009 5-year est.); Foreign born: 2.6% (2005-2009 5-year est.); Ancestry (includes multiple ancestries): 19.0% German, 15.9% English, 13.4% Irish, 10.5% American, 7.7% Swedish (2005-2009 5-year est.).
Economy: Employment by occupation: 2.8% management, 33.8% professional, 17.9% services, 15.2% sales, 0.0% farming, 4.8% construction, 25.5% production (2005-2009 5-year est.).
Income: Per capita income: $18,960 (2010); Median household income: $50,000 (2010); Average household income: $53,016 (2010); Percent of households with income of $100,000 or more: 4.8% (2010); Poverty rate: 14.8% (2005-2009 5-year est.).
Taxes: Total city taxes per capita: $26 (2007); City property taxes per capita: $26 (2007).
Education: Percent of population age 25 and over with: High school diploma (including GED) or higher: 84.5% (2010); Bachelor's degree or higher: 12.5% (2010); Master's degree or higher: 3.9% (2010).
School District(s)
Opdyke-Belle-Rive CCSD 5 (KG-08)
 2009-10 Enrollment: 190 . . . . (618) 756-2492
Housing: Homeownership rate: 86.5% (2010); Median home value: $70,455 (2010); Median contract rent: n/a per month (2005-2009 5-year est.); Median year structure built: 1975 (2005-2009 5-year est.).
Transportation: Commute to work: 95.8% car, 0.0% public transportation, 0.0% walk, 4.2% work from home (2005-2009 5-year est.); Travel time to work: 16.2% less than 15 minutes, 58.8% 15 to 30 minutes, 14.7% 30 to 45 minutes, 1.5% 45 to 60 minutes, 8.8% 60 minutes or more (2005-2009 5-year est.)

BLUFORD (village). Covers a land area of 1.456 square miles and a water area of 0.008 square miles. Located at 38.32° N. Lat; 88.73° W. Long. Elevation is 522 feet.
Population: 747 (1990); 785 (2000); 725 (2010); 692 (2015 projected); Race: 98.1% White, 0.0% Black, 0.3% Asian, 1.7% Other, 1.1% Hispanic of any race (2010); Density: 497.9 persons per square mile (2010); Average household size: 2.67 (2010); Median age: 38.2 (2010); Males per 100 females: 101.9 (2010); Marriage status: 29.1% never married, 57.4% now married, 6.9% widowed, 6.6% divorced (2005-2009 5-year est.); Foreign born: 0.0% (2005-2009 5-year est.); Ancestry (includes multiple ancestries): 31.8% English, 24.2% German, 15.1% Irish, 7.8% American, 5.3% French (2005-2009 5-year est.).

Economy: Single-family building permits issued: 0 (2010); Multi-family building permits issued: 0 (2010); Employment by occupation: 8.9% management, 8.6% professional, 20.2% services, 33.9% sales, 0.0% farming, 10.6% construction, 17.8% production (2005-2009 5-year est.).
Income: Per capita income: $20,083 (2010); Median household income: $45,667 (2010); Average household income: $54,136 (2010); Percent of households with income of $100,000 or more: 9.9% (2010); Poverty rate: 19.4% (2005-2009 5-year est.).
Taxes: Total city taxes per capita: $10 (2007); City property taxes per capita: $9 (2007).
Education: Percent of population age 25 and over with: High school diploma (including GED) or higher: 82.3% (2010); Bachelor's degree or higher: 6.8% (2010); Master's degree or higher: 1.8% (2010).
School District(s)
Bluford CCSD 114 (PK-08)
 2009-10 Enrollment: 320 . . . . (618) 732-8242
Farrington CCSD 99 (KG-08)
 2009-10 Enrollment: 64 . . . . (618) 755-4414
Webber Twp HSD 204 (09-12)
 2009-10 Enrollment: 154 . . . . (618) 732-6121
Housing: Homeownership rate: 86.4% (2010); Median home value: $62,045 (2010); Median contract rent: $388 per month (2005-2009 5-year est.); Median year structure built: 1970 (2005-2009 5-year est.).
Transportation: Commute to work: 95.4% car, 0.0% public transportation, 1.1% walk, 3.6% work from home (2005-2009 5-year est.); Travel time to work: 8.1% less than 15 minutes, 76.3% 15 to 30 minutes, 8.9% 30 to 45 minutes, 4.8% 45 to 60 minutes, 1.9% 60 minutes or more (2005-2009 5-year est.)

BONNIE (village). Covers a land area of 1.233 square miles and a water area of <.001 square miles. Located at 38.20° N. Lat; 88.90° W. Long. Elevation is 427 feet.
Population: 410 (1990); 424 (2000); 405 (2010); 392 (2015 projected); Race: 94.1% White, 1.7% Black, 0.0% Asian, 4.2% Other, 1.7% Hispanic of any race (2010); Density: 328.4 persons per square mile (2010); Average household size: 2.48 (2010); Median age: 39.7 (2010); Males per 100 females: 94.7 (2010); Marriage status: 20.4% never married, 56.2% now married, 8.8% widowed, 14.6% divorced (2005-2009 5-year est.); Foreign born: 1.7% (2005-2009 5-year est.); Ancestry (includes multiple ancestries): 24.5% German, 23.0% Irish, 18.9% American, 9.3% English, 3.7% Polish (2005-2009 5-year est.).
Economy: Single-family building permits issued: 0 (2010); Multi-family building permits issued: 0 (2010); Employment by occupation: 1.8% management, 10.6% professional, 18.6% services, 19.5% sales, 0.9% farming, 12.4% construction, 36.3% production (2005-2009 5-year est.).
Income: Per capita income: $20,231 (2010); Median household income: $45,938 (2010); Average household income: $50,184 (2010); Percent of households with income of $100,000 or more: 9.8% (2010); Poverty rate: 12.7% (2005-2009 5-year est.).
Taxes: Total city taxes per capita: $30 (2007); City property taxes per capita: $19 (2007).
Education: Percent of population age 25 and over with: High school diploma (including GED) or higher: 87.3% (2010); Bachelor's degree or higher: 4.6% (2010); Master's degree or higher: 1.4% (2010).
Housing: Homeownership rate: 84.7% (2010); Median home value: $61,905 (2010); Median contract rent: $300 per month (2005-2009 5-year est.); Median year structure built: 1974 (2005-2009 5-year est.).
Transportation: Commute to work: 96.5% car, 0.0% public transportation, 1.8% walk, 0.0% work from home (2005-2009 5-year est.); Travel time to work: 20.4% less than 15 minutes, 63.3% 15 to 30 minutes, 10.2% 30 to 45 minutes, 0.9% 45 to 60 minutes, 5.3% 60 minutes or more (2005-2009 5-year est.)

DIX (village). Aka Rome. Covers a land area of 2.094 square miles and a water area of 0.009 square miles. Located at 38.44° N. Lat; 88.94° W. Long. Elevation is 600 feet.
Population: 430 (1990); 494 (2000); 455 (2010); 431 (2015 projected); Race: 96.5% White, 0.7% Black, 1.1% Asian, 1.8% Other, 0.4% Hispanic of any race (2010); Density: 217.2 persons per square mile (2010); Average household size: 2.10 (2010); Median age: 43.4 (2010); Males per 100 females: 85.7 (2010); Marriage status: 19.8% never married, 42.3% now married, 14.5% widowed, 23.5% divorced (2005-2009 5-year est.); Foreign born: 0.3% (2005-2009 5-year est.); Ancestry (includes multiple ancestries): 18.3% German, 18.1% Irish, 13.4% English, 10.5% American, 5.2% Scottish (2005-2009 5-year est.).

Economy: Employment by occupation: 5.4% management, 11.5% professional, 27.0% services, 26.4% sales, 0.0% farming, 8.8% construction, 20.9% production (2005-2009 5-year est.).
Income: Per capita income: $19,573 (2010); Median household income: $28,056 (2010); Average household income: $40,876 (2010); Percent of households with income of $100,000 or more: 7.8% (2010); Poverty rate: 31.9% (2005-2009 5-year est.).
Taxes: Total city taxes per capita: $36 (2007); City property taxes per capita: $24 (2007).
Education: Percent of population age 25 and over with: High school diploma (including GED) or higher: 79.8% (2010); Bachelor's degree or higher: 9.7% (2010); Master's degree or higher: 0.9% (2010).

School District(s)
Rome CCSD 2 (PK-08)
   2009-10 Enrollment: 342 . . . . (618) 266-7214
Housing: Homeownership rate: 63.6% (2010); Median home value: $99,130 (2010); Median contract rent: $177 per month (2005-2009 5-year est.); Median year structure built: 1980 (2005-2009 5-year est.).
Transportation: Commute to work: 87.8% car, 0.0% public transportation, 0.0% walk, 9.4% work from home (2005-2009 5-year est.); Travel time to work: 23.8% less than 15 minutes, 43.7% 15 to 30 minutes, 8.7% 30 to 45 minutes, 2.4% 45 to 60 minutes, 21.4% 60 minutes or more (2005-2009 5-year est.)

INA (village). Covers a land area of 2.405 square miles and a water area of 0 square miles. Located at 38.15° N. Lat; 88.90° W. Long. Elevation is 430 feet.
Population: 722 (1990); 2,455 (2000); 2,528 (2010); 2,560 (2015 projected); Race: 41.8% White, 54.4% Black, 0.3% Asian, 3.5% Other, 8.5% Hispanic of any race (2010); Density: 1,050.9 persons per square mile (2010); Average household size: 2.56 (2010); Median age: 33.5 (2010); Males per 100 females: 579.6 (2010); Marriage status: 57.6% never married, 22.8% now married, 2.6% widowed, 17.0% divorced (2005-2009 5-year est.); Foreign born: 2.7% (2005-2009 5-year est.); Ancestry (includes multiple ancestries): 14.3% German, 13.6% Irish, 6.0% English, 4.0% Italian, 2.3% Polish (2005-2009 5-year est.).
Economy: Single-family building permits issued: 0 (2010); Multi-family building permits issued: 0 (2010); Employment by occupation: 16.7% management, 15.9% professional, 8.2% services, 28.8% sales, 0.0% farming, 10.7% construction, 19.7% production (2005-2009 5-year est.).
Income: Per capita income: $10,626 (2010); Median household income: $41,346 (2010); Average household income: $50,294 (2010); Percent of households with income of $100,000 or more: 10.4% (2010); Poverty rate: 13.1% (2005-2009 5-year est.).
Taxes: Total city taxes per capita: $9 (2007); City property taxes per capita: $8 (2007).
Education: Percent of population age 25 and over with: High school diploma (including GED) or higher: 50.4% (2010); Bachelor's degree or higher: 1.9% (2010); Master's degree or higher: 1.2% (2010).

School District(s)
Ina CCSD 8 (PK-08)
   2009-10 Enrollment: 106 . . . . (618) 437-5361

Two-year College(s)
Rend Lake College (Public)
   Fall 2009 Enrollment: 5,871 . . . . (618) 437-5321
   2010-11 Tuition: In-state $3,645; Out-of-state $4,800
Housing: Homeownership rate: 80.6% (2010); Median home value: $66,410 (2010); Median contract rent: $232 per month (2005-2009 5-year est.); Median year structure built: 1958 (2005-2009 5-year est.).
Transportation: Commute to work: 96.1% car, 0.0% public transportation, 2.6% walk, 1.3% work from home (2005-2009 5-year est.); Travel time to work: 23.0% less than 15 minutes, 52.7% 15 to 30 minutes, 11.9% 30 to 45 minutes, 0.9% 45 to 60 minutes, 11.5% 60 minutes or more (2005-2009 5-year est.)

MOUNT VERNON (city). County seat. Covers a land area of 11.521 square miles and a water area of 0.099 square miles. Located at 38.31° N. Lat; 88.90° W. Long. Elevation is 512 feet.
History: Mount Vernon was settled by people from the southern states. It grew slowly as the seat of Jefferson County after 1819.
Population: 17,465 (1990); 16,269 (2000); 15,774 (2010); 15,379 (2015 projected); Race: 84.4% White, 11.0% Black, 1.1% Asian, 3.5% Other, 1.8% Hispanic of any race (2010); Density: 1,369.1 persons per square mile (2010); Average household size: 2.22 (2010); Median age: 38.6 (2010); Males per 100 females: 87.9 (2010); Marriage status: 27.6% never

married, 46.7% now married, 11.6% widowed, 14.1% divorced (2005-2009 5-year est.); Foreign born: 2.7% (2005-2009 5-year est.); Ancestry (includes multiple ancestries): 25.2% German, 15.9% Irish, 13.2% English, 8.7% American, 2.9% Italian (2005-2009 5-year est.).
Economy: Single-family building permits issued: 0 (2010); Multi-family building permits issued: 0 (2010); Employment by occupation: 9.8% management, 17.6% professional, 20.3% services, 27.6% sales, 0.0% farming, 7.9% construction, 16.8% production (2005-2009 5-year est.).
Income: Per capita income: $19,846 (2010); Median household income: $33,001 (2010); Average household income: $44,750 (2010); Percent of households with income of $100,000 or more: 7.8% (2010); Poverty rate: 25.4% (2005-2009 5-year est.).
Taxes: Total city taxes per capita: $350 (2007); City property taxes per capita: $59 (2007).
Education: Percent of population age 25 and over with: High school diploma (including GED) or higher: 83.2% (2010); Bachelor's degree or higher: 17.2% (2010); Master's degree or higher: 6.8% (2010).

School District(s)
Bethel SD 82 (PK-08)
   2009-10 Enrollment: 163 . . . . (618) 244-8095
Dodds CCSD 7 (KG-08)
   2009-10 Enrollment: 137 . . . . (618) 244-8070
Franklin-Jefferson Co Sp Ed Dist (03-12)
   2009-10 Enrollment: n/a . . . . (618) 439-7231
Hamilton/Jefferson Roe (08-12)
   2009-10 Enrollment: n/a . . . . (618) 244-8040
Mcclellan CCSD 12 (KG-08)
   2009-10 Enrollment: 54 . . . . (618) 244-8072
Mount Vernon SD 80 (PK-08)
   2009-10 Enrollment: 1,756 . . . . (618) 244-8080
Mt Vernon Area Voc Center (11-12)
   2009-10 Enrollment: n/a . . . . (618) 246-5602
Mt Vernon Twp HSD 201 (09-12)
   2009-10 Enrollment: 1,358 . . . . (618) 246-5908
Summersville SD 79 (PK-08)
   2009-10 Enrollment: 296 . . . . (618) 244-8079
Housing: Homeownership rate: 63.0% (2010); Median home value: $66,964 (2010); Median contract rent: $372 per month (2005-2009 5-year est.); Median year structure built: 1963 (2005-2009 5-year est.).
Hospitals: Crossroads Community Hospital (55 beds); Good Samaritan Regional Health Center (175 beds)
Newspapers: Health Watch - Register News (Local news); Morning Sentinel (Regional news; Circulation 16,000); Mount Vernon Register-News (Local news; Circulation 15,000); Vernois News (Community news; Circulation 2,000)
Transportation: Commute to work: 87.9% car, 1.4% public transportation, 2.9% walk, 3.7% work from home (2005-2009 5-year est.); Travel time to work: 59.9% less than 15 minutes, 26.8% 15 to 30 minutes, 7.4% 30 to 45 minutes, 1.2% 45 to 60 minutes, 4.7% 60 minutes or more (2005-2009 5-year est.)
Airports: Mount Vernon (general aviation)
Additional Information Contacts
City of Mount Vernon . . . . (618) 242-5000
   http://www.mtvernon.com
Jefferson County Chamber of Commerce . . . . (618) 242-5725
   http://southernillinois.com

NASON (city). Covers a land area of 0.903 square miles and a water area of 0 square miles. Located at 38.17° N. Lat; 88.96° W. Long. Elevation is 436 feet.
Population: 235 (1990); 234 (2000); 243 (2010); 242 (2015 projected); Race: 98.8% White, 0.0% Black, 0.4% Asian, 0.8% Other, 0.4% Hispanic of any race (2010); Density: 269.0 persons per square mile (2010); Average household size: 2.48 (2010); Median age: 41.2 (2010); Males per 100 females: 109.5 (2010); Marriage status: 21.2% never married, 60.3% now married, 10.3% widowed, 8.2% divorced (2005-2009 5-year est.); Foreign born: 0.0% (2005-2009 5-year est.); Ancestry (includes multiple ancestries): 22.9% Irish, 20.5% German, 16.3% English, 10.2% American, 3.6% Italian (2005-2009 5-year est.).
Economy: Employment by occupation: 1.3% management, 3.8% professional, 7.7% services, 43.6% sales, 0.0% farming, 10.3% construction, 33.3% production (2005-2009 5-year est.).
Income: Per capita income: $21,975 (2010); Median household income: $51,613 (2010); Average household income: $54,439 (2010); Percent of

households with income of $100,000 or more: 8.2% (2010); Poverty rate: 5.4% (2005-2009 5-year est.).
Taxes: Total city taxes per capita: $17 (2007); City property taxes per capita: $8 (2007).
Education: Percent of population age 25 and over with: High school diploma (including GED) or higher: 89.9% (2010); Bachelor's degree or higher: 10.1% (2010); Master's degree or higher: 3.0% (2010).
Housing: Homeownership rate: 88.8% (2010); Median home value: $79,167 (2010); Median contract rent: n/a per month (2005-2009 5-year est.); Median year structure built: 1976 (2005-2009 5-year est.).
Transportation: Commute to work: 92.3% car, 0.0% public transportation, 2.6% walk, 2.6% work from home (2005-2009 5-year est.); Travel time to work: 5.3% less than 15 minutes, 77.6% 15 to 30 minutes, 6.6% 30 to 45 minutes, 5.3% 45 to 60 minutes, 5.3% 60 minutes or more (2005-2009 5-year est.)

OPDYKE (unincorporated postal area, zip code 62872). Covers a land area of 27.292 square miles and a water area of 0.033 square miles. Located at 38.28° N. Lat; 88.79° W. Long. Elevation is 515 feet.
Population: 1,327 (2000); Race: 98.9% White, 0.2% Black, 0.1% Asian, 0.8% Other, 3.3% Hispanic of any race (2000); Density: 48.6 persons per square mile (2000); Age: 33.5% under 18, 8.7% over 64 (2000); Marriage status: 18.3% never married, 69.1% now married, 5.1% widowed, 7.5% divorced (2000); Foreign born: 0.3% (2000); Ancestry (includes multiple ancestries): 20.9% German, 15.4% American, 10.4% Irish, 8.3% English (2000).
Economy: Employment by occupation: 10.8% management, 11.5% professional, 16.7% services, 22.3% sales, 0.7% farming, 12.5% construction, 25.6% production (2000).
Income: Per capita income: $14,881 (2000); Median household income: $38,854 (2000); Poverty rate: 12.7% (2000).
Education: Percent of population age 25 and over with: High school diploma (including GED) or higher: 76.8% (2000); Bachelor's degree or higher: 8.0% (2000).
School District(s)
Opdyke-Belle-Rive CCSD 5 (KG-08)
    2009-10 Enrollment: 190 . . . . (618) 756-2492
Housing: Homeownership rate: 92.0% (2000); Median home value: $68,700 (2000); Median contract rent: $241 per month (2000); Median year structure built: 1975 (2000).
Transportation: Commute to work: 93.1% car, 0.7% public transportation, 2.0% walk, 2.9% work from home (2000); Travel time to work: 23.6% less than 15 minutes, 57.8% 15 to 30 minutes, 10.8% 30 to 45 minutes, 3.0% 45 to 60 minutes, 4.9% 60 minutes or more (2000)

SCHELLER (unincorporated postal area, zip code 62883). Covers a land area of 38.171 square miles and a water area of 0.082 square miles. Located at 38.16° N. Lat; 89.11° W. Long. Elevation is 509 feet.
Population: 607 (2000); Race: 100.0% White, 0.0% Black, 0.0% Asian, 0.0% Other, 0.5% Hispanic of any race (2000); Density: 15.9 persons per square mile (2000); Age: 17.0% under 18, 20.5% over 64 (2000); Marriage status: 21.2% never married, 61.6% now married, 8.9% widowed, 8.3% divorced (2000); Foreign born: 0.0% (2000); Ancestry (includes multiple ancestries): 43.0% Polish, 24.3% German, 9.6% Irish, 8.9% American, 8.4% English (2000).
Economy: Employment by occupation: 11.5% management, 17.5% professional, 10.5% services, 15.4% sales, 2.1% farming, 10.8% construction, 32.2% production (2000).
Income: Per capita income: $21,207 (2000); Median household income: $43,021 (2000); Poverty rate: 1.4% (2000).
Education: Percent of population age 25 and over with: High school diploma (including GED) or higher: 80.9% (2000); Bachelor's degree or higher: 5.9% (2000).
Housing: Homeownership rate: 86.0% (2000); Median home value: $68,700 (2000); Median contract rent: $186 per month (2000); Median year structure built: 1972 (2000).
Transportation: Commute to work: 88.8% car, 0.0% public transportation, 4.0% walk, 5.8% work from home (2000); Travel time to work: 27.5% less than 15 minutes, 24.8% 15 to 30 minutes, 28.6% 30 to 45 minutes, 14.5% 45 to 60 minutes, 4.6% 60 minutes or more (2000)

TEXICO (unincorporated postal area, zip code 62889). Covers a land area of 34.835 square miles and a water area of 0.062 square miles. Located at 38.45° N. Lat; 88.82° W. Long. Elevation is 512 feet.

Population: 943 (2000); Race: 97.1% White, 1.8% Black, 0.0% Asian, 1.1% Other, 0.0% Hispanic of any race (2000); Density: 27.1 persons per square mile (2000); Age: 25.9% under 18, 13.4% over 64 (2000); Marriage status: 19.6% never married, 66.4% now married, 6.4% widowed, 7.7% divorced (2000); Foreign born: 0.4% (2000); Ancestry (includes multiple ancestries): 20.4% American, 16.9% English, 10.7% German, 8.6% Irish (2000).
Economy: Employment by occupation: 8.9% management, 10.2% professional, 14.9% services, 23.1% sales, 0.0% farming, 12.2% construction, 30.7% production (2000).
Income: Per capita income: $17,291 (2000); Median household income: $38,452 (2000); Poverty rate: 16.0% (2000).
Education: Percent of population age 25 and over with: High school diploma (including GED) or higher: 83.3% (2000); Bachelor's degree or higher: 8.1% (2000).
School District(s)
Field CCSD 3 (PK-08)
    2009-10 Enrollment: 303 . . . . (618) 755-4611
Housing: Homeownership rate: 89.7% (2000); Median home value: $43,200 (2000); Median contract rent: $341 per month (2000); Median year structure built: 1972 (2000).
Transportation: Commute to work: 94.4% car, 1.8% public transportation, 0.4% walk, 2.0% work from home (2000); Travel time to work: 9.1% less than 15 minutes, 58.1% 15 to 30 minutes, 15.9% 30 to 45 minutes, 4.6% 45 to 60 minutes, 12.3% 60 minutes or more (2000)

WALTONVILLE (village). Covers a land area of 0.958 square miles and a water area of 0.026 square miles. Located at 38.21° N. Lat; 89.04° W. Long. Elevation is 463 feet.
Population: 396 (1990); 422 (2000); 423 (2010); 418 (2015 projected); Race: 99.1% White, 0.0% Black, 0.0% Asian, 0.9% Other, 1.2% Hispanic of any race (2010); Density: 441.6 persons per square mile (2010); Average household size: 2.43 (2010); Median age: 36.9 (2010); Males per 100 females: 97.7 (2010); Marriage status: 24.8% never married, 58.1% now married, 8.3% widowed, 8.8% divorced (2005-2009 5-year est.); Foreign born: 1.6% (2005-2009 5-year est.); Ancestry (includes multiple ancestries): 20.5% German, 13.6% English, 12.7% Irish, 10.1% American, 7.4% Italian (2005-2009 5-year est.).
Economy: Employment by occupation: 4.6% management, 16.5% professional, 11.9% services, 27.8% sales, 0.0% farming, 16.5% construction, 22.7% production (2005-2009 5-year est.).
Income: Per capita income: $19,507 (2010); Median household income: $44,194 (2010); Average household income: $48,103 (2010); Percent of households with income of $100,000 or more: 9.2% (2010); Poverty rate: 13.1% (2005-2009 5-year est.).
Taxes: Total city taxes per capita: $16 (2007); City property taxes per capita: $16 (2007).
Education: Percent of population age 25 and over with: High school diploma (including GED) or higher: 81.5% (2010); Bachelor's degree or higher: 8.9% (2010); Master's degree or higher: 0.4% (2010).
School District(s)
Waltonville CUSD 1 (PK-12)
    2009-10 Enrollment: 391 . . . . (618) 279-7211
Housing: Homeownership rate: 79.9% (2010); Median home value: $73,889 (2010); Median contract rent: $228 per month (2005-2009 5-year est.); Median year structure built: 1970 (2005-2009 5-year est.).
Transportation: Commute to work: 94.6% car, 0.0% public transportation, 0.0% walk, 4.3% work from home (2005-2009 5-year est.); Travel time to work: 6.8% less than 15 minutes, 67.8% 15 to 30 minutes, 14.7% 30 to 45 minutes, 5.6% 45 to 60 minutes, 5.1% 60 minutes or more (2005-2009 5-year est.)

WOODLAWN (village). Covers a land area of 0.714 square miles and a water area of 0 square miles. Located at 38.33° N. Lat; 89.03° W. Long. Elevation is 492 feet.
Population: 582 (1990); 630 (2000); 667 (2010); 676 (2015 projected); Race: 98.7% White, 0.3% Black, 0.0% Asian, 1.0% Other, 0.6% Hispanic of any race (2010); Density: 934.1 persons per square mile (2010); Average household size: 2.58 (2010); Median age: 37.1 (2010); Males per 100 females: 95.0 (2010); Marriage status: 22.4% never married, 59.0% now married, 10.0% widowed, 8.6% divorced (2005-2009 5-year est.); Foreign born: 0.0% (2005-2009 5-year est.); Ancestry (includes multiple ancestries): 31.3% German, 17.3% Irish, 12.7% English, 10.0% Polish, 8.2% American (2005-2009 5-year est.).

Economy: Employment by occupation: 4.6% management, 16.5% professional, 10.9% services, 32.7% sales, 1.0% farming, 6.3% construction, 28.1% production (2005-2009 5-year est.).
Income: Per capita income: $22,776 (2010); Median household income: $48,622 (2010); Average household income: $60,550 (2010); Percent of households with income of $100,000 or more: 12.4% (2010); Poverty rate: 13.1% (2005-2009 5-year est.).
Taxes: Total city taxes per capita: $11 (2007); City property taxes per capita: $11 (2007).
Education: Percent of population age 25 and over with: High school diploma (including GED) or higher: 92.8% (2010); Bachelor's degree or higher: 17.4% (2010); Master's degree or higher: 6.7% (2010).

School District(s)
Woodlawn CCSD 4 (PK-08)
   2009-10 Enrollment: 368 . . . . (618) 735-2661
Woodlawn CHSD 205 (09-12)
   2009-10 Enrollment: 197 . . . . (618) 735-2631
Housing: Homeownership rate: 85.7% (2010); Median home value: $92,821 (2010); Median contract rent: $363 per month (2005-2009 5-year est.); Median year structure built: 1979 (2005-2009 5-year est.).
Transportation: Commute to work: 95.8% car, 0.0% public transportation, 1.4% walk, 1.4% work from home (2005-2009 5-year est.); Travel time to work: 35.2% less than 15 minutes, 53.0% 15 to 30 minutes, 7.8% 30 to 45 minutes, 1.4% 45 to 60 minutes, 2.5% 60 minutes or more (2005-2009 5-year est.)

Jersey County

Located in western Illinois; bounded on the south by the Mississippi River and the Missouri border, and on the west by the Illinois River. Covers a land area of 369.16 square miles, a water area of 7.86 square miles, and is located in the Central Time Zone at 39.08° N. Lat., 90.34° W. Long. The county was founded in 1839. County seat is Jerseyville.

Jersey County is part of the St. Louis, MO-IL Metropolitan Statistical Area. The entire metro area includes: Bond County, IL; Calhoun County, IL; Clinton County, IL; Jersey County, IL; Macoupin County, IL; Madison County, IL; Monroe County, IL; St. Clair County, IL; Crawford County, MO (pt.); Franklin County, MO; Jefferson County, MO; Lincoln County, MO; St. Charles County, MO; St. Louis County, MO; Warren County, MO; Washington County, MO; St. Louis city, MO

Weather Station: Jerseyville 2 SW									Elevation: 629 feet		
	Jan	Feb	Mar	Apr	May	Jun	Jul	Aug	Sep	Oct	Nov	Dec
High	37	42	53	65	74	83	87	86	79	67	54	40
Low	19	23	32	42	53	62	66	63	54	43	34	23
Precip	2.2	2.2	3.3	3.9	4.6	3.7	3.5	3.2	3.3	3.4	4.0	2.9
Snow	4.0	3.4	2.0	0.2	0.0	0.0	0.0	0.0	0.0	0.0	tr	0.8	3.1

High and Low temperatures in degrees Fahrenheit; Precipitation and Snow in inches

Population: 20,539 (1990); 21,668 (2000); 22,829 (2010); 23,280 (2015 projected); Race: 97.3% White, 1.2% Black, 0.3% Asian, 1.3% Other, 1.0% Hispanic of any race (2010); Density: 61.8 persons per square mile (2010); Average household size: 2.50 (2010); Median age: 38.2 (2010); Males per 100 females: 96.5 (2010).
Religion: Five largest groups: 20.1% Catholic Church, 6.8% American Baptist Churches in the USA, 6.2% Southern Baptist Convention, 4.9% Assemblies of God, 3.7% The United Methodist Church (2000).
Economy: Unemployment rate: 8.5% (August 2011); Total civilian labor force: 11,609 (August 2011); Leading industries: 21.9% retail trade; 18.0% health care and social assistance; 14.8% accommodation & food services (2009); Farms: 519 totaling 189,462 acres (2007); Companies that employ 500 or more persons: 1 (2009); Companies that employ 100 to 499 persons: 4 (2009); Companies that employ less than 100 persons: 455 (2009); Black-owned businesses: n/a (2007); Hispanic-owned businesses: n/a (2007); Asian-owned businesses: n/a (2007); Women-owned businesses: 697 (2007); Retail sales per capita: $11,969 (2010). Single-family building permits issued: 30 (2010); Multi-family building permits issued: 35 (2010).
Income: Per capita income: $25,224 (2010); Median household income: $53,424 (2010); Average household income: $64,681 (2010); Percent of households with income of $100,000 or more: 16.0% (2010); Poverty rate: 10.0% (2009); Bankruptcy rate: 3.96% (2010).
Taxes: Total county taxes per capita: $123 (2007); County property taxes per capita: $87 (2007).

Education: Percent of population age 25 and over with: High school diploma (including GED) or higher: 87.6% (2010); Bachelor's degree or higher: 15.6% (2010); Master's degree or higher: 4.7% (2010).
Housing: Homeownership rate: 78.8% (2010); Median home value: $108,287 (2010); Median contract rent: $416 per month (2005-2009 5-year est.); Median year structure built: 1970 (2005-2009 5-year est.).
Health: Birth rate: 120.2 per 10,000 population (2009); Death rate: 104.2 per 10,000 population (2009); Age-adjusted cancer mortality rate: 155.8 deaths per 100,000 population (2007); Number of physicians: 8.0 per 10,000 population (2008); Hospital beds: 29.9 per 10,000 population (2007); Hospital admissions: 841.4 per 10,000 population (2007).
Environment: Air Quality Index: 90.0% good, 9.6% moderate, 0.4% unhealthy for sensitive individuals, 0.0% unhealthy (percent of days in 2008)
Elections: 2008 Presidential election results: 47.6% Obama, 50.4% McCain, 1.0% Nader
National and State Parks: Pere Marquette State Park; Stump Lake State Fish And Waterfowl Manageme; The Glades State Fish And Waterfowl Manageme
Additional Information Contacts
Jersey County Government . . . . (618) 498-5571
   http://jerseycountyclerk-il.us
City of Jerseyville . . . . (618) 498-3312
   http://www.jerseyville-il.us
Jersey County Business Association . . . . (618) 639-5222
   http://www.jerseycounty.org

Jersey County Communities

DOW (unincorporated postal area, zip code 62022). Covers a land area of 17.512 square miles and a water area of 0.001 square miles. Located at 38.99° N. Lat; 90.34° W. Long. Elevation is 673 feet.
Population: 962 (2000); Race: 97.8% White, 0.7% Black, 0.5% Asian, 1.0% Other, 0.0% Hispanic of any race (2000); Density: 54.9 persons per square mile (2000); Age: 16.5% under 18, 14.9% over 64 (2000); Marriage status: 15.9% never married, 68.1% now married, 4.4% widowed, 11.6% divorced (2000); Foreign born: 2.0% (2000); Ancestry (includes multiple ancestries): 32.9% German, 14.1% American, 13.1% Irish, 8.0% English (2000).
Economy: Employment by occupation: 11.9% management, 22.2% professional, 15.9% services, 23.6% sales, 0.0% farming, 14.5% construction, 11.9% production (2000).
Income: Per capita income: $24,943 (2000); Median household income: $48,750 (2000); Poverty rate: 3.3% (2000).
Education: Percent of population age 25 and over with: High school diploma (including GED) or higher: 85.0% (2000); Bachelor's degree or higher: 11.5% (2000).

School District(s)
Jersey CUSD 100 (PK-12)
   2009-10 Enrollment: 2,862 . . . . (618) 498-5561
Housing: Homeownership rate: 94.0% (2000); Median home value: $81,500 (2000); Median contract rent: $425 per month (2000); Median year structure built: 1967 (2000).
Transportation: Commute to work: 90.2% car, 1.2% public transportation, 0.0% walk, 8.6% work from home (2000); Travel time to work: 9.4% less than 15 minutes, 37.9% 15 to 30 minutes, 30.3% 30 to 45 minutes, 14.6% 45 to 60 minutes, 7.8% 60 minutes or more (2000)

ELSAH (village). Covers a land area of 1.062 square miles and a water area of 0 square miles. Located at 38.95° N. Lat; 90.35° W. Long. Elevation is 433 feet.
History: The first settler in Elsah was Addision Greene in 1847, who chopped wood for the steamboats that came along the Mississippi River. The settlement of Jersey Landing developed and was purchased in 1853 by General James Semple, who changed its name to Elsah and built a distillery and two grist mills.
Population: 851 (1990); 635 (2000); 633 (2010); 631 (2015 projected); Race: 92.4% White, 3.6% Black, 0.9% Asian, 3.0% Other, 1.9% Hispanic of any race (2010); Density: 596.2 persons per square mile (2010); Average household size: 2.47 (2010); Median age: 25.2 (2010); Males per 100 females: 90.7 (2010); Marriage status: 80.8% never married, 13.9% now married, 1.1% widowed, 4.2% divorced (2005-2009 5-year est.); Foreign born: 10.3% (2005-2009 5-year est.); Ancestry (includes multiple ancestries): 39.2% German, 19.7% English, 14.4% Irish, 9.0% Scottish, 7.9% French (2005-2009 5-year est.).

Economy: Single-family building permits issued: 1 (2010); Multi-family building permits issued: 0 (2010); Employment by occupation: 9.3% management, 26.8% professional, 34.0% services, 24.7% sales, 0.7% farming, 1.0% construction, 3.6% production (2005-2009 5-year est.).
Income: Per capita income: $23,571 (2010); Median household income: $56,136 (2010); Average household income: $76,034 (2010); Percent of households with income of $100,000 or more: 15.1% (2010); Poverty rate: 7.9% (2005-2009 5-year est.).
Taxes: Total city taxes per capita: $30 (2007); City property taxes per capita: $20 (2007).
Education: Percent of population age 25 and over with: High school diploma (including GED) or higher: 88.4% (2010); Bachelor's degree or higher: 26.1% (2010); Master's degree or higher: 8.5% (2010).

Four-year College(s)
Principia College (Private, Not-for-profit)
    Fall 2009 Enrollment: 527 . . . . (618) 374-2131
    2010-11 Tuition: In-state $24,015; Out-of-state $24,015
Housing: Homeownership rate: 81.6% (2010); Median home value: $132,609 (2010); Median contract rent: $717 per month (2005-2009 5-year est.); Median year structure built: before 1940 (2005-2009 5-year est.).
Transportation: Commute to work: 23.3% car, 2.3% public transportation, 66.5% walk, 4.1% work from home (2005-2009 5-year est.); Travel time to work: 82.7% less than 15 minutes, 6.7% 15 to 30 minutes, 5.2% 30 to 45 minutes, 1.2% 45 to 60 minutes, 4.3% 60 minutes or more (2005-2009 5-year est.)

FIDELITY (village).
Covers a land area of 0.112 square miles and a water area of 0 square miles. Located at 39.15° N. Lat; 90.16° W. Long. Elevation is 636 feet.
Population: 66 (1990); 105 (2000); 102 (2010); 101 (2015 projected); Race: 98.0% White, 0.0% Black, 1.0% Asian, 1.0% Other, 1.0% Hispanic of any race (2010); Density: 914.3 persons per square mile (2010); Average household size: 2.68 (2010); Median age: 36.5 (2010); Males per 100 females: 108.2 (2010); Marriage status: 51.5% never married, 43.9% now married, 0.0% widowed, 4.5% divorced (2005-2009 5-year est.); Foreign born: 0.0% (2005-2009 5-year est.); Ancestry (includes multiple ancestries): 18.9% German, 12.6% Irish, 3.2% French (2005-2009 5-year est.).
Economy: Employment by occupation: 0.0% management, 10.3% professional, 34.5% services, 20.7% sales, 0.0% farming, 17.2% construction, 17.2% production (2005-2009 5-year est.).
Income: Per capita income: $18,318 (2010); Median household income: $50,000 (2010); Average household income: $50,658 (2010); Percent of households with income of $100,000 or more: 5.3% (2010); Poverty rate: 50.5% (2005-2009 5-year est.).
Taxes: Total city taxes per capita: $10 (2007); City property taxes per capita: $10 (2007).
Education: Percent of population age 25 and over with: High school diploma (including GED) or higher: 89.7% (2010); Bachelor's degree or higher: 17.6% (2010); Master's degree or higher: 5.9% (2010).
Housing: Homeownership rate: 81.6% (2010); Median home value: $117,857 (2010); Median contract rent: $375 per month (2005-2009 5-year est.); Median year structure built: 1977 (2005-2009 5-year est.).
Transportation: Commute to work: 100.0% car, 0.0% public transportation, 0.0% walk, 0.0% work from home (2005-2009 5-year est.); Travel time to work: 0.0% less than 15 minutes, 44.8% 15 to 30 minutes, 27.6% 30 to 45 minutes, 10.3% 45 to 60 minutes, 17.2% 60 minutes or more (2005-2009 5-year est.)

FIELDON (village).
Covers a land area of 0.199 square miles and a water area of 0 square miles. Located at 39.10° N. Lat; 90.50° W. Long. Elevation is 692 feet.
Population: 284 (1990); 271 (2000); 326 (2010); 347 (2015 projected); Race: 99.1% White, 0.0% Black, 0.3% Asian, 0.6% Other, 0.3% Hispanic of any race (2010); Density: 1,638.6 persons per square mile (2010); Average household size: 2.78 (2010); Median age: 38.3 (2010); Males per 100 females: 107.6 (2010); Marriage status: 12.7% never married, 58.7% now married, 12.7% widowed, 15.9% divorced (2005-2009 5-year est.); Foreign born: 0.0% (2005-2009 5-year est.); Ancestry (includes multiple ancestries): 38.0% German, 11.8% American, 10.9% French, 7.9% Irish, 5.7% Dutch (2005-2009 5-year est.).
Economy: Single-family building permits issued: 0 (2010); Multi-family building permits issued: 0 (2010); Employment by occupation: 11.5% management, 6.2% professional, 28.5% services, 10.0% sales, 2.3% farming, 6.9% construction, 34.6% production (2005-2009 5-year est.).

Income: Per capita income: $21,980 (2010); Median household income: $56,071 (2010); Average household income: $59,658 (2010); Percent of households with income of $100,000 or more: 11.1% (2010); Poverty rate: 10.6% (2005-2009 5-year est.).
Taxes: Total city taxes per capita: $37 (2007); City property taxes per capita: $29 (2007).
Education: Percent of population age 25 and over with: High school diploma (including GED) or higher: 91.1% (2010); Bachelor's degree or higher: 15.1% (2010); Master's degree or higher: 4.0% (2010).

School District(s)
Jersey CUSD 100 (PK-12)
    2009-10 Enrollment: 2,862 . . . . (618) 498-5561
Housing: Homeownership rate: 82.1% (2010); Median home value: $125,000 (2010); Median contract rent: $450 per month (2005-2009 5-year est.); Median year structure built: 1962 (2005-2009 5-year est.).
Transportation: Commute to work: 95.2% car, 0.0% public transportation, 0.0% walk, 3.2% work from home (2005-2009 5-year est.); Travel time to work: 14.0% less than 15 minutes, 24.0% 15 to 30 minutes, 30.6% 30 to 45 minutes, 7.4% 45 to 60 minutes, 24.0% 60 minutes or more (2005-2009 5-year est.)

GRAFTON (city).
Covers a land area of 4.056 square miles and a water area of 0 square miles. Located at 38.97° N. Lat; 90.43° W. Long. Elevation is 449 feet.
History: City suffered greatly during a devastating flood (1993). Incorporated 1837.
Population: 923 (1990); 609 (2000); 676 (2010); 697 (2015 projected); Race: 87.0% White, 10.8% Black, 0.1% Asian, 2.1% Other, 1.3% Hispanic of any race (2010); Density: 166.7 persons per square mile (2010); Average household size: 2.42 (2010); Median age: 37.4 (2010); Males per 100 females: 114.6 (2010); Marriage status: 23.3% never married, 62.8% now married, 5.6% widowed, 8.3% divorced (2005-2009 5-year est.); Foreign born: 1.2% (2005-2009 5-year est.); Ancestry (includes multiple ancestries): 23.4% English, 22.0% Irish, 18.8% German, 13.5% American, 5.7% Italian (2005-2009 5-year est.).
Economy: Single-family building permits issued: 2 (2010); Multi-family building permits issued: 0 (2010); Employment by occupation: 19.8% management, 25.0% professional, 17.0% services, 9.9% sales, 0.0% farming, 10.8% construction, 17.6% production (2005-2009 5-year est.).
Income: Per capita income: $31,900 (2010); Median household income: $61,198 (2010); Average household income: $81,419 (2010); Percent of households with income of $100,000 or more: 26.6% (2010); Poverty rate: 16.7% (2005-2009 5-year est.).
Taxes: Total city taxes per capita: $994 (2007); City property taxes per capita: $774 (2007).
Education: Percent of population age 25 and over with: High school diploma (including GED) or higher: 87.1% (2010); Bachelor's degree or higher: 18.2% (2010); Master's degree or higher: 5.0% (2010).

School District(s)
Jersey CUSD 100 (PK-12)
    2009-10 Enrollment: 2,862 . . . . (618) 498-5561
Housing: Homeownership rate: 75.7% (2010); Median home value: $109,574 (2010); Median contract rent: $338 per month (2005-2009 5-year est.); Median year structure built: 1982 (2005-2009 5-year est.).
Safety: Violent crime rate: 14.7 per 10,000 population; Property crime rate: 368.7 per 10,000 population (2010).
Transportation: Commute to work: 87.7% car, 0.0% public transportation, 2.5% walk, 6.8% work from home (2005-2009 5-year est.); Travel time to work: 27.5% less than 15 minutes, 19.9% 15 to 30 minutes, 24.2% 30 to 45 minutes, 14.9% 45 to 60 minutes, 13.6% 60 minutes or more (2005-2009 5-year est.)

JERSEYVILLE (city).
County seat. Covers a land area of 4.392 square miles and a water area of 0 square miles. Located at 39.12° N. Lat; 90.32° W. Long. Elevation is 659 feet.
History: Plotted 1834, incorporated 1855.
Population: 7,637 (1990); 7,984 (2000); 8,333 (2010); 8,472 (2015 projected); Race: 98.5% White, 0.1% Black, 0.2% Asian, 1.1% Other, 0.7% Hispanic of any race (2010); Density: 1,897.4 persons per square mile (2010); Average household size: 2.33 (2010); Median age: 39.1 (2010); Males per 100 females: 87.9 (2010); Marriage status: 27.8% never married, 51.5% now married, 10.6% widowed, 10.1% divorced (2005-2009 5-year est.); Foreign born: 1.9% (2005-2009 5-year est.); Ancestry (includes multiple ancestries): 38.4% German, 11.4% Irish, 9.7% English, 8.6% American, 3.4% Dutch (2005-2009 5-year est.).

Economy: Single-family building permits issued: 10 (2010); Multi-family building permits issued: 35 (2010); Employment by occupation: 11.4% management, 17.9% professional, 23.1% services, 27.5% sales, 0.3% farming, 7.7% construction, 12.1% production (2005-2009 5-year est.).
Income: Per capita income: $25,391 (2010); Median household income: $46,805 (2010); Average household income: $59,757 (2010); Percent of households with income of $100,000 or more: 14.8% (2010); Poverty rate: 9.0% (2005-2009 5-year est.).
Taxes: Total city taxes per capita: $204 (2007); City property taxes per capita: $68 (2007).
Education: Percent of population age 25 and over with: High school diploma (including GED) or higher: 83.9% (2010); Bachelor's degree or higher: 14.0% (2010); Master's degree or higher: 4.6% (2010).

School District(s)
Calhoun/Greene/Jersey/Macoupn Roe (07-12)
    2009-10 Enrollment: n/a . . . . (217) 854-4016
Jersey CUSD 100 (PK-12)
    2009-10 Enrollment: 2,862 . . . . (618) 498-5561
Housing: Homeownership rate: 69.9% (2010); Median home value: $95,141 (2010); Median contract rent: $420 per month (2005-2009 5-year est.); Median year structure built: 1960 (2005-2009 5-year est.).
Hospitals: Jersey Community Hospital (67 beds)
Safety: Violent crime rate: 44.7 per 10,000 population; Property crime rate: 283.6 per 10,000 population (2010).
Newspapers: Jersey County Star (Local news; Circulation 1,500); Quad County Edition of the Telegraph (Community news; Circulation 9,000)
Transportation: Commute to work: 96.3% car, 0.0% public transportation, 1.5% walk, 1.9% work from home (2005-2009 5-year est.); Travel time to work: 46.4% less than 15 minutes, 13.0% 15 to 30 minutes, 10.5% 30 to 45 minutes, 11.4% 45 to 60 minutes, 18.7% 60 minutes or more (2005-2009 5-year est.)
Additional Information Contacts
City of Jerseyville. . . . . (618) 498-3312
    http://www.jerseyville-il.us
Jersey County Business Association . . . . (618) 639-5222
    http://www.jerseycounty.org

OTTERVILLE (town). Covers a land area of 1.002 square miles and a water area of 0 square miles. Located at 39.05° N. Lat; 90.39° W. Long. Elevation is 627 feet.

Population: 115 (1990); 120 (2000); 130 (2010); 133 (2015 projected); Race: 99.2% White, 0.0% Black, 0.0% Asian, 0.8% Other, 1.5% Hispanic of any race (2010); Density: 129.8 persons per square mile (2010); Average household size: 2.71 (2010); Median age: 38.3 (2010); Males per 100 females: 116.7 (2010); Marriage status: 14.1% never married, 66.7% now married, 3.8% widowed, 15.4% divorced (2005-2009 5-year est.); Foreign born: 0.0% (2005-2009 5-year est.); Ancestry (includes multiple ancestries): 46.5% German, 14.9% English, 11.4% Irish, 5.3% Polish, 3.5% American (2005-2009 5-year est.).
Economy: Employment by occupation: 11.4% management, 0.0% professional, 14.3% services, 48.6% sales, 0.0% farming, 8.6% construction, 17.1% production (2005-2009 5-year est.).
Income: Per capita income: $20,957 (2010); Median household income: $52,083 (2010); Average household income: $56,667 (2010); Percent of households with income of $100,000 or more: 12.5% (2010); Poverty rate: 5.4% (2005-2009 5-year est.).
Taxes: Total city taxes per capita: $66 (2007); City property taxes per capita: $50 (2007).
Education: Percent of population age 25 and over with: High school diploma (including GED) or higher: 83.9% (2010); Bachelor's degree or higher: 8.0% (2010); Master's degree or higher: 3.4% (2010).
Housing: Homeownership rate: 87.5% (2010); Median home value: $96,364 (2010); Median contract rent: n/a per month (2005-2009 5-year est.); Median year structure built: before 1940 (2005-2009 5-year est.).
Transportation: Commute to work: 100.0% car, 0.0% public transportation, 0.0% walk, 0.0% work from home (2005-2009 5-year est.); Travel time to work: 17.1% less than 15 minutes, 48.6% 15 to 30 minutes, 22.9% 30 to 45 minutes, 11.4% 45 to 60 minutes, 0.0% 60 minutes or more (2005-2009 5-year est.)

Jo Daviess County

Located in northwestern Illinois; bounded on the north by Wisconsin, and on the west by the Mississippi River and the Iowa border; drained by the Apple, Plum, and Galena Rivers; includes Charles Mound, highest point in

the state (1,241 ft). Covers a land area of 601.08 square miles, a water area of 17.64 square miles, and is located in the Central Time Zone at 42.39° N. Lat., 90.23° W. Long. The county was founded in 1827. County seat is Galena.

Weather Station: Elizabeth 5 S   Elevation: 680 feet

	Jan	Feb	Mar	Apr	May	Jun	Jul	Aug	Sep	Oct	Nov	Dec
High	29	33	46	59	70	80	83	81	74	62	47	32
Low	10	14	25	35	45	56	59	57	48	37	27	14
Precip	1.2	na	2.4	3.4	3.9	4.9	3.4	4.6	3.5	2.7	2.8	1.8
Snow	9.0	na	2.4	1.0	tr	0.0	0.0	0.0	0.0	0.1	1.5	8.7

High and Low temperatures in degrees Fahrenheit; Precipitation and Snow in inches

Weather Station: Stockton 3 NNE   Elevation: 970 feet

	Jan	Feb	Mar	Apr	May	Jun	Jul	Aug	Sep	Oct	Nov	Dec
High	27	32	44	58	70	79	82	80	73	61	45	31
Low	11	15	26	37	48	58	61	59	50	39	29	16
Precip	1.1	1.4	2.2	3.5	3.8	5.0	3.5	4.8	3.8	2.9	2.6	1.7
Snow	9.2	7.1	4.4	1.6	0.1	0.0	0.0	0.0	0.0	0.3	1.8	9.3

High and Low temperatures in degrees Fahrenheit; Precipitation and Snow in inches

Population: 21,821 (1990); 22,289 (2000); 22,122 (2010); 21,861 (2015 projected); Race: 97.3% White, 0.8% Black, 0.3% Asian, 1.6% Other, 3.1% Hispanic of any race (2010); Density: 36.8 persons per square mile (2010); Average household size: 2.29 (2010); Median age: 43.2 (2010); Males per 100 females: 101.8 (2010).
Religion: Five largest groups: 50.0% Catholic Church, 10.6% The United Methodist Church, 10.5% Evangelical Lutheran Church in America, 2.7% Presbyterian Church (U.S.A.), 1.3% Lutheran Church—Missouri Synod (2000).
Economy: Unemployment rate: 6.6% (August 2011); Total civilian labor force: 13,433 (August 2011); Leading industries: 23.2% accommodation & food services; 16.5% manufacturing; 12.9% retail trade (2009); Farms: 1,016 totaling 281,457 acres (2007); Companies that employ 500 or more persons: 0 (2009); Companies that employ 100 to 499 persons: 14 (2009); Companies that employ less than 100 persons: 731 (2009); Black-owned businesses: n/a (2007); Hispanic-owned businesses: n/a (2007); Asian-owned businesses: n/a (2007); Women-owned businesses: 610 (2007); Retail sales per capita: $10,636 (2010). Single-family building permits issued: 37 (2010); Multi-family building permits issued: 0 (2010).
Income: Per capita income: $27,375 (2010); Median household income: $50,794 (2010); Average household income: $62,996 (2010); Percent of households with income of $100,000 or more: 13.8% (2010); Poverty rate: 10.5% (2009); Bankruptcy rate: 2.03% (2010).
Taxes: Total county taxes per capita: $187 (2007); County property taxes per capita: $178 (2007).
Education: Percent of population age 25 and over with: High school diploma (including GED) or higher: 88.6% (2010); Bachelor's degree or higher: 22.5% (2010); Master's degree or higher: 8.6% (2010).
Housing: Homeownership rate: 75.3% (2010); Median home value: $129,111 (2010); Median contract rent: $447 per month (2005-2009 5-year est.); Median year structure built: 1970 (2005-2009 5-year est.)
Health: Birth rate: 104.6 per 10,000 population (2009); Death rate: 106.9 per 10,000 population (2009); Age-adjusted cancer mortality rate: 177.8 deaths per 100,000 population (2007); Number of physicians: 6.8 per 10,000 population (2008); Hospital beds: 37.0 per 10,000 population (2007); Hospital admissions: 184.5 per 10,000 population (2007).
Elections: 2008 Presidential election results: 54.5% Obama, 44.0% McCain, 0.6% Nader
National and State Parks: Apple River Canyon State Park
Additional Information Contacts
Jo Daviess County Government . . . . (815) 777-0161
    http://www.jodaviess.org
Galena Area Chamber of Commerce . . . . (815) 777-9050
    http://www.galenachamber.com
Hanover Chamber of Commerce. (815) 591-3800
    http://hanover-il.com
Stockton Chamber of Commerce. (815) 947-2878
    http://www.stocktonil.com

Jo Daviess County Communities

APPLE RIVER (village). Covers a land area of 0.790 square miles and a water area of 0 square miles. Located at 42.50° N. Lat; 90.09° W. Long. Elevation is 1,010 feet.

Population: 414 (1990); 379 (2000); 378 (2010); 372 (2015 projected); Race: 97.1% White, 2.4% Black, 0.0% Asian, 0.5% Other, 0.5% Hispanic of any race (2010); Density: 478.3 persons per square mile (2010); Average household size: 2.42 (2010); Median age: 40.3 (2010); Males per 100 females: 103.2 (2010); Marriage status: 22.5% never married, 65.8% now married, 3.8% widowed, 7.9% divorced (2005-2009 5-year est.); Foreign born: 0.0% (2005-2009 5-year est.); Ancestry (includes multiple ancestries): 41.9% German, 19.7% Irish, 16.9% American, 11.8% English, 6.5% French (2005-2009 5-year est.).
Economy: Employment by occupation: 2.6% management, 13.2% professional, 10.1% services, 42.3% sales, 0.0% farming, 6.3% construction, 25.4% production (2005-2009 5-year est.).
Income: Per capita income: $28,551 (2010); Median household income: $51,667 (2010); Average household income: $68,237 (2010); Percent of households with income of $100,000 or more: 17.9% (2010); Poverty rate: 8.4% (2005-2009 5-year est.).
Taxes: Total city taxes per capita: $143 (2007); City property taxes per capita: $86 (2007).
Education: Percent of population age 25 and over with: High school diploma (including GED) or higher: 83.8% (2010); Bachelor's degree or higher: 13.5% (2010); Master's degree or higher: 3.1% (2010).

School District(s)

Warren CUSD 205 (PK-12)
    2009-10 Enrollment: 447 . . . . (815) 745-2653
Housing: Homeownership rate: 68.6% (2010); Median home value: $80,625 (2010); Median contract rent: $323 per month (2005-2009 5-year est.); Median year structure built: before 1940 (2005-2009 5-year est.).
Transportation: Commute to work: 93.0% car, 1.1% public transportation, 4.8% walk, 1.1% work from home (2005-2009 5-year est.); Travel time to work: 17.9% less than 15 minutes, 17.9% 15 to 30 minutes, 47.3% 30 to 45 minutes, 11.4% 45 to 60 minutes, 5.4% 60 minutes or more (2005-2009 5-year est.)

EAST DUBUQUE (city). Covers a land area of 2.062 square miles and a water area of 0.081 square miles. Located at 42.49° N. Lat; 90.64° W. Long. Elevation is 610 feet.

History: Incorporated 1857.
Population: 2,130 (1990); 1,995 (2000); 1,766 (2010); 1,671 (2015 projected); Race: 97.7% White, 0.9% Black, 0.4% Asian, 1.0% Other, 1.9% Hispanic of any race (2010); Density: 856.3 persons per square mile (2010); Average household size: 2.29 (2010); Median age: 39.4 (2010); Males per 100 females: 106.5 (2010); Marriage status: 24.2% never married, 53.1% now married, 4.2% widowed, 18.5% divorced (2005-2009 5-year est.); Foreign born: 0.3% (2005-2009 5-year est.); Ancestry (includes multiple ancestries): 49.7% German, 30.3% Irish, 7.3% Polish, 6.8% American, 4.3% English (2005-2009 5-year est.).
Economy: Single-family building permits issued: 1 (2010); Multi-family building permits issued: 0 (2010); Employment by occupation: 8.8% management, 10.3% professional, 20.4% services, 31.5% sales, 0.0% farming, 12.5% construction, 16.4% production (2005-2009 5-year est.).
Income: Per capita income: $25,756 (2010); Median household income: $51,064 (2010); Average household income: $58,773 (2010); Percent of households with income of $100,000 or more: 11.0% (2010); Poverty rate: 16.6% (2005-2009 5-year est.).
Taxes: Total city taxes per capita: $251 (2007); City property taxes per capita: $166 (2007).
Education: Percent of population age 25 and over with: High school diploma (including GED) or higher: 85.6% (2010); Bachelor's degree or higher: 14.9% (2010); Master's degree or higher: 4.7% (2010).

School District(s)

East Dubuque USD 119 (PK-12)
    2009-10 Enrollment: 683 . . . . (815) 747-3180
Housing: Homeownership rate: 72.1% (2010); Median home value: $124,401 (2010); Median contract rent: $399 per month (2005-2009 5-year est.); Median year structure built: 1957 (2005-2009 5-year est.).
Safety: Violent crime rate: 69.5 per 10,000 population; Property crime rate: 171.1 per 10,000 population (2010).
Newspapers: East Dubuque Register (Local news; Circulation 1,300)
Transportation: Commute to work: 96.4% car, 0.0% public transportation, 2.0% walk, 0.0% work from home (2005-2009 5-year est.); Travel time to work: 51.5% less than 15 minutes, 37.3% 15 to 30 minutes, 5.3% 30 to 45 minutes, 0.0% 45 to 60 minutes, 5.9% 60 minutes or more (2005-2009 5-year est.)

ELIZABETH (village). Covers a land area of 0.439 square miles and a water area of 0 square miles. Located at 42.31° N. Lat; 90.22° W. Long. Elevation is 801 feet.

History: Elizabeth was built on the site of the Apple River Fort, established during the Black Hawk War.
Population: 689 (1990); 682 (2000); 608 (2010); 574 (2015 projected); Race: 97.9% White, 0.5% Black, 0.2% Asian, 1.5% Other, 1.5% Hispanic of any race (2010); Density: 1,386.1 persons per square mile (2010); Average household size: 1.98 (2010); Median age: 47.7 (2010); Males per 100 females: 90.6 (2010); Marriage status: 13.2% never married, 50.2% now married, 18.6% widowed, 18.0% divorced (2005-2009 5-year est.); Foreign born: 3.2% (2005-2009 5-year est.); Ancestry (includes multiple ancestries): 40.5% German, 18.4% Irish, 13.4% American, 9.9% English, 5.7% French (2005-2009 5-year est.).
Economy: Employment by occupation: 12.8% management, 14.9% professional, 22.8% services, 18.7% sales, 2.8% farming, 18.7% construction, 9.3% production (2005-2009 5-year est.).
Income: Per capita income: $20,165 (2010); Median household income: $37,679 (2010); Average household income: $42,117 (2010); Percent of households with income of $100,000 or more: 3.8% (2010); Poverty rate: 10.3% (2005-2009 5-year est.).
Taxes: Total city taxes per capita: $126 (2007); City property taxes per capita: $69 (2007).
Education: Percent of population age 25 and over with: High school diploma (including GED) or higher: 88.4% (2010); Bachelor's degree or higher: 18.8% (2010); Master's degree or higher: 8.6% (2010).

School District(s)

Carroll/Jo Daviess/Stephenson Roe (06-12)
    2009-10 Enrollment: n/a . . . . (815) 947-3810
Jo Daviess-Carroll Area Voc Ctr (11-12)
    2009-10 Enrollment: n/a . . . . (815) 858-2203
Housing: Homeownership rate: 67.6% (2010); Median home value: $94,902 (2010); Median contract rent: $375 per month (2005-2009 5-year est.); Median year structure built: 1952 (2005-2009 5-year est.).
Safety: Violent crime rate: 0.0 per 10,000 population; Property crime rate: 205.4 per 10,000 population (2010).
Transportation: Commute to work: 89.2% car, 0.0% public transportation, 4.7% walk, 6.1% work from home (2005-2009 5-year est.); Travel time to work: 36.8% less than 15 minutes, 39.5% 15 to 30 minutes, 16.1% 30 to 45 minutes, 7.7% 45 to 60 minutes, 0.0% 60 minutes or more (2005-2009 5-year est.)

GALENA (city). County seat. Covers a land area of 3.735 square miles and a water area of <.001 square miles. Located at 42.41° N. Lat; 90.43° W. Long. Elevation is 633 feet.

History: The lead deposits in the Galena area interested French explorers in the 1700's. The town of Galena was laid out in 1826 and named for the mineral galena, the principal ore of lead. By this time the government was controlling the mineral lands and issuing leases. Smelter operations were responsible for Galena's early growth, and traffic on the old Fever River made it a trading center until the middle of the 1800's, when the lead veins were exhausted and the river silted in. Ulysses S. Grant was a resident of Galena when he was chosen to lead the Federal troops in the Civil War.
Population: 3,680 (1990); 3,460 (2000); 3,247 (2010); 3,135 (2015 projected); Race: 95.0% White, 0.9% Black, 0.6% Asian, 3.5% Other, 10.6% Hispanic of any race (2010); Density: 869.4 persons per square mile (2010); Average household size: 2.06 (2010); Median age: 45.6 (2010); Males per 100 females: 97.0 (2010); Marriage status: 22.9% never married, 50.8% now married, 12.8% widowed, 13.5% divorced (2005-2009 5-year est.); Foreign born: 12.0% (2005-2009 5-year est.); Ancestry (includes multiple ancestries): 52.1% German, 15.6% English, 14.3% Irish, 5.6% American, 5.2% Norwegian (2005-2009 5-year est.).
Economy: Single-family building permits issued: 3 (2010); Multi-family building permits issued: 0 (2010); Employment by occupation: 14.3% management, 14.5% professional, 23.2% services, 25.6% sales, 0.1% farming, 5.2% construction, 17.1% production (2005-2009 5-year est.).
Income: Per capita income: $25,929 (2010); Median household income: $46,073 (2010); Average household income: $53,758 (2010); Percent of households with income of $100,000 or more: 8.2% (2010); Poverty rate: 7.9% (2005-2009 5-year est.).
Taxes: Total city taxes per capita: $786 (2007); City property taxes per capita: $581 (2007).

Education: Percent of population age 25 and over with: High school diploma (including GED) or higher: 85.7% (2010); Bachelor's degree or higher: 25.3% (2010); Master's degree or higher: 9.8% (2010).

School District(s)

Galena USD 120 (PK-12)

    2009-10 Enrollment: 816 . . . . (815) 777-3086

Housing: Homeownership rate: 64.7% (2010); Median home value: $127,062 (2010); Median contract rent: $548 per month (2005-2009 5-year est.); Median year structure built: before 1940 (2005-2009 5-year est.).

Hospitals: Galena-Stauss Hospital & Healthcare Center

Newspapers: Galena Gazette (Local news; Circulation 5,800)

Transportation: Commute to work: 82.7% car, 0.0% public transportation, 12.3% walk, 4.9% work from home (2005-2009 5-year est.); Travel time to work: 64.2% less than 15 minutes, 23.3% 15 to 30 minutes, 8.1% 30 to 45 minutes, 1.8% 45 to 60 minutes, 2.7% 60 minutes or more (2005-2009 5-year est.)

Additional Information Contacts

Galena Area Chamber of Commerce . . . . (815) 777-9050

    http://www.galenachamber.com

HANOVER (village).

Covers a land area of 0.592 square miles and a water area of 0 square miles. Located at 42.25° N. Lat; 90.28° W. Long. Elevation is 627 feet.

History: Hanover's early development depended on mining. When this declined, the town built a dam across the Apple River and established a grist mill. When a woolen mill was added in 1864, the town became a textile center.

Population: 911 (1990); 836 (2000); 845 (2010); 842 (2015 projected); Race: 96.1% White, 0.6% Black, 0.2% Asian, 3.1% Other, 2.4% Hispanic of any race (2010); Density: 1,426.4 persons per square mile (2010); Average household size: 2.11 (2010); Median age: 43.1 (2010); Males per 100 females: 98.4 (2010); Marriage status: 28.0% never married, 50.9% now married, 11.7% widowed, 9.4% divorced (2005-2009 5-year est.); Foreign born: 2.2% (2005-2009 5-year est.); Ancestry (includes multiple ancestries): 31.9% German, 26.7% Irish, 20.0% English, 6.5% Norwegian, 6.3% Scottish (2005-2009 5-year est.).

Economy: Single-family building permits issued: 0 (2010); Multi-family building permits issued: 0 (2010); Employment by occupation: 5.7% management, 9.2% professional, 23.3% services, 23.8% sales, 2.8% farming, 9.4% construction, 25.7% production (2005-2009 5-year est.).

Income: Per capita income: $23,851 (2010); Median household income: $40,445 (2010); Average household income: $50,823 (2010); Percent of households with income of $100,000 or more: 9.7% (2010); Poverty rate: 15.2% (2005-2009 5-year est.).

Taxes: Total city taxes per capita: $149 (2007); City property taxes per capita: $145 (2007).

Education: Percent of population age 25 and over with: High school diploma (including GED) or higher: 86.3% (2010); Bachelor's degree or higher: 18.3% (2010); Master's degree or higher: 8.8% (2010).

School District(s)

Northwest Sp Ed District (06-12)

    2009-10 Enrollment: n/a . . . . (815) 232-0332

River Ridge CUSD 210 (PK-12)

    2009-10 Enrollment: 495 . . . . (815) 858-9005

Housing: Homeownership rate: 66.6% (2010); Median home value: $86,458 (2010); Median contract rent: $320 per month (2005-2009 5-year est.); Median year structure built: before 1940 (2005-2009 5-year est.).

Safety: Violent crime rate: 312.5 per 10,000 population; Property crime rate: 260.4 per 10,000 population (2010).

Transportation: Commute to work: 83.6% car, 1.0% public transportation, 8.8% walk, 4.0% work from home (2005-2009 5-year est.); Travel time to work: 44.8% less than 15 minutes, 29.7% 15 to 30 minutes, 14.6% 30 to 45 minutes, 5.4% 45 to 60 minutes, 5.4% 60 minutes or more (2005-2009 5-year est.)

Additional Information Contacts

Hanover Chamber of Commerce. (815) 591-3800

    http://hanover-il.com

MENOMINEE (village).

Covers a land area of 1.925 square miles and a water area of 0 square miles. Located at 42.47° N. Lat; 90.54° W. Long. Elevation is 761 feet.

Population: 267 (1990); 237 (2000); 194 (2010); 190 (2015 projected); Race: 97.9% White, 1.5% Black, 0.0% Asian, 0.5% Other, 2.6% Hispanic of any race (2010); Density: 100.8 persons per square mile (2010); Average household size: 2.73 (2010); Median age: 34.4 (2010); Males per

100 females: 110.9 (2010); Marriage status: 17.1% never married, 70.9% now married, 4.3% widowed, 7.7% divorced (2005-2009 5-year est.); Foreign born: 0.0% (2005-2009 5-year est.); Ancestry (includes multiple ancestries): 82.0% German, 21.1% Irish, 5.3% English, 4.5% Polish, 4.5% French (2005-2009 5-year est.).

Economy: Employment by occupation: 5.1% management, 29.1% professional, 22.8% services, 11.4% sales, 0.0% farming, 15.2% construction, 16.5% production (2005-2009 5-year est.).

Income: Per capita income: $24,643 (2010); Median household income: $57,237 (2010); Average household income: $72,817 (2010); Percent of households with income of $100,000 or more: 14.1% (2010); Poverty rate: 4.5% (2005-2009 5-year est.).

Taxes: Total city taxes per capita: $4 (2007); City property taxes per capita: $0 (2007).

Education: Percent of population age 25 and over with: High school diploma (including GED) or higher: 79.5% (2010); Bachelor's degree or higher: 9.4% (2010); Master's degree or higher: 1.6% (2010).

Housing: Homeownership rate: 76.1% (2010); Median home value: $142,500 (2010); Median contract rent: $319 per month (2005-2009 5-year est.); Median year structure built: 1970 (2005-2009 5-year est.).

Transportation: Commute to work: 91.1% car, 0.0% public transportation, 0.0% walk, 8.9% work from home (2005-2009 5-year est.); Travel time to work: 22.2% less than 15 minutes, 52.8% 15 to 30 minutes, 11.1% 30 to 45 minutes, 5.6% 45 to 60 minutes, 8.3% 60 minutes or more (2005-2009 5-year est.)

NORA (village).

Covers a land area of 0.906 square miles and a water area of 0 square miles. Located at 42.45° N. Lat; 89.94° W. Long. Elevation is 1,014 feet.

Population: 162 (1990); 118 (2000); 115 (2010); 113 (2015 projected); Race: 100.0% White, 0.0% Black, 0.0% Asian, 0.0% Other, 0.0% Hispanic of any race (2010); Density: 126.9 persons per square mile (2010); Average household size: 2.35 (2010); Median age: 40.6 (2010); Males per 100 females: 101.8 (2010); Marriage status: 7.8% never married, 80.5% now married, 6.5% widowed, 5.2% divorced (2005-2009 5-year est.); Foreign born: 0.0% (2005-2009 5-year est.); Ancestry (includes multiple ancestries): 47.6% German, 17.9% English, 11.9% Irish, 10.7% Czech, 8.3% Swiss (2005-2009 5-year est.).

Economy: Employment by occupation: 9.8% management, 9.8% professional, 11.5% services, 8.2% sales, 1.6% farming, 23.0% construction, 36.1% production (2005-2009 5-year est.).

Income: Per capita income: $33,281 (2010); Median household income: $67,045 (2010); Average household income: $74,898 (2010); Percent of households with income of $100,000 or more: 20.4% (2010); Poverty rate: 0.0% (2005-2009 5-year est.).

Taxes: Total city taxes per capita: $95 (2007); City property taxes per capita: $60 (2007).

Education: Percent of population age 25 and over with: High school diploma (including GED) or higher: 81.9% (2010); Bachelor's degree or higher: 7.2% (2010); Master's degree or higher: 1.2% (2010).

Housing: Homeownership rate: 73.5% (2010); Median home value: $122,222 (2010); Median contract rent: n/a per month (2005-2009 5-year est.); Median year structure built: 1945 (2005-2009 5-year est.).

Transportation: Commute to work: 100.0% car, 0.0% public transportation, 0.0% walk, 0.0% work from home (2005-2009 5-year est.); Travel time to work: 20.7% less than 15 minutes, 39.7% 15 to 30 minutes, 32.8% 30 to 45 minutes, 3.4% 45 to 60 minutes, 3.4% 60 minutes or more (2005-2009 5-year est.)

SCALES MOUND (village).

Covers a land area of 0.235 square miles and a water area of 0 square miles. Located at 42.47° N. Lat; 90.25° W. Long. Elevation is 955 feet.

Population: 398 (1990); 401 (2000); 410 (2010); 411 (2015 projected); Race: 97.3% White, 1.0% Black, 0.7% Asian, 1.0% Other, 2.4% Hispanic of any race (2010); Density: 1,747.9 persons per square mile (2010); Average household size: 2.32 (2010); Median age: 47.7 (2010); Males per 100 females: 109.2 (2010); Marriage status: 28.6% never married, 56.9% now married, 7.7% widowed, 6.8% divorced (2005-2009 5-year est.); Foreign born: 3.0% (2005-2009 5-year est.); Ancestry (includes multiple ancestries): 70.0% German, 20.8% English, 15.7% Irish, 4.9% Dutch, 3.5% American (2005-2009 5-year est.).

Economy: Single-family building permits issued: 0 (2010); Multi-family building permits issued: 0 (2010); Employment by occupation: 9.7% management, 8.4% professional, 21.7% services, 30.1% sales, 3.1% farming, 12.8% construction, 14.2% production (2005-2009 5-year est.).

Income: Per capita income: $26,337 (2010); Median household income: $52,865 (2010); Average household income: $63,446 (2010); Percent of households with income of $100,000 or more: 11.3% (2010); Poverty rate: 8.9% (2005-2009 5-year est.).

Taxes: Total city taxes per capita: $72 (2007); City property taxes per capita: $64 (2007).

Education: Percent of population age 25 and over with: High school diploma (including GED) or higher: 92.1% (2010); Bachelor's degree or higher: 24.8% (2010); Master's degree or higher: 10.2% (2010).

School District(s)

Scales Mound CUSD 211 (PK-12)

    2009-10 Enrollment: 250 . . . . (815) 845-2215

Housing: Homeownership rate: 83.1% (2010); Median home value: $161,957 (2010); Median contract rent: $400 per month (2005-2009 5-year est.); Median year structure built: before 1940 (2005-2009 5-year est.).

Transportation: Commute to work: 81.6% car, 0.0% public transportation, 12.1% walk, 6.3% work from home (2005-2009 5-year est.); Travel time to work: 25.4% less than 15 minutes, 42.5% 15 to 30 minutes, 22.3% 30 to 45 minutes, 1.6% 45 to 60 minutes, 8.3% 60 minutes or more (2005-2009 5-year est.)

STOCKTON (village). Aka Plum River. Covers a land area of 0.852 square miles and a water area of 0 square miles. Located at 42.35° N. Lat; 90.00° W. Long. Elevation is 994 feet.

History: Stockton was named by Alanson Parker, an early settler, who saw the prospects of this becoming a stock raising center, which it did near the end of the 1800's. Before the cattle came, Stockton was the home of lead smelters.

Population: 1,924 (1990); 1,926 (2000); 1,853 (2010); 1,801 (2015 projected); Race: 99.5% White, 0.1% Black, 0.1% Asian, 0.4% Other, 0.8% Hispanic of any race (2010); Density: 2,174.5 persons per square mile (2010); Average household size: 2.18 (2010); Median age: 41.9 (2010); Males per 100 females: 92.4 (2010); Marriage status: 30.7% never married, 44.8% now married, 12.9% widowed, 11.6% divorced (2005-2009 5-year est.); Foreign born: 1.5% (2005-2009 5-year est.); Ancestry (includes multiple ancestries): 47.5% German, 19.8% Irish, 13.0% American, 7.7% English, 7.5% Dutch (2005-2009 5-year est.).

Economy: Single-family building permits issued: 0 (2010); Multi-family building permits issued: 0 (2010); Employment by occupation: 6.2% management, 16.0% professional, 22.8% services, 23.1% sales, 0.5% farming, 4.3% construction, 27.0% production (2005-2009 5-year est.).

Income: Per capita income: $22,556 (2010); Median household income: $44,935 (2010); Average household income: $50,547 (2010); Percent of households with income of $100,000 or more: 7.0% (2010); Poverty rate: 13.5% (2005-2009 5-year est.).

Taxes: Total city taxes per capita: $119 (2007); City property taxes per capita: $110 (2007).

Education: Percent of population age 25 and over with: High school diploma (including GED) or higher: 89.5% (2010); Bachelor's degree or higher: 14.6% (2010); Master's degree or higher: 3.9% (2010).

School District(s)

Carroll/Jo Daviess/Stephenson Roe (06-12)

    2009-10 Enrollment: n/a . . . . (815) 947-3810

Stockton CUSD 206 (PK-12)

    2009-10 Enrollment: 609 . . . . (815) 947-3391

Housing: Homeownership rate: 72.0% (2010); Median home value: $94,630 (2010); Median contract rent: $416 per month (2005-2009 5-year est.); Median year structure built: 1944 (2005-2009 5-year est.).

Safety: Violent crime rate: 28.6 per 10,000 population; Property crime rate: 423.6 per 10,000 population (2010).

Transportation: Commute to work: 83.8% car, 0.5% public transportation, 7.7% walk, 6.8% work from home (2005-2009 5-year est.); Travel time to work: 58.7% less than 15 minutes, 9.8% 15 to 30 minutes, 16.3% 30 to 45 minutes, 5.9% 45 to 60 minutes, 9.4% 60 minutes or more (2005-2009 5-year est.)

Additional Information Contacts

Stockton Chamber of Commerce. (815) 947-2878

    http://www.stocktonil.com

WARREN (village). Covers a land area of 0.964 square miles and a water area of 0 square miles. Located at 42.49° N. Lat; 89.99° W. Long. Elevation is 981 feet.

History: Warren began in 1850 with the name of Courtland, but was renamed in 1853 to honor the son of Alexander Burnett, who had founded the town in 1843. Warren was located at the crossing of the Old Sucker

Trail with the Chicago-Galena Stagecoach Road, and later became a station on the railroad line between Galena and Chicago.

Population: 1,562 (1990); 1,496 (2000); 1,393 (2010); 1,332 (2015 projected); Race: 98.5% White, 0.9% Black, 0.0% Asian, 0.6% Other, 2.4% Hispanic of any race (2010); Density: 1,444.3 persons per square mile (2010); Average household size: 2.31 (2010); Median age: 41.7 (2010); Males per 100 females: 97.3 (2010); Marriage status: 20.3% never married, 63.6% now married, 7.5% widowed, 8.6% divorced (2005-2009 5-year est.); Foreign born: 2.2% (2005-2009 5-year est.); Ancestry (includes multiple ancestries): 43.7% German, 16.6% Irish, 14.9% English, 9.6% American, 7.1% Dutch (2005-2009 5-year est.).

Economy: Single-family building permits issued: 1 (2010); Multi-family building permits issued: 0 (2010); Employment by occupation: 4.7% management, 14.3% professional, 19.8% services, 23.1% sales, 1.2% farming, 8.7% construction, 28.3% production (2005-2009 5-year est.).

Income: Per capita income: $24,439 (2010); Median household income: $48,454 (2010); Average household income: $56,498 (2010); Percent of households with income of $100,000 or more: 11.6% (2010); Poverty rate: 14.7% (2005-2009 5-year est.).

Taxes: Total city taxes per capita: $163 (2007); City property taxes per capita: $90 (2007).

Education: Percent of population age 25 and over with: High school diploma (including GED) or higher: 85.3% (2010); Bachelor's degree or higher: 15.5% (2010); Master's degree or higher: 4.8% (2010).

School District(s)

Warren CUSD 205 (PK-12)

    2009-10 Enrollment: 447 . . . . (815) 745-2653

Housing: Homeownership rate: 79.3% (2010); Median home value: $98,784 (2010); Median contract rent: $323 per month (2005-2009 5-year est.); Median year structure built: 1952 (2005-2009 5-year est.).

Transportation: Commute to work: 94.5% car, 0.1% public transportation, 1.5% walk, 2.8% work from home (2005-2009 5-year est.); Travel time to work: 35.7% less than 15 minutes, 21.7% 15 to 30 minutes, 24.6% 30 to 45 minutes, 8.0% 45 to 60 minutes, 10.0% 60 minutes or more (2005-2009 5-year est.)

Johnson County

Located in southern Illinois, in the Ozarks; drained by the Cache River; includes part of Shawnee National Forest. Covers a land area of 344.63 square miles, a water area of 4.25 square miles, and is located in the Central Time Zone at 37.46° N. Lat., 88.89° W. Long. The county was founded in 1812. County seat is Vienna.

Population: 11,347 (1990); 12,878 (2000); 13,813 (2010); 14,116 (2015 projected); Race: 81.5% White, 15.9% Black, 0.1% Asian, 2.4% Other, 3.2% Hispanic of any race (2010); Density: 40.1 persons per square mile (2010); Average household size: 2.40 (2010); Median age: 36.0 (2010); Males per 100 females: 155.4 (2010).

Religion: Five largest groups: 21.5% Southern Baptist Convention, 5.2% The United Methodist Church, 1.5% Catholic Church, 1.1% Cumberland Presbyterian Church, 1.0% Churches of Christ (2000).

Economy: Unemployment rate: 10.2% (August 2011); Total civilian labor force: 5,276 (August 2011); Leading industries: 15.2% health care and social assistance; 14.2% retail trade; 10.3% accommodation & food services (2009); Farms: 568 totaling 100,499 acres (2007); Companies that employ 500 or more persons: 0 (2009); Companies that employ 100 to 499 persons: 1 (2009); Companies that employ less than 100 persons: 181 (2009); Black-owned businesses: n/a (2007); Hispanic-owned businesses: n/a (2007); Asian-owned businesses: n/a (2007); Women-owned businesses: 269 (2007); Retail sales per capita: $5,216 (2010). Single-family building permits issued: 1 (2010); Multi-family building permits issued: 2 (2010).

Income: Per capita income: $20,609 (2010); Median household income: $39,997 (2010); Average household income: $51,917 (2010); Percent of households with income of $100,000 or more: 9.9% (2010); Poverty rate: 16.9% (2009); Bankruptcy rate: 5.22% (2010).

Taxes: Total county taxes per capita: $84 (2007); County property taxes per capita: $84 (2007).

Education: Percent of population age 25 and over with: High school diploma (including GED) or higher: 75.3% (2010); Bachelor's degree or higher: 14.9% (2010); Master's degree or higher: 5.4% (2010).

Housing: Homeownership rate: 83.8% (2010); Median home value: $93,505 (2010); Median contract rent: $304 per month (2005-2009 5-year est.); Median year structure built: 1977 (2005-2009 5-year est.)

Health: Birth rate: 94.0 per 10,000 population (2009); Death rate: 87.4 per 10,000 population (2009); Age-adjusted cancer mortality rate: 219.4 deaths per 100,000 population (2007); Number of physicians: 2.9 per 10,000 population (2008); Hospital beds: 0.0 per 10,000 population (2007); Hospital admissions: 0.0 per 10,000 population (2007).

Elections: 2008 Presidential election results: 31.7% Obama, 66.3% McCain, 0.9% Nader

National and State Parks: Cache River State Natural Area; Ferne Clyffe State Park

Additional Information Contacts

Johnson County Government . . . . (618) 658-3611
    http://www.johnsoncountyil.com

Johnson County Communities

BELKNAP (village). Covers a land area of 1.035 square miles and a water area of 0 square miles. Located at 37.32° N. Lat; 88.94° W. Long. Elevation is 404 feet.

Population: 125 (1990); 133 (2000); 116 (2010); 108 (2015 projected); Race: 96.6% White, 0.0% Black, 0.0% Asian, 3.4% Other, 0.0% Hispanic of any race (2010); Density: 112.1 persons per square mile (2010); Average household size: 2.52 (2010); Median age: 37.8 (2010); Males per 100 females: 103.5 (2010); Marriage status: 24.2% never married, 51.5% now married, 15.2% widowed, 9.1% divorced (2005-2009 5-year est.); Foreign born: 0.0% (2005-2009 5-year est.); Ancestry (includes multiple ancestries): 32.4% American, 21.6% English, 21.6% Scotch-Irish, 18.9% Scottish, 13.5% Irish (2005-2009 5-year est.).

Economy: Employment by occupation: 0.0% management, 5.9% professional, 17.6% services, 64.7% sales, 0.0% farming, 11.8% construction, 0.0% production (2005-2009 5-year est.).

Income: Per capita income: $17,395 (2010); Median household income: $36,875 (2010); Average household income: $45,707 (2010); Percent of households with income of $100,000 or more: 4.3% (2010); Poverty rate: 8.3% (2005-2009 5-year est.).

Taxes: Total city taxes per capita: $42 (2007); City property taxes per capita: $42 (2007).

Education: Percent of population age 25 and over with: High school diploma (including GED) or higher: 84.8% (2010); Bachelor's degree or higher: 8.9% (2010); Master's degree or higher: 2.5% (2010).

Housing: Homeownership rate: 87.0% (2010); Median home value: $48,000 (2010); Median contract rent: n/a per month (2005-2009 5-year est.); Median year structure built: 1961 (2005-2009 5-year est.).

Transportation: Commute to work: 100.0% car, 0.0% public transportation, 0.0% walk, 0.0% work from home (2005-2009 5-year est.); Travel time to work: 0.0% less than 15 minutes, 11.8% 15 to 30 minutes, 47.1% 30 to 45 minutes, 5.9% 45 to 60 minutes, 35.3% 60 minutes or more (2005-2009 5-year est.)

BUNCOMBE (village). Covers a land area of 1.209 square miles and a water area of 0 square miles. Located at 37.47° N. Lat; 88.97° W. Long. Elevation is 518 feet.

Population: 208 (1990); 186 (2000); 182 (2010); 177 (2015 projected); Race: 98.9% White, 0.5% Black, 0.0% Asian, 0.5% Other, 0.0% Hispanic of any race (2010); Density: 150.5 persons per square mile (2010); Average household size: 2.52 (2010); Median age: 38.6 (2010); Males per 100 females: 93.6 (2010); Marriage status: 12.3% never married, 51.6% now married, 13.1% widowed, 23.0% divorced (2005-2009 5-year est.); Foreign born: 0.0% (2005-2009 5-year est.); Ancestry (includes multiple ancestries): 24.8% German, 21.7% Irish, 17.8% English, 12.7% American, 6.4% European (2005-2009 5-year est.).

Economy: Employment by occupation: 0.0% management, 15.6% professional, 11.1% services, 11.1% sales, 8.9% farming, 4.4% construction, 48.9% production (2005-2009 5-year est.).

Income: Per capita income: $19,621 (2010); Median household income: $43,382 (2010); Average household income: $48,908 (2010); Percent of households with income of $100,000 or more: 7.0% (2010); Poverty rate: 16.6% (2005-2009 5-year est.).

Taxes: Total city taxes per capita: $19 (2007); City property taxes per capita: $9 (2007).

Education: Percent of population age 25 and over with: High school diploma (including GED) or higher: 87.2% (2010); Bachelor's degree or higher: 8.0% (2010); Master's degree or higher: 0.0% (2010).

School District(s)

Buncombe Cons SD 43 (KG-08)
    2009-10 Enrollment: 78 . . . . (618) 658-8830

Lick Creek CCSD 16 (PK-08)
    2009-10 Enrollment: 120 . . . . (618) 833-2545

Housing: Homeownership rate: 88.7% (2010); Median home value: $78,333 (2010); Median contract rent: $313 per month (2005-2009 5-year est.); Median year structure built: 1944 (2005-2009 5-year est.).

Transportation: Commute to work: 93.3% car, 0.0% public transportation, 6.7% walk, 0.0% work from home (2005-2009 5-year est.); Travel time to work: 8.9% less than 15 minutes, 11.1% 15 to 30 minutes, 75.6% 30 to 45 minutes, 4.4% 45 to 60 minutes, 0.0% 60 minutes or more (2005-2009 5-year est.)

CYPRESS (village). Aka Whitehill. Covers a land area of 0.747 square miles and a water area of 0 square miles. Located at 37.36° N. Lat; 89.01° W. Long. Elevation is 390 feet.

Population: 275 (1990); 271 (2000); 244 (2010); 228 (2015 projected); Race: 97.1% White, 0.4% Black, 0.0% Asian, 2.5% Other, 0.0% Hispanic of any race (2010); Density: 326.5 persons per square mile (2010); Average household size: 2.49 (2010); Median age: 37.3 (2010); Males per 100 females: 108.5 (2010); Marriage status: 23.3% never married, 53.0% now married, 5.6% widowed, 18.1% divorced (2005-2009 5-year est.); Foreign born: 0.7% (2005-2009 5-year est.); Ancestry (includes multiple ancestries): 19.1% Irish, 13.8% American, 12.8% German, 5.9% French, 4.9% Dutch (2005-2009 5-year est.).

Economy: Employment by occupation: 5.8% management, 13.0% professional, 21.4% services, 27.3% sales, 0.0% farming, 11.0% construction, 21.4% production (2005-2009 5-year est.).

Income: Per capita income: $17,395 (2010); Median household income: $38,000 (2010); Average household income: $44,107 (2010); Percent of households with income of $100,000 or more: 4.1% (2010); Poverty rate: 16.4% (2005-2009 5-year est.).

Taxes: Total city taxes per capita: $34 (2007); City property taxes per capita: $31 (2007).

Education: Percent of population age 25 and over with: High school diploma (including GED) or higher: 85.5% (2010); Bachelor's degree or higher: 10.3% (2010); Master's degree or higher: 3.0% (2010).

School District(s)

Cypress SD 64 (PK-08)
    2009-10 Enrollment: 139 . . . . (618) 657-2525

Housing: Homeownership rate: 86.7% (2010); Median home value: $47,500 (2010); Median contract rent: n/a per month (2005-2009 5-year est.); Median year structure built: 1973 (2005-2009 5-year est.).

Transportation: Commute to work: 94.7% car, 0.0% public transportation, 2.0% walk, 3.3% work from home (2005-2009 5-year est.); Travel time to work: 22.1% less than 15 minutes, 30.3% 15 to 30 minutes, 31.7% 30 to 45 minutes, 10.3% 45 to 60 minutes, 5.5% 60 minutes or more (2005-2009 5-year est.)

GOREVILLE (village). Covers a land area of 1.630 square miles and a water area of 0.011 square miles. Located at 37.55° N. Lat; 88.97° W. Long. Elevation is 735 feet.

Population: 900 (1990); 938 (2000); 1,020 (2010); 1,041 (2015 projected); Race: 98.8% White, 0.0% Black, 0.0% Asian, 1.2% Other, 1.0% Hispanic of any race (2010); Density: 625.6 persons per square mile (2010); Average household size: 2.43 (2010); Median age: 39.3 (2010); Males per 100 females: 96.2 (2010); Marriage status: 20.8% never married, 54.7% now married, 7.4% widowed, 17.1% divorced (2005-2009 5-year est.); Foreign born: 0.0% (2005-2009 5-year est.); Ancestry (includes multiple ancestries): 22.7% German, 19.5% English, 12.6% American, 11.2% Irish, 3.7% Polish (2005-2009 5-year est.).

Economy: Single-family building permits issued: 1 (2010); Multi-family building permits issued: 2 (2010); Employment by occupation: 8.6% management, 16.8% professional, 26.2% services, 25.2% sales, 0.0% farming, 8.8% construction, 14.5% production (2005-2009 5-year est.).

Income: Per capita income: $20,258 (2010); Median household income: $44,375 (2010); Average household income: $49,887 (2010); Percent of households with income of $100,000 or more: 7.9% (2010); Poverty rate: 9.3% (2005-2009 5-year est.).

Taxes: Total city taxes per capita: $58 (2007); City property taxes per capita: $48 (2007).

Education: Percent of population age 25 and over with: High school diploma (including GED) or higher: 86.2% (2010); Bachelor's degree or higher: 18.3% (2010); Master's degree or higher: 6.5% (2010).

School District(s)

Five County Reg Voc Center (11-12)
    2009-10 Enrollment: n/a . . . . (618) 747-2703

Goreville CUD 1 (PK-12)

2009-10 Enrollment: 647 . . . . (618) 995-9831

Housing: Homeownership rate: 79.8% (2010); Median home value: $101,750 (2010); Median contract rent: $197 per month (2005-2009 5-year est.); Median year structure built: 1976 (2005-2009 5-year est.).

Newspapers: Goreville Gazette (Regional news; Circulation 800)

Transportation: Commute to work: 92.8% car, 0.4% public transportation, 2.0% walk, 3.7% work from home (2005-2009 5-year est.); Travel time to work: 31.6% less than 15 minutes, 28.4% 15 to 30 minutes, 24.8% 30 to 45 minutes, 10.9% 45 to 60 minutes, 4.3% 60 minutes or more (2005-2009 5-year est.)

GRANTSBURG (unincorporated postal area, zip code 62943).
Covers a land area of 32.210 square miles and a water area of 0.135 square miles. Located at 37.34° N. Lat; 88.73° W. Long. Elevation is 377 feet.

Population: 547 (2000); Race: 98.0% White, 0.0% Black, 0.0% Asian, 2.0% Other, 0.0% Hispanic of any race (2000); Density: 17.0 persons per square mile (2000); Age: 28.2% under 18, 21.0% over 64 (2000); Marriage status: 9.3% never married, 72.4% now married, 6.3% widowed, 12.0% divorced (2000); Foreign born: 0.9% (2000); Ancestry (includes multiple ancestries): 19.0% German, 17.3% Irish, 13.1% American, 5.5% Dutch (2000).

Economy: Employment by occupation: 18.3% management, 16.7% professional, 30.4% services, 17.5% sales, 2.1% farming, 7.1% construction, 7.9% production (2000).

Income: Per capita income: $15,316 (2000); Median household income: $29,539 (2000); Poverty rate: 16.0% (2000).

Education: Percent of population age 25 and over with: High school diploma (including GED) or higher: 76.2% (2000); Bachelor's degree or higher: 8.4% (2000).

Housing: Homeownership rate: 91.6% (2000); Median home value: $53,900 (2000); Median contract rent: $288 per month (2000); Median year structure built: 1962 (2000).

Transportation: Commute to work: 86.1% car, 0.0% public transportation, 0.0% walk, 6.1% work from home (2000); Travel time to work: 22.7% less than 15 minutes, 38.0% 15 to 30 minutes, 15.7% 30 to 45 minutes, 21.4% 45 to 60 minutes, 2.2% 60 minutes or more (2000)

NEW BURNSIDE (village). Covers a land area of 1.055 square miles and a water area of 0 square miles. Located at 37.57° N. Lat; 88.77° W. Long. Elevation is 541 feet.

History: New Burnside was founded in 1872 and named for Major General Ambrose E. Burnside, president of the Big Four Railroad. Fruit growing was an important industry.

Population: 259 (1990); 242 (2000); 243 (2010); 239 (2015 projected); Race: 96.3% White, 0.8% Black, 0.4% Asian, 2.5% Other, 1.2% Hispanic of any race (2010); Density: 230.3 persons per square mile (2010); Average household size: 2.61 (2010); Median age: 36.5 (2010); Males per 100 females: 100.8 (2010); Marriage status: 21.5% never married, 59.8% now married, 7.7% widowed, 11.0% divorced (2005-2009 5-year est.); Foreign born: 2.8% (2005-2009 5-year est.); Ancestry (includes multiple ancestries): 15.5% American, 12.4% French, 11.3% German, 9.2% Irish, 6.4% English (2005-2009 5-year est.).

Economy: Employment by occupation: 20.0% management, 15.3% professional, 15.3% services, 18.8% sales, 0.0% farming, 12.9% construction, 17.6% production (2005-2009 5-year est.).

Income: Per capita income: $21,310 (2010); Median household income: $41,618 (2010); Average household income: $60,081 (2010); Percent of households with income of $100,000 or more: 12.9% (2010); Poverty rate: 7.8% (2005-2009 5-year est.).

Taxes: Total city taxes per capita: $19 (2007); City property taxes per capita: $19 (2007).

Education: Percent of population age 25 and over with: High school diploma (including GED) or higher: 86.7% (2010); Bachelor's degree or higher: 10.8% (2010); Master's degree or higher: 1.9% (2010).

Housing: Homeownership rate: 88.2% (2010); Median home value: $76,000 (2010); Median contract rent: $131 per month (2005-2009 5-year est.); Median year structure built: 1958 (2005-2009 5-year est.).

Transportation: Commute to work: 98.8% car, 0.0% public transportation, 1.2% walk, 0.0% work from home (2005-2009 5-year est.); Travel time to work: 11.9% less than 15 minutes, 26.2% 15 to 30 minutes, 42.9% 30 to 45 minutes, 10.7% 45 to 60 minutes, 8.3% 60 minutes or more (2005-2009 5-year est.)

OZARK (unincorporated postal area, zip code 62972). Covers a land area of 19.848 square miles and a water area of 0.112 square miles. Located at 37.54° N. Lat; 88.74° W. Long. Elevation is 689 feet.

Population: 408 (2000); Race: 98.3% White, 0.0% Black, 0.0% Asian, 1.7% Other, 1.7% Hispanic of any race (2000); Density: 20.6 persons per square mile (2000); Age: 33.5% under 18, 7.4% over 64 (2000); Marriage status: 24.5% never married, 62.8% now married, 6.3% widowed, 6.3% divorced (2000); Foreign born: 1.7% (2000); Ancestry (includes multiple ancestries): 21.6% English, 19.5% German, 9.5% American, 7.2% Irish (2000).

Economy: Employment by occupation: 7.7% management, 6.5% professional, 10.7% services, 29.0% sales, 0.0% farming, 19.5% construction, 26.6% production (2000).

Income: Per capita income: $11,309 (2000); Median household income: $28,558 (2000); Poverty rate: 11.5% (2000).

Education: Percent of population age 25 and over with: High school diploma (including GED) or higher: 80.3% (2000); Bachelor's degree or higher: 3.9% (2000).

Housing: Homeownership rate: 91.6% (2000); Median home value: $52,900 (2000); Median contract rent: $265 per month (2000); Median year structure built: 1975 (2000).

Transportation: Commute to work: 95.1% car, 0.0% public transportation, 0.0% walk, 1.2% work from home (2000); Travel time to work: 11.7% less than 15 minutes, 27.2% 15 to 30 minutes, 10.5% 30 to 45 minutes, 19.1% 45 to 60 minutes, 31.5% 60 minutes or more (2000)

SIMPSON (village). Covers a land area of 0.522 square miles and a water area of 0 square miles. Located at 37.46° N. Lat; 88.75° W. Long. Elevation is 390 feet.

Population: 61 (1990); 54 (2000); 56 (2010); 59 (2015 projected); Race: 42.9% White, 53.6% Black, 0.0% Asian, 3.6% Other, 8.9% Hispanic of any race (2010); Density: 107.3 persons per square mile (2010); Average household size: 2.60 (2010); Median age: 32.4 (2010); Males per 100 females: 600.0 (2010); Marriage status: 9.5% never married, 66.7% now married, 9.5% widowed, 14.3% divorced (2005-2009 5-year est.); Foreign born: 11.5% (2005-2009 5-year est.); Ancestry (includes multiple ancestries): 30.8% Dutch, 11.5% German, 11.5% Scottish, 7.7% Canadian (2005-2009 5-year est.).

Economy: Employment by occupation: 85.7% management, 0.0% professional, 0.0% services, 0.0% sales, 0.0% farming, 0.0% construction, 14.3% production (2005-2009 5-year est.).

Income: Per capita income: $18,288 (2010); Median household income: $56,250 (2010); Average household income: $48,500 (2010); Percent of households with income of $100,000 or more: 0.0% (2010); Poverty rate: 30.8% (2005-2009 5-year est.).

Taxes: Total city taxes per capita: $17 (2007); City property taxes per capita: $0 (2007).

Education: Percent of population age 25 and over with: High school diploma (including GED) or higher: 52.4% (2010); Bachelor's degree or higher: 7.1% (2010); Master's degree or higher: 4.8% (2010).

Housing: Homeownership rate: 80.0% (2010); Median home value: $70,000 (2010); Median contract rent: n/a per month (2005-2009 5-year est.); Median year structure built: before 1940 (2005-2009 5-year est.).

Transportation: Commute to work: 57.1% car, 0.0% public transportation, 0.0% walk, 42.9% work from home (2005-2009 5-year est.); Travel time to work: 0.0% less than 15 minutes, 0.0% 15 to 30 minutes, 0.0% 30 to 45 minutes, 75.0% 45 to 60 minutes, 25.0% 60 minutes or more (2005-2009 5-year est.)

TUNNEL HILL (unincorporated postal area, zip code 62991). Covers a land area of 34.134 square miles and a water area of 0.038 square miles. Located at 37.54° N. Lat; 88.86° W. Long. Elevation is 636 feet.

Population: 685 (2000); Race: 100.0% White, 0.0% Black, 0.0% Asian, 0.0% Other, 0.4% Hispanic of any race (2000); Density: 20.1 persons per square mile (2000); Age: 22.0% under 18, 10.2% over 64 (2000); Marriage status: 16.9% never married, 66.9% now married, 8.1% widowed, 8.1% divorced (2000); Foreign born: 0.0% (2000); Ancestry (includes multiple ancestries): 26.6% Irish, 21.3% German, 13.3% English, 10.3% American (2000).

Economy: Employment by occupation: 13.6% management, 25.2% professional, 27.8% services, 17.7% sales, 1.0% farming, 7.0% construction, 7.7% production (2000).

Income: Per capita income: $20,884 (2000); Median household income: $40,893 (2000); Poverty rate: 11.2% (2000).

Education: Percent of population age 25 and over with: High school diploma (including GED) or higher: 84.6% (2000); Bachelor's degree or higher: 18.1% (2000).

School District(s)

New Simpson Hill SD 32 (PK-08)

    2009-10 Enrollment: 289 . . . . (618) 658-8536

Housing: Homeownership rate: 94.1% (2000); Median home value: $96,700 (2000); Median contract rent: $318 per month (2000); Median year structure built: 1988 (2000).

Transportation: Commute to work: 94.4% car, 1.2% public transportation, 0.0% walk, 3.6% work from home (2000); Travel time to work: 16.3% less than 15 minutes, 43.7% 15 to 30 minutes, 24.1% 30 to 45 minutes, 12.1% 45 to 60 minutes, 3.8% 60 minutes or more (2000)

VIENNA (city). County seat. Covers a land area of 2.240 square miles and a water area of 0.011 square miles. Located at 37.41° N. Lat; 88.89° W. Long. Elevation is 404 feet.

History: Incorporated 1837.

Population: 1,465 (1990); 1,234 (2000); 1,197 (2010); 1,169 (2015 projected); Race: 97.7% White, 0.1% Black, 0.1% Asian, 2.1% Other, 2.0% Hispanic of any race (2010); Density: 534.3 persons per square mile (2010); Average household size: 2.22 (2010); Median age: 39.3 (2010); Males per 100 females: 85.6 (2010); Marriage status: 24.0% never married, 40.1% now married, 15.7% widowed, 20.1% divorced (2005-2009 5-year est.); Foreign born: 1.0% (2005-2009 5-year est.); Ancestry (includes multiple ancestries): 35.4% German, 12.8% English, 12.7% Irish, 6.7% Scotch-Irish, 6.2% American (2005-2009 5-year est.).

Economy: Employment by occupation: 11.2% management, 21.2% professional, 31.2% services, 14.7% sales, 1.2% farming, 3.3% construction, 17.2% production (2005-2009 5-year est.).

Income: Per capita income: $17,999 (2010); Median household income: $29,276 (2010); Average household income: $39,803 (2010); Percent of households with income of $100,000 or more: 6.2% (2010); Poverty rate: 34.1% (2005-2009 5-year est.).

Taxes: Total city taxes per capita: $106 (2007); City property taxes per capita: $85 (2007).

Education: Percent of population age 25 and over with: High school diploma (including GED) or higher: 80.4% (2010); Bachelor's degree or higher: 14.7% (2010); Master's degree or higher: 5.1% (2010).

School District(s)

Five County Reg Voc System

    2009-10 Enrollment: n/a . . . . (618) 747-2703

Vienna HSD 133 (09-12)

    2009-10 Enrollment: 388 . . . . (618) 658-4461

Vienna SD 55 (PK-08)

    2009-10 Enrollment: 419 . . . . (618) 658-8638

Housing: Homeownership rate: 65.5% (2010); Median home value: $77,500 (2010); Median contract rent: $303 per month (2005-2009 5-year est.); Median year structure built: 1967 (2005-2009 5-year est.).

Newspapers: Vienna Times (National news; Circulation 2,800)

Transportation: Commute to work: 91.9% car, 1.9% public transportation, 2.4% walk, 1.0% work from home (2005-2009 5-year est.); Travel time to work: 37.0% less than 15 minutes, 28.0% 15 to 30 minutes, 21.2% 30 to 45 minutes, 10.9% 45 to 60 minutes, 3.0% 60 minutes or more (2005-2009 5-year est.)

Kane County

Located in northeastern Illinois; drained by the Fox River and Mill Creek. Covers a land area of 520.44 square miles, a water area of 3.64 square miles, and is located in the Central Time Zone at 41.91° N. Lat., 88.33° W. Long. The county was founded in 1836. County seat is Geneva.

Kane County is part of the Chicago-Joliet-Naperville, IL-IN-WI Metropolitan Statistical Area. The entire metro area includes: Chicago-Joliet-Naperville, IL Metropolitan Division (Cook County, IL; DeKalb County, IL; DuPage County, IL; Grundy County, IL; Kane County, IL; Kendall County, IL; McHenry County, IL; Will County, IL); Gary, IN Metropolitan Division (Jasper County, IN; Lake County, IN; Newton County, IN; Porter County, IN); Lake County-Kenosha County, IL-WI Metropolitan Division (Lake County, IL; Kenosha County, WI)

Weather Station: Aurora										Elevation: 640 feet		
	Jan	Feb	Mar	Apr	May	Jun	Jul	Aug	Sep	Oct	Nov	Dec
High	31	36	48	61	72	81	85	83	76	63	49	35
Low	14	18	28	38	48	58	63	61	53	41	31	19
Precip	1.6	1.7	2.3	3.7	3.9	4.0	4.2	4.3	3.6	3.0	3.3	2.3
Snow	9.6	6.8	2.8	0.6	0.0	0.0	0.0	0.0	0.0	tr	0.9	7.7

High and Low temperatures in degrees Fahrenheit; Precipitation and Snow in inches

Weather Station: Elgin										Elevation: 763 feet		
	Jan	Feb	Mar	Apr	May	Jun	Jul	Aug	Sep	Oct	Nov	Dec
High	29	34	45	58	70	79	83	82	75	62	47	33
Low	13	17	26	37	48	57	63	61	52	40	30	18
Precip	1.5	1.5	2.1	3.7	4.2	3.8	3.7	5.1	3.5	3.0	3.1	2.1
Snow	9.4	6.8	3.6	0.5	0.0	0.0	0.0	0.0	0.0	tr	0.8	8.1

High and Low temperatures in degrees Fahrenheit; Precipitation and Snow in inches

Population: 317,471 (1990); 404,119 (2000); 522,440 (2010); 572,947 (2015 projected); Race: 75.4% White, 5.2% Black, 3.2% Asian, 16.2% Other, 29.1% Hispanic of any race (2010); Density: 1,003.9 persons per square mile (2010); Average household size: 3.01 (2010); Median age: 32.9 (2010); Males per 100 females: 102.4 (2010).

Religion: Five largest groups: 34.4% Catholic Church, 3.7% Lutheran Church—Missouri Synod, 3.5% Evangelical Lutheran Church in America, 3.3% The United Methodist Church, 1.9% United Church of Christ (2000).

Economy: Unemployment rate: 9.9% (August 2011); Total civilian labor force: 270,681 (August 2011); Leading industries: 16.2% manufacturing; 13.5% retail trade; 12.2% health care and social assistance (2009); Farms: 759 totaling 192,372 acres (2007); Companies that employ 500 or more persons: 25 (2009); Companies that employ 100 to 499 persons: 245 (2009); Companies that employ less than 100 persons: 11,992 (2009); Black-owned businesses: 1,583 (2007); Hispanic-owned businesses: 2,935 (2007); Asian-owned businesses: 1,718 (2007); Women-owned businesses: 11,533 (2007); Retail sales per capita: $13,109 (2010). Single-family building permits issued: 527 (2010); Multi-family building permits issued: 38 (2010).

Income: Per capita income: $28,600 (2010); Median household income: $68,938 (2010); Average household income: $86,733 (2010); Percent of households with income of $100,000 or more: 28.6% (2010); Poverty rate: 9.4% (2009); Bankruptcy rate: 6.33% (2010).

Taxes: Total county taxes per capita: $195 (2007); County property taxes per capita: $164 (2007).

Education: Percent of population age 25 and over with: High school diploma (including GED) or higher: 82.8% (2010); Bachelor's degree or higher: 31.7% (2010); Master's degree or higher: 10.7% (2010).

Housing: Homeownership rate: 76.8% (2010); Median home value: $215,398 (2010); Median contract rent: $786 per month (2005-2009 5-year est.); Median year structure built: 1977 (2005-2009 5-year est.)

Health: Birth rate: 172.3 per 10,000 population (2009); Death rate: 54.9 per 10,000 population (2009); Age-adjusted cancer mortality rate: 169.1 deaths per 100,000 population (2007); Number of physicians: 14.6 per 10,000 population (2008); Hospital beds: 27.3 per 10,000 population (2007); Hospital admissions: 873.5 per 10,000 population (2007).

Environment: Air Quality Index: 94.6% good, 5.4% moderate, 0.0% unhealthy for sensitive individuals, 0.0% unhealthy (percent of days in 2008)

Elections: 2008 Presidential election results: 55.2% Obama, 43.4% McCain, 0.5% Nader

Additional Information Contacts

Kane County Government . . . . (630) 232-3400

    http://www.countyofkane.org

Aurora Hispanic Chamber of Commerce . . . . (630) 264-2422

    http://www.ahcc-il.com

Aurora Regional Chamber of Commerce . . . . (630) 256-3180

    http://www.aurorachamber.com

Batavia Chamber of Commerce . . . . (630) 879-7134

    http://www.bataviachamber.org

City of Aurora . . . . (630) 256-4636

    http://www.aurora-il.org

City of Batavia . . . . (630) 454-2000

    http://www.cityofbatavia.net

City of Elgin . . . . (847) 931-6100

    http://www.cityofelgin.org

City of Geneva . . . . (630) 232-7494

    http://www.geneva.il.us

City of Saint Charles . . . . (630) 377-4400

    http://www.stcharlesil.gov

Elgin Area Chamber of Commerce . . . . (847) 741-5660
  http://www.elginchamber.com
Geneva Chamber of Commerce . . . . (630) 232-6060
  http://www.genevachamber.com
Greater Montgomery Area Chamber of Commerce . . . . (630) 897-8137
  http://www.chamberofmontgomeryil.org
Hampshire Area Chamber of Commerce . . . . (847) 683-1122
  http://www.hampshirechamber.org
Northern Kane County Chamber of Commerce . . . . (847) 426-8565
  http://www.nkcchamber.com
St. Charles Chamber of Commerce . . . . (630) 584-8384
  http://www.stcharleschamber.com
Sugar Grove Chamber of Commerce & Industry . . . . (630) 466-7895
  http://www.sugargrovechamber.org
Village of Carpentersville . . . . (847) 426-3439
  http://vil.carpentersville.il.us
Village of Montgomery . . . . (630) 896-8080
  http://ci.montgomery.il.us
Village of North Aurora . . . . (630) 897-8228
  http://www.vil.north-aurora.il.us
Village of South Elgin . . . . (847) 742-5780
  http://www.southelgin.com
Village of West Dundee . . . . (847) 551-3800
  http://www.wdundee.org

Kane County Communities

AURORA (city). Covers a land area of 38.526 square miles and a water area of 0.893 square miles. Located at 41.76° N. Lat; 88.29° W. Long. Elevation is 679 feet.

History: Named for the Iroquoian translation of "constant dawn". Joseph McCarty of Elmira, New York, came to Illinois in 1834 and chose the site on the Fox River as superior to Chicago as a place to settle. Th e community of Aurora was platted in 1836 and a post office was soon established. Development along both sides of the river resulted in separate towns of East Aurora and West Aurora until 1857, when the two were joined in incorporation. Meanwhile, the Chicago, Burlington & Quincy Railroad had arrived with its tracks and shops, and with it a period of growth. Aurora, in 1881, was one of the first towns in the U.S. to have electric street lights.

Population: 102,513 (1990); 142,990 (2000); 179,187 (2010); 197,015 (2015 projected); Race: 62.6% White, 10.6% Black, 4.8% Asian, 22.0% Other, 40.0% Hispanic of any race (2010); Density: 4,651.1 persons per square mile (2010); Average household size: 3.10 (2010); Median age: 31.3 (2010); Males per 100 females: 102.9 (2010); Marriage status: 34.5% never married, 52.6% now married, 4.2% widowed, 8.6% divorced (2005-2009 5-year est.); Foreign born: 24.2% (2005-2009 5-year est.); Ancestry (includes multiple ancestries): 16.8% German, 9.7% Irish, 5.2% Polish, 4.9% Italian, 4.8% English (2005-2009 5-year est.).

Economy: Unemployment rate: 10.8% (August 2011); Total civilian labor force: 91,412 (August 2011); Single-family building permits issued: 71 (2010); Multi-family building permits issued: 0 (2010); Employment by occupation: 14.9% management, 17.2% professional, 14.8% services, 25.3% sales, 0.1% farming, 7.5% construction, 20.2% production (2005-2009 5-year est.).

Income: Per capita income: $25,929 (2010); Median household income: $63,571 (2010); Average household income: $80,584 (2010); Percent of households with income of $100,000 or more: 25.1% (2010); Poverty rate: 12.1% (2005-2009 5-year est.).

Taxes: Total city taxes per capita: $697 (2007); City property taxes per capita: $432 (2007).

Education: Percent of population age 25 and over with: High school diploma (including GED) or higher: 77.7% (2010); Bachelor's degree or higher: 32.8% (2010); Master's degree or higher: 11.3% (2010).

School District(s)

Aurora East USD 131 (PK-12)
  2009-10 Enrollment: 13,506 . . . . (630) 299-5554
Aurora West USD 129 (PK-12)
  2009-10 Enrollment: 12,508 . . . . (630) 301-5033
Indian Prairie CUSD 204 (PK-12)
  2009-10 Enrollment: 29,733 . . . . (630) 375-3000
Oswego CUSD 308 (PK-12)
  2009-10 Enrollment: 16,314 . . . . (630) 636-3080

Four-year College(s)

Aurora University (Private, Not-for-profit)
  Fall 2009 Enrollment: 4,355 . . . . (630) 892-6431
  2010-11 Tuition: In-state $18,700; Out-of-state $18,700

Vocational/Technical School(s)

Regency Beauty Institute-Aurora (Private, For-profit)
  Fall 2009 Enrollment: 153 . . . . (800) 787-6456
  2010-11 Tuition: $16,075

Housing: Homeownership rate: 70.5% (2010); Median home value: $180,242 (2010); Median contract rent: $819 per month (2005-2009 5-year est.); Median year structure built: 1979 (2005-2009 5-year est.).

Hospitals: Provena Mercy Medical Center (356 beds); Rush-Copley Medical Center (183 beds)

Safety: Violent crime rate: 36.4 per 10,000 population; Property crime rate: 216.2 per 10,000 population (2010).

Newspapers: Aurora Beacon-News (Local news; Circulation 36,000)

Transportation: Commute to work: 88.4% car, 4.9% public transportation, 1.3% walk, 3.0% work from home (2005-2009 5-year est.); Travel time to work: 23.3% less than 15 minutes, 35.3% 15 to 30 minutes, 19.2% 30 to 45 minutes, 9.3% 45 to 60 minutes, 12.9% 60 minutes or more (2005-2009 5-year est.)

Airports: Aurora Municipal (general aviation)

Additional Information Contacts

Aurora Hispanic Chamber of Commerce . . . . (630) 264-2422
  http://www.ahcc-il.com
Aurora Regional Chamber of Commerce . . . . (630) 256-3180
  http://www.aurorachamber.com
City of Aurora . . . . (630) 256-4636
  http://www.aurora-il.org

BATAVIA (city). Covers a land area of 9.046 square miles and a water area of 0.140 square miles. Located at 41.84° N. Lat; 88.30° W. Long. Elevation is 715 feet.

History: Batavia was settled in 1832 by people from New York, who chose the site for its water power, fertile soil, and surface limestone. They named the new town for their home in New York. Early Batavia had the nickname of Quarry City.

Population: 17,818 (1990); 23,866 (2000); 28,150 (2010); 30,640 (2015 projected); Race: 90.2% White, 2.9% Black, 2.4% Asian, 4.5% Other, 8.0% Hispanic of any race (2010); Density: 3,111.9 persons per square mile (2010); Average household size: 2.82 (2010); Median age: 34.2 (2010); Males per 100 females: 99.0 (2010); Marriage status: 25.3% never married, 62.1% now married, 4.4% widowed, 8.2% divorced (2005-2009 5-year est.); Foreign born: 4.6% (2005-2009 5-year est.); Ancestry (includes multiple ancestries): 35.8% German, 19.1% Irish, 11.9% English, 10.8% Polish, 9.2% Italian (2005-2009 5-year est.).

Economy: Unemployment rate: 8.2% (August 2011); Total civilian labor force: 15,023 (August 2011); Single-family building permits issued: 5 (2010); Multi-family building permits issued: 0 (2010); Employment by occupation: 21.9% management, 25.1% professional, 10.0% services, 28.1% sales, 0.1% farming, 5.9% construction, 8.8% production (2005-2009 5-year est.).

Income: Per capita income: $34,069 (2010); Median household income: $82,419 (2010); Average household income: $97,590 (2010); Percent of households with income of $100,000 or more: 38.2% (2010); Poverty rate: 5.9% (2005-2009 5-year est.).

Taxes: Total city taxes per capita: $407 (2007); City property taxes per capita: $218 (2007).

Education: Percent of population age 25 and over with: High school diploma (including GED) or higher: 94.8% (2010); Bachelor's degree or higher: 48.0% (2010); Master's degree or higher: 17.3% (2010).

School District(s)

Batavia USD 101 (PK-12)
  2009-10 Enrollment: 6,292 . . . . (630) 937-8834

Housing: Homeownership rate: 78.6% (2010); Median home value: $256,698 (2010); Median contract rent: $839 per month (2005-2009 5-year est.); Median year structure built: 1982 (2005-2009 5-year est.).

Safety: Violent crime rate: 14.4 per 10,000 population; Property crime rate: 183.4 per 10,000 population (2010).

Newspapers: Windmill Herald (Local news; Circulation 11,000)

Transportation: Commute to work: 84.4% car, 3.5% public transportation, 1.0% walk, 8.0% work from home (2005-2009 5-year est.); Travel time to work: 28.3% less than 15 minutes, 31.1% 15 to 30 minutes, 19.5% 30 to 45 minutes, 9.2% 45 to 60 minutes, 11.9% 60 minutes or more (2005-2009 5-year est.)

Additional Information Contacts

Batavia Chamber of Commerce . . . . (630) 879-7134
http://www.bataviachamber.org

City of Batavia . . . . (630) 454-2000
http://www.cityofbatavia.net

BIG ROCK (village). Covers a land area of 4.328 square miles and a water area of 0 square miles. Located at 41.75° N. Lat; 88.54° W. Long. Elevation is 709 feet.

History: Incorporated July 26, 2001.

Population: n/a (1990); n/a (2000); 1,126 (2010); n/a (2015 projected); Race: 97.0% White, 0.7% Black, 0.2% Asian, 2.1% Other, 2.0% Hispanic of any race (2010); Density: 260.2 persons per square mile (2010); Average household size: 2.75 (2010); Median age: 45.1 (2010); Males per 100 females: 109.3 (2010); Marriage status: 26.1% never married, 65.3% now married, 1.3% widowed, 7.3% divorced (2005-2009 5-year est.); Foreign born: 4.1% (2005-2009 5-year est.); Ancestry (includes multiple ancestries): 39.8% German, 21.3% Irish, 13.8% Polish, 7.5% Scottish, 6.0% Norwegian (2005-2009 5-year est.).

Economy: Employment by occupation: 15.5% management, 15.2% professional, 8.9% services, 19.2% sales, 0.0% farming, 17.5% construction, 23.6% production (2005-2009 5-year est.).

Income: Per capita income: n/a (2010); Median household income: n/a (2010); Average household income: n/a (2010); Percent of households with income of $100,000 or more: n/a (2010); Poverty rate: 4.4% (2005-2009 5-year est.).

Taxes: Total city taxes per capita: $3 (2007); City property taxes per capita: $0 (2007).

Education: Percent of population age 25 and over with: High school diploma (including GED) or higher: n/a (2010); Bachelor's degree or higher: n/a (2010); Master's degree or higher: n/a (2010).

School District(s)

Hinckley Big Rock CUSD 429 (PK-12)
2009-10 Enrollment: 761 . . . . (815) 286-7575

Housing: Homeownership rate: n/a (2010); Median home value: n/a (2010); Median contract rent: $886 per month (2005-2009 5-year est.); Median year structure built: 1964 (2005-2009 5-year est.).

Transportation: Commute to work: 90.2% car, 0.8% public transportation, 6.0% walk, 1.2% work from home (2005-2009 5-year est.); Travel time to work: 19.4% less than 15 minutes, 31.7% 15 to 30 minutes, 25.8% 30 to 45 minutes, 8.7% 45 to 60 minutes, 14.4% 60 minutes or more (2005-2009 5-year est.)

BURLINGTON (village). Covers a land area of 0.354 square miles and a water area of 0 square miles. Located at 42.05° N. Lat; 88.54° W. Long. Elevation is 925 feet.

Population: 431 (1990); 452 (2000); 538 (2010); 584 (2015 projected); Race: 95.0% White, 0.2% Black, 2.2% Asian, 2.6% Other, 2.2% Hispanic of any race (2010); Density: 1,520.1 persons per square mile (2010); Average household size: 2.74 (2010); Median age: 34.6 (2010); Males per 100 females: 92.8 (2010); Marriage status: 32.9% never married, 63.0% now married, 0.8% widowed, 3.4% divorced (2005-2009 5-year est.); Foreign born: 10.7% (2005-2009 5-year est.); Ancestry (includes multiple ancestries): 51.5% German, 11.1% Irish, 10.7% Scotch-Irish, 8.5% English, 8.1% Swedish (2005-2009 5-year est.).

Economy: Employment by occupation: 7.1% management, 24.4% professional, 20.4% services, 18.6% sales, 0.0% farming, 10.6% construction, 18.8% production (2005-2009 5-year est.).

Income: Per capita income: $27,810 (2010); Median household income: $68,396 (2010); Average household income: $77,015 (2010); Percent of households with income of $100,000 or more: 25.5% (2010); Poverty rate: 0.0% (2005-2009 5-year est.).

Taxes: Total city taxes per capita: $331 (2007); City property taxes per capita: $183 (2007).

Education: Percent of population age 25 and over with: High school diploma (including GED) or higher: 91.4% (2010); Bachelor's degree or higher: 16.3% (2010); Master's degree or higher: 6.2% (2010).

School District(s)

Central CUSD 301 (PK-12)
2009-10 Enrollment: 3,374 . . . . (847) 464-6005

Housing: Homeownership rate: 75.5% (2010); Median home value: $239,216 (2010); Median contract rent: $684 per month (2005-2009 5-year est.); Median year structure built: 1951 (2005-2009 5-year est.).

Transportation: Commute to work: 92.9% car, 1.1% public transportation, 6.0% walk, 0.0% work from home (2005-2009 5-year est.); Travel time to work: 30.2% less than 15 minutes, 35.7% 15 to 30 minutes, 8.0% 30 to 45 minutes, 17.5% 45 to 60 minutes, 8.6% 60 minutes or more (2005-2009 5-year est.)

CAMPTON HILLS (village). Covers a land area of 16.908 square miles and a water area of 0.082 square miles. Located at 41.93° N. Lat; 88.40° W. Long.

History: Incorporated May 14, 2007.

Population: n/a (1990); n/a (2000); 11,131 (2010); n/a (2015 projected); Race: 95.4% White, 0.5% Black, 1.8% Asian, 2.3% Other, 3.6% Hispanic of any race (2010); Density: 658.3 persons per square mile (2010); Average household size: 3.19 (2010); Median age: 42.4 (2010); Males per 100 females: 102.9 (2010); Marriage status: 23.1% never married, 69.4% now married, 3.5% widowed, 3.9% divorced (2005-2009 5-year est.); Foreign born: 8.5% (2005-2009 5-year est.); Ancestry (includes multiple ancestries): 32.0% German, 18.5% Irish, 15.7% Polish, 15.4% Italian, 8.1% English (2005-2009 5-year est.).

Economy: Employment by occupation: 27.1% management, 20.5% professional, 9.6% services, 25.6% sales, 0.2% farming, 4.9% construction, 12.2% production (2005-2009 5-year est.).

Income: Per capita income: n/a (2010); Median household income: n/a (2010); Average household income: n/a (2010); Percent of households with income of $100,000 or more: n/a (2010); Poverty rate: 0.9% (2005-2009 5-year est.).

Taxes: Total city taxes per capita: $1,023 (2007); City property taxes per capita: $566 (2007).

Education: Percent of population age 25 and over with: High school diploma (including GED) or higher: n/a (2010); Bachelor's degree or higher: n/a (2010); Master's degree or higher: n/a (2010).

Housing: Homeownership rate: n/a (2010); Median home value: n/a (2010); Median contract rent: $737 per month (2005-2009 5-year est.); Median year structure built: 1989 (2005-2009 5-year est.).

Safety: Violent crime rate: 2.1 per 10,000 population; Property crime rate: 64.7 per 10,000 population (2010).

Transportation: Commute to work: 86.8% car, 2.0% public transportation, 0.9% walk, 10.2% work from home (2005-2009 5-year est.); Travel time to work: 16.2% less than 15 minutes, 23.1% 15 to 30 minutes, 21.6% 30 to 45 minutes, 16.1% 45 to 60 minutes, 23.1% 60 minutes or more (2005-2009 5-year est.)

CARPENTERSVILLE (village). Covers a land area of 7.450 square miles and a water area of 0.148 square miles. Located at 42.12° N. Lat; 88.27° W. Long. Elevation is 889 feet.

History: Named for D. G. Carpenter, an early settler. Carpentersville was settled in 1834 by Angelo Carpenter of Massachusetts and his father and uncle. Carpenter built several mills and a store, and in 1851 he platted the town. An early industry was the Illinois Iron and Bolt Company.

Population: 23,869 (1990); 30,586 (2000); 38,438 (2010); 42,024 (2015 projected); Race: 60.7% White, 5.4% Black, 3.1% Asian, 30.9% Other, 49.6% Hispanic of any race (2010); Density: 5,159.4 persons per square mile (2010); Average household size: 3.55 (2010); Median age: 29.8 (2010); Males per 100 females: 104.7 (2010); Marriage status: 33.5% never married, 53.8% now married, 4.0% widowed, 8.6% divorced (2005-2009 5-year est.); Foreign born: 32.4% (2005-2009 5-year est.); Ancestry (includes multiple ancestries): 17.8% German, 9.2% Irish, 8.4% Polish, 5.4% Italian, 3.5% English (2005-2009 5-year est.).

Economy: Unemployment rate: 11.8% (August 2011); Total civilian labor force: 18,680 (August 2011); Single-family building permits issued: 35 (2010); Multi-family building permits issued: 0 (2010); Employment by occupation: 11.0% management, 12.2% professional, 18.2% services, 25.1% sales, 0.4% farming, 11.2% construction, 21.9% production (2005-2009 5-year est.).

Income: Per capita income: $21,352 (2010); Median household income: $63,252 (2010); Average household income: $75,797 (2010); Percent of households with income of $100,000 or more: 22.2% (2010); Poverty rate: 9.4% (2005-2009 5-year est.).

Taxes: Total city taxes per capita: $270 (2007); City property taxes per capita: $182 (2007).

Education: Percent of population age 25 and over with: High school diploma (including GED) or higher: 71.1% (2010); Bachelor's degree or higher: 16.8% (2010); Master's degree or higher: 4.7% (2010).

School District(s)

Barrington CUSD 220 (PK-12)
2009-10 Enrollment: 9,283 . . . . (847) 381-6300

CUSD 300 (PK-12)
   2009-10 Enrollment: 20,341 . . . . (847) 426-1300
Housing: Homeownership rate: 79.2% (2010); Median home value:
$158,111 (2010); Median contract rent: $837 per month (2005-2009 5-year
est.); Median year structure built: 1976 (2005-2009 5-year est.).
Safety: Violent crime rate: 11.2 per 10,000 population; Property crime rate:
150.8 per 10,000 population (2010).
Transportation: Commute to work: 93.2% car, 2.3% public transportation,
1.2% walk, 2.1% work from home (2005-2009 5-year est.); Travel time to
work: 16.5% less than 15 minutes, 30.6% 15 to 30 minutes, 29.6% 30 to 45
minutes, 12.6% 45 to 60 minutes, 10.7% 60 minutes or more (2005-2009
5-year est.)
Additional Information Contacts
Northern Kane County Chamber of Commerce. . . . . (847) 426-8565
   http://www.nkcchamber.com
Village of Carpentersville . . . . (847) 426-3439
   http://vil.carpentersville.il.us

DUNDEE (unincorporated postal area, zip code 60118). Aka West
Dundee. Covers a land area of 22.307 square miles and a water area of
0.373 square miles. Located at 42.02° N. Lat; 88.41° W. Long. Elevation is
919 feet.
Population: 14,739 (2000); Race: 95.1% White, 0.6% Black, 1.0% Asian,
3.3% Other, 3.2% Hispanic of any race (2000); Density: 660.7 persons per
square mile (2000); Age: 26.0% under 18, 9.3% over 64 (2000); Marriage
status: 20.8% never married, 65.7% now married, 4.1% widowed, 9.4%
divorced (2000); Foreign born: 7.9% (2000); Ancestry (includes multiple
ancestries): 35.3% German, 15.8% Irish, 13.0% Polish, 9.7% Italian, 9.1%
English (2000).
Economy: Employment by occupation: 22.8% management, 20.2%
professional, 8.1% services, 30.9% sales, 0.3% farming, 8.5%
construction, 9.2% production (2000).
Income: Per capita income: $31,260 (2000); Median household income:
$72,500 (2000); Poverty rate: 3.0% (2000).
Education: Percent of population age 25 and over with: High school
diploma (including GED) or higher: 91.4% (2000); Bachelor's degree or
higher: 37.0% (2000).
School District(s)
CUSD 300 (PK-12)
   2009-10 Enrollment: 20,341 . . . . (847) 426-1300
Housing: Homeownership rate: 82.4% (2000); Median home value:
$214,000 (2000); Median contract rent: $679 per month (2000); Median
year structure built: 1971 (2000).
Transportation: Commute to work: 90.4% car, 2.3% public transportation,
1.5% walk, 5.4% work from home (2000); Travel time to work: 25.5% less
than 15 minutes, 27.5% 15 to 30 minutes, 23.9% 30 to 45 minutes, 12.6%
45 to 60 minutes, 10.6% 60 minutes or more (2000)
Additional Information Contacts
Northern Kane County Chamber of Commerce. . . . . (847) 426-8565
   http://www.nkcchamber.com

EAST DUNDEE (village). Covers a land area of 2.679 square miles
and a water area of 0.235 square miles. Located at 42.10° N. Lat; 88.27°
W. Long. Elevation is 768 feet.
History: East Dundee was settled mainly by German immigrants who left
their home country during the 1848 Revolution.
Population: 2,838 (1990); 2,955 (2000); 3,187 (2010); 3,332 (2015
projected); Race: 90.3% White, 1.0% Black, 2.8% Asian, 5.9% Other, 6.2%
Hispanic of any race (2010); Density: 1,189.8 persons per square mile
(2010); Average household size: 2.45 (2010); Median age: 40.6 (2010);
Males per 100 females: 97.3 (2010); Marriage status: 25.4% never married,
59.7% now married, 7.9% widowed, 7.1% divorced (2005-2009 5-year
est.); Foreign born: 10.7% (2005-2009 5-year est.); Ancestry (includes
multiple ancestries): 35.0% German, 19.7% Irish, 13.6% English, 10.8%
Polish, 5.7% Italian (2005-2009 5-year est.).
Economy: Single-family building permits issued: 0 (2010); Multi-family
building permits issued: 0 (2010); Employment by occupation: 19.3%
management, 21.7% professional, 7.4% services, 23.7% sales, 0.0%
farming, 12.3% construction, 15.6% production (2005-2009 5-year est.).
Income: Per capita income: $35,388 (2010); Median household income:
$66,667 (2010); Average household income: $85,988 (2010); Percent of
households with income of $100,000 or more: 25.6% (2010); Poverty rate:
5.1% (2005-2009 5-year est.).
Taxes: Total city taxes per capita: $469 (2007); City property taxes per
capita: $216 (2007).

Education: Percent of population age 25 and over with: High school
diploma (including GED) or higher: 91.2% (2010); Bachelor's degree or
higher: 35.3% (2010); Master's degree or higher: 13.8% (2010).
Housing: Homeownership rate: 84.2% (2010); Median home value:
$207,175 (2010); Median contract rent: $911 per month (2005-2009 5-year
est.); Median year structure built: 1962 (2005-2009 5-year est.).
Transportation: Commute to work: 86.2% car, 1.7% public transportation,
4.1% walk, 5.0% work from home (2005-2009 5-year est.); Travel time to
work: 24.0% less than 15 minutes, 32.8% 15 to 30 minutes, 21.1% 30 to 45
minutes, 15.7% 45 to 60 minutes, 6.5% 60 minutes or more (2005-2009
5-year est.)

ELBURN (village). Covers a land area of 2.727 square miles and a
water area of 0 square miles. Located at 41.89° N. Lat; 88.46° W. Long.
Elevation is 853 feet.
History: Elburn began in 1854 when the Galena & Chicago Union Railroad
line was laid, and developed as a farming center. It is said that when
Lincoln visited Elburn in 1858, he was greeted by a group calling itself the
Lincoln True Hearts, pledging support.
Population: 1,762 (1990); 2,756 (2000); 3,511 (2010); 3,755 (2015
projected); Race: 96.1% White, 0.1% Black, 1.3% Asian, 2.5% Other, 3.4%
Hispanic of any race (2010); Density: 1,287.4 persons per square mile
(2010); Average household size: 2.72 (2010); Median age: 35.8 (2010);
Males per 100 females: 97.2 (2010); Marriage status: 26.1% never married,
63.4% now married, 2.8% widowed, 7.6% divorced (2005-2009 5-year
est.); Foreign born: 5.2% (2005-2009 5-year est.); Ancestry (includes
multiple ancestries): 50.1% German, 22.9% Irish, 12.6% Italian, 9.9%
Polish, 7.8% English (2005-2009 5-year est.).
Economy: Single-family building permits issued: 2 (2010); Multi-family
building permits issued: 0 (2010); Employment by occupation: 16.7%
management, 15.0% professional, 12.9% services, 32.2% sales, 0.0%
farming, 13.9% construction, 9.4% production (2005-2009 5-year est.).
Income: Per capita income: $36,340 (2010); Median household income:
$86,373 (2010); Average household income: $98,657 (2010); Percent of
households with income of $100,000 or more: 40.2% (2010); Poverty rate:
4.5% (2005-2009 5-year est.).
Taxes: Total city taxes per capita: $559 (2007); City property taxes per
capita: $160 (2007).
Education: Percent of population age 25 and over with: High school
diploma (including GED) or higher: 95.5% (2010); Bachelor's degree or
higher: 41.3% (2010); Master's degree or higher: 16.4% (2010).
School District(s)
Kaneland CUSD 302 (PK-12)
   2009-10 Enrollment: 4,746 . . . . (630) 365-5111
Housing: Homeownership rate: 84.0% (2010); Median home value:
$258,846 (2010); Median contract rent: $856 per month (2005-2009 5-year
est.); Median year structure built: 1998 (2005-2009 5-year est.).
Newspapers: Elburn Herald (Local news; Circulation 3,301)
Transportation: Commute to work: 89.6% car, 3.0% public transportation,
1.0% walk, 5.6% work from home (2005-2009 5-year est.); Travel time to
work: 18.6% less than 15 minutes, 29.6% 15 to 30 minutes, 21.4% 30 to 45
minutes, 14.0% 45 to 60 minutes, 16.4% 60 minutes or more (2005-2009
5-year est.)

ELGIN (city). Covers a land area of 25.003 square miles and a water
area of 0.386 square miles. Located at 42.03° N. Lat; 88.28° W. Long.
Elevation is 745 feet.
History: Named for a Scottish hymn, "Elgin," by James T. Gifford. Elgin
was settled in 1835 by James and Hezekiah Gifford from New York, who
dammed the river and built a sawmill and a gristmill. It was incorporated as
a village in 1847 and as a town in 1854. An early industry here was the
production of condensed milk, a process developed by Gail Borden. The
Elgin watch industry, which made the name of Elgin known around the
world, began in 1866, followed by the Elgin Watchmakers College which
opened in the 1920's.
Population: 78,650 (1990); 94,487 (2000); 104,109 (2010); 109,583 (2015
projected); Race: 65.0% White, 5.7% Black, 5.8% Asian, 23.6% Other,
44.1% Hispanic of any race (2010); Density: 4,163.9 persons per square
mile (2010); Average household size: 2.97 (2010); Median age: 32.8
(2010); Males per 100 females: 102.0 (2010); Marriage status: 34.2%
never married, 52.2% now married, 4.9% widowed, 8.8% divorced
(2005-2009 5-year est.); Foreign born: 25.6% (2005-2009 5-year est.);
Ancestry (includes multiple ancestries): 20.3% German, 10.3% Irish, 6.1%
Polish, 5.7% Italian, 5.5% English (2005-2009 5-year est.).

Economy: Unemployment rate: 11.0% (August 2011); Total civilian labor force: 57,814 (August 2011); Single-family building permits issued: 182 (2010); Multi-family building permits issued: 0 (2010); Employment by occupation: 11.4% management, 16.4% professional, 16.4% services, 24.4% sales, 0.5% farming, 9.2% construction, 21.7% production (2005-2009 5-year est.).

Income: Per capita income: $24,655 (2010); Median household income: $62,091 (2010); Average household income: $73,660 (2010); Percent of households with income of $100,000 or more: 21.3% (2010); Poverty rate: 10.9% (2005-2009 5-year est.).

Taxes: Total city taxes per capita: $507 (2007); City property taxes per capita: $400 (2007).

Education: Percent of population age 25 and over with: High school diploma (including GED) or higher: 77.5% (2010); Bachelor's degree or higher: 24.8% (2010); Master's degree or higher: 7.7% (2010).

School District(s)

Central CUSD 301 (PK-12)
　　2009-10 Enrollment: 3,374 . . . . (847) 464-6005
SD U-46 (PK-12)
　　2009-10 Enrollment: 41,446 . . . . (847) 888-5000

Four-year College(s)

Judson University (Private, Not-for-profit, Baptist)
　　Fall 2009 Enrollment: 1,231 . . . . (847) 628-2500
　　2010-11 Tuition: In-state $24,780; Out-of-state $24,780

Two-year College(s)

Elgin Community College (Public)
　　Fall 2009 Enrollment: 11,704 . . . . (847) 697-1000
　　2010-11 Tuition: In-state $8,252; Out-of-state $10,485

Vocational/Technical School(s)

Cannella School of Hair Design (Private, For-profit)
　　Fall 2009 Enrollment: 91 . . . . (708) 742-6611
　　2010-11 Tuition: $12,190
Regency Beauty Institute-Elgin (Private, For-profit)
　　Fall 2009 Enrollment: 76 . . . . (800) 787-6456
　　2010-11 Tuition: $16,075

Housing: Homeownership rate: 71.9% (2010); Median home value: $185,343 (2010); Median contract rent: $755 per month (2005-2009 5-year est.); Median year structure built: 1973 (2005-2009 5-year est.).

Hospitals: Provena Saint Joseph Hospital (260 beds); Sherman Hospital (353 beds)

Safety: Violent crime rate: 33.0 per 10,000 population; Property crime rate: 202.9 per 10,000 population (2010).

Newspapers: Courier-News (Local news; Circulation 33,240)

Transportation: Commute to work: 91.0% car, 2.3% public transportation, 2.3% walk, 2.7% work from home (2005-2009 5-year est.); Travel time to work: 25.1% less than 15 minutes, 30.7% 15 to 30 minutes, 24.0% 30 to 45 minutes, 9.4% 45 to 60 minutes, 10.8% 60 minutes or more (2005-2009 5-year est.)

Additional Information Contacts

City of Elgin . . . . (847) 931-6100
　　http://www.cityofelgin.org
Elgin Area Chamber of Commerce . . . . (847) 741-5660
　　http://www.elginchamber.com

GENEVA (city). County seat. Covers a land area of 8.407 square miles and a water area of 0.176 square miles. Located at 41.88° N. Lat; 88.31° W. Long. Elevation is 712 feet.

History: Named for Geneva, New York. Geneva was settled about 1832 by soldiers returning from the Black Hawk War and by pioneers heading west.

Population: 13,292 (1990); 19,515 (2000); 24,586 (2010); 27,120 (2015 projected); Race: 94.9% White, 1.4% Black, 2.0% Asian, 1.7% Other, 4.2% Hispanic of any race (2010); Density: 2,924.6 persons per square mile (2010); Average household size: 2.90 (2010); Median age: 34.3 (2010); Males per 100 females: 100.9 (2010); Marriage status: 27.6% never married, 60.8% now married, 3.9% widowed, 7.7% divorced (2005-2009 5-year est.); Foreign born: 4.5% (2005-2009 5-year est.); Ancestry (includes multiple ancestries): 30.1% German, 21.2% Irish, 13.8% Italian, 11.4% English, 10.0% Polish (2005-2009 5-year est.).

Economy: Single-family building permits issued: 5 (2010); Multi-family building permits issued: 0 (2010); Employment by occupation: 24.1% management, 25.4% professional, 8.9% services, 29.5% sales, 0.0% farming, 4.9% construction, 7.3% production (2005-2009 5-year est.).

Income: Per capita income: $37,643 (2010); Median household income: $89,412 (2010); Average household income: $110,379 (2010); Percent of households with income of $100,000 or more: 43.0% (2010); Poverty rate: 1.8% (2005-2009 5-year est.).

Taxes: Total city taxes per capita: $353 (2007); City property taxes per capita: $254 (2007).

Education: Percent of population age 25 and over with: High school diploma (including GED) or higher: 95.6% (2010); Bachelor's degree or higher: 56.3% (2010); Master's degree or higher: 21.8% (2010).

School District(s)

Geneva CUSD 304 (PK-12)
　　2009-10 Enrollment: 6,028 . . . . (630) 463-3000
Kane Roe (PK-12)
　　2009-10 Enrollment: n/a . . . . (630) 232-5955

Housing: Homeownership rate: 82.6% (2010); Median home value: $277,495 (2010); Median contract rent: $954 per month (2005-2009 5-year est.); Median year structure built: 1987 (2005-2009 5-year est.).

Hospitals: Delnor-Community Health System (118 beds)

Safety: Violent crime rate: 3.7 per 10,000 population; Property crime rate: 127.0 per 10,000 population (2010).

Newspapers: El Conquistador (Local news; Circulation 15,000); Kane County Chronicle (Local news; Circulation 14,000)

Transportation: Commute to work: 87.3% car, 4.7% public transportation, 1.2% walk, 6.0% work from home (2005-2009 5-year est.); Travel time to work: 35.5% less than 15 minutes, 21.5% 15 to 30 minutes, 18.9% 30 to 45 minutes, 10.0% 45 to 60 minutes, 14.1% 60 minutes or more (2005-2009 5-year est.)

Additional Information Contacts

City of Geneva . . . . (630) 232-7494
　　http://www.geneva.il.us
Geneva Chamber of Commerce . . . . (630) 232-6060
　　http://www.genevachamber.com

GILBERTS (village). Covers a land area of 3.214 square miles and a water area of 0.004 square miles. Located at 42.10° N. Lat; 88.36° W. Long. Elevation is 899 feet.

Population: 1,039 (1990); 1,279 (2000); 3,454 (2010); 3,893 (2015 projected); Race: 93.5% White, 0.4% Black, 2.8% Asian, 3.3% Other, 3.7% Hispanic of any race (2010); Density: 1,074.7 persons per square mile (2010); Average household size: 3.14 (2010); Median age: 35.3 (2010); Males per 100 females: 99.7 (2010); Marriage status: 28.2% never married, 60.1% now married, 4.6% widowed, 7.1% divorced (2005-2009 5-year est.); Foreign born: 23.9% (2005-2009 5-year est.); Ancestry (includes multiple ancestries): 16.5% German, 12.6% Irish, 12.5% Polish, 10.5% Italian, 4.4% American (2005-2009 5-year est.).

Economy: Single-family building permits issued: 46 (2010); Multi-family building permits issued: 17 (2010); Employment by occupation: 18.7% management, 25.0% professional, 13.1% services, 23.8% sales, 0.0% farming, 10.1% construction, 9.4% production (2005-2009 5-year est.).

Income: Per capita income: $38,075 (2010); Median household income: $102,210 (2010); Average household income: $119,281 (2010); Percent of households with income of $100,000 or more: 51.6% (2010); Poverty rate: 1.4% (2005-2009 5-year est.).

Taxes: Total city taxes per capita: $279 (2007); City property taxes per capita: $121 (2007).

Education: Percent of population age 25 and over with: High school diploma (including GED) or higher: 93.9% (2010); Bachelor's degree or higher: 33.7% (2010); Master's degree or higher: 11.5% (2010).

School District(s)

CUSD 300 (PK-12)
　　2009-10 Enrollment: 20,341 . . . . (847) 426-1300

Housing: Homeownership rate: 92.7% (2010); Median home value: $300,742 (2010); Median contract rent: $1,397 per month (2005-2009 5-year est.); Median year structure built: n/a (2005-2009 5-year est.).

Safety: Violent crime rate: 8.2 per 10,000 population; Property crime rate: 67.2 per 10,000 population (2010).

Transportation: Commute to work: 89.8% car, 5.2% public transportation, 0.0% walk, 4.4% work from home (2005-2009 5-year est.); Travel time to work: 16.7% less than 15 minutes, 20.4% 15 to 30 minutes, 29.7% 30 to 45 minutes, 15.9% 45 to 60 minutes, 17.2% 60 minutes or more (2005-2009 5-year est.)

Additional Information Contacts

Northern Kane County Chamber of Commerce . . . . (847) 426-8565
　　http://www.nkcchamber.com

HAMPSHIRE (village). Covers a land area of 4.877 square miles and a water area of 0 square miles. Located at 42.09° N. Lat; 88.52° W. Long. Elevation is 899 feet.

Population: 1,960 (1990); 2,900 (2000); 4,285 (2010); 4,865 (2015 projected); Race: 97.4% White, 0.1% Black, 0.2% Asian, 2.3% Other, 3.2% Hispanic of any race (2010); Density: 878.7 persons per square mile (2010); Average household size: 2.89 (2010); Median age: 32.6 (2010); Males per 100 females: 95.8 (2010); Marriage status: 21.7% never married, 65.0% now married, 2.1% widowed, 11.1% divorced (2005-2009 5-year est.); Foreign born: 3.2% (2005-2009 5-year est.); Ancestry (includes multiple ancestries): 43.0% German, 24.5% Irish, 13.9% Italian, 12.0% Polish, 8.1% English (2005-2009 5-year est.).

Economy: Single-family building permits issued: 1 (2010); Multi-family building permits issued: 2 (2010); Employment by occupation: 17.5% management, 15.3% professional, 17.5% services, 28.1% sales, 0.0% farming, 12.7% construction, 8.9% production (2005-2009 5-year est.).

Income: Per capita income: $26,813 (2010); Median household income: $69,710 (2010); Average household income: $77,240 (2010); Percent of households with income of $100,000 or more: 24.9% (2010); Poverty rate: 2.1% (2005-2009 5-year est.).

Taxes: Total city taxes per capita: $2,816 (2007); City property taxes per capita: $136 (2007).

Education: Percent of population age 25 and over with: High school diploma (including GED) or higher: 89.5% (2010); Bachelor's degree or higher: 22.6% (2010); Master's degree or higher: 5.8% (2010).

School District(s)
CUSD 300 (PK-12)
    2009-10 Enrollment: 20,341 . . . . (847) 426-1300

Housing: Homeownership rate: 80.7% (2010); Median home value: $185,376 (2010); Median contract rent: $774 per month (2005-2009 5-year est.); Median year structure built: 1994 (2005-2009 5-year est.).

Safety: Violent crime rate: 3.3 per 10,000 population; Property crime rate: 106.6 per 10,000 population (2010).

Transportation: Commute to work: 92.8% car, 1.1% public transportation, 2.1% walk, 3.7% work from home (2005-2009 5-year est.); Travel time to work: 23.0% less than 15 minutes, 26.4% 15 to 30 minutes, 20.1% 30 to 45 minutes, 13.9% 45 to 60 minutes, 16.6% 60 minutes or more (2005-2009 5-year est.)

Additional Information Contacts
Hampshire Area Chamber of Commerce. . . . . (847) 683-1122
    http://www.hampshirechamber.org

KANEVILLE (village). Covers a land area of 0.314 square miles and a water area of 0 square miles. Located at 41.83° N. Lat; 88.52° W. Long.

History: Incorporated November 2006.

Population: n/a (1990); n/a (2000); 484 (2010); n/a (2015 projected); Race: 96.5% White, 0.0% Black, 0.2% Asian, 3.3% Other, 6.0% Hispanic of any race (2010); Density: 1,541.4 persons per square mile (2010); Average household size: 2.55 (2010); Median age: 42.3 (2010); Males per 100 females: 105.1 (2010); Marriage status: 20.2% never married, 70.4% now married, 7.3% widowed, 2.2% divorced (2005-2009 5-year est.); Foreign born: 0.0% (2005-2009 5-year est.); Ancestry (includes multiple ancestries): 35.9% German, 12.9% American, 12.1% English, 11.9% Romanian, 8.5% European (2005-2009 5-year est.).

Economy: Employment by occupation: 29.1% management, 6.8% professional, 8.9% services, 21.1% sales, 0.0% farming, 24.5% construction, 9.7% production (2005-2009 5-year est.).

Income: Per capita income: n/a (2010); Median household income: n/a (2010); Average household income: n/a (2010); Percent of households with income of $100,000 or more: n/a (2010); Poverty rate: 0.0% (2005-2009 5-year est.).

Taxes: Total city taxes per capita: $133 (2007); City property taxes per capita: $120 (2007).

Education: Percent of population age 25 and over with: High school diploma (including GED) or higher: n/a (2010); Bachelor's degree or higher: n/a (2010); Master's degree or higher: n/a (2010).

Housing: Homeownership rate: n/a (2010); Median home value: n/a (2010); Median contract rent: n/a per month (2005-2009 5-year est.); Median year structure built: 1973 (2005-2009 5-year est.).

Transportation: Commute to work: 88.3% car, 0.0% public transportation, 0.0% walk, 4.3% work from home (2005-2009 5-year est.); Travel time to work: 18.2% less than 15 minutes, 46.4% 15 to 30 minutes, 30.9% 30 to 45 minutes, 4.5% 45 to 60 minutes, 0.0% 60 minutes or more (2005-2009 5-year est.)

LILY LAKE (village). Covers a land area of 2.246 square miles and a water area of <.001 square miles. Located at 41.94° N. Lat; 88.47° W. Long. Elevation is 961 feet.

Population: 714 (1990); 825 (2000); 1,070 (2010); 1,150 (2015 projected); Race: 97.0% White, 0.9% Black, 0.7% Asian, 1.4% Other, 2.0% Hispanic of any race (2010); Density: 476.4 persons per square mile (2010); Average household size: 3.10 (2010); Median age: 35.9 (2010); Males per 100 females: 103.8 (2010); Marriage status: 23.2% never married, 65.0% now married, 3.2% widowed, 8.6% divorced (2005-2009 5-year est.); Foreign born: 2.3% (2005-2009 5-year est.); Ancestry (includes multiple ancestries): 37.6% German, 16.3% Irish, 13.3% Italian, 12.8% Swedish, 8.4% Polish (2005-2009 5-year est.).

Economy: Employment by occupation: 11.8% management, 22.7% professional, 12.2% services, 30.6% sales, 0.0% farming, 11.8% construction, 10.7% production (2005-2009 5-year est.).

Income: Per capita income: $37,077 (2010); Median household income: $93,036 (2010); Average household income: $114,399 (2010); Percent of households with income of $100,000 or more: 44.3% (2010); Poverty rate: 3.4% (2005-2009 5-year est.).

Taxes: Total city taxes per capita: $140 (2007); City property taxes per capita: $0 (2007).

Education: Percent of population age 25 and over with: High school diploma (including GED) or higher: 95.3% (2010); Bachelor's degree or higher: 41.1% (2010); Master's degree or higher: 12.5% (2010).

Housing: Homeownership rate: 93.3% (2010); Median home value: $323,810 (2010); Median contract rent: $1,094 per month (2005-2009 5-year est.); Median year structure built: 1987 (2005-2009 5-year est.).

Transportation: Commute to work: 94.0% car, 1.2% public transportation, 0.0% walk, 4.3% work from home (2005-2009 5-year est.); Travel time to work: 9.7% less than 15 minutes, 40.4% 15 to 30 minutes, 22.3% 30 to 45 minutes, 9.7% 45 to 60 minutes, 17.8% 60 minutes or more (2005-2009 5-year est.)

MAPLE PARK (village). Covers a land area of 0.594 square miles and a water area of 0 square miles. Located at 41.90° N. Lat; 88.59° W. Long. Elevation is 863 feet.

Population: 690 (1990); 765 (2000); 1,373 (2010); 1,560 (2015 projected); Race: 96.5% White, 0.0% Black, 0.2% Asian, 3.3% Other, 3.7% Hispanic of any race (2010); Density: 2,311.8 persons per square mile (2010); Average household size: 2.76 (2010); Median age: 34.9 (2010); Males per 100 females: 107.1 (2010); Marriage status: 20.5% never married, 57.7% now married, 3.3% widowed, 18.6% divorced (2005-2009 5-year est.); Foreign born: 2.5% (2005-2009 5-year est.); Ancestry (includes multiple ancestries): 47.0% German, 23.9% Irish, 14.2% English, 12.8% Italian, 12.1% Polish (2005-2009 5-year est.).

Economy: Single-family building permits issued: 0 (2010); Multi-family building permits issued: 0 (2010); Employment by occupation: 11.7% management, 21.2% professional, 8.6% services, 26.0% sales, 0.0% farming, 18.9% construction, 13.6% production (2005-2009 5-year est.).

Income: Per capita income: $28,250 (2010); Median household income: $65,083 (2010); Average household income: $77,209 (2010); Percent of households with income of $100,000 or more: 25.9% (2010); Poverty rate: 7.8% (2005-2009 5-year est.).

Taxes: Total city taxes per capita: $326 (2007); City property taxes per capita: $185 (2007).

Education: Percent of population age 25 and over with: High school diploma (including GED) or higher: 94.1% (2010); Bachelor's degree or higher: 18.6% (2010); Master's degree or higher: 6.0% (2010).

School District(s)
Central CUSD 301 (PK-12)
    2009-10 Enrollment: 3,374 . . . . (847) 464-6005
Fox Valley Career Center (09-12)
    2009-10 Enrollment: n/a . . . . (630) 365-5113
Kaneland CUSD 302 (PK-12)
    2009-10 Enrollment: 4,746 . . . . (630) 365-5111

Housing: Homeownership rate: 79.9% (2010); Median home value: $182,432 (2010); Median contract rent: $701 per month (2005-2009 5-year est.); Median year structure built: 1974 (2005-2009 5-year est.).

Safety: Violent crime rate: 0.0 per 10,000 population; Property crime rate: 37.0 per 10,000 population (2010).

Transportation: Commute to work: 97.7% car, 0.0% public transportation, 0.4% walk, 1.9% work from home (2005-2009 5-year est.); Travel time to work: 13.3% less than 15 minutes, 27.3% 15 to 30 minutes, 31.1% 30 to 45

minutes, 14.8% 45 to 60 minutes, 13.5% 60 minutes or more (2005-2009 5-year est.)

MONTGOMERY (village).
Covers a land area of 6.415 square miles and a water area of 0.196 square miles. Located at 41.72° N. Lat; 88.32° W. Long. Elevation is 640 feet.

Population: 4,644 (1990); 5,471 (2000); 7,428 (2010); 8,587 (2015 projected); Race: 79.1% White, 6.7% Black, 1.4% Asian, 12.8% Other, 26.6% Hispanic of any race (2010); Density: 1,158.0 persons per square mile (2010); Average household size: 2.68 (2010); Median age: 33.6 (2010); Males per 100 females: 98.2 (2010); Marriage status: 28.3% never married, 53.5% now married, 8.1% widowed, 10.1% divorced (2005-2009 5-year est.); Foreign born: 10.3% (2005-2009 5-year est.); Ancestry (includes multiple ancestries): 28.4% German, 14.9% Irish, 9.6% English, 7.2% Polish, 6.5% Italian (2005-2009 5-year est.).

Economy: Single-family building permits issued: 67 (2010); Multi-family building permits issued: 0 (2010); Employment by occupation: 12.1% management, 16.7% professional, 14.2% services, 30.6% sales, 0.2% farming, 10.1% construction, 16.0% production (2005-2009 5-year est.).

Income: Per capita income: $25,147 (2010); Median household income: $60,000 (2010); Average household income: $67,330 (2010); Percent of households with income of $100,000 or more: 17.8% (2010); Poverty rate: 3.1% (2005-2009 5-year est.).

Taxes: Total city taxes per capita: $266 (2007); City property taxes per capita: $111 (2007).

Education: Percent of population age 25 and over with: High school diploma (including GED) or higher: 85.3% (2010); Bachelor's degree or higher: 19.8% (2010); Master's degree or higher: 5.3% (2010).

School District(s)
Aurora West USD 129 (PK-12)
    2009-10 Enrollment: 12,508 . . . . (630) 301-5033
Kaneland CUSD 302 (PK-12)
    2009-10 Enrollment: 4,746 . . . . (630) 365-5111
Oswego CUSD 308 (PK-12)
    2009-10 Enrollment: 16,314 . . . . (630) 636-3080

Housing: Homeownership rate: 76.3% (2010); Median home value: $171,831 (2010); Median contract rent: $831 per month (2005-2009 5-year est.); Median year structure built: 1989 (2005-2009 5-year est.).

Safety: Violent crime rate: 13.7 per 10,000 population; Property crime rate: 206.7 per 10,000 population (2010).

Transportation: Commute to work: 94.4% car, 2.2% public transportation, 0.0% walk, 2.2% work from home (2005-2009 5-year est.); Travel time to work: 23.0% less than 15 minutes, 42.9% 15 to 30 minutes, 15.4% 30 to 45 minutes, 8.0% 45 to 60 minutes, 10.7% 60 minutes or more (2005-2009 5-year est.)

Additional Information Contacts
Greater Montgomery Area Chamber of Commerce . . . . (630) 897-8137
    http://www.chamberofmontgomeryil.org
Village of Montgomery . . . . (630) 896-8080
    http://ci.montgomery.il.us

NORTH AURORA (village).
Covers a land area of 5.159 square miles and a water area of 0.147 square miles. Located at 41.80° N. Lat; 88.32° W. Long. Elevation is 679 feet.

Population: 6,673 (1990); 10,585 (2000); 14,830 (2010); 16,684 (2015 projected); Race: 81.9% White, 5.1% Black, 3.9% Asian, 9.1% Other, 16.2% Hispanic of any race (2010); Density: 2,874.6 persons per square mile (2010); Average household size: 2.72 (2010); Median age: 34.7 (2010); Males per 100 females: 101.1 (2010); Marriage status: 23.6% never married, 58.7% now married, 4.6% widowed, 13.1% divorced (2005-2009 5-year est.); Foreign born: 10.5% (2005-2009 5-year est.); Ancestry (includes multiple ancestries): 27.7% German, 14.7% Irish, 9.1% Polish, 8.2% Italian, 6.5% English (2005-2009 5-year est.).

Economy: Single-family building permits issued: 17 (2010); Multi-family building permits issued: 0 (2010); Employment by occupation: 19.7% management, 24.2% professional, 10.6% services, 25.0% sales, 0.3% farming, 6.3% construction, 14.0% production (2005-2009 5-year est.).

Income: Per capita income: $30,684 (2010); Median household income: $68,237 (2010); Average household income: $84,085 (2010); Percent of households with income of $100,000 or more: 27.3% (2010); Poverty rate: 6.3% (2005-2009 5-year est.).

Taxes: Total city taxes per capita: $387 (2007); City property taxes per capita: $217 (2007).

Education: Percent of population age 25 and over with: High school diploma (including GED) or higher: 89.8% (2010); Bachelor's degree or higher: 38.5% (2010); Master's degree or higher: 13.6% (2010).

School District(s)
Aurora West USD 129 (PK-12)
    2009-10 Enrollment: 12,508 . . . . (630) 301-5033

Vocational/Technical School(s)
Everest College-North Aurora (Private, For-profit)
    Fall 2009 Enrollment: 609 . . . . (630) 896-2140
    2010-11 Tuition: $15,193

Housing: Homeownership rate: 78.2% (2010); Median home value: $197,800 (2010); Median contract rent: $819 per month (2005-2009 5-year est.); Median year structure built: 1992 (2005-2009 5-year est.).

Safety: Violent crime rate: 21.5 per 10,000 population; Property crime rate: 173.9 per 10,000 population (2010).

Transportation: Commute to work: 90.0% car, 2.3% public transportation, 1.2% walk, 5.2% work from home (2005-2009 5-year est.); Travel time to work: 21.3% less than 15 minutes, 36.8% 15 to 30 minutes, 22.9% 30 to 45 minutes, 7.8% 45 to 60 minutes, 11.1% 60 minutes or more (2005-2009 5-year est.)

Additional Information Contacts
Village of North Aurora. . . . . (630) 897-8228
    http://www.vil.north-aurora.il.us

PINGREE GROVE (village).
Covers a land area of 0.616 square miles and a water area of 0 square miles. Located at 42.06° N. Lat; 88.41° W. Long. Elevation is 912 feet.

Population: 130 (1990); 124 (2000); 490 (2010); 544 (2015 projected); Race: 92.9% White, 0.4% Black, 2.7% Asian, 4.1% Other, 5.5% Hispanic of any race (2010); Density: 795.5 persons per square mile (2010); Average household size: 3.10 (2010); Median age: 37.9 (2010); Males per 100 females: 101.6 (2010); Marriage status: 13.2% never married, 76.1% now married, 4.2% widowed, 6.4% divorced (2005-2009 5-year est.); Foreign born: 8.8% (2005-2009 5-year est.); Ancestry (includes multiple ancestries): 29.0% German, 27.8% Polish, 26.1% Irish, 15.6% Italian, 6.3% American (2005-2009 5-year est.).

Economy: Single-family building permits issued: 25 (2010); Multi-family building permits issued: 14 (2010); Employment by occupation: 22.5% management, 30.4% professional, 3.4% services, 34.5% sales, 0.0% farming, 7.3% construction, 1.8% production (2005-2009 5-year est.).

Income: Per capita income: $33,271 (2010); Median household income: $93,333 (2010); Average household income: $103,165 (2010); Percent of households with income of $100,000 or more: 44.9% (2010); Poverty rate: 2.5% (2005-2009 5-year est.).

Taxes: Total city taxes per capita: $1,819 (2007); City property taxes per capita: $14 (2007).

Education: Percent of population age 25 and over with: High school diploma (including GED) or higher: 92.7% (2010); Bachelor's degree or higher: 31.8% (2010); Master's degree or higher: 9.1% (2010).

School District(s)
CUSD 300 (PK-12)
    2009-10 Enrollment: 20,341 . . . . (847) 426-1300

Housing: Homeownership rate: 89.9% (2010); Median home value: $313,953 (2010); Median contract rent: n/a per month (2005-2009 5-year est.); Median year structure built: 2005 (2005-2009 5-year est.).

Transportation: Commute to work: 95.8% car, 1.8% public transportation, 0.0% walk, 1.3% work from home (2005-2009 5-year est.); Travel time to work: 10.8% less than 15 minutes, 26.9% 15 to 30 minutes, 19.3% 30 to 45 minutes, 20.3% 45 to 60 minutes, 22.6% 60 minutes or more (2005-2009 5-year est.)

SAINT CHARLES (city).
Covers a land area of 13.990 square miles and a water area of 0.158 square miles. Located at 41.91° N. Lat; 88.31° W. Long. Elevation is 732 feet.

History: Named for Saint Charles Borromeo (1538-1584), an Italian cardinal. The community of St. Charles developed around a mill in the mid-1800's, and became a residential area for people moving out from Chicago.

Population: 24,173 (1990); 27,896 (2000); 32,785 (2010); 34,979 (2015 projected); Race: 89.9% White, 2.1% Black, 3.3% Asian, 4.6% Other, 8.9% Hispanic of any race (2010); Density: 2,343.4 persons per square mile (2010); Average household size: 2.66 (2010); Median age: 36.2 (2010); Males per 100 females: 101.7 (2010); Marriage status: 26.6% never married, 58.4% now married, 4.9% widowed, 10.2% divorced (2005-2009 5-year est.); Foreign born: 9.2% (2005-2009 5-year est.); Ancestry

(includes multiple ancestries): 32.4% German, 19.2% Irish, 14.3% Italian, 11.0% English, 10.8% Polish (2005-2009 5-year est.).
Economy: Unemployment rate: 8.7% (August 2011); Total civilian labor force: 19,005 (August 2011); Single-family building permits issued: 8 (2010); Multi-family building permits issued: 0 (2010); Employment by occupation: 21.1% management, 23.4% professional, 11.9% services, 29.8% sales, 0.0% farming, 6.5% construction, 7.4% production (2005-2009 5-year est.).
Income: Per capita income: $39,389 (2010); Median household income: $81,548 (2010); Average household income: $106,218 (2010); Percent of households with income of $100,000 or more: 38.3% (2010); Poverty rate: 4.9% (2005-2009 5-year est.).
Taxes: Total city taxes per capita: $730 (2007); City property taxes per capita: $352 (2007).
Education: Percent of population age 25 and over with: High school diploma (including GED) or higher: 93.4% (2010); Bachelor's degree or higher: 47.9% (2010); Master's degree or higher: 16.8% (2010).

School District(s)
Mid-Valley Special Ed Coop (KG-12)
   2009-10 Enrollment: n/a . . . . (630) 513-4400
St Charles CUSD 303 (PK-12)
   2009-10 Enrollment: 13,953 . . . . (630) 513-3030
Housing: Homeownership rate: 74.1% (2010); Median home value: $273,875 (2010); Median contract rent: $902 per month (2005-2009 5-year est.); Median year structure built: 1983 (2005-2009 5-year est.).
Newspapers: Batavia Republican (Community news; Circulation 3,200); The Farmside (Regional news; Circulation 1,563); Geneva Republican (Local news; Circulation 25,000); Saint Charles Republican (Community news; Circulation 16,500); West Chicago Press (Local news; Circulation 4,000); Winfield Press (Local news; Circulation 3,700)
Transportation: Commute to work: 87.4% car, 3.4% public transportation, 2.3% walk, 5.8% work from home (2005-2009 5-year est.); Travel time to work: 31.9% less than 15 minutes, 26.4% 15 to 30 minutes, 19.5% 30 to 45 minutes, 10.4% 45 to 60 minutes, 11.8% 60 minutes or more (2005-2009 5-year est.)
Additional Information Contacts
City of Saint Charles . . . . (630) 377-4400
   http://www.stcharlesil.gov
St. Charles Chamber of Commerce . . . . (630) 584-8384
   http://www.stcharleschamber.com

SLEEPY HOLLOW (village). Covers a land area of 2.011 square miles and a water area of 0.015 square miles. Located at 42.09° N. Lat; 88.31° W. Long. Elevation is 738 feet.
History: Various streets in the village are named after characters in Washington Irving's The Legend of Sleepy Hollow, including Headless Horseman Drive and Ichabod Crane Drive. Although it shares its name with Washington Irving's famous short story "The Legend of Sleepy Hollow", Sleepy Hollow, Illinois is not the original town about which Irving wrote. That distinction belongs to the town of Sleepy Hollow, New York, formerly known as North Tarrytown.
Population: 3,311 (1990); 3,553 (2000); 4,491 (2010); 4,942 (2015 projected); Race: 88.8% White, 0.7% Black, 5.1% Asian, 5.4% Other, 6.3% Hispanic of any race (2010); Density: 2,232.7 persons per square mile (2010); Average household size: 2.90 (2010); Median age: 36.3 (2010); Males per 100 females: 102.2 (2010); Marriage status: 18.9% never married, 70.8% now married, 2.7% widowed, 7.6% divorced (2005-2009 5-year est.); Foreign born: 3.5% (2005-2009 5-year est.); Ancestry (includes multiple ancestries): 37.4% German, 23.4% Irish, 11.7% English, 10.8% Italian, 10.3% Polish (2005-2009 5-year est.).
Economy: Single-family building permits issued: 0 (2010); Multi-family building permits issued: 0 (2010); Employment by occupation: 25.0% management, 23.7% professional, 7.5% services, 29.7% sales, 0.0% farming, 9.3% construction, 4.7% production (2005-2009 5-year est.).
Income: Per capita income: $35,891 (2010); Median household income: $91,833 (2010); Average household income: $104,096 (2010); Percent of households with income of $100,000 or more: 44.7% (2010); Poverty rate: 1.1% (2005-2009 5-year est.).
Taxes: Total city taxes per capita: $236 (2007); City property taxes per capita: $126 (2007).
Education: Percent of population age 25 and over with: High school diploma (including GED) or higher: 95.9% (2010); Bachelor's degree or higher: 47.3% (2010); Master's degree or higher: 16.6% (2010).

School District(s)
CUSD 300 (PK-12)
   2009-10 Enrollment: 20,341 . . . . (847) 426-1300
Housing: Homeownership rate: 84.8% (2010); Median home value: $308,917 (2010); Median contract rent: $1,070 per month (2005-2009 5-year est.); Median year structure built: 1981 (2005-2009 5-year est.).
Safety: Violent crime rate: 0.0 per 10,000 population; Property crime rate: 35.2 per 10,000 population (2010).
Transportation: Commute to work: 90.6% car, 0.8% public transportation, 0.0% walk, 6.8% work from home (2005-2009 5-year est.); Travel time to work: 14.9% less than 15 minutes, 23.5% 15 to 30 minutes, 33.1% 30 to 45 minutes, 18.3% 45 to 60 minutes, 10.2% 60 minutes or more (2005-2009 5-year est.)
Additional Information Contacts
Northern Kane County Chamber of Commerce . . . . (847) 426-8565
   http://www.nkcchamber.com

SOUTH ELGIN (village). Covers a land area of 6.288 square miles and a water area of 0.123 square miles. Located at 41.99° N. Lat; 88.30° W. Long. Elevation is 709 feet.
Population: 9,247 (1990); 16,100 (2000); 21,078 (2010); 23,286 (2015 projected); Race: 77.5% White, 4.0% Black, 9.6% Asian, 8.9% Other, 15.3% Hispanic of any race (2010); Density: 3,352.2 persons per square mile (2010); Average household size: 2.89 (2010); Median age: 33.2 (2010); Males per 100 females: 100.5 (2010); Marriage status: 26.8% never married, 57.7% now married, 4.1% widowed, 11.4% divorced (2005-2009 5-year est.); Foreign born: 11.0% (2005-2009 5-year est.); Ancestry (includes multiple ancestries): 30.9% German, 15.0% Irish, 14.4% Polish, 11.5% Italian, 7.3% English (2005-2009 5-year est.).
Economy: Single-family building permits issued: 1 (2010); Multi-family building permits issued: 0 (2010); Employment by occupation: 16.7% management, 20.7% professional, 14.4% services, 26.0% sales, 0.0% farming, 8.5% construction, 13.7% production (2005-2009 5-year est.).
Income: Per capita income: $32,080 (2010); Median household income: $76,736 (2010); Average household income: $93,647 (2010); Percent of households with income of $100,000 or more: 30.0% (2010); Poverty rate: 3.6% (2005-2009 5-year est.).
Taxes: Total city taxes per capita: $229 (2007); City property taxes per capita: $153 (2007).
Education: Percent of population age 25 and over with: High school diploma (including GED) or higher: 91.8% (2010); Bachelor's degree or higher: 31.4% (2010); Master's degree or higher: 8.4% (2010).

School District(s)
SD U-46 (PK-12)
   2009-10 Enrollment: 41,446 . . . . (847) 888-5000
St Charles CUSD 303 (PK-12)
   2009-10 Enrollment: 13,953 . . . . (630) 513-3030
Housing: Homeownership rate: 86.2% (2010); Median home value: $209,483 (2010); Median contract rent: $884 per month (2005-2009 5-year est.); Median year structure built: 1994 (2005-2009 5-year est.).
Safety: Violent crime rate: 8.3 per 10,000 population; Property crime rate: 106.3 per 10,000 population (2010).
Transportation: Commute to work: 94.3% car, 1.4% public transportation, 0.9% walk, 3.0% work from home (2005-2009 5-year est.); Travel time to work: 22.7% less than 15 minutes, 27.4% 15 to 30 minutes, 23.2% 30 to 45 minutes, 10.4% 45 to 60 minutes, 16.2% 60 minutes or more (2005-2009 5-year est.)
Additional Information Contacts
Elgin Area Chamber of Commerce . . . . (847) 741-5660
   http://www.elginchamber.com
Village of South Elgin . . . . (847) 742-5780
   http://www.southelgin.com

SUGAR GROVE (village). Covers a land area of 6.449 square miles and a water area of 0.015 square miles. Located at 41.77° N. Lat; 88.44° W. Long. Elevation is 719 feet.
Population: 2,522 (1990); 3,909 (2000); 6,115 (2010); 6,995 (2015 projected); Race: 92.6% White, 2.8% Black, 0.9% Asian, 3.7% Other, 6.5% Hispanic of any race (2010); Density: 948.2 persons per square mile (2010); Average household size: 2.83 (2010); Median age: 36.6 (2010); Males per 100 females: 103.0 (2010); Marriage status: 24.2% never married, 64.5% now married, 4.1% widowed, 7.3% divorced (2005-2009 5-year est.); Foreign born: 4.0% (2005-2009 5-year est.); Ancestry (includes multiple ancestries): 36.5% German, 15.5% Irish, 12.1% English, 9.8% Polish, 8.7% Italian (2005-2009 5-year est.).

Economy: Single-family building permits issued: 6 (2010); Multi-family building permits issued: 0 (2010); Employment by occupation: 21.2% management, 23.1% professional, 10.5% services, 30.1% sales, 0.9% farming, 7.4% construction, 6.7% production (2005-2009 5-year est.).
Income: Per capita income: $38,940 (2010); Median household income: $84,038 (2010); Average household income: $110,240 (2010); Percent of households with income of $100,000 or more: 37.4% (2010); Poverty rate: 2.0% (2005-2009 5-year est.).
Taxes: Total city taxes per capita: $256 (2007); City property taxes per capita: $125 (2007).
Education: Percent of population age 25 and over with: High school diploma (including GED) or higher: 96.3% (2010); Bachelor's degree or higher: 39.5% (2010); Master's degree or higher: 13.4% (2010).

School District(s)

Kaneland CUSD 302 (PK-12)
   2009-10 Enrollment: 4,746 . . . . (630) 365-5111

Two-year College(s)

Waubonsee Community College (Public)
   Fall 2009 Enrollment: 10,532. . . . . (630) 466-7900
   2010-11 Tuition: In-state $6,427; Out-of-state $7,082
Housing: Homeownership rate: 84.8% (2010); Median home value: $238,771 (2010); Median contract rent: $987 per month (2005-2009 5-year est.); Median year structure built: 2000 (2005-2009 5-year est.).
Safety: Violent crime rate: 5.7 per 10,000 population; Property crime rate: 69.4 per 10,000 population (2010).
Transportation: Commute to work: 87.1% car, 2.9% public transportation, 0.5% walk, 7.5% work from home (2005-2009 5-year est.); Travel time to work: 10.5% less than 15 minutes, 35.5% 15 to 30 minutes, 22.7% 30 to 45 minutes, 10.8% 45 to 60 minutes, 20.5% 60 minutes or more (2005-2009 5-year est.)

Additional Information Contacts

Sugar Grove Chamber of Commerce & Industry . . . . (630) 466-7895
   http://www.sugargrovechamber.org

VIRGIL (village). Covers a land area of 1.882 square miles and a water area of 0 square miles. Located at 41.95° N. Lat; 88.52° W. Long. Elevation is 869 feet.
Population: 263 (1990); 266 (2000); 381 (2010); 433 (2015 projected); Race: 97.4% White, 0.5% Black, 0.3% Asian, 1.8% Other, 2.9% Hispanic of any race (2010); Density: 202.5 persons per square mile (2010); Average household size: 2.93 (2010); Median age: 37.5 (2010); Males per 100 females: 110.5 (2010); Marriage status: 27.7% never married, 64.2% now married, 1.4% widowed, 6.8% divorced (2005-2009 5-year est.); Foreign born: 3.6% (2005-2009 5-year est.); Ancestry (includes multiple ancestries): 49.6% German, 18.8% Irish, 15.6% Polish, 10.9% Italian, 9.4% Swedish (2005-2009 5-year est.).
Economy: Employment by occupation: 6.9% management, 9.2% professional, 9.2% services, 26.7% sales, 1.4% farming, 26.3% construction, 20.3% production (2005-2009 5-year est.).
Income: Per capita income: $30,938 (2010); Median household income: $79,688 (2010); Average household income: $92,962 (2010); Percent of households with income of $100,000 or more: 30.0% (2010); Poverty rate: 7.4% (2005-2009 5-year est.).
Taxes: Total city taxes per capita: $19 (2007); City property taxes per capita: $0 (2007).
Education: Percent of population age 25 and over with: High school diploma (including GED) or higher: 90.8% (2010); Bachelor's degree or higher: 24.0% (2010); Master's degree or higher: 5.6% (2010).
Housing: Homeownership rate: 83.8% (2010); Median home value: $256,383 (2010); Median contract rent: $783 per month (2005-2009 5-year est.); Median year structure built: 1971 (2005-2009 5-year est.).
Transportation: Commute to work: 92.8% car, 0.0% public transportation, 3.4% walk, 1.0% work from home (2005-2009 5-year est.); Travel time to work: 25.9% less than 15 minutes, 19.5% 15 to 30 minutes, 42.0% 30 to 45 minutes, 7.3% 45 to 60 minutes, 5.4% 60 minutes or more (2005-2009 5-year est.)

WEST DUNDEE (village). Aka Dundee. Covers a land area of 2.660 square miles and a water area of 0.078 square miles. Located at 42.09° N. Lat; 88.28° W. Long. Elevation is 761 feet.
History: West Dundee was settled by Scots and English in the 1830's, and named for Dundee, Scotland. Allan Pinkerton (1819-1884) operated a coopers trade in West Dundee, but found a second career as a detective when his evidence resulted in the capture of some counterfeiters.

Population: 3,794 (1990); 5,428 (2000); 6,538 (2010); 7,034 (2015 projected); Race: 86.7% White, 1.7% Black, 4.5% Asian, 7.1% Other, 7.8% Hispanic of any race (2010); Density: 2,457.8 persons per square mile (2010); Average household size: 2.65 (2010); Median age: 35.6 (2010); Males per 100 females: 98.3 (2010); Marriage status: 25.8% never married, 62.0% now married, 2.6% widowed, 9.7% divorced (2005-2009 5-year est.); Foreign born: 10.4% (2005-2009 5-year est.); Ancestry (includes multiple ancestries): 36.2% German, 23.0% Irish, 18.4% Polish, 11.6% English, 6.4% Italian (2005-2009 5-year est.).
Economy: Single-family building permits issued: 0 (2010); Multi-family building permits issued: 0 (2010); Employment by occupation: 21.4% management, 19.7% professional, 13.2% services, 32.4% sales, 0.0% farming, 5.6% construction, 7.7% production (2005-2009 5-year est.).
Income: Per capita income: $35,270 (2010); Median household income: $74,130 (2010); Average household income: $93,911 (2010); Percent of households with income of $100,000 or more: 35.7% (2010); Poverty rate: 3.2% (2005-2009 5-year est.).
Taxes: Total city taxes per capita: $824 (2007); City property taxes per capita: $247 (2007).
Education: Percent of population age 25 and over with: High school diploma (including GED) or higher: 92.8% (2010); Bachelor's degree or higher: 40.9% (2010); Master's degree or higher: 13.4% (2010).

School District(s)

CUSD 300 (PK-12)
   2009-10 Enrollment: 20,341 . . . . (847) 426-1300

Two-year College(s)

Hair Professionals Academy of Cosmetology (Private, For-profit)
   Fall 2009 Enrollment: 291 . . . . (847) 836-5900
Housing: Homeownership rate: 76.1% (2010); Median home value: $257,310 (2010); Median contract rent: $1,082 per month (2005-2009 5-year est.); Median year structure built: 1985 (2005-2009 5-year est.).
Safety: Violent crime rate: 9.7 per 10,000 population; Property crime rate: 292.0 per 10,000 population (2010).
Transportation: Commute to work: 88.5% car, 1.9% public transportation, 2.0% walk, 6.5% work from home (2005-2009 5-year est.); Travel time to work: 26.0% less than 15 minutes, 28.0% 15 to 30 minutes, 21.1% 30 to 45 minutes, 13.4% 45 to 60 minutes, 11.4% 60 minutes or more (2005-2009 5-year est.)

Additional Information Contacts

Village of West Dundee . . . . (847) 551-3800
   http://www.wdundee.org

Kankakee County

Located in northeastern Illinois; bounded on the east by Indiana; drained by the Kankakee and Iroquois Rivers. Covers a land area of 676.75 square miles, a water area of 4.70 square miles, and is located in the Central Time Zone at 41.13° N. Lat., 87.84° W. Long. The county was founded in 1853. County seat is Kankakee.

Kankakee County is part of the Kankakee-Bradley, IL Metropolitan Statistical Area. The entire metro area includes: Kankakee County, IL

Weather Station: Kankakee Metro Wastwater										Elevation: 640 feet		
	Jan	Feb	Mar	Apr	May	Jun	Jul	Aug	Sep	Oct	Nov	Dec
High	33	37	48	61	73	82	85	83	78	65	51	37
Low	15	18	28	38	49	59	63	61	52	41	32	20
Precip	1.9	1.8	2.6	3.5	4.8	3.9	4.7	3.3	3.0	3.1	3.5	2.5
Snow	7.7	6.5	2.8	0.9	tr	0.0	0.0	0.0	0.0	tr	0.7	5.5

High and Low temperatures in degrees Fahrenheit; Precipitation and Snow in inches

Population: 96,255 (1990); 103,833 (2000); 114,177 (2010); 118,532 (2015 projected); Race: 78.7% White, 14.5% Black, 0.9% Asian, 5.9% Other, 7.7% Hispanic of any race (2010); Density: 168.7 persons per square mile (2010); Average household size: 2.59 (2010); Median age: 35.0 (2010); Males per 100 females: 95.9 (2010).
Religion: Five largest groups: 21.4% Catholic Church, 5.2% Church of the Nazarene, 4.6% The United Methodist Church, 4.5% Lutheran Church—Missouri Synod, 1.4% Southern Baptist Convention (2000).
Economy: Unemployment rate: 11.5% (August 2011); Total civilian labor force: 58,026 (August 2011); Leading industries: 18.5% health care and social assistance; 16.0% retail trade; 14.0% manufacturing (2009); Farms: 835 totaling 385,808 acres (2007); Companies that employ 500 or more persons: 6 (2009); Companies that employ 100 to 499 persons: 51 (2009); Companies that employ less than 100 persons: 2,367 (2009); Black-owned businesses: n/a (2007); Hispanic-owned businesses: n/a (2007);

Asian-owned businesses: n/a (2007); Women-owned businesses: 2,356 (2007); Retail sales per capita: $11,732 (2010). Single-family building permits issued: 59 (2010); Multi-family building permits issued: 12 (2010).
Income: Per capita income: $23,011 (2010); Median household income: $49,554 (2010); Average household income: $61,145 (2010); Percent of households with income of $100,000 or more: 14.8% (2010); Poverty rate: 15.1% (2009); Bankruptcy rate: 5.74% (2010).
Taxes: Total county taxes per capita: $121 (2007); County property taxes per capita: $115 (2007).
Education: Percent of population age 25 and over with: High school diploma (including GED) or higher: 85.5% (2010); Bachelor's degree or higher: 16.8% (2010); Master's degree or higher: 6.3% (2010).
Housing: Homeownership rate: 69.2% (2010); Median home value: $134,704 (2010); Median contract rent: $562 per month (2005-2009 5-year est.); Median year structure built: 1969 (2005-2009 5-year est.)
Health: Birth rate: 150.7 per 10,000 population (2009); Death rate: 95.7 per 10,000 population (2009); Age-adjusted cancer mortality rate: 224.7 deaths per 100,000 population (2007); Number of physicians: 14.7 per 10,000 population (2008); Hospital beds: 38.3 per 10,000 population (2007); Hospital admissions: 1,865.9 per 10,000 population (2007).
Elections: 2008 Presidential election results: 51.5% Obama, 46.9% McCain, 0.7% Nader
Additional Information Contacts

Kankakee County Government . . . . (815) 937-2990
    http://www.co.kankakee.il.us
City of Kankakee . . . . (815) 933-0480
    http://www.citykankakee-il.gov
Grant Park Chamber of Commerce . . . . (815) 465-6531
    http://grantparkchamber.org
Herscher Chamber of Commerce . . . . (815) 474-0044
    http://www.herscher.net
Kankakee County Chamber of Commerce . . . . (815) 932-2222
    http://business.kankakeecountychamber.com
Kankakee Regional Chamber of Commerce . . . . (815) 933-7721
    http://www.kankakee.org
Manteno Chamber of Commerce . . . . (815) 468-6226
    http://www.mantenochamber.com
Momence Chamber of Commerce . . . . (815) 472-4620
    http://www.momence.net
Village of Bourbonnais . . . . (815) 937-3570
    http://www.villageofbourbonnais.com
Village of Bradley . . . . (815) 932-2125
    http://www.bradleyil.org
Village of Manteno . . . . (815) 929-4800
    http://manteno.govoffice.com

Kankakee County Communities

AROMA PARK (village). Covers a land area of 1.200 square miles and a water area of 0.185 square miles. Located at 41.07° N. Lat; 87.80° W. Long. Elevation is 617 feet.
Population: 801 (1990); 821 (2000); 749 (2010); 733 (2015 projected); Race: 92.3% White, 4.5% Black, 0.0% Asian, 3.2% Other, 9.7% Hispanic of any race (2010); Density: 624.1 persons per square mile (2010); Average household size: 2.51 (2010); Median age: 41.0 (2010); Males per 100 females: 106.3 (2010); Marriage status: 20.1% never married, 53.8% now married, 7.3% widowed, 18.8% divorced (2005-2009 5-year est.); Foreign born: 0.6% (2005-2009 5-year est.); Ancestry (includes multiple ancestries): 27.4% German, 21.2% Irish, 13.3% French, 7.4% Polish, 5.7% English (2005-2009 5-year est.).
Economy: Single-family building permits issued: 0 (2010); Multi-family building permits issued: 0 (2010); Employment by occupation: 9.1% management, 12.9% professional, 16.3% services, 20.6% sales, 5.5% farming, 14.4% construction, 21.1% production (2005-2009 5-year est.).
Income: Per capita income: $23,234 (2010); Median household income: $47,460 (2010); Average household income: $59,817 (2010); Percent of households with income of $100,000 or more: 12.5% (2010); Poverty rate: 12.8% (2005-2009 5-year est.).
Taxes: Total city taxes per capita: $148 (2007); City property taxes per capita: $53 (2007).
Education: Percent of population age 25 and over with: High school diploma (including GED) or higher: 87.5% (2010); Bachelor's degree or higher: 12.1% (2010); Master's degree or higher: 5.4% (2010).

Kankakee SD 111 (PK-12)
    2009-10 Enrollment: 5,767 . . . . (815) 933-0700
Housing: Homeownership rate: 76.9% (2010); Median home value: $127,500 (2010); Median contract rent: $460 per month (2005-2009 5-year est.); Median year structure built: 1956 (2005-2009 5-year est.).
Transportation: Commute to work: 91.0% car, 0.8% public transportation, 6.4% walk, 1.8% work from home (2005-2009 5-year est.); Travel time to work: 34.6% less than 15 minutes, 41.1% 15 to 30 minutes, 7.1% 30 to 45 minutes, 11.0% 45 to 60 minutes, 6.3% 60 minutes or more (2005-2009 5-year est.)

BONFIELD (village). Covers a land area of 0.274 square miles and a water area of 0 square miles. Located at 41.14° N. Lat; 88.05° W. Long. Elevation is 630 feet.
Population: 299 (1990); 364 (2000); 390 (2010); 402 (2015 projected); Race: 98.2% White, 0.0% Black, 0.3% Asian, 1.5% Other, 1.0% Hispanic of any race (2010); Density: 1,423.8 persons per square mile (2010); Average household size: 2.87 (2010); Median age: 37.6 (2010); Males per 100 females: 104.2 (2010); Marriage status: 12.7% never married, 71.4% now married, 6.9% widowed, 9.0% divorced (2005-2009 5-year est.); Foreign born: 0.0% (2005-2009 5-year est.); Ancestry (includes multiple ancestries): 59.3% German, 13.6% Irish, 11.0% French, 8.9% Dutch, 7.6% American (2005-2009 5-year est.).
Economy: Single-family building permits issued: 0 (2010); Multi-family building permits issued: 0 (2010); Employment by occupation: 1.9% management, 14.4% professional, 11.5% services, 30.8% sales, 4.8% farming, 14.4% construction, 22.1% production (2005-2009 5-year est.).
Income: Per capita income: $25,617 (2010); Median household income: $62,931 (2010); Average household income: $73,529 (2010); Percent of households with income of $100,000 or more: 22.1% (2010); Poverty rate: 3.4% (2005-2009 5-year est.).
Taxes: Total city taxes per capita: $70 (2007); City property taxes per capita: $64 (2007).
Education: Percent of population age 25 and over with: High school diploma (including GED) or higher: 90.8% (2010); Bachelor's degree or higher: 11.1% (2010); Master's degree or higher: 3.1% (2010).

Herscher CUSD 2 (PK-12)
    2009-10 Enrollment: 2,068 . . . . (815) 426-2162
Housing: Homeownership rate: 85.3% (2010); Median home value: $195,455 (2010); Median contract rent: $636 per month (2005-2009 5-year est.); Median year structure built: 1962 (2005-2009 5-year est.).
Transportation: Commute to work: 90.2% car, 0.0% public transportation, 1.0% walk, 3.9% work from home (2005-2009 5-year est.); Travel time to work: 13.3% less than 15 minutes, 61.2% 15 to 30 minutes, 11.2% 30 to 45 minutes, 12.2% 45 to 60 minutes, 2.0% 60 minutes or more (2005-2009 5-year est.)

BOURBONNAIS (village). Covers a land area of 4.620 square miles and a water area of 0 square miles. Located at 41.16° N. Lat; 87.87° W. Long. Elevation is 650 feet.
History: Fur trader Noel La Vasseur established a trading post here in 1832, which drew French-Canadian settlers to the community named for Francois Bourbonnais. Bourbonnais was the first settlement on the Kankakee River.
Population: 14,215 (1990); 15,256 (2000); 17,429 (2010); 18,493 (2015 projected); Race: 88.8% White, 5.6% Black, 2.7% Asian, 2.9% Other, 3.3% Hispanic of any race (2010); Density: 3,772.5 persons per square mile (2010); Average household size: 2.56 (2010); Median age: 32.5 (2010); Males per 100 females: 91.3 (2010); Marriage status: 37.0% never married, 49.1% now married, 4.8% widowed, 9.0% divorced (2005-2009 5-year est.); Foreign born: 3.9% (2005-2009 5-year est.); Ancestry (includes multiple ancestries): 32.0% German, 14.4% Irish, 10.3% English, 10.2% French, 8.0% Polish (2005-2009 5-year est.).
Economy: Single-family building permits issued: 13 (2010); Multi-family building permits issued: 0 (2010); Employment by occupation: 13.3% management, 24.7% professional, 16.1% services, 27.1% sales, 0.1% farming, 6.2% construction, 12.4% production (2005-2009 5-year est.).
Income: Per capita income: $24,769 (2010); Median household income: $56,559 (2010); Average household income: $69,092 (2010); Percent of households with income of $100,000 or more: 16.9% (2010); Poverty rate: 9.0% (2005-2009 5-year est.).
Taxes: Total city taxes per capita: $149 (2007); City property taxes per capita: $113 (2007).

Education: Percent of population age 25 and over with: High school diploma (including GED) or higher: 92.2% (2010); Bachelor's degree or higher: 28.1% (2010); Master's degree or higher: 11.4% (2010).

School District(s)

Bourbonnais SD 53 (PK-08)
2009-10 Enrollment: 2,671 . . . . (815) 929-5100
Kankakee Area Career Center (11-12)
2009-10 Enrollment: n/a . . . . (815) 939-4971
St George CCSD 258 (PK-08)
2009-10 Enrollment: 481 . . . . (815) 802-3102

Four-year College(s)

Olivet Nazarene University (Private, Not-for-profit, Church of the Nazarene)
Fall 2009 Enrollment: 4,666. (815) 939-5011
2010-11 Tuition: In-state $25,590; Out-of-state $25,590

Housing: Homeownership rate: 64.0% (2010); Median home value: $165,508 (2010); Median contract rent: $627 per month (2005-2009 5-year est.); Median year structure built: 1978 (2005-2009 5-year est.).

Safety: Violent crime rate: 12.4 per 10,000 population; Property crime rate: 172.2 per 10,000 population (2010).

Newspapers: Daily Journal - Bourbonnais Bureau (Local news)

Transportation: Commute to work: 90.2% car, 1.4% public transportation, 4.7% walk, 2.2% work from home (2005-2009 5-year est.); Travel time to work: 53.1% less than 15 minutes, 28.7% 15 to 30 minutes, 9.2% 30 to 45 minutes, 2.8% 45 to 60 minutes, 6.2% 60 minutes or more (2005-2009 5-year est.)

Additional Information Contacts

Kankakee County Chamber of Commerce . . . . (815) 932-2222
http://business.kankakeecountychamber.com
Village of Bourbonnais. . . . . (815) 937-3570
http://www.villageofbourbonnais.com

BRADLEY (village).

Covers a land area of 3.781 square miles and a water area of 0.005 square miles. Located at 41.14° N. Lat; 87.85° W. Long. Elevation is 636 feet.

History: Bradley was known as North Kankakee when it was organized in 1892, but soon was renamed for resident and factory-owner David Bradley.

Population: 11,287 (1990); 12,784 (2000); 15,141 (2010); 16,052 (2015 projected); Race: 93.2% White, 2.4% Black, 0.9% Asian, 3.5% Other, 6.1% Hispanic of any race (2010); Density: 4,004.7 persons per square mile (2010); Average household size: 2.47 (2010); Median age: 34.7 (2010); Males per 100 females: 93.5 (2010); Marriage status: 30.5% never married, 48.0% now married, 8.3% widowed, 13.2% divorced (2005-2009 5-year est.); Foreign born: 1.4% (2005-2009 5-year est.); Ancestry (includes multiple ancestries): 28.2% German, 17.1% Irish, 15.0% French, 11.3% Italian, 8.3% English (2005-2009 5-year est.).

Economy: Single-family building permits issued: 8 (2010); Multi-family building permits issued: 10 (2010); Employment by occupation: 6.5% management, 19.3% professional, 17.8% services, 27.9% sales, 0.6% farming, 9.7% construction, 18.2% production (2005-2009 5-year est.).

Income: Per capita income: $23,566 (2010); Median household income: $49,445 (2010); Average household income: $58,668 (2010); Percent of households with income of $100,000 or more: 13.0% (2010); Poverty rate: 8.5% (2005-2009 5-year est.).

Taxes: Total city taxes per capita: $129 (2007); City property taxes per capita: $109 (2007).

Education: Percent of population age 25 and over with: High school diploma (including GED) or higher: 89.3% (2010); Bachelor's degree or higher: 14.1% (2010); Master's degree or higher: 5.0% (2010).

School District(s)

Bradley Bourbonnais CHSD 307 (09-12)
2009-10 Enrollment: 2,124 . . . . (815) 937-3707
Bradley SD 61 (PK-08)
2009-10 Enrollment: 1,556 . . . . (815) 933-3371

Vocational/Technical School(s)

Trend Setters College of Cosmetology (Private, For-profit)
Fall 2009 Enrollment: 75 . . . . (815) 932-5049
2010-11 Tuition: $18,425

Housing: Homeownership rate: 65.3% (2010); Median home value: $128,712 (2010); Median contract rent: $658 per month (2005-2009 5-year est.); Median year structure built: 1972 (2005-2009 5-year est.).

Safety: Violent crime rate: 31.1 per 10,000 population; Property crime rate: 527.4 per 10,000 population (2010).

Transportation: Commute to work: 93.1% car, 1.5% public transportation, 1.4% walk, 3.7% work from home (2005-2009 5-year est.); Travel time to work: 51.9% less than 15 minutes, 22.1% 15 to 30 minutes, 9.5% 30 to 45

minutes, 7.3% 45 to 60 minutes, 9.2% 60 minutes or more (2005-2009 5-year est.)

Additional Information Contacts

Village of Bradley. . . . . (815) 932-2125
http://www.bradleyil.org

BUCKINGHAM (village).

Covers a land area of 0.276 square miles and a water area of 0 square miles. Located at 41.04° N. Lat; 88.17° W. Long. Elevation is 656 feet.

Population: 340 (1990); 237 (2000); 262 (2010); 274 (2015 projected); Race: 95.0% White, 0.0% Black, 0.0% Asian, 5.0% Other, 1.5% Hispanic of any race (2010); Density: 950.0 persons per square mile (2010); Average household size: 2.82 (2010); Median age: 35.6 (2010); Males per 100 females: 101.5 (2010); Marriage status: 16.1% never married, 61.5% now married, 9.3% widowed, 13.0% divorced (2005-2009 5-year est.); Foreign born: 0.0% (2005-2009 5-year est.); Ancestry (includes multiple ancestries): 35.1% German, 22.5% Irish, 10.8% English, 7.7% French, 7.2% Dutch (2005-2009 5-year est.).

Economy: Single-family building permits issued: 0 (2010); Multi-family building permits issued: 0 (2010); Employment by occupation: 3.4% management, 13.8% professional, 13.8% services, 14.9% sales, 2.3% farming, 25.3% construction, 26.4% production (2005-2009 5-year est.).

Income: Per capita income: $27,061 (2010); Median household income: $68,382 (2010); Average household income: $74,839 (2010); Percent of households with income of $100,000 or more: 24.7% (2010); Poverty rate: 9.0% (2005-2009 5-year est.).

Taxes: Total city taxes per capita: $81 (2007); City property taxes per capita: $77 (2007).

Education: Percent of population age 25 and over with: High school diploma (including GED) or higher: 93.6% (2010); Bachelor's degree or higher: 12.9% (2010); Master's degree or higher: 5.3% (2010).

Housing: Homeownership rate: 84.9% (2010); Median home value: $137,903 (2010); Median contract rent: $375 per month (2005-2009 5-year est.); Median year structure built: 1965 (2005-2009 5-year est.).

Transportation: Commute to work: 92.8% car, 0.0% public transportation, 0.0% walk, 7.2% work from home (2005-2009 5-year est.); Travel time to work: 15.6% less than 15 minutes, 42.9% 15 to 30 minutes, 32.5% 30 to 45 minutes, 2.6% 45 to 60 minutes, 6.5% 60 minutes or more (2005-2009 5-year est.)

ESSEX (village).

Covers a land area of 2.030 square miles and a water area of 0.024 square miles. Located at 41.17° N. Lat; 88.19° W. Long. Elevation is 591 feet.

Population: 503 (1990); 554 (2000); 643 (2010); 683 (2015 projected); Race: 96.3% White, 0.0% Black, 0.2% Asian, 3.6% Other, 0.9% Hispanic of any race (2010); Density: 316.8 persons per square mile (2010); Average household size: 2.76 (2010); Median age: 36.0 (2010); Males per 100 females: 102.8 (2010); Marriage status: 22.7% never married, 62.4% now married, 4.9% widowed, 10.1% divorced (2005-2009 5-year est.); Foreign born: 2.2% (2005-2009 5-year est.); Ancestry (includes multiple ancestries): 40.1% German, 26.0% Polish, 15.5% Irish, 8.7% Croatian, 7.7% Norwegian (2005-2009 5-year est.).

Economy: Single-family building permits issued: 0 (2010); Multi-family building permits issued: 0 (2010); Employment by occupation: 7.8% management, 16.5% professional, 18.8% services, 18.8% sales, 0.0% farming, 17.0% construction, 21.1% production (2005-2009 5-year est.).

Income: Per capita income: $22,316 (2010); Median household income: $57,500 (2010); Average household income: $61,845 (2010); Percent of households with income of $100,000 or more: 13.7% (2010); Poverty rate: 5.0% (2005-2009 5-year est.).

Taxes: Total city taxes per capita: $64 (2007); City property taxes per capita: $31 (2007).

Education: Percent of population age 25 and over with: High school diploma (including GED) or higher: 90.4% (2010); Bachelor's degree or higher: 6.6% (2010); Master's degree or higher: 1.6% (2010).

Housing: Homeownership rate: 87.1% (2010); Median home value: $145,588 (2010); Median contract rent: $763 per month (2005-2009 5-year est.); Median year structure built: 1971 (2005-2009 5-year est.).

Transportation: Commute to work: 98.1% car, 0.0% public transportation, 0.0% walk, 1.9% work from home (2005-2009 5-year est.); Travel time to work: 12.0% less than 15 minutes, 36.1% 15 to 30 minutes, 41.3% 30 to 45 minutes, 3.4% 45 to 60 minutes, 7.2% 60 minutes or more (2005-2009 5-year est.)

GRANT PARK (village). Covers a land area of 0.618 square miles and a water area of 0.026 square miles. Located at 41.24° N. Lat; 87.64° W. Long. Elevation is 699 feet.
Population: 1,141 (1990); 1,358 (2000); 1,620 (2010); 1,742 (2015 projected); Race: 97.4% White, 0.1% Black, 0.4% Asian, 2.1% Other, 2.0% Hispanic of any race (2010); Density: 2,619.9 persons per square mile (2010); Average household size: 2.70 (2010); Median age: 36.4 (2010); Males per 100 females: 93.8 (2010); Marriage status: 24.4% never married, 59.1% now married, 5.8% widowed, 10.7% divorced (2005-2009 5-year est.); Foreign born: 0.4% (2005-2009 5-year est.); Ancestry (includes multiple ancestries): 48.1% German, 16.9% Irish, 15.1% Italian, 9.3% English, 6.5% French (2005-2009 5-year est.).
Economy: Single-family building permits issued: 0 (2010); Multi-family building permits issued: 0 (2010); Employment by occupation: 11.1% management, 15.5% professional, 12.4% services, 23.9% sales, 0.2% farming, 16.6% construction, 20.3% production (2005-2009 5-year est.).
Income: Per capita income: $26,956 (2010); Median household income: $61,935 (2010); Average household income: $72,883 (2010); Percent of households with income of $100,000 or more: 22.8% (2010); Poverty rate: 11.6% (2005-2009 5-year est.).
Taxes: Total city taxes per capita: $242 (2007); City property taxes per capita: $131 (2007).
Education: Percent of population age 25 and over with: High school diploma (including GED) or higher: 90.4% (2010); Bachelor's degree or higher: 10.3% (2010); Master's degree or higher: 2.2% (2010).

School District(s)
Grant Park CUSD 6 (PK-12)
   2009-10 Enrollment: 573 . . . . (815) 465-6013
Housing: Homeownership rate: 72.0% (2010); Median home value: $173,667 (2010); Median contract rent: $539 per month (2005-2009 5-year est.); Median year structure built: 1960 (2005-2009 5-year est.).
Safety: Violent crime rate: 29.1 per 10,000 population; Property crime rate: 69.9 per 10,000 population (2010).
Transportation: Commute to work: 89.0% car, 0.3% public transportation, 5.6% walk, 3.9% work from home (2005-2009 5-year est.); Travel time to work: 29.3% less than 15 minutes, 19.2% 15 to 30 minutes, 26.4% 30 to 45 minutes, 10.3% 45 to 60 minutes, 14.9% 60 minutes or more (2005-2009 5-year est.)
Additional Information Contacts
Grant Park Chamber of Commerce . . . . (815) 465-6531
   http://grantparkchamber.org

HERSCHER (village). Covers a land area of 1.725 square miles and a water area of 0 square miles. Located at 41.05° N. Lat; 88.09° W. Long. Elevation is 659 feet.
Population: 1,286 (1990); 1,523 (2000); 1,626 (2010); 1,674 (2015 projected); Race: 96.0% White, 0.4% Black, 0.9% Asian, 2.7% Other, 2.0% Hispanic of any race (2010); Density: 942.8 persons per square mile (2010); Average household size: 2.82 (2010); Median age: 33.0 (2010); Males per 100 females: 97.8 (2010); Marriage status: 30.3% never married, 55.4% now married, 5.9% widowed, 8.5% divorced (2005-2009 5-year est.); Foreign born: 1.9% (2005-2009 5-year est.); Ancestry (includes multiple ancestries): 38.1% German, 20.8% Irish, 15.3% French, 8.8% English, 8.2% Polish (2005-2009 5-year est.).
Economy: Single-family building permits issued: 3 (2010); Multi-family building permits issued: 0 (2010); Employment by occupation: 11.8% management, 15.1% professional, 16.5% services, 22.4% sales, 1.9% farming, 15.2% construction, 17.1% production (2005-2009 5-year est.).
Income: Per capita income: $22,311 (2010); Median household income: $56,696 (2010); Average household income: $63,523 (2010); Percent of households with income of $100,000 or more: 16.5% (2010); Poverty rate: 7.0% (2005-2009 5-year est.).
Taxes: Total city taxes per capita: $52 (2007); City property taxes per capita: $42 (2007).
Education: Percent of population age 25 and over with: High school diploma (including GED) or higher: 91.5% (2010); Bachelor's degree or higher: 21.7% (2010); Master's degree or higher: 7.4% (2010).

School District(s)
Herscher CUSD 2 (PK-12)
   2009-10 Enrollment: 2,068 . . . . (815) 426-2162
Housing: Homeownership rate: 76.6% (2010); Median home value: $163,821 (2010); Median contract rent: $606 per month (2005-2009 5-year est.); Median year structure built: 1968 (2005-2009 5-year est.).
Newspapers: Herscher Pilot (Local news; Circulation 2,200)

Transportation: Commute to work: 87.8% car, 0.2% public transportation, 8.7% walk, 2.1% work from home (2005-2009 5-year est.); Travel time to work: 33.5% less than 15 minutes, 20.4% 15 to 30 minutes, 26.3% 30 to 45 minutes, 7.5% 45 to 60 minutes, 12.4% 60 minutes or more (2005-2009 5-year est.)
Additional Information Contacts
Herscher Chamber of Commerce . . . . (815) 474-0044
   http://www.herscher.net

HOPKINS PARK (village). Aka Pembroke. Covers a land area of 3.661 square miles and a water area of 0 square miles. Located at 41.07° N. Lat; 87.60° W. Long. Elevation is 679 feet.
Population: 696 (1990); 711 (2000); 1,104 (2010); 1,170 (2015 projected); Race: 3.9% White, 90.5% Black, 0.4% Asian, 5.3% Other, 2.7% Hispanic of any race (2010); Density: 301.6 persons per square mile (2010); Average household size: 3.01 (2010); Median age: 28.6 (2010); Males per 100 females: 93.0 (2010); Marriage status: 46.3% never married, 16.2% now married, 19.0% widowed, 18.5% divorced (2005-2009 5-year est.); Foreign born: 0.0% (2005-2009 5-year est.); Ancestry (includes multiple ancestries): 2.2% American (2005-2009 5-year est.).
Economy: Single-family building permits issued: 0 (2010); Multi-family building permits issued: 0 (2010); Employment by occupation: 22.0% management, 23.5% professional, 28.0% services, 9.5% sales, 0.0% farming, 3.5% construction, 13.5% production (2005-2009 5-year est.).
Income: Per capita income: $10,079 (2010); Median household income: $23,304 (2010); Average household income: $30,926 (2010); Percent of households with income of $100,000 or more: 3.3% (2010); Poverty rate: 26.9% (2005-2009 5-year est.).
Taxes: Total city taxes per capita: $174 (2007); City property taxes per capita: $127 (2007).
Education: Percent of population age 25 and over with: High school diploma (including GED) or higher: 63.8% (2010); Bachelor's degree or higher: 6.0% (2010); Master's degree or higher: 1.1% (2010).

School District(s)
Pembroke CCSD 259 (PK-08)
   2009-10 Enrollment: 269 . . . . (815) 944-8168
Housing: Homeownership rate: 64.6% (2010); Median home value: $64,318 (2010); Median contract rent: $370 per month (2005-2009 5-year est.); Median year structure built: 1978 (2005-2009 5-year est.).
Transportation: Commute to work: 97.8% car, 0.0% public transportation, 0.0% walk, 0.0% work from home (2005-2009 5-year est.); Travel time to work: 24.6% less than 15 minutes, 30.2% 15 to 30 minutes, 32.4% 30 to 45 minutes, 10.6% 45 to 60 minutes, 2.2% 60 minutes or more (2005-2009 5-year est.)

IRWIN (village). Covers a land area of 0.068 square miles and a water area of 0 square miles. Located at 41.05° N. Lat; 87.98° W. Long. Elevation is 659 feet.
Population: 50 (1990); 92 (2000); 94 (2010); 95 (2015 projected); Race: 94.7% White, 2.1% Black, 0.0% Asian, 3.2% Other, 1.1% Hispanic of any race (2010); Density: 1,384.6 persons per square mile (2010); Average household size: 2.69 (2010); Median age: 38.1 (2010); Males per 100 females: 91.8 (2010); Marriage status: 43.9% never married, 31.7% now married, 7.3% widowed, 17.1% divorced (2005-2009 5-year est.); Foreign born: 0.0% (2005-2009 5-year est.); Ancestry (includes multiple ancestries): 42.2% Irish, 20.0% German, 13.3% Norwegian, 13.3% Polish, 11.1% Dutch (2005-2009 5-year est.).
Economy: Single-family building permits issued: 0 (2010); Multi-family building permits issued: 0 (2010); Employment by occupation: 9.1% management, 40.9% professional, 36.4% services, 0.0% sales, 9.1% farming, 4.5% construction, 0.0% production (2005-2009 5-year est.).
Income: Per capita income: $25,268 (2010); Median household income: $59,722 (2010); Average household income: $63,071 (2010); Percent of households with income of $100,000 or more: 14.3% (2010); Poverty rate: 4.4% (2005-2009 5-year est.).
Taxes: Total city taxes per capita: $45 (2007); City property taxes per capita: $45 (2007).
Education: Percent of population age 25 and over with: High school diploma (including GED) or higher: 88.1% (2010); Bachelor's degree or higher: 9.0% (2010); Master's degree or higher: 3.0% (2010).
Housing: Homeownership rate: 80.0% (2010); Median home value: $162,500 (2010); Median contract rent: n/a per month (2005-2009 5-year est.); Median year structure built: before 1940 (2005-2009 5-year est.).
Transportation: Commute to work: 81.8% car, 0.0% public transportation, 18.2% walk, 0.0% work from home (2005-2009 5-year est.); Travel time to

work: 27.3% less than 15 minutes, 50.0% 15 to 30 minutes, 13.6% 30 to 45 minutes, 0.0% 45 to 60 minutes, 9.1% 60 minutes or more (2005-2009 5-year est.)

KANKAKEE (city). County seat. Covers a land area of 12.274 square miles and a water area of 0.476 square miles. Located at 41.11° N. Lat; 87.86° W. Long. Elevation is 656 feet.

History: Kankakee developed around the Illinois Central Railroad depot, and was incorporated in 1855.

Population: 27,822 (1990); 27,491 (2000); 26,759 (2010); 26,615 (2015 projected); Race: 47.0% White, 39.8% Black, 0.3% Asian, 12.8% Other, 16.5% Hispanic of any race (2010); Density: 2,180.2 persons per square mile (2010); Average household size: 2.63 (2010); Median age: 33.3 (2010); Males per 100 females: 94.1 (2010); Marriage status: 42.8% never married, 38.1% now married, 7.1% widowed, 12.0% divorced (2005-2009 5-year est.); Foreign born: 8.8% (2005-2009 5-year est.); Ancestry (includes multiple ancestries): 14.4% German, 6.9% Irish, 6.5% French, 4.9% English, 3.3% American (2005-2009 5-year est.).

Economy: Unemployment rate: 16.2% (August 2011); Total civilian labor force: 12,253 (August 2011); Single-family building permits issued: 0 (2010); Multi-family building permits issued: 2 (2010); Employment by occupation: 5.7% management, 15.6% professional, 24.4% services, 19.8% sales, 3.2% farming, 6.7% construction, 24.6% production (2005-2009 5-year est.).

Income: Per capita income: $17,356 (2010); Median household income: $35,427 (2010); Average household income: $46,555 (2010); Percent of households with income of $100,000 or more: 7.7% (2010); Poverty rate: 31.4% (2005-2009 5-year est.).

Taxes: Total city taxes per capita: $565 (2007); City property taxes per capita: $418 (2007).

Education: Percent of population age 25 and over with: High school diploma (including GED) or higher: 75.2% (2010); Bachelor's degree or higher: 14.8% (2010); Master's degree or higher: 5.6% (2010).

School District(s)
Herscher CUSD 2 (PK-12)
 2009-10 Enrollment: 2,068 . . . . (815) 426-2162
Iroquois/Kankakee Roe (07-12)
 2009-10 Enrollment: n/a . . . . (815) 937-2950
Kankakee Area Spec Educ Coop (04-12)
 2009-10 Enrollment: n/a . . . . (815) 939-3651
Kankakee SD 111 (PK-12)
 2009-10 Enrollment: 5,767 . . . . (815) 933-0700

Two-year College(s)
Kankakee Community College (Public)
 Fall 2009 Enrollment: 4,298. (815) 802-8500
 2010-11 Tuition: In-state $5,125; Out-of-state $12,355

Housing: Homeownership rate: 54.2% (2010); Median home value: $98,388 (2010); Median contract rent: $505 per month (2005-2009 5-year est.); Median year structure built: 1953 (2005-2009 5-year est.).

Hospitals: Riverside Medical Center (336 beds); St. Mary's Hospital of Kankakee (210 beds)

Safety: Violent crime rate: 92.5 per 10,000 population; Property crime rate: 427.5 per 10,000 population (2010).

Newspapers: The Daily Journal (Community news; Circulation 9,000)

Transportation: Commute to work: 86.6% car, 4.6% public transportation, 4.0% walk, 3.1% work from home (2005-2009 5-year est.); Travel time to work: 45.8% less than 15 minutes, 30.5% 15 to 30 minutes, 12.9% 30 to 45 minutes, 4.7% 45 to 60 minutes, 6.1% 60 minutes or more (2005-2009 5-year est.); Amtrak: train service available.

Airports: Greater Kankakee (general aviation)

Additional Information Contacts
City of Kankakee . . . . (815) 933-0480
 http://www.citykankakee-il.gov
Kankakee Regional Chamber of Commerce . . . . (815) 933-7721
 http://www.kankakee.org

LIMESTONE (village). Covers a land area of 2.038 square miles and a water area of 0 square miles. Located at 41.13° N. Lat; 87.96° W. Long.
History: Incorporated 2006.

Population: n/a (1990); n/a (2000); 1,598 (2010); n/a (2015 projected); Race: 95.7% White, 0.5% Black, 0.6% Asian, 3.2% Other, 2.9% Hispanic of any race (2010); Density: 784.1 persons per square mile (2010); Average household size: 2.77 (2010); Median age: 40.3 (2010); Males per 100 females: 99.3 (2010); Marriage status: 25.1% never married, 60.5% now married, 5.1% widowed, 9.3% divorced (2005-2009 5-year est.);

Foreign born: 0.0% (2005-2009 5-year est.); Ancestry (includes multiple ancestries): 42.7% German, 23.1% French, 13.3% Irish, 11.1% Italian, 7.2% English (2005-2009 5-year est.).

Economy: Employment by occupation: 6.8% management, 16.9% professional, 21.6% services, 31.4% sales, 0.0% farming, 11.4% construction, 12.0% production (2005-2009 5-year est.).

Income: Per capita income: n/a (2010); Median household income: n/a (2010); Average household income: n/a (2010); Percent of households with income of $100,000 or more: n/a (2010); Poverty rate: 3.2% (2005-2009 5-year est.).

Taxes: Total city taxes per capita: $23 (2007); City property taxes per capita: $23 (2007).

Education: Percent of population age 25 and over with: High school diploma (including GED) or higher: n/a (2010); Bachelor's degree or higher: n/a (2010); Master's degree or higher: n/a (2010).

Housing: Homeownership rate: n/a (2010); Median home value: n/a (2010); Median contract rent: $645 per month (2005-2009 5-year est.); Median year structure built: 1971 (2005-2009 5-year est.).

Transportation: Commute to work: 96.9% car, 0.0% public transportation, 0.0% walk, 2.2% work from home (2005-2009 5-year est.); Travel time to work: 29.7% less than 15 minutes, 33.0% 15 to 30 minutes, 18.9% 30 to 45 minutes, 9.7% 45 to 60 minutes, 8.7% 60 minutes or more (2005-2009 5-year est.)

MANTENO (village). Covers a land area of 2.993 square miles and a water area of 0.032 square miles. Located at 41.25° N. Lat; 87.83° W. Long. Elevation is 686 feet.
History: Incorporated 1878.

Population: 4,304 (1990); 6,414 (2000); 8,196 (2010); 8,898 (2015 projected); Race: 94.8% White, 1.9% Black, 0.2% Asian, 3.1% Other, 5.6% Hispanic of any race (2010); Density: 2,738.3 persons per square mile (2010); Average household size: 2.46 (2010); Median age: 36.8 (2010); Males per 100 females: 98.0 (2010); Marriage status: 22.6% never married, 59.3% now married, 7.2% widowed, 10.9% divorced (2005-2009 5-year est.); Foreign born: 2.2% (2005-2009 5-year est.); Ancestry (includes multiple ancestries): 35.8% German, 20.8% Irish, 11.8% Italian, 10.7% English, 10.4% Polish (2005-2009 5-year est.).

Economy: Single-family building permits issued: 3 (2010); Multi-family building permits issued: 0 (2010); Employment by occupation: 12.0% management, 19.8% professional, 14.1% services, 26.4% sales, 0.0% farming, 11.2% construction, 16.4% production (2005-2009 5-year est.).

Income: Per capita income: $28,806 (2010); Median household income: $59,046 (2010); Average household income: $71,276 (2010); Percent of households with income of $100,000 or more: 21.8% (2010); Poverty rate: 6.6% (2005-2009 5-year est.).

Taxes: Total city taxes per capita: $350 (2007); City property taxes per capita: $236 (2007).

Education: Percent of population age 25 and over with: High school diploma (including GED) or higher: 89.5% (2010); Bachelor's degree or higher: 16.8% (2010); Master's degree or higher: 6.2% (2010).

School District(s)
Manteno CUSD 5 (PK-12)
 2009-10 Enrollment: 2,337 . . . . (815) 928-7000

Housing: Homeownership rate: 71.5% (2010); Median home value: $150,761 (2010); Median contract rent: $647 per month (2005-2009 5-year est.); Median year structure built: 1995 (2005-2009 5-year est.).

Transportation: Commute to work: 93.1% car, 2.0% public transportation, 1.0% walk, 3.2% work from home (2005-2009 5-year est.); Travel time to work: 26.5% less than 15 minutes, 32.9% 15 to 30 minutes, 20.0% 30 to 45 minutes, 4.7% 45 to 60 minutes, 15.9% 60 minutes or more (2005-2009 5-year est.)

Additional Information Contacts
Manteno Chamber of Commerce. . . . . (815) 468-6226
 http://www.mantenochamber.com
Village of Manteno . . . . (815) 929-4800
 http://manteno.govoffice.com

MOMENCE (city). Covers a land area of 1.369 square miles and a water area of 0.077 square miles. Located at 41.16° N. Lat; 87.66° W. Long. Elevation is 627 feet.
History: Momence, named for Isadore Momence, was laid out in 1844 on the Kankakee River. This was a camping place for travelers on the Hubbard Trail, who forded the Kankakee here.

Population: 2,975 (1990); 3,171 (2000); 3,180 (2010); 3,177 (2015 projected); Race: 84.6% White, 5.2% Black, 0.1% Asian, 10.1% Other,

19.1% Hispanic of any race (2010); Density: 2,322.8 persons per square mile (2010); Average household size: 2.55 (2010); Median age: 37.9 (2010); Males per 100 females: 91.8 (2010); Marriage status: 35.0% never married, 39.8% now married, 7.8% widowed, 17.3% divorced (2005-2009 5-year est.); Foreign born: 5.5% (2005-2009 5-year est.); Ancestry (includes multiple ancestries): 23.8% German, 19.3% Irish, 7.7% Italian, 6.8% English, 6.5% Polish (2005-2009 5-year est.).

Economy: Single-family building permits issued: 1 (2010); Multi-family building permits issued: 0 (2010); Employment by occupation: 8.7% management, 11.5% professional, 14.7% services, 33.2% sales, 2.7% farming, 8.2% construction, 20.9% production (2005-2009 5-year est.).

Income: Per capita income: $22,046 (2010); Median household income: $46,952 (2010); Average household income: $58,589 (2010); Percent of households with income of $100,000 or more: 12.7% (2010); Poverty rate: 15.7% (2005-2009 5-year est.).

Taxes: Total city taxes per capita: $109 (2007); City property taxes per capita: $91 (2007).

Education: Percent of population age 25 and over with: High school diploma (including GED) or higher: 81.0% (2010); Bachelor's degree or higher: 14.5% (2010); Master's degree or higher: 6.4% (2010).

School District(s)

Momence CUSD 1 (PK-12)

    2009-10 Enrollment: 1,151 . . . . (815) 472-3500

Housing: Homeownership rate: 66.0% (2010); Median home value: $141,139 (2010); Median contract rent: $495 per month (2005-2009 5-year est.); Median year structure built: 1944 (2005-2009 5-year est.).

Safety: Violent crime rate: 102.6 per 10,000 population; Property crime rate: 162.1 per 10,000 population (2010).

Newspapers: Momence Progress-Reporter (Local news; Circulation 2,200)

Transportation: Commute to work: 88.0% car, 1.2% public transportation, 5.1% walk, 3.5% work from home (2005-2009 5-year est.); Travel time to work: 57.8% less than 15 minutes, 25.4% 15 to 30 minutes, 9.0% 30 to 45 minutes, 2.6% 45 to 60 minutes, 5.2% 60 minutes or more (2005-2009 5-year est.)

Additional Information Contacts

Momence Chamber of Commerce. . . . . (815) 472-4620
    http://www.momence.net

REDDICK (village). Covers a land area of 0.234 square miles and a water area of 0 square miles. Located at 41.09° N. Lat; 88.24° W. Long. Elevation is 610 feet.

Population: 208 (1990); 219 (2000); 240 (2010); 251 (2015 projected); Race: 95.0% White, 0.0% Black, 0.0% Asian, 5.0% Other, 1.7% Hispanic of any race (2010); Density: 1,026.1 persons per square mile (2010); Average household size: 2.79 (2010); Median age: 35.4 (2010); Males per 100 females: 101.7 (2010); Marriage status: 18.7% never married, 69.5% now married, 6.4% widowed, 5.3% divorced (2005-2009 5-year est.); Foreign born: 0.0% (2005-2009 5-year est.); Ancestry (includes multiple ancestries): 45.1% Irish, 36.6% German, 13.6% Italian, 10.2% Polish, 8.5% English (2005-2009 5-year est.).

Economy: Employment by occupation: 6.2% management, 8.0% professional, 19.5% services, 26.5% sales, 0.0% farming, 19.5% construction, 20.4% production (2005-2009 5-year est.).

Income: Per capita income: $27,061 (2010); Median household income: $67,188 (2010); Average household income: $73,924 (2010); Percent of households with income of $100,000 or more: 23.3% (2010); Poverty rate: 0.0% (2005-2009 5-year est.).

Taxes: Total city taxes per capita: $51 (2007); City property taxes per capita: $51 (2007).

Education: Percent of population age 25 and over with: High school diploma (including GED) or higher: 93.0% (2010); Bachelor's degree or higher: 13.4% (2010); Master's degree or higher: 5.7% (2010).

School District(s)

Herscher CUSD 2 (PK-12)

    2009-10 Enrollment: 2,068 . . . . (815) 426-2162

Housing: Homeownership rate: 84.9% (2010); Median home value: $137,500 (2010); Median contract rent: n/a per month (2005-2009 5-year est.); Median year structure built: 1943 (2005-2009 5-year est.).

Transportation: Commute to work: 97.8% car, 0.0% public transportation, 2.2% walk, 0.0% work from home (2005-2009 5-year est.); Travel time to work: 17.6% less than 15 minutes, 27.5% 15 to 30 minutes, 23.1% 30 to 45 minutes, 5.5% 45 to 60 minutes, 26.4% 60 minutes or more (2005-2009 5-year est.)

SAINT ANNE (village). Covers a land area of 0.508 square miles and a water area of 0.007 square miles. Located at 41.02° N. Lat; 87.71° W. Long. Elevation is 666 feet.

History: In 1852 Father Charles Chiniquy and many of his French-Canadian parishioners immigrated here from Bourbonnais and founded the town of St. Anne.

Population: 1,153 (1990); 1,212 (2000); 1,184 (2010); 1,176 (2015 projected); Race: 84.7% White, 1.0% Black, 0.1% Asian, 14.2% Other, 15.3% Hispanic of any race (2010); Density: 2,330.2 persons per square mile (2010); Average household size: 2.57 (2010); Median age: 33.1 (2010); Males per 100 females: 96.7 (2010); Marriage status: 21.3% never married, 59.9% now married, 8.2% widowed, 10.6% divorced (2005-2009 5-year est.); Foreign born: 9.7% (2005-2009 5-year est.); Ancestry (includes multiple ancestries): 20.3% German, 15.4% Irish, 13.4% French, 7.3% Polish, 5.4% Canadian (2005-2009 5-year est.).

Economy: Single-family building permits issued: 0 (2010); Multi-family building permits issued: 0 (2010); Employment by occupation: 13.9% management, 8.4% professional, 17.0% services, 19.5% sales, 6.2% farming, 13.3% construction, 21.7% production (2005-2009 5-year est.).

Income: Per capita income: $18,865 (2010); Median household income: $43,168 (2010); Average household income: $48,701 (2010); Percent of households with income of $100,000 or more: 5.9% (2010); Poverty rate: 13.0% (2005-2009 5-year est.).

Taxes: Total city taxes per capita: $114 (2007); City property taxes per capita: $105 (2007).

Education: Percent of population age 25 and over with: High school diploma (including GED) or higher: 86.3% (2010); Bachelor's degree or higher: 13.2% (2010); Master's degree or higher: 4.1% (2010).

School District(s)

St Anne CCSD 256 (PK-08)

    2009-10 Enrollment: 360 . . . . (815) 427-8190

St Anne CHSD 302 (09-12)

    2009-10 Enrollment: 229 . . . . (815) 422-5022

Housing: Homeownership rate: 68.9% (2010); Median home value: $108,673 (2010); Median contract rent: $426 per month (2005-2009 5-year est.); Median year structure built: before 1940 (2005-2009 5-year est.).

Safety: Violent crime rate: 16.2 per 10,000 population; Property crime rate: 266.6 per 10,000 population (2010).

Newspapers: Record (Community news; Circulation 620)

Transportation: Commute to work: 98.1% car, 0.0% public transportation, 0.8% walk, 1.1% work from home (2005-2009 5-year est.); Travel time to work: 38.8% less than 15 minutes, 35.5% 15 to 30 minutes, 16.7% 30 to 45 minutes, 1.9% 45 to 60 minutes, 7.2% 60 minutes or more (2005-2009 5-year est.)

SAMMONS POINT (village). Covers a land area of 1.831 square miles and a water area of 0 square miles. Located at 41.03° N. Lat; 87.85° W. Long.

History: Initially incorporated as a village on March 21, 2006, it was disincorporated on August 8, 2007, and incorporated again on February 5, 2008.

Population: n/a (1990); n/a (2000); 279 (2010); n/a (2015 projected); Race: 96.1% White, 1.1% Black, 0.7% Asian, 2.2% Other, 2.2% Hispanic of any race (2010); Density: 152.4 persons per square mile (2010); Average household size: 2.71 (2010); Median age: 41.6 (2010); Males per 100 females: 95.1 (2010); Marriage status: 13.0% never married, 66.7% now married, 4.6% widowed, 15.7% divorced (2005-2009 5-year est.); Foreign born: 0.0% (2005-2009 5-year est.); Ancestry (includes multiple ancestries): 24.8% German, 20.5% Dutch, 9.4% Irish, 8.1% American, 4.7% French Canadian (2005-2009 5-year est.).

Economy: Single-family building permits issued: 1 (2010); Multi-family building permits issued: 0 (2010); Employment by occupation: 0.0% management, 0.0% professional, 6.7% services, 36.5% sales, 0.0% farming, 35.6% construction, 21.2% production (2005-2009 5-year est.).

Income: Per capita income: n/a (2010); Median household income: n/a (2010); Average household income: n/a (2010); Percent of households with income of $100,000 or more: n/a (2010); Poverty rate: 8.8% (2005-2009 5-year est.).

Taxes: Total city taxes per capita: $116 (2007); City property taxes per capita: $43 (2007).

Education: Percent of population age 25 and over with: High school diploma (including GED) or higher: n/a (2010); Bachelor's degree or higher: n/a (2010); Master's degree or higher: n/a (2010).

Housing: Homeownership rate: n/a (2010); Median home value: n/a (2010); Median contract rent: $570 per month (2005-2009 5-year est.); Median year structure built: 1971 (2005-2009 5-year est.).
Transportation: Commute to work: 100.0% car, 0.0% public transportation, 0.0% walk, 0.0% work from home (2005-2009 5-year est.); Travel time to work: 69.2% less than 15 minutes, 30.8% 15 to 30 minutes, 0.0% 30 to 45 minutes, 0.0% 45 to 60 minutes, 0.0% 60 minutes or more (2005-2009 5-year est.)

SUN RIVER TERRACE (village). Covers a land area of 0.454 square miles and a water area of 0.025 square miles. Located at 41.12° N. Lat; 87.73° W. Long. Elevation is 614 feet.

Population: 532 (1990); 383 (2000); 378 (2010); 377 (2015 projected); Race: 46.3% White, 51.3% Black, 0.5% Asian, 1.9% Other, 2.4% Hispanic of any race (2010); Density: 832.2 persons per square mile (2010); Average household size: 2.64 (2010); Median age: 33.4 (2010); Males per 100 females: 89.9 (2010); Marriage status: 27.2% never married, 42.1% now married, 18.5% widowed, 12.1% divorced (2005-2009 5-year est.); Foreign born: 2.8% (2005-2009 5-year est.); Ancestry (includes multiple ancestries): 4.7% Haitian, 1.9% African, 1.6% Arab (2005-2009 5-year est.).
Economy: Single-family building permits issued: 1 (2010); Multi-family building permits issued: 0 (2010); Employment by occupation: 3.5% management, 37.0% professional, 28.9% services, 19.7% sales, 0.0% farming, 0.0% construction, 11.0% production (2005-2009 5-year est.).
Income: Per capita income: $17,367 (2010); Median household income: $42,500 (2010); Average household income: $46,224 (2010); Percent of households with income of $100,000 or more: 7.7% (2010); Poverty rate: 18.5% (2005-2009 5-year est.).
Taxes: Total city taxes per capita: $213 (2007); City property taxes per capita: $62 (2007).
Education: Percent of population age 25 and over with: High school diploma (including GED) or higher: 84.5% (2010); Bachelor's degree or higher: 6.3% (2010); Master's degree or higher: 3.4% (2010).
Housing: Homeownership rate: 73.4% (2010); Median home value: $114,674 (2010); Median contract rent: $408 per month (2005-2009 5-year est.); Median year structure built: 1981 (2005-2009 5-year est.).
Transportation: Commute to work: 90.2% car, 9.8% public transportation, 0.0% walk, 0.0% work from home (2005-2009 5-year est.); Travel time to work: 20.8% less than 15 minutes, 35.3% 15 to 30 minutes, 27.7% 30 to 45 minutes, 1.7% 45 to 60 minutes, 14.5% 60 minutes or more (2005-2009 5-year est.)

UNION HILL (village). Covers a land area of 0.047 square miles and a water area of 0 square miles. Located at 41.10° N. Lat; 88.14° W. Long. Elevation is 617 feet.

Population: 37 (1990); 66 (2000); 75 (2010); 78 (2015 projected); Race: 94.7% White, 0.0% Black, 0.0% Asian, 5.3% Other, 1.3% Hispanic of any race (2010); Density: 1,611.2 persons per square mile (2010); Average household size: 2.78 (2010); Median age: 33.9 (2010); Males per 100 females: 97.4 (2010); Marriage status: 27.0% never married, 62.2% now married, 0.0% widowed, 10.8% divorced (2005-2009 5-year est.); Foreign born: 0.0% (2005-2009 5-year est.); Ancestry (includes multiple ancestries): 43.6% English, 23.6% German, 7.3% Irish, 7.3% European, 5.5% Italian (2005-2009 5-year est.).
Economy: Single-family building permits issued: 0 (2010); Multi-family building permits issued: 0 (2010); Employment by occupation: 7.4% management, 7.4% professional, 55.6% services, 3.7% sales, 0.0% farming, 0.0% construction, 25.9% production (2005-2009 5-year est.).
Income: Per capita income: $27,061 (2010); Median household income: $67,500 (2010); Average household income: $87,593 (2010); Percent of households with income of $100,000 or more: 25.9% (2010); Poverty rate: 0.0% (2005-2009 5-year est.).
Taxes: Total city taxes per capita: $0 (2007); City property taxes per capita: $0 (2007).
Education: Percent of population age 25 and over with: High school diploma (including GED) or higher: 92.0% (2010); Bachelor's degree or higher: 12.0% (2010); Master's degree or higher: 4.0% (2010).
Housing: Homeownership rate: 85.2% (2010); Median home value: $136,111 (2010); Median contract rent: n/a per month (2005-2009 5-year est.); Median year structure built: 1949 (2005-2009 5-year est.).
Transportation: Commute to work: 75.9% car, 0.0% public transportation, 9.3% walk, 14.8% work from home (2005-2009 5-year est.); Travel time to work: 30.4% less than 15 minutes, 10.9% 15 to 30 minutes, 41.3% 30 to 45

minutes, 17.4% 45 to 60 minutes, 0.0% 60 minutes or more (2005-2009 5-year est.)

Kendall County

Located in northeastern Illinois; drained by the Fox River. Covers a land area of 320.58 square miles, a water area of 2.09 square miles, and is located in the Central Time Zone at 41.64° N. Lat., 88.42° W. Long. The county was founded in 1841. County seat is Yorkville.

Kendall County is part of the Chicago-Joliet-Naperville, IL-IN-WI Metropolitan Statistical Area. The entire metro area includes: Chicago-Joliet-Naperville, IL Metropolitan Division (Cook County, IL; DeKalb County, IL; DuPage County, IL; Grundy County, IL; Kane County, IL; Kendall County, IL; McHenry County, IL; Will County, IL); Gary, IN Metropolitan Division (Jasper County, IN; Lake County, IN; Newton County, IN; Porter County, IN); Lake County-Kenosha County, IL-WI Metropolitan Division (Lake County, IL; Kenosha County, WI)

Population: 39,413 (1990); 54,544 (2000); 113,745 (2010); 142,927 (2015 projected); Race: 80.3% White, 6.1% Black, 2.8% Asian, 10.7% Other, 18.0% Hispanic of any race (2010); Density: 354.8 persons per square mile (2010); Average household size: 2.92 (2010); Median age: 31.0 (2010); Males per 100 females: 100.5 (2010).
Religion: Five largest groups: 17.9% Catholic Church, 4.3% The United Methodist Church, 3.6% Lutheran Church—Missouri Synod, 3.0% The Association of Free Lutheran Congregations, 2.3% Evangelical Lutheran Church in America (2000).
Economy: Unemployment rate: 9.4% (August 2011); Total civilian labor force: 60,000 (August 2011); Leading industries: 24.3% retail trade; 12.6% accommodation & food services; 11.8% manufacturing (2009); Farms: 424 totaling 166,872 acres (2007); Companies that employ 500 or more persons: 1 (2009); Companies that employ 100 to 499 persons: 33 (2009); Companies that employ less than 100 persons: 1,886 (2009); Black-owned businesses: 256 (2007); Hispanic-owned businesses: 774 (2007); Asian-owned businesses: n/a (2007); Women-owned businesses: 2,722 (2007); Retail sales per capita: $8,292 (2010). Single-family building permits issued: 171 (2010); Multi-family building permits issued: 6 (2010).
Income: Per capita income: $31,214 (2010); Median household income: $79,671 (2010); Average household income: $91,193 (2010); Percent of households with income of $100,000 or more: 32.9% (2010); Poverty rate: 4.2% (2009); Bankruptcy rate: 8.07% (2010).
Taxes: Total county taxes per capita: $183 (2007); County property taxes per capita: $156 (2007).
Education: Percent of population age 25 and over with: High school diploma (including GED) or higher: 92.4% (2010); Bachelor's degree or higher: 31.6% (2010); Master's degree or higher: 10.1% (2010).
Housing: Homeownership rate: 86.4% (2010); Median home value: $220,385 (2010); Median contract rent: $853 per month (2005-2009 5-year est.); Median year structure built: 1996 (2005-2009 5-year est.)
Health: Birth rate: 206.3 per 10,000 population (2009); Death rate: 40.7 per 10,000 population (2009); Age-adjusted cancer mortality rate: 194.2 deaths per 100,000 population (2007); Number of physicians: 6.4 per 10,000 population (2008); Hospital beds: 0.0 per 10,000 population (2007); Hospital admissions: 0.0 per 10,000 population (2007).
Elections: 2008 Presidential election results: 53.1% Obama, 45.8% McCain, 0.5% Nader
National and State Parks: Silver Springs State Park
Additional Information Contacts

Kendall County Government . . . . (630) 553-4104
  http://www.co.kendall.il.us
City of Plano. . . . . (630) 552-8275
  http://www.cityofplanoil.com
Oswego Chamber of Commerce . . . . (630) 554-3505
  http://www.oswegochamber.org
Plano Area Chamber of Commerce. . . . . (630) 552-7272
  http://www.planocommerce.org
United City of Yorkville. . . . . (630) 553-4350
  http://www.yorkville.il.us
Village of Oswego . . . . (630) 554-3618
  http://www.oswegoil.org
Yorkville Area Chamber of Commerce . . . . (630) 553-6853
  http://www.yorkvillechamber.org

Kendall County Communities

BOULDER HILL (CDP). Covers a land area of 1.458 square miles and a water area of 0.009 square miles. Located at 41.71° N. Lat; 88.33° W. Long. Elevation is 669 feet.
Population: 8,894 (1990); 8,169 (2000); 10,489 (2010); 12,967 (2015 projected); Race: 75.7% White, 7.7% Black, 1.5% Asian, 15.0% Other, 22.7% Hispanic of any race (2010); Density: 7,196.0 persons per square mile (2010); Average household size: 2.93 (2010); Median age: 30.6 (2010); Males per 100 females: 99.6 (2010); Marriage status: 25.6% never married, 61.8% now married, 4.4% widowed, 8.2% divorced (2005-2009 5-year est.); Foreign born: 7.5% (2005-2009 5-year est.); Ancestry (includes multiple ancestries): 28.7% German, 17.4% Irish, 8.3% English, 6.6% Italian, 6.1% Polish (2005-2009 5-year est.).
Economy: Employment by occupation: 11.5% management, 7.7% professional, 15.3% services, 35.5% sales, 0.0% farming, 10.6% construction, 19.4% production (2005-2009 5-year est.).
Income: Per capita income: $28,233 (2010); Median household income: $71,164 (2010); Average household income: $82,566 (2010); Percent of households with income of $100,000 or more: 26.8% (2010); Poverty rate: 4.5% (2005-2009 5-year est.).
Education: Percent of population age 25 and over with: High school diploma (including GED) or higher: 92.3% (2010); Bachelor's degree or higher: 29.5% (2010); Master's degree or higher: 9.6% (2010).
Housing: Homeownership rate: 90.6% (2010); Median home value: $170,335 (2010); Median contract rent: $1,066 per month (2005-2009 5-year est.); Median year structure built: 1971 (2005-2009 5-year est.).
Transportation: Commute to work: 96.1% car, 1.1% public transportation, 0.5% walk, 2.1% work from home (2005-2009 5-year est.); Travel time to work: 25.9% less than 15 minutes, 36.4% 15 to 30 minutes, 20.2% 30 to 45 minutes, 7.0% 45 to 60 minutes, 10.5% 60 minutes or more (2005-2009 5-year est.)

BRISTOL (unincorporated postal area, zip code 60512). Aka Bristol Station. Covers a land area of 10.460 square miles and a water area of 0 square miles. Located at 41.70° N. Lat; 88.41° W. Long. Elevation is 640 feet.
Population: 892 (2000); Race: 94.0% White, 0.0% Black, 4.5% Asian, 1.5% Other, 2.5% Hispanic of any race (2000); Density: 85.3 persons per square mile (2000); Age: 16.8% under 18, 17.5% over 64 (2000); Marriage status: 22.3% never married, 68.9% now married, 4.1% widowed, 4.7% divorced (2000); Foreign born: 9.2% (2000); Ancestry (includes multiple ancestries): 37.9% German, 18.3% Irish, 9.8% English, 6.2% Swedish (2000).
Economy: Employment by occupation: 12.0% management, 22.3% professional, 5.6% services, 26.3% sales, 0.0% farming, 18.2% construction, 15.6% production (2000).
Income: Per capita income: $28,669 (2000); Median household income: $65,625 (2000); Poverty rate: 1.5% (2000).
Education: Percent of population age 25 and over with: High school diploma (including GED) or higher: 88.0% (2000); Bachelor's degree or higher: 20.7% (2000).
School District(s)
Yorkville CUSD 115 (PK-12)
    2009-10 Enrollment: 5,119 . . . . (630) 553-4382
Housing: Homeownership rate: 92.9% (2000); Median home value: $176,700 (2000); Median contract rent: $442 per month (2000); Median year structure built: 1970 (2000).
Transportation: Commute to work: 93.9% car, 2.6% public transportation, 2.3% walk, 1.3% work from home (2000); Travel time to work: 12.2% less than 15 minutes, 46.1% 15 to 30 minutes, 10.6% 30 to 45 minutes, 4.4% 45 to 60 minutes, 26.7% 60 minutes or more (2000)

LISBON (village). Covers a land area of 0.310 square miles and a water area of 0 square miles. Located at 41.48° N. Lat; 88.48° W. Long. Elevation is 669 feet.
Population: 216 (1990); 248 (2000); 359 (2010); 453 (2015 projected); Race: 99.2% White, 0.0% Black, 0.0% Asian, 0.8% Other, 1.7% Hispanic of any race (2010); Density: 1,159.5 persons per square mile (2010); Average household size: 2.99 (2010); Median age: 31.0 (2010); Males per 100 females: 111.2 (2010); Marriage status: 30.8% never married, 56.3% now married, 8.4% widowed, 4.6% divorced (2005-2009 5-year est.); Foreign born: 6.6% (2005-2009 5-year est.); Ancestry (includes multiple ancestries): 37.7% Norwegian, 25.9% German, 9.2% English, 6.2% Irish, 5.2% Italian (2005-2009 5-year est.).

Economy: Single-family building permits issued: 0 (2010); Multi-family building permits issued: 0 (2010); Employment by occupation: 8.3% management, 13.4% professional, 33.8% services, 26.8% sales, 0.0% farming, 1.9% construction, 15.9% production (2005-2009 5-year est.).
Income: Per capita income: $28,011 (2010); Median household income: $71,429 (2010); Average household income: $82,458 (2010); Percent of households with income of $100,000 or more: 27.5% (2010); Poverty rate: 10.2% (2005-2009 5-year est.).
Taxes: Total city taxes per capita: $66 (2007); City property taxes per capita: $62 (2007).
Education: Percent of population age 25 and over with: High school diploma (including GED) or higher: 89.6% (2010); Bachelor's degree or higher: 22.5% (2010); Master's degree or higher: 5.6% (2010).
Housing: Homeownership rate: 80.8% (2010); Median home value: $193,421 (2010); Median contract rent: $733 per month (2005-2009 5-year est.); Median year structure built: 1965 (2005-2009 5-year est.).
Transportation: Commute to work: 81.3% car, 11.6% public transportation, 1.9% walk, 5.2% work from home (2005-2009 5-year est.); Travel time to work: 18.4% less than 15 minutes, 33.3% 15 to 30 minutes, 29.3% 30 to 45 minutes, 13.6% 45 to 60 minutes, 5.4% 60 minutes or more (2005-2009 5-year est.)

MILLBROOK (village). Covers a land area of 2.079 square miles and a water area of 0 square miles. Located at 41.59° N. Lat; 88.55° W. Long.
History: Incorporated November 5, 2002.
Population: n/a (1990); n/a (2000); 335 (2010); n/a (2015 projected); Race: 97.0% White, 0.9% Black, 0.3% Asian, 1.8% Other, 1.5% Hispanic of any race (2010); Density: 161.1 persons per square mile (2010); Average household size: 2.82 (2010); Median age: 43.1 (2010); Males per 100 females: 103.0 (2010); Marriage status: 24.6% never married, 69.5% now married, 2.7% widowed, 3.2% divorced (2005-2009 5-year est.); Foreign born: 2.7% (2005-2009 5-year est.); Ancestry (includes multiple ancestries): 59.8% German, 13.0% Irish, 13.0% English, 7.7% Norwegian, 5.0% Swedish (2005-2009 5-year est.).
Economy: Employment by occupation: 25.0% management, 22.4% professional, 8.6% services, 28.4% sales, 0.0% farming, 8.6% construction, 6.9% production (2005-2009 5-year est.).
Income: Per capita income: n/a (2010); Median household income: n/a (2010); Average household income: n/a (2010); Percent of households with income of $100,000 or more: n/a (2010); Poverty rate: 4.6% (2005-2009 5-year est.).
Taxes: Total city taxes per capita: $13 (2007); City property taxes per capita: $0 (2007).
Education: Percent of population age 25 and over with: High school diploma (including GED) or higher: n/a (2010); Bachelor's degree or higher: n/a (2010); Master's degree or higher: n/a (2010).
School District(s)
Newark CCSD 66 (PK-08)
    2009-10 Enrollment: 272 . . . . (815) 695-5143
Housing: Homeownership rate: n/a (2010); Median home value: n/a (2010); Median contract rent: n/a per month (2005-2009 5-year est.); Median year structure built: 1985 (2005-2009 5-year est.).
Transportation: Commute to work: 87.1% car, 0.0% public transportation, 5.2% walk, 5.2% work from home (2005-2009 5-year est.); Travel time to work: 28.2% less than 15 minutes, 42.7% 15 to 30 minutes, 10.0% 30 to 45 minutes, 7.3% 45 to 60 minutes, 11.8% 60 minutes or more (2005-2009 5-year est.)

MILLINGTON (village). Covers a land area of 0.557 square miles and a water area of 0.052 square miles. Located at 41.56° N. Lat; 88.60° W. Long. Elevation is 564 feet.
Population: 533 (1990); 458 (2000); 550 (2010); 650 (2015 projected); Race: 80.2% White, 13.3% Black, 1.5% Asian, 5.1% Other, 4.4% Hispanic of any race (2010); Density: 988.1 persons per square mile (2010); Average household size: 2.92 (2010); Median age: 30.9 (2010); Males per 100 females: 139.1 (2010); Marriage status: 28.1% never married, 60.1% now married, 2.4% widowed, 9.4% divorced (2005-2009 5-year est.); Foreign born: 5.9% (2005-2009 5-year est.); Ancestry (includes multiple ancestries): 39.3% German, 18.0% Irish, 8.7% English, 8.2% Scotch-Irish, 7.2% Swedish (2005-2009 5-year est.).
Economy: Employment by occupation: 7.6% management, 2.1% professional, 15.8% services, 24.1% sales, 0.0% farming, 28.9% construction, 21.6% production (2005-2009 5-year est.).
Income: Per capita income: $23,246 (2010); Median household income: $65,351 (2010); Average household income: $75,313 (2010); Percent of

households with income of $100,000 or more: 23.8% (2010); Poverty rate: 18.5% (2005-2009 5-year est.).

Taxes: Total city taxes per capita: $67 (2007); City property taxes per capita: $8 (2007).

Education: Percent of population age 25 and over with: High school diploma (including GED) or higher: 84.8% (2010); Bachelor's degree or higher: 18.9% (2010); Master's degree or higher: 5.1% (2010).

Housing: Homeownership rate: 80.6% (2010); Median home value: $202,381 (2010); Median contract rent: $694 per month (2005-2009 5-year est.); Median year structure built: 1972 (2005-2009 5-year est.).

Transportation: Commute to work: 97.8% car, 0.0% public transportation, 1.5% walk, 0.7% work from home (2005-2009 5-year est.); Travel time to work: 14.6% less than 15 minutes, 32.8% 15 to 30 minutes, 22.8% 30 to 45 minutes, 17.9% 45 to 60 minutes, 11.9% 60 minutes or more (2005-2009 5-year est.)

NEWARK (village).
Covers a land area of 1.133 square miles and a water area of <.001 square miles. Located at 41.53° N. Lat; 88.58° W. Long. Elevation is 673 feet.

Population: 870 (1990); 887 (2000); 1,183 (2010); 1,477 (2015 projected); Race: 96.2% White, 0.0% Black, 0.9% Asian, 2.9% Other, 3.1% Hispanic of any race (2010); Density: 1,044.0 persons per square mile (2010); Average household size: 2.70 (2010); Median age: 32.0 (2010); Males per 100 females: 114.3 (2010); Marriage status: 23.6% never married, 59.7% now married, 8.8% widowed, 7.9% divorced (2005-2009 5-year est.); Foreign born: 3.1% (2005-2009 5-year est.); Ancestry (includes multiple ancestries): 29.3% German, 22.0% Norwegian, 20.8% Irish, 19.4% English, 8.2% Polish (2005-2009 5-year est.).

Economy: Single-family building permits issued: 2 (2010); Multi-family building permits issued: 0 (2010); Employment by occupation: 9.6% management, 16.8% professional, 14.0% services, 26.5% sales, 0.0% farming, 13.6% construction, 19.6% production (2005-2009 5-year est.).

Income: Per capita income: $29,188 (2010); Median household income: $71,484 (2010); Average household income: $79,110 (2010); Percent of households with income of $100,000 or more: 24.9% (2010); Poverty rate: 1.3% (2005-2009 5-year est.).

Taxes: Total city taxes per capita: $147 (2007); City property taxes per capita: $45 (2007).

Education: Percent of population age 25 and over with: High school diploma (including GED) or higher: 89.7% (2010); Bachelor's degree or higher: 19.2% (2010); Master's degree or higher: 5.1% (2010).

School District(s)
Lisbon CCSD 90 (KG-08)
    2009-10 Enrollment: 120 . . . . (815) 736-6324
Newark CCSD 66 (PK-08)
    2009-10 Enrollment: 272 . . . . (815) 695-5143
Newark CHSD 18 (09-12)
    2009-10 Enrollment: 197 . . . . (815) 695-5164

Housing: Homeownership rate: 79.5% (2010); Median home value: $165,347 (2010); Median contract rent: $625 per month (2005-2009 5-year est.); Median year structure built: 1966 (2005-2009 5-year est.).

Transportation: Commute to work: 83.1% car, 4.0% public transportation, 4.8% walk, 6.4% work from home (2005-2009 5-year est.); Travel time to work: 21.3% less than 15 minutes, 29.5% 15 to 30 minutes, 26.2% 30 to 45 minutes, 5.6% 45 to 60 minutes, 17.4% 60 minutes or more (2005-2009 5-year est.)

OSWEGO (village).
Covers a land area of 6.582 square miles and a water area of 0.097 square miles. Located at 41.69° N. Lat; 88.34° W. Long. Elevation is 640 feet.

Population: 5,970 (1990); 13,326 (2000); 24,670 (2010); 31,384 (2015 projected); Race: 76.0% White, 10.2% Black, 4.4% Asian, 9.4% Other, 15.0% Hispanic of any race (2010); Density: 3,748.0 persons per square mile (2010); Average household size: 2.94 (2010); Median age: 31.1 (2010); Males per 100 females: 98.7 (2010); Marriage status: 22.8% never married, 66.6% now married, 4.0% widowed, 6.5% divorced (2005-2009 5-year est.); Foreign born: 7.1% (2005-2009 5-year est.); Ancestry (includes multiple ancestries): 29.7% German, 17.2% Irish, 10.6% Italian, 9.2% Polish, 7.6% English (2005-2009 5-year est.).

Economy: Unemployment rate: 8.6% (August 2011); Total civilian labor force: 16,322 (August 2011); Single-family building permits issued: 116 (2010); Multi-family building permits issued: 0 (2010); Employment by occupation: 19.1% management, 24.2% professional, 11.3% services, 28.0% sales, 0.0% farming, 8.1% construction, 9.2% production (2005-2009 5-year est.).

Income: Per capita income: $34,558 (2010); Median household income: $89,648 (2010); Average household income: $101,514 (2010); Percent of households with income of $100,000 or more: 40.9% (2010); Poverty rate: 3.5% (2005-2009 5-year est.).

Taxes: Total city taxes per capita: $180 (2007); City property taxes per capita: $38 (2007).

Education: Percent of population age 25 and over with: High school diploma (including GED) or higher: 95.4% (2010); Bachelor's degree or higher: 38.2% (2010); Master's degree or higher: 13.0% (2010).

School District(s)
Grundy/Kendall Roe (06-12)
    2009-10 Enrollment: n/a . . . . (815) 941-3247
Kendall Co Spec Educ Coop (01-12)
    2009-10 Enrollment: n/a . . . . (630) 553-5833
Oswego CUSD 308 (PK-12)
    2009-10 Enrollment: 16,314 . . . . (630) 636-3080

Vocational/Technical School(s)
Hair Professionals School of Cosmetology (Private, For-profit)
    Fall 2009 Enrollment: 120 . . . . (630) 554-2266
    2010-11 Tuition: $16,450

Housing: Homeownership rate: 87.9% (2010); Median home value: $231,248 (2010); Median contract rent: $1,042 per month (2005-2009 5-year est.); Median year structure built: 2000 (2005-2009 5-year est.).

Safety: Violent crime rate: 10.2 per 10,000 population; Property crime rate: 150.9 per 10,000 population (2010).

Newspapers: Oswego Ledger Sentinel (Community news; Circulation 5,100)

Transportation: Commute to work: 90.4% car, 4.5% public transportation, 0.5% walk, 3.7% work from home (2005-2009 5-year est.); Travel time to work: 21.5% less than 15 minutes, 27.6% 15 to 30 minutes, 20.5% 30 to 45 minutes, 14.7% 45 to 60 minutes, 15.8% 60 minutes or more (2005-2009 5-year est.)

Additional Information Contacts
Oswego Chamber of Commerce . . . . (630) 554-3505
    http://www.oswegochamber.org
Village of Oswego . . . . (630) 554-3618
    http://www.oswegoil.org

PLANO (city).
Covers a land area of 3.513 square miles and a water area of 0.042 square miles. Located at 41.66° N. Lat; 88.53° W. Long. Elevation is 650 feet.

History: Plano was settled by a group of Norwegian Quakers led by Kleng Peerson in 1835.

Population: 5,192 (1990); 5,633 (2000); 8,323 (2010); 10,433 (2015 projected); Race: 68.0% White, 1.0% Black, 0.9% Asian, 30.0% Other, 49.5% Hispanic of any race (2010); Density: 2,368.9 persons per square mile (2010); Average household size: 3.04 (2010); Median age: 29.7 (2010); Males per 100 females: 99.8 (2010); Marriage status: 25.3% never married, 60.4% now married, 4.0% widowed, 10.2% divorced (2005-2009 5-year est.); Foreign born: 19.2% (2005-2009 5-year est.); Ancestry (includes multiple ancestries): 15.6% German, 9.9% Irish, 9.3% Polish, 7.5% English, 7.2% Italian (2005-2009 5-year est.).

Economy: Single-family building permits issued: 6 (2010); Multi-family building permits issued: 0 (2010); Employment by occupation: 9.3% management, 13.9% professional, 12.1% services, 28.6% sales, 0.9% farming, 17.0% construction, 18.3% production (2005-2009 5-year est.).

Income: Per capita income: $21,560 (2010); Median household income: $56,734 (2010); Average household income: $65,333 (2010); Percent of households with income of $100,000 or more: 14.8% (2010); Poverty rate: 6.7% (2005-2009 5-year est.).

Taxes: Total city taxes per capita: $162 (2007); City property taxes per capita: $112 (2007).

Education: Percent of population age 25 and over with: High school diploma (including GED) or higher: 75.2% (2010); Bachelor's degree or higher: 16.9% (2010); Master's degree or higher: 4.1% (2010).

School District(s)
Grundy/Kendall Roe (06-12)
    2009-10 Enrollment: n/a . . . . (815) 941-3247
Plano CUSD 88 (PK-12)
    2009-10 Enrollment: 2,329 . . . . (630) 552-8978

Housing: Homeownership rate: 75.1% (2010); Median home value: $161,478 (2010); Median contract rent: $573 per month (2005-2009 5-year est.); Median year structure built: 1978 (2005-2009 5-year est.).

Safety: Violent crime rate: 13.9 per 10,000 population; Property crime rate: 145.1 per 10,000 population (2010).

Transportation: Commute to work: 94.7% car, 0.8% public transportation, 0.3% walk, 3.7% work from home (2005-2009 5-year est.); Travel time to work: 20.8% less than 15 minutes, 31.6% 15 to 30 minutes, 21.7% 30 to 45 minutes, 6.6% 45 to 60 minutes, 19.3% 60 minutes or more (2005-2009 5-year est.); Amtrak: train service available.

Additional Information Contacts

City of Plano... (630) 552-8275
    http://www.cityofplanoil.com
Plano Area Chamber of Commerce................... (630) 552-7272
    http://www.planocommerce.org

PLATTVILLE (village). Covers a land area of 2.273 square miles and a water area of 0 square miles. Located at 41.53° N. Lat; 88.38° W. Long.
History: Incorporated March 2006.
Population: n/a (1990); n/a (2000); 242 (2010); n/a (2015 projected); Race: 95.5% White, 0.0% Black, 0.0% Asian, 4.5% Other, 5.0% Hispanic of any race (2010); Density: 106.5 persons per square mile (2010); Average household size: 2.81 (2010); Median age: 38.0 (2010); Males per 100 females: 110.4 (2010); Marriage status: 30.9% never married, 52.5% now married, 10.3% widowed, 6.4% divorced (2005-2009 5-year est.); Foreign born: 0.0% (2005-2009 5-year est.); Ancestry (includes multiple ancestries): 48.9% German, 36.1% Irish, 22.3% English, 20.6% Polish, 8.2% Italian (2005-2009 5-year est.).
Economy: Employment by occupation: 10.4% management, 17.4% professional, 0.0% services, 40.3% sales, 7.6% farming, 2.1% construction, 22.2% production (2005-2009 5-year est.).
Income: Per capita income: n/a (2010); Median household income: n/a (2010); Average household income: n/a (2010); Percent of households with income of $100,000 or more: n/a (2010); Poverty rate: 6.0% (2005-2009 5-year est.).
Taxes: Total city taxes per capita: $10 (2007); City property taxes per capita: $7 (2007).
Education: Percent of population age 25 and over with: High school diploma (including GED) or higher: n/a (2010); Bachelor's degree or higher: n/a (2010); Master's degree or higher: n/a (2010).
Housing: Homeownership rate: n/a (2010); Median home value: n/a (2010); Median contract rent: $843 per month (2005-2009 5-year est.); Median year structure built: 1970 (2005-2009 5-year est.).
Transportation: Commute to work: 100.0% car, 0.0% public transportation, 0.0% walk, 0.0% work from home (2005-2009 5-year est.); Travel time to work: 7.6% less than 15 minutes, 51.4% 15 to 30 minutes, 13.9% 30 to 45 minutes, 18.1% 45 to 60 minutes, 9.0% 60 minutes or more (2005-2009 5-year est.)

YORKVILLE (city). County seat. Covers a land area of 7.043 square miles and a water area of 0.111 square miles. Located at 41.64° N. Lat; 88.44° W. Long. Elevation is 607 feet.
Population: 4,716 (1990); 6,189 (2000); 13,353 (2010); 16,643 (2015 projected); Race: 89.8% White, 2.1% Black, 1.3% Asian, 6.8% Other, 12.8% Hispanic of any race (2010); Density: 1,896.0 persons per square mile (2010); Average household size: 2.80 (2010); Median age: 31.3 (2010); Males per 100 females: 101.2 (2010); Marriage status: 29.5% never married, 58.4% now married, 3.1% widowed, 9.1% divorced (2005-2009 5-year est.); Foreign born: 5.4% (2005-2009 5-year est.); Ancestry (includes multiple ancestries): 32.5% German, 15.8% Irish, 11.0% English, 10.9% Italian, 7.8% Polish (2005-2009 5-year est.).
Economy: Single-family building permits issued: 42 (2010); Multi-family building permits issued: 6 (2010); Employment by occupation: 14.4% management, 20.4% professional, 16.4% services, 27.5% sales, 0.3% farming, 8.1% construction, 12.8% production (2005-2009 5-year est.).
Income: Per capita income: $31,233 (2010); Median household income: $76,561 (2010); Average household income: $87,495 (2010); Percent of households with income of $100,000 or more: 30.6% (2010); Poverty rate: 2.6% (2005-2009 5-year est.).
Taxes: Total city taxes per capita: $746 (2007); City property taxes per capita: $155 (2007).
Education: Percent of population age 25 and over with: High school diploma (including GED) or higher: 94.4% (2010); Bachelor's degree or higher: 29.9% (2010); Master's degree or higher: 10.4% (2010).
School District(s)
Grundy/Kendall Roe (06-12)
    2009-10 Enrollment: n/a .... (815) 941-3247
Yorkville CUSD 115 (PK-12)
    2009-10 Enrollment: 5,119 .... (630) 553-4382

Housing: Homeownership rate: 81.3% (2010); Median home value: $235,879 (2010); Median contract rent: $789 per month (2005-2009 5-year est.); Median year structure built: 1999 (2005-2009 5-year est.).
Safety: Violent crime rate: 9.9 per 10,000 population; Property crime rate: 117.7 per 10,000 population (2010).
Newspapers: Fox Valley Shopping News (Local news; Circulation 35,000); Kendall County Record (Community news; Circulation 4,650); Plano Record (Community news; Circulation 1,400); Sandwich Record (Community news; Circulation 4,950)
Transportation: Commute to work: 93.9% car, 0.8% public transportation, 0.5% walk, 4.8% work from home (2005-2009 5-year est.); Travel time to work: 19.5% less than 15 minutes, 23.6% 15 to 30 minutes, 26.3% 30 to 45 minutes, 15.0% 45 to 60 minutes, 15.5% 60 minutes or more (2005-2009 5-year est.)
Additional Information Contacts
United City of Yorkville........................... (630) 553-4350
    http://www.yorkville.il.us
Yorkville Area Chamber of Commerce .... (630) 553-6853
    http://www.yorkvillechamber.org

Knox County

Located in northwest central Illinois; drained by the Spoon River and Pope and Henderson Creeks. Covers a land area of 716.28 square miles, a water area of 3.42 square miles, and is located in the Central Time Zone at 40.94° N. Lat., 90.29° W. Long. The county was founded in 1825. County seat is Galesburg.

Knox County is part of the Galesburg, IL Micropolitan Statistical Area. The entire metro area includes: Knox County, IL; Warren County, IL

Weather Station: Galesburg   Elevation: 770 feet

	Jan	Feb	Mar	Apr	May	Jun	Jul	Aug	Sep	Oct	Nov	Dec
High	31	36	49	62	73	81	85	83	76	63	49	34
Low	16	20	30	41	52	61	66	64	55	43	32	20
Precip	1.5	1.6	2.7	3.7	4.3	4.0	4.3	4.2	3.5	2.7	2.9	2.4
Snow	7.4	5.2	2.0	1.3	tr	0.0	0.0	0.0	0.0	tr	0.8	6.0

High and Low temperatures in degrees Fahrenheit; Precipitation and Snow in inches

Population: 56,393 (1990); 55,836 (2000); 51,389 (2010); 49,140 (2015 projected); Race: 87.9% White, 7.1% Black, 1.0% Asian, 4.0% Other, 4.1% Hispanic of any race (2010); Density: 71.7 persons per square mile (2010); Average household size: 2.29 (2010); Median age: 40.6 (2010); Males per 100 females: 100.6 (2010).
Religion: Five largest groups: 10.4% Catholic Church, 7.0% The United Methodist Church, 5.6% Evangelical Lutheran Church in America, 3.0% Christian Church (Disciples of Christ), 2.5% Presbyterian Church (U.S.A.) (2000).
Economy: Unemployment rate: 8.5% (August 2011); Total civilian labor force: 26,031 (August 2011); Leading industries: 24.4% health care and social assistance; 21.9% retail trade; 11.5% accommodation & food services (2009); Farms: 904 totaling 362,951 acres (2007); Companies that employ 500 or more persons: 2 (2009); Companies that employ 100 to 499 persons: 24 (2009); Companies that employ less than 100 persons: 1,117 (2009); Black-owned businesses: n/a (2007); Hispanic-owned businesses: n/a (2007); Asian-owned businesses: n/a (2007); Women-owned businesses: 1,066 (2007); Retail sales per capita: $14,562 (2010). Single-family building permits issued: 7 (2010); Multi-family building permits issued: 0 (2010).
Income: Per capita income: $20,279 (2010); Median household income: $39,823 (2010); Average household income: $49,013 (2010); Percent of households with income of $100,000 or more: 7.7% (2010); Poverty rate: 13.2% (2009); Bankruptcy rate: 5.43% (2010).
Taxes: Total county taxes per capita: $138 (2007); County property taxes per capita: $121 (2007).
Education: Percent of population age 25 and over with: High school diploma (including GED) or higher: 84.6% (2010); Bachelor's degree or higher: 14.9% (2010); Master's degree or higher: 4.6% (2010).
Housing: Homeownership rate: 67.2% (2010); Median home value: $75,376 (2010); Median contract rent: $369 per month (2005-2009 5-year est.); Median year structure built: 1954 (2005-2009 5-year est.).
Health: Birth rate: 113.1 per 10,000 population (2009); Death rate: 127.4 per 10,000 population (2009); Age-adjusted cancer mortality rate: 225.1 deaths per 100,000 population (2007); Number of physicians: 18.9 per 10,000 population (2008); Hospital beds: 47.9 per 10,000 population (2007); Hospital admissions: 1,966.6 per 10,000 population (2007).

Elections: 2008 Presidential election results: 59.2% Obama, 39.3% McCain, 0.8% Nader

National and State Parks: Snakeden Hollow State Fish and Wildlife Area

Additional Information Contacts

Knox County Government . . . . (309) 343-3121
    http://www.co.knox.il.us

City of Galesburg . . . . (309) 343-4181
    http://www.ci.galesburg.il.us

Galesburg Area Chamber of Commerce . . . . (309) 343-1194
    http://www.galesburg.org

Knox County Communities

ABINGDON (city). Covers a land area of 1.459 square miles and a water area of 0 square miles. Located at 40.80° N. Lat; 90.40° W. Long. Elevation is 751 feet.

History: Incorporated 1857.

Population: 3,685 (1990); 3,612 (2000); 3,088 (2010); 2,885 (2015 projected); Race: 97.7% White, 0.6% Black, 0.1% Asian, 1.6% Other, 1.2% Hispanic of any race (2010); Density: 2,116.1 persons per square mile (2010); Average household size: 2.41 (2010); Median age: 40.9 (2010); Males per 100 females: 92.3 (2010); Marriage status: 16.3% never married, 53.6% now married, 14.1% widowed, 16.0% divorced (2005-2009 5-year est.); Foreign born: 0.0% (2005-2009 5-year est.); Ancestry (includes multiple ancestries): 32.9% German, 15.5% Irish, 13.6% English, 11.3% Swedish, 9.9% American (2005-2009 5-year est.).

Economy: Single-family building permits issued: 1 (2010); Multi-family building permits issued: 0 (2010); Employment by occupation: 11.8% management, 13.0% professional, 16.2% services, 25.3% sales, 0.0% farming, 6.4% construction, 27.3% production (2005-2009 5-year est.).

Income: Per capita income: $19,542 (2010); Median household income: $41,987 (2010); Average household income: $47,152 (2010); Percent of households with income of $100,000 or more: 6.0% (2010); Poverty rate: 14.4% (2005-2009 5-year est.).

Taxes: Total city taxes per capita: $69 (2007); City property taxes per capita: $65 (2007).

Education: Percent of population age 25 and over with: High school diploma (including GED) or higher: 84.3% (2010); Bachelor's degree or higher: 8.4% (2010); Master's degree or higher: 2.2% (2010).

School District(s)

Abingdon CUSD 217 (PK-12)
    2009-10 Enrollment: 779 . . . . (309) 462-2301

Housing: Homeownership rate: 75.7% (2010); Median home value: $62,414 (2010); Median contract rent: $307 per month (2005-2009 5-year est.); Median year structure built: 1946 (2005-2009 5-year est.).

Newspapers: Abingdon Argus (Community news; Circulation 2,050); Avon Sentinel (Community news; Circulation 850)

Transportation: Commute to work: 95.6% car, 0.0% public transportation, 0.6% walk, 2.2% work from home (2005-2009 5-year est.); Travel time to work: 37.6% less than 15 minutes, 42.6% 15 to 30 minutes, 7.8% 30 to 45 minutes, 2.2% 45 to 60 minutes, 9.8% 60 minutes or more (2005-2009 5-year est.)

ALTONA (village). Covers a land area of 1.016 square miles and a water area of 0 square miles. Located at 41.11° N. Lat; 90.16° W. Long. Elevation is 761 feet.

Population: 559 (1990); 570 (2000); 530 (2010); 510 (2015 projected); Race: 99.1% White, 0.0% Black, 0.2% Asian, 0.8% Other, 0.6% Hispanic of any race (2010); Density: 521.4 persons per square mile (2010); Average household size: 2.62 (2010); Median age: 39.3 (2010); Males per 100 females: 97.0 (2010); Marriage status: 24.2% never married, 59.2% now married, 9.5% widowed, 7.1% divorced (2005-2009 5-year est.); Foreign born: 0.9% (2005-2009 5-year est.); Ancestry (includes multiple ancestries): 27.1% German, 23.1% Swedish, 17.7% Dutch, 15.3% Irish, 7.8% English (2005-2009 5-year est.).

Economy: Employment by occupation: 7.2% management, 17.0% professional, 19.2% services, 25.3% sales, 0.0% farming, 5.7% construction, 25.7% production (2005-2009 5-year est.).

Income: Per capita income: $16,724 (2010); Median household income: $39,800 (2010); Average household income: $43,540 (2010); Percent of households with income of $100,000 or more: 3.0% (2010); Poverty rate: 8.9% (2005-2009 5-year est.).

Taxes: Total city taxes per capita: $43 (2007); City property taxes per capita: $37 (2007).

Education: Percent of population age 25 and over with: High school diploma (including GED) or higher: 89.0% (2010); Bachelor's degree or higher: 13.3% (2010); Master's degree or higher: 1.2% (2010).

School District(s)

R O W V a CUSD 208 (PK-12)
    2009-10 Enrollment: 743 . . . . (309) 483-3711

Housing: Homeownership rate: 80.7% (2010); Median home value: $67,073 (2010); Median contract rent: $404 per month (2005-2009 5-year est.); Median year structure built: 1944 (2005-2009 5-year est.).

Transportation: Commute to work: 92.5% car, 0.0% public transportation, 1.1% walk, 6.4% work from home (2005-2009 5-year est.); Travel time to work: 12.1% less than 15 minutes, 59.3% 15 to 30 minutes, 23.4% 30 to 45 minutes, 1.2% 45 to 60 minutes, 4.0% 60 minutes or more (2005-2009 5-year est.)

DAHINDA (unincorporated postal area, zip code 61428). Covers a land area of 33.362 square miles and a water area of 0.953 square miles. Located at 40.95° N. Lat; 90.12° W. Long. Elevation is 584 feet.

Population: 954 (2000); Race: 97.2% White, 0.0% Black, 0.0% Asian, 2.8% Other, 1.8% Hispanic of any race (2000); Density: 28.6 persons per square mile (2000); Age: 17.1% under 18, 21.7% over 64 (2000); Marriage status: 15.6% never married, 75.3% now married, 3.8% widowed, 5.3% divorced (2000); Foreign born: 2.2% (2000); Ancestry (includes multiple ancestries): 24.4% English, 19.5% German, 16.9% Irish, 13.5% American, 7.1% Swedish (2000).

Economy: Employment by occupation: 12.1% management, 17.5% professional, 8.8% services, 26.5% sales, 0.0% farming, 16.3% construction, 18.8% production (2000).

Income: Per capita income: $23,532 (2000); Median household income: $46,188 (2000); Poverty rate: 5.2% (2000).

Education: Percent of population age 25 and over with: High school diploma (including GED) or higher: 89.8% (2000); Bachelor's degree or higher: 17.8% (2000).

Housing: Homeownership rate: 89.8% (2000); Median home value: $92,900 (2000); Median contract rent: $355 per month (2000); Median year structure built: 1978 (2000).

Transportation: Commute to work: 96.7% car, 0.0% public transportation, 1.5% walk, 1.9% work from home (2000); Travel time to work: 12.8% less than 15 minutes, 36.6% 15 to 30 minutes, 31.1% 30 to 45 minutes, 8.9% 45 to 60 minutes, 10.6% 60 minutes or more (2000)

EAST GALESBURG (village). Covers a land area of 1.460 square miles and a water area of 0.051 square miles. Located at 40.94° N. Lat; 90.31° W. Long. Elevation is 774 feet.

Population: 887 (1990); 839 (2000); 663 (2010); 622 (2015 projected); Race: 96.4% White, 0.8% Black, 0.5% Asian, 2.4% Other, 2.1% Hispanic of any race (2010); Density: 454.1 persons per square mile (2010); Average household size: 2.12 (2010); Median age: 45.5 (2010); Males per 100 females: 93.9 (2010); Marriage status: 16.5% never married, 62.0% now married, 7.3% widowed, 14.2% divorced (2005-2009 5-year est.); Foreign born: 0.0% (2005-2009 5-year est.); Ancestry (includes multiple ancestries): 24.6% German, 16.2% English, 14.3% Irish, 11.7% Swedish, 7.6% American (2005-2009 5-year est.).

Economy: Single-family building permits issued: 1 (2010); Multi-family building permits issued: 0 (2010); Employment by occupation: 11.3% management, 19.6% professional, 18.4% services, 19.3% sales, 0.0% farming, 8.6% construction, 22.8% production (2005-2009 5-year est.).

Income: Per capita income: $32,560 (2010); Median household income: $48,856 (2010); Average household income: $68,522 (2010); Percent of households with income of $100,000 or more: 15.0% (2010); Poverty rate: 8.7% (2005-2009 5-year est.).

Taxes: Total city taxes per capita: $112 (2007); City property taxes per capita: $62 (2007).

Education: Percent of population age 25 and over with: High school diploma (including GED) or higher: 86.9% (2010); Bachelor's degree or higher: 22.5% (2010); Master's degree or higher: 8.2% (2010).

Housing: Homeownership rate: 57.5% (2010); Median home value: $81,429 (2010); Median contract rent: $362 per month (2005-2009 5-year est.); Median year structure built: 1965 (2005-2009 5-year est.).

Transportation: Commute to work: 95.8% car, 0.0% public transportation, 0.0% walk, 2.7% work from home (2005-2009 5-year est.); Travel time to work: 34.5% less than 15 minutes, 42.9% 15 to 30 minutes, 8.7% 30 to 45 minutes, 4.7% 45 to 60 minutes, 9.3% 60 minutes or more (2005-2009 5-year est.)

GALESBURG (city). County seat. Covers a land area of 16.896 square miles and a water area of 0.178 square miles. Located at 40.95° N. Lat; 90.36° W. Long. Elevation is 771 feet.

History: Galesburg was settled in 1836 on a site selected by an advance guard sent by Reverend George Washington Gale, a Presbyterian minister from New York who planned a town where morality and industry would rule. Among the early residents was the Ferris family, one of whom invented the ferris wheel, first shown at the Columbian Exposition in Chicago in 1893. Formerly Randall.

Population: 33,637 (1990); 33,706 (2000); 30,959 (2010); 29,569 (2015 projected); Race: 81.7% White, 11.2% Black, 1.4% Asian, 5.7% Other, 5.8% Hispanic of any race (2010); Density: 1,832.3 persons per square mile (2010); Average household size: 2.21 (2010); Median age: 38.9 (2010); Males per 100 females: 102.6 (2010); Marriage status: 34.0% never married, 44.5% now married, 8.0% widowed, 13.4% divorced (2005-2009 5-year est.); Foreign born: 2.9% (2005-2009 5-year est.); Ancestry (includes multiple ancestries): 20.0% German, 13.9% Irish, 11.5% English, 9.0% Swedish, 8.2% American (2005-2009 5-year est.).

Economy: Unemployment rate: 9.2% (August 2011); Total civilian labor force: 14,970 (August 2011); Single-family building permits issued: 0 (2010); Multi-family building permits issued: 0 (2010); Employment by occupation: 9.7% management, 17.3% professional, 22.5% services, 26.9% sales, 0.2% farming, 6.5% construction, 16.8% production (2005-2009 5-year est.).

Income: Per capita income: $18,570 (2010); Median household income: $34,536 (2010); Average household income: $44,583 (2010); Percent of households with income of $100,000 or more: 6.5% (2010); Poverty rate: 20.9% (2005-2009 5-year est.).

Taxes: Total city taxes per capita: $361 (2007); City property taxes per capita: $218 (2007).

Education: Percent of population age 25 and over with: High school diploma (including GED) or higher: 82.5% (2010); Bachelor's degree or higher: 15.2% (2010); Master's degree or higher: 5.3% (2010).

School District(s)

Galesburg Area Voc Ctr (11-12)
    2009-10 Enrollment: n/a . . . . (309) 343-3733
Galesburg CUSD 205 (PK-12)
    2009-10 Enrollment: 4,879 . . . . (309) 343-1151
Knox Roe (07-12)
    2009-10 Enrollment: n/a . . . . (309) 345-3832
Knox-Warren Spec Educ District (06-12)
    2009-10 Enrollment: n/a . . . . (309) 343-2143

Four-year College(s)

Knox College (Private, Not-for-profit)
    Fall 2009 Enrollment: 1,407. . . . . (309) 341-7000
    2010-11 Tuition: In-state $33,024; Out-of-state $33,024

Two-year College(s)

Carl Sandburg College (Public)
    Fall 2009 Enrollment: 2,661. . . . . (309) 344-2518
    2010-11 Tuition: In-state $5,265; Out-of-state $6,750

Housing: Homeownership rate: 60.1% (2010); Median home value: $68,515 (2010); Median contract rent: $372 per month (2005-2009 5-year est.); Median year structure built: 1952 (2005-2009 5-year est.).

Hospitals: Galesburg Cottage Hospital (170 beds); OSF St Mary Medical Center (156 beds)

Newspapers: Extra (Community news; Circulation 16,000); Galesburg Register-Mail (Local news; Circulation 17,948); Knoxville Journal - Galesburg Bureau (Local news); The Zephyr (Community news; Circulation 2,000)

Transportation: Commute to work: 89.2% car, 1.3% public transportation, 5.6% walk, 2.9% work from home (2005-2009 5-year est.); Travel time to work: 65.2% less than 15 minutes, 20.8% 15 to 30 minutes, 3.7% 30 to 45 minutes, 5.6% 45 to 60 minutes, 4.8% 60 minutes or more (2005-2009 5-year est.); Amtrak: train service available.

Airports: Galesburg Municipal (general aviation)

Additional Information Contacts

City of Galesburg . . . . (309) 343-4181
    http://www.ci.galesburg.il.us
Galesburg Area Chamber of Commerce . . . . (309) 343-1194
    http://www.galesburg.org

GILSON (unincorporated postal area, zip code 61436). Covers a land area of 64.363 square miles and a water area of 0.015 square miles. Located at 40.86° N. Lat; 90.22° W. Long. Elevation is 679 feet.

Population: 1,021 (2000); Race: 99.2% White, 0.0% Black, 0.8% Asian, 0.0% Other, 0.0% Hispanic of any race (2000); Density: 15.9 persons per square mile (2000); Age: 23.4% under 18, 12.6% over 64 (2000); Marriage status: 14.5% never married, 74.9% now married, 3.8% widowed, 6.8% divorced (2000); Foreign born: 0.8% (2000); Ancestry (includes multiple ancestries): 27.4% German, 17.5% American, 17.3% English, 15.6% Swedish, 9.3% Irish (2000).

Economy: Employment by occupation: 12.9% management, 5.1% professional, 11.6% services, 21.3% sales, 5.3% farming, 5.1% construction, 38.7% production (2000).

Income: Per capita income: $19,092 (2000); Median household income: $44,000 (2000); Poverty rate: 1.5% (2000).

Education: Percent of population age 25 and over with: High school diploma (including GED) or higher: 88.3% (2000); Bachelor's degree or higher: 8.7% (2000).

Housing: Homeownership rate: 87.1% (2000); Median home value: $68,400 (2000); Median contract rent: $211 per month (2000); Median year structure built: before 1940 (2000).

Transportation: Commute to work: 89.2% car, 0.0% public transportation, 0.0% walk, 9.7% work from home (2000); Travel time to work: 19.1% less than 15 minutes, 57.1% 15 to 30 minutes, 15.1% 30 to 45 minutes, 4.0% 45 to 60 minutes, 4.6% 60 minutes or more (2000)

HENDERSON (village). Aka Soperville. Covers a land area of 0.272 square miles and a water area of 0 square miles. Located at 41.02° N. Lat; 90.35° W. Long. Elevation is 817 feet.

Population: 290 (1990); 319 (2000); 285 (2010); 267 (2015 projected); Race: 98.2% White, 0.4% Black, 0.4% Asian, 1.1% Other, 1.4% Hispanic of any race (2010); Density: 1,047.4 persons per square mile (2010); Average household size: 2.36 (2010); Median age: 48.1 (2010); Males per 100 females: 109.6 (2010); Marriage status: 12.9% never married, 68.2% now married, 9.4% widowed, 9.4% divorced (2005-2009 5-year est.); Foreign born: 0.7% (2005-2009 5-year est.); Ancestry (includes multiple ancestries): 20.8% German, 18.8% Swedish, 17.7% Irish, 13.5% English, 5.9% Dutch (2005-2009 5-year est.).

Economy: Employment by occupation: 9.0% management, 33.1% professional, 3.8% services, 14.3% sales, 0.0% farming, 12.0% construction, 27.8% production (2005-2009 5-year est.).

Income: Per capita income: $31,578 (2010); Median household income: $51,500 (2010); Average household income: $75,517 (2010); Percent of households with income of $100,000 or more: 18.2% (2010); Poverty rate: 3.5% (2005-2009 5-year est.).

Taxes: Total city taxes per capita: $60 (2007); City property taxes per capita: $60 (2007).

Education: Percent of population age 25 and over with: High school diploma (including GED) or higher: 90.2% (2010); Bachelor's degree or higher: 19.6% (2010); Master's degree or higher: 6.1% (2010).

Housing: Homeownership rate: 82.6% (2010); Median home value: $91,000 (2010); Median contract rent: n/a per month (2005-2009 5-year est.); Median year structure built: 1972 (2005-2009 5-year est.).

Transportation: Commute to work: 98.4% car, 0.0% public transportation, 0.0% walk, 1.6% work from home (2005-2009 5-year est.); Travel time to work: 30.9% less than 15 minutes, 43.9% 15 to 30 minutes, 1.6% 30 to 45 minutes, 11.4% 45 to 60 minutes, 12.2% 60 minutes or more (2005-2009 5-year est.)

KNOXVILLE (city). Covers a land area of 2.198 square miles and a water area of 0 square miles. Located at 40.90° N. Lat; 90.28° W. Long. Elevation is 781 feet.

History: Incorporated 1832. Formerly the county seat.

Population: 3,244 (1990); 3,183 (2000); 2,856 (2010); 2,693 (2015 projected); Race: 97.7% White, 0.5% Black, 0.1% Asian, 1.8% Other, 1.0% Hispanic of any race (2010); Density: 1,299.2 persons per square mile (2010); Average household size: 2.40 (2010); Median age: 43.7 (2010); Males per 100 females: 87.8 (2010); Marriage status: 20.3% never married, 62.3% now married, 9.9% widowed, 7.5% divorced (2005-2009 5-year est.); Foreign born: 0.3% (2005-2009 5-year est.); Ancestry (includes multiple ancestries): 31.1% German, 18.4% Swedish, 17.5% Irish, 16.1% English, 7.7% American (2005-2009 5-year est.).

Economy: Single-family building permits issued: 4 (2010); Multi-family building permits issued: 0 (2010); Employment by occupation: 12.9% management, 18.7% professional, 16.7% services, 27.6% sales, 0.0% farming, 6.4% construction, 17.6% production (2005-2009 5-year est.).

Income: Per capita income: $22,225 (2010); Median household income: $49,092 (2010); Average household income: $54,529 (2010); Percent of

households with income of $100,000 or more: 8.7% (2010); Poverty rate: 10.0% (2005-2009 5-year est.).
Taxes: Total city taxes per capita: $153 (2007); City property taxes per capita: $115 (2007).
Education: Percent of population age 25 and over with: High school diploma (including GED) or higher: 85.4% (2010); Bachelor's degree or higher: 14.3% (2010); Master's degree or higher: 3.5% (2010).

School District(s)
Knoxville CUSD 202 (PK-12)
    2009-10 Enrollment: 1,108 . . . . (309) 289-2328
Housing: Homeownership rate: 79.4% (2010); Median home value: $87,182 (2010); Median contract rent: $347 per month (2005-2009 5-year est.); Median year structure built: 1961 (2005-2009 5-year est.).
Safety: Violent crime rate: 3.5 per 10,000 population; Property crime rate: 202.8 per 10,000 population (2010).
Transportation: Commute to work: 96.6% car, 1.6% public transportation, 0.0% walk, 1.8% work from home (2005-2009 5-year est.); Travel time to work: 50.7% less than 15 minutes, 29.3% 15 to 30 minutes, 2.8% 30 to 45 minutes, 11.8% 45 to 60 minutes, 5.5% 60 minutes or more (2005-2009 5-year est.)

MAQUON (village). Covers a land area of 0.161 square miles and a water area of 0 square miles. Located at 40.79° N. Lat; 90.16° W. Long. Elevation is 633 feet.
Population: 331 (1990); 318 (2000); 288 (2010); 275 (2015 projected); Race: 98.3% White, 0.0% Black, 0.7% Asian, 1.0% Other, 2.8% Hispanic of any race (2010); Density: 1,785.4 persons per square mile (2010); Average household size: 2.27 (2010); Median age: 40.0 (2010); Males per 100 females: 89.5 (2010); Marriage status: 21.7% never married, 53.7% now married, 10.0% widowed, 14.6% divorced (2005-2009 5-year est.); Foreign born: 0.0% (2005-2009 5-year est.); Ancestry (includes multiple ancestries): 23.1% German, 16.8% Irish, 13.8% English, 12.6% American, 7.8% French (2005-2009 5-year est.).
Economy: Single-family building permits issued: 0 (2010); Multi-family building permits issued: 0 (2010); Employment by occupation: 5.2% management, 16.3% professional, 24.4% services, 17.4% sales, 0.0% farming, 8.1% construction, 28.5% production (2005-2009 5-year est.).
Income: Per capita income: $19,757 (2010); Median household income: $39,662 (2010); Average household income: $44,902 (2010); Percent of households with income of $100,000 or more: 5.5% (2010); Poverty rate: 12.9% (2005-2009 5-year est.).
Taxes: Total city taxes per capita: $47 (2007); City property taxes per capita: $44 (2007).
Education: Percent of population age 25 and over with: High school diploma (including GED) or higher: 87.0% (2010); Bachelor's degree or higher: 10.9% (2010); Master's degree or higher: 2.1% (2010).
Housing: Homeownership rate: 74.0% (2010); Median home value: $63,158 (2010); Median contract rent: $263 per month (2005-2009 5-year est.); Median year structure built: before 1940 (2005-2009 5-year est.).
Transportation: Commute to work: 90.1% car, 0.0% public transportation, 0.6% walk, 9.3% work from home (2005-2009 5-year est.); Travel time to work: 15.1% less than 15 minutes, 30.1% 15 to 30 minutes, 10.3% 30 to 45 minutes, 27.4% 45 to 60 minutes, 17.1% 60 minutes or more (2005-2009 5-year est.)

ONEIDA (city). Covers a land area of 0.726 square miles and a water area of 0 square miles. Located at 41.07° N. Lat; 90.22° W. Long. Elevation is 814 feet.
Population: 723 (1990); 752 (2000); 719 (2010); 691 (2015 projected); Race: 97.2% White, 0.0% Black, 1.1% Asian, 1.7% Other, 2.2% Hispanic of any race (2010); Density: 990.4 persons per square mile (2010); Average household size: 2.50 (2010); Median age: 39.1 (2010); Males per 100 females: 98.1 (2010); Marriage status: 17.2% never married, 60.4% now married, 10.1% widowed, 12.3% divorced (2005-2009 5-year est.); Foreign born: 0.0% (2005-2009 5-year est.); Ancestry (includes multiple ancestries): 26.8% Irish, 20.0% German, 16.8% Swedish, 12.0% English, 9.6% American (2005-2009 5-year est.).
Economy: Employment by occupation: 7.9% management, 21.5% professional, 13.6% services, 23.7% sales, 0.0% farming, 15.2% construction, 18.0% production (2005-2009 5-year est.).
Income: Per capita income: $21,054 (2010); Median household income: $48,529 (2010); Average household income: $52,639 (2010); Percent of households with income of $100,000 or more: 8.3% (2010); Poverty rate: 10.8% (2005-2009 5-year est.).

Taxes: Total city taxes per capita: $53 (2007); City property taxes per capita: $53 (2007).
Education: Percent of population age 25 and over with: High school diploma (including GED) or higher: 94.1% (2010); Bachelor's degree or higher: 21.2% (2010); Master's degree or higher: 7.1% (2010).

School District(s)
R O W V a CUSD 208 (PK-12)
    2009-10 Enrollment: 743 . . . . (309) 483-3711
Housing: Homeownership rate: 71.9% (2010); Median home value: $75,283 (2010); Median contract rent: $442 per month (2005-2009 5-year est.); Median year structure built: 1954 (2005-2009 5-year est.).
Transportation: Commute to work: 95.6% car, 0.0% public transportation, 2.8% walk, 1.6% work from home (2005-2009 5-year est.); Travel time to work: 32.8% less than 15 minutes, 37.0% 15 to 30 minutes, 9.3% 30 to 45 minutes, 10.6% 45 to 60 minutes, 10.3% 60 minutes or more (2005-2009 5-year est.)

RIO (village). Covers a land area of 0.325 square miles and a water area of 0 square miles. Located at 41.11° N. Lat; 90.39° W. Long. Elevation is 778 feet.
Population: 260 (1990); 240 (2000); 227 (2010); 218 (2015 projected); Race: 98.7% White, 0.0% Black, 0.0% Asian, 1.3% Other, 2.2% Hispanic of any race (2010); Density: 697.7 persons per square mile (2010); Average household size: 2.61 (2010); Median age: 40.7 (2010); Males per 100 females: 99.1 (2010); Marriage status: 17.6% never married, 66.9% now married, 6.8% widowed, 8.8% divorced (2005-2009 5-year est.); Foreign born: 0.0% (2005-2009 5-year est.); Ancestry (includes multiple ancestries): 40.4% German, 23.3% Swedish, 17.6% English, 16.1% Irish, 8.3% Italian (2005-2009 5-year est.).
Economy: Employment by occupation: 21.5% management, 10.8% professional, 11.8% services, 23.7% sales, 0.0% farming, 10.8% construction, 21.5% production (2005-2009 5-year est.).
Income: Per capita income: $21,610 (2010); Median household income: $52,734 (2010); Average household income: $57,184 (2010); Percent of households with income of $100,000 or more: 3.4% (2010); Poverty rate: 3.7% (2005-2009 5-year est.).
Taxes: Total city taxes per capita: $39 (2007); City property taxes per capita: $39 (2007).
Education: Percent of population age 25 and over with: High school diploma (including GED) or higher: 92.1% (2010); Bachelor's degree or higher: 23.2% (2010); Master's degree or higher: 2.0% (2010).
Housing: Homeownership rate: 77.0% (2010); Median home value: $93,125 (2010); Median contract rent: n/a per month (2005-2009 5-year est.); Median year structure built: 1961 (2005-2009 5-year est.).
Transportation: Commute to work: 96.8% car, 0.0% public transportation, 3.2% walk, 0.0% work from home (2005-2009 5-year est.); Travel time to work: 21.5% less than 15 minutes, 50.5% 15 to 30 minutes, 15.1% 30 to 45 minutes, 7.5% 45 to 60 minutes, 5.4% 60 minutes or more (2005-2009 5-year est.)

SAINT AUGUSTINE (village). Covers a land area of 0.615 square miles and a water area of 0 square miles. Located at 40.72° N. Lat; 90.41° W. Long. Elevation is 643 feet.
Population: 151 (1990); 152 (2000); 130 (2010); 121 (2015 projected); Race: 97.7% White, 0.0% Black, 0.0% Asian, 2.3% Other, 0.8% Hispanic of any race (2010); Density: 211.4 persons per square mile (2010); Average household size: 2.36 (2010); Median age: 40.8 (2010); Males per 100 females: 88.4 (2010); Marriage status: 18.9% never married, 56.6% now married, 11.3% widowed, 13.2% divorced (2005-2009 5-year est.); Foreign born: 0.0% (2005-2009 5-year est.); Ancestry (includes multiple ancestries): 21.8% American, 14.5% German, 12.7% Swedish, 11.8% English, 7.3% Irish (2005-2009 5-year est.).
Economy: Single-family building permits issued: 0 (2010); Multi-family building permits issued: 0 (2010); Employment by occupation: 19.3% management, 0.0% professional, 31.6% services, 22.8% sales, 0.0% farming, 7.0% construction, 19.3% production (2005-2009 5-year est.).
Income: Per capita income: $19,826 (2010); Median household income: $43,500 (2010); Average household income: $46,136 (2010); Percent of households with income of $100,000 or more: 3.6% (2010); Poverty rate: 12.7% (2005-2009 5-year est.).
Taxes: Total city taxes per capita: $14 (2007); City property taxes per capita: $7 (2007).
Education: Percent of population age 25 and over with: High school diploma (including GED) or higher: 82.0% (2010); Bachelor's degree or higher: 4.5% (2010); Master's degree or higher: 0.0% (2010).

Housing: Homeownership rate: 80.0% (2010); Median home value: $55,385 (2010); Median contract rent: n/a per month (2005-2009 5-year est.); Median year structure built: 1952 (2005-2009 5-year est.).
Transportation: Commute to work: 96.4% car, 0.0% public transportation, 3.6% walk, 0.0% work from home (2005-2009 5-year est.); Travel time to work: 32.7% less than 15 minutes, 30.9% 15 to 30 minutes, 21.8% 30 to 45 minutes, 9.1% 45 to 60 minutes, 5.5% 60 minutes or more (2005-2009 5-year est.)

VICTORIA (village).
Covers a land area of 0.663 square miles and a water area of 0 square miles. Located at 41.03° N. Lat; 90.09° W. Long. Elevation is 833 feet.
Population: 315 (1990); 323 (2000); 322 (2010); 318 (2015 projected); Race: 99.1% White, 0.0% Black, 0.0% Asian, 0.9% Other, 0.9% Hispanic of any race (2010); Density: 485.4 persons per square mile (2010); Average household size: 2.60 (2010); Median age: 40.3 (2010); Males per 100 females: 102.5 (2010); Marriage status: 18.3% never married, 58.8% now married, 9.3% widowed, 13.6% divorced (2005-2009 5-year est.); Foreign born: 0.0% (2005-2009 5-year est.); Ancestry (includes multiple ancestries): 27.0% Irish, 24.2% German, 19.2% English, 12.9% Swedish, 10.1% American (2005-2009 5-year est.).
Economy: Single-family building permits issued: 0 (2010); Multi-family building permits issued: 0 (2010); Employment by occupation: 13.2% management, 1.4% professional, 18.8% services, 24.3% sales, 4.2% farming, 18.8% construction, 19.4% production (2005-2009 5-year est.).
Income: Per capita income: $15,836 (2010); Median household income: $33,000 (2010); Average household income: $40,847 (2010); Percent of households with income of $100,000 or more: 4.8% (2010); Poverty rate: 8.2% (2005-2009 5-year est.).
Taxes: Total city taxes per capita: $50 (2007); City property taxes per capita: $47 (2007).
Education: Percent of population age 25 and over with: High school diploma (including GED) or higher: 85.6% (2010); Bachelor's degree or higher: 6.9% (2010); Master's degree or higher: 2.3% (2010).
Housing: Homeownership rate: 73.4% (2010); Median home value: $88,824 (2010); Median contract rent: n/a per month (2005-2009 5-year est.); Median year structure built: before 1940 (2005-2009 5-year est.).
Transportation: Commute to work: 94.8% car, 0.0% public transportation, 1.5% walk, 3.7% work from home (2005-2009 5-year est.); Travel time to work: 19.4% less than 15 minutes, 39.5% 15 to 30 minutes, 33.3% 30 to 45 minutes, 6.2% 45 to 60 minutes, 1.6% 60 minutes or more (2005-2009 5-year est.)

WATAGA (village).
Covers a land area of 0.866 square miles and a water area of 0 square miles. Located at 41.02° N. Lat; 90.27° W. Long. Elevation is 830 feet.
Population: 888 (1990); 857 (2000); 796 (2010); 761 (2015 projected); Race: 97.4% White, 0.4% Black, 0.3% Asian, 2.0% Other, 1.8% Hispanic of any race (2010); Density: 919.1 persons per square mile (2010); Average household size: 2.50 (2010); Median age: 37.4 (2010); Males per 100 females: 88.2 (2010); Marriage status: 15.0% never married, 62.1% now married, 5.0% widowed, 17.9% divorced (2005-2009 5-year est.); Foreign born: 0.0% (2005-2009 5-year est.); Ancestry (includes multiple ancestries): 23.3% Irish, 18.6% German, 11.7% American, 11.3% English, 10.4% Swedish (2005-2009 5-year est.).
Economy: Single-family building permits issued: 1 (2010); Multi-family building permits issued: 0 (2010); Employment by occupation: 5.3% management, 11.8% professional, 19.0% services, 25.8% sales, 0.0% farming, 12.9% construction, 25.2% production (2005-2009 5-year est.).
Income: Per capita income: $20,745 (2010); Median household income: $45,938 (2010); Average household income: $50,893 (2010); Percent of households with income of $100,000 or more: 6.3% (2010); Poverty rate: 21.4% (2005-2009 5-year est.).
Taxes: Total city taxes per capita: $40 (2007); City property taxes per capita: $34 (2007).
Education: Percent of population age 25 and over with: High school diploma (including GED) or higher: 87.2% (2010); Bachelor's degree or higher: 12.2% (2010); Master's degree or higher: 2.4% (2010).
School District(s)
R O W V a CUSD 208 (PK-12)
    2009-10 Enrollment: 743 . . . . (309) 483-3711
Housing: Homeownership rate: 76.5% (2010); Median home value: $70,909 (2010); Median contract rent: $391 per month (2005-2009 5-year est.); Median year structure built: 1971 (2005-2009 5-year est.).

Transportation: Commute to work: 95.2% car, 0.0% public transportation, 0.8% walk, 1.4% work from home (2005-2009 5-year est.); Travel time to work: 30.0% less than 15 minutes, 44.9% 15 to 30 minutes, 10.6% 30 to 45 minutes, 9.4% 45 to 60 minutes, 5.1% 60 minutes or more (2005-2009 5-year est.)

WILLIAMSFIELD (village).
Covers a land area of 1.271 square miles and a water area of 0 square miles. Located at 40.92° N. Lat; 90.01° W. Long. Elevation is 705 feet.
Population: 621 (1990); 620 (2000); 545 (2010); 510 (2015 projected); Race: 98.7% White, 0.0% Black, 0.0% Asian, 1.3% Other, 0.9% Hispanic of any race (2010); Density: 428.9 persons per square mile (2010); Average household size: 2.45 (2010); Median age: 40.1 (2010); Males per 100 females: 99.6 (2010); Marriage status: 22.4% never married, 66.7% now married, 8.4% widowed, 2.5% divorced (2005-2009 5-year est.); Foreign born: 0.6% (2005-2009 5-year est.); Ancestry (includes multiple ancestries): 15.6% German, 11.7% Swedish, 11.4% American, 11.3% English, 7.9% Irish (2005-2009 5-year est.).
Economy: Employment by occupation: 8.9% management, 21.4% professional, 16.3% services, 28.0% sales, 0.0% farming, 9.7% construction, 15.6% production (2005-2009 5-year est.).
Income: Per capita income: $20,993 (2010); Median household income: $46,413 (2010); Average household income: $51,864 (2010); Percent of households with income of $100,000 or more: 5.9% (2010); Poverty rate: 6.9% (2005-2009 5-year est.).
Taxes: Total city taxes per capita: $44 (2007); City property taxes per capita: $37 (2007).
Education: Percent of population age 25 and over with: High school diploma (including GED) or higher: 91.9% (2010); Bachelor's degree or higher: 11.2% (2010); Master's degree or higher: 2.9% (2010).
School District(s)
Williamsfield CUSD 210 (PK-12)
    2009-10 Enrollment: 281 . . . . (309) 639-2219
Housing: Homeownership rate: 81.4% (2010); Median home value: $83,235 (2010); Median contract rent: $300 per month (2005-2009 5-year est.); Median year structure built: 1954 (2005-2009 5-year est.).
Transportation: Commute to work: 93.0% car, 0.0% public transportation, 3.5% walk, 3.5% work from home (2005-2009 5-year est.); Travel time to work: 23.4% less than 15 minutes, 29.4% 15 to 30 minutes, 28.6% 30 to 45 minutes, 10.1% 45 to 60 minutes, 8.5% 60 minutes or more (2005-2009 5-year est.)

YATES CITY (village).
Covers a land area of 0.587 square miles and a water area of 0 square miles. Located at 40.77° N. Lat; 90.01° W. Long. Elevation is 669 feet.
Population: 789 (1990); 725 (2000); 688 (2010); 658 (2015 projected); Race: 98.5% White, 0.7% Black, 0.0% Asian, 0.7% Other, 0.0% Hispanic of any race (2010); Density: 1,172.2 persons per square mile (2010); Average household size: 2.35 (2010); Median age: 40.8 (2010); Males per 100 females: 99.4 (2010); Marriage status: 20.3% never married, 60.5% now married, 7.7% widowed, 11.5% divorced (2005-2009 5-year est.); Foreign born: 0.0% (2005-2009 5-year est.); Ancestry (includes multiple ancestries): 33.1% German, 19.0% English, 16.5% American, 14.4% Irish, 7.9% French (2005-2009 5-year est.).
Economy: Employment by occupation: 12.5% management, 11.7% professional, 18.7% services, 21.3% sales, 0.0% farming, 22.4% construction, 13.3% production (2005-2009 5-year est.).
Income: Per capita income: $21,344 (2010); Median household income: $40,176 (2010); Average household income: $50,597 (2010); Percent of households with income of $100,000 or more: 6.8% (2010); Poverty rate: 6.4% (2005-2009 5-year est.).
Taxes: Total city taxes per capita: $115 (2007); City property taxes per capita: $64 (2007).
Education: Percent of population age 25 and over with: High school diploma (including GED) or higher: 89.0% (2010); Bachelor's degree or higher: 8.7% (2010); Master's degree or higher: 1.9% (2010).
Housing: Homeownership rate: 82.3% (2010); Median home value: $89,194 (2010); Median contract rent: $393 per month (2005-2009 5-year est.); Median year structure built: 1954 (2005-2009 5-year est.).
Transportation: Commute to work: 96.5% car, 0.0% public transportation, 0.8% walk, 2.7% work from home (2005-2009 5-year est.); Travel time to work: 22.3% less than 15 minutes, 12.1% 15 to 30 minutes, 39.1% 30 to 45 minutes, 25.1% 45 to 60 minutes, 1.4% 60 minutes or more (2005-2009 5-year est.)

La Salle County

Located in northern Illinois; drained by the Illinois, Fox, Vermilion, and Little Vermilion Rivers. Covers a land area of 1,134.92 square miles, a water area of 13.12 square miles, and is located in the Central Time Zone at 41.33° N. Lat., 88.90° W. Long. The county was founded in 1831. County seat is Ottawa.

La Salle County is part of the Ottawa-Streator, IL Micropolitan Statistical Area. The entire metro area includes: Bureau County, IL; La Salle County, IL; Putnam County, IL

Population: 106,913 (1990); 111,509 (2000); 112,913 (2010); 113,102 (2015 projected); Race: 93.3% White, 1.7% Black, 0.8% Asian, 4.1% Other, 7.5% Hispanic of any race (2010); Density: 99.5 persons per square mile (2010); Average household size: 2.45 (2010); Median age: 38.8 (2010); Males per 100 females: 97.0 (2010).
Religion: Five largest groups: 40.1% Catholic Church, 6.1% The United Methodist Church, 5.0% Evangelical Lutheran Church in America, 1.4% Presbyterian Church (U.S.A.), 1.3% Church of the Nazarene (2000).
Economy: Unemployment rate: 11.2% (August 2011); Total civilian labor force: 59,202 (August 2011); Leading industries: 17.7% retail trade; 16.1% health care and social assistance; 13.7% manufacturing (2009); Farms: 1,622 totaling 643,291 acres (2007); Companies that employ 500 or more persons: 4 (2009); Companies that employ 100 to 499 persons: 48 (2009); Companies that employ less than 100 persons: 2,797 (2009); Black-owned businesses: n/a (2007); Hispanic-owned businesses: n/a (2007); Asian-owned businesses: 276 (2007); Women-owned businesses: 2,291 (2007); Retail sales per capita: $15,147 (2010). Single-family building permits issued: 69 (2010); Multi-family building permits issued: 8 (2010).
Income: Per capita income: $24,279 (2010); Median household income: $49,427 (2010); Average household income: $60,139 (2010); Percent of households with income of $100,000 or more: 14.2% (2010); Poverty rate: 12.5% (2009); Bankruptcy rate: 6.47% (2010).
Taxes: Total county taxes per capita: $235 (2007); County property taxes per capita: $184 (2007).
Education: Percent of population age 25 and over with: High school diploma (including GED) or higher: 86.9% (2010); Bachelor's degree or higher: 15.7% (2010); Master's degree or higher: 4.7% (2010).
Housing: Homeownership rate: 74.3% (2010); Median home value: $119,437 (2010); Median contract rent: $472 per month (2005-2009 5-year est.); Median year structure built: 1958 (2005-2009 5-year est.)
Health: Birth rate: 131.8 per 10,000 population (2009); Death rate: 110.1 per 10,000 population (2009); Age-adjusted cancer mortality rate: 201.5 deaths per 100,000 population (2007); Number of physicians: 10.8 per 10,000 population (2008); Hospital beds: 29.0 per 10,000 population (2007); Hospital admissions: 1,165.0 per 10,000 population (2007).
Environment: Air Quality Index: 80.0% good, 20.0% moderate, 0.0% unhealthy for sensitive individuals, 0.0% unhealthy (percent of days in 2008)
Elections: 2008 Presidential election results: 54.7% Obama, 43.6% McCain, 0.8% Nader
National and State Parks: Buffalo Rock State Park; Illini State Park; La Salle Lake State Fish and Wildlife Area; Marseilles State Fish and Wildlife Area; Matthiessen State Park; Norwegian Settlers State Memorial; Starved Rock State Park
Additional Information Contacts
La Salle County Government. . . . . (815) 434-8200
  http://www.lasallecounty.org
City of La Salle. . . . . (815) 223-3755
  http://www.lasalle-il.gov
City of Mendota . . . . (815) 539-7459
  http://www.mendota.il.us
City of Ottawa . . . . (815) 433-0161
  http://www.cityofottawa.org
City of Peru . . . . (815) 223-0061
  http://www.peru.il.us
City of Streator. . . . . (815) 672-2517
  http://www.ci.streator.il.us/cms
Illinois River Area Chamber of Commerce. . . . . (815) 795-2323
  http://iracc.org
Illinois Valley Area Chamber of Commerce . . . . (815) 223-0227
  http://www.ivaced.org
Mendota Area Chamber of Commerce . . . . (815) 539-6507
  http://www.mendotachamber.com
Ottawa Area Chamber of Commerce. . . . . (815) 433-0084
  http://www.ottawachamberillinois.com
Streator Area Chamber of Commerce & Industry . . . . (815) 672-2921
  http://www.streatorchamber.com

La Salle County Communities

CEDAR POINT (village). Covers a land area of 1.022 square miles and a water area of 0 square miles. Located at 41.26° N. Lat; 89.12° W. Long. Elevation is 659 feet.
Population: 275 (1990); 262 (2000); 244 (2010); 229 (2015 projected); Race: 95.1% White, 0.4% Black, 2.0% Asian, 2.5% Other, 4.5% Hispanic of any race (2010); Density: 238.7 persons per square mile (2010); Average household size: 2.26 (2010); Median age: 42.9 (2010); Males per 100 females: 87.7 (2010); Marriage status: 21.0% never married, 54.3% now married, 7.8% widowed, 16.9% divorced (2005-2009 5-year est.); Foreign born: 0.0% (2005-2009 5-year est.); Ancestry (includes multiple ancestries): 28.8% German, 24.7% Italian, 14.2% Irish, 12.0% Polish, 11.6% American (2005-2009 5-year est.).
Economy: Single-family building permits issued: 0 (2010); Multi-family building permits issued: 0 (2010); Employment by occupation: 1.3% management, 7.7% professional, 23.1% services, 25.0% sales, 0.0% farming, 7.7% construction, 35.3% production (2005-2009 5-year est.).
Income: Per capita income: $30,336 (2010); Median household income: $56,250 (2010); Average household income: $67,963 (2010); Percent of households with income of $100,000 or more: 16.7% (2010); Poverty rate: 0.4% (2005-2009 5-year est.).
Taxes: Total city taxes per capita: $80 (2007); City property taxes per capita: $76 (2007).
Education: Percent of population age 25 and over with: High school diploma (including GED) or higher: 87.4% (2010); Bachelor's degree or higher: 20.0% (2010); Master's degree or higher: 5.7% (2010).
Housing: Homeownership rate: 76.9% (2010); Median home value: $122,059 (2010); Median contract rent: $441 per month (2005-2009 5-year est.); Median year structure built: 1952 (2005-2009 5-year est.).
Transportation: Commute to work: 98.0% car, 0.0% public transportation, 0.0% walk, 2.0% work from home (2005-2009 5-year est.); Travel time to work: 35.6% less than 15 minutes, 42.5% 15 to 30 minutes, 16.4% 30 to 45 minutes, 4.1% 45 to 60 minutes, 1.4% 60 minutes or more (2005-2009 5-year est.)

DANA (village). Covers a land area of 0.220 square miles and a water area of 0 square miles. Located at 40.95° N. Lat; 88.95° W. Long. Elevation is 669 feet.
Population: 165 (1990); 171 (2000); 175 (2010); 178 (2015 projected); Race: 99.4% White, 0.6% Black, 0.0% Asian, 0.0% Other, 2.3% Hispanic of any race (2010); Density: 796.6 persons per square mile (2010); Average household size: 2.54 (2010); Median age: 37.6 (2010); Males per 100 females: 110.8 (2010); Marriage status: 25.0% never married, 53.0% now married, 15.5% widowed, 6.5% divorced (2005-2009 5-year est.); Foreign born: 0.0% (2005-2009 5-year est.); Ancestry (includes multiple ancestries): 33.2% German, 21.6% American, 16.8% Norwegian, 11.2% Irish, 8.8% English (2005-2009 5-year est.).
Economy: Employment by occupation: 0.0% management, 2.8% professional, 36.4% services, 10.3% sales, 0.0% farming, 14.0% construction, 36.4% production (2005-2009 5-year est.).
Income: Per capita income: $20,129 (2010); Median household income: $41,964 (2010); Average household income: $51,594 (2010); Percent of households with income of $100,000 or more: 11.6% (2010); Poverty rate: 13.2% (2005-2009 5-year est.).
Taxes: Total city taxes per capita: $110 (2007); City property taxes per capita: $46 (2007).
Education: Percent of population age 25 and over with: High school diploma (including GED) or higher: 87.2% (2010); Bachelor's degree or higher: 10.3% (2010); Master's degree or higher: 0.0% (2010).
Housing: Homeownership rate: 81.2% (2010); Median home value: $67,273 (2010); Median contract rent: $189 per month (2005-2009 5-year est.); Median year structure built: 1954 (2005-2009 5-year est.).
Transportation: Commute to work: 92.4% car, 0.0% public transportation, 1.9% walk, 5.7% work from home (2005-2009 5-year est.); Travel time to work: 18.2% less than 15 minutes, 21.2% 15 to 30 minutes, 25.3% 30 to 45 minutes, 19.2% 45 to 60 minutes, 16.2% 60 minutes or more (2005-2009 5-year est.)

EARLVILLE (city). Covers a land area of 1.164 square miles and a water area of 0 square miles. Located at 41.58° N. Lat; 88.92° W. Long. Elevation is 705 feet.

History: Founded c.1854, incorporated 1869.

Population: 1,570 (1990); 1,778 (2000); 1,824 (2010); 1,832 (2015 projected); Race: 96.0% White, 0.2% Black, 0.4% Asian, 3.4% Other, 4.3% Hispanic of any race (2010); Density: 1,566.9 persons per square mile (2010); Average household size: 2.67 (2010); Median age: 35.5 (2010); Males per 100 females: 100.4 (2010); Marriage status: 24.6% never married, 57.1% now married, 5.8% widowed, 12.5% divorced (2005-2009 5-year est.); Foreign born: 1.7% (2005-2009 5-year est.); Ancestry (includes multiple ancestries): 37.0% German, 19.0% Irish, 11.8% English, 10.8% American, 7.0% Norwegian (2005-2009 5-year est.).

Economy: Single-family building permits issued: 0 (2010); Multi-family building permits issued: 0 (2010); Employment by occupation: 5.6% management, 12.0% professional, 17.8% services, 25.0% sales, 0.3% farming, 13.5% construction, 25.8% production (2005-2009 5-year est.).

Income: Per capita income: $22,355 (2010); Median household income: $52,679 (2010); Average household income: $60,000 (2010); Percent of households with income of $100,000 or more: 13.5% (2010); Poverty rate: 11.0% (2005-2009 5-year est.).

Taxes: Total city taxes per capita: $332 (2007); City property taxes per capita: $235 (2007).

Education: Percent of population age 25 and over with: High school diploma (including GED) or higher: 87.8% (2010); Bachelor's degree or higher: 14.2% (2010); Master's degree or higher: 5.0% (2010).

School District(s)

Earlville CUSD 9 (PK-12)

   2009-10 Enrollment: 459 . . . . (815) 246-8361

Serena CUSD 2 (KG-12)

   2009-10 Enrollment: 837 . . . . (815) 496-2850

Housing: Homeownership rate: 75.0% (2010); Median home value: $127,168 (2010); Median contract rent: $521 per month (2005-2009 5-year est.); Median year structure built: 1957 (2005-2009 5-year est.).

Newspapers: Somonauk Reporter (Local news; Circulation 1,000)

Transportation: Commute to work: 89.7% car, 0.3% public transportation, 3.8% walk, 2.7% work from home (2005-2009 5-year est.); Travel time to work: 21.1% less than 15 minutes, 22.1% 15 to 30 minutes, 29.1% 30 to 45 minutes, 13.4% 45 to 60 minutes, 14.3% 60 minutes or more (2005-2009 5-year est.)

GRAND RIDGE (village). Covers a land area of 0.474 square miles and a water area of 0 square miles. Located at 41.23° N. Lat; 88.83° W. Long. Elevation is 643 feet.

Population: 560 (1990); 546 (2000); 533 (2010); 523 (2015 projected); Race: 100.0% White, 0.0% Black, 0.0% Asian, 0.0% Other, 3.6% Hispanic of any race (2010); Density: 1,125.0 persons per square mile (2010); Average household size: 2.60 (2010); Median age: 36.3 (2010); Males per 100 females: 93.1 (2010); Marriage status: 19.0% never married, 66.3% now married, 8.4% widowed, 6.4% divorced (2005-2009 5-year est.); Foreign born: 3.6% (2005-2009 5-year est.); Ancestry (includes multiple ancestries): 40.6% Irish, 27.9% German, 10.8% English, 6.5% Slovak, 5.7% Czech (2005-2009 5-year est.).

Economy: Single-family building permits issued: 0 (2010); Multi-family building permits issued: 0 (2010); Employment by occupation: 8.9% management, 19.3% professional, 14.1% services, 25.9% sales, 0.0% farming, 13.3% construction, 18.5% production (2005-2009 5-year est.).

Income: Per capita income: $24,754 (2010); Median household income: $52,557 (2010); Average household income: $65,768 (2010); Percent of households with income of $100,000 or more: 15.6% (2010); Poverty rate: 4.4% (2005-2009 5-year est.).

Taxes: Total city taxes per capita: $85 (2007); City property taxes per capita: $85 (2007).

Education: Percent of population age 25 and over with: High school diploma (including GED) or higher: 88.8% (2010); Bachelor's degree or higher: 16.3% (2010); Master's degree or higher: 5.3% (2010).

School District(s)

Grand Ridge CCSD 95 (KG-08)

   2009-10 Enrollment: 341 . . . . (815) 249-6225

Housing: Homeownership rate: 78.0% (2010); Median home value: $122,115 (2010); Median contract rent: $525 per month (2005-2009 5-year est.); Median year structure built: before 1940 (2005-2009 5-year est.).

Transportation: Commute to work: 98.9% car, 0.0% public transportation, 1.1% walk, 0.0% work from home (2005-2009 5-year est.); Travel time to

work: 22.2% less than 15 minutes, 57.1% 15 to 30 minutes, 14.2% 30 to 45 minutes, 3.1% 45 to 60 minutes, 3.4% 60 minutes or more (2005-2009 5-year est.)

KANGLEY (village). Covers a land area of 0.338 square miles and a water area of 0 square miles. Located at 41.14° N. Lat; 88.87° W. Long. Elevation is 627 feet.

Population: 258 (1990); 287 (2000); 299 (2010); 299 (2015 projected); Race: 95.0% White, 0.3% Black, 0.0% Asian, 4.7% Other, 3.3% Hispanic of any race (2010); Density: 885.0 persons per square mile (2010); Average household size: 2.45 (2010); Median age: 42.6 (2010); Males per 100 females: 102.0 (2010); Marriage status: 25.6% never married, 61.4% now married, 6.5% widowed, 6.5% divorced (2005-2009 5-year est.); Foreign born: 0.3% (2005-2009 5-year est.); Ancestry (includes multiple ancestries): 22.3% German, 16.3% Irish, 14.2% Italian, 10.6% American, 8.4% English (2005-2009 5-year est.).

Economy: Single-family building permits issued: 0 (2010); Multi-family building permits issued: 0 (2010); Employment by occupation: 3.2% management, 13.5% professional, 16.1% services, 15.5% sales, 0.0% farming, 12.3% construction, 39.4% production (2005-2009 5-year est.).

Income: Per capita income: $21,434 (2010); Median household income: $48,043 (2010); Average household income: $52,623 (2010); Percent of households with income of $100,000 or more: 4.9% (2010); Poverty rate: 2.5% (2005-2009 5-year est.).

Taxes: Total city taxes per capita: $149 (2007); City property taxes per capita: $73 (2007).

Education: Percent of population age 25 and over with: High school diploma (including GED) or higher: 86.9% (2010); Bachelor's degree or higher: 13.1% (2010); Master's degree or higher: 2.8% (2010).

Housing: Homeownership rate: 87.7% (2010); Median home value: $111,364 (2010); Median contract rent: $474 per month (2005-2009 5-year est.); Median year structure built: before 1940 (2005-2009 5-year est.).

Transportation: Commute to work: 99.4% car, 0.0% public transportation, 0.0% walk, 0.6% work from home (2005-2009 5-year est.); Travel time to work: 55.3% less than 15 minutes, 20.1% 15 to 30 minutes, 22.6% 30 to 45 minutes, 0.0% 45 to 60 minutes, 1.9% 60 minutes or more (2005-2009 5-year est.)

LA SALLE (city). Aka La Salle-Peru. Covers a land area of 6.346 square miles and a water area of 0.093 square miles. Located at 41.34° N. Lat; 89.09° W. Long. Elevation is 571 feet.

History: La Salle was organized in 1827, and prospered with the opening of the Illinois & Michigan Canal in 1848. When the railroads replaced canal traffic, mining became an important industry for La Salle. The Matthiessen & Hegeler Zinc Company plant was established here in 1858. The town was named for La Salle, the French explorer of North America, who crossed this area in 1679.

Population: 10,091 (1990); 9,796 (2000); 9,524 (2010); 9,393 (2015 projected); Race: 90.7% White, 1.9% Black, 0.6% Asian, 6.8% Other, 12.0% Hispanic of any race (2010); Density: 1,500.7 persons per square mile (2010); Average household size: 2.28 (2010); Median age: 38.8 (2010); Males per 100 females: 98.4 (2010); Marriage status: 25.4% never married, 48.7% now married, 10.3% widowed, 15.6% divorced (2005-2009 5-year est.); Foreign born: 6.2% (2005-2009 5-year est.); Ancestry (includes multiple ancestries): 32.2% German, 16.7% Irish, 13.3% Polish, 13.0% Italian, 6.7% English (2005-2009 5-year est.).

Economy: Single-family building permits issued: 1 (2010); Multi-family building permits issued: 0 (2010); Employment by occupation: 8.0% management, 13.4% professional, 21.2% services, 28.7% sales, 1.0% farming, 7.6% construction, 20.1% production (2005-2009 5-year est.).

Income: Per capita income: $23,393 (2010); Median household income: $40,423 (2010); Average household income: $53,032 (2010); Percent of households with income of $100,000 or more: 10.2% (2010); Poverty rate: 25.1% (2005-2009 5-year est.).

Taxes: Total city taxes per capita: $480 (2007); City property taxes per capita: $285 (2007).

Education: Percent of population age 25 and over with: High school diploma (including GED) or higher: 85.7% (2010); Bachelor's degree or higher: 15.2% (2010); Master's degree or higher: 4.2% (2010).

School District(s)

Dimmick CCSD 175 (KG-08)

   2009-10 Enrollment: 101 . . . . (815) 223-2933

La Salle ESD 122 (PK-08)

   2009-10 Enrollment: 976 . . . . (815) 223-0786

La Salle-Peru Area Career Ctr (11-12)
2009-10 Enrollment: n/a . . . . (815) 223-2454
La Salle-Peru Twp HSD 120 (09-12)
2009-10 Enrollment: 1,204 . . . . (815) 223-1721

Vocational/Technical School(s)

Educators of Beauty (Private, For-profit)
Fall 2009 Enrollment: 66 . . . . (815) 223-7326
2010-11 Tuition: $16,575

Housing: Homeownership rate: 65.4% (2010); Median home value: $97,273 (2010); Median contract rent: $368 per month (2005-2009 5-year est.); Median year structure built: 1944 (2005-2009 5-year est.).

Safety: Violent crime rate: 18.2 per 10,000 population; Property crime rate: 171.0 per 10,000 population (2010).

Newspapers: Daily News Tribune (Local news; Circulation 19,525); NewsTribune (Local news; Circulation 19,447)

Transportation: Commute to work: 93.1% car, 0.6% public transportation, 2.1% walk, 3.6% work from home (2005-2009 5-year est.); Travel time to work: 60.5% less than 15 minutes, 26.1% 15 to 30 minutes, 8.6% 30 to 45 minutes, 1.3% 45 to 60 minutes, 3.5% 60 minutes or more (2005-2009 5-year est.)

Additional Information Contacts

City of La Salle. . . . . (815) 223-3755
http://www.lasalle-il.gov
Illinois Valley Area Chamber of Commerce . . . . (815) 223-0227
http://www.ivaced.org

LELAND (village). Covers a land area of 0.542 square miles and a water area of 0 square miles. Located at 41.61° N. Lat; 88.79° W. Long. Elevation is 696 feet.

Population: 895 (1990); 970 (2000); 966 (2010); 961 (2015 projected); Race: 95.8% White, 0.0% Black, 0.0% Asian, 4.2% Other, 5.2% Hispanic of any race (2010); Density: 1,780.7 persons per square mile (2010); Average household size: 2.65 (2010); Median age: 36.1 (2010); Males per 100 females: 98.8 (2010); Marriage status: 22.9% never married, 65.8% now married, 4.8% widowed, 6.6% divorced (2005-2009 5-year est.); Foreign born: 1.1% (2005-2009 5-year est.); Ancestry (includes multiple ancestries): 38.4% German, 19.7% Norwegian, 16.3% Irish, 14.6% English, 12.2% American (2005-2009 5-year est.).

Economy: Single-family building permits issued: 0 (2010); Multi-family building permits issued: 0 (2010); Employment by occupation: 5.6% management, 13.6% professional, 13.1% services, 19.2% sales, 0.0% farming, 30.4% construction, 18.1% production (2005-2009 5-year est.).

Income: Per capita income: $22,635 (2010); Median household income: $55,435 (2010); Average household income: $59,753 (2010); Percent of households with income of $100,000 or more: 9.9% (2010); Poverty rate: 9.1% (2005-2009 5-year est.).

Taxes: Total city taxes per capita: $228 (2007); City property taxes per capita: $124 (2007).

Education: Percent of population age 25 and over with: High school diploma (including GED) or higher: 91.1% (2010); Bachelor's degree or higher: 18.4% (2010); Master's degree or higher: 3.6% (2010).

School District(s)

Leland CUSD 1 (PK-12)
2009-10 Enrollment: 284 . . . . (815) 495-3821

Housing: Homeownership rate: 74.7% (2010); Median home value: $143,701 (2010); Median contract rent: $559 per month (2005-2009 5-year est.); Median year structure built: 1961 (2005-2009 5-year est.).

Transportation: Commute to work: 95.6% car, 0.0% public transportation, 3.3% walk, 1.1% work from home (2005-2009 5-year est.); Travel time to work: 24.5% less than 15 minutes, 24.5% 15 to 30 minutes, 18.2% 30 to 45 minutes, 18.2% 45 to 60 minutes, 14.6% 60 minutes or more (2005-2009 5-year est.)

LEONORE (village). Covers a land area of 0.086 square miles and a water area of 0 square miles. Located at 41.18° N. Lat; 88.98° W. Long. Elevation is 679 feet.

Population: 134 (1990); 110 (2000); 97 (2010); 93 (2015 projected); Race: 96.9% White, 2.1% Black, 0.0% Asian, 1.0% Other, 2.1% Hispanic of any race (2010); Density: 1,128.5 persons per square mile (2010); Average household size: 2.31 (2010); Median age: 45.3 (2010); Males per 100 females: 79.6 (2010); Marriage status: 25.0% never married, 58.8% now married, 0.0% widowed, 16.2% divorced (2005-2009 5-year est.); Foreign born: 4.6% (2005-2009 5-year est.); Ancestry (includes multiple ancestries): 65.5% German, 26.4% English, 18.4% Irish, 16.1% Scotch-Irish, 12.6% Italian (2005-2009 5-year est.).

Economy: Employment by occupation: 5.6% management, 8.3% professional, 19.4% services, 16.7% sales, 0.0% farming, 0.0% construction, 50.0% production (2005-2009 5-year est.).

Income: Per capita income: $23,420 (2010); Median household income: $46,667 (2010); Average household income: $51,488 (2010); Percent of households with income of $100,000 or more: 7.1% (2010); Poverty rate: 21.8% (2005-2009 5-year est.).

Taxes: Total city taxes per capita: $18 (2007); City property taxes per capita: $18 (2007).

Education: Percent of population age 25 and over with: High school diploma (including GED) or higher: 91.2% (2010); Bachelor's degree or higher: 13.2% (2010); Master's degree or higher: 2.9% (2010).

Housing: Homeownership rate: 81.0% (2010); Median home value: $83,333 (2010); Median contract rent: n/a per month (2005-2009 5-year est.); Median year structure built: before 1940 (2005-2009 5-year est.).

Transportation: Commute to work: 83.3% car, 0.0% public transportation, 16.7% walk, 0.0% work from home (2005-2009 5-year est.); Travel time to work: 36.1% less than 15 minutes, 27.8% 15 to 30 minutes, 16.7% 30 to 45 minutes, 5.6% 45 to 60 minutes, 13.9% 60 minutes or more (2005-2009 5-year est.)

LOSTANT (village). Covers a land area of 0.386 square miles and a water area of 0 square miles. Located at 41.14° N. Lat; 89.06° W. Long. Elevation is 696 feet.

Population: 510 (1990); 486 (2000); 494 (2010); 493 (2015 projected); Race: 97.6% White, 0.4% Black, 0.2% Asian, 1.8% Other, 1.6% Hispanic of any race (2010); Density: 1,280.4 persons per square mile (2010); Average household size: 2.43 (2010); Median age: 39.4 (2010); Males per 100 females: 98.4 (2010); Marriage status: 25.2% never married, 53.6% now married, 6.2% widowed, 15.0% divorced (2005-2009 5-year est.); Foreign born: 2.6% (2005-2009 5-year est.); Ancestry (includes multiple ancestries): 48.2% German, 19.9% Irish, 11.9% Polish, 10.1% English, 7.8% Italian (2005-2009 5-year est.).

Economy: Single-family building permits issued: 0 (2010); Multi-family building permits issued: 0 (2010); Employment by occupation: 2.9% management, 14.1% professional, 16.6% services, 24.9% sales, 0.0% farming, 8.3% construction, 33.2% production (2005-2009 5-year est.).

Income: Per capita income: $23,968 (2010); Median household income: $50,278 (2010); Average household income: $58,707 (2010); Percent of households with income of $100,000 or more: 11.8% (2010); Poverty rate: 3.9% (2005-2009 5-year est.).

Taxes: Total city taxes per capita: $77 (2007); City property taxes per capita: $75 (2007).

Education: Percent of population age 25 and over with: High school diploma (including GED) or higher: 91.7% (2010); Bachelor's degree or higher: 15.0% (2010); Master's degree or higher: 3.8% (2010).

School District(s)

Lostant CUSD 425 (KG-08)
2009-10 Enrollment: 87 . . . . (815) 368-3392

Housing: Homeownership rate: 82.8% (2010); Median home value: $94,815 (2010); Median contract rent: $650 per month (2005-2009 5-year est.); Median year structure built: 1944 (2005-2009 5-year est.).

Transportation: Commute to work: 85.9% car, 0.0% public transportation, 14.1% walk, 0.0% work from home (2005-2009 5-year est.); Travel time to work: 31.7% less than 15 minutes, 44.7% 15 to 30 minutes, 18.6% 30 to 45 minutes, 3.5% 45 to 60 minutes, 1.5% 60 minutes or more (2005-2009 5-year est.)

MARSEILLES (city). Covers a land area of 8.311 square miles and a water area of 0.387 square miles. Located at 41.32° N. Lat; 88.70° W. Long. Elevation is 518 feet.

History: Marseilles developed along a stretch of rapids on the Illinois River, providing water power for its early industries which included a paper mill.

Population: 4,834 (1990); 4,655 (2000); 4,671 (2010); 4,657 (2015 projected); Race: 96.9% White, 0.1% Black, 0.4% Asian, 2.6% Other, 2.7% Hispanic of any race (2010); Density: 562.0 persons per square mile (2010); Average household size: 2.43 (2010); Median age: 38.6 (2010); Males per 100 females: 94.5 (2010); Marriage status: 23.4% never married, 44.5% now married, 18.9% widowed, 13.2% divorced (2005-2009 5-year est.); Foreign born: 1.3% (2005-2009 5-year est.); Ancestry (includes multiple ancestries): 28.8% German, 18.0% Irish, 14.2% English, 9.7% American, 9.4% Norwegian (2005-2009 5-year est.).

Economy: Single-family building permits issued: 2 (2010); Multi-family building permits issued: 0 (2010); Employment by occupation: 7.9%

management, 24.9% professional, 18.8% services, 17.3% sales, 1.2% farming, 14.7% construction, 15.3% production (2005-2009 5-year est.).
Income: Per capita income: $22,926 (2010); Median household income: $48,476 (2010); Average household income: $56,151 (2010); Percent of households with income of $100,000 or more: 10.4% (2010); Poverty rate: 9.3% (2005-2009 5-year est.).
Taxes: Total city taxes per capita: $492 (2007); City property taxes per capita: $359 (2007).
Education: Percent of population age 25 and over with: High school diploma (including GED) or higher: 87.7% (2010); Bachelor's degree or higher: 11.5% (2010); Master's degree or higher: 3.1% (2010).

School District(s)
Marseilles ESD 150 (PK-08)
    2009-10 Enrollment: 656 . . . . (815) 795-2162
Miller Twp CCSD 210 (KG-08)
    2009-10 Enrollment: 224 . . . . (815) 357-8151
Housing: Homeownership rate: 75.1% (2010); Median home value: $106,416 (2010); Median contract rent: $529 per month (2005-2009 5-year est.); Median year structure built: 1951 (2005-2009 5-year est.).
Transportation: Commute to work: 95.0% car, 0.6% public transportation, 2.3% walk, 1.6% work from home (2005-2009 5-year est.); Travel time to work: 30.7% less than 15 minutes, 34.0% 15 to 30 minutes, 20.5% 30 to 45 minutes, 5.5% 45 to 60 minutes, 9.3% 60 minutes or more (2005-2009 5-year est.)
Additional Information Contacts
Illinois River Area Chamber of Commerce. . . . . (815) 795-2323
    http://iracc.org

MENDOTA (city). Covers a land area of 3.779 square miles and a water area of 0.096 square miles. Located at 41.54° N. Lat; 89.11° W. Long. Elevation is 741 feet.
History: Mendota developed as a trading and processing center for the produce of an agricultural area.
Population: 7,114 (1990); 7,272 (2000); 7,109 (2010); 7,008 (2015 projected); Race: 84.8% White, 0.6% Black, 0.7% Asian, 13.9% Other, 26.4% Hispanic of any race (2010); Density: 1,881.1 persons per square mile (2010); Average household size: 2.59 (2010); Median age: 37.1 (2010); Males per 100 females: 92.5 (2010); Marriage status: 28.4% never married, 53.0% now married, 10.8% widowed, 7.8% divorced (2005-2009 5-year est.); Foreign born: 10.3% (2005-2009 5-year est.); Ancestry (includes multiple ancestries): 32.2% German, 15.8% Irish, 9.9% English, 7.1% American, 3.8% Italian (2005-2009 5-year est.).
Economy: Single-family building permits issued: 3 (2010); Multi-family building permits issued: 0 (2010); Employment by occupation: 4.3% management, 11.0% professional, 16.7% services, 26.7% sales, 3.0% farming, 9.2% construction, 29.2% production (2005-2009 5-year est.).
Income: Per capita income: $21,987 (2010); Median household income: $47,563 (2010); Average household income: $56,700 (2010); Percent of households with income of $100,000 or more: 12.3% (2010); Poverty rate: 9.6% (2005-2009 5-year est.).
Taxes: Total city taxes per capita: $460 (2007); City property taxes per capita: $417 (2007).
Education: Percent of population age 25 and over with: High school diploma (including GED) or higher: 82.4% (2010); Bachelor's degree or higher: 14.8% (2010); Master's degree or higher: 6.4% (2010).

School District(s)
Mendota CCSD 289 (PK-08)
    2009-10 Enrollment: 1,313 . . . . (815) 539-7631
Mendota Twp HSD 280 (09-12)
    2009-10 Enrollment: 618 . . . . (815) 539-7446
Housing: Homeownership rate: 73.6% (2010); Median home value: $120,988 (2010); Median contract rent: $500 per month (2005-2009 5-year est.); Median year structure built: 1953 (2005-2009 5-year est.).
Hospitals: Mendota Community Hospital (32 beds)
Safety: Violent crime rate: 4.3 per 10,000 population; Property crime rate: 256.2 per 10,000 population (2010).
Newspapers: Mendota Reporter (Local news; Circulation 5,000)
Transportation: Commute to work: 85.7% car, 4.0% public transportation, 2.5% walk, 4.4% work from home (2005-2009 5-year est.); Travel time to work: 53.6% less than 15 minutes, 18.8% 15 to 30 minutes, 15.1% 30 to 45 minutes, 5.1% 45 to 60 minutes, 7.4% 60 minutes or more (2005-2009 5-year est.); Amtrak: train service available.
Additional Information Contacts
City of Mendota . . . . (815) 539-7459
    http://www.mendota.il.us

Mendota Area Chamber of Commerce . . . . (815) 539-6507
    http://www.mendotachamber.com

NAPLATE (village). Covers a land area of 0.112 square miles and a water area of 0 square miles. Located at 41.33° N. Lat; 88.87° W. Long. Elevation is 463 feet.
Population: 609 (1990); 523 (2000); 552 (2010); 584 (2015 projected); Race: 96.7% White, 0.2% Black, 0.2% Asian, 2.9% Other, 4.5% Hispanic of any race (2010); Density: 4,930.7 persons per square mile (2010); Average household size: 2.39 (2010); Median age: 39.5 (2010); Males per 100 females: 93.7 (2010); Marriage status: 36.1% never married, 45.6% now married, 5.0% widowed, 13.3% divorced (2005-2009 5-year est.); Foreign born: 0.5% (2005-2009 5-year est.); Ancestry (includes multiple ancestries): 32.0% Irish, 25.2% Italian, 24.6% German, 11.1% American, 9.5% English (2005-2009 5-year est.).
Economy: Employment by occupation: 4.5% management, 9.9% professional, 30.6% services, 24.5% sales, 0.0% farming, 7.6% construction, 22.9% production (2005-2009 5-year est.).
Income: Per capita income: $22,707 (2010); Median household income: $45,338 (2010); Average household income: $53,582 (2010); Percent of households with income of $100,000 or more: 11.7% (2010); Poverty rate: 6.8% (2005-2009 5-year est.).
Taxes: Total city taxes per capita: $31 (2007); City property taxes per capita: $19 (2007).
Education: Percent of population age 25 and over with: High school diploma (including GED) or higher: 86.4% (2010); Bachelor's degree or higher: 9.7% (2010); Master's degree or higher: 3.7% (2010).
Housing: Homeownership rate: 74.5% (2010); Median home value: $115,455 (2010); Median contract rent: $482 per month (2005-2009 5-year est.); Median year structure built: 1944 (2005-2009 5-year est.).
Transportation: Commute to work: 88.6% car, 0.0% public transportation, 9.1% walk, 1.0% work from home (2005-2009 5-year est.); Travel time to work: 46.7% less than 15 minutes, 38.5% 15 to 30 minutes, 9.2% 30 to 45 minutes, 3.0% 45 to 60 minutes, 2.6% 60 minutes or more (2005-2009 5-year est.)

NORTH UTICA (village). Aka Utica. Covers a land area of 1.506 square miles and a water area of 0 square miles. Located at 41.34° N. Lat; 89.01° W. Long. Elevation is 476 feet.
Population: 907 (1990); 977 (2000); 1,074 (2010); 1,109 (2015 projected); Race: 97.3% White, 0.2% Black, 0.3% Asian, 2.2% Other, 3.4% Hispanic of any race (2010); Density: 713.0 persons per square mile (2010); Average household size: 2.44 (2010); Median age: 40.2 (2010); Males per 100 females: 90.4 (2010); Marriage status: 19.5% never married, 67.5% now married, 5.3% widowed, 7.7% divorced (2005-2009 5-year est.); Foreign born: 4.4% (2005-2009 5-year est.); Ancestry (includes multiple ancestries): 34.8% German, 13.5% Italian, 12.7% Polish, 12.5% Irish, 10.7% English (2005-2009 5-year est.).
Economy: Single-family building permits issued: 10 (2010); Multi-family building permits issued: 0 (2010); Employment by occupation: 5.5% management, 21.8% professional, 27.5% services, 16.5% sales, 0.0% farming, 11.8% construction, 16.9% production (2005-2009 5-year est.).
Income: Per capita income: $31,282 (2010); Median household income: $61,264 (2010); Average household income: $79,067 (2010); Percent of households with income of $100,000 or more: 19.7% (2010); Poverty rate: 3.9% (2005-2009 5-year est.).
Taxes: Total city taxes per capita: $1,352 (2007); City property taxes per capita: $757 (2007).
Education: Percent of population age 25 and over with: High school diploma (including GED) or higher: 90.0% (2010); Bachelor's degree or higher: 16.2% (2010); Master's degree or higher: 4.3% (2010).
Housing: Homeownership rate: 80.0% (2010); Median home value: $140,809 (2010); Median contract rent: $576 per month (2005-2009 5-year est.); Median year structure built: 1969 (2005-2009 5-year est.).
Transportation: Commute to work: 95.7% car, 0.0% public transportation, 3.3% walk, 0.4% work from home (2005-2009 5-year est.); Travel time to work: 35.9% less than 15 minutes, 41.7% 15 to 30 minutes, 9.7% 30 to 45 minutes, 1.0% 45 to 60 minutes, 11.7% 60 minutes or more (2005-2009 5-year est.)

OGLESBY (city). Covers a land area of 4.001 square miles and a water area of 0 square miles. Located at 41.29° N. Lat; 89.06° W. Long. Elevation is 630 feet.

History: Oglesby developed as an industrial town, producing cement from the nearby limestone deposits. The town was named for Governor Richard J. Oglesby.
Population: 3,648 (1990); 3,647 (2000); 3,566 (2010); 3,515 (2015 projected); Race: 97.5% White, 0.5% Black, 0.3% Asian, 1.6% Other, 3.6% Hispanic of any race (2010); Density: 891.4 persons per square mile (2010); Average household size: 2.22 (2010); Median age: 41.8 (2010); Males per 100 females: 93.9 (2010); Marriage status: 21.1% never married, 59.9% now married, 12.0% widowed, 7.0% divorced (2005-2009 5-year est.); Foreign born: 1.8% (2005-2009 5-year est.); Ancestry (includes multiple ancestries): 27.3% German, 19.6% Italian, 17.1% Polish, 12.3% English, 10.2% Irish (2005-2009 5-year est.).
Economy: Single-family building permits issued: 4 (2010); Multi-family building permits issued: 0 (2010); Employment by occupation: 10.5% management, 18.5% professional, 13.3% services, 28.6% sales, 0.0% farming, 11.7% construction, 17.4% production (2005-2009 5-year est.).
Income: Per capita income: $24,662 (2010); Median household income: $42,468 (2010); Average household income: $54,698 (2010); Percent of households with income of $100,000 or more: 12.3% (2010); Poverty rate: 7.6% (2005-2009 5-year est.).
Taxes: Total city taxes per capita: $765 (2007); City property taxes per capita: $663 (2007).
Education: Percent of population age 25 and over with: High school diploma (including GED) or higher: 85.4% (2010); Bachelor's degree or higher: 13.1% (2010); Master's degree or higher: 3.5% (2010).

School District(s)
Oglesby ESD 125 (PK-08)
    2009-10 Enrollment: 617 . . . . (815) 883-9297
Two-year College(s)
Illinois Valley Community College (Public)
    Fall 2009 Enrollment: 4,529 . . . . (815) 224-2720
    2010-11 Tuition: In-state $7,819; Out-of-state $8,896
Housing: Homeownership rate: 76.8% (2010); Median home value: $102,850 (2010); Median contract rent: $450 per month (2005-2009 5-year est.); Median year structure built: 1947 (2005-2009 5-year est.).
Safety: Violent crime rate: 13.7 per 10,000 population; Property crime rate: 126.2 per 10,000 population (2010).
Transportation: Commute to work: 96.5% car, 0.0% public transportation, 0.0% walk, 3.0% work from home (2005-2009 5-year est.); Travel time to work: 39.5% less than 15 minutes, 39.5% 15 to 30 minutes, 11.2% 30 to 45 minutes, 5.1% 45 to 60 minutes, 4.7% 60 minutes or more (2005-2009 5-year est.)

OTTAWA (city). County seat. Covers a land area of 7.329 square miles and a water area of 0.334 square miles. Located at 41.34° N. Lat; 88.84° W. Long. Elevation is 482 feet.
History: Ottawa was laid out in 1830 by the Illinois & Michigan Canal commissioners. A settlement soon grew as the town was on the travel route between Chicago and the Illinois Valley. In 1858 Abraham Lincoln and Stephen Douglas held their first, highly-publicized debate in Ottawa.
Population: 17,954 (1990); 18,307 (2000); 18,630 (2010); 18,677 (2015 projected); Race: 93.9% White, 1.7% Black, 1.3% Asian, 3.1% Other, 6.6% Hispanic of any race (2010); Density: 2,541.9 persons per square mile (2010); Average household size: 2.34 (2010); Median age: 39.6 (2010); Males per 100 females: 92.1 (2010); Marriage status: 27.8% never married, 49.0% now married, 10.7% widowed, 12.5% divorced (2005-2009 5-year est.); Foreign born: 3.0% (2005-2009 5-year est.); Ancestry (includes multiple ancestries): 29.6% German, 22.7% Irish, 10.7% English, 10.0% Italian, 6.9% Norwegian (2005-2009 5-year est.).
Economy: Single-family building permits issued: 5 (2010); Multi-family building permits issued: 2 (2010); Employment by occupation: 11.8% management, 17.4% professional, 18.9% services, 24.4% sales, 0.1% farming, 9.9% construction, 17.5% production (2005-2009 5-year est.).
Income: Per capita income: $24,587 (2010); Median household income: $44,738 (2010); Average household income: $57,994 (2010); Percent of households with income of $100,000 or more: 14.3% (2010); Poverty rate: 11.9% (2005-2009 5-year est.).
Taxes: Total city taxes per capita: $389 (2007); City property taxes per capita: $283 (2007).
Education: Percent of population age 25 and over with: High school diploma (including GED) or higher: 88.1% (2010); Bachelor's degree or higher: 19.0% (2010); Master's degree or higher: 5.5% (2010).
School District(s)
Deer Park CCSD 82 (PK-08)
    2009-10 Enrollment: 72 . . . . (815) 434-6930

La Salle Roe (01-12)
    2009-10 Enrollment: n/a . . . . (815) 434-0780
Ottawa ESD 141 (PK-08)
    2009-10 Enrollment: 2,059 . . . . (815) 433-1133
Ottawa Twp HSD 140 (09-12)
    2009-10 Enrollment: 1,477 . . . . (815) 433-1323
Rutland CCSD 230 (KG-08)
    2009-10 Enrollment: 83 . . . . (815) 433-2949
Wallace CCSD 195 (KG-08)
    2009-10 Enrollment: 312 . . . . (815) 433-2986
Housing: Homeownership rate: 68.1% (2010); Median home value: $123,540 (2010); Median contract rent: $506 per month (2005-2009 5-year est.); Median year structure built: 1957 (2005-2009 5-year est.).
Hospitals: Community Hospital of Ottawa (124 beds)
Newspapers: Illinois Valley Thrif-T-Nikel (Community news; Circulation 19,000); Joy in Our Town - WWTO-TV (Regional news); Ottawa Daily Times (Local news; Circulation 13,879); The Times (Circulation 20,000); Town & Country (Local news; Circulation 19,500)
Transportation: Commute to work: 91.7% car, 0.4% public transportation, 4.1% walk, 2.2% work from home (2005-2009 5-year est.); Travel time to work: 51.8% less than 15 minutes, 23.6% 15 to 30 minutes, 10.5% 30 to 45 minutes, 6.3% 45 to 60 minutes, 8.0% 60 minutes or more (2005-2009 5-year est.)
Additional Information Contacts
City of Ottawa . . . . (815) 433-0161
    http://www.cityofottawa.org
Ottawa Area Chamber of Commerce . . . . (815) 433-0084
    http://www.ottawachamberillinois.com

PERU (city). Covers a land area of 5.941 square miles and a water area of 0.108 square miles. Located at 41.33° N. Lat; 89.12° W. Long. Elevation is 600 feet.
History: Peru's name is of Indian origin, meaning "plenty of everything." The town was founded in 1835 on the Illinois River, and became the terminus of the Illinois & Michigan Canal. River traffic influenced the development of Peru's early industries, which included the Peru Wheel Company and the Star Union Products Company.
Population: 9,318 (1990); 9,835 (2000); 9,685 (2010); 9,541 (2015 projected); Race: 94.5% White, 0.3% Black, 2.0% Asian, 3.2% Other, 6.4% Hispanic of any race (2010); Density: 1,630.2 persons per square mile (2010); Average household size: 2.27 (2010); Median age: 43.2 (2010); Males per 100 females: 89.8 (2010); Marriage status: 24.0% never married, 58.5% now married, 8.3% widowed, 9.2% divorced (2005-2009 5-year est.); Foreign born: 3.8% (2005-2009 5-year est.); Ancestry (includes multiple ancestries): 32.0% German, 19.1% Irish, 16.9% Polish, 14.5% Italian, 10.4% English (2005-2009 5-year est.).
Economy: Single-family building permits issued: 6 (2010); Multi-family building permits issued: 0 (2010); Employment by occupation: 11.6% management, 16.6% professional, 15.8% services, 29.8% sales, 0.3% farming, 6.9% construction, 19.0% production (2005-2009 5-year est.).
Income: Per capita income: $26,177 (2010); Median household income: $46,743 (2010); Average household income: $59,279 (2010); Percent of households with income of $100,000 or more: 12.4% (2010); Poverty rate: 9.7% (2005-2009 5-year est.).
Taxes: Total city taxes per capita: $195 (2007); City property taxes per capita: $71 (2007).
Education: Percent of population age 25 and over with: High school diploma (including GED) or higher: 86.8% (2010); Bachelor's degree or higher: 18.9% (2010); Master's degree or higher: 6.4% (2010).
School District(s)
Peru ESD 124 (PK-08)
    2009-10 Enrollment: 852 . . . . (815) 223-0486
Housing: Homeownership rate: 73.7% (2010); Median home value: $122,102 (2010); Median contract rent: $481 per month (2005-2009 5-year est.); Median year structure built: 1955 (2005-2009 5-year est.).
Hospitals: Illinois Valley Community Hospital
Safety: Violent crime rate: 10.3 per 10,000 population; Property crime rate: 267.5 per 10,000 population (2010).
Transportation: Commute to work: 95.7% car, 0.4% public transportation, 0.8% walk, 2.7% work from home (2005-2009 5-year est.); Travel time to work: 54.7% less than 15 minutes, 28.1% 15 to 30 minutes, 10.5% 30 to 45 minutes, 0.7% 45 to 60 minutes, 6.1% 60 minutes or more (2005-2009 5-year est.)
Airports: Illinois Valley Regional-Walter A Duncan Field (general aviation)
Additional Information Contacts

City of Peru . . . . (815) 223-0061
http://www.peru.il.us

RANSOM (village).
Covers a land area of 0.991 square miles and a water area of 0 square miles. Located at 41.15° N. Lat; 88.65° W. Long. Elevation is 705 feet.

Population: 438 (1990); 409 (2000); 412 (2010); 413 (2015 projected); Race: 97.6% White, 0.2% Black, 0.7% Asian, 1.5% Other, 2.4% Hispanic of any race (2010); Density: 415.6 persons per square mile (2010); Average household size: 2.65 (2010); Median age: 42.1 (2010); Males per 100 females: 95.3 (2010); Marriage status: 22.7% never married, 62.9% now married, 4.5% widowed, 9.8% divorced (2005-2009 5-year est.); Foreign born: 0.0% (2005-2009 5-year est.); Ancestry (includes multiple ancestries): 32.0% German, 22.5% Irish, 9.8% English, 6.9% Polish, 6.1% Italian (2005-2009 5-year est.).

Economy: Single-family building permits issued: 0 (2010); Multi-family building permits issued: 0 (2010); Employment by occupation: 6.3% management, 7.5% professional, 12.5% services, 25.6% sales, 0.0% farming, 11.9% construction, 36.3% production (2005-2009 5-year est.).

Income: Per capita income: $24,851 (2010); Median household income: $62,500 (2010); Average household income: $68,168 (2010); Percent of households with income of $100,000 or more: 17.8% (2010); Poverty rate: 10.5% (2005-2009 5-year est.).

Taxes: Total city taxes per capita: $75 (2007); City property taxes per capita: $72 (2007).

Education: Percent of population age 25 and over with: High school diploma (including GED) or higher: 89.1% (2010); Bachelor's degree or higher: 13.7% (2010); Master's degree or higher: 3.9% (2010).

School District(s)
Allen-Otter Creek CCSD 65 (KG-08)
    2009-10 Enrollment: 103 . . . . (815) 586-4611

Housing: Homeownership rate: 82.9% (2010); Median home value: $111,486 (2010); Median contract rent: $525 per month (2005-2009 5-year est.); Median year structure built: 1952 (2005-2009 5-year est.).

Transportation: Commute to work: 86.4% car, 1.9% public transportation, 8.4% walk, 1.3% work from home (2005-2009 5-year est.); Travel time to work: 28.9% less than 15 minutes, 33.6% 15 to 30 minutes, 18.4% 30 to 45 minutes, 7.2% 45 to 60 minutes, 11.8% 60 minutes or more (2005-2009 5-year est.)

RUTLAND (village).
Covers a land area of 0.820 square miles and a water area of 0 square miles. Located at 40.98° N. Lat; 89.04° W. Long. Elevation is 702 feet.

Population: 391 (1990); 354 (2000); 371 (2010); 377 (2015 projected); Race: 99.7% White, 0.0% Black, 0.0% Asian, 0.3% Other, 2.4% Hispanic of any race (2010); Density: 452.2 persons per square mile (2010); Average household size: 2.52 (2010); Median age: 38.5 (2010); Males per 100 females: 105.0 (2010); Marriage status: 24.8% never married, 66.4% now married, 4.0% widowed, 4.7% divorced (2005-2009 5-year est.); Foreign born: 5.4% (2005-2009 5-year est.); Ancestry (includes multiple ancestries): 39.7% German, 18.4% Irish, 6.7% French, 5.1% English, 4.1% American (2005-2009 5-year est.).

Economy: Employment by occupation: 9.2% management, 8.5% professional, 19.0% services, 17.6% sales, 0.7% farming, 14.4% construction, 30.7% production (2005-2009 5-year est.).

Income: Per capita income: $20,129 (2010); Median household income: $40,859 (2010); Average household income: $51,190 (2010); Percent of households with income of $100,000 or more: 10.9% (2010); Poverty rate: 6.3% (2005-2009 5-year est.).

Taxes: Total city taxes per capita: $99 (2007); City property taxes per capita: $42 (2007).

Education: Percent of population age 25 and over with: High school diploma (including GED) or higher: 87.2% (2010); Bachelor's degree or higher: 11.2% (2010); Master's degree or higher: 0.8% (2010).

Housing: Homeownership rate: 80.3% (2010); Median home value: $66,667 (2010); Median contract rent: $436 per month (2005-2009 5-year est.); Median year structure built: 1944 (2005-2009 5-year est.).

Transportation: Commute to work: 98.6% car, 0.0% public transportation, 0.0% walk, 1.4% work from home (2005-2009 5-year est.); Travel time to work: 52.7% less than 15 minutes, 22.6% 15 to 30 minutes, 14.4% 30 to 45 minutes, 4.1% 45 to 60 minutes, 6.2% 60 minutes or more (2005-2009 5-year est.)

SENECA (village).
Aka Crotty. Covers a land area of 3.307 square miles and a water area of 0.258 square miles. Located at 41.30° N. Lat; 88.60° W. Long. Elevation is 509 feet.

History: Seneca was built along the Illinois & Michigan Canal, and developed as a sawmill town.

Population: 1,966 (1990); 2,053 (2000); 2,069 (2010); 2,064 (2015 projected); Race: 97.8% White, 0.0% Black, 0.0% Asian, 2.1% Other, 3.3% Hispanic of any race (2010); Density: 625.6 persons per square mile (2010); Average household size: 2.69 (2010); Median age: 37.0 (2010); Males per 100 females: 96.1 (2010); Marriage status: 27.0% never married, 54.9% now married, 5.3% widowed, 12.8% divorced (2005-2009 5-year est.); Foreign born: 0.7% (2005-2009 5-year est.); Ancestry (includes multiple ancestries): 29.8% German, 20.5% Irish, 13.8% Norwegian, 9.0% English, 6.5% Italian (2005-2009 5-year est.).

Economy: Single-family building permits issued: 1 (2010); Multi-family building permits issued: 0 (2010); Employment by occupation: 12.9% management, 16.5% professional, 15.1% services, 21.9% sales, 0.9% farming, 10.2% construction, 22.6% production (2005-2009 5-year est.).

Income: Per capita income: $25,809 (2010); Median household income: $63,896 (2010); Average household income: $69,688 (2010); Percent of households with income of $100,000 or more: 19.6% (2010); Poverty rate: 5.5% (2005-2009 5-year est.).

Taxes: Total city taxes per capita: $393 (2007); City property taxes per capita: $271 (2007).

Education: Percent of population age 25 and over with: High school diploma (including GED) or higher: 89.2% (2010); Bachelor's degree or higher: 14.3% (2010); Master's degree or higher: 4.1% (2010).

School District(s)
Lasalle Putnam Alliance (04-12)
    2009-10 Enrollment: n/a . . . . (815) 433-6433
Seneca CCSD 170 (PK-08)
    2009-10 Enrollment: 544 . . . . (815) 357-8744
Seneca Twp HSD 160 (09-12)
    2009-10 Enrollment: 480 . . . . (815) 357-5000

Housing: Homeownership rate: 82.1% (2010); Median home value: $136,803 (2010); Median contract rent: $645 per month (2005-2009 5-year est.); Median year structure built: 1954 (2005-2009 5-year est.).

Transportation: Commute to work: 96.3% car, 0.0% public transportation, 0.8% walk, 2.9% work from home (2005-2009 5-year est.); Travel time to work: 31.7% less than 15 minutes, 37.2% 15 to 30 minutes, 19.5% 30 to 45 minutes, 6.3% 45 to 60 minutes, 5.3% 60 minutes or more (2005-2009 5-year est.)

SERENA (unincorporated postal area, zip code 60549).
Covers a land area of 24.144 square miles and a water area of 0 square miles. Located at 41.49° N. Lat; 88.75° W. Long. Elevation is 633 feet.

Population: 594 (2000); Race: 100.0% White, 0.0% Black, 0.0% Asian, 0.0% Other, 5.2% Hispanic of any race (2000); Density: 24.6 persons per square mile (2000); Age: 23.0% under 18, 10.6% over 64 (2000); Marriage status: 15.7% never married, 70.6% now married, 1.1% widowed, 12.5% divorced (2000); Foreign born: 0.0% (2000); Ancestry (includes multiple ancestries): 30.3% Norwegian, 22.8% Irish, 21.7% German, 18.5% English, 9.9% Italian (2000).

Economy: Employment by occupation: 25.0% management, 22.7% professional, 10.5% services, 18.4% sales, 0.0% farming, 16.1% construction, 7.2% production (2000).

Income: Per capita income: $20,022 (2000); Median household income: $52,000 (2000); Poverty rate: 6.5% (2000).

Education: Percent of population age 25 and over with: High school diploma (including GED) or higher: 93.7% (2000); Bachelor's degree or higher: 13.2% (2000).

School District(s)
Serena CUSD 2 (KG-12)
    2009-10 Enrollment: 837 . . . . (815) 496-2850

Housing: Homeownership rate: 79.5% (2000); Median home value: $126,400 (2000); Median contract rent: $443 per month (2000); Median year structure built: 1962 (2000).

Transportation: Commute to work: 95.1% car, 0.0% public transportation, 0.0% walk, 4.9% work from home (2000); Travel time to work: 15.6% less than 15 minutes, 49.8% 15 to 30 minutes, 23.9% 30 to 45 minutes, 10.7% 45 to 60 minutes, 0.0% 60 minutes or more (2000)

SHERIDAN (village). Covers a land area of 1.405 square miles and a water area of 0.040 square miles. Located at 41.52° N. Lat; 88.68° W. Long. Elevation is 594 feet.
Population: 1,517 (1990); 2,411 (2000); 1,991 (2010); 1,879 (2015 projected); Race: 44.6% White, 42.6% Black, 0.7% Asian, 12.2% Other, 13.7% Hispanic of any race (2010); Density: 1,416.6 persons per square mile (2010); Average household size: 2.88 (2010); Median age: 31.2 (2010); Males per 100 females: 396.5 (2010); Marriage status: 21.8% never married, 50.9% now married, 6.9% widowed, 20.5% divorced (2005-2009 5-year est.); Foreign born: 3.6% (2005-2009 5-year est.); Ancestry (includes multiple ancestries): 25.4% German, 21.7% English, 19.6% Irish, 12.8% Italian, 7.9% Norwegian (2005-2009 5-year est.).
Economy: Single-family building permits issued: 0 (2010); Multi-family building permits issued: 0 (2010); Employment by occupation: 6.8% management, 11.9% professional, 23.9% services, 12.3% sales, 3.1% farming, 13.6% construction, 28.4% production (2005-2009 5-year est.).
Income: Per capita income: $13,436 (2010); Median household income: $55,556 (2010); Average household income: $59,010 (2010); Percent of households with income of $100,000 or more: 11.8% (2010); Poverty rate: 12.5% (2005-2009 5-year est.).
Taxes: Total city taxes per capita: $18 (2007); City property taxes per capita: $7 (2007).
Education: Percent of population age 25 and over with: High school diploma (including GED) or higher: 64.1% (2010); Bachelor's degree or higher: 5.4% (2010); Master's degree or higher: 0.8% (2010).
School District(s)
Serena CUSD 2 (KG-12)
    2009-10 Enrollment: 837 . . . . (815) 496-2850
Housing: Homeownership rate: 74.3% (2010); Median home value: $137,379 (2010); Median contract rent: $400 per month (2005-2009 5-year est.); Median year structure built: 1959 (2005-2009 5-year est.).
Transportation: Commute to work: 94.9% car, 0.0% public transportation, 4.6% walk, 0.4% work from home (2005-2009 5-year est.); Travel time to work: 24.2% less than 15 minutes, 30.3% 15 to 30 minutes, 26.9% 30 to 45 minutes, 7.6% 45 to 60 minutes, 11.0% 60 minutes or more (2005-2009 5-year est.)

STREATOR (city). Covers a land area of 5.767 square miles and a water area of 0.013 square miles. Located at 41.12° N. Lat; 88.83° W. Long. Elevation is 620 feet.
History: Coal mining began in Streator in 1872, and the name of the town was changed from Unionville to Streator to honor the president of the coal company. Streator was sited near deposits of shale, clay, and sand which led to the manufacturing of glass.
Population: 14,861 (1990); 14,190 (2000); 13,636 (2010); 13,327 (2015 projected); Race: 93.8% White, 1.9% Black, 0.6% Asian, 3.8% Other, 9.3% Hispanic of any race (2010); Density: 2,364.6 persons per square mile (2010); Average household size: 2.38 (2010); Median age: 38.5 (2010); Males per 100 females: 93.4 (2010); Marriage status: 29.0% never married, 52.7% now married, 7.7% widowed, 10.6% divorced (2005-2009 5-year est.); Foreign born: 7.9% (2005-2009 5-year est.); Ancestry (includes multiple ancestries): 30.4% German, 19.3% Irish, 12.4% Slovak, 6.9% American, 6.8% English (2005-2009 5-year est.).
Economy: Single-family building permits issued: 4 (2010); Multi-family building permits issued: 6 (2010); Employment by occupation: 5.9% management, 10.0% professional, 19.2% services, 25.8% sales, 0.6% farming, 9.5% construction, 28.9% production (2005-2009 5-year est.).
Income: Per capita income: $21,093 (2010); Median household income: $41,714 (2010); Average household income: $50,187 (2010); Percent of households with income of $100,000 or more: 9.0% (2010); Poverty rate: 14.7% (2005-2009 5-year est.).
Taxes: Total city taxes per capita: $245 (2007); City property taxes per capita: $151 (2007).
Education: Percent of population age 25 and over with: High school diploma (including GED) or higher: 82.3% (2010); Bachelor's degree or higher: 11.1% (2010); Master's degree or higher: 3.4% (2010).
School District(s)
Streator ESD 44 (PK-08)
    2009-10 Enrollment: 1,972 . . . . (815) 672-2926
Streator Twp HSD 40 (09-12)
    2009-10 Enrollment: 971 . . . . (815) 672-0545
Woodland CUSD 5 (PK-12)
    2009-10 Enrollment: 497 . . . . (815) 672-5974

Housing: Homeownership rate: 71.3% (2010); Median home value: $75,538 (2010); Median contract rent: $438 per month (2005-2009 5-year est.); Median year structure built: 1951 (2005-2009 5-year est.).
Hospitals: St. Mary's Hospital (251 beds)
Newspapers: The Times-Press (Local news; Circulation 8,621)
Transportation: Commute to work: 92.4% car, 0.1% public transportation, 4.8% walk, 1.5% work from home (2005-2009 5-year est.); Travel time to work: 59.8% less than 15 minutes, 15.2% 15 to 30 minutes, 17.2% 30 to 45 minutes, 2.8% 45 to 60 minutes, 5.0% 60 minutes or more (2005-2009 5-year est.)
Additional Information Contacts
City of Streator . . . . (815) 672-2517
    http://www.ci.streator.il.us/cms
Streator Area Chamber of Commerce & Industry . . . . (815) 672-2921
    http://www.streatorchamber.com

TONICA (village). Covers a land area of 1.355 square miles and a water area of 0 square miles. Located at 41.21° N. Lat; 89.06° W. Long. Elevation is 659 feet.
Population: 794 (1990); 685 (2000); 705 (2010); 710 (2015 projected); Race: 98.2% White, 0.0% Black, 0.3% Asian, 1.6% Other, 5.1% Hispanic of any race (2010); Density: 520.3 persons per square mile (2010); Average household size: 2.28 (2010); Median age: 42.6 (2010); Males per 100 females: 98.6 (2010); Marriage status: 27.6% never married, 55.8% now married, 10.1% widowed, 6.6% divorced (2005-2009 5-year est.); Foreign born: 1.6% (2005-2009 5-year est.); Ancestry (includes multiple ancestries): 36.1% German, 21.2% Irish, 19.9% English, 14.1% Italian, 6.3% Polish (2005-2009 5-year est.).
Economy: Single-family building permits issued: 1 (2010); Multi-family building permits issued: 0 (2010); Employment by occupation: 8.9% management, 22.3% professional, 22.0% services, 14.9% sales, 0.0% farming, 14.9% construction, 17.0% production (2005-2009 5-year est.).
Income: Per capita income: $24,924 (2010); Median household income: $47,375 (2010); Average household income: $56,667 (2010); Percent of households with income of $100,000 or more: 10.7% (2010); Poverty rate: 6.9% (2005-2009 5-year est.).
Taxes: Total city taxes per capita: $456 (2007); City property taxes per capita: $452 (2007).
Education: Percent of population age 25 and over with: High school diploma (including GED) or higher: 88.7% (2010); Bachelor's degree or higher: 14.0% (2010); Master's degree or higher: 4.7% (2010).
School District(s)
Tonica CCSD 79 (PK-08)
    2009-10 Enrollment: 206 . . . . (815) 442-3420
Housing: Homeownership rate: 77.0% (2010); Median home value: $98,113 (2010); Median contract rent: $413 per month (2005-2009 5-year est.); Median year structure built: 1956 (2005-2009 5-year est.).
Newspapers: Tonica News (Local news; Circulation 1,150)
Transportation: Commute to work: 94.6% car, 0.0% public transportation, 1.1% walk, 3.6% work from home (2005-2009 5-year est.); Travel time to work: 19.3% less than 15 minutes, 55.4% 15 to 30 minutes, 17.8% 30 to 45 minutes, 1.5% 45 to 60 minutes, 5.9% 60 minutes or more (2005-2009 5-year est.)

TROY GROVE (village). Covers a land area of 0.687 square miles and a water area of 0 square miles. Located at 41.46° N. Lat; 89.08° W. Long. Elevation is 673 feet.
History: Troy Grove is the birthplace and boyhood home of James Butler "Wild Bill" Hickok (1837-1876), who toured with Buffalo Bill Cody in 1872-1873.
Population: 259 (1990); 305 (2000); 311 (2010); 311 (2015 projected); Race: 88.4% White, 0.0% Black, 6.8% Asian, 4.8% Other, 5.5% Hispanic of any race (2010); Density: 453.0 persons per square mile (2010); Average household size: 2.78 (2010); Median age: 34.7 (2010); Males per 100 females: 99.4 (2010); Marriage status: 22.5% never married, 62.7% now married, 7.1% widowed, 7.7% divorced (2005-2009 5-year est.); Foreign born: 2.8% (2005-2009 5-year est.); Ancestry (includes multiple ancestries): 33.2% German, 18.0% Irish, 10.9% Swedish, 10.0% Norwegian, 5.7% English (2005-2009 5-year est.).
Economy: Employment by occupation: 5.6% management, 26.4% professional, 16.0% services, 12.0% sales, 0.0% farming, 20.0% construction, 20.0% production (2005-2009 5-year est.).
Income: Per capita income: $27,346 (2010); Median household income: $68,056 (2010); Average household income: $77,254 (2010); Percent of

households with income of $100,000 or more: 17.0% (2010); Poverty rate: 15.6% (2005-2009 5-year est.).
Taxes: Total city taxes per capita: $43 (2007); City property taxes per capita: $7 (2007).
Education: Percent of population age 25 and over with: High school diploma (including GED) or higher: 90.6% (2010); Bachelor's degree or higher: 16.3% (2010); Master's degree or higher: 4.5% (2010).
Housing: Homeownership rate: 80.4% (2010); Median home value: $130,769 (2010); Median contract rent: $417 per month (2005-2009 5-year est.); Median year structure built: 1944 (2005-2009 5-year est.).
Transportation: Commute to work: 90.2% car, 0.0% public transportation, 8.1% walk, 0.0% work from home (2005-2009 5-year est.); Travel time to work: 48.8% less than 15 minutes, 15.4% 15 to 30 minutes, 8.1% 30 to 45 minutes, 2.4% 45 to 60 minutes, 25.2% 60 minutes or more (2005-2009 5-year est.)

UTICA (unincorporated postal area, zip code 61373). Aka North Utica. Covers a land area of 48.603 square miles and a water area of 0.177 square miles. Located at 41.41° N. Lat; 89.00° W. Long. Elevation is 476 feet.
Population: 1,998 (2000); Race: 97.5% White, 0.1% Black, 0.6% Asian, 1.8% Other, 1.1% Hispanic of any race (2000); Density: 41.1 persons per square mile (2000); Age: 26.8% under 18, 11.3% over 64 (2000); Marriage status: 19.6% never married, 66.9% now married, 5.8% widowed, 7.6% divorced (2000); Foreign born: 1.1% (2000); Ancestry (includes multiple ancestries): 32.8% German, 19.0% Irish, 12.5% English, 11.6% Polish, 10.9% Italian (2000).
Economy: Employment by occupation: 15.0% management, 14.4% professional, 13.0% services, 30.3% sales, 0.6% farming, 12.7% construction, 14.0% production (2000).
Income: Per capita income: $22,970 (2000); Median household income: $49,688 (2000); Poverty rate: 4.9% (2000).
Education: Percent of population age 25 and over with: High school diploma (including GED) or higher: 89.5% (2000); Bachelor's degree or higher: 16.5% (2000).

School District(s)
Waltham CCSD 185 (KG-08)
    2009-10 Enrollment: 239 . . . . (815) 667-4417
Housing: Homeownership rate: 82.0% (2000); Median home value: $120,900 (2000); Median contract rent: $448 per month (2000); Median year structure built: 1968 (2000).
Transportation: Commute to work: 92.0% car, 0.4% public transportation, 2.1% walk, 5.0% work from home (2000); Travel time to work: 37.3% less than 15 minutes, 43.6% 15 to 30 minutes, 7.9% 30 to 45 minutes, 2.2% 45 to 60 minutes, 9.0% 60 minutes or more (2000)

Lake County

Located in northeastern Illinois; bounded on the east by Lake Michigan, and on the north by Wisconsin; drained by the Fox and Des Plaines Rivers; includes many lakes. Covers a land area of 447.56 square miles, a water area of 920.39 square miles, and is located in the Central Time Zone at 42.31° N. Lat., 87.98° W. Long. The county was founded in 1839. County seat is Waukegan.

Lake County is part of the Chicago-Joliet-Naperville, IL-IN-WI Metropolitan Statistical Area. The entire metro area includes: Chicago-Joliet-Naperville, IL Metropolitan Division (Cook County, IL; DeKalb County, IL; DuPage County, IL; Grundy County, IL; Kane County, IL; Kendall County, IL; McHenry County, IL; Will County, IL); Gary, IN Metropolitan Division (Jasper County, IN; Lake County, IN; Newton County, IN; Porter County, IN); Lake County-Kenosha County, IL-WI Metropolitan Division (Lake County, IL; Kenosha County, WI)

Weather Station: Antioch   Elevation: 750 feet

	Jan	Feb	Mar	Apr	May	Jun	Jul	Aug	Sep	Oct	Nov	Dec
High	30	33	44	57	68	78	82	81	74	61	47	34
Low	13	16	26	37	46	56	62	61	53	41	30	19
Precip	1.6	1.5	1.9	3.2	4.1	4.1	3.8	4.3	3.6	2.9	2.9	2.1
Snow	11.1	9.1	5.6	1.5	tr	0.0	0.0	0.0	0.0	0.1	1.7	10.1

High and Low temperatures in degrees Fahrenheit; Precipitation and Snow in inches

Population: 516,418 (1990); 644,356 (2000); 721,415 (2010); 751,110 (2015 projected); Race: 75.1% White, 6.6% Black, 5.9% Asian, 12.4% Other, 20.3% Hispanic of any race (2010); Density: 1,611.9 persons per square mile (2010); Average household size: 2.93 (2010); Median age: 35.5 (2010); Males per 100 females: 100.2 (2010).
Religion: Five largest groups: 39.3% Catholic Church, 3.9% Jewish Estimate, 2.8% Independent, Non-Charismatic Churches, 2.5% Evangelical Lutheran Church in America, 1.6% Presbyterian Church (U.S.A.) (2000).
Economy: Unemployment rate: 9.1% (August 2011); Total civilian labor force: 366,853 (August 2011); Leading industries: 13.8% manufacturing; 13.5% retail trade; 10.6% wholesale trade (2009); Farms: 396 totaling 34,525 acres (2007); Companies that employ 500 or more persons: 71 (2009); Companies that employ 100 to 499 persons: 403 (2009); Companies that employ less than 100 persons: 19,031 (2009); Black-owned businesses: 2,622 (2007); Hispanic-owned businesses: 3,648 (2007); Asian-owned businesses: 3,994 (2007); Women-owned businesses: 19,571 (2007); Retail sales per capita: $23,068 (2010). Single-family building permits issued: 427 (2010); Multi-family building permits issued: 271 (2010).
Income: Per capita income: $36,996 (2010); Median household income: $80,402 (2010); Average household income: $109,773 (2010); Percent of households with income of $100,000 or more: 38.3% (2010); Poverty rate: 7.6% (2009); Bankruptcy rate: 6.11% (2010).
Taxes: Total county taxes per capita: $317 (2007); County property taxes per capita: $310 (2007).
Education: Percent of population age 25 and over with: High school diploma (including GED) or higher: 87.5% (2010); Bachelor's degree or higher: 41.0% (2010); Master's degree or higher: 16.5% (2010).
Housing: Homeownership rate: 78.6% (2010); Median home value: $261,854 (2010); Median contract rent: $824 per month (2005-2009 5-year est.); Median year structure built: 1979 (2005-2009 5-year est.)
Health: Birth rate: 141.2 per 10,000 population (2009); Death rate: 57.8 per 10,000 population (2009); Age-adjusted cancer mortality rate: 188.6 deaths per 100,000 population (2007); Number of physicians: 32.6 per 10,000 population (2008); Hospital beds: 18.5 per 10,000 population (2007); Hospital admissions: 871.3 per 10,000 population (2007).
Environment: Air Quality Index: 89.6% good, 10.4% moderate, 0.0% unhealthy for sensitive individuals, 0.0% unhealthy (percent of days in 2008)
Elections: 2008 Presidential election results: 59.3% Obama, 39.6% McCain, 0.5% Nader
National and State Parks: Chain O'Lakes State Park; Illinois Beach State Park; Volo Bog State Nature Preserve
Additional Information Contacts
Lake County Government . . . . (847) 377-2000
    http://www.lakecountyil.gov
Antioch Chamber of Commerce. (847) 395-2233
    http://www.antiochchamber.org
Buffalo Grove Area Chamber of Commerce . . . . (847) 541-7799
    http://www.buffalogrovechamber.org
City of Highland Park . . . . (847) 432-0800
    http://www.cityhpil.com
City of Lake Forest. . . . . (847) 234-2600
    http://www.cityoflakeforest.com
City of North Chicago. . . . . (847) 596-8600
    http://www.northchicago.org
City of Waukegan. . . . . (847) 599-2500
    http://www.waukeganweb.net
City of Zion. . . . . (847) 746-4000
    http://www.cityofzion.com
DBR Chamber of Commerce. . . . . (847) 945-4660
    http://www.dbrchamber.com
Fox Lake Area Chamber of Commerce . . . . (847) 587-7474
    http://www.discoverfoxlake.com
GLMV Area Chamber of Commerce . . . . (847) 680-0750
    http://www.glmvchamber.org
Grayslake Area Chamber of Commerce & Industry. . . . . . . (847) 223-6888
    http://www.grayslakechamber.com
Greater Lincolnshire Chamber of Commerce . . . . (847) 793-2409
    http://www.lincolnshirechamber.org
Highland Park Chamber of Commerce . . . . (847) 432-0284
    http://www.chamberhp.com
Highwood Chamber of Commerce. . . . . (847) 433-2100
    http://www.highwoodchamberofcommerce.com
Illinois Women's Chamber of Commerce
    http://www.uswomenschamber.com/html/illinois.htm
Lake County Chamber of Commerce . . . . (847) 249-3800
    http://www.lakecountychamber.com

Lake Forest/Lake Bluff Chamber of Commerce. . . . . (847) 234-4282
    http://www.lakeforestonline.com
Lake Zurich Area Chamber of Commerce . . . . (847) 438-5572
    http://www.lzacc.com
Lindenhurst/Lake Villa Chamber of Commerce . . . . (847) 356-8446
    http://www.llvchamber.com
Round Lake Area Chamber of Commerce & Industry . . . . . (847) 546-2002
    http://www.rlchamber.org
Village of Antioch. . . . . (847) 395-1000
    http://www.antioch.il.gov
Village of Beach Park. . . . . (847) 746-1770
    http://www.villageofbeachpark.com
Village of Buffalo Grove . . . . (847) 459-2525
    http://www.vbg.org
Village of Deerfield. . . . . (847) 945-5000
    http://www.deerfield.il.us
Village of Fox Lake . . . . (847) 587-2151
    http://www.foxlake.org
Village of Grayslake . . . . (847) 223-8515
    http://www.villageofgrayslake.com
Village of Gurnee . . . . (847) 599-7500
    http://www.gurnee.il.us
Village of Hawthorn Woods . . . . (847) 438-5500
    http://www.vhw.org
Village of Lake Bluff. . . . . (847) 234-0774
    http://www.lakebluff.org
Village of Lake Villa . . . . (847) 356-6100
    http://www.lake-villa.org
Village of Lake Zurich . . . . (847) 438-5141
    http://www.volz.org
Village of Libertyville . . . . (847) 362-2430
    http://www.libertyville.com/index.htm
Village of Lincolnshire . . . . (847) 883-8600
    http://www.village.lincolnshire.il.us
Village of Lindenhurst . . . . (847) 356-8252
    http://lindenhurstil.org
Village of Long Grove . . . . (847) 634-9440
    http://www.longgrove.net
Village of Mundelein. . . . . (847) 949-3200
    http://www.mundelein.org
Village of Round Lake . . . . (847) 546-5400
    http://www.eroundlake.com
Village of Round Lake Beach. . . . . (847) 546-2351
    http://www.villageofroundlakebeach.com
Village of Round Lake Park . . . . (847) 546-2790
    http://www.roundlakepark.us
Village of Vernon Hills . . . . (847) 367-3700
    http://www.vernonhills.org
Village of Wauconda . . . . (847) 526-9600
    http://www.wauconda-il.gov
Wauconda Area Chamber of Commerce. . . . . (847) 526-5580
    http://www.waucondachamber.org
Winthrop Harbor Chamber of Commerce
    http://www.cocwh.com
Zion Area Chamber of Commerce . . . . (847) 872-5405
    http://www.zionchamber.com

Lake County Communities

ANTIOCH (village). Covers a land area of 7.383 square miles and a water area of 0.262 square miles. Located at 42.47° N. Lat; 88.09° W. Long. Elevation is 784 feet.
History: Settled 1836, incorporated 1857.
Population: 6,395 (1990); 8,788 (2000); 12,462 (2010); 13,684 (2015 projected); Race: 93.8% White, 1.5% Black, 1.5% Asian, 3.3% Other, 7.2% Hispanic of any race (2010); Density: 1,688.0 persons per square mile (2010); Average household size: 2.72 (2010); Median age: 36.9 (2010); Males per 100 females: 96.7 (2010); Marriage status: 22.1% never married, 62.7% now married, 5.2% widowed, 10.0% divorced (2005-2009 5-year est.); Foreign born: 5.4% (2005-2009 5-year est.); Ancestry (includes multiple ancestries): 38.0% German, 22.6% Irish, 13.6% Polish, 9.9% English, 8.9% Italian (2005-2009 5-year est.).
Economy: Single-family building permits issued: 1 (2010); Multi-family building permits issued: 0 (2010); Employment by occupation: 18.8%

management, 24.4% professional, 11.5% services, 26.7% sales, 0.4% farming, 7.3% construction, 10.8% production (2005-2009 5-year est.).
Income: Per capita income: $33,282 (2010); Median household income: $71,328 (2010); Average household income: $90,305 (2010); Percent of households with income of $100,000 or more: 29.6% (2010); Poverty rate: 5.2% (2005-2009 5-year est.).
Taxes: Total city taxes per capita: $326 (2007); City property taxes per capita: $221 (2007).
Education: Percent of population age 25 and over with: High school diploma (including GED) or higher: 91.3% (2010); Bachelor's degree or higher: 28.3% (2010); Master's degree or higher: 9.9% (2010).

School District(s)
Antioch CCSD 34 (PK-08)
    2009-10 Enrollment: 3,158 . . . . (847) 838-8400
CHSD 117 (07-12)
    2009-10 Enrollment: 2,852 . . . . (847) 838-7170
Emmons SD 33 (KG-08)
    2009-10 Enrollment: 334 . . . . (847) 395-1105
Grass Lake SD 36 (PK-08)
    2009-10 Enrollment: 197 . . . . (847) 395-1550
Housing: Homeownership rate: 71.3% (2010); Median home value: $237,988 (2010); Median contract rent: $733 per month (2005-2009 5-year est.); Median year structure built: 1991 (2005-2009 5-year est.).
Safety: Violent crime rate: 3.5 per 10,000 population; Property crime rate: 207.5 per 10,000 population (2010).
Transportation: Commute to work: 90.9% car, 2.4% public transportation, 1.6% walk, 4.7% work from home (2005-2009 5-year est.); Travel time to work: 16.5% less than 15 minutes, 23.0% 15 to 30 minutes, 23.8% 30 to 45 minutes, 16.5% 45 to 60 minutes, 20.2% 60 minutes or more (2005-2009 5-year est.)
Additional Information Contacts
Antioch Chamber of Commerce. (847) 395-2233
    http://www.antiochchamber.org
Village of Antioch. . . . . (847) 395-1000
    http://www.antioch.il.gov

BANNOCKBURN (village). Covers a land area of 2.024 square miles and a water area of 0.008 square miles. Located at 42.19° N. Lat; 87.86° W. Long. Elevation is 686 feet.
Population: 1,388 (1990); 1,429 (2000); 1,378 (2010); 1,367 (2015 projected); Race: 89.1% White, 1.8% Black, 4.2% Asian, 4.9% Other, 5.9% Hispanic of any race (2010); Density: 680.9 persons per square mile (2010); Average household size: 2.88 (2010); Median age: 24.5 (2010); Males per 100 females: 96.3 (2010); Marriage status: 54.9% never married, 42.0% now married, 1.5% widowed, 1.7% divorced (2005-2009 5-year est.); Foreign born: 7.8% (2005-2009 5-year est.); Ancestry (includes multiple ancestries): 29.9% German, 11.8% Irish, 11.0% English, 7.0% Polish, 6.0% Swedish (2005-2009 5-year est.).
Economy: Single-family building permits issued: 0 (2010); Multi-family building permits issued: 0 (2010); Employment by occupation: 21.5% management, 19.1% professional, 13.3% services, 40.7% sales, 0.0% farming, 3.0% construction, 2.4% production (2005-2009 5-year est.).
Income: Per capita income: $43,619 (2010); Median household income: $133,333 (2010); Average household income: $181,605 (2010); Percent of households with income of $100,000 or more: 59.4% (2010); Poverty rate: 5.6% (2005-2009 5-year est.).
Taxes: Total city taxes per capita: $1,376 (2007); City property taxes per capita: $1,054 (2007).
Education: Percent of population age 25 and over with: High school diploma (including GED) or higher: 98.4% (2010); Bachelor's degree or higher: 72.6% (2010); Master's degree or higher: 31.3% (2010).

School District(s)
Bannockburn SD 106 (KG-08)
    2009-10 Enrollment: 205 . . . . (847) 945-5900
Housing: Homeownership rate: 87.4% (2010); Median home value: $796,196 (2010); Median contract rent: n/a per month (2005-2009 5-year est.); Median year structure built: 1958 (2005-2009 5-year est.).
Safety: Violent crime rate: 0.0 per 10,000 population; Property crime rate: 145.9 per 10,000 population (2010).
Transportation: Commute to work: 63.7% car, 3.0% public transportation, 19.0% walk, 10.9% work from home (2005-2009 5-year est.); Travel time to work: 35.4% less than 15 minutes, 33.4% 15 to 30 minutes, 17.4% 30 to 45 minutes, 3.9% 45 to 60 minutes, 9.9% 60 minutes or more (2005-2009 5-year est.)
Additional Information Contacts

DBR Chamber of Commerce . . . . (847) 945-4660
http://www.dbrchamber.com

BEACH PARK (village). Covers a land area of 6.419 square miles and a water area of 0 square miles. Located at 42.42° N. Lat; 87.84° W. Long. Elevation is 699 feet.

Population: 9,540 (1990); 10,072 (2000); 11,565 (2010); 12,211 (2015 projected); Race: 72.4% White, 9.3% Black, 2.7% Asian, 15.6% Other, 25.9% Hispanic of any race (2010); Density: 1,801.6 persons per square mile (2010); Average household size: 2.79 (2010); Median age: 37.6 (2010); Males per 100 females: 97.5 (2010); Marriage status: 28.3% never married, 54.1% now married, 6.2% widowed, 11.4% divorced (2005-2009 5-year est.); Foreign born: 12.1% (2005-2009 5-year est.); Ancestry (includes multiple ancestries): 23.6% German, 13.4% Irish, 9.1% Polish, 7.8% English, 4.9% Italian (2005-2009 5-year est.).
Economy: Single-family building permits issued: 23 (2010); Multi-family building permits issued: 0 (2010); Employment by occupation: 15.9% management, 16.6% professional, 15.2% services, 28.7% sales, 0.0% farming, 8.3% construction, 15.4% production (2005-2009 5-year est.).
Income: Per capita income: $28,749 (2010); Median household income: $69,769 (2010); Average household income: $79,709 (2010); Percent of households with income of $100,000 or more: 25.7% (2010); Poverty rate: 5.0% (2005-2009 5-year est.).
Taxes: Total city taxes per capita: $79 (2007); City property taxes per capita: $11 (2007).
Education: Percent of population age 25 and over with: High school diploma (including GED) or higher: 85.2% (2010); Bachelor's degree or higher: 19.4% (2010); Master's degree or higher: 7.2% (2010).

School District(s)
Beach Park CCSD 3 (PK-08)
    2009-10 Enrollment: 2,560 . . . . (847) 599-5005
Housing: Homeownership rate: 84.6% (2010); Median home value: $175,064 (2010); Median contract rent: $739 per month (2005-2009 5-year est.); Median year structure built: 1979 (2005-2009 5-year est.).
Transportation: Commute to work: 90.7% car, 2.6% public transportation, 0.2% walk, 3.6% work from home (2005-2009 5-year est.); Travel time to work: 20.2% less than 15 minutes, 39.2% 15 to 30 minutes, 21.7% 30 to 45 minutes, 7.9% 45 to 60 minutes, 11.0% 60 minutes or more (2005-2009 5-year est.)
Additional Information Contacts
Village of Beach Park . . . . (847) 746-1770
http://www.villageofbeachpark.com

BUFFALO GROVE (village). Covers a land area of 9.194 square miles and a water area of 0.020 square miles. Located at 42.16° N. Lat; 87.96° W. Long.

Population: 37,883 (1990); 42,909 (2000); 45,724 (2010); 46,665 (2015 projected); Race: 83.9% White, 0.7% Black, 12.4% Asian, 3.0% Other, 4.7% Hispanic of any race (2010); Density: 4,973.0 persons per square mile (2010); Average household size: 2.79 (2010); Median age: 39.6 (2010); Males per 100 females: 94.1 (2010); Marriage status: 23.2% never married, 63.8% now married, 5.3% widowed, 7.7% divorced (2005-2009 5-year est.); Foreign born: 24.9% (2005-2009 5-year est.); Ancestry (includes multiple ancestries): 17.4% Russian, 14.1% German, 10.7% Polish, 8.8% Irish, 5.5% English (2005-2009 5-year est.).
Economy: Unemployment rate: 8.0% (August 2011); Total civilian labor force: 24,161 (August 2011); Single-family building permits issued: 54 (2010); Multi-family building permits issued: 0 (2010); Employment by occupation: 25.5% management, 30.3% professional, 8.5% services, 27.5% sales, 0.1% farming, 2.9% construction, 5.2% production (2005-2009 5-year est.).
Income: Per capita income: $44,059 (2010); Median household income: $96,247 (2010); Average household income: $123,086 (2010); Percent of households with income of $100,000 or more: 47.6% (2010); Poverty rate: 3.3% (2005-2009 5-year est.).
Education: Percent of population age 25 and over with: High school diploma (including GED) or higher: 96.6% (2010); Bachelor's degree or higher: 59.7% (2010); Master's degree or higher: 23.4% (2010).

School District(s)
Aptakisic-Tripp CCSD 102 (PK-08)
    2009-10 Enrollment: 2,011 . . . . (847) 353-5650
Kildeer Countryside CCSD 96 (PK-08)
    2009-10 Enrollment: 3,157 . . . . (847) 459-4260
Township HSD 214 (09-12)
    2009-10 Enrollment: 12,241 . . . . (847) 718-7600

Wheeling CCSD 21 (PK-08)
    2009-10 Enrollment: 6,952 . . . . (847) 537-8270
Housing: Homeownership rate: 90.2% (2010); Median home value: $294,643 (2010); Median contract rent: $1,105 per month (2005-2009 5-year est.); Median year structure built: 1982 (2005-2009 5-year est.).
Safety: Violent crime rate: 1.9 per 10,000 population; Property crime rate: 92.5 per 10,000 population (2010).
Transportation: Commute to work: 89.3% car, 3.7% public transportation, 0.6% walk, 5.4% work from home (2005-2009 5-year est.); Travel time to work: 20.5% less than 15 minutes, 33.7% 15 to 30 minutes, 26.2% 30 to 45 minutes, 9.3% 45 to 60 minutes, 10.2% 60 minutes or more (2005-2009 5-year est.)
Additional Information Contacts
Buffalo Grove Area Chamber of Commerce . . . . (847) 541-7799
http://www.buffalogrovechamber.org
Village of Buffalo Grove . . . . (847) 459-2525
http://www.vbg.org

CHANNEL LAKE (CDP). Covers a land area of 1.949 square miles and a water area of 0.338 square miles. Located at 42.47° N. Lat; 88.14° W. Long. Elevation is 745 feet.

Population: 1,677 (1990); 1,785 (2000); 2,005 (2010); 2,092 (2015 projected); Race: 93.9% White, 0.4% Black, 1.0% Asian, 4.7% Other, 2.4% Hispanic of any race (2010); Density: 1,029.0 persons per square mile (2010); Average household size: 2.56 (2010); Median age: 41.7 (2010); Males per 100 females: 108.4 (2010); Marriage status: 31.8% never married, 48.4% now married, 6.9% widowed, 12.9% divorced (2005-2009 5-year est.); Foreign born: 0.4% (2005-2009 5-year est.); Ancestry (includes multiple ancestries): 40.7% German, 31.0% Irish, 11.3% Polish, 11.3% English, 8.9% American (2005-2009 5-year est.).
Economy: Employment by occupation: 9.0% management, 15.5% professional, 15.7% services, 30.8% sales, 0.0% farming, 18.1% construction, 10.8% production (2005-2009 5-year est.).
Income: Per capita income: $31,604 (2010); Median household income: $64,466 (2010); Average household income: $80,510 (2010); Percent of households with income of $100,000 or more: 23.6% (2010); Poverty rate: 8.3% (2005-2009 5-year est.).
Education: Percent of population age 25 and over with: High school diploma (including GED) or higher: 87.0% (2010); Bachelor's degree or higher: 20.0% (2010); Master's degree or higher: 5.9% (2010).
Housing: Homeownership rate: 83.4% (2010); Median home value: $191,265 (2010); Median contract rent: $659 per month (2005-2009 5-year est.); Median year structure built: 1957 (2005-2009 5-year est.).
Transportation: Commute to work: 87.2% car, 1.5% public transportation, 1.3% walk, 10.0% work from home (2005-2009 5-year est.); Travel time to work: 18.3% less than 15 minutes, 24.9% 15 to 30 minutes, 20.9% 30 to 45 minutes, 7.1% 45 to 60 minutes, 28.8% 60 minutes or more (2005-2009 5-year est.)

DEER PARK (village). Covers a land area of 3.646 square miles and a water area of 0.061 square miles. Located at 42.16° N. Lat; 88.08° W. Long. Elevation is 850 feet.

History: The Village of Deer Park was incorporated November 13, 1957. The village is located in both Lake & Cook Counties, east of the Village of Barrington, south of the Village of Lake Zurich, and it is 37 miles northwest of Chicago.
Population: 2,817 (1990); 3,102 (2000); 3,074 (2010); 3,048 (2015 projected); Race: 92.1% White, 0.5% Black, 5.9% Asian, 1.5% Other, 2.8% Hispanic of any race (2010); Density: 843.0 persons per square mile (2010); Average household size: 3.27 (2010); Median age: 37.2 (2010); Males per 100 females: 96.8 (2010); Marriage status: 25.6% never married, 68.3% now married, 3.3% widowed, 2.8% divorced (2005-2009 5-year est.); Foreign born: 7.4% (2005-2009 5-year est.); Ancestry (includes multiple ancestries): 29.6% German, 22.9% Irish, 17.9% Italian, 13.4% Polish, 7.9% English (2005-2009 5-year est.).
Economy: Single-family building permits issued: 5 (2010); Multi-family building permits issued: 0 (2010); Employment by occupation: 33.2% management, 20.8% professional, 6.6% services, 31.0% sales, 0.0% farming, 2.1% construction, 6.3% production (2005-2009 5-year est.).
Income: Per capita income: $54,356 (2010); Median household income: $127,123 (2010); Average household income: $180,480 (2010); Percent of households with income of $100,000 or more: 67.0% (2010); Poverty rate: 0.8% (2005-2009 5-year est.).
Taxes: Total city taxes per capita: $276 (2007); City property taxes per capita: $2 (2007).

Education: Percent of population age 25 and over with: High school diploma (including GED) or higher: 96.8% (2010); Bachelor's degree or higher: 58.4% (2010); Master's degree or higher: 23.9% (2010).
Housing: Homeownership rate: 97.5% (2010); Median home value: $391,250 (2010); Median contract rent: n/a per month (2005-2009 5-year est.); Median year structure built: 1982 (2005-2009 5-year est.).
Safety: Violent crime rate: 0.0 per 10,000 population; Property crime rate: 140.8 per 10,000 population (2010).
Transportation: Commute to work: 77.0% car, 8.2% public transportation, 0.4% walk, 13.7% work from home (2005-2009 5-year est.); Travel time to work: 23.9% less than 15 minutes, 26.8% 15 to 30 minutes, 23.3% 30 to 45 minutes, 9.2% 45 to 60 minutes, 16.9% 60 minutes or more (2005-2009 5-year est.)

DEERFIELD (village). Covers a land area of 5.483 square miles and a water area of 0.035 square miles. Located at 42.16° N. Lat; 87.85° W. Long. Elevation is 686 feet.
History: Named for the abundance of deer in the area. Incorporated 1903.
Population: 17,341 (1990); 18,420 (2000); 20,008 (2010); 20,531 (2015 projected); Race: 93.5% White, 0.3% Black, 4.2% Asian, 1.9% Other, 2.7% Hispanic of any race (2010); Density: 3,649.0 persons per square mile (2010); Average household size: 2.84 (2010); Median age: 40.0 (2010); Males per 100 females: 94.6 (2010); Marriage status: 21.2% never married, 67.2% now married, 5.3% widowed, 6.2% divorced (2005-2009 5-year est.); Foreign born: 7.7% (2005-2009 5-year est.); Ancestry (includes multiple ancestries): 19.4% Russian, 17.6% German, 11.5% American, 10.9% Polish, 9.4% Irish (2005-2009 5-year est.).
Economy: Single-family building permits issued: 27 (2010); Multi-family building permits issued: 0 (2010); Employment by occupation: 25.4% management, 38.4% professional, 7.6% services, 23.9% sales, 0.1% farming, 2.9% construction, 1.8% production (2005-2009 5-year est.).
Income: Per capita income: $59,119 (2010); Median household income: $128,043 (2010); Average household income: $169,059 (2010); Percent of households with income of $100,000 or more: 62.9% (2010); Poverty rate: 2.3% (2005-2009 5-year est.).
Taxes: Total city taxes per capita: $809 (2007); City property taxes per capita: $507 (2007).
Education: Percent of population age 25 and over with: High school diploma (including GED) or higher: 96.6% (2010); Bachelor's degree or higher: 71.4% (2010); Master's degree or higher: 34.9% (2010).

School District(s)
Deerfield SD 109 (PK-08)
    2009-10 Enrollment: 3,194 . . . . (847) 945-1844
Twp HSD 113 (09-12)
    2009-10 Enrollment: 3,737 . . . . (224) 765-1001
Four-year College(s)
Trinity International University (Private, Not-for-profit, Evangelical Free Church of America)
    Fall 2009 Enrollment: 2,730. . . . . (847) 945-8800
    2010-11 Tuition: In-state $23,370; Out-of-state $23,370
Housing: Homeownership rate: 91.4% (2010); Median home value: $465,182 (2010); Median contract rent: $1,302 per month (2005-2009 5-year est.); Median year structure built: 1966 (2005-2009 5-year est.).
Safety: Violent crime rate: 4.1 per 10,000 population; Property crime rate: 88.0 per 10,000 population (2010).
Transportation: Commute to work: 76.5% car, 12.0% public transportation, 1.1% walk, 8.6% work from home (2005-2009 5-year est.); Travel time to work: 27.8% less than 15 minutes, 28.2% 15 to 30 minutes, 19.0% 30 to 45 minutes, 10.1% 45 to 60 minutes, 14.9% 60 minutes or more (2005-2009 5-year est.)
Additional Information Contacts
DBR Chamber of Commerce. . . . . (847) 945-4660
    http://www.dbrchamber.com
Village of Deerfield. . . . . (847) 945-5000
    http://www.deerfield.il.us

FOREST LAKE (CDP). Covers a land area of 0.632 square miles and a water area of 0.062 square miles. Located at 42.20° N. Lat; 88.05° W. Long. Elevation is 814 feet.
Population: 997 (1990); 1,530 (2000); 1,863 (2010); 2,010 (2015 projected); Race: 92.5% White, 1.0% Black, 3.6% Asian, 3.0% Other, 4.8% Hispanic of any race (2010); Density: 2,948.7 persons per square mile (2010); Average household size: 3.01 (2010); Median age: 37.0 (2010); Males per 100 females: 98.0 (2010); Marriage status: 16.6% never married, 75.6% now married, 2.3% widowed, 5.5% divorced (2005-2009 5-year

est.); Foreign born: 27.7% (2005-2009 5-year est.); Ancestry (includes multiple ancestries): 31.0% German, 12.8% Polish, 9.2% Russian, 7.9% Italian, 5.6% Irish (2005-2009 5-year est.).
Economy: Employment by occupation: 23.9% management, 26.0% professional, 8.5% services, 27.4% sales, 0.0% farming, 5.7% construction, 8.4% production (2005-2009 5-year est.).
Income: Per capita income: $42,812 (2010); Median household income: $105,660 (2010); Average household income: $129,393 (2010); Percent of households with income of $100,000 or more: 53.9% (2010); Poverty rate: 1.6% (2005-2009 5-year est.).
Education: Percent of population age 25 and over with: High school diploma (including GED) or higher: 94.6% (2010); Bachelor's degree or higher: 48.1% (2010); Master's degree or higher: 13.7% (2010).
Housing: Homeownership rate: 92.2% (2010); Median home value: $283,026 (2010); Median contract rent: $1,240 per month (2005-2009 5-year est.); Median year structure built: 1976 (2005-2009 5-year est.).
Transportation: Commute to work: 87.3% car, 1.2% public transportation, 0.0% walk, 11.5% work from home (2005-2009 5-year est.); Travel time to work: 16.1% less than 15 minutes, 25.4% 15 to 30 minutes, 30.8% 30 to 45 minutes, 14.3% 45 to 60 minutes, 13.4% 60 minutes or more (2005-2009 5-year est.)

FORT SHERIDAN (unincorporated postal area, zip code 60037). Covers a land area of 0.450 square miles and a water area of 0 square miles. Located at 42.25° N. Lat; 87.81° W. Long.
Population: 901 (2000); Race: 82.5% White, 14.7% Black, 0.0% Asian, 2.8% Other, 3.8% Hispanic of any race (2000); Density: 2,002.2 persons per square mile (2000); Age: 47.0% under 18, 0.0% over 64 (2000); Marriage status: 7.1% never married, 89.8% now married, 0.0% widowed, 3.1% divorced (2000); Foreign born: 1.7% (2000); Ancestry (includes multiple ancestries): 26.1% German, 10.0% American, 9.8% Irish, 9.5% English (2000).
Economy: Employment by occupation: 9.2% management, 34.1% professional, 9.6% services, 36.0% sales, 0.0% farming, 5.4% construction, 5.7% production (2000).
Income: Per capita income: $16,727 (2000); Median household income: $46,750 (2000); Poverty rate: 0.0% (2000).
Education: Percent of population age 25 and over with: High school diploma (including GED) or higher: 98.7% (2000); Bachelor's degree or higher: 36.8% (2000).
Housing: Homeownership rate: 4.6% (2000); Median home value: $700,000 (2000); Median contract rent: $779 per month (2000); Median year structure built: 1961 (2000).
Transportation: Commute to work: 92.8% car, 0.0% public transportation, 1.9% walk, 3.9% work from home (2000); Travel time to work: 21.8% less than 15 minutes, 55.1% 15 to 30 minutes, 17.8% 30 to 45 minutes, 1.5% 45 to 60 minutes, 3.8% 60 minutes or more (2000)

FOX LAKE (village). Covers a land area of 7.348 square miles and a water area of 1.632 square miles. Located at 42.40° N. Lat; 88.17° W. Long. Elevation is 748 feet.
History: Fox Lake developed as a resort community for vacationers who enjoyed the numerous lakes in the area.
Population: 8,117 (1990); 9,178 (2000); 9,413 (2010); 9,552 (2015 projected); Race: 93.6% White, 0.8% Black, 1.1% Asian, 4.5% Other, 9.4% Hispanic of any race (2010); Density: 1,281.0 persons per square mile (2010); Average household size: 2.36 (2010); Median age: 39.6 (2010); Males per 100 females: 102.0 (2010); Marriage status: 28.7% never married, 47.7% now married, 6.5% widowed, 17.1% divorced (2005-2009 5-year est.); Foreign born: 5.4% (2005-2009 5-year est.); Ancestry (includes multiple ancestries): 31.3% German, 25.2% Irish, 22.0% Polish, 13.3% Italian, 6.2% English (2005-2009 5-year est.).
Economy: Single-family building permits issued: 0 (2010); Multi-family building permits issued: 0 (2010); Employment by occupation: 14.5% management, 15.3% professional, 14.4% services, 31.6% sales, 0.0% farming, 12.0% construction, 12.2% production (2005-2009 5-year est.).
Income: Per capita income: $28,802 (2010); Median household income: $58,175 (2010); Average household income: $67,780 (2010); Percent of households with income of $100,000 or more: 18.4% (2010); Poverty rate: 10.6% (2005-2009 5-year est.).
Taxes: Total city taxes per capita: $333 (2007); City property taxes per capita: $241 (2007).
Education: Percent of population age 25 and over with: High school diploma (including GED) or higher: 87.8% (2010); Bachelor's degree or higher: 16.0% (2010); Master's degree or higher: 6.0% (2010).

Fox Lake Gsd 114 (PK-08)

2009-10 Enrollment: 853 . . . . (847) 973-4027

Grant CHSD 124 (09-12)

2009-10 Enrollment: 1,816 . . . . (847) 587-2561

Housing: Homeownership rate: 68.9% (2010); Median home value: $174,728 (2010); Median contract rent: $745 per month (2005-2009 5-year est.); Median year structure built: 1975 (2005-2009 5-year est.).

Safety: Violent crime rate: 25.2 per 10,000 population; Property crime rate: 269.7 per 10,000 population (2010).

Transportation: Commute to work: 88.9% car, 3.2% public transportation, 1.4% walk, 5.0% work from home (2005-2009 5-year est.); Travel time to work: 14.8% less than 15 minutes, 21.9% 15 to 30 minutes, 23.4% 30 to 45 minutes, 16.3% 45 to 60 minutes, 23.7% 60 minutes or more (2005-2009 5-year est.)

Additional Information Contacts

Fox Lake Area Chamber of Commerce . . . . (847) 587-7474
  http://www.discoverfoxlake.com

Village of Fox Lake . . . . (847) 587-2151
  http://www.foxlake.org

FOX LAKE HILLS (CDP). Covers a land area of 1.328 square miles and a water area of 0.456 square miles. Located at 42.40° N. Lat; 88.12° W. Long. Elevation is 751 feet.

Population: 2,612 (1990); 2,561 (2000); 2,555 (2010); 2,553 (2015 projected); Race: 93.5% White, 3.0% Black, 0.7% Asian, 2.8% Other, 5.7% Hispanic of any race (2010); Density: 1,924.1 persons per square mile (2010); Average household size: 2.83 (2010); Median age: 40.0 (2010); Males per 100 females: 98.1 (2010); Marriage status: 25.6% never married, 52.6% now married, 6.8% widowed, 15.0% divorced (2005-2009 5-year est.); Foreign born: 4.8% (2005-2009 5-year est.); Ancestry (includes multiple ancestries): 35.2% German, 27.2% Irish, 24.0% Polish, 12.3% Italian, 9.0% Dutch (2005-2009 5-year est.).

Economy: Employment by occupation: 9.5% management, 10.9% professional, 11.6% services, 35.8% sales, 0.6% farming, 16.8% construction, 14.9% production (2005-2009 5-year est.).

Income: Per capita income: $32,567 (2010); Median household income: $81,250 (2010); Average household income: $92,742 (2010); Percent of households with income of $100,000 or more: 32.8% (2010); Poverty rate: 8.4% (2005-2009 5-year est.).

Education: Percent of population age 25 and over with: High school diploma (including GED) or higher: 90.8% (2010); Bachelor's degree or higher: 27.2% (2010); Master's degree or higher: 8.1% (2010).

Housing: Homeownership rate: 91.9% (2010); Median home value: $182,550 (2010); Median contract rent: $1,068 per month (2005-2009 5-year est.); Median year structure built: 1971 (2005-2009 5-year est.).

Transportation: Commute to work: 93.6% car, 0.0% public transportation, 0.0% walk, 5.6% work from home (2005-2009 5-year est.); Travel time to work: 15.1% less than 15 minutes, 14.9% 15 to 30 minutes, 27.8% 30 to 45 minutes, 20.7% 45 to 60 minutes, 21.5% 60 minutes or more (2005-2009 5-year est.)

GAGES LAKE (CDP). Covers a land area of 3.087 square miles and a water area of 0.219 square miles. Located at 42.35° N. Lat; 87.98° W. Long. Elevation is 768 feet.

Population: 8,138 (1990); 10,415 (2000); 10,618 (2010); 10,700 (2015 projected); Race: 80.4% White, 3.7% Black, 10.3% Asian, 5.6% Other, 8.1% Hispanic of any race (2010); Density: 3,439.8 persons per square mile (2010); Average household size: 2.85 (2010); Median age: 36.7 (2010); Males per 100 females: 96.8 (2010); Marriage status: 22.9% never married, 59.7% now married, 4.5% widowed, 12.8% divorced (2005-2009 5-year est.); Foreign born: 11.9% (2005-2009 5-year est.); Ancestry (includes multiple ancestries): 26.0% German, 17.9% Irish, 11.1% Polish, 10.6% English, 8.4% Italian (2005-2009 5-year est.).

Economy: Employment by occupation: 17.4% management, 18.9% professional, 7.9% services, 35.0% sales, 0.0% farming, 8.9% construction, 11.8% production (2005-2009 5-year est.).

Income: Per capita income: $36,880 (2010); Median household income: $88,018 (2010); Average household income: $105,003 (2010); Percent of households with income of $100,000 or more: 42.5% (2010); Poverty rate: 2.7% (2005-2009 5-year est.).

Education: Percent of population age 25 and over with: High school diploma (including GED) or higher: 94.8% (2010); Bachelor's degree or higher: 45.4% (2010); Master's degree or higher: 17.0% (2010).

Spec Educ Dist Lake County/Sedol (PK-12)

2009-10 Enrollment: n/a . . . . (847) 548-8470

Woodland CCSD 50 (PK-08)

2009-10 Enrollment: 6,835 . . . . (847) 596-5601

Housing: Homeownership rate: 82.1% (2010); Median home value: $235,224 (2010); Median contract rent: $1,011 per month (2005-2009 5-year est.); Median year structure built: 1982 (2005-2009 5-year est.).

Transportation: Commute to work: 91.6% car, 3.1% public transportation, 0.3% walk, 3.5% work from home (2005-2009 5-year est.); Travel time to work: 20.7% less than 15 minutes, 30.3% 15 to 30 minutes, 27.9% 30 to 45 minutes, 9.6% 45 to 60 minutes, 11.5% 60 minutes or more (2005-2009 5-year est.)

GRANDWOOD PARK (CDP). Covers a land area of 1.616 square miles and a water area of 0.015 square miles. Located at 42.39° N. Lat; 87.98° W. Long. Elevation is 745 feet.

Population: 2,439 (1990); 4,521 (2000); 4,900 (2010); 5,058 (2015 projected); Race: 78.6% White, 6.4% Black, 7.8% Asian, 7.2% Other, 9.4% Hispanic of any race (2010); Density: 3,032.9 persons per square mile (2010); Average household size: 2.90 (2010); Median age: 36.0 (2010); Males per 100 females: 96.2 (2010); Marriage status: 29.3% never married, 57.9% now married, 3.7% widowed, 9.1% divorced (2005-2009 5-year est.); Foreign born: 17.4% (2005-2009 5-year est.); Ancestry (includes multiple ancestries): 26.6% German, 16.3% Irish, 13.3% Polish, 8.2% English, 5.7% Italian (2005-2009 5-year est.).

Economy: Employment by occupation: 20.0% management, 21.1% professional, 10.1% services, 30.1% sales, 6.0% farming, 6.5% construction, 6.1% production (2005-2009 5-year est.).

Income: Per capita income: $41,549 (2010); Median household income: $89,543 (2010); Average household income: $120,602 (2010); Percent of households with income of $100,000 or more: 42.3% (2010); Poverty rate: 4.8% (2005-2009 5-year est.).

Education: Percent of population age 25 and over with: High school diploma (including GED) or higher: 94.1% (2010); Bachelor's degree or higher: 48.6% (2010); Master's degree or higher: 16.5% (2010).

Housing: Homeownership rate: 86.5% (2010); Median home value: $247,038 (2010); Median contract rent: $983 per month (2005-2009 5-year est.); Median year structure built: 1987 (2005-2009 5-year est.).

Transportation: Commute to work: 89.6% car, 1.4% public transportation, 6.1% walk, 2.9% work from home (2005-2009 5-year est.); Travel time to work: 20.4% less than 15 minutes, 28.3% 15 to 30 minutes, 27.8% 30 to 45 minutes, 12.2% 45 to 60 minutes, 11.2% 60 minutes or more (2005-2009 5-year est.)

GRAYSLAKE (village). Aka Grays Lake. Covers a land area of 9.398 square miles and a water area of 0.157 square miles. Located at 42.34° N. Lat; 88.03° W. Long. Elevation is 784 feet.

History: Named for William Gray, an early settler. College of Lake County here. Incorporated 1895.

Population: 8,307 (1990); 18,506 (2000); 25,008 (2010); 27,657 (2015 projected); Race: 84.9% White, 2.1% Black, 7.7% Asian, 5.3% Other, 8.8% Hispanic of any race (2010); Density: 2,661.1 persons per square mile (2010); Average household size: 2.97 (2010); Median age: 35.6 (2010); Males per 100 females: 97.1 (2010); Marriage status: 27.7% never married, 57.9% now married, 4.2% widowed, 10.1% divorced (2005-2009 5-year est.); Foreign born: 11.3% (2005-2009 5-year est.); Ancestry (includes multiple ancestries): 31.5% German, 20.7% Irish, 13.5% Polish, 9.6% Italian, 8.1% English (2005-2009 5-year est.).

Economy: Single-family building permits issued: 1 (2010); Multi-family building permits issued: 0 (2010); Employment by occupation: 23.0% management, 26.3% professional, 11.1% services, 28.0% sales, 0.2% farming, 5.7% construction, 5.7% production (2005-2009 5-year est.).

Income: Per capita income: $35,968 (2010); Median household income: $92,167 (2010); Average household income: $106,866 (2010); Percent of households with income of $100,000 or more: 43.6% (2010); Poverty rate: 4.7% (2005-2009 5-year est.).

Taxes: Total city taxes per capita: $162 (2007); City property taxes per capita: $95 (2007).

Education: Percent of population age 25 and over with: High school diploma (including GED) or higher: 94.8% (2010); Bachelor's degree or higher: 51.3% (2010); Master's degree or higher: 19.5% (2010).

Grayslake CCSD 46 (PK-08)

2009-10 Enrollment: 4,218 . . . . (847) 223-3650

Grayslake CHSD 127 (09-12)
  2009-10 Enrollment: 2,789 . . . . (847) 986-3400
Lake Co High Schools Tech Campus (11-12)
  2009-10 Enrollment: n/a . . . . (847) 543-6001
Lake Roe (06-12)
  2009-10 Enrollment: n/a . . . . (847) 543-7833
Prairie Crossing Charter School (KG-08)
  2009-10 Enrollment: 362 . . . . (847) 543-9722
Spec Educ Dist Lake County/Sedol (PK-12)
  2009-10 Enrollment: n/a . . . . (847) 548-8470

Two-year College(s)

College of Lake County (Public)
  Fall 2009 Enrollment: 18,092 . . . . (847) 543-2000
  2010-11 Tuition: In-state $6,888; Out-of-state $9,128
Housing: Homeownership rate: 82.3% (2010); Median home value: $233,489 (2010); Median contract rent: $778 per month (2005-2009 5-year est.); Median year structure built: 1993 (2005-2009 5-year est.).
Safety: Violent crime rate: 11.0 per 10,000 population; Property crime rate: 215.2 per 10,000 population (2010).
Newspapers: Antioch News Reporter (Regional news; Circulation 4,881); Fox Lake Press (Regional news; Circulation 5,579); Grayslake Times (Regional news; Circulation 4,326); Great Lakes Bulletin (Regional news); Gurnee Press (Regional news; Circulation 4,842); Lake Villa Record (Regional news; Circulation 2,742); Lake Zurich Enterprise (Local news; Circulation 3,721); Libertyville News (Regional news; Circulation 3,200); Lindenhurst News (Regional news; Circulation 2,711); Market/Journal (Community news; Circulation 90,162); Market/Journal II (Community news; Circulation 14,171); Market/Journal III (Community news; Circulation 10,338); Market/Journal V (Community news; Circulation 19,012); Market/Journal VI (Community news; Circulation 11,117); Market/Journal VII (Community news; Circulation 11,141); Market/Journal VIII (Community news; Circulation 11,141); Mundelein News (Regional news; Circulation 3,107); Vernon Hills News (Local news; Circulation 2,820); Wadsworth News (Regional news; Circulation 2,361)
Transportation: Commute to work: 87.9% car, 5.5% public transportation, 0.8% walk, 4.6% work from home (2005-2009 5-year est.); Travel time to work: 16.1% less than 15 minutes, 26.2% 15 to 30 minutes, 23.7% 30 to 45 minutes, 16.0% 45 to 60 minutes, 18.0% 60 minutes or more (2005-2009 5-year est.)

Additional Information Contacts
Grayslake Area Chamber of Commerce & Industry. . . . . . . (847) 223-6888
  http://www.grayslakechamber.com
Village of Grayslake. . . . . (847) 223-8515
  http://www.villageofgrayslake.com

GREAT LAKES (unincorporated postal area, zip code 60088).
Covers a land area of 2.362 square miles and a water area of 0 square miles. Located at 42.30° N. Lat; 87.85° W. Long. Elevation is 659 feet.
Population: 13,319 (2000); Race: 63.7% White, 20.7% Black, 5.0% Asian, 10.6% Other, 10.6% Hispanic of any race (2000); Density: 5,638.9 persons per square mile (2000); Age: 23.9% under 18, 0.1% over 64 (2000); Marriage status: 53.9% never married, 42.8% now married, 0.1% widowed, 3.3% divorced (2000); Foreign born: 6.8% (2000); Ancestry (includes multiple ancestries): 15.5% German, 12.2% Irish, 6.2% English, 6.1% American (2000).
Economy: Employment by occupation: 14.3% management, 24.0% professional, 22.2% services, 29.0% sales, 0.0% farming, 1.9% construction, 8.6% production (2000).
Income: Per capita income: $12,340 (2000); Median household income: $39,299 (2000); Poverty rate: 6.5% (2000).
Education: Percent of population age 25 and over with: High school diploma (including GED) or higher: 95.0% (2000); Bachelor's degree or higher: 17.6% (2000).

School District(s)

North Chicago SD 187 (PK-12)
  2009-10 Enrollment: 3,983 . . . . (847) 689-8150
Housing: Homeownership rate: 4.6% (2000); Median home value: $112,500 (2000); Median contract rent: $818 per month (2000); Median year structure built: 1968 (2000).
Hospitals: Naval Health Clinic: Great Lakes (186 beds)
Transportation: Commute to work: 39.6% car, 0.5% public transportation, 55.9% walk, 1.7% work from home (2000); Travel time to work: 76.1% less than 15 minutes, 16.0% 15 to 30 minutes, 3.2% 30 to 45 minutes, 2.4% 45 to 60 minutes, 2.2% 60 minutes or more (2000)

GREEN OAKS (village). Aka Oak Grove. Covers a land area of 4.004 square miles and a water area of 0.056 square miles. Located at 42.28° N. Lat; 87.91° W. Long. Elevation is 689 feet.
History: One of the earliest settlers was Thomas Madden, who bought some land about three miles east of the river in the year 1844; when the "Village Of Oak Grove" changed its name and founded Green Oaks in 1960, all 150 residents attended the celebration dinner.
Population: 2,357 (1990); 3,572 (2000); 4,126 (2010); 4,383 (2015 projected); Race: 81.9% White, 3.3% Black, 11.7% Asian, 3.1% Other, 5.5% Hispanic of any race (2010); Density: 1,030.4 persons per square mile (2010); Average household size: 2.67 (2010); Median age: 38.4 (2010); Males per 100 females: 98.5 (2010); Marriage status: 24.6% never married, 67.9% now married, 4.1% widowed, 3.4% divorced (2005-2009 5-year est.); Foreign born: 12.8% (2005-2009 5-year est.); Ancestry (includes multiple ancestries): 25.4% German, 17.1% Irish, 11.6% Polish, 8.0% English, 7.4% Italian (2005-2009 5-year est.).
Economy: Single-family building permits issued: 0 (2010); Multi-family building permits issued: 0 (2010); Employment by occupation: 34.7% management, 26.4% professional, 10.1% services, 22.4% sales, 0.0% farming, 4.1% construction, 2.4% production (2005-2009 5-year est.).
Income: Per capita income: $57,261 (2010); Median household income: $103,682 (2010); Average household income: $152,836 (2010); Percent of households with income of $100,000 or more: 51.4% (2010); Poverty rate: 2.4% (2005-2009 5-year est.).
Taxes: Total city taxes per capita: $114 (2007); City property taxes per capita: $85 (2007).
Education: Percent of population age 25 and over with: High school diploma (including GED) or higher: 97.2% (2010); Bachelor's degree or higher: 65.2% (2010); Master's degree or higher: 30.5% (2010).
Housing: Homeownership rate: 77.8% (2010); Median home value: $447,917 (2010); Median contract rent: n/a per month (2005-2009 5-year est.); Median year structure built: 1987 (2005-2009 5-year est.).
Transportation: Commute to work: 86.0% car, 4.3% public transportation, 0.4% walk, 8.7% work from home (2005-2009 5-year est.); Travel time to work: 24.7% less than 15 minutes, 37.4% 15 to 30 minutes, 14.6% 30 to 45 minutes, 10.1% 45 to 60 minutes, 13.2% 60 minutes or more (2005-2009 5-year est.)

Additional Information Contacts
GLMV Area Chamber of Commerce . . . . (847) 680-0750
  http://www.glmvchamber.org

GURNEE (village). Covers a land area of 13.401 square miles and a water area of 0.014 square miles. Located at 42.37° N. Lat; 87.93° W. Long. Elevation is 679 feet.
Population: 14,698 (1990); 28,834 (2000); 31,998 (2010); 33,591 (2015 projected); Race: 71.9% White, 7.0% Black, 13.3% Asian, 7.8% Other, 10.6% Hispanic of any race (2010); Density: 2,387.7 persons per square mile (2010); Average household size: 2.80 (2010); Median age: 36.8 (2010); Males per 100 females: 94.7 (2010); Marriage status: 26.4% never married, 60.6% now married, 4.9% widowed, 8.1% divorced (2005-2009 5-year est.); Foreign born: 16.6% (2005-2009 5-year est.); Ancestry (includes multiple ancestries): 24.5% German, 15.8% Irish, 10.3% Polish, 8.4% English, 8.1% Italian (2005-2009 5-year est.).
Economy: Unemployment rate: 9.4% (August 2011); Total civilian labor force: 17,073 (August 2011); Single-family building permits issued: 1 (2010); Multi-family building permits issued: 0 (2010); Employment by occupation: 22.5% management, 26.6% professional, 9.8% services, 28.7% sales, 0.1% farming, 4.8% construction, 7.6% production (2005-2009 5-year est.).
Income: Per capita income: $39,038 (2010); Median household income: $93,325 (2010); Average household income: $109,329 (2010); Percent of households with income of $100,000 or more: 46.3% (2010); Poverty rate: 5.1% (2005-2009 5-year est.).
Taxes: Total city taxes per capita: $227 (2007); City property taxes per capita: $15 (2007).
Education: Percent of population age 25 and over with: High school diploma (including GED) or higher: 95.1% (2010); Bachelor's degree or higher: 49.6% (2010); Master's degree or higher: 18.7% (2010).

School District(s)

Gurnee SD 56 (PK-08)
  2009-10 Enrollment: 2,158 . . . . (847) 336-0800
Warren Twp HSD 121 (09-12)
  2009-10 Enrollment: 4,397 . . . . (847) 662-1400

Woodland CCSD 50 (PK-08)

2009-10 Enrollment: 6,835 . . . . (847) 596-5601

Housing: Homeownership rate: 79.7% (2010); Median home value: $263,020 (2010); Median contract rent: $913 per month (2005-2009 5-year est.); Median year structure built: 1991 (2005-2009 5-year est.).

Safety: Violent crime rate: 9.2 per 10,000 population; Property crime rate: 448.8 per 10,000 population (2010).

Transportation: Commute to work: 91.4% car, 2.5% public transportation, 1.1% walk, 4.1% work from home (2005-2009 5-year est.); Travel time to work: 21.0% less than 15 minutes, 31.9% 15 to 30 minutes, 22.4% 30 to 45 minutes, 11.5% 45 to 60 minutes, 13.2% 60 minutes or more (2005-2009 5-year est.)

Additional Information Contacts

Lake County Chamber of Commerce . . . . (847) 249-3800
   http://www.lakecountychamber.com
Village of Gurnee . . . . (847) 599-7500
   http://www.gurnee.il.us

HAINESVILLE (village). Covers a land area of 1.743 square miles and a water area of 0.034 square miles. Located at 42.34° N. Lat; 88.06° W. Long. Elevation is 801 feet.

Population: 282 (1990); 2,129 (2000); 3,661 (2010); 4,013 (2015 projected); Race: 76.6% White, 3.1% Black, 4.7% Asian, 15.5% Other, 24.0% Hispanic of any race (2010); Density: 2,099.9 persons per square mile (2010); Average household size: 3.43 (2010); Median age: 31.7 (2010); Males per 100 females: 101.2 (2010); Marriage status: 19.0% never married, 63.2% now married, 3.9% widowed, 13.9% divorced (2005-2009 5-year est.); Foreign born: 25.0% (2005-2009 5-year est.); Ancestry (includes multiple ancestries): 26.0% German, 12.7% Polish, 12.2% Irish, 7.9% Italian, 6.4% Swedish (2005-2009 5-year est.).

Economy: Single-family building permits issued: 0 (2010); Multi-family building permits issued: 0 (2010); Employment by occupation: 19.0% management, 28.9% professional, 13.6% services, 28.3% sales, 0.0% farming, 4.0% construction, 6.2% production (2005-2009 5-year est.).

Income: Per capita income: $30,540 (2010); Median household income: $89,464 (2010); Average household income: $104,620 (2010); Percent of households with income of $100,000 or more: 41.7% (2010); Poverty rate: 6.6% (2005-2009 5-year est.).

Taxes: Total city taxes per capita: $259 (2007); City property taxes per capita: $145 (2007).

Education: Percent of population age 25 and over with: High school diploma (including GED) or higher: 85.5% (2010); Bachelor's degree or higher: 40.1% (2010); Master's degree or higher: 13.4% (2010).

School District(s)

Grayslake CCSD 46 (PK-08)

2009-10 Enrollment: 4,218 . . . . (847) 223-3650

Housing: Homeownership rate: 90.2% (2010); Median home value: $217,680 (2010); Median contract rent: $1,245 per month (2005-2009 5-year est.); Median year structure built: 1999 (2005-2009 5-year est.).

Transportation: Commute to work: 90.4% car, 3.9% public transportation, 0.0% walk, 3.8% work from home (2005-2009 5-year est.); Travel time to work: 10.8% less than 15 minutes, 20.5% 15 to 30 minutes, 26.1% 30 to 45 minutes, 21.6% 45 to 60 minutes, 21.0% 60 minutes or more (2005-2009 5-year est.)

HAWTHORN WOODS (village). Covers a land area of 5.359 square miles and a water area of 0.056 square miles. Located at 42.22° N. Lat; 88.05° W. Long. Elevation is 801 feet.

History: The village is located approximately 40 miles northwest of downtown Chicago. It was officially incorporated in 1958.

Population: 4,540 (1990); 6,002 (2000); 7,022 (2010); 7,507 (2015 projected); Race: 90.9% White, 0.7% Black, 5.8% Asian, 2.6% Other, 3.5% Hispanic of any race (2010); Density: 1,310.3 persons per square mile (2010); Average household size: 3.28 (2010); Median age: 37.9 (2010); Males per 100 females: 97.4 (2010); Marriage status: 22.8% never married, 71.4% now married, 1.4% widowed, 4.4% divorced (2005-2009 5-year est.); Foreign born: 10.9% (2005-2009 5-year est.); Ancestry (includes multiple ancestries): 30.7% German, 19.1% Irish, 12.1% Italian, 11.5% Polish, 9.5% English (2005-2009 5-year est.).

Economy: Single-family building permits issued: 4 (2010); Multi-family building permits issued: 0 (2010); Employment by occupation: 33.4% management, 25.6% professional, 6.7% services, 28.3% sales, 0.0% farming, 4.7% construction, 1.4% production (2005-2009 5-year est.).

Income: Per capita income: $59,728 (2010); Median household income: $153,283 (2010); Average household income: $196,064 (2010); Percent of

households with income of $100,000 or more: 71.8% (2010); Poverty rate: 2.0% (2005-2009 5-year est.).

Taxes: Total city taxes per capita: $404 (2007); City property taxes per capita: $170 (2007).

Education: Percent of population age 25 and over with: High school diploma (including GED) or higher: 95.6% (2010); Bachelor's degree or higher: 57.7% (2010); Master's degree or higher: 21.8% (2010).

School District(s)

Lake Zurich CUSD 95 (PK-12)

2009-10 Enrollment: 6,282 . . . . (847) 438-2831

Housing: Homeownership rate: 96.9% (2010); Median home value: $506,900 (2010); Median contract rent: $2,000+ per month (2005-2009 5-year est.); Median year structure built: 1989 (2005-2009 5-year est.).

Safety: Violent crime rate: 1.2 per 10,000 population; Property crime rate: 41.4 per 10,000 population (2010).

Transportation: Commute to work: 86.3% car, 2.3% public transportation, 1.1% walk, 9.4% work from home (2005-2009 5-year est.); Travel time to work: 11.3% less than 15 minutes, 25.4% 15 to 30 minutes, 30.3% 30 to 45 minutes, 17.7% 45 to 60 minutes, 15.3% 60 minutes or more (2005-2009 5-year est.)

Additional Information Contacts

Village of Hawthorn Woods . . . . (847) 438-5500
   http://www.vhw.org

HIGHLAND PARK (city). Covers a land area of 12.360 square miles and a water area of 0.006 square miles. Located at 42.18° N. Lat; 87.80° W. Long. Elevation is 696 feet.

History: Named for its train station, by the railroad company. The Green Bay House tavern was opened in 1834 on the Chicago-Milwaukee post road, where the city of Highland Park later developed. The name was given by the railroad company to their station here, and the town was incorporated under that name in 1867.

Population: 30,761 (1990); 31,365 (2000); 32,665 (2010); 33,023 (2015 projected); Race: 87.9% White, 1.8% Black, 2.5% Asian, 7.9% Other, 14.6% Hispanic of any race (2010); Density: 2,642.7 persons per square mile (2010); Average household size: 2.75 (2010); Median age: 40.8 (2010); Males per 100 females: 96.1 (2010); Marriage status: 19.9% never married, 66.8% now married, 6.1% widowed, 7.2% divorced (2005-2009 5-year est.); Foreign born: 11.5% (2005-2009 5-year est.); Ancestry (includes multiple ancestries): 18.6% Russian, 16.3% German, 9.6% Polish, 8.8% Irish, 8.5% Italian (2005-2009 5-year est.).

Economy: Unemployment rate: 6.2% (August 2011); Total civilian labor force: 16,209 (August 2011); Single-family building permits issued: 14 (2010); Multi-family building permits issued: 30 (2010); Employment by occupation: 24.6% management, 30.2% professional, 10.1% services, 27.9% sales, 0.0% farming, 3.4% construction, 3.8% production (2005-2009 5-year est.).

Income: Per capita income: $57,288 (2010); Median household income: $111,102 (2010); Average household income: $157,702 (2010); Percent of households with income of $100,000 or more: 54.7% (2010); Poverty rate: 4.3% (2005-2009 5-year est.).

Taxes: Total city taxes per capita: $979 (2007); City property taxes per capita: $409 (2007).

Education: Percent of population age 25 and over with: High school diploma (including GED) or higher: 92.0% (2010); Bachelor's degree or higher: 64.7% (2010); Master's degree or higher: 31.7% (2010).

School District(s)

North Shore SD 112 (PK-08)

2009-10 Enrollment: 4,609 . . . . (847) 681-6700

Northern Suburban Spec Ed Dist (PK-12)

2009-10 Enrollment: n/a . . . . (847) 831-5100

Twp HSD 113 (09-12)

2009-10 Enrollment: 3,737 . . . . (224) 765-1001

Housing: Homeownership rate: 81.7% (2010); Median home value: $529,130 (2010); Median contract rent: $1,081 per month (2005-2009 5-year est.); Median year structure built: 1960 (2005-2009 5-year est.).

Hospitals: Highland Park Hospital (239 beds)

Safety: Violent crime rate: 5.4 per 10,000 population; Property crime rate: 116.3 per 10,000 population (2010).

Transportation: Commute to work: 76.7% car, 10.3% public transportation, 2.3% walk, 9.6% work from home (2005-2009 5-year est.); Travel time to work: 30.2% less than 15 minutes, 27.9% 15 to 30 minutes, 18.4% 30 to 45 minutes, 9.1% 45 to 60 minutes, 14.4% 60 minutes or more (2005-2009 5-year est.)

Additional Information Contacts

City of Highland Park . . . . (847) 432-0800
　　http://www.cityhpil.com
Highland Park Chamber of Commerce . . . . (847) 432-0284
　　http://www.chamberhp.com

HIGHWOOD (city).
Covers a land area of 0.632 square miles and a water area of 0 square miles. Located at 42.20° N. Lat; 87.81° W. Long. Elevation is 676 feet.

History: Fort Sheridan decommissioned in 1990s. Incorporated 1886.

Population: 4,854 (1990); 4,143 (2000); 4,138 (2010); 4,152 (2015 projected); Race: 62.9% White, 1.7% Black, 2.9% Asian, 32.5% Other, 50.2% Hispanic of any race (2010); Density: 6,544.2 persons per square mile (2010); Average household size: 2.67 (2010); Median age: 36.8 (2010); Males per 100 females: 100.6 (2010); Marriage status: 34.3% never married, 49.2% now married, 3.8% widowed, 12.6% divorced (2005-2009 5-year est.); Foreign born: 51.0% (2005-2009 5-year est.); Ancestry (includes multiple ancestries): 15.0% Italian, 4.6% German, 4.5% Irish, 3.4% English, 2.9% Polish (2005-2009 5-year est.).

Economy: Single-family building permits issued: 1 (2010); Multi-family building permits issued: 0 (2010); Employment by occupation: 18.2% management, 16.1% professional, 29.1% services, 24.2% sales, 0.0% farming, 4.8% construction, 7.6% production (2005-2009 5-year est.).

Income: Per capita income: $29,635 (2010); Median household income: $52,404 (2010); Average household income: $79,584 (2010); Percent of households with income of $100,000 or more: 19.7% (2010); Poverty rate: 11.0% (2005-2009 5-year est.).

Taxes: Total city taxes per capita: $487 (2007); City property taxes per capita: $261 (2007).

Education: Percent of population age 25 and over with: High school diploma (including GED) or higher: 73.7% (2010); Bachelor's degree or higher: 32.8% (2010); Master's degree or higher: 15.7% (2010).

School District(s)
North Shore SD 112 (PK-08)
　　2009-10 Enrollment: 4,609 . . . . (847) 681-6700

Housing: Homeownership rate: 43.3% (2010); Median home value: $342,500 (2010); Median contract rent: $1,048 per month (2005-2009 5-year est.); Median year structure built: 1962 (2005-2009 5-year est.).

Safety: Violent crime rate: 16.9 per 10,000 population; Property crime rate: 86.5 per 10,000 population (2010).

Transportation: Commute to work: 68.0% car, 11.0% public transportation, 7.6% walk, 6.6% work from home (2005-2009 5-year est.); Travel time to work: 31.2% less than 15 minutes, 38.3% 15 to 30 minutes, 19.9% 30 to 45 minutes, 2.2% 45 to 60 minutes, 8.4% 60 minutes or more (2005-2009 5-year est.)

Additional Information Contacts
Highwood Chamber of Commerce. . . . . (847) 433-2100
　　http://www.highwoodchamberofcommerce.com

INDIAN CREEK (village).
Covers a land area of 0.267 square miles and a water area of 0 square miles. Located at 42.22° N. Lat; 87.97° W. Long. Elevation is 741 feet.

Population: 188 (1990); 194 (2000); 206 (2010); 210 (2015 projected); Race: 69.9% White, 1.9% Black, 15.0% Asian, 13.1% Other, 32.0% Hispanic of any race (2010); Density: 771.4 persons per square mile (2010); Average household size: 3.49 (2010); Median age: 32.5 (2010); Males per 100 females: 98.1 (2010); Marriage status: 19.5% never married, 70.0% now married, 3.7% widowed, 6.8% divorced (2005-2009 5-year est.); Foreign born: 24.3% (2005-2009 5-year est.); Ancestry (includes multiple ancestries): 17.8% German, 14.2% Irish, 9.4% Polish, 7.9% Russian, 6.3% English (2005-2009 5-year est.).

Economy: Single-family building permits issued: 0 (2010); Multi-family building permits issued: 0 (2010); Employment by occupation: 22.1% management, 29.6% professional, 3.1% services, 30.4% sales, 0.0% farming, 5.0% construction, 9.8% production (2005-2009 5-year est.).

Income: Per capita income: $29,699 (2010); Median household income: $92,708 (2010); Average household income: $103,136 (2010); Percent of households with income of $100,000 or more: 44.1% (2010); Poverty rate: 0.0% (2005-2009 5-year est.).

Taxes: Total city taxes per capita: $8 (2007); City property taxes per capita: $0 (2007).

Education: Percent of population age 25 and over with: High school diploma (including GED) or higher: 89.0% (2010); Bachelor's degree or higher: 47.2% (2010); Master's degree or higher: 15.0% (2010).

Housing: Homeownership rate: 78.0% (2010); Median home value: $270,588 (2010); Median contract rent: $2,000+ per month (2005-2009 5-year est.); Median year structure built: 2001 (2005-2009 5-year est.).

Transportation: Commute to work: 80.1% car, 9.9% public transportation, 1.1% walk, 8.5% work from home (2005-2009 5-year est.); Travel time to work: 13.0% less than 15 minutes, 23.6% 15 to 30 minutes, 28.0% 30 to 45 minutes, 11.5% 45 to 60 minutes, 23.9% 60 minutes or more (2005-2009 5-year est.)

INGLESIDE (unincorporated postal area, zip code 60041).
Part of the Village of Fox Lake. Covers a land area of 11.437 square miles and a water area of 0.538 square miles. Located at 42.37° N. Lat; 88.15° W. Long. Elevation is 764 feet.

Population: 9,286 (2000); Race: 96.8% White, 0.9% Black, 0.3% Asian, 2.0% Other, 1.7% Hispanic of any race (2000); Density: 811.9 persons per square mile (2000); Age: 26.5% under 18, 8.0% over 64 (2000); Marriage status: 23.8% never married, 62.3% now married, 4.8% widowed, 9.1% divorced (2000); Foreign born: 4.0% (2000); Ancestry (includes multiple ancestries): 36.1% German, 15.9% Polish, 15.1% Irish, 8.2% Italian (2000).

Economy: Employment by occupation: 10.9% management, 15.9% professional, 13.4% services, 30.8% sales, 0.0% farming, 14.7% construction, 14.2% production (2000).

Income: Per capita income: $24,726 (2000); Median household income: $59,874 (2000); Poverty rate: 3.8% (2000).

Education: Percent of population age 25 and over with: High school diploma (including GED) or higher: 88.8% (2000); Bachelor's degree or higher: 18.6% (2000).

School District(s)
Big Hollow SD 38 (PK-08)
　　2009-10 Enrollment: 1,681 . . . . (847) 740-1490
Gavin SD 37 (PK-08)
　　2009-10 Enrollment: 967 . . . . (847) 546-2916

Housing: Homeownership rate: 82.0% (2000); Median home value: $153,800 (2000); Median contract rent: $692 per month (2000); Median year structure built: 1961 (2000).

Transportation: Commute to work: 92.9% car, 2.0% public transportation, 0.9% walk, 4.1% work from home (2000); Travel time to work: 21.2% less than 15 minutes, 24.5% 15 to 30 minutes, 21.9% 30 to 45 minutes, 17.8% 45 to 60 minutes, 14.6% 60 minutes or more (2000)

KILDEER (village).
Covers a land area of 3.472 square miles and a water area of 0.046 square miles. Located at 42.18° N. Lat; 88.05° W. Long. Elevation is 778 feet.

History: A referendum for establishing the Village of Kildeer was held on March 22, 1958 and area residents voted to incorporate the new village with a population of 153, making it the 32nd municipality in Lake County. The polling place for this election was the home of Dorothea Huszagh. Brickman's immediate response was to file suit to have the referendum overturned.

Population: 2,748 (1990); 3,460 (2000); 4,209 (2010); 4,467 (2015 projected); Race: 90.9% White, 0.8% Black, 6.5% Asian, 1.9% Other, 4.7% Hispanic of any race (2010); Density: 1,212.4 persons per square mile (2010); Average household size: 3.15 (2010); Median age: 38.3 (2010); Males per 100 females: 99.0 (2010); Marriage status: 24.0% never married, 71.5% now married, 0.8% widowed, 3.7% divorced (2005-2009 5-year est.); Foreign born: 9.1% (2005-2009 5-year est.); Ancestry (includes multiple ancestries): 25.0% German, 13.4% English, 12.1% Irish, 11.5% American, 11.0% Polish (2005-2009 5-year est.).

Economy: Single-family building permits issued: 0 (2010); Multi-family building permits issued: 0 (2010); Employment by occupation: 40.1% management, 25.2% professional, 3.2% services, 26.5% sales, 0.0% farming, 2.2% construction, 2.8% production (2005-2009 5-year est.).

Income: Per capita income: $59,976 (2010); Median household income: $139,670 (2010); Average household income: $189,329 (2010); Percent of households with income of $100,000 or more: 68.7% (2010); Poverty rate: 1.7% (2005-2009 5-year est.).

Taxes: Total city taxes per capita: $308 (2007); City property taxes per capita: $213 (2007).

Education: Percent of population age 25 and over with: High school diploma (including GED) or higher: 97.3% (2010); Bachelor's degree or higher: 62.5% (2010); Master's degree or higher: 24.3% (2010).

Housing: Homeownership rate: 95.6% (2010); Median home value: $565,789 (2010); Median contract rent: n/a per month (2005-2009 5-year est.); Median year structure built: 1987 (2005-2009 5-year est.).

Safety: Violent crime rate: 2.4 per 10,000 population; Property crime rate: 96.8 per 10,000 population (2010).
Transportation: Commute to work: 87.0% car, 2.6% public transportation, 0.0% walk, 8.2% work from home (2005-2009 5-year est.); Travel time to work: 18.9% less than 15 minutes, 27.2% 15 to 30 minutes, 36.7% 30 to 45 minutes, 9.8% 45 to 60 minutes, 7.5% 60 minutes or more (2005-2009 5-year est.)

LAKE BARRINGTON (village).
Covers a land area of 5.336 square miles and a water area of 0.232 square miles. Located at 42.21° N. Lat; 88.16° W. Long. Elevation is 804 feet.
History: Established in 1959, borrowing its name from the town of Great Barrington, Massachusetts.
Population: 4,349 (1990); 4,757 (2000); 4,565 (2010); 4,556 (2015 projected); Race: 96.1% White, 0.6% Black, 1.3% Asian, 2.1% Other, 3.1% Hispanic of any race (2010); Density: 855.6 persons per square mile (2010); Average household size: 2.26 (2010); Median age: 52.8 (2010); Males per 100 females: 91.6 (2010); Marriage status: 14.3% never married, 67.2% now married, 10.7% widowed, 7.8% divorced (2005-2009 5-year est.); Foreign born: 6.8% (2005-2009 5-year est.); Ancestry (includes multiple ancestries): 32.3% German, 17.5% Irish, 14.1% English, 11.3% Italian, 9.8% Polish (2005-2009 5-year est.).
Economy: Single-family building permits issued: 2 (2010); Multi-family building permits issued: 0 (2010); Employment by occupation: 40.3% management, 20.9% professional, 2.5% services, 32.0% sales, 0.0% farming, 1.4% construction, 2.9% production (2005-2009 5-year est.).
Income: Per capita income: $63,244 (2010); Median household income: $106,612 (2010); Average household income: $142,936 (2010); Percent of households with income of $100,000 or more: 53.4% (2010); Poverty rate: 1.5% (2005-2009 5-year est.).
Taxes: Total city taxes per capita: $238 (2007); City property taxes per capita: $164 (2007).
Education: Percent of population age 25 and over with: High school diploma (including GED) or higher: 97.9% (2010); Bachelor's degree or higher: 58.9% (2010); Master's degree or higher: 27.1% (2010).
Housing: Homeownership rate: 95.9% (2010); Median home value: $378,909 (2010); Median contract rent: $1,295 per month (2005-2009 5-year est.); Median year structure built: 1984 (2005-2009 5-year est.).
Transportation: Commute to work: 74.0% car, 5.6% public transportation, 0.0% walk, 18.9% work from home (2005-2009 5-year est.); Travel time to work: 13.2% less than 15 minutes, 29.0% 15 to 30 minutes, 25.4% 30 to 45 minutes, 13.8% 45 to 60 minutes, 18.6% 60 minutes or more (2005-2009 5-year est.)

LAKE BLUFF (village).
Covers a land area of 4.059 square miles and a water area of 0.003 square miles. Located at 42.28° N. Lat; 87.84° W. Long. Elevation is 659 feet.
History: Lake Bluff began in 1874 as a Methodist camp-meeting ground.
Population: 5,650 (1990); 6,056 (2000); 5,875 (2010); 5,794 (2015 projected); Race: 90.6% White, 1.7% Black, 5.8% Asian, 1.9% Other, 2.5% Hispanic of any race (2010); Density: 1,447.4 persons per square mile (2010); Average household size: 2.77 (2010); Median age: 37.4 (2010); Males per 100 females: 96.5 (2010); Marriage status: 20.6% never married, 72.1% now married, 1.4% widowed, 5.8% divorced (2005-2009 5-year est.); Foreign born: 8.0% (2005-2009 5-year est.); Ancestry (includes multiple ancestries): 26.4% German, 22.6% English, 21.5% Irish, 9.7% Italian, 5.6% Russian (2005-2009 5-year est.).
Economy: Single-family building permits issued: 1 (2010); Multi-family building permits issued: 0 (2010); Employment by occupation: 31.5% management, 35.1% professional, 8.9% services, 22.1% sales, 0.0% farming, 0.8% construction, 1.6% production (2005-2009 5-year est.).
Income: Per capita income: $56,756 (2010); Median household income: $113,780 (2010); Average household income: $154,958 (2010); Percent of households with income of $100,000 or more: 55.3% (2010); Poverty rate: 1.3% (2005-2009 5-year est.).
Taxes: Total city taxes per capita: $900 (2007); City property taxes per capita: $463 (2007).
Education: Percent of population age 25 and over with: High school diploma (including GED) or higher: 98.5% (2010); Bachelor's degree or higher: 71.4% (2010); Master's degree or higher: 32.2% (2010).
School District(s)
Lake Bluff ESD 65 (PK-08)
    2009-10 Enrollment: 961 . . . . (847) 234-9400

Housing: Homeownership rate: 80.8% (2010); Median home value: $612,260 (2010); Median contract rent: $2,000+ per month (2005-2009 5-year est.); Median year structure built: 1965 (2005-2009 5-year est.).
Safety: Violent crime rate: 0.0 per 10,000 population; Property crime rate: 50.2 per 10,000 population (2010).
Transportation: Commute to work: 82.8% car, 9.1% public transportation, 2.6% walk, 4.8% work from home (2005-2009 5-year est.); Travel time to work: 37.6% less than 15 minutes, 25.8% 15 to 30 minutes, 8.7% 30 to 45 minutes, 9.6% 45 to 60 minutes, 18.2% 60 minutes or more (2005-2009 5-year est.)
Additional Information Contacts
Village of Lake Bluff . . . . (847) 234-0774
    http://www.lakebluff.org

LAKE CATHERINE (CDP).
Covers a land area of 1.064 square miles and a water area of 0.484 square miles. Located at 42.48° N. Lat; 88.12° W. Long. Elevation is 748 feet.
Population: 1,432 (1990); 1,490 (2000); 1,550 (2010); 1,718 (2015 projected); Race: 94.2% White, 0.9% Black, 1.2% Asian, 3.7% Other, 5.6% Hispanic of any race (2010); Density: 1,456.7 persons per square mile (2010); Average household size: 2.75 (2010); Median age: 37.7 (2010); Males per 100 females: 105.3 (2010); Marriage status: 24.8% never married, 62.9% now married, 7.8% widowed, 4.5% divorced (2005-2009 5-year est.); Foreign born: 3.5% (2005-2009 5-year est.); Ancestry (includes multiple ancestries): 29.7% German, 14.6% Irish, 12.0% Polish, 11.2% European, 8.3% American (2005-2009 5-year est.).
Economy: Employment by occupation: 11.2% management, 20.1% professional, 10.2% services, 28.9% sales, 0.0% farming, 17.9% construction, 11.7% production (2005-2009 5-year est.).
Income: Per capita income: $30,470 (2010); Median household income: $71,204 (2010); Average household income: $83,868 (2010); Percent of households with income of $100,000 or more: 26.8% (2010); Poverty rate: 8.7% (2005-2009 5-year est.).
Education: Percent of population age 25 and over with: High school diploma (including GED) or higher: 90.4% (2010); Bachelor's degree or higher: 20.6% (2010); Master's degree or higher: 6.7% (2010).
Housing: Homeownership rate: 88.3% (2010); Median home value: $219,257 (2010); Median contract rent: $928 per month (2005-2009 5-year est.); Median year structure built: 1949 (2005-2009 5-year est.).
Transportation: Commute to work: 93.4% car, 0.0% public transportation, 4.5% walk, 2.1% work from home (2005-2009 5-year est.); Travel time to work: 11.3% less than 15 minutes, 18.4% 15 to 30 minutes, 16.3% 30 to 45 minutes, 15.7% 45 to 60 minutes, 38.3% 60 minutes or more (2005-2009 5-year est.)

LAKE FOREST (city).
Covers a land area of 16.865 square miles and a water area of 0.048 square miles. Located at 42.23° N. Lat; 87.85° W. Long. Elevation is 689 feet.
History: Named for Lake Michigan and for the forests in the area. Lake Forest was laid out in 1856 by David Hotchkiss, a St. Louis landscape architect, for a company of Chicago businessmen who had purchased land here. The town grew around Lake Forest College, opened in 1857.
Population: 17,966 (1990); 20,059 (2000); 20,293 (2010); 20,363 (2015 projected); Race: 91.6% White, 1.5% Black, 5.0% Asian, 2.0% Other, 2.9% Hispanic of any race (2010); Density: 1,203.2 persons per square mile (2010); Average household size: 2.83 (2010); Median age: 40.3 (2010); Males per 100 females: 90.7 (2010); Marriage status: 26.9% never married, 62.8% now married, 5.3% widowed, 5.1% divorced (2005-2009 5-year est.); Foreign born: 8.9% (2005-2009 5-year est.); Ancestry (includes multiple ancestries): 27.0% German, 20.6% Irish, 15.8% English, 9.2% Italian, 6.3% Polish (2005-2009 5-year est.).
Economy: Single-family building permits issued: 7 (2010); Multi-family building permits issued: 0 (2010); Employment by occupation: 34.1% management, 22.3% professional, 7.9% services, 30.8% sales, 0.0% farming, 1.4% construction, 3.4% production (2005-2009 5-year est.).
Income: Per capita income: $70,911 (2010); Median household income: $159,647 (2010); Average household income: $212,119 (2010); Percent of households with income of $100,000 or more: 66.7% (2010); Poverty rate: 2.3% (2005-2009 5-year est.).
Taxes: Total city taxes per capita: $1,561 (2007); City property taxes per capita: $1,131 (2007).
Education: Percent of population age 25 and over with: High school diploma (including GED) or higher: 97.6% (2010); Bachelor's degree or higher: 76.3% (2010); Master's degree or higher: 37.7% (2010).

School District(s)

Lake Forest CHSD 115 (09-12)
  2009-10 Enrollment: 1,786 . . . . (847) 235-9657
Lake Forest SD 67 (KG-08)
  2009-10 Enrollment: 2,138 . . . . (847) 235-9657
Rondout SD 72 (KG-08)
  2009-10 Enrollment: 168 . . . . (847) 362-2021
Spec Educ Dist Lake County/Sedol (PK-12)
  2009-10 Enrollment: n/a . . . . (847) 548-8470

Four-year College(s)

Lake Forest College (Private, Not-for-profit)
  Fall 2009 Enrollment: 1,415 . . . . (847) 234-3100
  2010-11 Tuition: In-state $35,525; Out-of-state $35,525
Lake Forest Graduate School of Management (Private, Not-for-profit)
  Fall 2009 Enrollment: 769 . . . . (847) 234-5005

Housing: Homeownership rate: 87.6% (2010); Median home value: $822,463 (2010); Median contract rent: $1,156 per month (2005-2009 5-year est.); Median year structure built: 1973 (2005-2009 5-year est.).
Hospitals: Lake Forest Hospital (261 beds)
Transportation: Commute to work: 73.5% car, 9.0% public transportation, 5.3% walk, 10.8% work from home (2005-2009 5-year est.); Travel time to work: 29.1% less than 15 minutes, 25.9% 15 to 30 minutes, 19.0% 30 to 45 minutes, 7.6% 45 to 60 minutes, 18.4% 60 minutes or more (2005-2009 5-year est.)

Additional Information Contacts

City of Lake Forest . . . . (847) 234-2600
  http://www.cityoflakeforest.com
Lake Forest/Lake Bluff Chamber of Commerce . . . . (847) 234-4282
  http://www.lakeforestonline.com

LAKE VILLA (village).
Covers a land area of 5.724 square miles and a water area of 0.754 square miles. Located at 42.41° N. Lat; 88.08° W. Long. Elevation is 791 feet.
History: Lake Villa grew around a railroad station and the resort trade. It was the site of the Allendale Farm School, an experimental community founded in 1897 as a home for neglected boys.
Population: 3,273 (1990); 5,864 (2000); 7,779 (2010); 8,378 (2015 projected); Race: 86.2% White, 3.5% Black, 4.0% Asian, 6.3% Other, 10.1% Hispanic of any race (2010); Density: 1,359.0 persons per square mile (2010); Average household size: 2.80 (2010); Median age: 35.6 (2010); Males per 100 females: 97.9 (2010); Marriage status: 29.9% never married, 57.1% now married, 5.2% widowed, 7.9% divorced (2005-2009 5-year est.); Foreign born: 7.3% (2005-2009 5-year est.); Ancestry (includes multiple ancestries): 28.7% German, 21.2% Irish, 17.6% Polish, 8.2% Italian, 6.8% English (2005-2009 5-year est.).
Economy: Single-family building permits issued: 9 (2010); Multi-family building permits issued: 0 (2010); Employment by occupation: 23.6% management, 22.3% professional, 10.5% services, 28.1% sales, 0.0% farming, 7.0% construction, 8.6% production (2005-2009 5-year est.).
Income: Per capita income: $32,048 (2010); Median household income: $76,855 (2010); Average household income: $89,956 (2010); Percent of households with income of $100,000 or more: 32.5% (2010); Poverty rate: 2.3% (2005-2009 5-year est.).
Taxes: Total city taxes per capita: $286 (2007); City property taxes per capita: $191 (2007).
Education: Percent of population age 25 and over with: High school diploma (including GED) or higher: 92.5% (2010); Bachelor's degree or higher: 37.0% (2010); Master's degree or higher: 9.8% (2010).

School District(s)

CHSD 117 (07-12)
  2009-10 Enrollment: 2,852 . . . . (847) 838-7170
Lake Villa CCSD 41 (PK-08)
  2009-10 Enrollment: 3,266 . . . . (847) 356-2385

Housing: Homeownership rate: 78.9% (2010); Median home value: $231,257 (2010); Median contract rent: $858 per month (2005-2009 5-year est.); Median year structure built: 1995 (2005-2009 5-year est.).
Safety: Violent crime rate: 14.6 per 10,000 population; Property crime rate: 108.7 per 10,000 population (2010).
Transportation: Commute to work: 92.2% car, 3.9% public transportation, 0.6% walk, 3.1% work from home (2005-2009 5-year est.); Travel time to work: 14.6% less than 15 minutes, 23.7% 15 to 30 minutes, 27.1% 30 to 45 minutes, 15.4% 45 to 60 minutes, 19.3% 60 minutes or more (2005-2009 5-year est.)

Additional Information Contacts

Illinois Women's Chamber of Commerce . . . .
  http://www.uswomenschamber.com/html/illinois.htm
Village of Lake Villa . . . . (847) 356-6100
  http://www.lake-villa.org

LAKE ZURICH (village).
Covers a land area of 6.484 square miles and a water area of 0.359 square miles. Located at 42.19° N. Lat; 88.08° W. Long. Elevation is 876 feet.
Population: 15,857 (1990); 18,104 (2000); 20,708 (2010); 21,786 (2015 projected); Race: 89.1% White, 0.9% Black, 4.7% Asian, 5.3% Other, 8.6% Hispanic of any race (2010); Density: 3,193.9 persons per square mile (2010); Average household size: 3.12 (2010); Median age: 36.0 (2010); Males per 100 females: 99.6 (2010); Marriage status: 25.9% never married, 64.6% now married, 4.6% widowed, 4.9% divorced (2005-2009 5-year est.); Foreign born: 16.0% (2005-2009 5-year est.); Ancestry (includes multiple ancestries): 29.9% German, 18.7% Irish, 16.4% Polish, 11.0% Italian, 8.8% English (2005-2009 5-year est.).
Economy: Single-family building permits issued: 6 (2010); Multi-family building permits issued: 0 (2010); Employment by occupation: 22.4% management, 26.6% professional, 9.7% services, 28.2% sales, 0.0% farming, 5.4% construction, 7.7% production (2005-2009 5-year est.).
Income: Per capita income: $41,865 (2010); Median household income: $102,697 (2010); Average household income: $130,814 (2010); Percent of households with income of $100,000 or more: 51.6% (2010); Poverty rate: 1.5% (2005-2009 5-year est.).
Taxes: Total city taxes per capita: $497 (2007); City property taxes per capita: $378 (2007).
Education: Percent of population age 25 and over with: High school diploma (including GED) or higher: 94.3% (2010); Bachelor's degree or higher: 48.4% (2010); Master's degree or higher: 17.1% (2010).

School District(s)

Lake Zurich CUSD 95 (PK-12)
  2009-10 Enrollment: 6,282 . . . . (847) 438-2831

Housing: Homeownership rate: 90.9% (2010); Median home value: $315,568 (2010); Median contract rent: $976 per month (2005-2009 5-year est.); Median year structure built: 1983 (2005-2009 5-year est.).
Safety: Violent crime rate: 3.9 per 10,000 population; Property crime rate: 147.5 per 10,000 population (2010).
Transportation: Commute to work: 90.3% car, 2.6% public transportation, 0.8% walk, 4.5% work from home (2005-2009 5-year est.); Travel time to work: 18.5% less than 15 minutes, 24.0% 15 to 30 minutes, 30.7% 30 to 45 minutes, 16.2% 45 to 60 minutes, 10.7% 60 minutes or more (2005-2009 5-year est.)

Additional Information Contacts

Lake Zurich Area Chamber of Commerce . . . . (847) 438-5572
  http://www.lzacc.com
Village of Lake Zurich . . . . (847) 438-5141
  http://www.volz.org

LIBERTYVILLE (village).
Covers a land area of 8.772 square miles and a water area of 0.291 square miles. Located at 42.28° N. Lat; 87.96° W. Long. Elevation is 699 feet.
History: Named for the community's patriotism. Daniel Webster (1782-1852) was one of the first purchasers of land in Independence Grove, which changed its name to Libertyville in 1837 when the post office was established. Settlers and vacationists were attracted by the mineral springs in the area.
Population: 20,114 (1990); 20,742 (2000); 22,026 (2010); 22,824 (2015 projected); Race: 89.1% White, 1.4% Black, 6.2% Asian, 3.3% Other, 3.8% Hispanic of any race (2010); Density: 2,510.9 persons per square mile (2010); Average household size: 2.79 (2010); Median age: 40.5 (2010); Males per 100 females: 95.1 (2010); Marriage status: 25.9% never married, 59.0% now married, 7.4% widowed, 7.6% divorced (2005-2009 5-year est.); Foreign born: 8.8% (2005-2009 5-year est.); Ancestry (includes multiple ancestries): 32.6% German, 17.3% Irish, 11.9% English, 9.9% Italian, 8.8% Polish (2005-2009 5-year est.).
Economy: Single-family building permits issued: 17 (2010); Multi-family building permits issued: 0 (2010); Employment by occupation: 26.0% management, 32.0% professional, 7.3% services, 26.1% sales, 0.0% farming, 3.2% construction, 5.4% production (2005-2009 5-year est.).
Income: Per capita income: $49,648 (2010); Median household income: $106,587 (2010); Average household income: $140,341 (2010); Percent of households with income of $100,000 or more: 53.2% (2010); Poverty rate: 4.0% (2005-2009 5-year est.).

Taxes: Total city taxes per capita: $466 (2007); City property taxes per capita: $314 (2007).
Education: Percent of population age 25 and over with: High school diploma (including GED) or higher: 95.7% (2010); Bachelor's degree or higher: 60.9% (2010); Master's degree or higher: 27.7% (2010).

School District(s)
CHSD 128 (09-12)
    2009-10 Enrollment: 3,388 . . . . (847) 247-4510
Libertyville SD 70 (PK-08)
    2009-10 Enrollment: 2,595 . . . . (847) 362-9695
Oak Grove SD 68 (PK-08)
    2009-10 Enrollment: 982 . . . . (847) 367-4120

Vocational/Technical School(s)
Tricoci University of Beauty Culture (Private, For-profit)
    Fall 2009 Enrollment: 76 . . . . (630) 528-3336
    2010-11 Tuition: $16,650

Housing: Homeownership rate: 83.2% (2010); Median home value: $366,784 (2010); Median contract rent: $874 per month (2005-2009 5-year est.); Median year structure built: 1975 (2005-2009 5-year est.).
Hospitals: Condell Medical Center (305 beds)
Safety: Violent crime rate: 7.8 per 10,000 population; Property crime rate: 165.8 per 10,000 population (2010).
Transportation: Commute to work: 85.3% car, 4.3% public transportation, 1.3% walk, 7.6% work from home (2005-2009 5-year est.); Travel time to work: 30.9% less than 15 minutes, 35.2% 15 to 30 minutes, 12.8% 30 to 45 minutes, 10.3% 45 to 60 minutes, 10.8% 60 minutes or more (2005-2009 5-year est.)

Additional Information Contacts
GLMV Area Chamber of Commerce . . . . (847) 680-0750
    http://www.glmvchamber.org
Village of Libertyville . . . . (847) 362-2430
    http://www.libertyville.com/index.htm

LINCOLNSHIRE (village). Covers a land area of 4.406 square miles and a water area of 0.029 square miles. Located at 42.19° N. Lat; 87.91° W. Long. Elevation is 659 feet.

History: Lincolnshire was incorporated on August 5, 1957, from the unincorporated Half Day area when land was purchased to build a residential subdivision. The community underwent an aggressive era of expansion from 1983 to the 1990s.
Population: 5,497 (1990); 6,108 (2000); 7,221 (2010); 7,539 (2015 projected); Race: 87.0% White, 1.1% Black, 9.9% Asian, 2.0% Other, 3.6% Hispanic of any race (2010); Density: 1,638.8 persons per square mile (2010); Average household size: 2.75 (2010); Median age: 46.0 (2010); Males per 100 females: 94.7 (2010); Marriage status: 17.8% never married, 68.9% now married, 7.1% widowed, 6.2% divorced (2005-2009 5-year est.); Foreign born: 11.5% (2005-2009 5-year est.); Ancestry (includes multiple ancestries): 25.8% German, 16.2% Irish, 11.2% Polish, 8.7% Russian, 8.6% Italian (2005-2009 5-year est.).
Economy: Single-family building permits issued: 5 (2010); Multi-family building permits issued: 0 (2010); Employment by occupation: 40.2% management, 19.7% professional, 7.5% services, 28.3% sales, 0.0% farming, 0.7% construction, 3.6% production (2005-2009 5-year est.).
Income: Per capita income: $67,613 (2010); Median household income: $148,077 (2010); Average household income: $188,548 (2010); Percent of households with income of $100,000 or more: 67.9% (2010); Poverty rate: 2.4% (2005-2009 5-year est.).
Taxes: Total city taxes per capita: $996 (2007); City property taxes per capita: $196 (2007).
Education: Percent of population age 25 and over with: High school diploma (including GED) or higher: 97.1% (2010); Bachelor's degree or higher: 69.6% (2010); Master's degree or higher: 31.7% (2010).

School District(s)
Adlai E Stevenson HSD 125 (09-12)
    2009-10 Enrollment: 4,419 . . . . (847) 415-4000
Lincolnshire-Prairieview SD 103 (PK-08)
    2009-10 Enrollment: 1,439 . . . . (847) 295-4030

Housing: Homeownership rate: 95.4% (2010); Median home value: $573,401 (2010); Median contract rent: $1,928 per month (2005-2009 5-year est.); Median year structure built: 1980 (2005-2009 5-year est.).
Safety: Violent crime rate: 3.7 per 10,000 population; Property crime rate: 133.7 per 10,000 population (2010).
Transportation: Commute to work: 78.4% car, 8.0% public transportation, 1.2% walk, 11.8% work from home (2005-2009 5-year est.); Travel time to work: 20.5% less than 15 minutes, 36.1% 15 to 30 minutes, 20.3% 30 to 45

minutes, 8.9% 45 to 60 minutes, 14.3% 60 minutes or more (2005-2009 5-year est.)

Additional Information Contacts
Greater Lincolnshire Chamber of Commerce . . . . (847) 793-2409
    http://www.lincolnshirechamber.org
Village of Lincolnshire . . . . (847) 883-8600
    http://www.village.lincolnshire.il.us

LINDENHURST (village). Covers a land area of 3.721 square miles and a water area of 0.361 square miles. Located at 42.41° N. Lat; 88.02° W. Long. Elevation is 797 feet.

Population: 8,799 (1990); 12,539 (2000); 14,673 (2010); 15,617 (2015 projected); Race: 87.4% White, 2.4% Black, 5.4% Asian, 4.8% Other, 7.2% Hispanic of any race (2010); Density: 3,942.9 persons per square mile (2010); Average household size: 2.97 (2010); Median age: 35.4 (2010); Males per 100 females: 98.0 (2010); Marriage status: 25.2% never married, 63.2% now married, 4.2% widowed, 7.4% divorced (2005-2009 5-year est.); Foreign born: 6.9% (2005-2009 5-year est.); Ancestry (includes multiple ancestries): 32.5% German, 19.1% Irish, 13.4% Polish, 11.0% Italian, 10.2% English (2005-2009 5-year est.).
Economy: Single-family building permits issued: 0 (2010); Multi-family building permits issued: 0 (2010); Employment by occupation: 21.8% management, 21.8% professional, 9.3% services, 28.3% sales, 0.0% farming, 10.4% construction, 8.5% production (2005-2009 5-year est.).
Income: Per capita income: $33,610 (2010); Median household income: $89,064 (2010); Average household income: $99,857 (2010); Percent of households with income of $100,000 or more: 40.6% (2010); Poverty rate: 1.9% (2005-2009 5-year est.).
Taxes: Total city taxes per capita: $187 (2007); City property taxes per capita: $56 (2007).
Education: Percent of population age 25 and over with: High school diploma (including GED) or higher: 95.6% (2010); Bachelor's degree or higher: 41.5% (2010); Master's degree or higher: 11.6% (2010).

School District(s)
Lake Villa CCSD 41 (PK-08)
    2009-10 Enrollment: 3,266 . . . . (847) 356-2385
Millburn CCSD 24 (PK-08)
    2009-10 Enrollment: 1,614 . . . . (847) 356-8331

Housing: Homeownership rate: 91.9% (2010); Median home value: $225,516 (2010); Median contract rent: $1,080 per month (2005-2009 5-year est.); Median year structure built: 1991 (2005-2009 5-year est.).
Safety: Violent crime rate: 2.7 per 10,000 population; Property crime rate: 51.6 per 10,000 population (2010).
Transportation: Commute to work: 93.5% car, 1.4% public transportation, 0.2% walk, 4.0% work from home (2005-2009 5-year est.); Travel time to work: 13.6% less than 15 minutes, 23.6% 15 to 30 minutes, 26.3% 30 to 45 minutes, 17.0% 45 to 60 minutes, 19.5% 60 minutes or more (2005-2009 5-year est.)

Additional Information Contacts
Lindenhurst/Lake Villa Chamber of Commerce . . . . (847) 356-8446
    http://www.llvchamber.com
Village of Lindenhurst . . . . (847) 356-8252
    http://lindenhurstil.org

LONG GROVE (village). Aka Longgrove. Covers a land area of 12.275 square miles and a water area of 0.155 square miles. Located at 42.20° N. Lat; 88.00° W. Long. Elevation is 732 feet.

History: The village now has very strict building ordinances to preserve its "country atmosphere." There are no sidewalks, street lights or curbs throughout the villages many communities. The village was incorporated in 1956.
Population: 4,541 (1990); 6,735 (2000); 7,116 (2010); 7,508 (2015 projected); Race: 85.8% White, 0.9% Black, 10.9% Asian, 2.3% Other, 3.6% Hispanic of any race (2010); Density: 579.7 persons per square mile (2010); Average household size: 3.25 (2010); Median age: 40.9 (2010); Males per 100 females: 96.2 (2010); Marriage status: 22.7% never married, 72.7% now married, 1.4% widowed, 3.2% divorced (2005-2009 5-year est.); Foreign born: 16.1% (2005-2009 5-year est.); Ancestry (includes multiple ancestries): 19.1% German, 13.2% Irish, 12.4% Italian, 12.2% Polish, 9.2% Russian (2005-2009 5-year est.).
Economy: Single-family building permits issued: 2 (2010); Multi-family building permits issued: 0 (2010); Employment by occupation: 30.2% management, 29.4% professional, 8.6% services, 26.1% sales, 0.0% farming, 2.1% construction, 3.6% production (2005-2009 5-year est.).

Income: Per capita income: $60,169 (2010); Median household income: $156,604 (2010); Average household income: $199,316 (2010); Percent of households with income of $100,000 or more: 69.5% (2010); Poverty rate: 1.5% (2005-2009 5-year est.).

Taxes: Total city taxes per capita: $126 (2007); City property taxes per capita: $0 (2007).

Education: Percent of population age 25 and over with: High school diploma (including GED) or higher: 97.2% (2010); Bachelor's degree or higher: 64.0% (2010); Master's degree or higher: 29.0% (2010).

School District(s)

Kildeer Countryside CCSD 96 (PK-08)

    2009-10 Enrollment: 3,157 . . . . (847) 459-4260

Housing: Homeownership rate: 94.3% (2010); Median home value: $584,480 (2010); Median contract rent: n/a per month (2005-2009 5-year est.); Median year structure built: 1989 (2005-2009 5-year est.).

Transportation: Commute to work: 84.6% car, 6.2% public transportation, 0.0% walk, 8.0% work from home (2005-2009 5-year est.); Travel time to work: 13.1% less than 15 minutes, 31.0% 15 to 30 minutes, 28.3% 30 to 45 minutes, 12.3% 45 to 60 minutes, 15.3% 60 minutes or more (2005-2009 5-year est.)

Additional Information Contacts

Village of Long Grove . . . . (847) 634-9440
    http://www.longgrove.net

LONG LAKE (CDP). Covers a land area of 1.051 square miles and a water area of 0.606 square miles. Located at 42.37° N. Lat; 88.12° W. Long. Elevation is 751 feet.

Population: 2,743 (1990); 3,356 (2000); 4,054 (2010); 4,272 (2015 projected); Race: 85.8% White, 1.2% Black, 1.6% Asian, 11.4% Other, 22.7% Hispanic of any race (2010); Density: 3,857.5 persons per square mile (2010); Average household size: 2.95 (2010); Median age: 34.8 (2010); Males per 100 females: 105.0 (2010); Marriage status: 37.5% never married, 40.7% now married, 5.1% widowed, 16.7% divorced (2005-2009 5-year est.); Foreign born: 18.0% (2005-2009 5-year est.); Ancestry (includes multiple ancestries): 27.3% German, 13.8% Polish, 9.4% Irish, 8.7% American, 6.7% English (2005-2009 5-year est.).

Economy: Employment by occupation: 13.1% management, 6.3% professional, 12.1% services, 25.0% sales, 0.0% farming, 25.3% construction, 18.3% production (2005-2009 5-year est.).

Income: Per capita income: $26,128 (2010); Median household income: $69,880 (2010); Average household income: $77,114 (2010); Percent of households with income of $100,000 or more: 24.1% (2010); Poverty rate: 12.8% (2005-2009 5-year est.).

Education: Percent of population age 25 and over with: High school diploma (including GED) or higher: 79.9% (2010); Bachelor's degree or higher: 15.0% (2010); Master's degree or higher: 4.0% (2010).

Housing: Homeownership rate: 80.5% (2010); Median home value: $161,174 (2010); Median contract rent: $1,032 per month (2005-2009 5-year est.); Median year structure built: 1956 (2005-2009 5-year est.).

Transportation: Commute to work: 89.8% car, 6.6% public transportation, 0.0% walk, 3.7% work from home (2005-2009 5-year est.); Travel time to work: 16.2% less than 15 minutes, 25.7% 15 to 30 minutes, 19.8% 30 to 45 minutes, 20.7% 45 to 60 minutes, 17.6% 60 minutes or more (2005-2009 5-year est.)

METTAWA (village). Covers a land area of 5.467 square miles and a water area of 0.026 square miles. Located at 42.24° N. Lat; 87.91° W. Long. Elevation is 682 feet.

Population: 379 (1990); 367 (2000); 478 (2010); 510 (2015 projected); Race: 91.8% White, 1.9% Black, 2.9% Asian, 3.3% Other, 5.0% Hispanic of any race (2010); Density: 87.4 persons per square mile (2010); Average household size: 2.66 (2010); Median age: 46.1 (2010); Males per 100 females: 97.5 (2010); Marriage status: 23.8% never married, 67.4% now married, 5.7% widowed, 3.0% divorced (2005-2009 5-year est.); Foreign born: 17.6% (2005-2009 5-year est.); Ancestry (includes multiple ancestries): 28.4% German, 22.4% Irish, 9.2% Italian, 8.9% Nigerian, 8.5% Polish (2005-2009 5-year est.).

Economy: Single-family building permits issued: 0 (2010); Multi-family building permits issued: 0 (2010); Employment by occupation: 35.2% management, 15.3% professional, 22.3% services, 20.3% sales, 4.3% farming, 2.0% construction, 0.7% production (2005-2009 5-year est.).

Income: Per capita income: $66,610 (2010); Median household income: $133,088 (2010); Average household income: $180,044 (2010); Percent of households with income of $100,000 or more: 63.2% (2010); Poverty rate: 1.0% (2005-2009 5-year est.).

Taxes: Total city taxes per capita: $2,183 (2007); City property taxes per capita: $1,461 (2007).

Education: Percent of population age 25 and over with: High school diploma (including GED) or higher: 92.5% (2010); Bachelor's degree or higher: 57.6% (2010); Master's degree or higher: 24.8% (2010).

Housing: Homeownership rate: 91.2% (2010); Median home value: $600,000 (2010); Median contract rent: $1,750 per month (2005-2009 5-year est.); Median year structure built: 1985 (2005-2009 5-year est.).

Transportation: Commute to work: 72.0% car, 2.1% public transportation, 10.6% walk, 15.2% work from home (2005-2009 5-year est.); Travel time to work: 28.9% less than 15 minutes, 37.2% 15 to 30 minutes, 15.1% 30 to 45 minutes, 8.8% 45 to 60 minutes, 10.0% 60 minutes or more (2005-2009 5-year est.)

MUNDELEIN (village). Covers a land area of 8.623 square miles and a water area of 0.323 square miles. Located at 42.26° N. Lat; 88.00° W. Long. Elevation is 735 feet.

History: Named for Cardinal George William Mundelein (1872-1939), Archbishop of Chicago. The community here developed around the Sheldon School of Business Administration and was called Area, a reflection of the school's motto of "Ability, Reliability, Endurance, and Action." When this school was replaced by a Catholic seminary, the town name was changed to Mundelein for George Cardinal Mundelein, Archbishop of Chicago.

Population: 22,023 (1990); 30,935 (2000); 30,865 (2010); 31,322 (2015 projected); Race: 69.6% White, 2.1% Black, 9.7% Asian, 18.6% Other, 35.5% Hispanic of any race (2010); Density: 3,579.3 persons per square mile (2010); Average household size: 3.17 (2010); Median age: 33.9 (2010); Males per 100 females: 103.3 (2010); Marriage status: 31.4% never married, 57.7% now married, 3.3% widowed, 7.6% divorced (2005-2009 5-year est.); Foreign born: 29.8% (2005-2009 5-year est.); Ancestry (includes multiple ancestries): 21.3% German, 12.0% Irish, 9.9% Polish, 7.2% Italian, 5.0% English (2005-2009 5-year est.).

Economy: Unemployment rate: 8.2% (August 2011); Total civilian labor force: 17,910 (August 2011); Single-family building permits issued: 49 (2010); Multi-family building permits issued: 0 (2010); Employment by occupation: 18.9% management, 19.1% professional, 16.9% services, 26.2% sales, 0.1% farming, 6.1% construction, 12.8% production (2005-2009 5-year est.).

Income: Per capita income: $30,770 (2010); Median household income: $81,179 (2010); Average household income: $97,790 (2010); Percent of households with income of $100,000 or more: 35.6% (2010); Poverty rate: 4.0% (2005-2009 5-year est.).

Taxes: Total city taxes per capita: $542 (2007); City property taxes per capita: $277 (2007).

Education: Percent of population age 25 and over with: High school diploma (including GED) or higher: 83.1% (2010); Bachelor's degree or higher: 41.1% (2010); Master's degree or higher: 14.8% (2010).

School District(s)

Diamond Lake SD 76 (PK-08)

    2009-10 Enrollment: 1,151 . . . . (847) 566-9221

Fremont SD 79 (PK-08)

    2009-10 Enrollment: 2,119 . . . . (847) 566-0169

Mundelein Cons HSD 120 (09-12)

    2009-10 Enrollment: 2,256 . . . . (847) 949-2200

Mundelein ESD 75 (PK-08)

    2009-10 Enrollment: 1,876 . . . . (847) 949-2700

Four-year College(s)

University of Saint Mary of the Lake (Private, Not-for-profit, Roman Catholic)

    Fall 2009 Enrollment: 227 . . . . (847) 566-6401

Housing: Homeownership rate: 79.6% (2010); Median home value: $216,990 (2010); Median contract rent: $933 per month (2005-2009 5-year est.); Median year structure built: 1981 (2005-2009 5-year est.).

Safety: Violent crime rate: 3.5 per 10,000 population; Property crime rate: 124.1 per 10,000 population (2010).

Transportation: Commute to work: 88.6% car, 2.5% public transportation, 2.0% walk, 4.4% work from home (2005-2009 5-year est.); Travel time to work: 25.2% less than 15 minutes, 29.7% 15 to 30 minutes, 22.7% 30 to 45 minutes, 10.7% 45 to 60 minutes, 11.7% 60 minutes or more (2005-2009 5-year est.)

Additional Information Contacts

GLMV Area Chamber of Commerce . . . . (847) 680-0750
    http://www.glmvchamber.org

Village of Mundelein. . . . . (847) 949-3200
http://www.mundelein.org

NORTH BARRINGTON (village). Covers a land area of 4.389
square miles and a water area of 0.197 square miles. Located at 42.20° N.
Lat; 88.13° W. Long. Elevation is 791 feet.

History: The first settlers arrived in the 1830s and in 1854 the Chicago &
Northwestern Railroad built its first station in the Village of Barrington.
Subsequent generations have been attracted to the area by its appealing
natural resources, and its accessibility to the metropolitan area, which
provides a unique opportunity for countryside living with a proximity to
urban development.

Population: 2,013 (1990); 2,918 (2000); 3,182 (2010); 3,281 (2015
projected); Race: 95.5% White, 0.4% Black, 2.2% Asian, 1.9% Other, 2.8%
Hispanic of any race (2010); Density: 725.0 persons per square mile
(2010); Average household size: 2.94 (2010); Median age: 44.8 (2010);
Males per 100 females: 100.4 (2010); Marriage status: 19.8% never
married, 71.5% now married, 3.7% widowed, 5.0% divorced (2005-2009
5-year est.); Foreign born: 5.9% (2005-2009 5-year est.); Ancestry
(includes multiple ancestries): 26.3% German, 20.2% Irish, 13.7% Italian,
12.8% English, 7.0% Polish (2005-2009 5-year est.).

Economy: Single-family building permits issued: 2 (2010); Multi-family
building permits issued: 0 (2010); Employment by occupation: 35.3%
management, 26.8% professional, 4.7% services, 29.2% sales, 0.0%
farming, 2.0% construction, 2.0% production (2005-2009 5-year est.).

Income: Per capita income: $68,842 (2010); Median household income:
$149,775 (2010); Average household income: $202,482 (2010); Percent of
households with income of $100,000 or more: 71.3% (2010); Poverty rate:
2.0% (2005-2009 5-year est.).

Taxes: Total city taxes per capita: $208 (2007); City property taxes per
capita: $161 (2007).

Education: Percent of population age 25 and over with: High school
diploma (including GED) or higher: 98.1% (2010); Bachelor's degree or
higher: 65.1% (2010); Master's degree or higher: 25.8% (2010).

Housing: Homeownership rate: 97.0% (2010); Median home value:
$622,588 (2010); Median contract rent: $1,542 per month (2005-2009
5-year est.); Median year structure built: 1985 (2005-2009 5-year est.).

Transportation: Commute to work: 78.9% car, 9.9% public transportation,
0.0% walk, 8.8% work from home (2005-2009 5-year est.); Travel time to
work: 16.4% less than 15 minutes, 15.5% 15 to 30 minutes, 26.0% 30 to 45
minutes, 13.2% 45 to 60 minutes, 28.9% 60 minutes or more (2005-2009
5-year est.)

NORTH CHICAGO (city). Covers a land area of 7.832 square miles
and a water area of 0.013 square miles. Located at 42.32° N. Lat; 87.85°
W. Long. Elevation is 659 feet.

History: Named for its location north of Chicago. A sit-down strike at a
steel plant here in 1937 led to a U.S. Supreme Court decision (1939) ruling
sit-down strikes illegal. Incorporated 1895.

Population: 35,785 (1990); 35,918 (2000); 32,890 (2010); 32,212 (2015
projected); Race: 44.5% White, 34.5% Black, 4.3% Asian, 16.8% Other,
28.1% Hispanic of any race (2010); Density: 4,199.7 persons per square
mile (2010); Average household size: 3.26 (2010); Median age: 23.3
(2010); Males per 100 females: 147.3 (2010); Marriage status: 52.0%
never married, 36.4% now married, 3.6% widowed, 7.9% divorced
(2005-2009 5-year est.); Foreign born: 21.1% (2005-2009 5-year est.);
Ancestry (includes multiple ancestries): 10.9% German, 8.3% Irish, 3.2%
Italian, 2.5% English, 2.4% Polish (2005-2009 5-year est.).

Economy: Unemployment rate: 19.5% (August 2011); Total civilian labor
force: 9,750 (August 2011); Single-family building permits issued: 0 (2010);
Multi-family building permits issued: 0 (2010); Employment by occupation:
7.0% management, 15.6% professional, 21.6% services, 21.6% sales,
0.1% farming, 10.1% construction, 23.9% production (2005-2009 5-year
est.).

Income: Per capita income: $15,974 (2010); Median household income:
$43,587 (2010); Average household income: $57,916 (2010); Percent of
households with income of $100,000 or more: 11.6% (2010); Poverty rate:
16.0% (2005-2009 5-year est.).

Taxes: Total city taxes per capita: $278 (2007); City property taxes per
capita: $151 (2007).

Education: Percent of population age 25 and over with: High school
diploma (including GED) or higher: 76.2% (2010); Bachelor's degree or
higher: 15.7% (2010); Master's degree or higher: 6.2% (2010).

School District(s)
North Chicago SD 187 (PK-12)
    2009-10 Enrollment: 3,983 . . . . (847) 689-8150
Four-year College(s)
Rosalind Franklin University of Medicine and Science (Private,
Not-for-profit)
    Fall 2009 Enrollment: 1,915. (847) 578-3000
Housing: Homeownership rate: 41.5% (2010); Median home value:
$139,992 (2010); Median contract rent: $866 per month (2005-2009 5-year
est.); Median year structure built: 1967 (2005-2009 5-year est.).
Hospitals: North Chicago VA Medical Center
Transportation: Commute to work: 58.4% car, 2.9% public transportation,
22.2% walk, 13.8% work from home (2005-2009 5-year est.); Travel time to
work: 44.9% less than 15 minutes, 31.3% 15 to 30 minutes, 12.4% 30 to 45
minutes, 5.5% 45 to 60 minutes, 5.9% 60 minutes or more (2005-2009
5-year est.)
Additional Information Contacts
City of North Chicago. . . . . (847) 596-8600
http://www.northchicago.org

OLD MILL CREEK (village). Aka Mill Creek. Covers a land area of
10.113 square miles and a water area of 0.119 square miles. Located at
42.42° N. Lat; 87.98° W. Long. Elevation is 705 feet.
Population: 143 (1990); 251 (2000); 270 (2010); 279 (2015 projected);
Race: 84.4% White, 3.7% Black, 6.3% Asian, 5.6% Other, 7.8% Hispanic
of any race (2010); Density: 26.7 persons per square mile (2010); Average
household size: 2.81 (2010); Median age: 36.9 (2010); Males per 100
females: 100.0 (2010); Marriage status: 17.5% never married, 68.7% now
married, 5.8% widowed, 7.9% divorced (2005-2009 5-year est.); Foreign
born: 13.9% (2005-2009 5-year est.); Ancestry (includes multiple
ancestries): 20.1% German, 19.4% Irish, 13.2% English, 11.0% Polish,
9.3% French (2005-2009 5-year est.).
Economy: Single-family building permits issued: 1 (2010); Multi-family
building permits issued: 0 (2010); Employment by occupation: 21.3%
management, 29.5% professional, 12.6% services, 20.2% sales, 0.0%
farming, 8.2% construction, 8.2% production (2005-2009 5-year est.).
Income: Per capita income: $47,542 (2010); Median household income:
$100,000 (2010); Average household income: $129,896 (2010); Percent of
households with income of $100,000 or more: 50.0% (2010); Poverty rate:
3.6% (2005-2009 5-year est.).
Taxes: Total city taxes per capita: $306 (2007); City property taxes per
capita: $194 (2007).
Education: Percent of population age 25 and over with: High school
diploma (including GED) or higher: 96.5% (2010); Bachelor's degree or
higher: 48.8% (2010); Master's degree or higher: 18.0% (2010).
School District(s)
Millburn CCSD 24 (PK-08)
    2009-10 Enrollment: 1,614 . . . . (847) 356-8331
Housing: Homeownership rate: 83.3% (2010); Median home value:
$333,333 (2010); Median contract rent: $1,016 per month (2005-2009
5-year est.); Median year structure built: 1992 (2005-2009 5-year est.).
Transportation: Commute to work: 93.0% car, 3.2% public transportation,
0.0% walk, 3.7% work from home (2005-2009 5-year est.); Travel time to
work: 13.9% less than 15 minutes, 26.1% 15 to 30 minutes, 32.2% 30 to 45
minutes, 16.1% 45 to 60 minutes, 11.7% 60 minutes or more (2005-2009
5-year est.)

PARK CITY (city). Covers a land area of 1.150 square miles and a
water area of 0 square miles. Located at 42.35° N. Lat; 87.88° W. Long.
Elevation is 699 feet.
Population: 4,705 (1990); 6,637 (2000); 6,660 (2010); 6,678 (2015
projected); Race: 53.1% White, 6.7% Black, 9.3% Asian, 30.8% Other,
53.4% Hispanic of any race (2010); Density: 5,793.0 persons per square
mile (2010); Average household size: 2.78 (2010); Median age: 32.8
(2010); Males per 100 females: 101.4 (2010); Marriage status: 30.3%
never married, 55.8% now married, 3.7% widowed, 10.2% divorced
(2005-2009 5-year est.); Foreign born: 36.7% (2005-2009 5-year est.);
Ancestry (includes multiple ancestries): 8.7% German, 5.0% Polish, 4.0%
Irish, 2.9% Italian, 2.2% English (2005-2009 5-year est.).
Economy: Single-family building permits issued: 0 (2010); Multi-family
building permits issued: 0 (2010); Employment by occupation: 3.9%
management, 9.7% professional, 27.9% services, 26.7% sales, 0.0%
farming, 10.0% construction, 21.8% production (2005-2009 5-year est.).
Income: Per capita income: $21,386 (2010); Median household income:
$46,415 (2010); Average household income: $59,455 (2010); Percent of

households with income of $100,000 or more: 11.8% (2010); Poverty rate: 8.9% (2005-2009 5-year est.).
Taxes: Total city taxes per capita: $132 (2007); City property taxes per capita: $12 (2007).
Education: Percent of population age 25 and over with: High school diploma (including GED) or higher: 72.7% (2010); Bachelor's degree or higher: 19.1% (2010); Master's degree or higher: 6.9% (2010).
Housing: Homeownership rate: 68.1% (2010); Median home value: $29,690 (2010); Median contract rent: $681 per month (2005-2009 5-year est.); Median year structure built: 1983 (2005-2009 5-year est.).
Safety: Violent crime rate: 13.5 per 10,000 population; Property crime rate: 213.7 per 10,000 population (2010).
Transportation: Commute to work: 94.5% car, 0.6% public transportation, 2.0% walk, 2.5% work from home (2005-2009 5-year est.); Travel time to work: 33.4% less than 15 minutes, 31.2% 15 to 30 minutes, 25.1% 30 to 45 minutes, 7.2% 45 to 60 minutes, 3.0% 60 minutes or more (2005-2009 5-year est.)

RIVERWOODS (village). Covers a land area of 3.989 square miles and a water area of 0.011 square miles. Located at 42.17° N. Lat; 87.89° W. Long. Elevation is 656 feet.
History: Riverwoods was established on the banks of the Des Plaines River in 1949 by local steel magnate Edward L. Ryerson. Orphans of the Storm, an animal shelter founded in 1928 by famous dancer Irene Castle ia also a notable addition to this area.
Population: 3,000 (1990); 3,843 (2000); 4,055 (2010); 4,200 (2015 projected); Race: 91.6% White, 0.6% Black, 5.4% Asian, 2.4% Other, 3.3% Hispanic of any race (2010); Density: 1,016.5 persons per square mile (2010); Average household size: 2.93 (2010); Median age: 41.3 (2010); Males per 100 females: 96.1 (2010); Marriage status: 12.7% never married, 75.5% now married, 8.0% widowed, 3.8% divorced (2005-2009 5-year est.); Foreign born: 13.5% (2005-2009 5-year est.); Ancestry (includes multiple ancestries): 19.2% German, 15.9% Russian, 14.5% Polish, 12.0% Irish, 7.5% Italian (2005-2009 5-year est.).
Economy: Single-family building permits issued: 0 (2010); Multi-family building permits issued: 0 (2010); Employment by occupation: 29.4% management, 25.1% professional, 4.2% services, 31.2% sales, 0.0% farming, 2.4% construction, 7.7% production (2005-2009 5-year est.).
Income: Per capita income: $63,761 (2010); Median household income: $143,548 (2010); Average household income: $188,165 (2010); Percent of households with income of $100,000 or more: 66.8% (2010); Poverty rate: 6.8% (2005-2009 5-year est.).
Taxes: Total city taxes per capita: $754 (2007); City property taxes per capita: $320 (2007).
Education: Percent of population age 25 and over with: High school diploma (including GED) or higher: 97.1% (2010); Bachelor's degree or higher: 72.6% (2010); Master's degree or higher: 35.4% (2010).
Housing: Homeownership rate: 91.4% (2010); Median home value: $618,836 (2010); Median contract rent: $2,000+ per month (2005-2009 5-year est.); Median year structure built: 1975 (2005-2009 5-year est.).
Safety: Violent crime rate: 2.5 per 10,000 population; Property crime rate: 69.1 per 10,000 population (2010).
Transportation: Commute to work: 82.1% car, 5.8% public transportation, 0.5% walk, 10.8% work from home (2005-2009 5-year est.); Travel time to work: 27.6% less than 15 minutes, 37.9% 15 to 30 minutes, 22.2% 30 to 45 minutes, 3.7% 45 to 60 minutes, 8.5% 60 minutes or more (2005-2009 5-year est.)
Additional Information Contacts
DBR Chamber of Commerce . . . . (847) 945-4660
   http://www.dbrchamber.com

ROUND LAKE (village). Covers a land area of 3.520 square miles and a water area of 0.064 square miles. Located at 42.35° N. Lat; 88.10° W. Long. Elevation is 797 feet.
Population: 3,764 (1990); 5,842 (2000); 9,608 (2010); 10,558 (2015 projected); Race: 74.1% White, 2.6% Black, 3.2% Asian, 20.1% Other, 27.6% Hispanic of any race (2010); Density: 2,729.9 persons per square mile (2010); Average household size: 2.90 (2010); Median age: 34.9 (2010); Males per 100 females: 100.6 (2010); Marriage status: 27.0% never married, 61.9% now married, 3.1% widowed, 8.0% divorced (2005-2009 5-year est.); Foreign born: 26.0% (2005-2009 5-year est.); Ancestry (includes multiple ancestries): 16.3% German, 11.7% Polish, 10.6% Irish, 6.1% Italian, 3.3% English (2005-2009 5-year est.).
Economy: Single-family building permits issued: 17 (2010); Multi-family building permits issued: 0 (2010); Employment by occupation: 15.8%

management, 20.9% professional, 14.6% services, 26.7% sales, 0.0% farming, 8.8% construction, 13.2% production (2005-2009 5-year est.).
Income: Per capita income: $28,593 (2010); Median household income: $71,368 (2010); Average household income: $83,011 (2010); Percent of households with income of $100,000 or more: 28.7% (2010); Poverty rate: 11.6% (2005-2009 5-year est.).
Taxes: Total city taxes per capita: $268 (2007); City property taxes per capita: $163 (2007).
Education: Percent of population age 25 and over with: High school diploma (including GED) or higher: 78.7% (2010); Bachelor's degree or higher: 24.0% (2010); Master's degree or higher: 7.4% (2010).
School District(s)
Grayslake CCSD 46 (PK-08)
   2009-10 Enrollment: 4,218 . . . . (847) 223-3650
Round Lake CUSD 116 (PK-12)
   2009-10 Enrollment: 7,050 . . . . (847) 270-9001
Housing: Homeownership rate: 80.8% (2010); Median home value: $192,500 (2010); Median contract rent: $858 per month (2005-2009 5-year est.); Median year structure built: 2001 (2005-2009 5-year est.).
Safety: Violent crime rate: 18.4 per 10,000 population; Property crime rate: 93.8 per 10,000 population (2010).
Transportation: Commute to work: 91.9% car, 3.4% public transportation, 1.6% walk, 2.1% work from home (2005-2009 5-year est.); Travel time to work: 12.8% less than 15 minutes, 24.6% 15 to 30 minutes, 21.3% 30 to 45 minutes, 20.1% 45 to 60 minutes, 21.1% 60 minutes or more (2005-2009 5-year est.)
Additional Information Contacts
Round Lake Area Chamber of Commerce & Industry . . . . . (847) 546-2002
   http://www.rlchamber.org
Village of Round Lake . . . . (847) 546-5400
   http://www.eroundlake.com

ROUND LAKE BEACH (village). Covers a land area of 4.996 square miles and a water area of 0.100 square miles. Located at 42.37° N. Lat; 88.08° W. Long. Elevation is 764 feet.
History: Named for a small round lake close to the city. Incorporated 1937.
Population: 17,438 (1990); 25,859 (2000); 30,807 (2010); 33,126 (2015 projected); Race: 62.7% White, 3.9% Black, 2.6% Asian, 30.8% Other, 46.0% Hispanic of any race (2010); Density: 6,166.8 persons per square mile (2010); Average household size: 3.56 (2010); Median age: 31.8 (2010); Males per 100 females: 102.4 (2010); Marriage status: 32.6% never married, 56.9% now married, 2.6% widowed, 8.0% divorced (2005-2009 5-year est.); Foreign born: 26.9% (2005-2009 5-year est.); Ancestry (includes multiple ancestries): 15.9% German, 10.8% Irish, 9.6% Polish, 4.7% English, 3.2% Italian (2005-2009 5-year est.).
Economy: Unemployment rate: 10.3% (August 2011); Total civilian labor force: 14,393 (August 2011); Single-family building permits issued: 0 (2010); Multi-family building permits issued: 0 (2010); Employment by occupation: 8.5% management, 14.6% professional, 20.6% services, 26.6% sales, 0.5% farming, 12.1% construction, 17.1% production (2005-2009 5-year est.).
Income: Per capita income: $21,726 (2010); Median household income: $69,113 (2010); Average household income: $77,364 (2010); Percent of households with income of $100,000 or more: 23.9% (2010); Poverty rate: 14.0% (2005-2009 5-year est.).
Taxes: Total city taxes per capita: $308 (2007); City property taxes per capita: $176 (2007).
Education: Percent of population age 25 and over with: High school diploma (including GED) or higher: 75.3% (2010); Bachelor's degree or higher: 17.2% (2010); Master's degree or higher: 5.6% (2010).
School District(s)
Grayslake CCSD 46 (PK-08)
   2009-10 Enrollment: 4,218 . . . . (847) 223-3650
Round Lake CUSD 116 (PK-12)
   2009-10 Enrollment: 7,050 . . . . (847) 270-9001
Housing: Homeownership rate: 84.7% (2010); Median home value: $161,656 (2010); Median contract rent: $904 per month (2005-2009 5-year est.); Median year structure built: 1983 (2005-2009 5-year est.).
Safety: Violent crime rate: 23.1 per 10,000 population; Property crime rate: 234.9 per 10,000 population (2010).
Transportation: Commute to work: 92.6% car, 3.3% public transportation, 0.6% walk, 2.0% work from home (2005-2009 5-year est.); Travel time to work: 15.7% less than 15 minutes, 24.7% 15 to 30 minutes, 24.9% 30 to 45 minutes, 13.2% 45 to 60 minutes, 21.4% 60 minutes or more (2005-2009 5-year est.)

Additional Information Contacts
Round Lake Area Chamber of Commerce & Industry . . . . . (847) 546-2002
  http://www.rlchamber.org
Village of Round Lake Beach. . . . . (847) 546-2351
  http://www.villageofroundlakebeach.com

ROUND LAKE HEIGHTS (village). Aka Indian Hills. Covers a land area of 0.612 square miles and a water area of 0 square miles. Located at 42.38° N. Lat; 88.10° W. Long. Elevation is 784 feet.

Population: 1,251 (1990); 1,347 (2000); 2,136 (2010); 2,300 (2015 projected); Race: 75.4% White, 4.8% Black, 0.9% Asian, 18.9% Other, 27.9% Hispanic of any race (2010); Density: 3,489.8 persons per square mile (2010); Average household size: 2.97 (2010); Median age: 33.6 (2010); Males per 100 females: 98.5 (2010); Marriage status: 27.0% never married, 60.8% now married, 4.1% widowed, 8.1% divorced (2005-2009 5-year est.); Foreign born: 18.5% (2005-2009 5-year est.); Ancestry (includes multiple ancestries): 21.0% German, 14.6% Irish, 14.3% Polish, 7.4% Italian, 4.9% English (2005-2009 5-year est.).

Economy: Single-family building permits issued: 0 (2010); Multi-family building permits issued: 0 (2010); Employment by occupation: 9.1% management, 15.9% professional, 14.8% services, 27.1% sales, 0.2% farming, 14.4% construction, 18.4% production (2005-2009 5-year est.).

Income: Per capita income: $25,989 (2010); Median household income: $67,196 (2010); Average household income: $76,791 (2010); Percent of households with income of $100,000 or more: 22.5% (2010); Poverty rate: 4.6% (2005-2009 5-year est.).

Taxes: Total city taxes per capita: $131 (2007); City property taxes per capita: $50 (2007).

Education: Percent of population age 25 and over with: High school diploma (including GED) or higher: 85.7% (2010); Bachelor's degree or higher: 19.4% (2010); Master's degree or higher: 6.3% (2010).

School District(s)
Round Lake CUSD 116 (PK-12)
  2009-10 Enrollment: 7,050 . . . . (847) 270-9001
Housing: Homeownership rate: 84.7% (2010); Median home value: $141,342 (2010); Median contract rent: $1,038 per month (2005-2009 5-year est.); Median year structure built: 1988 (2005-2009 5-year est.).
Safety: Violent crime rate: 6.7 per 10,000 population; Property crime rate: 157.3 per 10,000 population (2010).
Transportation: Commute to work: 91.8% car, 2.2% public transportation, 1.7% walk, 2.4% work from home (2005-2009 5-year est.); Travel time to work: 13.3% less than 15 minutes, 21.7% 15 to 30 minutes, 24.3% 30 to 45 minutes, 21.2% 45 to 60 minutes, 19.5% 60 minutes or more (2005-2009 5-year est.)
Additional Information Contacts
Round Lake Area Chamber of Commerce & Industry . . . . . (847) 546-2002
  http://www.rlchamber.org

ROUND LAKE PARK (village). Covers a land area of 2.990 square miles and a water area of 0.055 square miles. Located at 42.34° N. Lat; 88.07° W. Long. Elevation is 791 feet.

History: Incorporated 1947.

Population: 4,034 (1990); 6,038 (2000); 7,968 (2010); 8,835 (2015 projected); Race: 68.7% White, 3.4% Black, 1.6% Asian, 26.3% Other, 37.7% Hispanic of any race (2010); Density: 2,664.9 persons per square mile (2010); Average household size: 2.87 (2010); Median age: 36.7 (2010); Males per 100 females: 100.5 (2010); Marriage status: 24.9% never married, 56.0% now married, 9.8% widowed, 9.3% divorced (2005-2009 5-year est.); Foreign born: 18.9% (2005-2009 5-year est.); Ancestry (includes multiple ancestries): 22.9% German, 16.0% Irish, 9.2% Polish, 6.5% Italian, 5.7% Norwegian (2005-2009 5-year est.).

Economy: Single-family building permits issued: 0 (2010); Multi-family building permits issued: 0 (2010); Employment by occupation: 8.3% management, 8.4% professional, 23.9% services, 32.3% sales, 0.6% farming, 9.6% construction, 17.0% production (2005-2009 5-year est.).

Income: Per capita income: $25,322 (2010); Median household income: $58,870 (2010); Average household income: $72,667 (2010); Percent of households with income of $100,000 or more: 19.0% (2010); Poverty rate: 12.4% (2005-2009 5-year est.).

Taxes: Total city taxes per capita: $223 (2007); City property taxes per capita: $128 (2007).

Education: Percent of population age 25 and over with: High school diploma (including GED) or higher: 78.6% (2010); Bachelor's degree or higher: 19.7% (2010); Master's degree or higher: 5.6% (2010).

School District(s)
Round Lake CUSD 116 (PK-12)
  2009-10 Enrollment: 7,050 . . . . (847) 270-9001
Housing: Homeownership rate: 82.7% (2010); Median home value: $170,909 (2010); Median contract rent: $936 per month (2005-2009 est.); Median year structure built: 1980 (2005-2009 5-year est.).
Transportation: Commute to work: 93.0% car, 0.9% public transportation, 4.3% walk, 1.3% work from home (2005-2009 5-year est.); Travel time to work: 18.7% less than 15 minutes, 31.2% 15 to 30 minutes, 20.4% 30 to 45 minutes, 13.6% 45 to 60 minutes, 16.1% 60 minutes or more (2005-2009 5-year est.)
Additional Information Contacts
Round Lake Area Chamber of Commerce & Industry . . . . . (847) 546-2002
  http://www.rlchamber.org
Village of Round Lake Park . . . . (847) 546-2790
  http://www.roundlakepark.us

THIRD LAKE (village). Covers a land area of 0.548 square miles and a water area of 0.252 square miles. Located at 42.36° N. Lat; 88.00° W. Long. Elevation is 771 feet.

Population: 1,116 (1990); 1,355 (2000); 1,685 (2010); 1,894 (2015 projected); Race: 84.9% White, 1.8% Black, 8.5% Asian, 4.7% Other, 7.2% Hispanic of any race (2010); Density: 3,077.5 persons per square mile (2010); Average household size: 3.23 (2010); Median age: 35.8 (2010); Males per 100 females: 98.2 (2010); Marriage status: 25.5% never married, 65.1% now married, 1.8% widowed, 7.5% divorced (2005-2009 5-year est.); Foreign born: 4.1% (2005-2009 5-year est.); Ancestry (includes multiple ancestries): 34.9% German, 25.1% Irish, 13.1% Polish, 12.4% English, 10.2% Italian (2005-2009 5-year est.).

Economy: Single-family building permits issued: 0 (2010); Multi-family building permits issued: 0 (2010); Employment by occupation: 23.2% management, 31.7% professional, 7.0% services, 22.8% sales, 0.0% farming, 7.0% construction, 8.5% production (2005-2009 5-year est.).

Income: Per capita income: $39,924 (2010); Median household income: $115,169 (2010); Average household income: $128,654 (2010); Percent of households with income of $100,000 or more: 60.3% (2010); Poverty rate: 4.1% (2005-2009 5-year est.).

Taxes: Total city taxes per capita: $73 (2007); City property taxes per capita: $41 (2007).

Education: Percent of population age 25 and over with: High school diploma (including GED) or higher: 96.5% (2010); Bachelor's degree or higher: 56.4% (2010); Master's degree or higher: 24.3% (2010).
Housing: Homeownership rate: 95.4% (2010); Median home value: $260,839 (2010); Median contract rent: $1,500 per month (2005-2009 5-year est.); Median year structure built: 1985 (2005-2009 5-year est.).
Transportation: Commute to work: 88.5% car, 4.7% public transportation, 0.0% walk, 4.8% work from home (2005-2009 5-year est.); Travel time to work: 20.4% less than 15 minutes, 28.8% 15 to 30 minutes, 24.5% 30 to 45 minutes, 13.3% 45 to 60 minutes, 13.0% 60 minutes or more (2005-2009 5-year est.)

TOWER LAKES (village). Covers a land area of 0.947 square miles and a water area of 0.120 square miles. Located at 42.23° N. Lat; 88.15° W. Long. Elevation is 781 feet.

Population: 1,360 (1990); 1,310 (2000); 1,225 (2010); 1,145 (2015 projected); Race: 94.7% White, 0.0% Black, 1.5% Asian, 3.8% Other, 2.0% Hispanic of any race (2010); Density: 1,293.4 persons per square mile (2010); Average household size: 2.95 (2010); Median age: 45.1 (2010); Males per 100 females: 95.7 (2010); Marriage status: 23.8% never married, 72.0% now married, 0.6% widowed, 3.6% divorced (2005-2009 5-year est.); Foreign born: 10.3% (2005-2009 5-year est.); Ancestry (includes multiple ancestries): 28.7% German, 24.4% Irish, 15.6% Polish, 11.4% Italian, 10.4% English (2005-2009 5-year est.).

Economy: Single-family building permits issued: 0 (2010); Multi-family building permits issued: 0 (2010); Employment by occupation: 28.6% management, 20.0% professional, 9.4% services, 37.2% sales, 0.0% farming, 2.8% construction, 2.0% production (2005-2009 5-year est.).

Income: Per capita income: $63,395 (2010); Median household income: $151,838 (2010); Average household income: $186,416 (2010); Percent of households with income of $100,000 or more: 68.4% (2010); Poverty rate: 1.1% (2005-2009 5-year est.).

Taxes: Total city taxes per capita: $401 (2007); City property taxes per capita: $319 (2007).

Education: Percent of population age 25 and over with: High school diploma (including GED) or higher: 98.1% (2010); Bachelor's degree or higher: 65.1% (2010); Master's degree or higher: 31.6% (2010).

Housing: Homeownership rate: 98.3% (2010); Median home value: $470,455 (2010); Median contract rent: n/a per month (2005-2009 5-year est.); Median year structure built: 1967 (2005-2009 5-year est.).
Transportation: Commute to work: 80.5% car, 8.3% public transportation, 0.7% walk, 10.0% work from home (2005-2009 5-year est.); Travel time to work: 14.5% less than 15 minutes, 24.2% 15 to 30 minutes, 22.2% 30 to 45 minutes, 9.9% 45 to 60 minutes, 29.2% 60 minutes or more (2005-2009 5-year est.)

VENETIAN VILLAGE (CDP). Covers a land area of 2.418 square miles and a water area of 0.696 square miles. Located at 42.39° N. Lat; 88.04° W. Long. Elevation is 797 feet.
Population: 2,516 (1990); 3,082 (2000); 3,389 (2010); 3,739 (2015 projected); Race: 86.2% White, 3.3% Black, 3.5% Asian, 7.0% Other, 9.5% Hispanic of any race (2010); Density: 1,401.5 persons per square mile (2010); Average household size: 2.93 (2010); Median age: 36.1 (2010); Males per 100 females: 99.0 (2010); Marriage status: 23.5% never married, 63.2% now married, 4.2% widowed, 9.1% divorced (2005-2009 5-year est.); Foreign born: 5.1% (2005-2009 5-year est.); Ancestry (includes multiple ancestries): 35.3% German, 21.3% Irish, 19.0% Polish, 10.3% Italian, 10.0% Swedish (2005-2009 5-year est.).
Economy: Employment by occupation: 16.2% management, 14.4% professional, 12.3% services, 25.5% sales, 0.8% farming, 16.8% construction, 14.0% production (2005-2009 5-year est.).
Income: Per capita income: $30,621 (2010); Median household income: $79,268 (2010); Average household income: $89,919 (2010); Percent of households with income of $100,000 or more: 32.2% (2010); Poverty rate: 0.7% (2005-2009 5-year est.).
Education: Percent of population age 25 and over with: High school diploma (including GED) or higher: 91.8% (2010); Bachelor's degree or higher: 32.3% (2010); Master's degree or higher: 9.6% (2010).
Housing: Homeownership rate: 88.7% (2010); Median home value: $202,078 (2010); Median contract rent: $989 per month (2005-2009 5-year est.); Median year structure built: 1969 (2005-2009 5-year est.).
Transportation: Commute to work: 96.2% car, 0.4% public transportation, 1.0% walk, 1.1% work from home (2005-2009 5-year est.); Travel time to work: 15.4% less than 15 minutes, 15.6% 15 to 30 minutes, 35.2% 30 to 45 minutes, 15.2% 45 to 60 minutes, 18.6% 60 minutes or more (2005-2009 5-year est.)

VERNON HILLS (village). Covers a land area of 7.429 square miles and a water area of 0.190 square miles. Located at 42.23° N. Lat; 87.96° W. Long. Elevation is 735 feet.
Population: 15,529 (1990); 20,120 (2000); 23,980 (2010); 25,041 (2015 projected); Race: 75.7% White, 1.6% Black, 17.1% Asian, 5.7% Other, 10.4% Hispanic of any race (2010); Density: 3,227.9 persons per square mile (2010); Average household size: 2.78 (2010); Median age: 36.7 (2010); Males per 100 females: 95.9 (2010); Marriage status: 25.4% never married, 61.6% now married, 4.6% widowed, 8.4% divorced (2005-2009 5-year est.); Foreign born: 27.0% (2005-2009 5-year est.); Ancestry (includes multiple ancestries): 16.7% German, 11.6% Irish, 9.8% Polish, 8.9% Russian, 7.1% Italian (2005-2009 5-year est.).
Economy: Single-family building permits issued: 4 (2010); Multi-family building permits issued: 231 (2010); Employment by occupation: 23.6% management, 27.1% professional, 11.0% services, 26.4% sales, 0.0% farming, 4.3% construction, 7.7% production (2005-2009 5-year est.).
Income: Per capita income: $41,705 (2010); Median household income: $91,726 (2010); Average household income: $115,767 (2010); Percent of households with income of $100,000 or more: 44.9% (2010); Poverty rate: 4.7% (2005-2009 5-year est.).
Taxes: Total city taxes per capita: $231 (2007); City property taxes per capita: $0 (2007).
Education: Percent of population age 25 and over with: High school diploma (including GED) or higher: 94.6% (2010); Bachelor's degree or higher: 58.5% (2010); Master's degree or higher: 22.6% (2010).
School District(s)
CHSD 128 (09-12)
    2009-10 Enrollment: 3,388 . . . . (847) 247-4510
Hawthorn CCSD 73 (PK-08)
    2009-10 Enrollment: 3,909 . . . . (847) 990-4244
Spec Educ Dist Lake County/Sedol (PK-12)
    2009-10 Enrollment: n/a . . . . (847) 548-8470
Housing: Homeownership rate: 80.0% (2010); Median home value: $292,155 (2010); Median contract rent: $1,092 per month (2005-2009 5-year est.); Median year structure built: 1985 (2005-2009 5-year est.).

Safety: Violent crime rate: 2.4 per 10,000 population; Property crime rate: 273.7 per 10,000 population (2010).
Newspapers: Chicago Tribune - Vernon Hills Bureau (Local news); Daily Herald - Vernon Hills Bureau (Local news)
Transportation: Commute to work: 89.3% car, 3.7% public transportation, 0.2% walk, 5.1% work from home (2005-2009 5-year est.); Travel time to work: 22.7% less than 15 minutes, 30.4% 15 to 30 minutes, 27.5% 30 to 45 minutes, 9.0% 45 to 60 minutes, 10.4% 60 minutes or more (2005-2009 5-year est.)
Additional Information Contacts
GLMV Area Chamber of Commerce . . . . (847) 680-0750
    http://www.glmvchamber.org
Village of Vernon Hills . . . . (847) 367-3700
    http://www.vernonhills.org

VOLO (village). Covers a land area of 2.791 square miles and a water area of 0.012 square miles. Located at 42.33° N. Lat; 88.16° W. Long. Elevation is 794 feet.
Population: 157 (1990); 180 (2000); 328 (2010); 367 (2015 projected); Race: 91.2% White, 0.6% Black, 3.4% Asian, 4.9% Other, 12.8% Hispanic of any race (2010); Density: 117.5 persons per square mile (2010); Average household size: 2.84 (2010); Median age: 38.5 (2010); Males per 100 females: 96.4 (2010); Marriage status: 19.2% never married, 64.3% now married, 4.0% widowed, 12.4% divorced (2005-2009 5-year est.); Foreign born: 9.1% (2005-2009 5-year est.); Ancestry (includes multiple ancestries): 31.8% German, 18.5% Polish, 17.7% Irish, 15.2% Italian, 6.9% English (2005-2009 5-year est.).
Economy: Single-family building permits issued: 74 (2010); Multi-family building permits issued: 0 (2010); Employment by occupation: 15.7% management, 24.3% professional, 9.9% services, 33.2% sales, 0.0% farming, 7.2% construction, 9.6% production (2005-2009 5-year est.).
Income: Per capita income: $35,648 (2010); Median household income: $88,125 (2010); Average household income: $98,609 (2010); Percent of households with income of $100,000 or more: 41.7% (2010); Poverty rate: 2.1% (2005-2009 5-year est.).
Taxes: Total city taxes per capita: $10,759 (2007); City property taxes per capita: $440 (2007).
Education: Percent of population age 25 and over with: High school diploma (including GED) or higher: 91.0% (2010); Bachelor's degree or higher: 30.0% (2010); Master's degree or higher: 9.0% (2010).
Housing: Homeownership rate: 81.7% (2010); Median home value: $269,444 (2010); Median contract rent: $975 per month (2005-2009 5-year est.); Median year structure built: 2005 (2005-2009 5-year est.).
Transportation: Commute to work: 89.8% car, 1.8% public transportation, 1.2% walk, 7.0% work from home (2005-2009 5-year est.); Travel time to work: 13.3% less than 15 minutes, 17.1% 15 to 30 minutes, 29.3% 30 to 45 minutes, 24.8% 45 to 60 minutes, 15.5% 60 minutes or more (2005-2009 5-year est.)

WADSWORTH (village). Covers a land area of 8.773 square miles and a water area of 0.037 square miles. Located at 42.43° N. Lat; 87.92° W. Long. Elevation is 705 feet.
Population: 2,570 (1990); 3,083 (2000); 3,833 (2010); 4,103 (2015 projected); Race: 88.5% White, 2.5% Black, 2.7% Asian, 6.3% Other, 8.5% Hispanic of any race (2010); Density: 436.9 persons per square mile (2010); Average household size: 2.89 (2010); Median age: 43.2 (2010); Males per 100 females: 100.3 (2010); Marriage status: 25.4% never married, 67.9% now married, 2.3% widowed, 4.4% divorced (2005-2009 5-year est.); Foreign born: 7.0% (2005-2009 5-year est.); Ancestry (includes multiple ancestries): 27.8% German, 18.4% Polish, 17.4% Irish, 12.7% English, 9.6% Italian (2005-2009 5-year est.).
Economy: Single-family building permits issued: 0 (2010); Multi-family building permits issued: 0 (2010); Employment by occupation: 22.3% management, 26.3% professional, 13.2% services, 23.1% sales, 0.0% farming, 9.1% construction, 6.0% production (2005-2009 5-year est.).
Income: Per capita income: $41,031 (2010); Median household income: $96,801 (2010); Average household income: $118,786 (2010); Percent of households with income of $100,000 or more: 48.0% (2010); Poverty rate: 0.9% (2005-2009 5-year est.).
Taxes: Total city taxes per capita: $93 (2007); City property taxes per capita: $27 (2007).
Education: Percent of population age 25 and over with: High school diploma (including GED) or higher: 94.9% (2010); Bachelor's degree or higher: 37.4% (2010); Master's degree or higher: 17.0% (2010).

School District(s)
Beach Park CCSD 3 (PK-08)
2009-10 Enrollment: 2,560 . . . . (847) 599-5005
Housing: Homeownership rate: 91.1% (2010); Median home value: $311,648 (2010); Median contract rent: $953 per month (2005-2009 5-year est.); Median year structure built: 1985 (2005-2009 5-year est.).
Transportation: Commute to work: 92.6% car, 3.0% public transportation, 0.0% walk, 3.1% work from home (2005-2009 5-year est.); Travel time to work: 18.7% less than 15 minutes, 36.6% 15 to 30 minutes, 18.9% 30 to 45 minutes, 8.4% 45 to 60 minutes, 17.5% 60 minutes or more (2005-2009 5-year est.)

WAUCONDA (village).
Covers a land area of 3.864 square miles and a water area of 0.419 square miles. Located at 42.26° N. Lat; 88.14° W. Long. Elevation is 804 feet.
History: Wauconda was settled in 1836 by Justus Bangs. The name he gave the village probably came from a favorite book of his, and was Indian in origin.
Population: 7,481 (1990); 9,448 (2000); 11,905 (2010); 12,757 (2015 projected); Race: 85.7% White, 0.7% Black, 2.7% Asian, 11.0% Other, 17.5% Hispanic of any race (2010); Density: 3,080.8 persons per square mile (2010); Average household size: 2.59 (2010); Median age: 39.5 (2010); Males per 100 females: 101.8 (2010); Marriage status: 29.2% never married, 56.5% now married, 4.7% widowed, 9.6% divorced (2005-2009 5-year est.); Foreign born: 16.3% (2005-2009 5-year est.); Ancestry (includes multiple ancestries): 26.9% German, 14.6% Irish, 11.2% Polish, 9.8% Italian, 7.4% English (2005-2009 5-year est.).
Economy: Single-family building permits issued: 39 (2010); Multi-family building permits issued: 0 (2010); Employment by occupation: 17.2% management, 17.1% professional, 15.2% services, 29.8% sales, 0.0% farming, 9.3% construction, 11.4% production (2005-2009 5-year est.).
Income: Per capita income: $32,822 (2010); Median household income: $70,994 (2010); Average household income: $84,846 (2010); Percent of households with income of $100,000 or more: 27.5% (2010); Poverty rate: 4.6% (2005-2009 5-year est.).
Taxes: Total city taxes per capita: $356 (2007); City property taxes per capita: $223 (2007).
Education: Percent of population age 25 and over with: High school diploma (including GED) or higher: 89.3% (2010); Bachelor's degree or higher: 27.6% (2010); Master's degree or higher: 8.5% (2010).
School District(s)
Wauconda CUSD 118 (PK-12)
2009-10 Enrollment: 4,401 . . . . (847) 526-7690
Housing: Homeownership rate: 82.8% (2010); Median home value: $223,289 (2010); Median contract rent: $783 per month (2005-2009 5-year est.); Median year structure built: 1987 (2005-2009 5-year est.).
Safety: Violent crime rate: 8.0 per 10,000 population; Property crime rate: 132.5 per 10,000 population (2010).
Transportation: Commute to work: 91.3% car, 1.9% public transportation, 1.1% walk, 2.9% work from home (2005-2009 5-year est.); Travel time to work: 22.3% less than 15 minutes, 27.1% 15 to 30 minutes, 25.0% 30 to 45 minutes, 12.1% 45 to 60 minutes, 13.5% 60 minutes or more (2005-2009 5-year est.)
Additional Information Contacts
Village of Wauconda . . . . (847) 526-9600
http://www.wauconda-il.gov
Wauconda Area Chamber of Commerce . . . . (847) 526-5580
http://www.waucondachamber.org

WAUKEGAN (city).
County seat. Covers a land area of 23.012 square miles and a water area of 0.079 square miles. Located at 42.37° N. Lat; 87.86° W. Long. Elevation is 653 feet.
History: Named for the Indian translation of "sheltering place". Waukegan began with the founding of Little Fort by the French in the 1700's, the present name being of Indian origin meaning "fort or trading post." Settlers came to Little Fort in 1835, and in 1846 it was designated as a U.S. port of entry. Waukegan was incorporated as a village in 1849, and as a city in 1859.
Population: 70,309 (1990); 87,901 (2000); 92,155 (2010); 94,001 (2015 projected); Race: 46.1% White, 16.0% Black, 4.1% Asian, 33.9% Other, 57.9% Hispanic of any race (2010); Density: 4,004.7 persons per square mile (2010); Average household size: 3.15 (2010); Median age: 32.0 (2010); Males per 100 females: 102.9 (2010); Marriage status: 36.9% never married, 48.2% now married, 5.2% widowed, 9.8% divorced (2005-2009 5-year est.); Foreign born: 33.4% (2005-2009 5-year est.);

Ancestry (includes multiple ancestries): 7.0% German, 4.6% Irish, 2.8% Italian, 2.5% Polish, 2.5% English (2005-2009 5-year est.).
Economy: Unemployment rate: 11.5% (August 2011); Total civilian labor force: 43,315 (August 2011); Single-family building permits issued: 17 (2010); Multi-family building permits issued: 10 (2010); Employment by occupation: 7.8% management, 11.6% professional, 22.2% services, 22.7% sales, 0.1% farming, 9.8% construction, 25.8% production (2005-2009 5-year est.).
Income: Per capita income: $19,205 (2010); Median household income: $48,669 (2010); Average household income: $60,619 (2010); Percent of households with income of $100,000 or more: 13.9% (2010); Poverty rate: 13.0% (2005-2009 5-year est.).
Taxes: Total city taxes per capita: $413 (2007); City property taxes per capita: $241 (2007).
Education: Percent of population age 25 and over with: High school diploma (including GED) or higher: 67.4% (2010); Bachelor's degree or higher: 18.0% (2010); Master's degree or higher: 6.5% (2010).
School District(s)
Waukegan CUSD 60 (PK-12)
2009-10 Enrollment: 16,660 . . . . (847) 336-3100
Housing: Homeownership rate: 56.0% (2010); Median home value: $151,724 (2010); Median contract rent: $701 per month (2005-2009 5-year est.); Median year structure built: 1963 (2005-2009 5-year est.).
Hospitals: Vista Health - Saint Therese Medical Center (388 beds); Vista Medical Center East (299 beds)
Newspapers: Antioch Review (Community news; Circulation 1,644); Deerfield Review (Community news; Circulation 5,282); Grayslake Review (Community news; Circulation 3,520); Gurnee Review (Community news; Circulation 3,694); Highland Park News (Community news; Circulation 7,392); Lake Forester (Community news; Circulation 6,811); Lake Villa/Lindenhurst Review (Community news; Circulation 2,381); Libertyville Review (Community news; Circulation 4,480); Lincolnshire Review (Community news); Mundelein Review (Community news; Circulation 2,538); News Sun (Local news; Circulation 21,299); Vernon Hills Review (Community news; Circulation 2,200)
Transportation: Commute to work: 90.1% car, 4.2% public transportation, 1.4% walk, 2.2% work from home (2005-2009 5-year est.); Travel time to work: 21.6% less than 15 minutes, 38.9% 15 to 30 minutes, 23.4% 30 to 45 minutes, 7.7% 45 to 60 minutes, 8.4% 60 minutes or more (2005-2009 5-year est.)
Airports: Waukegan Regional (general aviation)
Additional Information Contacts
City of Waukegan . . . . (847) 599-2500
http://www.waukeganweb.net

WINTHROP HARBOR (village).
Covers a land area of 4.309 square miles and a water area of 0.069 square miles. Located at 42.48° N. Lat; 87.82° W. Long. Elevation is 636 feet.
History: The Winthrop Harbor and Dock Company purchased land here in 1892, but plans to develop the harbor and town were abandoned. The community that grew here depended on dairying.
Population: 6,397 (1990); 6,670 (2000); 7,547 (2010); 7,863 (2015 projected); Race: 88.4% White, 2.6% Black, 2.2% Asian, 6.9% Other, 9.0% Hispanic of any race (2010); Density: 1,751.5 persons per square mile (2010); Average household size: 2.78 (2010); Median age: 37.9 (2010); Males per 100 females: 99.9 (2010); Marriage status: 28.7% never married, 56.5% now married, 5.6% widowed, 9.1% divorced (2005-2009 5-year est.); Foreign born: 2.9% (2005-2009 5-year est.); Ancestry (includes multiple ancestries): 32.4% German, 16.3% Irish, 14.2% Polish, 12.3% English, 5.1% Italian (2005-2009 5-year est.).
Economy: Single-family building permits issued: 1 (2010); Multi-family building permits issued: 0 (2010); Employment by occupation: 16.6% management, 18.5% professional, 16.4% services, 26.2% sales, 0.2% farming, 6.8% construction, 15.3% production (2005-2009 5-year est.).
Income: Per capita income: $28,561 (2010); Median household income: $70,280 (2010); Average household income: $79,283 (2010); Percent of households with income of $100,000 or more: 27.0% (2010); Poverty rate: 3.6% (2005-2009 5-year est.).
Taxes: Total city taxes per capita: $316 (2007); City property taxes per capita: $184 (2007).
Education: Percent of population age 25 and over with: High school diploma (including GED) or higher: 90.8% (2010); Bachelor's degree or higher: 21.5% (2010); Master's degree or higher: 7.8% (2010).

School District(s)

Winthrop Harbor SD 1 (KG-08)

2009-10 Enrollment: 669 . . . . (847) 731-3085

Housing: Homeownership rate: 81.6% (2010); Median home value: $184,135 (2010); Median contract rent: $780 per month (2005-2009 5-year est.); Median year structure built: 1976 (2005-2009 5-year est.).

Safety: Violent crime rate: 13.9 per 10,000 population; Property crime rate: 133.9 per 10,000 population (2010).

Transportation: Commute to work: 97.0% car, 0.2% public transportation, 0.5% walk, 1.6% work from home (2005-2009 5-year est.); Travel time to work: 24.8% less than 15 minutes, 30.5% 15 to 30 minutes, 17.6% 30 to 45 minutes, 15.7% 45 to 60 minutes, 11.4% 60 minutes or more (2005-2009 5-year est.)

Additional Information Contacts

Winthrop Harbor Chamber of Commerce . . . .
http://www.cocwh.com

ZION (city). Covers a land area of 8.197 square miles and a water area of 0 square miles. Located at 42.45° N. Lat; 87.84° W. Long. Elevation is 650 feet.

History: Named for Mount Zion in Palestine. Zion began as the dream of John Alexander Dowie (1847-1907), the Scottish founder of the Christian Catholic Apostolic Church, who planned Zion as a city where the tenets of the church would govern. In 1899 Dowie's followers began to settle here. Dowie was succeeded by Wilbur Glenn Voliva, who attempted to industrialize Zion, but the church owned all industries and commercial establishments. In 1939, after several bankruptcies, titles were transferred to individuals.

Population: 20,171 (1990); 22,866 (2000); 25,320 (2010); 26,354 (2015 projected); Race: 48.6% White, 30.3% Black, 2.4% Asian, 18.8% Other, 24.9% Hispanic of any race (2010); Density: 3,088.9 persons per square mile (2010); Average household size: 3.01 (2010); Median age: 32.4 (2010); Males per 100 females: 94.9 (2010); Marriage status: 35.6% never married, 49.0% now married, 4.0% widowed, 11.4% divorced (2005-2009 5-year est.); Foreign born: 12.9% (2005-2009 5-year est.); Ancestry (includes multiple ancestries): 13.5% German, 11.6% Irish, 5.2% English, 3.4% Polish, 3.0% Swedish (2005-2009 5-year est.).

Economy: Unemployment rate: 12.9% (August 2011); Total civilian labor force: 12,072 (August 2011); Single-family building permits issued: 10 (2010); Multi-family building permits issued: 0 (2010); Employment by occupation: 11.0% management, 14.6% professional, 20.5% services, 27.5% sales, 0.2% farming, 8.9% construction, 17.3% production (2005-2009 5-year est.).

Income: Per capita income: $21,204 (2010); Median household income: $52,225 (2010); Average household income: $63,782 (2010); Percent of households with income of $100,000 or more: 16.8% (2010); Poverty rate: 15.7% (2005-2009 5-year est.).

Taxes: Total city taxes per capita: $552 (2007); City property taxes per capita: $393 (2007).

Education: Percent of population age 25 and over with: High school diploma (including GED) or higher: 81.0% (2010); Bachelor's degree or higher: 18.3% (2010); Master's degree or higher: 7.1% (2010).

School District(s)

Lake Roe (06-12)

2009-10 Enrollment: n/a . . . . (847) 543-7833

Zion ESD 6 (PK-08)

2009-10 Enrollment: 2,681 . . . . (847) 872-5455

Zion-Benton Twp HSD 126 (09-12)

2009-10 Enrollment: 2,878 . . . . (847) 731-9792

Housing: Homeownership rate: 60.5% (2010); Median home value: $152,085 (2010); Median contract rent: $717 per month (2005-2009 5-year est.); Median year structure built: 1971 (2005-2009 5-year est.).

Hospitals: Midwestern Regional Medical Center (95 beds)

Newspapers: Bargaineer (Community news; Circulation 28,000); Zion-Benton News (Community news; Circulation 3,500)

Transportation: Commute to work: 91.0% car, 3.8% public transportation, 2.6% walk, 1.7% work from home (2005-2009 5-year est.); Travel time to work: 18.6% less than 15 minutes, 28.9% 15 to 30 minutes, 26.9% 30 to 45 minutes, 14.1% 45 to 60 minutes, 11.5% 60 minutes or more (2005-2009 5-year est.)

Additional Information Contacts

City of Zion . . . . (847) 746-4000
http://www.cityofzion.com

Zion Area Chamber of Commerce . . . . (847) 872-5405
http://www.zionchamber.com

Lawrence County

Located in southeastern Illinois; bounded on the east by the Wabash River and the Indiana border; drained by the Embarrass River. Covers a land area of 371.98 square miles, a water area of 1.96 square miles, and is located in the Central Time Zone at 38.72° N. Lat., 87.72° W. Long. The county was founded in 1821. County seat is Lawrenceville.

Population: 15,972 (1990); 15,452 (2000); 16,748 (2010); 17,134 (2015 projected); Race: 88.7% White, 9.3% Black, 0.2% Asian, 1.7% Other, 2.3% Hispanic of any race (2010); Density: 45.0 persons per square mile (2010); Average household size: 2.31 (2010); Median age: 44.3 (2010); Males per 100 females: 100.6 (2010).

Religion: Five largest groups: 15.2% The United Methodist Church, 10.2% Christian Churches and Churches of Christ, 5.2% Catholic Church, 5.1% Southern Baptist Convention, 2.5% The Wesleyan Church (2000).

Economy: Unemployment rate: 9.4% (August 2011); Total civilian labor force: 8,317 (August 2011); Leading industries: 20.4% health care and social assistance; 15.3% manufacturing; 13.8% retail trade (2009); Farms: 421 totaling 194,035 acres (2007); Companies that employ 500 or more persons: 0 (2009); Companies that employ 100 to 499 persons: 9 (2009); Companies that employ less than 100 persons: 293 (2009); Black-owned businesses: n/a (2007); Hispanic-owned businesses: n/a (2007); Asian-owned businesses: n/a (2007); Women-owned businesses: n/a (2007); Retail sales per capita: $6,025 (2010). Single-family building permits issued: 0 (2010); Multi-family building permits issued: 0 (2010).

Income: Per capita income: $20,552 (2010); Median household income: $37,443 (2010); Average household income: $47,985 (2010); Percent of households with income of $100,000 or more: 7.7% (2010); Poverty rate: 18.1% (2009); Bankruptcy rate: 3.40% (2010).

Taxes: Total county taxes per capita: $117 (2007); County property taxes per capita: $116 (2007).

Education: Percent of population age 25 and over with: High school diploma (including GED) or higher: 86.0% (2010); Bachelor's degree or higher: 11.8% (2010); Master's degree or higher: 4.0% (2010).

Housing: Homeownership rate: 75.8% (2010); Median home value: $57,916 (2010); Median contract rent: $302 per month (2005-2009 5-year est.); Median year structure built: 1958 (2005-2009 5-year est.)

Health: Birth rate: 96.3 per 10,000 population (2009); Death rate: 135.9 per 10,000 population (2009); Age-adjusted cancer mortality rate: 206.1 deaths per 100,000 population (2007); Number of physicians: 7.3 per 10,000 population (2008); Hospital beds: 21.1 per 10,000 population (2007); Hospital admissions: 639.2 per 10,000 population (2007).

Elections: 2008 Presidential election results: 46.1% Obama, 52.1% McCain, 0.9% Nader

National and State Parks: Lincoln Trail State Memorial; Red Hills State Park

Additional Information Contacts

Lawrence County Government . . . . (618) 943-2346
http://www.lawrencecountyillinois.com

Lawrence County Chamber of Commerce . . . . (618) 943-3516
http://www.lawrencecountychamberofcommerce.com

Lawrence County Communities

BIRDS (village). Covers a land area of 0.216 square miles and a water area of 0 square miles. Located at 38.83° N. Lat; 87.66° W. Long. Elevation is 436 feet.

Population: 160 (1990); 51 (2000); 46 (2010); 44 (2015 projected); Race: 80.4% White, 17.4% Black, 0.0% Asian, 2.2% Other, 2.2% Hispanic of any race (2010); Density: 212.5 persons per square mile (2010); Average household size: 2.32 (2010); Median age: 37.9 (2010); Males per 100 females: 84.0 (2010); Marriage status: 31.4% never married, 57.1% now married, 0.0% widowed, 11.4% divorced (2005-2009 5-year est.); Foreign born: 10.6% (2005-2009 5-year est.); Ancestry (includes multiple ancestries): 38.3% German, 31.9% Polish, 17.0% French, 6.4% Dutch, 6.4% Irish (2005-2009 5-year est.).

Economy: Employment by occupation: 0.0% management, 0.0% professional, 31.8% services, 54.5% sales, 0.0% farming, 0.0% construction, 13.6% production (2005-2009 5-year est.).

Income: Per capita income: $17,917 (2010); Median household income: $36,875 (2010); Average household income: $39,342 (2010); Percent of households with income of $100,000 or more: 0.0% (2010); Poverty rate: 10.6% (2005-2009 5-year est.).

Taxes: Total city taxes per capita: $40 (2007); City property taxes per capita: $20 (2007).

Education: Percent of population age 25 and over with: High school diploma (including GED) or higher: 90.9% (2010); Bachelor's degree or higher: 6.1% (2010); Master's degree or higher: 0.0% (2010).
Housing: Homeownership rate: 84.2% (2010); Median home value: $73,333 (2010); Median contract rent: n/a per month (2005-2009 5-year est.); Median year structure built: 1959 (2005-2009 5-year est.).
Transportation: Commute to work: 100.0% car, 0.0% public transportation, 0.0% walk, 0.0% work from home (2005-2009 5-year est.); Travel time to work: 22.7% less than 15 minutes, 40.9% 15 to 30 minutes, 0.0% 30 to 45 minutes, 36.4% 45 to 60 minutes, 0.0% 60 minutes or more (2005-2009 5-year est.)

BRIDGEPORT (city).

Covers a land area of 1.071 square miles and a water area of 0.025 square miles. Located at 38.71° N. Lat; 87.75° W. Long. Elevation is 446 feet.
History: Bridgeport was the center of an early oil boom, when a company built a pumping station and supply yards here.
Population: 2,118 (1990); 2,168 (2000); 2,159 (2010); 2,144 (2015 projected); Race: 92.7% White, 5.3% Black, 0.0% Asian, 2.0% Other, 1.8% Hispanic of any race (2010); Density: 2,015.6 persons per square mile (2010); Average household size: 2.34 (2010); Median age: 40.0 (2010); Males per 100 females: 107.6 (2010); Marriage status: 22.1% never married, 45.3% now married, 15.9% widowed, 16.7% divorced (2005-2009 5-year est.); Foreign born: 0.2% (2005-2009 5-year est.); Ancestry (includes multiple ancestries): 22.4% American, 10.1% English, 10.0% German, 9.2% Irish, 4.5% French (2005-2009 5-year est.).
Economy: Employment by occupation: 4.4% management, 12.9% professional, 31.6% services, 28.5% sales, 0.0% farming, 5.3% construction, 17.4% production (2005-2009 5-year est.).
Income: Per capita income: $17,802 (2010); Median household income: $35,654 (2010); Average household income: $42,545 (2010); Percent of households with income of $100,000 or more: 3.7% (2010); Poverty rate: 17.8% (2005-2009 5-year est.).
Taxes: Total city taxes per capita: $17 (2007); City property taxes per capita: $11 (2007).
Education: Percent of population age 25 and over with: High school diploma (including GED) or higher: 83.8% (2010); Bachelor's degree or higher: 6.2% (2010); Master's degree or higher: 2.1% (2010).

School District(s)
Red Hill CUSD 10 (PK-12)
   2009-10 Enrollment: 1,108 . . . . (618) 945-2061
Housing: Homeownership rate: 74.9% (2010); Median home value: $55,280 (2010); Median contract rent: $309 per month (2005-2009 5-year est.); Median year structure built: 1961 (2005-2009 5-year est.).
Newspapers: Bridgeport Leader (Local news; Circulation 6,000)
Transportation: Commute to work: 97.0% car, 0.0% public transportation, 3.0% walk, 0.0% work from home (2005-2009 5-year est.); Travel time to work: 55.4% less than 15 minutes, 28.6% 15 to 30 minutes, 12.7% 30 to 45 minutes, 2.4% 45 to 60 minutes, 0.8% 60 minutes or more (2005-2009 5-year est.)

LAWRENCEVILLE (city).

County seat. Covers a land area of 2.022 square miles and a water area of 0 square miles. Located at 38.72° N. Lat; 87.68° W. Long. Elevation is 469 feet.
History: The first settler here was Captain Toussaint Dubois, veteran of the American Revolution, who came about 1780 and planted an orchard. Jessie K. Dubois, the captain's son, was a friend of Abraham Lincoln and one of the pall bearers at his funeral. Lawrenceville was organized in 1821 and named for Captain James Lawrence, commander of the "Chesapeake" in the War of 1812, who said, "Don't give up the ship." Lawrenceville developed as an oil town in the early 1900's, and as the seat of Lawrence County.
Population: 4,902 (1990); 4,745 (2000); 5,779 (2010); 5,933 (2015 projected); Race: 87.7% White, 10.3% Black, 0.5% Asian, 1.6% Other, 3.6% Hispanic of any race (2010); Density: 2,858.3 persons per square mile (2010); Average household size: 2.17 (2010); Median age: 49.4 (2010); Males per 100 females: 83.5 (2010); Marriage status: 43.7% never married, 33.5% now married, 9.8% widowed, 13.0% divorced (2005-2009 5-year est.); Foreign born: 3.0% (2005-2009 5-year est.); Ancestry (includes multiple ancestries): 13.2% German, 12.0% Irish, 8.8% English, 5.8% American, 2.0% French (2005-2009 5-year est.).
Economy: Single-family building permits issued: 0 (2010); Multi-family building permits issued: 0 (2010); Employment by occupation: 4.4% management, 12.7% professional, 33.5% services, 15.9% sales, 2.2% farming, 12.3% construction, 19.0% production (2005-2009 5-year est.).

Income: Per capita income: $20,277 (2010); Median household income: $33,174 (2010); Average household income: $47,344 (2010); Percent of households with income of $100,000 or more: 8.8% (2010); Poverty rate: 27.6% (2005-2009 5-year est.).
Taxes: Total city taxes per capita: $122 (2007); City property taxes per capita: $105 (2007).
Education: Percent of population age 25 and over with: High school diploma (including GED) or higher: 86.6% (2010); Bachelor's degree or higher: 16.3% (2010); Master's degree or higher: 5.0% (2010).

School District(s)
Clay/Cwford/Jsper/Lwrnce/Rhland (PK-12)
   2009-10 Enrollment: n/a . . . . (618) 392-4631
Lawrence County CUD 20 (PK-12)
   2009-10 Enrollment: 1,322 . . . . (618) 943-2326
Housing: Homeownership rate: 66.6% (2010); Median home value: $54,760 (2010); Median contract rent: $291 per month (2005-2009 5-year est.); Median year structure built: 1955 (2005-2009 5-year est.).
Hospitals: Lawrence County Memorial Hospital (25 beds)
Safety: Violent crime rate: 35.7 per 10,000 population; Property crime rate: 142.8 per 10,000 population (2010).
Newspapers: Daily Record (Local news; Circulation 4,300); Lawrence County News (Community news; Circulation 900)
Transportation: Commute to work: 90.6% car, 0.0% public transportation, 4.1% walk, 2.0% work from home (2005-2009 5-year est.); Travel time to work: 52.1% less than 15 minutes, 31.0% 15 to 30 minutes, 4.6% 30 to 45 minutes, 3.2% 45 to 60 minutes, 9.1% 60 minutes or more (2005-2009 5-year est.)
Airports: Lawrenceville-Vincennes International (general aviation)
Additional Information Contacts
Lawrence County Chamber of Commerce. . . . . (618) 943-3516
   http://www.lawrencecountychamberofcommerce.com

RUSSELLVILLE (village).

Covers a land area of 0.459 square miles and a water area of 0 square miles. Located at 38.82° N. Lat; 87.53° W. Long. Elevation is 427 feet.
History: Russellville grew around a ferry that crossed the Wabash River here.
Population: 133 (1990); 119 (2000); 101 (2010); 96 (2015 projected); Race: 90.1% White, 5.9% Black, 0.0% Asian, 4.0% Other, 5.0% Hispanic of any race (2010); Density: 220.3 persons per square mile (2010); Average household size: 2.30 (2010); Median age: 41.3 (2010); Males per 100 females: 124.4 (2010); Marriage status: 18.8% never married, 43.8% now married, 20.3% widowed, 17.2% divorced (2005-2009 5-year est.); Foreign born: 0.0% (2005-2009 5-year est.); Ancestry (includes multiple ancestries): 18.3% German, 18.3% English, 5.6% Irish, 5.6% Scottish, 4.2% Pennsylvania German (2005-2009 5-year est.).
Economy: Employment by occupation: 17.4% management, 21.7% professional, 0.0% services, 17.4% sales, 0.0% farming, 30.4% construction, 13.0% production (2005-2009 5-year est.).
Income: Per capita income: $28,209 (2010); Median household income: $46,667 (2010); Average household income: $60,455 (2010); Percent of households with income of $100,000 or more: 18.2% (2010); Poverty rate: 32.4% (2005-2009 5-year est.).
Taxes: Total city taxes per capita: $0 (2007); City property taxes per capita: $0 (2007).
Education: Percent of population age 25 and over with: High school diploma (including GED) or higher: 91.7% (2010); Bachelor's degree or higher: 15.3% (2010); Master's degree or higher: 2.8% (2010).
Housing: Homeownership rate: 86.4% (2010); Median home value: $84,000 (2010); Median contract rent: $139 per month (2005-2009 5-year est.); Median year structure built: 1972 (2005-2009 5-year est.).
Transportation: Commute to work: 91.3% car, 0.0% public transportation, 8.7% walk, 0.0% work from home (2005-2009 5-year est.); Travel time to work: 8.7% less than 15 minutes, 60.9% 15 to 30 minutes, 0.0% 30 to 45 minutes, 0.0% 45 to 60 minutes, 30.4% 60 minutes or more (2005-2009 5-year est.)

SAINT FRANCISVILLE (city).

Covers a land area of 0.746 square miles and a water area of 0.034 square miles. Located at 38.59° N. Lat; 87.64° W. Long. Elevation is 466 feet.
Population: 851 (1990); 759 (2000); 699 (2010); 693 (2015 projected); Race: 98.0% White, 0.9% Black, 0.0% Asian, 1.1% Other, 0.1% Hispanic of any race (2010); Density: 936.9 persons per square mile (2010); Average household size: 2.39 (2010); Median age: 36.7 (2010); Males per 100 females: 111.8 (2010); Marriage status: 30.1% never married, 45.3%

now married, 11.3% widowed, 13.3% divorced (2005-2009 5-year est.); Foreign born: 0.0% (2005-2009 5-year est.); Ancestry (includes multiple ancestries): 27.3% German, 7.9% Dutch, 6.6% French, 6.3% Irish, 5.0% Italian (2005-2009 5-year est.).

Economy: Employment by occupation: 7.3% management, 16.9% professional, 24.1% services, 14.5% sales, 7.3% farming, 5.8% construction, 24.1% production (2005-2009 5-year est.).

Income: Per capita income: $15,541 (2010); Median household income: $31,132 (2010); Average household income: $37,910 (2010); Percent of households with income of $100,000 or more: 4.1% (2010); Poverty rate: 11.3% (2005-2009 5-year est.).

Taxes: Total city taxes per capita: $53 (2007); City property taxes per capita: $44 (2007).

Education: Percent of population age 25 and over with: High school diploma (including GED) or higher: 84.4% (2010); Bachelor's degree or higher: 7.3% (2010); Master's degree or higher: 2.4% (2010).

Housing: Homeownership rate: 77.8% (2010); Median home value: $37,297 (2010); Median contract rent: $248 per month (2005-2009 5-year est.); Median year structure built: before 1940 (2005-2009 5-year est.).

Transportation: Commute to work: 97.6% car, 0.0% public transportation, 2.4% walk, 0.0% work from home (2005-2009 5-year est.); Travel time to work: 17.6% less than 15 minutes, 65.5% 15 to 30 minutes, 9.4% 30 to 45 minutes, 0.0% 45 to 60 minutes, 7.6% 60 minutes or more (2005-2009 5-year est.)

SUMNER (city). Covers a land area of 1.031 square miles and a water area of 0 square miles. Located at 38.71° N. Lat; 87.86° W. Long. Elevation is 449 feet.

History: Incorporated 1887.

Population: 1,083 (1990); 1,022 (2000); 1,967 (2010); 2,211 (2015 projected); Race: 78.2% White, 20.4% Black, 0.0% Asian, 1.4% Other, 1.2% Hispanic of any race (2010); Density: 1,907.3 persons per square mile (2010); Average household size: 2.34 (2010); Median age: 46.4 (2010); Males per 100 females: 107.1 (2010); Marriage status: 23.0% never married, 53.9% now married, 11.8% widowed, 11.3% divorced (2005-2009 5-year est.); Foreign born: 0.0% (2005-2009 5-year est.); Ancestry (includes multiple ancestries): 24.4% American, 12.5% Irish, 12.4% German, 4.9% English, 4.2% Hungarian (2005-2009 5-year est.).

Economy: Employment by occupation: 5.6% management, 15.1% professional, 29.1% services, 15.7% sales, 0.0% farming, 4.3% construction, 30.1% production (2005-2009 5-year est.).

Income: Per capita income: $21,216 (2010); Median household income: $34,315 (2010); Average household income: $39,162 (2010); Percent of households with income of $100,000 or more: 2.6% (2010); Poverty rate: 23.7% (2005-2009 5-year est.).

Taxes: Total city taxes per capita: $4 (2007); City property taxes per capita: $4 (2007).

Education: Percent of population age 25 and over with: High school diploma (including GED) or higher: 74.9% (2010); Bachelor's degree or higher: 7.0% (2010); Master's degree or higher: 2.1% (2010).

School District(s)
Red Hill CUSD 10 (PK-12)
    2009-10 Enrollment: 1,108 . . . . (618) 945-2061

Housing: Homeownership rate: 76.4% (2010); Median home value: $47,103 (2010); Median contract rent: $281 per month (2005-2009 5-year est.); Median year structure built: 1957 (2005-2009 5-year est.).

Newspapers: Sumner Press (Regional news; Circulation 2,150)

Transportation: Commute to work: 97.1% car, 0.0% public transportation, 1.9% walk, 0.0% work from home (2005-2009 5-year est.); Travel time to work: 33.8% less than 15 minutes, 30.4% 15 to 30 minutes, 22.4% 30 to 45 minutes, 10.2% 45 to 60 minutes, 3.1% 60 minutes or more (2005-2009 5-year est.)

Lee County

Located in northern Illinois; drained by the Rock, Green, and Kyte Rivers. Covers a land area of 725.36 square miles, a water area of 3.92 square miles, and is located in the Central Time Zone at 41.77° N. Lat., 89.35° W. Long. The county was founded in 1839. County seat is Dixon.

Lee County is part of the Dixon, IL Micropolitan Statistical Area. The entire metro area includes: Lee County, IL

Weather Station: Dixon 1 NW										Elevation: 700 feet		
	Jan	Feb	Mar	Apr	May	Jun	Jul	Aug	Sep	Oct	Nov	Dec
High	29	34	46	60	71	80	83	81	75	62	48	33
Low	12	16	27	38	49	58	62	61	51	39	29	17
Precip	1.5	1.6	2.4	3.5	4.3	4.7	4.1	4.6	3.5	2.9	2.7	2.1
Snow	10.3	6.9	3.7	0.8	0.0	0.0	0.0	0.0	0.0	0.1	1.3	8.5

High and Low temperatures in degrees Fahrenheit; Precipitation and Snow in inches

Weather Station: Paw Paw 2 NW										Elevation: 950 feet		
	Jan	Feb	Mar	Apr	May	Jun	Jul	Aug	Sep	Oct	Nov	Dec
High	28	32	44	58	70	79	82	80	74	61	46	32
Low	12	16	25	36	47	58	61	59	51	39	29	16
Precip	1.3	1.4	2.1	3.1	4.5	4.0	4.1	4.3	3.6	2.8	3.0	2.0
Snow	8.8	6.5	3.9	0.8	tr	0.0	0.0	0.0	0.0	0.2	1.2	8.5

High and Low temperatures in degrees Fahrenheit; Precipitation and Snow in inches

Population: 34,392 (1990); 36,062 (2000); 35,133 (2010); 34,615 (2015 projected); Race: 92.4% White, 4.2% Black, 1.0% Asian, 2.5% Other, 4.5% Hispanic of any race (2010); Density: 48.4 persons per square mile (2010); Average household size: 2.45 (2010); Median age: 39.5 (2010); Males per 100 females: 101.1 (2010).

Religion: Five largest groups: 33.3% Catholic Church, 10.4% Evangelical Lutheran Church in America, 8.5% The United Methodist Church, 1.7% Southern Baptist Convention, 1.5% New Testament Association of Independent Baptist Churches and other Fundame

Economy: Unemployment rate: 9.6% (August 2011); Total civilian labor force: 18,254 (August 2011); Leading industries: 31.9% manufacturing; 14.5% retail trade; 12.7% health care and social assistance (2009); Farms: 898 totaling 395,624 acres (2007); Companies that employ 500 or more persons: 2 (2009); Companies that employ 100 to 499 persons: 17 (2009); Companies that employ less than 100 persons: 734 (2009); Black-owned businesses: n/a (2007); Hispanic-owned businesses: n/a (2007); Asian-owned businesses: n/a (2007); Women-owned businesses: 644 (2007); Retail sales per capita: $9,553 (2010). Single-family building permits issued: 29 (2010); Multi-family building permits issued: 0 (2010).

Income: Per capita income: $23,404 (2010); Median household income: $49,191 (2010); Average household income: $59,898 (2010); Percent of households with income of $100,000 or more: 13.1% (2010); Poverty rate: 10.5% (2009); Bankruptcy rate: 4.87% (2010).

Taxes: Total county taxes per capita: $180 (2007); County property taxes per capita: $116 (2007).

Education: Percent of population age 25 and over with: High school diploma (including GED) or higher: 85.3% (2010); Bachelor's degree or higher: 14.5% (2010); Master's degree or higher: 4.8% (2010).

Housing: Homeownership rate: 72.4% (2010); Median home value: $113,495 (2010); Median contract rent: $440 per month (2005-2009 5-year est.); Median year structure built: 1954 (2005-2009 5-year est.)

Health: Birth rate: 114.3 per 10,000 population (2009); Death rate: 101.4 per 10,000 population (2009); Age-adjusted cancer mortality rate: 277.2 deaths per 100,000 population (2007); Number of physicians: 16.3 per 10,000 population (2008); Hospital beds: 23.9 per 10,000 population (2007); Hospital admissions: 1,177.2 per 10,000 population (2007).

Elections: 2008 Presidential election results: 47.6% Obama, 50.6% McCain, 0.7% Nader

National and State Parks: Franklin Creek State Park; Green River State Wildlife Management Area; Hennepin Canal Parkway State Park

Additional Information Contacts

Lee County Government . . . . (815) 288-3309
    http://www.countyoflee.org
City of Dixon. . . . . (815) 288-1485
    http://discoverdixon.org
Dixon Area Chamber of Commerce & Industry . . . . (815) 284-3361
    http://www.dixonillinoischamber.com

Lee County Communities

AMBOY (city). Covers a land area of 1.258 square miles and a water area of 0 square miles. Located at 41.71° N. Lat; 89.33° W. Long. Elevation is 745 feet.

History: In Amboy in 1854, Scotch-Irish immigrants Samuel Carson and John T. Pirie opened a small grocery store which later became the firm of Carson Pirie Scott & Company.

Population: 2,377 (1990); 2,561 (2000); 2,487 (2010); 2,442 (2015 projected); Race: 96.8% White, 1.0% Black, 0.0% Asian, 2.3% Other, 4.1% Hispanic of any race (2010); Density: 1,976.6 persons per square mile (2010); Average household size: 2.50 (2010); Median age: 37.8 (2010);

Males per 100 females: 95.8 (2010); Marriage status: 24.3% never married, 43.4% now married, 17.0% widowed, 15.4% divorced (2005-2009 5-year est.); Foreign born: 1.3% (2005-2009 5-year est.); Ancestry (includes multiple ancestries): 44.1% German, 22.3% Irish, 12.5% English, 7.1% American, 4.4% French (2005-2009 5-year est.).

Economy: Single-family building permits issued: 1 (2010); Multi-family building permits issued: 0 (2010); Employment by occupation: 8.3% management, 10.6% professional, 22.2% services, 21.0% sales, 0.0% farming, 15.4% construction, 22.5% production (2005-2009 5-year est.).

Income: Per capita income: $21,796 (2010); Median household income: $44,349 (2010); Average household income: $55,201 (2010); Percent of households with income of $100,000 or more: 9.8% (2010); Poverty rate: 10.4% (2005-2009 5-year est.).

Taxes: Total city taxes per capita: $163 (2007); City property taxes per capita: $91 (2007).

Education: Percent of population age 25 and over with: High school diploma (including GED) or higher: 84.3% (2010); Bachelor's degree or higher: 9.8% (2010); Master's degree or higher: 3.0% (2010).

School District(s)
Amboy CUSD 272 (PK-12)
    2009-10 Enrollment: 935 . . . . (815) 857-2164

Housing: Homeownership rate: 69.9% (2010); Median home value: $100,794 (2010); Median contract rent: $408 per month (2005-2009 5-year est.); Median year structure built: 1959 (2005-2009 5-year est.).

Newspapers: Amboy News (Local news; Circulation 2,250)

Transportation: Commute to work: 86.1% car, 2.1% public transportation, 6.4% walk, 3.0% work from home (2005-2009 5-year est.); Travel time to work: 36.3% less than 15 minutes, 38.6% 15 to 30 minutes, 11.7% 30 to 45 minutes, 4.0% 45 to 60 minutes, 9.4% 60 minutes or more (2005-2009 5-year est.)

ASHTON (village). Covers a land area of 0.661 square miles and a water area of 0 square miles. Located at 41.86° N. Lat; 89.22° W. Long. Elevation is 823 feet.

Population: 1,042 (1990); 1,142 (2000); 1,179 (2010); 1,191 (2015 projected); Race: 96.1% White, 1.3% Black, 1.4% Asian, 1.3% Other, 4.4% Hispanic of any race (2010); Density: 1,783.6 persons per square mile (2010); Average household size: 2.59 (2010); Median age: 37.2 (2010); Males per 100 females: 93.0 (2010); Marriage status: 25.7% never married, 49.2% now married, 8.7% widowed, 16.4% divorced (2005-2009 5-year est.); Foreign born: 0.9% (2005-2009 5-year est.); Ancestry (includes multiple ancestries): 39.6% German, 24.0% Irish, 9.9% English, 9.6% American, 3.1% Swedish (2005-2009 5-year est.).

Economy: Single-family building permits issued: 0 (2010); Multi-family building permits issued: 0 (2010); Employment by occupation: 6.7% management, 7.6% professional, 10.6% services, 21.2% sales, 0.0% farming, 10.9% construction, 42.9% production (2005-2009 5-year est.).

Income: Per capita income: $22,176 (2010); Median household income: $49,080 (2010); Average household income: $57,810 (2010); Percent of households with income of $100,000 or more: 10.0% (2010); Poverty rate: 6.1% (2005-2009 5-year est.).

Taxes: Total city taxes per capita: $100 (2007); City property taxes per capita: $92 (2007).

Education: Percent of population age 25 and over with: High school diploma (including GED) or higher: 88.6% (2010); Bachelor's degree or higher: 13.0% (2010); Master's degree or higher: 3.8% (2010).

School District(s)
Ashton-Franklin Center CUSD 275 (PK-12)
    2009-10 Enrollment: 621 . . . . (815) 453-7461

Housing: Homeownership rate: 71.8% (2010); Median home value: $115,957 (2010); Median contract rent: $342 per month (2005-2009 5-year est.); Median year structure built: before 1940 (2005-2009 5-year est.).

Safety: Violent crime rate: 0.0 per 10,000 population; Property crime rate: 157.5 per 10,000 population (2010).

Newspapers: Ashton Gazette (Community news; Circulation 1,050)

Transportation: Commute to work: 91.2% car, 2.1% public transportation, 3.6% walk, 3.1% work from home (2005-2009 5-year est.); Travel time to work: 34.9% less than 15 minutes, 27.9% 15 to 30 minutes, 24.2% 30 to 45 minutes, 7.4% 45 to 60 minutes, 5.5% 60 minutes or more (2005-2009 5-year est.)

COMPTON (village). Covers a land area of 0.166 square miles and a water area of 0 square miles. Located at 41.69° N. Lat; 89.08° W. Long. Elevation is 968 feet.

Population: 343 (1990); 347 (2000); 370 (2010); 380 (2015 projected); Race: 97.8% White, 0.0% Black, 1.4% Asian, 0.8% Other, 0.8% Hispanic of any race (2010); Density: 2,230.8 persons per square mile (2010); Average household size: 2.66 (2010); Median age: 37.6 (2010); Males per 100 females: 103.3 (2010); Marriage status: 30.0% never married, 51.1% now married, 3.6% widowed, 15.2% divorced (2005-2009 5-year est.); Foreign born: 2.6% (2005-2009 5-year est.); Ancestry (includes multiple ancestries): 29.2% German, 26.2% Irish, 11.4% Scotch-Irish, 9.6% Dutch, 9.2% Polish (2005-2009 5-year est.).

Economy: Employment by occupation: 3.9% management, 14.7% professional, 18.6% services, 16.7% sales, 0.0% farming, 19.6% construction, 26.5% production (2005-2009 5-year est.).

Income: Per capita income: $22,299 (2010); Median household income: $55,682 (2010); Average household income: $58,094 (2010); Percent of households with income of $100,000 or more: 10.8% (2010); Poverty rate: 9.2% (2005-2009 5-year est.).

Taxes: Total city taxes per capita: $15 (2007); City property taxes per capita: $15 (2007).

Education: Percent of population age 25 and over with: High school diploma (including GED) or higher: 88.3% (2010); Bachelor's degree or higher: 10.8% (2010); Master's degree or higher: 4.3% (2010).

Housing: Homeownership rate: 79.9% (2010); Median home value: $143,750 (2010); Median contract rent: $500 per month (2005-2009 5-year est.); Median year structure built: before 1940 (2005-2009 5-year est.).

Transportation: Commute to work: 97.1% car, 0.0% public transportation, 0.0% walk, 2.9% work from home (2005-2009 5-year est.); Travel time to work: 9.1% less than 15 minutes, 35.4% 15 to 30 minutes, 16.2% 30 to 45 minutes, 21.2% 45 to 60 minutes, 18.2% 60 minutes or more (2005-2009 5-year est.)

DIXON (city). County seat. Covers a land area of 6.326 square miles and a water area of 0.421 square miles. Located at 41.84° N. Lat; 89.48° W. Long. Elevation is 682 feet.

History: Dixon was settled in 1830 by John Dixon, who operated a trading post and tavern. Industry soon came to Dixon because of the water power available from the Rock River.

Population: 15,718 (1990); 15,941 (2000); 14,671 (2010); 14,121 (2015 projected); Race: 87.3% White, 8.5% Black, 1.3% Asian, 2.9% Other, 5.9% Hispanic of any race (2010); Density: 2,319.1 persons per square mile (2010); Average household size: 2.29 (2010); Median age: 38.8 (2010); Males per 100 females: 105.3 (2010); Marriage status: 32.4% never married, 46.7% now married, 6.8% widowed, 14.0% divorced (2005-2009 5-year est.); Foreign born: 3.3% (2005-2009 5-year est.); Ancestry (includes multiple ancestries): 35.6% German, 18.2% Irish, 7.7% English, 7.1% American, 4.8% Dutch (2005-2009 5-year est.).

Economy: Single-family building permits issued: 8 (2010); Multi-family building permits issued: 0 (2010); Employment by occupation: 7.4% management, 17.6% professional, 18.8% services, 20.9% sales, 0.1% farming, 7.5% construction, 27.8% production (2005-2009 5-year est.).

Income: Per capita income: $20,874 (2010); Median household income: $43,301 (2010); Average household income: $52,094 (2010); Percent of households with income of $100,000 or more: 9.6% (2010); Poverty rate: 12.2% (2005-2009 5-year est.).

Taxes: Total city taxes per capita: $277 (2007); City property taxes per capita: $203 (2007).

Education: Percent of population age 25 and over with: High school diploma (including GED) or higher: 81.1% (2010); Bachelor's degree or higher: 14.1% (2010); Master's degree or higher: 4.5% (2010).

School District(s)
Dixon USD 170 (PK-12)
    2009-10 Enrollment: 2,874 . . . . (815) 284-7722
Lee/Ogle Roe (06-12)
    2009-10 Enrollment: n/a . . . . (815) 652-2054

Two-year College(s)
Sauk Valley Community College (Public)
    Fall 2009 Enrollment: 2,504 . . . . (815) 288-5511
    2010-11 Tuition: In-state $8,235; Out-of-state $9,323

Housing: Homeownership rate: 66.2% (2010); Median home value: $95,944 (2010); Median contract rent: $444 per month (2005-2009 5-year est.); Median year structure built: 1951 (2005-2009 5-year est.).

Hospitals: Katherine Shaw Bethea Hospital

Safety: Violent crime rate: 21.1 per 10,000 population; Property crime rate: 342.3 per 10,000 population (2010).

Newspapers: Telegraph (Local news; Circulation 9,448)

Transportation: Commute to work: 86.8% car, 4.1% public transportation, 1.8% walk, 5.0% work from home (2005-2009 5-year est.); Travel time to work: 55.9% less than 15 minutes, 26.5% 15 to 30 minutes, 9.2% 30 to 45 minutes, 3.1% 45 to 60 minutes, 5.2% 60 minutes or more (2005-2009 5-year est.)

Additional Information Contacts

City of Dixon . . . . (815) 288-1485
    http://discoverdixon.org
Dixon Area Chamber of Commerce & Industry . . . . (815) 284-3361
    http://www.dixonillinoischamber.com

FRANKLIN GROVE (village). Covers a land area of 0.371 square miles and a water area of 0 square miles. Located at 41.84° N. Lat; 89.30° W. Long. Elevation is 804 feet.

Population: 968 (1990); 1,052 (2000); 1,018 (2010); 999 (2015 projected); Race: 98.5% White, 0.1% Black, 0.2% Asian, 1.2% Other, 1.3% Hispanic of any race (2010); Density: 2,743.9 persons per square mile (2010); Average household size: 2.49 (2010); Median age: 41.9 (2010); Males per 100 females: 86.1 (2010); Marriage status: 19.2% never married, 48.2% now married, 26.7% widowed, 5.8% divorced (2005-2009 5-year est.); Foreign born: 5.8% (2005-2009 5-year est.); Ancestry (includes multiple ancestries): 43.8% German, 19.2% Irish, 15.8% English, 6.9% Dutch, 5.6% Polish (2005-2009 5-year est.).

Economy: Single-family building permits issued: 0 (2010); Multi-family building permits issued: 0 (2010); Employment by occupation: 6.7% management, 15.4% professional, 22.8% services, 25.9% sales, 0.0% farming, 12.4% construction, 16.9% production (2005-2009 5-year est.).

Income: Per capita income: $22,284 (2010); Median household income: $54,508 (2010); Average household income: $60,107 (2010); Percent of households with income of $100,000 or more: 13.9% (2010); Poverty rate: 15.3% (2005-2009 5-year est.).

Taxes: Total city taxes per capita: $85 (2007); City property taxes per capita: $56 (2007).

Education: Percent of population age 25 and over with: High school diploma (including GED) or higher: 87.2% (2010); Bachelor's degree or higher: 16.9% (2010); Master's degree or higher: 7.7% (2010).

School District(s)

Ashton-Franklin Center CUSD 275 (PK-12)
    2009-10 Enrollment: 621 . . . . (815) 453-7461

Housing: Homeownership rate: 67.4% (2010); Median home value: $110,648 (2010); Median contract rent: $538 per month (2005-2009 5-year est.); Median year structure built: before 1940 (2005-2009 5-year est.).

Safety: Violent crime rate: 30.4 per 10,000 population; Property crime rate: 172.1 per 10,000 population (2010).

Transportation: Commute to work: 92.9% car, 0.0% public transportation, 2.3% walk, 4.0% work from home (2005-2009 5-year est.); Travel time to work: 32.3% less than 15 minutes, 32.9% 15 to 30 minutes, 13.4% 30 to 45 minutes, 7.0% 45 to 60 minutes, 14.4% 60 minutes or more (2005-2009 5-year est.)

HARMON (village). Covers a land area of 0.142 square miles and a water area of 0 square miles. Located at 41.72° N. Lat; 89.55° W. Long. Elevation is 676 feet.

Population: 186 (1990); 149 (2000); 137 (2010); 132 (2015 projected); Race: 96.4% White, 0.0% Black, 0.0% Asian, 3.6% Other, 3.6% Hispanic of any race (2010); Density: 965.2 persons per square mile (2010); Average household size: 2.49 (2010); Median age: 46.5 (2010); Males per 100 females: 104.5 (2010); Marriage status: 33.2% never married, 53.8% now married, 4.3% widowed, 8.7% divorced (2005-2009 5-year est.); Foreign born: 0.0% (2005-2009 5-year est.); Ancestry (includes multiple ancestries): 37.7% German, 17.2% American, 12.7% Irish, 9.4% English (2005-2009 5-year est.).

Economy: Employment by occupation: 20.7% management, 8.6% professional, 25.0% services, 14.7% sales, 0.0% farming, 6.9% construction, 24.1% production (2005-2009 5-year est.).

Income: Per capita income: $29,620 (2010); Median household income: $60,417 (2010); Average household income: $67,636 (2010); Percent of households with income of $100,000 or more: 14.5% (2010); Poverty rate: 4.1% (2005-2009 5-year est.).

Taxes: Total city taxes per capita: $27 (2007); City property taxes per capita: $21 (2007).

Education: Percent of population age 25 and over with: High school diploma (including GED) or higher: 95.2% (2010); Bachelor's degree or higher: 16.2% (2010); Master's degree or higher: 5.7% (2010).

Housing: Homeownership rate: 78.2% (2010); Median home value: $117,308 (2010); Median contract rent: $397 per month (2005-2009 5-year est.); Median year structure built: before 1940 (2005-2009 5-year est.).

Transportation: Commute to work: 86.2% car, 0.0% public transportation, 6.9% walk, 6.9% work from home (2005-2009 5-year est.); Travel time to work: 14.8% less than 15 minutes, 62.0% 15 to 30 minutes, 10.2% 30 to 45 minutes, 7.4% 45 to 60 minutes, 5.6% 60 minutes or more (2005-2009 5-year est.)

LEE (village). Covers a land area of 0.223 square miles and a water area of 0 square miles. Located at 41.79° N. Lat; 88.94° W. Long. Elevation is 938 feet.

Population: 347 (1990); 313 (2000); 320 (2010); 320 (2015 projected); Race: 97.2% White, 0.3% Black, 0.3% Asian, 2.2% Other, 4.1% Hispanic of any race (2010); Density: 1,435.6 persons per square mile (2010); Average household size: 2.76 (2010); Median age: 34.7 (2010); Males per 100 females: 110.5 (2010); Marriage status: 33.2% never married, 47.2% now married, 2.8% widowed, 16.8% divorced (2005-2009 5-year est.); Foreign born: 0.9% (2005-2009 5-year est.); Ancestry (includes multiple ancestries): 38.3% German, 29.8% Irish, 21.3% English, 11.1% Norwegian, 8.3% Swedish (2005-2009 5-year est.).

Economy: Single-family building permits issued: 0 (2010); Multi-family building permits issued: 0 (2010); Employment by occupation: 7.8% management, 23.9% professional, 12.4% services, 9.2% sales, 6.4% farming, 16.1% construction, 24.3% production (2005-2009 5-year est.).

Income: Per capita income: $25,674 (2010); Median household income: $63,281 (2010); Average household income: $71,703 (2010); Percent of households with income of $100,000 or more: 19.8% (2010); Poverty rate: 7.3% (2005-2009 5-year est.).

Taxes: Total city taxes per capita: $175 (2007); City property taxes per capita: $70 (2007).

Education: Percent of population age 25 and over with: High school diploma (including GED) or higher: 92.8% (2010); Bachelor's degree or higher: 24.6% (2010); Master's degree or higher: 7.7% (2010).

Housing: Homeownership rate: 75.0% (2010); Median home value: $176,786 (2010); Median contract rent: $550 per month (2005-2009 5-year est.); Median year structure built: 1955 (2005-2009 5-year est.).

Transportation: Commute to work: 90.4% car, 0.0% public transportation, 4.1% walk, 0.9% work from home (2005-2009 5-year est.); Travel time to work: 19.0% less than 15 minutes, 29.6% 15 to 30 minutes, 28.2% 30 to 45 minutes, 7.9% 45 to 60 minutes, 15.3% 60 minutes or more (2005-2009 5-year est.)

NELSON (village). Covers a land area of 0.227 square miles and a water area of 0.005 square miles. Located at 41.79° N. Lat; 89.60° W. Long. Elevation is 653 feet.

Population: 200 (1990); 163 (2000); 168 (2010); 168 (2015 projected); Race: 98.8% White, 0.0% Black, 0.6% Asian, 0.6% Other, 1.8% Hispanic of any race (2010); Density: 741.1 persons per square mile (2010); Average household size: 2.55 (2010); Median age: 43.6 (2010); Males per 100 females: 97.6 (2010); Marriage status: 28.0% never married, 42.4% now married, 6.4% widowed, 23.2% divorced (2005-2009 5-year est.); Foreign born: 0.0% (2005-2009 5-year est.); Ancestry (includes multiple ancestries): 36.9% German, 10.1% Dutch, 6.7% Norwegian, 6.0% American, 5.4% Irish (2005-2009 5-year est.).

Economy: Employment by occupation: 8.6% management, 7.4% professional, 14.8% services, 19.8% sales, 0.0% farming, 6.2% construction, 43.2% production (2005-2009 5-year est.).

Income: Per capita income: $25,095 (2010); Median household income: $47,500 (2010); Average household income: $70,417 (2010); Percent of households with income of $100,000 or more: 13.6% (2010); Poverty rate: 13.4% (2005-2009 5-year est.).

Taxes: Total city taxes per capita: $25 (2007); City property taxes per capita: $25 (2007).

Education: Percent of population age 25 and over with: High school diploma (including GED) or higher: 80.6% (2010); Bachelor's degree or higher: 11.3% (2010); Master's degree or higher: 0.8% (2010).

School District(s)

Nelson Public SD No 8 (KG-08)
    2009-10 Enrollment: 31 . . . . (815) 251-4412

Housing: Homeownership rate: 86.4% (2010); Median home value: $89,286 (2010); Median contract rent: $341 per month (2005-2009 5-year est.); Median year structure built: 1946 (2005-2009 5-year est.).

Transportation: Commute to work: 97.3% car, 0.0% public transportation, 2.7% walk, 0.0% work from home (2005-2009 5-year est.); Travel time to

work: 38.4% less than 15 minutes, 46.6% 15 to 30 minutes, 6.8% 30 to 45 minutes, 8.2% 45 to 60 minutes, 0.0% 60 minutes or more (2005-2009 5-year est.)

PAW PAW (village). Aka Pawpaw. Covers a land area of 0.566 square miles and a water area of 0 square miles. Located at 41.68° N. Lat; 88.98° W. Long. Elevation is 945 feet.
Population: 833 (1990); 852 (2000); 879 (2010); 887 (2015 projected); Race: 98.5% White, 0.0% Black, 0.6% Asian, 0.9% Other, 1.4% Hispanic of any race (2010); Density: 1,554.0 persons per square mile (2010); Average household size: 2.46 (2010); Median age: 40.4 (2010); Males per 100 females: 100.2 (2010); Marriage status: 22.3% never married, 63.7% now married, 6.6% widowed, 7.4% divorced (2005-2009 5-year est.); Foreign born: 0.0% (2005-2009 5-year est.); Ancestry (includes multiple ancestries): 37.4% German, 16.4% Irish, 12.0% English, 11.4% Italian, 7.8% Scottish (2005-2009 5-year est.).
Economy: Single-family building permits issued: 0 (2010); Multi-family building permits issued: 0 (2010); Employment by occupation: 11.3% management, 18.3% professional, 20.8% services, 13.9% sales, 0.8% farming, 22.4% construction, 12.6% production (2005-2009 5-year est.).
Income: Per capita income: $21,619 (2010); Median household income: $46,250 (2010); Average household income: $53,473 (2010); Percent of households with income of $100,000 or more: 6.7% (2010); Poverty rate: 15.9% (2005-2009 5-year est.).
Taxes: Total city taxes per capita: $263 (2007); City property taxes per capita: $249 (2007).
Education: Percent of population age 25 and over with: High school diploma (including GED) or higher: 89.2% (2010); Bachelor's degree or higher: 9.4% (2010); Master's degree or higher: 2.0% (2010).

School District(s)
Paw Paw CUSD 271 (PK-12)
    2009-10 Enrollment: 306 . . . . (815) 627-2841
Housing: Homeownership rate: 80.4% (2010); Median home value: $136,779 (2010); Median contract rent: $575 per month (2005-2009 5-year est.); Median year structure built: 1953 (2005-2009 5-year est.).
Transportation: Commute to work: 89.4% car, 1.0% public transportation, 3.9% walk, 4.4% work from home (2005-2009 5-year est.); Travel time to work: 26.9% less than 15 minutes, 19.3% 15 to 30 minutes, 19.3% 30 to 45 minutes, 13.0% 45 to 60 minutes, 21.5% 60 minutes or more (2005-2009 5-year est.)

STEWARD (village). Covers a land area of 0.124 square miles and a water area of 0 square miles. Located at 41.84° N. Lat; 89.02° W. Long. Elevation is 820 feet.
Population: 282 (1990); 271 (2000); 276 (2010); 275 (2015 projected); Race: 97.5% White, 0.0% Black, 0.0% Asian, 2.5% Other, 4.7% Hispanic of any race (2010); Density: 2,221.1 persons per square mile (2010); Average household size: 2.76 (2010); Median age: 35.6 (2010); Males per 100 females: 107.5 (2010); Marriage status: 19.3% never married, 72.6% now married, 3.1% widowed, 4.9% divorced (2005-2009 5-year est.); Foreign born: 1.1% (2005-2009 5-year est.); Ancestry (includes multiple ancestries): 41.1% German, 16.3% Irish, 12.8% American, 9.9% English, 9.2% Norwegian (2005-2009 5-year est.).
Economy: Employment by occupation: 7.4% management, 18.4% professional, 3.7% services, 33.8% sales, 0.0% farming, 12.5% construction, 24.3% production (2005-2009 5-year est.).
Income: Per capita income: $24,993 (2010); Median household income: $62,121 (2010); Average household income: $70,525 (2010); Percent of households with income of $100,000 or more: 18.0% (2010); Poverty rate: 12.4% (2005-2009 5-year est.).
Taxes: Total city taxes per capita: $19 (2007); City property taxes per capita: $19 (2007).
Education: Percent of population age 25 and over with: High school diploma (including GED) or higher: 88.6% (2010); Bachelor's degree or higher: 19.4% (2010); Master's degree or higher: 6.3% (2010).

School District(s)
Steward ESD 220 (KG-08)
    2009-10 Enrollment: 81 . . . . (815) 396-2413
Housing: Homeownership rate: 77.0% (2010); Median home value: $151,667 (2010); Median contract rent: n/a per month (2005-2009 5-year est.); Median year structure built: before 1940 (2005-2009 5-year est.).
Transportation: Commute to work: 98.5% car, 0.0% public transportation, 1.5% walk, 0.0% work from home (2005-2009 5-year est.); Travel time to work: 20.6% less than 15 minutes, 36.8% 15 to 30 minutes, 30.1% 30 to 45

minutes, 8.8% 45 to 60 minutes, 3.7% 60 minutes or more (2005-2009 5-year est.)

SUBLETTE (village). Covers a land area of 0.350 square miles and a water area of 0 square miles. Located at 41.64° N. Lat; 89.23° W. Long. Elevation is 919 feet.
Population: 405 (1990); 456 (2000); 466 (2010); 465 (2015 projected); Race: 97.2% White, 0.4% Black, 0.0% Asian, 2.4% Other, 5.8% Hispanic of any race (2010); Density: 1,332.1 persons per square mile (2010); Average household size: 2.51 (2010); Median age: 39.5 (2010); Males per 100 females: 94.2 (2010); Marriage status: 24.3% never married, 60.6% now married, 7.4% widowed, 7.6% divorced (2005-2009 5-year est.); Foreign born: 4.0% (2005-2009 5-year est.); Ancestry (includes multiple ancestries): 67.6% German, 11.8% Irish, 11.1% Polish, 6.5% English, 5.8% French (2005-2009 5-year est.).
Economy: Employment by occupation: 12.9% management, 8.1% professional, 12.5% services, 22.1% sales, 0.0% farming, 12.5% construction, 31.7% production (2005-2009 5-year est.).
Income: Per capita income: $30,807 (2010); Median household income: $63,889 (2010); Average household income: $78,454 (2010); Percent of households with income of $100,000 or more: 25.8% (2010); Poverty rate: 2.0% (2005-2009 5-year est.).
Taxes: Total city taxes per capita: $67 (2007); City property taxes per capita: $51 (2007).
Education: Percent of population age 25 and over with: High school diploma (including GED) or higher: 90.6% (2010); Bachelor's degree or higher: 8.5% (2010); Master's degree or higher: 3.5% (2010).
Housing: Homeownership rate: 72.6% (2010); Median home value: $131,771 (2010); Median contract rent: $325 per month (2005-2009 5-year est.); Median year structure built: 1973 (2005-2009 5-year est.).
Transportation: Commute to work: 90.4% car, 0.0% public transportation, 3.3% walk, 3.3% work from home (2005-2009 5-year est.); Travel time to work: 42.7% less than 15 minutes, 35.9% 15 to 30 minutes, 11.5% 30 to 45 minutes, 2.3% 45 to 60 minutes, 7.6% 60 minutes or more (2005-2009 5-year est.)

WEST BROOKLYN (village). Covers a land area of 0.107 square miles and a water area of 0 square miles. Located at 41.69° N. Lat; 89.14° W. Long. Elevation is 945 feet.
Population: 164 (1990); 174 (2000); 176 (2010); 179 (2015 projected); Race: 94.9% White, 0.0% Black, 1.7% Asian, 3.4% Other, 3.4% Hispanic of any race (2010); Density: 1,647.8 persons per square mile (2010); Average household size: 2.67 (2010); Median age: 37.3 (2010); Males per 100 females: 89.2 (2010); Marriage status: 22.7% never married, 66.4% now married, 3.6% widowed, 7.3% divorced (2005-2009 5-year est.); Foreign born: 7.1% (2005-2009 5-year est.); Ancestry (includes multiple ancestries): 37.0% German, 15.0% Irish, 13.4% American, 7.9% English, 7.1% French (2005-2009 5-year est.).
Economy: Employment by occupation: 8.6% management, 7.4% professional, 23.5% services, 12.3% sales, 0.0% farming, 28.4% construction, 19.8% production (2005-2009 5-year est.).
Income: Per capita income: $23,955 (2010); Median household income: $61,250 (2010); Average household income: $62,652 (2010); Percent of households with income of $100,000 or more: 12.1% (2010); Poverty rate: 4.7% (2005-2009 5-year est.).
Taxes: Total city taxes per capita: $65 (2007); City property taxes per capita: $59 (2007).
Education: Percent of population age 25 and over with: High school diploma (including GED) or higher: 91.2% (2010); Bachelor's degree or higher: 8.8% (2010); Master's degree or higher: 2.7% (2010).
Housing: Homeownership rate: 74.2% (2010); Median home value: $125,000 (2010); Median contract rent: $667 per month (2005-2009 5-year est.); Median year structure built: before 1940 (2005-2009 5-year est.).
Transportation: Commute to work: 91.1% car, 0.0% public transportation, 6.3% walk, 2.5% work from home (2005-2009 5-year est.); Travel time to work: 33.8% less than 15 minutes, 23.4% 15 to 30 minutes, 15.6% 30 to 45 minutes, 0.0% 45 to 60 minutes, 27.3% 60 minutes or more (2005-2009 5-year est.)

Livingston County

Located in east central Illinois; drained by the Vermilion River. Covers a land area of 1,043.76 square miles, a water area of 1.67 square miles, and is located in the Central Time Zone at 40.90° N. Lat., 88.56° W. Long. The county was founded in 1837. County seat is Pontiac.

Livingston County is part of the Pontiac, IL Micropolitan Statistical Area. The entire metro area includes: Livingston County, IL

Weather Station: Pontiac   Elevation: 649 feet

	Jan	Feb	Mar	Apr	May	Jun	Jul	Aug	Sep	Oct	Nov	Dec
High	32	36	48	62	73	81	84	82	77	64	50	36
Low	16	20	29	40	50	61	64	63	54	42	32	20
Precip	1.9	1.6	2.8	3.3	3.9	3.6	4.1	3.7	3.0	3.0	3.2	2.5
Snow	8.0	6.8	2.8	0.8	0.0	0.0	0.0	0.0	0.0	tr	0.8	5.8

High and Low temperatures in degrees Fahrenheit; Precipitation and Snow in inches

Population: 39,301 (1990); 39,678 (2000); 37,400 (2010); 36,139 (2015 projected); Race: 91.7% White, 5.2% Black, 0.4% Asian, 2.7% Other, 3.0% Hispanic of any race (2010); Density: 35.8 persons per square mile (2010); Average household size: 2.47 (2010); Median age: 37.9 (2010); Males per 100 females: 97.6 (2010).
Religion: Five largest groups: 17.7% Catholic Church, 12.7% Evangelical Lutheran Church in America, 11.1% The United Methodist Church, 3.9% American Baptist Churches in the USA, 3.5% Apostolic Christian Church of America, Inc. (2000).
Economy: Unemployment rate: 8.5% (August 2011); Total civilian labor force: 19,188 (August 2011); Leading industries: 27.8% manufacturing; 17.0% health care and social assistance; 14.7% retail trade (2009); Farms: 1,319 totaling 628,502 acres (2007); Companies that employ 500 or more persons: 5 (2009); Companies that employ 100 to 499 persons: 17 (2009); Companies that employ less than 100 persons: 895 (2009); Black-owned businesses: n/a (2007); Hispanic-owned businesses: n/a (2007); Asian-owned businesses: 64 (2007); Women-owned businesses: 683 (2007); Retail sales per capita: $15,153 (2010). Single-family building permits issued: 29 (2010); Multi-family building permits issued: 0 (2010).
Income: Per capita income: $22,626 (2010); Median household income: $49,272 (2010); Average household income: $58,491 (2010); Percent of households with income of $100,000 or more: 12.9% (2010); Poverty rate: 11.2% (2009); Bankruptcy rate: 4.45% (2010).
Taxes: Total county taxes per capita: $168 (2007); County property taxes per capita: $166 (2007).
Education: Percent of population age 25 and over with: High school diploma (including GED) or higher: 83.9% (2010); Bachelor's degree or higher: 13.3% (2010); Master's degree or higher: 4.8% (2010).
Housing: Homeownership rate: 76.3% (2010); Median home value: $96,072 (2010); Median contract rent: $441 per month (2005-2009 5-year est.); Median year structure built: 1957 (2005-2009 5-year est.)
Health: Birth rate: 138.2 per 10,000 population (2009); Death rate: 114.1 per 10,000 population (2009); Age-adjusted cancer mortality rate: 224.0 deaths per 100,000 population (2007); Number of physicians: 9.5 per 10,000 population (2008); Hospital beds: 11.1 per 10,000 population (2007); Hospital admissions: 466.5 per 10,000 population (2007).
Elections: 2008 Presidential election results: 39.6% Obama, 58.8% McCain, 0.7% Nader

Additional Information Contacts

Livingston County Government . . . . (815) 844-2006
   http://www.livingstoncounty-il.org
City of Pontiac . . . . (815) 844-3396
   http://pontiac.org
Dwight Area Chamber of Commerce . . . . (815) 584-2091
   http://www.dwightchamber.net
Pontiac Area Chamber of Commerce . . . . (815) 844-5131
   http://www.pontiacchamber.org
Village of Dwight . . . . (815) 584-3077
   http://www.dwightillinois.org

Livingston County Communities

ANCONA (unincorporated postal area, zip code 61311). Covers a land area of 28.939 square miles and a water area of 0 square miles. Located at 41.04° N. Lat; 88.86° W. Long. Elevation is 620 feet.
Population: 353 (2000); Race: 96.8% White, 0.0% Black, 0.0% Asian, 3.2% Other, 7.6% Hispanic of any race (2000); Density: 12.2 persons per square mile (2000); Age: 28.9% under 18, 15.2% over 64 (2000); Marriage status: 20.3% never married, 69.0% now married, 4.6% widowed, 6.1% divorced (2000); Foreign born: 0.0% (2000); Ancestry (includes multiple ancestries): 29.8% German, 9.4% Irish, 8.5% English, 7.0% Norwegian, 6.7% Slovak (2000).
Economy: Employment by occupation: 18.5% management, 22.2% professional, 8.6% services, 11.1% sales, 1.2% farming, 16.7% construction, 21.6% production (2000).

Income: Per capita income: $23,007 (2000); Median household income: $55,500 (2000); Poverty rate: 11.7% (2000).
Education: Percent of population age 25 and over with: High school diploma (including GED) or higher: 80.5% (2000); Bachelor's degree or higher: 20.3% (2000).
Housing: Homeownership rate: 88.4% (2000); Median home value: $90,300 (2000); Median contract rent: n/a per month (2000); Median year structure built: before 1940 (2000).
Transportation: Commute to work: 80.9% car, 0.0% public transportation, 0.0% walk, 19.1% work from home (2000); Travel time to work: 35.1% less than 15 minutes, 35.1% 15 to 30 minutes, 22.1% 30 to 45 minutes, 0.0% 45 to 60 minutes, 7.6% 60 minutes or more (2000)

BLACKSTONE (unincorporated postal area, zip code 61313). Covers a land area of 44.936 square miles and a water area of 0 square miles. Located at 41.06° N. Lat; 88.66° W. Long. Elevation is 738 feet.
Population: 316 (2000); Race: 95.8% White, 4.2% Black, 0.0% Asian, 0.0% Other, 0.0% Hispanic of any race (2000); Density: 7.0 persons per square mile (2000); Age: 27.6% under 18, 12.0% over 64 (2000); Marriage status: 20.7% never married, 70.0% now married, 2.1% widowed, 7.1% divorced (2000); Foreign born: 0.3% (2000); Ancestry (includes multiple ancestries): 33.4% German, 12.0% American, 10.3% Irish, 8.4% English (2000).
Economy: Employment by occupation: 20.9% management, 18.6% professional, 21.9% services, 6.0% sales, 0.5% farming, 10.7% construction, 21.4% production (2000).
Income: Per capita income: $22,553 (2000); Median household income: $59,583 (2000); Poverty rate: 3.3% (2000).
Education: Percent of population age 25 and over with: High school diploma (including GED) or higher: 90.9% (2000); Bachelor's degree or higher: 19.0% (2000).
Housing: Homeownership rate: 81.3% (2000); Median home value: $86,300 (2000); Median contract rent: $392 per month (2000); Median year structure built: 1941 (2000).
Transportation: Commute to work: 88.2% car, 0.0% public transportation, 3.8% walk, 6.6% work from home (2000); Travel time to work: 23.9% less than 15 minutes, 58.9% 15 to 30 minutes, 8.6% 30 to 45 minutes, 2.5% 45 to 60 minutes, 6.1% 60 minutes or more (2000)

CAMPUS (village). Covers a land area of 0.099 square miles and a water area of 0 square miles. Located at 41.02° N. Lat; 88.30° W. Long. Elevation is 656 feet.
Population: 137 (1990); 145 (2000); 135 (2010); 128 (2015 projected); Race: 97.8% White, 0.0% Black, 0.0% Asian, 2.2% Other, 0.7% Hispanic of any race (2010); Density: 1,358.5 persons per square mile (2010); Average household size: 2.70 (2010); Median age: 34.7 (2010); Males per 100 females: 104.5 (2010); Marriage status: 63.9% never married, 29.6% now married, 1.9% widowed, 4.6% divorced (2005-2009 5-year est.); Foreign born: 1.5% (2005-2009 5-year est.); Ancestry (includes multiple ancestries): 50.0% German, 30.1% Irish, 16.2% Italian, 8.1% French, 5.1% English (2005-2009 5-year est.).
Economy: Employment by occupation: 0.0% management, 23.4% professional, 26.6% services, 12.5% sales, 6.3% farming, 10.9% construction, 20.3% production (2005-2009 5-year est.).
Income: Per capita income: $21,809 (2010); Median household income: $48,750 (2010); Average household income: $56,200 (2010); Percent of households with income of $100,000 or more: 6.0% (2010); Poverty rate: 25.7% (2005-2009 5-year est.).
Taxes: Total city taxes per capita: $90 (2007); City property taxes per capita: $83 (2007).
Education: Percent of population age 25 and over with: High school diploma (including GED) or higher: 89.4% (2010); Bachelor's degree or higher: 10.6% (2010); Master's degree or higher: 0.0% (2010).
Housing: Homeownership rate: 76.0% (2010); Median home value: $111,111 (2010); Median contract rent: $388 per month (2005-2009 5-year est.); Median year structure built: 1964 (2005-2009 5-year est.).
Transportation: Commute to work: 89.1% car, 0.0% public transportation, 10.9% walk, 0.0% work from home (2005-2009 5-year est.); Travel time to work: 28.1% less than 15 minutes, 23.4% 15 to 30 minutes, 12.5% 30 to 45 minutes, 28.1% 45 to 60 minutes, 7.8% 60 minutes or more (2005-2009 5-year est.)

CHATSWORTH (town). Covers a land area of 0.895 square miles and a water area of 0 square miles. Located at 40.75° N. Lat; 88.29° W. Long. Elevation is 735 feet.

History: Chatsworth was laid out in 1858, and devloped as a farming community and manufacturer of tiles and bricks from local clay.
Population: 1,206 (1990); 1,265 (2000); 1,158 (2010); 1,098 (2015 projected); Race: 98.3% White, 0.5% Black, 0.1% Asian, 1.1% Other, 1.9% Hispanic of any race (2010); Density: 1,293.3 persons per square mile (2010); Average household size: 2.35 (2010); Median age: 40.0 (2010); Males per 100 females: 97.3 (2010); Marriage status: 24.4% never married, 51.4% now married, 9.3% widowed, 14.9% divorced (2005-2009 5-year est.); Foreign born: 0.9% (2005-2009 5-year est.); Ancestry (includes multiple ancestries): 31.5% German, 21.4% Irish, 18.6% American, 9.8% English, 6.0% Italian (2005-2009 5-year est.).
Economy: Single-family building permits issued: 0 (2010); Multi-family building permits issued: 0 (2010); Employment by occupation: 4.8% management, 4.6% professional, 21.8% services, 29.8% sales, 1.7% farming, 5.5% construction, 31.9% production (2005-2009 5-year est.).
Income: Per capita income: $20,676 (2010); Median household income: $44,655 (2010); Average household income: $48,694 (2010); Percent of households with income of $100,000 or more: 7.7% (2010); Poverty rate: 25.6% (2005-2009 5-year est.).
Taxes: Total city taxes per capita: $121 (2007); City property taxes per capita: $117 (2007).
Education: Percent of population age 25 and over with: High school diploma (including GED) or higher: 85.0% (2010); Bachelor's degree or higher: 9.1% (2010); Master's degree or higher: 4.0% (2010).

School District(s)

Prairie Central CUSD 8 (PK-12)
    2009-10 Enrollment: 2,137 . . . . (815) 692-2504
Housing: Homeownership rate: 71.7% (2010); Median home value: $64,474 (2010); Median contract rent: $273 per month (2005-2009 5-year est.); Median year structure built: 1958 (2005-2009 5-year est.).
Transportation: Commute to work: 94.1% car, 0.2% public transportation, 0.6% walk, 1.5% work from home (2005-2009 5-year est.); Travel time to work: 54.7% less than 15 minutes, 15.3% 15 to 30 minutes, 19.0% 30 to 45 minutes, 4.3% 45 to 60 minutes, 6.7% 60 minutes or more (2005-2009 5-year est.)

CORNELL (village). Covers a land area of 0.636 square miles and a water area of 0 square miles. Located at 40.99° N. Lat; 88.73° W. Long. Elevation is 630 feet.
Population: 556 (1990); 511 (2000); 499 (2010); 488 (2015 projected); Race: 98.8% White, 0.4% Black, 0.0% Asian, 0.8% Other, 1.2% Hispanic of any race (2010); Density: 784.9 persons per square mile (2010); Average household size: 2.52 (2010); Median age: 36.9 (2010); Males per 100 females: 95.7 (2010); Marriage status: 20.5% never married, 67.7% now married, 5.8% widowed, 6.0% divorced (2005-2009 5-year est.); Foreign born: 0.0% (2005-2009 5-year est.); Ancestry (includes multiple ancestries): 44.5% German, 18.2% Irish, 14.2% English, 12.4% American, 4.1% Norwegian (2005-2009 5-year est.).
Economy: Single-family building permits issued: 1 (2010); Multi-family building permits issued: 0 (2010); Employment by occupation: 3.6% management, 13.8% professional, 28.1% services, 18.9% sales, 0.0% farming, 11.4% construction, 24.3% production (2005-2009 5-year est.).
Income: Per capita income: $25,901 (2010); Median household income: $62,054 (2010); Average household income: $65,051 (2010); Percent of households with income of $100,000 or more: 14.6% (2010); Poverty rate: 2.7% (2005-2009 5-year est.).
Taxes: Total city taxes per capita: $72 (2007); City property taxes per capita: $54 (2007).
Education: Percent of population age 25 and over with: High school diploma (including GED) or higher: 89.3% (2010); Bachelor's degree or higher: 8.8% (2010); Master's degree or higher: 1.8% (2010).

School District(s)

Cornell CCSD 426 (PK-08)
    2009-10 Enrollment: 115 . . . . (815) 358-2214
Housing: Homeownership rate: 78.3% (2010); Median home value: $71,379 (2010); Median contract rent: $415 per month (2005-2009 5-year est.); Median year structure built: 1956 (2005-2009 5-year est.).
Transportation: Commute to work: 92.0% car, 2.8% public transportation, 1.2% walk, 3.1% work from home (2005-2009 5-year est.); Travel time to work: 16.1% less than 15 minutes, 63.0% 15 to 30 minutes, 3.5% 30 to 45 minutes, 9.8% 45 to 60 minutes, 7.6% 60 minutes or more (2005-2009 5-year est.)

CULLOM (village). Covers a land area of 0.308 square miles and a water area of 0 square miles. Located at 40.87° N. Lat; 88.26° W. Long. Elevation is 682 feet.
Population: 568 (1990); 563 (2000); 533 (2010); 514 (2015 projected); Race: 98.1% White, 1.1% Black, 0.0% Asian, 0.8% Other, 0.4% Hispanic of any race (2010); Density: 1,729.7 persons per square mile (2010); Average household size: 2.25 (2010); Median age: 37.7 (2010); Males per 100 females: 93.8 (2010); Marriage status: 24.8% never married, 50.6% now married, 10.9% widowed, 13.7% divorced (2005-2009 5-year est.); Foreign born: 1.7% (2005-2009 5-year est.); Ancestry (includes multiple ancestries): 35.5% German, 21.5% English, 13.2% American, 8.9% Irish, 5.8% Italian (2005-2009 5-year est.).
Economy: Single-family building permits issued: 0 (2010); Multi-family building permits issued: 0 (2010); Employment by occupation: 5.9% management, 24.7% professional, 10.9% services, 28.5% sales, 1.3% farming, 8.8% construction, 20.1% production (2005-2009 5-year est.).
Income: Per capita income: $19,243 (2010); Median household income: $36,875 (2010); Average household income: $43,861 (2010); Percent of households with income of $100,000 or more: 5.1% (2010); Poverty rate: 7.9% (2005-2009 5-year est.).
Taxes: Total city taxes per capita: $75 (2007); City property taxes per capita: $70 (2007).
Education: Percent of population age 25 and over with: High school diploma (including GED) or higher: 86.1% (2010); Bachelor's degree or higher: 10.1% (2010); Master's degree or higher: 4.2% (2010).

School District(s)

Tri Point CUSD 6-J (PK-12)
    2009-10 Enrollment: 548 . . . . (815) 253-6299
Housing: Homeownership rate: 78.9% (2010); Median home value: $81,389 (2010); Median contract rent: $388 per month (2005-2009 5-year est.); Median year structure built: 1956 (2005-2009 5-year est.).
Transportation: Commute to work: 81.1% car, 0.0% public transportation, 7.0% walk, 8.8% work from home (2005-2009 5-year est.); Travel time to work: 31.9% less than 15 minutes, 23.2% 15 to 30 minutes, 21.7% 30 to 45 minutes, 8.7% 45 to 60 minutes, 14.5% 60 minutes or more (2005-2009 5-year est.)

DWIGHT (village). Covers a land area of 2.574 square miles and a water area of 0.008 square miles. Located at 41.09° N. Lat; 88.42° W. Long. Elevation is 630 feet.
History: In Dwight, Dr. Leslie Keeley, a Civil War surgeon, established the Keeley Institute for the treatment of alcoholism and drug addiction, and achieved much success and acclaim.
Population: 4,242 (1990); 4,363 (2000); 3,881 (2010); 3,642 (2015 projected); Race: 96.0% White, 0.9% Black, 0.2% Asian, 2.9% Other, 3.5% Hispanic of any race (2010); Density: 1,507.6 persons per square mile (2010); Average household size: 2.46 (2010); Median age: 37.0 (2010); Males per 100 females: 90.7 (2010); Marriage status: 21.9% never married, 53.5% now married, 15.1% widowed, 9.5% divorced (2005-2009 5-year est.); Foreign born: 1.7% (2005-2009 5-year est.); Ancestry (includes multiple ancestries): 31.9% German, 19.0% Irish, 12.3% English, 9.0% Italian, 6.2% Polish (2005-2009 5-year est.).
Economy: Single-family building permits issued: 2 (2010); Multi-family building permits issued: 0 (2010); Employment by occupation: 6.9% management, 20.2% professional, 23.4% services, 15.9% sales, 0.0% farming, 7.7% construction, 25.9% production (2005-2009 5-year est.).
Income: Per capita income: $23,560 (2010); Median household income: $45,718 (2010); Average household income: $60,137 (2010); Percent of households with income of $100,000 or more: 15.7% (2010); Poverty rate: 19.6% (2005-2009 5-year est.).
Taxes: Total city taxes per capita: $227 (2007); City property taxes per capita: $125 (2007).
Education: Percent of population age 25 and over with: High school diploma (including GED) or higher: 87.1% (2010); Bachelor's degree or higher: 12.0% (2010); Master's degree or higher: 4.5% (2010).

School District(s)

Dwight Common SD 232 (PK-08)
    2009-10 Enrollment: 629 . . . . (815) 584-6216
Dwight Twp HSD 230 (09-12)
    2009-10 Enrollment: 304 . . . . (815) 584-6216
Housing: Homeownership rate: 73.9% (2010); Median home value: $113,009 (2010); Median contract rent: $501 per month (2005-2009 5-year est.); Median year structure built: 1962 (2005-2009 5-year est.).

Safety: Violent crime rate: 7.1 per 10,000 population; Property crime rate: 71.0 per 10,000 population (2010).

Newspapers: Courier Press (Community news; Circulation 1,500); Dwight Star & Herald (Community news; Circulation 2,409)

Transportation: Commute to work: 94.5% car, 0.1% public transportation, 1.7% walk, 2.6% work from home (2005-2009 5-year est.); Travel time to work: 54.3% less than 15 minutes, 13.9% 15 to 30 minutes, 19.3% 30 to 45 minutes, 6.0% 45 to 60 minutes, 6.4% 60 minutes or more (2005-2009 5-year est.); Amtrak: train service available.

Additional Information Contacts

Dwight Area Chamber of Commerce . . . . (815) 584-2091
  http://www.dwightchamber.net
Village of Dwight . . . . (815) 584-3077
  http://www.dwightillinois.org

EMINGTON (village).
Covers a land area of 0.101 square miles and a water area of 0 square miles. Located at 40.97° N. Lat; 88.35° W. Long. Elevation is 715 feet.

Population: 135 (1990); 120 (2000); 111 (2010); 106 (2015 projected); Race: 98.2% White, 0.0% Black, 0.9% Asian, 0.9% Other, 0.9% Hispanic of any race (2010); Density: 1,095.8 persons per square mile (2010); Average household size: 2.71 (2010); Median age: 32.3 (2010); Males per 100 females: 109.4 (2010); Marriage status: 16.1% never married, 53.2% now married, 12.9% widowed, 17.7% divorced (2005-2009 5-year est.); Foreign born: 0.0% (2005-2009 5-year est.); Ancestry (includes multiple ancestries): 25.6% Irish, 16.7% German, 15.6% Polish, 7.8% American, 6.7% French (2005-2009 5-year est.).

Economy: Single-family building permits issued: 0 (2010); Multi-family building permits issued: 0 (2010); Employment by occupation: 5.0% management, 7.5% professional, 22.5% services, 22.5% sales, 0.0% farming, 12.5% construction, 30.0% production (2005-2009 5-year est.).

Income: Per capita income: $21,809 (2010); Median household income: $51,250 (2010); Average household income: $57,622 (2010); Percent of households with income of $100,000 or more: 9.8% (2010); Poverty rate: 14.4% (2005-2009 5-year est.).

Taxes: Total city taxes per capita: $62 (2007); City property taxes per capita: $62 (2007).

Education: Percent of population age 25 and over with: High school diploma (including GED) or higher: 89.2% (2010); Bachelor's degree or higher: 10.8% (2010); Master's degree or higher: 0.0% (2010).

Housing: Homeownership rate: 78.0% (2010); Median home value: $112,500 (2010); Median contract rent: $383 per month (2005-2009 5-year est.); Median year structure built: before 1940 (2005-2009 5-year est.).

Transportation: Commute to work: 100.0% car, 0.0% public transportation, 0.0% walk, 0.0% work from home (2005-2009 5-year est.); Travel time to work: 0.0% less than 15 minutes, 52.5% 15 to 30 minutes, 20.0% 30 to 45 minutes, 15.0% 45 to 60 minutes, 12.5% 60 minutes or more (2005-2009 5-year est.)

FAIRBURY (city).
Covers a land area of 1.297 square miles and a water area of 0 square miles. Located at 40.74° N. Lat; 88.51° W. Long. Elevation is 682 feet.

History: Incorporated 1890.

Population: 3,850 (1990); 3,968 (2000); 3,762 (2010); 3,615 (2015 projected); Race: 95.3% White, 0.5% Black, 0.7% Asian, 3.6% Other, 3.1% Hispanic of any race (2010); Density: 2,901.3 persons per square mile (2010); Average household size: 2.43 (2010); Median age: 38.2 (2010); Males per 100 females: 91.6 (2010); Marriage status: 21.9% never married, 55.2% now married, 13.8% widowed, 9.1% divorced (2005-2009 5-year est.); Foreign born: 1.2% (2005-2009 5-year est.); Ancestry (includes multiple ancestries): 44.6% German, 18.1% Irish, 12.8% American, 9.2% English, 8.6% Swiss (2005-2009 5-year est.).

Economy: Single-family building permits issued: 6 (2010); Multi-family building permits issued: 0 (2010); Employment by occupation: 6.8% management, 13.6% professional, 10.2% services, 29.3% sales, 0.0% farming, 16.9% construction, 23.2% production (2005-2009 5-year est.).

Income: Per capita income: $22,944 (2010); Median household income: $47,679 (2010); Average household income: $55,351 (2010); Percent of households with income of $100,000 or more: 11.2% (2010); Poverty rate: 5.3% (2005-2009 5-year est.).

Taxes: Total city taxes per capita: $196 (2007); City property taxes per capita: $184 (2007).

Education: Percent of population age 25 and over with: High school diploma (including GED) or higher: 84.6% (2010); Bachelor's degree or higher: 16.6% (2010); Master's degree or higher: 8.0% (2010).

School District(s)

Prairie Central CUSD 8 (PK-12)
  2009-10 Enrollment: 2,137 . . . . (815) 692-2504

Housing: Homeownership rate: 73.4% (2010); Median home value: $114,193 (2010); Median contract rent: $458 per month (2005-2009 5-year est.); Median year structure built: 1962 (2005-2009 5-year est.).

Newspapers: Blade (Community news; Circulation 3,400)

Transportation: Commute to work: 93.9% car, 0.0% public transportation, 3.3% walk, 2.8% work from home (2005-2009 5-year est.); Travel time to work: 60.6% less than 15 minutes, 20.8% 15 to 30 minutes, 9.7% 30 to 45 minutes, 6.8% 45 to 60 minutes, 2.2% 60 minutes or more (2005-2009 5-year est.)

FLANAGAN (village).
Covers a land area of 0.534 square miles and a water area of 0 square miles. Located at 40.87° N. Lat; 88.85° W. Long. Elevation is 673 feet.

Population: 989 (1990); 1,083 (2000); 996 (2010); 947 (2015 projected); Race: 98.2% White, 0.3% Black, 0.0% Asian, 1.5% Other, 0.2% Hispanic of any race (2010); Density: 1,865.8 persons per square mile (2010); Average household size: 2.23 (2010); Median age: 45.3 (2010); Males per 100 females: 84.4 (2010); Marriage status: 16.1% never married, 55.0% now married, 19.8% widowed, 9.0% divorced (2005-2009 5-year est.); Foreign born: 1.0% (2005-2009 5-year est.); Ancestry (includes multiple ancestries): 43.8% German, 16.3% Irish, 14.2% American, 8.2% English, 2.6% Italian (2005-2009 5-year est.).

Economy: Single-family building permits issued: 0 (2010); Multi-family building permits issued: 0 (2010); Employment by occupation: 8.4% management, 17.7% professional, 23.6% services, 25.7% sales, 0.6% farming, 10.1% construction, 13.8% production (2005-2009 5-year est.).

Income: Per capita income: $25,922 (2010); Median household income: $49,912 (2010); Average household income: $59,093 (2010); Percent of households with income of $100,000 or more: 12.4% (2010); Poverty rate: 7.1% (2005-2009 5-year est.).

Taxes: Total city taxes per capita: $38 (2007); City property taxes per capita: $37 (2007).

Education: Percent of population age 25 and over with: High school diploma (including GED) or higher: 91.1% (2010); Bachelor's degree or higher: 19.9% (2010); Master's degree or higher: 7.1% (2010).

School District(s)

Flanagan-Cornell Dist 74 (PK-12)
  2009-10 Enrollment: 363 . . . . (815) 796-2233

Housing: Homeownership rate: 77.3% (2010); Median home value: $92,644 (2010); Median contract rent: $502 per month (2005-2009 5-year est.); Median year structure built: 1955 (2005-2009 5-year est.).

Newspapers: Flanagan Home Times (Community news; Circulation 1,200)

Transportation: Commute to work: 87.7% car, 0.0% public transportation, 4.9% walk, 7.5% work from home (2005-2009 5-year est.); Travel time to work: 37.0% less than 15 minutes, 46.4% 15 to 30 minutes, 5.3% 30 to 45 minutes, 5.7% 45 to 60 minutes, 5.7% 60 minutes or more (2005-2009 5-year est.)

FORREST (village).
Covers a land area of 0.626 square miles and a water area of 0 square miles. Located at 40.75° N. Lat; 88.41° W. Long. Elevation is 686 feet.

History: Forrest was settled in 1836, but grew in the 1860's when German-Amish immigrants arrived.

Population: 1,198 (1990); 1,225 (2000); 1,186 (2010); 1,161 (2015 projected); Race: 94.0% White, 1.0% Black, 0.2% Asian, 4.8% Other, 3.7% Hispanic of any race (2010); Density: 1,894.2 persons per square mile (2010); Average household size: 2.70 (2010); Median age: 35.7 (2010); Males per 100 females: 97.0 (2010); Marriage status: 30.3% never married, 54.2% now married, 5.9% widowed, 9.7% divorced (2005-2009 5-year est.); Foreign born: 2.9% (2005-2009 5-year est.); Ancestry (includes multiple ancestries): 58.6% German, 23.2% Irish, 11.5% American, 9.8% English, 5.1% Polish (2005-2009 5-year est.).

Economy: Single-family building permits issued: 0 (2010); Multi-family building permits issued: 0 (2010); Employment by occupation: 10.0% management, 13.4% professional, 3.6% services, 32.3% sales, 2.3% farming, 19.3% construction, 19.1% production (2005-2009 5-year est.).

Income: Per capita income: $22,092 (2010); Median household income: $52,559 (2010); Average household income: $59,597 (2010); Percent of households with income of $100,000 or more: 11.4% (2010); Poverty rate: 13.4% (2005-2009 5-year est.).

Taxes: Total city taxes per capita: $188 (2007); City property taxes per capita: $99 (2007).

Education: Percent of population age 25 and over with: High school diploma (including GED) or higher: 83.9% (2010); Bachelor's degree or higher: 14.1% (2010); Master's degree or higher: 5.3% (2010).

School District(s)
Prairie Central CUSD 8 (PK-12)
    2009-10 Enrollment: 2,137 . . . . (815) 692-2504
Housing: Homeownership rate: 77.3% (2010); Median home value: $97,391 (2010); Median contract rent: $369 per month (2005-2009 5-year est.); Median year structure built: 1949 (2005-2009 5-year est.).
Transportation: Commute to work: 91.4% car, 0.0% public transportation, 7.0% walk, 1.5% work from home (2005-2009 5-year est.); Travel time to work: 58.1% less than 15 minutes, 17.1% 15 to 30 minutes, 14.7% 30 to 45 minutes, 2.7% 45 to 60 minutes, 7.3% 60 minutes or more (2005-2009 5-year est.)

GRAYMONT (unincorporated postal area, zip code 61743). Covers a land area of 15.916 square miles and a water area of 0 square miles. Located at 40.87° N. Lat; 88.77° W. Long. Elevation is 653 feet.
Population: 270 (2000); Race: 100.0% White, 0.0% Black, 0.0% Asian, 0.0% Other, 0.0% Hispanic of any race (2000); Density: 17.0 persons per square mile (2000); Age: 32.2% under 18, 11.4% over 64 (2000); Marriage status: 21.7% never married, 59.3% now married, 5.8% widowed, 13.2% divorced (2000); Foreign born: 0.0% (2000); Ancestry (includes multiple ancestries): 44.7% German, 15.7% English, 14.1% American, 9.4% Irish, 3.9% Scotch-Irish (2000).
Economy: Employment by occupation: 13.1% management, 12.4% professional, 25.5% services, 19.0% sales, 0.0% farming, 13.1% construction, 16.8% production (2000).
Income: Per capita income: $16,810 (2000); Median household income: $41,250 (2000); Poverty rate: 9.9% (2000).
Education: Percent of population age 25 and over with: High school diploma (including GED) or higher: 90.0% (2000); Bachelor's degree or higher: 14.7% (2000).

School District(s)
Rooks Creek CCSD 425 (KG-08)
    2009-10 Enrollment: 44 . . . . (815) 743-5346
Housing: Homeownership rate: 71.0% (2000); Median home value: $49,200 (2000); Median contract rent: $332 per month (2000); Median year structure built: before 1940 (2000).
Transportation: Commute to work: 82.8% car, 0.0% public transportation, 6.7% walk, 9.7% work from home (2000); Travel time to work: 50.4% less than 15 minutes, 25.6% 15 to 30 minutes, 9.9% 30 to 45 minutes, 9.1% 45 to 60 minutes, 5.0% 60 minutes or more (2000)

LONG POINT (village). Covers a land area of 0.188 square miles and a water area of 0 square miles. Located at 41.00° N. Lat; 88.89° W. Long. Elevation is 640 feet.
Population: 208 (1990); 247 (2000); 237 (2010); 230 (2015 projected); Race: 97.0% White, 1.3% Black, 0.4% Asian, 1.3% Other, 0.4% Hispanic of any race (2010); Density: 1,260.6 persons per square mile (2010); Average household size: 2.66 (2010); Median age: 40.7 (2010); Males per 100 females: 97.5 (2010); Marriage status: 27.0% never married, 63.3% now married, 5.6% widowed, 4.1% divorced (2005-2009 5-year est.); Foreign born: 0.4% (2005-2009 5-year est.); Ancestry (includes multiple ancestries): 45.5% German, 32.5% Irish, 24.6% Polish, 16.4% English, 9.0% Italian (2005-2009 5-year est.).
Economy: Employment by occupation: 11.7% management, 6.7% professional, 15.8% services, 25.8% sales, 0.0% farming, 8.3% construction, 31.7% production (2005-2009 5-year est.).
Income: Per capita income: $31,409 (2010); Median household income: $70,625 (2010); Average household income: $80,421 (2010); Percent of households with income of $100,000 or more: 22.5% (2010); Poverty rate: 6.7% (2005-2009 5-year est.).
Taxes: Total city taxes per capita: $33 (2007); City property taxes per capita: $29 (2007).
Education: Percent of population age 25 and over with: High school diploma (including GED) or higher: 91.3% (2010); Bachelor's degree or higher: 16.9% (2010); Master's degree or higher: 3.8% (2010).
Housing: Homeownership rate: 85.4% (2010); Median home value: $96,667 (2010); Median contract rent: $296 per month (2005-2009 5-year est.); Median year structure built: before 1940 (2005-2009 5-year est.).
Transportation: Commute to work: 89.8% car, 0.0% public transportation, 6.8% walk, 3.4% work from home (2005-2009 5-year est.); Travel time to work: 34.2% less than 15 minutes, 37.7% 15 to 30 minutes, 13.2% 30 to 45

minutes, 11.4% 45 to 60 minutes, 3.5% 60 minutes or more (2005-2009 5-year est.)

ODELL (village). Covers a land area of 1.115 square miles and a water area of 0.014 square miles. Located at 41.00° N. Lat; 88.52° W. Long. Elevation is 719 feet.
Population: 1,030 (1990); 1,014 (2000); 1,055 (2010); 1,064 (2015 projected); Race: 97.3% White, 0.1% Black, 0.4% Asian, 2.3% Other, 1.9% Hispanic of any race (2010); Density: 945.8 persons per square mile (2010); Average household size: 2.41 (2010); Median age: 38.0 (2010); Males per 100 females: 96.1 (2010); Marriage status: 34.3% never married, 51.7% now married, 5.4% widowed, 8.5% divorced (2005-2009 5-year est.); Foreign born: 1.1% (2005-2009 5-year est.); Ancestry (includes multiple ancestries): 46.4% German, 24.8% Irish, 10.1% English, 8.7% American, 5.6% Polish (2005-2009 5-year est.).
Economy: Single-family building permits issued: 1 (2010); Multi-family building permits issued: 0 (2010); Employment by occupation: 10.1% management, 15.0% professional, 16.6% services, 15.0% sales, 0.5% farming, 18.8% construction, 23.9% production (2005-2009 5-year est.).
Income: Per capita income: $22,198 (2010); Median household income: $46,484 (2010); Average household income: $53,567 (2010); Percent of households with income of $100,000 or more: 8.2% (2010); Poverty rate: 11.1% (2005-2009 5-year est.).
Taxes: Total city taxes per capita: $142 (2007); City property taxes per capita: $68 (2007).
Education: Percent of population age 25 and over with: High school diploma (including GED) or higher: 89.9% (2010); Bachelor's degree or higher: 12.7% (2010); Master's degree or higher: 4.4% (2010).

School District(s)
Odell CCSD 435 (PK-08)
    2009-10 Enrollment: 180 . . . . (815) 998-2272
Housing: Homeownership rate: 81.5% (2010); Median home value: $93,765 (2010); Median contract rent: $408 per month (2005-2009 5-year est.); Median year structure built: before 1940 (2005-2009 5-year est.).
Transportation: Commute to work: 90.3% car, 1.7% public transportation, 4.6% walk, 2.8% work from home (2005-2009 5-year est.); Travel time to work: 29.1% less than 15 minutes, 48.4% 15 to 30 minutes, 7.5% 30 to 45 minutes, 3.4% 45 to 60 minutes, 11.7% 60 minutes or more (2005-2009 5-year est.)

PONTIAC (city). County seat. Covers a land area of 5.243 square miles and a water area of 0.010 square miles. Located at 40.88° N. Lat; 88.63° W. Long. Elevation is 646 feet.
History: Pontiac was founded in 1837 and named for the Ottawa Chief Pontiac. Jesse W. Fell was a leader in the development of Pontiac, and chose the name for the town. Pontiac developed as the seat of Livingston County.
Population: 11,752 (1990); 11,864 (2000); 11,067 (2010); 10,690 (2015 projected); Race: 87.6% White, 8.5% Black, 0.6% Asian, 3.2% Other, 4.2% Hispanic of any race (2010); Density: 2,111.0 persons per square mile (2010); Average household size: 2.35 (2010); Median age: 36.1 (2010); Males per 100 females: 116.1 (2010); Marriage status: 32.1% never married, 50.3% now married, 4.0% widowed, 13.6% divorced (2005-2009 5-year est.); Foreign born: 2.4% (2005-2009 5-year est.); Ancestry (includes multiple ancestries): 30.7% German, 15.7% Irish, 10.5% American, 9.8% English, 4.6% Italian (2005-2009 5-year est.).
Economy: Single-family building permits issued: 2 (2010); Multi-family building permits issued: 0 (2010); Employment by occupation: 5.9% management, 16.9% professional, 27.4% services, 21.7% sales, 0.4% farming, 8.2% construction, 19.5% production (2005-2009 5-year est.).
Income: Per capita income: $20,624 (2010); Median household income: $43,524 (2010); Average household income: $52,182 (2010); Percent of households with income of $100,000 or more: 10.6% (2010); Poverty rate: 14.8% (2005-2009 5-year est.).
Taxes: Total city taxes per capita: $362 (2007); City property taxes per capita: $357 (2007).
Education: Percent of population age 25 and over with: High school diploma (including GED) or higher: 80.8% (2010); Bachelor's degree or higher: 14.3% (2010); Master's degree or higher: 4.9% (2010).

School District(s)
Livingston Area Career Cntr (11-12)
    2009-10 Enrollment: n/a . . . . (815) 842-2557
Livingston Co Spec Services Unit (01-12)
    2009-10 Enrollment: n/a . . . . (815) 844-7115

Pontiac CCSD 429 (PK-08)
   2009-10 Enrollment: 1,308 . . . . (815) 844-5632
Pontiac Twp HSD 90 (09-12)
   2009-10 Enrollment: 855 . . . . (815) 844-6113
Housing: Homeownership rate: 70.0% (2010); Median home value: $90,663 (2010); Median contract rent: $449 per month (2005-2009 5-year est.); Median year structure built: 1961 (2005-2009 5-year est.).
Hospitals: St. James OSF (89 beds)
Safety: Violent crime rate: 47.9 per 10,000 population; Property crime rate: 325.0 per 10,000 population (2010).
Newspapers: Pontiac Daily Leader (Local news; Circulation 6,200)
Transportation: Commute to work: 87.7% car, 0.9% public transportation, 6.6% walk, 2.0% work from home (2005-2009 5-year est.); Travel time to work: 67.9% less than 15 minutes, 16.4% 15 to 30 minutes, 7.8% 30 to 45 minutes, 5.3% 45 to 60 minutes, 2.6% 60 minutes or more (2005-2009 5-year est.); Amtrak: train service available.
Airports: Pontiac Municipal (general aviation)
Additional Information Contacts
City of Pontiac . . . . (815) 844-3396
   http://pontiac.org
Pontiac Area Chamber of Commerce . . . . (815) 844-5131
   http://www.pontiacchamber.org

SAUNEMIN (village). Covers a land area of 0.223 square miles and a water area of 0 square miles. Located at 40.89° N. Lat; 88.40° W. Long. Elevation is 689 feet.
Population: 399 (1990); 456 (2000); 472 (2010); 473 (2015 projected); Race: 98.3% White, 0.2% Black, 0.0% Asian, 1.5% Other, 2.1% Hispanic of any race (2010); Density: 2,117.7 persons per square mile (2010); Average household size: 2.90 (2010); Median age: 35.6 (2010); Males per 100 females: 112.6 (2010); Marriage status: 28.6% never married, 51.8% now married, 4.7% widowed, 14.9% divorced (2005-2009 5-year est.); Foreign born: 0.0% (2005-2009 5-year est.); Ancestry (includes multiple ancestries): 41.1% German, 23.7% Irish, 16.3% English, 8.9% American, 5.5% French (2005-2009 5-year est.).
Economy: Employment by occupation: 5.4% management, 11.4% professional, 23.5% services, 21.1% sales, 0.0% farming, 15.1% construction, 23.5% production (2005-2009 5-year est.).
Income: Per capita income: $23,226 (2010); Median household income: $63,315 (2010); Average household income: $67,745 (2010); Percent of households with income of $100,000 or more: 16.6% (2010); Poverty rate: 14.7% (2005-2009 5-year est.).
Taxes: Total city taxes per capita: $123 (2007); City property taxes per capita: $59 (2007).
Education: Percent of population age 25 and over with: High school diploma (including GED) or higher: 89.0% (2010); Bachelor's degree or higher: 10.0% (2010); Master's degree or higher: 2.1% (2010).
School District(s)
Saunemin CCSD 438 (PK-08)
   2009-10 Enrollment: 137 . . . . (815) 832-4421
Housing: Homeownership rate: 83.4% (2010); Median home value: $93,846 (2010); Median contract rent: $542 per month (2005-2009 5-year est.); Median year structure built: 1950 (2005-2009 5-year est.).
Transportation: Commute to work: 93.2% car, 0.0% public transportation, 0.0% walk, 1.2% work from home (2005-2009 5-year est.); Travel time to work: 6.3% less than 15 minutes, 61.3% 15 to 30 minutes, 13.8% 30 to 45 minutes, 6.9% 45 to 60 minutes, 11.9% 60 minutes or more (2005-2009 5-year est.)

STRAWN (village). Covers a land area of 0.142 square miles and a water area of 0 square miles. Located at 40.65° N. Lat; 88.39° W. Long. Elevation is 771 feet.
Population: 130 (1990); 104 (2000); 103 (2010); 103 (2015 projected); Race: 97.1% White, 1.9% Black, 0.0% Asian, 1.0% Other, 1.0% Hispanic of any race (2010); Density: 725.5 persons per square mile (2010); Average household size: 2.86 (2010); Median age: 35.3 (2010); Males per 100 females: 94.3 (2010); Marriage status: 13.2% never married, 71.4% now married, 8.8% widowed, 6.6% divorced (2005-2009 5-year est.); Foreign born: 0.0% (2005-2009 5-year est.); Ancestry (includes multiple ancestries): 49.6% Irish, 18.5% American, 17.8% German, 6.7% English, 5.2% Dutch (2005-2009 5-year est.).
Economy: Employment by occupation: 28.1% management, 21.9% professional, 10.9% services, 3.1% sales, 0.0% farming, 18.8% construction, 17.2% production (2005-2009 5-year est.).

Income: Per capita income: $27,644 (2010); Median household income: $72,917 (2010); Average household income: $79,931 (2010); Percent of households with income of $100,000 or more: 22.2% (2010); Poverty rate: 0.0% (2005-2009 5-year est.).
Taxes: Total city taxes per capita: $90 (2007); City property taxes per capita: $80 (2007).
Education: Percent of population age 25 and over with: High school diploma (including GED) or higher: 93.9% (2010); Bachelor's degree or higher: 18.2% (2010); Master's degree or higher: 7.6% (2010).
Housing: Homeownership rate: 80.6% (2010); Median home value: $98,000 (2010); Median contract rent: $333 per month (2005-2009 5-year est.); Median year structure built: before 1940 (2005-2009 5-year est.).
Transportation: Commute to work: 75.8% car, 0.0% public transportation, 21.0% walk, 3.2% work from home (2005-2009 5-year est.); Travel time to work: 46.7% less than 15 minutes, 25.0% 15 to 30 minutes, 10.0% 30 to 45 minutes, 10.0% 45 to 60 minutes, 8.3% 60 minutes or more (2005-2009 5-year est.)

Logan County

Located in central Illinois; drained by Salt and Kickapoo Creeks. Covers a land area of 618.14 square miles, a water area of 0.87 square miles, and is located in the Central Time Zone at 40.14° N. Lat., 89.36° W. Long. The county was founded in 1839. County seat is Lincoln.

Logan County is part of the Lincoln, IL Micropolitan Statistical Area. The entire metro area includes: Logan County, IL

Weather Station: Lincoln										Elevation: 583 feet		
	Jan	Feb	Mar	Apr	May	Jun	Jul	Aug	Sep	Oct	Nov	Dec
High	34	39	51	64	75	83	86	84	79	66	52	38
Low	17	21	30	40	51	61	64	62	53	41	32	21
Precip	2.0	1.6	2.7	3.7	4.1	3.9	5.0	3.9	3.0	3.3	3.3	2.6
Snow	6.1	4.9	1.8	0.5	0.0	0.0	0.0	0.0	0.0	tr	0.7	5.4

High and Low temperatures in degrees Fahrenheit; Precipitation and Snow in inches

Population: 30,798 (1990); 31,183 (2000); 29,620 (2010); 28,750 (2015 projected); Race: 90.2% White, 7.3% Black, 0.9% Asian, 1.6% Other, 1.9% Hispanic of any race (2010); Density: 47.9 persons per square mile (2010); Average household size: 2.39 (2010); Median age: 36.6 (2010); Males per 100 females: 101.1 (2010).
Religion: Five largest groups: 15.4% Christian Churches and Churches of Christ, 12.4% Catholic Church, 7.6% The United Methodist Church, 7.1% Lutheran Church—Missouri Synod, 6.1% Evangelical Lutheran Church in America (2000).
Economy: Unemployment rate: 8.3% (August 2011); Total civilian labor force: 13,704 (August 2011); Leading industries: 18.3% health care and social assistance; 15.1% retail trade; 12.8% manufacturing (2009); Farms: 710 totaling 320,356 acres (2007); Companies that employ 500 or more persons: 0 (2009); Companies that employ 100 to 499 persons: 11 (2009); Companies that employ less than 100 persons: 640 (2009); Black-owned businesses: n/a (2007); Hispanic-owned businesses: n/a (2007); Asian-owned businesses: n/a (2007); Women-owned businesses: 434 (2007); Retail sales per capita: $12,724 (2010). Single-family building permits issued: 17 (2010); Multi-family building permits issued: 0 (2010).
Income: Per capita income: $21,762 (2010); Median household income: $47,500 (2010); Average household income: $56,923 (2010); Percent of households with income of $100,000 or more: 12.1% (2010); Poverty rate: 13.8% (2009); Bankruptcy rate: 5.36% (2010).
Taxes: Total county taxes per capita: $97 (2007); County property taxes per capita: $93 (2007).
Education: Percent of population age 25 and over with: High school diploma (including GED) or higher: 84.8% (2010); Bachelor's degree or higher: 18.6% (2010); Master's degree or higher: 5.1% (2010).
Housing: Homeownership rate: 74.9% (2010); Median home value: $88,856 (2010); Median contract rent: $390 per month (2005-2009 5-year est.); Median year structure built: 1956 (2005-2009 5-year est.)
Health: Birth rate: 116.5 per 10,000 population (2009); Death rate: 105.5 per 10,000 population (2009); Age-adjusted cancer mortality rate: 223.1 deaths per 100,000 population (2007); Number of physicians: 5.3 per 10,000 population (2008); Hospital beds: 8.4 per 10,000 population (2007); Hospital admissions: 433.4 per 10,000 population (2007).
Elections: 2008 Presidential election results: 40.7% Obama, 57.6% McCain, 0.7% Nader
National and State Parks: Railsplitter State Park
Additional Information Contacts

Logan County Government . . . . (217) 732-4148
   http://www.co.logan.il.us
City of Lincoln . . . . (217) 735-2815
   http://www.cityoflincoln-il.gov
Lincoln/Logan County Chamber of Commerce . . . . (217) 735-2385
   http://www.lincolnillinois.com

Logan County Communities

ATLANTA (city). Covers a land area of 1.258 square miles and a water area of 0.008 square miles. Located at 40.26° N. Lat; 89.23° W. Long. Elevation is 709 feet.
History: Atlanta came into existence when the Chicago & Mississippi Railroad placed its tracks a mile away from the village of Newcastle, and the village moved to the railroad. The railroad station had been named Zenia, but town and railroad adopted the name of Atlanta in 1855.
Population: 1,622 (1990); 1,649 (2000); 1,632 (2010); 1,608 (2015 projected); Race: 99.1% White, 0.1% Black, 0.1% Asian, 0.7% Other, 0.7% Hispanic of any race (2010); Density: 1,297.0 persons per square mile (2010); Average household size: 2.34 (2010); Median age: 39.0 (2010); Males per 100 females: 92.5 (2010); Marriage status: 17.1% never married, 68.0% now married, 6.9% widowed, 8.1% divorced (2005-2009 5-year est.); Foreign born: 0.0% (2005-2009 5-year est.); Ancestry (includes multiple ancestries): 31.8% German, 21.8% American, 13.6% English, 11.3% Irish, 4.4% French (2005-2009 5-year est.).
Economy: Single-family building permits issued: 3 (2010); Multi-family building permits issued: 0 (2010); Employment by occupation: 12.0% management, 10.0% professional, 16.1% services, 29.5% sales, 0.3% farming, 16.2% construction, 16.0% production (2005-2009 5-year est.).
Income: Per capita income: $25,885 (2010); Median household income: $52,830 (2010); Average household income: $60,618 (2010); Percent of households with income of $100,000 or more: 13.8% (2010); Poverty rate: 8.9% (2005-2009 5-year est.).
Taxes: Total city taxes per capita: $170 (2007); City property taxes per capita: $80 (2007).
Education: Percent of population age 25 and over with: High school diploma (including GED) or higher: 88.5% (2010); Bachelor's degree or higher: 18.9% (2010); Master's degree or higher: 5.3% (2010).
School District(s)
Olympia CUSD 16 (PK-12)
   2009-10 Enrollment: 1,911 . . . . (309) 379-6011
Housing: Homeownership rate: 81.0% (2010); Median home value: $94,318 (2010); Median contract rent: $415 per month (2005-2009 5-year est.); Median year structure built: 1964 (2005-2009 5-year est.).
Transportation: Commute to work: 94.0% car, 0.0% public transportation, 2.8% walk, 2.0% work from home (2005-2009 5-year est.); Travel time to work: 24.4% less than 15 minutes, 34.9% 15 to 30 minutes, 29.9% 30 to 45 minutes, 7.0% 45 to 60 minutes, 3.9% 60 minutes or more (2005-2009 5-year est.)

BEASON (unincorporated postal area, zip code 62512). Covers a land area of 43.004 square miles and a water area of 0.004 square miles. Located at 40.13° N. Lat; 89.20° W. Long. Elevation is 640 feet.
Population: 552 (2000); Race: 100.0% White, 0.0% Black, 0.0% Asian, 0.0% Other, 0.9% Hispanic of any race (2000); Density: 12.8 persons per square mile (2000); Age: 28.7% under 18, 13.0% over 64 (2000); Marriage status: 18.6% never married, 71.6% now married, 4.4% widowed, 5.3% divorced (2000); Foreign born: 0.0% (2000); Ancestry (includes multiple ancestries): 37.8% German, 21.8% Irish, 17.3% American, 10.6% English (2000).
Economy: Employment by occupation: 2.8% management, 21.2% professional, 14.2% services, 12.2% sales, 7.6% farming, 2.4% construction, 39.6% production (2000).
Income: Per capita income: $19,329 (2000); Median household income: $57,875 (2000); Poverty rate: 1.7% (2000).
Education: Percent of population age 25 and over with: High school diploma (including GED) or higher: 91.6% (2000); Bachelor's degree or higher: 12.8% (2000).
Housing: Homeownership rate: 83.5% (2000); Median home value: $77,100 (2000); Median contract rent: $198 per month (2000); Median year structure built: 1941 (2000).
Transportation: Commute to work: 98.6% car, 0.0% public transportation, 0.0% walk, 1.4% work from home (2000); Travel time to work: 11.3% less than 15 minutes, 38.7% 15 to 30 minutes, 12.7% 30 to 45 minutes, 16.1% 45 to 60 minutes, 21.2% 60 minutes or more (2000)

BROADWELL (village). Covers a land area of 0.191 square miles and a water area of 0 square miles. Located at 40.06° N. Lat; 89.44° W. Long. Elevation is 591 feet.
Population: 146 (1990); 169 (2000); 166 (2010); 166 (2015 projected); Race: 45.8% White, 52.4% Black, 0.6% Asian, 1.2% Other, 7.8% Hispanic of any race (2010); Density: 868.5 persons per square mile (2010); Average household size: 2.61 (2010); Median age: 31.3 (2010); Males per 100 females: 201.8 (2010); Marriage status: 34.5% never married, 48.8% now married, 3.6% widowed, 13.1% divorced (2005-2009 5-year est.); Foreign born: 0.0% (2005-2009 5-year est.); Ancestry (includes multiple ancestries): 49.5% American, 14.3% German, 5.7% Dutch, 5.7% English, 1.9% Irish (2005-2009 5-year est.).
Economy: Single-family building permits issued: 0 (2010); Multi-family building permits issued: 0 (2010); Employment by occupation: 7.1% management, 3.6% professional, 21.4% services, 25.0% sales, 0.0% farming, 21.4% construction, 21.4% production (2005-2009 5-year est.).
Income: Per capita income: $14,127 (2010); Median household income: $70,000 (2010); Average household income: $81,111 (2010); Percent of households with income of $100,000 or more: 22.2% (2010); Poverty rate: 0.0% (2005-2009 5-year est.).
Taxes: Total city taxes per capita: $35 (2007); City property taxes per capita: $35 (2007).
Education: Percent of population age 25 and over with: High school diploma (including GED) or higher: 56.1% (2010); Bachelor's degree or higher: 3.3% (2010); Master's degree or higher: 0.0% (2010).
Housing: Homeownership rate: 83.3% (2010); Median home value: $90,000 (2010); Median contract rent: $388 per month (2005-2009 5-year est.); Median year structure built: 1960 (2005-2009 5-year est.).
Transportation: Commute to work: 100.0% car, 0.0% public transportation, 0.0% walk, 0.0% work from home (2005-2009 5-year est.); Travel time to work: 38.9% less than 15 minutes, 46.3% 15 to 30 minutes, 7.4% 30 to 45 minutes, 7.4% 45 to 60 minutes, 0.0% 60 minutes or more (2005-2009 5-year est.)

CHESTNUT (unincorporated postal area, zip code 62518). Covers a land area of 24.895 square miles and a water area of 0.025 square miles. Located at 40.05° N. Lat; 89.18° W. Long. Elevation is 617 feet.
Population: 468 (2000); Race: 100.0% White, 0.0% Black, 0.0% Asian, 0.0% Other, 0.0% Hispanic of any race (2000); Density: 18.8 persons per square mile (2000); Age: 21.2% under 18, 14.5% over 64 (2000); Marriage status: 21.5% never married, 71.0% now married, 3.5% widowed, 4.0% divorced (2000); Foreign born: 1.1% (2000); Ancestry (includes multiple ancestries): 37.8% German, 22.5% Irish, 7.6% English, 6.0% Dutch (2000).
Economy: Employment by occupation: 13.8% management, 16.3% professional, 21.1% services, 27.6% sales, 5.3% farming, 8.5% construction, 7.3% production (2000).
Income: Per capita income: $17,836 (2000); Median household income: $45,288 (2000); Poverty rate: 0.0% (2000).
Education: Percent of population age 25 and over with: High school diploma (including GED) or higher: 87.8% (2000); Bachelor's degree or higher: 23.1% (2000).
Housing: Homeownership rate: 85.6% (2000); Median home value: $62,500 (2000); Median contract rent: $359 per month (2000); Median year structure built: before 1940 (2000).
Transportation: Commute to work: 100.0% car, 0.0% public transportation, 0.0% walk, 0.0% work from home (2000); Travel time to work: 23.2% less than 15 minutes, 29.9% 15 to 30 minutes, 24.5% 30 to 45 minutes, 12.4% 45 to 60 minutes, 10.0% 60 minutes or more (2000)

ELKHART (village). Aka Elk Hart City. Covers a land area of 1.458 square miles and a water area of 0.008 square miles. Located at 40.02° N. Lat; 89.48° W. Long. Elevation is 594 feet.
History: Elkhart was the home of Richard J. Oglesby (1824-1899), a man of many occupations (farmer, carpenter, ropemaker, lawyer, miner, soldier) who served three times as the governor of Illinois, and as a U.S. senator.
Population: 475 (1990); 443 (2000); 419 (2010); 401 (2015 projected); Race: 99.3% White, 0.2% Black, 0.2% Asian, 0.2% Other, 1.0% Hispanic of any race (2010); Density: 287.4 persons per square mile (2010); Average household size: 2.49 (2010); Median age: 39.7 (2010); Males per 100 females: 94.0 (2010); Marriage status: 27.3% never married, 47.8% now married, 16.3% widowed, 8.7% divorced (2005-2009 5-year est.); Foreign born: 1.7% (2005-2009 5-year est.); Ancestry (includes multiple ancestries): 22.8% American, 22.5% German, 17.0% Irish, 8.1% English, 5.2% Scottish (2005-2009 5-year est.).

Economy: Single-family building permits issued: 1 (2010); Multi-family building permits issued: 0 (2010); Employment by occupation: 7.4% management, 16.6% professional, 10.9% services, 29.1% sales, 0.0% farming, 16.6% construction, 19.4% production (2005-2009 5-year est.).
Income: Per capita income: $28,546 (2010); Median household income: $65,341 (2010); Average household income: $70,164 (2010); Percent of households with income of $100,000 or more: 20.2% (2010); Poverty rate: 6.9% (2005-2009 5-year est.).
Taxes: Total city taxes per capita: $258 (2007); City property taxes per capita: $244 (2007).
Education: Percent of population age 25 and over with: High school diploma (including GED) or higher: 90.8% (2010); Bachelor's degree or higher: 23.2% (2010); Master's degree or higher: 2.2% (2010).
Housing: Homeownership rate: 78.6% (2010); Median home value: $93,600 (2010); Median contract rent: $338 per month (2005-2009 5-year est.); Median year structure built: 1951 (2005-2009 5-year est.).
Transportation: Commute to work: 89.4% car, 0.0% public transportation, 0.0% walk, 7.1% work from home (2005-2009 5-year est.); Travel time to work: 28.5% less than 15 minutes, 23.4% 15 to 30 minutes, 29.1% 30 to 45 minutes, 8.9% 45 to 60 minutes, 10.1% 60 minutes or more (2005-2009 5-year est.)

EMDEN (village). Covers a land area of 0.226 square miles and a water area of 0 square miles. Located at 40.29° N. Lat; 89.48° W. Long. Elevation is 591 feet.
Population: 488 (1990); 515 (2000); 466 (2010); 439 (2015 projected); Race: 97.6% White, 0.0% Black, 1.3% Asian, 1.1% Other, 0.6% Hispanic of any race (2010); Density: 2,062.1 persons per square mile (2010); Average household size: 2.57 (2010); Median age: 39.2 (2010); Males per 100 females: 84.9 (2010); Marriage status: 19.4% never married, 63.7% now married, 13.5% widowed, 3.4% divorced (2005-2009 5-year est.); Foreign born: 0.0% (2005-2009 5-year est.); Ancestry (includes multiple ancestries): 44.3% German, 31.5% American, 11.1% Irish, 7.0% English, 3.6% Scotch-Irish (2005-2009 5-year est.).
Economy: Single-family building permits issued: 0 (2010); Multi-family building permits issued: 0 (2010); Employment by occupation: 13.2% management, 7.0% professional, 10.5% services, 33.5% sales, 2.3% farming, 12.5% construction, 21.0% production (2005-2009 5-year est.).
Income: Per capita income: $22,284 (2010); Median household income: $47,035 (2010); Average household income: $56,561 (2010); Percent of households with income of $100,000 or more: 14.4% (2010); Poverty rate: 5.3% (2005-2009 5-year est.).
Taxes: Total city taxes per capita: $49 (2007); City property taxes per capita: $27 (2007).
Education: Percent of population age 25 and over with: High school diploma (including GED) or higher: 92.6% (2010); Bachelor's degree or higher: 19.9% (2010); Master's degree or higher: 2.6% (2010).
School District(s)
Hartsburg Emden CUSD 21 (KG-12)
    2009-10 Enrollment: 237 . . . . (217) 642-5244
Housing: Homeownership rate: 76.8% (2010); Median home value: $79,302 (2010); Median contract rent: $604 per month (2005-2009 5-year est.); Median year structure built: 1957 (2005-2009 5-year est.).
Transportation: Commute to work: 89.2% car, 0.0% public transportation, 4.4% walk, 6.0% work from home (2005-2009 5-year est.); Travel time to work: 28.6% less than 15 minutes, 60.3% 15 to 30 minutes, 10.3% 30 to 45 minutes, 0.9% 45 to 60 minutes, 0.0% 60 minutes or more (2005-2009 5-year est.)

HARTSBURG (village). Covers a land area of 0.145 square miles and a water area of 0 square miles. Located at 40.25° N. Lat; 89.44° W. Long. Elevation is 604 feet.
Population: 306 (1990); 358 (2000); 361 (2010); 366 (2015 projected); Race: 97.5% White, 0.0% Black, 0.0% Asian, 2.5% Other, 1.9% Hispanic of any race (2010); Density: 2,486.3 persons per square mile (2010); Average household size: 2.78 (2010); Median age: 37.8 (2010); Males per 100 females: 106.3 (2010); Marriage status: 16.4% never married, 55.3% now married, 14.3% widowed, 13.9% divorced (2005-2009 5-year est.); Foreign born: 1.0% (2005-2009 5-year est.); Ancestry (includes multiple ancestries): 46.7% German, 22.9% American, 6.5% Irish, 5.9% English, 3.9% Italian (2005-2009 5-year est.).
Economy: Single-family building permits issued: 1 (2010); Multi-family building permits issued: 0 (2010); Employment by occupation: 14.7% management, 3.1% professional, 16.3% services, 38.8% sales, 0.0% farming, 6.2% construction, 20.9% production (2005-2009 5-year est.).

Income: Per capita income: $27,170 (2010); Median household income: $67,241 (2010); Average household income: $74,462 (2010); Percent of households with income of $100,000 or more: 19.2% (2010); Poverty rate: 17.3% (2005-2009 5-year est.).
Taxes: Total city taxes per capita: $12 (2007); City property taxes per capita: $12 (2007).
Education: Percent of population age 25 and over with: High school diploma (including GED) or higher: 91.3% (2010); Bachelor's degree or higher: 21.6% (2010); Master's degree or higher: 3.7% (2010).
School District(s)
Hartsburg Emden CUSD 21 (KG-12)
    2009-10 Enrollment: 237 . . . . (217) 642-5244
Housing: Homeownership rate: 80.0% (2010); Median home value: $98,667 (2010); Median contract rent: $506 per month (2005-2009 5-year est.); Median year structure built: before 1940 (2005-2009 5-year est.).
Transportation: Commute to work: 95.3% car, 0.0% public transportation, 2.4% walk, 2.4% work from home (2005-2009 5-year est.); Travel time to work: 32.3% less than 15 minutes, 33.9% 15 to 30 minutes, 14.5% 30 to 45 minutes, 19.4% 45 to 60 minutes, 0.0% 60 minutes or more (2005-2009 5-year est.)

LATHAM (village). Covers a land area of 0.278 square miles and a water area of 0 square miles. Located at 39.96° N. Lat; 89.16° W. Long. Elevation is 614 feet.
Population: 482 (1990); 371 (2000); 328 (2010); 310 (2015 projected); Race: 99.7% White, 0.0% Black, 0.0% Asian, 0.3% Other, 0.3% Hispanic of any race (2010); Density: 1,179.1 persons per square mile (2010); Average household size: 2.50 (2010); Median age: 40.6 (2010); Males per 100 females: 103.7 (2010); Marriage status: 17.9% never married, 57.1% now married, 12.8% widowed, 12.2% divorced (2005-2009 5-year est.); Foreign born: 3.3% (2005-2009 5-year est.); Ancestry (includes multiple ancestries): 38.9% German, 23.9% American, 12.8% English, 6.8% Irish, 3.5% Scottish (2005-2009 5-year est.).
Economy: Single-family building permits issued: 0 (2010); Multi-family building permits issued: 0 (2010); Employment by occupation: 7.9% management, 11.9% professional, 11.1% services, 23.4% sales, 1.2% farming, 18.7% construction, 25.8% production (2005-2009 5-year est.).
Income: Per capita income: $29,135 (2010); Median household income: $65,948 (2010); Average household income: $73,168 (2010); Percent of households with income of $100,000 or more: 22.9% (2010); Poverty rate: 10.1% (2005-2009 5-year est.).
Taxes: Total city taxes per capita: $89 (2007); City property taxes per capita: $89 (2007).
Education: Percent of population age 25 and over with: High school diploma (including GED) or higher: 91.3% (2010); Bachelor's degree or higher: 17.5% (2010); Master's degree or higher: 3.5% (2010).
Housing: Homeownership rate: 79.4% (2010); Median home value: $85,263 (2010); Median contract rent: $310 per month (2005-2009 5-year est.); Median year structure built: 1951 (2005-2009 5-year est.).
Transportation: Commute to work: 90.0% car, 0.0% public transportation, 10.0% walk, 0.0% work from home (2005-2009 5-year est.); Travel time to work: 23.6% less than 15 minutes, 44.4% 15 to 30 minutes, 25.6% 30 to 45 minutes, 6.4% 45 to 60 minutes, 0.0% 60 minutes or more (2005-2009 5-year est.)

LINCOLN (city). County seat. Covers a land area of 5.919 square miles and a water area of 0 square miles. Located at 40.15° N. Lat; 89.36° W. Long. Elevation is 581 feet.
History: Lincoln was settled in 1853 on land owned by promoter Colonel Latham, who hired Springfield lawyer Abraham Lincoln to draw up the documents for the town lots and decided to name the town Lincoln. The seat of Logan County was changed from Mount Pulaski to Lincoln, which is the only town named for Lincoln with his knowledge and consent.
Population: 15,288 (1990); 15,369 (2000); 14,261 (2010); 13,713 (2015 projected); Race: 94.3% White, 2.3% Black, 1.4% Asian, 2.0% Other, 1.5% Hispanic of any race (2010); Density: 2,409.4 persons per square mile (2010); Average household size: 2.28 (2010); Median age: 38.0 (2010); Males per 100 females: 92.1 (2010); Marriage status: 38.7% never married, 40.5% now married, 7.4% widowed, 13.4% divorced (2005-2009 5-year est.); Foreign born: 1.0% (2005-2009 5-year est.); Ancestry (includes multiple ancestries): 31.1% German, 16.8% American, 13.9% Irish, 9.0% English, 3.2% Italian (2005-2009 5-year est.).
Economy: Single-family building permits issued: 2 (2010); Multi-family building permits issued: 0 (2010); Employment by occupation: 10.4%

management, 17.0% professional, 20.9% services, 25.5% sales, 1.2% farming, 10.5% construction, 14.5% production (2005-2009 5-year est.).
Income: Per capita income: $21,320 (2010); Median household income: $42,241 (2010); Average household income: $50,917 (2010); Percent of households with income of $100,000 or more: 9.3% (2010); Poverty rate: 15.0% (2005-2009 5-year est.).
Taxes: Total city taxes per capita: $155 (2007); City property taxes per capita: $105 (2007).
Education: Percent of population age 25 and over with: High school diploma (including GED) or higher: 88.1% (2010); Bachelor's degree or higher: 20.0% (2010); Master's degree or higher: 6.0% (2010).

School District(s)
Chester-East Lincoln CCSD 61 (PK-08)
    2009-10 Enrollment: 295 . . . . (217) 732-4136
Lincoln CHSD 404 (09-12)
    2009-10 Enrollment: 905 . . . . (217) 732-4131
Lincoln ESD 27 (PK-08)
    2009-10 Enrollment: 1,275 . . . . (217) 732-2522
Lincolnland Technical Ed Ctr (11-12)
    2009-10 Enrollment: n/a . . . . (217) 732-4131
West Lincoln-Broadwell ESD 92 (KG-08)
    2009-10 Enrollment: 156 . . . . (217) 732-2630

Four-year College(s)
Lincoln Christian University (Private, Not-for-profit, Christian Churches and Churches of Christ)
    Fall 2009 Enrollment: 993 . . . . (217) 732-3168
    2010-11 Tuition: In-state $13,680; Out-of-state $13,680
Lincoln College (Private, Not-for-profit)
    Fall 2009 Enrollment: 1,304 . . . . (217) 732-3155
    2010-11 Tuition: In-state $21,000; Out-of-state $21,000
Housing: Homeownership rate: 70.8% (2010); Median home value: $86,246 (2010); Median contract rent: $384 per month (2005-2009 5-year est.); Median year structure built: 1956 (2005-2009 5-year est.).
Hospitals: Abraham Lincoln Memorial Hospital (66 beds)
Safety: Violent crime rate: 47.6 per 10,000 population; Property crime rate: 466.7 per 10,000 population (2010).
Newspapers: Lincoln Courier (Local news; Circulation 7,000); Lincoln Daily News (Local news; Circulation 16,000); Logan County Shopper (Community news; Circulation 5,800)
Transportation: Commute to work: 87.3% car, 0.1% public transportation, 5.4% walk, 5.0% work from home (2005-2009 5-year est.); Travel time to work: 60.9% less than 15 minutes, 12.1% 15 to 30 minutes, 12.6% 30 to 45 minutes, 10.7% 45 to 60 minutes, 3.7% 60 minutes or more (2005-2009 5-year est.); Amtrak: train service available.
Additional Information Contacts
City of Lincoln . . . . (217) 735-2815
    http://www.cityoflincoln-il.gov
Lincoln/Logan County Chamber of Commerce . . . . (217) 735-2385
    http://www.lincolnillinois.com

MIDDLETOWN (village). Covers a land area of 0.240 square miles and a water area of 0 square miles. Located at 40.10° N. Lat; 89.59° W. Long. Elevation is 584 feet.
Population: 436 (1990); 434 (2000); 410 (2010); 391 (2015 projected); Race: 97.8% White, 0.0% Black, 0.5% Asian, 1.7% Other, 1.0% Hispanic of any race (2010); Density: 1,709.5 persons per square mile (2010); Average household size: 2.61 (2010); Median age: 37.6 (2010); Males per 100 females: 100.0 (2010); Marriage status: 14.6% never married, 64.9% now married, 12.7% widowed, 7.9% divorced (2005-2009 5-year est.); Foreign born: 0.0% (2005-2009 5-year est.); Ancestry (includes multiple ancestries): 49.4% American, 24.2% German, 11.1% Irish, 11.1% English, 2.3% Norwegian (2005-2009 5-year est.).
Economy: Employment by occupation: 8.8% management, 10.7% professional, 16.4% services, 32.1% sales, 0.0% farming, 10.1% construction, 22.0% production (2005-2009 5-year est.).
Income: Per capita income: $24,107 (2010); Median household income: $57,713 (2010); Average household income: $63,217 (2010); Percent of households with income of $100,000 or more: 11.5% (2010); Poverty rate: 18.9% (2005-2009 5-year est.).
Taxes: Total city taxes per capita: $23 (2007); City property taxes per capita: $21 (2007).
Education: Percent of population age 25 and over with: High school diploma (including GED) or higher: 91.3% (2010); Bachelor's degree or higher: 17.0% (2010); Master's degree or higher: 4.9% (2010).

School District(s)
New Holland-Middletown Ed 88 (KG-08)
    2009-10 Enrollment: 104 . . . . (217) 445-2421
Housing: Homeownership rate: 78.3% (2010); Median home value: $82,000 (2010); Median contract rent: $354 per month (2005-2009 5-year est.); Median year structure built: 1954 (2005-2009 5-year est.).
Transportation: Commute to work: 96.2% car, 0.0% public transportation, 3.2% walk, 0.0% work from home (2005-2009 5-year est.); Travel time to work: 10.8% less than 15 minutes, 43.9% 15 to 30 minutes, 33.8% 30 to 45 minutes, 6.4% 45 to 60 minutes, 5.1% 60 minutes or more (2005-2009 5-year est.)

MOUNT PULASKI (city). Covers a land area of 1.139 square miles and a water area of 0 square miles. Located at 40.01° N. Lat; 89.28° W. Long. Elevation is 663 feet.
History: Mount Pulaski served as the seat of Logan County from 1847 to 1853.
Population: 1,635 (1990); 1,701 (2000); 1,631 (2010); 1,574 (2015 projected); Race: 99.3% White, 0.0% Black, 0.0% Asian, 0.7% Other, 0.3% Hispanic of any race (2010); Density: 1,432.6 persons per square mile (2010); Average household size: 2.31 (2010); Median age: 42.3 (2010); Males per 100 females: 88.1 (2010); Marriage status: 17.9% never married, 51.6% now married, 20.1% widowed, 10.4% divorced (2005-2009 5-year est.); Foreign born: 0.6% (2005-2009 5-year est.); Ancestry (includes multiple ancestries): 37.4% German, 21.7% American, 17.6% Irish, 8.7% English, 4.1% French (2005-2009 5-year est.).
Economy: Single-family building permits issued: 0 (2010); Multi-family building permits issued: 0 (2010); Employment by occupation: 13.1% management, 16.3% professional, 8.9% services, 23.6% sales, 2.3% farming, 6.7% construction, 29.2% production (2005-2009 5-year est.).
Income: Per capita income: $22,777 (2010); Median household income: $46,069 (2010); Average household income: $53,070 (2010); Percent of households with income of $100,000 or more: 9.1% (2010); Poverty rate: 4.7% (2005-2009 5-year est.).
Taxes: Total city taxes per capita: $151 (2007); City property taxes per capita: $105 (2007).
Education: Percent of population age 25 and over with: High school diploma (including GED) or higher: 86.9% (2010); Bachelor's degree or higher: 21.4% (2010); Master's degree or higher: 6.9% (2010).

School District(s)
Mt Pulaski CUSD 23 (PK-12)
    2009-10 Enrollment: 557 . . . . (217) 792-7222
Housing: Homeownership rate: 81.5% (2010); Median home value: $90,559 (2010); Median contract rent: $361 per month (2005-2009 5-year est.); Median year structure built: 1951 (2005-2009 5-year est.).
Safety: Violent crime rate: 12.9 per 10,000 population; Property crime rate: 83.9 per 10,000 population (2010).
Newspapers: Mount Pulaski Weekly News (Community news; Circulation 1,650)
Transportation: Commute to work: 91.1% car, 0.0% public transportation, 4.2% walk, 2.4% work from home (2005-2009 5-year est.); Travel time to work: 32.2% less than 15 minutes, 29.5% 15 to 30 minutes, 23.0% 30 to 45 minutes, 10.4% 45 to 60 minutes, 5.0% 60 minutes or more (2005-2009 5-year est.)

NEW HOLLAND (village). Covers a land area of 0.287 square miles and a water area of 0 square miles. Located at 40.18° N. Lat; 89.58° W. Long. Elevation is 554 feet.
Population: 330 (1990); 318 (2000); 297 (2010); 287 (2015 projected); Race: 97.6% White, 0.3% Black, 0.0% Asian, 2.0% Other, 1.3% Hispanic of any race (2010); Density: 1,034.6 persons per square mile (2010); Average household size: 2.72 (2010); Median age: 34.9 (2010); Males per 100 females: 94.1 (2010); Marriage status: 9.9% never married, 61.4% now married, 15.8% widowed, 12.9% divorced (2005-2009 5-year est.); Foreign born: 0.0% (2005-2009 5-year est.); Ancestry (includes multiple ancestries): 33.7% German, 25.6% American, 15.0% English, 6.5% Irish, 4.9% Norwegian (2005-2009 5-year est.).
Economy: Employment by occupation: 9.0% management, 13.9% professional, 5.6% services, 48.6% sales, 1.4% farming, 7.6% construction, 13.9% production (2005-2009 5-year est.).
Income: Per capita income: $25,232 (2010); Median household income: $55,978 (2010); Average household income: $69,381 (2010); Percent of households with income of $100,000 or more: 20.2% (2010); Poverty rate: 2.1% (2005-2009 5-year est.).

Taxes: Total city taxes per capita: $42 (2007); City property taxes per capita: $38 (2007).
Education: Percent of population age 25 and over with: High school diploma (including GED) or higher: 91.8% (2010); Bachelor's degree or higher: 18.0% (2010); Master's degree or higher: 3.8% (2010).
Housing: Homeownership rate: 78.9% (2010); Median home value: $83,636 (2010); Median contract rent: $806 per month (2005-2009 5-year est.); Median year structure built: before 1940 (2005-2009 5-year est.).
Transportation: Commute to work: 92.4% car, 0.0% public transportation, 7.6% walk, 0.0% work from home (2005-2009 5-year est.); Travel time to work: 22.9% less than 15 minutes, 47.9% 15 to 30 minutes, 9.7% 30 to 45 minutes, 12.5% 45 to 60 minutes, 6.9% 60 minutes or more (2005-2009 5-year est.)

Macon County

Located in central Illinois; drained by the Sangamon River. Covers a land area of 580.52 square miles, a water area of 4.86 square miles, and is located in the Central Time Zone at 39.85° N. Lat., 88.95° W. Long. The county was founded in 1829. County seat is Decatur.

Macon County is part of the Decatur, IL Metropolitan Statistical Area. The entire metro area includes: Macon County, IL

Weather Station: Decatur   Elevation: 620 feet

	Jan	Feb	Mar	Apr	May	Jun	Jul	Aug	Sep	Oct	Nov	Dec
High	36	41	53	66	76	85	88	86	80	67	53	40
Low	19	23	32	42	52	61	65	64	56	44	35	24
Precip	2.2	2.0	2.7	3.7	4.6	4.0	3.8	3.7	3.1	3.4	3.4	2.7
Snow	6.0	4.3	1.9	0.2	tr	0.0	0.0	0.0	0.0	tr	0.7	5.0

High and Low temperatures in degrees Fahrenheit; Precipitation and Snow in inches

Population: 117,206 (1990); 114,706 (2000); 107,607 (2010); 103,879 (2015 projected); Race: 81.5% White, 14.8% Black, 1.0% Asian, 2.6% Other, 1.4% Hispanic of any race (2010); Density: 185.4 persons per square mile (2010); Average household size: 2.32 (2010); Median age: 39.3 (2010); Males per 100 females: 91.4 (2010).
Religion: Five largest groups: 9.3% Catholic Church, 6.8% The United Methodist Church, 5.7% Lutheran Church—Missouri Synod, 4.8% Southern Baptist Convention, 4.2% Christian Church (Disciples of Christ) (2000).
Economy: Unemployment rate: 10.7% (August 2011); Total civilian labor force: 54,651 (August 2011); Leading industries: 17.2% manufacturing; 16.9% health care and social assistance; 11.9% retail trade (2009); Farms: 708 totaling 290,603 acres (2007); Companies that employ 500 or more persons: 8 (2009); Companies that employ 100 to 499 persons: 52 (2009); Companies that employ less than 100 persons: 2,488 (2009); Black-owned businesses: n/a (2007); Hispanic-owned businesses: 56 (2007); Asian-owned businesses: 181 (2007); Women-owned businesses: 2,544 (2007); Retail sales per capita: $15,688 (2010). Single-family building permits issued: 95 (2010); Multi-family building permits issued: 6 (2010).
Income: Per capita income: $24,654 (2010); Median household income: $45,621 (2010); Average household income: $58,731 (2010); Percent of households with income of $100,000 or more: 13.6% (2010); Poverty rate: 15.1% (2009); Bankruptcy rate: 6.13% (2009).
Taxes: Total county taxes per capita: $162 (2007); County property taxes per capita: $160 (2007).
Education: Percent of population age 25 and over with: High school diploma (including GED) or higher: 87.0% (2010); Bachelor's degree or higher: 20.2% (2010); Master's degree or higher: 6.8% (2010).
Housing: Homeownership rate: 70.6% (2010); Median home value: $85,473 (2010); Median contract rent: $444 per month (2005-2009 5-year est.); Median year structure built: 1960 (2005-2009 5-year est.)
Health: Birth rate: 129.2 per 10,000 population (2009); Death rate: 109.0 per 10,000 population (2009); Age-adjusted cancer mortality rate: 215.6 deaths per 100,000 population (2007); Number of physicians: 24.1 per 10,000 population (2008); Hospital beds: 44.5 per 10,000 population (2007); Hospital admissions: 1,932.7 per 10,000 population (2007).
Environment: Air Quality Index: 84.2% good, 15.8% moderate, 0.0% unhealthy for sensitive individuals, 0.0% unhealthy (percent of days in 2008)
Elections: 2008 Presidential election results: 49.8% Obama, 48.7% McCain, 0.8% Nader
National and State Parks: Lincoln Trail Homestead State Park; Spitler Woods State Park
Additional Information Contacts

Macon County Government . . . . (217) 424-1305
  http://www.maconcounty-il.gov
City of Decatur . . . . (217) 424-2700
  http://www.ci.decatur.il.us
Mount Zion Chamber of Commerce. . . . . (217) 864-2526
  http://www.mtzionchamber.org

Macon County Communities

ARGENTA (village). Covers a land area of 0.560 square miles and a water area of 0 square miles. Located at 39.98° N. Lat; 88.82° W. Long. Elevation is 686 feet.
Population: 984 (1990); 921 (2000); 808 (2010); 758 (2015 projected); Race: 98.4% White, 0.1% Black, 0.0% Asian, 1.5% Other, 0.4% Hispanic of any race (2010); Density: 1,442.1 persons per square mile (2010); Average household size: 2.47 (2010); Median age: 38.6 (2010); Males per 100 females: 99.5 (2010); Marriage status: 22.7% never married, 54.8% now married, 10.5% widowed, 12.1% divorced (2005-2009 5-year est.); Foreign born: 1.7% (2005-2009 5-year est.); Ancestry (includes multiple ancestries): 28.6% German, 16.6% American, 13.3% Irish, 12.6% English, 6.0% French (2005-2009 5-year est.).
Economy: Single-family building permits issued: 1 (2010); Multi-family building permits issued: 0 (2010); Employment by occupation: 2.2% management, 22.0% professional, 8.6% services, 29.1% sales, 1.0% farming, 11.9% construction, 25.2% production (2005-2009 5-year est.).
Income: Per capita income: $26,500 (2010); Median household income: $62,005 (2010); Average household income: $65,352 (2010); Percent of households with income of $100,000 or more: 13.8% (2010); Poverty rate: 7.7% (2005-2009 5-year est.).
Taxes: Total city taxes per capita: $137 (2007); City property taxes per capita: $134 (2007).
Education: Percent of population age 25 and over with: High school diploma (including GED) or higher: 92.4% (2010); Bachelor's degree or higher: 12.7% (2010); Master's degree or higher: 3.3% (2010).
School District(s)
Argenta-Oreana CUSD 1 (PK-12)
    2009-10 Enrollment: 1,063 . . . . (217) 795-2313
Housing: Homeownership rate: 82.9% (2010); Median home value: $96,538 (2010); Median contract rent: $335 per month (2005-2009 5-year est.); Median year structure built: 1954 (2005-2009 5-year est.).
Transportation: Commute to work: 92.5% car, 0.0% public transportation, 1.3% walk, 0.0% work from home (2005-2009 5-year est.); Travel time to work: 28.7% less than 15 minutes, 44.5% 15 to 30 minutes, 19.5% 30 to 45 minutes, 3.3% 45 to 60 minutes, 4.0% 60 minutes or more (2005-2009 5-year est.)

BLUE MOUND (village). Covers a land area of 0.595 square miles and a water area of 0 square miles. Located at 39.70° N. Lat; 89.12° W. Long. Elevation is 623 feet.
Population: 1,226 (1990); 1,129 (2000); 1,015 (2010); 961 (2015 projected); Race: 99.5% White, 0.1% Black, 0.0% Asian, 0.4% Other, 0.2% Hispanic of any race (2010); Density: 1,707.2 persons per square mile (2010); Average household size: 2.44 (2010); Median age: 38.6 (2010); Males per 100 females: 91.9 (2010); Marriage status: 12.4% never married, 70.8% now married, 7.4% widowed, 9.5% divorced (2005-2009 5-year est.); Foreign born: 0.0% (2005-2009 5-year est.); Ancestry (includes multiple ancestries): 21.7% German, 21.1% American, 18.2% Irish, 13.9% English, 3.3% Italian (2005-2009 5-year est.).
Economy: Single-family building permits issued: 1 (2010); Multi-family building permits issued: 2 (2010); Employment by occupation: 7.5% management, 7.8% professional, 11.1% services, 28.2% sales, 0.5% farming, 22.3% construction, 22.6% production (2005-2009 5-year est.).
Income: Per capita income: $25,354 (2010); Median household income: $55,725 (2010); Average household income: $62,067 (2010); Percent of households with income of $100,000 or more: 13.7% (2010); Poverty rate: 10.0% (2005-2009 5-year est.).
Taxes: Total city taxes per capita: $133 (2007); City property taxes per capita: $104 (2007).
Education: Percent of population age 25 and over with: High school diploma (including GED) or higher: 91.9% (2010); Bachelor's degree or higher: 16.6% (2010); Master's degree or higher: 4.0% (2010).
School District(s)
Meridian CUSD 15 (PK-12)
    2009-10 Enrollment: 1,074 . . . . (217) 764-5269

Housing: Homeownership rate: 77.4% (2010); Median home value: $85,833 (2010); Median contract rent: $395 per month (2005-2009 5-year est.); Median year structure built: 1959 (2005-2009 5-year est.).
Safety: Violent crime rate: 40.2 per 10,000 population; Property crime rate: 170.7 per 10,000 population (2010).
Newspapers: Blue Mound Leader (Community news; Circulation 800)
Transportation: Commute to work: 92.2% car, 0.0% public transportation, 0.3% walk, 5.1% work from home (2005-2009 5-year est.); Travel time to work: 19.9% less than 15 minutes, 31.0% 15 to 30 minutes, 40.6% 30 to 45 minutes, 5.3% 45 to 60 minutes, 3.2% 60 minutes or more (2005-2009 5-year est.)

BOODY (unincorporated postal area, zip code 62514). Covers a land area of 4.047 square miles and a water area of 0 square miles. Located at 39.76° N. Lat; 89.05° W. Long. Elevation is 682 feet.
Population: 340 (2000); Race: 100.0% White, 0.0% Black, 0.0% Asian, 0.0% Other, 0.0% Hispanic of any race (2000); Density: 84.0 persons per square mile (2000); Age: 19.8% under 18, 9.7% over 64 (2000); Marriage status: 21.8% never married, 64.3% now married, 4.8% widowed, 9.1% divorced (2000); Foreign born: 0.0% (2000); Ancestry (includes multiple ancestries): 28.5% German, 28.2% English, 19.5% Irish, 19.1% American, 8.1% French (2000).
Economy: Employment by occupation: 3.8% management, 18.9% professional, 29.6% services, 18.9% sales, 0.0% farming, 25.8% construction, 3.1% production (2000).
Income: Per capita income: $17,957 (2000); Median household income: $39,875 (2000); Poverty rate: 2.0% (2000).
Education: Percent of population age 25 and over with: High school diploma (including GED) or higher: 96.3% (2000); Bachelor's degree or higher: 2.3% (2000).
Housing: Homeownership rate: 85.0% (2000); Median home value: $36,500 (2000); Median contract rent: n/a per month (2000); Median year structure built: before 1940 (2000).
Transportation: Commute to work: 91.2% car, 0.0% public transportation, 1.9% walk, 6.9% work from home (2000); Travel time to work: 2.0% less than 15 minutes, 75.0% 15 to 30 minutes, 18.9% 30 to 45 minutes, 4.1% 45 to 60 minutes, 0.0% 60 minutes or more (2000)

DECATUR (city). County seat. Covers a land area of 41.560 square miles and a water area of 4.317 square miles. Located at 39.85° N. Lat; 88.94° W. Long. Elevation is 673 feet.
History: Decatur was named and designated the seat of Macon County in 1829, though there was no settlement here at the time. In 1830 Abraham Lincoln and his family settled nearby, and in 1836 Richard J. Oglesby, who was to become a senator, three times governor of the state, and a friend of Lincoln's. First an agricultural center, manufacturing began in Decatur with the arrival of the railroad in 1854. Coal was discovered under the city in 1874.
Population: 85,750 (1990); 81,860 (2000); 75,427 (2010); 72,186 (2015 projected); Race: 74.9% White, 20.7% Black, 1.2% Asian, 3.2% Other, 1.7% Hispanic of any race (2010); Density: 1,814.9 persons per square mile (2010); Average household size: 2.25 (2010); Median age: 38.2 (2010); Males per 100 females: 88.8 (2010); Marriage status: 30.6% never married, 48.3% now married, 8.6% widowed, 12.5% divorced (2005-2009 5-year est.); Foreign born: 2.2% (2005-2009 5-year est.); Ancestry (includes multiple ancestries): 21.4% German, 13.5% Irish, 12.4% American, 10.6% English, 2.7% Italian (2005-2009 5-year est.).
Economy: Unemployment rate: 12.1% (August 2011); Total civilian labor force: 37,224 (August 2011); Single-family building permits issued: 20 (2010); Multi-family building permits issued: 0 (2010); Employment by occupation: 9.9% management, 20.7% professional, 19.1% services, 25.5% sales, 0.3% farming, 7.3% construction, 17.2% production (2005-2009 5-year est.).
Income: Per capita income: $22,337 (2010); Median household income: $39,478 (2010); Average household income: $51,940 (2010); Percent of households with income of $100,000 or more: 10.6% (2010); Poverty rate: 20.0% (2005-2009 5-year est.).
Taxes: Total city taxes per capita: $410 (2007); City property taxes per capita: $155 (2007).
Education: Percent of population age 25 and over with: High school diploma (including GED) or higher: 84.8% (2010); Bachelor's degree or higher: 19.8% (2010); Master's degree or higher: 6.7% (2010).

School District(s)
Decatur Area Technical Academy (11-12)
    2009-10 Enrollment: n/a . . . . (217) 424-3070

Decatur SD 61 (PK-12)
    2009-10 Enrollment: 9,189 . . . . (217) 424-3011
Heartland Region
    2009-10 Enrollment: n/a . . . . (217) 424-3071
Macon/Piatt Roe (01-12)
    2009-10 Enrollment: n/a . . . . (217) 872-3721
Four-year College(s)
Millikin University (Private, Not-for-profit, Presbyterian Church (USA))
    Fall 2009 Enrollment: 2,314. . . . . (217) 424-6211
    2010-11 Tuition: In-state $27,525; Out-of-state $27,525
Two-year College(s)
Mr John's School of Cosmetology Esthetics & Nails (Private, For-profit)
    Fall 2009 Enrollment: 79 . . . . (217) 423-8173
Richland Community College (Public)
    Fall 2009 Enrollment: 3,595. (217) 875-7200
    2010-11 Tuition: In-state $12,918; Out-of-state $13,911
Housing: Homeownership rate: 65.4% (2010); Median home value: $71,845 (2010); Median contract rent: $449 per month (2005-2009 5-year est.); Median year structure built: 1958 (2005-2009 5-year est.).
Hospitals: Decatur Memorial Hospital (314 beds); St. Mary's Hospital (371 beds)
Safety: Violent crime rate: 62.5 per 10,000 population; Property crime rate: 416.9 per 10,000 population (2010).
Newspapers: Decatur Tribune (Community news; Circulation 8,000); Herald & Review (Local news; Circulation 35,799); Prairie Shopper (Local news)
Transportation: Commute to work: 93.0% car, 1.6% public transportation, 2.5% walk, 1.3% work from home (2005-2009 5-year est.); Travel time to work: 52.5% less than 15 minutes, 35.7% 15 to 30 minutes, 5.1% 30 to 45 minutes, 3.9% 45 to 60 minutes, 2.8% 60 minutes or more (2005-2009 5-year est.)
Airports: Decatur (general aviation)
Additional Information Contacts
City of Decatur . . . . (217) 424-2700
    http://www.ci.decatur.il.us

FORSYTH (village). Covers a land area of 2.104 square miles and a water area of 0 square miles. Located at 39.92° N. Lat; 88.95° W. Long. Elevation is 679 feet.
Population: 1,766 (1990); 2,434 (2000); 2,961 (2010); 3,170 (2015 projected); Race: 95.3% White, 2.4% Black, 1.7% Asian, 0.6% Other, 1.0% Hispanic of any race (2010); Density: 1,407.0 persons per square mile (2010); Average household size: 2.51 (2010); Median age: 43.3 (2010); Males per 100 females: 94.7 (2010); Marriage status: 21.1% never married, 71.2% now married, 5.4% widowed, 2.3% divorced (2005-2009 5-year est.); Foreign born: 5.6% (2005-2009 5-year est.); Ancestry (includes multiple ancestries): 23.2% German, 14.1% Irish, 11.4% English, 10.0% American, 5.2% Polish (2005-2009 5-year est.).
Economy: Single-family building permits issued: 23 (2010); Multi-family building permits issued: 0 (2010); Employment by occupation: 25.9% management, 25.7% professional, 11.6% services, 19.4% sales, 0.0% farming, 5.7% construction, 11.8% production (2005-2009 5-year est.).
Income: Per capita income: $42,803 (2010); Median household income: $82,857 (2010); Average household income: $107,421 (2010); Percent of households with income of $100,000 or more: 39.8% (2010); Poverty rate: 8.6% (2005-2009 5-year est.).
Taxes: Total city taxes per capita: $229 (2007); City property taxes per capita: $150 (2007).
Education: Percent of population age 25 and over with: High school diploma (including GED) or higher: 95.0% (2010); Bachelor's degree or higher: 39.2% (2010); Master's degree or higher: 12.5% (2010).
School District(s)
Maroa Forsyth CUSD 2 (PK-12)
    2009-10 Enrollment: 1,190 . . . . (217) 794-3488
Housing: Homeownership rate: 85.2% (2010); Median home value: $183,140 (2010); Median contract rent: $524 per month (2005-2009 5-year est.); Median year structure built: 1991 (2005-2009 5-year est.).
Transportation: Commute to work: 93.3% car, 3.3% public transportation, 0.0% walk, 2.5% work from home (2005-2009 5-year est.); Travel time to work: 42.6% less than 15 minutes, 42.2% 15 to 30 minutes, 3.1% 30 to 45 minutes, 7.5% 45 to 60 minutes, 4.5% 60 minutes or more (2005-2009 5-year est.)

HARRISTOWN (village). Covers a land area of 1.856 square miles and a water area of 0 square miles. Located at 39.84° N. Lat; 89.06° W. Long. Elevation is 689 feet.
Population: 1,364 (1990); 1,338 (2000); 1,230 (2010); 1,169 (2015 projected); Race: 96.8% White, 1.1% Black, 0.2% Asian, 2.0% Other, 0.5% Hispanic of any race (2010); Density: 662.7 persons per square mile (2010); Average household size: 2.55 (2010); Median age: 41.8 (2010); Males per 100 females: 100.0 (2010); Marriage status: 16.8% never married, 62.8% now married, 8.6% widowed, 11.8% divorced (2005-2009 5-year est.); Foreign born: 0.5% (2005-2009 5-year est.); Ancestry (includes multiple ancestries): 27.2% German, 15.7% American, 12.4% English, 10.8% Irish, 3.3% Scotch-Irish (2005-2009 5-year est.).
Economy: Single-family building permits issued: 0 (2010); Multi-family building permits issued: 0 (2010); Employment by occupation: 9.0% management, 15.9% professional, 14.7% services, 29.6% sales, 0.0% farming, 16.3% construction, 14.5% production (2005-2009 5-year est.).
Income: Per capita income: $24,705 (2010); Median household income: $57,061 (2010); Average household income: $62,915 (2010); Percent of households with income of $100,000 or more: 13.1% (2010); Poverty rate: 8.7% (2005-2009 5-year est.).
Taxes: Total city taxes per capita: $21 (2007); City property taxes per capita: $13 (2007).
Education: Percent of population age 25 and over with: High school diploma (including GED) or higher: 86.7% (2010); Bachelor's degree or higher: 14.0% (2010); Master's degree or higher: 5.5% (2010).

School District(s)
Sangamon Valley CUSD 9 (PK-12)
    2009-10 Enrollment: 830 . . . . (217) 668-2338
Housing: Homeownership rate: 87.1% (2010); Median home value: $90,000 (2010); Median contract rent: $383 per month (2005-2009 5-year est.); Median year structure built: 1958 (2005-2009 5-year est.).
Transportation: Commute to work: 95.4% car, 0.4% public transportation, 0.0% walk, 4.3% work from home (2005-2009 5-year est.); Travel time to work: 22.7% less than 15 minutes, 62.9% 15 to 30 minutes, 8.6% 30 to 45 minutes, 2.8% 45 to 60 minutes, 3.0% 60 minutes or more (2005-2009 5-year est.)

LONG CREEK (village). Covers a land area of 2.658 square miles and a water area of 0 square miles. Located at 39.80° N. Lat; 88.85° W. Long. Elevation is 669 feet.
Population: 1,330 (1990); 1,364 (2000); 1,419 (2010); 1,435 (2015 projected); Race: 97.2% White, 0.6% Black, 0.9% Asian, 1.3% Other, 0.6% Hispanic of any race (2010); Density: 533.9 persons per square mile (2010); Average household size: 2.59 (2010); Median age: 43.1 (2010); Males per 100 females: 97.1 (2010); Marriage status: 16.2% never married, 72.6% now married, 5.8% widowed, 5.4% divorced (2005-2009 5-year est.); Foreign born: 0.8% (2005-2009 5-year est.); Ancestry (includes multiple ancestries): 35.8% German, 17.6% Irish, 15.9% English, 14.5% American, 3.7% Italian (2005-2009 5-year est.).
Economy: Single-family building permits issued: 3 (2010); Multi-family building permits issued: 0 (2010); Employment by occupation: 10.2% management, 18.2% professional, 19.6% services, 24.1% sales, 0.9% farming, 13.5% construction, 13.5% production (2005-2009 5-year est.).
Income: Per capita income: $30,199 (2010); Median household income: $67,092 (2010); Average household income: $78,647 (2010); Percent of households with income of $100,000 or more: 21.6% (2010); Poverty rate: 4.8% (2005-2009 5-year est.).
Taxes: Total city taxes per capita: $21 (2007); City property taxes per capita: $11 (2007).
Education: Percent of population age 25 and over with: High school diploma (including GED) or higher: 89.4% (2010); Bachelor's degree or higher: 17.0% (2010); Master's degree or higher: 6.2% (2010).
Housing: Homeownership rate: 90.3% (2010); Median home value: $121,311 (2010); Median contract rent: $481 per month (2005-2009 5-year est.); Median year structure built: 1972 (2005-2009 5-year est.).
Transportation: Commute to work: 92.8% car, 0.0% public transportation, 2.5% walk, 2.3% work from home (2005-2009 5-year est.); Travel time to work: 33.8% less than 15 minutes, 53.2% 15 to 30 minutes, 4.8% 30 to 45 minutes, 3.0% 45 to 60 minutes, 5.1% 60 minutes or more (2005-2009 5-year est.)

MACON (city). Covers a land area of 0.881 square miles and a water area of 0 square miles. Located at 39.70° N. Lat; 89.00° W. Long. Elevation is 715 feet.

Population: 1,376 (1990); 1,213 (2000); 1,108 (2010); 1,060 (2015 projected); Race: 98.9% White, 0.2% Black, 0.4% Asian, 0.5% Other, 0.7% Hispanic of any race (2010); Density: 1,257.1 persons per square mile (2010); Average household size: 2.41 (2010); Median age: 41.2 (2010); Males per 100 females: 92.7 (2010); Marriage status: 21.5% never married, 58.4% now married, 7.3% widowed, 12.7% divorced (2005-2009 5-year est.); Foreign born: 0.0% (2005-2009 5-year est.); Ancestry (includes multiple ancestries): 34.8% German, 23.0% American, 16.4% Irish, 11.7% English, 4.3% French (2005-2009 5-year est.).
Economy: Single-family building permits issued: 1 (2010); Multi-family building permits issued: 4 (2010); Employment by occupation: 10.8% management, 19.3% professional, 12.6% services, 29.2% sales, 0.0% farming, 16.1% construction, 12.0% production (2005-2009 5-year est.).
Income: Per capita income: $23,835 (2010); Median household income: $47,896 (2010); Average household income: $58,602 (2010); Percent of households with income of $100,000 or more: 11.6% (2010); Poverty rate: 7.5% (2005-2009 5-year est.).
Taxes: Total city taxes per capita: $179 (2007); City property taxes per capita: $163 (2007).
Education: Percent of population age 25 and over with: High school diploma (including GED) or higher: 92.5% (2010); Bachelor's degree or higher: 9.2% (2010); Master's degree or higher: 2.8% (2010).

School District(s)
Meridian CUSD 15 (PK-12)
    2009-10 Enrollment: 1,074 . . . . (217) 764-5269
Housing: Homeownership rate: 77.9% (2010); Median home value: $88,780 (2010); Median contract rent: $403 per month (2005-2009 5-year est.); Median year structure built: 1954 (2005-2009 5-year est.).
Transportation: Commute to work: 94.3% car, 0.0% public transportation, 3.3% walk, 2.1% work from home (2005-2009 5-year est.); Travel time to work: 28.5% less than 15 minutes, 44.5% 15 to 30 minutes, 15.8% 30 to 45 minutes, 4.8% 45 to 60 minutes, 6.3% 60 minutes or more (2005-2009 5-year est.)

MAROA (city). Covers a land area of 0.673 square miles and a water area of 0 square miles. Located at 40.03° N. Lat; 88.95° W. Long. Elevation is 725 feet.
Population: 1,621 (1990); 1,654 (2000); 1,547 (2010); 1,491 (2015 projected); Race: 98.8% White, 0.2% Black, 0.3% Asian, 0.6% Other, 1.0% Hispanic of any race (2010); Density: 2,297.3 persons per square mile (2010); Average household size: 2.44 (2010); Median age: 40.1 (2010); Males per 100 females: 101.2 (2010); Marriage status: 26.9% never married, 55.0% now married, 6.7% widowed, 11.4% divorced (2005-2009 5-year est.); Foreign born: 1.5% (2005-2009 5-year est.); Ancestry (includes multiple ancestries): 24.5% German, 22.5% American, 14.4% Irish, 12.3% English, 4.4% Dutch (2005-2009 5-year est.).
Economy: Single-family building permits issued: 2 (2010); Multi-family building permits issued: 0 (2010); Employment by occupation: 10.5% management, 17.9% professional, 15.4% services, 25.3% sales, 1.9% farming, 15.4% construction, 13.7% production (2005-2009 5-year est.).
Income: Per capita income: $27,170 (2010); Median household income: $54,318 (2010); Average household income: $66,224 (2010); Percent of households with income of $100,000 or more: 15.7% (2010); Poverty rate: 5.1% (2005-2009 5-year est.).
Taxes: Total city taxes per capita: $201 (2007); City property taxes per capita: $151 (2007).
Education: Percent of population age 25 and over with: High school diploma (including GED) or higher: 89.7% (2010); Bachelor's degree or higher: 14.2% (2010); Master's degree or higher: 2.7% (2010).

School District(s)
Maroa Forsyth CUSD 2 (PK-12)
    2009-10 Enrollment: 1,190 . . . . (217) 794-3488
Housing: Homeownership rate: 75.1% (2010); Median home value: $87,973 (2010); Median contract rent: $392 per month (2005-2009 5-year est.); Median year structure built: 1968 (2005-2009 5-year est.).
Safety: Violent crime rate: 39.0 per 10,000 population; Property crime rate: 117.0 per 10,000 population (2010).
Transportation: Commute to work: 96.8% car, 0.0% public transportation, 1.4% walk, 0.8% work from home (2005-2009 5-year est.); Travel time to work: 33.5% less than 15 minutes, 37.6% 15 to 30 minutes, 19.2% 30 to 45 minutes, 5.1% 45 to 60 minutes, 4.6% 60 minutes or more (2005-2009 5-year est.)

MOUNT ZION

MOUNT ZION (village). Covers a land area of 3.768 square miles and a water area of <.001 square miles. Located at 39.77° N. Lat; 88.87° W. Long. Elevation is 696 feet.

Population: 4,857 (1990); 4,845 (2000); 4,694 (2010); 4,658 (2015 projected); Race: 97.2% White, 0.1% Black, 1.4% Asian, 1.3% Other, 0.3% Hispanic of any race (2010); Density: 1,245.7 persons per square mile (2010); Average household size: 2.52 (2010); Median age: 40.6 (2010); Males per 100 females: 99.2 (2010); Marriage status: 18.1% never married, 69.3% now married, 3.6% widowed, 9.1% divorced (2005-2009 5-year est.); Foreign born: 1.0% (2005-2009 5-year est.); Ancestry (includes multiple ancestries): 27.0% German, 18.7% American, 15.6% English, 8.3% Irish, 5.7% Scottish (2005-2009 5-year est.).

Economy: Single-family building permits issued: 19 (2010); Multi-family building permits issued: 0 (2010); Employment by occupation: 17.5% management, 25.8% professional, 11.4% services, 22.3% sales, 0.7% farming, 9.3% construction, 13.1% production (2005-2009 5-year est.).

Income: Per capita income: $28,147 (2010); Median household income: $63,784 (2010); Average household income: $71,371 (2010); Percent of households with income of $100,000 or more: 20.1% (2010); Poverty rate: 2.9% (2005-2009 5-year est.).

Taxes: Total city taxes per capita: $219 (2007); City property taxes per capita: $152 (2007).

Education: Percent of population age 25 and over with: High school diploma (including GED) or higher: 92.8% (2010); Bachelor's degree or higher: 24.0% (2010); Master's degree or higher: 7.9% (2010).

School District(s)

Mt Zion CUSD 3 (PK-12)

    2009-10 Enrollment: 2,554 . . . . (217) 864-2366

Housing: Homeownership rate: 77.2% (2010); Median home value: $120,059 (2010); Median contract rent: $448 per month (2005-2009 5-year est.); Median year structure built: 1975 (2005-2009 5-year est.).

Safety: Violent crime rate: 7.7 per 10,000 population; Property crime rate: 103.6 per 10,000 population (2010).

Newspapers: Mount Zion Region News (Local news; Circulation 1,800)

Transportation: Commute to work: 96.6% car, 0.0% public transportation, 0.0% walk, 2.0% work from home (2005-2009 5-year est.); Travel time to work: 27.5% less than 15 minutes, 60.7% 15 to 30 minutes, 5.3% 30 to 45 minutes, 1.3% 45 to 60 minutes, 5.3% 60 minutes or more (2005-2009 5-year est.).

Additional Information Contacts

Mount Zion Chamber of Commerce. . . . . (217) 864-2526
    http://www.mtzionchamber.org

NIANTIC

NIANTIC (village). Covers a land area of 1.075 square miles and a water area of 0 square miles. Located at 39.85° N. Lat; 89.16° W. Long. Elevation is 604 feet.

Population: 699 (1990); 738 (2000); 655 (2010); 620 (2015 projected); Race: 98.9% White, 0.3% Black, 0.0% Asian, 0.8% Other, 0.6% Hispanic of any race (2010); Density: 609.5 persons per square mile (2010); Average household size: 2.55 (2010); Median age: 35.1 (2010); Males per 100 females: 96.1 (2010); Marriage status: 19.3% never married, 64.4% now married, 8.8% widowed, 7.5% divorced (2005-2009 5-year est.); Foreign born: 0.9% (2005-2009 5-year est.); Ancestry (includes multiple ancestries): 20.3% English, 20.0% Irish, 19.4% German, 17.0% American, 4.7% Italian (2005-2009 5-year est.).

Economy: Single-family building permits issued: 0 (2010); Multi-family building permits issued: 0 (2010); Employment by occupation: 8.2% management, 18.8% professional, 10.0% services, 21.4% sales, 2.9% farming, 14.1% construction, 24.6% production (2005-2009 5-year est.).

Income: Per capita income: $24,104 (2010); Median household income: $53,639 (2010); Average household income: $61,313 (2010); Percent of households with income of $100,000 or more: 12.5% (2010); Poverty rate: 1.6% (2005-2009 5-year est.).

Taxes: Total city taxes per capita: $103 (2007); City property taxes per capita: $63 (2007).

Education: Percent of population age 25 and over with: High school diploma (including GED) or higher: 92.9% (2010); Bachelor's degree or higher: 14.2% (2010); Master's degree or higher: 2.2% (2010).

School District(s)

Sangamon Valley CUSD 9 (PK-12)

    2009-10 Enrollment: 830 . . . . (217) 668-2338

Housing: Homeownership rate: 81.3% (2010); Median home value: $89,423 (2010); Median contract rent: $348 per month (2005-2009 5-year est.); Median year structure built: 1957 (2005-2009 5-year est.).

OAKLEY

OAKLEY (unincorporated postal area, zip code 62552). Covers a land area of 38.230 square miles and a water area of 0.004 square miles. Located at 39.87° N. Lat; 88.81° W. Long. Elevation is 689 feet.

Population: 1,063 (2000); Race: 100.0% White, 0.0% Black, 0.0% Asian, 0.0% Other, 0.0% Hispanic of any race (2000); Density: 27.8 persons per square mile (2000); Age: 19.7% under 18, 13.8% over 64 (2000); Marriage status: 13.9% never married, 75.1% now married, 2.7% widowed, 8.3% divorced (2000); Foreign born: 0.0% (2000); Ancestry (includes multiple ancestries): 22.4% German, 16.9% English, 10.9% American, 5.1% Irish (2000).

Economy: Employment by occupation: 7.5% management, 15.7% professional, 16.1% services, 25.7% sales, 1.4% farming, 17.3% construction, 16.3% production (2000).

Income: Per capita income: $19,102 (2000); Median household income: $49,228 (2000); Poverty rate: 3.3% (2000).

Education: Percent of population age 25 and over with: High school diploma (including GED) or higher: 82.6% (2000); Bachelor's degree or higher: 5.3% (2000).

Housing: Homeownership rate: 85.2% (2000); Median home value: $80,600 (2000); Median contract rent: $373 per month (2000); Median year structure built: 1965 (2000).

Transportation: Commute to work: 96.9% car, 0.0% public transportation, 1.2% walk, 2.0% work from home (2000); Travel time to work: 16.8% less than 15 minutes, 59.1% 15 to 30 minutes, 11.2% 30 to 45 minutes, 3.2% 45 to 60 minutes, 9.6% 60 minutes or more (2000)

OREANA

OREANA (village). Covers a land area of 0.500 square miles and a water area of 0 square miles. Located at 39.93° N. Lat; 88.86° W. Long. Elevation is 689 feet.

Population: 847 (1990); 892 (2000); 830 (2010); 797 (2015 projected); Race: 97.7% White, 0.1% Black, 0.4% Asian, 1.8% Other, 0.7% Hispanic of any race (2010); Density: 1,661.2 persons per square mile (2010); Average household size: 2.52 (2010); Median age: 40.9 (2010); Males per 100 females: 104.4 (2010); Marriage status: 18.8% never married, 69.7% now married, 4.8% widowed, 6.7% divorced (2005-2009 5-year est.); Foreign born: 0.0% (2005-2009 5-year est.); Ancestry (includes multiple ancestries): 31.9% German, 16.2% Irish, 15.0% English, 13.1% American, 6.3% French (2005-2009 5-year est.).

Economy: Single-family building permits issued: 0 (2010); Multi-family building permits issued: 0 (2010); Employment by occupation: 7.6% management, 21.5% professional, 16.6% services, 21.4% sales, 0.0% farming, 14.4% construction, 18.5% production (2005-2009 5-year est.).

Income: Per capita income: $26,938 (2010); Median household income: $62,059 (2010); Average household income: $67,924 (2010); Percent of households with income of $100,000 or more: 17.3% (2010); Poverty rate: 1.8% (2005-2009 5-year est.).

Taxes: Total city taxes per capita: $83 (2007); City property taxes per capita: $68 (2007).

Education: Percent of population age 25 and over with: High school diploma (including GED) or higher: 93.9% (2010); Bachelor's degree or higher: 14.0% (2010); Master's degree or higher: 4.2% (2010).

School District(s)

Argenta-Oreana CUSD 1 (PK-12)

    2009-10 Enrollment: 1,063 . . . . (217) 795-2313

Housing: Homeownership rate: 87.3% (2010); Median home value: $96,364 (2010); Median contract rent: $376 per month (2005-2009 5-year est.); Median year structure built: 1963 (2005-2009 5-year est.).

Transportation: Commute to work: 96.3% car, 0.0% public transportation, 0.6% walk, 2.6% work from home (2005-2009 5-year est.); Travel time to work: 42.8% less than 15 minutes, 41.7% 15 to 30 minutes, 5.9% 30 to 45 minutes, 3.8% 45 to 60 minutes, 5.9% 60 minutes or more (2005-2009 5-year est.)

WARRENSBURG

WARRENSBURG (village). Covers a land area of 0.678 square miles and a water area of 0 square miles. Located at 39.93° N. Lat; 89.06° W. Long. Elevation is 705 feet.

Population: 1,293 (1990); 1,289 (2000); 1,207 (2010); 1,162 (2015 projected); Race: 96.9% White, 0.9% Black, 0.1% Asian, 2.1% Other, 0.7% Hispanic of any race (2010); Density: 1,779.7 persons per square mile

(2010); Average household size: 2.56 (2010); Median age: 37.7 (2010); Males per 100 females: 98.2 (2010); Marriage status: 22.3% never married, 62.4% now married, 2.8% widowed, 12.5% divorced (2005-2009 5-year est.); Foreign born: 0.5% (2005-2009 5-year est.); Ancestry (includes multiple ancestries): 34.9% German, 18.5% Irish, 18.0% American, 11.6% English, 7.4% French (2005-2009 5-year est.).

Economy: Single-family building permits issued: 0 (2010); Multi-family building permits issued: 0 (2010); Employment by occupation: 9.3% management, 14.7% professional, 18.2% services, 24.7% sales, 0.0% farming, 14.3% construction, 18.7% production (2005-2009 5-year est.).

Income: Per capita income: $27,871 (2010); Median household income: $62,674 (2010); Average household income: $70,207 (2010); Percent of households with income of $100,000 or more: 17.7% (2010); Poverty rate: 6.7% (2005-2009 5-year est.).

Taxes: Total city taxes per capita: $114 (2007); City property taxes per capita: $110 (2007).

Education: Percent of population age 25 and over with: High school diploma (including GED) or higher: 91.3% (2010); Bachelor's degree or higher: 22.8% (2010); Master's degree or higher: 4.6% (2010).

School District(s)

Warrensburg-Latham CUSD 11 (PK-12)

2009-10 Enrollment: 1,074 . . . . (217) 672-3514

Housing: Homeownership rate: 75.5% (2010); Median home value: $105,476 (2010); Median contract rent: $331 per month (2005-2009 5-year est.); Median year structure built: 1970 (2005-2009 5-year est.).

Safety: Violent crime rate: 8.8 per 10,000 population; Property crime rate: 105.6 per 10,000 population (2010).

Transportation: Commute to work: 94.6% car, 0.3% public transportation, 1.0% walk, 3.5% work from home (2005-2009 5-year est.); Travel time to work: 21.2% less than 15 minutes, 64.8% 15 to 30 minutes, 6.9% 30 to 45 minutes, 3.6% 45 to 60 minutes, 3.5% 60 minutes or more (2005-2009 5-year est.)

Macoupin County

Located in southwest central Illinois; drained by Macoupin, Cahokia, and Otter Creeks. Covers a land area of 863.57 square miles, a water area of 4.04 square miles, and is located in the Central Time Zone at 39.23° N. Lat., 89.87° W. Long. The county was founded in 1829. County seat is Carlinville.

Macoupin County is part of the St. Louis, MO-IL Metropolitan Statistical Area. The entire metro area includes: Bond County, IL; Calhoun County, IL; Clinton County, IL; Jersey County, IL; Macoupin County, IL; Madison County, IL; Monroe County, IL; St. Clair County, IL; Crawford County, MO (pt.); Franklin County, MO; Jefferson County, MO; Lincoln County, MO; St. Charles County, MO; St. Louis County, MO; Warren County, MO; Washington County, MO; St. Louis city, MO

Weather Station: Carlinville										Elevation: 629 feet		
	Jan	Feb	Mar	Apr	May	Jun	Jul	Aug	Sep	Oct	Nov	Dec
High	36	42	53	65	75	84	87	86	79	67	53	40
Low	21	25	33	43	53	63	66	64	56	45	35	25
Precip	2.1	2.1	3.1	4.0	4.0	3.5	3.6	3.2	3.2	3.2	3.7	2.8
Snow	5.9	4.4	2.7	0.4	tr	0.0	0.0	0.0	0.0	tr	0.9	3.4

High and Low temperatures in degrees Fahrenheit; Precipitation and Snow in inches

Weather Station: Virden										Elevation: 674 feet		
	Jan	Feb	Mar	Apr	May	Jun	Jul	Aug	Sep	Oct	Nov	Dec
High	37	41	53	66	76	84	87	86	80	68	53	40
Low	21	25	33	44	54	63	67	65	57	46	36	24
Precip	1.9	2.1	2.8	3.5	4.2	3.8	3.5	2.7	2.9	3.1	3.5	2.5
Snow	5.1	5.6	3.0	0.4	0.0	0.0	0.0	0.0	0.0	tr	0.8	4.6

High and Low temperatures in degrees Fahrenheit; Precipitation and Snow in inches

Population: 47,679 (1990); 49,019 (2000); 48,021 (2010); 47,282 (2015 projected); Race: 97.3% White, 1.1% Black, 0.3% Asian, 1.3% Other, 1.0% Hispanic of any race (2010); Density: 55.6 persons per square mile (2010); Average household size: 2.44 (2010); Median age: 39.8 (2010); Males per 100 females: 95.6 (2010).

Religion: Five largest groups: 14.4% Catholic Church, 9.3% Southern Baptist Convention, 6.4% Lutheran Church—Missouri Synod, 6.2% The United Methodist Church, 2.5% United Church of Christ (2000).

Economy: Unemployment rate: 9.3% (August 2011); Total civilian labor force: 24,040 (August 2011); Leading industries: 20.3% health care and social assistance; 16.7% retail trade; 9.1% accommodation & food services

(2009); Farms: 1,187 totaling 394,228 acres (2007); Companies that employ 500 or more persons: 0 (2009); Companies that employ 100 to 499 persons: 13 (2009); Companies that employ less than 100 persons: 926 (2009); Black-owned businesses: n/a (2007); Hispanic-owned businesses: n/a (2007); Asian-owned businesses: n/a (2007); Women-owned businesses: 1,366 (2007); Retail sales per capita: $10,251 (2010). Single-family building permits issued: 42 (2010); Multi-family building permits issued: 6 (2010).

Income: Per capita income: $22,210 (2010); Median household income: $45,777 (2010); Average household income: $55,236 (2010); Percent of households with income of $100,000 or more: 11.0% (2010); Poverty rate: 12.1% (2009); Bankruptcy rate: 4.07% (2010).

Taxes: Total county taxes per capita: $57 (2007); County property taxes per capita: $56 (2007).

Education: Percent of population age 25 and over with: High school diploma (including GED) or higher: 87.0% (2010); Bachelor's degree or higher: 15.7% (2010); Master's degree or higher: 5.2% (2010).

Housing: Homeownership rate: 79.0% (2010); Median home value: $85,416 (2010); Median contract rent: $377 per month (2005-2009 5-year est.); Median year structure built: 1965 (2005-2009 5-year est.).

Health: Birth rate: 123.3 per 10,000 population (2009); Death rate: 118.3 per 10,000 population (2009); Age-adjusted cancer mortality rate: 203.8 deaths per 100,000 population (2007); Number of physicians: 4.8 per 10,000 population (2008); Hospital beds: 10.4 per 10,000 population (2007); Hospital admissions: 243.8 per 10,000 population (2007).

Environment: Air Quality Index: 95.8% good, 4.2% moderate, 0.0% unhealthy for sensitive individuals, 0.0% unhealthy (percent of days in 2008)

Elections: 2008 Presidential election results: 54.0% Obama, 44.2% McCain, 0.9% Nader

National and State Parks: Beaver Dam State Park

Additional Information Contacts

Macoupin County Government . . . . (217) 854-3214
   http://www.macoupincountyil.gov
Carlinville Community Chamber of Commerce . . . . (217) 854-2141
   http://carlinvillechamber.com
City of Carlinville . . . . (217) 854-4076
   http://www.cityofcarlinville.com
City of Staunton . . . . (618) 635-2233
   http://www.stauntonil.com
Coal Country Chamber of Commerce . . . . (217) 839-4888
   http://coalcountrychamber.com
Staunton Chamber of Commerce . . . . (618) 635-8356
   http://www.stauntonil.com/chamber/welcome.aspx
Virden Area Association of Commerce
   http://virdenonline.org

Macoupin County Communities

ATWATER (unincorporated postal area, zip code 62511). Covers a land area of 12.205 square miles and a water area of 0 square miles. Located at 39.34° N. Lat; 89.73° W. Long. Elevation is 633 feet.

Population: 176 (2000); Race: 100.0% White, 0.0% Black, 0.0% Asian, 0.0% Other, 0.0% Hispanic of any race (2000); Density: 14.4 persons per square mile (2000); Age: 16.9% under 18, 13.6% over 64 (2000); Marriage status: 14.2% never married, 66.5% now married, 11.6% widowed, 7.7% divorced (2000); Foreign born: 0.0% (2000); Ancestry (includes multiple ancestries): 37.3% German, 19.8% Irish, 14.1% Scotch-Irish, 9.6% English, 7.9% American (2000).

Economy: Employment by occupation: 16.5% management, 3.5% professional, 10.4% services, 37.4% sales, 0.0% farming, 10.4% construction, 21.7% production (2000).

Income: Per capita income: $19,332 (2000); Median household income: $33,958 (2000); Poverty rate: 0.0% (2000).

Education: Percent of population age 25 and over with: High school diploma (including GED) or higher: 82.1% (2000); Bachelor's degree or higher: 3.7% (2000).

Housing: Homeownership rate: 80.7% (2000); Median home value: $125,000 (2000); Median contract rent: n/a per month (2000); Median year structure built: 1973 (2000).

Transportation: Commute to work: 88.7% car, 0.0% public transportation, 0.0% walk, 11.3% work from home (2000); Travel time to work: 18.6% less than 15 minutes, 49.0% 15 to 30 minutes, 18.6% 30 to 45 minutes, 9.8% 45 to 60 minutes, 3.9% 60 minutes or more (2000)

BENLD (city). Covers a land area of 1.058 square miles and a water area of 0 square miles. Located at 39.09° N. Lat; 89.80° W. Long. Elevation is 633 feet.
History: Incorporated 1904; reincorporated 1930 as city.
Population: 1,604 (1990); 1,541 (2000); 1,427 (2010); 1,370 (2015 projected); Race: 97.3% White, 1.1% Black, 0.0% Asian, 1.6% Other, 2.0% Hispanic of any race (2010); Density: 1,348.2 persons per square mile (2010); Average household size: 2.28 (2010); Median age: 37.9 (2010); Males per 100 females: 91.8 (2010); Marriage status: 23.9% never married, 54.0% now married, 7.9% widowed, 14.2% divorced (2005-2009 5-year est.); Foreign born: 1.3% (2005-2009 5-year est.); Ancestry (includes multiple ancestries): 23.0% German, 18.9% Irish, 15.2% Italian, 10.0% French, 9.4% English (2005-2009 5-year est.).
Economy: Single-family building permits issued: 0 (2010); Multi-family building permits issued: 0 (2010); Employment by occupation: 10.5% management, 14.2% professional, 29.1% services, 22.3% sales, 0.0% farming, 9.8% construction, 14.1% production (2005-2009 5-year est.).
Income: Per capita income: $19,913 (2010); Median household income: $38,151 (2010); Average household income: $45,331 (2010); Percent of households with income of $100,000 or more: 6.9% (2010); Poverty rate: 15.7% (2005-2009 5-year est.).
Taxes: Total city taxes per capita: $149 (2007); City property taxes per capita: $61 (2007).
Education: Percent of population age 25 and over with: High school diploma (including GED) or higher: 83.1% (2010); Bachelor's degree or higher: 13.5% (2010); Master's degree or higher: 3.9% (2010).
Housing: Homeownership rate: 81.8% (2010); Median home value: $59,118 (2010); Median contract rent: $439 per month (2005-2009 5-year est.); Median year structure built: 1942 (2005-2009 5-year est.).
Transportation: Commute to work: 95.5% car, 0.3% public transportation, 0.5% walk, 3.7% work from home (2005-2009 5-year est.); Travel time to work: 32.7% less than 15 minutes, 24.8% 15 to 30 minutes, 17.9% 30 to 45 minutes, 10.8% 45 to 60 minutes, 13.9% 60 minutes or more (2005-2009 5-year est.)

BRIGHTON (village). Covers a land area of 1.610 square miles and a water area of 0.030 square miles. Located at 39.03° N. Lat; 90.14° W. Long. Elevation is 663 feet.
Population: 2,315 (1990); 2,196 (2000); 2,198 (2010); 2,185 (2015 projected); Race: 97.2% White, 0.7% Black, 0.8% Asian, 1.3% Other, 1.3% Hispanic of any race (2010); Density: 1,365.5 persons per square mile (2010); Average household size: 2.67 (2010); Median age: 38.2 (2010); Males per 100 females: 96.4 (2010); Marriage status: 26.1% never married, 57.8% now married, 7.5% widowed, 8.6% divorced (2005-2009 5-year est.); Foreign born: 1.4% (2005-2009 5-year est.); Ancestry (includes multiple ancestries): 38.5% German, 16.5% Irish, 10.7% English, 8.6% American, 5.0% Polish (2005-2009 5-year est.).
Economy: Single-family building permits issued: 3 (2010); Multi-family building permits issued: 0 (2010); Employment by occupation: 10.5% management, 14.2% professional, 20.5% services, 21.5% sales, 0.0% farming, 14.8% construction, 18.5% production (2005-2009 5-year est.).
Income: Per capita income: $19,931 (2010); Median household income: $46,272 (2010); Average household income: $54,032 (2010); Percent of households with income of $100,000 or more: 10.8% (2010); Poverty rate: 12.5% (2005-2009 5-year est.).
Taxes: Total city taxes per capita: $102 (2007); City property taxes per capita: $93 (2007).
Education: Percent of population age 25 and over with: High school diploma (including GED) or higher: 87.4% (2010); Bachelor's degree or higher: 11.8% (2010); Master's degree or higher: 3.6% (2010).
School District(s)
Southwestern CUSD 9 (PK-12)
    2009-10 Enrollment: 1,695 . . . . (618) 729-3221
Housing: Homeownership rate: 83.0% (2010); Median home value: $100,296 (2010); Median contract rent: $359 per month (2005-2009 5-year est.); Median year structure built: 1969 (2005-2009 5-year est.).
Newspapers: Southwestern Journal (Local news; Circulation 1,550); Southwestern Shoppers Guide (Community news; Circulation 8,600)
Transportation: Commute to work: 92.9% car, 2.4% public transportation, 0.7% walk, 3.3% work from home (2005-2009 5-year est.); Travel time to work: 22.1% less than 15 minutes, 41.9% 15 to 30 minutes, 13.9% 30 to 45 minutes, 8.4% 45 to 60 minutes, 13.8% 60 minutes or more (2005-2009 5-year est.)

BUNKER HILL (city). Covers a land area of 1.180 square miles and a water area of 0.023 square miles. Located at 39.04° N. Lat; 89.95° W. Long. Elevation is 663 feet.
History: Incorporated 1857.
Population: 1,737 (1990); 1,801 (2000); 1,651 (2010); 1,586 (2015 projected); Race: 96.5% White, 1.7% Black, 0.4% Asian, 1.5% Other, 0.6% Hispanic of any race (2010); Density: 1,399.7 persons per square mile (2010); Average household size: 2.52 (2010); Median age: 38.0 (2010); Males per 100 females: 91.8 (2010); Marriage status: 23.6% never married, 47.2% now married, 11.1% widowed, 18.0% divorced (2005-2009 5-year est.); Foreign born: 0.2% (2005-2009 5-year est.); Ancestry (includes multiple ancestries): 37.3% German, 14.3% Irish, 12.0% English, 11.7% American, 4.4% Italian (2005-2009 5-year est.).
Economy: Employment by occupation: 7.4% management, 14.0% professional, 17.0% services, 26.0% sales, 0.4% farming, 16.4% construction, 18.7% production (2005-2009 5-year est.).
Income: Per capita income: $23,036 (2010); Median household income: $51,742 (2010); Average household income: $59,275 (2010); Percent of households with income of $100,000 or more: 12.9% (2010); Poverty rate: 13.7% (2005-2009 5-year est.).
Taxes: Total city taxes per capita: $118 (2007); City property taxes per capita: $100 (2007).
Education: Percent of population age 25 and over with: High school diploma (including GED) or higher: 87.4% (2010); Bachelor's degree or higher: 16.2% (2010); Master's degree or higher: 3.4% (2010).
School District(s)
Bunker Hill CUSD 8 (PK-12)
    2009-10 Enrollment: 709 . . . . (618) 585-3116
Housing: Homeownership rate: 76.0% (2010); Median home value: $83,978 (2010); Median contract rent: $435 per month (2005-2009 5-year est.); Median year structure built: 1962 (2005-2009 5-year est.).
Safety: Violent crime rate: 87.9 per 10,000 population; Property crime rate: 158.3 per 10,000 population (2010).
Newspapers: Bunker Hill Gazette-News (Local news; Circulation 1,550); Southwest Advertiser (Local news; Circulation 7,700)
Transportation: Commute to work: 95.9% car, 0.0% public transportation, 0.7% walk, 3.1% work from home (2005-2009 5-year est.); Travel time to work: 22.1% less than 15 minutes, 25.6% 15 to 30 minutes, 29.4% 30 to 45 minutes, 16.2% 45 to 60 minutes, 6.6% 60 minutes or more (2005-2009 5-year est.)

CARLINVILLE (city). County seat. Covers a land area of 2.379 square miles and a water area of 0 square miles. Located at 39.28° N. Lat; 89.88° W. Long. Elevation is 620 feet.
History: Carlinville was the site of the "million-dollar courthouse" of Macoupin County, completed in 1870 at a cost of $1,380,500, and opposed by the taxpayers. Built of limestone, the courthouse was designed as two rectangles crossing at the center under a dome that rose 191 feet.
Population: 5,511 (1990); 5,685 (2000); 5,558 (2010); 5,470 (2015 projected); Race: 96.7% White, 1.8% Black, 0.2% Asian, 1.3% Other, 1.1% Hispanic of any race (2010); Density: 2,336.5 persons per square mile (2010); Average household size: 2.39 (2010); Median age: 39.3 (2010); Males per 100 females: 93.1 (2010); Marriage status: 34.1% never married, 44.7% now married, 5.4% widowed, 15.9% divorced (2005-2009 5-year est.); Foreign born: 0.5% (2005-2009 5-year est.); Ancestry (includes multiple ancestries): 37.5% German, 19.3% Irish, 16.8% English, 11.2% American, 7.7% Italian (2005-2009 5-year est.).
Economy: Employment by occupation: 9.7% management, 25.7% professional, 21.8% services, 22.4% sales, 0.5% farming, 7.1% construction, 12.7% production (2005-2009 5-year est.).
Income: Per capita income: $21,438 (2010); Median household income: $42,243 (2010); Average household income: $53,426 (2010); Percent of households with income of $100,000 or more: 11.5% (2010); Poverty rate: 11.7% (2005-2009 5-year est.).
Taxes: Total city taxes per capita: $99 (2007); City property taxes per capita: $85 (2007).
Education: Percent of population age 25 and over with: High school diploma (including GED) or higher: 85.5% (2010); Bachelor's degree or higher: 22.2% (2010); Master's degree or higher: 8.6% (2010).
School District(s)
Calhoun/Greene/Jersey/Macoupn Roe (07-12)
    2009-10 Enrollment: n/a . . . . (217) 854-4016
Carlinville CUSD 1 (PK-12)
    2009-10 Enrollment: 1,477 . . . . (217) 854-9823

Four-year College(s)
Blackburn College (Private, Not-for-profit, Presbyterian Church (USA))
Fall 2009 Enrollment: 607 . . . . (217) 854-3231
2010-11 Tuition: In-state $14,996; Out-of-state $14,996
Housing: Homeownership rate: 70.2% (2010); Median home value:
$85,370 (2010); Median contract rent: $387 per month (2005-2009 5-year
est.); Median year structure built: 1962 (2005-2009 5-year est.).
Hospitals: Carlinville Area Hospital (33 beds)
Safety: Violent crime rate: 24.0 per 10,000 population; Property crime rate:
296.4 per 10,000 population (2010).
Newspapers: Macoupin County Enquirer (Regional news; Circulation
4,900); Macoutin County Inquirer-Democrat (Community news; Circulation
2,500)
Transportation: Commute to work: 83.8% car, 0.0% public transportation,
8.7% walk, 4.8% work from home (2005-2009 5-year est.); Travel time to
work: 70.3% less than 15 minutes, 9.6% 15 to 30 minutes, 6.3% 30 to 45
minutes, 6.6% 45 to 60 minutes, 7.2% 60 minutes or more (2005-2009
5-year est.); Amtrak: train service available.
Additional Information Contacts
Carlinville Community Chamber of Commerce . . . . (217) 854-2141
http://carlinvillechamber.com
City of Carlinville . . . . (217) 854-4076
http://www.cityofcarlinville.com

CHESTERFIELD (village). Covers a land area of 0.541 square miles
and a water area of 0 square miles. Located at 39.25° N. Lat; 90.06° W.
Long. Elevation is 587 feet.
Population: 230 (1990); 223 (2000); 209 (2010); 202 (2015 projected);
Race: 96.2% White, 0.5% Black, 0.0% Asian, 3.3% Other, 1.0% Hispanic
of any race (2010); Density: 386.3 persons per square mile (2010);
Average household size: 2.68 (2010); Median age: 37.6 (2010); Males per
100 females: 99.0 (2010); Marriage status: 14.0% never married, 58.9%
now married, 5.6% widowed, 21.5% divorced (2005-2009 5-year est.);
Foreign born: 0.0% (2005-2009 5-year est.); Ancestry (includes multiple
ancestries): 22.6% German, 15.8% Irish, 12.0% English, 11.3% Scottish,
9.8% Dutch (2005-2009 5-year est.).
Economy: Employment by occupation: 11.1% management, 3.7%
professional, 22.2% services, 46.3% sales, 0.0% farming, 3.7%
construction, 13.0% production (2005-2009 5-year est.).
Income: Per capita income: $21,422 (2010); Median household income:
$45,000 (2010); Average household income: $52,692 (2010); Percent of
households with income of $100,000 or more: 9.0% (2010); Poverty rate:
25.6% (2005-2009 5-year est.).
Taxes: Total city taxes per capita: $50 (2007); City property taxes per
capita: $45 (2007).
Education: Percent of population age 25 and over with: High school
diploma (including GED) or higher: 87.1% (2010); Bachelor's degree or
higher: 9.3% (2010); Master's degree or higher: 2.1% (2010).
Housing: Homeownership rate: 83.3% (2010); Median home value:
$72,222 (2010); Median contract rent: n/a per month (2005-2009 5-year
est.); Median year structure built: 1960 (2005-2009 5-year est.).
Transportation: Commute to work: 94.2% car, 0.0% public transportation,
5.8% walk, 0.0% work from home (2005-2009 5-year est.); Travel time to
work: 5.8% less than 15 minutes, 48.1% 15 to 30 minutes, 7.7% 30 to 45
minutes, 7.7% 45 to 60 minutes, 30.8% 60 minutes or more (2005-2009
5-year est.)

DORCHESTER (village). Covers a land area of 0.715 square miles
and a water area of 0 square miles. Located at 39.08° N. Lat; 89.88° W.
Long. Elevation is 656 feet.
Population: 145 (1990); 142 (2000); 159 (2010); 164 (2015 projected);
Race: 97.5% White, 0.0% Black, 0.0% Asian, 2.5% Other, 1.3% Hispanic
of any race (2010); Density: 222.2 persons per square mile (2010);
Average household size: 2.36 (2010); Median age: 46.7 (2010); Males per
100 females: 101.3 (2010); Marriage status: 22.4% never married, 61.8%
now married, 2.6% widowed, 13.2% divorced (2005-2009 5-year est.);
Foreign born: 0.0% (2005-2009 5-year est.); Ancestry (includes multiple
ancestries): 46.1% German, 14.6% English, 6.7% American, 4.5% Irish,
4.5% Dutch (2005-2009 5-year est.).
Economy: Single-family building permits issued: 0 (2010); Multi-family
building permits issued: 0 (2010); Employment by occupation: 5.4%
management, 5.4% professional, 16.2% services, 40.5% sales, 0.0%
farming, 27.0% construction, 5.4% production (2005-2009 5-year est.).
Income: Per capita income: $27,979 (2010); Median household income:
$55,833 (2010); Average household income: $66,194 (2010); Percent of

households with income of $100,000 or more: 20.9% (2010); Poverty rate:
11.6% (2005-2009 5-year est.).
Taxes: Total city taxes per capita: $24 (2007); City property taxes per
capita: $24 (2007).
Education: Percent of population age 25 and over with: High school
diploma (including GED) or higher: 86.4% (2010); Bachelor's degree or
higher: 15.3% (2010); Master's degree or higher: 5.1% (2010).
Housing: Homeownership rate: 83.6% (2010); Median home value:
$74,286 (2010); Median contract rent: n/a per month (2005-2009 5-year
est.); Median year structure built: 1967 (2005-2009 5-year est.).
Transportation: Commute to work: 100.0% car, 0.0% public
transportation, 0.0% walk, 0.0% work from home (2005-2009 5-year est.);
Travel time to work: 32.3% less than 15 minutes, 32.3% 15 to 30 minutes,
22.6% 30 to 45 minutes, 12.9% 45 to 60 minutes, 0.0% 60 minutes or more
(2005-2009 5-year est.)

EAGARVILLE (village). Aka Eagerville. Covers a land area of 0.931
square miles and a water area of 0.002 square miles. Located at 39.11° N.
Lat; 89.78° W. Long. Elevation is 643 feet.
Population: 121 (1990); 128 (2000); 119 (2010); 117 (2015 projected);
Race: 97.5% White, 0.0% Black, 0.0% Asian, 2.5% Other, 1.7% Hispanic
of any race (2010); Density: 127.9 persons per square mile (2010);
Average household size: 2.43 (2010); Median age: 39.2 (2010); Males per
100 females: 105.2 (2010); Marriage status: 13.3% never married, 56.7%
now married, 1.7% widowed, 28.3% divorced (2005-2009 5-year est.);
Foreign born: 0.0% (2005-2009 5-year est.); Ancestry (includes multiple
ancestries): 62.0% German, 47.9% English, 21.1% Italian, 16.9% Welsh,
7.0% Irish (2005-2009 5-year est.).
Economy: Employment by occupation: 0.0% management, 0.0%
professional, 25.0% services, 15.0% sales, 0.0% farming, 35.0%
construction, 25.0% production (2005-2009 5-year est.).
Income: Per capita income: $21,501 (2010); Median household income:
$44,167 (2010); Average household income: $48,571 (2010); Percent of
households with income of $100,000 or more: 4.1% (2010); Poverty rate:
5.6% (2005-2009 5-year est.).
Taxes: Total city taxes per capita: $8 (2007); City property taxes per
capita: $8 (2007).
Education: Percent of population age 25 and over with: High school
diploma (including GED) or higher: 85.2% (2010); Bachelor's degree or
higher: 14.8% (2010); Master's degree or higher: 6.2% (2010).
Housing: Homeownership rate: 87.8% (2010); Median home value:
$95,714 (2010); Median contract rent: n/a per month (2005-2009 5-year
est.); Median year structure built: 1955 (2005-2009 5-year est.).
Transportation: Commute to work: 85.0% car, 0.0% public transportation,
0.0% walk, 15.0% work from home (2005-2009 5-year est.); Travel time to
work: 17.6% less than 15 minutes, 29.4% 15 to 30 minutes, 0.0% 30 to 45
minutes, 0.0% 45 to 60 minutes, 52.9% 60 minutes or more (2005-2009
5-year est.)

EAST GILLESPIE (village). Covers a land area of 0.318 square
miles and a water area of 0 square miles. Located at 39.13° N. Lat; 89.81°
W. Long. Elevation is 659 feet.
Population: 205 (1990); 234 (2000); 205 (2010); 198 (2015 projected);
Race: 97.6% White, 0.5% Black, 0.5% Asian, 1.5% Other, 1.5% Hispanic
of any race (2010); Density: 644.7 persons per square mile (2010);
Average household size: 2.47 (2010); Median age: 41.0 (2010); Males per
100 females: 95.2 (2010); Marriage status: 15.8% never married, 68.4%
now married, 6.6% widowed, 9.2% divorced (2005-2009 5-year est.);
Foreign born: 0.0% (2005-2009 5-year est.); Ancestry (includes multiple
ancestries): 29.9% German, 11.9% Irish, 11.9% Italian, 11.3% Scottish,
10.3% English (2005-2009 5-year est.).
Economy: Single-family building permits issued: 1 (2010); Multi-family
building permits issued: 0 (2010); Employment by occupation: 8.5%
management, 11.7% professional, 18.1% services, 19.1% sales, 0.0%
farming, 13.8% construction, 28.7% production (2005-2009 5-year est.).
Income: Per capita income: $21,986 (2010); Median household income:
$42,969 (2010); Average household income: $52,349 (2010); Percent of
households with income of $100,000 or more: 10.8% (2010); Poverty rate:
2.1% (2005-2009 5-year est.).
Taxes: Total city taxes per capita: $22 (2007); City property taxes per
capita: $18 (2007).
Education: Percent of population age 25 and over with: High school
diploma (including GED) or higher: 86.8% (2010); Bachelor's degree or
higher: 9.3% (2010); Master's degree or higher: 6.6% (2010).

Housing: Homeownership rate: 83.1% (2010); Median home value: $68,667 (2010); Median contract rent: $450 per month (2005-2009 5-year est.); Median year structure built: 1978 (2005-2009 5-year est.).
Transportation: Commute to work: 91.5% car, 4.3% public transportation, 0.0% walk, 0.0% work from home (2005-2009 5-year est.); Travel time to work: 22.3% less than 15 minutes, 35.1% 15 to 30 minutes, 24.5% 30 to 45 minutes, 9.6% 45 to 60 minutes, 8.5% 60 minutes or more (2005-2009 5-year est.)

GILLESPIE (city).
Covers a land area of 1.452 square miles and a water area of 0 square miles. Located at 39.12° N. Lat; 89.81° W. Long. Elevation is 659 feet.
Population: 3,628 (1990); 3,412 (2000); 3,048 (2010); 2,878 (2015 projected); Race: 97.4% White, 0.7% Black, 0.3% Asian, 1.6% Other, 1.3% Hispanic of any race (2010); Density: 2,098.6 persons per square mile (2010); Average household size: 2.30 (2010); Median age: 39.2 (2010); Males per 100 females: 91.1 (2010); Marriage status: 24.6% never married, 54.0% now married, 8.5% widowed, 12.9% divorced (2005-2009 5-year est.); Foreign born: 0.2% (2005-2009 5-year est.); Ancestry (includes multiple ancestries): 34.1% German, 20.5% Italian, 14.0% Irish, 11.1% English, 8.3% Polish (2005-2009 5-year est.).
Economy: Single-family building permits issued: 0 (2010); Multi-family building permits issued: 0 (2010); Employment by occupation: 15.6% management, 14.4% professional, 21.6% services, 26.0% sales, 0.0% farming, 10.3% construction, 12.1% production (2005-2009 5-year est.).
Income: Per capita income: $22,659 (2010); Median household income: $40,498 (2010); Average household income: $52,227 (2010); Percent of households with income of $100,000 or more: 11.2% (2010); Poverty rate: 16.8% (2005-2009 5-year est.).
Taxes: Total city taxes per capita: $175 (2007); City property taxes per capita: $85 (2007).
Education: Percent of population age 25 and over with: High school diploma (including GED) or higher: 89.0% (2010); Bachelor's degree or higher: 10.3% (2010); Master's degree or higher: 5.1% (2010).
School District(s)
Gillespie CUSD 7 (PK-12)
    2009-10 Enrollment: 1,263 . . . . (217) 839-2464
Housing: Homeownership rate: 76.5% (2010); Median home value: $72,153 (2010); Median contract rent: $370 per month (2005-2009 5-year est.); Median year structure built: 1951 (2005-2009 5-year est.).
Safety: Violent crime rate: 42.1 per 10,000 population; Property crime rate: 217.0 per 10,000 population (2010).
Newspapers: Gillespie Area News (Community news; Circulation 2,700)
Transportation: Commute to work: 94.5% car, 0.6% public transportation, 3.3% walk, 1.5% work from home (2005-2009 5-year est.); Travel time to work: 28.9% less than 15 minutes, 28.5% 15 to 30 minutes, 11.1% 30 to 45 minutes, 14.4% 45 to 60 minutes, 17.3% 60 minutes or more (2005-2009 5-year est.)
Additional Information Contacts
Coal Country Chamber of Commerce . . . . (217) 839-4888
    http://coalcountrychamber.com

GIRARD (city).
Covers a land area of 0.936 square miles and a water area of 0 square miles. Located at 39.44° N. Lat; 89.78° W. Long. Elevation is 669 feet.
History: Incorporated 1855.
Population: 2,164 (1990); 2,245 (2000); 2,110 (2010); 2,032 (2015 projected); Race: 98.2% White, 0.6% Black, 0.1% Asian, 1.0% Other, 2.2% Hispanic of any race (2010); Density: 2,254.6 persons per square mile (2010); Average household size: 2.45 (2010); Median age: 37.5 (2010); Males per 100 females: 96.8 (2010); Marriage status: 19.9% never married, 59.0% now married, 9.7% widowed, 11.4% divorced (2005-2009 5-year est.); Foreign born: 1.0% (2005-2009 5-year est.); Ancestry (includes multiple ancestries): 27.2% German, 19.2% Irish, 18.6% English, 8.3% American, 4.9% Swedish (2005-2009 5-year est.).
Economy: Employment by occupation: 9.0% management, 12.1% professional, 14.9% services, 25.5% sales, 0.0% farming, 19.4% construction, 19.2% production (2005-2009 5-year est.).
Income: Per capita income: $20,227 (2010); Median household income: $43,456 (2010); Average household income: $50,145 (2010); Percent of households with income of $100,000 or more: 8.6% (2010); Poverty rate: 16.2% (2005-2009 5-year est.).
Taxes: Total city taxes per capita: $63 (2007); City property taxes per capita: $32 (2007).

Education: Percent of population age 25 and over with: High school diploma (including GED) or higher: 86.4% (2010); Bachelor's degree or higher: 14.6% (2010); Master's degree or higher: 5.7% (2010).
School District(s)
Girard CUSD 3 (PK-12)
    2009-10 Enrollment: 655 . . . . (217) 627-2915
Housing: Homeownership rate: 71.6% (2010); Median home value: $78,483 (2010); Median contract rent: $318 per month (2005-2009 5-year est.); Median year structure built: 1967 (2005-2009 5-year est.).
Safety: Violent crime rate: 37.7 per 10,000 population; Property crime rate: 84.9 per 10,000 population (2010).
Newspapers: Girard Gazette (Local news; Circulation 1,400)
Transportation: Commute to work: 90.7% car, 0.0% public transportation, 6.3% walk, 2.0% work from home (2005-2009 5-year est.); Travel time to work: 30.8% less than 15 minutes, 22.6% 15 to 30 minutes, 24.1% 30 to 45 minutes, 16.0% 45 to 60 minutes, 6.5% 60 minutes or more (2005-2009 5-year est.)

HETTICK (village).
Covers a land area of 0.332 square miles and a water area of 0 square miles. Located at 39.35° N. Lat; 90.03° W. Long. Elevation is 597 feet.
Population: 211 (1990); 182 (2000); 176 (2010); 172 (2015 projected); Race: 100.0% White, 0.0% Black, 0.0% Asian, 0.0% Other, 0.0% Hispanic of any race (2010); Density: 530.8 persons per square mile (2010); Average household size: 2.38 (2010); Median age: 38.9 (2010); Males per 100 females: 93.4 (2010); Marriage status: 7.9% never married, 52.2% now married, 32.0% widowed, 7.9% divorced (2005-2009 5-year est.); Foreign born: 0.0% (2005-2009 5-year est.); Ancestry (includes multiple ancestries): 17.8% German, 11.4% Irish, 4.5% English, 3.8% American, 2.3% French (2005-2009 5-year est.).
Economy: Employment by occupation: 1.7% management, 14.5% professional, 23.1% services, 35.9% sales, 1.7% farming, 5.1% construction, 17.9% production (2005-2009 5-year est.).
Income: Per capita income: $26,924 (2010); Median household income: $52,500 (2010); Average household income: $64,392 (2010); Percent of households with income of $100,000 or more: 16.2% (2010); Poverty rate: 47.7% (2005-2009 5-year est.).
Taxes: Total city taxes per capita: $22 (2007); City property taxes per capita: $22 (2007).
Education: Percent of population age 25 and over with: High school diploma (including GED) or higher: 84.2% (2010); Bachelor's degree or higher: 5.8% (2010); Master's degree or higher: 2.5% (2010).
Housing: Homeownership rate: 81.1% (2010); Median home value: $100,000 (2010); Median contract rent: $184 per month (2005-2009 5-year est.); Median year structure built: before 1940 (2005-2009 5-year est.).
Transportation: Commute to work: 83.3% car, 0.0% public transportation, 10.5% walk, 6.1% work from home (2005-2009 5-year est.); Travel time to work: 22.4% less than 15 minutes, 35.5% 15 to 30 minutes, 27.1% 30 to 45 minutes, 10.3% 45 to 60 minutes, 4.7% 60 minutes or more (2005-2009 5-year est.)

LAKE KA-HO (village).
Covers a land area of 0.270 square miles and a water area of 0.053 square miles. Located at 39.11° N. Lat; 90.12° W. Long. Elevation is 650 feet.
History: Incorporated 2000.
Population: n/a (1990); n/a (2000); 237 (2010); n/a (2015 projected); Race: 98.3% White, 0.0% Black, 0.0% Asian, 1.7% Other, 0.4% Hispanic of any race (2010); Density: 877.8 persons per square mile (2010); Average household size: 1.99 (2010); Median age: 47.9 (2010); Males per 100 females: 119.4 (2010); Marriage status: 14.3% never married, 51.1% now married, 9.0% widowed, 25.6% divorced (2005-2009 5-year est.); Foreign born: 0.0% (2005-2009 5-year est.); Ancestry (includes multiple ancestries): 32.0% German, 18.3% English, 17.2% American, 15.4% Irish, 5.3% French (2005-2009 5-year est.).
Economy: Single-family building permits issued: 0 (2010); Multi-family building permits issued: 0 (2010); Employment by occupation: 0.0% management, 11.1% professional, 3.2% services, 36.5% sales, 4.8% farming, 12.7% construction, 31.7% production (2005-2009 5-year est.).
Income: Per capita income: n/a (2010); Median household income: n/a (2010); Average household income: n/a (2010); Percent of households with income of $100,000 or more: n/a (2010); Poverty rate: 3.0% (2005-2009 5-year est.).
Taxes: Total city taxes per capita: $40 (2007); City property taxes per capita: $16 (2007).

Education: Percent of population age 25 and over with: High school diploma (including GED) or higher: n/a (2010); Bachelor's degree or higher: n/a (2010); Master's degree or higher: n/a (2010).

Housing: Homeownership rate: n/a (2010); Median home value: n/a (2010); Median contract rent: n/a per month (2005-2009 5-year est.); Median year structure built: 1977 (2005-2009 5-year est.).

Transportation: Commute to work: 100.0% car, 0.0% public transportation, 0.0% walk, 0.0% work from home (2005-2009 5-year est.); Travel time to work: 32.8% less than 15 minutes, 7.8% 15 to 30 minutes, 17.2% 30 to 45 minutes, 26.6% 45 to 60 minutes, 15.6% 60 minutes or more (2005-2009 5-year est.)

MEDORA (village).

Covers a land area of 0.313 square miles and a water area of 0 square miles. Located at 39.17° N. Lat; 90.14° W. Long. Elevation is 610 feet.

Population: 420 (1990); 501 (2000); 470 (2010); 455 (2015 projected); Race: 96.6% White, 0.4% Black, 0.0% Asian, 3.0% Other, 1.3% Hispanic of any race (2010); Density: 1,499.7 persons per square mile (2010); Average household size: 2.67 (2010); Median age: 36.3 (2010); Males per 100 females: 93.4 (2010); Marriage status: 19.0% never married, 60.9% now married, 7.9% widowed, 12.1% divorced (2005-2009 5-year est.); Foreign born: 0.0% (2005-2009 5-year est.); Ancestry (includes multiple ancestries): 35.3% German, 29.1% English, 23.5% Irish, 13.2% American, 2.4% French Canadian (2005-2009 5-year est.).

Economy: Employment by occupation: 5.3% management, 12.8% professional, 24.5% services, 17.6% sales, 0.5% farming, 16.5% construction, 22.9% production (2005-2009 5-year est.).

Income: Per capita income: $21,422 (2010); Median household income: $46,818 (2010); Average household income: $56,065 (2010); Percent of households with income of $100,000 or more: 9.7% (2010); Poverty rate: 11.7% (2005-2009 5-year est.).

Taxes: Total city taxes per capita: $24 (2007); City property taxes per capita: $24 (2007).

Education: Percent of population age 25 and over with: High school diploma (including GED) or higher: 86.8% (2010); Bachelor's degree or higher: 9.6% (2010); Master's degree or higher: 2.6% (2010).

School District(s)

Southwestern CUSD 9 (PK-12)

    2009-10 Enrollment: 1,695 . . . . (618) 729-3221

Housing: Homeownership rate: 83.0% (2010); Median home value: $75,238 (2010); Median contract rent: $368 per month (2005-2009 5-year est.); Median year structure built: 1953 (2005-2009 5-year est.).

Transportation: Commute to work: 97.2% car, 0.0% public transportation, 2.8% walk, 0.0% work from home (2005-2009 5-year est.); Travel time to work: 19.1% less than 15 minutes, 24.7% 15 to 30 minutes, 30.9% 30 to 45 minutes, 18.0% 45 to 60 minutes, 7.3% 60 minutes or more (2005-2009 5-year est.)

MODESTO (village).

Covers a land area of 0.561 square miles and a water area of 0 square miles. Located at 39.47° N. Lat; 89.98° W. Long. Elevation is 679 feet.

Population: 240 (1990); 252 (2000); 250 (2010); 246 (2015 projected); Race: 99.2% White, 0.0% Black, 0.8% Asian, 0.0% Other, 0.0% Hispanic of any race (2010); Density: 445.7 persons per square mile (2010); Average household size: 2.53 (2010); Median age: 41.2 (2010); Males per 100 females: 98.4 (2010); Marriage status: 25.5% never married, 57.2% now married, 5.5% widowed, 11.7% divorced (2005-2009 5-year est.); Foreign born: 0.0% (2005-2009 5-year est.); Ancestry (includes multiple ancestries): 30.3% American, 25.0% German, 17.6% Irish, 15.4% English, 3.7% Swedish (2005-2009 5-year est.).

Economy: Employment by occupation: 11.5% management, 8.0% professional, 18.4% services, 28.7% sales, 2.3% farming, 23.0% construction, 8.0% production (2005-2009 5-year est.).

Income: Per capita income: $27,894 (2010); Median household income: $60,547 (2010); Average household income: $72,348 (2010); Percent of households with income of $100,000 or more: 15.2% (2010); Poverty rate: 8.3% (2005-2009 5-year est.).

Taxes: Total city taxes per capita: $24 (2007); City property taxes per capita: $24 (2007).

Education: Percent of population age 25 and over with: High school diploma (including GED) or higher: 90.3% (2010); Bachelor's degree or higher: 17.0% (2010); Master's degree or higher: 5.1% (2010).

Housing: Homeownership rate: 82.8% (2010); Median home value: $98,000 (2010); Median contract rent: $361 per month (2005-2009 5-year est.); Median year structure built: 1946 (2005-2009 5-year est.).

Transportation: Commute to work: 87.4% car, 0.0% public transportation, 8.0% walk, 4.6% work from home (2005-2009 5-year est.); Travel time to work: 24.1% less than 15 minutes, 47.0% 15 to 30 minutes, 8.4% 30 to 45 minutes, 13.3% 45 to 60 minutes, 7.2% 60 minutes or more (2005-2009 5-year est.)

MOUNT CLARE (village).

Covers a land area of 1.516 square miles and a water area of 0.036 square miles. Located at 39.10° N. Lat; 89.82° W. Long. Elevation is 643 feet.

Population: 297 (1990); 433 (2000); 429 (2010); 417 (2015 projected); Race: 96.5% White, 0.7% Black, 0.0% Asian, 2.8% Other, 0.5% Hispanic of any race (2010); Density: 282.9 persons per square mile (2010); Average household size: 2.34 (2010); Median age: 46.5 (2010); Males per 100 females: 78.8 (2010); Marriage status: 4.1% never married, 22.0% now married, 64.6% widowed, 9.3% divorced (2005-2009 5-year est.); Foreign born: 0.2% (2005-2009 5-year est.); Ancestry (includes multiple ancestries): 24.0% German, 22.1% Irish, 10.2% Italian, 9.7% Polish, 9.3% English (2005-2009 5-year est.).

Economy: Employment by occupation: 8.7% management, 22.0% professional, 22.0% services, 26.7% sales, 0.0% farming, 9.3% construction, 11.3% production (2005-2009 5-year est.).

Income: Per capita income: $21,240 (2010); Median household income: $43,672 (2010); Average household income: $54,018 (2010); Percent of households with income of $100,000 or more: 11.7% (2010); Poverty rate: 14.8% (2005-2009 5-year est.).

Taxes: Total city taxes per capita: $63 (2007); City property taxes per capita: $12 (2007).

Education: Percent of population age 25 and over with: High school diploma (including GED) or higher: 79.3% (2010); Bachelor's degree or higher: 11.0% (2010); Master's degree or higher: 2.8% (2010).

Housing: Homeownership rate: 84.7% (2010); Median home value: $65,000 (2010); Median contract rent: $378 per month (2005-2009 5-year est.); Median year structure built: before 1940 (2005-2009 5-year est.).

Transportation: Commute to work: 98.0% car, 0.0% public transportation, 0.0% walk, 2.0% work from home (2005-2009 5-year est.); Travel time to work: 28.6% less than 15 minutes, 42.2% 15 to 30 minutes, 14.3% 30 to 45 minutes, 13.6% 45 to 60 minutes, 1.4% 60 minutes or more (2005-2009 5-year est.)

MOUNT OLIVE (city).

Covers a land area of 1.104 square miles and a water area of 0 square miles. Located at 39.07° N. Lat; 89.72° W. Long. Elevation is 686 feet.

History: Mount Olive, an early coal-mining town, was connected with two labor organizers. Alexander Bradley (1866-1918) was a leader in union organization. "Mother" Jones (1830-1930), born Mary Harris in Ireland, was buried in Mount Olive.

Population: 2,126 (1990); 2,150 (2000); 2,087 (2010); 2,052 (2015 projected); Race: 98.1% White, 0.0% Black, 0.1% Asian, 1.7% Other, 1.1% Hispanic of any race (2010); Density: 1,891.2 persons per square mile (2010); Average household size: 2.45 (2010); Median age: 40.2 (2010); Males per 100 females: 97.6 (2010); Marriage status: 25.9% never married, 49.8% now married, 6.7% widowed, 17.5% divorced (2005-2009 5-year est.); Foreign born: 0.5% (2005-2009 5-year est.); Ancestry (includes multiple ancestries): 43.2% German, 13.8% Irish, 9.1% American, 8.9% English, 6.1% Italian (2005-2009 5-year est.).

Economy: Single-family building permits issued: 2 (2010); Multi-family building permits issued: 0 (2010); Employment by occupation: 10.0% management, 9.9% professional, 22.1% services, 29.8% sales, 0.5% farming, 11.0% construction, 16.7% production (2005-2009 5-year est.).

Income: Per capita income: $21,960 (2010); Median household income: $44,958 (2010); Average household income: $54,075 (2010); Percent of households with income of $100,000 or more: 8.2% (2010); Poverty rate: 14.1% (2005-2009 5-year est.).

Taxes: Total city taxes per capita: $199 (2007); City property taxes per capita: $86 (2007).

Education: Percent of population age 25 and over with: High school diploma (including GED) or higher: 85.9% (2010); Bachelor's degree or higher: 12.2% (2010); Master's degree or higher: 5.7% (2010).

School District(s)

Mount Olive CUSD 5 (PK-12)

    2009-10 Enrollment: 589 . . . . (217) 999-7831

Housing: Homeownership rate: 84.3% (2010); Median home value: $58,263 (2010); Median contract rent: $319 per month (2005-2009 5-year est.); Median year structure built: 1942 (2005-2009 5-year est.).

Newspapers: Mount Olive Herald (Regional news; Circulation 1,550)

Transportation: Commute to work: 94.7% car, 0.0% public transportation, 1.2% walk, 3.4% work from home (2005-2009 5-year est.); Travel time to work: 41.9% less than 15 minutes, 14.6% 15 to 30 minutes, 13.4% 30 to 45 minutes, 16.0% 45 to 60 minutes, 14.2% 60 minutes or more (2005-2009 5-year est.)

NILWOOD (town). Covers a land area of 0.465 square miles and a water area of 0 square miles. Located at 39.39° N. Lat; 89.80° W. Long. Elevation is 669 feet.
Population: 238 (1990); 284 (2000); 280 (2010); 279 (2015 projected); Race: 97.5% White, 0.0% Black, 1.1% Asian, 1.4% Other, 1.1% Hispanic of any race (2010); Density: 601.8 persons per square mile (2010); Average household size: 2.52 (2010); Median age: 37.3 (2010); Males per 100 females: 113.7 (2010); Marriage status: 12.8% never married, 56.1% now married, 7.3% widowed, 23.8% divorced (2005-2009 5-year est.); Foreign born: 0.0% (2005-2009 5-year est.); Ancestry (includes multiple ancestries): 32.4% German, 15.6% Irish, 10.2% English, 5.8% French, 5.3% American (2005-2009 5-year est.).
Economy: Employment by occupation: 11.7% management, 6.4% professional, 20.2% services, 33.0% sales, 5.3% farming, 10.6% construction, 12.8% production (2005-2009 5-year est.).
Income: Per capita income: $19,155 (2010); Median household income: $39,722 (2010); Average household income: $48,176 (2010); Percent of households with income of $100,000 or more: 9.0% (2010); Poverty rate: 13.3% (2005-2009 5-year est.).
Taxes: Total city taxes per capita: $29 (2007); City property taxes per capita: $29 (2007).
Education: Percent of population age 25 and over with: High school diploma (including GED) or higher: 82.4% (2010); Bachelor's degree or higher: 8.0% (2010); Master's degree or higher: 1.1% (2010).
Housing: Homeownership rate: 82.9% (2010); Median home value: $74,545 (2010); Median contract rent: n/a per month (2005-2009 5-year est.); Median year structure built: 1959 (2005-2009 5-year est.).
Transportation: Commute to work: 92.4% car, 0.0% public transportation, 2.2% walk, 5.4% work from home (2005-2009 5-year est.); Travel time to work: 26.4% less than 15 minutes, 34.5% 15 to 30 minutes, 14.9% 30 to 45 minutes, 18.4% 45 to 60 minutes, 5.7% 60 minutes or more (2005-2009 5-year est.)

PALMYRA (village). Covers a land area of 1.000 square miles and a water area of 0 square miles. Located at 39.43° N. Lat; 89.99° W. Long. Elevation is 673 feet.
Population: 727 (1990); 733 (2000); 743 (2010); 739 (2015 projected); Race: 98.4% White, 0.8% Black, 0.0% Asian, 0.8% Other, 0.3% Hispanic of any race (2010); Density: 742.9 persons per square mile (2010); Average household size: 2.18 (2010); Median age: 44.2 (2010); Males per 100 females: 97.6 (2010); Marriage status: 26.2% never married, 50.6% now married, 9.2% widowed, 13.9% divorced (2005-2009 5-year est.); Foreign born: 0.0% (2005-2009 5-year est.); Ancestry (includes multiple ancestries): 28.0% German, 19.2% Irish, 15.1% English, 13.3% American, 4.0% French (2005-2009 5-year est.).
Economy: Employment by occupation: 5.1% management, 15.7% professional, 12.7% services, 29.6% sales, 0.0% farming, 10.3% construction, 26.6% production (2005-2009 5-year est.).
Income: Per capita income: $20,253 (2010); Median household income: $36,350 (2010); Average household income: $44,267 (2010); Percent of households with income of $100,000 or more: 6.5% (2010); Poverty rate: 18.7% (2005-2009 5-year est.).
Taxes: Total city taxes per capita: $33 (2007); City property taxes per capita: $30 (2007).
Education: Percent of population age 25 and over with: High school diploma (including GED) or higher: 82.7% (2010); Bachelor's degree or higher: 10.8% (2010); Master's degree or higher: 3.3% (2010).

School District(s)
Northwestern CUSD 2 (PK-12)
    2009-10 Enrollment: 363 . . . . (217) 436-2210
Housing: Homeownership rate: 72.1% (2010); Median home value: $54,921 (2010); Median contract rent: $233 per month (2005-2009 5-year est.); Median year structure built: 1951 (2005-2009 5-year est.).
Transportation: Commute to work: 96.7% car, 0.0% public transportation, 3.3% walk, 0.0% work from home (2005-2009 5-year est.); Travel time to work: 18.8% less than 15 minutes, 29.2% 15 to 30 minutes, 13.1% 30 to 45 minutes, 18.5% 45 to 60 minutes, 20.4% 60 minutes or more (2005-2009 5-year est.)

PIASA (unincorporated postal area, zip code 62079). Covers a land area of 6.456 square miles and a water area of 0.031 square miles. Located at 39.11° N. Lat; 90.13° W. Long. Elevation is 594 feet.
Population: 180 (2000); Race: 100.0% White, 0.0% Black, 0.0% Asian, 0.0% Other, 0.0% Hispanic of any race (2000); Density: 27.9 persons per square mile (2000); Age: 27.5% under 18, 11.3% over 64 (2000); Marriage status: 12.0% never married, 75.2% now married, 4.8% widowed, 8.0% divorced (2000); Foreign born: 0.0% (2000); Ancestry (includes multiple ancestries): 42.5% German, 20.6% American, 8.8% English, 3.8% Irish (2000).
Economy: Employment by occupation: 27.6% management, 5.3% professional, 11.8% services, 39.5% sales, 0.0% farming, 0.0% construction, 15.8% production (2000).
Income: Per capita income: $25,089 (2000); Median household income: $66,000 (2000); Poverty rate: 3.8% (2000).
Education: Percent of population age 25 and over with: High school diploma (including GED) or higher: 79.3% (2000); Bachelor's degree or higher: 23.3% (2000).

School District(s)
Southwestern CUSD 9 (PK-12)
    2009-10 Enrollment: 1,695 . . . . (618) 729-3221
Housing: Homeownership rate: 73.0% (2000); Median home value: $98,600 (2000); Median contract rent: $225 per month (2000); Median year structure built: 1976 (2000).
Transportation: Commute to work: 100.0% car, 0.0% public transportation, 0.0% walk, 0.0% work from home (2000); Travel time to work: 35.5% less than 15 minutes, 40.8% 15 to 30 minutes, 6.6% 30 to 45 minutes, 17.1% 45 to 60 minutes, 0.0% 60 minutes or more (2000)

ROYAL LAKES (village). Aka Royal Lake. Covers a land area of 0.466 square miles and a water area of 0.046 square miles. Located at 39.11° N. Lat; 89.96° W. Long. Elevation is 623 feet.
Population: 272 (1990); 190 (2000); 179 (2010); 175 (2015 projected); Race: 81.0% White, 16.8% Black, 0.0% Asian, 2.2% Other, 0.6% Hispanic of any race (2010); Density: 384.5 persons per square mile (2010); Average household size: 2.56 (2010); Median age: 36.9 (2010); Males per 100 females: 108.1 (2010); Marriage status: 15.9% never married, 66.1% now married, 12.6% widowed, 5.4% divorced (2005-2009 5-year est.); Foreign born: 14.0% (2005-2009 5-year est.); Ancestry (includes multiple ancestries): 15.7% African, 2.4% German, 1.7% French, 1.4% Irish, 0.7% American (2005-2009 5-year est.).
Economy: Employment by occupation: 2.9% management, 0.0% professional, 17.5% services, 11.7% sales, 0.0% farming, 8.7% construction, 59.2% production (2005-2009 5-year est.).
Income: Per capita income: $18,933 (2010); Median household income: $40,000 (2010); Average household income: $46,464 (2010); Percent of households with income of $100,000 or more: 7.1% (2010); Poverty rate: 29.5% (2005-2009 5-year est.).
Taxes: Total city taxes per capita: $32 (2007); City property taxes per capita: $32 (2007).
Education: Percent of population age 25 and over with: High school diploma (including GED) or higher: 82.1% (2010); Bachelor's degree or higher: 10.6% (2010); Master's degree or higher: 0.8% (2010).
Housing: Homeownership rate: 78.6% (2010); Median home value: $95,833 (2010); Median contract rent: n/a per month (2005-2009 5-year est.); Median year structure built: 1975 (2005-2009 5-year est.).
Transportation: Commute to work: 84.7% car, 12.2% public transportation, 3.1% walk, 0.0% work from home (2005-2009 5-year est.); Travel time to work: 15.3% less than 15 minutes, 5.1% 15 to 30 minutes, 71.4% 30 to 45 minutes, 3.1% 45 to 60 minutes, 5.1% 60 minutes or more (2005-2009 5-year est.)

SAWYERVILLE (village). Covers a land area of 1.013 square miles and a water area of 0 square miles. Located at 39.07° N. Lat; 89.80° W. Long. Elevation is 630 feet.
Population: 312 (1990); 295 (2000); 268 (2010); 255 (2015 projected); Race: 97.8% White, 0.7% Black, 0.0% Asian, 1.5% Other, 0.7% Hispanic of any race (2010); Density: 264.5 persons per square mile (2010); Average household size: 2.41 (2010); Median age: 40.0 (2010); Males per 100 females: 106.2 (2010); Marriage status: 34.6% never married, 43.0% now married, 8.9% widowed, 13.6% divorced (2005-2009 5-year est.); Foreign born: 4.5% (2005-2009 5-year est.); Ancestry (includes multiple ancestries): 30.9% German, 25.3% Italian, 19.7% French, 10.4% Irish, 7.1% Slovak (2005-2009 5-year est.).

Economy: Employment by occupation: 27.0% management, 4.3% professional, 13.9% services, 12.2% sales, 0.0% farming, 26.1% construction, 16.5% production (2005-2009 5-year est.).
Income: Per capita income: $18,260 (2010); Median household income: $38,900 (2010); Average household income: $44,144 (2010); Percent of households with income of $100,000 or more: 6.3% (2010); Poverty rate: 30.1% (2005-2009 5-year est.).
Taxes: Total city taxes per capita: $21 (2007); City property taxes per capita: $21 (2007).
Education: Percent of population age 25 and over with: High school diploma (including GED) or higher: 82.9% (2010); Bachelor's degree or higher: 13.9% (2010); Master's degree or higher: 2.7% (2010).
Housing: Homeownership rate: 82.9% (2010); Median home value: $73,333 (2010); Median contract rent: $375 per month (2005-2009 5-year est.); Median year structure built: 1956 (2005-2009 5-year est.).
Transportation: Commute to work: 87.8% car, 5.2% public transportation, 0.0% walk, 7.0% work from home (2005-2009 5-year est.); Travel time to work: 34.6% less than 15 minutes, 15.0% 15 to 30 minutes, 9.3% 30 to 45 minutes, 28.0% 45 to 60 minutes, 13.1% 60 minutes or more (2005-2009 5-year est.)

SCOTTVILLE (village). Aka Scottsville. Covers a land area of 1.001 square miles and a water area of 0 square miles. Located at 39.47° N. Lat; 90.10° W. Long. Elevation is 659 feet.
Population: 165 (1990); 140 (2000); 127 (2010); 121 (2015 projected); Race: 99.2% White, 0.0% Black, 0.8% Asian, 0.0% Other, 0.8% Hispanic of any race (2010); Density: 126.9 persons per square mile (2010); Average household size: 2.54 (2010); Median age: 45.2 (2010); Males per 100 females: 101.6 (2010); Marriage status: 17.1% never married, 64.8% now married, 2.9% widowed, 15.2% divorced (2005-2009 5-year est.); Foreign born: 0.0% (2005-2009 5-year est.); Ancestry (includes multiple ancestries): 27.0% Irish, 26.2% German, 9.8% French, 9.0% Dutch, 4.9% American (2005-2009 5-year est.).
Economy: Employment by occupation: 7.4% management, 16.2% professional, 14.7% services, 14.7% sales, 5.9% farming, 5.9% construction, 35.3% production (2005-2009 5-year est.).
Income: Per capita income: $24,589 (2010); Median household income: $51,786 (2010); Average household income: $58,050 (2010); Percent of households with income of $100,000 or more: 10.0% (2010); Poverty rate: 12.6% (2005-2009 5-year est.).
Taxes: Total city taxes per capita: $29 (2007); City property taxes per capita: $29 (2007).
Education: Percent of population age 25 and over with: High school diploma (including GED) or higher: 83.1% (2010); Bachelor's degree or higher: 18.0% (2010); Master's degree or higher: 5.6% (2010).
Housing: Homeownership rate: 80.0% (2010); Median home value: $75,000 (2010); Median contract rent: n/a per month (2005-2009 5-year est.); Median year structure built: 1964 (2005-2009 5-year est.).
Transportation: Commute to work: 100.0% car, 0.0% public transportation, 0.0% walk, 0.0% work from home (2005-2009 5-year est.); Travel time to work: 9.1% less than 15 minutes, 43.6% 15 to 30 minutes, 30.9% 30 to 45 minutes, 3.6% 45 to 60 minutes, 12.7% 60 minutes or more (2005-2009 5-year est.)

SHIPMAN (village). Covers a land area of 1.321 square miles and a water area of 0.013 square miles. Located at 39.11° N. Lat; 90.04° W. Long. Elevation is 636 feet.
Population: 624 (1990); 655 (2000); 635 (2010); 619 (2015 projected); Race: 96.7% White, 1.6% Black, 0.5% Asian, 1.3% Other, 0.8% Hispanic of any race (2010); Density: 480.7 persons per square mile (2010); Average household size: 2.61 (2010); Median age: 36.8 (2010); Males per 100 females: 104.8 (2010); Marriage status: 9.3% never married, 71.8% now married, 5.8% widowed, 13.2% divorced (2005-2009 5-year est.); Foreign born: 2.5% (2005-2009 5-year est.); Ancestry (includes multiple ancestries): 33.1% German, 15.3% Scotch-Irish, 14.3% Irish, 12.2% American, 9.5% English (2005-2009 5-year est.).
Economy: Employment by occupation: 19.3% management, 6.3% professional, 17.0% services, 20.0% sales, 2.0% farming, 14.7% construction, 20.7% production (2005-2009 5-year est.).
Income: Per capita income: $22,162 (2010); Median household income: $48,316 (2010); Average household income: $58,282 (2010); Percent of households with income of $100,000 or more: 9.9% (2010); Poverty rate: 20.7% (2005-2009 5-year est.).
Taxes: Total city taxes per capita: $22 (2007); City property taxes per capita: $22 (2007).

Education: Percent of population age 25 and over with: High school diploma (including GED) or higher: 89.6% (2010); Bachelor's degree or higher: 18.2% (2010); Master's degree or higher: 3.5% (2010).

School District(s)
Southwestern CUSD 9 (PK-12)
   2009-10 Enrollment: 1,695 . . . . (618) 729-3221
Housing: Homeownership rate: 82.3% (2010); Median home value: $82,963 (2010); Median contract rent: $361 per month (2005-2009 5-year est.); Median year structure built: 1970 (2005-2009 5-year est.).
Transportation: Commute to work: 91.6% car, 0.0% public transportation, 3.7% walk, 4.7% work from home (2005-2009 5-year est.); Travel time to work: 22.6% less than 15 minutes, 22.6% 15 to 30 minutes, 32.2% 30 to 45 minutes, 9.5% 45 to 60 minutes, 13.1% 60 minutes or more (2005-2009 5-year est.)

STANDARD CITY (village). Aka South Standard. Covers a land area of 0.637 square miles and a water area of 0.003 square miles. Located at 39.35° N. Lat; 89.78° W. Long. Elevation is 640 feet.
Population: 128 (1990); 138 (2000); 132 (2010); 128 (2015 projected); Race: 97.7% White, 0.0% Black, 0.8% Asian, 1.5% Other, 1.5% Hispanic of any race (2010); Density: 207.3 persons per square mile (2010); Average household size: 2.59 (2010); Median age: 33.9 (2010); Males per 100 females: 94.1 (2010); Marriage status: 29.2% never married, 53.9% now married, 6.7% widowed, 10.1% divorced (2005-2009 5-year est.); Foreign born: 0.8% (2005-2009 5-year est.); Ancestry (includes multiple ancestries): 39.5% German, 27.9% English, 24.8% Italian, 16.3% Scottish, 4.7% American (2005-2009 5-year est.).
Economy: Employment by occupation: 0.0% management, 16.4% professional, 3.6% services, 47.3% sales, 0.0% farming, 20.0% construction, 12.7% production (2005-2009 5-year est.).
Income: Per capita income: $18,135 (2010); Median household income: $39,500 (2010); Average household income: $48,186 (2010); Percent of households with income of $100,000 or more: 9.8% (2010); Poverty rate: 31.8% (2005-2009 5-year est.).
Taxes: Total city taxes per capita: $22 (2007); City property taxes per capita: $15 (2007).
Education: Percent of population age 25 and over with: High school diploma (including GED) or higher: 84.1% (2010); Bachelor's degree or higher: 8.5% (2010); Master's degree or higher: 1.2% (2010).
Housing: Homeownership rate: 84.3% (2010); Median home value: $65,000 (2010); Median contract rent: $288 per month (2005-2009 5-year est.); Median year structure built: 1943 (2005-2009 5-year est.).
Transportation: Commute to work: 100.0% car, 0.0% public transportation, 0.0% walk, 0.0% work from home (2005-2009 5-year est.); Travel time to work: 11.8% less than 15 minutes, 49.0% 15 to 30 minutes, 0.0% 30 to 45 minutes, 21.6% 45 to 60 minutes, 17.6% 60 minutes or more (2005-2009 5-year est.)

STAUNTON (city). Covers a land area of 2.282 square miles and a water area of 0.027 square miles. Located at 39.01° N. Lat; 89.78° W. Long. Elevation is 620 feet.
History: Staunton was settled in 1817 by John Wood of Virginia, and a village was laid out in 1835. Staunton was named for one of its founders, and operated as a trading point for settlers. Later, coal mining was an important industry.
Population: 4,849 (1990); 5,030 (2000); 4,988 (2010); 4,942 (2015 projected); Race: 98.1% White, 0.3% Black, 0.7% Asian, 1.0% Other, 1.2% Hispanic of any race (2010); Density: 2,186.2 persons per square mile (2010); Average household size: 2.43 (2010); Median age: 38.7 (2010); Males per 100 females: 93.1 (2010); Marriage status: 25.6% never married, 53.2% now married, 9.3% widowed, 12.0% divorced (2005-2009 5-year est.); Foreign born: 1.9% (2005-2009 5-year est.); Ancestry (includes multiple ancestries): 44.5% German, 17.5% Italian, 7.6% Irish, 7.0% American, 6.7% English (2005-2009 5-year est.).
Economy: Single-family building permits issued: 3 (2010); Multi-family building permits issued: 6 (2010); Employment by occupation: 11.6% management, 15.2% professional, 19.9% services, 20.1% sales, 0.6% farming, 12.4% construction, 20.3% production (2005-2009 5-year est.).
Income: Per capita income: $21,148 (2010); Median household income: $44,399 (2010); Average household income: $51,889 (2010); Percent of households with income of $100,000 or more: 8.0% (2010); Poverty rate: 12.7% (2005-2009 5-year est.).
Taxes: Total city taxes per capita: $181 (2007); City property taxes per capita: $81 (2007).

Education: Percent of population age 25 and over with: High school diploma (including GED) or higher: 88.3% (2010); Bachelor's degree or higher: 16.7% (2010); Master's degree or higher: 5.5% (2010).

School District(s)

Staunton CUSD 6 (PK-12)

2009-10 Enrollment: 1,249 . . . . (618) 635-2962

Housing: Homeownership rate: 75.2% (2010); Median home value: $86,676 (2010); Median contract rent: $479 per month (2005-2009 5-year est.); Median year structure built: 1959 (2005-2009 5-year est.).

Hospitals: Community Memorial Hospital (49 beds)

Safety: Violent crime rate: 17.9 per 10,000 population; Property crime rate: 212.9 per 10,000 population (2010).

Newspapers: Staunton Star-Times (Local news; Circulation 3,995)

Transportation: Commute to work: 98.0% car, 0.0% public transportation, 1.4% walk, 0.7% work from home (2005-2009 5-year est.); Travel time to work: 38.8% less than 15 minutes, 19.5% 15 to 30 minutes, 21.9% 30 to 45 minutes, 12.4% 45 to 60 minutes, 7.4% 60 minutes or more (2005-2009 5-year est.)

Additional Information Contacts

City of Staunton . . . . (618) 635-2233
  http://www.stauntonil.com

Staunton Chamber of Commerce . . . . (618) 635-8356
  http://www.stauntonil.com/chamber/welcome.aspx

VIRDEN (city).

Covers a land area of 1.716 square miles and a water area of 0 square miles. Located at 39.50° N. Lat; 89.76° W. Long. Elevation is 686 feet.

History: Virden was a coal mining town and the location of the Virden riot in 1898 when mine operators refused to pay the rates established by the Illinois Coal Operators Association.

Population: 3,652 (1990); 3,488 (2000); 3,355 (2010); 3,269 (2015 projected); Race: 98.5% White, 0.2% Black, 0.2% Asian, 1.1% Other, 0.6% Hispanic of any race (2010); Density: 1,955.1 persons per square mile (2010); Average household size: 2.26 (2010); Median age: 40.7 (2010); Males per 100 females: 90.2 (2010); Marriage status: 23.8% never married, 55.6% now married, 6.0% widowed, 14.6% divorced (2005-2009 5-year est.); Foreign born: 0.4% (2005-2009 5-year est.); Ancestry (includes multiple ancestries): 29.5% German, 20.1% Irish, 17.1% English, 8.9% American, 7.9% Italian (2005-2009 5-year est.).

Economy: Employment by occupation: 8.4% management, 17.4% professional, 14.8% services, 29.6% sales, 0.0% farming, 15.2% construction, 14.5% production (2005-2009 5-year est.).

Income: Per capita income: $21,932 (2010); Median household income: $43,666 (2010); Average household income: $50,927 (2010); Percent of households with income of $100,000 or more: 8.6% (2010); Poverty rate: 13.4% (2005-2009 5-year est.).

Taxes: Total city taxes per capita: $70 (2007); City property taxes per capita: $63 (2007).

Education: Percent of population age 25 and over with: High school diploma (including GED) or higher: 87.4% (2010); Bachelor's degree or higher: 13.5% (2010); Master's degree or higher: 3.4% (2010).

School District(s)

Virden CUSD 4 (PK-12)

2009-10 Enrollment: 919 . . . . (217) 965-4226

Housing: Homeownership rate: 73.7% (2010); Median home value: $75,984 (2010); Median contract rent: $314 per month (2005-2009 5-year est.); Median year structure built: 1963 (2005-2009 5-year est.).

Newspapers: Northwestern News (Community news; Circulation 1,100); Panhandle Press (Community news; Circulation 1,200); Virden Recorder (Community news; Circulation 2,400)

Transportation: Commute to work: 94.7% car, 0.0% public transportation, 0.7% walk, 3.1% work from home (2005-2009 5-year est.); Travel time to work: 32.7% less than 15 minutes, 14.4% 15 to 30 minutes, 35.4% 30 to 45 minutes, 10.4% 45 to 60 minutes, 7.2% 60 minutes or more (2005-2009 5-year est.)

Additional Information Contacts

Virden Area Association of Commerce. . . . .
  http://virdenonline.org

WHITE CITY (village).

Covers a land area of 1.215 square miles and a water area of 0 square miles. Located at 39.07° N. Lat; 89.76° W. Long. Elevation is 653 feet.

Population: 229 (1990); 221 (2000); 214 (2010); 210 (2015 projected); Race: 97.7% White, 0.5% Black, 0.5% Asian, 1.4% Other, 0.5% Hispanic of any race (2010); Density: 176.1 persons per square mile (2010);

Average household size: 2.40 (2010); Median age: 42.4 (2010); Males per 100 females: 101.9 (2010); Marriage status: 20.4% never married, 58.7% now married, 5.3% widowed, 15.5% divorced (2005-2009 5-year est.); Foreign born: 0.0% (2005-2009 5-year est.); Ancestry (includes multiple ancestries): 40.7% German, 18.5% Irish, 13.7% French, 8.9% Scottish, 8.1% Croatian (2005-2009 5-year est.).

Economy: Single-family building permits issued: 0 (2010); Multi-family building permits issued: 0 (2010); Employment by occupation: 15.8% management, 23.3% professional, 12.5% services, 30.8% sales, 0.0% farming, 9.2% construction, 8.3% production (2005-2009 5-year est.).

Income: Per capita income: $20,182 (2010); Median household income: $41,250 (2010); Average household income: $48,624 (2010); Percent of households with income of $100,000 or more: 10.1% (2010); Poverty rate: 5.2% (2005-2009 5-year est.).

Taxes: Total city taxes per capita: $32 (2007); City property taxes per capita: $14 (2007).

Education: Percent of population age 25 and over with: High school diploma (including GED) or higher: 84.1% (2010); Bachelor's degree or higher: 7.6% (2010); Master's degree or higher: 1.3% (2010).

Housing: Homeownership rate: 84.3% (2010); Median home value: $86,923 (2010); Median contract rent: $256 per month (2005-2009 5-year est.); Median year structure built: 1966 (2005-2009 5-year est.).

Transportation: Commute to work: 100.0% car, 0.0% public transportation, 0.0% walk, 0.0% work from home (2005-2009 5-year est.); Travel time to work: 16.1% less than 15 minutes, 49.2% 15 to 30 minutes, 22.9% 30 to 45 minutes, 11.9% 45 to 60 minutes, 0.0% 60 minutes or more (2005-2009 5-year est.)

WILSONVILLE (village).

Covers a land area of 0.954 square miles and a water area of 0.024 square miles. Located at 39.07° N. Lat; 89.85° W. Long. Elevation is 643 feet.

Population: 609 (1990); 604 (2000); 592 (2010); 586 (2015 projected); Race: 97.5% White, 0.5% Black, 0.0% Asian, 2.0% Other, 0.5% Hispanic of any race (2010); Density: 620.8 persons per square mile (2010); Average household size: 2.46 (2010); Median age: 43.6 (2010); Males per 100 females: 86.2 (2010); Marriage status: 21.9% never married, 62.2% now married, 10.8% widowed, 5.1% divorced (2005-2009 5-year est.); Foreign born: 3.7% (2005-2009 5-year est.); Ancestry (includes multiple ancestries): 29.6% German, 18.6% Italian, 14.5% Irish, 13.3% English, 8.2% Croatian (2005-2009 5-year est.).

Economy: Employment by occupation: 7.8% management, 18.0% professional, 23.5% services, 21.2% sales, 0.0% farming, 15.7% construction, 13.8% production (2005-2009 5-year est.).

Income: Per capita income: $22,028 (2010); Median household income: $46,890 (2010); Average household income: $55,572 (2010); Percent of households with income of $100,000 or more: 11.7% (2010); Poverty rate: 16.3% (2005-2009 5-year est.).

Taxes: Total city taxes per capita: $24 (2007); City property taxes per capita: $22 (2007).

Education: Percent of population age 25 and over with: High school diploma (including GED) or higher: 83.6% (2010); Bachelor's degree or higher: 14.5% (2010); Master's degree or higher: 4.7% (2010).

Housing: Homeownership rate: 86.5% (2010); Median home value: $77,742 (2010); Median contract rent: $525 per month (2005-2009 5-year est.); Median year structure built: 1953 (2005-2009 5-year est.).

Transportation: Commute to work: 95.5% car, 0.0% public transportation, 4.5% walk, 0.0% work from home (2005-2009 5-year est.); Travel time to work: 9.5% less than 15 minutes, 31.8% 15 to 30 minutes, 34.3% 30 to 45 minutes, 12.4% 45 to 60 minutes, 11.9% 60 minutes or more (2005-2009 5-year est.)

Madison County

Located in southwestern Illinois; bounded on the west by the Mississippi River and the Missouri border; drained by Cahokia and Silver Creeks. Covers a land area of 725.02 square miles, a water area of 15.33 square miles, and is located in the Central Time Zone at 38.81° N. Lat., 90.01° W. Long. The county was founded in 1812. County seat is Edwardsville.

Madison County is part of the St. Louis, MO-IL Metropolitan Statistical Area. The entire metro area includes: Bond County, IL; Calhoun County, IL; Clinton County, IL; Jersey County, IL; Macoupin County, IL; Madison County, IL; Monroe County, IL; St. Clair County, IL; Crawford County, MO (pt.); Franklin County, MO; Jefferson County, MO; Lincoln County, MO; St.

Charles County, MO; St. Louis County, MO; Warren County, MO; Washington County, MO; St. Louis city, MO

Weather Station: Alton Melvin Price L&D   Elevation: 430 feet

	Jan	Feb	Mar	Apr	May	Jun	Jul	Aug	Sep	Oct	Nov	Dec
High	38	42	53	65	75	84	88	87	80	67	54	42
Low	22	25	35	45	56	65	69	68	60	47	37	26
Precip	2.4	2.3	3.2	4.2	5.1	3.6	3.8	3.3	3.1	3.2	3.8	2.9
Snow	1.4	1.8	0.8	0.2	0.0	0.0	0.0	0.0	0.0	tr	0.1	0.5

High and Low temperatures in degrees Fahrenheit; Precipitation and Snow in inches

Population: 249,238 (1990); 258,941 (2000); 269,509 (2010); 272,734 (2015 projected); Race: 88.6% White, 8.2% Black, 0.7% Asian, 2.6% Other, 2.3% Hispanic of any race (2010); Density: 371.7 persons per square mile (2010); Average household size: 2.42 (2010); Median age: 37.4 (2010); Males per 100 females: 94.2 (2010).
Religion: Five largest groups: 16.4% Catholic Church, 8.5% Southern Baptist Convention, 5.3% Lutheran Church—Missouri Synod, 4.3% United Church of Christ, 3.6% The United Methodist Church (2000).
Economy: Unemployment rate: 8.8% (August 2011); Total civilian labor force: 138,559 (August 2011); Leading industries: 15.8% health care and social assistance; 15.7% manufacturing; 15.1% retail trade (2009); Farms: 1,229 totaling 312,936 acres (2007); Companies that employ 500 or more persons: 16 (2009); Companies that employ 100 to 499 persons: 96 (2009); Companies that employ less than 100 persons: 5,876 (2009); Black-owned businesses: 569 (2007); Hispanic-owned businesses: 526 (2007); Asian-owned businesses: n/a (2007); Women-owned businesses: 5,762 (2007); Retail sales per capita: $13,492 (2010). Single-family building permits issued: 422 (2010); Multi-family building permits issued: 61 (2010).
Income: Per capita income: $26,184 (2010); Median household income: $51,752 (2010); Average household income: $64,280 (2010); Percent of households with income of $100,000 or more: 16.7% (2010); Poverty rate: 13.1% (2009); Bankruptcy rate: 5.55% (2010).
Taxes: Total county taxes per capita: $100 (2007); County property taxes per capita: $98 (2007).
Education: Percent of population age 25 and over with: High school diploma (including GED) or higher: 89.8% (2010); Bachelor's degree or higher: 23.1% (2010); Master's degree or higher: 8.1% (2010).
Housing: Homeownership rate: 74.3% (2010); Median home value: $111,236 (2010); Median contract rent: $508 per month (2005-2009 5-year est.); Median year structure built: 1965 (2005-2009 5-year est.)
Health: Birth rate: 132.9 per 10,000 population (2009); Death rate: 97.6 per 10,000 population (2009); Age-adjusted cancer mortality rate: 203.2 deaths per 100,000 population (2007); Number of physicians: 11.8 per 10,000 population (2008); Hospital beds: 43.1 per 10,000 population (2007); Hospital admissions: 1,214.2 per 10,000 population (2007).
Environment: Air Quality Index: 63.9% good, 34.6% moderate, 1.5% unhealthy for sensitive individuals, 0.0% unhealthy (percent of days in 2008)
Elections: 2008 Presidential election results: 53.7% Obama, 44.6% McCain, 0.8% Nader
National and State Parks: Horseshoe Lake State Park; Lovejoy State Memorial
Additional Information Contacts
Madison County Government . . . . (618) 692-6290
  http://www.co.madison.il.us
City of Alton . . . . (618) 463-3500
  http://www.alton-il.com
City of Collinsville. . . . . (618) 346-5200
  http://www2.collinsvilleil.org
City of Edwardsville . . . . (618) 692-7500
  http://www.cityofedwardsville.com
City of Granite City. . . . . (618) 452-6200
  http://www.granitecity.illinois.gov
City of Highland . . . . (618) 654-9891
  http://www.ci.highland.il.us
City of Troy. . . . . (618) 667-6741
  http://www.troyil.us
City of Wood River. . . . . (618) 251-3100
  http://www.woodriver.org
Collinsville Chamber of Commerce . . . . (618) 344-2884
  http://www.discovercollinsville.com
Edwardsville/Glen Carbon Chamber of Commerce . . . . . . (618) 656-7600
  http://www.edglenchamber.com

Highland Chamber of Commerce . . . . (618) 654-3721
  http://www.highlandillinois.com
River Bend Growth Association . . . . (618) 467-2280
  http://www.growthassociation.com
Southwestern Madison County Chamber of Commerce . . . (618) 876-6400
  http://www.chamberswmadisoncounty.com
Troy/Maryville/St. Jacob Area Chamber of Commerce . . . . (618) 667-8769
  http://www.troycoc.com
Village of Bethalto . . . . (618) 377-8051
  http://www.bethalto.com
Village of East Alton. . . . . (618) 259-7714
  http://www.eastaltonvillage.org
Village of Glen Carbon. . . . . (618) 288-1200
  http://www.glen-carbon.il.us
Village of Godfrey . . . . (618) 466-3324
  http://www.godfreyil.org
Village of Pontoon Beach. . . . . (618) 931-6100

Madison County Communities

ALHAMBRA (village). Covers a land area of 0.755 square miles and a water area of 0.006 square miles. Located at 38.88° N. Lat; 89.73° W. Long. Elevation is 564 feet.
Population: 709 (1990); 630 (2000); 704 (2010); 727 (2015 projected); Race: 98.3% White, 0.0% Black, 0.1% Asian, 1.6% Other, 1.1% Hispanic of any race (2010); Density: 932.4 persons per square mile (2010); Average household size: 2.50 (2010); Median age: 47.1 (2010); Males per 100 females: 93.4 (2010); Marriage status: 10.7% never married, 52.5% now married, 29.1% widowed, 7.6% divorced (2005-2009 5-year est.); Foreign born: 1.6% (2005-2009 5-year est.); Ancestry (includes multiple ancestries): 60.4% German, 17.0% Irish, 3.9% French, 3.9% English, 2.0% American (2005-2009 5-year est.).
Economy: Single-family building permits issued: 1 (2010); Multi-family building permits issued: 0 (2010); Employment by occupation: 11.9% management, 9.7% professional, 14.4% services, 28.4% sales, 0.0% farming, 17.6% construction, 18.0% production (2005-2009 5-year est.).
Income: Per capita income: $24,317 (2010); Median household income: $55,952 (2010); Average household income: $64,498 (2010); Percent of households with income of $100,000 or more: 15.0% (2010); Poverty rate: 0.0% (2005-2009 5-year est.).
Taxes: Total city taxes per capita: $105 (2007); City property taxes per capita: $102 (2007).
Education: Percent of population age 25 and over with: High school diploma (including GED) or higher: 85.5% (2010); Bachelor's degree or higher: 13.5% (2010); Master's degree or higher: 2.1% (2010).
School District(s)
Highland CUSD 5 (PK-12)
  2009-10 Enrollment: 3,107 . . . . (618) 654-2106
Housing: Homeownership rate: 86.2% (2010); Median home value: $138,851 (2010); Median contract rent: $458 per month (2005-2009 5-year est.); Median year structure built: 1958 (2005-2009 5-year est.).
Transportation: Commute to work: 92.6% car, 0.0% public transportation, 4.5% walk, 3.0% work from home (2005-2009 5-year est.); Travel time to work: 17.6% less than 15 minutes, 39.5% 15 to 30 minutes, 26.1% 30 to 45 minutes, 14.2% 45 to 60 minutes, 2.7% 60 minutes or more (2005-2009 5-year est.)

ALTON (city). Covers a land area of 15.645 square miles and a water area of 0.961 square miles. Located at 38.90° N. Lat; 90.16° W. Long. Elevation is 499 feet.
History: Alton's first known settler arrived about 1783, but significant settlement began between 1816 and 1818, when three towns were founded at this advantageous river location. One of these, planned by Colonel Rufus Easton and named for one of his sons, Alton, absorbed the other towns and was incorporated as a city in 1837. Alton was the site of the Lincoln-Shields duel in 1842, and the last Lincoln-Douglas debate in 1858.
Population: 32,996 (1990); 30,496 (2000); 29,266 (2010); 28,518 (2015 projected); Race: 70.7% White, 25.6% Black, 0.4% Asian, 3.3% Other, 2.1% Hispanic of any race (2010); Density: 1,870.6 persons per square mile (2010); Average household size: 2.30 (2010); Median age: 35.9 (2010); Males per 100 females: 91.6 (2010); Marriage status: 32.7% never married, 44.0% now married, 8.2% widowed, 15.0% divorced (2005-2009 5-year est.); Foreign born: 1.5% (2005-2009 5-year est.); Ancestry

(includes multiple ancestries): 24.9% German, 13.0% Irish, 11.9% English, 6.6% American, 4.5% Italian (2005-2009 5-year est.).
Economy: Unemployment rate: 11.5% (August 2011); Total civilian labor force: 13,937 (August 2011); Single-family building permits issued: 4 (2010); Multi-family building permits issued: 0 (2010); Employment by occupation: 8.1% management, 20.9% professional, 24.1% services, 23.2% sales, 0.2% farming, 6.6% construction, 17.0% production (2005-2009 5-year est.).
Income: Per capita income: $20,334 (2010); Median household income: $38,444 (2010); Average household income: $47,100 (2010); Percent of households with income of $100,000 or more: 7.8% (2010); Poverty rate: 21.3% (2005-2009 5-year est.).
Taxes: Total city taxes per capita: $339 (2007); City property taxes per capita: $175 (2007).
Education: Percent of population age 25 and over with: High school diploma (including GED) or higher: 87.7% (2010); Bachelor's degree or higher: 19.4% (2010); Master's degree or higher: 6.1% (2010).

School District(s)
Alton CUSD 11 (PK-12)
    2009-10 Enrollment: 6,653 . . . . (618) 474-2600
Vocational/Technical School(s)
CALC Institute of Technology (Private, For-profit)
    Fall 2009 Enrollment: 194 . . . . (618) 474-0616
Housing: Homeownership rate: 66.1% (2010); Median home value: $77,242 (2010); Median contract rent: $454 per month (2005-2009 5-year est.); Median year structure built: 1950 (2005-2009 5-year est.).
Hospitals: Alton Memorial Hospital (222 beds); Saint Anthony's Health Center (192 beds)
Safety: Violent crime rate: 60.3 per 10,000 population; Property crime rate: 438.6 per 10,000 population (2010).
Newspapers: Alton Telegraph (Local news; Circulation 27,600); The Telegraph (Regional news; Circulation 20,000)
Transportation: Commute to work: 93.4% car, 1.1% public transportation, 1.5% walk, 2.7% work from home (2005-2009 5-year est.); Travel time to work: 38.0% less than 15 minutes, 28.4% 15 to 30 minutes, 17.8% 30 to 45 minutes, 10.7% 45 to 60 minutes, 5.0% 60 minutes or more (2005-2009 5-year est.); Amtrak: train service available.
Airports: St Louis Regional (general aviation)
Additional Information Contacts
City of Alton . . . . (618) 463-3500
    http://www.alton-il.com

BETHALTO (village). Covers a land area of 6.578 square miles and a water area of 0 square miles. Located at 38.90° N. Lat; 90.04° W. Long. Elevation is 525 feet.
History: Incorporated 1869.
Population: 9,646 (1990); 9,454 (2000); 9,164 (2010); 9,040 (2015 projected); Race: 97.4% White, 0.8% Black, 0.4% Asian, 1.4% Other, 1.8% Hispanic of any race (2010); Density: 1,393.2 persons per square mile (2010); Average household size: 2.46 (2010); Median age: 37.3 (2010); Males per 100 females: 95.1 (2010); Marriage status: 20.4% never married, 53.9% now married, 10.6% widowed, 15.2% divorced (2005-2009 5-year est.); Foreign born: 0.9% (2005-2009 5-year est.); Ancestry (includes multiple ancestries): 36.2% German, 16.5% Irish, 11.5% English, 9.6% American, 6.7% Italian (2005-2009 5-year est.).
Economy: Single-family building permits issued: 19 (2010); Multi-family building permits issued: 0 (2010); Employment by occupation: 10.2% management, 20.3% professional, 13.2% services, 26.4% sales, 0.7% farming, 12.3% construction, 17.0% production (2005-2009 5-year est.).
Income: Per capita income: $24,194 (2010); Median household income: $52,804 (2010); Average household income: $59,825 (2010); Percent of households with income of $100,000 or more: 14.7% (2010); Poverty rate: 7.9% (2005-2009 5-year est.).
Taxes: Total city taxes per capita: $186 (2007); City property taxes per capita: $121 (2007).
Education: Percent of population age 25 and over with: High school diploma (including GED) or higher: 91.0% (2010); Bachelor's degree or higher: 15.7% (2010); Master's degree or higher: 6.5% (2010).

School District(s)
Bethalto CUSD 8 (PK-12)
    2009-10 Enrollment: 2,738 . . . . (618) 377-7200
Housing: Homeownership rate: 74.4% (2010); Median home value: $112,841 (2010); Median contract rent: $533 per month (2005-2009 5-year est.); Median year structure built: 1970 (2005-2009 5-year est.).

Safety: Violent crime rate: 10.1 per 10,000 population; Property crime rate: 28.3 per 10,000 population (2010).
Transportation: Commute to work: 95.9% car, 0.3% public transportation, 1.3% walk, 2.2% work from home (2005-2009 5-year est.); Travel time to work: 34.1% less than 15 minutes, 35.8% 15 to 30 minutes, 15.9% 30 to 45 minutes, 7.9% 45 to 60 minutes, 6.3% 60 minutes or more (2005-2009 5-year est.)
Additional Information Contacts
Village of Bethalto . . . . (618) 377-8051
    http://www.bethalto.com

COLLINSVILLE (city). Covers a land area of 13.594 square miles and a water area of 0.014 square miles. Located at 38.67° N. Lat; 89.99° W. Long. Elevation is 561 feet.
History: Named for William Collins and his family, founders of the town. Collinsville was settled in 1817 by William Collins and his brothers from Connecticut. Between the five brothers they operated a store, blacksmith shop, shoe shop, wagon shop, sawmill, tannery, distillery, and a church. Collinsville was incorporated as a village in 1856, and as a city in 1859. The arrival of the railroad in 1869 led to mining of a coal seam and building of an ore-smelting furnace.
Population: 23,754 (1990); 24,707 (2000); 26,206 (2010); 26,764 (2015 projected); Race: 88.9% White, 7.5% Black, 0.6% Asian, 3.0% Other, 3.3% Hispanic of any race (2010); Density: 1,927.7 persons per square mile (2010); Average household size: 2.30 (2010); Median age: 37.8 (2010); Males per 100 females: 95.9 (2010); Marriage status: 32.4% never married, 49.3% now married, 5.7% widowed, 12.6% divorced (2005-2009 5-year est.); Foreign born: 2.6% (2005-2009 5-year est.); Ancestry (includes multiple ancestries): 31.3% German, 16.4% Irish, 10.2% English, 8.3% Italian, 6.1% American (2005-2009 5-year est.).
Economy: Unemployment rate: 8.4% (August 2011); Total civilian labor force: 14,303 (August 2011); Single-family building permits issued: 3 (2010); Multi-family building permits issued: 0 (2010); Employment by occupation: 11.5% management, 20.5% professional, 19.3% services, 26.9% sales, 0.1% farming, 9.0% construction, 12.7% production (2005-2009 5-year est.).
Income: Per capita income: $26,132 (2010); Median household income: $51,085 (2010); Average household income: $60,202 (2010); Percent of households with income of $100,000 or more: 14.9% (2010); Poverty rate: 11.8% (2005-2009 5-year est.).
Taxes: Total city taxes per capita: $239 (2007); City property taxes per capita: $138 (2007).
Education: Percent of population age 25 and over with: High school diploma (including GED) or higher: 90.4% (2010); Bachelor's degree or higher: 24.1% (2010); Master's degree or higher: 7.6% (2010).

School District(s)
Collinsville Area Career Ctr (11-12)
    2009-10 Enrollment: n/a . . . . (618) 346-6320
Collinsville CUSD 10 (PK-12)
    2009-10 Enrollment: 6,623 . . . . (618) 346-6350
Two-year College(s)
Sanford-Brown College (Private, For-profit)
    Fall 2009 Enrollment: 612 . . . . (618) 344-5600
    2010-11 Tuition: In-state $16,321; Out-of-state $16,321
Housing: Homeownership rate: 67.8% (2010); Median home value: $116,058 (2010); Median contract rent: $533 per month (2005-2009 5-year est.); Median year structure built: 1968 (2005-2009 5-year est.).
Safety: Violent crime rate: 21.3 per 10,000 population; Property crime rate: 282.0 per 10,000 population (2010).
Newspapers: Collinsville Herald (Community news; Circulation 20,200); Collinsville Journal (Community news); Edwardsville Journal (Community news); Granite City Press Record Journal (Community news; Circulation 22,140); Granite City Press-Record (Community news)
Transportation: Commute to work: 92.8% car, 3.6% public transportation, 0.4% walk, 2.5% work from home (2005-2009 5-year est.); Travel time to work: 24.3% less than 15 minutes, 40.1% 15 to 30 minutes, 25.1% 30 to 45 minutes, 6.7% 45 to 60 minutes, 3.8% 60 minutes or more (2005-2009 5-year est.)
Additional Information Contacts
City of Collinsville . . . . (618) 346-5200
    http://www2.collinsvilleil.org
Collinsville Chamber of Commerce . . . . (618) 344-2884
    http://www.discovercollinsville.com

COTTAGE HILLS (unincorporated postal area, zip code 62018).
Covers a land area of 3.618 square miles and a water area of 0 square miles. Located at 38.90° N. Lat; 90.08° W. Long. Elevation is 512 feet.
Population: 4,387 (2000); Race: 94.4% White, 2.5% Black, 0.0% Asian, 3.1% Other, 0.6% Hispanic of any race (2000); Density: 1,212.5 persons per square mile (2000); Age: 27.2% under 18, 10.8% over 64 (2000); Marriage status: 28.0% never married, 52.3% now married, 6.1% widowed, 13.6% divorced (2000); Foreign born: 0.6% (2000); Ancestry (includes multiple ancestries): 23.9% German, 23.4% American, 8.0% Irish, 4.4% French (2000).
Economy: Employment by occupation: 5.3% management, 9.5% professional, 24.8% services, 25.8% sales, 0.0% farming, 14.9% construction, 19.7% production (2000).
Income: Per capita income: $13,242 (2000); Median household income: $29,898 (2000); Poverty rate: 17.3% (2000).
Education: Percent of population age 25 and over with: High school diploma (including GED) or higher: 75.0% (2000); Bachelor's degree or higher: 3.2% (2000).
Housing: Homeownership rate: 73.3% (2000); Median home value: $52,300 (2000); Median contract rent: $326 per month (2000); Median year structure built: 1962 (2000).
Transportation: Commute to work: 96.8% car, 0.0% public transportation, 2.1% walk, 0.7% work from home (2000); Travel time to work: 32.0% less than 15 minutes, 35.8% 15 to 30 minutes, 17.0% 30 to 45 minutes, 9.9% 45 to 60 minutes, 5.4% 60 minutes or more (2000)

DORSEY (unincorporated postal area, zip code 62021). Aka Dorsey's.
Covers a land area of 20.799 square miles and a water area of 0.041 square miles. Located at 38.97° N. Lat; 89.97° W. Long. Elevation is 587 feet.
Population: 965 (2000); Race: 100.0% White, 0.0% Black, 0.0% Asian, 0.0% Other, 0.0% Hispanic of any race (2000); Density: 46.4 persons per square mile (2000); Age: 24.5% under 18, 10.4% over 64 (2000); Marriage status: 17.6% never married, 70.9% now married, 3.7% widowed, 7.8% divorced (2000); Foreign born: 0.5% (2000); Ancestry (includes multiple ancestries): 41.5% German, 14.2% American, 12.1% Irish, 7.4% English, 5.7% Italian (2000).
Economy: Employment by occupation: 13.6% management, 14.5% professional, 10.9% services, 26.4% sales, 0.9% farming, 14.5% construction, 19.2% production (2000).
Income: Per capita income: $21,055 (2000); Median household income: $40,000 (2000); Poverty rate: 0.0% (2000).
Education: Percent of population age 25 and over with: High school diploma (including GED) or higher: 89.7% (2000); Bachelor's degree or higher: 17.5% (2000).
Housing: Homeownership rate: 95.1% (2000); Median home value: $85,700 (2000); Median contract rent: $375 per month (2000); Median year structure built: 1968 (2000).
Transportation: Commute to work: 96.8% car, 0.0% public transportation, 0.0% walk, 3.2% work from home (2000); Travel time to work: 20.0% less than 15 minutes, 46.5% 15 to 30 minutes, 22.7% 30 to 45 minutes, 9.3% 45 to 60 minutes, 1.5% 60 minutes or more (2000)

EAST ALTON (village). Covers a land area of 5.502 square miles and a water area of 0.131 square miles. Located at 38.88° N. Lat; 90.10° W. Long. Elevation is 436 feet.
History: In 1893 the Western Cartridge Company established a powder mill in East Alton and began the manufacture of ammunition.
Population: 7,222 (1990); 6,830 (2000); 6,488 (2010); 6,302 (2015 projected); Race: 94.8% White, 1.6% Black, 0.5% Asian, 3.1% Other, 1.8% Hispanic of any race (2010); Density: 1,179.1 persons per square mile (2010); Average household size: 2.24 (2010); Median age: 36.2 (2010); Males per 100 females: 94.3 (2010); Marriage status: 25.1% never married, 48.8% now married, 7.8% widowed, 18.4% divorced (2005-2009 5-year est.); Foreign born: 0.8% (2005-2009 5-year est.); Ancestry (includes multiple ancestries): 35.6% German, 15.0% Irish, 14.1% American, 9.2% English, 3.8% French (2005-2009 5-year est.).
Economy: Single-family building permits issued: 4 (2010); Multi-family building permits issued: 0 (2010); Employment by occupation: 7.6% management, 10.0% professional, 24.4% services, 26.6% sales, 0.0% farming, 8.1% construction, 23.4% production (2005-2009 5-year est.).
Income: Per capita income: $18,044 (2010); Median household income: $31,725 (2010); Average household income: $40,385 (2010); Percent of

households with income of $100,000 or more: 4.5% (2010); Poverty rate: 27.1% (2005-2009 5-year est.).
Taxes: Total city taxes per capita: $181 (2007); City property taxes per capita: $161 (2007).
Education: Percent of population age 25 and over with: High school diploma (including GED) or higher: 80.4% (2010); Bachelor's degree or higher: 8.3% (2010); Master's degree or higher: 1.5% (2010).
School District(s)
East Alton SD 13 (PK-08)
    2009-10 Enrollment: 820 . . . . (618) 433-2051
Housing: Homeownership rate: 57.4% (2010); Median home value: $72,468 (2010); Median contract rent: $416 per month (2005-2009 5-year est.); Median year structure built: 1953 (2005-2009 5-year est.).
Safety: Violent crime rate: 23.3 per 10,000 population; Property crime rate: 508.5 per 10,000 population (2010).
Transportation: Commute to work: 95.3% car, 1.4% public transportation, 1.2% walk, 0.9% work from home (2005-2009 5-year est.); Travel time to work: 39.0% less than 15 minutes, 30.3% 15 to 30 minutes, 15.1% 30 to 45 minutes, 12.0% 45 to 60 minutes, 3.6% 60 minutes or more (2005-2009 5-year est.)
Additional Information Contacts
Village of East Alton. . . . . (618) 259-7714
    http://www.eastaltonvillage.org

EDWARDSVILLE (city). County seat. Covers a land area of 13.872 square miles and a water area of 0.218 square miles. Located at 38.80° N. Lat; 89.95° W. Long. Elevation is 541 feet.
History: Edwardsville was settled by James Gillham of Kentucky in 1800. Some of his friends followed and a town was platted in 1813, named for Ninian Edwards, governor of Illinois Territory from 1809-1818. Edwardsville was incorporated in 1837.
Population: 17,105 (1990); 21,491 (2000); 22,832 (2010); 23,461 (2015 projected); Race: 85.9% White, 9.9% Black, 1.5% Asian, 2.7% Other, 1.5% Hispanic of any race (2010); Density: 1,645.9 persons per square mile (2010); Average household size: 2.38 (2010); Median age: 34.7 (2010); Males per 100 females: 90.4 (2010); Marriage status: 43.9% never married, 44.6% now married, 3.9% widowed, 7.6% divorced (2005-2009 5-year est.); Foreign born: 4.2% (2005-2009 5-year est.); Ancestry (includes multiple ancestries): 38.2% German, 15.1% Irish, 11.1% English, 4.8% Italian, 4.4% American (2005-2009 5-year est.).
Economy: Single-family building permits issued: 50 (2010); Multi-family building permits issued: 0 (2010); Employment by occupation: 17.7% management, 29.0% professional, 18.2% services, 24.0% sales, 0.0% farming, 3.6% construction, 7.5% production (2005-2009 5-year est.).
Income: Per capita income: $32,320 (2010); Median household income: $64,231 (2010); Average household income: $82,709 (2010); Percent of households with income of $100,000 or more: 26.8% (2010); Poverty rate: 12.0% (2005-2009 5-year est.).
Taxes: Total city taxes per capita: $422 (2007); City property taxes per capita: $364 (2007).
Education: Percent of population age 25 and over with: High school diploma (including GED) or higher: 95.3% (2010); Bachelor's degree or higher: 44.6% (2010); Master's degree or higher: 17.6% (2010).
School District(s)
Edwardsville CUSD 7 (PK-12)
    2009-10 Enrollment: 7,623 . . . . (618) 656-1182
Four-year College(s)
Southern Illinois University Edwardsville (Public)
    Fall 2009 Enrollment: 13,940 . . . . (618) 650-2000
    2010-11 Tuition: In-state $8,401; Out-of-state $17,703
Vocational/Technical School(s)
Alvareitas College of Cosmetology (Private, For-profit)
    Fall 2009 Enrollment: 44 . . . . (618) 656-2593
    2010-11 Tuition: $12,600
Housing: Homeownership rate: 71.4% (2010); Median home value: $141,848 (2010); Median contract rent: $654 per month (2005-2009 5-year est.); Median year structure built: 1973 (2005-2009 5-year est.).
Safety: Violent crime rate: 8.2 per 10,000 population; Property crime rate: 176.8 per 10,000 population (2010).
Newspapers: Edwardsville Intelligencer (Local news; Circulation 5,406); The Record (Regional news); St. Louis Post-Dispatch - Edwardsville Bureau (Local news; Circulation 490,000)
Transportation: Commute to work: 86.4% car, 5.8% public transportation, 2.7% walk, 3.7% work from home (2005-2009 5-year est.); Travel time to work: 35.1% less than 15 minutes, 27.9% 15 to 30 minutes, 23.2% 30 to 45

minutes, 9.8% 45 to 60 minutes, 4.0% 60 minutes or more (2005-2009 5-year est.)

Additional Information Contacts

City of Edwardsville . . . . (618) 692-7500
    http://www.cityofedwardsville.com

Edwardsville/Glen Carbon Chamber of Commerce . . . . (618) 656-7600
    http://www.edglenchamber.com

GLEN CARBON (village). Covers a land area of 7.417 square miles and a water area of 0.043 square miles. Located at 38.76° N. Lat; 89.96° W. Long. Elevation is 466 feet.

History: Incorporated 1892.

Population: 8,151 (1990); 10,425 (2000); 13,082 (2010); 14,105 (2015 projected); Race: 89.5% White, 6.4% Black, 2.1% Asian, 2.0% Other, 2.1% Hispanic of any race (2010); Density: 1,763.8 persons per square mile (2010); Average household size: 2.56 (2010); Median age: 35.9 (2010); Males per 100 females: 96.3 (2010); Marriage status: 27.6% never married, 59.4% now married, 6.3% widowed, 6.8% divorced (2005-2009 5-year est.); Foreign born: 5.7% (2005-2009 5-year est.); Ancestry (includes multiple ancestries): 35.7% German, 15.8% Irish, 10.8% English, 6.0% American, 5.3% French (2005-2009 5-year est.).

Economy: Single-family building permits issued: 43 (2010); Multi-family building permits issued: 0 (2010); Employment by occupation: 18.7% management, 31.6% professional, 12.9% services, 20.8% sales, 0.0% farming, 4.8% construction, 11.2% production (2005-2009 5-year est.).

Income: Per capita income: $34,852 (2010); Median household income: $74,270 (2010); Average household income: $89,512 (2010); Percent of households with income of $100,000 or more: 34.2% (2010); Poverty rate: 5.5% (2005-2009 5-year est.).

Taxes: Total city taxes per capita: $283 (2007); City property taxes per capita: $258 (2007).

Education: Percent of population age 25 and over with: High school diploma (including GED) or higher: 94.7% (2010); Bachelor's degree or higher: 49.0% (2010); Master's degree or higher: 18.9% (2010).

School District(s)

Edwardsville CUSD 7 (PK-12)
    2009-10 Enrollment: 7,623 . . . . (618) 656-1182

Housing: Homeownership rate: 75.5% (2010); Median home value: $175,737 (2010); Median contract rent: $657 per month (2005-2009 5-year est.); Median year structure built: 1986 (2005-2009 5-year est.).

Transportation: Commute to work: 94.8% car, 1.5% public transportation, 0.3% walk, 3.0% work from home (2005-2009 5-year est.); Travel time to work: 27.9% less than 15 minutes, 34.5% 15 to 30 minutes, 24.8% 30 to 45 minutes, 9.9% 45 to 60 minutes, 2.9% 60 minutes or more (2005-2009 5-year est.)

Additional Information Contacts

Village of Glen Carbon . . . . (618) 288-1200
    http://www.glen-carbon.il.us

GODFREY (village). Covers a land area of 34.481 square miles and a water area of 1.686 square miles. Located at 38.94° N. Lat; 90.20° W. Long. Elevation is 610 feet.

History: Godfrey grew around the Monticello College and Preparatory School for Girls, founded in 1835 by a retired Cape Cod sea captain, Benjamin Godfrey.

Population: 15,785 (1990); 16,286 (2000); 17,047 (2010); 17,378 (2015 projected); Race: 91.5% White, 6.1% Black, 0.7% Asian, 1.8% Other, 1.5% Hispanic of any race (2010); Density: 494.4 persons per square mile (2010); Average household size: 2.38 (2010); Median age: 42.5 (2010); Males per 100 females: 95.4 (2010); Marriage status: 23.2% never married, 56.7% now married, 10.5% widowed, 9.7% divorced (2005-2009 5-year est.); Foreign born: 0.7% (2005-2009 5-year est.); Ancestry (includes multiple ancestries): 38.5% German, 17.5% Irish, 14.7% English, 6.6% American, 4.0% French (2005-2009 5-year est.).

Economy: Single-family building permits issued: 28 (2010); Multi-family building permits issued: 12 (2010); Employment by occupation: 13.6% management, 20.8% professional, 16.3% services, 27.2% sales, 0.0% farming, 8.7% construction, 13.4% production (2005-2009 5-year est.).

Income: Per capita income: $29,918 (2010); Median household income: $60,076 (2010); Average household income: $72,636 (2010); Percent of households with income of $100,000 or more: 19.7% (2010); Poverty rate: 9.6% (2005-2009 5-year est.).

Taxes: Total city taxes per capita: $79 (2007); City property taxes per capita: $39 (2007).

Education: Percent of population age 25 and over with: High school diploma (including GED) or higher: 91.5% (2010); Bachelor's degree or higher: 28.3% (2010); Master's degree or higher: 11.0% (2010).

School District(s)

Alton CUSD 11 (PK-12)
    2009-10 Enrollment: 6,653 . . . . (618) 474-2600

Two-year College(s)

Lewis and Clark Community College (Public)
    Fall 2009 Enrollment: 8,179 . . . . (618) 468-7000
    2010-11 Tuition: In-state $7,784; Out-of-state $10,220

Vocational/Technical School(s)

Alvareitas College of Cosmetology (Private, For-profit)
    Fall 2009 Enrollment: 36 . . . . (618) 466-8952
    2010-11 Tuition: $12,600

Housing: Homeownership rate: 84.1% (2010); Median home value: $131,844 (2010); Median contract rent: $553 per month (2005-2009 5-year est.); Median year structure built: 1971 (2005-2009 5-year est.).

Transportation: Commute to work: 96.9% car, 0.2% public transportation, 0.5% walk, 1.9% work from home (2005-2009 5-year est.); Travel time to work: 35.4% less than 15 minutes, 29.6% 15 to 30 minutes, 14.7% 30 to 45 minutes, 14.2% 45 to 60 minutes, 6.1% 60 minutes or more (2005-2009 5-year est.)

Additional Information Contacts

River Bend Growth Association . . . . (618) 467-2280
    http://www.growthassociation.com

Village of Godfrey . . . . (618) 466-3324
    http://www.godfreyil.org

GRANITE CITY (city). Covers a land area of 16.683 square miles and a water area of 0.487 square miles. Located at 38.71° N. Lat; 90.13° W. Long. Elevation is 423 feet.

History: Farmers settled here in the early 1800's, but Granite City began when William F. Niedringhaus purchased land here for his National Enameling and Stamping Company plant. The American Steel Foundry followed, and in 1896 Granite City was incorporated, named for the granite ware produced there.

Population: 34,236 (1990); 31,301 (2000); 29,699 (2010); 28,933 (2015 projected); Race: 91.8% White, 3.5% Black, 0.5% Asian, 4.2% Other, 4.4% Hispanic of any race (2010); Density: 1,780.2 persons per square mile (2010); Average household size: 2.37 (2010); Median age: 38.5 (2010); Males per 100 females: 93.8 (2010); Marriage status: 26.0% never married, 51.2% now married, 9.4% widowed, 13.4% divorced (2005-2009 5-year est.); Foreign born: 2.4% (2005-2009 5-year est.); Ancestry (includes multiple ancestries): 25.8% German, 19.7% Irish, 9.7% English, 9.7% American, 5.7% Italian (2005-2009 5-year est.).

Economy: Unemployment rate: 10.0% (August 2011); Total civilian labor force: 15,049 (August 2011); Single-family building permits issued: 15 (2010); Multi-family building permits issued: 43 (2010); Employment by occupation: 10.8% management, 15.3% professional, 16.8% services, 29.0% sales, 0.1% farming, 10.9% construction, 17.2% production (2005-2009 5-year est.).

Income: Per capita income: $21,157 (2010); Median household income: $41,758 (2010); Average household income: $50,239 (2010); Percent of households with income of $100,000 or more: 8.0% (2010); Poverty rate: 15.1% (2005-2009 5-year est.).

Taxes: Total city taxes per capita: $390 (2007); City property taxes per capita: $242 (2007).

Education: Percent of population age 25 and over with: High school diploma (including GED) or higher: 84.4% (2010); Bachelor's degree or higher: 11.8% (2010); Master's degree or higher: 3.5% (2010).

School District(s)

Granite City CUSD 9 (PK-12)
    2009-10 Enrollment: 7,065 . . . . (618) 451-5800

Housing: Homeownership rate: 71.3% (2010); Median home value: $75,045 (2010); Median contract rent: $451 per month (2005-2009 5-year est.); Median year structure built: 1955 (2005-2009 5-year est.).

Hospitals: Gateway Regional Medical Center (393 beds)

Safety: Violent crime rate: 52.2 per 10,000 population; Property crime rate: 256.8 per 10,000 population (2010).

Transportation: Commute to work: 93.6% car, 1.2% public transportation, 2.3% walk, 2.1% work from home (2005-2009 5-year est.); Travel time to work: 31.7% less than 15 minutes, 37.1% 15 to 30 minutes, 21.7% 30 to 45 minutes, 7.5% 45 to 60 minutes, 2.0% 60 minutes or more (2005-2009 5-year est.)

Additional Information Contacts

City of Granite City. . . . . (618) 452-6200
    http://www.granitecity.illinois.gov
Southwestern Madison County Chamber of Commerce . . . (618) 876-6400
    http://www.chamberswmadisoncounty.com

GRANTFORK (village).
Covers a land area of 0.228 square miles and a water area of 0 square miles. Located at 38.83° N. Lat; 89.66° W. Long. Elevation is 535 feet.
Population: 276 (1990); 254 (2000); 271 (2010); 289 (2015 projected); Race: 98.2% White, 0.4% Black, 0.0% Asian, 1.5% Other, 2.2% Hispanic of any race (2010); Density: 1,186.5 persons per square mile (2010); Average household size: 2.63 (2010); Median age: 36.7 (2010); Males per 100 females: 99.3 (2010); Marriage status: 27.3% never married, 52.3% now married, 7.4% widowed, 13.1% divorced (2005-2009 5-year est.); Foreign born: 4.5% (2005-2009 5-year est.); Ancestry (includes multiple ancestries): 34.8% German, 22.2% American, 12.7% Irish, 5.0% English, 3.6% Scottish (2005-2009 5-year est.).
Economy: Single-family building permits issued: 0 (2010); Multi-family building permits issued: 0 (2010); Employment by occupation: 1.9% management, 10.6% professional, 27.9% services, 18.3% sales, 0.0% farming, 23.1% construction, 18.3% production (2005-2009 5-year est.).
Income: Per capita income: $28,518 (2010); Median household income: $66,406 (2010); Average household income: $71,748 (2010); Percent of households with income of $100,000 or more: 21.4% (2010); Poverty rate: 8.1% (2005-2009 5-year est.).
Taxes: Total city taxes per capita: $32 (2007); City property taxes per capita: $25 (2007).
Education: Percent of population age 25 and over with: High school diploma (including GED) or higher: 87.2% (2010); Bachelor's degree or higher: 15.1% (2010); Master's degree or higher: 4.5% (2010).
Housing: Homeownership rate: 87.4% (2010); Median home value: $130,000 (2010); Median contract rent: n/a per month (2005-2009 5-year est.); Median year structure built: 1975 (2005-2009 5-year est.).
Safety: Violent crime rate: 0.0 per 10,000 population; Property crime rate: 58.0 per 10,000 population (2010).
Transportation: Commute to work: 80.8% car, 3.8% public transportation, 0.0% walk, 10.6% work from home (2005-2009 5-year est.); Travel time to work: 20.4% less than 15 minutes, 39.8% 15 to 30 minutes, 21.5% 30 to 45 minutes, 11.8% 45 to 60 minutes, 6.5% 60 minutes or more (2005-2009 5-year est.)

HAMEL (village).
Covers a land area of 1.160 square miles and a water area of 0 square miles. Located at 38.88° N. Lat; 89.84° W. Long. Elevation is 545 feet.
Population: 530 (1990); 570 (2000); 600 (2010); 612 (2015 projected); Race: 97.3% White, 0.8% Black, 0.0% Asian, 1.8% Other, 1.2% Hispanic of any race (2010); Density: 517.1 persons per square mile (2010); Average household size: 2.46 (2010); Median age: 38.7 (2010); Males per 100 females: 96.7 (2010); Marriage status: 17.4% never married, 45.5% now married, 26.8% widowed, 10.4% divorced (2005-2009 5-year est.); Foreign born: 0.0% (2005-2009 5-year est.); Ancestry (includes multiple ancestries): 46.0% German, 6.8% French, 6.4% Irish, 5.9% English, 2.7% Italian (2005-2009 5-year est.).
Economy: Single-family building permits issued: 4 (2010); Multi-family building permits issued: 0 (2010); Employment by occupation: 5.7% management, 15.7% professional, 42.7% services, 23.1% sales, 0.0% farming, 1.4% construction, 11.4% production (2005-2009 5-year est.).
Income: Per capita income: $24,134 (2010); Median household income: $57,813 (2010); Average household income: $59,877 (2010); Percent of households with income of $100,000 or more: 13.1% (2010); Poverty rate: 1.1% (2005-2009 5-year est.).
Taxes: Total city taxes per capita: $161 (2007); City property taxes per capita: $49 (2007).
Education: Percent of population age 25 and over with: High school diploma (including GED) or higher: 89.3% (2010); Bachelor's degree or higher: 20.8% (2010); Master's degree or higher: 3.0% (2010).
School District(s)
Edwardsville CUSD 7 (PK-12)
    2009-10 Enrollment: 7,623 . . . . (618) 656-1182
Housing: Homeownership rate: 78.3% (2010); Median home value: $134,063 (2010); Median contract rent: $654 per month (2005-2009 5-year est.); Median year structure built: 1958 (2005-2009 5-year est.).
Transportation: Commute to work: 96.5% car, 0.0% public transportation, 1.4% walk, 2.0% work from home (2005-2009 5-year est.); Travel time to work: 9.4% less than 15 minutes, 35.9% 15 to 30 minutes, 20.0% 30 to 45

minutes, 33.2% 45 to 60 minutes, 1.5% 60 minutes or more (2005-2009 5-year est.)

HARTFORD (village).
Covers a land area of 3.898 square miles and a water area of 0.014 square miles. Located at 38.82° N. Lat; 90.09° W. Long. Elevation is 430 feet.
History: In 1915 the International Shoe Company established a tannery in Hartford, and the town developed around it.
Population: 1,690 (1990); 1,545 (2000); 1,496 (2010); 1,466 (2015 projected); Race: 97.6% White, 0.3% Black, 0.5% Asian, 1.7% Other, 1.2% Hispanic of any race (2010); Density: 383.8 persons per square mile (2010); Average household size: 2.30 (2010); Median age: 39.8 (2010); Males per 100 females: 100.8 (2010); Marriage status: 19.9% never married, 56.9% now married, 9.7% widowed, 13.6% divorced (2005-2009 5-year est.); Foreign born: 0.8% (2005-2009 5-year est.); Ancestry (includes multiple ancestries): 28.3% German, 15.7% Irish, 11.1% American, 9.3% English, 5.5% Dutch (2005-2009 5-year est.).
Economy: Single-family building permits issued: 0 (2010); Multi-family building permits issued: 0 (2010); Employment by occupation: 3.9% management, 14.8% professional, 18.2% services, 21.0% sales, 0.0% farming, 18.9% construction, 23.2% production (2005-2009 5-year est.).
Income: Per capita income: $19,470 (2010); Median household income: $38,686 (2010); Average household income: $44,677 (2010); Percent of households with income of $100,000 or more: 6.2% (2010); Poverty rate: 13.5% (2005-2009 5-year est.).
Taxes: Total city taxes per capita: $835 (2007); City property taxes per capita: $526 (2007).
Education: Percent of population age 25 and over with: High school diploma (including GED) or higher: 84.8% (2010); Bachelor's degree or higher: 4.4% (2010); Master's degree or higher: 1.0% (2010).
School District(s)
Wood River-Hartford ESD 15 (PK-08)
    2009-10 Enrollment: 830 . . . . (618) 254-0607
Housing: Homeownership rate: 77.8% (2010); Median home value: $60,000 (2010); Median contract rent: $467 per month (2005-2009 5-year est.); Median year structure built: 1951 (2005-2009 5-year est.).
Transportation: Commute to work: 90.6% car, 2.1% public transportation, 1.5% walk, 3.9% work from home (2005-2009 5-year est.); Travel time to work: 35.6% less than 15 minutes, 35.9% 15 to 30 minutes, 21.3% 30 to 45 minutes, 4.3% 45 to 60 minutes, 3.0% 60 minutes or more (2005-2009 5-year est.)

HIGHLAND (city).
Covers a land area of 5.405 square miles and a water area of 1.018 square miles. Located at 38.74° N. Lat; 89.67° W. Long. Elevation is 525 feet.
History: Highland was settled about 1804 by families from Kentucky and North Carolina. In 1831 a group of Swiss colonists led by Dr. Caspar Koepfli located in Highland, and the community became a dairy producer. A leading firm here in the early 1900's was the Wicks Organ Company.
Population: 7,847 (1990); 8,438 (2000); 9,058 (2010); 9,341 (2015 projected); Race: 98.3% White, 0.1% Black, 0.6% Asian, 1.1% Other, 2.3% Hispanic of any race (2010); Density: 1,675.8 persons per square mile (2010); Average household size: 2.40 (2010); Median age: 37.1 (2010); Males per 100 females: 91.5 (2010); Marriage status: 23.5% never married, 57.8% now married, 8.7% widowed, 10.0% divorced (2005-2009 5-year est.); Foreign born: 1.2% (2005-2009 5-year est.); Ancestry (includes multiple ancestries): 53.7% German, 13.9% Irish, 8.2% English, 6.6% American, 6.1% Swiss (2005-2009 5-year est.).
Economy: Single-family building permits issued: 16 (2010); Multi-family building permits issued: 0 (2010); Employment by occupation: 14.6% management, 18.1% professional, 17.0% services, 26.1% sales, 0.8% farming, 12.0% construction, 11.3% production (2005-2009 5-year est.).
Income: Per capita income: $26,502 (2010); Median household income: $52,545 (2010); Average household income: $64,694 (2010); Percent of households with income of $100,000 or more: 17.7% (2010); Poverty rate: 4.9% (2005-2009 5-year est.).
Taxes: Total city taxes per capita: $305 (2007); City property taxes per capita: $269 (2007).
Education: Percent of population age 25 and over with: High school diploma (including GED) or higher: 91.0% (2010); Bachelor's degree or higher: 25.7% (2010); Master's degree or higher: 8.6% (2010).
School District(s)
Highland CUSD 5 (PK-12)
    2009-10 Enrollment: 3,107 . . . . (618) 654-2106

Housing: Homeownership rate: 72.4% (2010); Median home value: $129,100 (2010); Median contract rent: $488 per month (2005-2009 5-year est.); Median year structure built: 1973 (2005-2009 5-year est.).
Hospitals: St. Joseph's Hospital (106 beds)
Safety: Violent crime rate: 9.1 per 10,000 population; Property crime rate: 195.1 per 10,000 population (2010).
Newspapers: Highland News Leader (Local news; Circulation 15,000)
Transportation: Commute to work: 92.6% car, 1.5% public transportation, 1.8% walk, 2.4% work from home (2005-2009 5-year est.); Travel time to work: 48.1% less than 15 minutes, 16.5% 15 to 30 minutes, 18.2% 30 to 45 minutes, 12.1% 45 to 60 minutes, 5.1% 60 minutes or more (2005-2009 5-year est.)
Additional Information Contacts
City of Highland . . . . (618) 654-9891
　http://www.ci.highland.il.us
Highland Chamber of Commerce . . . . (618) 654-3721
　http://www.highlandillinois.com

LIVINGSTON (village). Covers a land area of 1.061 square miles and a water area of 0.008 square miles. Located at 38.96° N. Lat; 89.76° W. Long. Elevation is 591 feet.
History: Incorporated 1905.
Population: 928 (1990); 825 (2000); 743 (2010); 705 (2015 projected); Race: 98.7% White, 0.0% Black, 0.0% Asian, 1.3% Other, 0.5% Hispanic of any race (2010); Density: 700.2 persons per square mile (2010); Average household size: 2.18 (2010); Median age: 39.7 (2010); Males per 100 females: 100.8 (2010); Marriage status: 26.8% never married, 58.9% now married, 3.9% widowed, 10.3% divorced (2005-2009 5-year est.); Foreign born: 0.9% (2005-2009 5-year est.); Ancestry (includes multiple ancestries): 29.7% German, 12.1% Irish, 10.6% English, 9.2% Italian, 4.0% French (2005-2009 5-year est.).
Economy: Single-family building permits issued: 0 (2010); Multi-family building permits issued: 0 (2010); Employment by occupation: 4.4% management, 19.3% professional, 17.1% services, 21.3% sales, 0.0% farming, 19.3% construction, 18.5% production (2005-2009 5-year est.).
Income: Per capita income: $25,406 (2010); Median household income: $51,658 (2010); Average household income: $55,528 (2010); Percent of households with income of $100,000 or more: 8.2% (2010); Poverty rate: 28.2% (2005-2009 5-year est.).
Taxes: Total city taxes per capita: $83 (2007); City property taxes per capita: $29 (2007).
Education: Percent of population age 25 and over with: High school diploma (including GED) or higher: 86.3% (2010); Bachelor's degree or higher: 8.6% (2010); Master's degree or higher: 3.3% (2010).
School District(s)
Staunton CUSD 6 (PK-12)
　2009-10 Enrollment: 1,249 . . . . (618) 635-2962
Housing: Homeownership rate: 79.2% (2010); Median home value: $74,915 (2010); Median contract rent: $454 per month (2005-2009 5-year est.); Median year structure built: 1952 (2005-2009 5-year est.).
Transportation: Commute to work: 90.8% car, 5.9% public transportation, 1.7% walk, 1.7% work from home (2005-2009 5-year est.); Travel time to work: 15.4% less than 15 minutes, 25.9% 15 to 30 minutes, 43.9% 30 to 45 minutes, 9.7% 45 to 60 minutes, 5.1% 60 minutes or more (2005-2009 5-year est.)

MADISON (city). Covers a land area of 7.011 square miles and a water area of 0.266 square miles. Located at 38.68° N. Lat; 90.15° W. Long. Elevation is 413 feet.
History: The Madison Land Syndicate was formed in 1887 by a group of St. Louis businessmen who promoted the construction of Merchants Bridge over the Mississippi River. An American Car and Foundry plant was built near the new bridge, and the town of Madison was incorporated in 1891 by the Land Syndicate.
Population: 5,215 (1990); 4,545 (2000); 4,578 (2010); 4,594 (2015 projected); Race: 43.9% White, 52.2% Black, 0.1% Asian, 3.8% Other, 3.7% Hispanic of any race (2010); Density: 653.0 persons per square mile (2010); Average household size: 2.47 (2010); Median age: 32.6 (2010); Males per 100 females: 96.7 (2010); Marriage status: 46.5% never married, 30.4% now married, 11.2% widowed, 12.0% divorced (2005-2009 5-year est.); Foreign born: 0.0% (2005-2009 5-year est.); Ancestry (includes multiple ancestries): 9.8% German, 7.5% European, 7.2% Irish, 4.2% Polish, 3.4% American (2005-2009 5-year est.).
Economy: Single-family building permits issued: 3 (2010); Multi-family building permits issued: 0 (2010); Employment by occupation: 2.4%

management, 11.3% professional, 22.2% services, 24.3% sales, 0.0% farming, 8.1% construction, 31.8% production (2005-2009 5-year est.).
Income: Per capita income: $15,646 (2010); Median household income: $29,882 (2010); Average household income: $38,580 (2010); Percent of households with income of $100,000 or more: 4.7% (2010); Poverty rate: 29.3% (2005-2009 5-year est.).
Taxes: Total city taxes per capita: $573 (2007); City property taxes per capita: $402 (2007).
Education: Percent of population age 25 and over with: High school diploma (including GED) or higher: 76.7% (2010); Bachelor's degree or higher: 7.5% (2010); Master's degree or higher: 2.8% (2010).
School District(s)
Madison CUSD 12 (PK-12)
　2009-10 Enrollment: 862 . . . . (618) 877-1712
Housing: Homeownership rate: 59.7% (2010); Median home value: $52,203 (2010); Median contract rent: $478 per month (2005-2009 5-year est.); Median year structure built: 1953 (2005-2009 5-year est.).
Transportation: Commute to work: 91.0% car, 5.1% public transportation, 0.8% walk, 1.1% work from home (2005-2009 5-year est.); Travel time to work: 44.9% less than 15 minutes, 34.3% 15 to 30 minutes, 16.1% 30 to 45 minutes, 3.4% 45 to 60 minutes, 1.4% 60 minutes or more (2005-2009 5-year est.)

MARINE (village). Covers a land area of 0.761 square miles and a water area of 0.019 square miles. Located at 38.78° N. Lat; 89.77° W. Long. Elevation is 522 feet.
Population: 972 (1990); 910 (2000); 922 (2010); 926 (2015 projected); Race: 97.2% White, 0.0% Black, 0.1% Asian, 2.7% Other, 1.1% Hispanic of any race (2010); Density: 1,212.1 persons per square mile (2010); Average household size: 2.44 (2010); Median age: 36.2 (2010); Males per 100 females: 94.1 (2010); Marriage status: 31.5% never married, 50.4% now married, 6.5% widowed, 11.6% divorced (2005-2009 5-year est.); Foreign born: 0.6% (2005-2009 5-year est.); Ancestry (includes multiple ancestries): 57.7% German, 20.9% Irish, 8.7% English, 3.8% Dutch, 3.7% Polish (2005-2009 5-year est.).
Economy: Single-family building permits issued: 0 (2010); Multi-family building permits issued: 0 (2010); Employment by occupation: 15.9% management, 12.5% professional, 20.3% services, 24.1% sales, 1.6% farming, 12.1% construction, 13.4% production (2005-2009 5-year est.).
Income: Per capita income: $25,293 (2010); Median household income: $49,741 (2010); Average household income: $62,242 (2010); Percent of households with income of $100,000 or more: 16.4% (2010); Poverty rate: 8.6% (2005-2009 5-year est.).
Taxes: Total city taxes per capita: $102 (2007); City property taxes per capita: $66 (2007).
Education: Percent of population age 25 and over with: High school diploma (including GED) or higher: 89.0% (2010); Bachelor's degree or higher: 14.2% (2010); Master's degree or higher: 5.2% (2010).
School District(s)
Triad CUSD 2 (PK-12)
　2009-10 Enrollment: 3,730 . . . . (618) 667-8851
Housing: Homeownership rate: 74.6% (2010); Median home value: $123,611 (2010); Median contract rent: $524 per month (2005-2009 5-year est.); Median year structure built: 1955 (2005-2009 5-year est.).
Transportation: Commute to work: 93.2% car, 0.0% public transportation, 5.7% walk, 0.5% work from home (2005-2009 5-year est.); Travel time to work: 20.8% less than 15 minutes, 44.2% 15 to 30 minutes, 21.1% 30 to 45 minutes, 10.5% 45 to 60 minutes, 3.4% 60 minutes or more (2005-2009 5-year est.)

MARYVILLE (village). Covers a land area of 4.667 square miles and a water area of 0.032 square miles. Located at 38.72° N. Lat; 89.95° W. Long. Elevation is 577 feet.
Population: 3,477 (1990); 4,651 (2000); 5,785 (2010); 6,221 (2015 projected); Race: 93.3% White, 3.3% Black, 1.0% Asian, 2.4% Other, 2.0% Hispanic of any race (2010); Density: 1,239.5 persons per square mile (2010); Average household size: 2.56 (2010); Median age: 38.5 (2010); Males per 100 females: 94.0 (2010); Marriage status: 26.6% never married, 58.4% now married, 5.7% widowed, 9.4% divorced (2005-2009 5-year est.); Foreign born: 1.6% (2005-2009 5-year est.); Ancestry (includes multiple ancestries): 36.0% German, 14.4% Irish, 10.1% English, 9.0% Italian, 7.3% American (2005-2009 5-year est.).
Economy: Single-family building permits issued: 75 (2010); Multi-family building permits issued: 3 (2010); Employment by occupation: 20.8%

management, 25.9% professional, 7.7% services, 30.1% sales, 0.0% farming, 6.8% construction, 8.7% production (2005-2009 5-year est.).
Income: Per capita income: $33,774 (2010); Median household income: $76,181 (2010); Average household income: $87,944 (2010); Percent of households with income of $100,000 or more: 30.3% (2010); Poverty rate: 5.7% (2005-2009 5-year est.).
Taxes: Total city taxes per capita: $289 (2007); City property taxes per capita: $180 (2007).
Education: Percent of population age 25 and over with: High school diploma (including GED) or higher: 93.4% (2010); Bachelor's degree or higher: 32.3% (2010); Master's degree or higher: 8.9% (2010).

School District(s)
Collinsville CUSD 10 (PK-12)
    2009-10 Enrollment: 6,623 . . . . (618) 346-6350
Housing: Homeownership rate: 84.3% (2010); Median home value: $161,106 (2010); Median contract rent: $496 per month (2005-2009 5-year est.); Median year structure built: 1993 (2005-2009 5-year est.).
Hospitals: Anderson Hospital (130 beds)
Transportation: Commute to work: 94.5% car, 0.4% public transportation, 1.0% walk, 3.3% work from home (2005-2009 5-year est.); Travel time to work: 22.3% less than 15 minutes, 34.6% 15 to 30 minutes, 29.1% 30 to 45 minutes, 10.7% 45 to 60 minutes, 3.3% 60 minutes or more (2005-2009 5-year est.)

MORO (unincorporated postal area, zip code 62067). Covers a land area of 16.810 square miles and a water area of 0.046 square miles. Located at 38.92° N. Lat; 90.01° W. Long. Elevation is 531 feet.
Population: 2,089 (2000); Race: 98.9% White, 0.0% Black, 0.0% Asian, 1.1% Other, 0.3% Hispanic of any race (2000); Density: 124.3 persons per square mile (2000); Age: 23.6% under 18, 15.6% over 64 (2000); Marriage status: 21.5% never married, 66.0% now married, 6.1% widowed, 6.4% divorced (2000); Foreign born: 1.0% (2000); Ancestry (includes multiple ancestries): 36.8% German, 14.2% English, 13.9% American, 6.3% Irish, 5.4% French (2000).
Economy: Employment by occupation: 17.8% management, 11.8% professional, 16.7% services, 21.2% sales, 0.8% farming, 13.3% construction, 18.3% production (2000).
Income: Per capita income: $18,510 (2000); Median household income: $38,491 (2000); Poverty rate: 9.3% (2000).
Education: Percent of population age 25 and over with: High school diploma (including GED) or higher: 81.3% (2000); Bachelor's degree or higher: 15.5% (2000).

School District(s)
Bethalto CUSD 8 (PK-12)
    2009-10 Enrollment: 2,738 . . . . (618) 377-7200
Edwardsville CUSD 7 (PK-12)
    2009-10 Enrollment: 7,623 . . . . (618) 656-1182
Housing: Homeownership rate: 85.4% (2000); Median home value: $78,200 (2000); Median contract rent: $334 per month (2000); Median year structure built: 1970 (2000).
Transportation: Commute to work: 91.1% car, 0.7% public transportation, 0.8% walk, 7.4% work from home (2000); Travel time to work: 21.1% less than 15 minutes, 47.6% 15 to 30 minutes, 20.8% 30 to 45 minutes, 5.1% 45 to 60 minutes, 5.4% 60 minutes or more (2000)

NEW DOUGLAS (village). Covers a land area of 1.068 square miles and a water area of 0 square miles. Located at 38.97° N. Lat; 89.66° W. Long. Elevation is 620 feet.
Population: 387 (1990); 369 (2000); 432 (2010); 458 (2015 projected); Race: 97.9% White, 0.0% Black, 0.2% Asian, 1.9% Other, 3.9% Hispanic of any race (2010); Density: 404.6 persons per square mile (2010); Average household size: 2.53 (2010); Median age: 39.4 (2010); Males per 100 females: 101.9 (2010); Marriage status: 23.4% never married, 61.9% now married, 3.7% widowed, 11.0% divorced (2005-2009 5-year est.); Foreign born: 0.0% (2005-2009 5-year est.); Ancestry (includes multiple ancestries): 46.5% German, 19.5% Irish, 13.2% Polish, 8.9% English, 8.1% American (2005-2009 5-year est.).
Economy: Single-family building permits issued: 2 (2010); Multi-family building permits issued: 0 (2010); Employment by occupation: 5.6% management, 4.3% professional, 13.6% services, 30.9% sales, 0.0% farming, 26.5% construction, 19.1% production (2005-2009 5-year est.).
Income: Per capita income: $24,812 (2010); Median household income: $56,250 (2010); Average household income: $62,968 (2010); Percent of households with income of $100,000 or more: 20.5% (2010); Poverty rate: 19.2% (2005-2009 5-year est.).

Taxes: Total city taxes per capita: $56 (2007); City property taxes per capita: $24 (2007).
Education: Percent of population age 25 and over with: High school diploma (including GED) or higher: 85.2% (2010); Bachelor's degree or higher: 13.1% (2010); Master's degree or higher: 5.1% (2010).

School District(s)
Highland CUSD 5 (PK-12)
    2009-10 Enrollment: 3,107 . . . . (618) 654-2106
Housing: Homeownership rate: 83.6% (2010); Median home value: $111,667 (2010); Median contract rent: $425 per month (2005-2009 5-year est.); Median year structure built: 1948 (2005-2009 5-year est.).
Transportation: Commute to work: 87.4% car, 2.0% public transportation, 1.3% walk, 9.3% work from home (2005-2009 5-year est.); Travel time to work: 13.1% less than 15 minutes, 27.0% 15 to 30 minutes, 29.2% 30 to 45 minutes, 16.1% 45 to 60 minutes, 14.6% 60 minutes or more (2005-2009 5-year est.)

PONTOON BEACH (village). Covers a land area of 8.182 square miles and a water area of 0.279 square miles. Located at 38.72° N. Lat; 90.06° W. Long. Elevation is 417 feet.
Population: 5,045 (1990); 5,620 (2000); 5,712 (2010); 5,736 (2015 projected); Race: 85.7% White, 10.1% Black, 0.6% Asian, 3.5% Other, 2.5% Hispanic of any race (2010); Density: 698.1 persons per square mile (2010); Average household size: 2.53 (2010); Median age: 35.3 (2010); Males per 100 females: 96.3 (2010); Marriage status: 21.3% never married, 60.5% now married, 5.1% widowed, 13.2% divorced (2005-2009 5-year est.); Foreign born: 6.5% (2005-2009 5-year est.); Ancestry (includes multiple ancestries): 27.8% German, 15.1% Irish, 11.4% English, 6.6% American, 5.0% French (2005-2009 5-year est.).
Economy: Single-family building permits issued: 0 (2010); Multi-family building permits issued: 0 (2010); Employment by occupation: 8.7% management, 15.9% professional, 12.0% services, 29.4% sales, 0.4% farming, 8.7% construction, 24.9% production (2005-2009 5-year est.).
Income: Per capita income: $22,985 (2010); Median household income: $48,376 (2010); Average household income: $58,260 (2010); Percent of households with income of $100,000 or more: 12.3% (2010); Poverty rate: 9.0% (2005-2009 5-year est.).
Taxes: Total city taxes per capita: $635 (2007); City property taxes per capita: $522 (2007).
Education: Percent of population age 25 and over with: High school diploma (including GED) or higher: 89.4% (2010); Bachelor's degree or higher: 12.3% (2010); Master's degree or higher: 4.5% (2010).
Housing: Homeownership rate: 75.2% (2010); Median home value: $88,498 (2010); Median contract rent: $527 per month (2005-2009 5-year est.); Median year structure built: 1981 (2005-2009 5-year est.).
Safety: Violent crime rate: 9.8 per 10,000 population; Property crime rate: 187.1 per 10,000 population (2010).
Transportation: Commute to work: 95.5% car, 0.0% public transportation, 0.6% walk, 1.9% work from home (2005-2009 5-year est.); Travel time to work: 25.3% less than 15 minutes, 40.9% 15 to 30 minutes, 19.9% 30 to 45 minutes, 9.0% 45 to 60 minutes, 4.8% 60 minutes or more (2005-2009 5-year est.)
Additional Information Contacts
Village of Pontoon Beach. . . . . (618) 931-6100

ROSEWOOD HEIGHTS (CDP). Covers a land area of 2.144 square miles and a water area of 0 square miles. Located at 38.89° N. Lat; 90.07° W. Long. Elevation is 548 feet.
Population: 4,596 (1990); 4,262 (2000); 4,181 (2010); 4,114 (2015 projected); Race: 97.5% White, 0.8% Black, 0.4% Asian, 1.3% Other, 0.8% Hispanic of any race (2010); Density: 1,950.2 persons per square mile (2010); Average household size: 2.41 (2010); Median age: 41.6 (2010); Males per 100 females: 91.8 (2010); Marriage status: 18.5% never married, 68.3% now married, 3.9% widowed, 9.3% divorced (2005-2009 5-year est.); Foreign born: 0.4% (2005-2009 5-year est.); Ancestry (includes multiple ancestries): 29.0% German, 18.9% Irish, 10.1% English, 9.4% Italian, 8.8% American (2005-2009 5-year est.).
Economy: Employment by occupation: 8.0% management, 13.0% professional, 13.5% services, 32.5% sales, 0.0% farming, 15.3% construction, 17.6% production (2005-2009 5-year est.).
Income: Per capita income: $25,928 (2010); Median household income: $57,386 (2010); Average household income: $62,187 (2010); Percent of households with income of $100,000 or more: 13.4% (2010); Poverty rate: 11.3% (2005-2009 5-year est.).

Education: Percent of population age 25 and over with: High school diploma (including GED) or higher: 93.1% (2010); Bachelor's degree or higher: 18.3% (2010); Master's degree or higher: 4.4% (2010).
Housing: Homeownership rate: 83.4% (2010); Median home value: $102,939 (2010); Median contract rent: $384 per month (2005-2009 5-year est.); Median year structure built: 1960 (2005-2009 5-year est.)
Transportation: Commute to work: 93.7% car, 0.0% public transportation, 1.3% walk, 3.9% work from home (2005-2009 5-year est.); Travel time to work: 40.6% less than 15 minutes, 24.6% 15 to 30 minutes, 22.9% 30 to 45 minutes, 9.0% 45 to 60 minutes, 2.9% 60 minutes or more (2005-2009 5-year est.)

ROXANA (village). Covers a land area of 6.801 square miles and a water area of 0.022 square miles. Located at 38.83° N. Lat; 90.06° W. Long. Elevation is 446 feet.
History: Incorporated 1921.
Population: 1,639 (1990); 1,547 (2000); 1,577 (2010); 1,573 (2015 projected); Race: 97.7% White, 0.6% Black, 0.2% Asian, 1.5% Other, 0.8% Hispanic of any race (2010); Density: 231.9 persons per square mile (2010); Average household size: 2.29 (2010); Median age: 37.0 (2010); Males per 100 females: 91.2 (2010); Marriage status: 28.0% never married, 54.0% now married, 6.3% widowed, 11.8% divorced (2005-2009 5-year est.); Foreign born: 0.6% (2005-2009 5-year est.); Ancestry (includes multiple ancestries): 28.6% German, 22.2% Irish, 10.7% American, 9.6% English, 5.7% French (2005-2009 5-year est.).
Economy: Single-family building permits issued: 0 (2010); Multi-family building permits issued: 0 (2010); Employment by occupation: 11.8% management, 17.1% professional, 25.6% services, 18.7% sales, 0.0% farming, 8.3% construction, 18.6% production (2005-2009 5-year est.).
Income: Per capita income: $24,438 (2010); Median household income: $46,563 (2010); Average household income: $56,030 (2010); Percent of households with income of $100,000 or more: 12.8% (2010); Poverty rate: 15.9% (2005-2009 5-year est.).
Taxes: Total city taxes per capita: $706 (2007); City property taxes per capita: $672 (2007).
Education: Percent of population age 25 and over with: High school diploma (including GED) or higher: 89.7% (2010); Bachelor's degree or higher: 11.3% (2010); Master's degree or higher: 6.1% (2010).

School District(s)
Roxana CUSD 1 (PK-12)
  2009-10 Enrollment: 1,995 . . . . (618) 254-7544
Housing: Homeownership rate: 70.8% (2010); Median home value: $72,336 (2010); Median contract rent: $456 per month (2005-2009 5-year est.); Median year structure built: 1947 (2005-2009 5-year est.).
Safety: Violent crime rate: 6.5 per 10,000 population; Property crime rate: 339.9 per 10,000 population (2010).
Transportation: Commute to work: 95.3% car, 1.0% public transportation, 1.7% walk, 1.5% work from home (2005-2009 5-year est.); Travel time to work: 34.9% less than 15 minutes, 35.6% 15 to 30 minutes, 16.5% 30 to 45 minutes, 9.2% 45 to 60 minutes, 3.8% 60 minutes or more (2005-2009 5-year est.)

SAINT JACOB (village). Covers a land area of 0.559 square miles and a water area of 0 square miles. Located at 38.71° N. Lat; 89.76° W. Long. Elevation is 512 feet.
History: St. Jacob was built near the site of Fort Chilton, established in 1812.
Population: 776 (1990); 801 (2000); 873 (2010); 899 (2015 projected); Race: 97.7% White, 0.0% Black, 0.1% Asian, 2.2% Other, 3.0% Hispanic of any race (2010); Density: 1,562.0 persons per square mile (2010); Average household size: 2.58 (2010); Median age: 37.7 (2010); Males per 100 females: 101.6 (2010); Marriage status: 15.0% never married, 75.7% now married, 3.2% widowed, 6.2% divorced (2005-2009 5-year est.); Foreign born: 0.3% (2005-2009 5-year est.); Ancestry (includes multiple ancestries): 56.6% German, 17.9% Irish, 5.6% Polish, 4.6% English, 4.5% American (2005-2009 5-year est.).
Economy: Single-family building permits issued: 3 (2010); Multi-family building permits issued: 3 (2010); Employment by occupation: 10.5% management, 14.5% professional, 16.2% services, 24.5% sales, 1.5% farming, 18.8% construction, 14.0% production (2005-2009 5-year est.).
Income: Per capita income: $28,015 (2010); Median household income: $59,536 (2010); Average household income: $72,300 (2010); Percent of households with income of $100,000 or more: 19.5% (2010); Poverty rate: 2.5% (2005-2009 5-year est.).

Taxes: Total city taxes per capita: $221 (2007); City property taxes per capita: $154 (2007).
Education: Percent of population age 25 and over with: High school diploma (including GED) or higher: 89.8% (2010); Bachelor's degree or higher: 17.8% (2010); Master's degree or higher: 7.6% (2010).

School District(s)
Triad CUSD 2 (PK-12)
  2009-10 Enrollment: 3,730 . . . . (618) 667-8851
Housing: Homeownership rate: 83.7% (2010); Median home value: $124,148 (2010); Median contract rent: $460 per month (2005-2009 5-year est.); Median year structure built: 1972 (2005-2009 5-year est.).
Transportation: Commute to work: 96.9% car, 0.0% public transportation, 1.9% walk, 1.2% work from home (2005-2009 5-year est.); Travel time to work: 16.8% less than 15 minutes, 30.2% 15 to 30 minutes, 39.2% 30 to 45 minutes, 9.8% 45 to 60 minutes, 4.1% 60 minutes or more (2005-2009 5-year est.)

SOUTH ROXANA (village). Covers a land area of 1.587 square miles and a water area of 0 square miles. Located at 38.82° N. Lat; 90.05° W. Long. Elevation is 440 feet.
Population: 1,961 (1990); 1,888 (2000); 1,971 (2010); 1,999 (2015 projected); Race: 97.0% White, 0.5% Black, 0.3% Asian, 2.2% Other, 0.8% Hispanic of any race (2010); Density: 1,242.3 persons per square mile (2010); Average household size: 2.57 (2010); Median age: 35.2 (2010); Males per 100 females: 96.3 (2010); Marriage status: 27.9% never married, 48.9% now married, 5.4% widowed, 17.8% divorced (2005-2009 5-year est.); Foreign born: 0.2% (2005-2009 5-year est.); Ancestry (includes multiple ancestries): 34.2% German, 20.1% Irish, 9.6% English, 7.1% American, 3.9% Dutch (2005-2009 5-year est.).
Economy: Single-family building permits issued: 0 (2010); Multi-family building permits issued: 0 (2010); Employment by occupation: 10.4% management, 6.0% professional, 18.5% services, 24.4% sales, 0.0% farming, 10.8% construction, 30.0% production (2005-2009 5-year est.).
Income: Per capita income: $18,238 (2010); Median household income: $39,022 (2010); Average household income: $47,115 (2010); Percent of households with income of $100,000 or more: 5.9% (2010); Poverty rate: 17.9% (2005-2009 5-year est.).
Taxes: Total city taxes per capita: $215 (2007); City property taxes per capita: $110 (2007).
Education: Percent of population age 25 and over with: High school diploma (including GED) or higher: 82.3% (2010); Bachelor's degree or higher: 5.0% (2010); Master's degree or higher: 1.9% (2010).

School District(s)
Roxana CUSD 1 (PK-12)
  2009-10 Enrollment: 1,995 . . . . (618) 254-7544
Housing: Homeownership rate: 74.7% (2010); Median home value: $63,556 (2010); Median contract rent: $504 per month (2005-2009 5-year est.); Median year structure built: 1964 (2005-2009 5-year est.).
Transportation: Commute to work: 92.9% car, 0.0% public transportation, 1.2% walk, 4.9% work from home (2005-2009 5-year est.); Travel time to work: 21.6% less than 15 minutes, 40.9% 15 to 30 minutes, 20.9% 30 to 45 minutes, 13.9% 45 to 60 minutes, 2.7% 60 minutes or more (2005-2009 5-year est.)

TROY (city). Covers a land area of 4.183 square miles and a water area of 0 square miles. Located at 38.72° N. Lat; 89.89° W. Long. Elevation is 561 feet.
History: Troy began as the community of Columbia, with a grist mill and tavern built by John G. Jarvis about 1814. When the property was purchased in 1819 by land speculators, it was renamed Troy, for the New York town. In 1857 Mechanicsburg, which had been platted in 1836, merged with Troy, and in 1891 Brookside did the same. Troy was incorporated as a city in 1892.
Population: 6,879 (1990); 8,524 (2000); 10,018 (2010); 10,439 (2015 projected); Race: 93.5% White, 2.6% Black, 0.7% Asian, 3.1% Other, 2.5% Hispanic of any race (2010); Density: 2,394.7 persons per square mile (2010); Average household size: 2.68 (2010); Median age: 35.1 (2010); Males per 100 females: 96.8 (2010); Marriage status: 27.9% never married, 55.6% now married, 5.2% widowed, 11.3% divorced (2005-2009 5-year est.); Foreign born: 1.8% (2005-2009 5-year est.); Ancestry (includes multiple ancestries): 37.5% German, 15.1% Irish, 8.5% English, 6.0% Italian, 5.5% American (2005-2009 5-year est.).
Economy: Single-family building permits issued: 40 (2010); Multi-family building permits issued: 0 (2010); Employment by occupation: 12.6%

management, 22.5% professional, 15.3% services, 29.6% sales, 0.0% farming, 7.6% construction, 12.3% production (2005-2009 5-year est.).
Income: Per capita income: $30,018 (2010); Median household income: $69,873 (2010); Average household income: $80,642 (2010); Percent of households with income of $100,000 or more: 25.0% (2010); Poverty rate: 6.1% (2005-2009 5-year est.).
Taxes: Total city taxes per capita: $181 (2007); City property taxes per capita: $129 (2007).
Education: Percent of population age 25 and over with: High school diploma (including GED) or higher: 93.7% (2010); Bachelor's degree or higher: 29.0% (2010); Master's degree or higher: 9.5% (2010).

School District(s)

Madison Roe (06-12)
    2009-10 Enrollment: n/a . . . . (618) 692-6200
Triad CUSD 2 (PK-12)
    2009-10 Enrollment: 3,730 . . . . (618) 667-8851
Housing: Homeownership rate: 76.6% (2010); Median home value: $146,506 (2010); Median contract rent: $507 per month (2005-2009 5-year est.); Median year structure built: 1987 (2005-2009 5-year est.).
Safety: Violent crime rate: 12.1 per 10,000 population; Property crime rate: 98.1 per 10,000 population (2010).
Newspapers: Times Tribune (Local news; Circulation 3,850)
Transportation: Commute to work: 94.0% car, 0.8% public transportation, 0.8% walk, 3.4% work from home (2005-2009 5-year est.); Travel time to work: 21.4% less than 15 minutes, 36.7% 15 to 30 minutes, 25.8% 30 to 45 minutes, 13.4% 45 to 60 minutes, 2.7% 60 minutes or more (2005-2009 5-year est.)
Additional Information Contacts
City of Troy. . . . . (618) 667-6741
    http://www.troyil.us
Troy/Maryville/St. Jacob Area Chamber of Commerce . . . . (618) 667-8769
    http://www.troycoc.com

VENICE (city).
Covers a land area of 1.875 square miles and a water area of 0 square miles. Located at 38.67° N. Lat; 90.16° W. Long. Elevation is 410 feet.
History: Before the construction of levees, Venice experienced frequent flooding of its streets, which led to its being named after the Italian city of waterways. A ferry landing was established here in 1804. The town was platted in 1841 and incorporated in 1873.
Population: 3,571 (1990); 2,528 (2000); 2,403 (2010); 2,332 (2015 projected); Race: 4.2% White, 94.5% Black, 0.0% Asian, 1.2% Other, 0.9% Hispanic of any race (2010); Density: 1,281.9 persons per square mile (2010); Average household size: 2.58 (2010); Median age: 30.1 (2010); Males per 100 females: 83.0 (2010); Marriage status: 48.4% never married, 28.1% now married, 11.3% widowed, 12.2% divorced (2005-2009 5-year est.); Foreign born: 2.4% (2005-2009 5-year est.); Ancestry (includes multiple ancestries): 2.2% African, 1.8% Italian, 1.6% American, 1.1% German, 0.4% Irish (2005-2009 5-year est.).
Economy: Single-family building permits issued: 2 (2010); Multi-family building permits issued: 0 (2010); Employment by occupation: 3.1% management, 10.8% professional, 18.9% services, 31.9% sales, 0.0% farming, 6.9% construction, 28.4% production (2005-2009 5-year est.).
Income: Per capita income: $14,147 (2010); Median household income: $23,708 (2010); Average household income: $36,515 (2010); Percent of households with income of $100,000 or more: 7.4% (2010); Poverty rate: 43.9% (2005-2009 5-year est.).
Taxes: Total city taxes per capita: $292 (2007); City property taxes per capita: $213 (2007).
Education: Percent of population age 25 and over with: High school diploma (including GED) or higher: 76.9% (2010); Bachelor's degree or higher: 7.0% (2010); Master's degree or higher: 1.4% (2010).

School District(s)

Venice CUSD 3 (KG-08)
    2009-10 Enrollment: 85 . . . . (618) 274-7953
Housing: Homeownership rate: 46.1% (2010); Median home value: $43,333 (2010); Median contract rent: $367 per month (2005-2009 5-year est.); Median year structure built: 1952 (2005-2009 5-year est.).
Transportation: Commute to work: 85.9% car, 10.1% public transportation, 1.1% walk, 1.9% work from home (2005-2009 5-year est.); Travel time to work: 21.5% less than 15 minutes, 50.1% 15 to 30 minutes, 24.3% 30 to 45 minutes, 2.3% 45 to 60 minutes, 1.7% 60 minutes or more (2005-2009 5-year est.)

WILLIAMSON (village).
Covers a land area of 1.518 square miles and a water area of 0.043 square miles. Located at 38.98° N. Lat; 89.76° W. Long. Elevation is 604 feet.
Population: 278 (1990); 251 (2000); 294 (2010); 313 (2015 projected); Race: 98.3% White, 0.0% Black, 0.0% Asian, 1.7% Other, 2.0% Hispanic of any race (2010); Density: 193.7 persons per square mile (2010); Average household size: 2.49 (2010); Median age: 44.1 (2010); Males per 100 females: 101.4 (2010); Marriage status: 30.3% never married, 49.5% now married, 10.1% widowed, 10.1% divorced (2005-2009 5-year est.); Foreign born: 0.0% (2005-2009 5-year est.); Ancestry (includes multiple ancestries): 32.4% German, 21.8% Italian, 10.1% English, 9.7% Irish, 5.5% Scotch-Irish (2005-2009 5-year est.).
Economy: Single-family building permits issued: 0 (2010); Multi-family building permits issued: 0 (2010); Employment by occupation: 2.4% management, 8.4% professional, 12.0% services, 30.1% sales, 0.0% farming, 8.4% construction, 38.6% production (2005-2009 5-year est.).
Income: Per capita income: $27,610 (2010); Median household income: $59,259 (2010); Average household income: $67,394 (2010); Percent of households with income of $100,000 or more: 19.5% (2010); Poverty rate: 27.3% (2005-2009 5-year est.).
Taxes: Total city taxes per capita: $41 (2007); City property taxes per capita: $37 (2007).
Education: Percent of population age 25 and over with: High school diploma (including GED) or higher: 87.1% (2010); Bachelor's degree or higher: 17.1% (2010); Master's degree or higher: 5.1% (2010).
Housing: Homeownership rate: 89.0% (2010); Median home value: $106,250 (2010); Median contract rent: $354 per month (2005-2009 5-year est.); Median year structure built: 1951 (2005-2009 5-year est.).
Transportation: Commute to work: 100.0% car, 0.0% public transportation, 0.0% walk, 0.0% work from home (2005-2009 5-year est.); Travel time to work: 24.1% less than 15 minutes, 36.7% 15 to 30 minutes, 21.5% 30 to 45 minutes, 12.7% 45 to 60 minutes, 5.1% 60 minutes or more (2005-2009 5-year est.)

WOOD RIVER (city).
Covers a land area of 6.056 square miles and a water area of 0.025 square miles. Located at 38.86° N. Lat; 90.08° W. Long. Elevation is 436 feet.
History: Named for a small stream that used to be in the city. Wood River was selected by the Standard Oil Company in 1907 as the site of its refinery because of the rail and river transportation available here.
Population: 11,628 (1990); 11,296 (2000); 10,962 (2010); 10,760 (2015 projected); Race: 97.1% White, 0.8% Black, 0.4% Asian, 1.7% Other, 2.1% Hispanic of any race (2010); Density: 1,810.0 persons per square mile (2010); Average household size: 2.29 (2010); Median age: 37.6 (2010); Males per 100 females: 91.6 (2010); Marriage status: 33.9% never married, 42.3% now married, 7.5% widowed, 16.3% divorced (2005-2009 5-year est.); Foreign born: 0.6% (2005-2009 5-year est.); Ancestry (includes multiple ancestries): 28.8% German, 16.2% Irish, 8.3% English, 7.8% American, 5.0% Italian (2005-2009 5-year est.).
Economy: Single-family building permits issued: 1 (2010); Multi-family building permits issued: 0 (2010); Employment by occupation: 7.9% management, 15.2% professional, 22.1% services, 26.8% sales, 0.0% farming, 11.5% construction, 16.6% production (2005-2009 5-year est.).
Income: Per capita income: $22,041 (2010); Median household income: $41,608 (2010); Average household income: $50,356 (2010); Percent of households with income of $100,000 or more: 9.6% (2010); Poverty rate: 17.2% (2005-2009 5-year est.).
Taxes: Total city taxes per capita: $316 (2007); City property taxes per capita: $219 (2007).
Education: Percent of population age 25 and over with: High school diploma (including GED) or higher: 89.8% (2010); Bachelor's degree or higher: 13.8% (2010); Master's degree or higher: 3.6% (2010).

School District(s)

East Alton-Wood River CHSD 14 (09-12)
    2009-10 Enrollment: 652 . . . . (618) 254-3151
Wood River-Hartford ESD 15 (PK-08)
    2009-10 Enrollment: 830 . . . . (618) 254-0607
Housing: Homeownership rate: 70.2% (2010); Median home value: $83,796 (2010); Median contract rent: $511 per month (2005-2009 5-year est.); Median year structure built: 1953 (2005-2009 5-year est.).
Safety: Violent crime rate: 40.8 per 10,000 population; Property crime rate: 501.5 per 10,000 population (2010).
Transportation: Commute to work: 94.9% car, 1.9% public transportation, 1.7% walk, 0.7% work from home (2005-2009 5-year est.); Travel time to

work: 33.6% less than 15 minutes, 37.5% 15 to 30 minutes, 18.6% 30 to 45 minutes, 9.2% 45 to 60 minutes, 1.2% 60 minutes or more (2005-2009 5-year est.)

Additional Information Contacts
City of Wood River . . . . (618) 251-3100
   http://www.woodriver.org

WORDEN (village). Covers a land area of 0.660 square miles and a water area of 0 square miles. Located at 38.93° N. Lat; 89.84° W. Long. Elevation is 568 feet.

History: Incorporated 1877.

Population: 900 (1990); 905 (2000); 933 (2010); 973 (2015 projected); Race: 98.8% White, 0.0% Black, 0.5% Asian, 0.6% Other, 2.5% Hispanic of any race (2010); Density: 1,412.7 persons per square mile (2010); Average household size: 2.35 (2010); Median age: 37.6 (2010); Males per 100 females: 95.6 (2010); Marriage status: 21.0% never married, 61.1% now married, 7.0% widowed, 10.9% divorced (2005-2009 5-year est.); Foreign born: 0.5% (2005-2009 5-year est.); Ancestry (includes multiple ancestries): 48.7% German, 15.8% Irish, 13.0% English, 6.3% American, 5.1% Scotch-Irish (2005-2009 5-year est.).

Economy: Single-family building permits issued: 4 (2010); Multi-family building permits issued: 0 (2010); Employment by occupation: 5.3% management, 14.2% professional, 15.2% services, 29.2% sales, 0.6% farming, 20.3% construction, 15.2% production (2005-2009 5-year est.).

Income: Per capita income: $24,688 (2010); Median household income: $48,097 (2010); Average household income: $58,350 (2010); Percent of households with income of $100,000 or more: 11.1% (2010); Poverty rate: 19.9% (2005-2009 5-year est.).

Taxes: Total city taxes per capita: $240 (2007); City property taxes per capita: $103 (2007).

Education: Percent of population age 25 and over with: High school diploma (including GED) or higher: 87.3% (2010); Bachelor's degree or higher: 9.5% (2010); Master's degree or higher: 2.9% (2010).

School District(s)
Edwardsville CUSD 7 (PK-12)
   2009-10 Enrollment: 7,623 . . . . (618) 656-1182

Housing: Homeownership rate: 79.1% (2010); Median home value: $85,957 (2010); Median contract rent: $355 per month (2005-2009 5-year est.); Median year structure built: 1962 (2005-2009 5-year est.).

Newspapers: Madison County Chronicle (Local news; Circulation 1,225)

Transportation: Commute to work: 94.9% car, 0.0% public transportation, 3.2% walk, 1.2% work from home (2005-2009 5-year est.); Travel time to work: 14.1% less than 15 minutes, 31.8% 15 to 30 minutes, 39.1% 30 to 45 minutes, 8.6% 45 to 60 minutes, 6.4% 60 minutes or more (2005-2009 5-year est.)

Marion County

Located in south central Illinois; drained by Skillet Fork, Crooked Creek, and a headstream of Kaskaskia River. Covers a land area of 572.26 square miles, a water area of 3.44 square miles, and is located in the Central Time Zone at 38.61° N. Lat., 88.99° W. Long. The county was founded in 1823. County seat is Salem.

Marion County is part of the Centralia, IL Micropolitan Statistical Area. The entire metro area includes: Marion County, IL

Weather Station: Salem Leckrone Arpt   Elevation: 569 feet

	Jan	Feb	Mar	Apr	May	Jun	Jul	Aug	Sep	Oct	Nov	Dec
High	39	44	55	67	76	85	88	87	80	69	55	42
Low	22	25	34	44	54	63	67	65	57	45	36	25
Precip	2.8	2.6	3.8	3.7	5.0	4.1	3.9	3.4	3.1	3.8	4.1	3.2
Snow	4.4	3.9	1.0	0.1	0.0	0.0	0.0	0.0	0.0	0.1	0.3	3.2

High and Low temperatures in degrees Fahrenheit; Precipitation and Snow in inches

Population: 41,561 (1990); 41,691 (2000); 39,271 (2010); 38,000 (2015 projected); Race: 93.3% White, 4.0% Black, 0.6% Asian, 2.1% Other, 1.2% Hispanic of any race (2010); Density: 68.6 persons per square mile (2010); Average household size: 2.42 (2010); Median age: 40.0 (2010); Males per 100 females: 93.1 (2010).

Religion: Five largest groups: 17.2% Southern Baptist Convention, 10.9% Christian Churches and Churches of Christ, 8.5% Catholic Church, 6.5% The United Methodist Church, 5.3% Lutheran Church—Missouri Synod (2000).

Economy: Unemployment rate: 11.3% (August 2011); Total civilian labor force: 18,110 (August 2011); Leading industries: 25.8% health care and

social assistance; 21.5% manufacturing; 14.3% retail trade (2009); Farms: 1,077 totaling 260,679 acres (2007); Companies that employ 500 or more persons: 1 (2009); Companies that employ 100 to 499 persons: 16 (2009); Companies that employ less than 100 persons: 956 (2009); Black-owned businesses: n/a (2007); Hispanic-owned businesses: n/a (2007); Asian-owned businesses: n/a (2007); Women-owned businesses: n/a (2007); Retail sales per capita: $11,900 (2010). Single-family building permits issued: 0 (2010); Multi-family building permits issued: 0 (2010).

Income: Per capita income: $20,430 (2010); Median household income: $40,502 (2010); Average household income: $50,014 (2010); Percent of households with income of $100,000 or more: 8.2% (2010); Poverty rate: 19.4% (2009); Bankruptcy rate: 4.32% (2010).

Taxes: Total county taxes per capita: $93 (2007); County property taxes per capita: $70 (2007).

Education: Percent of population age 25 and over with: High school diploma (including GED) or higher: 81.6% (2010); Bachelor's degree or higher: 13.2% (2010); Master's degree or higher: 4.7% (2010).

Housing: Homeownership rate: 72.9% (2010); Median home value: $64,988 (2010); Median contract rent: $367 per month (2005-2009 5-year est.); Median year structure built: 1967 (2005-2009 5-year est.).

Health: Birth rate: 124.3 per 10,000 population (2009); Death rate: 125.9 per 10,000 population (2009); Age-adjusted cancer mortality rate: 213.3 deaths per 100,000 population (2007); Number of physicians: 14.2 per 10,000 population (2008); Hospital beds: 35.1 per 10,000 population (2007); Hospital admissions: 2,114.7 per 10,000 population (2007).

Elections: 2008 Presidential election results: 48.1% Obama, 50.1% McCain, 1.0% Nader

National and State Parks: Stephen A Forbes State Park

Additional Information Contacts
Marion County Government . . . . (618) 548-3400

City of Centralia . . . . (618) 533-7623
   http://www.city.centralia.il.us
City of Salem . . . . (618) 548-2222
   http://www.salemil.us
Greater Salem Chamber of Commerce . . . . (618) 548-3010
   http://www.salemilchamber.com
The Greater Centralia Chamber of Commerce . . . . (618) 532-6789
   http://www.centraliail.com

Marion County Communities

ALMA (village). Covers a land area of 1.080 square miles and a water area of 0 square miles. Located at 38.72° N. Lat; 88.91° W. Long. Elevation is 623 feet.

Population: 419 (1990); 386 (2000); 350 (2010); 334 (2015 projected); Race: 98.6% White, 0.3% Black, 0.0% Asian, 1.1% Other, 0.0% Hispanic of any race (2010); Density: 324.1 persons per square mile (2010); Average household size: 2.40 (2010); Median age: 40.6 (2010); Males per 100 females: 98.9 (2010); Marriage status: 13.2% never married, 55.4% now married, 9.8% widowed, 21.6% divorced (2005-2009 5-year est.); Foreign born: 0.0% (2005-2009 5-year est.); Ancestry (includes multiple ancestries): 21.2% Irish, 16.9% American, 16.5% German, 7.8% English, 5.1% Czech (2005-2009 5-year est.).

Economy: Employment by occupation: 10.0% management, 8.8% professional, 23.8% services, 8.8% sales, 2.5% farming, 8.8% construction, 37.5% production (2005-2009 5-year est.).

Income: Per capita income: $24,682 (2010); Median household income: $41,724 (2010); Average household income: $59,332 (2010); Percent of households with income of $100,000 or more: 19.9% (2010); Poverty rate: 20.0% (2005-2009 5-year est.).

Taxes: Total city taxes per capita: $29 (2007); City property taxes per capita: $24 (2007).

Education: Percent of population age 25 and over with: High school diploma (including GED) or higher: 80.4% (2010); Bachelor's degree or higher: 6.0% (2010); Master's degree or higher: 0.4% (2010).

Housing: Homeownership rate: 80.1% (2010); Median home value: $76,667 (2010); Median contract rent: $303 per month (2005-2009 5-year est.); Median year structure built: 1961 (2005-2009 5-year est.).

Transportation: Commute to work: 93.8% car, 0.0% public transportation, 2.5% walk, 0.0% work from home (2005-2009 5-year est.); Travel time to work: 18.8% less than 15 minutes, 52.5% 15 to 30 minutes, 13.8% 30 to 45 minutes, 6.3% 45 to 60 minutes, 8.8% 60 minutes or more (2005-2009 5-year est.)

CENTRAL CITY (village).
Covers a land area of 0.580 square miles and a water area of 0 square miles. Located at 38.54° N. Lat; 89.12° W. Long. Elevation is 486 feet.

History: Central City was settled by German immigrants, and incorporated in 1857.

Population: 1,414 (1990); 1,371 (2000); 1,248 (2010); 1,197 (2015 projected); Race: 91.6% White, 2.5% Black, 1.1% Asian, 4.8% Other, 3.0% Hispanic of any race (2010); Density: 2,153.2 persons per square mile (2010); Average household size: 2.54 (2010); Median age: 34.6 (2010); Males per 100 females: 94.7 (2010); Marriage status: 29.7% never married, 51.3% now married, 7.3% widowed, 11.7% divorced (2005-2009 5-year est.); Foreign born: 0.8% (2005-2009 5-year est.); Ancestry (includes multiple ancestries): 26.5% German, 14.0% Irish, 12.6% English, 11.7% American, 5.0% Polish (2005-2009 5-year est.).

Economy: Employment by occupation: 4.4% management, 12.4% professional, 21.7% services, 35.7% sales, 0.0% farming, 6.5% construction, 19.4% production (2005-2009 5-year est.).

Income: Per capita income: $18,574 (2010); Median household income: $35,907 (2010); Average household income: $47,215 (2010); Percent of households with income of $100,000 or more: 5.5% (2010); Poverty rate: 18.4% (2005-2009 5-year est.).

Taxes: Total city taxes per capita: $90 (2007); City property taxes per capita: $19 (2007).

Education: Percent of population age 25 and over with: High school diploma (including GED) or higher: 79.4% (2010); Bachelor's degree or higher: 9.6% (2010); Master's degree or higher: 2.4% (2010).

Housing: Homeownership rate: 72.1% (2010); Median home value: $42,667 (2010); Median contract rent: $374 per month (2005-2009 5-year est.); Median year structure built: 1962 (2005-2009 5-year est.).

Safety: Violent crime rate: 0.0 per 10,000 population; Property crime rate: 256.8 per 10,000 population (2010).

Transportation: Commute to work: 96.0% car, 0.4% public transportation, 0.2% walk, 1.8% work from home (2005-2009 5-year est.); Travel time to work: 44.9% less than 15 minutes, 29.5% 15 to 30 minutes, 13.7% 30 to 45 minutes, 5.5% 45 to 60 minutes, 6.4% 60 minutes or more (2005-2009 5-year est.)

CENTRALIA (city).
Covers a land area of 7.502 square miles and a water area of 0.137 square miles. Located at 38.52° N. Lat; 89.13° W. Long. Elevation is 492 feet.

History: Centralia was laid out by the Illinois Central Railroad in 1853, and named for the company. Many early residents were of German descent. Since Centralia was located in a fruit-producing area, the railroad company was interested in refrigerated cars for shipping the fruit, and in 1868 the first such train began operation between Centralia and Chicago.

Population: 14,585 (1990); 14,136 (2000); 13,273 (2010); 12,878 (2015 projected); Race: 84.2% White, 11.5% Black, 0.8% Asian, 3.4% Other, 1.8% Hispanic of any race (2010); Density: 1,769.4 persons per square mile (2010); Average household size: 2.27 (2010); Median age: 40.3 (2010); Males per 100 females: 89.6 (2010); Marriage status: 29.4% never married, 45.9% now married, 10.3% widowed, 14.4% divorced (2005-2009 5-year est.); Foreign born: 1.4% (2005-2009 5-year est.); Ancestry (includes multiple ancestries): 24.9% German, 13.8% Irish, 13.0% English, 9.1% American, 3.8% French (2005-2009 5-year est.).

Economy: Single-family building permits issued: 0 (2010); Multi-family building permits issued: 0 (2010); Employment by occupation: 6.4% management, 15.1% professional, 27.1% services, 21.5% sales, 0.9% farming, 7.8% construction, 21.2% production (2005-2009 5-year est.).

Income: Per capita income: $19,257 (2010); Median household income: $34,708 (2010); Average household income: $45,078 (2010); Percent of households with income of $100,000 or more: 6.7% (2010); Poverty rate: 21.3% (2005-2009 5-year est.).

Taxes: Total city taxes per capita: $304 (2007); City property taxes per capita: $190 (2007).

Education: Percent of population age 25 and over with: High school diploma (including GED) or higher: 79.7% (2010); Bachelor's degree or higher: 15.8% (2010); Master's degree or higher: 6.2% (2010).

School District(s)
Central City SD 133 (PK-08)
    2009-10 Enrollment: 216 . . . . (618) 532-9521
Centralia HSD 200 (09-12)
    2009-10 Enrollment: 1,028 . . . . (618) 532-7391
Centralia SD 135 (PK-08)
    2009-10 Enrollment: 1,326 . . . . (618) 532-1907
Clinton/Marion/Washington Roe (01-12)
    2009-10 Enrollment: 30 . . . . (618) 594-2432
Grand Prairie CCSD 6 (KG-08)
    2009-10 Enrollment: 71 . . . . (618) 249-6289
Kaskaskia Spec Educ District (KG-12)
    2009-10 Enrollment: n/a . . . . (618) 532-4721
North Wamac SD 186 (KG-08)
    2009-10 Enrollment: 106 . . . . (618) 532-1826
Raccoon Cons SD 1 (PK-08)
    2009-10 Enrollment: 244 . . . . (618) 532-7329
Willow Grove SD 46 (PK-08)
    2009-10 Enrollment: 192 . . . . (618) 532-3313

Two-year College(s)
Kaskaskia College (Public)
    Fall 2009 Enrollment: 5,337. . . . . (618) 545-3000
    2010-11 Tuition: In-state $5,152; Out-of-state $11,232

Housing: Homeownership rate: 65.3% (2010); Median home value: $58,328 (2010); Median contract rent: $375 per month (2005-2009 5-year est.); Median year structure built: 1957 (2005-2009 5-year est.).

Hospitals: St. Mary's Good Samaritan (276 beds)

Safety: Violent crime rate: 76.3 per 10,000 population; Property crime rate: 608.1 per 10,000 population (2010).

Newspapers: The Morning Sentinel (Local news)

Transportation: Commute to work: 90.5% car, 0.4% public transportation, 3.9% walk, 1.7% work from home (2005-2009 5-year est.); Travel time to work: 53.0% less than 15 minutes, 24.3% 15 to 30 minutes, 11.3% 30 to 45 minutes, 5.0% 45 to 60 minutes, 6.4% 60 minutes or more (2005-2009 5-year est.); Amtrak: train service available.

Additional Information Contacts
City of Centralia . . . . (618) 533-7623
    http://www.city.centralia.il.us
The Greater Centralia Chamber of Commerce . . . . (618) 532-6789
    http://www.centraliail.com

IUKA (village).
Covers a land area of 0.792 square miles and a water area of 0.002 square miles. Located at 38.61° N. Lat; 88.78° W. Long. Elevation is 518 feet.

Population: 494 (1990); 598 (2000); 566 (2010); 544 (2015 projected); Race: 98.4% White, 0.2% Black, 0.4% Asian, 1.1% Other, 1.1% Hispanic of any race (2010); Density: 714.3 persons per square mile (2010); Average household size: 2.64 (2010); Median age: 36.1 (2010); Males per 100 females: 95.8 (2010); Marriage status: 15.5% never married, 50.8% now married, 13.8% widowed, 19.9% divorced (2005-2009 5-year est.); Foreign born: 0.0% (2005-2009 5-year est.); Ancestry (includes multiple ancestries): 19.4% Irish, 19.2% German, 13.5% American, 10.7% English, 4.8% Dutch (2005-2009 5-year est.).

Economy: Employment by occupation: 11.5% management, 13.9% professional, 29.7% services, 14.5% sales, 0.0% farming, 11.5% construction, 18.8% production (2005-2009 5-year est.).

Income: Per capita income: $16,769 (2010); Median household income: $34,459 (2010); Average household income: $44,977 (2010); Percent of households with income of $100,000 or more: 6.5% (2010); Poverty rate: 14.4% (2005-2009 5-year est.).

Taxes: Total city taxes per capita: $34 (2007); City property taxes per capita: $31 (2007).

Education: Percent of population age 25 and over with: High school diploma (including GED) or higher: 81.2% (2010); Bachelor's degree or higher: 6.4% (2010); Master's degree or higher: 2.2% (2010).

School District(s)
Iuka CCSD 7 (PK-08)
    2009-10 Enrollment: 268 . . . . (618) 323-6233

Housing: Homeownership rate: 82.7% (2010); Median home value: $55,588 (2010); Median contract rent: $245 per month (2005-2009 5-year est.); Median year structure built: 1963 (2005-2009 5-year est.).

Transportation: Commute to work: 95.1% car, 0.0% public transportation, 1.9% walk, 1.2% work from home (2005-2009 5-year est.); Travel time to work: 20.6% less than 15 minutes, 49.4% 15 to 30 minutes, 20.0% 30 to 45 minutes, 5.0% 45 to 60 minutes, 5.0% 60 minutes or more (2005-2009 5-year est.)

JUNCTION CITY (village).
Aka Glenridge. Covers a land area of 0.675 square miles and a water area of 0.018 square miles. Located at 38.58° N. Lat; 89.12° W. Long. Elevation is 492 feet.

Population: 539 (1990); 559 (2000); 575 (2010); 581 (2015 projected); Race: 97.4% White, 0.7% Black, 0.2% Asian, 1.7% Other, 0.5% Hispanic

of any race (2010); Density: 851.6 persons per square mile (2010); Average household size: 2.64 (2010); Median age: 37.5 (2010); Males per 100 females: 94.9 (2010); Marriage status: 23.1% never married, 59.2% now married, 1.6% widowed, 16.1% divorced (2005-2009 5-year est.); Foreign born: 4.2% (2005-2009 5-year est.); Ancestry (includes multiple ancestries): 40.4% German, 16.8% American, 14.9% Irish, 11.1% Polish, 9.5% English (2005-2009 5-year est.).
Economy: Employment by occupation: 0.0% management, 11.6% professional, 37.6% services, 17.5% sales, 0.0% farming, 5.3% construction, 28.1% production (2005-2009 5-year est.).
Income: Per capita income: $20,434 (2010); Median household income: $45,610 (2010); Average household income: $53,784 (2010); Percent of households with income of $100,000 or more: 8.7% (2010); Poverty rate: 19.6% (2005-2009 5-year est.).
Taxes: Total city taxes per capita: $26 (2007); City property taxes per capita: $18 (2007).
Education: Percent of population age 25 and over with: High school diploma (including GED) or higher: 74.0% (2010); Bachelor's degree or higher: 6.0% (2010); Master's degree or higher: 2.3% (2010).
Housing: Homeownership rate: 79.4% (2010); Median home value: $53,000 (2010); Median contract rent: $313 per month (2005-2009 5-year est.); Median year structure built: 1978 (2005-2009 5-year est.).
Transportation: Commute to work: 95.4% car, 0.0% public transportation, 0.0% walk, 2.9% work from home (2005-2009 5-year est.); Travel time to work: 25.6% less than 15 minutes, 49.8% 15 to 30 minutes, 14.5% 30 to 45 minutes, 1.7% 45 to 60 minutes, 8.4% 60 minutes or more (2005-2009 5-year est.)

KELL (village). Covers a land area of 1.010 square miles and a water area of 0 square miles. Located at 38.49° N. Lat; 88.90° W. Long. Elevation is 610 feet.
Population: 213 (1990); 231 (2000); 229 (2010); 223 (2015 projected); Race: 100.0% White, 0.0% Black, 0.0% Asian, 0.0% Other, 0.0% Hispanic of any race (2010); Density: 226.8 persons per square mile (2010); Average household size: 2.63 (2010); Median age: 39.0 (2010); Males per 100 females: 95.7 (2010); Marriage status: 16.9% never married, 62.8% now married, 8.1% widowed, 12.2% divorced (2005-2009 5-year est.); Foreign born: 7.6% (2005-2009 5-year est.); Ancestry (includes multiple ancestries): 24.0% English, 23.4% German, 15.2% American, 12.9% Irish, 2.9% French (2005-2009 5-year est.).
Economy: Employment by occupation: 2.1% management, 17.9% professional, 22.1% services, 18.9% sales, 13.7% farming, 5.3% construction, 20.0% production (2005-2009 5-year est.).
Income: Per capita income: $18,223 (2010); Median household income: $44,643 (2010); Average household income: $47,787 (2010); Percent of households with income of $100,000 or more: 5.7% (2010); Poverty rate: 11.7% (2005-2009 5-year est.).
Taxes: Total city taxes per capita: $27 (2007); City property taxes per capita: $27 (2007).
Education: Percent of population age 25 and over with: High school diploma (including GED) or higher: 86.8% (2010); Bachelor's degree or higher: 11.9% (2010); Master's degree or higher: 5.3% (2010).
School District(s)
Kell Cons SD 2 (PK-08)
    2009-10 Enrollment: 118 . . . . (618) 822-6234
Housing: Homeownership rate: 87.4% (2010); Median home value: $66,000 (2010); Median contract rent: n/a per month (2005-2009 5-year est.); Median year structure built: 1972 (2005-2009 5-year est.).
Transportation: Commute to work: 68.8% car, 0.0% public transportation, 20.4% walk, 7.5% work from home (2005-2009 5-year est.); Travel time to work: 33.7% less than 15 minutes, 52.3% 15 to 30 minutes, 14.0% 30 to 45 minutes, 0.0% 45 to 60 minutes, 0.0% 60 minutes or more (2005-2009 5-year est.)

KINMUNDY (city). Covers a land area of 1.031 square miles and a water area of 0 square miles. Located at 38.77° N. Lat; 88.85° W. Long. Elevation is 604 feet.
Population: 879 (1990); 892 (2000); 801 (2010); 757 (2015 projected); Race: 97.6% White, 0.4% Black, 0.0% Asian, 2.0% Other, 0.6% Hispanic of any race (2010); Density: 777.0 persons per square mile (2010); Average household size: 2.38 (2010); Median age: 39.1 (2010); Males per 100 females: 90.3 (2010); Marriage status: 18.5% never married, 52.7% now married, 9.4% widowed, 19.4% divorced (2005-2009 5-year est.); Foreign born: 1.1% (2005-2009 5-year est.); Ancestry (includes multiple

ancestries): 34.4% German, 24.1% Irish, 17.6% English, 12.1% American, 2.2% Polish (2005-2009 5-year est.).
Economy: Employment by occupation: 3.2% management, 19.8% professional, 20.0% services, 10.1% sales, 2.9% farming, 6.5% construction, 37.4% production (2005-2009 5-year est.).
Income: Per capita income: $18,750 (2010); Median household income: $35,517 (2010); Average household income: $44,033 (2010); Percent of households with income of $100,000 or more: 6.8% (2010); Poverty rate: 25.7% (2005-2009 5-year est.).
Taxes: Total city taxes per capita: $44 (2007); City property taxes per capita: $39 (2007).
Education: Percent of population age 25 and over with: High school diploma (including GED) or higher: 78.4% (2010); Bachelor's degree or higher: 7.3% (2010); Master's degree or higher: 0.5% (2010).
School District(s)
South Central CUD 401 (PK-12)
    2009-10 Enrollment: 693 . . . . (618) 547-3414
Housing: Homeownership rate: 73.2% (2010); Median home value: $48,750 (2010); Median contract rent: $328 per month (2005-2009 5-year est.); Median year structure built: 1964 (2005-2009 5-year est.).
Newspapers: Kinmundy Express (Community news; Circulation 900)
Transportation: Commute to work: 97.7% car, 0.0% public transportation, 1.4% walk, 0.0% work from home (2005-2009 5-year est.); Travel time to work: 19.8% less than 15 minutes, 47.1% 15 to 30 minutes, 15.9% 30 to 45 minutes, 8.3% 45 to 60 minutes, 9.0% 60 minutes or more (2005-2009 5-year est.)

ODIN (village). Covers a land area of 1.010 square miles and a water area of 0 square miles. Located at 38.61° N. Lat; 89.05° W. Long. Elevation is 528 feet.
History: Odin developed as a mining and agricultural center along the Illinois Central Railroad.
Population: 1,150 (1990); 1,122 (2000); 946 (2010); 898 (2015 projected); Race: 98.0% White, 1.1% Black, 0.1% Asian, 0.8% Other, 1.3% Hispanic of any race (2010); Density: 936.6 persons per square mile (2010); Average household size: 2.33 (2010); Median age: 40.1 (2010); Males per 100 females: 85.9 (2010); Marriage status: 24.8% never married, 46.0% now married, 12.8% widowed, 16.5% divorced (2005-2009 5-year est.); Foreign born: 0.6% (2005-2009 5-year est.); Ancestry (includes multiple ancestries): 26.7% German, 17.0% Irish, 7.6% American, 7.5% English, 4.9% Italian (2005-2009 5-year est.).
Economy: Single-family building permits issued: 0 (2010); Multi-family building permits issued: 0 (2010); Employment by occupation: 1.6% management, 14.2% professional, 33.5% services, 14.4% sales, 0.0% farming, 8.5% construction, 27.8% production (2005-2009 5-year est.).
Income: Per capita income: $20,516 (2010); Median household income: $40,387 (2010); Average household income: $50,637 (2010); Percent of households with income of $100,000 or more: 9.0% (2010); Poverty rate: 21.1% (2005-2009 5-year est.).
Taxes: Total city taxes per capita: $115 (2007); City property taxes per capita: $109 (2007).
Education: Percent of population age 25 and over with: High school diploma (including GED) or higher: 78.2% (2010); Bachelor's degree or higher: 10.1% (2010); Master's degree or higher: 2.8% (2010).
School District(s)
Odin CHSD 700 (09-12)
    2009-10 Enrollment: 81 . . . . (618) 775-8266
Odin SD 122 (KG-08)
    2009-10 Enrollment: 189 . . . . (618) 775-8266
Housing: Homeownership rate: 73.2% (2010); Median home value: $54,667 (2010); Median contract rent: $318 per month (2005-2009 5-year est.); Median year structure built: 1973 (2005-2009 5-year est.).
Transportation: Commute to work: 94.0% car, 1.4% public transportation, 3.0% walk, 1.6% work from home (2005-2009 5-year est.); Travel time to work: 24.5% less than 15 minutes, 44.5% 15 to 30 minutes, 14.2% 30 to 45 minutes, 12.6% 45 to 60 minutes, 4.2% 60 minutes or more (2005-2009 5-year est.)

PATOKA (village). Covers a land area of 1.100 square miles and a water area of 0 square miles. Located at 38.75° N. Lat; 89.09° W. Long. Elevation is 505 feet.
History: Patoka was named for an Indian chief. Oil was discovered in Patoka in 1937, bringing new growth to the town.
Population: 656 (1990); 633 (2000); 596 (2010); 575 (2015 projected); Race: 98.3% White, 0.3% Black, 0.2% Asian, 1.2% Other, 1.7% Hispanic

of any race (2010); Density: 541.8 persons per square mile (2010); Average household size: 2.26 (2010); Median age: 42.1 (2010); Males per 100 females: 96.1 (2010); Marriage status: 22.3% never married, 53.6% now married, 10.9% widowed, 13.2% divorced (2005-2009 5-year est.); Foreign born: 0.0% (2005-2009 5-year est.); Ancestry (includes multiple ancestries): 24.1% Irish, 20.3% English, 20.1% German, 15.7% American, 4.6% Italian (2005-2009 5-year est.).

Economy: Employment by occupation: 4.2% management, 15.4% professional, 27.9% services, 14.6% sales, 0.0% farming, 9.2% construction, 28.7% production (2005-2009 5-year est.).

Income: Per capita income: $19,327 (2010); Median household income: $36,200 (2010); Average household income: $43,968 (2010); Percent of households with income of $100,000 or more: 6.8% (2010); Poverty rate: 18.4% (2005-2009 5-year est.).

Taxes: Total city taxes per capita: $91 (2007); City property taxes per capita: $62 (2007).

Education: Percent of population age 25 and over with: High school diploma (including GED) or higher: 79.1% (2010); Bachelor's degree or higher: 4.7% (2010); Master's degree or higher: 2.1% (2010).

School District(s)

Patoka CUSD 100 (PK-12)
    2009-10 Enrollment: 289 . . . . (618) 432-5440

Housing: Homeownership rate: 78.4% (2010); Median home value: $58,810 (2010); Median contract rent: $305 per month (2005-2009 5-year est.); Median year structure built: 1963 (2005-2009 5-year est.).

Transportation: Commute to work: 97.9% car, 0.0% public transportation, 2.1% walk, 0.0% work from home (2005-2009 5-year est.); Travel time to work: 19.9% less than 15 minutes, 54.2% 15 to 30 minutes, 17.8% 30 to 45 minutes, 3.4% 45 to 60 minutes, 4.7% 60 minutes or more (2005-2009 5-year est.)

SALEM (city). County seat. Covers a land area of 6.100 square miles and a water area of 0.157 square miles. Located at 38.62° N. Lat; 88.94° W. Long. Elevation is 538 feet.

History: Salem was laid out in 1813 on the St. Louis-Vincennes stagecoach route, and incorporated in 1837. William Jennings Bryan (1860-1925) was born and grew up in Salem. Oil was discovered in Salem in 1939.

Population: 7,795 (1990); 7,909 (2000); 7,239 (2010); 6,895 (2015 projected); Race: 96.7% White, 1.0% Black, 1.1% Asian, 1.3% Other, 0.8% Hispanic of any race (2010); Density: 1,186.6 persons per square mile (2010); Average household size: 2.26 (2010); Median age: 40.4 (2010); Males per 100 females: 88.7 (2010); Marriage status: 27.1% never married, 51.1% now married, 11.5% widowed, 10.3% divorced (2005-2009 5-year est.); Foreign born: 2.0% (2005-2009 5-year est.); Ancestry (includes multiple ancestries): 23.5% German, 17.5% Irish, 12.3% English, 11.7% American, 3.8% Italian (2005-2009 5-year est.).

Economy: Single-family building permits issued: 0 (2010); Multi-family building permits issued: 0 (2010); Employment by occupation: 7.7% management, 21.5% professional, 17.1% services, 24.6% sales, 0.2% farming, 5.3% construction, 23.6% production (2005-2009 5-year est.).

Income: Per capita income: $18,772 (2010); Median household income: $36,008 (2010); Average household income: $43,472 (2010); Percent of households with income of $100,000 or more: 5.8% (2010); Poverty rate: 21.7% (2005-2009 5-year est.).

Taxes: Total city taxes per capita: $213 (2007); City property taxes per capita: $203 (2007).

Education: Percent of population age 25 and over with: High school diploma (including GED) or higher: 79.8% (2010); Bachelor's degree or higher: 14.1% (2010); Master's degree or higher: 4.4% (2010).

School District(s)

Clinton/Marion/Washington Roe (01-12)
    2009-10 Enrollment: 30 . . . . (618) 594-2432
Marion/Clinton/Wash Co Ctes
    2009-10 Enrollment: n/a . . . . (618) 548-6385
Salem CHSD 600 (09-12)
    2009-10 Enrollment: 826 . . . . (618) 548-0727
Salem SD 111 (PK-08)
    2009-10 Enrollment: 1,028 . . . . (618) 548-7702
Selmaville CCSD 10 (KG-08)
    2009-10 Enrollment: 222 . . . . (618) 548-2416

Housing: Homeownership rate: 64.3% (2010); Median home value: $67,579 (2010); Median contract rent: $374 per month (2005-2009 5-year est.); Median year structure built: 1969 (2005-2009 5-year est.).

Hospitals: Salem Township Hospital (46 beds)

Safety: Violent crime rate: 22.3 per 10,000 population; Property crime rate: 497.2 per 10,000 population (2010).

Newspapers: Salem Times-Commoner (Local news; Circulation 4,350); Town & County Crier (Local news; Circulation 15,000)

Transportation: Commute to work: 87.2% car, 1.2% public transportation, 4.3% walk, 4.2% work from home (2005-2009 5-year est.); Travel time to work: 60.2% less than 15 minutes, 17.0% 15 to 30 minutes, 11.8% 30 to 45 minutes, 5.8% 45 to 60 minutes, 5.2% 60 minutes or more (2005-2009 5-year est.)

Additional Information Contacts

City of Salem . . . . (618) 548-2222
    http://www.salemil.us
Greater Salem Chamber of Commerce . . . . (618) 548-3010
    http://www.salemilchamber.com

SANDOVAL (village). Covers a land area of 0.960 square miles and a water area of 0 square miles. Located at 38.61° N. Lat; 89.12° W. Long. Elevation is 509 feet.

History: Incorporated 1859.

Population: 1,535 (1990); 1,434 (2000); 1,245 (2010); 1,171 (2015 projected); Race: 98.0% White, 0.3% Black, 0.2% Asian, 1.4% Other, 1.2% Hispanic of any race (2010); Density: 1,297.1 persons per square mile (2010); Average household size: 2.53 (2010); Median age: 37.0 (2010); Males per 100 females: 92.7 (2010); Marriage status: 24.2% never married, 51.6% now married, 7.0% widowed, 17.2% divorced (2005-2009 5-year est.); Foreign born: 0.4% (2005-2009 5-year est.); Ancestry (includes multiple ancestries): 30.8% German, 17.7% Irish, 12.7% American, 6.4% Italian, 6.3% Dutch (2005-2009 5-year est.).

Economy: Single-family building permits issued: 0 (2010); Multi-family building permits issued: 0 (2010); Employment by occupation: 3.5% management, 17.5% professional, 35.2% services, 15.8% sales, 0.0% farming, 9.1% construction, 19.0% production (2005-2009 5-year est.).

Income: Per capita income: $19,000 (2010); Median household income: $40,574 (2010); Average household income: $48,996 (2010); Percent of households with income of $100,000 or more: 6.1% (2010); Poverty rate: 31.8% (2005-2009 5-year est.).

Taxes: Total city taxes per capita: $104 (2007); City property taxes per capita: $94 (2007).

Education: Percent of population age 25 and over with: High school diploma (including GED) or higher: 74.8% (2010); Bachelor's degree or higher: 7.0% (2010); Master's degree or higher: 2.3% (2010).

School District(s)

Sandoval CUSD 501 (PK-12)
    2009-10 Enrollment: 553 . . . . (618) 247-3233

Housing: Homeownership rate: 69.4% (2010); Median home value: $43,235 (2010); Median contract rent: $235 per month (2005-2009 5-year est.); Median year structure built: 1971 (2005-2009 5-year est.).

Transportation: Commute to work: 94.8% car, 0.0% public transportation, 3.4% walk, 1.8% work from home (2005-2009 5-year est.); Travel time to work: 31.0% less than 15 minutes, 47.5% 15 to 30 minutes, 8.9% 30 to 45 minutes, 1.6% 45 to 60 minutes, 11.0% 60 minutes or more (2005-2009 5-year est.)

VERNON (village). Covers a land area of 0.911 square miles and a water area of 0 square miles. Located at 38.80° N. Lat; 89.08° W. Long. Elevation is 515 feet.

History: Vernon developed as the center of a peach and pear growing area.

Population: 207 (1990); 178 (2000); 178 (2010); 177 (2015 projected); Race: 96.1% White, 0.0% Black, 2.2% Asian, 1.7% Other, 1.7% Hispanic of any race (2010); Density: 195.5 persons per square mile (2010); Average household size: 2.62 (2010); Median age: 39.7 (2010); Males per 100 females: 125.3 (2010); Marriage status: 15.9% never married, 72.6% now married, 3.5% widowed, 8.0% divorced (2005-2009 5-year est.); Foreign born: 0.0% (2005-2009 5-year est.); Ancestry (includes multiple ancestries): 25.2% American, 20.2% German, 16.8% Irish, 16.0% English, 9.2% Dutch (2005-2009 5-year est.).

Economy: Employment by occupation: 6.5% management, 0.0% professional, 21.7% services, 10.9% sales, 0.0% farming, 26.1% construction, 34.8% production (2005-2009 5-year est.).

Income: Per capita income: $20,883 (2010); Median household income: $48,636 (2010); Average household income: $53,897 (2010); Percent of households with income of $100,000 or more: 7.4% (2010); Poverty rate: 12.6% (2005-2009 5-year est.).

Taxes: Total city taxes per capita: $12 (2007); City property taxes per capita: $12 (2007).
Education: Percent of population age 25 and over with: High school diploma (including GED) or higher: 81.3% (2010); Bachelor's degree or higher: 8.9% (2010); Master's degree or higher: 3.3% (2010).
Housing: Homeownership rate: 86.8% (2010); Median home value: $69,000 (2010); Median contract rent: n/a per month (2005-2009 5-year est.); Median year structure built: before 1940 (2005-2009 5-year est.).
Transportation: Commute to work: 89.1% car, 0.0% public transportation, 6.5% walk, 4.3% work from home (2005-2009 5-year est.); Travel time to work: 25.0% less than 15 minutes, 40.9% 15 to 30 minutes, 25.0% 30 to 45 minutes, 4.5% 45 to 60 minutes, 4.5% 60 minutes or more (2005-2009 5-year est.)

WALNUT HILL (village). Covers a land area of 0.371 square miles and a water area of 0 square miles. Located at 38.47° N. Lat; 89.04° W. Long. Elevation is 568 feet.
Population: 133 (1990); 109 (2000); 100 (2010); 96 (2015 projected); Race: 97.0% White, 2.0% Black, 0.0% Asian, 1.0% Other, 0.0% Hispanic of any race (2010); Density: 269.9 persons per square mile (2010); Average household size: 2.56 (2010); Median age: 40.0 (2010); Males per 100 females: 108.3 (2010); Marriage status: 17.7% never married, 43.5% now married, 8.1% widowed, 30.6% divorced (2005-2009 5-year est.); Foreign born: 0.0% (2005-2009 5-year est.); Ancestry (includes multiple ancestries): 41.3% German, 33.1% Irish, 17.5% English, 1.3% Scottish, 1.3% American (2005-2009 5-year est.).
Economy: Employment by occupation: 0.0% management, 15.8% professional, 10.5% services, 31.6% sales, 0.0% farming, 28.1% construction, 14.0% production (2005-2009 5-year est.).
Income: Per capita income: $30,384 (2010); Median household income: $58,654 (2010); Average household income: $73,526 (2010); Percent of households with income of $100,000 or more: 15.4% (2010); Poverty rate: 31.3% (2005-2009 5-year est.).
Taxes: Total city taxes per capita: $19 (2007); City property taxes per capita: $19 (2007).
Education: Percent of population age 25 and over with: High school diploma (including GED) or higher: 89.7% (2010); Bachelor's degree or higher: 14.7% (2010); Master's degree or higher: 1.5% (2010).
Housing: Homeownership rate: 89.7% (2010); Median home value: $88,333 (2010); Median contract rent: $433 per month (2005-2009 5-year est.); Median year structure built: 1959 (2005-2009 5-year est.).
Transportation: Commute to work: 100.0% car, 0.0% public transportation, 0.0% walk, 0.0% work from home (2005-2009 5-year est.); Travel time to work: 45.6% less than 15 minutes, 50.9% 15 to 30 minutes, 0.0% 30 to 45 minutes, 0.0% 45 to 60 minutes, 3.5% 60 minutes or more (2005-2009 5-year est.)

WAMAC (city). Covers a land area of 1.508 square miles and a water area of 0 square miles. Located at 38.50° N. Lat; 89.14° W. Long.
History: Wamac was incorporated as a city in 1913. Its name was made from the first letters of the counties in which the town was situated—Washington, Marion, and Clinton.
Population: 1,501 (1990); 1,378 (2000); 1,259 (2010); 1,199 (2015 projected); Race: 96.4% White, 2.5% Black, 0.2% Asian, 1.0% Other, 1.7% Hispanic of any race (2010); Density: 834.7 persons per square mile (2010); Average household size: 2.34 (2010); Median age: 37.2 (2010); Males per 100 females: 97.3 (2010); Marriage status: 29.1% never married, 37.9% now married, 13.5% widowed, 19.5% divorced (2005-2009 5-year est.); Foreign born: 1.1% (2005-2009 5-year est.); Ancestry (includes multiple ancestries): 22.3% German, 14.8% American, 13.5% Irish, 5.4% English, 3.4% Dutch (2005-2009 5-year est.).
Economy: Single-family building permits issued: 0 (2010); Multi-family building permits issued: 0 (2010); Employment by occupation: 2.5% management, 6.1% professional, 31.6% services, 11.7% sales, 1.5% farming, 9.1% construction, 37.5% production (2005-2009 5-year est.).
Income: Per capita income: $18,143 (2010); Median household income: $33,564 (2010); Average household income: $42,807 (2010); Percent of households with income of $100,000 or more: 5.6% (2010); Poverty rate: 33.7% (2005-2009 5-year est.).
Taxes: Total city taxes per capita: $101 (2007); City property taxes per capita: $63 (2007).
Education: Percent of population age 25 and over with: High school diploma (including GED) or higher: 76.2% (2010); Bachelor's degree or higher: 5.0% (2010); Master's degree or higher: 1.8% (2010).

Housing: Homeownership rate: 66.7% (2010); Median home value: $36,952 (2010); Median contract rent: $340 per month (2005-2009 5-year est.); Median year structure built: 1961 (2005-2009 5-year est.).
Transportation: Commute to work: 86.5% car, 3.2% public transportation, 3.2% walk, 2.6% work from home (2005-2009 5-year est.); Travel time to work: 42.3% less than 15 minutes, 36.2% 15 to 30 minutes, 14.7% 30 to 45 minutes, 2.6% 45 to 60 minutes, 4.2% 60 minutes or more (2005-2009 5-year est.)

Marshall County

Located in north central Illinois; drained by the Illinois River and Sandy Creek. Covers a land area of 386.06 square miles, a water area of 12.45 square miles, and is located in the Central Time Zone at 41.04° N. Lat., 89.29° W. Long. The county was founded in 1839. County seat is Lacon.

Marshall County is part of the Peoria, IL Metropolitan Statistical Area. The entire metro area includes: Marshall County, IL; Peoria County, IL; Stark County, IL; Tazewell County, IL; Woodford County, IL

Weather Station: Lacon 1 N   Elevation: 459 feet

	Jan	Feb	Mar	Apr	May	Jun	Jul	Aug	Sep	Oct	Nov	Dec
High	34	38	51	64	75	84	87	86	79	66	52	38
Low	18	21	31	41	51	60	65	63	54	43	33	22
Precip	1.9	1.8	3.1	3.9	4.4	3.8	3.8	3.7	3.2	3.2	3.2	2.3
Snow	6.5	5.0	2.9	0.8	tr	0.0	0.0	0.0	0.0	tr	0.8	6.1

High and Low temperatures in degrees Fahrenheit; Precipitation and Snow in inches

Population: 12,846 (1990); 13,180 (2000); 12,550 (2010); 12,148 (2015 projected); Race: 96.5% White, 0.9% Black, 0.5% Asian, 2.1% Other, 2.8% Hispanic of any race (2010); Density: 32.5 persons per square mile (2010); Average household size: 2.41 (2010); Median age: 42.0 (2010); Males per 100 females: 97.8 (2010).
Religion: Five largest groups: 26.7% Catholic Church, 7.0% Evangelical Lutheran Church in America, 6.9% The United Methodist Church, 4.9% Christian Church (Disciples of Christ), 3.9% Lutheran Church—Missouri Synod (2000).
Economy: Unemployment rate: 8.0% (August 2011); Total civilian labor force: 7,312 (August 2011); Leading industries: 36.2% manufacturing; 16.8% health care and social assistance; 11.2% retail trade (2009); Farms: 500 totaling 204,584 acres (2007); Companies that employ 500 or more persons: 0 (2009); Companies that employ 100 to 499 persons: 4 (2009); Companies that employ less than 100 persons: 271 (2009); Black-owned businesses: n/a (2007); Hispanic-owned businesses: n/a (2007); Asian-owned businesses: n/a (2007); Women-owned businesses: n/a (2007); Retail sales per capita: $8,039 (2010). Single-family building permits issued: 13 (2010); Multi-family building permits issued: 0 (2010).
Income: Per capita income: $23,984 (2010); Median household income: $50,318 (2010); Average household income: $58,605 (2010); Percent of households with income of $100,000 or more: 11.9% (2010); Poverty rate: 10.4% (2009); Bankruptcy rate: 4.28% (2010).
Taxes: Total county taxes per capita: $192 (2007); County property taxes per capita: $162 (2007).
Education: Percent of population age 25 and over with: High school diploma (including GED) or higher: 89.4% (2010); Bachelor's degree or higher: 17.4% (2010); Master's degree or higher: 4.5% (2010).
Housing: Homeownership rate: 79.0% (2010); Median home value: $103,734 (2010); Median contract rent: $382 per month (2005-2009 5-year est.); Median year structure built: 1959 (2005-2009 5-year est.)
Health: Birth rate: 118.9 per 10,000 population (2009); Death rate: 140.9 per 10,000 population (2009); Age-adjusted cancer mortality rate: 239.0 deaths per 100,000 population (2007); Number of physicians: 3.9 per 10,000 population (2008); Hospital beds: 0.0 per 10,000 population (2007); Hospital admissions: 0.0 per 10,000 population (2007).
Elections: 2008 Presidential election results: 48.6% Obama, 49.7% McCain, 0.6% Nader
National and State Parks: Cameron National Wildlife Refuge; Marshall County State Conservation Areas; Sparland State Conservation Area
Additional Information Contacts
Marshall County Government . . . . (309) 246-6325
  http://www.marshallcountyillinois.com
Henry Area Chamber of Commerce . . . . (309) 364-3261
  http://www.henrychamber.org
Lacon Chamber of Commerce. . . . . (309) 246-5222
  http://www.laconchamber.com

Marshall County Communities

HENRY (city). Covers a land area of 1.395 square miles and a water area of 0.069 square miles. Located at 41.11° N. Lat; 89.36° W. Long. Elevation is 492 feet.

History: Founded in early 1840s; incorporated 1854.

Population: 2,662 (1990); 2,540 (2000); 2,437 (2010); 2,363 (2015 projected); Race: 95.5% White, 1.4% Black, 0.7% Asian, 2.5% Other, 1.3% Hispanic of any race (2010); Density: 1,747.5 persons per square mile (2010); Average household size: 2.37 (2010); Median age: 41.7 (2010); Males per 100 females: 92.5 (2010); Marriage status: 22.8% never married, 54.4% now married, 12.9% widowed, 9.8% divorced (2005-2009 5-year est.); Foreign born: 0.9% (2005-2009 5-year est.); Ancestry (includes multiple ancestries): 38.1% German, 18.3% Irish, 9.7% English, 8.2% American, 5.3% Italian (2005-2009 5-year est.).

Economy: Single-family building permits issued: 1 (2010); Multi-family building permits issued: 0 (2010); Employment by occupation: 13.2% management, 17.6% professional, 16.6% services, 21.4% sales, 1.8% farming, 8.4% construction, 21.0% production (2005-2009 5-year est.).

Income: Per capita income: $23,546 (2010); Median household income: $48,654 (2010); Average household income: $57,138 (2010); Percent of households with income of $100,000 or more: 10.3% (2010); Poverty rate: 13.1% (2005-2009 5-year est.).

Taxes: Total city taxes per capita: $132 (2007); City property taxes per capita: $125 (2007).

Education: Percent of population age 25 and over with: High school diploma (including GED) or higher: 87.1% (2010); Bachelor's degree or higher: 19.6% (2010); Master's degree or higher: 6.6% (2010).

School District(s)

Henry-Senachwine CUSD 5 (PK-12)

2009-10 Enrollment: 659 . . . . (309) 364-3614

Housing: Homeownership rate: 76.9% (2010); Median home value: $87,361 (2010); Median contract rent: $395 per month (2005-2009 5-year est.); Median year structure built: 1951 (2005-2009 5-year est.).

Safety: Violent crime rate: 37.7 per 10,000 population; Property crime rate: 213.8 per 10,000 population (2010).

Newspapers: Henry News Republican (Local news; Circulation 2,850); Wenona Index (Community news; Circulation 900)

Transportation: Commute to work: 92.8% car, 0.0% public transportation, 4.9% walk, 1.3% work from home (2005-2009 5-year est.); Travel time to work: 42.9% less than 15 minutes, 16.0% 15 to 30 minutes, 16.2% 30 to 45 minutes, 17.0% 45 to 60 minutes, 7.9% 60 minutes or more (2005-2009 5-year est.)

Additional Information Contacts

Henry Area Chamber of Commerce . . . . (309) 364-3261
http://www.henrychamber.org

HOPEWELL (village). Covers a land area of 1.125 square miles and a water area of 0 square miles. Located at 40.98° N. Lat; 89.45° W. Long. Elevation is 633 feet.

Population: 343 (1990); 396 (2000); 396 (2010); 394 (2015 projected); Race: 97.5% White, 0.8% Black, 0.0% Asian, 1.8% Other, 4.5% Hispanic of any race (2010); Density: 352.0 persons per square mile (2010); Average household size: 2.69 (2010); Median age: 40.5 (2010); Males per 100 females: 104.1 (2010); Marriage status: 13.6% never married, 74.3% now married, 2.3% widowed, 9.8% divorced (2005-2009 5-year est.); Foreign born: 1.4% (2005-2009 5-year est.); Ancestry (includes multiple ancestries): 48.0% German, 15.7% Irish, 10.9% American, 9.5% English, 7.6% Polish (2005-2009 5-year est.).

Economy: Single-family building permits issued: 3 (2010); Multi-family building permits issued: 0 (2010); Employment by occupation: 12.4% management, 29.7% professional, 8.8% services, 23.7% sales, 0.8% farming, 14.5% construction, 10.0% production (2005-2009 5-year est.).

Income: Per capita income: $21,800 (2010); Median household income: $49,674 (2010); Average household income: $58,452 (2010); Percent of households with income of $100,000 or more: 16.3% (2010); Poverty rate: 0.0% (2005-2009 5-year est.).

Taxes: Total city taxes per capita: $0 (2007); City property taxes per capita: $0 (2007).

Education: Percent of population age 25 and over with: High school diploma (including GED) or higher: 90.4% (2010); Bachelor's degree or higher: 16.4% (2010); Master's degree or higher: 5.0% (2010).

Housing: Homeownership rate: 84.4% (2010); Median home value: $116,176 (2010); Median contract rent: $292 per month (2005-2009 5-year est.); Median year structure built: 1979 (2005-2009 5-year est.).

Transportation: Commute to work: 100.0% car, 0.0% public transportation, 0.0% walk, 0.0% work from home (2005-2009 5-year est.); Travel time to work: 10.4% less than 15 minutes, 33.8% 15 to 30 minutes, 43.3% 30 to 45 minutes, 7.5% 45 to 60 minutes, 5.0% 60 minutes or more (2005-2009 5-year est.)

LA ROSE (village). Covers a land area of 0.220 square miles and a water area of 0 square miles. Located at 40.98° N. Lat; 89.23° W. Long. Elevation is 682 feet.

Population: 130 (1990); 159 (2000); 138 (2010); 130 (2015 projected); Race: 92.8% White, 0.7% Black, 0.0% Asian, 6.5% Other, 5.1% Hispanic of any race (2010); Density: 627.0 persons per square mile (2010); Average household size: 2.56 (2010); Median age: 39.0 (2010); Males per 100 females: 115.6 (2010); Marriage status: 21.5% never married, 67.7% now married, 0.0% widowed, 10.8% divorced (2005-2009 5-year est.); Foreign born: 0.0% (2005-2009 5-year est.); Ancestry (includes multiple ancestries): 53.6% German, 17.0% English, 10.7% Norwegian, 9.8% American, 6.3% Italian (2005-2009 5-year est.).

Economy: Employment by occupation: 16.7% management, 2.1% professional, 31.3% services, 18.8% sales, 0.0% farming, 14.6% construction, 16.7% production (2005-2009 5-year est.).

Income: Per capita income: $21,783 (2010); Median household income: $51,667 (2010); Average household income: $55,046 (2010); Percent of households with income of $100,000 or more: 5.6% (2010); Poverty rate: 12.5% (2005-2009 5-year est.).

Taxes: Total city taxes per capita: $74 (2007); City property taxes per capita: $74 (2007).

Education: Percent of population age 25 and over with: High school diploma (including GED) or higher: 89.4% (2010); Bachelor's degree or higher: 14.9% (2010); Master's degree or higher: 3.2% (2010).

Housing: Homeownership rate: 79.6% (2010); Median home value: $117,308 (2010); Median contract rent: $394 per month (2005-2009 5-year est.); Median year structure built: before 1940 (2005-2009 5-year est.).

Transportation: Commute to work: 100.0% car, 0.0% public transportation, 0.0% walk, 0.0% work from home (2005-2009 5-year est.); Travel time to work: 45.8% less than 15 minutes, 29.2% 15 to 30 minutes, 6.3% 30 to 45 minutes, 14.6% 45 to 60 minutes, 4.2% 60 minutes or more (2005-2009 5-year est.)

LACON (city). County seat. Covers a land area of 1.604 square miles and a water area of 0.044 square miles. Located at 41.02° N. Lat; 89.40° W. Long. Elevation is 476 feet.

History: Laid out as Columbia in 1826; incorporated 1839.

Population: 1,989 (1990); 1,979 (2000); 1,863 (2010); 1,770 (2015 projected); Race: 98.9% White, 0.1% Black, 0.1% Asian, 0.9% Other, 3.2% Hispanic of any race (2010); Density: 1,161.6 persons per square mile (2010); Average household size: 2.33 (2010); Median age: 44.4 (2010); Males per 100 females: 93.3 (2010); Marriage status: 27.1% never married, 52.4% now married, 10.5% widowed, 10.1% divorced (2005-2009 5-year est.); Foreign born: 4.3% (2005-2009 5-year est.); Ancestry (includes multiple ancestries): 34.7% German, 27.5% Irish, 19.1% English, 9.0% Italian, 6.8% American (2005-2009 5-year est.).

Economy: Single-family building permits issued: 0 (2010); Multi-family building permits issued: 0 (2010); Employment by occupation: 7.8% management, 14.7% professional, 18.5% services, 27.5% sales, 0.0% farming, 12.7% construction, 18.7% production (2005-2009 5-year est.).

Income: Per capita income: $24,447 (2010); Median household income: $53,082 (2010); Average household income: $57,800 (2010); Percent of households with income of $100,000 or more: 10.4% (2010); Poverty rate: 8.8% (2005-2009 5-year est.).

Taxes: Total city taxes per capita: $331 (2007); City property taxes per capita: $326 (2007).

Education: Percent of population age 25 and over with: High school diploma (including GED) or higher: 87.4% (2010); Bachelor's degree or higher: 17.0% (2010); Master's degree or higher: 3.3% (2010).

School District(s)

Midland CUSD 7 (PK-12)

2009-10 Enrollment: 823 . . . . (309) 463-2364

Housing: Homeownership rate: 78.2% (2010); Median home value: $114,593 (2010); Median contract rent: $397 per month (2005-2009 5-year est.); Median year structure built: 1953 (2005-2009 5-year est.).

Safety: Violent crime rate: 5.6 per 10,000 population; Property crime rate: 100.2 per 10,000 population (2010).

Newspapers: Illinois Valley Peach (Community news; Circulation 9,800); Lacon Home Journal (Community news; Circulation 2,400)

Transportation: Commute to work: 87.5% car, 0.0% public transportation, 9.9% walk, 2.0% work from home (2005-2009 5-year est.); Travel time to work: 36.8% less than 15 minutes, 23.2% 15 to 30 minutes, 22.6% 30 to 45 minutes, 5.8% 45 to 60 minutes, 11.6% 60 minutes or more (2005-2009 5-year est.)
Additional Information Contacts
Lacon Chamber of Commerce. . . . . (309) 246-5222
  http://www.laconchamber.com

SPARLAND (village). Covers a land area of 0.582 square miles and a water area of 0 square miles. Located at 41.03° N. Lat; 89.43° W. Long. Elevation is 472 feet.
Population: 412 (1990); 504 (2000); 516 (2010); 513 (2015 projected); Race: 97.3% White, 1.0% Black, 0.0% Asian, 1.7% Other, 4.7% Hispanic of any race (2010); Density: 885.9 persons per square mile (2010); Average household size: 2.70 (2010); Median age: 40.8 (2010); Males per 100 females: 106.4 (2010); Marriage status: 21.0% never married, 67.5% now married, 5.1% widowed, 6.4% divorced (2005-2009 5-year est.); Foreign born: 0.0% (2005-2009 5-year est.); Ancestry (includes multiple ancestries): 38.8% German, 23.7% Irish, 12.2% English, 8.2% Scottish, 6.1% American (2005-2009 5-year est.).
Economy: Employment by occupation: 3.6% management, 15.4% professional, 20.7% services, 25.4% sales, 0.0% farming, 7.7% construction, 27.2% production (2005-2009 5-year est.).
Income: Per capita income: $21,800 (2010); Median household income: $50,313 (2010); Average household income: $58,822 (2010); Percent of households with income of $100,000 or more: 16.2% (2010); Poverty rate: 11.2% (2005-2009 5-year est.).
Taxes: Total city taxes per capita: $55 (2007); City property taxes per capita: $47 (2007).
Education: Percent of population age 25 and over with: High school diploma (including GED) or higher: 89.9% (2010); Bachelor's degree or higher: 16.9% (2010); Master's degree or higher: 5.4% (2010).
School District(s)
Midland CUSD 7 (PK-12)
  2009-10 Enrollment: 823 . . . . (309) 463-2364
Housing: Homeownership rate: 84.8% (2010); Median home value: $116,667 (2010); Median contract rent: $440 per month (2005-2009 5-year est.); Median year structure built: 1944 (2005-2009 5-year est.).
Transportation: Commute to work: 100.0% car, 0.0% public transportation, 0.0% walk, 0.0% work from home (2005-2009 5-year est.); Travel time to work: 32.7% less than 15 minutes, 26.3% 15 to 30 minutes, 17.3% 30 to 45 minutes, 16.7% 45 to 60 minutes, 7.1% 60 minutes or more (2005-2009 5-year est.)

TOLUCA (city). Covers a land area of 1.062 square miles and a water area of 0 square miles. Located at 41.00° N. Lat; 89.13° W. Long. Elevation is 692 feet.
History: Incorporated 1894.
Population: 1,315 (1990); 1,339 (2000); 1,242 (2010); 1,194 (2015 projected); Race: 95.9% White, 0.2% Black, 0.7% Asian, 3.2% Other, 3.1% Hispanic of any race (2010); Density: 1,169.5 persons per square mile (2010); Average household size: 2.13 (2010); Median age: 45.3 (2010); Males per 100 females: 85.1 (2010); Marriage status: 21.9% never married, 52.2% now married, 10.9% widowed, 15.0% divorced (2005-2009 5-year est.); Foreign born: 2.1% (2005-2009 5-year est.); Ancestry (includes multiple ancestries): 43.6% German, 13.6% Italian, 10.4% Irish, 9.1% English, 5.6% American (2005-2009 5-year est.).
Economy: Single-family building permits issued: 0 (2010); Multi-family building permits issued: 0 (2010); Employment by occupation: 5.5% management, 12.3% professional, 15.7% services, 21.2% sales, 1.6% farming, 7.7% construction, 35.9% production (2005-2009 5-year est.).
Income: Per capita income: $24,596 (2010); Median household income: $44,463 (2010); Average household income: $55,096 (2010); Percent of households with income of $100,000 or more: 9.0% (2010); Poverty rate: 8.6% (2005-2009 5-year est.).
Taxes: Total city taxes per capita: $93 (2007); City property taxes per capita: $91 (2007).
Education: Percent of population age 25 and over with: High school diploma (including GED) or higher: 85.9% (2010); Bachelor's degree or higher: 14.6% (2010); Master's degree or higher: 3.9% (2010).
School District(s)
Fieldcrest CUSD 6 (PK-12)
  2009-10 Enrollment: 1,257 . . . . (309) 432-2177

Housing: Homeownership rate: 76.4% (2010); Median home value: $89,412 (2010); Median contract rent: $359 per month (2005-2009 5-year est.); Median year structure built: 1954 (2005-2009 5-year est.).
Transportation: Commute to work: 90.7% car, 0.0% public transportation, 6.0% walk, 1.5% work from home (2005-2009 5-year est.); Travel time to work: 42.7% less than 15 minutes, 15.7% 15 to 30 minutes, 19.7% 30 to 45 minutes, 13.0% 45 to 60 minutes, 8.9% 60 minutes or more (2005-2009 5-year est.)

VARNA (village). Covers a land area of 0.293 square miles and a water area of 0 square miles. Located at 41.03° N. Lat; 89.22° W. Long. Elevation is 728 feet.
Population: 408 (1990); 436 (2000); 392 (2010); 372 (2015 projected); Race: 98.0% White, 0.3% Black, 0.0% Asian, 1.8% Other, 4.3% Hispanic of any race (2010); Density: 1,338.1 persons per square mile (2010); Average household size: 2.46 (2010); Median age: 40.3 (2010); Males per 100 females: 95.0 (2010); Marriage status: 22.0% never married, 61.0% now married, 7.3% widowed, 9.8% divorced (2005-2009 5-year est.); Foreign born: 1.0% (2005-2009 5-year est.); Ancestry (includes multiple ancestries): 44.1% German, 13.7% Irish, 11.0% Italian, 10.0% American, 9.5% Swedish (2005-2009 5-year est.).
Economy: Employment by occupation: 9.5% management, 19.0% professional, 18.1% services, 30.0% sales, 0.0% farming, 9.5% construction, 13.8% production (2005-2009 5-year est.).
Income: Per capita income: $22,579 (2010); Median household income: $52,123 (2010); Average household income: $55,425 (2010); Percent of households with income of $100,000 or more: 8.2% (2010); Poverty rate: 11.2% (2005-2009 5-year est.).
Taxes: Total city taxes per capita: $118 (2007); City property taxes per capita: $40 (2007).
Education: Percent of population age 25 and over with: High school diploma (including GED) or higher: 88.7% (2010); Bachelor's degree or higher: 7.5% (2010); Master's degree or higher: 1.1% (2010).
School District(s)
Midland CUSD 7 (PK-12)
  2009-10 Enrollment: 823 . . . . (309) 463-2364
Housing: Homeownership rate: 79.2% (2010); Median home value: $95,000 (2010); Median contract rent: $348 per month (2005-2009 5-year est.); Median year structure built: before 1940 (2005-2009 5-year est.).
Newspapers: Lake Wildwood Sunbeam (Community news; Circulation 1,450)
Transportation: Commute to work: 92.5% car, 0.0% public transportation, 0.0% walk, 5.2% work from home (2005-2009 5-year est.); Travel time to work: 28.4% less than 15 minutes, 20.4% 15 to 30 minutes, 26.9% 30 to 45 minutes, 16.4% 45 to 60 minutes, 8.0% 60 minutes or more (2005-2009 5-year est.)

WENONA (city). Covers a land area of 0.672 square miles and a water area of 0 square miles. Located at 41.05° N. Lat; 89.05° W. Long. Elevation is 699 feet.
History: Wenona's early economy was based on soy beans and corn.
Population: 981 (1990); 1,065 (2000); 1,005 (2010); 967 (2015 projected); Race: 96.4% White, 0.5% Black, 0.1% Asian, 3.0% Other, 2.5% Hispanic of any race (2010); Density: 1,494.6 persons per square mile (2010); Average household size: 2.28 (2010); Median age: 39.4 (2010); Males per 100 females: 94.8 (2010); Marriage status: 29.8% never married, 50.8% now married, 8.3% widowed, 11.2% divorced (2005-2009 5-year est.); Foreign born: 2.2% (2005-2009 5-year est.); Ancestry (includes multiple ancestries): 36.1% German, 26.1% Irish, 8.4% English, 7.7% Italian, 6.5% Polish (2005-2009 5-year est.).
Economy: Single-family building permits issued: 0 (2010); Multi-family building permits issued: 0 (2010); Employment by occupation: 8.6% management, 6.8% professional, 25.4% services, 19.9% sales, 0.0% farming, 7.7% construction, 31.8% production (2005-2009 5-year est.).
Income: Per capita income: $20,430 (2010); Median household income: $39,030 (2010); Average household income: $46,705 (2010); Percent of households with income of $100,000 or more: 6.1% (2010); Poverty rate: 18.3% (2005-2009 5-year est.).
Taxes: Total city taxes per capita: $714 (2007); City property taxes per capita: $607 (2007).
Education: Percent of population age 25 and over with: High school diploma (including GED) or higher: 90.8% (2010); Bachelor's degree or higher: 15.3% (2010); Master's degree or higher: 3.9% (2010).

School District(s)

Fieldcrest CUSD 6 (PK-12)

    2009-10 Enrollment: 1,257 . . . . (309) 432-2177

Housing: Homeownership rate: 78.0% (2010); Median home value: $81,413 (2010); Median contract rent: $418 per month (2005-2009 5-year est.); Median year structure built: 1945 (2005-2009 5-year est.).

Transportation: Commute to work: 89.9% car, 1.1% public transportation, 4.1% walk, 0.0% work from home (2005-2009 5-year est.); Travel time to work: 45.5% less than 15 minutes, 23.6% 15 to 30 minutes, 13.4% 30 to 45 minutes, 6.1% 45 to 60 minutes, 11.4% 60 minutes or more (2005-2009 5-year est.)

Mason County

Located in central Illinois; bounded on the west by the Illinois River, and on the south by the Sangamon River and Salt Creek. Covers a land area of 538.94 square miles, a water area of 24.43 square miles, and is located in the Central Time Zone at 40.26° N. Lat., 89.91° W. Long. The county was founded in 1841. County seat is Havana.

Weather Station: Havana 4 NNE										Elevation: 459 feet		
	Jan	Feb	Mar	Apr	May	Jun	Jul	Aug	Sep	Oct	Nov	Dec
High	34	39	51	64	74	84	88	86	80	67	52	38
Low	16	20	30	40	51	61	65	62	52	41	31	20
Precip	2.1	2.1	2.8	3.6	4.5	4.2	3.9	3.8	3.2	3.0	3.2	2.8
Snow	9.3	7.5	3.1	1.1	tr	0.0	0.0	0.0	0.0	tr	1.0	7.5

High and Low temperatures in degrees Fahrenheit; Precipitation and Snow in inches

Weather Station: Mason City 1 W										Elevation: 584 feet		
	Jan	Feb	Mar	Apr	May	Jun	Jul	Aug	Sep	Oct	Nov	Dec
High	34	40	52	65	75	84	86	85	79	67	51	38
Low	18	22	31	42	52	62	65	63	55	44	33	22
Precip	1.7	1.6	2.3	3.5	4.0	4.0	4.4	3.5	3.1	2.9	3.2	2.3
Snow	4.4	3.8	1.7	0.5	0.0	0.0	0.0	0.0	0.0	tr	0.4	4.2

High and Low temperatures in degrees Fahrenheit; Precipitation and Snow in inches

Population: 16,269 (1990); 16,038 (2000); 14,936 (2010); 14,343 (2015 projected); Race: 97.8% White, 0.5% Black, 0.3% Asian, 1.4% Other, 0.9% Hispanic of any race (2010); Density: 27.7 persons per square mile (2010); Average household size: 2.44 (2010); Median age: 41.8 (2010); Males per 100 females: 95.7 (2010).

Religion: Five largest groups: 13.9% Lutheran Church—Missouri Synod, 9.1% The United Methodist Church, 6.6% Catholic Church, 4.7% American Baptist Churches in the USA, 4.1% Christian Churches and Churches of Christ (2000).

Economy: Unemployment rate: 10.6% (August 2011); Total civilian labor force: 7,789 (August 2011); Leading industries: 20.5% health care and social assistance; 16.2% retail trade; 10.6% accommodation & food services (2009); Farms: 447 totaling 273,362 acres (2007); Companies that employ 500 or more persons: 0 (2009); Companies that employ 100 to 499 persons: 1 (2009); Companies that employ less than 100 persons: 311 (2009); Black-owned businesses: n/a (2007); Hispanic-owned businesses: n/a (2007); Asian-owned businesses: n/a (2007); Women-owned businesses: 197 (2007); Retail sales per capita: $10,195 (2010). Single-family building permits issued: 8 (2010); Multi-family building permits issued: 0 (2010).

Income: Per capita income: $21,595 (2010); Median household income: $44,033 (2010); Average household income: $52,886 (2010); Percent of households with income of $100,000 or more: 9.1% (2010); Poverty rate: 12.5% (2009); Bankruptcy rate: 4.85% (2010).

Taxes: Total county taxes per capita: $204 (2007); County property taxes per capita: $167 (2007).

Education: Percent of population age 25 and over with: High school diploma (including GED) or higher: 85.3% (2010); Bachelor's degree or higher: 13.7% (2010); Master's degree or higher: 4.0% (2010).

Housing: Homeownership rate: 75.5% (2010); Median home value: $86,067 (2010); Median contract rent: $367 per month (2005-2009 5-year est.); Median year structure built: 1961 (2005-2009 5-year est.)

Health: Birth rate: 121.7 per 10,000 population (2009); Death rate: 129.2 per 10,000 population (2009); Age-adjusted cancer mortality rate: 202.7 deaths per 100,000 population (2007); Number of physicians: 6.0 per 10,000 population (2008); Hospital beds: 16.6 per 10,000 population (2007); Hospital admissions: 291.7 per 10,000 population (2007).

Elections: 2008 Presidential election results: 52.0% Obama, 46.1% McCain, 1.0% Nader

National and State Parks: Chautauqua National Wildlife Refuge; Chautauqua National Migratory Waterfowl Refuge; Mason County State Wildlife Refuge and Recreation; Sand Ridge State Forest

Additional Information Contacts

Mason County Government . . . . (309) 543-6661
    http://www.masoncountyil.org

Havana Area Chamber of Commerce . . . . (309) 543-3528
    http://www.scenichavana.com

Mason County Communities

BATH (village). Covers a land area of 0.365 square miles and a water area of <.001 square miles. Located at 40.19° N. Lat; 90.14° W. Long. Elevation is 463 feet.

History: Bath was surveyed in 1836 by Abraham Lincoln, who was then the Deputy Surveyor of Sangamon County. Bath served as the county seat from 1843 to 1851.

Population: 388 (1990); 310 (2000); 299 (2010); 291 (2015 projected); Race: 96.7% White, 0.7% Black, 0.0% Asian, 2.7% Other, 0.7% Hispanic of any race (2010); Density: 818.7 persons per square mile (2010); Average household size: 2.32 (2010); Median age: 39.5 (2010); Males per 100 females: 86.9 (2010); Marriage status: 22.5% never married, 45.4% now married, 12.5% widowed, 19.6% divorced (2005-2009 5-year est.); Foreign born: 0.9% (2005-2009 5-year est.); Ancestry (includes multiple ancestries): 27.9% German, 21.7% American, 16.4% Irish, 9.3% English, 3.4% Italian (2005-2009 5-year est.).

Economy: Single-family building permits issued: 0 (2010); Multi-family building permits issued: 0 (2010); Employment by occupation: 8.3% management, 10.0% professional, 30.0% services, 7.5% sales, 0.0% farming, 20.8% construction, 23.3% production (2005-2009 5-year est.).

Income: Per capita income: $18,903 (2010); Median household income: $38,056 (2010); Average household income: $44,147 (2010); Percent of households with income of $100,000 or more: 3.9% (2010); Poverty rate: 22.4% (2005-2009 5-year est.).

Taxes: Total city taxes per capita: $40 (2007); City property taxes per capita: $23 (2007).

Education: Percent of population age 25 and over with: High school diploma (including GED) or higher: 88.1% (2010); Bachelor's degree or higher: 10.4% (2010); Master's degree or higher: 5.0% (2010).

Housing: Homeownership rate: 80.6% (2010); Median home value: $66,154 (2010); Median contract rent: $389 per month (2005-2009 5-year est.); Median year structure built: 1957 (2005-2009 5-year est.).

Transportation: Commute to work: 98.3% car, 1.7% public transportation, 0.0% walk, 0.0% work from home (2005-2009 5-year est.); Travel time to work: 19.0% less than 15 minutes, 37.1% 15 to 30 minutes, 25.0% 30 to 45 minutes, 12.1% 45 to 60 minutes, 6.9% 60 minutes or more (2005-2009 5-year est.)

EASTON (village). Covers a land area of 0.233 square miles and a water area of 0 square miles. Located at 40.23° N. Lat; 89.84° W. Long. Elevation is 512 feet.

Population: 375 (1990); 373 (2000); 357 (2010); 344 (2015 projected); Race: 98.6% White, 0.0% Black, 0.3% Asian, 1.1% Other, 0.0% Hispanic of any race (2010); Density: 1,530.9 persons per square mile (2010); Average household size: 2.47 (2010); Median age: 45.4 (2010); Males per 100 females: 104.0 (2010); Marriage status: 14.3% never married, 68.8% now married, 6.1% widowed, 10.8% divorced (2005-2009 5-year est.); Foreign born: 0.0% (2005-2009 5-year est.); Ancestry (includes multiple ancestries): 42.5% German, 16.3% American, 12.4% English, 10.4% Irish, 4.4% French (2005-2009 5-year est.).

Economy: Single-family building permits issued: 0 (2010); Multi-family building permits issued: 0 (2010); Employment by occupation: 11.3% management, 14.9% professional, 14.9% services, 13.4% sales, 1.0% farming, 13.4% construction, 30.9% production (2005-2009 5-year est.).

Income: Per capita income: $18,250 (2010); Median household income: $37,143 (2010); Average household income: $44,618 (2010); Percent of households with income of $100,000 or more: 5.6% (2010); Poverty rate: 10.9% (2005-2009 5-year est.).

Taxes: Total city taxes per capita: $85 (2007); City property taxes per capita: $85 (2007).

Education: Percent of population age 25 and over with: High school diploma (including GED) or higher: 89.0% (2010); Bachelor's degree or higher: 20.5% (2010); Master's degree or higher: 4.2% (2010).

Housing: Homeownership rate: 82.6% (2010); Median home value: $88,636 (2010); Median contract rent: $338 per month (2005-2009 5-year est.); Median year structure built: 1941 (2005-2009 5-year est.).
Safety: Violent crime rate: 0.0 per 10,000 population; Property crime rate: 29.6 per 10,000 population (2010).
Transportation: Commute to work: 93.3% car, 0.0% public transportation, 4.6% walk, 1.0% work from home (2005-2009 5-year est.); Travel time to work: 40.1% less than 15 minutes, 18.8% 15 to 30 minutes, 16.1% 30 to 45 minutes, 5.2% 45 to 60 minutes, 19.8% 60 minutes or more (2005-2009 5-year est.)

FOREST CITY (village).
Covers a land area of 0.524 square miles and a water area of 0 square miles. Located at 40.37° N. Lat; 89.82° W. Long. Elevation is 492 feet.
Population: 321 (1990); 287 (2000); 236 (2010); 218 (2015 projected); Race: 97.5% White, 1.3% Black, 0.0% Asian, 1.3% Other, 1.3% Hispanic of any race (2010); Density: 450.5 persons per square mile (2010); Average household size: 2.71 (2010); Median age: 39.5 (2010); Males per 100 females: 107.0 (2010); Marriage status: 21.1% never married, 55.4% now married, 14.9% widowed, 8.6% divorced (2005-2009 5-year est.); Foreign born: 0.0% (2005-2009 5-year est.); Ancestry (includes multiple ancestries): 30.6% German, 27.0% American, 14.5% English, 12.9% Irish, 4.8% Italian (2005-2009 5-year est.).
Economy: Employment by occupation: 4.6% management, 9.2% professional, 17.2% services, 16.1% sales, 13.8% farming, 17.2% construction, 21.8% production (2005-2009 5-year est.).
Income: Per capita income: $19,983 (2010); Median household income: $44,079 (2010); Average household income: $52,902 (2010); Percent of households with income of $100,000 or more: 6.9% (2010); Poverty rate: 25.8% (2005-2009 5-year est.).
Taxes: Total city taxes per capita: $135 (2007); City property taxes per capita: $80 (2007).
Education: Percent of population age 25 and over with: High school diploma (including GED) or higher: 83.4% (2010); Bachelor's degree or higher: 12.7% (2010); Master's degree or higher: 1.9% (2010).
Housing: Homeownership rate: 79.3% (2010); Median home value: $94,000 (2010); Median contract rent: $543 per month (2005-2009 5-year est.); Median year structure built: 1948 (2005-2009 5-year est.).
Transportation: Commute to work: 93.3% car, 0.0% public transportation, 1.3% walk, 1.3% work from home (2005-2009 5-year est.); Travel time to work: 47.3% less than 15 minutes, 20.3% 15 to 30 minutes, 17.6% 30 to 45 minutes, 9.5% 45 to 60 minutes, 5.4% 60 minutes or more (2005-2009 5-year est.)

HAVANA (city).
County seat. Covers a land area of 2.628 square miles and a water area of 0.151 square miles. Located at 40.29° N. Lat; 90.06° W. Long. Elevation is 476 feet.
History: Havana grew up around the ferry across the Spoon River, established in 1824 by Major Ossian M. Ross. Havana shared in the prosperity brought by steamboat travel on the Illinois River, shipping grain and produce to market. Commercial fishing was important here in the early 1900's.
Population: 3,672 (1990); 3,577 (2000); 3,292 (2010); 3,148 (2015 projected); Race: 97.4% White, 0.5% Black, 0.8% Asian, 1.4% Other, 1.0% Hispanic of any race (2010); Density: 1,252.6 persons per square mile (2010); Average household size: 2.34 (2010); Median age: 41.5 (2010); Males per 100 females: 87.9 (2010); Marriage status: 22.1% never married, 51.4% now married, 10.7% widowed, 15.7% divorced (2005-2009 5-year est.); Foreign born: 1.6% (2005-2009 5-year est.); Ancestry (includes multiple ancestries): 31.7% German, 17.4% American, 13.4% Irish, 11.9% English, 4.1% French (2005-2009 5-year est.).
Economy: Single-family building permits issued: 1 (2010); Multi-family building permits issued: 0 (2010); Employment by occupation: 13.2% management, 22.4% professional, 21.5% services, 19.0% sales, 2.4% farming, 8.4% construction, 13.1% production (2005-2009 5-year est.).
Income: Per capita income: $20,318 (2010); Median household income: $35,602 (2010); Average household income: $47,517 (2010); Percent of households with income of $100,000 or more: 7.7% (2010); Poverty rate: 18.6% (2005-2009 5-year est.).
Taxes: Total city taxes per capita: $342 (2007); City property taxes per capita: $288 (2007).
Education: Percent of population age 25 and over with: High school diploma (including GED) or higher: 83.0% (2010); Bachelor's degree or higher: 15.1% (2010); Master's degree or higher: 5.0% (2010).

School District(s)
Havana CUSD 126 (PK-12)
   2009-10 Enrollment: 1,130 . . . . (309) 543-3384
Housing: Homeownership rate: 66.2% (2010); Median home value: $73,767 (2010); Median contract rent: $404 per month (2005-2009 5-year est.); Median year structure built: 1945 (2005-2009 5-year est.).
Hospitals: Mason District Hospital (48 beds)
Newspapers: Market Place (Community news; Circulation 6,300); Mason County Democrat (Community news; Circulation 6,300)
Transportation: Commute to work: 88.5% car, 0.0% public transportation, 6.1% walk, 2.4% work from home (2005-2009 5-year est.); Travel time to work: 64.3% less than 15 minutes, 8.3% 15 to 30 minutes, 10.6% 30 to 45 minutes, 7.4% 45 to 60 minutes, 9.4% 60 minutes or more (2005-2009 5-year est.)
Additional Information Contacts
Havana Area Chamber of Commerce . . . . (309) 543-3528
   http://www.scenichavana.com

KILBOURNE (village).
Covers a land area of 1.062 square miles and a water area of 0 square miles. Located at 40.15° N. Lat; 90.01° W. Long. Elevation is 495 feet.
Population: 358 (1990); 375 (2000); 334 (2010); 311 (2015 projected); Race: 96.4% White, 0.3% Black, 0.3% Asian, 3.0% Other, 1.2% Hispanic of any race (2010); Density: 314.5 persons per square mile (2010); Average household size: 2.42 (2010); Median age: 40.2 (2010); Males per 100 females: 107.5 (2010); Marriage status: 33.0% never married, 50.2% now married, 6.8% widowed, 10.0% divorced (2005-2009 5-year est.); Foreign born: 9.0% (2005-2009 5-year est.); Ancestry (includes multiple ancestries): 44.1% American, 17.2% German, 9.0% Irish, 3.9% English, 3.6% Dutch (2005-2009 5-year est.).
Economy: Employment by occupation: 6.0% management, 4.3% professional, 20.7% services, 7.8% sales, 0.0% farming, 12.9% construction, 48.3% production (2005-2009 5-year est.).
Income: Per capita income: $20,792 (2010); Median household income: $42,800 (2010); Average household income: $50,181 (2010); Percent of households with income of $100,000 or more: 10.1% (2010); Poverty rate: 22.6% (2005-2009 5-year est.).
Taxes: Total city taxes per capita: $36 (2007); City property taxes per capita: $31 (2007).
Education: Percent of population age 25 and over with: High school diploma (including GED) or higher: 86.2% (2010); Bachelor's degree or higher: 9.1% (2010); Master's degree or higher: 2.6% (2010).
Housing: Homeownership rate: 78.3% (2010); Median home value: $66,667 (2010); Median contract rent: $770 per month (2005-2009 5-year est.); Median year structure built: 1952 (2005-2009 5-year est.).
Transportation: Commute to work: 96.7% car, 0.0% public transportation, 0.0% walk, 1.6% work from home (2005-2009 5-year est.); Travel time to work: 17.5% less than 15 minutes, 54.2% 15 to 30 minutes, 5.0% 30 to 45 minutes, 12.5% 45 to 60 minutes, 10.8% 60 minutes or more (2005-2009 5-year est.)

MANITO (village).
Covers a land area of 1.539 square miles and a water area of 0 square miles. Located at 40.42° N. Lat; 89.78° W. Long. Elevation is 495 feet.
Population: 1,743 (1990); 1,733 (2000); 1,690 (2010); 1,651 (2015 projected); Race: 97.7% White, 1.2% Black, 0.1% Asian, 1.0% Other, 0.6% Hispanic of any race (2010); Density: 1,098.0 persons per square mile (2010); Average household size: 2.46 (2010); Median age: 40.0 (2010); Males per 100 females: 103.1 (2010); Marriage status: 25.9% never married, 60.8% now married, 5.7% widowed, 7.5% divorced (2005-2009 5-year est.); Foreign born: 0.2% (2005-2009 5-year est.); Ancestry (includes multiple ancestries): 30.3% German, 17.6% American, 10.7% Irish, 6.2% English, 4.8% French (2005-2009 5-year est.).
Economy: Single-family building permits issued: 0 (2010); Multi-family building permits issued: 0 (2010); Employment by occupation: 9.9% management, 17.9% professional, 19.6% services, 22.4% sales, 2.0% farming, 13.1% construction, 15.0% production (2005-2009 5-year est.).
Income: Per capita income: $21,976 (2010); Median household income: $48,211 (2010); Average household income: $54,112 (2010); Percent of households with income of $100,000 or more: 9.4% (2010); Poverty rate: 9.7% (2005-2009 5-year est.).
Taxes: Total city taxes per capita: $124 (2007); City property taxes per capita: $91 (2007).
Education: Percent of population age 25 and over with: High school diploma (including GED) or higher: 87.8% (2010); Bachelor's degree or higher: 12.8% (2010); Master's degree or higher: 3.6% (2010).

School District(s)
Midwest Central CUSD 191 (PK-12)
2009-10 Enrollment: 1,149 . . . . (309) 968-6868
Spring Lake CCSD 606 (KG-06)
2009-10 Enrollment: 73 . . . . (309) 545-2241
Housing: Homeownership rate: 75.7% (2010); Median home value: $110,897 (2010); Median contract rent: $393 per month (2005-2009 5-year est.); Median year structure built: 1965 (2005-2009 5-year est.).
Transportation: Commute to work: 96.4% car, 0.0% public transportation, 1.1% walk, 1.9% work from home (2005-2009 5-year est.); Travel time to work: 24.8% less than 15 minutes, 28.3% 15 to 30 minutes, 22.7% 30 to 45 minutes, 19.0% 45 to 60 minutes, 5.2% 60 minutes or more (2005-2009 5-year est.)

MASON CITY (city). Covers a land area of 0.984 square miles and a water area of 0 square miles. Located at 40.20° N. Lat; 89.69° W. Long. Elevation is 581 feet.
History: Incorporated 1869.
Population: 2,378 (1990); 2,558 (2000); 2,329 (2010); 2,230 (2015 projected); Race: 98.2% White, 0.1% Black, 0.2% Asian, 1.4% Other, 1.2% Hispanic of any race (2010); Density: 2,366.4 persons per square mile (2010); Average household size: 2.37 (2010); Median age: 42.5 (2010); Males per 100 females: 88.3 (2010); Marriage status: 21.1% never married, 52.5% now married, 15.0% widowed, 11.4% divorced (2005-2009 5-year est.); Foreign born: 1.7% (2005-2009 5-year est.); Ancestry (includes multiple ancestries): 31.8% German, 17.1% American, 12.3% English, 11.2% Irish, 4.4% Dutch (2005-2009 5-year est.).
Economy: Single-family building permits issued: 0 (2010); Multi-family building permits issued: 0 (2010); Employment by occupation: 10.1% management, 8.5% professional, 24.5% services, 20.3% sales, 1.1% farming, 6.4% construction, 29.0% production (2005-2009 5-year est.).
Income: Per capita income: $21,534 (2010); Median household income: $43,036 (2010); Average household income: $51,445 (2010); Percent of households with income of $100,000 or more: 7.5% (2010); Poverty rate: 18.2% (2005-2009 5-year est.).
Taxes: Total city taxes per capita: $101 (2007); City property taxes per capita: $92 (2007).
Education: Percent of population age 25 and over with: High school diploma (including GED) or higher: 87.0% (2010); Bachelor's degree or higher: 14.1% (2010); Master's degree or higher: 4.5% (2010).

School District(s)
Illini Central CUSD 189 (PK-12)
2009-10 Enrollment: 878 . . . . (217) 482-5180
Housing: Homeownership rate: 75.6% (2010); Median home value: $79,795 (2010); Median contract rent: $305 per month (2005-2009 5-year est.); Median year structure built: 1958 (2005-2009 5-year est.).
Newspapers: Mason City Banner Times (Local news; Circulation 20,000)
Transportation: Commute to work: 90.4% car, 0.0% public transportation, 3.3% walk, 2.9% work from home (2005-2009 5-year est.); Travel time to work: 47.5% less than 15 minutes, 14.3% 15 to 30 minutes, 17.0% 30 to 45 minutes, 12.9% 45 to 60 minutes, 8.3% 60 minutes or more (2005-2009 5-year est.)

SAN JOSE (village). Covers a land area of 0.511 square miles and a water area of 0 square miles. Located at 40.30° N. Lat; 89.60° W. Long.
Population: 573 (1990); 696 (2000); 661 (2010); 634 (2015 projected); Race: 97.4% White, 0.2% Black, 0.3% Asian, 2.1% Other, 2.9% Hispanic of any race (2010); Density: 1,292.9 persons per square mile (2010); Average household size: 2.67 (2010); Median age: 37.0 (2010); Males per 100 females: 94.4 (2010); Marriage status: 24.3% never married, 59.1% now married, 7.5% widowed, 9.1% divorced (2005-2009 5-year est.); Foreign born: 0.0% (2005-2009 5-year est.); Ancestry (includes multiple ancestries): 40.6% German, 22.6% American, 10.9% Irish, 10.8% English, 8.2% Dutch (2005-2009 5-year est.).
Economy: Single-family building permits issued: 1 (2010); Multi-family building permits issued: 0 (2010); Employment by occupation: 8.2% management, 14.5% professional, 11.3% services, 21.1% sales, 6.6% farming, 9.1% construction, 29.2% production (2005-2009 5-year est.).
Income: Per capita income: $22,476 (2010); Median household income: $52,419 (2010); Average household income: $60,141 (2010); Percent of households with income of $100,000 or more: 13.7% (2010); Poverty rate: 3.2% (2005-2009 5-year est.).
Education: Percent of population age 25 and over with: High school diploma (including GED) or higher: 88.5% (2010); Bachelor's degree or higher: 12.5% (2010); Master's degree or higher: 1.4% (2010).

Housing: Homeownership rate: 75.8% (2010); Median home value: $82,222 (2010); Median contract rent: $348 per month (2005-2009 5-year est.); Median year structure built: 1954 (2005-2009 5-year est.).
Transportation: Commute to work: 86.7% car, 0.0% public transportation, 1.3% walk, 10.1% work from home (2005-2009 5-year est.); Travel time to work: 13.7% less than 15 minutes, 26.0% 15 to 30 minutes, 30.3% 30 to 45 minutes, 21.7% 45 to 60 minutes, 8.3% 60 minutes or more (2005-2009 5-year est.).

TOPEKA (town). Covers a land area of 0.139 square miles and a water area of 0 square miles. Located at 40.33° N. Lat; 89.93° W. Long. Elevation is 472 feet.
Population: 93 (1990); 90 (2000); 79 (2010); 75 (2015 projected); Race: 98.7% White, 0.0% Black, 0.0% Asian, 1.3% Other, 1.3% Hispanic of any race (2010); Density: 568.8 persons per square mile (2010); Average household size: 2.47 (2010); Median age: 41.1 (2010); Males per 100 females: 125.7 (2010); Marriage status: 20.8% never married, 66.7% now married, 0.0% widowed, 12.5% divorced (2005-2009 5-year est.); Foreign born: 0.0% (2005-2009 5-year est.); Ancestry (includes multiple ancestries): 34.0% American, 10.0% German, 10.0% Irish, 8.0% Scotch-Irish, 4.0% French (2005-2009 5-year est.).
Economy: Employment by occupation: 0.0% management, 33.3% professional, 33.3% services, 11.1% sales, 0.0% farming, 0.0% construction, 22.2% production (2005-2009 5-year est.).
Income: Per capita income: $24,516 (2010); Median household income: $48,125 (2010); Average household income: $54,219 (2010); Percent of households with income of $100,000 or more: 12.5% (2010); Poverty rate: 24.0% (2005-2009 5-year est.).
Taxes: Total city taxes per capita: $0 (2007); City property taxes per capita: $0 (2007).
Education: Percent of population age 25 and over with: High school diploma (including GED) or higher: 75.4% (2010); Bachelor's degree or higher: 3.5% (2010); Master's degree or higher: 1.8% (2010).
Housing: Homeownership rate: 78.1% (2010); Median home value: $104,167 (2010); Median contract rent: n/a per month (2005-2009 5-year est.); Median year structure built: 1973 (2005-2009 5-year est.).
Transportation: Commute to work: 100.0% car, 0.0% public transportation, 0.0% walk, 0.0% work from home (2005-2009 5-year est.); Travel time to work: 25.9% less than 15 minutes, 33.3% 15 to 30 minutes, 29.6% 30 to 45 minutes, 11.1% 45 to 60 minutes, 0.0% 60 minutes or more (2005-2009 5-year est.)

Massac County

Located in southern Illinois; bounded on the south and east by the Ohio River and the Kentucky border, and on the northwest by the Cache River; includes part of Shawnee National Forest. Covers a land area of 239.05 square miles, a water area of 3.06 square miles, and is located in the Central Time Zone at 37.20° N. Lat., 88.74° W. Long. The county was founded in 1843. County seat is Metropolis.

Massac County is part of the Paducah, KY-IL Micropolitan Statistical Area. The entire metro area includes: Massac County, IL; Ballard County, KY; Livingston County, KY; McCracken County, KY

Weather Station: Brookport Dam 52											Elevation: 330 feet
	Jan	Feb	Mar	Apr	May	Jun	Jul	Aug	Sep	Oct	Nov	Dec
High	44	48	58	69	77	86	89	89	82	70	58	46
Low	26	30	37	47	56	64	69	67	59	47	38	29
Precip	3.5	3.9	4.1	4.6	5.0	4.1	4.2	2.8	3.5	4.0	4.2	4.6
Snow	2.1	2.4	0.6	tr	0.0	0.0	0.0	0.0	0.0	0.0	0.0	1.7

High and Low temperatures in degrees Fahrenheit; Precipitation and Snow in inches

Population: 14,752 (1990); 15,161 (2000); 15,048 (2010); 14,890 (2015 projected); Race: 91.2% White, 6.2% Black, 0.3% Asian, 2.3% Other, 1.5% Hispanic of any race (2010); Density: 62.9 persons per square mile (2010); Average household size: 2.33 (2010); Median age: 39.3 (2010); Males per 100 females: 92.8 (2010).
Religion: Five largest groups: 37.9% Southern Baptist Convention, 5.9% The United Methodist Church, 5.2% Evangelical Lutheran Church in America, 3.6% Churches of Christ, 2.5% United Church of Christ (2000).
Economy: Unemployment rate: 10.6% (August 2011); Total civilian labor force: 7,350 (August 2011); Leading industries: 15.1% health care and social assistance; 14.1% transportation & warehousing; 8.0% retail trade (2009); Farms: 400 totaling 89,693 acres (2007); Companies that employ 500 or more persons: 1 (2009); Companies that employ 100 to 499

persons: 6 (2009); Companies that employ less than 100 persons: 235 (2009); Black-owned businesses: n/a (2007); Hispanic-owned businesses: n/a (2007); Asian-owned businesses: n/a (2007); Women-owned businesses: 330 (2007); Retail sales per capita: $9,171 (2010). Single-family building permits issued: 1 (2010); Multi-family building permits issued: 0 (2010).
Income: Per capita income: $20,631 (2010); Median household income: $39,388 (2010); Average household income: $48,076 (2010); Percent of households with income of $100,000 or more: 9.5% (2010); Poverty rate: 16.4% (2009); Bankruptcy rate: 3.83% (2010).
Taxes: Total county taxes per capita: $185 (2007); County property taxes per capita: $185 (2007).
Education: Percent of population age 25 and over with: High school diploma (including GED) or higher: 82.9% (2010); Bachelor's degree or higher: 13.5% (2010); Master's degree or higher: 4.2% (2010).
Housing: Homeownership rate: 77.4% (2010); Median home value: $88,145 (2010); Median contract rent: $348 per month (2005-2009 5-year est.); Median year structure built: 1971 (2005-2009 5-year est.)
Health: Birth rate: 133.6 per 10,000 population (2009); Death rate: 132.3 per 10,000 population (2009); Age-adjusted cancer mortality rate: 291.1 deaths per 100,000 population (2007); Number of physicians: 4.7 per 10,000 population (2008); Hospital beds: 16.5 per 10,000 population (2007); Hospital admissions: 676.2 per 10,000 population (2007).
Elections: 2008 Presidential election results: 37.5% Obama, 60.8% McCain, 0.8% Nader
National and State Parks: Fort Massac State Park; Mermet Lake State Conservation Area
Additional Information Contacts
Massac County Government . . . . (618) 524-5213

Metropolis Chamber of Commerce . . . . (618) 524-2714
    http://www.metropolischamber.com

Massac County Communities

BROOKPORT (city). Covers a land area of 0.797 square miles and a water area of 0 square miles. Located at 37.12° N. Lat; 88.62° W. Long. Elevation is 338 feet.
History: Brookport developed as an agricultural trading center on the Ohio River. The flooding of the river in 1937 damaged much of Brookport.
Population: 1,090 (1990); 1,054 (2000); 1,117 (2010); 1,135 (2015 projected); Race: 90.7% White, 7.2% Black, 0.3% Asian, 1.9% Other, 2.5% Hispanic of any race (2010); Density: 1,400.8 persons per square mile (2010); Average household size: 2.34 (2010); Median age: 36.2 (2010); Males per 100 females: 94.6 (2010); Marriage status: 23.4% never married, 51.3% now married, 13.4% widowed, 11.9% divorced (2005-2009 5-year est.); Foreign born: 0.0% (2005-2009 5-year est.); Ancestry (includes multiple ancestries): 16.2% American, 14.7% German, 13.7% Irish, 5.2% English, 2.7% French (2005-2009 5-year est.).
Economy: Single-family building permits issued: 0 (2010); Multi-family building permits issued: 0 (2010); Employment by occupation: 7.0% management, 13.4% professional, 31.5% services, 23.8% sales, 1.3% farming, 10.4% construction, 12.4% production (2005-2009 5-year est.).
Income: Per capita income: $19,315 (2010); Median household income: $37,403 (2010); Average household income: $45,047 (2010); Percent of households with income of $100,000 or more: 6.9% (2010); Poverty rate: 15.3% (2005-2009 5-year est.).
Taxes: Total city taxes per capita: $77 (2007); City property taxes per capita: $35 (2007).
Education: Percent of population age 25 and over with: High school diploma (including GED) or higher: 81.6% (2010); Bachelor's degree or higher: 9.0% (2010); Master's degree or higher: 2.2% (2010).
School District(s)
Massac UD 1 (PK-12)
    2009-10 Enrollment: 2,317 . . . . (618) 524-9376
Housing: Homeownership rate: 79.5% (2010); Median home value: $70,377 (2010); Median contract rent: $218 per month (2005-2009 5-year est.); Median year structure built: 1960 (2005-2009 5-year est.).
Transportation: Commute to work: 96.6% car, 0.0% public transportation, 3.4% walk, 0.0% work from home (2005-2009 5-year est.); Travel time to work: 36.2% less than 15 minutes, 52.4% 15 to 30 minutes, 10.0% 30 to 45 minutes, 0.0% 45 to 60 minutes, 1.4% 60 minutes or more (2005-2009 5-year est.)

JOPPA (village). Covers a land area of 0.488 square miles and a water area of 0.008 square miles. Located at 37.20° N. Lat; 88.84° W. Long. Elevation is 354 feet.
Population: 492 (1990); 409 (2000); 361 (2010); 339 (2015 projected); Race: 94.7% White, 2.5% Black, 0.0% Asian, 2.8% Other, 2.2% Hispanic of any race (2010); Density: 739.9 persons per square mile (2010); Average household size: 2.49 (2010); Median age: 35.7 (2010); Males per 100 females: 106.3 (2010); Marriage status: 33.6% never married, 36.2% now married, 14.0% widowed, 16.2% divorced (2005-2009 5-year est.); Foreign born: 1.8% (2005-2009 5-year est.); Ancestry (includes multiple ancestries): 14.4% German, 12.6% Irish, 9.5% Dutch, 7.5% English, 5.9% American (2005-2009 5-year est.).
Economy: Employment by occupation: 2.5% management, 10.1% professional, 30.3% services, 38.7% sales, 0.0% farming, 0.0% construction, 18.5% production (2005-2009 5-year est.).
Income: Per capita income: $17,783 (2010); Median household income: $38,250 (2010); Average household income: $44,155 (2010); Percent of households with income of $100,000 or more: 6.9% (2010); Poverty rate: 49.6% (2005-2009 5-year est.).
Taxes: Total city taxes per capita: $39 (2007); City property taxes per capita: $27 (2007).
Education: Percent of population age 25 and over with: High school diploma (including GED) or higher: 79.9% (2010); Bachelor's degree or higher: 7.3% (2010); Master's degree or higher: 4.3% (2010).
School District(s)
Five County Reg Voc System
    2009-10 Enrollment: n/a . . . . (618) 747-2703
Joppa-Maple Grove UD 38 (PK-12)
    2009-10 Enrollment: 288 . . . . (618) 543-9023
Housing: Homeownership rate: 78.6% (2010); Median home value: $60,000 (2010); Median contract rent: $205 per month (2005-2009 5-year est.); Median year structure built: 1953 (2005-2009 5-year est.).
Transportation: Commute to work: 91.6% car, 0.0% public transportation, 6.7% walk, 1.7% work from home (2005-2009 5-year est.); Travel time to work: 26.5% less than 15 minutes, 40.2% 15 to 30 minutes, 24.8% 30 to 45 minutes, 8.5% 45 to 60 minutes, 0.0% 60 minutes or more (2005-2009 5-year est.)

METROPOLIS (city). County seat. Covers a land area of 5.005 square miles and a water area of 0.064 square miles. Located at 37.15° N. Lat; 88.72° W. Long. Elevation is 361 feet.
History: The first settlement in Metropolis was in 1796. This was platted in 1836 as the City of Massac. Metropolis City was platted in 1839 by William A. McBane and James H.G. Wilcox, who dreamed that their community would be a metropolis. Metropolis City was incorporated in 1845, and in 1892 the two communities united.
Population: 6,921 (1990); 6,482 (2000); 5,633 (2010); 5,243 (2015 projected); Race: 88.2% White, 9.4% Black, 0.1% Asian, 2.2% Other, 1.3% Hispanic of any race (2010); Density: 1,125.4 persons per square mile (2010); Average household size: 2.09 (2010); Median age: 42.6 (2010); Males per 100 females: 81.8 (2010); Marriage status: 16.4% never married, 56.2% now married, 13.4% widowed, 13.9% divorced (2005-2009 5-year est.); Foreign born: 0.9% (2005-2009 5-year est.); Ancestry (includes multiple ancestries): 20.3% German, 14.0% Irish, 7.8% English, 5.8% American, 4.4% Scottish (2005-2009 5-year est.).
Economy: Single-family building permits issued: 1 (2010); Multi-family building permits issued: 0 (2010); Employment by occupation: 9.0% management, 13.2% professional, 26.5% services, 23.4% sales, 0.0% farming, 12.5% construction, 15.5% production (2005-2009 5-year est.).
Income: Per capita income: $18,626 (2010); Median household income: $29,847 (2010); Average household income: $39,079 (2010); Percent of households with income of $100,000 or more: 5.4% (2010); Poverty rate: 18.1% (2005-2009 5-year est.).
Taxes: Total city taxes per capita: $157 (2007); City property taxes per capita: $60 (2007).
Education: Percent of population age 25 and over with: High school diploma (including GED) or higher: 80.4% (2010); Bachelor's degree or higher: 12.8% (2010); Master's degree or higher: 5.0% (2010).
School District(s)
Five County Reg Voc System
    2009-10 Enrollment: n/a . . . . (618) 747-2703
Joppa-Maple Grove UD 38 (PK-12)
    2009-10 Enrollment: 288 . . . . (618) 543-9023

Massac UD 1 (PK-12)
2009-10 Enrollment: 2,317 . . . . (618) 524-9376
Housing: Homeownership rate: 66.8% (2010); Median home value:
$74,983 (2010); Median contract rent: $343 per month (2005-2009 5-year
est.); Median year structure built: 1957 (2005-2009 5-year est.).
Hospitals: Massac Memorial Hospital (57 beds)
Safety: Violent crime rate: 70.2 per 10,000 population; Property crime rate:
433.4 per 10,000 population (2010).
Newspapers: Metropolis Planet (Community news; Circulation 5,533);
Southern Scene (Community news; Circulation 13,000)
Transportation: Commute to work: 92.9% car, 0.0% public transportation,
1.7% walk, 1.9% work from home (2005-2009 5-year est.); Travel time to
work: 51.2% less than 15 minutes, 35.7% 15 to 30 minutes, 8.7% 30 to 45
minutes, 0.4% 45 to 60 minutes, 4.0% 60 minutes or more (2005-2009
5-year est.)
Additional Information Contacts
Metropolis Chamber of Commerce . . . . (618) 524-2714
http://www.metropolischamber.com

McDonough County

Located in western Illinois; drained by the La Moine River. Covers a land
area of 589.27 square miles, a water area of 0.75 square miles, and is
located in the Central Time Zone at 40.47° N. Lat., 90.67° W. Long. The
county was founded in 1826. County seat is Macomb.

McDonough County is part of the Macomb, IL Micropolitan Statistical Area.
The entire metro area includes: McDonough County, IL

Population: 35,244 (1990); 32,913 (2000); 32,678 (2010); 32,279 (2015
projected); Race: 89.9% White, 4.7% Black, 3.3% Asian, 2.1% Other, 1.9%
Hispanic of any race (2010); Density: 55.5 persons per square mile (2010);
Average household size: 2.23 (2010); Median age: 26.7 (2010); Males per
100 females: 96.4 (2010).
Religion: Five largest groups: 7.8% The United Methodist Church, 6.8%
Catholic Church, 3.8% Presbyterian Church (U.S.A.), 3.6% Christian
Churches and Churches of Christ, 2.8% Assemblies of God (2000).
Economy: Unemployment rate: 8.6% (August 2011); Total civilian labor
force: 16,238 (August 2011); Leading industries: 20.9% health care and
social assistance; 17.9% retail trade; 15.9% accommodation & food
services (2009); Farms: 761 totaling 307,725 acres (2007); Companies that
employ 500 or more persons: 1 (2009); Companies that employ 100 to 499
persons: 11 (2009); Companies that employ less than 100 persons: 717
(2009); Black-owned businesses: n/a (2007); Hispanic-owned businesses:
n/a (2007); Asian-owned businesses: n/a (2007); Women-owned
businesses: n/a (2007); Retail sales per capita: $8,496 (2010).
Single-family building permits issued: 4 (2010); Multi-family building permits
issued: 5 (2010).
Income: Per capita income: $17,783 (2010); Median household income:
$36,989 (2010); Average household income: $46,675 (2010); Percent of
households with income of $100,000 or more: 8.3% (2010); Poverty rate:
22.6% (2009); Bankruptcy rate: 2.82% (2010).
Taxes: Total county taxes per capita: $127 (2007); County property taxes
per capita: $127 (2007).
Education: Percent of population age 25 and over with: High school
diploma (including GED) or higher: 92.8% (2010); Bachelor's degree or
higher: 36.4% (2010); Master's degree or higher: 16.5% (2010).
Housing: Homeownership rate: 61.9% (2010); Median home value:
$79,769 (2010); Median contract rent: $490 per month (2005-2009 5-year
est.); Median year structure built: 1965 (2005-2009 5-year est.)
Health: Birth rate: 93.4 per 10,000 population (2009); Death rate: 84.2 per
10,000 population (2009); Age-adjusted cancer mortality rate: 214.9 deaths
per 100,000 population (2007); Number of physicians: 12.5 per 10,000
population (2008); Hospital beds: 27.5 per 10,000 population (2007);
Hospital admissions: 958.0 per 10,000 population (2007).
Elections: 2008 Presidential election results: 52.0% Obama, 46.4%
McCain, 0.7% Nader
National and State Parks: Argyle Lake State Park
Additional Information Contacts
McDonough County Government . . . . (309) 833-2474

City of Macomb . . . . (309) 833-2575
http://www.cityofmacomb.com
Macomb Area Chamber of Commerce & Downtown Development Corp
(309) 837-4855
http://www.macombareachamber.com

Macomb Area Convention & Visitors Bureau. . . . . (309) 833-1315
http://www.makeitmacomb.com

McDonough County Communities

ADAIR (unincorporated postal area, zip code 61411). Covers a land
area of 38.024 square miles and a water area of 0.016 square miles.
Located at 40.40° N. Lat; 90.50° W. Long. Elevation is 646 feet.
Population: 419 (2000); Race: 100.0% White, 0.0% Black, 0.0% Asian,
0.0% Other, 0.0% Hispanic of any race (2000); Density: 11.0 persons per
square mile (2000); Age: 14.4% under 18, 22.2% over 64 (2000); Marriage
status: 22.0% never married, 58.8% now married, 10.4% widowed, 8.8%
divorced (2000); Foreign born: 0.0% (2000); Ancestry (includes multiple
ancestries): 21.0% English, 17.4% American, 15.4% German, 4.5%
Swedish (2000).
Economy: Employment by occupation: 19.4% management, 21.0%
professional, 9.7% services, 20.6% sales, 5.6% farming, 5.6%
construction, 18.1% production (2000).
Income: Per capita income: $20,915 (2000); Median household income:
$40,893 (2000); Poverty rate: 3.8% (2000).
Education: Percent of population age 25 and over with: High school
diploma (including GED) or higher: 84.5% (2000); Bachelor's degree or
higher: 13.8% (2000).
Housing: Homeownership rate: 72.2% (2000); Median home value:
$49,700 (2000); Median contract rent: $218 per month (2000); Median year
structure built: 1943 (2000).
Transportation: Commute to work: 91.1% car, 0.0% public transportation,
0.0% walk, 0.8% work from home (2000); Travel time to work: 26.8% less
than 15 minutes, 53.3% 15 to 30 minutes, 12.2% 30 to 45 minutes, 7.7%
45 to 60 minutes, 0.0% 60 minutes or more (2000)

BARDOLPH (village). Covers a land area of 0.595 square miles and a
water area of 0 square miles. Located at 40.49° N. Lat; 90.56° W. Long.
Elevation is 673 feet.
Population: 301 (1990); 253 (2000); 197 (2010); 175 (2015 projected);
Race: 99.0% White, 0.5% Black, 0.0% Asian, 0.5% Other, 0.0% Hispanic
of any race (2010); Density: 331.3 persons per square mile (2010);
Average household size: 2.63 (2010); Median age: 34.1 (2010); Males per
100 females: 97.0 (2010); Marriage status: 27.3% never married, 58.1%
now married, 2.3% widowed, 12.2% divorced (2005-2009 5-year est.);
Foreign born: 0.0% (2005-2009 5-year est.); Ancestry (includes multiple
ancestries): 22.7% English, 15.5% Irish, 15.0% German, 12.3% American,
4.5% Italian (2005-2009 5-year est.).
Economy: Employment by occupation: 1.2% management, 3.6%
professional, 36.9% services, 39.3% sales, 0.0% farming, 1.2%
construction, 17.9% production (2005-2009 5-year est.).
Income: Per capita income: $22,293 (2010); Median household income:
$49,464 (2010); Average household income: $55,833 (2010); Percent of
households with income of $100,000 or more: 10.7% (2010); Poverty rate:
28.6% (2005-2009 5-year est.).
Taxes: Total city taxes per capita: $43 (2007); City property taxes per
capita: $43 (2007).
Education: Percent of population age 25 and over with: High school
diploma (including GED) or higher: 90.2% (2010); Bachelor's degree or
higher: 14.6% (2010); Master's degree or higher: 3.3% (2010).
Housing: Homeownership rate: 72.0% (2010); Median home value:
$88,571 (2010); Median contract rent: $335 per month (2005-2009 5-year
est.); Median year structure built: before 1940 (2005-2009 5-year est.).
Transportation: Commute to work: 98.8% car, 0.0% public transportation,
0.0% walk, 0.0% work from home (2005-2009 5-year est.); Travel time to
work: 32.1% less than 15 minutes, 47.6% 15 to 30 minutes, 10.7% 30 to 45
minutes, 1.2% 45 to 60 minutes, 8.3% 60 minutes or more (2005-2009
5-year est.)

BLANDINSVILLE (village). Covers a land area of 0.885 square miles
and a water area of 0 square miles. Located at 40.55° N. Lat; 90.86° W.
Long. Elevation is 728 feet.
Population: 762 (1990); 777 (2000); 619 (2010); 560 (2015 projected);
Race: 97.7% White, 0.0% Black, 0.3% Asian, 1.9% Other, 1.0% Hispanic
of any race (2010); Density: 699.6 persons per square mile (2010);
Average household size: 2.28 (2010); Median age: 39.9 (2010); Males per
100 females: 104.3 (2010); Marriage status: 20.0% never married, 62.9%
now married, 4.7% widowed, 12.4% divorced (2005-2009 5-year est.);
Foreign born: 0.8% (2005-2009 5-year est.); Ancestry (includes multiple

ancestries): 29.4% German, 17.5% Irish, 12.0% English, 9.8% American, 5.2% Italian (2005-2009 5-year est.).
Economy: Employment by occupation: 10.5% management, 18.5% professional, 16.9% services, 19.9% sales, 7.0% farming, 6.7% construction, 20.4% production (2005-2009 5-year est.).
Income: Per capita income: $18,942 (2010); Median household income: $35,167 (2010); Average household income: $41,614 (2010); Percent of households with income of $100,000 or more: 3.0% (2010); Poverty rate: 10.4% (2005-2009 5-year est.).
Taxes: Total city taxes per capita: $49 (2007); City property taxes per capita: $46 (2007).
Education: Percent of population age 25 and over with: High school diploma (including GED) or higher: 91.7% (2010); Bachelor's degree or higher: 17.1% (2010); Master's degree or higher: 1.6% (2010).
Housing: Homeownership rate: 80.8% (2010); Median home value: $67,174 (2010); Median contract rent: $254 per month (2005-2009 5-year est.); Median year structure built: before 1940 (2005-2009 5-year est.).
Safety: Violent crime rate: 0.0 per 10,000 population; Property crime rate: 73.6 per 10,000 population (2010).
Transportation: Commute to work: 92.1% car, 0.0% public transportation, 4.1% walk, 2.7% work from home (2005-2009 5-year est.); Travel time to work: 38.2% less than 15 minutes, 36.8% 15 to 30 minutes, 16.0% 30 to 45 minutes, 5.1% 45 to 60 minutes, 3.9% 60 minutes or more (2005-2009 5-year est.)

BUSHNELL (city). Covers a land area of 2.047 square miles and a water area of 0.008 square miles. Located at 40.55° N. Lat; 90.50° W. Long. Elevation is 653 feet.
History: Incorporated 1865.
Population: 3,290 (1990); 3,221 (2000); 2,737 (2010); 2,512 (2015 projected); Race: 98.2% White, 0.1% Black, 0.1% Asian, 1.5% Other, 0.9% Hispanic of any race (2010); Density: 1,337.4 persons per square mile (2010); Average household size: 2.45 (2010); Median age: 35.8 (2010); Males per 100 females: 93.6 (2010); Marriage status: 20.0% never married, 60.4% now married, 10.7% widowed, 8.9% divorced (2005-2009 5-year est.); Foreign born: 0.3% (2005-2009 5-year est.); Ancestry (includes multiple ancestries): 31.9% German, 21.6% American, 14.1% English, 8.1% Irish, 5.5% Dutch (2005-2009 5-year est.).
Economy: Employment by occupation: 5.3% management, 17.1% professional, 14.0% services, 16.1% sales, 9.1% farming, 10.4% construction, 28.1% production (2005-2009 5-year est.).
Income: Per capita income: $17,205 (2010); Median household income: $34,715 (2010); Average household income: $42,209 (2010); Percent of households with income of $100,000 or more: 4.4% (2010); Poverty rate: 16.9% (2005-2009 5-year est.).
Taxes: Total city taxes per capita: $54 (2007); City property taxes per capita: $48 (2007).
Education: Percent of population age 25 and over with: High school diploma (including GED) or higher: 89.7% (2010); Bachelor's degree or higher: 15.5% (2010); Master's degree or higher: 5.6% (2010).
School District(s)
Bushnell Prairie City CUSD 170 (PK-12)
    2009-10 Enrollment: 818 . . . . (309) 772-9461
Housing: Homeownership rate: 74.6% (2010); Median home value: $54,700 (2010); Median contract rent: $303 per month (2005-2009 5-year est.); Median year structure built: 1958 (2005-2009 5-year est.).
Newspapers: McDonough Democrat (Community news; Circulation 5,000)
Transportation: Commute to work: 89.5% car, 1.7% public transportation, 2.3% walk, 2.2% work from home (2005-2009 5-year est.); Travel time to work: 42.1% less than 15 minutes, 35.6% 15 to 30 minutes, 8.5% 30 to 45 minutes, 8.4% 45 to 60 minutes, 5.5% 60 minutes or more (2005-2009 5-year est.)

COLCHESTER (city). Covers a land area of 0.995 square miles and a water area of 0 square miles. Located at 40.42° N. Lat; 90.79° W. Long. Elevation is 692 feet.
History: Incorporated 1867.
Population: 1,658 (1990); 1,493 (2000); 1,211 (2010); 1,100 (2015 projected); Race: 99.3% White, 0.0% Black, 0.0% Asian, 0.7% Other, 0.6% Hispanic of any race (2010); Density: 1,217.3 persons per square mile (2010); Average household size: 2.27 (2010); Median age: 39.8 (2010); Males per 100 females: 91.6 (2010); Marriage status: 28.4% never married, 54.9% now married, 7.8% widowed, 8.9% divorced (2005-2009 5-year est.); Foreign born: 2.3% (2005-2009 5-year est.); Ancestry (includes

multiple ancestries): 28.1% German, 11.6% Irish, 11.6% English, 9.9% American, 4.1% Italian (2005-2009 5-year est.).
Economy: Employment by occupation: 9.2% management, 19.2% professional, 14.0% services, 30.3% sales, 0.5% farming, 8.5% construction, 18.3% production (2005-2009 5-year est.).
Income: Per capita income: $20,849 (2010); Median household income: $39,026 (2010); Average household income: $47,481 (2010); Percent of households with income of $100,000 or more: 6.7% (2010); Poverty rate: 17.3% (2005-2009 5-year est.).
Taxes: Total city taxes per capita: $66 (2007); City property taxes per capita: $66 (2007).
Education: Percent of population age 25 and over with: High school diploma (including GED) or higher: 90.0% (2010); Bachelor's degree or higher: 16.5% (2010); Master's degree or higher: 4.1% (2010).
School District(s)
West Prairie CUSD 103 (PK-12)
    2009-10 Enrollment: 690 . . . . (309) 776-3180
Housing: Homeownership rate: 75.3% (2010); Median home value: $53,458 (2010); Median contract rent: $360 per month (2005-2009 5-year est.); Median year structure built: 1958 (2005-2009 5-year est.).
Transportation: Commute to work: 92.7% car, 0.0% public transportation, 2.3% walk, 4.2% work from home (2005-2009 5-year est.); Travel time to work: 27.5% less than 15 minutes, 51.7% 15 to 30 minutes, 11.1% 30 to 45 minutes, 1.3% 45 to 60 minutes, 8.5% 60 minutes or more (2005-2009 5-year est.)

GOOD HOPE (village). Covers a land area of 0.295 square miles and a water area of 0 square miles. Located at 40.55° N. Lat; 90.67° W. Long. Elevation is 709 feet.
History: When Good Hope was platted in 1866, it was called Sheridan by its founder, J.E. Morris. The town of Milan was laid out next to Sheridan the following year. Since both were served by the post office which was called Good Hope, that is the name that survived.
Population: 447 (1990); 415 (2000); 348 (2010); 317 (2015 projected); Race: 98.9% White, 0.0% Black, 0.6% Asian, 0.6% Other, 0.3% Hispanic of any race (2010); Density: 1,180.7 persons per square mile (2010); Average household size: 2.43 (2010); Median age: 37.1 (2010); Males per 100 females: 103.5 (2010); Marriage status: 24.8% never married, 60.3% now married, 7.0% widowed, 7.9% divorced (2005-2009 5-year est.); Foreign born: 3.1% (2005-2009 5-year est.); Ancestry (includes multiple ancestries): 23.5% German, 17.8% English, 16.4% American, 9.6% Irish, 4.0% Dutch (2005-2009 5-year est.).
Economy: Employment by occupation: 6.9% management, 20.7% professional, 19.5% services, 20.7% sales, 2.9% farming, 6.3% construction, 23.0% production (2005-2009 5-year est.).
Income: Per capita income: $20,829 (2010); Median household income: $47,885 (2010); Average household income: $51,346 (2010); Percent of households with income of $100,000 or more: 3.5% (2010); Poverty rate: 16.5% (2005-2009 5-year est.).
Taxes: Total city taxes per capita: $34 (2007); City property taxes per capita: $31 (2007).
Education: Percent of population age 25 and over with: High school diploma (including GED) or higher: 93.7% (2010); Bachelor's degree or higher: 30.3% (2010); Master's degree or higher: 9.0% (2010).
School District(s)
West Prairie CUSD 103 (PK-12)
    2009-10 Enrollment: 690 . . . . (309) 776-3180
Housing: Homeownership rate: 76.2% (2010); Median home value: $93,125 (2010); Median contract rent: $415 per month (2005-2009 5-year est.); Median year structure built: 1955 (2005-2009 5-year est.).
Transportation: Commute to work: 95.2% car, 0.0% public transportation, 2.4% walk, 2.4% work from home (2005-2009 5-year est.); Travel time to work: 39.6% less than 15 minutes, 47.6% 15 to 30 minutes, 4.9% 30 to 45 minutes, 6.7% 45 to 60 minutes, 1.2% 60 minutes or more (2005-2009 5-year est.)

INDUSTRY (village). Covers a land area of 0.471 square miles and a water area of <.001 square miles. Located at 40.32° N. Lat; 90.60° W. Long. Elevation is 659 feet.
History: The first settler in Industry was William Carter who came in 1826. The village was organized in the 1840's.
Population: 571 (1990); 540 (2000); 445 (2010); 405 (2015 projected); Race: 97.1% White, 0.2% Black, 1.6% Asian, 1.1% Other, 0.9% Hispanic of any race (2010); Density: 944.6 persons per square mile (2010); Average household size: 2.47 (2010); Median age: 38.3 (2010); Males per

100 females: 100.5 (2010); Marriage status: 13.3% never married, 74.1% now married, 6.8% widowed, 5.8% divorced (2005-2009 5-year est.); Foreign born: 4.6% (2005-2009 5-year est.); Ancestry (includes multiple ancestries): 18.7% German, 15.8% American, 11.6% Irish, 6.9% English, 2.5% British (2005-2009 5-year est.).

Economy: Employment by occupation: 6.0% management, 15.3% professional, 23.0% services, 31.1% sales, 0.9% farming, 8.9% construction, 14.9% production (2005-2009 5-year est.).

Income: Per capita income: $21,333 (2010); Median household income: $47,692 (2010); Average household income: $53,403 (2010); Percent of households with income of $100,000 or more: 9.4% (2010); Poverty rate: 14.7% (2005-2009 5-year est.).

Taxes: Total city taxes per capita: $30 (2007); City property taxes per capita: $28 (2007).

Education: Percent of population age 25 and over with: High school diploma (including GED) or higher: 93.4% (2010); Bachelor's degree or higher: 27.3% (2010); Master's degree or higher: 7.6% (2010).

School District(s)

Schuyler-Industry CUSD 5 (PK-12)

    2009-10 Enrollment: 1,223 . . . . (217) 322-4311

Housing: Homeownership rate: 78.9% (2010); Median home value: $84,000 (2010); Median contract rent: $268 per month (2005-2009 5-year est.); Median year structure built: 1945 (2005-2009 5-year est.).

Transportation: Commute to work: 85.0% car, 0.4% public transportation, 7.3% walk, 6.0% work from home (2005-2009 5-year est.); Travel time to work: 32.0% less than 15 minutes, 47.0% 15 to 30 minutes, 7.8% 30 to 45 minutes, 3.7% 45 to 60 minutes, 9.6% 60 minutes or more (2005-2009 5-year est.)

MACOMB (city). County seat. Covers a land area of 9.849 square miles and a water area of 0.401 square miles. Located at 40.46° N. Lat; 90.67° W. Long. Elevation is 705 feet.

History: Macomb was settled in 1830, incorporated as a village in 1841, and as a city in 1856. Many of the early settlers were from New England, and they named the town for Alexander Macomb, Commander-in-Chief of the U.S. Army from 1828 to 1841.

Population: 20,205 (1990); 18,558 (2000); 20,237 (2010); 20,762 (2015 projected); Race: 85.5% White, 7.2% Black, 4.6% Asian, 2.7% Other, 2.5% Hispanic of any race (2010); Density: 2,054.7 persons per square mile (2010); Average household size: 2.07 (2010); Median age: 23.7 (2010); Males per 100 females: 95.9 (2010); Marriage status: 65.6% never married, 25.2% now married, 3.8% widowed, 5.4% divorced (2005-2009 5-year est.); Foreign born: 5.3% (2005-2009 5-year est.); Ancestry (includes multiple ancestries): 26.0% German, 14.7% Irish, 13.4% American, 11.0% English, 8.0% Italian (2005-2009 5-year est.).

Economy: Single-family building permits issued: 4 (2010); Multi-family building permits issued: 5 (2010); Employment by occupation: 8.8% management, 24.6% professional, 21.4% services, 28.5% sales, 0.4% farming, 6.3% construction, 9.9% production (2005-2009 5-year est.).

Income: Per capita income: $15,084 (2010); Median household income: $30,510 (2010); Average household income: $41,010 (2010); Percent of households with income of $100,000 or more: 7.1% (2010); Poverty rate: 32.8% (2005-2009 5-year est.).

Taxes: Total city taxes per capita: $114 (2007); City property taxes per capita: $62 (2007).

Education: Percent of population age 25 and over with: High school diploma (including GED) or higher: 93.6% (2010); Bachelor's degree or higher: 45.9% (2010); Master's degree or higher: 22.3% (2010).

School District(s)

Hancock/Mcdonough Roe (07-12)

    2009-10 Enrollment: n/a . . . . (309) 837-4821

Macomb CUSD 185 (PK-12)

    2009-10 Enrollment: 1,908 . . . . (309) 833-4161

West Central II Spec Educ Coop (06-12)

    2009-10 Enrollment: n/a . . . . (309) 837-3911

Western Area Career System 265

    2009-10 Enrollment: n/a . . . . (309) 837-4821

Four-year College(s)

Western Illinois University (Public)

    Fall 2009 Enrollment: 12,679. . . . . (309) 295-1414

    2010-11 Tuition: In-state $10,149; Out-of-state $13,758

Housing: Homeownership rate: 48.8% (2010); Median home value: $87,634 (2010); Median contract rent: $540 per month (2005-2009 5-year est.); Median year structure built: 1968 (2005-2009 5-year est.).

Hospitals: McDonough District Hospital (113 beds)

Safety: Violent crime rate: 13.2 per 10,000 population; Property crime rate: 209.4 per 10,000 population (2010).

Newspapers: Macomb Eagle (Community news; Circulation 2,500); Macomb Journal (Local news; Circulation 7,000)

Transportation: Commute to work: 75.3% car, 3.1% public transportation, 15.2% walk, 4.5% work from home (2005-2009 5-year est.); Travel time to work: 78.9% less than 15 minutes, 13.6% 15 to 30 minutes, 3.7% 30 to 45 minutes, 1.5% 45 to 60 minutes, 2.3% 60 minutes or more (2005-2009 5-year est.); Amtrak: train service available.

Airports: Macomb Municipal (general aviation)

Additional Information Contacts

City of Macomb . . . . (309) 833-2575

    http://www.cityofmacomb.com

Macomb Area Chamber of Commerce & Downtown Development Corp

    (309) 837-4855

    http://www.macombareachamber.com

Macomb Area Convention & Visitors Bureau. . . . . (309) 833-1315

    http://www.makeitmacomb.com

PRAIRIE CITY (village). Covers a land area of 1.013 square miles and a water area of 0 square miles. Located at 40.62° N. Lat; 90.46° W. Long. Elevation is 669 feet.

Population: 497 (1990); 461 (2000); 409 (2010); 380 (2015 projected); Race: 97.1% White, 0.0% Black, 1.5% Asian, 1.5% Other, 1.0% Hispanic of any race (2010); Density: 403.9 persons per square mile (2010); Average household size: 2.67 (2010); Median age: 40.1 (2010); Males per 100 females: 98.5 (2010); Marriage status: 10.0% never married, 75.5% now married, 10.5% widowed, 3.9% divorced (2005-2009 5-year est.); Foreign born: 1.2% (2005-2009 5-year est.); Ancestry (includes multiple ancestries): 25.7% German, 19.3% American, 11.8% Irish, 11.4% Swedish, 3.3% English (2005-2009 5-year est.).

Economy: Employment by occupation: 2.6% management, 12.4% professional, 41.6% services, 16.5% sales, 0.0% farming, 7.9% construction, 19.1% production (2005-2009 5-year est.).

Income: Per capita income: $21,775 (2010); Median household income: $50,987 (2010); Average household income: $59,633 (2010); Percent of households with income of $100,000 or more: 13.3% (2010); Poverty rate: 11.0% (2005-2009 5-year est.).

Taxes: Total city taxes per capita: $33 (2007); City property taxes per capita: $33 (2007).

Education: Percent of population age 25 and over with: High school diploma (including GED) or higher: 91.3% (2010); Bachelor's degree or higher: 23.6% (2010); Master's degree or higher: 5.8% (2010).

Housing: Homeownership rate: 86.7% (2010); Median home value: $50,000 (2010); Median contract rent: $567 per month (2005-2009 5-year est.); Median year structure built: 1954 (2005-2009 5-year est.).

Transportation: Commute to work: 99.2% car, 0.0% public transportation, 0.0% walk, 0.0% work from home (2005-2009 5-year est.); Travel time to work: 36.1% less than 15 minutes, 47.0% 15 to 30 minutes, 11.3% 30 to 45 minutes, 3.4% 45 to 60 minutes, 2.3% 60 minutes or more (2005-2009 5-year est.)

SCIOTA (village). Covers a land area of 0.317 square miles and a water area of 0 square miles. Located at 40.56° N. Lat; 90.75° W. Long. Elevation is 758 feet.

Population: 68 (1990); 58 (2000); 42 (2010); 38 (2015 projected); Race: 100.0% White, 0.0% Black, 0.0% Asian, 0.0% Other, 0.0% Hispanic of any race (2010); Density: 132.3 persons per square mile (2010); Average household size: 2.47 (2010); Median age: 43.0 (2010); Males per 100 females: 90.9 (2010); Marriage status: 0.0% never married, 68.4% now married, 13.2% widowed, 18.4% divorced (2005-2009 5-year est.); Foreign born: 0.0% (2005-2009 5-year est.); Ancestry (includes multiple ancestries): 37.7% German, 32.1% English, 24.5% African, 7.5% Irish, 7.5% Dutch (2005-2009 5-year est.).

Economy: Employment by occupation: 0.0% management, 40.6% professional, 25.0% services, 18.8% sales, 0.0% farming, 6.3% construction, 9.4% production (2005-2009 5-year est.).

Income: Per capita income: $24,259 (2010); Median household income: $48,125 (2010); Average household income: $53,824 (2010); Percent of households with income of $100,000 or more: 11.8% (2010); Poverty rate: 2.0% (2005-2009 5-year est.).

Taxes: Total city taxes per capita: $38 (2007); City property taxes per capita: $38 (2007).

Education: Percent of population age 25 and over with: High school diploma (including GED) or higher: 96.3% (2010); Bachelor's degree or higher: 37.0% (2010); Master's degree or higher: 11.1% (2010).

School District(s)
West Prairie CUSD 103 (PK-12)

   2009-10 Enrollment: 690 . . . . (309) 776-3180

Housing: Homeownership rate: 70.6% (2010); Median home value: $90,000 (2010); Median contract rent: $517 per month (2005-2009 5-year est.); Median year structure built: 1947 (2005-2009 5-year est.).

Transportation: Commute to work: 76.7% car, 0.0% public transportation, 16.7% walk, 3.3% work from home (2005-2009 5-year est.); Travel time to work: 51.7% less than 15 minutes, 48.3% 15 to 30 minutes, 0.0% 30 to 45 minutes, 0.0% 45 to 60 minutes, 0.0% 60 minutes or more (2005-2009 5-year est.)

TENNESSEE (village). Covers a land area of 0.425 square miles and a water area of 0 square miles. Located at 40.41° N. Lat; 90.83° W. Long. Elevation is 686 feet.

Population: 127 (1990); 144 (2000); 125 (2010); 116 (2015 projected); Race: 97.6% White, 0.0% Black, 0.0% Asian, 2.4% Other, 0.0% Hispanic of any race (2010); Density: 294.5 persons per square mile (2010); Average household size: 2.40 (2010); Median age: 41.1 (2010); Males per 100 females: 115.5 (2010); Marriage status: 23.5% never married, 56.8% now married, 14.8% widowed, 4.9% divorced (2005-2009 5-year est.); Foreign born: 0.0% (2005-2009 5-year est.); Ancestry (includes multiple ancestries): 16.7% English, 13.3% German, 13.3% American, 12.2% Irish, 6.7% Scotch-Irish (2005-2009 5-year est.).

Economy: Employment by occupation: 5.9% management, 8.8% professional, 23.5% services, 26.5% sales, 0.0% farming, 35.3% construction, 0.0% production (2005-2009 5-year est.).

Income: Per capita income: $19,204 (2010); Median household income: $39,615 (2010); Average household income: $43,654 (2010); Percent of households with income of $100,000 or more: 3.8% (2010); Poverty rate: 18.9% (2005-2009 5-year est.).

Taxes: Total city taxes per capita: $45 (2007); City property taxes per capita: $30 (2007).

Education: Percent of population age 25 and over with: High school diploma (including GED) or higher: 90.9% (2010); Bachelor's degree or higher: 19.3% (2010); Master's degree or higher: 11.4% (2010).

Housing: Homeownership rate: 86.5% (2010); Median home value: $50,000 (2010); Median contract rent: n/a per month (2005-2009 5-year est.); Median year structure built: 1963 (2005-2009 5-year est.).

Transportation: Commute to work: 94.1% car, 0.0% public transportation, 0.0% walk, 0.0% work from home (2005-2009 5-year est.); Travel time to work: 17.6% less than 15 minutes, 61.8% 15 to 30 minutes, 17.6% 30 to 45 minutes, 0.0% 45 to 60 minutes, 2.9% 60 minutes or more (2005-2009 5-year est.)

McHenry County

Located in northeastern Illinois; bounded on the north by Wisconsin; drained by the Fox and Kishwaukee Rivers; includes many lakes. Covers a land area of 603.51 square miles, a water area of 7.62 square miles, and is located in the Central Time Zone at 42.29° N. Lat., 88.35° W. Long. The county was founded in 1836. County seat is Woodstock.

McHenry County is part of the Chicago-Joliet-Naperville, IL-IN-WI Metropolitan Statistical Area. The entire metro area includes: Chicago-Joliet-Naperville, IL Metropolitan Division (Cook County, IL; DeKalb County, IL; DuPage County, IL; Grundy County, IL; Kane County, IL; Kendall County, IL; McHenry County, IL; Will County, IL); Gary, IN Metropolitan Division (Jasper County, IN; Lake County, IN; Newton County, IN; Porter County, IN); Lake County-Kenosha County, IL-WI Metropolitan Division (Lake County, IL; Kenosha County, WI)

Weather Station: Marengo   Elevation: 819 feet

	Jan	Feb	Mar	Apr	May	Jun	Jul	Aug	Sep	Oct	Nov	Dec
High	29	33	45	59	71	81	84	82	76	62	47	33
Low	12	14	25	36	46	56	61	59	50	38	28	17
Precip	1.3	1.3	2.0	3.2	4.0	4.0	3.7	4.8	3.0	2.9	2.6	1.9
Snow	9.3	8.0	3.3	1.1	0.1	0.0	0.0	0.0	0.0	0.1	1.7	7.6

High and Low temperatures in degrees Fahrenheit; Precipitation and Snow in inches

Population: 183,241 (1990); 260,077 (2000); 326,542 (2010); 354,251 (2015 projected); Race: 89.9% White, 1.3% Black, 2.7% Asian, 6.1% Other, 11.8% Hispanic of any race (2010); Density: 541.1 persons per square mile (2010); Average household size: 2.91 (2010); Median age: 35.8 (2010); Males per 100 females: 100.9 (2010).

Religion: Five largest groups: 29.4% Catholic Church, 4.9% Evangelical Lutheran Church in America, 4.0% Lutheran Church—Missouri Synod, 2.6% The United Methodist Church, 2.1% United Church of Christ (2000).

Economy: Unemployment rate: 8.8% (August 2011); Total civilian labor force: 179,589 (August 2011); Leading industries: 21.2% manufacturing; 17.7% retail trade; 12.2% health care and social assistance (2009); Farms: 1,035 totaling 215,584 acres (2007); Companies that employ 500 or more persons: 9 (2009); Companies that employ 100 to 499 persons: 109 (2009); Companies that employ less than 100 persons: 7,692 (2009); Black-owned businesses: 196 (2007); Hispanic-owned businesses: 845 (2007); Asian-owned businesses: 946 (2007); Women-owned businesses: 8,533 (2007); Retail sales per capita: $13,855 (2010). Single-family building permits issued: 301 (2010); Multi-family building permits issued: 4 (2010).

Income: Per capita income: $32,003 (2010); Median household income: $77,442 (2010); Average household income: $93,146 (2010); Percent of households with income of $100,000 or more: 33.1% (2010); Poverty rate: 6.6% (2009); Bankruptcy rate: 7.36% (2010).

Taxes: Total county taxes per capita: $223 (2007); County property taxes per capita: $182 (2007).

Education: Percent of population age 25 and over with: High school diploma (including GED) or higher: 91.6% (2010); Bachelor's degree or higher: 32.0% (2010); Master's degree or higher: 10.2% (2010).

Housing: Homeownership rate: 84.7% (2010); Median home value: $226,797 (2010); Median contract rent: $854 per month (2005-2009 5-year est.); Median year structure built: 1985 (2005-2009 5-year est.)

Health: Birth rate: 140.5 per 10,000 population (2009); Death rate: 64.2 per 10,000 population (2009); Age-adjusted cancer mortality rate: 197.4 deaths per 100,000 population (2007); Number of physicians: 12.4 per 10,000 population (2008); Hospital beds: 11.3 per 10,000 population (2007); Hospital admissions: 650.7 per 10,000 population (2007).

Environment: Air Quality Index: 83.9% good, 16.1% moderate, 0.0% unhealthy for sensitive individuals, 0.0% unhealthy (percent of days in 2008)

Elections: 2008 Presidential election results: 51.9% Obama, 46.6% McCain, 0.7% Nader

National and State Parks: Moraine Hills State Park

Additional Information Contacts

McHenry County Government . . . . (815) 334-4000
    http://www.co.mchenry.il.us
Algonquin/Lake in the Hills Chamber of Commerce . . . . . . (847) 658-5300
    http://www.alchamber.com
Cary Grove Area Chamber of Commerce . . . . (847) 639-2800
    http://www.carygrovechamber.com
City of Crystal Lake . . . . (815) 459-2020
    http://www.crystallake.org
City of Harvard . . . . (815) 943-6468
    http://www.cityofharvard.org
City of Marengo . . . . (815) 568-7112
    http://www.cityofmarengo.com
City of McHenry . . . . (815) 363-2100
    http://www.ci.mchenry.il.us
City of Woodstock . . . . (815) 338-4300
    http://www.woodstock-il.com
Crystal Lake Chamber of Commerce . . . . (815) 459-1300
    http://www.clchamber.com
Harvard Chamber of Commerce . . . . (815) 943-4404
    http://www.harvcc.net
Huntley Area Chamber of Commerce & Industry . . . . (847) 669-0166
    http://www.huntleychamber.org
Island Lake Area Chamber of Commerce . . . . (847) 604-4522
    http://www.islandlakechamber.org
Marengo Union Chamber of Commerce . . . . (815) 568-6680
    http://www.marengo-union.com
McHenry Area Chamber of Commerce . . . . (815) 385-4300
    http://www.mchenrychamber.com
Richmond/Spring Grove Chamber of Commerce . . . . (815) 678-7742
    http://www.rsgchamber.com
Village of Algonquin . . . . (847) 658-2700
    http://www.algonquin.org
Village of Cary . . . . (847) 639-0003
    http://www.caryillinois.com
Village of Huntley . . . . (847) 515-5200
    http://www.huntley.il.us

Village of Island Lake. . . . . (847) 526-8764
   http://www.villageofislandlake.com
Village of Johnsburg . . . . (815) 385-6023
   http://www.johnsburg.org
Village of Lake in the Hills . . . . (847) 960-7400
   http://www.lith.org
Wonder Lake Chamber of Commerce . . . . (815) 728-0682
   http://www.wonderlake.org
Woodstock Chamber of Commerce & Industry . . . . (815) 338-2436
   http://www.woodstockilchamber.com

McHenry County Communities

ALGONQUIN (village). Covers a land area of 9.832 square miles and a water area of 0.164 square miles. Located at 42.16° N. Lat; 88.30° W. Long. Elevation is 741 feet.
Population: 12,745 (1990); 23,276 (2000); 30,534 (2010); 33,853 (2015 projected); Race: 88.5% White, 2.0% Black, 5.4% Asian, 4.1% Other, 7.1% Hispanic of any race (2010); Density: 3,105.6 persons per square mile (2010); Average household size: 3.03 (2010); Median age: 35.8 (2010); Males per 100 females: 99.0 (2010); Marriage status: 24.9% never married, 64.2% now married, 3.3% widowed, 7.5% divorced (2005-2009 5-year est.); Foreign born: 11.6% (2005-2009 5-year est.); Ancestry (includes multiple ancestries): 32.4% German, 17.8% Polish, 17.5% Irish, 13.5% Italian, 7.0% English (2005-2009 5-year est.).
Economy: Unemployment rate: 9.1% (August 2011); Total civilian labor force: 16,825 (August 2011); Single-family building permits issued: 2 (2010); Multi-family building permits issued: 0 (2010); Employment by occupation: 18.9% management, 23.6% professional, 8.2% services, 31.5% sales, 0.0% farming, 7.8% construction, 10.0% production (2005-2009 5-year est.).
Income: Per capita income: $37,154 (2010); Median household income: $95,809 (2010); Average household income: $112,590 (2010); Percent of households with income of $100,000 or more: 46.9% (2010); Poverty rate: 3.8% (2005-2009 5-year est.).
Taxes: Total city taxes per capita: $353 (2007); City property taxes per capita: $158 (2007).
Education: Percent of population age 25 and over with: High school diploma (including GED) or higher: 96.1% (2010); Bachelor's degree or higher: 41.9% (2010); Master's degree or higher: 12.9% (2010).
School District(s)
CUSD 300 (PK-12)
   2009-10 Enrollment: 20,341 . . . . (847) 426-1300
Cons SD 158 (PK-12)
   2009-10 Enrollment: 8,992 . . . . (847) 659-6158
Housing: Homeownership rate: 95.3% (2010); Median home value: $251,749 (2010); Median contract rent: $887 per month (2005-2009 5-year est.); Median year structure built: 1992 (2005-2009 5-year est.).
Safety: Violent crime rate: 25.6 per 10,000 population; Property crime rate: 171.5 per 10,000 population (2010).
Newspapers: Algonquin Countryside (Community news; Circulation 2,243); Cary-Grove Countryside (Community news; Circulation 2,442); Lake Zurich Courier (Local news; Circulation 4,279); Pioneer Press - Northwest/Barrington Bureau (Community news); Wauconda Leader (Regional news; Circulation 4,309).
Transportation: Commute to work: 90.5% car, 2.6% public transportation, 0.5% walk, 5.3% work from home (2005-2009 5-year est.); Travel time to work: 17.4% less than 15 minutes, 25.2% 15 to 30 minutes, 21.3% 30 to 45 minutes, 16.7% 45 to 60 minutes, 19.5% 60 minutes or more (2005-2009 5-year est.)
Additional Information Contacts
Algonquin/Lake in the Hills Chamber of Commerce . . . . . . (847) 658-5300
   http://www.alchamber.com
Village of Algonquin . . . . (847) 658-2700
   http://www.algonquin.org

BULL VALLEY (village). Covers a land area of 5.609 square miles and a water area of 0 square miles. Located at 42.31° N. Lat; 88.36° W. Long. Elevation is 922 feet.
Population: 699 (1990); 726 (2000); 941 (2010); 1,042 (2015 projected); Race: 92.9% White, 0.4% Black, 1.7% Asian, 5.0% Other, 8.6% Hispanic of any race (2010); Density: 167.8 persons per square mile (2010); Average household size: 2.88 (2010); Median age: 37.1 (2010); Males per 100 females: 96.5 (2010); Marriage status: 19.5% never married, 71.2% now married, 3.5% widowed, 5.8% divorced (2005-2009 5-year est.);

Foreign born: 2.0% (2005-2009 5-year est.); Ancestry (includes multiple ancestries): 43.6% German, 20.6% Irish, 13.7% English, 13.5% Italian, 9.6% Polish (2005-2009 5-year est.).
Economy: Single-family building permits issued: 0 (2010); Multi-family building permits issued: 0 (2010); Employment by occupation: 27.6% management, 24.8% professional, 7.8% services, 26.8% sales, 0.0% farming, 7.8% construction, 5.1% production (2005-2009 5-year est.).
Income: Per capita income: $39,498 (2010); Median household income: $78,804 (2010); Average household income: $113,558 (2010); Percent of households with income of $100,000 or more: 38.0% (2010); Poverty rate: 1.1% (2005-2009 5-year est.).
Taxes: Total city taxes per capita: $384 (2007); City property taxes per capita: $261 (2007).
Education: Percent of population age 25 and over with: High school diploma (including GED) or higher: 93.9% (2010); Bachelor's degree or higher: 39.7% (2010); Master's degree or higher: 17.5% (2010).
Housing: Homeownership rate: 89.9% (2010); Median home value: $278,169 (2010); Median contract rent: $852 per month (2005-2009 5-year est.); Median year structure built: 1983 (2005-2009 5-year est.).
Safety: Violent crime rate: 0.0 per 10,000 population; Property crime rate: 70.9 per 10,000 population (2010).
Transportation: Commute to work: 85.1% car, 4.3% public transportation, 0.0% walk, 10.6% work from home (2005-2009 5-year est.); Travel time to work: 14.4% less than 15 minutes, 26.2% 15 to 30 minutes, 11.7% 30 to 45 minutes, 18.5% 45 to 60 minutes, 29.3% 60 minutes or more (2005-2009 5-year est.)

CARY (village). Covers a land area of 5.253 square miles and a water area of 0.058 square miles. Located at 42.21° N. Lat; 88.24° W. Long. Elevation is 823 feet.
Population: 10,305 (1990); 15,531 (2000); 19,962 (2010); 22,028 (2015 projected); Race: 92.8% White, 0.6% Black, 2.2% Asian, 4.3% Other, 10.2% Hispanic of any race (2010); Density: 3,799.8 persons per square mile (2010); Average household size: 3.18 (2010); Median age: 34.6 (2010); Males per 100 females: 99.2 (2010); Marriage status: 27.5% never married, 61.8% now married, 3.3% widowed, 7.4% divorced (2005-2009 5-year est.); Foreign born: 12.3% (2005-2009 5-year est.); Ancestry (includes multiple ancestries): 34.3% German, 20.8% Irish, 14.8% Polish, 11.6% Italian, 8.1% English (2005-2009 5-year est.).
Economy: Single-family building permits issued: 1 (2010); Multi-family building permits issued: 0 (2010); Employment by occupation: 20.0% management, 23.6% professional, 13.7% services, 26.9% sales, 0.1% farming, 4.4% construction, 11.3% production (2005-2009 5-year est.).
Income: Per capita income: $32,048 (2010); Median household income: $87,311 (2010); Average household income: $101,986 (2010); Percent of households with income of $100,000 or more: 39.8% (2010); Poverty rate: 3.0% (2005-2009 5-year est.).
Taxes: Total city taxes per capita: $180 (2007); City property taxes per capita: $116 (2007).
Education: Percent of population age 25 and over with: High school diploma (including GED) or higher: 94.0% (2010); Bachelor's degree or higher: 42.9% (2010); Master's degree or higher: 14.3% (2010).
School District(s)
CHSD 155 (09-12)
   2009-10 Enrollment: 7,146 . . . . (815) 455-8500
Cary CCSD 26 (PK-08)
   2009-10 Enrollment: 3,251 . . . . (847) 639-7788
Housing: Homeownership rate: 91.7% (2010); Median home value: $243,147 (2010); Median contract rent: $859 per month (2005-2009 5-year est.); Median year structure built: 1987 (2005-2009 5-year est.).
Transportation: Commute to work: 85.8% car, 5.2% public transportation, 2.0% walk, 6.0% work from home (2005-2009 5-year est.); Travel time to work: 21.7% less than 15 minutes, 22.6% 15 to 30 minutes, 25.2% 30 to 45 minutes, 12.4% 45 to 60 minutes, 18.2% 60 minutes or more (2005-2009 5-year est.)
Additional Information Contacts
Cary Grove Area Chamber of Commerce . . . . (847) 639-2800
   http://www.carygrovechamber.com
Village of Cary . . . . (847) 639-0003
   http://www.caryillinois.com

CRYSTAL LAKE (city). Covers a land area of 16.243 square miles and a water area of 0.560 square miles. Located at 42.22° N. Lat; 88.33° W. Long. Elevation is 915 feet.

History: Named for the small lake around which the town developed. Crystal Lake was settled in 1825 when the Erie Canal opened, and grew when the Chicago & North Western Railroad arrived.
Population: 25,852 (1990); 38,000 (2000); 43,344 (2010); 45,903 (2015 projected); Race: 90.1% White, 1.1% Black, 3.4% Asian, 5.4% Other, 11.0% Hispanic of any race (2010); Density: 2,668.5 persons per square mile (2010); Average household size: 2.88 (2010); Median age: 35.5 (2010); Males per 100 females: 99.6 (2010); Marriage status: 28.0% never married, 55.9% now married, 6.0% widowed, 10.1% divorced (2005-2009 5-year est.); Foreign born: 10.4% (2005-2009 5-year est.); Ancestry (includes multiple ancestries): 32.7% German, 19.6% Irish, 14.2% Polish, 13.4% Italian, 8.0% English (2005-2009 5-year est.).
Economy: Unemployment rate: 9.2% (August 2011); Total civilian labor force: 22,469 (August 2011); Single-family building permits issued: 12 (2010); Multi-family building permits issued: 0 (2010); Employment by occupation: 14.2% management, 21.9% professional, 16.4% services, 30.1% sales, 0.0% farming, 6.6% construction, 10.8% production (2005-2009 5-year est.).
Income: Per capita income: $32,476 (2010); Median household income: $80,249 (2010); Average household income: $93,739 (2010); Percent of households with income of $100,000 or more: 34.6% (2010); Poverty rate: 4.5% (2005-2009 5-year est.).
Taxes: Total city taxes per capita: $381 (2007); City property taxes per capita: $299 (2007).
Education: Percent of population age 25 and over with: High school diploma (including GED) or higher: 94.2% (2010); Bachelor's degree or higher: 41.8% (2010); Master's degree or higher: 14.0% (2010).

School District(s)
CHSD 155 (09-12)
    2009-10 Enrollment: 7,146 . . . . (815) 455-8500
Crystal Lake CCSD 47 (PK-08)
    2009-10 Enrollment: 8,707 . . . . (815) 459-6070
Prairie Grove CSD 46 (PK-08)
    2009-10 Enrollment: 976 . . . . (815) 459-3023

Two-year College(s)
McHenry County College (Public)
    Fall 2009 Enrollment: 6,811. . . . . (815) 455-3700
    2010-11 Tuition: In-state $9,437; Out-of-state $10,477

Vocational/Technical School(s)
Cosmetology & Spa Institute (Private, For-profit)
    Fall 2009 Enrollment: 254 . . . . (815) 455-5900
    2010-11 Tuition: $16,000
First Institute Inc (Private, For-profit)
    Fall 2009 Enrollment: 155 . . . . (815) 459-3500
    2010-11 Tuition: $13,600

Housing: Homeownership rate: 83.3% (2010); Median home value: $221,678 (2010); Median contract rent: $975 per month (2005-2009 5-year est.); Median year structure built: 1982 (2005-2009 5-year est.).
Safety: Violent crime rate: 12.8 per 10,000 population; Property crime rate: 196.3 per 10,000 population (2010).
Newspapers: Northwest Herald (Local news; Circulation 33,800)
Transportation: Commute to work: 87.6% car, 2.9% public transportation, 1.8% walk, 6.5% work from home (2005-2009 5-year est.); Travel time to work: 31.3% less than 15 minutes, 24.7% 15 to 30 minutes, 14.3% 30 to 45 minutes, 10.9% 45 to 60 minutes, 18.7% 60 minutes or more (2005-2009 5-year est.)
Additional Information Contacts
City of Crystal Lake . . . . (815) 459-2020
    http://www.crystallake.org
Crystal Lake Chamber of Commerce. . . . . (815) 459-1300
    http://www.clchamber.com

FOX RIVER GROVE (village). Covers a land area of 1.660 square miles and a water area of 0.104 square miles. Located at 42.19° N. Lat; 88.21° W. Long. Elevation is 817 feet.
History: Fox River Grove developed as a summer resort town.
Population: 3,900 (1990); 4,862 (2000); 5,427 (2010); 5,649 (2015 projected); Race: 92.6% White, 1.0% Black, 3.0% Asian, 3.4% Other, 5.2% Hispanic of any race (2010); Density: 3,270.1 persons per square mile (2010); Average household size: 2.86 (2010); Median age: 37.8 (2010); Males per 100 females: 104.1 (2010); Marriage status: 29.3% never married, 57.9% now married, 4.2% widowed, 8.6% divorced (2005-2009 5-year est.); Foreign born: 5.6% (2005-2009 5-year est.); Ancestry (includes multiple ancestries): 33.0% German, 15.7% Irish, 15.5% Polish, 12.9% Italian, 8.1% English (2005-2009 5-year est.).

Economy: Single-family building permits issued: 0 (2010); Multi-family building permits issued: 0 (2010); Employment by occupation: 19.7% management, 22.9% professional, 12.4% services, 28.9% sales, 0.6% farming, 8.3% construction, 7.3% production (2005-2009 5-year est.).
Income: Per capita income: $34,647 (2010); Median household income: $76,812 (2010); Average household income: $99,055 (2010); Percent of households with income of $100,000 or more: 33.5% (2010); Poverty rate: 5.9% (2005-2009 5-year est.).
Taxes: Total city taxes per capita: $345 (2007); City property taxes per capita: $274 (2007).
Education: Percent of population age 25 and over with: High school diploma (including GED) or higher: 93.8% (2010); Bachelor's degree or higher: 36.6% (2010); Master's degree or higher: 9.1% (2010).

School District(s)
Fox River Grove Cons SD 3 (PK-08)
    2009-10 Enrollment: 527 . . . . (847) 516-5100
Housing: Homeownership rate: 85.8% (2010); Median home value: $261,211 (2010); Median contract rent: $810 per month (2005-2009 5-year est.); Median year structure built: 1975 (2005-2009 5-year est.).
Safety: Violent crime rate: 9.7 per 10,000 population; Property crime rate: 168.3 per 10,000 population (2010).
Transportation: Commute to work: 88.9% car, 5.7% public transportation, 2.0% walk, 2.2% work from home (2005-2009 5-year est.); Travel time to work: 18.8% less than 15 minutes, 34.0% 15 to 30 minutes, 16.5% 30 to 45 minutes, 15.8% 45 to 60 minutes, 15.0% 60 minutes or more (2005-2009 5-year est.)

GREENWOOD (village). Covers a land area of 1.559 square miles and a water area of 0 square miles. Located at 42.39° N. Lat; 88.38° W. Long. Elevation is 856 feet.
Population: 214 (1990); 244 (2000); 222 (2010); 228 (2015 projected); Race: 94.6% White, 0.5% Black, 0.9% Asian, 4.1% Other, 7.7% Hispanic of any race (2010); Density: 142.4 persons per square mile (2010); Average household size: 2.87 (2010); Median age: 39.8 (2010); Males per 100 females: 107.5 (2010); Marriage status: 22.7% never married, 58.3% now married, 4.5% widowed, 14.4% divorced (2005-2009 5-year est.); Foreign born: 2.6% (2005-2009 5-year est.); Ancestry (includes multiple ancestries): 49.7% German, 22.6% Irish, 9.7% Italian, 8.4% Polish, 7.7% Dutch (2005-2009 5-year est.).
Economy: Employment by occupation: 9.2% management, 18.4% professional, 11.8% services, 28.9% sales, 0.0% farming, 18.4% construction, 13.2% production (2005-2009 5-year est.).
Income: Per capita income: $27,275 (2010); Median household income: $63,393 (2010); Average household income: $77,695 (2010); Percent of households with income of $100,000 or more: 24.7% (2010); Poverty rate: 2.6% (2005-2009 5-year est.).
Taxes: Total city taxes per capita: $257 (2007); City property taxes per capita: $209 (2007).
Education: Percent of population age 25 and over with: High school diploma (including GED) or higher: 91.0% (2010); Bachelor's degree or higher: 22.6% (2010); Master's degree or higher: 6.5% (2010).
Housing: Homeownership rate: 90.9% (2010); Median home value: $218,182 (2010); Median contract rent: $575 per month (2005-2009 5-year est.); Median year structure built: before 1940 (2005-2009 5-year est.).
Transportation: Commute to work: 98.7% car, 0.0% public transportation, 0.0% walk, 1.3% work from home (2005-2009 5-year est.); Travel time to work: 16.0% less than 15 minutes, 49.3% 15 to 30 minutes, 20.0% 30 to 45 minutes, 2.7% 45 to 60 minutes, 12.0% 60 minutes or more (2005-2009 5-year est.)

HARVARD (city). Covers a land area of 5.337 square miles and a water area of 0 square miles. Located at 42.42° N. Lat; 88.61° W. Long. Elevation is 958 feet.
History: Incorporated 1867.
Population: 6,401 (1990); 7,996 (2000); 9,705 (2010); 10,541 (2015 projected); Race: 71.9% White, 1.1% Black, 1.8% Asian, 25.2% Other, 50.4% Hispanic of any race (2010); Density: 1,818.4 persons per square mile (2010); Average household size: 3.10 (2010); Median age: 32.8 (2010); Males per 100 females: 108.6 (2010); Marriage status: 31.4% never married, 49.4% now married, 4.8% widowed, 14.3% divorced (2005-2009 5-year est.); Foreign born: 20.1% (2005-2009 5-year est.); Ancestry (includes multiple ancestries): 23.2% German, 15.6% Irish, 7.8% Italian, 5.8% English, 5.0% American (2005-2009 5-year est.).
Economy: Single-family building permits issued: 2 (2010); Multi-family building permits issued: 0 (2010); Employment by occupation: 5.6%

management, 10.3% professional, 18.1% services, 19.7% sales, 1.8% farming, 11.8% construction, 32.7% production (2005-2009 5-year est.).
Income: Per capita income: $20,923 (2010); Median household income: $54,457 (2010); Average household income: $64,640 (2010); Percent of households with income of $100,000 or more: 13.8% (2010); Poverty rate: 19.7% (2005-2009 5-year est.).
Taxes: Total city taxes per capita: $349 (2007); City property taxes per capita: $259 (2007).
Education: Percent of population age 25 and over with: High school diploma (including GED) or higher: 75.1% (2010); Bachelor's degree or higher: 18.4% (2010); Master's degree or higher: 7.2% (2010).

School District(s)
Harvard CUSD 50 (PK-12)
    2009-10 Enrollment: 2,429 . . . . (815) 943-4022
Housing: Homeownership rate: 64.3% (2010); Median home value: $145,667 (2010); Median contract rent: $670 per month (2005-2009 5-year est.); Median year structure built: 1964 (2005-2009 5-year est.).
Hospitals: Mercy Harvard Hospital (46 beds)
Safety: Violent crime rate: 4.0 per 10,000 population; Property crime rate: 88.4 per 10,000 population (2010).
Transportation: Commute to work: 88.4% car, 4.8% public transportation, 2.4% walk, 2.3% work from home (2005-2009 5-year est.); Travel time to work: 22.2% less than 15 minutes, 28.5% 15 to 30 minutes, 28.4% 30 to 45 minutes, 10.9% 45 to 60 minutes, 10.0% 60 minutes or more (2005-2009 5-year est.)
Additional Information Contacts
City of Harvard. . . . . (815) 943-6468
    http://www.cityofharvard.org
Harvard Chamber of Commerce . . . . (815) 943-4404
    http://www.harvcc.net

HEBRON (village). Covers a land area of 0.685 square miles and a water area of 0 square miles. Located at 42.47° N. Lat; 88.43° W. Long. Elevation is 928 feet.
Population: 895 (1990); 1,038 (2000); 1,285 (2010); 1,401 (2015 projected); Race: 97.4% White, 0.2% Black, 0.1% Asian, 2.4% Other, 7.2% Hispanic of any race (2010); Density: 1,876.6 persons per square mile (2010); Average household size: 2.61 (2010); Median age: 35.9 (2010); Males per 100 females: 101.1 (2010); Marriage status: 26.2% never married, 52.0% now married, 8.4% widowed, 13.4% divorced (2005-2009 5-year est.); Foreign born: 4.6% (2005-2009 5-year est.); Ancestry (includes multiple ancestries): 36.5% German, 18.0% Irish, 12.4% American, 12.4% English, 10.8% Polish (2005-2009 5-year est.).
Economy: Single-family building permits issued: 1 (2010); Multi-family building permits issued: 0 (2010); Employment by occupation: 7.6% management, 18.6% professional, 17.6% services, 20.6% sales, 0.0% farming, 14.2% construction, 21.4% production (2005-2009 5-year est.).
Income: Per capita income: $24,667 (2010); Median household income: $56,973 (2010); Average household income: $64,599 (2010); Percent of households with income of $100,000 or more: 13.6% (2010); Poverty rate: 7.1% (2005-2009 5-year est.).
Taxes: Total city taxes per capita: $311 (2007); City property taxes per capita: $119 (2007).
Education: Percent of population age 25 and over with: High school diploma (including GED) or higher: 90.6% (2010); Bachelor's degree or higher: 14.5% (2010); Master's degree or higher: 5.2% (2010).

School District(s)
Alden Hebron SD 19 (PK-12)
    2009-10 Enrollment: 469 . . . . (815) 648-2886
Housing: Homeownership rate: 71.3% (2010); Median home value: $174,291 (2010); Median contract rent: $694 per month (2005-2009 5-year est.); Median year structure built: 1972 (2005-2009 5-year est.).
Transportation: Commute to work: 89.6% car, 1.4% public transportation, 7.6% walk, 0.9% work from home (2005-2009 5-year est.); Travel time to work: 28.0% less than 15 minutes, 30.0% 15 to 30 minutes, 17.1% 30 to 45 minutes, 9.3% 45 to 60 minutes, 15.5% 60 minutes or more (2005-2009 5-year est.)

HOLIDAY HILLS (village). Covers a land area of 0.947 square miles and a water area of 0.037 square miles. Located at 42.29° N. Lat; 88.22° W. Long. Elevation is 741 feet.
Population: 855 (1990); 831 (2000); 804 (2010); 794 (2015 projected); Race: 92.4% White, 2.0% Black, 0.5% Asian, 5.1% Other, 8.6% Hispanic of any race (2010); Density: 849.2 persons per square mile (2010); Average household size: 2.76 (2010); Median age: 36.8 (2010); Males per

100 females: 108.8 (2010); Marriage status: 24.2% never married, 62.1% now married, 3.8% widowed, 10.0% divorced (2005-2009 5-year est.); Foreign born: 3.9% (2005-2009 5-year est.); Ancestry (includes multiple ancestries): 43.6% German, 24.8% Irish, 13.1% Polish, 8.6% English, 5.7% American (2005-2009 5-year est.).
Economy: Single-family building permits issued: 0 (2010); Multi-family building permits issued: 0 (2010); Employment by occupation: 7.9% management, 12.2% professional, 19.3% services, 27.9% sales, 0.5% farming, 17.5% construction, 14.7% production (2005-2009 5-year est.).
Income: Per capita income: $27,651 (2010); Median household income: $73,992 (2010); Average household income: $76,022 (2010); Percent of households with income of $100,000 or more: 22.0% (2010); Poverty rate: 2.0% (2005-2009 5-year est.).
Taxes: Total city taxes per capita: $92 (2007); City property taxes per capita: $31 (2007).
Education: Percent of population age 25 and over with: High school diploma (including GED) or higher: 86.3% (2010); Bachelor's degree or higher: 16.8% (2010); Master's degree or higher: 3.8% (2010).
Housing: Homeownership rate: 90.0% (2010); Median home value: $169,068 (2010); Median contract rent: $921 per month (2005-2009 5-year est.); Median year structure built: 1965 (2005-2009 5-year est.).
Transportation: Commute to work: 94.8% car, 0.8% public transportation, 0.8% walk, 1.6% work from home (2005-2009 5-year est.); Travel time to work: 18.4% less than 15 minutes, 33.3% 15 to 30 minutes, 15.5% 30 to 45 minutes, 10.0% 45 to 60 minutes, 22.8% 60 minutes or more (2005-2009 5-year est.)

HUNTLEY (village). Covers a land area of 11.716 square miles and a water area of 0.032 square miles. Located at 42.16° N. Lat; 88.42° W. Long. Elevation is 889 feet.
Population: 2,695 (1990); 5,730 (2000); 16,552 (2010); 18,581 (2015 projected); Race: 91.8% White, 1.3% Black, 3.5% Asian, 3.4% Other, 6.2% Hispanic of any race (2010); Density: 1,412.8 persons per square mile (2010); Average household size: 2.76 (2010); Median age: 37.7 (2010); Males per 100 females: 97.1 (2010); Marriage status: 13.6% never married, 69.3% now married, 9.1% widowed, 8.1% divorced (2005-2009 5-year est.); Foreign born: 11.3% (2005-2009 5-year est.); Ancestry (includes multiple ancestries): 33.4% German, 16.1% Irish, 15.7% Polish, 14.9% Italian, 8.5% English (2005-2009 5-year est.).
Economy: Single-family building permits issued: 107 (2010); Multi-family building permits issued: 0 (2010); Employment by occupation: 18.2% management, 19.8% professional, 14.6% services, 34.7% sales, 0.4% farming, 5.2% construction, 7.1% production (2005-2009 5-year est.).
Income: Per capita income: $35,302 (2010); Median household income: $80,438 (2010); Average household income: $97,312 (2010); Percent of households with income of $100,000 or more: 32.7% (2010); Poverty rate: 4.0% (2005-2009 5-year est.).
Taxes: Total city taxes per capita: $450 (2007); City property taxes per capita: $219 (2007).
Education: Percent of population age 25 and over with: High school diploma (including GED) or higher: 92.9% (2010); Bachelor's degree or higher: 28.8% (2010); Master's degree or higher: 7.5% (2010).

School District(s)
Cons SD 158 (PK-12)
    2009-10 Enrollment: 8,992 . . . . (847) 659-6158
Housing: Homeownership rate: 86.0% (2010); Median home value: $257,656 (2010); Median contract rent: $890 per month (2005-2009 5-year est.); Median year structure built: 2002 (2005-2009 5-year est.).
Safety: Violent crime rate: 2.7 per 10,000 population; Property crime rate: 78.5 per 10,000 population (2010).
Transportation: Commute to work: 92.2% car, 2.4% public transportation, 0.5% walk, 4.5% work from home (2005-2009 5-year est.); Travel time to work: 14.8% less than 15 minutes, 22.4% 15 to 30 minutes, 19.5% 30 to 45 minutes, 18.5% 45 to 60 minutes, 24.8% 60 minutes or more (2005-2009 5-year est.)
Additional Information Contacts
Huntley Area Chamber of Commerce & Industry. . . . . (847) 669-0166
    http://www.huntleychamber.org
Village of Huntley . . . . (847) 515-5200
    http://www.huntley.il.us

ISLAND LAKE (village). Covers a land area of 2.854 square miles and a water area of 0.208 square miles. Located at 42.27° N. Lat; 88.20° W. Long.

Population: 4,839 (1990); 8,153 (2000); 9,499 (2010); 10,212 (2015 projected); Race: 90.1% White, 0.9% Black, 2.4% Asian, 6.6% Other, 12.9% Hispanic of any race (2010); Density: 3,327.8 persons per square mile (2010); Average household size: 2.89 (2010); Median age: 35.1 (2010); Males per 100 females: 99.5 (2010); Marriage status: 26.9% never married, 59.9% now married, 4.5% widowed, 8.8% divorced (2005-2009 5-year est.); Foreign born: 10.5% (2005-2009 5-year est.); Ancestry (includes multiple ancestries): 31.0% German, 16.9% Irish, 12.5% Polish, 10.1% Italian, 6.7% English (2005-2009 5-year est.).
Economy: Single-family building permits issued: 1 (2010); Multi-family building permits issued: 0 (2010); Employment by occupation: 13.7% management, 14.2% professional, 14.0% services, 28.3% sales, 0.0% farming, 16.0% construction, 13.7% production (2005-2009 5-year est.).
Income: Per capita income: $30,244 (2010); Median household income: $76,286 (2010); Average household income: $87,119 (2010); Percent of households with income of $100,000 or more: 29.8% (2010); Poverty rate: 6.3% (2005-2009 5-year est.).
Education: Percent of population age 25 and over with: High school diploma (including GED) or higher: 90.7% (2010); Bachelor's degree or higher: 27.5% (2010); Master's degree or higher: 7.3% (2010).

School District(s)
Wauconda CUSD 118 (PK-12)
    2009-10 Enrollment: 4,401 . . . . (847) 526-7690
Housing: Homeownership rate: 92.2% (2010); Median home value: $188,117 (2010); Median contract rent: $1,019 per month (2005-2009 5-year est.); Median year structure built: 1990 (2005-2009 5-year est.).
Transportation: Commute to work: 94.2% car, 1.3% public transportation, 1.0% walk, 1.8% work from home (2005-2009 5-year est.); Travel time to work: 15.2% less than 15 minutes, 22.2% 15 to 30 minutes, 24.5% 30 to 45 minutes, 19.8% 45 to 60 minutes, 18.4% 60 minutes or more (2005-2009 5-year est.)

Additional Information Contacts
Island Lake Area Chamber of Commerce . . . . (847) 604-4522
    http://www.islandlakechamber.org
Village of Island Lake. . . . . (847) 526-8764
    http://www.villageofislandlake.com

JOHNSBURG (village). Aka Sunnyside. Covers a land area of 5.537 square miles and a water area of 0.576 square miles. Located at 42.38° N. Lat; 88.23° W. Long. Elevation is 751 feet.
Population: 4,589 (1990); 5,391 (2000); 6,170 (2010); 6,593 (2015 projected); Race: 98.0% White, 0.2% Black, 0.4% Asian, 1.3% Other, 2.8% Hispanic of any race (2010); Density: 1,114.4 persons per square mile (2010); Average household size: 2.93 (2010); Median age: 38.7 (2010); Males per 100 females: 101.1 (2010); Marriage status: 29.5% never married, 58.1% now married, 4.8% widowed, 7.6% divorced (2005-2009 5-year est.); Foreign born: 2.6% (2005-2009 5-year est.); Ancestry (includes multiple ancestries): 42.5% German, 18.0% Irish, 10.6% Polish, 9.9% Italian, 7.6% English (2005-2009 5-year est.).
Economy: Single-family building permits issued: 12 (2010); Multi-family building permits issued: 0 (2010); Employment by occupation: 21.1% management, 15.9% professional, 13.6% services, 32.8% sales, 0.5% farming, 10.1% construction, 6.0% production (2005-2009 5-year est.).
Income: Per capita income: $31,359 (2010); Median household income: $75,139 (2010); Average household income: $91,934 (2010); Percent of households with income of $100,000 or more: 28.7% (2010); Poverty rate: 3.1% (2005-2009 5-year est.).
Taxes: Total city taxes per capita: $197 (2007); City property taxes per capita: $131 (2007).
Education: Percent of population age 25 and over with: High school diploma (including GED) or higher: 93.0% (2010); Bachelor's degree or higher: 28.9% (2010); Master's degree or higher: 9.8% (2010).

School District(s)
Johnsburg CUSD 12 (PK-12)
    2009-10 Enrollment: 2,482 . . . . (815) 385-6916
Housing: Homeownership rate: 91.3% (2010); Median home value: $259,459 (2010); Median contract rent: $1,045 per month (2005-2009 5-year est.); Median year structure built: 1981 (2005-2009 5-year est.).
Safety: Violent crime rate: 1.5 per 10,000 population; Property crime rate: 185.9 per 10,000 population (2010).
Transportation: Commute to work: 86.5% car, 3.5% public transportation, 1.1% walk, 5.9% work from home (2005-2009 5-year est.); Travel time to work: 22.7% less than 15 minutes, 31.5% 15 to 30 minutes, 14.8% 30 to 45 minutes, 11.3% 45 to 60 minutes, 19.8% 60 minutes or more (2005-2009 5-year est.)

Additional Information Contacts
Village of Johnsburg . . . . (815) 385-6023
    http://www.johnsburg.org

LAKE IN THE HILLS (village). Covers a land area of 9.404 square miles and a water area of 0.232 square miles. Located at 42.18° N. Lat; 88.34° W. Long. Elevation is 866 feet.
Population: 7,263 (1990); 23,152 (2000); 33,153 (2010); 36,557 (2015 projected); Race: 85.5% White, 3.3% Black, 6.4% Asian, 4.9% Other, 8.8% Hispanic of any race (2010); Density: 3,525.4 persons per square mile (2010); Average household size: 3.06 (2010); Median age: 33.0 (2010); Males per 100 females: 99.9 (2010); Marriage status: 26.0% never married, 61.3% now married, 2.2% widowed, 10.5% divorced (2005-2009 5-year est.); Foreign born: 15.6% (2005-2009 5-year est.); Ancestry (includes multiple ancestries): 27.7% German, 17.4% Polish, 15.8% Italian, 15.2% Irish, 5.1% English (2005-2009 5-year est.).
Economy: Unemployment rate: 8.9% (August 2011); Total civilian labor force: 17,048 (August 2011); Single-family building permits issued: 3 (2010); Multi-family building permits issued: 0 (2010); Employment by occupation: 18.2% management, 16.7% professional, 13.6% services, 28.9% sales, 0.0% farming, 10.4% construction, 12.2% production (2005-2009 5-year est.).
Income: Per capita income: $34,324 (2010); Median household income: $91,112 (2010); Average household income: $104,957 (2010); Percent of households with income of $100,000 or more: 41.9% (2010); Poverty rate: 4.2% (2005-2009 5-year est.).
Taxes: Total city taxes per capita: $289 (2007); City property taxes per capita: $181 (2007).
Education: Percent of population age 25 and over with: High school diploma (including GED) or higher: 95.0% (2010); Bachelor's degree or higher: 38.0% (2010); Master's degree or higher: 8.8% (2010).

School District(s)
CUSD 300 (PK-12)
    2009-10 Enrollment: 20,341 . . . . (847) 426-1300
Cons SD 158 (PK-12)
    2009-10 Enrollment: 8,992 . . . . (847) 659-6158
Housing: Homeownership rate: 92.6% (2010); Median home value: $234,657 (2010); Median contract rent: $973 per month (2005-2009 5-year est.); Median year structure built: 1994 (2005-2009 5-year est.).
Safety: Violent crime rate: 10.7 per 10,000 population; Property crime rate: 79.3 per 10,000 population (2010).
Transportation: Commute to work: 92.2% car, 1.7% public transportation, 0.3% walk, 5.6% work from home (2005-2009 5-year est.); Travel time to work: 15.0% less than 15 minutes, 20.0% 15 to 30 minutes, 22.2% 30 to 45 minutes, 17.8% 45 to 60 minutes, 24.9% 60 minutes or more (2005-2009 5-year est.)

Additional Information Contacts
Village of Lake in the Hills . . . . (847) 960-7400
    http://www.lith.org

LAKEMOOR (village). Covers a land area of 4.280 square miles and a water area of 0.221 square miles. Located at 42.33° N. Lat; 88.20° W. Long. Elevation is 761 feet.
Population: 1,638 (1990); 2,788 (2000); 3,702 (2010); 4,024 (2015 projected); Race: 93.0% White, 0.5% Black, 1.8% Asian, 4.6% Other, 7.0% Hispanic of any race (2010); Density: 864.9 persons per square mile (2010); Average household size: 2.66 (2010); Median age: 37.9 (2010); Males per 100 females: 104.9 (2010); Marriage status: 27.8% never married, 59.6% now married, 1.1% widowed, 11.6% divorced (2005-2009 5-year est.); Foreign born: 13.2% (2005-2009 5-year est.); Ancestry (includes multiple ancestries): 29.4% German, 22.9% Irish, 20.7% Polish, 14.0% Italian, 5.7% Swedish (2005-2009 5-year est.).
Economy: Single-family building permits issued: 0 (2010); Multi-family building permits issued: 0 (2010); Employment by occupation: 15.0% management, 15.0% professional, 18.0% services, 25.9% sales, 0.0% farming, 11.1% construction, 14.9% production (2005-2009 5-year est.).
Income: Per capita income: $30,645 (2010); Median household income: $69,664 (2010); Average household income: $81,146 (2010); Percent of households with income of $100,000 or more: 24.7% (2010); Poverty rate: 5.6% (2005-2009 5-year est.).
Taxes: Total city taxes per capita: $202 (2007); City property taxes per capita: $85 (2007).
Education: Percent of population age 25 and over with: High school diploma (including GED) or higher: 89.8% (2010); Bachelor's degree or higher: 18.2% (2010); Master's degree or higher: 4.3% (2010).

Housing: Homeownership rate: 83.1% (2010); Median home value: $204,508 (2010); Median contract rent: $979 per month (2005-2009 5-year est.); Median year structure built: 2000 (2005-2009 5-year est.).
Safety: Violent crime rate: 19.6 per 10,000 population; Property crime rate: 128.9 per 10,000 population (2010).
Transportation: Commute to work: 96.0% car, 0.8% public transportation, 1.2% walk, 0.8% work from home (2005-2009 5-year est.); Travel time to work: 12.7% less than 15 minutes, 30.0% 15 to 30 minutes, 19.5% 30 to 45 minutes, 14.3% 45 to 60 minutes, 23.4% 60 minutes or more (2005-2009 5-year est.)

LAKEWOOD (village). Covers a land area of 3.091 square miles and a water area of 0.294 square miles. Located at 42.22° N. Lat; 88.37° W. Long. Elevation is 889 feet.
History: The Village of Lakewood was incorporated on July 10, 1933. In 1993 the Village Board developed a vision statement which has become the basis for making decisions to preserve this way of life. The statement reads, "Lakewood will remain a friendly community providing families with quality living in a natural setting", adopted as our mission statement.
Population: 1,711 (1990); 2,337 (2000); 3,085 (2010); 3,349 (2015 projected); Race: 90.5% White, 1.5% Black, 3.0% Asian, 5.0% Other, 7.8% Hispanic of any race (2010); Density: 998.0 persons per square mile (2010); Average household size: 2.90 (2010); Median age: 37.3 (2010); Males per 100 females: 100.2 (2010); Marriage status: 17.7% never married, 70.2% now married, 6.1% widowed, 6.0% divorced (2005-2009 5-year est.); Foreign born: 7.3% (2005-2009 5-year est.); Ancestry (includes multiple ancestries): 37.5% German, 17.1% Polish, 15.3% Irish, 9.7% Italian, 7.7% English (2005-2009 5-year est.).
Economy: Single-family building permits issued: 0 (2010); Multi-family building permits issued: 0 (2010); Employment by occupation: 31.9% management, 13.5% professional, 12.0% services, 30.5% sales, 0.0% farming, 6.0% construction, 6.2% production (2005-2009 5-year est.).
Income: Per capita income: $45,155 (2010); Median household income: $104,362 (2010); Average household income: $130,965 (2010); Percent of households with income of $100,000 or more: 52.4% (2010); Poverty rate: 1.2% (2005-2009 5-year est.).
Taxes: Total city taxes per capita: $481 (2007); City property taxes per capita: $355 (2007).
Education: Percent of population age 25 and over with: High school diploma (including GED) or higher: 95.0% (2010); Bachelor's degree or higher: 50.8% (2010); Master's degree or higher: 19.4% (2010).
Housing: Homeownership rate: 95.7% (2010); Median home value: $290,604 (2010); Median contract rent: n/a per month (2005-2009 5-year est.); Median year structure built: 1995 (2005-2009 5-year est.).
Transportation: Commute to work: 84.5% car, 2.5% public transportation, 2.7% walk, 10.3% work from home (2005-2009 5-year est.); Travel time to work: 23.2% less than 15 minutes, 19.2% 15 to 30 minutes, 13.5% 30 to 45 minutes, 21.2% 45 to 60 minutes, 22.8% 60 minutes or more (2005-2009 5-year est.)

MARENGO (city). Covers a land area of 3.975 square miles and a water area of 0 square miles. Located at 42.25° N. Lat; 88.60° W. Long. Elevation is 833 feet.
History: Marengo was the birthplace of Egbert Van Alstyne who composed the songs "In the Shade of the Old Apple Tree," and "Pony Boy." An early industry here was the McGill Metal Products Plant, a manufacturer of mousetraps.
Population: 4,872 (1990); 6,355 (2000); 7,821 (2010); 8,527 (2015 projected); Race: 89.4% White, 0.8% Black, 0.4% Asian, 9.4% Other, 15.9% Hispanic of any race (2010); Density: 1,967.3 persons per square mile (2010); Average household size: 2.72 (2010); Median age: 35.3 (2010); Males per 100 females: 99.1 (2010); Marriage status: 23.7% never married, 57.4% now married, 7.2% widowed, 11.7% divorced (2005-2009 5-year est.); Foreign born: 7.5% (2005-2009 5-year est.); Ancestry (includes multiple ancestries): 37.7% German, 16.4% Irish, 10.5% Polish, 9.0% Italian, 7.3% English (2005-2009 5-year est.).
Economy: Single-family building permits issued: 2 (2010); Multi-family building permits issued: 0 (2010); Employment by occupation: 12.6% management, 17.5% professional, 17.4% services, 24.7% sales, 0.0% farming, 14.0% construction, 13.9% production (2005-2009 5-year est.).
Income: Per capita income: $27,660 (2010); Median household income: $63,837 (2010); Average household income: $75,186 (2010); Percent of households with income of $100,000 or more: 22.4% (2010); Poverty rate: 5.3% (2005-2009 5-year est.).

Taxes: Total city taxes per capita: $282 (2007); City property taxes per capita: $155 (2007).
Education: Percent of population age 25 and over with: High school diploma (including GED) or higher: 88.8% (2010); Bachelor's degree or higher: 17.5% (2010); Master's degree or higher: 5.5% (2010).
School District(s)
Marengo CHSD 154 (09-12)
   2009-10 Enrollment: 869 . . . . (815) 568-6511
Marengo-Union E Cons D 165 (PK-08)
   2009-10 Enrollment: 1,088 . . . . (815) 568-8323
Riley CCSD 18 (KG-08)
   2009-10 Enrollment: 320 . . . . (815) 568-8637
Housing: Homeownership rate: 71.9% (2010); Median home value: $186,358 (2010); Median contract rent: $747 per month (2005-2009 5-year est.); Median year structure built: 1971 (2005-2009 5-year est.).
Transportation: Commute to work: 93.1% car, 1.4% public transportation, 2.1% walk, 2.3% work from home (2005-2009 5-year est.); Travel time to work: 24.0% less than 15 minutes, 28.0% 15 to 30 minutes, 22.9% 30 to 45 minutes, 8.4% 45 to 60 minutes, 16.7% 60 minutes or more (2005-2009 5-year est.)
Additional Information Contacts
City of Marengo . . . . (815) 568-7112
   http://www.cityofmarengo.com
Marengo Union Chamber of Commerce . . . . (815) 568-6680
   http://www.marengo-union.com

MCCULLOM LAKE (village). Covers a land area of 0.280 square miles and a water area of 0 square miles. Located at 42.37° N. Lat; 88.29° W. Long. Elevation is 787 feet.
Population: 1,099 (1990); 1,038 (2000); 1,187 (2010); 1,257 (2015 projected); Race: 94.1% White, 1.4% Black, 0.6% Asian, 3.9% Other, 5.5% Hispanic of any race (2010); Density: 4,240.5 persons per square mile (2010); Average household size: 2.75 (2010); Median age: 36.6 (2010); Males per 100 females: 99.2 (2010); Marriage status: 23.1% never married, 64.1% now married, 3.8% widowed, 8.9% divorced (2005-2009 5-year est.); Foreign born: 5.6% (2005-2009 5-year est.); Ancestry (includes multiple ancestries): 24.5% German, 18.4% American, 18.0% Irish, 12.7% Swedish, 11.1% Polish (2005-2009 5-year est.).
Economy: Single-family building permits issued: 0 (2010); Multi-family building permits issued: 0 (2010); Employment by occupation: 23.8% management, 5.7% professional, 8.8% services, 33.4% sales, 0.0% farming, 14.4% construction, 13.9% production (2005-2009 5-year est.).
Income: Per capita income: $24,110 (2010); Median household income: $60,950 (2010); Average household income: $66,700 (2010); Percent of households with income of $100,000 or more: 13.5% (2010); Poverty rate: 6.9% (2005-2009 5-year est.).
Taxes: Total city taxes per capita: $188 (2007); City property taxes per capita: $142 (2007).
Education: Percent of population age 25 and over with: High school diploma (including GED) or higher: 89.7% (2010); Bachelor's degree or higher: 14.9% (2010); Master's degree or higher: 3.4% (2010).
Housing: Homeownership rate: 84.5% (2010); Median home value: $167,000 (2010); Median contract rent: $847 per month (2005-2009 5-year est.); Median year structure built: 1951 (2005-2009 5-year est.).
Transportation: Commute to work: 95.4% car, 1.0% public transportation, 0.5% walk, 3.1% work from home (2005-2009 5-year est.); Travel time to work: 32.0% less than 15 minutes, 21.8% 15 to 30 minutes, 8.6% 30 to 45 minutes, 5.7% 45 to 60 minutes, 31.9% 60 minutes or more (2005-2009 5-year est.)

MCHENRY (city). Covers a land area of 11.621 square miles and a water area of 0.491 square miles. Located at 42.33° N. Lat; 88.28° W. Long. Elevation is 797 feet.
History: Named for William McHenry (1774-1839), who fought in the Black Hawk War of 1832. McHenry began in 1836 when Dr. Christy C. Wheeler became the first postmaster and storekeeper. McHenry was located on the Chicago Pike route and entertained many travelers. Later the economy depended on butter, cheese, and pickle production.
Population: 17,677 (1990); 21,501 (2000); 25,957 (2010); 28,084 (2015 projected); Race: 90.3% White, 0.6% Black, 1.3% Asian, 7.7% Other, 12.1% Hispanic of any race (2010); Density: 2,233.7 persons per square mile (2010); Average household size: 2.69 (2010); Median age: 36.9 (2010); Males per 100 females: 97.1 (2010); Marriage status: 27.4% never married, 57.2% now married, 6.6% widowed, 8.8% divorced (2005-2009 5-year est.); Foreign born: 11.2% (2005-2009 5-year est.); Ancestry

(includes multiple ancestries): 35.9% German, 19.1% Irish, 16.8% Polish, 8.4% Italian, 8.3% English (2005-2009 5-year est.).
Economy: Unemployment rate: 9.4% (August 2011); Total civilian labor force: 15,229 (August 2011); Single-family building permits issued: 8 (2010); Multi-family building permits issued: 0 (2010); Employment by occupation: 13.1% management, 18.2% professional, 14.3% services, 30.6% sales, 0.0% farming, 9.1% construction, 14.7% production (2005-2009 5-year est.).
Income: Per capita income: $28,392 (2010); Median household income: $65,109 (2010); Average household income: $76,032 (2010); Percent of households with income of $100,000 or more: 24.1% (2010); Poverty rate: 6.7% (2005-2009 5-year est.).
Taxes: Total city taxes per capita: $198 (2007); City property taxes per capita: $171 (2007).
Education: Percent of population age 25 and over with: High school diploma (including GED) or higher: 89.9% (2010); Bachelor's degree or higher: 25.9% (2010); Master's degree or higher: 7.5% (2010).

School District(s)
Mchenry CCSD 15 (PK-08)
   2009-10 Enrollment: 4,981 . . . . (815) 385-7210
Mchenry CHSD 156 (09-12)
   2009-10 Enrollment: 2,568 . . . . (815) 385-7900
Housing: Homeownership rate: 78.5% (2010); Median home value: $191,383 (2010); Median contract rent: $863 per month (2005-2009 5-year est.); Median year structure built: 1983 (2005-2009 5-year est.).
Hospitals: Centegra Northern Illinois Medical Center (196 beds)
Safety: Violent crime rate: 13.5 per 10,000 population; Property crime rate: 197.3 per 10,000 population (2010).
Transportation: Commute to work: 94.0% car, 1.4% public transportation, 1.0% walk, 2.8% work from home (2005-2009 5-year est.); Travel time to work: 30.6% less than 15 minutes, 33.5% 15 to 30 minutes, 14.8% 30 to 45 minutes, 8.3% 45 to 60 minutes, 12.8% 60 minutes or more (2005-2009 5-year est.)
Additional Information Contacts
City of McHenry . . . . (815) 363-2100
   http://www.ci.mchenry.il.us
McHenry Area Chamber of Commerce . . . . (815) 385-4300
   http://www.mchenrychamber.com

OAKWOOD HILLS (village). Covers a land area of 1.129 square miles and a water area of 0.079 square miles. Located at 42.24° N. Lat; 88.24° W. Long. Elevation is 827 feet.
Population: 1,699 (1990); 2,194 (2000); 2,443 (2010); 2,569 (2015 projected); Race: 95.7% White, 1.1% Black, 1.0% Asian, 2.2% Other, 5.2% Hispanic of any race (2010); Density: 2,164.5 persons per square mile (2010); Average household size: 2.93 (2010); Median age: 35.8 (2010); Males per 100 females: 99.9 (2010); Marriage status: 24.6% never married, 65.2% now married, 2.8% widowed, 7.4% divorced (2005-2009 5-year est.); Foreign born: 8.1% (2005-2009 5-year est.); Ancestry (includes multiple ancestries): 44.8% German, 19.9% Irish, 19.5% Polish, 13.2% Italian, 7.8% Swedish (2005-2009 5-year est.).
Economy: Single-family building permits issued: 4 (2010); Multi-family building permits issued: 0 (2010); Employment by occupation: 17.5% management, 19.4% professional, 10.5% services, 31.3% sales, 0.0% farming, 12.0% construction, 9.2% production (2005-2009 5-year est.).
Income: Per capita income: $31,861 (2010); Median household income: $74,479 (2010); Average household income: $93,736 (2010); Percent of households with income of $100,000 or more: 32.7% (2010); Poverty rate: 3.8% (2005-2009 5-year est.).
Taxes: Total city taxes per capita: $129 (2007); City property taxes per capita: $104 (2007).
Education: Percent of population age 25 and over with: High school diploma (including GED) or higher: 92.7% (2010); Bachelor's degree or higher: 37.4% (2010); Master's degree or higher: 10.9% (2010).
Housing: Homeownership rate: 89.0% (2010); Median home value: $249,807 (2010); Median contract rent: $663 per month (2005-2009 5-year est.); Median year structure built: 1979 (2005-2009 5-year est.).
Safety: Violent crime rate: 4.2 per 10,000 population; Property crime rate: 79.5 per 10,000 population (2010).
Transportation: Commute to work: 92.6% car, 2.2% public transportation, 0.0% walk, 4.3% work from home (2005-2009 5-year est.); Travel time to work: 23.6% less than 15 minutes, 26.4% 15 to 30 minutes, 17.6% 30 to 45 minutes, 13.2% 45 to 60 minutes, 19.2% 60 minutes or more (2005-2009 5-year est.)

PISTAKEE HIGHLANDS (CDP). Aka Pistakee. Covers a land area of 1.437 square miles and a water area of 0.329 square miles. Located at 42.40° N. Lat; 88.21° W. Long. Elevation is 758 feet.
Population: 3,785 (1990); 3,812 (2000); 4,266 (2010); 4,514 (2015 projected); Race: 97.3% White, 0.3% Black, 0.1% Asian, 2.3% Other, 5.3% Hispanic of any race (2010); Density: 2,969.0 persons per square mile (2010); Average household size: 2.80 (2010); Median age: 37.8 (2010); Males per 100 females: 103.9 (2010); Marriage status: 23.2% never married, 56.1% now married, 5.7% widowed, 15.0% divorced (2005-2009 5-year est.); Foreign born: 1.7% (2005-2009 5-year est.); Ancestry (includes multiple ancestries): 38.5% German, 17.2% Irish, 15.3% Polish, 15.2% Italian, 8.8% English (2005-2009 5-year est.).
Economy: Employment by occupation: 10.3% management, 14.3% professional, 10.3% services, 35.5% sales, 0.0% farming, 16.2% construction, 13.5% production (2005-2009 5-year est.).
Income: Per capita income: $26,303 (2010); Median household income: $67,742 (2010); Average household income: $73,522 (2010); Percent of households with income of $100,000 or more: 23.0% (2010); Poverty rate: 2.3% (2005-2009 5-year est.).
Education: Percent of population age 25 and over with: High school diploma (including GED) or higher: 88.9% (2010); Bachelor's degree or higher: 14.3% (2010); Master's degree or higher: 3.4% (2010).
Housing: Homeownership rate: 93.1% (2010); Median home value: $167,003 (2010); Median contract rent: $1,136 per month (2005-2009 5-year est.); Median year structure built: 1965 (2005-2009 5-year est.).
Transportation: Commute to work: 96.0% car, 0.9% public transportation, 0.6% walk, 1.8% work from home (2005-2009 5-year est.); Travel time to work: 27.5% less than 15 minutes, 22.6% 15 to 30 minutes, 20.4% 30 to 45 minutes, 16.4% 45 to 60 minutes, 13.1% 60 minutes or more (2005-2009 5-year est.)

PORT BARRINGTON (village). Aka formerly Fox River Valley Gardens. Covers a land area of 0.979 square miles and a water area of 0.096 square miles. Located at 42.24° N. Lat; 88.19° W. Long. Elevation is 738 feet.
Population: 637 (1990); 788 (2000); 1,302 (2010); 1,456 (2015 projected); Race: 93.9% White, 1.3% Black, 1.8% Asian, 3.1% Other, 6.3% Hispanic of any race (2010); Density: 1,330.2 persons per square mile (2010); Average household size: 2.88 (2010); Median age: 37.5 (2010); Males per 100 females: 104.7 (2010); Marriage status: 15.9% never married, 77.3% now married, 1.5% widowed, 5.3% divorced (2005-2009 5-year est.); Foreign born: 11.7% (2005-2009 5-year est.); Ancestry (includes multiple ancestries): 30.9% German, 23.5% Polish, 15.3% Italian, 11.6% Irish, 9.1% Swedish (2005-2009 5-year est.).
Economy: Employment by occupation: 19.7% management, 23.6% professional, 4.3% services, 36.5% sales, 0.0% farming, 10.9% construction, 5.0% production (2005-2009 5-year est.).
Income: Per capita income: $42,886 (2010); Median household income: $97,089 (2010); Average household income: $123,520 (2010); Percent of households with income of $100,000 or more: 48.1% (2010); Poverty rate: 2.0% (2005-2009 5-year est.).
Education: Percent of population age 25 and over with: High school diploma (including GED) or higher: 93.6% (2010); Bachelor's degree or higher: 32.7% (2010); Master's degree or higher: 10.1% (2010).
Housing: Homeownership rate: 94.7% (2010); Median home value: $252,326 (2010); Median contract rent: $1,025 per month (2005-2009 5-year est.); Median year structure built: 1998 (2005-2009 5-year est.).
Transportation: Commute to work: 90.7% car, 3.4% public transportation, 0.6% walk, 5.3% work from home (2005-2009 5-year est.); Travel time to work: 10.5% less than 15 minutes, 27.9% 15 to 30 minutes, 24.3% 30 to 45 minutes, 19.2% 45 to 60 minutes, 18.0% 60 minutes or more (2005-2009 5-year est.)

PRAIRIE GROVE (village). Covers a land area of 4.633 square miles and a water area of 0.139 square miles. Located at 42.27° N. Lat; 88.26° W. Long. Elevation is 758 feet.
Population: 801 (1990); 960 (2000); 1,055 (2010); 1,116 (2015 projected); Race: 95.3% White, 0.9% Black, 1.1% Asian, 2.7% Other, 3.6% Hispanic of any race (2010); Density: 227.7 persons per square mile (2010); Average household size: 2.85 (2010); Median age: 38.4 (2010); Males per 100 females: 100.6 (2010); Marriage status: 25.1% never married, 60.4% now married, 2.7% widowed, 11.9% divorced (2005-2009 5-year est.); Foreign born: 8.7% (2005-2009 5-year est.); Ancestry (includes multiple

ancestries): 33.4% German, 15.6% Irish, 14.1% English, 13.5% Italian, 9.2% Polish (2005-2009 5-year est.).
Economy: Single-family building permits issued: 0 (2010); Multi-family building permits issued: 0 (2010); Employment by occupation: 19.3% management, 21.0% professional, 11.9% services, 34.3% sales, 0.0% farming, 9.4% construction, 4.0% production (2005-2009 5-year est.).
Income: Per capita income: $35,414 (2010); Median household income: $81,653 (2010); Average household income: $101,500 (2010); Percent of households with income of $100,000 or more: 37.5% (2010); Poverty rate: 3.5% (2005-2009 5-year est.).
Taxes: Total city taxes per capita: $260 (2007); City property taxes per capita: $193 (2007).
Education: Percent of population age 25 and over with: High school diploma (including GED) or higher: 93.3% (2010); Bachelor's degree or higher: 34.1% (2010); Master's degree or higher: 10.3% (2010).
Housing: Homeownership rate: 83.8% (2010); Median home value: $274,766 (2010); Median contract rent: $371 per month (2005-2009 5-year est.); Median year structure built: 1997 (2005-2009 5-year est.).
Transportation: Commute to work: 84.6% car, 3.9% public transportation, 1.3% walk, 9.6% work from home (2005-2009 5-year est.); Travel time to work: 20.1% less than 15 minutes, 29.8% 15 to 30 minutes, 11.5% 30 to 45 minutes, 20.0% 45 to 60 minutes, 18.6% 60 minutes or more (2005-2009 5-year est.)

RICHMOND (village).
Covers a land area of 1.360 square miles and a water area of 0 square miles. Located at 42.47° N. Lat; 88.30° W. Long. Elevation is 820 feet.
History: Richmond was settled in 1837, and developed around a grist mill.
Population: 1,083 (1990); 1,091 (2000); 1,442 (2010); 1,596 (2015 projected); Race: 97.8% White, 0.2% Black, 0.2% Asian, 1.8% Other, 5.7% Hispanic of any race (2010); Density: 1,060.4 persons per square mile (2010); Average household size: 2.62 (2010); Median age: 39.0 (2010); Males per 100 females: 95.1 (2010); Marriage status: 37.6% never married, 43.9% now married, 2.7% widowed, 15.8% divorced (2005-2009 5-year est.); Foreign born: 2.5% (2005-2009 5-year est.); Ancestry (includes multiple ancestries): 37.7% German, 20.9% Irish, 13.5% Swedish, 12.0% Polish, 7.4% English (2005-2009 5-year est.).
Economy: Single-family building permits issued: 13 (2010); Multi-family building permits issued: 0 (2010); Employment by occupation: 13.2% management, 24.8% professional, 13.2% services, 24.9% sales, 0.0% farming, 10.5% construction, 13.4% production (2005-2009 5-year est.).
Income: Per capita income: $34,152 (2010); Median household income: $69,471 (2010); Average household income: $89,755 (2010); Percent of households with income of $100,000 or more: 34.4% (2010); Poverty rate: 3.4% (2005-2009 5-year est.).
Taxes: Total city taxes per capita: $210 (2007); City property taxes per capita: $167 (2007).
Education: Percent of population age 25 and over with: High school diploma (including GED) or higher: 91.4% (2010); Bachelor's degree or higher: 31.8% (2010); Master's degree or higher: 13.1% (2010).

School District(s)
Nippersink SD 2 (PK-08)
    2009-10 Enrollment: 1,484 . . . . (815) 678-4242
Richmond-Burton CHSD 157 (09-12)
    2009-10 Enrollment: 783 . . . . (815) 678-4525
Housing: Homeownership rate: 74.5% (2010); Median home value: $215,652 (2010); Median contract rent: $701 per month (2005-2009 5-year est.); Median year structure built: 1986 (2005-2009 5-year est.).
Safety: Violent crime rate: 8.1 per 10,000 population; Property crime rate: 113.5 per 10,000 population (2010).
Transportation: Commute to work: 94.5% car, 0.8% public transportation, 0.3% walk, 4.4% work from home (2005-2009 5-year est.); Travel time to work: 24.8% less than 15 minutes, 15.9% 15 to 30 minutes, 20.4% 30 to 45 minutes, 19.0% 45 to 60 minutes, 19.8% 60 minutes or more (2005-2009 5-year est.)
Additional Information Contacts
Richmond/Spring Grove Chamber of Commerce . . . . (815) 678-7742
    http://www.rsgchamber.com

RINGWOOD (village).
Covers a land area of 2.338 square miles and a water area of 0 square miles. Located at 42.39° N. Lat; 88.30° W. Long. Elevation is 856 feet.
Population: 371 (1990); 471 (2000); 643 (2010); 706 (2015 projected); Race: 97.0% White, 0.2% Black, 0.6% Asian, 2.2% Other, 3.7% Hispanic of any race (2010); Density: 275.1 persons per square mile (2010);

Average household size: 3.00 (2010); Median age: 38.0 (2010); Males per 100 females: 101.6 (2010); Marriage status: 22.4% never married, 67.0% now married, 2.8% widowed, 7.7% divorced (2005-2009 5-year est.); Foreign born: 1.6% (2005-2009 5-year est.); Ancestry (includes multiple ancestries): 38.3% German, 18.7% Italian, 18.2% Irish, 17.6% Polish, 7.9% English (2005-2009 5-year est.).
Economy: Employment by occupation: 20.6% management, 15.7% professional, 16.8% services, 23.4% sales, 0.9% farming, 17.8% construction, 4.9% production (2005-2009 5-year est.).
Income: Per capita income: $29,854 (2010); Median household income: $80,612 (2010); Average household income: $88,855 (2010); Percent of households with income of $100,000 or more: 32.2% (2010); Poverty rate: 3.8% (2005-2009 5-year est.).
Taxes: Total city taxes per capita: $308 (2007); City property taxes per capita: $174 (2007).
Education: Percent of population age 25 and over with: High school diploma (including GED) or higher: 94.4% (2010); Bachelor's degree or higher: 29.6% (2010); Master's degree or higher: 14.7% (2010).

School District(s)
Johnsburg CUSD 12 (PK-12)
    2009-10 Enrollment: 2,482 . . . . (815) 385-6916
Housing: Homeownership rate: 89.3% (2010); Median home value: $272,642 (2010); Median contract rent: $1,007 per month (2005-2009 5-year est.); Median year structure built: 1979 (2005-2009 5-year est.).
Transportation: Commute to work: 94.5% car, 0.7% public transportation, 1.0% walk, 3.9% work from home (2005-2009 5-year est.); Travel time to work: 33.1% less than 15 minutes, 27.3% 15 to 30 minutes, 17.0% 30 to 45 minutes, 11.5% 45 to 60 minutes, 11.0% 60 minutes or more (2005-2009 5-year est.)

SPRING GROVE (village).
Covers a land area of 6.211 square miles and a water area of 0.025 square miles. Located at 42.45° N. Lat; 88.24° W. Long. Elevation is 764 feet.
Population: 1,725 (1990); 3,880 (2000); 5,817 (2010); 6,649 (2015 projected); Race: 96.1% White, 0.3% Black, 1.4% Asian, 2.2% Other, 2.6% Hispanic of any race (2010); Density: 936.5 persons per square mile (2010); Average household size: 3.27 (2010); Median age: 35.7 (2010); Males per 100 females: 100.9 (2010); Marriage status: 17.1% never married, 72.3% now married, 4.5% widowed, 6.1% divorced (2005-2009 5-year est.); Foreign born: 5.4% (2005-2009 5-year est.); Ancestry (includes multiple ancestries): 41.7% German, 23.0% Irish, 17.9% Polish, 12.7% Italian, 10.5% English (2005-2009 5-year est.).
Economy: Single-family building permits issued: 5 (2010); Multi-family building permits issued: 0 (2010); Employment by occupation: 26.0% management, 31.6% professional, 11.9% services, 20.5% sales, 0.0% farming, 4.5% construction, 5.4% production (2005-2009 5-year est.).
Income: Per capita income: $33,064 (2010); Median household income: $94,956 (2010); Average household income: $108,126 (2010); Percent of households with income of $100,000 or more: 46.1% (2010); Poverty rate: 1.7% (2005-2009 5-year est.).
Taxes: Total city taxes per capita: $299 (2007); City property taxes per capita: $113 (2007).
Education: Percent of population age 25 and over with: High school diploma (including GED) or higher: 94.8% (2010); Bachelor's degree or higher: 30.1% (2010); Master's degree or higher: 10.8% (2010).

School District(s)
Fox Lake Gsd 114 (PK-08)
    2009-10 Enrollment: 853 . . . . (847) 973-4027
Nippersink SD 2 (PK-08)
    2009-10 Enrollment: 1,484 . . . . (815) 678-4242
Housing: Homeownership rate: 95.9% (2010); Median home value: $316,270 (2010); Median contract rent: $908 per month (2005-2009 5-year est.); Median year structure built: 1996 (2005-2009 5-year est.).
Safety: Violent crime rate: 3.4 per 10,000 population; Property crime rate: 117.3 per 10,000 population (2010).
Transportation: Commute to work: 87.0% car, 2.2% public transportation, 1.3% walk, 8.5% work from home (2005-2009 5-year est.); Travel time to work: 12.3% less than 15 minutes, 31.5% 15 to 30 minutes, 19.7% 30 to 45 minutes, 14.7% 45 to 60 minutes, 21.7% 60 minutes or more (2005-2009 5-year est.)

TROUT VALLEY (village).
Covers a land area of 0.428 square miles and a water area of <.001 square miles. Located at 42.19° N. Lat; 88.25° W. Long. Elevation is 794 feet.

Population: 599 (1990); 599 (2000); 613 (2010); 647 (2015 projected); Race: 91.7% White, 1.0% Black, 1.3% Asian, 6.0% Other, 8.8% Hispanic of any race (2010); Density: 1,432.4 persons per square mile (2010); Average household size: 2.61 (2010); Median age: 42.4 (2010); Males per 100 females: 108.5 (2010); Marriage status: 27.4% never married, 67.9% now married, 1.5% widowed, 3.1% divorced (2005-2009 5-year est.); Foreign born: 5.2% (2005-2009 5-year est.); Ancestry (includes multiple ancestries): 35.7% Irish, 27.2% German, 18.9% English, 13.9% Italian, 11.4% Polish (2005-2009 5-year est.).
Economy: Employment by occupation: 18.5% management, 33.5% professional, 5.4% services, 36.9% sales, 0.0% farming, 4.2% construction, 1.5% production (2005-2009 5-year est.).
Income: Per capita income: $46,717 (2010); Median household income: $99,653 (2010); Average household income: $121,245 (2010); Percent of households with income of $100,000 or more: 49.8% (2010); Poverty rate: 1.2% (2005-2009 5-year est.).
Taxes: Total city taxes per capita: $18 (2007); City property taxes per capita: $0 (2007).
Education: Percent of population age 25 and over with: High school diploma (including GED) or higher: 97.0% (2010); Bachelor's degree or higher: 47.2% (2010); Master's degree or higher: 15.4% (2010).
Housing: Homeownership rate: 89.8% (2010); Median home value: $288,095 (2010); Median contract rent: $2,000 per month (2005-2009 5-year est.); Median year structure built: 1965 (2005-2009 5-year est.).
Transportation: Commute to work: 74.1% car, 10.6% public transportation, 0.0% walk, 10.6% work from home (2005-2009 5-year est.); Travel time to work: 26.8% less than 15 minutes, 17.1% 15 to 30 minutes, 10.5% 30 to 45 minutes, 15.4% 45 to 60 minutes, 30.3% 60 minutes or more (2005-2009 5-year est.)

UNION (village). Covers a land area of 0.606 square miles and a water area of 0 square miles. Located at 42.23° N. Lat; 88.54° W. Long. Elevation is 840 feet.
History: Illinois Railroad Museum here.
Population: 552 (1990); 576 (2000); 586 (2010); 597 (2015 projected); Race: 97.1% White, 0.0% Black, 0.9% Asian, 2.0% Other, 5.5% Hispanic of any race (2010); Density: 966.9 persons per square mile (2010); Average household size: 2.79 (2010); Median age: 39.3 (2010); Males per 100 females: 94.0 (2010); Marriage status: 34.7% never married, 49.8% now married, 4.5% widowed, 11.0% divorced (2005-2009 5-year est.); Foreign born: 0.0% (2005-2009 5-year est.); Ancestry (includes multiple ancestries): 59.6% German, 15.1% Irish, 10.8% Italian, 8.6% Russian, 6.6% English (2005-2009 5-year est.).
Economy: Single-family building permits issued: 0 (2010); Multi-family building permits issued: 0 (2010); Employment by occupation: 9.9% management, 13.9% professional, 26.4% services, 25.7% sales, 0.0% farming, 11.0% construction, 13.1% production (2005-2009 5-year est.).
Income: Per capita income: $27,031 (2010); Median household income: $69,196 (2010); Average household income: $75,512 (2010); Percent of households with income of $100,000 or more: 29.5% (2010); Poverty rate: 7.1% (2005-2009 5-year est.).
Taxes: Total city taxes per capita: $376 (2007); City property taxes per capita: $107 (2007).
Education: Percent of population age 25 and over with: High school diploma (including GED) or higher: 83.5% (2010); Bachelor's degree or higher: 15.1% (2010); Master's degree or higher: 4.2% (2010).

School District(s)
Mchenry Roe (08-12)
    2009-10 Enrollment: n/a . . . . (815) 334-4475
Spec Ed Dist of Mchenry Co-Sedom (PK-12)
    2009-10 Enrollment: n/a . . . . (815) 338-3622
Housing: Homeownership rate: 85.2% (2010); Median home value: $203,125 (2010); Median contract rent: $663 per month (2005-2009 5-year est.); Median year structure built: 1941 (2005-2009 5-year est.).
Transportation: Commute to work: 97.6% car, 0.0% public transportation, 0.5% walk, 0.8% work from home (2005-2009 5-year est.); Travel time to work: 23.6% less than 15 minutes, 28.7% 15 to 30 minutes, 20.1% 30 to 45 minutes, 15.3% 45 to 60 minutes, 12.3% 60 minutes or more (2005-2009 5-year est.)

WONDER LAKE (village). Aka Wonder Center. Covers a land area of 0.811 square miles and a water area of 0.005 square miles. Located at 42.38° N. Lat; 88.36° W. Long. Elevation is 837 feet.
Population: 1,057 (1990); 1,345 (2000); 1,853 (2010); 1,960 (2015 projected); Race: 94.7% White, 0.5% Black, 0.9% Asian, 3.9% Other, 7.2%

Hispanic of any race (2010); Density: 2,283.5 persons per square mile (2010); Average household size: 2.92 (2010); Median age: 37.5 (2010); Males per 100 females: 104.1 (2010); Marriage status: 21.8% never married, 64.2% now married, 4.8% widowed, 9.2% divorced (2005-2009 5-year est.); Foreign born: 2.6% (2005-2009 5-year est.); Ancestry (includes multiple ancestries): 41.2% German, 23.8% Irish, 18.6% Polish, 12.2% English, 7.8% Italian (2005-2009 5-year est.).
Economy: Single-family building permits issued: 2 (2010); Multi-family building permits issued: 0 (2010); Employment by occupation: 14.2% management, 18.0% professional, 10.2% services, 29.5% sales, 0.0% farming, 11.4% construction, 16.7% production (2005-2009 5-year est.).
Income: Per capita income: $27,513 (2010); Median household income: $70,661 (2010); Average household income: $79,735 (2010); Percent of households with income of $100,000 or more: 26.6% (2010); Poverty rate: 2.3% (2005-2009 5-year est.).
Taxes: Total city taxes per capita: $257 (2007); City property taxes per capita: $95 (2007).
Education: Percent of population age 25 and over with: High school diploma (including GED) or higher: 90.2% (2010); Bachelor's degree or higher: 19.7% (2010); Master's degree or higher: 6.0% (2010).
School District(s)
Harrison SD 36 (PK-08)
    2009-10 Enrollment: 474 . . . . (815) 653-2311
Housing: Homeownership rate: 91.1% (2010); Median home value: $197,120 (2010); Median contract rent: $844 per month (2005-2009 5-year est.); Median year structure built: 1980 (2005-2009 5-year est.).
Transportation: Commute to work: 96.5% car, 1.3% public transportation, 0.0% walk, 1.8% work from home (2005-2009 5-year est.); Travel time to work: 8.7% less than 15 minutes, 40.0% 15 to 30 minutes, 17.9% 30 to 45 minutes, 10.6% 45 to 60 minutes, 22.8% 60 minutes or more (2005-2009 5-year est.)

WOODSTOCK (city). County seat. Covers a land area of 10.656 square miles and a water area of 0 square miles. Located at 42.31° N. Lat; 88.44° W. Long. Elevation is 945 feet.
History: Woodstock was settled in the 1830's and 1840's by people from Vermont, who named it for the Vermont town. After 1844, Woodstock grew as the seat of McHenry County.
Population: 15,150 (1990); 20,151 (2000); 24,054 (2010); 26,086 (2015 projected); Race: 82.5% White, 1.8% Black, 2.9% Asian, 12.9% Other, 27.1% Hispanic of any race (2010); Density: 2,257.4 persons per square mile (2010); Average household size: 2.69 (2010); Median age: 35.0 (2010); Males per 100 females: 102.0 (2010); Marriage status: 29.8% never married, 55.1% now married, 5.4% widowed, 9.7% divorced (2005-2009 5-year est.); Foreign born: 17.1% (2005-2009 5-year est.); Ancestry (includes multiple ancestries): 29.8% German, 17.6% Irish, 7.8% Polish, 7.6% English, 6.3% Italian (2005-2009 5-year est.).
Economy: Single-family building permits issued: 102 (2010); Multi-family building permits issued: 4 (2010); Employment by occupation: 12.1% management, 19.6% professional, 15.0% services, 25.0% sales, 0.2% farming, 9.8% construction, 18.4% production (2005-2009 5-year est.).
Income: Per capita income: $27,158 (2010); Median household income: $58,239 (2010); Average household income: $72,596 (2010); Percent of households with income of $100,000 or more: 19.3% (2010); Poverty rate: 10.2% (2005-2009 5-year est.).
Taxes: Total city taxes per capita: $428 (2007); City property taxes per capita: $333 (2007).
Education: Percent of population age 25 and over with: High school diploma (including GED) or higher: 83.9% (2010); Bachelor's degree or higher: 27.3% (2010); Master's degree or higher: 9.3% (2010).
School District(s)
Mchenry Co Coop for Employ Educ
    2009-10 Enrollment: n/a . . . . (815) 334-0183
Spec Ed Dist of Mchenry Co-Sedom (PK-12)
    2009-10 Enrollment: n/a . . . . (815) 338-3622
Woodstock CUSD 200 (PK-12)
    2009-10 Enrollment: 6,467 . . . . (815) 337-5406
Housing: Homeownership rate: 64.9% (2010); Median home value: $190,700 (2010); Median contract rent: $786 per month (2005-2009 5-year est.); Median year structure built: 1983 (2005-2009 5-year est.).
Hospitals: Centegra Memorial Medical Center (154 beds)
Safety: Violent crime rate: 10.2 per 10,000 population; Property crime rate: 159.5 per 10,000 population (2010).
Newspapers: Independent Plus (Community news; Circulation 22,000); Woodstock Independent (Community news; Circulation 2,800)

Transportation: Commute to work: 86.9% car, 4.4% public transportation, 3.8% walk, 3.4% work from home (2005-2009 5-year est.); Travel time to work: 31.8% less than 15 minutes, 32.0% 15 to 30 minutes, 12.8% 30 to 45 minutes, 6.3% 45 to 60 minutes, 17.1% 60 minutes or more (2005-2009 5-year est.)
Additional Information Contacts
City of Woodstock . . . . (815) 338-4300
   http://www.woodstock-il.com
Woodstock Chamber of Commerce & Industry . . . . (815) 338-2436
   http://www.woodstockilchamber.com

McLean County

Located in central Illinois; drained by the Sangamon and Mackinaw Rivers; includes Lake Bloomington. Covers a land area of 1,183.53 square miles, a water area of 2.76 square miles, and is located in the Central Time Zone at 40.49° N. Lat., 88.88° W. Long. The county was founded in 1830. County seat is Bloomington.

McLean County is part of the Bloomington-Normal, IL Metropolitan Statistical Area. The entire metro area includes: McLean County, IL

Weather Station: Chenoa										Elevation: 711 feet		
	Jan	Feb	Mar	Apr	May	Jun	Jul	Aug	Sep	Oct	Nov	Dec
High	33	38	50	64	75	83	85	84	78	65	51	37
Low	17	20	30	40	51	61	64	62	54	43	33	21
Precip	1.7	1.3	2.9	3.3	4.0	3.8	3.5	3.2	2.9	3.1	2.9	2.2
Snow	5.0	5.5	1.8	0.9	tr	0.0	0.0	0.0	0.0	0.1	1.0	4.2

High and Low temperatures in degrees Fahrenheit; Precipitation and Snow in inches

Weather Station: Normal										Elevation: 785 feet		
	Jan	Feb	Mar	Apr	May	Jun	Jul	Aug	Sep	Oct	Nov	Dec
High	34	39	50	63	74	83	86	84	78	66	51	37
Low	17	21	29	40	51	61	65	63	54	43	32	21
Precip	2.1	1.9	2.8	3.7	4.4	4.0	4.1	4.0	3.0	3.3	3.2	2.5
Snow	6.1	5.3	1.8	0.8	tr	0.0	0.0	0.0	0.0	0.1	0.7	4.9

High and Low temperatures in degrees Fahrenheit; Precipitation and Snow in inches

Population: 129,180 (1990); 150,433 (2000); 167,733 (2010); 174,825 (2015 projected); Race: 86.2% White, 7.2% Black, 3.1% Asian, 3.5% Other, 3.6% Hispanic of any race (2010); Density: 141.7 persons per square mile (2010); Average household size: 2.44 (2010); Median age: 31.8 (2010); Males per 100 females: 94.9 (2010).
Religion: Five largest groups: 12.7% Catholic Church, 6.5% The United Methodist Church, 3.7% Lutheran Church—Missouri Synod, 3.7% Christian Churches and Churches of Christ, 2.9% Evangelical Lutheran Church in America (2000).
Economy: Unemployment rate: 7.4% (August 2011); Total civilian labor force: 90,961 (August 2011); Leading industries: 29.2% finance & insurance; 12.2% retail trade; 11.9% health care and social assistance (2009); Farms: 1,513 totaling 675,984 acres (2007); Companies that employ 500 or more persons: 9 (2009); Companies that employ 100 to 499 persons: 79 (2009); Companies that employ less than 100 persons: 3,603 (2009); Black-owned businesses: 682 (2007); Hispanic-owned businesses: 176 (2007); Asian-owned businesses: 501 (2007); Women-owned businesses: 3,787 (2007); Retail sales per capita: $16,202 (2010). Single-family building permits issued: 319 (2010); Multi-family building permits issued: 108 (2010).
Income: Per capita income: $27,666 (2010); Median household income: $56,992 (2010); Average household income: $71,499 (2010); Percent of households with income of $100,000 or more: 21.1% (2010); Poverty rate: 14.4% (2009); Bankruptcy rate: 4.34% (2010).
Taxes: Total county taxes per capita: $220 (2007); County property taxes per capita: $170 (2007).
Education: Percent of population age 25 and over with: High school diploma (including GED) or higher: 94.0% (2010); Bachelor's degree or higher: 39.9% (2010); Master's degree or higher: 12.0% (2010).
Housing: Homeownership rate: 67.9% (2010); Median home value: $143,145 (2010); Median contract rent: $578 per month (2005-2009 5-year est.); Median year structure built: 1976 (2005-2009 5-year est.)
Health: Birth rate: 137.4 per 10,000 population (2009); Death rate: 64.6 per 10,000 population (2009); Age-adjusted cancer mortality rate: 183.9 deaths per 100,000 population (2007); Number of physicians: 21.1 per 10,000 population (2008); Hospital beds: 22.6 per 10,000 population (2007); Hospital admissions: 1,009.2 per 10,000 population (2007).

Environment: Air Quality Index: 89.8% good, 10.2% moderate, 0.0% unhealthy for sensitive individuals, 0.0% unhealthy (percent of days in 2008)
Elections: 2008 Presidential election results: 49.8% Obama, 48.5% McCain, 0.7% Nader
National and State Parks: Moraine View State Park
Additional Information Contacts
McLean County Government . . . . (309) 888-5190
   http://www.mcleancountyil.gov
Bloomington-Normal Area Convention & Visitors Bureau . . (309) 665-0033
   http://www.bloomingtonnormalcvb.org
City of Bloomington . . . . (309) 434-2509
   http://www.cityblm.org/
LeRoy Business Development Group . . . . (309) 962-2030
   http://www.leroybiz.org
McLean County Chamber of Commerce . . . . (309) 829-6344
   http://www.mcleancochamber.org
Town of Normal . . . . (309) 454-2444
   http://www.normal.org

McLean County Communities

ANCHOR (village). Covers a land area of 0.193 square miles and a water area of 0 square miles. Located at 40.56° N. Lat; 88.53° W. Long. Elevation is 778 feet.
Population: 178 (1990); 175 (2000); 178 (2010); 181 (2015 projected); Race: 98.3% White, 0.6% Black, 0.0% Asian, 1.1% Other, 0.0% Hispanic of any race (2010); Density: 920.1 persons per square mile (2010); Average household size: 2.52 (2010); Median age: 40.0 (2010); Males per 100 females: 91.4 (2010); Marriage status: 17.4% never married, 57.6% now married, 6.5% widowed, 18.5% divorced (2005-2009 5-year est.); Foreign born: 0.0% (2005-2009 5-year est.); Ancestry (includes multiple ancestries): 31.4% German, 30.5% American, 15.3% Italian, 11.0% English, 9.3% Irish (2005-2009 5-year est.).
Economy: Single-family building permits issued: 0 (2010); Multi-family building permits issued: 0 (2010); Employment by occupation: 23.6% management, 3.6% professional, 10.9% services, 30.9% sales, 0.0% farming, 9.1% construction, 21.8% production (2005-2009 5-year est.).
Income: Per capita income: $28,149 (2010); Median household income: $63,281 (2010); Average household income: $68,514 (2010); Percent of households with income of $100,000 or more: 17.4% (2010); Poverty rate: 11.9% (2005-2009 5-year est.).
Taxes: Total city taxes per capita: $88 (2007); City property taxes per capita: $88 (2007).
Education: Percent of population age 25 and over with: High school diploma (including GED) or higher: 94.2% (2010); Bachelor's degree or higher: 19.2% (2010); Master's degree or higher: 4.2% (2010).
Housing: Homeownership rate: 78.3% (2010); Median home value: $127,778 (2010); Median contract rent: $464 per month (2005-2009 5-year est.); Median year structure built: 1959 (2005-2009 5-year est.).
Transportation: Commute to work: 96.4% car, 0.0% public transportation, 0.0% walk, 0.0% work from home (2005-2009 5-year est.); Travel time to work: 21.8% less than 15 minutes, 20.0% 15 to 30 minutes, 36.4% 30 to 45 minutes, 21.8% 45 to 60 minutes, 0.0% 60 minutes or more (2005-2009 5-year est.)

ARROWSMITH (village). Covers a land area of 0.203 square miles and a water area of 0 square miles. Located at 40.44° N. Lat; 88.63° W. Long. Elevation is 883 feet.
Population: 313 (1990); 298 (2000); 292 (2010); 291 (2015 projected); Race: 96.2% White, 0.3% Black, 0.3% Asian, 3.1% Other, 0.7% Hispanic of any race (2010); Density: 1,435.0 persons per square mile (2010); Average household size: 2.78 (2010); Median age: 33.8 (2010); Males per 100 females: 100.0 (2010); Marriage status: 24.0% never married, 65.5% now married, 5.4% widowed, 5.1% divorced (2005-2009 5-year est.); Foreign born: 2.1% (2005-2009 5-year est.); Ancestry (includes multiple ancestries): 28.2% American, 18.7% Irish, 16.1% German, 13.7% English, 5.5% Scottish (2005-2009 5-year est.).
Economy: Single-family building permits issued: 0 (2010); Multi-family building permits issued: 0 (2010); Employment by occupation: 16.4% management, 15.9% professional, 11.8% services, 19.5% sales, 3.6% farming, 21.0% construction, 11.8% production (2005-2009 5-year est.).
Income: Per capita income: $31,719 (2010); Median household income: $73,370 (2010); Average household income: $87,929 (2010); Percent of

households with income of $100,000 or more: 26.7% (2010); Poverty rate: 9.5% (2005-2009 5-year est.).

Taxes: Total city taxes per capita: $63 (2007); City property taxes per capita: $63 (2007).

Education: Percent of population age 25 and over with: High school diploma (including GED) or higher: 95.0% (2010); Bachelor's degree or higher: 25.4% (2010); Master's degree or higher: 7.2% (2010).

Housing: Homeownership rate: 81.9% (2010); Median home value: $132,353 (2010); Median contract rent: $525 per month (2005-2009 5-year est.); Median year structure built: 1953 (2005-2009 5-year est.).

Transportation: Commute to work: 86.0% car, 0.0% public transportation, 10.7% walk, 3.4% work from home (2005-2009 5-year est.); Travel time to work: 27.3% less than 15 minutes, 35.5% 15 to 30 minutes, 33.7% 30 to 45 minutes, 2.3% 45 to 60 minutes, 1.2% 60 minutes or more (2005-2009 5-year est.)

BELLFLOWER (village).
Covers a land area of 0.365 square miles and a water area of 0 square miles. Located at 40.34° N. Lat; 88.52° W. Long. Elevation is 784 feet.

Population: 405 (1990); 408 (2000); 402 (2010); 401 (2015 projected); Race: 94.8% White, 3.7% Black, 0.2% Asian, 1.2% Other, 0.2% Hispanic of any race (2010); Density: 1,101.6 persons per square mile (2010); Average household size: 2.58 (2010); Median age: 38.6 (2010); Males per 100 females: 104.1 (2010); Marriage status: 26.7% never married, 58.7% now married, 5.8% widowed, 8.8% divorced (2005-2009 5-year est.); Foreign born: 0.4% (2005-2009 5-year est.); Ancestry (includes multiple ancestries): 28.5% German, 26.9% American, 15.7% English, 7.9% Irish, 7.7% Italian (2005-2009 5-year est.).

Economy: Single-family building permits issued: 0 (2010); Multi-family building permits issued: 0 (2010); Employment by occupation: 15.8% management, 15.8% professional, 11.4% services, 24.1% sales, 1.8% farming, 13.2% construction, 18.0% production (2005-2009 5-year est.).

Income: Per capita income: $24,289 (2010); Median household income: $58,571 (2010); Average household income: $62,356 (2010); Percent of households with income of $100,000 or more: 15.4% (2010); Poverty rate: 8.3% (2005-2009 5-year est.).

Taxes: Total city taxes per capita: $44 (2007); City property taxes per capita: $42 (2007).

Education: Percent of population age 25 and over with: High school diploma (including GED) or higher: 92.8% (2010); Bachelor's degree or higher: 17.7% (2010); Master's degree or higher: 5.4% (2010).

Housing: Homeownership rate: 80.1% (2010); Median home value: $96,667 (2010); Median contract rent: $388 per month (2005-2009 5-year est.); Median year structure built: 1941 (2005-2009 5-year est.).

Transportation: Commute to work: 96.1% car, 0.0% public transportation, 0.4% walk, 0.9% work from home (2005-2009 5-year est.); Travel time to work: 8.8% less than 15 minutes, 26.1% 15 to 30 minutes, 42.0% 30 to 45 minutes, 13.7% 45 to 60 minutes, 9.3% 60 minutes or more (2005-2009 5-year est.)

BLOOMINGTON (city).
County seat. Covers a land area of 22.500 square miles and a water area of 0 square miles. Located at 40.47° N. Lat; 88.98° W. Long. Elevation is 797 feet.

History: Bloomington was laid out in 1831 on land belonging to James Allin, adjoining the settlement called Blooming Grove. Allin also donated land for the county courthouse. Bloomington's growth was given impetus by the founding in 1853 of Illinois Wesleyan University, and the arrival in 1854 of both the Illinois Central and the Chicago & Mississippi Railroads. Adlai Stevenson (1835-1914) practiced law in Bloomington before serving in Congress and as vice-president, and returned to Bloomington in 1900.

Population: 53,588 (1990); 64,808 (2000); 72,644 (2010); 76,404 (2015 projected); Race: 81.1% White, 9.5% Black, 4.8% Asian, 4.6% Other, 4.8% Hispanic of any race (2010); Density: 3,228.6 persons per square mile (2010); Average household size: 2.33 (2010); Median age: 33.9 (2010); Males per 100 females: 96.1 (2010); Marriage status: 32.5% never married, 52.1% now married, 4.6% widowed, 10.8% divorced (2005-2009 5-year est.); Foreign born: 6.3% (2005-2009 5-year est.); Ancestry (includes multiple ancestries): 30.5% German, 15.5% Irish, 11.7% English, 10.4% American, 4.0% Italian (2005-2009 5-year est.).

Economy: Unemployment rate: 7.8% (August 2011); Total civilian labor force: 41,618 (August 2011); Single-family building permits issued: 184 (2010); Multi-family building permits issued: 3 (2010); Employment by occupation: 17.1% management, 25.1% professional, 15.1% services, 28.7% sales, 0.3% farming, 6.0% construction, 7.8% production (2005-2009 5-year est.).

Income: Per capita income: $29,746 (2010); Median household income: $54,800 (2010); Average household income: $71,199 (2010); Percent of households with income of $100,000 or more: 20.8% (2010); Poverty rate: 11.4% (2005-2009 5-year est.).

Taxes: Total city taxes per capita: $590 (2007); City property taxes per capita: $239 (2007).

Education: Percent of population age 25 and over with: High school diploma (including GED) or higher: 93.3% (2010); Bachelor's degree or higher: 42.7% (2010); Master's degree or higher: 12.5% (2010).

School District(s)

Bloomington Area Career Center (11-12)
  2009-10 Enrollment: n/a . . . . (309) 829-8671
Bloomington SD 87 (PK-12)
  2009-10 Enrollment: 5,609 . . . . (309) 827-6031
De Witt Livingston Mclean Roe (07-12)
  2009-10 Enrollment: n/a . . . . (309) 888-5120
Mclean County USD 5 (PK-12)
  2009-10 Enrollment: 12,976 . . . . (309) 888-6970

Four-year College(s)

Illinois Wesleyan University (Private, Not-for-profit)
  Fall 2009 Enrollment: 2,066 . . . . (309) 556-1000
  2010-11 Tuition: In-state $35,256; Out-of-state $35,256

Vocational/Technical School(s)

Hairmasters Institute of Cosmetology (Private, For-profit)
  Fall 2009 Enrollment: 136 . . . . (309) 828-1884
  2010-11 Tuition: $13,500

Housing: Homeownership rate: 64.9% (2010); Median home value: $141,902 (2010); Median contract rent: $580 per month (2005-2009 5-year est.); Median year structure built: 1977 (2005-2009 5-year est.).

Hospitals: BroMenn Regional Medical Center (224 beds); St. Joseph Medical Center (182 beds)

Safety: Violent crime rate: 51.8 per 10,000 population; Property crime rate: 263.8 per 10,000 population (2010).

Newspapers: The Pantagraph (Local news; Circulation 49,659)

Transportation: Commute to work: 89.8% car, 1.9% public transportation, 3.7% walk, 3.4% work from home (2005-2009 5-year est.); Travel time to work: 59.7% less than 15 minutes, 30.2% 15 to 30 minutes, 4.5% 30 to 45 minutes, 2.7% 45 to 60 minutes, 2.9% 60 minutes or more (2005-2009 5-year est.); Amtrak: train service available.

Airports: Central IL Regional Airport at Bloomington-Normal (primary service)

Additional Information Contacts

Bloomington-Normal Area Convention & Visitors Bureau . . (309) 665-0033
  http://www.bloomingtonnormalcvb.org
City of Bloomington . . . . (309) 434-2509
  http://www.cityblm.org/
McLean County Chamber of Commerce . . . . (309) 829-6344
  http://www.mcleancochamber.org

CARLOCK (village).
Covers a land area of 0.244 square miles and a water area of 0 square miles. Located at 40.58° N. Lat; 89.13° W. Long. Elevation is 771 feet.

Population: 442 (1990); 456 (2000); 471 (2010); 483 (2015 projected); Race: 98.1% White, 0.4% Black, 0.6% Asian, 0.8% Other, 0.8% Hispanic of any race (2010); Density: 1,933.4 persons per square mile (2010); Average household size: 2.59 (2010); Median age: 38.0 (2010); Males per 100 females: 104.8 (2010); Marriage status: 18.6% never married, 65.0% now married, 5.1% widowed, 11.4% divorced (2005-2009 5-year est.); Foreign born: 0.4% (2005-2009 5-year est.); Ancestry (includes multiple ancestries): 46.7% German, 17.9% American, 10.7% Irish, 8.9% Swedish, 8.0% Scotch-Irish (2005-2009 5-year est.).

Economy: Single-family building permits issued: 0 (2010); Multi-family building permits issued: 0 (2010); Employment by occupation: 19.7% management, 16.4% professional, 13.9% services, 19.7% sales, 0.0% farming, 9.7% construction, 20.6% production (2005-2009 5-year est.).

Income: Per capita income: $28,516 (2010); Median household income: $66,176 (2010); Average household income: $73,324 (2010); Percent of households with income of $100,000 or more: 20.3% (2010); Poverty rate: 3.2% (2005-2009 5-year est.).

Taxes: Total city taxes per capita: $31 (2007); City property taxes per capita: $16 (2007).

Education: Percent of population age 25 and over with: High school diploma (including GED) or higher: 95.2% (2010); Bachelor's degree or higher: 31.3% (2010); Master's degree or higher: 6.4% (2010).

School District(s)
Mclean County USD 5 (PK-12)
　2009-10 Enrollment: 12,976 . . . . (309) 888-6970
Housing: Homeownership rate: 85.2% (2010); Median home value: $157,609 (2010); Median contract rent: $496 per month (2005-2009 5-year est.); Median year structure built: 1953 (2005-2009 5-year est.).
Transportation: Commute to work: 93.2% car, 0.0% public transportation, 3.6% walk, 3.2% work from home (2005-2009 5-year est.); Travel time to work: 25.1% less than 15 minutes, 60.0% 15 to 30 minutes, 8.8% 30 to 45 minutes, 2.3% 45 to 60 minutes, 3.7% 60 minutes or more (2005-2009 5-year est.)

CHENOA (city). Covers a land area of 1.253 square miles and a water area of 0.037 square miles. Located at 40.74° N. Lat; 88.72° W. Long. Elevation is 719 feet.
History: Chenoa was laid out in 1856 by Matthew T. Scott, and grew up around the junction of the Peoria & Oquawka and the Chicago & Mississippi Railroads. Chenoa is of Indian origin and means "white dove."
Population: 1,740 (1990); 1,845 (2000); 1,793 (2010); 1,774 (2015 projected); Race: 97.1% White, 0.2% Black, 0.5% Asian, 2.2% Other, 2.6% Hispanic of any race (2010); Density: 1,430.7 persons per square mile (2010); Average household size: 2.54 (2010); Median age: 34.8 (2010); Males per 100 females: 98.3 (2010); Marriage status: 27.2% never married, 55.3% now married, 5.6% widowed, 12.0% divorced (2005-2009 5-year est.); Foreign born: 4.5% (2005-2009 5-year est.); Ancestry (includes multiple ancestries): 37.0% German, 19.1% Irish, 10.7% English, 9.8% American, 3.8% Italian (2005-2009 5-year est.).
Economy: Single-family building permits issued: 0 (2010); Multi-family building permits issued: 2 (2010); Employment by occupation: 15.3% management, 11.2% professional, 23.4% services, 18.4% sales, 0.0% farming, 10.0% construction, 21.7% production (2005-2009 5-year est.).
Income: Per capita income: $22,608 (2010); Median household income: $50,068 (2010); Average household income: $57,724 (2010); Percent of households with income of $100,000 or more: 10.0% (2010); Poverty rate: 12.2% (2005-2009 5-year est.).
Taxes: Total city taxes per capita: $107 (2007); City property taxes per capita: $93 (2007).
Education: Percent of population age 25 and over with: High school diploma (including GED) or higher: 87.9% (2010); Bachelor's degree or higher: 17.0% (2010); Master's degree or higher: 4.8% (2010).
School District(s)
Prairie Central CUSD 8 (PK-12)
　2009-10 Enrollment: 2,137 . . . . (815) 692-2504
Housing: Homeownership rate: 82.5% (2010); Median home value: $102,326 (2010); Median contract rent: $485 per month (2005-2009 est.); Median year structure built: 1955 (2005-2009 5-year est.).
Transportation: Commute to work: 93.8% car, 0.0% public transportation, 2.0% walk, 1.8% work from home (2005-2009 5-year est.); Travel time to work: 25.6% less than 15 minutes, 32.0% 15 to 30 minutes, 29.2% 30 to 45 minutes, 4.4% 45 to 60 minutes, 8.8% 60 minutes or more (2005-2009 5-year est.)

COLFAX (village). Covers a land area of 0.541 square miles and a water area of 0 square miles. Located at 40.56° N. Lat; 88.61° W. Long. Elevation is 755 feet.
History: Site of defunct coal mine.
Population: 908 (1990); 989 (2000); 1,016 (2010); 1,032 (2015 projected); Race: 98.8% White, 0.0% Black, 0.0% Asian, 1.2% Other, 2.2% Hispanic of any race (2010); Density: 1,879.3 persons per square mile (2010); Average household size: 2.37 (2010); Median age: 41.0 (2010); Males per 100 females: 96.9 (2010); Marriage status: 25.1% never married, 45.6% now married, 20.0% widowed, 9.2% divorced (2005-2009 5-year est.); Foreign born: 0.8% (2005-2009 5-year est.); Ancestry (includes multiple ancestries): 36.9% German, 16.7% Irish, 15.5% American, 15.3% English, 2.0% Scottish (2005-2009 5-year est.).
Economy: Single-family building permits issued: 0 (2010); Multi-family building permits issued: 0 (2010); Employment by occupation: 14.9% management, 18.5% professional, 16.7% services, 26.6% sales, 0.0% farming, 14.7% construction, 8.6% production (2005-2009 5-year est.).
Income: Per capita income: $25,295 (2010); Median household income: $58,142 (2010); Average household income: $61,962 (2010); Percent of households with income of $100,000 or more: 12.7% (2010); Poverty rate: 2.0% (2005-2009 5-year est.).
Taxes: Total city taxes per capita: $125 (2007); City property taxes per capita: $62 (2007).

Education: Percent of population age 25 and over with: High school diploma (including GED) or higher: 87.7% (2010); Bachelor's degree or higher: 17.4% (2010); Master's degree or higher: 4.4% (2010).
School District(s)
Ridgeview CUSD 19 (PK-12)
　2009-10 Enrollment: 626 . . . . (309) 723-5111
Housing: Homeownership rate: 83.6% (2010); Median home value: $97,778 (2010); Median contract rent: $515 per month (2005-2009 est.); Median year structure built: 1956 (2005-2009 5-year est.).
Safety: Violent crime rate: 0.0 per 10,000 population; Property crime rate: 139.6 per 10,000 population (2010).
Transportation: Commute to work: 97.1% car, 0.0% public transportation, 0.5% walk, 2.3% work from home (2005-2009 5-year est.); Travel time to work: 21.2% less than 15 minutes, 31.9% 15 to 30 minutes, 39.2% 30 to 45 minutes, 6.0% 45 to 60 minutes, 1.6% 60 minutes or more (2005-2009 5-year est.)

COOKSVILLE (village). Covers a land area of 0.232 square miles and a water area of 0 square miles. Located at 40.54° N. Lat; 88.71° W. Long. Elevation is 768 feet.
Population: 211 (1990); 213 (2000); 210 (2010); 214 (2015 projected); Race: 98.1% White, 0.5% Black, 0.0% Asian, 1.4% Other, 0.0% Hispanic of any race (2010); Density: 905.0 persons per square mile (2010); Average household size: 2.53 (2010); Median age: 39.7 (2010); Males per 100 females: 92.7 (2010); Marriage status: 12.9% never married, 67.7% now married, 3.2% widowed, 16.1% divorced (2005-2009 5-year est.); Foreign born: 0.0% (2005-2009 5-year est.); Ancestry (includes multiple ancestries): 58.0% German, 15.2% Irish, 10.1% English, 8.7% American, 5.8% Czech (2005-2009 5-year est.).
Economy: Single-family building permits issued: 0 (2010); Multi-family building permits issued: 0 (2010); Employment by occupation: 7.5% management, 11.8% professional, 11.8% services, 25.8% sales, 0.0% farming, 20.4% construction, 22.6% production (2005-2009 5-year est.).
Income: Per capita income: $28,149 (2010); Median household income: $66,447 (2010); Average household income: $73,272 (2010); Percent of households with income of $100,000 or more: 19.8% (2010); Poverty rate: 2.9% (2005-2009 5-year est.).
Taxes: Total city taxes per capita: $109 (2007); City property taxes per capita: $99 (2007).
Education: Percent of population age 25 and over with: High school diploma (including GED) or higher: 95.1% (2010); Bachelor's degree or higher: 18.1% (2010); Master's degree or higher: 3.5% (2010).
Housing: Homeownership rate: 77.8% (2010); Median home value: $125,000 (2010); Median contract rent: n/a per month (2005-2009 est.); Median year structure built: before 1940 (2005-2009 5-year est.).
Transportation: Commute to work: 97.8% car, 0.0% public transportation, 0.0% walk, 2.2% work from home (2005-2009 5-year est.); Travel time to work: 17.8% less than 15 minutes, 61.1% 15 to 30 minutes, 13.3% 30 to 45 minutes, 2.2% 45 to 60 minutes, 5.6% 60 minutes or more (2005-2009 5-year est.)

CROPSEY (unincorporated postal area, zip code 61731). Covers a land area of 19.941 square miles and a water area of 0 square miles. Located at 40.60° N. Lat; 88.49° W. Long. Elevation is 801 feet.
Population: 254 (2000); Race: 100.0% White, 0.0% Black, 0.0% Asian, 0.0% Other, 0.0% Hispanic of any race (2000); Density: 12.7 persons per square mile (2000); Age: 37.1% under 18, 12.9% over 64 (2000); Marriage status: 20.8% never married, 66.9% now married, 12.3% widowed, 0.0% divorced (2000); Foreign born: 0.0% (2000); Ancestry (includes multiple ancestries): 48.7% German, 8.5% English, 7.1% European, 6.3% Irish (2000).
Economy: Employment by occupation: 18.9% management, 6.6% professional, 0.0% services, 0.0% sales, 11.3% farming, 19.8% construction, 43.4% production (2000).
Income: Per capita income: $14,385 (2000); Median household income: $42,625 (2000); Poverty rate: 37.9% (2000).
Education: Percent of population age 25 and over with: High school diploma (including GED) or higher: 72.4% (2000); Bachelor's degree or higher: 8.2% (2000).
Housing: Homeownership rate: 72.2% (2000); Median home value: $62,400 (2000); Median contract rent: $325 per month (2000); Median year structure built: before 1940 (2000).
Transportation: Commute to work: 86.8% car, 0.0% public transportation, 0.0% walk, 13.2% work from home (2000); Travel time to work: 18.5% less

than 15 minutes, 35.9% 15 to 30 minutes, 9.8% 30 to 45 minutes, 35.9% 45 to 60 minutes, 0.0% 60 minutes or more (2000)

DANVERS (village). Covers a land area of 0.864 square miles and a water area of 0 square miles. Located at 40.52° N. Lat; 89.17° W. Long. Elevation is 814 feet.

Population: 1,041 (1990); 1,183 (2000); 1,067 (2010); 1,015 (2015 projected); Race: 97.4% White, 1.2% Black, 0.1% Asian, 1.3% Other, 0.7% Hispanic of any race (2010); Density: 1,234.4 persons per square mile (2010); Average household size: 2.70 (2010); Median age: 34.2 (2010); Males per 100 females: 98.3 (2010); Marriage status: 19.6% never married, 65.8% now married, 7.3% widowed, 7.3% divorced (2005-2009 5-year est.); Foreign born: 2.8% (2005-2009 5-year est.); Ancestry (includes multiple ancestries): 35.9% German, 12.2% Irish, 10.7% English, 8.0% American, 4.7% French (2005-2009 5-year est.).
Economy: Single-family building permits issued: 0 (2010); Multi-family building permits issued: 0 (2010); Employment by occupation: 17.2% management, 19.5% professional, 11.9% services, 24.9% sales, 0.0% farming, 12.1% construction, 14.3% production (2005-2009 5-year est.).
Income: Per capita income: $29,090 (2010); Median household income: $73,801 (2010); Average household income: $78,076 (2010); Percent of households with income of $100,000 or more: 26.3% (2010); Poverty rate: 2.1% (2005-2009 5-year est.).
Taxes: Total city taxes per capita: $123 (2007); City property taxes per capita: $95 (2007).
Education: Percent of population age 25 and over with: High school diploma (including GED) or higher: 95.5% (2010); Bachelor's degree or higher: 24.2% (2010); Master's degree or higher: 6.2% (2010).

School District(s)

Olympia CUSD 16 (PK-12)

   2009-10 Enrollment: 1,911 . . . . (309) 379-6011
Housing: Homeownership rate: 85.8% (2010); Median home value: $138,619 (2010); Median contract rent: $439 per month (2005-2009 5-year est.); Median year structure built: 1955 (2005-2009 5-year est.).
Transportation: Commute to work: 89.6% car, 1.6% public transportation, 1.6% walk, 7.3% work from home (2005-2009 5-year est.); Travel time to work: 21.3% less than 15 minutes, 48.7% 15 to 30 minutes, 21.2% 30 to 45 minutes, 5.4% 45 to 60 minutes, 3.4% 60 minutes or more (2005-2009 5-year est.)

DOWNS (village). Covers a land area of 2.706 square miles and a water area of 0 square miles. Located at 40.39° N. Lat; 88.88° W. Long. Elevation is 804 feet.

Population: 692 (1990); 776 (2000); 816 (2010); 834 (2015 projected); Race: 97.4% White, 1.0% Black, 0.4% Asian, 1.2% Other, 0.5% Hispanic of any race (2010); Density: 301.6 persons per square mile (2010); Average household size: 2.80 (2010); Median age: 36.0 (2010); Males per 100 females: 103.5 (2010); Marriage status: 25.7% never married, 63.3% now married, 3.7% widowed, 7.2% divorced (2005-2009 5-year est.); Foreign born: 0.0% (2005-2009 5-year est.); Ancestry (includes multiple ancestries): 41.5% German, 14.1% American, 10.9% English, 9.3% Irish, 5.5% French (2005-2009 5-year est.).
Economy: Single-family building permits issued: 0 (2010); Multi-family building permits issued: 0 (2010); Employment by occupation: 8.8% management, 23.4% professional, 13.2% services, 30.5% sales, 0.4% farming, 14.5% construction, 9.2% production (2005-2009 5-year est.).
Income: Per capita income: $30,220 (2010); Median household income: $72,994 (2010); Average household income: $84,218 (2010); Percent of households with income of $100,000 or more: 27.5% (2010); Poverty rate: 3.9% (2005-2009 5-year est.).
Taxes: Total city taxes per capita: $381 (2007); City property taxes per capita: $379 (2007).
Education: Percent of population age 25 and over with: High school diploma (including GED) or higher: 94.1% (2010); Bachelor's degree or higher: 31.9% (2010); Master's degree or higher: 6.2% (2010).

School District(s)

Tri Valley CUSD 3 (PK-12)

   2009-10 Enrollment: 1,081 . . . . (309) 378-2351
Housing: Homeownership rate: 89.3% (2010); Median home value: $148,837 (2010); Median contract rent: $675 per month (2005-2009 5-year est.); Median year structure built: 1963 (2005-2009 5-year est.).
Transportation: Commute to work: 93.2% car, 0.0% public transportation, 0.6% walk, 4.6% work from home (2005-2009 5-year est.); Travel time to work: 30.2% less than 15 minutes, 54.2% 15 to 30 minutes, 8.9% 30 to 45

minutes, 2.8% 45 to 60 minutes, 3.9% 60 minutes or more (2005-2009 5-year est.)

ELLSWORTH (village). Covers a land area of 0.237 square miles and a water area of 0 square miles. Located at 40.44° N. Lat; 88.71° W. Long. Elevation is 866 feet.

Population: 224 (1990); 271 (2000); 269 (2010); 268 (2015 projected); Race: 96.3% White, 0.4% Black, 0.4% Asian, 3.0% Other, 0.4% Hispanic of any race (2010); Density: 1,137.2 persons per square mile (2010); Average household size: 2.77 (2010); Median age: 34.0 (2010); Males per 100 females: 102.3 (2010); Marriage status: 34.2% never married, 54.9% now married, 6.5% widowed, 4.3% divorced (2005-2009 5-year est.); Foreign born: 0.0% (2005-2009 5-year est.); Ancestry (includes multiple ancestries): 49.1% German, 15.9% American, 13.1% English, 11.2% Irish, 7.0% Polish (2005-2009 5-year est.).
Economy: Single-family building permits issued: 0 (2010); Multi-family building permits issued: 0 (2010); Employment by occupation: 1.8% management, 19.6% professional, 8.0% services, 35.7% sales, 5.4% farming, 16.1% construction, 13.4% production (2005-2009 5-year est.).
Income: Per capita income: $31,719 (2010); Median household income: $74,432 (2010); Average household income: $89,510 (2010); Percent of households with income of $100,000 or more: 26.8% (2010); Poverty rate: 1.4% (2005-2009 5-year est.).
Taxes: Total city taxes per capita: $78 (2007); City property taxes per capita: $58 (2007).
Education: Percent of population age 25 and over with: High school diploma (including GED) or higher: 95.2% (2010); Bachelor's degree or higher: 24.6% (2010); Master's degree or higher: 6.6% (2010).
Housing: Homeownership rate: 81.4% (2010); Median home value: $134,677 (2010); Median contract rent: $388 per month (2005-2009 5-year est.); Median year structure built: before 1940 (2005-2009 5-year est.).
Transportation: Commute to work: 100.0% car, 0.0% public transportation, 0.0% walk, 0.0% work from home (2005-2009 5-year est.); Travel time to work: 2.9% less than 15 minutes, 36.2% 15 to 30 minutes, 54.3% 30 to 45 minutes, 0.0% 45 to 60 minutes, 6.7% 60 minutes or more (2005-2009 5-year est.)

GRIDLEY (village). Covers a land area of 1.161 square miles and a water area of 0 square miles. Located at 40.74° N. Lat; 88.88° W. Long. Elevation is 755 feet.

History: Gridley was named for Asahel Gridley (1810-1881), a New Yorker who came to Illinois in 1831 and served in the Civil War as a brigadier general.
Population: 1,353 (1990); 1,411 (2000); 1,405 (2010); 1,423 (2015 projected); Race: 97.5% White, 0.3% Black, 0.4% Asian, 1.8% Other, 0.9% Hispanic of any race (2010); Density: 1,210.4 persons per square mile (2010); Average household size: 2.60 (2010); Median age: 35.2 (2010); Males per 100 females: 99.3 (2010); Marriage status: 22.9% never married, 64.6% now married, 6.4% widowed, 6.1% divorced (2005-2009 5-year est.); Foreign born: 1.3% (2005-2009 5-year est.); Ancestry (includes multiple ancestries): 56.0% German, 15.7% English, 15.2% Irish, 10.0% American, 5.5% Swiss (2005-2009 5-year est.).
Economy: Single-family building permits issued: 1 (2010); Multi-family building permits issued: 4 (2010); Employment by occupation: 12.4% management, 20.8% professional, 21.8% services, 22.4% sales, 1.6% farming, 4.9% construction, 16.1% production (2005-2009 5-year est.).
Income: Per capita income: $24,519 (2010); Median household income: $56,690 (2010); Average household income: $63,694 (2010); Percent of households with income of $100,000 or more: 16.7% (2010); Poverty rate: 4.6% (2005-2009 5-year est.).
Taxes: Total city taxes per capita: $122 (2007); City property taxes per capita: $115 (2007).
Education: Percent of population age 25 and over with: High school diploma (including GED) or higher: 91.8% (2010); Bachelor's degree or higher: 25.6% (2010); Master's degree or higher: 6.6% (2010).

School District(s)

El Paso-Gridley CUSD 11 (PK-12)

   2009-10 Enrollment: 1,298 . . . . (309) 527-4410
Housing: Homeownership rate: 79.4% (2010); Median home value: $111,257 (2010); Median contract rent: $507 per month (2005-2009 5-year est.); Median year structure built: 1961 (2005-2009 5-year est.).
Newspapers: Gridley Village Times (Local news)
Transportation: Commute to work: 90.1% car, 0.7% public transportation, 5.3% walk, 2.0% work from home (2005-2009 5-year est.); Travel time to work: 36.2% less than 15 minutes, 21.0% 15 to 30 minutes, 28.9% 30 to 45

minutes, 6.4% 45 to 60 minutes, 7.5% 60 minutes or more (2005-2009 5-year est.)

HEYWORTH (village). Covers a land area of 1.545 square miles and a water area of 0 square miles. Located at 40.31° N. Lat; 88.97° W. Long. Elevation is 755 feet.
Population: 1,703 (1990); 2,431 (2000); 2,564 (2010); 2,643 (2015 projected); Race: 96.9% White, 0.2% Black, 0.6% Asian, 2.3% Other, 1.2% Hispanic of any race (2010); Density: 1,659.7 persons per square mile (2010); Average household size: 2.68 (2010); Median age: 32.4 (2010); Males per 100 females: 97.1 (2010); Marriage status: 18.5% never married, 67.5% now married, 3.5% widowed, 10.5% divorced (2005-2009 5-year est.); Foreign born: 0.9% (2005-2009 5-year est.); Ancestry (includes multiple ancestries): 35.2% German, 17.0% American, 13.5% Irish, 10.6% English, 4.6% Scottish (2005-2009 5-year est.).
Economy: Single-family building permits issued: 5 (2010); Multi-family building permits issued: 2 (2010); Employment by occupation: 17.6% management, 15.7% professional, 13.3% services, 26.3% sales, 0.0% farming, 11.6% construction, 15.5% production (2005-2009 5-year est.).
Income: Per capita income: $27,435 (2010); Median household income: $65,506 (2010); Average household income: $73,091 (2010); Percent of households with income of $100,000 or more: 21.5% (2010); Poverty rate: 11.7% (2005-2009 5-year est.).
Taxes: Total city taxes per capita: $721 (2007); City property taxes per capita: $663 (2007).
Education: Percent of population age 25 and over with: High school diploma (including GED) or higher: 90.9% (2010); Bachelor's degree or higher: 20.8% (2010); Master's degree or higher: 3.9% (2010).
School District(s)
Heyworth CUSD 4 (PK-12)
    2009-10 Enrollment: 952 . . . . (309) 473-3727
Housing: Homeownership rate: 83.5% (2010); Median home value: $133,956 (2010); Median contract rent: $388 per month (2005-2009 5-year est.); Median year structure built: 1969 (2005-2009 5-year est.).
Newspapers: Heyworth Star (Community news; Circulation 1,150)
Transportation: Commute to work: 93.3% car, 0.0% public transportation, 3.4% walk, 2.5% work from home (2005-2009 5-year est.); Travel time to work: 22.4% less than 15 minutes, 56.8% 15 to 30 minutes, 12.9% 30 to 45 minutes, 5.6% 45 to 60 minutes, 2.3% 60 minutes or more (2005-2009 5-year est.)

HUDSON (village). Covers a land area of 0.665 square miles and a water area of 0 square miles. Located at 40.60° N. Lat; 88.98° W. Long. Elevation is 768 feet.
History: Hudson was settled in 1836 by a group of New Yorkers called the Hudson Colony.
Population: 1,097 (1990); 1,510 (2000); 1,424 (2010); 1,529 (2015 projected); Race: 98.0% White, 0.1% Black, 0.5% Asian, 1.5% Other, 1.5% Hispanic of any race (2010); Density: 2,142.7 persons per square mile (2010); Average household size: 2.96 (2010); Median age: 33.6 (2010); Males per 100 females: 96.7 (2010); Marriage status: 17.8% never married, 73.1% now married, 2.2% widowed, 7.0% divorced (2005-2009 5-year est.); Foreign born: 1.4% (2005-2009 5-year est.); Ancestry (includes multiple ancestries): 34.4% German, 19.2% Irish, 12.3% English, 8.9% American, 4.7% French (2005-2009 5-year est.).
Economy: Single-family building permits issued: 0 (2010); Multi-family building permits issued: 0 (2010); Employment by occupation: 14.7% management, 26.0% professional, 11.8% services, 28.3% sales, 0.6% farming, 10.4% construction, 8.2% production (2005-2009 5-year est.).
Income: Per capita income: $28,514 (2010); Median household income: $78,312 (2010); Average household income: $83,508 (2010); Percent of households with income of $100,000 or more: 28.9% (2010); Poverty rate: 5.7% (2005-2009 5-year est.).
Taxes: Total city taxes per capita: $121 (2007); City property taxes per capita: $37 (2007).
Education: Percent of population age 25 and over with: High school diploma (including GED) or higher: 95.4% (2010); Bachelor's degree or higher: 32.2% (2010); Master's degree or higher: 6.9% (2010).
School District(s)
Mclean County USD 5 (PK-12)
    2009-10 Enrollment: 12,976 . . . . (309) 888-6970
Housing: Homeownership rate: 92.3% (2010); Median home value: $140,107 (2010); Median contract rent: $400 per month (2005-2009 5-year est.); Median year structure built: 1983 (2005-2009 5-year est.).

Transportation: Commute to work: 96.3% car, 0.0% public transportation, 0.5% walk, 1.9% work from home (2005-2009 5-year est.); Travel time to work: 21.0% less than 15 minutes, 63.2% 15 to 30 minutes, 11.0% 30 to 45 minutes, 3.3% 45 to 60 minutes, 1.5% 60 minutes or more (2005-2009 5-year est.)

LE ROY (city). Aka Leroy. Covers a land area of 2.221 square miles and a water area of 0.016 square miles. Located at 40.34° N. Lat; 88.76° W. Long. Elevation is 791 feet.
History: Incorporated 1857.
Population: 2,980 (1990); 3,332 (2000); 3,582 (2010); 3,720 (2015 projected); Race: 98.3% White, 0.4% Black, 0.1% Asian, 1.2% Other, 1.9% Hispanic of any race (2010); Density: 1,612.9 persons per square mile (2010); Average household size: 2.53 (2010); Median age: 36.6 (2010); Males per 100 females: 96.2 (2010); Marriage status: 21.1% never married, 64.3% now married, 5.2% widowed, 9.4% divorced (2005-2009 5-year est.); Foreign born: 0.5% (2005-2009 5-year est.); Ancestry (includes multiple ancestries): 40.7% German, 22.6% Irish, 12.5% American, 11.5% English, 4.4% Scotch-Irish (2005-2009 5-year est.).
Economy: Single-family building permits issued: 6 (2010); Multi-family building permits issued: 0 (2010); Employment by occupation: 14.2% management, 17.5% professional, 18.7% services, 33.4% sales, 0.0% farming, 7.9% construction, 8.4% production (2005-2009 5-year est.).
Income: Per capita income: $25,749 (2010); Median household income: $58,710 (2010); Average household income: $66,023 (2010); Percent of households with income of $100,000 or more: 16.9% (2010); Poverty rate: 5.5% (2005-2009 5-year est.).
Taxes: Total city taxes per capita: $317 (2007); City property taxes per capita: $259 (2007).
Education: Percent of population age 25 and over with: High school diploma (including GED) or higher: 92.0% (2010); Bachelor's degree or higher: 22.6% (2010); Master's degree or higher: 5.5% (2010).
School District(s)
Leroy CUSD 2 (PK-12)
    2009-10 Enrollment: 837 . . . . (309) 962-4211
Housing: Homeownership rate: 78.6% (2010); Median home value: $132,776 (2010); Median contract rent: $485 per month (2005-2009 5-year est.); Median year structure built: 1971 (2005-2009 5-year est.).
Safety: Violent crime rate: 16.9 per 10,000 population; Property crime rate: 208.4 per 10,000 population (2010).
Newspapers: Le Roy Journal (Local news; Circulation 3,050)
Transportation: Commute to work: 90.6% car, 0.0% public transportation, 3.9% walk, 3.5% work from home (2005-2009 5-year est.); Travel time to work: 27.6% less than 15 minutes, 40.8% 15 to 30 minutes, 27.4% 30 to 45 minutes, 3.7% 45 to 60 minutes, 0.5% 60 minutes or more (2005-2009 5-year est.)
Additional Information Contacts
LeRoy Business Development Group . . . . (309) 962-2030
    http://www.leroybiz.org

LEXINGTON (city). Covers a land area of 1.050 square miles and a water area of 0 square miles. Located at 40.64° N. Lat; 88.78° W. Long. Elevation is 751 feet.
History: Lexington was settled in 1828 and named for the battlefield in Massachusetts. The town developed along the Chicago & Mississippi Railroad as a produce center.
Population: 1,900 (1990); 1,912 (2000); 1,909 (2010); 1,913 (2015 projected); Race: 98.5% White, 0.2% Black, 0.1% Asian, 1.3% Other, 0.8% Hispanic of any race (2010); Density: 1,817.4 persons per square mile (2010); Average household size: 2.48 (2010); Median age: 37.8 (2010); Males per 100 females: 95.8 (2010); Marriage status: 22.1% never married, 62.6% now married, 7.5% widowed, 7.8% divorced (2005-2009 5-year est.); Foreign born: 0.8% (2005-2009 5-year est.); Ancestry (includes multiple ancestries): 36.8% German, 17.4% American, 15.2% Irish, 11.4% English, 3.6% Swedish (2005-2009 5-year est.).
Economy: Single-family building permits issued: 2 (2010); Multi-family building permits issued: 0 (2010); Employment by occupation: 14.5% management, 16.6% professional, 13.5% services, 31.4% sales, 1.3% farming, 12.0% construction, 10.6% production (2005-2009 5-year est.).
Income: Per capita income: $24,055 (2010); Median household income: $50,345 (2010); Average household income: $59,852 (2010); Percent of households with income of $100,000 or more: 14.3% (2010); Poverty rate: 5.6% (2005-2009 5-year est.).
Taxes: Total city taxes per capita: $253 (2007); City property taxes per capita: $236 (2007).

Education: Percent of population age 25 and over with: High school diploma (including GED) or higher: 92.7% (2010); Bachelor's degree or higher: 22.8% (2010); Master's degree or higher: 4.9% (2010).

School District(s)

Lexington CUSD 7 (PK-12)
   2009-10 Enrollment: 540 . . . . (309) 365-4141
Housing: Homeownership rate: 80.7% (2010); Median home value: $133,333 (2010); Median contract rent: $488 per month (2005-2009 5-year est.); Median year structure built: 1967 (2005-2009 5-year est.).
Newspapers: Lexingtonian (Local news; Circulation 700)
Transportation: Commute to work: 89.3% car, 0.0% public transportation, 3.5% walk, 4.5% work from home (2005-2009 5-year est.); Travel time to work: 23.1% less than 15 minutes, 47.5% 15 to 30 minutes, 25.6% 30 to 45 minutes, 0.9% 45 to 60 minutes, 2.9% 60 minutes or more (2005-2009 5-year est.)

MCLEAN (village).
Covers a land area of 0.431 square miles and a water area of 0 square miles. Located at 40.31° N. Lat; 89.17° W. Long. Elevation is 709 feet.
Population: 797 (1990); 808 (2000); 763 (2010); 745 (2015 projected); Race: 96.3% White, 1.0% Black, 1.6% Asian, 1.0% Other, 0.0% Hispanic of any race (2010); Density: 1,769.7 persons per square mile (2010); Average household size: 2.50 (2010); Median age: 36.4 (2010); Males per 100 females: 90.8 (2010); Marriage status: 28.2% never married, 59.8% now married, 4.6% widowed, 7.5% divorced (2005-2009 5-year est.); Foreign born: 1.1% (2005-2009 5-year est.); Ancestry (includes multiple ancestries): 31.9% German, 14.4% American, 11.5% Irish, 11.3% English, 5.4% Scottish (2005-2009 5-year est.).
Economy: Single-family building permits issued: 0 (2010); Multi-family building permits issued: 0 (2010); Employment by occupation: 6.6% management, 10.2% professional, 17.0% services, 34.3% sales, 0.0% farming, 16.1% construction, 15.7% production (2005-2009 5-year est.).
Income: Per capita income: $22,456 (2010); Median household income: $54,127 (2010); Average household income: $56,115 (2010); Percent of households with income of $100,000 or more: 6.9% (2010); Poverty rate: 2.4% (2005-2009 5-year est.).
Taxes: Total city taxes per capita: $68 (2007); City property taxes per capita: $55 (2007).
Education: Percent of population age 25 and over with: High school diploma (including GED) or higher: 88.7% (2010); Bachelor's degree or higher: 11.1% (2010); Master's degree or higher: 3.1% (2010).
Housing: Homeownership rate: 88.2% (2010); Median home value: $100,714 (2010); Median contract rent: $507 per month (2005-2009 5-year est.); Median year structure built: 1953 (2005-2009 5-year est.).
Safety: Violent crime rate: 0.0 per 10,000 population; Property crime rate: 63.3 per 10,000 population (2010).
Transportation: Commute to work: 91.4% car, 0.0% public transportation, 5.3% walk, 2.6% work from home (2005-2009 5-year est.); Travel time to work: 25.2% less than 15 minutes, 47.1% 15 to 30 minutes, 16.7% 30 to 45 minutes, 1.9% 45 to 60 minutes, 9.0% 60 minutes or more (2005-2009 5-year est.)

NORMAL (town).
Covers a land area of 13.619 square miles and a water area of 0.062 square miles. Located at 40.51° N. Lat; 88.98° W. Long. Elevation is 801 feet.
History: Normal began as North Bloomington, but soon changed its name to Normal when the Illinois State Normal University was founded here in 1857.
Population: 40,139 (1990); 45,386 (2000); 50,021 (2010); 51,999 (2015 projected); Race: 84.7% White, 9.4% Black, 2.6% Asian, 3.3% Other, 3.5% Hispanic of any race (2010); Density: 3,672.9 persons per square mile (2010); Average household size: 2.39 (2010); Median age: 25.0 (2010); Males per 100 females: 90.1 (2010); Marriage status: 56.6% never married, 34.2% now married, 3.2% widowed, 6.0% divorced (2005-2009 5-year est.); Foreign born: 3.7% (2005-2009 5-year est.); Ancestry (includes multiple ancestries): 33.7% German, 17.0% Irish, 9.4% English, 7.5% American, 6.7% Italian (2005-2009 5-year est.).
Economy: Unemployment rate: 7.4% (August 2011); Total civilian labor force: 27,947 (August 2011); Single-family building permits issued: 80 (2010); Multi-family building permits issued: 97 (2010); Employment by occupation: 13.2% management, 23.1% professional, 19.9% services, 32.7% sales, 0.0% farming, 4.3% construction, 6.9% production (2005-2009 5-year est.).
Income: Per capita income: $21,362 (2010); Median household income: $47,617 (2010); Average household income: $59,632 (2010); Percent of

households with income of $100,000 or more: 15.7% (2010); Poverty rate: 24.8% (2005-2009 5-year est.).
Taxes: Total city taxes per capita: $465 (2007); City property taxes per capita: $146 (2007).
Education: Percent of population age 25 and over with: High school diploma (including GED) or higher: 95.5% (2010); Bachelor's degree or higher: 44.3% (2010); Master's degree or higher: 14.5% (2010).

School District(s)

Mclean County USD 5 (PK-12)
   2009-10 Enrollment: 12,976 . . . . (309) 888-6970

Four-year College(s)

Illinois State University (Public)
   Fall 2009 Enrollment: 21,184. . . . . (309) 438-2111
   2010-11 Tuition: In-state $11,417; Out-of-state $17,957

Two-year College(s)

Heartland Community College (Public)
   Fall 2009 Enrollment: 5,266. . . . . (309) 268-8000
   2010-11 Tuition: In-state $6,690; Out-of-state $9,930
Housing: Homeownership rate: 56.3% (2010); Median home value: $143,985 (2010); Median contract rent: $605 per month (2005-2009 5-year est.); Median year structure built: 1981 (2005-2009 5-year est.).
Hospitals: Bromenn Healthcare
Safety: Violent crime rate: 27.5 per 10,000 population; Property crime rate: 282.4 per 10,000 population (2010).
Newspapers: Normalite (Community news; Circulation 12,500)
Transportation: Commute to work: 82.9% car, 1.8% public transportation, 11.7% walk, 2.1% work from home (2005-2009 5-year est.); Travel time to work: 54.9% less than 15 minutes, 33.3% 15 to 30 minutes, 5.2% 30 to 45 minutes, 3.0% 45 to 60 minutes, 3.6% 60 minutes or more (2005-2009 5-year est.); Amtrak: train service available.
Airports: Central IL Regional Airport at Bloomington-Normal (primary service)
Additional Information Contacts
Town of Normal . . . . (309) 454-2444
   http://www.normal.org

SAYBROOK (village).
Covers a land area of 0.792 square miles and a water area of 0.027 square miles. Located at 40.42° N. Lat; 88.52° W. Long. Elevation is 801 feet.
Population: 767 (1990); 764 (2000); 754 (2010); 748 (2015 projected); Race: 98.8% White, 0.1% Black, 0.0% Asian, 1.1% Other, 0.3% Hispanic of any race (2010); Density: 951.7 persons per square mile (2010); Average household size: 2.41 (2010); Median age: 38.7 (2010); Males per 100 females: 93.3 (2010); Marriage status: 20.9% never married, 57.2% now married, 8.6% widowed, 13.3% divorced (2005-2009 5-year est.); Foreign born: 1.1% (2005-2009 5-year est.); Ancestry (includes multiple ancestries): 32.4% German, 31.0% American, 15.6% Irish, 8.0% English, 4.2% Polish (2005-2009 5-year est.).
Economy: Single-family building permits issued: 0 (2010); Multi-family building permits issued: 0 (2010); Employment by occupation: 5.2% management, 6.4% professional, 20.2% services, 29.8% sales, 2.0% farming, 17.9% construction, 18.5% production (2005-2009 5-year est.).
Income: Per capita income: $22,196 (2010); Median household income: $50,931 (2010); Average household income: $52,867 (2010); Percent of households with income of $100,000 or more: 7.0% (2010); Poverty rate: 4.0% (2005-2009 5-year est.).
Taxes: Total city taxes per capita: $53 (2007); City property taxes per capita: $45 (2007).
Education: Percent of population age 25 and over with: High school diploma (including GED) or higher: 91.3% (2010); Bachelor's degree or higher: 8.5% (2010); Master's degree or higher: 2.6% (2010).
Housing: Homeownership rate: 76.7% (2010); Median home value: $105,000 (2010); Median contract rent: $335 per month (2005-2009 5-year est.); Median year structure built: 1954 (2005-2009 5-year est.).
Transportation: Commute to work: 90.3% car, 0.0% public transportation, 2.4% walk, 6.5% work from home (2005-2009 5-year est.); Travel time to work: 35.8% less than 15 minutes, 22.3% 15 to 30 minutes, 22.3% 30 to 45 minutes, 13.2% 45 to 60 minutes, 6.3% 60 minutes or more (2005-2009 5-year est.)

SHIRLEY (unincorporated postal area, zip code 61772).
Covers a land area of 24.352 square miles and a water area of 0 square miles. Located at 40.40° N. Lat; 89.06° W. Long. Elevation is 764 feet.
Population: 388 (2000); Race: 94.9% White, 0.0% Black, 2.0% Asian, 3.1% Other, 3.1% Hispanic of any race (2000); Density: 15.9 persons per

square mile (2000); Age: 14.8% under 18, 14.5% over 64 (2000); Marriage status: 18.4% never married, 60.5% now married, 8.2% widowed, 12.8% divorced (2000); Foreign born: 2.0% (2000); Ancestry (includes multiple ancestries): 30.7% German, 23.6% American, 11.1% English, 6.3% Italian (2000).
Economy: Employment by occupation: 4.7% management, 16.8% professional, 23.7% services, 16.8% sales, 0.0% farming, 13.2% construction, 24.7% production (2000).
Income: Per capita income: $28,002 (2000); Median household income: $67,917 (2000); Poverty rate: 4.8% (2000).
Education: Percent of population age 25 and over with: High school diploma (including GED) or higher: 93.0% (2000); Bachelor's degree or higher: 22.4% (2000).
Housing: Homeownership rate: 85.2% (2000); Median home value: $80,800 (2000); Median contract rent: $425 per month (2000); Median year structure built: 1961 (2000).
Transportation: Commute to work: 97.4% car, 0.0% public transportation, 2.6% walk, 0.0% work from home (2000); Travel time to work: 11.1% less than 15 minutes, 75.8% 15 to 30 minutes, 3.2% 30 to 45 minutes, 10.0% 45 to 60 minutes, 0.0% 60 minutes or more (2000)

STANFORD (village).
Covers a land area of 0.383 square miles and a water area of 0 square miles. Located at 40.43° N. Lat; 89.22° W. Long. Elevation is 679 feet.
Population: 615 (1990); 670 (2000); 651 (2010); 645 (2015 projected); Race: 97.8% White, 0.0% Black, 0.0% Asian, 2.2% Other, 1.7% Hispanic of any race (2010); Density: 1,700.2 persons per square mile (2010); Average household size: 2.76 (2010); Median age: 31.9 (2010); Males per 100 females: 99.1 (2010); Marriage status: 29.9% never married, 51.6% now married, 6.2% widowed, 12.3% divorced (2005-2009 5-year est.); Foreign born: 0.0% (2005-2009 5-year est.); Ancestry (includes multiple ancestries): 32.7% American, 28.9% German, 10.7% English, 8.2% Irish, 1.8% Scotch-Irish (2005-2009 5-year est.).
Economy: Single-family building permits issued: 0 (2010); Multi-family building permits issued: 0 (2010); Employment by occupation: 6.9% management, 21.1% professional, 14.1% services, 28.8% sales, 0.0% farming, 6.6% construction, 22.4% production (2005-2009 5-year est.).
Income: Per capita income: $25,086 (2010); Median household income: $61,429 (2010); Average household income: $68,517 (2010); Percent of households with income of $100,000 or more: 15.7% (2010); Poverty rate: 26.0% (2005-2009 5-year est.).
Taxes: Total city taxes per capita: $161 (2007); City property taxes per capita: $90 (2007).
Education: Percent of population age 25 and over with: High school diploma (including GED) or higher: 91.3% (2010); Bachelor's degree or higher: 17.3% (2010); Master's degree or higher: 3.1% (2010).
School District(s)
Olympia CUSD 16 (PK-12)
    2009-10 Enrollment: 1,911 . . . . (309) 379-6011
Housing: Homeownership rate: 82.6% (2010); Median home value: $105,682 (2010); Median contract rent: $535 per month (2005-2009 5-year est.); Median year structure built: 1941 (2005-2009 5-year est.).
Transportation: Commute to work: 95.5% car, 0.0% public transportation, 0.0% walk, 2.5% work from home (2005-2009 5-year est.); Travel time to work: 10.3% less than 15 minutes, 51.7% 15 to 30 minutes, 31.3% 30 to 45 minutes, 3.4% 45 to 60 minutes, 3.2% 60 minutes or more (2005-2009 5-year est.)

TOWANDA (village).
Covers a land area of 0.695 square miles and a water area of 0 square miles. Located at 40.56° N. Lat; 88.89° W. Long. Elevation is 781 feet.
History: The first settler in Towanda was John Smith, who built a home in 1826 at Smith's Grove. The town of Towanda was laid out in 1854 when the railroad reached the community. The name is of Indian origin and means "where we bury our dead."
Population: 858 (1990); 493 (2000); 509 (2010); 520 (2015 projected); Race: 98.0% White, 0.4% Black, 0.6% Asian, 1.0% Other, 0.6% Hispanic of any race (2010); Density: 732.0 persons per square mile (2010); Average household size: 2.53 (2010); Median age: 39.4 (2010); Males per 100 females: 97.3 (2010); Marriage status: 30.3% never married, 54.4% now married, 6.6% widowed, 8.8% divorced (2005-2009 5-year est.); Foreign born: 0.0% (2005-2009 5-year est.); Ancestry (includes multiple ancestries): 30.9% German, 25.0% American, 16.5% English, 10.0% Irish, 6.0% Italian (2005-2009 5-year est.).

Economy: Single-family building permits issued: 0 (2010); Multi-family building permits issued: 0 (2010); Employment by occupation: 2.1% management, 11.9% professional, 10.6% services, 38.2% sales, 0.0% farming, 18.2% construction, 19.0% production (2005-2009 5-year est.).
Income: Per capita income: $29,414 (2010); Median household income: $68,155 (2010); Average household income: $75,659 (2010); Percent of households with income of $100,000 or more: 22.4% (2010); Poverty rate: 8.3% (2005-2009 5-year est.).
Taxes: Total city taxes per capita: $219 (2007); City property taxes per capita: $125 (2007).
Education: Percent of population age 25 and over with: High school diploma (including GED) or higher: 95.4% (2010); Bachelor's degree or higher: 25.7% (2010); Master's degree or higher: 5.7% (2010).
School District(s)
Mclean County USD 5 (PK-12)
    2009-10 Enrollment: 12,976 . . . . (309) 888-6970
Housing: Homeownership rate: 86.6% (2010); Median home value: $123,718 (2010); Median contract rent: $447 per month (2005-2009 5-year est.); Median year structure built: 1963 (2005-2009 5-year est.).
Transportation: Commute to work: 93.9% car, 0.0% public transportation, 3.2% walk, 2.9% work from home (2005-2009 5-year est.); Travel time to work: 33.8% less than 15 minutes, 48.4% 15 to 30 minutes, 0.8% 30 to 45 minutes, 6.6% 45 to 60 minutes, 10.4% 60 minutes or more (2005-2009 5-year est.)

Menard County

Located in central Illinois; drained by the Sangamon River and Salt Creek. Covers a land area of 314.25 square miles, a water area of 1.13 square miles, and is located in the Central Time Zone at 40.03° N. Lat., 89.81° W. Long. The county was founded in 1839. County seat is Petersburg.

Menard County is part of the Springfield, IL Metropolitan Statistical Area. The entire metro area includes: Menard County, IL; Sangamon County, IL

Population: 11,164 (1990); 12,486 (2000); 12,482 (2010); 12,419 (2015 projected); Race: 97.7% White, 1.1% Black, 0.2% Asian, 1.1% Other, 1.2% Hispanic of any race (2010); Density: 39.7 persons per square mile (2010); Average household size: 2.48 (2010); Median age: 40.6 (2010); Males per 100 females: 96.8 (2010).
Religion: Five largest groups: 11.4% Catholic Church, 10.7% Christian Churches and Churches of Christ, 8.4% Southern Baptist Convention, 6.2% Presbyterian Church (U.S.A.), 6.2% The United Methodist Church (2000).
Economy: Unemployment rate: 7.4% (August 2011); Total civilian labor force: 7,253 (August 2011); Leading industries: 22.4% retail trade; 11.9% accommodation & food services; 9.1% other services (except public administration) (2009); Farms: 411 totaling 168,594 acres (2007); Companies that employ 500 or more persons: 0 (2009); Companies that employ 100 to 499 persons: 0 (2009); Companies that employ less than 100 persons: 229 (2009); Black-owned businesses: n/a (2007); Hispanic-owned businesses: n/a (2007); Asian-owned businesses: n/a (2007); Women-owned businesses: n/a (2007); Retail sales per capita: $6,675 (2010). Single-family building permits issued: 9 (2010); Multi-family building permits issued: 0 (2010).
Income: Per capita income: $27,047 (2010); Median household income: $56,691 (2010); Average household income: $67,431 (2010); Percent of households with income of $100,000 or more: 17.1% (2010); Poverty rate: 9.3% (2009); Bankruptcy rate: 4.95% (2010).
Taxes: Total county taxes per capita: $248 (2007); County property taxes per capita: $219 (2007).
Education: Percent of population age 25 and over with: High school diploma (including GED) or higher: 91.9% (2010); Bachelor's degree or higher: 24.3% (2010); Master's degree or higher: 6.6% (2010).
Housing: Homeownership rate: 77.8% (2010); Median home value: $119,716 (2010); Median contract rent: $374 per month (2005-2009 5-year est.); Median year structure built: 1971 (2005-2009 5-year est.).
Health: Birth rate: 114.7 per 10,000 population (2009); Death rate: 112.3 per 10,000 population (2009); Age-adjusted cancer mortality rate: 186.1 deaths per 100,000 population (2007); Number of physicians: 5.6 per 10,000 population (2008); Hospital beds: 0.0 per 10,000 population (2007); Hospital admissions: 0.0 per 10,000 population (2007).
Elections: 2008 Presidential election results: 41.9% Obama, 56.8% McCain, 0.5% Nader
National and State Parks: Lincolns New Salem State Park
Additional Information Contacts

Menard County Government . . . . (217) 632-2415
   http://menardcountyil.com
Petersburg Chamber of Commerce . . . . (217) 632-7363
   http://www.petersburgilchamber.com

Menard County Communities

ATHENS (city). Covers a land area of 1.468 square miles and a water area of 0 square miles. Located at 39.96° N. Lat; 89.72° W. Long. Elevation is 600 feet.
History: Incorporated 1892.
Population: 1,570 (1990); 1,726 (2000); 1,813 (2010); 1,839 (2015 projected); Race: 97.6% White, 0.9% Black, 0.2% Asian, 1.3% Other, 1.9% Hispanic of any race (2010); Density: 1,234.7 persons per square mile (2010); Average household size: 2.47 (2010); Median age: 37.7 (2010); Males per 100 females: 92.5 (2010); Marriage status: 15.4% never married, 65.8% now married, 5.6% widowed, 13.2% divorced (2005-2009 5-year est.); Foreign born: 0.5% (2005-2009 5-year est.); Ancestry (includes multiple ancestries): 39.4% German, 16.4% American, 16.0% Irish, 11.0% English, 4.2% Scottish (2005-2009 5-year est.).
Economy: Single-family building permits issued: 1 (2010); Multi-family building permits issued: 0 (2010); Employment by occupation: 10.6% management, 22.4% professional, 12.3% services, 34.2% sales, 0.0% farming, 13.4% construction, 7.2% production (2005-2009 5-year est.).
Income: Per capita income: $25,341 (2010); Median household income: $55,104 (2010); Average household income: $62,163 (2010); Percent of households with income of $100,000 or more: 16.5% (2010); Poverty rate: 7.4% (2005-2009 5-year est.).
Taxes: Total city taxes per capita: $79 (2007); City property taxes per capita: $66 (2007).
Education: Percent of population age 25 and over with: High school diploma (including GED) or higher: 92.7% (2010); Bachelor's degree or higher: 19.1% (2010); Master's degree or higher: 6.7% (2010).
School District(s)
Athens CUSD 213 (PK-12)
   2009-10 Enrollment: 1,155 . . . . (217) 636-8761
Logan/Mason/Menard Roe (06-12)
   2009-10 Enrollment: n/a . . . . (217) 732-8388
Housing: Homeownership rate: 78.6% (2010); Median home value: $118,041 (2010); Median contract rent: $410 per month (2005-2009 5-year est.); Median year structure built: 1970 (2005-2009 5-year est.).
Transportation: Commute to work: 90.6% car, 0.0% public transportation, 1.1% walk, 7.3% work from home (2005-2009 5-year est.); Travel time to work: 11.6% less than 15 minutes, 37.3% 15 to 30 minutes, 37.0% 30 to 45 minutes, 6.9% 45 to 60 minutes, 7.2% 60 minutes or more (2005-2009 5-year est.)

GREENVIEW (village). Covers a land area of 0.850 square miles and a water area of 0 square miles. Located at 40.08° N. Lat; 89.74° W. Long. Elevation is 541 feet.
Population: 861 (1990); 862 (2000); 857 (2010); 853 (2015 projected); Race: 99.4% White, 0.4% Black, 0.2% Asian, 0.0% Other, 0.1% Hispanic of any race (2010); Density: 1,008.3 persons per square mile (2010); Average household size: 2.33 (2010); Median age: 38.5 (2010); Males per 100 females: 101.2 (2010); Marriage status: 27.1% never married, 58.9% now married, 4.5% widowed, 9.5% divorced (2005-2009 5-year est.); Foreign born: 0.0% (2005-2009 5-year est.); Ancestry (includes multiple ancestries): 34.8% German, 25.5% American, 14.5% English, 12.6% Irish, 4.9% Dutch (2005-2009 5-year est.).
Economy: Single-family building permits issued: 0 (2010); Multi-family building permits issued: 0 (2010); Employment by occupation: 10.1% management, 12.4% professional, 17.5% services, 38.4% sales, 2.2% farming, 11.5% construction, 7.9% production (2005-2009 5-year est.).
Income: Per capita income: $26,385 (2010); Median household income: $50,000 (2010); Average household income: $61,556 (2010); Percent of households with income of $100,000 or more: 13.0% (2010); Poverty rate: 5.3% (2005-2009 5-year est.).
Taxes: Total city taxes per capita: $38 (2007); City property taxes per capita: $32 (2007).
Education: Percent of population age 25 and over with: High school diploma (including GED) or higher: 88.7% (2010); Bachelor's degree or higher: 21.0% (2010); Master's degree or higher: 4.0% (2010).
School District(s)
Greenview CUSD 200 (KG-12)
   2009-10 Enrollment: 229 . . . . (217) 968-2295

Housing: Homeownership rate: 74.7% (2010); Median home value: $84,182 (2010); Median contract rent: $478 per month (2005-2009 5-year est.); Median year structure built: 1951 (2005-2009 5-year est.).
Transportation: Commute to work: 90.7% car, 0.0% public transportation, 6.8% walk, 2.5% work from home (2005-2009 5-year est.); Travel time to work: 17.4% less than 15 minutes, 30.4% 15 to 30 minutes, 40.8% 30 to 45 minutes, 5.3% 45 to 60 minutes, 6.0% 60 minutes or more (2005-2009 5-year est.)

OAKFORD (village). Covers a land area of 0.247 square miles and a water area of 0 square miles. Located at 40.10° N. Lat; 89.96° W. Long. Elevation is 495 feet.
Population: 246 (1990); 309 (2000); 288 (2010); 279 (2015 projected); Race: 98.3% White, 0.3% Black, 0.0% Asian, 1.4% Other, 1.4% Hispanic of any race (2010); Density: 1,164.4 persons per square mile (2010); Average household size: 2.44 (2010); Median age: 39.8 (2010); Males per 100 females: 105.7 (2010); Marriage status: 16.4% never married, 53.4% now married, 18.5% widowed, 11.6% divorced (2005-2009 5-year est.); Foreign born: 0.0% (2005-2009 5-year est.); Ancestry (includes multiple ancestries): 40.9% German, 23.6% English, 20.4% Irish, 12.4% Dutch, 12.4% American (2005-2009 5-year est.).
Economy: Employment by occupation: 4.7% management, 13.3% professional, 30.5% services, 16.4% sales, 0.8% farming, 2.3% construction, 32.0% production (2005-2009 5-year est.).
Income: Per capita income: $23,835 (2010); Median household income: $45,556 (2010); Average household income: $59,110 (2010); Percent of households with income of $100,000 or more: 9.3% (2010); Poverty rate: 9.9% (2005-2009 5-year est.).
Taxes: Total city taxes per capita: $17 (2007); City property taxes per capita: $17 (2007).
Education: Percent of population age 25 and over with: High school diploma (including GED) or higher: 91.1% (2010); Bachelor's degree or higher: 13.9% (2010); Master's degree or higher: 5.0% (2010).
Housing: Homeownership rate: 77.1% (2010); Median home value: $72,917 (2010); Median contract rent: $309 per month (2005-2009 5-year est.); Median year structure built: before 1940 (2005-2009 5-year est.).
Transportation: Commute to work: 91.6% car, 0.0% public transportation, 0.0% walk, 2.5% work from home (2005-2009 5-year est.); Travel time to work: 36.2% less than 15 minutes, 46.6% 15 to 30 minutes, 2.6% 30 to 45 minutes, 12.1% 45 to 60 minutes, 2.6% 60 minutes or more (2005-2009 5-year est.)

PETERSBURG (city). County seat. Covers a land area of 1.348 square miles and a water area of 0 square miles. Located at 40.01° N. Lat; 89.85° W. Long. Elevation is 512 feet.
History: Founded c.1836, incorporated 1841. Ann Rutledge's grave is here. Lincoln's New Salem (State Historic Site) is South.
Population: 2,354 (1990); 2,299 (2000); 2,213 (2010); 2,151 (2015 projected); Race: 95.7% White, 2.8% Black, 0.2% Asian, 1.4% Other, 1.4% Hispanic of any race (2010); Density: 1,641.8 persons per square mile (2010); Average household size: 2.21 (2010); Median age: 40.3 (2010); Males per 100 females: 86.6 (2010); Marriage status: 22.0% never married, 51.1% now married, 11.6% widowed, 15.3% divorced (2005-2009 5-year est.); Foreign born: 0.6% (2005-2009 5-year est.); Ancestry (includes multiple ancestries): 28.5% German, 23.8% American, 12.2% English, 11.8% Irish, 4.7% Scottish (2005-2009 5-year est.).
Economy: Single-family building permits issued: 3 (2010); Multi-family building permits issued: 0 (2010); Employment by occupation: 10.0% management, 26.5% professional, 23.7% services, 28.2% sales, 0.0% farming, 7.6% construction, 4.0% production (2005-2009 5-year est.).
Income: Per capita income: $23,729 (2010); Median household income: $44,220 (2010); Average household income: $54,065 (2010); Percent of households with income of $100,000 or more: 8.7% (2010); Poverty rate: 15.8% (2005-2009 5-year est.).
Taxes: Total city taxes per capita: $142 (2007); City property taxes per capita: $130 (2007).
Education: Percent of population age 25 and over with: High school diploma (including GED) or higher: 89.6% (2010); Bachelor's degree or higher: 24.6% (2010); Master's degree or higher: 4.4% (2010).
School District(s)
Porta CUSD 202 (PK-12)
   2009-10 Enrollment: 1,267 . . . . (217) 632-3803
Housing: Homeownership rate: 61.5% (2010); Median home value: $106,658 (2010); Median contract rent: $375 per month (2005-2009 5-year est.); Median year structure built: 1950 (2005-2009 5-year est.).

Newspapers: Menard County Review (Community news; Circulation 1,600); Petersburg Observer (Local news; Circulation 3,200)
Transportation: Commute to work: 88.7% car, 0.0% public transportation, 0.8% walk, 8.6% work from home (2005-2009 5-year est.); Travel time to work: 39.2% less than 15 minutes, 8.5% 15 to 30 minutes, 43.3% 30 to 45 minutes, 6.5% 45 to 60 minutes, 2.5% 60 minutes or more (2005-2009 5-year est.)
Additional Information Contacts
Petersburg Chamber of Commerce . . . . (217) 632-7363
   http://www.petersburgilchamber.com

TALLULA (village). Covers a land area of 0.528 square miles and a water area of 0 square miles. Located at 39.94° N. Lat; 89.93° W. Long. Elevation is 623 feet.
Population: 598 (1990); 638 (2000); 618 (2010); 609 (2015 projected); Race: 97.6% White, 1.1% Black, 0.2% Asian, 1.1% Other, 0.5% Hispanic of any race (2010); Density: 1,169.5 persons per square mile (2010); Average household size: 2.58 (2010); Median age: 39.6 (2010); Males per 100 females: 100.6 (2010); Marriage status: 28.0% never married, 54.8% now married, 7.8% widowed, 9.4% divorced (2005-2009 5-year est.); Foreign born: 0.0% (2005-2009 5-year est.); Ancestry (includes multiple ancestries): 31.7% German, 21.6% American, 14.9% Irish, 13.6% English, 10.7% Dutch (2005-2009 5-year est.).
Economy: Employment by occupation: 12.6% management, 17.2% professional, 34.8% services, 13.6% sales, 0.0% farming, 4.6% construction, 17.2% production (2005-2009 5-year est.).
Income: Per capita income: $24,502 (2010); Median household income: $49,167 (2010); Average household income: $61,438 (2010); Percent of households with income of $100,000 or more: 12.1% (2010); Poverty rate: 20.2% (2005-2009 5-year est.).
Taxes: Total city taxes per capita: $24 (2007); City property taxes per capita: $21 (2007).
Education: Percent of population age 25 and over with: High school diploma (including GED) or higher: 83.3% (2010); Bachelor's degree or higher: 14.0% (2010); Master's degree or higher: 7.7% (2010).

School District(s)
Porta CUSD 202 (PK-12)
   2009-10 Enrollment: 1,267 . . . . (217) 632-3803
Housing: Homeownership rate: 79.2% (2010); Median home value: $81,818 (2010); Median contract rent: $364 per month (2005-2009 5-year est.); Median year structure built: 1941 (2005-2009 5-year est.).
Transportation: Commute to work: 91.1% car, 0.0% public transportation, 1.0% walk, 7.5% work from home (2005-2009 5-year est.); Travel time to work: 20.7% less than 15 minutes, 28.4% 15 to 30 minutes, 39.9% 30 to 45 minutes, 8.9% 45 to 60 minutes, 2.2% 60 minutes or more (2005-2009 5-year est.)

Mercer County

Located in northwestern Illinois; bounded on the west by the Mississippi River and the Iowa border; drained by the Edwards River. Covers a land area of 561.02 square miles, a water area of 7.86 square miles, and is located in the Central Time Zone at 41.20° N. Lat., 90.73° W. Long. The county was founded in 1825. County seat is Aledo.

Mercer County is part of the Davenport-Moline-Rock Island, IA-IL Metropolitan Statistical Area. The entire metro area includes: Henry County, IL; Mercer County, IL; Rock Island County, IL; Scott County, IA

Weather Station: Aledo										Elevation: 720 feet	
	Jan	Feb	Mar	Apr	May	Jun	Jul	Aug	Sep	Oct	Nov	Dec
High	31	36	48	62	72	81	85	83	76	63	49	34
Low	15	18	28	39	50	60	63	62	53	42	31	18
Precip	1.4	1.5	2.4	3.7	4.3	4.5	4.0	4.5	3.3	3.0	2.3	2.0
Snow	6.8	4.5	2.7	0.8	tr	0.0	0.0	0.0	0.0	0.1	0.6	5.2

High and Low temperatures in degrees Fahrenheit; Precipitation and Snow in inches

Population: 17,290 (1990); 16,957 (2000); 16,432 (2010); 16,109 (2015 projected); Race: 97.2% White, 0.9% Black, 0.2% Asian, 1.6% Other, 1.8% Hispanic of any race (2010); Density: 29.3 persons per square mile (2010); Average household size: 2.49 (2010); Median age: 41.9 (2010); Males per 100 females: 98.0 (2010).
Religion: Five largest groups: 15.3% Catholic Church, 9.6% The United Methodist Church, 8.4% Evangelical Lutheran Church in America, 6.9% Presbyterian Church (U.S.A.), 3.4% American Baptist Churches in the USA (2000).

Economy: Unemployment rate: 7.6% (August 2011); Total civilian labor force: 8,653 (August 2011); Leading industries: 23.6% manufacturing; 16.4% retail trade; 16.2% health care and social assistance (2009); Farms: 785 totaling 306,306 acres (2007); Companies that employ 500 or more persons: 0 (2009); Companies that employ 100 to 499 persons: 2 (2009); Companies that employ less than 100 persons: 290 (2009); Black-owned businesses: n/a (2007); Hispanic-owned businesses: n/a (2007); Asian-owned businesses: n/a (2007); Women-owned businesses: 445 (2007); Retail sales per capita: $8,486 (2010). Single-family building permits issued: 10 (2010); Multi-family building permits issued: 0 (2010).
Income: Per capita income: $23,870 (2010); Median household income: $51,326 (2010); Average household income: $59,874 (2010); Percent of households with income of $100,000 or more: 12.4% (2010); Poverty rate: 9.4% (2009); Bankruptcy rate: 4.63% (2010).
Taxes: Total county taxes per capita: $175 (2007); County property taxes per capita: $175 (2007).
Education: Percent of population age 25 and over with: High school diploma (including GED) or higher: 89.2% (2010); Bachelor's degree or higher: 15.2% (2010); Master's degree or higher: 3.8% (2010).
Housing: Homeownership rate: 78.6% (2010); Median home value: $95,436 (2010); Median contract rent: $383 per month (2005-2009 5-year est.); Median year structure built: 1953 (2005-2009 5-year est.)
Health: Birth rate: 111.8 per 10,000 population (2009); Death rate: 110.6 per 10,000 population (2009); Age-adjusted cancer mortality rate: 172.6 deaths per 100,000 population (2007); Number of physicians: 6.1 per 10,000 population (2008); Hospital beds: 23.7 per 10,000 population (2007); Hospital admissions: 182.6 per 10,000 population (2007).
Elections: 2008 Presidential election results: 55.2% Obama, 43.3% McCain, 0.7% Nader
National and State Parks: Mark Twain National Wildlife Refuge
Additional Information Contacts
Mercer County Government . . . . (309) 582-2138
   http://mercercountyil.org
Aledo Area Chamber of Commerce . . . . (309) 582-5373
   http://aledochamber.org
City of Aledo . . . . (309) 582-7241
   http://www.aledo-il.org

Mercer County Communities

ALEDO (city). County seat. Covers a land area of 2.242 square miles and a water area of 0.014 square miles. Located at 41.20° N. Lat; 90.75° W. Long. Elevation is 735 feet.
History: Aledo developed as a trading center, and as the seat of Mercer County.
Population: 3,695 (1990); 3,613 (2000); 3,518 (2010); 3,472 (2015 projected); Race: 96.9% White, 1.5% Black, 0.3% Asian, 1.3% Other, 0.9% Hispanic of any race (2010); Density: 1,568.8 persons per square mile (2010); Average household size: 2.30 (2010); Median age: 45.0 (2010); Males per 100 females: 88.6 (2010); Marriage status: 16.6% never married, 60.7% now married, 14.3% widowed, 8.4% divorced (2005-2009 5-year est.); Foreign born: 0.2% (2005-2009 5-year est.); Ancestry (includes multiple ancestries): 19.5% German, 17.8% Irish, 12.1% Swedish, 10.7% English, 4.0% American (2005-2009 5-year est.).
Economy: Single-family building permits issued: 1 (2010); Multi-family building permits issued: 0 (2010); Employment by occupation: 9.3% management, 20.0% professional, 14.4% services, 28.4% sales, 0.7% farming, 10.6% construction, 16.5% production (2005-2009 5-year est.).
Income: Per capita income: $22,285 (2010); Median household income: $42,558 (2010); Average household income: $52,676 (2010); Percent of households with income of $100,000 or more: 9.6% (2010); Poverty rate: 14.7% (2005-2009 5-year est.).
Taxes: Total city taxes per capita: $216 (2007); City property taxes per capita: $212 (2007).
Education: Percent of population age 25 and over with: High school diploma (including GED) or higher: 87.5% (2010); Bachelor's degree or higher: 21.7% (2010); Master's degree or higher: 4.6% (2010).

School District(s)
Mercer County School District 404 (PK-12)
   2009-10 Enrollment: 1,376 . . . . (309) 582-2238
Housing: Homeownership rate: 72.8% (2010); Median home value: $92,837 (2010); Median contract rent: $426 per month (2005-2009 5-year est.); Median year structure built: 1944 (2005-2009 5-year est.).
Safety: Violent crime rate: 31.7 per 10,000 population; Property crime rate: 262.6 per 10,000 population (2010).

Newspapers: Times Record (Regional news; Circulation 3,200)
Transportation: Commute to work: 89.2% car, 0.0% public transportation, 3.6% walk, 6.9% work from home (2005-2009 5-year est.); Travel time to work: 61.0% less than 15 minutes, 7.8% 15 to 30 minutes, 12.6% 30 to 45 minutes, 12.9% 45 to 60 minutes, 5.7% 60 minutes or more (2005-2009 5-year est.)
Additional Information Contacts
City of Aledo . . . . (309) 582-7241
  http://www.aledo-il.org

JOY (village). Covers a land area of 0.420 square miles and a water area of 0 square miles. Located at 41.19° N. Lat; 90.88° W. Long. Elevation is 686 feet.
Population: 452 (1990); 373 (2000); 336 (2010); 321 (2015 projected); Race: 98.5% White, 0.0% Black, 0.0% Asian, 1.5% Other, 0.9% Hispanic of any race (2010); Density: 800.2 persons per square mile (2010); Average household size: 2.55 (2010); Median age: 38.0 (2010); Males per 100 females: 96.5 (2010); Marriage status: 21.0% never married, 61.6% now married, 8.3% widowed, 9.2% divorced (2005-2009 5-year est.); Foreign born: 0.0% (2005-2009 5-year est.); Ancestry (includes multiple ancestries): 30.6% German, 15.7% Irish, 11.4% American, 6.3% English, 4.6% Swedish (2005-2009 5-year est.).
Economy: Single-family building permits issued: 0 (2010); Multi-family building permits issued: 0 (2010); Employment by occupation: 11.0% management, 8.0% professional, 24.5% services, 16.6% sales, 0.0% farming, 14.1% construction, 25.8% production (2005-2009 5-year est.).
Income: Per capita income: $21,799 (2010); Median household income: $50,962 (2010); Average household income: $56,383 (2010); Percent of households with income of $100,000 or more: 8.3% (2010); Poverty rate: 9.6% (2005-2009 5-year est.).
Taxes: Total city taxes per capita: $129 (2007); City property taxes per capita: $93 (2007).
Education: Percent of population age 25 and over with: High school diploma (including GED) or higher: 89.1% (2010); Bachelor's degree or higher: 10.0% (2010); Master's degree or higher: 1.3% (2010).
School District(s)
Mercer County School District 404 (PK-12)
  2009-10 Enrollment: 1,376 . . . . (309) 582-2238
Housing: Homeownership rate: 78.0% (2010); Median home value: $72,105 (2010); Median contract rent: $253 per month (2005-2009 5-year est.); Median year structure built: before 1940 (2005-2009 5-year est.).
Transportation: Commute to work: 100.0% car, 0.0% public transportation, 0.0% walk, 0.0% work from home (2005-2009 5-year est.); Travel time to work: 34.6% less than 15 minutes, 32.1% 15 to 30 minutes, 5.8% 30 to 45 minutes, 19.2% 45 to 60 minutes, 8.3% 60 minutes or more (2005-2009 5-year est.)

KEITHSBURG (city). Covers a land area of 2.579 square miles and a water area of 0.599 square miles. Located at 41.10° N. Lat; 90.93° W. Long. Elevation is 545 feet.
History: Incorporated 1857.
Population: 747 (1990); 714 (2000); 688 (2010); 669 (2015 projected); Race: 97.2% White, 0.7% Black, 0.0% Asian, 2.0% Other, 0.4% Hispanic of any race (2010); Density: 266.8 persons per square mile (2010); Average household size: 2.47 (2010); Median age: 39.1 (2010); Males per 100 females: 95.5 (2010); Marriage status: 10.6% never married, 68.7% now married, 15.2% widowed, 5.5% divorced (2005-2009 5-year est.); Foreign born: 0.0% (2005-2009 5-year est.); Ancestry (includes multiple ancestries): 23.0% German, 14.4% Irish, 13.8% American, 7.5% Swedish, 6.5% English (2005-2009 5-year est.).
Economy: Single-family building permits issued: 0 (2010); Multi-family building permits issued: 0 (2010); Employment by occupation: 3.7% management, 15.8% professional, 17.9% services, 13.7% sales, 1.6% farming, 13.2% construction, 34.2% production (2005-2009 5-year est.).
Income: Per capita income: $18,998 (2010); Median household income: $40,902 (2010); Average household income: $47,347 (2010); Percent of households with income of $100,000 or more: 3.2% (2010); Poverty rate: 15.8% (2005-2009 5-year est.).
Taxes: Total city taxes per capita: $126 (2007); City property taxes per capita: $59 (2007).
Education: Percent of population age 25 and over with: High school diploma (including GED) or higher: 81.3% (2010); Bachelor's degree or higher: 9.1% (2010); Master's degree or higher: 3.0% (2010).

Housing: Homeownership rate: 80.6% (2010); Median home value: $52,830 (2010); Median contract rent: $294 per month (2005-2009 5-year est.); Median year structure built: 1951 (2005-2009 5-year est.).
Transportation: Commute to work: 93.4% car, 0.0% public transportation, 4.9% walk, 1.6% work from home (2005-2009 5-year est.); Travel time to work: 10.1% less than 15 minutes, 20.7% 15 to 30 minutes, 33.5% 30 to 45 minutes, 20.1% 45 to 60 minutes, 15.6% 60 minutes or more (2005-2009 5-year est.)

MATHERVILLE (village). Covers a land area of 0.392 square miles and a water area of 0.007 square miles. Located at 41.26° N. Lat; 90.60° W. Long. Elevation is 748 feet.
Population: 708 (1990); 772 (2000); 764 (2010); 755 (2015 projected); Race: 97.4% White, 0.0% Black, 0.4% Asian, 2.2% Other, 1.4% Hispanic of any race (2010); Density: 1,948.3 persons per square mile (2010); Average household size: 2.61 (2010); Median age: 34.6 (2010); Males per 100 females: 95.9 (2010); Marriage status: 20.6% never married, 63.2% now married, 4.3% widowed, 11.9% divorced (2005-2009 5-year est.); Foreign born: 1.4% (2005-2009 5-year est.); Ancestry (includes multiple ancestries): 26.3% German, 13.0% English, 7.8% Irish, 4.7% Polish, 4.2% Dutch (2005-2009 5-year est.).
Economy: Single-family building permits issued: 0 (2010); Multi-family building permits issued: 0 (2010); Employment by occupation: 5.1% management, 8.7% professional, 27.8% services, 18.4% sales, 0.0% farming, 14.3% construction, 25.7% production (2005-2009 5-year est.).
Income: Per capita income: $22,441 (2010); Median household income: $50,962 (2010); Average household income: $56,954 (2010); Percent of households with income of $100,000 or more: 12.6% (2010); Poverty rate: 11.4% (2005-2009 5-year est.).
Taxes: Total city taxes per capita: $92 (2007); City property taxes per capita: $30 (2007).
Education: Percent of population age 25 and over with: High school diploma (including GED) or higher: 89.0% (2010); Bachelor's degree or higher: 7.2% (2010); Master's degree or higher: 2.3% (2010).
School District(s)
Sherrard CUSD 200 (PK-12)
  2009-10 Enrollment: 1,656 . . . . (309) 593-4075
Housing: Homeownership rate: 75.1% (2010); Median home value: $76,970 (2010); Median contract rent: $358 per month (2005-2009 5-year est.); Median year structure built: 1963 (2005-2009 5-year est.).
Transportation: Commute to work: 93.5% car, 0.0% public transportation, 0.8% walk, 5.7% work from home (2005-2009 5-year est.); Travel time to work: 13.2% less than 15 minutes, 31.8% 15 to 30 minutes, 40.0% 30 to 45 minutes, 10.7% 45 to 60 minutes, 4.4% 60 minutes or more (2005-2009 5-year est.)

NEW BOSTON (city). Covers a land area of 0.940 square miles and a water area of 0.453 square miles. Located at 41.17° N. Lat; 90.99° W. Long. Elevation is 568 feet.
Population: 620 (1990); 632 (2000); 570 (2010); 539 (2015 projected); Race: 99.3% White, 0.7% Black, 0.0% Asian, 0.0% Other, 0.2% Hispanic of any race (2010); Density: 606.6 persons per square mile (2010); Average household size: 2.25 (2010); Median age: 46.1 (2010); Males per 100 females: 107.3 (2010); Marriage status: 23.0% never married, 55.1% now married, 4.7% widowed, 17.1% divorced (2005-2009 5-year est.); Foreign born: 0.0% (2005-2009 5-year est.); Ancestry (includes multiple ancestries): 34.0% German, 22.7% Irish, 8.0% Swedish, 6.6% English, 4.6% Norwegian (2005-2009 5-year est.).
Economy: Employment by occupation: 9.2% management, 6.9% professional, 17.1% services, 16.1% sales, 4.3% farming, 15.5% construction, 30.9% production (2005-2009 5-year est.).
Income: Per capita income: $22,449 (2010); Median household income: $39,943 (2010); Average household income: $50,771 (2010); Percent of households with income of $100,000 or more: 9.9% (2010); Poverty rate: 10.2% (2005-2009 5-year est.).
Taxes: Total city taxes per capita: $73 (2007); City property taxes per capita: $59 (2007).
Education: Percent of population age 25 and over with: High school diploma (including GED) or higher: 78.7% (2010); Bachelor's degree or higher: 3.4% (2010); Master's degree or higher: 1.1% (2010).
School District(s)
Mercer County School District 404 (PK-12)
  2009-10 Enrollment: 1,376 . . . . (309) 582-2238

Housing: Homeownership rate: 81.8% (2010); Median home value: $72,857 (2010); Median contract rent: $396 per month (2005-2009 5-year est.); Median year structure built: 1972 (2005-2009 5-year est.).
Transportation: Commute to work: 95.1% car, 0.0% public transportation, 0.0% walk, 0.0% work from home (2005-2009 5-year est.); Travel time to work: 10.2% less than 15 minutes, 35.5% 15 to 30 minutes, 29.6% 30 to 45 minutes, 8.9% 45 to 60 minutes, 15.8% 60 minutes or more (2005-2009 5-year est.)

NEW WINDSOR (unincorporated postal area, zip code 61465). Aka Windsor. Covers a land area of 36.425 square miles and a water area of 0.017 square miles. Located at 41.17° N. Lat; 90.68° W. Long. Elevation is 804 feet.
Population: 1,144 (2000); Race: 97.9% White, 0.0% Black, 0.5% Asian, 1.6% Other, 2.0% Hispanic of any race (2000); Density: 31.4 persons per square mile (2000); Age: 23.0% under 18, 19.9% over 64 (2000); Marriage status: 16.2% never married, 63.7% now married, 10.2% widowed, 10.0% divorced (2000); Foreign born: 0.5% (2000); Ancestry (includes multiple ancestries): 20.0% German, 18.0% Swedish, 14.9% Irish, 10.6% English (2000).
Economy: Employment by occupation: 10.2% management, 13.3% professional, 14.5% services, 22.7% sales, 2.8% farming, 11.4% construction, 25.1% production (2000).
Income: Per capita income: $19,286 (2000); Median household income: $40,069 (2000); Poverty rate: 12.0% (2000).
Education: Percent of population age 25 and over with: High school diploma (including GED) or higher: 86.8% (2000); Bachelor's degree or higher: 11.1% (2000).
Housing: Homeownership rate: 80.9% (2000); Median home value: $64,200 (2000); Median contract rent: $228 per month (2000); Median year structure built: 1948 (2000).
Transportation: Commute to work: 94.4% car, 0.0% public transportation, 0.6% walk, 2.8% work from home (2000); Travel time to work: 26.1% less than 15 minutes, 20.6% 15 to 30 minutes, 23.0% 30 to 45 minutes, 24.1% 45 to 60 minutes, 6.2% 60 minutes or more (2000)

NORTH HENDERSON (village). Covers a land area of 0.225 square miles and a water area of 0 square miles. Located at 41.09° N. Lat; 90.47° W. Long. Elevation is 774 feet.
Population: 184 (1990); 187 (2000); 177 (2010); 173 (2015 projected); Race: 98.9% White, 0.0% Black, 0.0% Asian, 1.1% Other, 4.0% Hispanic of any race (2010); Density: 787.8 persons per square mile (2010); Average household size: 2.53 (2010); Median age: 44.7 (2010); Males per 100 females: 105.8 (2010); Marriage status: 17.6% never married, 60.6% now married, 4.2% widowed, 17.6% divorced (2005-2009 5-year est.); Foreign born: 0.6% (2005-2009 5-year est.); Ancestry (includes multiple ancestries): 20.9% German, 16.6% Irish, 15.3% Swedish, 11.0% English, 6.7% French (2005-2009 5-year est.).
Economy: Employment by occupation: 4.0% management, 25.3% professional, 8.0% services, 25.3% sales, 0.0% farming, 10.7% construction, 26.7% production (2005-2009 5-year est.).
Income: Per capita income: $21,936 (2010); Median household income: $50,000 (2010); Average household income: $54,857 (2010); Percent of households with income of $100,000 or more: 10.0% (2010); Poverty rate: 19.6% (2005-2009 5-year est.).
Taxes: Total city taxes per capita: $54 (2007); City property taxes per capita: $16 (2007).
Education: Percent of population age 25 and over with: High school diploma (including GED) or higher: 93.1% (2010); Bachelor's degree or higher: 12.3% (2010); Master's degree or higher: 5.4% (2010).
Housing: Homeownership rate: 85.7% (2010); Median home value: $80,000 (2010); Median contract rent: $342 per month (2005-2009 5-year est.); Median year structure built: before 1940 (2005-2009 5-year est.).
Transportation: Commute to work: 97.3% car, 0.0% public transportation, 0.0% walk, 0.0% work from home (2005-2009 5-year est.); Travel time to work: 9.3% less than 15 minutes, 81.3% 15 to 30 minutes, 6.7% 30 to 45 minutes, 0.0% 45 to 60 minutes, 2.7% 60 minutes or more (2005-2009 5-year est.)

SEATON (village). Covers a land area of 1.568 square miles and a water area of 0 square miles. Located at 41.10° N. Lat; 90.80° W. Long. Elevation is 614 feet.
Population: 221 (1990); 242 (2000); 240 (2010); 239 (2015 projected); Race: 91.7% White, 7.5% Black, 0.0% Asian, 0.8% Other, 0.4% Hispanic of any race (2010); Density: 153.1 persons per square mile (2010);

Average household size: 2.58 (2010); Median age: 40.6 (2010); Males per 100 females: 96.7 (2010); Marriage status: 26.9% never married, 52.9% now married, 11.2% widowed, 9.0% divorced (2005-2009 5-year est.); Foreign born: 0.8% (2005-2009 5-year est.); Ancestry (includes multiple ancestries): 19.2% Swedish, 16.5% German, 12.4% Irish, 10.9% English, 8.3% Dutch (2005-2009 5-year est.).
Economy: Single-family building permits issued: 0 (2010); Multi-family building permits issued: 0 (2010); Employment by occupation: 14.4% management, 12.9% professional, 14.4% services, 17.4% sales, 0.0% farming, 8.3% construction, 32.6% production (2005-2009 5-year est.).
Income: Per capita income: $22,623 (2010); Median household income: $44,205 (2010); Average household income: $60,376 (2010); Percent of households with income of $100,000 or more: 11.8% (2010); Poverty rate: 10.5% (2005-2009 5-year est.).
Taxes: Total city taxes per capita: $30 (2007); City property taxes per capita: $30 (2007).
Education: Percent of population age 25 and over with: High school diploma (including GED) or higher: 92.5% (2010); Bachelor's degree or higher: 11.9% (2010); Master's degree or higher: 3.8% (2010).
Housing: Homeownership rate: 78.5% (2010); Median home value: $90,000 (2010); Median contract rent: n/a per month (2005-2009 5-year est.); Median year structure built: before 1940 (2005-2009 5-year est.).
Transportation: Commute to work: 90.6% car, 0.0% public transportation, 3.1% walk, 2.3% work from home (2005-2009 5-year est.); Travel time to work: 24.0% less than 15 minutes, 44.0% 15 to 30 minutes, 3.2% 30 to 45 minutes, 20.0% 45 to 60 minutes, 8.8% 60 minutes or more (2005-2009 5-year est.)

SHERRARD (village). Covers a land area of 0.419 square miles and a water area of 0 square miles. Located at 41.31° N. Lat; 90.50° W. Long. Elevation is 801 feet.
Population: 697 (1990); 694 (2000); 600 (2010); 559 (2015 projected); Race: 97.7% White, 0.3% Black, 0.0% Asian, 2.0% Other, 2.0% Hispanic of any race (2010); Density: 1,433.6 persons per square mile (2010); Average household size: 2.52 (2010); Median age: 39.4 (2010); Males per 100 females: 92.3 (2010); Marriage status: 20.1% never married, 61.0% now married, 8.1% widowed, 10.8% divorced (2005-2009 5-year est.); Foreign born: 0.0% (2005-2009 5-year est.); Ancestry (includes multiple ancestries): 23.6% German, 16.8% English, 16.5% Irish, 15.2% Swedish, 7.7% Polish (2005-2009 5-year est.).
Economy: Single-family building permits issued: 0 (2010); Multi-family building permits issued: 0 (2010); Employment by occupation: 7.7% management, 12.0% professional, 17.8% services, 24.6% sales, 0.0% farming, 19.5% construction, 18.3% production (2005-2009 5-year est.).
Income: Per capita income: $29,103 (2010); Median household income: $67,279 (2010); Average household income: $73,067 (2010); Percent of households with income of $100,000 or more: 16.8% (2010); Poverty rate: 4.1% (2005-2009 5-year est.).
Taxes: Total city taxes per capita: $46 (2007); City property taxes per capita: $38 (2007).
Education: Percent of population age 25 and over with: High school diploma (including GED) or higher: 94.2% (2010); Bachelor's degree or higher: 12.6% (2010); Master's degree or higher: 3.4% (2010).

School District(s)

Sherrard CUSD 200 (PK-12)
    2009-10 Enrollment: 1,656 . . . . (309) 593-4075
Housing: Homeownership rate: 82.4% (2010); Median home value: $86,667 (2010); Median contract rent: $360 per month (2005-2009 5-year est.); Median year structure built: 1954 (2005-2009 5-year est.).
Transportation: Commute to work: 90.1% car, 0.0% public transportation, 5.8% walk, 2.9% work from home (2005-2009 5-year est.); Travel time to work: 15.1% less than 15 minutes, 34.9% 15 to 30 minutes, 40.1% 30 to 45 minutes, 5.3% 45 to 60 minutes, 4.6% 60 minutes or more (2005-2009 5-year est.)

VIOLA (village). Covers a land area of 0.827 square miles and a water area of 0 square miles. Located at 41.20° N. Lat; 90.58° W. Long. Elevation is 791 feet.
History: Viola developed as a coal mining town.
Population: 964 (1990); 956 (2000); 907 (2010); 882 (2015 projected); Race: 96.1% White, 0.6% Black, 0.0% Asian, 3.3% Other, 4.1% Hispanic of any race (2010); Density: 1,096.6 persons per square mile (2010); Average household size: 2.54 (2010); Median age: 38.7 (2010); Males per 100 females: 92.6 (2010); Marriage status: 19.0% never married, 66.3% now married, 7.1% widowed, 7.6% divorced (2005-2009 5-year est.);

Foreign born: 0.0% (2005-2009 5-year est.); Ancestry (includes multiple ancestries): 29.1% German, 15.8% Irish, 10.5% Swedish, 7.7% English, 7.4% American (2005-2009 5-year est.).
Economy: Single-family building permits issued: 1 (2010); Multi-family building permits issued: 0 (2010); Employment by occupation: 11.1% management, 11.7% professional, 13.7% services, 24.6% sales, 0.0% farming, 19.0% construction, 19.8% production (2005-2009 5-year est.).
Income: Per capita income: $21,505 (2010); Median household income: $48,625 (2010); Average household income: $53,964 (2010); Percent of households with income of $100,000 or more: 9.2% (2010); Poverty rate: 6.4% (2005-2009 5-year est.).
Taxes: Total city taxes per capita: $51 (2007); City property taxes per capita: $45 (2007).
Education: Percent of population age 25 and over with: High school diploma (including GED) or higher: 88.3% (2010); Bachelor's degree or higher: 15.9% (2010); Master's degree or higher: 4.8% (2010).

School District(s)

Sherrard CUSD 200 (PK-12)
    2009-10 Enrollment: 1,656 . . . . (309) 593-4075
Housing: Homeownership rate: 80.7% (2010); Median home value: $92,093 (2010); Median contract rent: $332 per month (2005-2009 5-year est.); Median year structure built: before 1940 (2005-2009 5-year est.).
Transportation: Commute to work: 94.4% car, 0.0% public transportation, 0.8% walk, 3.9% work from home (2005-2009 5-year est.); Travel time to work: 28.2% less than 15 minutes, 30.6% 15 to 30 minutes, 25.0% 30 to 45 minutes, 14.7% 45 to 60 minutes, 1.5% 60 minutes or more (2005-2009 5-year est.)
Additional Information Contacts
Aledo Area Chamber of Commerce. . . . . (309) 582-5373
    http://aledochamber.org

WINDSOR (village). Aka New Windsor. Covers a land area of 0.442 square miles and a water area of 0 square miles. Located at 41.20° N. Lat; 90.44° W. Long. Elevation is 804 feet.
Population: 774 (1990); 720 (2000); 651 (2010); 617 (2015 projected); Race: 98.0% White, 0.0% Black, 0.8% Asian, 1.2% Other, 3.7% Hispanic of any race (2010); Density: 1,472.4 persons per square mile (2010); Average household size: 2.34 (2010); Median age: 45.2 (2010); Males per 100 females: 102.2 (2010); Marriage status: 21.0% never married, 63.4% now married, 5.8% widowed, 9.9% divorced (2005-2009 5-year est.); Foreign born: 2.3% (2005-2009 5-year est.); Ancestry (includes multiple ancestries): 38.7% German, 19.4% Irish, 16.4% English, 15.0% Swedish, 6.5% American (2005-2009 5-year est.).
Economy: Single-family building permits issued: 0 (2010); Multi-family building permits issued: 0 (2010); Employment by occupation: 8.0% management, 21.2% professional, 17.4% services, 23.5% sales, 0.0% farming, 5.5% construction, 24.4% production (2005-2009 5-year est.).
Income: Per capita income: $24,261 (2010); Median household income: $50,949 (2010); Average household income: $54,964 (2010); Percent of households with income of $100,000 or more: 8.3% (2010); Poverty rate: 7.1% (2005-2009 5-year est.).
Taxes: Total city taxes per capita: $73 (2007); City property taxes per capita: $42 (2007).
Education: Percent of population age 25 and over with: High school diploma (including GED) or higher: 90.3% (2010); Bachelor's degree or higher: 11.1% (2010); Master's degree or higher: 3.2% (2010).
Housing: Homeownership rate: 78.8% (2010); Median home value: $93,256 (2010); Median contract rent: $247 per month (2005-2009 5-year est.); Median year structure built: 1954 (2005-2009 5-year est.).
Transportation: Commute to work: 93.2% car, 0.0% public transportation, 1.9% walk, 1.9% work from home (2005-2009 5-year est.); Travel time to work: 21.9% less than 15 minutes, 18.5% 15 to 30 minutes, 36.1% 30 to 45 minutes, 16.9% 45 to 60 minutes, 6.6% 60 minutes or more (2005-2009 5-year est.)

Monroe County

Located in southwestern Illinois; bounded on the west by the Mississippi River and the Missouri border; drained by the Kaskaskia River. Covers a land area of 388.29 square miles, a water area of 9.42 square miles, and is located in the Central Time Zone at 38.32° N. Lat., 90.17° W. Long. The county was founded in 1816. County seat is Waterloo.

Monroe County is part of the St. Louis, MO-IL Metropolitan Statistical Area. The entire metro area includes: Bond County, IL; Calhoun County, IL;

Clinton County, IL; Jersey County, IL; Macoupin County, IL; Madison County, IL; Monroe County, IL; St. Clair County, IL; Crawford County, MO (pt.); Franklin County, MO; Jefferson County, MO; Lincoln County, MO; St. Charles County, MO; St. Louis County, MO; Warren County, MO; Washington County, MO; St. Louis city, MO

Population: 22,422 (1990); 27,619 (2000); 33,558 (2010); 36,058 (2015 projected); Race: 97.4% White, 1.1% Black, 0.3% Asian, 1.2% Other, 1.3% Hispanic of any race (2010); Density: 86.4 persons per square mile (2010); Average household size: 2.62 (2010); Median age: 37.4 (2010); Males per 100 females: 98.5 (2010).
Religion: Five largest groups: 35.4% Catholic Church, 18.3% United Church of Christ, 8.4% Lutheran Church—Missouri Synod, 6.2% Southern Baptist Convention, 0.7% The United Methodist Church (2000).
Economy: Unemployment rate: 6.7% (August 2011); Total civilian labor force: 18,478 (August 2011); Leading industries: 17.3% retail trade; 12.4% accommodation & food services; 12.2% health care and social assistance (2009); Farms: 678 totaling 178,134 acres (2007); Companies that employ 500 or more persons: 0 (2009); Companies that employ 100 to 499 persons: 7 (2009); Companies that employ less than 100 persons: 765 (2009); Black-owned businesses: n/a (2007); Hispanic-owned businesses: n/a (2007); Asian-owned businesses: n/a (2007); Women-owned businesses: 912 (2007); Retail sales per capita: $11,460 (2010). Single-family building permits issued: 131 (2010); Multi-family building permits issued: 0 (2010).
Income: Per capita income: $29,580 (2010); Median household income: $67,748 (2010); Average household income: $77,987 (2010); Percent of households with income of $100,000 or more: 24.8% (2010); Poverty rate: 5.0% (2009); Bankruptcy rate: 3.97% (2010).
Taxes: Total county taxes per capita: $217 (2007); County property taxes per capita: $217 (2007).
Education: Percent of population age 25 and over with: High school diploma (including GED) or higher: 91.1% (2010); Bachelor's degree or higher: 25.4% (2010); Master's degree or higher: 9.1% (2010).
Housing: Homeownership rate: 82.0% (2010); Median home value: $169,218 (2010); Median contract rent: $574 per month (2005-2009 5-year est.); Median year structure built: 1984 (2005-2009 5-year est.)
Health: Birth rate: 126.7 per 10,000 population (2009); Death rate: 84.5 per 10,000 population (2009); Age-adjusted cancer mortality rate: 180.0 deaths per 100,000 population (2007); Number of physicians: 6.1 per 10,000 population (2008); Hospital beds: 0.0 per 10,000 population (2007); Hospital admissions: 0.0 per 10,000 population (2007).
Elections: 2008 Presidential election results: 44.0% Obama, 54.6% McCain, 0.7% Nader
National and State Parks: Illinois Caverns State Natural Area
Additional Information Contacts
Monroe County Government . . . . (618) 939-8681
    http://www.monroecountyil.org
City of Columbia. . . . . (618) 281-7144
    http://www.columbiaillinois.com
City of Waterloo . . . . (618) 939-7184
    http://www.waterloo.il.us
Waterloo Chamber of Commerce . . . . (618) 939-5300
    http://www.enjoywaterloo.com

Monroe County Communities

COLUMBIA (city). Covers a land area of 9.414 square miles and a water area of 0.021 square miles. Located at 38.44° N. Lat; 90.20° W. Long. Elevation is 502 feet.
History: Columbia was established as a stop on the Kaskaskia-Cahokia trail. Many early residents were of German descent. The quarrying of Keokuk limestone began here in 1840.
Population: 6,110 (1990); 7,922 (2000); 9,441 (2010); 10,101 (2015 projected); Race: 95.3% White, 3.1% Black, 0.4% Asian, 1.2% Other, 1.5% Hispanic of any race (2010); Density: 1,002.9 persons per square mile (2010); Average household size: 2.47 (2010); Median age: 38.4 (2010); Males per 100 females: 96.2 (2010); Marriage status: 26.0% never married, 57.9% now married, 5.7% widowed, 10.4% divorced (2005-2009 5-year est.); Foreign born: 1.0% (2005-2009 5-year est.); Ancestry (includes multiple ancestries): 53.7% German, 15.1% Irish, 8.9% English, 8.7% French, 5.0% Polish (2005-2009 5-year est.).
Economy: Single-family building permits issued: 54 (2010); Multi-family building permits issued: 0 (2010); Employment by occupation: 16.1% management, 20.8% professional, 15.2% services, 27.1% sales, 0.2% farming, 13.0% construction, 7.6% production (2005-2009 5-year est.).

Income: Per capita income: $33,759 (2010); Median household income: $72,478 (2010); Average household income: $83,952 (2010); Percent of households with income of $100,000 or more: 29.1% (2010); Poverty rate: 3.3% (2005-2009 5-year est.).

Taxes: Total city taxes per capita: $326 (2007); City property taxes per capita: $186 (2007).

Education: Percent of population age 25 and over with: High school diploma (including GED) or higher: 93.0% (2010); Bachelor's degree or higher: 35.2% (2010); Master's degree or higher: 12.6% (2010).

School District(s)

Columbia CUSD 4 (PK-12)

   2009-10 Enrollment: 2,011 . . . . (618) 281-4772

Housing: Homeownership rate: 79.2% (2010); Median home value: $168,743 (2010); Median contract rent: $624 per month (2005-2009 5-year est.); Median year structure built: 1982 (2005-2009 5-year est.).

Safety: Violent crime rate: 6.3 per 10,000 population; Property crime rate: 142.9 per 10,000 population (2010).

Newspapers: Enterprise Journal (Community news; Circulation 3,900); Monroe County Clarion-Journal (Local news; Circulation 13,986)

Transportation: Commute to work: 95.8% car, 0.5% public transportation, 1.1% walk, 2.4% work from home (2005-2009 5-year est.); Travel time to work: 25.0% less than 15 minutes, 31.6% 15 to 30 minutes, 30.5% 30 to 45 minutes, 8.9% 45 to 60 minutes, 4.1% 60 minutes or more (2005-2009 5-year est.)

Additional Information Contacts

City of Columbia. . . . . (618) 281-7144
   http://www.columbiaillinois.com

FULTS (village). Covers a land area of 0.068 square miles and a water area of 0 square miles. Located at 38.16° N. Lat; 90.21° W. Long. Elevation is 394 feet.

History: Heavily damaged in floods of 1993.

Population: 43 (1990); 28 (2000); 19 (2010); 19 (2015 projected); Race: 100.0% White, 0.0% Black, 0.0% Asian, 0.0% Other, 0.0% Hispanic of any race (2010); Density: 279.0 persons per square mile (2010); Average household size: 3.17 (2010); Median age: 32.5 (2010); Males per 100 females: 46.2 (2010); Marriage status: 32.0% never married, 60.0% now married, 8.0% widowed, 0.0% divorced (2005-2009 5-year est.); Foreign born: 0.0% (2005-2009 5-year est.); Ancestry (includes multiple ancestries): 58.8% German, 14.7% English, 8.8% Italian, 8.8% French, 5.9% Irish (2005-2009 5-year est.).

Economy: Employment by occupation: 7.7% management, 0.0% professional, 7.7% services, 38.5% sales, 0.0% farming, 0.0% construction, 46.2% production (2005-2009 5-year est.).

Income: Per capita income: $22,989 (2010); Median household income: $75,000 (2010); Average household income: $82,500 (2010); Percent of households with income of $100,000 or more: 33.3% (2010); Poverty rate: 0.0% (2005-2009 5-year est.).

Taxes: Total city taxes per capita: $103 (2007); City property taxes per capita: $69 (2007).

Education: Percent of population age 25 and over with: High school diploma (including GED) or higher: 81.8% (2010); Bachelor's degree or higher: 9.1% (2010); Master's degree or higher: 0.0% (2010).

Housing: Homeownership rate: 83.3% (2010); Median home value: $175,000 (2010); Median contract rent: n/a per month (2005-2009 5-year est.); Median year structure built: before 1940 (2005-2009 5-year est.).

Transportation: Commute to work: 100.0% car, 0.0% public transportation, 0.0% walk, 0.0% work from home (2005-2009 5-year est.); Travel time to work: 23.1% less than 15 minutes, 30.8% 15 to 30 minutes, 0.0% 30 to 45 minutes, 0.0% 45 to 60 minutes, 46.2% 60 minutes or more (2005-2009 5-year est.).

HECKER (village). Covers a land area of 0.238 square miles and a water area of 0 square miles. Located at 38.30° N. Lat; 89.99° W. Long. Elevation is 472 feet.

Population: 534 (1990); 475 (2000); 509 (2010); 522 (2015 projected); Race: 99.2% White, 0.0% Black, 0.2% Asian, 0.6% Other, 0.2% Hispanic of any race (2010); Density: 2,136.5 persons per square mile (2010); Average household size: 2.66 (2010); Median age: 36.8 (2010); Males per 100 females: 98.8 (2010); Marriage status: 31.0% never married, 56.0% now married, 4.9% widowed, 8.0% divorced (2005-2009 5-year est.); Foreign born: 1.7% (2005-2009 5-year est.); Ancestry (includes multiple ancestries): 65.2% German, 18.0% Irish, 9.7% Swedish, 9.0% English, 5.9% French (2005-2009 5-year est.).

Economy: Single-family building permits issued: 0 (2010); Multi-family building permits issued: 0 (2010); Employment by occupation: 12.9% management, 17.3% professional, 14.9% services, 17.3% sales, 0.0% farming, 12.9% construction, 24.6% production (2005-2009 5-year est.).

Income: Per capita income: $30,726 (2010); Median household income: $68,910 (2010); Average household income: $79,908 (2010); Percent of households with income of $100,000 or more: 25.7% (2010); Poverty rate: 4.3% (2005-2009 5-year est.).

Taxes: Total city taxes per capita: $142 (2007); City property taxes per capita: $63 (2007).

Education: Percent of population age 25 and over with: High school diploma (including GED) or higher: 91.0% (2010); Bachelor's degree or higher: 11.0% (2010); Master's degree or higher: 4.0% (2010).

Housing: Homeownership rate: 85.3% (2010); Median home value: $162,500 (2010); Median contract rent: $391 per month (2005-2009 5-year est.); Median year structure built: 1958 (2005-2009 5-year est.).

Transportation: Commute to work: 86.9% car, 2.9% public transportation, 5.3% walk, 4.9% work from home (2005-2009 5-year est.); Travel time to work: 13.4% less than 15 minutes, 29.3% 15 to 30 minutes, 24.1% 30 to 45 minutes, 12.5% 45 to 60 minutes, 20.7% 60 minutes or more (2005-2009 5-year est.)

MAEYSTOWN (village). Covers a land area of 0.304 square miles and a water area of 0 square miles. Located at 38.22° N. Lat; 90.23° W. Long. Elevation is 469 feet.

Population: 143 (1990); 148 (2000); 156 (2010); 160 (2015 projected); Race: 98.1% White, 0.0% Black, 0.6% Asian, 1.3% Other, 1.3% Hispanic of any race (2010); Density: 513.6 persons per square mile (2010); Average household size: 2.69 (2010); Median age: 39.0 (2010); Males per 100 females: 100.0 (2010); Marriage status: 11.0% never married, 89.0% now married, 0.0% widowed, 0.0% divorced (2005-2009 5-year est.); Foreign born: 0.0% (2005-2009 5-year est.); Ancestry (includes multiple ancestries): 88.8% German, 14.2% Irish, 7.7% Swiss, 7.3% English, 3.9% French (2005-2009 5-year est.).

Economy: Employment by occupation: 24.4% management, 14.3% professional, 10.9% services, 21.8% sales, 16.8% farming, construction, 11.8% production (2005-2009 5-year est.).

Income: Per capita income: $21,576 (2010); Median household income: $52,778 (2010); Average household income: $59,052 (2010); Percent of households with income of $100,000 or more: 20.7% (2010); Poverty rate: 5.6% (2005-2009 5-year est.).

Taxes: Total city taxes per capita: $85 (2007); City property taxes per capita: $72 (2007).

Education: Percent of population age 25 and over with: High school diploma (including GED) or higher: 74.8% (2010); Bachelor's degree or higher: 9.0% (2010); Master's degree or higher: 0.0% (2010).

Housing: Homeownership rate: 89.7% (2010); Median home value: $145,455 (2010); Median contract rent: n/a per month (2005-2009 5-year est.); Median year structure built: before 1940 (2005-2009 5-year est.).

Transportation: Commute to work: 94.1% car, 0.0% public transportation, 0.0% walk, 5.9% work from home (2005-2009 5-year est.); Travel time to work: 2.7% less than 15 minutes, 38.4% 15 to 30 minutes, 20.5% 30 to 45 minutes, 15.2% 45 to 60 minutes, 23.2% 60 minutes or more (2005-2009 5-year est.)

VALMEYER (village). Aka Maeys. Covers a land area of 3.328 square miles and a water area of 0.026 square miles. Located at 38.30° N. Lat; 90.30° W. Long. Elevation is 735 feet.

History: Town established by Swiss farmers at the end of the 19th century on rich Mississippi bottom land. Town flooded twice in September and October of 1993, with 90% of the homes beyond repair. A new town was constructed two miles east of the old Valmeyer on 500 acres of former dairy lands.

Population: 1,117 (1990); 608 (2000); 1,009 (2010); 1,132 (2015 projected); Race: 97.2% White, 1.7% Black, 0.5% Asian, 0.6% Other, 1.0% Hispanic of any race (2010); Density: 303.2 persons per square mile (2010); Average household size: 2.83 (2010); Median age: 34.5 (2010); Males per 100 females: 93.3 (2010); Marriage status: 17.9% never married, 68.0% now married, 9.1% widowed, 5.0% divorced (2005-2009 5-year est.); Foreign born: 0.4% (2005-2009 5-year est.); Ancestry (includes multiple ancestries): 53.3% German, 16.5% Irish, 8.9% English, 6.5% Italian, 5.2% French (2005-2009 5-year est.).

Economy: Single-family building permits issued: 4 (2010); Multi-family building permits issued: 0 (2010); Employment by occupation: 10.6%

management, 20.2% professional, 13.1% services, 26.1% sales, 0.8% farming, 13.3% construction, 15.9% production (2005-2009 5-year est.).
Income: Per capita income: $24,131 (2010); Median household income: $60,634 (2010); Average household income: $67,430 (2010); Percent of households with income of $100,000 or more: 22.7% (2010); Poverty rate: 1.8% (2005-2009 5-year est.).
Taxes: Total city taxes per capita: $324 (2007); City property taxes per capita: $176 (2007).
Education: Percent of population age 25 and over with: High school diploma (including GED) or higher: 83.9% (2010); Bachelor's degree or higher: 16.6% (2010); Master's degree or higher: 3.7% (2010).

School District(s)
Valmeyer CUSD 3 (PK-12)
  2009-10 Enrollment: 260 . . . . (618) 935-2100
Housing: Homeownership rate: 84.6% (2010); Median home value: $159,140 (2010); Median contract rent: $383 per month (2005-2009 5-year est.); Median year structure built: 1998 (2005-2009 5-year est.).
Transportation: Commute to work: 96.6% car, 0.0% public transportation, 1.0% walk, 0.8% work from home (2005-2009 5-year est.); Travel time to work: 14.4% less than 15 minutes, 23.7% 15 to 30 minutes, 37.2% 30 to 45 minutes, 19.3% 45 to 60 minutes, 5.4% 60 minutes or more (2005-2009 5-year est.)

WATERLOO (city). County seat. Covers a land area of 5.567 square miles and a water area of 0.051 square miles. Located at 38.33° N. Lat; 90.15° W. Long. Elevation is 709 feet.
History: Waterloo was established on the trail from Fort Chartresto Cahokia, and developed as the seat of Monroe County. For a time it had a reputation as a place for quick marriages.
Population: 5,885 (1990); 7,614 (2000); 9,162 (2010); 9,815 (2015 projected); Race: 98.4% White, 0.1% Black, 0.3% Asian, 1.2% Other, 1.1% Hispanic of any race (2010); Density: 1,645.9 persons per square mile (2010); Average household size: 2.59 (2010); Median age: 36.6 (2010); Males per 100 females: 95.3 (2010); Marriage status: 24.6% never married, 59.1% now married, 7.9% widowed, 8.4% divorced (2005-2009 5-year est.); Foreign born: 2.2% (2005-2009 5-year est.); Ancestry (includes multiple ancestries): 49.1% German, 15.7% Irish, 11.8% English, 8.6% French, 7.6% American (2005-2009 5-year est.).
Economy: Single-family building permits issued: 45 (2010); Multi-family building permits issued: 0 (2010); Employment by occupation: 13.2% management, 16.1% professional, 21.9% services, 27.2% sales, 0.0% farming, 8.3% construction, 13.3% production (2005-2009 5-year est.).
Income: Per capita income: $27,384 (2010); Median household income: $61,490 (2010); Average household income: $71,368 (2010); Percent of households with income of $100,000 or more: 21.5% (2010); Poverty rate: 5.1% (2005-2009 5-year est.).
Taxes: Total city taxes per capita: $199 (2007); City property taxes per capita: $75 (2007).
Education: Percent of population age 25 and over with: High school diploma (including GED) or higher: 90.6% (2010); Bachelor's degree or higher: 23.3% (2010); Master's degree or higher: 7.8% (2010).

School District(s)
Waterloo CUSD 5 (PK-12)
  2009-10 Enrollment: 2,749 . . . . (618) 939-3453
Housing: Homeownership rate: 77.2% (2010); Median home value: $165,865 (2010); Median contract rent: $556 per month (2005-2009 5-year est.); Median year structure built: 1988 (2005-2009 5-year est.).
Safety: Violent crime rate: 3.0 per 10,000 population; Property crime rate: 80.4 per 10,000 population (2010).
Newspapers: Cahokia-Dupo Herald (Local news; Circulation 14,000); Herald (Local news; Circulation 14,000); Waterloo Republic-Times (Local news; Circulation 4,000); Waterloo Republic-Times Shopper (Community news; Circulation 13,000)
Transportation: Commute to work: 91.6% car, 1.0% public transportation, 2.6% walk, 4.5% work from home (2005-2009 5-year est.); Travel time to work: 32.1% less than 15 minutes, 15.6% 15 to 30 minutes, 27.9% 30 to 45 minutes, 15.8% 45 to 60 minutes, 8.6% 60 minutes or more (2005-2009 5-year est.)
Additional Information Contacts
City of Waterloo . . . . (618) 939-7184
  http://www.waterloo.il.us
Waterloo Chamber of Commerce . . . . (618) 939-5300
  http://www.enjoywaterloo.com

Montgomery County

Located in south central Illinois; drained by Shoal and Macoupin Creeks. Covers a land area of 703.80 square miles, a water area of 5.96 square miles, and is located in the Central Time Zone at 39.20° N. Lat., 89.50° W. Long. The county was founded in 1821. County seat is Hillsboro.

Weather Station: Hillsboro   Elevation: 629 feet

	Jan	Feb	Mar	Apr	May	Jun	Jul	Aug	Sep	Oct	Nov	Dec
High	39	44	55	68	77	86	90	88	82	69	55	42
Low	22	25	34	44	54	63	67	65	56	46	36	25
Precip	2.3	2.1	3.0	4.0	5.0	3.8	3.6	3.1	3.3	3.5	3.9	2.9
Snow	5.1	3.8	1.7	0.2	tr	0.0	0.0	0.0	0.0	tr	0.5	3.6

High and Low temperatures in degrees Fahrenheit; Precipitation and Snow in inches

Population: 30,728 (1990); 30,652 (2000); 29,647 (2010); 29,006 (2015 projected); Race: 94.1% White, 4.1% Black, 0.2% Asian, 1.5% Other, 1.3% Hispanic of any race (2010); Density: 42.1 persons per square mile (2010); Average household size: 2.40 (2010); Median age: 39.6 (2010); Males per 100 females: 107.3 (2010).
Religion: Five largest groups: 12.6% Southern Baptist Convention, 10.9% Catholic Church, 6.8% Lutheran Church—Missouri Synod, 5.0% The United Methodist Church, 4.4% Evangelical Lutheran Church in America (2000).
Economy: Unemployment rate: 11.9% (August 2011); Total civilian labor force: 13,912 (August 2011); Leading industries: 20.1% retail trade; 16.2% health care and social assistance; 12.4% accommodation & food services (2009); Farms: 1,029 totaling 347,765 acres (2007); Companies that employ 500 or more persons: 0 (2009); Companies that employ 100 to 499 persons: 8 (2009); Companies that employ less than 100 persons: 743 (2009); Black-owned businesses: n/a (2007); Hispanic-owned businesses: n/a (2007); Asian-owned businesses: n/a (2007); Women-owned businesses: 794 (2007); Retail sales per capita: $14,120 (2010). Single-family building permits issued: 24 (2010); Multi-family building permits issued: 0 (2010).
Income: Per capita income: $19,984 (2010); Median household income: $40,347 (2010); Average household income: $49,731 (2010); Percent of households with income of $100,000 or more: 8.6% (2010); Poverty rate: 14.9% (2009); Bankruptcy rate: 3.84% (2010).
Taxes: Total county taxes per capita: $114 (2007); County property taxes per capita: $108 (2007).
Education: Percent of population age 25 and over with: High school diploma (including GED) or higher: 82.8% (2010); Bachelor's degree or higher: 14.8% (2010); Master's degree or higher: 4.6% (2010).
Housing: Homeownership rate: 77.2% (2010); Median home value: $70,937 (2010); Median contract rent: $341 per month (2005-2009 5-year est.); Median year structure built: 1955 (2005-2009 5-year est.).
Health: Birth rate: 109.8 per 10,000 population (2009); Death rate: 118.3 per 10,000 population (2009); Age-adjusted cancer mortality rate: 203.0 deaths per 100,000 population (2007); Number of physicians: 6.4 per 10,000 population (2008); Hospital beds: 33.9 per 10,000 population (2007); Hospital admissions: 965.8 per 10,000 population (2007).
Elections: 2008 Presidential election results: 50.4% Obama, 47.8% McCain, 0.9% Nader
National and State Parks: Coffeen Lake State Fish and Wildlife Area
Additional Information Contacts
Montgomery County Government . . . . (217) 532-9530
  http://www.montgomeryco.com
Hillsboro Chamber of Commerce. . . . . (217) 532-3711
  http://www.hillsborochamber.net
Litchfield Chamber of Commerce . . . . (217) 324-2533
  http://www.litchfieldchamber.com
Nokomis Chamber of Commerce
  http://www.nokomisonline.com/coc

Montgomery County Communities

BUTLER (village). Covers a land area of 0.570 square miles and a water area of 0 square miles. Located at 39.19° N. Lat; 89.53° W. Long. Elevation is 630 feet.
Population: 165 (1990); 197 (2000); 198 (2010); 198 (2015 projected); Race: 99.0% White, 0.0% Black, 0.5% Asian, 0.5% Other, 0.5% Hispanic of any race (2010); Density: 347.5 persons per square mile (2010); Average household size: 2.54 (2010); Median age: 42.1 (2010); Males per 100 females: 102.0 (2010); Marriage status: 32.0% never married, 46.4% now married, 12.0% widowed, 9.6% divorced (2005-2009 5-year est.);

Foreign born: 9.6% (2005-2009 5-year est.); Ancestry (includes multiple ancestries): 17.8% American, 11.9% German, 9.6% Polish, 8.9% English, 5.9% Irish (2005-2009 5-year est.).
Economy: Employment by occupation: 1.4% management, 11.6% professional, 21.7% services, 24.6% sales, 0.0% farming, 23.2% construction, 17.4% production (2005-2009 5-year est.).
Income: Per capita income: $23,427 (2010); Median household income: $50,000 (2010); Average household income: $57,500 (2010); Percent of households with income of $100,000 or more: 11.5% (2010); Poverty rate: 16.3% (2005-2009 5-year est.).
Taxes: Total city taxes per capita: $36 (2007); City property taxes per capita: $31 (2007).
Education: Percent of population age 25 and over with: High school diploma (including GED) or higher: 90.6% (2010); Bachelor's degree or higher: 20.1% (2010); Master's degree or higher: 2.0% (2010).
Housing: Homeownership rate: 85.9% (2010); Median home value: $83,750 (2010); Median contract rent: n/a per month (2005-2009 5-year est.); Median year structure built: 1955 (2005-2009 5-year est.).
Transportation: Commute to work: 100.0% car, 0.0% public transportation, 0.0% walk, 0.0% work from home (2005-2009 5-year est.); Travel time to work: 15.4% less than 15 minutes, 52.3% 15 to 30 minutes, 12.3% 30 to 45 minutes, 7.7% 45 to 60 minutes, 12.3% 60 minutes or more (2005-2009 5-year est.)

COALTON (village).
Covers a land area of 0.519 square miles and a water area of 0 square miles. Located at 39.28° N. Lat; 89.30° W. Long. Elevation is 676 feet.
Population: 359 (1990); 307 (2000); 289 (2010); 280 (2015 projected); Race: 97.6% White, 0.0% Black, 0.7% Asian, 1.7% Other, 0.3% Hispanic of any race (2010); Density: 557.4 persons per square mile (2010); Average household size: 2.45 (2010); Median age: 39.0 (2010); Males per 100 females: 84.1 (2010); Marriage status: 27.1% never married, 58.6% now married, 4.9% widowed, 9.4% divorced (2005-2009 5-year est.); Foreign born: 1.6% (2005-2009 5-year est.); Ancestry (includes multiple ancestries): 30.8% German, 13.0% American, 11.1% English, 8.6% Irish, 4.1% Polish (2005-2009 5-year est.).
Economy: Employment by occupation: 16.3% management, 12.5% professional, 25.6% services, 16.9% sales, 3.1% farming, 9.4% construction, 16.3% production (2005-2009 5-year est.).
Income: Per capita income: $22,772 (2010); Median household income: $44,000 (2010); Average household income: $56,229 (2010); Percent of households with income of $100,000 or more: 10.2% (2010); Poverty rate: 9.3% (2005-2009 5-year est.).
Taxes: Total city taxes per capita: $23 (2007); City property taxes per capita: $23 (2007).
Education: Percent of population age 25 and over with: High school diploma (including GED) or higher: 91.2% (2010); Bachelor's degree or higher: 15.0% (2010); Master's degree or higher: 6.7% (2010).
Housing: Homeownership rate: 87.3% (2010); Median home value: $63,500 (2010); Median contract rent: n/a per month (2005-2009 5-year est.); Median year structure built: 1947 (2005-2009 5-year est.).
Transportation: Commute to work: 98.7% car, 0.0% public transportation, 1.3% walk, 0.0% work from home (2005-2009 5-year est.); Travel time to work: 51.0% less than 15 minutes, 21.7% 15 to 30 minutes, 8.3% 30 to 45 minutes, 7.6% 45 to 60 minutes, 11.5% 60 minutes or more (2005-2009 5-year est.)

COFFEEN (city).
Covers a land area of 1.032 square miles and a water area of 0 square miles. Located at 39.09° N. Lat; 89.39° W. Long. Elevation is 630 feet.
Population: 741 (1990); 709 (2000); 688 (2010); 675 (2015 projected); Race: 98.5% White, 0.0% Black, 0.6% Asian, 0.9% Other, 0.3% Hispanic of any race (2010); Density: 666.8 persons per square mile (2010); Average household size: 2.36 (2010); Median age: 42.4 (2010); Males per 100 females: 97.7 (2010); Marriage status: 24.8% never married, 45.0% now married, 7.2% widowed, 23.1% divorced (2005-2009 5-year est.); Foreign born: 0.0% (2005-2009 5-year est.); Ancestry (includes multiple ancestries): 18.4% German, 10.6% English, 9.7% Irish, 7.8% American, 3.7% French (2005-2009 5-year est.).
Economy: Employment by occupation: 9.3% management, 7.8% professional, 31.3% services, 21.5% sales, 0.0% farming, 11.6% construction, 18.5% production (2005-2009 5-year est.).
Income: Per capita income: $20,727 (2010); Median household income: $44,457 (2010); Average household income: $48,904 (2010); Percent of

households with income of $100,000 or more: 6.5% (2010); Poverty rate: 15.1% (2005-2009 5-year est.).
Taxes: Total city taxes per capita: $113 (2007); City property taxes per capita: $42 (2007).
Education: Percent of population age 25 and over with: High school diploma (including GED) or higher: 84.6% (2010); Bachelor's degree or higher: 9.3% (2010); Master's degree or higher: 1.4% (2010).
School District(s)
Hillsboro CUSD 3 (PK-12)
    2009-10 Enrollment: 1,954 . . . . (217) 532-2942
Housing: Homeownership rate: 81.5% (2010); Median home value: $55,238 (2010); Median contract rent: $268 per month (2005-2009 5-year est.); Median year structure built: 1954 (2005-2009 5-year est.).
Transportation: Commute to work: 94.8% car, 0.0% public transportation, 0.0% walk, 5.2% work from home (2005-2009 5-year est.); Travel time to work: 29.9% less than 15 minutes, 43.1% 15 to 30 minutes, 8.4% 30 to 45 minutes, 6.4% 45 to 60 minutes, 12.2% 60 minutes or more (2005-2009 5-year est.)

DONNELLSON (village).
Covers a land area of 0.238 square miles and a water area of 0 square miles. Located at 39.03° N. Lat; 89.47° W. Long. Elevation is 614 feet.
Population: 167 (1990); 243 (2000); 237 (2010); 233 (2015 projected); Race: 98.3% White, 0.4% Black, 0.0% Asian, 1.3% Other, 0.0% Hispanic of any race (2010); Density: 996.0 persons per square mile (2010); Average household size: 2.37 (2010); Median age: 45.4 (2010); Males per 100 females: 104.3 (2010); Marriage status: 19.1% never married, 41.8% now married, 7.2% widowed, 32.0% divorced (2005-2009 5-year est.); Foreign born: 2.8% (2005-2009 5-year est.); Ancestry (includes multiple ancestries): 15.4% German, 10.9% Irish, 8.5% Italian, 7.7% English, 2.4% Welsh (2005-2009 5-year est.).
Economy: Employment by occupation: 9.8% management, 4.3% professional, 18.5% services, 29.3% sales, 0.0% farming, 31.5% construction, 6.5% production (2005-2009 5-year est.).
Income: Per capita income: $22,473 (2010); Median household income: $44,545 (2010); Average household income: $52,400 (2010); Percent of households with income of $100,000 or more: 9.0% (2010); Poverty rate: 21.1% (2005-2009 5-year est.).
Taxes: Total city taxes per capita: $53 (2007); City property taxes per capita: $53 (2007).
Education: Percent of population age 25 and over with: High school diploma (including GED) or higher: 86.3% (2010); Bachelor's degree or higher: 13.7% (2010); Master's degree or higher: 2.3% (2010).
Housing: Homeownership rate: 85.0% (2010); Median home value: $58,125 (2010); Median contract rent: $342 per month (2005-2009 5-year est.); Median year structure built: 1944 (2005-2009 5-year est.).
Transportation: Commute to work: 100.0% car, 0.0% public transportation, 0.0% walk, 0.0% work from home (2005-2009 5-year est.); Travel time to work: 23.9% less than 15 minutes, 46.6% 15 to 30 minutes, 15.9% 30 to 45 minutes, 4.5% 45 to 60 minutes, 9.1% 60 minutes or more (2005-2009 5-year est.)

FARMERSVILLE (village).
Covers a land area of 0.988 square miles and a water area of 0.008 square miles. Located at 39.44° N. Lat; 89.65° W. Long. Elevation is 643 feet.
Population: 698 (1990); 768 (2000); 746 (2010); 731 (2015 projected); Race: 97.5% White, 0.5% Black, 1.5% Asian, 0.5% Other, 0.4% Hispanic of any race (2010); Density: 755.4 persons per square mile (2010); Average household size: 2.41 (2010); Median age: 36.8 (2010); Males per 100 females: 90.3 (2010); Marriage status: 23.2% never married, 62.0% now married, 5.0% widowed, 9.8% divorced (2005-2009 5-year est.); Foreign born: 2.6% (2005-2009 5-year est.); Ancestry (includes multiple ancestries): 23.0% German, 17.4% Irish, 10.7% American, 8.9% English, 5.7% Dutch (2005-2009 5-year est.).
Economy: Employment by occupation: 12.2% management, 10.5% professional, 12.2% services, 31.6% sales, 1.1% farming, 13.9% construction, 18.4% production (2005-2009 5-year est.).
Income: Per capita income: $23,809 (2010); Median household income: $49,202 (2010); Average household income: $57,233 (2010); Percent of households with income of $100,000 or more: 12.0% (2010); Poverty rate: 17.2% (2005-2009 5-year est.).
Taxes: Total city taxes per capita: $41 (2007); City property taxes per capita: $35 (2007).

Education: Percent of population age 25 and over with: High school diploma (including GED) or higher: 87.1% (2010); Bachelor's degree or higher: 16.9% (2010); Master's degree or higher: 4.0% (2010).

School District(s)
Panhandle CUSD 2 (PK-12)

   2009-10 Enrollment: 543 . . . . (217) 229-4215

Housing: Homeownership rate: 75.1% (2010); Median home value: $82,105 (2010); Median contract rent: $386 per month (2005-2009 5-year est.); Median year structure built: 1973 (2005-2009 5-year est.).

Transportation: Commute to work: 88.2% car, 1.9% public transportation, 1.3% walk, 5.5% work from home (2005-2009 5-year est.); Travel time to work: 23.4% less than 15 minutes, 29.2% 15 to 30 minutes, 21.4% 30 to 45 minutes, 9.2% 45 to 60 minutes, 16.7% 60 minutes or more (2005-2009 5-year est.)

FILLMORE (village).
Covers a land area of 0.774 square miles and a water area of 0 square miles. Located at 39.11° N. Lat; 89.27° W. Long. Elevation is 633 feet.

Population: 326 (1990); 362 (2000); 357 (2010); 350 (2015 projected); Race: 97.8% White, 0.0% Black, 0.3% Asian, 2.0% Other, 0.8% Hispanic of any race (2010); Density: 461.0 persons per square mile (2010); Average household size: 2.55 (2010); Median age: 39.2 (2010); Males per 100 females: 94.0 (2010); Marriage status: 22.4% never married, 66.7% now married, 5.9% widowed, 5.0% divorced (2005-2009 5-year est.); Foreign born: 1.2% (2005-2009 5-year est.); Ancestry (includes multiple ancestries): 10.9% American, 8.6% Irish, 7.6% German, 7.2% English, 2.0% Italian (2005-2009 5-year est.).

Economy: Employment by occupation: 2.3% management, 6.9% professional, 17.1% services, 40.6% sales, 1.1% farming, 13.7% construction, 18.3% production (2005-2009 5-year est.).

Income: Per capita income: $21,064 (2010); Median household income: $47,500 (2010); Average household income: $53,375 (2010); Percent of households with income of $100,000 or more: 7.1% (2010); Poverty rate: 13.9% (2005-2009 5-year est.).

Taxes: Total city taxes per capita: $39 (2007); City property taxes per capita: $39 (2007).

Education: Percent of population age 25 and over with: High school diploma (including GED) or higher: 81.5% (2010); Bachelor's degree or higher: 9.3% (2010); Master's degree or higher: 1.2% (2010).

Housing: Homeownership rate: 85.0% (2010); Median home value: $63,846 (2010); Median contract rent: $325 per month (2005-2009 5-year est.); Median year structure built: 1961 (2005-2009 5-year est.).

Transportation: Commute to work: 93.3% car, 0.0% public transportation, 0.0% walk, 4.5% work from home (2005-2009 5-year est.); Travel time to work: 19.4% less than 15 minutes, 25.3% 15 to 30 minutes, 30.6% 30 to 45 minutes, 11.2% 45 to 60 minutes, 13.5% 60 minutes or more (2005-2009 5-year est.)

HARVEL (village).
Covers a land area of 0.727 square miles and a water area of 0 square miles. Located at 39.35° N. Lat; 89.53° W. Long. Elevation is 636 feet.

Population: 213 (1990); 235 (2000); 236 (2010); 234 (2015 projected); Race: 97.9% White, 0.4% Black, 0.4% Asian, 1.3% Other, 0.8% Hispanic of any race (2010); Density: 324.6 persons per square mile (2010); Average household size: 2.54 (2010); Median age: 42.6 (2010); Males per 100 females: 100.0 (2010); Marriage status: 29.0% never married, 49.5% now married, 6.1% widowed, 15.4% divorced (2005-2009 5-year est.); Foreign born: 0.0% (2005-2009 5-year est.); Ancestry (includes multiple ancestries): 20.6% German, 7.4% English, 5.5% American, 3.2% Scottish, 2.9% French (2005-2009 5-year est.).

Economy: Employment by occupation: 9.6% management, 8.8% professional, 29.8% services, 18.4% sales, 3.5% farming, 7.9% construction, 21.9% production (2005-2009 5-year est.).

Income: Per capita income: $19,867 (2010); Median household income: $38,553 (2010); Average household income: $48,790 (2010); Percent of households with income of $100,000 or more: 10.8% (2010); Poverty rate: 35.8% (2005-2009 5-year est.).

Taxes: Total city taxes per capita: $116 (2007); City property taxes per capita: $99 (2007).

Education: Percent of population age 25 and over with: High school diploma (including GED) or higher: 90.1% (2010); Bachelor's degree or higher: 15.1% (2010); Master's degree or higher: 5.2% (2010).

Housing: Homeownership rate: 79.6% (2010); Median home value: $102,381 (2010); Median contract rent: $371 per month (2005-2009 5-year est.); Median year structure built: before 1940 (2005-2009 5-year est.).

Transportation: Commute to work: 100.0% car, 0.0% public transportation, 0.0% walk, 0.0% work from home (2005-2009 5-year est.); Travel time to work: 28.1% less than 15 minutes, 26.3% 15 to 30 minutes, 17.5% 30 to 45 minutes, 26.3% 45 to 60 minutes, 1.8% 60 minutes or more (2005-2009 5-year est.)

HILLSBORO (city).
County seat. Covers a land area of 3.588 square miles and a water area of 1.742 square miles. Located at 39.16° N. Lat; 89.48° W. Long. Elevation is 633 feet.

History: Incorporated 1855.

Population: 4,445 (1990); 4,359 (2000); 3,929 (2010); 3,715 (2015 projected); Race: 97.6% White, 0.6% Black, 0.4% Asian, 1.5% Other, 0.9% Hispanic of any race (2010); Density: 1,095.0 persons per square mile (2010); Average household size: 2.31 (2010); Median age: 39.2 (2010); Males per 100 females: 87.5 (2010); Marriage status: 33.0% never married, 40.9% now married, 9.4% widowed, 16.7% divorced (2005-2009 5-year est.); Foreign born: 3.3% (2005-2009 5-year est.); Ancestry (includes multiple ancestries): 20.0% German, 10.1% American, 9.9% Irish, 9.7% English, 5.0% Italian (2005-2009 5-year est.).

Economy: Employment by occupation: 6.0% management, 26.9% professional, 27.3% services, 17.8% sales, 0.0% farming, 12.1% construction, 9.8% production (2005-2009 5-year est.).

Income: Per capita income: $20,920 (2010); Median household income: $39,522 (2010); Average household income: $49,848 (2010); Percent of households with income of $100,000 or more: 8.0% (2010); Poverty rate: 8.7% (2005-2009 5-year est.).

Taxes: Total city taxes per capita: $183 (2007); City property taxes per capita: $122 (2007).

Education: Percent of population age 25 and over with: High school diploma (including GED) or higher: 88.8% (2010); Bachelor's degree or higher: 20.9% (2010); Master's degree or higher: 6.9% (2010).

School District(s)
Hillsboro CUSD 3 (PK-12)

   2009-10 Enrollment: 1,954 . . . . (217) 532-2942

Housing: Homeownership rate: 68.5% (2010); Median home value: $78,365 (2010); Median contract rent: $505 per month (2005-2009 5-year est.); Median year structure built: 1948 (2005-2009 5-year est.).

Hospitals: Hillsboro Area Hospital (100 beds)

Safety: Violent crime rate: 34.9 per 10,000 population; Property crime rate: 76.5 per 10,000 population (2010).

Newspapers: Hillsboro Journal (Local news; Circulation 6,566); M & M Journal (Local news; Circulation 21,945); Montgomery County News (Community news; Circulation 4,000); Raymond News (Local news; Circulation 655); Sorento News (Community news; Circulation 500)

Transportation: Commute to work: 92.9% car, 0.0% public transportation, 2.0% walk, 4.0% work from home (2005-2009 5-year est.); Travel time to work: 54.0% less than 15 minutes, 21.1% 15 to 30 minutes, 12.4% 30 to 45 minutes, 2.3% 45 to 60 minutes, 10.1% 60 minutes or more (2005-2009 5-year est.)

Additional Information Contacts

Hillsboro Chamber of Commerce. (217) 532-3711
   http://www.hillsborochamber.net

IRVING (village).
Covers a land area of 0.818 square miles and a water area of 0 square miles. Located at 39.20° N. Lat; 89.40° W. Long. Elevation is 656 feet.

Population: 516 (1990); 2,484 (2000); 2,517 (2010); 2,523 (2015 projected); Race: 56.2% White, 38.2% Black, 0.0% Asian, 5.6% Other, 7.7% Hispanic of any race (2010); Density: 3,078.5 persons per square mile (2010); Average household size: 2.56 (2010); Median age: 33.0 (2010); Males per 100 females: 529.3 (2010); Marriage status: 24.4% never married, 59.4% now married, 5.7% widowed, 10.5% divorced (2005-2009 5-year est.); Foreign born: 0.0% (2005-2009 5-year est.); Ancestry (includes multiple ancestries): 17.4% German, 13.8% English, 9.2% Irish, 7.9% American, 1.5% Russian (2005-2009 5-year est.).

Economy: Employment by occupation: 9.1% management, 7.8% professional, 13.6% services, 21.4% sales, 0.0% farming, 11.7% construction, 36.4% production (2005-2009 5-year est.).

Income: Per capita income: $14,214 (2010); Median household income: $41,702 (2010); Average household income: $47,492 (2010); Percent of households with income of $100,000 or more: 8.6% (2010); Poverty rate: 18.8% (2005-2009 5-year est.).

Taxes: Total city taxes per capita: $33 (2007); City property taxes per capita: $31 (2007).

Education: Percent of population age 25 and over with: High school diploma (including GED) or higher: 62.9% (2010); Bachelor's degree or higher: 3.0% (2010); Master's degree or higher: 1.0% (2010).
Housing: Homeownership rate: 82.2% (2010); Median home value: $79,310 (2010); Median contract rent: $275 per month (2005-2009 5-year est.); Median year structure built: before 1940 (2005-2009 5-year est.).
Safety: Violent crime rate: 21.4 per 10,000 population; Property crime rate: 149.6 per 10,000 population (2010).
Transportation: Commute to work: 95.3% car, 0.0% public transportation, 0.0% walk, 1.3% work from home (2005-2009 5-year est.); Travel time to work: 22.3% less than 15 minutes, 39.2% 15 to 30 minutes, 8.8% 30 to 45 minutes, 19.6% 45 to 60 minutes, 10.1% 60 minutes or more (2005-2009 5-year est.)

LITCHFIELD (city). Covers a land area of 5.091 square miles and a water area of 0.003 square miles. Located at 39.17° N. Lat; 89.65° W. Long. Elevation is 689 feet.

History: Litchfield was incorporated in 1859 and developed around a coal field. An early employer was the International Stove Company.
Population: 7,105 (1990); 6,815 (2000); 6,295 (2010); 6,033 (2015 projected); Race: 98.1% White, 0.2% Black, 0.3% Asian, 1.4% Other, 1.1% Hispanic of any race (2010); Density: 1,236.4 persons per square mile (2010); Average household size: 2.36 (2010); Median age: 39.9 (2010); Males per 100 females: 87.2 (2010); Marriage status: 24.2% never married, 56.4% now married, 8.1% widowed, 11.3% divorced (2005-2009 5-year est.); Foreign born: 0.9% (2005-2009 5-year est.); Ancestry (includes multiple ancestries): 31.6% German, 12.2% Irish, 10.6% English, 10.3% American, 4.5% Italian (2005-2009 5-year est.).
Economy: Employment by occupation: 8.4% management, 14.6% professional, 23.8% services, 27.0% sales, 0.5% farming, 13.1% construction, 12.6% production (2005-2009 5-year est.).
Income: Per capita income: $17,583 (2010); Median household income: $33,454 (2010); Average household income: $41,427 (2010); Percent of households with income of $100,000 or more: 5.2% (2010); Poverty rate: 17.8% (2005-2009 5-year est.).
Taxes: Total city taxes per capita: $304 (2007); City property taxes per capita: $273 (2007).
Education: Percent of population age 25 and over with: High school diploma (including GED) or higher: 80.1% (2010); Bachelor's degree or higher: 15.7% (2010); Master's degree or higher: 5.3% (2010).
School District(s)
Litchfield CUSD 12 (PK-12)
   2009-10 Enrollment: 1,506 . . . . (217) 324-2157
Vocational/Technical School(s)
Tri-County Beauty Academy (Private, For-profit)
   Fall 2009 Enrollment: 7 . . . . (217) 324-9062
   2010-11 Tuition: $11,025
Housing: Homeownership rate: 71.0% (2010); Median home value: $62,700 (2010); Median contract rent: $327 per month (2005-2009 5-year est.); Median year structure built: 1953 (2005-2009 5-year est.).
Hospitals: St. Francis Hospital (25 beds)
Safety: Violent crime rate: 32.4 per 10,000 population; Property crime rate: 353.3 per 10,000 population (2010).
Newspapers: News-Herald (Local news; Circulation 5,800)
Transportation: Commute to work: 91.8% car, 0.8% public transportation, 1.8% walk, 3.8% work from home (2005-2009 5-year est.); Travel time to work: 59.7% less than 15 minutes, 17.5% 15 to 30 minutes, 6.4% 30 to 45 minutes, 8.8% 45 to 60 minutes, 7.7% 60 minutes or more (2005-2009 5-year est.)
Additional Information Contacts
Litchfield Chamber of Commerce . . . . (217) 324-2533
   http://www.litchfieldchamber.com

NOKOMIS (city). Covers a land area of 1.300 square miles and a water area of 0 square miles. Located at 39.30° N. Lat; 89.28° W. Long. Elevation is 673 feet.

History: Incorporated 1867.
Population: 2,574 (1990); 2,389 (2000); 2,259 (2010); 2,182 (2015 projected); Race: 99.3% White, 0.0% Black, 0.0% Asian, 0.7% Other, 0.1% Hispanic of any race (2010); Density: 1,737.3 persons per square mile (2010); Average household size: 2.17 (2010); Median age: 44.0 (2010); Males per 100 females: 87.9 (2010); Marriage status: 18.8% never married, 65.3% now married, 9.6% widowed, 6.4% divorced (2005-2009 5-year est.); Foreign born: 1.0% (2005-2009 5-year est.); Ancestry (includes

multiple ancestries): 30.7% German, 15.1% Irish, 8.6% English, 5.7% American, 4.7% Italian (2005-2009 5-year est.).
Economy: Employment by occupation: 8.0% management, 18.2% professional, 22.7% services, 19.5% sales, 1.4% farming, 11.6% construction, 18.5% production (2005-2009 5-year est.).
Income: Per capita income: $20,533 (2010); Median household income: $35,943 (2010); Average household income: $44,944 (2010); Percent of households with income of $100,000 or more: 7.3% (2010); Poverty rate: 10.3% (2005-2009 5-year est.).
Taxes: Total city taxes per capita: $152 (2007); City property taxes per capita: $58 (2007).
Education: Percent of population age 25 and over with: High school diploma (including GED) or higher: 85.0% (2010); Bachelor's degree or higher: 13.4% (2010); Master's degree or higher: 5.5% (2010).
School District(s)
Nokomis CUSD 22 (PK-12)
   2009-10 Enrollment: 707 . . . . (217) 563-7311
Housing: Homeownership rate: 78.8% (2010); Median home value: $59,852 (2010); Median contract rent: $319 per month (2005-2009 5-year est.); Median year structure built: 1945 (2005-2009 5-year est.).
Newspapers: Free Press-Progress (Local news; Circulation 3,000)
Transportation: Commute to work: 91.3% car, 0.0% public transportation, 7.2% walk, 0.5% work from home (2005-2009 5-year est.); Travel time to work: 42.2% less than 15 minutes, 20.3% 15 to 30 minutes, 18.2% 30 to 45 minutes, 4.4% 45 to 60 minutes, 14.9% 60 minutes or more (2005-2009 5-year est.)
Additional Information Contacts
Nokomis Chamber of Commerce . . . .
   http://www.nokomisonline.com/coc

OHLMAN (village). Covers a land area of 0.269 square miles and a water area of 0 square miles. Located at 39.34° N. Lat; 89.21° W. Long. Elevation is 688 feet.

History: As of the 2000 Census, the village had a total population of 0. A recount in 2004 issued a revised population of 148.
Population: n/a (1990); n/a (2000); 135 (2010); n/a (2015 projected); Race: 98.5% White, 0.0% Black, 0.0% Asian, 1.5% Other, 0.0% Hispanic of any race (2010); Density: 501.9 persons per square mile (2010); Average household size: 2.29 (2010); Median age: 49.5 (2010); Males per 100 females: 101.5 (2010); Marriage status: 16.7% never married, 56.3% now married, 11.5% widowed, 15.6% divorced (2005-2009 5-year est.); Foreign born: 0.0% (2005-2009 5-year est.); Ancestry (includes multiple ancestries): 22.5% German, 16.2% English, 12.6% American, 12.6% Irish, 4.5% Italian (2005-2009 5-year est.).
Economy: Employment by occupation: 11.5% management, 0.0% professional, 34.6% services, 15.4% sales, 0.0% farming, 23.1% construction, 15.4% production (2005-2009 5-year est.).
Income: Per capita income: n/a (2010); Median household income: n/a (2010); Average household income: n/a (2010); Percent of households with income of $100,000 or more: n/a (2010); Poverty rate: 36.0% (2005-2009 5-year est.).
Taxes: Total city taxes per capita: $35 (2007); City property taxes per capita: $28 (2007).
Education: Percent of population age 25 and over with: High school diploma (including GED) or higher: n/a (2010); Bachelor's degree or higher: n/a (2010); Master's degree or higher: n/a (2010).
Housing: Homeownership rate: n/a (2010); Median home value: n/a (2010); Median contract rent: n/a per month (2005-2009 5-year est.); Median year structure built: before 1940 (2005-2009 5-year est.).
Transportation: Commute to work: 100.0% car, 0.0% public transportation, 0.0% walk, 0.0% work from home (2005-2009 5-year est.); Travel time to work: 38.5% less than 15 minutes, 46.2% 15 to 30 minutes, 7.7% 30 to 45 minutes, 0.0% 45 to 60 minutes, 7.7% 60 minutes or more (2005-2009 5-year est.)

PANAMA (village). Covers a land area of 0.337 square miles and a water area of <.001 square miles. Located at 39.03° N. Lat; 89.52° W. Long. Elevation is 591 feet.

Population: 297 (1990); 323 (2000); 309 (2010); 301 (2015 projected); Race: 98.4% White, 0.0% Black, 0.0% Asian, 1.6% Other, 0.0% Hispanic of any race (2010); Density: 916.7 persons per square mile (2010); Average household size: 2.40 (2010); Median age: 41.1 (2010); Males per 100 females: 94.3 (2010); Marriage status: 18.1% never married, 46.6% now married, 13.6% widowed, 21.7% divorced (2005-2009 5-year est.); Foreign born: 1.6% (2005-2009 5-year est.); Ancestry (includes multiple

ancestries): 19.2% German, 6.3% English, 5.1% Italian, 4.3% Irish, 4.3% American (2005-2009 5-year est.).
Economy: Employment by occupation: 18.0% management, 6.3% professional, 19.8% services, 27.0% sales, 0.0% farming, 4.5% construction, 24.3% production (2005-2009 5-year est.).
Income: Per capita income: $22,187 (2010); Median household income: $44,569 (2010); Average household income: $52,810 (2010); Percent of households with income of $100,000 or more: 10.9% (2010); Poverty rate: 18.4% (2005-2009 5-year est.).
Taxes: Total city taxes per capita: $59 (2007); City property taxes per capita: $28 (2007).
Education: Percent of population age 25 and over with: High school diploma (including GED) or higher: 83.4% (2010); Bachelor's degree or higher: 12.9% (2010); Master's degree or higher: 2.8% (2010).
Housing: Homeownership rate: 87.6% (2010); Median home value: $58,000 (2010); Median contract rent: $429 per month (2005-2009 5-year est.); Median year structure built: before 1940 (2005-2009 5-year est.).
Transportation: Commute to work: 96.2% car, 0.0% public transportation, 0.0% walk, 3.8% work from home (2005-2009 5-year est.); Travel time to work: 28.0% less than 15 minutes, 46.0% 15 to 30 minutes, 11.0% 30 to 45 minutes, 2.0% 45 to 60 minutes, 13.0% 60 minutes or more (2005-2009 5-year est.)

RAYMOND (village). Covers a land area of 1.255 square miles and a water area of 0 square miles. Located at 39.32° N. Lat; 89.57° W. Long. Elevation is 643 feet.
Population: 851 (1990); 927 (2000); 866 (2010); 831 (2015 projected); Race: 99.7% White, 0.0% Black, 0.0% Asian, 0.3% Other, 0.0% Hispanic of any race (2010); Density: 690.0 persons per square mile (2010); Average household size: 2.35 (2010); Median age: 40.9 (2010); Males per 100 females: 91.6 (2010); Marriage status: 25.3% never married, 58.6% now married, 8.4% widowed, 7.7% divorced (2005-2009 5-year est.); Foreign born: 0.0% (2005-2009 5-year est.); Ancestry (includes multiple ancestries): 35.0% German, 12.4% English, 12.3% Irish, 8.6% American, 2.9% Scotch-Irish (2005-2009 5-year est.).
Economy: Employment by occupation: 9.3% management, 16.2% professional, 16.4% services, 27.6% sales, 2.6% farming, 13.8% construction, 14.2% production (2005-2009 5-year est.).
Income: Per capita income: $22,234 (2010); Median household income: $46,047 (2010); Average household income: $52,209 (2010); Percent of households with income of $100,000 or more: 10.0% (2010); Poverty rate: 9.6% (2005-2009 5-year est.).
Taxes: Total city taxes per capita: $95 (2007); City property taxes per capita: $93 (2007).
Education: Percent of population age 25 and over with: High school diploma (including GED) or higher: 86.0% (2010); Bachelor's degree or higher: 20.6% (2010); Master's degree or higher: 8.1% (2010).

School District(s)
Panhandle CUSD 2 (PK-12)
    2009-10 Enrollment: 543 . . . . (217) 229-4215
Housing: Homeownership rate: 75.3% (2010); Median home value: $76,981 (2010); Median contract rent: $355 per month (2005-2009 5-year est.); Median year structure built: 1958 (2005-2009 5-year est.).
Safety: Violent crime rate: 0.0 per 10,000 population; Property crime rate: 11.4 per 10,000 population (2010).
Transportation: Commute to work: 94.4% car, 0.0% public transportation, 1.7% walk, 2.7% work from home (2005-2009 5-year est.); Travel time to work: 33.7% less than 15 minutes, 29.7% 15 to 30 minutes, 17.9% 30 to 45 minutes, 13.5% 45 to 60 minutes, 5.2% 60 minutes or more (2005-2009 5-year est.)

SCHRAM CITY (village). Covers a land area of 0.733 square miles and a water area of 0 square miles. Located at 39.16° N. Lat; 89.46° W. Long. Elevation is 607 feet.
Population: 682 (1990); 653 (2000); 580 (2010); 542 (2015 projected); Race: 99.0% White, 0.3% Black, 0.2% Asian, 0.5% Other, 0.2% Hispanic of any race (2010); Density: 791.5 persons per square mile (2010); Average household size: 2.41 (2010); Median age: 41.3 (2010); Males per 100 females: 100.0 (2010); Marriage status: 17.4% never married, 65.6% now married, 7.4% widowed, 9.6% divorced (2005-2009 5-year est.); Foreign born: 0.0% (2005-2009 5-year est.); Ancestry (includes multiple ancestries): 22.2% German, 13.3% Irish, 12.6% American, 11.5% Italian, 8.3% English (2005-2009 5-year est.).

Economy: Employment by occupation: 5.1% management, 11.3% professional, 32.5% services, 25.2% sales, 0.0% farming, 7.7% construction, 18.2% production (2005-2009 5-year est.).
Income: Per capita income: $20,720 (2010); Median household income: $41,585 (2010); Average household income: $49,842 (2010); Percent of households with income of $100,000 or more: 8.0% (2010); Poverty rate: 17.6% (2005-2009 5-year est.).
Taxes: Total city taxes per capita: $83 (2007); City property taxes per capita: $29 (2007).
Education: Percent of population age 25 and over with: High school diploma (including GED) or higher: 80.8% (2010); Bachelor's degree or higher: 7.2% (2010); Master's degree or higher: 2.9% (2010).
Housing: Homeownership rate: 81.9% (2010); Median home value: $57,955 (2010); Median contract rent: $295 per month (2005-2009 5-year est.); Median year structure built: 1950 (2005-2009 5-year est.).
Transportation: Commute to work: 94.7% car, 0.0% public transportation, 3.0% walk, 2.3% work from home (2005-2009 5-year est.); Travel time to work: 51.5% less than 15 minutes, 24.6% 15 to 30 minutes, 7.7% 30 to 45 minutes, 4.6% 45 to 60 minutes, 11.5% 60 minutes or more (2005-2009 5-year est.)

TAYLOR SPRINGS (village). Covers a land area of 0.861 square miles and a water area of 0.033 square miles. Located at 39.13° N. Lat; 89.49° W. Long. Elevation is 627 feet.
Population: 672 (1990); 583 (2000); 556 (2010); 543 (2015 projected); Race: 99.5% White, 0.0% Black, 0.0% Asian, 0.5% Other, 0.4% Hispanic of any race (2010); Density: 645.8 persons per square mile (2010); Average household size: 2.31 (2010); Median age: 47.7 (2010); Males per 100 females: 94.4 (2010); Marriage status: 15.8% never married, 44.5% now married, 24.0% widowed, 15.8% divorced (2005-2009 5-year est.); Foreign born: 0.7% (2005-2009 5-year est.); Ancestry (includes multiple ancestries): 14.6% German, 11.2% Irish, 6.9% English, 5.1% American, 3.6% Italian (2005-2009 5-year est.).
Economy: Employment by occupation: 6.6% management, 12.8% professional, 32.2% services, 20.9% sales, 0.0% farming, 10.4% construction, 17.1% production (2005-2009 5-year est.).
Income: Per capita income: $19,313 (2010); Median household income: $40,179 (2010); Average household income: $47,488 (2010); Percent of households with income of $100,000 or more: 8.3% (2010); Poverty rate: 19.8% (2005-2009 5-year est.).
Taxes: Total city taxes per capita: $74 (2007); City property taxes per capita: $60 (2007).
Education: Percent of population age 25 and over with: High school diploma (including GED) or higher: 82.9% (2010); Bachelor's degree or higher: 15.9% (2010); Master's degree or higher: 5.5% (2010).
Housing: Homeownership rate: 81.6% (2010); Median home value: $62,195 (2010); Median contract rent: $375 per month (2005-2009 5-year est.); Median year structure built: 1952 (2005-2009 5-year est.).
Transportation: Commute to work: 92.8% car, 0.0% public transportation, 1.5% walk, 3.1% work from home (2005-2009 5-year est.); Travel time to work: 60.1% less than 15 minutes, 23.4% 15 to 30 minutes, 4.8% 30 to 45 minutes, 10.1% 45 to 60 minutes, 1.6% 60 minutes or more (2005-2009 5-year est.)

WAGGONER (village). Covers a land area of 0.264 square miles and a water area of 0 square miles. Located at 39.37° N. Lat; 89.65° W. Long. Elevation is 640 feet.
Population: 221 (1990); 245 (2000); 255 (2010); 257 (2015 projected); Race: 99.2% White, 0.0% Black, 0.0% Asian, 0.8% Other, 0.0% Hispanic of any race (2010); Density: 967.7 persons per square mile (2010); Average household size: 2.71 (2010); Median age: 35.8 (2010); Males per 100 females: 100.8 (2010); Marriage status: 24.0% never married, 47.3% now married, 6.7% widowed, 22.0% divorced (2005-2009 5-year est.); Foreign born: 0.0% (2005-2009 5-year est.); Ancestry (includes multiple ancestries): 40.1% German, 29.7% Irish, 10.4% English, 4.2% French, 4.2% American (2005-2009 5-year est.).
Economy: Employment by occupation: 7.4% management, 14.8% professional, 14.8% services, 27.2% sales, 0.0% farming, 18.5% construction, 17.3% production (2005-2009 5-year est.).
Income: Per capita income: $17,969 (2010); Median household income: $43,250 (2010); Average household income: $48,963 (2010); Percent of households with income of $100,000 or more: 5.3% (2010); Poverty rate: 27.1% (2005-2009 5-year est.).
Taxes: Total city taxes per capita: $37 (2007); City property taxes per capita: $33 (2007).

Education: Percent of population age 25 and over with: High school diploma (including GED) or higher: 84.4% (2010); Bachelor's degree or higher: 3.6% (2010); Master's degree or higher: 2.4% (2010).
Housing: Homeownership rate: 78.7% (2010); Median home value: $56,667 (2010); Median contract rent: n/a per month (2005-2009 5-year est.); Median year structure built: 1955 (2005-2009 5-year est.).
Transportation: Commute to work: 93.7% car, 0.0% public transportation, 0.0% walk, 6.3% work from home (2005-2009 5-year est.); Travel time to work: 17.6% less than 15 minutes, 23.0% 15 to 30 minutes, 40.5% 30 to 45 minutes, 13.5% 45 to 60 minutes, 5.4% 60 minutes or more (2005-2009 5-year est.)

WALSHVILLE (village). Covers a land area of 0.256 square miles and a water area of 0 square miles. Located at 39.07° N. Lat; 89.61° W. Long. Elevation is 617 feet.
Population: 44 (1990); 89 (2000); 89 (2010); 89 (2015 projected); Race: 98.9% White, 0.0% Black, 0.0% Asian, 1.1% Other, 0.0% Hispanic of any race (2010); Density: 348.1 persons per square mile (2010); Average household size: 2.70 (2010); Median age: 43.6 (2010); Males per 100 females: 102.3 (2010); Marriage status: 38.5% never married, 53.8% now married, 0.0% widowed, 7.7% divorced (2005-2009 5-year est.); Foreign born: 0.0% (2005-2009 5-year est.); Ancestry (includes multiple ancestries): 23.9% German, 16.9% American, 11.3% English, 4.2% Hungarian, 4.2% Slovak (2005-2009 5-year est.).
Economy: Employment by occupation: 0.0% management, 2.4% professional, 19.5% services, 9.8% sales, 14.6% farming, 39.0% construction, 14.6% production (2005-2009 5-year est.).
Income: Per capita income: $23,933 (2010); Median household income: $58,929 (2010); Average household income: $80,758 (2010); Percent of households with income of $100,000 or more: 21.2% (2010); Poverty rate: 35.2% (2005-2009 5-year est.).
Taxes: Total city taxes per capita: $45 (2007); City property taxes per capita: $45 (2007).
Education: Percent of population age 25 and over with: High school diploma (including GED) or higher: 89.1% (2010); Bachelor's degree or higher: 25.0% (2010); Master's degree or higher: 10.9% (2010).
Housing: Homeownership rate: 87.9% (2010); Median home value: $108,333 (2010); Median contract rent: n/a per month (2005-2009 5-year est.); Median year structure built: 1985 (2005-2009 5-year est.).
Transportation: Commute to work: 100.0% car, 0.0% public transportation, 0.0% walk, 0.0% work from home (2005-2009 5-year est.); Travel time to work: 10.8% less than 15 minutes, 62.2% 15 to 30 minutes, 21.6% 30 to 45 minutes, 2.7% 45 to 60 minutes, 2.7% 60 minutes or more (2005-2009 5-year est.)

WENONAH (village). Covers a land area of 1.509 square miles and a water area of 0 square miles. Located at 39.32° N. Lat; 89.28° W. Long. Elevation is 673 feet.
Population: 40 (1990); 44 (2000); 48 (2010); 49 (2015 projected); Race: 97.9% White, 0.0% Black, 0.0% Asian, 2.1% Other, 0.0% Hispanic of any race (2010); Density: 31.8 persons per square mile (2010); Average household size: 2.67 (2010); Median age: 40.7 (2010); Males per 100 females: 77.8 (2010); Marriage status: 70.8% never married, 20.8% now married, 8.3% widowed, 0.0% divorced (2005-2009 5-year est.); Foreign born: 0.0% (2005-2009 5-year est.); Ancestry (includes multiple ancestries): 5.3% Irish (2005-2009 5-year est.).
Economy: Employment by occupation: n/a management, n/a professional, n/a services, n/a sales, n/a farming, n/a construction, n/a production (2005-2009 5-year est.).
Income: Per capita income: $19,061 (2010); Median household income: $55,000 (2010); Average household income: $54,722 (2010); Percent of households with income of $100,000 or more: 5.6% (2010); Poverty rate: 73.7% (2005-2009 5-year est.).
Taxes: Total city taxes per capita: $0 (2007); City property taxes per capita: $0 (2007).
Education: Percent of population age 25 and over with: High school diploma (including GED) or higher: 90.9% (2010); Bachelor's degree or higher: 18.2% (2010); Master's degree or higher: 6.1% (2010).
Housing: Homeownership rate: 83.3% (2010); Median home value: $72,500 (2010); Median contract rent: n/a per month (2005-2009 5-year est.); Median year structure built: 1988 (2005-2009 5-year est.).
Transportation: Commute to work: n/a car, n/a public transportation, n/a walk, n/a work from home (2005-2009 5-year est.); Travel time to work: n/a less than 15 minutes, n/a 15 to 30 minutes, n/a 30 to 45 minutes, n/a 45 to 60 minutes, n/a 60 minutes or more (2005-2009 5-year est.)

WITT (city). Covers a land area of 1.394 square miles and a water area of 0 square miles. Located at 39.25° N. Lat; 89.35° W. Long. Elevation is 663 feet.
Population: 866 (1990); 991 (2000); 1,045 (2010); 1,065 (2015 projected); Race: 99.5% White, 0.1% Black, 0.1% Asian, 0.3% Other, 0.6% Hispanic of any race (2010); Density: 749.6 persons per square mile (2010); Average household size: 2.25 (2010); Median age: 39.9 (2010); Males per 100 females: 90.0 (2010); Marriage status: 28.7% never married, 51.7% now married, 6.3% widowed, 13.2% divorced (2005-2009 5-year est.); Foreign born: 0.0% (2005-2009 5-year est.); Ancestry (includes multiple ancestries): 24.0% German, 8.6% English, 6.9% Irish, 6.8% American, 3.4% Yugoslavian (2005-2009 5-year est.).
Economy: Employment by occupation: 5.7% management, 6.8% professional, 30.9% services, 24.6% sales, 3.1% farming, 19.8% construction, 9.1% production (2005-2009 5-year est.).
Income: Per capita income: $17,960 (2010); Median household income: $32,339 (2010); Average household income: $39,898 (2010); Percent of households with income of $100,000 or more: 4.3% (2010); Poverty rate: 24.4% (2005-2009 5-year est.).
Taxes: Total city taxes per capita: $90 (2007); City property taxes per capita: $37 (2007).
Education: Percent of population age 25 and over with: High school diploma (including GED) or higher: 81.5% (2010); Bachelor's degree or higher: 12.7% (2010); Master's degree or higher: 4.4% (2010).

School District(s)
Hillsboro CUSD 3 (PK-12)
    2009-10 Enrollment: 1,954 . . . . (217) 532-2942
Housing: Homeownership rate: 78.3% (2010); Median home value: $56,250 (2010); Median contract rent: $178 per month (2005-2009 5-year est.); Median year structure built: 1955 (2005-2009 5-year est.).
Safety: Violent crime rate: 0.0 per 10,000 population; Property crime rate: 85.6 per 10,000 population (2010).
Transportation: Commute to work: 92.8% car, 0.0% public transportation, 0.0% walk, 7.2% work from home (2005-2009 5-year est.); Travel time to work: 23.8% less than 15 minutes, 36.9% 15 to 30 minutes, 14.7% 30 to 45 minutes, 13.1% 45 to 60 minutes, 11.6% 60 minutes or more (2005-2009 5-year est.)

Morgan County

Located in west central Illinois; bounded on the west by the Illinois River; includes part of Lake Meredosia. Covers a land area of 568.76 square miles, a water area of 3.51 square miles, and is located in the Central Time Zone at 39.71° N. Lat., 90.21° W. Long. The county was founded in 1823. County seat is Jacksonville.

Morgan County is part of the Jacksonville, IL Micropolitan Statistical Area. The entire metro area includes: Morgan County, IL; Scott County, IL

Weather Station: Jacksonville 2 E   Elevation: 609 feet

	Jan	Feb	Mar	Apr	May	Jun	Jul	Aug	Sep	Oct	Nov	Dec
High	36	40	52	64	74	83	86	85	79	67	53	39
Low	18	20	29	39	50	59	63	61	52	41	32	21
Precip	1.6	1.7	2.8	3.9	4.7	4.3	3.8	3.5	3.6	3.0	3.6	2.5
Snow	6.0	5.0	2.6	0.4	0.0	0.0	0.0	0.0	0.0	tr	0.6	5.6

High and Low temperatures in degrees Fahrenheit; Precipitation and Snow in inches

Population: 36,397 (1990); 36,616 (2000); 35,047 (2010); 34,108 (2015 projected); Race: 91.2% White, 5.6% Black, 0.7% Asian, 2.5% Other, 1.6% Hispanic of any race (2010); Density: 61.6 persons per square mile (2010); Average household size: 2.33 (2010); Median age: 38.9 (2010); Males per 100 females: 100.7 (2010).
Religion: Five largest groups: 11.2% Catholic Church, 7.3% The United Methodist Church, 6.3% Christian Church (Disciples of Christ), 5.4% Southern Baptist Convention, 5.3% Lutheran Church—Missouri Synod (2000).
Economy: Unemployment rate: 8.8% (August 2011); Total civilian labor force: 17,884 (August 2011); Leading industries: 20.5% health care and social assistance; 15.9% manufacturing; 15.4% retail trade (2009); Farms: 740 totaling 320,512 acres (2007); Companies that employ 500 or more persons: 3 (2009); Companies that employ 100 to 499 persons: 17 (2009); Companies that employ less than 100 persons: 870 (2009); Black-owned businesses: n/a (2007); Hispanic-owned businesses: n/a (2007); Asian-owned businesses: n/a (2007); Women-owned businesses: 708

(2007); Retail sales per capita: $13,547 (2010). Single-family building permits issued: 8 (2010); Multi-family building permits issued: 0 (2010).
Income: Per capita income: $22,196 (2010); Median household income: $44,416 (2010); Average household income: $55,117 (2010); Percent of households with income of $100,000 or more: 10.8% (2010); Poverty rate: 14.1% (2009); Bankruptcy rate: 4.29% (2010).
Taxes: Total county taxes per capita: $164 (2007); County property taxes per capita: $142 (2007).
Education: Percent of population age 25 and over with: High school diploma (including GED) or higher: 85.8% (2010); Bachelor's degree or higher: 20.7% (2010); Master's degree or higher: 6.9% (2010).
Housing: Homeownership rate: 70.4% (2010); Median home value: $87,333 (2010); Median contract rent: $401 per month (2005-2009 5-year est.); Median year structure built: 1961 (2005-2009 5-year est.)
Health: Birth rate: 118.1 per 10,000 population (2009); Death rate: 114.3 per 10,000 population (2009); Age-adjusted cancer mortality rate: 206.1 deaths per 100,000 population (2007); Number of physicians: 11.7 per 10,000 population (2008); Hospital beds: 31.7 per 10,000 population (2007); Hospital admissions: 1,143.7 per 10,000 population (2007).
Elections: 2008 Presidential election results: 48.6% Obama, 49.4% McCain, 1.0% Nader
Additional Information Contacts
Morgan County Government . . . . (217) 243-8581
  http://www.morgancounty-il.com
City of Jacksonville . . . . (217) 479-4600
  http://www.jacksonvilleil.com
Jacksonville Area Chamber of Commerce. . . . . (217) 245-2174
  http://www.jacksonvilleareachamber.org

Morgan County Communities

ALEXANDER (unincorporated postal area, zip code 62601). Covers a land area of 55.344 square miles and a water area of 0 square miles. Located at 39.75° N. Lat; 90.02° W. Long. Elevation is 659 feet.
Population: 512 (2000); Race: 97.7% White, 1.3% Black, 0.0% Asian, 1.0% Other, 0.0% Hispanic of any race (2000); Density: 9.3 persons per square mile (2000); Age: 25.0% under 18, 11.4% over 64 (2000); Marriage status: 20.1% never married, 63.8% now married, 4.6% widowed, 11.4% divorced (2000); Foreign born: 0.0% (2000); Ancestry (includes multiple ancestries): 23.3% German, 20.3% English, 10.9% Irish, 7.7% American, 3.8% Swedish (2000).
Economy: Employment by occupation: 22.6% management, 7.7% professional, 13.1% services, 26.2% sales, 4.5% farming, 12.8% construction, 13.1% production (2000).
Income: Per capita income: $19,414 (2000); Median household income: $46,932 (2000); Poverty rate: 6.2% (2000).
Education: Percent of population age 25 and over with: High school diploma (including GED) or higher: 86.3% (2000); Bachelor's degree or higher: 12.9% (2000).
School District(s)
Franklin CUSD 1 (PK-12)
  2009-10 Enrollment: 326 . . . . (217) 478-3011
Housing: Homeownership rate: 73.1% (2000); Median home value: $75,700 (2000); Median contract rent: $352 per month (2000); Median year structure built: 1945 (2000).
Transportation: Commute to work: 90.1% car, 0.0% public transportation, 1.8% walk, 8.1% work from home (2000); Travel time to work: 29.3% less than 15 minutes, 40.1% 15 to 30 minutes, 20.2% 30 to 45 minutes, 8.8% 45 to 60 minutes, 1.6% 60 minutes or more (2000)

CHAPIN (village). Covers a land area of 0.975 square miles and a water area of 0 square miles. Located at 39.76° N. Lat; 90.40° W. Long. Elevation is 620 feet.
Population: 632 (1990); 592 (2000); 476 (2010); 429 (2015 projected); Race: 98.5% White, 0.0% Black, 0.0% Asian, 1.5% Other, 0.2% Hispanic of any race (2010); Density: 488.1 persons per square mile (2010); Average household size: 2.55 (2010); Median age: 37.3 (2010); Males per 100 females: 106.1 (2010); Marriage status: 23.3% never married, 55.2% now married, 7.7% widowed, 13.8% divorced (2005-2009 5-year est.); Foreign born: 0.0% (2005-2009 5-year est.); Ancestry (includes multiple ancestries): 38.1% American, 28.9% German, 14.4% English, 6.0% Irish, 2.9% French (2005-2009 5-year est.).
Economy: Employment by occupation: 6.1% management, 12.7% professional, 28.3% services, 27.9% sales, 2.0% farming, 6.6% construction, 16.4% production (2005-2009 5-year est.).

Income: Per capita income: $23,115 (2010); Median household income: $56,629 (2010); Average household income: $59,011 (2010); Percent of households with income of $100,000 or more: 10.2% (2010); Poverty rate: 11.8% (2005-2009 5-year est.).
Taxes: Total city taxes per capita: $122 (2007); City property taxes per capita: $67 (2007).
Education: Percent of population age 25 and over with: High school diploma (including GED) or higher: 93.0% (2010); Bachelor's degree or higher: 13.2% (2010); Master's degree or higher: 1.3% (2010).
Housing: Homeownership rate: 86.6% (2010); Median home value: $68,718 (2010); Median contract rent: $289 per month (2005-2009 5-year est.); Median year structure built: 1962 (2005-2009 5-year est.).
Transportation: Commute to work: 95.1% car, 0.0% public transportation, 1.6% walk, 3.3% work from home (2005-2009 5-year est.); Travel time to work: 16.8% less than 15 minutes, 56.3% 15 to 30 minutes, 7.1% 30 to 45 minutes, 13.9% 45 to 60 minutes, 5.9% 60 minutes or more (2005-2009 5-year est.)

CONCORD (village). Covers a land area of 0.263 square miles and a water area of 0 square miles. Located at 39.81° N. Lat; 90.37° W. Long. Elevation is 594 feet.
Population: 172 (1990); 176 (2000); 167 (2010); 158 (2015 projected); Race: 99.4% White, 0.0% Black, 0.0% Asian, 0.6% Other, 0.0% Hispanic of any race (2010); Density: 636.0 persons per square mile (2010); Average household size: 2.57 (2010); Median age: 42.6 (2010); Males per 100 females: 101.2 (2010); Marriage status: 32.7% never married, 54.2% now married, 7.5% widowed, 5.6% divorced (2005-2009 5-year est.); Foreign born: 0.0% (2005-2009 5-year est.); Ancestry (includes multiple ancestries): 45.2% German, 18.5% American, 11.3% English, 10.5% Irish, 6.5% Swiss (2005-2009 5-year est.).
Economy: Employment by occupation: 18.2% management, 18.2% professional, 10.6% services, 18.2% sales, 0.0% farming, 7.6% construction, 27.3% production (2005-2009 5-year est.).
Income: Per capita income: $22,938 (2010); Median household income: $47,500 (2010); Average household income: $57,192 (2010); Percent of households with income of $100,000 or more: 12.3% (2010); Poverty rate: 0.0% (2005-2009 5-year est.).
Taxes: Total city taxes per capita: $69 (2007); City property taxes per capita: $69 (2007).
Education: Percent of population age 25 and over with: High school diploma (including GED) or higher: 92.2% (2010); Bachelor's degree or higher: 17.2% (2010); Master's degree or higher: 3.4% (2010).
School District(s)
Triopia CUSD 27 (PK-12)
  2009-10 Enrollment: 398 . . . . (217) 457-2283
Housing: Homeownership rate: 84.6% (2010); Median home value: $88,182 (2010); Median contract rent: n/a per month (2005-2009 5-year est.); Median year structure built: before 1940 (2005-2009 5-year est.).
Transportation: Commute to work: 100.0% car, 0.0% public transportation, 0.0% walk, 0.0% work from home (2005-2009 5-year est.); Travel time to work: 13.6% less than 15 minutes, 60.6% 15 to 30 minutes, 15.2% 30 to 45 minutes, 0.0% 45 to 60 minutes, 10.6% 60 minutes or more (2005-2009 5-year est.)

FRANKLIN (village). Covers a land area of 0.731 square miles and a water area of 0 square miles. Located at 39.62° N. Lat; 90.04° W. Long. Elevation is 682 feet.
Population: 681 (1990); 586 (2000); 473 (2010); 430 (2015 projected); Race: 97.7% White, 0.4% Black, 0.0% Asian, 1.9% Other, 1.9% Hispanic of any race (2010); Density: 646.8 persons per square mile (2010); Average household size: 2.53 (2010); Median age: 39.8 (2010); Males per 100 females: 97.9 (2010); Marriage status: 14.0% never married, 71.6% now married, 6.9% widowed, 7.6% divorced (2005-2009 5-year est.); Foreign born: 0.5% (2005-2009 5-year est.); Ancestry (includes multiple ancestries): 29.2% American, 19.8% German, 17.6% Irish, 6.5% Swedish, 4.9% English (2005-2009 5-year est.).
Economy: Employment by occupation: 4.7% management, 16.6% professional, 20.7% services, 18.6% sales, 0.7% farming, 14.9% construction, 23.7% production (2005-2009 5-year est.).
Income: Per capita income: $26,324 (2010); Median household income: $59,750 (2010); Average household income: $65,896 (2010); Percent of households with income of $100,000 or more: 18.2% (2010); Poverty rate: 11.3% (2005-2009 5-year est.).
Taxes: Total city taxes per capita: $43 (2007); City property taxes per capita: $43 (2007).

Education: Percent of population age 25 and over with: High school diploma (including GED) or higher: 90.7% (2010); Bachelor's degree or higher: 13.6% (2010); Master's degree or higher: 3.7% (2010).

School District(s)

Franklin CUSD 1 (PK-12)
    2009-10 Enrollment: 326 . . . . (217) 478-3011

Housing: Homeownership rate: 78.1% (2010); Median home value: $93,333 (2010); Median contract rent: $520 per month (2005-2009 5-year est.); Median year structure built: 1943 (2005-2009 5-year est.).

Newspapers: Franklin Times (Community news; Circulation 800); Murrayville Gazette (Local news; Circulation 800)

Transportation: Commute to work: 86.1% car, 0.0% public transportation, 6.0% walk, 3.6% work from home (2005-2009 5-year est.); Travel time to work: 20.3% less than 15 minutes, 38.0% 15 to 30 minutes, 19.9% 30 to 45 minutes, 10.0% 45 to 60 minutes, 11.8% 60 minutes or more (2005-2009 5-year est.)

JACKSONVILLE (city). County seat. Covers a land area of 10.133 square miles and a water area of 0.193 square miles. Located at 39.73° N. Lat; 90.23° W. Long. Elevation is 610 feet.

History: Jacksonville was founded in 1825, and named for Andrew Jackson. The first settlers were southerners, but they were followed by people from New England. Abolitionist sentiment was strong, and Jacksonville served as a station on the Underground Railroad. Both William Jennings Bryan (1883) and Stephen A. Douglas (1834) began their law practices in Jacksonville, and Abraham Lincoln was a frequent speaker here.

Population: 19,613 (1990); 18,940 (2000); 17,423 (2010); 16,662 (2015 projected); Race: 89.8% White, 5.9% Black, 1.1% Asian, 3.2% Other, 1.8% Hispanic of any race (2010); Density: 1,719.4 persons per square mile (2010); Average household size: 2.23 (2010); Median age: 38.0 (2010); Males per 100 females: 92.9 (2010); Marriage status: 34.5% never married, 45.4% now married, 7.7% widowed, 12.5% divorced (2005-2009 5-year est.); Foreign born: 1.4% (2005-2009 5-year est.); Ancestry (includes multiple ancestries): 24.2% German, 22.1% American, 15.5% Irish, 13.2% English, 2.3% Scotch-Irish (2005-2009 5-year est.).

Economy: Single-family building permits issued: 8 (2010); Multi-family building permits issued: 0 (2010); Employment by occupation: 11.2% management, 21.8% professional, 22.9% services, 26.2% sales, 0.5% farming, 5.3% construction, 12.0% production (2005-2009 5-year est.).

Income: Per capita income: $20,262 (2010); Median household income: $38,203 (2010); Average household income: $50,354 (2010); Percent of households with income of $100,000 or more: 9.6% (2010); Poverty rate: 20.5% (2005-2009 5-year est.).

Taxes: Total city taxes per capita: $312 (2007); City property taxes per capita: $206 (2007).

Education: Percent of population age 25 and over with: High school diploma (including GED) or higher: 85.4% (2010); Bachelor's degree or higher: 24.1% (2010); Master's degree or higher: 8.3% (2010).

School District(s)

Brown/Cass/Morgan/Scott Roe (07-12)
    2009-10 Enrollment: n/a . . . . (217) 243-1804
Four Rivers Spec Educ Dist (03-12)
    2009-10 Enrollment: n/a . . . . (217) 245-7174
Jacksonville SD 117 (PK-12)
    2009-10 Enrollment: 3,753 . . . . (217) 243-9411

Four-year College(s)

Illinois College (Private, Not-for-profit, Presbyterian Church (USA))
    Fall 2009 Enrollment: 894 . . . . (217) 245-3000
    2010-11 Tuition: In-state $22,800; Out-of-state $22,800
MacMurray College (Private, Not-for-profit, United Methodist)
    Fall 2009 Enrollment: 518 . . . . (217) 479-7000
    2010-11 Tuition: In-state $19,310; Out-of-state $19,310

Vocational/Technical School(s)

Mr John's School of Cosmetology & Nails (Private, For-profit)
    Fall 2009 Enrollment: 36 . . . . (217) 243-1744
    2010-11 Tuition: $13,045

Housing: Homeownership rate: 61.1% (2010); Median home value: $82,672 (2010); Median contract rent: $412 per month (2005-2009 5-year est.); Median year structure built: 1958 (2005-2009 5-year est.).

Hospitals: Passavant Area Hospital (99 beds)

Safety: Violent crime rate: 39.6 per 10,000 population; Property crime rate: 271.4 per 10,000 population (2010).

Newspapers: Jacksonville Journal Courier (Local news; Circulation 14,969); Shoppers Guide (Local news; Circulation 14,000)

Transportation: Commute to work: 86.3% car, 2.8% public transportation, 6.7% walk, 2.8% work from home (2005-2009 5-year est.); Travel time to work: 67.7% less than 15 minutes, 13.1% 15 to 30 minutes, 7.3% 30 to 45 minutes, 7.1% 45 to 60 minutes, 4.8% 60 minutes or more (2005-2009 5-year est.)

Airports: Jacksonville Municipal (general aviation)

Additional Information Contacts

City of Jacksonville . . . . (217) 479-4600
    http://www.jacksonvilleil.com
Jacksonville Area Chamber of Commerce. . . . . (217) 245-2174
    http://www.jacksonvilleareachamber.org

LYNNVILLE (village). Covers a land area of 0.079 square miles and a water area of 0 square miles. Located at 39.68° N. Lat; 90.34° W. Long. Elevation is 620 feet.

Population: 125 (1990); 137 (2000); 163 (2010); 172 (2015 projected); Race: 99.4% White, 0.0% Black, 0.0% Asian, 0.6% Other, 2.5% Hispanic of any race (2010); Density: 2,066.8 persons per square mile (2010); Average household size: 2.59 (2010); Median age: 42.1 (2010); Males per 100 females: 117.3 (2010); Marriage status: 51.4% never married, 22.5% now married, 9.4% widowed, 16.7% divorced (2005-2009 5-year est.); Foreign born: 0.0% (2005-2009 5-year est.); Ancestry (includes multiple ancestries): 32.5% Irish, 31.4% German, 23.7% American, 7.1% English, 3.0% Greek (2005-2009 5-year est.).

Economy: Employment by occupation: 6.3% management, 7.2% professional, 29.7% services, 21.6% sales, 0.0% farming, 5.4% construction, 29.7% production (2005-2009 5-year est.).

Income: Per capita income: $26,142 (2010); Median household income: $60,625 (2010); Average household income: $70,714 (2010); Percent of households with income of $100,000 or more: 15.9% (2010); Poverty rate: 14.2% (2005-2009 5-year est.).

Taxes: Total city taxes per capita: $15 (2007); City property taxes per capita: $15 (2007).

Education: Percent of population age 25 and over with: High school diploma (including GED) or higher: 92.4% (2010); Bachelor's degree or higher: 22.7% (2010); Master's degree or higher: 8.4% (2010).

Housing: Homeownership rate: 85.7% (2010); Median home value: $125,000 (2010); Median contract rent: $358 per month (2005-2009 5-year est.); Median year structure built: 1974 (2005-2009 5-year est.).

Transportation: Commute to work: 95.5% car, 0.0% public transportation, 4.5% walk, 0.0% work from home (2005-2009 5-year est.); Travel time to work: 23.4% less than 15 minutes, 55.0% 15 to 30 minutes, 7.2% 30 to 45 minutes, 9.9% 45 to 60 minutes, 4.5% 60 minutes or more (2005-2009 5-year est.)

MEREDOSIA (village). Covers a land area of 0.921 square miles and a water area of 0.078 square miles. Located at 39.83° N. Lat; 90.55° W. Long. Elevation is 446 feet.

History: The name of Meredosia is from the French "marais d'osier" meaning "swamp of the basket reeds." The town was located at the mouth of Meredosia Lake. The railroad connecting with the Illinois & Michigan Canal was constructed here in 1838, but the Canal continued to hold supremacy over the railroad until 1878.

Population: 1,166 (1990); 1,041 (2000); 864 (2010); 791 (2015 projected); Race: 99.5% White, 0.1% Black, 0.0% Asian, 0.3% Other, 0.1% Hispanic of any race (2010); Density: 938.1 persons per square mile (2010); Average household size: 2.28 (2010); Median age: 40.7 (2010); Males per 100 females: 97.7 (2010); Marriage status: 17.9% never married, 58.3% now married, 8.2% widowed, 15.6% divorced (2005-2009 5-year est.); Foreign born: 0.0% (2005-2009 5-year est.); Ancestry (includes multiple ancestries): 31.6% German, 25.0% American, 15.1% Irish, 11.1% English, 2.6% Swedish (2005-2009 5-year est.).

Economy: Single-family building permits issued: 0 (2010); Multi-family building permits issued: 0 (2010); Employment by occupation: 5.4% management, 19.1% professional, 14.7% services, 19.6% sales, 1.6% farming, 7.8% construction, 31.8% production (2005-2009 5-year est.).

Income: Per capita income: $19,618 (2010); Median household income: $37,981 (2010); Average household income: $45,026 (2010); Percent of households with income of $100,000 or more: 3.4% (2010); Poverty rate: 21.2% (2005-2009 5-year est.).

Taxes: Total city taxes per capita: $99 (2007); City property taxes per capita: $92 (2007).

Education: Percent of population age 25 and over with: High school diploma (including GED) or higher: 82.6% (2010); Bachelor's degree or higher: 5.3% (2010); Master's degree or higher: 2.8% (2010).

School District(s)

Meredosia-Chambersburg CUSD 11 (PK-12)

    2009-10 Enrollment: 310 . . . . (217) 584-1744

Housing: Homeownership rate: 80.2% (2010); Median home value: $51,250 (2010); Median contract rent: $246 per month (2005-2009 5-year est.); Median year structure built: 1960 (2005-2009 5-year est.).

Safety: Violent crime rate: 0.0 per 10,000 population; Property crime rate: 63.7 per 10,000 population (2010).

Transportation: Commute to work: 95.8% car, 0.0% public transportation, 0.0% walk, 2.6% work from home (2005-2009 5-year est.); Travel time to work: 45.0% less than 15 minutes, 28.2% 15 to 30 minutes, 17.4% 30 to 45 minutes, 2.4% 45 to 60 minutes, 7.0% 60 minutes or more (2005-2009 5-year est.)

MURRAYVILLE (village).

Covers a land area of 0.498 square miles and a water area of 0 square miles. Located at 39.58° N. Lat; 90.25° W. Long. Elevation is 692 feet.

Population: 673 (1990); 644 (2000); 748 (2010); 782 (2015 projected); Race: 98.3% White, 0.1% Black, 0.1% Asian, 1.5% Other, 0.0% Hispanic of any race (2010); Density: 1,501.1 persons per square mile (2010); Average household size: 2.60 (2010); Median age: 38.2 (2010); Males per 100 females: 102.2 (2010); Marriage status: 20.3% never married, 67.9% now married, 5.2% widowed, 6.5% divorced (2005-2009 5-year est.); Foreign born: 0.0% (2005-2009 5-year est.); Ancestry (includes multiple ancestries): 28.3% American, 22.6% English, 17.6% German, 11.7% Irish, 5.0% Scottish (2005-2009 5-year est.).

Economy: Employment by occupation: 3.6% management, 15.6% professional, 10.4% services, 36.7% sales, 0.6% farming, 18.2% construction, 14.9% production (2005-2009 5-year est.).

Income: Per capita income: $21,433 (2010); Median household income: $53,431 (2010); Average household income: $55,712 (2010); Percent of households with income of $100,000 or more: 6.6% (2010); Poverty rate: 13.9% (2005-2009 5-year est.).

Taxes: Total city taxes per capita: $106 (2007); City property taxes per capita: $63 (2007).

Education: Percent of population age 25 and over with: High school diploma (including GED) or higher: 89.9% (2010); Bachelor's degree or higher: 15.3% (2010); Master's degree or higher: 6.4% (2010).

School District(s)

Jacksonville SD 117 (PK-12)

    2009-10 Enrollment: 3,753 . . . . (217) 243-9411

Housing: Homeownership rate: 84.0% (2010); Median home value: $82,174 (2010); Median contract rent: $288 per month (2005-2009 5-year est.); Median year structure built: 1962 (2005-2009 5-year est.).

Transportation: Commute to work: 92.2% car, 0.0% public transportation, 1.0% walk, 1.0% work from home (2005-2009 5-year est.); Travel time to work: 19.5% less than 15 minutes, 59.7% 15 to 30 minutes, 5.8% 30 to 45 minutes, 5.8% 45 to 60 minutes, 9.2% 60 minutes or more (2005-2009 5-year est.)

SOUTH JACKSONVILLE (village).

Covers a land area of 1.653 square miles and a water area of 0.058 square miles. Located at 39.71° N. Lat; 90.23° W. Long. Elevation is 620 feet.

Population: 3,292 (1990); 3,475 (2000); 3,250 (2010); 3,122 (2015 projected); Race: 87.2% White, 9.1% Black, 1.2% Asian, 2.5% Other, 2.3% Hispanic of any race (2010); Density: 1,966.2 persons per square mile (2010); Average household size: 2.14 (2010); Median age: 42.3 (2010); Males per 100 females: 105.2 (2010); Marriage status: 24.1% never married, 52.6% now married, 7.2% widowed, 16.1% divorced (2005-2009 5-year est.); Foreign born: 1.1% (2005-2009 5-year est.); Ancestry (includes multiple ancestries): 35.8% German, 19.0% English, 18.2% Irish, 16.6% American, 4.9% Dutch (2005-2009 5-year est.).

Economy: Single-family building permits issued: 0 (2010); Multi-family building permits issued: 0 (2010); Employment by occupation: 14.7% management, 17.5% professional, 12.9% services, 33.5% sales, 0.0% farming, 7.7% construction, 13.7% production (2005-2009 5-year est.).

Income: Per capita income: $25,669 (2010); Median household income: $48,337 (2010); Average household income: $57,087 (2010); Percent of households with income of $100,000 or more: 11.4% (2010); Poverty rate: 16.7% (2005-2009 5-year est.).

Taxes: Total city taxes per capita: $182 (2007); City property taxes per capita: $141 (2007).

Education: Percent of population age 25 and over with: High school diploma (including GED) or higher: 84.3% (2010); Bachelor's degree or higher: 24.7% (2010); Master's degree or higher: 8.2% (2010).

Housing: Homeownership rate: 70.8% (2010); Median home value: $98,869 (2010); Median contract rent: $331 per month (2005-2009 est.); Median year structure built: 1968 (2005-2009 5-year est.).

Safety: Violent crime rate: 15.9 per 10,000 population; Property crime rate: 127.2 per 10,000 population (2010).

Transportation: Commute to work: 95.9% car, 0.0% public transportation, 0.0% walk, 1.4% work from home (2005-2009 5-year est.); Travel time to work: 65.9% less than 15 minutes, 16.9% 15 to 30 minutes, 4.9% 30 to 45 minutes, 8.9% 45 to 60 minutes, 3.4% 60 minutes or more (2005-2009 5-year est.)

WAVERLY (city).

Covers a land area of 1.032 square miles and a water area of 0 square miles. Located at 39.59° N. Lat; 89.95° W. Long. Elevation is 682 feet.

History: Incorporated 1867.

Population: 1,402 (1990); 1,346 (2000); 1,167 (2010); 1,088 (2015 projected); Race: 99.4% White, 0.0% Black, 0.1% Asian, 0.5% Other, 0.3% Hispanic of any race (2010); Density: 1,130.5 persons per square mile (2010); Average household size: 2.33 (2010); Median age: 40.3 (2010); Males per 100 females: 93.2 (2010); Marriage status: 16.8% never married, 57.0% now married, 13.8% widowed, 12.5% divorced (2005-2009 5-year est.); Foreign born: 0.6% (2005-2009 5-year est.); Ancestry (includes multiple ancestries): 30.4% American, 24.4% German, 11.5% Irish, 11.1% English, 2.8% French (2005-2009 5-year est.).

Economy: Single-family building permits issued: 0 (2010); Multi-family building permits issued: 0 (2010); Employment by occupation: 10.0% management, 9.6% professional, 19.7% services, 34.4% sales, 0.0% farming, 6.4% construction, 19.9% production (2005-2009 5-year est.).

Income: Per capita income: $23,990 (2010); Median household income: $47,150 (2010); Average household income: $54,905 (2010); Percent of households with income of $100,000 or more: 9.6% (2010); Poverty rate: 11.7% (2005-2009 5-year est.).

Taxes: Total city taxes per capita: $69 (2007); City property taxes per capita: $56 (2007).

Education: Percent of population age 25 and over with: High school diploma (including GED) or higher: 89.1% (2010); Bachelor's degree or higher: 13.4% (2010); Master's degree or higher: 5.5% (2010).

School District(s)

Waverly CUSD 6 (PK-12)

    2009-10 Enrollment: 389 . . . . (217) 435-8121

Housing: Homeownership rate: 82.6% (2010); Median home value: $71,630 (2010); Median contract rent: $371 per month (2005-2009 5-year est.); Median year structure built: 1950 (2005-2009 5-year est.).

Newspapers: Waverly Journal (Community news; Circulation 1,561)

Transportation: Commute to work: 89.5% car, 0.0% public transportation, 6.1% walk, 3.0% work from home (2005-2009 5-year est.); Travel time to work: 29.7% less than 15 minutes, 23.6% 15 to 30 minutes, 27.5% 30 to 45 minutes, 17.3% 45 to 60 minutes, 1.8% 60 minutes or more (2005-2009 5-year est.)

WOODSON (village).

Covers a land area of 0.387 square miles and a water area of 0 square miles. Located at 39.62° N. Lat; 90.22° W. Long. Elevation is 679 feet.

Population: 509 (1990); 559 (2000); 615 (2010); 633 (2015 projected); Race: 97.7% White, 0.3% Black, 0.3% Asian, 1.6% Other, 0.2% Hispanic of any race (2010); Density: 1,587.1 persons per square mile (2010); Average household size: 2.51 (2010); Median age: 40.2 (2010); Males per 100 females: 101.0 (2010); Marriage status: 8.3% never married, 80.6% now married, 5.3% widowed, 5.8% divorced (2005-2009 5-year est.); Foreign born: 3.2% (2005-2009 5-year est.); Ancestry (includes multiple ancestries): 32.6% American, 20.7% Irish, 18.1% German, 9.9% English, 7.8% Portuguese (2005-2009 5-year est.).

Economy: Employment by occupation: 12.0% management, 11.3% professional, 18.6% services, 28.1% sales, 1.1% farming, 8.8% construction, 20.1% production (2005-2009 5-year est.).

Income: Per capita income: $23,766 (2010); Median household income: $51,096 (2010); Average household income: $60,010 (2010); Percent of households with income of $100,000 or more: 14.3% (2010); Poverty rate: 3.8% (2005-2009 5-year est.).

Taxes: Total city taxes per capita: $139 (2007); City property taxes per capita: $74 (2007).

Education: Percent of population age 25 and over with: High school diploma (including GED) or higher: 90.8% (2010); Bachelor's degree or higher: 17.2% (2010); Master's degree or higher: 5.9% (2010).

Housing: Homeownership rate: 86.9% (2010); Median home value: $111,364 (2010); Median contract rent: $563 per month (2005-2009 5-year est.); Median year structure built: 1975 (2005-2009 5-year est.).
Transportation: Commute to work: 96.2% car, 0.0% public transportation, 0.0% walk, 3.8% work from home (2005-2009 5-year est.); Travel time to work: 19.9% less than 15 minutes, 61.4% 15 to 30 minutes, 8.0% 30 to 45 minutes, 5.6% 45 to 60 minutes, 5.2% 60 minutes or more (2005-2009 5-year est.)

Moultrie County

Located in central Illinois; drained by the Kaskaskia River. Covers a land area of 335.60 square miles, a water area of 8.87 square miles, and is located in the Central Time Zone at 39.63° N. Lat., 88.62° W. Long. The county was founded in 1843. County seat is Sullivan.

Population: 13,930 (1990); 14,287 (2000); 14,415 (2010); 14,411 (2015 projected); Race: 97.8% White, 0.7% Black, 0.3% Asian, 1.1% Other, 0.8% Hispanic of any race (2010); Density: 43.0 persons per square mile (2010); Average household size: 2.53 (2010); Median age: 39.0 (2010); Males per 100 females: 93.9 (2010).
Religion: Five largest groups: 10.0% Christian Church (Disciples of Christ), 7.4% The United Methodist Church, 6.0% Southern Baptist Convention, 4.2% Catholic Church, 3.1% Lutheran Church—Missouri Synod (2000).
Economy: Unemployment rate: 8.8% (August 2011); Total civilian labor force: 7,757 (August 2011); Leading industries: 17.7% health care and social assistance; 8.6% retail trade; 5.1% accommodation & food services (2009); Farms: 520 totaling 167,791 acres (2007); Companies that employ 500 or more persons: 1 (2009); Companies that employ 100 to 499 persons: 4 (2009); Companies that employ less than 100 persons: 311 (2009); Black-owned businesses: n/a (2007); Hispanic-owned businesses: n/a (2007); Asian-owned businesses: n/a (2007); Women-owned businesses: n/a (2007); Retail sales per capita: $5,240 (2010). Single-family building permits issued: 24 (2010); Multi-family building permits issued: 9 (2010).
Income: Per capita income: $23,022 (2010); Median household income: $48,504 (2010); Average household income: $58,057 (2010); Percent of households with income of $100,000 or more: 12.1% (2010); Poverty rate: 10.8% (2009); Bankruptcy rate: 4.09% (2010).
Taxes: Total county taxes per capita: $133 (2007); County property taxes per capita: $133 (2007).
Education: Percent of population age 25 and over with: High school diploma (including GED) or higher: 84.7% (2010); Bachelor's degree or higher: 18.2% (2010); Master's degree or higher: 4.7% (2010).
Housing: Homeownership rate: 77.3% (2010); Median home value: $109,752 (2010); Median contract rent: $408 per month (2005-2009 5-year est.); Median year structure built: 1960 (2005-2009 5-year est.)
Health: Birth rate: 134.1 per 10,000 population (2009); Death rate: 134.1 per 10,000 population (2009); Age-adjusted cancer mortality rate: 211.2 deaths per 100,000 population (2007); Number of physicians: 4.2 per 10,000 population (2008); Hospital beds: 0.0 per 10,000 population (2007); Hospital admissions: 0.0 per 10,000 population (2007).
Elections: 2008 Presidential election results: 42.6% Obama, 55.4% McCain, 0.9% Nader
National and State Parks: Kaskaskia River State Fish and Wildlife Management; West Okaw River State Fish and Wildlife Management
Additional Information Contacts
Moultrie County Government . . . . (217) 728-4389
   http://moultriecountyil.com
Sullivan Chamber of Commerce . . . . (217) 728-4223
   http://www.sullivanchamber.com

Moultrie County Communities

ALLENVILLE (village). Covers a land area of 0.582 square miles and a water area of 0 square miles. Located at 39.55° N. Lat; 88.53° W. Long. Elevation is 650 feet.
Population: 166 (1990); 154 (2000); 168 (2010); 173 (2015 projected); Race: 98.8% White, 0.0% Black, 0.0% Asian, 1.2% Other, 0.6% Hispanic of any race (2010); Density: 288.4 persons per square mile (2010); Average household size: 2.90 (2010); Median age: 46.9 (2010); Males per 100 females: 102.4 (2010); Marriage status: 18.3% never married, 71.2% now married, 2.9% widowed, 7.7% divorced (2005-2009 5-year est.); Foreign born: 0.0% (2005-2009 5-year est.); Ancestry (includes multiple

ancestries): 22.3% English, 19.8% German, 17.4% American, 16.5% Irish, 9.1% Polish (2005-2009 5-year est.).
Economy: Single-family building permits issued: 0 (2010); Multi-family building permits issued: 0 (2010); Employment by occupation: 4.5% management, 4.5% professional, 13.6% services, 28.8% sales, 0.0% farming, 22.7% construction, 25.8% production (2005-2009 5-year est.).
Income: Per capita income: $25,259 (2010); Median household income: $62,500 (2010); Average household income: $71,480 (2010); Percent of households with income of $100,000 or more: 20.4% (2010); Poverty rate: 1.7% (2005-2009 5-year est.).
Taxes: Total city taxes per capita: $20 (2007); City property taxes per capita: $20 (2007).
Education: Percent of population age 25 and over with: High school diploma (including GED) or higher: 83.9% (2010); Bachelor's degree or higher: 28.2% (2010); Master's degree or higher: 5.6% (2010).
Housing: Homeownership rate: 85.7% (2010); Median home value: $150,000 (2010); Median contract rent: n/a per month (2005-2009 5-year est.); Median year structure built: 1972 (2005-2009 5-year est.).
Transportation: Commute to work: 92.1% car, 0.0% public transportation, 0.0% walk, 3.2% work from home (2005-2009 5-year est.); Travel time to work: 27.9% less than 15 minutes, 49.2% 15 to 30 minutes, 6.6% 30 to 45 minutes, 8.2% 45 to 60 minutes, 8.2% 60 minutes or more (2005-2009 5-year est.)

BETHANY (village). Covers a land area of 0.972 square miles and a water area of 0.004 square miles. Located at 39.64° N. Lat; 88.73° W. Long. Elevation is 650 feet.
Population: 1,438 (1990); 1,287 (2000); 1,256 (2010); 1,234 (2015 projected); Race: 98.2% White, 0.3% Black, 0.0% Asian, 1.4% Other, 0.6% Hispanic of any race (2010); Density: 1,291.7 persons per square mile (2010); Average household size: 2.38 (2010); Median age: 42.9 (2010); Males per 100 females: 95.0 (2010); Marriage status: 14.2% never married, 65.4% now married, 6.0% widowed, 14.4% divorced (2005-2009 5-year est.); Foreign born: 0.7% (2005-2009 5-year est.); Ancestry (includes multiple ancestries): 21.5% German, 18.5% English, 13.3% Irish, 8.3% American, 3.0% Scottish (2005-2009 5-year est.).
Economy: Single-family building permits issued: 0 (2010); Multi-family building permits issued: 0 (2010); Employment by occupation: 6.6% management, 23.0% professional, 16.5% services, 19.7% sales, 1.6% farming, 8.8% construction, 23.8% production (2005-2009 5-year est.).
Income: Per capita income: $23,149 (2010); Median household income: $47,188 (2010); Average household income: $54,825 (2010); Percent of households with income of $100,000 or more: 9.3% (2010); Poverty rate: 8.6% (2005-2009 5-year est.).
Taxes: Total city taxes per capita: $53 (2007); City property taxes per capita: $48 (2007).
Education: Percent of population age 25 and over with: High school diploma (including GED) or higher: 91.3% (2010); Bachelor's degree or higher: 12.7% (2010); Master's degree or higher: 3.7% (2010).
School District(s)
Okaw Valley CUSD 302 (PK-12)
   2009-10 Enrollment: 565 . . . . (217) 665-3232
Housing: Homeownership rate: 84.1% (2010); Median home value: $103,077 (2010); Median contract rent: $375 per month (2005-2009 5-year est.); Median year structure built: 1958 (2005-2009 5-year est.).
Transportation: Commute to work: 93.7% car, 0.0% public transportation, 2.2% walk, 2.7% work from home (2005-2009 5-year est.); Travel time to work: 25.6% less than 15 minutes, 30.2% 15 to 30 minutes, 32.4% 30 to 45 minutes, 3.7% 45 to 60 minutes, 8.2% 60 minutes or more (2005-2009 5-year est.)

DALTON CITY (village). Covers a land area of 0.617 square miles and a water area of 0.003 square miles. Located at 39.71° N. Lat; 88.80° W. Long. Elevation is 689 feet.
Population: 600 (1990); 581 (2000); 564 (2010); 552 (2015 projected); Race: 97.5% White, 1.4% Black, 0.0% Asian, 1.1% Other, 2.1% Hispanic of any race (2010); Density: 914.1 persons per square mile (2010); Average household size: 2.61 (2010); Median age: 35.9 (2010); Males per 100 females: 97.9 (2010); Marriage status: 25.1% never married, 60.9% now married, 0.8% widowed, 13.2% divorced (2005-2009 5-year est.); Foreign born: 3.3% (2005-2009 5-year est.); Ancestry (includes multiple ancestries): 23.0% German, 22.9% American, 18.8% English, 5.7% French, 4.8% Italian (2005-2009 5-year est.).
Economy: Single-family building permits issued: 1 (2010); Multi-family building permits issued: 0 (2010); Employment by occupation: 8.5%

management, 8.1% professional, 20.8% services, 21.2% sales, 4.2% farming, 13.8% construction, 23.3% production (2005-2009 5-year est.).
Income: Per capita income: $22,876 (2010); Median household income: $56,439 (2010); Average household income: $59,919 (2010); Percent of households with income of $100,000 or more: 10.6% (2010); Poverty rate: 8.1% (2005-2009 5-year est.).
Taxes: Total city taxes per capita: $101 (2007); City property taxes per capita: $60 (2007).
Education: Percent of population age 25 and over with: High school diploma (including GED) or higher: 92.0% (2010); Bachelor's degree or higher: 8.0% (2010); Master's degree or higher: 1.7% (2010).
Housing: Homeownership rate: 79.2% (2010); Median home value: $104,231 (2010); Median contract rent: $409 per month (2005-2009 5-year est.); Median year structure built: 1956 (2005-2009 5-year est.).
Transportation: Commute to work: 95.4% car, 0.0% public transportation, 3.2% walk, 0.0% work from home (2005-2009 5-year est.); Travel time to work: 16.3% less than 15 minutes, 51.1% 15 to 30 minutes, 27.0% 30 to 45 minutes, 2.1% 45 to 60 minutes, 3.5% 60 minutes or more (2005-2009 5-year est.).

GAYS (village). Covers a land area of 0.409 square miles and a water area of 0 square miles. Located at 39.45° N. Lat; 88.49° W. Long. Elevation is 755 feet.
Population: 265 (1990); 259 (2000); 266 (2010); 272 (2015 projected); Race: 95.9% White, 1.9% Black, 0.4% Asian, 1.9% Other, 0.4% Hispanic of any race (2010); Density: 650.6 persons per square mile (2010); Average household size: 2.61 (2010); Median age: 40.9 (2010); Males per 100 females: 98.5 (2010); Marriage status: 28.1% never married, 61.2% now married, 5.0% widowed, 5.8% divorced (2005-2009 5-year est.); Foreign born: 0.0% (2005-2009 5-year est.); Ancestry (includes multiple ancestries): 23.5% German, 14.2% Irish, 12.1% American, 8.5% English, 5.7% French (2005-2009 5-year est.).
Economy: Single-family building permits issued: 0 (2010); Multi-family building permits issued: 0 (2010); Employment by occupation: 13.5% management, 9.0% professional, 18.6% services, 18.6% sales, 0.0% farming, 5.8% construction, 34.6% production (2005-2009 5-year est.).
Income: Per capita income: $25,200 (2010); Median household income: $54,000 (2010); Average household income: $60,760 (2010); Percent of households with income of $100,000 or more: 13.7% (2010); Poverty rate: 5.7% (2005-2009 5-year est.).
Taxes: Total city taxes per capita: $31 (2007); City property taxes per capita: $27 (2007).
Education: Percent of population age 25 and over with: High school diploma (including GED) or higher: 93.2% (2010); Bachelor's degree or higher: 20.9% (2010); Master's degree or higher: 5.1% (2010).
Housing: Homeownership rate: 83.3% (2010); Median home value: $100,781 (2010); Median contract rent: $385 per month (2005-2009 5-year est.); Median year structure built: 1947 (2005-2009 5-year est.).
Transportation: Commute to work: 94.4% car, 5.6% public transportation, 0.0% walk, 0.0% work from home (2005-2009 5-year est.); Travel time to work: 37.3% less than 15 minutes, 48.6% 15 to 30 minutes, 12.7% 30 to 45 minutes, 0.0% 45 to 60 minutes, 1.4% 60 minutes or more (2005-2009 5-year est.).

LOVINGTON (village). Covers a land area of 0.805 square miles and a water area of 0 square miles. Located at 39.71° N. Lat; 88.63° W. Long. Elevation is 679 feet.
History: Incorporated 1873.
Population: 1,143 (1990); 1,222 (2000); 1,204 (2010); 1,189 (2015 projected); Race: 97.1% White, 1.1% Black, 1.0% Asian, 0.8% Other, 0.6% Hispanic of any race (2010); Density: 1,496.1 persons per square mile (2010); Average household size: 2.42 (2010); Median age: 39.3 (2010); Males per 100 females: 98.7 (2010); Marriage status: 32.7% never married, 48.2% now married, 6.8% widowed, 12.3% divorced (2005-2009 5-year est.); Foreign born: 0.2% (2005-2009 5-year est.); Ancestry (includes multiple ancestries): 24.5% German, 14.0% Irish, 11.5% English, 8.0% American, 3.6% Welsh (2005-2009 5-year est.).
Economy: Single-family building permits issued: 0 (2010); Multi-family building permits issued: 0 (2010); Employment by occupation: 12.1% management, 10.0% professional, 16.2% services, 15.3% sales, 0.0% farming, 11.1% construction, 35.3% production (2005-2009 5-year est.).
Income: Per capita income: $24,540 (2010); Median household income: $47,624 (2010); Average household income: $58,440 (2010); Percent of households with income of $100,000 or more: 11.6% (2010); Poverty rate: 15.1% (2005-2009 5-year est.).

Taxes: Total city taxes per capita: $80 (2007); City property taxes per capita: $71 (2007).
Education: Percent of population age 25 and over with: High school diploma (including GED) or higher: 88.5% (2010); Bachelor's degree or higher: 13.9% (2010); Master's degree or higher: 4.1% (2010).
School District(s)
Lovington CUSD 303 (PK-12)
    2009-10 Enrollment: 278 . . . . (217) 873-4310
Housing: Homeownership rate: 73.4% (2010); Median home value: $90,484 (2010); Median contract rent: $359 per month (2005-2009 5-year est.); Median year structure built: 1948 (2005-2009 5-year est.).
Transportation: Commute to work: 93.7% car, 0.0% public transportation, 3.3% walk, 2.2% work from home (2005-2009 5-year est.); Travel time to work: 32.8% less than 15 minutes, 28.8% 15 to 30 minutes, 26.6% 30 to 45 minutes, 5.4% 45 to 60 minutes, 6.4% 60 minutes or more (2005-2009 5-year est.)

SULLIVAN (city). County seat. Covers a land area of 2.039 square miles and a water area of 0.004 square miles. Located at 39.59° N. Lat; 88.61° W. Long. Elevation is 673 feet.
History: Incorporated 1869.
Population: 4,410 (1990); 4,326 (2000); 4,342 (2010); 4,316 (2015 projected); Race: 97.0% White, 1.3% Black, 0.6% Asian, 1.0% Other, 0.7% Hispanic of any race (2010); Density: 2,129.3 persons per square mile (2010); Average household size: 2.24 (2010); Median age: 40.2 (2010); Males per 100 females: 86.4 (2010); Marriage status: 27.4% never married, 49.6% now married, 10.5% widowed, 12.6% divorced (2005-2009 5-year est.); Foreign born: 3.2% (2005-2009 5-year est.); Ancestry (includes multiple ancestries): 19.2% German, 15.1% Irish, 12.7% English, 12.6% American, 3.2% Swedish (2005-2009 5-year est.).
Economy: Single-family building permits issued: 6 (2010); Multi-family building permits issued: 7 (2010); Employment by occupation: 6.2% management, 19.4% professional, 26.0% services, 16.1% sales, 0.8% farming, 6.0% construction, 25.5% production (2005-2009 5-year est.).
Income: Per capita income: $22,335 (2010); Median household income: $41,722 (2010); Average household income: $49,574 (2010); Percent of households with income of $100,000 or more: 8.4% (2010); Poverty rate: 7.5% (2005-2009 5-year est.).
Taxes: Total city taxes per capita: $407 (2007); City property taxes per capita: $379 (2007).
Education: Percent of population age 25 and over with: High school diploma (including GED) or higher: 84.1% (2010); Bachelor's degree or higher: 19.7% (2010); Master's degree or higher: 6.0% (2010).
School District(s)
Eastern Il Area of Spec Educ (PK-12)
    2009-10 Enrollment: n/a . . . . (217) 348-7700
Sullivan CUSD 300 (PK-12)
    2009-10 Enrollment: 1,122 . . . . (217) 728-8341
Housing: Homeownership rate: 70.7% (2010); Median home value: $98,602 (2010); Median contract rent: $418 per month (2005-2009 5-year est.); Median year structure built: 1956 (2005-2009 5-year est.).
Newspapers: News-Progress (Regional news; Circulation 3,800)
Transportation: Commute to work: 89.3% car, 0.0% public transportation, 6.7% walk, 2.1% work from home (2005-2009 5-year est.); Travel time to work: 58.1% less than 15 minutes, 12.6% 15 to 30 minutes, 14.8% 30 to 45 minutes, 9.6% 45 to 60 minutes, 4.9% 60 minutes or more (2005-2009 5-year est.).
Additional Information Contacts
Sullivan Chamber of Commerce . . . . (217) 728-4223
    http://www.sullivanchamber.com

Ogle County

Located in northern Illinois; drained by the Rock, Leaf, and Kyte Rivers. Covers a land area of 758.83 square miles, a water area of 4.43 square miles, and is located in the Central Time Zone at 42.02° N. Lat., 89.30° W. Long. The county was founded in 1836. County seat is Oregon.

Ogle County is part of the Rochelle, IL Micropolitan Statistical Area. The entire metro area includes: Ogle County, IL

Weather Station: Rochelle   Elevation: 774 feet

	Jan	Feb	Mar	Apr	May	Jun	Jul	Aug	Sep	Oct	Nov	Dec
High	29	33	45	59	71	80	83	82	75	62	47	33
Low	12	16	26	37	48	58	61	60	51	39	29	16
Precip	1.4	1.5	1.9	3.2	4.0	4.1	3.5	4.3	3.3	2.9	2.5	1.9
Snow	6.1	4.4	2.5	0.6	0.0	0.0	0.0	0.0	0.0	tr	0.6	6.0

High and Low temperatures in degrees Fahrenheit; Precipitation and Snow in inches

Population: 45,957 (1990); 51,032 (2000); 55,723 (2010); 57,478 (2015 projected); Race: 92.8% White, 1.1% Black, 0.6% Asian, 5.5% Other, 9.2% Hispanic of any race (2010); Density: 73.4 persons per square mile (2010); Average household size: 2.60 (2010); Median age: 38.5 (2010); Males per 100 females: 98.5 (2010).

Religion: Five largest groups: 16.4% Catholic Church, 7.8% Evangelical Lutheran Church in America, 7.5% The United Methodist Church, 3.2% Presbyterian Church (U.S.A.), 2.6% Lutheran Church—Missouri Synod (2000).

Economy: Unemployment rate: 12.4% (August 2011); Total civilian labor force: 26,793 (August 2011); Leading industries: 27.3% manufacturing; 11.6% retail trade; 11.4% health care and social assistance (2009); Farms: 1,274 totaling 366,470 acres (2007); Companies that employ 500 or more persons: 3 (2009); Companies that employ 100 to 499 persons: 16 (2009); Companies that employ less than 100 persons: 1,084 (2009); Black-owned businesses: n/a (2007); Hispanic-owned businesses: n/a (2007); Asian-owned businesses: n/a (2007); Women-owned businesses: n/a (2007); Retail sales per capita: $9,109 (2010). Single-family building permits issued: 49 (2010); Multi-family building permits issued: 48 (2010).

Income: Per capita income: $25,052 (2010); Median household income: $54,388 (2010); Average household income: $65,371 (2010); Percent of households with income of $100,000 or more: 17.1% (2010); Poverty rate: 10.9% (2009); Bankruptcy rate: 4.91% (2010).

Taxes: Total county taxes per capita: $181 (2007); County property taxes per capita: $172 (2007).

Education: Percent of population age 25 and over with: High school diploma (including GED) or higher: 86.7% (2010); Bachelor's degree or higher: 17.1% (2010); Master's degree or higher: 5.6% (2010).

Housing: Homeownership rate: 74.2% (2010); Median home value: $140,661 (2010); Median contract rent: $468 per month (2005-2009 5-year est.); Median year structure built: 1967 (2005-2009 5-year est.)

Health: Birth rate: 120.0 per 10,000 population (2009); Death rate: 91.1 per 10,000 population (2009); Age-adjusted cancer mortality rate: 201.2 deaths per 100,000 population (2007); Number of physicians: 7.4 per 10,000 population (2008); Hospital beds: 4.5 per 10,000 population (2007); Hospital admissions: 147.6 per 10,000 population (2007).

Elections: 2008 Presidential election results: 45.3% Obama, 52.9% McCain, 0.8% Nader

National and State Parks: Lowden State Park; White Pines Forest State Park

Additional Information Contacts

Ogle County Government . . . . (815) 732-1110
    http://www.oglecounty.org
Byron Area Chamber of Commerce. . . . . (815) 234-5500
    http://www.byronchamber.org
City of Byron . . . . (815) 234-2762
    http://byron.govoffice.com
City of Rochelle . . . . (815) 562-6161
    http://www.cityofrochelle.net
Oregon Area Chamber of Commerce . . . . (815) 732-2100
    http://www.oregonil.com
Polo Chamber of Commerce . . . . (815) 946-3131
    http://www.poloil.org
Rochelle Area Chamber of Commerce . . . . (815) 562-4189
    http://www.rochellechamber.org

Ogle County Communities

ADELINE (village). Covers a land area of 0.269 square miles and a water area of 0 square miles. Located at 42.14° N. Lat; 89.49° W. Long. Elevation is 797 feet.

Population: 156 (1990); 139 (2000); 152 (2010); 164 (2015 projected); Race: 98.0% White, 0.7% Black, 0.0% Asian, 1.3% Other, 0.7% Hispanic of any race (2010); Density: 565.5 persons per square mile (2010); Average household size: 2.81 (2010); Median age: 41.4 (2010); Males per 100 females: 92.4 (2010); Marriage status: 31.7% never married, 48.5% now married, 2.0% widowed, 17.8% divorced (2005-2009 5-year est.); Foreign born: 0.0% (2005-2009 5-year est.); Ancestry (includes multiple

ancestries): 23.5% German, 18.3% Irish, 13.9% English, 5.2% American, 4.3% Swedish (2005-2009 5-year est.).

Economy: Employment by occupation: 0.0% management, 8.9% professional, 19.6% services, 17.9% sales, 0.0% farming, 25.0% construction, 28.6% production (2005-2009 5-year est.).

Income: Per capita income: $24,815 (2010); Median household income: $60,000 (2010); Average household income: $68,935 (2010); Percent of households with income of $100,000 or more: 20.4% (2010); Poverty rate: 17.6% (2005-2009 5-year est.).

Taxes: Total city taxes per capita: $49 (2007); City property taxes per capita: $35 (2007).

Education: Percent of population age 25 and over with: High school diploma (including GED) or higher: 91.1% (2010); Bachelor's degree or higher: 19.8% (2010); Master's degree or higher: 4.0% (2010).

Housing: Homeownership rate: 81.5% (2010); Median home value: $175,000 (2010); Median contract rent: n/a per month (2005-2009 5-year est.); Median year structure built: before 1940 (2005-2009 5-year est.).

Transportation: Commute to work: 96.3% car, 0.0% public transportation, 0.0% walk, 0.0% work from home (2005-2009 5-year est.); Travel time to work: 14.8% less than 15 minutes, 59.3% 15 to 30 minutes, 16.7% 30 to 45 minutes, 9.3% 45 to 60 minutes, 0.0% 60 minutes or more (2005-2009 5-year est.)

BAILEYVILLE (unincorporated postal area, zip code 61007). Covers a land area of 24.962 square miles and a water area of 0 square miles. Located at 42.19° N. Lat; 89.59° W. Long. Elevation is 925 feet.

Population: 548 (2000); Race: 100.0% White, 0.0% Black, 0.0% Asian, 0.0% Other, 0.0% Hispanic of any race (2000); Density: 22.0 persons per square mile (2000); Age: 22.0% under 18, 13.1% over 64 (2000); Marriage status: 12.9% never married, 79.6% now married, 2.4% widowed, 5.2% divorced (2000); Foreign born: 0.0% (2000); Ancestry (includes multiple ancestries): 52.1% German, 10.7% American, 7.5% Irish, 6.3% Polish, 5.9% Norwegian (2000).

Economy: Employment by occupation: 15.5% management, 12.6% professional, 9.1% services, 14.2% sales, 4.5% farming, 14.9% construction, 29.1% production (2000).

Income: Per capita income: $17,301 (2000); Median household income: $49,375 (2000); Poverty rate: 3.7% (2000).

Education: Percent of population age 25 and over with: High school diploma (including GED) or higher: 79.6% (2000); Bachelor's degree or higher: 11.9% (2000).

Housing: Homeownership rate: 84.7% (2000); Median home value: $96,300 (2000); Median contract rent: $419 per month (2000); Median year structure built: before 1940 (2000).

Transportation: Commute to work: 84.0% car, 0.0% public transportation, 0.0% walk, 16.0% work from home (2000); Travel time to work: 50.0% less than 15 minutes, 33.5% 15 to 30 minutes, 7.0% 30 to 45 minutes, 1.7% 45 to 60 minutes, 7.9% 60 minutes or more (2000)

BYRON (city). Covers a land area of 2.474 square miles and a water area of <.001 square miles. Located at 42.12° N. Lat; 89.26° W. Long. Elevation is 728 feet.

History: Byron was founded in 1835 by settlers from New England, and named for the English poet Lord Byron. Many houses in Byron were stations on the Underground Railroad, offering escape for slaves from the south.

Population: 2,381 (1990); 2,917 (2000); 3,515 (2010); 3,775 (2015 projected); Race: 96.4% White, 1.2% Black, 0.3% Asian, 2.0% Other, 2.5% Hispanic of any race (2010); Density: 1,421.0 persons per square mile (2010); Average household size: 2.59 (2010); Median age: 35.3 (2010); Males per 100 females: 91.0 (2010); Marriage status: 25.7% never married, 46.1% now married, 16.9% widowed, 11.3% divorced (2005-2009 5-year est.); Foreign born: 2.2% (2005-2009 5-year est.); Ancestry (includes multiple ancestries): 36.9% German, 13.4% Irish, 9.5% Italian, 8.2% English, 7.7% American (2005-2009 5-year est.).

Economy: Single-family building permits issued: 1 (2010); Multi-family building permits issued: 0 (2010); Employment by occupation: 7.9% management, 20.2% professional, 19.0% services, 32.0% sales, 0.0% farming, 6.2% construction, 14.6% production (2005-2009 5-year est.).

Income: Per capita income: $21,970 (2010); Median household income: $47,834 (2010); Average household income: $57,387 (2010); Percent of households with income of $100,000 or more: 12.2% (2010); Poverty rate: 9.3% (2005-2009 5-year est.).

Taxes: Total city taxes per capita: $957 (2007); City property taxes per capita: $873 (2007).

Education: Percent of population age 25 and over with: High school diploma (including GED) or higher: 90.4% (2010); Bachelor's degree or higher: 14.1% (2010); Master's degree or higher: 3.3% (2010).

School District(s)
Byron CUSD 226 (PK-12)

    2009-10 Enrollment: 1,653 . . . . (815) 234-5491
Housing: Homeownership rate: 61.7% (2010); Median home value: $134,597 (2010); Median contract rent: $530 per month (2005-2009 5-year est.); Median year structure built: 1985 (2005-2009 5-year est.).
Safety: Violent crime rate: 12.8 per 10,000 population; Property crime rate: 179.3 per 10,000 population (2010).
Transportation: Commute to work: 94.4% car, 0.0% public transportation, 2.6% walk, 1.0% work from home (2005-2009 5-year est.); Travel time to work: 26.1% less than 15 minutes, 29.3% 15 to 30 minutes, 27.6% 30 to 45 minutes, 5.1% 45 to 60 minutes, 11.8% 60 minutes or more (2005-2009 5-year est.)

Additional Information Contacts
Byron Area Chamber of Commerce . . . . (815) 234-5500
    http://www.byronchamber.org
City of Byron . . . . (815) 234-2762
    http://byron.govoffice.com

CHANA (unincorporated postal area, zip code 61015). Covers a land area of 40.799 square miles and a water area of 0.057 square miles. Located at 41.98° N. Lat; 89.21° W. Long. Elevation is 781 feet.
Population: 993 (2000); Race: 99.0% White, 0.3% Black, 0.0% Asian, 0.7% Other, 1.8% Hispanic of any race (2000); Density: 24.3 persons per square mile (2000); Age: 21.5% under 18, 11.2% over 64 (2000); Marriage status: 21.4% never married, 66.5% now married, 5.5% widowed, 6.6% divorced (2000); Foreign born: 0.2% (2000); Ancestry (includes multiple ancestries): 39.5% German, 12.1% English, 7.6% Irish, 5.6% Polish, 5.1% Norwegian (2000).
Economy: Employment by occupation: 12.4% management, 7.4% professional, 12.7% services, 23.3% sales, 0.0% farming, 20.5% construction, 23.7% production (2000).
Income: Per capita income: $20,508 (2000); Median household income: $49,000 (2000); Poverty rate: 0.7% (2000).
Education: Percent of population age 25 and over with: High school diploma (including GED) or higher: 86.7% (2000); Bachelor's degree or higher: 15.9% (2000).

School District(s)
Lee/Ogle Roe (06-12)

    2009-10 Enrollment: n/a . . . . (815) 652-2054
Ogle Co Education Cooperative (KG-12)

    2009-10 Enrollment: n/a . . . . (815) 234-2722
Housing: Homeownership rate: 80.3% (2000); Median home value: $114,400 (2000); Median contract rent: $342 per month (2000); Median year structure built: 1953 (2000).
Transportation: Commute to work: 97.8% car, 0.0% public transportation, 1.8% walk, 0.4% work from home (2000); Travel time to work: 8.5% less than 15 minutes, 40.0% 15 to 30 minutes, 28.9% 30 to 45 minutes, 11.4% 45 to 60 minutes, 11.2% 60 minutes or more (2000)

CRESTON (village). Covers a land area of 0.418 square miles and a water area of 0 square miles. Located at 41.93° N. Lat; 88.96° W. Long. Elevation is 906 feet.
Population: 581 (1990); 543 (2000); 618 (2010); 651 (2015 projected); Race: 83.5% White, 2.3% Black, 0.6% Asian, 13.6% Other, 25.6% Hispanic of any race (2010); Density: 1,478.8 persons per square mile (2010); Average household size: 2.88 (2010); Median age: 35.1 (2010); Males per 100 females: 110.2 (2010); Marriage status: 33.4% never married, 48.3% now married, 1.2% widowed, 17.1% divorced (2005-2009 5-year est.); Foreign born: 2.2% (2005-2009 5-year est.); Ancestry (includes multiple ancestries): 41.5% German, 20.7% Norwegian, 15.9% English, 13.8% Irish, 12.2% African (2005-2009 5-year est.).
Economy: Single-family building permits issued: 4 (2010); Multi-family building permits issued: 0 (2010); Employment by occupation: 6.3% management, 31.7% professional, 17.0% services, 23.3% sales, 0.0% farming, 3.7% construction, 17.9% production (2005-2009 5-year est.).
Income: Per capita income: $18,513 (2010); Median household income: $44,375 (2010); Average household income: $53,152 (2010); Percent of households with income of $100,000 or more: 10.9% (2010); Poverty rate: 6.5% (2005-2009 5-year est.).
Taxes: Total city taxes per capita: $145 (2007); City property taxes per capita: $27 (2007).

Education: Percent of population age 25 and over with: High school diploma (including GED) or higher: 80.4% (2010); Bachelor's degree or higher: 10.9% (2010); Master's degree or higher: 2.0% (2010).

School District(s)
Creston CCSD 161 (KG-08)

    2009-10 Enrollment: 128 . . . . (815) 384-3920
Housing: Homeownership rate: 62.6% (2010); Median home value: $130,645 (2010); Median contract rent: $731 per month (2005-2009 5-year est.); Median year structure built: 1952 (2005-2009 5-year est.).
Transportation: Commute to work: 94.9% car, 0.0% public transportation, 1.6% walk, 3.5% work from home (2005-2009 5-year est.); Travel time to work: 15.5% less than 15 minutes, 51.4% 15 to 30 minutes, 22.5% 30 to 45 minutes, 6.8% 45 to 60 minutes, 3.9% 60 minutes or more (2005-2009 5-year est.)

DAVIS JUNCTION (village). Covers a land area of 3.790 square miles and a water area of 0 square miles. Located at 42.10° N. Lat; 89.09° W. Long. Elevation is 791 feet.
Population: 356 (1990); 491 (2000); 779 (2010); 873 (2015 projected); Race: 92.9% White, 0.1% Black, 0.4% Asian, 6.5% Other, 7.1% Hispanic of any race (2010); Density: 205.6 persons per square mile (2010); Average household size: 2.90 (2010); Median age: 35.6 (2010); Males per 100 females: 96.2 (2010); Marriage status: 22.9% never married, 61.3% now married, 4.4% widowed, 11.4% divorced (2005-2009 5-year est.); Foreign born: 16.1% (2005-2009 5-year est.); Ancestry (includes multiple ancestries): 31.3% German, 11.3% Irish, 9.4% Swedish, 8.2% English, 4.8% Norwegian (2005-2009 5-year est.).
Economy: Single-family building permits issued: 5 (2010); Multi-family building permits issued: 0 (2010); Employment by occupation: 11.5% management, 13.2% professional, 12.8% services, 22.8% sales, 0.0% farming, 13.0% construction, 26.8% production (2005-2009 5-year est.).
Income: Per capita income: $26,199 (2010); Median household income: $67,061 (2010); Average household income: $74,935 (2010); Percent of households with income of $100,000 or more: 20.1% (2010); Poverty rate: 8.1% (2005-2009 5-year est.).
Taxes: Total city taxes per capita: $114 (2007); City property taxes per capita: $22 (2007).
Education: Percent of population age 25 and over with: High school diploma (including GED) or higher: 84.7% (2010); Bachelor's degree or higher: 15.9% (2010); Master's degree or higher: 3.6% (2010).
Housing: Homeownership rate: 88.1% (2010); Median home value: $162,288 (2010); Median contract rent: $293 per month (2005-2009 5-year est.); Median year structure built: 2001 (2005-2009 5-year est.).
Transportation: Commute to work: 95.6% car, 0.0% public transportation, 1.8% walk, 2.2% work from home (2005-2009 5-year est.); Travel time to work: 14.4% less than 15 minutes, 36.4% 15 to 30 minutes, 24.2% 30 to 45 minutes, 9.6% 45 to 60 minutes, 15.4% 60 minutes or more (2005-2009 5-year est.)

FORRESTON (village). Covers a land area of 0.831 square miles and a water area of 0 square miles. Located at 42.12° N. Lat; 89.58° W. Long. Elevation is 938 feet.
History: The first sauerkraut festival was held in Forreston in 1913.
Population: 1,372 (1990); 1,469 (2000); 1,503 (2010); 1,510 (2015 projected); Race: 98.6% White, 0.0% Black, 0.6% Asian, 0.8% Other, 1.8% Hispanic of any race (2010); Density: 1,808.3 persons per square mile (2010); Average household size: 2.45 (2010); Median age: 36.9 (2010); Males per 100 females: 94.7 (2010); Marriage status: 25.6% never married, 52.0% now married, 8.8% widowed, 13.6% divorced (2005-2009 5-year est.); Foreign born: 5.4% (2005-2009 5-year est.); Ancestry (includes multiple ancestries): 45.6% German, 16.0% Irish, 9.0% American, 8.8% English, 6.5% Dutch (2005-2009 5-year est.).
Economy: Single-family building permits issued: 0 (2010); Multi-family building permits issued: 0 (2010); Employment by occupation: 9.7% management, 13.8% professional, 19.0% services, 27.6% sales, 0.9% farming, 8.5% construction, 20.5% production (2005-2009 5-year est.).
Income: Per capita income: $20,748 (2010); Median household income: $42,304 (2010); Average household income: $49,866 (2010); Percent of households with income of $100,000 or more: 8.0% (2010); Poverty rate: 8.1% (2005-2009 5-year est.).
Taxes: Total city taxes per capita: $159 (2007); City property taxes per capita: $138 (2007).
Education: Percent of population age 25 and over with: High school diploma (including GED) or higher: 84.4% (2010); Bachelor's degree or higher: 15.0% (2010); Master's degree or higher: 4.8% (2010).

School District(s)
Forrestville Valley CUSD 221 (PK-12)
   2009-10 Enrollment: 898 . . . . (815) 938-2036
Housing: Homeownership rate: 75.6% (2010); Median home value: $106,452 (2010); Median contract rent: $501 per month (2005-2009 5-year est.); Median year structure built: 1957 (2005-2009 5-year est.).
Newspapers: Forreston Journal (Community news; Circulation 800)
Transportation: Commute to work: 87.0% car, 0.0% public transportation, 10.1% walk, 2.9% work from home (2005-2009 5-year est.); Travel time to work: 34.8% less than 15 minutes, 33.4% 15 to 30 minutes, 17.2% 30 to 45 minutes, 8.9% 45 to 60 minutes, 5.7% 60 minutes or more (2005-2009 5-year est.)

HILLCREST (village). Covers a land area of 0.557 square miles and a water area of 0 square miles. Located at 41.95° N. Lat; 89.06° W. Long. Elevation is 830 feet.

Population: 843 (1990); 1,158 (2000); 1,317 (2010); 1,388 (2015 projected); Race: 83.4% White, 2.5% Black, 0.7% Asian, 13.4% Other, 25.5% Hispanic of any race (2010); Density: 2,366.5 persons per square mile (2010); Average household size: 2.88 (2010); Median age: 35.0 (2010); Males per 100 females: 107.4 (2010); Marriage status: 23.7% never married, 60.4% now married, 2.4% widowed, 13.5% divorced (2005-2009 5-year est.); Foreign born: 17.0% (2005-2009 5-year est.); Ancestry (includes multiple ancestries): 21.0% German, 8.9% Irish, 7.2% English, 7.0% American, 4.4% Swedish (2005-2009 5-year est.).
Economy: Single-family building permits issued: 0 (2010); Multi-family building permits issued: 0 (2010); Employment by occupation: 4.6% management, 12.7% professional, 18.3% services, 20.3% sales, 0.7% farming, 16.4% construction, 27.0% production (2005-2009 5-year est.).
Income: Per capita income: $18,513 (2010); Median household income: $44,658 (2010); Average household income: $53,072 (2010); Percent of households with income of $100,000 or more: 10.7% (2010); Poverty rate: 4.2% (2005-2009 5-year est.).
Taxes: Total city taxes per capita: $43 (2007); City property taxes per capita: $30 (2007).
Education: Percent of population age 25 and over with: High school diploma (including GED) or higher: 80.4% (2010); Bachelor's degree or higher: 11.0% (2010); Master's degree or higher: 2.0% (2010).
Housing: Homeownership rate: 62.4% (2010); Median home value: $129,735 (2010); Median contract rent: $525 per month (2005-2009 5-year est.); Median year structure built: 1980 (2005-2009 5-year est.).
Transportation: Commute to work: 94.6% car, 0.0% public transportation, 1.6% walk, 3.2% work from home (2005-2009 5-year est.); Travel time to work: 40.2% less than 15 minutes, 35.2% 15 to 30 minutes, 16.5% 30 to 45 minutes, 2.5% 45 to 60 minutes, 5.7% 60 minutes or more (2005-2009 5-year est.)

LEAF RIVER (village). Covers a land area of 0.857 square miles and a water area of 0 square miles. Located at 42.12° N. Lat; 89.40° W. Long. Elevation is 725 feet.

Population: 546 (1990); 555 (2000); 549 (2010); 550 (2015 projected); Race: 96.7% White, 2.9% Black, 0.0% Asian, 0.4% Other, 0.4% Hispanic of any race (2010); Density: 640.6 persons per square mile (2010); Average household size: 2.59 (2010); Median age: 40.3 (2010); Males per 100 females: 97.5 (2010); Marriage status: 40.9% never married, 37.2% now married, 11.1% widowed, 10.8% divorced (2005-2009 5-year est.); Foreign born: 0.0% (2005-2009 5-year est.); Ancestry (includes multiple ancestries): 54.8% German, 10.5% American, 8.2% English, 7.0% Irish, 7.0% Hungarian (2005-2009 5-year est.).
Economy: Single-family building permits issued: 0 (2010); Multi-family building permits issued: 0 (2010); Employment by occupation: 2.8% management, 8.9% professional, 14.1% services, 20.2% sales, 0.0% farming, 8.1% construction, 46.0% production (2005-2009 5-year est.).
Income: Per capita income: $20,433 (2010); Median household income: $45,603 (2010); Average household income: $53,962 (2010); Percent of households with income of $100,000 or more: 9.0% (2010); Poverty rate: 5.5% (2005-2009 5-year est.).
Taxes: Total city taxes per capita: $88 (2007); City property taxes per capita: $27 (2007).
Education: Percent of population age 25 and over with: High school diploma (including GED) or higher: 87.0% (2010); Bachelor's degree or higher: 8.5% (2010); Master's degree or higher: 1.0% (2010).
Housing: Homeownership rate: 75.9% (2010); Median home value: $120,673 (2010); Median contract rent: $471 per month (2005-2009 5-year est.); Median year structure built: before 1940 (2005-2009 5-year est.).

Transportation: Commute to work: 99.2% car, 0.8% public transportation, 0.0% walk, 0.0% work from home (2005-2009 5-year est.); Travel time to work: 49.8% less than 15 minutes, 29.2% 15 to 30 minutes, 8.6% 30 to 45 minutes, 11.5% 45 to 60 minutes, 0.8% 60 minutes or more (2005-2009 5-year est.)

LINDENWOOD (unincorporated postal area, zip code 61049). Covers a land area of 17.773 square miles and a water area of 0 square miles. Located at 42.05° N. Lat; 89.02° W. Long. Elevation is 771 feet.

Population: 505 (2000); Race: 96.6% White, 0.4% Black, 0.2% Asian, 2.8% Other, 1.9% Hispanic of any race (2000); Density: 28.4 persons per square mile (2000); Age: 24.5% under 18, 14.8% over 64 (2000); Marriage status: 21.0% never married, 65.3% now married, 4.0% widowed, 9.7% divorced (2000); Foreign born: 1.9% (2000); Ancestry (includes multiple ancestries): 40.1% German, 11.0% Norwegian, 10.5% Irish, 10.3% English, 8.6% American (2000).
Economy: Employment by occupation: 9.4% management, 13.5% professional, 8.8% services, 31.6% sales, 3.0% farming, 12.1% construction, 21.5% production (2000).
Income: Per capita income: $22,639 (2000); Median household income: $47,625 (2000); Poverty rate: 3.6% (2000).
Education: Percent of population age 25 and over with: High school diploma (including GED) or higher: 88.1% (2000); Bachelor's degree or higher: 14.6% (2000).
School District(s)
Eswood CCSD 269 (KG-08)
   2009-10 Enrollment: 113 . . . . (815) 393-4477
Housing: Homeownership rate: 79.7% (2000); Median home value: $108,200 (2000); Median contract rent: $439 per month (2000); Median year structure built: before 1940 (2000).
Transportation: Commute to work: 84.2% car, 4.1% public transportation, 3.8% walk, 7.2% work from home (2000); Travel time to work: 18.1% less than 15 minutes, 37.0% 15 to 30 minutes, 28.9% 30 to 45 minutes, 5.9% 45 to 60 minutes, 10.0% 60 minutes or more (2000)

MONROE CENTER (village). Covers a land area of 1.207 square miles and a water area of 0 square miles. Located at 42.11° N. Lat; 89.00° W. Long. Elevation is 853 feet.

Population: n/a (1990); n/a (2000); 471 (2010); n/a (2015 projected); Race: 98.1% White, 0.2% Black, 0.0% Asian, 1.7% Other, 1.5% Hispanic of any race (2010); Density: 390.2 persons per square mile (2010); Average household size: 2.69 (2010); Median age: 36.6 (2010); Males per 100 females: 110.3 (2010); Marriage status: 25.6% never married, 57.3% now married, 2.6% widowed, 14.6% divorced (2005-2009 5-year est.); Foreign born: 0.5% (2005-2009 5-year est.); Ancestry (includes multiple ancestries): 43.7% German, 21.5% Irish, 15.1% English, 7.1% American, 5.4% Norwegian (2005-2009 5-year est.).
Economy: Single-family building permits issued: 0 (2010); Multi-family building permits issued: 0 (2010); Employment by occupation: 4.1% management, 13.3% professional, 13.3% services, 26.5% sales, 0.0% farming, 7.4% construction, 35.4% production (2005-2009 5-year est.).
Income: Per capita income: n/a (2010); Median household income: n/a (2010); Average household income: n/a (2010); Percent of households with income of $100,000 or more: n/a (2010); Poverty rate: 2.3% (2005-2009 5-year est.).
Taxes: Total city taxes per capita: $49 (2007); City property taxes per capita: $35 (2007).
Education: Percent of population age 25 and over with: High school diploma (including GED) or higher: n/a (2010); Bachelor's degree or higher: n/a (2010); Master's degree or higher: n/a (2010).
School District(s)
Meridian CUSD 223 (PK-12)
   2009-10 Enrollment: 1,972 . . . . (815) 645-2606
Housing: Homeownership rate: n/a (2010); Median home value: n/a (2010); Median contract rent: $479 per month (2005-2009 5-year est.); Median year structure built: 1956 (2005-2009 5-year est.).
Transportation: Commute to work: 94.0% car, 0.0% public transportation, 4.8% walk, 1.2% work from home (2005-2009 5-year est.); Travel time to work: 15.9% less than 15 minutes, 50.6% 15 to 30 minutes, 17.4% 30 to 45 minutes, 6.1% 45 to 60 minutes, 10.1% 60 minutes or more (2005-2009 5-year est.)

MOUNT MORRIS (village). Covers a land area of 1.166 square miles and a water area of 0 square miles. Located at 42.04° N. Lat; 89.43° W. Long. Elevation is 909 feet.

History: Mount Morris was settled in 1838 by a group from Maryland. The railroad bypassed Mount Morris, but the town continued to grow. An early industry was the Kable Brothers printing company founded in 1898.
Population: 2,934 (1990); 3,013 (2000); 3,032 (2010); 3,027 (2015 projected); Race: 95.9% White, 0.2% Black, 0.6% Asian, 3.3% Other, 4.5% Hispanic of any race (2010); Density: 2,601.4 persons per square mile (2010); Average household size: 2.28 (2010); Median age: 39.0 (2010); Males per 100 females: 95.4 (2010); Marriage status: 23.4% never married, 52.5% now married, 8.5% widowed, 15.6% divorced (2005-2009 5-year est.); Foreign born: 1.6% (2005-2009 5-year est.); Ancestry (includes multiple ancestries): 42.7% German, 18.6% Irish, 11.6% English, 7.3% American, 6.0% Italian (2005-2009 5-year est.).
Economy: Single-family building permits issued: 4 (2010); Multi-family building permits issued: 0 (2010); Employment by occupation: 8.1% management, 17.3% professional, 15.6% services, 32.7% sales, 0.0% farming, 8.5% construction, 17.9% production (2005-2009 5-year est.).
Income: Per capita income: $25,912 (2010); Median household income: $48,589 (2010); Average household income: $59,100 (2010); Percent of households with income of $100,000 or more: 12.5% (2010); Poverty rate: 15.7% (2005-2009 5-year est.).
Taxes: Total city taxes per capita: $214 (2007); City property taxes per capita: $149 (2007).
Education: Percent of population age 25 and over with: High school diploma (including GED) or higher: 89.8% (2010); Bachelor's degree or higher: 16.2% (2010); Master's degree or higher: 6.1% (2010).

School District(s)
Oregon CUSD 220 (PK-12)
    2009-10 Enrollment: 1,569 . . . . (815) 732-2186
Housing: Homeownership rate: 71.5% (2010); Median home value: $112,366 (2010); Median contract rent: $408 per month (2005-2009 5-year est.); Median year structure built: 1948 (2005-2009 5-year est.).
Safety: Violent crime rate: 3.3 per 10,000 population; Property crime rate: 166.4 per 10,000 population (2010).
Transportation: Commute to work: 88.0% car, 2.6% public transportation, 7.0% walk, 2.4% work from home (2005-2009 5-year est.); Travel time to work: 37.3% less than 15 minutes, 27.8% 15 to 30 minutes, 18.5% 30 to 45 minutes, 9.7% 45 to 60 minutes, 6.7% 60 minutes or more (2005-2009 5-year est.)

OREGON (city). County seat. Covers a land area of 2.031 square miles and a water area of 0.079 square miles. Located at 42.01° N. Lat; 89.33° W. Long. Elevation is 709 feet.
History: Oregon developed as a trading center and industrial town, and as the seat of Ogle County. It was also known as an artistic community, with the Eagle's Nest Art Colony established nearby in 1898.
Population: 4,110 (1990); 4,060 (2000); 4,023 (2010); 4,001 (2015 projected); Race: 93.3% White, 3.2% Black, 0.6% Asian, 2.9% Other, 3.1% Hispanic of any race (2010); Density: 1,980.3 persons per square mile (2010); Average household size: 2.27 (2010); Median age: 40.8 (2010); Males per 100 females: 95.0 (2010); Marriage status: 23.9% never married, 49.7% now married, 11.2% widowed, 15.3% divorced (2005-2009 5-year est.); Foreign born: 6.1% (2005-2009 5-year est.); Ancestry (includes multiple ancestries): 37.4% German, 13.3% Irish, 10.0% English, 8.8% American, 8.8% Polish (2005-2009 5-year est.).
Economy: Single-family building permits issued: 0 (2010); Multi-family building permits issued: 2 (2010); Employment by occupation: 7.8% management, 16.4% professional, 29.8% services, 20.6% sales, 0.9% farming, 7.4% construction, 17.2% production (2005-2009 5-year est.).
Income: Per capita income: $22,778 (2010); Median household income: $41,055 (2010); Average household income: $53,038 (2010); Percent of households with income of $100,000 or more: 12.7% (2010); Poverty rate: 6.9% (2005-2009 5-year est.).
Taxes: Total city taxes per capita: $146 (2007); City property taxes per capita: $95 (2007).
Education: Percent of population age 25 and over with: High school diploma (including GED) or higher: 82.7% (2010); Bachelor's degree or higher: 17.7% (2010); Master's degree or higher: 9.5% (2010).

School District(s)
Oregon CUSD 220 (PK-12)
    2009-10 Enrollment: 1,569 . . . . (815) 732-2186
Housing: Homeownership rate: 64.9% (2010); Median home value: $126,523 (2010); Median contract rent: $480 per month (2005-2009 5-year est.); Median year structure built: 1948 (2005-2009 5-year est.).
Newspapers: Mount Morris Times (Community news; Circulation 2,000); Ogle County Life (Community news; Circulation 12,000); Ogle County

News (Community news; Circulation 1,000); Oregon Republican Reporter (Community news; Circulation 1,000); Tri-County Press (Community news; Circulation 17,000)
Transportation: Commute to work: 82.8% car, 0.0% public transportation, 6.9% walk, 5.2% work from home (2005-2009 5-year est.); Travel time to work: 56.1% less than 15 minutes, 17.3% 15 to 30 minutes, 10.5% 30 to 45 minutes, 5.2% 45 to 60 minutes, 10.9% 60 minutes or more (2005-2009 5-year est.)
Additional Information Contacts
Oregon Area Chamber of Commerce . . . . (815) 732-2100
    http://www.oregonil.com

POLO (city). Covers a land area of 1.313 square miles and a water area of 0 square miles. Located at 41.98° N. Lat; 89.57° W. Long. Elevation is 863 feet.
History: The city of Polo was named for Venetian traveler Marco Polo, and developed as a trading center for a stock raising area.
Population: 2,531 (1990); 2,477 (2000); 2,481 (2010); 2,469 (2015 projected); Race: 98.1% White, 0.0% Black, 0.4% Asian, 1.5% Other, 2.4% Hispanic of any race (2010); Density: 1,889.2 persons per square mile (2010); Average household size: 2.35 (2010); Median age: 40.7 (2010); Males per 100 females: 94.3 (2010); Marriage status: 27.3% never married, 44.9% now married, 11.7% widowed, 16.1% divorced (2005-2009 5-year est.); Foreign born: 1.3% (2005-2009 5-year est.); Ancestry (includes multiple ancestries): 42.3% German, 12.8% Irish, 9.9% American, 7.3% English, 4.2% Dutch (2005-2009 5-year est.).
Economy: Single-family building permits issued: 0 (2010); Multi-family building permits issued: 0 (2010); Employment by occupation: 14.9% management, 13.4% professional, 14.1% services, 22.2% sales, 0.7% farming, 15.4% construction, 19.3% production (2005-2009 5-year est.).
Income: Per capita income: $22,465 (2010); Median household income: $45,200 (2010); Average household income: $52,800 (2010); Percent of households with income of $100,000 or more: 9.2% (2010); Poverty rate: 14.5% (2005-2009 5-year est.).
Taxes: Total city taxes per capita: $175 (2007); City property taxes per capita: $86 (2007).
Education: Percent of population age 25 and over with: High school diploma (including GED) or higher: 86.9% (2010); Bachelor's degree or higher: 12.1% (2010); Master's degree or higher: 3.6% (2010).

School District(s)
Polo CUSD 222 (PK-12)
    2009-10 Enrollment: 697 . . . . (815) 946-3815
Housing: Homeownership rate: 71.7% (2010); Median home value: $105,796 (2010); Median contract rent: $435 per month (2005-2009 5-year est.); Median year structure built: 1942 (2005-2009 5-year est.).
Transportation: Commute to work: 87.0% car, 0.0% public transportation, 6.8% walk, 5.0% work from home (2005-2009 5-year est.); Travel time to work: 29.5% less than 15 minutes, 45.8% 15 to 30 minutes, 14.7% 30 to 45 minutes, 2.5% 45 to 60 minutes, 7.4% 60 minutes or more (2005-2009 5-year est.)
Additional Information Contacts
Polo Chamber of Commerce . . . . (815) 946-3131
    http://www.poloil.org

ROCHELLE (city). Covers a land area of 7.474 square miles and a water area of 0.023 square miles. Located at 41.92° N. Lat; 89.06° W. Long. Elevation is 823 feet.
History: Rochelle developed as an agricultural center and the home of the Del Monte cannery. Charles Butterfield, composer of "When You and I Were Young, Maggie," and Francis Rose, who wrote "Just Before the Battle, Mother," both lived in Rochelle.
Population: 8,944 (1990); 9,424 (2000); 9,660 (2010); 9,753 (2015 projected); Race: 80.8% White, 2.6% Black, 1.1% Asian, 15.5% Other, 27.6% Hispanic of any race (2010); Density: 1,292.5 persons per square mile (2010); Average household size: 2.55 (2010); Median age: 35.4 (2010); Males per 100 females: 97.0 (2010); Marriage status: 32.7% never married, 48.1% now married, 7.3% widowed, 11.9% divorced (2005-2009 5-year est.); Foreign born: 12.3% (2005-2009 5-year est.); Ancestry (includes multiple ancestries): 29.6% German, 11.8% Irish, 8.3% English, 5.9% American, 5.8% Italian (2005-2009 5-year est.).
Economy: Single-family building permits issued: 11 (2010); Multi-family building permits issued: 46 (2010); Employment by occupation: 8.2% management, 10.8% professional, 16.0% services, 21.1% sales, 2.0% farming, 6.9% construction, 35.0% production (2005-2009 5-year est.).

Income: Per capita income: $21,520 (2010); Median household income: $46,070 (2010); Average household income: $54,975 (2010); Percent of households with income of $100,000 or more: 11.0% (2010); Poverty rate: 12.4% (2005-2009 5-year est.).

Taxes: Total city taxes per capita: $191 (2007); City property taxes per capita: $107 (2007).

Education: Percent of population age 25 and over with: High school diploma (including GED) or higher: 78.2% (2010); Bachelor's degree or higher: 15.5% (2010); Master's degree or higher: 4.8% (2010).

School District(s)

Rochelle CCSD 231 (PK-08)
   2009-10 Enrollment: 1,746 . . . . (815) 562-6363
Rochelle Twp HSD 212 (09-12)
   2009-10 Enrollment: 1,050 . . . . (815) 562-4161

Housing: Homeownership rate: 60.4% (2010); Median home value: $132,815 (2010); Median contract rent: $461 per month (2005-2009 5-year est.); Median year structure built: 1965 (2005-2009 5-year est.).

Hospitals: Rochelle Community Hospital (42 beds)

Newspapers: Rochelle News Leader (Local news; Circulation 5,500)

Transportation: Commute to work: 85.3% car, 1.4% public transportation, 9.0% walk, 3.7% work from home (2005-2009 5-year est.); Travel time to work: 57.3% less than 15 minutes, 11.9% 15 to 30 minutes, 17.2% 30 to 45 minutes, 8.1% 45 to 60 minutes, 5.6% 60 minutes or more (2005-2009 5-year est.)

Additional Information Contacts

City of Rochelle . . . . (815) 562-6161
   http://www.cityofrochelle.net
Rochelle Area Chamber of Commerce . . . . (815) 562-4189
   http://www.rochellechamber.org

STILLMAN VALLEY (village). Covers a land area of 0.548 square miles and a water area of 0 square miles. Located at 42.10° N. Lat; 89.18° W. Long. Elevation is 712 feet.

History: The Battle of Stillman's Run took place here in 1832, where a monument was placed to mark the dead.

Population: 874 (1990); 1,048 (2000); 1,224 (2010); 1,301 (2015 projected); Race: 96.2% White, 0.5% Black, 0.3% Asian, 2.9% Other, 2.6% Hispanic of any race (2010); Density: 2,234.0 persons per square mile (2010); Average household size: 2.68 (2010); Median age: 38.3 (2010); Males per 100 females: 94.9 (2010); Marriage status: 21.8% never married, 62.8% now married, 6.0% widowed, 9.4% divorced (2005-2009 5-year est.); Foreign born: 2.5% (2005-2009 5-year est.); Ancestry (includes multiple ancestries): 54.2% German, 13.0% English, 11.4% Irish, 10.1% Swedish, 5.1% Norwegian (2005-2009 5-year est.).

Economy: Single-family building permits issued: 1 (2010); Multi-family building permits issued: 0 (2010); Employment by occupation: 6.9% management, 19.3% professional, 16.8% services, 26.8% sales, 0.0% farming, 6.0% construction, 24.1% production (2005-2009 5-year est.).

Income: Per capita income: $24,667 (2010); Median household income: $55,948 (2010); Average household income: $65,071 (2010); Percent of households with income of $100,000 or more: 14.0% (2010); Poverty rate: 5.6% (2005-2009 5-year est.).

Taxes: Total city taxes per capita: $158 (2007); City property taxes per capita: $80 (2007).

Education: Percent of population age 25 and over with: High school diploma (including GED) or higher: 91.7% (2010); Bachelor's degree or higher: 16.7% (2010); Master's degree or higher: 5.6% (2010).

School District(s)

Meridian CUSD 223 (PK-12)
   2009-10 Enrollment: 1,972 . . . . (815) 645-2606

Housing: Homeownership rate: 77.2% (2010); Median home value: $162,316 (2010); Median contract rent: $636 per month (2005-2009 5-year est.); Median year structure built: 1968 (2005-2009 5-year est.).

Transportation: Commute to work: 94.0% car, 0.0% public transportation, 3.2% walk, 2.2% work from home (2005-2009 5-year est.); Travel time to work: 42.8% less than 15 minutes, 34.4% 15 to 30 minutes, 18.9% 30 to 45 minutes, 1.7% 45 to 60 minutes, 2.1% 60 minutes or more (2005-2009 5-year est.)

Peoria County

Located in central Illinois; bounded on the east and south by the Illinois River and Lake Peorio; drained by the Spoon River and Kickapoo Creek. Covers a land area of 619.52 square miles, a water area of 11.36 square miles, and is located in the Central Time Zone at 40.75° N. Lat., 89.66° W. Long. The county was founded in 1825. County seat is Peoria.

Peoria County is part of the Peoria, IL Metropolitan Statistical Area. The entire metro area includes: Marshall County, IL; Peoria County, IL; Stark County, IL; Tazewell County, IL; Woodford County, IL

Weather Station: Peoria Greater Peoria Arpt   Elevation: 651 feet

	Jan	Feb	Mar	Apr	May	Jun	Jul	Aug	Sep	Oct	Nov	Dec
High	33	38	50	63	73	82	86	84	77	64	50	36
Low	17	21	31	41	52	61	66	64	55	43	33	21
Precip	1.7	1.8	2.8	3.6	4.1	3.6	3.7	3.4	3.1	2.9	3.1	2.4
Snow	6.8	5.9	2.9	0.9	tr	tr	tr	0.0	tr	tr	1.3	6.5

High and Low temperatures in degrees Fahrenheit; Precipitation and Snow in inches

Weather Station: Princeville   Elevation: 734 feet

	Jan	Feb	Mar	Apr	May	Jun	Jul	Aug	Sep	Oct	Nov	Dec
High	32	37	49	63	73	82	85	83	77	65	50	36
Low	13	17	26	37	48	57	61	59	50	39	29	17
Precip	2.1	1.9	2.9	3.6	4.5	3.7	3.9	3.9	3.4	2.8	3.0	2.4
Snow	6.1	5.9	2.3	0.4	tr	0.0	0.0	0.0	0.0	tr	1.0	5.9

High and Low temperatures in degrees Fahrenheit; Precipitation and Snow in inches

Population: 182,827 (1990); 183,433 (2000); 184,190 (2010); 183,847 (2015 projected); Race: 76.5% White, 16.9% Black, 2.6% Asian, 4.0% Other, 3.0% Hispanic of any race (2010); Density: 297.3 persons per square mile (2010); Average household size: 2.39 (2010); Median age: 36.4 (2010); Males per 100 females: 93.6 (2010).

Religion: Five largest groups: 19.3% Catholic Church, 5.4% The United Methodist Church, 3.5% Evangelical Lutheran Church in America, 3.1% Lutheran Church—Missouri Synod, 2.0% Southern Baptist Convention (2000).

Economy: Unemployment rate: 9.2% (August 2011); Total civilian labor force: 101,125 (August 2011); Leading industries: 19.6% health care and social assistance; 10.3% retail trade; 9.5% manufacturing (2009); Farms: 877 totaling 259,204 acres (2007); Companies that employ 500 or more persons: 17 (2009); Companies that employ 100 to 499 persons: 113 (2009); Companies that employ less than 100 persons: 4,603 (2009); Black-owned businesses: n/a (2007); Hispanic-owned businesses: 161 (2007); Asian-owned businesses: 375 (2007); Women-owned businesses: 3,994 (2007); Retail sales per capita: $13,479 (2010). Single-family building permits issued: 252 (2010); Multi-family building permits issued: 203 (2010).

Income: Per capita income: $26,528 (2010); Median household income: $49,475 (2010); Average household income: $65,032 (2010); Percent of households with income of $100,000 or more: 17.4% (2010); Poverty rate: 16.8% (2009); Bankruptcy rate: 5.53% (2010).

Taxes: Total county taxes per capita: $144 (2007); County property taxes per capita: $111 (2007).

Education: Percent of population age 25 and over with: High school diploma (including GED) or higher: 87.5% (2010); Bachelor's degree or higher: 27.5% (2010); Master's degree or higher: 9.6% (2010).

Housing: Homeownership rate: 69.6% (2010); Median home value: $115,905 (2010); Median contract rent: $512 per month (2005-2009 5-year est.); Median year structure built: 1960 (2005-2009 5-year est.)

Health: Birth rate: 145.6 per 10,000 population (2009); Death rate: 92.0 per 10,000 population (2009); Age-adjusted cancer mortality rate: 201.7 deaths per 100,000 population (2007); Number of physicians: 50.7 per 10,000 population (2008); Hospital beds: 56.0 per 10,000 population (2007); Hospital admissions: 2,739.4 per 10,000 population (2007).

Environment: Air Quality Index: 73.8% good, 26.2% moderate, 0.0% unhealthy for sensitive individuals, 0.0% unhealthy (percent of days in 2008)

Elections: 2008 Presidential election results: 56.2% Obama, 42.3% McCain, 0.6% Nader

National and State Parks: Jubilee College State Park; Spring Branch State Conservation Area; Spring Lake State Park

Additional Information Contacts

Peoria County Government . . . . (309) 672-6056
   http://www.peoriacounty.org
Chillicothe Chamber of Commerce . . . . (309) 274-4556
   http://www.chillicothechamber.com
City of Chillicothe . . . . (309) 274-2020
   http://www.cityofchillicotheil.com
City of Peoria . . . . (309) 494-8565
   http://www.ci.peoria.il.us

Peoria Area Chamber of Commerce . . . . (309) 495-5900
    http://www.peoriachamber.org
Peoria Heights Chamber of Commerce. . . . . (309) 685-4812
    http://peoriaheightschamber.com

Peoria County Communities

BARTONVILLE (village). Covers a land area of 8.026 square miles
and a water area of 0.424 square miles. Located at 40.64° N. Lat; 89.66°
W. Long. Elevation is 505 feet.
History: Bartonville developed as a coal mining community, with factories
that manufactured steel wire and fence.
Population: 6,555 (1990); 6,310 (2000); 5,803 (2010); 5,570 (2015
projected); Race: 97.5% White, 0.3% Black, 0.6% Asian, 1.6% Other, 1.3%
Hispanic of any race (2010); Density: 723.0 persons per square mile
(2010); Average household size: 2.39 (2010); Median age: 40.3 (2010);
Males per 100 females: 95.3 (2010); Marriage status: 28.5% never married,
52.4% now married, 6.7% widowed, 12.4% divorced (2005-2009 5-year
est.); Foreign born: 0.8% (2005-2009 5-year est.); Ancestry (includes
multiple ancestries): 37.4% German, 17.2% Irish, 15.4% English, 8.9%
American, 6.8% Italian (2005-2009 5-year est.).
Economy: Single-family building permits issued: 1 (2010); Multi-family
building permits issued: 0 (2010); Employment by occupation: 6.2%
management, 14.1% professional, 19.6% services, 27.3% sales, 0.0%
farming, 13.7% construction, 19.1% production (2005-2009 5-year est.).
Income: Per capita income: $26,265 (2010); Median household income:
$53,852 (2010); Average household income: $62,612 (2010); Percent of
households with income of $100,000 or more: 13.3% (2010); Poverty rate:
4.8% (2005-2009 5-year est.).
Taxes: Total city taxes per capita: $294 (2007); City property taxes per
capita: $205 (2007).
Education: Percent of population age 25 and over with: High school
diploma (including GED) or higher: 85.0% (2010); Bachelor's degree or
higher: 12.7% (2010); Master's degree or higher: 2.5% (2010).
School District(s)
Bartonville SD 66 (PK-08)
    2009-10 Enrollment: 271 . . . . (309) 697-3253
Monroe SD 70 (KG-08)
    2009-10 Enrollment: 304 . . . . (309) 697-3120
Housing: Homeownership rate: 81.7% (2010); Median home value:
$104,910 (2010); Median contract rent: $499 per month (2005-2009 5-year
est.); Median year structure built: 1955 (2005-2009 5-year est.).
Safety: Violent crime rate: 44.0 per 10,000 population; Property crime rate:
351.7 per 10,000 population (2010).
Newspapers: Limestone Independent News (Local news; Circulation
2,000)
Transportation: Commute to work: 95.9% car, 0.0% public transportation,
1.3% walk, 1.0% work from home (2005-2009 5-year est.); Travel time to
work: 27.3% less than 15 minutes, 57.1% 15 to 30 minutes, 10.0% 30 to 45
minutes, 3.7% 45 to 60 minutes, 1.8% 60 minutes or more (2005-2009
5-year est.)

BELLEVUE (village). Covers a land area of 1.678 square miles and a
water area of 0 square miles. Located at 40.68° N. Lat; 89.66° W. Long.
Elevation is 676 feet.
History: Incorporated 1941.
Population: 1,675 (1990); 1,887 (2000); 1,692 (2010); 1,660 (2015
projected); Race: 94.9% White, 1.7% Black, 1.1% Asian, 2.3% Other, 2.1%
Hispanic of any race (2010); Density: 1,008.1 persons per square mile
(2010); Average household size: 2.47 (2010); Median age: 38.7 (2010);
Males per 100 females: 95.4 (2010); Marriage status: 25.3% never married,
54.6% now married, 5.1% widowed, 15.0% divorced (2005-2009 5-year
est.); Foreign born: 0.5% (2005-2009 5-year est.); Ancestry (includes
multiple ancestries): 30.5% German, 21.5% Irish, 11.7% English, 7.9%
American, 4.0% Dutch (2005-2009 5-year est.).
Economy: Single-family building permits issued: 2 (2010); Multi-family
building permits issued: 0 (2010); Employment by occupation: 6.1%
management, 12.1% professional, 21.9% services, 35.5% sales, 0.0%
farming, 5.7% construction, 18.6% production (2005-2009 5-year est.).
Income: Per capita income: $25,233 (2010); Median household income:
$48,665 (2010); Average household income: $62,536 (2010); Percent of
households with income of $100,000 or more: 12.1% (2010); Poverty rate:
19.5% (2005-2009 5-year est.).
Taxes: Total city taxes per capita: $80 (2007); City property taxes per
capita: $68 (2007).

Education: Percent of population age 25 and over with: High school
diploma (including GED) or higher: 83.2% (2010); Bachelor's degree or
higher: 11.7% (2010); Master's degree or higher: 2.7% (2010).
Housing: Homeownership rate: 83.2% (2010); Median home value:
$109,799 (2010); Median contract rent: $444 per month (2005-2009 5-year
est.); Median year structure built: 1959 (2005-2009 5-year est.).
Transportation: Commute to work: 92.5% car, 0.4% public transportation,
2.0% walk, 1.2% work from home (2005-2009 5-year est.); Travel time to
work: 30.2% less than 15 minutes, 49.5% 15 to 30 minutes, 12.9% 30 to 45
minutes, 0.3% 45 to 60 minutes, 7.1% 60 minutes or more (2005-2009
5-year est.)

BRIMFIELD (village). Covers a land area of 0.753 square miles and a
water area of 0.005 square miles. Located at 40.83° N. Lat; 89.88° W.
Long. Elevation is 702 feet.
Population: 811 (1990); 933 (2000); 969 (2010); 988 (2015 projected);
Race: 97.0% White, 0.2% Black, 0.2% Asian, 2.6% Other, 1.7% Hispanic
of any race (2010); Density: 1,286.5 persons per square mile (2010);
Average household size: 2.55 (2010); Median age: 36.5 (2010); Males per
100 females: 101.0 (2010); Marriage status: 21.0% never married, 59.8%
now married, 9.8% widowed, 9.4% divorced (2005-2009 5-year est.);
Foreign born: 1.1% (2005-2009 5-year est.); Ancestry (includes multiple
ancestries): 32.7% German, 14.7% English, 12.8% Irish, 12.0% American,
5.7% French (2005-2009 5-year est.).
Economy: Single-family building permits issued: 1 (2010); Multi-family
building permits issued: 0 (2010); Employment by occupation: 12.0%
management, 30.2% professional, 13.9% services, 22.4% sales, 0.5%
farming, 11.5% construction, 9.5% production (2005-2009 5-year est.).
Income: Per capita income: $28,189 (2010); Median household income:
$59,840 (2010); Average household income: $71,375 (2010); Percent of
households with income of $100,000 or more: 20.8% (2010); Poverty rate:
16.7% (2005-2009 5-year est.).
Taxes: Total city taxes per capita: $82 (2007); City property taxes per
capita: $52 (2007).
Education: Percent of population age 25 and over with: High school
diploma (including GED) or higher: 90.8% (2010); Bachelor's degree or
higher: 19.1% (2010); Master's degree or higher: 4.9% (2010).
School District(s)
Brimfield CUSD 309 (PK-12)
    2009-10 Enrollment: 729 . . . . (309) 446-3378
Housing: Homeownership rate: 83.7% (2010); Median home value:
$118,033 (2010); Median contract rent: $415 per month (2005-2009 5-year
est.); Median year structure built: 1958 (2005-2009 5-year est.).
Transportation: Commute to work: 85.3% car, 0.0% public transportation,
6.4% walk, 3.4% work from home (2005-2009 5-year est.); Travel time to
work: 22.9% less than 15 minutes, 47.1% 15 to 30 minutes, 25.2% 30 to 45
minutes, 1.0% 45 to 60 minutes, 3.8% 60 minutes or more (2005-2009
5-year est.)

CHILLICOTHE (city). Covers a land area of 4.940 square miles and a
water area of 0.283 square miles. Located at 40.92° N. Lat; 89.49° W.
Long. Elevation is 499 feet.
History: Incorporated 1861.
Population: 6,054 (1990); 5,996 (2000); 5,922 (2010); 5,882 (2015
projected); Race: 97.0% White, 0.1% Black, 0.3% Asian, 2.6% Other, 3.4%
Hispanic of any race (2010); Density: 1,198.8 persons per square mile
(2010); Average household size: 2.39 (2010); Median age: 37.6 (2010);
Males per 100 females: 93.0 (2010); Marriage status: 25.5% never married,
54.4% now married, 8.3% widowed, 11.8% divorced (2005-2009 5-year
est.); Foreign born: 1.6% (2005-2009 5-year est.); Ancestry (includes
multiple ancestries): 37.4% German, 19.0% Irish, 17.0% English, 7.1%
American, 3.6% Dutch (2005-2009 5-year est.).
Economy: Single-family building permits issued: 20 (2010); Multi-family
building permits issued: 0 (2010); Employment by occupation: 9.8%
management, 19.2% professional, 21.5% services, 19.2% sales, 0.7%
farming, 12.3% construction, 17.4% production (2005-2009 5-year est.).
Income: Per capita income: $25,744 (2010); Median household income:
$51,834 (2010); Average household income: $61,652 (2010); Percent of
households with income of $100,000 or more: 15.9% (2010); Poverty rate:
5.0% (2005-2009 5-year est.).
Taxes: Total city taxes per capita: $164 (2007); City property taxes per
capita: $107 (2007).
Education: Percent of population age 25 and over with: High school
diploma (including GED) or higher: 90.0% (2010); Bachelor's degree or
higher: 15.5% (2010); Master's degree or higher: 4.5% (2010).

School District(s)

Il Valley Central USD 321 (PK-12)

2009-10 Enrollment: 2,282 . . . . (309) 274-5418

Housing: Homeownership rate: 77.9% (2010); Median home value: $110,469 (2010); Median contract rent: $437 per month (2005-2009 5-year est.); Median year structure built: 1958 (2005-2009 5-year est.).

Transportation: Commute to work: 92.3% car, 0.4% public transportation, 1.4% walk, 3.5% work from home (2005-2009 5-year est.); Travel time to work: 38.7% less than 15 minutes, 33.2% 15 to 30 minutes, 20.5% 30 to 45 minutes, 1.2% 45 to 60 minutes, 6.3% 60 minutes or more (2005-2009 5-year est.)

Additional Information Contacts

Chillicothe Chamber of Commerce . . . . (309) 274-4556
http://www.chillicothechamber.com

City of Chillicothe . . . . (309) 274-2020
http://www.cityofchillicotheil.com

DUNLAP (village).

Covers a land area of 0.373 square miles and a water area of 0 square miles. Located at 40.86° N. Lat; 89.67° W. Long. Elevation is 735 feet.

Population: 985 (1990); 926 (2000); 984 (2010); 989 (2015 projected); Race: 96.7% White, 0.7% Black, 1.6% Asian, 0.9% Other, 2.2% Hispanic of any race (2010); Density: 2,637.8 persons per square mile (2010); Average household size: 2.68 (2010); Median age: 37.1 (2010); Males per 100 females: 100.8 (2010); Marriage status: 16.9% never married, 69.2% now married, 4.0% widowed, 9.9% divorced (2005-2009 5-year est.); Foreign born: 0.2% (2005-2009 5-year est.); Ancestry (includes multiple ancestries): 40.2% German, 22.4% English, 17.9% Irish, 10.1% American, 7.1% Swedish (2005-2009 5-year est.).

Economy: Employment by occupation: 19.6% management, 30.6% professional, 10.2% services, 23.5% sales, 0.3% farming, 6.0% construction, 9.7% production (2005-2009 5-year est.).

Income: Per capita income: $29,004 (2010); Median household income: $67,935 (2010); Average household income: $79,653 (2010); Percent of households with income of $100,000 or more: 25.9% (2010); Poverty rate: 2.1% (2005-2009 5-year est.).

Taxes: Total city taxes per capita: $73 (2007); City property taxes per capita: $68 (2007).

Education: Percent of population age 25 and over with: High school diploma (including GED) or higher: 92.8% (2010); Bachelor's degree or higher: 29.7% (2010); Master's degree or higher: 7.5% (2010).

School District(s)

Dunlap CUSD 323 (PK-12)

2009-10 Enrollment: 3,473 . . . . (309) 243-7716

Housing: Homeownership rate: 82.0% (2010); Median home value: $156,466 (2010); Median contract rent: $426 per month (2005-2009 5-year est.); Median year structure built: 1972 (2005-2009 5-year est.).

Hospitals: Greenview Regional Hospital (211 beds)

Transportation: Commute to work: 96.1% car, 0.5% public transportation, 1.3% walk, 2.1% work from home (2005-2009 5-year est.); Travel time to work: 30.2% less than 15 minutes, 53.5% 15 to 30 minutes, 11.3% 30 to 45 minutes, 2.5% 45 to 60 minutes, 2.5% 60 minutes or more (2005-2009 5-year est.)

EDELSTEIN (unincorporated postal area, zip code 61526).

Covers a land area of 33.664 square miles and a water area of 0.009 square miles. Located at 40.93° N. Lat; 89.62° W. Long. Elevation is 814 feet.

Population: 1,173 (2000); Race: 97.9% White, 0.0% Black, 0.0% Asian, 2.1% Other, 0.0% Hispanic of any race (2000); Density: 34.8 persons per square mile (2000); Age: 28.2% under 18, 12.1% over 64 (2000); Marriage status: 14.6% never married, 77.3% now married, 4.1% widowed, 4.0% divorced (2000); Foreign born: 0.5% (2000); Ancestry (includes multiple ancestries): 41.3% German, 18.8% English, 12.6% Irish, 5.7% American, 3.8% Swedish (2000).

Economy: Employment by occupation: 11.7% management, 20.8% professional, 9.2% services, 29.2% sales, 0.0% farming, 14.1% construction, 15.1% production (2000).

Income: Per capita income: $24,575 (2000); Median household income: $65,217 (2000); Poverty rate: 0.8% (2000).

Education: Percent of population age 25 and over with: High school diploma (including GED) or higher: 84.1% (2000); Bachelor's degree or higher: 17.0% (2000).

Housing: Homeownership rate: 96.1% (2000); Median home value: $123,600 (2000); Median contract rent: $275 per month (2000); Median year structure built: 1972 (2000).

Transportation: Commute to work: 94.8% car, 0.0% public transportation, 1.0% walk, 4.2% work from home (2000); Travel time to work: 24.7% less than 15 minutes, 46.6% 15 to 30 minutes, 19.8% 30 to 45 minutes, 5.2% 45 to 60 minutes, 3.7% 60 minutes or more (2000)

EDWARDS (unincorporated postal area, zip code 61528).

Covers a land area of 17.631 square miles and a water area of 0 square miles. Located at 40.77° N. Lat; 89.74° W. Long. Elevation is 525 feet.

Population: 1,608 (2000); Race: 97.8% White, 0.2% Black, 0.4% Asian, 1.6% Other, 1.3% Hispanic of any race (2000); Density: 91.2 persons per square mile (2000); Age: 25.7% under 18, 12.3% over 64 (2000); Marriage status: 21.0% never married, 67.6% now married, 5.2% widowed, 6.2% divorced (2000); Foreign born: 1.3% (2000); Ancestry (includes multiple ancestries): 35.3% German, 17.4% Irish, 17.1% English, 10.0% American, 6.0% French (2000).

Economy: Employment by occupation: 16.6% management, 21.9% professional, 15.4% services, 23.2% sales, 0.0% farming, 8.4% construction, 14.5% production (2000).

Income: Per capita income: $28,248 (2000); Median household income: $63,867 (2000); Poverty rate: 3.6% (2000).

Education: Percent of population age 25 and over with: High school diploma (including GED) or higher: 85.8% (2000); Bachelor's degree or higher: 29.5% (2000).

Housing: Homeownership rate: 92.4% (2000); Median home value: $136,800 (2000); Median contract rent: $328 per month (2000); Median year structure built: 1972 (2000).

Transportation: Commute to work: 95.2% car, 0.0% public transportation, 0.9% walk, 3.9% work from home (2000); Travel time to work: 18.3% less than 15 minutes, 63.8% 15 to 30 minutes, 13.0% 30 to 45 minutes, 2.6% 45 to 60 minutes, 2.3% 60 minutes or more (2000)

ELMWOOD (city).

Covers a land area of 1.233 square miles and a water area of 0 square miles. Located at 40.77° N. Lat; 89.96° W. Long. Elevation is 643 feet.

History: Incorporated 1867. Lorado Taft born here; his statue *PIONEERS OF THE PRAIRIESITAL (1928) IS IN CITY PARK.*

Population: 1,892 (1990); 1,945 (2000); 1,895 (2010); 1,874 (2015 projected); Race: 98.2% White, 0.3% Black, 0.2% Asian, 1.4% Other, 1.2% Hispanic of any race (2010); Density: 1,536.6 persons per square mile (2010); Average household size: 2.44 (2010); Median age: 37.7 (2010); Males per 100 females: 90.8 (2010); Marriage status: 22.2% never married, 63.2% now married, 9.8% widowed, 4.8% divorced (2005-2009 5-year est.); Foreign born: 0.6% (2005-2009 5-year est.); Ancestry (includes multiple ancestries): 43.5% German, 18.4% Irish, 13.3% English, 10.4% American, 7.8% Italian (2005-2009 5-year est.).

Economy: Employment by occupation: 9.7% management, 19.8% professional, 16.3% services, 28.0% sales, 0.5% farming, 9.7% construction, 16.0% production (2005-2009 5-year est.).

Income: Per capita income: $28,000 (2010); Median household income: $61,585 (2010); Average household income: $68,303 (2010); Percent of households with income of $100,000 or more: 17.7% (2010); Poverty rate: 6.5% (2005-2009 5-year est.).

Taxes: Total city taxes per capita: $165 (2007); City property taxes per capita: $148 (2007).

Education: Percent of population age 25 and over with: High school diploma (including GED) or higher: 89.8% (2010); Bachelor's degree or higher: 20.9% (2010); Master's degree or higher: 3.9% (2010).

School District(s)

Elmwood CUSD 322 (PK-12)

2009-10 Enrollment: 736 . . . . (309) 742-8464

Housing: Homeownership rate: 82.6% (2010); Median home value: $107,692 (2010); Median contract rent: $513 per month (2005-2009 5-year est.); Median year structure built: 1947 (2005-2009 5-year est.).

Safety: Violent crime rate: 32.2 per 10,000 population; Property crime rate: 134.3 per 10,000 population (2010).

Newspapers: Advertiser (Local news; Circulation 6,980); Home Shopper (Community news; Circulation 7,995); Tri County News-Elmwood Gazette Edition (Local news; Circulation 400); Tri County News-Yates City Banner Edition (Local news; Circulation 100); Tri-County News Princeville Telephone (Community news; Circulation 450); Tri-County News-Farmington Bugle Edition (Local news; Circulation 150); Tri-County News-Williamsfield Times Edition (Local news; Circulation 500)

Transportation: Commute to work: 93.8% car, 0.0% public transportation, 1.2% walk, 1.7% work from home (2005-2009 5-year est.); Travel time to work: 26.5% less than 15 minutes, 16.4% 15 to 30 minutes, 47.0% 30 to 45

minutes, 6.5% 45 to 60 minutes, 3.5% 60 minutes or more (2005-2009 5-year est.)

GLASFORD (village). Covers a land area of 0.883 square miles and a water area of 0 square miles. Located at 40.57° N. Lat; 89.81° W. Long. Elevation is 614 feet.
Population: 1,234 (1990); 1,076 (2000); 985 (2010); 948 (2015 projected); Race: 98.4% White, 0.0% Black, 0.0% Asian, 1.6% Other, 2.0% Hispanic of any race (2010); Density: 1,115.4 persons per square mile (2010); Average household size: 2.45 (2010); Median age: 37.8 (2010); Males per 100 females: 96.6 (2010); Marriage status: 23.1% never married, 55.7% now married, 6.9% widowed, 14.2% divorced (2005-2009 5-year est.); Foreign born: 0.5% (2005-2009 5-year est.); Ancestry (includes multiple ancestries): 36.2% German, 15.7% English, 12.0% American, 8.7% Irish, 3.2% Italian (2005-2009 5-year est.).
Economy: Single-family building permits issued: 0 (2010); Multi-family building permits issued: 0 (2010); Employment by occupation: 3.4% management, 12.8% professional, 17.4% services, 29.0% sales, 0.0% farming, 11.0% construction, 26.4% production (2005-2009 5-year est.).
Income: Per capita income: $23,375 (2010); Median household income: $48,864 (2010); Average household income: $56,922 (2010); Percent of households with income of $100,000 or more: 12.7% (2010); Poverty rate: 16.0% (2005-2009 5-year est.).
Taxes: Total city taxes per capita: $109 (2007); City property taxes per capita: $73 (2007).
Education: Percent of population age 25 and over with: High school diploma (including GED) or higher: 87.2% (2010); Bachelor's degree or higher: 10.9% (2010); Master's degree or higher: 2.9% (2010).
School District(s)
Illini Bluffs CUSD 327 (PK-12)
    2009-10 Enrollment: 995 . . . . (309) 389-2231
Housing: Homeownership rate: 81.8% (2010); Median home value: $94,675 (2010); Median contract rent: $409 per month (2005-2009 5-year est.); Median year structure built: 1957 (2005-2009 5-year est.).
Safety: Violent crime rate: 19.4 per 10,000 population; Property crime rate: 29.2 per 10,000 population (2010).
Newspapers: Glasford Gazette (Local news; Circulation 1,300)
Transportation: Commute to work: 96.8% car, 0.0% public transportation, 0.6% walk, 0.9% work from home (2005-2009 5-year est.); Travel time to work: 12.7% less than 15 minutes, 31.3% 15 to 30 minutes, 48.3% 30 to 45 minutes, 3.9% 45 to 60 minutes, 3.9% 60 minutes or more (2005-2009 5-year est.)

HANNA CITY (village). Aka Hanna. Covers a land area of 0.477 square miles and a water area of 0 square miles. Located at 40.69° N. Lat; 89.79° W. Long. Elevation is 728 feet.
Population: 1,248 (1990); 1,013 (2000); 988 (2010); 981 (2015 projected); Race: 85.9% White, 10.2% Black, 1.3% Asian, 2.5% Other, 1.9% Hispanic of any race (2010); Density: 2,071.3 persons per square mile (2010); Average household size: 2.51 (2010); Median age: 37.4 (2010); Males per 100 females: 120.5 (2010); Marriage status: 26.2% never married, 59.8% now married, 7.9% widowed, 6.1% divorced (2005-2009 5-year est.); Foreign born: 0.8% (2005-2009 5-year est.); Ancestry (includes multiple ancestries): 42.3% German, 14.4% English, 12.4% American, 9.1% Irish, 5.7% Polish (2005-2009 5-year est.).
Economy: Employment by occupation: 9.7% management, 18.8% professional, 15.9% services, 25.5% sales, 0.0% farming, 10.3% construction, 19.8% production (2005-2009 5-year est.).
Income: Per capita income: $27,631 (2010); Median household income: $63,911 (2010); Average household income: $72,347 (2010); Percent of households with income of $100,000 or more: 19.8% (2010); Poverty rate: 4.9% (2005-2009 5-year est.).
Taxes: Total city taxes per capita: $84 (2007); City property taxes per capita: $82 (2007).
Education: Percent of population age 25 and over with: High school diploma (including GED) or higher: 84.1% (2010); Bachelor's degree or higher: 8.6% (2010); Master's degree or higher: 0.6% (2010).
Housing: Homeownership rate: 85.7% (2010); Median home value: $126,374 (2010); Median contract rent: $525 per month (2005-2009 5-year est.); Median year structure built: 1965 (2005-2009 5-year est.).
Transportation: Commute to work: 94.0% car, 0.0% public transportation, 1.9% walk, 2.1% work from home (2005-2009 5-year est.); Travel time to work: 18.7% less than 15 minutes, 59.8% 15 to 30 minutes, 11.3% 30 to 45 minutes, 5.5% 45 to 60 minutes, 4.8% 60 minutes or more (2005-2009 5-year est.)

KINGSTON MINES (village). Covers a land area of 1.340 square miles and a water area of 0.103 square miles. Located at 40.55° N. Lat; 89.77° W. Long. Elevation is 463 feet.
Population: 293 (1990); 259 (2000); 238 (2010); 227 (2015 projected); Race: 97.9% White, 0.0% Black, 0.0% Asian, 2.1% Other, 2.5% Hispanic of any race (2010); Density: 177.6 persons per square mile (2010); Average household size: 2.53 (2010); Median age: 36.2 (2010); Males per 100 females: 93.5 (2010); Marriage status: 32.0% never married, 39.5% now married, 11.5% widowed, 17.0% divorced (2005-2009 5-year est.); Foreign born: 1.2% (2005-2009 5-year est.); Ancestry (includes multiple ancestries): 23.2% American, 18.9% German, 5.5% Irish, 3.9% English, 2.0% Dutch (2005-2009 5-year est.).
Economy: Single-family building permits issued: 0 (2010); Multi-family building permits issued: 0 (2010); Employment by occupation: 3.4% management, 9.3% professional, 25.4% services, 17.8% sales, 0.0% farming, 23.7% construction, 20.3% production (2005-2009 5-year est.).
Income: Per capita income: $22,666 (2010); Median household income: $52,885 (2010); Average household income: $57,872 (2010); Percent of households with income of $100,000 or more: 13.8% (2010); Poverty rate: 3.5% (2005-2009 5-year est.).
Taxes: Total city taxes per capita: $107 (2007); City property taxes per capita: $103 (2007).
Education: Percent of population age 25 and over with: High school diploma (including GED) or higher: 85.8% (2010); Bachelor's degree or higher: 9.9% (2010); Master's degree or higher: 2.5% (2010).
Housing: Homeownership rate: 84.0% (2010); Median home value: $98,235 (2010); Median contract rent: $294 per month (2005-2009 5-year est.); Median year structure built: 1948 (2005-2009 5-year est.).
Transportation: Commute to work: 100.0% car, 0.0% public transportation, 0.0% walk, 0.0% work from home (2005-2009 5-year est.); Travel time to work: 18.8% less than 15 minutes, 42.9% 15 to 30 minutes, 36.6% 30 to 45 minutes, 0.0% 45 to 60 minutes, 1.8% 60 minutes or more (2005-2009 5-year est.)

LAURA (unincorporated postal area, zip code 61451). Covers a land area of 22.326 square miles and a water area of 0.106 square miles. Located at 40.95° N. Lat; 89.94° W. Long. Elevation is 728 feet.
Population: 383 (2000); Race: 98.9% White, 0.0% Black, 0.0% Asian, 1.1% Other, 0.0% Hispanic of any race (2000); Density: 17.2 persons per square mile (2000); Age: 23.9% under 18, 8.8% over 64 (2000); Marriage status: 17.8% never married, 60.1% now married, 8.7% widowed, 13.4% divorced (2000); Foreign born: 0.0% (2000); Ancestry (includes multiple ancestries): 22.1% German, 15.2% English, 10.9% Irish, 7.7% French, 7.7% Swedish (2000).
Economy: Employment by occupation: 9.7% management, 2.2% professional, 14.0% services, 15.6% sales, 1.6% farming, 23.1% construction, 33.9% production (2000).
Income: Per capita income: $18,145 (2000); Median household income: $45,000 (2000); Poverty rate: 0.0% (2000).
Education: Percent of population age 25 and over with: High school diploma (including GED) or higher: 92.0% (2000); Bachelor's degree or higher: 12.5% (2000).
Housing: Homeownership rate: 82.2% (2000); Median home value: $49,200 (2000); Median contract rent: $200 per month (2000); Median year structure built: 1942 (2000).
Transportation: Commute to work: 93.0% car, 0.0% public transportation, 0.0% walk, 7.0% work from home (2000); Travel time to work: 14.5% less than 15 minutes, 26.6% 15 to 30 minutes, 46.2% 30 to 45 minutes, 8.7% 45 to 60 minutes, 4.0% 60 minutes or more (2000)

MAPLETON (village). Covers a land area of 0.718 square miles and a water area of 0 square miles. Located at 40.57° N. Lat; 89.72° W. Long. Elevation is 469 feet.
Population: 270 (1990); 227 (2000); 226 (2010); 224 (2015 projected); Race: 96.5% White, 1.3% Black, 0.0% Asian, 2.2% Other, 0.4% Hispanic of any race (2010); Density: 314.7 persons per square mile (2010); Average household size: 2.52 (2010); Median age: 44.2 (2010); Males per 100 females: 113.2 (2010); Marriage status: 13.1% never married, 63.4% now married, 6.0% widowed, 17.5% divorced (2005-2009 5-year est.); Foreign born: 1.4% (2005-2009 5-year est.); Ancestry (includes multiple ancestries): 32.0% German, 24.2% American, 14.2% Irish, 12.8% English, 4.1% French (2005-2009 5-year est.).
Economy: Single-family building permits issued: 0 (2010); Multi-family building permits issued: 0 (2010); Employment by occupation: 20.0%

management, 27.6% professional, 18.1% services, 15.2% sales, 0.0% farming, 6.7% construction, 12.4% production (2005-2009 5-year est.).
Income: Per capita income: $33,889 (2010); Median household income: $76,786 (2010); Average household income: $85,253 (2010); Percent of households with income of $100,000 or more: 28.1% (2010); Poverty rate: 3.2% (2005-2009 5-year est.).
Taxes: Total city taxes per capita: $105 (2007); City property taxes per capita: $89 (2007).
Education: Percent of population age 25 and over with: High school diploma (including GED) or higher: 91.3% (2010); Bachelor's degree or higher: 11.2% (2010); Master's degree or higher: 3.1% (2010).
Housing: Homeownership rate: 88.8% (2010); Median home value: $135,227 (2010); Median contract rent: $500 per month (2005-2009 5-year est.); Median year structure built: 1957 (2005-2009 5-year est.).
Transportation: Commute to work: 88.7% car, 0.0% public transportation, 2.8% walk, 1.9% work from home (2005-2009 5-year est.); Travel time to work: 34.6% less than 15 minutes, 44.2% 15 to 30 minutes, 13.5% 30 to 45 minutes, 0.0% 45 to 60 minutes, 7.7% 60 minutes or more (2005-2009 5-year est.)

NORWOOD (village). Aka Norwood Park. Covers a land area of 0.264 square miles and a water area of 0 square miles. Located at 40.70° N. Lat; 89.70° W. Long. Elevation is 696 feet.
Population: 517 (1990); 473 (2000); 392 (2010); 379 (2015 projected); Race: 90.1% White, 7.9% Black, 0.5% Asian, 1.5% Other, 1.0% Hispanic of any race (2010); Density: 1,482.5 persons per square mile (2010); Average household size: 2.71 (2010); Median age: 43.0 (2010); Males per 100 females: 100.0 (2010); Marriage status: 16.5% never married, 63.0% now married, 5.5% widowed, 15.0% divorced (2005-2009 5-year est.); Foreign born: 0.5% (2005-2009 5-year est.); Ancestry (includes multiple ancestries): 31.4% German, 19.0% Irish, 11.5% English, 9.5% French, 7.5% American (2005-2009 5-year est.).
Economy: Employment by occupation: 7.5% management, 19.1% professional, 17.6% services, 25.6% sales, 0.0% farming, 7.5% construction, 22.6% production (2005-2009 5-year est.).
Income: Per capita income: $21,353 (2010); Median household income: $57,759 (2010); Average household income: $59,894 (2010); Percent of households with income of $100,000 or more: 9.3% (2010); Poverty rate: 8.6% (2005-2009 5-year est.).
Taxes: Total city taxes per capita: $52 (2007); City property taxes per capita: $50 (2007).
Education: Percent of population age 25 and over with: High school diploma (including GED) or higher: 80.8% (2010); Bachelor's degree or higher: 10.1% (2010); Master's degree or higher: 2.9% (2010).
Housing: Homeownership rate: 94.1% (2010); Median home value: $123,125 (2010); Median contract rent: n/a per month (2005-2009 5-year est.); Median year structure built: 1957 (2005-2009 5-year est.).
Transportation: Commute to work: 99.5% car, 0.0% public transportation, 0.0% walk, 0.0% work from home (2005-2009 5-year est.); Travel time to work: 19.6% less than 15 minutes, 61.4% 15 to 30 minutes, 16.4% 30 to 45 minutes, 1.1% 45 to 60 minutes, 1.6% 60 minutes or more (2005-2009 5-year est.)

PEORIA (city). County seat. Covers a land area of 44.404 square miles and a water area of 2.230 square miles. Located at 40.72° N. Lat; 89.60° W. Long. Elevation is 502 feet.
History: Peoria began with the establishment by the French of Fort Pimiteoui on Lake Peoria in 1691. This trading post thrived for over a century, and the village which grew around it was at times called Au Pe, Le Pe, Opa, Au Pay, and Piorias. The American Fort Clark was erected here in 1813 and settlers from New England moved in. When Peoria County was created in 1825, the French-Indian name of Peoria was given to the community at Fort Clark, which became the county seat. Peoria was incorporated as a town in 1835, and received a city charter in 1845. In a speech in Peoria in 1854, following a talk by Stephen Douglas that lasted all afternoon, Abraham Lincoln first publicly denounced slavery.
Population: 114,341 (1990); 112,936 (2000); 113,823 (2010); 113,750 (2015 projected); Race: 66.3% White, 25.3% Black, 3.5% Asian, 4.9% Other, 3.7% Hispanic of any race (2010); Density: 2,563.4 persons per square mile (2010); Average household size: 2.35 (2010); Median age: 34.8 (2010); Males per 100 females: 91.7 (2010); Marriage status: 38.4% never married, 42.6% now married, 6.7% widowed, 12.3% divorced (2005-2009 5-year est.); Foreign born: 4.8% (2005-2009 5-year est.); Ancestry (includes multiple ancestries): 24.1% German, 13.8% Irish, 9.6% English, 4.8% American, 4.1% Italian (2005-2009 5-year est.).

Economy: Unemployment rate: 9.8% (August 2011); Total civilian labor force: 60,185 (August 2011); Single-family building permits issued: 146 (2010); Multi-family building permits issued: 203 (2010); Employment by occupation: 12.8% management, 25.9% professional, 19.4% services, 25.9% sales, 0.2% farming, 4.6% construction, 11.1% production (2005-2009 5-year est.).
Income: Per capita income: $24,932 (2010); Median household income: $44,369 (2010); Average household income: $60,564 (2010); Percent of households with income of $100,000 or more: 15.4% (2010); Poverty rate: 18.0% (2005-2009 5-year est.).
Taxes: Total city taxes per capita: $600 (2007); City property taxes per capita: $233 (2007).
Education: Percent of population age 25 and over with: High school diploma (including GED) or higher: 86.6% (2010); Bachelor's degree or higher: 31.9% (2010); Master's degree or higher: 11.8% (2010).

School District(s)
Dunlap CUSD 323 (PK-12)
    2009-10 Enrollment: 3,473 . . . . (309) 243-7716
Hollis Cons SD 328 (KG-08)
    2009-10 Enrollment: 143 . . . . (309) 697-1325
Limestone CHSD 310 (09-12)
    2009-10 Enrollment: 1,141 . . . . (309) 697-6271
Limestone Walters CCSD 316 (KG-08)
    2009-10 Enrollment: 198 . . . . (309) 697-3035
Norwood ESD 63 (PK-08)
    2009-10 Enrollment: 544 . . . . (309) 676-3523
Oak Grove SD 68 (PK-08)
    2009-10 Enrollment: 412 . . . . (309) 697-3367
Peoria Educ Reg for Empl Traing
    2009-10 Enrollment: n/a . . . . (309) 693-7373
Peoria Roe (06-12)
    2009-10 Enrollment: n/a . . . . (309) 672-6906
Peoria SD 150 (PK-12)
    2009-10 Enrollment: 13,951 . . . . (309) 672-6768
Pleasant Hill SD 69 (PK-08)
    2009-10 Enrollment: 231 . . . . (309) 637-6829
Pleasant Valley SD 62 (PK-08)
    2009-10 Enrollment: 491 . . . . (309) 673-6750

Four-year College(s)
Bradley University (Private, Not-for-profit)
    Fall 2009 Enrollment: 5,800 . . . . (309) 676-7611
    2010-11 Tuition: In-state $25,424; Out-of-state $25,424
Methodist College of Nursing (Private, Not-for-profit)
    Fall 2009 Enrollment: 198 . . . . (309) 672-5513
    2010-11 Tuition: In-state $11,700; Out-of-state $11,700
Midstate College (Private, For-profit)
    Fall 2009 Enrollment: 650 . . . . (309) 692-4092
    2010-11 Tuition: In-state $13,200; Out-of-state $13,200
Saint Francis Medical Center College of Nursing (Private, Not-for-profit, Roman Catholic)
    Fall 2009 Enrollment: 507 . . . . (309) 655-2201

Vocational/Technical School(s)
Regency Beauty Institute-Peoria (Private, For-profit)
    Fall 2009 Enrollment: 138 . . . . (800) 787-6456
    2010-11 Tuition: $16,075
Tricoci University of Beauty Culture (Private, For-profit)
    Fall 2009 Enrollment: 51 . . . . (630) 528-3336
    2010-11 Tuition: $15,450
Housing: Homeownership rate: 62.6% (2010); Median home value: $110,241 (2010); Median contract rent: $520 per month (2005-2009 5-year est.); Median year structure built: 1959 (2005-2009 5-year est.).
Hospitals: Methodist Medical Center of Illinois (330 beds); Proctor Hospital (175 beds); Saint Francis Medical Center (731 beds)
Safety: Violent crime rate: 76.6 per 10,000 population; Property crime rate: 450.7 per 10,000 population (2010).
Newspapers: Catholic Post (Regional news; Circulation 27,089); Chillicothe Times-Bulletin (Local news; Circulation 2,000); East Peoria Courier (Local news; Circulation 8,250); Journal Star (Regional news; Circulation 75,500); Morton Times-News (Local news; Circulation 2,700); Peoria Times-Observer (Local news; Circulation 18,320); Tazewell Times Extra (Community news; Circulation 3,150); Washington Reporter (Local news; Circulation 8,445); Washington Times Reporter (Local news; Circulation 2,700)
Transportation: Commute to work: 89.5% car, 2.6% public transportation, 3.1% walk, 3.1% work from home (2005-2009 5-year est.); Travel time to

work: 42.4% less than 15 minutes, 47.5% 15 to 30 minutes, 5.6% 30 to 45 minutes, 2.1% 45 to 60 minutes, 2.3% 60 minutes or more (2005-2009 5-year est.); Amtrak: train service available.
Airports: Greater Peoria Regional (primary service); Mount Hawley Auxiliary (general aviation)
Additional Information Contacts
City of Peoria . . . . (309) 494-8565
   http://www.ci.peoria.il.us
Peoria Area Chamber of Commerce . . . . (309) 495-5900
   http://www.peoriachamber.org

PEORIA HEIGHTS (village). Covers a land area of 2.644 square miles and a water area of 4.268 square miles. Located at 40.74° N. Lat; 89.57° W. Long. Elevation is 784 feet.

History: Incorporated 1898.
Population: 6,948 (1990); 6,635 (2000); 6,183 (2010); 5,973 (2015 projected); Race: 91.9% White, 2.9% Black, 1.4% Asian, 3.8% Other, 2.6% Hispanic of any race (2010); Density: 2,338.1 persons per square mile (2010); Average household size: 2.06 (2010); Median age: 39.8 (2010); Males per 100 females: 94.6 (2010); Marriage status: 30.6% never married, 42.8% now married, 6.0% widowed, 20.7% divorced (2005-2009 5-year est.); Foreign born: 1.7% (2005-2009 5-year est.); Ancestry (includes multiple ancestries): 34.0% German, 16.7% Irish, 12.1% English, 9.7% American, 5.3% French (2005-2009 5-year est.).
Economy: Single-family building permits issued: 0 (2010); Multi-family building permits issued: 0 (2010); Employment by occupation: 12.7% management, 14.8% professional, 21.2% services, 26.1% sales, 0.3% farming, 8.9% construction, 16.0% production (2005-2009 5-year est.).
Income: Per capita income: $26,189 (2010); Median household income: $43,097 (2010); Average household income: $54,255 (2010); Percent of households with income of $100,000 or more: 8.9% (2010); Poverty rate: 8.4% (2005-2009 5-year est.).
Taxes: Total city taxes per capita: $242 (2007); City property taxes per capita: $99 (2007).
Education: Percent of population age 25 and over with: High school diploma (including GED) or higher: 88.3% (2010); Bachelor's degree or higher: 18.2% (2010); Master's degree or higher: 4.9% (2010).
School District(s)
Peoria Heights CUSD 325 (PK-12)
   2009-10 Enrollment: 817 . . . . (309) 686-8800
Housing: Homeownership rate: 61.4% (2010); Median home value: $85,882 (2010); Median contract rent: $475 per month (2005-2009 5-year est.); Median year structure built: 1954 (2005-2009 5-year est.).
Transportation: Commute to work: 95.2% car, 2.4% public transportation, 0.4% walk, 1.6% work from home (2005-2009 5-year est.); Travel time to work: 37.1% less than 15 minutes, 47.4% 15 to 30 minutes, 6.9% 30 to 45 minutes, 4.3% 45 to 60 minutes, 4.3% 60 minutes or more (2005-2009 5-year est.)
Additional Information Contacts
Peoria Heights Chamber of Commerce . . . . (309) 685-4812
   http://peoriaheightschamber.com

PRINCEVILLE (village). Covers a land area of 1.308 square miles and a water area of 0 square miles. Located at 40.93° N. Lat; 89.75° W. Long. Elevation is 738 feet.

Population: 1,522 (1990); 1,621 (2000); 1,770 (2010); 1,835 (2015 projected); Race: 97.1% White, 0.1% Black, 0.2% Asian, 2.7% Other, 2.1% Hispanic of any race (2010); Density: 1,353.3 persons per square mile (2010); Average household size: 2.57 (2010); Median age: 36.1 (2010); Males per 100 females: 96.4 (2010); Marriage status: 26.5% never married, 56.5% now married, 6.3% widowed, 10.7% divorced (2005-2009 5-year est.); Foreign born: 0.7% (2005-2009 5-year est.); Ancestry (includes multiple ancestries): 45.9% German, 18.3% Irish, 10.4% English, 9.5% American, 3.1% French (2005-2009 5-year est.).
Economy: Single-family building permits issued: 2 (2010); Multi-family building permits issued: 0 (2010); Employment by occupation: 12.4% management, 18.8% professional, 15.6% services, 18.7% sales, 0.6% farming, 16.0% construction, 17.8% production (2005-2009 5-year est.).
Income: Per capita income: $26,657 (2010); Median household income: $59,145 (2010); Average household income: $68,650 (2010); Percent of households with income of $100,000 or more: 18.0% (2010); Poverty rate: 10.0% (2005-2009 5-year est.).
Taxes: Total city taxes per capita: $311 (2007); City property taxes per capita: $299 (2007).

Education: Percent of population age 25 and over with: High school diploma (including GED) or higher: 91.5% (2010); Bachelor's degree or higher: 16.4% (2010); Master's degree or higher: 6.3% (2010).
School District(s)
Princeville CUSD 326 (PK-12)
   2009-10 Enrollment: 787 . . . . (309) 385-2213
Housing: Homeownership rate: 81.1% (2010); Median home value: $122,612 (2010); Median contract rent: $430 per month (2005-2009 5-year est.); Median year structure built: 1958 (2005-2009 5-year est.).
Transportation: Commute to work: 94.2% car, 0.0% public transportation, 2.2% walk, 1.9% work from home (2005-2009 5-year est.); Travel time to work: 29.0% less than 15 minutes, 40.5% 15 to 30 minutes, 24.4% 30 to 45 minutes, 4.4% 45 to 60 minutes, 1.7% 60 minutes or more (2005-2009 5-year est.)

ROME (CDP). Covers a land area of 1.905 square miles and a water area of 0 square miles. Located at 40.87° N. Lat; 89.50° W. Long. Elevation is 463 feet.

Population: 1,860 (1990); 1,776 (2000); 1,625 (2010); 1,560 (2015 projected); Race: 98.1% White, 0.4% Black, 0.2% Asian, 1.2% Other, 1.9% Hispanic of any race (2010); Density: 853.2 persons per square mile (2010); Average household size: 2.48 (2010); Median age: 41.0 (2010); Males per 100 females: 102.6 (2010); Marriage status: 23.3% never married, 62.5% now married, 5.7% widowed, 8.5% divorced (2005-2009 5-year est.); Foreign born: 1.4% (2005-2009 5-year est.); Ancestry (includes multiple ancestries): 31.5% German, 15.4% English, 10.4% Irish, 7.0% French, 5.7% American (2005-2009 5-year est.).
Economy: Employment by occupation: 9.0% management, 6.9% professional, 15.6% services, 39.0% sales, 0.0% farming, 8.3% construction, 21.2% production (2005-2009 5-year est.).
Income: Per capita income: $24,007 (2010); Median household income: $52,861 (2010); Average household income: $60,200 (2010); Percent of households with income of $100,000 or more: 15.7% (2010); Poverty rate: 8.7% (2005-2009 5-year est.).
Education: Percent of population age 25 and over with: High school diploma (including GED) or higher: 88.6% (2010); Bachelor's degree or higher: 18.4% (2010); Master's degree or higher: 5.1% (2010).
Housing: Homeownership rate: 83.2% (2010); Median home value: $119,000 (2010); Median contract rent: $439 per month (2005-2009 5-year est.); Median year structure built: 1958 (2005-2009 5-year est.).
Transportation: Commute to work: 89.5% car, 0.0% public transportation, 0.0% walk, 6.5% work from home (2005-2009 5-year est.); Travel time to work: 28.9% less than 15 minutes, 44.2% 15 to 30 minutes, 23.5% 30 to 45 minutes, 0.0% 45 to 60 minutes, 3.3% 60 minutes or more (2005-2009 5-year est.)

TRIVOLI (unincorporated postal area, zip code 61569). Covers a land area of 38.577 square miles and a water area of 0.317 square miles. Located at 40.69° N. Lat; 89.89° W. Long. Elevation is 751 feet.

Population: 1,215 (2000); Race: 100.0% White, 0.0% Black, 0.0% Asian, 0.0% Other, 0.0% Hispanic of any race (2000); Density: 31.5 persons per square mile (2000); Age: 18.9% under 18, 21.2% over 64 (2000); Marriage status: 15.1% never married, 75.4% now married, 4.6% widowed, 4.8% divorced (2000); Foreign born: 0.0% (2000); Ancestry (includes multiple ancestries): 29.2% German, 16.9% English, 16.9% Irish, 7.8% American, 7.4% French (2000).
Economy: Employment by occupation: 16.6% management, 10.9% professional, 16.1% services, 26.0% sales, 0.0% farming, 14.9% construction, 15.6% production (2000).
Income: Per capita income: $24,636 (2000); Median household income: $53,542 (2000); Poverty rate: 3.9% (2000).
Education: Percent of population age 25 and over with: High school diploma (including GED) or higher: 92.5% (2000); Bachelor's degree or higher: 16.4% (2000).
Housing: Homeownership rate: 93.4% (2000); Median home value: $102,700 (2000); Median contract rent: $415 per month (2000); Median year structure built: 1963 (2000).
Transportation: Commute to work: 93.7% car, 0.0% public transportation, 1.9% walk, 4.4% work from home (2000); Travel time to work: 21.6% less than 15 minutes, 39.5% 15 to 30 minutes, 29.2% 30 to 45 minutes, 6.4% 45 to 60 minutes, 3.4% 60 minutes or more (2000)

WEST PEORIA (city). Covers a land area of 1.286 square miles and a water area of 0 square miles. Located at 40.69° N. Lat; 89.63° W. Long. Elevation is 594 feet.

History: Bradley University to East.
Population: 5,315 (1990); 4,762 (2000); 4,458 (2010); 4,353 (2015 projected); Race: 78.8% White, 16.2% Black, 1.1% Asian, 4.0% Other, 1.5% Hispanic of any race (2010); Density: 3,467.3 persons per square mile (2010); Average household size: 2.29 (2010); Median age: 37.0 (2010); Males per 100 females: 86.4 (2010); Marriage status: 30.1% never married, 51.2% now married, 7.1% widowed, 11.6% divorced (2005-2009 5-year est.); Foreign born: 2.8% (2005-2009 5-year est.); Ancestry (includes multiple ancestries): 38.7% German, 25.3% Irish, 8.8% English, 3.7% French, 3.4% Czech (2005-2009 5-year est.).
Economy: Employment by occupation: 6.9% management, 23.6% professional, 12.8% services, 29.9% sales, 2.0% farming, 8.2% construction, 16.6% production (2005-2009 5-year est.).
Income: Per capita income: $25,700 (2010); Median household income: $48,580 (2010); Average household income: $59,703 (2010); Percent of households with income of $100,000 or more: 14.7% (2010); Poverty rate: 11.1% (2005-2009 5-year est.).
Taxes: Total city taxes per capita: $45 (2007); City property taxes per capita: $31 (2007).
Education: Percent of population age 25 and over with: High school diploma (including GED) or higher: 87.0% (2010); Bachelor's degree or higher: 22.8% (2010); Master's degree or higher: 5.5% (2010).

School District(s)
Peoria SD 150 (PK-12)
    2009-10 Enrollment: 13,951 . . . . (309) 672-6768
Housing: Homeownership rate: 75.9% (2010); Median home value: $92,959 (2010); Median contract rent: $517 per month (2005-2009 5-year est.); Median year structure built: 1945 (2005-2009 5-year est.).
Transportation: Commute to work: 95.7% car, 1.1% public transportation, 0.0% walk, 0.3% work from home (2005-2009 5-year est.); Travel time to work: 49.3% less than 15 minutes, 39.4% 15 to 30 minutes, 4.6% 30 to 45 minutes, 2.6% 45 to 60 minutes, 4.2% 60 minutes or more (2005-2009 5-year est.)

Perry County

Located in southwestern Illinois; bounded partly on the east by the Little Muddy River; drained by Beaucoup and Galum Creeks. Covers a land area of 440.96 square miles, a water area of 5.85 square miles, and is located in the Central Time Zone at 38.05° N. Lat., 89.34° W. Long. The county was founded in 1827. County seat is Pinckneyville.

Weather Station: Du Quoin 4 SE									Elevation: 419 feet			
	Jan	Feb	Mar	Apr	May	Jun	Jul	Aug	Sep	Oct	Nov	Dec
High	41	46	56	68	77	85	88	88	81	69	56	44
Low	24	28	36	46	55	64	68	65	56	46	36	27
Precip	2.8	2.7	4.2	4.2	5.6	4.5	3.8	3.1	3.5	3.9	4.2	3.5
Snow	3.2	3.4	1.0	0.2	0.0	0.0	0.0	0.0	0.0	0.2	0.6	2.9

High and Low temperatures in degrees Fahrenheit; Precipitation and Snow in inches

Population: 21,412 (1990); 23,094 (2000); 22,388 (2010); 21,923 (2015 projected); Race: 88.5% White, 8.5% Black, 0.3% Asian, 2.7% Other, 2.1% Hispanic of any race (2010); Density: 50.8 persons per square mile (2010); Average household size: 2.37 (2010); Median age: 37.9 (2010); Males per 100 females: 116.6 (2010).
Religion: Five largest groups: 26.2% Southern Baptist Convention, 14.7% Catholic Church, 4.3% The United Methodist Church, 3.1% United Church of Christ, 2.5% Christian Church (Disciples of Christ) (2000).
Economy: Unemployment rate: 10.7% (August 2011); Total civilian labor force: 9,610 (August 2011); Leading industries: 19.7% health care and social assistance; 15.1% retail trade; 10.3% accommodation & food services (2009); Farms: 589 totaling 200,354 acres (2007); Companies that employ 500 or more persons: 0 (2009); Companies that employ 100 to 499 persons: 8 (2009); Companies that employ less than 100 persons: 408 (2009); Black-owned businesses: n/a (2007); Hispanic-owned businesses: n/a (2007); Asian-owned businesses: n/a (2007); Women-owned businesses: 286 (2007); Retail sales per capita: $8,955 (2010). Single-family building permits issued: 26 (2010); Multi-family building permits issued: 0 (2010).
Income: Per capita income: $19,969 (2010); Median household income: $41,239 (2010); Average household income: $49,415 (2010); Percent of households with income of $100,000 or more: 8.1% (2010); Poverty rate: 17.8% (2009); Bankruptcy rate: 5.29% (2010).
Taxes: Total county taxes per capita: $116 (2007); County property taxes per capita: $115 (2007).

Education: Percent of population age 25 and over with: High school diploma (including GED) or higher: 82.3% (2010); Bachelor's degree or higher: 12.8% (2010); Master's degree or higher: 4.0% (2010).
Housing: Homeownership rate: 78.8% (2010); Median home value: $69,359 (2010); Median contract rent: $319 per month (2005-2009 5-year est.); Median year structure built: 1965 (2005-2009 5-year est.)
Health: Birth rate: 116.4 per 10,000 population (2009); Death rate: 111.5 per 10,000 population (2009); Age-adjusted cancer mortality rate: 237.0 deaths per 100,000 population (2007); Number of physicians: 6.2 per 10,000 population (2008); Hospital beds: 44.3 per 10,000 population (2007); Hospital admissions: 855.5 per 10,000 population (2007).
Elections: 2008 Presidential election results: 47.0% Obama, 50.9% McCain, 0.9% Nader
National and State Parks: Pyramid State Park
Additional Information Contacts
Perry County Government . . . . (618) 357-5116
    http://www.perrycountyil.org
City of Du Quoin . . . . (618) 542-3841
    http://www.duquoin.org
City of Pinckneyville . . . . (618) 357-6916
    http://www.ci.pinckneyville.il.us
Du Quoin Chamber of Commerce . . . . (618) 542-9570
Pinckneyville Chamber of Commerce . . . . (618) 357-3243
    http://www.pinckneyville.com

Perry County Communities

CUTLER (village). Covers a land area of 0.474 square miles and a water area of 0 square miles. Located at 38.03° N. Lat; 89.56° W. Long. Elevation is 499 feet.
Population: 523 (1990); 543 (2000); 506 (2010); 487 (2015 projected); Race: 98.2% White, 0.0% Black, 0.0% Asian, 1.8% Other, 0.4% Hispanic of any race (2010); Density: 1,068.3 persons per square mile (2010); Average household size: 2.66 (2010); Median age: 33.1 (2010); Males per 100 females: 91.7 (2010); Marriage status: 34.7% never married, 49.3% now married, 4.1% widowed, 11.8% divorced (2005-2009 5-year est.); Foreign born: 0.4% (2005-2009 5-year est.); Ancestry (includes multiple ancestries): 40.0% German, 16.4% Irish, 10.3% English, 8.4% Scotch-Irish, 8.0% Italian (2005-2009 5-year est.).
Economy: Employment by occupation: 1.0% management, 10.0% professional, 17.4% services, 11.4% sales, 0.0% farming, 22.4% construction, 37.8% production (2005-2009 5-year est.).
Income: Per capita income: $22,641 (2010); Median household income: $42,703 (2010); Average household income: $60,737 (2010); Percent of households with income of $100,000 or more: 10.0% (2010); Poverty rate: 12.6% (2005-2009 5-year est.).
Taxes: Total city taxes per capita: $121 (2007); City property taxes per capita: $72 (2007).
Education: Percent of population age 25 and over with: High school diploma (including GED) or higher: 72.2% (2010); Bachelor's degree or higher: 8.3% (2010); Master's degree or higher: 0.3% (2010).
Housing: Homeownership rate: 79.5% (2010); Median home value: $46,744 (2010); Median contract rent: $281 per month (2005-2009 5-year est.); Median year structure built: 1963 (2005-2009 5-year est.).
Transportation: Commute to work: 97.4% car, 0.0% public transportation, 1.6% walk, 1.1% work from home (2005-2009 5-year est.); Travel time to work: 24.6% less than 15 minutes, 48.7% 15 to 30 minutes, 13.4% 30 to 45 minutes, 1.6% 45 to 60 minutes, 11.8% 60 minutes or more (2005-2009 5-year est.)

DU QUOIN (city). Covers a land area of 6.865 square miles and a water area of 0.067 square miles. Located at 38.00° N. Lat; 89.23° W. Long. Elevation is 459 feet.
History: Du Quoin developed as a coal mining town. It was named for Jean Baptiste Du Quoigne, chief of the Kaskaskia tribe.
Population: 6,773 (1990); 6,448 (2000); 6,145 (2010); 5,913 (2015 projected); Race: 92.8% White, 4.2% Black, 0.3% Asian, 2.7% Other, 1.6% Hispanic of any race (2010); Density: 895.2 persons per square mile (2010); Average household size: 2.24 (2010); Median age: 38.8 (2010); Males per 100 females: 92.9 (2010); Marriage status: 30.1% never married, 45.0% now married, 12.0% widowed, 12.9% divorced (2005-2009 5-year est.); Foreign born: 1.4% (2005-2009 5-year est.); Ancestry (includes multiple ancestries): 26.4% German, 11.7% Irish, 10.9% English, 7.8% American, 6.1% Italian (2005-2009 5-year est.).

Economy: Employment by occupation: 10.3% management, 18.5% professional, 21.4% services, 19.6% sales, 0.5% farming, 11.0% construction, 18.7% production (2005-2009 5-year est.).
Income: Per capita income: $18,859 (2010); Median household income: $35,328 (2010); Average household income: $43,142 (2010); Percent of households with income of $100,000 or more: 6.7% (2010); Poverty rate: 17.4% (2005-2009 5-year est.).
Taxes: Total city taxes per capita: $103 (2007); City property taxes per capita: $13 (2007).
Education: Percent of population age 25 and over with: High school diploma (including GED) or higher: 86.4% (2010); Bachelor's degree or higher: 17.4% (2010); Master's degree or higher: 5.1% (2010).

School District(s)
Duquoin CUSD 300 (PK-12)
    2009-10 Enrollment: 1,563 . . . . (618) 542-3856
Tri-County Sp Ed Jnt Agreement (PK-12)
    2009-10 Enrollment: n/a . . . . (618) 684-2109
Housing: Homeownership rate: 72.3% (2010); Median home value: $61,159 (2010); Median contract rent: $313 per month (2005-2009 5-year est.); Median year structure built: 1952 (2005-2009 5-year est.).
Hospitals: Marshall Browning Hospital (25 beds)
Safety: Violent crime rate: 16.1 per 10,000 population; Property crime rate: 188.0 per 10,000 population (2010).
Newspapers: Ashley News (Local news; Circulation 4,000); Du Quoin Evening Call (Local news; Circulation 4,350)
Transportation: Commute to work: 92.9% car, 0.0% public transportation, 2.7% walk, 3.7% work from home (2005-2009 5-year est.); Travel time to work: 42.9% less than 15 minutes, 19.2% 15 to 30 minutes, 15.9% 30 to 45 minutes, 18.3% 45 to 60 minutes, 3.6% 60 minutes or more (2005-2009 5-year est.); Amtrak: train service available.
Additional Information Contacts
City of Du Quoin. . . . . (618) 542-3841
    http://www.duquoin.org
Du Quoin Chamber of Commerce . . . . (618) 542-9570

PINCKNEYVILLE (city). County seat. Covers a land area of 3.161 square miles and a water area of 0.002 square miles. Located at 38.07° N. Lat; 89.38° W. Long. Elevation is 433 feet.
History: Pyramid State Park to South, created from reclaimed coal strip mines. Incorporated 1861.
Population: 4,021 (1990); 5,464 (2000); 5,252 (2010); 5,046 (2015 projected); Race: 73.1% White, 22.3% Black, 0.4% Asian, 4.2% Other, 4.3% Hispanic of any race (2010); Density: 1,661.5 persons per square mile (2010); Average household size: 2.23 (2010); Median age: 35.8 (2010); Males per 100 females: 172.3 (2010); Marriage status: 47.3% never married, 36.2% now married, 5.7% widowed, 10.8% divorced (2005-2009 5-year est.); Foreign born: 2.6% (2005-2009 5-year est.); Ancestry (includes multiple ancestries): 29.1% German, 8.3% American, 8.2% Irish, 6.2% English, 3.8% Polish (2005-2009 5-year est.).
Economy: Employment by occupation: 3.0% management, 21.4% professional, 24.0% services, 22.8% sales, 0.0% farming, 8.8% construction, 19.9% production (2005-2009 5-year est.).
Income: Per capita income: $18,868 (2010); Median household income: $38,470 (2010); Average household income: $47,729 (2010); Percent of households with income of $100,000 or more: 6.6% (2010); Poverty rate: 8.3% (2005-2009 5-year est.).
Taxes: Total city taxes per capita: $141 (2007); City property taxes per capita: $129 (2007).
Education: Percent of population age 25 and over with: High school diploma (including GED) or higher: 74.3% (2010); Bachelor's degree or higher: 10.4% (2010); Master's degree or higher: 4.2% (2010).

School District(s)
CCSD 204 (KG-08)
    2009-10 Enrollment: 165 . . . . (618) 357-2419
Pinckneyville CHSD 101 (09-12)
    2009-10 Enrollment: 483 . . . . (618) 357-5013
Pinckneyville SD 50 (PK-08)
    2009-10 Enrollment: 595 . . . . (618) 357-5161
Housing: Homeownership rate: 75.8% (2010); Median home value: $72,000 (2010); Median contract rent: $273 per month (2005-2009 5-year est.); Median year structure built: 1954 (2005-2009 5-year est.).
Hospitals: Pinckneyville Community Hospital (85 beds)
Safety: Violent crime rate: 13.2 per 10,000 population; Property crime rate: 49.0 per 10,000 population (2010).

Newspapers: Pinckneyville Democrat (Community news; Circulation 2,800)
Transportation: Commute to work: 87.2% car, 0.0% public transportation, 3.7% walk, 5.9% work from home (2005-2009 5-year est.); Travel time to work: 49.1% less than 15 minutes, 31.0% 15 to 30 minutes, 7.7% 30 to 45 minutes, 8.4% 45 to 60 minutes, 3.8% 60 minutes or more (2005-2009 5-year est.)
Additional Information Contacts
City of Pinckneyville. . . . . (618) 357-6916
    http://www.ci.pinckneyville.il.us
Pinckneyville Chamber of Commerce . . . . (618) 357-3243
    http://www.pinckneyville.com

SAINT JOHNS (village). Covers a land area of 0.703 square miles and a water area of 0.045 square miles. Located at 38.03° N. Lat; 89.24° W. Long. Elevation is 463 feet.
Population: 261 (1990); 218 (2000); 173 (2010); 166 (2015 projected); Race: 95.4% White, 2.3% Black, 0.0% Asian, 2.3% Other, 1.2% Hispanic of any race (2010); Density: 246.0 persons per square mile (2010); Average household size: 2.25 (2010); Median age: 39.0 (2010); Males per 100 females: 92.2 (2010); Marriage status: 7.3% never married, 60.7% now married, 8.9% widowed, 23.0% divorced (2005-2009 5-year est.); Foreign born: 0.0% (2005-2009 5-year est.); Ancestry (includes multiple ancestries): 29.5% Irish, 22.8% German, 15.6% English, 4.2% Dutch, 3.0% Italian (2005-2009 5-year est.).
Economy: Employment by occupation: 8.3% management, 8.3% professional, 33.3% services, 21.9% sales, 0.0% farming, 3.1% construction, 25.0% production (2005-2009 5-year est.).
Income: Per capita income: $19,271 (2010); Median household income: $31,538 (2010); Average household income: $40,357 (2010); Percent of households with income of $100,000 or more: 3.9% (2010); Poverty rate: 14.8% (2005-2009 5-year est.).
Taxes: Total city taxes per capita: $55 (2007); City property taxes per capita: $18 (2007).
Education: Percent of population age 25 and over with: High school diploma (including GED) or higher: 86.6% (2010); Bachelor's degree or higher: 15.1% (2010); Master's degree or higher: 4.2% (2010).
Housing: Homeownership rate: 75.3% (2010); Median home value: $55,714 (2010); Median contract rent: $263 per month (2005-2009 5-year est.); Median year structure built: 1979 (2005-2009 5-year est.).
Transportation: Commute to work: 100.0% car, 0.0% public transportation, 0.0% walk, 0.0% work from home (2005-2009 5-year est.); Travel time to work: 38.5% less than 15 minutes, 17.7% 15 to 30 minutes, 28.1% 30 to 45 minutes, 7.3% 45 to 60 minutes, 8.3% 60 minutes or more (2005-2009 5-year est.)

TAMAROA (village). Covers a land area of 0.983 square miles and a water area of 0 square miles. Located at 38.13° N. Lat; 89.22° W. Long. Elevation is 509 feet.
History: Tamaroa was named for the Tamaroa Indians that lived in this area.
Population: 786 (1990); 740 (2000); 741 (2010); 736 (2015 projected); Race: 97.8% White, 0.1% Black, 0.3% Asian, 1.8% Other, 0.1% Hispanic of any race (2010); Density: 754.1 persons per square mile (2010); Average household size: 2.39 (2010); Median age: 38.2 (2010); Males per 100 females: 96.6 (2010); Marriage status: 32.0% never married, 48.7% now married, 0.3% widowed, 19.0% divorced (2005-2009 5-year est.); Foreign born: 0.0% (2005-2009 5-year est.); Ancestry (includes multiple ancestries): 26.1% German, 16.6% English, 15.1% Irish, 9.0% American, 7.5% Polish (2005-2009 5-year est.).
Economy: Employment by occupation: 2.4% management, 16.4% professional, 17.4% services, 15.3% sales, 0.0% farming, 18.5% construction, 30.0% production (2005-2009 5-year est.).
Income: Per capita income: $20,605 (2010); Median household income: $42,500 (2010); Average household income: $48,605 (2010); Percent of households with income of $100,000 or more: 8.1% (2010); Poverty rate: 31.1% (2005-2009 5-year est.).
Taxes: Total city taxes per capita: $63 (2007); City property taxes per capita: $48 (2007).
Education: Percent of population age 25 and over with: High school diploma (including GED) or higher: 82.7% (2010); Bachelor's degree or higher: 9.6% (2010); Master's degree or higher: 3.7% (2010).

School District(s)
Tamaroa School Dist 5 (PK-08)
    2009-10 Enrollment: 112 . . . . (618) 496-5513

Housing: Homeownership rate: 83.5% (2010); Median home value: $54,906 (2010); Median contract rent: $285 per month (2005-2009 5-year est.); Median year structure built: 1975 (2005-2009 5-year est.).
Transportation: Commute to work: 91.0% car, 0.0% public transportation, 1.5% walk, 7.5% work from home (2005-2009 5-year est.); Travel time to work: 16.5% less than 15 minutes, 29.4% 15 to 30 minutes, 25.4% 30 to 45 minutes, 21.0% 45 to 60 minutes, 7.7% 60 minutes or more (2005-2009 5-year est.)

WILLISVILLE (village). Covers a land area of 0.377 square miles and a water area of 0 square miles. Located at 37.98° N. Lat; 89.59° W. Long. Elevation is 495 feet.
Population: 577 (1990); 694 (2000); 650 (2010); 626 (2015 projected); Race: 99.5% White, 0.2% Black, 0.0% Asian, 0.3% Other, 0.3% Hispanic of any race (2010); Density: 1,723.7 persons per square mile (2010); Average household size: 2.57 (2010); Median age: 35.0 (2010); Males per 100 females: 95.8 (2010); Marriage status: 24.5% never married, 54.4% now married, 9.5% widowed, 11.7% divorced (2005-2009 5-year est.); Foreign born: 0.0% (2005-2009 5-year est.); Ancestry (includes multiple ancestries): 41.1% German, 13.5% Irish, 13.4% English, 10.5% Italian, 8.2% French (2005-2009 5-year est.).
Economy: Employment by occupation: 10.8% management, 12.5% professional, 15.4% services, 9.7% sales, 0.0% farming, 18.3% construction, 33.3% production (2005-2009 5-year est.).
Income: Per capita income: $20,320 (2010); Median household income: $42,763 (2010); Average household income: $52,787 (2010); Percent of households with income of $100,000 or more: 6.3% (2010); Poverty rate: 16.7% (2005-2009 5-year est.).
Taxes: Total city taxes per capita: $109 (2007); City property taxes per capita: $47 (2007).
Education: Percent of population age 25 and over with: High school diploma (including GED) or higher: 80.4% (2010); Bachelor's degree or higher: 3.6% (2010); Master's degree or higher: 1.5% (2010).
Housing: Homeownership rate: 80.6% (2010); Median home value: $54,444 (2010); Median contract rent: $331 per month (2005-2009 5-year est.); Median year structure built: 1969 (2005-2009 5-year est.).
Transportation: Commute to work: 98.5% car, 0.0% public transportation, 0.0% walk, 1.5% work from home (2005-2009 5-year est.); Travel time to work: 29.4% less than 15 minutes, 29.0% 15 to 30 minutes, 18.6% 30 to 45 minutes, 6.3% 45 to 60 minutes, 16.7% 60 minutes or more (2005-2009 5-year est.)

Piatt County

Located in central Illinois; drained by the Sangamon River. Covers a land area of 440.02 square miles, a water area of 0.31 square miles, and is located in the Central Time Zone at 39.99° N. Lat., 88.57° W. Long. The county was founded in 1841. County seat is Monticello.

Piatt County is part of the Champaign-Urbana, IL Metropolitan Statistical Area. The entire metro area includes: Champaign County, IL; Ford County, IL; Piatt County, IL

Population: 15,548 (1990); 16,365 (2000); 16,544 (2010); 16,533 (2015 projected); Race: 97.4% White, 0.9% Black, 0.6% Asian, 1.1% Other, 1.0% Hispanic of any race (2010); Density: 37.6 persons per square mile (2010); Average household size: 2.45 (2010); Median age: 41.2 (2010); Males per 100 females: 96.7 (2010).
Religion: Five largest groups: 17.2% The United Methodist Church, 6.0% Southern Baptist Convention, 5.8% Christian Churches and Churches of Christ, 5.8% Catholic Church, 4.0% United Church of Christ (2000).
Economy: Unemployment rate: 8.5% (August 2011); Total civilian labor force: 8,329 (August 2011); Leading industries: 18.4% retail trade; 15.5% health care and social assistance; 14.1% accommodation & food services (2009); Farms: 480 totaling 267,265 acres (2007); Companies that employ 500 or more persons: 0 (2009); Companies that employ 100 to 499 persons: 3 (2009); Companies that employ less than 100 persons: 345 (2009); Black-owned businesses: n/a (2007); Hispanic-owned businesses: n/a (2007); Asian-owned businesses: n/a (2007); Women-owned businesses: n/a (2007); Retail sales per capita: $8,716 (2010). Single-family building permits issued: 31 (2010); Multi-family building permits issued: 10 (2010).
Income: Per capita income: $27,545 (2010); Median household income: $57,546 (2010); Average household income: $68,099 (2010); Percent of households with income of $100,000 or more: 16.8% (2010); Poverty rate: 6.7% (2009); Bankruptcy rate: 5.13% (2010).

Taxes: Total county taxes per capita: $209 (2007); County property taxes per capita: $191 (2007).
Education: Percent of population age 25 and over with: High school diploma (including GED) or higher: 92.1% (2010); Bachelor's degree or higher: 24.8% (2010); Master's degree or higher: 8.9% (2010).
Housing: Homeownership rate: 79.1% (2010); Median home value: $120,168 (2010); Median contract rent: $474 per month (2005-2009 5-year est.); Median year structure built: 1966 (2005-2009 5-year est.).
Health: Birth rate: 126.9 per 10,000 population (2009); Death rate: 96.7 per 10,000 population (2009); Age-adjusted cancer mortality rate: 168.1 deaths per 100,000 population (2007); Number of physicians: 5.5 per 10,000 population (2008); Hospital beds: 12.8 per 10,000 population (2007); Hospital admissions: 277.1 per 10,000 population (2007).
Elections: 2008 Presidential election results: 42.9% Obama, 55.5% McCain, 0.7% Nader
Additional Information Contacts

Piatt County Government . . . . (217) 762-9487
   http://www.piattcounty.org
City of Monticello . . . . (217) 762-2815
   http://www.cityofmonticello.net
Mansfield Chamber of Commerce . . . . (217) 489-3351
Monticello Chamber of Commerce . . . . (217) 762-7921
   http://www.monticellochamber.org

Piatt County Communities

ATWOOD (village). Covers a land area of 0.569 square miles and a water area of 0 square miles. Located at 39.80° N. Lat; 88.46° W. Long. Elevation is 669 feet.
Population: 1,314 (1990); 1,290 (2000); 1,192 (2010); 1,143 (2015 projected); Race: 97.9% White, 0.8% Black, 0.1% Asian, 1.2% Other, 1.7% Hispanic of any race (2010); Density: 2,093.7 persons per square mile (2010); Average household size: 2.50 (2010); Median age: 37.7 (2010); Males per 100 females: 91.9 (2010); Marriage status: 16.6% never married, 68.0% now married, 6.6% widowed, 8.8% divorced (2005-2009 5-year est.); Foreign born: 0.9% (2005-2009 5-year est.); Ancestry (includes multiple ancestries): 30.5% German, 23.1% American, 8.9% Irish, 7.5% English, 4.8% Dutch (2005-2009 5-year est.).
Economy: Single-family building permits issued: 1 (2010); Multi-family building permits issued: 0 (2010); Employment by occupation: 9.6% management, 6.7% professional, 21.9% services, 26.6% sales, 0.0% farming, 22.0% construction, 13.2% production (2005-2009 5-year est.).
Income: Per capita income: $21,934 (2010); Median household income: $43,407 (2010); Average household income: $54,921 (2010); Percent of households with income of $100,000 or more: 10.7% (2010); Poverty rate: 1.8% (2005-2009 5-year est.).
Taxes: Total city taxes per capita: $126 (2007); City property taxes per capita: $117 (2007).
Education: Percent of population age 25 and over with: High school diploma (including GED) or higher: 83.4% (2010); Bachelor's degree or higher: 13.5% (2010); Master's degree or higher: 3.1% (2010).
School District(s)
Atwood Hammond CUSD 39 (PK-12)
   2009-10 Enrollment: 424 . . . . (217) 578-3111
Housing: Homeownership rate: 79.4% (2010); Median home value: $94,857 (2010); Median contract rent: $372 per month (2005-2009 5-year est.); Median year structure built: 1956 (2005-2009 5-year est.).
Safety: Violent crime rate: 8.4 per 10,000 population; Property crime rate: 83.8 per 10,000 population (2010).
Newspapers: Atwood Herald (Local news; Circulation 1,000)
Transportation: Commute to work: 95.7% car, 0.0% public transportation, 2.1% walk, 1.4% work from home (2005-2009 5-year est.); Travel time to work: 39.2% less than 15 minutes, 28.6% 15 to 30 minutes, 10.2% 30 to 45 minutes, 18.0% 45 to 60 minutes, 4.0% 60 minutes or more (2005-2009 5-year est.)

BEMENT (village). Covers a land area of 0.812 square miles and a water area of 0 square miles. Located at 39.92° N. Lat; 88.57° W. Long. Elevation is 689 feet.
History: Incorporated 1874. Bryant Cottage State Historical Site.
Population: 1,676 (1990); 1,784 (2000); 1,717 (2010); 1,683 (2015 projected); Race: 95.2% White, 2.9% Black, 1.0% Asian, 0.9% Other, 0.3% Hispanic of any race (2010); Density: 2,114.6 persons per square mile (2010); Average household size: 2.44 (2010); Median age: 40.4 (2010); Males per 100 females: 101.3 (2010); Marriage status: 36.0% never

married, 40.7% now married, 14.5% widowed, 8.9% divorced (2005-2009 5-year est.); Foreign born: 1.4% (2005-2009 5-year est.); Ancestry (includes multiple ancestries): 25.8% German, 23.0% American, 12.5% Irish, 7.8% English, 3.2% French (2005-2009 5-year est.).
Economy: Single-family building permits issued: 1 (2010); Multi-family building permits issued: 10 (2010); Employment by occupation: 5.9% management, 9.4% professional, 24.4% services, 19.6% sales, 1.2% farming, 12.9% construction, 26.6% production (2005-2009 5-year est.).
Income: Per capita income: $23,432 (2010); Median household income: $50,500 (2010); Average household income: $58,044 (2010); Percent of households with income of $100,000 or more: 8.7% (2010); Poverty rate: 7.5% (2005-2009 5-year est.).
Taxes: Total city taxes per capita: $90 (2007); City property taxes per capita: $83 (2007).
Education: Percent of population age 25 and over with: High school diploma (including GED) or higher: 89.1% (2010); Bachelor's degree or higher: 14.5% (2010); Master's degree or higher: 4.9% (2010).

School District(s)
Bement CUSD 5 (PK-12)
    2009-10 Enrollment: 410 . . . . (217) 678-4200
Housing: Homeownership rate: 80.0% (2010); Median home value: $96,122 (2010); Median contract rent: $397 per month (2005-2009 5-year est.); Median year structure built: 1953 (2005-2009 5-year est.).
Newspapers: News Record (Local news; Circulation 1,500)
Transportation: Commute to work: 91.2% car, 0.0% public transportation, 3.8% walk, 1.3% work from home (2005-2009 5-year est.); Travel time to work: 37.4% less than 15 minutes, 20.4% 15 to 30 minutes, 29.8% 30 to 45 minutes, 7.6% 45 to 60 minutes, 4.8% 60 minutes or more (2005-2009 5-year est.)

CERRO GORDO (village). Covers a land area of 0.741 square miles and a water area of 0 square miles. Located at 39.89° N. Lat; 88.73° W. Long. Elevation is 745 feet.
History: Incorporated 1873.
Population: 1,436 (1990); 1,436 (2000); 1,398 (2010); 1,373 (2015 projected); Race: 98.9% White, 0.4% Black, 0.4% Asian, 0.4% Other, 1.0% Hispanic of any race (2010); Density: 1,886.7 persons per square mile (2010); Average household size: 2.53 (2010); Median age: 38.0 (2010); Males per 100 females: 95.0 (2010); Marriage status: 21.7% never married, 68.8% now married, 5.0% widowed, 4.5% divorced (2005-2009 5-year est.); Foreign born: 0.7% (2005-2009 5-year est.); Ancestry (includes multiple ancestries): 33.5% American, 27.7% German, 12.2% English, 11.3% Irish, 5.1% Dutch (2005-2009 5-year est.).
Economy: Single-family building permits issued: 0 (2010); Multi-family building permits issued: 0 (2010); Employment by occupation: 7.9% management, 19.0% professional, 8.4% services, 18.8% sales, 1.7% farming, 13.7% construction, 30.5% production (2005-2009 5-year est.).
Income: Per capita income: $21,110 (2010); Median household income: $49,643 (2010); Average household income: $53,555 (2010); Percent of households with income of $100,000 or more: 10.1% (2010); Poverty rate: 8.0% (2005-2009 5-year est.).
Taxes: Total city taxes per capita: $89 (2007); City property taxes per capita: $80 (2007).
Education: Percent of population age 25 and over with: High school diploma (including GED) or higher: 92.6% (2010); Bachelor's degree or higher: 13.3% (2010); Master's degree or higher: 3.1% (2010).

School District(s)
Cerro Gordo CUSD 100 (PK-12)
    2009-10 Enrollment: 626 . . . . (217) 763-5221
Housing: Homeownership rate: 79.3% (2010); Median home value: $104,595 (2010); Median contract rent: $468 per month (2005-2009 5-year est.); Median year structure built: 1962 (2005-2009 5-year est.).
Safety: Violent crime rate: 68.1 per 10,000 population; Property crime rate: 113.6 per 10,000 population (2010).
Transportation: Commute to work: 93.3% car, 0.0% public transportation, 2.9% walk, 1.1% work from home (2005-2009 5-year est.); Travel time to work: 22.0% less than 15 minutes, 52.4% 15 to 30 minutes, 21.6% 30 to 45 minutes, 2.6% 45 to 60 minutes, 1.5% 60 minutes or more (2005-2009 5-year est.)

CISCO (village). Covers a land area of 0.381 square miles and a water area of 0 square miles. Located at 40.01° N. Lat; 88.72° W. Long. Elevation is 689 feet.
Population: 280 (1990); 264 (2000); 266 (2010); 266 (2015 projected); Race: 96.6% White, 0.0% Black, 0.0% Asian, 3.4% Other, 1.1% Hispanic

of any race (2010); Density: 697.9 persons per square mile (2010); Average household size: 2.51 (2010); Median age: 38.8 (2010); Males per 100 females: 107.8 (2010); Marriage status: 14.0% never married, 66.0% now married, 10.2% widowed, 9.8% divorced (2005-2009 5-year est.); Foreign born: 0.8% (2005-2009 5-year est.); Ancestry (includes multiple ancestries): 42.1% American, 20.7% German, 16.8% English, 11.6% Irish, 5.5% Norwegian (2005-2009 5-year est.).
Economy: Single-family building permits issued: 0 (2010); Multi-family building permits issued: 0 (2010); Employment by occupation: 8.0% management, 20.0% professional, 5.6% services, 28.0% sales, 1.6% farming, 17.6% construction, 19.2% production (2005-2009 5-year est.).
Income: Per capita income: $24,181 (2010); Median household income: $56,667 (2010); Average household income: $62,288 (2010); Percent of households with income of $100,000 or more: 11.3% (2010); Poverty rate: 1.9% (2005-2009 5-year est.).
Taxes: Total city taxes per capita: $95 (2007); City property taxes per capita: $57 (2007).
Education: Percent of population age 25 and over with: High school diploma (including GED) or higher: 96.1% (2010); Bachelor's degree or higher: 19.9% (2010); Master's degree or higher: 6.6% (2010).
Housing: Homeownership rate: 74.5% (2010); Median home value: $129,000 (2010); Median contract rent: $493 per month (2005-2009 5-year est.); Median year structure built: before 1940 (2005-2009 5-year est.).
Transportation: Commute to work: 90.2% car, 0.0% public transportation, 4.9% walk, 4.9% work from home (2005-2009 5-year est.); Travel time to work: 23.1% less than 15 minutes, 44.4% 15 to 30 minutes, 22.2% 30 to 45 minutes, 10.3% 45 to 60 minutes, 0.0% 60 minutes or more (2005-2009 5-year est.)

DE LAND (village). Aka Deland. Covers a land area of 0.396 square miles and a water area of 0 square miles. Located at 40.12° N. Lat; 88.64° W. Long. Elevation is 702 feet.
Population: 458 (1990); 475 (2000); 495 (2010); 502 (2015 projected); Race: 97.4% White, 0.8% Black, 0.2% Asian, 1.6% Other, 1.6% Hispanic of any race (2010); Density: 1,248.5 persons per square mile (2010); Average household size: 2.61 (2010); Median age: 39.3 (2010); Males per 100 females: 99.6 (2010); Marriage status: 24.7% never married, 64.8% now married, 2.9% widowed, 7.6% divorced (2005-2009 5-year est.); Foreign born: 1.5% (2005-2009 5-year est.); Ancestry (includes multiple ancestries): 34.0% American, 28.3% German, 20.8% Irish, 9.6% English, 1.7% Italian (2005-2009 5-year est.).
Economy: Single-family building permits issued: 1 (2010); Multi-family building permits issued: 0 (2010); Employment by occupation: 6.0% management, 14.4% professional, 22.7% services, 27.3% sales, 0.0% farming, 7.9% construction, 21.8% production (2005-2009 5-year est.).
Income: Per capita income: $29,206 (2010); Median household income: $64,407 (2010); Average household income: $76,816 (2010); Percent of households with income of $100,000 or more: 18.4% (2010); Poverty rate: 6.2% (2005-2009 5-year est.).
Taxes: Total city taxes per capita: $56 (2007); City property taxes per capita: $56 (2007).
Education: Percent of population age 25 and over with: High school diploma (including GED) or higher: 91.3% (2010); Bachelor's degree or higher: 16.9% (2010); Master's degree or higher: 2.3% (2010).

School District(s)
Deland-Weldon CUSD 57 (PK-12)
    2009-10 Enrollment: 205 . . . . (217) 736-2311
Housing: Homeownership rate: 75.8% (2010); Median home value: $108,333 (2010); Median contract rent: $377 per month (2005-2009 5-year est.); Median year structure built: 1940 (2005-2009 5-year est.).
Transportation: Commute to work: 100.0% car, 0.0% public transportation, 0.0% walk, 0.0% work from home (2005-2009 5-year est.); Travel time to work: 24.4% less than 15 minutes, 16.9% 15 to 30 minutes, 45.1% 30 to 45 minutes, 12.7% 45 to 60 minutes, 0.9% 60 minutes or more (2005-2009 5-year est.)

HAMMOND (village). Covers a land area of 0.762 square miles and a water area of 0.006 square miles. Located at 39.79° N. Lat; 88.59° W. Long. Elevation is 673 feet.
Population: 527 (1990); 518 (2000); 514 (2010); 511 (2015 projected); Race: 96.5% White, 1.9% Black, 0.8% Asian, 0.8% Other, 0.6% Hispanic of any race (2010); Density: 674.5 persons per square mile (2010); Average household size: 2.37 (2010); Median age: 40.5 (2010); Males per 100 females: 115.1 (2010); Marriage status: 13.7% never married, 61.1% now married, 8.4% widowed, 16.8% divorced (2005-2009 5-year est.);

Foreign born: 0.0% (2005-2009 5-year est.); Ancestry (includes multiple ancestries): 32.8% American, 21.9% German, 11.9% English, 9.1% Irish, 7.7% Scottish (2005-2009 5-year est.).
Economy: Single-family building permits issued: 0 (2010); Multi-family building permits issued: 0 (2010); Employment by occupation: 10.0% management, 10.0% professional, 9.0% services, 20.0% sales, 0.0% farming, 25.0% construction, 26.0% production (2005-2009 5-year est.).
Income: Per capita income: $27,101 (2010); Median household income: $58,036 (2010); Average household income: $62,535 (2010); Percent of households with income of $100,000 or more: 13.4% (2010); Poverty rate: 14.7% (2005-2009 5-year est.).
Taxes: Total city taxes per capita: $85 (2007); City property taxes per capita: $77 (2007).
Education: Percent of population age 25 and over with: High school diploma (including GED) or higher: 91.6% (2010); Bachelor's degree or higher: 14.2% (2010); Master's degree or higher: 5.3% (2010).
Housing: Homeownership rate: 72.4% (2010); Median home value: $106,746 (2010); Median contract rent: $285 per month (2005-2009 5-year est.); Median year structure built: 1962 (2005-2009 5-year est.).
Transportation: Commute to work: 97.4% car, 0.0% public transportation, 1.5% walk, 0.0% work from home (2005-2009 5-year est.); Travel time to work: 16.8% less than 15 minutes, 43.4% 15 to 30 minutes, 16.3% 30 to 45 minutes, 18.9% 45 to 60 minutes, 4.6% 60 minutes or more (2005-2009 5-year est.)

MANSFIELD (village). Covers a land area of 0.511 square miles and a water area of 0.025 square miles. Located at 40.21° N. Lat; 88.50° W. Long. Elevation is 728 feet.

Population: 940 (1990); 949 (2000); 877 (2010); 841 (2015 projected); Race: 97.0% White, 0.1% Black, 2.1% Asian, 0.8% Other, 1.5% Hispanic of any race (2010); Density: 1,715.4 persons per square mile (2010); Average household size: 2.38 (2010); Median age: 40.9 (2010); Males per 100 females: 92.7 (2010); Marriage status: 28.1% never married, 53.9% now married, 10.0% widowed, 8.0% divorced (2005-2009 5-year est.); Foreign born: 0.1% (2005-2009 5-year est.); Ancestry (includes multiple ancestries): 24.0% German, 18.8% American, 15.4% Irish, 13.5% English, 4.1% Scotch-Irish (2005-2009 5-year est.).
Economy: Single-family building permits issued: 0 (2010); Multi-family building permits issued: 0 (2010); Employment by occupation: 12.1% management, 13.8% professional, 18.5% services, 20.4% sales, 0.0% farming, 18.3% construction, 17.0% production (2005-2009 5-year est.).
Income: Per capita income: $27,308 (2010); Median household income: $57,901 (2010); Average household income: $65,603 (2010); Percent of households with income of $100,000 or more: 12.7% (2010); Poverty rate: 8.4% (2005-2009 5-year est.).
Taxes: Total city taxes per capita: $137 (2007); City property taxes per capita: $93 (2007).
Education: Percent of population age 25 and over with: High school diploma (including GED) or higher: 90.8% (2010); Bachelor's degree or higher: 17.3% (2010); Master's degree or higher: 7.0% (2010).
School District(s)
Blue Ridge CUSD 18 (PK-12)
    2009-10 Enrollment: 859 . . . . (309) 928-9141
Housing: Homeownership rate: 76.2% (2010); Median home value: $98,372 (2010); Median contract rent: $379 per month (2005-2009 5-year est.); Median year structure built: 1969 (2005-2009 5-year est.).
Transportation: Commute to work: 91.1% car, 0.0% public transportation, 2.7% walk, 1.3% work from home (2005-2009 5-year est.); Travel time to work: 23.5% less than 15 minutes, 41.0% 15 to 30 minutes, 29.6% 30 to 45 minutes, 4.3% 45 to 60 minutes, 1.6% 60 minutes or more (2005-2009 5-year est.)
Additional Information Contacts
Mansfield Chamber of Commerce . . . . (217) 489-3351

MILMINE (unincorporated postal area, zip code 61855). Covers a land area of 5.535 square miles and a water area of 0 square miles. Located at 39.92° N. Lat; 88.67° W. Long. Elevation is 712 feet.

Population: 74 (2000); Race: 100.0% White, 0.0% Black, 0.0% Asian, 0.0% Other, 0.0% Hispanic of any race (2000); Density: 13.4 persons per square mile (2000); Age: 19.6% under 18, 16.1% over 64 (2000); Marriage status: 6.7% never married, 86.7% now married, 6.7% widowed, 0.0% divorced (2000); Foreign born: 0.0% (2000); Ancestry (includes multiple ancestries): 10.7% English, 10.7% American, 7.1% Norwegian, 7.1% French (2000).

Economy: Employment by occupation: 0.0% management, 13.0% professional, 17.4% services, 13.0% sales, 0.0% farming, 21.7% construction, 34.8% production (2000).
Income: Per capita income: $18,811 (2000); Median household income: $34,531 (2000); Poverty rate: 0.0% (2000).
Education: Percent of population age 25 and over with: High school diploma (including GED) or higher: 70.7% (2000); Bachelor's degree or higher: 0.0% (2000).
Housing: Homeownership rate: 77.8% (2000); Median home value: $58,100 (2000); Median contract rent: $225 per month (2000); Median year structure built: before 1940 (2000).
Transportation: Commute to work: 100.0% car, 0.0% public transportation, 0.0% walk, 0.0% work from home (2000); Travel time to work: 0.0% less than 15 minutes, 47.8% 15 to 30 minutes, 30.4% 30 to 45 minutes, 21.7% 45 to 60 minutes, 0.0% 60 minutes or more (2000)

MONTICELLO (city). County seat. Covers a land area of 2.979 square miles and a water area of 0 square miles. Located at 40.02° N. Lat; 88.57° W. Long. Elevation is 659 feet.

History: Incorporated 1841.
Population: 4,919 (1990); 5,138 (2000); 5,354 (2010); 5,412 (2015 projected); Race: 97.9% White, 0.4% Black, 0.7% Asian, 1.0% Other, 1.2% Hispanic of any race (2010); Density: 1,797.2 persons per square mile (2010); Average household size: 2.32 (2010); Median age: 43.1 (2010); Males per 100 females: 91.8 (2010); Marriage status: 14.6% never married, 64.3% now married, 8.4% widowed, 12.6% divorced (2005-2009 5-year est.); Foreign born: 2.4% (2005-2009 5-year est.); Ancestry (includes multiple ancestries): 30.5% German, 20.5% American, 16.6% English, 14.0% Irish, 5.3% Scotch-Irish (2005-2009 5-year est.).
Economy: Single-family building permits issued: 8 (2010); Multi-family building permits issued: 0 (2010); Employment by occupation: 13.1% management, 26.3% professional, 20.4% services, 19.6% sales, 0.7% farming, 7.1% construction, 12.8% production (2005-2009 5-year est.).
Income: Per capita income: $30,034 (2010); Median household income: $56,488 (2010); Average household income: $70,683 (2010); Percent of households with income of $100,000 or more: 19.5% (2010); Poverty rate: 8.3% (2005-2009 5-year est.).
Taxes: Total city taxes per capita: $140 (2007); City property taxes per capita: $111 (2007).
Education: Percent of population age 25 and over with: High school diploma (including GED) or higher: 92.4% (2010); Bachelor's degree or higher: 35.5% (2010); Master's degree or higher: 13.5% (2010).
School District(s)
Monticello CUSD 25 (PK-12)
    2009-10 Enrollment: 1,707 . . . . (217) 762-8511
Housing: Homeownership rate: 77.6% (2010); Median home value: $133,004 (2010); Median contract rent: $520 per month (2005-2009 5-year est.); Median year structure built: 1971 (2005-2009 5-year est.).
Hospitals: John & Mary Kirby Hospital (17 beds)
Safety: Violent crime rate: 22.5 per 10,000 population; Property crime rate: 108.6 per 10,000 population (2010).
Newspapers: Piatt County Journal-Republican (Community news; Circulation 3,800)
Transportation: Commute to work: 92.6% car, 0.0% public transportation, 3.9% walk, 3.0% work from home (2005-2009 5-year est.); Travel time to work: 49.2% less than 15 minutes, 22.6% 15 to 30 minutes, 25.2% 30 to 45 minutes, 0.9% 45 to 60 minutes, 2.1% 60 minutes or more (2005-2009 5-year est.)
Additional Information Contacts
City of Monticello . . . . (217) 762-2815
    http://www.cityofmonticello.net
Monticello Chamber of Commerce . . . . (217) 762-7921
    http://www.monticellochamber.org

WHITE HEATH (unincorporated postal area, zip code 61884). Covers a land area of 25.358 square miles and a water area of 0.081 square miles. Located at 40.10° N. Lat; 88.49° W. Long. Elevation is 722 feet.

Population: 1,172 (2000); Race: 100.0% White, 0.0% Black, 0.0% Asian, 0.0% Other, 0.0% Hispanic of any race (2000); Density: 46.2 persons per square mile (2000); Age: 32.7% under 18, 10.6% over 64 (2000); Marriage status: 23.3% never married, 70.5% now married, 2.4% widowed, 3.9% divorced (2000); Foreign born: 0.0% (2000); Ancestry (includes multiple ancestries): 18.5% German, 17.9% Irish, 15.5% American, 12.0% English, 3.7% Italian (2000).

Economy: Employment by occupation: 8.9% management, 19.7% professional, 12.2% services, 27.4% sales, 3.5% farming, 8.2% construction, 20.1% production (2000).
Income: Per capita income: $23,131 (2000); Median household income: $53,819 (2000); Poverty rate: 0.5% (2000).
Education: Percent of population age 25 and over with: High school diploma (including GED) or higher: 92.4% (2000); Bachelor's degree or higher: 28.1% (2000).

School District(s)
Monticello CUSD 25 (PK-12)
   2009-10 Enrollment: 1,707 . . . . (217) 762-8511
Housing: Homeownership rate: 87.7% (2000); Median home value: $128,800 (2000); Median contract rent: $360 per month (2000); Median year structure built: 1973 (2000).
Transportation: Commute to work: 93.8% car, 0.0% public transportation, 0.0% walk, 5.1% work from home (2000); Travel time to work: 18.4% less than 15 minutes, 47.8% 15 to 30 minutes, 19.5% 30 to 45 minutes, 3.3% 45 to 60 minutes, 11.0% 60 minutes or more (2000)

Pike County

Located in western Illinois; bounded on the west and southwest by the Mississippi River and the Missouri border, and on the east by the Illinois River. Covers a land area of 830.30 square miles, a water area of 18.57 square miles, and is located in the Central Time Zone at 39.62° N. Lat., 90.88° W. Long. The county was founded in 1821. County seat is Pittsfield.
Population: 17,577 (1990); 17,384 (2000); 16,406 (2010); 15,871 (2015 projected); Race: 97.1% White, 1.4% Black, 0.3% Asian, 1.2% Other, 0.9% Hispanic of any race (2010); Density: 19.8 persons per square mile (2010); Average household size: 2.40 (2010); Median age: 41.2 (2010); Males per 100 females: 97.6 (2010).
Religion: Five largest groups: 11.8% The United Methodist Church, 9.2% Christian Churches and Churches of Christ, 7.1% Southern Baptist Convention, 5.3% Christian Church (Disciples of Christ), 3.5% Assemblies of God (2000).
Economy: Unemployment rate: 7.3% (August 2011); Total civilian labor force: 8,953 (August 2011); Leading industries: 19.9% health care and social assistance; 18.8% retail trade; 11.8% accommodation & food services (2009); Farms: 967 totaling 389,808 acres (2007); Companies that employ 500 or more persons: 0 (2009); Companies that employ 100 to 499 persons: 5 (2009); Companies that employ less than 100 persons: 379 (2009); Black-owned businesses: n/a (2007); Hispanic-owned businesses: n/a (2007); Asian-owned businesses: n/a (2007); Women-owned businesses: n/a (2007); Retail sales per capita: $11,197 (2009). Single-family building permits issued: 15 (2010); Multi-family building permits issued: 0 (2010).
Income: Per capita income: $19,763 (2010); Median household income: $39,480 (2010); Average household income: $48,032 (2010); Percent of households with income of $100,000 or more: 6.7% (2010); Poverty rate: 17.1% (2009); Bankruptcy rate: 4.03% (2010).
Taxes: Total county taxes per capita: $136 (2007); County property taxes per capita: $119 (2007).
Education: Percent of population age 25 and over with: High school diploma (including GED) or higher: 84.6% (2010); Bachelor's degree or higher: 12.4% (2010); Master's degree or higher: 3.5% (2010).
Housing: Homeownership rate: 75.9% (2010); Median home value: $83,099 (2010); Median contract rent: $293 per month (2005-2009 5-year est.); Median year structure built: 1957 (2005-2009 5-year est.)
Health: Birth rate: 114.9 per 10,000 population (2009); Death rate: 125.4 per 10,000 population (2009); Age-adjusted cancer mortality rate: 191.9 deaths per 100,000 population (2007); Number of physicians: 6.1 per 10,000 population (2008); Hospital beds: 15.1 per 10,000 population (2007); Hospital admissions: 401.2 per 10,000 population (2007).
Elections: 2008 Presidential election results: 39.7% Obama, 58.5% McCain, 0.6% Nader
Additional Information Contacts
Pike County Government. . . . . (217) 285-6812
   http://www.pikeil.org
Pike County Chamber of Commerce . . . . (217) 285-2971
   http://www.pikeil.org

Pike County Communities

BARRY (city). Covers a land area of 1.142 square miles and a water area of 0 square miles. Located at 39.69° N. Lat; 91.04° W. Long. Elevation is 712 feet.
History: Barry developed as a trading center for a dairying and agricultural area.
Population: 1,440 (1990); 1,368 (2000); 1,293 (2010); 1,253 (2015 projected); Race: 98.6% White, 0.0% Black, 0.6% Asian, 0.8% Other, 1.2% Hispanic of any race (2010); Density: 1,132.4 persons per square mile (2010); Average household size: 2.28 (2010); Median age: 44.8 (2010); Males per 100 females: 86.6 (2010); Marriage status: 21.1% never married, 54.2% now married, 15.0% widowed, 9.7% divorced (2005-2009 5-year est.); Foreign born: 0.2% (2005-2009 5-year est.); Ancestry (includes multiple ancestries): 24.1% American, 23.9% German, 14.3% Irish, 13.6% English, 2.6% Swedish (2005-2009 5-year est.).
Economy: Single-family building permits issued: 2 (2010); Multi-family building permits issued: 0 (2010); Employment by occupation: 8.4% management, 13.4% professional, 28.9% services, 14.0% sales, 1.5% farming, 13.7% construction, 20.2% production (2005-2009 5-year est.).
Income: Per capita income: $18,612 (2010); Median household income: $31,354 (2010); Average household income: $43,886 (2010); Percent of households with income of $100,000 or more: 5.8% (2010); Poverty rate: 12.5% (2005-2009 5-year est.).
Taxes: Total city taxes per capita: $78 (2007); City property taxes per capita: $70 (2007).
Education: Percent of population age 25 and over with: High school diploma (including GED) or higher: 81.1% (2010); Bachelor's degree or higher: 10.7% (2010); Master's degree or higher: 3.2% (2010).
School District(s)
Western CUSD 12 (PK-12)
   2009-10 Enrollment: 676 . . . . (217) 335-2323
Housing: Homeownership rate: 74.0% (2010); Median home value: $86,000 (2010); Median contract rent: $260 per month (2005-2009 5-year est.); Median year structure built: 1941 (2005-2009 5-year est.).
Transportation: Commute to work: 88.8% car, 0.0% public transportation, 3.3% walk, 6.2% work from home (2005-2009 5-year est.); Travel time to work: 37.5% less than 15 minutes, 18.5% 15 to 30 minutes, 27.1% 30 to 45 minutes, 9.9% 45 to 60 minutes, 7.1% 60 minutes or more (2005-2009 5-year est.)

BAYLIS (village). Covers a land area of 0.479 square miles and a water area of 0 square miles. Located at 39.72° N. Lat; 90.90° W. Long. Elevation is 863 feet.
Population: 257 (1990); 265 (2000); 254 (2010); 246 (2015 projected); Race: 97.6% White, 0.0% Black, 0.4% Asian, 2.0% Other, 1.6% Hispanic of any race (2010); Density: 529.8 persons per square mile (2010); Average household size: 2.75 (2010); Median age: 37.6 (2010); Males per 100 females: 104.8 (2010); Marriage status: 18.3% never married, 62.8% now married, 5.5% widowed, 13.4% divorced (2005-2009 5-year est.); Foreign born: 0.0% (2005-2009 5-year est.); Ancestry (includes multiple ancestries): 28.4% American, 13.1% Irish, 13.1% English, 6.6% German, 5.5% French (2005-2009 5-year est.).
Economy: Employment by occupation: 14.3% management, 2.6% professional, 33.8% services, 14.3% sales, 0.0% farming, 2.6% construction, 32.5% production (2005-2009 5-year est.).
Income: Per capita income: $22,312 (2010); Median household income: $48,500 (2010); Average household income: $63,179 (2010); Percent of households with income of $100,000 or more: 10.9% (2010); Poverty rate: 0.0% (2005-2009 5-year est.).
Taxes: Total city taxes per capita: $104 (2007); City property taxes per capita: $20 (2007).
Education: Percent of population age 25 and over with: High school diploma (including GED) or higher: 84.1% (2010); Bachelor's degree or higher: 11.0% (2010); Master's degree or higher: 1.8% (2010).
Housing: Homeownership rate: 71.7% (2010); Median home value: $73,333 (2010); Median contract rent: n/a per month (2005-2009 5-year est.); Median year structure built: before 1940 (2005-2009 5-year est.).
Transportation: Commute to work: 92.2% car, 0.0% public transportation, 7.8% walk, 0.0% work from home (2005-2009 5-year est.); Travel time to work: 16.9% less than 15 minutes, 32.5% 15 to 30 minutes, 16.9% 30 to 45 minutes, 20.8% 45 to 60 minutes, 13.0% 60 minutes or more (2005-2009 5-year est.)

CHAMBERSBURG (unincorporated postal area, zip code 62323).
Covers a land area of 42.802 square miles and a water area of 0.058 square miles. Located at 39.81° N. Lat; 90.66° W. Long. Elevation is 466 feet.

Population: 294 (2000); Race: 99.1% White, 0.0% Black, 0.0% Asian, 0.9% Other, 0.0% Hispanic of any race (2000); Density: 6.9 persons per square mile (2000); Age: 23.5% under 18, 17.4% over 64 (2000); Marriage status: 18.0% never married, 73.9% now married, 3.2% widowed, 4.9% divorced (2000); Foreign born: 0.0% (2000); Ancestry (includes multiple ancestries): 47.7% German, 16.9% English, 14.0% Irish, 7.8% American (2000).

Economy: Employment by occupation: 19.2% management, 16.8% professional, 11.4% services, 13.8% sales, 1.8% farming, 9.6% construction, 27.5% production (2000).

Income: Per capita income: $18,810 (2000); Median household income: $31,875 (2000); Poverty rate: 3.8% (2000).

Education: Percent of population age 25 and over with: High school diploma (including GED) or higher: 91.1% (2000); Bachelor's degree or higher: 12.2% (2000).

Housing: Homeownership rate: 75.2% (2000); Median home value: $57,500 (2000); Median contract rent: $265 per month (2000); Median year structure built: 1951 (2000).

Transportation: Commute to work: 96.2% car, 0.0% public transportation, 1.3% walk, 2.5% work from home (2000); Travel time to work: 43.2% less than 15 minutes, 20.0% 15 to 30 minutes, 17.4% 30 to 45 minutes, 10.3% 45 to 60 minutes, 9.0% 60 minutes or more (2000)

DETROIT (village). Covers a land area of 0.239 square miles and a water area of 0 square miles. Located at 39.62° N. Lat; 90.67° W. Long. Elevation is 640 feet.

Population: 126 (1990); 93 (2000); 91 (2010); 89 (2015 projected); Race: 100.0% White, 0.0% Black, 0.0% Asian, 0.0% Other, 2.2% Hispanic of any race (2010); Density: 380.4 persons per square mile (2010); Average household size: 2.53 (2010); Median age: 41.8 (2010); Males per 100 females: 71.7 (2010); Marriage status: 22.7% never married, 70.5% now married, 0.0% widowed, 6.8% divorced (2005-2009 5-year est.); Foreign born: 0.0% (2005-2009 5-year est.); Ancestry (includes multiple ancestries): 7.7% German, 7.7% American, 5.8% English, 5.8% Canadian, 5.8% French (2005-2009 5-year est.).

Economy: Employment by occupation: 40.0% management, 0.0% professional, 6.7% services, 23.3% sales, 0.0% farming, 30.0% construction, 0.0% production (2005-2009 5-year est.).

Income: Per capita income: $20,472 (2010); Median household income: $47,857 (2010); Average household income: $51,111 (2010); Percent of households with income of $100,000 or more: 5.6% (2010); Poverty rate: 19.2% (2005-2009 5-year est.).

Taxes: Total city taxes per capita: $11 (2007); City property taxes per capita: $0 (2007).

Education: Percent of population age 25 and over with: High school diploma (including GED) or higher: 84.1% (2010); Bachelor's degree or higher: 4.8% (2010); Master's degree or higher: 3.2% (2010).

Housing: Homeownership rate: 75.0% (2010); Median home value: $115,000 (2010); Median contract rent: n/a per month (2005-2009 5-year est.); Median year structure built: before 1940 (2005-2009 5-year est.).

Transportation: Commute to work: 83.3% car, 0.0% public transportation, 16.7% walk, 0.0% work from home (2005-2009 5-year est.); Travel time to work: 30.0% less than 15 minutes, 13.3% 15 to 30 minutes, 33.3% 30 to 45 minutes, 13.3% 45 to 60 minutes, 10.0% 60 minutes or more (2005-2009 5-year est.)

EL DARA (village). Covers a land area of 0.967 square miles and a water area of 0 square miles. Located at 39.62° N. Lat; 90.99° W. Long. Elevation is 735 feet.

Population: 94 (1990); 89 (2000); 86 (2010); 83 (2015 projected); Race: 98.8% White, 0.0% Black, 1.2% Asian, 0.0% Other, 0.0% Hispanic of any race (2010); Density: 88.9 persons per square mile (2010); Average household size: 2.53 (2010); Median age: 45.8 (2010); Males per 100 females: 95.5 (2010); Marriage status: 44.1% never married, 51.2% now married, 1.6% widowed, 3.1% divorced (2005-2009 5-year est.); Foreign born: 0.0% (2005-2009 5-year est.); Ancestry (includes multiple ancestries): 73.5% Irish, 12.1% English, 7.6% American, 6.8% Italian, 6.1% German (2005-2009 5-year est.).

Economy: Employment by occupation: 3.4% management, 3.4% professional, 63.6% services, 20.5% sales, 0.0% farming, 0.0% construction, 9.1% production (2005-2009 5-year est.).

Income: Per capita income: $16,918 (2010); Median household income: $40,000 (2010); Average household income: $44,044 (2010); Percent of households with income of $100,000 or more: 5.9% (2010); Poverty rate: 0.0% (2005-2009 5-year est.).

Taxes: Total city taxes per capita: $12 (2007); City property taxes per capita: $12 (2007).

Education: Percent of population age 25 and over with: High school diploma (including GED) or higher: 88.5% (2010); Bachelor's degree or higher: 16.4% (2010); Master's degree or higher: 6.6% (2010).

Housing: Homeownership rate: 79.4% (2010); Median home value: $92,500 (2010); Median contract rent: n/a per month (2005-2009 5-year est.); Median year structure built: 1949 (2005-2009 5-year est.).

Transportation: Commute to work: 100.0% car, 0.0% public transportation, 0.0% walk, 0.0% work from home (2005-2009 5-year est.); Travel time to work: 58.0% less than 15 minutes, 13.6% 15 to 30 minutes, 19.3% 30 to 45 minutes, 9.1% 45 to 60 minutes, 0.0% 60 minutes or more (2005-2009 5-year est.)

FLORENCE (village). Covers a land area of 0.203 square miles and a water area of 0 square miles. Located at 39.62° N. Lat; 90.61° W. Long. Elevation is 453 feet.

Population: 45 (1990); 71 (2000); 71 (2010); 70 (2015 projected); Race: 100.0% White, 0.0% Black, 0.0% Asian, 0.0% Other, 1.4% Hispanic of any race (2010); Density: 350.4 persons per square mile (2010); Average household size: 2.54 (2010); Median age: 39.5 (2010); Males per 100 females: 69.0 (2010); Marriage status: 30.8% never married, 43.6% now married, 12.8% widowed, 12.8% divorced (2005-2009 5-year est.); Foreign born: 7.7% (2005-2009 5-year est.); Ancestry (includes multiple ancestries): 46.2% German, 10.3% Irish, 7.7% American, 5.1% Polish, 5.1% Italian (2005-2009 5-year est.).

Economy: Employment by occupation: 0.0% management, 0.0% professional, 83.3% services, 0.0% sales, 0.0% farming, 0.0% construction, 16.7% production (2005-2009 5-year est.).

Income: Per capita income: $20,472 (2010); Median household income: $50,000 (2010); Average household income: $53,750 (2010); Percent of households with income of $100,000 or more: 7.1% (2010); Poverty rate: 43.6% (2005-2009 5-year est.).

Taxes: Total city taxes per capita: $60 (2007); City property taxes per capita: $45 (2007).

Education: Percent of population age 25 and over with: High school diploma (including GED) or higher: 79.2% (2010); Bachelor's degree or higher: 2.1% (2010); Master's degree or higher: 2.1% (2010).

Housing: Homeownership rate: 75.0% (2010); Median home value: $106,250 (2010); Median contract rent: n/a per month (2005-2009 5-year est.); Median year structure built: 1968 (2005-2009 5-year est.).

Transportation: Commute to work: 100.0% car, 0.0% public transportation, 0.0% walk, 0.0% work from home (2005-2009 5-year est.); Travel time to work: 0.0% less than 15 minutes, 83.3% 15 to 30 minutes, 0.0% 30 to 45 minutes, 16.7% 45 to 60 minutes, 0.0% 60 minutes or more (2005-2009 5-year est.)

GRIGGSVILLE (city). Covers a land area of 1.035 square miles and a water area of 0 square miles. Located at 39.70° N. Lat; 90.72° W. Long. Elevation is 705 feet.

History: Incorporated 1878.

Population: 1,218 (1990); 1,258 (2000); 1,195 (2010); 1,163 (2015 projected); Race: 99.3% White, 0.1% Black, 0.1% Asian, 0.5% Other, 0.3% Hispanic of any race (2010); Density: 1,154.2 persons per square mile (2010); Average household size: 2.55 (2010); Median age: 38.7 (2010); Males per 100 females: 92.7 (2010); Marriage status: 26.3% never married, 54.9% now married, 4.0% widowed, 14.8% divorced (2005-2009 5-year est.); Foreign born: 0.6% (2005-2009 5-year est.); Ancestry (includes multiple ancestries): 30.0% German, 20.7% Irish, 17.9% English, 15.1% American, 5.4% Italian (2005-2009 5-year est.).

Economy: Single-family building permits issued: 0 (2010); Multi-family building permits issued: 0 (2010); Employment by occupation: 13.4% management, 8.9% professional, 21.6% services, 28.4% sales, 0.0% farming, 10.1% construction, 17.6% production (2005-2009 5-year est.).

Income: Per capita income: $20,244 (2010); Median household income: $44,808 (2010); Average household income: $51,471 (2010); Percent of households with income of $100,000 or more: 7.5% (2010); Poverty rate: 34.0% (2005-2009 5-year est.).

Taxes: Total city taxes per capita: $175 (2007); City property taxes per capita: $88 (2007).
Education: Percent of population age 25 and over with: High school diploma (including GED) or higher: 88.5% (2010); Bachelor's degree or higher: 12.8% (2010); Master's degree or higher: 3.7% (2010).
School District(s)
Griggsville-Perry CUSD 4 (PK-12)
    2009-10 Enrollment: 418 . . . . (217) 833-2352
Housing: Homeownership rate: 74.6% (2010); Median home value: $79,130 (2010); Median contract rent: $284 per month (2005-2009 5-year est.); Median year structure built: 1955 (2005-2009 5-year est.).
Transportation: Commute to work: 95.4% car, 0.0% public transportation, 3.9% walk, 0.7% work from home (2005-2009 5-year est.); Travel time to work: 44.9% less than 15 minutes, 36.2% 15 to 30 minutes, 9.4% 30 to 45 minutes, 3.9% 45 to 60 minutes, 5.5% 60 minutes or more (2005-2009 5-year est.)

HULL (village). Aka Hulls. Covers a land area of 1.836 square miles and a water area of 0.010 square miles. Located at 39.70° N. Lat; 91.20° W. Long. Elevation is 469 feet.
Population: 514 (1990); 474 (2000); 417 (2010); 390 (2015 projected); Race: 97.8% White, 0.0% Black, 0.5% Asian, 1.7% Other, 1.2% Hispanic of any race (2010); Density: 227.2 persons per square mile (2010); Average household size: 2.38 (2010); Median age: 40.7 (2010); Males per 100 females: 102.4 (2010); Marriage status: 19.6% never married, 56.5% now married, 14.0% widowed, 9.8% divorced (2005-2009 5-year est.); Foreign born: 0.0% (2005-2009 5-year est.); Ancestry (includes multiple ancestries): 32.2% German, 23.9% American, 12.3% Irish, 10.1% English, 4.3% Italian (2005-2009 5-year est.).
Economy: Single-family building permits issued: 0 (2010); Multi-family building permits issued: 0 (2010); Employment by occupation: 10.7% management, 7.9% professional, 13.1% services, 35.5% sales, 0.0% farming, 18.2% construction, 14.5% production (2005-2009 5-year est.).
Income: Per capita income: $19,640 (2010); Median household income: $39,257 (2010); Average household income: $45,900 (2010); Percent of households with income of $100,000 or more: 6.9% (2010); Poverty rate: 16.6% (2005-2009 5-year est.).
Taxes: Total city taxes per capita: $23 (2007); City property taxes per capita: $23 (2007).
Education: Percent of population age 25 and over with: High school diploma (including GED) or higher: 86.0% (2010); Bachelor's degree or higher: 19.4% (2010); Master's degree or higher: 6.4% (2010).
School District(s)
Western CUSD 12 (PK-12)
    2009-10 Enrollment: 676 . . . . (217) 335-2323
Housing: Homeownership rate: 77.1% (2010); Median home value: $76,400 (2010); Median contract rent: $350 per month (2005-2009 5-year est.); Median year structure built: 1953 (2005-2009 5-year est.).
Transportation: Commute to work: 88.5% car, 0.0% public transportation, 6.7% walk, 1.0% work from home (2005-2009 5-year est.); Travel time to work: 15.5% less than 15 minutes, 51.0% 15 to 30 minutes, 25.7% 30 to 45 minutes, 7.8% 45 to 60 minutes, 0.0% 60 minutes or more (2005-2009 5-year est.)

KINDERHOOK (village). Covers a land area of 0.884 square miles and a water area of 0 square miles. Located at 39.70° N. Lat; 91.15° W. Long. Elevation is 486 feet.
Population: 269 (1990); 249 (2000); 228 (2010); 219 (2015 projected); Race: 98.2% White, 0.0% Black, 0.0% Asian, 1.8% Other, 2.2% Hispanic of any race (2010); Density: 257.9 persons per square mile (2010); Average household size: 2.43 (2010); Median age: 39.3 (2010); Males per 100 females: 100.0 (2010); Marriage status: 17.3% never married, 61.8% now married, 5.2% widowed, 15.7% divorced (2005-2009 5-year est.); Foreign born: 0.0% (2005-2009 5-year est.); Ancestry (includes multiple ancestries): 26.5% Irish, 26.1% German, 10.1% English, 9.7% American, 3.8% Swedish (2005-2009 5-year est.).
Economy: Employment by occupation: 2.9% management, 5.1% professional, 29.2% services, 12.4% sales, 2.2% farming, 9.5% construction, 38.7% production (2005-2009 5-year est.).
Income: Per capita income: $21,976 (2010); Median household income: $46,250 (2010); Average household income: $53,617 (2010); Percent of households with income of $100,000 or more: 8.5% (2010); Poverty rate: 2.1% (2005-2009 5-year est.).
Taxes: Total city taxes per capita: $17 (2007); City property taxes per capita: $13 (2007).

Education: Percent of population age 25 and over with: High school diploma (including GED) or higher: 87.2% (2010); Bachelor's degree or higher: 16.5% (2010); Master's degree or higher: 4.9% (2010).
School District(s)
Western CUSD 12 (PK-12)
    2009-10 Enrollment: 676 . . . . (217) 335-2323
Housing: Homeownership rate: 79.8% (2010); Median home value: $75,000 (2010); Median contract rent: $363 per month (2005-2009 5-year est.); Median year structure built: 1942 (2005-2009 5-year est.).
Transportation: Commute to work: 89.8% car, 0.0% public transportation, 2.9% walk, 0.0% work from home (2005-2009 5-year est.); Travel time to work: 28.5% less than 15 minutes, 35.0% 15 to 30 minutes, 29.2% 30 to 45 minutes, 7.3% 45 to 60 minutes, 0.0% 60 minutes or more (2005-2009 5-year est.)

MILTON (village). Covers a land area of 0.375 square miles and a water area of 0 square miles. Located at 39.56° N. Lat; 90.64° W. Long. Elevation is 666 feet.
Population: 270 (1990); 274 (2000); 260 (2010); 257 (2015 projected); Race: 99.6% White, 0.0% Black, 0.0% Asian, 0.4% Other, 0.8% Hispanic of any race (2010); Density: 693.6 persons per square mile (2010); Average household size: 2.59 (2010); Median age: 36.3 (2010); Males per 100 females: 98.5 (2010); Marriage status: 20.2% never married, 68.5% now married, 4.8% widowed, 6.5% divorced (2005-2009 5-year est.); Foreign born: 0.0% (2005-2009 5-year est.); Ancestry (includes multiple ancestries): 30.5% German, 24.2% American, 8.2% English, 7.1% Irish, 2.2% Dutch (2005-2009 5-year est.).
Economy: Employment by occupation: 11.2% management, 2.4% professional, 19.2% services, 18.4% sales, 23.2% farming, 10.4% construction, 15.2% production (2005-2009 5-year est.).
Income: Per capita income: $21,394 (2010); Median household income: $46,250 (2010); Average household income: $53,611 (2010); Percent of households with income of $100,000 or more: 6.1% (2010); Poverty rate: 33.8% (2005-2009 5-year est.).
Taxes: Total city taxes per capita: $8 (2007); City property taxes per capita: $8 (2007).
Education: Percent of population age 25 and over with: High school diploma (including GED) or higher: 87.4% (2010); Bachelor's degree or higher: 3.0% (2010); Master's degree or higher: 0.6% (2010).
Housing: Homeownership rate: 83.8% (2010); Median home value: $96,667 (2010); Median contract rent: $225 per month (2005-2009 5-year est.); Median year structure built: 1976 (2005-2009 5-year est.).
Transportation: Commute to work: 100.0% car, 0.0% public transportation, 0.0% walk, 0.0% work from home (2005-2009 5-year est.); Travel time to work: 21.6% less than 15 minutes, 68.8% 15 to 30 minutes, 7.2% 30 to 45 minutes, 2.4% 45 to 60 minutes, 0.0% 60 minutes or more (2005-2009 5-year est.)

NEBO (village). Covers a land area of 0.423 square miles and a water area of 0.006 square miles. Located at 39.44° N. Lat; 90.78° W. Long. Elevation is 482 feet.
Population: 400 (1990); 408 (2000); 391 (2010); 381 (2015 projected); Race: 98.5% White, 0.0% Black, 0.0% Asian, 1.5% Other, 2.6% Hispanic of any race (2010); Density: 924.7 persons per square mile (2010); Average household size: 2.57 (2010); Median age: 38.6 (2010); Males per 100 females: 103.6 (2010); Marriage status: 26.4% never married, 48.8% now married, 14.4% widowed, 10.4% divorced (2005-2009 5-year est.); Foreign born: 0.0% (2005-2009 5-year est.); Ancestry (includes multiple ancestries): 16.2% American, 13.4% Irish, 11.2% German, 4.2% Scottish, 3.7% English (2005-2009 5-year est.).
Economy: Employment by occupation: 2.0% management, 5.9% professional, 20.6% services, 21.1% sales, 4.4% farming, 12.7% construction, 33.3% production (2005-2009 5-year est.).
Income: Per capita income: $22,137 (2010); Median household income: $48,696 (2010); Average household income: $59,260 (2010); Percent of households with income of $100,000 or more: 13.2% (2010); Poverty rate: 23.9% (2005-2009 5-year est.).
Taxes: Total city taxes per capita: $41 (2007); City property taxes per capita: $41 (2007).
Education: Percent of population age 25 and over with: High school diploma (including GED) or higher: 83.3% (2010); Bachelor's degree or higher: 9.7% (2010); Master's degree or higher: 1.5% (2010).
Housing: Homeownership rate: 84.2% (2010); Median home value: $56,552 (2010); Median contract rent: $250 per month (2005-2009 5-year est.); Median year structure built: 1960 (2005-2009 5-year est.).

Transportation: Commute to work: 97.3% car, 2.7% public transportation, 0.0% walk, 0.0% work from home (2005-2009 5-year est.); Travel time to work: 10.2% less than 15 minutes, 29.9% 15 to 30 minutes, 35.8% 30 to 45 minutes, 11.2% 45 to 60 minutes, 12.8% 60 minutes or more (2005-2009 5-year est.)

NEW CANTON (town). Covers a land area of 0.778 square miles and a water area of 0 square miles. Located at 39.63° N. Lat; 91.09° W. Long. Elevation is 476 feet.
Population: 405 (1990); 417 (2000); 383 (2010); 368 (2015 projected); Race: 99.5% White, 0.0% Black, 0.0% Asian, 0.5% Other, 0.5% Hispanic of any race (2010); Density: 492.1 persons per square mile (2010); Average household size: 2.41 (2010); Median age: 43.3 (2010); Males per 100 females: 85.9 (2010); Marriage status: 24.0% never married, 52.3% now married, 14.9% widowed, 8.8% divorced (2005-2009 5-year est.); Foreign born: 2.0% (2005-2009 5-year est.); Ancestry (includes multiple ancestries): 32.2% German, 20.1% Irish, 12.7% English, 12.7% American, 4.6% Polish (2005-2009 5-year est.).
Economy: Employment by occupation: 4.2% management, 10.6% professional, 23.9% services, 31.7% sales, 2.8% farming, 5.6% construction, 21.1% production (2005-2009 5-year est.).
Income: Per capita income: $18,473 (2010); Median household income: $34,423 (2010); Average household income: $44,151 (2010); Percent of households with income of $100,000 or more: 4.4% (2010); Poverty rate: 12.2% (2005-2009 5-year est.).
Taxes: Total city taxes per capita: $23 (2007); City property taxes per capita: $20 (2007).
Education: Percent of population age 25 and over with: High school diploma (including GED) or higher: 87.6% (2010); Bachelor's degree or higher: 12.4% (2010); Master's degree or higher: 2.5% (2010).
Housing: Homeownership rate: 78.0% (2010); Median home value: $56,129 (2010); Median contract rent: $411 per month (2005-2009 5-year est.); Median year structure built: 1957 (2005-2009 5-year est.).
Transportation: Commute to work: 93.0% car, 0.0% public transportation, 0.0% walk, 4.2% work from home (2005-2009 5-year est.); Travel time to work: 25.0% less than 15 minutes, 14.0% 15 to 30 minutes, 23.5% 30 to 45 minutes, 33.1% 45 to 60 minutes, 4.4% 60 minutes or more (2005-2009 5-year est.)

NEW SALEM (village). Covers a land area of 1.043 square miles and a water area of 0 square miles. Located at 39.70° N. Lat; 90.84° W. Long. Elevation is 784 feet.
Population: 147 (1990); 136 (2000); 129 (2010); 125 (2015 projected); Race: 97.7% White, 0.0% Black, 0.0% Asian, 2.3% Other, 0.8% Hispanic of any race (2010); Density: 123.7 persons per square mile (2010); Average household size: 2.67 (2010); Median age: 38.0 (2010); Males per 100 females: 98.5 (2010); Marriage status: 40.5% never married, 42.2% now married, 5.2% widowed, 12.1% divorced (2005-2009 5-year est.); Foreign born: 0.0% (2005-2009 5-year est.); Ancestry (includes multiple ancestries): 24.3% Irish, 20.9% American, 16.2% German, 13.5% Dutch, 8.8% English (2005-2009 5-year est.).
Economy: Employment by occupation: 3.8% management, 28.8% professional, 26.9% services, 3.8% sales, 0.0% farming, 15.4% construction, 21.2% production (2005-2009 5-year est.).
Income: Per capita income: $22,086 (2010); Median household income: $47,273 (2010); Average household income: $59,531 (2010); Percent of households with income of $100,000 or more: 10.4% (2010); Poverty rate: 24.5% (2005-2009 5-year est.).
Taxes: Total city taxes per capita: $8 (2007); City property taxes per capita: $8 (2007).
Education: Percent of population age 25 and over with: High school diploma (including GED) or higher: 88.4% (2010); Bachelor's degree or higher: 12.8% (2010); Master's degree or higher: 3.5% (2010).
Housing: Homeownership rate: 72.9% (2010); Median home value: $76,667 (2010); Median contract rent: n/a per month (2005-2009 5-year est.); Median year structure built: 1949 (2005-2009 5-year est.).
Transportation: Commute to work: 92.3% car, 0.0% public transportation, 7.7% walk, 0.0% work from home (2005-2009 5-year est.); Travel time to work: 28.8% less than 15 minutes, 46.2% 15 to 30 minutes, 21.2% 30 to 45 minutes, 0.0% 45 to 60 minutes, 3.8% 60 minutes or more (2005-2009 5-year est.)

PEARL (village). Covers a land area of 1.507 square miles and a water area of 0.087 square miles. Located at 39.45° N. Lat; 90.62° W. Long. Elevation is 459 feet.

Population: 177 (1990); 187 (2000); 172 (2010); 164 (2015 projected); Race: 97.7% White, 0.0% Black, 0.0% Asian, 2.3% Other, 0.0% Hispanic of any race (2010); Density: 114.2 persons per square mile (2010); Average household size: 2.53 (2010); Median age: 41.0 (2010); Males per 100 females: 97.7 (2010); Marriage status: 23.7% never married, 39.0% now married, 8.5% widowed, 28.8% divorced (2005-2009 5-year est.); Foreign born: 0.0% (2005-2009 5-year est.); Ancestry (includes multiple ancestries): 35.0% American, 20.4% Scottish, 16.5% English, 12.6% Irish, 10.7% German (2005-2009 5-year est.).
Economy: Employment by occupation: 10.7% management, 10.7% professional, 28.6% services, 0.0% sales, 28.6% farming, 0.0% construction, 21.4% production (2005-2009 5-year est.).
Income: Per capita income: $24,358 (2010); Median household income: $40,000 (2010); Average household income: $59,596 (2010); Percent of households with income of $100,000 or more: 11.8% (2010); Poverty rate: 30.1% (2005-2009 5-year est.).
Taxes: Total city taxes per capita: $40 (2007); City property taxes per capita: $34 (2007).
Education: Percent of population age 25 and over with: High school diploma (including GED) or higher: 79.5% (2010); Bachelor's degree or higher: 6.0% (2010); Master's degree or higher: 0.9% (2010).
Housing: Homeownership rate: 82.4% (2010); Median home value: $56,000 (2010); Median contract rent: $282 per month (2005-2009 5-year est.); Median year structure built: 1947 (2005-2009 5-year est.).
Transportation: Commute to work: 88.0% car, 0.0% public transportation, 12.0% walk, 0.0% work from home (2005-2009 5-year est.); Travel time to work: 44.0% less than 15 minutes, 12.0% 15 to 30 minutes, 16.0% 30 to 45 minutes, 0.0% 45 to 60 minutes, 28.0% 60 minutes or more (2005-2009 5-year est.)

PERRY (village). Covers a land area of 0.382 square miles and a water area of 0 square miles. Located at 39.78° N. Lat; 90.74° W. Long. Elevation is 591 feet.
Population: 491 (1990); 437 (2000); 411 (2010); 396 (2015 projected); Race: 98.5% White, 0.0% Black, 0.2% Asian, 1.2% Other, 0.0% Hispanic of any race (2010); Density: 1,075.5 persons per square mile (2010); Average household size: 2.36 (2010); Median age: 42.0 (2010); Males per 100 females: 96.7 (2010); Marriage status: 16.8% never married, 54.3% now married, 14.3% widowed, 14.6% divorced (2005-2009 5-year est.); Foreign born: 0.0% (2005-2009 5-year est.); Ancestry (includes multiple ancestries): 22.3% English, 22.1% German, 16.7% American, 5.6% Irish, 4.3% French (2005-2009 5-year est.).
Economy: Single-family building permits issued: 1 (2010); Multi-family building permits issued: 0 (2010); Employment by occupation: 7.1% management, 15.7% professional, 14.3% services, 23.8% sales, 1.4% farming, 21.0% construction, 16.7% production (2005-2009 5-year est.).
Income: Per capita income: $21,362 (2010); Median household income: $40,000 (2010); Average household income: $49,555 (2010); Percent of households with income of $100,000 or more: 8.6% (2010); Poverty rate: 33.3% (2005-2009 5-year est.).
Taxes: Total city taxes per capita: $39 (2007); City property taxes per capita: $22 (2007).
Education: Percent of population age 25 and over with: High school diploma (including GED) or higher: 87.8% (2010); Bachelor's degree or higher: 8.3% (2010); Master's degree or higher: 3.5% (2010).
School District(s)
Griggsville-Perry CUSD 4 (PK-12)
    2009-10 Enrollment: 418 . . . . (217) 833-2352
Housing: Homeownership rate: 75.9% (2010); Median home value: $67,619 (2010); Median contract rent: $238 per month (2005-2009 5-year est.); Median year structure built: 1961 (2005-2009 5-year est.).
Transportation: Commute to work: 95.7% car, 0.0% public transportation, 1.9% walk, 1.0% work from home (2005-2009 5-year est.); Travel time to work: 22.3% less than 15 minutes, 33.0% 15 to 30 minutes, 19.9% 30 to 45 minutes, 16.0% 45 to 60 minutes, 8.7% 60 minutes or more (2005-2009 5-year est.)

PITTSFIELD (city). County seat. Covers a land area of 3.574 square miles and a water area of 0.045 square miles. Located at 39.61° N. Lat; 90.80° W. Long. Elevation is 732 feet.
History: Pittsfield was founded in 1833 by settlers from Pittsfield, Massachusetts. The town developed as the seat of Pike County, and as a pork-packing center, using barrels made of white oak that grew around the town. John Hay (1838-1905), Secretary of State under Presidents McKinley and Theodore Roosevelt, was a resident of Pittsfield for several years.

Population: 4,193 (1990); 4,211 (2000); 4,002 (2010); 3,885 (2015 projected); Race: 94.3% White, 3.7% Black, 0.5% Asian, 1.4% Other, 0.8% Hispanic of any race (2010); Density: 1,119.7 persons per square mile (2010); Average household size: 2.21 (2010); Median age: 43.3 (2010); Males per 100 females: 97.0 (2010); Marriage status: 28.2% never married, 51.6% now married, 11.1% widowed, 9.0% divorced (2005-2009 5-year est.); Foreign born: 2.5% (2005-2009 5-year est.); Ancestry (includes multiple ancestries): 27.8% German, 18.4% American, 13.9% English, 12.9% Irish, 2.6% French (2005-2009 5-year est.).
Economy: Single-family building permits issued: 2 (2010); Multi-family building permits issued: 0 (2010); Employment by occupation: 8.3% management, 14.8% professional, 25.2% services, 27.4% sales, 1.4% farming, 6.9% construction, 16.0% production (2005-2009 5-year est.).
Income: Per capita income: $19,717 (2010); Median household income: $35,699 (2010); Average household income: $44,585 (2010); Percent of households with income of $100,000 or more: 5.1% (2010); Poverty rate: 12.9% (2005-2009 5-year est.).
Taxes: Total city taxes per capita: $76 (2007); City property taxes per capita: $73 (2007).
Education: Percent of population age 25 and over with: High school diploma (including GED) or higher: 85.0% (2010); Bachelor's degree or higher: 17.2% (2010); Master's degree or higher: 4.3% (2010).

School District(s)
Pikeland CUSD 10 (PK-12)
    2009-10 Enrollment: 1,358 . . . . (217) 285-2147
Housing: Homeownership rate: 72.0% (2010); Median home value: $95,865 (2010); Median contract rent: $295 per month (2005-2009 5-year est.); Median year structure built: 1959 (2005-2009 5-year est.).
Hospitals: Illinois Community Hospital (37 beds)
Safety: Violent crime rate: 0.0 per 10,000 population; Property crime rate: 13.9 per 10,000 population (2010).
Newspapers: Pike County Express (Local news; Circulation 4,100); Pike Press (Community news; Circulation 7,850)
Transportation: Commute to work: 83.6% car, 0.0% public transportation, 5.1% walk, 5.3% work from home (2005-2009 5-year est.); Travel time to work: 67.5% less than 15 minutes, 13.5% 15 to 30 minutes, 10.3% 30 to 45 minutes, 4.1% 45 to 60 minutes, 4.6% 60 minutes or more (2005-2009 5-year est.)
Airports: Pittsfield Penstone Municipal (general aviation)
Additional Information Contacts
Pike County Chamber of Commerce . . . . (217) 285-2971
    http://www.pikeil.org

PLEASANT HILL (village). Covers a land area of 0.763 square miles and a water area of 0.023 square miles. Located at 39.44° N. Lat; 90.87° W. Long. Elevation is 469 feet.
Population: 1,124 (1990); 1,047 (2000); 977 (2010); 941 (2015 projected); Race: 97.9% White, 0.0% Black, 0.0% Asian, 2.1% Other, 0.9% Hispanic of any race (2010); Density: 1,281.0 persons per square mile (2010); Average household size: 2.35 (2010); Median age: 40.9 (2010); Males per 100 females: 93.8 (2010); Marriage status: 21.4% never married, 56.9% now married, 11.5% widowed, 10.2% divorced (2005-2009 5-year est.); Foreign born: 0.9% (2005-2009 5-year est.); Ancestry (includes multiple ancestries): 22.8% German, 22.6% American, 10.5% Irish, 8.6% English, 5.2% Scottish (2005-2009 5-year est.).
Economy: Employment by occupation: 6.5% management, 11.0% professional, 22.8% services, 28.4% sales, 5.6% farming, 7.8% construction, 17.9% production (2005-2009 5-year est.).
Income: Per capita income: $15,834 (2010); Median household income: $32,422 (2010); Average household income: $37,918 (2010); Percent of households with income of $100,000 or more: 3.7% (2010); Poverty rate: 18.2% (2005-2009 5-year est.).
Taxes: Total city taxes per capita: $39 (2007); City property taxes per capita: $37 (2007).
Education: Percent of population age 25 and over with: High school diploma (including GED) or higher: 78.5% (2010); Bachelor's degree or higher: 10.7% (2010); Master's degree or higher: 3.4% (2010).

School District(s)
Pleasant Hill CUSD 3 (PK-12)
    2009-10 Enrollment: 327 . . . . (217) 734-2311
Housing: Homeownership rate: 77.4% (2010); Median home value: $72,105 (2010); Median contract rent: $345 per month (2005-2009 5-year est.); Median year structure built: 1965 (2005-2009 5-year est.).
Newspapers: Weekly Messenger (Local news; Circulation 1,500)

Transportation: Commute to work: 94.0% car, 0.0% public transportation, 2.1% walk, 2.6% work from home (2005-2009 5-year est.); Travel time to work: 24.5% less than 15 minutes, 30.8% 15 to 30 minutes, 30.8% 30 to 45 minutes, 3.3% 45 to 60 minutes, 10.6% 60 minutes or more (2005-2009 5-year est.)

ROCKPORT (unincorporated postal area, zip code 62370). Covers a land area of 55.630 square miles and a water area of 0.377 square miles. Located at 39.51° N. Lat; 90.99° W. Long. Elevation is 489 feet.
Population: 641 (2000); Race: 100.0% White, 0.0% Black, 0.0% Asian, 0.0% Other, 0.0% Hispanic of any race (2000); Density: 11.5 persons per square mile (2000); Age: 29.7% under 18, 8.3% over 64 (2000); Marriage status: 25.4% never married, 60.1% now married, 5.4% widowed, 9.1% divorced (2000); Foreign born: 0.9% (2000); Ancestry (includes multiple ancestries): 28.6% American, 16.3% German, 7.1% English, 6.3% Irish (2000).
Economy: Employment by occupation: 13.7% management, 8.5% professional, 18.6% services, 22.9% sales, 7.3% farming, 7.6% construction, 21.3% production (2000).
Income: Per capita income: $14,348 (2000); Median household income: $33,036 (2000); Poverty rate: 10.4% (2000).
Education: Percent of population age 25 and over with: High school diploma (including GED) or higher: 83.3% (2000); Bachelor's degree or higher: 2.5% (2000).
Housing: Homeownership rate: 81.7% (2000); Median home value: $51,700 (2000); Median contract rent: $225 per month (2000); Median year structure built: 1954 (2000).
Transportation: Commute to work: 95.0% car, 0.0% public transportation, 0.0% walk, 4.3% work from home (2000); Travel time to work: 18.2% less than 15 minutes, 41.6% 15 to 30 minutes, 14.9% 30 to 45 minutes, 9.1% 45 to 60 minutes, 16.2% 60 minutes or more (2000)

TIME (village). Covers a land area of 0.436 square miles and a water area of 0 square miles. Located at 39.56° N. Lat; 90.72° W. Long. Elevation is 692 feet.
Population: 36 (1990); 29 (2000); 32 (2010); 32 (2015 projected); Race: 100.0% White, 0.0% Black, 0.0% Asian, 0.0% Other, 0.0% Hispanic of any race (2010); Density: 73.4 persons per square mile (2010); Average household size: 2.67 (2010); Median age: 45.0 (2010); Males per 100 females: 68.4 (2010); Marriage status: 0.0% never married, 90.3% now married, 0.0% widowed, 9.7% divorced (2005-2009 5-year est.); Foreign born: 0.0% (2005-2009 5-year est.); Ancestry (includes multiple ancestries): 84.9% English, 17.0% German, 7.5% American, 1.9% Scotch-Irish (2005-2009 5-year est.).
Economy: Employment by occupation: 40.0% management, 0.0% professional, 50.0% services, 10.0% sales, 0.0% farming, 0.0% construction, 0.0% production (2005-2009 5-year est.).
Income: Per capita income: $20,904 (2010); Median household income: $50,000 (2010); Average household income: $56,458 (2010); Percent of households with income of $100,000 or more: 8.3% (2010); Poverty rate: 1.9% (2005-2009 5-year est.).
Taxes: Total city taxes per capita: $0 (2007); City property taxes per capita: $0 (2007).
Education: Percent of population age 25 and over with: High school diploma (including GED) or higher: 87.0% (2010); Bachelor's degree or higher: 0.0% (2010); Master's degree or higher: 0.0% (2010).
Housing: Homeownership rate: 75.0% (2010); Median home value: $95,000 (2010); Median contract rent: n/a per month (2005-2009 5-year est.); Median year structure built: 2005 (2005-2009 5-year est.).
Transportation: Commute to work: 60.0% car, 0.0% public transportation, 0.0% walk, 40.0% work from home (2005-2009 5-year est.); Travel time to work: 83.3% less than 15 minutes, 16.7% 15 to 30 minutes, 0.0% 30 to 45 minutes, 0.0% 45 to 60 minutes, 0.0% 60 minutes or more (2005-2009 5-year est.)

VALLEY CITY (village). Covers a land area of 0.196 square miles and a water area of 0.013 square miles. Located at 39.70° N. Lat; 90.65° W. Long. Elevation is 486 feet.
Population: 23 (1990); 14 (2000); 15 (2010); 15 (2015 projected); Race: 100.0% White, 0.0% Black, 0.0% Asian, 0.0% Other, 0.0% Hispanic of any race (2010); Density: 76.6 persons per square mile (2010); Average household size: 2.50 (2010); Median age: 32.5 (2010); Males per 100 females: 87.5 (2010); Marriage status: n/a never married, n/a now married, n/a widowed, n/a divorced (2005-2009 5-year est.); Foreign born: n/a

(2005-2009 5-year est.); Ancestry (includes multiple ancestries): n/a (2005-2009 5-year est.).
Economy: Employment by occupation: n/a management, n/a professional, n/a services, n/a sales, n/a farming, n/a construction, n/a production (2005-2009 5-year est.).
Income: Per capita income: $19,528 (2010); Median household income: $35,000 (2010); Average household income: $62,917 (2010); Percent of households with income of $100,000 or more: 16.7% (2010); Poverty rate: n/a (2005-2009 5-year est.).
Taxes: Total city taxes per capita: $77 (2007); City property taxes per capita: $77 (2007).
Education: Percent of population age 25 and over with: High school diploma (including GED) or higher: 100.0% (2010); Bachelor's degree or higher: 33.3% (2010); Master's degree or higher: 11.1% (2010).
Housing: Homeownership rate: 66.7% (2010); Median home value: $80,000 (2010); Median contract rent: n/a per month (2005-2009 5-year est.); Median year structure built: n/a (2005-2009 5-year est.).
Transportation: Commute to work: n/a car, n/a public transportation, n/a walk, n/a work from home (2005-2009 5-year est.); Travel time to work: n/a less than 15 minutes, n/a 15 to 30 minutes, n/a 30 to 45 minutes, n/a 45 to 60 minutes, n/a 60 minutes or more (2005-2009 5-year est.)

Pope County

Located in southeastern Illinois, partly in the Ozarks; bounded on the east by the Ohio River and the Kentucky border; drained by tributaries of the Ohio River; includes part of Shawnee National Forest. Covers a land area of 370.86 square miles, a water area of 3.77 square miles, and is located in the Central Time Zone at 37.41° N. Lat., 88.57° W. Long. The county was founded in 1816. County seat is Golconda.

Weather Station: Dixon Springs Agr Center										Elevation: 540 feet		
	Jan	Feb	Mar	Apr	May	Jun	Jul	Aug	Sep	Oct	Nov	Dec
High	44	50	59	70	78	86	89	89	83	72	59	47
Low	26	30	38	47	56	64	68	66	58	47	39	30
Precip	3.6	3.5	4.5	4.6	5.5	4.1	4.2	3.3	3.6	3.7	4.4	4.5
Snow	2.5	3.1	0.7	tr	0.0	0.0	0.0	0.0	0.0	0.2	tr	1.1

High and Low temperatures in degrees Fahrenheit; Precipitation and Snow in inches

Weather Station: Smithland Lock & Dam										Elevation: 356 feet		
	Jan	Feb	Mar	Apr	May	Jun	Jul	Aug	Sep	Oct	Nov	Dec
High	42	47	57	68	77	85	89	88	81	70	58	46
Low	25	28	36	45	55	64	68	67	59	47	37	28
Precip	3.4	3.8	4.2	4.5	5.1	4.2	4.3	2.7	3.6	3.9	4.1	4.6
Snow	1.6	1.5	0.4	tr	0.0	0.0	0.0	0.0	0.0	tr	tr	1.6

High and Low temperatures in degrees Fahrenheit; Precipitation and Snow in inches

Population: 4,373 (1990); 4,413 (2000); 4,029 (2010); 3,824 (2015 projected); Race: 92.5% White, 4.2% Black, 0.3% Asian, 3.1% Other, 1.2% Hispanic of any race (2010); Density: 10.9 persons per square mile (2010); Average household size: 2.26 (2010); Median age: 44.3 (2010); Males per 100 females: 101.3 (2010).
Religion: Five largest groups: 33.7% Southern Baptist Convention, 4.5% The United Methodist Church, 2.7% Lutheran Church—Missouri Synod, 2.6% Church of God (Cleveland, Tennessee), 0.9% Presbyterian Church (U.S.A.) (2000).
Economy: Unemployment rate: 10.1% (August 2011); Total civilian labor force: 1,993 (August 2011); Leading industries: 55.7% health care and social assistance; 18.0% retail trade; 4.0% construction (2009); Farms: 346 totaling 60,809 acres (2007); Companies that employ 500 or more persons: 0 (2009); Companies that employ 100 to 499 persons: 0 (2009); Companies that employ less than 100 persons: 62 (2009); Black-owned businesses: n/a (2007); Hispanic-owned businesses: n/a (2007); Asian-owned businesses: n/a (2007); Women-owned businesses: n/a (2007); Retail sales per capita: $2,282 (2010). Single-family building permits issued: 0 (2010); Multi-family building permits issued: 0 (2010).
Income: Per capita income: $19,857 (2010); Median household income: $36,881 (2010); Average household income: $46,700 (2010); Percent of households with income of $100,000 or more: 6.7% (2010); Poverty rate: 18.0% (2009); Bankruptcy rate: 1.57% (2010).
Taxes: Total county taxes per capita: $131 (2007); County property taxes per capita: $131 (2007).
Education: Percent of population age 25 and over with: High school diploma (including GED) or higher: 82.8% (2010); Bachelor's degree or higher: 13.3% (2010); Master's degree or higher: 5.6% (2010).

Housing: Homeownership rate: 81.2% (2010); Median home value: $86,012 (2010); Median contract rent: $257 per month (2005-2009 5-year est.); Median year structure built: 1971 (2005-2009 5-year est.)
Health: Birth rate: 102.7 per 10,000 population (2009); Death rate: 102.7 per 10,000 population (2009); Age-adjusted cancer mortality rate: 172.5 (Unreliable) deaths per 100,000 population (2007); Number of physicians: 0.0 per 10,000 population (2008); Hospital beds: 0.0 per 10,000 population (2007); Hospital admissions: 0.0 per 10,000 population (2007).
Elections: 2008 Presidential election results: 37.9% Obama, 60.2% McCain, 1.3% Nader
National and State Parks: Dixon Springs State Park; Dog Island State Wetlands; Millstone Bluff National Register Site; Shawnee National Forest
Additional Information Contacts
Pope County Government . . . . (618) 683-4466

Golconda Pope County Chamber . . . . (618) 683-9702

Pope County Communities

EDDYVILLE (village). Covers a land area of 0.287 square miles and a water area of 0 square miles. Located at 37.50° N. Lat; 88.58° W. Long. Elevation is 699 feet.
Population: 151 (1990); 153 (2000); 149 (2010); 141 (2015 projected); Race: 97.3% White, 0.0% Black, 0.0% Asian, 2.7% Other, 0.7% Hispanic of any race (2010); Density: 519.2 persons per square mile (2010); Average household size: 2.29 (2010); Median age: 47.4 (2010); Males per 100 females: 115.9 (2010); Marriage status: 29.6% never married, 27.8% now married, 27.8% widowed, 14.8% divorced (2005-2009 5-year est.); Foreign born: 0.0% (2005-2009 5-year est.); Ancestry (includes multiple ancestries): 40.6% Irish, 34.4% German, 20.3% English, 10.9% Dutch, 7.8% Scotch-Irish (2005-2009 5-year est.).
Economy: Employment by occupation: 0.0% management, 21.6% professional, 54.1% services, 16.2% sales, 0.0% farming, 8.1% construction, 0.0% production (2005-2009 5-year est.).
Income: Per capita income: $20,233 (2010); Median household income: $38,500 (2010); Average household income: $45,192 (2010); Percent of households with income of $100,000 or more: 3.1% (2010); Poverty rate: 39.1% (2005-2009 5-year est.).
Taxes: Total city taxes per capita: $42 (2007); City property taxes per capita: $14 (2007).
Education: Percent of population age 25 and over with: High school diploma (including GED) or higher: 85.1% (2010); Bachelor's degree or higher: 10.5% (2010); Master's degree or higher: 4.4% (2010).
Housing: Homeownership rate: 81.5% (2010); Median home value: $98,750 (2010); Median contract rent: $193 per month (2005-2009 5-year est.); Median year structure built: 1978 (2005-2009 5-year est.).
Transportation: Commute to work: 86.5% car, 0.0% public transportation, 13.5% walk, 0.0% work from home (2005-2009 5-year est.); Travel time to work: 27.0% less than 15 minutes, 54.1% 15 to 30 minutes, 0.0% 30 to 45 minutes, 18.9% 45 to 60 minutes, 0.0% 60 minutes or more (2005-2009 5-year est.)

GOLCONDA (city). County seat. Covers a land area of 0.564 square miles and a water area of 0.026 square miles. Located at 37.36° N. Lat; 88.48° W. Long. Elevation is 354 feet.
History: Incorporated 1845.
Population: 877 (1990); 726 (2000); 624 (2010); 579 (2015 projected); Race: 96.0% White, 1.6% Black, 0.3% Asian, 2.1% Other, 0.5% Hispanic of any race (2010); Density: 1,106.2 persons per square mile (2010); Average household size: 2.07 (2010); Median age: 46.8 (2010); Males per 100 females: 86.3 (2010); Marriage status: 25.8% never married, 35.7% now married, 9.2% widowed, 29.3% divorced (2005-2009 5-year est.); Foreign born: 0.0% (2005-2009 5-year est.); Ancestry (includes multiple ancestries): 39.2% German, 16.9% Irish, 8.0% Italian, 5.4% English, 3.6% Scotch-Irish (2005-2009 5-year est.).
Economy: Single-family building permits issued: 0 (2010); Multi-family building permits issued: 0 (2010); Employment by occupation: 18.6% management, 7.5% professional, 36.8% services, 13.5% sales, 0.0% farming, 7.5% construction, 16.0% production (2005-2009 5-year est.).
Income: Per capita income: $20,422 (2010); Median household income: $30,833 (2010); Average household income: $41,568 (2010); Percent of households with income of $100,000 or more: 6.8% (2010); Poverty rate: 33.0% (2005-2009 5-year est.).
Taxes: Total city taxes per capita: $112 (2007); City property taxes per capita: $92 (2007).

Education: Percent of population age 25 and over with: High school diploma (including GED) or higher: 74.1% (2010); Bachelor's degree or higher: 11.9% (2010); Master's degree or higher: 5.3% (2010).

School District(s)

Pope Co CUD 1 (PK-12)

  2009-10 Enrollment: 556 . . . . (618) 683-2301

Housing: Homeownership rate: 63.4% (2010); Median home value: $62,000 (2010); Median contract rent: $248 per month (2005-2009 5-year est.); Median year structure built: 1953 (2005-2009 5-year est.).

Newspapers: Herald-Enterprise (Local news; Circulation 2,000)

Transportation: Commute to work: 83.5% car, 0.0% public transportation, 8.8% walk, 5.4% work from home (2005-2009 5-year est.); Travel time to work: 39.1% less than 15 minutes, 8.5% 15 to 30 minutes, 40.2% 30 to 45 minutes, 3.9% 45 to 60 minutes, 8.2% 60 minutes or more (2005-2009 5-year est.)

Additional Information Contacts

Golconda Pope County Chamber . . . . (618) 683-9702

HEROD (unincorporated postal area, zip code 62947). Covers a land area of 68.806 square miles and a water area of 0.144 square miles. Located at 37.56° N. Lat; 88.39° W. Long. Elevation is 423 feet.

Population: 597 (2000); Race: 98.8% White, 0.0% Black, 0.0% Asian, 1.2% Other, 0.0% Hispanic of any race (2000); Density: 8.7 persons per square mile (2000); Age: 23.2% under 18, 6.6% over 64 (2000); Marriage status: 28.7% never married, 54.9% now married, 2.8% widowed, 13.6% divorced (2000); Foreign born: 8.1% (2000); Ancestry (includes multiple ancestries): 14.0% American, 10.7% German, 10.5% Irish, 8.1% Swiss (2000).

Economy: Employment by occupation: 13.1% management, 13.1% professional, 12.7% services, 15.0% sales, 0.0% farming, 28.1% construction, 18.0% production (2000).

Income: Per capita income: $18,727 (2000); Median household income: $35,769 (2000); Poverty rate: 7.4% (2000).

Education: Percent of population age 25 and over with: High school diploma (including GED) or higher: 91.0% (2000); Bachelor's degree or higher: 19.3% (2000).

Housing: Homeownership rate: 90.2% (2000); Median home value: $36,400 (2000); Median contract rent: $275 per month (2000); Median year structure built: 1971 (2000).

Transportation: Commute to work: 95.7% car, 0.0% public transportation, 0.0% walk, 2.3% work from home (2000); Travel time to work: 7.9% less than 15 minutes, 54.5% 15 to 30 minutes, 15.4% 30 to 45 minutes, 13.7% 45 to 60 minutes, 8.6% 60 minutes or more (2000)

Pulaski County

Located in southern Illinois; bounded on the south by the Ohio River and the Kentucky border; drained by the Cache River. Covers a land area of 200.79 square miles, a water area of 2.55 square miles, and is located in the Central Time Zone at 37.19° N. Lat., 89.13° W. Long. The county was founded in 1843. County seat is Mound City.

Population: 7,523 (1990); 7,348 (2000); 6,202 (2010); 5,629 (2015 projected); Race: 66.1% White, 30.6% Black, 1.0% Asian, 2.3% Other, 1.9% Hispanic of any race (2010); Density: 30.9 persons per square mile (2010); Average household size: 2.39 (2010); Median age: 39.9 (2010); Males per 100 females: 91.4 (2010).

Religion: Five largest groups: 30.5% Southern Baptist Convention, 8.4% Catholic Church, 6.8% The United Methodist Church, 3.0% Conservative Congregational Christian Conference, 2.8% Churches of Christ (2000).

Economy: Unemployment rate: 10.9% (August 2011); Total civilian labor force: 2,807 (August 2011); Leading industries: 19.3% health care and social assistance; 9.0% retail trade; 6.1% finance & insurance (2009); Farms: 276 totaling 101,189 acres (2007); Companies that employ 500 or more persons: 0 (2009); Companies that employ 100 to 499 persons: 1 (2009); Companies that employ less than 100 persons: 98 (2009); Black-owned businesses: n/a (2007); Hispanic-owned businesses: n/a (2007); Asian-owned businesses: n/a (2007); Women-owned businesses: n/a (2007); Retail sales per capita: $3,427 (2010). Single-family building permits issued: 8 (2010); Multi-family building permits issued: 0 (2010).

Income: Per capita income: $17,747 (2010); Median household income: $32,590 (2010); Average household income: $42,241 (2010); Percent of households with income of $100,000 or more: 7.3% (2010); Poverty rate: 25.1% (2009); Bankruptcy rate: 8.47% (2010).

Taxes: Total county taxes per capita: $168 (2007); County property taxes per capita: $158 (2007).

Education: Percent of population age 25 and over with: High school diploma (including GED) or higher: 77.1% (2010); Bachelor's degree or higher: 9.0% (2010); Master's degree or higher: 2.5% (2010).

Housing: Homeownership rate: 74.4% (2010); Median home value: $44,278 (2010); Median contract rent: $260 per month (2005-2009 5-year est.); Median year structure built: 1961 (2005-2009 5-year est.)

Health: Birth rate: 131.9 per 10,000 population (2009); Death rate: 123.8 per 10,000 population (2009); Age-adjusted cancer mortality rate: 370.3 deaths per 100,000 population (2007); Number of physicians: 0.0 per 10,000 population (2008); Hospital beds: 0.0 per 10,000 population (2007); Hospital admissions: 0.0 per 10,000 population (2007).

Elections: 2008 Presidential election results: 50.1% Obama, 48.7% McCain, 0.6% Nader

Additional Information Contacts

Pulaski County Government . . . . (618) 748-9360
  http://pulaskicountyil.net

Pulaski County Communities

GRAND CHAIN (unincorporated postal area, zip code 62941). Aka New Grand Chain. Covers a land area of 35.579 square miles and a water area of 0.817 square miles. Located at 37.24° N. Lat; 88.99° W. Long. Elevation is 394 feet.

Population: 890 (2000); Race: 90.7% White, 6.0% Black, 0.0% Asian, 3.3% Other, 0.0% Hispanic of any race (2000); Density: 25.0 persons per square mile (2000); Age: 24.1% under 18, 16.9% over 64 (2000); Marriage status: 13.9% never married, 66.7% now married, 8.7% widowed, 10.7% divorced (2000); Foreign born: 0.4% (2000); Ancestry (includes multiple ancestries): 27.6% German, 16.6% Irish, 14.6% English, 6.3% American (2000).

Economy: Employment by occupation: 10.9% management, 15.6% professional, 20.3% services, 17.4% sales, 1.0% farming, 16.6% construction, 18.1% production (2000).

Income: Per capita income: $19,028 (2000); Median household income: $38,173 (2000); Poverty rate: 14.6% (2000).

Education: Percent of population age 25 and over with: High school diploma (including GED) or higher: 82.8% (2000); Bachelor's degree or higher: 8.1% (2000).

School District(s)

Jamp Spec Educ Services (02-12)

  2009-10 Enrollment: n/a . . . . (618) 634-9800

Housing: Homeownership rate: 84.7% (2000); Median home value: $51,500 (2000); Median contract rent: $244 per month (2000); Median year structure built: 1968 (2000).

Transportation: Commute to work: 91.6% car, 1.5% public transportation, 1.3% walk, 4.3% work from home (2000); Travel time to work: 23.8% less than 15 minutes, 29.1% 15 to 30 minutes, 24.1% 30 to 45 minutes, 13.1% 45 to 60 minutes, 9.9% 60 minutes or more (2000)

KARNAK (village). Covers a land area of 1.813 square miles and a water area of 0 square miles. Located at 37.29° N. Lat; 88.97° W. Long. Elevation is 341 feet.

History: Karnak was established as a company town for a logging and milling industry.

Population: 581 (1990); 619 (2000); 509 (2010); 456 (2015 projected); Race: 90.0% White, 9.2% Black, 0.0% Asian, 0.8% Other, 3.7% Hispanic of any race (2010); Density: 280.7 persons per square mile (2010); Average household size: 2.44 (2010); Median age: 38.3 (2010); Males per 100 females: 84.4 (2010); Marriage status: 15.3% never married, 73.2% now married, 6.5% widowed, 5.0% divorced (2005-2009 5-year est.); Foreign born: 1.0% (2005-2009 5-year est.); Ancestry (includes multiple ancestries): 21.7% German, 11.6% Irish, 10.6% English, 8.2% American, 5.2% Scotch-Irish (2005-2009 5-year est.).

Economy: Employment by occupation: 6.2% management, 10.3% professional, 30.4% services, 24.2% sales, 0.0% farming, 8.4% construction, 20.5% production (2005-2009 5-year est.).

Income: Per capita income: $20,973 (2010); Median household income: $39,773 (2010); Average household income: $49,713 (2010); Percent of households with income of $100,000 or more: 8.6% (2010); Poverty rate: 13.0% (2005-2009 5-year est.).

Taxes: Total city taxes per capita: $19 (2007); City property taxes per capita: $9 (2007).

Education: Percent of population age 25 and over with: High school diploma (including GED) or higher: 77.7% (2010); Bachelor's degree or higher: 9.4% (2010); Master's degree or higher: 1.6% (2010).

Housing: Homeownership rate: 78.0% (2010); Median home value: $48,049 (2010); Median contract rent: $400 per month (2005-2009 5-year est.); Median year structure built: 1960 (2005-2009 5-year est.).
Transportation: Commute to work: 89.9% car, 0.0% public transportation, 7.9% walk, 1.1% work from home (2005-2009 5-year est.); Travel time to work: 20.1% less than 15 minutes, 33.7% 15 to 30 minutes, 26.5% 30 to 45 minutes, 17.0% 45 to 60 minutes, 2.7% 60 minutes or more (2005-2009 5-year est.)

MOUND CITY (city). County seat. Covers a land area of 0.711 square miles and a water area of 0.050 square miles. Located at 37.08° N. Lat; 89.16° W. Long. Elevation is 318 feet.

History: Important Union naval base in Civil War. National cemetery is nearby. City severely damaged in 1937 flood. Incorporated 1857.
Population: 765 (1990); 692 (2000); 590 (2010); 533 (2015 projected); Race: 51.5% White, 47.3% Black, 0.0% Asian, 1.2% Other, 1.4% Hispanic of any race (2010); Density: 830.0 persons per square mile (2010); Average household size: 2.41 (2010); Median age: 34.7 (2010); Males per 100 females: 74.0 (2010); Marriage status: 39.3% never married, 42.4% now married, 7.1% widowed, 11.2% divorced (2005-2009 5-year est.); Foreign born: 0.9% (2005-2009 5-year est.); Ancestry (includes multiple ancestries): 7.4% German, 4.2% American, 4.1% Irish, 3.2% French, 2.8% English (2005-2009 5-year est.).
Economy: Single-family building permits issued: 0 (2010); Multi-family building permits issued: 0 (2010); Employment by occupation: 8.8% management, 9.4% professional, 28.3% services, 7.8% sales, 0.0% farming, 2.3% construction, 43.3% production (2005-2009 5-year est.).
Income: Per capita income: $15,166 (2010); Median household income: $22,442 (2010); Average household income: $36,977 (2010); Percent of households with income of $100,000 or more: 8.2% (2010); Poverty rate: 38.8% (2005-2009 5-year est.).
Taxes: Total city taxes per capita: $206 (2007); City property taxes per capita: $62 (2007).
Education: Percent of population age 25 and over with: High school diploma (including GED) or higher: 71.5% (2010); Bachelor's degree or higher: 7.1% (2010); Master's degree or higher: 0.5% (2010).
Housing: Homeownership rate: 56.1% (2010); Median home value: $32,500 (2010); Median contract rent: $208 per month (2005-2009 5-year est.); Median year structure built: 1963 (2005-2009 5-year est.).
Transportation: Commute to work: 83.4% car, 11.3% public transportation, 4.3% walk, 1.0% work from home (2005-2009 5-year est.); Travel time to work: 42.8% less than 15 minutes, 24.1% 15 to 30 minutes, 9.7% 30 to 45 minutes, 6.0% 45 to 60 minutes, 17.4% 60 minutes or more (2005-2009 5-year est.)

MOUNDS (city). Covers a land area of 1.216 square miles and a water area of 0 square miles. Located at 37.11° N. Lat; 89.19° W. Long. Elevation is 325 feet.

History: Incorporated 1904.
Population: 1,407 (1990); 1,117 (2000); 928 (2010); 837 (2015 projected); Race: 32.2% White, 63.9% Black, 0.2% Asian, 3.7% Other, 1.0% Hispanic of any race (2010); Density: 763.4 persons per square mile (2010); Average household size: 2.49 (2010); Median age: 35.8 (2010); Males per 100 females: 84.5 (2010); Marriage status: 35.1% never married, 21.8% now married, 20.7% widowed, 22.3% divorced (2005-2009 5-year est.); Foreign born: 1.2% (2005-2009 5-year est.); Ancestry (includes multiple ancestries): 4.0% American, 3.2% Irish, 2.3% African, 2.1% German, 1.1% Scottish (2005-2009 5-year est.).
Economy: Single-family building permits issued: 0 (2010); Multi-family building permits issued: 0 (2010); Employment by occupation: 6.7% management, 10.8% professional, 38.6% services, 28.3% sales, 0.0% farming, 0.9% construction, 14.8% production (2005-2009 5-year est.).
Income: Per capita income: $15,627 (2010); Median household income: $23,442 (2010); Average household income: $37,088 (2010); Percent of households with income of $100,000 or more: 5.4% (2010); Poverty rate: 47.5% (2005-2009 5-year est.).
Taxes: Total city taxes per capita: $102 (2007); City property taxes per capita: $16 (2007).
Education: Percent of population age 25 and over with: High school diploma (including GED) or higher: 75.0% (2010); Bachelor's degree or higher: 8.4% (2010); Master's degree or higher: 3.5% (2010).

School District(s)
Meridian CUSD 101 (PK-12)
    2009-10 Enrollment: 655 . . . . (618) 342-6776

Housing: Homeownership rate: 65.3% (2010); Median home value: $30,123 (2010); Median contract rent: $235 per month (2005-2009 5-year est.); Median year structure built: 1941 (2005-2009 5-year est.).
Newspapers: Pulaski Enterprise (Community news; Circulation 4,789)
Transportation: Commute to work: 88.6% car, 4.1% public transportation, 6.8% walk, 0.5% work from home (2005-2009 5-year est.); Travel time to work: 45.0% less than 15 minutes, 29.4% 15 to 30 minutes, 9.2% 30 to 45 minutes, 12.4% 45 to 60 minutes, 4.1% 60 minutes or more (2005-2009 5-year est.)

NEW GRAND CHAIN (village). Aka Grand Chain. Covers a land area of 1.058 square miles and a water area of 0 square miles. Located at 37.25° N. Lat; 89.02° W. Long. Elevation is 410 feet.

History: New Grand Chain was named for a row of rocks in the Ohio River, where the town was first located. It was moved in 1872 to be on the new railroad line.
Population: 273 (1990); 233 (2000); 196 (2010); 176 (2015 projected); Race: 82.1% White, 15.3% Black, 0.0% Asian, 2.6% Other, 0.5% Hispanic of any race (2010); Density: 185.2 persons per square mile (2010); Average household size: 2.36 (2010); Median age: 46.9 (2010); Males per 100 females: 100.0 (2010); Marriage status: 12.9% never married, 65.8% now married, 9.7% widowed, 11.6% divorced (2005-2009 5-year est.); Foreign born: 5.7% (2005-2009 5-year est.); Ancestry (includes multiple ancestries): 17.1% English, 14.3% German, 11.9% Irish, 7.6% Italian, 4.3% American (2005-2009 5-year est.).
Economy: Employment by occupation: 5.2% management, 32.3% professional, 25.0% services, 24.0% sales, 0.0% farming, 6.3% construction, 7.3% production (2005-2009 5-year est.).
Income: Per capita income: $19,991 (2010); Median household income: $41,094 (2010); Average household income: $51,747 (2010); Percent of households with income of $100,000 or more: 10.8% (2010); Poverty rate: 21.4% (2005-2009 5-year est.).
Taxes: Total city taxes per capita: $14 (2007); City property taxes per capita: $14 (2007).
Education: Percent of population age 25 and over with: High school diploma (including GED) or higher: 84.5% (2010); Bachelor's degree or higher: 9.9% (2010); Master's degree or higher: 3.5% (2010).
Housing: Homeownership rate: 80.7% (2010); Median home value: $51,875 (2010); Median contract rent: $279 per month (2005-2009 5-year est.); Median year structure built: 1982 (2005-2009 5-year est.).
Transportation: Commute to work: 95.8% car, 0.0% public transportation, 2.1% walk, 2.1% work from home (2005-2009 5-year est.); Travel time to work: 14.9% less than 15 minutes, 20.2% 15 to 30 minutes, 38.3% 30 to 45 minutes, 11.7% 45 to 60 minutes, 14.9% 60 minutes or more (2005-2009 5-year est.)

OLMSTED (village). Covers a land area of 1.680 square miles and a water area of 0.045 square miles. Located at 37.18° N. Lat; 89.08° W. Long. Elevation is 358 feet.

Population: 358 (1990); 299 (2000); 268 (2010); 251 (2015 projected); Race: 86.2% White, 11.6% Black, 0.4% Asian, 1.9% Other, 0.7% Hispanic of any race (2010); Density: 159.5 persons per square mile (2010); Average household size: 2.37 (2010); Median age: 42.6 (2010); Males per 100 females: 88.7 (2010); Marriage status: 11.2% never married, 66.3% now married, 8.2% widowed, 14.2% divorced (2005-2009 5-year est.); Foreign born: 0.0% (2005-2009 5-year est.); Ancestry (includes multiple ancestries): 15.8% American, 10.7% German, 10.1% English, 9.5% Irish, 4.7% French (2005-2009 5-year est.).
Economy: Employment by occupation: 3.9% management, 24.3% professional, 20.4% services, 16.5% sales, 0.0% farming, 11.7% construction, 23.3% production (2005-2009 5-year est.).
Income: Per capita income: $19,532 (2010); Median household income: $36,406 (2010); Average household income: $46,748 (2010); Percent of households with income of $100,000 or more: 10.6% (2010); Poverty rate: 23.7% (2005-2009 5-year est.).
Taxes: Total city taxes per capita: $108 (2007); City property taxes per capita: $18 (2007).
Education: Percent of population age 25 and over with: High school diploma (including GED) or higher: 79.7% (2010); Bachelor's degree or higher: 3.8% (2010); Master's degree or higher: 0.5% (2010).
Housing: Homeownership rate: 78.8% (2010); Median home value: $51,364 (2010); Median contract rent: $141 per month (2005-2009 5-year est.); Median year structure built: 1955 (2005-2009 5-year est.).
Transportation: Commute to work: 97.9% car, 0.0% public transportation, 0.0% walk, 0.0% work from home (2005-2009 5-year est.); Travel time to

work: 16.5% less than 15 minutes, 47.4% 15 to 30 minutes, 9.3% 30 to 45 minutes, 16.5% 45 to 60 minutes, 10.3% 60 minutes or more (2005-2009 5-year est.)

PULASKI (village). Covers a land area of 1.275 square miles and a water area of 0 square miles. Located at 37.21° N. Lat; 89.20° W. Long. Elevation is 344 feet.
Population: 361 (1990); 274 (2000); 200 (2010); 182 (2015 projected); Race: 51.0% White, 36.0% Black, 10.0% Asian, 3.0% Other, 7.5% Hispanic of any race (2010); Density: 156.9 persons per square mile (2010); Average household size: 2.35 (2010); Median age: 37.1 (2010); Males per 100 females: 177.8 (2010); Marriage status: 33.6% never married, 36.8% now married, 19.4% widowed, 10.1% divorced (2005-2009 5-year est.); Foreign born: 0.0% (2005-2009 5-year est.); Ancestry (includes multiple ancestries): 11.9% German, 6.3% English, 3.2% Irish, 3.2% Dutch, 2.1% African (2005-2009 5-year est.).
Economy: Single-family building permits issued: 0 (2010); Multi-family building permits issued: 0 (2010); Employment by occupation: 8.7% management, 10.7% professional, 39.8% services, 16.5% sales, 6.8% farming, 6.8% construction, 10.7% production (2005-2009 5-year est.).
Income: Per capita income: $16,873 (2010); Median household income: $28,750 (2010); Average household income: $39,035 (2010); Percent of households with income of $100,000 or more: 5.3% (2010); Poverty rate: 50.4% (2005-2009 5-year est.).
Taxes: Total city taxes per capita: $119 (2007); City property taxes per capita: $12 (2007).
Education: Percent of population age 25 and over with: High school diploma (including GED) or higher: 70.0% (2010); Bachelor's degree or higher: 15.0% (2010); Master's degree or higher: 2.9% (2010).
Housing: Homeownership rate: 82.5% (2010); Median home value: $41,667 (2010); Median contract rent: $261 per month (2005-2009 5-year est.); Median year structure built: 1966 (2005-2009 5-year est.).
Transportation: Commute to work: 73.8% car, 8.7% public transportation, 8.7% walk, 0.0% work from home (2005-2009 5-year est.); Travel time to work: 59.2% less than 15 minutes, 6.8% 15 to 30 minutes, 4.9% 30 to 45 minutes, 20.4% 45 to 60 minutes, 8.7% 60 minutes or more (2005-2009 5-year est.)

ULLIN (village). Covers a land area of 2.863 square miles and a water area of 0 square miles. Located at 37.27° N. Lat; 89.18° W. Long. Elevation is 341 feet.
Population: 602 (1990); 779 (2000); 683 (2010); 618 (2015 projected); Race: 65.4% White, 28.6% Black, 3.1% Asian, 2.9% Other, 2.5% Hispanic of any race (2010); Density: 238.5 persons per square mile (2010); Average household size: 2.19 (2010); Median age: 41.1 (2010); Males per 100 females: 107.0 (2010); Marriage status: 19.0% never married, 59.1% now married, 11.4% widowed, 10.6% divorced (2005-2009 5-year est.); Foreign born: 17.4% (2005-2009 5-year est.); Ancestry (includes multiple ancestries): 16.2% German, 6.0% American, 4.2% French, 3.2% Irish, 2.5% English (2005-2009 5-year est.).
Economy: Single-family building permits issued: 0 (2010); Multi-family building permits issued: 0 (2010); Employment by occupation: 4.2% management, 29.3% professional, 23.4% services, 21.0% sales, 0.0% farming, 8.4% construction, 13.8% production (2005-2009 5-year est.).
Income: Per capita income: $16,790 (2010); Median household income: $28,409 (2010); Average household income: $36,491 (2010); Percent of households with income of $100,000 or more: 4.5% (2010); Poverty rate: 22.4% (2005-2009 5-year est.).
Taxes: Total city taxes per capita: $13 (2007); City property taxes per capita: $13 (2007).
Education: Percent of population age 25 and over with: High school diploma (including GED) or higher: 78.4% (2010); Bachelor's degree or higher: 12.1% (2010); Master's degree or higher: 1.9% (2010).

School District(s)
Alxndr/John/Masc/Pulski/Union Roe (06-12)
    2009-10 Enrollment: n/a . . . . (618) 634-2292
Century CUSD 100 (PK-12)
    2009-10 Enrollment: 466 . . . . (618) 845-3447
Two-year College(s)
Shawnee Community College (Public)
    Fall 2009 Enrollment: 2,834 . . . . (618) 634-3200
    2010-11 Tuition: In-state $3,930; Out-of-state $4,350
Housing: Homeownership rate: 75.1% (2010); Median home value: $43,421 (2010); Median contract rent: $451 per month (2005-2009 5-year est.); Median year structure built: 1964 (2005-2009 5-year est.).

Transportation: Commute to work: 82.6% car, 0.0% public transportation, 3.0% walk, 6.0% work from home (2005-2009 5-year est.); Travel time to work: 17.8% less than 15 minutes, 45.9% 15 to 30 minutes, 18.5% 30 to 45 minutes, 8.3% 45 to 60 minutes, 9.6% 60 minutes or more (2005-2009 5-year est.)

VILLA RIDGE (unincorporated postal area, zip code 62996). Covers a land area of 26.870 square miles and a water area of 0.031 square miles. Located at 37.15° N. Lat; 89.16° W. Long. Elevation is 387 feet.
Population: 759 (2000); Race: 70.9% White, 25.7% Black, 1.1% Asian, 2.3% Other, 0.9% Hispanic of any race (2000); Density: 28.2 persons per square mile (2000); Age: 26.0% under 18, 9.3% over 64 (2000); Marriage status: 17.3% never married, 71.5% now married, 3.9% widowed, 7.3% divorced (2000); Foreign born: 2.0% (2000); Ancestry (includes multiple ancestries): 24.5% American, 12.8% Irish, 10.9% German, 8.6% English (2000).
Economy: Employment by occupation: 13.7% management, 8.1% professional, 16.3% services, 32.8% sales, 1.5% farming, 10.7% construction, 16.8% production (2000).
Income: Per capita income: $13,995 (2000); Median household income: $26,513 (2000); Poverty rate: 12.9% (2000).
Education: Percent of population age 25 and over with: High school diploma (including GED) or higher: 70.3% (2000); Bachelor's degree or higher: 3.7% (2000).
Housing: Homeownership rate: 89.1% (2000); Median home value: $48,000 (2000); Median contract rent: $232 per month (2000); Median year structure built: 1970 (2000).
Transportation: Commute to work: 93.5% car, 0.0% public transportation, 0.0% walk, 6.5% work from home (2000); Travel time to work: 31.5% less than 15 minutes, 41.6% 15 to 30 minutes, 18.2% 30 to 45 minutes, 6.4% 45 to 60 minutes, 2.3% 60 minutes or more (2000)

Putnam County

Located in north central Illinois; bounded on the north and west by the Illinois River. Covers a land area of 159.80 square miles, a water area of 12.45 square miles, and is located in the Central Time Zone at 41.22° N. Lat., 89.27° W. Long. The county was founded in 1825. County seat is Hennepin.

Putnam County is part of the Ottawa-Streator, IL Micropolitan Statistical Area. The entire metro area includes: Bureau County, IL; La Salle County, IL; Putnam County, IL

Weather Station: Hennepin Power Plant										Elevation: 459 feet	
	Jan	Feb	Mar	Apr	May	Jun	Jul	Aug	Sep	Oct	Nov	Dec
High	33	37	49	62	74	83	86	85	78	65	50	36
Low	14	17	28	38	48	58	62	60	52	40	30	18
Precip	1.3	1.4	2.0	3.1	3.5	3.8	4.1	4.4	3.5	2.7	2.7	na
Snow	5.0	4.4	na	0.2	0.0	0.0	0.0	0.0	0.0	tr	0.2	5.0

High and Low temperatures in degrees Fahrenheit; Precipitation and Snow in inches

Population: 5,730 (1990); 6,086 (2000); 6,008 (2010); 5,945 (2015 projected); Race: 96.8% White, 0.7% Black, 0.3% Asian, 2.1% Other, 4.4% Hispanic of any race (2010); Density: 37.6 persons per square mile (2010); Average household size: 2.47 (2010); Median age: 42.5 (2010); Males per 100 females: 100.5 (2010).
Religion: Five largest groups: 27.1% Catholic Church, 6.7% United Church of Christ, 5.3% The United Methodist Church, 4.6% Evangelical Lutheran Church in America, 1.1% Friends (Quakers) (2000).
Economy: Unemployment rate: 9.8% (August 2011); Total civilian labor force: 3,192 (August 2011); Leading industries: 27.6% manufacturing; 11.7% construction; 8.2% retail trade (2009); Farms: 167 totaling 62,705 acres (2007); Companies that employ 500 or more persons: 0 (2009); Companies that employ 100 to 499 persons: 2 (2009); Companies that employ less than 100 persons: 133 (2009); Black-owned businesses: n/a (2007); Hispanic-owned businesses: n/a (2007); Asian-owned businesses: n/a (2007); Women-owned businesses: n/a (2007); Retail sales per capita: $4,169 (2010). Single-family building permits issued: 15 (2010); Multi-family building permits issued: 0 (2010).
Income: Per capita income: $26,558 (2010); Median household income: $57,820 (2010); Average household income: $65,454 (2010); Percent of households with income of $100,000 or more: 15.4% (2010); Poverty rate: 8.5% (2009); Bankruptcy rate: 5.84% (2010).
Taxes: Total county taxes per capita: $196 (2007); County property taxes per capita: $187 (2007).

Education: Percent of population age 25 and over with: High school diploma (including GED) or higher: 88.4% (2010); Bachelor's degree or higher: 14.8% (2010); Master's degree or higher: 5.1% (2010).
Housing: Homeownership rate: 81.6% (2010); Median home value: $130,189 (2010); Median contract rent: $440 per month (2005-2009 5-year est.); Median year structure built: 1971 (2005-2009 5-year est.)
Health: Birth rate: 99.9 per 10,000 population (2009); Death rate: 91.5 per 10,000 population (2009); Age-adjusted cancer mortality rate: 227.4 (Unreliable) deaths per 100,000 population (2007); Number of physicians: 1.7 per 10,000 population (2008); Hospital beds: 0.0 per 10,000 population (2007); Hospital admissions: 0.0 per 10,000 population (2007).
Elections: 2008 Presidential election results: 56.9% Obama, 41.3% McCain, 0.9% Nader
National and State Parks: Donnelley State Fish and Wildlife Area; Fox Run State Conservation Area
Additional Information Contacts
Putnam County Government . . . . (815) 925-7129

Putnam County Communities

GRANVILLE (village). Covers a land area of 0.957 square miles and a water area of 0 square miles. Located at 41.26° N. Lat; 89.22° W. Long. Elevation is 686 feet.
History: Incorporated 1861.
Population: 1,407 (1990); 1,414 (2000); 1,415 (2010); 1,413 (2015 projected); Race: 96.8% White, 0.2% Black, 0.5% Asian, 2.5% Other, 6.1% Hispanic of any race (2010); Density: 1,477.8 persons per square mile (2010); Average household size: 2.37 (2010); Median age: 40.2 (2010); Males per 100 females: 88.9 (2010); Marriage status: 22.5% never married, 59.6% now married, 8.4% widowed, 9.5% divorced (2005-2009 5-year est.); Foreign born: 2.4% (2005-2009 5-year est.); Ancestry (includes multiple ancestries): 39.3% German, 19.9% Italian, 14.1% Irish, 11.5% English, 9.8% Polish (2005-2009 5-year est.).
Economy: Single-family building permits issued: 1 (2010); Multi-family building permits issued: 0 (2010); Employment by occupation: 9.3% management, 11.1% professional, 16.3% services, 20.2% sales, 0.0% farming, 15.8% construction, 27.4% production (2005-2009 5-year est.).
Income: Per capita income: $25,166 (2010); Median household income: $49,368 (2010); Average household income: $59,740 (2010); Percent of households with income of $100,000 or more: 15.3% (2010); Poverty rate: 14.7% (2005-2009 5-year est.).
Taxes: Total city taxes per capita: $83 (2007); City property taxes per capita: $68 (2007).
Education: Percent of population age 25 and over with: High school diploma (including GED) or higher: 88.1% (2010); Bachelor's degree or higher: 12.0% (2010); Master's degree or higher: 4.3% (2010).
School District(s)
Putnam County CUSD 535 (PK-12)
    2009-10 Enrollment: 933 . . . . (815) 882-2800
Housing: Homeownership rate: 79.5% (2010); Median home value: $121,123 (2010); Median contract rent: $405 per month (2005-2009 5-year est.); Median year structure built: 1963 (2005-2009 5-year est.).
Safety: Violent crime rate: 0.0 per 10,000 population; Property crime rate: 22.7 per 10,000 population (2010).
Newspapers: Putnam County Record (Community news; Circulation 3,200)
Transportation: Commute to work: 96.7% car, 0.0% public transportation, 2.2% walk, 1.1% work from home (2005-2009 5-year est.); Travel time to work: 35.6% less than 15 minutes, 45.7% 15 to 30 minutes, 9.3% 30 to 45 minutes, 5.2% 45 to 60 minutes, 4.2% 60 minutes or more (2005-2009 5-year est.)

HENNEPIN (village). County seat. Covers a land area of 5.223 square miles and a water area of 0.360 square miles. Located at 41.25° N. Lat; 89.33° W. Long. Elevation is 502 feet.
History: Hennepin was named for Father Louis Hennepin, an early missionary pilot who guided explorers on the waterways.
Population: 669 (1990); 707 (2000); 710 (2010); 704 (2015 projected); Race: 97.5% White, 0.8% Black, 1.0% Asian, 0.7% Other, 4.6% Hispanic of any race (2010); Density: 135.9 persons per square mile (2010); Average household size: 2.36 (2010); Median age: 44.5 (2010); Males per 100 females: 100.0 (2010); Marriage status: 21.8% never married, 64.0% now married, 7.1% widowed, 7.1% divorced (2005-2009 5-year est.); Foreign born: 1.3% (2005-2009 5-year est.); Ancestry (includes multiple

ancestries): 46.2% German, 19.5% Irish, 19.0% Polish, 13.9% Italian, 12.0% English (2005-2009 5-year est.).
Economy: Single-family building permits issued: 1 (2010); Multi-family building permits issued: 0 (2010); Employment by occupation: 8.9% management, 7.6% professional, 20.9% services, 26.0% sales, 1.9% farming, 12.2% construction, 22.5% production (2005-2009 5-year est.).
Income: Per capita income: $28,962 (2010); Median household income: $55,986 (2010); Average household income: $68,917 (2010); Percent of households with income of $100,000 or more: 18.7% (2010); Poverty rate: 7.9% (2005-2009 5-year est.).
Taxes: Total city taxes per capita: $66 (2007); City property taxes per capita: $64 (2007).
Education: Percent of population age 25 and over with: High school diploma (including GED) or higher: 86.9% (2010); Bachelor's degree or higher: 13.3% (2010); Master's degree or higher: 4.7% (2010).
School District(s)
Putnam County CUSD 535 (PK-12)
    2009-10 Enrollment: 933 . . . . (815) 882-2800
Housing: Homeownership rate: 80.3% (2010); Median home value: $143,667 (2010); Median contract rent: $472 per month (2005-2009 5-year est.); Median year structure built: 1971 (2005-2009 5-year est.).
Transportation: Commute to work: 86.2% car, 0.0% public transportation, 5.1% walk, 8.7% work from home (2005-2009 5-year est.); Travel time to work: 44.0% less than 15 minutes, 36.0% 15 to 30 minutes, 6.5% 30 to 45 minutes, 2.2% 45 to 60 minutes, 11.4% 60 minutes or more (2005-2009 5-year est.)

MAGNOLIA (village). Covers a land area of 0.298 square miles and a water area of 0 square miles. Located at 41.11° N. Lat; 89.19° W. Long. Elevation is 663 feet.
Population: 262 (1990); 279 (2000); 277 (2010); 275 (2015 projected); Race: 96.8% White, 2.2% Black, 0.4% Asian, 0.7% Other, 0.4% Hispanic of any race (2010); Density: 930.2 persons per square mile (2010); Average household size: 2.54 (2010); Median age: 40.6 (2010); Males per 100 females: 97.9 (2010); Marriage status: 24.3% never married, 60.5% now married, 0.5% widowed, 14.6% divorced (2005-2009 5-year est.); Foreign born: 0.0% (2005-2009 5-year est.); Ancestry (includes multiple ancestries): 28.5% German, 9.4% Swedish, 8.3% American, 7.6% Italian, 7.2% Irish (2005-2009 5-year est.).
Economy: Single-family building permits issued: 0 (2010); Multi-family building permits issued: 0 (2010); Employment by occupation: 15.7% management, 1.7% professional, 20.7% services, 11.6% sales, 0.0% farming, 16.5% construction, 33.9% production (2005-2009 5-year est.).
Income: Per capita income: $27,744 (2010); Median household income: $64,500 (2010); Average household income: $72,798 (2010); Percent of households with income of $100,000 or more: 16.5% (2010); Poverty rate: 4.7% (2005-2009 5-year est.).
Taxes: Total city taxes per capita: $109 (2007); City property taxes per capita: $65 (2007).
Education: Percent of population age 25 and over with: High school diploma (including GED) or higher: 87.0% (2010); Bachelor's degree or higher: 17.6% (2010); Master's degree or higher: 5.2% (2010).
Housing: Homeownership rate: 79.8% (2010); Median home value: $107,759 (2010); Median contract rent: $372 per month (2005-2009 5-year est.); Median year structure built: before 1940 (2005-2009 5-year est.).
Transportation: Commute to work: 100.0% car, 0.0% public transportation, 0.0% walk, 0.0% work from home (2005-2009 5-year est.); Travel time to work: 12.6% less than 15 minutes, 25.2% 15 to 30 minutes, 36.0% 30 to 45 minutes, 16.2% 45 to 60 minutes, 9.9% 60 minutes or more (2005-2009 5-year est.)

MARK (village). Covers a land area of 0.812 square miles and a water area of 0 square miles. Located at 41.26° N. Lat; 89.24° W. Long. Elevation is 689 feet.
Population: 399 (1990); 491 (2000); 485 (2010); 479 (2015 projected); Race: 97.9% White, 0.2% Black, 0.0% Asian, 1.9% Other, 7.0% Hispanic of any race (2010); Density: 597.5 persons per square mile (2010); Average household size: 2.65 (2010); Median age: 40.4 (2010); Males per 100 females: 93.2 (2010); Marriage status: 25.5% never married, 59.8% now married, 5.7% widowed, 9.0% divorced (2005-2009 5-year est.); Foreign born: 0.4% (2005-2009 5-year est.); Ancestry (includes multiple ancestries): 37.3% German, 31.4% Italian, 17.4% Polish, 9.7% English, 6.3% American (2005-2009 5-year est.).
Economy: Single-family building permits issued: 3 (2010); Multi-family building permits issued: 0 (2010); Employment by occupation: 14.9%

management, 18.2% professional, 15.3% services, 13.1% sales, 0.0% farming, 8.4% construction, 30.2% production (2005-2009 5-year est.).
Income: Per capita income: $24,925 (2010); Median household income: $57,176 (2010); Average household income: $65,180 (2010); Percent of households with income of $100,000 or more: 13.8% (2010); Poverty rate: 5.5% (2005-2009 5-year est.).
Taxes: Total city taxes per capita: $64 (2007); City property taxes per capita: $40 (2007).
Education: Percent of population age 25 and over with: High school diploma (including GED) or higher: 86.1% (2010); Bachelor's degree or higher: 11.5% (2010); Master's degree or higher: 1.8% (2010).
Housing: Homeownership rate: 85.1% (2010); Median home value: $132,143 (2010); Median contract rent: $479 per month (2005-2009 5-year est.); Median year structure built: 1956 (2005-2009 5-year est.).
Transportation: Commute to work: 100.0% car, 0.0% public transportation, 0.0% walk, 0.0% work from home (2005-2009 5-year est.); Travel time to work: 23.3% less than 15 minutes, 52.4% 15 to 30 minutes, 14.9% 30 to 45 minutes, 0.0% 45 to 60 minutes, 9.5% 60 minutes or more (2005-2009 5-year est.)

MCNABB (village). Covers a land area of 0.199 square miles and a water area of 0 square miles. Located at 41.17° N. Lat; 89.20° W. Long. Elevation is 686 feet.
Population: 310 (1990); 310 (2000); 307 (2010); 305 (2015 projected); Race: 97.1% White, 2.0% Black, 0.3% Asian, 0.7% Other, 0.3% Hispanic of any race (2010); Density: 1,540.3 persons per square mile (2010); Average household size: 2.54 (2010); Median age: 40.8 (2010); Males per 100 females: 100.7 (2010); Marriage status: 20.5% never married, 73.1% now married, 2.3% widowed, 4.1% divorced (2005-2009 5-year est.); Foreign born: 0.0% (2005-2009 5-year est.); Ancestry (includes multiple ancestries): 59.3% German, 26.9% Irish, 16.2% Italian, 6.7% Norwegian, 5.7% Swedish (2005-2009 5-year est.).
Economy: Single-family building permits issued: 0 (2010); Multi-family building permits issued: 0 (2010); Employment by occupation: 9.4% management, 11.8% professional, 13.4% services, 18.1% sales, 0.0% farming, 13.4% construction, 33.9% production (2005-2009 5-year est.).
Income: Per capita income: $27,744 (2010); Median household income: $62,500 (2010); Average household income: $68,740 (2010); Percent of households with income of $100,000 or more: 15.7% (2010); Poverty rate: 15.5% (2005-2009 5-year est.).
Taxes: Total city taxes per capita: $60 (2007); City property taxes per capita: $57 (2007).
Education: Percent of population age 25 and over with: High school diploma (including GED) or higher: 87.4% (2010); Bachelor's degree or higher: 17.7% (2010); Master's degree or higher: 4.7% (2010).
School District(s)
Putnam County CUSD 535 (PK-12)
    2009-10 Enrollment: 933 . . . . (815) 882-2800
Housing: Homeownership rate: 80.2% (2010); Median home value: $109,559 (2010); Median contract rent: $420 per month (2005-2009 5-year est.); Median year structure built: 1960 (2005-2009 5-year est.).
Transportation: Commute to work: 89.5% car, 0.0% public transportation, 5.6% walk, 0.8% work from home (2005-2009 5-year est.); Travel time to work: 30.9% less than 15 minutes, 32.5% 15 to 30 minutes, 22.0% 30 to 45 minutes, 11.4% 45 to 60 minutes, 3.3% 60 minutes or more (2005-2009 5-year est.)

PUTNAM (unincorporated postal area, zip code 61560). Covers a land area of 33.771 square miles and a water area of 0.505 square miles. Located at 41.19° N. Lat; 89.43° W. Long. Elevation is 518 feet.
Population: 705 (2000); Race: 98.9% White, 0.3% Black, 0.0% Asian, 0.8% Other, 1.6% Hispanic of any race (2000); Density: 20.9 persons per square mile (2000); Age: 15.9% under 18, 19.8% over 64 (2000); Marriage status: 19.6% never married, 71.3% now married, 5.6% widowed, 3.6% divorced (2000); Foreign born: 0.5% (2000); Ancestry (includes multiple ancestries): 36.0% German, 15.6% Irish, 12.4% Polish, 12.0% English, 7.1% Swedish (2000).
Economy: Employment by occupation: 16.0% management, 15.7% professional, 7.1% services, 16.3% sales, 1.3% farming, 15.7% construction, 27.9% production (2000).
Income: Per capita income: $21,515 (2000); Median household income: $46,917 (2000); Poverty rate: 5.0% (2000).
Education: Percent of population age 25 and over with: High school diploma (including GED) or higher: 93.3% (2000); Bachelor's degree or higher: 20.3% (2000).

Housing: Homeownership rate: 90.3% (2000); Median home value: $118,200 (2000); Median contract rent: $275 per month (2000); Median year structure built: 1982 (2000).
Transportation: Commute to work: 88.3% car, 2.0% public transportation, 4.0% walk, 5.7% work from home (2000); Travel time to work: 24.2% less than 15 minutes, 40.9% 15 to 30 minutes, 7.5% 30 to 45 minutes, 12.1% 45 to 60 minutes, 15.3% 60 minutes or more (2000)

STANDARD (village). Covers a land area of 0.565 square miles and a water area of 0 square miles. Located at 41.25° N. Lat; 89.17° W. Long. Elevation is 679 feet.
Population: 260 (1990); 256 (2000); 236 (2010); 226 (2015 projected); Race: 98.3% White, 0.0% Black, 0.0% Asian, 1.7% Other, 4.7% Hispanic of any race (2010); Density: 417.8 persons per square mile (2010); Average household size: 2.51 (2010); Median age: 42.0 (2010); Males per 100 females: 103.4 (2010); Marriage status: 21.3% never married, 57.3% now married, 10.0% widowed, 11.4% divorced (2005-2009 5-year est.); Foreign born: 4.8% (2005-2009 5-year est.); Ancestry (includes multiple ancestries): 42.3% German, 29.0% Italian, 7.7% Irish, 7.3% Danish, 6.0% Swedish (2005-2009 5-year est.).
Economy: Single-family building permits issued: 0 (2010); Multi-family building permits issued: 0 (2010); Employment by occupation: 0.0% management, 16.4% professional, 11.7% services, 25.0% sales, 0.0% farming, 4.7% construction, 42.2% production (2005-2009 5-year est.).
Income: Per capita income: $25,829 (2010); Median household income: $65,714 (2010); Average household income: $65,053 (2010); Percent of households with income of $100,000 or more: 7.4% (2010); Poverty rate: 6.9% (2005-2009 5-year est.).
Taxes: Total city taxes per capita: $79 (2007); City property taxes per capita: $51 (2007).
Education: Percent of population age 25 and over with: High school diploma (including GED) or higher: 84.8% (2010); Bachelor's degree or higher: 13.3% (2010); Master's degree or higher: 5.5% (2010).
Housing: Homeownership rate: 79.8% (2010); Median home value: $112,500 (2010); Median contract rent: $416 per month (2005-2009 5-year est.); Median year structure built: 1948 (2005-2009 5-year est.).
Transportation: Commute to work: 99.2% car, 0.0% public transportation, 0.0% walk, 0.8% work from home (2005-2009 5-year est.); Travel time to work: 25.8% less than 15 minutes, 50.8% 15 to 30 minutes, 16.1% 30 to 45 minutes, 0.0% 45 to 60 minutes, 7.3% 60 minutes or more (2005-2009 5-year est.)

Randolph County

Located in southwestern Illinois; bounded on the west and south by the Mississippi River and the Missouri border; drained by the Kaskaskia River. Covers a land area of 578.42 square miles, a water area of 18.84 square miles, and is located in the Central Time Zone at 38.07° N. Lat., 89.79° W. Long. The county was founded in 1795. County seat is Chester.

Weather Station: Kaskaskia River Nav Lock										Elevation: 379 feet		
	Jan	Feb	Mar	Apr	May	Jun	Jul	Aug	Sep	Oct	Nov	Dec
High	42	47	57	69	79	87	91	90	83	70	57	44
Low	22	25	34	44	54	63	67	65	57	45	35	25
Precip	2.0	2.2	3.3	3.6	5.1	3.8	3.7	3.4	3.5	3.7	3.9	3.3
Snow	1.5	2.1	0.2	0.1	0.0	0.0	0.0	0.0	0.0	0.0	0.4	1.6

High and Low temperatures in degrees Fahrenheit; Precipitation and Snow in inches

Weather Station: Sparta 1 W										Elevation: 535 feet		
	Jan	Feb	Mar	Apr	May	Jun	Jul	Aug	Sep	Oct	Nov	Dec
High	41	46	56	67	76	85	89	88	81	70	56	43
Low	23	27	34	44	54	63	67	65	56	46	36	26
Precip	2.6	2.6	4.0	4.1	5.2	3.8	3.8	3.0	2.9	3.6	4.3	3.0
Snow	3.7	3.8	1.1	0.2	0.0	0.0	0.0	0.0	0.0	tr	0.6	3.1

High and Low temperatures in degrees Fahrenheit; Precipitation and Snow in inches

Population: 34,583 (1990); 33,893 (2000); 32,431 (2010); 31,536 (2015 projected); Race: 88.1% White, 9.4% Black, 0.2% Asian, 2.2% Other, 1.8% Hispanic of any race (2010); Density: 56.1 persons per square mile (2010); Average household size: 2.41 (2010); Median age: 38.1 (2010); Males per 100 females: 115.8 (2010).
Religion: Five largest groups: 18.8% Catholic Church, 18.5% Lutheran Church—Missouri Synod, 7.9% Southern Baptist Convention, 5.5% Evangelical Lutheran Church in America, 4.1% The United Methodist Church (2000).

Economy: Unemployment rate: 8.3% (August 2011); Total civilian labor force: 15,659 (August 2011); Leading industries: 27.7% manufacturing; 21.0% health care and social assistance; 13.6% retail trade (2009); Farms: 833 totaling 252,926 acres (2007); Companies that employ 500 or more persons: 2 (2009); Companies that employ 100 to 499 persons: 14 (2009); Companies that employ less than 100 persons: 665 (2009); Black-owned businesses: n/a (2007); Hispanic-owned businesses: n/a (2007); Asian-owned businesses: n/a (2007); Women-owned businesses: 757 (2007); Retail sales per capita: $12,540 (2010). Single-family building permits issued: 38 (2010); Multi-family building permits issued: 12 (2010).
Income: Per capita income: $21,008 (2010); Median household income: $45,041 (2010); Average household income: $53,693 (2010); Percent of households with income of $100,000 or more: 9.3% (2010); Poverty rate: 13.3% (2009); Bankruptcy rate: 3.15% (2010).
Taxes: Total county taxes per capita: $126 (2007); County property taxes per capita: $125 (2007).
Education: Percent of population age 25 and over with: High school diploma (including GED) or higher: 79.3% (2010); Bachelor's degree or higher: 12.1% (2010); Master's degree or higher: 3.7% (2010).
Housing: Homeownership rate: 77.6% (2010); Median home value: $81,377 (2010); Median contract rent: $373 per month (2005-2009 5-year est.); Median year structure built: 1966 (2005-2009 5-year est.).
Health: Birth rate: 118.4 per 10,000 population (2009); Death rate: 111.1 per 10,000 population (2009); Age-adjusted cancer mortality rate: 187.1 deaths per 100,000 population (2007); Number of physicians: 10.7 per 10,000 population (2008); Hospital beds: 149.9 per 10,000 population (2007); Hospital admissions: 1,172.5 per 10,000 population (2007).
Environment: Air Quality Index: 92.8% good, 7.2% moderate, 0.0% unhealthy for sensitive individuals, 0.0% unhealthy (percent of days in 2008)
Elections: 2008 Presidential election results: 48.6% Obama, 49.6% McCain, 0.9% Nader
National and State Parks: Baldwin Lake State Fish and Wildlife Area; Fort Chartres State Park; Fort Kaskaskia State Park; Modoc Rock Shelter National Historic Site; Randolph County State Conservation Area
Additional Information Contacts
Randolph County Government . . . . (618) 826-5000
    http://www.randolphco.org/gov
Chester Chamber of Commerce . . . . (618) 826-2721
    http://www.chesterill.com/chamber
City of Chester . . . . (618) 826-2326
    http://www.chesterill.com
Red Bud Chamber of Commerce . . . . (618) 282-3505
    http://www.redbudchamber.com
Sparta Area Chamber of Commerce . . . . (618) 317-7222
    http://spartailchamber.com
Steeleville Chamber of Commerce . . . . (618) 965-3134

Randolph County Communities

BALDWIN (village). Covers a land area of 0.669 square miles and a water area of 0 square miles. Located at 38.18° N. Lat; 89.84° W. Long. Elevation is 459 feet.
Population: 426 (1990); 3,627 (2000); 3,420 (2010); 3,329 (2015 projected); Race: 38.3% White, 54.9% Black, 0.2% Asian, 6.7% Other, 7.7% Hispanic of any race (2010); Density: 5,112.3 persons per square mile (2010); Average household size: 2.53 (2010); Median age: 32.0 (2010); Males per 100 females: 575.9 (2010); Marriage status: 21.2% never married, 63.6% now married, 10.0% widowed, 5.3% divorced (2005-2009 5-year est.); Foreign born: 5.7% (2005-2009 5-year est.); Ancestry (includes multiple ancestries): 41.6% German, 16.2% Irish, 16.2% American, 10.0% Other Arab, 1.9% French (2005-2009 5-year est.).
Economy: Single-family building permits issued: 0 (2010); Multi-family building permits issued: 0 (2010); Employment by occupation: 5.9% management, 19.3% professional, 17.6% services, 18.2% sales, 0.0% farming, 13.4% construction, 25.7% production (2005-2009 5-year est.).
Income: Per capita income: $14,549 (2010); Median household income: $40,259 (2010); Average household income: $46,829 (2010); Percent of households with income of $100,000 or more: 7.9% (2010); Poverty rate: 7.4% (2005-2009 5-year est.).
Taxes: Total city taxes per capita: $142 (2007); City property taxes per capita: $51 (2007).
Education: Percent of population age 25 and over with: High school diploma (including GED) or higher: 50.5% (2010); Bachelor's degree or higher: 3.7% (2010); Master's degree or higher: 0.3% (2010).

Housing: Homeownership rate: 84.2% (2010); Median home value: $64,032 (2010); Median contract rent: $400 per month (2005-2009 5-year est.); Median year structure built: 1951 (2005-2009 5-year est.).
Transportation: Commute to work: 97.3% car, 0.0% public transportation, 0.5% walk, 2.2% work from home (2005-2009 5-year est.); Travel time to work: 18.9% less than 15 minutes, 29.4% 15 to 30 minutes, 13.3% 30 to 45 minutes, 27.2% 45 to 60 minutes, 11.1% 60 minutes or more (2005-2009 5-year est.)

CHESTER (city). County seat. Covers a land area of 5.893 square miles and a water area of 0.012 square miles. Located at 37.91° N. Lat; 89.82° W. Long. Elevation is 669 feet.
History: Chester was established in 1819 as a commercial rival for Kaskaskia by a land company from Cincinnati.
Population: 8,185 (1990); 5,185 (2000); 5,030 (2010); 4,913 (2015 projected); Race: 97.1% White, 1.4% Black, 0.2% Asian, 1.4% Other, 0.5% Hispanic of any race (2010); Density: 853.6 persons per square mile (2010); Average household size: 2.31 (2010); Median age: 40.8 (2010); Males per 100 females: 99.5 (2010); Marriage status: 51.7% never married, 30.4% now married, 5.6% widowed, 12.4% divorced (2005-2009 5-year est.); Foreign born: 3.3% (2005-2009 5-year est.); Ancestry (includes multiple ancestries): 20.0% German, 6.2% Irish, 5.5% English, 3.5% French, 3.1% American (2005-2009 5-year est.).
Economy: Single-family building permits issued: 5 (2010); Multi-family building permits issued: 0 (2010); Employment by occupation: 5.9% management, 17.2% professional, 23.7% services, 21.8% sales, 0.6% farming, 10.3% construction, 20.6% production (2005-2009 5-year est.).
Income: Per capita income: $25,182 (2010); Median household income: $47,601 (2010); Average household income: $61,091 (2010); Percent of households with income of $100,000 or more: 12.8% (2010); Poverty rate: 8.9% (2005-2009 5-year est.).
Taxes: Total city taxes per capita: $154 (2007); City property taxes per capita: $92 (2007).
Education: Percent of population age 25 and over with: High school diploma (including GED) or higher: 82.1% (2010); Bachelor's degree or higher: 15.8% (2010); Master's degree or higher: 4.6% (2010).
School District(s)
Chester CUSD 139 (PK-12)
    2009-10 Enrollment: 954 . . . . (618) 826-4509
Housing: Homeownership rate: 74.7% (2010); Median home value: $77,617 (2010); Median contract rent: $351 per month (2005-2009 5-year est.); Median year structure built: 1955 (2005-2009 5-year est.).
Hospitals: Memorial Hospital (25 beds)
Safety: Violent crime rate: 37.8 per 10,000 population; Property crime rate: 134.2 per 10,000 population (2010).
Newspapers: Randolph Herald Tribune (Local news; Circulation 3,500)
Transportation: Commute to work: 94.2% car, 2.7% public transportation, 2.5% walk, 0.6% work from home (2005-2009 5-year est.); Travel time to work: 69.7% less than 15 minutes, 16.6% 15 to 30 minutes, 6.7% 30 to 45 minutes, 3.2% 45 to 60 minutes, 3.8% 60 minutes or more (2005-2009 5-year est.)
Additional Information Contacts
Chester Chamber of Commerce . . . . (618) 826-2721
    http://www.chesterill.com/chamber
City of Chester . . . . (618) 826-2326
    http://www.chesterill.com

COULTERVILLE (village). Covers a land area of 0.566 square miles and a water area of 0 square miles. Located at 38.18° N. Lat; 89.60° W. Long. Elevation is 551 feet.
History: Incorporated 1874.
Population: 986 (1990); 1,230 (2000); 1,040 (2010); 957 (2015 projected); Race: 96.0% White, 1.1% Black, 0.3% Asian, 2.7% Other, 0.2% Hispanic of any race (2010); Density: 1,838.5 persons per square mile (2010); Average household size: 2.39 (2010); Median age: 37.4 (2010); Males per 100 females: 93.3 (2010); Marriage status: 28.9% never married, 49.7% now married, 8.2% widowed, 13.2% divorced (2005-2009 5-year est.); Foreign born: 0.1% (2005-2009 5-year est.); Ancestry (includes multiple ancestries): 35.9% German, 26.4% Irish, 12.4% English, 8.3% French, 4.4% Scotch-Irish (2005-2009 5-year est.).
Economy: Employment by occupation: 4.2% management, 17.7% professional, 22.6% services, 21.9% sales, 1.2% farming, 9.9% construction, 22.4% production (2005-2009 5-year est.).
Income: Per capita income: $17,755 (2010); Median household income: $33,358 (2010); Average household income: $42,953 (2010); Percent of

households with income of $100,000 or more: 5.7% (2010); Poverty rate: 22.8% (2005-2009 5-year est.).
Taxes: Total city taxes per capita: $145 (2007); City property taxes per capita: $59 (2007).
Education: Percent of population age 25 and over with: High school diploma (including GED) or higher: 84.4% (2010); Bachelor's degree or higher: 8.2% (2010); Master's degree or higher: 2.9% (2010).
School District(s)
Coulterville USD 1 (KG-12)
   2009-10 Enrollment: 219 . . . . (618) 758-2881
Housing: Homeownership rate: 79.1% (2010); Median home value: $53,077 (2010); Median contract rent: $333 per month (2005-2009 5-year est.); Median year structure built: 1958 (2005-2009 5-year est.).
Transportation: Commute to work: 93.3% car, 0.0% public transportation, 5.0% walk, 1.7% work from home (2005-2009 5-year est.); Travel time to work: 31.7% less than 15 minutes, 23.0% 15 to 30 minutes, 15.5% 30 to 45 minutes, 5.6% 45 to 60 minutes, 24.2% 60 minutes or more (2005-2009 5-year est.)

ELLIS GROVE (village). Aka Ellisgrove. Covers a land area of 0.465 square miles and a water area of 0 square miles. Located at 38.01° N. Lat; 89.90° W. Long. Elevation is 548 feet.

History: Fort Kaskaskia State Historical Site nearby.
Population: 372 (1990); 381 (2000); 371 (2010); 361 (2015 projected); Race: 98.9% White, 0.0% Black, 0.0% Asian, 1.1% Other, 0.3% Hispanic of any race (2010); Density: 797.9 persons per square mile (2010); Average household size: 2.63 (2010); Median age: 35.8 (2010); Males per 100 females: 93.2 (2010); Marriage status: 28.9% never married, 52.3% now married, 6.5% widowed, 12.3% divorced (2005-2009 5-year est.); Foreign born: 0.0% (2005-2009 5-year est.); Ancestry (includes multiple ancestries): 46.0% German, 21.2% Irish, 10.6% French, 10.0% American, 5.6% English (2005-2009 5-year est.).
Economy: Employment by occupation: 1.9% management, 3.7% professional, 34.0% services, 24.7% sales, 1.9% farming, 9.9% construction, 24.1% production (2005-2009 5-year est.).
Income: Per capita income: $23,864 (2010); Median household income: $57,440 (2010); Average household income: $63,954 (2010); Percent of households with income of $100,000 or more: 13.5% (2010); Poverty rate: 14.5% (2005-2009 5-year est.).
Taxes: Total city taxes per capita: $101 (2007); City property taxes per capita: $35 (2007).
Education: Percent of population age 25 and over with: High school diploma (including GED) or higher: 82.8% (2010); Bachelor's degree or higher: 16.3% (2010); Master's degree or higher: 10.3% (2010).
Housing: Homeownership rate: 83.7% (2010); Median home value: $80,000 (2010); Median contract rent: $452 per month (2005-2009 5-year est.); Median year structure built: 1975 (2005-2009 5-year est.).
Transportation: Commute to work: 95.7% car, 0.0% public transportation, 1.9% walk, 1.9% work from home (2005-2009 5-year est.); Travel time to work: 24.5% less than 15 minutes, 54.1% 15 to 30 minutes, 13.2% 30 to 45 minutes, 3.8% 45 to 60 minutes, 4.4% 60 minutes or more (2005-2009 5-year est.)

EVANSVILLE (village). Covers a land area of 0.741 square miles and a water area of 0.018 square miles. Located at 38.09° N. Lat; 89.93° W. Long. Elevation is 390 feet.

Population: 861 (1990); 724 (2000); 650 (2010); 609 (2015 projected); Race: 98.8% White, 0.5% Black, 0.2% Asian, 0.6% Other, 0.9% Hispanic of any race (2010); Density: 877.0 persons per square mile (2010); Average household size: 2.34 (2010); Median age: 38.9 (2010); Males per 100 females: 94.6 (2010); Marriage status: 20.5% never married, 53.8% now married, 10.8% widowed, 14.9% divorced (2005-2009 5-year est.); Foreign born: 0.5% (2005-2009 5-year est.); Ancestry (includes multiple ancestries): 40.1% German, 14.3% Irish, 10.6% French, 10.6% American, 6.6% Italian (2005-2009 5-year est.).
Economy: Single-family building permits issued: 3 (2010); Multi-family building permits issued: 0 (2010); Employment by occupation: 7.4% management, 16.7% professional, 16.0% services, 16.0% sales, 1.2% farming, 10.5% construction, 32.3% production (2005-2009 5-year est.).
Income: Per capita income: $21,785 (2010); Median household income: $42,105 (2010); Average household income: $51,195 (2010); Percent of households with income of $100,000 or more: 6.2% (2010); Poverty rate: 8.5% (2005-2009 5-year est.).
Taxes: Total city taxes per capita: $153 (2007); City property taxes per capita: $69 (2007).

Education: Percent of population age 25 and over with: High school diploma (including GED) or higher: 82.5% (2010); Bachelor's degree or higher: 7.2% (2010); Master's degree or higher: 3.3% (2010).
School District(s)
Perandoe Spec Educ District (KG-12)
   2009-10 Enrollment: n/a . . . . (618) 282-6251
Sparta CUSD 140 (PK-12)
   2009-10 Enrollment: 1,398 . . . . (618) 443-5331
Housing: Homeownership rate: 78.5% (2010); Median home value: $69,074 (2010); Median contract rent: $408 per month (2005-2009 5-year est.); Median year structure built: 1954 (2005-2009 5-year est.).
Transportation: Commute to work: 91.6% car, 1.2% public transportation, 3.2% walk, 0.0% work from home (2005-2009 5-year est.); Travel time to work: 26.5% less than 15 minutes, 23.7% 15 to 30 minutes, 20.5% 30 to 45 minutes, 13.3% 45 to 60 minutes, 16.1% 60 minutes or more (2005-2009 5-year est.)

KASKASKIA (village). Covers a land area of 0.108 square miles and a water area of 0 square miles. Located at 37.92° N. Lat; 89.91° W. Long.

History: Second-smallest incorporated community in Illinois.
Population: n/a (1990); n/a (2000); 14 (2010); n/a (2015 projected); Race: 71.4% White, 0.0% Black, 0.0% Asian, 28.6% Other, 28.6% Hispanic of any race (2010); Density: 129.6 persons per square mile (2010); Average household size: 3.50 (2010); Median age: 38.5 (2010); Males per 100 females: 250.0 (2010); Marriage status: n/a never married, n/a now married, n/a widowed, n/a divorced (2005-2009 5-year est.); Foreign born: n/a (2005-2009 5-year est.); Ancestry (includes multiple ancestries): n/a (2005-2009 5-year est.).
Economy: Employment by occupation: n/a management, n/a professional, n/a services, n/a sales, n/a farming, n/a construction, n/a production (2005-2009 5-year est.).
Income: Per capita income: n/a (2010); Median household income: n/a (2010); Average household income: n/a (2010); Percent of households with income of $100,000 or more: n/a (2010); Poverty rate: n/a (2005-2009 5-year est.).
Education: Percent of population age 25 and over with: High school diploma (including GED) or higher: n/a (2010); Bachelor's degree or higher: n/a (2010); Master's degree or higher: n/a (2010).
Housing: Homeownership rate: n/a (2010); Median home value: n/a (2010); Median contract rent: n/a per month (2005-2009 5-year est.); Median year structure built: n/a (2005-2009 5-year est.).
Transportation: Commute to work: n/a car, n/a public transportation, n/a walk, n/a work from home (2005-2009 5-year est.); Travel time to work: n/a less than 15 minutes, n/a 15 to 30 minutes, n/a 30 to 45 minutes, n/a 45 to 60 minutes, n/a 60 minutes or more (2005-2009 5-year est.)

MODOC (unincorporated postal area, zip code 62261). Covers a land area of 31.259 square miles and a water area of 0.032 square miles. Located at 37.98° N. Lat; 90.00° W. Long. Elevation is 397 feet.

Population: 221 (2000); Race: 100.0% White, 0.0% Black, 0.0% Asian, 0.0% Other, 0.0% Hispanic of any race (2000); Density: 7.1 persons per square mile (2000); Age: 32.8% under 18, 11.2% over 64 (2000); Marriage status: 20.8% never married, 58.9% now married, 7.1% widowed, 13.1% divorced (2000); Foreign born: 0.0% (2000); Ancestry (includes multiple ancestries): 37.6% German, 24.0% American, 11.6% French, 3.6% Scottish (2000).
Economy: Employment by occupation: 7.3% management, 16.5% professional, 14.7% services, 14.7% sales, 0.0% farming, 14.7% construction, 32.1% production (2000).
Income: Per capita income: $15,081 (2000); Median household income: $34,286 (2000); Poverty rate: 2.9% (2000).
Education: Percent of population age 25 and over with: High school diploma (including GED) or higher: 77.6% (2000); Bachelor's degree or higher: 12.2% (2000).
Housing: Homeownership rate: 91.6% (2000); Median home value: $43,300 (2000); Median contract rent: $2,000+ per month (2000); Median year structure built: 1967 (2000).
Transportation: Commute to work: 93.6% car, 0.0% public transportation, 0.0% walk, 6.4% work from home (2000); Travel time to work: 25.5% less than 15 minutes, 30.4% 15 to 30 minutes, 31.4% 30 to 45 minutes, 0.0% 45 to 60 minutes, 12.7% 60 minutes or more (2000)

PERCY (village). Covers a land area of 0.880 square miles and a water area of 0 square miles. Located at 38.01° N. Lat; 89.61° W. Long. Elevation is 472 feet.

Population: 966 (1990); 942 (2000); 813 (2010); 753 (2015 projected); Race: 99.3% White, 0.1% Black, 0.0% Asian, 0.6% Other, 1.5% Hispanic of any race (2010); Density: 924.0 persons per square mile (2010); Average household size: 2.31 (2010); Median age: 38.8 (2010); Males per 100 females: 93.1 (2010); Marriage status: 26.6% never married, 45.5% now married, 10.2% widowed, 17.8% divorced (2005-2009 5-year est.); Foreign born: 1.4% (2005-2009 5-year est.); Ancestry (includes multiple ancestries): 34.6% German, 16.6% English, 12.6% Irish, 8.9% Scotch-Irish, 6.5% American (2005-2009 5-year est.).

Economy: Employment by occupation: 1.9% management, 13.8% professional, 16.4% services, 19.9% sales, 0.0% farming, 7.4% construction, 40.5% production (2005-2009 5-year est.).

Income: Per capita income: $19,161 (2010); Median household income: $36,438 (2010); Average household income: $44,109 (2010); Percent of households with income of $100,000 or more: 4.6% (2010); Poverty rate: 35.4% (2005-2009 5-year est.).

Taxes: Total city taxes per capita: $42 (2007); City property taxes per capita: $36 (2007).

Education: Percent of population age 25 and over with: High school diploma (including GED) or higher: 80.3% (2010); Bachelor's degree or higher: 10.0% (2010); Master's degree or higher: 1.6% (2010).

Housing: Homeownership rate: 75.0% (2010); Median home value: $60,204 (2010); Median contract rent: $347 per month (2005-2009 5-year est.); Median year structure built: 1964 (2005-2009 5-year est.).

Newspapers: County Journal (Local news; Circulation 7,100)

Transportation: Commute to work: 93.4% car, 1.3% public transportation, 0.0% walk, 3.3% work from home (2005-2009 5-year est.); Travel time to work: 47.4% less than 15 minutes, 22.7% 15 to 30 minutes, 20.6% 30 to 45 minutes, 2.1% 45 to 60 minutes, 7.2% 60 minutes or more (2005-2009 5-year est.)

PRAIRIE DU ROCHER (village). Aka Prairie Du Rocher. Covers a land area of 0.570 square miles and a water area of 0 square miles. Located at 38.08° N. Lat; 90.09° W. Long. Elevation is 394 feet.

History: Prairie du Rocher was founded in the early 1700's by people brought to the area by John Law, a Scotch promoter who organized a company and was granted a charter for the Louisiana Territory.

Population: 540 (1990); 613 (2000); 597 (2010); 591 (2015 projected); Race: 98.3% White, 0.0% Black, 0.0% Asian, 1.7% Other, 0.2% Hispanic of any race (2010); Density: 1,048.1 persons per square mile (2010); Average household size: 2.54 (2010); Median age: 33.5 (2010); Males per 100 females: 88.9 (2010); Marriage status: 21.9% never married, 60.1% now married, 7.8% widowed, 10.2% divorced (2005-2009 5-year est.); Foreign born: 0.0% (2005-2009 5-year est.); Ancestry (includes multiple ancestries): 56.1% German, 22.5% French, 12.4% Irish, 9.2% American, 8.9% English (2005-2009 5-year est.).

Economy: Single-family building permits issued: 0 (2010); Multi-family building permits issued: 0 (2010); Employment by occupation: 10.3% management, 11.4% professional, 17.1% services, 30.4% sales, 0.0% farming, 8.0% construction, 22.8% production (2005-2009 5-year est.).

Income: Per capita income: $22,075 (2010); Median household income: $50,605 (2010); Average household income: $56,617 (2010); Percent of households with income of $100,000 or more: 7.7% (2010); Poverty rate: 8.7% (2005-2009 5-year est.).

Taxes: Total city taxes per capita: $108 (2007); City property taxes per capita: $31 (2007).

Education: Percent of population age 25 and over with: High school diploma (including GED) or higher: 80.0% (2010); Bachelor's degree or higher: 12.0% (2010); Master's degree or higher: 3.7% (2010).

School District(s)

Prairie Du Rocher CCSD 134 (PK-08)
    2009-10 Enrollment: 193 . . . . (618) 284-3530

Housing: Homeownership rate: 73.6% (2010); Median home value: $80,294 (2010); Median contract rent: $350 per month (2005-2009 5-year est.); Median year structure built: 1960 (2005-2009 5-year est.).

Safety: Violent crime rate: 0.0 per 10,000 population; Property crime rate: 0.0 per 10,000 population (2010).

Transportation: Commute to work: 92.2% car, 0.0% public transportation, 4.9% walk, 2.9% work from home (2005-2009 5-year est.); Travel time to work: 18.1% less than 15 minutes, 29.4% 15 to 30 minutes, 16.8% 30 to 45 minutes, 16.8% 45 to 60 minutes, 18.9% 60 minutes or more (2005-2009 5-year est.)

RED BUD (city). Covers a land area of 2.104 square miles and a water area of 0.007 square miles. Located at 38.21° N. Lat; 89.99° W. Long. Elevation is 472 feet.

History: Red Bud was named for the red-bud trees that once covered the town site.

Population: 3,329 (1990); 3,422 (2000); 3,604 (2010); 3,624 (2015 projected); Race: 98.6% White, 0.0% Black, 0.2% Asian, 1.2% Other, 0.8% Hispanic of any race (2010); Density: 1,712.8 persons per square mile (2010); Average household size: 2.43 (2010); Median age: 40.2 (2010); Males per 100 females: 91.1 (2010); Marriage status: 20.8% never married, 57.4% now married, 9.4% widowed, 12.4% divorced (2005-2009 5-year est.); Foreign born: 0.6% (2005-2009 5-year est.); Ancestry (includes multiple ancestries): 58.4% German, 15.0% Irish, 11.2% French, 8.7% English, 6.1% American (2005-2009 5-year est.).

Economy: Single-family building permits issued: 6 (2010); Multi-family building permits issued: 0 (2010); Employment by occupation: 11.2% management, 17.9% professional, 18.6% services, 26.5% sales, 0.6% farming, 8.1% construction, 17.1% production (2005-2009 5-year est.).

Income: Per capita income: $23,145 (2010); Median household income: $50,584 (2010); Average household income: $57,025 (2010); Percent of households with income of $100,000 or more: 10.6% (2010); Poverty rate: 16.1% (2005-2009 5-year est.).

Taxes: Total city taxes per capita: $164 (2007); City property taxes per capita: $135 (2007).

Education: Percent of population age 25 and over with: High school diploma (including GED) or higher: 84.5% (2010); Bachelor's degree or higher: 17.1% (2010); Master's degree or higher: 4.1% (2010).

School District(s)

Beck Area Career Center (09-12)
    2009-10 Enrollment: n/a . . . . (618) 473-2222
Monroe/Randolph Roe (06-12)
    2009-10 Enrollment: n/a . . . . (618) 939-5650
Red Bud CUSD 132 (PK-12)
    2009-10 Enrollment: 1,067 . . . . (618) 282-3507

Vocational/Technical School(s)

Beck Area Career Center-Red Bud (Public)
    Fall 2009 Enrollment: 97 . . . . (618) 473-2222
    2010-11 Tuition: $11,950

Housing: Homeownership rate: 75.6% (2010); Median home value: $121,922 (2010); Median contract rent: $494 per month (2005-2009 5-year est.); Median year structure built: 1968 (2005-2009 5-year est.).

Hospitals: Red Bud Regional Hospital (202 beds)

Safety: Violent crime rate: 75.0 per 10,000 population; Property crime rate: 105.6 per 10,000 population (2010).

Newspapers: North County News (Local news; Circulation 4,000)

Transportation: Commute to work: 90.6% car, 0.8% public transportation, 3.4% walk, 3.4% work from home (2005-2009 5-year est.); Travel time to work: 41.1% less than 15 minutes, 18.4% 15 to 30 minutes, 19.0% 30 to 45 minutes, 11.3% 45 to 60 minutes, 10.2% 60 minutes or more (2005-2009 5-year est.)

Additional Information Contacts

Red Bud Chamber of Commerce. . . . . (618) 282-3505
    http://www.redbudchamber.com

ROCKWOOD (village). Covers a land area of 0.211 square miles and a water area of 0 square miles. Located at 37.83° N. Lat; 89.69° W. Long. Elevation is 381 feet.

History: Early settlers in Rockwood provided river steamers with wood for fuel, and built flatboats for transporting cargo.

Population: 55 (1990); 41 (2000); 41 (2010); 41 (2015 projected); Race: 100.0% White, 0.0% Black, 0.0% Asian, 0.0% Other, 0.0% Hispanic of any race (2010); Density: 193.9 persons per square mile (2010); Average household size: 2.56 (2010); Median age: 40.0 (2010); Males per 100 females: 95.2 (2010); Marriage status: 30.6% never married, 22.4% now married, 34.7% widowed, 12.2% divorced (2005-2009 5-year est.); Foreign born: 0.0% (2005-2009 5-year est.); Ancestry (includes multiple ancestries): 40.8% German, 32.7% Irish, 18.4% Dutch, 8.2% Polish, 4.1% French (2005-2009 5-year est.).

Economy: Employment by occupation: 6.7% management, 0.0% professional, 0.0% services, 53.3% sales, 0.0% farming, 26.7% construction, 13.3% production (2005-2009 5-year est.).

Income: Per capita income: $21,380 (2010); Median household income: $55,000 (2010); Average household income: $57,031 (2010); Percent of

households with income of $100,000 or more: 6.3% (2010); Poverty rate: 53.1% (2005-2009 5-year est.).
Taxes: Total city taxes per capita: $50 (2007); City property taxes per capita: $50 (2007).
Education: Percent of population age 25 and over with: High school diploma (including GED) or higher: 88.0% (2010); Bachelor's degree or higher: 20.0% (2010); Master's degree or higher: 4.0% (2010).
Housing: Homeownership rate: 93.8% (2010); Median home value: $95,000 (2010); Median contract rent: n/a per month (2005-2009 5-year est.); Median year structure built: 1966 (2005-2009 5-year est.).
Transportation: Commute to work: 93.3% car, 0.0% public transportation, 0.0% walk, 0.0% work from home (2005-2009 5-year est.); Travel time to work: 0.0% less than 15 minutes, 80.0% 15 to 30 minutes, 0.0% 30 to 45 minutes, 20.0% 45 to 60 minutes, 0.0% 60 minutes or more (2005-2009 5-year est.)

RUMA (village). Covers a land area of 0.410 square miles and a water area of 0 square miles. Located at 38.13° N. Lat; 89.99° W. Long. Elevation is 443 feet.
Population: 272 (1990); 260 (2000); 274 (2010); 276 (2015 projected); Race: 98.2% White, 0.0% Black, 0.4% Asian, 1.5% Other, 0.0% Hispanic of any race (2010); Density: 668.1 persons per square mile (2010); Average household size: 2.48 (2010); Median age: 43.5 (2010); Males per 100 females: 97.1 (2010); Marriage status: 25.7% never married, 60.0% now married, 7.8% widowed, 6.5% divorced (2005-2009 5-year est.); Foreign born: 0.4% (2005-2009 5-year est.); Ancestry (includes multiple ancestries): 68.3% German, 32.7% French, 9.7% English, 6.5% Irish, 5.0% American (2005-2009 5-year est.).
Economy: Single-family building permits issued: 1 (2010); Multi-family building permits issued: 0 (2010); Employment by occupation: 9.8% management, 14.7% professional, 6.3% services, 44.1% sales, 0.0% farming, 4.9% construction, 20.3% production (2005-2009 5-year est.).
Income: Per capita income: $22,534 (2010); Median household income: $49,625 (2010); Average household income: $58,452 (2010); Percent of households with income of $100,000 or more: 14.3% (2010); Poverty rate: 5.4% (2005-2009 5-year est.).
Taxes: Total city taxes per capita: $112 (2007); City property taxes per capita: $35 (2007).
Education: Percent of population age 25 and over with: High school diploma (including GED) or higher: 82.2% (2010); Bachelor's degree or higher: 11.2% (2010); Master's degree or higher: 5.1% (2010).
School District(s)
Monroe/Randolph Roe (06-12)
    2009-10 Enrollment: n/a . . . . (618) 939-5650
Housing: Homeownership rate: 81.9% (2010); Median home value: $110,417 (2010); Median contract rent: $617 per month (2005-2009 5-year est.); Median year structure built: 1989 (2005-2009 5-year est.).
Safety: Violent crime rate: 0.0 per 10,000 population; Property crime rate: 132.5 per 10,000 population (2010).
Transportation: Commute to work: 84.4% car, 0.0% public transportation, 9.2% walk, 5.0% work from home (2005-2009 5-year est.); Travel time to work: 40.3% less than 15 minutes, 5.2% 15 to 30 minutes, 25.4% 30 to 45 minutes, 15.7% 45 to 60 minutes, 13.4% 60 minutes or more (2005-2009 5-year est.)

SPARTA (city). Covers a land area of 9.033 square miles and a water area of 0.150 square miles. Located at 38.12° N. Lat; 89.70° W. Long. Elevation is 528 feet.
History: Incorporated 1847.
Population: 4,942 (1990); 4,486 (2000); 3,955 (2010); 3,698 (2015 projected); Race: 83.1% White, 13.0% Black, 0.5% Asian, 3.5% Other, 1.8% Hispanic of any race (2010); Density: 437.8 persons per square mile (2010); Average household size: 2.36 (2010); Median age: 39.2 (2010); Males per 100 females: 85.2 (2010); Marriage status: 22.9% never married, 54.4% now married, 10.3% widowed, 12.4% divorced (2005-2009 5-year est.); Foreign born: 1.1% (2005-2009 5-year est.); Ancestry (includes multiple ancestries): 34.8% German, 12.3% English, 12.1% Irish, 5.9% Italian, 4.2% French (2005-2009 5-year est.).
Economy: Single-family building permits issued: 0 (2010); Multi-family building permits issued: 12 (2010); Employment by occupation: 11.8% management, 17.0% professional, 21.1% services, 14.7% sales, 0.0% farming, 8.1% construction, 27.3% production (2005-2009 5-year est.).
Income: Per capita income: $18,811 (2010); Median household income: $38,177 (2010); Average household income: $44,658 (2010); Percent of

households with income of $100,000 or more: 6.4% (2010); Poverty rate: 19.2% (2005-2009 5-year est.).
Taxes: Total city taxes per capita: $327 (2007); City property taxes per capita: $207 (2007).
Education: Percent of population age 25 and over with: High school diploma (including GED) or higher: 87.7% (2010); Bachelor's degree or higher: 15.9% (2010); Master's degree or higher: 6.0% (2010).
School District(s)
Sparta CUSD 140 (PK-12)
    2009-10 Enrollment: 1,398 . . . . (618) 443-5331
Housing: Homeownership rate: 69.4% (2010); Median home value: $64,977 (2010); Median contract rent: $344 per month (2005-2009 5-year est.); Median year structure built: 1962 (2005-2009 5-year est.).
Hospitals: Sparta Community Hospital (39 beds)
Safety: Violent crime rate: 23.5 per 10,000 population; Property crime rate: 233.1 per 10,000 population (2010).
Newspapers: Sparta News-Plaindealer (Community news; Circulation 5,000)
Transportation: Commute to work: 97.0% car, 0.0% public transportation, 1.8% walk, 0.8% work from home (2005-2009 5-year est.); Travel time to work: 55.2% less than 15 minutes, 21.0% 15 to 30 minutes, 5.4% 30 to 45 minutes, 6.2% 45 to 60 minutes, 12.1% 60 minutes or more (2005-2009 5-year est.)
Additional Information Contacts
Sparta Area Chamber of Commerce . . . . (618) 317-7222
    http://spartailchamber.com

STEELEVILLE (village). Covers a land area of 1.304 square miles and a water area of 0.008 square miles. Located at 38.00° N. Lat; 89.65° W. Long. Elevation is 413 feet.
History: Incorporated 1851.
Population: 2,113 (1990); 2,077 (2000); 1,969 (2010); 1,891 (2015 projected); Race: 98.3% White, 0.1% Black, 0.5% Asian, 1.1% Other, 1.0% Hispanic of any race (2010); Density: 1,510.2 persons per square mile (2010); Average household size: 2.26 (2010); Median age: 42.1 (2010); Males per 100 females: 89.1 (2010); Marriage status: 14.9% never married, 58.6% now married, 12.0% widowed, 14.6% divorced (2005-2009 5-year est.); Foreign born: 0.1% (2005-2009 5-year est.); Ancestry (includes multiple ancestries): 56.9% German, 8.4% French, 8.1% Irish, 7.5% English, 5.8% American (2005-2009 5-year est.).
Economy: Single-family building permits issued: 1 (2010); Multi-family building permits issued: 0 (2010); Employment by occupation: 9.4% management, 11.2% professional, 17.3% services, 27.0% sales, 0.0% farming, 15.2% construction, 19.9% production (2005-2009 5-year est.).
Income: Per capita income: $22,529 (2010); Median household income: $41,879 (2010); Average household income: $51,480 (2010); Percent of households with income of $100,000 or more: 9.7% (2010); Poverty rate: 8.8% (2005-2009 5-year est.).
Taxes: Total city taxes per capita: $302 (2007); City property taxes per capita: $142 (2007).
Education: Percent of population age 25 and over with: High school diploma (including GED) or higher: 83.5% (2010); Bachelor's degree or higher: 12.3% (2010); Master's degree or higher: 2.6% (2010).
School District(s)
Steeleville CUSD 138 (PK-12)
    2009-10 Enrollment: 444 . . . . (618) 965-3432
Housing: Homeownership rate: 77.3% (2010); Median home value: $86,364 (2010); Median contract rent: $373 per month (2005-2009 5-year est.); Median year structure built: 1960 (2005-2009 5-year est.).
Newspapers: Steeleville Ledger (Local news; Circulation 1,350)
Transportation: Commute to work: 95.5% car, 0.0% public transportation, 2.8% walk, 1.2% work from home (2005-2009 5-year est.); Travel time to work: 43.1% less than 15 minutes, 26.9% 15 to 30 minutes, 8.5% 30 to 45 minutes, 9.8% 45 to 60 minutes, 11.6% 60 minutes or more (2005-2009 5-year est.)
Additional Information Contacts
Steeleville Chamber of Commerce . . . . (618) 965-3134

TILDEN (village). Covers a land area of 0.965 square miles and a water area of 0.010 square miles. Located at 38.21° N. Lat; 89.68° W. Long. Elevation is 525 feet.
Population: 919 (1990); 922 (2000); 765 (2010); 699 (2015 projected); Race: 98.8% White, 0.0% Black, 0.0% Asian, 1.2% Other, 2.7% Hispanic of any race (2010); Density: 792.5 persons per square mile (2010); Average household size: 2.46 (2010); Median age: 35.0 (2010); Males per

100 females: 98.2 (2010); Marriage status: 22.7% never married, 60.7% now married, 9.3% widowed, 7.3% divorced (2005-2009 5-year est.); Foreign born: 0.0% (2005-2009 5-year est.); Ancestry (includes multiple ancestries): 35.4% German, 23.7% Irish, 13.1% English, 10.7% American, 9.7% French (2005-2009 5-year est.).

Economy: Employment by occupation: 10.9% management, 9.1% professional, 20.0% services, 18.1% sales, 1.1% farming, 15.5% construction, 25.3% production (2005-2009 5-year est.).

Income: Per capita income: $19,287 (2010); Median household income: $42,383 (2010); Average household income: $47,420 (2010); Percent of households with income of $100,000 or more: 4.5% (2010); Poverty rate: 27.2% (2005-2009 5-year est.).

Taxes: Total city taxes per capita: $103 (2007); City property taxes per capita: $51 (2007).

Education: Percent of population age 25 and over with: High school diploma (including GED) or higher: 81.3% (2010); Bachelor's degree or higher: 6.2% (2010); Master's degree or higher: 2.2% (2010).

School District(s)

Sparta CUSD 140 (PK-12)

    2009-10 Enrollment: 1,398 . . . . (618) 443-5331

Housing: Homeownership rate: 71.1% (2010); Median home value: $46,833 (2010); Median contract rent: $321 per month (2005-2009 5-year est.); Median year structure built: 1974 (2005-2009 5-year est.).

Transportation: Commute to work: 97.7% car, 0.0% public transportation, 2.3% walk, 0.0% work from home (2005-2009 5-year est.); Travel time to work: 33.7% less than 15 minutes, 22.5% 15 to 30 minutes, 9.7% 30 to 45 minutes, 15.1% 45 to 60 minutes, 19.0% 60 minutes or more (2005-2009 5-year est.)

WALSH (unincorporated postal area, zip code 62297). Covers a land area of 22.664 square miles and a water area of 0.064 square miles. Located at 38.05° N. Lat; 89.80° W. Long. Elevation is 479 feet.

Population: 411 (2000); Race: 100.0% White, 0.0% Black, 0.0% Asian, 0.0% Other, 0.0% Hispanic of any race (2000); Density: 18.1 persons per square mile (2000); Age: 21.0% under 18, 20.5% over 64 (2000); Marriage status: 18.8% never married, 76.1% now married, 5.2% widowed, 0.0% divorced (2000); Foreign born: 0.0% (2000); Ancestry (includes multiple ancestries): 51.7% German, 13.8% Irish, 8.8% Italian, 7.5% American, 7.0% Scotch-Irish (2000).

Economy: Employment by occupation: 2.5% management, 8.7% professional, 10.6% services, 23.0% sales, 0.0% farming, 20.5% construction, 34.8% production (2000).

Income: Per capita income: $17,737 (2000); Median household income: $50,197 (2000); Poverty rate: 2.8% (2000).

Education: Percent of population age 25 and over with: High school diploma (including GED) or higher: 77.8% (2000); Bachelor's degree or higher: 6.6% (2000).

Housing: Homeownership rate: 96.2% (2000); Median home value: $68,600 (2000); Median contract rent: n/a per month (2000); Median year structure built: 1947 (2000).

Transportation: Commute to work: 94.4% car, 0.0% public transportation, 5.6% walk, 0.0% work from home (2000); Travel time to work: 8.1% less than 15 minutes, 47.8% 15 to 30 minutes, 21.1% 30 to 45 minutes, 4.3% 45 to 60 minutes, 18.6% 60 minutes or more (2000)

Richland County

Located in southeastern Illinois; bounded partly on the west by the Little Wabash River; drained by the Fox River and Bonpas Creek. Covers a land area of 360.14 square miles, a water area of 1.87 square miles, and is located in the Central Time Zone at 38.72° N. Lat., 88.09° W. Long. The county was founded in 1841. County seat is Olney.

Weather Station: Olney 2 S										Elevation: 479 feet		
	Jan	Feb	Mar	Apr	May	Jun	Jul	Aug	Sep	Oct	Nov	Dec
High	39	44	54	66	76	85	88	87	81	69	55	42
Low	22	26	34	44	54	63	66	65	57	45	36	26
Precip	3.2	2.7	4.4	4.4	5.6	4.1	4.2	3.3	3.2	4.0	4.5	3.9
Snow	4.3	3.0	1.4	tr	0.0	0.0	0.0	0.0	0.0	tr	0.5	3.7

High and Low temperatures in degrees Fahrenheit; Precipitation and Snow in inches

Population: 16,545 (1990); 16,149 (2000); 15,389 (2010); 14,859 (2015 projected); Race: 97.2% White, 0.8% Black, 0.6% Asian, 1.4% Other, 1.0% Hispanic of any race (2010); Density: 42.7 persons per square mile (2010); Average household size: 2.35 (2010); Median age: 41.1 (2010); Males per 100 females: 92.6 (2010).

Religion: Five largest groups: 14.8% Catholic Church, 13.6% Christian Churches and Churches of Christ, 10.1% The United Methodist Church, 4.7% Southern Baptist Convention, 3.9% Evangelical Lutheran Church in America (2000).

Economy: Unemployment rate: 9.3% (August 2011); Total civilian labor force: 7,222 (August 2011); Leading industries: 19.4% transportation & warehousing; 18.4% health care and social assistance; 13.9% retail trade (2009); Farms: 579 totaling 202,860 acres (2007); Companies that employ 500 or more persons: 1 (2009); Companies that employ 100 to 499 persons: 4 (2009); Companies that employ less than 100 persons: 467 (2009); Black-owned businesses: n/a (2007); Hispanic-owned businesses: n/a (2007); Asian-owned businesses: n/a (2007); Women-owned businesses: 320 (2007); Retail sales per capita: $11,868 (2010). Single-family building permits issued: 10 (2010); Multi-family building permits issued: 0 (2010).

Income: Per capita income: $20,272 (2010); Median household income: $37,898 (2010); Average household income: $48,286 (2010); Percent of households with income of $100,000 or more: 8.3% (2010); Poverty rate: 15.1% (2009); Bankruptcy rate: 3.25% (2010).

Taxes: Total county taxes per capita: $114 (2007); County property taxes per capita: $79 (2007).

Education: Percent of population age 25 and over with: High school diploma (including GED) or higher: 88.5% (2010); Bachelor's degree or higher: 18.3% (2010); Master's degree or higher: 5.5% (2010).

Housing: Homeownership rate: 75.3% (2010); Median home value: $90,108 (2010); Median contract rent: $367 per month (2005-2009 5-year est.); Median year structure built: 1966 (2005-2009 5-year est.)

Health: Birth rate: 123.0 per 10,000 population (2009); Death rate: 146.9 per 10,000 population (2009); Age-adjusted cancer mortality rate: 189.7 deaths per 100,000 population (2007); Number of physicians: 18.1 per 10,000 population (2008); Hospital beds: 71.8 per 10,000 population (2007); Hospital admissions: 2,088.5 per 10,000 population (2007).

Elections: 2008 Presidential election results: 41.6% Obama, 56.6% McCain, 0.8% Nader

Additional Information Contacts

Richland County Government . . . . (618) 392-3111

City of Olney . . . . (618) 395-7302
    http://www.ci.olney.il.us
Olney and The Greater Richland County Chamber of Commerce. . . . (618) 392-2241
    http://www.olneychamber.com

Richland County Communities

CALHOUN (village). Covers a land area of 1.047 square miles and a water area of 0 square miles. Located at 38.65° N. Lat; 88.04° W. Long. Elevation is 541 feet.

Population: 232 (1990); 222 (2000); 202 (2010); 190 (2015 projected); Race: 98.0% White, 0.0% Black, 1.0% Asian, 1.0% Other, 0.0% Hispanic of any race (2010); Density: 192.8 persons per square mile (2010); Average household size: 2.43 (2010); Median age: 41.1 (2010); Males per 100 females: 102.0 (2010); Marriage status: 17.3% never married, 60.9% now married, 9.5% widowed, 12.3% divorced (2005-2009 5-year est.); Foreign born: 0.0% (2005-2009 5-year est.); Ancestry (includes multiple ancestries): 32.5% German, 23.7% Irish, 10.3% English, 4.6% American, 4.6% Scotch-Irish (2005-2009 5-year est.).

Economy: Employment by occupation: 8.9% management, 12.9% professional, 15.3% services, 15.3% sales, 0.0% farming, 25.0% construction, 22.6% production (2005-2009 5-year est.).

Income: Per capita income: $18,925 (2010); Median household income: $38,750 (2010); Average household income: $45,873 (2010); Percent of households with income of $100,000 or more: 7.2% (2010); Poverty rate: 5.2% (2005-2009 5-year est.).

Taxes: Total city taxes per capita: $18 (2007); City property taxes per capita: $18 (2007).

Education: Percent of population age 25 and over with: High school diploma (including GED) or higher: 88.9% (2010); Bachelor's degree or higher: 12.5% (2010); Master's degree or higher: 4.2% (2010).

Housing: Homeownership rate: 85.5% (2010); Median home value: $71,000 (2010); Median contract rent: $275 per month (2005-2009 5-year est.); Median year structure built: 1972 (2005-2009 5-year est.).

Transportation: Commute to work: 85.7% car, 0.0% public transportation, 5.0% walk, 0.0% work from home (2005-2009 5-year est.); Travel time to work: 45.4% less than 15 minutes, 37.8% 15 to 30 minutes, 14.3% 30 to 45

minutes, 2.5% 45 to 60 minutes, 0.0% 60 minutes or more (2005-2009 5-year est.)

CLAREMONT (village). Covers a land area of 1.135 square miles and a water area of 0 square miles. Located at 38.72° N. Lat; 87.97° W. Long. Elevation is 509 feet.

Population: 256 (1990); 212 (2000); 210 (2010); 208 (2015 projected); Race: 97.1% White, 0.0% Black, 1.0% Asian, 1.9% Other, 0.0% Hispanic of any race (2010); Density: 185.0 persons per square mile (2010); Average household size: 2.59 (2010); Median age: 40.9 (2010); Males per 100 females: 100.0 (2010); Marriage status: 9.7% never married, 66.7% now married, 5.8% widowed, 17.9% divorced (2005-2009 5-year est.); Foreign born: 0.0% (2005-2009 5-year est.); Ancestry (includes multiple ancestries): 28.9% German, 12.8% Irish, 8.3% American, 6.4% English, 2.3% Swedish (2005-2009 5-year est.).
Economy: Employment by occupation: 7.7% management, 0.7% professional, 17.6% services, 21.1% sales, 0.0% farming, 2.8% construction, 50.0% production (2005-2009 5-year est.).
Income: Per capita income: $17,196 (2010); Median household income: $40,921 (2010); Average household income: $44,938 (2010); Percent of households with income of $100,000 or more: 4.9% (2010); Poverty rate: 28.4% (2005-2009 5-year est.).
Taxes: Total city taxes per capita: $19 (2007); City property taxes per capita: $19 (2007).
Education: Percent of population age 25 and over with: High school diploma (including GED) or higher: 87.1% (2010); Bachelor's degree or higher: 12.1% (2010); Master's degree or higher: 5.0% (2010).
Housing: Homeownership rate: 87.7% (2010); Median home value: $121,154 (2010); Median contract rent: n/a per month (2005-2009 5-year est.); Median year structure built: 1961 (2005-2009 5-year est.).
Transportation: Commute to work: 99.3% car, 0.0% public transportation, 0.0% walk, 0.0% work from home (2005-2009 5-year est.); Travel time to work: 73.6% less than 15 minutes, 8.6% 15 to 30 minutes, 12.9% 30 to 45 minutes, 0.0% 45 to 60 minutes, 5.0% 60 minutes or more (2005-2009 5-year est.)

DUNDAS (unincorporated postal area, zip code 62425). Covers a land area of 43.742 square miles and a water area of 0.009 square miles. Located at 38.83° N. Lat; 88.09° W. Long. Elevation is 472 feet.

Population: 716 (2000); Race: 100.0% White, 0.0% Black, 0.0% Asian, 0.0% Other, 2.0% Hispanic of any race (2000); Density: 16.4 persons per square mile (2000); Age: 32.8% under 18, 24.4% over 64 (2000); Marriage status: 17.0% never married, 69.7% now married, 9.8% widowed, 3.4% divorced (2000); Foreign born: 0.0% (2000); Ancestry (includes multiple ancestries): 36.3% German, 16.0% American, 13.6% English, 10.3% Irish (2000).
Economy: Employment by occupation: 15.1% management, 18.3% professional, 12.3% services, 25.4% sales, 4.6% farming, 10.9% construction, 13.4% production (2000).
Income: Per capita income: $14,419 (2000); Median household income: $32,222 (2000); Poverty rate: 6.0% (2000).
Education: Percent of population age 25 and over with: High school diploma (including GED) or higher: 80.6% (2000); Bachelor's degree or higher: 9.3% (2000).
Housing: Homeownership rate: 91.2% (2000); Median home value: $55,700 (2000); Median contract rent: $253 per month (2000); Median year structure built: 1963 (2000).
Transportation: Commute to work: 90.1% car, 0.0% public transportation, 0.0% walk, 9.9% work from home (2000); Travel time to work: 43.8% less than 15 minutes, 35.2% 15 to 30 minutes, 14.8% 30 to 45 minutes, 3.1% 45 to 60 minutes, 3.1% 60 minutes or more (2000)

NOBLE (village). Covers a land area of 1.024 square miles and a water area of 0.005 square miles. Located at 38.69° N. Lat; 88.22° W. Long. Elevation is 476 feet.

Population: 757 (1990); 746 (2000); 664 (2010); 622 (2015 projected); Race: 99.1% White, 0.0% Black, 0.0% Asian, 0.9% Other, 1.5% Hispanic of any race (2010); Density: 648.6 persons per square mile (2010); Average household size: 2.41 (2010); Median age: 37.0 (2010); Males per 100 females: 101.2 (2010); Marriage status: 26.3% never married, 66.2% now married, 3.8% widowed, 3.6% divorced (2005-2009 5-year est.); Foreign born: 0.7% (2005-2009 5-year est.); Ancestry (includes multiple ancestries): 30.3% German, 18.7% English, 11.7% Irish, 6.7% American, 2.5% Scotch-Irish (2005-2009 5-year est.).

Economy: Single-family building permits issued: 3 (2010); Multi-family building permits issued: 0 (2010); Employment by occupation: 4.6% management, 6.6% professional, 11.8% services, 33.8% sales, 1.0% farming, 20.0% construction, 22.3% production (2005-2009 5-year est.).
Income: Per capita income: $19,802 (2010); Median household income: $42,050 (2010); Average household income: $48,609 (2010); Percent of households with income of $100,000 or more: 8.0% (2010); Poverty rate: 10.2% (2005-2009 5-year est.).
Taxes: Total city taxes per capita: $78 (2007); City property taxes per capita: $68 (2007).
Education: Percent of population age 25 and over with: High school diploma (including GED) or higher: 86.6% (2010); Bachelor's degree or higher: 18.9% (2010); Master's degree or higher: 6.0% (2010).

School District(s)
West Richland CUSD 2 (PK-12)
    2009-10 Enrollment: 380 . . . . (618) 723-2334
Housing: Homeownership rate: 76.7% (2010); Median home value: $69,250 (2010); Median contract rent: $421 per month (2005-2009 5-year est.); Median year structure built: 1957 (2005-2009 5-year est.).
Newspapers: County Commoner (Local news; Circulation 1,300)
Transportation: Commute to work: 98.3% car, 0.0% public transportation, 0.7% walk, 0.0% work from home (2005-2009 5-year est.); Travel time to work: 36.1% less than 15 minutes, 33.8% 15 to 30 minutes, 19.6% 30 to 45 minutes, 2.0% 45 to 60 minutes, 8.4% 60 minutes or more (2005-2009 5-year est.)

OLNEY (city). County seat. Covers a land area of 5.760 square miles and a water area of <.001 square miles. Located at 38.73° N. Lat; 88.08° W. Long. Elevation is 479 feet.

History: Olney was named for John Olney, lawyer and officer in the Civil War. It developed as a shipping and trading center, and as the seat of Richland County. In 1902 a naturalist brought a pair of albino squirrels to Olney and set them loose. Soon Olney became known as "the home of white squirrels," as thousands of these squirrels took up residence in the parks and gardens.
Population: 9,096 (1990); 8,631 (2000); 7,972 (2010); 7,568 (2015 projected); Race: 96.3% White, 1.3% Black, 0.7% Asian, 1.7% Other, 1.3% Hispanic of any race (2010); Density: 1,384.0 persons per square mile (2010); Average household size: 2.21 (2010); Median age: 41.1 (2010); Males per 100 females: 86.3 (2010); Marriage status: 21.5% never married, 52.8% now married, 12.7% widowed, 12.9% divorced (2005-2009 5-year est.); Foreign born: 2.3% (2005-2009 5-year est.); Ancestry (includes multiple ancestries): 26.9% German, 12.3% English, 11.1% American, 10.8% Irish, 3.1% Italian (2005-2009 5-year est.).
Economy: Single-family building permits issued: 7 (2010); Multi-family building permits issued: 0 (2010); Employment by occupation: 11.6% management, 18.0% professional, 18.2% services, 24.2% sales, 1.6% farming, 6.4% construction, 20.0% production (2005-2009 5-year est.).
Income: Per capita income: $18,859 (2010); Median household income: $32,490 (2010); Average household income: $42,522 (2010); Percent of households with income of $100,000 or more: 6.8% (2010); Poverty rate: 18.6% (2005-2009 5-year est.).
Taxes: Total city taxes per capita: $182 (2007); City property taxes per capita: $161 (2007).
Education: Percent of population age 25 and over with: High school diploma (including GED) or higher: 88.1% (2010); Bachelor's degree or higher: 19.2% (2010); Master's degree or higher: 6.4% (2010).

School District(s)
Clay/Cwford/Jsper/Lwrnce/Rhland (PK-12)
    2009-10 Enrollment: n/a . . . . (618) 392-4631
East Richland CUSD 1 (PK-12)
    2009-10 Enrollment: 2,127 . . . . (618) 395-2324
Two-year College(s)
Illinois Eastern Community Colleges-Olney Central College (Public)
    Fall 2009 Enrollment: 1,627. . . . . (618) 393-2982
    2010-11 Tuition: In-state $6,808; Out-of-state $9,081
Housing: Homeownership rate: 67.1% (2010); Median home value: $77,717 (2010); Median contract rent: $377 per month (2005-2009 5-year est.); Median year structure built: 1961 (2005-2009 5-year est.).
Hospitals: Richland Memorial Hospital (135 beds)
Safety: Violent crime rate: 31.5 per 10,000 population; Property crime rate: 376.2 per 10,000 population (2010).
Newspapers: Olney Daily Mail (Regional news; Circulation 5,000)
Transportation: Commute to work: 94.4% car, 0.3% public transportation, 1.7% walk, 2.4% work from home (2005-2009 5-year est.); Travel time to

work: 68.6% less than 15 minutes, 13.1% 15 to 30 minutes, 8.6% 30 to 45 minutes, 4.2% 45 to 60 minutes, 5.5% 60 minutes or more (2005-2009 5-year est.)

Airports: Olney-Noble (general aviation)

Additional Information Contacts

City of Olney . . . . (618) 395-7302
   http://www.ci.olney.il.us
Olney and The Greater Richland County Chamber of Commerce. . . . (618) 392-2241
   http://www.olneychamber.com

PARKERSBURG (village). Covers a land area of 0.746 square miles and a water area of 0 square miles. Located at 38.59° N. Lat; 88.05° W. Long. Elevation is 479 feet.

Population: 223 (1990); 234 (2000); 212 (2010); 199 (2015 projected); Race: 98.1% White, 0.0% Black, 1.4% Asian, 0.5% Other, 0.0% Hispanic of any race (2010); Density: 284.1 persons per square mile (2010); Average household size: 2.44 (2010); Median age: 38.7 (2010); Males per 100 females: 98.1 (2010); Marriage status: 15.3% never married, 61.6% now married, 7.4% widowed, 15.8% divorced (2005-2009 5-year est.); Foreign born: 0.0% (2005-2009 5-year est.); Ancestry (includes multiple ancestries): 22.1% German, 10.5% Irish, 9.0% English, 5.2% American, 4.1% Italian (2005-2009 5-year est.).

Economy: Employment by occupation: 2.1% management, 5.2% professional, 16.5% services, 26.8% sales, 1.0% farming, 6.2% construction, 42.3% production (2005-2009 5-year est.).

Income: Per capita income: $18,925 (2010); Median household income: $39,500 (2010); Average household income: $46,092 (2010); Percent of households with income of $100,000 or more: 6.9% (2010); Poverty rate: 24.7% (2005-2009 5-year est.).

Taxes: Total city taxes per capita: $18 (2007); City property taxes per capita: $18 (2007).

Education: Percent of population age 25 and over with: High school diploma (including GED) or higher: 88.4% (2010); Bachelor's degree or higher: 12.2% (2010); Master's degree or higher: 4.1% (2010).

Housing: Homeownership rate: 85.1% (2010); Median home value: $73,333 (2010); Median contract rent: n/a per month (2005-2009 5-year est.); Median year structure built: 1960 (2005-2009 5-year est.).

Transportation: Commute to work: 100.0% car, 0.0% public transportation, 0.0% walk, 0.0% work from home (2005-2009 5-year est.); Travel time to work: 30.7% less than 15 minutes, 64.8% 15 to 30 minutes, 0.0% 30 to 45 minutes, 2.3% 45 to 60 minutes, 2.3% 60 minutes or more (2005-2009 5-year est.)

Rock Island County

Located in northwestern Illinois; bounded on the north and west by the Mississippi River and the Iowa border, and partly on the east by the Rock River. Covers a land area of 426.75 square miles, a water area of 24.40 square miles, and is located in the Central Time Zone at 41.49° N. Lat., 90.50° W. Long. The county was founded in 1831. County seat is Rock Island.

Rock Island County is part of the Davenport-Moline-Rock Island, IA-IL Metropolitan Statistical Area. The entire metro area includes: Henry County, IL; Mercer County, IL; Rock Island County, IL; Scott County, IA

Weather Station: Moline Quad City Arpt										Elevation: 591 feet		
	Jan	Feb	Mar	Apr	May	Jun	Jul	Aug	Sep	Oct	Nov	Dec
High	31	36	49	62	73	82	86	84	77	64	49	35
Low	15	19	29	40	50	60	65	63	54	42	31	19
Precip	1.5	1.6	2.8	3.5	4.3	4.4	4.2	4.6	3.0	3.0	2.5	2.2
Snow	9.2	6.7	4.1	1.2	tr	tr	tr	0.0	tr	0.1	1.2	8.8

High and Low temperatures in degrees Fahrenheit; Precipitation and Snow in inches

Weather Station: Rock Island L&D 15										Elevation: 567 feet		
	Jan	Feb	Mar	Apr	May	Jun	Jul	Aug	Sep	Oct	Nov	Dec
High	32	36	49	62	72	81	84	83	77	64	49	35
Low	17	20	31	42	53	64	68	66	57	45	33	20
Precip	1.5	1.6	2.6	3.6	4.9	5.1	4.1	3.9	2.8	2.7	2.4	1.9
Snow	na	na	0.6	0.1	0.0	0.0	0.0	0.0	0.0	tr	0.5	na

High and Low temperatures in degrees Fahrenheit; Precipitation and Snow in inches

Population: 148,723 (1990); 149,374 (2000); 146,750 (2010); 144,833 (2015 projected); Race: 82.6% White, 7.7% Black, 2.1% Asian, 7.6% Other, 10.7% Hispanic of any race (2010); Density: 343.9 persons per

square mile (2010); Average household size: 2.36 (2010); Median age: 38.2 (2010); Males per 100 females: 95.7 (2010).

Religion: Five largest groups: 18.7% Catholic Church, 4.5% Evangelical Lutheran Church in America, 3.9% The United Methodist Church, 3.5% Lutheran Church—Missouri Synod, 2.4% International Church of the Foursquare Gospel (2000).

Economy: Unemployment rate: 7.8% (August 2011); Total civilian labor force: 79,022 (August 2011); Leading industries: 15.3% health care and social assistance; 13.1% manufacturing; 13.0% retail trade (2009); Farms: 700 totaling 178,623 acres (2007); Companies that employ 500 or more persons: 10 (2009); Companies that employ 100 to 499 persons: 88 (2009); Companies that employ less than 100 persons: 3,255 (2009); Black-owned businesses: 482 (2007); Hispanic-owned businesses: 272 (2007); Asian-owned businesses: n/a (2007); Women-owned businesses: 2,749 (2007); Retail sales per capita: $13,339 (2010). Single-family building permits issued: 80 (2010); Multi-family building permits issued: 157 (2010).

Income: Per capita income: $24,515 (2010); Median household income: $46,677 (2010); Average household income: $58,967 (2010); Percent of households with income of $100,000 or more: 14.0% (2010); Poverty rate: 11.2% (2009); Bankruptcy rate: 4.34% (2010).

Taxes: Total county taxes per capita: $138 (2007); County property taxes per capita: $122 (2007).

Education: Percent of population age 25 and over with: High school diploma (including GED) or higher: 86.9% (2010); Bachelor's degree or higher: 20.4% (2010); Master's degree or higher: 6.7% (2010).

Housing: Homeownership rate: 71.1% (2010); Median home value: $104,044 (2010); Median contract rent: $484 per month (2005-2009 5-year est.); Median year structure built: 1958 (2005-2009 5-year est.)

Health: Birth rate: 135.2 per 10,000 population (2009); Death rate: 99.0 per 10,000 population (2009); Age-adjusted cancer mortality rate: 191.1 deaths per 100,000 population (2007); Number of physicians: 18.1 per 10,000 population (2008); Hospital beds: 28.8 per 10,000 population (2007); Hospital admissions: 1,494.0 per 10,000 population (2007).

Environment: Air Quality Index: 95.8% good, 4.2% moderate, 0.0% unhealthy for sensitive individuals, 0.0% unhealthy (percent of days in 2008)

Elections: 2008 Presidential election results: 61.7% Obama, 37.1% McCain, 0.6% Nader

National and State Parks: Black Hawk State Historical Site; Campbells Island State Park

Additional Information Contacts

Rock Island County Government . . . . (309) 558-3569
   http://www.rockislandcounty.org
City of East Moline . . . . (309) 752-1581
   http://www.eastmoline.com
City of Moline . . . . (309) 524-2004
   http://www.moline.il.us
City of Rock Island . . . . (309) 732-2000
   http://www.rigov.org
City of Silvis . . . . (309) 792-9181
   http://www.silvisil.org
Illinois Quad City Chamber of Commerce . . . . (309) 757-5416
   http://www.quadcitieschamber.com
Milan Chamber of Commerce . . . . (309) 716-8144
   http://www.milanilchamber.org
Village of Milan . . . . (309) 787-8500
   http://www.milanil.org

Rock Island County Communities

ANDALUSIA (village). Covers a land area of 0.717 square miles and a water area of 0.004 square miles. Located at 41.44° N. Lat; 90.72° W. Long. Elevation is 574 feet.

History: Andalusia was the location on the Mississippi River of Clark's Ferry which gave passage to Buffalo, Iowa, to thousands of settlers in the 1830's.

Population: 967 (1990); 1,050 (2000); 992 (2010); 963 (2015 projected); Race: 96.5% White, 0.7% Black, 0.1% Asian, 2.7% Other, 2.5% Hispanic of any race (2010); Density: 1,382.6 persons per square mile (2010); Average household size: 2.54 (2010); Median age: 41.1 (2010); Males per 100 females: 100.8 (2010); Marriage status: 15.2% never married, 69.9% now married, 7.4% widowed, 7.4% divorced (2005-2009 5-year est.); Foreign born: 1.0% (2005-2009 5-year est.); Ancestry (includes multiple

ancestries): 41.6% German, 24.0% Irish, 12.2% Swedish, 9.1% English, 7.3% Belgian (2005-2009 5-year est.).
Economy: Single-family building permits issued: 5 (2010); Multi-family building permits issued: 0 (2010); Employment by occupation: 12.5% management, 19.1% professional, 11.3% services, 27.5% sales, 0.0% farming, 12.5% construction, 17.2% production (2005-2009 5-year est.).
Income: Per capita income: $28,109 (2010); Median household income: $61,483 (2010); Average household income: $70,575 (2010); Percent of households with income of $100,000 or more: 20.5% (2010); Poverty rate: 4.4% (2005-2009 5-year est.).
Taxes: Total city taxes per capita: $206 (2007); City property taxes per capita: $117 (2007).
Education: Percent of population age 25 and over with: High school diploma (including GED) or higher: 93.1% (2010); Bachelor's degree or higher: 17.2% (2010); Master's degree or higher: 7.8% (2010).

School District(s)
Rockridge CUSD 300 (PK-12)
    2009-10 Enrollment: 1,298 . . . . (309) 793-8001
Housing: Homeownership rate: 88.0% (2010); Median home value: $124,138 (2010); Median contract rent: $427 per month (2005-2009 5-year est.); Median year structure built: 1969 (2005-2009 5-year est.).
Transportation: Commute to work: 96.3% car, 0.0% public transportation, 0.0% walk, 3.7% work from home (2005-2009 5-year est.); Travel time to work: 15.1% less than 15 minutes, 69.9% 15 to 30 minutes, 9.7% 30 to 45 minutes, 0.0% 45 to 60 minutes, 5.4% 60 minutes or more (2005-2009 5-year est.)

CARBON CLIFF (village). Covers a land area of 2.041 square miles and a water area of 0 square miles. Located at 41.49° N. Lat; 90.39° W. Long. Elevation is 604 feet.
Population: 1,674 (1990); 1,689 (2000); 1,773 (2010); 1,800 (2015 projected); Race: 89.7% White, 3.8% Black, 0.5% Asian, 6.0% Other, 5.1% Hispanic of any race (2010); Density: 868.5 persons per square mile (2010); Average household size: 2.41 (2010); Median age: 33.3 (2010); Males per 100 females: 92.7 (2010); Marriage status: 28.9% never married, 40.0% now married, 5.6% widowed, 25.5% divorced (2005-2009 5-year est.); Foreign born: 4.5% (2005-2009 5-year est.); Ancestry (includes multiple ancestries): 31.6% German, 15.5% Irish, 6.4% Italian, 5.6% Swedish, 5.5% English (2005-2009 5-year est.).
Economy: Single-family building permits issued: 0 (2010); Multi-family building permits issued: 0 (2010); Employment by occupation: 13.7% management, 7.8% professional, 18.2% services, 25.3% sales, 0.6% farming, 9.9% construction, 24.6% production (2005-2009 5-year est.).
Income: Per capita income: $21,122 (2010); Median household income: $43,485 (2010); Average household income: $51,009 (2010); Percent of households with income of $100,000 or more: 9.2% (2010); Poverty rate: 30.9% (2005-2009 5-year est.).
Taxes: Total city taxes per capita: $260 (2007); City property taxes per capita: $193 (2007).
Education: Percent of population age 25 and over with: High school diploma (including GED) or higher: 86.0% (2010); Bachelor's degree or higher: 12.9% (2010); Master's degree or higher: 3.8% (2010).

School District(s)
Black Hawk Area Sp Ed District (07-12)
    2009-10 Enrollment: n/a . . . . (309) 796-2500
Housing: Homeownership rate: 70.6% (2010); Median home value: $106,364 (2010); Median contract rent: $540 per month (2005-2009 5-year est.); Median year structure built: 1970 (2005-2009 5-year est.).
Transportation: Commute to work: 85.1% car, 11.1% public transportation, 0.8% walk, 2.5% work from home (2005-2009 5-year est.); Travel time to work: 18.9% less than 15 minutes, 46.6% 15 to 30 minutes, 19.7% 30 to 45 minutes, 6.2% 45 to 60 minutes, 8.6% 60 minutes or more (2005-2009 5-year est.)

COAL VALLEY (village). Covers a land area of 2.861 square miles and a water area of 0 square miles. Located at 41.44° N. Lat; 90.45° W. Long. Elevation is 623 feet.
Population: 3,548 (1990); 3,606 (2000); 3,696 (2010); 3,788 (2015 projected); Race: 95.4% White, 1.6% Black, 0.5% Asian, 2.5% Other, 3.8% Hispanic of any race (2010); Density: 1,291.9 persons per square mile (2010); Average household size: 2.57 (2010); Median age: 38.6 (2010); Males per 100 females: 103.6 (2010); Marriage status: 21.4% never married, 58.3% now married, 5.3% widowed, 15.0% divorced (2005-2009 5-year est.); Foreign born: 1.6% (2005-2009 5-year est.); Ancestry

(includes multiple ancestries): 32.4% German, 13.8% Irish, 13.3% English, 9.3% Swedish, 6.7% Belgian (2005-2009 5-year est.).
Economy: Single-family building permits issued: 10 (2010); Multi-family building permits issued: 0 (2010); Employment by occupation: 11.6% management, 18.5% professional, 15.3% services, 29.3% sales, 0.0% farming, 6.1% construction, 19.2% production (2005-2009 5-year est.).
Income: Per capita income: $27,123 (2010); Median household income: $59,317 (2010); Average household income: $70,523 (2010); Percent of households with income of $100,000 or more: 21.7% (2010); Poverty rate: 9.4% (2005-2009 5-year est.).
Taxes: Total city taxes per capita: $137 (2007); City property taxes per capita: $58 (2007).
Education: Percent of population age 25 and over with: High school diploma (including GED) or higher: 88.5% (2010); Bachelor's degree or higher: 20.5% (2010); Master's degree or higher: 7.5% (2010).

School District(s)
Moline USD 40 (PK-12)
    2009-10 Enrollment: 7,397 . . . . (309) 743-1600
Housing: Homeownership rate: 93.1% (2010); Median home value: $124,311 (2010); Median contract rent: $509 per month (2005-2009 5-year est.); Median year structure built: 1973 (2005-2009 5-year est.).
Safety: Violent crime rate: 2.5 per 10,000 population; Property crime rate: 124.2 per 10,000 population (2010).
Transportation: Commute to work: 98.3% car, 0.0% public transportation, 0.5% walk, 0.6% work from home (2005-2009 5-year est.); Travel time to work: 20.9% less than 15 minutes, 58.9% 15 to 30 minutes, 16.5% 30 to 45 minutes, 0.0% 45 to 60 minutes, 3.7% 60 minutes or more (2005-2009 5-year est.)

CORDOVA (village). Covers a land area of 0.562 square miles and a water area of 0.005 square miles. Located at 41.67° N. Lat; 90.32° W. Long. Elevation is 591 feet.
Population: 678 (1990); 633 (2000); 661 (2010); 669 (2015 projected); Race: 96.8% White, 0.3% Black, 0.2% Asian, 2.7% Other, 2.3% Hispanic of any race (2010); Density: 1,175.7 persons per square mile (2010); Average household size: 2.51 (2010); Median age: 42.5 (2010); Males per 100 females: 107.9 (2010); Marriage status: 23.3% never married, 62.4% now married, 10.0% widowed, 4.2% divorced (2005-2009 5-year est.); Foreign born: 0.6% (2005-2009 5-year est.); Ancestry (includes multiple ancestries): 33.3% German, 12.5% Swedish, 12.3% Irish, 12.2% English, 5.7% Belgian (2005-2009 5-year est.).
Economy: Single-family building permits issued: 0 (2010); Multi-family building permits issued: 0 (2010); Employment by occupation: 12.9% management, 10.2% professional, 14.8% services, 24.0% sales, 0.0% farming, 14.8% construction, 23.4% production (2005-2009 5-year est.).
Income: Per capita income: $31,825 (2010); Median household income: $64,231 (2010); Average household income: $79,380 (2010); Percent of households with income of $100,000 or more: 22.1% (2010); Poverty rate: 5.9% (2005-2009 5-year est.).
Taxes: Total city taxes per capita: $404 (2007); City property taxes per capita: $368 (2007).
Education: Percent of population age 25 and over with: High school diploma (including GED) or higher: 91.9% (2010); Bachelor's degree or higher: 22.2% (2010); Master's degree or higher: 5.5% (2010).
Housing: Homeownership rate: 84.0% (2010); Median home value: $145,536 (2010); Median contract rent: $475 per month (2005-2009 5-year est.); Median year structure built: 1973 (2005-2009 5-year est.).
Transportation: Commute to work: 97.8% car, 0.9% public transportation, 0.0% walk, 0.0% work from home (2005-2009 5-year est.); Travel time to work: 30.8% less than 15 minutes, 31.1% 15 to 30 minutes, 31.4% 30 to 45 minutes, 4.9% 45 to 60 minutes, 1.8% 60 minutes or more (2005-2009 5-year est.)

COYNE CENTER (CDP). Covers a land area of 1.793 square miles and a water area of 0 square miles. Located at 41.40° N. Lat; 90.56° W. Long. Elevation is 748 feet.
Population: 1,137 (1990); 906 (2000); 863 (2010); 838 (2015 projected); Race: 97.1% White, 1.3% Black, 0.2% Asian, 1.4% Other, 1.6% Hispanic of any race (2010); Density: 481.4 persons per square mile (2010); Average household size: 2.40 (2010); Median age: 43.2 (2010); Males per 100 females: 93.5 (2010); Marriage status: 22.5% never married, 53.7% now married, 8.1% widowed, 15.7% divorced (2005-2009 5-year est.); Foreign born: 0.0% (2005-2009 5-year est.); Ancestry (includes multiple ancestries): 21.3% German, 18.9% Irish, 14.5% American, 11.6% Swedish, 11.0% Belgian (2005-2009 5-year est.).

Economy: Employment by occupation: 5.2% management, 9.2% professional, 9.8% services, 43.8% sales, 2.6% farming, 4.6% construction, 24.7% production (2005-2009 5-year est.).
Income: Per capita income: $28,311 (2010); Median household income: $58,488 (2010); Average household income: $68,893 (2010); Percent of households with income of $100,000 or more: 17.8% (2010); Poverty rate: 1.5% (2005-2009 5-year est.).
Education: Percent of population age 25 and over with: High school diploma (including GED) or higher: 90.8% (2010); Bachelor's degree or higher: 20.2% (2010); Master's degree or higher: 6.0% (2010).
Housing: Homeownership rate: 93.9% (2010); Median home value: $121,364 (2010); Median contract rent: n/a per month (2005-2009 5-year est.); Median year structure built: 1962 (2005-2009 5-year est.).
Transportation: Commute to work: 94.6% car, 0.0% public transportation, 2.8% walk, 2.6% work from home (2005-2009 5-year est.); Travel time to work: 36.9% less than 15 minutes, 34.8% 15 to 30 minutes, 22.5% 30 to 45 minutes, 3.7% 45 to 60 minutes, 2.1% 60 minutes or more (2005-2009 5-year est.)

EAST MOLINE (city). Covers a land area of 9.017 square miles and a water area of 0 square miles. Located at 41.51° N. Lat; 90.43° W. Long. Elevation is 702 feet.

History: East Moline was incorporated as a city in 1907, and developed as an industrial center for nearby Moline and Rock Island. An International Harvester plant was a major employer.
Population: 20,575 (1990); 20,333 (2000); 20,207 (2010); 20,054 (2015 projected); Race: 76.9% White, 6.1% Black, 4.9% Asian, 12.1% Other, 18.4% Hispanic of any race (2010); Density: 2,240.9 persons per square mile (2010); Average household size: 2.33 (2010); Median age: 37.7 (2010); Males per 100 females: 93.0 (2010); Marriage status: 32.4% never married, 46.0% now married, 9.6% widowed, 11.9% divorced (2005-2009 5-year est.); Foreign born: 10.4% (2005-2009 5-year est.); Ancestry (includes multiple ancestries): 23.2% German, 11.8% Irish, 8.5% English, 5.8% Swedish, 4.2% Italian (2005-2009 5-year est.).
Economy: Single-family building permits issued: 3 (2010); Multi-family building permits issued: 84 (2010); Employment by occupation: 12.7% management, 19.4% professional, 16.9% services, 24.9% sales, 0.1% farming, 6.7% construction, 19.4% production (2005-2009 5-year est.).
Income: Per capita income: $22,031 (2010); Median household income: $42,760 (2010); Average household income: $51,800 (2010); Percent of households with income of $100,000 or more: 10.5% (2010); Poverty rate: 15.8% (2005-2009 5-year est.).
Taxes: Total city taxes per capita: $346 (2007); City property taxes per capita: $237 (2007).
Education: Percent of population age 25 and over with: High school diploma (including GED) or higher: 85.7% (2010); Bachelor's degree or higher: 19.4% (2010); Master's degree or higher: 6.3% (2010).

School District(s)
East Moline SD 37 (PK-08)
    2009-10 Enrollment: 2,545 . . . . (309) 792-2887
Moline USD 40 (PK-12)
    2009-10 Enrollment: 7,397 . . . . (309) 743-1600
United Twp Area Career Ctr (11-12)
    2009-10 Enrollment: n/a . . . . (309) 752-1691
United Twp HSD 30 (09-12)
    2009-10 Enrollment: 1,736 . . . . (309) 752-1611

Vocational/Technical School(s)
La James International College (Private, For-profit)
    Fall 2009 Enrollment: 36 . . . . (309) 755-1313
    2010-11 Tuition: $16,925

Housing: Homeownership rate: 67.0% (2010); Median home value: $99,863 (2010); Median contract rent: $464 per month (2005-2009 5-year est.); Median year structure built: 1962 (2005-2009 5-year est.).
Safety: Violent crime rate: 35.9 per 10,000 population; Property crime rate: 273.4 per 10,000 population (2010).
Transportation: Commute to work: 95.0% car, 0.5% public transportation, 1.7% walk, 1.4% work from home (2005-2009 5-year est.); Travel time to work: 32.1% less than 15 minutes, 52.3% 15 to 30 minutes, 11.5% 30 to 45 minutes, 1.8% 45 to 60 minutes, 2.4% 60 minutes or more (2005-2009 5-year est.)
Additional Information Contacts
City of East Moline . . . . (309) 752-1581
    http://www.eastmoline.com

HAMPTON (village). Covers a land area of 1.580 square miles and a water area of 0 square miles. Located at 41.55° N. Lat; 90.40° W. Long. Elevation is 587 feet.

Population: 1,626 (1990); 1,626 (2000); 1,659 (2010); 1,674 (2015 projected); Race: 95.1% White, 0.4% Black, 0.1% Asian, 4.4% Other, 4.9% Hispanic of any race (2010); Density: 1,049.7 persons per square mile (2010); Average household size: 2.53 (2010); Median age: 41.3 (2010); Males per 100 females: 96.6 (2010); Marriage status: 19.6% never married, 64.5% now married, 5.3% widowed, 10.6% divorced (2005-2009 5-year est.); Foreign born: 1.2% (2005-2009 5-year est.); Ancestry (includes multiple ancestries): 28.4% German, 19.7% Irish, 9.1% English, 9.1% Swedish, 7.0% Belgian (2005-2009 5-year est.).
Economy: Single-family building permits issued: 3 (2010); Multi-family building permits issued: 0 (2010); Employment by occupation: 11.6% management, 16.7% professional, 17.7% services, 27.3% sales, 0.3% farming, 8.6% construction, 17.9% production (2005-2009 5-year est.).
Income: Per capita income: $32,059 (2010); Median household income: $69,656 (2010); Average household income: $81,133 (2010); Percent of households with income of $100,000 or more: 28.6% (2010); Poverty rate: 7.0% (2005-2009 5-year est.).
Taxes: Total city taxes per capita: $733 (2007); City property taxes per capita: $638 (2007).
Education: Percent of population age 25 and over with: High school diploma (including GED) or higher: 89.5% (2010); Bachelor's degree or higher: 20.6% (2010); Master's degree or higher: 9.1% (2010).

School District(s)
Hampton SD 29 (KG-08)
    2009-10 Enrollment: 256 . . . . (309) 755-0693

Housing: Homeownership rate: 87.6% (2010); Median home value: $119,500 (2010); Median contract rent: $359 per month (2005-2009 5-year est.); Median year structure built: 1974 (2005-2009 5-year est.).
Transportation: Commute to work: 95.7% car, 0.0% public transportation, 0.2% walk, 3.3% work from home (2005-2009 5-year est.); Travel time to work: 29.3% less than 15 minutes, 50.7% 15 to 30 minutes, 15.3% 30 to 45 minutes, 2.3% 45 to 60 minutes, 2.4% 60 minutes or more (2005-2009 5-year est.)

HILLSDALE (village). Covers a land area of 0.754 square miles and a water area of 0.025 square miles. Located at 41.61° N. Lat; 90.17° W. Long. Elevation is 581 feet.

Population: 557 (1990); 588 (2000); 530 (2010); 503 (2015 projected); Race: 94.2% White, 0.6% Black, 0.2% Asian, 5.1% Other, 3.8% Hispanic of any race (2010); Density: 703.2 persons per square mile (2010); Average household size: 2.62 (2010); Median age: 36.6 (2010); Males per 100 females: 95.6 (2010); Marriage status: 23.3% never married, 50.1% now married, 7.6% widowed, 19.0% divorced (2005-2009 5-year est.); Foreign born: 1.6% (2005-2009 5-year est.); Ancestry (includes multiple ancestries): 28.9% German, 26.1% Irish, 11.5% American, 5.7% Swedish, 5.4% English (2005-2009 5-year est.).
Economy: Employment by occupation: 11.2% management, 7.6% professional, 10.0% services, 38.6% sales, 0.0% farming, 8.0% construction, 24.7% production (2005-2009 5-year est.).
Income: Per capita income: $23,279 (2010); Median household income: $53,226 (2010); Average household income: $61,139 (2010); Percent of households with income of $100,000 or more: 12.4% (2010); Poverty rate: 10.5% (2005-2009 5-year est.).
Taxes: Total city taxes per capita: $98 (2007); City property taxes per capita: $46 (2007).
Education: Percent of population age 25 and over with: High school diploma (including GED) or higher: 87.7% (2010); Bachelor's degree or higher: 6.2% (2010); Master's degree or higher: 2.9% (2010).
Housing: Homeownership rate: 79.2% (2010); Median home value: $101,111 (2010); Median contract rent: $435 per month (2005-2009 5-year est.); Median year structure built: 1963 (2005-2009 5-year est.).
Transportation: Commute to work: 91.6% car, 0.0% public transportation, 0.8% walk, 7.6% work from home (2005-2009 5-year est.); Travel time to work: 27.2% less than 15 minutes, 24.6% 15 to 30 minutes, 42.2% 30 to 45 minutes, 4.3% 45 to 60 minutes, 1.7% 60 minutes or more (2005-2009 5-year est.)

ILLINOIS CITY (unincorporated postal area, zip code 61259). Covers a land area of 61.147 square miles and a water area of 0.376 square miles. Located at 41.36° N. Lat; 90.92° W. Long. Elevation is 764 feet.

Population: 1,209 (2000); Race: 95.5% White, 0.0% Black, 0.5% Asian, 4.0% Other, 3.1% Hispanic of any race (2000); Density: 19.8 persons per square mile (2000); Age: 21.0% under 18, 15.1% over 64 (2000); Marriage status: 18.7% never married, 74.0% now married, 3.4% widowed, 4.0% divorced (2000); Foreign born: 0.9% (2000); Ancestry (includes multiple ancestries): 26.9% German, 12.9% English, 9.8% Irish, 7.0% Swedish (2000).

Economy: Employment by occupation: 10.1% management, 15.3% professional, 11.5% services, 26.8% sales, 1.9% farming, 11.2% construction, 23.3% production (2000).

Income: Per capita income: $21,311 (2000); Median household income: $46,741 (2000); Poverty rate: 3.8% (2000).

Education: Percent of population age 25 and over with: High school diploma (including GED) or higher: 78.3% (2000); Bachelor's degree or higher: 15.7% (2000).

School District(s)
Rockridge CUSD 300 (PK-12)
    2009-10 Enrollment: 1,298 . . . . (309) 793-8001

Housing: Homeownership rate: 83.4% (2000); Median home value: $107,400 (2000); Median contract rent: $438 per month (2000); Median year structure built: 1955 (2000).

Transportation: Commute to work: 95.9% car, 0.0% public transportation, 0.6% walk, 3.5% work from home (2000); Travel time to work: 9.5% less than 15 minutes, 56.6% 15 to 30 minutes, 26.1% 30 to 45 minutes, 5.9% 45 to 60 minutes, 2.0% 60 minutes or more (2000)

MILAN (village). Covers a land area of 5.537 square miles and a water area of 0.514 square miles. Located at 41.44° N. Lat; 90.56° W. Long. Elevation is 568 feet.

History: Incorporated 1865.

Population: 6,077 (1990); 5,348 (2000); 5,102 (2010); 4,982 (2015 projected); Race: 85.0% White, 10.2% Black, 0.5% Asian, 4.3% Other, 4.3% Hispanic of any race (2010); Density: 921.4 persons per square mile (2010); Average household size: 2.26 (2010); Median age: 37.0 (2010); Males per 100 females: 105.8 (2010); Marriage status: 25.6% never married, 52.0% now married, 9.6% widowed, 12.8% divorced (2005-2009 5-year est.); Foreign born: 2.0% (2005-2009 5-year est.); Ancestry (includes multiple ancestries): 27.8% German, 15.7% Irish, 11.1% English, 7.9% American, 5.7% Swedish (2005-2009 5-year est.).

Economy: Single-family building permits issued: 6 (2010); Multi-family building permits issued: 0 (2010); Employment by occupation: 6.6% management, 16.5% professional, 15.2% services, 28.1% sales, 0.1% farming, 12.7% construction, 20.8% production (2005-2009 5-year est.).

Income: Per capita income: $22,181 (2010); Median household income: $41,297 (2010); Average household income: $51,274 (2010); Percent of households with income of $100,000 or more: 10.3% (2010); Poverty rate: 14.5% (2005-2009 5-year est.).

Taxes: Total city taxes per capita: $476 (2007); City property taxes per capita: $453 (2007).

Education: Percent of population age 25 and over with: High school diploma (including GED) or higher: 82.8% (2010); Bachelor's degree or higher: 9.6% (2010); Master's degree or higher: 2.0% (2010).

School District(s)
Rock Island SD 41 (PK-12)
    2009-10 Enrollment: 6,225 . . . . (309) 793-5900
Sherrard CUSD 200 (PK-12)
    2009-10 Enrollment: 1,656 . . . . (309) 593-4075

Housing: Homeownership rate: 68.3% (2010); Median home value: $84,479 (2010); Median contract rent: $462 per month (2005-2009 5-year est.); Median year structure built: 1963 (2005-2009 5-year est.).

Safety: Violent crime rate: 21.5 per 10,000 population; Property crime rate: 253.7 per 10,000 population (2010).

Transportation: Commute to work: 93.3% car, 0.0% public transportation, 3.7% walk, 1.4% work from home (2005-2009 5-year est.); Travel time to work: 33.2% less than 15 minutes, 53.1% 15 to 30 minutes, 11.2% 30 to 45 minutes, 0.0% 45 to 60 minutes, 2.5% 60 minutes or more (2005-2009 5-year est.)

Additional Information Contacts
Milan Chamber of Commerce . . . . (309) 716-8144
    http://www.milanilchamber.org
Village of Milan. . . . . (309) 787-8500
    http://www.milanil.org

MOLINE (city). Covers a land area of 15.599 square miles and a water area of 0.222 square miles. Located at 41.49° N. Lat; 90.50° W. Long. Elevation is 577 feet.

History: Moline was laid out in 1843. An early resident was John Deere, who had been producing plows in Grand Detour, but moved to Moline for the availability of steel for his machinery. The John Deere plants founded here soon became a major employer. Moline was incorporated as a town in 1848, and as a city in 1872.

Population: 43,798 (1990); 43,768 (2000); 42,621 (2010); 41,881 (2015 projected); Race: 84.1% White, 3.7% Black, 2.8% Asian, 9.3% Other, 15.6% Hispanic of any race (2010); Density: 2,732.2 persons per square mile (2010); Average household size: 2.35 (2010); Median age: 38.6 (2010); Males per 100 females: 93.4 (2010); Marriage status: 27.0% never married, 53.4% now married, 7.1% widowed, 12.5% divorced (2005-2009 5-year est.); Foreign born: 8.6% (2005-2009 5-year est.); Ancestry (includes multiple ancestries): 27.2% German, 15.0% Irish, 10.0% English, 8.0% Swedish, 6.5% Belgian (2005-2009 5-year est.).

Economy: Unemployment rate: 7.2% (August 2011); Total civilian labor force: 23,648 (August 2011); Single-family building permits issued: 0 (2010); Multi-family building permits issued: 0 (2010); Employment by occupation: 11.8% management, 16.9% professional, 20.9% services, 25.9% sales, 0.1% farming, 6.5% construction, 17.9% production (2005-2009 5-year est.).

Income: Per capita income: $25,490 (2010); Median household income: $46,710 (2010); Average household income: $60,024 (2010); Percent of households with income of $100,000 or more: 14.0% (2010); Poverty rate: 10.2% (2005-2009 5-year est.).

Taxes: Total city taxes per capita: $649 (2007); City property taxes per capita: $366 (2007).

Education: Percent of population age 25 and over with: High school diploma (including GED) or higher: 88.0% (2010); Bachelor's degree or higher: 24.4% (2010); Master's degree or higher: 7.9% (2010).

School District(s)
Moline USD 40 (PK-12)
    2009-10 Enrollment: 7,397 . . . . (309) 743-1600
Rock Island Roe
    2009-10 Enrollment: n/a . . . . (309) 736-1111
Rock Island SD 41 (PK-12)
    2009-10 Enrollment: 6,225 . . . . (309) 793-5900

Two-year College(s)
Black Hawk College (Public)
    Fall 2009 Enrollment: 6,267. . . . . (309) 796-5000
    2010-11 Tuition: In-state $6,075; Out-of-state $6,075
Brown Mackie College-Quad Cities (Private, For-profit)
    Fall 2009 Enrollment: 246 . . . . (309) 762-2100
    2010-11 Tuition: In-state $8,679; Out-of-state $8,679

Housing: Homeownership rate: 68.7% (2010); Median home value: $103,174 (2010); Median contract rent: $512 per month (2005-2009 5-year est.); Median year structure built: 1954 (2005-2009 5-year est.).

Safety: Violent crime rate: 50.8 per 10,000 population; Property crime rate: 349.8 per 10,000 population (2010).

Newspapers: Dispatch (Community news; Circulation 31,716)

Transportation: Commute to work: 93.8% car, 0.8% public transportation, 2.4% walk, 2.0% work from home (2005-2009 5-year est.); Travel time to work: 44.4% less than 15 minutes, 45.5% 15 to 30 minutes, 5.7% 30 to 45 minutes, 2.3% 45 to 60 minutes, 2.2% 60 minutes or more (2005-2009 5-year est.); Amtrak: train service available.

Airports: Quad City International (primary service/small hub)

Additional Information Contacts
City of Moline . . . . (309) 524-2004
    http://www.moline.il.us
Illinois Quad City Chamber of Commerce . . . . (309) 757-5416
    http://www.quadcitieschamber.com

OAK GROVE (village). Aka Oak Grove Park. Covers a land area of 0.631 square miles and a water area of 0 square miles. Located at 41.41° N. Lat; 90.57° W. Long. Elevation is 722 feet.

Population: 201 (1990); 1,318 (2000); 1,318 (2010); 1,304 (2015 projected); Race: 55.5% White, 37.6% Black, 0.2% Asian, 6.7% Other, 7.1% Hispanic of any race (2010); Density: 2,088.2 persons per square mile (2010); Average household size: 2.59 (2010); Median age: 32.3 (2010); Males per 100 females: 181.0 (2010); Marriage status: 32.9% never married, 32.0% now married, 3.2% widowed, 31.8% divorced (2005-2009 5-year est.); Foreign born: 1.6% (2005-2009 5-year est.);

Ancestry (includes multiple ancestries): 28.0% German, 22.0% Irish, 11.1% English, 7.2% Scottish, 7.0% American (2005-2009 5-year est.).
Economy: Single-family building permits issued: 0 (2010); Multi-family building permits issued: 0 (2010); Employment by occupation: 6.3% management, 6.6% professional, 29.7% services, 31.3% sales, 0.0% farming, 6.9% construction, 19.4% production (2005-2009 5-year est.).
Income: Per capita income: $22,718 (2010); Median household income: $61,268 (2010); Average household income: $68,601 (2010); Percent of households with income of $100,000 or more: 20.7% (2010); Poverty rate: 13.9% (2005-2009 5-year est.).
Taxes: Total city taxes per capita: $17 (2007); City property taxes per capita: $14 (2007).
Education: Percent of population age 25 and over with: High school diploma (including GED) or higher: 76.5% (2010); Bachelor's degree or higher: 10.3% (2010); Master's degree or higher: 3.2% (2010).
Housing: Homeownership rate: 72.4% (2010); Median home value: $118,632 (2010); Median contract rent: $484 per month (2005-2009 5-year est.); Median year structure built: 1971 (2005-2009 5-year est.).
Transportation: Commute to work: 95.6% car, 3.1% public transportation, 1.3% walk, 0.0% work from home (2005-2009 5-year est.); Travel time to work: 15.3% less than 15 minutes, 58.8% 15 to 30 minutes, 17.2% 30 to 45 minutes, 0.0% 45 to 60 minutes, 8.8% 60 minutes or more (2005-2009 5-year est.)

PORT BYRON (village). Covers a land area of 2.311 square miles and a water area of 0 square miles. Located at 41.61° N. Lat; 90.33° W. Long. Elevation is 600 feet.
Population: 1,098 (1990); 1,535 (2000); 1,619 (2010); 1,648 (2015 projected); Race: 96.8% White, 0.2% Black, 0.1% Asian, 2.9% Other, 2.9% Hispanic of any race (2010); Density: 700.7 persons per square mile (2010); Average household size: 2.53 (2010); Median age: 40.5 (2010); Males per 100 females: 104.9 (2010); Marriage status: 21.2% never married, 63.5% now married, 4.7% widowed, 10.7% divorced (2005-2009 5-year est.); Foreign born: 2.6% (2005-2009 5-year est.); Ancestry (includes multiple ancestries): 37.3% German, 16.4% English, 11.5% Irish, 6.7% Italian, 6.4% Swedish (2005-2009 5-year est.).
Economy: Single-family building permits issued: 3 (2010); Multi-family building permits issued: 3 (2010); Employment by occupation: 14.6% management, 21.8% professional, 14.0% services, 24.8% sales, 0.0% farming, 13.1% construction, 11.7% production (2005-2009 5-year est.).
Income: Per capita income: $32,292 (2010); Median household income: $64,196 (2010); Average household income: $81,495 (2010); Percent of households with income of $100,000 or more: 26.4% (2010); Poverty rate: 9.0% (2005-2009 5-year est.).
Taxes: Total city taxes per capita: $320 (2007); City property taxes per capita: $269 (2007).
Education: Percent of population age 25 and over with: High school diploma (including GED) or higher: 91.8% (2010); Bachelor's degree or higher: 24.3% (2010); Master's degree or higher: 9.1% (2010).
School District(s)
Riverdale CUSD 100 (PK-12)
   2009-10 Enrollment: 1,182 . . . . (309) 523-3184
Housing: Homeownership rate: 86.7% (2010); Median home value: $142,262 (2010); Median contract rent: $361 per month (2005-2009 5-year est.); Median year structure built: 1968 (2005-2009 5-year est.).
Transportation: Commute to work: 93.4% car, 0.0% public transportation, 1.5% walk, 3.9% work from home (2005-2009 5-year est.); Travel time to work: 24.4% less than 15 minutes, 48.6% 15 to 30 minutes, 21.1% 30 to 45 minutes, 3.9% 45 to 60 minutes, 2.0% 60 minutes or more (2005-2009 5-year est.)

RAPIDS CITY (village). Covers a land area of 1.530 square miles and a water area of 0 square miles. Located at 41.58° N. Lat; 90.34° W. Long. Elevation is 581 feet.
Population: 934 (1990); 953 (2000); 998 (2010); 1,016 (2015 projected); Race: 96.9% White, 0.2% Black, 0.0% Asian, 2.9% Other, 3.0% Hispanic of any race (2010); Density: 652.4 persons per square mile (2010); Average household size: 2.53 (2010); Median age: 40.4 (2010); Males per 100 females: 104.9 (2010); Marriage status: 18.5% never married, 65.4% now married, 7.3% widowed, 8.8% divorced (2005-2009 5-year est.); Foreign born: 2.0% (2005-2009 5-year est.); Ancestry (includes multiple ancestries): 32.7% German, 20.2% Irish, 12.7% English, 9.0% American, 4.1% French (2005-2009 5-year est.).
Economy: Single-family building permits issued: 0 (2010); Multi-family building permits issued: 0 (2010); Employment by occupation: 12.7%

management, 26.5% professional, 5.9% services, 28.5% sales, 0.0% farming, 8.4% construction, 18.1% production (2005-2009 5-year est.).
Income: Per capita income: $32,292 (2010); Median household income: $64,244 (2010); Average household income: $81,352 (2010); Percent of households with income of $100,000 or more: 26.4% (2010); Poverty rate: 1.9% (2005-2009 5-year est.).
Taxes: Total city taxes per capita: $178 (2007); City property taxes per capita: $107 (2007).
Education: Percent of population age 25 and over with: High school diploma (including GED) or higher: 91.6% (2010); Bachelor's degree or higher: 23.9% (2010); Master's degree or higher: 8.8% (2010).
Housing: Homeownership rate: 86.8% (2010); Median home value: $142,233 (2010); Median contract rent: $527 per month (2005-2009 5-year est.); Median year structure built: 1971 (2005-2009 5-year est.).
Transportation: Commute to work: 98.6% car, 0.0% public transportation, 0.0% walk, 1.4% work from home (2005-2009 5-year est.); Travel time to work: 11.5% less than 15 minutes, 74.9% 15 to 30 minutes, 12.6% 30 to 45 minutes, 0.9% 45 to 60 minutes, 0.0% 60 minutes or more (2005-2009 5-year est.)

REYNOLDS (village). Covers a land area of 0.369 square miles and a water area of 0 square miles. Located at 41.33° N. Lat; 90.67° W. Long. Elevation is 810 feet.
Population: 600 (1990); 508 (2000); 488 (2010); 478 (2015 projected); Race: 98.6% White, 0.4% Black, 0.2% Asian, 0.8% Other, 1.2% Hispanic of any race (2010); Density: 1,323.4 persons per square mile (2010); Average household size: 2.49 (2010); Median age: 39.0 (2010); Males per 100 females: 95.2 (2010); Marriage status: 17.8% never married, 68.0% now married, 5.1% widowed, 9.1% divorced (2005-2009 5-year est.); Foreign born: 0.0% (2005-2009 5-year est.); Ancestry (includes multiple ancestries): 26.2% Irish, 23.8% German, 14.1% Polish, 10.1% English, 4.5% American (2005-2009 5-year est.).
Economy: Single-family building permits issued: 0 (2010); Multi-family building permits issued: 0 (2010); Employment by occupation: 19.5% management, 13.7% professional, 21.7% services, 19.9% sales, 0.0% farming, 5.3% construction, 19.9% production (2005-2009 5-year est.).
Income: Per capita income: $28,477 (2010); Median household income: $61,111 (2010); Average household income: $69,681 (2010); Percent of households with income of $100,000 or more: 19.9% (2010); Poverty rate: 14.7% (2005-2009 5-year est.).
Taxes: Total city taxes per capita: $41 (2007); City property taxes per capita: $41 (2007).
Education: Percent of population age 25 and over with: High school diploma (including GED) or higher: 92.9% (2010); Bachelor's degree or higher: 19.8% (2010); Master's degree or higher: 5.0% (2010).
School District(s)
Rockridge CUSD 300 (PK-12)
   2009-10 Enrollment: 1,298 . . . . (309) 793-8001
Housing: Homeownership rate: 82.7% (2010); Median home value: $110,256 (2010); Median contract rent: $450 per month (2005-2009 5-year est.); Median year structure built: 1954 (2005-2009 5-year est.).
Transportation: Commute to work: 90.5% car, 0.0% public transportation, 8.2% walk, 1.4% work from home (2005-2009 5-year est.); Travel time to work: 18.0% less than 15 minutes, 30.9% 15 to 30 minutes, 46.5% 30 to 45 minutes, 2.3% 45 to 60 minutes, 2.3% 60 minutes or more (2005-2009 5-year est.)

ROCK ISLAND (city). Aka Quad Cities. County seat. Covers a land area of 15.924 square miles and a water area of 1.223 square miles. Located at 41.48° N. Lat; 90.57° W. Long. Elevation is 561 feet.
History: Rock Island developed from a community called Stephenson, whose name was changed in 1841. Rock Island was a steamboat port until the Rock Island Railroad Company completed a bridge across the Mississippi in 1855 and rail began to replace water as the means of transportation of goods. The Farmall Works of the International Harvester Company was established in Rock Island. The limestone island that became the location of the Rock Island Arsenal first served as a prison for Confederate soldiers, with more than 12,000 at a time confined here.
Population: 40,511 (1990); 39,684 (2000); 38,118 (2010); 37,220 (2015 projected); Race: 74.9% White, 17.2% Black, 1.5% Asian, 6.5% Other, 7.4% Hispanic of any race (2010); Density: 2,393.7 persons per square mile (2010); Average household size: 2.27 (2010); Median age: 37.1 (2010); Males per 100 females: 92.5 (2010); Marriage status: 35.3% never married, 44.6% now married, 7.6% widowed, 12.5% divorced (2005-2009 5-year est.); Foreign born: 5.0% (2005-2009 5-year est.); Ancestry

(includes multiple ancestries): 23.3% German, 13.0% Irish, 7.4% English, 6.3% Swedish, 4.8% American (2005-2009 5-year est.).
Economy: Unemployment rate: 8.7% (August 2011); Total civilian labor force: 19,893 (August 2011); Single-family building permits issued: 9 (2010); Multi-family building permits issued: 70 (2010); Employment by occupation: 10.7% management, 19.3% professional, 16.8% services, 26.9% sales, 0.3% farming, 8.1% construction, 18.0% production (2005-2009 5-year est.).
Income: Per capita income: $22,546 (2010); Median household income: $41,753 (2010); Average household income: $53,789 (2010); Percent of households with income of $100,000 or more: 11.1% (2010); Poverty rate: 17.5% (2005-2009 5-year est.).
Taxes: Total city taxes per capita: $515 (2007); City property taxes per capita: $328 (2007).
Education: Percent of population age 25 and over with: High school diploma (including GED) or higher: 86.3% (2010); Bachelor's degree or higher: 21.5% (2010); Master's degree or higher: 7.2% (2010).

School District(s)
Rock Island SD 41 (PK-12)
   2009-10 Enrollment: 6,225 . . . . (309) 793-5900

Four-year College(s)
Augustana College (Private, Not-for-profit, Evangelical Lutheran Church)
   Fall 2009 Enrollment: 2,472 . . . . (309) 794-7000
   2010-11 Tuition: In-state $32,235; Out-of-state $32,235
Trinity College of Nursing and Health Sciences (Private, Not-for-profit)
   Fall 2009 Enrollment: 264 . . . . (309) 779-7700
   2010-11 Tuition: In-state $13,532; Out-of-state $13,532
Housing: Homeownership rate: 66.8% (2010); Median home value: $91,913 (2010); Median contract rent: $444 per month (2005-2009 5-year est.); Median year structure built: 1951 (2005-2009 5-year est.).
Hospitals: Trinity Medical Center (338 beds)
Safety: Violent crime rate: 81.8 per 10,000 population; Property crime rate: 348.0 per 10,000 population (2010).
Newspapers: Leader (Local news; Circulation 53,000); Rock Island Argus (Community news; Circulation 12,729)
Transportation: Commute to work: 87.8% car, 2.9% public transportation, 6.0% walk, 2.2% work from home (2005-2009 5-year est.); Travel time to work: 47.9% less than 15 minutes, 40.1% 15 to 30 minutes, 6.8% 30 to 45 minutes, 2.3% 45 to 60 minutes, 2.9% 60 minutes or more (2005-2009 5-year est.); Amtrak: bus service available.
Additional Information Contacts
City of Rock Island . . . . (309) 732-2000
   http://www.rigov.org

ROCK ISLAND ARSENAL (CDP). Covers a land area of 1.595 square miles and a water area of 0.968 square miles. Located at 41.51° N. Lat; 90.53° W. Long.
Population: 212 (1990); 145 (2000); 125 (2010); 119 (2015 projected); Race: 68.8% White, 18.4% Black, 0.0% Asian, 12.8% Other, 1.6% Hispanic of any race (2010); Density: 78.4 persons per square mile (2010); Average household size: 3.38 (2010); Median age: 24.8 (2010); Males per 100 females: 101.6 (2010); Marriage status: 16.7% never married, 56.1% now married, 15.2% widowed, 12.1% divorced (2005-2009 5-year est.); Foreign born: 28.7% (2005-2009 5-year est.); Ancestry (includes multiple ancestries): 38.9% German, 23.1% Norwegian, 23.1% Swedish (2005-2009 5-year est.).
Economy: Employment by occupation: 39.6% management, 16.7% professional, 0.0% services, 0.0% sales, 22.9% farming, 0.0% construction, 20.8% production (2005-2009 5-year est.).
Income: Per capita income: $19,520 (2010); Median household income: $54,167 (2010); Average household income: $65,946 (2010); Percent of households with income of $100,000 or more: 13.5% (2010); Poverty rate: 0.0% (2005-2009 5-year est.).
Education: Percent of population age 25 and over with: High school diploma (including GED) or higher: 80.6% (2010); Bachelor's degree or higher: 11.3% (2010); Master's degree or higher: 3.2% (2010).
Housing: Homeownership rate: 0.0% (2010); Median home value: n/a (2010); Median contract rent: n/a per month (2005-2009 5-year est.); Median year structure built: 1950 (2005-2009 5-year est.).
Transportation: Commute to work: 100.0% car, 0.0% public transportation, 0.0% walk, 0.0% work from home (2005-2009 5-year est.); Travel time to work: 32.8% less than 15 minutes, 50.0% 15 to 30 minutes, 17.2% 30 to 45 minutes, 0.0% 45 to 60 minutes, 0.0% 60 minutes or more (2005-2009 5-year est.)

SILVIS (city). Covers a land area of 3.646 square miles and a water area of 0 square miles. Located at 41.50° N. Lat; 90.41° W. Long. Elevation is 594 feet.
History: Incorporated 1906.
Population: 7,048 (1990); 7,269 (2000); 7,302 (2010); 7,296 (2015 projected); Race: 83.6% White, 4.3% Black, 1.4% Asian, 10.7% Other, 14.5% Hispanic of any race (2010); Density: 2,002.9 persons per square mile (2010); Average household size: 2.37 (2010); Median age: 37.1 (2010); Males per 100 females: 94.3 (2010); Marriage status: 24.7% never married, 48.6% now married, 11.9% widowed, 14.9% divorced (2005-2009 5-year est.); Foreign born: 5.0% (2005-2009 5-year est.); Ancestry (includes multiple ancestries): 27.8% German, 11.7% Irish, 8.4% English, 7.8% Swedish, 6.6% Belgian (2005-2009 5-year est.).
Economy: Single-family building permits issued: 5 (2010); Multi-family building permits issued: 0 (2010); Employment by occupation: 9.1% management, 18.3% professional, 17.0% services, 25.8% sales, 0.9% farming, 9.6% construction, 19.3% production (2005-2009 5-year est.).
Income: Per capita income: $21,543 (2010); Median household income: $43,251 (2010); Average household income: $51,079 (2010); Percent of households with income of $100,000 or more: 10.5% (2010); Poverty rate: 11.1% (2005-2009 5-year est.).
Taxes: Total city taxes per capita: $623 (2007); City property taxes per capita: $453 (2007).
Education: Percent of population age 25 and over with: High school diploma (including GED) or higher: 82.2% (2010); Bachelor's degree or higher: 11.8% (2010); Master's degree or higher: 3.8% (2010).

School District(s)
Carbon Cliff-Barstow SD 36 (PK-08)
   2009-10 Enrollment: 286 . . . . (309) 792-2002
East Moline SD 37 (PK-08)
   2009-10 Enrollment: 2,545 . . . . (309) 792-2887
Silvis SD 34 (PK-08)
   2009-10 Enrollment: 623 . . . . (309) 792-9325
Housing: Homeownership rate: 64.1% (2010); Median home value: $104,777 (2010); Median contract rent: $478 per month (2005-2009 5-year est.); Median year structure built: 1966 (2005-2009 5-year est.).
Hospitals: Genesis Medical Center-Illini Campus (150 beds)
Safety: Violent crime rate: 36.2 per 10,000 population; Property crime rate: 412.8 per 10,000 population (2010).
Newspapers: Hola America (Community news; Circulation 10,000)
Transportation: Commute to work: 95.1% car, 0.4% public transportation, 1.1% walk, 3.1% work from home (2005-2009 5-year est.); Travel time to work: 34.5% less than 15 minutes, 41.9% 15 to 30 minutes, 19.0% 30 to 45 minutes, 3.0% 45 to 60 minutes, 1.6% 60 minutes or more (2005-2009 5-year est.)
Additional Information Contacts
City of Silvis . . . . (309) 792-9181
   http://www.silvisil.org

TAYLOR RIDGE (unincorporated postal area, zip code 61284). Covers a land area of 56.358 square miles and a water area of 0.198 square miles. Located at 41.40° N. Lat; 90.73° W. Long. Elevation is 771 feet.
Population: 3,439 (2000); Race: 98.6% White, 0.9% Black, 0.0% Asian, 0.5% Other, 0.7% Hispanic of any race (2000); Density: 61.0 persons per square mile (2000); Age: 26.9% under 18, 10.6% over 64 (2000); Marriage status: 18.4% never married, 69.0% now married, 5.9% widowed, 6.7% divorced (2000); Foreign born: 0.1% (2000); Ancestry (includes multiple ancestries): 34.4% German, 12.5% Irish, 9.3% English, 7.5% American, 6.1% Belgian (2000).
Economy: Employment by occupation: 16.2% management, 19.3% professional, 8.8% services, 28.1% sales, 0.2% farming, 8.6% construction, 18.8% production (2000).
Income: Per capita income: $26,077 (2000); Median household income: $62,882 (2000); Poverty rate: 5.0% (2000).
Education: Percent of population age 25 and over with: High school diploma (including GED) or higher: 88.9% (2000); Bachelor's degree or higher: 19.1% (2000).

School District(s)
Rockridge CUSD 300 (PK-12)
   2009-10 Enrollment: 1,298 . . . . (309) 793-8001
Housing: Homeownership rate: 91.8% (2000); Median home value: $109,800 (2000); Median contract rent: $378 per month (2000); Median year structure built: 1969 (2000).

Transportation: Commute to work: 94.8% car, 0.1% public transportation, 0.8% walk, 4.1% work from home (2000); Travel time to work: 12.8% less than 15 minutes, 54.4% 15 to 30 minutes, 26.8% 30 to 45 minutes, 2.7% 45 to 60 minutes, 3.3% 60 minutes or more (2000)

Saline County

Located in southeastern Illinois, partly in the Ozarks; drained by the Saline River; includes part of Shawnee National Forest. Covers a land area of 383.31 square miles, a water area of 3.67 square miles, and is located in the Central Time Zone at 37.75° N. Lat., 88.54° W. Long. The county was founded in 1847. County seat is Harrisburg.

Saline County is part of the Harrisburg, IL Micropolitan Statistical Area. The entire metro area includes: Saline County, IL

Weather Station: Harrisburg   Elevation: 365 feet

	Jan	Feb	Mar	Apr	May	Jun	Jul	Aug	Sep	Oct	Nov	Dec
High	41	47	57	69	78	86	89	89	82	71	58	46
Low	24	27	35	45	55	64	67	66	57	45	37	28
Precip	3.4	2.8	4.3	4.4	4.9	4.3	3.9	2.9	3.2	3.9	4.1	4.2
Snow	1.3	1.6	0.6	tr	0.0	0.0	0.0	0.0	0.0	tr	0.1	0.6

High and Low temperatures in degrees Fahrenheit; Precipitation and Snow in inches

Population: 26,551 (1990); 26,733 (2000); 25,859 (2010); 25,327 (2015 projected); Race: 93.1% White, 4.5% Black, 0.3% Asian, 2.2% Other, 1.4% Hispanic of any race (2010); Density: 67.5 persons per square mile (2010); Average household size: 2.30 (2010); Median age: 40.2 (2010); Males per 100 females: 94.5 (2010).
Religion: Five largest groups: 41.1% Southern Baptist Convention, 4.3% The United Methodist Church, 4.3% Catholic Church, 1.6% Church of God (Cleveland, Tennessee), 1.4% Christian Churches and Churches of Christ (2000).
Economy: Unemployment rate: 9.6% (August 2011); Total civilian labor force: 13,229 (August 2011); Leading industries: 21.7% health care and social assistance; 17.9% mining; 16.5% retail trade (2009); Farms: 497 totaling 117,233 acres (2007); Companies that employ 500 or more persons: 1 (2009); Companies that employ 100 to 499 persons: 7 (2009); Companies that employ less than 100 persons: 594 (2009); Black-owned businesses: n/a (2007); Hispanic-owned businesses: n/a (2007); Asian-owned businesses: n/a (2007); Women-owned businesses: 497 (2007); Retail sales per capita: $12,782 (2010). Single-family building permits issued: 0 (2010); Multi-family building permits issued: 0 (2010).
Income: Per capita income: $19,189 (2010); Median household income: $35,072 (2010); Average household income: $45,500 (2010); Percent of households with income of $100,000 or more: 7.4% (2010); Poverty rate: 16.6% (2009); Bankruptcy rate: 5.99% (2010).
Taxes: Total county taxes per capita: $148 (2007); County property taxes per capita: $100 (2007).
Education: Percent of population age 25 and over with: High school diploma (including GED) or higher: 81.9% (2010); Bachelor's degree or higher: 14.0% (2010); Master's degree or higher: 5.2% (2010).
Housing: Homeownership rate: 72.6% (2010); Median home value: $59,023 (2010); Median contract rent: $310 per month (2005-2009 5-year est.); Median year structure built: 1964 (2005-2009 5-year est.)
Health: Birth rate: 125.9 per 10,000 population (2009); Death rate: 148.4 per 10,000 population (2009); Age-adjusted cancer mortality rate: 253.7 deaths per 100,000 population (2007); Number of physicians: 12.4 per 10,000 population (2008); Hospital beds: 38.1 per 10,000 population (2007); Hospital admissions: 1,687.9 per 10,000 population (2007).
Elections: 2008 Presidential election results: 44.5% Obama, 53.4% McCain, 1.1% Nader
National and State Parks: Saline County State Conservation Area
Additional Information Contacts
Saline County Government . . . . (618) 252-6905

City of Harrisburg. . . . . (618) 253-7740
   http://thecityofharrisburgil.com
Saline County Chamber of Commerce . . . . (618) 252-4192
   http://salinecountychamber.org

Saline County Communities

CARRIER MILLS (village). Aka Carriers Mills. Covers a land area of 1.238 square miles and a water area of 0.005 square miles. Located at 37.68° N. Lat; 88.62° W. Long. Elevation is 387 feet.

History: Carriers (or Carrier) Mills was named for William H. Carrier who built a sawmill here in 1870. The town developed around the mining industry.
Population: 1,991 (1990); 1,886 (2000); 1,767 (2010); 1,714 (2015 projected); Race: 85.9% White, 11.4% Black, 0.3% Asian, 2.5% Other, 1.1% Hispanic of any race (2010); Density: 1,426.8 persons per square mile (2010); Average household size: 2.29 (2010); Median age: 41.0 (2010); Males per 100 females: 86.8 (2010); Marriage status: 18.3% never married, 46.6% now married, 22.3% widowed, 12.8% divorced (2005-2009 5-year est.); Foreign born: 1.1% (2005-2009 5-year est.); Ancestry (includes multiple ancestries): 15.1% Irish, 9.6% German, 8.1% English, 3.7% American, 3.2% Scotch-Irish (2005-2009 5-year est.).
Economy: Employment by occupation: 7.6% management, 18.6% professional, 22.6% services, 30.1% sales, 2.4% farming, 8.7% construction, 10.0% production (2005-2009 5-year est.).
Income: Per capita income: $18,806 (2010); Median household income: $34,577 (2010); Average household income: $43,581 (2010); Percent of households with income of $100,000 or more: 7.1% (2010); Poverty rate: 19.2% (2005-2009 5-year est.).
Taxes: Total city taxes per capita: $27 (2007); City property taxes per capita: $27 (2007).
Education: Percent of population age 25 and over with: High school diploma (including GED) or higher: 79.3% (2010); Bachelor's degree or higher: 10.0% (2010); Master's degree or higher: 4.4% (2010).
School District(s)
Carrier Mills-Stonefort CUSD 2 (PK-12)
   2009-10 Enrollment: 456 . . . . (618) 994-2392
Housing: Homeownership rate: 74.8% (2010); Median home value: $47,876 (2010); Median contract rent: $259 per month (2005-2009 5-year est.); Median year structure built: 1964 (2005-2009 5-year est.).
Safety: Violent crime rate: 78.0 per 10,000 population; Property crime rate: 167.0 per 10,000 population (2010).
Transportation: Commute to work: 95.5% car, 0.0% public transportation, 1.2% walk, 0.0% work from home (2005-2009 5-year est.); Travel time to work: 19.0% less than 15 minutes, 50.4% 15 to 30 minutes, 19.4% 30 to 45 minutes, 8.1% 45 to 60 minutes, 3.1% 60 minutes or more (2005-2009 5-year est.)

ELDORADO (city). Covers a land area of 2.304 square miles and a water area of 0.032 square miles. Located at 37.81° N. Lat; 88.44° W. Long. Elevation is 394 feet.
History: Incorporated 1873.
Population: 4,645 (1990); 4,534 (2000); 4,284 (2010); 4,168 (2015 projected); Race: 97.3% White, 0.6% Black, 0.0% Asian, 2.1% Other, 2.0% Hispanic of any race (2010); Density: 1,859.3 persons per square mile (2010); Average household size: 2.21 (2010); Median age: 41.8 (2010); Males per 100 females: 86.7 (2010); Marriage status: 20.8% never married, 55.0% now married, 8.1% widowed, 16.1% divorced (2005-2009 5-year est.); Foreign born: 0.9% (2005-2009 5-year est.); Ancestry (includes multiple ancestries): 26.0% Irish, 20.7% German, 13.5% American, 6.5% English, 3.1% Italian (2005-2009 5-year est.).
Economy: Employment by occupation: 13.1% management, 18.0% professional, 21.5% services, 20.7% sales, 0.7% farming, 14.0% construction, 12.1% production (2005-2009 5-year est.).
Income: Per capita income: $15,262 (2010); Median household income: $27,362 (2010); Average household income: $34,542 (2010); Percent of households with income of $100,000 or more: 2.4% (2010); Poverty rate: 23.1% (2005-2009 5-year est.).
Taxes: Total city taxes per capita: $122 (2007); City property taxes per capita: $55 (2007).
Education: Percent of population age 25 and over with: High school diploma (including GED) or higher: 75.1% (2010); Bachelor's degree or higher: 11.2% (2010); Master's degree or higher: 4.3% (2010).
School District(s)
Eldorado CUSD 4 (PK-12)
   2009-10 Enrollment: 1,246 . . . . (618) 273-6394
Housing: Homeownership rate: 67.2% (2010); Median home value: $43,438 (2010); Median contract rent: $271 per month (2005-2009 5-year est.); Median year structure built: 1955 (2005-2009 5-year est.).
Hospitals: Ferrell Hospital (51 beds)
Newspapers: Eldorado Daily Journal (Local news; Circulation 18,000)
Transportation: Commute to work: 89.0% car, 0.3% public transportation, 3.7% walk, 4.0% work from home (2005-2009 5-year est.); Travel time to work: 47.9% less than 15 minutes, 30.4% 15 to 30 minutes, 9.2% 30 to 45

minutes, 8.1% 45 to 60 minutes, 4.3% 60 minutes or more (2005-2009 5-year est.)

Additional Information Contacts
Saline County Chamber of Commerce . . . . (618) 252-4192
 http://salinecountychamber.org

GALATIA (village). Covers a land area of 1.961 square miles and a water area of 0.016 square miles. Located at 37.84° N. Lat; 88.61° W. Long. Elevation is 420 feet.
Population: 983 (1990); 1,013 (2000); 951 (2010); 924 (2015 projected); Race: 98.3% White, 0.2% Black, 0.0% Asian, 1.5% Other, 0.5% Hispanic of any race (2010); Density: 484.9 persons per square mile (2010); Average household size: 2.30 (2010); Median age: 40.6 (2010); Males per 100 females: 83.6 (2010); Marriage status: 20.2% never married, 53.5% now married, 14.2% widowed, 12.1% divorced (2005-2009 5-year est.); Foreign born: 0.2% (2005-2009 5-year est.); Ancestry (includes multiple ancestries): 19.3% Irish, 13.4% German, 9.7% American, 8.8% English, 5.2% Italian (2005-2009 5-year est.).
Economy: Employment by occupation: 5.2% management, 13.7% professional, 31.4% services, 18.6% sales, 1.0% farming, 11.8% construction, 18.3% production (2005-2009 5-year est.).
Income: Per capita income: $18,017 (2010); Median household income: $32,982 (2010); Average household income: $41,253 (2010); Percent of households with income of $100,000 or more: 5.9% (2010); Poverty rate: 25.0% (2005-2009 5-year est.).
Taxes: Total city taxes per capita: $26 (2007); City property taxes per capita: $26 (2007).
Education: Percent of population age 25 and over with: High school diploma (including GED) or higher: 80.8% (2010); Bachelor's degree or higher: 9.7% (2010); Master's degree or higher: 4.5% (2010).

School District(s)
Galatia CUSD 1 (PK-12)
 2009-10 Enrollment: 420 . . . . (618) 268-4194
Housing: Homeownership rate: 72.6% (2010); Median home value: $67,606 (2010); Median contract rent: $238 per month (2005-2009 5-year est.); Median year structure built: 1967 (2005-2009 5-year est.).
Transportation: Commute to work: 90.8% car, 0.7% public transportation, 4.7% walk, 2.7% work from home (2005-2009 5-year est.); Travel time to work: 38.0% less than 15 minutes, 38.3% 15 to 30 minutes, 14.6% 30 to 45 minutes, 5.2% 45 to 60 minutes, 3.8% 60 minutes or more (2005-2009 5-year est.)

HARRISBURG (city). County seat. Covers a land area of 6.239 square miles and a water area of 0.141 square miles. Located at 37.73° N. Lat; 88.54° W. Long. Elevation is 397 feet.
History: Harrisburg was platted in 1853 and developed as an industrial center with planing, flour, and woolen mills founded in the late 1800's. Coal mining began in 1905.
Population: 9,592 (1990); 9,860 (2000); 9,445 (2010); 9,210 (2015 projected); Race: 88.7% White, 8.0% Black, 0.6% Asian, 2.8% Other, 2.0% Hispanic of any race (2010); Density: 1,513.8 persons per square mile (2010); Average household size: 2.21 (2010); Median age: 38.5 (2010); Males per 100 females: 97.0 (2010); Marriage status: 28.7% never married, 49.9% now married, 10.3% widowed, 11.2% divorced (2005-2009 5-year est.); Foreign born: 0.6% (2005-2009 5-year est.); Ancestry (includes multiple ancestries): 17.2% Irish, 14.6% German, 11.1% American, 10.1% English, 4.5% Scotch-Irish (2005-2009 5-year est.).
Economy: Employment by occupation: 7.7% management, 21.1% professional, 24.6% services, 20.6% sales, 0.3% farming, 14.3% construction, 11.4% production (2005-2009 5-year est.).
Income: Per capita income: $18,145 (2010); Median household income: $32,492 (2010); Average household income: $42,610 (2010); Percent of households with income of $100,000 or more: 6.1% (2010); Poverty rate: 25.8% (2005-2009 5-year est.).
Taxes: Total city taxes per capita: $164 (2007); City property taxes per capita: $132 (2007).
Education: Percent of population age 25 and over with: High school diploma (including GED) or higher: 80.5% (2010); Bachelor's degree or higher: 13.2% (2010); Master's degree or higher: 5.0% (2010).

School District(s)
Edwd/Gltn/Hdin/Pop/Slne/Wbh/wn/wh (06-12)
 2009-10 Enrollment: n/a . . . . (618) 253-5581
Harrisburg CUSD 3 (PK-12)
 2009-10 Enrollment: 2,204 . . . . (618) 253-7637

Two-year College(s)
Southeastern Illinois College (Public)
 Fall 2009 Enrollment: 2,941 . . . . (618) 252-5400
 2010-11 Tuition: In-state $3,960; Out-of-state $4,320
Housing: Homeownership rate: 64.9% (2010); Median home value: $52,188 (2010); Median contract rent: $338 per month (2005-2009 5-year est.); Median year structure built: 1955 (2005-2009 5-year est.).
Hospitals: Harrisburg Medical Center (86 beds)
Newspapers: American Weekend - Daily Register (Community news); Daily Register (Regional news; Circulation 6,100); The Daily Register (Local news; Circulation 3,500)
Transportation: Commute to work: 91.5% car, 0.0% public transportation, 3.7% walk, 2.4% work from home (2005-2009 5-year est.); Travel time to work: 52.5% less than 15 minutes, 24.3% 15 to 30 minutes, 10.1% 30 to 45 minutes, 8.5% 45 to 60 minutes, 4.7% 60 minutes or more (2005-2009 5-year est.)

Additional Information Contacts
City of Harrisburg . . . . (618) 253-7740
 http://thecityofharrisburgil.com
Saline County Chamber of Commerce . . . . (618) 252-4192
 http://salinecountychamber.org

MUDDY (village). Covers a land area of 0.263 square miles and a water area of 0 square miles. Located at 37.76° N. Lat; 88.51° W. Long. Elevation is 371 feet.
Population: 108 (1990); 78 (2000); 81 (2010); 80 (2015 projected); Race: 96.3% White, 1.2% Black, 0.0% Asian, 2.5% Other, 1.2% Hispanic of any race (2010); Density: 308.3 persons per square mile (2010); Average household size: 2.38 (2010); Median age: 42.2 (2010); Males per 100 females: 102.5 (2010); Marriage status: 32.8% never married, 37.3% now married, 7.5% widowed, 22.4% divorced (2005-2009 5-year est.); Foreign born: 0.0% (2005-2009 5-year est.); Ancestry (includes multiple ancestries): 45.2% Irish, 25.0% Italian, 13.1% German, 7.1% English, 3.6% Polish (2005-2009 5-year est.).
Economy: Single-family building permits issued: 0 (2010); Multi-family building permits issued: 0 (2010); Employment by occupation: 11.1% management, 8.3% professional, 47.2% services, 5.6% sales, 8.3% farming, 11.1% construction, 8.3% production (2005-2009 5-year est.).
Income: Per capita income: $34,615 (2010); Median household income: $60,000 (2010); Average household income: $88,235 (2010); Percent of households with income of $100,000 or more: 26.5% (2010); Poverty rate: 45.0% (2005-2009 5-year est.).
Taxes: Total city taxes per capita: $135 (2007); City property taxes per capita: $122 (2007).
Education: Percent of population age 25 and over with: High school diploma (including GED) or higher: 86.4% (2010); Bachelor's degree or higher: 16.9% (2010); Master's degree or higher: 5.1% (2010).
Housing: Homeownership rate: 76.5% (2010); Median home value: $107,143 (2010); Median contract rent: $183 per month (2005-2009 5-year est.); Median year structure built: 1943 (2005-2009 5-year est.).
Transportation: Commute to work: 93.9% car, 0.0% public transportation, 0.0% walk, 0.0% work from home (2005-2009 5-year est.); Travel time to work: 78.8% less than 15 minutes, 12.1% 15 to 30 minutes, 0.0% 30 to 45 minutes, 0.0% 45 to 60 minutes, 9.1% 60 minutes or more (2005-2009 5-year est.)

RALEIGH (village). Covers a land area of 1.974 square miles and a water area of 0 square miles. Located at 37.82° N. Lat; 88.53° W. Long. Elevation is 410 feet.
Population: 305 (1990); 330 (2000); 315 (2010); 306 (2015 projected); Race: 99.0% White, 0.0% Black, 0.0% Asian, 1.0% Other, 0.0% Hispanic of any race (2010); Density: 159.5 persons per square mile (2010); Average household size: 2.40 (2010); Median age: 38.9 (2010); Males per 100 females: 101.9 (2010); Marriage status: 22.7% never married, 51.2% now married, 7.1% widowed, 19.0% divorced (2005-2009 5-year est.); Foreign born: 0.0% (2005-2009 5-year est.); Ancestry (includes multiple ancestries): 22.2% Irish, 13.8% German, 6.6% French, 5.7% Lithuanian, 5.5% American (2005-2009 5-year est.).
Economy: Employment by occupation: 7.7% management, 20.5% professional, 5.1% services, 23.7% sales, 0.0% farming, 17.3% construction, 25.6% production (2005-2009 5-year est.).
Income: Per capita income: $20,104 (2010); Median household income: $37,917 (2010); Average household income: $48,206 (2010); Percent of households with income of $100,000 or more: 7.6% (2010); Poverty rate: 10.9% (2005-2009 5-year est.).

Taxes: Total city taxes per capita: $19 (2007); City property taxes per capita: $19 (2007).

Education: Percent of population age 25 and over with: High school diploma (including GED) or higher: 90.4% (2010); Bachelor's degree or higher: 19.6% (2010); Master's degree or higher: 5.3% (2010).

Housing: Homeownership rate: 83.2% (2010); Median home value: $75,333 (2010); Median contract rent: $261 per month (2005-2009 5-year est.); Median year structure built: 1962 (2005-2009 5-year est.).

Transportation: Commute to work: 96.7% car, 0.0% public transportation, 0.0% walk, 3.3% work from home (2005-2009 5-year est.); Travel time to work: 42.9% less than 15 minutes, 25.9% 15 to 30 minutes, 4.1% 30 to 45 minutes, 6.1% 45 to 60 minutes, 21.1% 60 minutes or more (2005-2009 5-year est.)

Sangamon County

Located in central Illinois; drained by the Sangamon River and its South Fork; includes Lake Springfield. Covers a land area of 868.18 square miles, a water area of 8.82 square miles, and is located in the Central Time Zone at 39.76° N. Lat., 89.64° W. Long. The county was founded in 1821. County seat is Springfield.

Sangamon County is part of the Springfield, IL Metropolitan Statistical Area. The entire metro area includes: Menard County, IL; Sangamon County, IL

Weather Station: Springfield Capital Arpt										Elevation: 585 feet		
	Jan	Feb	Mar	Apr	May	Jun	Jul	Aug	Sep	Oct	Nov	Dec
High	35	40	52	64	75	83	86	85	79	66	52	39
Low	19	23	32	42	53	62	66	64	55	44	34	23
Precip	1.8	1.8	2.7	3.5	4.0	4.3	3.8	3.2	2.8	3.2	3.2	2.5
Snow	6.3	5.6	2.7	0.5	tr	0.0	tr	0.0	0.0	tr	0.8	5.4

High and Low temperatures in degrees Fahrenheit; Precipitation and Snow in inches

Population: 178,386 (1990); 188,951 (2000); 195,977 (2010); 198,129 (2015 projected); Race: 85.3% White, 11.0% Black, 1.3% Asian, 2.4% Other, 1.4% Hispanic of any race (2010); Density: 225.7 persons per square mile (2010); Average household size: 2.31 (2010); Median age: 38.9 (2010); Males per 100 females: 92.1 (2010).

Religion: Five largest groups: 19.5% Catholic Church, 7.9% Assemblies of God, 6.0% The United Methodist Church, 4.3% Lutheran Church—Missouri Synod, 3.9% Christian Churches and Churches of Christ (2000).

Economy: Unemployment rate: 7.5% (August 2011); Total civilian labor force: 113,336 (August 2011); Leading industries: 23.0% health care and social assistance; 14.7% retail trade; 10.7% accommodation & food services (2009); Farms: 1,153 totaling 518,153 acres (2007); Companies that employ 500 or more persons: 9 (2009); Companies that employ 100 to 499 persons: 105 (2009); Companies that employ less than 100 persons: 5,026 (2009); Black-owned businesses: 1,025 (2007); Hispanic-owned businesses: n/a (2007); Asian-owned businesses: n/a (2007); Women-owned businesses: 4,828 (2007); Retail sales per capita: $15,170 (2010). Single-family building permits issued: 277 (2010); Multi-family building permits issued: 113 (2010).

Income: Per capita income: $28,108 (2010); Median household income: $51,000 (2010); Average household income: $65,714 (2010); Percent of households with income of $100,000 or more: 17.0% (2010); Poverty rate: 13.1% (2009); Bankruptcy rate: 4.54% (2010).

Taxes: Total county taxes per capita: $132 (2007); County property taxes per capita: $124 (2007).

Education: Percent of population age 25 and over with: High school diploma (including GED) or higher: 91.2% (2010); Bachelor's degree or higher: 29.5% (2010); Master's degree or higher: 10.4% (2010).

Housing: Homeownership rate: 73.4% (2010); Median home value: $115,429 (2010); Median contract rent: $509 per month (2005-2009 5-year est.); Median year structure built: 1972 (2005-2009 5-year est.)

Health: Birth rate: 133.8 per 10,000 population (2009); Death rate: 93.7 per 10,000 population (2009); Age-adjusted cancer mortality rate: 202.4 deaths per 100,000 population (2007); Number of physicians: 52.8 per 10,000 population (2008); Hospital beds: 53.3 per 10,000 population (2007); Hospital admissions: 2,349.7 per 10,000 population (2007).

Environment: Air Quality Index: 92.9% good, 7.1% moderate, 0.0% unhealthy for sensitive individuals, 0.0% unhealthy (percent of days in 2008)

Elections: 2008 Presidential election results: 51.4% Obama, 47.0% McCain, 0.7% Nader

National and State Parks: Lincoln Home National Historic Site; Lincolns Tomb State Historic Site; Sangchris Lake State Park

Additional Information Contacts

Sangamon County Government . . . . (217) 753-6600
  http://www.co.sangamon.il.us
Chatham Area Chamber of Commerce . . . . (217) 483-6450
  http://www.chatham-il-chamber.com
City of Springfield . . . . (217) 789-2000
  http://www.springfield.il.us
Illinois Chamber of Commerce . . . . (217) 522-5512
  http://www.ilchamber.org
Pawnee Chamber of Commerce . . . . (217) 625-8270
  http://www.pawneechamber.org
Springfield Convention & Visitors Bureau . . . . (217) 789-2360
  http://www.visit-springfieldillinois.com
The Greater Springfield Chamber of Commerce . . . . (217) 525-1173
  http://www.gscc.org
Village of Chatham . . . . (217) 483-2451
  http://www.chathamil.net

Sangamon County Communities

AUBURN (city). Covers a land area of 3.156 square miles and a water area of 0 square miles. Located at 39.58° N. Lat; 89.74° W. Long. Elevation is 627 feet.

History: Incorporated 1865.

Population: 3,865 (1990); 4,317 (2000); 4,241 (2010); 4,207 (2015 projected); Race: 98.1% White, 0.4% Black, 0.3% Asian, 1.3% Other, 0.7% Hispanic of any race (2010); Density: 1,343.9 persons per square mile (2010); Average household size: 2.55 (2010); Median age: 34.2 (2010); Males per 100 females: 91.2 (2010); Marriage status: 26.7% never married, 54.7% now married, 10.9% widowed, 7.7% divorced (2005-2009 5-year est.); Foreign born: 0.3% (2005-2009 5-year est.); Ancestry (includes multiple ancestries): 39.1% German, 18.8% Irish, 12.0% American, 10.5% English, 8.3% French (2005-2009 5-year est.).

Economy: Single-family building permits issued: 3 (2010); Multi-family building permits issued: 0 (2010); Employment by occupation: 11.0% management, 10.5% professional, 20.7% services, 31.4% sales, 2.1% farming, 9.5% construction, 14.8% production (2005-2009 5-year est.).

Income: Per capita income: $25,365 (2010); Median household income: $55,330 (2010); Average household income: $64,735 (2010); Percent of households with income of $100,000 or more: 14.1% (2010); Poverty rate: 12.2% (2005-2009 5-year est.).

Taxes: Total city taxes per capita: $56 (2007); City property taxes per capita: $41 (2007).

Education: Percent of population age 25 and over with: High school diploma (including GED) or higher: 91.0% (2010); Bachelor's degree or higher: 21.0% (2010); Master's degree or higher: 4.4% (2010).

School District(s)

Auburn CUSD 10 (PK-12)
  2009-10 Enrollment: 1,532 . . . . (217) 438-6164

Housing: Homeownership rate: 78.8% (2010); Median home value: $121,084 (2010); Median contract rent: $465 per month (2005-2009 5-year est.); Median year structure built: 1968 (2005-2009 5-year est.).

Newspapers: Auburn Citizen (Local news); Divernon News (Local news); Pawnee Post (Local news; Circulation 800); Rochester Times (Local news; Circulation 925)

Transportation: Commute to work: 94.7% car, 0.0% public transportation, 1.7% walk, 2.6% work from home (2005-2009 5-year est.); Travel time to work: 24.0% less than 15 minutes, 37.6% 15 to 30 minutes, 33.4% 30 to 45 minutes, 1.1% 45 to 60 minutes, 3.9% 60 minutes or more (2005-2009 5-year est.)

BERLIN (village). Covers a land area of 0.996 square miles and a water area of 0 square miles. Located at 39.75° N. Lat; 89.90° W. Long. Elevation is 636 feet.

Population: 180 (1990); 140 (2000); 151 (2010); 152 (2015 projected); Race: 99.3% White, 0.0% Black, 0.0% Asian, 0.7% Other, 1.3% Hispanic of any race (2010); Density: 151.7 persons per square mile (2010); Average household size: 2.52 (2010); Median age: 45.6 (2010); Males per 100 females: 104.1 (2010); Marriage status: 23.8% never married, 62.9% now married, 7.0% widowed, 6.3% divorced (2005-2009 5-year est.); Foreign born: 0.0% (2005-2009 5-year est.); Ancestry (includes multiple ancestries): 34.5% German, 17.0% English, 16.4% Irish, 14.6% American, 4.7% Russian (2005-2009 5-year est.).

Economy: Employment by occupation: 5.6% management, 10.0% professional, 21.1% services, 24.4% sales, 0.0% farming, 6.7% construction, 32.2% production (2005-2009 5-year est.).
Income: Per capita income: $29,602 (2010); Median household income: $66,250 (2010); Average household income: $72,042 (2010); Percent of households with income of $100,000 or more: 21.7% (2010); Poverty rate: 14.0% (2005-2009 5-year est.).
Taxes: Total city taxes per capita: $14 (2007); City property taxes per capita: $7 (2007).
Education: Percent of population age 25 and over with: High school diploma (including GED) or higher: 92.9% (2010); Bachelor's degree or higher: 22.1% (2010); Master's degree or higher: 9.7% (2010).
Housing: Homeownership rate: 81.7% (2010); Median home value: $159,375 (2010); Median contract rent: $313 per month (2005-2009 5-year est.); Median year structure built: 1989 (2005-2009 5-year est.).
Transportation: Commute to work: 93.3% car, 0.0% public transportation, 4.4% walk, 2.2% work from home (2005-2009 5-year est.); Travel time to work: 20.5% less than 15 minutes, 26.1% 15 to 30 minutes, 42.0% 30 to 45 minutes, 11.4% 45 to 60 minutes, 0.0% 60 minutes or more (2005-2009 5-year est.)

BUFFALO (village). Covers a land area of 0.369 square miles and a water area of 0 square miles. Located at 39.85° N. Lat; 89.40° W. Long. Elevation is 614 feet.
Population: 503 (1990); 491 (2000); 471 (2010); 462 (2015 projected); Race: 97.5% White, 0.2% Black, 0.2% Asian, 2.1% Other, 0.8% Hispanic of any race (2010); Density: 1,277.9 persons per square mile (2010); Average household size: 2.51 (2010); Median age: 41.3 (2010); Males per 100 females: 101.3 (2010); Marriage status: 22.6% never married, 57.6% now married, 7.1% widowed, 12.8% divorced (2005-2009 5-year est.); Foreign born: 0.0% (2005-2009 5-year est.); Ancestry (includes multiple ancestries): 37.1% German, 30.2% Irish, 20.8% English, 12.2% American, 8.6% Dutch (2005-2009 5-year est.).
Economy: Single-family building permits issued: 0 (2010); Multi-family building permits issued: 0 (2010); Employment by occupation: 7.4% management, 13.7% professional, 14.7% services, 25.5% sales, 0.5% farming, 22.1% construction, 16.2% production (2005-2009 5-year est.).
Income: Per capita income: $27,705 (2010); Median household income: $63,176 (2010); Average household income: $68,556 (2010); Percent of households with income of $100,000 or more: 22.5% (2010); Poverty rate: 11.2% (2005-2009 5-year est.).
Taxes: Total city taxes per capita: $116 (2007); City property taxes per capita: $42 (2007).
Education: Percent of population age 25 and over with: High school diploma (including GED) or higher: 92.1% (2010); Bachelor's degree or higher: 16.7% (2010); Master's degree or higher: 4.3% (2010).
School District(s)
Tri City CUSD 1 (PK-12)
    2009-10 Enrollment: 544 . . . . (217) 364-4811
Housing: Homeownership rate: 84.5% (2010); Median home value: $131,429 (2010); Median contract rent: $304 per month (2005-2009 5-year est.); Median year structure built: 1955 (2005-2009 5-year est.).
Transportation: Commute to work: 95.8% car, 0.0% public transportation, 0.0% walk, 0.0% work from home (2005-2009 5-year est.); Travel time to work: 5.7% less than 15 minutes, 60.9% 15 to 30 minutes, 24.5% 30 to 45 minutes, 4.2% 45 to 60 minutes, 4.7% 60 minutes or more (2005-2009 5-year est.)

CANTRALL (village). Covers a land area of 0.255 square miles and a water area of 0 square miles. Located at 39.93° N. Lat; 89.67° W. Long. Elevation is 594 feet.
Population: 123 (1990); 139 (2000); 114 (2010); 115 (2015 projected); Race: 99.1% White, 0.0% Black, 0.0% Asian, 0.9% Other, 0.0% Hispanic of any race (2010); Density: 447.2 persons per square mile (2010); Average household size: 2.85 (2010); Median age: 39.0 (2010); Males per 100 females: 93.2 (2010); Marriage status: 24.7% never married, 63.9% now married, 5.2% widowed, 6.2% divorced (2005-2009 5-year est.); Foreign born: 0.9% (2005-2009 5-year est.); Ancestry (includes multiple ancestries): 34.2% German, 23.7% Irish, 14.9% English, 8.8% Italian, 7.0% American (2005-2009 5-year est.).
Economy: Employment by occupation: 0.0% management, 28.9% professional, 19.7% services, 30.3% sales, 0.0% farming, 9.2% construction, 11.8% production (2005-2009 5-year est.).
Income: Per capita income: $27,293 (2010); Median household income: $66,667 (2010); Average household income: $75,688 (2010); Percent of

households with income of $100,000 or more: 25.0% (2010); Poverty rate: 0.0% (2005-2009 5-year est.).
Taxes: Total city taxes per capita: $22 (2007); City property taxes per capita: $22 (2007).
Education: Percent of population age 25 and over with: High school diploma (including GED) or higher: 93.3% (2010); Bachelor's degree or higher: 34.7% (2010); Master's degree or higher: 9.3% (2010).
School District(s)
Athens CUSD 213 (PK-12)
    2009-10 Enrollment: 1,155 . . . . (217) 636-8761
Housing: Homeownership rate: 90.0% (2010); Median home value: $166,667 (2010); Median contract rent: n/a per month (2005-2009 5-year est.); Median year structure built: 1974 (2005-2009 5-year est.).
Transportation: Commute to work: 97.4% car, 0.0% public transportation, 2.6% walk, 0.0% work from home (2005-2009 5-year est.); Travel time to work: 5.3% less than 15 minutes, 71.1% 15 to 30 minutes, 21.1% 30 to 45 minutes, 2.6% 45 to 60 minutes, 0.0% 60 minutes or more (2005-2009 5-year est.)

CHATHAM (village). Covers a land area of 4.965 square miles and a water area of 0.003 square miles. Located at 39.67° N. Lat; 89.69° W. Long. Elevation is 600 feet.
Population: 6,443 (1990); 8,583 (2000); 10,325 (2010); 11,064 (2015 projected); Race: 96.4% White, 1.5% Black, 0.9% Asian, 1.2% Other, 0.8% Hispanic of any race (2010); Density: 2,079.5 persons per square mile (2010); Average household size: 2.69 (2010); Median age: 36.0 (2010); Males per 100 females: 96.6 (2010); Marriage status: 22.2% never married, 64.2% now married, 3.1% widowed, 10.5% divorced (2005-2009 5-year est.); Foreign born: 1.8% (2005-2009 5-year est.); Ancestry (includes multiple ancestries): 44.0% German, 19.7% Irish, 16.3% English, 8.8% American, 5.7% Italian (2005-2009 5-year est.).
Economy: Single-family building permits issued: 49 (2010); Multi-family building permits issued: 10 (2010); Employment by occupation: 15.5% management, 31.7% professional, 11.2% services, 28.8% sales, 0.7% farming, 5.9% construction, 6.1% production (2005-2009 5-year est.).
Income: Per capita income: $29,810 (2010); Median household income: $71,886 (2010); Average household income: $80,405 (2010); Percent of households with income of $100,000 or more: 25.4% (2010); Poverty rate: 2.4% (2005-2009 5-year est.).
Taxes: Total city taxes per capita: $175 (2007); City property taxes per capita: $104 (2007).
Education: Percent of population age 25 and over with: High school diploma (including GED) or higher: 96.1% (2010); Bachelor's degree or higher: 36.4% (2010); Master's degree or higher: 10.0% (2010).
School District(s)
Ball Chatham CUSD 5 (PK-12)
    2009-10 Enrollment: 4,383 . . . . (217) 483-2416
Housing: Homeownership rate: 86.6% (2010); Median home value: $138,436 (2010); Median contract rent: $573 per month (2005-2009 5-year est.); Median year structure built: 1988 (2005-2009 5-year est.).
Safety: Violent crime rate: 12.8 per 10,000 population; Property crime rate: 122.4 per 10,000 population (2010).
Newspapers: Chatham Clarion (Community news; Circulation 1,900)
Transportation: Commute to work: 95.8% car, 0.0% public transportation, 0.0% walk, 3.8% work from home (2005-2009 5-year est.); Travel time to work: 19.5% less than 15 minutes, 55.2% 15 to 30 minutes, 18.2% 30 to 45 minutes, 2.5% 45 to 60 minutes, 4.6% 60 minutes or more (2005-2009 5-year est.)
Additional Information Contacts
Chatham Area Chamber of Commerce . . . . (217) 483-6450
    http://www.chatham-il-chamber.com
Village of Chatham. . . . . (217) 483-2451
    http://www.chathamil.net

CLEAR LAKE (village). Covers a land area of 0.093 square miles and a water area of 0 square miles. Located at 39.81° N. Lat; 89.56° W. Long. Elevation is 574 feet.
Population: 231 (1990); 267 (2000); 226 (2010); 210 (2015 projected); Race: 94.2% White, 2.7% Black, 0.9% Asian, 2.2% Other, 1.3% Hispanic of any race (2010); Density: 2,430.8 persons per square mile (2010); Average household size: 2.60 (2010); Median age: 36.0 (2010); Males per 100 females: 101.8 (2010); Marriage status: 27.3% never married, 52.5% now married, 5.1% widowed, 15.2% divorced (2005-2009 5-year est.); Foreign born: 2.7% (2005-2009 5-year est.); Ancestry (includes multiple

ancestries): 16.8% German, 15.0% American, 10.6% Irish, 7.1% French, 5.3% Italian (2005-2009 5-year est.).
Economy: Employment by occupation: 4.8% management, 6.5% professional, 21.0% services, 38.7% sales, 0.0% farming, 11.3% construction, 17.7% production (2005-2009 5-year est.).
Income: Per capita income: $16,963 (2010); Median household income: $41,618 (2010); Average household income: $43,391 (2010); Percent of households with income of $100,000 or more: 2.3% (2010); Poverty rate: 7.1% (2005-2009 5-year est.).
Taxes: Total city taxes per capita: $12 (2007); City property taxes per capita: $8 (2007).
Education: Percent of population age 25 and over with: High school diploma (including GED) or higher: 78.9% (2010); Bachelor's degree or higher: 16.4% (2010); Master's degree or higher: 1.3% (2010).
Housing: Homeownership rate: 90.8% (2010); Median home value: $27,778 (2010); Median contract rent: $342 per month (2005-2009 5-year est.); Median year structure built: 1984 (2005-2009 5-year est.).
Transportation: Commute to work: 98.4% car, 0.0% public transportation, 1.6% walk, 0.0% work from home (2005-2009 5-year est.); Travel time to work: 38.7% less than 15 minutes, 56.5% 15 to 30 minutes, 4.8% 30 to 45 minutes, 0.0% 45 to 60 minutes, 0.0% 60 minutes or more (2005-2009 5-year est.)

CURRAN (village). Covers a land area of 2.068 square miles and a water area of 0 square miles. Located at 39.74° N. Lat; 89.77° W. Long. Elevation is 623 feet.
History: Incorporated 2005.
Population: n/a (1990); n/a (2000); 212 (2010); n/a (2015 projected); Race: 97.6% White, 0.0% Black, 2.8% Asian, -0.5% Other, 0.5% Hispanic of any race (2010); Density: 102.5 persons per square mile (2010); Average household size: 2.38 (2010); Median age: 44.3 (2010); Males per 100 females: 94.5 (2010); Marriage status: 22.1% never married, 62.8% now married, 13.6% widowed, 1.5% divorced (2005-2009 5-year est.); Foreign born: 0.0% (2005-2009 5-year est.); Ancestry (includes multiple ancestries): 41.7% Irish, 37.9% German, 21.4% English, 7.3% American, 5.8% French (2005-2009 5-year est.).
Economy: Employment by occupation: 10.3% management, 3.4% professional, 17.1% services, 37.0% sales, 0.0% farming, 3.4% construction, 28.8% production (2005-2009 5-year est.).
Income: Per capita income: n/a (2010); Median household income: n/a (2010); Average household income: n/a (2010); Percent of households with income of $100,000 or more: n/a (2010); Poverty rate: 6.3% (2005-2009 5-year est.).
Taxes: Total city taxes per capita: $33 (2007); City property taxes per capita: $17 (2007).
Education: Percent of population age 25 and over with: High school diploma (including GED) or higher: n/a (2010); Bachelor's degree or higher: n/a (2010); Master's degree or higher: n/a (2010).
Housing: Homeownership rate: n/a (2010); Median home value: n/a (2010); Median contract rent: n/a per month (2005-2009 5-year est.); Median year structure built: 1984 (2005-2009 5-year est.).
Transportation: Commute to work: 96.6% car, 0.0% public transportation, 0.0% walk, 1.4% work from home (2005-2009 5-year est.); Travel time to work: 9.0% less than 15 minutes, 50.0% 15 to 30 minutes, 29.2% 30 to 45 minutes, 11.8% 45 to 60 minutes, 0.0% 60 minutes or more (2005-2009 5-year est.)

DAWSON (village). Covers a land area of 0.871 square miles and a water area of 0 square miles. Located at 39.85° N. Lat; 89.46° W. Long. Elevation is 600 feet.
Population: 536 (1990); 466 (2000); 399 (2010); 375 (2015 projected); Race: 97.7% White, 0.0% Black, 0.0% Asian, 2.3% Other, 0.5% Hispanic of any race (2010); Density: 458.1 persons per square mile (2010); Average household size: 2.44 (2010); Median age: 41.7 (2010); Males per 100 females: 90.0 (2010); Marriage status: 22.0% never married, 60.5% now married, 6.4% widowed, 11.1% divorced (2005-2009 5-year est.); Foreign born: 0.0% (2005-2009 5-year est.); Ancestry (includes multiple ancestries): 39.0% German, 14.5% English, 11.6% Irish, 9.1% Scottish, 6.6% American (2005-2009 5-year est.).
Economy: Single-family building permits issued: 0 (2010); Multi-family building permits issued: 0 (2010); Employment by occupation: 2.1% management, 9.6% professional, 20.0% services, 32.9% sales, 0.0% farming, 22.1% construction, 13.3% production (2005-2009 5-year est.).
Income: Per capita income: $30,883 (2010); Median household income: $72,917 (2010); Average household income: $74,645 (2010); Percent of

households with income of $100,000 or more: 19.1% (2010); Poverty rate: 15.8% (2005-2009 5-year est.).
Taxes: Total city taxes per capita: $104 (2007); City property taxes per capita: $26 (2007).
Education: Percent of population age 25 and over with: High school diploma (including GED) or higher: 93.4% (2010); Bachelor's degree or higher: 15.3% (2010); Master's degree or higher: 2.8% (2010).
Housing: Homeownership rate: 77.8% (2010); Median home value: $105,000 (2010); Median contract rent: $404 per month (2005-2009 5-year est.); Median year structure built: 1964 (2005-2009 5-year est.).
Transportation: Commute to work: 97.1% car, 1.3% public transportation, 0.0% walk, 1.7% work from home (2005-2009 5-year est.); Travel time to work: 18.3% less than 15 minutes, 58.7% 15 to 30 minutes, 20.4% 30 to 45 minutes, 0.0% 45 to 60 minutes, 2.6% 60 minutes or more (2005-2009 5-year est.)

DIVERNON (village). Covers a land area of 0.797 square miles and a water area of 0.002 square miles. Located at 39.56° N. Lat; 89.65° W. Long. Elevation is 614 feet.
History: Incorporated 1900.
Population: 1,230 (1990); 1,201 (2000); 1,097 (2010); 1,053 (2015 projected); Race: 98.3% White, 0.5% Black, 0.1% Asian, 1.1% Other, 1.9% Hispanic of any race (2010); Density: 1,376.8 persons per square mile (2010); Average household size: 2.44 (2010); Median age: 38.8 (2010); Males per 100 females: 93.5 (2010); Marriage status: 17.3% never married, 55.6% now married, 15.3% widowed, 11.9% divorced (2005-2009 5-year est.); Foreign born: 0.2% (2005-2009 5-year est.); Ancestry (includes multiple ancestries): 33.7% German, 13.3% Irish, 9.7% American, 8.7% English, 6.8% Italian (2005-2009 5-year est.).
Economy: Single-family building permits issued: 0 (2010); Multi-family building permits issued: 0 (2010); Employment by occupation: 12.6% management, 19.0% professional, 15.9% services, 24.4% sales, 2.6% farming, 10.1% construction, 15.3% production (2005-2009 5-year est.).
Income: Per capita income: $28,070 (2010); Median household income: $57,707 (2010); Average household income: $68,211 (2010); Percent of households with income of $100,000 or more: 16.2% (2010); Poverty rate: 0.9% (2005-2009 5-year est.).
Taxes: Total city taxes per capita: $23 (2007); City property taxes per capita: $20 (2007).
Education: Percent of population age 25 and over with: High school diploma (including GED) or higher: 93.1% (2010); Bachelor's degree or higher: 17.3% (2010); Master's degree or higher: 6.4% (2010).
School District(s)
Auburn CUSD 10 (PK-12)
    2009-10 Enrollment: 1,532 . . . . (217) 438-6164
Housing: Homeownership rate: 81.1% (2010); Median home value: $115,157 (2010); Median contract rent: $398 per month (2005-2009 5-year est.); Median year structure built: 1957 (2005-2009 5-year est.).
Safety: Violent crime rate: 9.0 per 10,000 population; Property crime rate: 260.8 per 10,000 population (2010).
Transportation: Commute to work: 96.0% car, 0.0% public transportation, 1.4% walk, 1.6% work from home (2005-2009 5-year est.); Travel time to work: 11.9% less than 15 minutes, 53.1% 15 to 30 minutes, 25.7% 30 to 45 minutes, 5.4% 45 to 60 minutes, 3.9% 60 minutes or more (2005-2009 5-year est.)

GLENARM (unincorporated postal area, zip code 62536). Covers a land area of 7.817 square miles and a water area of 0.066 square miles. Located at 39.64° N. Lat; 89.65° W. Long. Elevation is 600 feet.
Population: 942 (2000); Race: 100.0% White, 0.0% Black, 0.0% Asian, 0.0% Other, 0.0% Hispanic of any race (2000); Density: 120.5 persons per square mile (2000); Age: 22.2% under 18, 7.5% over 64 (2000); Marriage status: 13.4% never married, 76.0% now married, 3.3% widowed, 7.3% divorced (2000); Foreign born: 1.1% (2000); Ancestry (includes multiple ancestries): 35.2% German, 24.4% Irish, 19.7% English, 8.0% American, 7.7% Dutch (2000).
Economy: Employment by occupation: 16.6% management, 31.0% professional, 4.9% services, 27.9% sales, 1.9% farming, 12.7% construction, 5.0% production (2000).
Income: Per capita income: $27,618 (2000); Median household income: $62,382 (2000); Poverty rate: 0.8% (2000).
Education: Percent of population age 25 and over with: High school diploma (including GED) or higher: 94.0% (2000); Bachelor's degree or higher: 32.4% (2000).

Housing: Homeownership rate: 89.0% (2000); Median home value: $118,500 (2000); Median contract rent: $668 per month (2000); Median year structure built: 1982 (2000).
Transportation: Commute to work: 93.2% car, 0.0% public transportation, 0.0% walk, 6.8% work from home (2000); Travel time to work: 16.2% less than 15 minutes, 59.5% 15 to 30 minutes, 18.0% 30 to 45 minutes, 6.3% 45 to 60 minutes, 0.0% 60 minutes or more (2000)

GRANDVIEW (village). Covers a land area of 0.341 square miles and a water area of 0 square miles. Located at 39.81° N. Lat; 89.62° W. Long. Elevation is 597 feet.
History: Incorporated 1939.
Population: 1,640 (1990); 1,537 (2000); 1,334 (2010); 1,249 (2015 projected); Race: 90.5% White, 7.1% Black, 0.0% Asian, 2.4% Other, 0.7% Hispanic of any race (2010); Density: 3,906.9 persons per square mile (2010); Average household size: 2.31 (2010); Median age: 39.6 (2010); Males per 100 females: 93.9 (2010); Marriage status: 26.8% never married, 50.2% now married, 9.8% widowed, 13.2% divorced (2005-2009 5-year est.); Foreign born: 1.1% (2005-2009 5-year est.); Ancestry (includes multiple ancestries): 29.7% German, 18.0% Irish, 12.8% American, 10.1% English, 7.4% Italian (2005-2009 5-year est.).
Economy: Single-family building permits issued: 0 (2010); Multi-family building permits issued: 0 (2010); Employment by occupation: 7.1% management, 8.2% professional, 16.6% services, 47.6% sales, 0.0% farming, 8.9% construction, 11.5% production (2005-2009 5-year est.).
Income: Per capita income: $19,493 (2010); Median household income: $39,709 (2010); Average household income: $45,139 (2010); Percent of households with income of $100,000 or more: 4.0% (2010); Poverty rate: 10.1% (2005-2009 5-year est.).
Taxes: Total city taxes per capita: $51 (2007); City property taxes per capita: $27 (2007).
Education: Percent of population age 25 and over with: High school diploma (including GED) or higher: 82.3% (2010); Bachelor's degree or higher: 8.7% (2010); Master's degree or higher: 1.9% (2010).
Housing: Homeownership rate: 80.1% (2010); Median home value: $77,059 (2010); Median contract rent: $506 per month (2005-2009 5-year est.); Median year structure built: 1954 (2005-2009 5-year est.).
Safety: Violent crime rate: 72.4 per 10,000 population; Property crime rate: 246.2 per 10,000 population (2010).
Transportation: Commute to work: 91.6% car, 1.9% public transportation, 3.2% walk, 2.9% work from home (2005-2009 5-year est.); Travel time to work: 47.0% less than 15 minutes, 38.6% 15 to 30 minutes, 5.9% 30 to 45 minutes, 3.1% 45 to 60 minutes, 5.5% 60 minutes or more (2005-2009 5-year est.)

ILLIOPOLIS (village). Covers a land area of 0.452 square miles and a water area of 0 square miles. Located at 39.85° N. Lat; 89.24° W. Long. Elevation is 604 feet.
Population: 947 (1990); 916 (2000); 828 (2010); 796 (2015 projected); Race: 97.7% White, 0.4% Black, 0.0% Asian, 1.9% Other, 0.1% Hispanic of any race (2010); Density: 1,832.2 persons per square mile (2010); Average household size: 2.46 (2010); Median age: 37.9 (2010); Males per 100 females: 94.8 (2010); Marriage status: 26.5% never married, 51.6% now married, 4.9% widowed, 16.9% divorced (2005-2009 5-year est.); Foreign born: 0.9% (2005-2009 5-year est.); Ancestry (includes multiple ancestries): 39.9% German, 29.7% Irish, 15.9% English, 9.6% American, 3.2% Dutch (2005-2009 5-year est.).
Economy: Single-family building permits issued: 1 (2010); Multi-family building permits issued: 0 (2010); Employment by occupation: 8.8% management, 16.1% professional, 7.1% services, 23.8% sales, 3.1% farming, 6.2% construction, 34.8% production (2005-2009 5-year est.).
Income: Per capita income: $26,965 (2010); Median household income: $56,633 (2010); Average household income: $65,766 (2010); Percent of households with income of $100,000 or more: 14.0% (2010); Poverty rate: 7.8% (2005-2009 5-year est.).
Taxes: Total city taxes per capita: $113 (2007); City property taxes per capita: $26 (2007).
Education: Percent of population age 25 and over with: High school diploma (including GED) or higher: 92.3% (2010); Bachelor's degree or higher: 14.9% (2010); Master's degree or higher: 4.9% (2010).

School District(s)
Sangamon Valley CUSD 9 (PK-12)
    2009-10 Enrollment: 830 . . . . (217) 668-2338

Housing: Homeownership rate: 78.6% (2010); Median home value: $86,400 (2010); Median contract rent: $421 per month (2005-2009 5-year est.); Median year structure built: 1949 (2005-2009 5-year est.).
Newspapers: County Line Observer (Community news; Circulation 700)
Transportation: Commute to work: 93.6% car, 0.0% public transportation, 2.2% walk, 3.7% work from home (2005-2009 5-year est.); Travel time to work: 43.5% less than 15 minutes, 14.1% 15 to 30 minutes, 37.3% 30 to 45 minutes, 3.2% 45 to 60 minutes, 1.9% 60 minutes or more (2005-2009 5-year est.)

JEROME (village). Covers a land area of 0.371 square miles and a water area of 0 square miles. Located at 39.76° N. Lat; 89.67° W. Long. Elevation is 600 feet.
Population: 1,530 (1990); 1,414 (2000); 1,337 (2010); 1,283 (2015 projected); Race: 78.5% White, 14.2% Black, 3.0% Asian, 4.3% Other, 3.5% Hispanic of any race (2010); Density: 3,599.5 persons per square mile (2010); Average household size: 2.07 (2010); Median age: 40.9 (2010); Males per 100 females: 90.2 (2010); Marriage status: 28.8% never married, 45.7% now married, 10.0% widowed, 15.4% divorced (2005-2009 5-year est.); Foreign born: 3.3% (2005-2009 5-year est.); Ancestry (includes multiple ancestries): 32.1% German, 20.9% Irish, 13.8% English, 9.1% American, 7.0% Italian (2005-2009 5-year est.).
Economy: Single-family building permits issued: 0 (2010); Multi-family building permits issued: 0 (2010); Employment by occupation: 20.0% management, 18.0% professional, 12.8% services, 36.1% sales, 0.0% farming, 4.7% construction, 8.4% production (2005-2009 5-year est.).
Income: Per capita income: $25,280 (2010); Median household income: $46,679 (2010); Average household income: $52,365 (2010); Percent of households with income of $100,000 or more: 7.7% (2010); Poverty rate: 5.3% (2005-2009 5-year est.).
Taxes: Total city taxes per capita: $72 (2007); City property taxes per capita: $22 (2007).
Education: Percent of population age 25 and over with: High school diploma (including GED) or higher: 92.5% (2010); Bachelor's degree or higher: 24.4% (2010); Master's degree or higher: 6.9% (2010).
Housing: Homeownership rate: 76.6% (2010); Median home value: $98,047 (2010); Median contract rent: $575 per month (2005-2009 5-year est.); Median year structure built: 1954 (2005-2009 5-year est.).
Transportation: Commute to work: 94.5% car, 0.4% public transportation, 2.4% walk, 1.0% work from home (2005-2009 5-year est.); Travel time to work: 48.7% less than 15 minutes, 44.9% 15 to 30 minutes, 2.4% 30 to 45 minutes, 2.9% 45 to 60 minutes, 1.1% 60 minutes or more (2005-2009 5-year est.)

LELAND GROVE (city). Covers a land area of 0.627 square miles and a water area of 0 square miles. Located at 39.77° N. Lat; 89.68° W. Long. Elevation is 600 feet.
Population: 1,644 (1990); 1,592 (2000); 1,481 (2010); 1,462 (2015 projected); Race: 95.9% White, 1.5% Black, 0.9% Asian, 1.7% Other, 1.1% Hispanic of any race (2010); Density: 2,363.2 persons per square mile (2010); Average household size: 2.31 (2010); Median age: 48.4 (2010); Males per 100 females: 88.2 (2010); Marriage status: 20.0% never married, 66.6% now married, 5.6% widowed, 7.8% divorced (2005-2009 5-year est.); Foreign born: 3.7% (2005-2009 5-year est.); Ancestry (includes multiple ancestries): 31.6% German, 25.6% Irish, 20.5% English, 7.8% Scotch-Irish, 7.6% Italian (2005-2009 5-year est.).
Economy: Single-family building permits issued: 23 (2010); Multi-family building permits issued: 0 (2010); Employment by occupation: 21.6% management, 49.4% professional, 4.9% services, 21.4% sales, 0.0% farming, 2.1% construction, 0.6% production (2005-2009 5-year est.).
Income: Per capita income: $56,524 (2010); Median household income: $94,196 (2010); Average household income: $131,310 (2010); Percent of households with income of $100,000 or more: 47.0% (2010); Poverty rate: 3.2% (2005-2009 5-year est.).
Taxes: Total city taxes per capita: $355 (2007); City property taxes per capita: $283 (2007).
Education: Percent of population age 25 and over with: High school diploma (including GED) or higher: 97.8% (2010); Bachelor's degree or higher: 66.2% (2010); Master's degree or higher: 33.5% (2010).
Housing: Homeownership rate: 92.2% (2010); Median home value: $226,685 (2010); Median contract rent: $629 per month (2005-2009 5-year est.); Median year structure built: 1953 (2005-2009 5-year est.).
Safety: Violent crime rate: 0.0 per 10,000 population; Property crime rate: 156.3 per 10,000 population (2010).

Transportation: Commute to work: 91.6% car, 0.7% public transportation, 0.0% walk, 5.9% work from home (2005-2009 5-year est.); Travel time to work: 58.2% less than 15 minutes, 33.1% 15 to 30 minutes, 2.9% 30 to 45 minutes, 1.1% 45 to 60 minutes, 4.6% 60 minutes or more (2005-2009 5-year est.)

LOAMI (village). Covers a land area of 0.977 square miles and a water area of 0.004 square miles. Located at 39.67° N. Lat; 89.84° W. Long. Elevation is 633 feet.
Population: 826 (1990); 804 (2000); 771 (2010); 756 (2015 projected); Race: 98.4% White, 0.4% Black, 0.5% Asian, 0.6% Other, 1.2% Hispanic of any race (2010); Density: 788.8 persons per square mile (2010); Average household size: 2.56 (2010); Median age: 37.9 (2010); Males per 100 females: 95.2 (2010); Marriage status: 24.3% never married, 50.9% now married, 5.4% widowed, 19.4% divorced (2005-2009 5-year est.); Foreign born: 0.8% (2005-2009 5-year est.); Ancestry (includes multiple ancestries): 21.8% German, 20.4% English, 16.1% American, 12.4% Irish, 7.3% French (2005-2009 5-year est.).
Economy: Single-family building permits issued: 2 (2010); Multi-family building permits issued: 0 (2010); Employment by occupation: 7.0% management, 11.3% professional, 25.0% services, 24.5% sales, 0.0% farming, 26.5% construction, 5.7% production (2005-2009 5-year est.).
Income: Per capita income: $26,411 (2010); Median household income: $60,417 (2010); Average household income: $67,550 (2010); Percent of households with income of $100,000 or more: 18.3% (2010); Poverty rate: 21.3% (2005-2009 5-year est.).
Taxes: Total city taxes per capita: $117 (2007); City property taxes per capita: $53 (2007).
Education: Percent of population age 25 and over with: High school diploma (including GED) or higher: 92.5% (2010); Bachelor's degree or higher: 14.3% (2010); Master's degree or higher: 1.5% (2010).
School District(s)
New Berlin CUSD 16 (PK-12)
   2009-10 Enrollment: 823 . . . . (217) 488-6111
Housing: Homeownership rate: 89.4% (2010); Median home value: $93,902 (2010); Median contract rent: $431 per month (2005-2009 5-year est.); Median year structure built: 1975 (2005-2009 5-year est.).
Safety: Violent crime rate: 0.0 per 10,000 population; Property crime rate: 51.5 per 10,000 population (2010).
Transportation: Commute to work: 94.3% car, 0.0% public transportation, 0.0% walk, 5.7% work from home (2005-2009 5-year est.); Travel time to work: 6.3% less than 15 minutes, 47.5% 15 to 30 minutes, 36.9% 30 to 45 minutes, 3.0% 45 to 60 minutes, 6.3% 60 minutes or more (2005-2009 5-year est.)

MECHANICSBURG (village). Covers a land area of 0.379 square miles and a water area of 0 square miles. Located at 39.80° N. Lat; 89.39° W. Long. Elevation is 591 feet.
Population: 538 (1990); 456 (2000); 405 (2010); 381 (2015 projected); Race: 98.3% White, 0.2% Black, 0.5% Asian, 1.0% Other, 0.2% Hispanic of any race (2010); Density: 1,068.6 persons per square mile (2010); Average household size: 2.58 (2010); Median age: 35.7 (2010); Males per 100 females: 99.5 (2010); Marriage status: 31.4% never married, 48.9% now married, 2.7% widowed, 17.0% divorced (2005-2009 5-year est.); Foreign born: 3.3% (2005-2009 5-year est.); Ancestry (includes multiple ancestries): 31.3% German, 13.7% Irish, 11.8% American, 11.6% English, 9.0% Slovak (2005-2009 5-year est.).
Economy: Single-family building permits issued: 2 (2010); Multi-family building permits issued: 0 (2010); Employment by occupation: 10.8% management, 8.5% professional, 11.2% services, 48.8% sales, 0.8% farming, 15.4% construction, 4.6% production (2005-2009 5-year est.).
Income: Per capita income: $25,267 (2010); Median household income: $57,267 (2010); Average household income: $65,478 (2010); Percent of households with income of $100,000 or more: 15.9% (2010); Poverty rate: 6.0% (2005-2009 5-year est.).
Taxes: Total city taxes per capita: $258 (2007); City property taxes per capita: $210 (2007).
Education: Percent of population age 25 and over with: High school diploma (including GED) or higher: 82.4% (2010); Bachelor's degree or higher: 7.5% (2010); Master's degree or higher: 1.5% (2010).
Housing: Homeownership rate: 85.4% (2010); Median home value: $90,476 (2010); Median contract rent: $393 per month (2005-2009 5-year est.); Median year structure built: 1962 (2005-2009 5-year est.).
Transportation: Commute to work: 96.6% car, 0.0% public transportation, 0.0% walk, 3.4% work from home (2005-2009 5-year est.); Travel time to

work: 3.1% less than 15 minutes, 53.5% 15 to 30 minutes, 33.9% 30 to 45 minutes, 6.3% 45 to 60 minutes, 3.1% 60 minutes or more (2005-2009 5-year est.)

NEW BERLIN (village). Covers a land area of 1.108 square miles and a water area of 0 square miles. Located at 39.72° N. Lat; 89.91° W. Long. Elevation is 650 feet.
Population: 810 (1990); 1,030 (2000); 1,128 (2010); 1,167 (2015 projected); Race: 97.9% White, 0.6% Black, 0.0% Asian, 1.5% Other, 1.0% Hispanic of any race (2010); Density: 1,017.7 persons per square mile (2010); Average household size: 2.35 (2010); Median age: 37.0 (2010); Males per 100 females: 92.8 (2010); Marriage status: 25.1% never married, 55.5% now married, 7.1% widowed, 12.3% divorced (2005-2009 5-year est.); Foreign born: 0.3% (2005-2009 5-year est.); Ancestry (includes multiple ancestries): 41.3% German, 22.0% Irish, 16.8% English, 8.2% Italian, 4.8% American (2005-2009 5-year est.).
Economy: Single-family building permits issued: 0 (2010); Multi-family building permits issued: 0 (2010); Employment by occupation: 18.9% management, 21.9% professional, 10.2% services, 27.5% sales, 0.0% farming, 11.3% construction, 10.2% production (2005-2009 5-year est.).
Income: Per capita income: $26,583 (2010); Median household income: $53,125 (2010); Average household income: $62,667 (2010); Percent of households with income of $100,000 or more: 11.9% (2010); Poverty rate: 12.7% (2005-2009 5-year est.).
Taxes: Total city taxes per capita: $181 (2007); City property taxes per capita: $173 (2007).
Education: Percent of population age 25 and over with: High school diploma (including GED) or higher: 90.4% (2010); Bachelor's degree or higher: 22.2% (2010); Master's degree or higher: 8.4% (2010).
School District(s)
New Berlin CUSD 16 (PK-12)
   2009-10 Enrollment: 823 . . . . (217) 488-6111
Housing: Homeownership rate: 84.1% (2010); Median home value: $118,169 (2010); Median contract rent: $427 per month (2005-2009 5-year est.); Median year structure built: 1976 (2005-2009 5-year est.).
Transportation: Commute to work: 87.9% car, 0.0% public transportation, 4.2% walk, 5.8% work from home (2005-2009 5-year est.); Travel time to work: 21.3% less than 15 minutes, 41.2% 15 to 30 minutes, 29.2% 30 to 45 minutes, 4.0% 45 to 60 minutes, 4.3% 60 minutes or more (2005-2009 5-year est.)

PAWNEE (village). Covers a land area of 1.192 square miles and a water area of 0 square miles. Located at 39.59° N. Lat; 89.58° W. Long. Elevation is 604 feet.
History: Incorporated 1891.
Population: 2,430 (1990); 2,647 (2000); 2,421 (2010); 2,359 (2015 projected); Race: 98.4% White, 0.3% Black, 0.1% Asian, 1.1% Other, 0.4% Hispanic of any race (2010); Density: 2,031.4 persons per square mile (2010); Average household size: 2.51 (2010); Median age: 37.2 (2010); Males per 100 females: 94.5 (2010); Marriage status: 18.9% never married, 58.0% now married, 7.7% widowed, 15.4% divorced (2005-2009 5-year est.); Foreign born: 0.2% (2005-2009 5-year est.); Ancestry (includes multiple ancestries): 37.8% German, 19.5% English, 18.7% Irish, 13.9% American, 5.5% Italian (2005-2009 5-year est.).
Economy: Single-family building permits issued: 2 (2010); Multi-family building permits issued: 0 (2010); Employment by occupation: 15.5% management, 21.2% professional, 14.0% services, 30.5% sales, 0.6% farming, 7.7% construction, 10.5% production (2005-2009 5-year est.).
Income: Per capita income: $27,852 (2010); Median household income: $59,787 (2010); Average household income: $69,595 (2010); Percent of households with income of $100,000 or more: 19.2% (2010); Poverty rate: 6.0% (2005-2009 5-year est.).
Taxes: Total city taxes per capita: $162 (2007); City property taxes per capita: $118 (2007).
Education: Percent of population age 25 and over with: High school diploma (including GED) or higher: 91.9% (2010); Bachelor's degree or higher: 20.2% (2010); Master's degree or higher: 6.1% (2010).
School District(s)
Pawnee CUSD 11 (PK-12)
   2009-10 Enrollment: 706 . . . . (217) 625-2471
Housing: Homeownership rate: 85.6% (2010); Median home value: $105,442 (2010); Median contract rent: $547 per month (2005-2009 5-year est.); Median year structure built: 1965 (2005-2009 5-year est.).
Safety: Violent crime rate: 15.9 per 10,000 population; Property crime rate: 123.3 per 10,000 population (2010).

Transportation: Commute to work: 96.4% car, 0.0% public transportation, 0.5% walk, 2.0% work from home (2005-2009 5-year est.); Travel time to work: 14.0% less than 15 minutes, 45.9% 15 to 30 minutes, 32.8% 30 to 45 minutes, 2.9% 45 to 60 minutes, 4.4% 60 minutes or more (2005-2009 5-year est.)

Additional Information Contacts
Pawnee Chamber of Commerce . . . . (217) 625-8270
http://www.pawneechamber.org

PLEASANT PLAINS (village). Covers a land area of 1.241 square miles and a water area of 0 square miles. Located at 39.87° N. Lat; 89.92° W. Long. Elevation is 610 feet.
Population: 751 (1990); 777 (2000); 708 (2010); 677 (2015 projected); Race: 95.3% White, 2.7% Black, 0.1% Asian, 1.8% Other, 1.0% Hispanic of any race (2010); Density: 570.4 persons per square mile (2010); Average household size: 2.66 (2010); Median age: 36.1 (2010); Males per 100 females: 95.6 (2010); Marriage status: 17.9% never married, 69.8% now married, 4.6% widowed, 7.7% divorced (2005-2009 5-year est.); Foreign born: 0.5% (2005-2009 5-year est.); Ancestry (includes multiple ancestries): 27.0% German, 23.5% Irish, 16.5% American, 12.2% English, 3.9% Scottish (2005-2009 5-year est.).
Economy: Single-family building permits issued: 1 (2010); Multi-family building permits issued: 0 (2010); Employment by occupation: 10.6% management, 19.0% professional, 13.0% services, 38.2% sales, 1.5% farming, 11.5% construction, 6.2% production (2005-2009 5-year est.).
Income: Per capita income: $26,519 (2010); Median household income: $62,500 (2010); Average household income: $70,620 (2010); Percent of households with income of $100,000 or more: 17.7% (2010); Poverty rate: 6.5% (2005-2009 5-year est.).
Taxes: Total city taxes per capita: $110 (2007); City property taxes per capita: $98 (2007).
Education: Percent of population age 25 and over with: High school diploma (including GED) or higher: 93.3% (2010); Bachelor's degree or higher: 17.9% (2010); Master's degree or higher: 4.3% (2010).
School District(s)
Pleasant Plains CUSD 8 (PK-12)
    2009-10 Enrollment: 1,359 . . . . (217) 626-1041
Housing: Homeownership rate: 86.1% (2010); Median home value: $128,158 (2010); Median contract rent: $437 per month (2005-2009 5-year est.); Median year structure built: 1967 (2005-2009 5-year est.).
Transportation: Commute to work: 90.8% car, 0.0% public transportation, 5.8% walk, 2.5% work from home (2005-2009 5-year est.); Travel time to work: 21.5% less than 15 minutes, 44.9% 15 to 30 minutes, 26.7% 30 to 45 minutes, 5.4% 45 to 60 minutes, 1.4% 60 minutes or more (2005-2009 5-year est.)

RIVERTON (village). Covers a land area of 2.036 square miles and a water area of 0.035 square miles. Located at 39.84° N. Lat; 89.54° W. Long. Elevation is 571 feet.
History: Incorporated 1873.
Population: 2,981 (1990); 3,048 (2000); 2,801 (2010); 2,703 (2015 projected); Race: 98.6% White, 0.0% Black, 0.1% Asian, 1.2% Other, 1.2% Hispanic of any race (2010); Density: 1,376.1 persons per square mile (2010); Average household size: 2.41 (2010); Median age: 36.6 (2010); Males per 100 females: 94.8 (2010); Marriage status: 20.9% never married, 53.9% now married, 9.6% widowed, 15.7% divorced (2005-2009 5-year est.); Foreign born: 5.7% (2005-2009 5-year est.); Ancestry (includes multiple ancestries): 38.8% German, 13.3% Irish, 12.9% Italian, 12.3% English, 10.0% American (2005-2009 5-year est.).
Economy: Single-family building permits issued: 4 (2010); Multi-family building permits issued: 0 (2010); Employment by occupation: 16.1% management, 23.3% professional, 13.4% services, 30.6% sales, 0.0% farming, 6.9% construction, 9.7% production (2005-2009 5-year est.).
Income: Per capita income: $26,853 (2010); Median household income: $54,223 (2010); Average household income: $64,877 (2010); Percent of households with income of $100,000 or more: 16.4% (2010); Poverty rate: 17.2% (2005-2009 5-year est.).
Taxes: Total city taxes per capita: $44 (2007); City property taxes per capita: $41 (2007).
Education: Percent of population age 25 and over with: High school diploma (including GED) or higher: 92.8% (2010); Bachelor's degree or higher: 20.4% (2010); Master's degree or higher: 4.9% (2010).
School District(s)
Riverton CUSD 14 (PK-12)
    2009-10 Enrollment: 1,535 . . . . (217) 629-6009

Housing: Homeownership rate: 78.0% (2010); Median home value: $107,631 (2010); Median contract rent: $478 per month (2005-2009 5-year est.); Median year structure built: 1977 (2005-2009 5-year est.).
Newspapers: Tri-City Register (Community news; Circulation 600); Williamsville Sun (Community news; Circulation 400)
Transportation: Commute to work: 97.1% car, 0.5% public transportation, 1.2% walk, 1.2% work from home (2005-2009 5-year est.); Travel time to work: 24.5% less than 15 minutes, 56.5% 15 to 30 minutes, 14.7% 30 to 45 minutes, 3.5% 45 to 60 minutes, 0.8% 60 minutes or more (2005-2009 5-year est.)

ROCHESTER (village). Covers a land area of 2.107 square miles and a water area of 0.011 square miles. Located at 39.75° N. Lat; 89.54° W. Long. Elevation is 558 feet.
Population: 2,894 (1990); 2,893 (2000); 2,812 (2010); 2,865 (2015 projected); Race: 97.9% White, 0.8% Black, 0.2% Asian, 1.1% Other, 0.7% Hispanic of any race (2010); Density: 1,334.5 persons per square mile (2010); Average household size: 2.66 (2010); Median age: 44.1 (2010); Males per 100 females: 97.9 (2010); Marriage status: 17.4% never married, 66.0% now married, 7.8% widowed, 8.8% divorced (2005-2009 5-year est.); Foreign born: 1.6% (2005-2009 5-year est.); Ancestry (includes multiple ancestries): 34.2% German, 18.2% Irish, 18.2% English, 11.6% American, 5.6% Italian (2005-2009 5-year est.).
Economy: Single-family building permits issued: 10 (2010); Multi-family building permits issued: 4 (2010); Employment by occupation: 16.3% management, 38.9% professional, 8.5% services, 27.9% sales, 0.0% farming, 3.0% construction, 5.4% production (2005-2009 5-year est.).
Income: Per capita income: $34,284 (2010); Median household income: $76,707 (2010); Average household income: $91,307 (2010); Percent of households with income of $100,000 or more: 31.9% (2010); Poverty rate: 1.1% (2005-2009 5-year est.).
Taxes: Total city taxes per capita: $177 (2007); City property taxes per capita: $66 (2007).
Education: Percent of population age 25 and over with: High school diploma (including GED) or higher: 94.7% (2010); Bachelor's degree or higher: 40.6% (2010); Master's degree or higher: 13.7% (2010).
School District(s)
Rochester CUSD 3a (PK-12)
    2009-10 Enrollment: 2,276 . . . . (217) 498-6210
Housing: Homeownership rate: 93.1% (2010); Median home value: $161,909 (2010); Median contract rent: $428 per month (2005-2009 5-year est.); Median year structure built: 1977 (2005-2009 5-year est.).
Safety: Violent crime rate: 0.0 per 10,000 population; Property crime rate: 144.6 per 10,000 population (2010).
Transportation: Commute to work: 87.8% car, 0.0% public transportation, 0.0% walk, 9.0% work from home (2005-2009 5-year est.); Travel time to work: 20.1% less than 15 minutes, 65.9% 15 to 30 minutes, 6.8% 30 to 45 minutes, 2.2% 45 to 60 minutes, 5.0% 60 minutes or more (2005-2009 5-year est.)

SHERMAN (village). Covers a land area of 3.076 square miles and a water area of 0.050 square miles. Located at 39.89° N. Lat; 89.60° W. Long. Elevation is 581 feet.
Population: 2,169 (1990); 2,871 (2000); 3,555 (2010); 3,765 (2015 projected); Race: 97.1% White, 0.4% Black, 1.1% Asian, 1.4% Other, 0.5% Hispanic of any race (2010); Density: 1,155.9 persons per square mile (2010); Average household size: 2.69 (2010); Median age: 41.5 (2010); Males per 100 females: 95.3 (2010); Marriage status: 18.6% never married, 57.8% now married, 13.4% widowed, 10.1% divorced (2005-2009 5-year est.); Foreign born: 2.0% (2005-2009 5-year est.); Ancestry (includes multiple ancestries): 35.4% German, 20.8% Irish, 17.8% English, 9.8% American, 9.6% Italian (2005-2009 5-year est.).
Economy: Single-family building permits issued: 33 (2010); Multi-family building permits issued: 0 (2010); Employment by occupation: 23.4% management, 21.5% professional, 16.3% services, 24.9% sales, 0.0% farming, 9.8% construction, 4.1% production (2005-2009 5-year est.).
Income: Per capita income: $33,413 (2010); Median household income: $81,612 (2010); Average household income: $92,532 (2010); Percent of households with income of $100,000 or more: 33.9% (2010); Poverty rate: 5.4% (2005-2009 5-year est.).
Taxes: Total city taxes per capita: $340 (2007); City property taxes per capita: $328 (2007).
Education: Percent of population age 25 and over with: High school diploma (including GED) or higher: 94.7% (2010); Bachelor's degree or higher: 34.5% (2010); Master's degree or higher: 10.9% (2010).

Williamsville CUSD 15 (PK-12)
  2009-10 Enrollment: 1,402 . . . . (217) 566-2014
Housing: Homeownership rate: 86.5% (2010); Median home value: $160,121 (2010); Median contract rent: $666 per month (2005-2009 5-year est.); Median year structure built: 1989 (2005-2009 5-year est.).
Safety: Violent crime rate: 12.7 per 10,000 population; Property crime rate: 98.9 per 10,000 population (2010).
Transportation: Commute to work: 95.0% car, 0.0% public transportation, 0.0% walk, 4.2% work from home (2005-2009 5-year est.); Travel time to work: 29.9% less than 15 minutes, 59.9% 15 to 30 minutes, 6.4% 30 to 45 minutes, 0.9% 45 to 60 minutes, 2.8% 60 minutes or more (2005-2009 5-year est.)

SOUTHERN VIEW (village). Covers a land area of 0.527 square miles and a water area of 0 square miles. Located at 39.75° N. Lat; 89.65° W. Long. Elevation is 610 feet.
Population: 1,896 (1990); 1,695 (2000); 1,460 (2010); 1,400 (2015 projected); Race: 94.7% White, 1.6% Black, 0.5% Asian, 3.2% Other, 2.5% Hispanic of any race (2010); Density: 2,772.2 persons per square mile (2010); Average household size: 2.03 (2010); Median age: 42.4 (2010); Males per 100 females: 87.7 (2010); Marriage status: 34.4% never married, 41.8% now married, 7.5% widowed, 16.3% divorced (2005-2009 5-year est.); Foreign born: 2.1% (2005-2009 5-year est.); Ancestry (includes multiple ancestries): 27.4% German, 17.6% English, 15.7% Irish, 10.0% American, 7.0% Scotch-Irish (2005-2009 5-year est.).
Economy: Single-family building permits issued: 0 (2010); Multi-family building permits issued: 0 (2010); Employment by occupation: 9.7% management, 25.8% professional, 12.8% services, 30.7% sales, 0.0% farming, 14.6% construction, 6.4% production (2005-2009 5-year est.).
Income: Per capita income: $21,900 (2010); Median household income: $41,074 (2010); Average household income: $45,571 (2010); Percent of households with income of $100,000 or more: 3.7% (2010); Poverty rate: 4.8% (2005-2009 5-year est.).
Taxes: Total city taxes per capita: $124 (2007); City property taxes per capita: $45 (2007).
Education: Percent of population age 25 and over with: High school diploma (including GED) or higher: 90.8% (2010); Bachelor's degree or higher: 18.8% (2010); Master's degree or higher: 5.8% (2010).
Housing: Homeownership rate: 72.2% (2010); Median home value: $84,088 (2010); Median contract rent: $577 per month (2005-2009 5-year est.); Median year structure built: 1954 (2005-2009 5-year est.).
Safety: Violent crime rate: 18.6 per 10,000 population; Property crime rate: 298.3 per 10,000 population (2010).
Transportation: Commute to work: 95.6% car, 0.6% public transportation, 0.4% walk, 2.9% work from home (2005-2009 5-year est.); Travel time to work: 45.6% less than 15 minutes, 47.0% 15 to 30 minutes, 1.9% 30 to 45 minutes, 2.1% 45 to 60 minutes, 3.3% 60 minutes or more (2005-2009 5-year est.)

SPAULDING (village). Covers a land area of 0.777 square miles and a water area of 0.002 square miles. Located at 39.86° N. Lat; 89.54° W. Long. Elevation is 581 feet.
Population: 477 (1990); 559 (2000); 577 (2010); 587 (2015 projected); Race: 97.7% White, 0.7% Black, 0.2% Asian, 1.4% Other, 1.2% Hispanic of any race (2010); Density: 742.6 persons per square mile (2010); Average household size: 2.66 (2010); Median age: 38.8 (2010); Males per 100 females: 96.9 (2010); Marriage status: 21.8% never married, 66.4% now married, 2.8% widowed, 9.0% divorced (2005-2009 5-year est.); Foreign born: 0.5% (2005-2009 5-year est.); Ancestry (includes multiple ancestries): 34.5% German, 18.1% American, 15.4% Irish, 11.8% English, 7.6% Dutch (2005-2009 5-year est.).
Economy: Single-family building permits issued: 0 (2010); Multi-family building permits issued: 0 (2010); Employment by occupation: 13.7% management, 28.1% professional, 13.7% services, 22.7% sales, 0.0% farming, 15.1% construction, 6.8% production (2005-2009 5-year est.).
Income: Per capita income: $31,614 (2010); Median household income: $74,265 (2010); Average household income: $85,933 (2010); Percent of households with income of $100,000 or more: 29.5% (2010); Poverty rate: 2.0% (2005-2009 5-year est.).
Taxes: Total city taxes per capita: $25 (2007); City property taxes per capita: $12 (2007).
Education: Percent of population age 25 and over with: High school diploma (including GED) or higher: 93.4% (2010); Bachelor's degree or higher: 21.9% (2010); Master's degree or higher: 7.1% (2010).

Housing: Homeownership rate: 88.5% (2010); Median home value: $130,769 (2010); Median contract rent: $518 per month (2005-2009 5-year est.); Median year structure built: 1990 (2005-2009 5-year est.).
Transportation: Commute to work: 98.9% car, 0.0% public transportation, 0.8% walk, 0.0% work from home (2005-2009 5-year est.); Travel time to work: 17.8% less than 15 minutes, 70.1% 15 to 30 minutes, 7.6% 30 to 45 minutes, 1.9% 45 to 60 minutes, 2.7% 60 minutes or more (2005-2009 5-year est.)

SPRINGFIELD (city). Aka Southlawn. County seat. Covers a land area of 54.001 square miles and a water area of 6.307 square miles. Located at 39.78° N. Lat; 89.65° W. Long. Elevation is 597 feet.
History: Springfield's history is closely linked with Abraham Lincoln, who practiced law here from 1837 to 1861. The first settlers here were Elisha Kelly and his brothers, and in 1821 Springfield received its name, from nearby Spring Creek, and became the seat of the new Sangamon County, with the courthouse built in John Kelly's field. Due to Lincoln's leadership, Springfield was chosen for the state capital in 1837, and was incorporated as a city in 1840. Coal mining became an important industry after 1867.
Population: 108,997 (1990); 111,454 (2000); 116,211 (2010); 117,855 (2015 projected); Race: 78.8% White, 16.6% Black, 1.7% Asian, 2.9% Other, 1.6% Hispanic of any race (2010); Density: 2,152.0 persons per square mile (2010); Average household size: 2.20 (2010); Median age: 38.8 (2010); Males per 100 females: 90.3 (2010); Marriage status: 32.5% never married, 47.0% now married, 6.8% widowed, 13.7% divorced (2005-2009 5-year est.); Foreign born: 3.0% (2005-2009 5-year est.); Ancestry (includes multiple ancestries): 28.0% German, 15.4% Irish, 11.7% English, 7.6% American, 6.5% Italian (2005-2009 5-year est.).
Economy: Unemployment rate: 8.1% (August 2011); Total civilian labor force: 67,794 (August 2011); Single-family building permits issued: 106 (2010); Multi-family building permits issued: 99 (2010); Employment by occupation: 15.1% management, 24.5% professional, 18.5% services, 29.4% sales, 0.2% farming, 5.7% construction, 6.6% production (2005-2009 5-year est.).
Income: Per capita income: $27,321 (2010); Median household income: $45,797 (2010); Average household income: $60,973 (2010); Percent of households with income of $100,000 or more: 14.7% (2010); Poverty rate: 15.8% (2005-2009 5-year est.).
Taxes: Total city taxes per capita: $467 (2007); City property taxes per capita: $195 (2007).
Education: Percent of population age 25 and over with: High school diploma (including GED) or higher: 90.4% (2010); Bachelor's degree or higher: 31.2% (2010); Master's degree or higher: 11.7% (2010).
School District(s)
Capital Area Career Center (12-12)
  2009-10 Enrollment: n/a . . . . (217) 529-5431
Sangamon Area Spec Ed Dist (01-12)
  2009-10 Enrollment: n/a . . . . (217) 786-3250
Sangamon Roe (07-12)
  2009-10 Enrollment: n/a . . . . (217) 753-6620
Springfield SD 186 (PK-12)
  2009-10 Enrollment: 15,110 . . . . (217) 525-3002
Four-year College(s)
St Johns College (Private, Not-for-profit, Roman Catholic)
  Fall 2009 Enrollment: 79 . . . . (217) 525-5628
University of Illinois at Springfield (Public)
  Fall 2009 Enrollment: 4,977 . . . . (217) 206-6600
  2010-11 Tuition: In-state $8,101; Out-of-state $15,421
Two-year College(s)
Lincoln Land Community College (Public)
  Fall 2009 Enrollment: 7,677 . . . . (217) 786-2200
  2010-11 Tuition: In-state $5,310; Out-of-state $7,800
Springfield College in Illinois (Private, Not-for-profit, Roman Catholic)
  Fall 2009 Enrollment: 559 . . . . (217) 525-1420
Vocational/Technical School(s)
Capital Area School of Practical Nursing (Public)
  Fall 2009 Enrollment: 205 . . . . (217) 585-2160
  2010-11 Tuition: $6,965
Midwest Technical Institute (Private, For-profit)
  Fall 2009 Enrollment: 903 . . . . (217) 527-8324
  2010-11 Tuition: $12,320
St Johns Hospital School of Clinical Lab Science (Private, Not-for-profit, Roman Catholic)
  Fall 2009 Enrollment: 6 . . . . (217) 757-6788

University of Spa & Cosmetology Arts (Private, For-profit)
    Fall 2009 Enrollment: 223 . . . . (217) 753-8990
    2010-11 Tuition: $13,100
Housing: Homeownership rate: 67.0% (2010); Median home value: $106,850 (2010); Median contract rent: $516 per month (2005-2009 5-year est.); Median year structure built: 1971 (2005-2009 5-year est.).
Hospitals: Andrew McFarland Mental Health Center (118 beds); Memorial Medical Center (444 beds); St. John's Hospital (742 beds)
Safety: Violent crime rate: 123.7 per 10,000 population; Property crime rate: 644.6 per 10,000 population (2010).
Newspapers: Catholic Times (Regional news; Circulation 49,700); Chicago Sun-Times - Springfield Bureau (Regional news); Chicago Tribune - Springfield Bureau (Local news); Herald & Review - Springfield Bureau (Local news); Pure News USA (Regional news; Circulation 50,000); Small Newspaper Group - Springfield Bureau (Local news; Circulation 100,000); St. Louis Post-Dispatch - Springfield Bureau (Local news); State Journal-Register (Community news; Circulation 63,674)
Transportation: Commute to work: 92.0% car, 2.1% public transportation, 2.3% walk, 2.3% work from home (2005-2009 5-year est.); Travel time to work: 45.3% less than 15 minutes, 44.2% 15 to 30 minutes, 5.8% 30 to 45 minutes, 1.9% 45 to 60 minutes, 2.9% 60 minutes or more (2005-2009 5-year est.); Amtrak: train service available.
Airports: Abraham Lincoln Capital (primary service)
Additional Information Contacts
City of Springfield. . . . . (217) 789-2000
    http://www.springfield.il.us
Illinois Chamber of Commerce. . . . . (217) 522-5512
    http://www.ilchamber.org
Springfield Convention & Visitors Bureau . . . . (217) 789-2360
    http://www.visit-springfieldillinois.com
The Greater Springfield Chamber of Commerce . . . . (217) 525-1173
    http://www.gscc.org

THAYER (village). Covers a land area of 0.601 square miles and a water area of 0 square miles. Located at 39.53° N. Lat; 89.76° W. Long. Elevation is 643 feet.
Population: 730 (1990); 750 (2000); 682 (2010); 654 (2015 projected); Race: 99.3% White, 0.1% Black, 0.0% Asian, 0.6% Other, 1.2% Hispanic of any race (2010); Density: 1,135.2 persons per square mile (2010); Average household size: 2.66 (2010); Median age: 34.9 (2010); Males per 100 females: 100.0 (2010); Marriage status: 20.7% never married, 61.8% now married, 4.6% widowed, 12.9% divorced (2005-2009 5-year est.); Foreign born: 0.0% (2005-2009 5-year est.); Ancestry (includes multiple ancestries): 41.8% German, 16.7% American, 14.9% Irish, 13.7% English, 5.5% Italian (2005-2009 5-year est.).
Economy: Single-family building permits issued: 1 (2010); Multi-family building permits issued: 0 (2010); Employment by occupation: 9.4% management, 11.1% professional, 12.5% services, 36.1% sales, 0.0% farming, 13.2% construction, 17.7% production (2005-2009 5-year est.).
Income: Per capita income: $25,080 (2010); Median household income: $60,938 (2010); Average household income: $66,582 (2010); Percent of households with income of $100,000 or more: 14.5% (2010); Poverty rate: 4.3% (2005-2009 5-year est.).
Taxes: Total city taxes per capita: $39 (2007); City property taxes per capita: $23 (2007).
Education: Percent of population age 25 and over with: High school diploma (including GED) or higher: 86.9% (2010); Bachelor's degree or higher: 12.6% (2010); Master's degree or higher: 1.4% (2010).
Housing: Homeownership rate: 88.7% (2010); Median home value: $123,101 (2010); Median contract rent: $525 per month (2005-2009 5-year est.); Median year structure built: 1957 (2005-2009 5-year est.).
Transportation: Commute to work: 95.4% car, 0.0% public transportation, 0.0% walk, 4.6% work from home (2005-2009 5-year est.); Travel time to work: 21.6% less than 15 minutes, 21.9% 15 to 30 minutes, 43.1% 30 to 45 minutes, 4.5% 45 to 60 minutes, 8.9% 60 minutes or more (2005-2009 5-year est.)

WILLIAMSVILLE (village). Covers a land area of 1.242 square miles and a water area of 0 square miles. Located at 39.95° N. Lat; 89.55° W. Long. Elevation is 600 feet.
Population: 1,280 (1990); 1,439 (2000); 1,414 (2010); 1,442 (2015 projected); Race: 97.9% White, 0.4% Black, 0.4% Asian, 1.3% Other, 0.8% Hispanic of any race (2010); Density: 1,138.9 persons per square mile (2010); Average household size: 2.61 (2010); Median age: 37.0 (2010); Males per 100 females: 92.9 (2010); Marriage status: 23.2% never married,

59.1% now married, 4.8% widowed, 12.8% divorced (2005-2009 5-year est.); Foreign born: 1.3% (2005-2009 5-year est.); Ancestry (includes multiple ancestries): 38.4% German, 18.4% Irish, 14.0% English, 13.6% American, 8.2% Italian (2005-2009 5-year est.).
Economy: Single-family building permits issued: 2 (2010); Multi-family building permits issued: 0 (2010); Employment by occupation: 13.9% management, 24.5% professional, 15.3% services, 28.5% sales, 0.0% farming, 8.7% construction, 9.0% production (2005-2009 5-year est.).
Income: Per capita income: $24,253 (2010); Median household income: $57,624 (2010); Average household income: $63,113 (2010); Percent of households with income of $100,000 or more: 15.1% (2010); Poverty rate: 4.0% (2005-2009 5-year est.).
Taxes: Total city taxes per capita: $189 (2007); City property taxes per capita: $134 (2007).
Education: Percent of population age 25 and over with: High school diploma (including GED) or higher: 90.2% (2010); Bachelor's degree or higher: 20.5% (2010); Master's degree or higher: 4.9% (2010).

School District(s)
Williamsville CUSD 15 (PK-12)
    2009-10 Enrollment: 1,402 . . . . (217) 566-2014
Housing: Homeownership rate: 83.2% (2010); Median home value: $129,367 (2010); Median contract rent: $454 per month (2005-2009 5-year est.); Median year structure built: 1974 (2005-2009 5-year est.).
Transportation: Commute to work: 96.9% car, 0.5% public transportation, 1.1% walk, 1.5% work from home (2005-2009 5-year est.); Travel time to work: 18.5% less than 15 minutes, 60.0% 15 to 30 minutes, 15.5% 30 to 45 minutes, 5.0% 45 to 60 minutes, 1.1% 60 minutes or more (2005-2009 5-year est.)

Schuyler County

Located in western Illinois; bounded on the southeast by the Illinois River; drained by the La Moine River. Covers a land area of 437.31 square miles, a water area of 4.07 square miles, and is located in the Central Time Zone at 40.14° N. Lat., 90.57° W. Long. The county was founded in 1825. County seat is Rushville.

Weather Station: Rushville   Elevation: 660 feet

	Jan	Feb	Mar	Apr	May	Jun	Jul	Aug	Sep	Oct	Nov	Dec
High	34	39	51	63	73	82	86	85	78	66	52	38
Low	18	22	31	42	52	61	66	63	55	44	33	21
Precip	1.7	1.9	2.6	3.9	5.0	4.3	4.0	3.7	3.5	3.2	3.1	2.4
Snow	3.5	3.3	1.2	0.4	0.0	0.0	0.0	0.0	0.0	tr	0.4	3.1

High and Low temperatures in degrees Fahrenheit; Precipitation and Snow in inches

Population: 7,498 (1990); 7,189 (2000); 6,858 (2010); 6,645 (2015 projected); Race: 96.8% White, 1.6% Black, 0.2% Asian, 1.4% Other, 1.2% Hispanic of any race (2010); Density: 15.7 persons per square mile (2010); Average household size: 2.34 (2010); Median age: 42.7 (2010); Males per 100 females: 99.1 (2010).
Religion: Five largest groups: 15.9% The United Methodist Church, 8.9% Christian Churches and Churches of Christ, 6.6% Christian Church (Disciples of Christ), 5.8% Southern Baptist Convention, 4.1% Catholic Church (2000).
Economy: Unemployment rate: 6.4% (August 2011); Total civilian labor force: 4,366 (August 2011); Leading industries: 10.5% accommodation & food services; 8.6% wholesale trade; 8.1% other services (except public administration) (2009); Farms: 534 totaling 207,457 acres (2007); Companies that employ 500 or more persons: 0 (2009); Companies that employ 100 to 499 persons: 1 (2009); Companies that employ less than 100 persons: 153 (2009); Black-owned businesses: n/a (2007); Hispanic-owned businesses: n/a (2007); Asian-owned businesses: n/a (2007); Women-owned businesses: n/a (2007); Retail sales per capita: $9,784 (2010). Single-family building permits issued: n/a (2010); Multi-family building permits issued: n/a (2010).
Income: Per capita income: $23,109 (2010); Median household income: $45,122 (2010); Average household income: $54,737 (2010); Percent of households with income of $100,000 or more: 9.0% (2010); Poverty rate: 13.3% (2009); Bankruptcy rate: 3.19% (2010).
Taxes: Total county taxes per capita: $146 (2007); County property taxes per capita: $146 (2007).
Education: Percent of population age 25 and over with: High school diploma (including GED) or higher: 87.9% (2010); Bachelor's degree or higher: 14.3% (2010); Master's degree or higher: 3.5% (2010).

Housing: Homeownership rate: 77.6% (2010); Median home value: $73,066 (2010); Median contract rent: $326 per month (2005-2009 5-year est.); Median year structure built: 1965 (2005-2009 5-year est.)
Health: Birth rate: 118.9 per 10,000 population (2009); Death rate: 142.6 per 10,000 population (2009); Age-adjusted cancer mortality rate: 158.3 (Unreliable) deaths per 100,000 population (2007); Number of physicians: 4.4 per 10,000 population (2008); Hospital beds: 76.3 per 10,000 population (2007); Hospital admissions: 738.9 per 10,000 population (2007).
Elections: 2008 Presidential election results: 49.7% Obama, 47.9% McCain, 1.2% Nader
National and State Parks: Weinborg-King State Park
Additional Information Contacts
Schuyler County Government . . . . (217) 322-4734
    http://www.schuylercountyillinois.com
Rushville Area Chamber of Commerce & Main Street. . . . . (217) 322-3689

Schuyler County Communities

BROWNING (village). Covers a land area of 0.310 square miles and a water area of 0 square miles. Located at 40.12° N. Lat; 90.37° W. Long. Elevation is 449 feet.
Population: 193 (1990); 130 (2000); 117 (2010); 111 (2015 projected); Race: 98.3% White, 0.0% Black, 0.0% Asian, 1.7% Other, 1.7% Hispanic of any race (2010); Density: 377.1 persons per square mile (2010); Average household size: 2.34 (2010); Median age: 46.6 (2010); Males per 100 females: 105.3 (2010); Marriage status: 26.6% never married, 67.9% now married, 3.7% widowed, 1.8% divorced (2005-2009 5-year est.); Foreign born: 0.0% (2005-2009 5-year est.); Ancestry (includes multiple ancestries): 45.9% Irish, 33.6% German, 19.9% American, 6.2% English, 6.2% Scotch-Irish (2005-2009 5-year est.).
Economy: Employment by occupation: 8.1% management, 8.1% professional, 41.9% services, 24.2% sales, 0.0% farming, 17.7% construction, 0.0% production (2005-2009 5-year est.).
Income: Per capita income: $19,447 (2010); Median household income: $39,500 (2010); Average household income: $44,400 (2010); Percent of households with income of $100,000 or more: 4.0% (2010); Poverty rate: 23.3% (2005-2009 5-year est.).
Taxes: Total city taxes per capita: $71 (2007); City property taxes per capita: $63 (2007).
Education: Percent of population age 25 and over with: High school diploma (including GED) or higher: 74.2% (2010); Bachelor's degree or higher: 3.4% (2010); Master's degree or higher: 1.1% (2010).
Housing: Homeownership rate: 86.0% (2010); Median home value: $46,250 (2010); Median contract rent: n/a per month (2005-2009 5-year est.); Median year structure built: 1955 (2005-2009 5-year est.).
Transportation: Commute to work: 100.0% car, 0.0% public transportation, 0.0% walk, 0.0% work from home (2005-2009 5-year est.); Travel time to work: 17.7% less than 15 minutes, 54.8% 15 to 30 minutes, 0.0% 30 to 45 minutes, 8.1% 45 to 60 minutes, 19.4% 60 minutes or more (2005-2009 5-year est.)

CAMDEN (village). Covers a land area of 0.762 square miles and a water area of 0 square miles. Located at 40.15° N. Lat; 90.77° W. Long. Elevation is 600 feet.
Population: 115 (1990); 97 (2000); 89 (2010); 86 (2015 projected); Race: 98.9% White, 0.0% Black, 0.0% Asian, 1.1% Other, 1.1% Hispanic of any race (2010); Density: 116.8 persons per square mile (2010); Average household size: 2.41 (2010); Median age: 36.6 (2010); Males per 100 females: 107.0 (2010); Marriage status: 15.3% never married, 65.3% now married, 5.6% widowed, 13.9% divorced (2005-2009 5-year est.); Foreign born: 0.0% (2005-2009 5-year est.); Ancestry (includes multiple ancestries): 79.7% American, 7.6% Irish, 6.3% German (2005-2009 5-year est.).
Economy: Employment by occupation: 14.3% management, 0.0% professional, 14.3% services, 20.0% sales, 0.0% farming, 0.0% construction, 51.4% production (2005-2009 5-year est.).
Income: Per capita income: $17,804 (2010); Median household income: $34,167 (2010); Average household income: $43,919 (2010); Percent of households with income of $100,000 or more: 8.1% (2010); Poverty rate: 41.8% (2005-2009 5-year est.).
Taxes: Total city taxes per capita: $0 (2007); City property taxes per capita: $0 (2007).

Education: Percent of population age 25 and over with: High school diploma (including GED) or higher: 78.7% (2010); Bachelor's degree or higher: 13.1% (2010); Master's degree or higher: 4.9% (2010).
Housing: Homeownership rate: 78.4% (2010); Median home value: $70,000 (2010); Median contract rent: n/a per month (2005-2009 5-year est.); Median year structure built: 1945 (2005-2009 5-year est.).
Transportation: Commute to work: 74.3% car, 0.0% public transportation, 20.0% walk, 0.0% work from home (2005-2009 5-year est.); Travel time to work: 25.7% less than 15 minutes, 28.6% 15 to 30 minutes, 45.7% 30 to 45 minutes, 0.0% 45 to 60 minutes, 0.0% 60 minutes or more (2005-2009 5-year est.)

FREDERICK (unincorporated postal area, zip code 62639). Covers a land area of 34.538 square miles and a water area of 1.058 square miles. Located at 40.04° N. Lat; 90.46° W. Long. Elevation is 446 feet.
Population: 341 (2000); Race: 97.4% White, 0.0% Black, 0.0% Asian, 2.6% Other, 2.6% Hispanic of any race (2000); Density: 9.9 persons per square mile (2000); Age: 24.9% under 18, 14.9% over 64 (2000); Marriage status: 27.4% never married, 61.4% now married, 3.2% widowed, 8.1% divorced (2000); Foreign born: 0.0% (2000); Ancestry (includes multiple ancestries): 24.1% German, 10.6% English, 9.7% Irish, 8.3% Italian, 6.6% British (2000).
Economy: Employment by occupation: 11.6% management, 16.3% professional, 21.8% services, 25.2% sales, 0.0% farming, 3.4% construction, 21.8% production (2000).
Income: Per capita income: $16,011 (2000); Median household income: $38,125 (2000); Poverty rate: 20.3% (2000).
Education: Percent of population age 25 and over with: High school diploma (including GED) or higher: 90.1% (2000); Bachelor's degree or higher: 8.3% (2000).
Housing: Homeownership rate: 92.6% (2000); Median home value: $43,700 (2000); Median contract rent: n/a per month (2000); Median year structure built: 1951 (2000).
Transportation: Commute to work: 95.0% car, 0.0% public transportation, 0.0% walk, 0.0% work from home (2000); Travel time to work: 37.1% less than 15 minutes, 42.1% 15 to 30 minutes, 5.0% 30 to 45 minutes, 0.0% 45 to 60 minutes, 15.7% 60 minutes or more (2000)

HUNTSVILLE (unincorporated postal area, zip code 62344). Covers a land area of 37.078 square miles and a water area of 0 square miles. Located at 40.18° N. Lat; 90.81° W. Long. Elevation is 659 feet.
Population: 185 (2000); Race: 100.0% White, 0.0% Black, 0.0% Asian, 0.0% Other, 0.0% Hispanic of any race (2000); Density: 5.0 persons per square mile (2000); Age: 29.3% under 18, 2.4% over 64 (2000); Marriage status: 23.6% never married, 61.5% now married, 3.1% widowed, 11.8% divorced (2000); Foreign born: 0.0% (2000); Ancestry (includes multiple ancestries): 39.9% English, 32.2% German, 21.2% American, 10.6% Irish, 5.3% Dutch (2000).
Economy: Employment by occupation: 26.4% management, 21.8% professional, 16.4% services, 14.5% sales, 4.5% farming, 4.5% construction, 11.8% production (2000).
Income: Per capita income: $10,976 (2000); Median household income: $38,542 (2000); Poverty rate: 4.8% (2000).
Education: Percent of population age 25 and over with: High school diploma (including GED) or higher: 79.3% (2000); Bachelor's degree or higher: 12.4% (2000).
Housing: Homeownership rate: 69.1% (2000); Median home value: $58,000 (2000); Median contract rent: $125 per month (2000); Median year structure built: 1948 (2000).
Transportation: Commute to work: 100.0% car, 0.0% public transportation, 0.0% walk, 0.0% work from home (2000); Travel time to work: 20.0% less than 15 minutes, 25.5% 15 to 30 minutes, 20.0% 30 to 45 minutes, 6.4% 45 to 60 minutes, 28.2% 60 minutes or more (2000)

LITTLETON (village). Covers a land area of 1.163 square miles and a water area of 0 square miles. Located at 40.23° N. Lat; 90.61° W. Long. Elevation is 679 feet.
Population: 181 (1990); 197 (2000); 186 (2010); 180 (2015 projected); Race: 90.3% White, 8.6% Black, 0.0% Asian, 1.1% Other, 1.1% Hispanic of any race (2010); Density: 159.9 persons per square mile (2010); Average household size: 2.51 (2010); Median age: 42.5 (2010); Males per 100 females: 102.2 (2010); Marriage status: 24.7% never married, 54.1% now married, 2.6% widowed, 18.6% divorced (2005-2009 5-year est.); Foreign born: 0.0% (2005-2009 5-year est.); Ancestry (includes multiple

ancestries): 47.3% American, 17.6% Irish, 16.9% German, 2.4% English, 1.7% Dutch (2005-2009 5-year est.).
Economy: Employment by occupation: 2.6% management, 4.7% professional, 11.4% services, 23.8% sales, 1.6% farming, 15.0% construction, 40.9% production (2005-2009 5-year est.).
Income: Per capita income: $28,524 (2010); Median household income: $58,000 (2010); Average household income: $66,757 (2010); Percent of households with income of $100,000 or more: 13.5% (2010); Poverty rate: 15.2% (2005-2009 5-year est.).
Taxes: Total city taxes per capita: $31 (2007); City property taxes per capita: $16 (2007).
Education: Percent of population age 25 and over with: High school diploma (including GED) or higher: 89.2% (2010); Bachelor's degree or higher: 15.4% (2010); Master's degree or higher: 1.5% (2010).
Housing: Homeownership rate: 79.7% (2010); Median home value: $98,333 (2010); Median contract rent: n/a per month (2005-2009 5-year est.); Median year structure built: before 1940 (2005-2009 5-year est.).
Transportation: Commute to work: 96.7% car, 0.0% public transportation, 2.2% walk, 1.1% work from home (2005-2009 5-year est.); Travel time to work: 35.4% less than 15 minutes, 37.6% 15 to 30 minutes, 25.4% 30 to 45 minutes, 0.0% 45 to 60 minutes, 1.7% 60 minutes or more (2005-2009 5-year est.)

RUSHVILLE (city). County seat. Covers a land area of 1.572 square miles and a water area of 0 square miles. Located at 40.12° N. Lat; 90.56° W. Long. Elevation is 676 feet.
History: Rushville was founded in 1825 as Rushton. Both names honor Dr. William Rush, a Philadelphia physician.
Population: 3,342 (1990); 3,212 (2000); 3,049 (2010); 2,950 (2015 projected); Race: 98.2% White, 0.3% Black, 0.0% Asian, 1.5% Other, 1.0% Hispanic of any race (2010); Density: 1,939.9 persons per square mile (2010); Average household size: 2.21 (2010); Median age: 43.9 (2010); Males per 100 females: 91.3 (2010); Marriage status: 20.1% never married, 60.0% now married, 10.6% widowed, 9.3% divorced (2005-2009 5-year est.); Foreign born: 4.4% (2005-2009 5-year est.); Ancestry (includes multiple ancestries): 22.6% German, 19.1% American, 14.8% English, 12.2% Irish, 3.8% Dutch (2005-2009 5-year est.).
Economy: Employment by occupation: 8.1% management, 15.5% professional, 20.7% services, 19.7% sales, 1.6% farming, 12.4% construction, 22.0% production (2005-2009 5-year est.).
Income: Per capita income: $22,118 (2010); Median household income: $40,309 (2010); Average household income: $50,156 (2010); Percent of households with income of $100,000 or more: 8.3% (2010); Poverty rate: 12.7% (2005-2009 5-year est.).
Taxes: Total city taxes per capita: $113 (2007); City property taxes per capita: $110 (2007).
Education: Percent of population age 25 and over with: High school diploma (including GED) or higher: 88.4% (2010); Bachelor's degree or higher: 15.2% (2010); Master's degree or higher: 4.1% (2010).

School District(s)
Schuyler-Industry CUSD 5 (PK-12)
　2009-10 Enrollment: 1,223 . . . . (217) 322-4311
Housing: Homeownership rate: 72.3% (2010); Median home value: $67,469 (2010); Median contract rent: $346 per month (2005-2009 5-year est.); Median year structure built: 1969 (2005-2009 5-year est.).
Hospitals: Culberton Memorial Hospital (64 beds)
Safety: Violent crime rate: 6.8 per 10,000 population; Property crime rate: 145.3 per 10,000 population (2010).
Newspapers: Rushville Times (Community news; Circulation 3,669)
Transportation: Commute to work: 88.3% car, 0.0% public transportation, 7.8% walk, 2.4% work from home (2005-2009 5-year est.); Travel time to work: 46.2% less than 15 minutes, 27.6% 15 to 30 minutes, 18.9% 30 to 45 minutes, 3.0% 45 to 60 minutes, 4.3% 60 minutes or more (2005-2009 5-year est.)
Additional Information Contacts
Rushville Area Chamber of Commerce & Main Street. . . . . (217) 322-3689

Scott County

Located in west central Illinois; bounded on the west by the Illinois River; drained by Sandy and Mauvaise Terre Creeks. Covers a land area of 250.92 square miles, a water area of 1.85 square miles, and is located in the Central Time Zone at 39.64° N. Lat., 90.47° W. Long. The county was founded in 1839. County seat is Winchester.

Scott County is part of the Jacksonville, IL Micropolitan Statistical Area. The entire metro area includes: Morgan County, IL; Scott County, IL

Population: 5,644 (1990); 5,537 (2000); 5,120 (2010); 4,889 (2015 projected); Race: 99.3% White, 0.1% Black, 0.1% Asian, 0.5% Other, 0.4% Hispanic of any race (2010); Density: 20.4 persons per square mile (2010); Average household size: 2.42 (2010); Median age: 42.4 (2010); Males per 100 females: 94.5 (2010).
Religion: Five largest groups: 17.9% American Baptist Churches in the USA, 17.2% Southern Baptist Convention, 9.5% Lutheran Church—Missouri Synod, 8.7% Catholic Church, 8.1% The United Methodist Church (2000).
Economy: Unemployment rate: 7.6% (August 2011); Total civilian labor force: 2,730 (August 2011); Leading industries: 18.4% manufacturing; 16.8% retail trade; 9.4% accommodation & food services (2009); Farms: 350 totaling 135,731 acres (2007); Companies that employ 500 or more persons: 0 (2009); Companies that employ 100 to 499 persons: 0 (2009); Companies that employ less than 100 persons: 77 (2009); Black-owned businesses: n/a (2007); Hispanic-owned businesses: n/a (2007); Asian-owned businesses: n/a (2007); Women-owned businesses: n/a (2007); Retail sales per capita: $6,251 (2010). Single-family building permits issued: n/a (2010); Multi-family building permits issued: n/a (2010).
Income: Per capita income: $21,596 (2010); Median household income: $45,529 (2010); Average household income: $52,635 (2010); Percent of households with income of $100,000 or more: 9.0% (2010); Poverty rate: 10.4% (2009); Bankruptcy rate: 5.39% (2010).
Taxes: Total county taxes per capita: $266 (2007); County property taxes per capita: $258 (2007).
Education: Percent of population age 25 and over with: High school diploma (including GED) or higher: 87.9% (2010); Bachelor's degree or higher: 14.9% (2010); Master's degree or higher: 2.9% (2010).
Housing: Homeownership rate: 76.4% (2010); Median home value: $83,663 (2010); Median contract rent: $283 per month (2005-2009 5-year est.); Median year structure built: 1963 (2005-2009 5-year est.).
Health: Birth rate: 113.6 per 10,000 population (2009); Death rate: 109.8 per 10,000 population (2009); Age-adjusted cancer mortality rate: 292.4 deaths per 100,000 population (2007); Number of physicians: 3.8 per 10,000 population (2008); Hospital beds: 0.0 per 10,000 population (2007); Hospital admissions: 0.0 per 10,000 population (2007).
Elections: 2008 Presidential election results: 41.9% Obama, 56.0% McCain, 0.8% Nader
Additional Information Contacts
Scott County Government . . . . (217) 742-3178
　http://scottco.org

Scott County Communities

ALSEY (village). Covers a land area of 0.557 square miles and a water area of 0.010 square miles. Located at 39.56° N. Lat; 90.43° W. Long. Elevation is 630 feet.
Population: 253 (1990); 246 (2000); 218 (2010); 202 (2015 projected); Race: 98.6% White, 0.0% Black, 0.5% Asian, 0.9% Other, 0.0% Hispanic of any race (2010); Density: 391.4 persons per square mile (2010); Average household size: 2.60 (2010); Median age: 39.8 (2010); Males per 100 females: 96.4 (2010); Marriage status: 20.4% never married, 62.1% now married, 11.2% widowed, 6.3% divorced (2005-2009 5-year est.); Foreign born: 1.1% (2005-2009 5-year est.); Ancestry (includes multiple ancestries): 34.4% American, 23.0% German, 12.6% English, 9.6% Irish, 4.8% Italian (2005-2009 5-year est.).
Economy: Employment by occupation: 4.7% management, 12.3% professional, 35.8% services, 8.5% sales, 0.0% farming, 10.4% construction, 28.3% production (2005-2009 5-year est.).
Income: Per capita income: $23,086 (2010); Median household income: $54,630 (2010); Average household income: $60,089 (2010); Percent of households with income of $100,000 or more: 8.3% (2010); Poverty rate: 27.0% (2005-2009 5-year est.).
Taxes: Total city taxes per capita: $54 (2007); City property taxes per capita: $13 (2007).
Education: Percent of population age 25 and over with: High school diploma (including GED) or higher: 88.3% (2010); Bachelor's degree or higher: 11.0% (2010); Master's degree or higher: 2.1% (2010).
Housing: Homeownership rate: 82.1% (2010); Median home value: $80,833 (2010); Median contract rent: $444 per month (2005-2009 5-year est.); Median year structure built: 1941 (2005-2009 5-year est.).
Transportation: Commute to work: 99.1% car, 0.0% public transportation, 0.9% walk, 0.0% work from home (2005-2009 5-year est.); Travel time to

work: 17.0% less than 15 minutes, 13.2% 15 to 30 minutes, 44.3% 30 to 45 minutes, 6.6% 45 to 60 minutes, 18.9% 60 minutes or more (2005-2009 5-year est.)

BLUFFS (village). Covers a land area of 1.015 square miles and a water area of 0 square miles. Located at 39.74° N. Lat; 90.53° W. Long. Elevation is 469 feet.
Population: 774 (1990); 748 (2000); 598 (2010); 541 (2015 projected); Race: 99.2% White, 0.0% Black, 0.2% Asian, 0.7% Other, 0.0% Hispanic of any race (2010); Density: 589.1 persons per square mile (2010); Average household size: 2.40 (2010); Median age: 40.1 (2010); Males per 100 females: 93.5 (2010); Marriage status: 13.0% never married, 70.7% now married, 8.5% widowed, 7.8% divorced (2005-2009 5-year est.); Foreign born: 0.3% (2005-2009 5-year est.); Ancestry (includes multiple ancestries): 29.3% German, 21.4% American, 19.3% Irish, 12.1% English, 4.5% Italian (2005-2009 5-year est.).
Economy: Employment by occupation: 13.2% management, 15.4% professional, 19.6% services, 20.9% sales, 0.0% farming, 1.3% construction, 29.6% production (2005-2009 5-year est.).
Income: Per capita income: $25,540 (2010); Median household income: $49,063 (2010); Average household income: $60,151 (2010); Percent of households with income of $100,000 or more: 15.3% (2010); Poverty rate: 11.1% (2005-2009 5-year est.).
Taxes: Total city taxes per capita: $76 (2007); City property taxes per capita: $28 (2007).
Education: Percent of population age 25 and over with: High school diploma (including GED) or higher: 90.8% (2010); Bachelor's degree or higher: 16.3% (2010); Master's degree or higher: 3.6% (2010).
School District(s)
Scott-Morgan CUSD 2 (PK-12)
    2009-10 Enrollment: 251 . . . . (217) 754-3351
Housing: Homeownership rate: 79.5% (2010); Median home value: $78,286 (2010); Median contract rent: $229 per month (2005-2009 5-year est.); Median year structure built: 1961 (2005-2009 5-year est.).
Newspapers: Bluffs Times (Community news; Circulation 2,850); Meredosia Budget (Community news; Circulation 2,850)
Transportation: Commute to work: 97.7% car, 0.0% public transportation, 1.6% walk, 0.0% work from home (2005-2009 5-year est.); Travel time to work: 34.7% less than 15 minutes, 29.5% 15 to 30 minutes, 27.3% 30 to 45 minutes, 1.3% 45 to 60 minutes, 7.1% 60 minutes or more (2005-2009 5-year est.)

EXETER (village). Covers a land area of 0.690 square miles and a water area of 0 square miles. Located at 39.71° N. Lat; 90.49° W. Long. Elevation is 554 feet.
Population: 59 (1990); 70 (2000); 69 (2010); 67 (2015 projected); Race: 100.0% White, 0.0% Black, 0.0% Asian, 0.0% Other, 1.4% Hispanic of any race (2010); Density: 100.1 persons per square mile (2010); Average household size: 2.65 (2010); Median age: 44.6 (2010); Males per 100 females: 155.6 (2010); Marriage status: 41.3% never married, 27.8% now married, 3.2% widowed, 27.8% divorced (2005-2009 5-year est.); Foreign born: 0.0% (2005-2009 5-year est.); Ancestry (includes multiple ancestries): 24.2% American, 11.4% German, 4.5% English, 3.8% Italian, 3.8% Irish (2005-2009 5-year est.).
Economy: Employment by occupation: 1.9% management, 4.6% professional, 1.9% services, 14.8% sales, 0.0% farming, 39.8% construction, 37.0% production (2005-2009 5-year est.).
Income: Per capita income: $22,731 (2010); Median household income: $53,125 (2010); Average household income: $54,519 (2010); Percent of households with income of $100,000 or more: 7.7% (2010); Poverty rate: 6.1% (2005-2009 5-year est.).
Taxes: Total city taxes per capita: $29 (2007); City property taxes per capita: $15 (2007).
Education: Percent of population age 25 and over with: High school diploma (including GED) or higher: 87.7% (2010); Bachelor's degree or higher: 14.0% (2010); Master's degree or higher: 3.5% (2010).
Housing: Homeownership rate: 73.1% (2010); Median home value: $85,000 (2010); Median contract rent: n/a per month (2005-2009 5-year est.); Median year structure built: 1993 (2005-2009 5-year est.).
Transportation: Commute to work: 99.1% car, 0.9% public transportation, 0.0% walk, 0.0% work from home (2005-2009 5-year est.); Travel time to work: 6.5% less than 15 minutes, 44.4% 15 to 30 minutes, 7.4% 30 to 45 minutes, 0.0% 45 to 60 minutes, 41.7% 60 minutes or more (2005-2009 5-year est.)

GLASGOW (village). Covers a land area of 1.011 square miles and a water area of 0 square miles. Located at 39.55° N. Lat; 90.48° W. Long. Elevation is 584 feet.
Population: 163 (1990); 170 (2000); 167 (2010); 163 (2015 projected); Race: 99.4% White, 0.0% Black, 0.0% Asian, 0.6% Other, 0.0% Hispanic of any race (2010); Density: 165.1 persons per square mile (2010); Average household size: 2.30 (2010); Median age: 44.1 (2010); Males per 100 females: 92.0 (2010); Marriage status: 8.9% never married, 74.4% now married, 1.1% widowed, 15.6% divorced (2005-2009 5-year est.); Foreign born: 0.0% (2005-2009 5-year est.); Ancestry (includes multiple ancestries): 36.0% Irish, 25.4% American, 14.0% German, 7.9% Welsh, 7.0% English (2005-2009 5-year est.).
Economy: Employment by occupation: 15.2% management, 10.6% professional, 10.6% services, 31.8% sales, 3.0% farming, 9.1% construction, 19.7% production (2005-2009 5-year est.).
Income: Per capita income: $20,390 (2010); Median household income: $41,750 (2010); Average household income: $50,599 (2010); Percent of households with income of $100,000 or more: 8.5% (2010); Poverty rate: 11.4% (2005-2009 5-year est.).
Taxes: Total city taxes per capita: $6 (2007); City property taxes per capita: $6 (2007).
Education: Percent of population age 25 and over with: High school diploma (including GED) or higher: 87.2% (2010); Bachelor's degree or higher: 17.1% (2010); Master's degree or higher: 4.3% (2010).
Housing: Homeownership rate: 73.2% (2010); Median home value: $87,500 (2010); Median contract rent: n/a per month (2005-2009 5-year est.); Median year structure built: 1972 (2005-2009 5-year est.).
Transportation: Commute to work: 95.5% car, 0.0% public transportation, 3.0% walk, 1.5% work from home (2005-2009 5-year est.); Travel time to work: 16.9% less than 15 minutes, 30.8% 15 to 30 minutes, 49.2% 30 to 45 minutes, 1.5% 45 to 60 minutes, 1.5% 60 minutes or more (2005-2009 5-year est.)

MANCHESTER (village). Covers a land area of 1.036 square miles and a water area of 0 square miles. Located at 39.54° N. Lat; 90.32° W. Long. Elevation is 686 feet.
Population: 347 (1990); 354 (2000); 329 (2010); 311 (2015 projected); Race: 99.7% White, 0.0% Black, 0.0% Asian, 0.3% Other, 0.0% Hispanic of any race (2010); Density: 317.7 persons per square mile (2010); Average household size: 2.57 (2010); Median age: 40.5 (2010); Males per 100 females: 112.3 (2010); Marriage status: 26.0% never married, 59.9% now married, 6.9% widowed, 7.2% divorced (2005-2009 5-year est.); Foreign born: 0.0% (2005-2009 5-year est.); Ancestry (includes multiple ancestries): 29.4% German, 24.7% American, 17.6% English, 11.2% Irish, 5.0% Scottish (2005-2009 5-year est.).
Economy: Employment by occupation: 10.4% management, 10.9% professional, 21.4% services, 27.1% sales, 0.0% farming, 10.4% construction, 19.8% production (2005-2009 5-year est.).
Income: Per capita income: $17,442 (2010); Median household income: $41,250 (2010); Average household income: $44,160 (2010); Percent of households with income of $100,000 or more: 3.9% (2010); Poverty rate: 1.8% (2005-2009 5-year est.).
Taxes: Total city taxes per capita: $26 (2007); City property taxes per capita: $26 (2007).
Education: Percent of population age 25 and over with: High school diploma (including GED) or higher: 89.0% (2010); Bachelor's degree or higher: 10.1% (2010); Master's degree or higher: 3.1% (2010).
Housing: Homeownership rate: 83.6% (2010); Median home value: $79,565 (2010); Median contract rent: $207 per month (2005-2009 5-year est.); Median year structure built: 1962 (2005-2009 5-year est.).
Transportation: Commute to work: 86.2% car, 0.0% public transportation, 7.5% walk, 6.3% work from home (2005-2009 5-year est.); Travel time to work: 15.3% less than 15 minutes, 65.0% 15 to 30 minutes, 11.7% 30 to 45 minutes, 6.1% 45 to 60 minutes, 1.8% 60 minutes or more (2005-2009 5-year est.)

NAPLES (town). Covers a land area of 0.605 square miles and a water area of 0 square miles. Located at 39.75° N. Lat; 90.60° W. Long. Elevation is 440 feet.
History: It was in Naples that the steamboat "Olitippa" was built on the Illinois River, before regular steamboat service began.
Population: 130 (1990); 134 (2000); 125 (2010); 122 (2015 projected); Race: 99.2% White, 0.0% Black, 0.0% Asian, 0.8% Other, 1.6% Hispanic of any race (2010); Density: 206.7 persons per square mile (2010);

Average household size: 2.66 (2010); Median age: 39.2 (2010); Males per 100 females: 92.3 (2010); Marriage status: 14.6% never married, 75.0% now married, 0.0% widowed, 10.4% divorced (2005-2009 5-year est.); Foreign born: 0.0% (2005-2009 5-year est.); Ancestry (includes multiple ancestries): 27.9% Polish, 23.0% German, 21.3% Irish, 21.3% Scotch-Irish, 6.6% English (2005-2009 5-year est.).
Economy: Employment by occupation: 27.6% management, 48.3% professional, 0.0% services, 6.9% sales, 10.3% farming, 6.9% construction, 0.0% production (2005-2009 5-year est.).
Income: Per capita income: $22,731 (2010); Median household income: $55,833 (2010); Average household income: $56,702 (2010); Percent of households with income of $100,000 or more: 10.6% (2010); Poverty rate: 6.6% (2005-2009 5-year est.).
Taxes: Total city taxes per capita: $63 (2007); City property taxes per capita: $63 (2007).
Education: Percent of population age 25 and over with: High school diploma (including GED) or higher: 85.1% (2010); Bachelor's degree or higher: 13.8% (2010); Master's degree or higher: 1.1% (2010).
Housing: Homeownership rate: 72.3% (2010); Median home value: $80,000 (2010); Median contract rent: n/a per month (2005-2009 5-year est.); Median year structure built: 1984 (2005-2009 5-year est.).
Transportation: Commute to work: 95.5% car, 0.0% public transportation, 4.5% walk, 0.0% work from home (2005-2009 5-year est.); Travel time to work: 50.0% less than 15 minutes, 9.1% 15 to 30 minutes, 18.2% 30 to 45 minutes, 4.5% 45 to 60 minutes, 18.2% 60 minutes or more (2005-2009 5-year est.)

WINCHESTER (city). County seat. Covers a land area of 1.064 square miles and a water area of 0 square miles. Located at 39.63° N. Lat; 90.45° W. Long. Elevation is 541 feet.

History: A grist mill was operating in Winchester in 1824. When the town was platted in 1830, so the story is told, the surveyor allowed a resident from Kentucky to name the townsite in exchange for a jug of whiskey. Stephen A. Douglas taught school and began his legal career here in 1833. Winchester developed as the seat of Scott County.
Population: 1,770 (1990); 1,650 (2000); 1,606 (2010); 1,566 (2015 projected); Race: 99.4% White, 0.1% Black, 0.1% Asian, 0.4% Other, 0.2% Hispanic of any race (2010); Density: 1,510.0 persons per square mile (2010); Average household size: 2.28 (2010); Median age: 45.4 (2010); Males per 100 females: 88.5 (2010); Marriage status: 21.2% never married, 55.9% now married, 9.7% widowed, 13.3% divorced (2005-2009 5-year est.); Foreign born: 0.1% (2005-2009 5-year est.); Ancestry (includes multiple ancestries): 23.1% German, 20.9% English, 18.9% American, 16.6% Irish, 3.3% Dutch (2005-2009 5-year est.).
Economy: Employment by occupation: 7.6% management, 18.5% professional, 19.3% services, 21.9% sales, 3.7% farming, 13.2% construction, 15.9% production (2005-2009 5-year est.).
Income: Per capita income: $20,390 (2010); Median household income: $39,853 (2010); Average household income: $47,937 (2010); Percent of households with income of $100,000 or more: 7.0% (2010); Poverty rate: 13.4% (2005-2009 5-year est.).
Taxes: Total city taxes per capita: $131 (2007); City property taxes per capita: $99 (2007).
Education: Percent of population age 25 and over with: High school diploma (including GED) or higher: 87.4% (2010); Bachelor's degree or higher: 17.0% (2010); Master's degree or higher: 3.3% (2010).

School District(s)
Winchester CUSD 1 (PK-12)
    2009-10 Enrollment: 722 . . . . (217) 742-3175
Housing: Homeownership rate: 73.5% (2010); Median home value: $89,412 (2010); Median contract rent: $307 per month (2005-2009 5-year est.); Median year structure built: 1958 (2005-2009 5-year est.).
Newspapers: Scott County Times (Community news; Circulation 1,800)
Transportation: Commute to work: 88.6% car, 0.6% public transportation, 6.1% walk, 4.3% work from home (2005-2009 5-year est.); Travel time to work: 32.4% less than 15 minutes, 33.7% 15 to 30 minutes, 17.9% 30 to 45 minutes, 6.6% 45 to 60 minutes, 9.4% 60 minutes or more (2005-2009 5-year est.)

Shelby County

Located in central Illinois; drained by the South Fork of the Sangamon River, and by the Kaskaskia and Little Wabash Rivers. Covers a land area of 758.51 square miles, a water area of 9.54 square miles, and is located in the Central Time Zone at 39.38° N. Lat., 88.79° W. Long. The county was founded in 1827. County seat is Shelbyville.

Weather Station: Windsor   Elevation: 689 feet

	Jan	Feb	Mar	Apr	May	Jun	Jul	Aug	Sep	Oct	Nov	Dec
High	36	41	53	66	76	84	87	86	80	68	53	40
Low	21	24	33	43	54	62	66	64	56	45	35	25
Precip	2.3	2.0	3.1	3.9	4.4	3.7	3.7	3.1	3.1	3.5	4.0	2.9
Snow	6.2	4.1	2.2	0.2	0.0	0.0	0.0	0.0	0.0	tr	1.1	4.8

High and Low temperatures in degrees Fahrenheit; Precipitation and Snow in inches

Population: 22,261 (1990); 22,893 (2000); 21,627 (2010); 20,959 (2015 projected); Race: 98.0% White, 0.7% Black, 0.3% Asian, 1.0% Other, 0.8% Hispanic of any race (2010); Density: 28.5 persons per square mile (2010); Average household size: 2.45 (2010); Median age: 41.4 (2010); Males per 100 females: 98.9 (2010).
Religion: Five largest groups: 13.3% Christian Churches and Churches of Christ, 11.7% The United Methodist Church, 7.7% Lutheran Church—Missouri Synod, 7.6% Catholic Church, 3.9% Southern Baptist Convention (2000).
Economy: Unemployment rate: 9.3% (August 2011); Total civilian labor force: 11,086 (August 2011); Leading industries: 24.0% manufacturing; 17.0% health care and social assistance; 13.1% retail trade (2009); Farms: 1,185 totaling 387,288 acres (2007); Companies that employ 500 or more persons: 1 (2009); Companies that employ 100 to 499 persons: 4 (2009); Companies that employ less than 100 persons: 452 (2009); Black-owned businesses: n/a (2007); Hispanic-owned businesses: n/a (2007); Asian-owned businesses: n/a (2007); Women-owned businesses: n/a (2007); Retail sales per capita: $7,544 (2010). Single-family building permits issued: 53 (2010); Multi-family building permits issued: 46 (2010).
Income: Per capita income: $21,676 (2010); Median household income: $45,482 (2010); Average household income: $53,478 (2010); Percent of households with income of $100,000 or more: 9.6% (2010); Poverty rate: 10.9% (2009); Bankruptcy rate: 2.55% (2010).
Taxes: Total county taxes per capita: $171 (2007); County property taxes per capita: $167 (2007).
Education: Percent of population age 25 and over with: High school diploma (including GED) or higher: 86.9% (2010); Bachelor's degree or higher: 14.8% (2010); Master's degree or higher: 5.0% (2010).
Housing: Homeownership rate: 78.7% (2010); Median home value: $82,847 (2010); Median contract rent: $335 per month (2005-2009 5-year est.); Median year structure built: 1960 (2005-2009 5-year est.)
Health: Birth rate: 125.7 per 10,000 population (2009); Death rate: 110.1 per 10,000 population (2009); Age-adjusted cancer mortality rate: 208.1 deaths per 100,000 population (2007); Number of physicians: 5.0 per 10,000 population (2008); Hospital beds: 20.7 per 10,000 population (2007); Hospital admissions: 701.5 per 10,000 population (2007).
Elections: 2008 Presidential election results: 39.1% Obama, 58.9% McCain, 1.0% Nader
National and State Parks: Eagle Creek State Park; Hidden Springs State Forest; Wolf Creek State Park
Additional Information Contacts
Shelby County Government. . . . . (217) 774-4421
    http://shelbycounty-il.com
Greater Shelbyville Chamber of Commerce . . . . (217) 774-2221
    http://www.shelbyvillechamberofcommerce.com

Shelby County Communities

COWDEN (village). Covers a land area of 0.401 square miles and a water area of 0 square miles. Located at 39.24° N. Lat; 88.86° W. Long. Elevation is 597 feet.
Population: 599 (1990); 612 (2000); 574 (2010); 545 (2015 projected); Race: 96.5% White, 1.7% Black, 0.0% Asian, 1.7% Other, 0.2% Hispanic of any race (2010); Density: 1,431.5 persons per square mile (2010); Average household size: 2.57 (2010); Median age: 35.4 (2010); Males per 100 females: 97.3 (2010); Marriage status: 20.8% never married, 42.4% now married, 21.6% widowed, 15.1% divorced (2005-2009 5-year est.); Foreign born: 0.0% (2005-2009 5-year est.); Ancestry (includes multiple ancestries): 28.5% German, 21.8% English, 5.9% Irish, 4.4% Dutch, 3.2% Portuguese (2005-2009 5-year est.).
Economy: Single-family building permits issued: 0 (2010); Multi-family building permits issued: 0 (2010); Employment by occupation: 8.2% management, 15.5% professional, 11.3% services, 24.7% sales, 7.2% farming, 2.1% construction, 30.9% production (2005-2009 5-year est.).

Income: Per capita income: $17,353 (2010); Median household income: $35,192 (2010); Average household income: $43,957 (2010); Percent of households with income of $100,000 or more: 5.8% (2010); Poverty rate: 20.6% (2005-2009 5-year est.).

Taxes: Total city taxes per capita: $61 (2007); City property taxes per capita: $61 (2007).

Education: Percent of population age 25 and over with: High school diploma (including GED) or higher: 85.4% (2010); Bachelor's degree or higher: 8.0% (2010); Master's degree or higher: 3.0% (2010).

School District(s)

Cowden-Herrick CUSD 3a (PK-12)

    2009-10 Enrollment: 438 . . . . (217) 783-2126

Housing: Homeownership rate: 80.3% (2010); Median home value: $49,773 (2010); Median contract rent: $378 per month (2005-2009 5-year est.); Median year structure built: 1967 (2005-2009 5-year est.).

Transportation: Commute to work: 95.9% car, 0.0% public transportation, 0.0% walk, 4.1% work from home (2005-2009 5-year est.); Travel time to work: 17.2% less than 15 minutes, 62.4% 15 to 30 minutes, 11.8% 30 to 45 minutes, 6.5% 45 to 60 minutes, 2.2% 60 minutes or more (2005-2009 5-year est.)

FINDLAY (village). Covers a land area of 0.919 square miles and a water area of 0 square miles. Located at 39.52° N. Lat; 88.75° W. Long. Elevation is 679 feet.

Population: 787 (1990); 723 (2000); 672 (2010); 642 (2015 projected); Race: 95.1% White, 4.0% Black, 0.3% Asian, 0.6% Other, 0.7% Hispanic of any race (2010); Density: 731.2 persons per square mile (2010); Average household size: 2.31 (2010); Median age: 41.8 (2010); Males per 100 females: 96.5 (2010); Marriage status: 28.1% never married, 56.2% now married, 6.5% widowed, 9.3% divorced (2005-2009 5-year est.); Foreign born: 0.0% (2005-2009 5-year est.); Ancestry (includes multiple ancestries): 22.0% German, 14.0% American, 11.5% Irish, 7.3% English, 4.3% Scotch-Irish (2005-2009 5-year est.).

Economy: Single-family building permits issued: 0 (2010); Multi-family building permits issued: 0 (2010); Employment by occupation: 9.8% management, 7.0% professional, 25.3% services, 16.2% sales, 1.0% farming, 12.0% construction, 28.7% production (2005-2009 5-year est.).

Income: Per capita income: $18,328 (2010); Median household income: $34,100 (2010); Average household income: $41,692 (2010); Percent of households with income of $100,000 or more: 5.8% (2010); Poverty rate: 16.2% (2005-2009 5-year est.).

Taxes: Total city taxes per capita: $174 (2007); City property taxes per capita: $171 (2007).

Education: Percent of population age 25 and over with: High school diploma (including GED) or higher: 85.9% (2010); Bachelor's degree or higher: 16.5% (2010); Master's degree or higher: 4.9% (2010).

School District(s)

Okaw Valley CUSD 302 (PK-12)

    2009-10 Enrollment: 565 . . . . (217) 665-3232

Housing: Homeownership rate: 72.2% (2010); Median home value: $68,205 (2010); Median contract rent: $149 per month (2005-2009 5-year est.); Median year structure built: 1960 (2005-2009 5-year est.).

Transportation: Commute to work: 93.6% car, 0.0% public transportation, 2.3% walk, 4.1% work from home (2005-2009 5-year est.); Travel time to work: 17.5% less than 15 minutes, 37.1% 15 to 30 minutes, 22.7% 30 to 45 minutes, 19.2% 45 to 60 minutes, 3.5% 60 minutes or more (2005-2009 5-year est.)

HERRICK (village). Covers a land area of 0.363 square miles and a water area of 0 square miles. Located at 39.21° N. Lat; 88.98° W. Long. Elevation is 600 feet.

Population: 466 (1990); 524 (2000); 507 (2010); 501 (2015 projected); Race: 99.6% White, 0.0% Black, 0.0% Asian, 0.4% Other, 0.4% Hispanic of any race (2010); Density: 1,396.0 persons per square mile (2010); Average household size: 2.63 (2010); Median age: 33.5 (2010); Males per 100 females: 107.8 (2010); Marriage status: 30.2% never married, 48.1% now married, 13.0% widowed, 8.6% divorced (2005-2009 5-year est.); Foreign born: 0.0% (2005-2009 5-year est.); Ancestry (includes multiple ancestries): 28.5% German, 12.9% English, 5.7% Irish, 5.0% French, 3.4% Dutch (2005-2009 5-year est.).

Economy: Employment by occupation: 5.1% management, 14.6% professional, 20.2% services, 14.0% sales, 6.7% farming, 14.6% construction, 24.7% production (2005-2009 5-year est.).

Income: Per capita income: $19,416 (2010); Median household income: $39,662 (2010); Average household income: $49,080 (2010); Percent of

households with income of $100,000 or more: 7.8% (2010); Poverty rate: 22.4% (2005-2009 5-year est.).

Taxes: Total city taxes per capita: $85 (2007); City property taxes per capita: $37 (2007).

Education: Percent of population age 25 and over with: High school diploma (including GED) or higher: 68.4% (2010); Bachelor's degree or higher: 4.0% (2010); Master's degree or higher: 2.3% (2010).

School District(s)

Cowden-Herrick CUSD 3a (PK-12)

    2009-10 Enrollment: 438 . . . . (217) 783-2126

Housing: Homeownership rate: 80.3% (2010); Median home value: $58,077 (2010); Median contract rent: $356 per month (2005-2009 5-year est.); Median year structure built: 1958 (2005-2009 5-year est.).

Transportation: Commute to work: 81.5% car, 0.0% public transportation, 8.7% walk, 1.2% work from home (2005-2009 5-year est.); Travel time to work: 22.8% less than 15 minutes, 29.8% 15 to 30 minutes, 21.1% 30 to 45 minutes, 14.0% 45 to 60 minutes, 12.3% 60 minutes or more (2005-2009 5-year est.)

LAKEWOOD (unincorporated postal area, zip code 62438). Covers a land area of 26.118 square miles and a water area of 0 square miles. Located at 39.31° N. Lat; 88.87° W. Long. Elevation is 627 feet.

Population: 404 (2000); Race: 100.0% White, 0.0% Black, 0.0% Asian, 0.0% Other, 1.1% Hispanic of any race (2000); Density: 15.5 persons per square mile (2000); Age: 28.9% under 18, 12.8% over 64 (2000); Marriage status: 20.5% never married, 71.8% now married, 0.0% widowed, 7.8% divorced (2000); Foreign born: 0.0% (2000); Ancestry (includes multiple ancestries): 12.6% American, 10.5% German, 8.5% English, 3.6% Irish, 2.9% European (2000).

Economy: Employment by occupation: 17.0% management, 4.8% professional, 6.1% services, 15.7% sales, 4.3% farming, 13.0% construction, 39.1% production (2000).

Income: Per capita income: $16,951 (2000); Median household income: $38,750 (2000); Poverty rate: 7.6% (2000).

Education: Percent of population age 25 and over with: High school diploma (including GED) or higher: 90.3% (2000); Bachelor's degree or higher: 5.9% (2000).

Housing: Homeownership rate: 82.5% (2000); Median home value: $46,000 (2000); Median contract rent: $320 per month (2000); Median year structure built: 1955 (2000).

Transportation: Commute to work: 93.0% car, 0.0% public transportation, 0.0% walk, 7.0% work from home (2000); Travel time to work: 16.6% less than 15 minutes, 49.3% 15 to 30 minutes, 13.3% 30 to 45 minutes, 10.0% 45 to 60 minutes, 10.9% 60 minutes or more (2000)

MODE (unincorporated postal area, zip code 62444). Covers a land area of 20.301 square miles and a water area of 0 square miles. Located at 39.43° N. Lat; 88.80° W. Long. Elevation is 627 feet.

Population: 339 (2000); Race: 100.0% White, 0.0% Black, 0.0% Asian, 0.0% Other, 0.0% Hispanic of any race (2000); Density: 16.7 persons per square mile (2000); Age: 15.8% under 18, 16.1% over 64 (2000); Marriage status: 8.2% never married, 66.3% now married, 5.8% widowed, 19.6% divorced (2000); Foreign born: 0.0% (2000); Ancestry (includes multiple ancestries): 21.4% American, 16.7% German, 12.0% Irish, 11.4% English (2000).

Economy: Employment by occupation: 9.6% management, 9.0% professional, 15.4% services, 9.6% sales, 10.3% farming, 9.0% construction, 37.2% production (2000).

Income: Per capita income: $18,500 (2000); Median household income: $32,083 (2000); Poverty rate: 16.1% (2000).

Education: Percent of population age 25 and over with: High school diploma (including GED) or higher: 61.8% (2000); Bachelor's degree or higher: 8.1% (2000).

Housing: Homeownership rate: 86.6% (2000); Median home value: $56,700 (2000); Median contract rent: $205 per month (2000); Median year structure built: 1964 (2000).

Transportation: Commute to work: 100.0% car, 0.0% public transportation, 0.0% walk, 0.0% work from home (2000); Travel time to work: 11.5% less than 15 minutes, 20.5% 15 to 30 minutes, 48.7% 30 to 45 minutes, 4.5% 45 to 60 minutes, 14.7% 60 minutes or more (2000)

MOWEAQUA (village). Covers a land area of 1.118 square miles and a water area of 0 square miles. Located at 39.62° N. Lat; 89.01° W. Long. Elevation is 633 feet.

History: Incorporated 1877.

Population: 1,840 (1990); 1,923 (2000); 1,843 (2010); 1,777 (2015 projected); Race: 98.8% White, 0.3% Black, 0.2% Asian, 0.8% Other, 1.0% Hispanic of any race (2010); Density: 1,648.5 persons per square mile (2010); Average household size: 2.36 (2010); Median age: 43.0 (2010); Males per 100 females: 85.2 (2010); Marriage status: 20.8% never married, 57.8% now married, 8.7% widowed, 12.6% divorced (2005-2009 5-year est.); Foreign born: 0.0% (2005-2009 5-year est.); Ancestry (includes multiple ancestries): 29.6% German, 17.0% English, 11.3% Irish, 7.5% American, 4.3% Dutch (2005-2009 5-year est.).
Economy: Single-family building permits issued: 0 (2010); Multi-family building permits issued: 0 (2010); Employment by occupation: 9.2% management, 23.5% professional, 15.0% services, 23.7% sales, 1.8% farming, 9.1% construction, 17.7% production (2005-2009 5-year est.).
Income: Per capita income: $21,878 (2010); Median household income: $46,194 (2010); Average household income: $53,269 (2010); Percent of households with income of $100,000 or more: 9.9% (2010); Poverty rate: 6.8% (2005-2009 5-year est.).
Taxes: Total city taxes per capita: $139 (2007); City property taxes per capita: $72 (2007).
Education: Percent of population age 25 and over with: High school diploma (including GED) or higher: 84.8% (2010); Bachelor's degree or higher: 17.8% (2010); Master's degree or higher: 7.6% (2010).

School District(s)
Central a & M CUD 21 (PK-12)
    2009-10 Enrollment: 930 . . . . (217) 226-4042
Housing: Homeownership rate: 76.6% (2010); Median home value: $86,182 (2010); Median contract rent: $399 per month (2005-2009 5-year est.); Median year structure built: 1958 (2005-2009 5-year est.).
Safety: Violent crime rate: 0.0 per 10,000 population; Property crime rate: 16.7 per 10,000 population (2010).
Transportation: Commute to work: 93.5% car, 0.0% public transportation, 2.0% walk, 4.1% work from home (2005-2009 5-year est.); Travel time to work: 24.9% less than 15 minutes, 37.9% 15 to 30 minutes, 30.1% 30 to 45 minutes, 4.0% 45 to 60 minutes, 3.0% 60 minutes or more (2005-2009 5-year est.)

OCONEE (village). Covers a land area of 0.360 square miles and a water area of 0 square miles. Located at 39.28° N. Lat; 89.10° W. Long. Elevation is 669 feet.
Population: 201 (1990); 202 (2000); 196 (2010); 192 (2015 projected); Race: 98.5% White, 0.0% Black, 1.0% Asian, 0.5% Other, 1.0% Hispanic of any race (2010); Density: 544.1 persons per square mile (2010); Average household size: 2.61 (2010); Median age: 42.1 (2010); Males per 100 females: 104.2 (2010); Marriage status: 11.9% never married, 76.2% now married, 4.9% widowed, 7.0% divorced (2005-2009 5-year est.); Foreign born: 0.0% (2005-2009 5-year est.); Ancestry (includes multiple ancestries): 46.9% German, 15.8% American, 14.5% English, 4.8% Dutch, 3.5% Croatian (2005-2009 5-year est.).
Economy: Single-family building permits issued: 0 (2010); Multi-family building permits issued: 0 (2010); Employment by occupation: 5.7% management, 4.6% professional, 16.1% services, 24.1% sales, 0.0% farming, 6.9% construction, 42.5% production (2005-2009 5-year est.).
Income: Per capita income: $20,709 (2010); Median household income: $48,816 (2010); Average household income: $55,367 (2010); Percent of households with income of $100,000 or more: 2.7% (2010); Poverty rate: 32.0% (2005-2009 5-year est.).
Taxes: Total city taxes per capita: $26 (2007); City property taxes per capita: $26 (2007).
Education: Percent of population age 25 and over with: High school diploma (including GED) or higher: 84.6% (2010); Bachelor's degree or higher: 3.7% (2010); Master's degree or higher: 0.7% (2010).
Housing: Homeownership rate: 86.7% (2010); Median home value: $87,333 (2010); Median contract rent: $243 per month (2005-2009 5-year est.); Median year structure built: 1957 (2005-2009 5-year est.).
Transportation: Commute to work: 97.7% car, 0.0% public transportation, 2.3% walk, 0.0% work from home (2005-2009 5-year est.); Travel time to work: 13.8% less than 15 minutes, 36.8% 15 to 30 minutes, 19.5% 30 to 45 minutes, 26.4% 45 to 60 minutes, 3.4% 60 minutes or more (2005-2009 5-year est.)

SHELBYVILLE (city). County seat. Covers a land area of 3.696 square miles and a water area of 0.185 square miles. Located at 39.40° N. Lat; 88.80° W. Long. Elevation is 640 feet.
History: Incorporated 1839.

Population: 4,990 (1990); 4,971 (2000); 4,582 (2010); 4,378 (2015 projected); Race: 97.8% White, 0.4% Black, 0.5% Asian, 1.4% Other, 1.2% Hispanic of any race (2010); Density: 1,239.8 persons per square mile (2010); Average household size: 2.25 (2010); Median age: 42.4 (2010); Males per 100 females: 94.3 (2010); Marriage status: 26.8% never married, 52.5% now married, 10.8% widowed, 9.9% divorced (2005-2009 5-year est.); Foreign born: 1.0% (2005-2009 5-year est.); Ancestry (includes multiple ancestries): 31.5% German, 14.2% Irish, 11.9% English, 9.6% American, 3.9% French (2005-2009 5-year est.).
Economy: Single-family building permits issued: 3 (2010); Multi-family building permits issued: 46 (2010); Employment by occupation: 14.2% management, 14.9% professional, 22.2% services, 12.4% sales, 0.0% farming, 9.4% construction, 26.9% production (2005-2009 5-year est.).
Income: Per capita income: $21,802 (2010); Median household income: $40,238 (2010); Average household income: $49,230 (2010); Percent of households with income of $100,000 or more: 8.5% (2010); Poverty rate: 15.0% (2005-2009 5-year est.).
Taxes: Total city taxes per capita: $178 (2007); City property taxes per capita: $173 (2007).
Education: Percent of population age 25 and over with: High school diploma (including GED) or higher: 87.6% (2010); Bachelor's degree or higher: 17.7% (2010); Master's degree or higher: 7.1% (2010).

School District(s)
Clk Cls Cmbn Dglas Edgr Mltr Shlb (06-12)
    2009-10 Enrollment: n/a . . . . (217) 348-0151
Shelbyville CUSD 4 (PK-12)
    2009-10 Enrollment: 1,261 . . . . (217) 774-4626
Housing: Homeownership rate: 69.3% (2010); Median home value: $81,845 (2010); Median contract rent: $329 per month (2005-2009 5-year est.); Median year structure built: 1949 (2005-2009 5-year est.).
Hospitals: Shelby Memorial Hospital (54 beds)
Newspapers: Shelbyville Daily Union (Local news; Circulation 12,000)
Transportation: Commute to work: 85.8% car, 1.0% public transportation, 6.7% walk, 5.3% work from home (2005-2009 5-year est.); Travel time to work: 59.2% less than 15 minutes, 17.7% 15 to 30 minutes, 9.0% 30 to 45 minutes, 10.9% 45 to 60 minutes, 3.1% 60 minutes or more (2005-2009 5-year est.)
Additional Information Contacts
Greater Shelbyville Chamber of Commerce . . . . (217) 774-2221
    http://www.shelbyvillechamberofcommerce.com

SIGEL (town). Covers a land area of 0.273 square miles and a water area of 0.008 square miles. Located at 39.22° N. Lat; 88.49° W. Long. Elevation is 636 feet.
Population: 364 (1990); 386 (2000); 378 (2010); 370 (2015 projected); Race: 98.4% White, 0.0% Black, 0.5% Asian, 1.1% Other, 1.3% Hispanic of any race (2010); Density: 1,382.4 persons per square mile (2010); Average household size: 2.92 (2010); Median age: 33.6 (2010); Males per 100 females: 106.6 (2010); Marriage status: 28.7% never married, 45.8% now married, 11.2% widowed, 14.3% divorced (2005-2009 5-year est.); Foreign born: 0.0% (2005-2009 5-year est.); Ancestry (includes multiple ancestries): 55.9% German, 8.6% Scottish, 8.6% Irish, 5.8% English, 4.8% American (2005-2009 5-year est.).
Economy: Single-family building permits issued: 0 (2010); Multi-family building permits issued: 0 (2010); Employment by occupation: 10.9% management, 12.2% professional, 18.6% services, 27.6% sales, 2.6% farming, 7.1% construction, 21.2% production (2005-2009 5-year est.).
Income: Per capita income: $20,547 (2010); Median household income: $48,828 (2010); Average household income: $60,698 (2010); Percent of households with income of $100,000 or more: 14.0% (2010); Poverty rate: 12.8% (2005-2009 5-year est.).
Taxes: Total city taxes per capita: $47 (2007); City property taxes per capita: $45 (2007).
Education: Percent of population age 25 and over with: High school diploma (including GED) or higher: 89.2% (2010); Bachelor's degree or higher: 19.4% (2010); Master's degree or higher: 7.8% (2010).
Housing: Homeownership rate: 78.3% (2010); Median home value: $108,333 (2010); Median contract rent: $340 per month (2005-2009 5-year est.); Median year structure built: 1961 (2005-2009 5-year est.).
Transportation: Commute to work: 92.3% car, 0.0% public transportation, 2.6% walk, 3.9% work from home (2005-2009 5-year est.); Travel time to work: 38.3% less than 15 minutes, 45.0% 15 to 30 minutes, 13.4% 30 to 45 minutes, 0.0% 45 to 60 minutes, 3.4% 60 minutes or more (2005-2009 5-year est.)

STEWARDSON (village). Covers a land area of 0.605 square miles and a water area of 0 square miles. Located at 39.26° N. Lat; 88.62° W. Long. Elevation is 643 feet.
Population: 672 (1990); 747 (2000); 732 (2010); 718 (2015 projected); Race: 99.3% White, 0.0% Black, 0.1% Asian, 0.5% Other, 0.0% Hispanic of any race (2010); Density: 1,210.2 persons per square mile (2010); Average household size: 2.46 (2010); Median age: 37.0 (2010); Males per 100 females: 99.5 (2010); Marriage status: 18.8% never married, 63.7% now married, 4.6% widowed, 12.9% divorced (2005-2009 5-year est.); Foreign born: 0.0% (2005-2009 5-year est.); Ancestry (includes multiple ancestries): 39.6% German, 6.8% English, 6.6% Irish, 4.8% American, 2.0% French (2005-2009 5-year est.).
Economy: Single-family building permits issued: 0 (2010); Multi-family building permits issued: 0 (2010); Employment by occupation: 12.1% management, 21.3% professional, 9.3% services, 28.3% sales, 0.0% farming, 2.3% construction, 26.7% production (2005-2009 5-year est.).
Income: Per capita income: $20,020 (2010); Median household income: $41,471 (2010); Average household income: $49,933 (2010); Percent of households with income of $100,000 or more: 7.0% (2010); Poverty rate: 7.5% (2005-2009 5-year est.).
Taxes: Total city taxes per capita: $43 (2007); City property taxes per capita: $43 (2007).
Education: Percent of population age 25 and over with: High school diploma (including GED) or higher: 87.7% (2010); Bachelor's degree or higher: 13.7% (2010); Master's degree or higher: 4.2% (2010).
Housing: Homeownership rate: 74.8% (2010); Median home value: $72,553 (2010); Median contract rent: $358 per month (2005-2009 5-year est.); Median year structure built: 1961 (2005-2009 5-year est.).
Transportation: Commute to work: 94.6% car, 0.0% public transportation, 1.9% walk, 0.0% work from home (2005-2009 5-year est.); Travel time to work: 21.2% less than 15 minutes, 50.1% 15 to 30 minutes, 17.7% 30 to 45 minutes, 6.2% 45 to 60 minutes, 4.8% 60 minutes or more (2005-2009 5-year est.)

STRASBURG (village). Covers a land area of 0.528 square miles and a water area of 0 square miles. Located at 39.35° N. Lat; 88.61° W. Long. Elevation is 636 feet.
Population: 478 (1990); 603 (2000); 572 (2010); 558 (2015 projected); Race: 99.1% White, 0.0% Black, 0.2% Asian, 0.7% Other, 0.0% Hispanic of any race (2010); Density: 1,083.2 persons per square mile (2010); Average household size: 2.57 (2010); Median age: 48.8 (2010); Males per 100 females: 89.4 (2010); Marriage status: 11.7% never married, 49.8% now married, 32.4% widowed, 6.0% divorced (2005-2009 5-year est.); Foreign born: 3.2% (2005-2009 5-year est.); Ancestry (includes multiple ancestries): 33.8% German, 13.6% Irish, 12.4% English, 7.2% American, 2.6% Egyptian (2005-2009 5-year est.).
Economy: Single-family building permits issued: 0 (2010); Multi-family building permits issued: 0 (2010); Employment by occupation: 8.6% management, 24.0% professional, 10.7% services, 23.2% sales, 0.0% farming, 8.2% construction, 25.3% production (2005-2009 5-year est.).
Income: Per capita income: $20,388 (2010); Median household income: $47,857 (2010); Average household income: $55,319 (2010); Percent of households with income of $100,000 or more: 9.2% (2010); Poverty rate: 7.1% (2005-2009 5-year est.).
Taxes: Total city taxes per capita: $69 (2007); City property taxes per capita: $26 (2007).
Education: Percent of population age 25 and over with: High school diploma (including GED) or higher: 88.7% (2010); Bachelor's degree or higher: 17.2% (2010); Master's degree or higher: 4.9% (2010).
School District(s)
Stewardson-Strasburg CUD 5a (PK-12)
    2009-10 Enrollment: 423 . . . . (217) 682-3355
Housing: Homeownership rate: 89.8% (2010); Median home value: $90,000 (2010); Median contract rent: n/a per month (2005-2009 5-year est.); Median year structure built: 1946 (2005-2009 5-year est.).
Transportation: Commute to work: 96.7% car, 0.0% public transportation, 1.4% walk, 1.9% work from home (2005-2009 5-year est.); Travel time to work: 15.0% less than 15 minutes, 42.7% 15 to 30 minutes, 37.4% 30 to 45 minutes, 4.9% 45 to 60 minutes, 0.0% 60 minutes or more (2005-2009 5-year est.)

TOWER HILL (village). Covers a land area of 1.003 square miles and a water area of 0 square miles. Located at 39.38° N. Lat; 88.96° W. Long. Elevation is 659 feet.

Population: 601 (1990); 609 (2000); 589 (2010); 579 (2015 projected); Race: 98.3% White, 0.0% Black, 0.2% Asian, 1.5% Other, 0.7% Hispanic of any race (2010); Density: 587.2 persons per square mile (2010); Average household size: 2.53 (2010); Median age: 37.2 (2010); Males per 100 females: 90.6 (2010); Marriage status: 17.1% never married, 63.5% now married, 2.4% widowed, 17.1% divorced (2005-2009 5-year est.); Foreign born: 0.0% (2005-2009 5-year est.); Ancestry (includes multiple ancestries): 19.3% German, 9.8% English, 6.5% Irish, 4.0% Italian, 2.6% Scottish (2005-2009 5-year est.).
Economy: Employment by occupation: 10.1% management, 4.7% professional, 19.1% services, 27.2% sales, 5.1% farming, 8.2% construction, 25.7% production (2005-2009 5-year est.).
Income: Per capita income: $17,148 (2010); Median household income: $37,550 (2010); Average household income: $43,433 (2010); Percent of households with income of $100,000 or more: 4.7% (2010); Poverty rate: 29.5% (2005-2009 5-year est.).
Taxes: Total city taxes per capita: $77 (2007); City property taxes per capita: $59 (2007).
Education: Percent of population age 25 and over with: High school diploma (including GED) or higher: 83.6% (2010); Bachelor's degree or higher: 8.9% (2010); Master's degree or higher: 4.2% (2010).
Housing: Homeownership rate: 77.3% (2010); Median home value: $40,714 (2010); Median contract rent: n/a per month (2005-2009 5-year est.); Median year structure built: 1956 (2005-2009 5-year est.).
Transportation: Commute to work: 82.7% car, 0.0% public transportation, 2.9% walk, 14.4% work from home (2005-2009 5-year est.); Travel time to work: 42.3% less than 15 minutes, 36.1% 15 to 30 minutes, 5.3% 30 to 45 minutes, 5.3% 45 to 60 minutes, 11.1% 60 minutes or more (2005-2009 5-year est.)

WINDSOR (city). Covers a land area of 0.618 square miles and a water area of 0 square miles. Located at 39.43° N. Lat; 88.59° W. Long. Elevation is 702 feet.
History: Incorporated 1869.
Population: 1,143 (1990); 1,125 (2000); 1,046 (2010); 1,011 (2015 projected); Race: 98.7% White, 0.0% Black, 0.0% Asian, 1.3% Other, 0.5% Hispanic of any race (2010); Density: 1,692.5 persons per square mile (2010); Average household size: 2.47 (2010); Median age: 40.1 (2010); Males per 100 females: 94.4 (2010); Marriage status: 23.1% never married, 57.1% now married, 10.9% widowed, 9.0% divorced (2005-2009 5-year est.); Foreign born: 0.0% (2005-2009 5-year est.); Ancestry (includes multiple ancestries): 24.4% German, 11.2% English, 10.2% Irish, 9.8% American, 2.5% Scotch-Irish (2005-2009 5-year est.).
Economy: Employment by occupation: 7.3% management, 9.3% professional, 21.6% services, 22.1% sales, 1.0% farming, 8.7% construction, 29.9% production (2005-2009 5-year est.).
Income: Per capita income: $20,344 (2010); Median household income: $44,712 (2010); Average household income: $50,177 (2010); Percent of households with income of $100,000 or more: 8.0% (2010); Poverty rate: 11.1% (2005-2009 5-year est.).
Taxes: Total city taxes per capita: $100 (2007); City property taxes per capita: $53 (2007).
Education: Percent of population age 25 and over with: High school diploma (including GED) or higher: 84.9% (2010); Bachelor's degree or higher: 13.3% (2010); Master's degree or higher: 2.1% (2010).
School District(s)
Windsor CUSD 1 (PK-12)
    2009-10 Enrollment: 430 . . . . (217) 459-2636
Housing: Homeownership rate: 79.9% (2010); Median home value: $73,824 (2010); Median contract rent: $329 per month (2005-2009 5-year est.); Median year structure built: 1957 (2005-2009 5-year est.).
Transportation: Commute to work: 90.4% car, 0.0% public transportation, 1.5% walk, 6.3% work from home (2005-2009 5-year est.); Travel time to work: 17.9% less than 15 minutes, 58.9% 15 to 30 minutes, 13.2% 30 to 45 minutes, 4.5% 45 to 60 minutes, 5.5% 60 minutes or more (2005-2009 5-year est.)

Saint Clair County

Located in southwestern Illinois; bounded on the northwest by the Mississippi River and the Missouri border; also drained by the Kaskaskia River and Silver Creek. Covers a land area of 663.81 square miles, a water area of 10.15 square miles, and is located in the Central Time Zone at 38.53° N. Lat., 90.00° W. Long. The county was founded in 1790. County seat is Belleville.

Saint Clair County is part of the St. Louis, MO-IL Metropolitan Statistical Area. The entire metro area includes: Bond County, IL; Calhoun County, IL; Clinton County, IL; Jersey County, IL; Macoupin County, IL; Madison County, IL; Monroe County, IL; St. Clair County, IL; Crawford County, MO (pt.); Franklin County, MO; Jefferson County, MO; Lincoln County, MO; St. Charles County, MO; St. Louis County, MO; Warren County, MO; Washington County, MO; St. Louis city, MO

Weather Station: Belleville Scott AFB — Elevation: 442 feet

	Jan	Feb	Mar	Apr	May	Jun	Jul	Aug	Sep	Oct	Nov	Dec
High	42	47	58	69	78	86	89	89	82	71	57	44
Low	24	27	36	45	55	63	67	65	56	46	37	27
Precip	2.3	2.2	3.2	3.9	4.8	4.2	3.8	3.2	3.3	3.5	3.8	2.8
Snow	4.5	3.2	1.6	0.4	0.0	0.0	0.0	0.0	0.0	0.0	0.4	3.0

High and Low temperatures in degrees Fahrenheit; Precipitation and Snow in inches

Weather Station: Cahokia — Elevation: 399 feet

	Jan	Feb	Mar	Apr	May	Jun	Jul	Aug	Sep	Oct	Nov	Dec
High	41	46	56	68	77	85	89	87	81	70	57	44
Low	23	26	34	45	55	64	68	66	58	46	36	25
Precip	2.5	2.6	3.4	3.8	4.5	4.0	4.4	3.5	3.2	3.4	3.7	3.0
Snow	5.0	3.8	1.9	0.2	0.0	0.0	0.0	0.0	0.0	tr	0.6	3.9

High and Low temperatures in degrees Fahrenheit; Precipitation and Snow in inches

Population: 262,852 (1990); 256,082 (2000); 263,504 (2010); 265,535 (2015 projected); Race: 66.2% White, 29.3% Black, 1.2% Asian, 3.3% Other, 2.8% Hispanic of any race (2010); Density: 397.0 persons per square mile (2010); Average household size: 2.53 (2010); Median age: 35.7 (2010); Males per 100 females: 91.5 (2010).
Religion: Five largest groups: 20.6% Catholic Church, 6.6% Southern Baptist Convention, 4.3% United Church of Christ, 2.7% The United Methodist Church, 1.9% Lutheran Church—Missouri Synod (2000).
Economy: Unemployment rate: 10.7% (August 2011); Total civilian labor force: 125,654 (August 2011); Leading industries: 18.6% health care and social assistance; 17.3% retail trade; 12.9% accommodation & food services (2009); Farms: 895 totaling 306,533 acres (2007); Companies that employ 500 or more persons: 13 (2009); Companies that employ 100 to 499 persons: 84 (2009); Companies that employ less than 100 persons: 5,389 (2009); Black-owned businesses: 2,306 (2007); Hispanic-owned businesses: 253 (2007); Asian-owned businesses: 453 (2007); Women-owned businesses: 5,692 (2007); Retail sales per capita: $11,939 (2010). Single-family building permits issued: 621 (2010); Multi-family building permits issued: 402 (2010).
Income: Per capita income: $24,200 (2010); Median household income: $48,366 (2010); Average household income: $61,752 (2010); Percent of households with income of $100,000 or more: 15.7% (2010); Poverty rate: 17.1% (2009); Bankruptcy rate: 5.73% (2010).
Taxes: Total county taxes per capita: $112 (2007); County property taxes per capita: $107 (2007).
Education: Percent of population age 25 and over with: High school diploma (including GED) or higher: 87.5% (2010); Bachelor's degree or higher: 23.8% (2010); Master's degree or higher: 8.7% (2010).
Housing: Homeownership rate: 67.7% (2010); Median home value: $106,091 (2010); Median contract rent: $495 per month (2005-2009 5-year est.); Median year structure built: 1968 (2005-2009 5-year est.)
Health: Birth rate: 147.3 per 10,000 population (2009); Death rate: 94.3 per 10,000 population (2009); Age-adjusted cancer mortality rate: 209.9 deaths per 100,000 population (2007); Number of physicians: 18.3 per 10,000 population (2008); Hospital beds: 33.7 per 10,000 population (2007); Hospital admissions: 1,389.1 per 10,000 population (2007).
Environment: Air Quality Index: 71.1% good, 28.6% moderate, 0.3% unhealthy for sensitive individuals, 0.0% unhealthy (percent of days in 2008)
Elections: 2008 Presidential election results: 60.6% Obama, 38.1% McCain, 0.6% Nader
National and State Parks: Cahokia Mounds State Park; Holten State Park
Additional Information Contacts
Saint Clair County Government . . . . (618) 277-6600
http://www.co.st-clair.il.us
Cahokia Area Chamber of Commerce . . . . (618) 332-4258
http://www.cahokiachamber.org
City of Belleville . . . . (618) 233-6810
http://www.belleville.net
City of East Saint Louis . . . . (618) 482-6600
http://www.cesl.us

City of Fairview Heights . . . . (618) 489-2000
http://www.fairviewheightscity.com
City of Mascoutah . . . . (618) 566-2964
http://www.mascoutah.com
City of O'Fallon . . . . (618) 624-4500
http://www.ofallon.org
Fairview Heights Chamber of Commerce . . . . (618) 397-3127
http://www.fairviewheightschamber.org
Greater Belleville Chamber of Commerce . . . . (618) 233-2015
http://www.bellevillechamber.org
Lebanon Chamber of Commerce . . . . (618) 537-8420
http://lebanonil.org/chamber.html
O'Fallon-Shiloh Chamber of Commerce . . . . (618) 632-3377
http://www.ofallonchamber.com
O'Fallon-Shiloh Chamber of Commerce . . . . (618) 632-3377
http://www.shilohchamber.org
Smithton Chamber of Commerce . . . . (618) 473-3366
http://smithtonchamber.ning.com
Swansea Chamber of Commerce . . . . (618) 233-3938
http://www.swanseachamber.org
Village of Cahokia . . . . (618) 337-9500
http://cahokiaillinois.org
Village of Shiloh . . . . (618) 632-1022
http://www.shilohil.org
Village of Swansea . . . . (618) 234-0044
http://www.swanseail.org

Saint Clair County Communities

ALORTON (village). Covers a land area of 1.779 square miles and a water area of 0 square miles. Located at 38.58° N. Lat; 90.11° W. Long. Elevation is 417 feet.
History: Incorporated 1944.
Population: 2,960 (1990); 2,749 (2000); 2,622 (2010); 2,554 (2015 projected); Race: 2.3% White, 95.5% Black, 0.0% Asian, 2.1% Other, 1.4% Hispanic of any race (2010); Density: 1,473.9 persons per square mile (2010); Average household size: 2.89 (2010); Median age: 28.0 (2010); Males per 100 females: 87.2 (2010); Marriage status: 45.1% never married, 34.2% now married, 9.6% widowed, 11.0% divorced (2005-2009 5-year est.); Foreign born: 0.0% (2005-2009 5-year est.); Ancestry (includes multiple ancestries): 2.0% African, 1.0% American, 0.6% German, 0.6% Irish, 0.4% English (2005-2009 5-year est.).
Economy: Employment by occupation: 4.4% management, 3.3% professional, 25.8% services, 8.4% sales, 0.0% farming, 4.0% construction, 54.1% production (2005-2009 5-year est.).
Income: Per capita income: $11,700 (2010); Median household income: $21,979 (2010); Average household income: $34,294 (2010); Percent of households with income of $100,000 or more: 4.6% (2010); Poverty rate: 47.9% (2005-2009 5-year est.).
Taxes: Total city taxes per capita: $181 (2007); City property taxes per capita: $66 (2007).
Education: Percent of population age 25 and over with: High school diploma (including GED) or higher: 69.4% (2010); Bachelor's degree or higher: 6.6% (2010); Master's degree or higher: 1.3% (2010).
School District(s)
East St Louis SD 189 (PK-12)
2009-10 Enrollment: 8,141 . . . . (618) 646-3009
Housing: Homeownership rate: 45.6% (2010); Median home value: $50,917 (2010); Median contract rent: $451 per month (2005-2009 5-year est.); Median year structure built: 1968 (2005-2009 5-year est.).
Transportation: Commute to work: 77.7% car, 4.0% public transportation, 0.0% walk, 1.3% work from home (2005-2009 5-year est.); Travel time to work: 34.0% less than 15 minutes, 23.5% 15 to 30 minutes, 14.8% 30 to 45 minutes, 26.0% 45 to 60 minutes, 1.7% 60 minutes or more (2005-2009 5-year est.)

BELLEVILLE (city). County seat. Covers a land area of 18.854 square miles and a water area of 0.128 square miles. Located at 38.52° N. Lat; 89.99° W. Long. Elevation is 515 feet.
History: Named for the French translation of "beautiful city," by George Blair. Settlers came to Belleville early in the 1800's, and in 1814 the settlement became the seat of St. Clair County, succeeding Cahokia. The town was incorporated in 1819. The discovery of coal in 1828 brought many German immigrants to Belleville, which came to be known as Dutch Town.

Population: 43,445 (1990); 41,410 (2000); 39,931 (2010); 39,149 (2015 projected); Race: 74.9% White, 20.9% Black, 1.1% Asian, 3.1% Other, 2.1% Hispanic of any race (2010); Density: 2,117.9 persons per square mile (2010); Average household size: 2.22 (2010); Median age: 38.4 (2010); Males per 100 females: 89.3 (2010); Marriage status: 34.4% never married, 44.2% now married, 7.4% widowed, 13.9% divorced (2005-2009 5-year est.); Foreign born: 1.5% (2005-2009 5-year est.); Ancestry (includes multiple ancestries): 34.9% German, 13.9% Irish, 8.4% English, 5.0% French, 4.6% American (2005-2009 5-year est.).
Economy: Unemployment rate: 11.3% (August 2011); Total civilian labor force: 21,791 (August 2011); Single-family building permits issued: 48 (2010); Multi-family building permits issued: 0 (2010); Employment by occupation: 12.9% management, 17.6% professional, 21.2% services, 27.2% sales, 0.3% farming, 8.7% construction, 12.0% production (2005-2009 5-year est.).
Income: Per capita income: $22,875 (2010); Median household income: $42,102 (2010); Average household income: $51,581 (2010); Percent of households with income of $100,000 or more: 9.6% (2010); Poverty rate: 12.3% (2005-2009 5-year est.).
Taxes: Total city taxes per capita: $497 (2007); City property taxes per capita: $339 (2007).
Education: Percent of population age 25 and over with: High school diploma (including GED) or higher: 89.2% (2010); Bachelor's degree or higher: 20.9% (2010); Master's degree or higher: 6.8% (2010).

School District(s)
Belle Valley SD 119 (PK-08)
   2009-10 Enrollment: 876 . . . . (618) 234-7723
Belleville Area Special Services (KG-12)
   2009-10 Enrollment: n/a . . . . (618) 355-4700
Belleville SD 118 (PK-08)
   2009-10 Enrollment: 3,695 . . . . (618) 233-2830
Belleville Twp HSD 201 (09-12)
   2009-10 Enrollment: 5,032 . . . . (618) 222-8241
East St Louis SD 189 (PK-12)
   2009-10 Enrollment: 8,141 . . . . (618) 646-3009
Harmony Emge SD 175 (PK-08)
   2009-10 Enrollment: 755 . . . . (618) 397-8444
Signal Hill SD 181 (PK-08)
   2009-10 Enrollment: 374 . . . . (618) 397-0325
St Clair Roe (06-12)
   2009-10 Enrollment: n/a . . . . (618) 825-3900
Whiteside SD 115 (PK-08)
   2009-10 Enrollment: 1,388 . . . . (618) 239-0000

Two-year College(s)
Southwestern Illinois College (Public)
   Fall 2009 Enrollment: 14,440. . . . . (618) 235-2700
   2010-11 Tuition: In-state $6,104; Out-of-state $9,968

Vocational/Technical School(s)
Alvareitas College of Cosmetology (Private, For-profit)
   Fall 2009 Enrollment: 18 . . . . (618) 257-9193
   2010-11 Tuition: $12,600
Housing: Homeownership rate: 61.2% (2010); Median home value: $91,977 (2010); Median contract rent: $479 per month (2005-2009 5-year est.); Median year structure built: 1957 (2005-2009 5-year est.).
Hospitals: 375th Medical Group Hospital (161 beds); Memorial Hospital (313 beds); St. Elizabeth's Hospital (498 beds)
Newspapers: Belleville News-Democrat (Local news; Circulation 53,365); Cahokia Journal (Local news; Circulation 13,000); Cahokia-Dupo Journal (Local news; Circulation 13,700); East St. Louis Journal (Local news; Circulation 20,990); The Messenger (Regional news; Circulation 14,000); O'Fallon Journal (Community news; Circulation 7,912); St. Louis Post-Dispatch - Belleville Bureau (Local news)
Transportation: Commute to work: 89.2% car, 5.0% public transportation, 1.4% walk, 2.9% work from home (2005-2009 5-year est.); Travel time to work: 32.7% less than 15 minutes, 36.6% 15 to 30 minutes, 17.1% 30 to 45 minutes, 8.9% 45 to 60 minutes, 4.7% 60 minutes or more (2005-2009 5-year est.)
Airports: Scott AFB/Midamerica (primary service)
Additional Information Contacts
City of Belleville . . . . (618) 233-6810
   http://www.belleville.net
Greater Belleville Chamber of Commerce . . . . (618) 233-2015
   http://www.bellevillechamber.org

BROOKLYN (village). Aka Lovejoy. Covers a land area of 0.843 square miles and a water area of 0 square miles. Located at 38.65° N. Lat; 90.16° W. Long. Elevation is 413 feet.
History: When it was incorporated in 1874 Brooklyn was called Lovejoy, in honor of Abolitionist editor Elijah P. Lovejoy.
Population: 1,144 (1990); 676 (2000); 550 (2010); 503 (2015 projected); Race: 0.7% White, 97.6% Black, 0.0% Asian, 1.6% Other, 0.5% Hispanic of any race (2010); Density: 652.5 persons per square mile (2010); Average household size: 2.46 (2010); Median age: 29.9 (2010); Males per 100 females: 71.9 (2010); Marriage status: 43.2% never married, 29.3% now married, 17.8% widowed, 9.7% divorced (2005-2009 5-year est.); Foreign born: 0.0% (2005-2009 5-year est.); Ancestry (includes multiple ancestries): 0.8% African, 0.8% Irish, 0.8% Welsh (2005-2009 5-year est.).
Economy: Employment by occupation: 8.8% management, 18.6% professional, 37.2% services, 18.6% sales, 0.0% farming, 3.5% construction, 13.3% production (2005-2009 5-year est.).
Income: Per capita income: $9,238 (2010); Median household income: $19,412 (2010); Average household income: $22,545 (2010); Percent of households with income of $100,000 or more: 0.0% (2010); Poverty rate: 34.8% (2005-2009 5-year est.).
Taxes: Total city taxes per capita: $417 (2007); City property taxes per capita: $63 (2007).
Education: Percent of population age 25 and over with: High school diploma (including GED) or higher: 68.7% (2010); Bachelor's degree or higher: 5.7% (2010); Master's degree or higher: 0.6% (2010).

School District(s)
Brooklyn UD 188 (PK-12)
   2009-10 Enrollment: 156 . . . . (618) 271-1028
Housing: Homeownership rate: 52.7% (2010); Median home value: $60,606 (2010); Median contract rent: $173 per month (2005-2009 5-year est.); Median year structure built: 1965 (2005-2009 5-year est.).
Safety: Violent crime rate: 556.5 per 10,000 population; Property crime rate: 982.0 per 10,000 population (2010).
Transportation: Commute to work: 76.2% car, 14.3% public transportation, 9.5% walk, 0.0% work from home (2005-2009 5-year est.); Travel time to work: 34.3% less than 15 minutes, 47.6% 15 to 30 minutes, 2.9% 30 to 45 minutes, 7.6% 45 to 60 minutes, 7.6% 60 minutes or more (2005-2009 5-year est.)

CAHOKIA (village). Aka Maplewood Park. Covers a land area of 9.609 square miles and a water area of 0.367 square miles. Located at 38.56° N. Lat; 90.17° W. Long. Elevation is 407 feet.
History: Named for an Indian tribe of the Illinois Confederacy. Cahokia began with a mission established in 1699 by Jean Francois Buisson de St. Cosme of the Seminary of Foreign Missions, and a trading post developed around the mission. In 1809 county lines were redrawn so that Cahokia served as the seat of a territory that later was divided into 80 northern counties.
Population: 17,550 (1990); 16,391 (2000); 14,975 (2010); 14,365 (2015 projected); Race: 45.6% White, 50.6% Black, 0.3% Asian, 3.5% Other, 2.7% Hispanic of any race (2010); Density: 1,558.4 persons per square mile (2010); Average household size: 2.81 (2010); Median age: 31.4 (2010); Males per 100 females: 88.5 (2010); Marriage status: 40.6% never married, 40.6% now married, 7.0% widowed, 11.8% divorced (2005-2009 5-year est.); Foreign born: 1.4% (2005-2009 5-year est.); Ancestry (includes multiple ancestries): 10.0% German, 8.9% Irish, 6.0% European, 5.5% English, 4.0% American (2005-2009 5-year est.).
Economy: Single-family building permits issued: 0 (2010); Multi-family building permits issued: 0 (2010); Employment by occupation: 4.4% management, 10.7% professional, 32.4% services, 29.4% sales, 0.2% farming, 7.5% construction, 15.5% production (2005-2009 5-year est.).
Income: Per capita income: $14,486 (2010); Median household income: $32,988 (2010); Average household income: $40,698 (2010); Percent of households with income of $100,000 or more: 4.0% (2010); Poverty rate: 24.2% (2005-2009 5-year est.).
Taxes: Total city taxes per capita: $384 (2007); City property taxes per capita: $239 (2007).
Education: Percent of population age 25 and over with: High school diploma (including GED) or higher: 78.9% (2010); Bachelor's degree or higher: 7.5% (2010); Master's degree or higher: 2.6% (2010).

School District(s)
Cahokia CUSD 187 (PK-12)
   2009-10 Enrollment: 4,585 . . . . (618) 332-3700

Housing: Homeownership rate: 66.6% (2010); Median home value: $52,756 (2010); Median contract rent: $497 per month (2005-2009 5-year est.); Median year structure built: 1959 (2005-2009 5-year est.).
Safety: Violent crime rate: 39.1 per 10,000 population; Property crime rate: 582.8 per 10,000 population (2010).
Transportation: Commute to work: 90.3% car, 6.3% public transportation, 1.6% walk, 1.2% work from home (2005-2009 5-year est.); Travel time to work: 27.1% less than 15 minutes, 44.9% 15 to 30 minutes, 21.7% 30 to 45 minutes, 3.5% 45 to 60 minutes, 2.7% 60 minutes or more (2005-2009 5-year est.)
Airports: Saint Louis Downtown (general aviation)
Additional Information Contacts
Cahokia Area Chamber of Commerce . . . . (618) 332-4258
   http://www.cahokiachamber.org
Village of Cahokia . . . . (618) 337-9500
   http://cahokiaillinois.org

CASEYVILLE (village). Covers a land area of 6.211 square miles and a water area of 0 square miles. Located at 38.63° N. Lat; 90.03° W. Long. Elevation is 453 feet.
Population: 5,001 (1990); 4,310 (2000); 4,161 (2010); 4,158 (2015 projected); Race: 84.9% White, 11.0% Black, 0.5% Asian, 3.6% Other, 4.0% Hispanic of any race (2010); Density: 670.0 persons per square mile (2010); Average household size: 2.41 (2010); Median age: 40.2 (2010); Males per 100 females: 92.0 (2010); Marriage status: 20.6% never married, 50.8% now married, 11.3% widowed, 17.3% divorced (2005-2009 5-year est.); Foreign born: 3.1% (2005-2009 5-year est.); Ancestry (includes multiple ancestries): 27.7% German, 11.6% Irish, 9.5% English, 7.2% American, 4.6% European (2005-2009 5-year est.).
Economy: Single-family building permits issued: 3 (2010); Multi-family building permits issued: 0 (2010); Employment by occupation: 11.8% management, 17.3% professional, 17.9% services, 20.3% sales, 1.6% farming, 12.4% construction, 18.9% production (2005-2009 5-year est.).
Income: Per capita income: $20,035 (2010); Median household income: $40,074 (2010); Average household income: $48,617 (2010); Percent of households with income of $100,000 or more: 7.5% (2010); Poverty rate: 12.7% (2005-2009 5-year est.).
Taxes: Total city taxes per capita: $607 (2007); City property taxes per capita: $377 (2007).
Education: Percent of population age 25 and over with: High school diploma (including GED) or higher: 83.0% (2010); Bachelor's degree or higher: 14.4% (2010); Master's degree or higher: 4.0% (2010).
School District(s)
Collinsville CUSD 10 (PK-12)
   2009-10 Enrollment: 6,623 . . . . (618) 346-6350
Housing: Homeownership rate: 80.1% (2010); Median home value: $83,927 (2010); Median contract rent: $442 per month (2005-2009 5-year est.); Median year structure built: 1960 (2005-2009 5-year est.).
Safety: Violent crime rate: 40.9 per 10,000 population; Property crime rate: 245.3 per 10,000 population (2010).
Transportation: Commute to work: 93.9% car, 0.4% public transportation, 2.6% walk, 3.0% work from home (2005-2009 5-year est.); Travel time to work: 24.2% less than 15 minutes, 49.2% 15 to 30 minutes, 21.1% 30 to 45 minutes, 1.3% 45 to 60 minutes, 4.2% 60 minutes or more (2005-2009 5-year est.)

CENTREVILLE (city). Covers a land area of 4.333 square miles and a water area of 0 square miles. Located at 38.58° N. Lat; 90.10° W. Long. Elevation is 413 feet.
Population: 7,413 (1990); 5,951 (2000); 5,662 (2010); 5,519 (2015 projected); Race: 3.5% White, 94.8% Black, 0.0% Asian, 1.7% Other, 0.6% Hispanic of any race (2010); Density: 1,306.6 persons per square mile (2010); Average household size: 2.72 (2010); Median age: 30.1 (2010); Males per 100 females: 86.0 (2010); Marriage status: 43.3% never married, 28.2% now married, 13.9% widowed, 14.6% divorced (2005-2009 5-year est.); Foreign born: 0.0% (2005-2009 5-year est.); Ancestry (includes multiple ancestries): 0.9% African, 0.9% Polish, 0.4% Irish, 0.4% German, 0.2% Norwegian (2005-2009 5-year est.).
Economy: Single-family building permits issued: 0 (2010); Multi-family building permits issued: 0 (2010); Employment by occupation: 2.2% management, 17.2% professional, 23.7% services, 30.3% sales, 2.1% farming, 5.3% construction, 19.2% production (2005-2009 5-year est.).
Income: Per capita income: $13,910 (2010); Median household income: $27,255 (2010); Average household income: $37,794 (2010); Percent of

households with income of $100,000 or more: 5.3% (2010); Poverty rate: 39.3% (2005-2009 5-year est.).
Taxes: Total city taxes per capita: $279 (2007); City property taxes per capita: $173 (2007).
Education: Percent of population age 25 and over with: High school diploma (including GED) or higher: 76.4% (2010); Bachelor's degree or higher: 12.9% (2010); Master's degree or higher: 5.2% (2010).
School District(s)
Cahokia CUSD 187 (PK-12)
   2009-10 Enrollment: 4,585 . . . . (618) 332-3700
Housing: Homeownership rate: 57.9% (2010); Median home value: $58,235 (2010); Median contract rent: $270 per month (2005-2009 5-year est.); Median year structure built: 1958 (2005-2009 5-year est.).
Hospitals: Touchette Regional Hospital (114 beds)
Transportation: Commute to work: 87.5% car, 8.7% public transportation, 3.3% walk, 0.5% work from home (2005-2009 5-year est.); Travel time to work: 23.6% less than 15 minutes, 46.3% 15 to 30 minutes, 19.9% 30 to 45 minutes, 2.5% 45 to 60 minutes, 7.7% 60 minutes or more (2005-2009 5-year est.)

DUPO (village). Aka Sugar Loaf Heights. Covers a land area of 4.426 square miles and a water area of 0 square miles. Located at 38.51° N. Lat; 90.20° W. Long. Elevation is 417 feet.
History: The name of Dupo is a shortened form of Prairie du Pont, which is a French term meaning "meadow of the bridge." Oil was discovered near Dupo in 1928 and a brief period of fast growth ensued.
Population: 3,634 (1990); 3,933 (2000); 4,196 (2010); 4,248 (2015 projected); Race: 96.8% White, 0.9% Black, 0.3% Asian, 2.0% Other, 0.9% Hispanic of any race (2010); Density: 948.0 persons per square mile (2010); Average household size: 2.46 (2010); Median age: 36.2 (2010); Males per 100 females: 94.8 (2010); Marriage status: 31.9% never married, 47.6% now married, 7.6% widowed, 12.8% divorced (2005-2009 5-year est.); Foreign born: 0.8% (2005-2009 5-year est.); Ancestry (includes multiple ancestries): 36.0% German, 18.3% Irish, 8.1% English, 6.0% Italian, 5.4% French (2005-2009 5-year est.).
Economy: Single-family building permits issued: 3 (2010); Multi-family building permits issued: 0 (2010); Employment by occupation: 8.4% management, 16.4% professional, 23.5% services, 28.5% sales, 0.0% farming, 8.5% construction, 14.8% production (2005-2009 5-year est.).
Income: Per capita income: $25,446 (2010); Median household income: $56,460 (2010); Average household income: $62,276 (2010); Percent of households with income of $100,000 or more: 12.9% (2010); Poverty rate: 11.6% (2005-2009 5-year est.).
Taxes: Total city taxes per capita: $241 (2007); City property taxes per capita: $109 (2007).
Education: Percent of population age 25 and over with: High school diploma (including GED) or higher: 83.9% (2010); Bachelor's degree or higher: 13.3% (2010); Master's degree or higher: 3.7% (2010).
School District(s)
Dupo CUSD 196 (PK-12)
   2009-10 Enrollment: 1,189 . . . . (618) 286-3812
Housing: Homeownership rate: 73.7% (2010); Median home value: $92,657 (2010); Median contract rent: $465 per month (2005-2009 5-year est.); Median year structure built: 1959 (2005-2009 5-year est.).
Transportation: Commute to work: 93.5% car, 1.6% public transportation, 0.0% walk, 4.7% work from home (2005-2009 5-year est.); Travel time to work: 22.2% less than 15 minutes, 46.6% 15 to 30 minutes, 15.4% 30 to 45 minutes, 9.8% 45 to 60 minutes, 6.0% 60 minutes or more (2005-2009 5-year est.)

EAST CARONDELET (village). Covers a land area of 1.251 square miles and a water area of 0.412 square miles. Located at 38.54° N. Lat; 90.23° W. Long. Elevation is 410 feet.
History: Damaged in floods of 1993.
Population: 644 (1990); 267 (2000); 246 (2010); 236 (2015 projected); Race: 96.3% White, 0.8% Black, 0.0% Asian, 2.8% Other, 0.0% Hispanic of any race (2010); Density: 196.7 persons per square mile (2010); Average household size: 2.80 (2010); Median age: 34.5 (2010); Males per 100 females: 93.7 (2010); Marriage status: 45.7% never married, 47.0% now married, 3.4% widowed, 3.9% divorced (2005-2009 5-year est.); Foreign born: 0.0% (2005-2009 5-year est.); Ancestry (includes multiple ancestries): 60.0% German, 41.6% Italian, 26.8% Irish, 1.5% Swedish, 1.2% English (2005-2009 5-year est.).
Economy: Single-family building permits issued: 0 (2010); Multi-family building permits issued: 0 (2010); Employment by occupation: 4.2%

management, 9.8% professional, 12.6% services, 15.7% sales, 0.0% farming, 3.5% construction, 54.2% production (2005-2009 5-year est.).
Income: Per capita income: $21,512 (2010); Median household income: $49,167 (2010); Average household income: $62,074 (2010); Percent of households with income of $100,000 or more: 8.0% (2010); Poverty rate: 5.5% (2005-2009 5-year est.).
Taxes: Total city taxes per capita: $82 (2007); City property taxes per capita: $33 (2007).
Education: Percent of population age 25 and over with: High school diploma (including GED) or higher: 73.0% (2010); Bachelor's degree or higher: 2.5% (2010); Master's degree or higher: 0.0% (2010).
Housing: Homeownership rate: 78.4% (2010); Median home value: $57,727 (2010); Median contract rent: $427 per month (2005-2009 5-year est.); Median year structure built: 1956 (2005-2009 5-year est.).
Transportation: Commute to work: 100.0% car, 0.0% public transportation, 0.0% walk, 0.0% work from home (2005-2009 5-year est.); Travel time to work: 9.5% less than 15 minutes, 17.8% 15 to 30 minutes, 66.9% 30 to 45 minutes, 2.5% 45 to 60 minutes, 3.3% 60 minutes or more (2005-2009 5-year est.)

EAST SAINT LOUIS (city). Covers a land area of 14.063 square miles and a water area of 0.367 square miles. Located at 38.61° N. Lat; 90.12° W. Long. Elevation is 417 feet.
History: Settlement across the Mississippi River from St. Louis, Missouri, was achieved by Captain James Piggott who established ferry service here in 1795. A village called Illinoistown was platted near the ferry dock in 1816. When Illinoistown was incorporated in 1859, a town called East St. Louis had been established nearby. In 1861 the charter of Illinoistown was extended to include the new town, and the name was changed to East St. Louis. Near the end of the 19th century, East St. Louis changed from a river town to an industrial center.
Population: 40,944 (1990); 31,542 (2000); 27,992 (2010); 26,626 (2015 projected); Race: 1.6% White, 96.7% Black, 0.1% Asian, 1.5% Other, 1.1% Hispanic of any race (2010); Density: 1,990.5 persons per square mile (2010); Average household size: 2.70 (2010); Median age: 31.1 (2010); Males per 100 females: 83.5 (2010); Marriage status: 51.4% never married, 24.8% now married, 10.8% widowed, 13.0% divorced (2005-2009 5-year est.); Foreign born: 0.2% (2005-2009 5-year est.); Ancestry (includes multiple ancestries): 1.9% African, 0.6% American, 0.5% Irish, 0.4% German, 0.3% French (2005-2009 5-year est.).
Economy: Unemployment rate: 18.5% (August 2011); Total civilian labor force: 10,204 (August 2011); Single-family building permits issued: 8 (2010); Multi-family building permits issued: 30 (2010); Employment by occupation: 7.8% management, 15.3% professional, 35.6% services, 22.7% sales, 0.0% farming, 4.1% construction, 14.6% production (2005-2009 5-year est.).
Income: Per capita income: $13,104 (2010); Median household income: $24,853 (2010); Average household income: $35,479 (2010); Percent of households with income of $100,000 or more: 5.4% (2010); Poverty rate: 38.6% (2005-2009 5-year est.).
Taxes: Total city taxes per capita: $499 (2007); City property taxes per capita: $329 (2007).
Education: Percent of population age 25 and over with: High school diploma (including GED) or higher: 76.3% (2010); Bachelor's degree or higher: 11.8% (2010); Master's degree or higher: 3.7% (2010).
School District(s)
East St Louis SD 189 (PK-12)
    2009-10 Enrollment: 8,141 . . . . (618) 646-3009
Vocational/Technical School(s)
Vees School of Beauty Culture (Private, For-profit)
    Fall 2009 Enrollment: 42 . . . . (618) 274-1751
    2010-11 Tuition: $12,160
Housing: Homeownership rate: 52.9% (2010); Median home value: $57,280 (2010); Median contract rent: $282 per month (2005-2009 5-year est.); Median year structure built: 1954 (2005-2009 5-year est.).
Safety: Violent crime rate: 582.5 per 10,000 population; Property crime rate: 892.6 per 10,000 population (2010).
Newspapers: East Saint Louis Monitor (Local news; Circulation 5,400)
Transportation: Commute to work: 81.1% car, 13.2% public transportation, 1.4% walk, 3.3% work from home (2005-2009 5-year est.); Travel time to work: 29.7% less than 15 minutes, 41.8% 15 to 30 minutes, 19.2% 30 to 45 minutes, 5.1% 45 to 60 minutes, 4.2% 60 minutes or more (2005-2009 5-year est.)
Additional Information Contacts

City of East Saint Louis . . . . (618) 482-6600
    http://www.cesl.us

FAIRMONT CITY (village). Covers a land area of 2.405 square miles and a water area of 0 square miles. Located at 38.65° N. Lat; 90.10° W. Long. Elevation is 420 feet.
History: Fairmont City came into being in 1910 when the Pennsylvania Railroad built a roundhouse here. First called Willow Town, the name was changed to Fairmont City when it was incorporated in 1914.
Population: 2,140 (1990); 2,436 (2000); 2,643 (2010); 2,748 (2015 projected); Race: 59.3% White, 1.7% Black, 0.1% Asian, 39.0% Other, 67.9% Hispanic of any race (2010); Density: 1,099.2 persons per square mile (2010); Average household size: 2.79 (2010); Median age: 32.3 (2010); Males per 100 females: 112.6 (2010); Marriage status: 29.5% never married, 57.0% now married, 6.5% widowed, 7.0% divorced (2005-2009 5-year est.); Foreign born: 34.0% (2005-2009 5-year est.); Ancestry (includes multiple ancestries): 7.1% German, 5.3% Irish, 3.3% American, 3.2% European, 2.9% Italian (2005-2009 5-year est.).
Economy: Employment by occupation: 4.5% management, 3.4% professional, 22.8% services, 18.6% sales, 4.2% farming, 7.3% construction, 39.2% production (2005-2009 5-year est.).
Income: Per capita income: $14,045 (2010); Median household income: $31,310 (2010); Average household income: $39,302 (2010); Percent of households with income of $100,000 or more: 3.3% (2010); Poverty rate: 38.5% (2005-2009 5-year est.).
Taxes: Total city taxes per capita: $94 (2007); City property taxes per capita: $20 (2007).
Education: Percent of population age 25 and over with: High school diploma (including GED) or higher: 57.5% (2010); Bachelor's degree or higher: 7.9% (2010); Master's degree or higher: 2.4% (2010).
Housing: Homeownership rate: 73.3% (2010); Median home value: $54,224 (2010); Median contract rent: $347 per month (2005-2009 5-year est.); Median year structure built: 1954 (2005-2009 5-year est.).
Safety: Violent crime rate: 4.5 per 10,000 population; Property crime rate: 293.3 per 10,000 population (2010).
Transportation: Commute to work: 90.9% car, 0.4% public transportation, 0.6% walk, 1.5% work from home (2005-2009 5-year est.); Travel time to work: 29.6% less than 15 minutes, 48.5% 15 to 30 minutes, 16.6% 30 to 45 minutes, 3.2% 45 to 60 minutes, 2.1% 60 minutes or more (2005-2009 5-year est.)

FAIRVIEW HEIGHTS (city). Aka Fairview. Covers a land area of 11.148 square miles and a water area of 0.065 square miles. Located at 38.59° N. Lat; 89.99° W. Long. Elevation is 584 feet.
History: Named to promote the town as a good place to live. Also known as Fairview. Formerly called Lincoln Heights.
Population: 15,019 (1990); 15,034 (2000); 15,900 (2010); 16,083 (2015 projected); Race: 72.2% White, 21.8% Black, 2.7% Asian, 3.3% Other, 2.6% Hispanic of any race (2010); Density: 1,426.3 persons per square mile (2010); Average household size: 2.39 (2010); Median age: 40.3 (2010); Males per 100 females: 92.0 (2010); Marriage status: 26.8% never married, 55.8% now married, 6.8% widowed, 10.6% divorced (2005-2009 5-year est.); Foreign born: 2.2% (2005-2009 5-year est.); Ancestry (includes multiple ancestries): 27.7% German, 12.6% Irish, 9.6% English, 6.0% American, 4.4% Italian (2005-2009 5-year est.).
Economy: Single-family building permits issued: 49 (2010); Multi-family building permits issued: 9 (2010); Employment by occupation: 12.8% management, 23.0% professional, 16.0% services, 28.7% sales, 0.0% farming, 9.6% construction, 9.9% production (2005-2009 5-year est.).
Income: Per capita income: $28,450 (2010); Median household income: $57,009 (2010); Average household income: $67,897 (2010); Percent of households with income of $100,000 or more: 18.1% (2010); Poverty rate: 7.7% (2005-2009 5-year est.).
Taxes: Total city taxes per capita: $356 (2007); City property taxes per capita: $0 (2007).
Education: Percent of population age 25 and over with: High school diploma (including GED) or higher: 89.3% (2010); Bachelor's degree or higher: 29.8% (2010); Master's degree or higher: 11.0% (2010).
School District(s)
Grant CCSD 110 (PK-08)
    2009-10 Enrollment: 751 . . . . (618) 398-5577
Pontiac-W Holliday SD 105 (PK-08)
    2009-10 Enrollment: 763 . . . . (618) 233-2320

Vocational/Technical School(s)
Regency Beauty Institute-Fairview Heights (Private, For-profit)
Fall 2009 Enrollment: 152 . . . . (800) 787-6456
2010-11 Tuition: $16,075
Housing: Homeownership rate: 76.4% (2010); Median home value: $119,008 (2010); Median contract rent: $684 per month (2005-2009 5-year est.); Median year structure built: 1973 (2005-2009 5-year est.).
Safety: Violent crime rate: 22.1 per 10,000 population; Property crime rate: 570.8 per 10,000 population (2010).
Transportation: Commute to work: 93.0% car, 3.8% public transportation, 1.0% walk, 0.9% work from home (2005-2009 5-year est.); Travel time to work: 26.6% less than 15 minutes, 44.2% 15 to 30 minutes, 17.4% 30 to 45 minutes, 6.9% 45 to 60 minutes, 4.8% 60 minutes or more (2005-2009 5-year est.)
Additional Information Contacts
City of Fairview Heights . . . . (618) 489-2000
http://www.fairviewheightscity.com
Fairview Heights Chamber of Commerce . . . . (618) 397-3127
http://www.fairviewheightschamber.org

FAYETTEVILLE (village). Covers a land area of 0.255 square miles and a water area of 0 square miles. Located at 38.37° N. Lat; 89.79° W. Long. Elevation is 413 feet.
Population: 402 (1990); 384 (2000); 434 (2010); 452 (2015 projected); Race: 97.9% White, 0.0% Black, 0.2% Asian, 1.8% Other, 1.4% Hispanic of any race (2010); Density: 1,699.5 persons per square mile (2010); Average household size: 2.73 (2010); Median age: 38.6 (2010); Males per 100 females: 107.7 (2010); Marriage status: 33.1% never married, 56.2% now married, 4.5% widowed, 6.2% divorced (2005-2009 5-year est.); Foreign born: 0.0% (2005-2009 5-year est.); Ancestry (includes multiple ancestries): 59.0% German, 19.3% Irish, 10.5% Dutch, 6.4% French, 4.3% Polish (2005-2009 5-year est.).
Economy: Single-family building permits issued: 0 (2010); Multi-family building permits issued: 0 (2010); Employment by occupation: 8.2% management, 7.2% professional, 21.5% services, 24.1% sales, 0.0% farming, 5.6% construction, 33.3% production (2005-2009 5-year est.).
Income: Per capita income: $31,210 (2010); Median household income: $73,558 (2010); Average household income: $83,522 (2010); Percent of households with income of $100,000 or more: 28.9% (2010); Poverty rate: 27.9% (2005-2009 5-year est.).
Taxes: Total city taxes per capita: $155 (2007); City property taxes per capita: $74 (2007).
Education: Percent of population age 25 and over with: High school diploma (including GED) or higher: 90.0% (2010); Bachelor's degree or higher: 19.0% (2010); Master's degree or higher: 3.8% (2010).
Housing: Homeownership rate: 84.9% (2010); Median home value: $120,192 (2010); Median contract rent: $375 per month (2005-2009 5-year est.); Median year structure built: 1976 (2005-2009 5-year est.).
Transportation: Commute to work: 94.8% car, 0.0% public transportation, 0.0% walk, 4.2% work from home (2005-2009 5-year est.); Travel time to work: 21.2% less than 15 minutes, 25.0% 15 to 30 minutes, 25.0% 30 to 45 minutes, 12.0% 45 to 60 minutes, 16.8% 60 minutes or more (2005-2009 5-year est.)

FREEBURG (village). Covers a land area of 3.187 square miles and a water area of 0.051 square miles. Located at 38.42° N. Lat; 89.91° W. Long. Elevation is 509 feet.
History: Incorporated 1859.
Population: 3,490 (1990); 3,872 (2000); 3,963 (2010); 3,994 (2015 projected); Race: 98.5% White, 0.1% Black, 0.2% Asian, 1.2% Other, 1.3% Hispanic of any race (2010); Density: 1,243.6 persons per square mile (2010); Average household size: 2.58 (2010); Median age: 38.9 (2010); Males per 100 females: 92.1 (2010); Marriage status: 21.8% never married, 58.4% now married, 9.8% widowed, 10.0% divorced (2005-2009 5-year est.); Foreign born: 0.4% (2005-2009 5-year est.); Ancestry (includes multiple ancestries): 56.0% German, 13.6% Irish, 7.2% French, 6.7% English, 5.9% American (2005-2009 5-year est.).
Economy: Single-family building permits issued: 3 (2010); Multi-family building permits issued: 25 (2010); Employment by occupation: 14.6% management, 26.0% professional, 10.4% services, 28.4% sales, 0.0% farming, 9.6% construction, 10.9% production (2005-2009 5-year est.).
Income: Per capita income: $27,849 (2010); Median household income: $62,680 (2010); Average household income: $72,997 (2010); Percent of households with income of $100,000 or more: 20.2% (2010); Poverty rate: 10.9% (2005-2009 5-year est.).

Taxes: Total city taxes per capita: $163 (2007); City property taxes per capita: $71 (2007).
Education: Percent of population age 25 and over with: High school diploma (including GED) or higher: 91.8% (2010); Bachelor's degree or higher: 21.8% (2010); Master's degree or higher: 8.0% (2010).
School District(s)
Freeburg CCSD 70 (PK-08)
2009-10 Enrollment: 773 . . . . (618) 539-3188
Freeburg CHSD 77 (09-12)
2009-10 Enrollment: 672 . . . . (618) 539-5533
Housing: Homeownership rate: 82.1% (2010); Median home value: $139,614 (2010); Median contract rent: $561 per month (2005-2009 5-year est.); Median year structure built: 1987 (2005-2009 5-year est.).
Newspapers: Freeburg Tribune (Local news; Circulation 2,800)
Transportation: Commute to work: 92.7% car, 1.9% public transportation, 0.6% walk, 4.7% work from home (2005-2009 5-year est.); Travel time to work: 21.6% less than 15 minutes, 36.5% 15 to 30 minutes, 23.8% 30 to 45 minutes, 12.3% 45 to 60 minutes, 5.7% 60 minutes or more (2005-2009 5-year est.)

LEBANON (city). Covers a land area of 2.146 square miles and a water area of 0.002 square miles. Located at 38.60° N. Lat; 89.81° W. Long. Elevation is 512 feet.
History: Lebanon was platted in the early 1800's. It grew as the site of McKendree College, organized in 1818 by the Methodist Church. Both Abraham Lincoln and Charles Dickens were guests at the Mermaid Inn, built in 1830 in Lebanon.
Population: 3,839 (1990); 3,523 (2000); 4,420 (2010); 4,756 (2015 projected); Race: 81.9% White, 14.5% Black, 0.4% Asian, 3.2% Other, 1.4% Hispanic of any race (2010); Density: 2,059.3 persons per square mile (2010); Average household size: 2.40 (2010); Median age: 33.8 (2010); Males per 100 females: 86.3 (2010); Marriage status: 34.7% never married, 43.4% now married, 12.2% widowed, 9.7% divorced (2005-2009 5-year est.); Foreign born: 2.0% (2005-2009 5-year est.); Ancestry (includes multiple ancestries): 40.4% German, 11.0% Irish, 8.2% English, 4.1% Italian, 3.8% French (2005-2009 5-year est.).
Economy: Single-family building permits issued: 9 (2010); Multi-family building permits issued: 17 (2010); Employment by occupation: 12.7% management, 21.9% professional, 18.5% services, 31.2% sales, 0.0% farming, 9.1% construction, 6.6% production (2005-2009 5-year est.).
Income: Per capita income: $23,658 (2010); Median household income: $51,304 (2010); Average household income: $60,018 (2010); Percent of households with income of $100,000 or more: 14.4% (2010); Poverty rate: 12.5% (2005-2009 5-year est.).
Taxes: Total city taxes per capita: $121 (2007); City property taxes per capita: $67 (2007).
Education: Percent of population age 25 and over with: High school diploma (including GED) or higher: 90.0% (2010); Bachelor's degree or higher: 31.3% (2010); Master's degree or higher: 13.8% (2010).
School District(s)
Lebanon CUSD 9 (PK-12)
2009-10 Enrollment: 672 . . . . (618) 537-4611
Four-year College(s)
McKendree University (Private, Not-for-profit, United Methodist)
Fall 2009 Enrollment: 3,284 . . . . (618) 537-4481
2010-11 Tuition: In-state $23,130; Out-of-state $23,130
Housing: Homeownership rate: 64.8% (2010); Median home value: $123,671 (2010); Median contract rent: $363 per month (2005-2009 5-year est.); Median year structure built: 1964 (2005-2009 5-year est.).
Newspapers: Lebanon Advertiser (International news; Circulation 1,542)
Transportation: Commute to work: 85.7% car, 1.0% public transportation, 5.1% walk, 6.0% work from home (2005-2009 5-year est.); Travel time to work: 34.4% less than 15 minutes, 31.6% 15 to 30 minutes, 22.5% 30 to 45 minutes, 3.8% 45 to 60 minutes, 7.7% 60 minutes or more (2005-2009 5-year est.)
Additional Information Contacts
Lebanon Chamber of Commerce. (618) 537-8420
http://lebanonil.org/chamber.html

LENZBURG (village). Covers a land area of 1.235 square miles and a water area of 0.059 square miles. Located at 38.28° N. Lat; 89.81° W. Long. Elevation is 443 feet.
Population: 510 (1990); 577 (2000); 552 (2010); 539 (2015 projected); Race: 99.5% White, 0.0% Black, 0.0% Asian, 0.5% Other, 0.7% Hispanic of any race (2010); Density: 446.9 persons per square mile (2010);

Average household size: 2.56 (2010); Median age: 35.6 (2010); Males per 100 females: 100.7 (2010); Marriage status: 20.0% never married, 64.3% now married, 4.9% widowed, 10.8% divorced (2005-2009 5-year est.); Foreign born: 0.7% (2005-2009 5-year est.); Ancestry (includes multiple ancestries): 44.1% German, 16.0% Irish, 12.5% English, 9.7% American, 8.9% French (2005-2009 5-year est.).
Economy: Employment by occupation: 7.2% management, 12.9% professional, 25.4% services, 18.7% sales, 0.0% farming, 11.5% construction, 24.4% production (2005-2009 5-year est.).
Income: Per capita income: $22,819 (2010); Median household income: $53,819 (2010); Average household income: $58,113 (2010); Percent of households with income of $100,000 or more: 10.2% (2010); Poverty rate: 17.1% (2005-2009 5-year est.).
Taxes: Total city taxes per capita: $83 (2007); City property taxes per capita: $20 (2007).
Education: Percent of population age 25 and over with: High school diploma (including GED) or higher: 84.0% (2010); Bachelor's degree or higher: 5.1% (2010); Master's degree or higher: 1.1% (2010).
Housing: Homeownership rate: 81.5% (2010); Median home value: $79,091 (2010); Median contract rent: $403 per month (2005-2009 5-year est.); Median year structure built: 1965 (2005-2009 5-year est.).
Transportation: Commute to work: 94.2% car, 0.0% public transportation, 2.9% walk, 1.5% work from home (2005-2009 5-year est.); Travel time to work: 13.8% less than 15 minutes, 31.5% 15 to 30 minutes, 27.6% 30 to 45 minutes, 16.3% 45 to 60 minutes, 10.8% 60 minutes or more (2005-2009 5-year est.)

MARISSA (village). Covers a land area of 3.717 square miles and a water area of 0.195 square miles. Located at 38.24° N. Lat; 89.75° W. Long. Elevation is 453 feet.
History: Incorporated 1882.
Population: 2,441 (1990); 2,141 (2000); 1,984 (2010); 1,916 (2015 projected); Race: 98.4% White, 0.3% Black, 0.3% Asian, 1.0% Other, 1.0% Hispanic of any race (2010); Density: 533.8 persons per square mile (2010); Average household size: 2.37 (2010); Median age: 36.9 (2010); Males per 100 females: 92.2 (2010); Marriage status: 18.4% never married, 59.3% now married, 10.3% widowed, 12.1% divorced (2005-2009 5-year est.); Foreign born: 0.7% (2005-2009 5-year est.); Ancestry (includes multiple ancestries): 31.4% German, 22.8% Irish, 12.7% American, 11.8% English, 4.1% Dutch (2005-2009 5-year est.).
Economy: Single-family building permits issued: 0 (2010); Multi-family building permits issued: 0 (2010); Employment by occupation: 6.3% management, 13.4% professional, 17.4% services, 29.1% sales, 0.0% farming, 12.5% construction, 21.2% production (2005-2009 5-year est.).
Income: Per capita income: $21,896 (2010); Median household income: $44,594 (2010); Average household income: $51,962 (2010); Percent of households with income of $100,000 or more: 10.3% (2010); Poverty rate: 16.4% (2005-2009 5-year est.).
Taxes: Total city taxes per capita: $98 (2007); City property taxes per capita: $30 (2007).
Education: Percent of population age 25 and over with: High school diploma (including GED) or higher: 84.8% (2010); Bachelor's degree or higher: 12.9% (2010); Master's degree or higher: 2.7% (2010).
School District(s)
Marissa CUSD 40 (PK-12)
    2009-10 Enrollment: 592 . . . . (618) 295-2313
Housing: Homeownership rate: 77.4% (2010); Median home value: $69,180 (2010); Median contract rent: $329 per month (2005-2009 5-year est.); Median year structure built: 1951 (2005-2009 5-year est.).
Safety: Violent crime rate: 30.5 per 10,000 population; Property crime rate: 259.5 per 10,000 population (2010).
Newspapers: This Week in Marissa (Community news; Circulation 780)
Transportation: Commute to work: 92.0% car, 1.1% public transportation, 2.9% walk, 3.1% work from home (2005-2009 5-year est.); Travel time to work: 33.0% less than 15 minutes, 25.8% 15 to 30 minutes, 13.1% 30 to 45 minutes, 13.6% 45 to 60 minutes, 14.5% 60 minutes or more (2005-2009 5-year est.)

MASCOUTAH (city). Covers a land area of 8.638 square miles and a water area of 0.061 square miles. Located at 38.49° N. Lat; 89.80° W. Long. Elevation is 430 feet.
History: Incorporated 1839.
Population: 5,770 (1990); 5,659 (2000); 6,650 (2010); 7,010 (2015 projected); Race: 92.3% White, 2.8% Black, 1.1% Asian, 3.8% Other, 2.0% Hispanic of any race (2010); Density: 769.9 persons per square mile

(2010); Average household size: 2.49 (2010); Median age: 38.5 (2010); Males per 100 females: 91.6 (2010); Marriage status: 25.9% never married, 53.9% now married, 7.9% widowed, 12.3% divorced (2005-2009 5-year est.); Foreign born: 1.8% (2005-2009 5-year est.); Ancestry (includes multiple ancestries): 37.5% German, 15.0% Irish, 9.5% English, 6.0% Polish, 5.4% Scottish (2005-2009 5-year est.).
Economy: Single-family building permits issued: 82 (2010); Multi-family building permits issued: 0 (2010); Employment by occupation: 15.4% management, 22.6% professional, 16.2% services, 26.0% sales, 0.0% farming, 4.6% construction, 15.1% production (2005-2009 5-year est.).
Income: Per capita income: $26,830 (2010); Median household income: $58,985 (2010); Average household income: $67,352 (2010); Percent of households with income of $100,000 or more: 16.0% (2010); Poverty rate: 12.2% (2005-2009 5-year est.).
Taxes: Total city taxes per capita: $314 (2007); City property taxes per capita: $209 (2007).
Education: Percent of population age 25 and over with: High school diploma (including GED) or higher: 90.0% (2010); Bachelor's degree or higher: 22.1% (2010); Master's degree or higher: 8.8% (2010).
School District(s)
Mascoutah CUD 19 (PK-12)
    2009-10 Enrollment: 3,447 . . . . (618) 566-7414
Housing: Homeownership rate: 72.3% (2010); Median home value: $121,218 (2010); Median contract rent: $448 per month (2005-2009 5-year est.); Median year structure built: 1970 (2005-2009 5-year est.).
Safety: Violent crime rate: 5.9 per 10,000 population; Property crime rate: 138.9 per 10,000 population (2010).
Newspapers: Clinton County News (Community news; Circulation 1,800); Fairview Heights Tribune (Community news; Circulation 1,200); Herald Publications (Local news; Circulation 2,400); Herald Scott Flier (Community news; Circulation 5,000)
Transportation: Commute to work: 88.7% car, 2.9% public transportation, 3.7% walk, 1.9% work from home (2005-2009 5-year est.); Travel time to work: 33.7% less than 15 minutes, 34.1% 15 to 30 minutes, 18.5% 30 to 45 minutes, 7.9% 45 to 60 minutes, 5.8% 60 minutes or more (2005-2009 5-year est.)
Additional Information Contacts
City of Mascoutah . . . . (618) 566-2964
    http://www.mascoutah.com

MILLSTADT (village). Covers a land area of 1.112 square miles and a water area of 0 square miles. Located at 38.45° N. Lat; 90.09° W. Long. Elevation is 617 feet.
History: Incorporated 1878.
Population: 2,774 (1990); 2,794 (2000); 2,876 (2010); 2,918 (2015 projected); Race: 98.3% White, 0.0% Black, 0.2% Asian, 1.4% Other, 0.6% Hispanic of any race (2010); Density: 2,585.6 persons per square mile (2010); Average household size: 2.49 (2010); Median age: 38.8 (2010); Males per 100 females: 95.2 (2010); Marriage status: 11.0% never married, 70.7% now married, 10.0% widowed, 8.3% divorced (2005-2009 5-year est.); Foreign born: 0.8% (2005-2009 5-year est.); Ancestry (includes multiple ancestries): 58.0% German, 10.4% Irish, 8.0% English, 6.7% French, 5.2% Italian (2005-2009 5-year est.).
Economy: Single-family building permits issued: 11 (2010); Multi-family building permits issued: 0 (2010); Employment by occupation: 12.4% management, 22.3% professional, 15.0% services, 26.2% sales, 0.5% farming, 8.1% construction, 15.4% production (2005-2009 5-year est.).
Income: Per capita income: $29,405 (2010); Median household income: $63,274 (2010); Average household income: $73,050 (2010); Percent of households with income of $100,000 or more: 23.2% (2010); Poverty rate: 2.0% (2005-2009 5-year est.).
Taxes: Total city taxes per capita: $213 (2007); City property taxes per capita: $190 (2007).
Education: Percent of population age 25 and over with: High school diploma (including GED) or higher: 89.6% (2010); Bachelor's degree or higher: 22.4% (2010); Master's degree or higher: 6.5% (2010).
School District(s)
Millstadt CCSD 160 (PK-08)
    2009-10 Enrollment: 901 . . . . (618) 476-1803
Housing: Homeownership rate: 80.1% (2010); Median home value: $151,152 (2010); Median contract rent: $511 per month (2005-2009 5-year est.); Median year structure built: 1981 (2005-2009 5-year est.).
Safety: Violent crime rate: 23.4 per 10,000 population; Property crime rate: 114.3 per 10,000 population (2010).

Transportation: Commute to work: 95.0% car, 0.0% public transportation, 0.0% walk, 5.0% work from home (2005-2009 5-year est.); Travel time to work: 21.3% less than 15 minutes, 44.4% 15 to 30 minutes, 22.4% 30 to 45 minutes, 7.3% 45 to 60 minutes, 4.6% 60 minutes or more (2005-2009 5-year est.)

NEW ATHENS (village).
Covers a land area of 1.725 square miles and a water area of 0.111 square miles. Located at 38.32° N. Lat; 89.87° W. Long. Elevation is 397 feet.

History: Incorporated 1869.

Population: 2,010 (1990); 1,981 (2000); 1,938 (2010); 1,920 (2015 projected); Race: 97.7% White, 0.8% Black, 0.4% Asian, 1.1% Other, 1.0% Hispanic of any race (2010); Density: 1,123.4 persons per square mile (2010); Average household size: 2.41 (2010); Median age: 39.0 (2010); Males per 100 females: 88.7 (2010); Marriage status: 23.5% never married, 59.7% now married, 8.2% widowed, 8.6% divorced (2005-2009 5-year est.); Foreign born: 1.4% (2005-2009 5-year est.); Ancestry (includes multiple ancestries): 52.7% German, 15.0% Irish, 7.4% English, 4.8% French, 4.6% Italian (2005-2009 5-year est.).

Economy: Single-family building permits issued: 0 (2010); Multi-family building permits issued: 0 (2010); Employment by occupation: 9.5% management, 12.5% professional, 21.7% services, 21.0% sales, 0.0% farming, 16.0% construction, 19.3% production (2005-2009 5-year est.).

Income: Per capita income: $24,175 (2010); Median household income: $50,588 (2010); Average household income: $59,804 (2010); Percent of households with income of $100,000 or more: 12.6% (2010); Poverty rate: 9.8% (2005-2009 5-year est.).

Taxes: Total city taxes per capita: $145 (2007); City property taxes per capita: $78 (2007).

Education: Percent of population age 25 and over with: High school diploma (including GED) or higher: 85.8% (2010); Bachelor's degree or higher: 13.7% (2010); Master's degree or higher: 3.5% (2010).

School District(s)
New Athens CUSD 60 (PK-12)
    2009-10 Enrollment: 618 . . . . (618) 475-2174

Housing: Homeownership rate: 80.8% (2010); Median home value: $105,422 (2010); Median contract rent: $377 per month (2005-2009 5-year est.); Median year structure built: 1954 (2005-2009 5-year est.).

Safety: Violent crime rate: 0.0 per 10,000 population; Property crime rate: 91.0 per 10,000 population (2010).

Newspapers: Journal-Messenger (Community news; Circulation 2,800)

Transportation: Commute to work: 92.4% car, 0.5% public transportation, 3.7% walk, 1.6% work from home (2005-2009 5-year est.); Travel time to work: 22.8% less than 15 minutes, 21.3% 15 to 30 minutes, 27.8% 30 to 45 minutes, 14.3% 45 to 60 minutes, 13.8% 60 minutes or more (2005-2009 5-year est.)

O'FALLON (city).
Covers a land area of 10.913 square miles and a water area of 0.012 square miles. Located at 38.59° N. Lat; 89.91° W. Long. Elevation is 548 feet.

History: O'Fallon developed in 1854 along the railroad route. Named for the owner of the land on which the town was sited, it grew as a residential community.

Population: 17,169 (1990); 21,910 (2000); 26,194 (2010); 28,028 (2015 projected); Race: 79.5% White, 13.7% Black, 3.1% Asian, 3.7% Other, 2.7% Hispanic of any race (2010); Density: 2,400.2 persons per square mile (2010); Average household size: 2.58 (2010); Median age: 36.7 (2010); Males per 100 females: 93.2 (2010); Marriage status: 28.9% never married, 59.1% now married, 4.1% widowed, 7.9% divorced (2005-2009 5-year est.); Foreign born: 4.0% (2005-2009 5-year est.); Ancestry (includes multiple ancestries): 31.8% German, 13.6% Irish, 13.4% English, 6.6% American, 5.8% Italian (2005-2009 5-year est.).

Economy: Unemployment rate: 8.2% (August 2011); Total civilian labor force: 14,201 (August 2011); Single-family building permits issued: 140 (2010); Multi-family building permits issued: 232 (2010); Employment by occupation: 18.8% management, 25.8% professional, 15.0% services, 28.9% sales, 0.4% farming, 5.6% construction, 5.5% production (2005-2009 5-year est.).

Income: Per capita income: $31,852 (2010); Median household income: $68,373 (2010); Average household income: $82,505 (2010); Percent of households with income of $100,000 or more: 27.9% (2010); Poverty rate: 6.8% (2005-2009 5-year est.).

Taxes: Total city taxes per capita: $308 (2007); City property taxes per capita: $179 (2007).

Education: Percent of population age 25 and over with: High school diploma (including GED) or higher: 95.1% (2010); Bachelor's degree or higher: 42.8% (2010); Master's degree or higher: 18.4% (2010).

School District(s)
Central SD 104 (PK-08)
    2009-10 Enrollment: 511 . . . . (618) 632-6336
O Fallon CCSD 90 (PK-08)
    2009-10 Enrollment: 3,522 . . . . (618) 632-3666
O Fallon Twp HSD 203 (09-12)
    2009-10 Enrollment: 2,524 . . . . (618) 632-3507

Housing: Homeownership rate: 69.3% (2010); Median home value: $150,533 (2010); Median contract rent: $676 per month (2005-2009 5-year est.); Median year structure built: 1987 (2005-2009 5-year est.).

Safety: Violent crime rate: 11.7 per 10,000 population; Property crime rate: 250.5 per 10,000 population (2010).

Newspapers: O'Fallon Progress (Community news; Circulation 6,000)

Transportation: Commute to work: 94.0% car, 1.2% public transportation, 1.0% walk, 3.4% work from home (2005-2009 5-year est.); Travel time to work: 29.2% less than 15 minutes, 43.1% 15 to 30 minutes, 16.6% 30 to 45 minutes, 7.3% 45 to 60 minutes, 3.8% 60 minutes or more (2005-2009 5-year est.)

Additional Information Contacts
City of O'Fallon . . . . (618) 624-4500
    http://www.ofallon.org
O'Fallon-Shiloh Chamber of Commerce . . . . (618) 632-3377
    http://www.ofallonchamber.com

SAINT LIBORY (village).
Covers a land area of 0.943 square miles and a water area of 0 square miles. Located at 38.36° N. Lat; 89.71° W. Long. Elevation is 407 feet.

Population: 590 (1990); 583 (2000); 555 (2010); 543 (2015 projected); Race: 96.8% White, 1.3% Black, 0.0% Asian, 2.0% Other, 0.5% Hispanic of any race (2010); Density: 588.4 persons per square mile (2010); Average household size: 2.71 (2010); Median age: 34.4 (2010); Males per 100 females: 92.0 (2010); Marriage status: 24.5% never married, 48.7% now married, 12.8% widowed, 13.9% divorced (2005-2009 5-year est.); Foreign born: 0.0% (2005-2009 5-year est.); Ancestry (includes multiple ancestries): 69.4% German, 8.0% Polish, 4.5% Irish, 3.5% English, 2.8% Scottish (2005-2009 5-year est.).

Economy: Single-family building permits issued: 2 (2010); Multi-family building permits issued: 0 (2010); Employment by occupation: 14.5% management, 21.5% professional, 17.5% services, 22.5% sales, 0.0% farming, 6.0% construction, 18.0% production (2005-2009 5-year est.).

Income: Per capita income: $24,632 (2010); Median household income: $55,515 (2010); Average household income: $68,183 (2010); Percent of households with income of $100,000 or more: 18.5% (2010); Poverty rate: 6.6% (2005-2009 5-year est.).

Taxes: Total city taxes per capita: $26 (2007); City property taxes per capita: $18 (2007).

Education: Percent of population age 25 and over with: High school diploma (including GED) or higher: 86.4% (2010); Bachelor's degree or higher: 8.5% (2010); Master's degree or higher: 2.8% (2010).

School District(s)
St Libory Cons SD 30 (PK-08)
    2009-10 Enrollment: 110 . . . . (618) 768-4923

Housing: Homeownership rate: 82.0% (2010); Median home value: $123,810 (2010); Median contract rent: $178 per month (2005-2009 5-year est.); Median year structure built: 1959 (2005-2009 5-year est.).

Transportation: Commute to work: 95.5% car, 0.0% public transportation, 3.0% walk, 0.0% work from home (2005-2009 5-year est.); Travel time to work: 20.5% less than 15 minutes, 24.5% 15 to 30 minutes, 35.0% 30 to 45 minutes, 13.0% 45 to 60 minutes, 7.0% 60 minutes or more (2005-2009 5-year est.)

SAUGET (village).
Aka Monsanto. Covers a land area of 4.130 square miles and a water area of 0.319 square miles. Located at 38.58° N. Lat; 90.16° W. Long. Elevation is 410 feet.

History: Formerly called Monsanto.

Population: 273 (1990); 249 (2000); 256 (2010); 259 (2015 projected); Race: 69.5% White, 29.3% Black, 0.4% Asian, 0.8% Other, 0.8% Hispanic of any race (2010); Density: 62.0 persons per square mile (2010); Average household size: 2.44 (2010); Median age: 36.4 (2010); Males per 100 females: 86.9 (2010); Marriage status: 24.5% never married, 48.5% now married, 12.0% widowed, 15.0% divorced (2005-2009 5-year est.); Foreign born: 0.0% (2005-2009 5-year est.); Ancestry (includes multiple

ancestries): 16.9% German, 14.1% European, 12.4% Irish, 12.0% French, 11.2% English (2005-2009 5-year est.).

Economy: Employment by occupation: 1.6% management, 7.8% professional, 30.2% services, 31.0% sales, 0.0% farming, 14.0% construction, 15.5% production (2005-2009 5-year est.).

Income: Per capita income: $20,826 (2010); Median household income: $40,114 (2010); Average household income: $50,524 (2010); Percent of households with income of $100,000 or more: 9.5% (2010); Poverty rate: 8.4% (2005-2009 5-year est.).

Taxes: Total city taxes per capita: $30,066 (2007); City property taxes per capita: $28,678 (2007).

Education: Percent of population age 25 and over with: High school diploma (including GED) or higher: 83.3% (2010); Bachelor's degree or higher: 12.5% (2010); Master's degree or higher: 4.2% (2010).

Housing: Homeownership rate: 59.0% (2010); Median home value: $56,364 (2010); Median contract rent: $438 per month (2005-2009 5-year est.); Median year structure built: 1962 (2005-2009 5-year est.).

Safety: Violent crime rate: 720.3 per 10,000 population; Property crime rate: 2,457.6 per 10,000 population (2010).

Transportation: Commute to work: 86.7% car, 1.6% public transportation, 9.4% walk, 2.3% work from home (2005-2009 5-year est.); Travel time to work: 42.4% less than 15 minutes, 20.8% 15 to 30 minutes, 24.8% 30 to 45 minutes, 8.8% 45 to 60 minutes, 3.2% 60 minutes or more (2005-2009 5-year est.)

SCOTT AFB (CDP).

Covers a land area of 3.755 square miles and a water area of 0 square miles. Located at 38.54° N. Lat; 89.85° W. Long.

Population: 7,245 (1990); 2,707 (2000); 2,023 (2010); 1,849 (2015 projected); Race: 82.6% White, 10.5% Black, 2.2% Asian, 4.7% Other, 3.8% Hispanic of any race (2010); Density: 538.8 persons per square mile (2010); Average household size: 3.85 (2010); Median age: 24.1 (2010); Males per 100 females: 98.7 (2010); Marriage status: 42.4% never married, 56.0% now married, 0.7% widowed, 0.9% divorced (2005-2009 5-year est.); Foreign born: 3.3% (2005-2009 5-year est.); Ancestry (includes multiple ancestries): 12.0% Italian, 11.9% German, 10.1% Irish, 7.8% American, 7.8% Scottish (2005-2009 5-year est.).

Economy: Employment by occupation: 21.4% management, 19.1% professional, 28.4% services, 15.6% sales, 6.2% farming, 0.0% construction, 9.3% production (2005-2009 5-year est.).

Income: Per capita income: $20,723 (2010); Median household income: $70,192 (2010); Average household income: $80,857 (2010); Percent of households with income of $100,000 or more: 21.4% (2010); Poverty rate: 1.8% (2005-2009 5-year est.).

Education: Percent of population age 25 and over with: High school diploma (including GED) or higher: 99.0% (2010); Bachelor's degree or higher: 49.0% (2010); Master's degree or higher: 19.3% (2010).

School District(s)

Mascoutah CUD 19 (PK-12)
    2009-10 Enrollment: 3,447 . . . . (618) 566-7414

Housing: Homeownership rate: 11.6% (2010); Median home value: $42,609 (2010); Median contract rent: $1,085 per month (2005-2009 5-year est.); Median year structure built: 1960 (2005-2009 5-year est.).

Newspapers: Command Post (Local news; Circulation 14,300)

Transportation: Commute to work: 76.1% car, 3.2% public transportation, 14.7% walk, 3.4% work from home (2005-2009 5-year est.); Travel time to work: 66.4% less than 15 minutes, 20.9% 15 to 30 minutes, 7.8% 30 to 45 minutes, 1.6% 45 to 60 minutes, 3.3% 60 minutes or more (2005-2009 5-year est.)

SHILOH (village).

Covers a land area of 10.054 square miles and a water area of 0.033 square miles. Located at 38.55° N. Lat; 89.91° W. Long. Elevation is 663 feet.

Population: 4,935 (1990); 7,643 (2000); 8,794 (2010); 9,294 (2015 projected); Race: 77.0% White, 17.5% Black, 1.8% Asian, 3.7% Other, 2.8% Hispanic of any race (2010); Density: 874.7 persons per square mile (2010); Average household size: 2.56 (2010); Median age: 34.3 (2010); Males per 100 females: 99.0 (2010); Marriage status: 26.8% never married, 60.2% now married, 3.8% widowed, 9.3% divorced (2005-2009 5-year est.); Foreign born: 7.2% (2005-2009 5-year est.); Ancestry (includes multiple ancestries): 29.9% German, 14.1% Irish, 8.4% English, 5.8% French, 5.6% Italian (2005-2009 5-year est.).

Economy: Single-family building permits issued: 63 (2010); Multi-family building permits issued: 89 (2010); Employment by occupation: 15.3% management, 24.3% professional, 16.7% services, 29.6% sales, 0.0% farming, 6.3% construction, 7.7% production (2005-2009 5-year est.).

Income: Per capita income: $31,728 (2010); Median household income: $67,429 (2010); Average household income: $83,418 (2010); Percent of households with income of $100,000 or more: 28.7% (2010); Poverty rate: 6.2% (2005-2009 5-year est.).

Taxes: Total city taxes per capita: $198 (2007); City property taxes per capita: $108 (2007).

Education: Percent of population age 25 and over with: High school diploma (including GED) or higher: 95.1% (2010); Bachelor's degree or higher: 36.8% (2010); Master's degree or higher: 15.5% (2010).

School District(s)

Shiloh Village SD 85 (PK-08)
    2009-10 Enrollment: 543 . . . . (618) 632-7434

Housing: Homeownership rate: 67.4% (2010); Median home value: $154,056 (2010); Median contract rent: $608 per month (2005-2009 5-year est.); Median year structure built: 1994 (2005-2009 5-year est.).

Safety: Violent crime rate: 17.9 per 10,000 population; Property crime rate: 187.2 per 10,000 population (2010).

Transportation: Commute to work: 93.1% car, 3.1% public transportation, 1.0% walk, 2.5% work from home (2005-2009 5-year est.); Travel time to work: 33.9% less than 15 minutes, 37.5% 15 to 30 minutes, 16.3% 30 to 45 minutes, 7.9% 45 to 60 minutes, 4.3% 60 minutes or more (2005-2009 5-year est.)

Additional Information Contacts

O'Fallon-Shiloh Chamber of Commerce . . . . (618) 632-3377
    http://www.shilohchamber.org
Village of Shiloh . . . . (618) 632-1022
    http://www.shilohil.org

SMITHTON (village).

Covers a land area of 1.672 square miles and a water area of 0.006 square miles. Located at 38.40° N. Lat; 89.99° W. Long. Elevation is 476 feet.

Population: 1,796 (1990); 2,248 (2000); 2,888 (2010); 3,141 (2015 projected); Race: 97.3% White, 0.3% Black, 0.5% Asian, 1.8% Other, 0.2% Hispanic of any race (2010); Density: 1,727.2 persons per square mile (2010); Average household size: 2.63 (2010); Median age: 37.8 (2010); Males per 100 females: 92.4 (2010); Marriage status: 18.1% never married, 63.2% now married, 8.0% widowed, 10.7% divorced (2005-2009 5-year est.); Foreign born: 0.8% (2005-2009 5-year est.); Ancestry (includes multiple ancestries): 47.4% German, 15.3% Irish, 11.1% English, 6.9% American, 6.5% French (2005-2009 5-year est.).

Economy: Single-family building permits issued: 26 (2010); Multi-family building permits issued: 0 (2010); Employment by occupation: 19.6% management, 19.4% professional, 14.9% services, 24.2% sales, 0.3% farming, 8.6% construction, 12.9% production (2005-2009 5-year est.).

Income: Per capita income: $26,188 (2010); Median household income: $65,995 (2010); Average household income: $70,101 (2010); Percent of households with income of $100,000 or more: 18.4% (2010); Poverty rate: 6.3% (2005-2009 5-year est.).

Taxes: Total city taxes per capita: $194 (2007); City property taxes per capita: $94 (2007).

Education: Percent of population age 25 and over with: High school diploma (including GED) or higher: 89.0% (2010); Bachelor's degree or higher: 17.6% (2010); Master's degree or higher: 3.7% (2010).

School District(s)

Smithton CCSD 130 (PK-08)
    2009-10 Enrollment: 502 . . . . (618) 233-6863

Housing: Homeownership rate: 87.3% (2010); Median home value: $135,534 (2010); Median contract rent: $442 per month (2005-2009 5-year est.); Median year structure built: 1989 (2005-2009 5-year est.).

Safety: Violent crime rate: 0.0 per 10,000 population; Property crime rate: 70.4 per 10,000 population (2010).

Transportation: Commute to work: 94.9% car, 1.9% public transportation, 1.8% walk, 0.9% work from home (2005-2009 5-year est.); Travel time to work: 13.8% less than 15 minutes, 36.6% 15 to 30 minutes, 28.6% 30 to 45 minutes, 12.6% 45 to 60 minutes, 8.4% 60 minutes or more (2005-2009 5-year est.)

Additional Information Contacts

Smithton Chamber of Commerce . . . . (618) 473-3366
    http://smithtonchamber.ning.com

SUMMERFIELD (village).

Covers a land area of 0.420 square miles and a water area of 0 square miles. Located at 38.59° N. Lat; 89.75° W. Long. Elevation is 479 feet.

Population: 509 (1990); 472 (2000); 557 (2010); 590 (2015 projected); Race: 93.5% White, 3.9% Black, 0.0% Asian, 2.5% Other, 1.3% Hispanic

of any race (2010); Density: 1,324.7 persons per square mile (2010); Average household size: 2.80 (2010); Median age: 37.0 (2010); Males per 100 females: 104.0 (2010); Marriage status: 26.3% never married, 59.7% now married, 3.9% widowed, 10.1% divorced (2005-2009 5-year est.); Foreign born: 1.7% (2005-2009 5-year est.); Ancestry (includes multiple ancestries): 33.9% German, 23.2% Irish, 17.9% American, 9.5% Scotch-Irish, 9.0% English (2005-2009 5-year est.).
Economy: Single-family building permits issued: 0 (2010); Multi-family building permits issued: 0 (2010); Employment by occupation: 5.3% management, 10.1% professional, 28.0% services, 23.8% sales, 1.1% farming, 10.6% construction, 21.2% production (2005-2009 5-year est.).
Income: Per capita income: $23,457 (2010); Median household income: $54,167 (2010); Average household income: $64,774 (2010); Percent of households with income of $100,000 or more: 10.1% (2010); Poverty rate: 9.8% (2005-2009 5-year est.).
Taxes: Total city taxes per capita: $103 (2007); City property taxes per capita: $43 (2007).
Education: Percent of population age 25 and over with: High school diploma (including GED) or higher: 82.2% (2010); Bachelor's degree or higher: 13.9% (2010); Master's degree or higher: 4.6% (2010).

School District(s)
Lebanon CUSD 9 (PK-12)
    2009-10 Enrollment: 672 . . . . (618) 537-4611
Housing: Homeownership rate: 81.9% (2010); Median home value: $106,439 (2010); Median contract rent: $450 per month (2005-2009 5-year est.); Median year structure built: 1970 (2005-2009 5-year est.).
Transportation: Commute to work: 92.3% car, 4.9% public transportation, 0.0% walk, 1.1% work from home (2005-2009 5-year est.); Travel time to work: 28.2% less than 15 minutes, 23.8% 15 to 30 minutes, 27.1% 30 to 45 minutes, 15.5% 45 to 60 minutes, 5.5% 60 minutes or more (2005-2009 5-year est.)

SWANSEA (village). Covers a land area of 5.073 square miles and a water area of 0.020 square miles. Located at 38.54° N. Lat; 89.98° W. Long. Elevation is 545 feet.
History: Incorporated 1895.
Population: 9,325 (1990); 10,579 (2000); 10,992 (2010); 11,144 (2015 projected); Race: 84.8% White, 11.0% Black, 1.8% Asian, 2.4% Other, 1.7% Hispanic of any race (2010); Density: 2,167.0 persons per square mile (2010); Average household size: 2.54 (2010); Median age: 38.0 (2010); Males per 100 females: 90.6 (2010); Marriage status: 25.4% never married, 57.3% now married, 8.6% widowed, 8.7% divorced (2005-2009 5-year est.); Foreign born: 3.4% (2005-2009 5-year est.); Ancestry (includes multiple ancestries): 41.7% German, 14.4% Irish, 11.4% English, 5.0% French, 4.5% Italian (2005-2009 5-year est.).
Economy: Single-family building permits issued: 118 (2010); Multi-family building permits issued: 0 (2010); Employment by occupation: 16.8% management, 25.2% professional, 14.9% services, 28.5% sales, 0.0% farming, 7.0% construction, 7.6% production (2005-2009 5-year est.).
Income: Per capita income: $29,629 (2010); Median household income: $58,706 (2010); Average household income: $76,638 (2010); Percent of households with income of $100,000 or more: 22.8% (2010); Poverty rate: 4.7% (2005-2009 5-year est.).
Taxes: Total city taxes per capita: $170 (2007); City property taxes per capita: $78 (2007).
Education: Percent of population age 25 and over with: High school diploma (including GED) or higher: 90.6% (2010); Bachelor's degree or higher: 31.3% (2010); Master's degree or higher: 11.8% (2010).

School District(s)
High Mount SD 116 (PK-08)
    2009-10 Enrollment: 440 . . . . (618) 233-1054
Wolf Branch SD 113 (KG-08)
    2009-10 Enrollment: 871 . . . . (618) 277-2100
Housing: Homeownership rate: 78.2% (2010); Median home value: $141,552 (2010); Median contract rent: $581 per month (2005-2009 5-year est.); Median year structure built: 1984 (2005-2009 5-year est.).
Safety: Violent crime rate: 9.9 per 10,000 population; Property crime rate: 183.4 per 10,000 population (2010).
Newspapers: Belleville Journal (Local news; Circulation 34,009); East St. Louis News Journal (Community news; Circulation 20,990)
Transportation: Commute to work: 90.6% car, 4.9% public transportation, 0.6% walk, 2.9% work from home (2005-2009 5-year est.); Travel time to work: 32.3% less than 15 minutes, 31.9% 15 to 30 minutes, 20.8% 30 to 45 minutes, 10.6% 45 to 60 minutes, 4.5% 60 minutes or more (2005-2009 5-year est.)

Additional Information Contacts
Swansea Chamber of Commerce . . . . (618) 233-3938
    http://www.swanseachamber.org
Village of Swansea . . . . (618) 234-0044
    http://www.swanseail.org

WASHINGTON PARK (village). Covers a land area of 2.451 square miles and a water area of 0 square miles. Located at 38.63° N. Lat; 90.09° W. Long. Elevation is 410 feet.
History: Incorporated 1917.
Population: 7,431 (1990); 5,345 (2000); 4,899 (2010); 4,687 (2015 projected); Race: 5.4% White, 92.3% Black, 0.1% Asian, 2.2% Other, 2.3% Hispanic of any race (2010); Density: 1,998.4 persons per square mile (2010); Average household size: 3.05 (2010); Median age: 28.0 (2010); Males per 100 females: 84.0 (2010); Marriage status: 62.5% never married, 24.1% now married, 5.0% widowed, 8.3% divorced (2005-2009 5-year est.); Foreign born: 2.0% (2005-2009 5-year est.); Ancestry (includes multiple ancestries): 3.1% German, 2.3% Italian, 1.9% Jamaican, 1.3% Polish, 1.2% Irish (2005-2009 5-year est.).
Economy: Single-family building permits issued: 0 (2010); Multi-family building permits issued: 0 (2010); Employment by occupation: 2.8% management, 10.1% professional, 29.0% services, 25.4% sales, 3.1% farming, 8.3% construction, 21.3% production (2005-2009 5-year est.).
Income: Per capita income: $10,940 (2010); Median household income: $25,357 (2010); Average household income: $32,746 (2010); Percent of households with income of $100,000 or more: 3.2% (2010); Poverty rate: 45.4% (2005-2009 5-year est.).
Taxes: Total city taxes per capita: $968 (2007); City property taxes per capita: $229 (2007).
Education: Percent of population age 25 and over with: High school diploma (including GED) or higher: 72.6% (2010); Bachelor's degree or higher: 5.2% (2010); Master's degree or higher: 1.4% (2010).

School District(s)
East St Louis SD 189 (PK-12)
    2009-10 Enrollment: 8,141 . . . . (618) 646-3009
Housing: Homeownership rate: 56.7% (2010); Median home value: $46,213 (2010); Median contract rent: $479 per month (2005-2009 5-year est.); Median year structure built: 1955 (2005-2009 5-year est.).
Transportation: Commute to work: 80.8% car, 15.9% public transportation, 0.0% walk, 0.9% work from home (2005-2009 5-year est.); Travel time to work: 13.0% less than 15 minutes, 47.1% 15 to 30 minutes, 19.9% 30 to 45 minutes, 9.8% 45 to 60 minutes, 10.1% 60 minutes or more (2005-2009 5-year est.)

Stark County

Located in north central Illinois; drained by the Spoon River and Indian Creek. Covers a land area of 287.94 square miles, a water area of 0.28 square miles, and is located in the Central Time Zone at 41.09° N. Lat., 89.80° W. Long. The county was founded in 1839. County seat is Toulon.

Stark County is part of the Peoria, IL Metropolitan Statistical Area. The entire metro area includes: Marshall County, IL; Peoria County, IL; Stark County, IL; Tazewell County, IL; Woodford County, IL

Population: 6,534 (1990); 6,332 (2000); 6,118 (2010); 5,996 (2015 projected); Race: 98.2% White, 0.2% Black, 0.2% Asian, 1.4% Other, 1.2% Hispanic of any race (2010); Density: 21.2 persons per square mile (2010); Average household size: 2.41 (2010); Median age: 42.9 (2010); Males per 100 females: 92.0 (2010).
Religion: Five largest groups: 14.6% Apostolic Christian Church of America, Inc., 14.3% The United Methodist Church, 13.6% Catholic Church, 4.4% New Testament Association of Independent Baptist Churches and other Fundamental Baptist Associations, 3
Economy: Unemployment rate: 8.2% (August 2011); Total civilian labor force: 2,925 (August 2011); Leading industries: 19.2% manufacturing; 15.3% retail trade; 10.4% wholesale trade (2009); Farms: 372 totaling 169,775 acres (2007); Companies that employ 500 or more persons: 0 (2009); Companies that employ 100 to 499 persons: 1 (2009); Companies that employ less than 100 persons: 125 (2009); Black-owned businesses: n/a (2007); Hispanic-owned businesses: n/a (2007); Asian-owned businesses: n/a (2007); Women-owned businesses: n/a (2007); Retail sales per capita: $6,561 (2010). Single-family building permits issued: 0 (2010); Multi-family building permits issued: 0 (2010).
Income: Per capita income: $21,575 (2010); Median household income: $44,179 (2010); Average household income: $52,195 (2010); Percent of

households with income of $100,000 or more: 8.7% (2010); Poverty rate: 11.5% (2009); Bankruptcy rate: 4.67% (2010).

Taxes: Total county taxes per capita: $134 (2007); County property taxes per capita: $134 (2007).

Education: Percent of population age 25 and over with: High school diploma (including GED) or higher: 88.2% (2010); Bachelor's degree or higher: 16.2% (2010); Master's degree or higher: 3.6% (2010).

Housing: Homeownership rate: 76.0% (2010); Median home value: $84,667 (2010); Median contract rent: $339 per month (2005-2009 5-year est.); Median year structure built: 1944 (2005-2009 5-year est.)

Health: Birth rate: 129.6 per 10,000 population (2009); Death rate: 136.2 per 10,000 population (2009); Age-adjusted cancer mortality rate: 165.6 (Unreliable) deaths per 100,000 population (2007); Number of physicians: 1.6 per 10,000 population (2008); Hospital beds: 0.0 per 10,000 population (2007); Hospital admissions: 0.0 per 10,000 population (2007).

Elections: 2008 Presidential election results: 46.7% Obama, 52.0% McCain, 0.6% Nader

Additional Information Contacts

Stark County Government . . . . (309) 286-5911
   http://starkco.illinois.gov
Wyoming Chamber of Commerce . . . . (309) 695-2900
   http://www.wyoming-chamber.org

Stark County Communities

BRADFORD (village). Covers a land area of 0.397 square miles and a water area of 0 square miles. Located at 41.17° N. Lat; 89.65° W. Long. Elevation is 807 feet.

Population: 836 (1990); 787 (2000); 742 (2010); 723 (2015 projected); Race: 98.4% White, 0.0% Black, 0.5% Asian, 1.1% Other, 1.1% Hispanic of any race (2010); Density: 1,871.3 persons per square mile (2010); Average household size: 2.41 (2010); Median age: 40.5 (2010); Males per 100 females: 93.7 (2010); Marriage status: 21.9% never married, 62.1% now married, 6.6% widowed, 9.4% divorced (2005-2009 5-year est.); Foreign born: 0.0% (2005-2009 5-year est.); Ancestry (includes multiple ancestries): 43.0% German, 13.2% Irish, 10.0% English, 8.0% American, 6.1% Swedish (2005-2009 5-year est.).

Economy: Employment by occupation: 9.4% management, 8.2% professional, 17.2% services, 25.5% sales, 3.0% farming, 13.1% construction, 23.6% production (2005-2009 5-year est.).

Income: Per capita income: $22,056 (2010); Median household income: $43,115 (2010); Average household income: $52,808 (2010); Percent of households with income of $100,000 or more: 9.1% (2010); Poverty rate: 22.4% (2005-2009 5-year est.).

Taxes: Total city taxes per capita: $132 (2007); City property taxes per capita: $65 (2007).

Education: Percent of population age 25 and over with: High school diploma (including GED) or higher: 86.9% (2010); Bachelor's degree or higher: 13.3% (2010); Master's degree or higher: 2.8% (2010).

School District(s)

Bradford CUSD 1 (PK-08)
   2009-10 Enrollment: 229 . . . . (309) 897-2801

Housing: Homeownership rate: 80.8% (2010); Median home value: $80,303 (2010); Median contract rent: $309 per month (2005-2009 5-year est.); Median year structure built: before 1940 (2005-2009 5-year est.).

Transportation: Commute to work: 94.3% car, 1.5% public transportation, 3.4% walk, 0.8% work from home (2005-2009 5-year est.); Travel time to work: 17.8% less than 15 minutes, 32.0% 15 to 30 minutes, 25.1% 30 to 45 minutes, 13.5% 45 to 60 minutes, 11.6% 60 minutes or more (2005-2009 5-year est.)

Airports: Rinkenberger RLA (general aviation)

LA FAYETTE (village). Aka Lafayette. Covers a land area of 0.184 square miles and a water area of 0 square miles. Located at 41.11° N. Lat; 89.97° W. Long. Elevation is 797 feet.

Population: 231 (1990); 227 (2000); 207 (2010); 196 (2015 projected); Race: 97.6% White, 0.0% Black, 0.5% Asian, 1.9% Other, 1.0% Hispanic of any race (2010); Density: 1,126.3 persons per square mile (2010); Average household size: 2.59 (2010); Median age: 40.4 (2010); Males per 100 females: 84.8 (2010); Marriage status: 35.9% never married, 42.5% now married, 3.9% widowed, 17.7% divorced (2005-2009 5-year est.); Foreign born: 0.4% (2005-2009 5-year est.); Ancestry (includes multiple ancestries): 24.8% Swedish, 16.9% American, 16.1% German, 14.0% Norwegian, 13.6% English (2005-2009 5-year est.).

Economy: Employment by occupation: 7.3% management, 7.3% professional, 21.8% services, 25.8% sales, 0.0% farming, 6.5% construction, 31.5% production (2005-2009 5-year est.).

Income: Per capita income: $22,863 (2010); Median household income: $54,000 (2010); Average household income: $64,594 (2010); Percent of households with income of $100,000 or more: 10.0% (2010); Poverty rate: 17.0% (2005-2009 5-year est.).

Taxes: Total city taxes per capita: $54 (2007); City property taxes per capita: $54 (2007).

Education: Percent of population age 25 and over with: High school diploma (including GED) or higher: 91.7% (2010); Bachelor's degree or higher: 11.7% (2010); Master's degree or higher: 0.7% (2010).

Housing: Homeownership rate: 72.5% (2010); Median home value: $68,235 (2010); Median contract rent: n/a per month (2005-2009 5-year est.); Median year structure built: before 1940 (2005-2009 5-year est.).

Newspapers: Prairie Shopper (Community news; Circulation 5,851)

Transportation: Commute to work: 93.4% car, 0.0% public transportation, 6.6% walk, 0.0% work from home (2005-2009 5-year est.); Travel time to work: 29.5% less than 15 minutes, 34.4% 15 to 30 minutes, 20.5% 30 to 45 minutes, 9.8% 45 to 60 minutes, 5.7% 60 minutes or more (2005-2009 5-year est.)

SPEER (unincorporated postal area, zip code 61479). Covers a land area of 13.178 square miles and a water area of 0 square miles. Located at 40.99° N. Lat; 89.65° W. Long. Elevation is 741 feet.

Population: 169 (2000); Race: 100.0% White, 0.0% Black, 0.0% Asian, 0.0% Other, 0.0% Hispanic of any race (2000); Density: 12.8 persons per square mile (2000); Age: 16.5% under 18, 12.0% over 64 (2000); Marriage status: 12.5% never married, 79.2% now married, 8.3% widowed, 0.0% divorced (2000); Foreign born: 0.0% (2000); Ancestry (includes multiple ancestries): 42.4% German, 19.6% French, 19.6% Irish, 13.3% Scottish, 12.0% English (2000).

Economy: Employment by occupation: 7.2% management, 7.2% professional, 15.9% services, 34.8% sales, 0.0% farming, 0.0% construction, 34.8% production (2000).

Income: Per capita income: $19,389 (2000); Median household income: $35,455 (2000); Poverty rate: 0.0% (2000).

Education: Percent of population age 25 and over with: High school diploma (including GED) or higher: 85.7% (2000); Bachelor's degree or higher: 4.0% (2000).

Housing: Homeownership rate: 78.9% (2000); Median home value: $70,800 (2000); Median contract rent: $397 per month (2000); Median year structure built: before 1940 (2000).

Transportation: Commute to work: 89.9% car, 0.0% public transportation, 10.1% walk, 0.0% work from home (2000); Travel time to work: 33.3% less than 15 minutes, 58.0% 15 to 30 minutes, 8.7% 30 to 45 minutes, 0.0% 45 to 60 minutes, 0.0% 60 minutes or more (2000)

TOULON (city). County seat. Covers a land area of 0.889 square miles and a water area of 0 square miles. Located at 41.09° N. Lat; 89.86° W. Long. Elevation is 728 feet.

History: Incorporated 1859.

Population: 1,341 (1990); 1,400 (2000); 1,416 (2010); 1,421 (2015 projected); Race: 97.9% White, 0.6% Black, 0.1% Asian, 1.5% Other, 0.5% Hispanic of any race (2010); Density: 1,593.5 persons per square mile (2010); Average household size: 2.26 (2010); Median age: 47.0 (2010); Males per 100 females: 81.5 (2010); Marriage status: 16.2% never married, 56.5% now married, 16.8% widowed, 10.5% divorced (2005-2009 5-year est.); Foreign born: 0.3% (2005-2009 5-year est.); Ancestry (includes multiple ancestries): 31.5% German, 19.4% American, 15.4% English, 12.9% Irish, 7.9% Swedish (2005-2009 5-year est.).

Economy: Employment by occupation: 7.5% management, 23.8% professional, 12.5% services, 19.3% sales, 1.4% farming, 11.1% construction, 24.3% production (2005-2009 5-year est.).

Income: Per capita income: $20,963 (2010); Median household income: $39,912 (2010); Average household income: $48,478 (2010); Percent of households with income of $100,000 or more: 7.6% (2010); Poverty rate: 14.4% (2005-2009 5-year est.).

Taxes: Total city taxes per capita: $98 (2007); City property taxes per capita: $82 (2007).

Education: Percent of population age 25 and over with: High school diploma (including GED) or higher: 87.8% (2010); Bachelor's degree or higher: 17.7% (2010); Master's degree or higher: 5.9% (2010).

School District(s)

Stark County CUSD 100 (PK-12)

2009-10 Enrollment: 869 . . . . (309) 695-6123

Housing: Homeownership rate: 73.4% (2010); Median home value: $77,303 (2010); Median contract rent: $345 per month (2005-2009 5-year est.); Median year structure built: 1951 (2005-2009 5-year est.).

Transportation: Commute to work: 83.9% car, 0.0% public transportation, 6.8% walk, 5.4% work from home (2005-2009 5-year est.); Travel time to work: 44.9% less than 15 minutes, 18.6% 15 to 30 minutes, 15.8% 30 to 45 minutes, 9.6% 45 to 60 minutes, 11.1% 60 minutes or more (2005-2009 5-year est.)

WYOMING (city). Covers a land area of 0.742 square miles and a water area of 0 square miles. Located at 41.06° N. Lat; 89.77° W. Long. Elevation is 699 feet.

History: Incorporated 1865.

Population: 1,462 (1990); 1,424 (2000); 1,435 (2010); 1,432 (2015 projected); Race: 98.7% White, 0.1% Black, 0.1% Asian, 1.0% Other, 0.3% Hispanic of any race (2010); Density: 1,933.0 persons per square mile (2010); Average household size: 2.34 (2010); Median age: 42.7 (2010); Males per 100 females: 90.1 (2010); Marriage status: 19.7% never married, 58.3% now married, 10.4% widowed, 11.7% divorced (2005-2009 5-year est.); Foreign born: 0.8% (2005-2009 5-year est.); Ancestry (includes multiple ancestries): 23.2% German, 21.8% Irish, 14.8% English, 12.0% American, 5.9% Dutch (2005-2009 5-year est.).

Economy: Employment by occupation: 8.2% management, 10.8% professional, 16.5% services, 29.4% sales, 0.0% farming, 6.3% construction, 28.9% production (2005-2009 5-year est.).

Income: Per capita income: $20,046 (2010); Median household income: $38,894 (2010); Average household income: $46,462 (2010); Percent of households with income of $100,000 or more: 6.4% (2010); Poverty rate: 14.3% (2005-2009 5-year est.).

Taxes: Total city taxes per capita: $123 (2007); City property taxes per capita: $113 (2007).

Education: Percent of population age 25 and over with: High school diploma (including GED) or higher: 87.0% (2010); Bachelor's degree or higher: 16.3% (2010); Master's degree or higher: 3.8% (2010).

School District(s)

Stark County CUSD 100 (PK-12)

2009-10 Enrollment: 869 . . . . (309) 695-6123

Housing: Homeownership rate: 77.0% (2010); Median home value: $88,482 (2010); Median contract rent: $346 per month (2005-2009 5-year est.); Median year structure built: 1951 (2005-2009 5-year est.).

Transportation: Commute to work: 93.0% car, 0.0% public transportation, 2.2% walk, 3.2% work from home (2005-2009 5-year est.); Travel time to work: 37.7% less than 15 minutes, 15.4% 15 to 30 minutes, 22.5% 30 to 45 minutes, 15.2% 45 to 60 minutes, 9.2% 60 minutes or more (2005-2009 5-year est.)

Additional Information Contacts

Wyoming Chamber of Commerce . . . . (309) 695-2900
http://www.wyoming-chamber.org

Stephenson County

Located in northern Illinois; bounded on the north by Wisconsin; drained by the Pecatonica River. Covers a land area of 564.18 square miles, a water area of 0.54 square miles, and is located in the Central Time Zone at 42.34° N. Lat., 89.64° W. Long. The county was founded in 1837. County seat is Freeport.

Stephenson County is part of the Freeport, IL Micropolitan Statistical Area. The entire metro area includes: Stephenson County, IL

Weather Station: Freeport Waste Wtr Plt   Elevation: 750 feet

	Jan	Feb	Mar	Apr	May	Jun	Jul	Aug	Sep	Oct	Nov	Dec
High	28	33	45	59	70	80	83	81	74	61	47	32
Low	11	15	26	37	48	58	62	60	50	39	29	16
Precip	1.4	1.5	2.0	3.3	4.0	4.5	3.6	4.5	3.8	2.8	2.6	1.8
Snow	8.8	6.4	3.4	1.0	tr	0.0	0.0	0.0	0.0	tr	1.5	9.0

High and Low temperatures in degrees Fahrenheit; Precipitation and Snow in inches

Population: 48,052 (1990); 48,979 (2000); 45,942 (2010); 44,224 (2015 projected); Race: 87.4% White, 8.0% Black, 0.9% Asian, 3.6% Other, 2.7% Hispanic of any race (2010); Density: 81.4 persons per square mile (2010); Average household size: 2.40 (2010); Median age: 41.0 (2010); Males per 100 females: 93.2 (2010).

Religion: Five largest groups: 17.1% Catholic Church, 11.6% The United Methodist Church, 5.2% Evangelical Lutheran Church in America, 4.7% United Church of Christ, 4.0% Lutheran Church—Missouri Synod (2000).

Economy: Unemployment rate: 10.0% (August 2011); Total civilian labor force: 24,204 (August 2011); Leading industries: 19.0% health care and social assistance; 17.5% manufacturing; 16.0% retail trade (2009); Farms: 1,178 totaling 337,932 acres (2007); Companies that employ 500 or more persons: 3 (2009); Companies that employ 100 to 499 persons: 20 (2009); Companies that employ less than 100 persons: 1,084 (2009); Black-owned businesses: n/a (2007); Hispanic-owned businesses: 41 (2007); Asian-owned businesses: n/a (2007); Women-owned businesses: n/a (2007); Retail sales per capita: $12,421 (2010). Single-family building permits issued: 27 (2010); Multi-family building permits issued: 0 (2010).

Income: Per capita income: $22,106 (2010); Median household income: $44,131 (2010); Average household income: $53,356 (2010); Percent of households with income of $100,000 or more: 9.8% (2010); Poverty rate: 13.0% (2009); Bankruptcy rate: 4.73% (2010).

Taxes: Total county taxes per capita: $163 (2007); County property taxes per capita: $129 (2007).

Education: Percent of population age 25 and over with: High school diploma (including GED) or higher: 87.6% (2010); Bachelor's degree or higher: 16.6% (2010); Master's degree or higher: 5.7% (2010).

Housing: Homeownership rate: 73.9% (2010); Median home value: $97,467 (2010); Median contract rent: $407 per month (2005-2009 5-year est.); Median year structure built: 1956 (2005-2009 5-year est.)

Health: Birth rate: 121.0 per 10,000 population (2009); Death rate: 114.1 per 10,000 population (2009); Age-adjusted cancer mortality rate: 187.1 deaths per 100,000 population (2007); Number of physicians: 13.9 per 10,000 population (2008); Hospital beds: 33.6 per 10,000 population (2007); Hospital admissions: 1,339.2 per 10,000 population (2007).

Elections: 2008 Presidential election results: 52.5% Obama, 45.9% McCain, 0.7% Nader

National and State Parks: Lake Le-Aqua-Na State Park

Additional Information Contacts

Stephenson County Government. (815) 235-8277
http://www.co.stephenson.il.us

City of Freeport . . . . (815) 235-8200
http://www.ci.freeport.il.us

Freeport Area Chamber of Commerce . . . . (815) 233-1350
http://www.freeportilchamber.com

Stephenson County Communities

CEDARVILLE (village). Covers a land area of 0.449 square miles and a water area of 0 square miles. Located at 42.37° N. Lat; 89.63° W. Long. Elevation is 866 feet.

History: Cedarville was the birthplace and burial place of Jane Addams (1860-1935), whose parents built a house here in 1850 and raised their family on the homestead. John Addams operated a mill.

Population: 753 (1990); 719 (2000); 634 (2010); 594 (2015 projected); Race: 96.8% White, 0.9% Black, 1.3% Asian, 0.9% Other, 0.9% Hispanic of any race (2010); Density: 1,410.7 persons per square mile (2010); Average household size: 2.47 (2010); Median age: 45.9 (2010); Males per 100 females: 100.0 (2010); Marriage status: 22.3% never married, 63.0% now married, 0.8% widowed, 13.9% divorced (2005-2009 5-year est.); Foreign born: 2.6% (2005-2009 5-year est.); Ancestry (includes multiple ancestries): 61.2% German, 17.1% Irish, 11.9% English, 9.5% American, 5.5% Swedish (2005-2009 5-year est.).

Economy: Single-family building permits issued: 0 (2010); Multi-family building permits issued: 0 (2010); Employment by occupation: 9.7% management, 20.5% professional, 8.3% services, 20.2% sales, 0.4% farming, 13.2% construction, 27.7% production (2005-2009 5-year est.).

Income: Per capita income: $27,479 (2010); Median household income: $57,863 (2010); Average household income: $67,101 (2010); Percent of households with income of $100,000 or more: 16.0% (2010); Poverty rate: 6.2% (2005-2009 5-year est.).

Taxes: Total city taxes per capita: $110 (2007); City property taxes per capita: $100 (2007).

Education: Percent of population age 25 and over with: High school diploma (including GED) or higher: 91.1% (2010); Bachelor's degree or higher: 21.0% (2010); Master's degree or higher: 9.1% (2010).

Housing: Homeownership rate: 89.1% (2010); Median home value: $119,086 (2010); Median contract rent: $441 per month (2005-2009 5-year est.); Median year structure built: 1959 (2005-2009 5-year est.).

Transportation: Commute to work: 92.6% car, 0.0% public transportation, 2.3% walk, 5.0% work from home (2005-2009 5-year est.); Travel time to work: 33.2% less than 15 minutes, 54.2% 15 to 30 minutes, 9.7% 30 to 45 minutes, 1.1% 45 to 60 minutes, 1.8% 60 minutes or more (2005-2009 5-year est.)

DAKOTA (village). Covers a land area of 0.288 square miles and a water area of 0 square miles. Located at 42.38° N. Lat; 89.52° W. Long. Elevation is 945 feet.
Population: 560 (1990); 499 (2000); 451 (2010); 425 (2015 projected); Race: 97.6% White, 0.4% Black, 0.9% Asian, 1.1% Other, 0.9% Hispanic of any race (2010); Density: 1,565.3 persons per square mile (2010); Average household size: 2.65 (2010); Median age: 39.6 (2010); Males per 100 females: 99.6 (2010); Marriage status: 29.4% never married, 52.6% now married, 8.7% widowed, 9.3% divorced (2005-2009 5-year est.); Foreign born: 2.6% (2005-2009 5-year est.); Ancestry (includes multiple ancestries): 56.2% German, 10.4% English, 9.2% Irish, 9.0% American, 8.0% Swiss (2005-2009 5-year est.).
Economy: Single-family building permits issued: 0 (2010); Multi-family building permits issued: 0 (2010); Employment by occupation: 7.1% management, 17.5% professional, 13.0% services, 19.7% sales, 2.2% farming, 11.5% construction, 29.0% production (2005-2009 5-year est.).
Income: Per capita income: $22,132 (2010); Median household income: $48,929 (2010); Average household income: $59,338 (2010); Percent of households with income of $100,000 or more: 10.6% (2010); Poverty rate: 9.0% (2005-2009 5-year est.).
Taxes: Total city taxes per capita: $21 (2007); City property taxes per capita: $21 (2007).
Education: Percent of population age 25 and over with: High school diploma (including GED) or higher: 89.3% (2010); Bachelor's degree or higher: 6.1% (2010); Master's degree or higher: 1.3% (2010).
School District(s)
Dakota CUSD 201 (PK-12)
   2009-10 Enrollment: 917 . . . . (815) 449-2832
Housing: Homeownership rate: 75.9% (2010); Median home value: $98,800 (2010); Median contract rent: $348 per month (2005-2009 5-year est.); Median year structure built: 1947 (2005-2009 5-year est.).
Transportation: Commute to work: 86.0% car, 0.0% public transportation, 3.4% walk, 7.2% work from home (2005-2009 5-year est.); Travel time to work: 28.2% less than 15 minutes, 47.3% 15 to 30 minutes, 11.8% 30 to 45 minutes, 2.4% 45 to 60 minutes, 10.2% 60 minutes or more (2005-2009 5-year est.)

DAVIS (village). Covers a land area of 0.428 square miles and a water area of 0 square miles. Located at 42.42° N. Lat; 89.41° W. Long. Elevation is 889 feet.
Population: 608 (1990); 662 (2000); 708 (2010); 722 (2015 projected); Race: 98.0% White, 0.1% Black, 0.1% Asian, 1.7% Other, 1.7% Hispanic of any race (2010); Density: 1,654.2 persons per square mile (2010); Average household size: 2.51 (2010); Median age: 44.2 (2010); Males per 100 females: 101.1 (2010); Marriage status: 25.4% never married, 61.3% now married, 7.4% widowed, 5.9% divorced (2005-2009 5-year est.); Foreign born: 0.0% (2005-2009 5-year est.); Ancestry (includes multiple ancestries): 54.2% German, 13.7% Norwegian, 8.7% Swiss, 7.5% American, 6.5% English (2005-2009 5-year est.).
Economy: Single-family building permits issued: 0 (2010); Multi-family building permits issued: 0 (2010); Employment by occupation: 7.7% management, 24.5% professional, 7.2% services, 21.2% sales, 1.7% farming, 16.5% construction, 21.2% production (2005-2009 5-year est.).
Income: Per capita income: $29,295 (2010); Median household income: $66,544 (2010); Average household income: $73,227 (2010); Percent of households with income of $100,000 or more: 22.0% (2010); Poverty rate: 7.5% (2005-2009 5-year est.).
Taxes: Total city taxes per capita: $585 (2007); City property taxes per capita: $580 (2007).
Education: Percent of population age 25 and over with: High school diploma (including GED) or higher: 90.3% (2010); Bachelor's degree or higher: 22.2% (2010); Master's degree or higher: 6.1% (2010).
Housing: Homeownership rate: 90.8% (2010); Median home value: $140,556 (2010); Median contract rent: $458 per month (2005-2009 5-year est.); Median year structure built: 1962 (2005-2009 5-year est.).
Transportation: Commute to work: 96.3% car, 1.1% public transportation, 0.0% walk, 1.7% work from home (2005-2009 5-year est.); Travel time to work: 25.3% less than 15 minutes, 30.5% 15 to 30 minutes, 31.7% 30 to 45

minutes, 7.0% 45 to 60 minutes, 5.5% 60 minutes or more (2005-2009 5-year est.)

FREEPORT (city). County seat. Covers a land area of 11.413 square miles and a water area of 0.010 square miles. Located at 42.29° N. Lat; 89.63° W. Long. Elevation is 778 feet.
History: Freeport was settled in 1835 by William "Tutty" Baker and his wife. The name reportedly came from Baker's generosity in sharing his food with anyone who came along. Miners returning from the Galena lead mines joined the Bakers, and Freeport became the seat of Stephenson County. It was here that the second Lincoln-Douglas debate took place in 1858.
Population: 26,316 (1990); 26,443 (2000); 24,338 (2010); 23,248 (2015 projected); Race: 79.2% White, 14.2% Black, 1.2% Asian, 5.3% Other, 3.7% Hispanic of any race (2010); Density: 2,132.4 persons per square mile (2010); Average household size: 2.27 (2010); Median age: 40.1 (2010); Males per 100 females: 88.3 (2010); Marriage status: 28.1% never married, 48.9% now married, 9.9% widowed, 13.2% divorced (2005-2009 5-year est.); Foreign born: 2.4% (2005-2009 5-year est.); Ancestry (includes multiple ancestries): 40.1% German, 11.8% Irish, 9.7% English, 8.1% American, 4.4% Dutch (2005-2009 5-year est.).
Economy: Unemployment rate: 12.0% (August 2011); Total civilian labor force: 12,401 (August 2011); Single-family building permits issued: 0 (2010); Multi-family building permits issued: 0 (2010); Employment by occupation: 10.5% management, 15.4% professional, 20.0% services, 28.8% sales, 0.4% farming, 5.2% construction, 19.7% production (2005-2009 5-year est.).
Income: Per capita income: $20,137 (2010); Median household income: $37,537 (2010); Average household income: $46,172 (2010); Percent of households with income of $100,000 or more: 6.5% (2010); Poverty rate: 17.1% (2005-2009 5-year est.).
Taxes: Total city taxes per capita: $285 (2007); City property taxes per capita: $143 (2007).
Education: Percent of population age 25 and over with: High school diploma (including GED) or higher: 86.4% (2010); Bachelor's degree or higher: 18.3% (2010); Master's degree or higher: 6.1% (2010).
School District(s)
Career & Tech Educ Consortium
   2009-10 Enrollment: n/a . . . . (815) 232-0709
Carroll/Jo Daviess/Stephenson Roe (06-12)
   2009-10 Enrollment: n/a . . . . (815) 947-3810
Freeport SD 145 (PK-12)
   2009-10 Enrollment: 4,290 . . . . (815) 232-0300
Two-year College(s)
Highland Community College (Public)
   Fall 2009 Enrollment: 2,455. (815) 235-6121
   2010-11 Tuition: In-state $3,792; Out-of-state $3,984
Housing: Homeownership rate: 67.4% (2010); Median home value: $79,689 (2010); Median contract rent: $412 per month (2005-2009 5-year est.); Median year structure built: 1954 (2005-2009 5-year est.).
Hospitals: FHN Memorial Hospital (194 beds)
Safety: Violent crime rate: 20.2 per 10,000 population; Property crime rate: 362.5 per 10,000 population (2010).
Newspapers: Advertizer Shopping News (Local news; Circulation 22,800); The Journal-Standard (Local news; Circulation 36,000)
Transportation: Commute to work: 89.1% car, 2.2% public transportation, 4.5% walk, 2.9% work from home (2005-2009 5-year est.); Travel time to work: 66.6% less than 15 minutes, 13.5% 15 to 30 minutes, 8.6% 30 to 45 minutes, 6.9% 45 to 60 minutes, 4.3% 60 minutes or more (2005-2009 5-year est.)
Airports: Albertus (general aviation)
Additional Information Contacts
City of Freeport . . . . (815) 235-8200
   http://www.ci.freeport.il.us
Freeport Area Chamber of Commerce . . . . (815) 233-1350
   http://www.freeportilchamber.com

GERMAN VALLEY (village). Covers a land area of 0.487 square miles and a water area of 0 square miles. Located at 42.21° N. Lat; 89.47° W. Long. Elevation is 823 feet.
Population: 507 (1990); 481 (2000); 431 (2010); 407 (2015 projected); Race: 99.3% White, 0.0% Black, 0.2% Asian, 0.5% Other, 3.0% Hispanic of any race (2010); Density: 885.2 persons per square mile (2010); Average household size: 2.63 (2010); Median age: 40.9 (2010); Males per 100 females: 95.0 (2010); Marriage status: 19.1% never married, 70.1%

now married, 5.4% widowed, 5.4% divorced (2005-2009 5-year est.); Foreign born: 0.4% (2005-2009 5-year est.); Ancestry (includes multiple ancestries): 57.6% German, 14.6% American, 10.5% Irish, 7.2% English, 4.7% Swiss (2005-2009 5-year est.).

Economy: Single-family building permits issued: 0 (2010); Multi-family building permits issued: 0 (2010); Employment by occupation: 5.8% management, 20.2% professional, 14.8% services, 27.4% sales, 0.0% farming, 13.5% construction, 18.4% production (2005-2009 5-year est.).

Income: Per capita income: $23,910 (2010); Median household income: $51,829 (2010); Average household income: $64,192 (2010); Percent of households with income of $100,000 or more: 13.4% (2010); Poverty rate: 7.2% (2005-2009 5-year est.).

Taxes: Total city taxes per capita: $94 (2007); City property taxes per capita: $92 (2007).

Education: Percent of population age 25 and over with: High school diploma (including GED) or higher: 93.0% (2010); Bachelor's degree or higher: 11.6% (2010); Master's degree or higher: 3.7% (2010).

School District(s)
Forrestville Valley CUSD 221 (PK-12)
    2009-10 Enrollment: 898 . . . . (815) 938-2036

Housing: Homeownership rate: 81.1% (2010); Median home value: $123,214 (2010); Median contract rent: $138 per month (2005-2009 5-year est.); Median year structure built: 1960 (2005-2009 5-year est.).

Transportation: Commute to work: 91.6% car, 0.0% public transportation, 2.8% walk, 4.2% work from home (2005-2009 5-year est.); Travel time to work: 11.7% less than 15 minutes, 54.9% 15 to 30 minutes, 21.4% 30 to 45 minutes, 8.3% 45 to 60 minutes, 3.9% 60 minutes or more (2005-2009 5-year est.)

KENT (unincorporated postal area, zip code 61044). Covers a land area of 14.493 square miles and a water area of 0 square miles. Located at 42.32° N. Lat; 89.91° W. Long. Elevation is 899 feet.

Population: 234 (2000); Race: 100.0% White, 0.0% Black, 0.0% Asian, 0.0% Other, 0.0% Hispanic of any race (2000); Density: 16.1 persons per square mile (2000); Age: 19.2% under 18, 5.3% over 64 (2000); Marriage status: 17.3% never married, 77.2% now married, 3.1% widowed, 2.4% divorced (2000); Foreign born: 0.0% (2000); Ancestry (includes multiple ancestries): 76.8% German, 16.6% Dutch, 15.9% English, 10.6% Irish, 4.6% Swedish (2000).

Economy: Employment by occupation: 28.7% management, 4.3% professional, 7.0% services, 24.3% sales, 0.0% farming, 8.7% construction, 27.0% production (2000).

Income: Per capita income: $24,019 (2000); Median household income: $44,000 (2000); Poverty rate: 0.0% (2000).

Education: Percent of population age 25 and over with: High school diploma (including GED) or higher: 90.9% (2000); Bachelor's degree or higher: 6.4% (2000).

Housing: Homeownership rate: 89.8% (2000); Median home value: $65,000 (2000); Median contract rent: n/a per month (2000); Median year structure built: before 1940 (2000).

Transportation: Commute to work: 82.7% car, 0.0% public transportation, 4.5% walk, 12.7% work from home (2000); Travel time to work: 38.5% less than 15 minutes, 28.1% 15 to 30 minutes, 30.2% 30 to 45 minutes, 0.0% 45 to 60 minutes, 3.1% 60 minutes or more (2000)

LENA (village). Covers a land area of 2.139 square miles and a water area of 0 square miles. Located at 42.37° N. Lat; 89.82° W. Long. Elevation is 948 feet.

History: Lena was known as one of the first places in the United States where Camembert and Brie cheeses were made.

Population: 2,794 (1990); 2,887 (2000); 2,714 (2010); 2,621 (2015 projected); Race: 97.8% White, 0.1% Black, 0.1% Asian, 2.0% Other, 2.2% Hispanic of any race (2010); Density: 1,269.1 persons per square mile (2010); Average household size: 2.41 (2010); Median age: 40.9 (2010); Males per 100 females: 93.3 (2010); Marriage status: 24.9% never married, 52.4% now married, 8.6% widowed, 14.0% divorced (2005-2009 5-year est.); Foreign born: 0.0% (2005-2009 5-year est.); Ancestry (includes multiple ancestries): 54.0% German, 20.4% Irish, 10.9% English, 10.5% American, 2.8% Swiss (2005-2009 5-year est.).

Economy: Single-family building permits issued: 1 (2010); Multi-family building permits issued: 0 (2010); Employment by occupation: 13.3% management, 18.9% professional, 12.9% services, 23.2% sales, 1.3% farming, 13.9% construction, 16.5% production (2005-2009 5-year est.).

Income: Per capita income: $21,818 (2010); Median household income: $45,123 (2010); Average household income: $52,871 (2010); Percent of

households with income of $100,000 or more: 8.2% (2010); Poverty rate: 4.9% (2005-2009 5-year est.).

Taxes: Total city taxes per capita: $238 (2007); City property taxes per capita: $224 (2007).

Education: Percent of population age 25 and over with: High school diploma (including GED) or higher: 89.5% (2010); Bachelor's degree or higher: 14.3% (2010); Master's degree or higher: 6.5% (2010).

School District(s)
Lena Winslow CUSD 202 (PK-12)
    2009-10 Enrollment: 951 . . . . (815) 369-3100

Housing: Homeownership rate: 77.0% (2010); Median home value: $115,692 (2010); Median contract rent: $365 per month (2005-2009 5-year est.); Median year structure built: 1966 (2005-2009 5-year est.).

Transportation: Commute to work: 91.8% car, 0.0% public transportation, 3.9% walk, 3.8% work from home (2005-2009 5-year est.); Travel time to work: 35.1% less than 15 minutes, 35.3% 15 to 30 minutes, 11.4% 30 to 45 minutes, 6.5% 45 to 60 minutes, 11.7% 60 minutes or more (2005-2009 5-year est.)

MCCONNELL (unincorporated postal area, zip code 61050). Covers a land area of 13.223 square miles and a water area of 0 square miles. Located at 42.44° N. Lat; 89.72° W. Long. Elevation is 778 feet.

Population: 447 (2000); Race: 100.0% White, 0.0% Black, 0.0% Asian, 0.0% Other, 0.0% Hispanic of any race (2000); Density: 33.8 persons per square mile (2000); Age: 20.2% under 18, 18.0% over 64 (2000); Marriage status: 16.1% never married, 67.4% now married, 4.9% widowed, 11.7% divorced (2000); Foreign born: 2.8% (2000); Ancestry (includes multiple ancestries): 50.6% German, 13.7% Irish, 10.7% English, 9.9% Swiss, 9.4% American (2000).

Economy: Employment by occupation: 23.5% management, 11.3% professional, 9.0% services, 21.3% sales, 1.8% farming, 12.2% construction, 20.8% production (2000).

Income: Per capita income: $16,634 (2000); Median household income: $32,143 (2000); Poverty rate: 11.8% (2000).

Education: Percent of population age 25 and over with: High school diploma (including GED) or higher: 85.0% (2000); Bachelor's degree or higher: 2.2% (2000).

Housing: Homeownership rate: 83.5% (2000); Median home value: $65,000 (2000); Median contract rent: $325 per month (2000); Median year structure built: before 1940 (2000).

Transportation: Commute to work: 84.7% car, 0.0% public transportation, 0.0% walk, 15.3% work from home (2000); Travel time to work: 26.9% less than 15 minutes, 34.6% 15 to 30 minutes, 25.3% 30 to 45 minutes, 7.1% 45 to 60 minutes, 6.0% 60 minutes or more (2000)

ORANGEVILLE (village). Covers a land area of 0.642 square miles and a water area of 0 square miles. Located at 42.46° N. Lat; 89.64° W. Long. Elevation is 820 feet.

Population: 637 (1990); 751 (2000); 723 (2010); 696 (2015 projected); Race: 98.2% White, 0.6% Black, 0.0% Asian, 1.2% Other, 1.7% Hispanic of any race (2010); Density: 1,125.3 persons per square mile (2010); Average household size: 2.51 (2010); Median age: 38.4 (2010); Males per 100 females: 102.5 (2010); Marriage status: 23.0% never married, 65.6% now married, 3.3% widowed, 8.1% divorced (2005-2009 5-year est.); Foreign born: 0.0% (2005-2009 5-year est.); Ancestry (includes multiple ancestries): 69.3% German, 13.3% Irish, 11.8% Swiss, 6.3% English, 5.3% Polish (2005-2009 5-year est.).

Economy: Single-family building permits issued: 0 (2010); Multi-family building permits issued: 0 (2010); Employment by occupation: 11.1% management, 14.8% professional, 16.9% services, 28.4% sales, 0.0% farming, 7.1% construction, 21.8% production (2005-2009 5-year est.).

Income: Per capita income: $18,745 (2010); Median household income: $42,159 (2010); Average household income: $47,318 (2010); Percent of households with income of $100,000 or more: 3.5% (2010); Poverty rate: 8.6% (2005-2009 5-year est.).

Taxes: Total city taxes per capita: $525 (2007); City property taxes per capita: $523 (2007).

Education: Percent of population age 25 and over with: High school diploma (including GED) or higher: 87.8% (2010); Bachelor's degree or higher: 12.6% (2010); Master's degree or higher: 4.6% (2010).

School District(s)
Orangeville CUSD 203 (PK-12)
    2009-10 Enrollment: 447 . . . . (815) 789-4450

Housing: Homeownership rate: 75.7% (2010); Median home value: $107,143 (2010); Median contract rent: $406 per month (2005-2009 5-year est.); Median year structure built: 1958 (2005-2009 5-year est.).
Transportation: Commute to work: 88.9% car, 0.0% public transportation, 7.4% walk, 2.2% work from home (2005-2009 5-year est.); Travel time to work: 31.1% less than 15 minutes, 53.7% 15 to 30 minutes, 6.1% 30 to 45 minutes, 3.7% 45 to 60 minutes, 5.5% 60 minutes or more (2005-2009 5-year est.)

PEARL CITY (village). Covers a land area of 0.567 square miles and a water area of 0.009 square miles. Located at 42.26° N. Lat; 89.82° W. Long. Elevation is 833 feet.

Population: 700 (1990); 780 (2000); 723 (2010); 712 (2015 projected); Race: 98.1% White, 0.3% Black, 0.1% Asian, 1.5% Other, 0.8% Hispanic of any race (2010); Density: 1,276.1 persons per square mile (2010); Average household size: 2.70 (2010); Median age: 38.8 (2010); Males per 100 females: 94.4 (2010); Marriage status: 21.1% never married, 55.4% now married, 7.5% widowed, 16.0% divorced (2005-2009 5-year est.); Foreign born: 1.2% (2005-2009 5-year est.); Ancestry (includes multiple ancestries): 50.7% German, 12.3% Irish, 6.4% American, 5.9% English, 5.0% Norwegian (2005-2009 5-year est.).
Economy: Single-family building permits issued: 0 (2010); Multi-family building permits issued: 0 (2010); Employment by occupation: 14.8% management, 18.5% professional, 17.1% services, 20.6% sales, 2.3% farming, 8.7% construction, 18.0% production (2005-2009 5-year est.).
Income: Per capita income: $21,188 (2010); Median household income: $49,706 (2010); Average household income: $57,719 (2010); Percent of households with income of $100,000 or more: 10.3% (2010); Poverty rate: 6.1% (2005-2009 5-year est.).
Taxes: Total city taxes per capita: $527 (2007); City property taxes per capita: $523 (2007).
Education: Percent of population age 25 and over with: High school diploma (including GED) or higher: 89.4% (2010); Bachelor's degree or higher: 14.1% (2010); Master's degree or higher: 2.9% (2010).
School District(s)
Pearl City CUSD 200 (PK-12)
    2009-10 Enrollment: 522 . . . . (815) 443-2715
Housing: Homeownership rate: 77.9% (2010); Median home value: $118,750 (2010); Median contract rent: $358 per month (2005-2009 5-year est.); Median year structure built: 1968 (2005-2009 5-year est.).
Transportation: Commute to work: 92.1% car, 0.0% public transportation, 5.5% walk, 1.7% work from home (2005-2009 5-year est.); Travel time to work: 30.3% less than 15 minutes, 45.9% 15 to 30 minutes, 11.2% 30 to 45 minutes, 4.9% 45 to 60 minutes, 7.8% 60 minutes or more (2005-2009 5-year est.)

RIDOTT (village). Covers a land area of 0.105 square miles and a water area of 0 square miles. Located at 42.29° N. Lat; 89.47° W. Long. Elevation is 758 feet.

Population: 156 (1990); 159 (2000); 155 (2010); 150 (2015 projected); Race: 98.7% White, 0.0% Black, 0.0% Asian, 1.3% Other, 1.9% Hispanic of any race (2010); Density: 1,480.7 persons per square mile (2010); Average household size: 2.61 (2010); Median age: 44.7 (2010); Males per 100 females: 106.7 (2010); Marriage status: 19.1% never married, 66.1% now married, 5.2% widowed, 9.6% divorced (2005-2009 5-year est.); Foreign born: 0.7% (2005-2009 5-year est.); Ancestry (includes multiple ancestries): 35.8% German, 19.0% Swedish, 15.3% Italian, 9.5% American, 6.6% English (2005-2009 5-year est.).
Economy: Employment by occupation: 12.8% management, 0.0% professional, 23.4% services, 23.4% sales, 0.0% farming, 12.8% construction, 27.7% production (2005-2009 5-year est.).
Income: Per capita income: $27,929 (2010); Median household income: $62,500 (2010); Average household income: $68,686 (2010); Percent of households with income of $100,000 or more: 20.3% (2010); Poverty rate: 12.4% (2005-2009 5-year est.).
Taxes: Total city taxes per capita: $40 (2007); City property taxes per capita: $33 (2007).
Education: Percent of population age 25 and over with: High school diploma (including GED) or higher: 91.2% (2010); Bachelor's degree or higher: 14.2% (2010); Master's degree or higher: 4.4% (2010).
Housing: Homeownership rate: 79.7% (2010); Median home value: $143,750 (2010); Median contract rent: n/a per month (2005-2009 5-year est.); Median year structure built: before 1940 (2005-2009 5-year est.).
Transportation: Commute to work: 89.4% car, 0.0% public transportation, 0.0% walk, 0.0% work from home (2005-2009 5-year est.); Travel time to

work: 8.5% less than 15 minutes, 40.4% 15 to 30 minutes, 31.9% 30 to 45 minutes, 2.1% 45 to 60 minutes, 17.0% 60 minutes or more (2005-2009 5-year est.)

ROCK CITY (village). Covers a land area of 0.143 square miles and a water area of 0 square miles. Located at 42.41° N. Lat; 89.46° W. Long. Elevation is 909 feet.

Population: 331 (1990); 313 (2000); 290 (2010); 279 (2015 projected); Race: 95.9% White, 0.3% Black, 1.0% Asian, 2.8% Other, 1.4% Hispanic of any race (2010); Density: 2,034.4 persons per square mile (2010); Average household size: 2.66 (2010); Median age: 38.9 (2010); Males per 100 females: 93.3 (2010); Marriage status: 28.6% never married, 59.0% now married, 8.7% widowed, 3.7% divorced (2005-2009 5-year est.); Foreign born: 0.0% (2005-2009 5-year est.); Ancestry (includes multiple ancestries): 30.7% German, 25.8% American, 14.6% Irish, 11.2% European, 4.6% Swedish (2005-2009 5-year est.).
Economy: Single-family building permits issued: 0 (2010); Multi-family building permits issued: 0 (2010); Employment by occupation: 15.2% management, 5.1% professional, 21.8% services, 16.8% sales, 1.0% farming, 4.6% construction, 35.5% production (2005-2009 5-year est.).
Income: Per capita income: $24,505 (2010); Median household income: $51,705 (2010); Average household income: $64,151 (2010); Percent of households with income of $100,000 or more: 17.4% (2010); Poverty rate: 3.4% (2005-2009 5-year est.).
Taxes: Total city taxes per capita: $22 (2007); City property taxes per capita: $10 (2007).
Education: Percent of population age 25 and over with: High school diploma (including GED) or higher: 88.5% (2010); Bachelor's degree or higher: 13.1% (2010); Master's degree or higher: 3.1% (2010).
Housing: Homeownership rate: 79.8% (2010); Median home value: $123,148 (2010); Median contract rent: $300 per month (2005-2009 5-year est.); Median year structure built: 1962 (2005-2009 5-year est.).
Transportation: Commute to work: 96.4% car, 0.0% public transportation, 2.0% walk, 1.0% work from home (2005-2009 5-year est.); Travel time to work: 17.4% less than 15 minutes, 26.7% 15 to 30 minutes, 41.0% 30 to 45 minutes, 9.7% 45 to 60 minutes, 5.1% 60 minutes or more (2005-2009 5-year est.)

WINSLOW (village). Covers a land area of 0.446 square miles and a water area of 0 square miles. Located at 42.49° N. Lat; 89.79° W. Long. Elevation is 774 feet.

Population: 317 (1990); 345 (2000); 330 (2010); 320 (2015 projected); Race: 97.0% White, 0.3% Black, 0.0% Asian, 2.7% Other, 2.1% Hispanic of any race (2010); Density: 739.4 persons per square mile (2010); Average household size: 2.68 (2010); Median age: 37.5 (2010); Males per 100 females: 102.5 (2010); Marriage status: 23.8% never married, 61.7% now married, 9.8% widowed, 4.7% divorced (2005-2009 5-year est.); Foreign born: 2.1% (2005-2009 5-year est.); Ancestry (includes multiple ancestries): 58.7% German, 17.3% Irish, 10.6% Norwegian, 9.2% English, 8.1% American (2005-2009 5-year est.).
Economy: Single-family building permits issued: 1 (2010); Multi-family building permits issued: 0 (2010); Employment by occupation: 4.2% management, 7.0% professional, 21.0% services, 32.9% sales, 0.0% farming, 12.6% construction, 22.4% production (2005-2009 5-year est.).
Income: Per capita income: $19,858 (2010); Median household income: $56,010 (2010); Average household income: $54,675 (2010); Percent of households with income of $100,000 or more: 6.5% (2010); Poverty rate: 3.2% (2005-2009 5-year est.).
Taxes: Total city taxes per capita: $148 (2007); City property taxes per capita: $142 (2007).
Education: Percent of population age 25 and over with: High school diploma (including GED) or higher: 84.7% (2010); Bachelor's degree or higher: 8.4% (2010); Master's degree or higher: 0.9% (2010).
Housing: Homeownership rate: 74.8% (2010); Median home value: $93,077 (2010); Median contract rent: $417 per month (2005-2009 5-year est.); Median year structure built: before 1940 (2005-2009 5-year est.).
Transportation: Commute to work: 78.5% car, 0.0% public transportation, 7.4% walk, 14.1% work from home (2005-2009 5-year est.); Travel time to work: 33.6% less than 15 minutes, 43.1% 15 to 30 minutes, 6.0% 30 to 45 minutes, 0.0% 45 to 60 minutes, 17.2% 60 minutes or more (2005-2009 5-year est.)

Tazewell County

Located in central Illinois; bounded on the northwest by the Illinois River; drained by the Mackinaw River. Covers a land area of 648.86 square miles, a water area of 9.03 square miles, and is located in the Central Time Zone at 40.55° N. Lat., 89.54° W. Long. The county was founded in 1827. County seat is Pekin.

Tazewell County is part of the Peoria, IL Metropolitan Statistical Area. The entire metro area includes: Marshall County, IL; Peoria County, IL; Stark County, IL; Tazewell County, IL; Woodford County, IL

Population: 123,692 (1990); 128,485 (2000); 132,452 (2010); 133,865 (2015 projected); Race: 96.3% White, 1.4% Black, 0.7% Asian, 1.6% Other, 1.5% Hispanic of any race (2010); Density: 204.1 persons per square mile (2010); Average household size: 2.43 (2010); Median age: 39.0 (2010); Males per 100 females: 96.9 (2010).
Religion: Five largest groups: 11.0% Catholic Church, 5.8% The United Methodist Church, 5.2% Lutheran Church—Missouri Synod, 3.0% Southern Baptist Convention, 2.2% Christian Churches and Churches of Christ (2000).
Economy: Unemployment rate: 8.0% (August 2011); Total civilian labor force: 75,052 (August 2011); Leading industries: 17.4% manufacturing; 15.1% retail trade; 14.7% accommodation & food services (2009); Farms: 998 totaling 329,268 acres (2007); Companies that employ 500 or more persons: 6 (2009); Companies that employ 100 to 499 persons: 61 (2009); Companies that employ less than 100 persons: 2,769 (2009); Black-owned businesses: 94 (2007); Hispanic-owned businesses: n/a (2007); Asian-owned businesses: n/a (2007); Women-owned businesses: 2,761 (2007); Retail sales per capita: $17,106 (2010). Single-family building permits issued: 240 (2010); Multi-family building permits issued: 2 (2010).
Income: Per capita income: $27,099 (2010); Median household income: $55,331 (2010); Average household income: $66,402 (2010); Percent of households with income of $100,000 or more: 17.4% (2010); Poverty rate: 8.3% (2009); Bankruptcy rate: 5.97% (2010).
Taxes: Total county taxes per capita: $114 (2007); County property taxes per capita: $61 (2007).
Education: Percent of population age 25 and over with: High school diploma (including GED) or higher: 90.5% (2010); Bachelor's degree or higher: 24.0% (2010); Master's degree or higher: 6.5% (2010).
Housing: Homeownership rate: 78.1% (2010); Median home value: $124,211 (2010); Median contract rent: $484 per month (2005-2009 5-year est.); Median year structure built: 1965 (2005-2009 5-year est.)
Health: Birth rate: 132.3 per 10,000 population (2009); Death rate: 101.2 per 10,000 population (2009); Age-adjusted cancer mortality rate: 187.2 deaths per 100,000 population (2007); Number of physicians: 12.3 per 10,000 population (2008); Hospital beds: 14.3 per 10,000 population (2007); Hospital admissions: 413.3 per 10,000 population (2007).
Environment: Air Quality Index: 99.1% good, 0.9% moderate, 0.0% unhealthy for sensitive individuals, 0.0% unhealthy (percent of days in 2008)
Elections: 2008 Presidential election results: 46.0% Obama, 52.1% McCain, 0.8% Nader
National and State Parks: Fort Creve Coeur State Park
Additional Information Contacts

Tazewell County Government . . . . (309) 477-2272
    http://www.tazewell.com
City of East Peoria . . . . (309) 698-4715
    http://www.cityofeastpeoria.com
City of Pekin . . . . (309) 477-2300
    http://www.ci.pekin.il.us
City of Washington . . . . (309) 444-3196
    http://ci.washington.il.us
East Peoria Chamber of Commerce . . . . (309) 699-6212
    http://www.epcc.org
Morton Chamber of Commerce . . . . (309) 263-2491
    http://www.mortonchamber.org
Pekin Area Chamber of Commerce . . . . (309) 346-2106
    http://www.pekinchamber.com
Village of Morton . . . . (309) 266-5361
    http://www.morton-il.gov
Washington Chamber of Commerce . . . . (309) 444-9921
    http://www.washingtoncoc.com

Tazewell County Communities

ARMINGTON (village). Covers a land area of 0.287 square miles and a water area of 0 square miles. Located at 40.33° N. Lat; 89.31° W. Long. Elevation is 630 feet.
Population: 344 (1990); 368 (2000); 400 (2010); 418 (2015 projected); Race: 98.5% White, 0.5% Black, 0.3% Asian, 0.8% Other, 2.0% Hispanic of any race (2010); Density: 1,395.3 persons per square mile (2010); Average household size: 2.76 (2010); Median age: 38.0 (2010); Males per 100 females: 109.4 (2010); Marriage status: 23.1% never married, 51.6% now married, 14.3% widowed, 11.0% divorced (2005-2009 5-year est.); Foreign born: 0.4% (2005-2009 5-year est.); Ancestry (includes multiple ancestries): 34.5% German, 22.9% American, 9.7% Irish, 9.2% Dutch, 8.8% English (2005-2009 5-year est.).
Economy: Single-family building permits issued: 0 (2010); Multi-family building permits issued: 0 (2010); Employment by occupation: 8.6% management, 11.1% professional, 8.6% services, 23.7% sales, 5.1% farming, 10.6% construction, 32.3% production (2005-2009 5-year est.).
Income: Per capita income: $26,268 (2010); Median household income: $62,500 (2010); Average household income: $74,190 (2010); Percent of households with income of $100,000 or more: 21.4% (2010); Poverty rate: 23.0% (2005-2009 5-year est.).
Taxes: Total city taxes per capita: $150 (2007); City property taxes per capita: $79 (2007).
Education: Percent of population age 25 and over with: High school diploma (including GED) or higher: 93.8% (2010); Bachelor's degree or higher: 30.0% (2010); Master's degree or higher: 4.7% (2010).
Housing: Homeownership rate: 86.2% (2010); Median home value: $120,455 (2010); Median contract rent: $406 per month (2005-2009 5-year est.); Median year structure built: before 1940 (2005-2009 5-year est.).
Transportation: Commute to work: 96.3% car, 0.0% public transportation, 1.1% walk, 0.0% work from home (2005-2009 5-year est.); Travel time to work: 16.9% less than 15 minutes, 15.9% 15 to 30 minutes, 36.0% 30 to 45 minutes, 20.1% 45 to 60 minutes, 11.1% 60 minutes or more (2005-2009 5-year est.)

CREVE COEUR (village). Covers a land area of 4.059 square miles and a water area of 0.376 square miles. Located at 40.64° N. Lat; 89.59° W. Long. Elevation is 686 feet.
History: Incorporated 1921. Nearby is site of old Fort Creve Coeur, built 1680 by La Salle.
Population: 5,935 (1990); 5,448 (2000); 5,120 (2010); 4,959 (2015 projected); Race: 96.3% White, 0.4% Black, 0.1% Asian, 3.1% Other, 2.6% Hispanic of any race (2010); Density: 1,261.4 persons per square mile (2010); Average household size: 2.38 (2010); Median age: 37.8 (2010); Males per 100 females: 97.3 (2010); Marriage status: 29.1% never married, 51.4% now married, 3.4% widowed, 16.0% divorced (2005-2009 5-year est.); Foreign born: 2.5% (2005-2009 5-year est.); Ancestry (includes multiple ancestries): 29.0% German, 14.2% Irish, 13.8% American, 9.4% English, 5.0% Italian (2005-2009 5-year est.).
Economy: Single-family building permits issued: 0 (2010); Multi-family building permits issued: 0 (2010); Employment by occupation: 12.4% management, 7.3% professional, 13.4% services, 28.3% sales, 0.0% farming, 7.5% construction, 31.1% production (2005-2009 5-year est.).
Income: Per capita income: $19,261 (2010); Median household income: $41,043 (2010); Average household income: $45,930 (2010); Percent of households with income of $100,000 or more: 4.0% (2010); Poverty rate: 7.5% (2005-2009 5-year est.).
Taxes: Total city taxes per capita: $105 (2007); City property taxes per capita: $100 (2007).
Education: Percent of population age 25 and over with: High school diploma (including GED) or higher: 86.9% (2010); Bachelor's degree or higher: 7.4% (2010); Master's degree or higher: 2.0% (2010).

School District(s)
Creve Coeur SD 76 (PK-08)
    2009-10 Enrollment: 669 . . . . (309) 698-3600
Tazewell Roe (08-12)
    2009-10 Enrollment: n/a . . . . (309) 477-2290
Housing: Homeownership rate: 77.2% (2010); Median home value: $78,776 (2010); Median contract rent: $496 per month (2005-2009 5-year est.); Median year structure built: 1956 (2005-2009 5-year est.).
Transportation: Commute to work: 94.4% car, 0.9% public transportation, 1.6% walk, 1.4% work from home (2005-2009 5-year est.); Travel time to work: 29.2% less than 15 minutes, 57.8% 15 to 30 minutes, 9.5% 30 to 45

minutes, 1.6% 45 to 60 minutes, 2.0% 60 minutes or more (2005-2009 5-year est.)

DEER CREEK (village). Covers a land area of 0.314 square miles and a water area of 0 square miles. Located at 40.62° N. Lat; 89.33° W. Long. Elevation is 761 feet.

Population: 630 (1990); 605 (2000); 698 (2010); 741 (2015 projected); Race: 96.7% White, 0.4% Black, 0.9% Asian, 2.0% Other, 0.6% Hispanic of any race (2010); Density: 2,219.9 persons per square mile (2010); Average household size: 2.57 (2010); Median age: 37.7 (2010); Males per 100 females: 103.5 (2010); Marriage status: 14.9% never married, 68.5% now married, 6.1% widowed, 10.6% divorced (2005-2009 5-year est.); Foreign born: 1.6% (2005-2009 5-year est.); Ancestry (includes multiple ancestries): 44.8% German, 18.4% English, 11.6% Irish, 7.9% American, 5.6% Dutch (2005-2009 5-year est.).

Economy: Single-family building permits issued: 1 (2010); Multi-family building permits issued: 0 (2010); Employment by occupation: 11.7% management, 19.2% professional, 14.6% services, 23.5% sales, 1.7% farming, 4.9% construction, 24.4% production (2005-2009 5-year est.).

Income: Per capita income: $30,566 (2010); Median household income: $61,824 (2010); Average household income: $77,390 (2010); Percent of households with income of $100,000 or more: 20.2% (2010); Poverty rate: 3.3% (2005-2009 5-year est.).

Taxes: Total city taxes per capita: $473 (2007); City property taxes per capita: $408 (2007).

Education: Percent of population age 25 and over with: High school diploma (including GED) or higher: 94.3% (2010); Bachelor's degree or higher: 24.3% (2010); Master's degree or higher: 8.5% (2010).

School District(s)
Deer Creek-Mackinaw CUSD 701 (PK-12)
    2009-10 Enrollment: 1,139 . . . . (309) 359-8965

Housing: Homeownership rate: 85.3% (2010); Median home value: $140,500 (2010); Median contract rent: $574 per month (2005-2009 5-year est.); Median year structure built: 1958 (2005-2009 5-year est.).

Transportation: Commute to work: 93.1% car, 0.0% public transportation, 4.2% walk, 1.8% work from home (2005-2009 5-year est.); Travel time to work: 34.8% less than 15 minutes, 34.5% 15 to 30 minutes, 21.3% 30 to 45 minutes, 6.4% 45 to 60 minutes, 3.0% 60 minutes or more (2005-2009 5-year est.)

DELAVAN (city). Covers a land area of 0.711 square miles and a water area of 0 square miles. Located at 40.37° N. Lat; 89.54° W. Long. Elevation is 617 feet.

History: Founded 1837, incorporated 1888.

Population: 1,670 (1990); 1,825 (2000); 1,808 (2010); 1,794 (2015 projected); Race: 97.5% White, 0.8% Black, 0.2% Asian, 1.6% Other, 0.4% Hispanic of any race (2010); Density: 2,543.5 persons per square mile (2010); Average household size: 2.60 (2010); Median age: 36.2 (2010); Males per 100 females: 95.7 (2010); Marriage status: 22.7% never married, 60.1% now married, 6.2% widowed, 11.0% divorced (2005-2009 5-year est.); Foreign born: 0.2% (2005-2009 5-year est.); Ancestry (includes multiple ancestries): 40.9% German, 16.5% American, 15.8% Irish, 7.1% English, 3.1% Italian (2005-2009 5-year est.).

Economy: Single-family building permits issued: 1 (2010); Multi-family building permits issued: 0 (2010); Employment by occupation: 9.7% management, 14.6% professional, 18.5% services, 24.7% sales, 1.2% farming, 10.6% construction, 20.7% production (2005-2009 5-year est.).

Income: Per capita income: $24,242 (2010); Median household income: $50,161 (2010); Average household income: $62,816 (2010); Percent of households with income of $100,000 or more: 13.8% (2010); Poverty rate: 16.0% (2005-2009 5-year est.).

Taxes: Total city taxes per capita: $145 (2007); City property taxes per capita: $95 (2007).

Education: Percent of population age 25 and over with: High school diploma (including GED) or higher: 90.9% (2010); Bachelor's degree or higher: 21.2% (2010); Master's degree or higher: 5.3% (2010).

School District(s)
Delavan CUSD 703 (PK-12)
    2009-10 Enrollment: 482 . . . . (309) 244-8283

Housing: Homeownership rate: 80.3% (2010); Median home value: $100,429 (2010); Median contract rent: $360 per month (2005-2009 5-year est.); Median year structure built: 1954 (2005-2009 5-year est.).

Safety: Violent crime rate: 23.0 per 10,000 population; Property crime rate: 212.9 per 10,000 population (2010).

Newspapers: Delavan Times (National news; Circulation 1,400)

Transportation: Commute to work: 90.3% car, 0.0% public transportation, 5.4% walk, 3.2% work from home (2005-2009 5-year est.); Travel time to work: 25.9% less than 15 minutes, 33.4% 15 to 30 minutes, 24.9% 30 to 45 minutes, 12.9% 45 to 60 minutes, 2.9% 60 minutes or more (2005-2009 5-year est.)

EAST PEORIA (city). Covers a land area of 18.812 square miles and a water area of 2.215 square miles. Located at 40.66° N. Lat; 89.54° W. Long. Elevation is 463 feet.

History: East Peoria developed as an industrial and residential neighbor of Peoria. The Caterpillar Tractor Company plant was a major industry.

Population: 22,946 (1990); 22,638 (2000); 23,074 (2010); 23,158 (2015 projected); Race: 96.5% White, 0.6% Black, 0.9% Asian, 2.0% Other, 1.8% Hispanic of any race (2010); Density: 1,226.5 persons per square mile (2010); Average household size: 2.29 (2010); Median age: 41.3 (2010); Males per 100 females: 94.4 (2010); Marriage status: 23.7% never married, 57.5% now married, 8.5% widowed, 10.4% divorced (2005-2009 5-year est.); Foreign born: 2.1% (2005-2009 5-year est.); Ancestry (includes multiple ancestries): 30.3% German, 20.1% American, 13.4% Irish, 11.8% English, 3.5% French (2005-2009 5-year est.).

Economy: Single-family building permits issued: 33 (2010); Multi-family building permits issued: 0 (2010); Employment by occupation: 11.0% management, 20.1% professional, 19.6% services, 22.3% sales, 0.1% farming, 10.1% construction, 16.9% production (2005-2009 5-year est.).

Income: Per capita income: $25,574 (2010); Median household income: $50,162 (2010); Average household income: $58,978 (2010); Percent of households with income of $100,000 or more: 13.5% (2010); Poverty rate: 7.4% (2005-2009 5-year est.).

Taxes: Total city taxes per capita: $561 (2007); City property taxes per capita: $249 (2007).

Education: Percent of population age 25 and over with: High school diploma (including GED) or higher: 88.2% (2010); Bachelor's degree or higher: 20.2% (2010); Master's degree or higher: 4.6% (2010).

School District(s)
East Peoria CHSD 309 (09-12)
    2009-10 Enrollment: 1,215 . . . . (309) 694-8300
East Peoria SD 86 (PK-08)
    2009-10 Enrollment: 1,817 . . . . (309) 427-5100
Riverview CCSD 2 (PK-08)
    2009-10 Enrollment: 259 . . . . (309) 822-8550
Robein SD 85 (PK-08)
    2009-10 Enrollment: 200 . . . . (309) 694-1409
Tazewell Roe (08-12)
    2009-10 Enrollment: n/a . . . . (309) 477-2290

Two-year College(s)
Illinois Central College (Public)
    Fall 2009 Enrollment: 13,049. (309) 694-5422
    2010-11 Tuition: In-state $6,150; Out-of-state $6,150

Vocational/Technical School(s)
Oehrlein School of Cosmetology (Private, For-profit)
    Fall 2009 Enrollment: 81 . . . . (309) 699-1561
    2010-11 Tuition: $13,225

Housing: Homeownership rate: 76.3% (2010); Median home value: $122,395 (2010); Median contract rent: $446 per month (2005-2009 5-year est.); Median year structure built: 1962 (2005-2009 5-year est.).

Safety: Violent crime rate: 52.1 per 10,000 population; Property crime rate: 333.1 per 10,000 population (2010).

Transportation: Commute to work: 95.3% car, 0.4% public transportation, 1.8% walk, 1.8% work from home (2005-2009 5-year est.); Travel time to work: 34.6% less than 15 minutes, 49.8% 15 to 30 minutes, 10.0% 30 to 45 minutes, 2.2% 45 to 60 minutes, 3.4% 60 minutes or more (2005-2009 5-year est.)

Additional Information Contacts
City of East Peoria . . . . (309) 698-4715
    http://www.cityofeastpeoria.com
East Peoria Chamber of Commerce . . . . (309) 699-6212
    http://www.epcc.org

GREEN VALLEY (village). Covers a land area of 0.308 square miles and a water area of 0 square miles. Located at 40.40° N. Lat; 89.64° W. Long. Elevation is 538 feet.

Population: 770 (1990); 728 (2000); 685 (2010); 668 (2015 projected); Race: 99.0% White, 0.3% Black, 0.1% Asian, 0.6% Other, 0.7% Hispanic of any race (2010); Density: 2,221.1 persons per square mile (2010); Average household size: 2.67 (2010); Median age: 34.4 (2010); Males per

100 females: 86.1 (2010); Marriage status: 21.4% never married, 65.5% now married, 6.5% widowed, 6.5% divorced (2005-2009 5-year est.); Foreign born: 0.0% (2005-2009 5-year est.); Ancestry (includes multiple ancestries): 35.5% American, 32.8% German, 8.7% Irish, 8.1% Italian, 7.2% English (2005-2009 5-year est.).
Economy: Single-family building permits issued: 0 (2010); Multi-family building permits issued: 0 (2010); Employment by occupation: 16.1% management, 10.0% professional, 18.3% services, 21.5% sales, 0.0% farming, 11.8% construction, 22.2% production (2005-2009 5-year est.).
Income: Per capita income: $21,747 (2010); Median household income: $50,000 (2010); Average household income: $57,054 (2010); Percent of households with income of $100,000 or more: 12.7% (2010); Poverty rate: 10.2% (2005-2009 5-year est.).
Taxes: Total city taxes per capita: $49 (2007); City property taxes per capita: $45 (2007).
Education: Percent of population age 25 and over with: High school diploma (including GED) or higher: 89.0% (2010); Bachelor's degree or higher: 17.9% (2010); Master's degree or higher: 5.5% (2010).

School District(s)
Midwest Central CUSD 191 (PK-12)
    2009-10 Enrollment: 1,149 . . . . (309) 968-6868
Housing: Homeownership rate: 83.7% (2010); Median home value: $99,318 (2010); Median contract rent: $395 per month (2005-2009 5-year est.); Median year structure built: 1954 (2005-2009 5-year est.).
Transportation: Commute to work: 95.0% car, 0.0% public transportation, 0.0% walk, 5.0% work from home (2005-2009 5-year est.); Travel time to work: 22.3% less than 15 minutes, 36.6% 15 to 30 minutes, 29.4% 30 to 45 minutes, 11.7% 45 to 60 minutes, 0.0% 60 minutes or more (2005-2009 5-year est.)

GROVELAND (unincorporated postal area, zip code 61535). Covers a land area of 8.063 square miles and a water area of 0.077 square miles. Located at 40.60° N. Lat; 89.55° W. Long. Elevation is 771 feet.
Population: 1,398 (2000); Race: 97.9% White, 0.0% Black, 0.0% Asian, 2.1% Other, 0.0% Hispanic of any race (2000); Density: 173.4 persons per square mile (2000); Age: 29.1% under 18, 7.0% over 64 (2000); Marriage status: 16.9% never married, 74.7% now married, 4.4% widowed, 4.0% divorced (2000); Foreign born: 0.0% (2000); Ancestry (includes multiple ancestries): 45.9% German, 13.3% Irish, 12.8% English, 6.8% Italian, 4.5% American (2000).
Economy: Employment by occupation: 14.1% management, 38.7% professional, 10.1% services, 27.2% sales, 0.0% farming, 4.7% construction, 5.3% production (2000).
Income: Per capita income: $28,588 (2000); Median household income: $61,359 (2000); Poverty rate: 2.1% (2000).
Education: Percent of population age 25 and over with: High school diploma (including GED) or higher: 96.2% (2000); Bachelor's degree or higher: 32.3% (2000).
Housing: Homeownership rate: 92.5% (2000); Median home value: $141,100 (2000); Median contract rent: $478 per month (2000); Median year structure built: 1973 (2000).
Transportation: Commute to work: 95.6% car, 1.8% public transportation, 1.7% walk, 0.9% work from home (2000); Travel time to work: 29.1% less than 15 minutes, 54.2% 15 to 30 minutes, 8.5% 30 to 45 minutes, 5.8% 45 to 60 minutes, 2.4% 60 minutes or more (2000)

HOPEDALE (village). Covers a land area of 0.537 square miles and a water area of 0.004 square miles. Located at 40.42° N. Lat; 89.41° W. Long. Elevation is 643 feet.
Population: 814 (1990); 929 (2000); 967 (2010); 985 (2015 projected); Race: 99.3% White, 0.1% Black, 0.0% Asian, 0.6% Other, 0.4% Hispanic of any race (2010); Density: 1,800.5 persons per square mile (2010); Average household size: 2.69 (2010); Median age: 39.3 (2010); Males per 100 females: 96.5 (2010); Marriage status: 18.9% never married, 65.8% now married, 8.1% widowed, 7.2% divorced (2005-2009 5-year est.); Foreign born: 0.4% (2005-2009 5-year est.); Ancestry (includes multiple ancestries): 36.5% German, 18.8% American, 14.7% Irish, 8.8% English, 4.9% Welsh (2005-2009 5-year est.).
Economy: Single-family building permits issued: 1 (2010); Multi-family building permits issued: 0 (2010); Employment by occupation: 14.6% management, 24.9% professional, 12.3% services, 20.3% sales, 2.7% farming, 16.7% construction, 8.4% production (2005-2009 5-year est.).
Income: Per capita income: $26,726 (2010); Median household income: $61,473 (2010); Average household income: $74,145 (2010); Percent of

households with income of $100,000 or more: 20.6% (2010); Poverty rate: 3.9% (2005-2009 5-year est.).
Taxes: Total city taxes per capita: $236 (2007); City property taxes per capita: $149 (2007).
Education: Percent of population age 25 and over with: High school diploma (including GED) or higher: 91.2% (2010); Bachelor's degree or higher: 24.1% (2010); Master's degree or higher: 4.1% (2010).
Housing: Homeownership rate: 82.9% (2010); Median home value: $143,351 (2010); Median contract rent: $389 per month (2005-2009 5-year est.); Median year structure built: 1957 (2005-2009 5-year est.).
Hospitals: Hopedale Medical Complex
Transportation: Commute to work: 90.5% car, 0.0% public transportation, 5.0% walk, 2.5% work from home (2005-2009 5-year est.); Travel time to work: 32.6% less than 15 minutes, 28.8% 15 to 30 minutes, 30.8% 30 to 45 minutes, 6.9% 45 to 60 minutes, 0.8% 60 minutes or more (2005-2009 5-year est.)

MACKINAW (village). Covers a land area of 1.255 square miles and a water area of 0.030 square miles. Located at 40.53° N. Lat; 89.35° W. Long. Elevation is 682 feet.
Population: 1,345 (1990); 1,452 (2000); 1,397 (2010); 1,372 (2015 projected); Race: 96.1% White, 0.3% Black, 0.4% Asian, 3.3% Other, 1.9% Hispanic of any race (2010); Density: 1,113.4 persons per square mile (2010); Average household size: 2.52 (2010); Median age: 35.8 (2010); Males per 100 females: 98.4 (2010); Marriage status: 25.4% never married, 61.9% now married, 4.9% widowed, 7.8% divorced (2005-2009 5-year est.); Foreign born: 0.9% (2005-2009 5-year est.); Ancestry (includes multiple ancestries): 32.5% German, 16.4% American, 13.4% Scotch-Irish, 9.9% English, 9.9% Irish (2005-2009 5-year est.).
Economy: Single-family building permits issued: 2 (2010); Multi-family building permits issued: 2 (2010); Employment by occupation: 7.5% management, 18.4% professional, 16.2% services, 20.2% sales, 0.0% farming, 18.6% construction, 19.1% production (2005-2009 5-year est.).
Income: Per capita income: $25,381 (2010); Median household income: $53,417 (2010); Average household income: $63,192 (2010); Percent of households with income of $100,000 or more: 14.3% (2010); Poverty rate: 4.2% (2005-2009 5-year est.).
Taxes: Total city taxes per capita: $176 (2007); City property taxes per capita: $107 (2007).
Education: Percent of population age 25 and over with: High school diploma (including GED) or higher: 89.9% (2010); Bachelor's degree or higher: 19.5% (2010); Master's degree or higher: 3.2% (2010).
School District(s)
Deer Creek-Mackinaw CUSD 701 (PK-12)
    2009-10 Enrollment: 1,139 . . . . (309) 359-8965
Housing: Homeownership rate: 79.2% (2010); Median home value: $119,706 (2010); Median contract rent: $578 per month (2005-2009 5-year est.); Median year structure built: 1957 (2005-2009 5-year est.).
Transportation: Commute to work: 94.8% car, 0.0% public transportation, 0.8% walk, 3.5% work from home (2005-2009 5-year est.); Travel time to work: 23.5% less than 15 minutes, 41.7% 15 to 30 minutes, 20.6% 30 to 45 minutes, 10.7% 45 to 60 minutes, 3.6% 60 minutes or more (2005-2009 5-year est.)

MARQUETTE HEIGHTS (city). Covers a land area of 1.641 square miles and a water area of 0 square miles. Located at 40.61° N. Lat; 89.60° W. Long. Elevation is 620 feet.
Population: 3,080 (1990); 2,794 (2000); 2,858 (2010); 2,855 (2015 projected); Race: 97.8% White, 0.5% Black, 0.4% Asian, 1.4% Other, 1.5% Hispanic of any race (2010); Density: 1,741.7 persons per square mile (2010); Average household size: 2.73 (2010); Median age: 37.2 (2010); Males per 100 females: 99.0 (2010); Marriage status: 19.9% never married, 59.8% now married, 6.6% widowed, 13.7% divorced (2005-2009 5-year est.); Foreign born: 1.9% (2005-2009 5-year est.); Ancestry (includes multiple ancestries): 33.6% German, 13.4% Irish, 12.1% American, 11.9% English, 5.1% French (2005-2009 5-year est.).
Economy: Single-family building permits issued: 2 (2010); Multi-family building permits issued: 0 (2010); Employment by occupation: 7.8% management, 12.5% professional, 13.8% services, 31.3% sales, 0.0% farming, 10.9% construction, 23.6% production (2005-2009 5-year est.).
Income: Per capita income: $22,431 (2010); Median household income: $55,251 (2010); Average household income: $61,431 (2010); Percent of households with income of $100,000 or more: 11.4% (2010); Poverty rate: 5.7% (2005-2009 5-year est.).

Taxes: Total city taxes per capita: $212 (2007); City property taxes per capita: $118 (2007).

Education: Percent of population age 25 and over with: High school diploma (including GED) or higher: 91.0% (2010); Bachelor's degree or higher: 12.8% (2010); Master's degree or higher: 4.8% (2010).

School District(s)

N Pekin & Marquette Hght SD 102 (PK-08)

    2009-10 Enrollment: 688 . . . . (309) 382-2172

Housing: Homeownership rate: 91.1% (2010); Median home value: $99,439 (2010); Median contract rent: $583 per month (2005-2009 5-year est.); Median year structure built: 1961 (2005-2009 5-year est.).

Transportation: Commute to work: 97.5% car, 0.0% public transportation, 0.0% walk, 1.5% work from home (2005-2009 5-year est.); Travel time to work: 24.7% less than 15 minutes, 62.0% 15 to 30 minutes, 9.1% 30 to 45 minutes, 0.9% 45 to 60 minutes, 3.4% 60 minutes or more (2005-2009 5-year est.)

MINIER (village). Covers a land area of 0.625 square miles and a water area of 0 square miles. Located at 40.43° N. Lat; 89.31° W. Long. Elevation is 636 feet.

Population: 1,179 (1990); 1,244 (2000); 1,302 (2010); 1,331 (2015 projected); Race: 98.5% White, 0.3% Black, 0.2% Asian, 0.9% Other, 1.8% Hispanic of any race (2010); Density: 2,084.0 persons per square mile (2010); Average household size: 2.47 (2010); Median age: 39.1 (2010); Males per 100 females: 95.5 (2010); Marriage status: 23.6% never married, 53.8% now married, 8.4% widowed, 14.2% divorced (2005-2009 5-year est.); Foreign born: 2.0% (2005-2009 5-year est.); Ancestry (includes multiple ancestries): 33.7% German, 22.9% Irish, 18.4% American, 12.5% English, 5.1% Scottish (2005-2009 5-year est.).

Economy: Single-family building permits issued: 1 (2010); Multi-family building permits issued: 0 (2010); Employment by occupation: 11.5% management, 13.9% professional, 21.9% services, 22.9% sales, 0.0% farming, 11.4% construction, 18.5% production (2005-2009 5-year est.).

Income: Per capita income: $24,568 (2010); Median household income: $52,788 (2010); Average household income: $59,867 (2010); Percent of households with income of $100,000 or more: 12.0% (2010); Poverty rate: 5.7% (2005-2009 5-year est.).

Taxes: Total city taxes per capita: $232 (2007); City property taxes per capita: $145 (2007).

Education: Percent of population age 25 and over with: High school diploma (including GED) or higher: 88.9% (2010); Bachelor's degree or higher: 18.8% (2010); Master's degree or higher: 2.4% (2010).

School District(s)

Olympia CUSD 16 (PK-12)

    2009-10 Enrollment: 1,911 . . . . (309) 379-6011

Housing: Homeownership rate: 78.7% (2010); Median home value: $121,089 (2010); Median contract rent: $422 per month (2005-2009 5-year est.); Median year structure built: 1957 (2005-2009 5-year est.).

Newspapers: Olympia Review (Local news; Circulation 7,000)

Transportation: Commute to work: 91.6% car, 1.1% public transportation, 4.4% walk, 1.9% work from home (2005-2009 5-year est.); Travel time to work: 27.5% less than 15 minutes, 17.9% 15 to 30 minutes, 47.0% 30 to 45 minutes, 5.4% 45 to 60 minutes, 2.1% 60 minutes or more (2005-2009 5-year est.)

MORTON (village). Covers a land area of 12.182 square miles and a water area of 0.044 square miles. Located at 40.61° N. Lat; 89.46° W. Long. Elevation is 715 feet.

History: Incorporated 1877.

Population: 14,148 (1990); 15,198 (2000); 15,901 (2010); 16,176 (2015 projected); Race: 96.7% White, 0.2% Black, 1.9% Asian, 1.2% Other, 1.2% Hispanic of any race (2010); Density: 1,305.3 persons per square mile (2010); Average household size: 2.41 (2010); Median age: 41.0 (2010); Males per 100 females: 94.0 (2010); Marriage status: 19.5% never married, 63.6% now married, 8.0% widowed, 8.9% divorced (2005-2009 5-year est.); Foreign born: 2.0% (2005-2009 5-year est.); Ancestry (includes multiple ancestries): 43.7% German, 15.7% English, 12.5% Irish, 9.5% American, 4.4% Italian (2005-2009 5-year est.).

Economy: Single-family building permits issued: 40 (2010); Multi-family building permits issued: 0 (2010); Employment by occupation: 19.7% management, 28.1% professional, 11.5% services, 24.8% sales, 0.2% farming, 6.7% construction, 9.1% production (2005-2009 5-year est.).

Income: Per capita income: $32,405 (2010); Median household income: $65,528 (2010); Average household income: $79,689 (2010); Percent of

households with income of $100,000 or more: 25.3% (2010); Poverty rate: 6.5% (2005-2009 5-year est.).

Taxes: Total city taxes per capita: $157 (2007); City property taxes per capita: $84 (2007).

Education: Percent of population age 25 and over with: High school diploma (including GED) or higher: 94.7% (2010); Bachelor's degree or higher: 41.1% (2010); Master's degree or higher: 11.2% (2010).

School District(s)

Morton CUSD 709 (PK-12)

    2009-10 Enrollment: 2,784 . . . . (309) 263-2581

Housing: Homeownership rate: 79.4% (2010); Median home value: $167,138 (2010); Median contract rent: $623 per month (2005-2009 5-year est.); Median year structure built: 1973 (2005-2009 5-year est.).

Safety: Violent crime rate: 5.0 per 10,000 population; Property crime rate: 104.3 per 10,000 population (2010).

Newspapers: Morton Courier (Community news; Circulation 8,700)

Transportation: Commute to work: 94.7% car, 0.1% public transportation, 2.1% walk, 2.4% work from home (2005-2009 5-year est.); Travel time to work: 38.3% less than 15 minutes, 45.3% 15 to 30 minutes, 10.4% 30 to 45 minutes, 3.6% 45 to 60 minutes, 2.4% 60 minutes or more (2005-2009 5-year est.)

Additional Information Contacts

Morton Chamber of Commerce . . . . (309) 263-2491
    http://www.mortonchamber.org

Village of Morton . . . . (309) 266-5361
    http://www.morton-il.gov

NORTH PEKIN (village). Covers a land area of 1.157 square miles and a water area of 0.028 square miles. Located at 40.61° N. Lat; 89.62° W. Long. Elevation is 482 feet.

Population: 1,582 (1990); 1,574 (2000); 1,440 (2010); 1,395 (2015 projected); Race: 96.7% White, 0.1% Black, 0.8% Asian, 2.3% Other, 0.5% Hispanic of any race (2010); Density: 1,244.1 persons per square mile (2010); Average household size: 2.57 (2010); Median age: 37.3 (2010); Males per 100 females: 101.7 (2010); Marriage status: 20.4% never married, 61.9% now married, 8.6% widowed, 9.1% divorced (2005-2009 5-year est.); Foreign born: 0.3% (2005-2009 5-year est.); Ancestry (includes multiple ancestries): 29.7% German, 19.9% American, 12.1% Irish, 7.6% English, 3.8% Dutch (2005-2009 5-year est.).

Economy: Single-family building permits issued: 7 (2010); Multi-family building permits issued: 0 (2010); Employment by occupation: 10.3% management, 16.0% professional, 18.6% services, 22.3% sales, 0.2% farming, 9.3% construction, 23.3% production (2005-2009 5-year est.).

Income: Per capita income: $21,520 (2010); Median household income: $49,481 (2010); Average household income: $54,684 (2010); Percent of households with income of $100,000 or more: 9.1% (2010); Poverty rate: 7.3% (2005-2009 5-year est.).

Taxes: Total city taxes per capita: $149 (2007); City property taxes per capita: $127 (2007).

Education: Percent of population age 25 and over with: High school diploma (including GED) or higher: 90.2% (2010); Bachelor's degree or higher: 7.1% (2010); Master's degree or higher: 1.4% (2010).

School District(s)

N Pekin & Marquette Hght SD 102 (PK-08)

    2009-10 Enrollment: 688 . . . . (309) 382-2172

Housing: Homeownership rate: 87.2% (2010); Median home value: $88,333 (2010); Median contract rent: $527 per month (2005-2009 5-year est.); Median year structure built: 1958 (2005-2009 5-year est.).

Transportation: Commute to work: 97.0% car, 0.0% public transportation, 1.3% walk, 1.4% work from home (2005-2009 5-year est.); Travel time to work: 36.7% less than 15 minutes, 49.1% 15 to 30 minutes, 8.2% 30 to 45 minutes, 1.3% 45 to 60 minutes, 4.6% 60 minutes or more (2005-2009 5-year est.)

PEKIN (city). County seat. Covers a land area of 13.150 square miles and a water area of 0.596 square miles. Located at 40.56° N. Lat; 89.63° W. Long. Elevation is 502 feet.

History: Pekin was settled by pioneers of English descent who came from Virginia, Kentucky, and Tennessee. Abraham Lincoln argued many of his legal cases in the courthouse at Pekin. Incorporated 1948.

Population: 33,227 (1990); 33,857 (2000); 34,017 (2010); 33,988 (2015 projected); Race: 95.4% White, 2.6% Black, 0.5% Asian, 1.5% Other, 1.8% Hispanic of any race (2010); Density: 2,586.9 persons per square mile (2010); Average household size: 2.33 (2010); Median age: 37.7 (2010); Males per 100 females: 95.8 (2010); Marriage status: 25.9% never married,

51.0% now married, 8.2% widowed, 14.8% divorced (2005-2009 5-year est.); Foreign born: 1.4% (2005-2009 5-year est.); Ancestry (includes multiple ancestries): 32.9% German, 18.7% American, 13.4% Irish, 10.7% English, 5.2% Italian (2005-2009 5-year est.).

Economy: Unemployment rate: 9.9% (August 2011); Total civilian labor force: 18,162 (August 2011); Single-family building permits issued: 30 (2010); Multi-family building permits issued: 0 (2010); Employment by occupation: 10.5% management, 16.9% professional, 21.0% services, 25.4% sales, 0.4% farming, 7.3% construction, 18.5% production (2005-2009 5-year est.).

Income: Per capita income: $24,168 (2010); Median household income: $45,803 (2010); Average household income: $56,832 (2010); Percent of households with income of $100,000 or more: 12.4% (2010); Poverty rate: 12.8% (2005-2009 5-year est.).

Taxes: Total city taxes per capita: $326 (2007); City property taxes per capita: $167 (2007).

Education: Percent of population age 25 and over with: High school diploma (including GED) or higher: 87.9% (2010); Bachelor's degree or higher: 17.8% (2010); Master's degree or higher: 5.8% (2010).

School District(s)

Pekin CSD 303 (09-12)
    2009-10 Enrollment: 2,109 . . . . (309) 477-4222
Pekin Psd 108 (PK-08)
    2009-10 Enrollment: 3,695 . . . . (309) 477-4700
Rankin CSD 98 (KG-08)
    2009-10 Enrollment: 207 . . . . (309) 346-3182
Tazewell Co Area Efe Rds
    2009-10 Enrollment: n/a . . . . (309) 353-5011
Tazewell-Mason Cntys Sp Ed Assoc (PK-12)
    2009-10 Enrollment: n/a . . . . (309) 347-5164

Housing: Homeownership rate: 70.3% (2010); Median home value: $98,481 (2010); Median contract rent: $430 per month (2005-2009 5-year est.); Median year structure built: 1960 (2005-2009 5-year est.).

Hospitals: Pekin Hospital (125 beds)

Safety: Violent crime rate: 34.9 per 10,000 population; Property crime rate: 253.9 per 10,000 population (2010).

Newspapers: Pekin Daily Times (Local news; Circulation 9,000)

Transportation: Commute to work: 93.5% car, 0.2% public transportation, 3.2% walk, 1.9% work from home (2005-2009 5-year est.); Travel time to work: 40.6% less than 15 minutes, 39.5% 15 to 30 minutes, 14.2% 30 to 45 minutes, 3.3% 45 to 60 minutes, 2.4% 60 minutes or more (2005-2009 5-year est.)

Additional Information Contacts

City of Pekin. . . . . (309) 477-2300
    http://www.ci.pekin.il.us
Pekin Area Chamber of Commerce . . . . (309) 346-2106
    http://www.pekinchamber.com

SOUTH PEKIN (village). Covers a land area of 0.429 square miles and a water area of 0 square miles. Located at 40.49° N. Lat; 89.65° W. Long. Elevation is 515 feet.

History: Incorporated 1917.

Population: 1,185 (1990); 1,162 (2000); 922 (2010); 837 (2015 projected); Race: 99.3% White, 0.2% Black, 0.1% Asian, 0.3% Other, 2.3% Hispanic of any race (2010); Density: 2,148.9 persons per square mile (2010); Average household size: 2.69 (2010); Median age: 32.8 (2010); Males per 100 females: 96.2 (2010); Marriage status: 26.0% never married, 55.2% now married, 5.8% widowed, 13.0% divorced (2005-2009 5-year est.); Foreign born: 1.1% (2005-2009 5-year est.); Ancestry (includes multiple ancestries): 28.9% American, 27.8% German, 11.7% Irish, 5.4% English, 4.4% Polish (2005-2009 5-year est.).

Economy: Single-family building permits issued: 1 (2010); Multi-family building permits issued: 0 (2010); Employment by occupation: 4.9% management, 14.9% professional, 18.5% services, 30.3% sales, 0.0% farming, 14.3% construction, 17.1% production (2005-2009 5-year est.).

Income: Per capita income: $20,706 (2010); Median household income: $52,140 (2010); Average household income: $55,689 (2010); Percent of households with income of $100,000 or more: 7.9% (2010); Poverty rate: 14.4% (2005-2009 5-year est.).

Taxes: Total city taxes per capita: $152 (2007); City property taxes per capita: $96 (2007).

Education: Percent of population age 25 and over with: High school diploma (including GED) or higher: 82.7% (2010); Bachelor's degree or higher: 4.1% (2010); Master's degree or higher: 0.7% (2010).

School District(s)

South Pekin SD 137 (PK-08)
    2009-10 Enrollment: 240 . . . . (309) 348-3695

Housing: Homeownership rate: 81.2% (2010); Median home value: $76,835 (2010); Median contract rent: $439 per month (2005-2009 5-year est.); Median year structure built: 1964 (2005-2009 5-year est.).

Safety: Violent crime rate: 67.2 per 10,000 population; Property crime rate: 151.1 per 10,000 population (2010).

Transportation: Commute to work: 98.0% car, 0.0% public transportation, 2.0% walk, 0.0% work from home (2005-2009 5-year est.); Travel time to work: 29.0% less than 15 minutes, 31.3% 15 to 30 minutes, 30.3% 30 to 45 minutes, 5.3% 45 to 60 minutes, 4.1% 60 minutes or more (2005-2009 5-year est.)

TREMONT (village). Covers a land area of 0.953 square miles and a water area of 0 square miles. Located at 40.52° N. Lat; 89.49° W. Long. Elevation is 643 feet.

Population: 2,088 (1990); 2,029 (2000); 2,013 (2010); 2,015 (2015 projected); Race: 99.3% White, 0.2% Black, 0.2% Asian, 0.3% Other, 1.5% Hispanic of any race (2010); Density: 2,112.0 persons per square mile (2010); Average household size: 2.60 (2010); Median age: 36.5 (2010); Males per 100 females: 97.2 (2010); Marriage status: 19.6% never married, 67.1% now married, 8.1% widowed, 5.2% divorced (2005-2009 5-year est.); Foreign born: 1.1% (2005-2009 5-year est.); Ancestry (includes multiple ancestries): 45.1% German, 16.8% American, 14.6% English, 7.2% Irish, 5.1% French (2005-2009 5-year est.).

Economy: Single-family building permits issued: 1 (2010); Multi-family building permits issued: 0 (2010); Employment by occupation: 17.1% management, 27.8% professional, 14.0% services, 21.4% sales, 0.0% farming, 5.8% construction, 13.9% production (2005-2009 5-year est.).

Income: Per capita income: $29,740 (2010); Median household income: $68,121 (2010); Average household income: $77,410 (2010); Percent of households with income of $100,000 or more: 24.6% (2010); Poverty rate: 1.2% (2005-2009 5-year est.).

Taxes: Total city taxes per capita: $120 (2007); City property taxes per capita: $104 (2007).

Education: Percent of population age 25 and over with: High school diploma (including GED) or higher: 95.0% (2010); Bachelor's degree or higher: 29.0% (2010); Master's degree or higher: 7.2% (2010).

School District(s)

Tremont CUSD 702 (PK-12)
    2009-10 Enrollment: 1,012 . . . . (309) 925-3461

Housing: Homeownership rate: 79.7% (2010); Median home value: $141,886 (2010); Median contract rent: $624 per month (2005-2009 5-year est.); Median year structure built: 1967 (2005-2009 5-year est.).

Transportation: Commute to work: 89.7% car, 0.0% public transportation, 5.0% walk, 3.6% work from home (2005-2009 5-year est.); Travel time to work: 46.7% less than 15 minutes, 29.9% 15 to 30 minutes, 19.4% 30 to 45 minutes, 3.2% 45 to 60 minutes, 0.8% 60 minutes or more (2005-2009 5-year est.)

WASHINGTON (city). Covers a land area of 7.476 square miles and a water area of 0.012 square miles. Located at 40.70° N. Lat; 89.42° W. Long. Elevation is 761 feet.

History: Incorporated 1857.

Population: 10,778 (1990); 10,841 (2000); 12,281 (2010); 12,865 (2015 projected); Race: 97.9% White, 0.3% Black, 0.5% Asian, 1.3% Other, 1.0% Hispanic of any race (2010); Density: 1,642.7 persons per square mile (2010); Average household size: 2.49 (2010); Median age: 38.4 (2010); Males per 100 females: 95.7 (2010); Marriage status: 20.1% never married, 64.3% now married, 5.9% widowed, 9.7% divorced (2005-2009 5-year est.); Foreign born: 1.8% (2005-2009 5-year est.); Ancestry (includes multiple ancestries): 35.3% German, 16.4% Irish, 15.0% English, 12.8% American, 4.5% Italian (2005-2009 5-year est.).

Economy: Single-family building permits issued: 82 (2010); Multi-family building permits issued: 0 (2010); Employment by occupation: 14.0% management, 24.2% professional, 14.9% services, 24.1% sales, 0.8% farming, 10.0% construction, 12.0% production (2005-2009 5-year est.).

Income: Per capita income: $29,795 (2010); Median household income: $63,111 (2010); Average household income: $74,407 (2010); Percent of households with income of $100,000 or more: 21.4% (2010); Poverty rate: 6.1% (2005-2009 5-year est.).

Taxes: Total city taxes per capita: $258 (2007); City property taxes per capita: $91 (2007).

Education: Percent of population age 25 and over with: High school diploma (including GED) or higher: 94.4% (2010); Bachelor's degree or higher: 35.1% (2010); Master's degree or higher: 9.6% (2010).

School District(s)

Central SD 51 (PK-08)
  2009-10 Enrollment: 1,029 . . . . (309) 444-3943
District 50 Schools (PK-08)
  2009-10 Enrollment: 798 . . . . (309) 745-8914
Washington CHSD 308 (09-12)
  2009-10 Enrollment: 1,210 . . . . (309) 444-7704
Washington SD 52 (PK-08)
  2009-10 Enrollment: 830 . . . . (309) 444-4182

Housing: Homeownership rate: 80.6% (2010); Median home value: $137,637 (2010); Median contract rent: $552 per month (2005-2009 5-year est.); Median year structure built: 1970 (2005-2009 5-year est.).

Newspapers: Washington Courier (Community news); Woodford Courier (Community news)

Transportation: Commute to work: 96.8% car, 0.1% public transportation, 1.2% walk, 1.9% work from home (2005-2009 5-year est.); Travel time to work: 25.3% less than 15 minutes, 50.2% 15 to 30 minutes, 16.9% 30 to 45 minutes, 3.9% 45 to 60 minutes, 3.7% 60 minutes or more (2005-2009 5-year est.)

Additional Information Contacts

City of Washington. . . . . (309) 444-3196
  http://ci.washington.il.us
Washington Chamber of Commerce . . . . (309) 444-9921
  http://www.washingtoncoc.com

Union County

Located in southern Illinois; bounded on the west by the Mississippi River and the Missouri border; drained by the Cache River; includes part of Shawnee National Forest. Covers a land area of 416.16 square miles, a water area of 5.97 square miles, and is located in the Central Time Zone at 37.46° N. Lat., 89.24° W. Long. The county was founded in 1818. County seat is Jonesboro.

Weather Station: Anna 2 NNE									Elevation: 600 feet		
	Jan	Feb	Mar	Apr	May	Jun	Jul	Aug	Sep	Oct	Nov	Dec
High	43	48	58	69	77	85	89	89	81	70	58	46
Low	25	28	36	45	55	63	67	66	57	46	37	28
Precip	3.7	3.5	4.6	4.5	5.9	4.4	3.4	3.2	3.3	4.3	4.8	4.5
Snow	3.4	3.9	1.1	0.1	0.0	0.0	0.0	0.0	0.0	0.1	0.3	2.6

High and Low temperatures in degrees Fahrenheit; Precipitation and Snow in inches

Population: 17,619 (1990); 18,293 (2000); 18,202 (2010); 18,066 (2015 projected); Race: 94.9% White, 1.1% Black, 0.4% Asian, 3.6% Other, 4.0% Hispanic of any race (2010); Density: 43.7 persons per square mile (2010); Average household size: 2.36 (2010); Median age: 40.7 (2010); Males per 100 females: 94.9 (2010).

Religion: Five largest groups: 43.8% Southern Baptist Convention, 7.7% Catholic Church, 5.1% Evangelical Lutheran Church in America, 2.0% Christian Churches and Churches of Christ, 2.0% The United Methodist Church (2000).

Economy: Unemployment rate: 11.1% (August 2011); Total civilian labor force: 8,239 (August 2011); Leading industries: 36.5% health care and social assistance; 19.2% retail trade; 10.3% manufacturing (2009); Farms: 620 totaling 122,362 acres (2007); Companies that employ 500 or more persons: 0 (2009); Companies that employ 100 to 499 persons: 6 (2009); Companies that employ less than 100 persons: 353 (2009); Black-owned businesses: n/a (2007); Hispanic-owned businesses: 71 (2007); Asian-owned businesses: n/a (2007); Women-owned businesses: n/a (2007); Retail sales per capita: $9,565 (2010). Single-family building permits issued: 27 (2010); Multi-family building permits issued: 0 (2010).

Income: Per capita income: $20,082 (2010); Median household income: $37,892 (2010); Average household income: $48,175 (2010); Percent of households with income of $100,000 or more: 9.0% (2010); Poverty rate: 20.0% (2009); Bankruptcy rate: 5.60% (2010).

Taxes: Total county taxes per capita: $127 (2007); County property taxes per capita: $126 (2007).

Education: Percent of population age 25 and over with: High school diploma (including GED) or higher: 80.9% (2010); Bachelor's degree or higher: 19.6% (2010); Master's degree or higher: 7.7% (2010).

Housing: Homeownership rate: 74.1% (2010); Median home value: $84,696 (2010); Median contract rent: $299 per month (2005-2009 5-year est.); Median year structure built: 1968 (2005-2009 5-year est.)

Health: Birth rate: 133.9 per 10,000 population (2009); Death rate: 127.2 per 10,000 population (2009); Age-adjusted cancer mortality rate: 193.1 deaths per 100,000 population (2007); Number of physicians: 11.6 per 10,000 population (2008); Hospital beds: 69.5 per 10,000 population (2007); Hospital admissions: 942.4 per 10,000 population (2007).

Elections: 2008 Presidential election results: 43.0% Obama, 54.9% McCain, 0.8% Nader

National and State Parks: Larue-Pine Hills National Natural Landmark; Trail of Tears State Forest; Union County State Conservation Area; Union County State Forest

Additional Information Contacts

Union County Government . . . . (618) 833-5711
  http://blog.unioncountyil.gov
City of Anna . . . . (618) 833-8528
  http://www.cityofanna.org

Union County Communities

ALTO PASS (village). Covers a land area of 2.150 square miles and a water area of 0.025 square miles. Located at 37.57° N. Lat; 89.31° W. Long. Elevation is 748 feet.

Population: 417 (1990); 388 (2000); 404 (2010); 408 (2015 projected); Race: 94.6% White, 0.2% Black, 0.0% Asian, 5.2% Other, 7.7% Hispanic of any race (2010); Density: 187.9 persons per square mile (2010); Average household size: 2.44 (2010); Median age: 41.1 (2010); Males per 100 females: 99.0 (2010); Marriage status: 21.3% never married, 54.2% now married, 10.5% widowed, 14.0% divorced (2005-2009 5-year est.); Foreign born: 11.7% (2005-2009 5-year est.); Ancestry (includes multiple ancestries): 17.2% Irish, 16.0% English, 11.2% German, 6.9% American, 3.4% British (2005-2009 5-year est.).

Economy: Employment by occupation: 7.6% management, 22.0% professional, 17.4% services, 12.9% sales, 2.3% farming, 15.9% construction, 22.0% production (2005-2009 5-year est.).

Income: Per capita income: $22,077 (2010); Median household income: $44,792 (2010); Average household income: $54,879 (2010); Percent of households with income of $100,000 or more: 10.9% (2010); Poverty rate: 32.1% (2005-2009 5-year est.).

Taxes: Total city taxes per capita: $59 (2007); City property taxes per capita: $31 (2007).

Education: Percent of population age 25 and over with: High school diploma (including GED) or higher: 87.2% (2010); Bachelor's degree or higher: 30.4% (2010); Master's degree or higher: 11.4% (2010).

Housing: Homeownership rate: 84.2% (2010); Median home value: $86,429 (2010); Median contract rent: n/a per month (2005-2009 5-year est.); Median year structure built: 1967 (2005-2009 5-year est.).

Transportation: Commute to work: 91.7% car, 0.0% public transportation, 1.5% walk, 6.8% work from home (2005-2009 5-year est.); Travel time to work: 26.8% less than 15 minutes, 30.1% 15 to 30 minutes, 22.8% 30 to 45 minutes, 4.9% 45 to 60 minutes, 15.4% 60 minutes or more (2005-2009 5-year est.)

ANNA (city). Covers a land area of 3.380 square miles and a water area of 0.009 square miles. Located at 37.46° N. Lat; 89.24° W. Long. Elevation is 630 feet.

History: Incorporated 1865.

Population: 4,854 (1990); 5,136 (2000); 4,543 (2010); 4,275 (2015 projected); Race: 95.0% White, 2.4% Black, 0.2% Asian, 2.3% Other, 1.9% Hispanic of any race (2010); Density: 1,343.9 persons per square mile (2010); Average household size: 2.09 (2010); Median age: 43.4 (2010); Males per 100 females: 89.4 (2010); Marriage status: 29.7% never married, 44.8% now married, 8.8% widowed, 16.7% divorced (2005-2009 5-year est.); Foreign born: 1.3% (2005-2009 5-year est.); Ancestry (includes multiple ancestries): 23.4% German, 11.9% Irish, 9.5% American, 7.6% English, 2.1% Italian (2005-2009 5-year est.).

Economy: Single-family building permits issued: 4 (2010); Multi-family building permits issued: 0 (2010); Employment by occupation: 10.9% management, 18.1% professional, 20.5% services, 20.3% sales, 0.0% farming, 10.2% construction, 20.0% production (2005-2009 5-year est.).

Income: Per capita income: $18,479 (2010); Median household income: $29,261 (2010); Average household income: $39,917 (2010); Percent of households with income of $100,000 or more: 6.7% (2010); Poverty rate: 26.8% (2005-2009 5-year est.).

Taxes: Total city taxes per capita: $59 (2007); City property taxes per capita: $50 (2007).

Education: Percent of population age 25 and over with: High school diploma (including GED) or higher: 74.4% (2010); Bachelor's degree or higher: 19.1% (2010); Master's degree or higher: 10.1% (2010).

School District(s)

Anna CCSD 37 (KG-08)
  2009-10 Enrollment: 649 . . . . (618) 833-6812
Anna Jonesboro CHSD 81 (09-12)
  2009-10 Enrollment: 542 . . . . (618) 833-8421
Five County Reg Voc System
  2009-10 Enrollment: n/a . . . . (618) 747-2703
Tri-County Sp Ed Jnt Agreement (PK-12)
  2009-10 Enrollment: n/a . . . . (618) 684-2109

Housing: Homeownership rate: 56.6% (2010); Median home value: $76,486 (2010); Median contract rent: $277 per month (2005-2009 5-year est.); Median year structure built: 1961 (2005-2009 5-year est.).
Hospitals: Union County Hospital District (58 beds)
Newspapers: Gazette-Democrat (Local news; Circulation 4,400); Monday's Pub (Community news; Circulation 19,500)
Transportation: Commute to work: 91.5% car, 0.0% public transportation, 4.6% walk, 1.2% work from home (2005-2009 5-year est.); Travel time to work: 59.7% less than 15 minutes, 9.0% 15 to 30 minutes, 20.6% 30 to 45 minutes, 8.0% 45 to 60 minutes, 2.7% 60 minutes or more (2005-2009 5-year est.)

Additional Information Contacts
City of Anna . . . . (618) 833-8528
  http://www.cityofanna.org

COBDEN (village). Covers a land area of 1.228 square miles and a water area of 0 square miles. Located at 37.53° N. Lat; 89.25° W. Long. Elevation is 587 feet.

History: Cobden was named for an English director of the railroad. The town grew as a fruit shipping station on the Illinois Central Railroad.
Population: 1,092 (1990); 1,116 (2000); 1,111 (2010); 1,098 (2015 projected); Race: 87.6% White, 1.2% Black, 0.2% Asian, 11.1% Other, 18.6% Hispanic of any race (2010); Density: 904.6 persons per square mile (2010); Average household size: 2.40 (2010); Median age: 39.9 (2010); Males per 100 females: 90.6 (2010); Marriage status: 28.8% never married, 40.5% now married, 15.3% widowed, 15.4% divorced (2005-2009 5-year est.); Foreign born: 12.3% (2005-2009 5-year est.); Ancestry (includes multiple ancestries): 17.7% German, 12.0% Irish, 9.5% English, 3.9% American, 2.3% Scotch-Irish (2005-2009 5-year est.).
Economy: Single-family building permits issued: 0 (2010); Multi-family building permits issued: 0 (2010); Employment by occupation: 5.2% management, 29.0% professional, 11.0% services, 30.3% sales, 5.4% farming, 6.6% construction, 12.4% production (2005-2009 5-year est.).
Income: Per capita income: $16,456 (2010); Median household income: $31,351 (2010); Average household income: $39,780 (2010); Percent of households with income of $100,000 or more: 5.8% (2010); Poverty rate: 30.3% (2005-2009 5-year est.).
Taxes: Total city taxes per capita: $64 (2007); City property taxes per capita: $35 (2007).
Education: Percent of population age 25 and over with: High school diploma (including GED) or higher: 73.3% (2010); Bachelor's degree or higher: 21.0% (2010); Master's degree or higher: 6.5% (2010).

School District(s)

Cobden Sud 17 (KG-12)
  2009-10 Enrollment: 579 . . . . (618) 893-2313
Five County Reg Voc System
  2009-10 Enrollment: n/a . . . . (618) 747-2703

Housing: Homeownership rate: 75.2% (2010); Median home value: $71,404 (2010); Median contract rent: $204 per month (2005-2009 5-year est.); Median year structure built: 1948 (2005-2009 5-year est.).
Safety: Violent crime rate: 9.3 per 10,000 population; Property crime rate: 65.4 per 10,000 population (2010).
Transportation: Commute to work: 95.0% car, 0.0% public transportation, 0.0% walk, 3.7% work from home (2005-2009 5-year est.); Travel time to work: 19.1% less than 15 minutes, 30.6% 15 to 30 minutes, 34.6% 30 to 45 minutes, 5.2% 45 to 60 minutes, 10.6% 60 minutes or more (2005-2009 5-year est.)

DONGOLA (village). Covers a land area of 1.106 square miles and a water area of 0.030 square miles. Located at 37.36° N. Lat; 89.16° W. Long. Elevation is 394 feet.

Population: 728 (1990); 806 (2000); 780 (2010); 762 (2015 projected); Race: 95.1% White, 0.1% Black, 0.5% Asian, 4.2% Other, 0.3% Hispanic

of any race (2010); Density: 705.3 persons per square mile (2010); Average household size: 2.39 (2010); Median age: 35.2 (2010); Males per 100 females: 93.5 (2010); Marriage status: 24.2% never married, 53.6% now married, 10.5% widowed, 11.7% divorced (2005-2009 5-year est.); Foreign born: 1.9% (2005-2009 5-year est.); Ancestry (includes multiple ancestries): 20.7% Irish, 14.7% German, 10.8% American, 5.8% Dutch, 4.5% English (2005-2009 5-year est.).
Economy: Employment by occupation: 6.9% management, 21.2% professional, 17.5% services, 24.0% sales, 2.3% farming, 10.6% construction, 17.5% production (2005-2009 5-year est.).
Income: Per capita income: $15,848 (2010); Median household income: $32,188 (2010); Average household income: $38,357 (2010); Percent of households with income of $100,000 or more: 5.0% (2010); Poverty rate: 33.3% (2005-2009 5-year est.).
Taxes: Total city taxes per capita: $46 (2007); City property taxes per capita: $46 (2007).
Education: Percent of population age 25 and over with: High school diploma (including GED) or higher: 82.3% (2010); Bachelor's degree or higher: 11.6% (2010); Master's degree or higher: 4.7% (2010).

School District(s)

Dongola USD 66 (PK-12)
  2009-10 Enrollment: 273 . . . . (618) 827-3841

Housing: Homeownership rate: 70.7% (2010); Median home value: $59,153 (2010); Median contract rent: $270 per month (2005-2009 5-year est.); Median year structure built: 1959 (2005-2009 5-year est.).
Newspapers: Dongola Tri-County Record (Regional news)
Transportation: Commute to work: 79.3% car, 0.0% public transportation, 12.2% walk, 8.5% work from home (2005-2009 5-year est.); Travel time to work: 36.4% less than 15 minutes, 32.3% 15 to 30 minutes, 14.9% 30 to 45 minutes, 7.2% 45 to 60 minutes, 9.2% 60 minutes or more (2005-2009 5-year est.)

JONESBORO (city). County seat. Covers a land area of 1.914 square miles and a water area of 0 square miles. Located at 37.45° N. Lat; 89.26° W. Long. Elevation is 564 feet.

History: Jonesboro was platted in 1816 and named for a physician who was a resident there.
Population: 1,810 (1990); 1,853 (2000); 1,666 (2010); 1,580 (2015 projected); Race: 95.6% White, 1.1% Black, 0.7% Asian, 2.5% Other, 2.4% Hispanic of any race (2010); Density: 870.3 persons per square mile (2010); Average household size: 2.39 (2010); Median age: 39.9 (2010); Males per 100 females: 91.5 (2010); Marriage status: 39.0% never married, 40.8% now married, 5.4% widowed, 14.8% divorced (2005-2009 5-year est.); Foreign born: 0.4% (2005-2009 5-year est.); Ancestry (includes multiple ancestries): 18.2% German, 12.0% Irish, 9.7% American, 6.5% English, 1.9% Dutch (2005-2009 5-year est.).
Economy: Single-family building permits issued: 1 (2010); Multi-family building permits issued: 0 (2010); Employment by occupation: 9.7% management, 27.6% professional, 17.3% services, 28.7% sales, 0.9% farming, 5.7% construction, 10.2% production (2005-2009 5-year est.).
Income: Per capita income: $18,952 (2010); Median household income: $37,123 (2010); Average household income: $45,890 (2010); Percent of households with income of $100,000 or more: 6.4% (2010); Poverty rate: 39.2% (2005-2009 5-year est.).
Taxes: Total city taxes per capita: $44 (2007); City property taxes per capita: $38 (2007).
Education: Percent of population age 25 and over with: High school diploma (including GED) or higher: 83.5% (2010); Bachelor's degree or higher: 18.3% (2010); Master's degree or higher: 6.2% (2010).

School District(s)

Jonesboro CCSD 43 (PK-08)
  2009-10 Enrollment: 366 . . . . (618) 833-6651

Housing: Homeownership rate: 72.7% (2010); Median home value: $66,522 (2010); Median contract rent: $258 per month (2005-2009 5-year est.); Median year structure built: 1964 (2005-2009 5-year est.).
Transportation: Commute to work: 92.6% car, 0.8% public transportation, 1.6% walk, 2.2% work from home (2005-2009 5-year est.); Travel time to work: 53.5% less than 15 minutes, 21.2% 15 to 30 minutes, 18.6% 30 to 45 minutes, 3.4% 45 to 60 minutes, 3.3% 60 minutes or more (2005-2009 5-year est.)

MILL CREEK (village). Aka Millcreek. Covers a land area of 0.366 square miles and a water area of 0.009 square miles. Located at 37.34° N. Lat; 89.25° W. Long. Elevation is 381 feet.

Population: 87 (1990); 76 (2000); 89 (2010); 94 (2015 projected); Race: 96.6% White, 0.0% Black, 1.1% Asian, 2.2% Other, 2.2% Hispanic of any race (2010); Density: 243.2 persons per square mile (2010); Average household size: 2.62 (2010); Median age: 32.5 (2010); Males per 100 females: 97.8 (2010); Marriage status: 20.6% never married, 60.3% now married, 7.4% widowed, 11.8% divorced (2005-2009 5-year est.); Foreign born: 2.6% (2005-2009 5-year est.); Ancestry (includes multiple ancestries): 8.8% Irish, 5.3% German, 1.8% Dutch (2005-2009 5-year est.).
Economy: Employment by occupation: 0.0% management, 3.8% professional, 21.2% services, 23.1% sales, 0.0% farming, 46.2% construction, 5.8% production (2005-2009 5-year est.).
Income: Per capita income: $19,874 (2010); Median household income: $35,000 (2010); Average household income: $49,412 (2010); Percent of households with income of $100,000 or more: 11.8% (2010); Poverty rate: 52.6% (2005-2009 5-year est.).
Taxes: Total city taxes per capita: $13 (2007); City property taxes per capita: $13 (2007).
Education: Percent of population age 25 and over with: High school diploma (including GED) or higher: 87.3% (2010); Bachelor's degree or higher: 20.0% (2010); Master's degree or higher: 9.1% (2010).
Housing: Homeownership rate: 88.2% (2010); Median home value: $96,000 (2010); Median contract rent: $237 per month (2005-2009 5-year est.); Median year structure built: 1964 (2005-2009 5-year est.).
Transportation: Commute to work: 94.2% car, 0.0% public transportation, 0.0% walk, 0.0% work from home (2005-2009 5-year est.); Travel time to work: 5.8% less than 15 minutes, 34.6% 15 to 30 minutes, 59.6% 30 to 45 minutes, 0.0% 45 to 60 minutes, 0.0% 60 minutes or more (2005-2009 5-year est.)

WOLF LAKE (unincorporated postal area, zip code 62998). Covers a land area of 41.246 square miles and a water area of 0.528 square miles. Located at 37.50° N. Lat; 89.44° W. Long. Elevation is 354 feet.
Population: 491 (2000); Race: 100.0% White, 0.0% Black, 0.0% Asian, 0.0% Other, 0.0% Hispanic of any race (2000); Density: 11.9 persons per square mile (2000); Age: 23.6% under 18, 8.1% over 64 (2000); Marriage status: 30.6% never married, 51.7% now married, 6.6% widowed, 11.0% divorced (2000); Foreign born: 0.0% (2000); Ancestry (includes multiple ancestries): 21.0% American, 16.9% German, 7.9% English, 7.2% Irish, 4.2% Scotch-Irish (2000).
Economy: Employment by occupation: 4.9% management, 3.3% professional, 24.6% services, 20.2% sales, 3.8% farming, 18.0% construction, 25.1% production (2000).
Income: Per capita income: $17,343 (2000); Median household income: $32,833 (2000); Poverty rate: 19.4% (2000).
Education: Percent of population age 25 and over with: High school diploma (including GED) or higher: 78.4% (2000); Bachelor's degree or higher: 17.3% (2000).

School District(s)
Shawnee CUSD 84 (PK-12)
   2009-10 Enrollment: 460 . . . . (618) 833-5709
Housing: Homeownership rate: 80.4% (2000); Median home value: $50,000 (2000); Median contract rent: $250 per month (2000); Median year structure built: 1963 (2000).
Transportation: Commute to work: 100.0% car, 0.0% public transportation, 0.0% walk, 0.0% work from home (2000); Travel time to work: 37.6% less than 15 minutes, 34.4% 15 to 30 minutes, 0.0% 30 to 45 minutes, 8.9% 45 to 60 minutes, 19.1% 60 minutes or more (2000)

Vermilion County

Located in eastern Illinois; bounded on the east by Indiana; drained by the Vermilion and Little Vermilion Rivers; includes Lake Vermilion. Covers a land area of 899.08 square miles, a water area of 3.06 square miles, and is located in the Central Time Zone at 40.15° N. Lat., 87.69° W. Long. The county was founded in 1826. County seat is Danville.

Vermilion County is part of the Danville, IL Metropolitan Statistical Area. The entire metro area includes: Vermilion County, IL

Weather Station: Danville										Elevation: 558 feet	
	Jan	Feb	Mar	Apr	May	Jun	Jul	Aug	Sep	Oct	Nov	Dec
High	35	40	52	65	75	83	86	84	79	66	52	39
Low	19	23	32	42	51	60	65	63	55	44	34	23
Precip	2.2	2.2	3.0	4.0	4.5	4.5	4.6	3.5	2.9	3.6	3.8	2.8
Snow	4.5	4.4	2.1	0.2	tr	0.0	0.0	0.0	0.0	0.2	0.6	4.0

High and Low temperatures in degrees Fahrenheit; Precipitation and Snow in inches

Weather Station: Hoopeston 1 NE										Elevation: 709 feet	
	Jan	Feb	Mar	Apr	May	Jun	Jul	Aug	Sep	Oct	Nov	Dec
High	34	38	50	63	74	83	85	84	78	65	51	37
Low	19	22	31	41	52	61	65	63	55	44	34	23
Precip	1.8	1.9	2.8	3.6	4.4	4.3	4.4	4.0	2.8	3.5	3.1	2.3
Snow	5.5	4.9	1.5	0.4	tr	0.0	0.0	0.0	0.0	0.1	0.6	4.8

High and Low temperatures in degrees Fahrenheit; Precipitation and Snow in inches

Population: 88,257 (1990); 83,919 (2000); 80,060 (2010); 77,667 (2015 projected); Race: 83.4% White, 11.9% Black, 0.7% Asian, 4.0% Other, 3.8% Hispanic of any race (2010); Density: 89.0 persons per square mile (2010); Average household size: 2.40 (2010); Median age: 38.5 (2010); Males per 100 females: 97.3 (2010).
Religion: Five largest groups: 7.6% Christian Churches and Churches of Christ, 7.0% Catholic Church, 6.1% The United Methodist Church, 2.7% Church of the Nazarene, 2.6% Lutheran Church—Missouri Synod (2000).
Economy: Unemployment rate: 10.6% (August 2011); Total civilian labor force: 36,372 (August 2011); Leading industries: 20.3% manufacturing; 19.2% health care and social assistance; 13.8% retail trade (2009); Farms: 1,014 totaling 457,375 acres (2007); Companies that employ 500 or more persons: 6 (2009); Companies that employ 100 to 499 persons: 35 (2009); Companies that employ less than 100 persons: 1,496 (2009); Black-owned businesses: n/a (2007); Hispanic-owned businesses: n/a (2007); Asian-owned businesses: n/a (2007); Women-owned businesses: 1,661 (2007); Retail sales per capita: $11,180 (2010). Single-family building permits issued: 10 (2010); Multi-family building permits issued: 3 (2010).
Income: Per capita income: $19,947 (2010); Median household income: $40,202 (2010); Average household income: $49,086 (2010); Percent of households with income of $100,000 or more: 8.3% (2010); Poverty rate: 21.7% (2009); Bankruptcy rate: 5.41% (2010).
Taxes: Total county taxes per capita: $145 (2007); County property taxes per capita: $124 (2007).
Education: Percent of population age 25 and over with: High school diploma (including GED) or higher: 85.3% (2010); Bachelor's degree or higher: 13.1% (2010); Master's degree or higher: 4.3% (2010).
Housing: Homeownership rate: 72.4% (2010); Median home value: $68,403 (2010); Median contract rent: $395 per month (2005-2009 5-year est.); Median year structure built: 1955 (2005-2009 5-year est.)
Health: Birth rate: 132.1 per 10,000 population (2009); Death rate: 117.5 per 10,000 population (2009); Age-adjusted cancer mortality rate: 214.5 deaths per 100,000 population (2007); Number of physicians: 12.4 per 10,000 population (2008); Hospital beds: 74.7 per 10,000 population (2007); Hospital admissions: 1,425.5 per 10,000 population (2007).
Elections: 2008 Presidential election results: 49.4% Obama, 48.8% McCain, 0.8% Nader
National and State Parks: Kickapoo State Park; Middle Fork State Fish and Wildlife Areas
Additional Information Contacts
Vermilion County Government . . . . (217) 554-1900
   http://www.co.vermilion.il.us
City of Danville . . . . (217) 431-2304
   http://www.cityofdanville.org
City of Hoopeston . . . . (217) 283-6990
   http://www.hoopeston-il.gov
Danville Area Convention & Visitors' Bureau . . . . (217) 442-2096
   http://danvilleareainfo.com
Hoopeston Chamber of Commerce . . . . (217) 283-7873

Vermilion County Communities

ALLERTON (village). Covers a land area of 0.645 square miles and a water area of 0 square miles. Located at 39.91° N. Lat; 87.93° W. Long. Elevation is 702 feet.
Population: 274 (1990); 293 (2000); 306 (2010); 310 (2015 projected); Race: 99.0% White, 0.0% Black, 0.0% Asian, 1.0% Other, 1.0% Hispanic of any race (2010); Density: 474.5 persons per square mile (2010); Average household size: 2.55 (2010); Median age: 43.8 (2010); Males per 100 females: 98.7 (2010); Marriage status: 25.5% never married, 53.8% now married, 5.4% widowed, 15.2% divorced (2005-2009 5-year est.); Foreign born: 0.0% (2005-2009 5-year est.); Ancestry (includes multiple ancestries): 52.5% American, 19.8% German, 12.9% Irish, 5.5% Dutch, 3.7% English (2005-2009 5-year est.).
Economy: Single-family building permits issued: 0 (2010); Multi-family building permits issued: 0 (2010); Employment by occupation: 7.6% management, 15.3% professional, 4.6% services, 38.2% sales, 1.5% farming, 18.3% construction, 14.5% production (2005-2009 5-year est.).

Income: Per capita income: $28,219 (2010); Median household income: $58,594 (2010); Average household income: $69,500 (2010); Percent of households with income of $100,000 or more: 20.8% (2010); Poverty rate: 8.3% (2005-2009 5-year est.).

Taxes: Total city taxes per capita: $11 (2007); City property taxes per capita: $11 (2007).

Education: Percent of population age 25 and over with: High school diploma (including GED) or higher: 95.0% (2010); Bachelor's degree or higher: 19.6% (2010); Master's degree or higher: 4.1% (2010).

Housing: Homeownership rate: 82.5% (2010); Median home value: $94,167 (2010); Median contract rent: $379 per month (2005-2009 5-year est.); Median year structure built: 1964 (2005-2009 5-year est.).

Transportation: Commute to work: 96.2% car, 0.0% public transportation, 2.3% walk, 1.5% work from home (2005-2009 5-year est.); Travel time to work: 8.5% less than 15 minutes, 15.5% 15 to 30 minutes, 24.8% 30 to 45 minutes, 45.0% 45 to 60 minutes, 6.2% 60 minutes or more (2005-2009 5-year est.)

ALVAN (village). Aka Alvin. Covers a land area of 0.795 square miles and a water area of 0 square miles. Located at 40.30° N. Lat; 87.60° W. Long. Elevation is 653 feet.

History: Alvin was platted in 1876. The village developed around a grain elevator.

Population: 339 (1990); 316 (2000); 291 (2010); 276 (2015 projected); Race: 99.0% White, 0.0% Black, 0.3% Asian, 0.7% Other, 0.0% Hispanic of any race (2010); Density: 365.8 persons per square mile (2010); Average household size: 2.72 (2010); Median age: 37.4 (2010); Males per 100 females: 96.6 (2010); Marriage status: 28.9% never married, 50.0% now married, 7.5% widowed, 13.7% divorced (2005-2009 5-year est.); Foreign born: 0.0% (2005-2009 5-year est.); Ancestry (includes multiple ancestries): 35.1% American, 18.5% Irish, 10.4% German, 9.0% Italian, 8.2% English (2005-2009 5-year est.).

Economy: Employment by occupation: 3.5% management, 3.5% professional, 10.4% services, 14.5% sales, 0.0% farming, 26.6% construction, 41.6% production (2005-2009 5-year est.).

Income: Per capita income: $19,831 (2010); Median household income: $46,250 (2010); Average household income: $52,897 (2010); Percent of households with income of $100,000 or more: 5.6% (2010); Poverty rate: 8.4% (2005-2009 5-year est.).

Taxes: Total city taxes per capita: $16 (2007); City property taxes per capita: $13 (2007).

Education: Percent of population age 25 and over with: High school diploma (including GED) or higher: 90.1% (2010); Bachelor's degree or higher: 10.4% (2010); Master's degree or higher: 3.1% (2010).

Housing: Homeownership rate: 79.4% (2010); Median home value: $70,714 (2010); Median contract rent: $386 per month (2005-2009 5-year est.); Median year structure built: 1963 (2005-2009 5-year est.).

Transportation: Commute to work: 98.2% car, 0.0% public transportation, 1.8% walk, 0.0% work from home (2005-2009 5-year est.); Travel time to work: 10.5% less than 15 minutes, 59.6% 15 to 30 minutes, 20.5% 30 to 45 minutes, 2.3% 45 to 60 minutes, 7.0% 60 minutes or more (2005-2009 5-year est.)

ARMSTRONG (unincorporated postal area, zip code 61812). Covers a land area of 27.238 square miles and a water area of 0 square miles. Located at 40.27° N. Lat; 87.88° W. Long. Elevation is 696 feet.

Population: 420 (2000); Race: 96.8% White, 3.0% Black, 0.0% Asian, 0.2% Other, 0.7% Hispanic of any race (2000); Density: 15.4 persons per square mile (2000); Age: 25.3% under 18, 16.4% over 64 (2000); Marriage status: 17.3% never married, 63.0% now married, 9.9% widowed, 9.9% divorced (2000); Foreign born: 1.0% (2000); Ancestry (includes multiple ancestries): 20.6% German, 11.2% English, 6.7% American, 4.2% Irish (2000).

Economy: Employment by occupation: 14.4% management, 14.4% professional, 10.8% services, 14.9% sales, 2.1% farming, 13.9% construction, 29.4% production (2000).

Income: Per capita income: $17,395 (2000); Median household income: $34,091 (2000); Poverty rate: 4.0% (2000).

Education: Percent of population age 25 and over with: High school diploma (including GED) or higher: 90.7% (2000); Bachelor's degree or higher: 11.7% (2000).

School District(s)

Armstrong Twp HSD 225 (09-12)

    2009-10 Enrollment: 166 . . . . (217) 569-2122

Armstrong-Ellis Cons SD 61 (PK-08)

    2009-10 Enrollment: 105 . . . . (217) 569-2115

Housing: Homeownership rate: 82.4% (2000); Median home value: $55,400 (2000); Median contract rent: $313 per month (2000); Median year structure built: 1957 (2000).

Transportation: Commute to work: 86.8% car, 0.0% public transportation, 0.5% walk, 11.6% work from home (2000); Travel time to work: 11.9% less than 15 minutes, 26.2% 15 to 30 minutes, 40.5% 30 to 45 minutes, 14.3% 45 to 60 minutes, 7.1% 60 minutes or more (2000)

BELGIUM (village). Covers a land area of 0.423 square miles and a water area of 0 square miles. Located at 40.06° N. Lat; 87.63° W. Long. Elevation is 653 feet.

History: Many of the early residents of Belgium were from the country of Belgium. The village was incorporated in 1909, with coal mining as the major industry.

Population: 511 (1990); 466 (2000); 447 (2010); 431 (2015 projected); Race: 97.3% White, 0.2% Black, 0.0% Asian, 2.5% Other, 1.3% Hispanic of any race (2010); Density: 1,056.3 persons per square mile (2010); Average household size: 2.37 (2010); Median age: 39.5 (2010); Males per 100 females: 89.4 (2010); Marriage status: 25.1% never married, 49.9% now married, 6.8% widowed, 18.3% divorced (2005-2009 5-year est.); Foreign born: 1.4% (2005-2009 5-year est.); Ancestry (includes multiple ancestries): 23.3% Irish, 22.7% American, 15.5% German, 7.4% French, 6.6% Italian (2005-2009 5-year est.).

Economy: Single-family building permits issued: 0 (2010); Multi-family building permits issued: 0 (2010); Employment by occupation: 5.9% management, 6.4% professional, 18.3% services, 26.5% sales, 0.0% farming, 18.7% construction, 24.2% production (2005-2009 5-year est.).

Income: Per capita income: $20,507 (2010); Median household income: $39,500 (2010); Average household income: $48,585 (2010); Percent of households with income of $100,000 or more: 6.9% (2010); Poverty rate: 20.5% (2005-2009 5-year est.).

Taxes: Total city taxes per capita: $32 (2007); City property taxes per capita: $15 (2007).

Education: Percent of population age 25 and over with: High school diploma (including GED) or higher: 85.0% (2010); Bachelor's degree or higher: 8.1% (2010); Master's degree or higher: 2.0% (2010).

Housing: Homeownership rate: 78.8% (2010); Median home value: $70,294 (2010); Median contract rent: $287 per month (2005-2009 5-year est.); Median year structure built: 1971 (2005-2009 5-year est.).

Safety: Violent crime rate: 0.0 per 10,000 population; Property crime rate: 0.0 per 10,000 population (2010).

Transportation: Commute to work: 96.3% car, 0.0% public transportation, 0.0% walk, 2.8% work from home (2005-2009 5-year est.); Travel time to work: 35.5% less than 15 minutes, 46.4% 15 to 30 minutes, 11.8% 30 to 45 minutes, 5.2% 45 to 60 minutes, 0.9% 60 minutes or more (2005-2009 5-year est.)

BISMARCK (village). Covers a land area of 0.679 square miles and a water area of 0 square miles. Located at 40.26° N. Lat; 87.61° W. Long. Elevation is 646 feet.

Population: 542 (1990); 542 (2000); 525 (2010); 509 (2015 projected); Race: 98.5% White, 0.2% Black, 0.0% Asian, 1.3% Other, 0.2% Hispanic of any race (2010); Density: 772.8 persons per square mile (2010); Average household size: 2.65 (2010); Median age: 38.0 (2010); Males per 100 females: 93.7 (2010); Marriage status: 24.5% never married, 65.6% now married, 5.0% widowed, 5.0% divorced (2005-2009 5-year est.); Foreign born: 0.7% (2005-2009 5-year est.); Ancestry (includes multiple ancestries): 30.5% American, 20.0% German, 11.4% Irish, 4.4% Scotch-Irish, 3.2% Dutch (2005-2009 5-year est.).

Economy: Single-family building permits issued: 0 (2010); Multi-family building permits issued: 0 (2010); Employment by occupation: 6.9% management, 18.9% professional, 18.3% services, 29.6% sales, 0.0% farming, 7.2% construction, 19.2% production (2005-2009 5-year est.).

Income: Per capita income: $23,080 (2010); Median household income: $54,808 (2010); Average household income: $60,343 (2010); Percent of households with income of $100,000 or more: 15.2% (2010); Poverty rate: 1.9% (2005-2009 5-year est.).

Taxes: Total city taxes per capita: $2 (2007); City property taxes per capita: $0 (2007).

Education: Percent of population age 25 and over with: High school diploma (including GED) or higher: 90.8% (2010); Bachelor's degree or higher: 13.8% (2010); Master's degree or higher: 5.2% (2010).

School District(s)

Bismarck Henning CUSD (KG-12)
   2009-10 Enrollment: 933 . . . . (217) 759-7261
Housing: Homeownership rate: 83.2% (2010); Median home value: $81,600 (2010); Median contract rent: $550 per month (2005-2009 5-year est.); Median year structure built: 1959 (2005-2009 5-year est.).
Transportation: Commute to work: 83.7% car, 0.0% public transportation, 6.9% walk, 8.2% work from home (2005-2009 5-year est.); Travel time to work: 34.5% less than 15 minutes, 46.7% 15 to 30 minutes, 16.8% 30 to 45 minutes, 0.0% 45 to 60 minutes, 2.0% 60 minutes or more (2005-2009 5-year est.)

CATLIN (village). Covers a land area of 0.785 square miles and a water area of 0.004 square miles. Located at 40.06° N. Lat; 87.70° W. Long. Elevation is 659 feet.
Population: 2,203 (1990); 2,087 (2000); 1,887 (2010); 1,790 (2015 projected); Race: 98.7% White, 0.1% Black, 0.1% Asian, 1.2% Other, 0.5% Hispanic of any race (2010); Density: 2,402.5 persons per square mile (2010); Average household size: 2.46 (2010); Median age: 39.0 (2010); Males per 100 females: 90.6 (2010); Marriage status: 15.5% never married, 73.1% now married, 6.4% widowed, 5.0% divorced (2005-2009 5-year est.); Foreign born: 0.9% (2005-2009 5-year est.); Ancestry (includes multiple ancestries): 21.3% German, 17.9% American, 10.1% Irish, 9.4% English, 6.4% French (2005-2009 5-year est.).
Economy: Single-family building permits issued: 1 (2010); Multi-family building permits issued: 3 (2010); Employment by occupation: 11.4% management, 19.2% professional, 19.9% services, 25.5% sales, 0.4% farming, 8.0% construction, 15.6% production (2005-2009 5-year est.).
Income: Per capita income: $21,815 (2010); Median household income: $47,966 (2010); Average household income: $53,773 (2010); Percent of households with income of $100,000 or more: 8.4% (2010); Poverty rate: 3.9% (2005-2009 5-year est.).
Taxes: Total city taxes per capita: $70 (2007); City property taxes per capita: $66 (2007).
Education: Percent of population age 25 and over with: High school diploma (including GED) or higher: 92.2% (2010); Bachelor's degree or higher: 18.0% (2010); Master's degree or higher: 6.9% (2010).

School District(s)

Catlin CUSD 5 (PK-12)
   2009-10 Enrollment: 535 . . . . (217) 427-2116
Housing: Homeownership rate: 79.7% (2010); Median home value: $84,907 (2010); Median contract rent: $601 per month (2005-2009 5-year est.); Median year structure built: 1966 (2005-2009 5-year est.).
Safety: Violent crime rate: 4.8 per 10,000 population; Property crime rate: 53.3 per 10,000 population (2010).
Transportation: Commute to work: 94.3% car, 0.0% public transportation, 2.9% walk, 2.9% work from home (2005-2009 5-year est.); Travel time to work: 35.5% less than 15 minutes, 42.8% 15 to 30 minutes, 11.1% 30 to 45 minutes, 4.4% 45 to 60 minutes, 6.2% 60 minutes or more (2005-2009 5-year est.)

COLLISON (unincorporated postal area, zip code 61831). Covers a land area of 11.691 square miles and a water area of 0 square miles. Located at 40.21° N. Lat; 87.78° W. Long. Elevation is 692 feet.
Population: 180 (2000); Race: 100.0% White, 0.0% Black, 0.0% Asian, 0.0% Other, 0.0% Hispanic of any race (2000); Density: 15.4 persons per square mile (2000); Age: 24.5% under 18, 10.9% over 64 (2000); Marriage status: 15.8% never married, 65.0% now married, 7.5% widowed, 11.7% divorced (2000); Foreign born: 0.0% (2000); Ancestry (includes multiple ancestries): 19.7% American, 17.7% Irish, 17.0% German, 8.2% English (2000).
Economy: Employment by occupation: 5.1% management, 10.3% professional, 7.7% services, 41.0% sales, 2.6% farming, 9.0% construction, 24.4% production (2000).
Income: Per capita income: $16,937 (2000); Median household income: $42,750 (2000); Poverty rate: 8.8% (2000).
Education: Percent of population age 25 and over with: High school diploma (including GED) or higher: 82.7% (2000); Bachelor's degree or higher: 11.5% (2000).
Housing: Homeownership rate: 87.9% (2000); Median home value: $63,000 (2000); Median contract rent: $263 per month (2000); Median year structure built: 1950 (2000).
Transportation: Commute to work: 96.2% car, 0.0% public transportation, 0.0% walk, 3.8% work from home (2000); Travel time to work: 12.0% less than 15 minutes, 36.0% 15 to 30 minutes, 44.0% 30 to 45 minutes, 5.3% 45 to 60 minutes, 2.7% 60 minutes or more (2000)

DANVILLE (city). County seat. Covers a land area of 17.003 square miles and a water area of 0.095 square miles. Located at 40.13° N. Lat; 87.62° W. Long. Elevation is 600 feet.
History: Danville had its beginning when a salt works was established in 1824. The town was laid out nearby in 1827 by Dan Beckwith, on land donated by him and Guy W. Smith, and the town was named for Beckwith.
Population: 35,622 (1990); 33,904 (2000); 32,300 (2010); 31,229 (2015 projected); Race: 66.7% White, 26.8% Black, 1.1% Asian, 5.4% Other, 5.8% Hispanic of any race (2010); Density: 1,899.6 persons per square mile (2010); Average household size: 2.37 (2010); Median age: 36.4 (2010); Males per 100 females: 99.0 (2010); Marriage status: 33.5% never married, 43.3% now married, 9.1% widowed, 14.1% divorced (2005-2009 5-year est.); Foreign born: 3.1% (2005-2009 5-year est.); Ancestry (includes multiple ancestries): 16.9% American, 14.7% German, 8.1% Irish, 7.0% English, 2.3% French (2005-2009 5-year est.).
Economy: Unemployment rate: 12.1% (August 2011); Total civilian labor force: 13,354 (August 2011); Single-family building permits issued: 5 (2010); Multi-family building permits issued: 0 (2010); Employment by occupation: 10.3% management, 17.2% professional, 18.4% services, 23.3% sales, 0.0% farming, 7.9% construction, 22.9% production (2005-2009 5-year est.).
Income: Per capita income: $18,168 (2010); Median household income: $34,058 (2010); Average household income: $44,710 (2010); Percent of households with income of $100,000 or more: 7.3% (2010); Poverty rate: 26.7% (2005-2009 5-year est.).
Taxes: Total city taxes per capita: $438 (2007); City property taxes per capita: $196 (2007).
Education: Percent of population age 25 and over with: High school diploma (including GED) or higher: 82.6% (2010); Bachelor's degree or higher: 15.1% (2010); Master's degree or higher: 4.8% (2010).

School District(s)

Danville CCSD 118 (PK-12)
   2009-10 Enrollment: 6,222 . . . . (217) 444-1004
Oakwood CUSD 76 (PK-12)
   2009-10 Enrollment: 1,159 . . . . (217) 354-4355
Vermilion Assoc for Spec Educ (KG-12)
   2009-10 Enrollment: n/a . . . . (217) 443-8273
Vermilion Voc Ed Deliver System
   2009-10 Enrollment: n/a . . . . (217) 443-8742
Vermillion Roe (06-12)
   2009-10 Enrollment: n/a . . . . (217) 431-2668

Four-year College(s)

Lakeview College of Nursing (Private, Not-for-profit)
   Fall 2009 Enrollment: 278 . . . . (217) 443-5238

Two-year College(s)

Danville Area Community College (Public)
   Fall 2009 Enrollment: 3,584 . . . . (217) 443-3222
   2010-11 Tuition: In-state $5,610; Out-of-state $5,610

Vocational/Technical School(s)

Concept College of Cosmetology (Private, For-profit)
   Fall 2009 Enrollment: 51 . . . . (217) 442-9329
   2010-11 Tuition: $13,000
Housing: Homeownership rate: 63.3% (2010); Median home value: $61,154 (2010); Median contract rent: $404 per month (2005-2009 5-year est.); Median year structure built: 1952 (2005-2009 5-year est.).
Hospitals: Danville Veterans Affairs Medical Center (350 beds); Provena United Samaritans Medical Center (210 beds)
Safety: Violent crime rate: 108.9 per 10,000 population; Property crime rate: 681.9 per 10,000 population (2010).
Newspapers: Commercial-News (Community news); News-Gazette - Danville Bureau (Regional news)
Transportation: Commute to work: 91.4% car, 1.2% public transportation, 2.8% walk, 2.1% work from home (2005-2009 5-year est.); Travel time to work: 60.6% less than 15 minutes, 27.1% 15 to 30 minutes, 7.1% 30 to 45 minutes, 2.9% 45 to 60 minutes, 2.3% 60 minutes or more (2005-2009 5-year est.); Amtrak: bus service available.
Airports: Vermilion Regional (general aviation)
Additional Information Contacts
City of Danville . . . . (217) 431-2304
   http://www.cityofdanville.org
Danville Area Convention & Visitors' Bureau . . . . (217) 442-2096
   http://danvilleareainfo.com

FAIRMOUNT (village). Covers a land area of 0.311 square miles and a water area of 0 square miles. Located at 40.04° N. Lat; 87.83° W. Long. Elevation is 666 feet.
Population: 716 (1990); 640 (2000); 596 (2010); 576 (2015 projected); Race: 97.8% White, 0.5% Black, 0.2% Asian, 1.5% Other, 0.8% Hispanic of any race (2010); Density: 1,914.1 persons per square mile (2010); Average household size: 2.46 (2010); Median age: 39.6 (2010); Males per 100 females: 96.1 (2010); Marriage status: 21.7% never married, 56.7% now married, 11.3% widowed, 10.4% divorced (2005-2009 5-year est.); Foreign born: 0.0% (2005-2009 5-year est.); Ancestry (includes multiple ancestries): 43.1% American, 12.3% German, 9.5% English, 3.4% Irish, 3.4% Dutch (2005-2009 5-year est.).
Economy: Employment by occupation: 3.1% management, 14.6% professional, 22.4% services, 26.5% sales, 0.0% farming, 3.7% construction, 29.6% production (2005-2009 5-year est.).
Income: Per capita income: $23,724 (2010); Median household income: $54,452 (2010); Average household income: $57,562 (2010); Percent of households with income of $100,000 or more: 8.3% (2010); Poverty rate: 8.5% (2005-2009 5-year est.).
Taxes: Total city taxes per capita: $33 (2007); City property taxes per capita: $33 (2007).
Education: Percent of population age 25 and over with: High school diploma (including GED) or higher: 84.9% (2010); Bachelor's degree or higher: 6.2% (2010); Master's degree or higher: 2.2% (2010).
Housing: Homeownership rate: 84.7% (2010); Median home value: $74,000 (2010); Median contract rent: $395 per month (2005-2009 5-year est.); Median year structure built: 1943 (2005-2009 5-year est.).
Safety: Violent crime rate: 0.0 per 10,000 population; Property crime rate: 16.2 per 10,000 population (2010).
Transportation: Commute to work: 92.5% car, 0.0% public transportation, 4.4% walk, 2.0% work from home (2005-2009 5-year est.); Travel time to work: 24.0% less than 15 minutes, 28.8% 15 to 30 minutes, 40.6% 30 to 45 minutes, 4.5% 45 to 60 minutes, 2.1% 60 minutes or more (2005-2009 5-year est.)

FITHIAN (village). Covers a land area of 0.387 square miles and a water area of 0 square miles. Located at 40.11° N. Lat; 87.87° W. Long. Elevation is 663 feet.
Population: 512 (1990); 506 (2000); 416 (2010); 382 (2015 projected); Race: 99.0% White, 0.2% Black, 0.0% Asian, 0.7% Other, 0.7% Hispanic of any race (2010); Density: 1,076.1 persons per square mile (2010); Average household size: 2.55 (2010); Median age: 37.4 (2010); Males per 100 females: 105.9 (2010); Marriage status: 23.8% never married, 59.8% now married, 1.9% widowed, 14.6% divorced (2005-2009 5-year est.); Foreign born: 1.0% (2005-2009 5-year est.); Ancestry (includes multiple ancestries): 43.6% American, 31.6% German, 13.6% Irish, 5.9% English, 4.5% Lithuanian (2005-2009 5-year est.).
Economy: Single-family building permits issued: 0 (2010); Multi-family building permits issued: 0 (2010); Employment by occupation: 8.1% management, 11.4% professional, 15.1% services, 25.4% sales, 0.0% farming, 14.3% construction, 25.7% production (2005-2009 5-year est.).
Income: Per capita income: $24,098 (2010); Median household income: $58,088 (2010); Average household income: $61,856 (2010); Percent of households with income of $100,000 or more: 10.4% (2010); Poverty rate: 5.1% (2005-2009 5-year est.).
Taxes: Total city taxes per capita: $93 (2007); City property taxes per capita: $47 (2007).
Education: Percent of population age 25 and over with: High school diploma (including GED) or higher: 94.8% (2010); Bachelor's degree or higher: 10.0% (2010); Master's degree or higher: 1.9% (2010).
School District(s)
Oakwood CUSD 76 (PK-12)
    2009-10 Enrollment: 1,159 . . . . (217) 354-4355
Housing: Homeownership rate: 77.9% (2010); Median home value: $82,174 (2010); Median contract rent: $453 per month (2005-2009 5-year est.); Median year structure built: 1949 (2005-2009 5-year est.).
Safety: Violent crime rate: 0.0 per 10,000 population; Property crime rate: 0.0 per 10,000 population (2010).
Transportation: Commute to work: 93.2% car, 0.0% public transportation, 1.9% walk, 3.4% work from home (2005-2009 5-year est.); Travel time to work: 10.6% less than 15 minutes, 41.3% 15 to 30 minutes, 40.2% 30 to 45 minutes, 3.9% 45 to 60 minutes, 3.9% 60 minutes or more (2005-2009 5-year est.)

GEORGETOWN (city). Covers a land area of 1.612 square miles and a water area of 0 square miles. Located at 39.97° N. Lat; 87.63° W. Long. Elevation is 669 feet.
History: Georgetown was settled by Quakers from Tennessee and North Carolina. The town was laid out in 1827.
Population: 3,684 (1990); 3,628 (2000); 3,439 (2010); 3,329 (2015 projected); Race: 95.9% White, 2.0% Black, 0.0% Asian, 2.1% Other, 1.5% Hispanic of any race (2010); Density: 2,133.4 persons per square mile (2010); Average household size: 2.44 (2010); Median age: 36.4 (2010); Males per 100 females: 92.1 (2010); Marriage status: 27.5% never married, 43.9% now married, 7.6% widowed, 21.1% divorced (2005-2009 5-year est.); Foreign born: 1.7% (2005-2009 5-year est.); Ancestry (includes multiple ancestries): 27.9% American, 21.2% German, 9.5% English, 6.9% Irish, 2.7% Polish (2005-2009 5-year est.).
Economy: Single-family building permits issued: 1 (2010); Multi-family building permits issued: 0 (2010); Employment by occupation: 4.4% management, 12.0% professional, 25.2% services, 21.0% sales, 0.0% farming, 10.5% construction, 26.9% production (2005-2009 5-year est.).
Income: Per capita income: $18,778 (2010); Median household income: $41,365 (2010); Average household income: $45,872 (2010); Percent of households with income of $100,000 or more: 6.7% (2010); Poverty rate: 18.0% (2005-2009 5-year est.).
Taxes: Total city taxes per capita: $69 (2007); City property taxes per capita: $38 (2007).
Education: Percent of population age 25 and over with: High school diploma (including GED) or higher: 84.8% (2010); Bachelor's degree or higher: 7.9% (2010); Master's degree or higher: 2.4% (2010).
School District(s)
Georgetown-Ridge Farm CUD 4 (PK-12)
    2009-10 Enrollment: 1,176 . . . . (217) 662-8488
Housing: Homeownership rate: 75.2% (2010); Median home value: $59,132 (2010); Median contract rent: $380 per month (2005-2009 5-year est.); Median year structure built: 1952 (2005-2009 5-year est.).
Safety: Violent crime rate: 23.8 per 10,000 population; Property crime rate: 214.5 per 10,000 population (2010).
Newspapers: Independent News (Local news; Circulation 17,253)
Transportation: Commute to work: 87.8% car, 0.9% public transportation, 6.5% walk, 4.8% work from home (2005-2009 5-year est.); Travel time to work: 23.6% less than 15 minutes, 41.4% 15 to 30 minutes, 27.4% 30 to 45 minutes, 5.2% 45 to 60 minutes, 2.5% 60 minutes or more (2005-2009 5-year est.)

HENNING (village). Covers a land area of 1.524 square miles and a water area of 0 square miles. Located at 40.30° N. Lat; 87.70° W. Long. Elevation is 686 feet.
Population: 273 (1990); 241 (2000); 221 (2010); 210 (2015 projected); Race: 99.1% White, 0.0% Black, 0.0% Asian, 0.9% Other, 0.0% Hispanic of any race (2010); Density: 145.0 persons per square mile (2010); Average household size: 2.73 (2010); Median age: 38.7 (2010); Males per 100 females: 102.8 (2010); Marriage status: 18.8% never married, 71.4% now married, 0.0% widowed, 9.9% divorced (2005-2009 5-year est.); Foreign born: 0.0% (2005-2009 5-year est.); Ancestry (includes multiple ancestries): 23.7% German, 22.4% American, 16.8% Irish, 8.2% English, 3.9% Dutch (2005-2009 5-year est.).
Economy: Single-family building permits issued: 0 (2010); Multi-family building permits issued: 0 (2010); Employment by occupation: 8.3% management, 16.7% professional, 15.0% services, 11.7% sales, 1.7% farming, 18.3% construction, 28.3% production (2005-2009 5-year est.).
Income: Per capita income: $19,872 (2010); Median household income: $46,719 (2010); Average household income: $53,457 (2010); Percent of households with income of $100,000 or more: 6.2% (2010); Poverty rate: 9.1% (2005-2009 5-year est.).
Taxes: Total city taxes per capita: $39 (2007); City property taxes per capita: $39 (2007).
Education: Percent of population age 25 and over with: High school diploma (including GED) or higher: 89.9% (2010); Bachelor's degree or higher: 10.1% (2010); Master's degree or higher: 2.7% (2010).
Housing: Homeownership rate: 79.0% (2010); Median home value: $72,727 (2010); Median contract rent: n/a per month (2005-2009 5-year est.); Median year structure built: 1957 (2005-2009 5-year est.).
Safety: Violent crime rate: 0.0 per 10,000 population; Property crime rate: 0.0 per 10,000 population (2010).
Transportation: Commute to work: 100.0% car, 0.0% public transportation, 0.0% walk, 0.0% work from home (2005-2009 5-year est.);

Travel time to work: 12.7% less than 15 minutes, 46.6% 15 to 30 minutes, 24.6% 30 to 45 minutes, 7.6% 45 to 60 minutes, 8.5% 60 minutes or more (2005-2009 5-year est.)

HOOPESTON (city).
Covers a land area of 3.117 square miles and a water area of 0 square miles. Located at 40.46° N. Lat; 87.67° W. Long. Elevation is 725 feet.

History: Townsites were laid out on the Hoope farm, near the intersection of two railway lines, in 1871. Hoopeston grew rapidly as a canning center.

Population: 5,891 (1990); 5,965 (2000); 5,624 (2010); 5,412 (2015 projected); Race: 89.2% White, 1.1% Black, 0.2% Asian, 9.5% Other, 9.7% Hispanic of any race (2010); Density: 1,804.4 persons per square mile (2010); Average household size: 2.41 (2010); Median age: 40.1 (2010); Males per 100 females: 99.2 (2010); Marriage status: 25.9% never married, 51.3% now married, 9.8% widowed, 12.9% divorced (2005-2009 5-year est.); Foreign born: 4.4% (2005-2009 5-year est.); Ancestry (includes multiple ancestries): 30.2% American, 24.8% German, 9.1% English, 6.1% Irish, 2.7% Scottish (2005-2009 5-year est.).

Economy: Single-family building permits issued: 1 (2010); Multi-family building permits issued: 0 (2010); Employment by occupation: 3.5% management, 17.0% professional, 21.7% services, 22.4% sales, 0.6% farming, 14.4% construction, 20.4% production (2005-2009 5-year est.).

Income: Per capita income: $17,741 (2010); Median household income: $35,810 (2010); Average household income: $44,625 (2010); Percent of households with income of $100,000 or more: 6.6% (2010); Poverty rate: 26.7% (2005-2009 5-year est.).

Taxes: Total city taxes per capita: $245 (2007); City property taxes per capita: $98 (2007).

Education: Percent of population age 25 and over with: High school diploma (including GED) or higher: 83.3% (2010); Bachelor's degree or higher: 9.2% (2010); Master's degree or higher: 3.7% (2010).

School District(s)
Hoopeston Area CUSD 11 (PK-12)
   2009-10 Enrollment: 1,381 . . . . (217) 283-6668

Housing: Homeownership rate: 69.8% (2010); Median home value: $60,367 (2010); Median contract rent: $366 per month (2005-2009 5-year est.); Median year structure built: 1948 (2005-2009 5-year est.).

Hospitals: Hoopeston Community Memorial Hospital (25 beds)

Safety: Violent crime rate: 41.8 per 10,000 population; Property crime rate: 377.7 per 10,000 population (2010).

Newspapers: Chronicle (Community news; Circulation 2,205)

Transportation: Commute to work: 91.8% car, 0.0% public transportation, 3.0% walk, 5.2% work from home (2005-2009 5-year est.); Travel time to work: 54.1% less than 15 minutes, 7.8% 15 to 30 minutes, 18.0% 30 to 45 minutes, 10.3% 45 to 60 minutes, 9.9% 60 minutes or more (2005-2009 5-year est.)

Additional Information Contacts
City of Hoopeston . . . . (217) 283-6990
   http://www.hoopeston-il.gov
Hoopeston Chamber of Commerce . . . . (217) 283-7873

INDIANOLA (village).
Covers a land area of 0.386 square miles and a water area of 0 square miles. Located at 39.92° N. Lat; 87.74° W. Long. Elevation is 673 feet.

Population: 336 (1990); 207 (2000); 201 (2010); 196 (2015 projected); Race: 98.0% White, 0.0% Black, 1.0% Asian, 1.0% Other, 0.5% Hispanic of any race (2010); Density: 520.2 persons per square mile (2010); Average household size: 2.61 (2010); Median age: 40.5 (2010); Males per 100 females: 91.4 (2010); Marriage status: 16.4% never married, 64.6% now married, 9.0% widowed, 10.1% divorced (2005-2009 5-year est.); Foreign born: 2.1% (2005-2009 5-year est.); Ancestry (includes multiple ancestries): 21.4% American, 20.5% German, 13.7% English, 9.0% Irish, 8.1% Scottish (2005-2009 5-year est.).

Economy: Employment by occupation: 9.3% management, 3.7% professional, 15.7% services, 23.1% sales, 0.0% farming, 14.8% construction, 33.3% production (2005-2009 5-year est.).

Income: Per capita income: $22,131 (2010); Median household income: $47,917 (2010); Average household income: $57,045 (2010); Percent of households with income of $100,000 or more: 14.3% (2010); Poverty rate: 6.6% (2005-2009 5-year est.).

Taxes: Total city taxes per capita: $27 (2007); City property taxes per capita: $27 (2007).

Education: Percent of population age 25 and over with: High school diploma (including GED) or higher: 88.5% (2010); Bachelor's degree or higher: 7.2% (2010); Master's degree or higher: 2.9% (2010).

Housing: Homeownership rate: 83.1% (2010); Median home value: $82,857 (2010); Median contract rent: n/a per month (2005-2009 5-year est.); Median year structure built: 1960 (2005-2009 5-year est.).

Safety: Violent crime rate: 0.0 per 10,000 population; Property crime rate: 0.0 per 10,000 population (2010).

Transportation: Commute to work: 96.1% car, 0.0% public transportation, 0.0% walk, 3.9% work from home (2005-2009 5-year est.); Travel time to work: 7.1% less than 15 minutes, 27.3% 15 to 30 minutes, 43.4% 30 to 45 minutes, 12.1% 45 to 60 minutes, 10.1% 60 minutes or more (2005-2009 5-year est.)

MUNCIE (village).
Covers a land area of 0.180 square miles and a water area of 0 square miles. Located at 40.11° N. Lat; 87.84° W. Long. Elevation is 646 feet.

Population: 182 (1990); 155 (2000); 162 (2010); 164 (2015 projected); Race: 98.8% White, 0.0% Black, 0.0% Asian, 1.2% Other, 0.6% Hispanic of any race (2010); Density: 898.3 persons per square mile (2010); Average household size: 2.49 (2010); Median age: 43.3 (2010); Males per 100 females: 92.9 (2010); Marriage status: 17.9% never married, 62.1% now married, 7.6% widowed, 12.4% divorced (2005-2009 5-year est.); Foreign born: 0.0% (2005-2009 5-year est.); Ancestry (includes multiple ancestries): 28.7% American, 21.6% German, 16.4% Polish, 14.0% Irish, 6.4% English (2005-2009 5-year est.).

Economy: Single-family building permits issued: 0 (2010); Multi-family building permits issued: 0 (2010); Employment by occupation: 6.0% management, 15.7% professional, 6.0% services, 31.3% sales, 1.2% farming, 26.5% construction, 13.3% production (2005-2009 5-year est.).

Income: Per capita income: $22,108 (2010); Median household income: $49,531 (2010); Average household income: $53,385 (2010); Percent of households with income of $100,000 or more: 7.7% (2010); Poverty rate: 18.7% (2005-2009 5-year est.).

Taxes: Total city taxes per capita: $13 (2007); City property taxes per capita: $13 (2007).

Education: Percent of population age 25 and over with: High school diploma (including GED) or higher: 88.7% (2010); Bachelor's degree or higher: 20.9% (2010); Master's degree or higher: 7.8% (2010).

Housing: Homeownership rate: 83.1% (2010); Median home value: $115,385 (2010); Median contract rent: n/a per month (2005-2009 5-year est.); Median year structure built: 1951 (2005-2009 5-year est.).

Transportation: Commute to work: 100.0% car, 0.0% public transportation, 0.0% walk, 0.0% work from home (2005-2009 5-year est.); Travel time to work: 14.8% less than 15 minutes, 35.8% 15 to 30 minutes, 38.3% 30 to 45 minutes, 7.4% 45 to 60 minutes, 3.7% 60 minutes or more (2005-2009 5-year est.)

OAKWOOD (village).
Covers a land area of 0.899 square miles and a water area of 0 square miles. Located at 40.11° N. Lat; 87.77° W. Long. Elevation is 646 feet.

Population: 1,535 (1990); 1,502 (2000); 1,421 (2010); 1,387 (2015 projected); Race: 99.3% White, 0.1% Black, 0.1% Asian, 0.5% Other, 0.4% Hispanic of any race (2010); Density: 1,579.8 persons per square mile (2010); Average household size: 2.40 (2010); Median age: 38.8 (2010); Males per 100 females: 95.2 (2010); Marriage status: 23.4% never married, 47.0% now married, 7.6% widowed, 22.0% divorced (2005-2009 5-year est.); Foreign born: 0.4% (2005-2009 5-year est.); Ancestry (includes multiple ancestries): 35.0% American, 14.4% German, 8.1% Irish, 6.5% English, 3.3% Scottish (2005-2009 5-year est.).

Economy: Single-family building permits issued: 0 (2010); Multi-family building permits issued: 0 (2010); Employment by occupation: 6.9% management, 18.9% professional, 21.3% services, 19.4% sales, 1.5% farming, 8.4% construction, 23.7% production (2005-2009 5-year est.).

Income: Per capita income: $22,810 (2010); Median household income: $49,750 (2010); Average household income: $54,827 (2010); Percent of households with income of $100,000 or more: 8.9% (2010); Poverty rate: 22.1% (2005-2009 5-year est.).

Taxes: Total city taxes per capita: $86 (2007); City property taxes per capita: $6 (2007).

Education: Percent of population age 25 and over with: High school diploma (including GED) or higher: 90.6% (2010); Bachelor's degree or higher: 11.5% (2010); Master's degree or higher: 3.7% (2010).

School District(s)
Oakwood CUSD 76 (PK-12)
   2009-10 Enrollment: 1,159 . . . . (217) 354-4355

Housing: Homeownership rate: 83.5% (2010); Median home value: $74,659 (2010); Median contract rent: $446 per month (2005-2009 5-year est.); Median year structure built: 1972 (2005-2009 5-year est.).
Safety: Violent crime rate: 0.0 per 10,000 population; Property crime rate: 106.8 per 10,000 population (2010).
Transportation: Commute to work: 93.1% car, 0.0% public transportation, 4.0% walk, 1.8% work from home (2005-2009 5-year est.); Travel time to work: 20.8% less than 15 minutes, 50.0% 15 to 30 minutes, 17.5% 30 to 45 minutes, 6.3% 45 to 60 minutes, 5.4% 60 minutes or more (2005-2009 5-year est.)

POTOMAC (village). Covers a land area of 0.483 square miles and a water area of 0 square miles. Located at 40.30° N. Lat; 87.80° W. Long. Elevation is 669 feet.
Population: 753 (1990); 681 (2000); 661 (2010); 654 (2015 projected); Race: 97.4% White, 0.0% Black, 0.0% Asian, 2.6% Other, 2.0% Hispanic of any race (2010); Density: 1,367.2 persons per square mile (2010); Average household size: 2.68 (2010); Median age: 37.1 (2010); Males per 100 females: 99.7 (2010); Marriage status: 20.9% never married, 63.4% now married, 9.4% widowed, 6.3% divorced (2005-2009 5-year est.); Foreign born: 0.0% (2005-2009 5-year est.); Ancestry (includes multiple ancestries): 29.5% American, 18.4% German, 9.8% Irish, 4.6% Dutch, 4.5% English (2005-2009 5-year est.).
Economy: Single-family building permits issued: 0 (2010); Multi-family building permits issued: 0 (2010); Employment by occupation: 1.6% management, 9.7% professional, 21.5% services, 30.2% sales, 0.6% farming, 11.2% construction, 25.2% production (2005-2009 5-year est.).
Income: Per capita income: $20,498 (2010); Median household income: $50,192 (2010); Average household income: $54,868 (2010); Percent of households with income of $100,000 or more: 9.3% (2010); Poverty rate: 8.8% (2005-2009 5-year est.).
Taxes: Total city taxes per capita: $107 (2007); City property taxes per capita: $47 (2007).
Education: Percent of population age 25 and over with: High school diploma (including GED) or higher: 90.6% (2010); Bachelor's degree or higher: 10.4% (2010); Master's degree or higher: 4.2% (2010).

School District(s)
Potomac CUSD 10 (PK-08)
  2009-10 Enrollment: 160 . . . . (217) 987-6155
Housing: Homeownership rate: 84.2% (2010); Median home value: $60,500 (2010); Median contract rent: $433 per month (2005-2009 5-year est.); Median year structure built: 1949 (2005-2009 5-year est.).
Safety: Violent crime rate: 0.0 per 10,000 population; Property crime rate: 62.1 per 10,000 population (2010).
Transportation: Commute to work: 95.0% car, 0.0% public transportation, 3.5% walk, 1.6% work from home (2005-2009 5-year est.); Travel time to work: 14.1% less than 15 minutes, 28.1% 15 to 30 minutes, 38.7% 30 to 45 minutes, 12.5% 45 to 60 minutes, 6.7% 60 minutes or more (2005-2009 5-year est.)

RANKIN (village). Covers a land area of 0.572 square miles and a water area of 0 square miles. Located at 40.46° N. Lat; 87.89° W. Long. Elevation is 722 feet.
Population: 619 (1990); 617 (2000); 559 (2010); 531 (2015 projected); Race: 90.0% White, 0.2% Black, 0.7% Asian, 9.1% Other, 8.6% Hispanic of any race (2010); Density: 976.9 persons per square mile (2010); Average household size: 2.50 (2010); Median age: 37.7 (2010); Males per 100 females: 103.3 (2010); Marriage status: 26.5% never married, 44.9% now married, 12.7% widowed, 15.9% divorced (2005-2009 5-year est.); Foreign born: 0.0% (2005-2009 5-year est.); Ancestry (includes multiple ancestries): 28.1% German, 24.6% American, 23.4% Irish, 8.9% Italian, 8.3% English (2005-2009 5-year est.).
Economy: Single-family building permits issued: 0 (2010); Multi-family building permits issued: 0 (2010); Employment by occupation: 0.0% management, 10.1% professional, 22.9% services, 20.3% sales, 0.0% farming, 20.3% construction, 26.4% production (2005-2009 5-year est.).
Income: Per capita income: $16,790 (2010); Median household income: $34,730 (2010); Average household income: $42,243 (2010); Percent of households with income of $100,000 or more: 3.6% (2010); Poverty rate: 11.2% (2005-2009 5-year est.).
Taxes: Total city taxes per capita: $94 (2007); City property taxes per capita: $47 (2007).
Education: Percent of population age 25 and over with: High school diploma (including GED) or higher: 84.5% (2010); Bachelor's degree or higher: 7.3% (2010); Master's degree or higher: 3.4% (2010).

Housing: Homeownership rate: 81.7% (2010); Median home value: $57,632 (2010); Median contract rent: $365 per month (2005-2009 5-year est.); Median year structure built: before 1940 (2005-2009 5-year est.).
Safety: Violent crime rate: 17.5 per 10,000 population; Property crime rate: 0.0 per 10,000 population (2010).
Transportation: Commute to work: 100.0% car, 0.0% public transportation, 0.0% walk, 0.0% work from home (2005-2009 5-year est.); Travel time to work: 22.2% less than 15 minutes, 38.0% 15 to 30 minutes, 22.6% 30 to 45 minutes, 8.6% 45 to 60 minutes, 8.6% 60 minutes or more (2005-2009 5-year est.)

RIDGE FARM (village). Covers a land area of 3.127 square miles and a water area of 0 square miles. Located at 39.89° N. Lat; 87.65° W. Long. Elevation is 702 feet.
History: Ridge Farm was platted in 1853 and incorporated as a village in 1874. It developed as a trading center.
Population: 939 (1990); 912 (2000); 806 (2010); 755 (2015 projected); Race: 99.5% White, 0.0% Black, 0.0% Asian, 0.5% Other, 0.6% Hispanic of any race (2010); Density: 257.7 persons per square mile (2010); Average household size: 2.44 (2010); Median age: 37.9 (2010); Males per 100 females: 98.0 (2010); Marriage status: 18.7% never married, 58.0% now married, 7.8% widowed, 15.5% divorced (2005-2009 5-year est.); Foreign born: 0.0% (2005-2009 5-year est.); Ancestry (includes multiple ancestries): 23.8% American, 22.3% German, 13.3% Irish, 6.5% English, 4.2% Dutch (2005-2009 5-year est.).
Economy: Single-family building permits issued: 0 (2010); Multi-family building permits issued: 0 (2010); Employment by occupation: 9.4% management, 14.7% professional, 8.9% services, 33.5% sales, 0.0% farming, 13.5% construction, 20.1% production (2005-2009 5-year est.).
Income: Per capita income: $19,584 (2010); Median household income: $40,223 (2010); Average household income: $47,591 (2010); Percent of households with income of $100,000 or more: 8.2% (2010); Poverty rate: 20.2% (2005-2009 5-year est.).
Taxes: Total city taxes per capita: $97 (2007); City property taxes per capita: $94 (2007).
Education: Percent of population age 25 and over with: High school diploma (including GED) or higher: 87.8% (2010); Bachelor's degree or higher: 11.9% (2010); Master's degree or higher: 2.8% (2010).

School District(s)
Georgetown-Ridge Farm CUD 4 (PK-12)
  2009-10 Enrollment: 1,176 . . . . (217) 662-8488
Housing: Homeownership rate: 80.1% (2010); Median home value: $61,042 (2010); Median contract rent: $403 per month (2005-2009 5-year est.); Median year structure built: 1955 (2005-2009 5-year est.).
Safety: Violent crime rate: 0.0 per 10,000 population; Property crime rate: 35.9 per 10,000 population (2010).
Transportation: Commute to work: 93.9% car, 0.0% public transportation, 3.1% walk, 1.8% work from home (2005-2009 5-year est.); Travel time to work: 23.9% less than 15 minutes, 26.2% 15 to 30 minutes, 28.6% 30 to 45 minutes, 16.1% 45 to 60 minutes, 5.2% 60 minutes or more (2005-2009 5-year est.)

ROSSVILLE (village). Covers a land area of 1.345 square miles and a water area of 0 square miles. Located at 40.38° N. Lat; 87.66° W. Long. Elevation is 689 feet.
History: Rossville was laid out in 1857 and named for early settler Jacob Ross. The site at the intersection of two roads had previously been called Henpeck.
Population: 1,334 (1990); 1,217 (2000); 1,160 (2010); 1,121 (2015 projected); Race: 96.5% White, 0.4% Black, 0.1% Asian, 3.0% Other, 2.8% Hispanic of any race (2010); Density: 862.7 persons per square mile (2010); Average household size: 2.24 (2010); Median age: 41.8 (2010); Males per 100 females: 89.5 (2010); Marriage status: 26.6% never married, 59.4% now married, 5.7% widowed, 8.3% divorced (2005-2009 5-year est.); Foreign born: 0.7% (2005-2009 5-year est.); Ancestry (includes multiple ancestries): 29.9% German, 19.2% English, 14.5% American, 13.4% Irish, 3.3% Italian (2005-2009 5-year est.).
Economy: Single-family building permits issued: 0 (2010); Multi-family building permits issued: 0 (2010); Employment by occupation: 8.0% management, 12.6% professional, 14.4% services, 32.0% sales, 3.4% farming, 12.5% construction, 17.0% production (2005-2009 5-year est.).
Income: Per capita income: $21,615 (2010); Median household income: $43,094 (2010); Average household income: $48,559 (2010); Percent of households with income of $100,000 or more: 7.2% (2010); Poverty rate: 15.8% (2005-2009 5-year est.).

Taxes: Total city taxes per capita: $27 (2007); City property taxes per capita: $22 (2007).
Education: Percent of population age 25 and over with: High school diploma (including GED) or higher: 87.8% (2010); Bachelor's degree or higher: 13.9% (2010); Master's degree or higher: 3.0% (2010).
School District(s)
Rossville-Alvin CUSD 7 (PK-08)
    2009-10 Enrollment: 240 . . . . (217) 748-6666
Housing: Homeownership rate: 77.6% (2010); Median home value: $77,541 (2010); Median contract rent: $393 per month (2005-2009 5-year est.); Median year structure built: before 1940 (2005-2009 5-year est.).
Transportation: Commute to work: 95.9% car, 0.0% public transportation, 0.3% walk, 3.3% work from home (2005-2009 5-year est.); Travel time to work: 23.9% less than 15 minutes, 25.8% 15 to 30 minutes, 43.7% 30 to 45 minutes, 2.0% 45 to 60 minutes, 4.6% 60 minutes or more (2005-2009 5-year est.)

SIDELL (village). Covers a land area of 0.928 square miles and a water area of 0 square miles. Located at 39.91° N. Lat; 87.82° W. Long. Elevation is 682 feet.
Population: 584 (1990); 626 (2000); 536 (2010); 499 (2015 projected); Race: 99.1% White, 0.2% Black, 0.0% Asian, 0.7% Other, 0.4% Hispanic of any race (2010); Density: 577.7 persons per square mile (2010); Average household size: 2.59 (2010); Median age: 38.8 (2010); Males per 100 females: 97.1 (2010); Marriage status: 30.8% never married, 52.1% now married, 7.5% widowed, 9.5% divorced (2005-2009 5-year est.); Foreign born: 0.0% (2005-2009 5-year est.); Ancestry (includes multiple ancestries): 19.0% American, 12.9% German, 12.1% Irish, 11.5% English, 2.7% Scotch-Irish (2005-2009 5-year est.).
Economy: Single-family building permits issued: 0 (2010); Multi-family building permits issued: 0 (2010); Employment by occupation: 9.6% management, 7.3% professional, 29.7% services, 19.6% sales, 0.0% farming, 7.8% construction, 26.0% production (2005-2009 5-year est.).
Income: Per capita income: $20,521 (2010); Median household income: $44,329 (2010); Average household income: $53,563 (2010); Percent of households with income of $100,000 or more: 9.7% (2010); Poverty rate: 7.4% (2005-2009 5-year est.).
Taxes: Total city taxes per capita: $42 (2007); City property taxes per capita: $37 (2007).
Education: Percent of population age 25 and over with: High school diploma (including GED) or higher: 86.3% (2010); Bachelor's degree or higher: 9.4% (2010); Master's degree or higher: 1.7% (2010).
School District(s)
Jamaica CUSD 12 (PK-12)
    2009-10 Enrollment: 434 . . . . (217) 288-9306
Housing: Homeownership rate: 83.1% (2010); Median home value: $67,143 (2010); Median contract rent: $246 per month (2005-2009 5-year est.); Median year structure built: before 1940 (2005-2009 5-year est.).
Safety: Violent crime rate: 0.0 per 10,000 population; Property crime rate: 0.0 per 10,000 population (2010).
Newspapers: Sidell Reporter (Community news; Circulation 900)
Transportation: Commute to work: 95.4% car, 0.0% public transportation, 1.4% walk, 3.2% work from home (2005-2009 5-year est.); Travel time to work: 23.1% less than 15 minutes, 21.2% 15 to 30 minutes, 30.2% 30 to 45 minutes, 22.6% 45 to 60 minutes, 2.8% 60 minutes or more (2005-2009 5-year est.)

TILTON (village). Covers a land area of 3.098 square miles and a water area of 0.028 square miles. Located at 40.09° N. Lat; 87.64° W. Long. Elevation is 643 feet.
History: Incorporated 1884.
Population: 3,263 (1990); 2,976 (2000); 2,813 (2010); 2,693 (2015 projected); Race: 96.7% White, 0.8% Black, 0.3% Asian, 2.2% Other, 1.5% Hispanic of any race (2010); Density: 907.9 persons per square mile (2010); Average household size: 2.25 (2010); Median age: 42.2 (2010); Males per 100 females: 87.4 (2010); Marriage status: 27.3% never married, 48.6% now married, 11.0% widowed, 13.1% divorced (2005-2009 5-year est.); Foreign born: 0.7% (2005-2009 5-year est.); Ancestry (includes multiple ancestries): 36.7% American, 14.2% German, 9.9% Irish, 8.8% English, 2.8% Italian (2005-2009 5-year est.).
Economy: Single-family building permits issued: 0 (2010); Multi-family building permits issued: 0 (2010); Employment by occupation: 9.6% management, 5.7% professional, 17.5% services, 31.4% sales, 0.0% farming, 9.6% construction, 26.2% production (2005-2009 5-year est.).

Income: Per capita income: $18,890 (2010); Median household income: $38,392 (2010); Average household income: $42,633 (2010); Percent of households with income of $100,000 or more: 4.5% (2010); Poverty rate: 7.9% (2005-2009 5-year est.).
Taxes: Total city taxes per capita: $202 (2007); City property taxes per capita: $92 (2007).
Education: Percent of population age 25 and over with: High school diploma (including GED) or higher: 85.4% (2010); Bachelor's degree or higher: 6.1% (2010); Master's degree or higher: 0.5% (2010).
Housing: Homeownership rate: 77.7% (2010); Median home value: $59,911 (2010); Median contract rent: $410 per month (2005-2009 5-year est.); Median year structure built: 1956 (2005-2009 5-year est.).
Safety: Violent crime rate: 36.6 per 10,000 population; Property crime rate: 169.5 per 10,000 population (2010).
Transportation: Commute to work: 97.5% car, 0.0% public transportation, 2.5% walk, 0.0% work from home (2005-2009 5-year est.); Travel time to work: 31.8% less than 15 minutes, 48.8% 15 to 30 minutes, 14.4% 30 to 45 minutes, 2.7% 45 to 60 minutes, 2.3% 60 minutes or more (2005-2009 5-year est.)

WESTVILLE (village). Covers a land area of 1.595 square miles and a water area of 0 square miles. Located at 40.04° N. Lat; 87.63° W. Long. Elevation is 669 feet.
History: Westville was named for W.P. and E.A. West, who laid out the town in 1873. Coal mining was the first major industry.
Population: 3,387 (1990); 3,175 (2000); 2,929 (2010); 2,810 (2015 projected); Race: 97.5% White, 0.2% Black, 0.0% Asian, 2.3% Other, 1.3% Hispanic of any race (2010); Density: 1,836.3 persons per square mile (2010); Average household size: 2.26 (2010); Median age: 40.7 (2010); Males per 100 females: 93.0 (2010); Marriage status: 22.9% never married, 54.2% now married, 12.6% widowed, 10.4% divorced (2005-2009 5-year est.); Foreign born: 1.1% (2005-2009 5-year est.); Ancestry (includes multiple ancestries): 24.1% American, 19.3% German, 9.3% Irish, 8.7% English, 7.8% French (2005-2009 5-year est.).
Economy: Single-family building permits issued: 2 (2010); Multi-family building permits issued: 0 (2010); Employment by occupation: 5.8% management, 11.6% professional, 18.2% services, 37.0% sales, 0.0% farming, 10.3% construction, 17.1% production (2005-2009 5-year est.).
Income: Per capita income: $22,174 (2010); Median household income: $41,124 (2010); Average household income: $50,195 (2010); Percent of households with income of $100,000 or more: 6.4% (2010); Poverty rate: 11.2% (2005-2009 5-year est.).
Taxes: Total city taxes per capita: $10 (2007); City property taxes per capita: $4 (2007).
Education: Percent of population age 25 and over with: High school diploma (including GED) or higher: 85.7% (2010); Bachelor's degree or higher: 8.9% (2010); Master's degree or higher: 2.4% (2010).
School District(s)
Westville CUSD 2 (PK-12)
    2009-10 Enrollment: 1,249 . . . . (217) 267-3141
Housing: Homeownership rate: 80.0% (2010); Median home value: $67,176 (2010); Median contract rent: $404 per month (2005-2009 5-year est.); Median year structure built: 1953 (2005-2009 5-year est.).
Safety: Violent crime rate: 47.9 per 10,000 population; Property crime rate: 157.4 per 10,000 population (2010).
Transportation: Commute to work: 88.1% car, 0.0% public transportation, 10.3% walk, 0.8% work from home (2005-2009 5-year est.); Travel time to work: 30.9% less than 15 minutes, 50.7% 15 to 30 minutes, 8.5% 30 to 45 minutes, 5.7% 45 to 60 minutes, 4.2% 60 minutes or more (2005-2009 5-year est.)

Wabash County

Located in southeastern Illinois; bounded on the east and south by the Wabash River, and the Indiana border. Covers a land area of 223.47 square miles, a water area of 4.29 square miles, and is located in the Central Time Zone at 38.43° N. Lat., 87.81° W. Long. The county was founded in 1824. County seat is Mount Carmel.

Weather Station: Mount Carmel   Elevation: 430 feet

	Jan	Feb	Mar	Apr	May	Jun	Jul	Aug	Sep	Oct	Nov	Dec
High	41	45	55	67	76	85	89	88	81	70	56	43
Low	22	25	34	44	54	63	66	64	56	44	35	25
Precip	3.0	3.0	4.0	4.3	6.0	4.0	4.0	3.3	3.1	3.6	4.1	3.4
Snow	2.6	3.3	1.0	tr	0.0	0.0	0.0	0.0	0.0	0.1	tr	3.0

High and Low temperatures in degrees Fahrenheit; Precipitation and Snow in inches

Population: 13,111 (1990); 12,937 (2000); 11,899 (2010); 11,333 (2015 projected); Race: 96.6% White, 0.7% Black, 0.9% Asian, 1.8% Other, 1.1% Hispanic of any race (2010); Density: 53.2 persons per square mile (2010); Average household size: 2.40 (2010); Median age: 40.0 (2010); Males per 100 females: 96.4 (2010).

Religion: Five largest groups: 12.7% Catholic Church, 9.9% The United Methodist Church, 9.6% Christian Churches and Churches of Christ, 5.2% Christian Church (Disciples of Christ), 4.3% Southern Baptist Convention (2000).

Economy: Unemployment rate: 9.5% (August 2011); Total civilian labor force: 6,048 (August 2011); Leading industries: 28.3% health care and social assistance; 15.2% retail trade; 9.8% accommodation & food services (2009); Farms: 225 totaling 114,361 acres (2007); Companies that employ 500 or more persons: 0 (2009); Companies that employ 100 to 499 persons: 4 (2009); Companies that employ less than 100 persons: 271 (2009); Black-owned businesses: n/a (2007); Hispanic-owned businesses: n/a (2007); Asian-owned businesses: n/a (2007); Women-owned businesses: 146 (2007); Retail sales per capita: $8,450 (2010). Single-family building permits issued: 1 (2010); Multi-family building permits issued: 0 (2010).

Income: Per capita income: $22,381 (2010); Median household income: $44,339 (2010); Average household income: $53,871 (2010); Percent of households with income of $100,000 or more: 9.8% (2010); Poverty rate: 12.7% (2009); Bankruptcy rate: 2.77% (2010).

Taxes: Total county taxes per capita: $126 (2007); County property taxes per capita: $125 (2007).

Education: Percent of population age 25 and over with: High school diploma (including GED) or higher: 87.4% (2010); Bachelor's degree or higher: 15.1% (2010); Master's degree or higher: 5.0% (2010).

Housing: Homeownership rate: 73.9% (2010); Median home value: $62,553 (2010); Median contract rent: $336 per month (2005-2009 5-year est.); Median year structure built: 1962 (2005-2009 5-year est.)

Health: Birth rate: 128.4 per 10,000 population (2009); Death rate: 122.5 per 10,000 population (2009); Age-adjusted cancer mortality rate: 205.7 deaths per 100,000 population (2007); Number of physicians: 8.3 per 10,000 population (2008); Hospital beds: 20.5 per 10,000 population (2007); Hospital admissions: 467.1 per 10,000 population (2007).

Environment: Air Quality Index: 100.0% good, 0.0% moderate, 0.0% unhealthy for sensitive individuals, 0.0% unhealthy (percent of days in 2008)

Elections: 2008 Presidential election results: 42.6% Obama, 56.3% McCain, 0.5% Nader

National and State Parks: Beall Woods State Conservation and Natural Area

Additional Information Contacts
Wabash County Government . . . . (618) 262-4561

City of Mount Carmel . . . . (618) 262-4822
  http://www.cityofmtcarmel.com
Wabash County Chamber of Commerce . . . . (618) 262-5116
  http://www.wabashcountychamber.com

Wabash County Communities

ALLENDALE (village). Aka Orio. Covers a land area of 0.301 square miles and a water area of 0 square miles. Located at 38.52° N. Lat; 87.71° W. Long. Elevation is 492 feet.
Population: 476 (1990); 528 (2000); 481 (2010); 454 (2015 projected); Race: 97.3% White, 1.2% Black, 0.0% Asian, 1.5% Other, 0.8% Hispanic of any race (2010); Density: 1,599.2 persons per square mile (2010); Average household size: 2.58 (2010); Median age: 41.3 (2010); Males per 100 females: 106.4 (2010); Marriage status: 13.8% never married, 73.7% now married, 4.5% widowed, 8.1% divorced (2005-2009 5-year est.); Foreign born: 0.0% (2005-2009 5-year est.); Ancestry (includes multiple ancestries): 15.4% German, 11.9% American, 8.0% Dutch, 7.8% English, 6.8% Irish (2005-2009 5-year est.).
Economy: Single-family building permits issued: 1 (2010); Multi-family building permits issued: 0 (2010); Employment by occupation: 3.5% management, 11.7% professional, 14.4% services, 26.1% sales, 1.9% farming, 11.3% construction, 31.1% production (2005-2009 5-year est.).
Income: Per capita income: $20,914 (2010); Median household income: $47,581 (2010); Average household income: $54,547 (2010); Percent of households with income of $100,000 or more: 6.6% (2010); Poverty rate: 14.9% (2005-2009 5-year est.).

Taxes: Total city taxes per capita: $26 (2007); City property taxes per capita: $26 (2007).
Education: Percent of population age 25 and over with: High school diploma (including GED) or higher: 90.1% (2010); Bachelor's degree or higher: 15.2% (2010); Master's degree or higher: 4.4% (2010).
School District(s)
Allendale CCSD 17 (PK-08)
  2009-10 Enrollment: 108 . . . . (618) 299-3161
Housing: Homeownership rate: 83.0% (2010); Median home value: $65,313 (2010); Median contract rent: $279 per month (2005-2009 5-year est.); Median year structure built: 1977 (2005-2009 5-year est.).
Transportation: Commute to work: 97.2% car, 0.0% public transportation, 0.8% walk, 0.0% work from home (2005-2009 5-year est.); Travel time to work: 22.5% less than 15 minutes, 39.5% 15 to 30 minutes, 26.1% 30 to 45 minutes, 4.7% 45 to 60 minutes, 7.1% 60 minutes or more (2005-2009 5-year est.)

BELLMONT (village). Covers a land area of 0.365 square miles and a water area of 0 square miles. Located at 38.38° N. Lat; 87.90° W. Long. Elevation is 446 feet.
Population: 271 (1990); 297 (2000); 319 (2010); 327 (2015 projected); Race: 96.9% White, 0.3% Black, 0.9% Asian, 1.9% Other, 0.6% Hispanic of any race (2010); Density: 874.2 persons per square mile (2010); Average household size: 2.47 (2010); Median age: 39.5 (2010); Males per 100 females: 118.5 (2010); Marriage status: 20.2% never married, 62.8% now married, 0.0% widowed, 17.0% divorced (2005-2009 5-year est.); Foreign born: 5.6% (2005-2009 5-year est.); Ancestry (includes multiple ancestries): 29.2% German, 11.5% English, 10.1% Irish, 5.2% American, 1.7% Dutch (2005-2009 5-year est.).
Economy: Employment by occupation: 9.2% management, 20.2% professional, 13.4% services, 22.7% sales, 2.5% farming, 4.2% construction, 27.7% production (2005-2009 5-year est.).
Income: Per capita income: $19,285 (2010); Median household income: $37,813 (2010); Average household income: $47,733 (2010); Percent of households with income of $100,000 or more: 8.5% (2010); Poverty rate: 15.6% (2005-2009 5-year est.).
Taxes: Total city taxes per capita: $17 (2007); City property taxes per capita: $17 (2007).
Education: Percent of population age 25 and over with: High school diploma (including GED) or higher: 88.6% (2010); Bachelor's degree or higher: 14.5% (2010); Master's degree or higher: 4.1% (2010).
Housing: Homeownership rate: 81.4% (2010); Median home value: $60,769 (2010); Median contract rent: $211 per month (2005-2009 5-year est.); Median year structure built: 1959 (2005-2009 5-year est.).
Transportation: Commute to work: 95.8% car, 0.0% public transportation, 2.5% walk, 0.0% work from home (2005-2009 5-year est.); Travel time to work: 24.4% less than 15 minutes, 42.0% 15 to 30 minutes, 17.6% 30 to 45 minutes, 11.8% 45 to 60 minutes, 4.2% 60 minutes or more (2005-2009 5-year est.)

KEENSBURG (village). Covers a land area of 0.258 square miles and a water area of 0 square miles. Located at 38.35° N. Lat; 87.86° W. Long. Elevation is 436 feet.
Population: 238 (1990); 252 (2000); 246 (2010); 241 (2015 projected); Race: 99.2% White, 0.0% Black, 0.0% Asian, 0.8% Other, 0.0% Hispanic of any race (2010); Density: 955.3 persons per square mile (2010); Average household size: 2.41 (2010); Median age: 44.7 (2010); Males per 100 females: 93.7 (2010); Marriage status: 15.0% never married, 65.0% now married, 9.2% widowed, 10.8% divorced (2005-2009 5-year est.); Foreign born: 0.0% (2005-2009 5-year est.); Ancestry (includes multiple ancestries): 16.2% German, 12.0% English, 7.0% Dutch, 4.2% French, 4.2% Russian (2005-2009 5-year est.).
Economy: Employment by occupation: 0.0% management, 5.5% professional, 12.3% services, 13.7% sales, 0.0% farming, 6.8% construction, 61.6% production (2005-2009 5-year est.).
Income: Per capita income: $25,330 (2010); Median household income: $58,065 (2010); Average household income: $61,593 (2010); Percent of households with income of $100,000 or more: 12.7% (2010); Poverty rate: 0.0% (2005-2009 5-year est.).
Taxes: Total city taxes per capita: $12 (2007); City property taxes per capita: $12 (2007).
Education: Percent of population age 25 and over with: High school diploma (including GED) or higher: 89.2% (2010); Bachelor's degree or higher: 17.7% (2010); Master's degree or higher: 5.4% (2010).

Housing: Homeownership rate: 77.5% (2010); Median home value: $51,333 (2010); Median contract rent: $238 per month (2005-2009 5-year est.); Median year structure built: 1962 (2005-2009 5-year est.).
Transportation: Commute to work: 98.6% car, 0.0% public transportation, 0.0% walk, 0.0% work from home (2005-2009 5-year est.); Travel time to work: 12.3% less than 15 minutes, 34.2% 15 to 30 minutes, 50.7% 30 to 45 minutes, 2.7% 45 to 60 minutes, 0.0% 60 minutes or more (2005-2009 5-year est.)

MOUNT CARMEL (city). Aka Sugar Creek. County seat. Covers a land area of 4.617 square miles and a water area of 0.153 square miles. Located at 38.41° N. Lat; 87.76° W. Long. Elevation is 449 feet.

History: Mount Carmel was founded in 1818 by Rev. Thomas S. Hinde of Ohio, who hoped for a "moral, temperate, and industrious village." A mussel and pearl industry began here in 1900.
Population: 8,353 (1990); 7,982 (2000); 6,936 (2010); 6,427 (2015 projected); Race: 96.4% White, 0.7% Black, 1.0% Asian, 1.8% Other, 1.3% Hispanic of any race (2010); Density: 1,502.2 persons per square mile (2010); Average household size: 2.32 (2010); Median age: 39.9 (2010); Males per 100 females: 92.1 (2010); Marriage status: 24.0% never married, 53.9% now married, 10.0% widowed, 12.0% divorced (2005-2009 5-year est.); Foreign born: 0.7% (2005-2009 5-year est.); Ancestry (includes multiple ancestries): 28.2% German, 13.9% English, 13.5% American, 11.9% Irish, 2.9% Scottish (2005-2009 5-year est.).
Economy: Single-family building permits issued: 0 (2010); Multi-family building permits issued: 0 (2010); Employment by occupation: 11.1% management, 11.7% professional, 20.2% services, 20.3% sales, 0.4% farming, 8.1% construction, 28.2% production (2005-2009 5-year est.).
Income: Per capita income: $22,450 (2010); Median household income: $41,795 (2010); Average household income: $52,422 (2010); Percent of households with income of $100,000 or more: 9.9% (2010); Poverty rate: 16.9% (2005-2009 5-year est.).
Taxes: Total city taxes per capita: $206 (2007); City property taxes per capita: $151 (2007).
Education: Percent of population age 25 and over with: High school diploma (including GED) or higher: 85.6% (2010); Bachelor's degree or higher: 15.7% (2010); Master's degree or higher: 5.7% (2010).

School District(s)
Wabash CUSD 348 (PK-12)
    2009-10 Enrollment: 1,780 . . . . (618) 262-4181
Two-year College(s)
Illinois Eastern Community Colleges-Wabash Valley College (Public)
    Fall 2009 Enrollment: 4,810. . . . . (618) 393-2982
    2010-11 Tuition: In-state $6,808; Out-of-state $9,081
Housing: Homeownership rate: 68.0% (2010); Median home value: $60,237 (2010); Median contract rent: $345 per month (2005-2009 5-year est.); Median year structure built: 1958 (2005-2009 5-year est.).
Hospitals: Wabash General Hospital (56 beds)
Safety: Violent crime rate: 29.1 per 10,000 population; Property crime rate: 157.7 per 10,000 population (2010).
Newspapers: Daily Republican Register (Local news; Circulation 4,300)
Transportation: Commute to work: 93.8% car, 0.0% public transportation, 1.7% walk, 4.2% work from home (2005-2009 5-year est.); Travel time to work: 62.2% less than 15 minutes, 19.8% 15 to 30 minutes, 9.0% 30 to 45 minutes, 5.5% 45 to 60 minutes, 3.6% 60 minutes or more (2005-2009 5-year est.)
Additional Information Contacts
City of Mount Carmel . . . . (618) 262-4822
    http://www.cityofmtcarmel.com
Wabash County Chamber of Commerce . . . . (618) 262-5116
    http://www.wabashcountychamber.com

Warren County

Located in western Illinois; drained by Henderson Creek. Covers a land area of 542.52 square miles, a water area of 0.65 square miles, and is located in the Central Time Zone at 40.87° N. Lat., 90.62° W. Long. The county was founded in 1825. County seat is Monmouth.

Warren County is part of the Galesburg, IL Micropolitan Statistical Area. The entire metro area includes: Knox County, IL; Warren County, IL

Weather Station: Monmouth											Elevation: 745 feet	
	Jan	Feb	Mar	Apr	May	Jun	Jul	Aug	Sep	Oct	Nov	Dec
High	33	38	51	64	75	83	86	85	78	66	51	36
Low	16	20	30	41	51	60	64	62	54	43	32	20
Precip	1.6	1.8	2.7	3.8	4.5	4.3	4.1	4.3	3.8	3.0	2.8	2.3
Snow	7.1	5.6	3.0	1.3	0.0	0.0	0.0	0.0	0.0	0.1	1.3	6.5

High and Low temperatures in degrees Fahrenheit; Precipitation and Snow in inches

Population: 19,181 (1990); 18,735 (2000); 17,390 (2010); 16,696 (2015 projected); Race: 92.7% White, 2.1% Black, 0.7% Asian, 4.4% Other, 5.6% Hispanic of any race (2010); Density: 32.1 persons per square mile (2010); Average household size: 2.42 (2010); Median age: 38.1 (2010); Males per 100 females: 92.8 (2010).
Religion: Five largest groups: 11.0% Catholic Church, 9.7% The United Methodist Church, 7.2% Presbyterian Church (U.S.A.), 5.1% Christian Churches and Churches of Christ, 4.6% Christian Church (Disciples of Christ) (2000).
Economy: Unemployment rate: 7.3% (August 2011); Total civilian labor force: 9,342 (August 2011); Leading industries: 30.8% manufacturing; 15.2% health care and social assistance; 10.2% retail trade (2009); Farms: 644 totaling 294,907 acres (2007); Companies that employ 500 or more persons: 2 (2009); Companies that employ 100 to 499 persons: 2 (2009); Companies that employ less than 100 persons: 362 (2009); Black-owned businesses: n/a (2007); Hispanic-owned businesses: n/a (2007); Asian-owned businesses: n/a (2007); Women-owned businesses: 394 (2007); Retail sales per capita: $9,117 (2010). Single-family building permits issued: 37 (2010); Multi-family building permits issued: 20 (2010).
Income: Per capita income: $21,383 (2010); Median household income: $46,510 (2010); Average household income: $55,324 (2010); Percent of households with income of $100,000 or more: 11.3% (2010); Poverty rate: 13.6% (2009); Bankruptcy rate: 4.19% (2010).
Taxes: Total county taxes per capita: $120 (2007); County property taxes per capita: $119 (2007).
Education: Percent of population age 25 and over with: High school diploma (including GED) or higher: 87.3% (2010); Bachelor's degree or higher: 19.2% (2010); Master's degree or higher: 5.5% (2010).
Housing: Homeownership rate: 73.3% (2010); Median home value: $85,795 (2010); Median contract rent: $352 per month (2005-2009 5-year est.); Median year structure built: 1951 (2005-2009 5-year est.)
Health: Birth rate: 123.5 per 10,000 population (2009); Death rate: 111.4 per 10,000 population (2009); Age-adjusted cancer mortality rate: 191.0 deaths per 100,000 population (2007); Number of physicians: 8.0 per 10,000 population (2008); Hospital beds: 38.7 per 10,000 population (2007); Hospital admissions: 251.8 per 10,000 population (2007).
Elections: 2008 Presidential election results: 53.4% Obama, 45.3% McCain, 0.7% Nader
Additional Information Contacts
Warren County Government . . . . (309) 734-8592
    http://www.warrencountyil.com
City of Monmouth. . . . . (309) 734-2141
    http://cityofmonmouth.com
Monmouth Area Chamber of Commerce . . . . (309) 734-3181
    http://monmouthilchamber.com
Roseville Chamber of Commerce
    http://roseville-il.org

Warren County Communities

ALEXIS (village). Covers a land area of 0.485 square miles and a water area of 0 square miles. Located at 41.06° N. Lat; 90.55° W. Long. Elevation is 699 feet.

Population: 921 (1990); 863 (2000); 705 (2010); 677 (2015 projected); Race: 98.9% White, 0.0% Black, 0.0% Asian, 1.1% Other, 2.7% Hispanic of any race (2010); Density: 1,452.9 persons per square mile (2010); Average household size: 2.40 (2010); Median age: 44.5 (2010); Males per 100 females: 98.0 (2010); Marriage status: 14.5% never married, 59.7% now married, 8.7% widowed, 17.2% divorced (2005-2009 5-year est.); Foreign born: 1.7% (2005-2009 5-year est.); Ancestry (includes multiple ancestries): 15.5% Swedish, 14.1% German, 13.7% Irish, 13.5% English, 4.8% Dutch (2005-2009 5-year est.).
Economy: Single-family building permits issued: 0 (2010); Multi-family building permits issued: 0 (2010); Employment by occupation: 8.1% management, 18.3% professional, 11.3% services, 30.9% sales, 0.6% farming, 8.9% construction, 21.9% production (2005-2009 5-year est.).
Income: Per capita income: $22,127 (2010); Median household income: $47,543 (2010); Average household income: $52,918 (2010); Percent of

households with income of $100,000 or more: 8.2% (2010); Poverty rate: 6.4% (2005-2009 5-year est.).

Taxes: Total city taxes per capita: $68 (2007); City property taxes per capita: $27 (2007).

Education: Percent of population age 25 and over with: High school diploma (including GED) or higher: 91.8% (2010); Bachelor's degree or higher: 12.9% (2010); Master's degree or higher: 4.1% (2010).

School District(s)

United CUSD 304 (PK-12)

    2009-10 Enrollment: 921 . . . . (309) 482-3344

Housing: Homeownership rate: 79.2% (2010); Median home value: $86,111 (2010); Median contract rent: $312 per month (2005-2009 5-year est.); Median year structure built: 1960 (2005-2009 5-year est.).

Transportation: Commute to work: 91.7% car, 0.4% public transportation, 4.8% walk, 2.4% work from home (2005-2009 5-year est.); Travel time to work: 30.5% less than 15 minutes, 32.1% 15 to 30 minutes, 18.2% 30 to 45 minutes, 10.5% 45 to 60 minutes, 8.7% 60 minutes or more (2005-2009 5-year est.)

BERWICK (unincorporated postal area, zip code 61417). Covers a land area of 28.943 square miles and a water area of 0 square miles. Located at 40.78° N. Lat; 90.52° W. Long. Elevation is 709 feet.

Population: 324 (2000); Race: 100.0% White, 0.0% Black, 0.0% Asian, 0.0% Other, 0.0% Hispanic of any race (2000); Density: 11.2 persons per square mile (2000); Age: 14.0% under 18, 12.2% over 64 (2000); Marriage status: 17.6% never married, 69.3% now married, 3.0% widowed, 10.1% divorced (2000); Foreign born: 0.0% (2000); Ancestry (includes multiple ancestries): 31.3% American, 11.9% English, 8.8% Swedish, 6.1% Irish, 4.9% German (2000).

Economy: Employment by occupation: 23.2% management, 6.2% professional, 10.0% services, 19.9% sales, 1.4% farming, 8.5% construction, 30.8% production (2000).

Income: Per capita income: $19,834 (2000); Median household income: $40,268 (2000); Poverty rate: 3.1% (2000).

Education: Percent of population age 25 and over with: High school diploma (including GED) or higher: 91.6% (2000); Bachelor's degree or higher: 10.4% (2000).

Housing: Homeownership rate: 72.1% (2000); Median home value: $48,300 (2000); Median contract rent: $269 per month (2000); Median year structure built: before 1940 (2000).

Transportation: Commute to work: 86.4% car, 0.0% public transportation, 2.4% walk, 11.2% work from home (2000); Travel time to work: 31.7% less than 15 minutes, 13.1% 15 to 30 minutes, 43.7% 30 to 45 minutes, 6.0% 45 to 60 minutes, 5.5% 60 minutes or more (2000)

CAMERON (unincorporated postal area, zip code 61423). Covers a land area of 53.529 square miles and a water area of 0 square miles. Located at 40.88° N. Lat; 90.50° W. Long. Elevation is 771 feet.

Population: 779 (2000); Race: 100.0% White, 0.0% Black, 0.0% Asian, 0.0% Other, 2.9% Hispanic of any race (2000); Density: 14.6 persons per square mile (2000); Age: 26.1% under 18, 11.9% over 64 (2000); Marriage status: 19.0% never married, 74.4% now married, 2.2% widowed, 4.3% divorced (2000); Foreign born: 0.0% (2000); Ancestry (includes multiple ancestries): 23.9% American, 17.7% German, 16.9% Irish, 13.9% English, 12.0% Swedish (2000).

Economy: Employment by occupation: 11.3% management, 16.9% professional, 17.3% services, 14.9% sales, 2.9% farming, 5.6% construction, 31.1% production (2000).

Income: Per capita income: $19,469 (2000); Median household income: $47,596 (2000); Poverty rate: 6.0% (2000).

Education: Percent of population age 25 and over with: High school diploma (including GED) or higher: 85.8% (2000); Bachelor's degree or higher: 10.7% (2000).

Housing: Homeownership rate: 89.0% (2000); Median home value: $75,000 (2000); Median contract rent: $304 per month (2000); Median year structure built: 1952 (2000).

Transportation: Commute to work: 95.8% car, 0.0% public transportation, 0.7% walk, 2.8% work from home (2000); Travel time to work: 15.3% less than 15 minutes, 59.6% 15 to 30 minutes, 7.2% 30 to 45 minutes, 0.7% 45 to 60 minutes, 17.2% 60 minutes or more (2000)

GERLAW (unincorporated postal area, zip code 61435). Covers a land area of 9.520 square miles and a water area of 0 square miles. Located at 40.97° N. Lat; 90.54° W. Long. Elevation is 735 feet.

Population: 85 (2000); Race: 100.0% White, 0.0% Black, 0.0% Asian, 0.0% Other, 0.0% Hispanic of any race (2000); Density: 8.9 persons per square mile (2000); Age: 31.6% under 18, 14.0% over 64 (2000); Marriage status: 27.9% never married, 62.8% now married, 0.0% widowed, 9.3% divorced (2000); Foreign born: 0.0% (2000); Ancestry (includes multiple ancestries): 29.8% American, 26.3% English, 19.3% German, 14.0% Swedish, 5.3% Scandinavian (2000).

Economy: Employment by occupation: 33.3% management, 12.5% professional, 0.0% services, 41.7% sales, 0.0% farming, 0.0% construction, 12.5% production (2000).

Income: Per capita income: $14,618 (2000); Median household income: $29,063 (2000); Poverty rate: 7.0% (2000).

Education: Percent of population age 25 and over with: High school diploma (including GED) or higher: 91.7% (2000); Bachelor's degree or higher: 8.3% (2000).

Housing: Homeownership rate: 63.6% (2000); Median home value: $105,000 (2000); Median contract rent: n/a per month (2000); Median year structure built: before 1940 (2000).

Transportation: Commute to work: 66.7% car, 0.0% public transportation, 12.5% walk, 20.8% work from home (2000); Travel time to work: 31.6% less than 15 minutes, 68.4% 15 to 30 minutes, 0.0% 30 to 45 minutes, 0.0% 45 to 60 minutes, 0.0% 60 minutes or more (2000)

KIRKWOOD (village). Covers a land area of 0.909 square miles and a water area of 0 square miles. Located at 40.86° N. Lat; 90.75° W. Long. Elevation is 741 feet.

Population: 902 (1990); 794 (2000); 667 (2010); 612 (2015 projected); Race: 96.4% White, 0.1% Black, 0.4% Asian, 3.0% Other, 2.5% Hispanic of any race (2010); Density: 734.0 persons per square mile (2010); Average household size: 2.58 (2010); Median age: 39.4 (2010); Males per 100 females: 93.3 (2010); Marriage status: 29.7% never married, 50.1% now married, 7.2% widowed, 13.1% divorced (2005-2009 5-year est.); Foreign born: 0.0% (2005-2009 5-year est.); Ancestry (includes multiple ancestries): 23.7% German, 14.4% Irish, 8.7% Swedish, 6.9% American, 6.1% Dutch (2005-2009 5-year est.).

Economy: Single-family building permits issued: 0 (2010); Multi-family building permits issued: 0 (2010); Employment by occupation: 7.0% management, 10.0% professional, 19.2% services, 20.5% sales, 4.1% farming, 7.6% construction, 31.6% production (2005-2009 5-year est.).

Income: Per capita income: $17,798 (2010); Median household income: $40,875 (2010); Average household income: $45,830 (2010); Percent of households with income of $100,000 or more: 3.9% (2010); Poverty rate: 14.1% (2005-2009 5-year est.).

Taxes: Total city taxes per capita: $31 (2007); City property taxes per capita: $31 (2007).

Education: Percent of population age 25 and over with: High school diploma (including GED) or higher: 91.9% (2010); Bachelor's degree or higher: 11.0% (2010); Master's degree or higher: 2.7% (2010).

Housing: Homeownership rate: 79.5% (2010); Median home value: $75,484 (2010); Median contract rent: $281 per month (2005-2009 5-year est.); Median year structure built: before 1940 (2005-2009 5-year est.).

Transportation: Commute to work: 91.1% car, 0.0% public transportation, 5.3% walk, 3.6% work from home (2005-2009 5-year est.); Travel time to work: 26.9% less than 15 minutes, 39.6% 15 to 30 minutes, 22.0% 30 to 45 minutes, 1.2% 45 to 60 minutes, 10.4% 60 minutes or more (2005-2009 5-year est.)

LITTLE YORK (village). Covers a land area of 0.258 square miles and a water area of 0 square miles. Located at 41.01° N. Lat; 90.74° W. Long. Elevation is 614 feet.

Population: 349 (1990); 269 (2000); 238 (2010); 220 (2015 projected); Race: 98.3% White, 0.0% Black, 0.4% Asian, 1.3% Other, 1.7% Hispanic of any race (2010); Density: 923.1 persons per square mile (2010); Average household size: 2.59 (2010); Median age: 39.6 (2010); Males per 100 females: 98.3 (2010); Marriage status: 22.3% never married, 47.7% now married, 13.2% widowed, 16.8% divorced (2005-2009 5-year est.); Foreign born: 0.0% (2005-2009 5-year est.); Ancestry (includes multiple ancestries): 25.2% German, 16.1% Irish, 11.2% English, 9.9% Swedish, 5.8% American (2005-2009 5-year est.).

Economy: Single-family building permits issued: 0 (2010); Multi-family building permits issued: 0 (2010); Employment by occupation: 14.8% management, 2.8% professional, 19.4% services, 17.6% sales, 4.6% farming, 9.3% construction, 31.5% production (2005-2009 5-year est.).

Income: Per capita income: $22,384 (2010); Median household income: $52,083 (2010); Average household income: $57,527 (2010); Percent of

households with income of $100,000 or more: 13.0% (2010); Poverty rate: 12.8% (2005-2009 5-year est.).

Taxes: Total city taxes per capita: $32 (2007); City property taxes per capita: $24 (2007).

Education: Percent of population age 25 and over with: High school diploma (including GED) or higher: 87.0% (2010); Bachelor's degree or higher: 14.8% (2010); Master's degree or higher: 4.9% (2010).

Housing: Homeownership rate: 72.8% (2010); Median home value: $79,333 (2010); Median contract rent: $313 per month (2005-2009 5-year est.); Median year structure built: 1947 (2005-2009 5-year est.).

Transportation: Commute to work: 90.5% car, 0.0% public transportation, 3.2% walk, 6.3% work from home (2005-2009 5-year est.); Travel time to work: 24.7% less than 15 minutes, 34.8% 15 to 30 minutes, 18.0% 30 to 45 minutes, 4.5% 45 to 60 minutes, 18.0% 60 minutes or more (2005-2009 5-year est.)

MONMOUTH (city). County seat. Covers a land area of 4.029 square miles and a water area of 0.021 square miles. Located at 40.91° N. Lat; 90.64° W. Long. Elevation is 761 feet.

History: Monmouth was named in remembrance of the Revolutionary War battle that took place at Monmouth, New Jersey. Monmouth was established in 1831, and grew as the seat of Warren County.

Population: 9,495 (1990); 9,841 (2000); 9,406 (2010); 9,165 (2015 projected); Race: 88.6% White, 3.5% Black, 0.9% Asian, 6.9% Other, 8.7% Hispanic of any race (2010); Density: 2,334.3 persons per square mile (2010); Average household size: 2.39 (2010); Median age: 32.9 (2010); Males per 100 females: 89.0 (2010); Marriage status: 36.8% never married, 42.9% now married, 8.1% widowed, 12.1% divorced (2005-2009 5-year est.); Foreign born: 3.9% (2005-2009 5-year est.); Ancestry (includes multiple ancestries): 21.0% German, 15.2% Irish, 8.6% English, 8.3% Swedish, 6.4% American (2005-2009 5-year est.).

Economy: Single-family building permits issued: 22 (2010); Multi-family building permits issued: 20 (2010); Employment by occupation: 5.3% management, 16.6% professional, 24.8% services, 18.9% sales, 0.9% farming, 5.9% construction, 27.7% production (2005-2009 5-year est.).

Income: Per capita income: $19,695 (2010); Median household income: $44,082 (2010); Average household income: $53,056 (2010); Percent of households with income of $100,000 or more: 10.6% (2010); Poverty rate: 20.6% (2005-2009 5-year est.).

Taxes: Total city taxes per capita: $195 (2007); City property taxes per capita: $169 (2007).

Education: Percent of population age 25 and over with: High school diploma (including GED) or higher: 84.0% (2010); Bachelor's degree or higher: 20.5% (2010); Master's degree or higher: 6.3% (2010).

School District(s)
Henderson/Mercer/Warren Roe (07-12)
   2009-10 Enrollment: 35 . . . . (309) 734-6822
Monmouth-Roseville CUSD 238 (PK-12)
   2009-10 Enrollment: 1,718 . . . . (309) 734-4712
United CUSD 304 (PK-12)
   2009-10 Enrollment: 921 . . . . (309) 482-3344

Four-year College(s)
Monmouth College (Private, Not-for-profit)
   Fall 2009 Enrollment: 1,379 . . . . (309) 457-2311
   2010-11 Tuition: In-state $26,900; Out-of-state $26,900

Housing: Homeownership rate: 69.2% (2010); Median home value: $72,270 (2010); Median contract rent: $352 per month (2005-2009 5-year est.); Median year structure built: 1946 (2005-2009 5-year est.).

Hospitals: Community Medical Center (68 beds)

Safety: Violent crime rate: 61.6 per 10,000 population; Property crime rate: 520.2 per 10,000 population (2010).

Newspapers: Daily Review Atlas (Local news; Circulation 3,750); The Register-Mail - Monmouth Bureau (Local news)

Transportation: Commute to work: 83.4% car, 0.4% public transportation, 10.3% walk, 4.3% work from home (2005-2009 5-year est.); Travel time to work: 69.6% less than 15 minutes, 16.6% 15 to 30 minutes, 6.5% 30 to 45 minutes, 2.0% 45 to 60 minutes, 5.3% 60 minutes or more (2005-2009 5-year est.)

Additional Information Contacts
City of Monmouth . . . . (309) 734-2141
   http://cityofmonmouth.com
Monmouth Area Chamber of Commerce . . . . (309) 734-3181
   http://monmouthilchamber.com

ROSEVILLE (village). Covers a land area of 0.812 square miles and a water area of 0 square miles. Located at 40.73° N. Lat; 90.66° W. Long. Elevation is 745 feet.

History: Roseville grew as a trading center and shipping point for oats and soy beans. The town was first called Hat Grove, referring to the shape of a particular grove of trees.

Population: 1,151 (1990); 1,083 (2000); 948 (2010); 901 (2015 projected); Race: 99.1% White, 0.3% Black, 0.2% Asian, 0.4% Other, 0.9% Hispanic of any race (2010); Density: 1,167.1 persons per square mile (2010); Average household size: 2.29 (2010); Median age: 47.0 (2010); Males per 100 females: 85.9 (2010); Marriage status: 24.0% never married, 52.4% now married, 11.7% widowed, 12.0% divorced (2005-2009 5-year est.); Foreign born: 1.9% (2005-2009 5-year est.); Ancestry (includes multiple ancestries): 25.9% German, 25.8% Irish, 19.7% English, 16.6% Swedish, 3.4% American (2005-2009 5-year est.).

Economy: Single-family building permits issued: 0 (2010); Multi-family building permits issued: 0 (2010); Employment by occupation: 13.6% management, 16.1% professional, 24.8% services, 21.7% sales, 0.0% farming, 8.9% construction, 14.9% production (2005-2009 5-year est.).

Income: Per capita income: $22,690 (2010); Median household income: $45,377 (2010); Average household income: $52,552 (2010); Percent of households with income of $100,000 or more: 9.9% (2010); Poverty rate: 8.3% (2005-2009 5-year est.).

Taxes: Total city taxes per capita: $58 (2007); City property taxes per capita: $54 (2007).

Education: Percent of population age 25 and over with: High school diploma (including GED) or higher: 85.6% (2010); Bachelor's degree or higher: 21.0% (2010); Master's degree or higher: 5.5% (2010).

School District(s)
Monmouth-Roseville CUSD 238 (PK-12)
   2009-10 Enrollment: 1,718 . . . . (309) 734-4712

Housing: Homeownership rate: 79.5% (2010); Median home value: $82,295 (2010); Median contract rent: $309 per month (2005-2009 5-year est.); Median year structure built: 1954 (2005-2009 5-year est.).

Newspapers: Roseville Independent (Community news; Circulation 950)

Transportation: Commute to work: 89.6% car, 0.5% public transportation, 7.6% walk, 2.2% work from home (2005-2009 5-year est.); Travel time to work: 47.0% less than 15 minutes, 25.1% 15 to 30 minutes, 19.0% 30 to 45 minutes, 0.4% 45 to 60 minutes, 8.6% 60 minutes or more (2005-2009 5-year est.)

Additional Information Contacts
Roseville Chamber of Commerce . . . .
   http://roseville-il.org

SMITHSHIRE (unincorporated postal area, zip code 61478). Covers a land area of 36.926 square miles and a water area of 0 square miles. Located at 40.77° N. Lat; 90.76° W. Long. Elevation is 735 feet.

Population: 337 (2000); Race: 100.0% White, 0.0% Black, 0.0% Asian, 0.0% Other, 0.7% Hispanic of any race (2000); Density: 9.1 persons per square mile (2000); Age: 22.2% under 18, 18.5% over 64 (2000); Marriage status: 11.6% never married, 72.6% now married, 11.2% widowed, 4.6% divorced (2000); Foreign born: 0.7% (2000); Ancestry (includes multiple ancestries): 19.9% German, 13.2% American, 12.3% English, 8.3% Irish (2000).

Economy: Employment by occupation: 6.9% management, 13.8% professional, 19.2% services, 27.7% sales, 3.1% farming, 6.9% construction, 22.3% production (2000).

Income: Per capita income: $19,660 (2000); Median household income: $36,250 (2000); Poverty rate: 8.9% (2000).

Education: Percent of population age 25 and over with: High school diploma (including GED) or higher: 74.5% (2000); Bachelor's degree or higher: 6.9% (2000).

Housing: Homeownership rate: 82.5% (2000); Median home value: $38,600 (2000); Median contract rent: $186 per month (2000); Median year structure built: 1947 (2000).

Transportation: Commute to work: 83.8% car, 0.0% public transportation, 2.3% walk, 13.8% work from home (2000); Travel time to work: 20.5% less than 15 minutes, 35.7% 15 to 30 minutes, 35.7% 30 to 45 minutes, 8.0% 45 to 60 minutes, 0.0% 60 minutes or more (2000)

Washington County

Located in southwestern Illinois; bounded on the north by the Kaskaskia River; drained by the Little Muddy River. Covers a land area of 562.61

square miles, a water area of 1.51 square miles, and is located in the Central Time Zone at 38.36° N. Lat., 89.37° W. Long. The county was founded in 1818. County seat is Nashville.

Weather Station: Nashville 4 NE   Elevation: 515 feet

	Jan	Feb	Mar	Apr	May	Jun	Jul	Aug	Sep	Oct	Nov	Dec
High	39	44	55	67	76	85	88	87	80	69	55	42
Low	23	27	35	45	55	64	68	66	58	47	37	27
Precip	2.3	2.3	3.4	3.7	4.7	3.8	3.9	2.6	3.3	3.4	3.6	2.8
Snow	4.2	4.3	1.0	0.1	0.0	0.0	0.0	0.0	0.0	0.1	0.6	3.5

High and Low temperatures in degrees Fahrenheit; Precipitation and Snow in inches

Population: 14,965 (1990); 15,148 (2000); 14,654 (2010); 14,329 (2015 projected); Race: 97.6% White, 0.9% Black, 0.2% Asian, 1.2% Other, 1.2% Hispanic of any race (2010); Density: 26.0 persons per square mile (2010); Average household size: 2.52 (2010); Median age: 40.3 (2010); Males per 100 females: 98.8 (2010).
Religion: Five largest groups: 30.0% Catholic Church, 18.3% Lutheran Church—Missouri Synod, 15.5% United Church of Christ, 6.8% Southern Baptist Convention, 4.9% The United Methodist Church (2000).
Economy: Unemployment rate: 7.3% (August 2011); Total civilian labor force: 8,601 (August 2011); Leading industries: 31.9% manufacturing; 10.3% transportation & warehousing; 10.3% retail trade (2009); Farms: 779 totaling 353,903 acres (2007); Companies that employ 500 or more persons: 1 (2009); Companies that employ 100 to 499 persons: 5 (2009); Companies that employ less than 100 persons: 390 (2009); Black-owned businesses: n/a (2007); Hispanic-owned businesses: n/a (2007); Asian-owned businesses: n/a (2007); Women-owned businesses: n/a (2007); Retail sales per capita: $17,570 (2010). Single-family building permits issued: 29 (2010); Multi-family building permits issued: 2 (2010).
Income: Per capita income: $24,138 (2010); Median household income: $50,707 (2010); Average household income: $61,091 (2010); Percent of households with income of $100,000 or more: 12.8% (2010); Poverty rate: 9.6% (2009); Bankruptcy rate: 2.65% (2010).
Taxes: Total county taxes per capita: $147 (2007); County property taxes per capita: $147 (2007).
Education: Percent of population age 25 and over with: High school diploma (including GED) or higher: 85.0% (2010); Bachelor's degree or higher: 16.2% (2010); Master's degree or higher: 5.7% (2010).
Housing: Homeownership rate: 80.0% (2010); Median home value: $103,842 (2010); Median contract rent: $355 per month (2005-2009 5-year est.); Median year structure built: 1964 (2005-2009 5-year est.)
Health: Birth rate: 130.5 per 10,000 population (2009); Death rate: 110.6 per 10,000 population (2009); Age-adjusted cancer mortality rate: 158.5 deaths per 100,000 population (2007); Number of physicians: 6.8 per 10,000 population (2008); Hospital beds: 39.4 per 10,000 population (2007); Hospital admissions: 243.8 per 10,000 population (2007).
Elections: 2008 Presidential election results: 42.1% Obama, 56.4% McCain, 0.7% Nader
National and State Parks: Washington County State Conservation Area
Additional Information Contacts
Washington County Government.....................(618) 327-4800

Nashville Chamber of Commerce ....(618) 327-3700
  http://nashvilleilchamber.com
Okawville Chamber of Commerce...................(618) 243-5694
  http://www.okawvillecc.com

Washington County Communities

ADDIEVILLE (village). Covers a land area of 1.053 square miles and a water area of 0 square miles. Located at 38.39° N. Lat; 89.48° W. Long. Elevation is 469 feet.
Population: 257 (1990); 267 (2000); 239 (2010); 225 (2015 projected); Race: 98.3% White, 0.0% Black, 0.0% Asian, 1.7% Other, 1.3% Hispanic of any race (2010); Density: 227.0 persons per square mile (2010); Average household size: 2.52 (2010); Median age: 43.8 (2010); Males per 100 females: 107.8 (2010); Marriage status: 25.0% never married, 57.1% now married, 10.4% widowed, 7.5% divorced (2005-2009 5-year est.); Foreign born: 1.7% (2005-2009 5-year est.); Ancestry (includes multiple ancestries): 57.9% German, 11.7% Irish, 8.7% Polish, 7.0% Italian, 3.3% European (2005-2009 5-year est.).
Economy: Employment by occupation: 4.0% management, 19.9% professional, 13.2% services, 29.8% sales, 0.0% farming, 17.2% construction, 15.9% production (2005-2009 5-year est.).

Income: Per capita income: $24,206 (2010); Median household income: $48,750 (2010); Average household income: $59,789 (2010); Percent of households with income of $100,000 or more: 14.7% (2010); Poverty rate: 5.2% (2005-2009 5-year est.).
Taxes: Total city taxes per capita: $62 (2007); City property taxes per capita: $62 (2007).
Education: Percent of population age 25 and over with: High school diploma (including GED) or higher: 85.4% (2010); Bachelor's degree or higher: 20.5% (2010); Master's degree or higher: 9.4% (2010).
Housing: Homeownership rate: 84.2% (2010); Median home value: $100,000 (2010); Median contract rent: n/a per month (2005-2009 5-year est.); Median year structure built: 1947 (2005-2009 5-year est.).
Transportation: Commute to work: 96.0% car, 0.0% public transportation, 0.0% walk, 4.0% work from home (2005-2009 5-year est.); Travel time to work: 39.3% less than 15 minutes, 16.6% 15 to 30 minutes, 20.7% 30 to 45 minutes, 15.2% 45 to 60 minutes, 8.3% 60 minutes or more (2005-2009 5-year est.)

ASHLEY (city). Covers a land area of 1.107 square miles and a water area of 0.022 square miles. Located at 38.32° N. Lat; 89.18° W. Long. Elevation is 548 feet.
History: Ashley was named for early settler John Ashley.
Population: 583 (1990); 613 (2000); 570 (2010); 549 (2015 projected); Race: 97.4% White, 0.7% Black, 0.0% Asian, 1.9% Other, 1.4% Hispanic of any race (2010); Density: 514.8 persons per square mile (2010); Average household size: 2.49 (2010); Median age: 37.9 (2010); Males per 100 females: 102.8 (2010); Marriage status: 27.9% never married, 52.2% now married, 8.1% widowed, 11.7% divorced (2005-2009 5-year est.); Foreign born: 1.8% (2005-2009 5-year est.); Ancestry (includes multiple ancestries): 29.5% German, 17.1% Polish, 13.3% Irish, 9.0% American, 4.7% French (2005-2009 5-year est.).
Economy: Single-family building permits issued: 0 (2010); Multi-family building permits issued: 0 (2010); Employment by occupation: 5.5% management, 9.8% professional, 24.0% services, 18.5% sales, 1.2% farming, 14.2% construction, 26.8% production (2005-2009 5-year est.).
Income: Per capita income: $18,039 (2010); Median household income: $38,424 (2010); Average household income: $44,072 (2010); Percent of households with income of $100,000 or more: 6.6% (2010); Poverty rate: 22.4% (2005-2009 5-year est.).
Taxes: Total city taxes per capita: $80 (2007); City property taxes per capita: $73 (2007).
Education: Percent of population age 25 and over with: High school diploma (including GED) or higher: 83.7% (2010); Bachelor's degree or higher: 7.3% (2010); Master's degree or higher: 1.3% (2010).
School District(s)
Ashley CCSD 15 (PK-08)
  2009-10 Enrollment: 147 ....(618) 485-6611
Housing: Homeownership rate: 81.2% (2010); Median home value: $55,102 (2010); Median contract rent: $309 per month (2005-2009 5-year est.); Median year structure built: 1958 (2005-2009 5-year est.).
Transportation: Commute to work: 98.4% car, 0.0% public transportation, 1.6% walk, 0.0% work from home (2005-2009 5-year est.); Travel time to work: 22.9% less than 15 minutes, 48.1% 15 to 30 minutes, 11.6% 30 to 45 minutes, 3.5% 45 to 60 minutes, 14.0% 60 minutes or more (2005-2009 5-year est.)

DU BOIS (village). Covers a land area of 1.068 square miles and a water area of 0 square miles. Located at 38.22° N. Lat; 89.21° W. Long. Elevation is 522 feet.
Population: 216 (1990); 222 (2000); 205 (2010); 199 (2015 projected); Race: 94.6% White, 4.4% Black, 0.0% Asian, 1.0% Other, 2.0% Hispanic of any race (2010); Density: 191.9 persons per square mile (2010); Average household size: 2.42 (2010); Median age: 52.5 (2010); Males per 100 females: 95.2 (2010); Marriage status: 33.5% never married, 55.5% now married, 5.5% widowed, 5.5% divorced (2005-2009 5-year est.); Foreign born: 0.0% (2005-2009 5-year est.); Ancestry (includes multiple ancestries): 68.3% Polish, 44.2% German, 16.1% Irish, 3.5% English, 3.0% Italian (2005-2009 5-year est.).
Economy: Single-family building permits issued: 1 (2010); Multi-family building permits issued: 0 (2010); Employment by occupation: 3.0% management, 0.0% professional, 16.8% services, 20.8% sales, 3.0% farming, 18.8% construction, 37.6% production (2005-2009 5-year est.).
Income: Per capita income: $18,957 (2010); Median household income: $43,250 (2010); Average household income: $55,261 (2010); Percent of

households with income of $100,000 or more: 6.0% (2010); Poverty rate: 6.0% (2005-2009 5-year est.).

Taxes: Total city taxes per capita: $76 (2007); City property taxes per capita: $66 (2007).

Education: Percent of population age 25 and over with: High school diploma (including GED) or higher: 65.6% (2010); Bachelor's degree or higher: 3.2% (2010); Master's degree or higher: 2.5% (2010).

Housing: Homeownership rate: 89.6% (2010); Median home value: $74,000 (2010); Median contract rent: $294 per month (2005-2009 5-year est.); Median year structure built: 1953 (2005-2009 5-year est.).

Transportation: Commute to work: 97.9% car, 0.0% public transportation, 0.0% walk, 2.1% work from home (2005-2009 5-year est.); Travel time to work: 2.2% less than 15 minutes, 21.7% 15 to 30 minutes, 46.7% 30 to 45 minutes, 2.2% 45 to 60 minutes, 27.2% 60 minutes or more (2005-2009 5-year est.)

HOYLETON (village).
Covers a land area of 0.750 square miles and a water area of 0 square miles. Located at 38.44° N. Lat; 89.27° W. Long. Elevation is 518 feet.

Population: 508 (1990); 520 (2000); 485 (2010); 463 (2015 projected); Race: 92.6% White, 5.8% Black, 0.4% Asian, 1.2% Other, 0.6% Hispanic of any race (2010); Density: 646.3 persons per square mile (2010); Average household size: 2.57 (2010); Median age: 35.9 (2010); Males per 100 females: 102.1 (2010); Marriage status: 51.6% never married, 41.9% now married, 2.6% widowed, 3.9% divorced (2005-2009 5-year est.); Foreign born: 0.0% (2005-2009 5-year est.); Ancestry (includes multiple ancestries): 42.2% German, 6.5% Italian, 6.3% English, 5.6% Irish, 4.9% French (2005-2009 5-year est.).

Economy: Single-family building permits issued: 0 (2010); Multi-family building permits issued: 0 (2010); Employment by occupation: 7.9% management, 9.9% professional, 12.6% services, 26.5% sales, 0.0% farming, 4.3% construction, 38.7% production (2005-2009 5-year est.).

Income: Per capita income: $24,442 (2010); Median household income: $52,885 (2010); Average household income: $66,691 (2010); Percent of households with income of $100,000 or more: 14.5% (2010); Poverty rate: 32.5% (2005-2009 5-year est.).

Taxes: Total city taxes per capita: $124 (2007); City property taxes per capita: $62 (2007).

Education: Percent of population age 25 and over with: High school diploma (including GED) or higher: 85.4% (2010); Bachelor's degree or higher: 17.8% (2010); Master's degree or higher: 4.2% (2010).

School District(s)
Hoyleton Cons SD 29 (KG-08)
    2009-10 Enrollment: 72 . . . . (618) 493-7787
Kaskaskia Spec Educ District (KG-12)
    2009-10 Enrollment: n/a . . . . (618) 532-4721

Housing: Homeownership rate: 78.0% (2010); Median home value: $76,829 (2010); Median contract rent: $328 per month (2005-2009 5-year est.); Median year structure built: 1946 (2005-2009 5-year est.).

Transportation: Commute to work: 90.7% car, 0.0% public transportation, 2.4% walk, 6.1% work from home (2005-2009 5-year est.); Travel time to work: 26.8% less than 15 minutes, 44.6% 15 to 30 minutes, 15.6% 30 to 45 minutes, 3.9% 45 to 60 minutes, 9.1% 60 minutes or more (2005-2009 5-year est.)

IRVINGTON (village).
Covers a land area of 0.838 square miles and a water area of 0 square miles. Located at 38.43° N. Lat; 89.16° W. Long. Elevation is 531 feet.

History: Irvington was a major strawberry-producing center in the 1890's, when special trains took the produce to Chicago.

Population: 857 (1990); 736 (2000); 649 (2010); 605 (2015 projected); Race: 96.9% White, 0.5% Black, 0.6% Asian, 2.0% Other, 0.5% Hispanic of any race (2010); Density: 774.7 persons per square mile (2010); Average household size: 2.61 (2010); Median age: 34.7 (2010); Males per 100 females: 103.4 (2010); Marriage status: 13.7% never married, 73.0% now married, 3.2% widowed, 10.1% divorced (2005-2009 5-year est.); Foreign born: 5.4% (2005-2009 5-year est.); Ancestry (includes multiple ancestries): 44.9% German, 18.0% Irish, 7.7% English, 6.8% Polish, 5.0% Czechoslovakian (2005-2009 5-year est.).

Economy: Single-family building permits issued: 0 (2010); Multi-family building permits issued: 0 (2010); Employment by occupation: 12.9% management, 10.5% professional, 15.6% services, 18.6% sales, 4.5% farming, 3.9% construction, 33.9% production (2005-2009 5-year est.).

Income: Per capita income: $23,261 (2010); Median household income: $56,530 (2010); Average household income: $60,542 (2010); Percent of

households with income of $100,000 or more: 11.6% (2010); Poverty rate: 6.1% (2005-2009 5-year est.).

Taxes: Total city taxes per capita: $40 (2007); City property taxes per capita: $40 (2007).

Education: Percent of population age 25 and over with: High school diploma (including GED) or higher: 88.8% (2010); Bachelor's degree or higher: 16.1% (2010); Master's degree or higher: 4.4% (2010).

School District(s)
Irvington CCSD 11 (KG-08)
    2009-10 Enrollment: 85 . . . . (618) 249-6761

Housing: Homeownership rate: 72.3% (2010); Median home value: $80,851 (2010); Median contract rent: $379 per month (2005-2009 5-year est.); Median year structure built: 1970 (2005-2009 5-year est.).

Transportation: Commute to work: 99.1% car, 0.0% public transportation, 0.0% walk, 0.0% work from home (2005-2009 5-year est.); Travel time to work: 15.1% less than 15 minutes, 41.2% 15 to 30 minutes, 31.1% 30 to 45 minutes, 4.0% 45 to 60 minutes, 8.6% 60 minutes or more (2005-2009 5-year est.)

NASHVILLE (city).
County seat. Covers a land area of 2.681 square miles and a water area of 0.089 square miles. Located at 38.34° N. Lat; 89.38° W. Long. Elevation is 518 feet.

History: Incorporated 1853.

Population: 3,280 (1990); 3,147 (2000); 3,029 (2010); 2,957 (2015 projected); Race: 98.6% White, 0.3% Black, 0.3% Asian, 0.8% Other, 1.6% Hispanic of any race (2010); Density: 1,129.9 persons per square mile (2010); Average household size: 2.38 (2010); Median age: 40.2 (2010); Males per 100 females: 90.3 (2010); Marriage status: 27.6% never married, 54.4% now married, 11.0% widowed, 7.0% divorced (2005-2009 5-year est.); Foreign born: 0.0% (2005-2009 5-year est.); Ancestry (includes multiple ancestries): 57.0% German, 13.8% Polish, 12.7% Irish, 10.7% English, 9.6% American (2005-2009 5-year est.).

Economy: Single-family building permits issued: 3 (2010); Multi-family building permits issued: 2 (2010); Employment by occupation: 14.2% management, 25.2% professional, 16.2% services, 17.7% sales, 1.0% farming, 11.5% construction, 14.1% production (2005-2009 5-year est.).

Income: Per capita income: $27,287 (2010); Median household income: $51,713 (2010); Average household income: $64,615 (2010); Percent of households with income of $100,000 or more: 15.3% (2010); Poverty rate: 14.9% (2005-2009 5-year est.).

Taxes: Total city taxes per capita: $113 (2007); City property taxes per capita: $94 (2007).

Education: Percent of population age 25 and over with: High school diploma (including GED) or higher: 88.4% (2010); Bachelor's degree or higher: 25.2% (2010); Master's degree or higher: 10.4% (2010).

School District(s)
Nashville CCSD 49 (PK-08)
    2009-10 Enrollment: 585 . . . . (618) 327-3055
Nashville CHSD 99 (09-12)
    2009-10 Enrollment: 512 . . . . (618) 327-8286

Housing: Homeownership rate: 71.6% (2010); Median home value: $114,950 (2010); Median contract rent: $410 per month (2005-2009 5-year est.); Median year structure built: 1959 (2005-2009 5-year est.).

Hospitals: Washington County Hospital (61 beds)

Newspapers: Nashville News (Local news; Circulation 5,400)

Transportation: Commute to work: 92.6% car, 1.8% public transportation, 1.1% walk, 4.5% work from home (2005-2009 5-year est.); Travel time to work: 55.3% less than 15 minutes, 11.0% 15 to 30 minutes, 21.3% 30 to 45 minutes, 4.5% 45 to 60 minutes, 7.9% 60 minutes or more (2005-2009 5-year est.)

Additional Information Contacts
Nashville Chamber of Commerce . . . . (618) 327-3700
    http://nashvilleilchamber.com

NEW MINDEN (village).
Covers a land area of 0.275 square miles and a water area of 0 square miles. Located at 38.43° N. Lat; 89.36° W. Long. Elevation is 453 feet.

Population: 219 (1990); 204 (2000); 201 (2010); 199 (2015 projected); Race: 98.0% White, 1.5% Black, 0.5% Asian, 0.0% Other, 4.5% Hispanic of any race (2010); Density: 730.9 persons per square mile (2010); Average household size: 2.48 (2010); Median age: 38.4 (2010); Males per 100 females: 84.4 (2010); Marriage status: 18.4% never married, 63.2% now married, 9.6% widowed, 8.8% divorced (2005-2009 5-year est.); Foreign born: 1.3% (2005-2009 5-year est.); Ancestry (includes multiple

ancestries): 55.2% German, 10.4% Polish, 9.1% American, 8.4% English, 7.1% Irish (2005-2009 5-year est.).
Economy: Employment by occupation: 14.4% management, 10.0% professional, 15.6% services, 27.8% sales, 0.0% farming, 10.0% construction, 22.2% production (2005-2009 5-year est.).
Income: Per capita income: $23,652 (2010); Median household income: $53,500 (2010); Average household income: $62,840 (2010); Percent of households with income of $100,000 or more: 9.9% (2010); Poverty rate: 0.7% (2005-2009 5-year est.).
Taxes: Total city taxes per capita: $25 (2007); City property taxes per capita: $15 (2007).
Education: Percent of population age 25 and over with: High school diploma (including GED) or higher: 83.2% (2010); Bachelor's degree or higher: 18.3% (2010); Master's degree or higher: 4.6% (2010).
Housing: Homeownership rate: 86.4% (2010); Median home value: $83,333 (2010); Median contract rent: $500 per month (2005-2009 5-year est.); Median year structure built: 1954 (2005-2009 5-year est.).
Transportation: Commute to work: 91.1% car, 1.1% public transportation, 1.1% walk, 5.6% work from home (2005-2009 5-year est.); Travel time to work: 34.1% less than 15 minutes, 29.4% 15 to 30 minutes, 10.6% 30 to 45 minutes, 15.3% 45 to 60 minutes, 10.6% 60 minutes or more (2005-2009 5-year est.)

OAKDALE (village). Covers a land area of 1.660 square miles and a water area of 0 square miles. Located at 38.26° N. Lat; 89.50° W. Long. Elevation is 518 feet.
Population: 206 (1990); 213 (2000); 222 (2010); 224 (2015 projected); Race: 96.8% White, 0.0% Black, 0.5% Asian, 2.7% Other, 0.0% Hispanic of any race (2010); Density: 133.7 persons per square mile (2010); Average household size: 2.64 (2010); Median age: 40.9 (2010); Males per 100 females: 93.0 (2010); Marriage status: 33.8% never married, 51.0% now married, 6.4% widowed, 8.8% divorced (2005-2009 5-year est.); Foreign born: 2.2% (2005-2009 5-year est.); Ancestry (includes multiple ancestries): 32.4% German, 16.4% Irish, 12.4% American, 10.5% Polish, 8.4% English (2005-2009 5-year est.).
Economy: Employment by occupation: 1.5% management, 9.8% professional, 23.3% services, 30.8% sales, 0.0% farming, 17.3% construction, 17.3% production (2005-2009 5-year est.).
Income: Per capita income: $27,895 (2010); Median household income: $56,250 (2010); Average household income: $73,899 (2010); Percent of households with income of $100,000 or more: 20.2% (2010); Poverty rate: 13.5% (2005-2009 5-year est.).
Taxes: Total city taxes per capita: $29 (2007); City property taxes per capita: $29 (2007).
Education: Percent of population age 25 and over with: High school diploma (including GED) or higher: 91.8% (2010); Bachelor's degree or higher: 19.7% (2010); Master's degree or higher: 6.8% (2010).
School District(s)
Oakdale CCSD 1 (KG-08)
    2009-10 Enrollment: 86 . . . . (618) 329-5292
Housing: Homeownership rate: 86.9% (2010); Median home value: $118,750 (2010); Median contract rent: $458 per month (2005-2009 5-year est.); Median year structure built: 1961 (2005-2009 5-year est.).
Transportation: Commute to work: 94.7% car, 0.0% public transportation, 3.0% walk, 0.0% work from home (2005-2009 5-year est.); Travel time to work: 25.6% less than 15 minutes, 45.9% 15 to 30 minutes, 9.8% 30 to 45 minutes, 14.3% 45 to 60 minutes, 4.5% 60 minutes or more (2005-2009 5-year est.)

OKAWVILLE (village). Covers a land area of 2.027 square miles and a water area of 0 square miles. Located at 38.43° N. Lat; 89.54° W. Long. Elevation is 440 feet.
Population: 1,304 (1990); 1,355 (2000); 1,328 (2010); 1,301 (2015 projected); Race: 97.4% White, 1.0% Black, 0.2% Asian, 1.4% Other, 0.5% Hispanic of any race (2010); Density: 655.3 persons per square mile (2010); Average household size: 2.39 (2010); Median age: 38.9 (2010); Males per 100 females: 100.0 (2010); Marriage status: 18.2% never married, 58.9% now married, 8.0% widowed, 14.9% divorced (2005-2009 5-year est.); Foreign born: 0.8% (2005-2009 5-year est.); Ancestry (includes multiple ancestries): 54.3% German, 17.3% Irish, 8.6% English, 4.9% French, 4.8% American (2005-2009 5-year est.).
Economy: Single-family building permits issued: 5 (2010); Multi-family building permits issued: 0 (2010); Employment by occupation: 13.1% management, 16.5% professional, 19.2% services, 13.3% sales, 0.5% farming, 15.5% construction, 21.9% production (2005-2009 5-year est.).

Income: Per capita income: $24,911 (2010); Median household income: $48,169 (2010); Average household income: $59,419 (2010); Percent of households with income of $100,000 or more: 12.1% (2010); Poverty rate: 9.5% (2005-2009 5-year est.).
Taxes: Total city taxes per capita: $106 (2007); City property taxes per capita: $103 (2007).
Education: Percent of population age 25 and over with: High school diploma (including GED) or higher: 83.8% (2010); Bachelor's degree or higher: 19.9% (2010); Master's degree or higher: 6.9% (2010).
School District(s)
West Washington Co CUD 10 (KG-12)
    2009-10 Enrollment: 540 . . . . (618) 243-6454
Housing: Homeownership rate: 76.4% (2010); Median home value: $111,000 (2010); Median contract rent: $344 per month (2005-2009 5-year est.); Median year structure built: 1962 (2005-2009 5-year est.).
Newspapers: Okawville Times (Regional news; Circulation 2,200)
Transportation: Commute to work: 92.7% car, 0.2% public transportation, 5.5% walk, 0.7% work from home (2005-2009 5-year est.); Travel time to work: 28.7% less than 15 minutes, 24.9% 15 to 30 minutes, 24.2% 30 to 45 minutes, 14.2% 45 to 60 minutes, 8.0% 60 minutes or more (2005-2009 5-year est.)
Additional Information Contacts
Okawville Chamber of Commerce . . . . (618) 243-5694
    http://www.okawvillecc.com

RADOM (village). Covers a land area of 1.037 square miles and a water area of 0 square miles. Located at 38.28° N. Lat; 89.19° W. Long. Elevation is 535 feet.
Population: 174 (1990); 395 (2000); 376 (2010); 364 (2015 projected); Race: 94.7% White, 4.3% Black, 0.0% Asian, 1.1% Other, 1.6% Hispanic of any race (2010); Density: 362.6 persons per square mile (2010); Average household size: 2.43 (2010); Median age: 52.3 (2010); Males per 100 females: 83.4 (2010); Marriage status: 18.6% never married, 53.9% now married, 16.1% widowed, 11.4% divorced (2005-2009 5-year est.); Foreign born: 0.9% (2005-2009 5-year est.); Ancestry (includes multiple ancestries): 48.6% Polish, 25.7% German, 13.8% English, 11.3% Irish, 4.9% Italian (2005-2009 5-year est.).
Economy: Employment by occupation: 9.3% management, 17.8% professional, 14.0% services, 6.5% sales, 1.9% farming, 19.6% construction, 30.8% production (2005-2009 5-year est.).
Income: Per capita income: $18,957 (2010); Median household income: $41,667 (2010); Average household income: $50,656 (2010); Percent of households with income of $100,000 or more: 4.9% (2010); Poverty rate: 12.0% (2005-2009 5-year est.).
Taxes: Total city taxes per capita: $44 (2007); City property taxes per capita: $41 (2007).
Education: Percent of population age 25 and over with: High school diploma (including GED) or higher: 66.7% (2010); Bachelor's degree or higher: 3.9% (2010); Master's degree or higher: 2.5% (2010).
Housing: Homeownership rate: 90.2% (2010); Median home value: $75,238 (2010); Median contract rent: $238 per month (2005-2009 5-year est.); Median year structure built: 1975 (2005-2009 5-year est.).
Transportation: Commute to work: 89.0% car, 0.0% public transportation, 0.0% walk, 8.0% work from home (2005-2009 5-year est.); Travel time to work: 9.8% less than 15 minutes, 43.5% 15 to 30 minutes, 33.7% 30 to 45 minutes, 0.0% 45 to 60 minutes, 13.0% 60 minutes or more (2005-2009 5-year est.)

RICHVIEW (village). Covers a land area of 1.112 square miles and a water area of 0 square miles. Located at 38.37° N. Lat; 89.18° W. Long. Elevation is 541 feet.
Population: 325 (1990); 308 (2000); 287 (2010); 273 (2015 projected); Race: 94.4% White, 1.4% Black, 0.3% Asian, 3.8% Other, 2.8% Hispanic of any race (2010); Density: 258.1 persons per square mile (2010); Average household size: 2.56 (2010); Median age: 39.1 (2010); Males per 100 females: 105.0 (2010); Marriage status: 22.0% never married, 64.0% now married, 5.6% widowed, 8.4% divorced (2005-2009 5-year est.); Foreign born: 2.4% (2005-2009 5-year est.); Ancestry (includes multiple ancestries): 43.9% German, 15.9% Irish, 7.1% Polish, 6.8% English, 3.0% Austrian (2005-2009 5-year est.).
Economy: Single-family building permits issued: 0 (2010); Multi-family building permits issued: 0 (2010); Employment by occupation: 5.0% management, 37.0% professional, 16.8% services, 21.0% sales, 0.0% farming, 4.2% construction, 16.0% production (2005-2009 5-year est.).

Income: Per capita income: $19,774 (2010); Median household income: $39,565 (2010); Average household income: $51,295 (2010); Percent of households with income of $100,000 or more: 6.3% (2010); Poverty rate: 24.7% (2005-2009 5-year est.).

Taxes: Total city taxes per capita: $96 (2007); City property taxes per capita: $51 (2007).

Education: Percent of population age 25 and over with: High school diploma (including GED) or higher: 84.7% (2010); Bachelor's degree or higher: 15.9% (2010); Master's degree or higher: 4.8% (2010).

Housing: Homeownership rate: 80.4% (2010); Median home value: $58,261 (2010); Median contract rent: $221 per month (2005-2009 5-year est.); Median year structure built: 1973 (2005-2009 5-year est.).

Transportation: Commute to work: 90.5% car, 0.0% public transportation, 7.6% walk, 0.0% work from home (2005-2009 5-year est.); Travel time to work: 21.0% less than 15 minutes, 61.9% 15 to 30 minutes, 13.3% 30 to 45 minutes, 3.8% 45 to 60 minutes, 0.0% 60 minutes or more (2005-2009 5-year est.)

VENEDY (village). Covers a land area of 0.286 square miles and a water area of 0 square miles. Located at 38.39° N. Lat; 89.64° W. Long. Elevation is 453 feet.

Population: 158 (1990); 137 (2000); 129 (2010); 124 (2015 projected); Race: 98.4% White, 0.0% Black, 0.0% Asian, 1.6% Other, 0.8% Hispanic of any race (2010); Density: 451.2 persons per square mile (2010); Average household size: 2.63 (2010); Median age: 43.2 (2010); Males per 100 females: 118.6 (2010); Marriage status: 17.2% never married, 71.3% now married, 9.8% widowed, 1.6% divorced (2005-2009 5-year est.); Foreign born: 2.2% (2005-2009 5-year est.); Ancestry (includes multiple ancestries): 79.6% German, 6.6% Irish, 4.4% Portuguese, 3.6% Czechoslovakian, 1.5% Dutch (2005-2009 5-year est.).

Economy: Employment by occupation: 15.4% management, 7.7% professional, 3.8% services, 29.5% sales, 0.0% farming, 19.2% construction, 24.4% production (2005-2009 5-year est.).

Income: Per capita income: $20,555 (2010); Median household income: $46,250 (2010); Average household income: $48,980 (2010); Percent of households with income of $100,000 or more: 8.2% (2010); Poverty rate: 4.4% (2005-2009 5-year est.).

Taxes: Total city taxes per capita: $60 (2007); City property taxes per capita: $45 (2007).

Education: Percent of population age 25 and over with: High school diploma (including GED) or higher: 85.9% (2010); Bachelor's degree or higher: 13.0% (2010); Master's degree or higher: 3.3% (2010).

Housing: Homeownership rate: 83.7% (2010); Median home value: $130,357 (2010); Median contract rent: $288 per month (2005-2009 5-year est.); Median year structure built: 1954 (2005-2009 5-year est.).

Transportation: Commute to work: 80.8% car, 0.0% public transportation, 7.7% walk, 11.5% work from home (2005-2009 5-year est.); Travel time to work: 34.8% less than 15 minutes, 23.2% 15 to 30 minutes, 23.2% 30 to 45 minutes, 11.6% 45 to 60 minutes, 7.2% 60 minutes or more (2005-2009 5-year est.)

Wayne County

Located in southeastern Illinois; drained by the Little Wabash River. Covers a land area of 713.90 square miles, a water area of 1.66 square miles, and is located in the Central Time Zone at 38.41° N. Lat., 88.40° W. Long. The county was founded in 1819. County seat is Fairfield.

Weather Station: Fairfield Radio Wfiw										Elevation: 430 feet		
	Jan	Feb	Mar	Apr	May	Jun	Jul	Aug	Sep	Oct	Nov	Dec
High	39	44	55	67	76	85	88	87	81	68	55	42
Low	23	26	34	44	53	62	66	64	56	44	35	26
Precip	3.0	2.8	4.5	4.4	4.9	3.7	3.6	3.1	2.7	4.0	4.1	3.5
Snow	3.7	4.0	1.6	0.1	0.0	0.0	0.0	0.0	0.0	0.1	0.3	3.7

High and Low temperatures in degrees Fahrenheit; Precipitation and Snow in inches

Population: 17,241 (1990); 17,151 (2000); 16,417 (2010); 15,997 (2015 projected); Race: 97.6% White, 0.8% Black, 0.5% Asian, 1.1% Other, 0.9% Hispanic of any race (2010); Density: 23.0 persons per square mile (2010); Average household size: 2.32 (2010); Median age: 40.7 (2010); Males per 100 females: 95.7 (2010).

Religion: Five largest groups: 23.5% Southern Baptist Convention, 12.6% Christian Churches and Churches of Christ, 8.4% The United Methodist Church, 3.6% Cumberland Presbyterian Church, 1.8% National Association of Free Will Baptists (2000).

Economy: Unemployment rate: 8.3% (August 2011); Total civilian labor force: 8,131 (August 2011); Leading industries: 24.7% health care and social assistance; 19.5% retail trade; 7.3% accommodation & food services (2009); Farms: 1,233 totaling 333,255 acres (2007); Companies that employ 500 or more persons: 1 (2009); Companies that employ 100 to 499 persons: 3 (2009); Companies that employ less than 100 persons: 347 (2009); Black-owned businesses: n/a (2007); Hispanic-owned businesses: n/a (2007); Asian-owned businesses: n/a (2007); Women-owned businesses: 393 (2007); Retail sales per capita: $9,410 (2010). Single-family building permits issued: 1 (2010); Multi-family building permits issued: 0 (2010).

Income: Per capita income: $20,165 (2010); Median household income: $38,444 (2010); Average household income: $46,950 (2010); Percent of households with income of $100,000 or more: 6.6% (2010); Poverty rate: 14.6% (2009); Bankruptcy rate: 3.41% (2010).

Taxes: Total county taxes per capita: $105 (2007); County property taxes per capita: $77 (2007).

Education: Percent of population age 25 and over with: High school diploma (including GED) or higher: 81.7% (2010); Bachelor's degree or higher: 12.4% (2010); Master's degree or higher: 4.0% (2010).

Housing: Homeownership rate: 78.3% (2010); Median home value: $60,465 (2010); Median contract rent: $290 per month (2005-2009 5-year est.); Median year structure built: 1967 (2005-2009 5-year est.)

Health: Birth rate: 117.8 per 10,000 population (2009); Death rate: 125.2 per 10,000 population (2009); Age-adjusted cancer mortality rate: 209.8 deaths per 100,000 population (2007); Number of physicians: 6.7 per 10,000 population (2008); Hospital beds: 98.2 per 10,000 population (2007); Hospital admissions: 1,007.6 per 10,000 population (2007).

Elections: 2008 Presidential election results: 31.6% Obama, 66.8% McCain, 0.6% Nader

National and State Parks: Sam Dale Lake State Conservation Area

Additional Information Contacts

Wayne County Government . . . . (618) 842-5182

City of Fairfield . . . . (618) 842-3871
    http://www.fairfield-il.com
Fairfield Chamber of Commerce . . . . (618) 842-6116
    http://fairfieldillinoischamber.com

Wayne County Communities

BARNHILL (unincorporated postal area, zip code 62809). Aka Barn Hill. Covers a land area of 14.526 square miles and a water area of 0.026 square miles. Located at 38.26° N. Lat; 88.34° W. Long. Elevation is 397 feet.

Population: 239 (2000); Race: 98.6% White, 0.0% Black, 0.0% Asian, 1.4% Other, 2.7% Hispanic of any race (2000); Density: 16.5 persons per square mile (2000); Age: 22.8% under 18, 13.7% over 64 (2000); Marriage status: 11.1% never married, 72.2% now married, 4.4% widowed, 12.2% divorced (2000); Foreign born: 0.0% (2000); Ancestry (includes multiple ancestries): 27.9% American, 13.2% English, 9.6% German, 5.5% Irish (2000).

Economy: Employment by occupation: 14.0% management, 11.4% professional, 5.3% services, 25.4% sales, 0.0% farming, 9.6% construction, 34.2% production (2000).

Income: Per capita income: $16,212 (2000); Median household income: $31,250 (2000); Poverty rate: 6.4% (2000).

Education: Percent of population age 25 and over with: High school diploma (including GED) or higher: 80.1% (2000); Bachelor's degree or higher: 8.7% (2000).

Housing: Homeownership rate: 83.7% (2000); Median home value: $33,100 (2000); Median contract rent: $267 per month (2000); Median year structure built: 1968 (2000).

Transportation: Commute to work: 89.1% car, 1.8% public transportation, 5.5% walk, 1.8% work from home (2000); Travel time to work: 51.9% less than 15 minutes, 26.9% 15 to 30 minutes, 5.6% 30 to 45 minutes, 10.2% 45 to 60 minutes, 5.6% 60 minutes or more (2000)

CISNE (village). Covers a land area of 0.638 square miles and a water area of 0 square miles. Located at 38.51° N. Lat; 88.43° W. Long. Elevation is 459 feet.

Population: 645 (1990); 673 (2000); 638 (2010); 618 (2015 projected); Race: 97.2% White, 1.9% Black, 0.3% Asian, 0.6% Other, 0.5% Hispanic of any race (2010); Density: 999.9 persons per square mile (2010); Average household size: 2.20 (2010); Median age: 41.6 (2010); Males per

100 females: 87.6 (2010); Marriage status: 21.4% never married, 52.7% now married, 10.0% widowed, 16.0% divorced (2005-2009 5-year est.); Foreign born: 0.0% (2005-2009 5-year est.); Ancestry (includes multiple ancestries): 20.5% German, 9.2% English, 7.5% Irish, 3.1% American, 2.7% Polish (2005-2009 5-year est.).
Economy: Employment by occupation: 8.5% management, 9.4% professional, 14.0% services, 24.8% sales, 8.8% farming, 3.4% construction, 31.1% production (2005-2009 5-year est.).
Income: Per capita income: $19,835 (2010); Median household income: $33,415 (2010); Average household income: $43,280 (2010); Percent of households with income of $100,000 or more: 4.3% (2010); Poverty rate: 13.8% (2005-2009 5-year est.).
Taxes: Total city taxes per capita: $20 (2007); City property taxes per capita: $17 (2007).
Education: Percent of population age 25 and over with: High school diploma (including GED) or higher: 75.4% (2010); Bachelor's degree or higher: 13.2% (2010); Master's degree or higher: 3.5% (2010).

School District(s)
North Wayne CUSD 200 (PK-12)
    2009-10 Enrollment: 430 . . . . (618) 673-2151
Wayne City CUSD 100 (PK-12)
    2009-10 Enrollment: 575 . . . . (618) 895-3103
Housing: Homeownership rate: 79.6% (2010); Median home value: $52,239 (2010); Median contract rent: $244 per month (2005-2009 5-year est.); Median year structure built: 1957 (2005-2009 5-year est.).
Transportation: Commute to work: 95.7% car, 0.0% public transportation, 0.0% walk, 4.3% work from home (2005-2009 5-year est.); Travel time to work: 35.9% less than 15 minutes, 56.7% 15 to 30 minutes, 3.8% 30 to 45 minutes, 1.6% 45 to 60 minutes, 1.9% 60 minutes or more (2005-2009 5-year est.)

FAIRFIELD (city). Aka Thomas Prairie. County seat. Covers a land area of 3.616 square miles and a water area of 0.034 square miles. Located at 38.38° N. Lat; 88.36° W. Long. Elevation is 440 feet.
History: Fairfield was established in 1819, and developed as the seat of Wayne County. Clothing and automobile parts manufacturing were early industries.
Population: 5,573 (1990); 5,421 (2000); 5,175 (2010); 5,029 (2015 projected); Race: 97.6% White, 0.4% Black, 0.9% Asian, 1.1% Other, 0.9% Hispanic of any race (2010); Density: 1,430.9 persons per square mile (2010); Average household size: 2.08 (2010); Median age: 44.0 (2010); Males per 100 females: 85.3 (2010); Marriage status: 24.6% never married, 49.4% now married, 9.2% widowed, 16.7% divorced (2005-2009 5-year est.); Foreign born: 1.7% (2005-2009 5-year est.); Ancestry (includes multiple ancestries): 19.2% English, 15.5% German, 13.1% American, 12.7% Irish, 2.6% Italian (2005-2009 5-year est.).
Economy: Single-family building permits issued: 1 (2010); Multi-family building permits issued: 0 (2010); Employment by occupation: 5.6% management, 15.4% professional, 20.6% services, 23.1% sales, 0.7% farming, 9.9% construction, 24.7% production (2005-2009 5-year est.).
Income: Per capita income: $21,751 (2010); Median household income: $34,173 (2010); Average household income: $45,896 (2010); Percent of households with income of $100,000 or more: 6.8% (2010); Poverty rate: 21.8% (2005-2009 5-year est.).
Taxes: Total city taxes per capita: $186 (2007); City property taxes per capita: $151 (2007).
Education: Percent of population age 25 and over with: High school diploma (including GED) or higher: 81.3% (2010); Bachelor's degree or higher: 14.8% (2010); Master's degree or higher: 5.3% (2010).

School District(s)
Fairfield Comm H S Dist 225 (09-12)
    2009-10 Enrollment: 476 . . . . (618) 842-2649
Fairfield Psd 112 (PK-08)
    2009-10 Enrollment: 700 . . . . (618) 842-6501
Jasper CCSD 17 (KG-08)
    2009-10 Enrollment: 164 . . . . (618) 842-3048
New Hope CCSD 6 (PK-08)
    2009-10 Enrollment: 190 . . . . (618) 842-3296

Two-year College(s)
Illinois Eastern Community Colleges-Frontier Community Coll (Public)
    Fall 2009 Enrollment: 2,009 . . . . (618) 393-2982
    2010-11 Tuition: In-state $6,808; Out-of-state $9,081
Housing: Homeownership rate: 68.7% (2010); Median home value: $59,162 (2010); Median contract rent: $311 per month (2005-2009 5-year est.); Median year structure built: 1958 (2005-2009 5-year est.).

Hospitals: Fairfield Memorial Hospital (80 beds)
Safety: Violent crime rate: 22.0 per 10,000 population; Property crime rate: 186.1 per 10,000 population (2010).
Newspapers: Wayne County Press (Local news; Circulation 8,125)
Transportation: Commute to work: 88.4% car, 2.4% public transportation, 7.7% walk, 0.4% work from home (2005-2009 5-year est.); Travel time to work: 70.5% less than 15 minutes, 16.5% 15 to 30 minutes, 6.8% 30 to 45 minutes, 4.7% 45 to 60 minutes, 1.5% 60 minutes or more (2005-2009 5-year est.)
Additional Information Contacts
City of Fairfield . . . . (618) 842-3871
    http://www.fairfield-il.com
Fairfield Chamber of Commerce . . . . (618) 842-6116
    http://fairfieldillinoischamber.com

GEFF (unincorporated postal area, zip code 62842). Aka Jeffersonville. Covers a land area of 41.983 square miles and a water area of 0.010 square miles. Located at 38.44° N. Lat; 88.41° W. Long. Elevation is 459 feet.
Population: 840 (2000); Race: 97.6% White, 0.0% Black, 0.0% Asian, 2.4% Other, 2.3% Hispanic of any race (2000); Density: 20.0 persons per square mile (2000); Age: 25.7% under 18, 18.4% over 64 (2000); Marriage status: 18.2% never married, 65.1% now married, 9.0% widowed, 7.6% divorced (2000); Foreign born: 0.2% (2000); Ancestry (includes multiple ancestries): 16.0% American, 12.6% German, 10.3% English, 7.4% Irish (2000).
Economy: Employment by occupation: 15.8% management, 7.0% professional, 16.8% services, 14.2% sales, 4.8% farming, 8.6% construction, 32.9% production (2000).
Income: Per capita income: $14,504 (2000); Median household income: $30,040 (2000); Poverty rate: 10.9% (2000).
Education: Percent of population age 25 and over with: High school diploma (including GED) or higher: 74.5% (2000); Bachelor's degree or higher: 8.2% (2000).

School District(s)
Geff CCSD 14 (KG-08)
    2009-10 Enrollment: 88 . . . . (618) 897-2465
Housing: Homeownership rate: 85.3% (2000); Median home value: $39,800 (2000); Median contract rent: $252 per month (2000); Median year structure built: 1966 (2000).
Transportation: Commute to work: 93.0% car, 0.0% public transportation, 0.0% walk, 6.5% work from home (2000); Travel time to work: 35.9% less than 15 minutes, 35.7% 15 to 30 minutes, 19.4% 30 to 45 minutes, 4.9% 45 to 60 minutes, 4.1% 60 minutes or more (2000)

GOLDEN GATE (village). Aka Goldengate. Covers a land area of 0.077 square miles and a water area of 0 square miles. Located at 38.35° N. Lat; 88.20° W. Long. Elevation is 397 feet.
Population: 90 (1990); 100 (2000); 92 (2010); 90 (2015 projected); Race: 98.9% White, 0.0% Black, 0.0% Asian, 1.1% Other, 2.2% Hispanic of any race (2010); Density: 1,202.1 persons per square mile (2010); Average household size: 2.56 (2010); Median age: 36.7 (2010); Males per 100 females: 130.0 (2010); Marriage status: 32.7% never married, 32.7% now married, 27.3% widowed, 7.3% divorced (2005-2009 5-year est.); Foreign born: 0.0% (2005-2009 5-year est.); Ancestry (includes multiple ancestries): 45.6% English, 10.5% German, 10.5% Irish, 8.8% Welsh (2005-2009 5-year est.).
Economy: Employment by occupation: 0.0% management, 6.1% professional, 0.0% services, 18.2% sales, 0.0% farming, 12.1% construction, 63.6% production (2005-2009 5-year est.).
Income: Per capita income: $16,018 (2010); Median household income: $36,500 (2010); Average household income: $41,528 (2010); Percent of households with income of $100,000 or more: 5.6% (2010); Poverty rate: 17.5% (2005-2009 5-year est.).
Taxes: Total city taxes per capita: $41 (2007); City property taxes per capita: $41 (2007).
Education: Percent of population age 25 and over with: High school diploma (including GED) or higher: 81.0% (2010); Bachelor's degree or higher: 7.9% (2010); Master's degree or higher: 0.0% (2010).
Housing: Homeownership rate: 83.3% (2010); Median home value: $40,000 (2010); Median contract rent: n/a per month (2005-2009 5-year est.); Median year structure built: 1948 (2005-2009 5-year est.).
Transportation: Commute to work: 100.0% car, 0.0% public transportation, 0.0% walk, 0.0% work from home (2005-2009 5-year est.); Travel time to work: 12.1% less than 15 minutes, 87.9% 15 to 30 minutes,

0.0% 30 to 45 minutes, 0.0% 45 to 60 minutes, 0.0% 60 minutes or more (2005-2009 5-year est.)

JEFFERSONVILLE (village). Aka Geff. Covers a land area of 1.020 square miles and a water area of 0 square miles. Located at 38.44° N. Lat; 88.40° W. Long. Elevation is 459 feet.

History: Also known as Geff.

Population: 311 (1990); 366 (2000); 355 (2010); 348 (2015 projected); Race: 97.7% White, 0.8% Black, 0.6% Asian, 0.8% Other, 2.3% Hispanic of any race (2010); Density: 348.0 persons per square mile (2010); Average household size: 2.48 (2010); Median age: 34.9 (2010); Males per 100 females: 101.7 (2010); Marriage status: 21.6% never married, 47.4% now married, 12.9% widowed, 18.1% divorced (2005-2009 5-year est.); Foreign born: 1.9% (2005-2009 5-year est.); Ancestry (includes multiple ancestries): 19.3% American, 13.4% German, 6.2% English, 5.7% Irish, 3.2% Dutch (2005-2009 5-year est.).

Economy: Employment by occupation: 1.5% management, 28.4% professional, 14.7% services, 20.6% sales, 2.9% farming, 8.8% construction, 23.0% production (2005-2009 5-year est.).

Income: Per capita income: $17,998 (2010); Median household income: $36,641 (2010); Average household income: $44,790 (2010); Percent of households with income of $100,000 or more: 7.0% (2010); Poverty rate: 10.0% (2005-2009 5-year est.).

Taxes: Total city taxes per capita: $11 (2007); City property taxes per capita: $8 (2007).

Education: Percent of population age 25 and over with: High school diploma (including GED) or higher: 84.4% (2010); Bachelor's degree or higher: 11.2% (2010); Master's degree or higher: 3.1% (2010).

Housing: Homeownership rate: 83.2% (2010); Median home value: $50,417 (2010); Median contract rent: $234 per month (2005-2009 5-year est.); Median year structure built: 1970 (2005-2009 5-year est.).

Transportation: Commute to work: 98.5% car, 0.0% public transportation, 1.5% walk, 0.0% work from home (2005-2009 5-year est.); Travel time to work: 64.4% less than 15 minutes, 17.8% 15 to 30 minutes, 5.4% 30 to 45 minutes, 3.5% 45 to 60 minutes, 8.9% 60 minutes or more (2005-2009 5-year est.)

JOHNSONVILLE (village). Covers a land area of 0.212 square miles and a water area of 0 square miles. Located at 38.52° N. Lat; 88.53° W. Long. Elevation is 541 feet.

Population: 68 (1990); 69 (2000); 66 (2010); 64 (2015 projected); Race: 93.9% White, 3.0% Black, 1.5% Asian, 1.5% Other, 0.0% Hispanic of any race (2010); Density: 311.7 persons per square mile (2010); Average household size: 2.44 (2010); Median age: 40.0 (2010); Males per 100 females: 112.9 (2010); Marriage status: 26.5% never married, 47.1% now married, 0.0% widowed, 26.5% divorced (2005-2009 5-year est.); Foreign born: 0.0% (2005-2009 5-year est.); Ancestry (includes multiple ancestries): 12.3% German, 12.3% Irish (2005-2009 5-year est.).

Economy: Employment by occupation: 9.1% management, 13.6% professional, 18.2% services, 13.6% sales, 9.1% farming, 0.0% construction, 36.4% production (2005-2009 5-year est.).

Income: Per capita income: $21,828 (2010); Median household income: $48,750 (2010); Average household income: $55,185 (2010); Percent of households with income of $100,000 or more: 11.1% (2010); Poverty rate: 47.4% (2005-2009 5-year est.).

Taxes: Total city taxes per capita: $15 (2007); City property taxes per capita: $15 (2007).

Education: Percent of population age 25 and over with: High school diploma (including GED) or higher: 85.4% (2010); Bachelor's degree or higher: 14.6% (2010); Master's degree or higher: 2.1% (2010).

School District(s)
North Wayne CUSD 200 (PK-12)
    2009-10 Enrollment: 430 . . . . (618) 673-2151

Housing: Homeownership rate: 88.9% (2010); Median home value: $60,000 (2010); Median contract rent: n/a per month (2005-2009 5-year est.); Median year structure built: 1990 (2005-2009 5-year est.).

Transportation: Commute to work: 100.0% car, 0.0% public transportation, 0.0% walk, 0.0% work from home (2005-2009 5-year est.); Travel time to work: 13.6% less than 15 minutes, 86.4% 15 to 30 minutes, 0.0% 30 to 45 minutes, 0.0% 45 to 60 minutes, 0.0% 60 minutes or more (2005-2009 5-year est.)

KEENES (village). Covers a land area of 0.130 square miles and a water area of 0 square miles. Located at 38.33° N. Lat; 88.64° W. Long. Elevation is 449 feet.

Population: 62 (1990); 99 (2000); 101 (2010); 101 (2015 projected); Race: 97.0% White, 2.0% Black, 0.0% Asian, 1.0% Other, 1.0% Hispanic of any race (2010); Density: 777.6 persons per square mile (2010); Average household size: 2.66 (2010); Median age: 38.9 (2010); Males per 100 females: 98.0 (2010); Marriage status: 22.6% never married, 54.8% now married, 0.0% widowed, 22.6% divorced (2005-2009 5-year est.); Foreign born: 0.0% (2005-2009 5-year est.); Ancestry (includes multiple ancestries): 9.2% English, 8.4% American, 4.2% German, 2.5% Irish (2005-2009 5-year est.).

Economy: Employment by occupation: 0.0% management, 0.0% professional, 12.2% services, 26.5% sales, 8.2% farming, 6.1% construction, 46.9% production (2005-2009 5-year est.).

Income: Per capita income: $20,780 (2010); Median household income: $55,000 (2010); Average household income: $53,553 (2010); Percent of households with income of $100,000 or more: 10.5% (2010); Poverty rate: 1.7% (2005-2009 5-year est.).

Taxes: Total city taxes per capita: $10 (2007); City property taxes per capita: $10 (2007).

Education: Percent of population age 25 and over with: High school diploma (including GED) or higher: 78.3% (2010); Bachelor's degree or higher: 10.1% (2010); Master's degree or higher: 4.3% (2010).

Housing: Homeownership rate: 86.8% (2010); Median home value: $58,000 (2010); Median contract rent: $292 per month (2005-2009 5-year est.); Median year structure built: 1967 (2005-2009 5-year est.).

Transportation: Commute to work: 95.9% car, 0.0% public transportation, 0.0% walk, 4.1% work from home (2005-2009 5-year est.); Travel time to work: 0.0% less than 15 minutes, 38.3% 15 to 30 minutes, 34.0% 30 to 45 minutes, 27.7% 45 to 60 minutes, 0.0% 60 minutes or more (2005-2009 5-year est.)

MOUNT ERIE (village). Covers a land area of 0.389 square miles and a water area of 0 square miles. Located at 38.51° N. Lat; 88.23° W. Long. Elevation is 499 feet.

Population: 155 (1990); 105 (2000); 98 (2010); 94 (2015 projected); Race: 98.0% White, 0.0% Black, 0.0% Asian, 2.0% Other, 1.0% Hispanic of any race (2010); Density: 251.7 persons per square mile (2010); Average household size: 2.45 (2010); Median age: 43.1 (2010); Males per 100 females: 96.0 (2010); Marriage status: 22.9% never married, 66.7% now married, 4.2% widowed, 6.3% divorced (2005-2009 5-year est.); Foreign born: 0.0% (2005-2009 5-year est.); Ancestry (includes multiple ancestries): 15.2% German, 14.6% English, 11.4% American, 9.5% Irish, 3.2% French (2005-2009 5-year est.).

Economy: Employment by occupation: 8.2% management, 16.5% professional, 14.1% services, 28.2% sales, 2.4% farming, 11.8% construction, 18.8% production (2005-2009 5-year est.).

Income: Per capita income: $16,696 (2010); Median household income: $30,714 (2010); Average household income: $38,750 (2010); Percent of households with income of $100,000 or more: 2.5% (2010); Poverty rate: 20.3% (2005-2009 5-year est.).

Taxes: Total city taxes per capita: $39 (2007); City property taxes per capita: $39 (2007).

Education: Percent of population age 25 and over with: High school diploma (including GED) or higher: 77.3% (2010); Bachelor's degree or higher: 13.3% (2010); Master's degree or higher: 4.0% (2010).

School District(s)
North Wayne CUSD 200 (PK-12)
    2009-10 Enrollment: 430 . . . . (618) 673-2151

Housing: Homeownership rate: 80.0% (2010); Median home value: $66,667 (2010); Median contract rent: n/a per month (2005-2009 5-year est.); Median year structure built: 1974 (2005-2009 5-year est.).

Transportation: Commute to work: 95.0% car, 0.0% public transportation, 2.5% walk, 0.0% work from home (2005-2009 5-year est.); Travel time to work: 33.8% less than 15 minutes, 35.0% 15 to 30 minutes, 18.8% 30 to 45 minutes, 0.0% 45 to 60 minutes, 12.5% 60 minutes or more (2005-2009 5-year est.)

RINARD (unincorporated postal area, zip code 62878). Covers a land area of 44.117 square miles and a water area of 0.011 square miles. Located at 38.57° N. Lat; 88.49° W. Long. Elevation is 459 feet.

Population: 463 (2000); Race: 100.0% White, 0.0% Black, 0.0% Asian, 0.0% Other, 0.0% Hispanic of any race (2000); Density: 10.5 persons per square mile (2000); Age: 21.2% under 18, 20.8% over 64 (2000); Marriage status: 12.5% never married, 63.7% now married, 11.0% widowed, 12.8% divorced (2000); Foreign born: 0.0% (2000); Ancestry (includes multiple ancestries): 18.6% American, 14.1% German, 4.3% English, 3.8% Irish (2000).

Economy: Employment by occupation: 14.1% management, 22.4% professional, 13.5% services, 5.7% sales, 0.0% farming, 10.4% construction, 33.9% production (2000).

Income: Per capita income: $16,474 (2000); Median household income: $33,000 (2000); Poverty rate: 7.4% (2000).

Education: Percent of population age 25 and over with: High school diploma (including GED) or higher: 65.6% (2000); Bachelor's degree or higher: 11.8% (2000).

Housing: Homeownership rate: 85.1% (2000); Median home value: $36,100 (2000); Median contract rent: $196 per month (2000); Median year structure built: 1958 (2000).

Transportation: Commute to work: 92.0% car, 2.1% public transportation, 0.0% walk, 5.9% work from home (2000); Travel time to work: 14.2% less than 15 minutes, 45.5% 15 to 30 minutes, 27.3% 30 to 45 minutes, 5.1% 45 to 60 minutes, 8.0% 60 minutes or more (2000)

SIMS (village). Covers a land area of 1.200 square miles and a water area of 0 square miles. Located at 38.36° N. Lat; 88.53° W. Long. Elevation is 410 feet.

Population: 338 (1990); 273 (2000); 256 (2010); 249 (2015 projected); Race: 94.9% White, 3.9% Black, 0.0% Asian, 1.2% Other, 1.2% Hispanic of any race (2010); Density: 213.3 persons per square mile (2010); Average household size: 2.46 (2010); Median age: 39.6 (2010); Males per 100 females: 100.0 (2010); Marriage status: 17.2% never married, 78.1% now married, 4.6% widowed, 0.0% divorced (2005-2009 5-year est.); Foreign born: 1.6% (2005-2009 5-year est.); Ancestry (includes multiple ancestries): 19.8% Irish, 14.4% English, 8.6% American, 5.9% German, 2.7% Dutch (2005-2009 5-year est.).

Economy: Employment by occupation: 0.0% management, 5.9% professional, 24.7% services, 28.2% sales, 0.0% farming, 15.3% construction, 25.9% production (2005-2009 5-year est.).

Income: Per capita income: $19,491 (2010); Median household income: $39,688 (2010); Average household income: $46,803 (2010); Percent of households with income of $100,000 or more: 3.8% (2010); Poverty rate: 8.0% (2005-2009 5-year est.).

Taxes: Total city taxes per capita: $19 (2007); City property taxes per capita: $19 (2007).

Education: Percent of population age 25 and over with: High school diploma (including GED) or higher: 80.4% (2010); Bachelor's degree or higher: 6.1% (2010); Master's degree or higher: 1.1% (2010).

Housing: Homeownership rate: 78.8% (2010); Median home value: $57,143 (2010); Median contract rent: $267 per month (2005-2009 5-year est.); Median year structure built: 1961 (2005-2009 5-year est.).

Transportation: Commute to work: 90.1% car, 0.0% public transportation, 4.9% walk, 0.0% work from home (2005-2009 5-year est.); Travel time to work: 39.5% less than 15 minutes, 34.6% 15 to 30 minutes, 9.9% 30 to 45 minutes, 13.6% 45 to 60 minutes, 2.5% 60 minutes or more (2005-2009 5-year est.)

WAYNE CITY (village). Covers a land area of 1.677 square miles and a water area of 0 square miles. Located at 38.34° N. Lat; 88.59° W. Long. Elevation is 433 feet.

Population: 1,186 (1990); 1,089 (2000); 1,059 (2010); 1,044 (2015 projected); Race: 97.5% White, 0.9% Black, 0.1% Asian, 1.4% Other, 0.7% Hispanic of any race (2010); Density: 631.4 persons per square mile (2010); Average household size: 2.31 (2010); Median age: 36.9 (2010); Males per 100 females: 93.6 (2010); Marriage status: 21.4% never married, 57.1% now married, 12.6% widowed, 8.9% divorced (2005-2009 5-year est.); Foreign born: 0.8% (2005-2009 5-year est.); Ancestry (includes multiple ancestries): 20.0% German, 14.8% English, 13.0% Irish, 4.3% Dutch, 3.1% Scottish (2005-2009 5-year est.).

Economy: Employment by occupation: 23.0% management, 9.9% professional, 7.8% services, 26.4% sales, 1.5% farming, 4.6% construction, 26.8% production (2005-2009 5-year est.).

Income: Per capita income: $20,084 (2010); Median household income: $38,309 (2010); Average household income: $45,671 (2010); Percent of households with income of $100,000 or more: 6.6% (2010); Poverty rate: 13.2% (2005-2009 5-year est.).

Taxes: Total city taxes per capita: $79 (2007); City property taxes per capita: $79 (2007).

Education: Percent of population age 25 and over with: High school diploma (including GED) or higher: 78.7% (2010); Bachelor's degree or higher: 11.3% (2010); Master's degree or higher: 2.4% (2010).

School District(s)

Wayne City CUSD 100 (PK-12)

    2009-10 Enrollment: 575 . . . . (618) 895-3103

Housing: Homeownership rate: 73.8% (2010); Median home value: $58,909 (2010); Median contract rent: $252 per month (2005-2009 5-year est.); Median year structure built: 1964 (2005-2009 5-year est.).

Transportation: Commute to work: 97.4% car, 0.0% public transportation, 1.7% walk, 0.9% work from home (2005-2009 5-year est.); Travel time to work: 28.3% less than 15 minutes, 42.3% 15 to 30 minutes, 19.7% 30 to 45 minutes, 2.4% 45 to 60 minutes, 7.2% 60 minutes or more (2005-2009 5-year est.)

White County

Located in southeastern Illinois; bounded on the east by the Wabash River and the Indiana border; drained by the Little Wabash River. Covers a land area of 494.87 square miles, a water area of 6.83 square miles, and is located in the Central Time Zone at 38.10° N. Lat., 88.18° W. Long. The county was founded in 1815. County seat is Carmi.

Weather Station: Fulton L&D #13   Elevation: 591 feet

	Jan	Feb	Mar	Apr	May	Jun	Jul	Aug	Sep	Oct	Nov	Dec
High	29	33	45	59	70	80	83	82	75	62	47	33
Low	13	16	27	39	50	60	64	63	54	42	31	18
Precip	1.2	1.4	2.3	3.1	3.6	4.2	3.2	4.1	2.9	2.9	2.5	1.8
Snow	3.1	1.7	0.4	0.5	0.0	0.0	0.0	0.0	0.0	0.0	0.2	1.5

High and Low temperatures in degrees Fahrenheit; Precipitation and Snow in inches

Weather Station: Morrison   Elevation: 603 feet

	Jan	Feb	Mar	Apr	May	Jun	Jul	Aug	Sep	Oct	Nov	Dec
High	31	35	47	61	73	82	85	83	76	64	49	35
Low	12	16	27	37	49	58	62	60	51	39	29	17
Precip	1.5	1.6	2.6	3.3	4.1	4.4	3.9	4.8	3.0	2.9	2.8	2.1
Snow	10.0	6.9	3.3	1.0	0.0	0.0	0.0	0.0	0.0	tr	1.5	8.5

High and Low temperatures in degrees Fahrenheit; Precipitation and Snow in inches

Population: 16,522 (1990); 15,371 (2000); 14,583 (2010); 14,146 (2015 projected); Race: 97.1% White, 0.8% Black, 0.2% Asian, 1.9% Other, 1.0% Hispanic of any race (2010); Density: 29.5 persons per square mile (2010); Average household size: 2.25 (2010); Median age: 42.3 (2010); Males per 100 females: 91.6 (2010).

Religion: Five largest groups: 17.7% Southern Baptist Convention, 13.0% Christian Churches and Churches of Christ, 10.7% The United Methodist Church, 5.4% Catholic Church, 2.9% Independent, Charismatic Churches (2000).

Economy: Unemployment rate: 7.8% (August 2011); Total civilian labor force: 7,832 (August 2011); Leading industries: 16.7% health care and social assistance; 14.5% retail trade; 9.5% accommodation & food services (2009); Farms: 481 totaling 296,989 acres (2007); Companies that employ 500 or more persons: 0 (2009); Companies that employ 100 to 499 persons: 4 (2009); Companies that employ less than 100 persons: 368 (2009); Black-owned businesses: n/a (2007); Hispanic-owned businesses: n/a (2007); Asian-owned businesses: n/a (2007); Women-owned businesses: n/a (2007); Retail sales per capita: $10,495 (2010). Single-family building permits issued: 0 (2010); Multi-family building permits issued: 0 (2010).

Income: Per capita income: $21,168 (2010); Median household income: $37,392 (2010); Average household income: $47,865 (2010); Percent of households with income of $100,000 or more: 7.9% (2010); Poverty rate: 15.5% (2009); Bankruptcy rate: 2.87% (2010).

Taxes: Total county taxes per capita: $75 (2007); County property taxes per capita: $75 (2007).

Education: Percent of population age 25 and over with: High school diploma (including GED) or higher: 81.5% (2010); Bachelor's degree or higher: 13.0% (2010); Master's degree or higher: 4.1% (2010).

Housing: Homeownership rate: 76.8% (2010); Median home value: $51,431 (2010); Median contract rent: $287 per month (2005-2009 5-year est.); Median year structure built: 1959 (2005-2009 5-year est.)

Health: Birth rate: 124.1 per 10,000 population (2009); Death rate: 148.0 per 10,000 population (2009); Age-adjusted cancer mortality rate: 199.9 deaths per 100,000 population (2007); Number of physicians: 4.1 per 10,000 population (2008); Hospital beds: 0.0 per 10,000 population (2007); Hospital admissions: 0.0 per 10,000 population (2007).

Elections: 2008 Presidential election results: 44.5% Obama, 53.5% McCain, 1.0% Nader

Additional Information Contacts

White County Government. . . . . (618) 382-7211
   http://www.whitecounty-il.gov
City of Carmi . . . . (618) 384-2001
   http://www.cityofcarmi.com
Grayville Chamber of Commerce. . . . . (618) 375-7518

White County Communities

BURNT PRAIRIE (village). Aka Liberty. Covers a land area of 0.080 square miles and a water area of 0 square miles. Located at 38.25° N. Lat; 88.25° W. Long. Elevation is 446 feet.
Population: 71 (1990); 58 (2000); 57 (2010); 54 (2015 projected); Race: 100.0% White, 0.0% Black, 0.0% Asian, 0.0% Other, 1.8% Hispanic of any race (2010); Density: 715.7 persons per square mile (2010); Average household size: 2.19 (2010); Median age: 41.4 (2010); Males per 100 females: 103.6 (2010); Marriage status: 19.1% never married, 66.0% now married, 4.3% widowed, 10.6% divorced (2005-2009 5-year est.); Foreign born: 0.0% (2005-2009 5-year est.); Ancestry (includes multiple ancestries): 22.4% German, 19.0% English, 10.3% Polish (2005-2009 5-year est.).
Economy: Employment by occupation: 13.3% management, 0.0% professional, 16.7% services, 16.7% sales, 6.7% farming, 33.3% construction, 13.3% production (2005-2009 5-year est.).
Income: Per capita income: $21,045 (2010); Median household income: $35,000 (2010); Average household income: $49,327 (2010); Percent of households with income of $100,000 or more: 11.5% (2010); Poverty rate: 24.1% (2005-2009 5-year est.).
Taxes: Total city taxes per capita: $211 (2007); City property taxes per capita: $18 (2007).
Education: Percent of population age 25 and over with: High school diploma (including GED) or higher: 82.9% (2010); Bachelor's degree or higher: 9.8% (2010); Master's degree or higher: 2.4% (2010).
Housing: Homeownership rate: 84.6% (2010); Median home value: $45,000 (2010); Median contract rent: n/a per month (2005-2009 5-year est.); Median year structure built: before 1940 (2005-2009 5-year est.).
Transportation: Commute to work: 85.7% car, 0.0% public transportation, 0.0% walk, 14.3% work from home (2005-2009 5-year est.); Travel time to work: 41.7% less than 15 minutes, 41.7% 15 to 30 minutes, 16.7% 30 to 45 minutes, 0.0% 45 to 60 minutes, 0.0% 60 minutes or more (2005-2009 5-year est.)

CARMI (city). County seat. Covers a land area of 2.478 square miles and a water area of 0.034 square miles. Located at 38.08° N. Lat; 88.16° W. Long. Elevation is 394 feet.
History: Carmi, platted in 1816, developed as the seat of White County.
Population: 5,684 (1990); 5,422 (2000); 5,081 (2010); 4,898 (2015 projected); Race: 96.9% White, 1.5% Black, 0.2% Asian, 1.4% Other, 0.9% Hispanic of any race (2010); Density: 2,050.1 persons per square mile (2010); Average household size: 2.14 (2010); Median age: 43.2 (2010); Males per 100 females: 86.5 (2010); Marriage status: 18.7% never married, 56.5% now married, 14.2% widowed, 10.6% divorced (2005-2009 5-year est.); Foreign born: 1.5% (2005-2009 5-year est.); Ancestry (includes multiple ancestries): 26.1% German, 21.2% American, 11.8% Irish, 10.7% English, 2.7% French (2005-2009 5-year est.).
Economy: Employment by occupation: 5.3% management, 15.6% professional, 20.2% services, 21.5% sales, 0.4% farming, 9.3% construction, 27.6% production (2005-2009 5-year est.).
Income: Per capita income: $19,124 (2010); Median household income: $31,289 (2010); Average household income: $40,807 (2010); Percent of households with income of $100,000 or more: 5.6% (2010); Poverty rate: 12.7% (2005-2009 5-year est.).
Taxes: Total city taxes per capita: $140 (2007); City property taxes per capita: $41 (2007).
Education: Percent of population age 25 and over with: High school diploma (including GED) or higher: 78.8% (2010); Bachelor's degree or higher: 12.4% (2010); Master's degree or higher: 4.2% (2010).
School District(s)
Carmi-White County CUSD 5 (PK-12)
   2009-10 Enrollment: 1,394 . . . . (618) 382-2341
Housing: Homeownership rate: 68.5% (2010); Median home value: $46,314 (2010); Median contract rent: $307 per month (2005-2009 5-year est.); Median year structure built: 1956 (2005-2009 5-year est.).
Hospitals: White County Medical Center (49 beds)

Newspapers: Carmi Times & Weekly Times (Local news; Circulation 3,900); Weekly Times (National news; Circulation 500); White County Shopper News (National news; Circulation 500)
Transportation: Commute to work: 91.5% car, 0.0% public transportation, 3.7% walk, 2.7% work from home (2005-2009 5-year est.); Travel time to work: 55.1% less than 15 minutes, 12.3% 15 to 30 minutes, 13.9% 30 to 45 minutes, 6.6% 45 to 60 minutes, 12.1% 60 minutes or more (2005-2009 5-year est.)
Additional Information Contacts
City of Carmi . . . . (618) 384-2001
   http://www.cityofcarmi.com

CROSSVILLE (village). Covers a land area of 0.642 square miles and a water area of 0 square miles. Located at 38.16° N. Lat; 88.06° W. Long. Elevation is 410 feet.
Population: 805 (1990); 782 (2000); 737 (2010); 708 (2015 projected); Race: 97.7% White, 0.0% Black, 0.0% Asian, 2.3% Other, 1.6% Hispanic of any race (2010); Density: 1,147.1 persons per square mile (2010); Average household size: 2.30 (2010); Median age: 42.1 (2010); Males per 100 females: 100.3 (2010); Marriage status: 21.1% never married, 52.2% now married, 10.8% widowed, 15.9% divorced (2005-2009 5-year est.); Foreign born: 0.0% (2005-2009 5-year est.); Ancestry (includes multiple ancestries): 18.6% German, 18.1% American, 17.3% Irish, 8.9% French, 8.4% English (2005-2009 5-year est.).
Economy: Single-family building permits issued: 0 (2010); Multi-family building permits issued: 0 (2010); Employment by occupation: 9.3% management, 9.6% professional, 17.6% services, 20.3% sales, 1.8% farming, 8.7% construction, 32.8% production (2005-2009 5-year est.).
Income: Per capita income: $23,555 (2010); Median household income: $44,052 (2010); Average household income: $53,547 (2010); Percent of households with income of $100,000 or more: 9.1% (2010); Poverty rate: 21.4% (2005-2009 5-year est.).
Taxes: Total city taxes per capita: $91 (2007); City property taxes per capita: $59 (2007).
Education: Percent of population age 25 and over with: High school diploma (including GED) or higher: 80.2% (2010); Bachelor's degree or higher: 12.1% (2010); Master's degree or higher: 1.7% (2010).
School District(s)
Carmi-White County CUSD 5 (PK-12)
   2009-10 Enrollment: 1,394 . . . . (618) 382-2341
Housing: Homeownership rate: 79.7% (2010); Median home value: $54,898 (2010); Median contract rent: $272 per month (2005-2009 5-year est.); Median year structure built: 1957 (2005-2009 5-year est.).
Transportation: Commute to work: 97.2% car, 0.0% public transportation, 1.2% walk, 1.6% work from home (2005-2009 5-year est.); Travel time to work: 42.1% less than 15 minutes, 30.7% 15 to 30 minutes, 15.2% 30 to 45 minutes, 4.7% 45 to 60 minutes, 7.3% 60 minutes or more (2005-2009 5-year est.)

ENFIELD (village). Covers a land area of 1.160 square miles and a water area of 0 square miles. Located at 38.09° N. Lat; 88.34° W. Long. Elevation is 486 feet.
History: Enfield was settled in 1813.
Population: 683 (1990); 625 (2000); 601 (2010); 589 (2015 projected); Race: 98.8% White, 0.2% Black, 0.0% Asian, 1.0% Other, 0.3% Hispanic of any race (2010); Density: 518.1 persons per square mile (2010); Average household size: 2.31 (2010); Median age: 41.5 (2010); Males per 100 females: 93.2 (2010); Marriage status: 23.5% never married, 51.3% now married, 5.9% widowed, 19.3% divorced (2005-2009 5-year est.); Foreign born: 1.5% (2005-2009 5-year est.); Ancestry (includes multiple ancestries): 27.7% German, 23.3% Irish, 14.7% American, 12.0% English, 4.4% Scotch-Irish (2005-2009 5-year est.).
Economy: Employment by occupation: 6.7% management, 8.6% professional, 27.6% services, 12.7% sales, 3.4% farming, 14.2% construction, 26.9% production (2005-2009 5-year est.).
Income: Per capita income: $23,590 (2010); Median household income: $38,625 (2010); Average household income: $53,287 (2010); Percent of households with income of $100,000 or more: 10.8% (2010); Poverty rate: 33.2% (2005-2009 5-year est.).
Taxes: Total city taxes per capita: $91 (2007); City property taxes per capita: $89 (2007).
Education: Percent of population age 25 and over with: High school diploma (including GED) or higher: 79.3% (2010); Bachelor's degree or higher: 12.4% (2010); Master's degree or higher: 4.8% (2010).

Norris City-Omaha-Enfield CUSD 3 (PK-12)
2009-10 Enrollment: 734 . . . . (618) 378-3222
Housing: Homeownership rate: 85.3% (2010); Median home value: $48,696 (2010); Median contract rent: $246 per month (2005-2009 5-year est.); Median year structure built: 1959 (2005-2009 5-year est.).
Transportation: Commute to work: 93.4% car, 0.0% public transportation, 4.3% walk, 1.2% work from home (2005-2009 5-year est.); Travel time to work: 44.7% less than 15 minutes, 26.7% 15 to 30 minutes, 12.2% 30 to 45 minutes, 9.4% 45 to 60 minutes, 7.1% 60 minutes or more (2005-2009 5-year est.)

GRAYVILLE (city). Covers a land area of 1.489 square miles and a water area of 0.043 square miles. Located at 38.25° N. Lat; 87.99° W. Long.
Population: 2,044 (1990); 1,725 (2000); 1,569 (2010); 1,489 (2015 projected); Race: 98.0% White, 0.1% Black, 0.1% Asian, 1.8% Other, 0.4% Hispanic of any race (2010); Density: 1,053.4 persons per square mile (2010); Average household size: 2.20 (2010); Median age: 45.2 (2010); Males per 100 females: 87.5 (2010); Marriage status: 16.2% never married, 66.8% now married, 7.6% widowed, 9.4% divorced (2005-2009 5-year est.); Foreign born: 0.0% (2005-2009 5-year est.); Ancestry (includes multiple ancestries): 23.3% German, 16.1% English, 15.8% American, 14.4% Irish, 2.3% Scottish (2005-2009 5-year est.).
Economy: Single-family building permits issued: 0 (2010); Multi-family building permits issued: 0 (2010); Employment by occupation: 18.7% management, 13.3% professional, 22.7% services, 19.2% sales, 0.0% farming, 3.6% construction, 22.5% production (2005-2009 5-year est.).
Income: Per capita income: $22,877 (2010); Median household income: $41,913 (2010); Average household income: $51,355 (2010); Percent of households with income of $100,000 or more: 8.8% (2010); Poverty rate: 18.9% (2005-2009 5-year est.).
Taxes: Total city taxes per capita: $195 (2007); City property taxes per capita: $152 (2007).
Education: Percent of population age 25 and over with: High school diploma (including GED) or higher: 83.6% (2010); Bachelor's degree or higher: 9.3% (2010); Master's degree or higher: 3.1% (2010).
Grayville CUSD 1 (PK-12)
2009-10 Enrollment: 330 . . . . (618) 375-7214
Housing: Homeownership rate: 75.5% (2010); Median home value: $49,398 (2010); Median contract rent: $335 per month (2005-2009 5-year est.); Median year structure built: 1955 (2005-2009 5-year est.).
Safety: Violent crime rate: 96.5 per 10,000 population; Property crime rate: 154.4 per 10,000 population (2010).
Transportation: Commute to work: 94.3% car, 0.0% public transportation, 2.2% walk, 2.5% work from home (2005-2009 5-year est.); Travel time to work: 51.9% less than 15 minutes, 18.0% 15 to 30 minutes, 12.1% 30 to 45 minutes, 10.8% 45 to 60 minutes, 7.2% 60 minutes or more (2005-2009 5-year est.)
Additional Information Contacts
Grayville Chamber of Commerce . . . . (618) 375-7518

MAUNIE (village). Covers a land area of 0.161 square miles and a water area of 0 square miles. Located at 38.03° N. Lat; 88.04° W. Long. Elevation is 371 feet.
Population: 119 (1990); 177 (2000); 168 (2010); 157 (2015 projected); Race: 94.0% White, 1.2% Black, 0.6% Asian, 4.2% Other, 0.0% Hispanic of any race (2010); Density: 1,040.5 persons per square mile (2010); Average household size: 2.37 (2010); Median age: 43.5 (2010); Males per 100 females: 97.6 (2010); Marriage status: 31.1% never married, 31.1% now married, 7.8% widowed, 30.0% divorced (2005-2009 5-year est.); Foreign born: 0.0% (2005-2009 5-year est.); Ancestry (includes multiple ancestries): 41.9% Irish, 40.3% German, 13.7% English, 5.6% French, 4.8% Dutch (2005-2009 5-year est.).
Economy: Employment by occupation: 8.3% management, 16.7% professional, 33.3% services, 4.2% sales, 0.0% farming, 0.0% construction, 37.5% production (2005-2009 5-year est.).
Income: Per capita income: $22,057 (2010); Median household income: $44,167 (2010); Average household income: $53,521 (2010); Percent of households with income of $100,000 or more: 7.0% (2010); Poverty rate: 47.6% (2005-2009 5-year est.).
Taxes: Total city taxes per capita: $17 (2007); City property taxes per capita: $11 (2007).

Education: Percent of population age 25 and over with: High school diploma (including GED) or higher: 81.5% (2010); Bachelor's degree or higher: 12.6% (2010); Master's degree or higher: 2.5% (2010).
Housing: Homeownership rate: 80.3% (2010); Median home value: $34,091 (2010); Median contract rent: $461 per month (2005-2009 5-year est.); Median year structure built: 1949 (2005-2009 5-year est.).
Transportation: Commute to work: 95.8% car, 0.0% public transportation, 0.0% walk, 4.2% work from home (2005-2009 5-year est.); Travel time to work: 34.8% less than 15 minutes, 30.4% 15 to 30 minutes, 4.3% 30 to 45 minutes, 8.7% 45 to 60 minutes, 21.7% 60 minutes or more (2005-2009 5-year est.)

MILL SHOALS (village). Covers a land area of 0.783 square miles and a water area of 0 square miles. Located at 38.24° N. Lat; 88.34° W. Long. Elevation is 381 feet.
Population: 300 (1990); 235 (2000); 220 (2010); 207 (2015 projected); Race: 98.6% White, 0.0% Black, 0.9% Asian, 0.5% Other, 0.0% Hispanic of any race (2010); Density: 280.8 persons per square mile (2010); Average household size: 2.18 (2010); Median age: 43.0 (2010); Males per 100 females: 94.7 (2010); Marriage status: 9.0% never married, 78.9% now married, 4.0% widowed, 8.0% divorced (2005-2009 5-year est.); Foreign born: 0.9% (2005-2009 5-year est.); Ancestry (includes multiple ancestries): 25.0% German, 20.7% Irish, 15.9% Polish, 11.2% English, 11.2% American (2005-2009 5-year est.).
Economy: Employment by occupation: 5.2% management, 8.3% professional, 18.8% services, 19.8% sales, 1.0% farming, 6.3% construction, 40.6% production (2005-2009 5-year est.).
Income: Per capita income: $21,074 (2010); Median household income: $36,974 (2010); Average household income: $46,436 (2010); Percent of households with income of $100,000 or more: 7.9% (2010); Poverty rate: 11.3% (2005-2009 5-year est.).
Taxes: Total city taxes per capita: $34 (2007); City property taxes per capita: $34 (2007).
Education: Percent of population age 25 and over with: High school diploma (including GED) or higher: 77.4% (2010); Bachelor's degree or higher: 7.3% (2010); Master's degree or higher: 1.8% (2010).
Edwd/Gltn/Hdin/Pop/Slne/Wbh/wn/wh (06-12)
2009-10 Enrollment: n/a . . . . (618) 253-5581
Housing: Homeownership rate: 83.2% (2010); Median home value: $41,429 (2010); Median contract rent: $132 per month (2005-2009 5-year est.); Median year structure built: 1948 (2005-2009 5-year est.).
Transportation: Commute to work: 96.8% car, 0.0% public transportation, 3.2% walk, 0.0% work from home (2005-2009 5-year est.); Travel time to work: 24.2% less than 15 minutes, 47.4% 15 to 30 minutes, 8.4% 30 to 45 minutes, 15.8% 45 to 60 minutes, 4.2% 60 minutes or more (2005-2009 5-year est.)

NORRIS CITY (village). Covers a land area of 1.159 square miles and a water area of 0 square miles. Located at 37.98° N. Lat; 88.32° W. Long. Elevation is 420 feet.
History: Norris City was named for pioneer settler William Norris. It developed as an agricultural and coal mining trading area.
Population: 1,341 (1990); 1,057 (2000); 902 (2010); 837 (2015 projected); Race: 97.6% White, 0.0% Black, 0.4% Asian, 2.0% Other, 0.1% Hispanic of any race (2010); Density: 777.9 persons per square mile (2010); Average household size: 2.10 (2010); Median age: 41.1 (2010); Males per 100 females: 87.9 (2010); Marriage status: 26.3% never married, 53.0% now married, 7.6% widowed, 13.1% divorced (2005-2009 5-year est.); Foreign born: 0.0% (2005-2009 5-year est.); Ancestry (includes multiple ancestries): 20.7% German, 19.8% Irish, 19.0% English, 5.5% Welsh, 4.1% Polish (2005-2009 5-year est.).
Economy: Employment by occupation: 4.3% management, 18.5% professional, 31.6% services, 14.2% sales, 2.3% farming, 10.6% construction, 18.5% production (2005-2009 5-year est.).
Income: Per capita income: $17,521 (2010); Median household income: $27,949 (2010); Average household income: $36,727 (2010); Percent of households with income of $100,000 or more: 2.1% (2010); Poverty rate: 14.0% (2005-2009 5-year est.).
Taxes: Total city taxes per capita: $111 (2007); City property taxes per capita: $111 (2007).
Education: Percent of population age 25 and over with: High school diploma (including GED) or higher: 83.4% (2010); Bachelor's degree or higher: 9.8% (2010); Master's degree or higher: 3.3% (2010).

Norris City-Omaha-Enfield CUSD 3 (PK-12)
2009-10 Enrollment: 734 . . . . (618) 378-3222
Ohio & Wabash Valley Reg Voc Sys
2009-10 Enrollment: n/a . . . . (618) 378-2274
Wabash & Ohio Valley Sp Ed Dist (KG-12)
2009-10 Enrollment: n/a . . . . (618) 378-2131
Housing: Homeownership rate: 75.6% (2010); Median home value:
$41,868 (2010); Median contract rent: $279 per month (2005-2009 5-year
est.); Median year structure built: 1956 (2005-2009 5-year est.).
Newspapers: Norris City Banner (Community news; Circulation 1,304)
Transportation: Commute to work: 92.2% car, 2.3% public transportation,
0.7% walk, 3.7% work from home (2005-2009 5-year est.); Travel time to
work: 35.2% less than 15 minutes, 26.2% 15 to 30 minutes, 16.9% 30 to 45
minutes, 7.9% 45 to 60 minutes, 13.8% 60 minutes or more (2005-2009
5-year est.)

PHILLIPSTOWN (village). Covers a land area of 0.271 square miles
and a water area of 0 square miles. Located at 38.14° N. Lat; 88.02° W.
Long. Elevation is 545 feet.
Population: 48 (1990); 28 (2000); 29 (2010); 28 (2015 projected); Race:
96.6% White, 0.0% Black, 0.0% Asian, 3.4% Other, 0.0% Hispanic of any
race (2010); Density: 107.0 persons per square mile (2010); Average
household size: 2.23 (2010); Median age: 46.0 (2010); Males per 100
females: 107.1 (2010); Marriage status: 21.6% never married, 78.4% now
married, 0.0% widowed, 0.0% divorced (2005-2009 5-year est.); Foreign
born: 0.0% (2005-2009 5-year est.); Ancestry (includes multiple
ancestries): 71.4% German, 46.9% Irish (2005-2009 5-year est.).
Economy: Employment by occupation: 3.7% management, 37.0%
professional, 3.7% services, 18.5% sales, 7.4% farming, 22.2%
construction, 7.4% production (2005-2009 5-year est.).
Income: Per capita income: $22,383 (2010); Median household income:
$47,500 (2010); Average household income: $52,308 (2010); Percent of
households with income of $100,000 or more: 7.7% (2010); Poverty rate:
0.0% (2005-2009 5-year est.).
Taxes: Total city taxes per capita: $0 (2007); City property taxes per
capita: $0 (2007).
Education: Percent of population age 25 and over with: High school
diploma (including GED) or higher: 90.5% (2010); Bachelor's degree or
higher: 9.5% (2010); Master's degree or higher: 4.8% (2010).
Housing: Homeownership rate: 76.9% (2010); Median home value:
$46,667 (2010); Median contract rent: n/a per month (2005-2009 5-year
est.); Median year structure built: 1968 (2005-2009 5-year est.).
Transportation: Commute to work: 92.6% car, 0.0% public transportation,
0.0% walk, 7.4% work from home (2005-2009 5-year est.); Travel time to
work: 12.0% less than 15 minutes, 24.0% 15 to 30 minutes, 32.0% 30 to 45
minutes, 32.0% 45 to 60 minutes, 0.0% 60 minutes or more (2005-2009
5-year est.)

SPRINGERTON (village). Aka Springer. Covers a land area of 0.125
square miles and a water area of 0 square miles. Located at 38.17° N. Lat;
88.35° W. Long. Elevation is 394 feet.
Population: 164 (1990); 134 (2000); 135 (2010); 133 (2015 projected);
Race: 98.5% White, 0.0% Black, 0.0% Asian, 1.5% Other, 0.0% Hispanic
of any race (2010); Density: 1,076.7 persons per square mile (2010);
Average household size: 2.22 (2010); Median age: 42.7 (2010); Males per
100 females: 90.1 (2010); Marriage status: 17.4% never married, 50.7%
now married, 7.2% widowed, 24.6% divorced (2005-2009 5-year est.);
Foreign born: 0.0% (2005-2009 5-year est.); Ancestry (includes multiple
ancestries): 19.0% Irish, 17.9% English, 14.3% German, 9.5% American,
6.0% European (2005-2009 5-year est.).
Economy: Employment by occupation: 0.0% management, 6.5%
professional, 67.7% services, 12.9% sales, 3.2% farming, 0.0%
construction, 9.7% production (2005-2009 5-year est.).
Income: Per capita income: $23,295 (2010); Median household income:
$35,625 (2010); Average household income: $55,551 (2010); Percent of
households with income of $100,000 or more: 8.5% (2010); Poverty rate:
17.9% (2005-2009 5-year est.).
Taxes: Total city taxes per capita: $0 (2007); City property taxes per
capita: $0 (2007).
Education: Percent of population age 25 and over with: High school
diploma (including GED) or higher: 80.9% (2010); Bachelor's degree or
higher: 8.5% (2010); Master's degree or higher: 3.2% (2010).
Housing: Homeownership rate: 83.1% (2010); Median home value:
$43,000 (2010); Median contract rent: n/a per month (2005-2009 5-year
est.); Median year structure built: 1952 (2005-2009 5-year est.).

Transportation: Commute to work: 100.0% car, 0.0% public
transportation, 0.0% walk, 0.0% work from home (2005-2009 5-year est.);
Travel time to work: 12.9% less than 15 minutes, 45.2% 15 to 30 minutes,
9.7% 30 to 45 minutes, 32.3% 45 to 60 minutes, 0.0% 60 minutes or more
(2005-2009 5-year est.)

Whiteside County

Located in northwestern Illinois; bounded on the northwest by the
Mississippi River and the Iowa border; drained by the Rock River. Covers a
land area of 684.77 square miles, a water area of 12.24 square miles, and
is located in the Central Time Zone at 41.77° N. Lat., 89.86° W. Long. The
county was founded in 1836. County seat is Morrison.

Whiteside County is part of the Sterling, IL Micropolitan Statistical Area.
The entire metro area includes: Whiteside County, IL

Weather Station: Fulton L&D #13   Elevation: 591 feet

	Jan	Feb	Mar	Apr	May	Jun	Jul	Aug	Sep	Oct	Nov	Dec
High	29	33	45	59	70	80	83	82	75	62	47	33
Low	13	16	27	39	50	60	64	63	54	42	31	18
Precip	1.2	1.4	2.3	3.1	3.6	4.2	3.2	4.1	2.9	2.9	2.5	1.8
Snow	3.1	1.7	0.4	0.5	0.0	0.0	0.0	0.0	0.0	0.0	0.2	1.5

High and Low temperatures in degrees Fahrenheit; Precipitation and Snow in inches

Weather Station: Morrison   Elevation: 603 feet

	Jan	Feb	Mar	Apr	May	Jun	Jul	Aug	Sep	Oct	Nov	Dec
High	31	35	47	61	73	82	85	83	76	64	49	35
Low	12	16	27	37	49	58	62	60	51	39	29	17
Precip	1.5	1.6	2.6	3.3	4.1	4.4	3.9	4.8	3.0	2.9	2.8	2.1
Snow	10.0	6.9	3.3	1.0	0.0	0.0	0.0	0.0	0.0	tr	1.5	8.5

High and Low temperatures in degrees Fahrenheit; Precipitation and Snow in inches

Population: 60,186 (1990); 60,653 (2000); 59,062 (2010); 58,092 (2015
projected); Race: 91.3% White, 1.5% Black, 0.5% Asian, 6.7% Other,
10.0% Hispanic of any race (2010); Density: 86.3 persons per square mile
(2010); Average household size: 2.46 (2010); Median age: 40.2 (2010);
Males per 100 females: 96.1 (2010).
Religion: Five largest groups: 22.7% Catholic Church, 8.4% The United
Methodist Church, 6.6% Evangelical Lutheran Church in America, 5.6%
Reformed Church in America, 3.2% Lutheran Church—Missouri Synod
(2000).
Economy: Unemployment rate: 9.9% (August 2011); Total civilian labor
force: 30,326 (August 2011); Leading industries: 21.9% manufacturing;
20.5% health care and social assistance; 15.6% retail trade (2009); Farms:
1,132 totaling 405,333 acres (2007); Companies that employ 500 or more
persons: 3 (2009); Companies that employ 100 to 499 persons: 20 (2009);
Companies that employ less than 100 persons: 1,264 (2009); Black-owned
businesses: n/a (2007); Hispanic-owned businesses: n/a (2007);
Asian-owned businesses: n/a (2007); Women-owned businesses: 961
(2007); Retail sales per capita: $12,195 (2010). Single-family building
permits issued: 50 (2010); Multi-family building permits issued: 0 (2010).
Income: Per capita income: $22,595 (2010); Median household income:
$46,120 (2010); Average household income: $55,943 (2010); Percent of
households with income of $100,000 or more: 10.3% (2010); Poverty rate:
11.8% (2009); Bankruptcy rate: 3.95% (2010).
Taxes: Total county taxes per capita: $123 (2007); County property taxes
per capita: $118 (2007).
Education: Percent of population age 25 and over with: High school
diploma (including GED) or higher: 84.6% (2010); Bachelor's degree or
higher: 14.5% (2010); Master's degree or higher: 4.5% (2010).
Housing: Homeownership rate: 74.4% (2010); Median home value:
$90,877 (2010); Median contract rent: $439 per month (2005-2009 5-year
est.); Median year structure built: 1959 (2005-2009 5-year est.)
Health: Birth rate: 128.7 per 10,000 population (2009); Death rate: 110.2
per 10,000 population (2009); Age-adjusted cancer mortality rate: 184.6
deaths per 100,000 population (2007); Number of physicians: 12.2 per
10,000 population (2008); Hospital beds: 27.0 per 10,000 population
(2007); Hospital admissions: 985.4 per 10,000 population (2007).
Elections: 2008 Presidential election results: 58.0% Obama, 40.4%
McCain, 0.9% Nader
National and State Parks: Big Bend State Conservation Area;
Morrison-Rockwood State Park; Prophetstown State Park
Additional Information Contacts
Whiteside County Government . . . . (815) 772-5100
http://www.whiteside.org

City of Rock Falls . . . . (815) 622-1100
   http://www.rockfalls61071.com
City of Sterling . . . . (815) 632-6621
   http://ci.sterling.il.us/main
Fulton Chamber of Commerce. . . . . (815) 589-4545
   http://www.cityoffulton.us/chamber/chamber-of-commerce.html
Morrison Chamber of Commerce. (815) 772-3757
   http://www.morrisonchamber.com
Prophetstown Main Street . . . . (815) 537-5139
   http://www.prophetstown.us
Prophetstown/Lyndon Area Chamber of Commerce . . . . . . (815) 537-5754
   http://www.prophetstown.us/community.php
Rock Falls Chamber of Commerce . . . . (815) 625-4500
   http://www.rockfallschamber.com
Sauk Valley Area Chamber of Commerce. . . . . (815) 625-2400
   http://www.saukvalleyareachamber.com

Whiteside County Communities

ALBANY (village). Covers a land area of 1.000 square miles and a water area of 0 square miles. Located at 41.78° N. Lat; 90.21° W. Long. Elevation is 614 feet.
Population: 835 (1990); 895 (2000); 893 (2010); 895 (2015 projected); Race: 98.0% White, 1.3% Black, 0.0% Asian, 0.7% Other, 0.7% Hispanic of any race (2010); Density: 892.8 persons per square mile (2010); Average household size: 2.47 (2010); Median age: 39.4 (2010); Males per 100 females: 98.0 (2010); Marriage status: 26.3% never married, 61.2% now married, 6.3% widowed, 6.1% divorced (2005-2009 5-year est.); Foreign born: 4.2% (2005-2009 5-year est.); Ancestry (includes multiple ancestries): 40.6% German, 14.6% Irish, 12.3% Dutch, 8.3% Swedish, 7.7% American (2005-2009 5-year est.).
Economy: Single-family building permits issued: 1 (2010); Multi-family building permits issued: 0 (2010); Employment by occupation: 13.4% management, 22.9% professional, 10.4% services, 21.5% sales, 0.0% farming, 9.8% construction, 22.1% production (2005-2009 5-year est.).
Income: Per capita income: $23,774 (2010); Median household income: $53,360 (2010); Average household income: $59,204 (2010); Percent of households with income of $100,000 or more: 12.7% (2010); Poverty rate: 4.5% (2005-2009 5-year est.).
Taxes: Total city taxes per capita: $188 (2007); City property taxes per capita: $128 (2007).
Education: Percent of population age 25 and over with: High school diploma (including GED) or higher: 90.8% (2010); Bachelor's degree or higher: 15.9% (2010); Master's degree or higher: 3.1% (2010).
Housing: Homeownership rate: 88.4% (2010); Median home value: $99,074 (2010); Median contract rent: $425 per month (2005-2009 5-year est.); Median year structure built: 1962 (2005-2009 5-year est.).
Safety: Violent crime rate: 0.0 per 10,000 population; Property crime rate: 261.7 per 10,000 population (2010).
Transportation: Commute to work: 92.3% car, 0.0% public transportation, 3.3% walk, 3.6% work from home (2005-2009 5-year est.); Travel time to work: 30.7% less than 15 minutes, 45.5% 15 to 30 minutes, 16.8% 30 to 45 minutes, 4.8% 45 to 60 minutes, 2.3% 60 minutes or more (2005-2009 5-year est.)

COLETA (village). Covers a land area of 0.455 square miles and a water area of 0 square miles. Located at 41.90° N. Lat; 89.80° W. Long. Elevation is 817 feet.
Population: 154 (1990); 155 (2000); 179 (2010); 179 (2015 projected); Race: 94.4% White, 1.7% Black, 0.0% Asian, 3.9% Other, 6.7% Hispanic of any race (2010); Density: 393.8 persons per square mile (2010); Average household size: 2.67 (2010); Median age: 44.1 (2010); Males per 100 females: 98.9 (2010); Marriage status: 27.2% never married, 53.6% now married, 1.6% widowed, 17.6% divorced (2005-2009 5-year est.); Foreign born: 2.1% (2005-2009 5-year est.); Ancestry (includes multiple ancestries): 47.6% German, 23.4% Irish, 5.5% English, 5.5% American, 3.4% Belgian (2005-2009 5-year est.).
Economy: Employment by occupation: 4.4% management, 29.4% professional, 16.2% services, 29.4% sales, 2.9% farming, 7.4% construction, 10.3% production (2005-2009 5-year est.).
Income: Per capita income: $21,438 (2010); Median household income: $51,875 (2010); Average household income: $57,463 (2010); Percent of households with income of $100,000 or more: 11.9% (2010); Poverty rate: 2.8% (2005-2009 5-year est.).

Taxes: Total city taxes per capita: $26 (2007); City property taxes per capita: $6 (2007).
Education: Percent of population age 25 and over with: High school diploma (including GED) or higher: 93.4% (2010); Bachelor's degree or higher: 12.3% (2010); Master's degree or higher: 5.7% (2010).
Housing: Homeownership rate: 82.1% (2010); Median home value: $127,500 (2010); Median contract rent: n/a per month (2005-2009 5-year est.); Median year structure built: before 1940 (2005-2009 5-year est.).
Transportation: Commute to work: 100.0% car, 0.0% public transportation, 0.0% walk, 0.0% work from home (2005-2009 5-year est.); Travel time to work: 14.5% less than 15 minutes, 66.1% 15 to 30 minutes, 16.1% 30 to 45 minutes, 3.2% 45 to 60 minutes, 0.0% 60 minutes or more (2005-2009 5-year est.)

DEER GROVE (village). Covers a land area of 0.456 square miles and a water area of 0 square miles. Located at 41.60° N. Lat; 89.69° W. Long. Elevation is 646 feet.
Population: 44 (1990); 48 (2000); 46 (2010); 45 (2015 projected); Race: 95.7% White, 0.0% Black, 0.0% Asian, 4.3% Other, 4.3% Hispanic of any race (2010); Density: 101.0 persons per square mile (2010); Average household size: 2.88 (2010); Median age: 26.3 (2010); Males per 100 females: 100.0 (2010); Marriage status: 2.6% never married, 76.3% now married, 7.9% widowed, 13.2% divorced (2005-2009 5-year est.); Foreign born: 0.0% (2005-2009 5-year est.); Ancestry (includes multiple ancestries): 60.0% German, 25.0% Dutch, 16.7% Irish, 8.3% Norwegian, 8.3% French (2005-2009 5-year est.).
Economy: Employment by occupation: 0.0% management, 0.0% professional, 13.3% services, 40.0% sales, 0.0% farming, 0.0% construction, 46.7% production (2005-2009 5-year est.).
Income: Per capita income: $21,610 (2010); Median household income: $62,500 (2010); Average household income: $79,844 (2010); Percent of households with income of $100,000 or more: 18.8% (2010); Poverty rate: 24.1% (2005-2009 5-year est.).
Taxes: Total city taxes per capita: $42 (2007); City property taxes per capita: $21 (2007).
Education: Percent of population age 25 and over with: High school diploma (including GED) or higher: 87.5% (2010); Bachelor's degree or higher: 16.7% (2010); Master's degree or higher: 0.0% (2010).
Housing: Homeownership rate: 75.0% (2010); Median home value: $116,667 (2010); Median contract rent: n/a per month (2005-2009 5-year est.); Median year structure built: before 1940 (2005-2009 5-year est.).
Transportation: Commute to work: 93.3% car, 0.0% public transportation, 0.0% walk, 0.0% work from home (2005-2009 5-year est.); Travel time to work: 6.7% less than 15 minutes, 93.3% 15 to 30 minutes, 0.0% 30 to 45 minutes, 0.0% 45 to 60 minutes, 0.0% 60 minutes or more (2005-2009 5-year est.)

ERIE (village). Covers a land area of 1.403 square miles and a water area of 0.009 square miles. Located at 41.65° N. Lat; 90.07° W. Long. Elevation is 591 feet.
History: Incorporated 1872.
Population: 1,580 (1990); 1,589 (2000); 1,586 (2010); 1,577 (2015 projected); Race: 98.0% White, 0.3% Black, 0.1% Asian, 1.7% Other, 1.1% Hispanic of any race (2010); Density: 1,130.6 persons per square mile (2010); Average household size: 2.56 (2010); Median age: 39.3 (2010); Males per 100 females: 95.6 (2010); Marriage status: 24.2% never married, 60.9% now married, 6.7% widowed, 8.2% divorced (2005-2009 5-year est.); Foreign born: 0.6% (2005-2009 5-year est.); Ancestry (includes multiple ancestries): 40.7% German, 18.9% Irish, 11.2% English, 10.2% Dutch, 8.5% Swedish (2005-2009 5-year est.).
Economy: Single-family building permits issued: 0 (2010); Multi-family building permits issued: 0 (2010); Employment by occupation: 9.1% management, 18.1% professional, 17.9% services, 18.1% sales, 1.6% farming, 11.6% construction, 23.5% production (2005-2009 5-year est.).
Income: Per capita income: $24,068 (2010); Median household income: $53,264 (2010); Average household income: $61,797 (2010); Percent of households with income of $100,000 or more: 13.9% (2010); Poverty rate: 6.2% (2005-2009 5-year est.).
Taxes: Total city taxes per capita: $200 (2007); City property taxes per capita: $121 (2007).
Education: Percent of population age 25 and over with: High school diploma (including GED) or higher: 90.4% (2010); Bachelor's degree or higher: 16.7% (2010); Master's degree or higher: 4.4% (2010).

School District(s)

Erie CUSD 1 (PK-12)

   2009-10 Enrollment: 699 . . . . (309) 659-2239

Housing: Homeownership rate: 80.5% (2010); Median home value: $108,201 (2010); Median contract rent: $379 per month (2005-2009 5-year est.); Median year structure built: 1962 (2005-2009 5-year est.).

Newspapers: Review (Regional news; Circulation 1,700)

Transportation: Commute to work: 94.8% car, 0.0% public transportation, 1.7% walk, 2.1% work from home (2005-2009 5-year est.); Travel time to work: 33.3% less than 15 minutes, 27.2% 15 to 30 minutes, 25.7% 30 to 45 minutes, 10.4% 45 to 60 minutes, 3.3% 60 minutes or more (2005-2009 5-year est.)

FENTON (unincorporated postal area, zip code 61251). Covers a land area of 17.109 square miles and a water area of 0 square miles. Located at 41.73° N. Lat; 90.06° W. Long. Elevation is 620 feet.

Population: 317 (2000); Race: 100.0% White, 0.0% Black, 0.0% Asian, 0.0% Other, 0.0% Hispanic of any race (2000); Density: 18.5 persons per square mile (2000); Age: 29.2% under 18, 9.4% over 64 (2000); Marriage status: 24.2% never married, 70.3% now married, 3.7% widowed, 1.9% divorced (2000); Foreign born: 0.0% (2000); Ancestry (includes multiple ancestries): 23.1% English, 21.3% Irish, 14.6% German, 13.7% Scotch-Irish, 12.9% Dutch (2000).

Economy: Employment by occupation: 13.4% management, 12.7% professional, 15.9% services, 8.9% sales, 5.1% farming, 10.8% construction, 33.1% production (2000).

Income: Per capita income: $15,537 (2000); Median household income: $47,813 (2000); Poverty rate: 0.0% (2000).

Education: Percent of population age 25 and over with: High school diploma (including GED) or higher: 90.7% (2000); Bachelor's degree or higher: 11.8% (2000).

Housing: Homeownership rate: 85.7% (2000); Median home value: $66,200 (2000); Median contract rent: $225 per month (2000); Median year structure built: before 1940 (2000).

Transportation: Commute to work: 100.0% car, 0.0% public transportation, 0.0% walk, 0.0% work from home (2000); Travel time to work: 19.7% less than 15 minutes, 40.1% 15 to 30 minutes, 26.1% 30 to 45 minutes, 10.8% 45 to 60 minutes, 3.2% 60 minutes or more (2000)

FULTON (city). Covers a land area of 2.272 square miles and a water area of 0.071 square miles. Located at 41.86° N. Lat; 90.15° W. Long. Elevation is 650 feet.

History: The name of Fulton honors the inventor of the steamboat, and the city itself owes its early development to river commerce. Later it became the center of an agricultural area, producing tomatoes and cucumbers.

Population: 3,708 (1990); 3,881 (2000); 3,755 (2010); 3,676 (2015 projected); Race: 96.9% White, 1.2% Black, 0.6% Asian, 1.2% Other, 1.8% Hispanic of any race (2010); Density: 1,652.6 persons per square mile (2010); Average household size: 2.31 (2010); Median age: 43.0 (2010); Males per 100 females: 97.2 (2010); Marriage status: 21.7% never married, 54.8% now married, 7.2% widowed, 16.3% divorced (2005-2009 5-year est.); Foreign born: 2.2% (2005-2009 5-year est.); Ancestry (includes multiple ancestries): 36.2% German, 30.1% Dutch, 14.4% Irish, 10.2% English, 6.8% American (2005-2009 5-year est.).

Economy: Single-family building permits issued: 1 (2010); Multi-family building permits issued: 0 (2010); Employment by occupation: 5.7% management, 20.0% professional, 14.3% services, 25.6% sales, 2.1% farming, 9.3% construction, 23.0% production (2005-2009 5-year est.).

Income: Per capita income: $22,737 (2010); Median household income: $42,333 (2010); Average household income: $53,117 (2010); Percent of households with income of $100,000 or more: 7.7% (2010); Poverty rate: 8.1% (2005-2009 5-year est.).

Taxes: Total city taxes per capita: $94 (2007); City property taxes per capita: $72 (2007).

Education: Percent of population age 25 and over with: High school diploma (including GED) or higher: 85.4% (2010); Bachelor's degree or higher: 16.4% (2010); Master's degree or higher: 4.7% (2010).

School District(s)

River Bend CUSD 2 (PK-12)

   2009-10 Enrollment: 1,026 . . . . (815) 589-2711

Housing: Homeownership rate: 76.3% (2010); Median home value: $95,897 (2010); Median contract rent: $363 per month (2005-2009 5-year est.); Median year structure built: 1954 (2005-2009 5-year est.).

Safety: Violent crime rate: 15.9 per 10,000 population; Property crime rate: 143.0 per 10,000 population (2010).

Newspapers: Fulton Journal (Local news; Circulation 2,300); Whiteside Shopper (Local news; Circulation 3,400)

Transportation: Commute to work: 94.1% car, 0.0% public transportation, 3.6% walk, 0.6% work from home (2005-2009 5-year est.); Travel time to work: 52.3% less than 15 minutes, 32.5% 15 to 30 minutes, 8.0% 30 to 45 minutes, 3.7% 45 to 60 minutes, 3.5% 60 minutes or more (2005-2009 5-year est.)

Additional Information Contacts

Fulton Chamber of Commerce . . . . (815) 589-4545

   http://www.cityoffulton.us/chamber/chamber-of-commerce.html

---

LYNDON (village). Covers a land area of 0.821 square miles and a water area of 0 square miles. Located at 41.71° N. Lat; 89.92° W. Long. Elevation is 614 feet.

Population: 615 (1990); 566 (2000); 559 (2010); 554 (2015 projected); Race: 95.2% White, 0.0% Black, 0.2% Asian, 4.7% Other, 1.8% Hispanic of any race (2010); Density: 681.0 persons per square mile (2010); Average household size: 2.50 (2010); Median age: 41.7 (2010); Males per 100 females: 106.3 (2010); Marriage status: 23.2% never married, 51.9% now married, 5.0% widowed, 19.9% divorced (2005-2009 5-year est.); Foreign born: 0.0% (2005-2009 5-year est.); Ancestry (includes multiple ancestries): 29.0% German, 21.1% Irish, 14.0% English, 8.9% Dutch, 4.1% Italian (2005-2009 5-year est.).

Economy: Single-family building permits issued: 2 (2010); Multi-family building permits issued: 0 (2010); Employment by occupation: 7.6% management, 12.2% professional, 23.5% services, 17.4% sales, 0.0% farming, 16.8% construction, 22.3% production (2005-2009 5-year est.).

Income: Per capita income: $19,843 (2010); Median household income: $44,130 (2010); Average household income: $49,833 (2010); Percent of households with income of $100,000 or more: 7.6% (2010); Poverty rate: 7.8% (2005-2009 5-year est.).

Taxes: Total city taxes per capita: $110 (2007); City property taxes per capita: $105 (2007).

Education: Percent of population age 25 and over with: High school diploma (including GED) or higher: 82.1% (2010); Bachelor's degree or higher: 8.0% (2010); Master's degree or higher: 3.6% (2010).

Housing: Homeownership rate: 86.2% (2010); Median home value: $79,706 (2010); Median contract rent: $404 per month (2005-2009 5-year est.); Median year structure built: 1956 (2005-2009 5-year est.).

Transportation: Commute to work: 97.8% car, 1.2% public transportation, 0.0% walk, 0.9% work from home (2005-2009 5-year est.); Travel time to work: 23.0% less than 15 minutes, 38.4% 15 to 30 minutes, 22.3% 30 to 45 minutes, 6.9% 45 to 60 minutes, 9.4% 60 minutes or more (2005-2009 5-year est.)

MORRISON (city). County seat. Covers a land area of 2.141 square miles and a water area of 0 square miles. Located at 41.80° N. Lat; 89.96° W. Long. Elevation is 679 feet.

History: Morrison developed when the Chicago & North Western Railway built its station here. It was in Morrison in 1874 that James Sargent installed the first time lock in the First National Bank of Morrison.

Population: 4,534 (1990); 4,447 (2000); 4,308 (2010); 4,245 (2015 projected); Race: 97.1% White, 1.1% Black, 0.1% Asian, 1.8% Other, 2.4% Hispanic of any race (2010); Density: 2,012.6 persons per square mile (2010); Average household size: 2.30 (2010); Median age: 43.0 (2010); Males per 100 females: 94.8 (2010); Marriage status: 27.2% never married, 50.7% now married, 12.2% widowed, 9.9% divorced (2005-2009 5-year est.); Foreign born: 1.3% (2005-2009 5-year est.); Ancestry (includes multiple ancestries): 38.6% German, 23.2% Dutch, 18.7% Irish, 11.1% English, 4.5% American (2005-2009 5-year est.).

Economy: Single-family building permits issued: 4 (2010); Multi-family building permits issued: 0 (2010); Employment by occupation: 12.0% management, 15.2% professional, 26.5% services, 21.6% sales, 0.5% farming, 10.3% construction, 13.9% production (2005-2009 5-year est.).

Income: Per capita income: $23,584 (2010); Median household income: $47,619 (2010); Average household income: $56,820 (2010); Percent of households with income of $100,000 or more: 9.7% (2010); Poverty rate: 4.3% (2005-2009 5-year est.).

Taxes: Total city taxes per capita: $186 (2007); City property taxes per capita: $126 (2007).

Education: Percent of population age 25 and over with: High school diploma (including GED) or higher: 89.9% (2010); Bachelor's degree or higher: 18.8% (2010); Master's degree or higher: 6.8% (2010).

School District(s)

Morrison CUSD 6 (PK-12)
  2009-10 Enrollment: 1,128 . . . . (815) 772-2064

Two-year College(s)

Morrison Institute of Technology (Private, Not-for-profit)
  Fall 2009 Enrollment: 103 . . . . (815) 772-7218
  2010-11 Tuition: In-state $14,640; Out-of-state $14,640

Housing: Homeownership rate: 78.3% (2010); Median home value: $95,672 (2010); Median contract rent: $414 per month (2005-2009 5-year est.); Median year structure built: 1949 (2005-2009 5-year est.).

Hospitals: Morrison Community Hospital (76 beds)

Safety: Violent crime rate: 11.8 per 10,000 population; Property crime rate: 179.0 per 10,000 population (2010).

Newspapers: Whiteside News Sentinel (Local news; Circulation 3,000)

Transportation: Commute to work: 93.6% car, 0.0% public transportation, 3.5% walk, 1.8% work from home (2005-2009 5-year est.); Travel time to work: 49.5% less than 15 minutes, 27.3% 15 to 30 minutes, 10.4% 30 to 45 minutes, 5.4% 45 to 60 minutes, 7.4% 60 minutes or more (2005-2009 5-year est.)

Additional Information Contacts

Morrison Chamber of Commerce. (815) 772-3757
  http://www.morrisonchamber.com

PROPHETSTOWN (city).

Covers a land area of 1.363 square miles and a water area of 0.021 square miles. Located at 41.67° N. Lat; 89.93° W. Long. Elevation is 620 feet.

History: The name of Prophetstown refers to the Indian prophet White Cloud, who warned his people about the loss of their lands. The town was founded on the Rock River, where White Cloud had lived.

Population: 1,924 (1990); 2,023 (2000); 2,017 (2010); 1,994 (2015 projected); Race: 97.5% White, 1.1% Black, 0.0% Asian, 1.3% Other, 0.9% Hispanic of any race (2010); Density: 1,480.1 persons per square mile (2010); Average household size: 2.31 (2010); Median age: 45.5 (2010); Males per 100 females: 93.8 (2010); Marriage status: 26.2% never married, 48.9% now married, 14.5% widowed, 10.5% divorced (2005-2009 5-year est.); Foreign born: 0.3% (2005-2009 5-year est.); Ancestry (includes multiple ancestries): 43.1% German, 13.1% Irish, 10.2% English, 7.6% American, 6.2% Dutch (2005-2009 5-year est.).

Economy: Single-family building permits issued: 0 (2010); Multi-family building permits issued: 0 (2010); Employment by occupation: 4.0% management, 19.9% professional, 18.5% services, 14.9% sales, 1.1% farming, 13.7% construction, 27.8% production (2005-2009 5-year est.).

Income: Per capita income: $23,796 (2010); Median household income: $44,924 (2010); Average household income: $57,425 (2010); Percent of households with income of $100,000 or more: 12.5% (2010); Poverty rate: 16.3% (2005-2009 5-year est.).

Taxes: Total city taxes per capita: $133 (2007); City property taxes per capita: $120 (2007).

Education: Percent of population age 25 and over with: High school diploma (including GED) or higher: 90.4% (2010); Bachelor's degree or higher: 17.8% (2010); Master's degree or higher: 4.7% (2010).

School District(s)

Prophetstown-Lyndon-Tampico CUSD3 (PK-12)
  2009-10 Enrollment: 1,015 . . . . (815) 537-5101

Housing: Homeownership rate: 77.9% (2010); Median home value: $90,408 (2010); Median contract rent: $390 per month (2005-2009 5-year est.); Median year structure built: 1952 (2005-2009 5-year est.).

Transportation: Commute to work: 92.3% car, 0.8% public transportation, 4.4% walk, 0.5% work from home (2005-2009 5-year est.); Travel time to work: 40.2% less than 15 minutes, 27.2% 15 to 30 minutes, 23.8% 30 to 45 minutes, 3.9% 45 to 60 minutes, 5.0% 60 minutes or more (2005-2009 5-year est.)

Additional Information Contacts

Prophetstown Main Street . . . . (815) 537-5139
  http://www.prophetstown.us
Prophetstown/Lyndon Area Chamber of Commerce . . . . . . (815) 537-5754
  http://www.prophetstown.us/community.php

ROCK FALLS (city).

Covers a land area of 3.317 square miles and a water area of 0.114 square miles. Located at 41.77° N. Lat; 89.69° W. Long. Elevation is 646 feet.

History: Rock Falls was platted in 1837. Development came when a dam was built across the river, and later when a feeder canal connected Rock Falls and the Rock River with the Illinois & Mississippi Canal.

Population: 9,950 (1990); 9,580 (2000); 9,151 (2010); 8,926 (2015 projected); Race: 90.6% White, 1.3% Black, 0.3% Asian, 7.9% Other, 13.3% Hispanic of any race (2010); Density: 2,758.7 persons per square mile (2010); Average household size: 2.37 (2010); Median age: 38.0 (2010); Males per 100 females: 93.0 (2010); Marriage status: 29.8% never married, 46.4% now married, 9.5% widowed, 14.3% divorced (2005-2009 5-year est.); Foreign born: 3.1% (2005-2009 5-year est.); Ancestry (includes multiple ancestries): 28.8% German, 16.9% Irish, 8.1% American, 8.0% English, 4.7% Swedish (2005-2009 5-year est.).

Economy: Single-family building permits issued: 4 (2010); Multi-family building permits issued: 0 (2010); Employment by occupation: 5.8% management, 9.7% professional, 20.5% services, 28.2% sales, 0.1% farming, 9.6% construction, 26.0% production (2005-2009 5-year est.).

Income: Per capita income: $19,683 (2010); Median household income: $39,223 (2010); Average household income: $46,531 (2010); Percent of households with income of $100,000 or more: 5.9% (2010); Poverty rate: 19.9% (2005-2009 5-year est.).

Taxes: Total city taxes per capita: $143 (2007); City property taxes per capita: $81 (2007).

Education: Percent of population age 25 and over with: High school diploma (including GED) or higher: 77.7% (2010); Bachelor's degree or higher: 8.2% (2010); Master's degree or higher: 3.2% (2010).

School District(s)

East Coloma SD 12 (KG-08)
  2009-10 Enrollment: 273 . . . . (815) 625-4400
Montmorency CCSD 145 (PK-08)
  2009-10 Enrollment: 350 . . . . (815) 625-6616
Riverdale SD 14 (PK-08)
  2009-10 Enrollment: 82 . . . . (815) 625-5280
Rock Falls ESD 13 (PK-08)
  2009-10 Enrollment: 1,037 . . . . (815) 626-2604
Rock Falls Twp HSD 301 (09-12)
  2009-10 Enrollment: 682 . . . . (815) 625-3886

Housing: Homeownership rate: 65.3% (2010); Median home value: $74,000 (2010); Median contract rent: $445 per month (2005-2009 5-year est.); Median year structure built: 1957 (2005-2009 5-year est.).

Safety: Violent crime rate: 23.0 per 10,000 population; Property crime rate: 415.8 per 10,000 population (2010).

Transportation: Commute to work: 92.8% car, 0.8% public transportation, 4.1% walk, 1.1% work from home (2005-2009 5-year est.); Travel time to work: 55.0% less than 15 minutes, 31.1% 15 to 30 minutes, 8.6% 30 to 45 minutes, 3.1% 45 to 60 minutes, 2.3% 60 minutes or more (2005-2009 5-year est.)

Additional Information Contacts

City of Rock Falls . . . . (815) 622-1100
  http://www.rockfalls61071.com
Rock Falls Chamber of Commerce . . . . (815) 625-4500
  http://www.rockfallschamber.com

STERLING (city).

Covers a land area of 4.672 square miles and a water area of 0.188 square miles. Located at 41.79° N. Lat; 89.69° W. Long. Elevation is 659 feet.

History: Sterling originated in 1839 from the union of Chatham and Harrisburg in the hopes that the new town would become the seat of Whiteside County. Though Sterling was chosen, it soon lost the honor to Morrison.

Population: 15,602 (1990); 15,451 (2000); 14,793 (2010); 14,414 (2015 projected); Race: 80.8% White, 3.2% Black, 1.1% Asian, 14.8% Other, 21.9% Hispanic of any race (2010); Density: 3,166.2 persons per square mile (2010); Average household size: 2.42 (2010); Median age: 37.3 (2010); Males per 100 females: 93.0 (2010); Marriage status: 28.6% never married, 45.7% now married, 9.2% widowed, 16.5% divorced (2005-2009 5-year est.); Foreign born: 3.9% (2005-2009 5-year est.); Ancestry (includes multiple ancestries): 29.0% German, 16.5% Irish, 5.4% English, 4.9% American, 4.3% Dutch (2005-2009 5-year est.).

Economy: Single-family building permits issued: 4 (2010); Multi-family building permits issued: 0 (2010); Employment by occupation: 9.6% management, 14.7% professional, 19.8% services, 25.7% sales, 0.0% farming, 6.0% construction, 24.1% production (2005-2009 5-year est.).

Income: Per capita income: $21,701 (2010); Median household income: $43,322 (2010); Average household income: $52,564 (2010); Percent of households with income of $100,000 or more: 8.7% (2010); Poverty rate: 14.7% (2005-2009 5-year est.).

Taxes: Total city taxes per capita: $325 (2007); City property taxes per capita: $200 (2007).

Education: Percent of population age 25 and over with: High school diploma (including GED) or higher: 82.7% (2010); Bachelor's degree or higher: 15.7% (2010); Master's degree or higher: 4.8% (2010).

School District(s)

Sterling CUSD 5 (PK-12)
2009-10 Enrollment: 3,604 . . . . (815) 626-5050
Whiteside Area Career (11-12)
2009-10 Enrollment: n/a . . . . (815) 626-5810
Whiteside Roe (08-10)
2009-10 Enrollment: n/a . . . . (815) 625-1495

Vocational/Technical School(s)

Educators of Beauty (Private, For-profit)
Fall 2009 Enrollment: 30 . . . . (815) 625-0247
2010-11 Tuition: $16,675

Housing: Homeownership rate: 64.2% (2010); Median home value: $82,256 (2010); Median contract rent: $478 per month (2005-2009 5-year est.); Median year structure built: 1956 (2005-2009 5-year est.).

Hospitals: CGH Medical Center (139 beds)

Safety: Violent crime rate: 28.3 per 10,000 population; Property crime rate: 435.1 per 10,000 population (2010).

Newspapers: Daily Gazette (Local news; Circulation 12,206); Sauk Valley Sunday (Community news; Circulation 15,000); The Telegraph (Local news; Circulation 8,972)

Transportation: Commute to work: 90.7% car, 1.8% public transportation, 3.6% walk, 1.8% work from home (2005-2009 5-year est.); Travel time to work: 58.9% less than 15 minutes, 26.8% 15 to 30 minutes, 8.2% 30 to 45 minutes, 2.7% 45 to 60 minutes, 3.3% 60 minutes or more (2005-2009 5-year est.)

Airports: Whiteside County-Jos H Bittorf Field (general aviation)

Additional Information Contacts

City of Sterling . . . . (815) 632-6621
http://ci.sterling.il.us/main
Sauk Valley Area Chamber of Commerce . . . . (815) 625-2400
http://www.saukvalleyareachamber.com

TAMPICO (village). Covers a land area of 0.398 square miles and a water area of 0 square miles. Located at 41.63° N. Lat; 89.78° W. Long. Elevation is 640 feet.

History: Birthplace of Ronald Reagan.

Population: 815 (1990); 772 (2000); 732 (2010); 707 (2015 projected); Race: 98.9% White, 0.3% Black, 0.0% Asian, 0.8% Other, 2.9% Hispanic of any race (2010); Density: 1,840.7 persons per square mile (2010); Average household size: 2.60 (2010); Median age: 36.2 (2010); Males per 100 females: 107.4 (2010); Marriage status: 33.0% never married, 48.5% now married, 5.4% widowed, 13.2% divorced (2005-2009 5-year est.); Foreign born: 0.0% (2005-2009 5-year est.); Ancestry (includes multiple ancestries): 25.6% German, 19.9% American, 10.3% Irish, 5.5% English, 3.9% Belgian (2005-2009 5-year est.).

Economy: Single-family building permits issued: 0 (2010); Multi-family building permits issued: 0 (2010); Employment by occupation: 10.4% management, 9.2% professional, 18.7% services, 23.5% sales, 3.2% farming, 11.4% construction, 23.5% production (2005-2009 5-year est.).

Income: Per capita income: $18,994 (2010); Median household income: $45,398 (2010); Average household income: $49,146 (2010); Percent of households with income of $100,000 or more: 6.4% (2010); Poverty rate: 19.8% (2005-2009 5-year est.).

Taxes: Total city taxes per capita: $84 (2007); City property taxes per capita: $76 (2007).

Education: Percent of population age 25 and over with: High school diploma (including GED) or higher: 85.1% (2010); Bachelor's degree or higher: 11.3% (2010); Master's degree or higher: 1.1% (2010).

School District(s)

Prophetstown-Lyndon-Tampico CUSD3 (PK-12)
2009-10 Enrollment: 1,015 . . . . (815) 537-5101

Housing: Homeownership rate: 77.9% (2010); Median home value: $80,758 (2010); Median contract rent: $375 per month (2005-2009 5-year est.); Median year structure built: before 1940 (2005-2009 5-year est.).

Transportation: Commute to work: 96.1% car, 0.0% public transportation, 0.0% walk, 0.7% work from home (2005-2009 5-year est.); Travel time to work: 32.0% less than 15 minutes, 39.5% 15 to 30 minutes, 20.6% 30 to 45 minutes, 2.5% 45 to 60 minutes, 5.5% 60 minutes or more (2005-2009 5-year est.)

Will County

Located in northeastern Illinois; bounded on the east by Indiana; drained by the Des Plaines, Du Page, and Kankakee Rivers. Covers a land area of 836.94 square miles, a water area of 12.45 square miles, and is located in the Central Time Zone at 41.52° N. Lat., 88.03° W. Long. The county was founded in 1836. County seat is Joliet.

Will County is part of the Chicago-Joliet-Naperville, IL-IN-WI Metropolitan Statistical Area. The entire metro area includes: Chicago-Joliet-Naperville, IL Metropolitan Division (Cook County, IL; DeKalb County, IL; DuPage County, IL; Grundy County, IL; Kane County, IL; Kendall County, IL; McHenry County, IL; Will County, IL); Gary, IN Metropolitan Division (Jasper County, IN; Lake County, IN; Newton County, IN; Porter County, IN); Lake County-Kenosha County, IL-WI Metropolitan Division (Lake County, IL; Kenosha County, WI)

Weather Station: Joliet Brandon Rd Dam								Elevation: 542 feet			
	Jan	Feb	Mar	Apr	May	Jun	Jul	Aug	Sep	Oct	Nov	Dec
High	31	36	47	60	71	81	84	83	76	63	49	35
Low	16	19	29	39	49	59	64	62	54	42	32	20
Precip	1.7	1.7	2.3	3.5	4.0	3.7	4.3	3.9	3.2	3.0	3.0	2.2
Snow	na	na	1.0	0.1	0.0	0.0	0.0	0.0	0.0	0.0	0.1	3.3

High and Low temperatures in degrees Fahrenheit; Precipitation and Snow in inches

Population: 357,313 (1990); 502,266 (2000); 704,288 (2010); 789,440 (2015 projected); Race: 76.0% White, 10.8% Black, 4.0% Asian, 9.2% Other, 15.6% Hispanic of any race (2010); Density: 841.5 persons per square mile (2010); Average household size: 2.97 (2010); Median age: 33.4 (2010); Males per 100 females: 99.9 (2010).

Religion: Five largest groups: 38.9% Catholic Church, 2.3% Evangelical Lutheran Church in America, 2.0% The United Methodist Church, 1.9% Lutheran Church—Missouri Synod, 1.3% United Church of Christ (2000).

Economy: Unemployment rate: 10.3% (August 2011); Total civilian labor force: 367,943 (August 2011); Leading industries: 15.2% retail trade; 11.3% health care and social assistance; 11.3% accommodation & food services (2009); Farms: 877 totaling 220,851 acres (2007); Companies that employ 500 or more persons: 25 (2009); Companies that employ 100 to 499 persons: 270 (2009); Companies that employ less than 100 persons: 13,505 (2009); Black-owned businesses: 3,671 (2007); Hispanic-owned businesses: 2,819 (2007); Asian-owned businesses: 2,765 (2007); Women-owned businesses: 15,591 (2007); Retail sales per capita: $10,806 (2010). Single-family building permits issued: 492 (2010); Multi-family building permits issued: 126 (2010).

Income: Per capita income: $30,327 (2010); Median household income: $75,740 (2010); Average household income: $90,606 (2010); Percent of households with income of $100,000 or more: 32.5% (2010); Poverty rate: 7.0% (2009); Bankruptcy rate: 8.21% (2010).

Taxes: Total county taxes per capita: $208 (2007); County property taxes per capita: $203 (2007).

Education: Percent of population age 25 and over with: High school diploma (including GED) or higher: 89.2% (2010); Bachelor's degree or higher: 30.1% (2010); Master's degree or higher: 9.8% (2010).

Housing: Homeownership rate: 85.1% (2010); Median home value: $208,248 (2010); Median contract rent: $721 per month (2005-2009 5-year est.); Median year structure built: 1986 (2005-2009 5-year est.)

Health: Birth rate: 157.2 per 10,000 population (2009); Death rate: 54.0 per 10,000 population (2009); Age-adjusted cancer mortality rate: 195.5 deaths per 100,000 population (2007); Number of physicians: 12.5 per 10,000 population (2008); Hospital beds: 10.6 per 10,000 population (2007); Hospital admissions: 610.5 per 10,000 population (2007).

Environment: Air Quality Index: 94.0% good, 6.0% moderate, 0.0% unhealthy for sensitive individuals, 0.0% unhealthy (percent of days in 2008)

Elections: 2008 Presidential election results: 56.0% Obama, 42.8% McCain, 0.6% Nader

National and State Parks: Channahon Parkway State Park; Des Plaines State Conservation Area; Kankakee River State Park; Midewin National Tallgrass Prairie

Additional Information Contacts

Will County Government . . . . (815) 722-5515
http://www.willcountyillinois.com
Bolingbrook Area Chamber of Commerce . . . . (630) 226-8420
http://bolingbrook.org
City of Braidwood . . . . (815) 458-2333
http://www.braidwood.us

City of Crest Hill . . . . (815) 741-5100
    http://www.cityofcresthill.com
City of Joliet . . . . (815) 724-4000
    http://www.cityofjoliet.info
City of Lockport . . . . (815) 838-0549
    http://www.cityoflockport.net
City of Wilmington . . . . (815) 476-2175
    http://www.wilmington-il.com
Crete Area Chamber of Commerce . . . . (708) 672-9216
    http://www.cretechamber.com
Frankfort Chamber of Commerce . . . . (815) 469-3356
    http://www.frankfortchamber.com
Homer Township Chamber of Commerce . . . . (708) 301-8111
    http://www.homerchamber.com
Joliet Region Chamber of Commerce & Industry . . . . (815) 727-5371
    http://www.jolietchamber.com
Lockport Area Chamber of Commerce . . . . (815) 838-3357
    http://www.lockportchamber.com
Manhattan Chamber of Commerce . . . . (815) 478-3811
    http://www.manhattan-il.com
Mokena Chamber of Commerce . . . . (708) 479-2468
    http://www.mokena.com
Monee Area Chamber of Commerce . . . . (708) 212-4133
    http://www.moneechamber.com
New Lenox Chamber of Commerce . . . . (815) 485-4241
    http://www.newlenoxchamber.com
Peotone Chamber of Commerce . . . . (708) 258-9450
    http://www.peotonechamber.com
Plainfield Area Chamber of Commerce . . . . (815) 436-4431
    http://www.plainfieldchamber.com
Romeoville Area Chamber of Commerce . . . . (815) 886-2076
    http://www.romeovillechamber.org
Shorewood Area Chamber of Commerce . . . . (815) 725-2900
    http://www.shorewoodchamber.com
Village of Bolingbrook . . . . (630) 226-8400
    http://www.bolingbrook.com
Village of Channahon . . . . (815) 467-6644
    http://www.channahon.org
Village of Crete . . . . (708) 672-5431
    http://www.villageofcrete.org
Village of Frankfort . . . . (815) 469-2177
    http://www.villageoffrankfort.com
Village of Mokena . . . . (708) 479-3900
    http://www.mokena.org
Village of New Lenox . . . . (815) 462-6400
    http://www.newlenox.net
Village of Plainfield . . . . (815) 436-7093
    http://www.plainfield-il.org
Village of Romeoville . . . . (815) 866-7200
    http://www.romeoville.org
Village of Shorewood . . . . (815) 725-2150
    http://www.vil.shorewood.il.us
Village of Steger . . . . (708) 754-3395
    http://www.villageofsteger.com
Village of University Park . . . . (708) 534-6451
    http://www.university-park-il.com
Will County Center for Economic Development . . . . (815) 723-1800
    http://www.c-e-d.org
Wilmington Chamber of Commerce . . . . (815) 476-5991
    http://wilmingtonilchamber.org

Will County Communities

BEECHER (village). Covers a land area of 2.108 square miles and a water area of 0 square miles. Located at 41.34° N. Lat; 87.62° W. Long. Elevation is 735 feet.
History: Beecher was platted in 1870 when the Chicago & Eastern Illinois Railway was being built here. The village was named for Henry Ward Beecher.
Population: 2,105 (1990); 2,033 (2000); 2,565 (2010); 2,834 (2015 projected); Race: 96.1% White, 0.1% Black, 0.7% Asian, 3.1% Other, 3.9% Hispanic of any race (2010); Density: 1,216.8 persons per square mile (2010); Average household size: 2.43 (2010); Median age: 42.8 (2010); Males per 100 females: 92.0 (2010); Marriage status: 29.1% never married, 57.3% now married, 4.4% widowed, 9.3% divorced (2005-2009 5-year

est.); Foreign born: 4.2% (2005-2009 5-year est.); Ancestry (includes multiple ancestries): 30.3% German, 24.0% Irish, 18.1% Italian, 11.0% Polish, 8.1% English (2005-2009 5-year est.).
Economy: Single-family building permits issued: 15 (2010); Multi-family building permits issued: 0 (2010); Employment by occupation: 15.5% management, 21.5% professional, 16.5% services, 20.7% sales, 1.8% farming, 8.1% construction, 15.8% production (2005-2009 5-year est.).
Income: Per capita income: $25,616 (2010); Median household income: $54,951 (2010); Average household income: $62,198 (2010); Percent of households with income of $100,000 or more: 15.4% (2010); Poverty rate: 5.3% (2005-2009 5-year est.).
Taxes: Total city taxes per capita: $461 (2007); City property taxes per capita: $201 (2007).
Education: Percent of population age 25 and over with: High school diploma (including GED) or higher: 87.2% (2010); Bachelor's degree or higher: 19.3% (2010); Master's degree or higher: 6.9% (2010).
School District(s)
Beecher CUSD 200u (KG-12)
    2009-10 Enrollment: 1,144 . . . . (708) 946-2266
Housing: Homeownership rate: 81.5% (2010); Median home value: $190,138 (2010); Median contract rent: $655 per month (2005-2009 5-year est.); Median year structure built: 1978 (2005-2009 5-year est.).
Safety: Violent crime rate: 6.3 per 10,000 population; Property crime rate: 129.8 per 10,000 population (2010).
Transportation: Commute to work: 92.6% car, 2.1% public transportation, 1.6% walk, 3.6% work from home (2005-2009 5-year est.); Travel time to work: 23.9% less than 15 minutes, 21.4% 15 to 30 minutes, 19.8% 30 to 45 minutes, 19.9% 45 to 60 minutes, 15.0% 60 minutes or more (2005-2009 5-year est.)

BOLINGBROOK (village). Covers a land area of 20.506 square miles and a water area of 0.237 square miles. Located at 41.69° N. Lat; 88.08° W. Long. Elevation is 702 feet.
Population: 41,386 (1990); 56,321 (2000); 71,674 (2010); 78,969 (2015 projected); Race: 51.8% White, 23.9% Black, 8.8% Asian, 15.5% Other, 25.2% Hispanic of any race (2010); Density: 3,495.2 persons per square mile (2010); Average household size: 3.21 (2010); Median age: 32.2 (2010); Males per 100 females: 99.9 (2010); Marriage status: 30.2% never married, 60.1% now married, 3.1% widowed, 6.6% divorced (2005-2009 5-year est.); Foreign born: 22.7% (2005-2009 5-year est.); Ancestry (includes multiple ancestries): 15.0% German, 11.3% Irish, 9.9% Polish, 6.2% Italian, 4.5% English (2005-2009 5-year est.).
Economy: Unemployment rate: 9.9% (August 2011); Total civilian labor force: 40,030 (August 2011); Single-family building permits issued: 37 (2010); Multi-family building permits issued: 63 (2010); Employment by occupation: 15.2% management, 20.4% professional, 17.1% services, 26.4% sales, 0.1% farming, 6.8% construction, 13.9% production (2005-2009 5-year est.).
Income: Per capita income: $29,560 (2010); Median household income: $82,643 (2010); Average household income: $94,809 (2010); Percent of households with income of $100,000 or more: 36.6% (2010); Poverty rate: 5.7% (2005-2009 5-year est.).
Taxes: Total city taxes per capita: $599 (2007); City property taxes per capita: $194 (2007).
Education: Percent of population age 25 and over with: High school diploma (including GED) or higher: 89.3% (2010); Bachelor's degree or higher: 35.1% (2010); Master's degree or higher: 10.3% (2010).
School District(s)
Indian Prairie CUSD 204 (PK-12)
    2009-10 Enrollment: 29,733 . . . . (630) 375-3000
Plainfield SD 202 (PK-12)
    2009-10 Enrollment: 29,254 . . . . (815) 254-4005
Valley View CUSD 365u (PK-12)
    2009-10 Enrollment: 18,133 . . . . (815) 886-2700
Will Roe (06-12)
    2009-10 Enrollment: n/a . . . . (815) 740-8360
Housing: Homeownership rate: 86.9% (2010); Median home value: $196,886 (2010); Median contract rent: $816 per month (2005-2009 5-year est.); Median year structure built: 1986 (2005-2009 5-year est.).
Newspapers: Chicago China News Digest (Circulation 10,000)
Transportation: Commute to work: 90.0% car, 3.7% public transportation, 1.0% walk, 3.3% work from home (2005-2009 5-year est.); Travel time to work: 20.3% less than 15 minutes, 26.4% 15 to 30 minutes, 24.8% 30 to 45 minutes, 13.9% 45 to 60 minutes, 14.6% 60 minutes or more (2005-2009 5-year est.)

Airports: Bolingbrook's Clow International (general aviation)
Additional Information Contacts
Bolingbrook Area Chamber of Commerce . . . . (630) 226-8420
   http://bolingbrook.org
Village of Bolingbrook . . . . (630) 226-8400
   http://www.bolingbrook.com

BRAIDWOOD (city). Covers a land area of 4.629 square miles and a water area of 0.126 square miles. Located at 41.27° N. Lat; 88.21° W. Long. Elevation is 574 feet.

History: Braidwood was a crowded coal-mining town in the 1880's, with many mining syndicates operating. The first coal vein was discovered in 1865 by settler William Henneberry. By 1873 Braidwood was incorporated as a city.

Population: 3,658 (1990); 5,203 (2000); 6,976 (2010); 7,864 (2015 projected); Race: 95.5% White, 0.4% Black, 0.5% Asian, 3.6% Other, 6.5% Hispanic of any race (2010); Density: 1,507.0 persons per square mile (2010); Average household size: 2.82 (2010); Median age: 33.5 (2010); Males per 100 females: 100.7 (2010); Marriage status: 30.5% never married, 53.3% now married, 7.2% widowed, 9.0% divorced (2005-2009 5-year est.); Foreign born: 1.2% (2005-2009 5-year est.); Ancestry (includes multiple ancestries): 28.8% German, 21.6% Irish, 10.2% Italian, 10.1% Polish, 8.4% English (2005-2009 5-year est.).

Economy: Single-family building permits issued: 1 (2010); Multi-family building permits issued: 0 (2010); Employment by occupation: 10.1% management, 9.5% professional, 20.6% services, 22.3% sales, 0.0% farming, 18.1% construction, 19.3% production (2005-2009 5-year est.).

Income: Per capita income: $26,473 (2010); Median household income: $65,324 (2010); Average household income: $74,631 (2010); Percent of households with income of $100,000 or more: 23.9% (2010); Poverty rate: 11.1% (2005-2009 5-year est.).

Taxes: Total city taxes per capita: $781 (2007); City property taxes per capita: $649 (2007).

Education: Percent of population age 25 and over with: High school diploma (including GED) or higher: 87.4% (2010); Bachelor's degree or higher: 10.9% (2010); Master's degree or higher: 2.6% (2010).

School District(s)
Reed Custer CUSD 255u (PK-12)
   2009-10 Enrollment: 1,804 . . . . (815) 458-2307
Housing: Homeownership rate: 86.1% (2010); Median home value: $141,451 (2010); Median contract rent: $595 per month (2005-2009 5-year est.); Median year structure built: 1991 (2005-2009 5-year est.).
Safety: Violent crime rate: 11.6 per 10,000 population; Property crime rate: 175.7 per 10,000 population (2010).
Transportation: Commute to work: 96.3% car, 0.0% public transportation, 1.3% walk, 1.0% work from home (2005-2009 5-year est.); Travel time to work: 25.6% less than 15 minutes, 23.6% 15 to 30 minutes, 21.7% 30 to 45 minutes, 10.9% 45 to 60 minutes, 18.3% 60 minutes or more (2005-2009 5-year est.)
Additional Information Contacts
City of Braidwood. . . . . (815) 458-2333
   http://www.braidwood.us

CHANNAHON (village). Covers a land area of 7.207 square miles and a water area of 0.669 square miles. Located at 41.43° N. Lat; 88.21° W. Long. Elevation is 528 feet.

History: Channahon was settled in 1832 and developed when the Illinois & Michigan Canal was built. Early industries included grain shipping, quarrying, and the manufacture of farm equipment.

Population: 5,088 (1990); 7,344 (2000); 11,245 (2010); 12,869 (2015 projected); Race: 95.1% White, 0.5% Black, 0.6% Asian, 3.9% Other, 7.4% Hispanic of any race (2010); Density: 1,560.3 persons per square mile (2010); Average household size: 3.12 (2010); Median age: 33.3 (2010); Males per 100 females: 102.8 (2010); Marriage status: 24.9% never married, 65.1% now married, 3.2% widowed, 6.8% divorced (2005-2009 5-year est.); Foreign born: 2.1% (2005-2009 5-year est.); Ancestry (includes multiple ancestries): 28.3% German, 26.1% Irish, 17.2% Italian, 15.3% Polish, 8.1% English (2005-2009 5-year est.).

Economy: Single-family building permits issued: 4 (2010); Multi-family building permits issued: 0 (2010); Employment by occupation: 14.4% management, 18.7% professional, 16.3% services, 24.1% sales, 0.0% farming, 12.9% construction, 13.7% production (2005-2009 5-year est.).

Income: Per capita income: $30,236 (2010); Median household income: $87,136 (2010); Average household income: $94,293 (2010); Percent of

households with income of $100,000 or more: 38.7% (2010); Poverty rate: 2.1% (2005-2009 5-year est.).

Taxes: Total city taxes per capita: $1,011 (2007); City property taxes per capita: $526 (2007).

Education: Percent of population age 25 and over with: High school diploma (including GED) or higher: 93.5% (2010); Bachelor's degree or higher: 22.1% (2010); Master's degree or higher: 5.6% (2010).

School District(s)
Channahon SD 17 (PK-08)
   2009-10 Enrollment: 1,581 . . . . (815) 467-4315
Housing: Homeownership rate: 91.1% (2010); Median home value: $210,099 (2010); Median contract rent: $981 per month (2005-2009 5-year est.); Median year structure built: 1995 (2005-2009 5-year est.).
Transportation: Commute to work: 94.1% car, 1.0% public transportation, 0.7% walk, 3.5% work from home (2005-2009 5-year est.); Travel time to work: 26.4% less than 15 minutes, 31.7% 15 to 30 minutes, 18.7% 30 to 45 minutes, 10.7% 45 to 60 minutes, 12.5% 60 minutes or more (2005-2009 5-year est.)
Additional Information Contacts
Village of Channahon. . . . . (815) 467-6644
   http://www.channahon.org

CREST HILL (city). Covers a land area of 7.161 square miles and a water area of 0.106 square miles. Located at 41.56° N. Lat; 88.10° W. Long. Elevation is 643 feet.

Population: 10,628 (1990); 13,329 (2000); 16,862 (2010); 18,699 (2015 projected); Race: 68.4% White, 19.4% Black, 2.6% Asian, 9.6% Other, 17.7% Hispanic of any race (2010); Density: 2,354.6 persons per square mile (2010); Average household size: 2.38 (2010); Median age: 33.9 (2010); Males per 100 females: 134.4 (2010); Marriage status: 32.8% never married, 49.5% now married, 5.2% widowed, 12.4% divorced (2005-2009 5-year est.); Foreign born: 9.4% (2005-2009 5-year est.); Ancestry (includes multiple ancestries): 19.5% German, 13.7% Polish, 12.7% Irish, 8.5% Italian, 4.9% English (2005-2009 5-year est.).

Economy: Single-family building permits issued: 0 (2010); Multi-family building permits issued: 6 (2010); Employment by occupation: 12.0% management, 14.2% professional, 18.6% services, 27.6% sales, 0.0% farming, 10.9% construction, 16.7% production (2005-2009 5-year est.).

Income: Per capita income: $28,787 (2010); Median household income: $61,077 (2010); Average household income: $72,496 (2010); Percent of households with income of $100,000 or more: 18.2% (2010); Poverty rate: 8.2% (2005-2009 5-year est.).

Taxes: Total city taxes per capita: $147 (2007); City property taxes per capita: $72 (2007).

Education: Percent of population age 25 and over with: High school diploma (including GED) or higher: 79.4% (2010); Bachelor's degree or higher: 16.1% (2010); Master's degree or higher: 4.5% (2010).

School District(s)
Chaney-Monge SD 88 (KG-08)
   2009-10 Enrollment: 494 . . . . (815) 722-6673
Richland Gsd 88a (PK-08)
   2009-10 Enrollment: 944 . . . . (815) 744-7288
Housing: Homeownership rate: 70.2% (2010); Median home value: $150,714 (2010); Median contract rent: $756 per month (2005-2009 5-year est.); Median year structure built: 1992 (2005-2009 5-year est.).
Transportation: Commute to work: 96.0% car, 1.9% public transportation, 0.2% walk, 1.3% work from home (2005-2009 5-year est.); Travel time to work: 26.3% less than 15 minutes, 34.4% 15 to 30 minutes, 13.7% 30 to 45 minutes, 11.4% 45 to 60 minutes, 14.3% 60 minutes or more (2005-2009 5-year est.)
Additional Information Contacts
City of Crest Hill . . . . (815) 741-5100
   http://www.cityofcresthill.com

CRETE (village). Covers a land area of 6.378 square miles and a water area of 0.025 square miles. Located at 41.45° N. Lat; 87.61° W. Long. Elevation is 728 feet.

History: Crete was laid out in 1849 by William Wood, operator of a tavern for travelers on the Chicago-Vincennes Road.

Population: 6,952 (1990); 7,346 (2000); 8,055 (2010); 8,612 (2015 projected); Race: 78.2% White, 16.7% Black, 1.0% Asian, 4.1% Other, 7.2% Hispanic of any race (2010); Density: 1,263.0 persons per square mile (2010); Average household size: 2.66 (2010); Median age: 39.8 (2010); Males per 100 females: 96.9 (2010); Marriage status: 22.5% never married, 62.1% now married, 7.7% widowed, 7.6% divorced (2005-2009

5-year est.); Foreign born: 5.8% (2005-2009 5-year est.); Ancestry (includes multiple ancestries): 26.2% German, 12.2% Irish, 11.2% Polish, 9.0% English, 8.4% Italian (2005-2009 5-year est.).
Economy: Single-family building permits issued: 0 (2010); Multi-family building permits issued: 0 (2010); Employment by occupation: 25.4% management, 18.1% professional, 13.1% services, 21.2% sales, 0.0% farming, 13.1% construction, 9.0% production (2005-2009 5-year est.).
Income: Per capita income: $35,167 (2010); Median household income: $76,591 (2010); Average household income: $94,075 (2010); Percent of households with income of $100,000 or more: 33.0% (2010); Poverty rate: 3.5% (2005-2009 5-year est.).
Taxes: Total city taxes per capita: $398 (2007); City property taxes per capita: $342 (2007).
Education: Percent of population age 25 and over with: High school diploma (including GED) or higher: 93.7% (2010); Bachelor's degree or higher: 30.8% (2010); Master's degree or higher: 11.8% (2010).

School District(s)
Crete Monee CUSD 201u (PK-12)
   2009-10 Enrollment: 5,245 . . . . (708) 367-8300
Housing: Homeownership rate: 90.5% (2010); Median home value: $187,413 (2010); Median contract rent: $646 per month (2005-2009 5-year est.); Median year structure built: 1979 (2005-2009 5-year est.).
Safety: Violent crime rate: 10.9 per 10,000 population; Property crime rate: 201.0 per 10,000 population (2010).
Transportation: Commute to work: 87.9% car, 6.0% public transportation, 1.7% walk, 4.4% work from home (2005-2009 5-year est.); Travel time to work: 20.6% less than 15 minutes, 22.5% 15 to 30 minutes, 28.5% 30 to 45 minutes, 11.6% 45 to 60 minutes, 16.8% 60 minutes or more (2005-2009 5-year est.)
Additional Information Contacts
Crete Area Chamber of Commerce . . . . (708) 672-9216
  http://www.cretechamber.com
Village of Crete . . . . (708) 672-5431
  http://www.villageofcrete.org

CRYSTAL LAWNS (CDP). Covers a land area of 0.993 square miles and a water area of 0 square miles. Located at 41.57° N. Lat; 88.15° W. Long. Elevation is 604 feet.
Population: 2,925 (1990); 2,933 (2000); 3,356 (2010); 3,852 (2015 projected); Race: 87.3% White, 3.3% Black, 2.1% Asian, 7.3% Other, 13.1% Hispanic of any race (2010); Density: 3,380.6 persons per square mile (2010); Average household size: 2.90 (2010); Median age: 35.4 (2010); Males per 100 females: 96.5 (2010); Marriage status: 32.0% never married, 55.1% now married, 4.4% widowed, 8.4% divorced (2005-2009 5-year est.); Foreign born: 8.0% (2005-2009 5-year est.); Ancestry (includes multiple ancestries): 35.3% German, 19.7% Irish, 13.2% Italian, 12.2% Polish, 8.9% English (2005-2009 5-year est.).
Economy: Employment by occupation: 9.8% management, 13.4% professional, 22.3% services, 29.0% sales, 0.0% farming, 12.8% construction, 12.6% production (2005-2009 5-year est.).
Income: Per capita income: $25,684 (2010); Median household income: $69,534 (2010); Average household income: $74,418 (2010); Percent of households with income of $100,000 or more: 21.1% (2010); Poverty rate: 15.2% (2005-2009 5-year est.).
Education: Percent of population age 25 and over with: High school diploma (including GED) or higher: 89.9% (2010); Bachelor's degree or higher: 23.6% (2010); Master's degree or higher: 6.5% (2010).
Housing: Homeownership rate: 95.0% (2010); Median home value: $178,988 (2010); Median contract rent: $718 per month (2005-2009 5-year est.); Median year structure built: 1964 (2005-2009 5-year est.).
Transportation: Commute to work: 94.6% car, 0.0% public transportation, 0.0% walk, 4.6% work from home (2005-2009 5-year est.); Travel time to work: 30.0% less than 15 minutes, 33.6% 15 to 30 minutes, 16.6% 30 to 45 minutes, 9.2% 45 to 60 minutes, 10.7% 60 minutes or more (2005-2009 5-year est.)

ELWOOD (village). Covers a land area of 2.711 square miles and a water area of 0 square miles. Located at 41.41° N. Lat; 88.11° W. Long. Elevation is 646 feet.
Population: 1,022 (1990); 1,620 (2000); 2,714 (2010); 3,150 (2015 projected); Race: 96.1% White, 0.2% Black, 0.7% Asian, 3.0% Other, 7.5% Hispanic of any race (2010); Density: 1,001.1 persons per square mile (2010); Average household size: 2.56 (2010); Median age: 36.3 (2010); Males per 100 females: 95.5 (2010); Marriage status: 18.5% never married, 68.8% now married, 6.2% widowed, 6.5% divorced (2005-2009 5-year

est.); Foreign born: 0.7% (2005-2009 5-year est.); Ancestry (includes multiple ancestries): 36.9% German, 36.9% Irish, 14.6% Italian, 8.8% Polish, 8.1% English (2005-2009 5-year est.).
Economy: Single-family building permits issued: 0 (2010); Multi-family building permits issued: 0 (2010); Employment by occupation: 10.2% management, 16.9% professional, 14.3% services, 23.8% sales, 0.0% farming, 14.7% construction, 20.1% production (2005-2009 5-year est.).
Income: Per capita income: $29,212 (2010); Median household income: $65,880 (2010); Average household income: $74,873 (2010); Percent of households with income of $100,000 or more: 24.3% (2010); Poverty rate: 4.8% (2005-2009 5-year est.).
Taxes: Total city taxes per capita: $2,968 (2007); City property taxes per capita: $2,459 (2007).
Education: Percent of population age 25 and over with: High school diploma (including GED) or higher: 90.0% (2010); Bachelor's degree or higher: 13.6% (2010); Master's degree or higher: 4.1% (2010).

School District(s)
Elwood CCSD 203 (KG-08)
   2009-10 Enrollment: 439 . . . . (815) 423-5588
Housing: Homeownership rate: 85.7% (2010); Median home value: $172,044 (2010); Median contract rent: $706 per month (2005-2009 5-year est.); Median year structure built: 1995 (2005-2009 5-year est.).
Transportation: Commute to work: 94.7% car, 2.6% public transportation, 0.4% walk, 2.3% work from home (2005-2009 5-year est.); Travel time to work: 20.4% less than 15 minutes, 37.3% 15 to 30 minutes, 24.2% 30 to 45 minutes, 8.7% 45 to 60 minutes, 9.5% 60 minutes or more (2005-2009 5-year est.)

FAIRMONT (CDP). Covers a land area of 1.648 square miles and a water area of 0 square miles. Located at 41.56° N. Lat; 88.06° W. Long. Elevation is 633 feet.
Population: 2,774 (1990); 2,563 (2000); 2,986 (2010); 3,244 (2015 projected); Race: 43.2% White, 39.2% Black, 0.4% Asian, 17.2% Other, 18.9% Hispanic of any race (2010); Density: 1,812.4 persons per square mile (2010); Average household size: 2.94 (2010); Median age: 33.3 (2010); Males per 100 females: 101.2 (2010); Marriage status: 31.7% never married, 44.9% now married, 8.4% widowed, 15.0% divorced (2005-2009 5-year est.); Foreign born: 7.3% (2005-2009 5-year est.); Ancestry (includes multiple ancestries): 7.3% Irish, 7.2% German, 6.4% Polish, 5.2% Italian, 2.7% American (2005-2009 5-year est.).
Economy: Employment by occupation: 5.5% management, 9.1% professional, 18.6% services, 26.2% sales, 0.0% farming, 8.4% construction, 32.3% production (2005-2009 5-year est.).
Income: Per capita income: $22,092 (2010); Median household income: $51,539 (2010); Average household income: $64,857 (2010); Percent of households with income of $100,000 or more: 16.8% (2010); Poverty rate: 21.3% (2005-2009 5-year est.).
Education: Percent of population age 25 and over with: High school diploma (including GED) or higher: 78.7% (2010); Bachelor's degree or higher: 8.4% (2010); Master's degree or higher: 3.3% (2010).
Housing: Homeownership rate: 72.4% (2010); Median home value: $120,347 (2010); Median contract rent: $623 per month (2005-2009 5-year est.); Median year structure built: 1956 (2005-2009 5-year est.).
Transportation: Commute to work: 98.0% car, 0.0% public transportation, 0.9% walk, 1.1% work from home (2005-2009 5-year est.); Travel time to work: 10.0% less than 15 minutes, 46.9% 15 to 30 minutes, 32.1% 30 to 45 minutes, 4.4% 45 to 60 minutes, 6.6% 60 minutes or more (2005-2009 5-year est.)

FRANKFORT (village). Covers a land area of 10.907 square miles and a water area of 0 square miles. Located at 41.49° N. Lat; 87.85° W. Long. Elevation is 761 feet.
History: Frankfort's name was never spelled "Frankfurt" even though it was named after Frankfurt am Main in Germany. It was commonly known as "Frankfort Station" after the opening of the Joliet & Northern Indiana Railroad through the township in 1855. The local residents incorporated as a village in 1879. After that it was simply known as "Frankfort.
Population: 7,827 (1990); 10,391 (2000); 13,990 (2010); 15,677 (2015 projected); Race: 90.4% White, 3.6% Black, 3.1% Asian, 3.0% Other, 5.4% Hispanic of any race (2010); Density: 1,282.7 persons per square mile (2010); Average household size: 2.94 (2010); Median age: 37.9 (2010); Males per 100 females: 94.9 (2010); Marriage status: 22.1% never married, 70.0% now married, 3.3% widowed, 4.6% divorced (2005-2009 5-year est.); Foreign born: 4.3% (2005-2009 5-year est.); Ancestry (includes

multiple ancestries): 26.1% Irish, 25.7% German, 15.3% Polish, 13.8% Italian, 7.8% English (2005-2009 5-year est.).

Economy: Single-family building permits issued: 35 (2010); Multi-family building permits issued: 0 (2010); Employment by occupation: 22.2% management, 32.9% professional, 8.6% services, 21.8% sales, 0.2% farming, 7.6% construction, 6.8% production (2005-2009 5-year est.).

Income: Per capita income: $39,695 (2010); Median household income: $98,183 (2010); Average household income: $117,450 (2010); Percent of households with income of $100,000 or more: 48.8% (2010); Poverty rate: 1.8% (2005-2009 5-year est.).

Taxes: Total city taxes per capita: $264 (2007); City property taxes per capita: $201 (2007).

Education: Percent of population age 25 and over with: High school diploma (including GED) or higher: 94.8% (2010); Bachelor's degree or higher: 41.5% (2010); Master's degree or higher: 17.5% (2010).

School District(s)

Frankfort CCSD 157c (PK-08)
    2009-10 Enrollment: 2,466 . . . . (815) 469-5922
Lincoln Way CHSD 210 (09-12)
    2009-10 Enrollment: 7,346 . . . . (815) 462-2100
Lincoln-Way Area Spec Ja Dist (PK-12)
    2009-10 Enrollment: n/a . . . . (815) 806-4600
Peotone CUSD 207u (PK-12)
    2009-10 Enrollment: 2,085 . . . . (708) 258-0991
Summit Hill SD 161 (PK-08)
    2009-10 Enrollment: 3,662 . . . . (815) 469-9103

Housing: Homeownership rate: 92.6% (2010); Median home value: $319,498 (2010); Median contract rent: $816 per month (2005-2009 5-year est.); Median year structure built: 1997 (2005-2009 5-year est.).

Safety: Violent crime rate: 7.8 per 10,000 population; Property crime rate: 158.5 per 10,000 population (2010).

Transportation: Commute to work: 85.5% car, 8.4% public transportation, 0.3% walk, 5.1% work from home (2005-2009 5-year est.); Travel time to work: 20.9% less than 15 minutes, 24.8% 15 to 30 minutes, 17.2% 30 to 45 minutes, 14.8% 45 to 60 minutes, 22.3% 60 minutes or more (2005-2009 5-year est.)

Additional Information Contacts

Frankfort Chamber of Commerce . . . . (815) 469-3356
    http://www.frankfortchamber.com
Village of Frankfort. . . . . (815) 469-2177
    http://www.villageoffrankfort.com

FRANKFORT SQUARE (CDP). Covers a land area of 2.096 square miles and a water area of 0 square miles. Located at 41.51° N. Lat; 87.80° W. Long. Elevation is 709 feet.

Population: 6,317 (1990); 7,766 (2000); 10,631 (2010); 12,028 (2015 projected); Race: 90.9% White, 1.6% Black, 2.8% Asian, 4.7% Other, 8.1% Hispanic of any race (2010); Density: 5,072.3 persons per square mile (2010); Average household size: 3.38 (2010); Median age: 30.0 (2010); Males per 100 females: 98.3 (2010); Marriage status: 26.1% never married, 63.5% now married, 4.4% widowed, 6.0% divorced (2005-2009 5-year est.); Foreign born: 4.4% (2005-2009 5-year est.); Ancestry (includes multiple ancestries): 31.8% German, 29.5% Irish, 23.3% Polish, 15.1% Italian, 7.3% English (2005-2009 5-year est.).

Economy: Employment by occupation: 14.2% management, 20.2% professional, 11.1% services, 29.9% sales, 0.0% farming, 13.5% construction, 11.1% production (2005-2009 5-year est.).

Income: Per capita income: $28,406 (2010); Median household income: $89,272 (2010); Average household income: $95,975 (2010); Percent of households with income of $100,000 or more: 39.5% (2010); Poverty rate: 3.5% (2005-2009 5-year est.).

Education: Percent of population age 25 and over with: High school diploma (including GED) or higher: 95.7% (2010); Bachelor's degree or higher: 28.6% (2010); Master's degree or higher: 7.2% (2010).

Housing: Homeownership rate: 97.1% (2010); Median home value: $240,367 (2010); Median contract rent: n/a per month (2005-2009 5-year est.); Median year structure built: 1982 (2005-2009 5-year est.).

Transportation: Commute to work: 86.4% car, 9.5% public transportation, 0.3% walk, 3.0% work from home (2005-2009 5-year est.); Travel time to work: 25.1% less than 15 minutes, 27.1% 15 to 30 minutes, 15.3% 30 to 45 minutes, 10.5% 45 to 60 minutes, 22.0% 60 minutes or more (2005-2009 5-year est.)

GODLEY (village). Covers a land area of 1.086 square miles and a water area of 0 square miles. Located at 41.23° N. Lat; 88.24° W. Long. Elevation is 587 feet.

History: Godley began as a coal town settled by Scotch, Irish, and Welsh miners in the 1880's. The population declined when the mines closed in the early 1900's.

Population: 322 (1990); 594 (2000); 790 (2010); 896 (2015 projected); Race: 94.6% White, 0.1% Black, 0.8% Asian, 4.6% Other, 8.0% Hispanic of any race (2010); Density: 727.4 persons per square mile (2010); Average household size: 2.65 (2010); Median age: 33.6 (2010); Males per 100 females: 99.5 (2010); Marriage status: 41.0% never married, 32.5% now married, 7.4% widowed, 19.1% divorced (2005-2009 5-year est.); Foreign born: 0.5% (2005-2009 5-year est.); Ancestry (includes multiple ancestries): 31.1% Irish, 23.3% German, 7.7% Italian, 6.5% English, 5.8% Czech (2005-2009 5-year est.).

Economy: Single-family building permits issued: 10 (2010); Multi-family building permits issued: 0 (2010); Employment by occupation: 2.9% management, 4.6% professional, 17.4% services, 23.7% sales, 0.0% farming, 24.9% construction, 26.6% production (2005-2009 5-year est.).

Income: Per capita income: $26,434 (2010); Median household income: $60,041 (2010); Average household income: $70,295 (2010); Percent of households with income of $100,000 or more: 25.3% (2010); Poverty rate: 26.0% (2005-2009 5-year est.).

Taxes: Total city taxes per capita: $38 (2007); City property taxes per capita: $10 (2007).

Education: Percent of population age 25 and over with: High school diploma (including GED) or higher: 84.3% (2010); Bachelor's degree or higher: 9.5% (2010); Master's degree or higher: 4.6% (2010).

Housing: Homeownership rate: 82.5% (2010); Median home value: $136,176 (2010); Median contract rent: $726 per month (2005-2009 5-year est.); Median year structure built: 1986 (2005-2009 5-year est.).

Transportation: Commute to work: 90.5% car, 6.6% public transportation, 1.4% walk, 0.0% work from home (2005-2009 5-year est.); Travel time to work: 21.3% less than 15 minutes, 33.4% 15 to 30 minutes, 21.0% 30 to 45 minutes, 4.6% 45 to 60 minutes, 19.6% 60 minutes or more (2005-2009 5-year est.)

HOMER GLEN (CDP). Aka formerly Goodings Grove. Covers a land area of 9.420 square miles and a water area of 0.009 square miles. Located at 41.62° N. Lat; 87.94° W. Long. Elevation is 758 feet.

Population: 14,054 (1990); 17,084 (2000); 18,924 (2010); 20,434 (2015 projected); Race: 94.3% White, 0.4% Black, 2.6% Asian, 2.7% Other, 6.7% Hispanic of any race (2010); Density: 2,008.9 persons per square mile (2010); Average household size: 3.32 (2010); Median age: 34.0 (2010); Males per 100 females: 100.2 (2010); Marriage status: 28.0% never married, 62.6% now married, 4.3% widowed, 5.2% divorced (2005-2009 5-year est.); Foreign born: 11.0% (2005-2009 5-year est.); Ancestry (includes multiple ancestries): 28.6% Polish, 25.7% Irish, 19.7% German, 15.8% Italian, 4.2% English (2005-2009 5-year est.).

Economy: Unemployment rate: 8.4% (August 2011); Total civilian labor force: 14,573 (August 2011); Employment by occupation: 17.9% management, 22.2% professional, 13.6% services, 26.6% sales, 0.3% farming, 10.6% construction, 8.9% production (2005-2009 5-year est.).

Income: Per capita income: $36,320 (2010); Median household income: $103,457 (2010); Average household income: $120,224 (2010); Percent of households with income of $100,000 or more: 52.4% (2010); Poverty rate: 3.3% (2005-2009 5-year est.).

Education: Percent of population age 25 and over with: High school diploma (including GED) or higher: 93.7% (2010); Bachelor's degree or higher: 34.8% (2010); Master's degree or higher: 11.7% (2010).

School District(s)

Homer CCSD 33c (PK-08)
    2009-10 Enrollment: 3,638 . . . . (708) 226-7600
Will County SD 92 (PK-08)
    2009-10 Enrollment: 1,802 . . . . (815) 838-8031

Housing: Homeownership rate: 97.8% (2010); Median home value: $287,444 (2010); Median contract rent: $1,564 per month (2005-2009 5-year est.); Median year structure built: 1987 (2005-2009 5-year est.).

Transportation: Commute to work: 92.7% car, 3.6% public transportation, 1.1% walk, 2.0% work from home (2005-2009 5-year est.); Travel time to work: 17.0% less than 15 minutes, 23.0% 15 to 30 minutes, 27.5% 30 to 45 minutes, 14.4% 45 to 60 minutes, 18.1% 60 minutes or more (2005-2009 5-year est.)

Additional Information Contacts

Homer Township Chamber of Commerce . . . . (708) 301-8111
   http://www.homerchamber.com

INGALLS PARK (CDP). Covers a land area of 1.081 square miles and a water area of 0 square miles. Located at 41.52° N. Lat; 88.03° W. Long. Elevation is 610 feet.

Population: 3,189 (1990); 3,082 (2000); 3,402 (2010); 3,688 (2015 projected); Race: 78.8% White, 7.1% Black, 0.3% Asian, 13.8% Other, 28.0% Hispanic of any race (2010); Density: 3,146.3 persons per square mile (2010); Average household size: 2.46 (2010); Median age: 34.0 (2010); Males per 100 females: 105.1 (2010); Marriage status: 29.1% never married, 49.2% now married, 4.1% widowed, 17.5% divorced (2005-2009 5-year est.); Foreign born: 14.3% (2005-2009 5-year est.); Ancestry (includes multiple ancestries): 23.4% Irish, 20.8% German, 7.2% Italian, 5.0% French, 4.0% Polish (2005-2009 5-year est.).
Economy: Employment by occupation: 7.2% management, 9.5% professional, 26.1% services, 19.3% sales, 0.0% farming, 9.2% construction, 28.6% production (2005-2009 5-year est.).
Income: Per capita income: $22,752 (2010); Median household income: $49,582 (2010); Average household income: $55,948 (2010); Percent of households with income of $100,000 or more: 9.0% (2010); Poverty rate: 13.5% (2005-2009 5-year est.).
Education: Percent of population age 25 and over with: High school diploma (including GED) or higher: 84.6% (2010); Bachelor's degree or higher: 7.6% (2010); Master's degree or higher: 3.4% (2010).
Housing: Homeownership rate: 76.6% (2010); Median home value: $113,689 (2010); Median contract rent: $719 per month (2005-2009 5-year est.); Median year structure built: 1950 (2005-2009 5-year est.).
Transportation: Commute to work: 96.3% car, 0.0% public transportation, 0.7% walk, 1.0% work from home (2005-2009 5-year est.); Travel time to work: 39.4% less than 15 minutes, 23.8% 15 to 30 minutes, 12.7% 30 to 45 minutes, 11.5% 45 to 60 minutes, 12.6% 60 minutes or more (2005-2009 5-year est.)

JOLIET (city). County seat. Covers a land area of 38.059 square miles and a water area of 0.286 square miles. Located at 41.53° N. Lat; 88.10° W. Long. Elevation is 541 feet.

History: Named for Louis Joliet (1645-1700), French-Canadian explorer. The town of Joliet was laid out in 1834 with the name of Juliet (a neighboring village was Romeo) and incorporated in 1837 as the seat of Will County. Industry bloomed in Joliet when the Illinois & Michigan Canal was completed here in 1848. Limestone from the Joliet quarries was shipped across the country. Steel manufacturing in the late 1800's was replaced by the production of wallpaper as a leading industry.
Population: 82,008 (1990); 106,221 (2000); 144,356 (2010); 160,857 (2015 projected); Race: 65.6% White, 15.7% Black, 1.7% Asian, 17.0% Other, 29.1% Hispanic of any race (2010); Density: 3,792.9 persons per square mile (2010); Average household size: 2.85 (2010); Median age: 32.4 (2010); Males per 100 females: 99.9 (2010); Marriage status: 32.7% never married, 51.4% now married, 5.5% widowed, 10.4% divorced (2005-2009 5-year est.); Foreign born: 15.0% (2005-2009 5-year est.); Ancestry (includes multiple ancestries): 16.1% German, 14.1% Irish, 9.2% Polish, 9.0% Italian, 4.6% English (2005-2009 5-year est.).
Economy: Unemployment rate: 13.0% (August 2011); Total civilian labor force: 73,435 (August 2011); Single-family building permits issued: 78 (2010); Multi-family building permits issued: 6 (2010); Employment by occupation: 10.2% management, 14.5% professional, 19.5% services, 26.2% sales, 0.3% farming, 9.7% construction, 19.6% production (2005-2009 5-year est.).
Income: Per capita income: $23,257 (2010); Median household income: $57,582 (2010); Average household income: $67,490 (2010); Percent of households with income of $100,000 or more: 19.1% (2010); Poverty rate: 12.2% (2005-2009 5-year est.).
Taxes: Total city taxes per capita: $453 (2007); City property taxes per capita: $211 (2007).
Education: Percent of population age 25 and over with: High school diploma (including GED) or higher: 81.6% (2010); Bachelor's degree or higher: 22.2% (2010); Master's degree or higher: 7.1% (2010).

School District(s)
Grundy/Kendall Roe (06-12)
   2009-10 Enrollment: n/a . . . . (815) 941-3247
Joliet Psd 86 (PK-08)
   2009-10 Enrollment: 10,127 . . . . (815) 740-3196
Joliet Twp HSD 204 (09-12)
   2009-10 Enrollment: 5,791 . . . . (815) 727-6970

Laraway CCSD 70c (PK-08)
   2009-10 Enrollment: 328 . . . . (815) 727-5115
Minooka CCSD 201 (PK-08)
   2009-10 Enrollment: 3,940 . . . . (815) 467-6121
Plainfield SD 202 (PK-12)
   2009-10 Enrollment: 29,254 . . . . (815) 254-4005
S Will Co Coop for Spec Ed (KG-12)
   2009-10 Enrollment: n/a . . . . (815) 741-7777
Troy CCSD 30c (PK-08)
   2009-10 Enrollment: 4,432 . . . . (815) 577-6760
Union SD 81 (KG-08)
   2009-10 Enrollment: 116 . . . . (815) 726-5218
Will Roe (06-12)
   2009-10 Enrollment: n/a . . . . (815) 740-8360

Four-year College(s)
University of St Francis (Private, Not-for-profit, Roman Catholic)
   Fall 2009 Enrollment: 3,352 . . . . (815) 740-3360
   2010-11 Tuition: In-state $24,742; Out-of-state $24,742

Two-year College(s)
Joliet Junior College (Public)
   Fall 2009 Enrollment: 15,288 . . . . (815) 729-9020
   2010-11 Tuition: In-state $7,821; Out-of-state $8,684

Vocational/Technical School(s)
Professionals Choice Hair Design Academy (Private, For-profit)
   Fall 2009 Enrollment: 66 . . . . (815) 741-8224
   2010-11 Tuition: $13,700
Regency Beauty Institute-Joliet (Private, For-profit)
   Fall 2009 Enrollment: 154 . . . . (800) 787-6456
   2010-11 Tuition: $16,075

Housing: Homeownership rate: 74.2% (2010); Median home value: $160,060 (2010); Median contract rent: $654 per month (2005-2009 5-year est.); Median year structure built: 1969 (2005-2009 5-year est.).
Hospitals: Silver Cross Hospital (297 beds); St. Joseph Medical Center (452 beds); Stateville Correctional Center Hospital (32 beds)
Safety: Violent crime rate: 36.0 per 10,000 population; Property crime rate: 278.0 per 10,000 population (2010).
Newspapers: The Herald News (Local news; Circulation 44,344); KSKJ Boyce - Amerikanski Slovenec (National news; Circulation 11,000); Times Weekly Newspaper (Local news; Circulation 30,000)
Transportation: Commute to work: 91.1% car, 2.5% public transportation, 1.9% walk, 3.0% work from home (2005-2009 5-year est.); Travel time to work: 25.0% less than 15 minutes, 29.2% 15 to 30 minutes, 20.0% 30 to 45 minutes, 10.8% 45 to 60 minutes, 14.9% 60 minutes or more (2005-2009 5-year est.); Amtrak: train service available.

Additional Information Contacts
City of Joliet . . . . (815) 724-4000
   http://www.cityofjoliet.info
Joliet Region Chamber of Commerce & Industry . . . . (815) 727-5371
   http://www.jolietchamber.com
Will County Center for Economic Development . . . . (815) 723-1800
   http://www.c-e-d.org

LAKEWOOD SHORES (CDP). Covers a land area of 2.321 square miles and a water area of 0.423 square miles. Located at 41.26° N. Lat; 88.13° W. Long. Elevation is 564 feet.

Population: 1,606 (1990); 1,487 (2000); 1,617 (2010); 1,717 (2015 projected); Race: 95.9% White, 0.1% Black, 0.5% Asian, 3.5% Other, 3.8% Hispanic of any race (2010); Density: 696.7 persons per square mile (2010); Average household size: 2.77 (2010); Median age: 36.0 (2010); Males per 100 females: 107.3 (2010); Marriage status: 23.8% never married, 67.7% now married, 1.2% widowed, 7.2% divorced (2005-2009 5-year est.); Foreign born: 0.6% (2005-2009 5-year est.); Ancestry (includes multiple ancestries): 39.3% Irish, 30.7% German, 9.2% Polish, 8.4% Italian, 7.6% American (2005-2009 5-year est.).
Economy: Employment by occupation: 5.9% management, 5.3% professional, 25.5% services, 25.7% sales, 0.0% farming, 9.1% construction, 28.4% production (2005-2009 5-year est.).
Income: Per capita income: $24,310 (2010); Median household income: $61,258 (2010); Average household income: $66,943 (2010); Percent of households with income of $100,000 or more: 16.6% (2010); Poverty rate: 1.1% (2005-2009 5-year est.).
Education: Percent of population age 25 and over with: High school diploma (including GED) or higher: 84.2% (2010); Bachelor's degree or higher: 9.7% (2010); Master's degree or higher: 4.8% (2010).

Housing: Homeownership rate: 89.9% (2010); Median home value: $145,978 (2010); Median contract rent: n/a per month (2005-2009 5-year est.); Median year structure built: 1959 (2005-2009 5-year est.).
Transportation: Commute to work: 96.8% car, 0.0% public transportation, 0.0% walk, 3.2% work from home (2005-2009 5-year est.); Travel time to work: 22.1% less than 15 minutes, 24.6% 15 to 30 minutes, 35.8% 30 to 45 minutes, 12.9% 45 to 60 minutes, 4.7% 60 minutes or more (2005-2009 5-year est.)

LOCKPORT (city). Covers a land area of 7.084 square miles and a water area of 0.011 square miles. Located at 41.58° N. Lat; 88.04° W. Long. Elevation is 594 feet.
History: Named for the locks on the Illinois and Michigan Canal. Lockport developed as a shipping and transfer point on the Illinois & Michigan Canal. This was the location of the lock that controlled the volume of water from Lake Michigan. The canal company offices were located here also.
Population: 11,341 (1990); 15,191 (2000); 20,784 (2010); 23,111 (2015 projected); Race: 91.1% White, 3.0% Black, 1.0% Asian, 4.8% Other, 9.4% Hispanic of any race (2010); Density: 2,933.8 persons per square mile (2010); Average household size: 2.73 (2010); Median age: 34.9 (2010); Males per 100 females: 99.4 (2010); Marriage status: 28.3% never married, 58.2% now married, 4.1% widowed, 9.4% divorced (2005-2009 5-year est.); Foreign born: 5.8% (2005-2009 5-year est.); Ancestry (includes multiple ancestries): 28.6% German, 24.4% Polish, 22.6% Irish, 15.5% Italian, 6.3% English (2005-2009 5-year est.).
Economy: Unemployment rate: 10.6% (August 2011); Total civilian labor force: 14,248 (August 2011); Single-family building permits issued: 35 (2010); Multi-family building permits issued: 0 (2010); Employment by occupation: 15.4% management, 19.9% professional, 16.5% services, 28.0% sales, 0.0% farming, 9.3% construction, 10.8% production (2005-2009 5-year est.).
Income: Per capita income: $29,558 (2010); Median household income: $69,460 (2010); Average household income: $80,722 (2010); Percent of households with income of $100,000 or more: 24.4% (2010); Poverty rate: 6.7% (2005-2009 5-year est.).
Taxes: Total city taxes per capita: $334 (2007); City property taxes per capita: $234 (2007).
Education: Percent of population age 25 and over with: High school diploma (including GED) or higher: 90.8% (2010); Bachelor's degree or higher: 25.4% (2010); Master's degree or higher: 9.0% (2010).
School District(s)
Fairmont SD 89 (PK-08)
    2009-10 Enrollment: 304 . . . . (815) 726-6318
Homer CCSD 33c (PK-08)
    2009-10 Enrollment: 3,638 . . . . (708) 226-7600
Lockport SD 91 (PK-08)
    2009-10 Enrollment: 677 . . . . (815) 838-0737
Lockport Twp HSD 205 (09-12)
    2009-10 Enrollment: 3,872 . . . . (815) 588-8100
Taft SD 90 (PK-08)
    2009-10 Enrollment: 339 . . . . (815) 838-0408
Will County SD 92 (PK-08)
    2009-10 Enrollment: 1,802 . . . . (815) 838-8031
Housing: Homeownership rate: 81.0% (2010); Median home value: $195,502 (2010); Median contract rent: $723 per month (2005-2009 5-year est.); Median year structure built: 1985 (2005-2009 5-year est.).
Safety: Violent crime rate: 13.5 per 10,000 population; Property crime rate: 120.1 per 10,000 population (2010).
Transportation: Commute to work: 90.1% car, 3.8% public transportation, 2.1% walk, 3.1% work from home (2005-2009 5-year est.); Travel time to work: 23.1% less than 15 minutes, 25.3% 15 to 30 minutes, 25.4% 30 to 45 minutes, 12.1% 45 to 60 minutes, 14.1% 60 minutes or more (2005-2009 5-year est.)
Additional Information Contacts
City of Lockport . . . . (815) 838-0549
    http://www.cityoflockport.net
Lockport Area Chamber of Commerce . . . . (815) 838-3357
    http://www.lockportchamber.com

MANHATTAN (village). Covers a land area of 3.366 square miles and a water area of 0 square miles. Located at 41.42° N. Lat; 87.98° W. Long. Elevation is 682 feet.
Population: 2,149 (1990); 3,330 (2000); 6,449 (2010); 7,363 (2015 projected); Race: 94.0% White, 0.5% Black, 0.2% Asian, 5.2% Other, 6.5% Hispanic of any race (2010); Density: 1,915.9 persons per square mile

(2010); Average household size: 2.91 (2010); Median age: 31.8 (2010); Males per 100 females: 104.5 (2010); Marriage status: 24.9% never married, 64.2% now married, 2.6% widowed, 8.3% divorced (2005-2009 5-year est.); Foreign born: 1.2% (2005-2009 5-year est.); Ancestry (includes multiple ancestries): 33.6% Irish, 30.5% German, 18.3% Italian, 15.2% Polish, 7.2% Czech (2005-2009 5-year est.).
Economy: Single-family building permits issued: 10 (2010); Multi-family building permits issued: 0 (2010); Employment by occupation: 13.1% management, 18.0% professional, 15.3% services, 29.5% sales, 0.0% farming, 17.6% construction, 6.5% production (2005-2009 5-year est.).
Income: Per capita income: $28,369 (2010); Median household income: $73,752 (2010); Average household income: $82,598 (2010); Percent of households with income of $100,000 or more: 30.1% (2010); Poverty rate: 2.4% (2005-2009 5-year est.).
Taxes: Total city taxes per capita: $231 (2007); City property taxes per capita: $167 (2007).
Education: Percent of population age 25 and over with: High school diploma (including GED) or higher: 94.5% (2010); Bachelor's degree or higher: 21.5% (2010); Master's degree or higher: 4.8% (2010).
School District(s)
Manhattan SD 114 (PK-08)
    2009-10 Enrollment: 1,301 . . . . (815) 478-0191
Peotone CUSD 207u (PK-12)
    2009-10 Enrollment: 2,085 . . . . (708) 258-0991
Housing: Homeownership rate: 78.4% (2010); Median home value: $210,338 (2010); Median contract rent: $765 per month (2005-2009 5-year est.); Median year structure built: 1996 (2005-2009 5-year est.).
Safety: Violent crime rate: 7.6 per 10,000 population; Property crime rate: 45.8 per 10,000 population (2010).
Transportation: Commute to work: 92.1% car, 4.7% public transportation, 1.8% walk, 1.4% work from home (2005-2009 5-year est.); Travel time to work: 20.8% less than 15 minutes, 27.7% 15 to 30 minutes, 24.4% 30 to 45 minutes, 11.9% 45 to 60 minutes, 15.1% 60 minutes or more (2005-2009 5-year est.)
Additional Information Contacts
Manhattan Chamber of Commerce . . . . (815) 478-3811
    http://www.manhattan-il.com

MOKENA (village). Covers a land area of 5.995 square miles and a water area of 0.004 square miles. Located at 41.53° N. Lat; 87.87° W. Long. Elevation is 705 feet.
Population: 7,878 (1990); 14,583 (2000); 19,645 (2010); 22,405 (2015 projected); Race: 93.6% White, 1.0% Black, 2.7% Asian, 2.7% Other, 6.0% Hispanic of any race (2010); Density: 3,276.7 persons per square mile (2010); Average household size: 3.14 (2010); Median age: 33.5 (2010); Males per 100 females: 100.3 (2010); Marriage status: 30.1% never married, 59.6% now married, 4.8% widowed, 5.5% divorced (2005-2009 5-year est.); Foreign born: 3.8% (2005-2009 5-year est.); Ancestry (includes multiple ancestries): 31.1% German, 27.5% Irish, 19.0% Polish, 15.1% Italian, 5.9% English (2005-2009 5-year est.).
Economy: Single-family building permits issued: 45 (2010); Multi-family building permits issued: 0 (2010); Employment by occupation: 17.5% management, 21.2% professional, 10.9% services, 31.3% sales, 0.0% farming, 10.7% construction, 8.3% production (2005-2009 5-year est.).
Income: Per capita income: $34,585 (2010); Median household income: $93,895 (2010); Average household income: $108,629 (2010); Percent of households with income of $100,000 or more: 45.5% (2010); Poverty rate: 1.6% (2005-2009 5-year est.).
Taxes: Total city taxes per capita: $139 (2007); City property taxes per capita: $67 (2007).
Education: Percent of population age 25 and over with: High school diploma (including GED) or higher: 95.1% (2010); Bachelor's degree or higher: 37.0% (2010); Master's degree or higher: 13.4% (2010).
School District(s)
Mokena SD 159 (PK-08)
    2009-10 Enrollment: 2,081 . . . . (708) 342-4900
Summit Hill SD 161 (PK-08)
    2009-10 Enrollment: 3,662 . . . . (815) 469-9103
Housing: Homeownership rate: 89.4% (2010); Median home value: $272,976 (2010); Median contract rent: $897 per month (2005-2009 5-year est.); Median year structure built: 1994 (2005-2009 5-year est.).
Safety: Violent crime rate: 6.1 per 10,000 population; Property crime rate: 109.4 per 10,000 population (2010).
Transportation: Commute to work: 84.2% car, 11.2% public transportation, 1.0% walk, 2.6% work from home (2005-2009 5-year est.);

Travel time to work: 17.0% less than 15 minutes, 27.9% 15 to 30 minutes, 21.1% 30 to 45 minutes, 11.1% 45 to 60 minutes, 22.9% 60 minutes or more (2005-2009 5-year est.)

Additional Information Contacts
Mokena Chamber of Commerce . . . . (708) 479-2468
   http://www.mokena.com
Village of Mokena . . . . (708) 479-3900
   http://www.mokena.org

MONEE (village). Covers a land area of 3.100 square miles and a water area of 0 square miles. Located at 41.41° N. Lat; 87.74° W. Long. Elevation is 797 feet.

Population: 1,458 (1990); 2,924 (2000); 4,470 (2010); 5,145 (2015 projected); Race: 86.1% White, 6.9% Black, 1.3% Asian, 5.7% Other, 5.2% Hispanic of any race (2010); Density: 1,442.1 persons per square mile (2010); Average household size: 2.51 (2010); Median age: 38.5 (2010); Males per 100 females: 101.5 (2010); Marriage status: 18.7% never married, 67.7% now married, 7.6% widowed, 6.0% divorced (2005-2009 5-year est.); Foreign born: 2.5% (2005-2009 5-year est.); Ancestry (includes multiple ancestries): 32.1% German, 25.8% Irish, 13.5% Polish, 10.5% Italian, 5.1% English (2005-2009 5-year est.).
Economy: Single-family building permits issued: 0 (2010); Multi-family building permits issued: 0 (2010); Employment by occupation: 13.8% management, 15.8% professional, 16.8% services, 21.9% sales, 0.0% farming, 15.5% construction, 16.1% production (2005-2009 5-year est.).
Income: Per capita income: $37,188 (2010); Median household income: $76,451 (2010); Average household income: $93,440 (2010); Percent of households with income of $100,000 or more: 32.2% (2010); Poverty rate: 2.9% (2005-2009 5-year est.).
Taxes: Total city taxes per capita: $733 (2007); City property taxes per capita: $564 (2007).
Education: Percent of population age 25 and over with: High school diploma (including GED) or higher: 90.2% (2010); Bachelor's degree or higher: 23.9% (2010); Master's degree or higher: 8.4% (2010).

School District(s)
Crete Monee CUSD 201u (PK-12)
   2009-10 Enrollment: 5,245 . . . . (708) 367-8300
Will Roe (06-12)
   2009-10 Enrollment: n/a . . . . (815) 740-8360
Housing: Homeownership rate: 87.5% (2010); Median home value: $189,359 (2010); Median contract rent: $558 per month (2005-2009 5-year est.); Median year structure built: 1999 (2005-2009 5-year est.).
Transportation: Commute to work: 84.7% car, 6.1% public transportation, 0.0% walk, 7.8% work from home (2005-2009 5-year est.); Travel time to work: 27.1% less than 15 minutes, 26.9% 15 to 30 minutes, 11.7% 30 to 45 minutes, 10.6% 45 to 60 minutes, 23.7% 60 minutes or more (2005-2009 5-year est.)
Airports: Bult Field (general aviation)
Additional Information Contacts
Monee Area Chamber of Commerce . . . . (708) 212-4133
   http://www.moneechamber.com

NEW LENOX (village). Covers a land area of 10.094 square miles and a water area of 0.018 square miles. Located at 41.50° N. Lat; 87.97° W. Long. Elevation is 669 feet.

History: New Lenox was first settled in the 1820's along Hickory Creek.
Population: 11,574 (1990); 17,771 (2000); 23,526 (2010); 26,605 (2015 projected); Race: 95.5% White, 0.5% Black, 0.7% Asian, 3.3% Other, 6.0% Hispanic of any race (2010); Density: 2,330.7 persons per square mile (2010); Average household size: 3.05 (2010); Median age: 33.2 (2010); Males per 100 females: 96.0 (2010); Marriage status: 25.1% never married, 64.0% now married, 3.8% widowed, 7.1% divorced (2005-2009 5-year est.); Foreign born: 2.7% (2005-2009 5-year est.); Ancestry (includes multiple ancestries): 32.3% German, 26.0% Irish, 19.5% Polish, 18.2% Italian, 7.2% English (2005-2009 5-year est.).
Economy: Single-family building permits issued: 23 (2010); Multi-family building permits issued: 0 (2010); Employment by occupation: 15.8% management, 23.7% professional, 10.5% services, 28.1% sales, 0.2% farming, 11.5% construction, 10.3% production (2005-2009 5-year est.).
Income: Per capita income: $31,673 (2010); Median household income: $85,843 (2010); Average household income: $96,525 (2010); Percent of households with income of $100,000 or more: 38.0% (2010); Poverty rate: 2.9% (2005-2009 5-year est.).
Taxes: Total city taxes per capita: $126 (2007); City property taxes per capita: $93 (2007).

Education: Percent of population age 25 and over with: High school diploma (including GED) or higher: 94.0% (2010); Bachelor's degree or higher: 28.4% (2010); Master's degree or higher: 9.3% (2010).

School District(s)
Lincoln Way CHSD 210 (09-12)
   2009-10 Enrollment: 7,346 . . . . (815) 462-2100
Lincoln-Way Area Spec Ed Ja Dist (PK-12)
   2009-10 Enrollment: n/a . . . . (815) 806-4600
New Lenox SD 122 (PK-08)
   2009-10 Enrollment: 5,667 . . . . (815) 485-2169

Vocational/Technical School(s)
Capri Beauty College (Private, For-profit)
   Fall 2009 Enrollment: 50 . . . . (815) 485-3020
   2010-11 Tuition: $17,600
Housing: Homeownership rate: 90.3% (2010); Median home value: $239,765 (2010); Median contract rent: $814 per month (2005-2009 5-year est.); Median year structure built: 1993 (2005-2009 5-year est.).
Safety: Violent crime rate: 4.0 per 10,000 population; Property crime rate: 107.6 per 10,000 population (2010).
Transportation: Commute to work: 88.0% car, 7.1% public transportation, 0.3% walk, 4.2% work from home (2005-2009 5-year est.); Travel time to work: 21.9% less than 15 minutes, 28.5% 15 to 30 minutes, 20.2% 30 to 45 minutes, 9.2% 45 to 60 minutes, 20.2% 60 minutes or more (2005-2009 5-year est.)
Additional Information Contacts
New Lenox Chamber of Commerce. . . . . (815) 485-4241
   http://www.newlenoxchamber.com
Village of New Lenox . . . . (815) 462-6400
   http://www.newlenox.net

PEOTONE (village). Covers a land area of 1.516 square miles and a water area of 0.003 square miles. Located at 41.32° N. Lat; 87.79° W. Long. Elevation is 705 feet.

History: Incorporated 1869.
Population: 3,094 (1990); 3,385 (2000); 4,427 (2010); 4,944 (2015 projected); Race: 95.1% White, 1.3% Black, 0.6% Asian, 3.0% Other, 3.8% Hispanic of any race (2010); Density: 2,919.6 persons per square mile (2010); Average household size: 2.67 (2010); Median age: 35.7 (2010); Males per 100 females: 94.3 (2010); Marriage status: 27.8% never married, 60.6% now married, 4.2% widowed, 7.4% divorced (2005-2009 5-year est.); Foreign born: 0.7% (2005-2009 5-year est.); Ancestry (includes multiple ancestries): 34.2% German, 26.7% Irish, 13.3% English, 11.2% Italian, 10.7% Polish (2005-2009 5-year est.).
Economy: Single-family building permits issued: 5 (2010); Multi-family building permits issued: 0 (2010); Employment by occupation: 13.7% management, 23.0% professional, 11.8% services, 27.2% sales, 0.0% farming, 13.1% construction, 11.2% production (2005-2009 5-year est.).
Income: Per capita income: $30,288 (2010); Median household income: $69,831 (2010); Average household income: $80,730 (2010); Percent of households with income of $100,000 or more: 26.7% (2010); Poverty rate: 3.1% (2005-2009 5-year est.).
Taxes: Total city taxes per capita: $303 (2007); City property taxes per capita: $161 (2007).
Education: Percent of population age 25 and over with: High school diploma (including GED) or higher: 91.1% (2010); Bachelor's degree or higher: 23.8% (2010); Master's degree or higher: 5.7% (2010).

School District(s)
Peotone CUSD 207u (PK-12)
   2009-10 Enrollment: 2,085 . . . . (708) 258-0991
Housing: Homeownership rate: 74.5% (2010); Median home value: $206,556 (2010); Median contract rent: $676 per month (2005-2009 5-year est.); Median year structure built: 1975 (2005-2009 5-year est.).
Safety: Violent crime rate: 4.6 per 10,000 population; Property crime rate: 112.0 per 10,000 population (2010).
Newspapers: Crete Record (Community news; Circulation 5,000); Daily Journal - Peotone Bureau (Local news); Grant Park Gazette (Community news; Circulation 20,000); Manhattan American (Community news; Circulation 8,500); Manteno News (Community news)
Transportation: Commute to work: 92.1% car, 2.5% public transportation, 1.6% walk, 1.6% work from home (2005-2009 5-year est.); Travel time to work: 34.1% less than 15 minutes, 23.9% 15 to 30 minutes, 18.6% 30 to 45 minutes, 4.7% 45 to 60 minutes, 18.7% 60 minutes or more (2005-2009 5-year est.)
Additional Information Contacts

Peotone Chamber of Commerce . . . . (708) 258-9450
http://www.peotonechamber.com

PLAINFIELD (village). Covers a land area of 11.612 square miles and a water area of 0.835 square miles. Located at 41.61° N. Lat; 88.20° W. Long. Elevation is 617 feet.

History: Plainfield began as a trading post founded by the Frenchman Du Pazhe about 1790, and later operated by Vetel Vermette for the American Fur Trading Company. The town grew around a cabin built by Captain James Walker in 1829, and was first known as Walker's Grove. The name of Plainfield refers to the flat prairie setting.

Population: 6,409 (1990); 13,038 (2000); 26,040 (2010); 29,879 (2015 projected); Race: 87.1% White, 3.0% Black, 4.6% Asian, 5.4% Other, 10.4% Hispanic of any race (2010); Density: 2,242.6 persons per square mile (2010); Average household size: 3.23 (2010); Median age: 32.0 (2010); Males per 100 females: 99.4 (2010); Marriage status: 23.6% never married, 65.2% now married, 5.2% widowed, 6.0% divorced (2005-2009 5-year est.); Foreign born: 11.2% (2005-2009 5-year est.); Ancestry (includes multiple ancestries): 25.1% German, 20.2% Irish, 14.7% Italian, 14.4% Polish, 7.6% English (2005-2009 5-year est.).

Economy: Unemployment rate: 9.6% (August 2011); Total civilian labor force: 20,260 (August 2011); Single-family building permits issued: 59 (2010); Multi-family building permits issued: 0 (2010); Employment by occupation: 23.5% management, 25.6% professional, 11.2% services, 26.8% sales, 0.0% farming, 5.0% construction, 7.9% production (2005-2009 5-year est.).

Income: Per capita income: $34,357 (2010); Median household income: $97,437 (2010); Average household income: $110,993 (2010); Percent of households with income of $100,000 or more: 47.8% (2010); Poverty rate: 2.8% (2005-2009 5-year est.).

Taxes: Total city taxes per capita: $338 (2007); City property taxes per capita: $134 (2007).

Education: Percent of population age 25 and over with: High school diploma (including GED) or higher: 96.6% (2010); Bachelor's degree or higher: 43.8% (2010); Master's degree or higher: 11.5% (2010).

School District(s)

Oswego CUSD 308 (PK-12)
    2009-10 Enrollment: 16,314 . . . . (630) 636-3080
Plainfield SD 202 (PK-12)
    2009-10 Enrollment: 29,254 . . . . (815) 254-4005
Troy CCSD 30c (PK-08)
    2009-10 Enrollment: 4,432 . . . . (815) 577-6760

Housing: Homeownership rate: 92.6% (2010); Median home value: $268,333 (2010); Median contract rent: $1,060 per month (2005-2009 5-year est.); Median year structure built: 2001 (2005-2009 5-year est.).

Safety: Violent crime rate: 5.2 per 10,000 population; Property crime rate: 127.2 per 10,000 population (2010).

Newspapers: Enterprise (Local news; Circulation 6,000); Plainfield Sun (Local news; Circulation 15,000)

Transportation: Commute to work: 90.5% car, 3.4% public transportation, 0.6% walk, 4.8% work from home (2005-2009 5-year est.); Travel time to work: 15.2% less than 15 minutes, 22.3% 15 to 30 minutes, 22.0% 30 to 45 minutes, 15.9% 45 to 60 minutes, 24.6% 60 minutes or more (2005-2009 5-year est.)

Additional Information Contacts

Plainfield Area Chamber of Commerce . . . . (815) 436-4431
http://www.plainfieldchamber.com
Village of Plainfield . . . . (815) 436-7093
http://www.plainfield-il.org

PRESTON HEIGHTS (CDP). Covers a land area of 1.494 square miles and a water area of 0 square miles. Located at 41.49° N. Lat; 88.07° W. Long. Elevation is 630 feet.

Population: 2,563 (1990); 2,527 (2000); 3,065 (2010); 3,397 (2015 projected); Race: 19.4% White, 72.9% Black, 0.2% Asian, 7.5% Other, 8.9% Hispanic of any race (2010); Density: 2,051.4 persons per square mile (2010); Average household size: 2.89 (2010); Median age: 31.2 (2010); Males per 100 females: 93.7 (2010); Marriage status: 43.5% never married, 40.7% now married, 6.0% widowed, 9.8% divorced (2005-2009 5-year est.); Foreign born: 2.9% (2005-2009 5-year est.); Ancestry (includes multiple ancestries): 9.6% German, 5.7% Irish, 3.5% Italian, 3.0% American, 2.1% Haitian (2005-2009 5-year est.).

Economy: Employment by occupation: 4.5% management, 4.4% professional, 36.6% services, 24.8% sales, 0.0% farming, 7.1% construction, 22.6% production (2005-2009 5-year est.).

Income: Per capita income: $20,521 (2010); Median household income: $45,399 (2010); Average household income: $59,147 (2010); Percent of households with income of $100,000 or more: 14.2% (2010); Poverty rate: 13.1% (2005-2009 5-year est.).

Education: Percent of population age 25 and over with: High school diploma (including GED) or higher: 77.2% (2010); Bachelor's degree or higher: 11.0% (2010); Master's degree or higher: 2.3% (2010).

Housing: Homeownership rate: 66.3% (2010); Median home value: $109,217 (2010); Median contract rent: $671 per month (2005-2009 est.); Median year structure built: 1964 (2005-2009 5-year est.).

Transportation: Commute to work: 92.6% car, 4.8% public transportation, 0.0% walk, 2.5% work from home (2005-2009 5-year est.); Travel time to work: 26.0% less than 15 minutes, 43.7% 15 to 30 minutes, 13.1% 30 to 45 minutes, 8.1% 45 to 60 minutes, 9.1% 60 minutes or more (2005-2009 5-year est.)

ROCKDALE (village). Covers a land area of 0.794 square miles and a water area of 0 square miles. Located at 41.50° N. Lat; 88.11° W. Long. Elevation is 551 feet.

History: Incorporated 1903.

Population: 1,725 (1990); 1,888 (2000); 2,474 (2010); 2,792 (2015 projected); Race: 72.4% White, 1.3% Black, 0.7% Asian, 25.6% Other, 36.7% Hispanic of any race (2010); Density: 3,115.4 persons per square mile (2010); Average household size: 2.49 (2010); Median age: 34.6 (2010); Males per 100 females: 103.1 (2010); Marriage status: 32.6% never married, 45.2% now married, 7.7% widowed, 14.5% divorced (2005-2009 5-year est.); Foreign born: 14.3% (2005-2009 5-year est.); Ancestry (includes multiple ancestries): 16.9% German, 13.7% Irish, 11.9% Italian, 9.8% Polish, 5.7% English (2005-2009 5-year est.).

Economy: Single-family building permits issued: 0 (2010); Multi-family building permits issued: 0 (2010); Employment by occupation: 4.1% management, 13.5% professional, 17.4% services, 30.1% sales, 0.0% farming, 14.4% construction, 20.5% production (2005-2009 5-year est.).

Income: Per capita income: $20,330 (2010); Median household income: $43,113 (2010); Average household income: $50,584 (2010); Percent of households with income of $100,000 or more: 8.9% (2010); Poverty rate: 10.0% (2005-2009 5-year est.).

Taxes: Total city taxes per capita: $254 (2007); City property taxes per capita: $71 (2007).

Education: Percent of population age 25 and over with: High school diploma (including GED) or higher: 79.4% (2010); Bachelor's degree or higher: 9.9% (2010); Master's degree or higher: 2.6% (2010).

School District(s)

Rockdale SD 84 (PK-08)
    2009-10 Enrollment: 275 . . . . (815) 725-5321

Housing: Homeownership rate: 62.3% (2010); Median home value: $123,696 (2010); Median contract rent: $664 per month (2005-2009 5-year est.); Median year structure built: 1955 (2005-2009 5-year est.).

Transportation: Commute to work: 88.6% car, 4.8% public transportation, 3.6% walk, 2.4% work from home (2005-2009 5-year est.); Travel time to work: 36.2% less than 15 minutes, 31.7% 15 to 30 minutes, 15.3% 30 to 45 minutes, 9.5% 45 to 60 minutes, 7.3% 60 minutes or more (2005-2009 5-year est.)

ROMEOVILLE (village). Aka Romeo. Covers a land area of 14.514 square miles and a water area of 0.381 square miles. Located at 41.64° N. Lat; 88.10° W. Long. Elevation is 617 feet.

History: Named for the hero of Shakespeare's "Romeo and Juliet". Romeoville developed along the Illinois & Michigan Canal. An early industry was the Globe Oil Refinery.

Population: 15,337 (1990); 21,153 (2000); 34,162 (2010); 39,055 (2015 projected); Race: 78.3% White, 6.8% Black, 4.1% Asian, 10.9% Other, 20.7% Hispanic of any race (2010); Density: 2,353.8 persons per square mile (2010); Average household size: 2.81 (2010); Median age: 33.0 (2010); Males per 100 females: 99.7 (2010); Marriage status: 31.5% never married, 55.1% now married, 3.8% widowed, 9.6% divorced (2005-2009 5-year est.); Foreign born: 18.1% (2005-2009 5-year est.); Ancestry (includes multiple ancestries): 18.1% German, 15.3% Irish, 14.5% Polish, 10.9% Italian, 3.0% English (2005-2009 5-year est.).

Economy: Unemployment rate: 10.4% (August 2011); Total civilian labor force: 22,291 (August 2011); Single-family building permits issued: 9 (2010); Multi-family building permits issued: 0 (2010); Employment by occupation: 11.7% management, 17.1% professional, 15.2% services, 29.1% sales, 0.0% farming, 9.6% construction, 17.3% production (2005-2009 5-year est.).

Income: Per capita income: $25,012 (2010); Median household income: $64,515 (2010); Average household income: $71,419 (2010); Percent of households with income of $100,000 or more: 17.8% (2010); Poverty rate: 6.0% (2005-2009 5-year est.).

Taxes: Total city taxes per capita: $609 (2007); City property taxes per capita: $318 (2007).

Education: Percent of population age 25 and over with: High school diploma (including GED) or higher: 87.3% (2010); Bachelor's degree or higher: 22.8% (2010); Master's degree or higher: 5.6% (2010).

School District(s)

Valley View CUSD 365u (PK-12)
  2009-10 Enrollment: 18,133 . . . . (815) 886-2700
Wilco Area Career Center (11-12)
  2009-10 Enrollment: n/a . . . . (815) 838-6941

Four-year College(s)

Lewis University (Private, Not-for-profit, Roman Catholic)
  Fall 2009 Enrollment: 5,847 . . . . (815) 838-0500
  2010-11 Tuition: In-state $23,780; Out-of-state $23,780

Housing: Homeownership rate: 86.3% (2010); Median home value: $173,370 (2010); Median contract rent: $1,005 per month (2005-2009 5-year est.); Median year structure built: 1994 (2005-2009 5-year est.).

Safety: Violent crime rate: 8.0 per 10,000 population; Property crime rate: 195.2 per 10,000 population (2010).

Newspapers: Catholic Explorer (Regional news; Circulation 25,000)

Transportation: Commute to work: 89.9% car, 2.4% public transportation, 2.7% walk, 3.1% work from home (2005-2009 5-year est.); Travel time to work: 17.9% less than 15 minutes, 24.0% 15 to 30 minutes, 26.6% 30 to 45 minutes, 14.3% 45 to 60 minutes, 17.2% 60 minutes or more (2005-2009 5-year est.)

Airports: Lewis University (general aviation)

Additional Information Contacts

Romeoville Area Chamber of Commerce . . . . (815) 886-2076
  http://www.romeovillechamber.org
Village of Romeoville . . . . (815) 866-7200
  http://www.romeoville.org

SHOREWOOD (village). Covers a land area of 3.887 square miles and a water area of 0.065 square miles. Located at 41.51° N. Lat; 88.20° W. Long. Elevation is 577 feet.

Population: 6,415 (1990); 7,686 (2000); 11,342 (2010); 13,026 (2015 projected); Race: 86.5% White, 3.8% Black, 1.4% Asian, 8.3% Other, 10.5% Hispanic of any race (2010); Density: 2,917.6 persons per square mile (2010); Average household size: 2.91 (2010); Median age: 35.9 (2010); Males per 100 females: 98.4 (2010); Marriage status: 26.5% never married, 61.0% now married, 4.4% widowed, 8.1% divorced (2005-2009 5-year est.); Foreign born: 4.4% (2005-2009 5-year est.); Ancestry (includes multiple ancestries): 26.9% German, 21.1% Irish, 15.4% Italian, 12.4% Polish, 6.2% English (2005-2009 5-year est.).

Economy: Single-family building permits issued: 78 (2010); Multi-family building permits issued: 51 (2010); Employment by occupation: 19.9% management, 22.4% professional, 9.8% services, 28.6% sales, 0.0% farming, 10.1% construction, 9.2% production (2005-2009 5-year est.).

Income: Per capita income: $32,823 (2010); Median household income: $82,564 (2010); Average household income: $95,540 (2010); Percent of households with income of $100,000 or more: 37.5% (2010); Poverty rate: 5.0% (2005-2009 5-year est.).

Taxes: Total city taxes per capita: $291 (2007); City property taxes per capita: $87 (2007).

Education: Percent of population age 25 and over with: High school diploma (including GED) or higher: 94.0% (2010); Bachelor's degree or higher: 38.2% (2010); Master's degree or higher: 11.2% (2010).

School District(s)

Minooka CCSD 201 (PK-08)
  2009-10 Enrollment: 3,940 . . . . (815) 467-6121
Troy CCSD 30c (PK-08)
  2009-10 Enrollment: 4,432 . . . . (815) 577-6760

Housing: Homeownership rate: 95.8% (2010); Median home value: $202,038 (2010); Median contract rent: $1,159 per month (2005-2009 5-year est.); Median year structure built: 1998 (2005-2009 5-year est.).

Safety: Violent crime rate: 9.0 per 10,000 population; Property crime rate: 103.2 per 10,000 population (2010).

Transportation: Commute to work: 93.5% car, 3.4% public transportation, 0.2% walk, 2.7% work from home (2005-2009 5-year est.); Travel time to work: 19.1% less than 15 minutes, 31.4% 15 to 30 minutes, 16.3% 30 to 45

minutes, 15.3% 45 to 60 minutes, 17.9% 60 minutes or more (2005-2009 5-year est.)

Additional Information Contacts

Shorewood Area Chamber of Commerce . . . . (815) 725-2900
  http://www.shorewoodchamber.com
Village of Shorewood . . . . (815) 725-2150
  http://www.vil.shorewood.il.us

STEGER (village). Covers a land area of 3.524 square miles and a water area of 0 square miles. Located at 41.47° N. Lat; 87.63° W. Long.

History: Steger grew up around the piano factory founded by John V. Steger.

Population: 9,386 (1990); 9,682 (2000); 10,635 (2010); 11,216 (2015 projected); Race: 80.0% White, 11.1% Black, 0.7% Asian, 8.1% Other, 11.4% Hispanic of any race (2010); Density: 3,017.7 persons per square mile (2010); Average household size: 2.49 (2010); Median age: 35.5 (2010); Males per 100 females: 100.1 (2010); Marriage status: 31.9% never married, 49.5% now married, 6.4% widowed, 12.3% divorced (2005-2009 5-year est.); Foreign born: 3.6% (2005-2009 5-year est.); Ancestry (includes multiple ancestries): 22.9% German, 17.2% Italian, 17.0% Irish, 11.5% Polish, 5.9% English (2005-2009 5-year est.).

Economy: Single-family building permits issued: 0 (2010); Multi-family building permits issued: 0 (2010); Employment by occupation: 8.6% management, 15.2% professional, 19.4% services, 20.8% sales, 0.2% farming, 15.1% construction, 20.6% production (2005-2009 5-year est.).

Income: Per capita income: $22,862 (2010); Median household income: $48,293 (2010); Average household income: $56,679 (2010); Percent of households with income of $100,000 or more: 13.7% (2010); Poverty rate: 9.0% (2005-2009 5-year est.).

Taxes: Total city taxes per capita: $241 (2007); City property taxes per capita: $157 (2007).

Education: Percent of population age 25 and over with: High school diploma (including GED) or higher: 85.0% (2010); Bachelor's degree or higher: 12.7% (2010); Master's degree or higher: 4.3% (2010).

School District(s)

Steger SD 194 (PK-08)
  2009-10 Enrollment: 1,609 . . . . (708) 755-0022

Housing: Homeownership rate: 66.9% (2010); Median home value: $130,400 (2010); Median contract rent: $658 per month (2005-2009 5-year est.); Median year structure built: 1965 (2005-2009 5-year est.).

Safety: Violent crime rate: 27.0 per 10,000 population; Property crime rate: 321.6 per 10,000 population (2010).

Transportation: Commute to work: 87.6% car, 5.1% public transportation, 1.2% walk, 3.5% work from home (2005-2009 5-year est.); Travel time to work: 27.7% less than 15 minutes, 32.4% 15 to 30 minutes, 17.7% 30 to 45 minutes, 8.1% 45 to 60 minutes, 14.0% 60 minutes or more (2005-2009 5-year est.)

Additional Information Contacts

Village of Steger . . . . (708) 754-3395
  http://www.villageofsteger.com

SYMERTON (village). Covers a land area of 0.051 square miles and a water area of 0 square miles. Located at 41.32° N. Lat; 88.05° W. Long. Elevation is 640 feet.

Population: 110 (1990); 106 (2000); 171 (2010); 198 (2015 projected); Race: 97.1% White, 0.0% Black, 0.0% Asian, 2.9% Other, 4.7% Hispanic of any race (2010); Density: 3,329.8 persons per square mile (2010); Average household size: 2.90 (2010); Median age: 37.3 (2010); Males per 100 females: 92.1 (2010); Marriage status: 31.2% never married, 48.4% now married, 2.2% widowed, 18.3% divorced (2005-2009 5-year est.); Foreign born: 3.9% (2005-2009 5-year est.); Ancestry (includes multiple ancestries): 50.8% Irish, 49.2% German, 5.5% Belgian, 5.5% French, 4.7% Polish (2005-2009 5-year est.).

Economy: Single-family building permits issued: 1 (2010); Multi-family building permits issued: 0 (2010); Employment by occupation: 0.0% management, 30.3% professional, 18.2% services, 6.1% sales, 0.0% farming, 39.4% construction, 6.1% production (2005-2009 5-year est.).

Income: Per capita income: $34,558 (2010); Median household income: $85,119 (2010); Average household income: $99,661 (2010); Percent of households with income of $100,000 or more: 28.8% (2010); Poverty rate: 5.5% (2005-2009 5-year est.).

Taxes: Total city taxes per capita: $26 (2007); City property taxes per capita: $9 (2007).

Education: Percent of population age 25 and over with: High school diploma (including GED) or higher: 86.2% (2010); Bachelor's degree or higher: 22.4% (2010); Master's degree or higher: 12.9% (2010).
Housing: Homeownership rate: 91.5% (2010); Median home value: $200,000 (2010); Median contract rent: n/a per month (2005-2009 5-year est.); Median year structure built: before 1940 (2005-2009 5-year est.).
Transportation: Commute to work: 93.9% car, 0.0% public transportation, 0.0% walk, 6.1% work from home (2005-2009 5-year est.); Travel time to work: 6.5% less than 15 minutes, 45.2% 15 to 30 minutes, 22.6% 30 to 45 minutes, 9.7% 45 to 60 minutes, 16.1% 60 minutes or more (2005-2009 5-year est.)

UNIVERSITY PARK (village). Aka Park Forest South. Covers a land area of 9.758 square miles and a water area of 0.008 square miles. Located at 41.43° N. Lat; 87.69° W. Long. Elevation is 771 feet.

History: Seat of Governors State University.
Population: 6,225 (1990); 6,662 (2000); 7,449 (2010); 8,000 (2015 projected); Race: 13.6% White, 81.2% Black, 0.4% Asian, 4.8% Other, 3.6% Hispanic of any race (2010); Density: 763.4 persons per square mile (2010); Average household size: 2.97 (2010); Median age: 31.1 (2010); Males per 100 females: 88.4 (2010); Marriage status: 39.1% never married, 46.0% now married, 5.3% widowed, 9.6% divorced (2005-2009 5-year est.); Foreign born: 1.7% (2005-2009 5-year est.); Ancestry (includes multiple ancestries): 3.6% Italian, 2.4% Irish, 1.5% African, 1.5% Polish, 1.5% German (2005-2009 5-year est.).
Economy: Single-family building permits issued: 0 (2010); Multi-family building permits issued: 0 (2010); Employment by occupation: 9.5% management, 17.7% professional, 21.5% services, 22.2% sales, 0.0% farming, 8.0% construction, 21.2% production (2005-2009 5-year est.).
Income: Per capita income: $25,185 (2010); Median household income: $62,791 (2010); Average household income: $74,775 (2010); Percent of households with income of $100,000 or more: 22.6% (2010); Poverty rate: 17.9% (2005-2009 5-year est.).
Taxes: Total city taxes per capita: $1,348 (2007); City property taxes per capita: $1,099 (2007).
Education: Percent of population age 25 and over with: High school diploma (including GED) or higher: 94.2% (2010); Bachelor's degree or higher: 30.0% (2010); Master's degree or higher: 12.9% (2010).

School District(s)
Crete Monee CUSD 201u (PK-12)
    2009-10 Enrollment: 5,245 . . . . (708) 367-8300

Four-year College(s)
Governors State University (Public)
    Fall 2009 Enrollment: 5,674. . . . . (708) 534-5000
Housing: Homeownership rate: 65.7% (2010); Median home value: $131,938 (2010); Median contract rent: $779 per month (2005-2009 5-year est.); Median year structure built: 1975 (2005-2009 5-year est.).
Transportation: Commute to work: 84.7% car, 9.2% public transportation, 1.2% walk, 3.1% work from home (2005-2009 5-year est.); Travel time to work: 15.8% less than 15 minutes, 19.3% 15 to 30 minutes, 25.0% 30 to 45 minutes, 11.8% 45 to 60 minutes, 28.0% 60 minutes or more (2005-2009 5-year est.)
Additional Information Contacts
Village of University Park. . . . . (708) 534-6451
    http://www.university-park-il.com

WILLOWBROOK (CDP). Covers a land area of 3.376 square miles and a water area of 0.016 square miles. Located at 41.45° N. Lat; 87.54° W. Long. Elevation is 715 feet.

Population: 1,837 (1990); 2,130 (2000); 2,540 (2010); 2,799 (2015 projected); Race: 58.7% White, 35.7% Black, 1.5% Asian, 4.1% Other, 8.0% Hispanic of any race (2010); Density: 752.5 persons per square mile (2010); Average household size: 2.94 (2010); Median age: 44.4 (2010); Males per 100 females: 100.5 (2010); Marriage status: 20.9% never married, 69.4% now married, 3.2% widowed, 6.6% divorced (2005-2009 5-year est.); Foreign born: 5.3% (2005-2009 5-year est.); Ancestry (includes multiple ancestries): 24.0% German, 15.0% Polish, 14.8% Irish, 9.5% Italian, 6.6% Swedish (2005-2009 5-year est.).
Economy: Employment by occupation: 20.8% management, 19.4% professional, 8.5% services, 39.1% sales, 0.0% farming, 7.2% construction, 5.1% production (2005-2009 5-year est.).
Income: Per capita income: $41,925 (2010); Median household income: $107,109 (2010); Average household income: $122,963 (2010); Percent of households with income of $100,000 or more: 55.3% (2010); Poverty rate: 1.9% (2005-2009 5-year est.).

Education: Percent of population age 25 and over with: High school diploma (including GED) or higher: 93.3% (2010); Bachelor's degree or higher: 37.3% (2010); Master's degree or higher: 17.2% (2010).
Housing: Homeownership rate: 98.4% (2010); Median home value: $310,093 (2010); Median contract rent: n/a per month (2005-2009 5-year est.); Median year structure built: 1986 (2005-2009 5-year est.).
Transportation: Commute to work: 88.0% car, 3.2% public transportation, 1.5% walk, 7.3% work from home (2005-2009 5-year est.); Travel time to work: 7.1% less than 15 minutes, 39.9% 15 to 30 minutes, 25.8% 30 to 45 minutes, 8.9% 45 to 60 minutes, 18.3% 60 minutes or more (2005-2009 5-year est.)

WILMINGTON (city). Covers a land area of 4.214 square miles and a water area of 0.310 square miles. Located at 41.30° N. Lat; 88.14° W. Long. Elevation is 545 feet.

History: Wilmington was laid out in the 1840's by Thomas Fox, who called it Winchester. In 1854 it was incorporated as a village with the name of Wilmington. The village grew around grist, saw, and carding mills operated by Fox.
Population: 4,872 (1990); 5,134 (2000); 5,984 (2010); 6,501 (2015 projected); Race: 94.8% White, 1.3% Black, 0.5% Asian, 3.5% Other, 4.3% Hispanic of any race (2010); Density: 1,420.0 persons per square mile (2010); Average household size: 2.46 (2010); Median age: 36.0 (2010); Males per 100 females: 95.6 (2010); Marriage status: 26.4% never married, 50.8% now married, 8.7% widowed, 14.2% divorced (2005-2009 5-year est.); Foreign born: 1.4% (2005-2009 5-year est.); Ancestry (includes multiple ancestries): 26.1% German, 21.9% Irish, 13.7% English, 10.1% Polish, 6.4% Italian (2005-2009 5-year est.).
Economy: Single-family building permits issued: 1 (2010); Multi-family building permits issued: 0 (2010); Employment by occupation: 11.1% management, 11.5% professional, 17.6% services, 26.8% sales, 0.0% farming, 13.9% construction, 19.1% production (2005-2009 5-year est.).
Income: Per capita income: $25,859 (2010); Median household income: $52,273 (2010); Average household income: $62,485 (2010); Percent of households with income of $100,000 or more: 16.8% (2010); Poverty rate: 3.7% (2005-2009 5-year est.).
Taxes: Total city taxes per capita: $321 (2007); City property taxes per capita: $193 (2007).
Education: Percent of population age 25 and over with: High school diploma (including GED) or higher: 87.4% (2010); Bachelor's degree or higher: 11.2% (2010); Master's degree or higher: 3.8% (2010).

School District(s)
S Will Co Coop for Spec Ed (KG-12)
    2009-10 Enrollment: n/a . . . . (815) 741-7777
Wilmington CUSD 209u (PK-12)
    2009-10 Enrollment: 1,469 . . . . (815) 926-1751
Housing: Homeownership rate: 70.5% (2010); Median home value: $139,185 (2010); Median contract rent: $431 per month (2005-2009 5-year est.); Median year structure built: 1971 (2005-2009 5-year est.).
Newspapers: Braidwood Journal (Local news; Circulation 2,000); Braidwood Journal - Wilmington Bureau (Community news; Circulation 2,000); Free Press Advocate (Local news; Circulation 21,000); Outdoor Times (Regional news; Circulation 150,000); Prairie Shopper (Local news; Circulation 2,000)
Transportation: Commute to work: 93.5% car, 0.0% public transportation, 0.0% walk, 2.0% work from home (2005-2009 5-year est.); Travel time to work: 29.7% less than 15 minutes, 31.4% 15 to 30 minutes, 23.6% 30 to 45 minutes, 2.6% 45 to 60 minutes, 12.7% 60 minutes or more (2005-2009 5-year est.)
Additional Information Contacts
City of Wilmington . . . . (815) 476-2175
    http://www.wilmington-il.com
Wilmington Chamber of Commerce. . . . . (815) 476-5991
    http://wilmingtonilchamber.org

Williamson County

Located in southern Illinois; drained by the Big Muddy and South Fork of the Saline River; includes Crab Orchard Lake. Covers a land area of 423.41 square miles, a water area of 20.96 square miles, and is located in the Central Time Zone at 37.74° N. Lat., 88.97° W. Long. The county was founded in 1839. County seat is Marion.

Williamson County is part of the Marion-Herrin, IL Micropolitan Statistical Area. The entire metro area includes: Williamson County, IL

Population: 57,733 (1990); 61,296 (2000); 65,249 (2010); 66,771 (2015 projected); Race: 93.7% White, 3.4% Black, 0.8% Asian, 2.2% Other, 1.6% Hispanic of any race (2010); Density: 154.1 persons per square mile (2010); Average household size: 2.31 (2010); Median age: 38.2 (2010); Males per 100 females: 94.6 (2010).
Religion: Five largest groups: 24.4% Southern Baptist Convention, 7.6% Catholic Church, 5.3% The United Methodist Church, 2.9% Christian Churches and Churches of Christ, 2.5% American Baptist Churches in the USA (2000).
Economy: Unemployment rate: 8.8% (August 2011); Total civilian labor force: 34,795 (August 2011); Leading industries: 26.0% health care and social assistance; 16.5% retail trade; 11.5% accommodation & food services (2009); Farms: 616 totaling 94,124 acres (2007); Companies that employ 500 or more persons: 3 (2009); Companies that employ 100 to 499 persons: 31 (2009); Companies that employ less than 100 persons: 1,587 (2009); Black-owned businesses: n/a (2007); Hispanic-owned businesses: 56 (2007); Asian-owned businesses: n/a (2007); Women-owned businesses: 1,632 (2007); Retail sales per capita: $14,776 (2010). Single-family building permits issued: 78 (2010); Multi-family building permits issued: 50 (2010).
Income: Per capita income: $22,481 (2010); Median household income: $40,162 (2010); Average household income: $52,307 (2010); Percent of households with income of $100,000 or more: 10.6% (2010); Poverty rate: 18.3% (2009); Bankruptcy rate: 6.04% (2010).
Taxes: Total county taxes per capita: $113 (2007); County property taxes per capita: $112 (2007).
Education: Percent of population age 25 and over with: High school diploma (including GED) or higher: 87.9% (2010); Bachelor's degree or higher: 19.4% (2010); Master's degree or higher: 6.7% (2010).
Housing: Homeownership rate: 72.7% (2010); Median home value: $80,979 (2010); Median contract rent: $418 per month (2005-2009 5-year est.); Median year structure built: 1972 (2005-2009 5-year est.)
Health: Birth rate: 126.4 per 10,000 population (2009); Death rate: 112.8 per 10,000 population (2009); Age-adjusted cancer mortality rate: 224.3 deaths per 100,000 population (2007); Number of physicians: 18.3 per 10,000 population (2008); Hospital beds: 46.8 per 10,000 population (2007); Hospital admissions: 2,314.8 per 10,000 population (2007).
Elections: 2008 Presidential election results: 41.9% Obama, 56.4% McCain, 0.7% Nader
National and State Parks: Crab Orchard National Wildlife Refuge
Additional Information Contacts
Williamson County Government . . . . (618) 997-1301
  http://www.williamsoncountycourthouse.com
Carterville Chamber of Commerce . . . . (618) 985-6942
  http://www.cartervillechamber.com
City of Herrin . . . . (618) 942-3175
  http://www.herrinillinois.com
City of Marion . . . . (618) 997-6281
  http://www.cityofmarionil.gov
Herrin Chamber of Commerce. . . . . (618) 942-5163
  http://www.herrinillinois.com
Marion Chamber of Commerce . . . . (618) 997-6311
  http://www.marionillinois.com

Williamson County Communities

BUSH (village). Covers a land area of 0.461 square miles and a water area of 0.006 square miles. Located at 37.84° N. Lat; 89.13° W. Long. Elevation is 410 feet.
Population: 351 (1990); 257 (2000); 243 (2010); 237 (2015 projected); Race: 96.3% White, 1.6% Black, 0.0% Asian, 2.1% Other, 0.8% Hispanic of any race (2010); Density: 527.6 persons per square mile (2010); Average household size: 2.21 (2010); Median age: 36.1 (2010); Males per 100 females: 100.8 (2010); Marriage status: 22.8% never married, 53.8% now married, 5.1% widowed, 18.3% divorced (2005-2009 5-year est.); Foreign born: 0.0% (2005-2009 5-year est.); Ancestry (includes multiple ancestries): 26.1% Irish, 19.8% English, 14.0% German, 7.7% Dutch, 7.7% American (2005-2009 5-year est.).
Economy: Employment by occupation: 6.3% management, 1.3% professional, 15.0% services, 25.0% sales, 0.0% farming, 17.5% construction, 35.0% production (2005-2009 5-year est.).
Income: Per capita income: $16,082 (2010); Median household income: $26,429 (2010); Average household income: $35,114 (2010); Percent of households with income of $100,000 or more: 3.6% (2010); Poverty rate: 10.9% (2005-2009 5-year est.).

Taxes: Total city taxes per capita: $57 (2007); City property taxes per capita: $27 (2007).
Education: Percent of population age 25 and over with: High school diploma (including GED) or higher: 77.8% (2010); Bachelor's degree or higher: 8.0% (2010); Master's degree or higher: 1.2% (2010).
Housing: Homeownership rate: 70.9% (2010); Median home value: $37,143 (2010); Median contract rent: $500 per month (2005-2009 5-year est.); Median year structure built: 1967 (2005-2009 5-year est.).
Transportation: Commute to work: 97.5% car, 0.0% public transportation, 0.0% walk, 0.0% work from home (2005-2009 5-year est.); Travel time to work: 23.8% less than 15 minutes, 40.0% 15 to 30 minutes, 28.7% 30 to 45 minutes, 0.0% 45 to 60 minutes, 7.5% 60 minutes or more (2005-2009 5-year est.)

CAMBRIA (village). Covers a land area of 1.365 square miles and a water area of 0.010 square miles. Located at 37.78° N. Lat; 89.11° W. Long. Elevation is 423 feet.
Population: 1,358 (1990); 1,330 (2000); 1,371 (2010); 1,384 (2015 projected); Race: 95.3% White, 1.9% Black, 0.3% Asian, 2.5% Other, 1.8% Hispanic of any race (2010); Density: 1,004.3 persons per square mile (2010); Average household size: 2.32 (2010); Median age: 34.5 (2010); Males per 100 females: 93.4 (2010); Marriage status: 28.8% never married, 48.9% now married, 7.8% widowed, 14.5% divorced (2005-2009 5-year est.); Foreign born: 3.6% (2005-2009 5-year est.); Ancestry (includes multiple ancestries): 24.2% Irish, 20.9% German, 18.8% English, 5.5% American, 4.4% Dutch (2005-2009 5-year est.).
Economy: Single-family building permits issued: 13 (2010); Multi-family building permits issued: 0 (2010); Employment by occupation: 9.7% management, 20.5% professional, 26.3% services, 23.4% sales, 0.0% farming, 9.7% construction, 10.4% production (2005-2009 5-year est.).
Income: Per capita income: $22,014 (2010); Median household income: $41,220 (2010); Average household income: $51,208 (2010); Percent of households with income of $100,000 or more: 10.6% (2010); Poverty rate: 29.7% (2005-2009 5-year est.).
Taxes: Total city taxes per capita: $99 (2007); City property taxes per capita: $32 (2007).
Education: Percent of population age 25 and over with: High school diploma (including GED) or higher: 86.1% (2010); Bachelor's degree or higher: 22.3% (2010); Master's degree or higher: 7.6% (2010).
Housing: Homeownership rate: 69.1% (2010); Median home value: $74,464 (2010); Median contract rent: $423 per month (2005-2009 5-year est.); Median year structure built: 1975 (2005-2009 5-year est.).
Transportation: Commute to work: 96.4% car, 0.0% public transportation, 0.7% walk, 2.9% work from home (2005-2009 5-year est.); Travel time to work: 38.1% less than 15 minutes, 55.2% 15 to 30 minutes, 3.0% 30 to 45 minutes, 0.7% 45 to 60 minutes, 3.0% 60 minutes or more (2005-2009 5-year est.)

CARTERVILLE (city). Covers a land area of 4.347 square miles and a water area of 0.010 square miles. Located at 37.76° N. Lat; 89.08° W. Long. Elevation is 449 feet.
History: Incorporated 1892.
Population: 4,293 (1990); 4,616 (2000); 4,951 (2010); 5,089 (2015 projected); Race: 93.4% White, 3.3% Black, 1.0% Asian, 2.3% Other, 1.0% Hispanic of any race (2010); Density: 1,138.9 persons per square mile (2010); Average household size: 2.32 (2010); Median age: 34.8 (2010); Males per 100 females: 93.5 (2010); Marriage status: 22.1% never married, 58.8% now married, 5.8% widowed, 13.4% divorced (2005-2009 5-year est.); Foreign born: 0.0% (2005-2009 5-year est.); Ancestry (includes multiple ancestries): 29.9% German, 19.3% Irish, 18.6% English, 10.7% Italian, 5.7% Scotch-Irish (2005-2009 5-year est.).
Economy: Single-family building permits issued: 15 (2010); Multi-family building permits issued: 0 (2010); Employment by occupation: 9.2% management, 32.9% professional, 17.3% services, 26.0% sales, 0.5% farming, 6.2% construction, 8.0% production (2005-2009 5-year est.).
Income: Per capita income: $23,577 (2010); Median household income: $43,005 (2010); Average household income: $54,851 (2010); Percent of households with income of $100,000 or more: 13.2% (2010); Poverty rate: 18.3% (2005-2009 5-year est.).
Taxes: Total city taxes per capita: $219 (2007); City property taxes per capita: $68 (2007).
Education: Percent of population age 25 and over with: High school diploma (including GED) or higher: 91.3% (2010); Bachelor's degree or higher: 31.7% (2010); Master's degree or higher: 10.8% (2010).

School District(s)

Carterville CUSD 5 (KG-12)

   2009-10 Enrollment: 1,802 . . . . (618) 985-4826

Two-year College(s)

John A Logan College (Public)

   Fall 2009 Enrollment: 8,568. (618) 985-3741

   2010-11 Tuition: In-state $6,480; Out-of-state $8,370

Housing: Homeownership rate: 66.0% (2010); Median home value: $88,899 (2010); Median contract rent: $449 per month (2005-2009 5-year est.); Median year structure built: 1973 (2005-2009 5-year est.).

Transportation: Commute to work: 93.9% car, 0.0% public transportation, 1.2% walk, 3.4% work from home (2005-2009 5-year est.); Travel time to work: 27.4% less than 15 minutes, 57.7% 15 to 30 minutes, 6.9% 30 to 45 minutes, 1.7% 45 to 60 minutes, 6.4% 60 minutes or more (2005-2009 5-year est.)

Additional Information Contacts

Carterville Chamber of Commerce . . . . (618) 985-6942

   http://www.cartervillechamber.com

COLP (village). Covers a land area of 0.142 square miles and a water area of 0 square miles. Located at 37.80° N. Lat; 89.07° W. Long. Elevation is 400 feet.

Population: 235 (1990); 224 (2000); 257 (2010); 268 (2015 projected); Race: 86.0% White, 12.5% Black, 0.0% Asian, 1.6% Other, 0.4% Hispanic of any race (2010); Density: 1,808.7 persons per square mile (2010); Average household size: 2.31 (2010); Median age: 37.8 (2010); Males per 100 females: 90.4 (2010); Marriage status: 29.7% never married, 32.4% now married, 17.1% widowed, 20.7% divorced (2005-2009 5-year est.); Foreign born: 5.1% (2005-2009 5-year est.); Ancestry (includes multiple ancestries): 14.6% American, 14.6% Irish, 10.2% English, 5.1% German, 5.1% Dutch (2005-2009 5-year est.).

Economy: Employment by occupation: 3.1% management, 31.3% professional, 46.9% services, 6.3% sales, 0.0% farming, 3.1% construction, 9.4% production (2005-2009 5-year est.).

Income: Per capita income: $20,903 (2010); Median household income: $40,625 (2010); Average household income: $48,086 (2010); Percent of households with income of $100,000 or more: 8.1% (2010); Poverty rate: 32.8% (2005-2009 5-year est.).

Taxes: Total city taxes per capita: $26 (2007); City property taxes per capita: $13 (2007).

Education: Percent of population age 25 and over with: High school diploma (including GED) or higher: 82.2% (2010); Bachelor's degree or higher: 13.0% (2010); Master's degree or higher: 4.7% (2010).

Housing: Homeownership rate: 87.4% (2010); Median home value: $68,095 (2010); Median contract rent: $225 per month (2005-2009 5-year est.); Median year structure built: 1945 (2005-2009 5-year est.).

Transportation: Commute to work: 96.8% car, 0.0% public transportation, 3.2% walk, 0.0% work from home (2005-2009 5-year est.); Travel time to work: 19.4% less than 15 minutes, 67.7% 15 to 30 minutes, 12.9% 30 to 45 minutes, 0.0% 45 to 60 minutes, 0.0% 60 minutes or more (2005-2009 5-year est.)

CRAINVILLE (village). Covers a land area of 1.397 square miles and a water area of 0 square miles. Located at 37.74° N. Lat; 89.06° W. Long. Elevation is 469 feet.

Population: 1,030 (1990); 992 (2000); 969 (2010); 999 (2015 projected); Race: 95.8% White, 2.8% Black, 0.1% Asian, 1.3% Other, 0.4% Hispanic of any race (2010); Density: 693.5 persons per square mile (2010); Average household size: 2.21 (2010); Median age: 35.1 (2010); Males per 100 females: 91.9 (2010); Marriage status: 25.4% never married, 49.3% now married, 11.1% widowed, 14.1% divorced (2005-2009 5-year est.); Foreign born: 5.4% (2005-2009 5-year est.); Ancestry (includes multiple ancestries): 28.2% German, 24.3% Irish, 18.3% English, 7.0% Scottish, 5.4% Italian (2005-2009 5-year est.).

Economy: Single-family building permits issued: 7 (2010); Multi-family building permits issued: 3 (2010); Employment by occupation: 11.1% management, 17.0% professional, 17.3% services, 38.6% sales, 0.0% farming, 7.5% construction, 8.3% production (2005-2009 5-year est.).

Income: Per capita income: $22,488 (2010); Median household income: $39,009 (2010); Average household income: $48,628 (2010); Percent of households with income of $100,000 or more: 10.5% (2010); Poverty rate: 15.1% (2005-2009 5-year est.).

Taxes: Total city taxes per capita: $120 (2007); City property taxes per capita: $35 (2007).

Education: Percent of population age 25 and over with: High school diploma (including GED) or higher: 93.0% (2010); Bachelor's degree or higher: 28.9% (2010); Master's degree or higher: 8.9% (2010).

Housing: Homeownership rate: 62.9% (2010); Median home value: $87,407 (2010); Median contract rent: $427 per month (2005-2009 5-year est.); Median year structure built: 1977 (2005-2009 5-year est.).

Transportation: Commute to work: 94.9% car, 0.5% public transportation, 0.8% walk, 2.5% work from home (2005-2009 5-year est.); Travel time to work: 49.7% less than 15 minutes, 38.8% 15 to 30 minutes, 7.3% 30 to 45 minutes, 2.3% 45 to 60 minutes, 1.9% 60 minutes or more (2005-2009 5-year est.)

CREAL SPRINGS (city). Covers a land area of 0.990 square miles and a water area of 0.007 square miles. Located at 37.62° N. Lat; 88.83° W. Long. Elevation is 509 feet.

Population: 851 (1990); 702 (2000); 712 (2010); 717 (2015 projected); Race: 96.6% White, 0.3% Black, 0.1% Asian, 2.9% Other, 2.7% Hispanic of any race (2010); Density: 719.2 persons per square mile (2010); Average household size: 2.40 (2010); Median age: 39.8 (2010); Males per 100 females: 98.3 (2010); Marriage status: 15.7% never married, 61.2% now married, 12.1% widowed, 11.0% divorced (2005-2009 5-year est.); Foreign born: 1.7% (2005-2009 5-year est.); Ancestry (includes multiple ancestries): 24.9% English, 23.7% German, 13.7% American, 11.0% Irish, 4.2% French (2005-2009 5-year est.).

Economy: Employment by occupation: 9.1% management, 10.8% professional, 20.4% services, 27.4% sales, 0.0% farming, 15.6% construction, 16.7% production (2005-2009 5-year est.).

Income: Per capita income: $20,136 (2010); Median household income: $35,188 (2010); Average household income: $50,077 (2010); Percent of households with income of $100,000 or more: 7.2% (2010); Poverty rate: 19.2% (2005-2009 5-year est.).

Taxes: Total city taxes per capita: $73 (2007); City property taxes per capita: $67 (2007).

Education: Percent of population age 25 and over with: High school diploma (including GED) or higher: 79.8% (2010); Bachelor's degree or higher: 14.0% (2010); Master's degree or higher: 4.3% (2010).

School District(s)

Marion CUSD 2 (PK-12)

   2009-10 Enrollment: 3,941 . . . . (618) 993-2321

Housing: Homeownership rate: 85.2% (2010); Median home value: $74,000 (2010); Median contract rent: $303 per month (2005-2009 5-year est.); Median year structure built: 1957 (2005-2009 5-year est.).

Transportation: Commute to work: 95.8% car, 0.0% public transportation, 4.2% walk, 0.0% work from home (2005-2009 5-year est.); Travel time to work: 13.7% less than 15 minutes, 36.9% 15 to 30 minutes, 35.1% 30 to 45 minutes, 5.4% 45 to 60 minutes, 8.9% 60 minutes or more (2005-2009 5-year est.)

ENERGY (village). Covers a land area of 1.186 square miles and a water area of 0.009 square miles. Located at 37.77° N. Lat; 89.02° W. Long. Elevation is 459 feet.

Population: 1,105 (1990); 1,175 (2000); 1,498 (2010); 1,619 (2015 projected); Race: 96.2% White, 1.2% Black, 1.5% Asian, 1.1% Other, 0.9% Hispanic of any race (2010); Density: 1,263.3 persons per square mile (2010); Average household size: 2.30 (2010); Median age: 42.0 (2010); Males per 100 females: 88.0 (2010); Marriage status: 19.5% never married, 51.2% now married, 10.2% widowed, 19.1% divorced (2005-2009 5-year est.); Foreign born: 0.0% (2005-2009 5-year est.); Ancestry (includes multiple ancestries): 24.3% German, 22.9% Irish, 22.0% English, 7.4% Italian, 4.4% American (2005-2009 5-year est.).

Economy: Single-family building permits issued: 1 (2010); Multi-family building permits issued: 0 (2010); Employment by occupation: 18.5% management, 11.6% professional, 17.0% services, 29.3% sales, 0.0% farming, 8.4% construction, 15.2% production (2005-2009 5-year est.).

Income: Per capita income: $24,163 (2010); Median household income: $47,558 (2010); Average household income: $58,354 (2010); Percent of households with income of $100,000 or more: 12.6% (2010); Poverty rate: 18.6% (2005-2009 5-year est.).

Taxes: Total city taxes per capita: $151 (2007); City property taxes per capita: $81 (2007).

Education: Percent of population age 25 and over with: High school diploma (including GED) or higher: 90.4% (2010); Bachelor's degree or higher: 28.1% (2010); Master's degree or higher: 8.8% (2010).

Housing: Homeownership rate: 69.3% (2010); Median home value: $116,783 (2010); Median contract rent: $366 per month (2005-2009 5-year est.); Median year structure built: 1978 (2005-2009 5-year est.).
Safety: Violent crime rate: 16.7 per 10,000 population; Property crime rate: 150.4 per 10,000 population (2010).
Transportation: Commute to work: 97.9% car, 0.0% public transportation, 1.5% walk, 0.0% work from home (2005-2009 5-year est.); Travel time to work: 50.9% less than 15 minutes, 33.6% 15 to 30 minutes, 8.5% 30 to 45 minutes, 1.8% 45 to 60 minutes, 5.2% 60 minutes or more (2005-2009 5-year est.)

HERRIN (city). Covers a land area of 8.202 square miles and a water area of 0.174 square miles. Located at 37.80° N. Lat; 89.02° W. Long. Elevation is 420 feet.
History: Coal mining began in Herrin in 1895. It was incorporated as a village in 1898 and as a city in 1900.
Population: 11,097 (1990); 11,298 (2000); 11,619 (2010); 11,716 (2015 projected); Race: 94.8% White, 1.4% Black, 1.2% Asian, 2.5% Other, 1.5% Hispanic of any race (2010); Density: 1,416.6 persons per square mile (2010); Average household size: 2.22 (2010); Median age: 38.9 (2010); Males per 100 females: 87.6 (2010); Marriage status: 24.4% never married, 51.4% now married, 10.0% widowed, 14.2% divorced (2005-2009 5-year est.); Foreign born: 0.9% (2005-2009 5-year est.); Ancestry (includes multiple ancestries): 24.0% German, 18.3% English, 18.0% Irish, 10.6% American, 9.1% Italian (2005-2009 5-year est.).
Economy: Single-family building permits issued: 28 (2010); Multi-family building permits issued: 12 (2010); Employment by occupation: 10.3% management, 19.1% professional, 22.8% services, 29.2% sales, 0.2% farming, 7.1% construction, 11.2% production (2005-2009 5-year est.).
Income: Per capita income: $19,749 (2010); Median household income: $33,966 (2010); Average household income: $44,449 (2010); Percent of households with income of $100,000 or more: 8.2% (2010); Poverty rate: 17.1% (2005-2009 5-year est.).
Taxes: Total city taxes per capita: $210 (2007); City property taxes per capita: $87 (2007).
Education: Percent of population age 25 and over with: High school diploma (including GED) or higher: 88.2% (2010); Bachelor's degree or higher: 19.3% (2010); Master's degree or higher: 6.1% (2010).
School District(s)
Herrin CUSD 4 (PK-12)
    2009-10 Enrollment: 2,500 . . . . (618) 988-8024
Housing: Homeownership rate: 69.9% (2010); Median home value: $63,707 (2010); Median contract rent: $405 per month (2005-2009 5-year est.); Median year structure built: 1960 (2005-2009 5-year est.).
Hospitals: Herrin Hospital (92 beds)
Safety: Violent crime rate: 140.1 per 10,000 population; Property crime rate: 376.0 per 10,000 population (2010).
Newspapers: Spokesman (Community news; Circulation 2,100); Spokesman Sunday (Community news; Circulation 10,200)
Transportation: Commute to work: 92.4% car, 0.3% public transportation, 3.0% walk, 2.2% work from home (2005-2009 5-year est.); Travel time to work: 42.7% less than 15 minutes, 38.2% 15 to 30 minutes, 13.4% 30 to 45 minutes, 3.6% 45 to 60 minutes, 2.2% 60 minutes or more (2005-2009 5-year est.)
Additional Information Contacts
City of Herrin . . . . (618) 942-3175
    http://www.herrinillinois.com
Herrin Chamber of Commerce . . . . (618) 942-5163
    http://www.herrinillinois.com

HURST (city). Covers a land area of 0.861 square miles and a water area of 0 square miles. Located at 37.83° N. Lat; 89.14° W. Long. Elevation is 390 feet.
Population: 843 (1990); 805 (2000); 771 (2010); 753 (2015 projected); Race: 96.5% White, 1.6% Black, 0.0% Asian, 1.9% Other, 1.0% Hispanic of any race (2010); Density: 895.6 persons per square mile (2010); Average household size: 2.21 (2010); Median age: 37.0 (2010); Males per 100 females: 94.2 (2010); Marriage status: 18.8% never married, 54.7% now married, 7.9% widowed, 18.6% divorced (2005-2009 5-year est.); Foreign born: 0.0% (2005-2009 5-year est.); Ancestry (includes multiple ancestries): 27.0% German, 22.7% Irish, 16.4% English, 10.8% Dutch, 6.5% Scotch-Irish (2005-2009 5-year est.).
Economy: Single-family building permits issued: 0 (2010); Multi-family building permits issued: 0 (2010); Employment by occupation: 5.6%

management, 14.8% professional, 10.6% services, 17.3% sales, 0.0% farming, 23.7% construction, 28.1% production (2005-2009 5-year est.).
Income: Per capita income: $16,083 (2010); Median household income: $26,625 (2010); Average household income: $35,709 (2010); Percent of households with income of $100,000 or more: 4.0% (2010); Poverty rate: 18.8% (2005-2009 5-year est.).
Taxes: Total city taxes per capita: $61 (2007); City property taxes per capita: $51 (2007).
Education: Percent of population age 25 and over with: High school diploma (including GED) or higher: 77.6% (2010); Bachelor's degree or higher: 8.8% (2010); Master's degree or higher: 2.1% (2010).
Housing: Homeownership rate: 71.1% (2010); Median home value: $37,753 (2010); Median contract rent: $322 per month (2005-2009 5-year est.); Median year structure built: 1955 (2005-2009 5-year est.).
Transportation: Commute to work: 99.4% car, 0.0% public transportation, 0.0% walk, 0.6% work from home (2005-2009 5-year est.); Travel time to work: 16.2% less than 15 minutes, 58.8% 15 to 30 minutes, 17.1% 30 to 45 minutes, 3.8% 45 to 60 minutes, 4.1% 60 minutes or more (2005-2009 5-year est.)

JOHNSTON CITY (city). Covers a land area of 1.953 square miles and a water area of 0.058 square miles. Located at 37.82° N. Lat; 88.92° W. Long. Elevation is 430 feet.
History: Incorporated 1896.
Population: 3,770 (1990); 3,557 (2000); 3,548 (2010); 3,543 (2015 projected); Race: 98.6% White, 0.1% Black, 0.1% Asian, 1.1% Other, 1.4% Hispanic of any race (2010); Density: 1,816.3 persons per square mile (2010); Average household size: 2.26 (2010); Median age: 39.3 (2010); Males per 100 females: 87.8 (2010); Marriage status: 24.5% never married, 52.8% now married, 4.8% widowed, 17.9% divorced (2005-2009 5-year est.); Foreign born: 0.6% (2005-2009 5-year est.); Ancestry (includes multiple ancestries): 23.7% German, 21.2% English, 17.4% Irish, 6.9% American, 5.1% Scottish (2005-2009 5-year est.).
Economy: Single-family building permits issued: 0 (2010); Multi-family building permits issued: 0 (2010); Employment by occupation: 2.1% management, 8.4% professional, 27.9% services, 32.8% sales, 0.0% farming, 7.4% construction, 21.4% production (2005-2009 5-year est.).
Income: Per capita income: $16,815 (2010); Median household income: $32,473 (2010); Average household income: $37,810 (2010); Percent of households with income of $100,000 or more: 2.3% (2010); Poverty rate: 25.5% (2005-2009 5-year est.).
Taxes: Total city taxes per capita: $170 (2007); City property taxes per capita: $93 (2007).
Education: Percent of population age 25 and over with: High school diploma (including GED) or higher: 82.7% (2010); Bachelor's degree or higher: 8.8% (2010); Master's degree or higher: 3.9% (2010).
School District(s)
Franklin/Williamson Roe (PK-12)
    2009-10 Enrollment: 108 . . . . (618) 438-9711
Johnston City CUSD 1 (PK-12)
    2009-10 Enrollment: 1,202 . . . . (618) 983-8021
Housing: Homeownership rate: 75.1% (2010); Median home value: $51,105 (2010); Median contract rent: $231 per month (2005-2009 5-year est.); Median year structure built: 1951 (2005-2009 5-year est.).
Transportation: Commute to work: 97.6% car, 0.0% public transportation, 1.3% walk, 1.1% work from home (2005-2009 5-year est.); Travel time to work: 32.8% less than 15 minutes, 60.9% 15 to 30 minutes, 2.3% 30 to 45 minutes, 1.4% 45 to 60 minutes, 2.6% 60 minutes or more (2005-2009 5-year est.)

MARION (city). County seat. Covers a land area of 12.826 square miles and a water area of 0.697 square miles. Located at 37.73° N. Lat; 88.93° W. Long. Elevation is 423 feet.
History: Marion was established in the mid-1800's. Early residents were Robert G. Ingersoll and John A. Logan, both of whom became colonels serving in the Civil War.
Population: 14,971 (1990); 16,035 (2000); 16,361 (2010); 16,531 (2015 projected); Race: 90.0% White, 6.3% Black, 1.2% Asian, 2.5% Other, 2.0% Hispanic of any race (2010); Density: 1,275.6 persons per square mile (2010); Average household size: 2.21 (2010); Median age: 38.5 (2010); Males per 100 females: 89.4 (2010); Marriage status: 23.9% never married, 49.8% now married, 9.9% widowed, 16.3% divorced (2005-2009 5-year est.); Foreign born: 2.3% (2005-2009 5-year est.); Ancestry (includes multiple ancestries): 22.7% German, 15.7% English, 14.6% Irish, 9.3% American, 4.4% Italian (2005-2009 5-year est.).

Economy: Single-family building permits issued: 14 (2010); Multi-family building permits issued: 35 (2010); Employment by occupation: 9.9% management, 24.2% professional, 23.2% services, 24.7% sales, 0.8% farming, 7.0% construction, 10.3% production (2005-2009 5-year est.).
Income: Per capita income: $23,572 (2010); Median household income: $36,535 (2010); Average household income: $52,692 (2010); Percent of households with income of $100,000 or more: 10.9% (2010); Poverty rate: 18.4% (2005-2009 5-year est.).
Taxes: Total city taxes per capita: $575 (2007); City property taxes per capita: $203 (2007).
Education: Percent of population age 25 and over with: High school diploma (including GED) or higher: 87.8% (2010); Bachelor's degree or higher: 18.5% (2010); Master's degree or higher: 6.5% (2010).

School District(s)

Crab Orchard CUSD 3 (PK-12)
    2009-10 Enrollment: 445 . . . . (618) 982-2181
Marion CUSD 2 (PK-12)
    2009-10 Enrollment: 3,941 . . . . (618) 993-2321
Williamson Co Spec Educ District (PK-12)
    2009-10 Enrollment: n/a . . . . (618) 993-2138

Housing: Homeownership rate: 63.7% (2010); Median home value: $83,699 (2010); Median contract rent: $433 per month (2005-2009 5-year est.); Median year structure built: 1973 (2005-2009 5-year est.).
Hospitals: Heartland Regional Medical Center (92 beds); US Penitentiary Infirmary; Veterans Affairs Medical Center (39 beds)
Newspapers: Marion Daily Republican (Community news; Circulation 3,500); Williamson County Extra (Community news; Circulation 20,000)
Transportation: Commute to work: 93.6% car, 0.1% public transportation, 2.8% walk, 3.0% work from home (2005-2009 5-year est.); Travel time to work: 50.8% less than 15 minutes, 28.8% 15 to 30 minutes, 11.5% 30 to 45 minutes, 6.0% 45 to 60 minutes, 2.8% 60 minutes or more (2005-2009 5-year est.)
Airports: Williamson County Regional (commercial service)
Additional Information Contacts

City of Marion . . . . (618) 997-6281
    http://www.cityofmarionil.gov
Marion Chamber of Commerce . . . . (618) 997-6311
    http://www.marionillinois.com

PITTSBURG (village).

Covers a land area of 2.085 square miles and a water area of 0.027 square miles. Located at 37.77° N. Lat; 88.85° W. Long. Elevation is 466 feet.
Population: 602 (1990); 575 (2000); 672 (2010); 714 (2015 projected); Race: 97.5% White, 1.5% Black, 0.1% Asian, 0.9% Other, 0.7% Hispanic of any race (2010); Density: 322.3 persons per square mile (2010); Average household size: 2.45 (2010); Median age: 39.0 (2010); Males per 100 females: 104.9 (2010); Marriage status: 16.2% never married, 66.2% now married, 10.9% widowed, 6.6% divorced (2005-2009 5-year est.); Foreign born: 2.3% (2005-2009 5-year est.); Ancestry (includes multiple ancestries): 29.9% German, 25.5% Irish, 14.7% English, 11.6% French, 9.3% American (2005-2009 5-year est.).
Economy: Employment by occupation: 9.2% management, 26.9% professional, 16.1% services, 22.6% sales, 0.0% farming, 6.9% construction, 18.4% production (2005-2009 5-year est.).
Income: Per capita income: $29,554 (2010); Median household income: $45,446 (2010); Average household income: $72,664 (2010); Percent of households with income of $100,000 or more: 17.2% (2010); Poverty rate: 13.8% (2005-2009 5-year est.).
Taxes: Total city taxes per capita: $83 (2007); City property taxes per capita: $40 (2007).
Education: Percent of population age 25 and over with: High school diploma (including GED) or higher: 89.0% (2010); Bachelor's degree or higher: 14.3% (2010); Master's degree or higher: 4.3% (2010).

School District(s)

Johnston City CUSD 1 (PK-12)
    2009-10 Enrollment: 1,202 . . . . (618) 983-8021

Housing: Homeownership rate: 89.4% (2010); Median home value: $74,000 (2010); Median contract rent: $363 per month (2005-2009 5-year est.); Median year structure built: 1949 (2005-2009 5-year est.).
Transportation: Commute to work: 99.0% car, 0.0% public transportation, 0.0% walk, 0.0% work from home (2005-2009 5-year est.); Travel time to work: 10.7% less than 15 minutes, 55.3% 15 to 30 minutes, 21.6% 30 to 45 minutes, 6.9% 45 to 60 minutes, 5.5% 60 minutes or more (2005-2009 5-year est.)

SPILLERTOWN (village).

Covers a land area of 0.311 square miles and a water area of 0 square miles. Located at 37.76° N. Lat; 88.91° W. Long. Elevation is 482 feet.
Population: 249 (1990); 220 (2000); 229 (2010); 242 (2015 projected); Race: 97.4% White, 1.7% Black, 0.0% Asian, 0.9% Other, 2.2% Hispanic of any race (2010); Density: 736.5 persons per square mile (2010); Average household size: 2.57 (2010); Median age: 36.1 (2010); Males per 100 females: 99.1 (2010); Marriage status: 17.5% never married, 55.2% now married, 6.3% widowed, 21.0% divorced (2005-2009 5-year est.); Foreign born: 1.2% (2005-2009 5-year est.); Ancestry (includes multiple ancestries): 23.8% Irish, 23.8% German, 10.4% English, 6.7% American, 5.5% French (2005-2009 5-year est.).
Economy: Employment by occupation: 5.9% management, 14.1% professional, 29.4% services, 27.1% sales, 0.0% farming, 10.6% construction, 12.9% production (2005-2009 5-year est.).
Income: Per capita income: $20,740 (2010); Median household income: $40,735 (2010); Average household income: $54,242 (2010); Percent of households with income of $100,000 or more: 11.2% (2010); Poverty rate: 16.5% (2005-2009 5-year est.).
Taxes: Total city taxes per capita: $32 (2007); City property taxes per capita: $23 (2007).
Education: Percent of population age 25 and over with: High school diploma (including GED) or higher: 83.2% (2010); Bachelor's degree or higher: 10.3% (2010); Master's degree or higher: 3.9% (2010).
Housing: Homeownership rate: 83.1% (2010); Median home value: $70,909 (2010); Median contract rent: $417 per month (2005-2009 5-year est.); Median year structure built: 1963 (2005-2009 5-year est.).
Transportation: Commute to work: 97.6% car, 0.0% public transportation, 0.0% walk, 0.0% work from home (2005-2009 5-year est.); Travel time to work: 42.7% less than 15 minutes, 36.6% 15 to 30 minutes, 13.4% 30 to 45 minutes, 0.0% 45 to 60 minutes, 7.3% 60 minutes or more (2005-2009 5-year est.)

STONEFORT (village).

Covers a land area of 1.461 square miles and a water area of 0.003 square miles. Located at 37.61° N. Lat; 88.70° W. Long. Elevation is 410 feet.
History: Stonefort was built on the ruins of an old stone fort, a prehistoric structure on a cliff with a stone barricade on the approachable side. In 1872 the town was moved to take advantage of the arrival of the railroad.
Population: 301 (1990); 292 (2000); 321 (2010); 330 (2015 projected); Race: 96.9% White, 1.6% Black, 0.0% Asian, 1.6% Other, 2.5% Hispanic of any race (2010); Density: 219.8 persons per square mile (2010); Average household size: 2.53 (2010); Median age: 37.3 (2010); Males per 100 females: 91.1 (2010); Marriage status: 28.4% never married, 48.7% now married, 8.6% widowed, 14.2% divorced (2005-2009 5-year est.); Foreign born: 0.8% (2005-2009 5-year est.); Ancestry (includes multiple ancestries): 38.1% Irish, 8.8% Scottish, 8.8% German, 8.4% English, 6.3% American (2005-2009 5-year est.).
Economy: Employment by occupation: 0.0% management, 5.1% professional, 25.5% services, 48.0% sales, 2.0% farming, 9.2% construction, 10.2% production (2005-2009 5-year est.).
Income: Per capita income: $23,167 (2010); Median household income: $49,135 (2010); Average household income: $60,925 (2010); Percent of households with income of $100,000 or more: 14.2% (2010); Poverty rate: 9.2% (2005-2009 5-year est.).
Taxes: Total city taxes per capita: $21 (2007); City property taxes per capita: $21 (2007).
Education: Percent of population age 25 and over with: High school diploma (including GED) or higher: 83.3% (2010); Bachelor's degree or higher: 11.6% (2010); Master's degree or higher: 4.7% (2010).
Housing: Homeownership rate: 85.8% (2010); Median home value: $72,500 (2010); Median contract rent: $233 per month (2005-2009 5-year est.); Median year structure built: 1974 (2005-2009 5-year est.).
Transportation: Commute to work: 97.8% car, 0.0% public transportation, 0.0% walk, 2.2% work from home (2005-2009 5-year est.); Travel time to work: 15.4% less than 15 minutes, 53.8% 15 to 30 minutes, 15.4% 30 to 45 minutes, 9.9% 45 to 60 minutes, 5.5% 60 minutes or more (2005-2009 5-year est.)

WHITEASH (village).

Covers a land area of 0.870 square miles and a water area of 0.024 square miles. Located at 37.78° N. Lat; 88.92° W. Long.
Population: 249 (1990); 268 (2000); 215 (2010); 224 (2015 projected); Race: 96.7% White, 1.4% Black, 0.5% Asian, 1.4% Other, 1.9% Hispanic

of any race (2010); Density: 247.2 persons per square mile (2010); Average household size: 2.53 (2010); Median age: 37.3 (2010); Males per 100 females: 100.9 (2010); Marriage status: 18.1% never married, 62.9% now married, 4.1% widowed, 14.9% divorced (2005-2009 5-year est.); Foreign born: 1.2% (2005-2009 5-year est.); Ancestry (includes multiple ancestries): 24.8% German, 20.1% English, 19.7% Irish, 7.9% Dutch, 5.5% French (2005-2009 5-year est.).

Economy: Employment by occupation: 7.6% management, 11.8% professional, 41.2% services, 18.5% sales, 0.0% farming, 10.1% construction, 10.9% production (2005-2009 5-year est.).

Income: Per capita income: $19,602 (2010); Median household income: $35,469 (2010); Average household income: $46,059 (2010); Percent of households with income of $100,000 or more: 8.2% (2010); Poverty rate: 31.9% (2005-2009 5-year est.).

Taxes: Total city taxes per capita: $11 (2007); City property taxes per capita: $7 (2007).

Education: Percent of population age 25 and over with: High school diploma (including GED) or higher: 83.0% (2010); Bachelor's degree or higher: 11.6% (2010); Master's degree or higher: 3.4% (2010).

Housing: Homeownership rate: 83.5% (2010); Median home value: $83,846 (2010); Median contract rent: $388 per month (2005-2009 5-year est.); Median year structure built: 1981 (2005-2009 5-year est.).

Transportation: Commute to work: 96.6% car, 0.0% public transportation, 0.0% walk, 1.7% work from home (2005-2009 5-year est.); Travel time to work: 38.8% less than 15 minutes, 50.0% 15 to 30 minutes, 6.9% 30 to 45 minutes, 2.6% 45 to 60 minutes, 1.7% 60 minutes or more (2005-2009 5-year est.)

Winnebago County

Located in northern Illinois; bounded on the north by Wisconsin; drained by the Rock, Pecatonica, and Kishwaukee Rivers. Covers a land area of 513.74 square miles, a water area of 5.54 square miles, and is located in the Central Time Zone at 42.31° N. Lat., 89.08° W. Long. The county was founded in 1836. County seat is Rockford.

Winnebago County is part of the Rockford, IL Metropolitan Statistical Area. The entire metro area includes: Boone County, IL; Winnebago County, IL

Weather Station: Rockford Greater Rockford Arpt   Elevation: 680 feet

	Jan	Feb	Mar	Apr	May	Jun	Jul	Aug	Sep	Oct	Nov	Dec
High	29	34	46	60	71	80	84	82	75	62	47	33
Low	13	17	27	37	48	58	63	61	52	40	30	18
Precip	1.4	1.4	2.3	3.3	3.9	4.7	3.8	4.7	3.5	2.6	2.6	2.0
Snow	10.3	7.6	5.0	1.1	tr	tr	tr	tr	tr	0.1	1.7	10.8

High and Low temperatures in degrees Fahrenheit; Precipitation and Snow in inches

Population: 252,913 (1990); 278,418 (2000); 304,411 (2010); 315,272 (2015 projected); Race: 78.8% White, 11.3% Black, 2.0% Asian, 7.8% Other, 10.7% Hispanic of any race (2010); Density: 592.5 persons per square mile (2010); Average household size: 2.55 (2010); Median age: 36.8 (2010); Males per 100 females: 97.1 (2010).

Religion: Five largest groups: 22.2% Catholic Church, 7.1% Evangelical Lutheran Church in America, 3.6% The United Methodist Church, 2.4% Assemblies of God, 2.0% Lutheran Church—Missouri Synod (2000).

Economy: Unemployment rate: 13.1% (August 2011); Total civilian labor force: 143,675 (August 2011); Leading industries: 20.3% manufacturing; 16.6% health care and social assistance; 12.5% retail trade (2009); Farms: 860 totaling 183,615 acres (2007); Companies that employ 500 or more persons: 18 (2009); Companies that employ 100 to 499 persons: 175 (2009); Companies that employ less than 100 persons: 6,576 (2009); Black-owned businesses: 1,665 (2007); Hispanic-owned businesses: 563 (2007); Asian-owned businesses: 650 (2007); Women-owned businesses: 6,844 (2007); Retail sales per capita: $13,966 (2010). Single-family building permits issued: 251 (2010); Multi-family building permits issued: 6 (2010).

Income: Per capita income: $23,743 (2010); Median household income: $48,508 (2010); Average household income: $60,964 (2010); Percent of households with income of $100,000 or more: 14.1% (2010); Poverty rate: 17.7% (2009); Bankruptcy rate: 7.69% (2010).

Taxes: Total county taxes per capita: $230 (2007); County property taxes per capita: $116 (2007).

Education: Percent of population age 25 and over with: High school diploma (including GED) or higher: 82.7% (2010); Bachelor's degree or higher: 19.9% (2010); Master's degree or higher: 6.6% (2010).

Housing: Homeownership rate: 70.7% (2010); Median home value: $120,979 (2010); Median contract rent: $533 per month (2005-2009 5-year est.); Median year structure built: 1967 (2005-2009 5-year est.)

Health: Birth rate: 141.1 per 10,000 population (2009); Death rate: 86.2 per 10,000 population (2009); Age-adjusted cancer mortality rate: 185.0 deaths per 100,000 population (2007); Number of physicians: 24.3 per 10,000 population (2008); Hospital beds: 33.9 per 10,000 population (2007); Hospital admissions: 1,450.1 per 10,000 population (2007).

Environment: Air Quality Index: 92.6% good, 7.1% moderate, 0.3% unhealthy for sensitive individuals, 0.0% unhealthy (percent of days in 2008)

Elections: 2008 Presidential election results: 55.6% Obama, 42.8% McCain, 0.6% Nader

National and State Parks: Rock Cut State Park

Additional Information Contacts

Winnebago County Government . . . . (815) 319-4250
   http://www.co.winnebago.il.us
City of Loves Park . . . . (815) 654-5030
   http://www.loves-park.il.us
City of Rockford . . . . (815) 987-5590
   http://www.rockfordil.gov
City of South Beloit . . . . (815) 389-3023
   http://www.southbeloit.org
Rockford Chamber of Commerce . . . . (815) 987-8100
   http://www.rockfordchamber.com
Rockton Chamber of Commerce . . . . (815) 624-7625
   http://www.rocktonchamber.com
Roscoe Area Chamber of Commerce . . . . (815) 623-9065
   http://www.roscoechamber.com
The Parks Chamber of Commerce . . . . (815) 633-3999
   http://www.parkschamber.com
Village of Machesney Park . . . . (815) 877-5432
   http://www.machesney-park.il.us
Village of Rockton . . . . (815) 624-7600
   http://rocktonvillage.com
Village of Roscoe . . . . (815) 623-2829
   http://www.villageofroscoe.com

Winnebago County Communities

CHERRY VALLEY (village). Covers a land area of 3.757 square miles and a water area of 0.049 square miles. Located at 42.23° N. Lat; 88.96° W. Long. Elevation is 728 feet.

Population: 1,819 (1990); 2,191 (2000); 2,940 (2010); 3,124 (2015 projected); Race: 93.6% White, 1.8% Black, 2.3% Asian, 2.3% Other, 4.0% Hispanic of any race (2010); Density: 782.6 persons per square mile (2010); Average household size: 2.60 (2010); Median age: 40.9 (2010); Males per 100 females: 100.0 (2010); Marriage status: 24.1% never married, 57.0% now married, 7.5% widowed, 11.4% divorced (2005-2009 5-year est.); Foreign born: 8.0% (2005-2009 5-year est.); Ancestry (includes multiple ancestries): 24.2% German, 15.7% American, 12.6% Irish, 8.7% Italian, 8.6% Swedish (2005-2009 5-year est.).

Economy: Employment by occupation: 11.2% management, 21.4% professional, 15.1% services, 26.2% sales, 0.0% farming, 13.9% construction, 12.1% production (2005-2009 5-year est.).

Income: Per capita income: $30,054 (2010); Median household income: $70,511 (2010); Average household income: $78,502 (2010); Percent of households with income of $100,000 or more: 25.4% (2010); Poverty rate: 8.4% (2005-2009 5-year est.).

Taxes: Total city taxes per capita: $70 (2007); City property taxes per capita: $15 (2007).

Education: Percent of population age 25 and over with: High school diploma (including GED) or higher: 91.2% (2010); Bachelor's degree or higher: 24.3% (2010); Master's degree or higher: 5.9% (2010).

School District(s)

Rockford SD 205 (PK-12)
  2009-10 Enrollment: 29,071 . . . . (815) 966-3101

Housing: Homeownership rate: 84.3% (2010); Median home value: $146,703 (2010); Median contract rent: $581 per month (2005-2009 5-year est.); Median year structure built: 1991 (2005-2009 5-year est.).

Transportation: Commute to work: 95.9% car, 0.0% public transportation, 0.3% walk, 2.5% work from home (2005-2009 5-year est.); Travel time to work: 29.7% less than 15 minutes, 43.7% 15 to 30 minutes, 13.2% 30 to 45 minutes, 5.5% 45 to 60 minutes, 7.9% 60 minutes or more (2005-2009 5-year est.)

DURAND (village). Covers a land area of 0.900 square miles and a water area of 0 square miles. Located at 42.43° N. Lat; 89.32° W. Long. Elevation is 771 feet.
Population: 1,156 (1990); 1,081 (2000); 1,267 (2010); 1,350 (2015 projected); Race: 95.9% White, 0.8% Black, 0.0% Asian, 3.3% Other, 1.4% Hispanic of any race (2010); Density: 1,407.5 persons per square mile (2010); Average household size: 2.45 (2010); Median age: 39.6 (2010); Males per 100 females: 90.0 (2010); Marriage status: 28.1% never married, 56.9% now married, 4.4% widowed, 10.7% divorced (2005-2009 5-year est.); Foreign born: 1.2% (2005-2009 5-year est.); Ancestry (includes multiple ancestries): 47.2% German, 19.5% Irish, 11.0% English, 9.6% Swedish, 8.4% American (2005-2009 5-year est.).
Economy: Employment by occupation: 11.5% management, 12.1% professional, 20.1% services, 26.9% sales, 0.5% farming, 9.0% construction, 19.9% production (2005-2009 5-year est.).
Income: Per capita income: $23,025 (2010); Median household income: $53,101 (2010); Average household income: $59,250 (2010); Percent of households with income of $100,000 or more: 13.5% (2010); Poverty rate: 10.4% (2005-2009 5-year est.).
Taxes: Total city taxes per capita: $142 (2007); City property taxes per capita: $63 (2007).
Education: Percent of population age 25 and over with: High school diploma (including GED) or higher: 87.3% (2010); Bachelor's degree or higher: 17.2% (2010); Master's degree or higher: 5.0% (2010).
School District(s)
Durand CUSD 322 (PK-12)
    2009-10 Enrollment: 621 . . . . (815) 248-2171
Housing: Homeownership rate: 72.7% (2010); Median home value: $118,716 (2010); Median contract rent: $423 per month (2005-2009 5-year est.); Median year structure built: 1970 (2005-2009 5-year est.).
Safety: Violent crime rate: 28.0 per 10,000 population; Property crime rate: 168.2 per 10,000 population (2010).
Newspapers: Durand Volunteer (Community news; Circulation 2,000)
Transportation: Commute to work: 95.2% car, 0.0% public transportation, 2.6% walk, 1.7% work from home (2005-2009 5-year est.); Travel time to work: 24.8% less than 15 minutes, 19.0% 15 to 30 minutes, 44.3% 30 to 45 minutes, 8.4% 45 to 60 minutes, 3.4% 60 minutes or more (2005-2009 5-year est.)

LAKE SUMMERSET (CDP). Covers a land area of 2.071 square miles and a water area of 0.425 square miles. Located at 42.44° N. Lat; 89.39° W. Long. Elevation is 860 feet.
Population: 1,296 (1990); 2,061 (2000); 2,557 (2010); 2,745 (2015 projected); Race: 98.4% White, 0.5% Black, 0.2% Asian, 0.9% Other, 1.1% Hispanic of any race (2010); Density: 1,234.8 persons per square mile (2010); Average household size: 2.54 (2010); Median age: 46.3 (2010); Males per 100 females: 93.9 (2010); Marriage status: 13.8% never married, 71.7% now married, 9.0% widowed, 5.4% divorced (2005-2009 5-year est.); Foreign born: 3.5% (2005-2009 5-year est.); Ancestry (includes multiple ancestries): 33.4% German, 17.3% Irish, 11.9% Swedish, 8.3% Italian, 7.2% Polish (2005-2009 5-year est.).
Economy: Employment by occupation: 16.3% management, 22.7% professional, 21.2% services, 16.5% sales, 0.0% farming, 10.1% construction, 13.2% production (2005-2009 5-year est.).
Income: Per capita income: $30,133 (2010); Median household income: $65,371 (2010); Average household income: $76,272 (2010); Percent of households with income of $100,000 or more: 21.8% (2010); Poverty rate: 0.4% (2005-2009 5-year est.).
Education: Percent of population age 25 and over with: High school diploma (including GED) or higher: 94.3% (2010); Bachelor's degree or higher: 28.4% (2010); Master's degree or higher: 8.1% (2010).
Housing: Homeownership rate: 94.0% (2010); Median home value: $144,675 (2010); Median contract rent: $393 per month (2005-2009 5-year est.); Median year structure built: 1987 (2005-2009 5-year est.).
Transportation: Commute to work: 92.0% car, 0.0% public transportation, 0.0% walk, 8.0% work from home (2005-2009 5-year est.); Travel time to work: 7.9% less than 15 minutes, 28.0% 15 to 30 minutes, 24.4% 30 to 45 minutes, 11.5% 45 to 60 minutes, 28.3% 60 minutes or more (2005-2009 5-year est.)

LOVES PARK (city). Covers a land area of 14.450 square miles and a water area of 0.368 square miles. Located at 42.32° N. Lat; 89.02° W. Long. Elevation is 728 feet.
History: Incorporated 1947.

Population: 16,327 (1990); 20,044 (2000); 23,728 (2010); 25,108 (2015 projected); Race: 89.6% White, 3.6% Black, 2.6% Asian, 4.2% Other, 4.6% Hispanic of any race (2010); Density: 1,642.1 persons per square mile (2010); Average household size: 2.46 (2010); Median age: 36.9 (2010); Males per 100 females: 96.7 (2010); Marriage status: 25.3% never married, 54.9% now married, 6.0% widowed, 13.8% divorced (2005-2009 5-year est.); Foreign born: 7.2% (2005-2009 5-year est.); Ancestry (includes multiple ancestries): 26.3% German, 15.7% Irish, 12.1% American, 10.3% Swedish, 9.8% English (2005-2009 5-year est.).
Economy: Single-family building permits issued: 27 (2010); Multi-family building permits issued: 0 (2010); Employment by occupation: 9.6% management, 18.3% professional, 16.1% services, 30.7% sales, 0.1% farming, 7.1% construction, 18.1% production (2005-2009 5-year est.).
Income: Per capita income: $23,256 (2010); Median household income: $49,543 (2010); Average household income: $57,226 (2010); Percent of households with income of $100,000 or more: 10.0% (2010); Poverty rate: 8.4% (2005-2009 5-year est.).
Taxes: Total city taxes per capita: $71 (2007); City property taxes per capita: $5 (2007).
Education: Percent of population age 25 and over with: High school diploma (including GED) or higher: 88.3% (2010); Bachelor's degree or higher: 19.2% (2010); Master's degree or higher: 5.9% (2010).
School District(s)
Boone/Winnebago Roe (06-12)
    2009-10 Enrollment: n/a . . . . (815) 636-3060
Harlem UD 122 (PK-12)
    2009-10 Enrollment: 7,752 . . . . (815) 654-4500
Housing: Homeownership rate: 70.4% (2010); Median home value: $119,033 (2010); Median contract rent: $571 per month (2005-2009 5-year est.); Median year structure built: 1982 (2005-2009 5-year est.).
Safety: Violent crime rate: 34.9 per 10,000 population; Property crime rate: 350.4 per 10,000 population (2010).
Transportation: Commute to work: 94.7% car, 0.2% public transportation, 1.2% walk, 3.3% work from home (2005-2009 5-year est.); Travel time to work: 37.6% less than 15 minutes, 46.9% 15 to 30 minutes, 6.6% 30 to 45 minutes, 4.3% 45 to 60 minutes, 4.7% 60 minutes or more (2005-2009 5-year est.)
Additional Information Contacts
City of Loves Park . . . . (815) 654-5030
    http://www.loves-park.il.us
The Parks Chamber of Commerce . . . . (815) 633-3999
    http://www.parkschamber.com

MACHESNEY PARK (village). Covers a land area of 12.008 square miles and a water area of 0.381 square miles. Located at 42.35° N. Lat; 89.04° W. Long. Elevation is 741 feet.
Population: 19,112 (1990); 20,759 (2000); 22,852 (2010); 23,530 (2015 projected); Race: 93.7% White, 2.0% Black, 1.0% Asian, 3.4% Other, 3.9% Hispanic of any race (2010); Density: 1,903.1 persons per square mile (2010); Average household size: 2.66 (2010); Median age: 37.1 (2010); Males per 100 females: 99.7 (2010); Marriage status: 26.3% never married, 55.1% now married, 6.1% widowed, 12.5% divorced (2005-2009 5-year est.); Foreign born: 3.8% (2005-2009 5-year est.); Ancestry (includes multiple ancestries): 30.6% German, 17.8% Irish, 13.2% American, 10.1% English, 8.6% Swedish (2005-2009 5-year est.).
Economy: Employment by occupation: 10.4% management, 12.4% professional, 15.4% services, 29.8% sales, 0.0% farming, 9.9% construction, 22.0% production (2005-2009 5-year est.).
Income: Per capita income: $22,378 (2010); Median household income: $53,000 (2010); Average household income: $59,712 (2010); Percent of households with income of $100,000 or more: 10.6% (2010); Poverty rate: 8.5% (2005-2009 5-year est.).
Taxes: Total city taxes per capita: $51 (2007); City property taxes per capita: $29 (2007).
Education: Percent of population age 25 and over with: High school diploma (including GED) or higher: 82.3% (2010); Bachelor's degree or higher: 11.8% (2010); Master's degree or higher: 3.1% (2010).
School District(s)
Harlem UD 122 (PK-12)
    2009-10 Enrollment: 7,752 . . . . (815) 654-4500
Housing: Homeownership rate: 83.1% (2010); Median home value: $119,917 (2010); Median contract rent: $635 per month (2005-2009 5-year est.); Median year structure built: 1972 (2005-2009 5-year est.).
Safety: Violent crime rate: 26.0 per 10,000 population; Property crime rate: 311.2 per 10,000 population (2010).

Newspapers: Channooka Weekly Trading Post (Community news; Circulation 4,000); Chanooka Weekly (Local news; Circulation 1,500); Durand/Stephenson Gazette (Community news; Circulation 4,416); Gazette (Community news; Circulation 8,730); North Suburban Herald (Community news; Circulation 1,568); Northern Ogle County Tempo (Local news; Circulation 4,800); Parks Journal (Community news; Circulation 20,600); Pecatonica/Winnebago Gazette (Local news; Circulation 7,141); Post Journal (Community news; Circulation 14,550); Rockford Journal (Community news; Circulation 5,500); Senior Courier (Local news; Circulation 10,000)

Transportation: Commute to work: 96.4% car, 0.2% public transportation, 0.5% walk, 1.9% work from home (2005-2009 5-year est.); Travel time to work: 31.1% less than 15 minutes, 45.9% 15 to 30 minutes, 14.4% 30 to 45 minutes, 3.3% 45 to 60 minutes, 5.2% 60 minutes or more (2005-2009 5-year est.)

Additional Information Contacts

Village of Machesney Park . . . . (815) 877-5432
http://www.machesney-park.il.us

NEW MILFORD (village). Covers a land area of 1.089 square miles and a water area of 0.025 square miles. Located at 42.18° N. Lat; 89.07° W. Long.

Population: 662 (1990); 541 (2000); 597 (2010); 615 (2015 projected); Race: 93.1% White, 1.7% Black, 1.5% Asian, 3.7% Other, 2.2% Hispanic of any race (2010); Density: 548.0 persons per square mile (2010); Average household size: 2.44 (2010); Median age: 43.0 (2010); Males per 100 females: 101.0 (2010); Marriage status: 15.0% never married, 68.5% now married, 4.9% widowed, 11.6% divorced (2005-2009 5-year est.); Foreign born: 4.2% (2005-2009 5-year est.); Ancestry (includes multiple ancestries): 30.4% German, 15.1% English, 13.0% Swedish, 11.1% Irish, 6.2% American (2005-2009 5-year est.).

Economy: Employment by occupation: 8.8% management, 19.4% professional, 20.1% services, 15.3% sales, 0.0% farming, 7.8% construction, 28.6% production (2005-2009 5-year est.).

Income: Per capita income: $26,409 (2010); Median household income: $56,250 (2010); Average household income: $64,888 (2010); Percent of households with income of $100,000 or more: 15.1% (2010); Poverty rate: 13.5% (2005-2009 5-year est.).

Taxes: Total city taxes per capita: $77 (2007); City property taxes per capita: $7 (2007).

Education: Percent of population age 25 and over with: High school diploma (including GED) or higher: 83.3% (2010); Bachelor's degree or higher: 14.0% (2010); Master's degree or higher: 5.3% (2010).

Housing: Homeownership rate: 91.0% (2010); Median home value: $106,908 (2010); Median contract rent: $475 per month (2005-2009 5-year est.); Median year structure built: 1988 (2005-2009 5-year est.).

Transportation: Commute to work: 95.1% car, 0.0% public transportation, 0.0% walk, 4.9% work from home (2005-2009 5-year est.); Travel time to work: 20.3% less than 15 minutes, 56.2% 15 to 30 minutes, 11.6% 30 to 45 minutes, 3.2% 45 to 60 minutes, 8.8% 60 minutes or more (2005-2009 5-year est.)

PECATONICA (village). Covers a land area of 1.243 square miles and a water area of 0.018 square miles. Located at 42.31° N. Lat; 89.35° W. Long. Elevation is 771 feet.

History: Incorporated 1869.

Population: 1,838 (1990); 1,997 (2000); 2,352 (2010); 2,512 (2015 projected); Race: 97.8% White, 0.3% Black, 0.1% Asian, 1.8% Other, 0.9% Hispanic of any race (2010); Density: 1,893.0 persons per square mile (2010); Average household size: 2.53 (2010); Median age: 37.3 (2010); Males per 100 females: 93.3 (2010); Marriage status: 21.3% never married, 58.5% now married, 7.1% widowed, 13.1% divorced (2005-2009 5-year est.); Foreign born: 0.2% (2005-2009 5-year est.); Ancestry (includes multiple ancestries): 40.6% German, 17.6% Irish, 12.9% American, 11.0% Swedish, 7.3% Dutch (2005-2009 5-year est.).

Economy: Single-family building permits issued: 0 (2010); Multi-family building permits issued: 0 (2010); Employment by occupation: 12.4% management, 10.6% professional, 19.7% services, 28.4% sales, 0.7% farming, 12.8% construction, 15.5% production (2005-2009 5-year est.).

Income: Per capita income: $23,609 (2010); Median household income: $55,196 (2010); Average household income: $59,618 (2010); Percent of households with income of $100,000 or more: 10.9% (2010); Poverty rate: 8.3% (2005-2009 5-year est.).

Taxes: Total city taxes per capita: $141 (2007); City property taxes per capita: $55 (2007).

Education: Percent of population age 25 and over with: High school diploma (including GED) or higher: 90.0% (2010); Bachelor's degree or higher: 13.5% (2010); Master's degree or higher: 4.8% (2010).

School District(s)

Pecatonica CUSD 321 (PK-12)
2009-10 Enrollment: 972 . . . . (815) 239-1639

Housing: Homeownership rate: 81.3% (2010); Median home value: $127,731 (2010); Median contract rent: $488 per month (2005-2009 5-year est.); Median year structure built: 1959 (2005-2009 5-year est.).

Transportation: Commute to work: 91.9% car, 0.0% public transportation, 1.0% walk, 4.5% work from home (2005-2009 5-year est.); Travel time to work: 22.5% less than 15 minutes, 28.2% 15 to 30 minutes, 39.3% 30 to 45 minutes, 3.1% 45 to 60 minutes, 6.8% 60 minutes or more (2005-2009 5-year est.)

ROCKFORD (city). County seat. Covers a land area of 56.005 square miles and a water area of 0.713 square miles. Located at 42.27° N. Lat; 89.07° W. Long. Elevation is 715 feet.

History: Rockford was named for the ford across the Rock River where the stagecoach crossed before the town was built. Rockford was settled by New Englanders after Germanicus Kent and Thatcher Blake of Galena laid out the town and opened a sawmill. The availability of water power accounted for Rockford's growth, and it was incorporated in 1839 along with a village that had grown up on the other side of the river. In the 1850's both the Rockford Water Power Company and the Manny Company, producer of reaper-mower machines, were founded. After 1852, when the Chicago & Galena Union Railroad arrived, many people of Swedish descent settled here.

Population: 146,309 (1990); 150,115 (2000); 156,386 (2010); 158,758 (2015 projected); Race: 67.4% White, 18.6% Black, 2.4% Asian, 11.5% Other, 16.3% Hispanic of any race (2010); Density: 2,792.3 persons per square mile (2010); Average household size: 2.48 (2010); Median age: 35.8 (2010); Males per 100 females: 95.0 (2010); Marriage status: 34.4% never married, 44.8% now married, 7.9% widowed, 12.9% divorced (2005-2009 5-year est.); Foreign born: 10.1% (2005-2009 5-year est.); Ancestry (includes multiple ancestries): 20.5% German, 11.1% Irish, 8.5% Swedish, 7.9% American, 7.0% English (2005-2009 5-year est.).

Economy: Unemployment rate: 15.2% (August 2011); Total civilian labor force: 71,897 (August 2011); Single-family building permits issued: 24 (2010); Multi-family building permits issued: 2 (2010); Employment by occupation: 9.9% management, 17.5% professional, 18.8% services, 26.1% sales, 0.0% farming, 6.4% construction, 21.3% production (2005-2009 5-year est.).

Income: Per capita income: $21,387 (2010); Median household income: $40,497 (2010); Average household income: $53,558 (2010); Percent of households with income of $100,000 or more: 10.5% (2010); Poverty rate: 21.9% (2005-2009 5-year est.).

Taxes: Total city taxes per capita: $431 (2007); City property taxes per capita: $325 (2007).

Education: Percent of population age 25 and over with: High school diploma (including GED) or higher: 78.5% (2010); Bachelor's degree or higher: 19.9% (2010); Master's degree or higher: 6.8% (2010).

School District(s)

Boone/Winnebago Roe (06-12)
2009-10 Enrollment: n/a . . . . (815) 636-3060
Career Educ Assoc of N Central Illinois
2009-10 Enrollment: n/a . . . . (815) 921-1651
Rockford SD 205 (PK-12)
2009-10 Enrollment: 29,071 . . . . (815) 966-3101

Four-year College(s)

Rasmussen College-Rockford (Private, For-profit)
Fall 2009 Enrollment: 881 . . . . (815) 316-4800
2010-11 Tuition: In-state $13,560; Out-of-state $13,560
Rockford College (Private, Not-for-profit)
Fall 2009 Enrollment: 1,341 . . . . (815) 226-4050
2010-11 Tuition: In-state $24,750; Out-of-state $24,750
Saint Anthony College of Nursing (Private, Not-for-profit, Roman Catholic)
Fall 2009 Enrollment: 188 . . . . (815) 395-5091

Two-year College(s)

Rock Valley College (Public)
Fall 2009 Enrollment: 8,659 . . . . (815) 921-7821
2010-11 Tuition: In-state $8,160; Out-of-state $14,630
Rockford Career College (Private, For-profit)
Fall 2009 Enrollment: 752 . . . . (815) 965-8616
2010-11 Tuition: In-state $8,480; Out-of-state $8,480

Vocational/Technical School(s)

Educators of Beauty (Private, For-profit)
Fall 2009 Enrollment: 55 . . . . (815) 639-9200
2010-11 Tuition: $16,575

Regency Beauty Institute-Rockford (Private, For-profit)
Fall 2009 Enrollment: 178 . . . . (800) 787-6456
2010-11 Tuition: $16,075

Tricoci University of Beauty Culture (Private, For-profit)
Fall 2009 Enrollment: 45 . . . . (630) 528-3336
2010-11 Tuition: $15,450

Housing: Homeownership rate: 62.0% (2010); Median home value: $100,619 (2010); Median contract rent: $523 per month (2005-2009 5-year est.); Median year structure built: 1959 (2005-2009 5-year est.).

Hospitals: H. Douglas Singer Mental Health & Development Center (80 beds); Rockford Memorial Hospital (396 beds); St. Anthony Medical Center (254 beds); Swedish American Hospital (357 beds)

Safety: Violent crime rate: 145.5 per 10,000 population; Property crime rate: 499.7 per 10,000 population (2010).

Newspapers: The Observer (Regional news; Circulation 32,500); Rock River Times (Regional news; Circulation 19,000); Rockford Labor News (National news; Circulation 20,000); Rockford Register Star (Local news; Circulation 86,000)

Transportation: Commute to work: 92.4% car, 1.4% public transportation, 1.9% walk, 3.0% work from home (2005-2009 5-year est.); Travel time to work: 36.8% less than 15 minutes, 43.6% 15 to 30 minutes, 10.2% 30 to 45 minutes, 3.4% 45 to 60 minutes, 5.9% 60 minutes or more (2005-2009 5-year est.); Amtrak: train service available.

Airports: Chicago/Rockford International (primary service)

Additional Information Contacts

City of Rockford . . . . (815) 987-5590
http://www.rockfordil.gov

Rockford Chamber of Commerce . . . . (815) 987-8100
http://www.rockfordchamber.com

ROCKTON (village). Covers a land area of 3.518 square miles and a water area of 0.182 square miles. Located at 42.45° N. Lat; 89.06° W. Long. Elevation is 738 feet.

History: Incorporated 1847.

Population: 3,530 (1990); 5,296 (2000); 6,097 (2010); 6,450 (2015 projected); Race: 96.2% White, 0.8% Black, 0.9% Asian, 2.1% Other, 2.6% Hispanic of any race (2010); Density: 1,733.2 persons per square mile (2010); Average household size: 2.74 (2010); Median age: 36.2 (2010); Males per 100 females: 98.0 (2010); Marriage status: 22.4% never married, 64.8% now married, 4.8% widowed, 8.1% divorced (2005-2009 5-year est.); Foreign born: 2.4% (2005-2009 5-year est.); Ancestry (includes multiple ancestries): 33.0% German, 15.0% Irish, 10.0% American, 9.0% Italian, 9.0% English (2005-2009 5-year est.).

Economy: Employment by occupation: 21.2% management, 21.4% professional, 14.0% services, 29.4% sales, 0.0% farming, 7.8% construction, 6.2% production (2005-2009 5-year est.).

Income: Per capita income: $26,606 (2010); Median household income: $62,312 (2010); Average household income: $73,158 (2010); Percent of households with income of $100,000 or more: 21.4% (2010); Poverty rate: 1.3% (2005-2009 5-year est.).

Taxes: Total city taxes per capita: $218 (2007); City property taxes per capita: $146 (2007).

Education: Percent of population age 25 and over with: High school diploma (including GED) or higher: 92.3% (2010); Bachelor's degree or higher: 28.4% (2010); Master's degree or higher: 9.9% (2010).

School District(s)

Hononegah Chd 207 (09-12)
2009-10 Enrollment: 2,169 . . . . (815) 624-5010

Rockton SD 140 (PK-08)
2009-10 Enrollment: 1,569 . . . . (815) 624-7143

Housing: Homeownership rate: 78.8% (2010); Median home value: $148,538 (2010); Median contract rent: $534 per month (2005-2009 5-year est.); Median year structure built: 1991 (2005-2009 5-year est.).

Transportation: Commute to work: 94.1% car, 0.0% public transportation, 1.0% walk, 4.0% work from home (2005-2009 5-year est.); Travel time to work: 27.3% less than 15 minutes, 41.0% 15 to 30 minutes, 22.4% 30 to 45 minutes, 2.3% 45 to 60 minutes, 7.0% 60 minutes or more (2005-2009 5-year est.)

Additional Information Contacts

Rockton Chamber of Commerce . . . . (815) 624-7625
http://www.rocktonchamber.com

Village of Rockton . . . . (815) 624-7600
http://rocktonvillage.com

ROSCOE (village). Covers a land area of 9.249 square miles and a water area of 0.072 square miles. Located at 42.41° N. Lat; 89.01° W. Long. Elevation is 738 feet.

Population: 2,632 (1990); 6,244 (2000); 9,706 (2010); 10,678 (2015 projected); Race: 94.5% White, 2.3% Black, 0.7% Asian, 2.4% Other, 3.4% Hispanic of any race (2010); Density: 1,049.4 persons per square mile (2010); Average household size: 2.82 (2010); Median age: 36.4 (2010); Males per 100 females: 99.5 (2010); Marriage status: 21.1% never married, 64.7% now married, 3.4% widowed, 10.7% divorced (2005-2009 5-year est.); Foreign born: 3.8% (2005-2009 5-year est.); Ancestry (includes multiple ancestries): 30.5% German, 19.7% American, 14.1% Irish, 10.4% English, 7.7% Italian (2005-2009 5-year est.).

Economy: Employment by occupation: 11.5% management, 23.1% professional, 15.9% services, 27.8% sales, 0.0% farming, 7.3% construction, 14.4% production (2005-2009 5-year est.).

Income: Per capita income: $27,556 (2010); Median household income: $68,762 (2010); Average household income: $78,030 (2010); Percent of households with income of $100,000 or more: 21.1% (2010); Poverty rate: 2.7% (2005-2009 5-year est.).

Taxes: Total city taxes per capita: $147 (2007); City property taxes per capita: $97 (2007).

Education: Percent of population age 25 and over with: High school diploma (including GED) or higher: 91.2% (2010); Bachelor's degree or higher: 21.7% (2010); Master's degree or higher: 6.0% (2010).

School District(s)

Kinnikinnick CCSD 131 (PK-08)
2009-10 Enrollment: 2,113 . . . . (815) 623-2837

Housing: Homeownership rate: 84.0% (2010); Median home value: $162,214 (2010); Median contract rent: $725 per month (2005-2009 5-year est.); Median year structure built: 1996 (2005-2009 5-year est.).

Transportation: Commute to work: 94.3% car, 0.2% public transportation, 0.9% walk, 3.6% work from home (2005-2009 5-year est.); Travel time to work: 18.3% less than 15 minutes, 52.2% 15 to 30 minutes, 22.2% 30 to 45 minutes, 3.6% 45 to 60 minutes, 3.7% 60 minutes or more (2005-2009 5-year est.)

Additional Information Contacts

Roscoe Area Chamber of Commerce . . . . (815) 623-9065
http://www.roscoechamber.com

Village of Roscoe . . . . (815) 623-2829
http://www.villageofroscoe.com

SOUTH BELOIT (city). Covers a land area of 3.960 square miles and a water area of 0.125 square miles. Located at 42.48° N. Lat; 89.03° W. Long. Elevation is 738 feet.

History: Incorporated 1917.

Population: 4,376 (1990); 5,397 (2000); 6,160 (2010); 6,436 (2015 projected); Race: 87.2% White, 3.8% Black, 0.9% Asian, 8.1% Other, 10.8% Hispanic of any race (2010); Density: 1,555.5 persons per square mile (2010); Average household size: 2.52 (2010); Median age: 35.9 (2010); Males per 100 females: 102.3 (2010); Marriage status: 22.9% never married, 56.6% now married, 7.6% widowed, 12.9% divorced (2005-2009 5-year est.); Foreign born: 5.9% (2005-2009 5-year est.); Ancestry (includes multiple ancestries): 30.6% German, 14.1% Irish, 12.7% American, 10.4% English, 9.8% Italian (2005-2009 5-year est.).

Economy: Employment by occupation: 5.1% management, 18.2% professional, 14.7% services, 28.0% sales, 0.0% farming, 8.2% construction, 25.8% production (2005-2009 5-year est.).

Income: Per capita income: $21,659 (2010); Median household income: $46,096 (2010); Average household income: $53,889 (2010); Percent of households with income of $100,000 or more: 10.2% (2010); Poverty rate: 14.2% (2005-2009 5-year est.).

Taxes: Total city taxes per capita: $291 (2007); City property taxes per capita: $180 (2007).

Education: Percent of population age 25 and over with: High school diploma (including GED) or higher: 78.6% (2010); Bachelor's degree or higher: 11.1% (2010); Master's degree or higher: 3.3% (2010).

School District(s)

County of Winnebago SD 320 (PK-12)
2009-10 Enrollment: 1,095 . . . . (815) 389-3478

Prairie Hill CCSD 133 (KG-08)
2009-10 Enrollment: 734 . . . . (815) 389-4694

Housing: Homeownership rate: 69.2% (2010); Median home value: $114,924 (2010); Median contract rent: $505 per month (2005-2009 5-year est.); Median year structure built: 1985 (2005-2009 5-year est.).
Transportation: Commute to work: 96.0% car, 0.0% public transportation, 1.5% walk, 1.7% work from home (2005-2009 5-year est.); Travel time to work: 35.2% less than 15 minutes, 31.8% 15 to 30 minutes, 17.3% 30 to 45 minutes, 6.3% 45 to 60 minutes, 9.4% 60 minutes or more (2005-2009 5-year est.); Amtrak: bus service available.
Additional Information Contacts
City of South Beloit . . . . (815) 389-3023
    http://www.southbeloit.org

WINNEBAGO (village). Covers a land area of 1.392 square miles and a water area of 0 square miles. Located at 42.26° N. Lat; 89.24° W. Long. Elevation is 869 feet.
Population: 2,172 (1990); 2,958 (2000); 3,471 (2010); 3,722 (2015 projected); Race: 96.8% White, 2.2% Black, 0.2% Asian, 0.8% Other, 2.0% Hispanic of any race (2010); Density: 2,493.9 persons per square mile (2010); Average household size: 2.97 (2010); Median age: 33.6 (2010); Males per 100 females: 95.1 (2010); Marriage status: 25.4% never married, 65.0% now married, 3.0% widowed, 6.6% divorced (2005-2009 5-year est.); Foreign born: 1.3% (2005-2009 5-year est.); Ancestry (includes multiple ancestries): 43.0% German, 16.4% English, 15.1% Irish, 9.7% American, 9.0% Swedish (2005-2009 5-year est.).
Economy: Single-family building permits issued: 1 (2010); Multi-family building permits issued: 0 (2010); Employment by occupation: 10.9% management, 25.0% professional, 14.4% services, 23.0% sales, 0.4% farming, 7.7% construction, 18.6% production (2005-2009 5-year est.).
Income: Per capita income: $25,859 (2010); Median household income: $71,483 (2010); Average household income: $76,938 (2010); Percent of households with income of $100,000 or more: 25.0% (2010); Poverty rate: 4.0% (2005-2009 5-year est.).
Taxes: Total city taxes per capita: $163 (2007); City property taxes per capita: $118 (2007).
Education: Percent of population age 25 and over with: High school diploma (including GED) or higher: 88.9% (2010); Bachelor's degree or higher: 18.6% (2010); Master's degree or higher: 5.7% (2010).

School District(s)
Winnebago CUSD 323 (PK-12)
    2009-10 Enrollment: 1,653 . . . . (815) 335-2456
Housing: Homeownership rate: 87.0% (2010); Median home value: $134,891 (2010); Median contract rent: $582 per month (2005-2009 5-year est.); Median year structure built: 1983 (2005-2009 5-year est.).
Safety: Violent crime rate: 3.1 per 10,000 population; Property crime rate: 173.5 per 10,000 population (2010).
Transportation: Commute to work: 93.1% car, 0.5% public transportation, 0.0% walk, 6.1% work from home (2005-2009 5-year est.); Travel time to work: 26.2% less than 15 minutes, 51.2% 15 to 30 minutes, 15.6% 30 to 45 minutes, 2.9% 45 to 60 minutes, 4.1% 60 minutes or more (2005-2009 5-year est.)

Woodford County

Located in central Illinois; bounded on the west by the Illinois River; drained by the Mackinaw River. Covers a land area of 527.95 square miles, a water area of 14.79 square miles, and is located in the Central Time Zone at 40.78° N. Lat., 89.22° W. Long. The county was founded in 1841. County seat is Eureka.

Woodford County is part of the Peoria, IL Metropolitan Statistical Area. The entire metro area includes: Marshall County, IL; Peoria County, IL; Stark County, IL; Tazewell County, IL; Woodford County, IL

Weather Station: Minonk   Elevation: 750 feet

	Jan	Feb	Mar	Apr	May	Jun	Jul	Aug	Sep	Oct	Nov	Dec
High	32	37	49	62	73	83	86	84	78	65	50	36
Low	15	19	28	39	49	59	63	60	52	41	31	19
Precip	2.0	1.9	2.9	3.6	4.2	3.7	3.8	3.5	3.4	3.0	3.5	2.4
Snow	6.5	6.7	2.9	0.9	tr	0.0	0.0	0.0	0.0	tr	0.8	6.2

High and Low temperatures in degrees Fahrenheit; Precipitation and Snow in inches

Population: 32,653 (1990); 35,469 (2000); 39,201 (2010); 40,898 (2015 projected); Race: 97.0% White, 1.2% Black, 0.6% Asian, 1.2% Other, 1.3% Hispanic of any race (2010); Density: 74.3 persons per square mile (2010); Average household size: 2.63 (2010); Median age: 37.5 (2010); Males per 100 females: 96.6 (2010).

Religion: Five largest groups: 15.9% Catholic Church, 7.4% The United Methodist Church, 7.3% Apostolic Christian Church of America, Inc., 4.3% United Church of Christ, 4.0% Lutheran Church—Missouri Synod (2000).
Economy: Unemployment rate: 6.5% (August 2011); Total civilian labor force: 22,032 (August 2011); Leading industries: 23.4% manufacturing; 15.9% health care and social assistance; 11.9% retail trade (2009); Farms: 932 totaling 288,400 acres (2007); Companies that employ 500 or more persons: 0 (2009); Companies that employ 100 to 499 persons: 14 (2009); Companies that employ less than 100 persons: 772 (2009); Black-owned businesses: n/a (2007); Hispanic-owned businesses: n/a (2007); Asian-owned businesses: n/a (2007); Women-owned businesses: n/a (2007); Retail sales per capita: $10,126 (2010). Single-family building permits issued: 65 (2010); Multi-family building permits issued: 18 (2010).
Income: Per capita income: $28,582 (2010); Median household income: $65,357 (2010); Average household income: $76,992 (2010); Percent of households with income of $100,000 or more: 22.8% (2010); Poverty rate: 6.8% (2009); Bankruptcy rate: 3.63% (2010).
Taxes: Total county taxes per capita: $117 (2007); County property taxes per capita: $74 (2007).
Education: Percent of population age 25 and over with: High school diploma (including GED) or higher: 92.3% (2010); Bachelor's degree or higher: 25.6% (2010); Master's degree or higher: 9.0% (2010).
Housing: Homeownership rate: 81.9% (2010); Median home value: $140,494 (2010); Median contract rent: $495 per month (2005-2009 5-year est.); Median year structure built: 1969 (2005-2009 5-year est.)
Health: Birth rate: 139.2 per 10,000 population (2009); Death rate: 87.7 per 10,000 population (2009); Age-adjusted cancer mortality rate: 212.9 deaths per 100,000 population (2007); Number of physicians: 11.9 per 10,000 population (2008); Hospital beds: 6.6 per 10,000 population (2007); Hospital admissions: 135.1 per 10,000 population (2007).
Elections: 2008 Presidential election results: 35.9% Obama, 62.6% McCain, 0.7% Nader
National and State Parks: Woodford County State Conservation Area
Additional Information Contacts
Woodford County Government . . . . (309) 467-2822
    http://www.woodford-county.org

Woodford County Communities

BAY VIEW GARDENS (village). Covers a land area of 0.178 square miles and a water area of 0 square miles. Located at 40.81° N. Lat; 89.51° W. Long. Elevation is 525 feet.
Population: 418 (1990); 366 (2000); 369 (2010); 372 (2015 projected); Race: 99.2% White, 0.3% Black, 0.0% Asian, 0.5% Other, 2.7% Hispanic of any race (2010); Density: 2,073.8 persons per square mile (2010); Average household size: 2.65 (2010); Median age: 37.9 (2010); Males per 100 females: 113.3 (2010); Marriage status: 28.0% never married, 50.6% now married, 6.9% widowed, 14.5% divorced (2005-2009 5-year est.); Foreign born: 0.0% (2005-2009 5-year est.); Ancestry (includes multiple ancestries): 23.2% German, 15.6% American, 12.8% English, 10.8% Dutch, 7.3% Irish (2005-2009 5-year est.).
Economy: Single-family building permits issued: 0 (2010); Multi-family building permits issued: 0 (2010); Employment by occupation: 9.5% management, 11.9% professional, 28.1% services, 21.9% sales, 0.0% farming, 4.8% construction, 23.8% production (2005-2009 5-year est.).
Income: Per capita income: $21,813 (2010); Median household income: $47,214 (2010); Average household income: $56,457 (2010); Percent of households with income of $100,000 or more: 9.4% (2010); Poverty rate: 17.9% (2005-2009 5-year est.).
Taxes: Total city taxes per capita: $58 (2007); City property taxes per capita: $14 (2007).
Education: Percent of population age 25 and over with: High school diploma (including GED) or higher: 85.7% (2010); Bachelor's degree or higher: 9.8% (2010); Master's degree or higher: 6.5% (2010).
Housing: Homeownership rate: 82.7% (2010); Median home value: $114,732 (2010); Median contract rent: $430 per month (2005-2009 5-year est.); Median year structure built: 1965 (2005-2009 5-year est.).
Transportation: Commute to work: 99.0% car, 0.0% public transportation, 0.0% walk, 1.0% work from home (2005-2009 5-year est.); Travel time to work: 13.1% less than 15 minutes, 67.7% 15 to 30 minutes, 13.1% 30 to 45 minutes, 2.0% 45 to 60 minutes, 4.0% 60 minutes or more (2005-2009 5-year est.)

BENSON (village). Covers a land area of 0.174 square miles and a water area of 0 square miles. Located at 40.85° N. Lat; 89.12° W. Long. Elevation is 764 feet.

Population: 415 (1990); 408 (2000); 450 (2010); 473 (2015 projected); Race: 99.3% White, 0.2% Black, 0.0% Asian, 0.4% Other, 0.9% Hispanic of any race (2010); Density: 2,579.3 persons per square mile (2010); Average household size: 2.53 (2010); Median age: 37.3 (2010); Males per 100 females: 105.5 (2010); Marriage status: 23.6% never married, 65.9% now married, 5.1% widowed, 5.4% divorced (2005-2009 5-year est.); Foreign born: 0.5% (2005-2009 5-year est.); Ancestry (includes multiple ancestries): 56.6% German, 13.3% Irish, 7.7% English, 6.7% American, 6.3% Swedish (2005-2009 5-year est.).

Economy: Single-family building permits issued: 0 (2010); Multi-family building permits issued: 0 (2010); Employment by occupation: 7.9% management, 12.3% professional, 14.8% services, 30.5% sales, 1.0% farming, 13.3% construction, 20.2% production (2005-2009 5-year est.).

Income: Per capita income: $22,795 (2010); Median household income: $52,604 (2010); Average household income: $57,626 (2010); Percent of households with income of $100,000 or more: 11.8% (2010); Poverty rate: 5.5% (2005-2009 5-year est.).

Taxes: Total city taxes per capita: $73 (2007); City property taxes per capita: $68 (2007).

Education: Percent of population age 25 and over with: High school diploma (including GED) or higher: 92.4% (2010); Bachelor's degree or higher: 19.9% (2010); Master's degree or higher: 7.6% (2010).

School District(s)
Roanoke Benson CUSD 60 (PK-12)
2009-10 Enrollment: 607 . . . . (309) 923-8921

Housing: Homeownership rate: 83.1% (2010); Median home value: $100,000 (2010); Median contract rent: $431 per month (2005-2009 5-year est.); Median year structure built: 1942 (2005-2009 5-year est.).

Transportation: Commute to work: 93.9% car, 0.0% public transportation, 2.5% walk, 1.5% work from home (2005-2009 5-year est.); Travel time to work: 27.3% less than 15 minutes, 27.8% 15 to 30 minutes, 23.7% 30 to 45 minutes, 17.0% 45 to 60 minutes, 4.1% 60 minutes or more (2005-2009 5-year est.)

CONGERVILLE (village). Covers a land area of 0.757 square miles and a water area of 0.004 square miles. Located at 40.61° N. Lat; 89.20° W. Long. Elevation is 748 feet.

Population: 452 (1990); 466 (2000); 534 (2010); 568 (2015 projected); Race: 97.8% White, 0.0% Black, 0.7% Asian, 1.5% Other, 0.0% Hispanic of any race (2010); Density: 705.1 persons per square mile (2010); Average household size: 2.86 (2010); Median age: 36.6 (2010); Males per 100 females: 105.4 (2010); Marriage status: 26.0% never married, 64.5% now married, 1.5% widowed, 8.1% divorced (2005-2009 5-year est.); Foreign born: 0.0% (2005-2009 5-year est.); Ancestry (includes multiple ancestries): 68.2% German, 14.6% Swiss, 10.5% American, 9.0% Irish, 3.0% French (2005-2009 5-year est.).

Economy: Single-family building permits issued: 1 (2010); Multi-family building permits issued: 0 (2010); Employment by occupation: 17.0% management, 15.7% professional, 11.9% services, 23.6% sales, 2.8% farming, 14.8% construction, 14.2% production (2005-2009 5-year est.).

Income: Per capita income: $28,841 (2010); Median household income: $67,540 (2010); Average household income: $82,981 (2010); Percent of households with income of $100,000 or more: 20.9% (2010); Poverty rate: 2.2% (2005-2009 5-year est.).

Taxes: Total city taxes per capita: $50 (2007); City property taxes per capita: $44 (2007).

Education: Percent of population age 25 and over with: High school diploma (including GED) or higher: 96.4% (2010); Bachelor's degree or higher: 19.7% (2010); Master's degree or higher: 6.8% (2010).

School District(s)
Eureka CUD 140 (PK-12)
2009-10 Enrollment: 1,622 . . . . (309) 467-3737

Housing: Homeownership rate: 83.4% (2010); Median home value: $174,324 (2010); Median contract rent: $487 per month (2005-2009 5-year est.); Median year structure built: 1969 (2005-2009 5-year est.).

Transportation: Commute to work: 94.2% car, 0.0% public transportation, 3.8% walk, 1.9% work from home (2005-2009 5-year est.); Travel time to work: 34.5% less than 15 minutes, 39.1% 15 to 30 minutes, 20.8% 30 to 45 minutes, 5.5% 45 to 60 minutes, 0.0% 60 minutes or more (2005-2009 5-year est.)

EL PASO (city). Covers a land area of 1.545 square miles and a water area of 0 square miles. Located at 40.73° N. Lat; 89.01° W. Long. Elevation is 751 feet.

History: El Paso was the home of Lester Pfister who developed a hybrid corn that gave a high yield.

Population: 2,547 (1990); 2,695 (2000); 2,932 (2010); 3,035 (2015 projected); Race: 98.3% White, 0.6% Black, 0.2% Asian, 0.9% Other, 1.5% Hispanic of any race (2010); Density: 1,897.2 persons per square mile (2010); Average household size: 2.57 (2010); Median age: 36.0 (2010); Males per 100 females: 95.9 (2010); Marriage status: 25.6% never married, 54.0% now married, 6.4% widowed, 14.1% divorced (2005-2009 5-year est.); Foreign born: 2.0% (2005-2009 5-year est.); Ancestry (includes multiple ancestries): 33.7% German, 18.4% Irish, 15.3% American, 14.5% English, 6.8% Italian (2005-2009 5-year est.).

Economy: Single-family building permits issued: 0 (2010); Multi-family building permits issued: 2 (2010); Employment by occupation: 9.9% management, 13.1% professional, 16.8% services, 29.7% sales, 1.7% farming, 12.2% construction, 16.6% production (2005-2009 5-year est.).

Income: Per capita income: $27,904 (2010); Median household income: $63,173 (2010); Average household income: $72,820 (2010); Percent of households with income of $100,000 or more: 18.5% (2010); Poverty rate: 6.7% (2005-2009 5-year est.).

Taxes: Total city taxes per capita: $199 (2007); City property taxes per capita: $158 (2007).

Education: Percent of population age 25 and over with: High school diploma (including GED) or higher: 90.5% (2010); Bachelor's degree or higher: 24.3% (2010); Master's degree or higher: 7.7% (2010).

School District(s)
El Paso-Gridley CUSD 11 (PK-12)
2009-10 Enrollment: 1,298 . . . . (309) 527-4410

Housing: Homeownership rate: 74.8% (2010); Median home value: $123,059 (2010); Median contract rent: $546 per month (2005-2009 5-year est.); Median year structure built: 1960 (2005-2009 5-year est.).

Safety: Violent crime rate: 10.5 per 10,000 population; Property crime rate: 70.1 per 10,000 population (2010).

Newspapers: El Paso Journal (Regional news; Circulation 1,175)

Transportation: Commute to work: 92.6% car, 0.0% public transportation, 2.9% walk, 2.8% work from home (2005-2009 5-year est.); Travel time to work: 38.3% less than 15 minutes, 27.7% 15 to 30 minutes, 25.8% 30 to 45 minutes, 5.7% 45 to 60 minutes, 2.5% 60 minutes or more (2005-2009 5-year est.)

EUREKA (city). County seat. Covers a land area of 2.690 square miles and a water area of 0.048 square miles. Located at 40.71° N. Lat; 89.27° W. Long. Elevation is 768 feet.

History: Eureka was settled in the 1830's, and developed around Eureka College, which began in 1848 as a seminary founded by the Disciples of Christ. Eureka was named the seat of Woodford County in 1896.

Population: 4,724 (1990); 4,871 (2000); 4,983 (2010); 5,129 (2015 projected); Race: 95.1% White, 3.0% Black, 0.8% Asian, 1.2% Other, 1.8% Hispanic of any race (2010); Density: 1,852.1 persons per square mile (2010); Average household size: 2.41 (2010); Median age: 33.9 (2010); Males per 100 females: 88.9 (2010); Marriage status: 29.9% never married, 48.3% now married, 13.9% widowed, 7.8% divorced (2005-2009 5-year est.); Foreign born: 0.4% (2005-2009 5-year est.); Ancestry (includes multiple ancestries): 48.6% German, 13.9% Irish, 13.0% American, 9.2% English, 6.9% Swiss (2005-2009 5-year est.).

Economy: Single-family building permits issued: 8 (2010); Multi-family building permits issued: 10 (2010); Employment by occupation: 12.2% management, 26.0% professional, 13.7% services, 22.6% sales, 1.4% farming, 6.7% construction, 17.4% production (2005-2009 5-year est.).

Income: Per capita income: $27,953 (2010); Median household income: $59,075 (2010); Average household income: $75,080 (2010); Percent of households with income of $100,000 or more: 20.1% (2010); Poverty rate: 9.7% (2005-2009 5-year est.).

Taxes: Total city taxes per capita: $94 (2007); City property taxes per capita: $54 (2007).

Education: Percent of population age 25 and over with: High school diploma (including GED) or higher: 89.7% (2010); Bachelor's degree or higher: 26.2% (2010); Master's degree or higher: 9.4% (2010).

School District(s)
Eureka CUD 140 (PK-12)
2009-10 Enrollment: 1,622 . . . . (309) 467-3737

Four-year College(s)

Eureka College (Private, Not-for-profit, Christian Church (Disciples of Christ))

    Fall 2009 Enrollment: 766 . . . . (309) 467-3721

    2010-11 Tuition: In-state $18,045; Out-of-state $18,045

Housing: Homeownership rate: 70.6% (2010); Median home value: $126,099 (2010); Median contract rent: $339 per month (2005-2009 5-year est.); Median year structure built: 1969 (2005-2009 5-year est.).

Hospitals: Eureka Community Hospital (25 beds)

Safety: Violent crime rate: 18.4 per 10,000 population; Property crime rate: 173.4 per 10,000 population (2010).

Newspapers: Woodford County Journal (Local news; Circulation 1,810); Woodford Star (Local news; Circulation 14,000)

Transportation: Commute to work: 91.8% car, 0.0% public transportation, 4.4% walk, 3.1% work from home (2005-2009 5-year est.); Travel time to work: 33.2% less than 15 minutes, 38.5% 15 to 30 minutes, 24.3% 30 to 45 minutes, 1.8% 45 to 60 minutes, 2.3% 60 minutes or more (2005-2009 5-year est.)

GERMANTOWN HILLS (village). Aka Oak Grove Park. Covers a land area of 1.285 square miles and a water area of 0.043 square miles. Located at 40.76° N. Lat; 89.46° W. Long. Elevation is 804 feet.

Population: 1,293 (1990); 2,111 (2000); 2,833 (2010); 3,059 (2015 projected); Race: 96.3% White, 0.6% Black, 1.6% Asian, 1.4% Other, 1.2% Hispanic of any race (2010); Density: 2,205.2 persons per square mile (2010); Average household size: 2.93 (2010); Median age: 35.8 (2010); Males per 100 females: 96.1 (2010); Marriage status: 24.5% never married, 66.8% now married, 2.4% widowed, 6.3% divorced (2005-2009 5-year est.); Foreign born: 1.4% (2005-2009 5-year est.); Ancestry (includes multiple ancestries): 44.3% German, 20.3% Irish, 8.0% English, 8.0% American, 4.2% Polish (2005-2009 5-year est.).

Economy: Single-family building permits issued: 6 (2010); Multi-family building permits issued: 2 (2010); Employment by occupation: 21.9% management, 32.2% professional, 8.3% services, 26.0% sales, 0.0% farming, 4.0% construction, 7.6% production (2005-2009 5-year est.).

Income: Per capita income: $35,589 (2010); Median household income: $90,323 (2010); Average household income: $104,187 (2010); Percent of households with income of $100,000 or more: 42.5% (2010); Poverty rate: 2.2% (2005-2009 5-year est.).

Taxes: Total city taxes per capita: $90 (2007); City property taxes per capita: $76 (2007).

Education: Percent of population age 25 and over with: High school diploma (including GED) or higher: 96.7% (2010); Bachelor's degree or higher: 45.1% (2010); Master's degree or higher: 18.8% (2010).

School District(s)

Germantown Hills SD 69 (PK-08)

    2009-10 Enrollment: 950 . . . . (309) 383-2121

Housing: Homeownership rate: 92.4% (2010); Median home value: $193,922 (2010); Median contract rent: $760 per month (2005-2009 5-year est.); Median year structure built: 1995 (2005-2009 5-year est.).

Transportation: Commute to work: 95.1% car, 0.0% public transportation, 0.0% walk, 4.2% work from home (2005-2009 5-year est.); Travel time to work: 17.0% less than 15 minutes, 62.7% 15 to 30 minutes, 16.6% 30 to 45 minutes, 3.0% 45 to 60 minutes, 0.7% 60 minutes or more (2005-2009 5-year est.)

GOODFIELD (village). Covers a land area of 1.447 square miles and a water area of 0.007 square miles. Located at 40.62° N. Lat; 89.27° W. Long. Elevation is 741 feet.

Population: 588 (1990); 686 (2000); 793 (2010); 843 (2015 projected); Race: 98.1% White, 0.1% Black, 0.1% Asian, 1.6% Other, 0.1% Hispanic of any race (2010); Density: 548.1 persons per square mile (2010); Average household size: 2.94 (2010); Median age: 31.5 (2010); Males per 100 females: 103.3 (2010); Marriage status: 22.0% never married, 71.9% now married, 3.5% widowed, 2.6% divorced (2005-2009 5-year est.); Foreign born: 0.4% (2005-2009 5-year est.); Ancestry (includes multiple ancestries): 59.6% German, 9.0% European, 8.5% English, 8.1% Swiss, 6.5% Irish (2005-2009 5-year est.).

Economy: Single-family building permits issued: 3 (2010); Multi-family building permits issued: 0 (2010); Employment by occupation: 28.5% management, 23.3% professional, 13.7% services, 19.0% sales, 0.0% farming, 4.9% construction, 10.6% production (2005-2009 5-year est.).

Income: Per capita income: $27,129 (2010); Median household income: $73,843 (2010); Average household income: $79,944 (2010); Percent of

households with income of $100,000 or more: 24.9% (2010); Poverty rate: 1.6% (2005-2009 5-year est.).

Taxes: Total city taxes per capita: $440 (2007); City property taxes per capita: $311 (2007).

Education: Percent of population age 25 and over with: High school diploma (including GED) or higher: 92.5% (2010); Bachelor's degree or higher: 24.5% (2010); Master's degree or higher: 6.4% (2010).

School District(s)

Eureka CUD 140 (PK-12)

    2009-10 Enrollment: 1,622 . . . . (309) 467-3737

Housing: Homeownership rate: 83.3% (2010); Median home value: $139,041 (2010); Median contract rent: $358 per month (2005-2009 5-year est.); Median year structure built: 1974 (2005-2009 5-year est.).

Transportation: Commute to work: 94.0% car, 0.0% public transportation, 1.3% walk, 2.1% work from home (2005-2009 5-year est.); Travel time to work: 33.0% less than 15 minutes, 45.4% 15 to 30 minutes, 18.0% 30 to 45 minutes, 3.5% 45 to 60 minutes, 0.0% 60 minutes or more (2005-2009 5-year est.)

KAPPA (village). Covers a land area of 0.228 square miles and a water area of 0 square miles. Located at 40.67° N. Lat; 89.00° W. Long. Elevation is 738 feet.

Population: 134 (1990); 170 (2000); 188 (2010); 196 (2015 projected); Race: 97.9% White, 0.5% Black, 0.0% Asian, 1.6% Other, 1.6% Hispanic of any race (2010); Density: 826.3 persons per square mile (2010); Average household size: 2.65 (2010); Median age: 44.6 (2010); Males per 100 females: 104.3 (2010); Marriage status: 28.7% never married, 42.1% now married, 6.1% widowed, 23.2% divorced (2005-2009 5-year est.); Foreign born: 0.0% (2005-2009 5-year est.); Ancestry (includes multiple ancestries): 42.1% Irish, 25.2% German, 12.6% American, 5.4% English, 2.9% Italian (2005-2009 5-year est.).

Economy: Single-family building permits issued: 2 (2010); Multi-family building permits issued: 0 (2010); Employment by occupation: 5.5% management, 26.6% professional, 9.4% services, 14.8% sales, 0.0% farming, 15.6% construction, 28.1% production (2005-2009 5-year est.).

Income: Per capita income: $28,402 (2010); Median household income: $75,000 (2010); Average household income: $87,417 (2010); Percent of households with income of $100,000 or more: 33.3% (2010); Poverty rate: 32.8% (2005-2009 5-year est.).

Taxes: Total city taxes per capita: $197 (2007); City property taxes per capita: $47 (2007).

Education: Percent of population age 25 and over with: High school diploma (including GED) or higher: 89.0% (2010); Bachelor's degree or higher: 22.8% (2010); Master's degree or higher: 7.4% (2010).

Housing: Homeownership rate: 78.3% (2010); Median home value: $137,500 (2010); Median contract rent: $631 per month (2005-2009 5-year est.); Median year structure built: 1986 (2005-2009 5-year est.).

Transportation: Commute to work: 93.6% car, 0.0% public transportation, 4.0% walk, 2.4% work from home (2005-2009 5-year est.); Travel time to work: 27.0% less than 15 minutes, 32.8% 15 to 30 minutes, 13.1% 30 to 45 minutes, 20.5% 45 to 60 minutes, 6.6% 60 minutes or more (2005-2009 5-year est.)

LOWPOINT (unincorporated postal area, zip code 61545). Aka Low Point. Covers a land area of 31.763 square miles and a water area of 0.031 square miles. Located at 40.87° N. Lat; 89.37° W. Long.

Population: 651 (2000); Race: 100.0% White, 0.0% Black, 0.0% Asian, 0.0% Other, 0.0% Hispanic of any race (2000); Density: 20.5 persons per square mile (2000); Age: 29.6% under 18, 12.6% over 64 (2000); Marriage status: 19.7% never married, 66.8% now married, 8.5% widowed, 5.0% divorced (2000); Foreign born: 0.0% (2000); Ancestry (includes multiple ancestries): 48.5% German, 15.5% English, 8.4% Irish, 5.3% Swiss (2000).

Economy: Employment by occupation: 13.2% management, 16.5% professional, 15.9% services, 14.7% sales, 2.4% farming, 13.2% construction, 24.3% production (2000).

Income: Per capita income: $16,658 (2000); Median household income: $44,167 (2000); Poverty rate: 8.2% (2000).

Education: Percent of population age 25 and over with: High school diploma (including GED) or higher: 82.0% (2000); Bachelor's degree or higher: 9.9% (2000).

Housing: Homeownership rate: 86.2% (2000); Median home value: $69,000 (2000); Median contract rent: $444 per month (2000); Median year structure built: 1941 (2000).

Transportation: Commute to work: 94.3% car, 0.0% public transportation, 2.1% walk, 1.8% work from home (2000); Travel time to work: 24.4% less than 15 minutes, 36.0% 15 to 30 minutes, 17.4% 30 to 45 minutes, 12.8% 45 to 60 minutes, 9.5% 60 minutes or more (2000)

METAMORA (village). Covers a land area of 1.389 square miles and a water area of 0.002 square miles. Located at 40.79° N. Lat; 89.36° W. Long. Elevation is 817 feet.

History: Former capital of Woodford county. Old courthouse is now state memorial to Lincoln, who often argued cases here. Incorporated 1845.
Population: 2,597 (1990); 2,700 (2000); 2,904 (2010); 3,113 (2015 projected); Race: 96.7% White, 2.6% Black, 0.1% Asian, 0.6% Other, 0.9% Hispanic of any race (2010); Density: 2,091.4 persons per square mile (2010); Average household size: 2.46 (2010); Median age: 41.9 (2010); Males per 100 females: 90.6 (2010); Marriage status: 24.1% never married, 54.8% now married, 12.8% widowed, 8.3% divorced (2005-2009 5-year est.); Foreign born: 0.9% (2005-2009 5-year est.); Ancestry (includes multiple ancestries): 56.3% German, 10.7% American, 10.7% Irish, 7.8% English, 5.4% French (2005-2009 5-year est.).
Economy: Single-family building permits issued: 6 (2010); Multi-family building permits issued: 4 (2010); Employment by occupation: 17.3% management, 27.7% professional, 14.5% services, 21.7% sales, 0.0% farming, 7.3% construction, 11.4% production (2005-2009 5-year est.).
Income: Per capita income: $23,211 (2010); Median household income: $54,677 (2010); Average household income: $59,236 (2010); Percent of households with income of $100,000 or more: 11.6% (2010); Poverty rate: 6.1% (2005-2009 5-year est.).
Taxes: Total city taxes per capita: $158 (2007); City property taxes per capita: $155 (2007).
Education: Percent of population age 25 and over with: High school diploma (including GED) or higher: 91.3% (2010); Bachelor's degree or higher: 27.0% (2010); Master's degree or higher: 6.1% (2010).

School District(s)
Central Il Voc Ed Coop
   2009-10 Enrollment: n/a . . . . (309) 367-2783
County of Woodford School (09-12)
   2009-10 Enrollment: 983 . . . . (309) 367-4151
Metamora CCSD 1 (PK-08)
   2009-10 Enrollment: 861 . . . . (309) 367-2361
Housing: Homeownership rate: 77.6% (2010); Median home value: $140,806 (2010); Median contract rent: $509 per month (2005-2009 5-year est.); Median year structure built: 1974 (2005-2009 5-year est.).
Newspapers: Metamora Herald (Community news; Circulation 3,300); Washburn Leader (Community news; Circulation 3,600); Woodford County Shopper (Community news; Circulation 7,500)
Transportation: Commute to work: 90.9% car, 0.0% public transportation, 2.2% walk, 3.7% work from home (2005-2009 5-year est.); Travel time to work: 29.0% less than 15 minutes, 40.4% 15 to 30 minutes, 18.7% 30 to 45 minutes, 7.1% 45 to 60 minutes, 4.8% 60 minutes or more (2005-2009 5-year est.)

MINONK (city). Covers a land area of 1.366 square miles and a water area of 0 square miles. Located at 40.90° N. Lat; 89.03° W. Long. Elevation is 741 feet.

History: Incorporated 1867.
Population: 2,008 (1990); 2,168 (2000); 2,243 (2010); 2,289 (2015 projected); Race: 97.9% White, 0.1% Black, 0.0% Asian, 2.0% Other, 2.8% Hispanic of any race (2010); Density: 1,642.5 persons per square mile (2010); Average household size: 2.52 (2010); Median age: 38.7 (2010); Males per 100 females: 94.7 (2010); Marriage status: 20.7% never married, 56.9% now married, 13.5% widowed, 8.9% divorced (2005-2009 5-year est.); Foreign born: 1.7% (2005-2009 5-year est.); Ancestry (includes multiple ancestries): 45.3% German, 14.2% Irish, 12.2% American, 10.6% English, 8.5% Polish (2005-2009 5-year est.).
Economy: Single-family building permits issued: 2 (2010); Multi-family building permits issued: 0 (2010); Employment by occupation: 4.3% management, 17.2% professional, 18.4% services, 25.9% sales, 0.4% farming, 7.7% construction, 26.1% production (2005-2009 5-year est.).
Income: Per capita income: $22,869 (2010); Median household income: $53,807 (2010); Average household income: $58,789 (2010); Percent of households with income of $100,000 or more: 11.9% (2010); Poverty rate: 10.3% (2005-2009 5-year est.).
Taxes: Total city taxes per capita: $340 (2007); City property taxes per capita: $266 (2007).
Education: Percent of population age 25 and over with: High school diploma (including GED) or higher: 90.4% (2010); Bachelor's degree or higher: 18.1% (2010); Master's degree or higher: 7.9% (2010).

School District(s)
Fieldcrest CUSD 6 (PK-12)
   2009-10 Enrollment: 1,257 . . . . (309) 432-2177
Housing: Homeownership rate: 77.1% (2010); Median home value: $93,117 (2010); Median contract rent: $389 per month (2005-2009 5-year est.); Median year structure built: 1952 (2005-2009 5-year est.).
Newspapers: Minonk News-Dispatch (Local news; Circulation 750)
Transportation: Commute to work: 94.7% car, 0.0% public transportation, 1.5% walk, 1.7% work from home (2005-2009 5-year est.); Travel time to work: 45.6% less than 15 minutes, 15.3% 15 to 30 minutes, 26.3% 30 to 45 minutes, 4.6% 45 to 60 minutes, 8.2% 60 minutes or more (2005-2009 5-year est.)

PANOLA (village). Covers a land area of 0.202 square miles and a water area of 0 square miles. Located at 40.78° N. Lat; 89.02° W. Long. Elevation is 735 feet.

Population: 43 (1990); 33 (2000); 39 (2010); 41 (2015 projected); Race: 94.9% White, 5.1% Black, 0.0% Asian, 0.0% Other, 0.0% Hispanic of any race (2010); Density: 193.2 persons per square mile (2010); Average household size: 2.79 (2010); Median age: 41.4 (2010); Males per 100 females: 129.4 (2010); Marriage status: 8.8% never married, 82.4% now married, 0.0% widowed, 8.8% divorced (2005-2009 5-year est.); Foreign born: 0.0% (2005-2009 5-year est.); Ancestry (includes multiple ancestries): 76.3% German, 15.8% English, 7.9% Irish, 5.3% Scottish, 2.6% Swedish (2005-2009 5-year est.).
Economy: Employment by occupation: 50.0% management, 0.0% professional, 15.0% services, 20.0% sales, 0.0% farming, 15.0% construction, 0.0% production (2005-2009 5-year est.).
Income: Per capita income: $27,137 (2010); Median household income: $62,500 (2010); Average household income: $71,786 (2010); Percent of households with income of $100,000 or more: 28.6% (2010); Poverty rate: 7.9% (2005-2009 5-year est.).
Taxes: Total city taxes per capita: $29 (2007); City property taxes per capita: $0 (2007).
Education: Percent of population age 25 and over with: High school diploma (including GED) or higher: 97.0% (2010); Bachelor's degree or higher: 21.2% (2010); Master's degree or higher: 6.1% (2010).
Housing: Homeownership rate: 78.6% (2010); Median home value: $125,000 (2010); Median contract rent: n/a per month (2005-2009 5-year est.); Median year structure built: 1970 (2005-2009 5-year est.).
Transportation: Commute to work: 100.0% car, 0.0% public transportation, 0.0% walk, 0.0% work from home (2005-2009 5-year est.); Travel time to work: 40.0% less than 15 minutes, 0.0% 15 to 30 minutes, 60.0% 30 to 45 minutes, 0.0% 45 to 60 minutes, 0.0% 60 minutes or more (2005-2009 5-year est.)

ROANOKE (village). Covers a land area of 0.910 square miles and a water area of 0.037 square miles. Located at 40.79° N. Lat; 89.20° W. Long. Elevation is 732 feet.

History: Incorporated 1874.
Population: 1,932 (1990); 1,994 (2000); 2,098 (2010); 2,152 (2015 projected); Race: 98.9% White, 0.4% Black, 0.1% Asian, 0.7% Other, 0.1% Hispanic of any race (2010); Density: 2,306.3 persons per square mile (2010); Average household size: 2.57 (2010); Median age: 37.0 (2010); Males per 100 females: 96.4 (2010); Marriage status: 18.0% never married, 66.9% now married, 6.6% widowed, 8.4% divorced (2005-2009 5-year est.); Foreign born: 0.5% (2005-2009 5-year est.); Ancestry (includes multiple ancestries): 53.6% German, 11.1% American, 8.9% Irish, 7.6% Swiss, 6.9% Italian (2005-2009 5-year est.).
Economy: Single-family building permits issued: 4 (2010); Multi-family building permits issued: 0 (2010); Employment by occupation: 8.1% management, 21.2% professional, 19.4% services, 23.6% sales, 0.7% farming, 7.2% construction, 19.9% production (2005-2009 5-year est.).
Income: Per capita income: $26,089 (2010); Median household income: $55,234 (2010); Average household income: $67,544 (2010); Percent of households with income of $100,000 or more: 16.6% (2010); Poverty rate: 5.3% (2005-2009 5-year est.).
Taxes: Total city taxes per capita: $85 (2007); City property taxes per capita: $77 (2007).
Education: Percent of population age 25 and over with: High school diploma (including GED) or higher: 92.8% (2010); Bachelor's degree or higher: 17.8% (2010); Master's degree or higher: 5.7% (2010).

School District(s)
Roanoke Benson CUSD 60 (PK-12)
   2009-10 Enrollment: 607 . . . . (309) 923-8921

Housing: Homeownership rate: 82.2% (2010); Median home value: $122,468 (2010); Median contract rent: $462 per month (2005-2009 5-year est.); Median year structure built: 1956 (2005-2009 5-year est.).
Newspapers: Roanoke Review (Community news; Circulation 1,025)
Transportation: Commute to work: 94.8% car, 0.0% public transportation, 2.2% walk, 1.2% work from home (2005-2009 5-year est.); Travel time to work: 36.8% less than 15 minutes, 29.5% 15 to 30 minutes, 27.5% 30 to 45 minutes, 3.7% 45 to 60 minutes, 2.5% 60 minutes or more (2005-2009 5-year est.)

SECOR (village). Covers a land area of 0.355 square miles and a water area of 0 square miles. Located at 40.74° N. Lat; 89.13° W. Long. Elevation is 732 feet.
Population: 391 (1990); 379 (2000); 387 (2010); 397 (2015 projected); Race: 98.4% White, 0.8% Black, 0.3% Asian, 0.5% Other, 0.3% Hispanic of any race (2010); Density: 1,091.2 persons per square mile (2010); Average household size: 2.74 (2010); Median age: 36.9 (2010); Males per 100 females: 95.5 (2010); Marriage status: 22.5% never married, 54.3% now married, 3.8% widowed, 19.4% divorced (2005-2009 5-year est.); Foreign born: 0.7% (2005-2009 5-year est.); Ancestry (includes multiple ancestries): 38.6% German, 30.6% American, 7.7% Irish, 7.7% Italian, 3.6% French (2005-2009 5-year est.).
Economy: Single-family building permits issued: 0 (2010); Multi-family building permits issued: 0 (2010); Employment by occupation: 6.4% management, 8.4% professional, 15.3% services, 21.2% sales, 3.4% farming, 13.8% construction, 31.5% production (2005-2009 5-year est.).
Income: Per capita income: $26,747 (2010); Median household income: $57,267 (2010); Average household income: $71,064 (2010); Percent of households with income of $100,000 or more: 17.0% (2010); Poverty rate: 7.7% (2005-2009 5-year est.).
Taxes: Total city taxes per capita: $123 (2007); City property taxes per capita: $123 (2007).
Education: Percent of population age 25 and over with: High school diploma (including GED) or higher: 90.1% (2010); Bachelor's degree or higher: 11.8% (2010); Master's degree or higher: 4.9% (2010).
Housing: Homeownership rate: 80.1% (2010); Median home value: $118,548 (2010); Median contract rent: $379 per month (2005-2009 5-year est.); Median year structure built: 1954 (2005-2009 5-year est.).
Transportation: Commute to work: 94.9% car, 0.0% public transportation, 0.0% walk, 5.1% work from home (2005-2009 5-year est.); Travel time to work: 25.7% less than 15 minutes, 32.1% 15 to 30 minutes, 24.6% 30 to 45 minutes, 15.5% 45 to 60 minutes, 2.1% 60 minutes or more (2005-2009 5-year est.)

SPRING BAY (village). Covers a land area of 0.806 square miles and a water area of 0.331 square miles. Located at 40.82° N. Lat; 89.52° W. Long. Elevation is 469 feet.
Population: 469 (1990); 436 (2000); 450 (2010); 455 (2015 projected); Race: 96.7% White, 1.6% Black, 0.7% Asian, 1.1% Other, 0.7% Hispanic of any race (2010); Density: 558.3 persons per square mile (2010); Average household size: 2.54 (2010); Median age: 43.0 (2010); Males per 100 females: 99.1 (2010); Marriage status: 24.6% never married, 53.5% now married, 3.5% widowed, 18.3% divorced (2005-2009 5-year est.); Foreign born: 0.9% (2005-2009 5-year est.); Ancestry (includes multiple ancestries): 34.8% German, 19.8% Irish, 13.5% American, 8.8% Polish, 8.3% English (2005-2009 5-year est.).
Economy: Single-family building permits issued: 1 (2010); Multi-family building permits issued: 0 (2010); Employment by occupation: 4.7% management, 10.9% professional, 17.8% services, 28.1% sales, 1.6% farming, 17.5% construction, 19.4% production (2005-2009 5-year est.).

Income: Per capita income: $27,313 (2010); Median household income: $62,972 (2010); Average household income: $69,605 (2010); Percent of households with income of $100,000 or more: 18.6% (2010); Poverty rate: 6.8% (2005-2009 5-year est.).
Taxes: Total city taxes per capita: $23 (2007); City property taxes per capita: $21 (2007).
Education: Percent of population age 25 and over with: High school diploma (including GED) or higher: 93.6% (2010); Bachelor's degree or higher: 21.9% (2010); Master's degree or higher: 9.1% (2010).
Housing: Homeownership rate: 86.4% (2010); Median home value: $134,574 (2010); Median contract rent: $479 per month (2005-2009 5-year est.); Median year structure built: 1974 (2005-2009 5-year est.).
Transportation: Commute to work: 95.9% car, 0.0% public transportation, 2.9% walk, 1.3% work from home (2005-2009 5-year est.); Travel time to work: 12.9% less than 15 minutes, 54.7% 15 to 30 minutes, 23.8% 30 to 45 minutes, 7.4% 45 to 60 minutes, 1.3% 60 minutes or more (2005-2009 5-year est.)

WASHBURN (village). Covers a land area of 0.727 square miles and a water area of 0 square miles. Located at 40.92° N. Lat; 89.29° W. Long. Elevation is 686 feet.
Population: 1,154 (1990); 1,147 (2000); 1,102 (2010); 1,088 (2015 projected); Race: 94.8% White, 1.0% Black, 0.2% Asian, 4.0% Other, 2.2% Hispanic of any race (2010); Density: 1,514.8 persons per square mile (2010); Average household size: 2.61 (2010); Median age: 34.9 (2010); Males per 100 females: 102.6 (2010); Marriage status: 23.3% never married, 55.8% now married, 8.1% widowed, 12.8% divorced (2005-2009 5-year est.); Foreign born: 0.0% (2005-2009 5-year est.); Ancestry (includes multiple ancestries): 41.8% German, 15.4% Irish, 13.1% American, 12.2% English, 3.6% Italian (2005-2009 5-year est.).
Economy: Single-family building permits issued: 0 (2010); Multi-family building permits issued: 0 (2010); Employment by occupation: 10.9% management, 21.4% professional, 13.8% services, 24.7% sales, 0.0% farming, 8.9% construction, 20.4% production (2005-2009 5-year est.).
Income: Per capita income: $27,480 (2010); Median household income: $63,911 (2010); Average household income: $72,316 (2010); Percent of households with income of $100,000 or more: 20.9% (2010); Poverty rate: 8.8% (2005-2009 5-year est.).
Taxes: Total city taxes per capita: $207 (2007); City property taxes per capita: $205 (2007).
Education: Percent of population age 25 and over with: High school diploma (including GED) or higher: 89.0% (2010); Bachelor's degree or higher: 15.9% (2010); Master's degree or higher: 7.6% (2010).
School District(s)
Lowpoint-Washburn CUSD 21 (PK-12)
    2009-10 Enrollment: 425 . . . . (309) 248-7522
Marshall/Putnam/Woodford/Roe (06-12)
    2009-10 Enrollment: n/a . . . . (309) 248-8212
Housing: Homeownership rate: 77.0% (2010); Median home value: $97,792 (2010); Median contract rent: $376 per month (2005-2009 5-year est.); Median year structure built: 1944 (2005-2009 5-year est.).
Safety: Violent crime rate: 0.0 per 10,000 population; Property crime rate: 36.5 per 10,000 population (2010).
Transportation: Commute to work: 92.0% car, 0.0% public transportation, 4.9% walk, 0.6% work from home (2005-2009 5-year est.); Travel time to work: 32.4% less than 15 minutes, 26.5% 15 to 30 minutes, 20.3% 30 to 45 minutes, 16.2% 45 to 60 minutes, 4.6% 60 minutes or more (2005-2009 5-year est.);

A

Abingdon city *Knox County*, 205
Adair postal area *McDonough County*, 279
Adams County, 1 - 4
Addieville village *Washington County*, 402
Addison village *Du Page County*, 107
Adeline village *Ogle County*, 315
Albany village *Whiteside County*, 412
Albers village *Clinton County*, 41
Albion city *Edwards County*, 121
Aledo city *Mercer County*, 299
Alexander County, 5 - 6
Alexander postal area *Morgan County*, 310
Alexis village *Warren County*, 399
Algonquin village *McHenry County*, 283
Alhambra village *Madison County*, 259
Allendale village *Wabash County*, 398
Allenville village *Moultrie County*, 313
Allerton village *Vermilion County*, 391
Alma village *Marion County*, 268
Alorton village *Saint Clair County*, 370
Alpha village *Henry County*, 159
Alsey village *Scott County*, 364
Alsip village *Cook County*, 50
Altamont city *Effingham County*, 122
Alto Pass village *Union County*, 389
Alton city *Madison County*, 259
Altona village *Knox County*, 205
Alvan village *Vermilion County*, 392
Amboy city *Lee County*, 235
Anchor village *McLean County*, 291
Ancona postal area *Livingston County*, 239
Andalusia village *Rock Island County*, 347
Andover village *Henry County*, 159
Anna city *Union County*, 389
Annapolis postal area *Crawford County*, 93
Annawan village *Henry County*, 159
Antioch village *Lake County*, 217
Apple River village *Jo Daviess County*, 181
Arcola city *Douglas County*, 103
Arenzville village *Cass County*, 24
Argenta village *Macon County*, 247
Arlington Heights village *Cook County*, 51
Arlington village *Bureau County*, 13
Armington village *Tazewell County*, 384
Armstrong postal area *Vermilion County*, 392
Aroma Park village *Kankakee County*, 196
Arrowsmith village *McLean County*, 291
Arthur village *Douglas County*, 104
Ashkum village *Iroquois County*, 164
Ashland village *Cass County*, 24
Ashley city *Washington County*, 402
Ashmore village *Coles County*, 45
Ashton village *Lee County*, 236
Assumption city *Christian County*, 33
Astoria town *Fulton County*, 135
Athens city *Menard County*, 298
Atkinson town *Henry County*, 160
Atlanta city *Logan County*, 244
Atwater postal area *Macoupin County*, 251
Atwood village *Piatt County*, 327
Auburn city *Sangamon County*, 355
Augusta village *Hancock County*, 150
Aurora city *Kane County*, 188
Ava city *Jackson County*, 170
Aviston village *Clinton County*, 42
Avon village *Fulton County*, 135

B

Baileyville postal area *Ogle County*, 315
Baldwin village *Randolph County*, 341
Banner village *Fulton County*, 135
Bannockburn village *Lake County*, 217
Bardolph village *McDonough County*, 279
Barnhill postal area *Wayne County*, 405
Barrington Hills village *Cook County*, 51
Barrington village *Cook County*, 51
Barry city *Pike County*, 330
Bartelso village *Clinton County*, 42
Bartlett village *Du Page County*, 107
Bartonville village *Peoria County*, 320
Basco village *Hancock County*, 151
Batavia city *Kane County*, 188
Batchtown village *Calhoun County*, 20
Bath village *Mason County*, 275
Bay View Gardens village *Woodford County*, 434
Baylis village *Pike County*, 330
Beach Park village *Lake County*, 218
Beardstown city *Cass County*, 25
Beason postal area *Logan County*, 244
Beaverville village *Iroquois County*, 164
Beckemeyer village *Clinton County*, 42
Bedford Park village *Cook County*, 52
Beecher City village *Effingham County*, 123
Beecher village *Will County*, 416
Belgium village *Vermilion County*, 392
Belknap village *Johnson County*, 185
Belle Prairie City town *Hamilton County*, 149
Belle Rive village *Jefferson County*, 176
Belleville city *Saint Clair County*, 370
Bellevue village *Peoria County*, 320
Bellflower village *McLean County*, 292
Bellmont village *Wabash County*, 398
Bellwood village *Cook County*, 52
Belvidere city *Boone County*, 10
Bement village *Piatt County*, 327
Benld city *Macoupin County*, 252
Bensenville village *Du Page County*, 107
Benson village *Woodford County*, 435
Bentley town *Hancock County*, 151
Benton city *Franklin County*, 130
Berkeley village *Cook County*, 52
Berlin village *Sangamon County*, 355
Berwick postal area *Warren County*, 400
Berwyn city *Cook County*, 53
Bethalto village *Madison County*, 260
Bethany village *Moultrie County*, 313
Big Rock village *Kane County*, 189
Biggsville village *Henderson County*, 156
Bingham village *Fayette County*, 125
Birds village *Lawrence County*, 233
Bishop Hill village *Henry County*, 160
Bismarck village *Vermilion County*, 392
Blackstone postal area *Livingston County*, 239
Blandinsville village *McDonough County*, 279
Bloomingdale village *Du Page County*, 108
Bloomington city *McLean County*, 292
Blue Island city *Cook County*, 53
Blue Mound village *Macon County*, 247
Bluffs village *Scott County*, 365
Bluford village *Jefferson County*, 176
Bolingbrook village *Will County*, 416
Bond County, 7 - 8
Bondville village *Champaign County*, 26

Bone Gap village *Edwards County*, 121
Bonfield village *Kankakee County*, 196
Bonnie village *Jefferson County*, 176
Boody postal area *Macon County*, 248
Boone County, 9 - 10
Boulder Hill CDP *Kendall County*, 202
Bourbonnais village *Kankakee County*, 196
Bowen village *Hancock County*, 151
Braceville village *Grundy County*, 145
Bradford village *Stark County*, 379
Bradley village *Kankakee County*, 197
Braidwood city *Will County*, 417
Breese city *Clinton County*, 42
Bridgeport city *Lawrence County*, 234
Bridgeview village *Cook County*, 53
Brighton village *Macoupin County*, 252
Brimfield village *Peoria County*, 320
Bristol postal area *Kendall County*, 202
Broadlands village *Champaign County*, 26
Broadview village *Cook County*, 54
Broadwell village *Logan County*, 244
Brocton village *Edgar County*, 118
Brookfield village *Cook County*, 54
Brooklyn village *Saint Clair County*, 371
Brookport city *Massac County*, 278
Broughton village *Hamilton County*, 149
Brown County, 11 - 12
Browning village *Schuyler County*, 363
Browns village *Edwards County*, 121
Brownstown village *Fayette County*, 125
Brussels village *Calhoun County*, 20
Bryant village *Fulton County*, 136
Buckingham village *Kankakee County*, 197
Buckley village *Iroquois County*, 164
Buckner village *Franklin County*, 131
Buda village *Bureau County*, 14
Buffalo Grove village *Lake County*, 218
Buffalo village *Sangamon County*, 356
Bull Valley village *McHenry County*, 283
Bulpitt village *Christian County*, 34
Buncombe village *Johnson County*, 185
Bunker Hill city *Macoupin County*, 252
Bureau County, 13 - 18
Bureau Junction village *Bureau County*, 14
Burlington village *Kane County*, 189
Burnham village *Cook County*, 55
Burnside postal area *Hancock County*, 151
Burnt Prairie village *White County*, 409
Burr Ridge village *Du Page County*, 108
Bush village *Williamson County*, 426
Bushnell city *McDonough County*, 280
Butler village *Montgomery County*, 304
Byron city *Ogle County*, 315

C

Cabery village *Ford County*, 128
Cahokia village *Saint Clair County*, 371
Cairo city *Alexander County*, 6
Caledonia village *Boone County*, 10
Calhoun County, 19 - 20
Calhoun village *Richland County*, 345
Calumet City city *Cook County*, 55
Calumet Park village *Cook County*, 55
Camargo village *Douglas County*, 104
Cambria village *Williamson County*, 426
Cambridge village *Henry County*, 160
Camden village *Schuyler County*, 363

CDP = Census Designated Place

Cameron postal area *Warren County*, 400
Camp Point village *Adams County*, 1
Campbell Hill village *Jackson County*, 170
Campton Hills village *Kane County*, 189
Campus village *Livingston County*, 239
Canton city *Fulton County*, 136
Cantrall village *Sangamon County*, 356
Capron village *Boone County*, 10
Carbon Cliff village *Rock Island County*, 348
Carbon Hill village *Grundy County*, 145
Carbondale city *Jackson County*, 170
Carlinville city *Macoupin County*, 252
Carlock village *McLean County*, 292
Carlyle city *Clinton County*, 43
Carman postal area *Henderson County*, 156
Carmi city *White County*, 409
Carol Stream village *Du Page County*, 108
Carpentersville village *Kane County*, 189
Carrier Mills village *Saline County*, 353
Carroll County, 21 - 23
Carrollton city *Greene County*, 142
Carterville city *Williamson County*, 426
Carthage city *Hancock County*, 151
Cary village *McHenry County*, 283
Casey city *Clark County*, 37
Caseyville village *Saint Clair County*, 372
Cass County, 24
Catlin village *Vermilion County*, 393
Cave-In-Rock village *Hardin County*, 155
Cedar Point village *La Salle County*, 209
Cedarville village *Stephenson County*, 380
Central City village *Marion County*, 269
Centralia city *Marion County*, 269
Centreville city *Saint Clair County*, 372
Cerro Gordo village *Piatt County*, 328
Chadwick village *Carroll County*, 22
Chambersburg postal area *Pike County*, 331
Champaign County, 25 - 32
Champaign city *Champaign County*, 27
Chana postal area *Ogle County*, 316
Chandlerville village *Cass County*, 25
Channahon village *Will County*, 417
Channel Lake CDP *Lake County*, 218
Chapin village *Morgan County*, 310
Charleston city *Coles County*, 46
Chatham village *Sangamon County*, 356
Chatsworth town *Livingston County*, 239
Chebanse village *Iroquois County*, 164
Chenoa city *McLean County*, 293
Cherry Valley village *Winnebago County*, 430
Cherry village *Bureau County*, 14
Chester city *Randolph County*, 341
Chesterfield village *Macoupin County*, 253
Chestnut postal area *Logan County*, 244
Chicago Heights city *Cook County*, 58
Chicago Ridge village *Cook County*, 59
Chicago city *Cook County*, 56
Chillicothe city *Peoria County*, 320
Chrisman city *Edgar County*, 118
Christian County, 33 - 36
Christopher city *Franklin County*, 131
Cicero town *Cook County*, 59
Cisco village *Piatt County*, 328
Cisne village *Wayne County*, 405
Cissna Park village *Iroquois County*, 165
Clare postal area *De Kalb County*, 99
Claremont village *Richland County*, 346
Clarendon Hills village *Du Page County*, 109

Clark County, 37 - 38
Clay City village *Clay County*, 39
Clay County, 39 - 40
Clayton village *Adams County*, 1
Clear Lake village *Sangamon County*, 356
Cleveland village *Henry County*, 160
Clifton village *Iroquois County*, 165
Clinton County, 41 - 44
Clinton city *De Witt County*, 97
Coal City village *Grundy County*, 145
Coal Valley village *Rock Island County*, 348
Coalton village *Montgomery County*, 305
Coatsburg village *Adams County*, 2
Cobden village *Union County*, 390
Coffeen city *Montgomery County*, 305
Colchester city *McDonough County*, 280
Coles County, 45 - 46
Coleta village *Whiteside County*, 412
Colfax village *McLean County*, 293
Collinsville city *Madison County*, 260
Collison postal area *Vermilion County*, 393
Colona city *Henry County*, 161
Colp village *Williamson County*, 427
Columbia city *Monroe County*, 302
Columbus village *Adams County*, 2
Compton village *Lee County*, 236
Concord village *Morgan County*, 310
Congerville village *Woodford County*, 435
Cook County, 47 - 91
Cooksville village *McLean County*, 293
Cordova village *Rock Island County*, 348
Cornell village *Livingston County*, 240
Cortland town *De Kalb County*, 99
Cottage Hills postal area *Madison County*, 261
Coulterville village *Randolph County*, 341
Country Club Hills city *Cook County*, 60
Countryside city *Cook County*, 60
Cowden village *Shelby County*, 366
Coyne Center CDP *Rock Island County*, 348
Crainville village *Williamson County*, 427
Crawford County, 92 - 94
Creal Springs city *Williamson County*, 427
Crescent City village *Iroquois County*, 165
Crest Hill city *Will County*, 417
Creston village *Ogle County*, 316
Crestwood village *Cook County*, 60
Crete village *Will County*, 417
Creve Coeur village *Tazewell County*, 384
Cropsey postal area *McLean County*, 293
Crossville village *White County*, 409
Crystal Lake city *McHenry County*, 283
Crystal Lawns CDP *Will County*, 418
Cuba city *Fulton County*, 136
Cullom village *Livingston County*, 240
Cumberland County, 95
Curran village *Sangamon County*, 357
Cutler village *Perry County*, 325
Cypress village *Johnson County*, 185

D

Dahinda postal area *Knox County*, 205
Dahlgren village *Hamilton County*, 149
Dakota village *Stephenson County*, 381
Dale postal area *Hamilton County*, 149
Dallas City city *Hancock County*, 152
Dalton City village *Moultrie County*, 313
Dalzell village *Bureau County*, 14

Damiansville village *Clinton County*, 43
Dana village *La Salle County*, 209
Danforth village *Iroquois County*, 165
Danvers village *McLean County*, 294
Danville city *Vermilion County*, 393
Darien city *Du Page County*, 109
Davis Junction village *Ogle County*, 316
Davis village *Stephenson County*, 381
Dawson village *Sangamon County*, 357
De Kalb County, 98 - 102
De Land village *Piatt County*, 328
De Pue village *Bureau County*, 15
De Soto village *Jackson County*, 171
De Witt County, 96 - 97
De Witt village *De Witt County*, 97
Decatur city *Macon County*, 248
Deer Creek village *Tazewell County*, 385
Deer Grove village *Whiteside County*, 412
Deer Park village *Lake County*, 218
Deerfield village *Lake County*, 219
DeKalb city *De Kalb County*, 99
Delavan city *Tazewell County*, 385
Dennison postal area *Clark County*, 38
Des Plaines city *Cook County*, 60
Detroit village *Pike County*, 331
Dewey postal area *Champaign County*, 27
Dewitt postal area *De Witt County*, 97
Diamond village *Grundy County*, 146
Dieterich village *Effingham County*, 123
Divernon village *Sangamon County*, 357
Dix village *Jefferson County*, 176
Dixmoor village *Cook County*, 61
Dixon city *Lee County*, 236
Dolton village *Cook County*, 61
Dongola village *Union County*, 390
Donnellson village *Montgomery County*, 305
Donovan village *Iroquois County*, 166
Dorchester village *Macoupin County*, 253
Dorsey postal area *Madison County*, 261
Douglas County, 103 - 104
Dover village *Bureau County*, 15
Dow postal area *Jersey County*, 179
Dowell village *Jackson County*, 171
Downers Grove village *Du Page County*, 109
Downs village *McLean County*, 294
Du Bois village *Washington County*, 402
Du Page County, 105 - 117
Du Quoin city *Perry County*, 325
Dundas postal area *Richland County*, 346
Dundee postal area *Kane County*, 190
Dunfermline village *Fulton County*, 136
Dunlap village *Peoria County*, 321
Dupo village *Saint Clair County*, 372
Durand village *Winnebago County*, 431
Dwight village *Livingston County*, 240

E

Eagarville village *Macoupin County*, 253
Earlville city *La Salle County*, 210
East Alton village *Madison County*, 261
East Brooklyn village *Grundy County*, 146
East Cape Girardeau village *Alexander County*, 6
East Carondelet village *Saint Clair County*, 372
East Dubuque city *Jo Daviess County*, 182
East Dundee village *Kane County*, 190
East Galesburg village *Knox County*, 205

CDP = Census Designated Place

CDP = Census Designated Place

Libertyville village *Lake County*, 225
Lily Lake village *Kane County*, 192
Lima village *Adams County*, 3
Limestone village *Kankakee County*, 199
Lincoln city *Logan County*, 245
Lincolnshire village *Lake County*, 226
Lincolnwood village *Cook County*, 72
Lindenhurst village *Lake County*, 226
Lindenwood postal area *Ogle County*, 317
Lisbon village *Kendall County*, 202
Lisle village *Du Page County*, 112
Litchfield city *Montgomery County*, 307
Little York village *Warren County*, 400
Littleton village *Schuyler County*, 363
Liverpool village *Fulton County*, 138
Livingston County, 238 - 242
Livingston village *Madison County*, 264
Loami village *Sangamon County*, 359
Lockport city *Will County*, 421
Loda village *Iroquois County*, 167
Logan County, 243 - 246
Lomax village *Henderson County*, 157
Lombard village *Du Page County*, 112
London Mills village *Fulton County*, 138
Long Creek village *Macon County*, 249
Long Grove village *Lake County*, 226
Long Lake CDP *Lake County*, 227
Long Point village *Livingston County*, 242
Longview village *Champaign County*, 29
Loraine village *Adams County*, 3
Lostant village *La Salle County*, 211
Louisville village *Clay County*, 40
Loves Park city *Winnebago County*, 431
Lovington village *Moultrie County*, 314
Lowpoint postal area *Woodford County*, 436
Ludlow village *Champaign County*, 29
Lyndon village *Whiteside County*, 413
Lynn Center postal area *Henry County*, 162
Lynnville village *Morgan County*, 311
Lynwood village *Cook County*, 72
Lyons village *Cook County*, 72

M

Macedonia village *Hamilton County*, 149
Machesney Park village *Winnebago County*, 431
Mackinaw village *Tazewell County*, 386
Macomb city *McDonough County*, 281
Macon County, 247 - 250
Macon city *Macon County*, 249
Macoupin County, 251 - 257
Madison County, 258 - 267
Madison city *Madison County*, 264
Maeystown village *Monroe County*, 303
Magnolia village *Putnam County*, 339
Mahomet village *Champaign County*, 29
Makanda village *Jackson County*, 172
Malden village *Bureau County*, 16
Malta village *De Kalb County*, 101
Manchester village *Scott County*, 365
Manhattan village *Will County*, 421
Manito village *Mason County*, 276
Manlius village *Bureau County*, 16
Mansfield village *Piatt County*, 329
Manteno village *Kankakee County*, 199
Maple Park village *Kane County*, 192
Mapleton village *Peoria County*, 322
Maquon village *Knox County*, 207

Marengo city *McHenry County*, 287
Marietta village *Fulton County*, 138
Marine village *Madison County*, 264
Marion County, 268 - 271
Marion city *Williamson County*, 428
Marissa village *Saint Clair County*, 375
Mark village *Putnam County*, 339
Markham city *Cook County*, 73
Maroa city *Macon County*, 249
Marquette Heights city *Tazewell County*, 386
Marseilles city *La Salle County*, 211
Marshall County, 272 - 274
Marshall city *Clark County*, 38
Martinsville city *Clark County*, 38
Martinton village *Iroquois County*, 167
Maryville village *Madison County*, 264
Mascoutah city *Saint Clair County*, 375
Mason City city *Mason County*, 277
Mason County, 275 - 276
Mason town *Effingham County*, 124
Massac County, 277 - 278
Matherville village *Mercer County*, 300
Matteson village *Cook County*, 73
Mattoon city *Coles County*, 47
Maunie village *White County*, 410
Maywood village *Cook County*, 73
Mazon village *Grundy County*, 147
McClure village *Alexander County*, 6
McConnell postal area *Stephenson County*, 382
McCook village *Cook County*, 74
McCullom Lake village *McHenry County*, 287
McDonough County, 279 - 281
McHenry County, 282 - 290
McHenry city *McHenry County*, 287
McLean County, 291 - 296
McLean village *McLean County*, 296
McLeansboro city *Hamilton County*, 150
McNabb village *Putnam County*, 340
Mechanicsburg village *Sangamon County*, 359
Media village *Henderson County*, 157
Medinah postal area *Du Page County*, 113
Medora village *Macoupin County*, 255
Melrose Park village *Cook County*, 74
Melvin village *Ford County*, 129
Menard County, 297 - 298
Mendon village *Adams County*, 3
Mendota city *La Salle County*, 212
Menominee village *Jo Daviess County*, 183
Mercer County, 299 - 301
Meredosia village *Morgan County*, 311
Merrionette Park village *Cook County*, 74
Metamora village *Woodford County*, 437
Metcalf village *Edgar County*, 119
Metropolis city *Massac County*, 278
Mettawa village *Lake County*, 227
Michael postal area *Calhoun County*, 21
Middletown village *Logan County*, 246
Midlothian village *Cook County*, 74
Milan village *Rock Island County*, 350
Milford village *Iroquois County*, 167
Mill Creek village *Union County*, 390
Mill Shoals village *White County*, 410
Millbrook village *Kendall County*, 202
Milledgeville village *Carroll County*, 22
Miller City postal area *Alexander County*, 6
Millington village *Kendall County*, 202

Millstadt village *Saint Clair County*, 375
Milmine postal area *Piatt County*, 329
Milton village *Pike County*, 332
Mineral village *Bureau County*, 16
Minier village *Tazewell County*, 387
Minonk city *Woodford County*, 437
Minooka village *Grundy County*, 147
Mode postal area *Shelby County*, 367
Modesto village *Macoupin County*, 255
Modoc postal area *Randolph County*, 342
Mokena village *Will County*, 421
Moline city *Rock Island County*, 350
Momence city *Kankakee County*, 199
Monee village *Will County*, 422
Monmouth city *Warren County*, 401
Monroe Center village *Ogle County*, 317
Monroe County, 302 - 303
Montgomery County, 304 - 308
Montgomery village *Kane County*, 193
Monticello city *Piatt County*, 329
Montrose village *Effingham County*, 124
Morgan County, 309 - 312
Moro postal area *Madison County*, 265
Morris city *Grundy County*, 147
Morrison city *Whiteside County*, 413
Morrisonville village *Christian County*, 35
Morton Grove village *Cook County*, 75
Morton village *Tazewell County*, 387
Moultrie County, 313
Mound City city *Pulaski County*, 337
Mound Station village *Brown County*, 12
Mounds city *Pulaski County*, 337
Mount Auburn village *Christian County*, 35
Mount Carmel city *Wabash County*, 399
Mount Carroll city *Carroll County*, 23
Mount Clare village *Macoupin County*, 255
Mount Erie village *Wayne County*, 407
Mount Morris village *Ogle County*, 317
Mount Olive city *Macoupin County*, 255
Mount Prospect village *Cook County*, 75
Mount Pulaski city *Logan County*, 246
Mount Sterling city *Brown County*, 12
Mount Vernon city *Jefferson County*, 177
Mount Zion village *Macon County*, 250
Moweaqua village *Shelby County*, 367
Mozier postal area *Calhoun County*, 21
Muddy village *Saline County*, 354
Mulberry Grove village *Bond County*, 8
Mulkeytown postal area *Franklin County*, 132
Muncie village *Vermilion County*, 395
Mundelein village *Lake County*, 227
Murphysboro city *Jackson County*, 172
Murrayville village *Morgan County*, 312

N

Naperville city *Du Page County*, 113
Naplate village *La Salle County*, 212
Naples town *Scott County*, 365
Nashville city *Washington County*, 403
Nason city *Jefferson County*, 177
Nauvoo city *Hancock County*, 153
Nebo village *Pike County*, 332
Nelson village *Lee County*, 237
Neoga city *Cumberland County*, 96
Neponset village *Bureau County*, 17
New Athens village *Saint Clair County*, 376
New Baden village *Clinton County*, 44
New Bedford village *Bureau County*, 17

CDP = Census Designated Place

New Berlin village *Sangamon County*, 359
New Boston city *Mercer County*, 300
New Burnside village *Johnson County*, 186
New Canton town *Pike County*, 333
New Douglas village *Madison County*, 265
New Grand Chain village *Pulaski County*, 337
New Haven village *Gallatin County*, 141
New Holland village *Logan County*, 246
New Lenox village *Will County*, 422
New Milford village *Winnebago County*, 432
New Minden village *Washington County*, 403
New Salem village *Pike County*, 333
New Windsor postal area *Mercer County*, 301
Newark village *Kendall County*, 203
Newman city *Douglas County*, 105
Newton city *Jasper County*, 174
Niantic village *Macon County*, 250
Niles village *Cook County*, 76
Nilwood town *Macoupin County*, 256
Niota postal area *Hancock County*, 153
Noble village *Richland County*, 346
Nokomis city *Montgomery County*, 307
Nora village *Jo Daviess County*, 183
Normal town *McLean County*, 296
Norridge village *Cook County*, 76
Norris City village *White County*, 410
Norris village *Fulton County*, 139
North Aurora village *Kane County*, 193
North Barrington village *Lake County*, 228
North Chicago city *Lake County*, 228
North City village *Franklin County*, 132
North Henderson village *Mercer County*, 301
North Pekin village *Tazewell County*, 387
North Riverside village *Cook County*, 76
North Utica village *La Salle County*, 212
Northbrook village *Cook County*, 77
Northfield village *Cook County*, 77
Northlake city *Cook County*, 77
Norwood village *Peoria County*, 323

O

O'Fallon city *Saint Clair County*, 376
Oak Brook village *Du Page County*, 113
Oak Forest city *Cook County*, 78
Oak Grove village *Rock Island County*, 350
Oak Lawn village *Cook County*, 78
Oak Park village *Cook County*, 79
Oakbrook Terrace city *Du Page County*, 114
Oakdale village *Washington County*, 404
Oakford village *Menard County*, 298
Oakland city *Coles County*, 47
Oakley postal area *Macon County*, 250
Oakwood Hills village *McHenry County*, 288
Oakwood village *Vermilion County*, 395
Oblong village *Crawford County*, 93
Oconee village *Shelby County*, 368
Odell village *Livingston County*, 242
Odin village *Marion County*, 270
Ogden village *Champaign County*, 29
Ogle County, 314 - 318
Oglesby city *La Salle County*, 212
Ohio village *Bureau County*, 17
Ohlman village *Montgomery County*, 307
Okawville village *Washington County*, 404
Old Mill Creek village *Lake County*, 228
Old Ripley village *Bond County*, 8
Old Shawneetown village *Gallatin County*, 141

Olive Branch postal area *Alexander County*, 7
Olmsted village *Pulaski County*, 337
Olney city *Richland County*, 346
Olympia Fields village *Cook County*, 79
Omaha village *Gallatin County*, 141
Onarga village *Iroquois County*, 167
Oneida city *Knox County*, 207
Opdyke postal area *Jefferson County*, 178
Opheim postal area *Henry County*, 162
Oquawka village *Henderson County*, 158
Orangeville village *Stephenson County*, 382
Oreana village *Macon County*, 250
Oregon city *Ogle County*, 318
Orient city *Franklin County*, 132
Orion village *Henry County*, 163
Orland Hills village *Cook County*, 79
Orland Park village *Cook County*, 80
Osco postal area *Henry County*, 163
Oswego village *Kendall County*, 203
Ottawa city *La Salle County*, 213
Otterville town *Jersey County*, 181
Owaneco village *Christian County*, 35
Ozark postal area *Johnson County*, 186

P

Palatine village *Cook County*, 80
Palestine village *Crawford County*, 94
Palmer village *Christian County*, 35
Palmyra village *Macoupin County*, 256
Paloma postal area *Adams County*, 4
Palos Heights city *Cook County*, 80
Palos Hills city *Cook County*, 81
Palos Park village *Cook County*, 81
Pana city *Christian County*, 36
Panama village *Montgomery County*, 307
Panola village *Woodford County*, 437
Papineau village *Iroquois County*, 168
Paris city *Edgar County*, 119
Park City city *Lake County*, 228
Park Forest village *Cook County*, 81
Park Ridge city *Cook County*, 82
Parkersburg village *Richland County*, 347
Patoka village *Marion County*, 270
Paw Paw village *Lee County*, 238
Pawnee village *Sangamon County*, 359
Paxton city *Ford County*, 129
Payson village *Adams County*, 4
Pearl City village *Stephenson County*, 383
Pearl village *Pike County*, 333
Pecatonica village *Winnebago County*, 432
Pekin city *Tazewell County*, 387
Penfield postal area *Champaign County*, 30
Peoria County, 319 - 324
Peoria Heights village *Peoria County*, 324
Peoria city *Peoria County*, 323
Peotone village *Will County*, 422
Percy village *Randolph County*, 342
Perry County, 325 - 326
Perry village *Pike County*, 333
Peru city *La Salle County*, 213
Pesotum village *Champaign County*, 30
Petersburg city *Menard County*, 298
Phillipstown village *White County*, 411
Philo village *Champaign County*, 30
Phoenix village *Cook County*, 82
Piasa postal area *Macoupin County*, 256
Piatt County, 327 - 329
Pierron village *Bond County*, 8

Pike County, 330 - 334
Pinckneyville city *Perry County*, 326
Pingree Grove village *Kane County*, 193
Piper City village *Ford County*, 129
Pistakee Highlands CDP *McHenry County*, 288
Pittsburg village *Williamson County*, 429
Pittsfield city *Pike County*, 333
Plainfield village *Will County*, 423
Plainville village *Adams County*, 4
Plano city *Kendall County*, 203
Plattville village *Kendall County*, 204
Pleasant Hill village *Pike County*, 334
Pleasant Plains village *Sangamon County*, 360
Plymouth village *Hancock County*, 154
Pocahontas village *Bond County*, 9
Polo city *Ogle County*, 318
Pomona postal area *Jackson County*, 173
Pontiac city *Livingston County*, 242
Pontoon Beach village *Madison County*, 265
Pontoosuc village *Hancock County*, 154
Pope County, 335
Poplar Grove village *Boone County*, 11
Port Barrington village *McHenry County*, 288
Port Byron village *Rock Island County*, 351
Posen village *Cook County*, 82
Potomac village *Vermilion County*, 396
Prairie City village *McDonough County*, 281
Prairie du Rocher village *Randolph County*, 343
Prairie Grove village *McHenry County*, 288
Preston Heights CDP *Will County*, 423
Princeton city *Bureau County*, 17
Princeville village *Peoria County*, 324
Prophetstown city *Whiteside County*, 414
Prospect Heights city *Cook County*, 83
Pulaski County, 336 - 337
Pulaski village *Pulaski County*, 338
Putnam County, 338 - 339
Putnam postal area *Putnam County*, 340

Q

Quincy city *Adams County*, 4

R

Radom village *Washington County*, 404
Raleigh village *Saline County*, 354
Ramsey village *Fayette County*, 126
Randolph County, 340 - 344
Rankin village *Vermilion County*, 396
Ransom village *La Salle County*, 214
Rantoul village *Champaign County*, 30
Rapids City village *Rock Island County*, 351
Raritan village *Henderson County*, 158
Raymond village *Montgomery County*, 308
Red Bud city *Randolph County*, 343
Reddick village *Kankakee County*, 200
Redmon village *Edgar County*, 120
Reynolds village *Rock Island County*, 351
Richland County, 345 - 346
Richmond village *McHenry County*, 289
Richton Park village *Cook County*, 83
Richview village *Washington County*, 404
Ridge Farm village *Vermilion County*, 396
Ridgway village *Gallatin County*, 141
Ridott village *Stephenson County*, 383
Rinard postal area *Wayne County*, 407
Ringwood village *McHenry County*, 289

CDP = Census Designated Place

CDP = Census Designated Place

Comparative
Statistics

Population

Place	1990	2000	2010 Estimate	2015 Projection
Addison village *Du Page Co.*	33,723	35,914	36,688	36,774
Algonquin village *McHenry Co.*	12,745	23,276	30,534	33,853
Alton city *Madison Co.*	32,996	30,496	29,266	28,518
Arlington Heights village *Cook Co.*	75,201	76,031	72,264	70,290
Aurora city *Kane Co.*	102,513	142,990	179,187	197,015
Bartlett village *Du Page Co.*	19,814	36,706	39,652	41,374
Batavia city *Kane Co.*	17,818	23,866	28,150	30,640
Belleville city *Saint Clair Co.*	43,445	41,410	39,931	39,149
Belvidere city *Boone Co.*	16,801	20,820	25,273	27,582
Berwyn city *Cook Co.*	45,426	54,016	50,481	48,959
Bloomington city *McLean Co.*	53,588	64,808	72,644	76,404
Bolingbrook village *Will Co.*	41,386	56,321	71,674	78,969
Buffalo Grove village *Lake Co.*	37,883	42,909	45,724	46,665
Burbank city *Cook Co.*	27,600	27,902	26,344	25,665
Calumet City city *Cook Co.*	37,803	39,071	37,604	36,997
Carol Stream village *Du Page Co.*	32,079	40,438	40,534	40,817
Carpentersville village *Kane Co.*	23,869	30,586	38,438	42,024
Champaign city *Champaign Co.*	65,449	67,518	76,962	80,417
Chicago city *Cook Co.*	2,783,726	2,896,016	2,848,389	2,814,480
Chicago Heights city *Cook Co.*	33,156	32,776	30,609	29,628
Cicero town *Cook Co.*	67,436	85,616	81,668	79,702
Collinsville city *Madison Co.*	23,754	24,707	26,206	26,764
Crystal Lake city *McHenry Co.*	25,852	38,000	43,344	45,903
Danville city *Vermilion Co.*	35,622	33,904	32,300	31,229
Darien city *Du Page Co.*	21,678	22,860	23,312	23,435
DeKalb city *De Kalb Co.*	36,443	39,018	46,971	50,210
Decatur city *Macon Co.*	85,750	81,860	75,427	72,186
Des Plaines city *Cook Co.*	54,783	58,720	59,116	59,197
Dolton village *Cook Co.*	24,035	25,614	23,861	23,036
Downers Grove village *Du Page Co.*	48,477	48,724	47,318	46,451
East Saint Louis city *Saint Clair Co.*	40,944	31,542	27,992	26,626
Elgin city *Kane Co.*	78,650	94,487	104,109	109,583
Elk Grove Village village *Cook Co.*	33,624	34,727	32,506	31,456
Elmhurst city *Du Page Co.*	42,108	42,762	42,564	42,102
Elmwood Park village *Cook Co.*	23,206	25,405	23,983	23,381
Evanston city *Cook Co.*	73,233	74,239	79,418	81,431
Freeport city *Stephenson Co.*	26,316	26,443	24,338	23,248
Galesburg city *Knox Co.*	33,637	33,706	30,959	29,569
Geneva city *Kane Co.*	13,292	19,515	24,586	27,120
Glen Ellyn village *Du Page Co.*	26,153	26,999	26,875	26,463
Glendale Heights village *Du Page Co.*	28,241	31,765	31,512	31,155
Glenview village *Cook Co.*	40,177	41,847	44,607	44,466
Granite City city *Madison Co.*	34,236	31,301	29,699	28,933
Grayslake village *Lake Co.*	8,307	18,506	25,008	27,657
Gurnee village *Lake Co.*	14,698	28,834	31,998	33,591
Hanover Park village *Cook Co.*	32,993	38,278	37,977	37,758
Harvey city *Cook Co.*	29,771	30,000	27,753	26,755
Highland Park city *Lake Co.*	30,761	31,365	32,665	33,023
Hoffman Estates village *Cook Co.*	46,320	49,495	49,845	49,785
Joliet city *Will Co.*	82,008	106,221	144,356	160,857

Place	1990	2000	2010 Estimate	2015 Projection
Kankakee city *Kankakee Co.*	27,822	27,491	26,759	26,615
Lake in the Hills village *McHenry Co.*	7,263	23,152	33,153	36,557
Lansing village *Cook Co.*	28,446	28,332	26,726	25,965
Lombard village *Du Page Co.*	40,229	42,322	41,791	41,335
Loves Park city *Winnebago Co.*	16,327	20,044	23,728	25,108
Maywood village *Cook Co.*	27,139	26,987	24,114	22,882
McHenry city *McHenry Co.*	17,677	21,501	25,957	28,084
Moline city *Rock Island Co.*	43,798	43,768	42,621	41,881
Mount Prospect village *Cook Co.*	53,114	56,265	54,473	53,579
Mundelein village *Lake Co.*	22,023	30,935	30,865	31,322
Naperville city *Du Page Co.*	90,506	128,358	147,227	155,212
New Lenox village *Will Co.*	11,574	17,771	23,526	26,605
Niles village *Cook Co.*	28,533	30,068	29,858	29,815
Normal town *McLean Co.*	40,139	45,386	50,021	51,999
North Chicago city *Lake Co.*	35,785	35,918	32,890	32,212
Northbrook village *Cook Co.*	33,020	33,435	32,899	32,821
O'Fallon city *Saint Clair Co.*	17,169	21,910	26,194	28,028
Oak Forest city *Cook Co.*	26,662	28,051	27,580	27,460
Oak Lawn village *Cook Co.*	56,325	55,245	52,284	50,899
Oak Park village *Cook Co.*	53,648	52,524	48,529	46,694
Orland Park village *Cook Co.*	38,946	51,077	55,374	57,081
Oswego village *Kendall Co.*	5,970	13,326	24,670	31,384
Palatine village *Cook Co.*	58,182	65,479	66,045	65,903
Park Ridge city *Cook Co.*	37,075	37,775	35,872	34,794
Pekin city *Tazewell Co.*	33,227	33,857	34,017	33,988
Peoria city *Peoria Co.*	114,341	112,936	113,823	113,750
Plainfield village *Will Co.*	6,409	13,038	26,040	29,879
Quincy city *Adams Co.*	41,151	40,366	39,376	38,766
Rock Island city *Rock Island Co.*	40,511	39,684	38,118	37,220
Rockford city *Winnebago Co.*	146,309	150,115	156,386	158,758
Rolling Meadows city *Cook Co.*	23,056	24,604	23,929	23,772
Romeoville village *Will Co.*	15,337	21,153	34,162	39,055
Round Lake Beach village *Lake Co.*	17,438	25,859	30,807	33,126
Saint Charles city *Kane Co.*	24,173	27,896	32,785	34,979
Schaumburg village *Cook Co.*	68,706	75,386	74,583	73,841
Skokie village *Cook Co.*	59,432	63,348	66,192	67,326
Springfield city *Sangamon Co.*	108,997	111,454	116,211	117,855
Streamwood village *Cook Co.*	31,724	36,407	35,561	35,205
Tinley Park village *Cook Co.*	38,640	48,401	53,896	56,003
Urbana city *Champaign Co.*	37,214	36,395	39,263	40,118
Vernon Hills village *Lake Co.*	15,529	20,120	23,980	25,041
Waukegan city *Lake Co.*	70,309	87,901	92,155	94,001
West Chicago city *Du Page Co.*	15,874	23,469	26,382	27,552
Westmont village *Du Page Co.*	22,443	24,554	24,583	24,429
Wheaton city *Du Page Co.*	52,280	55,416	53,627	52,569
Wheeling village *Cook Co.*	30,008	34,496	34,369	34,062
Wilmette village *Cook Co.*	26,685	27,651	27,504	27,369
Woodridge village *Du Page Co.*	27,524	30,934	34,216	34,557
Woodstock city *McHenry Co.*	15,150	20,151	24,054	26,086
Zion city *Lake Co.*	20,171	22,866	25,320	26,354

Physical Characteristics

Place	Density (persons per square mile)	Land Area (square miles)	Water Area (square miles)	Elevation (feet)
Addison village *Du Page Co.*	3,889.7	9.43	0.05	689
Algonquin village *McHenry Co.*	3,105.6	9.83	0.16	741
Alton city *Madison Co.*	1,870.6	15.64	0.96	499
Arlington Heights village *Cook Co.*	4,403.8	16.41	0.03	702
Aurora city *Kane Co.*	4,651.1	38.53	0.89	679
Bartlett village *Du Page Co.*	2,676.7	14.81	0.14	n/a
Batavia city *Kane Co.*	3,111.9	9.05	0.14	715
Belleville city *Saint Clair Co.*	2,117.9	18.85	0.13	515
Belvidere city *Boone Co.*	2,786.2	9.07	0.05	781
Berwyn city *Cook Co.*	12,968.1	3.89	0.00	617
Bloomington city *McLean Co.*	3,228.6	22.50	0.00	797
Bolingbrook village *Will Co.*	3,495.2	20.51	0.24	702
Buffalo Grove village *Lake Co.*	4,973.0	9.19	0.02	n/a
Burbank city *Cook Co.*	6,313.3	4.17	0.00	620
Calumet City city *Cook Co.*	5,176.1	7.26	0.12	591
Carol Stream village *Du Page Co.*	4,556.6	8.90	0.03	758
Carpentersville village *Kane Co.*	5,159.4	7.45	0.15	889
Champaign city *Champaign Co.*	4,530.6	16.99	0.02	738
Chicago city *Cook Co.*	12,540.6	227.13	6.87	587
Chicago Heights city *Cook Co.*	3,198.0	9.57	0.01	659
Cicero town *Cook Co.*	13,969.9	5.85	0.00	604
Collinsville city *Madison Co.*	1,927.7	13.59	0.01	561
Crystal Lake city *McHenry Co.*	2,668.5	16.24	0.56	915
Danville city *Vermilion Co.*	1,899.6	17.00	0.10	600
Darien city *Du Page Co.*	3,857.4	6.04	0.07	751
DeKalb city *De Kalb Co.*	3,724.6	12.61	0.01	880
Decatur city *Macon Co.*	1,814.9	41.56	4.32	673
Des Plaines city *Cook Co.*	4,098.6	14.42	0.11	633
Dolton village *Cook Co.*	5,242.5	4.55	0.12	604
Downers Grove village *Du Page Co.*	3,321.5	14.25	0.01	741
East Saint Louis city *Saint Clair Co.*	1,990.5	14.06	0.37	417
Elgin city *Kane Co.*	4,163.9	25.00	0.39	745
Elk Grove Village village *Cook Co.*	2,944.6	11.04	0.06	686
Elmhurst city *Du Page Co.*	4,146.7	10.26	0.00	686
Elmwood Park village *Cook Co.*	12,582.4	1.91	0.00	643
Evanston city *Cook Co.*	10,252.7	7.75	0.02	614
Freeport city *Stephenson Co.*	2,132.4	11.41	0.01	778
Galesburg city *Knox Co.*	1,832.3	16.90	0.18	771
Geneva city *Kane Co.*	2,924.6	8.41	0.18	712
Glen Ellyn village *Du Page Co.*	4,061.9	6.62	0.02	741
Glendale Heights village *Du Page Co.*	5,831.0	5.40	0.00	761
Glenview village *Cook Co.*	3,316.5	13.45	0.04	653
Granite City city *Madison Co.*	1,780.2	16.68	0.49	423
Grayslake village *Lake Co.*	2,661.1	9.40	0.16	784
Gurnee village *Lake Co.*	2,387.7	13.40	0.01	679
Hanover Park village *Cook Co.*	5,590.1	6.79	0.00	n/a
Harvey city *Cook Co.*	4,479.5	6.20	0.00	604
Highland Park city *Lake Co.*	2,642.7	12.36	0.01	696
Hoffman Estates village *Cook Co.*	2,528.9	19.71	0.16	784
Joliet city *Will Co.*	3,792.9	38.06	0.29	541

Place	Density (persons per square mile)	Land Area (square miles)	Water Area (square miles)	Elevation (feet)
Kankakee city *Kankakee Co.*	2,180.2	12.27	0.48	656
Lake in the Hills village *McHenry Co.*	3,525.4	9.40	0.23	866
Lansing village *Cook Co.*	3,951.3	6.76	0.06	630
Lombard village *Du Page Co.*	4,315.0	9.69	0.01	719
Loves Park city *Winnebago Co.*	1,642.1	14.45	0.37	728
Maywood village *Cook Co.*	8,904.7	2.71	0.00	627
McHenry city *McHenry Co.*	2,233.7	11.62	0.49	797
Moline city *Rock Island Co.*	2,732.2	15.60	0.22	577
Mount Prospect village *Cook Co.*	5,337.5	10.21	0.04	669
Mundelein village *Lake Co.*	3,579.3	8.62	0.32	735
Naperville city *Du Page Co.*	4,161.7	35.38	0.14	709
New Lenox village *Will Co.*	2,330.7	10.09	0.02	669
Niles village *Cook Co.*	5,082.1	5.88	0.00	636
Normal town *McLean Co.*	3,672.9	13.62	0.06	801
North Chicago city *Lake Co.*	4,199.7	7.83	0.01	659
Northbrook village *Cook Co.*	2,546.6	12.92	0.05	646
O'Fallon city *Saint Clair Co.*	2,400.2	10.91	0.01	548
Oak Forest city *Cook Co.*	4,882.0	5.65	0.05	673
Oak Lawn village *Cook Co.*	6,082.8	8.60	0.00	597
Oak Park village *Cook Co.*	10,323.5	4.70	0.00	620
Orland Park village *Cook Co.*	2,892.9	19.14	0.29	705
Oswego village *Kendall Co.*	3,748.0	6.58	0.10	640
Palatine village *Cook Co.*	5,090.8	12.97	0.13	741
Park Ridge city *Cook Co.*	5,103.8	7.03	0.04	643
Pekin city *Tazewell Co.*	2,586.9	13.15	0.60	502
Peoria city *Peoria Co.*	2,563.4	44.40	2.23	502
Plainfield village *Will Co.*	2,242.6	11.61	0.83	617
Quincy city *Adams Co.*	2,693.5	14.62	0.03	568
Rock Island city *Rock Island Co.*	2,393.7	15.92	1.22	561
Rockford city *Winnebago Co.*	2,792.3	56.01	0.71	715
Rolling Meadows city *Cook Co.*	4,386.7	5.45	0.00	719
Romeoville village *Will Co.*	2,353.8	14.51	0.38	617
Round Lake Beach village *Lake Co.*	6,166.8	5.00	0.10	764
Saint Charles city *Kane Co.*	2,343.4	13.99	0.16	732
Schaumburg village *Cook Co.*	3,924.9	19.00	0.12	794
Skokie village *Cook Co.*	6,591.9	10.04	0.00	607
Springfield city *Sangamon Co.*	2,152.0	54.00	6.31	597
Streamwood village *Cook Co.*	4,873.1	7.30	0.03	807
Tinley Park village *Cook Co.*	3,604.3	14.95	0.04	699
Urbana city *Champaign Co.*	3,741.6	10.49	0.01	728
Vernon Hills village *Lake Co.*	3,227.9	7.43	0.19	735
Waukegan city *Lake Co.*	4,004.7	23.01	0.08	653
West Chicago city *Du Page Co.*	1,906.4	13.84	0.00	784
Westmont village *Du Page Co.*	5,020.3	4.90	0.01	748
Wheaton city *Du Page Co.*	4,779.1	11.22	0.04	758
Wheeling village *Cook Co.*	4,091.4	8.40	0.04	650
Wilmette village *Cook Co.*	5,108.5	5.38	0.01	636
Woodridge village *Du Page Co.*	4,111.1	8.32	0.02	732
Woodstock city *McHenry Co.*	2,257.4	10.66	0.00	945
Zion city *Lake Co.*	3,088.9	8.20	0.00	650

NOTE: Population Density figures as of 2010; Land Area and Water Area figures as of 2000.

Population by Race/Hispanic Origin

Place	White (%)	Black (%)	Asian (%)	Other (%)	Hispanic (%)
Addison village *Du Page Co.*	69.2	3.5	8.2	19.1	39.0
Algonquin village *McHenry Co.*	88.5	2.0	5.4	4.1	7.1
Alton city *Madison Co.*	70.7	25.6	0.4	3.3	2.1
Arlington Heights village *Cook Co.*	87.9	1.1	7.3	3.7	6.3
Aurora city *Kane Co.*	62.6	10.6	4.8	22.0	40.0
Bartlett village *Du Page Co.*	81.4	2.9	11.1	4.6	8.6
Batavia city *Kane Co.*	90.2	2.9	2.4	4.5	8.0
Belleville city *Saint Clair Co.*	74.9	20.9	1.1	3.1	2.1
Belvidere city *Boone Co.*	72.0	2.8	1.2	24.0	34.3
Berwyn city *Cook Co.*	61.3	1.6	2.7	34.4	55.9
Bloomington city *McLean Co.*	81.1	9.5	4.8	4.6	4.8
Bolingbrook village *Will Co.*	51.8	23.9	8.8	15.5	25.2
Buffalo Grove village *Lake Co.*	83.9	0.7	12.4	3.0	4.7
Burbank city *Cook Co.*	86.0	0.4	2.2	11.4	17.3
Calumet City city *Cook Co.*	31.6	56.2	0.6	11.5	15.3
Carol Stream village *Du Page Co.*	71.2	5.5	15.3	8.1	13.8
Carpentersville village *Kane Co.*	60.7	5.4	3.1	30.9	49.6
Champaign city *Champaign Co.*	69.4	15.3	9.2	6.1	6.4
Chicago city *Cook Co.*	41.4	34.6	4.9	19.0	29.5
Chicago Heights city *Cook Co.*	41.7	35.7	0.7	21.8	31.3
Cicero town *Cook Co.*	43.7	1.3	0.6	54.5	86.1
Collinsville city *Madison Co.*	88.9	7.5	0.6	3.0	3.3
Crystal Lake city *McHenry Co.*	90.1	1.1	3.4	5.4	11.0
Danville city *Vermilion Co.*	66.7	26.8	1.1	5.4	5.8
Darien city *Du Page Co.*	80.1	4.0	12.2	3.6	6.1
DeKalb city *De Kalb Co.*	72.2	12.4	5.4	10.0	13.7
Decatur city *Macon Co.*	74.9	20.7	1.2	3.2	1.7
Des Plaines city *Cook Co.*	78.6	1.5	9.8	10.1	20.4
Dolton village *Cook Co.*	13.1	83.4	0.5	2.9	3.3
Downers Grove village *Du Page Co.*	86.4	2.9	7.4	3.3	5.4
East Saint Louis city *Saint Clair Co.*	1.6	96.7	0.1	1.5	1.1
Elgin city *Kane Co.*	65.0	5.7	5.8	23.6	44.1
Elk Grove Village village *Cook Co.*	82.9	1.6	9.9	5.6	8.7
Elmhurst city *Du Page Co.*	91.5	1.6	4.0	2.8	5.4
Elmwood Park village *Cook Co.*	87.4	0.7	2.8	9.1	17.0
Evanston city *Cook Co.*	65.0	19.1	7.6	8.3	8.8
Freeport city *Stephenson Co.*	79.2	14.2	1.2	5.3	3.7
Galesburg city *Knox Co.*	81.7	11.2	1.4	5.7	5.8
Geneva city *Kane Co.*	94.9	1.4	2.0	1.7	4.2
Glen Ellyn village *Du Page Co.*	85.6	3.2	5.6	5.6	7.5
Glendale Heights village *Du Page Co.*	54.2	7.1	22.5	16.2	26.8
Glenview village *Cook Co.*	77.6	5.4	12.2	4.7	7.6
Granite City city *Madison Co.*	91.8	3.5	0.5	4.2	4.4
Grayslake village *Lake Co.*	84.9	2.1	7.7	5.3	8.8
Gurnee village *Lake Co.*	71.9	7.0	13.3	7.8	10.6
Hanover Park village *Cook Co.*	59.6	7.1	15.1	18.1	33.6
Harvey city *Cook Co.*	11.0	73.6	0.6	14.8	19.5
Highland Park city *Lake Co.*	87.9	1.8	2.5	7.9	14.6
Hoffman Estates village *Cook Co.*	67.3	4.8	18.9	9.0	15.1
Joliet city *Will Co.*	65.6	15.7	1.7	17.0	29.1

Place	White (%)	Black (%)	Asian (%)	Other (%)	Hispanic (%)
Kankakee city *Kankakee Co.*	47.0	39.8	0.3	12.8	16.5
Lake in the Hills village *McHenry Co.*	85.5	3.3	6.4	4.9	8.8
Lansing village *Cook Co.*	79.7	15.4	0.9	4.1	8.4
Lombard village *Du Page Co.*	82.5	4.0	8.4	5.1	8.2
Loves Park city *Winnebago Co.*	89.6	3.6	2.6	4.2	4.6
Maywood village *Cook Co.*	10.4	79.2	0.3	10.1	14.8
McHenry city *McHenry Co.*	90.3	0.6	1.3	7.7	12.1
Moline city *Rock Island Co.*	84.1	3.7	2.8	9.3	15.6
Mount Prospect village *Cook Co.*	75.7	1.9	13.7	8.7	16.7
Mundelein village *Lake Co.*	69.6	2.1	9.7	18.6	35.5
Naperville city *Du Page Co.*	77.1	5.1	14.0	3.7	6.0
New Lenox village *Will Co.*	95.5	0.5	0.7	3.3	6.0
Niles village *Cook Co.*	76.9	0.6	17.2	5.3	6.8
Normal town *McLean Co.*	84.7	9.4	2.6	3.3	3.5
North Chicago city *Lake Co.*	44.5	34.5	4.3	16.8	28.1
Northbrook village *Cook Co.*	87.9	0.6	9.8	1.7	2.1
O'Fallon city *Saint Clair Co.*	79.5	13.7	3.1	3.7	2.7
Oak Forest city *Cook Co.*	86.6	4.7	3.5	5.1	9.0
Oak Lawn village *Cook Co.*	90.5	1.8	2.2	5.5	7.9
Oak Park village *Cook Co.*	66.2	23.0	5.0	5.8	5.8
Orland Park village *Cook Co.*	92.8	0.8	3.6	2.8	4.7
Oswego village *Kendall Co.*	76.0	10.2	4.4	9.4	15.0
Palatine village *Cook Co.*	80.1	1.9	9.4	8.7	17.8
Park Ridge city *Cook Co.*	93.8	0.3	3.5	2.4	4.2
Pekin city *Tazewell Co.*	95.4	2.6	0.5	1.5	1.8
Peoria city *Peoria Co.*	66.3	25.3	3.5	4.9	3.7
Plainfield village *Will Co.*	87.1	3.0	4.6	5.4	10.4
Quincy city *Adams Co.*	92.2	4.9	0.5	2.4	1.1
Rock Island city *Rock Island Co.*	74.9	17.2	1.5	6.5	7.4
Rockford city *Winnebago Co.*	67.4	18.6	2.4	11.5	16.3
Rolling Meadows city *Cook Co.*	76.9	2.9	8.6	11.6	23.5
Romeoville village *Will Co.*	78.3	6.8	4.1	10.9	20.7
Round Lake Beach village *Lake Co.*	62.7	3.9	2.6	30.8	46.0
Saint Charles city *Kane Co.*	89.9	2.1	3.3	4.6	8.9
Schaumburg village *Cook Co.*	71.3	3.6	19.7	5.3	8.2
Skokie village *Cook Co.*	61.8	5.5	25.6	7.1	7.4
Springfield city *Sangamon Co.*	78.8	16.6	1.7	2.9	1.6
Streamwood village *Cook Co.*	68.6	4.4	12.0	15.0	24.9
Tinley Park village *Cook Co.*	90.5	3.4	2.9	3.3	5.4
Urbana city *Champaign Co.*	64.4	14.2	15.7	5.7	4.9
Vernon Hills village *Lake Co.*	75.7	1.6	17.1	5.7	10.4
Waukegan city *Lake Co.*	46.1	16.0	4.1	33.9	57.9
West Chicago city *Du Page Co.*	76.8	1.7	1.9	19.6	56.5
Westmont village *Du Page Co.*	72.5	7.0	14.3	6.1	8.9
Wheaton city *Du Page Co.*	87.3	3.8	5.6	3.3	5.2
Wheeling village *Cook Co.*	67.5	2.3	11.1	19.1	32.8
Wilmette village *Cook Co.*	88.5	0.6	8.9	2.1	2.5
Woodridge village *Du Page Co.*	67.7	10.5	14.5	7.3	12.6
Woodstock city *McHenry Co.*	82.5	1.8	2.9	12.9	27.1
Zion city *Lake Co.*	48.6	30.3	2.4	18.8	24.9

NOTE: Data as of 2010; (1) Figures do not include multiple race combinations; (2) Persons of Hispanic Origin may be of any race

Avg. Household Size, Median Age, Male/Female Ratio & Foreign Born

Place	Average Household Size (persons)	Median Age (years)	Male/Female Ratio (males per 100 females)	Foreign Born (%)
Addison village *Du Page Co.*	3.05	36.3	103.5	34.9
Algonquin village *McHenry Co.*	3.03	35.8	99.0	11.6
Alton city *Madison Co.*	2.38	35.9	91.6	1.5
Arlington Heights village *Cook Co.*	2.47	41.9	93.8	17.0
Aurora city *Kane Co.*	3.13	31.3	102.9	24.2
Bartlett village *Du Page Co.*	3.02	36.3	98.8	14.6
Batavia city *Kane Co.*	2.88	34.2	99.0	4.6
Belleville city *Saint Clair Co.*	2.30	38.4	89.3	1.5
Belvidere city *Boone Co.*	2.79	33.2	100.0	14.6
Berwyn city *Cook Co.*	2.81	36.0	97.2	25.0
Bloomington city *McLean Co.*	2.42	33.9	96.1	6.3
Bolingbrook village *Will Co.*	3.22	32.2	99.9	22.7
Buffalo Grove village *Lake Co.*	2.80	39.6	94.1	24.9
Burbank city *Cook Co.*	3.03	38.2	97.0	30.4
Calumet City city *Cook Co.*	2.65	35.6	89.1	7.5
Carol Stream village *Du Page Co.*	2.96	34.8	99.7	20.1
Carpentersville village *Kane Co.*	3.55	29.8	104.7	32.4
Champaign city *Champaign Co.*	2.48	26.4	105.8	9.6
Chicago city *Cook Co.*	2.72	34.8	96.4	21.0
Chicago Heights city *Cook Co.*	3.11	32.3	97.6	12.9
Cicero town *Cook Co.*	3.80	28.6	106.1	43.7
Collinsville city *Madison Co.*	2.31	37.8	95.9	2.6
Crystal Lake city *McHenry Co.*	2.89	35.5	99.6	10.4
Danville city *Vermilion Co.*	2.54	36.4	99.0	3.1
Darien city *Du Page Co.*	2.57	44.3	96.1	18.7
DeKalb city *De Kalb Co.*	3.02	24.4	99.2	10.6
Decatur city *Macon Co.*	2.36	38.2	88.8	2.2
Des Plaines city *Cook Co.*	2.62	41.7	95.2	27.4
Dolton village *Cook Co.*	3.04	34.2	89.2	2.3
Downers Grove village *Du Page Co.*	2.52	41.7	95.1	9.3
East Saint Louis city *Saint Clair Co.*	2.73	31.1	83.5	0.2
Elgin city *Kane Co.*	3.02	32.8	102.0	25.6
Elk Grove Village village *Cook Co.*	2.57	40.8	95.5	19.1
Elmhurst city *Du Page Co.*	2.71	40.8	95.2	12.0
Elmwood Park village *Cook Co.*	2.63	41.2	92.6	27.6
Evanston city *Cook Co.*	2.53	35.2	90.8	15.0
Freeport city *Stephenson Co.*	2.34	40.1	88.3	2.4
Galesburg city *Knox Co.*	2.56	38.9	102.6	2.9
Geneva city *Kane Co.*	2.96	34.3	100.9	4.5
Glen Ellyn village *Du Page Co.*	2.63	38.8	97.1	9.8
Glendale Heights village *Du Page Co.*	2.95	35.3	104.8	34.3
Glenview village *Cook Co.*	2.72	39.8	94.0	21.3
Granite City city *Madison Co.*	2.39	38.5	93.8	2.4
Grayslake village *Lake Co.*	2.97	35.6	97.1	11.3
Gurnee village *Lake Co.*	2.81	36.8	94.7	16.6
Hanover Park village *Cook Co.*	3.34	33.4	104.5	37.0
Harvey city *Cook Co.*	3.36	29.6	94.0	9.3
Highland Park city *Lake Co.*	2.76	40.8	96.1	11.5
Hoffman Estates village *Cook Co.*	2.86	36.9	98.6	26.9
Joliet city *Will Co.*	2.93	32.4	99.9	15.0

Place	Average Household Size (persons)	Median Age (years)	Male/Female Ratio (males per 100 females)	Foreign Born (%)
Kankakee city Kankakee Co.	2.81	33.3	94.1	8.8
Lake in the Hills village McHenry Co.	3.06	33.0	99.9	15.6
Lansing village Cook Co.	2.47	39.8	92.1	5.2
Lombard village Du Page Co.	2.55	40.5	97.2	14.0
Loves Park city Winnebago Co.	2.46	36.9	96.7	7.2
Maywood village Cook Co.	3.43	32.4	89.7	9.6
McHenry city McHenry Co.	2.71	36.9	97.1	11.2
Moline city Rock Island Co.	2.37	38.6	93.4	8.6
Mount Prospect village Cook Co.	2.62	39.2	100.1	30.1
Mundelein village Lake Co.	3.19	33.9	103.3	29.8
Naperville city Du Page Co.	2.95	35.5	97.2	15.4
New Lenox village Will Co.	3.06	33.2	96.0	2.7
Niles village Cook Co.	2.56	49.7	87.6	42.0
Normal town McLean Co.	2.92	25.0	90.1	3.7
North Chicago city Lake Co.	4.72	23.3	147.3	21.1
Northbrook village Cook Co.	2.72	46.1	93.3	16.3
O'Fallon city Saint Clair Co.	2.60	36.7	93.2	4.0
Oak Forest city Cook Co.	2.85	38.1	99.8	7.7
Oak Lawn village Cook Co.	2.45	43.5	89.9	14.5
Oak Park village Cook Co.	2.25	39.3	89.0	9.9
Orland Park village Cook Co.	2.73	42.5	92.8	12.8
Oswego village Kendall Co.	2.94	31.1	98.7	7.1
Palatine village Cook Co.	2.57	37.7	99.6	23.2
Park Ridge city Cook Co.	2.67	44.9	91.4	15.3
Pekin city Tazewell Co.	2.43	37.7	95.8	1.4
Peoria city Peoria Co.	2.49	34.8	91.7	4.8
Plainfield village Will Co.	3.24	32.0	99.4	11.2
Quincy city Adams Co.	2.40	39.6	90.5	1.4
Rock Island city Rock Island Co.	2.46	37.1	92.5	5.0
Rockford city Winnebago Co.	2.55	35.8	95.0	10.1
Rolling Meadows city Cook Co.	2.73	37.7	102.3	24.8
Romeoville village Will Co.	2.87	33.0	99.7	18.1
Round Lake Beach village Lake Co.	3.57	31.8	102.4	26.9
Saint Charles city Kane Co.	2.72	36.2	101.7	9.2
Schaumburg village Cook Co.	2.45	39.0	97.1	23.4
Skokie village Cook Co.	2.79	44.0	91.3	39.2
Springfield city Sangamon Co.	2.25	38.8	90.3	3.0
Streamwood village Cook Co.	2.93	36.2	100.0	29.2
Tinley Park village Cook Co.	2.79	38.1	95.6	8.3
Urbana city Champaign Co.	2.58	25.3	117.4	15.6
Vernon Hills village Lake Co.	2.78	36.7	95.9	27.0
Waukegan city Lake Co.	3.21	32.0	102.9	33.4
West Chicago city Du Page Co.	3.55	32.9	111.3	35.8
Westmont village Du Page Co.	2.49	40.7	91.4	21.6
Wheaton city Du Page Co.	2.84	37.9	95.9	9.1
Wheeling village Cook Co.	2.71	38.2	98.5	39.0
Wilmette village Cook Co.	2.79	42.8	92.7	14.4
Woodridge village Du Page Co.	2.69	37.3	101.3	20.0
Woodstock city McHenry Co.	2.75	35.0	102.0	17.1
Zion city Lake Co.	3.06	32.4	94.9	12.9

NOTE: Average Household Size, Median Age, and Male/Female Ratio figures as of 2010. Foreign Born figures are 2005-2009 5-year estimates.

Five Largest Ancestry Groups

Place	Group 1	Group 2	Group 3	Group 4	Group 5
Addison village *Du Page Co.*	Italian (15.6%)	Polish (13.0%)	German (10.6%)	Irish (7.4%)	Greek (3.8%)
Algonquin village *McHenry Co.*	German (32.4%)	Polish (17.8%)	Irish (17.5%)	Italian (13.5%)	English (7.0%)
Alton city *Madison Co.*	German (24.9%)	Irish (13.0%)	English (11.9%)	American (6.6%)	Italian (4.5%)
Arlington Heights village *Cook Co.*	German (27.0%)	Irish (19.7%)	Polish (17.4%)	Italian (12.3%)	English (7.4%)
Aurora city *Kane Co.*	German (16.8%)	Irish (9.7%)	Polish (5.2%)	Italian (4.9%)	English (4.8%)
Bartlett village *Du Page Co.*	German (29.5%)	Italian (17.2%)	Irish (16.8%)	Polish (14.7%)	English (6.1%)
Batavia city *Kane Co.*	German (35.8%)	Irish (19.1%)	English (11.9%)	Polish (10.8%)	Italian (9.2%)
Belleville city *Saint Clair Co.*	German (34.9%)	Irish (13.9%)	English (8.4%)	French (5.0%)	American (4.6%)
Belvidere city *Boone Co.*	German (20.2%)	Irish (12.2%)	American (9.3%)	English (8.0%)	Italian (5.5%)
Berwyn city *Cook Co.*	Polish (9.4%)	German (9.2%)	Italian (9.1%)	Irish (8.8%)	Czech (3.5%)
Bloomington city *McLean Co.*	German (30.5%)	Irish (15.5%)	English (11.7%)	American (10.4%)	Italian (4.0%)
Bolingbrook village *Will Co.*	German (15.0%)	Irish (11.3%)	Polish (9.9%)	Italian (6.2%)	English (4.5%)
Buffalo Grove village *Lake Co.*	Russian (17.4%)	German (14.1%)	Polish (10.7%)	Irish (8.8%)	English (5.5%)
Burbank city *Cook Co.*	Polish (33.1%)	Irish (13.6%)	German (11.9%)	Italian (9.5%)	Lithuanian (3.4%)
Calumet City city *Cook Co.*	Polish (6.5%)	German (4.6%)	Irish (2.9%)	Italian (1.9%)	American (1.4%)
Carol Stream village *Du Page Co.*	German (24.2%)	Irish (16.2%)	Italian (12.7%)	Polish (11.6%)	English (6.2%)
Carpentersville village *Kane Co.*	German (17.8%)	Irish (9.2%)	Polish (8.4%)	Italian (5.4%)	English (3.5%)
Champaign city *Champaign Co.*	German (22.9%)	Irish (13.9%)	English (9.2%)	American (8.7%)	Polish (5.2%)
Chicago city *Cook Co.*	German (7.8%)	Irish (7.6%)	Polish (6.8%)	Italian (3.8%)	English (2.4%)
Chicago Heights city *Cook Co.*	Italian (9.8%)	German (8.0%)	Irish (5.2%)	Polish (5.0%)	English (1.7%)
Cicero town *Cook Co.*	Polish (3.1%)	Irish (2.9%)	German (2.7%)	Italian (2.1%)	Czech (1.2%)
Collinsville city *Madison Co.*	German (31.3%)	Irish (16.4%)	English (10.2%)	Italian (8.3%)	American (6.1%)
Crystal Lake city *McHenry Co.*	German (32.7%)	Irish (19.6%)	Polish (14.2%)	Italian (13.4%)	English (8.0%)
Danville city *Vermilion Co.*	American (16.9%)	German (14.7%)	Irish (8.1%)	English (7.0%)	French (2.3%)
Darien city *Du Page Co.*	German (21.2%)	Irish (17.8%)	Polish (16.0%)	Italian (14.6%)	Czech (5.2%)
DeKalb city *De Kalb Co.*	German (25.7%)	Irish (15.5%)	Polish (7.8%)	English (7.5%)	Italian (7.1%)
Decatur city *Macon Co.*	German (21.4%)	Irish (13.5%)	American (12.4%)	English (10.6%)	Italian (2.7%)
Des Plaines city *Cook Co.*	German (20.3%)	Polish (17.4%)	Irish (13.3%)	Italian (10.2%)	English (3.9%)
Dolton village *Cook Co.*	American (2.1%)	German (2.0%)	Polish (1.6%)	African (1.4%)	Irish (0.9%)
Downers Grove village *Du Page Co.*	German (26.7%)	Irish (20.6%)	Polish (16.5%)	Italian (14.7%)	English (9.7%)
East Saint Louis city *Saint Clair Co.*	African (1.9%)	American (0.6%)	Irish (0.5%)	German (0.4%)	French (0.3%)
Elgin city *Kane Co.*	German (20.3%)	Irish (10.3%)	Polish (6.1%)	Italian (5.7%)	English (5.5%)
Elk Grove Village village *Cook Co.*	German (22.7%)	Polish (19.5%)	Irish (18.2%)	Italian (13.8%)	English (6.2%)
Elmhurst city *Du Page Co.*	German (28.9%)	Irish (19.5%)	Italian (14.5%)	Polish (11.4%)	English (6.4%)
Elmwood Park village *Cook Co.*	Polish (23.8%)	Italian (23.7%)	German (13.6%)	Irish (12.8%)	English (3.2%)
Evanston city *Cook Co.*	German (17.5%)	Irish (13.2%)	English (9.0%)	Polish (6.7%)	Italian (5.5%)
Freeport city *Stephenson Co.*	German (40.1%)	Irish (11.8%)	English (9.7%)	American (8.1%)	Dutch (4.4%)
Galesburg city *Knox Co.*	German (20.0%)	Irish (13.9%)	English (11.5%)	Swedish (9.0%)	American (8.2%)
Geneva city *Kane Co.*	German (30.1%)	Irish (21.2%)	Italian (13.8%)	English (11.4%)	Polish (10.0%)
Glen Ellyn village *Du Page Co.*	German (30.0%)	Irish (25.2%)	English (12.2%)	Italian (11.9%)	Polish (8.3%)
Glendale Heights village *Du Page Co.*	German (14.1%)	Irish (9.3%)	Polish (8.8%)	Italian (7.3%)	English (3.0%)
Glenview village *Cook Co.*	German (19.1%)	Irish (16.0%)	Polish (12.4%)	Italian (7.1%)	English (7.1%)
Granite City city *Madison Co.*	German (25.8%)	Irish (19.7%)	English (9.7%)	American (9.7%)	Italian (5.7%)
Grayslake village *Lake Co.*	German (31.5%)	Irish (20.7%)	Polish (13.5%)	Italian (9.6%)	English (8.1%)
Gurnee village *Lake Co.*	German (24.5%)	Irish (15.8%)	Polish (10.3%)	English (8.4%)	Italian (8.1%)
Hanover Park village *Cook Co.*	German (15.0%)	Polish (9.6%)	Irish (9.0%)	Italian (6.8%)	English (4.5%)
Harvey city *Cook Co.*	German (1.7%)	Irish (1.1%)	Jamaican (0.8%)	African (0.8%)	American (0.8%)
Highland Park city *Lake Co.*	Russian (18.6%)	German (16.3%)	Polish (9.6%)	Irish (8.8%)	Italian (8.5%)
Hoffman Estates village *Cook Co.*	German (19.8%)	Polish (15.3%)	Irish (12.1%)	Italian (10.0%)	English (5.1%)
Joliet city *Will Co.*	German (16.1%)	Irish (14.1%)	Polish (9.2%)	Italian (9.0%)	English (4.6%)

Place	Group 1	Group 2	Group 3	Group 4	Group 5
Kankakee city *Kankakee Co.*	German (14.4%)	Irish (6.9%)	French (6.5%)	English (4.9%)	American (3.3%)
Lake in the Hills village *McHenry Co.*	German (27.7%)	Polish (17.4%)	Italian (15.8%)	Irish (15.2%)	English (5.1%)
Lansing village *Cook Co.*	German (17.8%)	Polish (15.4%)	Irish (14.3%)	Dutch (10.6%)	Italian (6.5%)
Lombard village *Du Page Co.*	German (26.6%)	Irish (20.4%)	Italian (14.1%)	Polish (13.0%)	English (7.8%)
Loves Park city *Winnebago Co.*	German (26.3%)	Irish (15.7%)	American (12.1%)	Swedish (10.3%)	English (9.8%)
Maywood village *Cook Co.*	African (1.5%)	Irish (1.2%)	German (1.1%)	Italian (0.7%)	Barbadian (0.4%)
McHenry city *McHenry Co.*	German (35.9%)	Irish (19.1%)	Polish (16.8%)	Italian (8.4%)	English (8.3%)
Moline city *Rock Island Co.*	German (27.2%)	Irish (15.0%)	English (10.0%)	Swedish (8.0%)	Belgian (6.5%)
Mount Prospect village *Cook Co.*	German (24.0%)	Polish (18.1%)	Irish (13.6%)	Italian (9.4%)	English (4.2%)
Mundelein village *Lake Co.*	German (21.3%)	Irish (12.0%)	Polish (9.9%)	Italian (7.2%)	English (5.0%)
Naperville city *Du Page Co.*	German (24.2%)	Irish (17.7%)	Polish (11.0%)	Italian (10.2%)	English (8.8%)
New Lenox village *Will Co.*	German (32.3%)	Irish (26.0%)	Polish (19.5%)	Italian (18.2%)	English (7.2%)
Niles village *Cook Co.*	Polish (21.1%)	German (13.4%)	Italian (8.8%)	Irish (8.7%)	ACS (4.9%)
Normal town *McLean Co.*	German (33.7%)	Irish (17.0%)	English (9.4%)	American (7.5%)	Italian (6.7%)
North Chicago city *Lake Co.*	German (10.9%)	Irish (8.3%)	Italian (3.2%)	English (2.5%)	Polish (2.4%)
Northbrook village *Cook Co.*	German (15.7%)	Russian (12.7%)	Irish (10.8%)	Polish (10.0%)	English (8.3%)
O'Fallon city *Saint Clair Co.*	German (31.8%)	Irish (13.6%)	English (13.4%)	American (6.6%)	Italian (5.8%)
Oak Forest city *Cook Co.*	Irish (28.6%)	German (22.9%)	Polish (19.5%)	Italian (14.8%)	Swedish (5.3%)
Oak Lawn village *Cook Co.*	Irish (26.8%)	Polish (21.4%)	German (18.2%)	Italian (11.4%)	Lithuanian (3.9%)
Oak Park village *Cook Co.*	German (20.8%)	Irish (19.2%)	English (9.5%)	Italian (8.4%)	Polish (7.6%)
Orland Park village *Cook Co.*	Irish (27.1%)	Polish (20.6%)	German (20.3%)	Italian (14.0%)	English (4.2%)
Oswego village *Kendall Co.*	German (29.7%)	Irish (17.2%)	Italian (10.6%)	Polish (9.2%)	English (7.6%)
Palatine village *Cook Co.*	German (22.9%)	Irish (16.0%)	Polish (13.5%)	Italian (10.6%)	English (5.4%)
Park Ridge city *Cook Co.*	German (23.7%)	Irish (22.2%)	Polish (21.0%)	Italian (15.5%)	English (7.2%)
Pekin city *Tazewell Co.*	German (32.9%)	American (18.7%)	Irish (13.4%)	English (10.7%)	Italian (5.2%)
Peoria city *Peoria Co.*	German (24.1%)	Irish (13.8%)	English (9.6%)	American (4.8%)	Italian (4.1%)
Plainfield village *Will Co.*	German (25.1%)	Irish (20.2%)	Italian (14.7%)	Polish (14.4%)	English (7.6%)
Quincy city *Adams Co.*	German (41.6%)	Irish (14.0%)	American (11.3%)	English (9.6%)	French (2.5%)
Rock Island city *Rock Island Co.*	German (23.3%)	Irish (13.0%)	English (7.4%)	Swedish (6.3%)	American (4.8%)
Rockford city *Winnebago Co.*	German (20.5%)	Irish (11.1%)	Swedish (8.5%)	American (7.9%)	English (7.0%)
Rolling Meadows city *Cook Co.*	German (24.0%)	Polish (13.0%)	Irish (11.2%)	Italian (9.0%)	English (5.9%)
Romeoville village *Will Co.*	German (18.1%)	Irish (15.3%)	Polish (14.5%)	Italian (10.9%)	English (3.0%)
Round Lake Beach village *Lake Co.*	German (15.9%)	Irish (10.8%)	Polish (9.6%)	English (4.7%)	Italian (3.2%)
Saint Charles city *Kane Co.*	German (32.4%)	Irish (19.2%)	Italian (14.3%)	English (11.0%)	Polish (10.8%)
Schaumburg village *Cook Co.*	German (23.4%)	Polish (17.0%)	Irish (13.9%)	Italian (13.2%)	English (5.8%)
Skokie village *Cook Co.*	German (10.1%)	Russian (7.8%)	Polish (6.6%)	ACS (6.3%)	Irish (6.2%)
Springfield city *Sangamon Co.*	German (28.0%)	Irish (15.4%)	English (11.7%)	American (7.6%)	Italian (6.5%)
Streamwood village *Cook Co.*	German (17.1%)	Polish (12.3%)	Italian (10.3%)	Irish (10.1%)	English (2.8%)
Tinley Park village *Cook Co.*	Irish (26.9%)	German (23.7%)	Polish (18.9%)	Italian (12.9%)	English (6.0%)
Urbana city *Champaign Co.*	German (19.0%)	Irish (10.4%)	American (8.9%)	English (8.1%)	Polish (4.7%)
Vernon Hills village *Lake Co.*	German (16.7%)	Irish (11.6%)	Polish (9.8%)	Russian (8.9%)	Italian (7.7%)
Waukegan city *Lake Co.*	German (7.0%)	Irish (4.6%)	Italian (2.8%)	Polish (2.5%)	English (2.5%)
West Chicago city *Du Page Co.*	German (15.4%)	Irish (8.1%)	Polish (6.1%)	Italian (5.0%)	English (3.9%)
Westmont village *Du Page Co.*	German (19.7%)	Polish (13.5%)	Irish (13.4%)	Italian (8.5%)	Czech (5.3%)
Wheaton city *Du Page Co.*	German (30.5%)	Irish (18.6%)	English (13.0%)	Italian (10.4%)	Polish (9.8%)
Wheeling village *Cook Co.*	German (14.2%)	Polish (10.7%)	Irish (8.0%)	Russian (7.4%)	Italian (4.1%)
Wilmette village *Cook Co.*	Irish (22.2%)	German (21.4%)	English (11.2%)	Polish (7.5%)	Russian (6.7%)
Woodridge village *Du Page Co.*	German (19.6%)	Irish (13.3%)	Polish (12.8%)	Italian (9.3%)	English (6.5%)
Woodstock city *McHenry Co.*	German (29.8%)	Irish (17.6%)	Polish (7.8%)	English (7.6%)	Italian (6.3%)
Zion city *Lake Co.*	German (13.5%)	Irish (11.6%)	English (5.2%)	Polish (3.4%)	Swedish (3.0%)

NOTE: Values are 2005-2009 5-year estimates; "French" excludes Basque; ACS = Assyrian/Chaldean/Syriac; Please refer to the Explanation of Data for more information.

Marriage Status

Place	Never Married (%)	Now Married (%)	Widowed (%)	Divorced (%)
Addison village *Du Page Co.*	32.2	56.6	4.8	6.5
Algonquin village *McHenry Co.*	24.9	64.2	3.3	7.5
Alton city *Madison Co.*	32.7	44.0	8.2	15.0
Arlington Heights village *Cook Co.*	23.4	61.3	7.7	7.6
Aurora city *Kane Co.*	34.5	52.6	4.2	8.6
Bartlett village *Du Page Co.*	23.2	66.5	3.6	6.8
Batavia city *Kane Co.*	25.3	62.1	4.4	8.2
Belleville city *Saint Clair Co.*	34.4	44.2	7.4	13.9
Belvidere city *Boone Co.*	30.1	53.6	6.4	9.9
Berwyn city *Cook Co.*	38.3	45.7	6.2	9.8
Bloomington city *McLean Co.*	32.5	52.1	4.6	10.8
Bolingbrook village *Will Co.*	30.2	60.1	3.1	6.6
Buffalo Grove village *Lake Co.*	23.2	63.8	5.3	7.7
Burbank city *Cook Co.*	31.9	54.3	6.8	7.0
Calumet City city *Cook Co.*	39.4	41.0	7.6	12.0
Carol Stream village *Du Page Co.*	31.2	56.9	4.6	7.3
Carpentersville village *Kane Co.*	33.5	53.8	4.0	8.6
Champaign city *Champaign Co.*	55.9	34.5	3.2	6.4
Chicago city *Cook Co.*	46.0	39.3	6.0	8.8
Chicago Heights city *Cook Co.*	42.6	41.7	7.5	8.2
Cicero town *Cook Co.*	36.3	53.5	4.4	5.8
Collinsville city *Madison Co.*	32.4	49.3	5.7	12.6
Crystal Lake city *McHenry Co.*	28.0	55.9	6.0	10.1
Danville city *Vermilion Co.*	33.5	43.3	9.1	14.1
Darien city *Du Page Co.*	24.1	61.4	6.0	8.6
DeKalb city *De Kalb Co.*	61.9	28.9	3.2	6.0
Decatur city *Macon Co.*	30.6	48.3	8.6	12.5
Des Plaines city *Cook Co.*	25.9	54.7	9.5	9.9
Dolton village *Cook Co.*	42.7	39.0	5.7	12.6
Downers Grove village *Du Page Co.*	26.9	56.8	7.3	9.0
East Saint Louis city *Saint Clair Co.*	51.4	24.8	10.8	13.0
Elgin city *Kane Co.*	34.2	52.2	4.9	8.8
Elk Grove Village village *Cook Co.*	27.8	59.1	5.5	7.6
Elmhurst city *Du Page Co.*	26.1	59.9	7.0	7.0
Elmwood Park village *Cook Co.*	34.5	47.2	9.1	9.2
Evanston city *Cook Co.*	40.0	45.8	6.0	8.2
Freeport city *Stephenson Co.*	28.1	48.9	9.9	13.2
Galesburg city *Knox Co.*	34.0	44.5	8.0	13.4
Geneva city *Kane Co.*	27.6	60.8	3.9	7.7
Glen Ellyn village *Du Page Co.*	23.3	61.5	6.9	8.4
Glendale Heights village *Du Page Co.*	32.2	54.2	4.7	8.9
Glenview village *Cook Co.*	21.5	64.9	7.9	5.7
Granite City city *Madison Co.*	26.0	51.2	9.4	13.4
Grayslake village *Lake Co.*	27.7	57.9	4.2	10.1
Gurnee village *Lake Co.*	26.4	60.6	4.9	8.1
Hanover Park village *Cook Co.*	30.6	58.6	2.7	8.1
Harvey city *Cook Co.*	46.8	35.5	7.4	10.4
Highland Park city *Lake Co.*	19.9	66.8	6.1	7.2
Hoffman Estates village *Cook Co.*	26.8	60.5	5.1	7.6
Joliet city *Will Co.*	32.7	51.4	5.5	10.4

Place	Never Married (%)	Now Married (%)	Widowed (%)	Divorced (%)
Kankakee city *Kankakee Co.*	42.8	38.1	7.1	12.0
Lake in the Hills village *McHenry Co.*	26.0	61.3	2.2	10.5
Lansing village *Cook Co.*	30.9	52.2	7.7	9.2
Lombard village *Du Page Co.*	28.6	54.7	8.3	8.4
Loves Park city *Winnebago Co.*	25.3	54.9	6.0	13.8
Maywood village *Cook Co.*	44.4	38.6	6.8	10.2
McHenry city *McHenry Co.*	27.4	57.2	6.6	8.8
Moline city *Rock Island Co.*	27.0	53.4	7.1	12.5
Mount Prospect village *Cook Co.*	27.6	58.8	7.0	6.6
Mundelein village *Lake Co.*	31.4	57.7	3.3	7.6
Naperville city *Du Page Co.*	26.2	63.5	3.9	6.4
New Lenox village *Will Co.*	25.1	64.0	3.8	7.1
Niles village *Cook Co.*	26.8	54.3	11.8	7.0
Normal town *McLean Co.*	56.6	34.2	3.2	6.0
North Chicago city *Lake Co.*	52.0	36.4	3.6	7.9
Northbrook village *Cook Co.*	20.9	65.5	6.4	7.2
O'Fallon city *Saint Clair Co.*	28.9	59.1	4.1	7.9
Oak Forest city *Cook Co.*	29.7	56.2	5.2	8.9
Oak Lawn village *Cook Co.*	30.3	51.3	9.8	8.6
Oak Park village *Cook Co.*	31.2	53.5	4.7	10.6
Orland Park village *Cook Co.*	25.1	58.8	9.0	7.1
Oswego village *Kendall Co.*	22.8	66.6	4.0	6.5
Palatine village *Cook Co.*	29.2	56.6	5.2	9.1
Park Ridge city *Cook Co.*	22.6	62.8	7.7	6.9
Pekin city *Tazewell Co.*	25.9	51.0	8.2	14.8
Peoria city *Peoria Co.*	38.4	42.6	6.7	12.3
Plainfield village *Will Co.*	23.6	65.2	5.2	6.0
Quincy city *Adams Co.*	29.9	48.4	9.7	11.9
Rock Island city *Rock Island Co.*	35.3	44.6	7.6	12.5
Rockford city *Winnebago Co.*	34.4	44.8	7.9	12.9
Rolling Meadows city *Cook Co.*	28.5	56.2	5.1	10.2
Romeoville village *Will Co.*	31.5	55.1	3.8	9.6
Round Lake Beach village *Lake Co.*	32.6	56.9	2.6	8.0
Saint Charles city *Kane Co.*	26.6	58.4	4.9	10.2
Schaumburg village *Cook Co.*	30.5	53.2	6.4	9.9
Skokie village *Cook Co.*	29.0	56.9	7.6	6.6
Springfield city *Sangamon Co.*	32.5	47.0	6.8	13.7
Streamwood village *Cook Co.*	27.5	60.0	4.7	7.8
Tinley Park village *Cook Co.*	28.3	55.6	7.5	8.6
Urbana city *Champaign Co.*	62.2	28.8	3.6	5.4
Vernon Hills village *Lake Co.*	25.4	61.6	4.6	8.4
Waukegan city *Lake Co.*	36.9	48.2	5.2	9.8
West Chicago city *Du Page Co.*	33.0	58.0	3.1	5.9
Westmont village *Du Page Co.*	28.5	51.6	10.1	9.8
Wheaton city *Du Page Co.*	32.9	54.4	5.6	7.2
Wheeling village *Cook Co.*	30.4	55.3	5.8	8.5
Wilmette village *Cook Co.*	21.3	66.3	6.5	5.9
Woodridge village *Du Page Co.*	32.8	55.2	3.3	8.8
Woodstock city *McHenry Co.*	29.8	55.1	5.4	9.7
Zion city *Lake Co.*	35.6	49.0	4.0	11.4

NOTE: Values are 2005-2009 5-year estimates.

Employment and Building Permits Issued

Place	Unemployment Rate (%)	Total Civilian Labor Force	Single-Family Building Permits	Multi-Family Building Permits
Addison village *Du Page Co.*	10.0	19,685	1	0
Algonquin village *McHenry Co.*	9.1	16,825	2	0
Alton city *Madison Co.*	11.5	13,937	4	0
Arlington Heights village *Cook Co.*	7.8	40,764	13	0
Aurora city *Kane Co.*	10.8	91,412	71	0
Bartlett village *Du Page Co.*	8.5	24,328	1	0
Batavia city *Kane Co.*	8.2	15,023	5	0
Belleville city *Saint Clair Co.*	11.3	21,791	48	0
Belvidere city *Boone Co.*	15.8	12,761	8	0
Berwyn city *Cook Co.*	11.6	25,268	0	0
Bloomington city *McLean Co.*	7.8	41,618	184	3
Bolingbrook village *Will Co.*	9.9	40,030	37	63
Buffalo Grove village *Lake Co.*	8.0	24,161	54	0
Burbank city *Cook Co.*	10.4	14,347	8	0
Calumet City city *Cook Co.*	14.3	18,199	0	0
Carol Stream village *Du Page Co.*	9.3	23,086	11	0
Carpentersville village *Kane Co.*	11.8	18,680	35	0
Champaign city *Champaign Co.*	9.3	40,723	63	266
Chicago city *Cook Co.*	11.7	1,333,308	164	1,713
Chicago Heights city *Cook Co.*	15.7	13,398	0	0
Cicero town *Cook Co.*	12.6	32,046	0	0
Collinsville city *Madison Co.*	8.4	14,303	3	0
Crystal Lake city *McHenry Co.*	9.2	22,469	12	0
Danville city *Vermilion Co.*	12.1	13,354	5	0
Darien city *Du Page Co.*	n/a	n/a	1	0
DeKalb city *De Kalb Co.*	10.1	24,905	3	0
Decatur city *Macon Co.*	12.1	37,224	20	0
Des Plaines city *Cook Co.*	9.4	29,981	37	0
Dolton village *Cook Co.*	15.6	12,453	3	0
Downers Grove village *Du Page Co.*	7.8	27,130	24	0
East Saint Louis city *Saint Clair Co.*	18.5	10,204	8	30
Elgin city *Kane Co.*	11.0	57,814	182	0
Elk Grove Village village *Cook Co.*	8.2	19,795	1	0
Elmhurst city *Du Page Co.*	7.2	24,860	46	183
Elmwood Park village *Cook Co.*	10.5	13,137	1	0
Evanston city *Cook Co.*	8.0	42,728	10	146
Freeport city *Stephenson Co.*	12.0	12,401	0	0
Galesburg city *Knox Co.*	9.2	14,970	0	0
Geneva city *Kane Co.*	n/a	n/a	5	0
Glen Ellyn village *Du Page Co.*	7.8	14,540	13	0
Glendale Heights village *Du Page Co.*	10.2	18,944	0	0
Glenview village *Cook Co.*	7.3	23,953	14	0
Granite City city *Madison Co.*	10.0	15,049	15	43
Grayslake village *Lake Co.*	n/a	n/a	1	0
Gurnee village *Lake Co.*	9.4	17,073	1	0
Hanover Park village *Cook Co.*	10.4	20,649	20	0
Harvey city *Cook Co.*	17.3	11,264	0	0
Highland Park city *Lake Co.*	6.2	16,209	14	30
Hoffman Estates village *Cook Co.*	8.3	30,980	10	0
Joliet city *Will Co.*	13.0	73,435	78	6

Place	Unemployment Rate (%)	Total Civilian Labor Force	Single-Family Building Permits	Multi-Family Building Permits
Kankakee city *Kankakee Co.*	16.2	12,253	0	2
Lake in the Hills village *McHenry Co.*	8.9	17,048	3	0
Lansing village *Cook Co.*	11.0	14,138	0	0
Lombard village *Du Page Co.*	9.5	24,479	5	0
Loves Park city *Winnebago Co.*	n/a	n/a	27	0
Maywood village *Cook Co.*	17.3	11,947	0	0
McHenry city *McHenry Co.*	9.4	15,229	8	0
Moline city *Rock Island Co.*	7.2	23,648	0	0
Mount Prospect village *Cook Co.*	7.8	29,702	3	0
Mundelein village *Lake Co.*	8.2	17,910	49	0
Naperville city *Du Page Co.*	7.9	76,727	94	0
New Lenox village *Will Co.*	n/a	n/a	23	0
Niles village *Cook Co.*	9.1	14,039	3	0
Normal town *McLean Co.*	7.4	27,947	80	97
North Chicago city *Lake Co.*	19.5	9,750	0	0
Northbrook village *Cook Co.*	7.7	17,090	24	0
O'Fallon city *Saint Clair Co.*	8.2	14,201	140	232
Oak Forest city *Cook Co.*	10.3	15,840	4	0
Oak Lawn village *Cook Co.*	11.3	26,535	5	0
Oak Park village *Cook Co.*	8.0	32,312	2	0
Orland Park village *Cook Co.*	8.8	28,792	38	0
Oswego village *Kendall Co.*	8.6	16,322	116	0
Palatine village *Cook Co.*	7.7	39,943	16	0
Park Ridge city *Cook Co.*	8.1	19,110	8	0
Pekin city *Tazewell Co.*	9.9	18,162	30	0
Peoria city *Peoria Co.*	9.8	60,185	146	203
Plainfield village *Will Co.*	9.6	20,260	59	0
Quincy city *Adams Co.*	7.4	22,124	50	88
Rock Island city *Rock Island Co.*	8.7	19,893	9	70
Rockford city *Winnebago Co.*	15.2	71,897	24	2
Rolling Meadows city *Cook Co.*	n/a	n/a	1	0
Romeoville village *Will Co.*	10.4	22,291	9	0
Round Lake Beach village *Lake Co.*	10.3	14,393	0	0
Saint Charles city *Kane Co.*	8.7	19,005	8	0
Schaumburg village *Cook Co.*	8.7	44,682	0	0
Skokie village *Cook Co.*	8.7	33,874	2	0
Springfield city *Sangamon Co.*	8.1	67,794	106	99
Streamwood village *Cook Co.*	9.7	21,838	6	0
Tinley Park village *Cook Co.*	8.6	32,740	8	0
Urbana city *Champaign Co.*	9.9	19,501	28	2
Vernon Hills village *Lake Co.*	n/a	n/a	4	231
Waukegan city *Lake Co.*	11.5	43,315	17	10
West Chicago city *Du Page Co.*	10.3	14,395	6	0
Westmont village *Du Page Co.*	8.8	13,541	4	0
Wheaton city *Du Page Co.*	8.1	29,477	18	0
Wheeling village *Cook Co.*	8.5	21,553	9	0
Wilmette village *Cook Co.*	7.1	12,592	24	0
Woodridge village *Du Page Co.*	9.0	20,163	5	0
Woodstock city *McHenry Co.*	n/a	n/a	102	4
Zion city *Lake Co.*	12.9	12,072	10	0

NOTE: Unemployment Rate and Civilian Labor Force as of August 2011; Building permit data covers 2010; n/a not available.

Employment by Occupation

Place	Sales (%)	Prof. (%)	Mgmt (%)	Svcs (%)	Prod. (%)	Constr. (%)
Addison village *Du Page Co.*	29.1	12.3	12.9	12.9	21.1	11.7
Algonquin village *McHenry Co.*	31.5	23.6	18.9	8.2	10.0	7.8
Alton city *Madison Co.*	23.2	20.9	8.1	24.1	17.0	6.6
Arlington Heights village *Cook Co.*	29.3	26.1	22.9	9.6	7.0	5.2
Aurora city *Kane Co.*	25.3	17.2	14.9	14.8	20.2	7.5
Bartlett village *Du Page Co.*	31.6	20.0	22.4	10.8	8.4	6.8
Batavia city *Kane Co.*	28.1	25.1	21.9	10.0	8.8	5.9
Belleville city *Saint Clair Co.*	27.2	17.6	12.9	21.2	12.0	8.7
Belvidere city *Boone Co.*	25.0	12.1	7.0	12.9	32.1	10.6
Berwyn city *Cook Co.*	26.6	15.6	10.0	20.5	17.7	9.6
Bloomington city *McLean Co.*	28.7	25.1	17.1	15.1	7.8	6.0
Bolingbrook village *Will Co.*	26.4	20.4	15.2	17.1	13.9	6.8
Buffalo Grove village *Lake Co.*	27.5	30.3	25.5	8.5	5.2	2.9
Burbank city *Cook Co.*	26.2	10.2	8.6	16.6	21.4	17.0
Calumet City city *Cook Co.*	29.8	14.2	9.6	17.8	21.2	7.3
Carol Stream village *Du Page Co.*	32.5	18.8	13.8	15.0	11.7	8.0
Carpentersville village *Kane Co.*	25.1	12.2	11.0	18.2	21.9	11.2
Champaign city *Champaign Co.*	23.3	33.9	10.7	19.8	8.1	3.9
Chicago city *Cook Co.*	24.6	21.1	14.4	19.4	13.8	6.5
Chicago Heights city *Cook Co.*	28.1	16.5	7.8	21.5	16.5	9.5
Cicero town *Cook Co.*	21.4	5.8	5.2	20.8	34.1	12.4
Collinsville city *Madison Co.*	26.9	20.5	11.5	19.3	12.7	9.0
Crystal Lake city *McHenry Co.*	30.1	21.9	14.2	16.4	10.8	6.6
Danville city *Vermilion Co.*	23.3	17.2	10.3	18.4	22.9	7.9
Darien city *Du Page Co.*	28.8	24.9	20.4	11.4	8.1	6.2
DeKalb city *De Kalb Co.*	28.5	25.0	9.3	19.8	11.4	5.8
Decatur city *Macon Co.*	25.5	20.7	9.9	19.1	17.2	7.3
Des Plaines city *Cook Co.*	29.0	19.2	15.3	15.7	12.4	8.4
Dolton village *Cook Co.*	32.7	16.7	10.4	18.1	15.7	6.4
Downers Grove village *Du Page Co.*	29.1	28.5	20.6	9.6	6.4	5.7
East Saint Louis city *Saint Clair Co.*	22.7	15.3	7.8	35.6	14.6	4.1
Elgin city *Kane Co.*	24.4	16.4	11.4	16.4	21.7	9.2
Elk Grove Village village *Cook Co.*	33.4	19.3	17.9	13.0	9.5	6.9
Elmhurst city *Du Page Co.*	27.8	26.5	20.7	11.2	7.0	6.6
Elmwood Park village *Cook Co.*	29.4	16.5	10.9	18.0	14.7	10.5
Evanston city *Cook Co.*	20.3	41.4	20.5	10.0	4.8	2.9
Freeport city *Stephenson Co.*	28.8	15.4	10.5	20.0	19.7	5.2
Galesburg city *Knox Co.*	26.9	17.3	9.7	22.5	16.8	6.5
Geneva city *Kane Co.*	29.5	25.4	24.1	8.9	7.3	4.9
Glen Ellyn village *Du Page Co.*	25.0	28.2	26.9	10.9	5.1	3.7
Glendale Heights village *Du Page Co.*	31.9	16.4	12.0	12.8	19.2	7.7
Glenview village *Cook Co.*	27.3	29.9	24.5	9.8	4.5	4.0
Granite City city *Madison Co.*	29.0	15.3	10.8	16.8	17.2	10.9
Grayslake village *Lake Co.*	28.0	26.3	23.0	11.1	5.7	5.7
Gurnee village *Lake Co.*	28.7	26.6	22.5	9.8	7.6	4.8
Hanover Park village *Cook Co.*	30.1	14.0	12.0	18.1	17.9	7.9
Harvey city *Cook Co.*	28.9	12.3	3.8	26.2	18.5	9.8
Highland Park city *Lake Co.*	27.9	30.2	24.6	10.1	3.8	3.4
Hoffman Estates village *Cook Co.*	28.2	23.7	21.0	11.2	9.9	5.8
Joliet city *Will Co.*	26.2	14.5	10.2	19.5	19.6	9.7

Place	Sales (%)	Prof. (%)	Mgmt (%)	Svcs (%)	Prod. (%)	Constr. (%)
Kankakee city *Kankakee Co.*	19.8	15.6	5.7	24.4	24.6	6.7
Lake in the Hills village *McHenry Co.*	28.9	16.7	18.2	13.6	12.2	10.4
Lansing village *Cook Co.*	30.5	17.9	10.7	15.6	15.2	9.9
Lombard village *Du Page Co.*	32.8	25.7	15.5	9.3	9.3	7.3
Loves Park city *Winnebago Co.*	30.7	18.3	9.6	16.1	18.1	7.1
Maywood village *Cook Co.*	28.7	13.5	6.6	20.8	22.9	7.4
McHenry city *McHenry Co.*	30.6	18.2	13.1	14.3	14.7	9.1
Moline city *Rock Island Co.*	25.9	16.9	11.8	20.9	17.9	6.5
Mount Prospect village *Cook Co.*	26.4	22.3	17.3	13.8	13.0	7.1
Mundelein village *Lake Co.*	26.2	19.1	18.9	16.9	12.8	6.1
Naperville city *Du Page Co.*	27.7	31.7	24.7	8.8	3.8	3.1
New Lenox village *Will Co.*	28.1	23.7	15.8	10.5	10.3	11.5
Niles village *Cook Co.*	30.6	20.7	11.0	15.3	13.1	9.3
Normal town *McLean Co.*	32.7	23.1	13.2	19.9	6.9	4.3
North Chicago city *Lake Co.*	21.6	15.6	7.0	21.6	23.9	10.1
Northbrook village *Cook Co.*	28.7	31.7	28.9	5.0	3.5	2.1
O'Fallon city *Saint Clair Co.*	28.9	25.8	18.8	15.0	5.5	5.6
Oak Forest city *Cook Co.*	29.3	20.2	11.1	16.6	11.7	11.2
Oak Lawn village *Cook Co.*	27.8	20.2	13.0	15.3	12.2	11.4
Oak Park village *Cook Co.*	22.3	40.6	20.9	9.1	4.5	2.5
Orland Park village *Cook Co.*	29.2	21.7	20.1	13.6	8.1	7.3
Oswego village *Kendall Co.*	28.0	24.2	19.1	11.3	9.2	8.1
Palatine village *Cook Co.*	28.2	23.2	19.9	12.5	10.6	5.6
Park Ridge city *Cook Co.*	27.3	28.0	24.9	10.3	3.9	5.7
Pekin city *Tazewell Co.*	25.4	16.9	10.5	21.0	18.5	7.3
Peoria city *Peoria Co.*	25.9	25.9	12.8	19.4	11.1	4.6
Plainfield village *Will Co.*	26.8	25.6	23.5	11.2	7.9	5.0
Quincy city *Adams Co.*	25.4	18.9	11.2	23.0	15.5	5.8
Rock Island city *Rock Island Co.*	26.9	19.3	10.7	16.8	18.0	8.1
Rockford city *Winnebago Co.*	26.1	17.5	9.9	18.8	21.3	6.4
Rolling Meadows city *Cook Co.*	27.8	16.6	18.4	16.2	11.8	8.9
Romeoville village *Will Co.*	29.1	17.1	11.7	15.2	17.3	9.6
Round Lake Beach village *Lake Co.*	26.6	14.6	8.5	20.6	17.1	12.1
Saint Charles city *Kane Co.*	29.8	23.4	21.1	11.9	7.4	6.5
Schaumburg village *Cook Co.*	28.9	24.5	21.3	10.8	9.1	5.4
Skokie village *Cook Co.*	26.1	29.3	15.5	12.8	11.3	4.9
Springfield city *Sangamon Co.*	29.4	24.5	15.1	18.5	6.6	5.7
Streamwood village *Cook Co.*	30.3	17.5	14.2	15.3	14.0	8.4
Tinley Park village *Cook Co.*	29.1	20.7	14.7	13.5	12.1	9.8
Urbana city *Champaign Co.*	22.0	40.9	8.0	19.2	6.9	2.7
Vernon Hills village *Lake Co.*	26.4	27.1	23.6	11.0	7.7	4.3
Waukegan city *Lake Co.*	22.7	11.6	7.8	22.2	25.8	9.8
West Chicago city *Du Page Co.*	22.3	14.9	10.4	15.7	23.0	12.3
Westmont village *Du Page Co.*	24.6	27.4	16.2	15.3	8.9	7.6
Wheaton city *Du Page Co.*	27.7	31.6	20.5	11.3	5.3	3.6
Wheeling village *Cook Co.*	26.5	17.4	13.0	17.4	18.8	6.9
Wilmette village *Cook Co.*	23.4	38.4	27.7	5.8	2.9	1.8
Woodridge village *Du Page Co.*	29.3	24.1	16.0	13.9	10.3	6.1
Woodstock city *McHenry Co.*	25.0	19.6	12.1	15.0	18.4	9.8
Zion city *Lake Co.*	27.5	14.6	11.0	20.5	17.3	8.9

NOTE: Values are 2005-2009 5-year estimates.

Educational Attainment

Place	High School Diploma including Equivalency	Bachelor's Degree or Higher	Masters's Degree or Higher
	Percent of Population 25 Years and Over with:		
Addison village *Du Page Co.*	77.8	21.1	6.3
Algonquin village *McHenry Co.*	96.1	41.9	12.9
Alton city *Madison Co.*	87.7	19.4	6.1
Arlington Heights village *Cook Co.*	94.4	50.0	18.3
Aurora city *Kane Co.*	77.7	32.8	11.3
Bartlett village *Du Page Co.*	94.4	41.7	12.7
Batavia city *Kane Co.*	94.8	48.0	17.3
Belleville city *Saint Clair Co.*	89.2	20.9	6.8
Belvidere city *Boone Co.*	80.4	11.9	2.5
Berwyn city *Cook Co.*	80.4	20.8	7.5
Bloomington city *McLean Co.*	93.3	42.7	12.5
Bolingbrook village *Will Co.*	89.3	35.1	10.3
Buffalo Grove village *Lake Co.*	96.6	59.7	23.4
Burbank city *Cook Co.*	80.1	11.7	3.9
Calumet City city *Cook Co.*	85.7	16.8	4.8
Carol Stream village *Du Page Co.*	92.3	35.1	10.8
Carpentersville village *Kane Co.*	71.1	16.8	4.7
Champaign city *Champaign Co.*	92.5	47.8	24.3
Chicago city *Cook Co.*	77.7	30.0	12.1
Chicago Heights city *Cook Co.*	77.1	15.4	5.4
Cicero town *Cook Co.*	54.4	7.8	2.9
Collinsville city *Madison Co.*	90.4	24.1	7.6
Crystal Lake city *McHenry Co.*	94.2	41.8	14.0
Danville city *Vermilion Co.*	82.6	15.1	4.8
Darien city *Du Page Co.*	94.2	44.9	18.4
DeKalb city *De Kalb Co.*	91.2	37.1	16.7
Decatur city *Macon Co.*	84.8	19.8	6.7
Des Plaines city *Cook Co.*	86.4	28.4	9.7
Dolton village *Cook Co.*	87.4	18.5	4.4
Downers Grove village *Du Page Co.*	94.7	48.6	20.5
East Saint Louis city *Saint Clair Co.*	76.3	11.8	3.7
Elgin city *Kane Co.*	77.5	24.8	7.7
Elk Grove Village village *Cook Co.*	93.1	35.5	10.4
Elmhurst city *Du Page Co.*	93.6	48.1	20.1
Elmwood Park village *Cook Co.*	84.7	22.9	7.7
Evanston city *Cook Co.*	93.9	66.4	36.1
Freeport city *Stephenson Co.*	86.4	18.3	6.1
Galesburg city *Knox Co.*	82.5	15.2	5.3
Geneva city *Kane Co.*	95.6	56.3	21.8
Glen Ellyn village *Du Page Co.*	95.2	60.1	24.8
Glendale Heights village *Du Page Co.*	86.1	29.3	8.1
Glenview village *Cook Co.*	95.6	56.7	24.9
Granite City city *Madison Co.*	84.4	11.8	3.5
Grayslake village *Lake Co.*	94.8	51.3	19.5
Gurnee village *Lake Co.*	95.1	49.6	18.7
Hanover Park village *Cook Co.*	83.8	25.8	6.3
Harvey city *Cook Co.*	75.6	10.2	3.1
Highland Park city *Lake Co.*	92.0	64.7	31.7
Hoffman Estates village *Cook Co.*	92.6	40.4	13.8
Joliet city *Will Co.*	81.6	22.2	7.1

Place	Percent of Population 25 Years and Over with:		
	High School Diploma including Equivalency	Bachelor's Degree or Higher	Masters's Degree or Higher
Kankakee city Kankakee Co.	75.2	14.8	5.6
Lake in the Hills village McHenry Co.	95.0	38.0	8.8
Lansing village Cook Co.	90.6	21.8	6.5
Lombard village Du Page Co.	92.2	38.2	13.1
Loves Park city Winnebago Co.	88.3	19.2	5.9
Maywood village Cook Co.	80.5	13.1	5.0
McHenry city McHenry Co.	89.9	25.9	7.5
Moline city Rock Island Co.	88.0	24.4	7.9
Mount Prospect village Cook Co.	88.8	39.6	13.9
Mundelein village Lake Co.	83.1	41.1	14.8
Naperville city Du Page Co.	97.2	62.5	25.8
New Lenox village Will Co.	94.0	28.4	9.3
Niles village Cook Co.	86.1	29.3	10.7
Normal town McLean Co.	95.5	44.3	14.5
North Chicago city Lake Co.	76.2	15.7	6.2
Northbrook village Cook Co.	96.9	65.6	28.8
O'Fallon city Saint Clair Co.	95.1	42.8	18.4
Oak Forest city Cook Co.	92.0	25.6	8.0
Oak Lawn village Cook Co.	88.0	24.5	8.2
Oak Park village Cook Co.	96.2	66.0	33.4
Orland Park village Cook Co.	93.2	35.6	13.6
Oswego village Kendall Co.	95.4	38.2	13.0
Palatine village Cook Co.	91.8	45.5	15.9
Park Ridge city Cook Co.	94.5	50.1	20.6
Pekin city Tazewell Co.	87.9	17.8	5.8
Peoria city Peoria Co.	86.6	31.9	11.8
Plainfield village Will Co.	96.6	43.8	11.5
Quincy city Adams Co.	89.1	23.1	7.8
Rock Island city Rock Island Co.	86.3	21.5	7.2
Rockford city Winnebago Co.	78.5	19.9	6.8
Rolling Meadows city Cook Co.	86.7	34.2	10.6
Romeoville village Will Co.	87.3	22.8	5.6
Round Lake Beach village Lake Co.	75.3	17.2	5.6
Saint Charles city Kane Co.	93.4	47.9	16.8
Schaumburg village Cook Co.	94.5	42.8	13.8
Skokie village Cook Co.	91.2	47.3	19.9
Springfield city Sangamon Co.	90.4	31.2	11.7
Streamwood village Cook Co.	89.1	31.4	8.9
Tinley Park village Cook Co.	92.6	28.5	9.1
Urbana city Champaign Co.	92.7	56.9	34.6
Vernon Hills village Lake Co.	94.6	58.5	22.6
Waukegan city Lake Co.	67.4	18.0	6.5
West Chicago city Du Page Co.	74.0	24.8	7.7
Westmont village Du Page Co.	91.2	42.1	16.4
Wheaton city Du Page Co.	95.9	60.3	25.5
Wheeling village Cook Co.	85.9	35.8	12.3
Wilmette village Cook Co.	97.8	75.6	40.5
Woodridge village Du Page Co.	93.0	44.2	16.3
Woodstock city McHenry Co.	83.9	27.3	9.3
Zion city Lake Co.	81.0	18.3	7.1

NOTE: Data as of 2010

Income and Poverty

Place	Average Household Income ($)	Median Household Income ($)	Per Capita Income ($)	Households w/$100,000+ Income (%)	Poverty Rate (%)
Addison village *Du Page Co.*	74,022	59,689	24,394	21.8	11.3
Algonquin village *McHenry Co.*	112,590	95,809	37,154	46.9	3.8
Alton city *Madison Co.*	47,100	38,444	20,334	7.8	21.3
Arlington Heights village *Cook Co.*	98,137	77,984	40,083	37.0	3.6
Aurora city *Kane Co.*	80,584	63,571	25,929	25.1	12.1
Bartlett village *Du Page Co.*	111,160	94,711	36,972	45.9	3.2
Batavia city *Kane Co.*	97,590	82,419	34,069	38.2	5.9
Belleville city *Saint Clair Co.*	51,581	42,102	22,875	9.6	12.3
Belvidere city *Boone Co.*	53,215	46,332	19,241	9.0	14.1
Berwyn city *Cook Co.*	62,151	50,915	22,142	15.4	11.2
Bloomington city *McLean Co.*	71,199	54,800	29,746	20.8	11.4
Bolingbrook village *Will Co.*	94,809	82,643	29,560	36.6	5.7
Buffalo Grove village *Lake Co.*	123,086	96,247	44,059	47.6	3.3
Burbank city *Cook Co.*	69,092	60,382	23,076	20.5	9.9
Calumet City city *Cook Co.*	53,036	44,426	20,087	10.6	16.8
Carol Stream village *Du Page Co.*	88,911	77,054	30,147	33.6	7.4
Carpentersville village *Kane Co.*	75,797	63,252	21,352	22.2	9.4
Champaign city *Champaign Co.*	53,786	39,158	22,287	12.3	27.2
Chicago city *Cook Co.*	66,345	47,233	24,664	18.1	20.8
Chicago Heights city *Cook Co.*	54,410	42,624	17,757	12.6	23.6
Cicero town *Cook Co.*	53,484	45,087	14,097	9.6	16.1
Collinsville city *Madison Co.*	60,202	51,085	26,132	14.9	11.8
Crystal Lake city *McHenry Co.*	93,739	80,249	32,476	34.6	4.5
Danville city *Vermilion Co.*	44,710	34,058	18,168	7.3	26.7
Darien city *Du Page Co.*	98,153	78,075	38,329	35.4	3.3
DeKalb city *De Kalb Co.*	51,358	40,164	18,244	11.7	28.2
Decatur city *Macon Co.*	51,940	39,478	22,337	10.6	20.0
Des Plaines city *Cook Co.*	74,582	63,250	28,695	22.8	6.6
Dolton village *Cook Co.*	61,149	53,190	20,171	13.7	16.1
Downers Grove village *Du Page Co.*	91,201	72,780	36,375	32.9	3.8
East Saint Louis city *Saint Clair Co.*	35,479	24,853	13,104	5.4	38.6
Elgin city *Kane Co.*	73,660	62,091	24,655	21.3	10.9
Elk Grove Village village *Cook Co.*	86,828	72,357	34,166	29.8	3.6
Elmhurst city *Du Page Co.*	106,112	82,709	39,575	39.1	3.2
Elmwood Park village *Cook Co.*	69,527	57,068	26,586	20.3	8.8
Evanston city *Cook Co.*	96,174	66,038	38,730	32.3	9.7
Freeport city *Stephenson Co.*	46,172	37,537	20,137	6.5	17.1
Galesburg city *Knox Co.*	44,583	34,536	18,570	6.5	20.9
Geneva city *Kane Co.*	110,379	89,412	37,643	43.0	1.8
Glen Ellyn village *Du Page Co.*	108,667	79,896	41,503	39.2	4.4
Glendale Heights village *Du Page Co.*	73,850	64,658	25,111	20.5	9.1
Glenview village *Cook Co.*	124,698	87,533	46,130	43.1	3.8
Granite City city *Madison Co.*	50,239	41,758	21,157	8.0	15.1
Grayslake village *Lake Co.*	106,866	92,167	35,968	43.6	4.7
Gurnee village *Lake Co.*	109,329	93,325	39,038	46.3	5.1
Hanover Park village *Cook Co.*	89,972	78,521	26,943	32.1	10.3
Harvey city *Cook Co.*	45,015	35,782	13,729	7.3	31.9
Highland Park city *Lake Co.*	157,702	111,102	57,288	54.7	4.3
Hoffman Estates village *Cook Co.*	90,469	71,913	31,785	31.0	5.7
Joliet city *Will Co.*	67,490	57,582	23,257	19.1	12.2

Place	Average Household Income ($)	Median Household Income ($)	Per Capita Income ($)	Households w/$100,000+ Income (%)	Poverty Rate (%)
Kankakee city *Kankakee Co.*	46,555	35,427	17,356	7.7	31.4
Lake in the Hills village *McHenry Co.*	104,957	91,112	34,324	41.9	4.2
Lansing village *Cook Co.*	64,426	54,586	26,029	15.5	10.6
Lombard village *Du Page Co.*	81,125	67,669	32,064	25.7	3.3
Loves Park city *Winnebago Co.*	57,226	49,543	23,256	10.0	8.4
Maywood village *Cook Co.*	59,076	48,543	17,351	14.6	15.2
McHenry city *McHenry Co.*	76,032	65,109	28,392	24.1	6.7
Moline city *Rock Island Co.*	60,024	46,710	25,490	14.0	10.2
Mount Prospect village *Cook Co.*	82,441	66,829	31,503	27.7	5.9
Mundelein village *Lake Co.*	97,790	81,179	30,770	35.6	4.0
Naperville city *Du Page Co.*	124,373	101,695	42,321	51.0	3.3
New Lenox village *Will Co.*	96,525	85,843	31,673	38.0	2.9
Niles village *Cook Co.*	71,036	59,428	28,661	21.1	6.3
Normal town *McLean Co.*	59,632	47,617	21,362	15.7	24.8
North Chicago city *Lake Co.*	57,916	43,587	15,974	11.6	16.0
Northbrook village *Cook Co.*	138,996	100,171	51,472	50.1	2.9
O'Fallon city *Saint Clair Co.*	82,505	68,373	31,852	27.9	6.8
Oak Forest city *Cook Co.*	81,669	71,307	28,836	27.7	6.7
Oak Lawn village *Cook Co.*	69,676	56,142	28,644	20.7	6.6
Oak Park village *Cook Co.*	101,221	71,401	45,311	34.2	5.6
Orland Park village *Cook Co.*	101,411	83,513	37,220	38.8	3.8
Oswego village *Kendall Co.*	101,514	89,648	34,558	40.9	3.5
Palatine village *Cook Co.*	97,994	77,830	38,198	35.0	7.5
Park Ridge city *Cook Co.*	109,621	85,331	41,561	40.7	2.5
Pekin city *Tazewell Co.*	56,832	45,803	24,168	12.4	12.8
Peoria city *Peoria Co.*	60,564	44,369	24,932	15.4	18.0
Plainfield village *Will Co.*	110,993	97,437	34,357	47.8	2.8
Quincy city *Adams Co.*	49,995	38,749	21,522	8.2	17.1
Rock Island city *Rock Island Co.*	53,789	41,753	22,546	11.1	17.5
Rockford city *Winnebago Co.*	53,558	40,497	21,387	10.5	21.9
Rolling Meadows city *Cook Co.*	85,526	69,384	31,625	28.2	7.0
Romeoville village *Will Co.*	71,419	64,515	25,012	17.8	6.0
Round Lake Beach village *Lake Co.*	77,364	69,113	21,726	23.9	14.0
Saint Charles city *Kane Co.*	106,218	81,548	39,389	38.3	4.9
Schaumburg village *Cook Co.*	88,134	72,953	36,119	30.1	4.5
Skokie village *Cook Co.*	87,041	68,367	31,422	29.7	7.6
Springfield city *Sangamon Co.*	60,973	45,797	27,321	14.7	15.8
Streamwood village *Cook Co.*	89,571	77,738	30,673	30.7	6.1
Tinley Park village *Cook Co.*	88,522	77,970	31,992	32.9	5.7
Urbana city *Champaign Co.*	47,245	33,124	19,232	9.3	30.4
Vernon Hills village *Lake Co.*	115,767	91,726	41,705	44.9	4.7
Waukegan city *Lake Co.*	60,619	48,669	19,205	13.9	13.0
West Chicago city *Du Page Co.*	89,867	72,819	25,365	30.8	12.1
Westmont village *Du Page Co.*	85,304	64,497	35,003	26.2	8.2
Wheaton city *Du Page Co.*	109,281	82,561	39,279	39.1	4.8
Wheeling village *Cook Co.*	81,902	67,287	30,366	25.8	8.1
Wilmette village *Cook Co.*	165,112	120,375	59,264	58.4	2.1
Woodridge village *Du Page Co.*	90,986	73,855	33,984	32.1	6.3
Woodstock city *McHenry Co.*	72,596	58,239	27,158	19.3	10.2
Zion city *Lake Co.*	63,782	52,225	21,204	16.8	15.7

NOTE: Data as of 2010 except for Poverty Rates which are 2005-2009 5-year estimates; (1) Percentage of population with income below the poverty level

Taxes

Place	Total City Taxes Per Capita ($)	City Property Taxes Per Capita ($)
Addison village *Du Page Co.*	506	252
Algonquin village *McHenry Co.*	353	158
Alton city *Madison Co.*	339	175
Arlington Heights village *Cook Co.*	840	573
Aurora city *Kane Co.*	697	432
Bartlett village *Du Page Co.*	n/a	n/a
Batavia city *Kane Co.*	407	218
Belleville city *Saint Clair Co.*	497	339
Belvidere city *Boone Co.*	204	173
Berwyn city *Cook Co.*	665	432
Bloomington city *McLean Co.*	590	239
Bolingbrook village *Will Co.*	599	194
Buffalo Grove village *Lake Co.*	n/a	n/a
Burbank city *Cook Co.*	464	251
Calumet City city *Cook Co.*	723	450
Carol Stream village *Du Page Co.*	237	13
Carpentersville village *Kane Co.*	270	182
Champaign city *Champaign Co.*	592	247
Chicago city *Cook Co.*	720	128
Chicago Heights city *Cook Co.*	592	411
Cicero town *Cook Co.*	828	502
Collinsville city *Madison Co.*	239	138
Crystal Lake city *McHenry Co.*	381	299
Danville city *Vermilion Co.*	438	196
Darien city *Du Page Co.*	166	66
DeKalb city *De Kalb Co.*	528	232
Decatur city *Macon Co.*	410	155
Des Plaines city *Cook Co.*	815	487
Dolton village *Cook Co.*	452	263
Downers Grove village *Du Page Co.*	599	309
East Saint Louis city *Saint Clair Co.*	499	329
Elgin city *Kane Co.*	507	400
Elk Grove Village village *Cook Co.*	990	474
Elmhurst city *Du Page Co.*	590	315
Elmwood Park village *Cook Co.*	629	418
Evanston city *Cook Co.*	991	545
Freeport city *Stephenson Co.*	285	143
Galesburg city *Knox Co.*	361	218
Geneva city *Kane Co.*	353	254
Glen Ellyn village *Du Page Co.*	454	295
Glendale Heights village *Du Page Co.*	407	231
Glenview village *Cook Co.*	1,066	786
Granite City city *Madison Co.*	390	242
Grayslake village *Lake Co.*	162	95
Gurnee village *Lake Co.*	227	15
Hanover Park village *Cook Co.*	436	278
Harvey city *Cook Co.*	435	293
Highland Park city *Lake Co.*	979	409
Hoffman Estates village *Cook Co.*	1,063	800
Joliet city *Will Co.*	453	211

Place	Total City Taxes Per Capita ($)	City Property Taxes Per Capita ($)
Kankakee city *Kankakee Co.*	565	418
Lake in the Hills village *McHenry Co.*	289	181
Lansing village *Cook Co.*	733	586
Lombard village *Du Page Co.*	486	166
Loves Park city *Winnebago Co.*	71	5
Maywood village *Cook Co.*	868	711
McHenry city *McHenry Co.*	198	171
Moline city *Rock Island Co.*	649	366
Mount Prospect village *Cook Co.*	701	444
Mundelein village *Lake Co.*	542	277
Naperville city *Du Page Co.*	499	290
New Lenox village *Will Co.*	126	93
Niles village *Cook Co.*	786	209
Normal town *McLean Co.*	465	146
North Chicago city *Lake Co.*	278	151
Northbrook village *Cook Co.*	762	415
O'Fallon city *Saint Clair Co.*	308	179
Oak Forest city *Cook Co.*	419	336
Oak Lawn village *Cook Co.*	484	333
Oak Park village *Cook Co.*	909	632
Orland Park village *Cook Co.*	635	378
Oswego village *Kendall Co.*	180	38
Palatine village *Cook Co.*	617	429
Park Ridge city *Cook Co.*	740	409
Pekin city *Tazewell Co.*	326	167
Peoria city *Peoria Co.*	600	233
Plainfield village *Will Co.*	338	134
Quincy city *Adams Co.*	304	83
Rock Island city *Rock Island Co.*	515	328
Rockford city *Winnebago Co.*	431	325
Rolling Meadows city *Cook Co.*	787	428
Romeoville village *Will Co.*	609	318
Round Lake Beach village *Lake Co.*	308	176
Saint Charles city *Kane Co.*	730	352
Schaumburg village *Cook Co.*	671	33
Skokie village *Cook Co.*	700	410
Springfield city *Sangamon Co.*	467	195
Streamwood village *Cook Co.*	365	188
Tinley Park village *Cook Co.*	422	350
Urbana city *Champaign Co.*	394	166
Vernon Hills village *Lake Co.*	231	0
Waukegan city *Lake Co.*	413	241
West Chicago city *Du Page Co.*	303	141
Westmont village *Du Page Co.*	418	173
Wheaton city *Du Page Co.*	469	318
Wheeling village *Cook Co.*	638	373
Wilmette village *Cook Co.*	743	406
Woodridge village *Du Page Co.*	368	179
Woodstock city *McHenry Co.*	428	333
Zion city *Lake Co.*	552	393

NOTE: Data as of 2007.

Housing

Place	Homeownership Rate (%)	Median Home Value ($)	Median Year Structure Built	Median Rent ($/month)
Addison village *Du Page Co.*	70.8	256,749	1973	801
Algonquin village *McHenry Co.*	95.3	251,749	1992	887
Alton city *Madison Co.*	66.1	77,242	1950	454
Arlington Heights village *Cook Co.*	78.1	316,035	1971	967
Aurora city *Kane Co.*	70.5	180,242	1979	819
Bartlett village *Du Page Co.*	94.2	269,580	1991	918
Batavia city *Kane Co.*	78.6	256,698	1982	839
Belleville city *Saint Clair Co.*	61.2	91,977	1957	479
Belvidere city *Boone Co.*	70.1	126,453	1969	554
Berwyn city *Cook Co.*	65.5	208,765	before 1940	739
Bloomington city *McLean Co.*	64.9	141,902	1977	580
Bolingbrook village *Will Co.*	86.9	196,886	1986	816
Buffalo Grove village *Lake Co.*	90.2	294,643	1982	1,105
Burbank city *Cook Co.*	85.9	209,295	1964	849
Calumet City city *Cook Co.*	68.4	125,187	1965	733
Carol Stream village *Du Page Co.*	72.4	234,246	1983	859
Carpentersville village *Kane Co.*	79.2	158,111	1976	837
Champaign city *Champaign Co.*	46.5	128,319	1974	629
Chicago city *Cook Co.*	47.7	229,010	1945	737
Chicago Heights city *Cook Co.*	67.2	128,182	1956	645
Cicero town *Cook Co.*	59.9	180,540	before 1940	667
Collinsville city *Madison Co.*	67.8	116,058	1968	533
Crystal Lake city *McHenry Co.*	83.3	221,678	1982	975
Danville city *Vermilion Co.*	63.3	61,154	1952	404
Darien city *Du Page Co.*	83.1	289,056	1977	921
DeKalb city *De Kalb Co.*	44.2	158,641	1975	668
Decatur city *Macon Co.*	65.4	71,845	1958	449
Des Plaines city *Cook Co.*	80.5	250,068	1965	861
Dolton village *Cook Co.*	83.3	129,370	1964	794
Downers Grove village *Du Page Co.*	79.0	286,650	1971	888
East Saint Louis city *Saint Clair Co.*	52.9	57,280	1954	282
Elgin city *Kane Co.*	71.9	185,343	1973	755
Elk Grove Village village *Cook Co.*	78.7	257,083	1974	887
Elmhurst city *Du Page Co.*	83.2	340,584	1958	1,022
Elmwood Park village *Cook Co.*	68.7	258,341	1954	783
Evanston city *Cook Co.*	55.7	334,802	1943	972
Freeport city *Stephenson Co.*	67.4	79,689	1954	412
Galesburg city *Knox Co.*	60.1	68,515	1952	372
Geneva city *Kane Co.*	82.6	277,495	1987	954
Glen Ellyn village *Du Page Co.*	76.5	364,216	1967	749
Glendale Heights village *Du Page Co.*	71.0	209,659	1977	925
Glenview village *Cook Co.*	79.6	448,127	1972	1,273
Granite City city *Madison Co.*	71.3	75,045	1955	451
Grayslake village *Lake Co.*	82.3	233,489	1993	778
Gurnee village *Lake Co.*	79.7	263,020	1991	913
Hanover Park village *Cook Co.*	84.9	204,868	1976	871
Harvey city *Cook Co.*	61.2	94,775	1958	676
Highland Park city *Lake Co.*	81.7	529,130	1960	1,081
Hoffman Estates village *Cook Co.*	78.8	252,012	1976	953
Joliet city *Will Co.*	74.2	160,060	1969	654

Place	Homeownership Rate (%)	Median Home Value ($)	Median Year Structure Built	Median Rent ($/month)
Kankakee city *Kankakee Co.*	54.2	98,388	1953	505
Lake in the Hills village *McHenry Co.*	92.6	234,657	1994	973
Lansing village *Cook Co.*	78.1	156,491	1964	764
Lombard village *Du Page Co.*	76.9	243,396	1969	997
Loves Park city *Winnebago Co.*	70.4	119,033	1982	571
Maywood village *Cook Co.*	66.7	160,144	1942	676
McHenry city *McHenry Co.*	78.5	191,383	1983	863
Moline city *Rock Island Co.*	68.7	103,174	1954	512
Mount Prospect village *Cook Co.*	73.4	282,300	1968	825
Mundelein village *Lake Co.*	79.6	216,990	1981	933
Naperville city *Du Page Co.*	82.5	335,587	1987	979
New Lenox village *Will Co.*	90.3	239,765	1993	814
Niles village *Cook Co.*	79.8	286,449	1964	817
Normal town *McLean Co.*	56.3	143,985	1981	605
North Chicago city *Lake Co.*	41.5	139,992	1967	866
Northbrook village *Cook Co.*	92.2	494,977	1972	1,548
O'Fallon city *Saint Clair Co.*	69.3	150,533	1987	676
Oak Forest city *Cook Co.*	83.5	195,996	1973	803
Oak Lawn village *Cook Co.*	85.0	210,387	1965	799
Oak Park village *Cook Co.*	59.8	313,591	before 1940	853
Orland Park village *Cook Co.*	92.5	269,771	1987	864
Oswego village *Kendall Co.*	87.9	231,248	2000	1,042
Palatine village *Cook Co.*	72.8	263,579	1977	929
Park Ridge city *Cook Co.*	89.0	433,080	1958	1,098
Pekin city *Tazewell Co.*	70.3	98,481	1960	430
Peoria city *Peoria Co.*	62.6	110,241	1959	520
Plainfield village *Will Co.*	92.6	268,333	2001	1,060
Quincy city *Adams Co.*	67.3	82,915	1953	402
Rock Island city *Rock Island Co.*	66.8	91,913	1951	444
Rockford city *Winnebago Co.*	62.0	100,619	1959	523
Rolling Meadows city *Cook Co.*	80.1	235,593	1971	930
Romeoville village *Will Co.*	86.3	173,370	1994	1,005
Round Lake Beach village *Lake Co.*	84.7	161,656	1983	904
Saint Charles city *Kane Co.*	74.1	273,875	1983	902
Schaumburg village *Cook Co.*	72.2	234,089	1977	1,015
Skokie village *Cook Co.*	77.9	307,588	1957	898
Springfield city *Sangamon Co.*	67.0	106,850	1971	516
Streamwood village *Cook Co.*	90.7	197,684	1980	1,205
Tinley Park village *Cook Co.*	88.1	228,742	1984	825
Urbana city *Champaign Co.*	38.6	128,807	1972	611
Vernon Hills village *Lake Co.*	80.0	292,155	1985	1,092
Waukegan city *Lake Co.*	56.0	151,724	1963	701
West Chicago city *Du Page Co.*	73.1	248,716	1975	746
Westmont village *Du Page Co.*	59.7	274,599	1976	827
Wheaton city *Du Page Co.*	74.2	302,273	1974	973
Wheeling village *Cook Co.*	72.5	220,762	1977	882
Wilmette village *Cook Co.*	88.8	611,440	1954	1,283
Woodridge village *Du Page Co.*	69.5	252,310	1979	888
Woodstock city *McHenry Co.*	64.9	190,700	1983	786
Zion city *Lake Co.*	60.5	152,085	1971	717

NOTE: Homeownership Rate and Median Home Value as of 2010; Median Rent and Median Age of Housing are 2005-2009 5-year estimates.

Commute to Work

Place	Automobile (%)	Public Transportation (%)	Walk (%)	Work from Home (%)
Addison village *Du Page Co.*	92.9	2.8	0.7	2.1
Algonquin village *McHenry Co.*	90.5	2.6	0.5	5.3
Alton city *Madison Co.*	93.4	1.1	1.5	2.7
Arlington Heights village *Cook Co.*	86.3	6.6	2.0	3.8
Aurora city *Kane Co.*	88.4	4.9	1.3	3.0
Bartlett village *Du Page Co.*	89.8	3.8	0.7	4.8
Batavia city *Kane Co.*	84.4	3.5	1.0	8.0
Belleville city *Saint Clair Co.*	89.2	5.0	1.4	2.9
Belvidere city *Boone Co.*	92.4	0.4	1.9	1.9
Berwyn city *Cook Co.*	83.8	11.0	3.2	1.3
Bloomington city *McLean Co.*	89.8	1.9	3.7	3.4
Bolingbrook village *Will Co.*	90.0	3.7	1.0	3.3
Buffalo Grove village *Lake Co.*	89.3	3.7	0.6	5.4
Burbank city *Cook Co.*	93.3	3.6	1.1	1.4
Calumet City city *Cook Co.*	84.7	11.1	1.8	2.0
Carol Stream village *Du Page Co.*	92.4	2.8	0.8	3.2
Carpentersville village *Kane Co.*	93.2	2.3	1.2	2.1
Champaign city *Champaign Co.*	73.3	6.6	12.6	3.7
Chicago city *Cook Co.*	61.6	26.4	5.7	3.7
Chicago Heights city *Cook Co.*	88.8	6.9	1.3	0.6
Cicero town *Cook Co.*	84.4	9.7	3.6	0.9
Collinsville city *Madison Co.*	92.8	3.6	0.4	2.5
Crystal Lake city *McHenry Co.*	87.6	2.9	1.8	6.5
Danville city *Vermilion Co.*	91.4	1.2	2.8	2.1
Darien city *Du Page Co.*	89.8	4.2	1.2	3.5
DeKalb city *De Kalb Co.*	81.0	3.5	9.9	4.1
Decatur city *Macon Co.*	93.0	1.6	2.5	1.3
Des Plaines city *Cook Co.*	88.5	6.1	1.4	3.0
Dolton village *Cook Co.*	85.5	11.6	0.3	2.1
Downers Grove village *Du Page Co.*	79.7	10.5	2.4	6.3
East Saint Louis city *Saint Clair Co.*	81.1	13.2	1.4	3.3
Elgin city *Kane Co.*	91.0	2.3	2.3	2.7
Elk Grove Village village *Cook Co.*	93.1	2.7	0.7	2.6
Elmhurst city *Du Page Co.*	83.4	8.2	2.9	4.6
Elmwood Park village *Cook Co.*	83.2	11.5	2.1	2.3
Evanston city *Cook Co.*	58.4	19.5	11.2	7.0
Freeport city *Stephenson Co.*	89.1	2.2	4.5	2.9
Galesburg city *Knox Co.*	89.2	1.3	5.6	2.9
Geneva city *Kane Co.*	87.3	4.7	1.2	6.0
Glen Ellyn village *Du Page Co.*	74.9	12.5	4.0	6.5
Glendale Heights village *Du Page Co.*	96.1	1.4	0.9	1.0
Glenview village *Cook Co.*	82.0	10.3	1.2	5.8
Granite City city *Madison Co.*	93.6	1.2	2.3	2.1
Grayslake village *Lake Co.*	87.9	5.5	0.8	4.6
Gurnee village *Lake Co.*	91.4	2.5	1.1	4.1
Hanover Park village *Cook Co.*	90.0	3.2	1.2	3.0
Harvey city *Cook Co.*	83.2	12.7	1.6	1.5
Highland Park city *Lake Co.*	76.7	10.3	2.3	9.6
Hoffman Estates village *Cook Co.*	91.8	3.1	1.0	3.0
Joliet city *Will Co.*	91.1	2.5	1.9	3.0

Place	Automobile (%)	Public Transportation (%)	Walk (%)	Work from Home (%)
Kankakee city Kankakee Co.	86.6	4.6	4.0	3.1
Lake in the Hills village McHenry Co.	92.2	1.7	0.3	5.6
Lansing village Cook Co.	90.8	6.0	1.2	0.9
Lombard village Du Page Co.	88.9	4.7	1.8	3.1
Loves Park city Winnebago Co.	94.7	0.2	1.2	3.3
Maywood village Cook Co.	84.7	8.5	2.9	3.2
McHenry city McHenry Co.	94.0	1.4	1.0	2.8
Moline city Rock Island Co.	93.8	0.8	2.4	2.0
Mount Prospect village Cook Co.	85.2	6.8	2.6	3.2
Mundelein village Lake Co.	88.6	2.5	2.0	4.4
Naperville city Du Page Co.	81.0	9.4	1.6	6.7
New Lenox village Will Co.	88.0	7.1	0.3	4.2
Niles village Cook Co.	87.5	6.7	2.1	2.2
Normal town McLean Co.	82.9	1.8	11.7	2.1
North Chicago city Lake Co.	58.4	2.9	22.2	13.8
Northbrook village Cook Co.	81.8	8.7	1.1	7.0
O'Fallon city Saint Clair Co.	94.0	1.2	1.0	3.4
Oak Forest city Cook Co.	88.3	9.8	0.3	1.3
Oak Lawn village Cook Co.	87.7	7.6	2.1	1.6
Oak Park village Cook Co.	66.4	21.4	4.1	5.6
Orland Park village Cook Co.	88.6	5.9	1.5	3.6
Oswego village Kendall Co.	90.4	4.5	0.5	3.7
Palatine village Cook Co.	88.4	4.8	1.4	4.5
Park Ridge city Cook Co.	79.4	11.2	2.7	6.0
Pekin city Tazewell Co.	93.5	0.2	3.2	1.9
Peoria city Peoria Co.	89.5	2.6	3.1	3.1
Plainfield village Will Co.	90.5	3.4	0.6	4.8
Quincy city Adams Co.	91.2	1.2	3.7	3.2
Rock Island city Rock Island Co.	87.8	2.9	6.0	2.2
Rockford city Winnebago Co.	92.4	1.4	1.9	3.0
Rolling Meadows city Cook Co.	87.7	5.1	1.2	4.2
Romeoville village Will Co.	89.9	2.4	2.7	3.1
Round Lake Beach village Lake Co.	92.6	3.3	0.6	2.0
Saint Charles city Kane Co.	87.4	3.4	2.3	5.8
Schaumburg village Cook Co.	92.1	3.6	0.7	2.6
Skokie village Cook Co.	84.5	8.1	2.4	3.6
Springfield city Sangamon Co.	92.0	2.1	2.3	2.3
Streamwood village Cook Co.	93.4	3.2	0.6	1.8
Tinley Park village Cook Co.	87.1	8.1	1.4	2.4
Urbana city Champaign Co.	60.0	12.2	18.9	3.4
Vernon Hills village Lake Co.	89.3	3.7	0.2	5.1
Waukegan city Lake Co.	90.1	4.2	1.4	2.2
West Chicago city Du Page Co.	91.6	1.9	3.0	2.0
Westmont village Du Page Co.	82.1	10.5	1.7	4.0
Wheaton city Du Page Co.	79.0	8.6	5.2	6.6
Wheeling village Cook Co.	90.7	2.5	1.6	3.3
Wilmette village Cook Co.	70.8	16.5	2.7	8.1
Woodridge village Du Page Co.	88.6	4.3	0.9	4.3
Woodstock city McHenry Co.	86.9	4.4	3.8	3.4
Zion city Lake Co.	91.0	3.8	2.6	1.7

NOTE: Values are 2005-2009 5-year estimates.

Travel Time to Work

Place	Less than 15 Minutes (%)	15 to 30 Minutes (%)	30 to 45 Minutes (%)	45 to 60 Minutes (%)	60 Minutes or More (%)
Addison village *Du Page Co.*	25.5	36.3	24.5	6.6	7.1
Algonquin village *McHenry Co.*	17.4	25.2	21.3	16.7	19.5
Alton city *Madison Co.*	38.0	28.4	17.8	10.7	5.0
Arlington Heights village *Cook Co.*	22.6	34.1	23.6	9.6	9.9
Aurora city *Kane Co.*	23.3	35.3	19.2	9.3	12.9
Bartlett village *Du Page Co.*	14.5	30.0	28.8	14.1	12.7
Batavia city *Kane Co.*	28.3	31.1	19.5	9.2	11.9
Belleville city *Saint Clair Co.*	32.7	36.6	17.1	8.9	4.7
Belvidere city *Boone Co.*	31.3	25.7	19.3	10.6	13.2
Berwyn city *Cook Co.*	18.3	28.4	28.4	12.8	12.1
Bloomington city *McLean Co.*	59.7	30.2	4.5	2.7	2.9
Bolingbrook village *Will Co.*	20.3	26.4	24.8	13.9	14.6
Buffalo Grove village *Lake Co.*	20.5	33.7	26.2	9.3	10.2
Burbank city *Cook Co.*	21.9	26.6	25.6	12.9	12.9
Calumet City city *Cook Co.*	13.6	23.1	26.2	15.3	21.9
Carol Stream village *Du Page Co.*	22.9	30.0	27.8	7.7	11.6
Carpentersville village *Kane Co.*	16.5	30.6	29.6	12.6	10.7
Champaign city *Champaign Co.*	53.3	38.7	4.7	1.9	1.5
Chicago city *Cook Co.*	13.5	27.9	29.2	14.1	15.3
Chicago Heights city *Cook Co.*	37.0	25.0	14.5	9.6	13.9
Cicero town *Cook Co.*	14.8	30.9	28.1	13.5	12.7
Collinsville city *Madison Co.*	24.3	40.1	25.1	6.7	3.8
Crystal Lake city *McHenry Co.*	31.3	24.7	14.3	10.9	18.7
Danville city *Vermilion Co.*	60.6	27.1	7.1	2.9	2.3
Darien city *Du Page Co.*	19.1	31.1	27.5	10.8	11.6
DeKalb city *De Kalb Co.*	53.0	21.5	10.9	7.5	7.2
Decatur city *Macon Co.*	52.5	35.7	5.1	3.9	2.8
Des Plaines city *Cook Co.*	21.0	36.1	25.4	9.4	8.2
Dolton village *Cook Co.*	9.8	23.2	30.6	15.9	20.6
Downers Grove village *Du Page Co.*	25.2	33.3	20.8	10.5	10.2
East Saint Louis city *Saint Clair Co.*	29.7	41.8	19.2	5.1	4.2
Elgin city *Kane Co.*	25.1	30.7	24.0	9.4	10.8
Elk Grove Village village *Cook Co.*	27.6	36.8	20.5	7.1	8.0
Elmhurst city *Du Page Co.*	28.3	30.5	21.7	8.7	10.8
Elmwood Park village *Cook Co.*	21.2	24.4	31.3	13.2	9.9
Evanston city *Cook Co.*	26.9	24.5	21.2	15.5	11.9
Freeport city *Stephenson Co.*	66.6	13.5	8.6	6.9	4.3
Galesburg city *Knox Co.*	65.2	20.8	3.7	5.6	4.8
Geneva city *Kane Co.*	35.5	21.5	18.9	10.0	14.1
Glen Ellyn village *Du Page Co.*	24.0	31.0	19.3	10.9	14.7
Glendale Heights village *Du Page Co.*	24.2	35.0	23.1	7.4	10.3
Glenview village *Cook Co.*	22.3	30.6	26.8	10.6	9.6
Granite City city *Madison Co.*	31.7	37.1	21.7	7.5	2.0
Grayslake village *Lake Co.*	16.1	26.2	23.7	16.0	18.0
Gurnee village *Lake Co.*	21.0	31.9	22.4	11.5	13.2
Hanover Park village *Cook Co.*	17.2	40.7	23.1	10.4	8.7
Harvey city *Cook Co.*	15.3	31.5	25.6	13.6	14.0
Highland Park city *Lake Co.*	30.2	27.9	18.4	9.1	14.4
Hoffman Estates village *Cook Co.*	19.1	34.7	25.7	10.8	9.7
Joliet city *Will Co.*	25.0	29.2	20.0	10.8	14.9

Place	Less than 15 Minutes (%)	15 to 30 Minutes (%)	30 to 45 Minutes (%)	45 to 60 Minutes (%)	60 Minutes or More (%)
Kankakee city Kankakee Co.	45.8	30.5	12.9	4.7	6.1
Lake in the Hills village McHenry Co.	15.0	20.0	22.2	17.8	24.9
Lansing village Cook Co.	22.7	27.9	18.3	12.8	18.3
Lombard village Du Page Co.	24.7	33.1	22.4	9.5	10.3
Loves Park city Winnebago Co.	37.6	46.9	6.6	4.3	4.7
Maywood village Cook Co.	20.9	31.9	27.8	8.5	10.9
McHenry city McHenry Co.	30.6	33.5	14.8	8.3	12.8
Moline city Rock Island Co.	44.4	45.5	5.7	2.3	2.2
Mount Prospect village Cook Co.	23.1	32.7	25.5	8.3	10.4
Mundelein village Lake Co.	25.2	29.7	22.7	10.7	11.7
Naperville city Du Page Co.	21.5	28.7	19.9	9.9	19.9
New Lenox village Will Co.	21.9	28.5	20.2	9.2	20.2
Niles village Cook Co.	24.1	33.9	24.4	8.6	8.9
Normal town McLean Co.	54.9	33.3	5.2	3.0	3.6
North Chicago city Lake Co.	44.9	31.3	12.4	5.5	5.9
Northbrook village Cook Co.	25.8	27.8	21.3	11.0	14.1
O'Fallon city Saint Clair Co.	29.2	43.1	16.6	7.3	3.8
Oak Forest city Cook Co.	19.5	30.4	21.4	12.2	16.5
Oak Lawn village Cook Co.	23.9	25.6	24.1	12.2	14.2
Oak Park village Cook Co.	19.7	23.2	32.7	14.9	9.5
Orland Park village Cook Co.	19.3	26.6	24.0	12.0	18.1
Oswego village Kendall Co.	21.5	27.6	20.5	14.7	15.8
Palatine village Cook Co.	20.7	34.6	25.9	9.9	8.9
Park Ridge city Cook Co.	26.3	27.6	26.2	11.2	8.8
Pekin city Tazewell Co.	40.6	39.5	14.2	3.3	2.4
Peoria city Peoria Co.	42.4	47.5	5.6	2.1	2.3
Plainfield village Will Co.	15.2	22.3	22.0	15.9	24.6
Quincy city Adams Co.	66.9	26.6	3.8	1.2	1.5
Rock Island city Rock Island Co.	47.9	40.1	6.8	2.3	2.9
Rockford city Winnebago Co.	36.8	43.6	10.2	3.4	5.9
Rolling Meadows city Cook Co.	26.2	40.6	17.6	7.8	7.9
Romeoville village Will Co.	17.9	24.0	26.6	14.3	17.2
Round Lake Beach village Lake Co.	15.7	24.7	24.9	13.2	21.4
Saint Charles city Kane Co.	31.9	26.4	19.5	10.4	11.8
Schaumburg village Cook Co.	23.0	35.3	23.3	9.8	8.7
Skokie village Cook Co.	23.6	34.2	21.4	10.3	10.6
Springfield city Sangamon Co.	45.3	44.2	5.8	1.9	2.9
Streamwood village Cook Co.	15.1	35.2	27.9	9.7	12.0
Tinley Park village Cook Co.	22.0	26.1	20.9	11.4	19.6
Urbana city Champaign Co.	55.6	35.9	5.2	1.1	2.2
Vernon Hills village Lake Co.	22.7	30.4	27.5	9.0	10.4
Waukegan city Lake Co.	21.6	38.9	23.4	7.7	8.4
West Chicago city Du Page Co.	30.3	37.1	17.6	7.1	8.0
Westmont village Du Page Co.	24.6	29.5	20.3	11.8	13.8
Wheaton city Du Page Co.	31.7	29.1	17.0	7.8	14.4
Wheeling village Cook Co.	25.7	35.5	27.1	5.4	6.3
Wilmette village Cook Co.	21.9	25.4	21.9	14.4	16.4
Woodridge village Du Page Co.	18.2	35.7	20.9	12.8	12.4
Woodstock city McHenry Co.	31.8	32.0	12.8	6.3	17.1
Zion city Lake Co.	18.6	28.9	26.9	14.1	11.5

NOTE: Values are 2005-2009 5-year estimates.

Crime

Place	Violent Crime Rate (crimes per 10,000 population)	Property Crime Rate (crimes per 10,000 population)
Addison village *Du Page Co.*	18.3	226.1
Algonquin village *McHenry Co.*	25.6	171.5
Alton city *Madison Co.*	60.3	438.6
Arlington Heights village *Cook Co.*	5.7	160.1
Aurora city *Kane Co.*	36.4	216.2
Bartlett village *Du Page Co.*	4.9	86.8
Batavia city *Kane Co.*	14.4	183.4
Belleville city *Saint Clair Co.*	n/a	n/a
Belvidere city *Boone Co.*	25.1	192.8
Berwyn city *Cook Co.*	42.1	257.9
Bloomington city *McLean Co.*	51.8	263.8
Bolingbrook village *Will Co.*	n/a	n/a
Buffalo Grove village *Lake Co.*	1.9	92.5
Burbank city *Cook Co.*	24.7	225.2
Calumet City city *Cook Co.*	68.6	748.3
Carol Stream village *Du Page Co.*	11.1	145.8
Carpentersville village *Kane Co.*	11.2	150.8
Champaign city *Champaign Co.*	n/a	n/a
Chicago city *Cook Co.*	n/a	423.6
Chicago Heights city *Cook Co.*	n/a	n/a
Cicero town *Cook Co.*	n/a	n/a
Collinsville city *Madison Co.*	21.3	282.0
Crystal Lake city *McHenry Co.*	12.8	196.3
Danville city *Vermilion Co.*	108.9	681.9
Darien city *Du Page Co.*	5.4	125.4
DeKalb city *De Kalb Co.*	35.2	271.1
Decatur city *Macon Co.*	62.5	416.9
Des Plaines city *Cook Co.*	10.1	129.7
Dolton village *Cook Co.*	n/a	n/a
Downers Grove village *Du Page Co.*	8.4	194.8
East Saint Louis city *Saint Clair Co.*	582.5	892.6
Elgin city *Kane Co.*	33.0	202.9
Elk Grove Village village *Cook Co.*	11.6	230.5
Elmhurst city *Du Page Co.*	4.8	141.9
Elmwood Park village *Cook Co.*	12.3	159.8
Evanston city *Cook Co.*	27.5	271.4
Freeport city *Stephenson Co.*	20.2	362.5
Galesburg city *Knox Co.*	n/a	n/a
Geneva city *Kane Co.*	3.7	127.0
Glen Ellyn village *Du Page Co.*	3.7	144.3
Glendale Heights village *Du Page Co.*	12.4	184.6
Glenview village *Cook Co.*	n/a	n/a
Granite City city *Madison Co.*	52.2	256.8
Grayslake village *Lake Co.*	11.0	215.2
Gurnee village *Lake Co.*	9.2	448.8
Hanover Park village *Cook Co.*	13.5	148.2
Harvey city *Cook Co.*	146.0	643.1
Highland Park city *Lake Co.*	5.4	116.3
Hoffman Estates village *Cook Co.*	10.8	140.0
Joliet city *Will Co.*	36.0	278.0

Place	Violent Crime Rate (crimes per 10,000 population)	Property Crime Rate (crimes per 10,000 population)
Kankakee city *Kankakee Co.*	92.5	427.5
Lake in the Hills village *McHenry Co.*	10.7	79.3
Lansing village *Cook Co.*	n/a	n/a
Lombard village *Du Page Co.*	12.5	280.0
Loves Park city *Winnebago Co.*	34.9	350.4
Maywood village *Cook Co.*	90.4	393.5
McHenry city *McHenry Co.*	13.5	197.3
Moline city *Rock Island Co.*	50.8	349.8
Mount Prospect village *Cook Co.*	6.7	127.6
Mundelein village *Lake Co.*	3.5	124.1
Naperville city *Du Page Co.*	n/a	n/a
New Lenox village *Will Co.*	4.0	107.6
Niles village *Cook Co.*	n/a	n/a
Normal town *McLean Co.*	27.5	282.4
North Chicago city *Lake Co.*	n/a	n/a
Northbrook village *Cook Co.*	2.4	134.6
O'Fallon city *Saint Clair Co.*	11.7	250.5
Oak Forest city *Cook Co.*	14.3	167.9
Oak Lawn village *Cook Co.*	17.1	214.1
Oak Park village *Cook Co.*	36.5	327.8
Orland Park village *Cook Co.*	4.2	210.5
Oswego village *Kendall Co.*	10.2	150.9
Palatine village *Cook Co.*	5.2	135.3
Park Ridge city *Cook Co.*	4.1	157.2
Pekin city *Tazewell Co.*	34.9	253.9
Peoria city *Peoria Co.*	76.6	450.7
Plainfield village *Will Co.*	5.2	127.2
Quincy city *Adams Co.*	47.0	338.3
Rock Island city *Rock Island Co.*	81.8	348.0
Rockford city *Winnebago Co.*	145.5	499.7
Rolling Meadows city *Cook Co.*	n/a	n/a
Romeoville village *Will Co.*	8.0	195.2
Round Lake Beach village *Lake Co.*	23.1	234.9
Saint Charles city *Kane Co.*	n/a	n/a
Schaumburg village *Cook Co.*	12.1	325.2
Skokie village *Cook Co.*	23.8	272.4
Springfield city *Sangamon Co.*	123.7	644.6
Streamwood village *Cook Co.*	9.6	190.6
Tinley Park village *Cook Co.*	8.2	163.6
Urbana city *Champaign Co.*	73.4	315.0
Vernon Hills village *Lake Co.*	2.4	273.7
Waukegan city *Lake Co.*	n/a	n/a
West Chicago city *Du Page Co.*	11.0	136.4
Westmont village *Du Page Co.*	11.7	138.2
Wheaton city *Du Page Co.*	4.5	145.8
Wheeling village *Cook Co.*	17.5	179.4
Wilmette village *Cook Co.*	n/a	n/a
Woodridge village *Du Page Co.*	14.1	125.7
Woodstock city *McHenry Co.*	10.2	159.5
Zion city *Lake Co.*	n/a	n/a

NOTE: Data as of 2010.

Education

Illinois Public School Educational Profile

Category	Value	Category	Value
Schools *(2009-2010)*	4,405	**Diploma Recipients** *(2008-2009)*	131,670
Instructional Level		White, Non-Hispanic	82,749
Primary	2,566	Black, Non-Hispanic	21,887
Middle	787	Asian/Pacific Islander, Non-Hispanic	5,600
High	841	American Indian/Alaskan Native, Non-Hisp.	242
Other/Not Reported	211	Hispanic	19,616
Curriculum		**Staff** *(2009-2010)*	
Regular	4,017	Teachers (FTE)	138,321.9
Special Education	147	Salary[1] ($)	63,005
Vocational	53	Librarians/Media Specialists (FTE)	1,727.2
Alternative	188	Guidance Counselors (FTE)	3,155.3
Type		**Ratios** *(2009-2010)*	
Magnet	104	Number of Students per Teacher	15.2 to 1
Charter	39	Number of Students per Librarian	1,218.3 to 1
Title I Eligible	3,194	Number of Students per Guidance Counselor	666.9 to 1
School-wide Title I	1,371	**Finances** *(2007-2008)*	
Students *(2009-2010)*	2,104,175	Current Expenditures ($ per student)	
Gender (%)		Total	10,353
Male	51.3	Instruction	6,086
Female	48.7	Support Services	3,940
Race/Ethnicity (%)		Other	327
White, Non-Hispanic	52.6	General Revenue ($ per student)	
Black, Non-Hispanic	18.9	Total	12,035
Asian/Pacific Islander	4.2	From Federal Sources	947
American Indian/Alaskan Native	0.2	From State Sources	3,753
Hispanic	21.1	From Local Sources	7,335
Special Programs (%)		Long-Term Debt ($ per student)	
Individual Education Program (IEP)	14.9	At beginning of fiscal year	7,670
English Language Learner (ELL)	8.5	At end of fiscal year	8,212
Eligible for Free Lunch Program	37.2	**College Entrance Exam Scores**	
Eligible for Reduced-Price Lunch Program	5.8	SAT Reasoning Test™ *(2011)*	
Average Freshman Grad. Rate (%) *(2008-2009)*	77.7	Participation Rate (%)	5
White, Non-Hispanic	85.7	Mean Critical Reading Score	599
Black, Non-Hispanic	60.8	Mean Math Score	617
Asian/Pacific Islander, Non-Hispanic	92.9	Mean Writing Score	591
American Indian/Alaskan Native, Non-Hisp.	70.6	ACT *(2011)*	
Hispanic	68.8	Participation Rate (%)	100
High School Drop-out Rate (%) *(2008-2009)*	11.5	Mean Composite Score	20.9
White, Non-Hispanic	8.0	Mean English Score	20.6
Black, Non-Hispanic	20.0	Mean Math Score	20.9
Asian/Pacific Islander, Non-Hispanic	8.2	Mean Reading Score	20.8
American Indian/Alaskan Native, Non-Hisp.	15.3	Mean Science Score	20.7
Hispanic	13.4		

Note: For an explanation of data, please refer to the User's Guide in the front of the book; (1) Average salary for classroom teachers in 2010-11

Number of Schools

Rank	Number	District Name	City
1	633	City of Chicago SD 299	Chicago
2	58	School District U-46	Elgin
3	54	Rockford SD 205	Rockford
4	38	Peoria SD 150	Peoria
5	35	Springfield SD 186	Springfield
6	33	Indian Prairie CUSD 204	Aurora
7	30	Plainfield SD 202	Plainfield
8	27	Community Unit SD 300	Carpentersville
8	27	Schaumburg CCSD 54	Schaumburg
10	24	Decatur SD 61	Decatur
10	24	East St Louis SD 189	E Saint Louis
10	24	Waukegan CUSD 60	Waukegan
13	21	Joliet Public SD 86	Joliet
13	21	Mclean County Unit Dist No 5	Normal
13	21	Naperville CUD 203	Naperville
16	20	Community Unit SD 200	Wheaton
16	20	Oswego Community Unit SD 308	Oswego
16	20	Palatine CCSD 15	Palatine
16	20	Valley View CUSD #365U	Romeoville
20	19	Moline Unit SD 40	Moline
21	18	Champaign Community Unit SD 4	Champaign
22	17	Aurora East Unit SD 131	Aurora
22	17	Aurora West Unit SD 129	Aurora
22	17	Evanston CCSD 65	Evanston
22	17	Saint Charles CUSD 303	Saint Charles
26	16	Cicero SD 99	Cicero
26	16	Rock Island SD 41	Rock Island
28	14	Community CSD 59	Arlington Hgts
28	14	Edwardsville CUSD 7	Edwardsville
30	13	Cook County SD 130	Blue Island
30	13	Downers Grove Grade SD 58	Downers Grove
30	13	Elmhurst SD 205	Elmhurst
30	13	Kankakee SD 111	Kankakee
30	13	Wheeling CCSD 21	Wheeling
35	12	Barrington CUSD 220	Barrington
35	12	Crystal Lake CCSD 47	Crystal Lake
35	12	Dekalb Community Unit SD 428	Dekalb
35	12	New Lenox SD 122	New Lenox
35	12	North Shore SD 112	Highland Park
35	12	Quincy SD 172	Quincy
35	12	Woodstock CUSD 200	Woodstock
42	11	Alton Community Unit SD 11	Alton
42	11	Belleville SD 118	Belleville
42	11	Belvidere CUSD 100	Belvidere
42	11	Cahokia Community Unit SD 187	Cahokia
42	11	Chicago Heights SD 170	Chicago Heights
42	11	Collinsville CUSD 10	Collinsville
42	11	Community Consolidated SD 62	Des Plaines
42	11	Danville CCSD 118	Danville
42	11	Dolton SD 148	Riverdale
42	11	Freeport SD 145	Freeport
42	11	Granite City CUSD 9	Granite City
42	11	Harlem Unit Dist 122	Machesney Park
42	11	Jacksonville SD 117	Jacksonville
42	11	Pekin Public SD 108	Pekin
56	10	Crete Monee CUSD 201u	Crete
56	10	Galesburg CUSD 205	Galesburg
56	10	Geneva Community Unit SD 304	Geneva
56	10	Maywood-Melrose Park-Broadview-89	Melrose Park
56	10	North Chicago SD 187	North Chicago
56	10	Oak Park Elem SD 97	Oak Park
56	10	Orland SD 135	Orland Park
56	10	Township High SD 214	Arlington Hgts
64	9	Arlington Hgts SD 25	Arlington Hgts
64	9	Bloomington SD 87	Bloomington
64	9	CCSD 181	Westmont
64	9	Community Consolidated SD 46	Grayslake
64	9	Round Lake Area Schs - Dist 116	Round Lake
64	9	Urbana SD 116	Urbana
64	9	Yorkville Community Unit SD 115	Yorkville
71	8	Addison SD 4	Addison
71	8	Batavia Unit SD 101	Batavia
71	8	Berwyn South SD 100	Berwyn
71	8	Burbank SD 111	Burbank
71	8	Community Consolidated SD 93	Bloomingdale
71	8	Consolidated SD 158	Algonquin
71	8	Glenview CCSD 34	Glenview
71	8	Harvey SD 152	Harvey
71	8	Jersey CUSD 100	Jerseyville
71	8	Lake Zurich CUSD 95	Lake Zurich
71	8	Mchenry CCSD 15	Mchenry
71	8	Park Ridge CCSD 64	Park Ridge
71	8	Prairie-Hills Elem SD 144	Markham
71	8	School District 45 Dupage County	Villa Park
71	8	West Chicago Elem SD 33	West Chicago
86	7	Bellwood SD 88	Bellwood
86	7	Bethalto SD 8	Bethalto
86	7	Central Community Unit SD 301	Burlington
86	7	Dunlap CUSD 323	Dunlap
86	7	East Maine SD 63	Des Plaines
86	7	East Peoria SD 86	East Peoria
86	7	Effingham Community Unit SD 40	Effingham
86	7	Highland Community Unit SD 5	Highland
86	7	Kildeer Countryside CCSD 96	Buffalo Grove
86	7	Kirby SD 140	Tinley Park
86	7	Lombard SD 44	Lombard
86	7	Marion Community Unit SD 2	Marion
86	7	Massac Unit District #1	Metropolis
86	7	Matteson Elem SD 162	Matteson
86	7	Monmouth-Roseville CUSD 238	Monmouth
86	7	O'Fallon CCSD 90	O Fallon
86	7	Oak Lawn-Hometown SD 123	Oak Lawn
86	7	Prairie Central CUSD 8	Fairbury
86	7	Sterling CUD 5	Sterling
86	7	Summit Hill SD 161	Frankfort
86	7	Sycamore CUSD 427	Sycamore
86	7	Township HSD 211	Palatine
86	7	Troy Community CSD 30C	Plainfield
86	7	Woodridge SD 68	Woodridge
86	7	Zion Elementary SD 6	Zion
111	6	Berkeley SD 87	Berkeley
111	6	Bourbonnais SD 53	Bourbonnais
111	6	Cary CCSD 26	Cary
111	6	Charleston CUSD 1	Charleston
111	6	Clinton CUSD 15	Clinton
111	6	Deerfield SD 109	Deerfield
111	6	Dolton SD 149	Calumet City
111	6	Geneseo Community Unit SD 228	Geneseo
111	6	Hawthorn CCSD 73	Vernon Hills
111	6	Illinois Valley CUD 321	Chillicothe
111	6	Indian Springs SD 109	Justice
111	6	Kaneland CUSD 302	Maple Park
111	6	Kewanee Community Unit SD 229	Kewanee
111	6	La Grange SD 102	La Grange Park
111	6	Litchfield CUSD 12	Litchfield
111	6	Lyons SD 103	Lyons
111	6	Minooka Community CSD 201	Minooka
111	6	Morton CUSD 709	Morton
111	6	North Boone CUSD 200	Poplar Grove
111	6	Park Forest SD 163	Park Forest
111	6	Peotone CUSD 207U	Peotone
111	6	Sandwich CUSD 430	Sandwich
111	6	Sherrard Community Unit SD 200	Sherrard
111	6	Southwestern CUSD 9	Piasa
111	6	Taylorville CUSD 3	Taylorville
111	6	Triad Community Unit SD 2	Troy
111	6	Wauconda Community Unit SD 118	Wauconda
111	6	Wilmette SD 39	Wilmette
139	5	Antioch CCSD 34	Antioch
139	5	Auburn CUSD 10	Auburn
139	5	Ball Chatham CUSD 5	Chatham
139	5	Beach Park CCSD 3	Beach Park
139	5	Beardstown CUSD 15	Beardstown
139	5	Bensenville SD 2	Bensenville
139	5	Bond County CUSD 2	Greenville
139	5	Canton Union SD 66	Canton
139	5	Coal City CUSD 1	Coal City
139	5	Dixon Unit SD 170	Dixon
139	5	East Moline SD 37	East Moline
139	5	Elem SD 159	Matteson
139	5	Elmwood Park CUSD 401	Elmwood Park
139	5	Eureka C U Dist 140	Eureka
139	5	Evergreen Park Elem SD 124	Evergreen Park
139	5	Flossmoor SD 161	Chicago Heights
139	5	Genoa Kingston CUSD 424	Genoa
139	5	Glen Ellyn CCSD 89	Glen Ellyn
139	5	Glen Ellyn SD 41	Glen Ellyn
139	5	Harvard CUSD 50	Harvard
139	5	Herscher Community Unit SD 2	Herscher
139	5	Hillsboro Community Unit SD 3	Hillsboro
139	5	Homer Community CSD 33c	Homer Glen
139	5	Lake Forest SD 67	Lake Forest
139	5	Lake Villa CCSD 41	Lake Villa
139	5	Lansing SD 158	Lansing
139	5	Libertyville SD 70	Libertyville
139	5	Macomb Community Unit SD 185	Macomb
139	5	Mahomet-Seymour CUSD 3	Mahomet
139	5	Maine Township HSD 207	Park Ridge
139	5	Mannheim SD 83	Franklin Park
139	5	Marquardt SD 15	Glendale Hgts
139	5	Mattoon CUSD 2	Mattoon
139	5	Monticello CUSD 25	Monticello
139	5	Mount Zion Community Unit SD 3	Mount Zion
139	5	North Palos SD 117	Palos Hills
139	5	Olympia CUSD 16	Stanford
139	5	Ottawa Elem SD 141	Ottawa
139	5	Plano Community Unit SD 88	Plano
139	5	Posen-Robbins Elem SD 143-5	Posen
139	5	Rantoul City SD 137	Rantoul
139	5	Ridgeland SD 122	Oak Lawn
139	5	Riverside SD 96	Riverside
139	5	Rochelle Community CD 231	Rochelle
139	5	Streator Elem SD 44	Streator
139	5	Summit SD 104	Summit
139	5	Tinley Park CCSD 146	Tinley Park
139	5	Winnebago CUSD 323	Winnebago
139	5	Winnetka SD 36	Winnetka
188	4	Alsip-Hazelgreen-Oak Lawn SD 126	Alsip
188	4	Aptakisic-Tripp CCSD 102	Buffalo Grove
188	4	Berwyn North SD 98	Berwyn
188	4	Bremen Community HS District 228	Midlothian
188	4	Channahon SD 17	Channahon
188	4	Community High SD 117	Lake Villa
188	4	Community High SD 155	Crystal Lake
188	4	Community High SD 218	Oak Lawn
188	4	Forest Ridge SD 142	Oak Forest
188	4	Frankfort Community Unit SD 168	West Frankfort
188	4	Glenbard Twp HSD 87	Glen Ellyn
188	4	Gurnee SD 56	Gurnee
188	4	Harrisburg CUSD 3	Harrisburg
188	4	Herrin CUSD 4	Herrin
188	4	Homewood SD 153	Homewood
188	4	J S Morton HS District 201	Cicero
188	4	Johnsburg CUSD 12	Johnsburg
188	4	Kinnikinnick CCSD 131	Roscoe
188	4	Lemont-Bromberek CSD 113A	Lemont
188	4	Lincoln Way Community HSD 210	New Lenox
188	4	Lisle CUSD 202	Lisle
188	4	Manteno Community Unit SD 5	Manteno
188	4	Mascoutah CUD 19	Mascoutah
188	4	Meridian CUSD 223	Stillman Valley
188	4	Midlothian SD 143	Midlothian
188	4	Mount Prospect SD 57	Mount Prospect
188	4	Mount Vernon SD 80	Mount Vernon
188	4	Mundelein Elem SD 75	Mundelein
188	4	Murphysboro CUSD 186	Murphysboro
188	4	Northbrook SD 28	Northbrook
188	4	Northfield Twp High SD 225	Glenview
188	4	Oregon CUSD 220	Oregon
188	4	Paxton-Buckley-Loda CUD 10	Paxton
188	4	Reed Custer CUSD 255U	Braidwood
188	4	Robinson CUSD 2	Robinson
188	4	Rochester CUSD 3A	Rochester
188	4	Roxana Community Unit SD 1	Roxana
188	4	Skokie SD 68	Skokie
188	4	South Holland SD 151	South Holland
188	4	Steger SD 194	Steger
188	4	Tolono CUSD 7	Tolono
188	4	Vandalia CUSD 203	Vandalia
188	4	Wabash CUSD 348	Mount Carmel
188	4	Waterloo CUSD 5	Waterloo
188	4	West Harvey-Dixmoor PSD 147	Harvey
188	4	Western Springs SD 101	Western Springs
188	4	Westmont CUSD 201	Westmont
188	4	Will County SD 92	Lockport
188	4	Woodland CCSD 50	Gurnee
237	3	Belleville Twp HSD 201	Belleville
237	3	Big Hollow SD 38	Ingleside
237	3	Bloom Twp High SD 206	Chicago Heights
237	3	Bradley SD 61	Bradley
237	3	Byron Community Unit SD 226	Byron
237	3	Carterville CUSD 5	Carterville
237	3	Columbia Community Unit SD 4	Columbia
237	3	Community CSD 168	Sauk Village
237	3	Cons High SD 230	Orland Park
237	3	Darien SD 61	Darien
237	3	Du Quoin CUSD 300	Du Quoin
237	3	East Richland CUSD 1	Olney
237	3	Frankfort CCSD 157C	Frankfort

Note: This section only includes districts with 1,500 or more students; All categories are ranked from high to low

237	3	Fremont SD 79	Mundelein
237	3	Joliet Twp HSD 204	Joliet
237	3	Keeneyville SD 20	Hanover Park
237	3	Mokena SD 159	Mokena
237	3	Niles Twp Community High SD 219	Skokie
237	3	Palos Community CSD 118	Palos Park
237	3	Proviso Twp HSD 209	Forest Park
237	3	Queen Bee SD 16	Glendale Hgts
237	3	Rich Twp HS District 227	Olympia Fields
237	3	Riverton CUSD 14	Riverton
237	3	Rockton SD 140	Rockton
237	3	Skokie SD 69	Skokie
237	3	Thornton Twp HSD 205	South Holland
263	2	Community High SD 128	Vernon Hills
263	2	Community High SD 99	Downers Grove
263	2	Du Page High SD 88	Addison
263	2	Grayslake Com High SD 127	Grayslake
263	2	Hinsdale Twp HSD 86	Hinsdale
263	2	Leyden Community HSD 212	Franklin Park
263	2	Mchenry Community HSD 156	Mchenry
263	2	Millburn CCSD 24	Old Mill Creek
263	2	New Trier Twp HSD 203	Northfield
263	2	Thornton Fractional HSD 215	Calumet City
263	2	Township High SD 113	Highland Park
263	2	Zion-Benton Twp HSD 126	Zion
275	1	Adlai E Stevenson Dist 125	Lincolnshire
275	1	Argo Community HSD 217	Summit
275	1	Bradley Bourbonnais CHSD 307	Bradley
275	1	Community High SD 94	West Chicago
275	1	Evanston Twp HSD 202	Evanston
275	1	Fenton Community HSD 100	Bensenville
275	1	Grant Community HS District 124	Fox Lake
275	1	Homewood Flossmoor CHSD 233	Flossmoor
275	1	Hononegah Community HSD 207	Rockton
275	1	Lake Forest CHSD 115	Lake Forest
275	1	Lake Park Community HSD 108	Roselle
275	1	Lemont Twp HSD 210	Lemont
275	1	Lockport Twp HSD 205	Lockport
275	1	Lyons Twp HSD 204	La Grange
275	1	Minooka Community HS District 111	Minooka
275	1	Mundelein Cons High SD 120	Mundelein
275	1	O'Fallon Twp High SD 203	O Fallon
275	1	Oak Lawn Community HSD 229	Oak Lawn
275	1	Oak Park & River Forest Dist 200	Oak Park
275	1	Pekin Community HSD 303	Pekin
275	1	Reavis Twp HSD 220	Burbank
275	1	United Twp HS District 30	East Moline
275	1	Warren Twp High SD 121	Gurnee

Number of Teachers

Rank	Number	District Name	City
1	24,760.3	City of Chicago SD 299	Chicago
2	2,326.7	School District U-46	Elgin
3	1,908.6	Indian Prairie CUSD 204	Aurora
4	1,839.5	Rockford SD 205	Rockford
5	1,700.2	Plainfield SD 202	Plainfield
6	1,175.2	Community Unit SD 300	Carpentersville
7	1,130.0	Springfield SD 186	Springfield
8	1,092.4	Waukegan CUSD 60	Waukegan
9	1,057.9	Valley View CUSD #365U	Romeoville
10	1,055.2	Naperville CUD 203	Naperville
11	995.7	Schaumburg CCSD 54	Schaumburg
12	978.3	Peoria SD 150	Peoria
13	881.7	Saint Charles CUSD 303	Saint Charles
14	867.2	Community Unit SD 200	Wheaton
15	841.3	Mclean County Unit Dist No 5	Normal
16	829.7	Oswego Community Unit SD 308	Oswego
17	816.6	Township HSD 211	Palatine
18	753.5	Township High SD 214	Arlington Hgts
19	752.0	Aurora East Unit SD 131	Aurora
20	736.9	Cicero SD 99	Cicero
21	711.8	Champaign Community Unit SD 4	Champaign
22	711.6	Palatine CCSD 15	Palatine
23	703.2	Aurora West Unit SD 129	Aurora
24	618.7	Joliet Public SD 86	Joliet
25	577.2	Barrington CUSD 220	Barrington
26	566.6	Evanston CCSD 65	Evanston
27	563.8	Crystal Lake CCSD 47	Crystal Lake
28	559.9	East St Louis SD 189	E Saint Louis
29	552.8	Consolidated SD 158	Algonquin
30	535.5	Elmhurst SD 205	Elmhurst
31	531.1	Belvidere CUSD 100	Belvidere
32	524.7	Glenbard Twp HSD 87	Glen Ellyn
33	518.4	Cons High SD 230	Orland Park
34	505.5	Maine Township HSD 207	Park Ridge
35	502.4	Harlem Unit Dist 122	Machesney Park
36	502.1	Decatur SD 61	Decatur
37	487.5	Wheeling CCSD 21	Wheeling
38	480.7	Edwardsville CUSD 7	Edwardsville
39	476.1	Woodland CCSD 50	Gurnee
40	467.4	Alton Community Unit SD 11	Alton
41	461.3	Moline Unit SD 40	Moline
42	457.7	Community CSD 59	Arlington Hgts
43	454.2	Lincoln Way Community HSD 210	New Lenox
44	453.5	J S Morton HS District 201	Cicero
45	437.0	Quincy SD 172	Quincy
46	424.6	Thornton Twp HSD 205	South Holland
47	411.8	Community High SD 155	Crystal Lake
48	391.0	Collinsville CUSD 10	Collinsville
49	390.8	Lake Zurich CUSD 95	Lake Zurich
50	389.2	Oak Park Elem SD 97	Oak Park
51	387.5	Round Lake Area Schs - Dist 116	Round Lake
52	385.9	Rock Island SD 41	Rock Island
53	384.9	Woodstock CUSD 200	Woodstock
54	384.7	Danville CCSD 118	Danville
55	370.4	North Shore SD 112	Highland Park
56	369.8	Batavia Unit SD 101	Batavia
57	367.1	Bloomington SD 87	Bloomington
58	367.0	Geneva Community Unit SD 304	Geneva
59	364.0	Granite City CUSD 9	Granite City
60	361.9	Dekalb Community Unit SD 428	Dekalb
61	353.5	Community High SD 218	Oak Lawn
62	352.4	Orland SD 135	Orland Park
63	351.2	Northfield Twp High SD 225	Glenview
64	349.1	Niles Twp Community High SD 219	Skokie
65	347.0	Community Consolidated SD 62	Des Plaines
66	346.9	Urbana SD 116	Urbana
67	346.3	Arlington Hgts SD 25	Arlington Hgts
67	346.3	Kankakee SD 111	Kankakee
69	341.9	Glenview CCSD 34	Glenview
70	340.8	Crete Monee CUSD 201u	Crete
71	337.1	Joliet Twp HSD 204	Joliet
72	336.9	New Trier Twp HSD 203	Northfield
73	330.0	Maywood-Melrose Park-Broadview-89	Melrose Park
74	328.3	Yorkville Community Unit SD 115	Yorkville
75	321.9	Community High SD 99	Downers Grove
76	317.0	Park Ridge CCSD 64	Park Ridge
77	316.5	Freeport SD 145	Freeport
78	311.9	Bremen Community HS District 228	Midlothian
79	298.3	Wilmette SD 39	Wilmette
80	297.1	Cahokia Community Unit SD 187	Cahokia
81	296.1	Hinsdale Twp HSD 86	Hinsdale
82	294.8	Kaneland CUSD 302	Maple Park
83	291.1	Community Consolidated SD 93	Bloomingdale
84	288.9	Cook County SD 130	Blue Island
85	287.5	New Lenox SD 122	New Lenox
86	280.4	Proviso Twp HSD 209	Forest Park
87	279.6	Belleville Twp HSD 201	Belleville
88	279.1	Mchenry CCSD 15	Mchenry
89	278.8	CCSD 181	Westmont
90	278.1	Galesburg CUSD 205	Galesburg
90	278.1	Rich Twp HS District 227	Olympia Fields
92	277.1	Downers Grove Grade SD 58	Downers Grove
93	274.9	Wauconda Community Unit SD 118	Wauconda
94	271.5	Adlai E Stevenson Dist 125	Lincolnshire
95	266.3	Kirby SD 140	Tinley Park
96	265.8	Du Page High SD 88	Addison
97	264.3	Community Consolidated SD 46	Grayslake
98	263.9	Addison SD 4	Addison
99	263.3	Troy Community CSD 30C	Plainfield
100	262.7	Berwyn South SD 100	Berwyn
101	260.4	East Maine SD 63	Des Plaines
102	253.2	Hawthorn CCSD 73	Vernon Hills
103	251.2	Jacksonville SD 117	Jacksonville
104	248.9	Pekin Public SD 108	Pekin
105	248.6	West Chicago Elem SD 33	West Chicago
106	248.5	Township High SD 113	Highland Park
107	246.0	Warren Twp High SD 121	Gurnee
108	245.7	Ball Chatham CUSD 5	Chatham
109	242.1	Lyons Twp HSD 204	La Grange
110	238.3	North Chicago SD 187	North Chicago
111	237.0	Burbank SD 111	Burbank
112	236.5	Glen Ellyn SD 41	Glen Ellyn
113	236.2	Dolton SD 148	Riverdale
114	233.9	Triad Community Unit SD 2	Troy
115	230.1	La Grange SD 102	La Grange Park
116	229.4	Deerfield SD 109	Deerfield
117	228.6	Belleville SD 118	Belleville
118	228.1	Sycamore CUSD 427	Sycamore
119	226.8	School District 45 Dupage County	Villa Park
120	226.0	Matteson Elem SD 162	Matteson
121	225.3	Mattoon CUSD 2	Mattoon
122	225.0	Central Community Unit SD 301	Burlington
123	221.2	Evanston Twp HSD 202	Evanston
124	219.0	Leyden Community HSD 212	Franklin Park
125	218.9	Oak Lawn-Hometown SD 123	Oak Lawn
126	218.1	Sterling CUD 5	Sterling
127	217.3	Kildeer Countryside CCSD 96	Buffalo Grove
128	217.1	Community High SD 128	Vernon Hills
129	216.2	Homer Community CSD 33c	Homer Glen
129	216.2	Lombard SD 44	Lombard
131	215.4	Marion Community Unit SD 2	Marion
132	210.7	Summit Hill SD 161	Frankfort
133	207.0	O'Fallon CCSD 90	O Fallon
134	205.1	Lockport Twp HSD 205	Lockport
135	202.1	Chicago Heights SD 170	Chicago Heights
136	200.2	Oak Park & River Forest Dist 200	Oak Park
136	200.2	Thornton Fractional HSD 215	Calumet City
138	198.0	Mascoutah CUD 19	Mascoutah
139	197.7	Mannheim SD 83	Franklin Park
140	196.1	Lake Villa CCSD 41	Lake Villa
141	194.9	Minooka Community CSD 201	Minooka
142	193.8	Community High SD 117	Lake Villa
143	193.6	Grayslake Com High SD 127	Grayslake
144	192.0	Cary CCSD 26	Cary
144	192.0	Highland Community Unit SD 5	Highland
146	189.4	Antioch CCSD 34	Antioch
147	188.9	Indian Springs SD 109	Justice
148	186.1	Woodridge SD 68	Woodridge
149	185.2	Prairie-Hills Elem SD 144	Markham
150	184.1	Dunlap CUSD 323	Dunlap
151	180.5	Bloom Twp High SD 206	Chicago Heights
152	180.1	Charleston CUSD 1	Charleston
153	179.5	Zion Elementary SD 6	Zion
154	178.6	Elmwood Park CUSD 401	Elmwood Park
155	178.0	Lyons SD 103	Lyons
156	177.9	East Moline SD 37	East Moline
157	177.3	Flossmoor SD 161	Chicago Heights
158	177.0	Dixon Unit SD 170	Dixon
159	176.5	Berwyn North SD 98	Berwyn
159	176.5	Bethalto CUSD 8	Bethalto
161	176.4	Effingham Community Unit SD 40	Effingham
162	176.1	North Palos SD 117	Palos Hills
163	175.5	Lake Forest SD 67	Lake Forest
164	175.2	Canton Union SD 66	Canton
165	174.8	Homewood Flossmoor CHSD 233	Flossmoor
166	174.4	Morton CUSD 709	Morton
167	173.0	Dolton SD 149	Calumet City
168	172.7	Mahomet-Seymour CUSD 3	Mahomet
169	170.6	Winnetka SD 36	Winnetka
170	168.1	Marquardt SD 15	Glendale Hgts
171	165.5	Berkeley SD 87	Berkeley
172	165.4	Waterloo CUSD 5	Waterloo
173	164.5	Sandwich CUSD 430	Sandwich
174	164.3	Jersey CUSD 100	Jerseyville
175	163.9	Lake Park Community HSD 108	Roselle
176	163.6	Prairie Central CUSD 8	Fairbury
177	162.0	Harvey SD 152	Harvey
178	161.3	Tinley Park CCSD 146	Tinley Park
179	160.6	Bourbonnais SD 53	Bourbonnais
180	159.5	Manteno Community Unit SD 5	Manteno
181	159.3	Libertyville SD 70	Libertyville
182	159.2	Geneseo Community Unit SD 228	Geneseo
183	159.0	Northbrook SD 28	Northbrook
184	158.6	Beach Park CCSD 3	Beach Park
185	158.2	Bellwood SD 88	Bellwood
185	158.2	Johnsburg CUSD 12	Johnsburg
187	157.9	Frankfort CCSD 157C	Frankfort
188	156.4	Mchenry Community HSD 156	Mchenry
189	155.0	Zion-Benton Twp HSD 126	Zion
190	151.9	Plano Community Unit SD 88	Plano
191	151.6	Taylorville CUSD 3	Taylorville
192	150.3	Aptakisic-Tripp CCSD 102	Buffalo Grove
193	150.1	Gurnee SD 56	Gurnee
194	149.0	Lansing SD 158	Lansing
195	147.2	Harvard CUSD 50	Harvard
196	145.5	Homewood SD 153	Homewood
197	145.3	Bensenville SD 2	Bensenville
198	144.8	O'Fallon Twp High SD 203	O Fallon
199	144.0	Lemont-Bromberek CSD 113A	Lemont

Note: This section only includes districts with 1,500 or more students; All categories are ranked from high to low

199	144.0	Massac Unit District #1	Metropolis
201	143.1	Clinton CUSD 15	Clinton
202	142.4	Evergreen Park Elem SD 124	Evergreen Park
203	141.8	Rochester CUSD 3A	Rochester
204	140.6	Ottawa Elem SD 141	Ottawa
205	139.7	Illinois Valley CUD 321	Chillicothe
206	139.4	Coal City CUSD 1	Coal City
207	139.2	Glen Ellyn CCSD 89	Glen Ellyn
208	138.5	East Richland CUSD 1	Olney
209	137.3	Genoa Kingston CUSD 424	Genoa
210	137.2	Murphysboro CUSD 186	Murphysboro
211	136.4	Mount Prospect SD 57	Mount Prospect
212	135.1	Mundelein Elem SD 75	Mundelein
213	134.6	Park Forest SD 163	Park Forest
214	132.9	Mount Zion Community Unit SD 3	Mount Zion
215	132.1	Streator Elem SD 44	Streator
216	131.7	Harrisburg CUSD 3	Harrisburg
216	131.7	Midlothian SD 143	Midlothian
216	131.7	Minooka Community HS District 111	Minooka
219	131.2	Palos Community CSD 118	Palos Park
219	131.2	Rochelle Community CD 231	Rochelle
221	131.0	Elem SD 159	Matteson
222	130.9	Lake Forest CHSD 115	Lake Forest
223	130.2	Queen Bee SD 16	Glendale Hgts
224	129.5	Steger SD 194	Steger
225	129.3	Skokie SD 68	Skokie
226	128.9	Macomb Community Unit SD 185	Macomb
227	128.5	Peotone CUSD 207U	Peotone
228	128.0	Fremont SD 79	Mundelein
229	127.7	Olympia CUSD 16	Stanford
230	126.8	Byron Community Unit SD 226	Byron
231	126.1	Ridgeland SD 122	Oak Lawn
232	126.0	Herscher Community Unit SD 2	Herscher
233	125.3	Sherrard Community Unit SD 200	Sherrard
234	125.0	Roxana Community Unit SD 1	Roxana
235	124.6	Pekin Community HSD 303	Pekin
236	124.0	Herrin CUSD 4	Herrin
237	123.0	Monmouth-Roseville CUSD 238	Monmouth
238	122.1	Bond County CUSD 2	Greenville
239	122.0	Hononegah Community HSD 207	Rockton
240	121.6	Community High SD 94	West Chicago
241	121.0	East Peoria SD 86	East Peoria
242	119.5	Mundelein Cons High SD 120	Mundelein
243	118.4	Kinnikinnick CCSD 131	Roscoe
244	117.9	Winnebago CUSD 323	Winnebago
245	116.8	Alsip-Hazelgreen-Oak Lawn SD 126	Alsip
246	115.9	North Boone CUSD 200	Poplar Grove
247	114.8	Millburn CCSD 24	Old Mill Creek
248	114.7	Tolono CUSD 7	Tolono
249	114.2	Reed Custer CUSD 255U	Braidwood
250	114.0	Oak Lawn Community HSD 229	Oak Lawn
251	113.5	Lisle CUSD 202	Lisle
251	113.5	Meridian CUSD 223	Stillman Valley
253	113.3	Bradley Bourbonnais CHSD 307	Bradley
254	112.5	Hillsboro Community Unit SD 3	Hillsboro
254	112.5	Skokie SD 69	Skokie
256	111.6	Wabash CUSD 348	Mount Carmel
257	111.4	Vandalia CUSD 203	Vandalia
258	111.3	Monticello CUSD 25	Monticello
259	110.5	Columbia Community Unit SD 4	Columbia
260	110.4	Paxton-Buckley-Loda CUD 10	Paxton
261	110.0	Carterville CUSD 5	Carterville
261	110.0	Robinson CUSD 2	Robinson
263	109.7	Frankfort Community Unit SD 168	West Frankfort
264	109.0	Community CSD 168	Sauk Village
265	108.0	Mount Vernon SD 80	Mount Vernon
266	107.8	Beardstown CUSD 15	Beardstown
267	106.9	Southwestern CUSD 9	Piasa
268	106.6	Argo Community HSD 217	Summit
269	106.5	Keeneyville SD 20	Hanover Park
269	106.5	Will County SD 92	Lockport
271	106.3	Westmont CUSD 201	Westmont
272	104.8	Big Hollow SD 38	Ingleside
272	104.8	Rantoul City SD 137	Rantoul
274	104.0	Mokena SD 159	Mokena
275	103.2	Oregon CUSD 220	Oregon
276	102.6	Bradley SD 61	Bradley
277	102.5	Darien SD 61	Darien
277	102.5	Forest Ridge SD 142	Oak Forest
277	102.5	Kewanee Community Unit SD 229	Kewanee
280	102.4	Rockton SD 140	Rockton
281	102.0	Posen-Robbins Elem SD 143-5	Posen
281	102.0	Riverside SD 96	Riverside
281	102.0	South Holland SD 151	South Holland
284	101.1	Reavis Twp HSD 220	Burbank
285	101.0	Summit SD 104	Summit
286	100.7	Du Quoin CUSD 300	Du Quoin
287	99.5	Eureka C U Dist 140	Eureka
288	97.6	Fenton Community HSD 100	Bensenville
289	96.9	Western Springs SD 101	Western Springs
290	96.2	Lemont Twp HSD 210	Lemont
291	93.4	Grant Community HS District 124	Fox Lake
292	89.9	Auburn CUSD 10	Auburn
293	89.0	West Harvey-Dixmoor PSD 147	Harvey
294	87.8	United Twp HS District 30	East Moline
295	85.3	Riverton CUSD 14	Riverton
296	83.5	Litchfield CUSD 12	Litchfield
297	79.0	Channahon SD 17	Channahon

Number of Students

Rank	Number	District Name	City
1	407,157	City of Chicago SD 299	Chicago
2	41,446	School District U-46	Elgin
3	29,733	Indian Prairie CUSD 204	Aurora
4	29,254	Plainfield SD 202	Plainfield
5	29,071	Rockford SD 205	Rockford
6	20,341	Community Unit SD 300	Carpentersville
7	18,133	Valley View CUSD #365U	Romeoville
8	17,977	Naperville CUD 203	Naperville
9	16,660	Waukegan CUSD 60	Waukegan
10	16,314	Oswego Community Unit SD 308	Oswego
11	15,110	Springfield SD 186	Springfield
12	14,313	Schaumburg CCSD 54	Schaumburg
13	13,953	Saint Charles CUSD 303	Saint Charles
14	13,951	Peoria SD 150	Peoria
15	13,732	Cicero SD 99	Cicero
16	13,506	Aurora East Unit SD 131	Aurora
17	13,488	Community Unit SD 200	Wheaton
18	12,976	Mclean County Unit Dist No 5	Normal
19	12,749	Township HSD 211	Palatine
20	12,508	Aurora West Unit SD 129	Aurora
21	12,241	Township High SD 214	Arlington Hgts
22	12,214	Palatine CCSD 15	Palatine
23	10,127	Joliet Public SD 86	Joliet
24	9,458	Champaign Community Unit SD 4	Champaign
25	9,283	Barrington CUSD 220	Barrington
26	9,189	Decatur SD 61	Decatur
27	9,068	Belvidere CUSD 100	Belvidere
28	8,992	Consolidated SD 158	Algonquin
29	8,985	Glenbard Twp HSD 87	Glen Ellyn
30	8,707	Crystal Lake CCSD 47	Crystal Lake
31	8,671	Cons High SD 230	Orland Park
32	8,489	J S Morton HS District 201	Cicero
33	8,221	Elmhurst SD 205	Elmhurst
34	8,141	East St Louis SD 189	E Saint Louis
35	7,752	Harlem Unit Dist 122	Machesney Park
36	7,623	Edwardsville CUSD 7	Edwardsville
37	7,397	Moline Unit SD 40	Moline
38	7,346	Lincoln Way Community HSD 210	New Lenox
39	7,146	Community High SD 155	Crystal Lake
40	7,081	Quincy SD 172	Quincy
41	7,065	Granite City CUSD 9	Granite City
42	7,050	Round Lake Area Schs - Dist 116	Round Lake
43	6,972	Maine Township HSD 207	Park Ridge
44	6,952	Wheeling CCSD 21	Wheeling
45	6,835	Woodland CCSD 50	Gurnee
46	6,812	Evanston CCSD 65	Evanston
47	6,653	Alton Community Unit SD 11	Alton
48	6,623	Collinsville CUSD 10	Collinsville
49	6,467	Woodstock CUSD 200	Woodstock
50	6,292	Batavia Unit SD 101	Batavia
51	6,282	Lake Zurich CUSD 95	Lake Zurich
52	6,255	Community CSD 59	Arlington Hgts
53	6,225	Rock Island SD 41	Rock Island
54	6,222	Danville CCSD 118	Danville
55	6,179	Thornton Twp HSD 205	South Holland
56	6,028	Geneva Community Unit SD 304	Geneva
57	6,018	Dekalb Community Unit SD 428	Dekalb
58	5,826	Community High SD 218	Oak Lawn
59	5,791	Joliet Twp HSD 204	Joliet
60	5,767	Kankakee SD 111	Kankakee
61	5,667	New Lenox SD 122	New Lenox
62	5,640	Maywood-Melrose Park-Broadview-89	Melrose Park
63	5,609	Bloomington SD 87	Bloomington
64	5,533	Bremen Community HS District 228	Midlothian
65	5,466	Orland SD 135	Orland Park
66	5,464	Oak Park Elem SD 97	Oak Park
67	5,254	Community High SD 99	Downers Grove
68	5,245	Crete Monee CUSD 201u	Crete
69	5,198	Proviso Twp HSD 209	Forest Park
70	5,137	Arlington Hgts SD 25	Arlington Hgts
71	5,119	Yorkville Community Unit SD 115	Yorkville
72	5,032	Belleville Twp HSD 201	Belleville
73	4,981	Mchenry CCSD 15	Mchenry
74	4,947	Downers Grove Grade SD 58	Downers Grove
75	4,879	Galesburg CUSD 205	Galesburg
76	4,803	Northfield Twp High SD 225	Glenview
77	4,798	Niles Twp Community High SD 219	Skokie
78	4,759	Community Consolidated SD 62	Des Plaines
79	4,746	Kaneland CUSD 302	Maple Park
80	4,621	Glenview CCSD 34	Glenview
81	4,609	North Shore SD 112	Highland Park
82	4,585	Cahokia Community Unit SD 187	Cahokia
83	4,560	Hinsdale Twp HSD 86	Hinsdale
84	4,432	Troy Community CSD 30C	Plainfield
85	4,419	Adlai E Stevenson Dist 125	Lincolnshire
86	4,401	Wauconda Community Unit SD 118	Wauconda
87	4,397	Warren Twp High SD 121	Gurnee
88	4,383	Ball Chatham CUSD 5	Chatham
89	4,372	Addison SD 4	Addison
90	4,291	Park Ridge CCSD 64	Park Ridge
91	4,290	Freeport SD 145	Freeport
92	4,242	West Chicago Elem SD 33	West Chicago
93	4,218	Community Consolidated SD 46	Grayslake
94	4,143	New Trier Twp HSD 203	Northfield
95	4,124	Urbana SD 116	Urbana
96	4,110	Du Page High SD 88	Addison
97	4,048	CCSD 181	Westmont
98	4,032	Rich Twp HS District 227	Olympia Fields
99	4,002	Community Consolidated SD 93	Bloomingdale
100	3,983	North Chicago SD 187	North Chicago
101	3,941	Marion Community Unit SD 2	Marion
102	3,940	Minooka Community CSD 201	Minooka
103	3,937	Cook County SD 130	Blue Island
104	3,928	Kirby SD 140	Tinley Park
105	3,909	Hawthorn CCSD 73	Vernon Hills
106	3,890	Lyons Twp HSD 204	La Grange
107	3,872	Lockport Twp HSD 205	Lockport
108	3,814	Sycamore CUSD 427	Sycamore
109	3,753	Jacksonville SD 117	Jacksonville
110	3,737	Township High SD 113	Highland Park
111	3,730	Triad Community Unit SD 2	Troy
112	3,723	Wilmette SD 39	Wilmette
113	3,695	Belleville SD 118	Belleville
113	3,695	Pekin Public SD 108	Pekin
115	3,678	Thornton Fractional HSD 215	Calumet City
116	3,677	Glen Ellyn SD 41	Glen Ellyn
117	3,662	Summit Hill SD 161	Frankfort
118	3,638	Homer Community CSD 33c	Homer Glen
119	3,604	Sterling CUD 5	Sterling
120	3,601	Berwyn South SD 100	Berwyn
121	3,569	East Maine SD 63	Des Plaines
122	3,523	Mattoon CUSD 2	Mattoon
123	3,522	O'Fallon CCSD 90	O Fallon
124	3,513	Bloom Twp High SD 206	Chicago Heights
125	3,497	Leyden Community HSD 212	Franklin Park
126	3,473	Dunlap CUSD 323	Dunlap
127	3,447	Mascoutah CUD 19	Mascoutah
128	3,439	Berwyn North SD 98	Berwyn
129	3,397	Dolton SD 149	Calumet City
130	3,392	School District 45 Dupage County	Villa Park
131	3,388	Community High SD 128	Vernon Hills
132	3,374	Central Community Unit SD 301	Burlington
133	3,373	Chicago Heights SD 170	Chicago Heights
134	3,296	Matteson Elem SD 162	Matteson
135	3,266	Burbank SD 111	Burbank
135	3,266	Lake Villa CCSD 41	Lake Villa
137	3,256	Oak Park & River Forest Dist 200	Oak Park
138	3,251	Cary CCSD 26	Cary
139	3,194	Deerfield SD 109	Deerfield
140	3,158	Antioch CCSD 34	Antioch
141	3,157	Kildeer Countryside CCSD 96	Buffalo Grove
142	3,128	Oak Lawn-Hometown SD 123	Oak Lawn
143	3,107	Highland Community Unit SD 5	Highland
144	3,095	Lombard SD 44	Lombard
145	3,079	North Palos SD 117	Palos Hills
146	3,065	Woodridge SD 68	Woodridge
147	3,057	Indian Springs SD 109	Justice
148	3,054	Evanston Twp HSD 202	Evanston
149	3,040	La Grange SD 102	La Grange Park

Note: This section only includes districts with 1,500 or more students; All categories are ranked from high to low

150	2,946	Elmwood Park CUSD 401	Elmwood Park
151	2,931	Prairie-Hills Elem SD 144	Markham
152	2,925	Lake Park Community HSD 108	Roselle
153	2,905	Berkeley SD 87	Berkeley
154	2,893	Homewood Flossmoor CHSD 233	Flossmoor
155	2,892	Charleston CUSD 1	Charleston
156	2,888	Bellwood SD 88	Bellwood
157	2,878	Zion-Benton Twp HSD 126	Zion
158	2,877	Effingham Community Unit SD 40	Effingham
159	2,874	Dixon Unit SD 170	Dixon
160	2,871	Taylorville CUSD 3	Taylorville
161	2,862	Jersey CUSD 100	Jerseyville
162	2,852	Community High SD 117	Lake Villa
163	2,836	Mahomet-Seymour CUSD 3	Mahomet
164	2,789	Grayslake Com High SD 127	Grayslake
165	2,784	Morton CUSD 709	Morton
166	2,749	Waterloo CUSD 5	Waterloo
167	2,738	Bethalto CUSD 8	Bethalto
168	2,719	Geneseo Community Unit SD 228	Geneseo
169	2,705	Mannheim SD 83	Franklin Park
170	2,681	Zion Elementary SD 6	Zion
171	2,671	Bourbonnais SD 53	Bourbonnais
172	2,666	Marquardt SD 15	Glendale Hgts
173	2,658	Canton Union SD 66	Canton
174	2,635	Dolton SD 148	Riverdale
175	2,607	Harvey SD 152	Harvey
176	2,595	Libertyville SD 70	Libertyville
177	2,593	Lemont-Bromberek CSD 113A	Lemont
178	2,568	Mchenry Community HSD 156	Mchenry
179	2,560	Beach Park CCSD 3	Beach Park
180	2,554	Mount Zion Community Unit SD 3	Mount Zion
181	2,545	East Moline SD 37	East Moline
182	2,524	O'Fallon Twp High SD 203	O Fallon
183	2,500	Herrin CUSD 4	Herrin
184	2,482	Johnsburg CUSD 12	Johnsburg
185	2,466	Frankfort CCSD 157C	Frankfort
186	2,461	Sandwich CUSD 430	Sandwich
187	2,459	Minooka Community HS District 111	Minooka
188	2,452	Lyons SD 103	Lyons
189	2,429	Harvard CUSD 50	Harvard
190	2,343	Tinley Park CCSD 146	Tinley Park
191	2,337	Manteno Community Unit SD 5	Manteno
192	2,334	Flossmoor SD 161	Chicago Heights
193	2,329	Plano Community Unit SD 88	Plano
194	2,317	Massac Unit District #1	Metropolis
195	2,294	Ridgeland SD 122	Oak Lawn
196	2,282	Illinois Valley CUD 321	Chillicothe
197	2,276	Rochester CUSD 3A	Rochester
198	2,256	Mundelein Cons High SD 120	Mundelein
199	2,204	Harrisburg CUSD 3	Harrisburg
200	2,183	Community High SD 94	West Chicago
201	2,169	Hononegah Community HSD 207	Rockton
202	2,160	Lansing SD 158	Lansing
203	2,158	Gurnee SD 56	Gurnee
204	2,152	Coal City CUSD 1	Coal City
205	2,147	Murphysboro CUSD 186	Murphysboro
206	2,145	Mount Prospect SD 57	Mount Prospect
207	2,138	Lake Forest SD 67	Lake Forest
208	2,137	Prairie Central CUSD 8	Fairbury
209	2,127	East Richland CUSD 1	Olney
210	2,124	Bradley Bourbonnais CHSD 307	Bradley
211	2,119	Fremont SD 79	Mundelein
212	2,113	Kinnikinnick CCSD 131	Roscoe
213	2,109	Pekin Community HSD 303	Pekin
214	2,104	Elem SD 159	Matteson
215	2,094	Bensenville SD 2	Bensenville
216	2,085	Peotone CUSD 207U	Peotone
217	2,084	Clinton CUSD 15	Clinton
218	2,081	Mokena SD 159	Mokena
219	2,068	Herscher Community Unit SD 2	Herscher
220	2,059	Glen Ellyn CCSD 89	Glen Ellyn
220	2,059	Ottawa Elem SD 141	Ottawa
222	2,052	Queen Bee SD 16	Glendale Hgts
223	2,044	Bond County CUSD 2	Greenville
224	2,020	Genoa Kingston CUSD 424	Genoa
225	2,011	Aptakisic-Tripp CCSD 102	Buffalo Grove
225	2,011	Columbia Community Unit SD 4	Columbia
227	1,995	Roxana Community Unit SD 1	Roxana
228	1,984	Frankfort Community Unit SD 168	West Frankfort
229	1,976	Midlothian SD 143	Midlothian
230	1,972	Meridian CUSD 223	Stillman Valley
230	1,972	Streator Elem SD 44	Streator
232	1,966	Homewood SD 153	Homewood
233	1,954	Hillsboro Community Unit SD 3	Hillsboro
234	1,930	Winnetka SD 36	Winnetka
235	1,911	Olympia CUSD 16	Stanford
236	1,909	Reavis Twp HSD 220	Burbank
237	1,908	Macomb Community Unit SD 185	Macomb
238	1,883	Evergreen Park Elem SD 124	Evergreen Park
238	1,883	Oak Lawn Community HSD 229	Oak Lawn
240	1,876	Mundelein Elem SD 75	Mundelein
241	1,873	Palos Community CSD 118	Palos Park
242	1,870	Posen-Robbins Elem SD 143-5	Posen
243	1,843	Argo Community HSD 217	Summit
244	1,841	Park Forest SD 163	Park Forest
245	1,838	Kewanee Community Unit SD 229	Kewanee
246	1,817	East Peoria SD 86	East Peoria
247	1,816	Grant Community HS District 124	Fox Lake
248	1,804	Reed Custer CUSD 255U	Braidwood
249	1,802	Carterville CUSD 5	Carterville
249	1,802	Will County SD 92	Lockport
251	1,786	Lake Forest CHSD 115	Lake Forest
252	1,780	Wabash CUSD 348	Mount Carmel
253	1,766	North Boone CUSD 200	Poplar Grove
254	1,756	Mount Vernon SD 80	Mount Vernon
255	1,746	Rochelle Community CD 231	Rochelle
256	1,737	Summit SD 104	Summit
257	1,736	United Twp HS District 30	East Moline
258	1,718	Monmouth-Roseville CUSD 238	Monmouth
259	1,713	Vandalia CUSD 203	Vandalia
260	1,710	Northbrook SD 28	Northbrook
261	1,707	Monticello CUSD 25	Monticello
262	1,705	Skokie SD 69	Skokie
263	1,695	Southwestern CUSD 9	Piasa
264	1,681	Big Hollow SD 38	Ingleside
265	1,676	Community CSD 168	Sauk Village
265	1,676	Skokie SD 68	Skokie
267	1,660	Tolono CUSD 7	Tolono
268	1,656	Sherrard Community Unit SD 200	Sherrard
269	1,653	Byron Community Unit SD 226	Byron
269	1,653	Winnebago CUSD 323	Winnebago
271	1,652	Forest Ridge SD 142	Oak Forest
272	1,646	Robinson CUSD 2	Robinson
273	1,623	Keeneyville SD 20	Hanover Park
274	1,622	Eureka C U Dist 140	Eureka
275	1,620	Darien SD 61	Darien
276	1,614	Millburn CCSD 24	Old Mill Creek
277	1,609	Steger SD 194	Steger
278	1,598	Rantoul City SD 137	Rantoul
279	1,590	Beardstown CUSD 15	Beardstown
280	1,589	Lisle CUSD 202	Lisle
281	1,581	Channahon SD 17	Channahon
282	1,569	Alsip-Hazelgreen-Oak Lawn SD 126	Alsip
282	1,569	Oregon CUSD 220	Oregon
282	1,569	Rockton SD 140	Rockton
285	1,566	Western Springs SD 101	Western Springs
286	1,563	Du Quoin CUSD 300	Du Quoin
287	1,556	Bradley SD 61	Bradley
288	1,547	South Holland SD 151	South Holland
289	1,535	Riverton CUSD 14	Riverton
289	1,535	Westmont CUSD 201	Westmont
291	1,533	Paxton-Buckley-Loda CUD 10	Paxton
292	1,532	Auburn CUSD 10	Auburn
293	1,526	Fenton Community HSD 100	Bensenville
294	1,523	Riverside SD 96	Riverside
295	1,508	West Harvey-Dixmoor PSD 147	Harvey
296	1,507	Lemont Twp HSD 210	Lemont
297	1,506	Litchfield CUSD 12	Litchfield

Male Students

Rank	Percent	District Name	City
1	54.3	Central Community Unit SD 301	Burlington
1	54.3	Harvard CUSD 50	Harvard
3	54.1	Midlothian SD 143	Midlothian
4	53.8	Antioch CCSD 34	Antioch
5	53.6	Bond County CUSD 2	Greenville
5	53.6	Northbrook SD 28	Northbrook
5	53.6	Winnebago CUSD 323	Winnebago
5	53.6	Winnetka SD 36	Winnetka
9	53.5	O'Fallon CCSD 90	O Fallon
9	53.5	Western Springs SD 101	Western Springs
11	53.4	East Moline SD 37	East Moline
11	53.4	Peotone CUSD 207U	Peotone
13	53.3	Sandwich CUSD 430	Sandwich
13	53.3	Waterloo CUSD 5	Waterloo
15	53.2	East Peoria SD 86	East Peoria
16	53.1	Alton Community Unit SD 11	Alton
16	53.1	Community High SD 117	Lake Villa
16	53.1	Fremont SD 79	Mundelein
16	53.1	Mount Prospect SD 57	Mount Prospect
16	53.1	Oregon CUSD 220	Oregon
16	53.1	Yorkville Community Unit SD 115	Yorkville
22	53.0	Argo Community HSD 217	Summit
22	53.0	Homer Community CSD 33c	Homer Glen
22	53.0	Taylorville CUSD 3	Taylorville
25	52.9	Bethalto CUSD 8	Bethalto
25	52.9	Cook County SD 130	Blue Island
25	52.9	Fenton Community HSD 100	Bensenville
25	52.9	North Chicago SD 187	North Chicago
29	52.8	Berwyn North SD 98	Berwyn
29	52.8	New Trier Twp HSD 203	Northfield
29	52.8	Prairie Central CUSD 8	Fairbury
29	52.8	Will County SD 92	Lockport
29	52.8	Woodstock CUSD 200	Woodstock
34	52.7	Beardstown CUSD 15	Beardstown
34	52.7	Collinsville CUSD 10	Collinsville
34	52.7	Community CSD 59	Arlington Hgts
34	52.7	Evergreen Park Elem SD 124	Evergreen Park
34	52.7	Kaneland CUSD 302	Maple Park
34	52.7	Warren Twp High SD 121	Gurnee
40	52.6	Champaign Community Unit SD 4	Champaign
40	52.6	Coal City CUSD 1	Coal City
40	52.6	Flossmoor SD 161	Chicago Heights
40	52.6	Harlem Unit Dist 122	Machesney Park
40	52.6	Marion Community Unit SD 2	Marion
40	52.6	Morton CUSD 709	Morton
40	52.6	Posen-Robbins Elem SD 143-5	Posen
47	52.5	Community Consolidated SD 93	Bloomingdale
47	52.5	Du Quoin CUSD 300	Du Quoin
47	52.5	Grant Community HS District 124	Fox Lake
47	52.5	Mannheim SD 83	Franklin Park
47	52.5	Mount Vernon SD 80	Mount Vernon
47	52.5	Northfield Twp High SD 225	Glenview
47	52.5	Rockton SD 140	Rockton
54	52.4	Bloomington SD 87	Bloomington
54	52.4	Columbia Community Unit SD 4	Columbia
54	52.4	Effingham Community Unit SD 40	Effingham
54	52.4	Eureka C U Dist 140	Eureka
54	52.4	Glen Ellyn SD 41	Glen Ellyn
54	52.4	Lake Park Community HSD 108	Roselle
54	52.4	Lemont-Bromberek CSD 113A	Lemont
54	52.4	Mascoutah CUD 19	Mascoutah
54	52.4	Mundelein Cons High SD 120	Mundelein
54	52.4	Tolono CUSD 7	Tolono
64	52.3	Charleston CUSD 1	Charleston
64	52.3	Darien SD 61	Darien
64	52.3	Grayslake Com High SD 127	Grayslake
64	52.3	Hillsboro Community Unit SD 3	Hillsboro
64	52.3	Wauconda Community Unit SD 118	Wauconda
64	52.3	Zion Elementary SD 6	Zion
70	52.2	Alsip-Hazelgreen-Oak Lawn SD 126	Alsip
70	52.2	Belleville SD 118	Belleville
70	52.2	Carterville CUSD 5	Carterville
70	52.2	Community Consolidated SD 46	Grayslake
70	52.2	Edwardsville CUSD 7	Edwardsville
70	52.2	Illinois Valley CUD 321	Chillicothe
70	52.2	Orland SD 135	Orland Park
70	52.2	Queen Bee SD 16	Glendale Hgts
70	52.2	Rich Twp HS District 227	Olympia Fields
70	52.2	Ridgeland SD 122	Oak Lawn
70	52.2	Rochester CUSD 3A	Rochester
70	52.2	Roxana Community Unit SD 1	Roxana
70	52.2	Tinley Park CCSD 146	Tinley Park
70	52.2	Woodland CCSD 50	Gurnee
84	52.1	Community High SD 155	Crystal Lake
84	52.1	Community High SD 218	Oak Lawn
84	52.1	Deerfield SD 109	Deerfield
84	52.1	Galesburg CUSD 205	Galesburg
84	52.1	Herscher Community Unit SD 2	Herscher
84	52.1	Homewood SD 153	Homewood
84	52.1	Johnsburg CUSD 12	Johnsburg
84	52.1	Lisle CUSD 202	Lisle
84	52.1	Minooka Community HS District 111	Minooka
84	52.1	Saint Charles CUSD 303	Saint Charles
84	52.1	Thornton Fractional HSD 215	Calumet City
95	52.0	Community Consolidated SD 62	Des Plaines
95	52.0	Lake Forest SD 67	Lake Forest
95	52.0	Lansing SD 158	Lansing
95	52.0	Manteno Community Unit SD 5	Manteno
95	52.0	New Lenox SD 122	New Lenox

Note: This section only includes districts with 1,500 or more students; All categories are ranked from high to low

95	52.0	Oswego Community Unit SD 308	Oswego
95	52.0	Riverside SD 96	Riverside
95	52.0	Round Lake Area Schs - Dist 116	Round Lake
95	52.0	Schaumburg CCSD 54	Schaumburg
95	52.0	Sycamore CUSD 427	Sycamore
105	51.9	Berkeley SD 87	Berkeley
105	51.9	Canton Union SD 66	Canton
105	51.9	Elmwood Park CUSD 401	Elmwood Park
105	51.9	Indian Springs SD 109	Justice
105	51.9	Mchenry CCSD 15	Mchenry
105	51.9	Millburn CCSD 24	Old Mill Creek
105	51.9	Oak Lawn-Hometown SD 123	Oak Lawn
112	51.8	Community High SD 99	Downers Grove
112	51.8	Frankfort CCSD 157C	Frankfort
112	51.8	Genoa Kingston CUSD 424	Genoa
112	51.8	Joliet Public SD 86	Joliet
112	51.8	Lake Forest CHSD 115	Lake Forest
112	51.8	Leyden Community HSD 212	Franklin Park
112	51.8	Minooka Community CSD 201	Minooka
119	51.7	Crete Monee CUSD 201u	Crete
119	51.7	Lyons SD 103	Lyons
119	51.7	Mount Zion Community Unit SD 3	Mount Zion
119	51.7	Oak Park & River Forest Dist 200	Oak Park
119	51.7	Plainfield SD 202	Plainfield
119	51.7	School District U-46	Elgin
119	51.7	Sherrard Community Unit SD 200	Sherrard
119	51.7	Southwestern CUSD 9	Piasa
127	51.6	Community Unit SD 200	Wheaton
127	51.6	Cons High SD 230	Orland Park
127	51.6	Consolidated SD 158	Algonquin
127	51.6	Downers Grove Grade SD 58	Downers Grove
127	51.6	Lake Zurich CUSD 95	Lake Zurich
127	51.6	Macomb Community Unit SD 185	Macomb
127	51.6	Olympia CUSD 16	Stanford
127	51.6	Quincy SD 172	Quincy
127	51.6	Rantoul City SD 137	Rantoul
136	51.5	Belleville Twp HSD 201	Belleville
136	51.5	Crystal Lake CCSD 47	Crystal Lake
136	51.5	East Maine SD 63	Des Plaines
136	51.5	Glenbard Twp HSD 87	Glen Ellyn
136	51.5	Granite City CUSD 9	Granite City
136	51.5	Gurnee SD 56	Gurnee
136	51.5	J S Morton HS District 201	Cicero
136	51.5	North Palos SD 117	Palos Hills
136	51.5	North Shore SD 112	Highland Park
136	51.5	Palatine CCSD 15	Palatine
136	51.5	Triad Community Unit SD 2	Troy
136	51.5	Wabash CUSD 348	Mount Carmel
148	51.4	Ball Chatham CUSD 5	Chatham
148	51.4	Barrington CUSD 220	Barrington
148	51.4	Batavia Unit SD 101	Batavia
148	51.4	Bradley SD 61	Bradley
148	51.4	Chicago Heights SD 170	Chicago Heights
148	51.4	Indian Prairie CUSD 204	Aurora
148	51.4	Kankakee SD 111	Kankakee
148	51.4	La Grange SD 102	La Grange Park
148	51.4	Park Ridge CCSD 64	Park Ridge
148	51.4	Reavis Twp HSD 220	Burbank
148	51.4	School District 45 Dupage County	Villa Park
148	51.4	Township High SD 113	Highland Park
148	51.4	West Chicago Elem SD 33	West Chicago
148	51.4	Wheeling CCSD 21	Wheeling
162	51.3	Bradley Bourbonnais CHSD 307	Bradley
162	51.3	Burbank SD 111	Burbank
162	51.3	CCSD 181	Westmont
162	51.3	Frankfort Community Unit SD 168	West Frankfort
162	51.3	Glen Ellyn CCSD 89	Glen Ellyn
162	51.3	Hinsdale Twp HSD 86	Hinsdale
162	51.3	Jacksonville SD 117	Jacksonville
162	51.3	Kinnikinnick CCSD 131	Roscoe
162	51.3	Maine Township HSD 207	Park Ridge
162	51.3	Maywood-Melrose Park-Broadview-89	Melrose Park
162	51.3	Naperville CUD 203	Naperville
162	51.3	Oak Lawn Community HSD 229	Oak Lawn
162	51.3	Park Forest SD 163	Park Forest
162	51.3	Springfield SD 186	Springfield
162	51.3	Township HSD 211	Palatine
177	51.2	Belvidere CUSD 100	Belvidere
177	51.2	Community High SD 128	Vernon Hills
177	51.2	Community Unit SD 300	Carpentersville
177	51.2	Geneseo Community Unit SD 228	Geneseo
177	51.2	Mclean County Unit Dist No 5	Normal
177	51.2	Niles Twp Community High SD 219	Skokie
177	51.2	Pekin Community HSD 303	Pekin
177	51.2	Robinson CUSD 2	Robinson
177	51.2	Skokie SD 69	Skokie
177	51.2	South Holland SD 151	South Holland
177	51.2	Summit Hill SD 161	Frankfort
177	51.2	Township High SD 214	Arlington Hgts
189	51.1	Arlington Hgts SD 25	Arlington Hgts
189	51.1	Channahon SD 17	Channahon
189	51.1	Cicero SD 99	Cicero
189	51.1	Dekalb Community Unit SD 428	Dekalb
189	51.1	Glenview CCSD 34	Glenview
189	51.1	Massac Unit District #1	Metropolis
189	51.1	Mattoon CUSD 2	Mattoon
189	51.1	Moline Unit SD 40	Moline
189	51.1	Paxton-Buckley-Loda CUD 10	Paxton
189	51.1	Rockford SD 205	Rockford
189	51.1	Valley View CUSD #365U	Romeoville
189	51.1	Waukegan CUSD 60	Waukegan
201	51.0	Addison SD 4	Addison
201	51.0	Aurora East Unit SD 131	Aurora
201	51.0	Cary CCSD 26	Cary
201	51.0	Du Page High SD 88	Addison
201	51.0	Dunlap CUSD 323	Dunlap
201	51.0	East Richland CUSD 1	Olney
201	51.0	Forest Ridge SD 142	Oak Forest
201	51.0	Mundelein Elem SD 75	Mundelein
201	51.0	Plano Community Unit SD 88	Plano
201	51.0	West Harvey-Dixmoor PSD 147	Harvey
201	51.0	Westmont CUSD 201	Westmont
212	50.9	Bourbonnais SD 53	Bourbonnais
212	50.9	Evanston CCSD 65	Evanston
212	50.9	Joliet Twp HSD 204	Joliet
212	50.9	Lincoln Way Community HSD 210	New Lenox
212	50.9	Monticello CUSD 25	Monticello
212	50.9	Summit SD 104	Summit
218	50.8	Adlai E Stevenson Dist 125	Lincolnshire
218	50.8	Bloom Twp High SD 206	Chicago Heights
218	50.8	Elem SD 159	Matteson
218	50.8	Elmhurst SD 205	Elmhurst
218	50.8	Hawthorn CCSD 73	Vernon Hills
218	50.8	Highland Community Unit SD 5	Highland
218	50.8	Kirby SD 140	Tinley Park
218	50.8	Lake Villa CCSD 41	Lake Villa
218	50.8	Lombard SD 44	Lombard
218	50.8	Mchenry Community HSD 156	Mchenry
218	50.8	Mokena SD 159	Mokena
218	50.8	Zion-Benton Twp HSD 126	Zion
230	50.7	Aptakisic-Tripp CCSD 102	Buffalo Grove
230	50.7	Beach Park CCSD 3	Beach Park
230	50.7	Bremen Community HS District 228	Midlothian
230	50.7	Geneva Community Unit SD 304	Geneva
230	50.7	Lemont Twp HSD 210	Lemont
230	50.7	Matteson Elem SD 162	Matteson
230	50.7	Rochelle Community CD 231	Rochelle
237	50.6	Berwyn South SD 100	Berwyn
237	50.6	Big Hollow SD 38	Ingleside
237	50.6	Cahokia Community Unit SD 187	Cahokia
237	50.6	Community High SD 94	West Chicago
237	50.6	Decatur SD 61	Decatur
237	50.6	Pekin Public SD 108	Pekin
237	50.6	Reed Custer CUSD 255U	Braidwood
237	50.6	Skokie SD 68	Skokie
237	50.6	Vandalia CUSD 203	Vandalia
246	50.5	Auburn CUSD 10	Auburn
246	50.5	Community CSD 168	Sauk Village
246	50.5	Keeneyville SD 20	Hanover Park
246	50.5	North Boone CUSD 200	Poplar Grove
246	50.5	Ottawa Elem SD 141	Ottawa
251	50.4	Bensenville SD 2	Bensenville
251	50.4	City of Chicago SD 299	Chicago
251	50.4	Dolton SD 148	Riverdale
251	50.4	Homewood Flossmoor CHSD 233	Flossmoor
251	50.4	Kewanee Community Unit SD 229	Kewanee
251	50.4	O'Fallon Twp High SD 203	O Fallon
251	50.4	Peoria SD 150	Peoria
251	50.4	Rock Island SD 41	Rock Island
251	50.4	Steger SD 194	Steger
251	50.4	Urbana SD 116	Urbana
261	50.3	Freeport SD 145	Freeport
261	50.3	Kildeer Countryside CCSD 96	Buffalo Grove
261	50.3	Litchfield CUSD 12	Litchfield
261	50.3	Oak Park Elem SD 97	Oak Park
265	50.2	Bellwood SD 88	Bellwood
265	50.2	Herrin CUSD 4	Herrin
265	50.2	Jersey CUSD 100	Jerseyville
265	50.2	Libertyville SD 70	Libertyville
265	50.2	Lyons Twp HSD 204	La Grange
265	50.2	Mahomet-Seymour CUSD 3	Mahomet
265	50.2	Streator Elem SD 44	Streator
265	50.2	Troy Community CSD 30C	Plainfield
273	50.1	Evanston Twp HSD 202	Evanston
274	50.0	Aurora West Unit SD 129	Aurora
274	50.0	Marquardt SD 15	Glendale Hgts
274	50.0	Sterling CUD 5	Sterling
274	50.0	Woodridge SD 68	Woodridge
278	49.9	Harvey SD 152	Harvey
278	49.9	Meridian CUSD 223	Stillman Valley
280	49.8	Dixon Unit SD 170	Dixon
280	49.8	Dolton SD 149	Calumet City
280	49.8	Lockport Twp HSD 205	Lockport
280	49.8	Murphysboro CUSD 186	Murphysboro
284	49.7	Byron Community Unit SD 226	Byron
284	49.7	Clinton CUSD 15	Clinton
284	49.7	Monmouth-Roseville CUSD 238	Monmouth
287	49.6	Prairie-Hills Elem SD 144	Markham
287	49.6	United Twp HS District 30	East Moline
289	49.5	Hononegah Community HSD 207	Rockton
289	49.5	Proviso Twp HSD 209	Forest Park
289	49.5	Riverton CUSD 14	Riverton
292	49.4	Wilmette SD 39	Wilmette
293	49.3	Danville CCSD 118	Danville
294	49.2	Harrisburg CUSD 3	Harrisburg
294	49.2	Palos Community CSD 118	Palos Park
296	48.9	Thornton Twp HSD 205	South Holland
297	48.8	East St Louis SD 189	E Saint Louis

Female Students

Rank	Percent	District Name	City
1	51.2	East St Louis SD 189	E Saint Louis
2	51.1	Thornton Twp HSD 205	South Holland
3	50.8	Harrisburg CUSD 3	Harrisburg
3	50.8	Palos Community CSD 118	Palos Park
5	50.7	Danville CCSD 118	Danville
6	50.6	Wilmette SD 39	Wilmette
7	50.5	Hononegah Community HSD 207	Rockton
7	50.5	Proviso Twp HSD 209	Forest Park
7	50.5	Riverton CUSD 14	Riverton
10	50.4	Prairie-Hills Elem SD 144	Markham
10	50.4	United Twp HS District 30	East Moline
12	50.3	Byron Community Unit SD 226	Byron
12	50.3	Clinton CUSD 15	Clinton
12	50.3	Monmouth-Roseville CUSD 238	Monmouth
15	50.2	Dixon Unit SD 170	Dixon
15	50.2	Dolton SD 149	Calumet City
15	50.2	Lockport Twp HSD 205	Lockport
15	50.2	Murphysboro CUSD 186	Murphysboro
19	50.1	Harvey SD 152	Harvey
19	50.1	Meridian CUSD 223	Stillman Valley
21	50.0	Aurora West Unit SD 129	Aurora
21	50.0	Marquardt SD 15	Glendale Hgts
21	50.0	Sterling CUD 5	Sterling
21	50.0	Woodridge SD 68	Woodridge
25	49.9	Evanston Twp HSD 202	Evanston
26	49.8	Bellwood SD 88	Bellwood
26	49.8	Herrin CUSD 4	Herrin
26	49.8	Jersey CUSD 100	Jerseyville
26	49.8	Libertyville SD 70	Libertyville
26	49.8	Lyons Twp HSD 204	La Grange
26	49.8	Mahomet-Seymour CUSD 3	Mahomet
26	49.8	Streator Elem SD 44	Streator
26	49.8	Troy Community CSD 30C	Plainfield
34	49.7	Freeport SD 145	Freeport
34	49.7	Kildeer Countryside CCSD 96	Buffalo Grove
34	49.7	Litchfield CUSD 12	Litchfield
34	49.7	Oak Park Elem SD 97	Oak Park
38	49.6	Bensenville SD 2	Bensenville
38	49.6	City of Chicago SD 299	Chicago
38	49.6	Dolton SD 148	Riverdale
38	49.6	Homewood Flossmoor CHSD 233	Flossmoor
38	49.6	Kewanee Community Unit SD 229	Kewanee
38	49.6	O'Fallon Twp High SD 203	O Fallon
38	49.6	Peoria SD 150	Peoria
38	49.6	Rock Island SD 41	Rock Island
38	49.6	Steger SD 194	Steger
38	49.6	Urbana SD 116	Urbana
48	49.5	Auburn CUSD 10	Auburn
48	49.5	Community CSD 168	Sauk Village

Note: This section only includes districts with 1,500 or more students; All categories are ranked from high to low

48	49.5	Keeneyville SD 20	Hanover Park
48	49.5	North Boone CUSD 200	Poplar Grove
48	49.5	Ottawa Elem SD 141	Ottawa
53	49.4	Berwyn South SD 100	Berwyn
53	49.4	Big Hollow SD 38	Ingleside
53	49.4	Cahokia Community Unit SD 187	Cahokia
53	49.4	Community High SD 94	West Chicago
53	49.4	Decatur SD 61	Decatur
53	49.4	Pekin Public SD 108	Pekin
53	49.4	Reed Custer CUSD 255U	Braidwood
53	49.4	Skokie SD 68	Skokie
53	49.4	Vandalia CUSD 203	Vandalia
62	49.3	Aptakisic-Tripp CCSD 102	Buffalo Grove
62	49.3	Beach Park CCSD 3	Beach Park
62	49.3	Bremen Community HS District 228	Midlothian
62	49.3	Geneva Community Unit SD 304	Geneva
62	49.3	Lemont Twp HSD 210	Lemont
62	49.3	Matteson Elem SD 162	Matteson
62	49.3	Rochelle Community CD 231	Rochelle
69	49.2	Adlai E Stevenson Dist 125	Lincolnshire
69	49.2	Bloom Twp High SD 206	Chicago Heights
69	49.2	Elem SD 159	Matteson
69	49.2	Elmhurst SD 205	Elmhurst
69	49.2	Hawthorn CCSD 73	Vernon Hills
69	49.2	Highland Community Unit SD 5	Highland
69	49.2	Kirby SD 140	Tinley Park
69	49.2	Lake Villa CCSD 41	Lake Villa
69	49.2	Lombard SD 44	Lombard
69	49.2	Mchenry Community HSD 156	Mchenry
69	49.2	Mokena SD 159	Mokena
69	49.2	Zion-Benton Twp HSD 126	Zion
81	49.1	Bourbonnais SD 53	Bourbonnais
81	49.1	Evanston CCSD 65	Evanston
81	49.1	Joliet Twp HSD 204	Joliet
81	49.1	Lincoln Way Community HSD 210	New Lenox
81	49.1	Monticello CUSD 25	Monticello
81	49.1	Summit SD 104	Summit
87	49.0	Addison SD 4	Addison
87	49.0	Aurora East Unit SD 131	Aurora
87	49.0	Cary CCSD 26	Cary
87	49.0	Du Page High SD 88	Addison
87	49.0	Dunlap CUSD 323	Dunlap
87	49.0	East Richland CUSD 1	Olney
87	49.0	Forest Ridge SD 142	Oak Forest
87	49.0	Mundelein Elem SD 75	Mundelein
87	49.0	Plano Community Unit SD 88	Plano
87	49.0	West Harvey-Dixmoor PSD 147	Harvey
87	49.0	Westmont CUSD 201	Westmont
98	48.9	Arlington Hgts SD 25	Arlington Hgts
98	48.9	Channahon SD 17	Channahon
98	48.9	Cicero SD 99	Cicero
98	48.9	Dekalb Community Unit SD 428	Dekalb
98	48.9	Glenview CCSD 34	Glenview
98	48.9	Massac Unit District #1	Metropolis
98	48.9	Mattoon CUSD 2	Mattoon
98	48.9	Moline Unit SD 40	Moline
98	48.9	Paxton-Buckley-Loda CUD 10	Paxton
98	48.9	Rockford SD 205	Rockford
98	48.9	Valley View CUSD #365U	Romeoville
98	48.9	Waukegan CUSD 60	Waukegan
110	48.8	Belvidere CUSD 100	Belvidere
110	48.8	Community High SD 128	Vernon Hills
110	48.8	Community Unit SD 300	Carpentersville
110	48.8	Geneseo Community Unit SD 228	Geneseo
110	48.8	Mclean County Unit Dist No 5	Normal
110	48.8	Niles Twp Community High SD 219	Skokie
110	48.8	Pekin Community HSD 303	Pekin
110	48.8	Robinson CUSD 2	Robinson
110	48.8	Skokie SD 69	Skokie
110	48.8	South Holland SD 151	South Holland
110	48.8	Summit Hill SD 161	Frankfort
110	48.8	Township High SD 214	Arlington Hgts
122	48.7	Bradley Bourbonnais CHSD 307	Bradley
122	48.7	Burbank SD 111	Burbank
122	48.7	CCSD 181	Westmont
122	48.7	Frankfort Community Unit SD 168	West Frankfort
122	48.7	Glen Ellyn CCSD 89	Glen Ellyn
122	48.7	Hinsdale Twp HSD 86	Hinsdale
122	48.7	Jacksonville SD 117	Jacksonville
122	48.7	Kinnikinnick CCSD 131	Roscoe
122	48.7	Maine Township HSD 207	Park Ridge
122	48.7	Maywood-Melrose Park-Broadview-89	Melrose Park
122	48.7	Naperville CUD 203	Naperville
122	48.7	Oak Lawn Community HSD 229	Oak Lawn
122	48.7	Park Forest SD 163	Park Forest
122	48.7	Springfield SD 186	Springfield
122	48.7	Township HSD 211	Palatine
137	48.6	Ball Chatham CUSD 5	Chatham
137	48.6	Barrington CUSD 220	Barrington
137	48.6	Batavia Unit SD 101	Batavia
137	48.6	Bradley SD 61	Bradley
137	48.6	Chicago Heights SD 170	Chicago Heights
137	48.6	Indian Prairie CUSD 204	Aurora
137	48.6	Kankakee SD 111	Kankakee
137	48.6	La Grange SD 102	La Grange Park
137	48.6	Park Ridge CCSD 64	Park Ridge
137	48.6	Reavis Twp HSD 220	Burbank
137	48.6	School District 45 Dupage County	Villa Park
137	48.6	Township High SD 113	Highland Park
137	48.6	West Chicago Elem SD 33	West Chicago
137	48.6	Wheeling CCSD 21	Wheeling
151	48.5	Belleville Twp HSD 201	Belleville
151	48.5	Crystal Lake CCSD 47	Crystal Lake
151	48.5	East Maine SD 63	Des Plaines
151	48.5	Glenbard Twp HSD 87	Glen Ellyn
151	48.5	Granite City CUSD 9	Granite City
151	48.5	Gurnee SD 56	Gurnee
151	48.5	J S Morton HS District 201	Cicero
151	48.5	North Palos SD 117	Palos Hills
151	48.5	North Shore SD 112	Highland Park
151	48.5	Palatine CCSD 15	Palatine
151	48.5	Triad Community Unit SD 2	Troy
151	48.5	Wabash CUSD 348	Mount Carmel
163	48.4	Community Unit SD 200	Wheaton
163	48.4	Cons High SD 230	Orland Park
163	48.4	Consolidated SD 158	Algonquin
163	48.4	Downers Grove Grade SD 58	Downers Grove
163	48.4	Lake Zurich CUSD 95	Lake Zurich
163	48.4	Macomb Community Unit SD 185	Macomb
163	48.4	Olympia CUSD 16	Stanford
163	48.4	Quincy SD 172	Quincy
163	48.4	Rantoul City SD 137	Rantoul
172	48.3	Crete Monee CUSD 201u	Crete
172	48.3	Lyons SD 103	Lyons
172	48.3	Mount Zion Community Unit SD 3	Mount Zion
172	48.3	Oak Park & River Forest Dist 200	Oak Park
172	48.3	Plainfield SD 202	Plainfield
172	48.3	School District U-46	Elgin
172	48.3	Sherrard Community Unit SD 200	Sherrard
172	48.3	Southwestern CUSD 9	Piasa
180	48.2	Community High SD 99	Downers Grove
180	48.2	Frankfort CCSD 157C	Frankfort
180	48.2	Genoa Kingston CUSD 424	Genoa
180	48.2	Joliet Public SD 86	Joliet
180	48.2	Lake Forest CHSD 115	Lake Forest
180	48.2	Leyden Community HSD 212	Franklin Park
180	48.2	Minooka Community CSD 201	Minooka
187	48.1	Berkeley SD 87	Berkeley
187	48.1	Canton Union SD 66	Canton
187	48.1	Elmwood Park CUSD 401	Elmwood Park
187	48.1	Indian Springs SD 109	Justice
187	48.1	Mchenry CCSD 15	Mchenry
187	48.1	Millburn CCSD 24	Old Mill Creek
187	48.1	Oak Lawn-Hometown SD 123	Oak Lawn
194	48.0	Community Consolidated SD 62	Des Plaines
194	48.0	Lake Forest SD 67	Lake Forest
194	48.0	Lansing SD 158	Lansing
194	48.0	Manteno Community Unit SD 5	Manteno
194	48.0	New Lenox SD 122	New Lenox
194	48.0	Oswego Community Unit SD 308	Oswego
194	48.0	Riverside SD 96	Riverside
194	48.0	Round Lake Area Schs - Dist 116	Round Lake
194	48.0	Schaumburg CCSD 54	Schaumburg
194	48.0	Sycamore CUSD 427	Sycamore
204	47.9	Community High SD 155	Crystal Lake
204	47.9	Community High SD 218	Oak Lawn
204	47.9	Deerfield SD 109	Deerfield
204	47.9	Galesburg CUSD 205	Galesburg
204	47.9	Herscher Community Unit SD 2	Herscher
204	47.9	Homewood SD 153	Homewood
204	47.9	Johnsburg CUSD 12	Johnsburg
204	47.9	Lisle CUSD 202	Lisle
204	47.9	Minooka Community HS District 111	Minooka
204	47.9	Saint Charles CUSD 303	Saint Charles
204	47.9	Thornton Fractional HSD 215	Calumet City
215	47.8	Alsip-Hazelgreen-Oak Lawn SD 126	Alsip
215	47.8	Belleville SD 118	Belleville
215	47.8	Carterville CUSD 5	Carterville
215	47.8	Community Consolidated SD 46	Grayslake
215	47.8	Edwardsville CUSD 7	Edwardsville
215	47.8	Illinois Valley CUD 321	Chillicothe
215	47.8	Orland SD 135	Orland Park
215	47.8	Queen Bee SD 16	Glendale Hgts
215	47.8	Rich Twp HS District 227	Olympia Fields
215	47.8	Ridgeland SD 122	Oak Lawn
215	47.8	Rochester CUSD 3A	Rochester
215	47.8	Roxana Community Unit SD 1	Roxana
215	47.8	Tinley Park CCSD 146	Tinley Park
215	47.8	Woodland CCSD 50	Gurnee
229	47.7	Charleston CUSD 1	Charleston
229	47.7	Darien SD 61	Darien
229	47.7	Grayslake Com High SD 127	Grayslake
229	47.7	Hillsboro Community Unit SD 3	Hillsboro
229	47.7	Wauconda Community Unit SD 118	Wauconda
229	47.7	Zion Elementary SD 6	Zion
235	47.6	Bloomington SD 87	Bloomington
235	47.6	Columbia Community Unit SD 4	Columbia
235	47.6	Effingham Community Unit SD 40	Effingham
235	47.6	Eureka C U Dist 140	Eureka
235	47.6	Glen Ellyn SD 41	Glen Ellyn
235	47.6	Lake Park Community HSD 108	Roselle
235	47.6	Lemont-Bromberek CSD 113A	Lemont
235	47.6	Mascoutah CUD 19	Mascoutah
235	47.6	Mundelein Cons High SD 120	Mundelein
235	47.6	Tolono CUSD 7	Tolono
245	47.5	Community Consolidated SD 93	Bloomingdale
245	47.5	Du Quoin CUSD 300	Du Quoin
245	47.5	Grant Community HS District 124	Fox Lake
245	47.5	Mannheim SD 83	Franklin Park
245	47.5	Mount Vernon SD 80	Mount Vernon
245	47.5	Northfield Twp High SD 225	Glenview
245	47.5	Rockton SD 140	Rockton
252	47.4	Champaign Community Unit SD 4	Champaign
252	47.4	Coal City CUSD 1	Coal City
252	47.4	Flossmoor SD 161	Chicago Heights
252	47.4	Harlem Unit Dist 122	Machesney Park
252	47.4	Marion Community Unit SD 2	Marion
252	47.4	Morton CUSD 709	Morton
252	47.4	Posen-Robbins Elem SD 143-5	Posen
259	47.3	Beardstown CUSD 15	Beardstown
259	47.3	Collinsville CUSD 10	Collinsville
259	47.3	Community CSD 59	Arlington Hgts
259	47.3	Evergreen Park Elem SD 124	Evergreen Park
259	47.3	Kaneland CUSD 302	Maple Park
259	47.3	Warren Twp High SD 121	Gurnee
265	47.2	Berwyn North SD 98	Berwyn
265	47.2	New Trier Twp HSD 203	Northfield
265	47.2	Prairie Central CUSD 8	Fairbury
265	47.2	Will County SD 92	Lockport
265	47.2	Woodstock CUSD 200	Woodstock
270	47.1	Bethalto CUSD 8	Bethalto
270	47.1	Cook County SD 130	Blue Island
270	47.1	Fenton Community HSD 100	Bensenville
270	47.1	North Chicago SD 187	North Chicago
274	47.0	Argo Community HSD 217	Summit
274	47.0	Homer Community CSD 33c	Homer Glen
274	47.0	Taylorville CUSD 3	Taylorville
277	46.9	Alton Community Unit SD 11	Alton
277	46.9	Community High SD 117	Lake Villa
277	46.9	Fremont SD 79	Mundelein
277	46.9	Mount Prospect SD 57	Mount Prospect
277	46.9	Oregon CUSD 220	Oregon
277	46.9	Yorkville Community Unit SD 115	Yorkville
283	46.8	East Peoria SD 86	East Peoria
284	46.7	Sandwich CUSD 430	Sandwich
284	46.7	Waterloo CUSD 5	Waterloo
286	46.6	East Moline SD 37	East Moline
286	46.6	Peotone CUSD 207U	Peotone
288	46.5	O'Fallon CCSD 90	O Fallon
288	46.5	Western Springs SD 101	Western Springs
290	46.4	Bond County CUSD 2	Greenville
290	46.4	Northbrook SD 28	Northbrook
290	46.4	Winnebago CUSD 323	Winnebago
290	46.4	Winnetka SD 36	Winnetka
294	46.2	Antioch CCSD 34	Antioch
295	45.9	Midlothian SD 143	Midlothian
296	45.7	Central Community Unit SD 301	Burlington
296	45.7	Harvard CUSD 50	Harvard

Note: This section only includes districts with 1,500 or more students; All categories are ranked from high to low

Individual Education Program Students

Rank	Percent	District Name	City
1	24.6	Evergreen Park Elem SD 124	Evergreen Park
2	22.8	Belleville SD 118	Belleville
3	22.7	Streator Elem SD 44	Streator
4	22.3	Alton Community Unit SD 11	Alton
5	22.1	Riverton CUSD 14	Riverton
6	21.8	Springfield SD 186	Springfield
7	21.7	Murphysboro CUSD 186	Murphysboro
7	21.7	Pekin Public SD 108	Pekin
9	21.3	Jacksonville SD 117	Jacksonville
10	21.1	Urbana SD 116	Urbana
11	21.0	Frankfort Community Unit SD 168	West Frankfort
11	21.0	Mount Vernon SD 80	Mount Vernon
13	20.9	Peoria SD 150	Peoria
14	20.6	Bloom Twp High SD 206	Chicago Heights
14	20.6	Prairie Central CUSD 8	Fairbury
16	20.5	Macomb Community Unit SD 185	Macomb
17	20.3	Big Hollow SD 38	Ingleside
18	20.1	Cahokia Community Unit SD 187	Cahokia
18	20.1	Charleston CUSD 1	Charleston
20	20.0	Elmwood Park CUSD 401	Elmwood Park
21	19.9	Tinley Park CCSD 146	Tinley Park
22	19.7	Beach Park CCSD 3	Beach Park
23	19.4	Auburn CUSD 10	Auburn
23	19.4	Belleville Twp HSD 201	Belleville
23	19.4	Du Quoin CUSD 300	Du Quoin
26	19.3	Collinsville CUSD 10	Collinsville
27	19.2	Bradley SD 61	Bradley
28	19.1	Crete Monee CUSD 201u	Crete
28	19.1	Mchenry CCSD 15	Mchenry
30	19.0	Joliet Twp HSD 204	Joliet
31	18.9	Ottawa Elem SD 141	Ottawa
31	18.9	Proviso Twp HSD 209	Forest Park
33	18.7	Beardstown CUSD 15	Beardstown
33	18.7	Harrisburg CUSD 3	Harrisburg
33	18.7	Park Forest SD 163	Park Forest
33	18.7	Robinson CUSD 2	Robinson
37	18.6	Carterville CUSD 5	Carterville
38	18.5	Clinton CUSD 15	Clinton
38	18.5	Community CSD 168	Sauk Village
38	18.5	Keeneyville SD 20	Hanover Park
41	18.4	Kewanee Community Unit SD 229	Kewanee
41	18.4	Skokie SD 68	Skokie
43	18.3	Granite City CUSD 9	Granite City
43	18.3	Rich Twp HS District 227	Olympia Fields
45	18.1	Cook County SD 130	Blue Island
46	18.0	Herrin CUSD 4	Herrin
47	17.9	Addison SD 4	Addison
47	17.9	Wabash CUSD 348	Mount Carmel
49	17.8	Bond County CUSD 2	Greenville
49	17.8	Canton Union SD 66	Canton
49	17.8	Effingham Community Unit SD 40	Effingham
49	17.8	Lansing SD 158	Lansing
53	17.7	Highland Community Unit SD 5	Highland
53	17.7	Ridgeland SD 122	Oak Lawn
55	17.6	Cary CCSD 26	Cary
55	17.6	Champaign Community Unit SD 4	Champaign
55	17.6	Illinois Valley CUD 321	Chillicothe
55	17.6	Marion Community Unit SD 2	Marion
55	17.6	Mundelein Cons High SD 120	Mundelein
55	17.6	Sterling CUD 5	Sterling
61	17.5	Homewood SD 153	Homewood
61	17.5	O'Fallon CCSD 90	O Fallon
63	17.4	Jersey CUSD 100	Jerseyville
63	17.4	Quincy SD 172	Quincy
63	17.4	Westmont CUSD 201	Westmont
66	17.2	Bethalto CUSD 8	Bethalto
66	17.2	Decatur SD 61	Decatur
68	17.1	East Peoria SD 86	East Peoria
68	17.1	Prairie-Hills Elem SD 144	Markham
70	17.0	Rantoul City SD 137	Rantoul
70	17.0	Rochelle Community CD 231	Rochelle
72	16.9	Orland SD 135	Orland Park
72	16.9	Triad Community Unit SD 2	Troy
72	16.9	Vandalia CUSD 203	Vandalia
72	16.9	Winnetka SD 36	Winnetka
76	16.8	Community Consolidated SD 46	Grayslake
76	16.8	Evanston Twp HSD 202	Evanston
76	16.8	Midlothian SD 143	Midlothian
79	16.7	Bremen Community HS District 228	Midlothian
79	16.7	East Moline SD 37	East Moline
79	16.7	La Grange SD 102	La Grange Park
79	16.7	Mattoon CUSD 2	Mattoon
79	16.7	Oak Park Elem SD 97	Oak Park
84	16.6	Bloomington SD 87	Bloomington
84	16.6	Joliet Public SD 86	Joliet
84	16.6	Lake Forest CHSD 115	Lake Forest
87	16.5	Kildeer Countryside CCSD 96	Buffalo Grove
87	16.5	Manteno Community Unit SD 5	Manteno
87	16.5	North Chicago SD 187	North Chicago
87	16.5	Oak Park & River Forest Dist 200	Oak Park
87	16.5	Park Ridge CCSD 64	Park Ridge
87	16.5	Round Lake Area Schs - Dist 116	Round Lake
87	16.5	Taylorville CUSD 3	Taylorville
87	16.5	Woodland CCSD 50	Gurnee
95	16.4	Community Unit SD 200	Wheaton
95	16.4	Gurnee SD 56	Gurnee
95	16.4	Lake Villa CCSD 41	Lake Villa
95	16.4	New Trier Twp HSD 203	Northfield
95	16.4	Olympia CUSD 16	Stanford
95	16.4	Palos Community CSD 118	Palos Park
95	16.4	Plano Community Unit SD 88	Plano
95	16.4	Rock Island SD 41	Rock Island
95	16.4	Roxana Community Unit SD 1	Roxana
95	16.4	United Twp HS District 30	East Moline
105	16.3	Community High SD 218	Oak Lawn
105	16.3	Eureka C U Dist 140	Eureka
107	16.2	Riverside SD 96	Riverside
107	16.2	Southwestern CUSD 9	Piasa
107	16.2	Township High SD 113	Highland Park
107	16.2	Western Springs SD 101	Western Springs
111	16.1	North Shore SD 112	Highland Park
111	16.1	Zion-Benton Twp HSD 126	Zion
113	16.0	Antioch CCSD 34	Antioch
113	16.0	Lisle CUSD 202	Lisle
113	16.0	Mchenry Community HSD 156	Mchenry
113	16.0	Zion Elementary SD 6	Zion
117	15.9	Downers Grove Grade SD 58	Downers Grove
117	15.9	Elmhurst SD 205	Elmhurst
117	15.9	Grant Community HS District 124	Fox Lake
117	15.9	Millburn CCSD 24	Old Mill Creek
121	15.8	Arlington Hgts SD 25	Arlington Hgts
121	15.8	Bradley Bourbonnais CHSD 307	Bradley
121	15.8	Kankakee SD 111	Kankakee
121	15.8	Lake Zurich CUSD 95	Lake Zurich
121	15.8	Paxton-Buckley-Loda CUD 10	Paxton
121	15.8	School District 45 Dupage County	Villa Park
127	15.7	Glenview CCSD 34	Glenview
127	15.7	Pekin Community HSD 303	Pekin
129	15.6	Community Consolidated SD 93	Bloomingdale
129	15.6	Homer Community CSD 33c	Homer Glen
129	15.6	West Harvey-Dixmoor PSD 147	Harvey
132	15.5	Litchfield CUSD 12	Litchfield
132	15.5	Mascoutah CUD 19	Mascoutah
134	15.4	Dixon Unit SD 170	Dixon
134	15.4	Maine Township HSD 207	Park Ridge
134	15.4	Reed Custer CUSD 255U	Braidwood
137	15.3	Community Unit SD 300	Carpentersville
137	15.3	Leyden Community HSD 212	Franklin Park
139	15.2	Mclean County Unit Dist No 5	Normal
139	15.2	Monmouth-Roseville CUSD 238	Monmouth
139	15.2	Oak Lawn-Hometown SD 123	Oak Lawn
139	15.2	Woodridge SD 68	Woodridge
143	15.1	Berwyn North SD 98	Berwyn
143	15.1	Community Consolidated SD 62	Des Plaines
143	15.1	Deerfield SD 109	Deerfield
143	15.1	Evanston CCSD 65	Evanston
143	15.1	Fenton Community HSD 100	Bensenville
143	15.1	Galesburg CUSD 205	Galesburg
143	15.1	Harlem Unit Dist 122	Machesney Park
143	15.1	Harvard CUSD 50	Harvard
143	15.1	Sandwich CUSD 430	Sandwich
152	15.0	Consolidated SD 158	Algonquin
152	15.0	Hillsboro Community Unit SD 3	Hillsboro
152	15.0	Kinnikinnick CCSD 131	Roscoe
152	15.0	Mundelein Elem SD 75	Mundelein
152	15.0	Thornton Fractional HSD 215	Calumet City
152	15.0	Woodstock CUSD 200	Woodstock
158	14.9	Danville CCSD 118	Danville
158	14.9	East Richland CUSD 1	Olney
158	14.9	Lombard SD 44	Lombard
161	14.8	Elem SD 159	Matteson
161	14.8	Kirby SD 140	Tinley Park
161	14.8	Rockford SD 205	Rockford
164	14.7	Matteson Elem SD 162	Matteson
164	14.7	Mokena SD 159	Mokena
164	14.7	Niles Twp Community High SD 219	Skokie
164	14.7	Oregon CUSD 220	Oregon
168	14.6	Barrington CUSD 220	Barrington
168	14.6	Belvidere CUSD 100	Belvidere
168	14.6	Lyons SD 103	Lyons
168	14.6	Steger SD 194	Steger
172	14.5	Du Page High SD 88	Addison
172	14.5	Morton CUSD 709	Morton
174	14.4	Aurora East Unit SD 131	Aurora
174	14.4	Berwyn South SD 100	Berwyn
174	14.4	Burbank SD 111	Burbank
174	14.4	Crystal Lake CCSD 47	Crystal Lake
174	14.4	Darien SD 61	Darien
174	14.4	Geneva Community Unit SD 304	Geneva
174	14.4	Mannheim SD 83	Franklin Park
174	14.4	Rochester CUSD 3A	Rochester
174	14.4	Will County SD 92	Lockport
183	14.3	Byron Community Unit SD 226	Byron
183	14.3	Lake Forest SD 67	Lake Forest
183	14.3	Oswego Community Unit SD 308	Oswego
183	14.3	Summit SD 104	Summit
183	14.3	Tolono CUSD 7	Tolono
188	14.2	East Maine SD 63	Des Plaines
188	14.2	East St Louis SD 189	E Saint Louis
188	14.2	Hawthorn CCSD 73	Vernon Hills
188	14.2	Lockport Twp HSD 205	Lockport
188	14.2	Monticello CUSD 25	Monticello
188	14.2	Schaumburg CCSD 54	Schaumburg
194	14.1	Community High SD 117	Lake Villa
194	14.1	Freeport SD 145	Freeport
194	14.1	Glen Ellyn CCSD 89	Glen Ellyn
194	14.1	Saint Charles CUSD 303	Saint Charles
194	14.1	Thornton Twp HSD 205	South Holland
194	14.1	Yorkville Community Unit SD 115	Yorkville
200	14.0	Aptakisic-Tripp CCSD 102	Buffalo Grove
200	14.0	Community CSD 59	Arlington Hgts
200	14.0	Forest Ridge SD 142	Oak Forest
200	14.0	North Boone CUSD 200	Poplar Grove
204	13.9	Community High SD 99	Downers Grove
204	13.9	Lake Park Community HSD 108	Roselle
204	13.9	Moline Unit SD 40	Moline
207	13.8	Channahon SD 17	Channahon
207	13.8	Township High SD 214	Arlington Hgts
207	13.8	Valley View CUSD #365U	Romeoville
207	13.8	West Chicago Elem SD 33	West Chicago
207	13.8	Wilmette SD 39	Wilmette
212	13.7	Alsip-Hazelgreen-Oak Lawn SD 126	Alsip
212	13.7	Chicago Heights SD 170	Chicago Heights
212	13.7	Minooka Community HS District 111	Minooka
212	13.7	Wauconda Community Unit SD 118	Wauconda
216	13.6	Summit Hill SD 161	Frankfort
216	13.6	Waukegan CUSD 60	Waukegan
218	13.5	Bellwood SD 88	Bellwood
218	13.5	Frankfort CCSD 157C	Frankfort
218	13.5	Sherrard Community Unit SD 200	Sherrard
221	13.4	Berkeley SD 87	Berkeley
221	13.4	Minooka Community CSD 201	Minooka
221	13.4	Rockton SD 140	Rockton
221	13.4	South Holland SD 151	South Holland
225	13.3	Bourbonnais SD 53	Bourbonnais
225	13.3	Coal City CUSD 1	Coal City
225	13.3	Grayslake Com High SD 127	Grayslake
225	13.3	Herscher Community Unit SD 2	Herscher
225	13.3	Massac Unit District #1	Metropolis
225	13.3	New Lenox SD 122	New Lenox
231	13.2	Ball Chatham CUSD 5	Chatham
231	13.2	Central Community Unit SD 301	Burlington
231	13.2	Cons High SD 230	Orland Park
231	13.2	Glenbard Twp HSD 87	Glen Ellyn
231	13.2	Homewood Flossmoor CHSD 233	Flossmoor
231	13.2	School District U-46	Elgin
231	13.2	Skokie SD 69	Skokie
231	13.2	Waterloo CUSD 5	Waterloo
239	13.1	Dekalb Community Unit SD 428	Dekalb
239	13.1	Maywood-Melrose Park-Broadview-89	Melrose Park
239	13.1	Township HSD 211	Palatine
242	13.0	Argo Community HSD 217	Summit
242	13.0	Aurora West Unit SD 129	Aurora
242	13.0	North Palos SD 117	Palos Hills
242	13.0	Queen Bee SD 16	Glendale Hgts
246	12.9	Troy Community CSD 30C	Plainfield
247	12.8	Community High SD 94	West Chicago
247	12.8	Fremont SD 79	Mundelein
249	12.7	City of Chicago SD 299	Chicago

Note: This section only includes districts with 1,500 or more students; All categories are ranked from high to low

249	12.7	Glen Ellyn SD 41	Glen Ellyn
249	12.7	Indian Springs SD 109	Justice
249	12.7	Kaneland CUSD 302	Maple Park
249	12.7	O'Fallon Twp High SD 203	O Fallon
249	12.7	Palatine CCSD 15	Palatine
255	12.6	CCSD 181	Westmont
255	12.6	Community High SD 155	Crystal Lake
255	12.6	Mount Prospect SD 57	Mount Prospect
255	12.6	Winnebago CUSD 323	Winnebago
259	12.4	J S Morton HS District 201	Cicero
260	12.3	Flossmoor SD 161	Chicago Heights
260	12.3	Oak Lawn Community HSD 229	Oak Lawn
260	12.3	Plainfield SD 202	Plainfield
260	12.3	Wheeling CCSD 21	Wheeling
264	12.2	Batavia Unit SD 101	Batavia
264	12.2	Cicero SD 99	Cicero
264	12.2	Dunlap CUSD 323	Dunlap
264	12.2	Harvey SD 152	Harvey
264	12.2	Mahomet-Seymour CUSD 3	Mahomet
269	12.1	Columbia Community Unit SD 4	Columbia
270	12.0	Peotone CUSD 207U	Peotone
271	11.9	Adlai E Stevenson Dist 125	Lincolnshire
271	11.9	Community High SD 128	Vernon Hills
271	11.9	Hononegah Community HSD 207	Rockton
271	11.9	Lincoln Way Community HSD 210	New Lenox
275	11.8	Johnsburg CUSD 12	Johnsburg
276	11.7	Northbrook SD 28	Northbrook
277	11.6	Warren Twp High SD 121	Gurnee
278	11.5	Dolton SD 149	Calumet City
279	11.4	Dolton SD 148	Riverdale
280	11.3	Lyons Twp HSD 204	La Grange
281	11.2	Geneseo Community Unit SD 228	Geneseo
281	11.2	Meridian CUSD 223	Stillman Valley
281	11.2	Northfield Twp High SD 225	Glenview
284	11.1	Bensenville SD 2	Bensenville
284	11.1	Naperville CUD 203	Naperville
286	10.8	Edwardsville CUSD 7	Edwardsville
286	10.8	Sycamore CUSD 427	Sycamore
288	10.7	Hinsdale Twp HSD 86	Hinsdale
289	10.6	Indian Prairie CUSD 204	Aurora
290	10.5	Genoa Kingston CUSD 424	Genoa
291	10.2	Lemont-Bromberek CSD 113A	Lemont
291	10.2	Mount Zion Community Unit SD 3	Mount Zion
291	10.2	Posen-Robbins Elem SD 143-5	Posen
294	10.0	Reavis Twp HSD 220	Burbank
295	8.5	Marquardt SD 15	Glendale Hgts
296	7.9	Lemont Twp HSD 210	Lemont
297	7.5	Libertyville SD 70	Libertyville

English Language Learner Students

Rank	Percent	District Name	City
1	57.6	West Chicago Elem SD 33	West Chicago
2	52.5	Cicero SD 99	Cicero
3	48.6	Bensenville SD 2	Bensenville
4	42.3	Wheeling CCSD 21	Wheeling
5	42.1	Community Consolidated SD 62	Des Plaines
6	37.3	Aurora East Unit SD 131	Aurora
7	36.0	Community CSD 59	Arlington Hgts
8	33.9	East Maine SD 63	Des Plaines
9	33.7	Addison SD 4	Addison
10	32.8	Waukegan CUSD 60	Waukegan
11	32.6	Berkeley SD 87	Berkeley
12	32.1	Summit SD 104	Summit
13	30.1	Harvard CUSD 50	Harvard
14	28.9	Queen Bee SD 16	Glendale Hgts
15	28.8	Mannheim SD 83	Franklin Park
16	28.7	Beardstown CUSD 15	Beardstown
17	26.2	Maywood-Melrose Park-Broadview-89	Melrose Park
18	25.8	Posen-Robbins Elem SD 143-5	Posen
19	24.8	Round Lake Area Schs - Dist 116	Round Lake
20	24.0	Indian Springs SD 109	Justice
21	23.7	Cook County SD 130	Blue Island
22	23.6	School District 45 Dupage County	Villa Park
23	23.0	Burbank SD 111	Burbank
24	22.7	School District U-46	Elgin
25	22.2	Marquardt SD 15	Glendale Hgts
25	22.2	Palatine CCSD 15	Palatine
27	21.7	Ridgeland SD 122	Oak Lawn
28	20.9	Mundelein Elem SD 75	Mundelein
29	20.8	North Chicago SD 187	North Chicago
30	20.3	Joliet Public SD 86	Joliet
31	20.0	Zion Elementary SD 6	Zion
32	19.9	Alsip-Hazelgreen-Oak Lawn SD 126	Alsip
33	18.9	Berwyn South SD 100	Berwyn
34	18.7	Rochelle Community CD 231	Rochelle
35	17.7	North Shore SD 112	Highland Park
36	17.6	Aurora West Unit SD 129	Aurora
37	17.4	Lyons SD 103	Lyons
38	17.3	Schaumburg CCSD 54	Schaumburg
39	17.1	Gurnee SD 56	Gurnee
40	17.0	Hawthorn CCSD 73	Vernon Hills
41	16.9	Keeneyville SD 20	Hanover Park
41	16.9	South Holland SD 151	South Holland
43	16.8	Woodridge SD 68	Woodridge
44	16.6	Berwyn North SD 98	Berwyn
45	16.5	Aptakisic-Tripp CCSD 102	Buffalo Grove
46	15.2	Skokie SD 69	Skokie
47	15.1	Community Consolidated SD 93	Bloomingdale
48	14.7	Skokie SD 68	Skokie
49	14.5	Glenview CCSD 34	Glenview
50	13.2	North Palos SD 117	Palos Hills
51	12.8	City of Chicago SD 299	Chicago
51	12.8	Darien SD 61	Darien
51	12.8	Evanston CCSD 65	Evanston
51	12.8	Woodstock CUSD 200	Woodstock
55	12.6	Beach Park CCSD 3	Beach Park
56	12.2	Community Unit SD 300	Carpentersville
57	12.0	Urbana SD 116	Urbana
58	11.4	Glen Ellyn SD 41	Glen Ellyn
58	11.4	Tinley Park CCSD 146	Tinley Park
60	11.1	Plano Community Unit SD 88	Plano
60	11.1	Wauconda Community Unit SD 118	Wauconda
62	10.9	Bellwood SD 88	Bellwood
62	10.9	Rockford SD 205	Rockford
64	10.5	Fremont SD 79	Mundelein
65	10.4	Lombard SD 44	Lombard
65	10.4	Monmouth-Roseville CUSD 238	Monmouth
65	10.4	Rantoul City SD 137	Rantoul
68	10.3	Mchenry CCSD 15	Mchenry
68	10.3	Valley View CUSD #365U	Romeoville
70	9.8	Kildeer Countryside CCSD 96	Buffalo Grove
71	9.7	Moline Unit SD 40	Moline
71	9.7	North Boone CUSD 200	Poplar Grove
73	9.4	East Moline SD 37	East Moline
74	9.3	Kewanee Community Unit SD 229	Kewanee
74	9.3	Plainfield SD 202	Plainfield
76	9.1	Belvidere CUSD 100	Belvidere
76	9.1	Community Unit SD 200	Wheaton
76	9.1	Mount Prospect SD 57	Mount Prospect
76	9.1	Reavis Twp HSD 220	Burbank
80	8.9	Elmwood Park CUSD 401	Elmwood Park
81	8.8	Barrington CUSD 220	Barrington
82	8.7	Kankakee SD 111	Kankakee
83	8.6	Evergreen Park Elem SD 124	Evergreen Park
84	8.4	Community High SD 94	West Chicago
84	8.4	Steger SD 194	Steger
86	8.3	Community Consolidated SD 46	Grayslake
86	8.3	Dekalb Community Unit SD 428	Dekalb
86	8.3	Woodland CCSD 50	Gurnee
89	8.2	Lansing SD 158	Lansing
90	8.1	Big Hollow SD 38	Ingleside
91	7.9	Cary CCSD 26	Cary
91	7.9	Indian Prairie CUSD 204	Aurora
93	7.8	Arlington Hgts SD 25	Arlington Hgts
94	7.5	Crystal Lake CCSD 47	Crystal Lake
94	7.5	Lemont-Bromberek CSD 113A	Lemont
96	7.4	Rock Island SD 41	Rock Island
97	7.3	Oak Lawn-Hometown SD 123	Oak Lawn
98	7.2	Forest Ridge SD 142	Oak Forest
99	7.1	J S Morton HS District 201	Cicero
100	7.0	Champaign Community Unit SD 4	Champaign
100	7.0	Streator Elem SD 44	Streator
102	6.7	Bradley SD 61	Bradley
103	6.6	Collinsville CUSD 10	Collinsville
103	6.6	West Harvey-Dixmoor PSD 147	Harvey
105	6.5	Chicago Heights SD 170	Chicago Heights
106	6.4	Palos Community CSD 118	Palos Park
107	6.3	Bloomington SD 87	Bloomington
108	6.2	Niles Twp Community High SD 219	Skokie
109	6.1	Genoa Kingston CUSD 424	Genoa
110	6.0	Glen Ellyn CCSD 89	Glen Ellyn
110	6.0	Sandwich CUSD 430	Sandwich
112	5.8	Yorkville Community Unit SD 115	Yorkville
113	5.7	Sterling CUD 5	Sterling
114	5.5	Argo Community HSD 217	Summit
114	5.5	Lake Villa CCSD 41	Lake Villa
114	5.5	Township High SD 214	Arlington Hgts
117	5.1	Township HSD 211	Palatine
118	5.0	Du Page High SD 88	Addison
118	5.0	Meridian CUSD 223	Stillman Valley
118	5.0	Proviso Twp HSD 209	Forest Park
121	4.9	Elmhurst SD 205	Elmhurst
122	4.8	La Grange SD 102	La Grange Park
122	4.8	Maine Township HSD 207	Park Ridge
124	4.7	Fenton Community HSD 100	Bensenville
124	4.7	Glenbard Twp HSD 87	Glen Ellyn
126	4.6	Leyden Community HSD 212	Franklin Park
127	4.5	Riverside SD 96	Riverside
128	4.3	Saint Charles CUSD 303	Saint Charles
128	4.3	Troy Community CSD 30C	Plainfield
130	4.2	Dunlap CUSD 323	Dunlap
130	4.2	Westmont CUSD 201	Westmont
132	4.1	Central Community Unit SD 301	Burlington
132	4.1	Peoria SD 150	Peoria
134	3.9	Community CSD 168	Sauk Village
134	3.9	Downers Grove Grade SD 58	Downers Grove
136	3.8	Winnebago CUSD 323	Winnebago
137	3.6	Batavia Unit SD 101	Batavia
137	3.6	Dolton SD 148	Riverdale
137	3.6	Joliet Twp HSD 204	Joliet
137	3.6	Naperville CUD 203	Naperville
137	3.6	Orland SD 135	Orland Park
142	3.5	Prairie-Hills Elem SD 144	Markham
143	3.4	Consolidated SD 158	Algonquin
143	3.4	Northfield Twp High SD 225	Glenview
145	3.3	Mclean County Unit Dist No 5	Normal
145	3.3	Oswego Community Unit SD 308	Oswego
147	3.1	Antioch CCSD 34	Antioch
147	3.1	Lisle CUSD 202	Lisle
147	3.1	Mundelein Cons High SD 120	Mundelein
147	3.1	Paxton-Buckley-Loda CUD 10	Paxton
151	3.0	Community High SD 218	Oak Lawn
151	3.0	Flossmoor SD 161	Chicago Heights
151	3.0	Northbrook SD 28	Northbrook
154	2.9	Adlai E Stevenson Dist 125	Lincolnshire
154	2.9	Kaneland CUSD 302	Maple Park
154	2.9	Sycamore CUSD 427	Sycamore
154	2.9	Wilmette SD 39	Wilmette
158	2.8	Evanston Twp HSD 202	Evanston
158	2.8	Lake Zurich CUSD 95	Lake Zurich
158	2.8	Oregon CUSD 220	Oregon
158	2.8	Summit Hill SD 161	Frankfort
162	2.7	Kirby SD 140	Tinley Park
162	2.7	Ottawa Elem SD 141	Ottawa
162	2.7	Zion-Benton Twp HSD 126	Zion
165	2.6	Minooka Community CSD 201	Minooka
166	2.5	Warren Twp High SD 121	Gurnee
167	2.4	Freeport SD 145	Freeport
167	2.4	Harlem Unit Dist 122	Machesney Park
167	2.4	Mchenry Community HSD 156	Mchenry
167	2.4	Murphysboro CUSD 186	Murphysboro
171	2.3	Macomb Community Unit SD 185	Macomb
171	2.3	Oak Lawn Community HSD 229	Oak Lawn
173	2.2	CCSD 181	Westmont
173	2.2	Community High SD 99	Downers Grove
173	2.2	Effingham Community Unit SD 40	Effingham
173	2.2	Mokena SD 159	Mokena
173	2.2	Will County SD 92	Lockport
178	2.1	Park Ridge CCSD 64	Park Ridge
179	2.0	Danville CCSD 118	Danville
179	2.0	Harvey SD 152	Harvey
179	2.0	Township High SD 113	Highland Park
182	1.8	Hinsdale Twp HSD 86	Hinsdale
182	1.8	Minooka Community HS District 111	Minooka
184	1.7	Oak Park Elem SD 97	Oak Park
184	1.7	Rockton SD 140	Rockton
186	1.6	Bremen Community HS District 228	Midlothian
186	1.6	Community High SD 128	Vernon Hills
186	1.6	Mascoutah CUD 19	Mascoutah
186	1.6	Matteson Elem SD 162	Matteson
186	1.6	New Trier Twp HSD 203	Northfield
191	1.5	Bloom Twp High SD 206	Chicago Heights
191	1.5	Millburn CCSD 24	Old Mill Creek
193	1.4	Cons High SD 230	Orland Park
193	1.4	Elem SD 159	Matteson
193	1.4	Granite City CUSD 9	Granite City
193	1.4	Lake Park Community HSD 108	Roselle
197	1.3	Bradley Bourbonnais CHSD 307	Bradley
197	1.3	Crete Monee CUSD 201u	Crete
197	1.3	Libertyville SD 70	Libertyville

Note: This section only includes districts with 1,500 or more students; All categories are ranked from high to low

200	1.2	Geneva Community Unit SD 304	Geneva
200	1.2	United Twp HS District 30	East Moline
202	1.1	Lyons Twp HSD 204	La Grange
202	1.1	Thornton Twp HSD 205	South Holland
204	1.0	Bourbonnais SD 53	Bourbonnais
204	1.0	Community High SD 155	Crystal Lake
204	1.0	Homer Community CSD 33c	Homer Glen
207	0.9	Channahon SD 17	Channahon
207	0.9	Deerfield SD 109	Deerfield
207	0.9	Grayslake Com High SD 127	Grayslake
207	0.9	Lockport Twp HSD 205	Lockport
207	0.9	Marion Community Unit SD 2	Marion
212	0.8	Decatur SD 61	Decatur
212	0.8	East Peoria SD 86	East Peoria
212	0.8	Edwardsville CUSD 7	Edwardsville
212	0.8	Hononegah Community HSD 207	Rockton
212	0.8	Kinnikinnick CCSD 131	Roscoe
217	0.7	Galesburg CUSD 205	Galesburg
217	0.7	Grant Community HS District 124	Fox Lake
217	0.7	Homewood SD 153	Homewood
217	0.7	Lake Forest SD 67	Lake Forest
217	0.7	Rochester CUSD 3A	Rochester
222	0.6	Byron Community Unit SD 226	Byron
222	0.6	Charleston CUSD 1	Charleston
222	0.6	Illinois Valley CUD 321	Chillicothe
222	0.6	Jacksonville SD 117	Jacksonville
222	0.6	Thornton Fractional HSD 215	Calumet City
227	0.5	Lincoln Way Community HSD 210	New Lenox
227	0.5	Mahomet-Seymour CUSD 3	Mahomet
227	0.5	Manteno Community Unit SD 5	Manteno
227	0.5	Mattoon CUSD 2	Mattoon
227	0.5	Morton CUSD 709	Morton
227	0.5	Winnetka SD 36	Winnetka
233	0.4	Dixon Unit SD 170	Dixon
233	0.4	East St Louis SD 189	E Saint Louis
233	0.4	Frankfort CCSD 157C	Frankfort
233	0.4	Southwestern CUSD 9	Piasa
233	0.4	Springfield SD 186	Springfield
233	0.4	Triad Community Unit SD 2	Troy
239	0.3	Alton Community Unit SD 11	Alton
239	0.3	Auburn CUSD 10	Auburn
239	0.3	Bethalto CUSD 8	Bethalto
239	0.3	Canton Union SD 66	Canton
239	0.3	Columbia Community Unit SD 4	Columbia
239	0.3	Oak Park & River Forest Dist 200	Oak Park
239	0.3	Olympia CUSD 16	Stanford
246	0.2	Belleville SD 118	Belleville
246	0.2	Bond County CUSD 2	Greenville
246	0.2	Community High SD 117	Lake Villa
246	0.2	Herscher Community Unit SD 2	Herscher
246	0.2	Highland Community Unit SD 5	Highland
246	0.2	Lemont Twp HSD 210	Lemont
246	0.2	Midlothian SD 143	Midlothian
246	0.2	Mount Zion Community Unit SD 3	Mount Zion
246	0.2	New Lenox SD 122	New Lenox
246	0.2	O'Fallon CCSD 90	O Fallon
246	0.2	O'Fallon Twp High SD 203	O Fallon
246	0.2	Park Forest SD 163	Park Forest
246	0.2	Pekin Public SD 108	Pekin
246	0.2	Peotone CUSD 207U	Peotone
246	0.2	Quincy SD 172	Quincy
246	0.2	Wabash CUSD 348	Mount Carmel
262	0.1	Ball Chatham CUSD 5	Chatham
262	0.1	Cahokia Community Unit SD 187	Cahokia
262	0.1	Coal City CUSD 1	Coal City
262	0.1	Frankfort Community Unit SD 168	West Frankfort
262	0.1	Lake Forest CHSD 115	Lake Forest
262	0.1	Litchfield CUSD 12	Litchfield
262	0.1	Mount Vernon SD 80	Mount Vernon
262	0.1	Rich Twp HS District 227	Olympia Fields
262	0.1	Riverton CUSD 14	Riverton
262	0.1	Roxana Community Unit SD 1	Roxana
262	0.1	Sherrard Community Unit SD 200	Sherrard
262	0.1	Taylorville CUSD 3	Taylorville
262	0.1	Vandalia CUSD 203	Vandalia
262	0.1	Waterloo CUSD 5	Waterloo
276	0.0	Belleville Twp HSD 201	Belleville
276	0.0	Carterville CUSD 5	Carterville
276	0.0	Clinton CUSD 15	Clinton
276	0.0	Dolton SD 149	Calumet City
276	0.0	Du Quoin CUSD 300	Du Quoin
276	0.0	East Richland CUSD 1	Olney
276	0.0	Eureka C U Dist 140	Eureka
276	0.0	Geneseo Community Unit SD 228	Geneseo
276	0.0	Harrisburg CUSD 3	Harrisburg
276	0.0	Herrin CUSD 4	Herrin
276	0.0	Hillsboro Community Unit SD 3	Hillsboro
276	0.0	Homewood Flossmoor CHSD 233	Flossmoor
276	0.0	Jersey CUSD 100	Jerseyville
276	0.0	Johnsburg CUSD 12	Johnsburg
276	0.0	Massac Unit District #1	Metropolis
276	0.0	Monticello CUSD 25	Monticello
276	0.0	Pekin Community HSD 303	Pekin
276	0.0	Prairie Central CUSD 8	Fairbury
276	0.0	Reed Custer CUSD 255U	Braidwood
276	0.0	Robinson CUSD 2	Robinson
276	0.0	Tolono CUSD 7	Tolono
276	0.0	Western Springs SD 101	Western Springs

Students Eligible for Free Lunch

Rank	Percent	District Name	City
1	88.9	West Harvey-Dixmoor PSD 147	Harvey
2	88.8	East St Louis SD 189	E Saint Louis
3	87.4	Chicago Heights SD 170	Chicago Heights
4	84.5	Prairie-Hills Elem SD 144	Markham
5	82.6	Community CSD 168	Sauk Village
6	82.1	Harvey SD 152	Harvey
7	80.9	Park Forest SD 163	Park Forest
8	78.1	Bellwood SD 88	Bellwood
9	77.9	Dolton SD 148	Riverdale
10	77.3	Cicero SD 99	Cicero
11	77.0	Dolton SD 149	Calumet City
12	74.3	Kankakee SD 111	Kankakee
12	74.3	Zion Elementary SD 6	Zion
14	73.4	Berwyn North SD 98	Berwyn
15	72.6	Aurora East Unit SD 131	Aurora
16	72.4	Mount Vernon SD 80	Mount Vernon
16	72.4	South Holland SD 151	South Holland
18	72.2	Cahokia Community Unit SD 187	Cahokia
19	71.0	Posen-Robbins Elem SD 143-5	Posen
20	70.8	North Chicago SD 187	North Chicago
21	70.5	City of Chicago SD 299	Chicago
22	70.2	Bloom Twp High SD 206	Chicago Heights
23	69.4	Rantoul City SD 137	Rantoul
24	68.8	Joliet Public SD 86	Joliet
25	68.2	Cook County SD 130	Blue Island
25	68.2	Peoria SD 150	Peoria
27	67.9	J S Morton HS District 201	Cicero
28	67.2	Thornton Twp HSD 205	South Holland
29	66.8	Maywood-Melrose Park-Broadview-89	Melrose Park
30	65.5	Rockford SD 205	Rockford
31	64.2	Danville CCSD 118	Danville
32	62.6	Rich Twp HS District 227	Olympia Fields
33	61.3	Summit SD 104	Summit
34	60.7	Waukegan CUSD 60	Waukegan
35	60.3	Thornton Fractional HSD 215	Calumet City
36	58.5	Round Lake Area Schs - Dist 116	Round Lake
37	57.6	Berwyn South SD 100	Berwyn
38	57.3	Matteson Elem SD 162	Matteson
39	56.7	Berkeley SD 87	Berkeley
40	55.1	Lansing SD 158	Lansing
41	55.0	Springfield SD 186	Springfield
42	54.8	Urbana SD 116	Urbana
43	54.5	Freeport SD 145	Freeport
44	53.9	Crete Monee CUSD 201u	Crete
45	53.6	Kewanee Community Unit SD 229	Kewanee
46	52.9	East Moline SD 37	East Moline
47	52.8	Murphysboro CUSD 186	Murphysboro
48	52.1	Beardstown CUSD 15	Beardstown
48	52.1	Lyons SD 103	Lyons
50	52.0	Proviso Twp HSD 209	Forest Park
51	51.6	Joliet Twp HSD 204	Joliet
52	50.9	Steger SD 194	Steger
53	50.8	Monmouth-Roseville CUSD 238	Monmouth
54	50.6	Rock Island SD 41	Rock Island
55	50.5	Herrin CUSD 4	Herrin
56	50.3	Streator Elem SD 44	Streator
57	50.2	Galesburg CUSD 205	Galesburg
58	49.2	Harvard CUSD 50	Harvard
59	48.9	Alton Community Unit SD 11	Alton
59	48.9	Elem SD 159	Matteson
61	48.8	Belleville SD 118	Belleville
62	48.3	Frankfort Community Unit SD 168	West Frankfort
63	48.1	Mannheim SD 83	Franklin Park
64	47.9	Pekin Public SD 108	Pekin
65	47.6	Granite City CUSD 9	Granite City
66	47.3	Champaign Community Unit SD 4	Champaign
67	46.8	Midlothian SD 143	Midlothian
68	46.6	Argo Community HSD 217	Summit
69	46.5	West Chicago Elem SD 33	West Chicago
70	46.1	Bensenville SD 2	Bensenville
71	45.6	Marquardt SD 15	Glendale Hgts
72	45.1	School District U-46	Elgin
73	44.4	Community High SD 218	Oak Lawn
73	44.4	Harrisburg CUSD 3	Harrisburg
75	44.2	Aurora West Unit SD 129	Aurora
76	43.7	Addison SD 4	Addison
76	43.7	Roxana Community Unit SD 1	Roxana
78	43.3	Collinsville CUSD 10	Collinsville
78	43.3	Jacksonville SD 117	Jacksonville
80	42.9	Quincy SD 172	Quincy
80	42.9	Vandalia CUSD 203	Vandalia
82	42.8	Massac Unit District #1	Metropolis
83	42.7	Bloomington SD 87	Bloomington
84	42.1	Skokie SD 69	Skokie
85	41.5	Indian Springs SD 109	Justice
86	41.1	Valley View CUSD #365U	Romeoville
87	40.7	United Twp HS District 30	East Moline
88	40.6	Ottawa Elem SD 141	Ottawa
89	40.2	Du Quoin CUSD 300	Du Quoin
90	40.1	Bradley SD 61	Bradley
91	39.9	Belvidere CUSD 100	Belvidere
92	39.7	Marion Community Unit SD 2	Marion
93	39.5	Ridgeland SD 122	Oak Lawn
94	39.2	East Richland CUSD 1	Olney
95	39.1	Burbank SD 111	Burbank
96	38.7	Rochelle Community CD 231	Rochelle
97	38.5	Fenton Community HSD 100	Bensenville
98	38.4	Sterling CUD 5	Sterling
99	38.2	Keeneyville SD 20	Hanover Park
99	38.2	Moline Unit SD 40	Moline
101	38.1	Mattoon CUSD 2	Mattoon
102	37.3	Zion-Benton Twp HSD 126	Zion
103	37.2	Robinson CUSD 2	Robinson
104	36.2	Community CSD 59	Arlington Hgts
105	34.9	Canton Union SD 66	Canton
105	34.9	Litchfield CUSD 12	Litchfield
107	34.7	Skokie SD 68	Skokie
108	34.5	Hillsboro Community Unit SD 3	Hillsboro
109	34.1	Dekalb Community Unit SD 428	Dekalb
109	34.1	East Maine SD 63	Des Plaines
111	33.8	Jersey CUSD 100	Jerseyville
112	33.7	Community Consolidated SD 62	Des Plaines
113	33.3	Beach Park CCSD 3	Beach Park
114	33.2	Taylorville CUSD 3	Taylorville
114	33.2	Wheeling CCSD 21	Wheeling
116	33.1	Evanston Twp HSD 202	Evanston
117	32.8	East Peoria SD 86	East Peoria
118	32.6	Clinton CUSD 15	Clinton
119	32.2	Macomb Community Unit SD 185	Macomb
119	32.2	Riverton CUSD 14	Riverton
121	32.0	Dixon Unit SD 170	Dixon
121	32.0	Leyden Community HSD 212	Franklin Park
123	31.9	Bond County CUSD 2	Greenville
124	31.8	Bethalto CUSD 8	Bethalto
125	31.6	Evanston CCSD 65	Evanston
126	30.9	School District 45 Dupage County	Villa Park
127	30.8	Community Unit SD 300	Carpentersville
128	30.7	Elmwood Park CUSD 401	Elmwood Park
129	30.2	Charleston CUSD 1	Charleston
130	30.1	Du Page High SD 88	Addison
130	30.1	Oregon CUSD 220	Oregon
132	29.9	Queen Bee SD 16	Glendale Hgts
133	29.5	Harlem Unit Dist 122	Machesney Park
133	29.5	Wabash CUSD 348	Mount Carmel
135	29.1	Belleville Twp HSD 201	Belleville
135	29.1	Westmont CUSD 201	Westmont
137	28.5	Prairie Central CUSD 8	Fairbury
138	28.4	Flossmoor SD 161	Chicago Heights
138	28.4	Oak Lawn-Hometown SD 123	Oak Lawn
140	27.9	Evergreen Park Elem SD 124	Evergreen Park
141	27.7	Woodstock CUSD 200	Woodstock
142	27.6	Pekin Community HSD 303	Pekin
143	27.5	Paxton-Buckley-Loda CUD 10	Paxton
144	27.2	North Palos SD 117	Palos Hills
145	26.8	Palatine CCSD 15	Palatine
146	26.7	Reed Custer CUSD 255U	Braidwood
147	26.1	Bourbonnais SD 53	Bourbonnais
148	25.3	North Boone CUSD 200	Poplar Grove
149	25.2	Alsip-Hazelgreen-Oak Lawn SD 126	Alsip

Note: This section only includes districts with 1,500 or more students; All categories are ranked from high to low

150	24.8	Effingham Community Unit SD 40	Effingham
151	23.8	Bradley Bourbonnais CHSD 307	Bradley
152	23.4	Woodridge SD 68	Woodridge
153	23.1	Southwestern CUSD 9	Piasa
154	22.1	Lombard SD 44	Lombard
155	22.0	Genoa Kingston CUSD 424	Genoa
156	21.5	Olympia CUSD 16	Stanford
156	21.5	Plano Community Unit SD 88	Plano
158	21.4	Mundelein Cons High SD 120	Mundelein
159	21.0	Sandwich CUSD 430	Sandwich
160	20.9	Highland Community Unit SD 5	Highland
160	20.9	Homewood SD 153	Homewood
162	20.6	Tinley Park CCSD 146	Tinley Park
163	20.2	Tolono CUSD 7	Tolono
164	19.7	Forest Ridge SD 142	Oak Forest
164	19.7	Troy Community CSD 30C	Plainfield
166	19.6	Wauconda Community Unit SD 118	Wauconda
167	19.3	Auburn CUSD 10	Auburn
167	19.3	Grant Community HS District 124	Fox Lake
169	19.2	Mchenry CCSD 15	Mchenry
169	19.2	Woodland CCSD 50	Gurnee
171	19.1	Darien SD 61	Darien
172	18.8	Manteno Community Unit SD 5	Manteno
173	18.6	Herscher Community Unit SD 2	Herscher
174	18.5	Community Unit SD 200	Wheaton
175	18.3	Illinois Valley CUD 321	Chillicothe
176	17.5	Hawthorn CCSD 73	Vernon Hills
176	17.5	Oak Park Elem SD 97	Oak Park
178	17.2	Township HSD 211	Palatine
179	16.4	Coal City CUSD 1	Coal City
180	16.3	Eureka C U Dist 140	Eureka
181	16.1	Glenbard Twp HSD 87	Glen Ellyn
181	16.1	Township High SD 214	Arlington Hgts
183	15.8	Mclean County Unit Dist No 5	Normal
184	15.6	Oak Park & River Forest Dist 200	Oak Park
185	15.5	Sherrard Community Unit SD 200	Sherrard
186	15.4	Oswego Community Unit SD 308	Oswego
187	15.2	Meridian CUSD 223	Stillman Valley
187	15.2	Rockton SD 140	Rockton
189	14.9	Carterville CUSD 5	Carterville
190	14.7	Community Consolidated SD 46	Grayslake
190	14.7	Winnebago CUSD 323	Winnebago
192	14.6	Glenview CCSD 34	Glenview
193	14.1	Mahomet-Seymour CUSD 3	Mahomet
194	14.0	Antioch CCSD 34	Antioch
195	13.9	Lake Villa CCSD 41	Lake Villa
196	13.6	Lisle CUSD 202	Lisle
197	13.4	Geneseo Community Unit SD 228	Geneseo
197	13.4	O'Fallon CCSD 90	O Fallon
199	13.1	Community High SD 99	Downers Grove
200	12.9	Triad Community Unit SD 2	Troy
201	12.7	Mundelein Elem SD 75	Mundelein
201	12.7	Waterloo CUSD 5	Waterloo
203	12.6	Edwardsville CUSD 7	Edwardsville
203	12.6	La Grange SD 102	La Grange Park
205	12.4	Minooka Community CSD 201	Minooka
206	12.1	Barrington CUSD 220	Barrington
207	11.4	Big Hollow SD 38	Ingleside
207	11.4	Hononegah Community HSD 207	Rockton
207	11.4	Sycamore CUSD 427	Sycamore
210	11.3	Crystal Lake CCSD 47	Crystal Lake
211	10.8	North Shore SD 112	Highland Park
212	10.7	Johnsburg CUSD 12	Johnsburg
212	10.7	Morton CUSD 709	Morton
214	10.5	Kinnikinnick CCSD 131	Roscoe
215	10.4	Mount Zion Community Unit SD 3	Mount Zion
216	10.1	Mascoutah CUD 19	Mascoutah
217	9.4	Cary CCSD 26	Cary
218	9.3	Peotone CUSD 207U	Peotone
219	9.1	Monticello CUSD 25	Monticello
219	9.1	O'Fallon Twp High SD 203	O Fallon
221	9.0	Lemont-Bromberek CSD 113A	Lemont
222	8.8	Elmhurst SD 205	Elmhurst
223	8.5	Ball Chatham CUSD 5	Chatham
223	8.5	Palos Community CSD 118	Palos Park
225	7.8	Batavia Unit SD 101	Batavia
226	7.7	Mokena SD 159	Mokena
226	7.7	New Lenox SD 122	New Lenox
226	7.7	Will County SD 92	Lockport
229	7.6	Plainfield SD 202	Plainfield
230	7.3	Community High SD 155	Crystal Lake
231	7.2	Saint Charles CUSD 303	Saint Charles
232	6.9	Indian Prairie CUSD 204	Aurora
233	6.8	Central Community Unit SD 301	Burlington
234	6.7	Channahon SD 17	Channahon
235	6.6	Columbia Community Unit SD 4	Columbia
236	6.5	Consolidated SD 158	Algonquin
237	6.4	Dunlap CUSD 323	Dunlap
238	6.1	Lake Zurich CUSD 95	Lake Zurich
239	5.7	Riverside SD 96	Riverside
239	5.7	Summit Hill SD 161	Frankfort
241	5.6	Arlington Hgts SD 25	Arlington Hgts
242	5.4	Kildeer Countryside CCSD 96	Buffalo Grove
243	4.4	Kaneland CUSD 302	Maple Park
244	4.1	Aptakisic-Tripp CCSD 102	Buffalo Grove
244	4.1	Lincoln Way Community HSD 210	New Lenox
246	3.6	Naperville CUD 203	Naperville
247	3.3	Byron Community Unit SD 226	Byron
247	3.3	Lemont Twp HSD 210	Lemont
247	3.3	Rochester CUSD 3A	Rochester
250	3.2	Downers Grove Grade SD 58	Downers Grove
251	2.8	Millburn CCSD 24	Old Mill Creek
252	2.5	Mount Prospect SD 57	Mount Prospect
253	2.2	Decatur SD 61	Decatur
254	0.0	Bremen Community HS District 228	Midlothian
254	0.0	CCSD 181	Westmont
254	0.0	Community Consolidated SD 93	Bloomingdale
254	0.0	Community High SD 117	Lake Villa
254	0.0	Community High SD 94	West Chicago
254	0.0	Cons High SD 230	Orland Park
254	0.0	Deerfield SD 109	Deerfield
254	0.0	Frankfort CCSD 157C	Frankfort
254	0.0	Fremont SD 79	Mundelein
254	0.0	Geneva Community Unit SD 304	Geneva
254	0.0	Glen Ellyn CCSD 89	Glen Ellyn
254	0.0	Glen Ellyn SD 41	Glen Ellyn
254	0.0	Grayslake Com High SD 127	Grayslake
254	0.0	Gurnee SD 56	Gurnee
254	0.0	Hinsdale Twp HSD 86	Hinsdale
254	0.0	Homer Community CSD 33c	Homer Glen
254	0.0	Kirby SD 140	Tinley Park
254	0.0	Lake Forest CHSD 115	Lake Forest
254	0.0	Lake Forest SD 67	Lake Forest
254	0.0	Lake Park Community HSD 108	Roselle
254	0.0	Lockport Twp HSD 205	Lockport
254	0.0	Lyons Twp HSD 204	La Grange
254	0.0	Maine Township HSD 207	Park Ridge
254	0.0	Minooka Community HS District 111	Minooka
254	0.0	Niles Twp Community High SD 219	Skokie
254	0.0	Northbrook SD 28	Northbrook
254	0.0	Orland SD 135	Orland Park
254	0.0	Park Ridge CCSD 64	Park Ridge
254	0.0	Schaumburg CCSD 54	Schaumburg
254	0.0	Warren Twp High SD 121	Gurnee
254	0.0	Western Springs SD 101	Western Springs
254	0.0	Wilmette SD 39	Wilmette
254	0.0	Winnetka SD 36	Winnetka
254	0.0	Yorkville Community Unit SD 115	Yorkville
n/a	n/a	Adlai E Stevenson Dist 125	Lincolnshire
n/a	n/a	Community High SD 128	Vernon Hills
n/a	n/a	Homewood Flossmoor CHSD 233	Flossmoor
n/a	n/a	Libertyville SD 70	Libertyville
n/a	n/a	Mchenry Community HSD 156	Mchenry
n/a	n/a	New Trier Twp HSD 203	Northfield
n/a	n/a	Northfield Twp High SD 225	Glenview
n/a	n/a	Oak Lawn Community HSD 229	Oak Lawn
n/a	n/a	Reavis Twp HSD 220	Burbank
n/a	n/a	Township High SD 113	Highland Park

Students Eligible for Reduced-Price Lunch

Rank	Percent	District Name	City
1	17.1	Thornton Twp HSD 205	South Holland
2	14.2	Berwyn South SD 100	Berwyn
3	14.1	Summit SD 104	Summit
4	13.9	Mannheim SD 83	Franklin Park
5	13.8	J S Morton HS District 201	Cicero
6	12.6	Lyons SD 103	Lyons
7	12.3	Steger SD 194	Steger
8	12.2	Berkeley SD 87	Berkeley
9	12.1	Marquardt SD 15	Glendale Hgts
10	11.8	Quincy SD 172	Quincy
11	11.2	Skokie SD 69	Skokie
11	11.2	Valley View CUSD #365U	Romeoville
13	11.0	East Richland CUSD 1	Olney
14	10.8	Canton Union SD 66	Canton
14	10.8	Mascoutah CUD 19	Mascoutah
16	10.7	Taylorville CUSD 3	Taylorville
17	10.6	Kewanee Community Unit SD 229	Kewanee
18	10.4	Lansing SD 158	Lansing
18	10.4	Pekin Public SD 108	Pekin
20	10.3	Matteson Elem SD 162	Matteson
20	10.3	Prairie Central CUSD 8	Fairbury
20	10.3	Zion Elementary SD 6	Zion
23	10.1	Belleville SD 118	Belleville
23	10.1	Olympia CUSD 16	Stanford
25	10.0	Beardstown CUSD 15	Beardstown
25	10.0	East Moline SD 37	East Moline
25	10.0	Joliet Twp HSD 204	Joliet
28	9.9	Berwyn North SD 98	Berwyn
29	9.7	Crete Monee CUSD 201u	Crete
30	9.6	Aurora East Unit SD 131	Aurora
30	9.6	Collinsville CUSD 10	Collinsville
30	9.6	Dolton SD 149	Calumet City
30	9.6	Rantoul City SD 137	Rantoul
34	9.3	Argo Community HSD 217	Summit
34	9.3	Cicero SD 99	Cicero
34	9.3	Genoa Kingston CUSD 424	Genoa
34	9.3	Harrisburg CUSD 3	Harrisburg
34	9.3	Waukegan CUSD 60	Waukegan
39	9.2	North Boone CUSD 200	Poplar Grove
39	9.2	Southwestern CUSD 9	Piasa
39	9.2	United Twp HS District 30	East Moline
42	9.1	Evergreen Park Elem SD 124	Evergreen Park
43	9.0	East Maine SD 63	Des Plaines
43	9.0	Evanston Twp HSD 202	Evanston
43	9.0	Round Lake Area Schs - Dist 116	Round Lake
46	8.8	Belvidere CUSD 100	Belvidere
46	8.8	Herrin CUSD 4	Herrin
46	8.8	Robinson CUSD 2	Robinson
46	8.8	Rockford SD 205	Rockford
46	8.8	South Holland SD 151	South Holland
51	8.7	Monmouth-Roseville CUSD 238	Monmouth
51	8.7	Murphysboro CUSD 186	Murphysboro
51	8.7	Ridgeland SD 122	Oak Lawn
51	8.7	West Chicago Elem SD 33	West Chicago
51	8.7	Woodstock CUSD 200	Woodstock
56	8.6	Bloomington SD 87	Bloomington
56	8.6	Roxana Community Unit SD 1	Roxana
58	8.5	Cook County SD 130	Blue Island
58	8.5	Dixon Unit SD 170	Dixon
58	8.5	Granite City CUSD 9	Granite City
58	8.5	Joliet Public SD 86	Joliet
58	8.5	Zion-Benton Twp HSD 126	Zion
63	8.4	Community Consolidated SD 62	Des Plaines
63	8.4	Rich Twp HS District 227	Olympia Fields
63	8.4	Thornton Fractional HSD 215	Calumet City
66	8.3	Harlem Unit Dist 122	Machesney Park
66	8.3	Litchfield CUSD 12	Litchfield
66	8.3	Pekin Community HSD 303	Pekin
66	8.3	Wabash CUSD 348	Mount Carmel
70	8.2	Bensenville SD 2	Bensenville
70	8.2	Bradley SD 61	Bradley
70	8.2	Community CSD 59	Arlington Hgts
70	8.2	Skokie SD 68	Skokie
74	8.1	Geneseo Community Unit SD 228	Geneseo
75	8.0	Hillsboro Community Unit SD 3	Hillsboro
75	8.0	Sterling CUD 5	Sterling
75	8.0	Streator Elem SD 44	Streator
78	7.9	Beach Park CCSD 3	Beach Park
78	7.9	Jacksonville SD 117	Jacksonville
78	7.9	Wheeling CCSD 21	Wheeling
81	7.8	Homewood SD 153	Homewood
81	7.8	Jersey CUSD 100	Jerseyville
81	7.8	Leyden Community HSD 212	Franklin Park
81	7.8	Mount Vernon SD 80	Mount Vernon
85	7.7	Belleville Twp HSD 201	Belleville
85	7.7	Galesburg CUSD 205	Galesburg
85	7.7	Peoria SD 150	Peoria
88	7.6	Charleston CUSD 1	Charleston
88	7.6	Community High SD 218	Oak Lawn
88	7.6	Mattoon CUSD 2	Mattoon
88	7.6	Vandalia CUSD 203	Vandalia
92	7.5	Massac Unit District #1	Metropolis
92	7.5	North Chicago SD 187	North Chicago
94	7.4	Elmwood Park CUSD 401	Elmwood Park
94	7.4	Moline Unit SD 40	Moline
94	7.4	Mundelein Elem SD 75	Mundelein
94	7.4	Prairie-Hills Elem SD 144	Markham
98	7.3	Bellwood SD 88	Bellwood

Note: This section only includes districts with 1,500 or more students; All categories are ranked from high to low

98	7.3	Burbank SD 111	Burbank
98	7.3	Evanston CCSD 65	Evanston
98	7.3	Woodridge SD 68	Woodridge
102	7.2	City of Chicago SD 299	Chicago
102	7.2	Rock Island SD 41	Rock Island
102	7.2	Troy Community CSD 30C	Plainfield
105	7.1	Addison SD 4	Addison
105	7.1	Auburn CUSD 10	Auburn
105	7.1	Aurora West Unit SD 129	Aurora
108	7.0	Kankakee SD 111	Kankakee
108	7.0	Mundelein Cons High SD 120	Mundelein
110	6.9	Alton Community Unit SD 11	Alton
110	6.9	Midlothian SD 143	Midlothian
110	6.9	Oak Lawn-Hometown SD 123	Oak Lawn
110	6.9	Urbana SD 116	Urbana
114	6.8	Alsip-Hazelgreen-Oak Lawn SD 126	Alsip
115	6.7	Bradley Bourbonnais CHSD 307	Bradley
115	6.7	Community CSD 168	Sauk Village
115	6.7	Park Forest SD 163	Park Forest
115	6.7	Sandwich CUSD 430	Sandwich
119	6.6	Dolton SD 148	Riverdale
119	6.6	Ottawa Elem SD 141	Ottawa
121	6.5	Bethalto CUSD 8	Bethalto
121	6.5	Danville CCSD 118	Danville
121	6.5	Macomb Community Unit SD 185	Macomb
124	6.4	Dekalb Community Unit SD 428	Dekalb
124	6.4	Frankfort Community Unit SD 168	West Frankfort
124	6.4	Proviso Twp HSD 209	Forest Park
124	6.4	Riverton CUSD 14	Riverton
124	6.4	Springfield SD 186	Springfield
129	6.3	Champaign Community Unit SD 4	Champaign
129	6.3	Fenton Community HSD 100	Bensenville
129	6.3	Highland Community Unit SD 5	Highland
132	6.2	Effingham Community Unit SD 40	Effingham
132	6.2	Freeport SD 145	Freeport
134	6.1	Elem SD 159	Matteson
134	6.1	Keeneyville SD 20	Hanover Park
134	6.1	Lake Villa CCSD 41	Lake Villa
134	6.1	School District U-46	Elgin
134	6.1	Sherrard Community Unit SD 200	Sherrard
134	6.1	Tolono CUSD 7	Tolono
140	6.0	East Peoria SD 86	East Peoria
140	6.0	Marion Community Unit SD 2	Marion
142	5.9	Bloom Twp High SD 206	Chicago Heights
142	5.9	Community Unit SD 300	Carpentersville
142	5.9	Du Page High SD 88	Addison
142	5.9	Indian Springs SD 109	Justice
142	5.9	Monticello CUSD 25	Monticello
142	5.9	Rochelle Community CD 231	Rochelle
148	5.6	Bond County CUSD 2	Greenville
148	5.6	Forest Ridge SD 142	Oak Forest
148	5.6	Rockton SD 140	Rockton
151	5.5	Clinton CUSD 15	Clinton
151	5.5	Maywood-Melrose Park-Broadview-89	Melrose Park
151	5.5	Township HSD 211	Palatine
154	5.3	Paxton-Buckley-Loda CUD 10	Paxton
155	5.1	Herscher Community Unit SD 2	Herscher
155	5.1	Oregon CUSD 220	Oregon
155	5.1	Waterloo CUSD 5	Waterloo
158	4.9	Grant Community HS District 124	Fox Lake
158	4.9	School District 45 Dupage County	Villa Park
160	4.8	Du Quoin CUSD 300	Du Quoin
160	4.8	Eureka C U Dist 140	Eureka
160	4.8	Posen-Robbins Elem SD 143-5	Posen
163	4.7	Channahon SD 17	Channahon
163	4.7	Kinnikinnick CCSD 131	Roscoe
163	4.7	Mchenry CCSD 15	Mchenry
163	4.7	Tinley Park CCSD 146	Tinley Park
167	4.6	Antioch CCSD 34	Antioch
167	4.6	Chicago Heights SD 170	Chicago Heights
167	4.6	Illinois Valley CUD 321	Chillicothe
167	4.6	Oswego Community Unit SD 308	Oswego
167	4.6	Triad Community Unit SD 2	Troy
167	4.6	Woodland CCSD 50	Gurnee
173	4.5	Community High SD 99	Downers Grove
173	4.5	Lombard SD 44	Lombard
173	4.5	Manteno Community Unit SD 5	Manteno
173	4.5	Oak Park Elem SD 97	Oak Park
173	4.5	Township High SD 214	Arlington Hgts
178	4.4	Cahokia Community Unit SD 187	Cahokia
178	4.4	Hawthorn CCSD 73	Vernon Hills
178	4.4	Palatine CCSD 15	Palatine
181	4.3	Community Consolidated SD 46	Grayslake
181	4.3	Winnebago CUSD 323	Winnebago
183	4.2	Big Hollow SD 38	Ingleside
183	4.2	Edwardsville CUSD 7	Edwardsville
183	4.2	Harvard CUSD 50	Harvard
186	4.1	Coal City CUSD 1	Coal City
186	4.1	Darien SD 61	Darien
186	4.1	Plano Community Unit SD 88	Plano
189	4.0	Bourbonnais SD 53	Bourbonnais
189	4.0	Consolidated SD 158	Algonquin
189	4.0	Hononegah Community HSD 207	Rockton
189	4.0	Lisle CUSD 202	Lisle
193	3.9	Community Unit SD 200	Wheaton
193	3.9	Flossmoor SD 161	Chicago Heights
195	3.7	Carterville CUSD 5	Carterville
195	3.7	O'Fallon CCSD 90	O Fallon
195	3.7	Wauconda Community Unit SD 118	Wauconda
195	3.7	Westmont CUSD 201	Westmont
199	3.6	Queen Bee SD 16	Glendale Hgts
199	3.6	Reed Custer CUSD 255U	Braidwood
201	3.5	Aptakisic-Tripp CCSD 102	Buffalo Grove
201	3.5	Oak Park & River Forest Dist 200	Oak Park
203	3.4	New Lenox SD 122	New Lenox
203	3.4	Will County SD 92	Lockport
205	3.3	Glenview CCSD 34	Glenview
205	3.3	Johnsburg CUSD 12	Johnsburg
207	3.2	Mahomet-Seymour CUSD 3	Mahomet
208	3.1	Mclean County Unit Dist No 5	Normal
209	3.0	Barrington CUSD 220	Barrington
209	3.0	Crystal Lake CCSD 47	Crystal Lake
211	2.9	Columbia Community Unit SD 4	Columbia
211	2.9	Meridian CUSD 223	Stillman Valley
211	2.9	Mount Zion Community Unit SD 3	Mount Zion
211	2.9	O'Fallon Twp High SD 203	O Fallon
215	2.8	Minooka Community CSD 201	Minooka
215	2.8	Saint Charles CUSD 303	Saint Charles
217	2.7	Glenbard Twp HSD 87	Glen Ellyn
217	2.7	Lemont-Bromberek CSD 113A	Lemont
217	2.7	North Palos SD 117	Palos Hills
220	2.6	Sycamore CUSD 427	Sycamore
220	2.6	West Harvey-Dixmoor PSD 147	Harvey
222	2.4	Plainfield SD 202	Plainfield
223	2.3	Ball Chatham CUSD 5	Chatham
223	2.3	La Grange SD 102	La Grange Park
225	2.2	Arlington Hgts SD 25	Arlington Hgts
225	2.2	Dunlap CUSD 323	Dunlap
225	2.2	Lake Zurich CUSD 95	Lake Zurich
225	2.2	Peotone CUSD 207U	Peotone
229	2.0	Batavia Unit SD 101	Batavia
230	1.9	Cary CCSD 26	Cary
230	1.9	Community High SD 155	Crystal Lake
230	1.9	Elmhurst SD 205	Elmhurst
230	1.9	Riverside SD 96	Riverside
234	1.8	Central Community Unit SD 301	Burlington
234	1.8	Indian Prairie CUSD 204	Aurora
234	1.8	Palos Community CSD 118	Palos Park
237	1.7	Lincoln Way Community HSD 210	New Lenox
237	1.7	Mokena SD 159	Mokena
239	1.5	Harvey SD 152	Harvey
240	1.4	Morton CUSD 709	Morton
241	1.3	Kaneland CUSD 302	Maple Park
241	1.3	Millburn CCSD 24	Old Mill Creek
241	1.3	Rochester CUSD 3A	Rochester
244	1.1	Lemont Twp HSD 210	Lemont
245	1.0	Kildeer Countryside CCSD 96	Buffalo Grove
245	1.0	North Shore SD 112	Highland Park
247	0.9	Summit Hill SD 161	Frankfort
248	0.7	Naperville CUD 203	Naperville
249	0.6	Byron Community Unit SD 226	Byron
249	0.6	Downers Grove Grade SD 58	Downers Grove
251	0.4	Mount Prospect SD 57	Mount Prospect
252	0.3	Decatur SD 61	Decatur
253	0.0	Bremen Community HS District 228	Midlothian
253	0.0	CCSD 181	Westmont
253	0.0	Community Consolidated SD 93	Bloomingdale
253	0.0	Community High SD 117	Lake Villa
253	0.0	Community High SD 94	West Chicago
253	0.0	Cons High SD 230	Orland Park
253	0.0	Deerfield SD 109	Deerfield
253	0.0	East St Louis SD 189	E Saint Louis
253	0.0	Frankfort CCSD 157C	Frankfort
253	0.0	Fremont SD 79	Mundelein
253	0.0	Geneva Community Unit SD 304	Geneva
253	0.0	Glen Ellyn CCSD 89	Glen Ellyn
253	0.0	Glen Ellyn SD 41	Glen Ellyn
253	0.0	Grayslake Com High SD 127	Grayslake
253	0.0	Gurnee SD 56	Gurnee
253	0.0	Hinsdale Twp HSD 86	Hinsdale
253	0.0	Homer Community CSD 33c	Homer Glen
253	0.0	Kirby SD 140	Tinley Park
253	0.0	Lake Forest CHSD 115	Lake Forest
253	0.0	Lake Forest SD 67	Lake Forest
253	0.0	Lake Park Community HSD 108	Roselle
253	0.0	Lockport Twp HSD 205	Lockport
253	0.0	Lyons Twp HSD 204	La Grange
253	0.0	Maine Township HSD 207	Park Ridge
253	0.0	Minooka Community HS District 111	Minooka
253	0.0	Niles Twp Community High SD 219	Skokie
253	0.0	Northbrook SD 28	Northbrook
253	0.0	Orland SD 135	Orland Park
253	0.0	Park Ridge CCSD 64	Park Ridge
253	0.0	Schaumburg CCSD 54	Schaumburg
253	0.0	Warren Twp High SD 121	Gurnee
253	0.0	Western Springs SD 101	Western Springs
253	0.0	Wilmette SD 39	Wilmette
253	0.0	Winnetka SD 36	Winnetka
253	0.0	Yorkville Community Unit SD 115	Yorkville
n/a	n/a	Adlai E Stevenson Dist 125	Lincolnshire
n/a	n/a	Community High SD 128	Vernon Hills
n/a	n/a	Homewood Flossmoor CHSD 233	Flossmoor
n/a	n/a	Libertyville SD 70	Libertyville
n/a	n/a	Mchenry Community HSD 156	Mchenry
n/a	n/a	New Trier Twp HSD 203	Northfield
n/a	n/a	Northfield Twp High SD 225	Glenview
n/a	n/a	Oak Lawn Community HSD 229	Oak Lawn
n/a	n/a	Reavis Twp HSD 220	Burbank
n/a	n/a	Township High SD 113	Highland Park

Student/Teacher Ratio

(number of students per teacher)

Rank	Number	District Name	City
1	10.8	Northbrook SD 28	Northbrook
2	11.2	Dolton SD 148	Riverdale
3	11.3	Winnetka SD 36	Winnetka
4	11.9	Urbana SD 116	Urbana
5	12.0	Evanston CCSD 65	Evanston
6	12.2	Lake Forest SD 67	Lake Forest
7	12.3	New Trier Twp HSD 203	Northfield
8	12.4	North Shore SD 112	Highland Park
8	12.4	Steger SD 194	Steger
10	12.5	Wilmette SD 39	Wilmette
11	13.0	Byron Community Unit SD 226	Byron
11	13.0	Skokie SD 68	Skokie
13	13.1	Prairie Central CUSD 8	Fairbury
14	13.2	Evergreen Park Elem SD 124	Evergreen Park
14	13.2	Flossmoor SD 161	Chicago Heights
14	13.2	La Grange SD 102	La Grange Park
14	13.2	Sherrard Community Unit SD 200	Sherrard
18	13.3	Champaign Community Unit SD 4	Champaign
18	13.3	Rochelle Community CD 231	Rochelle
20	13.4	Alsip-Hazelgreen-Oak Lawn SD 126	Alsip
20	13.4	Aptakisic-Tripp CCSD 102	Buffalo Grove
20	13.4	Springfield SD 186	Springfield
23	13.5	Glenview CCSD 34	Glenview
23	13.5	Homewood SD 153	Homewood
23	13.5	Park Ridge CCSD 64	Park Ridge
26	13.6	Cook County SD 130	Blue Island
26	13.6	Freeport SD 145	Freeport
26	13.6	Lake Forest CHSD 115	Lake Forest
29	13.7	Berwyn South SD 100	Berwyn
29	13.7	Community CSD 59	Arlington Hgts
29	13.7	Community Consolidated SD 62	Des Plaines
29	13.7	Community Consolidated SD 93	Bloomingdale
29	13.7	East Maine SD 63	Des Plaines
29	13.7	Mannheim SD 83	Franklin Park
29	13.7	Niles Twp Community High SD 219	Skokie
29	13.7	Northfield Twp High SD 225	Glenview
29	13.7	Park Forest SD 163	Park Forest
38	13.8	Burbank SD 111	Burbank
38	13.8	Evanston Twp HSD 202	Evanston
38	13.8	Lyons SD 103	Lyons
38	13.8	Maine Township HSD 207	Park Ridge
42	13.9	Deerfield SD 109	Deerfield
42	13.9	Mundelein Elem SD 75	Mundelein
42	13.9	Paxton-Buckley-Loda CUD 10	Paxton
45	14.0	Lisle CUSD 202	Lisle
45	14.0	Monmouth-Roseville CUSD 238	Monmouth
45	14.0	Oak Park Elem SD 97	Oak Park

Note: This section only includes districts with 1,500 or more students; All categories are ranked from high to low

45	14.0	Winnebago CUSD 323	Winnebago
49	14.1	Millburn CCSD 24	Old Mill Creek
50	14.2	Alton Community Unit SD 11	Alton
51	14.3	East Moline SD 37	East Moline
51	14.3	Lombard SD 44	Lombard
51	14.3	Oak Lawn-Hometown SD 123	Oak Lawn
51	14.3	Palos Community CSD 118	Palos Park
51	14.3	Peoria SD 150	Peoria
51	14.3	Wheeling CCSD 21	Wheeling
57	14.4	Bensenville SD 2	Bensenville
57	14.4	Grayslake Com High SD 127	Grayslake
57	14.4	Gurnee SD 56	Gurnee
57	14.4	Schaumburg CCSD 54	Schaumburg
57	14.4	Westmont CUSD 201	Westmont
57	14.4	Woodland CCSD 50	Gurnee
63	14.5	CCSD 181	Westmont
63	14.5	East St Louis SD 189	E Saint Louis
63	14.5	Kildeer Countryside CCSD 96	Buffalo Grove
63	14.5	Lansing SD 158	Lansing
63	14.5	Rich Twp HS District 227	Olympia Fields
63	14.5	Tinley Park CCSD 146	Tinley Park
63	14.5	Tolono CUSD 7	Tolono
70	14.6	Clinton CUSD 15	Clinton
70	14.6	Matteson Elem SD 162	Matteson
70	14.6	Ottawa Elem SD 141	Ottawa
70	14.6	Thornton Twp HSD 205	South Holland
74	14.7	Beardstown CUSD 15	Beardstown
74	14.7	Community High SD 117	Lake Villa
74	14.7	Genoa Kingston CUSD 424	Genoa
74	14.7	Manteno Community Unit SD 5	Manteno
78	14.8	Arlington Hgts SD 25	Arlington Hgts
78	14.8	Glen Ellyn CCSD 89	Glen Ellyn
78	14.8	Kirby SD 140	Tinley Park
78	14.8	Macomb Community Unit SD 185	Macomb
78	14.8	Pekin Public SD 108	Pekin
83	14.9	Jacksonville SD 117	Jacksonville
83	14.9	Riverside SD 96	Riverside
83	14.9	Streator Elem SD 44	Streator
83	14.9	Zion Elementary SD 6	Zion
87	15.0	Central Community Unit SD 301	Burlington
87	15.0	East Peoria SD 86	East Peoria
87	15.0	Midlothian SD 143	Midlothian
87	15.0	Olympia CUSD 16	Stanford
87	15.0	Robinson CUSD 2	Robinson
87	15.0	Sandwich CUSD 430	Sandwich
87	15.0	School District 45 Dupage County	Villa Park
87	15.0	Township High SD 113	Highland Park
95	15.2	Bradley SD 61	Bradley
95	15.2	Canton Union SD 66	Canton
95	15.2	Keeneyville SD 20	Hanover Park
95	15.2	North Boone CUSD 200	Poplar Grove
95	15.2	Oregon CUSD 220	Oregon
95	15.2	Rantoul City SD 137	Rantoul
95	15.2	Skokie SD 69	Skokie
95	15.2	South Holland SD 151	South Holland
103	15.3	Bloomington SD 87	Bloomington
103	15.3	Monticello CUSD 25	Monticello
103	15.3	Plano Community Unit SD 88	Plano
103	15.3	Rockton SD 140	Rockton
103	15.3	Waukegan CUSD 60	Waukegan
108	15.4	Cahokia Community Unit SD 187	Cahokia
108	15.4	Coal City CUSD 1	Coal City
108	15.4	Community CSD 168	Sauk Village
108	15.4	Crete Monee CUSD 201u	Crete
108	15.4	Crystal Lake CCSD 47	Crystal Lake
108	15.4	East Richland CUSD 1	Olney
108	15.4	Elmhurst SD 205	Elmhurst
108	15.4	Harlem Unit Dist 122	Machesney Park
108	15.4	Hawthorn CCSD 73	Vernon Hills
108	15.4	Hinsdale Twp HSD 86	Hinsdale
108	15.4	Mclean County Unit Dist No 5	Normal
108	15.4	Vandalia CUSD 203	Vandalia
120	15.5	Bethalto CUSD 8	Bethalto
120	15.5	Du Page High SD 88	Addison
120	15.5	Du Quoin CUSD 300	Du Quoin
120	15.5	Glen Ellyn SD 41	Glen Ellyn
120	15.5	Orland SD 135	Orland Park
125	15.6	Community High SD 128	Vernon Hills
125	15.6	Community Unit SD 200	Wheaton
125	15.6	Fenton Community HSD 100	Bensenville
125	15.6	Frankfort CCSD 157C	Frankfort
125	15.6	Indian Prairie CUSD 204	Aurora
125	15.6	Mattoon CUSD 2	Mattoon
125	15.6	Murphysboro CUSD 186	Murphysboro
125	15.6	Township HSD 211	Palatine
125	15.6	Yorkville Community Unit SD 115	Yorkville
134	15.7	Johnsburg CUSD 12	Johnsburg
134	15.7	Lemont Twp HSD 210	Lemont
134	15.7	Mount Prospect SD 57	Mount Prospect
137	15.8	Darien SD 61	Darien
137	15.8	Prairie-Hills Elem SD 144	Markham
137	15.8	Queen Bee SD 16	Glendale Hgts
137	15.8	Reed Custer CUSD 255U	Braidwood
137	15.8	Rockford SD 205	Rockford
137	15.8	Saint Charles CUSD 303	Saint Charles
143	15.9	Edwardsville CUSD 7	Edwardsville
143	15.9	Marquardt SD 15	Glendale Hgts
143	15.9	Southwestern CUSD 9	Piasa
143	15.9	Triad Community Unit SD 2	Troy
143	15.9	Wabash CUSD 348	Mount Carmel
148	16.0	Big Hollow SD 38	Ingleside
148	16.0	Community Consolidated SD 46	Grayslake
148	16.0	Leyden Community HSD 212	Franklin Park
148	16.0	Moline Unit SD 40	Moline
148	16.0	Morton CUSD 709	Morton
148	16.0	Roxana Community Unit SD 1	Roxana
148	16.0	Wauconda Community Unit SD 118	Wauconda
155	16.1	Barrington CUSD 220	Barrington
155	16.1	Beach Park CCSD 3	Beach Park
155	16.1	Charleston CUSD 1	Charleston
155	16.1	Elem SD 159	Matteson
155	16.1	Forest Ridge SD 142	Oak Forest
155	16.1	Harvey SD 152	Harvey
155	16.1	Kaneland CUSD 302	Maple Park
155	16.1	Lake Zurich CUSD 95	Lake Zurich
155	16.1	Lyons Twp HSD 204	La Grange
155	16.1	Massac Unit District #1	Metropolis
155	16.1	Rochester CUSD 3A	Rochester
155	16.1	Rock Island SD 41	Rock Island
167	16.2	Belleville SD 118	Belleville
167	16.2	Danville CCSD 118	Danville
167	16.2	Dixon Unit SD 170	Dixon
167	16.2	Highland Community Unit SD 5	Highland
167	16.2	Indian Springs SD 109	Justice
167	16.2	Lincoln Way Community HSD 210	New Lenox
167	16.2	Peotone CUSD 207U	Peotone
167	16.2	Quincy SD 172	Quincy
167	16.2	Township High SD 214	Arlington Hgts
167	16.2	Western Springs SD 101	Western Springs
177	16.3	Adlai E Stevenson Dist 125	Lincolnshire
177	16.3	Community High SD 99	Downers Grove
177	16.3	Consolidated SD 158	Algonquin
177	16.3	Effingham Community Unit SD 40	Effingham
177	16.3	Eureka C U Dist 140	Eureka
177	16.3	Illinois Valley CUD 321	Chillicothe
177	16.3	Libertyville SD 70	Libertyville
177	16.3	Mount Vernon SD 80	Mount Vernon
177	16.3	Oak Park & River Forest Dist 200	Oak Park
186	16.4	Carterville CUSD 5	Carterville
186	16.4	City of Chicago SD 299	Chicago
186	16.4	Geneva Community Unit SD 304	Geneva
186	16.4	Herscher Community Unit SD 2	Herscher
186	16.4	Joliet Public SD 86	Joliet
186	16.4	Mahomet-Seymour CUSD 3	Mahomet
186	16.4	Mchenry Community HSD 156	Mchenry
193	16.5	Community High SD 218	Oak Lawn
193	16.5	Elmwood Park CUSD 401	Elmwood Park
193	16.5	Harvard CUSD 50	Harvard
193	16.5	Oak Lawn Community HSD 229	Oak Lawn
193	16.5	Sterling CUD 5	Sterling
193	16.5	Woodridge SD 68	Woodridge
199	16.6	Addison SD 4	Addison
199	16.6	Bourbonnais SD 53	Bourbonnais
199	16.6	Dekalb Community Unit SD 428	Dekalb
199	16.6	Fremont SD 79	Mundelein
199	16.6	Homewood Flossmoor CHSD 233	Flossmoor
199	16.6	Waterloo CUSD 5	Waterloo
205	16.7	Antioch CCSD 34	Antioch
205	16.7	Bond County CUSD 2	Greenville
205	16.7	Chicago Heights SD 170	Chicago Heights
205	16.7	Cons High SD 230	Orland Park
205	16.7	Harrisburg CUSD 3	Harrisburg
205	16.7	Kankakee SD 111	Kankakee
205	16.7	Lake Villa CCSD 41	Lake Villa
205	16.7	North Chicago SD 187	North Chicago
205	16.7	Sycamore CUSD 427	Sycamore
214	16.8	Homer Community CSD 33c	Homer Glen
214	16.8	Troy Community CSD 30C	Plainfield
214	16.8	Woodstock CUSD 200	Woodstock
217	16.9	Cary CCSD 26	Cary
217	16.9	Collinsville CUSD 10	Collinsville
217	16.9	Pekin Community HSD 303	Pekin
217	16.9	West Harvey-Dixmoor PSD 147	Harvey
217	16.9	Will County SD 92	Lockport
222	17.0	Auburn CUSD 10	Auburn
222	17.0	Batavia Unit SD 101	Batavia
222	17.0	Naperville CUD 203	Naperville
222	17.0	O'Fallon CCSD 90	O Fallon
226	17.1	Belvidere CUSD 100	Belvidere
226	17.1	Geneseo Community Unit SD 228	Geneseo
226	17.1	Glenbard Twp HSD 87	Glen Ellyn
226	17.1	Maywood-Melrose Park-Broadview-89	Melrose Park
226	17.1	Valley View CUSD #365U	Romeoville
226	17.1	West Chicago Elem SD 33	West Chicago
232	17.2	Joliet Twp HSD 204	Joliet
232	17.2	Palatine CCSD 15	Palatine
232	17.2	Plainfield SD 202	Plainfield
232	17.2	Summit SD 104	Summit
236	17.3	Argo Community HSD 217	Summit
236	17.3	Community Unit SD 300	Carpentersville
238	17.4	Community High SD 155	Crystal Lake
238	17.4	Hillsboro Community Unit SD 3	Hillsboro
238	17.4	Jersey CUSD 100	Jerseyville
238	17.4	Mascoutah CUD 19	Mascoutah
238	17.4	Meridian CUSD 223	Stillman Valley
238	17.4	O'Fallon Twp High SD 203	O Fallon
238	17.4	Summit Hill SD 161	Frankfort
245	17.5	Galesburg CUSD 205	Galesburg
245	17.5	North Palos SD 117	Palos Hills
247	17.6	Berkeley SD 87	Berkeley
248	17.7	Bremen Community HS District 228	Midlothian
249	17.8	Aurora West Unit SD 129	Aurora
249	17.8	Ball Chatham CUSD 5	Chatham
249	17.8	Hononegah Community HSD 207	Rockton
249	17.8	Kinnikinnick CCSD 131	Roscoe
249	17.8	Lake Park Community HSD 108	Roselle
249	17.8	Mchenry CCSD 15	Mchenry
249	17.8	School District U-46	Elgin
256	17.9	Downers Grove Grade SD 58	Downers Grove
256	17.9	Kewanee Community Unit SD 229	Kewanee
256	17.9	Warren Twp High SD 121	Gurnee
259	18.0	Aurora East Unit SD 131	Aurora
259	18.0	Belleville Twp HSD 201	Belleville
259	18.0	Community High SD 94	West Chicago
259	18.0	Lemont-Bromberek CSD 113A	Lemont
259	18.0	Litchfield CUSD 12	Litchfield
259	18.0	Riverton CUSD 14	Riverton
265	18.1	Frankfort Community Unit SD 168	West Frankfort
266	18.2	Columbia Community Unit SD 4	Columbia
266	18.2	Ridgeland SD 122	Oak Lawn
266	18.2	Round Lake Area Schs - Dist 116	Round Lake
269	18.3	Bellwood SD 88	Bellwood
269	18.3	Decatur SD 61	Decatur
269	18.3	Marion Community Unit SD 2	Marion
269	18.3	Posen-Robbins Elem SD 143-5	Posen
273	18.4	Thornton Fractional HSD 215	Calumet City
274	18.5	Proviso Twp HSD 209	Forest Park
275	18.6	Cicero SD 99	Cicero
275	18.6	Zion-Benton Twp HSD 126	Zion
277	18.7	Bradley Bourbonnais CHSD 307	Bradley
277	18.7	J S Morton HS District 201	Cicero
277	18.7	Minooka Community HS District 111	Minooka
280	18.9	Dunlap CUSD 323	Dunlap
280	18.9	Lockport Twp HSD 205	Lockport
280	18.9	Mundelein Cons High SD 120	Mundelein
280	18.9	Reavis Twp HSD 220	Burbank
280	18.9	Taylorville CUSD 3	Taylorville
285	19.2	Mount Zion Community Unit SD 3	Mount Zion
286	19.4	Granite City CUSD 9	Granite City
286	19.4	Grant Community HS District 124	Fox Lake
288	19.5	Berwyn North SD 98	Berwyn
288	19.5	Bloom Twp High SD 206	Chicago Heights
290	19.6	Dolton SD 149	Calumet City
291	19.7	New Lenox SD 122	New Lenox
291	19.7	Oswego Community Unit SD 308	Oswego
293	19.8	United Twp HS District 30	East Moline
294	20.0	Channahon SD 17	Channahon
294	20.0	Mokena SD 159	Mokena
296	20.2	Herrin CUSD 4	Herrin
296	20.2	Minooka Community CSD 201	Minooka

Note: This section only includes districts with 1,500 or more students; All categories are ranked from high to low

Student/Librarian Ratio

(number of students per librarian)

Rank	Number	District Name	City
1	292.8	Dolton SD 148	Riverdale
2	377.0	West Harvey-Dixmoor PSD 147	Harvey
3	383.8	Westmont CUSD 201	Westmont
4	392.3	Alsip-Hazelgreen-Oak Lawn SD 126	Alsip
5	397.3	Lisle CUSD 202	Lisle
6	402.2	Aptakisic-Tripp CCSD 102	Buffalo Grove
7	411.8	Glen Ellyn CCSD 89	Glen Ellyn
8	412.3	Downers Grove Grade SD 58	Downers Grove
9	418.8	Bensenville SD 2	Bensenville
10	419.0	Skokie SD 68	Skokie
11	420.8	Elem SD 159	Matteson
12	426.8	Monticello CUSD 25	Monticello
13	427.5	Northbrook SD 28	Northbrook
14	429.5	Monmouth-Roseville CUSD 238	Monmouth
15	431.6	New Trier Twp HSD 203	Northfield
16	432.6	Community Consolidated SD 62	Des Plaines
17	437.9	Woodridge SD 68	Woodridge
18	443.2	North Shore SD 112	Highland Park
19	454.1	Evanston CCSD 65	Evanston
20	468.6	Tinley Park CCSD 146	Tinley Park
21	469.0	Mundelein Elem SD 75	Mundelein
22	482.5	Winnetka SD 36	Winnetka
23	491.5	Homewood SD 153	Homewood
24	500.3	Community Consolidated SD 93	Bloomingdale
25	506.0	CCSD 181	Westmont
26	506.7	La Grange SD 102	La Grange Park
27	507.1	Matteson Elem SD 162	Matteson
28	509.0	East Moline SD 37	East Moline
29	509.9	East Maine SD 63	Des Plaines
30	511.0	Paxton-Buckley-Loda CUD 10	Paxton
31	511.7	Riverton CUSD 14	Riverton
32	513.0	Queen Bee SD 16	Glendale Hgts
33	515.2	New Lenox SD 122	New Lenox
34	515.5	Urbana SD 116	Urbana
35	519.0	Libertyville SD 70	Libertyville
36	522.0	Western Springs SD 101	Western Springs
37	524.9	Cook County SD 130	Blue Island
38	526.2	Kildeer Countryside CCSD 96	Buffalo Grove
39	532.3	Deerfield SD 109	Deerfield
40	533.2	Marquardt SD 15	Glendale Hgts
41	534.2	Bourbonnais SD 53	Bourbonnais
42	536.3	Mount Prospect SD 57	Mount Prospect
43	541.8	Cary CCSD 26	Cary
44	546.4	Oak Park Elem SD 97	Oak Park
45	546.6	Orland SD 135	Orland Park
46	548.7	Robinson CUSD 2	Robinson
47	551.0	Harrisburg CUSD 3	Harrisburg
48	553.3	Tolono CUSD 7	Tolono
49	561.1	Kirby SD 140	Tinley Park
50	568.3	Skokie SD 69	Skokie
51	570.8	Arlington Hgts SD 25	Arlington Hgts
52	572.1	Park Ridge CCSD 64	Park Ridge
53	577.6	Glenview CCSD 34	Glenview
54	578.4	Charleston CUSD 1	Charleston
55	579.3	Wheeling CCSD 21	Wheeling
56	587.9	Woodstock CUSD 200	Woodstock
57	595.8	Palatine CCSD 15	Palatine
58	600.7	Will County SD 92	Lockport
59	601.3	Reed Custer CUSD 255U	Braidwood
60	606.0	West Chicago Elem SD 33	West Chicago
61	610.6	Prairie Central CUSD 8	Fairbury
62	616.5	Mahomet-Seymour CUSD 3	Mahomet
63	617.9	Mclean County Unit Dist No 5	Normal
64	620.5	Johnsburg CUSD 12	Johnsburg
64	620.5	Wilmette SD 39	Wilmette
66	622.6	Mchenry CCSD 15	Mchenry
67	622.8	Township High SD 113	Highland Park
68	624.3	Palos Community CSD 118	Palos Park
69	625.2	Harlem Unit Dist 122	Machesney Park
70	630.5	Champaign Community Unit SD 4	Champaign
71	632.4	Elmhurst SD 205	Elmhurst
72	651.4	Hinsdale Twp HSD 86	Hinsdale
73	656.7	Minooka Community CSD 201	Minooka
74	669.8	Geneva Community Unit SD 304	Geneva
75	672.5	Moline Unit SD 40	Moline
76	672.8	Lombard SD 44	Lombard
77	674.4	Community Unit SD 200	Wheaton
78	685.8	Hawthorn CCSD 73	Vernon Hills
79	689.3	Herscher Community Unit SD 2	Herscher
80	691.6	Bremen Community HS District 228	Midlothian
81	694.7	Clinton CUSD 15	Clinton
82	696.0	Morton CUSD 709	Morton
83	701.1	Bloomington SD 87	Bloomington
84	706.3	Fremont SD 79	Mundelein
85	719.3	Gurnee SD 56	Gurnee
86	720.0	Lansing SD 158	Lansing
87	725.6	Crystal Lake CCSD 47	Crystal Lake
88	733.5	Wauconda Community Unit SD 118	Wauconda
89	735.4	Glen Ellyn SD 41	Glen Ellyn
90	750.2	Saint Charles CUSD 303	Saint Charles
91	761.5	Riverside SD 96	Riverside
92	763.0	Fenton Community HSD 100	Bensenville
93	769.8	North Palos SD 117	Palos Hills
94	773.6	Barrington CUSD 220	Barrington
95	780.6	Oswego Community Unit SD 308	Oswego
96	781.8	Aurora West Unit SD 129	Aurora
97	782.0	Oak Lawn-Hometown SD 123	Oak Lawn
98	784.5	Oregon CUSD 220	Oregon
99	785.0	Naperville CUD 203	Naperville
100	785.3	Lake Zurich CUSD 95	Lake Zurich
101	786.5	Batavia Unit SD 101	Batavia
102	791.0	Kaneland CUSD 302	Maple Park
103	799.7	Niles Twp Community High SD 219	Skokie
104	800.5	Northfield Twp High SD 225	Glenview
105	809.7	Harvard CUSD 50	Harvard
106	811.5	Keeneyville SD 20	Hanover Park
107	813.2	Galesburg CUSD 205	Galesburg
108	849.5	Indian Prairie CUSD 204	Aurora
109	849.9	Township HSD 211	Palatine
110	851.3	Mount Zion Community Unit SD 3	Mount Zion
111	861.8	Mascoutah CUD 19	Mascoutah
112	874.3	Leyden Community HSD 212	Franklin Park
113	876.6	Ball Chatham CUSD 5	Chatham
114	880.8	Mattoon CUSD 2	Mattoon
115	882.7	Thornton Twp HSD 205	South Holland
116	893.0	Lake Forest CHSD 115	Lake Forest
117	898.5	Glenbard Twp HSD 87	Glen Ellyn
118	901.7	Mannheim SD 83	Franklin Park
119	911.2	Valley View CUSD #365U	Romeoville
120	920.5	Park Forest SD 163	Park Forest
121	930.7	Yorkville Community Unit SD 115	Yorkville
122	941.5	Oak Lawn Community HSD 229	Oak Lawn
123	954.0	Macomb Community Unit SD 185	Macomb
124	955.5	Olympia CUSD 16	Stanford
125	977.0	Hillsboro Community Unit SD 3	Hillsboro
126	980.9	Cicero SD 99	Cicero
127	986.0	Meridian CUSD 223	Stillman Valley
128	997.5	Roxana Community Unit SD 1	Roxana
129	1,018.0	Evanston Twp HSD 202	Evanston
130	1,022.0	Bond County CUSD 2	Greenville
131	1,035.7	Highland Community Unit SD 5	Highland
132	1,052.9	Joliet Twp HSD 204	Joliet
133	1,063.5	East Richland CUSD 1	Olney
134	1,066.8	Belvidere CUSD 100	Belvidere
135	1,073.5	Murphysboro CUSD 186	Murphysboro
136	1,085.3	Oak Park & River Forest Dist 200	Oak Park
137	1,091.5	Community High SD 94	West Chicago
138	1,093.0	Addison SD 4	Addison
139	1,108.8	Alton Community Unit SD 11	Alton
140	1,123.8	Community Unit SD 300	Carpentersville
141	1,129.3	Community High SD 128	Vernon Hills
142	1,138.0	Rochester CUSD 3A	Rochester
143	1,142.2	Community High SD 99	Downers Grove
144	1,146.3	Berwyn North SD 98	Berwyn
145	1,162.0	Maine Township HSD 207	Park Ridge
146	1,164.5	Plano Community Unit SD 88	Plano
147	1,226.0	Lyons SD 103	Lyons
148	1,229.5	Minooka Community HS District 111	Minooka
149	1,250.0	Herrin CUSD 4	Herrin
150	1,258.0	Belleville Twp HSD 201	Belleville
151	1,284.0	Mchenry Community HSD 156	Mchenry
152	1,294.8	Geneseo Community Unit SD 228	Geneseo
153	1,296.7	Lyons Twp HSD 204	La Grange
154	1,301.2	Schaumburg CCSD 54	Schaumburg
155	1,313.7	Marion Community Unit SD 2	Marion
156	1,344.0	Rich Twp HS District 227	Olympia Fields
157	1,367.0	Woodland CCSD 50	Gurnee
158	1,369.0	Bethalto CUSD 8	Bethalto
159	1,374.5	Waterloo CUSD 5	Waterloo
160	1,394.5	Grayslake Com High SD 127	Grayslake
161	1,406.0	Community Consolidated SD 46	Grayslake
162	1,413.7	Decatur SD 61	Decatur
163	1,430.0	Freeport SD 145	Freeport
164	1,431.0	Jersey CUSD 100	Jerseyville
165	1,435.5	Taylorville CUSD 3	Taylorville
166	1,438.5	Effingham Community Unit SD 40	Effingham
167	1,445.2	Cons High SD 230	Orland Park
168	1,446.5	Homewood Flossmoor CHSD 233	Flossmoor
169	1,456.5	Community High SD 218	Oak Lawn
170	1,462.5	Lake Park Community HSD 108	Roselle
171	1,506.0	Litchfield CUSD 12	Litchfield
172	1,507.0	Lemont Twp HSD 210	Lemont
173	1,511.0	Springfield SD 186	Springfield
174	1,532.0	Auburn CUSD 10	Auburn
175	1,539.7	Plainfield SD 202	Plainfield
176	1,556.0	Bradley SD 61	Bradley
177	1,569.0	Rockton SD 140	Rockton
178	1,590.0	Beardstown CUSD 15	Beardstown
179	1,609.0	Steger SD 194	Steger
180	1,614.0	Millburn CCSD 24	Old Mill Creek
181	1,620.0	Darien SD 61	Darien
182	1,622.0	Eureka C U Dist 140	Eureka
183	1,628.2	East St Louis SD 189	E Saint Louis
184	1,633.0	Burbank SD 111	Burbank
185	1,652.0	Forest Ridge SD 142	Oak Forest
186	1,653.0	Byron Community Unit SD 226	Byron
187	1,656.0	Sherrard Community Unit SD 200	Sherrard
188	1,666.0	Waukegan CUSD 60	Waukegan
189	1,687.0	Central Community Unit SD 301	Burlington
190	1,695.0	Southwestern CUSD 9	Piasa
191	1,696.0	School District 45 Dupage County	Villa Park
192	1,697.8	J S Morton HS District 201	Cicero
193	1,713.0	Vandalia CUSD 203	Vandalia
194	1,736.0	United Twp HS District 30	East Moline
195	1,736.5	Dunlap CUSD 323	Dunlap
196	1,746.0	Rochelle Community CD 231	Rochelle
197	1,756.5	Bloom Twp High SD 206	Chicago Heights
198	1,766.0	North Boone CUSD 200	Poplar Grove
199	1,780.0	Wabash CUSD 348	Mount Carmel
200	1,786.5	Community High SD 155	Crystal Lake
201	1,802.0	Carterville CUSD 5	Carterville
202	1,816.0	Grant Community HS District 124	Fox Lake
203	1,817.0	East Peoria SD 86	East Peoria
204	1,838.0	Kewanee Community Unit SD 229	Kewanee
205	1,839.0	Thornton Fractional HSD 215	Calumet City
206	1,865.0	Triad Community Unit SD 2	Troy
207	1,870.0	Posen-Robbins Elem SD 143-5	Posen
208	1,876.5	Jacksonville SD 117	Jacksonville
209	1,909.0	Reavis Twp HSD 220	Burbank
210	1,936.0	Lockport Twp HSD 205	Lockport
211	1,972.0	Streator Elem SD 44	Streator
212	2,011.0	Columbia Community Unit SD 4	Columbia
213	2,020.0	Genoa Kingston CUSD 424	Genoa
214	2,040.2	Township High SD 214	Arlington Hgts
215	2,055.0	Du Page High SD 88	Addison
216	2,059.0	Ottawa Elem SD 141	Ottawa
217	2,066.3	Winnebago CUSD 323	Winnebago
218	2,076.5	Rockford SD 205	Rockford
219	2,085.0	Peotone CUSD 207U	Peotone
220	2,109.0	Pekin Community HSD 303	Pekin
221	2,124.0	Bradley Bourbonnais CHSD 307	Bradley
222	2,138.0	Lake Forest SD 67	Lake Forest
223	2,152.0	Coal City CUSD 1	Coal City
224	2,169.0	Hononegah Community HSD 207	Rockton
225	2,198.5	Warren Twp High SD 121	Gurnee
226	2,209.5	Adlai E Stevenson Dist 125	Lincolnshire
227	2,248.0	Consolidated SD 158	Algonquin
228	2,256.0	Mundelein Cons High SD 120	Mundelein
229	2,317.0	Massac Unit District #1	Metropolis
230	2,325.2	Peoria SD 150	Peoria
231	2,334.0	Flossmoor SD 161	Chicago Heights
232	2,337.0	Manteno Community Unit SD 5	Manteno
233	2,448.7	Lincoln Way Community HSD 210	New Lenox
234	2,524.0	O'Fallon Twp High SD 203	O Fallon
235	2,560.0	Beach Park CCSD 3	Beach Park
236	2,593.0	Lemont-Bromberek CSD 113A	Lemont
237	2,599.0	Proviso Twp HSD 209	Forest Park
238	2,607.0	Harvey SD 152	Harvey
239	2,658.0	Canton Union SD 66	Canton
240	2,852.0	Community High SD 117	Lake Villa
241	2,874.0	Dixon Unit SD 170	Dixon
242	2,878.0	Zion-Benton Twp HSD 126	Zion
243	2,888.0	Bellwood SD 88	Bellwood
244	2,946.0	Elmwood Park CUSD 401	Elmwood Park
245	3,057.0	Indian Springs SD 109	Justice
246	3,127.5	Community CSD 59	Arlington Hgts
247	3,158.0	Antioch CCSD 34	Antioch
248	3,188.2	School District U-46	Elgin

Note: This section only includes districts with 1,500 or more students; All categories are ranked from high to low

249	3,266.0	Lake Villa CCSD 41	Lake Villa
250	3,311.5	Collinsville CUSD 10	Collinsville
251	3,522.0	O'Fallon CCSD 90	O Fallon
252	3,525.0	Round Lake Area Schs - Dist 116	Round Lake
253	3,601.0	Berwyn South SD 100	Berwyn
254	3,604.0	Sterling CUD 5	Sterling
255	3,662.0	Summit Hill SD 161	Frankfort
256	3,811.5	Edwardsville CUSD 7	Edwardsville
257	3,814.0	Sycamore CUSD 427	Sycamore
258	4,432.0	Troy Community CSD 30C	Plainfield
259	4,564.0	Illinois Valley CUD 321	Chillicothe
260	4,585.0	Cahokia Community Unit SD 187	Cahokia
261	5,063.5	Joliet Public SD 86	Joliet
262	5,245.0	Crete Monee CUSD 201u	Crete
263	5,640.0	Maywood-Melrose Park-Broadview-89	Melrose Park
264	5,767.0	Kankakee SD 111	Kankakee
265	6,018.0	Dekalb Community Unit SD 428	Dekalb
266	6,222.0	Danville CCSD 118	Danville
267	6,225.0	Rock Island SD 41	Rock Island
268	6,753.0	Aurora East Unit SD 131	Aurora
269	7,065.0	Granite City CUSD 9	Granite City
270	7,081.0	Quincy SD 172	Quincy
271	7,682.2	City of Chicago SD 299	Chicago
272	18,475.0	Pekin Public SD 108	Pekin
n/a	n/a	Argo Community HSD 217	Summit
n/a	n/a	Belleville SD 118	Belleville
n/a	n/a	Berkeley SD 87	Berkeley
n/a	n/a	Big Hollow SD 38	Ingleside
n/a	n/a	Channahon SD 17	Channahon
n/a	n/a	Chicago Heights SD 170	Chicago Heights
n/a	n/a	Community CSD 168	Sauk Village
n/a	n/a	Dolton SD 149	Calumet City
n/a	n/a	Du Quoin CUSD 300	Du Quoin
n/a	n/a	Evergreen Park Elem SD 124	Evergreen Park
n/a	n/a	Frankfort CCSD 157C	Frankfort
n/a	n/a	Frankfort Community Unit SD 168	West Frankfort
n/a	n/a	Homer Community CSD 33c	Homer Glen
n/a	n/a	Kinnikinnick CCSD 131	Roscoe
n/a	n/a	Midlothian SD 143	Midlothian
n/a	n/a	Mokena SD 159	Mokena
n/a	n/a	Mount Vernon SD 80	Mount Vernon
n/a	n/a	North Chicago SD 187	North Chicago
n/a	n/a	Prairie-Hills Elem SD 144	Markham
n/a	n/a	Rantoul City SD 137	Rantoul
n/a	n/a	Ridgeland SD 122	Oak Lawn
n/a	n/a	Sandwich CUSD 430	Sandwich
n/a	n/a	South Holland SD 151	South Holland
n/a	n/a	Summit SD 104	Summit
n/a	n/a	Zion Elementary SD 6	Zion

Student/Counselor Ratio

(number of students per counselor)

Rank	Number	District Name	City
1	203.6	Evanston Twp HSD 202	Evanston
2	207.6	Township High SD 113	Highland Park
3	217.1	Hinsdale Twp HSD 86	Hinsdale
4	218.3	Northfield Twp High SD 225	Glenview
5	221.0	Adlai E Stevenson Dist 125	Lincolnshire
6	223.3	Lake Forest CHSD 115	Lake Forest
7	224.6	Township High SD 214	Arlington Hgts
8	228.6	Maine Township HSD 207	Park Ridge
9	232.4	Grayslake Com High SD 127	Grayslake
10	238.4	Fenton Community HSD 100	Bensenville
11	238.7	Niles Twp Community High SD 219	Skokie
12	242.0	Community High SD 128	Vernon Hills
13	249.4	Lyons Twp HSD 204	La Grange
14	250.7	Mundelein Cons High SD 120	Mundelein
15	256.9	Du Page High SD 88	Addison
16	260.2	Township HSD 211	Palatine
17	262.7	Community High SD 99	Downers Grove
18	263.0	Homewood Flossmoor CHSD 233	Flossmoor
19	263.3	Argo Community HSD 217	Summit
20	264.3	Glenbard Twp HSD 87	Glen Ellyn
21	264.8	Community High SD 218	Oak Lawn
22	268.7	Thornton Twp HSD 205	South Holland
23	269.0	Leyden Community HSD 212	Franklin Park
23	269.0	Oak Lawn Community HSD 229	Oak Lawn
25	270.2	Bloom Twp High SD 206	Chicago Heights
26	271.3	Oak Park & River Forest Dist 200	Oak Park
27	278.8	Cons High SD 230	Orland Park
28	288.0	Rich Twp HS District 227	Olympia Fields
29	292.5	Lake Park Community HSD 108	Roselle
30	297.8	Lockport Twp HSD 205	Lockport
31	301.3	Pekin Community HSD 303	Pekin
32	305.8	Proviso Twp HSD 209	Forest Park
33	307.6	Lemont Twp HSD 210	Lemont
34	314.4	J S Morton HS District 201	Cicero
35	321.0	Mchenry Community HSD 156	Mchenry
36	324.8	Community High SD 155	Crystal Lake
37	333.7	Sterling CUD 5	Sterling
38	333.9	Lincoln Way Community HSD 210	New Lenox
39	334.4	Thornton Fractional HSD 215	Calumet City
40	340.9	Reavis Twp HSD 220	Burbank
41	347.2	United Twp HS District 30	East Moline
42	348.7	Oregon CUSD 220	Oregon
43	351.3	Minooka Community HS District 111	Minooka
44	352.1	Community High SD 117	Lake Villa
45	354.0	Bradley Bourbonnais CHSD 307	Bradley
46	363.2	Grant Community HS District 124	Fox Lake
47	363.6	East Moline SD 37	East Moline
48	363.8	Community High SD 94	West Chicago
49	366.4	Warren Twp High SD 121	Gurnee
50	373.6	Joliet Twp HSD 204	Joliet
51	376.5	Litchfield CUSD 12	Litchfield
52	393.3	East St Louis SD 189	E Saint Louis
53	395.2	Bremen Community HS District 228	Midlothian
54	411.1	Zion-Benton Twp HSD 126	Zion
55	411.5	Robinson CUSD 2	Robinson
56	413.3	Byron Community Unit SD 226	Byron
57	414.8	Marion Community Unit SD 2	Marion
58	419.0	Monmouth-Roseville CUSD 238	Monmouth
59	420.7	O'Fallon Twp High SD 203	O Fallon
60	433.8	Hononegah Community HSD 207	Rockton
61	435.8	Sherrard Community Unit SD 200	Sherrard
62	436.5	Rochelle Community CD 231	Rochelle
63	450.5	Carterville CUSD 5	Carterville
64	456.7	Elmhurst SD 205	Elmhurst
65	457.5	Belleville Twp HSD 201	Belleville
66	477.0	Macomb Community Unit SD 185	Macomb
67	479.0	Dixon Unit SD 170	Dixon
68	479.5	Effingham Community Unit SD 40	Effingham
69	493.0	Meridian CUSD 223	Stillman Valley
70	499.4	Naperville CUD 203	Naperville
71	507.1	Illinois Valley CUD 321	Chillicothe
72	507.7	City of Chicago SD 299	Chicago
73	511.7	Riverton CUSD 14	Riverton
74	514.8	Ottawa Elem SD 141	Ottawa
75	516.8	Harlem Unit Dist 122	Machesney Park
76	521.0	Clinton CUSD 15	Clinton
77	529.7	Lisle CUSD 202	Lisle
78	540.5	Decatur SD 61	Decatur
79	543.8	Geneseo Community Unit SD 228	Geneseo
80	543.9	Community Unit SD 200	Wheaton
81	546.1	Barrington CUSD 220	Barrington
82	547.9	Ball Chatham CUSD 5	Chatham
83	556.4	Champaign Community Unit SD 4	Champaign
84	578.4	Charleston CUSD 1	Charleston
85	578.8	Dunlap CUSD 323	Dunlap
86	582.3	Plano Community Unit SD 88	Plano
87	587.9	Woodstock CUSD 200	Woodstock
88	589.1	Urbana SD 116	Urbana
89	590.1	Quincy SD 172	Quincy
90	591.9	New Trier Twp HSD 203	Northfield
91	593.3	Wabash CUSD 348	Mount Carmel
92	594.5	Rockford SD 205	Rockford
93	612.9	Freeport SD 145	Freeport
94	619.4	Indian Prairie CUSD 204	Aurora
95	620.5	Johnsburg CUSD 12	Johnsburg
96	625.0	Herrin CUSD 4	Herrin
97	625.5	Jacksonville SD 117	Jacksonville
98	638.5	Mount Zion Community Unit SD 3	Mount Zion
99	640.8	Waukegan CUSD 60	Waukegan
100	651.3	Hillsboro Community Unit SD 3	Hillsboro
101	655.6	Crete Monee CUSD 201u	Crete
102	656.2	Community Unit SD 300	Carpentersville
103	664.5	Canton Union SD 66	Canton
104	665.0	Roxana Community Unit SD 1	Roxana
105	666.8	Belvidere CUSD 100	Belvidere
106	667.6	Saint Charles CUSD 303	Saint Charles
107	670.3	Columbia Community Unit SD 4	Columbia
108	672.5	Moline Unit SD 40	Moline
109	673.3	Genoa Kingston CUSD 424	Genoa
110	678.0	Kaneland CUSD 302	Maple Park
111	681.3	Bond County CUSD 2	Greenville
112	685.2	Vandalia CUSD 203	Vandalia
113	689.4	Mascoutah CUD 19	Mascoutah
114	696.0	Morton CUSD 709	Morton
115	697.4	Valley View CUSD #365U	Romeoville
116	698.0	Lake Zurich CUSD 95	Lake Zurich
117	704.6	Mattoon CUSD 2	Mattoon
118	707.8	Olympia CUSD 16	Stanford
119	709.2	Geneva Community Unit SD 304	Geneva
120	716.4	Dekalb Community Unit SD 428	Dekalb
121	717.3	Coal City CUSD 1	Coal City
122	726.3	Berkeley SD 87	Berkeley
123	727.6	Homer Community CSD 33c	Homer Glen
124	733.5	Wauconda Community Unit SD 118	Wauconda
125	738.0	Bloomington SD 87	Bloomington
126	739.0	Pekin Public SD 108	Pekin
127	754.0	West Harvey-Dixmoor PSD 147	Harvey
128	758.7	Rochester CUSD 3A	Rochester
129	762.8	Sycamore CUSD 427	Sycamore
130	767.5	Westmont CUSD 201	Westmont
131	776.8	Highland Community Unit SD 5	Highland
132	778.1	Rock Island SD 41	Rock Island
133	781.5	Du Quoin CUSD 300	Du Quoin
134	795.0	Beardstown CUSD 15	Beardstown
135	796.5	Batavia Unit SD 101	Batavia
136	796.6	North Chicago SD 187	North Chicago
137	811.0	Eureka C U Dist 140	Eureka
137	811.0	Mclean County Unit Dist No 5	Normal
139	820.3	Sandwich CUSD 430	Sandwich
140	823.9	Oswego Community Unit SD 308	Oswego
141	826.5	Winnebago CUSD 323	Winnebago
142	830.0	Tolono CUSD 7	Tolono
143	847.0	Edwardsville CUSD 7	Edwardsville
144	847.5	Southwestern CUSD 9	Piasa
145	853.2	Yorkville Community Unit SD 115	Yorkville
146	864.3	Lemont-Bromberek CSD 113A	Lemont
147	878.0	Mount Vernon SD 80	Mount Vernon
148	902.0	Reed Custer CUSD 255U	Braidwood
149	916.3	Waterloo CUSD 5	Waterloo
150	932.5	Triad Community Unit SD 2	Troy
151	934.8	Manteno Community Unit SD 5	Manteno
152	945.3	Mahomet-Seymour CUSD 3	Mahomet
153	954.0	Jersey CUSD 100	Jerseyville
154	961.2	Kankakee SD 111	Kankakee
155	982.0	Elmwood Park CUSD 401	Elmwood Park
156	996.5	Peoria SD 150	Peoria
157	1,010.9	School District U-46	Elgin
158	1,031.7	Lombard SD 44	Lombard
159	1,034.0	Herscher Community Unit SD 2	Herscher
160	1,037.0	Danville CCSD 118	Danville
161	1,038.9	Aurora East Unit SD 131	Aurora
162	1,042.5	Peotone CUSD 207U	Peotone
163	1,047.0	Bensenville SD 2	Bensenville
164	1,063.5	East Richland CUSD 1	Olney
165	1,068.5	Prairie Central CUSD 8	Fairbury
166	1,073.5	Murphysboro CUSD 186	Murphysboro
167	1,095.7	Plainfield SD 202	Plainfield
168	1,102.0	Harrisburg CUSD 3	Harrisburg
169	1,103.3	Massac Unit District #1	Metropolis
170	1,108.8	Alton Community Unit SD 11	Alton
171	1,124.0	Consolidated SD 158	Algonquin
172	1,124.7	Central Community Unit SD 301	Burlington
173	1,167.0	Flossmoor SD 161	Chicago Heights
174	1,175.0	Round Lake Area Schs - Dist 116	Round Lake
175	1,177.5	Granite City CUSD 9	Granite City
176	1,214.5	Harvard CUSD 50	Harvard
177	1,219.8	Galesburg CUSD 205	Galesburg
178	1,225.7	Glen Ellyn SD 41	Glen Ellyn
179	1,236.8	Downers Grove Grade SD 58	Downers Grove
180	1,369.0	Bethalto CUSD 8	Bethalto
181	1,389.8	Aurora West Unit SD 129	Aurora
182	1,435.5	Taylorville CUSD 3	Taylorville
183	1,528.3	Cahokia Community Unit SD 187	Cahokia
184	1,532.0	Auburn CUSD 10	Auburn
185	1,532.5	Woodridge SD 68	Woodridge
186	1,533.0	Paxton-Buckley-Loda CUD 10	Paxton
187	1,578.5	Kildeer Countryside CCSD 96	Buffalo Grove
188	1,652.0	Forest Ridge SD 142	Oak Forest
189	1,655.8	Collinsville CUSD 10	Collinsville
190	1,698.5	Dolton SD 149	Calumet City
191	1,707.0	Monticello CUSD 25	Monticello
192	1,766.0	North Boone CUSD 200	Poplar Grove
193	1,774.4	Deerfield SD 109	Deerfield
194	1,800.5	Berwyn South SD 100	Berwyn
195	1,817.0	East Peoria SD 86	East Peoria
196	1,831.0	Summit Hill SD 161	Frankfort
197	1,838.0	Kewanee Community Unit SD 229	Kewanee

Note: This section only includes districts with 1,500 or more students; All categories are ranked from high to low

198	1,876.0	Mundelein Elem SD 75	Mundelein
199	1,984.0	Frankfort Community Unit SD 168	West Frankfort
200	2,052.0	Queen Bee SD 16	Glendale Hgts
201	2,113.0	Kinnikinnick CCSD 131	Roscoe
202	2,121.0	West Chicago Elem SD 33	West Chicago
203	2,182.2	Kirby SD 140	Tinley Park
204	2,216.0	Troy Community CSD 30C	Plainfield
205	2,671.0	Bourbonnais SD 53	Bourbonnais
206	2,681.9	Park Ridge CCSD 64	Park Ridge
207	2,733.0	Orland SD 135	Orland Park
208	2,833.5	New Lenox SD 122	New Lenox
209	3,158.0	Antioch CCSD 34	Antioch
210	3,392.0	School District 45 Dupage County	Villa Park
211	4,071.3	Palatine CCSD 15	Palatine
212	4,372.0	Addison SD 4	Addison
213	5,345.0	Lake Forest SD 67	Lake Forest
214	6,255.0	Community CSD 59	Arlington Hgts
215	7,156.5	Schaumburg CCSD 54	Schaumburg
n/a	n/a	Alsip-Hazelgreen-Oak Lawn SD 126	Alsip
n/a	n/a	Aptakisic-Tripp CCSD 102	Buffalo Grove
n/a	n/a	Arlington Hgts SD 25	Arlington Hgts
n/a	n/a	Beach Park CCSD 3	Beach Park
n/a	n/a	Belleville SD 118	Belleville
n/a	n/a	Bellwood SD 88	Bellwood
n/a	n/a	Berwyn North SD 98	Berwyn
n/a	n/a	Big Hollow SD 38	Ingleside
n/a	n/a	Bradley SD 61	Bradley
n/a	n/a	Burbank SD 111	Burbank
n/a	n/a	CCSD 181	Westmont
n/a	n/a	Cary CCSD 26	Cary
n/a	n/a	Channahon SD 17	Channahon
n/a	n/a	Chicago Heights SD 170	Chicago Heights
n/a	n/a	Cicero SD 99	Cicero
n/a	n/a	Community CSD 168	Sauk Village
n/a	n/a	Community Consolidated SD 46	Grayslake
n/a	n/a	Community Consolidated SD 62	Des Plaines
n/a	n/a	Community Consolidated SD 93	Bloomingdale
n/a	n/a	Cook County SD 130	Blue Island
n/a	n/a	Crystal Lake CCSD 47	Crystal Lake
n/a	n/a	Darien SD 61	Darien
n/a	n/a	Dolton SD 148	Riverdale
n/a	n/a	East Maine SD 63	Des Plaines
n/a	n/a	Elem SD 159	Matteson
n/a	n/a	Evanston CCSD 65	Evanston
n/a	n/a	Evergreen Park Elem SD 124	Evergreen Park
n/a	n/a	Frankfort CCSD 157C	Frankfort
n/a	n/a	Fremont SD 79	Mundelein
n/a	n/a	Glen Ellyn CCSD 89	Glen Ellyn
n/a	n/a	Glenview CCSD 34	Glenview
n/a	n/a	Gurnee SD 56	Gurnee
n/a	n/a	Harvey SD 152	Harvey
n/a	n/a	Hawthorn CCSD 73	Vernon Hills
n/a	n/a	Homewood SD 153	Homewood
n/a	n/a	Indian Springs SD 109	Justice
n/a	n/a	Joliet Public SD 86	Joliet
n/a	n/a	Keeneyville SD 20	Hanover Park
n/a	n/a	La Grange SD 102	La Grange Park
n/a	n/a	Lake Villa CCSD 41	Lake Villa
n/a	n/a	Lansing SD 158	Lansing
n/a	n/a	Libertyville SD 70	Libertyville
n/a	n/a	Lyons SD 103	Lyons
n/a	n/a	Mannheim SD 83	Franklin Park
n/a	n/a	Marquardt SD 15	Glendale Hgts
n/a	n/a	Matteson Elem SD 162	Matteson
n/a	n/a	Maywood-Melrose Park-Broadview-89	Melrose Park
n/a	n/a	Mchenry CCSD 15	Mchenry
n/a	n/a	Midlothian SD 143	Midlothian
n/a	n/a	Millburn CCSD 24	Old Mill Creek
n/a	n/a	Minooka Community CSD 201	Minooka
n/a	n/a	Mokena SD 159	Mokena
n/a	n/a	Mount Prospect SD 57	Mount Prospect
n/a	n/a	North Palos SD 117	Palos Hills
n/a	n/a	North Shore SD 112	Highland Park
n/a	n/a	Northbrook SD 28	Northbrook
n/a	n/a	O'Fallon CCSD 90	O Fallon
n/a	n/a	Oak Lawn-Hometown SD 123	Oak Lawn
n/a	n/a	Oak Park Elem SD 97	Oak Park
n/a	n/a	Palos Community CSD 118	Palos Park
n/a	n/a	Park Forest SD 163	Park Forest
n/a	n/a	Posen-Robbins Elem SD 143-5	Posen
n/a	n/a	Prairie-Hills Elem SD 144	Markham
n/a	n/a	Rantoul City SD 137	Rantoul
n/a	n/a	Ridgeland SD 122	Oak Lawn
n/a	n/a	Riverside SD 96	Riverside
n/a	n/a	Rockton SD 140	Rockton
n/a	n/a	Skokie SD 68	Skokie
n/a	n/a	Skokie SD 69	Skokie
n/a	n/a	South Holland SD 151	South Holland
n/a	n/a	Springfield SD 186	Springfield
n/a	n/a	Steger SD 194	Steger
n/a	n/a	Streator Elem SD 44	Streator
n/a	n/a	Summit SD 104	Summit
n/a	n/a	Tinley Park CCSD 146	Tinley Park
n/a	n/a	Western Springs SD 101	Western Springs
n/a	n/a	Wheeling CCSD 21	Wheeling
n/a	n/a	Will County SD 92	Lockport
n/a	n/a	Wilmette SD 39	Wilmette
n/a	n/a	Winnetka SD 36	Winnetka
n/a	n/a	Woodland CCSD 50	Gurnee
n/a	n/a	Zion Elementary SD 6	Zion

Current Expenditures per Student

Rank	Dollars	District Name	City
1	21,179	Evanston Twp HSD 202	Evanston
2	20,128	Niles Twp Community High SD 219	Skokie
3	19,849	Township High SD 113	Highland Park
4	19,142	New Trier Twp HSD 203	Northfield
5	19,106	Lake Forest CHSD 115	Lake Forest
6	17,688	Northfield Twp High SD 225	Glenview
7	17,352	Oak Park & River Forest Dist 200	Oak Park
8	17,020	Maine Township HSD 207	Park Ridge
9	16,615	Community High SD 128	Vernon Hills
10	15,997	Township High SD 214	Arlington Hgts
11	15,504	Northbrook SD 28	Northbrook
12	15,475	Fenton Community HSD 100	Bensenville
13	15,200	Adlai E Stevenson Dist 125	Lincolnshire
14	15,085	Leyden Community HSD 212	Franklin Park
15	15,064	Lisle CUSD 202	Lisle
16	15,021	Township HSD 211	Palatine
17	14,978	Hinsdale Twp HSD 86	Hinsdale
18	14,779	Lyons Twp HSD 204	La Grange
19	14,258	Evanston CCSD 65	Evanston
20	14,251	Community High SD 218	Oak Lawn
21	14,028	Skokie SD 68	Skokie
22	13,961	Winnetka SD 36	Winnetka
23	13,857	Community High SD 117	Lake Villa
24	13,737	Westmont CUSD 201	Westmont
25	13,736	Lemont Twp HSD 210	Lemont
26	13,670	Homewood Flossmoor CHSD 233	Flossmoor
27	13,651	Lake Forest SD 67	Lake Forest
28	13,435	Community High SD 99	Downers Grove
29	13,331	Bremen Community HS District 228	Midlothian
30	13,321	Du Page High SD 88	Addison
31	13,291	Bloom Twp High SD 206	Chicago Heights
32	13,197	Oak Lawn Community HSD 229	Oak Lawn
33	13,067	Joliet Twp HSD 204	Joliet
34	12,926	Aptakisic-Tripp CCSD 102	Buffalo Grove
35	12,831	Urbana SD 116	Urbana
36	12,822	North Shore SD 112	Highland Park
37	12,808	Lake Park Community HSD 108	Roselle
38	12,755	Rich Twp HS District 227	Olympia Fields
39	12,741	Argo Community HSD 217	Summit
40	12,272	Proviso Twp HSD 209	Forest Park
41	12,230	Oak Park Elem SD 97	Oak Park
42	12,220	CCSD 181	Westmont
43	12,200	Community CSD 59	Arlington Hgts
44	12,113	Thornton Twp HSD 205	South Holland
45	12,089	Wilmette SD 39	Wilmette
46	12,043	Lombard SD 44	Lombard
47	12,006	Park Ridge CCSD 64	Park Ridge
48	11,999	Tinley Park CCSD 146	Tinley Park
49	11,909	Community Consolidated SD 62	Des Plaines
50	11,891	Cons High SD 230	Orland Park
50	11,891	Wheeling CCSD 21	Wheeling
52	11,862	Barrington CUSD 220	Barrington
53	11,710	Grayslake Com High SD 127	Grayslake
54	11,631	Kildeer Countryside CCSD 96	Buffalo Grove
55	11,581	Glenview CCSD 34	Glenview
56	11,542	East St Louis SD 189	E Saint Louis
57	11,541	Elmhurst SD 205	Elmhurst
58	11,411	Park Forest SD 163	Park Forest
59	11,359	Community High SD 94	West Chicago
60	11,317	Community Consolidated SD 93	Bloomingdale
61	11,302	Glen Ellyn CCSD 89	Glen Ellyn
62	11,241	Reavis Twp HSD 220	Burbank
63	11,138	Schaumburg CCSD 54	Schaumburg
64	11,072	Byron Community Unit SD 226	Byron
65	11,069	North Chicago SD 187	North Chicago
66	11,045	Orland SD 135	Orland Park
67	11,039	Mundelein Cons High SD 120	Mundelein
68	10,999	Naperville CUD 203	Naperville
69	10,991	Riverside SD 96	Riverside
70	10,952	Community Unit SD 200	Wheaton
71	10,941	Dolton SD 148	Riverdale
72	10,931	Arlington Hgts SD 25	Arlington Hgts
73	10,924	Reed Custer CUSD 255U	Braidwood
74	10,859	Glenbard Twp HSD 87	Glen Ellyn
75	10,852	Mannheim SD 83	Franklin Park
76	10,824	Zion-Benton Twp HSD 126	Zion
77	10,819	Deerfield SD 109	Deerfield
78	10,811	Peoria SD 150	Peoria
79	10,790	North Palos SD 117	Palos Hills
80	10,769	Downers Grove Grade SD 58	Downers Grove
81	10,742	Crete Monee CUSD 201u	Crete
82	10,620	Woodridge SD 68	Woodridge
83	10,611	West Harvey-Dixmoor PSD 147	Harvey
84	10,602	Thornton Fractional HSD 215	Calumet City
85	10,601	Hawthorn CCSD 73	Vernon Hills
86	10,593	Glen Ellyn SD 41	Glen Ellyn
87	10,566	Palos Community CSD 118	Palos Park
88	10,546	Summit SD 104	Summit
89	10,542	Lockport Twp HSD 205	Lockport
90	10,534	Bensenville SD 2	Bensenville
91	10,522	Mchenry Community HSD 156	Mchenry
92	10,508	Matteson Elem SD 162	Matteson
93	10,453	Palatine CCSD 15	Palatine
94	10,432	Central Community Unit SD 301	Burlington
95	10,427	School District 45 Dupage County	Villa Park
96	10,419	Community High SD 155	Crystal Lake
97	10,392	City of Chicago SD 299	Chicago
98	10,337	Geneva Community Unit SD 304	Geneva
99	10,334	Elem SD 159	Matteson
100	10,234	Cahokia Community Unit SD 187	Cahokia
101	10,223	Valley View CUSD #365U	Romeoville
102	10,206	Skokie SD 69	Skokie
103	10,139	Lincoln Way Community HSD 210	New Lenox
104	10,134	Lake Zurich CUSD 95	Lake Zurich
105	10,125	Bloomington SD 87	Bloomington
106	10,106	Homewood SD 153	Homewood
107	10,093	Keeneyville SD 20	Hanover Park
108	10,086	Evergreen Park Elem SD 124	Evergreen Park
109	10,067	East Maine SD 63	Des Plaines
110	10,048	Macomb Community Unit SD 185	Macomb
111	10,036	Marquardt SD 15	Glendale Hgts
112	10,013	J S Morton HS District 201	Cicero
113	9,980	Gurnee SD 56	Gurnee
114	9,968	Freeport SD 145	Freeport
115	9,920	Zion Elementary SD 6	Zion
116	9,912	Mattoon CUSD 2	Mattoon
117	9,881	Dekalb Community Unit SD 428	Dekalb
118	9,871	Cook County SD 130	Blue Island
119	9,816	Champaign Community Unit SD 4	Champaign
120	9,815	Saint Charles CUSD 303	Saint Charles
121	9,802	Kankakee SD 111	Kankakee
122	9,777	Oak Lawn-Hometown SD 123	Oak Lawn
123	9,776	Rockford SD 205	Rockford
124	9,754	Springfield SD 186	Springfield
125	9,748	Woodstock CUSD 200	Woodstock
126	9,730	Steger SD 194	Steger
127	9,722	Lyons SD 103	Lyons
128	9,718	West Chicago Elem SD 33	West Chicago
129	9,683	Belleville Twp HSD 201	Belleville
130	9,679	Elmwood Park CUSD 401	Elmwood Park
131	9,676	La Grange SD 102	La Grange Park
132	9,624	Warren Twp High SD 121	Gurnee
133	9,618	Libertyville SD 70	Libertyville
134	9,593	Kaneland CUSD 302	Maple Park
134	9,593	Streator Elem SD 44	Streator
136	9,563	Dolton SD 149	Calumet City
137	9,560	Mount Vernon SD 80	Mount Vernon
138	9,546	Ottawa Elem SD 141	Ottawa
139	9,524	Alton Community Unit SD 11	Alton
140	9,519	Chicago Heights SD 170	Chicago Heights
141	9,487	Harvey SD 152	Harvey
142	9,480	Wauconda Community Unit SD 118	Wauconda
143	9,463	Community Consolidated SD 46	Grayslake
144	9,435	Mascoutah CUD 19	Mascoutah
145	9,426	Johnsburg CUSD 12	Johnsburg
146	9,422	Morton CUSD 709	Morton
147	9,408	School District U-46	Elgin

Note: This section only includes districts with 1,500 or more students; All categories are ranked from high to low

148	9,405	Hononegah Community HSD 207	Rockton
149	9,371	Flossmoor SD 161	Chicago Heights
150	9,298	East Moline SD 37	East Moline
151	9,297	Homer Community CSD 33c	Homer Glen
152	9,283	Mount Prospect SD 57	Mount Prospect
153	9,280	Waukegan CUSD 60	Waukegan
154	9,256	Sycamore CUSD 427	Sycamore
155	9,250	Minooka Community HS District 111	Minooka
155	9,250	Woodland CCSD 50	Gurnee
157	9,249	Grant Community HS District 124	Fox Lake
157	9,249	Maywood-Melrose Park-Broadview-89	Melrose Park
159	9,190	Joliet Public SD 86	Joliet
160	9,156	Fremont SD 79	Mundelein
161	9,127	Cary CCSD 26	Cary
162	9,089	Burbank SD 111	Burbank
163	9,075	Indian Prairie CUSD 204	Aurora
164	9,055	Alsip-Hazelgreen-Oak Lawn SD 126	Alsip
165	9,045	Beach Park CCSD 3	Beach Park
166	9,030	Belleville SD 118	Belleville
167	9,025	Millburn CCSD 24	Old Mill Creek
168	9,018	Rock Island SD 41	Rock Island
169	8,953	Moline Unit SD 40	Moline
170	8,933	Dixon Unit SD 170	Dixon
171	8,931	Queen Bee SD 16	Glendale Hgts
172	8,923	Frankfort CCSD 157C	Frankfort
173	8,887	Batavia Unit SD 101	Batavia
174	8,886	Community CSD 168	Sauk Village
175	8,881	Danville CCSD 118	Danville
176	8,879	Jacksonville SD 117	Jacksonville
177	8,867	Community Unit SD 300	Carpentersville
178	8,824	Winnebago CUSD 323	Winnebago
179	8,786	Prairie Central CUSD 8	Fairbury
180	8,784	Quincy SD 172	Quincy
181	8,763	Olympia CUSD 16	Stanford
182	8,760	Edwardsville CUSD 7	Edwardsville
183	8,710	Jersey CUSD 100	Jerseyville
184	8,695	South Holland SD 151	South Holland
185	8,687	Mundelein Elem SD 75	Mundelein
186	8,685	Lemont-Bromberek CSD 113A	Lemont
187	8,662	Granite City CUSD 9	Granite City
188	8,654	Coal City CUSD 1	Coal City
189	8,641	Murphysboro CUSD 186	Murphysboro
190	8,621	Western Springs SD 101	Western Springs
191	8,617	Aurora West Unit SD 129	Aurora
192	8,579	Berwyn South SD 100	Berwyn
193	8,577	Prairie-Hills Elem SD 144	Markham
194	8,567	Bellwood SD 88	Bellwood
195	8,543	United Twp HS District 30	East Moline
196	8,528	Consolidated SD 158	Algonquin
197	8,519	Harvard CUSD 50	Harvard
198	8,495	Darien SD 61	Darien
199	8,494	Herscher Community Unit SD 2	Herscher
200	8,481	East Peoria SD 86	East Peoria
201	8,471	Kirby SD 140	Tinley Park
202	8,465	Roxana Community Unit SD 1	Roxana
203	8,438	Effingham Community Unit SD 40	Effingham
204	8,435	O'Fallon Twp High SD 203	O Fallon
205	8,422	Southwestern CUSD 9	Piasa
206	8,385	Decatur SD 61	Decatur
207	8,353	Sterling CUD 5	Sterling
208	8,339	Plainfield SD 202	Plainfield
209	8,326	Mclean County Unit Dist No 5	Normal
210	8,310	Bradley SD 61	Bradley
211	8,307	Belvidere CUSD 100	Belvidere
212	8,306	Pekin Public SD 108	Pekin
213	8,285	Harlem Unit Dist 122	Machesney Park
214	8,251	Bethalto CUSD 8	Bethalto
215	8,248	Crystal Lake CCSD 47	Crystal Lake
216	8,232	Forest Ridge SD 142	Oak Forest
217	8,198	Hillsboro Community Unit SD 3	Hillsboro
218	8,188	Highland Community Unit SD 5	Highland
219	8,184	Will County SD 92	Lockport
220	8,182	Robinson CUSD 2	Robinson
221	8,176	Collinsville CUSD 10	Collinsville
222	8,152	Tolono CUSD 7	Tolono
223	8,131	Oregon CUSD 220	Oregon
224	8,120	Pekin Community HSD 303	Pekin
225	8,119	Aurora East Unit SD 131	Aurora
225	8,119	Charleston CUSD 1	Charleston
227	8,084	Addison SD 4	Addison
228	8,047	Canton Union SD 66	Canton
229	8,030	Peotone CUSD 207U	Peotone
230	8,026	Bradley Bourbonnais CHSD 307	Bradley
231	8,018	Rantoul City SD 137	Rantoul
232	8,016	Sherrard Community Unit SD 200	Sherrard
233	8,009	Berkeley SD 87	Berkeley
234	8,005	O'Fallon CCSD 90	O Fallon
235	8,000	Troy Community CSD 30C	Plainfield
236	7,994	Oswego Community Unit SD 308	Oswego
237	7,963	Du Quoin CUSD 300	Du Quoin
238	7,894	Manteno Community Unit SD 5	Manteno
239	7,874	Sandwich CUSD 430	Sandwich
240	7,868	Posen-Robbins Elem SD 143-5	Posen
241	7,867	Triad Community Unit SD 2	Troy
242	7,861	Round Lake Area Schs - Dist 116	Round Lake
243	7,802	Mahomet-Seymour CUSD 3	Mahomet
244	7,799	Mchenry CCSD 15	Mchenry
245	7,794	Rochelle Community CD 231	Rochelle
246	7,757	Geneseo Community Unit SD 228	Geneseo
247	7,750	East Richland CUSD 1	Olney
248	7,746	Rockton SD 140	Rockton
249	7,744	Clinton CUSD 15	Clinton
250	7,706	Yorkville Community Unit SD 115	Yorkville
251	7,656	Monticello CUSD 25	Monticello
252	7,654	Lansing SD 158	Lansing
253	7,651	Columbia Community Unit SD 4	Columbia
254	7,646	Cicero SD 99	Cicero
255	7,644	Paxton-Buckley-Loda CUD 10	Paxton
256	7,635	Genoa Kingston CUSD 424	Genoa
257	7,570	Ridgeland SD 122	Oak Lawn
258	7,554	North Boone CUSD 200	Poplar Grove
259	7,551	Antioch CCSD 34	Antioch
260	7,525	Indian Springs SD 109	Justice
261	7,524	Illinois Valley CUD 321	Chillicothe
262	7,501	New Lenox SD 122	New Lenox
263	7,487	Waterloo CUSD 5	Waterloo
264	7,483	Bourbonnais SD 53	Bourbonnais
265	7,482	Berwyn North SD 98	Berwyn
266	7,445	Massac Unit District #1	Metropolis
267	7,432	Plano Community Unit SD 88	Plano
268	7,390	Eureka C U Dist 140	Eureka
268	7,390	Monmouth-Roseville CUSD 238	Monmouth
270	7,369	Galesburg CUSD 205	Galesburg
271	7,339	Bond County CUSD 2	Greenville
272	7,336	Harrisburg CUSD 3	Harrisburg
273	7,320	Meridian CUSD 223	Stillman Valley
274	7,281	Vandalia CUSD 203	Vandalia
275	7,273	Beardstown CUSD 15	Beardstown
276	7,265	Litchfield CUSD 12	Litchfield
277	7,241	Carterville CUSD 5	Carterville
278	7,130	Lake Villa CCSD 41	Lake Villa
279	7,127	Frankfort Community Unit SD 168	West Frankfort
280	7,070	Marion Community Unit SD 2	Marion
281	7,051	Ball Chatham CUSD 5	Chatham
282	7,045	Mokena SD 159	Mokena
283	7,023	Summit Hill SD 161	Frankfort
284	7,009	Wabash CUSD 348	Mount Carmel
285	6,947	Midlothian SD 143	Midlothian
286	6,877	Minooka Community CSD 201	Minooka
287	6,821	Kewanee Community Unit SD 229	Kewanee
288	6,715	Herrin CUSD 4	Herrin
289	6,629	Kinnikinnick CCSD 131	Roscoe
290	6,531	Dunlap CUSD 323	Dunlap
291	6,493	Mount Zion Community Unit SD 3	Mount Zion
292	6,403	Big Hollow SD 38	Ingleside
293	6,343	Riverton CUSD 14	Riverton
294	6,293	Taylorville CUSD 3	Taylorville
295	6,164	Auburn CUSD 10	Auburn
296	6,161	Rochester CUSD 3A	Rochester
297	6,122	Channahon SD 17	Channahon

Total General Revenue per Student

Rank	Dollars	District Name	City
1	27,300	Niles Twp Community High SD 219	Skokie
2	24,495	Township High SD 113	Highland Park
3	23,972	Lake Forest CHSD 115	Lake Forest
4	23,425	New Trier Twp HSD 203	Northfield
5	23,177	Evanston Twp HSD 202	Evanston
6	23,122	Oak Park & River Forest Dist 200	Oak Park
7	23,033	Community High SD 128	Vernon Hills
8	22,244	Northfield Twp High SD 225	Glenview
9	21,067	Adlai E Stevenson Dist 125	Lincolnshire
10	20,218	Leyden Community HSD 212	Franklin Park
11	18,956	Northbrook SD 28	Northbrook
12	18,894	Township HSD 211	Palatine
13	18,777	Winnetka SD 36	Winnetka
14	18,550	Maine Township HSD 207	Park Ridge
15	18,351	Lisle CUSD 202	Lisle
16	18,113	Fenton Community HSD 100	Bensenville
17	18,085	Skokie SD 68	Skokie
18	17,935	Township High SD 214	Arlington Hgts
19	17,823	Hinsdale Twp HSD 86	Hinsdale
20	17,727	Homewood Flossmoor CHSD 233	Flossmoor
21	17,391	Argo Community HSD 217	Summit
22	17,316	Grayslake Com High SD 127	Grayslake
23	17,161	Community High SD 218	Oak Lawn
24	16,708	Lyons Twp HSD 204	La Grange
25	16,366	Byron Community Unit SD 226	Byron
26	16,360	Lemont Twp HSD 210	Lemont
27	16,330	Rich Twp HS District 227	Olympia Fields
28	16,329	Evanston CCSD 65	Evanston
29	16,318	Bremen Community HS District 228	Midlothian
30	16,151	North Shore SD 112	Highland Park
31	16,108	Community High SD 117	Lake Villa
32	15,978	Thornton Twp HSD 205	South Holland
33	15,942	Lake Park Community HSD 108	Roselle
34	15,858	Mannheim SD 83	Franklin Park
35	15,750	Joliet Twp HSD 204	Joliet
36	15,664	Grant Community HS District 124	Fox Lake
37	15,614	Oak Lawn Community HSD 229	Oak Lawn
38	15,604	Aptakisic-Tripp CCSD 102	Buffalo Grove
39	15,588	Du Page High SD 88	Addison
40	15,567	Community High SD 99	Downers Grove
41	15,511	Westmont CUSD 201	Westmont
42	15,456	Minooka Community HS District 111	Minooka
43	15,377	Park Ridge CCSD 64	Park Ridge
44	15,201	Community Consolidated SD 62	Des Plaines
45	15,183	Community CSD 59	Arlington Hgts
46	15,182	Lake Forest SD 67	Lake Forest
47	15,054	Kildeer Countryside CCSD 96	Buffalo Grove
48	14,972	Cons High SD 230	Orland Park
49	14,881	Lombard SD 44	Lombard
50	14,803	Community Consolidated SD 93	Bloomingdale
51	14,697	Reavis Twp HSD 220	Burbank
52	14,599	Riverside SD 96	Riverside
53	14,543	Woodridge SD 68	Woodridge
54	14,439	CCSD 181	Westmont
55	14,421	Summit SD 104	Summit
56	14,412	Deerfield SD 109	Deerfield
57	14,351	Barrington CUSD 220	Barrington
58	14,257	Proviso Twp HSD 209	Forest Park
59	14,238	Mundelein Cons High SD 120	Mundelein
60	14,135	Tinley Park CCSD 146	Tinley Park
61	14,124	Arlington Hgts SD 25	Arlington Hgts
62	14,087	Schaumburg CCSD 54	Schaumburg
63	14,085	Zion-Benton Twp HSD 126	Zion
64	14,067	Community High SD 94	West Chicago
65	14,004	Bloom Twp High SD 206	Chicago Heights
66	13,945	West Harvey-Dixmoor PSD 147	Harvey
67	13,942	Glenbard Twp HSD 87	Glen Ellyn
68	13,824	Wheeling CCSD 21	Wheeling
69	13,663	Palos Community CSD 118	Palos Park
70	13,615	Lincoln Way Community HSD 210	New Lenox
71	13,591	Bensenville SD 2	Bensenville
72	13,560	Glenview CCSD 34	Glenview
73	13,496	Warren Twp High SD 121	Gurnee
74	13,451	Oak Park Elem SD 97	Oak Park
75	13,407	Elmhurst SD 205	Elmhurst
76	13,399	Geneva Community Unit SD 304	Geneva
77	13,299	Elmwood Park CUSD 401	Elmwood Park
78	13,271	Lockport Twp HSD 205	Lockport
79	13,197	Coal City CUSD 1	Coal City
80	13,180	Dolton SD 148	Riverdale
81	13,172	Central Community Unit SD 301	Burlington
82	13,117	Alsip-Hazelgreen-Oak Lawn SD 126	Alsip
83	13,049	Orland SD 135	Orland Park
84	13,018	Urbana SD 116	Urbana
85	13,001	Naperville CUD 203	Naperville
86	12,949	Park Forest SD 163	Park Forest
87	12,904	Marquardt SD 15	Glendale Hgts
88	12,898	Mchenry Community HSD 156	Mchenry
89	12,861	Hawthorn CCSD 73	Vernon Hills
90	12,839	Community High SD 155	Crystal Lake
91	12,812	Evergreen Park Elem SD 124	Evergreen Park
92	12,800	Thornton Fractional HSD 215	Calumet City
93	12,796	Woodstock CUSD 200	Woodstock
94	12,647	Skokie SD 69	Skokie
95	12,591	Lake Zurich CUSD 95	Lake Zurich
96	12,564	Glen Ellyn SD 41	Glen Ellyn
97	12,473	Glen Ellyn CCSD 89	Glen Ellyn

Note: This section only includes districts with 1,500 or more students; All categories are ranked from high to low

98	12,464	South Holland SD 151	South Holland
99	12,453	Wilmette SD 39	Wilmette
100	12,439	East St Louis SD 189	E Saint Louis
101	12,391	Frankfort CCSD 157C	Frankfort
102	12,326	East Maine SD 63	Des Plaines
103	12,297	Saint Charles CUSD 303	Saint Charles
104	12,160	Gurnee SD 56	Gurnee
105	12,126	Fremont SD 79	Mundelein
106	12,039	Homer Community CSD 33c	Homer Glen
107	11,904	Crete Monee CUSD 201u	Crete
108	11,888	City of Chicago SD 299	Chicago
109	11,886	Kaneland CUSD 302	Maple Park
110	11,874	Community Unit SD 200	Wheaton
111	11,869	Hononegah Community HSD 207	Rockton
112	11,868	North Palos SD 117	Palos Hills
113	11,863	School District 45 Dupage County	Villa Park
114	11,843	Valley View CUSD #365U	Romeoville
115	11,814	Burbank SD 111	Burbank
116	11,799	Homewood SD 153	Homewood
117	11,756	Libertyville SD 70	Libertyville
118	11,744	Flossmoor SD 161	Chicago Heights
119	11,709	North Chicago SD 187	North Chicago
120	11,644	Belleville Twp HSD 201	Belleville
121	11,632	Troy Community CSD 30C	Plainfield
122	11,627	Macomb Community Unit SD 185	Macomb
122	11,627	Sycamore CUSD 427	Sycamore
124	11,617	Mascoutah CUD 19	Mascoutah
125	11,563	Harvey SD 152	Harvey
126	11,549	Elem SD 159	Matteson
127	11,478	Oak Lawn-Hometown SD 123	Oak Lawn
128	11,428	Springfield SD 186	Springfield
129	11,426	Lansing SD 158	Lansing
130	11,410	Rockford SD 205	Rockford
131	11,398	Chicago Heights SD 170	Chicago Heights
132	11,390	Downers Grove Grade SD 58	Downers Grove
133	11,371	Batavia Unit SD 101	Batavia
134	11,354	Keeneyville SD 20	Hanover Park
135	11,311	Ridgeland SD 122	Oak Lawn
136	11,277	Palatine CCSD 15	Palatine
137	11,259	La Grange SD 102	La Grange Park
138	11,257	Peoria SD 150	Peoria
139	11,241	J S Morton HS District 201	Cicero
140	11,236	United Twp HS District 30	East Moline
141	11,204	Woodland CCSD 50	Gurnee
142	11,201	Will County SD 92	Lockport
143	11,184	West Chicago Elem SD 33	West Chicago
144	11,162	Cahokia Community Unit SD 187	Cahokia
145	11,131	Morton CUSD 709	Morton
146	11,121	Lyons SD 103	Lyons
147	11,110	Matteson Elem SD 162	Matteson
148	11,063	O'Fallon Twp High SD 203	O Fallon
149	11,046	Dolton SD 149	Calumet City
150	11,013	Rock Island SD 41	Rock Island
151	11,000	Freeport SD 145	Freeport
152	10,976	Kirby SD 140	Tinley Park
153	10,938	Bloomington SD 87	Bloomington
154	10,928	Mount Prospect SD 57	Mount Prospect
155	10,899	Yorkville Community Unit SD 115	Yorkville
156	10,892	Wauconda Community Unit SD 118	Wauconda
157	10,891	Community Consolidated SD 46	Grayslake
158	10,830	Community CSD 168	Sauk Village
159	10,827	Oswego Community Unit SD 308	Oswego
160	10,822	Plano Community Unit SD 88	Plano
161	10,701	Queen Bee SD 16	Glendale Hgts
162	10,700	Champaign Community Unit SD 4	Champaign
163	10,686	Reed Custer CUSD 255U	Braidwood
164	10,648	East Moline SD 37	East Moline
165	10,630	Kankakee SD 111	Kankakee
166	10,609	Dekalb Community Unit SD 428	Dekalb
167	10,554	Indian Prairie CUSD 204	Aurora
168	10,552	Community Unit SD 300	Carpentersville
169	10,547	Big Hollow SD 38	Ingleside
170	10,489	Mundelein Elem SD 75	Mundelein
171	10,486	East Peoria SD 86	East Peoria
172	10,426	Cook County SD 130	Blue Island
173	10,423	Moline Unit SD 40	Moline
174	10,414	Steger SD 194	Steger
175	10,393	Manteno Community Unit SD 5	Manteno
176	10,357	Zion Elementary SD 6	Zion
177	10,350	Murphysboro CUSD 186	Murphysboro
178	10,325	Johnsburg CUSD 12	Johnsburg
179	10,284	Consolidated SD 158	Algonquin
180	10,267	Mchenry CCSD 15	Mchenry
181	10,260	Mount Vernon SD 80	Mount Vernon
182	10,240	Canton Union SD 66	Canton
183	10,207	School District U-46	Elgin
184	10,194	Ottawa Elem SD 141	Ottawa
185	10,188	Darien SD 61	Darien
186	10,171	Pekin Community HSD 303	Pekin
187	10,167	Harvard CUSD 50	Harvard
188	10,156	Winnebago CUSD 323	Winnebago
189	10,137	Round Lake Area Schs - Dist 116	Round Lake
190	10,080	Sterling CUD 5	Sterling
191	10,077	Danville CCSD 118	Danville
192	10,063	Monticello CUSD 25	Monticello
193	10,041	Belleville SD 118	Belleville
194	10,036	Berkeley SD 87	Berkeley
195	9,980	Crystal Lake CCSD 47	Crystal Lake
196	9,978	Edwardsville CUSD 7	Edwardsville
197	9,960	Beach Park CCSD 3	Beach Park
198	9,921	Joliet Public SD 86	Joliet
199	9,895	Mattoon CUSD 2	Mattoon
200	9,885	Western Springs SD 101	Western Springs
201	9,879	Harlem Unit Dist 122	Machesney Park
202	9,852	Aurora West Unit SD 129	Aurora
203	9,843	Decatur SD 61	Decatur
204	9,841	Antioch CCSD 34	Antioch
204	9,841	Maywood-Melrose Park-Broadview-89	Melrose Park
206	9,810	North Boone CUSD 200	Poplar Grove
207	9,809	Waukegan CUSD 60	Waukegan
208	9,779	Charleston CUSD 1	Charleston
208	9,779	Du Quoin CUSD 300	Du Quoin
210	9,747	Dixon Unit SD 170	Dixon
211	9,742	Oregon CUSD 220	Oregon
212	9,705	Prairie Central CUSD 8	Fairbury
213	9,692	Plainfield SD 202	Plainfield
214	9,691	Summit Hill SD 161	Frankfort
215	9,678	Bradley Bourbonnais CHSD 307	Bradley
216	9,653	Alton Community Unit SD 11	Alton
217	9,640	Waterloo CUSD 5	Waterloo
218	9,591	Clinton CUSD 15	Clinton
219	9,584	Forest Ridge SD 142	Oak Forest
220	9,568	Cary CCSD 26	Cary
221	9,563	Prairie-Hills Elem SD 144	Markham
222	9,562	Roxana Community Unit SD 1	Roxana
223	9,516	Bellwood SD 88	Bellwood
224	9,479	Rochelle Community CD 231	Rochelle
225	9,453	Robinson CUSD 2	Robinson
226	9,445	Streator Elem SD 44	Streator
227	9,444	Berwyn South SD 100	Berwyn
228	9,442	Vandalia CUSD 203	Vandalia
229	9,434	Pekin Public SD 108	Pekin
230	9,389	Highland Community Unit SD 5	Highland
231	9,377	Jacksonville SD 117	Jacksonville
232	9,374	Dunlap CUSD 323	Dunlap
233	9,368	Rantoul City SD 137	Rantoul
234	9,362	Herscher Community Unit SD 2	Herscher
235	9,353	Millburn CCSD 24	Old Mill Creek
236	9,345	Sandwich CUSD 430	Sandwich
237	9,299	Channahon SD 17	Channahon
238	9,291	Quincy SD 172	Quincy
239	9,281	Mahomet-Seymour CUSD 3	Mahomet
240	9,265	New Lenox SD 122	New Lenox
241	9,235	Berwyn North SD 98	Berwyn
242	9,219	Peotone CUSD 207U	Peotone
243	9,213	Olympia CUSD 16	Stanford
244	9,196	Rockton SD 140	Rockton
245	9,180	Genoa Kingston CUSD 424	Genoa
246	9,177	Belvidere CUSD 100	Belvidere
247	9,172	Addison SD 4	Addison
248	9,144	Ball Chatham CUSD 5	Chatham
249	9,139	Indian Springs SD 109	Justice
250	9,129	Hillsboro Community Unit SD 3	Hillsboro
250	9,129	Triad Community Unit SD 2	Troy
252	9,128	Galesburg CUSD 205	Galesburg
253	9,105	Lake Villa CCSD 41	Lake Villa
254	9,100	Columbia Community Unit SD 4	Columbia
255	9,093	Cicero SD 99	Cicero
256	9,072	Meridian CUSD 223	Stillman Valley
257	9,061	Collinsville CUSD 10	Collinsville
257	9,061	Paxton-Buckley-Loda CUD 10	Paxton
259	9,056	Beardstown CUSD 15	Beardstown
260	9,042	Lemont-Bromberek CSD 113A	Lemont
261	9,032	Litchfield CUSD 12	Litchfield
262	9,023	Eureka C U Dist 140	Eureka
263	9,020	Jersey CUSD 100	Jerseyville
264	9,017	Geneseo Community Unit SD 228	Geneseo
264	9,017	Sherrard Community Unit SD 200	Sherrard
266	8,964	Tolono CUSD 7	Tolono
267	8,950	Bethalto CUSD 8	Bethalto
268	8,946	Effingham Community Unit SD 40	Effingham
269	8,923	O'Fallon CCSD 90	O Fallon
270	8,913	Bradley SD 61	Bradley
271	8,844	Mokena SD 159	Mokena
272	8,798	Midlothian SD 143	Midlothian
273	8,772	Granite City CUSD 9	Granite City
274	8,770	East Richland CUSD 1	Olney
275	8,767	Posen-Robbins Elem SD 143-5	Posen
276	8,755	Kewanee Community Unit SD 229	Kewanee
277	8,729	Illinois Valley CUD 321	Chillicothe
278	8,609	Minooka Community CSD 201	Minooka
279	8,600	Marion Community Unit SD 2	Marion
280	8,398	Carterville CUSD 5	Carterville
281	8,384	Rochester CUSD 3A	Rochester
282	8,361	Herrin CUSD 4	Herrin
283	8,326	Aurora East Unit SD 131	Aurora
284	8,315	Southwestern CUSD 9	Piasa
285	8,287	Harrisburg CUSD 3	Harrisburg
286	8,252	Massac Unit District #1	Metropolis
287	8,225	Monmouth-Roseville CUSD 238	Monmouth
288	8,159	Mclean County Unit Dist No 5	Normal
289	8,127	Bourbonnais SD 53	Bourbonnais
290	8,125	Bond County CUSD 2	Greenville
291	8,061	Mount Zion Community Unit SD 3	Mount Zion
292	8,036	Auburn CUSD 10	Auburn
293	8,020	Wabash CUSD 348	Mount Carmel
294	7,823	Kinnikinnick CCSD 131	Roscoe
295	7,720	Frankfort Community Unit SD 168	West Frankfort
296	7,681	Riverton CUSD 14	Riverton
297	7,217	Taylorville CUSD 3	Taylorville

Long-Term Debt per Student (end of FY)

Rank	Dollars	District Name	City
1	35,552	Lemont Twp HSD 210	Lemont
2	34,455	Lake Forest CHSD 115	Lake Forest
3	32,147	Minooka Community HS District 111	Minooka
4	31,128	Winnetka SD 36	Winnetka
5	29,745	Lincoln Way Community HSD 210	New Lenox
6	29,385	Niles Twp Community High SD 219	Skokie
7	28,613	Geneva Community Unit SD 304	Geneva
8	27,960	Big Hollow SD 38	Ingleside
9	26,536	Grayslake Com High SD 127	Grayslake
10	25,871	Oswego Community Unit SD 308	Oswego
11	25,661	Grant Community HS District 124	Fox Lake
12	24,747	Minooka Community CSD 201	Minooka
13	21,701	New Lenox SD 122	New Lenox
14	21,278	Du Page High SD 88	Addison
15	20,999	Frankfort CCSD 157C	Frankfort
16	20,985	O'Fallon Twp High SD 203	O Fallon
17	20,764	Kaneland CUSD 302	Maple Park
18	20,611	Northfield Twp High SD 225	Glenview
19	20,610	Woodstock CUSD 200	Woodstock
20	20,404	CCSD 181	Westmont
21	20,018	Troy Community CSD 30C	Plainfield
22	19,800	Summit SD 104	Summit
23	19,216	Crete Monee CUSD 201u	Crete
24	18,484	Edwardsville CUSD 7	Edwardsville
25	18,104	Wauconda Community Unit SD 118	Wauconda
26	17,953	Lake Park Community HSD 108	Roselle
27	17,904	Batavia Unit SD 101	Batavia
28	17,533	Township High SD 113	Highland Park
29	17,426	Triad Community Unit SD 2	Troy
30	17,318	Yorkville Community Unit SD 115	Yorkville
31	16,975	Summit Hill SD 161	Frankfort
32	16,743	Elmhurst SD 205	Elmhurst
32	16,743	Waterloo CUSD 5	Waterloo
34	16,629	Elem SD 159	Matteson
35	16,589	Oak Lawn-Hometown SD 123	Oak Lawn
36	16,565	Byron Community Unit SD 226	Byron
37	15,966	Central Community Unit SD 301	Burlington
38	15,631	Manteno Community Unit SD 5	Manteno
39	15,500	Consolidated SD 158	Algonquin
40	15,265	Community Unit SD 300	Carpentersville
41	15,235	Belleville Twp HSD 201	Belleville
42	14,733	Valley View CUSD #365U	Romeoville
43	14,577	Millburn CCSD 24	Old Mill Creek
44	14,527	Mchenry Community HSD 156	Mchenry
45	14,485	Mclean County Unit Dist No 5	Normal
46	14,411	Fremont SD 79	Mundelein
47	14,219	Plainfield SD 202	Plainfield

Note: This section only includes districts with 1,500 or more students; All categories are ranked from high to low

48	14,116	Columbia Community Unit SD 4	Columbia
49	14,091	Rich Twp HS District 227	Olympia Fields
50	14,089	Community Unit SD 200	Wheaton
51	13,514	Plano Community Unit SD 88	Plano
52	13,442	Community Consolidated SD 46	Grayslake
53	13,368	Sycamore CUSD 427	Sycamore
54	13,366	Robinson CUSD 2	Robinson
55	12,970	Tinley Park CCSD 146	Tinley Park
56	12,624	Dunlap CUSD 323	Dunlap
57	12,519	Community High SD 99	Downers Grove
58	12,460	Warren Twp High SD 121	Gurnee
59	12,298	Rochester CUSD 3A	Rochester
60	12,151	Indian Prairie CUSD 204	Aurora
61	12,078	Woodland CCSD 50	Gurnee
62	12,053	Saint Charles CUSD 303	Saint Charles
63	11,953	Ridgeland SD 122	Oak Lawn
64	11,824	Joliet Twp HSD 204	Joliet
65	11,648	Community High SD 128	Vernon Hills
66	11,620	Highland Community Unit SD 5	Highland
67	11,552	Peotone CUSD 207U	Peotone
68	11,504	City of Chicago SD 299	Chicago
69	11,491	Barrington CUSD 220	Barrington
70	10,800	Lake Zurich CUSD 95	Lake Zurich
71	10,641	Community High SD 94	West Chicago
72	10,422	Cons High SD 230	Orland Park
73	10,409	O'Fallon CCSD 90	O Fallon
74	10,016	La Grange SD 102	La Grange Park
75	9,890	Hawthorn CCSD 73	Vernon Hills
76	9,704	Skokie SD 69	Skokie
77	9,547	North Boone CUSD 200	Poplar Grove
78	9,542	Aurora West Unit SD 129	Aurora
79	9,304	Proviso Twp HSD 209	Forest Park
80	9,090	Gurnee SD 56	Gurnee
81	9,089	Lockport Twp HSD 205	Lockport
82	9,047	Community High SD 117	Lake Villa
83	8,846	Bond County CUSD 2	Greenville
84	8,657	Lisle CUSD 202	Lisle
85	8,621	Belvidere CUSD 100	Belvidere
86	8,611	Forest Ridge SD 142	Oak Forest
87	8,551	Tolono CUSD 7	Tolono
88	8,506	Western Springs SD 101	Western Springs
89	8,466	School District 45 Dupage County	Villa Park
90	8,335	School District U-46	Elgin
91	8,315	Hononegah Community HSD 207	Rockton
92	8,299	Vandalia CUSD 203	Vandalia
93	8,272	Roxana Community Unit SD 1	Roxana
94	8,230	J S Morton HS District 201	Cicero
95	8,155	Cary CCSD 26	Cary
96	8,071	Orland SD 135	Orland Park
97	8,023	Berwyn South SD 100	Berwyn
98	8,010	Evanston Twp HSD 202	Evanston
99	7,935	Alton Community Unit SD 11	Alton
100	7,918	North Shore SD 112	Highland Park
101	7,697	North Palos SD 117	Palos Hills
102	7,689	Mahomet-Seymour CUSD 3	Mahomet
103	7,656	Matteson Elem SD 162	Matteson
104	7,629	Wheeling CCSD 21	Wheeling
105	7,587	Adlai E Stevenson Dist 125	Lincolnshire
106	7,563	Lemont-Bromberek CSD 113A	Lemont
107	7,523	Mannheim SD 83	Franklin Park
108	7,511	Lake Villa CCSD 41	Lake Villa
109	7,501	Monticello CUSD 25	Monticello
110	7,218	Berkeley SD 87	Berkeley
111	7,177	Channahon SD 17	Channahon
112	7,064	Beach Park CCSD 3	Beach Park
113	7,025	Urbana SD 116	Urbana
114	6,985	Arlington Hgts SD 25	Arlington Hgts
114	6,985	Thornton Fractional HSD 215	Calumet City
116	6,927	Evanston CCSD 65	Evanston
117	6,923	West Harvey-Dixmoor PSD 147	Harvey
118	6,919	Olympia CUSD 16	Stanford
119	6,890	Ball Chatham CUSD 5	Chatham
120	6,889	Dekalb Community Unit SD 428	Dekalb
121	6,875	Homewood Flossmoor CHSD 233	Flossmoor
122	6,861	Coal City CUSD 1	Coal City
123	6,835	Bloomington SD 87	Bloomington
124	6,755	Aurora East Unit SD 131	Aurora
125	6,754	Joliet Public SD 86	Joliet
126	6,748	Du Quoin CUSD 300	Du Quoin
127	6,727	Mundelein Elem SD 75	Mundelein
128	6,709	Oak Park Elem SD 97	Oak Park
129	6,669	Round Lake Area Schs - Dist 116	Round Lake
130	6,618	Oak Park & River Forest Dist 200	Oak Park
131	6,587	Lombard SD 44	Lombard
132	6,556	Zion-Benton Twp HSD 126	Zion
133	6,527	Homewood SD 153	Homewood
134	6,357	East Peoria SD 86	East Peoria
135	6,215	Community High SD 218	Oak Lawn
136	6,089	Bloom Twp High SD 206	Chicago Heights
137	6,042	Elmwood Park CUSD 401	Elmwood Park
138	6,035	Glenview CCSD 34	Glenview
139	5,998	Bellwood SD 88	Bellwood
140	5,960	Bremen Community HS District 228	Midlothian
141	5,940	Burbank SD 111	Burbank
142	5,928	Johnsburg CUSD 12	Johnsburg
143	5,911	Addison SD 4	Addison
144	5,908	Deerfield SD 109	Deerfield
145	5,868	East Maine SD 63	Des Plaines
146	5,854	Glen Ellyn SD 41	Glen Ellyn
147	5,812	Glen Ellyn CCSD 89	Glen Ellyn
148	5,788	Herscher Community Unit SD 2	Herscher
149	5,741	Oak Lawn Community HSD 229	Oak Lawn
150	5,615	Dolton SD 148	Riverdale
151	5,570	Queen Bee SD 16	Glendale Hgts
152	5,450	Argo Community HSD 217	Summit
153	5,426	Riverton CUSD 14	Riverton
154	5,404	Pekin Community HSD 303	Pekin
155	5,379	Mokena SD 159	Mokena
156	5,362	Leyden Community HSD 212	Franklin Park
157	5,326	Dolton SD 149	Calumet City
158	5,284	Freeport SD 145	Freeport
159	5,272	Genoa Kingston CUSD 424	Genoa
160	5,260	Evergreen Park Elem SD 124	Evergreen Park
161	5,196	Skokie SD 68	Skokie
162	5,158	Alsip-Hazelgreen-Oak Lawn SD 126	Alsip
163	5,054	East Richland CUSD 1	Olney
164	4,962	Keeneyville SD 20	Hanover Park
165	4,941	Park Ridge CCSD 64	Park Ridge
166	4,924	Winnebago CUSD 323	Winnebago
167	4,908	Collinsville CUSD 10	Collinsville
167	4,908	Prairie Central CUSD 8	Fairbury
169	4,824	Westmont CUSD 201	Westmont
170	4,799	Jersey CUSD 100	Jerseyville
171	4,767	Bourbonnais SD 53	Bourbonnais
172	4,745	Mount Prospect SD 57	Mount Prospect
173	4,724	Wilmette SD 39	Wilmette
174	4,687	Glenbard Twp HSD 87	Glen Ellyn
175	4,675	East St Louis SD 189	E Saint Louis
176	4,669	Carterville CUSD 5	Carterville
177	4,660	Litchfield CUSD 12	Litchfield
178	4,641	Will County SD 92	Lockport
179	4,565	Antioch CCSD 34	Antioch
180	4,472	Mattoon CUSD 2	Mattoon
181	4,465	Lyons SD 103	Lyons
182	4,421	Cook County SD 130	Blue Island
183	4,416	Zion Elementary SD 6	Zion
184	4,383	Paxton-Buckley-Loda CUD 10	Paxton
185	4,337	Lansing SD 158	Lansing
186	4,311	New Trier Twp HSD 203	Northfield
187	4,239	Palatine CCSD 15	Palatine
188	4,227	Meridian CUSD 223	Stillman Valley
189	4,215	Mundelein Cons High SD 120	Mundelein
190	4,211	Harlem Unit Dist 122	Machesney Park
191	4,171	Kinnikinnick CCSD 131	Roscoe
192	4,117	Southwestern CUSD 9	Piasa
193	4,089	Herrin CUSD 4	Herrin
194	4,037	Steger SD 194	Steger
195	4,027	Community High SD 155	Crystal Lake
196	4,023	Hillsboro Community Unit SD 3	Hillsboro
197	3,995	Kildeer Countryside CCSD 96	Buffalo Grove
198	3,982	Belleville SD 118	Belleville
199	3,977	Maywood-Melrose Park-Broadview-89	Melrose Park
200	3,925	Sterling CUD 5	Sterling
201	3,896	Township HSD 211	Palatine
202	3,837	Woodridge SD 68	Woodridge
203	3,786	Community CSD 59	Arlington Hgts
204	3,689	Mchenry CCSD 15	Mchenry
205	3,650	Charleston CUSD 1	Charleston
206	3,640	Mount Zion Community Unit SD 3	Mount Zion
207	3,614	Community Consolidated SD 93	Bloomingdale
208	3,580	Thornton Twp HSD 205	South Holland
209	3,567	Marquardt SD 15	Glendale Hgts
210	3,492	Quincy SD 172	Quincy
211	3,456	Massac Unit District #1	Metropolis
212	3,427	Bethalto CUSD 8	Bethalto
213	3,394	Cicero SD 99	Cicero
214	3,382	Reavis Twp HSD 220	Burbank
215	3,372	Crystal Lake CCSD 47	Crystal Lake
216	3,337	Libertyville SD 70	Libertyville
217	3,327	Rockford SD 205	Rockford
218	3,324	Posen-Robbins Elem SD 143-5	Posen
219	3,321	Beardstown CUSD 15	Beardstown
220	3,263	Lyons Twp HSD 204	La Grange
221	3,228	Waukegan CUSD 60	Waukegan
222	3,199	Rock Island SD 41	Rock Island
223	3,130	Chicago Heights SD 170	Chicago Heights
224	3,096	Darien SD 61	Darien
225	3,093	Sherrard Community Unit SD 200	Sherrard
226	3,089	Sandwich CUSD 430	Sandwich
227	3,083	Geneseo Community Unit SD 228	Geneseo
228	3,025	Effingham Community Unit SD 40	Effingham
229	2,966	Indian Springs SD 109	Justice
230	2,951	Aptakisic-Tripp CCSD 102	Buffalo Grove
231	2,927	Berwyn North SD 98	Berwyn
232	2,915	Rochelle Community CD 231	Rochelle
233	2,894	Murphysboro CUSD 186	Murphysboro
234	2,803	Taylorville CUSD 3	Taylorville
235	2,802	Kankakee SD 111	Kankakee
236	2,758	North Chicago SD 187	North Chicago
237	2,712	Illinois Valley CUD 321	Chillicothe
238	2,687	Kirby SD 140	Tinley Park
239	2,670	East Moline SD 37	East Moline
240	2,641	West Chicago Elem SD 33	West Chicago
241	2,546	Streator Elem SD 44	Streator
242	2,531	Harrisburg CUSD 3	Harrisburg
243	2,311	Palos Community CSD 118	Palos Park
244	2,292	Township High SD 214	Arlington Hgts
245	2,285	Rockton SD 140	Rockton
246	2,211	Champaign Community Unit SD 4	Champaign
247	2,147	Maine Township HSD 207	Park Ridge
248	2,139	Harvey SD 152	Harvey
249	2,109	Ottawa Elem SD 141	Ottawa
250	2,103	Mount Vernon SD 80	Mount Vernon
251	2,063	Wabash CUSD 348	Mount Carmel
252	2,059	Hinsdale Twp HSD 86	Hinsdale
253	2,055	Midlothian SD 143	Midlothian
254	2,050	Harvard CUSD 50	Harvard
255	2,023	Frankfort Community Unit SD 168	West Frankfort
256	1,989	Fenton Community HSD 100	Bensenville
257	1,986	Oregon CUSD 220	Oregon
258	1,941	Bradley Bourbonnais CHSD 307	Bradley
259	1,842	Granite City CUSD 9	Granite City
260	1,681	Prairie-Hills Elem SD 144	Markham
261	1,605	Lake Forest SD 67	Lake Forest
262	1,573	Bensenville SD 2	Bensenville
263	1,563	Cahokia Community Unit SD 187	Cahokia
264	1,549	Decatur SD 61	Decatur
265	1,539	United Twp HS District 30	East Moline
266	1,482	Kewanee Community Unit SD 229	Kewanee
267	1,471	Danville CCSD 118	Danville
268	1,470	Canton Union SD 66	Canton
269	1,453	Clinton CUSD 15	Clinton
270	1,421	South Holland SD 151	South Holland
271	1,396	Park Forest SD 163	Park Forest
272	1,369	Springfield SD 186	Springfield
273	1,361	Auburn CUSD 10	Auburn
274	1,351	Macomb Community Unit SD 185	Macomb
275	1,230	Eureka C U Dist 140	Eureka
276	1,210	Peoria SD 150	Peoria
277	1,192	Moline Unit SD 40	Moline
278	1,159	Schaumburg CCSD 54	Schaumburg
279	1,133	Flossmoor SD 161	Chicago Heights
280	1,113	Dixon Unit SD 170	Dixon
281	982	Downers Grove Grade SD 58	Downers Grove
281	982	Galesburg CUSD 205	Galesburg
283	961	Marion Community Unit SD 2	Marion
284	905	Bradley SD 61	Bradley
285	557	Morton CUSD 709	Morton
286	549	Naperville CUD 203	Naperville
287	448	Community CSD 168	Sauk Village
288	378	Pekin Public SD 108	Pekin
289	86	Homer Community CSD 33c	Homer Glen
290	0	Community Consolidated SD 62	Des Plaines
290	0	Jacksonville SD 117	Jacksonville
290	0	Mascoutah CUD 19	Mascoutah
290	0	Monmouth-Roseville CUSD 238	Monmouth
290	0	Northbrook SD 28	Northbrook
290	0	Rantoul City SD 137	Rantoul
290	0	Reed Custer CUSD 255U	Braidwood
290	0	Riverside SD 96	Riverside

Note: This section only includes districts with 1,500 or more students; All categories are ranked from high to low

Number of Diploma Recipients

Rank	Number	District Name	City
1	20,082	City of Chicago SD 299	Chicago
2	2,895	Township HSD 211	Palatine
3	2,894	Township High SD 214	Arlington Hgts
4	2,455	School District U-46	Elgin
5	2,207	Cons High SD 230	Orland Park
6	2,054	Glenbard Twp HSD 87	Glen Ellyn
7	1,643	Plainfield SD 202	Plainfield
8	1,636	Lincoln Way Community HSD 210	New Lenox
9	1,611	Community High SD 155	Crystal Lake
10	1,579	Naperville CUD 203	Naperville
11	1,538	J S Morton HS District 201	Cicero
12	1,453	Maine Township HSD 207	Park Ridge
13	1,367	Rockford SD 205	Rockford
14	1,326	Community Unit SD 300	Carpentersville
15	1,229	Community High SD 99	Downers Grove
16	1,174	Niles Twp Community High SD 219	Skokie
17	1,171	Belleville Twp HSD 201	Belleville
18	1,152	Northfield Twp High SD 225	Glenview
19	1,140	Valley View CUSD #365U	Romeoville
20	1,130	Thornton Twp HSD 205	South Holland
21	1,129	Adlai E Stevenson Dist 125	Lincolnshire
22	1,116	Community High SD 218	Oak Lawn
23	1,110	Community Unit SD 200	Wheaton
24	1,081	Bremen Community HS District 228	Midlothian
25	1,059	Hinsdale Twp HSD 86	Hinsdale
26	1,037	Saint Charles CUSD 303	Saint Charles
27	1,022	New Trier Twp HSD 203	Northfield
28	998	Rich Twp HS District 227	Olympia Fields
29	897	Du Page High SD 88	Addison
30	893	Proviso Twp HSD 209	Forest Park
31	887	Lyons Twp HSD 204	La Grange
32	871	Joliet Twp HSD 204	Joliet
33	859	Township High SD 113	Highland Park
34	848	Warren Twp High SD 121	Gurnee
35	846	Community High SD 128	Vernon Hills
36	843	Lockport Twp HSD 205	Lockport
37	833	Peoria SD 150	Peoria
38	811	Waukegan CUSD 60	Waukegan
39	795	Oswego Community Unit SD 308	Oswego
40	771	Mclean County Unit Dist No 5	Normal
41	725	Lake Park Community HSD 108	Roselle
42	711	Oak Park & River Forest Dist 200	Oak Park
43	699	Leyden Community HSD 212	Franklin Park
44	692	Barrington CUSD 220	Barrington
45	684	Springfield SD 186	Springfield
46	636	Community High SD 117	Lake Villa
46	636	Homewood Flossmoor CHSD 233	Flossmoor
48	635	Evanston Twp HSD 202	Evanston
49	623	Aurora West Unit SD 129	Aurora
50	620	Thornton Fractional HSD 215	Calumet City
51	606	Mchenry Community HSD 156	Mchenry
52	599	Elmhurst SD 205	Elmhurst
53	596	Grayslake Com High SD 127	Grayslake
54	594	Bloom Twp High SD 206	Chicago Heights
55	578	Champaign Community Unit SD 4	Champaign
56	563	Edwardsville CUSD 7	Edwardsville
56	563	O'Fallon Twp High SD 203	O Fallon
58	525	Minooka Community HS District 111	Minooka
59	509	Aurora East Unit SD 131	Aurora
60	499	Lake Zurich CUSD 95	Lake Zurich
61	490	Harlem Unit Dist 122	Machesney Park
62	488	Zion-Benton Twp HSD 126	Zion
63	484	Mundelein Cons High SD 120	Mundelein
64	478	Geneva Community Unit SD 304	Geneva
65	472	Moline Unit SD 40	Moline
66	467	Alton Community Unit SD 11	Alton
66	467	Quincy SD 172	Quincy
68	455	East St Louis SD 189	E Saint Louis
69	448	Pekin Community HSD 303	Pekin
70	447	Decatur SD 61	Decatur
71	446	Bradley Bourbonnais CHSD 307	Bradley
72	443	Batavia Unit SD 101	Batavia
73	441	Belvidere CUSD 100	Belvidere
74	440	Woodstock CUSD 200	Woodstock
75	436	Community High SD 94	West Chicago
76	428	Collinsville CUSD 10	Collinsville
77	427	Hononegah Community HSD 207	Rockton
78	418	Granite City CUSD 9	Granite City
79	414	Lake Forest CHSD 115	Lake Forest
80	407	Oak Lawn Community HSD 229	Oak Lawn
81	402	Reavis Twp HSD 220	Burbank
82	392	Consolidated SD 158	Algonquin
82	392	Grant Community HS District 124	Fox Lake
84	367	United Twp HS District 30	East Moline
85	365	Argo Community HSD 217	Summit
86	354	Lemont Twp HSD 210	Lemont
87	350	Ball Chatham CUSD 5	Chatham
87	350	Dekalb Community Unit SD 428	Dekalb
89	348	Crete Monee CUSD 201u	Crete
90	321	Triad Community Unit SD 2	Troy
91	310	Rock Island SD 41	Rock Island
91	310	Round Lake Area Schs - Dist 116	Round Lake
93	307	Fenton Community HSD 100	Bensenville
94	306	Bloomington SD 87	Bloomington
95	305	Wauconda Community Unit SD 118	Wauconda
96	302	Yorkville Community Unit SD 115	Yorkville
97	294	Sycamore CUSD 427	Sycamore
98	290	Freeport SD 145	Freeport
99	284	Jacksonville SD 117	Jacksonville
100	277	Danville CCSD 118	Danville
101	272	Kaneland CUSD 302	Maple Park
102	261	Galesburg CUSD 205	Galesburg
103	243	Marion Community Unit SD 2	Marion
104	240	Kankakee SD 111	Kankakee
105	233	Highland Community Unit SD 5	Highland
106	232	Mattoon CUSD 2	Mattoon
107	231	Jersey CUSD 100	Jerseyville
108	230	Central Community Unit SD 301	Burlington
109	228	Dunlap CUSD 323	Dunlap
110	225	Sterling CUD 5	Sterling
111	224	Effingham Community Unit SD 40	Effingham
112	222	Cahokia Community Unit SD 187	Cahokia
112	222	Urbana SD 116	Urbana
112	222	Waterloo CUSD 5	Waterloo
115	218	Geneseo Community Unit SD 228	Geneseo
116	213	Mahomet-Seymour CUSD 3	Mahomet
117	209	Johnsburg CUSD 12	Johnsburg
118	207	Mascoutah CUD 19	Mascoutah
118	207	Taylorville CUSD 3	Taylorville
120	205	Morton CUSD 709	Morton
121	202	Elmwood Park CUSD 401	Elmwood Park
122	194	Dixon Unit SD 170	Dixon
123	190	Mount Zion Community Unit SD 3	Mount Zion
124	188	Charleston CUSD 1	Charleston
124	188	Sandwich CUSD 430	Sandwich
126	181	Bethalto CUSD 8	Bethalto
127	172	Peotone CUSD 207U	Peotone
128	171	Manteno Community Unit SD 5	Manteno
129	164	Reed Custer CUSD 255U	Braidwood
130	162	Illinois Valley CUD 321	Chillicothe
131	161	Canton Union SD 66	Canton
132	158	Prairie Central CUSD 8	Fairbury
133	157	Olympia CUSD 16	Stanford
134	153	Harvard CUSD 50	Harvard
135	152	Herscher Community Unit SD 2	Herscher
136	151	North Chicago SD 187	North Chicago
136	151	Rochester CUSD 3A	Rochester
138	150	Murphysboro CUSD 186	Murphysboro
138	150	Winnebago CUSD 323	Winnebago
140	148	Coal City CUSD 1	Coal City
140	148	Massac Unit District #1	Metropolis
140	148	Oregon CUSD 220	Oregon
143	144	Wabash CUSD 348	Mount Carmel
144	143	East Richland CUSD 1	Olney
145	142	Byron Community Unit SD 226	Byron
145	142	Herrin CUSD 4	Herrin
147	141	Columbia Community Unit SD 4	Columbia
148	138	Macomb Community Unit SD 185	Macomb
149	133	Meridian CUSD 223	Stillman Valley
149	133	Vandalia CUSD 203	Vandalia
151	132	Plano Community Unit SD 88	Plano
151	132	Roxana Community Unit SD 1	Roxana
153	131	Lisle CUSD 202	Lisle
154	126	Eureka C U Dist 140	Eureka
155	125	Harrisburg CUSD 3	Harrisburg
156	122	Tolono CUSD 7	Tolono
157	121	Carterville CUSD 5	Carterville
158	117	Genoa Kingston CUSD 424	Genoa
158	117	Monticello CUSD 25	Monticello
160	116	Bond County CUSD 2	Greenville
161	113	Robinson CUSD 2	Robinson
162	111	Westmont CUSD 201	Westmont
163	108	Hillsboro Community Unit SD 3	Hillsboro
163	108	Paxton-Buckley-Loda CUD 10	Paxton
163	108	Sherrard Community Unit SD 200	Sherrard
163	108	Southwestern CUSD 9	Piasa
167	105	Kewanee Community Unit SD 229	Kewanee
168	104	North Boone CUSD 200	Poplar Grove
169	103	Du Quoin CUSD 300	Du Quoin
170	101	Monmouth-Roseville CUSD 238	Monmouth
171	95	Frankfort Community Unit SD 168	West Frankfort
172	94	Riverton CUSD 14	Riverton
173	92	Litchfield CUSD 12	Litchfield
174	89	Auburn CUSD 10	Auburn
175	88	Beardstown CUSD 15	Beardstown
176	25	Indian Prairie CUSD 204	Aurora
n/a	n/a	Addison SD 4	Addison
n/a	n/a	Alsip-Hazelgreen-Oak Lawn SD 126	Alsip
n/a	n/a	Antioch CCSD 34	Antioch
n/a	n/a	Aptakisic-Tripp CCSD 102	Buffalo Grove
n/a	n/a	Arlington Hgts SD 25	Arlington Hgts
n/a	n/a	Beach Park CCSD 3	Beach Park
n/a	n/a	Belleville SD 118	Belleville
n/a	n/a	Bellwood SD 88	Bellwood
n/a	n/a	Bensenville SD 2	Bensenville
n/a	n/a	Berkeley SD 87	Berkeley
n/a	n/a	Berwyn North SD 98	Berwyn
n/a	n/a	Berwyn South SD 100	Berwyn
n/a	n/a	Big Hollow SD 38	Ingleside
n/a	n/a	Bourbonnais SD 53	Bourbonnais
n/a	n/a	Bradley SD 61	Bradley
n/a	n/a	Burbank SD 111	Burbank
n/a	n/a	CCSD 181	Westmont
n/a	n/a	Cary CCSD 26	Cary
n/a	n/a	Channahon SD 17	Channahon
n/a	n/a	Chicago Heights SD 170	Chicago Heights
n/a	n/a	Cicero SD 99	Cicero
n/a	n/a	Clinton CUSD 15	Clinton
n/a	n/a	Community CSD 168	Sauk Village
n/a	n/a	Community CSD 59	Arlington Hgts
n/a	n/a	Community Consolidated SD 46	Grayslake
n/a	n/a	Community Consolidated SD 62	Des Plaines
n/a	n/a	Community Consolidated SD 93	Bloomingdale
n/a	n/a	Cook County SD 130	Blue Island
n/a	n/a	Crystal Lake CCSD 47	Crystal Lake
n/a	n/a	Darien SD 61	Darien
n/a	n/a	Deerfield SD 109	Deerfield
n/a	n/a	Dolton SD 148	Riverdale
n/a	n/a	Dolton SD 149	Calumet City
n/a	n/a	Downers Grove Grade SD 58	Downers Grove
n/a	n/a	East Maine SD 63	Des Plaines
n/a	n/a	East Moline SD 37	East Moline
n/a	n/a	East Peoria SD 86	East Peoria
n/a	n/a	Elem SD 159	Matteson
n/a	n/a	Evanston CCSD 65	Evanston
n/a	n/a	Evergreen Park Elem SD 124	Evergreen Park
n/a	n/a	Flossmoor SD 161	Chicago Heights
n/a	n/a	Forest Ridge SD 142	Oak Forest
n/a	n/a	Frankfort CCSD 157C	Frankfort
n/a	n/a	Fremont SD 79	Mundelein
n/a	n/a	Glen Ellyn CCSD 89	Glen Ellyn
n/a	n/a	Glen Ellyn SD 41	Glen Ellyn
n/a	n/a	Glenview CCSD 34	Glenview
n/a	n/a	Gurnee SD 56	Gurnee
n/a	n/a	Harvey SD 152	Harvey
n/a	n/a	Hawthorn CCSD 73	Vernon Hills
n/a	n/a	Homer Community CSD 33c	Homer Glen
n/a	n/a	Homewood SD 153	Homewood
n/a	n/a	Indian Springs SD 109	Justice
n/a	n/a	Joliet Public SD 86	Joliet
n/a	n/a	Keeneyville SD 20	Hanover Park
n/a	n/a	Kildeer Countryside CCSD 96	Buffalo Grove
n/a	n/a	Kinnikinnick CCSD 131	Roscoe
n/a	n/a	Kirby SD 140	Tinley Park
n/a	n/a	La Grange SD 102	La Grange Park
n/a	n/a	Lake Forest SD 67	Lake Forest
n/a	n/a	Lake Villa CCSD 41	Lake Villa
n/a	n/a	Lansing SD 158	Lansing
n/a	n/a	Lemont-Bromberek CSD 113A	Lemont
n/a	n/a	Libertyville SD 70	Libertyville
n/a	n/a	Lombard SD 44	Lombard
n/a	n/a	Lyons SD 103	Lyons
n/a	n/a	Mannheim SD 83	Franklin Park
n/a	n/a	Marquardt SD 15	Glendale Hgts
n/a	n/a	Matteson Elem SD 162	Matteson
n/a	n/a	Maywood-Melrose Park-Broadview-89	Melrose Park
n/a	n/a	Mchenry CCSD 15	Mchenry
n/a	n/a	Midlothian SD 143	Midlothian
n/a	n/a	Millburn CCSD 24	Old Mill Creek

Note: This section only includes districts with 1,500 or more students; All categories are ranked from high to low

n/a	n/a	Minooka Community CSD 201	Minooka
n/a	n/a	Mokena SD 159	Mokena
n/a	n/a	Mount Prospect SD 57	Mount Prospect
n/a	n/a	Mount Vernon SD 80	Mount Vernon
n/a	n/a	Mundelein Elem SD 75	Mundelein
n/a	n/a	New Lenox SD 122	New Lenox
n/a	n/a	North Palos SD 117	Palos Hills
n/a	n/a	North Shore SD 112	Highland Park
n/a	n/a	Northbrook SD 28	Northbrook
n/a	n/a	O'Fallon CCSD 90	O Fallon
n/a	n/a	Oak Lawn-Hometown SD 123	Oak Lawn
n/a	n/a	Oak Park Elem SD 97	Oak Park
n/a	n/a	Orland SD 135	Orland Park
n/a	n/a	Ottawa Elem SD 141	Ottawa
n/a	n/a	Palatine CCSD 15	Palatine
n/a	n/a	Palos Community CSD 118	Palos Park
n/a	n/a	Park Forest SD 163	Park Forest
n/a	n/a	Park Ridge CCSD 64	Park Ridge
n/a	n/a	Pekin Public SD 108	Pekin
n/a	n/a	Posen-Robbins Elem SD 143-5	Posen
n/a	n/a	Prairie-Hills Elem SD 144	Markham
n/a	n/a	Queen Bee SD 16	Glendale Hgts
n/a	n/a	Rantoul City SD 137	Rantoul
n/a	n/a	Ridgeland SD 122	Oak Lawn
n/a	n/a	Riverside SD 96	Riverside
n/a	n/a	Rochelle Community CD 231	Rochelle
n/a	n/a	Rockton SD 140	Rockton
n/a	n/a	Schaumburg CCSD 54	Schaumburg
n/a	n/a	School District 45 Dupage County	Villa Park
n/a	n/a	Skokie SD 68	Skokie
n/a	n/a	Skokie SD 69	Skokie
n/a	n/a	South Holland SD 151	South Holland
n/a	n/a	Steger SD 194	Steger
n/a	n/a	Streator Elem SD 44	Streator
n/a	n/a	Summit Hill SD 161	Frankfort
n/a	n/a	Summit SD 104	Summit
n/a	n/a	Tinley Park CCSD 146	Tinley Park
n/a	n/a	Troy Community CSD 30C	Plainfield
n/a	n/a	West Chicago Elem SD 33	West Chicago
n/a	n/a	West Harvey-Dixmoor PSD 147	Harvey
n/a	n/a	Western Springs SD 101	Western Springs
n/a	n/a	Wheeling CCSD 21	Wheeling
n/a	n/a	Will County SD 92	Lockport
n/a	n/a	Wilmette SD 39	Wilmette
n/a	n/a	Winnetka SD 36	Winnetka
n/a	n/a	Woodland CCSD 50	Gurnee
n/a	n/a	Woodridge SD 68	Woodridge
n/a	n/a	Zion Elementary SD 6	Zion

High School Drop-out Rate

Rank	Percent	District Name	City
1	30.3	East St Louis SD 189	E Saint Louis
2	30.1	Decatur SD 61	Decatur
3	28.1	Cahokia Community Unit SD 187	Cahokia
4	27.4	Rock Island SD 41	Rock Island
5	26.8	North Chicago SD 187	North Chicago
6	26.0	Adlai E Stevenson Dist 125	Lincolnshire
7	25.4	North Boone CUSD 200	Poplar Grove
8	22.7	Lockport Twp HSD 205	Lockport
8	22.7	Rockford SD 205	Rockford
10	22.0	Kankakee SD 111	Kankakee
10	22.0	Thornton Twp HSD 205	South Holland
12	21.5	Aurora East Unit SD 131	Aurora
13	19.8	Peoria SD 150	Peoria
14	18.9	Danville CCSD 118	Danville
15	18.4	Champaign Community Unit SD 4	Champaign
16	17.8	Waukegan CUSD 60	Waukegan
17	17.3	Thornton Fractional HSD 215	Calumet City
18	16.9	Freeport SD 145	Freeport
19	16.7	Kewanee Community Unit SD 229	Kewanee
20	16.3	Frankfort Community Unit SD 168	West Frankfort
21	15.8	Bloom Twp High SD 206	Chicago Heights
22	15.5	Beardstown CUSD 15	Beardstown
22	15.5	Crete Monee CUSD 201u	Crete
24	15.3	Round Lake Area Schs - Dist 116	Round Lake
25	15.2	Granite City CUSD 9	Granite City
25	15.2	Monticello CUSD 25	Monticello
27	15.0	City of Chicago SD 299	Chicago
28	14.7	Galesburg CUSD 205	Galesburg
29	14.1	Riverton CUSD 14	Riverton
30	13.9	Urbana SD 116	Urbana
31	13.7	Valley View CUSD #365U	Romeoville
32	13.6	Bloomington SD 87	Bloomington
33	13.4	Alton Community Unit SD 11	Alton
33	13.4	Aurora West Unit SD 129	Aurora
33	13.4	Vandalia CUSD 203	Vandalia
36	13.1	J S Morton HS District 201	Cicero
37	12.5	Dixon Unit SD 170	Dixon
38	12.3	Harlem Unit Dist 122	Machesney Park
38	12.3	Moline Unit SD 40	Moline
38	12.3	Rich Twp HS District 227	Olympia Fields
41	12.0	Harvard CUSD 50	Harvard
41	12.0	Proviso Twp HSD 209	Forest Park
43	11.9	Belvidere CUSD 100	Belvidere
44	11.8	Herrin CUSD 4	Herrin
45	11.7	Roxana Community Unit SD 1	Roxana
46	11.5	Mascoutah CUD 19	Mascoutah
47	11.4	Effingham Community Unit SD 40	Effingham
47	11.4	Joliet Twp HSD 204	Joliet
49	11.3	United Twp HS District 30	East Moline
50	11.2	Dekalb Community Unit SD 428	Dekalb
50	11.2	Robinson CUSD 2	Robinson
52	11.1	Sterling CUD 5	Sterling
53	11.0	Springfield SD 186	Springfield
54	10.8	Plano Community Unit SD 88	Plano
55	10.7	Mattoon CUSD 2	Mattoon
56	10.6	Collinsville CUSD 10	Collinsville
57	10.5	Marion Community Unit SD 2	Marion
58	10.4	Murphysboro CUSD 186	Murphysboro
59	10.3	Hillsboro Community Unit SD 3	Hillsboro
59	10.3	Zion-Benton Twp HSD 126	Zion
61	10.1	Canton Union SD 66	Canton
61	10.1	Charleston CUSD 1	Charleston
61	10.1	Lake Park Community HSD 108	Roselle
61	10.1	Taylorville CUSD 3	Taylorville
65	10.0	Manteno Community Unit SD 5	Manteno
66	9.9	Massac Unit District #1	Metropolis
67	9.6	Du Quoin CUSD 300	Du Quoin
68	9.5	Pekin Community HSD 303	Pekin
69	9.3	Argo Community HSD 217	Summit
69	9.3	Evanston Twp HSD 202	Evanston
71	9.1	Harrisburg CUSD 3	Harrisburg
71	9.1	Leyden Community HSD 212	Franklin Park
71	9.1	School District U-46	Elgin
74	9.0	Bethalto CUSD 8	Bethalto
74	9.0	Litchfield CUSD 12	Litchfield
74	9.0	Wauconda Community Unit SD 118	Wauconda
77	8.9	Elmwood Park CUSD 401	Elmwood Park
78	8.8	Community Unit SD 300	Carpentersville
78	8.8	Jacksonville SD 117	Jacksonville
78	8.8	Sherrard Community Unit SD 200	Sherrard
81	8.7	Quincy SD 172	Quincy
82	8.6	Wabash CUSD 348	Mount Carmel
83	8.4	Paxton-Buckley-Loda CUD 10	Paxton
84	8.3	Homewood Flossmoor CHSD 233	Flossmoor
84	8.3	Macomb Community Unit SD 185	Macomb
86	8.2	Auburn CUSD 10	Auburn
87	8.1	Belleville Twp HSD 201	Belleville
87	8.1	East Richland CUSD 1	Olney
87	8.1	Meridian CUSD 223	Stillman Valley
87	8.1	O'Fallon Twp High SD 203	O Fallon
87	8.1	Plainfield SD 202	Plainfield
87	8.1	Woodstock CUSD 200	Woodstock
93	8.0	Community High SD 94	West Chicago
93	8.0	Mclean County Unit Dist No 5	Normal
93	8.0	Monmouth-Roseville CUSD 238	Monmouth
96	7.8	Bond County CUSD 2	Greenville
96	7.8	Bremen Community HS District 228	Midlothian
96	7.8	Peotone CUSD 207U	Peotone
99	7.7	Hononegah Community HSD 207	Rockton
100	7.5	Sandwich CUSD 430	Sandwich
101	7.1	Grant Community HS District 124	Fox Lake
102	6.9	Genoa Kingston CUSD 424	Genoa
102	6.9	Prairie Central CUSD 8	Fairbury
104	6.8	Mount Zion Community Unit SD 3	Mount Zion
105	6.7	Rochester CUSD 3A	Rochester
106	6.6	Bradley Bourbonnais CHSD 307	Bradley
106	6.6	Olympia CUSD 16	Stanford
108	6.5	Ball Chatham CUSD 5	Chatham
109	6.3	Fenton Community HSD 100	Bensenville
109	6.3	Highland Community Unit SD 5	Highland
109	6.3	Illinois Valley CUD 321	Chillicothe
109	6.3	Oregon CUSD 220	Oregon
109	6.3	Reavis Twp HSD 220	Burbank
109	6.3	Reed Custer CUSD 255U	Braidwood
109	6.3	Westmont CUSD 201	Westmont
116	6.1	Community High SD 218	Oak Lawn
116	6.1	Du Page High SD 88	Addison
118	6.0	Jersey CUSD 100	Jerseyville
118	6.0	Oswego Community Unit SD 308	Oswego
120	5.9	Clinton CUSD 15	Clinton
120	5.9	Mundelein Cons High SD 120	Mundelein
120	5.9	Southwestern CUSD 9	Piasa
120	5.9	Yorkville Community Unit SD 115	Yorkville
124	5.8	Carterville CUSD 5	Carterville
124	5.8	Oak Park & River Forest Dist 200	Oak Park
126	5.7	Mchenry Community HSD 156	Mchenry
127	5.6	Batavia Unit SD 101	Batavia
127	5.6	Coal City CUSD 1	Coal City
129	5.5	Eureka C U Dist 140	Eureka
129	5.5	Indian Prairie CUSD 204	Aurora
129	5.5	Johnsburg CUSD 12	Johnsburg
129	5.5	Lisle CUSD 202	Lisle
129	5.5	Oak Lawn Community HSD 229	Oak Lawn
134	5.4	Community High SD 117	Lake Villa
134	5.4	Naperville CUD 203	Naperville
136	5.3	Dunlap CUSD 323	Dunlap
137	5.2	Herscher Community Unit SD 2	Herscher
137	5.2	Triad Community Unit SD 2	Troy
137	5.2	Warren Twp High SD 121	Gurnee
140	5.1	Central Community Unit SD 301	Burlington
140	5.1	Community Unit SD 200	Wheaton
140	5.1	Glenbard Twp HSD 87	Glen Ellyn
143	5.0	Community High SD 155	Crystal Lake
144	4.8	Grayslake Com High SD 127	Grayslake
144	4.8	Morton CUSD 709	Morton
146	4.7	Consolidated SD 158	Algonquin
146	4.7	Saint Charles CUSD 303	Saint Charles
148	4.5	Byron Community Unit SD 226	Byron
148	4.5	Maine Township HSD 207	Park Ridge
150	4.3	Edwardsville CUSD 7	Edwardsville
150	4.3	Mahomet-Seymour CUSD 3	Mahomet
150	4.3	Township HSD 211	Palatine
153	4.2	Winnebago CUSD 323	Winnebago
154	4.1	Community High SD 99	Downers Grove
155	3.8	Kaneland CUSD 302	Maple Park
156	3.7	Lyons Twp HSD 204	La Grange
156	3.7	Waterloo CUSD 5	Waterloo
158	3.6	Lake Zurich CUSD 95	Lake Zurich
159	3.5	Geneseo Community Unit SD 228	Geneseo
159	3.5	Hinsdale Twp HSD 86	Hinsdale
161	3.4	Lemont Twp HSD 210	Lemont
161	3.4	Township High SD 214	Arlington Hgts
163	3.2	Lincoln Way Community HSD 210	New Lenox
163	3.2	Niles Twp Community High SD 219	Skokie
165	3.1	Barrington CUSD 220	Barrington
165	3.1	Sycamore CUSD 427	Sycamore
167	3.0	Columbia Community Unit SD 4	Columbia
168	2.9	Elmhurst SD 205	Elmhurst
168	2.9	Tolono CUSD 7	Tolono
170	2.8	Geneva Community Unit SD 304	Geneva
171	2.6	Community High SD 128	Vernon Hills
172	2.5	Cons High SD 230	Orland Park
173	2.4	Lake Forest CHSD 115	Lake Forest
173	2.4	Township High SD 113	Highland Park
175	2.1	New Trier Twp HSD 203	Northfield
176	2.0	Northfield Twp High SD 225	Glenview
n/a	n/a	Minooka Community HS District 111	Minooka
n/a	n/a	Addison SD 4	Addison
n/a	n/a	Alsip-Hazelgreen-Oak Lawn SD 126	Alsip
n/a	n/a	Antioch CCSD 34	Antioch
n/a	n/a	Aptakisic-Tripp CCSD 102	Buffalo Grove
n/a	n/a	Arlington Hgts SD 25	Arlington Hgts
n/a	n/a	Beach Park CCSD 3	Beach Park
n/a	n/a	Belleville SD 118	Belleville
n/a	n/a	Bellwood SD 88	Bellwood
n/a	n/a	Bensenville SD 2	Bensenville
n/a	n/a	Berkeley SD 87	Berkeley
n/a	n/a	Berwyn North SD 98	Berwyn
n/a	n/a	Berwyn South SD 100	Berwyn
n/a	n/a	Big Hollow SD 38	Ingleside
n/a	n/a	Bourbonnais SD 53	Bourbonnais
n/a	n/a	Bradley SD 61	Bradley
n/a	n/a	Burbank SD 111	Burbank
n/a	n/a	CCSD 181	Westmont
n/a	n/a	Cary CCSD 26	Cary
n/a	n/a	Channahon SD 17	Channahon
n/a	n/a	Chicago Heights SD 170	Chicago Heights
n/a	n/a	Cicero SD 99	Cicero
n/a	n/a	Community CSD 168	Sauk Village

Note: This section only includes districts with 1,500 or more students; All categories are ranked from high to low

n/a	n/a	Community CSD 59	Arlington Hgts
n/a	n/a	Community Consolidated SD 46	Grayslake
n/a	n/a	Community Consolidated SD 62	Des Plaines
n/a	n/a	Community Consolidated SD 93	Bloomingdale
n/a	n/a	Cook County SD 130	Blue Island
n/a	n/a	Crystal Lake CCSD 47	Crystal Lake
n/a	n/a	Darien SD 61	Darien
n/a	n/a	Deerfield SD 109	Deerfield
n/a	n/a	Dolton SD 148	Riverdale
n/a	n/a	Dolton SD 149	Calumet City
n/a	n/a	Downers Grove Grade SD 58	Downers Grove
n/a	n/a	East Maine SD 63	Des Plaines
n/a	n/a	East Moline SD 37	East Moline
n/a	n/a	East Peoria SD 86	East Peoria
n/a	n/a	Elem SD 159	Matteson
n/a	n/a	Evanston CCSD 65	Evanston
n/a	n/a	Evergreen Park Elem SD 124	Evergreen Park
n/a	n/a	Flossmoor SD 161	Chicago Heights
n/a	n/a	Forest Ridge SD 142	Oak Forest
n/a	n/a	Frankfort CCSD 157C	Frankfort
n/a	n/a	Fremont SD 79	Mundelein
n/a	n/a	Glen Ellyn CCSD 89	Glen Ellyn
n/a	n/a	Glen Ellyn SD 41	Glen Ellyn
n/a	n/a	Glenview CCSD 34	Glenview
n/a	n/a	Gurnee SD 56	Gurnee
n/a	n/a	Harvey SD 152	Harvey
n/a	n/a	Hawthorn CCSD 73	Vernon Hills
n/a	n/a	Homer Community CSD 33c	Homer Glen
n/a	n/a	Homewood SD 153	Homewood
n/a	n/a	Indian Springs SD 109	Justice
n/a	n/a	Joliet Public SD 86	Joliet
n/a	n/a	Keeneyville SD 20	Hanover Park
n/a	n/a	Kildeer Countryside CCSD 96	Buffalo Grove
n/a	n/a	Kinnikinnick CCSD 131	Roscoe
n/a	n/a	Kirby SD 140	Tinley Park
n/a	n/a	La Grange SD 102	La Grange Park
n/a	n/a	Lake Forest SD 67	Lake Forest
n/a	n/a	Lake Villa CCSD 41	Lake Villa
n/a	n/a	Lansing SD 158	Lansing
n/a	n/a	Lemont-Bromberek CSD 113A	Lemont
n/a	n/a	Libertyville SD 70	Libertyville
n/a	n/a	Lombard SD 44	Lombard
n/a	n/a	Lyons SD 103	Lyons
n/a	n/a	Mannheim SD 83	Franklin Park
n/a	n/a	Marquardt SD 15	Glendale Hgts
n/a	n/a	Matteson Elem SD 162	Matteson
n/a	n/a	Maywood-Melrose Park-Broadview-89	Melrose Park
n/a	n/a	Mchenry CCSD 15	Mchenry
n/a	n/a	Midlothian SD 143	Midlothian
n/a	n/a	Millburn CCSD 24	Old Mill Creek
n/a	n/a	Minooka Community CSD 201	Minooka
n/a	n/a	Mokena SD 159	Mokena
n/a	n/a	Mount Prospect SD 57	Mount Prospect
n/a	n/a	Mount Vernon SD 80	Mount Vernon
n/a	n/a	Mundelein Elem SD 75	Mundelein
n/a	n/a	New Lenox SD 122	New Lenox
n/a	n/a	North Palos SD 117	Palos Hills
n/a	n/a	North Shore SD 112	Highland Park
n/a	n/a	Northbrook SD 28	Northbrook
n/a	n/a	O'Fallon CCSD 90	O Fallon
n/a	n/a	Oak Lawn-Hometown SD 123	Oak Lawn
n/a	n/a	Oak Park Elem SD 97	Oak Park
n/a	n/a	Orland SD 135	Orland Park
n/a	n/a	Ottawa Elem SD 141	Ottawa
n/a	n/a	Palatine CCSD 15	Palatine
n/a	n/a	Palos Community CSD 118	Palos Park
n/a	n/a	Park Forest SD 163	Park Forest
n/a	n/a	Park Ridge CCSD 64	Park Ridge
n/a	n/a	Pekin Public SD 108	Pekin
n/a	n/a	Posen-Robbins Elem SD 143-5	Posen
n/a	n/a	Prairie-Hills Elem SD 144	Markham
n/a	n/a	Queen Bee SD 16	Glendale Hgts
n/a	n/a	Rantoul City SD 137	Rantoul
n/a	n/a	Ridgeland SD 122	Oak Lawn
n/a	n/a	Riverside SD 96	Riverside
n/a	n/a	Rochelle Community CD 231	Rochelle
n/a	n/a	Rockton SD 140	Rockton
n/a	n/a	Schaumburg CCSD 54	Schaumburg
n/a	n/a	School District 45 Dupage County	Villa Park
n/a	n/a	Skokie SD 68	Skokie
n/a	n/a	Skokie SD 69	Skokie
n/a	n/a	South Holland SD 151	South Holland
n/a	n/a	Steger SD 194	Steger
n/a	n/a	Streator Elem SD 44	Streator
n/a	n/a	Summit Hill SD 161	Frankfort
n/a	n/a	Summit SD 104	Summit
n/a	n/a	Tinley Park CCSD 146	Tinley Park
n/a	n/a	Troy Community CSD 30C	Plainfield
n/a	n/a	West Chicago Elem SD 33	West Chicago
n/a	n/a	West Harvey-Dixmoor PSD 147	Harvey
n/a	n/a	Western Springs SD 101	Western Springs
n/a	n/a	Wheeling CCSD 21	Wheeling
n/a	n/a	Will County SD 92	Lockport
n/a	n/a	Wilmette SD 39	Wilmette
n/a	n/a	Winnetka SD 36	Winnetka
n/a	n/a	Woodland CCSD 50	Gurnee
n/a	n/a	Woodridge SD 68	Woodridge
n/a	n/a	Zion Elementary SD 6	Zion

Average Freshman Graduation Rate

Rank	Percent	District Name	City
1	100.0	Auburn CUSD 10	Auburn
1	100.0	Central Community Unit SD 301	Burlington
1	100.0	Community High SD 117	Lake Villa
1	100.0	Dunlap CUSD 323	Dunlap
1	100.0	Maine Township HSD 207	Park Ridge
1	100.0	Naperville CUD 203	Naperville
1	100.0	Tolono CUSD 7	Tolono
1	100.0	Yorkville Community Unit SD 115	Yorkville
9	99.2	Ball Chatham CUSD 5	Chatham
10	98.1	Johnsburg CUSD 12	Johnsburg
11	98.0	Elmhurst SD 205	Elmhurst
11	98.0	Sycamore CUSD 427	Sycamore
13	97.8	Plano Community Unit SD 88	Plano
14	97.6	Reed Custer CUSD 255U	Braidwood
15	97.3	Mahomet-Seymour CUSD 3	Mahomet
16	97.2	Columbia Community Unit SD 4	Columbia
16	97.2	Peotone CUSD 207U	Peotone
16	97.2	Saint Charles CUSD 303	Saint Charles
19	96.9	Lake Zurich CUSD 95	Lake Zurich
19	96.9	Plainfield SD 202	Plainfield
21	96.8	Barrington CUSD 220	Barrington
21	96.8	Geneva Community Unit SD 304	Geneva
23	96.7	Community Unit SD 200	Wheaton
24	96.6	Byron Community Unit SD 226	Byron
25	96.5	Kaneland CUSD 302	Maple Park
26	96.2	Edwardsville CUSD 7	Edwardsville
27	96.1	Coal City CUSD 1	Coal City
28	95.9	Monticello CUSD 25	Monticello
29	95.8	Triad Community Unit SD 2	Troy
30	95.1	Consolidated SD 158	Algonquin
31	94.5	Effingham Community Unit SD 40	Effingham
32	94.4	Jacksonville SD 117	Jacksonville
32	94.4	Rochester CUSD 3A	Rochester
34	94.3	Winnebago CUSD 323	Winnebago
35	93.6	Morton CUSD 709	Morton
36	93.3	Oswego Community Unit SD 308	Oswego
37	92.6	Eureka C U Dist 140	Eureka
38	92.5	Waterloo CUSD 5	Waterloo
39	91.6	Mascoutah CUD 19	Mascoutah
40	91.4	Community Unit SD 300	Carpentersville
40	91.4	Genoa Kingston CUSD 424	Genoa
42	90.9	Jersey CUSD 100	Jerseyville
43	90.8	Geneseo Community Unit SD 228	Geneseo
44	90.5	Illinois Valley CUD 321	Chillicothe
45	90.3	Lisle CUSD 202	Lisle
46	90.2	Oregon CUSD 220	Oregon
47	89.9	East Richland CUSD 1	Olney
48	89.4	Herscher Community Unit SD 2	Herscher
49	89.0	Carterville CUSD 5	Carterville
50	88.8	Crete Monee CUSD 201u	Crete
51	88.7	Olympia CUSD 16	Stanford
52	88.4	Wauconda Community Unit SD 118	Wauconda
53	88.1	Manteno Community Unit SD 5	Manteno
54	87.9	Batavia Unit SD 101	Batavia
54	87.9	Macomb Community Unit SD 185	Macomb
56	87.8	Paxton-Buckley-Loda CUD 10	Paxton
57	87.4	Sandwich CUSD 430	Sandwich
58	86.8	Mount Zion Community Unit SD 3	Mount Zion
58	86.8	Woodstock CUSD 200	Woodstock
60	86.3	Roxana Community Unit SD 1	Roxana
61	86.2	Alton Community Unit SD 11	Alton
61	86.2	Wabash CUSD 348	Mount Carmel
63	85.6	Mclean County Unit Dist No 5	Normal
64	85.3	Highland Community Unit SD 5	Highland
65	85.1	Du Quoin CUSD 300	Du Quoin
66	84.7	Mattoon CUSD 2	Mattoon
66	84.7	Meridian CUSD 223	Stillman Valley
68	84.6	Valley View CUSD #365U	Romeoville
69	83.2	Prairie Central CUSD 8	Fairbury
70	83.1	Robinson CUSD 2	Robinson
71	82.9	Collinsville CUSD 10	Collinsville
72	82.5	Dekalb Community Unit SD 428	Dekalb
73	81.6	Westmont CUSD 201	Westmont
74	81.5	Beardstown CUSD 15	Beardstown
75	81.4	Charleston CUSD 1	Charleston
76	81.1	Murphysboro CUSD 186	Murphysboro
77	80.6	Champaign Community Unit SD 4	Champaign
78	80.5	Elmwood Park CUSD 401	Elmwood Park
79	80.2	School District U-46	Elgin
79	80.2	Taylorville CUSD 3	Taylorville
81	80.0	Moline Unit SD 40	Moline
81	80.0	Sherrard Community Unit SD 200	Sherrard
83	79.6	Massac Unit District #1	Metropolis
83	79.6	Vandalia CUSD 203	Vandalia
85	79.4	North Boone CUSD 200	Poplar Grove
86	78.6	Marion Community Unit SD 2	Marion
87	78.4	Freeport SD 145	Freeport
88	78.2	Canton Union SD 66	Canton
89	77.8	Quincy SD 172	Quincy
90	77.7	Harvard CUSD 50	Harvard
91	77.0	Riverton CUSD 14	Riverton
92	76.7	Dixon Unit SD 170	Dixon
93	76.5	Sterling CUD 5	Sterling
94	76.1	Southwestern CUSD 9	Piasa
95	75.8	Bond County CUSD 2	Greenville
96	75.5	Kewanee Community Unit SD 229	Kewanee
97	75.4	Frankfort Community Unit SD 168	West Frankfort
98	74.9	Harrisburg CUSD 3	Harrisburg
99	74.5	Bethalto CUSD 8	Bethalto
100	74.2	Harlem Unit Dist 122	Machesney Park
100	74.2	Litchfield CUSD 12	Litchfield
102	72.8	Herrin CUSD 4	Herrin
103	71.4	Peoria SD 150	Peoria
104	68.8	Hillsboro Community Unit SD 3	Hillsboro
105	67.4	Round Lake Area Schs - Dist 116	Round Lake
106	65.7	Granite City CUSD 9	Granite City
107	65.5	Bloomington SD 87	Bloomington
108	65.3	Galesburg CUSD 205	Galesburg
109	65.2	Waukegan CUSD 60	Waukegan
110	65.0	Belvidere CUSD 100	Belvidere
111	64.8	Aurora West Unit SD 129	Aurora
112	64.2	Rock Island SD 41	Rock Island
113	63.2	Urbana SD 116	Urbana
114	60.8	City of Chicago SD 299	Chicago
115	59.6	Springfield SD 186	Springfield
116	59.1	Aurora East Unit SD 131	Aurora
117	58.4	Danville CCSD 118	Danville
118	58.0	Cahokia Community Unit SD 187	Cahokia
119	57.3	Decatur SD 61	Decatur
120	55.2	Kankakee SD 111	Kankakee
121	55.0	Rockford SD 205	Rockford
122	54.0	East St Louis SD 189	E Saint Louis
123	52.4	North Chicago SD 187	North Chicago
n/a	n/a	Addison SD 4	Addison
n/a	n/a	Adlai E Stevenson Dist 125	Lincolnshire
n/a	n/a	Alsip-Hazelgreen-Oak Lawn SD 126	Alsip
n/a	n/a	Antioch CCSD 34	Antioch
n/a	n/a	Aptakisic-Tripp CCSD 102	Buffalo Grove
n/a	n/a	Argo Community HSD 217	Summit
n/a	n/a	Arlington Hgts SD 25	Arlington Hgts
n/a	n/a	Beach Park CCSD 3	Beach Park
n/a	n/a	Belleville SD 118	Belleville
n/a	n/a	Belleville Twp HSD 201	Belleville
n/a	n/a	Bellwood SD 88	Bellwood
n/a	n/a	Bensenville SD 2	Bensenville
n/a	n/a	Berkeley SD 87	Berkeley
n/a	n/a	Berwyn North SD 98	Berwyn
n/a	n/a	Berwyn South SD 100	Berwyn
n/a	n/a	Big Hollow SD 38	Ingleside
n/a	n/a	Bloom Twp High SD 206	Chicago Heights
n/a	n/a	Bourbonnais SD 53	Bourbonnais
n/a	n/a	Bradley Bourbonnais CHSD 307	Bradley
n/a	n/a	Bradley SD 61	Bradley
n/a	n/a	Bremen Community HS District 228	Midlothian
n/a	n/a	Burbank SD 111	Burbank
n/a	n/a	CCSD 181	Westmont
n/a	n/a	Cary CCSD 26	Cary
n/a	n/a	Channahon SD 17	Channahon
n/a	n/a	Chicago Heights SD 170	Chicago Heights

Note: This section only includes districts with 1,500 or more students; All categories are ranked from high to low

		District	City
n/a	n/a	Cicero SD 99	Cicero
n/a	n/a	Clinton CUSD 15	Clinton
n/a	n/a	Community CSD 168	Sauk Village
n/a	n/a	Community CSD 59	Arlington Hgts
n/a	n/a	Community Consolidated SD 46	Grayslake
n/a	n/a	Community Consolidated SD 62	Des Plaines
n/a	n/a	Community Consolidated SD 93	Bloomingdale
n/a	n/a	Community High SD 128	Vernon Hills
n/a	n/a	Community High SD 155	Crystal Lake
n/a	n/a	Community High SD 218	Oak Lawn
n/a	n/a	Community High SD 94	West Chicago
n/a	n/a	Community High SD 99	Downers Grove
n/a	n/a	Cons High SD 230	Orland Park
n/a	n/a	Cook County SD 130	Blue Island
n/a	n/a	Crystal Lake CCSD 47	Crystal Lake
n/a	n/a	Darien SD 61	Darien
n/a	n/a	Deerfield SD 109	Deerfield
n/a	n/a	Dolton SD 148	Riverdale
n/a	n/a	Dolton SD 149	Calumet City
n/a	n/a	Downers Grove Grade SD 58	Downers Grove
n/a	n/a	Du Page High SD 88	Addison
n/a	n/a	East Maine SD 63	Des Plaines
n/a	n/a	East Moline SD 37	East Moline
n/a	n/a	East Peoria SD 86	East Peoria
n/a	n/a	Elem SD 159	Matteson
n/a	n/a	Evanston CCSD 65	Evanston
n/a	n/a	Evanston Twp HSD 202	Evanston
n/a	n/a	Evergreen Park Elem SD 124	Evergreen Park
n/a	n/a	Fenton Community HSD 100	Bensenville
n/a	n/a	Flossmoor SD 161	Chicago Heights
n/a	n/a	Forest Ridge SD 142	Oak Forest
n/a	n/a	Frankfort CCSD 157C	Frankfort
n/a	n/a	Fremont SD 79	Mundelein
n/a	n/a	Glen Ellyn CCSD 89	Glen Ellyn
n/a	n/a	Glen Ellyn SD 41	Glen Ellyn
n/a	n/a	Glenbard Twp HSD 87	Glen Ellyn
n/a	n/a	Glenview CCSD 34	Glenview
n/a	n/a	Grant Community HS District 124	Fox Lake
n/a	n/a	Grayslake Com High SD 127	Grayslake
n/a	n/a	Gurnee SD 56	Gurnee
n/a	n/a	Harvey SD 152	Harvey
n/a	n/a	Hawthorn CCSD 73	Vernon Hills
n/a	n/a	Hinsdale Twp HSD 86	Hinsdale
n/a	n/a	Homer Community CSD 33c	Homer Glen
n/a	n/a	Homewood Flossmoor CHSD 233	Flossmoor
n/a	n/a	Homewood SD 153	Homewood
n/a	n/a	Hononegah Community HSD 207	Rockton
n/a	n/a	Indian Prairie CUSD 204	Aurora
n/a	n/a	Indian Springs SD 109	Justice
n/a	n/a	J S Morton HS District 201	Cicero
n/a	n/a	Joliet Public SD 86	Joliet
n/a	n/a	Joliet Twp HSD 204	Joliet
n/a	n/a	Keeneyville SD 20	Hanover Park
n/a	n/a	Kildeer Countryside CCSD 96	Buffalo Grove
n/a	n/a	Kinnikinnick CCSD 131	Roscoe
n/a	n/a	Kirby SD 140	Tinley Park
n/a	n/a	La Grange SD 102	La Grange Park
n/a	n/a	Lake Forest CHSD 115	Lake Forest
n/a	n/a	Lake Forest SD 67	Lake Forest
n/a	n/a	Lake Park Community HSD 108	Roselle
n/a	n/a	Lake Villa CCSD 41	Lake Villa
n/a	n/a	Lansing SD 158	Lansing
n/a	n/a	Lemont Twp HSD 210	Lemont
n/a	n/a	Lemont-Bromberek CSD 113A	Lemont
n/a	n/a	Leyden Community HSD 212	Franklin Park
n/a	n/a	Libertyville SD 70	Libertyville
n/a	n/a	Lincoln Way Community HSD 210	New Lenox
n/a	n/a	Lockport Twp HSD 205	Lockport
n/a	n/a	Lombard SD 44	Lombard
n/a	n/a	Lyons SD 103	Lyons
n/a	n/a	Lyons Twp HSD 204	La Grange
n/a	n/a	Mannheim SD 83	Franklin Park
n/a	n/a	Marquardt SD 15	Glendale Hgts
n/a	n/a	Matteson Elem SD 162	Matteson
n/a	n/a	Maywood-Melrose Park-Broadview-89	Melrose Park
n/a	n/a	Mchenry CCSD 15	Mchenry
n/a	n/a	Mchenry Community HSD 156	Mchenry
n/a	n/a	Midlothian SD 143	Midlothian
n/a	n/a	Millburn CCSD 24	Old Mill Creek
n/a	n/a	Minooka Community CSD 201	Minooka
n/a	n/a	Minooka Community HS District 111	Minooka
n/a	n/a	Mokena SD 159	Mokena
n/a	n/a	Monmouth-Roseville CUSD 238	Monmouth
n/a	n/a	Mount Prospect SD 57	Mount Prospect
n/a	n/a	Mount Vernon SD 80	Mount Vernon
n/a	n/a	Mundelein Cons High SD 120	Mundelein
n/a	n/a	Mundelein Elem SD 75	Mundelein
n/a	n/a	New Lenox SD 122	New Lenox
n/a	n/a	New Trier Twp HSD 203	Northfield
n/a	n/a	Niles Twp Community High SD 219	Skokie
n/a	n/a	North Palos SD 117	Palos Hills
n/a	n/a	North Shore SD 112	Highland Park
n/a	n/a	Northbrook SD 28	Northbrook
n/a	n/a	Northfield Twp High SD 225	Glenview
n/a	n/a	O'Fallon CCSD 90	O Fallon
n/a	n/a	O'Fallon Twp High SD 203	O Fallon
n/a	n/a	Oak Lawn Community HSD 229	Oak Lawn
n/a	n/a	Oak Lawn-Hometown SD 123	Oak Lawn
n/a	n/a	Oak Park & River Forest Dist 200	Oak Park
n/a	n/a	Oak Park Elem SD 97	Oak Park
n/a	n/a	Orland SD 135	Orland Park
n/a	n/a	Ottawa Elem SD 141	Ottawa
n/a	n/a	Palatine CCSD 15	Palatine
n/a	n/a	Palos Community CSD 118	Palos Park
n/a	n/a	Park Forest SD 163	Park Forest
n/a	n/a	Park Ridge CCSD 64	Park Ridge
n/a	n/a	Pekin Community HSD 303	Pekin
n/a	n/a	Pekin Public SD 108	Pekin
n/a	n/a	Posen-Robbins Elem SD 143-5	Posen
n/a	n/a	Prairie-Hills Elem SD 144	Markham
n/a	n/a	Proviso Twp HSD 209	Forest Park
n/a	n/a	Queen Bee SD 16	Glendale Hgts
n/a	n/a	Rantoul City SD 137	Rantoul
n/a	n/a	Reavis Twp HSD 220	Burbank
n/a	n/a	Rich Twp HS District 227	Olympia Fields
n/a	n/a	Ridgeland SD 122	Oak Lawn
n/a	n/a	Riverside SD 96	Riverside
n/a	n/a	Rochelle Community CD 231	Rochelle
n/a	n/a	Rockton SD 140	Rockton
n/a	n/a	Schaumburg CCSD 54	Schaumburg
n/a	n/a	School District 45 Dupage County	Villa Park
n/a	n/a	Skokie SD 68	Skokie
n/a	n/a	Skokie SD 69	Skokie
n/a	n/a	South Holland SD 151	South Holland
n/a	n/a	Steger SD 194	Steger
n/a	n/a	Streator Elem SD 44	Streator
n/a	n/a	Summit Hill SD 161	Frankfort
n/a	n/a	Summit SD 104	Summit
n/a	n/a	Thornton Fractional HSD 215	Calumet City
n/a	n/a	Thornton Twp HSD 205	South Holland
n/a	n/a	Tinley Park CCSD 146	Tinley Park
n/a	n/a	Township HSD 211	Palatine
n/a	n/a	Township High SD 113	Highland Park
n/a	n/a	Township High SD 214	Arlington Hgts
n/a	n/a	Troy Community CSD 30C	Plainfield
n/a	n/a	United Twp HS District 30	East Moline
n/a	n/a	Warren Twp High SD 121	Gurnee
n/a	n/a	West Chicago Elem SD 33	West Chicago
n/a	n/a	West Harvey-Dixmoor PSD 147	Harvey
n/a	n/a	Western Springs SD 101	Western Springs
n/a	n/a	Wheeling CCSD 21	Wheeling
n/a	n/a	Will County SD 92	Lockport
n/a	n/a	Wilmette SD 39	Wilmette
n/a	n/a	Winnetka SD 36	Winnetka
n/a	n/a	Woodland CCSD 50	Gurnee
n/a	n/a	Woodridge SD 68	Woodridge
n/a	n/a	Zion Elementary SD 6	Zion
n/a	n/a	Zion-Benton Twp HSD 126	Zion

Note: This section only includes districts with 1,500 or more students; All categories are ranked from high to low

Illinois
Grade 4
Public Schools

Overall Results

- In 2011, the average score of fourth-grade students in Illinois was 239. This was not significantly different from the average score of 240 for public school students in the nation.
- The average score for students in Illinois in 2011 (239) was not significantly different from their average score in 2009 (238) and was higher than their average score in 2000 (223).
- In 2011, the score gap between students in Illinois at the 75th percentile and students at the 25th percentile was 41 points. This performance gap was not significantly different from that of 2000 (42 points).
- The percentage of students in Illinois who performed at or above the NAEP *Proficient* level was 38 percent in 2011. This percentage was not significantly different from that in 2009 (38 percent) and was greater than that in 2000 (20 percent).
- The percentage of students in Illinois who performed at or above the NAEP *Basic* level was 80 percent in 2011. This percentage was not significantly different from that in 2009 (80 percent) and was greater than that in 2000 (63 percent).

Achievement-Level Percentages and Average Score Results

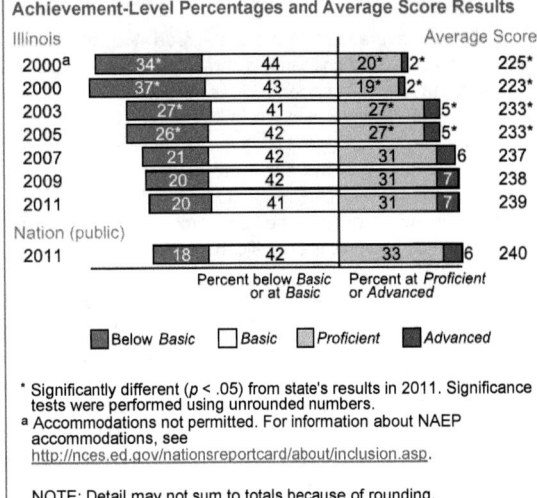

* Significantly different (*p* < .05) from state's results in 2011. Significance tests were performed using unrounded numbers.
a Accommodations not permitted. For information about NAEP accommodations, see http://nces.ed.gov/nationsreportcard/about/inclusion.asp.

NOTE: Detail may not sum to totals because of rounding.

Compare the Average Score in 2011 to Other States/Jurisdictions

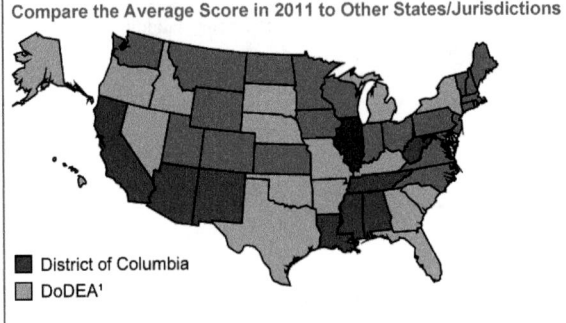

- ■ District of Columbia
- ■ DoDEA[1]

[1] Department of Defense Education Activity (overseas and domestic schools).

In 2011, the average score in Illinois (239) was
- lower than those in 23 states/jurisdictions
- higher than those in 9 states/jurisdictions
- not significantly different from those in 19 states/jurisdictions

Average Scores for State/Jurisdiction and Nation (public)

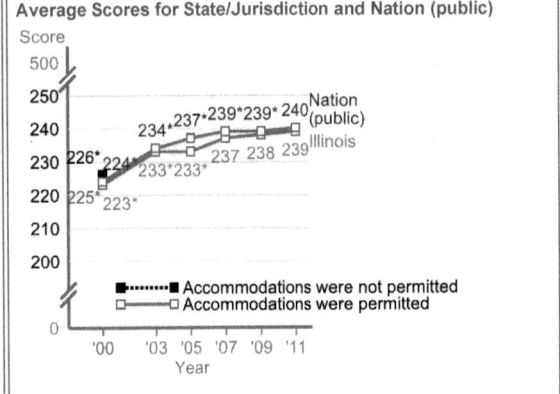

* Significantly different (*p* < .05) from 2011. Significance tests were performed using unrounded numbers.

NOTE: For information about NAEP accommodations, see http://nces.ed.gov/nationsreportcard/about/inclusion.asp.

Results for Student Groups in 2011

Reporting groups	Percent of students	Avg. score	Percentages at or above Basic	Proficient	Percent at Advanced
Race/Ethnicity					
White	53	249	90	51	10
Black	19	219	58	14	2
Hispanic	20	226	70	20	1
Asian	4	258	94	65	20
American Indian/Alaska Native	#	‡	‡	‡	‡
Native Hawaiian/Pacific Islander	#	‡	‡	‡	‡
Two or more races	3	244	85	45	8
Gender					
Male	52	240	81	39	8
Female	48	238	79	37	6
National School Lunch Program					
Eligible	49	225	67	20	1
Not eligible	51	252	92	56	12

Rounds to zero. ‡ Reporting standards not met.

NOTE: Detail may not sum to totals because of rounding, and because the "Information not available" category for the National School Lunch Program, which provides free/reduced-price lunches, is not displayed. Black includes African American and Hispanic includes Latino. Race categories exclude Hispanic origin.

Score Gaps for Student Groups

- In 2011, Black students had an average score that was 29 points lower than White students. This performance gap was not significantly different from that in 2000 (33 points).
- In 2011, Hispanic students had an average score that was 22 points lower than White students. This performance gap was not significantly different from that in 2000 (24 points).
- In 2011, male students in Illinois had an average score that was not significantly different from female students.
- In 2011, students who were eligible for free/reduced-price school lunch, an indicator of low family income, had an average score that was 27 points lower than students who were not eligible for free/reduced-price school lunch. This performance gap was not significantly different from that in 2000 (25 points).

NOTE: Statistical comparisons are calculated on the basis of unrounded scale scores or percentages.
SOURCE: U.S. Department of Education, Institute of Education Sciences, National Center for Education Statistics, National Assessment of Educational Progress (NAEP), various years, 2000–2011 Mathematics Assessments.

The Nation's Report Card Mathematics 2011 State Snapshot Report

Illinois
Grade 8
Public Schools

Overall Results

- In 2011, the average score of eighth-grade students in Illinois was 283. This was not significantly different from the average score of 283 for public school students in the nation.
- The average score for students in Illinois in 2011 (283) was not significantly different from their average score in 2009 (282) and was higher than their average score in 1990 (261).
- In 2011, the score gap between students in Illinois at the 75th percentile and students at the 25th percentile was 47 points. This performance gap was not significantly different from that of 1990 (49 points).
- The percentage of students in Illinois who performed at or above the NAEP *Proficient* level was 33 percent in 2011. This percentage was not significantly different from that in 2009 (33 percent) and was greater than that in 1990 (15 percent).
- The percentage of students in Illinois who performed at or above the NAEP *Basic* level was 73 percent in 2011. This percentage was not significantly different from that in 2009 (73 percent) and was greater than that in 1990 (50 percent).

Achievement-Level Percentages and Average Score Results

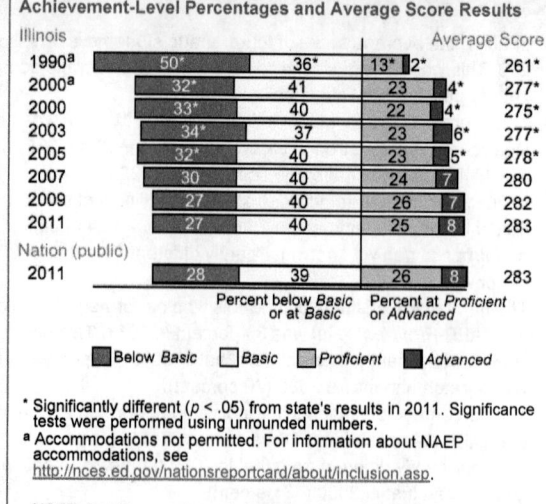

Illinois					Average Score
1990ª	50*	36*	13*	2*	261*
2000ª	32*	41	23	4*	277*
2000	33*	40	22	4*	275*
2003	34*	37	23	6*	277*
2005	32*	40	23	5*	278*
2007	30	40	24	7	280
2009	27	40	26	7	282
2011	27	40	25	8	283
Nation (public)					
2011	28	39	26	8	283

Percent below *Basic* or at *Basic*   Percent at *Proficient* or *Advanced*

■ Below *Basic*   ☐ *Basic*   ▨ *Proficient*   ■ *Advanced*

* Significantly different (*p* < .05) from state's results in 2011. Significance tests were performed using unrounded numbers.
ª Accommodations not permitted. For information about NAEP accommodations, see http://nces.ed.gov/nationsreportcard/about/inclusion.asp.

NOTE: Detail may not sum to totals because of rounding.

Compare the Average Score in 2011 to Other States/Jurisdictions

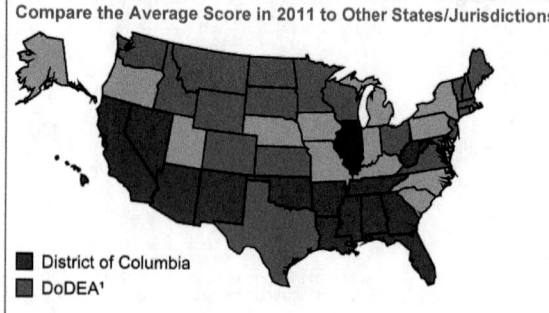

■ District of Columbia
■ DoDEA[1]

[1] Department of Defense Education Activity (overseas and domestic schools).

In 2011, the average score in Illinois (283) was
- lower than those in 21 states/jurisdictions
- higher than those in 15 states/jurisdictions
- not significantly different from those in 15 states/jurisdictions

Average Scores for State/Jurisdiction and Nation (public)

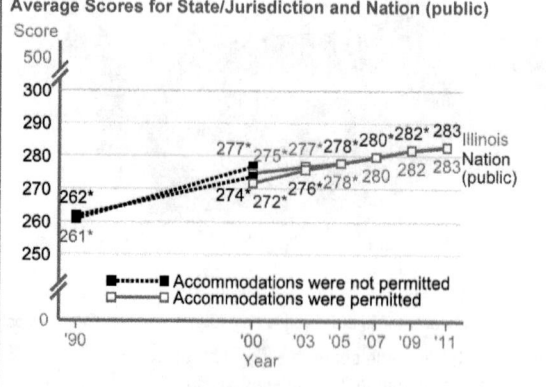

Score

277* 275* 277* 278* 280* 282* 283 Illinois
262*
261*
274* 272* 276* 278* 280 282 283 Nation (public)

■ Accommodations were not permitted
☐ Accommodations were permitted

'90 '00 '03 '05 '07 '09 '11
Year

* Significantly different (*p* < .05) from 2011. Significance tests were performed using unrounded numbers.

NOTE: For information about NAEP accommodations, see http://nces.ed.gov/nationsreportcard/about/inclusion.asp.

Results for Student Groups in 2011

Reporting groups	Percent of students	Avg. score	Percentages at or above Basic	Proficient	Percent at Advanced
Race/Ethnicity					
White	51	294	84	44	11
Black	18	260	48	10	1
Hispanic	24	272	64	19	3
Asian	4	315	93	68	32
American Indian/Alaska Native	#	‡	‡	‡	‡
Native Hawaiian/Pacific Islander	#	‡	‡	‡	‡
Two or more races	2	281	70	33	7
Gender					
Male	51	283	72	33	10
Female	49	283	74	32	7
National School Lunch Program					
Eligible	48	269	61	17	2
Not eligible	52	296	84	47	14

Rounds to zero.   ‡ Reporting standards not met.

NOTE: Detail may not sum to totals because of rounding, and because the "Information not available" category for the National School Lunch Program, which provides free/reduced-price lunches, is not displayed. Black includes African American and Hispanic includes Latino. Race categories exclude Hispanic origin.

Score Gaps for Student Groups

- In 2011, Black students had an average score that was 33 points lower than White students. This performance gap was not significantly different from that in 1990 (38 points).
- In 2011, Hispanic students had an average score that was 22 points lower than White students. This performance gap was not significantly different from that in 1990 (33 points).
- In 2011, male students in Illinois had an average score that was not significantly different from female students.
- In 2011, students who were eligible for free/reduced-price school lunch, an indicator of low family income, had an average score that was 27 points lower than students who were not eligible for free/reduced-price school lunch. This performance gap was not significantly different from that in 2000 (30 points).

ies NATIONAL CENTER FOR EDUCATION STATISTICS
Institute of Education Sciences

NOTE: Statistical comparisons are calculated on the basis of unrounded scale scores or percentages.
SOURCE: U.S. Department of Education, Institute of Education Sciences, National Center for Education Statistics, National Assessment of Educational Progress (NAEP), various years, 1990–2011 Mathematics Assessments.

Mathematics 2009
State Snapshot Report

Illinois
Grade 12
Public Schools

Overall Results

- In 2009, the average score of twelfth-grade students in Illinois was 154. This was not significantly different from the average score of 152 for public school students in the nation.
- The percentage of students in Illinois who performed at or above the NAEP *Proficient* level was 26 percent in 2009. This percentage was not significantly different from the nation (25 percent).
- The percentage of students in Illinois who performed at or above the NAEP *Basic* level was 67 percent in 2009. This percentage was not significantly different from the nation (63 percent).

Achievement-Level Percentages and Average Score Results

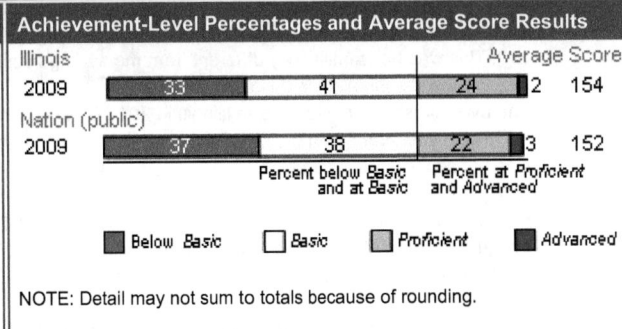

NOTE: Detail may not sum to totals because of rounding.

Compare the Average Score in 2009 to Other States/Jurisdictions

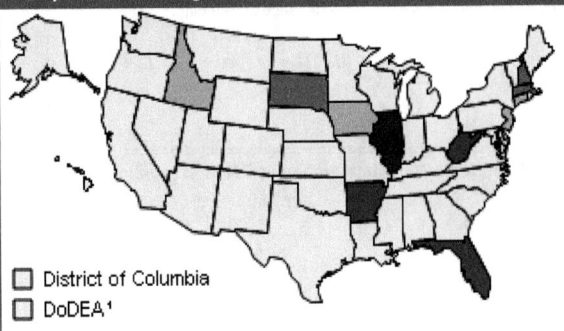

- District of Columbia
- DoDEA[1]

[1] Department of Defense Education Activity (domestic and overseas schools).

In 2009, the average score in **Illinois** was
- lower than those in 3 states/jurisdictions
- higher than those in 3 states/jurisdictions
- not significantly different from those in 4 states/jurisdictions
- 41 states/jurisdictions did not participate

Average Scores for State/Jurisdiction and Nation (public)

Illinois: 154
Nation (public): 152

Results for Student Groups in 2009

Reporting Groups	Percent of students	Avg. score	Basic	Proficient	Advanced
Gender					
Male	50	156	67	29	2
Female	50	153	66	24	1
Race/Ethnicity					
White	64	162	76	32	2
Black	16	130	38	6	1
Hispanic	14	141	48	13	#
Asian/Pacific Islander	4	171	82	46	4
American Indian/Alaska Native	#	‡	‡	‡	‡

(Percentages at or above / Percent at Advanced headers)

Rounds to zero. ‡ Reporting standards not met.

NOTE: Detail may not sum to totals because of rounding, and the "Unclassified" category for race/ethnicity are not displayed.

Score Gaps for Student Groups

- In 2009, male students in Illinois had an average score that was not significantly different from female students.
- In 2009, Black students had an average score that was 32 points lower than White students. This performance gap was not significantly different from the nation (29 points).
- In 2009, Hispanic students had an average score that was 20 points lower than White students. This performance gap was not significantly different from the nation (23 points).

NOTE: Statistical comparisons are calculated on the basis of unrounded scale scores or percentages. The national results are based on nationally representative samples of twelfth-graders from 1,670 schools. State results in NAEP mathematics are reported for twelfth-grade public school students in the 11 states that volunteered to participate in the first twelfth-grade state pilot program in 2009: Arkansas, Connecticut, Florida, Idaho, Illinois, Iowa, Massachusetts, New Hampshire, New Jersey, South Dakota, and West Virginia.
SOURCE: U.S. Department of Education, Institute of Education Sciences, National Center for Education Statistics, National Assessment of Educational Progress (NAEP), 2009 Mathematics Assessment.

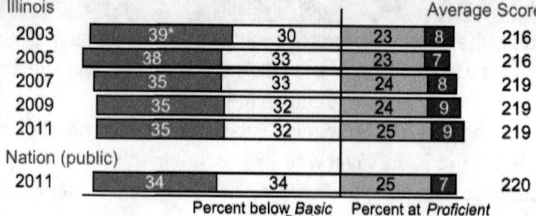

The Nation's Report Card
Reading
2011 State Snapshot Report

Illinois
Grade 4
Public Schools

Overall Results

- In 2011, the average score of fourth-grade students in Illinois was 219. This was not significantly different from the average score of 220 for public school students in the nation.
- The average score for students in Illinois in 2011 (219) was not significantly different from their average score in 2009 (219) and was not significantly different from their average score in 2003 (216).
- In 2011, the score gap between students in Illinois at the 75th percentile and students at the 25th percentile was 49 points. This performance gap was not significantly different from that of 2003 (53 points).
- The percentage of students in Illinois who performed at or above the NAEP *Proficient* level was 33 percent in 2011. This percentage was not significantly different from that in 2009 (32 percent) and was not significantly different from that in 2003 (31 percent).
- The percentage of students in Illinois who performed at or above the NAEP *Basic* level was 65 percent in 2011. This percentage was not significantly different from that in 2009 (65 percent) and was greater than that in 2003 (61 percent).

Achievement-Level Percentages and Average Score Results

Illinois					Average Score
2003	39*	30	23	8	216
2005	38	33	23	7	216
2007	35	33	24	8	219
2009	35	32	24	9	219
2011	35	32	25	9	219
Nation (public)					
2011	34	34	25	7	220

Percent below *Basic* or at *Basic*   Percent at *Proficient* or *Advanced*

■ Below *Basic*   □ *Basic*   ▨ *Proficient*   ■ *Advanced*

* Significantly different (*p* < .05) from state's results in 2011. Significance tests were performed using unrounded numbers.

NOTE: Detail may not sum to totals because of rounding.

Compare the Average Score in 2011 to Other States/Jurisdictions

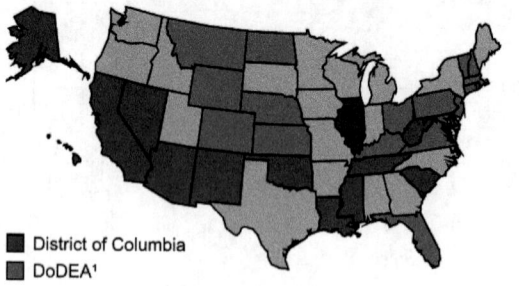

■ District of Columbia
■ DoDEA[1]

[1] Department of Defense Education Activity (overseas and domestic schools).

In 2011, the average score in **Illinois** (219) was
- lower than those in 20 states/jurisdictions
- higher than those in 13 states/jurisdictions
- not significantly different from those in 18 states/jurisdictions

Average Scores for State/Jurisdiction and Nation (public)

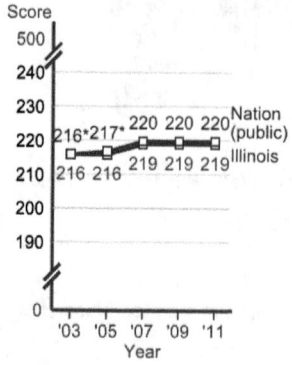

* Significantly different (*p* < .05) from 2011. Significance tests were performed using unrounded numbers.

Results for Student Groups in 2011

Reporting groups	Percent of students	Avg. score	Percentages at or above		Percent at Advanced
			Basic	Proficient	
Race/Ethnicity					
White	53	231	78	45	12
Black	20	198	42	12	2
Hispanic	19	204	49	18	2
Asian	4	237	84	53	17
American Indian/Alaska Native	#	‡	‡	‡	‡
Native Hawaiian/Pacific Islander	#	‡	‡	‡	‡
Two or more races	3	225	70	43	14
Gender					
Male	52	217	63	31	7
Female	48	222	68	36	10
National School Lunch Program					
Eligible	49	203	48	16	2
Not eligible	51	235	82	49	15

Rounds to zero.   ‡ Reporting standards not met.

NOTE: Detail may not sum to totals because of rounding, and because the "Information not available" category for the National School Lunch Program, which provides free/reduced-price lunches, is not displayed. Black includes African American and Hispanic includes Latino. Race categories exclude Hispanic origin.

Score Gaps for Student Groups

- In 2011, Black students had an average score that was 33 points lower than White students. This performance gap was not significantly different from that in 2003 (34 points).
- In 2011, Hispanic students had an average score that was 27 points lower than White students. This performance gap was not significantly different from that in 2003 (31 points).
- In 2011, female students in Illinois had an average score that was higher than male students by 6 points.
- In 2011, students who were eligible for free/reduced-price school lunch, an indicator of low family income, had an average score that was 32 points lower than students who were not eligible for free/reduced-price school lunch. This performance gap was not significantly different from that in 2003 (35 points).

NATIONAL CENTER FOR EDUCATION STATISTICS
Institute of Education Sciences

NOTE: Statistical comparisons are calculated on the basis of unrounded scale scores or percentages.
SOURCE: U.S. Department of Education, Institute of Education Sciences, National Center for Education Statistics, National Assessment of Educational Progress (NAEP), various years, 2003–2011 Reading Assessments.

The Nation's Report Card
Reading
2011 State Snapshot Report

Illinois
Grade 8
Public Schools

Overall Results

- In 2011, the average score of eighth-grade students in Illinois was 266. This was higher than the average score of 264 for public school students in the nation.
- The average score for students in Illinois in 2011 (266) was not significantly different from their average score in 2009 (265) and was not significantly different from their average score in 2003 (266).
- In 2011, the score gap between students in Illinois at the 75th percentile and students at the 25th percentile was 44 points. This performance gap was not significantly different from that of 2003 (44 points).
- The percentage of students in Illinois who performed at or above the NAEP *Proficient* level was 34 percent in 2011. This percentage was not significantly different from that in 2009 (33 percent) and was not significantly different from that in 2003 (35 percent).
- The percentage of students in Illinois who performed at or above the NAEP *Basic* level was 77 percent in 2011. This percentage was not significantly different from that in 2009 (77 percent) and was not significantly different from that in 2003 (77 percent).

Achievement-Level Percentages and Average Score Results

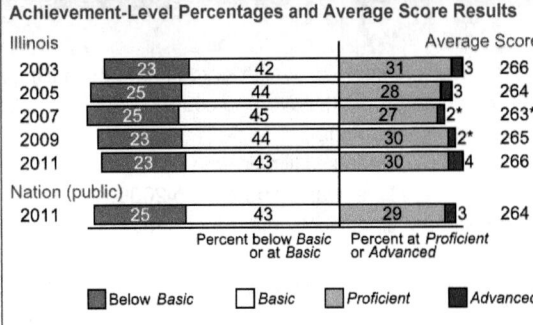

Illinois — Average Score

Year	Below Basic	Basic	Proficient	Advanced	Average Score
2003	23	42	31	3	266
2005	25	44	28	3	264
2007	25	45	27	2*	263*
2009	23	44	30	2*	265
2011	23	43	30	4	266

Nation (public)
| 2011 | 25 | 43 | 29 | 3 | 264 |

Percent below *Basic* or at *Basic*   Percent at *Proficient* or *Advanced*

■ Below *Basic*   ☐ *Basic*   ■ *Proficient*   ■ *Advanced*

* Significantly different (*p* < .05) from state's results in 2011. Significance tests were performed using unrounded numbers.

NOTE: Detail may not sum to totals because of rounding.

Compare the Average Score in 2011 to Other States/Jurisdictions

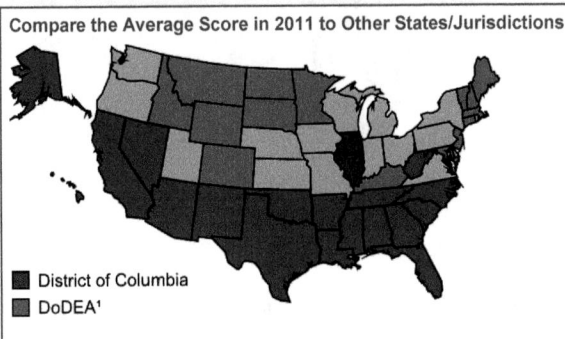

■ District of Columbia
■ DoDEA[1]

[1] Department of Defense Education Activity (overseas and domestic schools).

In 2011, the average score in Illinois (266) was
- lower than those in 16 states/jurisdictions
- higher than those in 19 states/jurisdictions
- not significantly different from those in 16 states/jurisdictions

Average Scores for State/Jurisdiction and Nation (public)

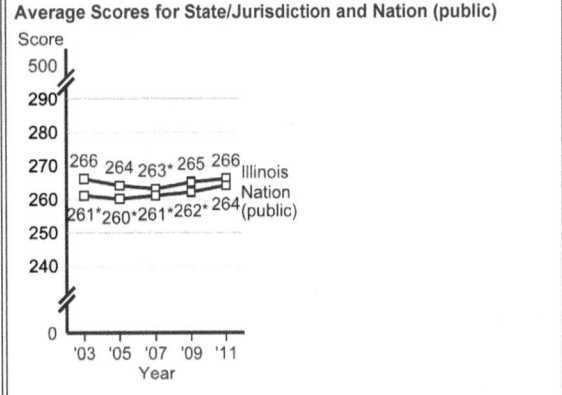

Illinois: 266, 264, 263*, 265, 266
Nation (public): 261*, 260*, 261*, 262*, 264

* Significantly different (*p* < .05) from 2011. Significance tests were performed using unrounded numbers.

Results for Student Groups in 2011

Reporting groups	Percent of students	Avg. score	Percentages at or above Basic	Percentages at or above Proficient	Percent at Advanced
Race/Ethnicity					
White	51	274	85	44	5
Black	18	249	62	15	1
Hispanic	23	257	69	23	2
Asian	4	281	89	54	11
American Indian/Alaska Native	#	‡	‡	‡	‡
Native Hawaiian/Pacific Islander	#	‡	‡	‡	‡
Two or more races	2	263	72	31	3
Gender					
Male	51	261	72	29	3
Female	49	271	82	39	5
National School Lunch Program					
Eligible	48	253	66	19	1
Not eligible	52	277	87	48	6

\# Rounds to zero.   ‡ Reporting standards not met.

NOTE: Detail may not sum to totals because of rounding, and because the "Information not available" category for the National School Lunch Program, which provides free/reduced-price lunches, is not displayed. Black includes African American and Hispanic includes Latino. Race categories exclude Hispanic origin.

Score Gaps for Student Groups

- In 2011, Black students had an average score that was 25 points lower than White students. This performance gap was not significantly different from that in 2003 (29 points).
- In 2011, Hispanic students had an average score that was 17 points lower than White students. This performance gap was narrower than that in 2003 (26 points).
- In 2011, female students in Illinois had an average score that was higher than male students by 10 points.
- In 2011, students who were eligible for free/reduced-price school lunch, an indicator of low family income, had an average score that was 24 points lower than students who were not eligible for free/reduced-price school lunch. This performance gap was not significantly different from that in 2003 (27 points).

ies NATIONAL CENTER FOR EDUCATION STATISTICS
Institute of Education Sciences

NOTE: Statistical comparisons are calculated on the basis of unrounded scale scores or percentages.
SOURCE: U.S. Department of Education, Institute of Education Sciences, National Center for Education Statistics, National Assessment of Educational Progress (NAEP), various years, 2003–2011 Reading Assessments.

Illinois
Grade 12
Public Schools

Reading 2009

State Snapshot Report

Overall Results

- In 2009, the average score of twelfth-grade students in Illinois was 292. This was higher than the average score of 287 for public school students in the nation.
- The percentage of students in Illinois who performed at or above the NAEP *Proficient* level was 40 percent in 2009. This percentage was not significantly different from the nation (37 percent).
- The percentage of students in Illinois who performed at or above the NAEP *Basic* level was 78 percent in 2009. This percentage was greater than the nation (73 percent).

Achievement-Level Percentages and Average Score Results

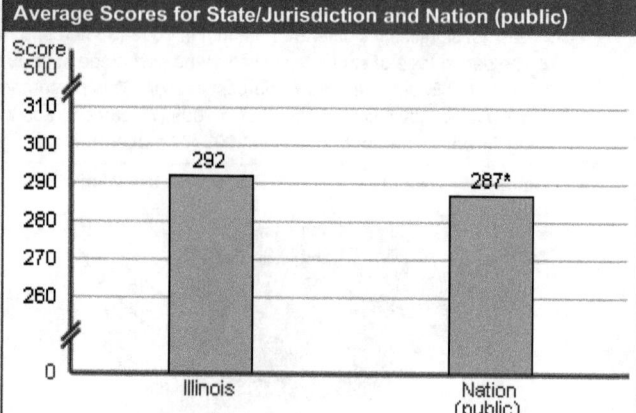

Average Score

Illinois 2009	22 38 35 5		292
Nation (public) 2009	27* 37 31* 5		287*

Percent below *Basic* and at *Basic* Percent at *Proficient* and *Advanced*

■ Below *Basic* □ *Basic* ■ *Proficient* ■ *Advanced*

* Significantly different (*p* < .05) from Illinois.

NOTE: Detail may not sum to totals because of rounding.

Compare the Average Score in 2009 to Other States/Jurisdictions

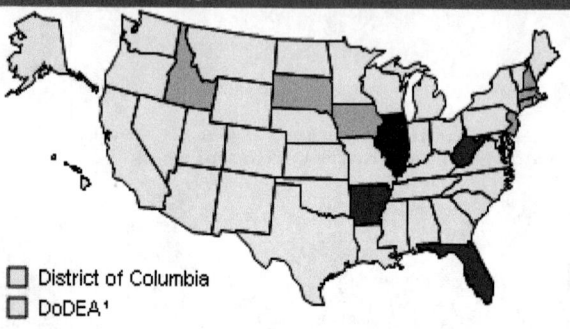

☐ District of Columbia
☐ DoDEA¹

¹ Department of Defense Education Activity (domestic and overseas schools).

In 2009, the average score in **Illinois** was
- lower than that in 0 states/jurisdictions
- higher than those in 3 states/jurisdictions
- not significantly different from those in 7 states/jurisdictions
- 41 states/jurisdictions did not participate

Average Scores for State/Jurisdiction and Nation (public)

Score
500
310
300 292   287*
290
280
270
260
0   Illinois   Nation (public)

* Significantly different (*p* < .05) from Illinois.

Results for Student Groups in 2009

Reporting Groups	Percent of students	Avg. score	Percentages at or above Basic	Proficient	Percent at Advanced
Gender					
Male	49	286	73	34	3
Female	51	297	84	46	7
Race/Ethnicity					
White	63	299	85	48	6
Black	16	273	60	20	1
Hispanic	15	276	65	24	1
Asian/Pacific Islander	5	308	89	61	13
American Indian/Alaska Native	#	‡	‡	‡	‡

\# Rounds to zero.   ‡ Reporting standards not met.

NOTE: Detail may not sum to totals because of rounding, and the "Unclassified" category for race/ethnicity are not displayed.

Score Gaps for Student Groups

- In 2009, female students in Illinois had an average score that was higher than male students.
- In 2009, Black students had an average score that was 26 points lower than White students. This performance gap was not significantly different from the nation (27 points).
- In 2009, Hispanic students had an average score that was 22 points lower than White students. This performance gap was not significantly different from the nation (22 points).

NOTE: Statistical comparisons are calculated on the basis of unrounded scale scores or percentages. The national results are based on nationally representative samples of twelfth-graders from 1,670 schools. State results in NAEP reading are reported for twelfth-grade public school students in the 11 states that volunteered to participate in the first twelfth-grade state pilot program in 2009: Arkansas, Connecticut, Florida, Idaho, Illinois, Iowa, Massachusetts, New Hampshire, New Jersey, South Dakota, and West Virginia.
SOURCE: U.S. Department of Education, Institute of Education Sciences, National Center for Education Statistics, National Assessment of Educational Progress (NAEP), 2009 Reading Assessment.

The National Assessment of Educational Progress (NAEP) assesses writing for three purposes identified in the NAEP framework: narrative, informative, and persuasive. The NAEP writing scale ranges from 0 to 300.

Overall Writing Results for Illinois

- Illinois' average score (160) in 2007 was higher than that of the nation's public schools (154).[1]
- Of the 45 states and one other jurisdiction that participated in the 2007 eighth-grade assessment, students' average scale score in Illinois was higher than those in 27 jurisdictions, not significantly different from those in 14 jurisdictions, and lower than those in 4 jurisdictions.[2]
- The percentage of students in Illinois who performed at or above the NAEP *Proficient* level was 37 percent in 2007. This percentage was greater than that in the nation (31 percent).
- The percentage of students in Illinois who performed at or above the NAEP *Basic* level was 90 percent in 2007. This percentage was greater than that in the nation (87 percent).

Percentages at NAEP Achievement Levels and Average Score

Illinois (public)					Average Score
2007	10	53	35	2	160
Nation (public)					
2007	13*	57*	29*	2	154*

Percent below *Basic*   Percent at *Basic, Proficient,* and *Advanced*

■ Below *Basic*   □ *Basic*   ▨ *Proficient*   ■ *Advanced*

NOTE: The NAEP grade 8 writing achievement levels correspond to the following scale points: Below *Basic*, 113 or lower; *Basic*, 114–172; *Proficient*, 173–223; *Advanced*, 224 or above.

Performance of NAEP Reporting Groups in Illinois: 2007

Reporting groups	Percent of students	Average score	Percent below *Basic*	Percent of students at or above *Basic*	Percent of students at or above *Proficient*	Percent *Advanced*
Male	51	150↑	15↓	85↑	27↑	1
Female	49	170↑	5↓	95↑	48↑	4
White	58	169↑	6↓	94↑	48↑	3
Black	19	142	19	81	18	#
Hispanic	18	143	18	82	17	#
Asian/Pacific Islander	4	180↑	2	98	60↑	8
American Indian/Alaska Native	#↓	‡	‡	‡	‡	‡
Eligible for National School Lunch Program	40	142	19	81	17	#
Not eligible for National School Lunch Program	60	172↑	5↓	95↑	51↑	4

Average Score Gaps Between Selected Groups

- In 2007, male students in Illinois had an average score that was lower than that of female students by 19 points. This performance gap was not significantly different from that of the nation (20 points).
- In 2007, Black students had an average score that was lower than that of White students by 27 points. This performance gap was wider than that of the nation (22 points).
- In 2007, Hispanic students had an average score that was lower than that of White students by 26 points. This performance gap was not significantly different from that of the nation (21 points).
- In 2007, students who were eligible for free/reduced-price school lunch, an indicator of poverty, had an average score that was lower than that of students who were not eligible for free/reduced-price school lunch by 29 points. This performance gap was wider than that of the nation (23 points).
- In 2007, the score gap between students at the 75th percentile and students at the 25th percentile was 47 points. This performance gap was not significantly different from that of the nation (46 points).

Writing Scores at Selected Percentiles: 2007

Jurisdiction	25th Percentile	50th Percentile	75th Percentile
Illinois	138	162	185
Nation (public)	132*	156*	178*

NOTE: Scores at selected percentiles on the NAEP writing scale indicate how well students at lower, middle, and higher levels performed. For example, the data above show that 75 percent of students in public schools nationally scored below 178, while 75 percent of students in Illinois scored below 185.

Rounds to zero.   ‡ Reporting standards not met.
* Significantly different from Illinois.   ↑ Significantly higher than nation (public). ↓ Significantly lower than nation (public).
[1] Comparisons (higher/lower/narrower/wider/not different) are based on statistical tests. The .05 level with appropriate adjustments for multiple comparisons was used for testing statistical significance. Statistical comparisons are calculated on the basis of unrounded scale scores or percentages. Comparisons across jurisdictions and comparisons with the nation or within a jurisdiction across years may be affected by differences in exclusion rates for students with disabilities (SD) and English language learners (ELL). The exclusion rates for SD and ELL in Illinois were 2 percent and 1 percent in 2007, respectively. For more information on NAEP significance testing, see http://nces.ed.gov/nationsreportcard/writing/interpret-results.asp#statistical.
[2] "Jurisdiction" refers to states, the District of Columbia, and the Department of Defense Education Activity schools.
NOTE: Detail may not sum to totals because of rounding and because the "Information not available" category for the National School Lunch Program, which provides free and reduced-price lunches, and the "Unclassified" category for race/ethnicity are not displayed. Visit http://nces.ed.gov/nationsreportcard/states/ for additional results and detailed information.
SOURCE: U.S. Department of Education, Institute of Education Sciences, National Center for Education Statistics, National Assessment of Educational Progress (NAEP), 2007 Writing Assessment.

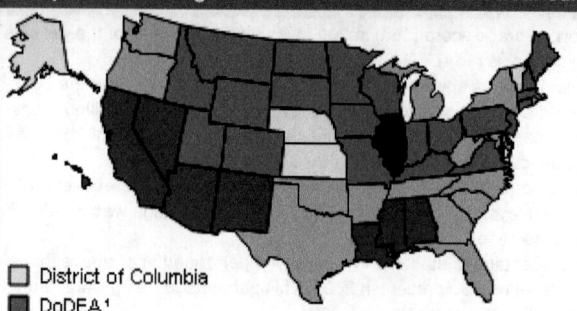

The Nation's Report Card Science 2009
State Snapshot Report

Illinois
Grade 4
Public Schools

2009 Science Assessment Content

Guided by a new framework, the NAEP science assessment was updated in 2009 to keep the content current with key developments in science, curriculum standards, assessments, and research. The 2009 framework organizes science content into three broad content areas. **Physical science** includes concepts related to properties and changes of matter, forms of energy, energy transfer and conservation, position and motion of objects, and forces affecting motion. **Life science** includes concepts related to organization and development, matter and energy transformations, interdependence, heredity and reproduction, and evolution and diversity. **Earth and space sciences** includes concepts related to objects in the universe, the history of the Earth, properties of Earth materials, tectonics, energy in Earth systems, climate and weather, and biogeochemical cycles.

The 2009 science assessment was composed of 143 questions at grade 4, 162 at grade 8, and 179 at grade 12. Students responded to only a portion of the questions, which included both multiple-choice questions and questions that required a written response.

Compare the Average Score in 2009 to Other States/Jurisdictions

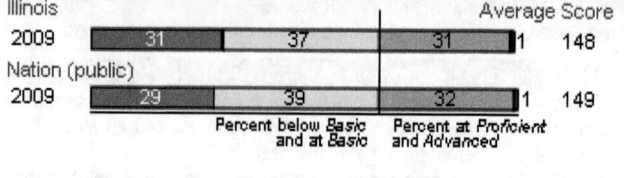

☐ District of Columbia
■ DoDEA[1]

[1] Department of Defense Education Activity (overseas and domestic schools).

In 2009, the average score in **Illinois** was
- lower than those in 23 states/jurisdictions
- higher than those in 8 states/jurisdictions
- not significantly different from those in 15 states/jurisdictions
- 5 states/jurisdictions did not participate

Overall Results

- In 2009, the average score of fourth-grade students in Illinois was 148. This was not significantly different from the average score of 149 for public school students in the nation.
- The percentage of students in Illinois who performed at or above the NAEP *Proficient* level was 32 percent in 2009. This percentage was not significantly different from the nation (32 percent).
- The percentage of students in Illinois who performed at or above the NAEP *Basic* level was 69 percent in 2009. This percentage was not significantly different from the nation (71 percent).

Achievement-Level Percentages and Average Score Results

				Average Score
Illinois 2009	31	37	31	1 148
Nation (public) 2009	29	39	32	1 149

Percent below *Basic* and at *Basic*   Percent at *Proficient* and *Advanced*

■ Below *Basic*   ☐ *Basic*   ■ *Proficient*   ■ *Advanced*

NOTE: Detail may not sum to totals because of rounding.

Results for Student Groups in 2009

Reporting Groups	Percent of students	Avg. score	Percentages at or above Basic	Proficient	Percent at Advanced
Gender					
Male	50	148	69	34	1
Female	50	147	69	30	1
Race/Ethnicity					
White	51	164	87	48	1
Black	19	120	37	9	#
Hispanic	22	129	51	10	#
Asian/Pacific Islander	5	166	86	51	3
American Indian/Alaska Native	#	‡	‡	‡	‡
National School Lunch Program					
Eligible	46	129	50	14	#
Not eligible	53	163	86	48	1

Rounds to zero.   ‡ Reporting standards not met.

NOTE: Detail may not sum to totals because of rounding, and because the "Information not available" category for the National School Lunch Program, which provides free/reduced-price lunches, and the "Unclassified" category for race/ethnicity are not displayed.

Score Gaps for Student Groups

- In 2009, male students in Illinois had an average score that was not significantly different from female students.
- In 2009, Black students had an average score that was 44 points lower than White students. This performance gap was wider than the nation (35 points).
- In 2009, Hispanic students had an average score that was 35 points lower than White students. This performance gap was not significantly different from the nation (32 points).
- In 2009, students who were eligible for free/reduced-price school lunch, an indicator of low family income, had an average score that was 34 points lower than students who were not eligible for free/reduced-price school lunch. This performance gap was wider than the nation (29 points).

NOTE: Statistical comparisons are calculated on the basis of unrounded scale scores or percentages.
SOURCE: U.S. Department of Education, Institute of Education Sciences, National Center for Education Statistics, National Assessment of Educational Progress (NAEP), 2009 Science Assessment.

:**ies** NATIONAL CENTER FOR EDUCATION STATISTICS
Institute of Education Sciences

The **Nation's** Report Card   **Science** 2009
State Snapshot Report

Illinois
Grade 8
Public Schools

2009 Science Assessment Content

Guided by a new framework, the NAEP science assessment was updated in 2009 to keep the content current with key developments in science, curriculum standards, assessments, and research. The 2009 framework organizes science content into three broad content areas. **Physical science** includes concepts related to properties and changes of matter, forms of energy, energy transfer and conservation, position and motion of objects, and forces affecting motion. **Life science** includes concepts related to organization and development, matter and energy transformations, interdependence, heredity and reproduction, and evolution and diversity. **Earth and space sciences** includes concepts related to objects in the universe, the history of the Earth, properties of Earth materials, tectonics, energy in Earth systems, climate and weather, and biogeochemical cycles.

The 2009 science assessment was composed of 143 questions at grade 4, 162 at grade 8, and 179 at grade 12. Students responded to only a portion of the questions, which included both multiple-choice questions and questions that required a written response.

Compare the Average Score in 2009 to Other States/Jurisdictions

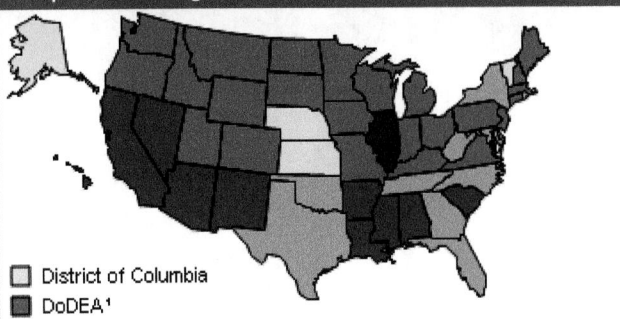

☐ District of Columbia
■ DoDEA[1]

[1] Department of Defense Education Activity (overseas and domestic schools).

In 2009, the average score in **Illinois** was
- lower than those in 25 states/jurisdictions
- higher than those in 10 states/jurisdictions
- not significantly different from those in 11 states/jurisdictions
- 5 states/jurisdictions did not participate

Overall Results

- In 2009, the average score of eighth-grade students in Illinois was 148. This was not significantly different from the average score of 149 for public school students in the nation.
- The percentage of students in Illinois who performed at or above the NAEP *Proficient* level was 28 percent in 2009. This percentage was not significantly different from the nation (29 percent).
- The percentage of students in Illinois who performed at or above the NAEP *Basic* level was 61 percent in 2009. This percentage was not significantly different from the nation (62 percent).

Achievement-Level Percentages and Average Score Results

				Average Score
Illinois 2009	39	33	27	1 148
Nation (public) 2009	38	33	28	1 149

Percent below *Basic* and at *Basic*   Percent at *Proficient* and *Advanced*

■ Below *Basic*   ☐ *Basic*   ■ *Proficient*   ■ *Advanced*

NOTE: Detail may not sum to totals because of rounding.

Results for Student Groups in 2009

Reporting Groups	Percent of students	Avg. score	Percentages at or above		Percent at Advanced
			Basic	*Proficient*	
Gender					
Male	51	150	64	32	2
Female	49	146	58	25	1
Race/Ethnicity					
White	58	162	79	41	2
Black	19	118	23	4	#
Hispanic	18	131	40	10	#
Asian/Pacific Islander	4	167	80	48	5
American Indian/Alaska Native	#	‡	‡	‡	‡
National School Lunch Program					
Eligible	39	127	35	9	#
Not eligible	61	161	78	41	2

Rounds to zero.   ‡ Reporting standards not met.

NOTE: Detail may not sum to totals because of rounding, and because the "Information not available" category for the National School Lunch Program, which provides free/reduced-price lunches, and the "Unclassified" category for race/ethnicity are not displayed.

Score Gaps for Student Groups

- In 2009, male students in Illinois had an average score that was higher than female students.
- In 2009, Black students had an average score that was 44 points lower than White students. This performance gap was wider than the nation (36 points).
- In 2009, Hispanic students had an average score that was 30 points lower than White students. This performance gap was not significantly different from the nation (30 points).
- In 2009, students who were eligible for free/reduced-price school lunch, an indicator of low family income, had an average score that was 34 points lower than students who were not eligible for free/reduced-price school lunch. This performance gap was wider than the nation (28 points).

NOTE: Statistical comparisons are calculated on the basis of unrounded scale scores or percentages.
SOURCE: U.S. Department of Education, Institute of Education Sciences, National Center for Education Statistics, National Assessment of Educational Progress (NAEP), 2009 Science Assessment.

ILLINOIS STANDARDS ACHIEVEMENT TEST (ISAT)

The following tables show the percentages of student scores in each of four performance levels. These levels were established with the help of Illinois educators who teach the grade levels and learning areas tested. Due to rounding, the sum of the percentages in the four performance levels may not always equal 100.

Level 1 -- Academic Warning -   Student work demonstrates limited knowledge and skills in the subject. Because of major gaps in learning, students apply knowledge and skills ineffectively.

Level 2 -- Below Standards -   Student work demonstrates basic knowledge and skills in the subject. However, because of gaps in learning, students apply knowledge and skills in limited ways.

Level 3 -- Meets Standards -   Student work demonstrates proficient knowledge and skills in the subject. Students effectively apply knowledge and skills to solve problems.

Level 4 -- Exceeds Standards -   Student work demonstrates advanced knowledge and skills in the subject. Students creatively apply knowledge and skills to solve problems and evaluate the results.

Grade 3

Grade 3 - All

Levels	Reading				Mathematics			
	1	2	3	4	1	2	3	4
	5.8	19.5	47.6	27.1	2.9	9.8	43.2	44.1

Grade 3 - Gender

Levels	Reading				Mathematics			
	1	2	3	4	1	2	3	4
Male	7.4	21.0	46.5	25.1	3.3	9.9	41.2	45.6
Female	4.2	17.8	48.8	29.2	2.4	9.8	45.2	42.6

Grade 3 - Racial/Ethnic Background

Levels	Reading				Mathematics			
	1	2	3	4	1	2	3	4
White	2.6	12.3	48.2	37.0	1.1	4.9	37.2	56.8
Black	10.8	28.6	47.3	13.2	7.3	18.8	51.0	22.9
Hispanic	9.3	29.3	47.6	13.8	3.6	14.3	52.5	29.5
Asian	2.5	8.4	42.5	46.6	1.2	3.0	24.3	71.5
Native Hawaiian/Pacific Islander	2.7	14.4	46.8	36.0	0.0	4.4	40.7	54.9
American Indian	7.1	21.7	51.8	19.4	3.2	12.4	45.8	38.5
Two or More Races	3.9	16.8	47.2	32.0	1.8	8.7	42.2	47.4

Grade 3 - Limited-English-Proficient

Levels	Reading				Mathematics			
	1	2	3	4	1	2	3	4
	15.4	42.1	37.7	4.8	6.0	20.6	55.5	18.0

Grade 3 - Migrant

Levels	Reading				Mathematics			
	1	2	3	4	1	2	3	4
	18.4	42.9	34.7	4.1	10.0	26.0	48.0	16.0

Grade 3 - Students with Disabilities

Levels	Reading				Mathematics			
	1	2	3	4	1	2	3	4
IEP	20.9	35.2	33.4	10.4	9.2	21.3	46.9	22.5
Non-IEP	3.6	17.2	49.6	29.5	2.0	8.2	42.6	47.2

Grade 3 - Economically Disadvantaged

Levels	Reading				Mathematics			
	1	2	3	4	1	2	3	4
Free/Reduced Price Lunch	9.4	28.2	48.3	14.1	4.8	15.3	51.7	28.2
Not Eligible	1.8	9.9	46.8	41.4	0.8	3.8	33.7	61.6

Grade 4

Grade 4 - All

Levels	Reading				Mathematics				Science			
	1	2	3	4	1	2	3	4	1	2	3	4
	0.9	24.3	44.5	30.2	1.2	11.1	60.1	27.6	3.5	17.2	58.4	21.0

Grade 4 - Gender

Levels	Reading				Mathematics				Science			
	1	2	3	4	1	2	3	4	1	2	3	4
Male	1.2	27.6	44.1	27.1	1.5	11.6	58.3	28.6	3.8	16.9	56.6	22.6
Female	0.6	21.0	44.9	33.5	0.9	10.5	61.9	26.7	3.1	17.5	60.2	19.2

Grade 4 - Racial/Ethnic Background

Levels	Reading				Mathematics				Science			
	1	2	3	4	1	2	3	4	1	2	3	4
White	0.4	14.7	44.3	40.5	0.6	5.8	56.6	37.0	1.1	8.5	60.2	30.2
Black	1.9	40.5	44.3	13.3	2.7	20.9	65.4	11.0	8.2	33.4	52.6	5.7
Hispanic	1.3	35.3	46.4	16.9	1.6	16.1	67.1	15.3	5.4	25.3	59.7	9.7
Asian	0.4	10.4	37.3	52.0	0.6	3.8	41.2	54.3	2.0	7.8	53.1	37.2
Native Hawaiian/Pacific Islander	0.0	21.3	42.5	36.2	3.1	7.1	55.9	33.9	4.7	13.3	53.9	28.1
American Indian	1.1	32.7	43.7	22.4	1.4	13.0	66.4	19.2	3.7	22.2	58.8	15.3
Two or More Races	0.9	19.6	44.2	35.3	0.9	10.5	57.1	31.5	1.9	14.6	58.8	24.6

Grade 4 - Limited-English-Proficient

Levels	Reading				Mathematics				Science			
	1	2	3	4	1	2	3	4	1	2	3	4
	3.2	62.9	30.6	3.2	3.7	29.7	61.2	5.4	13.3	41.5	43.2	2.0

Grade 4 - Migrant

Levels	Reading				Mathematics				Science			
	1	2	3	4	1	2	3	4	1	2	3	4
	1.9	46.3	42.6	9.3	3.6	16.1	75.0	5.4	10.7	26.8	62.5	0.0

Grade 4 - Students with Disabilities

Levels	Reading				Mathematics				Science			
	1	2	3	4	1	2	3	4	1	2	3	4
IEP	4.9	56.0	29.4	9.8	5.7	29.0	55.0	10.3	9.9	31.2	50.1	8.8
Non-IEP	0.3	19.6	46.8	33.3	0.5	8.4	60.9	30.2	2.5	15.1	59.6	22.8

Grade 4 - Economically Disadvantaged

Levels	Reading				Mathematics				Science			
	1	2	3	4	1	2	3	4	1	2	3	4
Free/Reduced Price Lunch	1.5	36.3	46.5	15.7	1.9	17.2	66.5	14.3	5.9	26.6	58.4	9.2
Not Eligible	0.3	11.8	42.4	45.5	0.4	4.6	53.3	41.6	1.0	7.3	58.4	33.3

Grade 5

Grade 5 - All

Levels	Reading				Mathematics			
	1	2	3	4	1	2	3	4
	0.4	23.2	49.1	27.3	0.5	15.5	64.6	19.4

Grade 5 - Gender

Levels	Reading				Mathematics			
	1	2	3	4	1	2	3	4
Male	0.5	26.1	48.8	24.6	0.6	16.5	63.0	19.9
Female	0.2	20.1	49.4	30.2	0.4	14.5	66.3	18.8

Grade 5 - Racial/Ethnic Background

Levels	Reading				Mathematics			
	1	2	3	4	1	2	3	4
White	0.2	13.7	49.8	36.3	0.2	8.9	64.9	25.9
Black	0.8	38.5	48.3	12.4	1.3	29.5	62.5	6.6
Hispanic	0.6	34.7	49.5	15.3	0.6	20.8	68.7	9.8
Asian	0.2	9.8	41.2	48.7	0.4	5.1	48.0	46.5
Native Hawaiian/Pacific Islander	0.0	13.3	49.2	37.5	0.0	10.8	58.5	30.8
American Indian	0.7	28.7	47.9	22.8	0.2	19.7	62.9	17.1
Two or More Races	0.2	18.1	49.4	32.2	0.3	13.4	63.9	22.3

Grade 5 - Limited-English-Proficient

Levels	Reading				Mathematics			
	1	2	3	4	1	2	3	4
	1.8	70.0	25.9	2.2	2.0	43.0	52.3	2.6

Grade 5 - Migrant

Levels	Reading				Mathematics			
	1	2	3	4	1	2	3	4
	2.3	62.8	34.9	0.0	0.0	44.4	55.6	0.0

Grade 5 - Students with Disabilities

Levels	Reading				Mathematics			
	1	2	3	4	1	2	3	4
IEP	2.2	59.6	31.6	6.7	2.5	42.1	50.4	5.0
Non-IEP	0.1	17.7	51.8	30.5	0.2	11.4	66.8	21.6

Grade 5 - Economically Disadvantaged

Levels	Reading				Mathematics			
	1	2	3	4	1	2	3	4
Free/Reduced Price Lunch	0.6	35.3	50.2	13.9	0.8	23.7	67.0	8.5
Not Eligible	0.1	10.9	48.0	41.0	0.2	7.2	62.2	30.5

Grade 6

Grade 6 - All

Levels	Reading				Mathematics			
	1	2	3	4	1	2	3	4
	0.2	15.7	56.8	27.3	0.6	15.5	58.0	25.9

Grade 6 - Gender

Levels	Reading				Mathematics			
	1	2	3	4	1	2	3	4
Male	0.3	19.1	57.1	23.5	0.7	16.8	56.2	26.3
Female	0.1	12.2	56.5	31.3	0.5	14.0	59.9	25.6

Grade 6 - Racial/Ethnic Background

Levels	Reading				Mathematics			
	1	2	3	4	1	2	3	4
White	0.1	9.4	54.7	35.8	0.3	8.9	56.8	34.0
Black	0.4	28.1	60.0	11.4	1.3	30.1	58.6	10.0
Hispanic	0.2	21.7	61.6	16.4	0.7	20.5	63.8	15.1
Asian	0.1	6.0	41.5	52.4	0.2	4.7	38.4	56.6
Native Hawaiian/Pacific Islander	0.0	10.7	55.7	33.6	0.8	9.0	56.6	33.6
American Indian	0.4	18.1	60.4	21.1	0.8	18.1	60.5	20.5
Two or More Races	0.1	12.9	55.1	31.8	0.4	13.3	57.1	29.1

Grade 6 - Limited-English-Proficient

Levels	Reading				Mathematics			
	1	2	3	4	1	2	3	4
	0.9	57.6	39.3	2.2	2.5	46.6	47.4	3.6

Grade 6 - Migrant

Levels	Reading				Mathematics			
	1	2	3	4	1	2	3	4
	2.7	37.8	56.8	2.7	2.7	37.8	54.1	5.4

Grade 6 - Students with Disabilities

Levels	Reading				Mathematics			
	1	2	3	4	1	2	3	4
IEP	1.3	51.5	41.8	5.4	3.1	46.0	45.0	5.9
Non-IEP	0.0	10.3	59.1	30.6	0.2	10.9	60.0	28.9

Grade 6 - Economically Disadvantaged

Levels	Reading				Mathematics			
	1	2	3	4	1	2	3	4
Free/Reduced Price Lunch	0.3	24.5	61.2	13.9	0.9	24.0	62.0	13.1
Not Eligible	0.1	7.0	52.4	40.5	0.2	7.0	54.1	38.7

Grade 7

Grade 7 - All

Levels	Reading				Mathematics				Science			
	1	2	3	4	1	2	3	4	1	2	3	4
	0.4	20.8	58.0	20.8	2.2	13.5	53.9	30.4	5.7	12.4	57.8	24.1

Grade 7 - Gender

Levels	Reading				Mathematics				Science			
	1	2	3	4	1	2	3	4	1	2	3	4
Male	0.6	24.9	56.8	17.7	2.8	15.0	51.7	30.5	6.8	12.4	54.5	26.4
Female	0.2	16.5	59.3	24.1	1.5	12.0	56.2	30.3	4.6	12.4	61.3	21.7

Grade 7 - Racial/Ethnic Background

Levels	Reading				Mathematics				Science			
	1	2	3	4	1	2	3	4	1	2	3	4
White	0.2	14.4	58.3	27.1	1.1	8.5	51.4	38.9	2.9	6.8	55.9	34.5
Black	0.9	34.3	55.7	9.1	4.9	24.4	58.3	12.4	12.3	22.9	58.4	6.5
Hispanic	0.5	26.6	60.9	11.9	2.6	17.7	59.8	19.9	7.5	17.9	63.3	11.3
Asian	0.2	8.2	48.9	42.6	0.8	4.8	33.6	60.9	2.4	5.3	50.2	42.0
Native Hawaiian/Pacific Islander	0.0	13.6	57.4	29.0	0.6	7.1	50.0	42.3	4.2	7.7	59.5	28.6
American Indian	1.0	30.4	55.5	13.1	3.5	19.3	56.4	20.7	8.3	16.3	59.1	16.3
Two or More Races	0.3	19.2	57.6	22.9	2.1	13.3	52.6	32.0	4.8	11.3	55.9	28.1

Grade 7 - Limited-English-Proficient

Levels	Reading				Mathematics				Science			
	1	2	3	4	1	2	3	4	1	2	3	4
	2.3	66.0	30.6	1.1	8.1	40.5	47.0	4.3	22.8	37.2	38.8	1.3

Grade 7 - Migrant

Levels	Reading				Mathematics				Science			
	1	2	3	4	1	2	3	4	1	2	3	4
	2.8	47.2	47.2	2.8	10.8	24.3	56.8	8.1	35.1	16.2	43.2	5.4

Grade 7 - Students with Disabilities

Levels	Reading				Mathematics				Science			
	1	2	3	4	1	2	3	4	1	2	3	4
IEP	2.4	61.2	33.0	3.4	11.1	39.7	42.9	6.2	20.4	27.0	46.1	6.5
Non-IEP	0.1	14.8	61.7	23.4	0.9	9.7	55.5	33.9	3.5	10.2	59.5	26.7

Grade 7 - Economically Disadvantaged

Levels	Reading				Mathematics				Science			
	1	2	3	4	1	2	3	4	1	2	3	4
Free/Reduced Price Lunch	0.7	31.0	58.3	10.0	3.5	20.6	59.4	16.4	9.2	19.3	61.1	10.4
Not Eligible	0.1	11.2	57.7	30.9	0.9	6.9	48.7	43.4	2.4	5.9	54.7	36.9

Grade 8

Grade 8 - All

Levels	Reading				Mathematics			
	1	2	3	4	1	2	3	4
	0.2	14.8	74.9	10.1	0.4	13.3	54.5	31.8

Grade 8 - Gender

Levels	Reading				Mathematics			
	1	2	3	4	1	2	3	4
Male	0.3	17.9	73.0	8.9	0.5	15.1	53.1	31.3
Female	0.1	11.6	76.8	11.5	0.3	11.5	56.0	32.2

Grade 8 - Racial/Ethnic Background

Levels	Reading				Mathematics			
	1	2	3	4	1	2	3	4
White	0.1	9.7	75.9	14.3	0.3	8.4	50.9	40.5
Black	0.3	25.6	71.7	2.4	0.8	25.4	60.6	13.2
Hispanic	0.2	19.7	76.0	4.1	0.5	17.0	61.8	20.8
Asian	0.1	5.9	70.6	23.4	0.2	3.7	34.3	61.9
Native Hawaiian/Pacific Islander	0.6	9.7	73.3	16.4	1.2	8.5	48.5	41.8
American Indian	0.0	20.8	74.0	5.2	1.1	19.4	55.3	24.2
Two or More Races	0.1	14.3	73.4	12.2	0.6	11.8	54.3	33.3

Grade 8 - Limited-English-Proficient

Levels	Reading				Mathematics			
	1	2	3	4	1	2	3	4
	0.8	55.5	43.4	0.2	1.4	39.5	53.8	5.3

Grade 8 - Migrant

Levels	Reading				Mathematics			
	1	2	3	4	1	2	3	4
	4.3	47.8	47.8	0.0	7.7	38.5	38.5	15.4

Grade 8 - Students with Disabilities

Levels	Reading				Mathematics			
	1	2	3	4	1	2	3	4
IEP	1.0	51.5	46.2	1.3	2.4	46.6	45.3	5.7
Non-IEP	0.1	9.4	79.1	11.4	0.1	8.5	55.8	35.6

Grade 8 - Economically Disadvantaged

Levels	Reading				Mathematics			
	1	2	3	4	1	2	3	4
Free/Reduced Price Lunch	0.3	22.7	73.5	3.4	0.7	20.6	61.3	17.4
Not Eligible	0.1	7.8	76.1	16.1	0.2	6.8	48.4	44.6

PRAIRIE STATE ACHIEVEMENT EXAMINATION (PSAE)

The following tables show the percentages of student scores in each of four performance levels. These levels were established with the help of Illinois educators who teach the grade levels and learning areas tested. Due to rounding, the sum of the percentages in the four performance levels may not always equal 100.

Level 1 -- Academic Warning -   Student work demonstrates limited knowledge and skills in the subject. Because of major gaps in learning, students apply knowledge and skills ineffectively.

Level 2 -- Below Standards -   Student work demonstrates basic knowledge and skills in the subject. However, because of gaps in learning, students apply knowledge and skills in limited ways.

Level 3 -- Meets Standards -   Student work demonstrates proficient knowledge and skills in the subject. Students effectively apply knowledge and skills to solve problems.

Level 4 -- Exceeds Standards -   Student work demonstrates advanced knowledge and skills in the subject. Students creatively apply knowledge and skills to solve problems and evaluate the results.

Grade 11

Grade 11 - All

Levels	Reading				Mathematics				Science			
	1	2	3	4	1	2	3	4	1	2	3	4
	10.1	38.9	40.7	10.4	10.0	38.7	43.1	8.2	8.6	42.2	39.6	9.6

Grade 11 - Gender

Levels	Reading				Mathematics				Science			
	1	2	3	4	1	2	3	4	1	2	3	4
Male	12.7	39.3	38.2	9.8	10.6	35.9	43.3	10.2	9.0	38.6	40.1	12.3
Female	7.5	38.5	43.2	10.9	9.4	41.5	42.9	6.2	8.1	45.8	39.2	6.9

Grade 11 - Racial/Ethnic Background

Levels	Reading				Mathematics				Science			
	1	2	3	4	1	2	3	4	1	2	3	4
White	6.1	29.6	49.4	14.9	5.3	29.8	53.5	11.4	4.2	31.3	50.4	14.0
Black	18.5	56.7	23.2	1.6	23.0	56.8	19.6	0.6	19.9	63.2	16.2	0.7
Hispanic	14.7	52.2	30.0	3.1	13.2	51.9	33.0	1.9	11.9	58.1	27.7	2.2
Asian	6.7	27.3	46.3	19.7	3.2	19.0	52.0	25.7	3.9	25.7	49.3	21.2
Native Hawaiian/Pacific Islander	8.0	43.8	41.6	6.6	5.8	40.1	46.7	7.3	2.9	49.6	38.7	8.8
American Indian	12.5	42.4	36.7	8.4	11.9	42.5	40.3	5.3	8.6	48.1	38.0	5.3
Two or More Races	7.6	35.9	43.6	12.9	8.5	38.6	44.1	8.7	6.5	40.2	41.8	11.5

Grade 11 - Limited-English-Proficient

Levels	Reading				Mathematics				Science			
	1	2	3	4	1	2	3	4	1	2	3	4
	55.5	41.0	3.3	0.3	35.8	51.3	11.8	1.2	35.9	57.7	6.2	0.2

Grade 11 - Migrant

Levels	Reading				Mathematics				Science			
	1	2	3	4	1	2	3	4	1	2	3	4
	25.9	51.9	14.8	7.4	14.3	67.9	17.9	0.0	21.4	60.7	17.9	0.0

Grade 11 - Students with Disabilities

Levels	Reading				Mathematics				Science			
	1	2	3	4	1	2	3	4	1	2	3	4
IEP	46.5	37.9	13.4	2.2	46.1	41.8	11.2	0.9	39.6	46.9	11.5	2.1
Non-IEP	5.2	39.0	44.3	11.4	5.2	38.3	47.4	9.1	4.5	41.6	43.4	10.6

Grade 11 - Economically Disadvantaged

Levels	Reading				Mathematics				Science			
	1	2	3	4	1	2	3	4	1	2	3	4
Free/Reduced Price Lunch	17.1	53.1	27.3	2.6	17.8	53.4	27.3	1.5	15.6	59.0	23.6	1.8
Not Eligible	5.5	29.7	49.4	15.4	5.0	29.1	53.4	12.5	4.0	31.3	50.0	14.6

ILLINOIS ALTERNATE ASSESSMENT (IAA)

The Illinois Alternate Assessment (IAA) is administered to students with disabilities whose Individualized Education Programs (IEPs) indicate that participation in the ISAT or PSAE would not be appropriate. The table below presents the percentages of student scores in each of four performance levels.

Level 1 -- Entry -   Students do not demonstrate knowledge and skills in the subject through links to the Illinois Learning Standards.

Level 2 --Foundational -   Students demonstrate emerging knowledge and skills in the subject as linked to the Illinois Learning Standards. Students exhibit an ability to reproduce knowledge and skills.

Level 3 -- Satisfactory -   Students demonstrate basic knowledge and skills in the subject through links to the Illinois Learning Standards. Students exhibit an ability to associate their knowledge and skills.

Level 4 -- Mastery -   Students demonstrate knowledge and skills in the subject through links to the Illinois Learning Standards. Students exhibit the ability to apply their knowledge and skills.

Grade 3

Grade 3 - All

Levels	Reading				Mathematics			
	1	2	3	4	1	2	3	4
	19.8	29.9	37.2	13.1	23.1	20.0	29.2	27.6

Grade 3 - Gender

Levels	Reading				Mathematics			
	1	2	3	4	1	2	3	4
Male	19.4	30.8	36.5	13.4	22.9	20.6	28.1	28.3
Female	20.7	27.6	39.0	12.7	23.6	18.5	31.5	26.4

Grade 3 - Racial/Ethnic Background

Levels	Reading				Mathematics			
	1	2	3	4	1	2	3	4
White	18.6	28.8	35.8	16.8	21.4	19.6	30.6	28.3
Black	23.1	29.4	36.7	10.9	26.8	19.7	27.3	26.3
Hispanic	17.5	31.2	42.1	9.2	22.3	21.0	28.0	28.8
Asian	32.8	31.3	32.8	3.0	27.9	27.9	26.5	17.6
Native Hawaiian/Pacific Islander								
American Indian								
Two or More Races	18.0	29.5	39.3	13.1	21.3	9.8	32.8	36.1

Grade 3 - Limited-English-Proficient

Levels	Reading				Mathematics			
	1	2	3	4	1	2	3	4
	18.0	28.8	44.1	9.0	21.1	22.0	30.0	26.9

Grade 3 - Economically Disadvantaged

Levels	Reading				Mathematics			
	1	2	3	4	1	2	3	4
Free/Reduced Price Lunch	17.7	28.5	38.9	14.9	21.6	17.9	29.7	30.7
Not Eligible	22.4	31.5	35.2	10.9	25.0	22.7	28.5	23.9

Grade 4

Grade 4 - All

Levels	Reading				Mathematics				Science			
	1	2	3	4	1	2	3	4	1	2	3	4
	21.2	24.6	38.3	15.9	14.8	18.5	50.1	16.6	12.8	19.1	27.6	40.5

Grade 4 - Gender

Levels	Reading				Mathematics				Science			
	1	2	3	4	1	2	3	4	1	2	3	4
Male	21.8	24.4	38.0	15.8	15.1	17.9	49.6	17.4	12.2	19.7	27.4	40.7
Female	20.3	24.6	39.1	16.0	14.3	19.2	51.2	15.3	14.0	18.1	27.8	40.1

Grade 4 - Racial/Ethnic Background

Levels	Reading				Mathematics				Science			
	1	2	3	4	1	2	3	4	1	2	3	4
White	18.2	22.8	41.9	17.1	11.8	17.2	52.2	18.8	10.1	17.6	27.6	44.7
Black	23.9	25.6	35.0	15.5	18.3	18.5	47.8	15.5	17.8	17.8	28.2	36.2
Hispanic	22.3	26.2	36.5	15.0	17.0	18.9	49.6	14.5	13.3	21.1	27.0	38.6
Asian	28.2	33.8	28.2	9.9	16.9	26.8	46.5	9.9	12.7	26.8	33.8	26.8
Native Hawaiian/Pacific Islander												
American Indian												
Two or More Races	29.3	19.0	36.2	15.5	17.2	19.0	44.8	19.0	13.8	29.3	19.0	37.9

Grade 4 - Limited-English-Proficient

Levels	Reading				Mathematics				Science			
	1	2	3	4	1	2	3	4	1	2	3	4
	18.7	30.9	38.3	12.2	13.5	18.3	53.9	14.3	12.2	17.8	30.4	39.6

Grade 4 - Economically Disadvantaged

Levels	Reading				Mathematics				Science			
	1	2	3	4	1	2	3	4	1	2	3	4
Free/Reduced Price Lunch	17.5	23.6	40.1	18.9	13.1	15.6	53.1	18.2	11.3	17.0	26.5	45.2
Not Eligible	26.1	25.8	35.9	12.1	17.0	22.3	46.1	14.6	14.8	21.8	29.1	34.3

Grade 5

Grade 5 - All

Levels	Reading				Mathematics			
	1	2	3	4	1	2	3	4
	23.7	21.3	21.8	33.1	13.5	22.6	43.5	20.4

Grade 5 - Gender

Levels	Reading				Mathematics			
	1	2	3	4	1	2	3	4
Male	23.1	22.2	22.6	32.1	13.1	23.0	42.8	21.1
Female	25.1	19.5	20.1	35.3	14.2	21.9	44.9	18.9

Grade 5 - Racial/Ethnic Background

Levels	Reading				Mathematics			
	1	2	3	4	1	2	3	4
White	22.4	20.9	21.4	35.3	12.0	22.9	43.7	21.4
Black	23.9	21.1	24.5	30.4	15.4	20.5	43.8	20.3
Hispanic	25.3	22.7	19.9	32.0	14.2	23.6	42.7	19.4
Asian	39.2	20.3	13.5	27.0	17.8	28.8	41.1	12.3
Native Hawaiian/Pacific Islander								
American Indian								
Two or More Races	17.5	19.3	28.1	35.1	12.3	21.1	43.9	22.8

Grade 5 - Limited-English-Proficient

Levels	Reading				Mathematics			
	1	2	3	4	1	2	3	4
	21.8	24.0	22.3	31.8	11.8	21.9	43.8	22.5

Grade 5 - Economically Disadvantaged

Levels	Reading				Mathematics			
	1	2	3	4	1	2	3	4
Free/Reduced Price Lunch	20.8	20.6	21.6	37.0	12.2	18.9	45.5	23.3
Not Eligible	27.3	22.2	22.1	28.4	14.9	27.1	41.1	16.9

Grade 6

Grade 6 - All

Levels	Reading				Mathematics			
	1	2	3	4	1	2	3	4
	13.9	21.1	34.4	30.6	11.9	14.7	36.3	37.1

Grade 6 - Gender

Levels	Reading				Mathematics			
	1	2	3	4	1	2	3	4
Male	14.1	21.1	34.3	30.5	11.4	14.7	35.1	38.7
Female	13.8	21.0	34.3	31.0	12.8	14.7	38.3	34.2

Grade 6 - Racial/Ethnic Background

Levels	Reading				Mathematics			
	1	2	3	4	1	2	3	4
White	11.4	21.5	34.8	32.3	8.6	16.4	38.4	36.7
Black	17.3	17.9	35.6	29.3	15.6	11.4	34.8	38.2
Hispanic	15.8	22.1	31.9	30.2	15.6	14.8	32.9	36.7
Asian	16.4	32.7	38.2	12.7	10.9	14.5	38.2	36.4
Native Hawaiian/Pacific Islander								
American Indian								
Two or More Races	11.3	22.6	26.4	39.6	9.4	15.1	35.8	39.6

Grade 6 - Limited-English-Proficient

Levels	Reading				Mathematics			
	1	2	3	4	1	2	3	4
	17.6	21.6	33.0	27.8	17.0	13.6	36.4	33.0

Grade 6 - Economically Disadvantaged

Levels	Reading				Mathematics			
	1	2	3	4	1	2	3	4
Free/Reduced Price Lunch	11.4	20.2	34.7	33.7	10.1	11.9	36.7	41.2
Not Eligible	16.8	22.1	34.0	27.1	13.9	17.9	35.9	32.4

Grade 7

Grade 7 - All

Levels	Reading				Mathematics				Science			
	1	2	3	4	1	2	3	4	1	2	3	4
	15.1	20.5	39.3	25.0	15.2	11.9	45.5	27.4	8.3	15.7	28.8	47.2

Grade 7 - Gender

Levels	Reading				Mathematics				Science			
	1	2	3	4	1	2	3	4	1	2	3	4
Male	14.8	20.2	38.9	26.1	15.3	11.0	44.6	29.0	8.0	15.0	28.5	48.5
Female	15.8	21.3	40.0	22.9	15.0	13.5	47.0	24.5	8.8	17.0	29.3	44.8

Grade 7 - Racial/Ethnic Background

Levels	Reading				Mathematics				Science			
	1	2	3	4	1	2	3	4	1	2	3	4
White	14.2	18.6	39.5	27.6	14.7	11.4	45.9	28.1	7.9	14.0	28.3	49.7
Black	15.0	20.3	40.2	24.5	14.6	11.5	45.3	28.7	8.1	16.2	29.1	46.5
Hispanic	16.2	24.3	38.8	20.8	16.2	14.0	43.9	25.9	7.5	18.3	30.5	43.7
Asian	21.0	32.3	38.7	8.1	22.6	14.5	51.6	11.3	16.1	17.7	35.5	30.6
Native Hawaiian/Pacific Islander												
American Indian												
Two or More Races	17.0	19.1	29.8	34.0	14.9	6.4	42.6	36.2	10.6	17.0	17.0	55.3

Grade 7- Limited-English-Proficient

Levels	Reading				Mathematics				Science			
	1	2	3	4	1	2	3	4	1	2	3	4
	19.0	24.7	39.7	16.7	15.5	17.8	44.8	21.8	10.3	17.8	33.9	37.9

Grade 7 - Economically Disadvantaged

Levels	Reading				Mathematics				Science			
	1	2	3	4	1	2	3	4	1	2	3	4
Free/Reduced Price Lunch	11.4	19.3	42.0	27.3	11.0	12.0	46.1	30.8	5.5	13.2	29.4	51.9
Not Eligible	19.8	22.0	36.0	22.2	20.4	11.6	44.8	23.2	11.6	18.9	28.0	41.4

Grade 8

Grade 8 - All

Levels	Reading				Mathematics			
	1	2	3	4	1	2	3	4
	15.5	15.0	35.5	34.1	10.6	17.6	37.4	34.4

Grade 8 - Gender

Levels	Reading				Mathematics			
	1	2	3	4	1	2	3	4
Male	14.3	15.8	35.9	34.1	9.5	17.4	38.0	35.0
Female	17.3	13.6	34.9	34.3	12.3	17.8	36.5	33.4

Grade 8 - Racial/Ethnic Background

Levels	Reading				Mathematics			
	1	2	3	4	1	2	3	4
White	12.9	14.3	34.6	38.2	9.0	16.8	38.7	35.5
Black	17.8	15.4	35.9	30.9	11.8	18.2	36.5	33.5
Hispanic	15.5	17.3	38.5	28.8	9.7	20.0	37.6	32.7
Asian	31.9	13.0	33.3	21.7	27.5	13.0	29.0	30.4
Native Hawaiian/Pacific Islander								
American Indian								
Two or More Races	11.1	8.3	33.3	47.2	11.4	5.7	37.1	45.7

Grade 8 - Limited-English-Proficient

Levels	Reading				Mathematics			
	1	2	3	4	1	2	3	4
	18.9	15.9	36.4	28.8	13.6	16.7	34.8	34.8

Grade 8 - Economically Disadvantaged

Levels	Reading				Mathematics			
	1	2	3	4	1	2	3	4
Free/Reduced Price Lunch	13.5	12.5	36.9	37.0	9.0	14.7	38.6	37.6
Not Eligible	17.9	17.9	33.7	30.6	12.4	21.1	36.0	30.5

Grade 11

Grade 11 - All

Levels	Reading				Mathematics				Science			
	1	2	3	4	1	2	3	4	1	2	3	4
	12.6	19.2	39.4	28.8	14.2	13.7	49.8	22.3	12.8	12.3	25.4	49.6

Grade 11 - Gender

Levels	Reading				Mathematics				Science			
	1	2	3	4	1	2	3	4	1	2	3	4
Male	12.3	20.0	37.6	30.0	15.2	12.7	47.7	24.4	13.3	12.5	22.7	51.4
Female	12.7	17.3	42.1	27.8	12.8	14.6	52.9	19.8	11.9	11.5	29.0	47.6

Grade 11 - Racial/Ethnic Background

Levels	Reading				Mathematics				Science			
	1	2	3	4	1	2	3	4	1	2	3	4
White	11.6	18.7	38.6	31.0	13.1	13.8	50.7	22.3	11.2	13.2	23.6	52.0
Black	11.0	18.9	42.5	27.6	15.2	12.7	50.8	21.2	13.3	10.8	26.8	49.0
Hispanic	16.0	19.5	38.2	26.3	13.9	13.1	48.7	24.3	14.5	11.9	26.7	46.9
Asian	22.2	17.8	31.1	28.9	24.4	11.1	40.0	24.4	22.7	9.1	31.8	36.4
Native Hawaiian/Pacific Islander												
American Indian	8.3	16.7	58.3	16.7	8.3	8.3	50.0	33.3	8.3	0.0	25.0	66.7
Two or More Races	16.7	20.0	30.0	33.3	13.3	26.7	36.7	23.3	16.7	10.0	26.7	46.7

Grade 11 - Limited-English-Proficient

Levels	Reading				Mathematics				Science			
	1	2	3	4	1	2	3	4	1	2	3	4
	21.7	22.6	34.9	20.8	17.0	11.3	52.8	18.9	16.0	15.1	25.5	43.4

Grade 11 - Economically Disadvantaged

Levels	Reading				Mathematics				Science			
	1	2	3	4	1	2	3	4	1	2	3	4
Free/Reduced Price Lunch	9.2	15.7	42.2	32.8	9.8	10.1	54.4	25.7	9.2	9.0	26.3	55.5
Not Eligible	16.1	22.7	36.6	24.6	18.8	17.4	45.0	18.7	16.5	15.7	24.5	43.4

Ancestry

Acadian/Cajun

Top 10 Places Sorted by Number
Based on all places, regardless of population

Place	Number	%
Chicago (city) Cook County	68	0.00
Decatur (city) Macon County	42	0.05
Springfield (city) Sangamon County	41	0.04
North Chicago (city) Lake County	37	0.10
Carbondale (city) Jackson County	31	0.15
Effingham (city) Effingham County	25	0.20
Hanover Park (village) Cook County	20	0.05
Villa Park (village) Du Page County	18	0.08
Rockford (city) Winnebago County	18	0.01
Swansea (village) Saint Clair County	15	0.14

Top 10 Places Sorted by Percent
Based on all places, regardless of population

Place	Number	%
Dunfermline (village) Fulton County	2	0.78
Marine (village) Madison County	4	0.45
Wapella (village) De Witt County	3	0.45
Manito (village) Mason County	7	0.41
North Utica (village) La Salle County	3	0.32
North City (village) Franklin County	2	0.31
Mount Sterling (city) Brown County	6	0.29
Effingham (city) Effingham County	25	0.20
Milledgeville (village) Carroll County	2	0.20
Scott AFB (cdp) Saint Clair County	5	0.18

Top 10 Places Sorted by Percent
Based on places with populations of 10,000 or more

Place	Number	%
Effingham (city) Effingham County	25	0.20
Carbondale (city) Jackson County	31	0.15
Swansea (village) Saint Clair County	15	0.14
North Chicago (city) Lake County	37	0.10
Godfrey (village) Madison County	15	0.09
Villa Park (village) Du Page County	18	0.08
Algonquin (village) McHenry County	14	0.06
Deerfield (village) Lake County	12	0.06
Decatur (city) Macon County	42	0.05
Hanover Park (village) Cook County	20	0.05

Afghan

Top 10 Places Sorted by Number
Based on all places, regardless of population

Place	Number	%
Chicago (city) Cook County	381	0.01
Champaign (city) Champaign County	41	0.06
Naperville (city) Du Page County	31	0.02
Morton Grove (village) Cook County	22	0.10
Wheaton (city) Du Page County	16	0.03
Park City (city) Lake County	14	0.20
Skokie (village) Cook County	14	0.02
Evergreen Park (village) Cook County	11	0.05
Urbana (city) Champaign County	11	0.03
Deer Park (village) Lake County	10	0.31

Top 10 Places Sorted by Percent
Based on all places, regardless of population

Place	Number	%
Deer Park (village) Lake County	10	0.31
Park City (city) Lake County	14	0.20
Morton Grove (village) Cook County	22	0.10
Lincolnwood (village) Cook County	9	0.07
Champaign (city) Champaign County	41	0.06
Evergreen Park (village) Cook County	11	0.05
Wheaton (city) Du Page County	16	0.03
Urbana (city) Champaign County	11	0.03
Lake in the Hills (village) McHenry County	8	0.03
Wilmette (village) Cook County	8	0.03

Top 10 Places Sorted by Percent
Based on places with populations of 10,000 or more

Place	Number	%
Morton Grove (village) Cook County	22	0.10
Lincolnwood (village) Cook County	9	0.07
Champaign (city) Champaign County	41	0.06
Evergreen Park (village) Cook County	11	0.05
Wheaton (city) Du Page County	16	0.03
Urbana (city) Champaign County	11	0.03
Lake in the Hills (village) McHenry County	8	0.03
Wilmette (village) Cook County	8	0.03
Naperville (city) Du Page County	31	0.02
Skokie (village) Cook County	14	0.02

African American/Black

Top 10 Places Sorted by Number
Based on all places, regardless of population

Place	Number	%
Chicago (city) Cook County	1,084,221	37.44
East Saint Louis (city) Saint Clair County	30,983	98.23
Peoria (city) Peoria County	29,553	26.17
Rockford (city) Winnebago County	27,596	18.38
Harvey (city) Cook County	24,232	80.77
Maywood (village) Cook County	22,612	83.79
Dolton (village) Cook County	21,293	83.13
Calumet City (city) Cook County	21,043	53.86
Joliet (city) Will County	20,012	18.84
Springfield (city) Sangamon County	18,072	16.21

Top 10 Places Sorted by Percent
Based on all places, regardless of population

Place	Number	%
Brooklyn (village) Saint Clair County	671	99.26
East Saint Louis (city) Saint Clair County	30,983	98.23
Alorton (village) Saint Clair County	2,692	97.93
Ford Heights (village) Cook County	3,332	96.41
Centreville (city) Saint Clair County	5,723	96.17
Robbins (village) Cook County	6,354	95.76
Phoenix (village) Cook County	2,046	94.85
Venice (city) Madison County	2,377	94.03
Hopkins Park (village) Kankakee County	665	93.53
Washington Park (village) Saint Clair County	4,952	92.65

Top 10 Places Sorted by Percent
Based on places with populations of 10,000 or more

Place	Number	%
East Saint Louis (city) Saint Clair County	30,983	98.23
Riverdale (village) Cook County	13,151	87.35
Maywood (village) Cook County	22,612	83.79
Country Club Hills (city) Cook County	13,468	83.30
Dolton (village) Cook County	21,293	83.13
Bellwood (village) Cook County	16,995	82.76
Harvey (city) Cook County	24,232	80.77
Markham (city) Cook County	10,089	79.94
Hazel Crest (village) Cook County	11,482	77.50
Matteson (village) Cook County	8,284	64.08

African American/Black: Not Hispanic

Top 10 Places Sorted by Number
Based on all places, regardless of population

Place	Number	%
Chicago (city) Cook County	1,068,054	36.88
East Saint Louis (city) Saint Clair County	30,845	97.79
Peoria (city) Peoria County	29,235	25.89
Rockford (city) Winnebago County	27,162	18.09
Harvey (city) Cook County	24,027	80.09
Maywood (village) Cook County	22,485	83.32
Dolton (village) Cook County	21,159	82.61
Calumet City (city) Cook County	20,855	53.38
Joliet (city) Will County	19,763	18.61
Springfield (city) Sangamon County	17,932	16.09

Top 10 Places Sorted by Percent
Based on all places, regardless of population

Place	Number	%
Brooklyn (village) Saint Clair County	668	98.82
East Saint Louis (city) Saint Clair County	30,845	97.79
Alorton (village) Saint Clair County	2,683	97.60
Centreville (city) Saint Clair County	5,695	95.70
Ford Heights (village) Cook County	3,305	95.63
Robbins (village) Cook County	6,317	95.21
Phoenix (village) Cook County	2,031	94.16
Venice (city) Madison County	2,364	93.51
Hopkins Park (village) Kankakee County	664	93.39
Washington Park (village) Saint Clair County	4,929	92.22

Top 10 Places Sorted by Percent
Based on places with populations of 10,000 or more

Place	Number	%
East Saint Louis (city) Saint Clair County	30,845	97.79
Riverdale (village) Cook County	13,066	86.79
Maywood (village) Cook County	22,485	83.32
Country Club Hills (city) Cook County	13,379	82.74
Dolton (village) Cook County	21,159	82.61
Bellwood (village) Cook County	16,848	82.05
Harvey (city) Cook County	24,027	80.09
Markham (city) Cook County	10,030	79.48
Hazel Crest (village) Cook County	11,384	76.84
Matteson (village) Cook County	8,194	63.38

African American/Black: Hispanic

Top 10 Places Sorted by Number
Based on all places, regardless of population

Place	Number	%
Chicago (city) Cook County	16,167	0.56
Waukegan (city) Lake County	822	0.94
Aurora (city) Kane County	715	0.50
Elgin (city) Kane County	487	0.52
Rockford (city) Winnebago County	434	0.29
Evanston (city) Cook County	377	0.51
Cicero (town) Cook County	374	0.44
Peoria (city) Peoria County	318	0.28
North Chicago (city) Lake County	289	0.80
Joliet (city) Will County	249	0.23

Top 10 Places Sorted by Percent
Based on all places, regardless of population

Place	Number	%
Simpson (village) Johnson County	4	7.41
Ullin (village) Pulaski County	14	1.80
Scales Mound (village) Jo Daviess County	6	1.50
Jeffersonville (village) Wayne County	5	1.37
Karnak (village) Pulaski County	8	1.29
Old Mill Creek (village) Lake County	3	1.20
Detroit (village) Pike County	1	1.08
Mound City (city) Pulaski County	7	1.01
Waukegan (city) Lake County	822	0.94
Sauk Village (village) Cook County	94	0.90

Top 10 Places Sorted by Percent
Based on places with populations of 10,000 or more

Place	Number	%
Waukegan (city) Lake County	822	0.94
Sauk Village (village) Cook County	94	0.90
Zion (city) Lake County	198	0.87
North Chicago (city) Lake County	289	0.80
Bellwood (village) Cook County	147	0.72
Matteson (village) Cook County	90	0.70
Forest Park (village) Cook County	108	0.69

Notes: (cdp) census designated place; Refer to the User's Guide in the front of the book for more detailed information.

Place	Number	%
Harvey (city) Cook County	205	0.68
Park Forest (village) Cook County	156	0.66
Hazel Crest (village) Cook County	98	0.66

African, sub-Saharan

Top 10 Places Sorted by Number
Based on all places, regardless of population

Place	Number	%
Chicago (city) Cook County	36,985	1.28
Rockford (city) Winnebago County	1,481	0.99
Peoria (city) Peoria County	1,264	1.12
Bolingbrook (village) Will County	1,084	1.92
Springfield (city) Sangamon County	996	0.89
Oak Park (village) Cook County	899	1.71
Evanston (city) Cook County	899	1.21
Waukegan (city) Lake County	827	0.94
Champaign (city) Champaign County	798	1.18
Harvey (city) Cook County	757	2.51

Top 10 Places Sorted by Percent
Based on all places, regardless of population

Place	Number	%
Elsah (village) Jersey County	41	6.56
Olympia Fields (village) Cook County	253	5.36
Pulaski (village) Pulaski County	15	5.14
Glenwood (village) Cook County	434	4.80
Makanda (village) Jackson County	18	4.42
Mounds (city) Pulaski County	44	3.93
Justice (village) Cook County	470	3.89
Flossmoor (village) Cook County	324	3.49
Phoenix (village) Cook County	74	3.45
Country Club Hills (city) Cook County	542	3.35

Top 10 Places Sorted by Percent
Based on places with populations of 10,000 or more

Place	Number	%
Justice (village) Cook County	470	3.89
Country Club Hills (city) Cook County	542	3.35
Cahokia (village) Saint Clair County	511	3.10
Riverdale (village) Cook County	406	2.71
Dolton (village) Cook County	655	2.54
Harvey (city) Cook County	757	2.51
South Holland (village) Cook County	543	2.44
Matteson (village) Cook County	303	2.35
Hazel Crest (village) Cook County	330	2.24
Bellwood (village) Cook County	412	2.01

African, Subsaharan: African

Top 10 Places Sorted by Number
Based on all places, regardless of population

Place	Number	%
Chicago (city) Cook County	26,959	0.93
Rockford (city) Winnebago County	1,432	0.96
Peoria (city) Peoria County	1,071	0.95
Harvey (city) Cook County	757	2.51
Evanston (city) Cook County	659	0.89
Springfield (city) Sangamon County	653	0.58
Bolingbrook (village) Will County	614	1.09
Waukegan (city) Lake County	609	0.69
Oak Park (village) Cook County	601	1.14
Champaign (city) Champaign County	545	0.80

Top 10 Places Sorted by Percent
Based on all places, regardless of population

Place	Number	%
Pulaski (village) Pulaski County	15	5.14
Glenwood (village) Cook County	414	4.58
Makanda (village) Jackson County	18	4.42
Mounds (city) Pulaski County	44	3.93
Justice (village) Cook County	431	3.56

Place	Number	%
Phoenix (village) Cook County	69	3.22
Cahokia (village) Saint Clair County	511	3.10
Country Club Hills (city) Cook County	501	3.09
Hillside (village) Cook County	236	2.86
Harvey (city) Cook County	757	2.51

Top 10 Places Sorted by Percent
Based on places with populations of 10,000 or more

Place	Number	%
Justice (village) Cook County	431	3.56
Cahokia (village) Saint Clair County	511	3.10
Country Club Hills (city) Cook County	501	3.09
Harvey (city) Cook County	757	2.51
Matteson (village) Cook County	268	2.08
South Holland (village) Cook County	420	1.89
Riverdale (village) Cook County	264	1.76
Bellwood (village) Cook County	359	1.75
Dolton (village) Cook County	414	1.61
Hazel Crest (village) Cook County	213	1.45

African, Subsaharan: Cape Verdean

Top 10 Places Sorted by Number
Based on all places, regardless of population

Place	Number	%
Chicago (city) Cook County	66	0.00
Bolingbrook (village) Will County	23	0.04
Beach Park (village) Lake County	13	0.13
Kankakee (city) Kankakee County	11	0.04
Richton Park (village) Cook County	10	0.08
Orland Park (village) Cook County	8	0.02
North Chicago (city) Lake County	6	0.02
Evanston (city) Cook County	6	0.01
Glendale Heights (village) Du Page County	4	0.01

Top 10 Places Sorted by Percent
Based on all places, regardless of population

Place	Number	%
Beach Park (village) Lake County	13	0.13
Richton Park (village) Cook County	10	0.08
Bolingbrook (village) Will County	23	0.04
Kankakee (city) Kankakee County	11	0.04
Orland Park (village) Cook County	8	0.02
North Chicago (city) Lake County	6	0.02
Evanston (city) Cook County	6	0.01
Glendale Heights (village) Du Page County	4	0.01
Chicago (city) Cook County	66	0.00

Top 10 Places Sorted by Percent
Based on places with populations of 10,000 or more

Place	Number	%
Richton Park (village) Cook County	10	0.08
Bolingbrook (village) Will County	23	0.04
Kankakee (city) Kankakee County	11	0.04
Orland Park (village) Cook County	8	0.02
North Chicago (city) Lake County	6	0.02
Evanston (city) Cook County	6	0.01
Glendale Heights (village) Du Page County	4	0.01
Chicago (city) Cook County	66	0.00

African, Subsaharan: Ethiopian

Top 10 Places Sorted by Number
Based on all places, regardless of population

Place	Number	%
Chicago (city) Cook County	1,186	0.04
Springfield (city) Sangamon County	73	0.07
Evanston (city) Cook County	67	0.09
Flossmoor (village) Cook County	55	0.59
Forest Park (village) Cook County	38	0.24
Elgin (city) Kane County	38	0.04
Glen Ellyn (village) Du Page County	37	0.14

Place	Number	%
Romeoville (village) Will County	33	0.16
Alsip (village) Cook County	27	0.14
Glenview (village) Cook County	21	0.05

Top 10 Places Sorted by Percent
Based on all places, regardless of population

Place	Number	%
Elsah (village) Jersey County	4	0.64
Flossmoor (village) Cook County	55	0.59
Forest Park (village) Cook County	38	0.24
Coulterville (village) Randolph County	2	0.19
Romeoville (village) Will County	33	0.16
Glen Ellyn (village) Du Page County	37	0.14
Alsip (village) Cook County	27	0.14
Evanston (city) Cook County	67	0.09
South Holland (village) Cook County	19	0.09
Springfield (city) Sangamon County	73	0.07

Top 10 Places Sorted by Percent
Based on places with populations of 10,000 or more

Place	Number	%
Forest Park (village) Cook County	38	0.24
Romeoville (village) Will County	33	0.16
Glen Ellyn (village) Du Page County	37	0.14
Alsip (village) Cook County	27	0.14
Evanston (city) Cook County	67	0.09
South Holland (village) Cook County	19	0.09
Springfield (city) Sangamon County	73	0.07
Bellwood (village) Cook County	14	0.07
Glenview (village) Cook County	21	0.05
Glendale Heights (village) Du Page County	15	0.05

African, Subsaharan: Ghanian

Top 10 Places Sorted by Number
Based on all places, regardless of population

Place	Number	%
Chicago (city) Cook County	1,522	0.05
Bolingbrook (village) Will County	301	0.53
Waukegan (city) Lake County	155	0.18
River Forest (village) Cook County	65	0.56
Evanston (city) Cook County	53	0.07
Springfield (city) Sangamon County	48	0.04
Romeoville (village) Will County	46	0.22
Olympia Fields (village) Cook County	42	0.89
Crete (village) Will County	40	0.55
Naperville (city) Du Page County	40	0.03

Top 10 Places Sorted by Percent
Based on all places, regardless of population

Place	Number	%
Olympia Fields (village) Cook County	42	0.89
River Forest (village) Cook County	65	0.56
Crete (village) Will County	40	0.55
Bolingbrook (village) Will County	301	0.53
Sun River Terrace (village) Kankakee County	2	0.48
Romeoville (village) Will County	46	0.22
Effingham (city) Effingham County	26	0.21
Bellwood (village) Cook County	39	0.19
Hazel Crest (village) Cook County	28	0.19
Richton Park (village) Cook County	23	0.19

Top 10 Places Sorted by Percent
Based on places with populations of 10,000 or more

Place	Number	%
River Forest (village) Cook County	65	0.56
Bolingbrook (village) Will County	301	0.53
Romeoville (village) Will County	46	0.22
Effingham (city) Effingham County	26	0.21
Bellwood (village) Cook County	39	0.19
Hazel Crest (village) Cook County	28	0.19
Richton Park (village) Cook County	23	0.19

Notes: (cdp) census designated place; Refer to the User's Guide in the front of the book for more detailed information.

Waukegan (city) Lake County	155	0.18
Lake in the Hills (village) McHenry County	39	0.17
Forest Park (village) Cook County	17	0.11

African, Subsaharan: Kenyan

Top 10 Places Sorted by Number
Based on all places, regardless of population

Place	Number	%
Chicago (city) Cook County	130	0.00
Forest Park (village) Cook County	38	0.24
Urbana (city) Champaign County	32	0.09
Oak Park (village) Cook County	27	0.05
Normal (town) McLean County	26	0.06
Evanston (city) Cook County	25	0.03
Wheaton (city) Du Page County	24	0.04
Macomb (city) McDonough County	19	0.10
Schaumburg (village) Cook County	19	0.03
Dolton (village) Cook County	17	0.07

Top 10 Places Sorted by Percent
Based on all places, regardless of population

Place	Number	%
Elsah (village) Jersey County	4	0.64
Forest Park (village) Cook County	38	0.24
Macomb (city) McDonough County	19	0.10
Urbana (city) Champaign County	32	0.09
Heyworth (village) McLean County	2	0.08
Dolton (village) Cook County	17	0.07
Rolling Meadows (city) Cook County	17	0.07
Murphysboro (city) Jackson County	9	0.07
Normal (town) McLean County	26	0.06
Oak Park (village) Cook County	27	0.05

Top 10 Places Sorted by Percent
Based on places with populations of 10,000 or more

Place	Number	%
Forest Park (village) Cook County	38	0.24
Macomb (city) McDonough County	19	0.10
Urbana (city) Champaign County	32	0.09
Dolton (village) Cook County	17	0.07
Rolling Meadows (city) Cook County	17	0.07
Murphysboro (city) Jackson County	9	0.07
Normal (town) McLean County	26	0.06
Oak Park (village) Cook County	27	0.05
Hinsdale (village) Du Page County	9	0.05
Rantoul (village) Champaign County	7	0.05

African, Subsaharan: Liberian

Top 10 Places Sorted by Number
Based on all places, regardless of population

Place	Number	%
Chicago (city) Cook County	171	0.01
Riverdale (village) Cook County	120	0.80
Champaign (city) Champaign County	95	0.14
Aurora (city) Kane County	74	0.05
Springfield (city) Sangamon County	57	0.05
Decatur (city) Macon County	28	0.03
Gurnee (village) Lake County	21	0.07
Woodridge (village) Du Page County	20	0.06
Kankakee (city) Kankakee County	17	0.06
Rock Island (city) Rock Island County	15	0.04

Top 10 Places Sorted by Percent
Based on all places, regardless of population

Place	Number	%
Riverdale (village) Cook County	120	0.80
Champaign (city) Champaign County	95	0.14
Gurnee (village) Lake County	21	0.07
Woodridge (village) Du Page County	20	0.06
Kankakee (city) Kankakee County	17	0.06

Aurora (city) Kane County	74	0.05
Springfield (city) Sangamon County	57	0.05
Rock Island (city) Rock Island County	15	0.04
Glendale Heights (village) Du Page County	14	0.04
Decatur (city) Macon County	28	0.03

Top 10 Places Sorted by Percent
Based on places with populations of 10,000 or more

Place	Number	%
Riverdale (village) Cook County	120	0.80
Champaign (city) Champaign County	95	0.14
Gurnee (village) Lake County	21	0.07
Woodridge (village) Du Page County	20	0.06
Kankakee (city) Kankakee County	17	0.06
Aurora (city) Kane County	74	0.05
Springfield (city) Sangamon County	57	0.05
Rock Island (city) Rock Island County	15	0.04
Glendale Heights (village) Du Page County	14	0.04
Decatur (city) Macon County	28	0.03

African, Subsaharan: Nigerian

Top 10 Places Sorted by Number
Based on all places, regardless of population

Place	Number	%
Chicago (city) Cook County	5,464	0.19
Dolton (village) Cook County	224	0.87
Oak Park (village) Cook County	185	0.35
Calumet City (city) Cook County	179	0.46
Olympia Fields (village) Cook County	159	3.37
Skokie (village) Cook County	148	0.23
Springfield (city) Sangamon County	137	0.12
Carbondale (city) Jackson County	132	0.64
Urbana (city) Champaign County	119	0.33
Bolingbrook (village) Will County	114	0.20

Top 10 Places Sorted by Percent
Based on all places, regardless of population

Place	Number	%
Olympia Fields (village) Cook County	159	3.37
Elsah (village) Jersey County	14	2.24
Woodland (village) Iroquois County	5	1.54
Flossmoor (village) Cook County	104	1.12
Dolton (village) Cook County	224	0.87
Burnham (village) Cook County	30	0.72
Carbondale (city) Jackson County	132	0.64
Hazel Crest (village) Cook County	79	0.54
Homewood (village) Cook County	98	0.50
Calumet City (city) Cook County	179	0.46

Top 10 Places Sorted by Percent
Based on places with populations of 10,000 or more

Place	Number	%
Dolton (village) Cook County	224	0.87
Carbondale (city) Jackson County	132	0.64
Hazel Crest (village) Cook County	79	0.54
Homewood (village) Cook County	98	0.50
Calumet City (city) Cook County	179	0.46
Oak Park (village) Cook County	185	0.35
Urbana (city) Champaign County	119	0.33
Lansing (village) Cook County	89	0.32
Matteson (village) Cook County	35	0.27
Country Club Hills (city) Cook County	41	0.25

African, Subsaharan: Senegalese

Top 10 Places Sorted by Number
Based on all places, regardless of population

Place	Number	%
Oswego (village) Kendall County	26	0.20
Chicago (city) Cook County	26	0.00
Mount Prospect (village) Cook County	13	0.02

| Broadview (village) Cook County | 9 | 0.11 |

Top 10 Places Sorted by Percent
Based on all places, regardless of population

Place	Number	%
Oswego (village) Kendall County	26	0.20
Broadview (village) Cook County	9	0.11
Mount Prospect (village) Cook County	13	0.02
Chicago (city) Cook County	26	0.00

Top 10 Places Sorted by Percent
Based on places with populations of 10,000 or more

Place	Number	%
Oswego (village) Kendall County	26	0.20
Mount Prospect (village) Cook County	13	0.02
Chicago (city) Cook County	26	0.00

African, Subsaharan: Sierra Leonean

Top 10 Places Sorted by Number
Based on all places, regardless of population

Place	Number	%
Chicago (city) Cook County	55	0.00
South Holland (village) Cook County	30	0.13
Peoria (city) Peoria County	29	0.03
Wheaton (city) Du Page County	20	0.04
Rock Island (city) Rock Island County	16	0.04
Morton (village) Tazewell County	12	0.08

Top 10 Places Sorted by Percent
Based on all places, regardless of population

Place	Number	%
South Holland (village) Cook County	30	0.13
Morton (village) Tazewell County	12	0.08
Wheaton (city) Du Page County	20	0.04
Rock Island (city) Rock Island County	16	0.04
Peoria (city) Peoria County	29	0.03
Chicago (city) Cook County	55	0.00

Top 10 Places Sorted by Percent
Based on places with populations of 10,000 or more

Place	Number	%
South Holland (village) Cook County	30	0.13
Morton (village) Tazewell County	12	0.08
Wheaton (city) Du Page County	20	0.04
Rock Island (city) Rock Island County	16	0.04
Peoria (city) Peoria County	29	0.03
Chicago (city) Cook County	55	0.00

African, Subsaharan: Somalian

Top 10 Places Sorted by Number
Based on all places, regardless of population

Place	Number	%
Chicago (city) Cook County	222	0.01
De Kalb (city) De Kalb County	63	0.16
Bloomington (city) McLean County	20	0.03
Springfield (city) Sangamon County	7	0.01

Top 10 Places Sorted by Percent
Based on all places, regardless of population

Place	Number	%
De Kalb (city) De Kalb County	63	0.16
Bloomington (city) McLean County	20	0.03
Chicago (city) Cook County	222	0.01
Springfield (city) Sangamon County	7	0.01

Top 10 Places Sorted by Percent
Based on places with populations of 10,000 or more

Place	Number	%
De Kalb (city) De Kalb County	63	0.16
Bloomington (city) McLean County	20	0.03
Chicago (city) Cook County	222	0.01
Springfield (city) Sangamon County	7	0.01

African, Subsaharan: South African

Top 10 Places Sorted by Number
Based on all places, regardless of population

Place	Number	%
Chicago (city) Cook County	223	0.01
Schaumburg (village) Cook County	84	0.11
Buffalo Grove (village) Lake County	68	0.16
Wheaton (city) Du Page County	65	0.12
Highland Park (city) Lake County	64	0.20
Aurora (city) Kane County	61	0.04
Urbana (city) Champaign County	59	0.16
Palatine (village) Cook County	55	0.08
Skokie (village) Cook County	43	0.07
Decatur (city) Macon County	43	0.05

Top 10 Places Sorted by Percent
Based on all places, regardless of population

Place	Number	%
Burlington (village) Kane County	2	0.43
Riverwoods (village) Lake County	11	0.29
Dongola (village) Union County	2	0.25
Highland Park (city) Lake County	64	0.20
Westmont (village) Du Page County	42	0.17
Buffalo Grove (village) Lake County	68	0.16
Urbana (city) Champaign County	59	0.16
Northfield (village) Cook County	8	0.15
Olympia Fields (village) Cook County	7	0.15
Inverness (village) Cook County	8	0.13

Top 10 Places Sorted by Percent
Based on places with populations of 10,000 or more

Place	Number	%
Highland Park (city) Lake County	64	0.20
Westmont (village) Du Page County	42	0.17
Buffalo Grove (village) Lake County	68	0.16
Urbana (city) Champaign County	59	0.16
Wheaton (city) Du Page County	65	0.12
Lake Forest (city) Lake County	24	0.12
Schaumburg (village) Cook County	84	0.11
Gages Lake (cdp) Lake County	12	0.11
Deerfield (village) Lake County	17	0.09
Palatine (village) Cook County	55	0.08

African, Subsaharan: Sudanese

Top 10 Places Sorted by Number
Based on all places, regardless of population

Place	Number	%
Chicago (city) Cook County	117	0.00
Justice (village) Cook County	30	0.25
Chicago Heights (city) Cook County	9	0.03
Peoria (city) Peoria County	9	0.01
Champaign (city) Champaign County	6	0.01
Macomb (city) McDonough County	4	0.02

Top 10 Places Sorted by Percent
Based on all places, regardless of population

Place	Number	%
Justice (village) Cook County	30	0.25
Chicago Heights (city) Cook County	9	0.03
Macomb (city) McDonough County	4	0.02
Peoria (city) Peoria County	9	0.01

| **Champaign** (city) Champaign County | 6 | 0.01 |
| **Chicago** (city) Cook County | 117 | 0.00 |

Top 10 Places Sorted by Percent
Based on places with populations of 10,000 or more

Place	Number	%
Justice (village) Cook County	30	0.25
Chicago Heights (city) Cook County	9	0.03
Macomb (city) McDonough County	4	0.02
Peoria (city) Peoria County	9	0.01
Champaign (city) Champaign County	6	0.01
Chicago (city) Cook County	117	0.00

African, Subsaharan: Ugandan

Top 10 Places Sorted by Number
Based on all places, regardless of population

Place	Number	%
Evanston (city) Cook County	27	0.04
Chicago (city) Cook County	24	0.00
Elmhurst (city) Du Page County	15	0.03
Mount Prospect (village) Cook County	13	0.02
Urbana (city) Champaign County	6	0.02

Top 10 Places Sorted by Percent
Based on all places, regardless of population

Place	Number	%
Evanston (city) Cook County	27	0.04
Elmhurst (city) Du Page County	15	0.03
Mount Prospect (village) Cook County	13	0.02
Urbana (city) Champaign County	6	0.02
Chicago (city) Cook County	24	0.00

Top 10 Places Sorted by Percent
Based on places with populations of 10,000 or more

Place	Number	%
Evanston (city) Cook County	27	0.04
Elmhurst (city) Du Page County	15	0.03
Mount Prospect (village) Cook County	13	0.02
Urbana (city) Champaign County	6	0.02
Chicago (city) Cook County	24	0.00

African, Subsaharan: Zairian

Top 10 Places Sorted by Number
Based on all places, regardless of population

Place	Number	%
Champaign (city) Champaign County	7	0.01

Top 10 Places Sorted by Percent
Based on all places, regardless of population

Place	Number	%
Champaign (city) Champaign County	7	0.01

Top 10 Places Sorted by Percent
Based on places with populations of 10,000 or more

Place	Number	%
Champaign (city) Champaign County	7	0.01

African, Subsaharan: Zimbabwean

Top 10 Places Sorted by Number
Based on all places, regardless of population

Place	Number	%
Chicago (city) Cook County	64	0.00
Glenview (village) Cook County	27	0.06
Forest Park (village) Cook County	15	0.10
Champaign (city) Champaign County	12	0.02

Mount Prospect (village) Cook County	12	0.02
Edwardsville (city) Madison County	10	0.05
Bolingbrook (village) Will County	10	0.02
Aurora (city) Kane County	9	0.01
Woodridge (village) Du Page County	8	0.03
Galesburg (city) Knox County	8	0.02

Top 10 Places Sorted by Percent
Based on all places, regardless of population

Place	Number	%
Coalton (village) Montgomery County	4	1.34
Forest Park (village) Cook County	15	0.10
Peru (city) La Salle County	7	0.07
Glenview (village) Cook County	27	0.06
Edwardsville (city) Madison County	10	0.05
Woodridge (village) Du Page County	8	0.03
Champaign (city) Champaign County	12	0.02
Mount Prospect (village) Cook County	12	0.02
Bolingbrook (village) Will County	10	0.02
Galesburg (city) Knox County	8	0.02

Top 10 Places Sorted by Percent
Based on places with populations of 10,000 or more

Place	Number	%
Forest Park (village) Cook County	15	0.10
Glenview (village) Cook County	27	0.06
Edwardsville (city) Madison County	10	0.05
Woodridge (village) Du Page County	8	0.03
Champaign (city) Champaign County	12	0.02
Mount Prospect (village) Cook County	12	0.02
Bolingbrook (village) Will County	10	0.02
Galesburg (city) Knox County	8	0.02
Kankakee (city) Kankakee County	6	0.02
Aurora (city) Kane County	9	0.01

African, Subsaharan: Other

Top 10 Places Sorted by Number
Based on all places, regardless of population

Place	Number	%
Chicago (city) Cook County	756	0.03
De Kalb (city) De Kalb County	58	0.15
Waukegan (city) Lake County	53	0.06
Aurora (city) Kane County	39	0.03
Zion (city) Lake County	34	0.15
Carbondale (city) Jackson County	30	0.14
Peoria (city) Peoria County	25	0.02
Murphysboro (city) Jackson County	23	0.17
Addison (village) Du Page County	23	0.06
Belleville (city) Saint Clair County	23	0.05

Top 10 Places Sorted by Percent
Based on all places, regardless of population

Place	Number	%
Elsah (village) Jersey County	5	0.80
Lebanon (city) Saint Clair County	9	0.26
Flossmoor (village) Cook County	22	0.24
Shawneetown (city) Gallatin County	3	0.22
Mount Pulaski (city) Logan County	3	0.18
Murphysboro (city) Jackson County	23	0.17
Beardstown (city) Cass County	10	0.17
De Kalb (city) De Kalb County	58	0.15
Zion (city) Lake County	34	0.15
Riverdale (village) Cook County	22	0.15

Top 10 Places Sorted by Percent
Based on places with populations of 10,000 or more

Place	Number	%
Murphysboro (city) Jackson County	23	0.17
De Kalb (city) De Kalb County	58	0.15
Zion (city) Lake County	34	0.15
Riverdale (village) Cook County	22	0.15

Notes: (cdp) census designated place; Refer to the User's Guide in the front of the book for more detailed information.

Place	Number	%
Carbondale (city) Jackson County	30	0.14
Lansing (village) Cook County	21	0.07
Forest Park (village) Cook County	11	0.07
Hazel Crest (village) Cook County	10	0.07
Justice (village) Cook County	9	0.07
Waukegan (city) Lake County	53	0.06

Alaska Native tribes, specified

Top 10 Places Sorted by Number
Based on all places, regardless of population

Place	Number	%
Chicago (city) Cook County	68	0.00
Aurora (city) Kane County	11	0.01
Belleville (city) Saint Clair County	10	0.02
North Chicago (city) Lake County	9	0.03
Naperville (city) Du Page County	7	0.01
Loves Park (city) Winnebago County	6	0.03
Lincoln (city) Logan County	5	0.03
Lansing (village) Cook County	5	0.02
Evanston (city) Cook County	5	0.01
Fairmont (cdp) Will County	4	0.16

Top 10 Places Sorted by Percent
Based on all places, regardless of population

Place	Number	%
Coleta (village) Whiteside County	2	1.29
Saint Johns (village) Perry County	2	0.92
Browning (village) Schuyler County	1	0.77
Kansas (village) Edgar County	3	0.36
Tiskilwa (village) Bureau County	2	0.25
Dawson (village) Sangamon County	1	0.21
Buffalo (village) Sangamon County	1	0.20
McCullom Lake (village) McHenry County	2	0.19
Wilsonville (village) Macoupin County	1	0.17
Fairmont (cdp) Will County	4	0.16

Top 10 Places Sorted by Percent
Based on places with populations of 10,000 or more

Place	Number	%
Beach Park (village) Lake County	4	0.04
North Chicago (city) Lake County	9	0.03
Loves Park (city) Winnebago County	6	0.03
Lincoln (city) Logan County	5	0.03
Rantoul (village) Champaign County	4	0.03
Herrin (city) Williamson County	3	0.03
Belleville (city) Saint Clair County	10	0.02
Lansing (village) Cook County	5	0.02
Batavia (city) Kane County	4	0.02
Country Club Hills (city) Cook County	4	0.02

Alaska Native: Alaska Athabascan

Top 10 Places Sorted by Number
Based on all places, regardless of population

Place	Number	%
Chicago (city) Cook County	9	0.00
Belleville (city) Saint Clair County	7	0.02
Naperville (city) Du Page County	4	0.00
Freeport (city) Stephenson County	3	0.01
Lansing (village) Cook County	3	0.01
Aurora (city) Kane County	3	0.00
Bloomington (city) McLean County	3	0.00
Kildeer (village) Lake County	2	0.06
Bridgeview (village) Cook County	2	0.01
Wilsonville (village) Macoupin County	1	0.17

Top 10 Places Sorted by Percent
Based on all places, regardless of population

Place	Number	%
Wilsonville (village) Macoupin County	1	0.17
Kildeer (village) Lake County	2	0.06

Place	Number	%
Zeigler (city) Franklin County	1	0.06
Fairmont City (village) Saint Clair County	1	0.04
Belleville (city) Saint Clair County	7	0.02
Fairfield (city) Wayne County	1	0.02
Savoy (village) Champaign County	1	0.02
Freeport (city) Stephenson County	3	0.01
Lansing (village) Cook County	3	0.01
Bridgeview (village) Cook County	2	0.01

Top 10 Places Sorted by Percent
Based on places with populations of 10,000 or more

Place	Number	%
Belleville (city) Saint Clair County	7	0.02
Freeport (city) Stephenson County	3	0.01
Lansing (village) Cook County	3	0.01
Bridgeview (village) Cook County	2	0.01
Hinsdale (village) Du Page County	1	0.01
Lincoln (city) Logan County	1	0.01
New Lenox (village) Will County	1	0.01
Ottawa (city) La Salle County	1	0.01
Warrenville (city) Du Page County	1	0.01
Washington (city) Tazewell County	1	0.01

Alaska Native: Aleut

Top 10 Places Sorted by Number
Based on all places, regardless of population

Place	Number	%
Chicago (city) Cook County	11	0.00
Beach Park (village) Lake County	4	0.04
Downers Grove (village) Du Page County	4	0.01
Herrin (city) Williamson County	3	0.03
Fairmont (cdp) Will County	2	0.08
Marshall (city) Clark County	2	0.05
Bourbonnais (village) Kankakee County	2	0.01
Woodridge (village) Du Page County	2	0.01
Aurora (city) Kane County	2	0.00
Champaign (city) Champaign County	2	0.00

Top 10 Places Sorted by Percent
Based on all places, regardless of population

Place	Number	%
Coleta (village) Whiteside County	1	0.65
Fairmont (cdp) Will County	2	0.08
Channel Lake (cdp) Lake County	1	0.06
Marshall (city) Clark County	2	0.05
Beach Park (village) Lake County	4	0.04
Herrin (city) Williamson County	3	0.03
Carlyle (city) Clinton County	1	0.03
Round Lake Park (village) Lake County	1	0.02
Downers Grove (village) Du Page County	4	0.01
Bourbonnais (village) Kankakee County	2	0.01

Top 10 Places Sorted by Percent
Based on places with populations of 10,000 or more

Place	Number	%
Beach Park (village) Lake County	4	0.04
Herrin (city) Williamson County	3	0.03
Downers Grove (village) Du Page County	4	0.01
Bourbonnais (village) Kankakee County	2	0.01
Woodridge (village) Du Page County	2	0.01
Hinsdale (village) Du Page County	1	0.01
Homewood (village) Cook County	1	0.01
Macomb (city) McDonough County	1	0.01
River Forest (village) Cook County	1	0.01
Chicago (city) Cook County	11	0.00

Alaska Native: Eskimo

Top 10 Places Sorted by Number
Based on all places, regardless of population

Place	Number	%
Chicago (city) Cook County	32	0.00
Loves Park (city) Winnebago County	6	0.03
Rantoul (village) Champaign County	4	0.03
Batavia (city) Kane County	4	0.02
Country Club Hills (city) Cook County	4	0.02
North Chicago (city) Lake County	4	0.01
Aurora (city) Kane County	4	0.00
Kansas (village) Edgar County	3	0.36
Tremont (village) Tazewell County	3	0.15
Oregon (city) Ogle County	3	0.07

Top 10 Places Sorted by Percent
Based on all places, regardless of population

Place	Number	%
Saint Johns (village) Perry County	2	0.92
Browning (village) Schuyler County	1	0.77
Coleta (village) Whiteside County	1	0.65
Kansas (village) Edgar County	3	0.36
Tiskilwa (village) Bureau County	2	0.25
Dawson (village) Sangamon County	1	0.21
Buffalo (village) Sangamon County	1	0.20
Tremont (village) Tazewell County	3	0.15
Wapella (village) De Witt County	1	0.15
Fairmont (cdp) Will County	2	0.08

Top 10 Places Sorted by Percent
Based on places with populations of 10,000 or more

Place	Number	%
Loves Park (city) Winnebago County	6	0.03
Rantoul (village) Champaign County	4	0.03
Batavia (city) Kane County	4	0.02
Country Club Hills (city) Cook County	4	0.02
Grayslake (village) Lake County	3	0.02
North Chicago (city) Lake County	4	0.01
Belleville (city) Saint Clair County	3	0.01
East Peoria (city) Tazewell County	3	0.01
Moline (city) Rock Island County	3	0.01
Lake in the Hills (village) McHenry County	2	0.01

Alaska Native: Tlingit-Haida

Top 10 Places Sorted by Number
Based on all places, regardless of population

Place	Number	%
Chicago (city) Cook County	15	0.00
O'Fallon (city) Saint Clair County	4	0.02
Evanston (city) Cook County	4	0.01
La Grange (village) Cook County	3	0.02
Lincoln (city) Logan County	3	0.02
McCullom Lake (village) McHenry County	2	0.19
Lemont (village) Cook County	2	0.02
Lansing (village) Cook County	2	0.01
Aurora (city) Kane County	2	0.00
Bolingbrook (village) Will County	2	0.00

Top 10 Places Sorted by Percent
Based on all places, regardless of population

Place	Number	%
McCullom Lake (village) McHenry County	2	0.19
Elsah (village) Jersey County	1	0.16
O'Fallon (city) Saint Clair County	4	0.02
La Grange (village) Cook County	3	0.02
Lincoln (city) Logan County	3	0.02
Lemont (village) Cook County	2	0.02
Lake Bluff (village) Lake County	1	0.02
Evanston (city) Cook County	4	0.01
Lansing (village) Cook County	2	0.01

Notes: (cdp) census designated place; Refer to the User's Guide in the front of the book for more detailed information.

Brookfield (village) Cook County   1   0.01

Top 10 Places Sorted by Percent
Based on places with populations of 10,000 or more

Place	Number	%
O'Fallon (city) Saint Clair County	4	0.02
La Grange (village) Cook County	3	0.02
Lincoln (city) Logan County	3	0.02
Lemont (village) Cook County	2	0.02
Evanston (city) Cook County	4	0.01
Lansing (village) Cook County	2	0.01
Brookfield (village) Cook County	1	0.01
Fairview Heights (city) Saint Clair County	1	0.01
Marion (city) Williamson County	1	0.01
Mattoon (city) Coles County	1	0.01

Alaska Native: All other tribes

Top 10 Places Sorted by Number
Based on all places, regardless of population

Place	Number	%
Pekin (city) Tazewell County	4	0.01
Harvard (city) McHenry County	3	0.04
North Chicago (city) Lake County	3	0.01
Lombard (village) Du Page County	2	0.00
Carthage (city) Hancock County	1	0.04
Chicago (city) Cook County	1	0.00
Villa Park (village) Du Page County	1	0.00
Wheaton (city) Du Page County	1	0.00

Top 10 Places Sorted by Percent
Based on all places, regardless of population

Place	Number	%
Harvard (city) McHenry County	3	0.04
Carthage (city) Hancock County	1	0.04
Pekin (city) Tazewell County	4	0.01
North Chicago (city) Lake County	3	0.01
Lombard (village) Du Page County	2	0.00
Chicago (city) Cook County	1	0.00
Villa Park (village) Du Page County	1	0.00
Wheaton (city) Du Page County	1	0.00

Top 10 Places Sorted by Percent
Based on places with populations of 10,000 or more

Place	Number	%
Pekin (city) Tazewell County	4	0.01
North Chicago (city) Lake County	3	0.01
Lombard (village) Du Page County	2	0.00
Chicago (city) Cook County	1	0.00
Villa Park (village) Du Page County	1	0.00
Wheaton (city) Du Page County	1	0.00

Alaska Native tribes, not specified

Top 10 Places Sorted by Number
Based on all places, regardless of population

Place	Number	%
Chicago (city) Cook County	8	0.00
Gurnee (village) Lake County	3	0.01
Cicero (town) Cook County	3	0.00
Plymouth (village) Hancock County	1	0.18
Hodgkins (village) Cook County	1	0.05
Fairfield (city) Wayne County	1	0.02
Lincolnshire (village) Lake County	1	0.02
Park City (city) Lake County	1	0.02
Savoy (village) Champaign County	1	0.02
Tuscola (city) Douglas County	1	0.02

Top 10 Places Sorted by Percent
Based on all places, regardless of population

Place	Number	%
Plymouth (village) Hancock County	1	0.18
Hodgkins (village) Cook County	1	0.05
Fairfield (city) Wayne County	1	0.02
Lincolnshire (village) Lake County	1	0.02
Park City (city) Lake County	1	0.02
Savoy (village) Champaign County	1	0.02
Tuscola (city) Douglas County	1	0.02
Gurnee (village) Lake County	3	0.01
Calumet Park (village) Cook County	1	0.01
Herrin (city) Williamson County	1	0.01

Top 10 Places Sorted by Percent
Based on places with populations of 10,000 or more

Place	Number	%
Gurnee (village) Lake County	3	0.01
Herrin (city) Williamson County	1	0.01
Ottawa (city) La Salle County	1	0.01
Chicago (city) Cook County	8	0.00
Cicero (town) Cook County	3	0.00
Aurora (city) Kane County	1	0.00
Belleville (city) Saint Clair County	1	0.00
Belvidere (city) Boone County	1	0.00
Decatur (city) Macon County	1	0.00
East Moline (city) Rock Island County	1	0.00

American Indian or Alaska Native, not specified

Top 10 Places Sorted by Number
Based on all places, regardless of population

Place	Number	%
Chicago (city) Cook County	9,741	0.34
Cicero (town) Cook County	592	0.69
Aurora (city) Kane County	461	0.32
Waukegan (city) Lake County	442	0.50
Rockford (city) Winnebago County	432	0.29
Elgin (city) Kane County	347	0.37
Joliet (city) Will County	324	0.31
Peoria (city) Peoria County	277	0.25
Springfield (city) Sangamon County	268	0.24
Evanston (city) Cook County	206	0.28

Top 10 Places Sorted by Percent
Based on all places, regardless of population

Place	Number	%
Long Point (village) Livingston County	7	2.83
Muddy (village) Saline County	2	2.56
Royal Lakes (village) Macoupin County	4	2.11
Palmer (village) Christian County	5	2.02
Eddyville (village) Pope County	3	1.96
West Brooklyn (village) Lee County	3	1.72
Emington (village) Livingston County	2	1.67
Vergennes (village) Jackson County	8	1.63
Ellsworth (village) McLean County	4	1.48
Winslow (village) Stephenson County	5	1.45

Top 10 Places Sorted by Percent
Based on places with populations of 10,000 or more

Place	Number	%
Cicero (town) Cook County	592	0.69
Round Lake Beach (village) Lake County	146	0.56
North Chicago (city) Lake County	183	0.51
Blue Island (city) Cook County	120	0.51
Waukegan (city) Lake County	442	0.50
Bensenville (village) Du Page County	97	0.47
Mount Vernon (city) Jefferson County	70	0.43
Centralia (city) Marion County	61	0.43
Sauk Village (village) Cook County	45	0.43
Granite City (city) Madison County	130	0.42

Albanian

Top 10 Places Sorted by Number
Based on all places, regardless of population

Place	Number	%
Chicago (city) Cook County	1,368	0.05
Addison (village) Du Page County	267	0.75
Elmwood Park (village) Cook County	202	0.80
Naperville (city) Du Page County	180	0.14
Carol Stream (village) Du Page County	148	0.37
Mount Prospect (village) Cook County	148	0.26
Summit (village) Cook County	144	1.35
Elgin (city) Kane County	116	0.12
Glen Ellyn (village) Du Page County	111	0.41
Joliet (city) Will County	98	0.09

Top 10 Places Sorted by Percent
Based on all places, regardless of population

Place	Number	%
Hindsboro (village) Douglas County	8	2.25
Newark (village) Kendall County	16	1.76
Hampton (village) Rock Island County	27	1.69
Greenup (village) Cumberland County	24	1.57
Summit (village) Cook County	144	1.35
Sandwich (city) De Kalb County	88	1.35
Cordova (village) Rock Island County	8	1.28
Bull Valley (village) McHenry County	8	1.15
Andalusia (village) Rock Island County	12	1.13
Roscoe (village) Winnebago County	69	1.09

Top 10 Places Sorted by Percent
Based on places with populations of 10,000 or more

Place	Number	%
Summit (village) Cook County	144	1.35
Elmwood Park (village) Cook County	202	0.80
Addison (village) Du Page County	267	0.75
Lyons (village) Cook County	74	0.73
Justice (village) Cook County	57	0.47
Bridgeview (village) Cook County	70	0.46
Glen Ellyn (village) Du Page County	111	0.41
Carol Stream (village) Du Page County	148	0.37
Hickory Hills (city) Cook County	52	0.37
Palos Hills (city) Cook County	64	0.36

Alsatian

Top 10 Places Sorted by Number
Based on all places, regardless of population

Place	Number	%
Chicago (city) Cook County	137	0.00
Flossmoor (village) Cook County	55	0.59
Naperville (city) Du Page County	30	0.02
Oak Park (village) Cook County	28	0.05
Niles (village) Cook County	24	0.08
Princeton (city) Bureau County	21	0.28
Lake Forest (city) Lake County	20	0.10
Plainfield (village) Will County	18	0.14
Elmhurst (city) Du Page County	16	0.04
Springfield (city) Sangamon County	16	0.01

Top 10 Places Sorted by Percent
Based on all places, regardless of population

Place	Number	%
Flossmoor (village) Cook County	55	0.59
Princeton (city) Bureau County	21	0.28
Aroma Park (village) Kankakee County	2	0.24
Hopedale (village) Tazewell County	2	0.21
Genoa (city) De Kalb County	8	0.18
Sheldon (village) Iroquois County	2	0.17
Lake Bluff (village) Lake County	9	0.15
Metamora (village) Woodford County	4	0.15
Plainfield (village) Will County	18	0.14

Marengo (city) McHenry County	9	0.14

Top 10 Places Sorted by Percent
Based on places with populations of 10,000 or more

Place	Number	%
Plainfield (village) Will County	18	0.14
Lake Forest (city) Lake County	20	0.10
River Forest (village) Cook County	12	0.10
Niles (village) Cook County	24	0.08
Park Forest (village) Cook County	13	0.06
Lemont (village) Cook County	8	0.06
Oak Park (village) Cook County	28	0.05
Wilmette (village) Cook County	14	0.05
Saint Charles (city) Kane County	13	0.05
Hinsdale (village) Du Page County	8	0.05

American Indian tribes, specified

Top 10 Places Sorted by Number
Based on all places, regardless of population

Place	Number	%
Chicago (city) Cook County	10,059	0.35
Rockford (city) Winnebago County	793	0.53
Aurora (city) Kane County	493	0.34
Cicero (town) Cook County	464	0.54
North Chicago (city) Lake County	410	1.14
Peoria (city) Peoria County	408	0.36
Waukegan (city) Lake County	396	0.45
Springfield (city) Sangamon County	377	0.34
Elgin (city) Kane County	344	0.36
Joliet (city) Will County	329	0.31

Top 10 Places Sorted by Percent
Based on all places, regardless of population

Place	Number	%
Topeka (village) Mason County	4	4.44
Dunfermline (village) Fulton County	8	3.05
Venedy (village) Washington County	4	2.92
Junction (village) Gallatin County	4	2.88
Dongola (village) Union County	22	2.73
Otterville (town) Jersey County	3	2.50
Wilmington (village) Greene County	3	2.50
Alsey (village) Scott County	6	2.44
Shawneetown (city) Gallatin County	32	2.27
Maunie (village) White County	4	2.26

Top 10 Places Sorted by Percent
Based on places with populations of 10,000 or more

Place	Number	%
North Chicago (city) Lake County	410	1.14
Zion (city) Lake County	212	0.93
Rantoul (village) Champaign County	100	0.78
Beach Park (village) Lake County	70	0.69
Carpentersville (village) Kane County	186	0.61
Round Lake Beach (village) Lake County	157	0.61
Sauk Village (village) Cook County	64	0.61
Granite City (city) Madison County	186	0.59
Murphysboro (city) Jackson County	77	0.58
Romeoville (village) Will County	121	0.57

American Indian: Apache

Top 10 Places Sorted by Number
Based on all places, regardless of population

Place	Number	%
Chicago (city) Cook County	278	0.01
Rockford (city) Winnebago County	30	0.02
Peoria (city) Peoria County	20	0.02
North Chicago (city) Lake County	17	0.05
Aurora (city) Kane County	15	0.01
Naperville (city) Du Page County	15	0.01
Burbank (city) Cook County	13	0.05

Chicago Heights (city) Cook County	13	0.04
Springfield (city) Sangamon County	13	0.01
Jacksonville (city) Morgan County	12	0.06

Top 10 Places Sorted by Percent
Based on all places, regardless of population

Place	Number	%
Banner (village) Fulton County	3	2.01
Mapleton (village) Peoria County	2	0.88
Vermont (village) Fulton County	5	0.63
Maunie (village) White County	1	0.56
Elsah (village) Jersey County	3	0.47
Chesterfield (village) Macoupin County	1	0.45
Tonica (village) La Salle County	3	0.44
Owaneco (village) Christian County	1	0.39
Old Shawneetown (village) Gallatin County	1	0.36
Lee (village) Lee County	1	0.32

Top 10 Places Sorted by Percent
Based on places with populations of 10,000 or more

Place	Number	%
Jacksonville (city) Morgan County	12	0.06
Lockport (city) Will County	9	0.06
Chicago Ridge (village) Cook County	8	0.06
Swansea (village) Saint Clair County	6	0.06
North Chicago (city) Lake County	17	0.05
Burbank (city) Cook County	13	0.05
Romeoville (village) Will County	10	0.05
Centralia (city) Marion County	7	0.05
Chicago Heights (city) Cook County	13	0.04
Carpentersville (village) Kane County	11	0.04

American Indian: Blackfeet

Top 10 Places Sorted by Number
Based on all places, regardless of population

Place	Number	%
Chicago (city) Cook County	425	0.01
Rockford (city) Winnebago County	62	0.04
Peoria (city) Peoria County	33	0.03
North Chicago (city) Lake County	29	0.08
Aurora (city) Kane County	28	0.02
Calumet City (city) Cook County	24	0.06
Evanston (city) Cook County	22	0.03
Rock Island (city) Rock Island County	21	0.05
Pekin (city) Tazewell County	19	0.06
Decatur (city) Macon County	19	0.02

Top 10 Places Sorted by Percent
Based on all places, regardless of population

Place	Number	%
Alsey (village) Scott County	3	1.22
Tower Hill (village) Shelby County	5	0.82
New Douglas (village) Madison County	3	0.81
Longview (village) Champaign County	1	0.65
Crossville (village) White County	5	0.64
Ferris (village) Hancock County	1	0.60
Tamms (village) Alexander County	4	0.55
Grafton (city) Jersey County	3	0.49
Patoka (village) Marion County	3	0.47
Greenfield (city) Greene County	5	0.42

Top 10 Places Sorted by Percent
Based on places with populations of 10,000 or more

Place	Number	%
Rantoul (village) Champaign County	11	0.09
North Chicago (city) Lake County	29	0.08
Zion (city) Lake County	18	0.08
Forest Park (village) Cook County	13	0.08
Murphysboro (city) Jackson County	11	0.08
Matteson (village) Cook County	10	0.08
Country Club Hills (city) Cook County	11	0.07

Kewanee (city) Henry County	9	0.07
Richton Park (village) Cook County	9	0.07
Calumet City (city) Cook County	24	0.06

American Indian: Cherokee

Top 10 Places Sorted by Number
Based on all places, regardless of population

Place	Number	%
Chicago (city) Cook County	2,337	0.08
Rockford (city) Winnebago County	346	0.23
Peoria (city) Peoria County	221	0.20
Springfield (city) Sangamon County	207	0.19
North Chicago (city) Lake County	175	0.49
Aurora (city) Kane County	164	0.11
Decatur (city) Macon County	140	0.17
Granite City (city) Madison County	115	0.37
Joliet (city) Will County	115	0.11
Waukegan (city) Lake County	113	0.13

Top 10 Places Sorted by Percent
Based on all places, regardless of population

Place	Number	%
Junction (village) Gallatin County	4	2.88
Otterville (town) Jersey County	3	2.50
Wilmington (village) Greene County	3	2.50
Belknap (village) Johnson County	3	2.26
Panama (village) Montgomery County	7	2.17
Dongola (village) Union County	16	1.99
Alvin (village) Vermilion County	6	1.90
Kilbourne (village) Mason County	7	1.87
Simpson (village) Johnson County	1	1.85
Gorham (village) Jackson County	4	1.56

Top 10 Places Sorted by Percent
Based on places with populations of 10,000 or more

Place	Number	%
North Chicago (city) Lake County	175	0.49
Zion (city) Lake County	89	0.39
Murphysboro (city) Jackson County	52	0.39
Granite City (city) Madison County	115	0.37
Mount Vernon (city) Jefferson County	61	0.37
Carbondale (city) Jackson County	70	0.34
Rantoul (village) Champaign County	42	0.33
O'Fallon (city) Saint Clair County	68	0.31
Beach Park (village) Lake County	31	0.31
Cahokia (village) Saint Clair County	48	0.29

American Indian: Cheyenne

Top 10 Places Sorted by Number
Based on all places, regardless of population

Place	Number	%
Chicago (city) Cook County	44	0.00
University Park (village) Will County	6	0.09
Rockford (city) Winnebago County	6	0.00
Waukegan (city) Lake County	5	0.01
Topeka (village) Mason County	4	4.44
South Beloit (city) Winnebago County	4	0.07
Yorkville (city) Kendall County	4	0.06
Wood River (city) Madison County	4	0.04
Joliet (city) Will County	4	0.00
Peoria (city) Peoria County	4	0.00

Top 10 Places Sorted by Percent
Based on all places, regardless of population

Place	Number	%
Topeka (village) Mason County	4	4.44
Lynnville (village) Morgan County	1	0.73
La Rose (village) Marshall County	1	0.63
Maunie (village) White County	1	0.56
Thawville (village) Iroquois County	1	0.39

	Number	%
Hanover (village) Jo Daviess County	1	0.12
Lakemoor (village) McHenry County	3	0.11
Hardin (village) Calhoun County	1	0.10
University Park (village) Will County	6	0.09
Energy (village) Williamson County	1	0.09

Top 10 Places Sorted by Percent
Based on places with populations of 10,000 or more

Place	Number	%
Wood River (city) Madison County	4	0.04
Pontiac (city) Livingston County	3	0.03
Crest Hill (city) Will County	3	0.02
Goodings Grove (cdp) Will County	3	0.02
Macomb (city) McDonough County	3	0.02
Waukegan (city) Lake County	5	0.01
North Chicago (city) Lake County	3	0.01
Orland Park (village) Cook County	3	0.01
Zion (city) Lake County	3	0.01
Alton (city) Madison County	2	0.01

American Indian: Chickasaw

Top 10 Places Sorted by Number
Based on all places, regardless of population

Place	Number	%
Chicago (city) Cook County	46	0.00
Forest Park (village) Cook County	5	0.03
Ottawa (city) La Salle County	5	0.03
Belleville (city) Saint Clair County	5	0.01
Evanston (city) Cook County	5	0.01
El Paso (city) Woodford County	4	0.15
Caseyville (village) Saint Clair County	4	0.09
Jacksonville (city) Morgan County	4	0.02
Morton Grove (village) Cook County	4	0.02
Bolingbrook (village) Will County	4	0.01

Top 10 Places Sorted by Percent
Based on all places, regardless of population

Place	Number	%
Donovan (village) Iroquois County	1	0.28
Mackinaw (village) Tazewell County	3	0.21
Hecker (village) Monroe County	1	0.21
El Paso (city) Woodford County	4	0.15
Colfax (village) McLean County	1	0.10
Elkville (village) Jackson County	1	0.10
Stillman Valley (village) Ogle County	1	0.10
Caseyville (village) Saint Clair County	4	0.09
Hillcrest (village) Ogle County	1	0.09
Ashland (village) Cass County	1	0.07

Top 10 Places Sorted by Percent
Based on places with populations of 10,000 or more

Place	Number	%
Forest Park (village) Cook County	5	0.03
Ottawa (city) La Salle County	5	0.03
Jacksonville (city) Morgan County	4	0.02
Morton Grove (village) Cook County	4	0.02
Bourbonnais (village) Kankakee County	3	0.02
Godfrey (village) Madison County	3	0.02
Glen Carbon (village) Madison County	2	0.02
Murphysboro (city) Jackson County	2	0.02
Belleville (city) Saint Clair County	5	0.01
Evanston (city) Cook County	5	0.01

American Indian: Chippewa

Top 10 Places Sorted by Number
Based on all places, regardless of population

Place	Number	%
Chicago (city) Cook County	636	0.02
Waukegan (city) Lake County	33	0.04
Rockford (city) Winnebago County	31	0.02
Zion (city) Lake County	29	0.13
Round Lake Beach (village) Lake County	29	0.11
Berwyn (city) Cook County	28	0.05
Elgin (city) Kane County	24	0.03
Joliet (city) Will County	23	0.02
Evanston (city) Cook County	22	0.03
Aurora (city) Kane County	22	0.02

Top 10 Places Sorted by Percent
Based on all places, regardless of population

Place	Number	%
Dunfermline (village) Fulton County	4	1.53
Thomson (village) Carroll County	5	0.89
Donovan (village) Iroquois County	2	0.57
Waltonville (village) Jefferson County	2	0.47
Greenwood (village) McHenry County	1	0.41
Round Lake Heights (village) Lake County	5	0.37
Toulon (city) Stark County	5	0.36
Rankin (village) Vermilion County	2	0.32
Andalusia (village) Rock Island County	3	0.29
Stillman Valley (village) Ogle County	3	0.29

Top 10 Places Sorted by Percent
Based on places with populations of 10,000 or more

Place	Number	%
Zion (city) Lake County	29	0.13
Round Lake Beach (village) Lake County	29	0.11
Beach Park (village) Lake County	10	0.10
Lindenhurst (village) Lake County	10	0.08
Sycamore (city) De Kalb County	10	0.08
Gurnee (village) Lake County	19	0.07
Darien (city) Du Page County	16	0.07
Carpentersville (village) Kane County	17	0.06
Worth (village) Cook County	7	0.06
Lyons (village) Cook County	6	0.06

American Indian: Choctaw

Top 10 Places Sorted by Number
Based on all places, regardless of population

Place	Number	%
Chicago (city) Cook County	401	0.01
North Chicago (city) Lake County	20	0.06
Rockford (city) Winnebago County	19	0.01
Elgin (city) Kane County	18	0.02
Springfield (city) Sangamon County	18	0.02
Waukegan (city) Lake County	16	0.02
Aurora (city) Kane County	16	0.01
Berwyn (city) Cook County	14	0.03
Tinley Park (village) Cook County	14	0.03
Burbank (city) Cook County	12	0.04

Top 10 Places Sorted by Percent
Based on all places, regardless of population

Place	Number	%
Venedy (village) Washington County	2	1.46
Whiteash (village) Williamson County	3	1.12
Bath (village) Mason County	2	0.65
Bay View Gardens (village) Woodford County	2	0.55
Alma (village) Marion County	2	0.52
Mill Shoals (village) White County	1	0.43
Donnellson (village) Montgomery County	1	0.41
Morrisonville (village) Christian County	4	0.37
Thompsonville (village) Franklin County	2	0.35
Lakewood Shores (cdp) Will County	5	0.34

Top 10 Places Sorted by Percent
Based on places with populations of 10,000 or more

Place	Number	%
Glen Carbon (village) Madison County	9	0.09
Country Club Hills (city) Cook County	11	0.07
Barrington (village) Cook County	7	0.07

	Number	%
North Chicago (city) Lake County	20	0.06
Rantoul (village) Champaign County	8	0.06
Burbank (city) Cook County	12	0.04
Maywood (village) Cook County	12	0.04
Carpentersville (village) Kane County	11	0.04
O'Fallon (city) Saint Clair County	8	0.04
Ottawa (city) La Salle County	7	0.04

American Indian: Colville

Top 10 Places Sorted by Number
Based on all places, regardless of population

Place	Number	%
Monmouth (city) Warren County	4	0.04
Bloomington (city) McLean County	3	0.00
Chicago (city) Cook County	3	0.00
Jacksonville (city) Morgan County	1	0.01
Lemont (village) Cook County	1	0.01
Cicero (town) Cook County	1	0.00
East Moline (city) Rock Island County	1	0.00
Springfield (city) Sangamon County	1	0.00

Top 10 Places Sorted by Percent
Based on all places, regardless of population

Place	Number	%
Monmouth (city) Warren County	4	0.04
Jacksonville (city) Morgan County	1	0.01
Lemont (village) Cook County	1	0.01
Bloomington (city) McLean County	3	0.00
Chicago (city) Cook County	3	0.00
Cicero (town) Cook County	1	0.00
East Moline (city) Rock Island County	1	0.00
Springfield (city) Sangamon County	1	0.00

Top 10 Places Sorted by Percent
Based on places with populations of 10,000 or more

Place	Number	%
Jacksonville (city) Morgan County	1	0.01
Lemont (village) Cook County	1	0.01
Bloomington (city) McLean County	3	0.00
Chicago (city) Cook County	3	0.00
Cicero (town) Cook County	1	0.00
East Moline (city) Rock Island County	1	0.00
Springfield (city) Sangamon County	1	0.00

American Indian: Comanche

Top 10 Places Sorted by Number
Based on all places, regardless of population

Place	Number	%
Chicago (city) Cook County	53	0.00
Round Lake Beach (village) Lake County	7	0.03
Rockdale (village) Will County	5	0.26
Bourbonnais (village) Kankakee County	5	0.03
East Peoria (city) Tazewell County	5	0.02
Zion (city) Lake County	5	0.02
Belleville (city) Saint Clair County	5	0.01
De Kalb (city) De Kalb County	5	0.01
North Chicago (city) Lake County	5	0.01
Palatine (village) Cook County	5	0.01

Top 10 Places Sorted by Percent
Based on all places, regardless of population

Place	Number	%
Smithfield (village) Fulton County	1	0.47
Rockdale (village) Will County	5	0.26
Ohio (village) Bureau County	1	0.19
Enfield (village) White County	1	0.16
Grand Tower (city) Jackson County	1	0.16
Pierron (village) Bond County	1	0.15
Schram City (village) Montgomery County	1	0.15
Gifford (village) Champaign County	1	0.12

Notes: (cdp) census designated place; Refer to the User's Guide in the front of the book for more detailed information.

Place	Number	%
Mansfield (village) Piatt County	1	0.11
Tilton (village) Vermilion County	3	0.10

Top 10 Places Sorted by Percent
Based on places with populations of 10,000 or more

Place	Number	%
Round Lake Beach (village) Lake County	7	0.03
Bourbonnais (village) Kankakee County	5	0.03
East Peoria (city) Tazewell County	5	0.02
Zion (city) Lake County	5	0.02
Forest Park (village) Cook County	3	0.02
Mount Vernon (city) Jefferson County	3	0.02
Norridge (village) Cook County	3	0.02
Belleville (city) Saint Clair County	5	0.01
De Kalb (city) De Kalb County	5	0.01
North Chicago (city) Lake County	5	0.01

American Indian: Cree

Top 10 Places Sorted by Number
Based on all places, regardless of population

Place	Number	%
Chicago (city) Cook County	62	0.00
Evanston (city) Cook County	6	0.01
Schaumburg (village) Cook County	6	0.01
Marion (city) Williamson County	5	0.03
Rockford (city) Winnebago County	5	0.01
Midlothian (village) Cook County	4	0.03
Oak Park (village) Cook County	4	0.01
Wyoming (city) Stark County	3	0.21
Worth (village) Cook County	3	0.03
Brookfield (village) Cook County	3	0.02

Top 10 Places Sorted by Percent
Based on all places, regardless of population

Place	Number	%
Wyoming (city) Stark County	3	0.21
Poplar Grove (village) Boone County	2	0.15
Mulberry Grove (village) Bond County	1	0.15
Rockdale (village) Will County	2	0.11
Shabbona (village) De Kalb County	1	0.11
Oakland (city) Coles County	1	0.10
Amboy (city) Lee County	2	0.08
Beecher (village) Will County	1	0.05
Stone Park (village) Cook County	2	0.04
Marion (city) Williamson County	5	0.03

Top 10 Places Sorted by Percent
Based on places with populations of 10,000 or more

Place	Number	%
Marion (city) Williamson County	5	0.03
Midlothian (village) Cook County	4	0.03
Worth (village) Cook County	3	0.03
Brookfield (village) Cook County	3	0.02
Riverdale (village) Cook County	3	0.02
Beach Park (village) Lake County	2	0.02
Plainfield (village) Will County	2	0.02
Evanston (city) Cook County	6	0.01
Schaumburg (village) Cook County	6	0.01
Oak Park (village) Cook County	4	0.01

American Indian: Creek

Top 10 Places Sorted by Number
Based on all places, regardless of population

Place	Number	%
Chicago (city) Cook County	102	0.00
Joliet (city) Will County	12	0.01
Woodridge (village) Du Page County	8	0.03
Cicero (town) Cook County	8	0.01
Springfield (city) Sangamon County	7	0.01
Waukegan (city) Lake County	7	0.01

Place	Number	%
Rosewood Heights (cdp) Madison County	6	0.14
Zion (city) Lake County	6	0.03
Naperville (city) Du Page County	6	0.00
Channel Lake (cdp) Lake County	5	0.28

Top 10 Places Sorted by Percent
Based on all places, regardless of population

Place	Number	%
Elliott (village) Ford County	4	1.17
Royal Lakes (village) Macoupin County	1	0.53
Arlington (village) Bureau County	1	0.47
Varna (village) Marshall County	2	0.46
Channel Lake (cdp) Lake County	5	0.28
Crossville (village) White County	2	0.26
Ellis Grove (village) Randolph County	1	0.26
Leland Grove (city) Sangamon County	4	0.25
Danvers (village) McLean County	3	0.25
Dakota (village) Stephenson County	1	0.20

Top 10 Places Sorted by Percent
Based on places with populations of 10,000 or more

Place	Number	%
Sauk Village (village) Cook County	4	0.04
Woodridge (village) Du Page County	8	0.03
Zion (city) Lake County	6	0.03
Palos Hills (city) Cook County	5	0.03
Justice (village) Cook County	3	0.02
Matteson (village) Cook County	3	0.02
Sterling (city) Whiteside County	3	0.02
Joliet (city) Will County	12	0.01
Cicero (town) Cook County	8	0.01
Springfield (city) Sangamon County	7	0.01

American Indian: Crow

Top 10 Places Sorted by Number
Based on all places, regardless of population

Place	Number	%
Chicago (city) Cook County	22	0.00
Aurora (city) Kane County	6	0.00
Rockford (city) Winnebago County	5	0.00
Roanoke (village) Woodford County	4	0.20
Gages Lake (cdp) Lake County	4	0.04
Alton (city) Madison County	4	0.01
North Chicago (city) Lake County	4	0.01
Sherman (village) Sangamon County	3	0.10
Metropolis (city) Massac County	3	0.05
Troy (city) Madison County	3	0.04

Top 10 Places Sorted by Percent
Based on all places, regardless of population

Place	Number	%
West Brooklyn (village) Lee County	2	1.15
Roanoke (village) Woodford County	4	0.20
Sherman (village) Sangamon County	3	0.10
Leland (village) La Salle County	1	0.10
Rushville (city) Schuyler County	2	0.06
Maroa (city) Macon County	1	0.06
Metropolis (city) Massac County	3	0.05
Gages Lake (cdp) Lake County	4	0.04
Troy (city) Madison County	3	0.04
Coal City (village) Grundy County	2	0.04

Top 10 Places Sorted by Percent
Based on places with populations of 10,000 or more

Place	Number	%
Gages Lake (cdp) Lake County	4	0.04
Midlothian (village) Cook County	3	0.02
Oswego (village) Kendall County	3	0.02
Herrin (city) Williamson County	2	0.02
Alton (city) Madison County	4	0.01
North Chicago (city) Lake County	4	0.01

Place	Number	%
Des Plaines (city) Cook County	3	0.01
East Moline (city) Rock Island County	2	0.01
Mount Vernon (city) Jefferson County	2	0.01
Bourbonnais (village) Kankakee County	1	0.01

American Indian: Delaware

Top 10 Places Sorted by Number
Based on all places, regardless of population

Place	Number	%
Chicago (city) Cook County	26	0.00
Romeoville (village) Will County	6	0.03
Watseka (city) Iroquois County	5	0.09
Decatur (city) Macon County	5	0.01
Hoffman Estates (village) Cook County	5	0.01
Bolingbrook (village) Will County	4	0.01
Mount Prospect (village) Cook County	3	0.01
Pekin (city) Tazewell County	3	0.01
Naperville (city) Du Page County	3	0.00
Rockford (city) Winnebago County	3	0.00

Top 10 Places Sorted by Percent
Based on all places, regardless of population

Place	Number	%
Saint Libory (village) Saint Clair County	2	0.34
Atkinson (town) Henry County	2	0.20
Crossville (village) White County	1	0.13
Beckemeyer (village) Clinton County	1	0.10
New Berlin (village) Sangamon County	1	0.10
Watseka (city) Iroquois County	5	0.09
Clifton (village) Iroquois County	1	0.08
Crystal Lawns (cdp) Will County	2	0.07
Winnebago (village) Winnebago County	2	0.07
Cuba (city) Fulton County	1	0.07

Top 10 Places Sorted by Percent
Based on places with populations of 10,000 or more

Place	Number	%
Romeoville (village) Will County	6	0.03
Decatur (city) Macon County	5	0.01
Hoffman Estates (village) Cook County	5	0.01
Bolingbrook (village) Will County	4	0.01
Mount Prospect (village) Cook County	3	0.01
Pekin (city) Tazewell County	3	0.01
Belvidere (city) Boone County	2	0.01
Jacksonville (city) Morgan County	1	0.01
Palos Hills (city) Cook County	1	0.01
Prospect Heights (city) Cook County	1	0.01

American Indian: Houma

Top 10 Places Sorted by Number
Based on all places, regardless of population

Place	Number	%
Chicago (city) Cook County	5	0.00
Wheaton (city) Du Page County	4	0.01
Norris City (village) White County	2	0.19
Peoria (city) Peoria County	2	0.00
Harvard (city) McHenry County	1	0.01
Aurora (city) Kane County	1	0.00
Bensenville (village) Du Page County	1	0.00
Glenview (village) Cook County	1	0.00

Top 10 Places Sorted by Percent
Based on all places, regardless of population

Place	Number	%
Norris City (village) White County	2	0.19
Wheaton (city) Du Page County	4	0.01
Harvard (city) McHenry County	1	0.01
Chicago (city) Cook County	5	0.00
Peoria (city) Peoria County	2	0.00
Aurora (city) Kane County	1	0.00

Notes: (cdp) census designated place; Refer to the User's Guide in the front of the book for more detailed information.

Bensenville (village) Du Page County	1	0.00
Glenview (village) Cook County	1	0.00

Top 10 Places Sorted by Percent
Based on places with populations of 10,000 or more

Place	Number	%
Wheaton (city) Du Page County	4	0.01
Chicago (city) Cook County	5	0.00
Peoria (city) Peoria County	2	0.00
Aurora (city) Kane County	1	0.00
Bensenville (village) Du Page County	1	0.00
Glenview (village) Cook County	1	0.00

American Indian: Iroquois

Top 10 Places Sorted by Number
Based on all places, regardless of population

Place	Number	%
Chicago (city) Cook County	401	0.01
Rockford (city) Winnebago County	25	0.02
Lansing (village) Cook County	21	0.07
De Kalb (city) De Kalb County	12	0.03
Des Plaines (city) Cook County	12	0.02
Oak Park (village) Cook County	12	0.02
Cicero (town) Cook County	12	0.01
Villa Park (village) Du Page County	11	0.05
Crystal Lake (city) McHenry County	11	0.03
Wheeling (village) Cook County	11	0.03

Top 10 Places Sorted by Percent
Based on all places, regardless of population

Place	Number	%
Whiteash (village) Williamson County	3	1.12
Calhoun (village) Richland County	2	0.90
Mount Auburn (village) Christian County	4	0.78
Magnolia (village) Putnam County	2	0.72
Hanover (village) Jo Daviess County	5	0.60
Thawville (village) Iroquois County	1	0.39
San Jose (village) Mason County	2	0.29
Pittsburg (village) Williamson County	1	0.17
Hinckley (village) De Kalb County	3	0.15
Genoa (city) De Kalb County	6	0.14

Top 10 Places Sorted by Percent
Based on places with populations of 10,000 or more

Place	Number	%
Lansing (village) Cook County	21	0.07
Villa Park (village) Du Page County	11	0.05
Lockport (city) Will County	7	0.05
Plainfield (village) Will County	6	0.05
Gages Lake (cdp) Lake County	5	0.05
Bloomingdale (village) Du Page County	8	0.04
Evergreen Park (village) Cook County	8	0.04
Lake Zurich (village) Lake County	8	0.04
Ottawa (city) La Salle County	7	0.04
South Elgin (village) Kane County	7	0.04

American Indian: Kiowa

Top 10 Places Sorted by Number
Based on all places, regardless of population

Place	Number	%
Chicago (city) Cook County	18	0.00
Effingham (city) Effingham County	7	0.06
Bloomington (city) McLean County	4	0.01
Mount Morris (village) Ogle County	3	0.10
Litchfield (city) Montgomery County	3	0.04
Marine (village) Madison County	2	0.22
Clay City (village) Clay County	2	0.20
Chicago Heights (city) Cook County	2	0.01
O'Fallon (city) Saint Clair County	2	0.01
Merrionette Park (village) Cook County	1	0.05

Top 10 Places Sorted by Percent
Based on all places, regardless of population

Place	Number	%
Marine (village) Madison County	2	0.22
Clay City (village) Clay County	2	0.20
Mount Morris (village) Ogle County	3	0.10
Effingham (city) Effingham County	7	0.06
Merrionette Park (village) Cook County	1	0.05
Mount Olive (city) Macoupin County	1	0.05
Litchfield (city) Montgomery County	3	0.04
Byron (city) Ogle County	1	0.03
Staunton (city) Macoupin County	1	0.02
Bloomington (city) McLean County	4	0.01

Top 10 Places Sorted by Percent
Based on places with populations of 10,000 or more

Place	Number	%
Effingham (city) Effingham County	7	0.06
Bloomington (city) McLean County	4	0.01
Chicago Heights (city) Cook County	2	0.01
O'Fallon (city) Saint Clair County	2	0.01
Alsip (village) Cook County	1	0.01
Barrington (village) Cook County	1	0.01
Gages Lake (cdp) Lake County	1	0.01
Hickory Hills (city) Cook County	1	0.01
Marion (city) Williamson County	1	0.01
Chicago (city) Cook County	18	0.00

American Indian: Latin American Indians

Top 10 Places Sorted by Number
Based on all places, regardless of population

Place	Number	%
Chicago (city) Cook County	3,250	0.11
Cicero (town) Cook County	249	0.29
Waukegan (city) Lake County	125	0.14
Aurora (city) Kane County	125	0.09
Elgin (city) Kane County	113	0.12
Rockford (city) Winnebago County	107	0.07
Berwyn (city) Cook County	75	0.14
Joliet (city) Will County	67	0.06
Chicago Heights (city) Cook County	53	0.16
Blue Island (city) Cook County	51	0.22

Top 10 Places Sorted by Percent
Based on all places, regardless of population

Place	Number	%
Mark (village) Putnam County	7	1.43
Shawneetown (city) Gallatin County	14	0.99
Trout Valley (village) McHenry County	4	0.67
Tallula (village) Menard County	4	0.63
Nelson (village) Lee County	1	0.61
Allerton (village) Vermilion County	1	0.34
Rochelle (city) Ogle County	31	0.33
Rosemont (village) Cook County	14	0.33
Stone Park (village) Cook County	16	0.31
Cicero (town) Cook County	249	0.29

Top 10 Places Sorted by Percent
Based on places with populations of 10,000 or more

Place	Number	%
Cicero (town) Cook County	249	0.29
Northlake (city) Cook County	27	0.23
Blue Island (city) Cook County	51	0.22
Melrose Park (village) Cook County	45	0.19
Chicago Heights (city) Cook County	53	0.16
Bensenville (village) Du Page County	33	0.16
Franklin Park (village) Cook County	31	0.16
Summit (village) Cook County	17	0.16
Waukegan (city) Lake County	125	0.14
Berwyn (city) Cook County	75	0.14

American Indian: Lumbee

Top 10 Places Sorted by Number
Based on all places, regardless of population

Place	Number	%
Chicago (city) Cook County	26	0.00
Peoria (city) Peoria County	6	0.01
Naperville (city) Du Page County	5	0.00
Orland Hills (village) Cook County	4	0.06
Romeoville (village) Will County	4	0.02
Waukegan (city) Lake County	4	0.00
Worden (village) Madison County	3	0.33
Northlake (city) Cook County	3	0.03
Swansea (village) Saint Clair County	3	0.03
Riverdale (village) Cook County	3	0.02

Top 10 Places Sorted by Percent
Based on all places, regardless of population

Place	Number	%
Worden (village) Madison County	3	0.33
Valmeyer (village) Monroe County	2	0.33
Greenview (village) Menard County	1	0.12
Edinburg (village) Christian County	1	0.09
Orland Hills (village) Cook County	4	0.06
Bellevue (village) Peoria County	1	0.05
Eureka (city) Woodford County	2	0.04
Northlake (city) Cook County	3	0.03
Swansea (village) Saint Clair County	3	0.03
Stickney (village) Cook County	2	0.03

Top 10 Places Sorted by Percent
Based on places with populations of 10,000 or more

Place	Number	%
Northlake (city) Cook County	3	0.03
Swansea (village) Saint Clair County	3	0.03
Romeoville (village) Will County	4	0.02
Riverdale (village) Cook County	3	0.02
Peoria (city) Peoria County	6	0.01
Crystal Lake (city) McHenry County	3	0.01
Collinsville (city) Madison County	2	0.01
Granite City (city) Madison County	2	0.01
North Chicago (city) Lake County	2	0.01
Wilmette (village) Cook County	2	0.01

American Indian: Menominee

Top 10 Places Sorted by Number
Based on all places, regardless of population

Place	Number	%
Chicago (city) Cook County	183	0.01
Springfield (city) Sangamon County	9	0.01
Rock Island (city) Rock Island County	7	0.02
Rockford (city) Winnebago County	7	0.00
Lyons (village) Cook County	6	0.06
Antioch (village) Lake County	5	0.06
Barrington (village) Cook County	5	0.05
Franklin Park (village) Cook County	5	0.03
Berwyn (city) Cook County	5	0.01
Crystal Lake (city) McHenry County	5	0.01

Top 10 Places Sorted by Percent
Based on all places, regardless of population

Place	Number	%
Buffalo (village) Sangamon County	4	0.81
Cave-In-Rock (village) Hardin County	1	0.29
Lyndon (village) Whiteside County	1	0.18
Carlinville (city) Macoupin County	4	0.07
Lyons (village) Cook County	6	0.06
Antioch (village) Lake County	5	0.06
South Beloit (city) Winnebago County	3	0.06
Channel Lake (cdp) Lake County	1	0.06
Hampton (village) Rock Island County	1	0.06

Notes: (cdp) census designated place; Refer to the User's Guide in the front of the book for more detailed information.

Barrington (village) Cook County   5   0.05

Top 10 Places Sorted by Percent
Based on places with populations of 10,000 or more

Place	Number	%
Lyons (village) Cook County	6	0.06
Barrington (village) Cook County	5	0.05
Franklin Park (village) Cook County	5	0.03
Cary (village) McHenry County	4	0.03
Schiller Park (village) Cook County	4	0.03
Rock Island (city) Rock Island County	7	0.02
Bradley (village) Kankakee County	3	0.02
Cahokia (village) Saint Clair County	3	0.02
Chicago Ridge (village) Cook County	3	0.02
Crestwood (village) Cook County	2	0.02

American Indian: Navajo

Top 10 Places Sorted by Number
Based on all places, regardless of population

Place	Number	%
Chicago (city) Cook County	245	0.01
Rockford (city) Winnebago County	21	0.01
North Chicago (city) Lake County	20	0.06
Aurora (city) Kane County	20	0.01
Boulder Hill (cdp) Kendall County	11	0.13
Carpentersville (village) Kane County	10	0.03
Bridgeview (village) Cook County	9	0.06
Zion (city) Lake County	9	0.04
Schaumburg (village) Cook County	9	0.01
Park Forest (village) Cook County	8	0.03

Top 10 Places Sorted by Percent
Based on all places, regardless of population

Place	Number	%
Galatia (village) Saline County	6	0.59
Redmon (village) Edgar County	1	0.50
Gulf Port (village) Henderson County	1	0.48
White City (village) Macoupin County	1	0.45
West City (village) Franklin County	3	0.42
Raleigh (village) Saline County	1	0.30
Blue Mound (village) Macon County	2	0.18
Andover (village) Henry County	1	0.17
Stone Park (village) Cook County	7	0.14
Hillsboro (city) Montgomery County	6	0.14

Top 10 Places Sorted by Percent
Based on places with populations of 10,000 or more

Place	Number	%
North Chicago (city) Lake County	20	0.06
Bridgeview (village) Cook County	9	0.06
Zion (city) Lake County	9	0.04
Godfrey (village) Madison County	7	0.04
Carpentersville (village) Kane County	10	0.03
Park Forest (village) Cook County	8	0.03
Homewood (village) Cook County	5	0.03
Crest Hill (city) Will County	4	0.03
Frankfort (village) Will County	3	0.03
Palos Heights (city) Cook County	3	0.03

American Indian: Osage

Top 10 Places Sorted by Number
Based on all places, regardless of population

Place	Number	%
Chicago (city) Cook County	20	0.00
Lombard (village) Du Page County	7	0.02
Midlothian (village) Cook County	4	0.03
Rockford (city) Winnebago County	4	0.00
Itasca (village) Du Page County	3	0.04
Swansea (village) Saint Clair County	3	0.03
Deerfield (village) Lake County	3	0.02

Granite City (city) Madison County	3	0.01
Machesney Park (village) Winnebago County	3	0.01
Aurora (city) Kane County	3	0.00

Top 10 Places Sorted by Percent
Based on all places, regardless of population

Place	Number	%
Media (village) Henderson County	1	0.77
East Cape Girardeau (village) Alexander County	2	0.46
Dunfermline (village) Fulton County	1	0.38
Sawyerville (village) Macoupin County	1	0.34
Mounds (city) Pulaski County	2	0.18
Roseville (village) Warren County	1	0.09
Minier (village) Tazewell County	1	0.08
Poplar Grove (village) Boone County	1	0.07
Grayville (city) White County	1	0.06
Teutopolis (village) Effingham County	1	0.06

Top 10 Places Sorted by Percent
Based on places with populations of 10,000 or more

Place	Number	%
Midlothian (village) Cook County	4	0.03
Swansea (village) Saint Clair County	3	0.03
Lombard (village) Du Page County	7	0.02
Deerfield (village) Lake County	3	0.02
Worth (village) Cook County	2	0.02
Granite City (city) Madison County	3	0.01
Machesney Park (village) Winnebago County	3	0.01
Charleston (city) Coles County	2	0.01
Collinsville (city) Madison County	2	0.01
Mattoon (city) Coles County	2	0.01

American Indian: Ottawa

Top 10 Places Sorted by Number
Based on all places, regardless of population

Place	Number	%
Chicago (city) Cook County	40	0.00
Bloomingdale (village) Du Page County	5	0.02
Round Lake Beach (village) Lake County	5	0.02
Rockford (city) Winnebago County	5	0.00
Lemont (village) Cook County	4	0.03
Schaumburg (village) Cook County	4	0.01
Aurora (city) Kane County	4	0.00
Cicero (town) Cook County	4	0.00
Elburn (village) Kane County	3	0.11
Westchester (village) Cook County	3	0.02

Top 10 Places Sorted by Percent
Based on all places, regardless of population

Place	Number	%
Livingston (village) Madison County	1	0.12
Elburn (village) Kane County	3	0.11
Brimfield (village) Peoria County	1	0.11
Crainville (village) Williamson County	1	0.10
Oakwood Hills (village) McHenry County	2	0.09
Diamond (village) Grundy County	1	0.07
Lake Catherine (cdp) Lake County	1	0.07
Fisher (village) Champaign County	1	0.06
Elmwood (city) Peoria County	1	0.05
South Beloit (city) Winnebago County	2	0.04

Top 10 Places Sorted by Percent
Based on places with populations of 10,000 or more

Place	Number	%
Lemont (village) Cook County	4	0.03
Bloomingdale (village) Du Page County	5	0.02
Round Lake Beach (village) Lake County	5	0.02
Westchester (village) Cook County	3	0.02
Bradley (village) Kankakee County	2	0.02
Washington (city) Tazewell County	2	0.02
Schaumburg (village) Cook County	4	0.01

De Kalb (city) De Kalb County	3	0.01
Orland Park (village) Cook County	3	0.01
Villa Park (village) Du Page County	3	0.01

American Indian: Paiute

Top 10 Places Sorted by Number
Based on all places, regardless of population

Place	Number	%
Chicago (city) Cook County	10	0.00
Rockford (city) Winnebago County	4	0.00
Decatur (city) Macon County	3	0.00
Burbank (city) Cook County	2	0.01
Energy (village) Williamson County	1	0.09
Toluca (city) Marshall County	1	0.07
Brookfield (village) Cook County	1	0.01
Cary (village) McHenry County	1	0.01
Mattoon (city) Coles County	1	0.01
Troy (city) Madison County	1	0.01

Top 10 Places Sorted by Percent
Based on all places, regardless of population

Place	Number	%
Energy (village) Williamson County	1	0.09
Toluca (city) Marshall County	1	0.07
Burbank (city) Cook County	2	0.01
Brookfield (village) Cook County	1	0.01
Cary (village) McHenry County	1	0.01
Mattoon (city) Coles County	1	0.01
Troy (city) Madison County	1	0.01
Chicago (city) Cook County	10	0.00
Rockford (city) Winnebago County	4	0.00
Decatur (city) Macon County	3	0.00

Top 10 Places Sorted by Percent
Based on places with populations of 10,000 or more

Place	Number	%
Burbank (city) Cook County	2	0.01
Brookfield (village) Cook County	1	0.01
Cary (village) McHenry County	1	0.01
Mattoon (city) Coles County	1	0.01
Chicago (city) Cook County	10	0.00
Rockford (city) Winnebago County	4	0.00
Decatur (city) Macon County	3	0.00
Champaign (city) Champaign County	1	0.00
Des Plaines (city) Cook County	1	0.00
Mundelein (village) Lake County	1	0.00

American Indian: Pima

Top 10 Places Sorted by Number
Based on all places, regardless of population

Place	Number	%
Chicago (city) Cook County	21	0.00
Carpentersville (village) Kane County	6	0.02
Lake in the Hills (village) McHenry County	5	0.02
Glen Ellyn (village) Du Page County	4	0.01
Peoria (city) Peoria County	3	0.00
West Frankfort (city) Franklin County	2	0.02
Freeport (city) Stephenson County	2	0.01
McHenry (city) McHenry County	2	0.01
Berwyn (city) Cook County	2	0.00
Des Plaines (city) Cook County	2	0.00

Top 10 Places Sorted by Percent
Based on all places, regardless of population

Place	Number	%
Middletown (village) Logan County	1	0.23
Carpentersville (village) Kane County	6	0.02
Lake in the Hills (village) McHenry County	5	0.02
West Frankfort (city) Franklin County	2	0.02
Park City (city) Lake County	1	0.02

Notes: (cdp) census designated place; Refer to the User's Guide in the front of the book for more detailed information.

Spring Valley (city) Bureau County	1	0.02
Glen Ellyn (village) Du Page County	4	0.01
Freeport (city) Stephenson County	2	0.01
McHenry (city) McHenry County	2	0.01
Pontiac (city) Livingston County	1	0.01

Top 10 Places Sorted by Percent
Based on places with populations of 10,000 or more

Place	Number	%
Carpentersville (village) Kane County	6	0.02
Lake in the Hills (village) McHenry County	5	0.02
Glen Ellyn (village) Du Page County	4	0.01
Freeport (city) Stephenson County	2	0.01
McHenry (city) McHenry County	2	0.01
Pontiac (city) Livingston County	1	0.01
Chicago (city) Cook County	21	0.00
Peoria (city) Peoria County	3	0.00
Berwyn (city) Cook County	2	0.00
Des Plaines (city) Cook County	2	0.00

American Indian: Potawatomi

Top 10 Places Sorted by Number
Based on all places, regardless of population

Place	Number	%
Chicago (city) Cook County	105	0.00
Bloomington (city) McLean County	20	0.03
Elgin (city) Kane County	12	0.01
Bolingbrook (village) Will County	11	0.02
Woodstock (city) McHenry County	7	0.03
South Elgin (village) Kane County	6	0.04
Rock Island (city) Rock Island County	6	0.02
Belleville (city) Saint Clair County	6	0.01
Chillicothe (city) Peoria County	5	0.08
Lindenhurst (village) Lake County	5	0.04

Top 10 Places Sorted by Percent
Based on all places, regardless of population

Place	Number	%
Kappa (village) Woodford County	2	1.18
Yale (village) Jasper County	1	1.03
Maquon (village) Knox County	2	0.63
Papineau (village) Iroquois County	1	0.51
Sherrard (village) Mercer County	3	0.43
Okawville (village) Washington County	2	0.15
Thornton (village) Cook County	3	0.12
Crainville (village) Williamson County	1	0.10
Chebanse (village) Iroquois County	1	0.09
Chillicothe (city) Peoria County	5	0.08

Top 10 Places Sorted by Percent
Based on places with populations of 10,000 or more

Place	Number	%
South Elgin (village) Kane County	6	0.04
Lindenhurst (village) Lake County	5	0.04
Bloomington (city) McLean County	20	0.03
Woodstock (city) McHenry County	7	0.03
Northlake (city) Cook County	3	0.03
Bolingbrook (village) Will County	11	0.02
Rock Island (city) Rock Island County	6	0.02
East Peoria (city) Tazewell County	5	0.02
Kankakee (city) Kankakee County	5	0.02
Charleston (city) Coles County	4	0.02

American Indian: Pueblo

Top 10 Places Sorted by Number
Based on all places, regardless of population

Place	Number	%
Chicago (city) Cook County	103	0.00
Hazel Crest (village) Cook County	7	0.05
Lockport (city) Will County	7	0.05

Cicero (town) Cook County	7	0.01
Godfrey (village) Madison County	5	0.03
Lisle (village) Du Page County	5	0.02
Machesney Park (village) Winnebago County	5	0.02
Hoffman Estates (village) Cook County	5	0.01
Wheaton (city) Du Page County	5	0.01
Shawneetown (city) Gallatin County	4	0.28

Top 10 Places Sorted by Percent
Based on all places, regardless of population

Place	Number	%
Rock Island Arsenal (cdp) Rock Island County	2	1.38
Dowell (village) Jackson County	2	0.45
Wyanet (village) Bureau County	3	0.29
Shawneetown (city) Gallatin County	4	0.28
Hillsdale (village) Rock Island County	1	0.17
New Athens (village) Saint Clair County	3	0.15
Millstadt (village) Saint Clair County	4	0.14
Lena (village) Stephenson County	3	0.10
Posen (village) Cook County	4	0.08
Ford Heights (village) Cook County	2	0.06

Top 10 Places Sorted by Percent
Based on places with populations of 10,000 or more

Place	Number	%
Hazel Crest (village) Cook County	7	0.05
Lockport (city) Will County	7	0.05
Sauk Village (village) Cook County	4	0.04
Godfrey (village) Madison County	5	0.03
River Grove (village) Cook County	3	0.03
Lisle (village) Du Page County	5	0.02
Machesney Park (village) Winnebago County	5	0.02
Herrin (city) Williamson County	2	0.02
Cicero (town) Cook County	7	0.01
Hoffman Estates (village) Cook County	5	0.01

American Indian: Puget Sound Salish

Top 10 Places Sorted by Number
Based on all places, regardless of population

Place	Number	%
Peoria (city) Peoria County	4	0.00
Dupo (village) Saint Clair County	3	0.08
Granite City (city) Madison County	3	0.01
Chicago (city) Cook County	3	0.00
Shiloh (village) Saint Clair County	2	0.03
North Chicago (city) Lake County	2	0.01
Evanston (city) Cook County	2	0.00
Warrenville (city) Du Page County	1	0.01
De Kalb (city) De Kalb County	1	0.00
Springfield (city) Sangamon County	1	0.00

Top 10 Places Sorted by Percent
Based on all places, regardless of population

Place	Number	%
Dupo (village) Saint Clair County	3	0.08
Shiloh (village) Saint Clair County	2	0.03
Granite City (city) Madison County	3	0.01
North Chicago (city) Lake County	2	0.01
Warrenville (city) Du Page County	1	0.01
Peoria (city) Peoria County	4	0.00
Chicago (city) Cook County	3	0.00
Evanston (city) Cook County	2	0.00
De Kalb (city) De Kalb County	1	0.00
Springfield (city) Sangamon County	1	0.00

Top 10 Places Sorted by Percent
Based on places with populations of 10,000 or more

Place	Number	%
Granite City (city) Madison County	3	0.01
North Chicago (city) Lake County	2	0.01
Warrenville (city) Du Page County	1	0.01

Peoria (city) Peoria County	4	0.00
Chicago (city) Cook County	3	0.00
Evanston (city) Cook County	2	0.00
De Kalb (city) De Kalb County	1	0.00
Springfield (city) Sangamon County	1	0.00

American Indian: Seminole

Top 10 Places Sorted by Number
Based on all places, regardless of population

Place	Number	%
Chicago (city) Cook County	81	0.00
Evanston (city) Cook County	12	0.05
Jacksonville (city) Morgan County	9	0.05
Rockford (city) Winnebago County	9	0.01
North Chicago (city) Lake County	6	0.02
Oak Park (village) Cook County	6	0.01
Springfield (city) Sangamon County	6	0.01
Mascoutah (city) Saint Clair County	5	0.09
Forest Park (village) Cook County	4	0.03
Round Lake Beach (village) Lake County	4	0.02

Top 10 Places Sorted by Percent
Based on all places, regardless of population

Place	Number	%
Franklin (village) Morgan County	2	0.34
De Land (village) Piatt County	1	0.21
Benld (city) Macoupin County	3	0.19
Princeville (village) Peoria County	3	0.19
Lovington (village) Moultrie County	2	0.16
Hopedale (village) Tazewell County	1	0.11
New Baden (village) Clinton County	3	0.10
Prophetstown (city) Whiteside County	2	0.10
Mascoutah (city) Saint Clair County	5	0.09
Gillespie (city) Macoupin County	3	0.09

Top 10 Places Sorted by Percent
Based on places with populations of 10,000 or more

Place	Number	%
Jacksonville (city) Morgan County	9	0.05
Forest Park (village) Cook County	4	0.03
Sauk Village (village) Cook County	3	0.03
Evanston (city) Cook County	12	0.02
North Chicago (city) Lake County	6	0.02
Round Lake Beach (village) Lake County	4	0.02
Matteson (village) Cook County	3	0.02
Rockford (city) Winnebago County	9	0.01
Oak Park (village) Cook County	6	0.01
Springfield (city) Sangamon County	6	0.01

American Indian: Shoshone

Top 10 Places Sorted by Number
Based on all places, regardless of population

Place	Number	%
Chicago (city) Cook County	15	0.00
Granite City (city) Madison County	7	0.02
Flossmoor (village) Cook County	6	0.06
Round Lake Beach (village) Lake County	4	0.02
Lockport (city) Will County	2	0.01
Rolling Meadows (city) Cook County	2	0.01
Saint Charles (city) Kane County	2	0.01
Berwyn (city) Cook County	2	0.00
Peoria (city) Peoria County	2	0.00
Milledgeville (village) Carroll County	1	0.10

Top 10 Places Sorted by Percent
Based on all places, regardless of population

Place	Number	%
Milledgeville (village) Carroll County	1	0.10
Rosiclare (city) Hardin County	1	0.08
Flossmoor (village) Cook County	6	0.06

Peoria (city) Peoria County	4	0.00
Chicago (city) Cook County	3	0.00
Evanston (city) Cook County	2	0.00
De Kalb (city) De Kalb County	1	0.00
Springfield (city) Sangamon County	1	0.00

Notes: (cdp) census designated place; Refer to the User's Guide in the front of the book for more detailed information.

Place	Number	%
Granite City (city) Madison County	7	0.02
Round Lake Beach (village) Lake County	4	0.02
Auburn (city) Sangamon County	1	0.02
Berkeley (village) Cook County	1	0.02
Lockport (city) Will County	2	0.01
Rolling Meadows (city) Cook County	2	0.01
Saint Charles (city) Kane County	2	0.01

Top 10 Places Sorted by Percent
Based on places with populations of 10,000 or more

Place	Number	%
Granite City (city) Madison County	7	0.02
Round Lake Beach (village) Lake County	4	0.02
Lockport (city) Will County	2	0.01
Rolling Meadows (city) Cook County	2	0.01
Saint Charles (city) Kane County	2	0.01
Bradley (village) Kankakee County	1	0.01
Bridgeview (village) Cook County	1	0.01
Dixon (city) Lee County	1	0.01
Streator (city) La Salle County	1	0.01
Westchester (village) Cook County	1	0.01

American Indian: Sioux

Top 10 Places Sorted by Number
Based on all places, regardless of population

Place	Number	%
Chicago (city) Cook County	439	0.02
Rockford (city) Winnebago County	41	0.03
Aurora (city) Kane County	37	0.03
Springfield (city) Sangamon County	33	0.03
Rock Island (city) Rock Island County	32	0.08
Peoria (city) Peoria County	27	0.02
North Chicago (city) Lake County	25	0.07
Moline (city) Rock Island County	22	0.05
Waukegan (city) Lake County	21	0.02
Cicero (town) Cook County	20	0.02

Top 10 Places Sorted by Percent
Based on all places, regardless of population

Place	Number	%
Ellsworth (village) McLean County	4	1.48
West City (village) Franklin County	8	1.12
Malden (village) Bureau County	3	0.87
Dongola (village) Union County	6	0.74
Nebo (village) Pike County	3	0.74
Bartelso (village) Clinton County	4	0.67
Bath (village) Mason County	2	0.65
Camargo (village) Douglas County	3	0.64
Mount Auburn (village) Christian County	3	0.58
West Point (village) Hancock County	1	0.51

Top 10 Places Sorted by Percent
Based on places with populations of 10,000 or more

Place	Number	%
Godfrey (village) Madison County	14	0.09
Rock Island (city) Rock Island County	32	0.08
North Chicago (city) Lake County	25	0.07
East Moline (city) Rock Island County	15	0.07
Beach Park (village) Lake County	6	0.06
Moline (city) Rock Island County	22	0.05
Belvidere (city) Boone County	11	0.05
Park Forest (village) Cook County	11	0.05
Dixon (city) Lee County	8	0.05
Sterling (city) Whiteside County	7	0.05

American Indian: Tohono O'Odham

Top 10 Places Sorted by Number
Based on all places, regardless of population

Place	Number	%
Chicago (city) Cook County	11	0.00

Place	Number	%
Mendota (city) La Salle County	4	0.06
Addison (village) Du Page County	4	0.01
East Dundee (village) Kane County	3	0.10
Flora (city) Clay County	2	0.04
McHenry (city) McHenry County	2	0.01
Rolling Meadows (city) Cook County	2	0.01
Des Plaines (city) Cook County	2	0.00
Peoria (city) Peoria County	2	0.00
Long Creek (village) Macon County	1	0.07

Top 10 Places Sorted by Percent
Based on all places, regardless of population

Place	Number	%
East Dundee (village) Kane County	3	0.10
Long Creek (village) Macon County	1	0.07
Mendota (city) La Salle County	4	0.06
Earlville (city) La Salle County	1	0.06
Flora (city) Clay County	2	0.04
Girard (city) Macoupin County	1	0.04
Addison (village) Du Page County	4	0.01
McHenry (city) McHenry County	2	0.01
Rolling Meadows (city) Cook County	2	0.01
Princeton (city) Bureau County	1	0.01

Top 10 Places Sorted by Percent
Based on places with populations of 10,000 or more

Place	Number	%
Addison (village) Du Page County	4	0.01
McHenry (city) McHenry County	2	0.01
Rolling Meadows (city) Cook County	2	0.01
Chicago (city) Cook County	11	0.00
Des Plaines (city) Cook County	2	0.00
Peoria (city) Peoria County	2	0.00
Carpentersville (village) Kane County	1	0.00
Elgin (city) Kane County	1	0.00
Elk Grove Village (village) Cook County	1	0.00
Lansing (village) Cook County	1	0.00

American Indian: Ute

Top 10 Places Sorted by Number
Based on all places, regardless of population

Place	Number	%
Chicago (city) Cook County	12	0.00
Hodgkins (village) Cook County	5	0.23
Hinsdale (village) Du Page County	4	0.02
Rockford (city) Winnebago County	4	0.00
Aurora (city) Kane County	3	0.00
Creve Coeur (village) Tazewell County	1	0.02
Hawthorn Woods (village) Lake County	1	0.02
Forest Park (village) Cook County	1	0.01
Alton (city) Madison County	1	0.00
Evergreen Park (village) Cook County	1	0.00

Top 10 Places Sorted by Percent
Based on all places, regardless of population

Place	Number	%
Hodgkins (village) Cook County	5	0.23
Hinsdale (village) Du Page County	4	0.02
Creve Coeur (village) Tazewell County	1	0.02
Hawthorn Woods (village) Lake County	1	0.02
Forest Park (village) Cook County	1	0.01
Chicago (city) Cook County	12	0.00
Rockford (city) Winnebago County	4	0.00
Aurora (city) Kane County	3	0.00
Alton (city) Madison County	1	0.00
Evergreen Park (village) Cook County	1	0.00

Top 10 Places Sorted by Percent
Based on places with populations of 10,000 or more

Place	Number	%
Hinsdale (village) Du Page County	4	0.02

Place	Number	%
Forest Park (village) Cook County	1	0.01
Chicago (city) Cook County	12	0.00
Rockford (city) Winnebago County	4	0.00
Aurora (city) Kane County	3	0.00
Alton (city) Madison County	1	0.00
Evergreen Park (village) Cook County	1	0.00
Kankakee (city) Kankakee County	1	0.00
Lisle (village) Du Page County	1	0.00
Villa Park (village) Du Page County	1	0.00

American Indian: Yakama

Top 10 Places Sorted by Number
Based on all places, regardless of population

Place	Number	%
Chicago (city) Cook County	3	0.00
Carol Stream (village) Du Page County	2	0.00
Rockton (village) Winnebago County	1	0.02
Alton (city) Madison County	1	0.00
Aurora (city) Kane County	1	0.00
Evanston (city) Cook County	1	0.00
Niles (village) Cook County	1	0.00

Top 10 Places Sorted by Percent
Based on all places, regardless of population

Place	Number	%
Rockton (village) Winnebago County	1	0.02
Chicago (city) Cook County	3	0.00
Carol Stream (village) Du Page County	2	0.00
Alton (city) Madison County	1	0.00
Aurora (city) Kane County	1	0.00
Evanston (city) Cook County	1	0.00
Niles (village) Cook County	1	0.00

Top 10 Places Sorted by Percent
Based on places with populations of 10,000 or more

Place	Number	%
Chicago (city) Cook County	3	0.00
Carol Stream (village) Du Page County	2	0.00
Alton (city) Madison County	1	0.00
Aurora (city) Kane County	1	0.00
Evanston (city) Cook County	1	0.00
Niles (village) Cook County	1	0.00

American Indian: Yaqui

Top 10 Places Sorted by Number
Based on all places, regardless of population

Place	Number	%
Chicago (city) Cook County	14	0.00
Hoopeston (city) Vermilion County	5	0.08
Willowbrook (village) Du Page County	5	0.06
Fairview Heights (city) Saint Clair County	4	0.03
Warrenville (city) Du Page County	4	0.03
Oak Forest (city) Cook County	4	0.01
Lake of the Woods (cdp) Champaign County	3	0.10
East Moline (city) Rock Island County	3	0.01
Lombard (village) Du Page County	3	0.01
North Chicago (city) Lake County	3	0.01

Top 10 Places Sorted by Percent
Based on all places, regardless of population

Place	Number	%
Lake of the Woods (cdp) Champaign County	3	0.10
Hoopeston (city) Vermilion County	5	0.08
Central City (village) Marion County	1	0.07
Willowbrook (village) Du Page County	5	0.06
Rosewood Heights (cdp) Madison County	2	0.05
Fairview Heights (city) Saint Clair County	4	0.03
Warrenville (city) Du Page County	4	0.03
Crete (village) Will County	2	0.03
Riverside (village) Cook County	2	0.02

Caseyville (village) Saint Clair County   1   0.02

Top 10 Places Sorted by Percent
Based on places with populations of 10,000 or more

Place	Number	%
Fairview Heights (city) Saint Clair County	4	0.03
Warrenville (city) Du Page County	4	0.03
Oak Forest (city) Cook County	4	0.01
East Moline (city) Rock Island County	3	0.01
Lombard (village) Du Page County	3	0.01
North Chicago (city) Lake County	3	0.01
Blue Island (city) Cook County	2	0.01
Cary (village) McHenry County	1	0.01
Morris (city) Grundy County	1	0.01
Richton Park (village) Cook County	1	0.01

American Indian: Yuman

Top 10 Places Sorted by Number
Based on all places, regardless of population

Place	Number	%
Chicago (city) Cook County	7	0.00
North Chicago (city) Lake County	2	0.01
Glenview (village) Cook County	2	0.01
Cortland (town) De Kalb County	1	0.05
Flora (city) Clay County	1	0.02
Chicago Ridge (village) Cook County	1	0.01
Mattoon (city) Coles County	1	0.01
Des Plaines (city) Cook County	1	0.01
Urbana (city) Champaign County	1	0.00

Top 10 Places Sorted by Percent
Based on all places, regardless of population

Place	Number	%
Cortland (town) De Kalb County	1	0.05
Flora (city) Clay County	1	0.02
North Chicago (city) Lake County	2	0.01
Chicago Ridge (village) Cook County	1	0.01
Mattoon (city) Coles County	1	0.01
Chicago (city) Cook County	7	0.00
Glenview (village) Cook County	2	0.00
Des Plaines (city) Cook County	1	0.00
Urbana (city) Champaign County	1	0.00

Top 10 Places Sorted by Percent
Based on places with populations of 10,000 or more

Place	Number	%
North Chicago (city) Lake County	2	0.01
Chicago Ridge (village) Cook County	1	0.01
Mattoon (city) Coles County	1	0.01
Chicago (city) Cook County	7	0.00
Glenview (village) Cook County	2	0.00
Des Plaines (city) Cook County	1	0.00
Urbana (city) Champaign County	1	0.00

American Indian: All other tribes

Top 10 Places Sorted by Number
Based on all places, regardless of population

Place	Number	%
Chicago (city) Cook County	612	0.02
Rockford (city) Winnebago County	40	0.03
North Chicago (city) Lake County	39	0.11
Joliet (city) Will County	36	0.03
Cicero (town) Cook County	31	0.04
Elgin (city) Kane County	31	0.03
Waukegan (city) Lake County	25	0.03
Springfield (city) Sangamon County	21	0.02
Aurora (city) Kane County	21	0.03
Romeoville (village) Will County	20	0.09

Top 10 Places Sorted by Percent
Based on all places, regardless of population

Place	Number	%
Union Hill (village) Kankakee County	1	1.52
Marietta (village) Fulton County	2	1.33
Williamson (village) Madison County	3	1.20
Kane (village) Greene County	5	1.09
Middletown (village) Logan County	4	0.92
Thebes (village) Alexander County	4	0.84
Fillmore (village) Montgomery County	3	0.83
Spaulding (village) Sangamon County	4	0.72
Magnolia (village) Putnam County	2	0.72
Loraine (village) Adams County	2	0.55

Top 10 Places Sorted by Percent
Based on places with populations of 10,000 or more

Place	Number	%
North Chicago (city) Lake County	39	0.11
Romeoville (village) Will County	20	0.09
Zion (city) Lake County	20	0.09
Westmont (village) Du Page County	19	0.08
Kankakee (city) Kankakee County	18	0.07
La Grange (village) Cook County	11	0.07
Lyons (village) Cook County	7	0.07
Sauk Village (village) Cook County	7	0.07
Roselle (village) Du Page County	14	0.06
Brookfield (village) Cook County	11	0.06

American Indian tribes, not specified

Top 10 Places Sorted by Number
Based on all places, regardless of population

Place	Number	%
Chicago (city) Cook County	1,394	0.05
Aurora (city) Kane County	81	0.06
Rockford (city) Winnebago County	75	0.05
Cicero (town) Cook County	65	0.08
Joliet (city) Will County	50	0.05
Peoria (city) Peoria County	46	0.04
Springfield (city) Sangamon County	41	0.04
Waukegan (city) Lake County	38	0.04
Champaign (city) Champaign County	35	0.05
De Kalb (city) De Kalb County	30	0.08

Top 10 Places Sorted by Percent
Based on all places, regardless of population

Place	Number	%
Belknap (village) Johnson County	3	2.26
Oakdale (village) Washington County	3	1.41
Medora (village) Macoupin County	6	1.20
Smithboro (village) Bond County	2	1.00
East Brooklyn (village) Grundy County	1	0.81
Bonnie (village) Jefferson County	3	0.71
Tennessee (village) McDonough County	1	0.69
Coleta (village) Whiteside County	1	0.65
Vernon (village) Marion County	1	0.56
Roberts (village) Ford County	2	0.52

Top 10 Places Sorted by Percent
Based on places with populations of 10,000 or more

Place	Number	%
Centralia (city) Marion County	17	0.12
Blue Island (city) Cook County	25	0.11
Herrin (city) Williamson County	11	0.10
Edwardsville (city) Madison County	20	0.09
Zion (city) Lake County	20	0.09
Wood Dale (city) Du Page County	12	0.09
Cicero (town) Cook County	65	0.08
De Kalb (city) De Kalb County	30	0.08
Matteson (village) Cook County	10	0.08
Richton Park (village) Cook County	10	0.08

Arab

Top 10 Places Sorted by Number
Based on all places, regardless of population

Place	Number	%
Chicago (city) Cook County	14,971	0.52
Oak Lawn (village) Cook County	2,142	3.87
Peoria (city) Peoria County	1,576	1.40
Burbank (city) Cook County	1,273	4.58
Bridgeview (village) Cook County	1,104	7.18
Chicago Ridge (village) Cook County	963	6.94
Orland Park (village) Cook County	960	1.88
Naperville (city) Du Page County	948	0.74
Hickory Hills (city) Cook County	763	5.48
Skokie (village) Cook County	592	0.93

Top 10 Places Sorted by Percent
Based on places, regardless of population

Place	Number	%
Bridgeview (village) Cook County	1,104	7.18
Chicago Ridge (village) Cook County	963	6.94
Hickory Hills (city) Cook County	763	5.48
Burbank (city) Cook County	1,273	4.58
Oak Brook (village) Du Page County	358	4.24
Justice (village) Cook County	507	4.19
Oak Lawn (village) Cook County	2,142	3.87
Palos Hills (city) Cook County	578	3.26
Hanna City (village) Peoria County	32	3.18
Orland Hills (village) Cook County	179	2.61

Top 10 Places Sorted by Percent
Based on places with populations of 10,000 or more

Place	Number	%
Bridgeview (village) Cook County	1,104	7.18
Chicago Ridge (village) Cook County	963	6.94
Hickory Hills (city) Cook County	763	5.48
Burbank (city) Cook County	1,273	4.58
Justice (village) Cook County	507	4.19
Oak Lawn (village) Cook County	2,142	3.87
Palos Hills (city) Cook County	578	3.26
Worth (village) Cook County	288	2.58
Schiller Park (village) Cook County	234	1.99
Alsip (village) Cook County	388	1.95

Arab: Arab/Arabic

Top 10 Places Sorted by Number
Based on all places, regardless of population

Place	Number	%
Chicago (city) Cook County	5,458	0.19
Oak Lawn (village) Cook County	1,070	1.93
Burbank (city) Cook County	788	2.83
Bridgeview (village) Cook County	743	4.83
Chicago Ridge (village) Cook County	539	3.88
Orland Park (village) Cook County	401	0.78
Hickory Hills (city) Cook County	381	2.73
Alsip (village) Cook County	338	1.70
Tinley Park (village) Cook County	324	0.67
Justice (village) Cook County	290	2.40

Top 10 Places Sorted by Percent
Based on all places, regardless of population

Place	Number	%
Bridgeview (village) Cook County	743	4.83
Chicago Ridge (village) Cook County	539	3.88
Burbank (city) Cook County	788	2.83
Hickory Hills (city) Cook County	381	2.73
Justice (village) Cook County	290	2.40
Orland Hills (village) Cook County	140	2.04
Davis Junction (village) Ogle County	9	1.98
Oak Lawn (village) Cook County	1,070	1.93
Worth (village) Cook County	201	1.80

Notes: (cdp) census designated place; Refer to the User's Guide in the front of the book for more detailed information.

Place	Number	%
Alsip (village) Cook County	338	1.70

Top 10 Places Sorted by Percent
Based on places with populations of 10,000 or more

Place	Number	%
Bridgeview (village) Cook County	743	4.83
Chicago Ridge (village) Cook County	539	3.88
Burbank (city) Cook County	788	2.83
Hickory Hills (city) Cook County	381	2.73
Justice (village) Cook County	290	2.40
Oak Lawn (village) Cook County	1,070	1.93
Worth (village) Cook County	201	1.80
Alsip (village) Cook County	338	1.70
Palos Hills (city) Cook County	253	1.42
Orland Park (village) Cook County	401	0.78

Arab: Egyptian

Top 10 Places Sorted by Number
Based on all places, regardless of population

Place	Number	%
Chicago (city) Cook County	556	0.02
Naperville (city) Du Page County	147	0.11
Downers Grove (village) Du Page County	143	0.29
Urbana (city) Champaign County	111	0.31
Oak Brook (village) Du Page County	109	1.29
Aurora (city) Kane County	106	0.07
Evanston (city) Cook County	90	0.12
Arlington Heights (village) Cook County	73	0.10
Palos Hills (city) Cook County	68	0.38
Burr Ridge (village) Du Page County	64	0.62

Top 10 Places Sorted by Percent
Based on all places, regardless of population

Place	Number	%
Oak Brook (village) Du Page County	109	1.29
Willow Springs (village) Cook County	48	0.97
Roscoe (village) Winnebago County	48	0.76
Savoy (village) Champaign County	28	0.65
Manhattan (village) Will County	22	0.65
De Land (village) Piatt County	3	0.63
Burr Ridge (village) Du Page County	64	0.62
Willowbrook (village) Du Page County	56	0.62
Lena (village) Stephenson County	17	0.59
Berkeley (village) Cook County	26	0.50

Top 10 Places Sorted by Percent
Based on places with populations of 10,000 or more

Place	Number	%
Burr Ridge (village) Du Page County	64	0.62
River Forest (village) Cook County	52	0.45
Justice (village) Cook County	50	0.41
Palos Hills (city) Cook County	68	0.38
Urbana (city) Champaign County	111	0.31
Norridge (village) Cook County	46	0.31
Downers Grove (village) Du Page County	143	0.29
Bridgeview (village) Cook County	45	0.29
Lisle (village) Du Page County	52	0.25
Hickory Hills (city) Cook County	29	0.21

Arab: Iraqi

Top 10 Places Sorted by Number
Based on all places, regardless of population

Place	Number	%
Chicago (city) Cook County	931	0.03
Skokie (village) Cook County	244	0.39
Springfield (city) Sangamon County	68	0.06
Des Plaines (city) Cook County	58	0.10
Niles (village) Cook County	52	0.17
Arlington Heights (village) Cook County	44	0.06
Morton Grove (village) Cook County	41	0.18
Romeoville (village) Will County	39	0.18
Streamwood (village) Cook County	30	0.08
Naperville (city) Du Page County	27	0.02

Top 10 Places Sorted by Percent
Based on all places, regardless of population

Place	Number	%
Lee (village) Lee County	6	2.21
Skokie (village) Cook County	244	0.39
East Dundee (village) Kane County	6	0.21
Morton Grove (village) Cook County	41	0.18
Romeoville (village) Will County	39	0.18
Niles (village) Cook County	52	0.17
Oglesby (city) La Salle County	6	0.17
Riverdale (village) Cook County	21	0.14
Des Plaines (city) Cook County	58	0.10
Stockton (village) Jo Daviess County	2	0.10

Top 10 Places Sorted by Percent
Based on places with populations of 10,000 or more

Place	Number	%
Skokie (village) Cook County	244	0.39
Morton Grove (village) Cook County	41	0.18
Romeoville (village) Will County	39	0.18
Niles (village) Cook County	52	0.17
Riverdale (village) Cook County	21	0.14
Des Plaines (city) Cook County	58	0.10
Libertyville (village) Lake County	18	0.09
Streamwood (village) Cook County	30	0.08
Springfield (city) Sangamon County	68	0.06
Arlington Heights (village) Cook County	44	0.06

Arab: Jordanian

Top 10 Places Sorted by Number
Based on all places, regardless of population

Place	Number	%
Chicago (city) Cook County	1,078	0.04
Oak Lawn (village) Cook County	194	0.35
Chicago Ridge (village) Cook County	192	1.38
Morton Grove (village) Cook County	189	0.84
Oak Forest (city) Cook County	138	0.49
Des Plaines (city) Cook County	104	0.18
Palos Hills (city) Cook County	102	0.57
Burbank (city) Cook County	96	0.35
Naperville (city) Du Page County	91	0.07
Niles (village) Cook County	89	0.30

Top 10 Places Sorted by Percent
Based on all places, regardless of population

Place	Number	%
Chicago Ridge (village) Cook County	192	1.38
Savanna (city) Carroll County	31	0.88
Morton Grove (village) Cook County	189	0.84
Hickory Hills (city) Cook County	82	0.59
Odell (village) Livingston County	6	0.59
Palos Hills (city) Cook County	102	0.57
Lincolnshire (village) Lake County	31	0.50
Oak Forest (city) Cook County	138	0.49
Bridgeview (village) Cook County	65	0.42
Oak Lawn (village) Cook County	194	0.35

Top 10 Places Sorted by Percent
Based on places with populations of 10,000 or more

Place	Number	%
Chicago Ridge (village) Cook County	192	1.38
Morton Grove (village) Cook County	189	0.84
Hickory Hills (city) Cook County	82	0.59
Palos Hills (city) Cook County	102	0.57
Oak Forest (city) Cook County	138	0.49
Bridgeview (village) Cook County	65	0.42
Oak Lawn (village) Cook County	194	0.35

Place	Number	%
Burbank (city) Cook County	96	0.35
Niles (village) Cook County	89	0.30
Schiller Park (village) Cook County	33	0.28

Arab: Lebanese

Top 10 Places Sorted by Number
Based on all places, regardless of population

Place	Number	%
Chicago (city) Cook County	2,027	0.07
Peoria (city) Peoria County	1,300	1.15
Naperville (city) Du Page County	374	0.29
East Peoria (city) Tazewell County	187	0.82
Aurora (city) Kane County	169	0.12
Schaumburg (village) Cook County	160	0.21
Wheaton (city) Du Page County	135	0.24
Springfield (city) Sangamon County	115	0.10
Evanston (city) Cook County	107	0.14
Normal (town) McLean County	95	0.21

Top 10 Places Sorted by Percent
Based on all places, regardless of population

Place	Number	%
Hanna City (village) Peoria County	32	3.18
Magnolia (village) Putnam County	7	2.19
Spring Bay (village) Woodford County	7	1.53
Rome (cdp) Peoria County	24	1.38
Yates City (village) Knox County	10	1.38
Mapleton (village) Peoria County	3	1.33
Peoria (city) Peoria County	1,300	1.15
North Riverside (village) Cook County	73	1.08
Oakbrook Terrace (city) Du Page County	24	1.00
West Peoria (city) Peoria County	47	0.98

Top 10 Places Sorted by Percent
Based on places with populations of 10,000 or more

Place	Number	%
Peoria (city) Peoria County	1,300	1.15
East Peoria (city) Tazewell County	187	0.82
Streator (city) La Salle County	78	0.55
Warrenville (city) Du Page County	72	0.55
River Forest (village) Cook County	60	0.52
Western Springs (village) Cook County	57	0.45
Plainfield (village) Will County	51	0.39
Villa Park (village) Du Page County	82	0.37
Morris (city) Grundy County	42	0.35
Westmont (village) Du Page County	78	0.32

Arab: Moroccan

Top 10 Places Sorted by Number
Based on all places, regardless of population

Place	Number	%
Chicago (city) Cook County	733	0.03
Skokie (village) Cook County	67	0.11
Lisle (village) Du Page County	60	0.28
Oak Lawn (village) Cook County	50	0.09
Berwyn (city) Cook County	45	0.08
Aurora (city) Kane County	27	0.02
Carol Stream (village) Du Page County	26	0.07
Buffalo Grove (village) Lake County	25	0.06
De Kalb (city) De Kalb County	24	0.06
Rock Island (city) Rock Island County	24	0.06

Top 10 Places Sorted by Percent
Based on all places, regardless of population

Place	Number	%
Lisle (village) Du Page County	60	0.28
Skokie (village) Cook County	67	0.11
River Grove (village) Cook County	11	0.10
Oak Lawn (village) Cook County	50	0.09
Berwyn (city) Cook County	45	0.08

Notes: (cdp) census designated place; Refer to the User's Guide in the front of the book for more detailed information.

Place	Number	%
Carol Stream (village) Du Page County	26	0.07
Glendale Heights (village) Du Page County	22	0.07
Highland Park (city) Lake County	21	0.07
Buffalo Grove (village) Lake County	25	0.06
De Kalb (city) De Kalb County	24	0.06

Top 10 Places Sorted by Percent
Based on places with populations of 10,000 or more

Place	Number	%
Lisle (village) Du Page County	60	0.28
Skokie (village) Cook County	67	0.11
River Grove (village) Cook County	11	0.10
Oak Lawn (village) Cook County	50	0.09
Berwyn (city) Cook County	45	0.08
Carol Stream (village) Du Page County	26	0.07
Glendale Heights (village) Du Page County	22	0.07
Highland Park (city) Lake County	21	0.07
Buffalo Grove (village) Lake County	25	0.06
De Kalb (city) De Kalb County	24	0.06

Arab: Palestinian

Top 10 Places Sorted by Number
Based on all places, regardless of population

Place	Number	%
Chicago (city) Cook County	2,052	0.07
Oak Lawn (village) Cook County	577	1.04
Orland Park (village) Cook County	394	0.77
Burbank (city) Cook County	311	1.12
Hickory Hills (city) Cook County	203	1.46
Chicago Ridge (village) Cook County	183	1.32
Palos Hills (city) Cook County	155	0.87
Bridgeview (village) Cook County	141	0.92
Goodings Grove (cdp) Will County	111	0.65
Summit (village) Cook County	106	1.00

Top 10 Places Sorted by Percent
Based on all places, regardless of population

Place	Number	%
Dunlap (village) Peoria County	19	2.11
Hickory Hills (city) Cook County	203	1.46
Chicago Ridge (village) Cook County	183	1.32
Burbank (city) Cook County	311	1.12
Oak Lawn (village) Cook County	577	1.04
Long Grove (village) Lake County	68	1.03
Summit (village) Cook County	106	1.00
Bridgeview (village) Cook County	141	0.92
Palos Hills (city) Cook County	155	0.87
Justice (village) Cook County	94	0.78

Top 10 Places Sorted by Percent
Based on places with populations of 10,000 or more

Place	Number	%
Hickory Hills (city) Cook County	203	1.46
Chicago Ridge (village) Cook County	183	1.32
Burbank (city) Cook County	311	1.12
Oak Lawn (village) Cook County	577	1.04
Summit (village) Cook County	106	1.00
Bridgeview (village) Cook County	141	0.92
Palos Hills (city) Cook County	155	0.87
Justice (village) Cook County	94	0.78
Orland Park (village) Cook County	394	0.77
Goodings Grove (cdp) Will County	111	0.65

Arab: Syrian

Top 10 Places Sorted by Number
Based on all places, regardless of population

Place	Number	%
Chicago (city) Cook County	1,124	0.04
Oak Lawn (village) Cook County	114	0.21
Peoria (city) Peoria County	104	0.09

Place	Number	%
Schaumburg (village) Cook County	92	0.12
Bridgeview (village) Cook County	91	0.59
Elgin (city) Kane County	89	0.09
Rockford (city) Winnebago County	86	0.06
Naperville (city) Du Page County	78	0.06
Oak Brook (village) Du Page County	74	0.88
Normal (town) McLean County	69	0.15

Top 10 Places Sorted by Percent
Based on all places, regardless of population

Place	Number	%
West Dundee (village) Kane County	50	0.93
Oak Brook (village) Du Page County	74	0.88
Rosemont (village) Cook County	30	0.72
Cairo (city) Alexander County	26	0.71
Kampsville (village) Calhoun County	2	0.68
Westville (village) Vermilion County	20	0.62
Summerfield (village) Saint Clair County	3	0.61
Bridgeview (village) Cook County	91	0.59
Burr Ridge (village) Du Page County	57	0.55
Willowbrook (village) Du Page County	45	0.50

Top 10 Places Sorted by Percent
Based on places with populations of 10,000 or more

Place	Number	%
Bridgeview (village) Cook County	91	0.59
Burr Ridge (village) Du Page County	57	0.55
Schiller Park (village) Cook County	35	0.30
Lake Forest (city) Lake County	51	0.25
Rolling Meadows (city) Cook County	58	0.24
Oak Lawn (village) Cook County	114	0.21
Algonquin (village) McHenry County	47	0.20
Northbrook (village) Cook County	60	0.18
Edwardsville (city) Madison County	37	0.18
Brookfield (village) McLean County	33	0.17

Arab: Other

Top 10 Places Sorted by Number
Based on all places, regardless of population

Place	Number	%
Chicago (city) Cook County	1,012	0.03
Bartlett (village) Du Page County	67	0.18
Schaumburg (village) Cook County	66	0.09
Carbondale (city) Jackson County	65	0.31
Justice (village) Cook County	60	0.50
Macomb (city) McDonough County	57	0.31
Oak Lawn (village) Cook County	45	0.08
Lyons (village) Cook County	44	0.43
Skokie (village) Cook County	44	0.07
Willowbrook (village) Du Page County	40	0.44

Top 10 Places Sorted by Percent
Based on all places, regardless of population

Place	Number	%
Tiskilwa (village) Bureau County	10	1.27
Standard (village) Putnam County	3	1.16
Lerna (village) Coles County	3	0.93
Justice (village) Cook County	60	0.50
Rome (cdp) Peoria County	8	0.46
Willowbrook (village) Du Page County	40	0.44
Lyons (village) Cook County	44	0.43
Grandwood Park (cdp) Lake County	17	0.38
Tilden (village) Randolph County	3	0.32
Carbondale (city) Jackson County	65	0.31

Top 10 Places Sorted by Percent
Based on places with populations of 10,000 or more

Place	Number	%
Justice (village) Cook County	60	0.50
Lyons (village) Cook County	44	0.43
Carbondale (city) Jackson County	65	0.31

Place	Number	%
Macomb (city) McDonough County	57	0.31
Bartlett (village) Du Page County	67	0.18
Hickory Hills (city) Cook County	25	0.18
Niles (village) Cook County	39	0.13
Chicago Ridge (village) Cook County	18	0.13
Bridgeview (village) Cook County	19	0.12
La Grange Park (village) Cook County	16	0.12

Armenian

Top 10 Places Sorted by Number
Based on all places, regardless of population

Place	Number	%
Chicago (city) Cook County	1,674	0.06
Skokie (village) Cook County	301	0.48
Waukegan (city) Lake County	252	0.29
Lake Forest (city) Lake County	234	1.17
Morton Grove (village) Cook County	169	0.75
Wheeling (village) Cook County	165	0.48
Northbrook (village) Cook County	159	0.48
Hoffman Estates (village) Cook County	137	0.27
Glenview (village) Cook County	136	0.33
Evanston (city) Cook County	136	0.18

Top 10 Places Sorted by Percent
Based on all places, regardless of population

Place	Number	%
Galatia (village) Saline County	36	3.44
Menominee (village) Jo Daviess County	8	3.31
Radom (village) Washington County	10	2.40
Kenilworth (village) Cook County	38	1.52
Trout Valley (village) McHenry County	7	1.18
Lake Forest (city) Lake County	234	1.17
Lakemoor (village) McHenry County	31	1.13
Lily Lake (village) Kane County	9	1.08
Willow Springs (village) Cook County	48	0.97
Enfield (village) White County	6	0.93

Top 10 Places Sorted by Percent
Based on places with populations of 10,000 or more

Place	Number	%
Lake Forest (city) Lake County	234	1.17
Lincolnwood (village) Cook County	98	0.79
Morton Grove (village) Cook County	169	0.75
River Forest (village) Cook County	57	0.49
Skokie (village) Cook County	301	0.48
Wheeling (village) Cook County	165	0.48
Northbrook (village) Cook County	159	0.48
Bloomingdale (village) Du Page County	98	0.45
Gurnee (village) Lake County	121	0.42
Lindenhurst (village) Lake County	50	0.40

Asian

Top 10 Places Sorted by Number
Based on all places, regardless of population

Place	Number	%
Chicago (city) Cook County	143,175	4.94
Skokie (village) Cook County	14,565	22.99
Naperville (city) Du Page County	13,377	10.42
Schaumburg (village) Cook County	11,373	15.09
Hoffman Estates (village) Cook County	8,046	16.26
Glendale Heights (village) Du Page County	6,764	21.29
Mount Prospect (village) Cook County	6,731	11.96
Urbana (city) Champaign County	5,661	15.55
Palatine (village) Cook County	5,439	8.31
Morton Grove (village) Cook County	5,345	23.81

Top 10 Places Sorted by Percent
Based on all places, regardless of population

Place	Number	%
Morton Grove (village) Cook County	5,345	23.81

Place	Number	%
Skokie (village) Cook County	14,565	22.99
Lincolnwood (village) Cook County	2,822	22.83
Oak Brook (village) Du Page County	1,881	21.62
Glendale Heights (village) Du Page County	6,764	21.29
Hoffman Estates (village) Cook County	8,046	16.26
South Barrington (village) Cook County	594	15.80
Urbana (city) Champaign County	5,661	15.55
Schaumburg (village) Cook County	11,373	15.09
Niles (village) Cook County	4,098	13.63

Top 10 Places Sorted by Percent
Based on places with populations of 10,000 or more

Place	Number	%
Morton Grove (village) Cook County	5,345	23.81
Skokie (village) Cook County	14,565	22.99
Lincolnwood (village) Cook County	2,822	22.83
Glendale Heights (village) Du Page County	6,764	21.29
Hoffman Estates (village) Cook County	8,046	16.26
Urbana (city) Champaign County	5,661	15.55
Schaumburg (village) Cook County	11,373	15.09
Niles (village) Cook County	4,098	13.63
Hanover Park (village) Cook County	4,991	13.04
Vernon Hills (village) Lake County	2,579	12.82

Asian: Bangladeshi

Top 10 Places Sorted by Number
Based on all places, regardless of population

Place	Number	%
Chicago (city) Cook County	376	0.01
Skokie (village) Cook County	32	0.05
Naperville (city) Du Page County	25	0.02
Springfield (city) Sangamon County	25	0.02
Bolingbrook (village) Will County	24	0.04
Palatine (village) Cook County	21	0.03
Carbondale (city) Jackson County	18	0.09
Mount Prospect (village) Cook County	15	0.03
Schaumburg (village) Cook County	13	0.02
O'Fallon (city) Saint Clair County	11	0.05

Top 10 Places Sorted by Percent
Based on all places, regardless of population

Place	Number	%
South Barrington (village) Cook County	7	0.19
Genoa (city) De Kalb County	5	0.12
Carbondale (city) Jackson County	18	0.09
Lake Villa (village) Lake County	5	0.09
Bridgeview (village) Cook County	9	0.06
Skokie (village) Cook County	32	0.05
O'Fallon (city) Saint Clair County	11	0.05
Carlinville (city) Macoupin County	3	0.05
Park City (city) Lake County	3	0.05
Bolingbrook (village) Will County	24	0.04

Top 10 Places Sorted by Percent
Based on places with populations of 10,000 or more

Place	Number	%
Carbondale (city) Jackson County	18	0.09
Bridgeview (village) Cook County	9	0.06
Skokie (village) Cook County	32	0.05
O'Fallon (city) Saint Clair County	11	0.05
Bolingbrook (village) Will County	24	0.04
Forest Park (village) Cook County	6	0.04
Lindenhurst (village) Lake County	5	0.04
Palatine (village) Cook County	21	0.03
Mount Prospect (village) Cook County	15	0.03
Roselle (village) Du Page County	8	0.03

Asian: Cambodian

Top 10 Places Sorted by Number
Based on all places, regardless of population

Place	Number	%
Chicago (city) Cook County	1,751	0.06
Joliet (city) Will County	95	0.09
Carol Stream (village) Du Page County	93	0.23
Glendale Heights (village) Du Page County	91	0.29
Mundelein (village) Lake County	83	0.27
Bolingbrook (village) Will County	75	0.13
Skokie (village) Cook County	73	0.12
Wheaton (city) Du Page County	70	0.13
Elgin (city) Kane County	69	0.07
Hanover Park (village) Cook County	68	0.18

Top 10 Places Sorted by Percent
Based on all places, regardless of population

Place	Number	%
Park City (city) Lake County	40	0.60
Cortland (town) De Kalb County	7	0.34
Lee (village) Lee County	1	0.32
Glendale Heights (village) Du Page County	91	0.29
Mundelein (village) Lake County	83	0.27
Warrenville (city) Du Page County	32	0.24
Carol Stream (village) Du Page County	93	0.23
Industry (village) McDonough County	1	0.19
Hanover Park (village) Cook County	68	0.18
Wheeling (village) Cook County	50	0.14

Top 10 Places Sorted by Percent
Based on places with populations of 10,000 or more

Place	Number	%
Glendale Heights (village) Du Page County	91	0.29
Mundelein (village) Lake County	83	0.27
Warrenville (city) Du Page County	32	0.24
Carol Stream (village) Du Page County	93	0.23
Hanover Park (village) Cook County	68	0.18
Wheeling (village) Cook County	50	0.14
Bolingbrook (village) Will County	75	0.13
Wheaton (city) Du Page County	70	0.13
Skokie (village) Cook County	73	0.12
Franklin Park (village) Cook County	21	0.11

Asian: Chinese, except Taiwanese

Top 10 Places Sorted by Number
Based on all places, regardless of population

Place	Number	%
Chicago (city) Cook County	33,701	1.16
Naperville (city) Du Page County	4,072	3.17
Urbana (city) Champaign County	2,034	5.59
Skokie (village) Cook County	1,702	2.69
Evanston (city) Cook County	1,464	1.97
Schaumburg (village) Cook County	1,403	1.86
Champaign (city) Champaign County	1,251	1.85
Hoffman Estates (village) Cook County	907	1.83
Palatine (village) Cook County	882	1.35
Arlington Heights (village) Cook County	818	1.08

Top 10 Places Sorted by Percent
Based on all places, regardless of population

Place	Number	%
Urbana (city) Champaign County	2,034	5.59
Ullin (village) Pulaski County	37	4.75
Oak Brook (village) Du Page County	316	3.63
Calhoun (village) Richland County	8	3.60
Vernon Hills (village) Lake County	649	3.23
Old Mill Creek (village) Lake County	8	3.19
Naperville (city) Du Page County	4,072	3.17
Lisle (village) Du Page County	645	3.05
South Barrington (village) Cook County	110	2.93

Place	Number	%
Westmont (village) Du Page County	710	2.89

Top 10 Places Sorted by Percent
Based on places with populations of 10,000 or more

Place	Number	%
Urbana (city) Champaign County	2,034	5.59
Vernon Hills (village) Lake County	649	3.23
Naperville (city) Du Page County	4,072	3.17
Lisle (village) Du Page County	645	3.05
Westmont (village) Du Page County	710	2.89
Skokie (village) Cook County	1,702	2.69
Wilmette (village) Cook County	734	2.65
Darien (city) Du Page County	530	2.32
Morton Grove (village) Cook County	511	2.28
Lincolnwood (village) Cook County	268	2.17

Asian: Filipino

Top 10 Places Sorted by Number
Based on all places, regardless of population

Place	Number	%
Chicago (city) Cook County	32,266	1.11
Skokie (village) Cook County	3,594	5.67
Waukegan (city) Lake County	2,008	2.28
Glendale Heights (village) Du Page County	1,926	6.06
Morton Grove (village) Cook County	1,569	6.99
Bolingbrook (village) Will County	1,529	2.71
Hanover Park (village) Cook County	1,274	3.33
Schaumburg (village) Cook County	1,196	1.59
Bartlett (village) Du Page County	1,149	3.13
Carol Stream (village) Du Page County	1,127	2.79

Top 10 Places Sorted by Percent
Based on all places, regardless of population

Place	Number	%
Morton Grove (village) Cook County	1,569	6.99
Glendale Heights (village) Du Page County	1,926	6.06
Skokie (village) Cook County	3,594	5.67
Strawn (village) Livingston County	5	4.81
Old Mill Creek (village) Lake County	12	4.78
Lincolnwood (village) Cook County	575	4.65
Darien (city) Du Page County	930	4.07
Park City (city) Lake County	229	3.45
Gurnee (village) Lake County	977	3.39
Hanover Park (village) Cook County	1,274	3.33

Top 10 Places Sorted by Percent
Based on places with populations of 10,000 or more

Place	Number	%
Morton Grove (village) Cook County	1,569	6.99
Glendale Heights (village) Du Page County	1,926	6.06
Skokie (village) Cook County	3,594	5.67
Lincolnwood (village) Cook County	575	4.65
Darien (city) Du Page County	930	4.07
Gurnee (village) Lake County	977	3.39
Hanover Park (village) Cook County	1,274	3.33
Niles (village) Cook County	958	3.19
Bartlett (village) Du Page County	1,149	3.13
Streamwood (village) Cook County	1,109	3.05

Asian: Hmong

Top 10 Places Sorted by Number
Based on all places, regardless of population

Place	Number	%
Chicago (city) Cook County	173	0.01
Aurora (city) Kane County	95	0.07
Danville (city) Vermilion County	35	0.10
Wheaton (city) Du Page County	20	0.04
Champaign (city) Champaign County	19	0.03
Dixon (city) Lee County	17	0.11
Carpentersville (village) Kane County	15	0.05

Place	Number	%
Rockford (city) Winnebago County	12	0.01
Plainfield (village) Will County	10	0.08
Goodings Grove (cdp) Will County	10	0.06

Top 10 Places Sorted by Percent
Based on all places, regardless of population

Place	Number	%
Hainesville (village) Lake County	5	0.23
Dixon (city) Lee County	17	0.11
Danville (city) Vermilion County	35	0.10
Plainfield (village) Will County	10	0.08
Aurora (city) Kane County	95	0.07
Goodings Grove (cdp) Will County	10	0.06
Winfield (village) Du Page County	5	0.06
Carpentersville (village) Kane County	15	0.05
Norridge (village) Cook County	8	0.05
Warrenville (city) Du Page County	7	0.05

Top 10 Places Sorted by Percent
Based on places with populations of 10,000 or more

Place	Number	%
Dixon (city) Lee County	17	0.11
Danville (city) Vermilion County	35	0.10
Plainfield (village) Will County	10	0.08
Aurora (city) Kane County	95	0.07
Goodings Grove (cdp) Will County	10	0.06
Carpentersville (village) Kane County	15	0.05
Norridge (village) Cook County	8	0.05
Warrenville (city) Du Page County	7	0.05
Wheaton (city) Du Page County	20	0.04
Rolling Meadows (city) Cook County	10	0.04

Asian: Indian

Top 10 Places Sorted by Number
Based on all places, regardless of population

Place	Number	%
Chicago (city) Cook County	27,889	0.96
Naperville (city) Du Page County	5,261	4.10
Schaumburg (village) Cook County	5,006	6.64
Skokie (village) Cook County	4,142	6.54
Hoffman Estates (village) Cook County	3,371	6.81
Mount Prospect (village) Cook County	3,325	5.91
Glendale Heights (village) Du Page County	2,840	8.94
Des Plaines (city) Cook County	2,339	3.98
Hanover Park (village) Cook County	2,313	6.04
Palatine (village) Cook County	2,229	3.40

Top 10 Places Sorted by Percent
Based on all places, regardless of population

Place	Number	%
Oak Brook (village) Du Page County	949	10.91
Glendale Heights (village) Du Page County	2,840	8.94
South Barrington (village) Cook County	273	7.26
Morton Grove (village) Cook County	1,565	6.97
Hoffman Estates (village) Cook County	3,371	6.81
Schaumburg (village) Cook County	5,006	6.64
Skokie (village) Cook County	4,142	6.54
Lincolnwood (village) Cook County	795	6.43
Burr Ridge (village) Du Page County	664	6.38
Hanover Park (village) Cook County	2,313	6.04

Top 10 Places Sorted by Percent
Based on places with populations of 10,000 or more

Place	Number	%
Glendale Heights (village) Du Page County	2,840	8.94
Morton Grove (village) Cook County	1,565	6.97
Hoffman Estates (village) Cook County	3,371	6.81
Schaumburg (village) Cook County	5,006	6.64
Skokie (village) Cook County	4,142	6.54
Lincolnwood (village) Cook County	795	6.43
Burr Ridge (village) Du Page County	664	6.38

Place	Number	%
Hanover Park (village) Cook County	2,313	6.04
Mount Prospect (village) Cook County	3,325	5.91
Woodridge (village) Du Page County	1,769	5.72

Asian: Indonesian

Top 10 Places Sorted by Number
Based on all places, regardless of population

Place	Number	%
Chicago (city) Cook County	359	0.01
Urbana (city) Champaign County	77	0.21
Skokie (village) Cook County	47	0.07
Schaumburg (village) Cook County	36	0.05
Naperville (city) Du Page County	24	0.02
Carbondale (city) Jackson County	21	0.10
Peoria (city) Peoria County	21	0.02
Arlington Heights (village) Cook County	19	0.02
Champaign (city) Champaign County	18	0.03
Hoffman Estates (village) Cook County	17	0.03

Top 10 Places Sorted by Percent
Based on all places, regardless of population

Place	Number	%
Neponset (village) Bureau County	5	0.96
Saint Libory (village) Saint Clair County	5	0.86
Elsah (village) Jersey County	3	0.47
New Millford (village) Winnebago County	2	0.37
Havana (city) Mason County	8	0.22
Urbana (city) Champaign County	77	0.21
Wayne (village) Kane County	4	0.19
Clarendon Hills (village) Du Page County	10	0.13
Tiskilwa (village) Bureau County	1	0.13
Carbondale (city) Jackson County	21	0.10

Top 10 Places Sorted by Percent
Based on places with populations of 10,000 or more

Place	Number	%
Urbana (city) Champaign County	77	0.21
Carbondale (city) Jackson County	21	0.10
Skokie (village) Cook County	47	0.07
Lincolnwood (village) Cook County	8	0.06
Schaumburg (village) Cook County	36	0.05
De Kalb (city) De Kalb County	14	0.04
Romeoville (village) Will County	9	0.04
La Grange (village) Cook County	6	0.04
Champaign (city) Champaign County	18	0.03
Hoffman Estates (village) Cook County	17	0.03

Asian: Japanese

Top 10 Places Sorted by Number
Based on all places, regardless of population

Place	Number	%
Chicago (city) Cook County	7,114	0.25
Schaumburg (village) Cook County	1,214	1.61
Arlington Heights (village) Cook County	1,108	1.46
Hoffman Estates (village) Cook County	796	1.61
Elk Grove Village (village) Cook County	676	1.95
Buffalo Grove (village) Lake County	600	1.40
Evanston (city) Cook County	597	0.80
Skokie (village) Cook County	494	0.78
Palatine (village) Cook County	490	0.75
Mount Prospect (village) Cook County	408	0.73

Top 10 Places Sorted by Percent
Based on all places, regardless of population

Place	Number	%
Belknap (village) Johnson County	9	6.77
Elk Grove Village (village) Cook County	676	1.95
Schaumburg (village) Cook County	1,214	1.61
Hoffman Estates (village) Cook County	796	1.61
Arlington Heights (village) Cook County	1,108	1.46

Place	Number	%
Buffalo Grove (village) Lake County	600	1.40
Troy Grove (village) La Salle County	4	1.31
Kempton (village) Ford County	3	1.28
Rose Hill (village) Jasper County	1	1.27
Wilmette (village) Cook County	348	1.26

Top 10 Places Sorted by Percent
Based on places with populations of 10,000 or more

Place	Number	%
Elk Grove Village (village) Cook County	676	1.95
Schaumburg (village) Cook County	1,214	1.61
Hoffman Estates (village) Cook County	796	1.61
Arlington Heights (village) Cook County	1,108	1.46
Buffalo Grove (village) Lake County	600	1.40
Wilmette (village) Cook County	348	1.26
Lincolnwood (village) Cook County	151	1.22
Carbondale (city) Jackson County	229	1.11
Glenview (village) Cook County	406	0.97
Urbana (city) Champaign County	316	0.87

Asian: Korean

Top 10 Places Sorted by Number
Based on all places, regardless of population

Place	Number	%
Chicago (city) Cook County	12,867	0.44
Skokie (village) Cook County	2,557	4.04
Glenview (village) Cook County	1,929	4.61
Schaumburg (village) Cook County	1,641	2.18
Northbrook (village) Cook County	1,520	4.55
Mount Prospect (village) Cook County	1,232	2.19
Naperville (city) Du Page County	1,215	0.95
Hoffman Estates (village) Cook County	1,144	2.31
Urbana (city) Champaign County	1,139	3.13
Buffalo Grove (village) Lake County	1,135	2.65

Top 10 Places Sorted by Percent
Based on all places, regardless of population

Place	Number	%
Belknap (village) Johnson County	9	6.77
Panola (village) Woodford County	2	6.06
Savoy (village) Champaign County	233	5.21
Morton Grove (village) Cook County	1,065	4.74
Lincolnwood (village) Cook County	586	4.74
Glenview (village) Cook County	1,929	4.61
Northbrook (village) Cook County	1,520	4.55
Skokie (village) Cook County	2,557	4.04
Niles (village) Cook County	949	3.16
Urbana (city) Champaign County	1,139	3.13

Top 10 Places Sorted by Percent
Based on places with populations of 10,000 or more

Place	Number	%
Morton Grove (village) Cook County	1,065	4.74
Lincolnwood (village) Cook County	586	4.74
Glenview (village) Cook County	1,929	4.61
Northbrook (village) Cook County	1,520	4.55
Skokie (village) Cook County	2,557	4.04
Niles (village) Cook County	949	3.16
Urbana (city) Champaign County	1,139	3.13
Vernon Hills (village) Lake County	626	3.11
Buffalo Grove (village) Lake County	1,135	2.65
Wilmette (village) Cook County	701	2.54

Asian: Laotian

Top 10 Places Sorted by Number
Based on all places, regardless of population

Place	Number	%
Elgin (city) Kane County	1,507	1.59
Rockford (city) Winnebago County	1,085	0.72
Chicago (city) Cook County	517	0.02

	Number	%
South Elgin (village) Kane County	380	2.36
Joliet (city) Will County	222	0.21
Hanover Park (village) Cook County	147	0.38
Aurora (city) Kane County	125	0.09
Streamwood (village) Cook County	67	0.18
Champaign (city) Champaign County	66	0.10
Carpentersville (village) Kane County	65	0.21

Top 10 Places Sorted by Percent
Based on all places, regardless of population

Place	Number	%
South Elgin (village) Kane County	380	2.36
De Pue (village) Bureau County	36	1.95
Elgin (city) Kane County	1,507	1.59
Ullin (village) Pulaski County	11	1.41
Cherry Valley (village) Winnebago County	23	1.05
Arlington (village) Bureau County	2	0.95
La Fayette (village) Stark County	2	0.88
Rockford (city) Winnebago County	1,085	0.72
North Aurora (village) Kane County	56	0.53
Hanover Park (village) Cook County	147	0.38

Top 10 Places Sorted by Percent
Based on places with populations of 10,000 or more

Place	Number	%
South Elgin (village) Kane County	380	2.36
Elgin (city) Kane County	1,507	1.59
Rockford (city) Winnebago County	1,085	0.72
North Aurora (village) Kane County	56	0.53
Hanover Park (village) Cook County	147	0.38
Loves Park (city) Winnebago County	51	0.25
Joliet (city) Will County	222	0.21
Carpentersville (village) Kane County	65	0.21
Markham (city) Cook County	26	0.21
Streamwood (village) Cook County	67	0.18

Asian: Malaysian

Top 10 Places Sorted by Number
Based on all places, regardless of population

Place	Number	%
Chicago (city) Cook County	186	0.01
Carbondale (city) Jackson County	55	0.27
Urbana (city) Champaign County	33	0.09
Champaign (city) Champaign County	27	0.04
Schaumburg (village) Cook County	20	0.03
De Kalb (city) De Kalb County	18	0.05
Skokie (village) Cook County	17	0.03
Evanston (city) Cook County	17	0.02
Lisle (village) Du Page County	11	0.05
Macomb (city) McDonough County	10	0.05

Top 10 Places Sorted by Percent
Based on all places, regardless of population

Place	Number	%
Davis Junction (village) Ogle County	2	0.41
Kampsville (village) Calhoun County	1	0.33
Carbondale (city) Jackson County	55	0.27
Bluffs (village) Scott County	1	0.13
Green Oaks (village) Lake County	4	0.11
Urbana (city) Champaign County	33	0.09
Savoy (village) Champaign County	3	0.07
De Soto (village) Jackson County	1	0.06
Teutopolis (village) Effingham County	1	0.06
De Kalb (city) De Kalb County	18	0.05

Top 10 Places Sorted by Percent
Based on places with populations of 10,000 or more

Place	Number	%
Carbondale (city) Jackson County	55	0.27
Urbana (city) Champaign County	33	0.09
De Kalb (city) De Kalb County	18	0.05

	Number	%
Lisle (village) Du Page County	11	0.05
Macomb (city) McDonough County	10	0.05
Champaign (city) Champaign County	27	0.04
Rolling Meadows (city) Cook County	9	0.04
Forest Park (village) Cook County	6	0.04
Justice (village) Cook County	5	0.04
Gages Lake (cdp) Lake County	4	0.04

Asian: Pakistani

Top 10 Places Sorted by Number
Based on all places, regardless of population

Place	Number	%
Chicago (city) Cook County	7,606	0.26
Skokie (village) Cook County	804	1.27
Naperville (city) Du Page County	403	0.31
Glendale Heights (village) Du Page County	354	1.11
Hanover Park (village) Cook County	351	0.92
Hoffman Estates (village) Cook County	351	0.71
Schaumburg (village) Cook County	326	0.43
Lombard (village) Du Page County	285	0.67
Bolingbrook (village) Will County	256	0.45
Carol Stream (village) Du Page County	245	0.61

Top 10 Places Sorted by Percent
Based on all places, regardless of population

Place	Number	%
Lincolnwood (village) Cook County	203	1.64
Skokie (village) Cook County	804	1.27
Oak Brook (village) Du Page County	107	1.23
Glendale Heights (village) Du Page County	354	1.11
Burr Ridge (village) Du Page County	97	0.93
Hanover Park (village) Cook County	351	0.92
Bensenville (village) Du Page County	187	0.90
Oakbrook Terrace (city) Du Page County	19	0.83
Hoffman Estates (village) Cook County	351	0.71
Lombard (village) Du Page County	285	0.67

Top 10 Places Sorted by Percent
Based on places with populations of 10,000 or more

Place	Number	%
Lincolnwood (village) Cook County	203	1.64
Skokie (village) Cook County	804	1.27
Glendale Heights (village) Du Page County	354	1.11
Burr Ridge (village) Du Page County	97	0.93
Hanover Park (village) Cook County	351	0.92
Bensenville (village) Du Page County	187	0.90
Hoffman Estates (village) Cook County	351	0.71
Lombard (village) Du Page County	285	0.67
Morton Grove (village) Cook County	146	0.65
Glen Ellyn (village) Du Page County	174	0.64

Asian: Sri Lankan

Top 10 Places Sorted by Number
Based on all places, regardless of population

Place	Number	%
Chicago (city) Cook County	144	0.00
Urbana (city) Champaign County	46	0.13
Skokie (village) Cook County	26	0.04
Naperville (city) Du Page County	22	0.02
Tinley Park (village) Cook County	14	0.03
Hoffman Estates (village) Cook County	13	0.03
Normal (town) McLean County	12	0.03
Lisle (village) Du Page County	11	0.05
Wheeling (village) Cook County	11	0.03
Darien (city) Du Page County	10	0.04

Top 10 Places Sorted by Percent
Based on all places, regardless of population

Place	Number	%
Mettawa (village) Lake County	1	0.27

	Number	%
Clifton (village) Iroquois County	2	0.15
Urbana (city) Champaign County	46	0.13
Savoy (village) Champaign County	5	0.11
Oak Brook (village) Du Page County	8	0.09
Willowbrook (village) Du Page County	7	0.08
River Forest (village) Cook County	8	0.07
Long Grove (village) Lake County	4	0.06
Lisle (village) Du Page County	11	0.05
Skokie (village) Cook County	26	0.04

Top 10 Places Sorted by Percent
Based on places with populations of 10,000 or more

Place	Number	%
Urbana (city) Champaign County	46	0.13
River Forest (village) Cook County	8	0.07
Lisle (village) Du Page County	11	0.05
Skokie (village) Cook County	26	0.04
Darien (city) Du Page County	10	0.04
Woodstock (city) McHenry County	8	0.04
Lindenhurst (village) Lake County	5	0.04
Tinley Park (village) Cook County	14	0.03
Hoffman Estates (village) Cook County	13	0.03
Normal (town) McLean County	12	0.03

Asian: Taiwanese

Top 10 Places Sorted by Number
Based on all places, regardless of population

Place	Number	%
Chicago (city) Cook County	669	0.02
Naperville (city) Du Page County	455	0.35
Urbana (city) Champaign County	260	0.71
Evanston (city) Cook County	161	0.22
Schaumburg (village) Cook County	109	0.14
Champaign (city) Champaign County	96	0.14
Skokie (village) Cook County	81	0.13
Hoffman Estates (village) Cook County	79	0.16
Oak Brook (village) Du Page County	77	0.88
Wilmette (village) Cook County	68	0.25

Top 10 Places Sorted by Percent
Based on all places, regardless of population

Place	Number	%
Oak Brook (village) Du Page County	77	0.88
Urbana (city) Champaign County	260	0.71
South Barrington (village) Cook County	26	0.69
Naperville (city) Du Page County	455	0.35
Lisle (village) Du Page County	66	0.31
Savoy (village) Champaign County	14	0.31
Leland Grove (city) Sangamon County	5	0.31
Third Lake (village) Lake County	4	0.30
Willowbrook (village) Du Page County	25	0.28
Wilmette (village) Cook County	68	0.25

Top 10 Places Sorted by Percent
Based on places with populations of 10,000 or more

Place	Number	%
Urbana (city) Champaign County	260	0.71
Naperville (city) Du Page County	455	0.35
Lisle (village) Du Page County	66	0.31
Wilmette (village) Cook County	68	0.25
Darien (city) Du Page County	56	0.24
Evanston (city) Cook County	161	0.22
Westmont (village) Du Page County	54	0.22
Carbondale (city) Jackson County	43	0.21
Vernon Hills (village) Lake County	36	0.18
Northbrook (village) Cook County	57	0.17

Notes: (cdp) census designated place; Refer to the User's Guide in the front of the book for more detailed information.

Asian: Thai

Top 10 Places Sorted by Number
Based on all places, regardless of population

Place	Number	%
Chicago (city) Cook County	2,385	0.08
Skokie (village) Cook County	243	0.38
Champaign (city) Champaign County	124	0.18
Morton Grove (village) Cook County	97	0.43
Urbana (city) Champaign County	92	0.25
Wilmette (village) Cook County	91	0.33
Evanston (city) Cook County	88	0.12
Elgin (city) Kane County	84	0.09
Glenview (village) Cook County	83	0.20
Darien (city) Du Page County	79	0.35

Top 10 Places Sorted by Percent
Based on all places, regardless of population

Place	Number	%
Damiansville (village) Clinton County	3	0.82
Lincolnwood (village) Cook County	62	0.50
Morton Grove (village) Cook County	97	0.43
Keyesport (village) Clinton County	2	0.42
Ullin (village) Pulaski County	3	0.39
Skokie (village) Cook County	243	0.38
Sims (village) Wayne County	1	0.37
Darien (city) Du Page County	79	0.35
Wilmette (village) Cook County	91	0.33
Bellevue (village) Peoria County	6	0.32

Top 10 Places Sorted by Percent
Based on places with populations of 10,000 or more

Place	Number	%
Lincolnwood (village) Cook County	62	0.50
Morton Grove (village) Cook County	97	0.43
Skokie (village) Cook County	243	0.38
Darien (city) Du Page County	79	0.35
Wilmette (village) Cook County	91	0.33
Forest Park (village) Cook County	43	0.27
Urbana (city) Champaign County	92	0.25
Glenview (village) Cook County	83	0.20
Carbondale (city) Jackson County	41	0.20
Niles (village) Cook County	57	0.19

Asian: Vietnamese

Top 10 Places Sorted by Number
Based on all places, regardless of population

Place	Number	%
Chicago (city) Cook County	8,925	0.31
Glendale Heights (village) Du Page County	805	2.53
Carol Stream (village) Du Page County	605	1.50
Rockford (city) Winnebago County	531	0.35
Wheaton (city) Du Page County	462	0.83
Champaign (city) Champaign County	416	0.62
Peoria (city) Peoria County	382	0.34
Skokie (village) Cook County	326	0.51
Aurora (city) Kane County	243	0.17
Elgin (city) Kane County	221	0.23

Top 10 Places Sorted by Percent
Based on all places, regardless of population

Place	Number	%
Glendale Heights (village) Du Page County	805	2.53
Carol Stream (village) Du Page County	605	1.50
Calhoun (village) Richland County	3	1.35
Volo (village) Lake County	2	1.11
Wheaton (city) Du Page County	462	0.83
Dunlap (village) Peoria County	7	0.76
New Millford (village) Winnebago County	4	0.74
Champaign (city) Champaign County	416	0.62
Lincolnwood (village) Cook County	74	0.60

| **Northlake** (city) Cook County | 71 | 0.60 |

Top 10 Places Sorted by Percent
Based on places with populations of 10,000 or more

Place	Number	%
Glendale Heights (village) Du Page County	805	2.53
Carol Stream (village) Du Page County	605	1.50
Wheaton (city) Du Page County	462	0.83
Champaign (city) Champaign County	416	0.62
Lincolnwood (village) Cook County	74	0.60
Northlake (city) Cook County	71	0.60
Urbana (city) Champaign County	196	0.54
Addison (village) Du Page County	193	0.54
Skokie (village) Cook County	326	0.51
East Moline (city) Rock Island County	98	0.48

Asian: Other Asian, specified

Top 10 Places Sorted by Number
Based on all places, regardless of population

Place	Number	%
Chicago (city) Cook County	404	0.01
Macomb (city) McDonough County	35	0.19
Evanston (city) Cook County	24	0.03
Schaumburg (village) Cook County	23	0.03
Urbana (city) Champaign County	21	0.06
Naperville (city) Du Page County	21	0.02
Niles (village) Cook County	20	0.07
De Kalb (city) De Kalb County	20	0.05
Skokie (village) Cook County	19	0.03
Peoria (city) Peoria County	19	0.02

Top 10 Places Sorted by Percent
Based on all places, regardless of population

Place	Number	%
Minonk (city) Woodford County	9	0.42
Bull Valley (village) McHenry County	2	0.28
Kane (village) Greene County	1	0.22
Macomb (city) McDonough County	35	0.19
Minier (village) Tazewell County	2	0.16
White Hall (city) Greene County	4	0.15
Third Lake (village) Lake County	2	0.15
Oak Brook (village) Du Page County	12	0.14
Mound City (city) Pulaski County	1	0.14
Orangeville (village) Stephenson County	1	0.13

Top 10 Places Sorted by Percent
Based on places with populations of 10,000 or more

Place	Number	%
Macomb (city) McDonough County	35	0.19
Glen Carbon (village) Madison County	8	0.08
Niles (village) Cook County	20	0.07
Urbana (city) Champaign County	21	0.06
Bourbonnais (village) Kankakee County	9	0.06
Markham (city) Cook County	7	0.06
Schiller Park (village) Cook County	7	0.06
De Kalb (city) De Kalb County	20	0.05
Wheeling (village) Cook County	16	0.05
Kewanee (city) Henry County	6	0.05

Asian: Other Asian, not specified

Top 10 Places Sorted by Number
Based on all places, regardless of population

Place	Number	%
Chicago (city) Cook County	5,843	0.20
Skokie (village) Cook County	372	0.59
Elgin (city) Kane County	247	0.26
Aurora (city) Kane County	205	0.14
Rockford (city) Winnebago County	204	0.14
Naperville (city) Du Page County	201	0.16
Schaumburg (village) Cook County	182	0.24

Hoffman Estates (village) Cook County	144	0.29
Evanston (city) Cook County	133	0.18
Champaign (city) Champaign County	119	0.18

Top 10 Places Sorted by Percent
Based on all places, regardless of population

Place	Number	%
Bannockburn (village) Lake County	27	1.89
Springerton (village) White County	2	1.49
Vergennes (village) Jackson County	4	0.81
Mound Station (village) Brown County	1	0.79
Clear Lake (village) Sangamon County	2	0.75
Lincolnwood (village) Cook County	85	0.69
Mechanicsburg (village) Sangamon County	3	0.66
Kampsville (village) Calhoun County	2	0.66
Justice (village) Cook County	77	0.63
Ferris (village) Hancock County	1	0.60

Top 10 Places Sorted by Percent
Based on places with populations of 10,000 or more

Place	Number	%
Lincolnwood (village) Cook County	85	0.69
Justice (village) Cook County	77	0.63
Skokie (village) Cook County	372	0.59
Chicago Ridge (village) Cook County	71	0.50
Niles (village) Cook County	112	0.37
Bridgeview (village) Cook County	57	0.37
Hickory Hills (city) Cook County	52	0.37
Glendale Heights (village) Du Page County	113	0.36
Alsip (village) Cook County	68	0.34
Schiller Park (village) Cook County	39	0.33

Assyrian/Chaldean/Syriac

Top 10 Places Sorted by Number
Based on all places, regardless of population

Place	Number	%
Chicago (city) Cook County	7,121	0.25
Skokie (village) Cook County	2,381	3.76
Morton Grove (village) Cook County	496	2.21
Niles (village) Cook County	458	1.52
Lincolnwood (village) Cook County	438	3.54
Elgin (city) Kane County	334	0.36
Schaumburg (village) Cook County	272	0.37
Mount Prospect (village) Cook County	220	0.39
Glenview (village) Cook County	203	0.49
Elk Grove Village (village) Cook County	169	0.49

Top 10 Places Sorted by Percent
Based on all places, regardless of population

Place	Number	%
Skokie (village) Cook County	2,381	3.76
Lincolnwood (village) Cook County	438	3.54
Golf (village) Cook County	13	2.88
Henderson (village) Knox County	9	2.54
Morton Grove (village) Cook County	496	2.21
Niles (village) Cook County	458	1.52
Mettawa (village) Lake County	3	0.93
Itasca (village) Du Page County	51	0.62
Willow Springs (village) Cook County	29	0.59
Winfield (village) Du Page County	49	0.55

Top 10 Places Sorted by Percent
Based on places with populations of 10,000 or more

Place	Number	%
Skokie (village) Cook County	2,381	3.76
Lincolnwood (village) Cook County	438	3.54
Morton Grove (village) Cook County	496	2.21
Niles (village) Cook County	458	1.52
Glenview (village) Cook County	203	0.49
Elk Grove Village (village) Cook County	169	0.49
Streamwood (village) Cook County	161	0.44

Notes: (cdp) census designated place; Refer to the User's Guide in the front of the book for more detailed information.

Place	Number	%
Mount Prospect (village) Cook County	220	0.39
Schaumburg (village) Cook County	272	0.37
Elgin (city) Kane County	334	0.36

Australian

Top 10 Places Sorted by Number
Based on all places, regardless of population

Place	Number	%
Chicago (city) Cook County	486	0.02
Aurora (city) Kane County	59	0.04
Wheaton (city) Du Page County	53	0.10
Elgin (city) Kane County	52	0.06
Washington (city) Tazewell County	50	0.46
Evanston (city) Cook County	49	0.07
Naperville (city) Du Page County	49	0.04
Schaumburg (village) Cook County	48	0.06
Lincolnshire (village) Lake County	41	0.66
Savoy (village) Champaign County	40	0.93

Top 10 Places Sorted by Percent
Based on all places, regardless of population

Place	Number	%
Bannockburn (village) Lake County	37	2.60
Trout Valley (village) McHenry County	6	1.01
Savoy (village) Champaign County	40	0.93
Mettawa (village) Lake County	3	0.93
Lincolnshire (village) Lake County	41	0.66
Saunemin (village) Livingston County	3	0.61
Plano (city) Kendall County	31	0.57
Inverness (village) Cook County	31	0.49
Washington (city) Tazewell County	50	0.46
Wonder Lake (cdp) McHenry County	35	0.46

Top 10 Places Sorted by Percent
Based on places with populations of 10,000 or more

Place	Number	%
Washington (city) Tazewell County	50	0.46
Lockport (city) Will County	40	0.27
Frankfort (village) Will County	16	0.16
River Forest (village) Cook County	17	0.15
Grayslake (village) Lake County	26	0.14
Mokena (village) Will County	20	0.14
Centralia (city) Marion County	19	0.13
Goodings Grove (cdp) Will County	19	0.11
Wheaton (city) Du Page County	53	0.10
Palos Hills (city) Cook County	17	0.10

Austrian

Top 10 Places Sorted by Number
Based on all places, regardless of population

Place	Number	%
Chicago (city) Cook County	8,080	0.28
Naperville (city) Du Page County	806	0.63
Arlington Heights (village) Cook County	712	0.94
Schaumburg (village) Cook County	640	0.86
Orland Park (village) Cook County	628	1.23
Oak Lawn (village) Cook County	619	1.12
Northbrook (village) Cook County	510	1.53
Evanston (city) Cook County	482	0.65
Des Plaines (city) Cook County	462	0.79
Highland Park (city) Lake County	456	1.45

Top 10 Places Sorted by Percent
Based on all places, regardless of population

Place	Number	%
Burnt Prairie (village) White County	2	4.35
Ringwood (village) McHenry County	17	3.83
Liverpool (village) Fulton County	3	3.16
Spaulding (village) Sangamon County	17	3.05
Eagarville (village) Macoupin County	3	2.50

Place	Number	%
Rockbridge (village) Greene County	4	2.22
Browning (village) Schuyler County	3	2.21
Coffeen (city) Montgomery County	16	2.15
Whiteash (village) Williamson County	6	2.14
New Douglas (village) Madison County	7	1.82

Top 10 Places Sorted by Percent
Based on places with populations of 10,000 or more

Place	Number	%
Deerfield (village) Lake County	312	1.69
Palos Heights (city) Cook County	188	1.66
Northbrook (village) Cook County	510	1.53
Highland Park (city) Lake County	456	1.45
Crestwood (village) Cook County	155	1.38
Evergreen Park (village) Cook County	280	1.34
Wood Dale (city) Du Page County	173	1.24
Orland Park (village) Cook County	628	1.23
Oak Forest (city) Cook County	321	1.15
Hickory Hills (city) Cook County	159	1.14

Basque

Top 10 Places Sorted by Number
Based on all places, regardless of population

Place	Number	%
Chicago (city) Cook County	141	0.00
Woodridge (village) Du Page County	89	0.29
Highland Park (city) Lake County	40	0.13
Waukegan (city) Lake County	35	0.04
Oak Park (village) Cook County	27	0.05
Naperville (city) Du Page County	21	0.02
Aurora (city) Kane County	17	0.01
Normal (town) McLean County	16	0.04
Libertyville (village) Lake County	15	0.07
Arlington Heights (village) Cook County	15	0.02

Top 10 Places Sorted by Percent
Based on all places, regardless of population

Place	Number	%
Sauget (village) Saint Clair County	1	0.54
Woodridge (village) Du Page County	89	0.29
Highland Park (city) Lake County	40	0.13
Minooka (village) Grundy County	4	0.10
McCullom Lake (village) McHenry County	1	0.10
Island Lake (village) McHenry County	7	0.09
Libertyville (village) Lake County	15	0.07
Oak Park (village) Cook County	27	0.05
Waukegan (city) Lake County	35	0.04
Normal (town) McLean County	16	0.04

Top 10 Places Sorted by Percent
Based on places with populations of 10,000 or more

Place	Number	%
Woodridge (village) Du Page County	89	0.29
Highland Park (city) Lake County	40	0.13
Libertyville (village) Lake County	15	0.07
Oak Park (village) Cook County	27	0.05
Waukegan (city) Lake County	35	0.04
Normal (town) McLean County	16	0.04
Collinsville (city) Madison County	10	0.04
Lake Zurich (village) Lake County	8	0.04
Chicago Ridge (village) Cook County	6	0.04
Glenview (village) Cook County	13	0.03

Belgian

Top 10 Places Sorted by Number
Based on all places, regardless of population

Place	Number	%
Moline (city) Rock Island County	2,686	6.14
Chicago (city) Cook County	2,366	0.08
East Moline (city) Rock Island County	1,490	7.32

Place	Number	%
Rock Island (city) Rock Island County	1,480	3.73
Kewanee (city) Henry County	805	6.22
Geneseo (city) Henry County	635	9.68
Silvis (city) Rock Island County	476	6.51
Peoria (city) Peoria County	380	0.34
Atkinson (town) Henry County	340	33.86
Rockford (city) Winnebago County	325	0.22

Top 10 Places Sorted by Percent
Based on all places, regardless of population

Place	Number	%
Atkinson (town) Henry County	340	33.86
Annawan (town) Henry County	290	33.56
Mineral (village) Bureau County	58	21.25
Deer Grove (village) Whiteside County	6	11.32
Geneseo (city) Henry County	635	9.68
Sherrard (village) Mercer County	65	9.45
Hooppole (village) Henry County	15	9.20
Sheffield (village) Bureau County	79	8.49
Apple River (village) Jo Daviess County	33	8.21
Reynolds (village) Rock Island County	40	7.98

Top 10 Places Sorted by Percent
Based on places with populations of 10,000 or more

Place	Number	%
East Moline (city) Rock Island County	1,490	7.32
Kewanee (city) Henry County	805	6.22
Moline (city) Rock Island County	2,686	6.14
Rock Island (city) Rock Island County	1,480	3.73
Geneva (city) Kane County	222	1.14
Saint Charles (city) Kane County	229	0.82
Oswego (village) Kendall County	109	0.82
Winnetka (village) Cook County	92	0.74
Rolling Meadows (city) Cook County	170	0.69
Lake Zurich (village) Lake County	99	0.55

Brazilian

Top 10 Places Sorted by Number
Based on all places, regardless of population

Place	Number	%
Chicago (city) Cook County	833	0.03
Urbana (city) Champaign County	101	0.28
Peoria (city) Peoria County	97	0.09
Libertyville (village) Lake County	79	0.38
Evanston (city) Cook County	76	0.10
Palatine (village) Cook County	73	0.11
Hawthorn Woods (village) Lake County	46	0.72
Oak Park (village) Cook County	42	0.08
Berwyn (city) Cook County	41	0.08
Lake Zurich (village) Lake County	40	0.22

Top 10 Places Sorted by Percent
Based on all places, regardless of population

Place	Number	%
Coleta (village) Whiteside County	9	5.63
Ivesdale (village) Champaign County	4	1.26
Chesterfield (village) Macoupin County	3	1.24
Spillertown (village) Williamson County	2	0.91
Hawthorn Woods (village) Lake County	46	0.72
Kangley (village) La Salle County	2	0.67
Burlington (village) Kane County	3	0.65
Stickney (village) Cook County	37	0.60
Savoy (village) Champaign County	26	0.60
Avon (village) Fulton County	4	0.44

Top 10 Places Sorted by Percent
Based on places with populations of 10,000 or more

Place	Number	%
Libertyville (village) Lake County	79	0.38
Urbana (city) Champaign County	101	0.28
Lake Zurich (village) Lake County	40	0.22

Notes: (cdp) census designated place; Refer to the User's Guide in the front of the book for more detailed information.

Place	Number	%
Morton (village) Tazewell County	30	0.20
Hinsdale (village) Du Page County	33	0.19
Bridgeview (village) Cook County	28	0.18
Schiller Park (village) Cook County	21	0.18
Vernon Hills (village) Lake County	29	0.14
Grayslake (village) Lake County	25	0.14
Mundelein (village) Lake County	37	0.12

British

Top 10 Places Sorted by Number
Based on all places, regardless of population

Place	Number	%
Chicago (city) Cook County	4,653	0.16
Naperville (city) Du Page County	711	0.55
Evanston (city) Cook County	596	0.80
Wheaton (city) Du Page County	515	0.93
Rockford (city) Winnebago County	491	0.33
Champaign (city) Champaign County	474	0.70
Aurora (city) Kane County	434	0.30
Peoria (city) Peoria County	347	0.31
Urbana (city) Champaign County	309	0.85
Decatur (city) Macon County	290	0.35

Top 10 Places Sorted by Percent
Based on all places, regardless of population

Place	Number	%
Liverpool (village) Fulton County	10	10.53
New Salem (village) Pike County	9	6.00
Walshville (village) Montgomery County	4	4.71
Parkersburg (village) Richland County	9	4.41
Bannockburn (village) Lake County	51	3.58
Rio (village) Knox County	8	3.20
East Galesburg (village) Knox County	24	2.93
Huey (village) Clinton County	5	2.53
Shabbona (village) De Kalb County	24	2.52
Hettick (village) Macoupin County	4	2.11

Top 10 Places Sorted by Percent
Based on places with populations of 10,000 or more

Place	Number	%
Winnetka (village) Cook County	144	1.16
Wheaton (city) Du Page County	515	0.93
Barrington (village) Cook County	91	0.91
Urbana (city) Champaign County	309	0.85
Evanston (city) Cook County	596	0.80
Rantoul (village) Champaign County	99	0.77
Vernon Hills (village) Lake County	155	0.75
Matteson (village) Cook County	97	0.75
Champaign (city) Champaign County	474	0.70
Batavia (city) Kane County	167	0.70

Bulgarian

Top 10 Places Sorted by Number
Based on all places, regardless of population

Place	Number	%
Chicago (city) Cook County	2,045	0.07
Schiller Park (village) Cook County	244	2.07
Skokie (village) Cook County	208	0.33
Mount Prospect (village) Cook County	164	0.29
Des Plaines (city) Cook County	149	0.25
Rosemont (village) Cook County	119	2.85
Elmwood Park (village) Cook County	106	0.42
Schaumburg (village) Cook County	103	0.14
Roselle (village) Du Page County	89	0.38
Naperville (city) Du Page County	83	0.06

Top 10 Places Sorted by Percent
Based on all places, regardless of population

Place	Number	%
Rosemont (village) Cook County	119	2.85

Place	Number	%
Schiller Park (village) Cook County	244	2.07
Nelson (village) Lee County	3	2.00
Ogden (village) Champaign County	7	0.95
River Grove (village) Cook County	82	0.77
Hanover (village) Jo Daviess County	6	0.76
Northfield (village) Cook County	38	0.69
Fairmont (cdp) Will County	16	0.61
Kenilworth (village) Cook County	14	0.56
Berkeley (village) Cook County	27	0.51

Top 10 Places Sorted by Percent
Based on places with populations of 10,000 or more

Place	Number	%
Schiller Park (village) Cook County	244	2.07
River Grove (village) Cook County	82	0.77
Elmwood Park (village) Cook County	106	0.42
Roselle (village) Du Page County	89	0.38
Grayslake (village) Lake County	64	0.35
Skokie (village) Cook County	208	0.33
Mount Prospect (village) Cook County	164	0.29
Wood Dale (city) Du Page County	39	0.28
Burr Ridge (village) Du Page County	28	0.27
Glen Carbon (village) Madison County	28	0.27

Canadian

Top 10 Places Sorted by Number
Based on all places, regardless of population

Place	Number	%
Chicago (city) Cook County	2,050	0.07
Naperville (city) Du Page County	554	0.43
Arlington Heights (village) Cook County	248	0.33
Wheaton (city) Du Page County	190	0.34
Rockford (city) Winnebago County	181	0.12
Elgin (city) Kane County	173	0.18
Champaign (city) Champaign County	168	0.25
Highland Park (city) Lake County	165	0.53
Aurora (city) Kane County	163	0.11
Bolingbrook (village) Will County	162	0.29

Top 10 Places Sorted by Percent
Based on all places, regardless of population

Place	Number	%
Sims (village) Wayne County	13	4.98
Hebron (village) McHenry County	23	2.28
Raleigh (village) Saline County	8	2.26
Bellmont (village) Wabash County	6	1.98
Mapleton (village) Peoria County	4	1.77
Trout Valley (village) McHenry County	10	1.68
Allendale (village) Wabash County	9	1.66
Joppa (village) Massac County	6	1.57
Pistakee Highlands (cdp) McHenry County	53	1.38
Allenville (village) Moultrie County	2	1.18

Top 10 Places Sorted by Percent
Based on places with populations of 10,000 or more

Place	Number	%
River Forest (village) Cook County	93	0.80
Winnetka (village) Cook County	68	0.55
Highland Park (city) Lake County	165	0.53
Cary (village) McHenry County	75	0.49
Barrington (village) Cook County	48	0.48
Hinsdale (village) Du Page County	82	0.47
Naperville (city) Du Page County	554	0.43
Vernon Hills (village) Lake County	89	0.43
Lansing (village) Cook County	117	0.42
Deerfield (village) Lake County	77	0.42

Carpatho Rusyn

Top 10 Places Sorted by Number
Based on all places, regardless of population

Place	Number	%
Chicago (city) Cook County	37	0.00
Westchester (village) Cook County	15	0.09
Crystal Lake (city) McHenry County	10	0.03
Orland Park (village) Cook County	10	0.02
Sterling (city) Whiteside County	9	0.06
Fairbury (city) Livingston County	7	0.18
Mount Olive (city) Macoupin County	6	0.28
Burnham (village) Cook County	5	0.12
Benld (city) Macoupin County	3	0.19
Leaf River (village) Ogle County	2	0.36

Top 10 Places Sorted by Percent
Based on all places, regardless of population

Place	Number	%
Leaf River (village) Ogle County	2	0.36
Mount Olive (city) Macoupin County	6	0.28
Benld (city) Macoupin County	3	0.19
Fairbury (city) Livingston County	7	0.18
Burnham (village) Cook County	5	0.12
Westchester (village) Cook County	15	0.09
Sterling (city) Whiteside County	9	0.06
Crystal Lake (city) McHenry County	10	0.03
Orland Park (village) Cook County	10	0.02
Chicago (city) Cook County	37	0.00

Top 10 Places Sorted by Percent
Based on places with populations of 10,000 or more

Place	Number	%
Westchester (village) Cook County	15	0.09
Sterling (city) Whiteside County	9	0.06
Crystal Lake (city) McHenry County	10	0.03
Orland Park (village) Cook County	10	0.02
Chicago (city) Cook County	37	0.00

Celtic

Top 10 Places Sorted by Number
Based on all places, regardless of population

Place	Number	%
Chicago (city) Cook County	269	0.01
Cahokia (village) Saint Clair County	59	0.36
Woodstock (city) McHenry County	42	0.21
Champaign (city) Champaign County	42	0.06
Springfield (city) Sangamon County	42	0.04
Arlington Heights (village) Cook County	33	0.04
Rockford (city) Winnebago County	32	0.02
West Chicago (city) Du Page County	31	0.13
Oak Park (village) Cook County	31	0.06
New Lenox (village) Will County	30	0.17

Top 10 Places Sorted by Percent
Based on all places, regardless of population

Place	Number	%
Ellsworth (village) McLean County	3	1.11
Timberlane (village) Boone County	2	1.00
Lerna (village) Coles County	3	0.93
Red Bud (city) Randolph County	27	0.81
Lewistown (city) Fulton County	17	0.68
Ransom (village) La Salle County	3	0.65
Elliott (village) Ford County	2	0.58
Makanda (village) Jackson County	2	0.49
Griggsville (city) Pike County	6	0.47
Tolono (village) Champaign County	11	0.41

Notes: (cdp) census designated place; Refer to the User's Guide in the front of the book for more detailed information.

Top 10 Places Sorted by Percent
Based on places with populations of 10,000 or more

Place	Number	%
Cahokia (village) Saint Clair County	59	0.36
Woodstock (city) McHenry County	42	0.21
New Lenox (village) Will County	30	0.17
Brookfield (village) Cook County	26	0.14
West Chicago (city) Du Page County	31	0.13
Morton (village) Tazewell County	18	0.12
Charleston (city) Coles County	20	0.10
Zion (city) Lake County	19	0.08
Bellwood (village) Cook County	15	0.07
Champaign (city) Champaign County	42	0.06

Croatian

Top 10 Places Sorted by Number
Based on all places, regardless of population

Place	Number	%
Chicago (city) Cook County	7,819	0.27
Joliet (city) Will County	1,536	1.45
Orland Park (village) Cook County	868	1.70
Oak Lawn (village) Cook County	713	1.29
Naperville (city) Du Page County	680	0.53
Lansing (village) Cook County	564	2.00
Tinley Park (village) Cook County	543	1.12
Downers Grove (village) Du Page County	488	1.00
Crest Hill (city) Will County	437	3.35
Berwyn (city) Cook County	415	0.77

Top 10 Places Sorted by Percent
Based on all places, regardless of population

Place	Number	%
McCook (village) Cook County	37	16.30
Mount Clare (village) Macoupin County	31	7.58
Norris (village) Fulton County	16	7.27
Saint David (village) Fulton County	42	6.94
Sawyerville (village) Macoupin County	21	6.60
Matherville (village) Mercer County	36	4.67
White City (village) Macoupin County	9	4.57
Dunfermline (village) Fulton County	11	4.28
Bryant (village) Fulton County	12	4.08
Mount Olive (city) Macoupin County	83	3.85

Top 10 Places Sorted by Percent
Based on places with populations of 10,000 or more

Place	Number	%
Crest Hill (city) Will County	437	3.35
Lansing (village) Cook County	564	2.00
Palos Hills (city) Cook County	351	1.98
Goodings Grove (cdp) Will County	316	1.85
Canton (city) Fulton County	264	1.73
Crestwood (village) Cook County	193	1.72
Orland Park (village) Cook County	868	1.70
Sauk Village (village) Cook County	175	1.68
Lyons (village) Cook County	157	1.55
Lemont (village) Cook County	202	1.53

Cypriot

Top 10 Places Sorted by Number
Based on all places, regardless of population

Place	Number	%
Chicago (city) Cook County	52	0.00
Carbondale (city) Jackson County	25	0.12
Lincolnwood (village) Cook County	18	0.15
Brookfield (village) Cook County	18	0.09
Des Plaines (city) Cook County	17	0.03
Murphysboro (city) Jackson County	15	0.11
Evanston (city) Cook County	9	0.01
Urbana (city) Champaign County	8	0.02
Naperville (city) Du Page County	8	0.01

Place	Number	%
Palatine (village) Cook County	8	0.01

Top 10 Places Sorted by Percent
Based on all places, regardless of population

Place	Number	%
East Dundee (village) Kane County	7	0.24
Lincolnwood (village) Cook County	18	0.15
Carbondale (city) Jackson County	25	0.12
Murphysboro (city) Jackson County	15	0.11
Brookfield (village) Cook County	18	0.09
La Grange Park (village) Cook County	6	0.05
Des Plaines (city) Cook County	17	0.03
Norridge (village) Cook County	4	0.03
Urbana (city) Champaign County	8	0.02
Evanston (city) Cook County	9	0.01

Top 10 Places Sorted by Percent
Based on places with populations of 10,000 or more

Place	Number	%
Lincolnwood (village) Cook County	18	0.15
Carbondale (city) Jackson County	25	0.12
Murphysboro (city) Jackson County	15	0.11
Brookfield (village) Cook County	18	0.09
La Grange Park (village) Cook County	6	0.05
Des Plaines (city) Cook County	17	0.03
Norridge (village) Cook County	4	0.03
Urbana (city) Champaign County	8	0.02
Evanston (city) Cook County	9	0.01
Naperville (city) Du Page County	8	0.01

Czech

Top 10 Places Sorted by Number
Based on all places, regardless of population

Place	Number	%
Chicago (city) Cook County	13,790	0.48
Berwyn (city) Cook County	2,982	5.52
Naperville (city) Du Page County	2,803	2.18
Downers Grove (village) Du Page County	2,563	5.27
Brookfield (village) Cook County	1,802	9.48
Cicero (town) Cook County	1,714	2.00
Bolingbrook (village) Will County	1,532	2.71
Woodridge (village) Du Page County	1,396	4.49
Wheaton (city) Du Page County	1,366	2.46
Schaumburg (village) Cook County	1,356	1.82

Top 10 Places Sorted by Percent
Based on all places, regardless of population

Place	Number	%
Forest View (village) Cook County	130	16.33
Stickney (village) Cook County	792	12.88
North Riverside (village) Cook County	790	11.73
East Brooklyn (village) Grundy County	10	9.80
Lyons (village) Cook County	991	9.78
Brookfield (village) Cook County	1,802	9.48
White City (village) Macoupin County	17	8.63
La Grange Park (village) Cook County	1,072	8.10
Indian Head Park (village) Cook County	285	7.45
Westchester (village) Cook County	1,194	7.17

Top 10 Places Sorted by Percent
Based on places with populations of 10,000 or more

Place	Number	%
Lyons (village) Cook County	991	9.78
Brookfield (village) Cook County	1,802	9.48
La Grange Park (village) Cook County	1,072	8.10
Westchester (village) Cook County	1,194	7.17
Berwyn (city) Cook County	2,982	5.52
La Grange (village) Cook County	853	5.42
Downers Grove (village) Du Page County	2,563	5.27
Darien (city) Du Page County	1,176	5.12
Burr Ridge (village) Du Page County	493	4.77

Place	Number	%
Woodridge (village) Du Page County	1,396	4.49

Czechoslovakian

Top 10 Places Sorted by Number
Based on all places, regardless of population

Place	Number	%
Chicago (city) Cook County	3,296	0.11
Naperville (city) Du Page County	827	0.64
Berwyn (city) Cook County	717	1.33
Downers Grove (village) Du Page County	374	0.77
Brookfield (village) Cook County	318	1.67
Arlington Heights (village) Cook County	292	0.38
Wheaton (city) Du Page County	288	0.52
Aurora (city) Kane County	282	0.20
Elgin (city) Kane County	265	0.28
Westchester (village) Cook County	260	1.56

Top 10 Places Sorted by Percent
Based on all places, regardless of population

Place	Number	%
Stickney (village) Cook County	203	3.30
Johnsburg (village) McHenry County	149	2.75
North Riverside (village) Cook County	183	2.72
Forest View (village) Cook County	21	2.64
Jeisyville (village) Christian County	2	2.22
Makanda (village) Jackson County	8	1.97
Cherry (village) Bureau County	10	1.95
Dowell (village) Jackson County	9	1.93
La Grange Park (village) Cook County	250	1.89
Donnellson (village) Montgomery County	4	1.79

Top 10 Places Sorted by Percent
Based on places with populations of 10,000 or more

Place	Number	%
La Grange Park (village) Cook County	250	1.89
Brookfield (village) Cook County	318	1.67
Burr Ridge (village) Du Page County	170	1.65
Lyons (village) Cook County	164	1.62
Westchester (village) Cook County	260	1.56
Berwyn (city) Cook County	717	1.33
Western Springs (village) Cook County	131	1.04
La Grange (village) Cook County	159	1.01
Darien (city) Du Page County	225	0.98
Villa Park (village) Du Page County	197	0.88

Danish

Top 10 Places Sorted by Number
Based on all places, regardless of population

Place	Number	%
Chicago (city) Cook County	5,922	0.20
Naperville (city) Du Page County	1,328	1.04
Rockford (city) Winnebago County	847	0.57
Aurora (city) Kane County	757	0.53
Palatine (village) Cook County	728	1.12
Arlington Heights (village) Cook County	667	0.88
Schaumburg (village) Cook County	617	0.83
Downers Grove (village) Du Page County	602	1.24
Crystal Lake (city) McHenry County	568	1.50
Des Plaines (city) Cook County	558	0.95

Top 10 Places Sorted by Percent
Based on all places, regardless of population

Place	Number	%
New Bedford (village) Bureau County	9	9.89
Nelson (village) Lee County	12	8.00
Dwight (village) Livingston County	315	7.19
Sciota (village) McDonough County	3	6.67
Kinsman (village) Grundy County	8	6.56
Prairie Grove (village) McHenry County	66	6.24
Greenwood (village) McHenry County	16	6.04

Notes: (cdp) census designated place; Refer to the User's Guide in the front of the book for more detailed information.

East Brooklyn (village) Grundy County	6	5.88
Hebron (village) McHenry County	54	5.35
McNabb (village) Putnam County	15	5.23

Top 10 Places Sorted by Percent
Based on places with populations of 10,000 or more

Place	Number	%
Lindenhurst (village) Lake County	230	1.82
Grayslake (village) Lake County	318	1.72
Crystal Lake (city) McHenry County	568	1.50
Oswego (village) Kendall County	198	1.49
Morris (city) Grundy County	170	1.42
Cary (village) McHenry County	208	1.35
Sycamore (city) De Kalb County	152	1.25
Downers Grove (village) Du Page County	602	1.24
Bradley (village) Kankakee County	156	1.23
Warrenville (city) Du Page County	157	1.19

Dutch

Top 10 Places Sorted by Number
Based on all places, regardless of population

Place	Number	%
Chicago (city) Cook County	11,906	0.41
Lansing (village) Cook County	3,857	13.70
Naperville (city) Du Page County	2,808	2.19
South Holland (village) Cook County	2,718	12.20
Tinley Park (village) Cook County	2,566	5.31
Rockford (city) Winnebago County	2,264	1.51
Springfield (city) Sangamon County	2,001	1.78
Aurora (city) Kane County	1,831	1.27
Peoria (city) Peoria County	1,821	1.61
Orland Park (village) Cook County	1,658	3.24

Top 10 Places Sorted by Percent
Based on all places, regardless of population

Place	Number	%
Fulton (city) Whiteside County	1,451	37.29
Wilmington (village) Greene County	26	23.21
Morrison (city) Whiteside County	1,021	23.19
Media (village) Henderson County	16	14.04
Lansing (village) Cook County	3,857	13.70
Strawn (village) Livingston County	15	13.04
Albany (village) Whiteside County	118	12.91
Cypress (village) Johnson County	30	12.61
South Holland (village) Cook County	2,718	12.20
Adeline (village) Ogle County	17	12.06

Top 10 Places Sorted by Percent
Based on places with populations of 10,000 or more

Place	Number	%
Lansing (village) Cook County	3,857	13.70
South Holland (village) Cook County	2,718	12.20
Palos Heights (city) Cook County	1,032	9.12
Tinley Park (village) Cook County	2,566	5.31
Oak Forest (city) Cook County	1,439	5.15
Frankfort (village) Will County	474	4.63
Worth (village) Cook County	500	4.48
Crestwood (village) Cook County	466	4.15
Mokena (village) Will County	563	3.84
Bradley (village) Kankakee County	463	3.64

Eastern European

Top 10 Places Sorted by Number
Based on all places, regardless of population

Place	Number	%
Chicago (city) Cook County	3,388	0.12
Highland Park (city) Lake County	797	2.54
Skokie (village) Cook County	603	0.95
Evanston (city) Cook County	585	0.79
Buffalo Grove (village) Lake County	521	1.22

Deerfield (village) Lake County	444	2.40
Glencoe (village) Cook County	387	4.38
Wilmette (village) Cook County	338	1.22
Northbrook (village) Cook County	331	0.99
Oak Park (village) Cook County	200	0.38

Top 10 Places Sorted by Percent
Based on all places, regardless of population

Place	Number	%
Smithfield (village) Fulton County	15	7.18
Glencoe (village) Cook County	387	4.38
Highland Park (city) Lake County	797	2.54
Deerfield (village) Lake County	444	2.40
Riverwoods (village) Lake County	58	1.54
Mineral (village) Bureau County	4	1.47
Buffalo Grove (village) Lake County	521	1.22
Wilmette (village) Cook County	338	1.22
Lincolnwood (village) Cook County	133	1.08
Northbrook (village) Cook County	331	0.99

Top 10 Places Sorted by Percent
Based on places with populations of 10,000 or more

Place	Number	%
Highland Park (city) Lake County	797	2.54
Deerfield (village) Lake County	444	2.40
Buffalo Grove (village) Lake County	521	1.22
Wilmette (village) Cook County	338	1.22
Lincolnwood (village) Cook County	133	1.08
Northbrook (village) Cook County	331	0.99
Skokie (village) Cook County	603	0.95
Winnetka (village) Cook County	115	0.93
Evanston (city) Cook County	585	0.79
Vernon Hills (village) Lake County	86	0.42

English

Top 10 Places Sorted by Number
Based on all places, regardless of population

Place	Number	%
Chicago (city) Cook County	57,579	1.99
Springfield (city) Sangamon County	13,288	11.84
Naperville (city) Du Page County	12,672	9.88
Rockford (city) Winnebago County	11,885	7.94
Peoria (city) Peoria County	9,938	8.80
Aurora (city) Kane County	8,014	5.58
Decatur (city) Macon County	7,668	9.34
Wheaton (city) Du Page County	7,150	12.90
Champaign (city) Champaign County	7,102	10.46
Bloomington (city) McLean County	7,025	10.80

Top 10 Places Sorted by Percent
Based on all places, regardless of population

Place	Number	%
Hanaford (village) Franklin County	2	100.00
Simpson (village) Johnson County	22	38.60
Garrett (village) Douglas County	64	31.53
La Prairie (village) Adams County	17	30.91
Neponset (village) Bureau County	154	30.62
Florence (village) Pike County	18	30.51
Manchester (village) Scott County	95	26.54
Albion (city) Edwards County	499	25.01
Waggoner (village) Montgomery County	74	24.67
Golf (village) Cook County	111	24.56

Top 10 Places Sorted by Percent
Based on places with populations of 10,000 or more

Place	Number	%
Winnetka (village) Cook County	2,271	18.33
Lake Forest (city) Lake County	3,288	16.43
Washington (city) Tazewell County	1,713	15.73
Hinsdale (village) Du Page County	2,430	13.90
Jacksonville (city) Morgan County	2,612	13.80

Godfrey (village) Madison County	2,220	13.60
Glen Ellyn (village) Du Page County	3,588	13.27
Morton (village) Tazewell County	1,985	13.19
East Peoria (city) Tazewell County	3,013	13.16
Marion (city) Williamson County	2,104	13.16

Estonian

Top 10 Places Sorted by Number
Based on all places, regardless of population

Place	Number	%
Chicago (city) Cook County	233	0.01
Crestwood (village) Cook County	55	0.49
Arlington Heights (village) Cook County	46	0.06
Naperville (city) Du Page County	45	0.04
Glen Ellyn (village) Du Page County	44	0.16
Grayslake (village) Lake County	35	0.19
Schaumburg (village) Cook County	31	0.04
Evanston (city) Cook County	30	0.04
Springfield (city) Sangamon County	28	0.02
Glencoe (village) Cook County	27	0.31

Top 10 Places Sorted by Percent
Based on all places, regardless of population

Place	Number	%
Third Lake (village) Lake County	7	0.52
Crestwood (village) Cook County	55	0.49
Barrington Hills (village) Cook County	14	0.34
Glencoe (village) Cook County	27	0.31
Riverwoods (village) Lake County	10	0.27
Long Lake (cdp) Lake County	9	0.26
Oakwood Hills (village) McHenry County	5	0.23
Burr Ridge (village) Du Page County	23	0.22
Grayslake (village) Lake County	35	0.19
Fox River Grove (village) McHenry County	9	0.18

Top 10 Places Sorted by Percent
Based on places with populations of 10,000 or more

Place	Number	%
Crestwood (village) Cook County	55	0.49
Burr Ridge (village) Du Page County	23	0.22
Grayslake (village) Lake County	35	0.19
Glen Ellyn (village) Du Page County	44	0.16
La Grange (village) Cook County	25	0.16
Woodstock (city) McHenry County	23	0.11
Canton (city) Fulton County	16	0.10
Mundelein (village) Lake County	26	0.09
Western Springs (village) Cook County	11	0.09
Northbrook (village) Cook County	25	0.07

European

Top 10 Places Sorted by Number
Based on all places, regardless of population

Place	Number	%
Chicago (city) Cook County	7,652	0.26
Evanston (city) Cook County	1,153	1.55
Springfield (city) Sangamon County	1,134	1.01
Naperville (city) Du Page County	962	0.75
Champaign (city) Champaign County	936	1.38
Peoria (city) Peoria County	853	0.76
Wheaton (city) Du Page County	768	1.39
Decatur (city) Macon County	729	0.89
Aurora (city) Kane County	635	0.44
Highland Park (city) Lake County	627	2.00

Top 10 Places Sorted by Percent
Based on all places, regardless of population

Place	Number	%
Cleveland (village) Henry County	24	9.56
Menominee (village) Jo Daviess County	14	5.79
Alhambra (village) Madison County	34	5.28

Havana (city) Mason County	169	4.72
Scott AFB (cdp) Saint Clair County	130	4.67
Cypress (village) Johnson County	11	4.62
Buncombe (village) Johnson County	9	4.43
Lee (village) Lee County	12	4.41
Campus (village) Livingston County	5	4.20
Wilsonville (village) Macoupin County	24	3.91

Top 10 Places Sorted by Percent
Based on places with populations of 10,000 or more

Place	Number	%
Wood River (city) Madison County	299	2.67
Winnetka (village) Cook County	321	2.59
Deerfield (village) Lake County	478	2.58
Godfrey (village) Madison County	415	2.54
Highland Park (city) Lake County	627	2.00
Sycamore (city) De Kalb County	215	1.77
Evanston (city) Cook County	1,153	1.55
O'Fallon (city) Saint Clair County	318	1.45
Carbondale (city) Jackson County	296	1.43
Wheaton (city) Du Page County	768	1.39

Finnish

Top 10 Places Sorted by Number
Based on all places, regardless of population

Place	Number	%
Chicago (city) Cook County	2,163	0.07
Waukegan (city) Lake County	635	0.72
Zion (city) Lake County	423	1.84
Gurnee (village) Lake County	384	1.34
Naperville (city) Du Page County	381	0.30
Rockford (city) Winnebago County	271	0.18
Winthrop Harbor (village) Lake County	266	4.00
Aurora (city) Kane County	253	0.18
Arlington Heights (village) Cook County	218	0.29
Mundelein (village) Lake County	217	0.71

Top 10 Places Sorted by Percent
Based on all places, regardless of population

Place	Number	%
Winthrop Harbor (village) Lake County	266	4.00
Wadsworth (village) Lake County	114	3.78
Kempton (village) Ford County	7	2.64
Lake Catherine (cdp) Lake County	34	2.36
Pingree Grove (village) Kane County	2	2.17
Old Mill Creek (village) Lake County	6	1.98
Beach Park (village) Lake County	187	1.92
Zion (city) Lake County	423	1.84
Vergennes (village) Jackson County	9	1.84
Spring Grove (village) McHenry County	69	1.81

Top 10 Places Sorted by Percent
Based on places with populations of 10,000 or more

Place	Number	%
Zion (city) Lake County	423	1.84
Gurnee (village) Lake County	384	1.34
Gages Lake (cdp) Lake County	114	1.09
McHenry (city) McHenry County	174	0.81
Waukegan (city) Lake County	635	0.72
Mundelein (village) Lake County	217	0.71
Streamwood (village) Cook County	211	0.57
Bloomingdale (village) Du Page County	122	0.57
De Kalb (city) De Kalb County	217	0.56
Grayslake (village) Lake County	104	0.56

French, except Basque

Top 10 Places Sorted by Number
Based on all places, regardless of population

Place	Number	%
Chicago (city) Cook County	24,043	0.83

Naperville (city) Du Page County	3,566	2.78
Rockford (city) Winnebago County	3,501	2.34
Springfield (city) Sangamon County	2,959	2.64
Aurora (city) Kane County	2,482	1.73
Peoria (city) Peoria County	2,428	2.15
Joliet (city) Will County	2,207	2.08
Belleville (city) Saint Clair County	2,141	5.08
Bloomington (city) McLean County	2,019	3.10
Decatur (city) Macon County	1,898	2.31

Top 10 Places Sorted by Percent
Based on all places, regardless of population

Place	Number	%
Prairie du Rocher (village) Randolph County	191	30.96
Ashkum (village) Iroquois County	152	21.35
Beaverville (village) Iroquois County	79	20.63
Campus (village) Livingston County	24	20.17
Saint Anne (village) Kankakee County	238	19.75
Irwin (village) Kankakee County	12	19.05
Donovan (village) Iroquois County	73	18.48
West Brooklyn (village) Lee County	32	17.88
Chebanse (village) Iroquois County	203	17.29
Clifton (village) Iroquois County	228	17.19

Top 10 Places Sorted by Percent
Based on places with populations of 10,000 or more

Place	Number	%
Bradley (village) Kankakee County	1,713	13.46
Bourbonnais (village) Kankakee County	1,854	12.08
Kankakee (city) Kankakee County	1,786	6.48
Collinsville (city) Madison County	1,336	5.47
Fairview Heights (city) Saint Clair County	817	5.34
O'Fallon (city) Saint Clair County	1,146	5.24
Ottawa (city) La Salle County	953	5.19
Belleville (city) Saint Clair County	2,141	5.08
Godfrey (village) Madison County	723	4.43
Granite City (city) Madison County	1,310	4.14

French Canadian

Top 10 Places Sorted by Number
Based on all places, regardless of population

Place	Number	%
Chicago (city) Cook County	4,945	0.17
Naperville (city) Du Page County	811	0.63
Aurora (city) Kane County	669	0.47
Bradley (village) Kankakee County	639	5.02
Rockford (city) Winnebago County	546	0.36
Kankakee (city) Kankakee County	496	1.80
Elgin (city) Kane County	454	0.48
Evanston (city) Cook County	376	0.51
Schaumburg (village) Cook County	373	0.50
Peoria (city) Peoria County	368	0.33

Top 10 Places Sorted by Percent
Based on all places, regardless of population

Place	Number	%
Beaverville (village) Iroquois County	46	12.01
Martinton (village) Iroquois County	34	8.72
Irwin (village) Kankakee County	4	6.35
Anchor (village) McLean County	10	6.13
Saint Anne (village) Kankakee County	62	5.15
Bradley (village) Kankakee County	639	5.02
Clifton (village) Iroquois County	65	4.90
Compton (village) Lee County	16	4.73
Buckingham (village) Kankakee County	9	3.88
Papineau (village) Iroquois County	7	3.83

Top 10 Places Sorted by Percent
Based on places with populations of 10,000 or more

Place	Number	%
Bradley (village) Kankakee County	639	5.02

Bourbonnais (village) Kankakee County	337	2.20
Kankakee (city) Kankakee County	496	1.80
Barrington (village) Cook County	131	1.31
Cary (village) McHenry County	194	1.26
Lemont (village) Cook County	132	1.00
Crest Hill (city) Will County	124	0.95
Glen Ellyn (village) Du Page County	244	0.90
Gurnee (village) Lake County	252	0.88
Geneva (city) Kane County	171	0.87

German

Top 10 Places Sorted by Number
Based on all places, regardless of population

Place	Number	%
Chicago (city) Cook County	189,618	6.55
Naperville (city) Du Page County	34,638	27.00
Rockford (city) Winnebago County	29,443	19.67
Springfield (city) Sangamon County	27,385	24.41
Aurora (city) Kane County	25,070	17.46
Peoria (city) Peoria County	24,774	21.94
Arlington Heights (village) Cook County	20,899	27.46
Elgin (city) Kane County	20,620	21.96
Joliet (city) Will County	19,079	17.97
Schaumburg (village) Cook County	18,501	24.83

Top 10 Places Sorted by Percent
Based on all places, regardless of population

Place	Number	%
Fults (village) Monroe County	38	100.00
Hanaford (village) Franklin County	2	100.00
Teutopolis (village) Effingham County	1,106	71.08
Sigel (town) Shelby County	270	69.77
Aviston (village) Clinton County	855	69.12
Germantown (village) Clinton County	769	68.91
Saint Libory (village) Saint Clair County	395	67.18
Bartelso (village) Clinton County	409	65.97
Brussels (village) Calhoun County	91	65.00
Harmon (village) Lee County	101	64.33

Top 10 Places Sorted by Percent
Based on places with populations of 10,000 or more

Place	Number	%
Morton (village) Tazewell County	6,055	40.25
Washington (city) Tazewell County	4,330	39.76
Swansea (village) Saint Clair County	4,089	39.27
Effingham (city) Effingham County	4,633	37.25
McHenry (city) McHenry County	7,904	36.65
Quincy (city) Adams County	14,757	36.64
Freeport (city) Stephenson County	9,600	36.31
Gages Lake (cdp) Lake County	3,676	35.15
Crystal Lake (city) McHenry County	13,035	34.45
Godfrey (village) Madison County	5,575	34.16

German Russian

Top 10 Places Sorted by Number
Based on all places, regardless of population

Place	Number	%
Chicago (city) Cook County	73	0.00
Rockton (village) Winnebago County	25	0.47
Buffalo Grove (village) Lake County	19	0.04
North Chicago (city) Lake County	16	0.04
Bellwood (village) Cook County	11	0.05
Fox River Grove (village) McHenry County	9	0.18
Midlothian (village) Cook County	9	0.06
Park Forest (village) Cook County	9	0.04
Naperville (city) Du Page County	9	0.01
Burr Ridge (village) Du Page County	7	0.07

Notes: (cdp) census designated place; Refer to the User's Guide in the front of the book for more detailed information.

Top 10 Places Sorted by Percent
Based on all places, regardless of population

Place	Number	%
Rockton (village) Winnebago County	25	0.47
Phoenix (village) Cook County	4	0.19
Fox River Grove (village) McHenry County	9	0.18
Thornton (village) Cook County	4	0.15
Wyoming (city) Stark County	2	0.14
Burr Ridge (village) Du Page County	7	0.07
Midlothian (village) Cook County	9	0.06
Glencoe (village) Cook County	5	0.06
Bellwood (village) Cook County	11	0.05
Herrin (city) Williamson County	5	0.05

Top 10 Places Sorted by Percent
Based on places with populations of 10,000 or more

Place	Number	%
Burr Ridge (village) Du Page County	7	0.07
Midlothian (village) Cook County	9	0.06
Bellwood (village) Cook County	11	0.05
Herrin (city) Williamson County	5	0.05
Buffalo Grove (village) Lake County	19	0.04
North Chicago (city) Lake County	16	0.04
Park Forest (village) Cook County	9	0.04
West Chicago (city) Du Page County	7	0.03
Loves Park (city) Winnebago County	5	0.03
Gages Lake (cdp) Lake County	3	0.03

Greek

Top 10 Places Sorted by Number
Based on all places, regardless of population

Place	Number	%
Chicago (city) Cook County	18,249	0.63
Orland Park (village) Cook County	1,797	3.52
Skokie (village) Cook County	1,706	2.69
Mount Prospect (village) Cook County	1,654	2.92
Naperville (city) Du Page County	1,606	1.25
Arlington Heights (village) Cook County	1,442	1.89
Des Plaines (city) Cook County	1,423	2.42
Glenview (village) Cook County	1,420	3.41
Oak Lawn (village) Cook County	1,378	2.49
Park Ridge (city) Cook County	1,288	3.41

Top 10 Places Sorted by Percent
Based on all places, regardless of population

Place	Number	%
Lincolnwood (village) Cook County	963	7.79
Greenwood (village) McHenry County	20	7.55
South Barrington (village) Cook County	274	7.35
Palos Hills (city) Cook County	1,141	6.43
Palos Park (village) Cook County	276	6.10
Bedford Park (village) Cook County	33	5.87
Cleveland (village) Henry County	12	4.78
Oak Brook (village) Du Page County	383	4.53
Harwood Heights (village) Cook County	357	4.34
Long Grove (village) Lake County	280	4.23

Top 10 Places Sorted by Percent
Based on places with populations of 10,000 or more

Place	Number	%
Lincolnwood (village) Cook County	963	7.79
Palos Hills (city) Cook County	1,141	6.43
Morton Grove (village) Cook County	859	3.83
Norridge (village) Cook County	556	3.78
Orland Park (village) Cook County	1,797	3.52
Glenview (village) Cook County	1,420	3.41
Park Ridge (city) Cook County	1,288	3.41
Niles (village) Cook County	990	3.28
Westchester (village) Cook County	491	2.95
Lake Forest (city) Lake County	586	2.93

Guyanese

Top 10 Places Sorted by Number
Based on all places, regardless of population

Place	Number	%
Chicago (city) Cook County	370	0.01
University Park (village) Will County	74	1.12
Hanover Park (village) Cook County	56	0.15
Rockford (city) Winnebago County	41	0.03
North Chicago (city) Lake County	28	0.08
Freeport (city) Stephenson County	26	0.10
Skokie (village) Cook County	16	0.03
Cortland (town) De Kalb County	15	0.73
Oak Park (village) Cook County	15	0.03
Bolingbrook (village) Will County	13	0.02

Top 10 Places Sorted by Percent
Based on all places, regardless of population

Place	Number	%
University Park (village) Will County	74	1.12
Dalton City (village) Moultrie County	5	0.82
Cortland (town) De Kalb County	15	0.73
Rankin (village) Vermilion County	2	0.33
Hanover Park (village) Cook County	56	0.15
Saint Joseph (village) Champaign County	4	0.14
River Grove (village) Cook County	12	0.11
Freeport (city) Stephenson County	26	0.10
North Chicago (city) Lake County	28	0.08
Bellwood (village) Cook County	12	0.06

Top 10 Places Sorted by Percent
Based on places with populations of 10,000 or more

Place	Number	%
Hanover Park (village) Cook County	56	0.15
River Grove (village) Cook County	12	0.11
Freeport (city) Stephenson County	26	0.10
North Chicago (city) Lake County	28	0.08
Bellwood (village) Cook County	12	0.06
Prospect Heights (city) Cook County	8	0.05
Matteson (village) Cook County	6	0.05
Rockford (city) Winnebago County	41	0.03
Skokie (village) Cook County	16	0.03
Oak Park (village) Cook County	15	0.03

Hawaii Native/Pacific Islander

Top 10 Places Sorted by Number
Based on all places, regardless of population

Place	Number	%
Chicago (city) Cook County	4,661	0.16
North Chicago (city) Lake County	184	0.51
Evanston (city) Cook County	150	0.20
Elgin (city) Kane County	133	0.14
Rockford (city) Winnebago County	131	0.09
Aurora (city) Kane County	126	0.09
Waukegan (city) Lake County	119	0.14
Peoria (city) Peoria County	107	0.09
Naperville (city) Du Page County	103	0.08
Skokie (village) Cook County	94	0.15

Top 10 Places Sorted by Percent
Based on all places, regardless of population

Place	Number	%
Gulf Port (village) Henderson County	5	2.42
Freeman Spur (village) Franklin County	6	2.20
Bannockburn (village) Lake County	26	1.82
Plymouth (village) Hancock County	10	1.78
Gays (village) Moultrie County	4	1.54
Troy Grove (village) La Salle County	4	1.31
Standard (village) Putnam County	3	1.17
Saint Libory (village) Saint Clair County	5	0.86
Loami (village) Sangamon County	6	0.75

Stronghurst (village) Henderson County	6	0.67

Top 10 Places Sorted by Percent
Based on places with populations of 10,000 or more

Place	Number	%
North Chicago (city) Lake County	184	0.51
Lake Forest (city) Lake County	75	0.37
De Kalb (city) De Kalb County	84	0.22
Evanston (city) Cook County	150	0.20
Crest Hill (city) Will County	26	0.20
O'Fallon (city) Saint Clair County	41	0.19
Urbana (city) Champaign County	67	0.18
Murphysboro (city) Jackson County	23	0.17
Gages Lake (cdp) Lake County	18	0.17
Chicago (city) Cook County	4,661	0.16

Hawaii Native/Pacific Islander: Melanesian

Top 10 Places Sorted by Number
Based on all places, regardless of population

Place	Number	%
Chicago (city) Cook County	23	0.00
Crete (village) Will County	4	0.05
Sauk Village (village) Cook County	4	0.04
Alsip (village) Cook County	4	0.02
Libertyville (village) Lake County	4	0.02
Bloomington (city) McLean County	4	0.01
De Kalb (city) De Kalb County	3	0.01
Glendale Heights (village) Du Page County	3	0.01
Carbon Cliff (village) Rock Island County	2	0.12
Bolingbrook (village) Will County	2	0.00

Top 10 Places Sorted by Percent
Based on all places, regardless of population

Place	Number	%
East Gillespie (village) Macoupin County	1	0.43
Carbon Cliff (village) Rock Island County	2	0.12
Crete (village) Will County	4	0.05
Sauk Village (village) Cook County	4	0.04
Alsip (village) Cook County	4	0.02
Libertyville (village) Lake County	4	0.02
South Beloit (city) Winnebago County	1	0.02
Tuscola (city) Douglas County	1	0.02
Bloomington (city) McLean County	4	0.01
De Kalb (city) De Kalb County	3	0.01

Top 10 Places Sorted by Percent
Based on places with populations of 10,000 or more

Place	Number	%
Sauk Village (village) Cook County	4	0.04
Alsip (village) Cook County	4	0.02
Libertyville (village) Lake County	4	0.02
Bloomington (city) McLean County	4	0.01
De Kalb (city) De Kalb County	3	0.01
Glendale Heights (village) Du Page County	3	0.01
Wood Dale (city) Du Page County	1	0.01
Chicago (city) Cook County	23	0.00
Bolingbrook (village) Will County	2	0.00
Springfield (city) Sangamon County	2	0.00

Hawaii Native/Pacific Islander: Fijian

Top 10 Places Sorted by Number
Based on all places, regardless of population

Place	Number	%
Chicago (city) Cook County	19	0.00
Crete (village) Will County	4	0.05
Sauk Village (village) Cook County	4	0.04
Alsip (village) Cook County	4	0.02
Libertyville (village) Lake County	4	0.02
Bloomington (city) McLean County	4	0.01
Glendale Heights (village) Du Page County	3	0.01

Place	Number	%
Carbon Cliff (village) Rock Island County	2	0.12
Bolingbrook (village) Will County	2	0.00
Springfield (city) Sangamon County	2	0.00

Top 10 Places Sorted by Percent
Based on all places, regardless of population

Place	Number	%
Carbon Cliff (village) Rock Island County	2	0.12
Crete (village) Will County	4	0.05
Sauk Village (village) Cook County	4	0.04
Alsip (village) Cook County	4	0.02
Libertyville (village) Lake County	4	0.02
South Beloit (city) Winnebago County	1	0.02
Bloomington (city) McLean County	4	0.01
Glendale Heights (village) Du Page County	3	0.01
Wood Dale (city) Du Page County	1	0.01
Chicago (city) Cook County	19	0.00

Top 10 Places Sorted by Percent
Based on places with populations of 10,000 or more

Place	Number	%
Sauk Village (village) Cook County	4	0.04
Alsip (village) Cook County	4	0.02
Libertyville (village) Lake County	4	0.02
Bloomington (city) McLean County	4	0.01
Glendale Heights (village) Du Page County	3	0.01
Wood Dale (city) Du Page County	1	0.01
Chicago (city) Cook County	19	0.00
Bolingbrook (village) Will County	2	0.00
Springfield (city) Sangamon County	2	0.00
Aurora (city) Kane County	1	0.00

Hawaii Native/Pacific Islander: Other Melanesian

Top 10 Places Sorted by Number
Based on all places, regardless of population

Place	Number	%
Chicago (city) Cook County	4	0.00
De Kalb (city) De Kalb County	3	0.01
East Gillespie (village) Macoupin County	1	0.43
Tuscola (city) Douglas County	1	0.02
Berwyn (city) Cook County	1	0.00
Wheaton (city) Du Page County	1	0.00

Top 10 Places Sorted by Percent
Based on all places, regardless of population

Place	Number	%
East Gillespie (village) Macoupin County	1	0.43
Tuscola (city) Douglas County	1	0.02
De Kalb (city) De Kalb County	3	0.01
Chicago (city) Cook County	4	0.00
Berwyn (city) Cook County	1	0.00
Wheaton (city) Du Page County	1	0.00

Top 10 Places Sorted by Percent
Based on places with populations of 10,000 or more

Place	Number	%
De Kalb (city) De Kalb County	3	0.01
Chicago (city) Cook County	4	0.00
Berwyn (city) Cook County	1	0.00
Wheaton (city) Du Page County	1	0.00

Hawaii Native/Pacific Islander: Micronesian

Top 10 Places Sorted by Number
Based on all places, regardless of population

Place	Number	%
Chicago (city) Cook County	663	0.02
North Chicago (city) Lake County	66	0.18

Place	Number	%
Aurora (city) Kane County	35	0.02
Cicero (town) Cook County	29	0.03
Evanston (city) Cook County	27	0.04
Elgin (city) Kane County	23	0.02
Belleville (city) Saint Clair County	19	0.05
Waukegan (city) Lake County	15	0.02
Woodridge (village) Du Page County	13	0.04
Peoria (city) Peoria County	13	0.01

Top 10 Places Sorted by Percent
Based on all places, regardless of population

Place	Number	%
Gays (village) Moultrie County	4	1.54
Troy Grove (village) La Salle County	4	1.31
Loami (village) Sangamon County	6	0.75
Mulberry Grove (village) Bond County	4	0.60
Makanda (village) Jackson County	2	0.48
Tonica (village) La Salle County	3	0.44
Cordova (village) Rock Island County	2	0.32
Evansville (village) Randolph County	2	0.28
Scott AFB (cdp) Saint Clair County	6	0.22
Sheffield (village) Bureau County	2	0.21

Top 10 Places Sorted by Percent
Based on places with populations of 10,000 or more

Place	Number	%
North Chicago (city) Lake County	66	0.18
Murphysboro (city) Jackson County	9	0.07
Belleville (city) Saint Clair County	19	0.05
Evanston (city) Cook County	27	0.04
Woodridge (village) Du Page County	13	0.04
O'Fallon (city) Saint Clair County	9	0.04
Zion (city) Lake County	9	0.04
Homewood (village) Cook County	7	0.04
Riverdale (village) Cook County	6	0.04
Wood Dale (city) Du Page County	5	0.04

Hawaii Native/Pacific Islander: Guamanian or Chamorro

Top 10 Places Sorted by Number
Based on all places, regardless of population

Place	Number	%
Chicago (city) Cook County	637	0.02
North Chicago (city) Lake County	55	0.15
Cicero (town) Cook County	29	0.03
Evanston (city) Cook County	26	0.04
Aurora (city) Kane County	23	0.02
Elgin (city) Kane County	23	0.02
Belleville (city) Saint Clair County	18	0.04
Waukegan (city) Lake County	15	0.02
Woodridge (village) Du Page County	12	0.04
Peoria (city) Peoria County	12	0.01

Top 10 Places Sorted by Percent
Based on all places, regardless of population

Place	Number	%
Gays (village) Moultrie County	4	1.54
Troy Grove (village) La Salle County	4	1.31
Loami (village) Sangamon County	6	0.75
Makanda (village) Jackson County	2	0.48
Tonica (village) La Salle County	3	0.44
Cordova (village) Rock Island County	2	0.32
Evansville (village) Randolph County	2	0.28
Scott AFB (cdp) Saint Clair County	6	0.22
Sheffield (village) Bureau County	2	0.21
De Land (village) Piatt County	1	0.21

Top 10 Places Sorted by Percent
Based on places with populations of 10,000 or more

Place	Number	%
North Chicago (city) Lake County	55	0.15

Place	Number	%
Evanston (city) Cook County	26	0.04
Belleville (city) Saint Clair County	18	0.04
Woodridge (village) Du Page County	12	0.04
O'Fallon (city) Saint Clair County	9	0.04
Zion (city) Lake County	9	0.04
Riverdale (village) Cook County	6	0.04
Murphysboro (city) Jackson County	5	0.04
Wood Dale (city) Du Page County	5	0.04
Swansea (village) Saint Clair County	4	0.04

Hawaii Native/Pacific Islander: Other Micronesian

Top 10 Places Sorted by Number
Based on all places, regardless of population

Place	Number	%
Chicago (city) Cook County	26	0.00
Aurora (city) Kane County	12	0.01
North Chicago (city) Lake County	11	0.03
Park City (city) Lake County	9	0.14
Homewood (village) Cook County	7	0.04
Danville (city) Vermilion County	5	0.01
Mulberry Grove (village) Bond County	4	0.60
Murphysboro (city) Jackson County	4	0.03
Hoffman Estates (village) Cook County	4	0.01
Warrenville (city) Du Page County	3	0.02

Top 10 Places Sorted by Percent
Based on all places, regardless of population

Place	Number	%
Mulberry Grove (village) Bond County	4	0.60
Park City (city) Lake County	9	0.14
Payson (village) Adams County	1	0.09
Clifton (village) Iroquois County	1	0.08
Homewood (village) Cook County	7	0.04
Tolono (village) Champaign County	1	0.04
North Chicago (city) Lake County	11	0.03
Murphysboro (city) Jackson County	4	0.03
Mount Carmel (city) Wabash County	2	0.03
Salem (city) Marion County	2	0.03

Top 10 Places Sorted by Percent
Based on places with populations of 10,000 or more

Place	Number	%
Homewood (village) Cook County	7	0.04
North Chicago (city) Lake County	11	0.03
Murphysboro (city) Jackson County	4	0.03
Warrenville (city) Du Page County	3	0.02
Aurora (city) Kane County	12	0.01
Danville (city) Vermilion County	5	0.01
Hoffman Estates (village) Cook County	4	0.01
Bartlett (village) Du Page County	2	0.01
Charleston (city) Coles County	2	0.01
Darien (city) Du Page County	2	0.01

Hawaii Native/Pacific Islander: Polynesian

Top 10 Places Sorted by Number
Based on all places, regardless of population

Place	Number	%
Chicago (city) Cook County	1,303	0.04
North Chicago (city) Lake County	72	0.20
Rockford (city) Winnebago County	71	0.05
Peoria (city) Peoria County	49	0.04
Waukegan (city) Lake County	47	0.05
Schaumburg (village) Cook County	41	0.05
Elgin (city) Kane County	41	0.04
Springfield (city) Sangamon County	41	0.04
Evanston (city) Cook County	40	0.05
Joliet (city) Will County	39	0.04

Notes: (cdp) census designated place; Refer to the User's Guide in the front of the book for more detailed information.

Top 10 Places Sorted by Percent
Based on all places, regardless of population

Place	Number	%
Gulf Port (village) Henderson County	5	2.42
Freeman Spur (village) Franklin County	6	2.20
Standard (village) Putnam County	3	1.17
De Witt (village) De Witt County	1	0.53
Alhambra (village) Madison County	3	0.48
Nauvoo (city) Hancock County	5	0.47
Saint Johns (village) Perry County	1	0.46
Colp (village) Williamson County	1	0.45
Watson (village) Effingham County	3	0.41
Lisbon (village) Kendall County	1	0.40

Top 10 Places Sorted by Percent
Based on places with populations of 10,000 or more

Place	Number	%
North Chicago (city) Lake County	72	0.20
Gages Lake (cdp) Lake County	18	0.17
Crest Hill (city) Will County	19	0.14
O'Fallon (city) Saint Clair County	23	0.10
Lyons (village) Cook County	9	0.09
Park Forest (village) Cook County	19	0.08
Rantoul (village) Champaign County	10	0.08
Richton Park (village) Cook County	10	0.08
De Kalb (city) De Kalb County	29	0.07
Edwardsville (city) Madison County	14	0.07

Hawaii Native/Pacific Islander: Native Hawaiian

Top 10 Places Sorted by Number
Based on all places, regardless of population

Place	Number	%
Chicago (city) Cook County	643	0.02
North Chicago (city) Lake County	60	0.17
Waukegan (city) Lake County	34	0.04
Rockford (city) Winnebago County	33	0.02
Peoria (city) Peoria County	30	0.03
Evanston (city) Cook County	27	0.04
Joliet (city) Will County	27	0.03
Des Plaines (city) Cook County	23	0.04
Elgin (city) Kane County	23	0.02
Springfield (city) Sangamon County	23	0.02

Top 10 Places Sorted by Percent
Based on all places, regardless of population

Place	Number	%
Gulf Port (village) Henderson County	5	2.42
Freeman Spur (village) Franklin County	6	2.20
Standard (village) Putnam County	3	1.17
Nauvoo (city) Hancock County	5	0.47
Colp (village) Williamson County	1	0.45
Watson (village) Effingham County	3	0.41
Lisbon (village) Kendall County	1	0.40
Old Mill Creek (village) Lake County	1	0.40
Cullom (village) Livingston County	2	0.36
Forest Lake (cdp) Lake County	5	0.33

Top 10 Places Sorted by Percent
Based on places with populations of 10,000 or more

Place	Number	%
North Chicago (city) Lake County	60	0.17
Crest Hill (city) Will County	13	0.10
Gages Lake (cdp) Lake County	10	0.10
O'Fallon (city) Saint Clair County	18	0.08
Lyons (village) Cook County	8	0.08
Rantoul (village) Champaign County	9	0.07
Fairview Heights (city) Saint Clair County	9	0.06
Effingham (city) Effingham County	7	0.06
Belleville (city) Saint Clair County	20	0.05
Urbana (city) Champaign County	17	0.05

Hawaii Native/Pacific Islander: Samoan

Top 10 Places Sorted by Number
Based on all places, regardless of population

Place	Number	%
Chicago (city) Cook County	618	0.02
Rockford (city) Winnebago County	36	0.02
De Kalb (city) De Kalb County	23	0.06
Peoria (city) Peoria County	19	0.02
Schaumburg (village) Cook County	18	0.02
Elgin (city) Kane County	17	0.02
Springfield (city) Sangamon County	17	0.02
Park Forest (village) Cook County	13	0.06
Waukegan (city) Lake County	13	0.01
Rock Island (city) Rock Island County	12	0.03

Top 10 Places Sorted by Percent
Based on all places, regardless of population

Place	Number	%
De Witt (village) De Witt County	1	0.53
Saint Johns (village) Perry County	1	0.46
Cherry (village) Bureau County	2	0.39
Danforth (village) Iroquois County	2	0.34
Rosiclare (city) Hardin County	3	0.25
East Galesburg (village) Knox County	2	0.24
Smithton (village) Saint Clair County	5	0.22
German Valley (village) Stephenson County	1	0.21
Wilsonville (village) Macoupin County	1	0.17
Alhambra (village) Madison County	1	0.16

Top 10 Places Sorted by Percent
Based on places with populations of 10,000 or more

Place	Number	%
Gages Lake (cdp) Lake County	7	0.07
De Kalb (city) De Kalb County	23	0.06
Park Forest (village) Cook County	13	0.06
Crest Hill (city) Will County	6	0.05
McHenry (city) McHenry County	8	0.04
Dixon (city) Lee County	7	0.04
Centralia (city) Marion County	5	0.04
Richton Park (village) Cook County	5	0.04
Rock Island (city) Rock Island County	12	0.03
North Chicago (city) Lake County	11	0.03

Hawaii Native/Pacific Islander: Tongan

Top 10 Places Sorted by Number
Based on all places, regardless of population

Place	Number	%
West Chicago (city) Du Page County	7	0.03
Chicago (city) Cook County	7	0.00
Mount Carmel (city) Wabash County	4	0.05
Mount Vernon (city) Jefferson County	4	0.02
Oak Park (village) Cook County	3	0.01
Wheeling (village) Cook County	3	0.01
Alhambra (village) Madison County	2	0.32
Eureka (city) Woodford County	2	0.04
Park Ridge (city) Cook County	2	0.01
Savoy (village) Champaign County	1	0.02

Top 10 Places Sorted by Percent
Based on all places, regardless of population

Place	Number	%
Alhambra (village) Madison County	2	0.32
Mount Carmel (city) Wabash County	4	0.05
Eureka (city) Woodford County	2	0.04
West Chicago (city) Du Page County	7	0.03
Mount Vernon (city) Jefferson County	4	0.02
Savoy (village) Champaign County	1	0.02
Oak Park (village) Cook County	3	0.01
Wheeling (village) Cook County	3	0.01
Park Ridge (city) Cook County	2	0.01

Place	Number	%
Chicago (city) Cook County	7	0.00

Top 10 Places Sorted by Percent
Based on places with populations of 10,000 or more

Place	Number	%
West Chicago (city) Du Page County	7	0.03
Mount Vernon (city) Jefferson County	4	0.02
Oak Park (village) Cook County	3	0.01
Wheeling (village) Cook County	3	0.01
Park Ridge (city) Cook County	2	0.01
Chicago (city) Cook County	7	0.00
Arlington Heights (village) Cook County	1	0.00
Chicago Heights (city) Cook County	1	0.00
North Chicago (city) Lake County	1	0.00
O'Fallon (city) Saint Clair County	1	0.00

Hawaii Native/Pacific Islander: Other Polynesian

Top 10 Places Sorted by Number
Based on all places, regardless of population

Place	Number	%
Chicago (city) Cook County	35	0.00
Wheaton (city) Du Page County	5	0.01
Mokena (village) Will County	4	0.03
Champaign (city) Champaign County	4	0.01
Evanston (city) Cook County	4	0.01
Mount Olive (city) Macoupin County	3	0.14
Richton Park (village) Cook County	3	0.02
Blue Island (city) Cook County	3	0.01
Schaumburg (village) Cook County	3	0.00
Bartonville (village) Peoria County	2	0.03

Top 10 Places Sorted by Percent
Based on all places, regardless of population

Place	Number	%
Mount Olive (city) Macoupin County	3	0.14
Mokena (village) Will County	4	0.03
Bartonville (village) Peoria County	2	0.03
Stickney (village) Cook County	2	0.03
Casey (city) Clark County	1	0.03
Gibson (city) Ford County	1	0.03
Sleepy Hollow (village) Kane County	1	0.03
Richton Park (village) Cook County	3	0.02
Manteno (village) Kankakee County	1	0.02
Mascoutah (city) Saint Clair County	1	0.02

Top 10 Places Sorted by Percent
Based on places with populations of 10,000 or more

Place	Number	%
Mokena (village) Will County	4	0.03
Richton Park (village) Cook County	3	0.02
Wheaton (city) Du Page County	5	0.01
Champaign (city) Champaign County	4	0.01
Evanston (city) Cook County	4	0.01
Blue Island (city) Cook County	3	0.01
Crystal Lake (city) McHenry County	2	0.01
La Grange (village) Cook County	2	0.01
Wheeling (village) Cook County	2	0.01
Forest Park (village) Cook County	1	0.01

Hawaii Native/Pacific Islander: Other Pacific Islander, specified

Top 10 Places Sorted by Number
Based on all places, regardless of population

Place	Number	%
Chicago (city) Cook County	132	0.00
Minonk (city) Woodford County	9	0.42
Batavia (city) Kane County	8	0.03
Joliet (city) Will County	8	0.01
West Frankfort (city) Franklin County	6	0.07

Notes: (cdp) census designated place; Refer to the User's Guide in the front of the book for more detailed information.

Place	Number	%
Kewanee (city) Henry County	6	0.05
Dixon (city) Lee County	6	0.04
Godfrey (village) Madison County	6	0.04
New Lenox (village) Will County	6	0.03
Berwyn (city) Cook County	6	0.01

Top 10 Places Sorted by Percent
Based on all places, regardless of population

Place	Number	%
Minonk (city) Woodford County	9	0.42
White Hall (city) Greene County	4	0.15
Mound City (city) Pulaski County	1	0.14
West Frankfort (city) Franklin County	6	0.07
Harristown (village) Macon County	1	0.07
Kewanee (city) Henry County	6	0.05
Dixon (city) Lee County	6	0.04
Godfrey (village) Madison County	6	0.04
Beach Park (village) Lake County	4	0.04
Lynwood (village) Cook County	3	0.04

Top 10 Places Sorted by Percent
Based on places with populations of 10,000 or more

Place	Number	%
Kewanee (city) Henry County	6	0.05
Dixon (city) Lee County	6	0.04
Godfrey (village) Madison County	6	0.04
Beach Park (village) Lake County	4	0.04
Batavia (city) Kane County	8	0.03
New Lenox (village) Will County	6	0.03
McHenry (city) McHenry County	5	0.02
Ottawa (city) La Salle County	4	0.02
Lake Zurich (village) Lake County	3	0.02
Palos Hills (city) Cook County	3	0.02

Hawaii Native/Pacific Islander: Other Pacific Islander, not specified

Top 10 Places Sorted by Number
Based on all places, regardless of population

Place	Number	%
Chicago (city) Cook County	2,540	0.09
Evanston (city) Cook County	80	0.11
Naperville (city) Du Page County	78	0.06
Lake Forest (city) Lake County	71	0.35
Elgin (city) Kane County	69	0.07
Skokie (village) Cook County	68	0.11
Aurora (city) Kane County	67	0.05
Waukegan (city) Lake County	56	0.06
Rockford (city) Winnebago County	50	0.03
Champaign (city) Champaign County	48	0.07

Top 10 Places Sorted by Percent
Based on all places, regardless of population

Place	Number	%
Bannockburn (village) Lake County	26	1.82
Plymouth (village) Hancock County	10	1.78
Saint Libory (village) Saint Clair County	5	0.86
Sparland (village) Marshall County	3	0.60
Sidney (village) Champaign County	5	0.47
Stronghurst (village) Henderson County	4	0.45
Lanark (city) Carroll County	7	0.44
Warsaw (city) Hancock County	7	0.39
Lake Forest (city) Lake County	71	0.35
South Barrington (village) Cook County	12	0.32

Top 10 Places Sorted by Percent
Based on places with populations of 10,000 or more

Place	Number	%
Lake Forest (city) Lake County	71	0.35
North Chicago (city) Lake County	46	0.13
Evanston (city) Cook County	80	0.11
Skokie (village) Cook County	68	0.11

Place	Number	%
De Kalb (city) De Kalb County	43	0.11
Streamwood (village) Cook County	40	0.11
Darien (city) Du Page County	26	0.11
Lincolnwood (village) Cook County	13	0.11
Glendale Heights (village) Du Page County	33	0.10
Carpentersville (village) Kane County	30	0.10

Hispanic or Latino

Top 10 Places Sorted by Number
Based on all places, regardless of population

Place	Number	%
Chicago (city) Cook County	753,644	26.02
Cicero (town) Cook County	66,299	77.44
Aurora (city) Kane County	46,557	32.56
Waukegan (city) Lake County	39,396	44.82
Elgin (city) Kane County	32,430	34.32
Berwyn (city) Cook County	20,543	38.03
Joliet (city) Will County	19,552	18.41
Rockford (city) Winnebago County	15,278	10.18
Melrose Park (village) Cook County	12,485	53.88
Carpentersville (village) Kane County	12,410	40.57

Top 10 Places Sorted by Percent
Based on all places, regardless of population

Place	Number	%
Stone Park (village) Cook County	4,057	79.13
Cicero (town) Cook County	66,299	77.44
Fairmont City (village) Saint Clair County	1,349	55.38
Melrose Park (village) Cook County	12,485	53.88
West Chicago (city) Du Page County	11,405	48.60
Summit (village) Cook County	5,156	48.47
De Pue (village) Bureau County	843	45.77
Waukegan (city) Lake County	39,396	44.82
Hodgkins (village) Cook County	933	43.72
Carpentersville (village) Kane County	12,410	40.57

Top 10 Places Sorted by Percent
Based on places with populations of 10,000 or more

Place	Number	%
Cicero (town) Cook County	66,299	77.44
Melrose Park (village) Cook County	12,485	53.88
West Chicago (city) Du Page County	11,405	48.60
Summit (village) Cook County	5,156	48.47
Waukegan (city) Lake County	39,396	44.82
Carpentersville (village) Kane County	12,410	40.57
Franklin Park (village) Cook County	7,399	38.07
Berwyn (city) Cook County	20,543	38.03
Blue Island (city) Cook County	8,899	37.93
Bensenville (village) Du Page County	7,690	37.14

Hispanic: Central American

Top 10 Places Sorted by Number
Based on all places, regardless of population

Place	Number	%
Chicago (city) Cook County	23,339	0.81
Waukegan (city) Lake County	2,082	2.37
Cicero (town) Cook County	879	1.03
Berwyn (city) Cook County	350	0.65
Aurora (city) Kane County	329	0.23
Elgin (city) Kane County	295	0.31
Glendale Heights (village) Du Page County	290	0.91
Carpentersville (village) Kane County	282	0.92
Skokie (village) Cook County	271	0.43
Hanover Park (village) Cook County	270	0.71

Top 10 Places Sorted by Percent
Based on all places, regardless of population

Place	Number	%
Stone Park (village) Cook County	166	3.24
Waukegan (city) Lake County	2,082	2.37

Place	Number	%
Spillertown (village) Williamson County	3	1.36
Northlake (city) Cook County	146	1.23
Highwood (city) Lake County	50	1.21
Park City (city) Lake County	73	1.10
Bensenville (village) Du Page County	226	1.09
Melrose Park (village) Cook County	243	1.05
Cicero (town) Cook County	879	1.03
Godley (village) Will County	6	1.01

Top 10 Places Sorted by Percent
Based on places with populations of 10,000 or more

Place	Number	%
Waukegan (city) Lake County	2,082	2.37
Northlake (city) Cook County	146	1.23
Bensenville (village) Du Page County	226	1.09
Melrose Park (village) Cook County	243	1.05
Cicero (town) Cook County	879	1.03
Carpentersville (village) Kane County	282	0.92
Glendale Heights (village) Du Page County	290	0.91
Franklin Park (village) Cook County	175	0.90
Rolling Meadows (city) Cook County	214	0.87
Chicago (city) Cook County	23,339	0.81

Hispanic: Costa Rican

Top 10 Places Sorted by Number
Based on all places, regardless of population

Place	Number	%
Chicago (city) Cook County	609	0.02
Rockford (city) Winnebago County	42	0.03
Champaign (city) Champaign County	29	0.04
Des Plaines (city) Cook County	15	0.03
Wheaton (city) Du Page County	15	0.03
Evanston (city) Cook County	13	0.02
Aurora (city) Kane County	12	0.01
Cicero (town) Cook County	12	0.01
Hanover Park (village) Cook County	11	0.03
Lombard (village) Du Page County	11	0.03

Top 10 Places Sorted by Percent
Based on all places, regardless of population

Place	Number	%
Spillertown (village) Williamson County	3	1.36
Godley (village) Will County	6	1.01
Campbell Hill (village) Jackson County	1	0.30
Sidney (village) Champaign County	2	0.19
Findlay (village) Shelby County	1	0.14
Aroma Park (village) Kankakee County	1	0.12
White Hall (city) Greene County	3	0.11
New Berlin (village) Sangamon County	1	0.10
Caseyville (village) Saint Clair County	4	0.09
Lakewood (village) McHenry County	2	0.09

Top 10 Places Sorted by Percent
Based on places with populations of 10,000 or more

Place	Number	%
Lincolnwood (village) Cook County	8	0.06
Midlothian (village) Cook County	7	0.05
Summit (village) Cook County	5	0.05
Champaign (city) Champaign County	29	0.04
Romeoville (village) Will County	8	0.04
Schiller Park (village) Cook County	5	0.04
Lyons (village) Cook County	4	0.04
Rockford (city) Winnebago County	42	0.03
Des Plaines (city) Cook County	15	0.03
Wheaton (city) Du Page County	15	0.03

Notes: (cdp) census designated place; Refer to the User's Guide in the front of the book for more detailed information.

Hispanic: Guatemalan

Top 10 Places Sorted by Number
Based on all places, regardless of population

Place	Number	%
Chicago (city) Cook County	13,610	0.47
Cicero (town) Cook County	478	0.56
Glendale Heights (village) Du Page County	219	0.69
Addison (village) Du Page County	189	0.53
Waukegan (city) Lake County	189	0.22
Bensenville (village) Du Page County	187	0.90
Melrose Park (village) Cook County	177	0.76
Berwyn (city) Cook County	169	0.31
Stone Park (village) Cook County	129	2.52
Franklin Park (village) Cook County	127	0.65

Top 10 Places Sorted by Percent
Based on all places, regardless of population

Place	Number	%
Stone Park (village) Cook County	129	2.52
Northlake (city) Cook County	112	0.94
Bensenville (village) Du Page County	187	0.90
Coatsburg (village) Adams County	2	0.88
Melrose Park (village) Cook County	177	0.76
Glendale Heights (village) Du Page County	219	0.69
Dalton City (village) Moultrie County	4	0.69
Troy Grove (village) La Salle County	2	0.66
Franklin Park (village) Cook County	127	0.65
Park City (city) Lake County	38	0.57

Top 10 Places Sorted by Percent
Based on places with populations of 10,000 or more

Place	Number	%
Northlake (city) Cook County	112	0.94
Bensenville (village) Du Page County	187	0.90
Melrose Park (village) Cook County	177	0.76
Glendale Heights (village) Du Page County	219	0.69
Franklin Park (village) Cook County	127	0.65
Cicero (town) Cook County	478	0.56
Addison (village) Du Page County	189	0.53
Chicago (city) Cook County	13,610	0.47
Schiller Park (village) Cook County	43	0.36
Hanover Park (village) Cook County	123	0.32

Hispanic: Honduran

Top 10 Places Sorted by Number
Based on all places, regardless of population

Place	Number	%
Chicago (city) Cook County	3,049	0.11
Waukegan (city) Lake County	1,287	1.46
Cicero (town) Cook County	134	0.16
North Chicago (city) Lake County	73	0.20
Aurora (city) Kane County	58	0.04
Zion (city) Lake County	53	0.23
Berwyn (city) Cook County	51	0.09
Skokie (village) Cook County	50	0.08
Rockford (city) Winnebago County	49	0.03
Elgin (city) Kane County	32	0.03

Top 10 Places Sorted by Percent
Based on all places, regardless of population

Place	Number	%
Waukegan (city) Lake County	1,287	1.46
Cobden (village) Union County	5	0.45
Dakota (village) Stephenson County	2	0.40
Park City (city) Lake County	20	0.30
De Pue (village) Bureau County	5	0.27
Hurst (city) Williamson County	2	0.25
Zion (city) Lake County	53	0.23
Highwood (city) Lake County	9	0.22
Chenoa (city) McLean County	4	0.22

| **North Chicago** (city) Lake County | 73 | 0.20 |

Top 10 Places Sorted by Percent
Based on places with populations of 10,000 or more

Place	Number	%
Waukegan (city) Lake County	1,287	1.46
Zion (city) Lake County	53	0.23
North Chicago (city) Lake County	73	0.20
Cicero (town) Cook County	134	0.16
Beach Park (village) Lake County	12	0.12
Chicago (city) Cook County	3,049	0.11
Northlake (city) Cook County	13	0.11
Franklin Park (village) Cook County	20	0.10
Sauk Village (village) Cook County	10	0.10
Berwyn (city) Cook County	51	0.09

Hispanic: Nicaraguan

Top 10 Places Sorted by Number
Based on all places, regardless of population

Place	Number	%
Chicago (city) Cook County	778	0.03
Cicero (town) Cook County	44	0.05
Aurora (city) Kane County	37	0.03
North Chicago (city) Lake County	27	0.08
Waukegan (city) Lake County	26	0.03
Palatine (village) Cook County	24	0.04
Melrose Park (village) Cook County	22	0.09
Oak Park (village) Cook County	21	0.04
Skokie (village) Cook County	17	0.03
Champaign (city) Champaign County	16	0.02

Top 10 Places Sorted by Percent
Based on all places, regardless of population

Place	Number	%
Jerome (village) Sangamon County	3	0.21
Amboy (city) Lee County	4	0.16
Kenilworth (village) Cook County	3	0.12
Forest Park (village) Cook County	15	0.10
Melrose Park (village) Cook County	22	0.09
North Chicago (city) Lake County	27	0.08
Green Oaks (village) Lake County	3	0.08
Pistakee Highlands (cdp) McHenry County	3	0.08
Lewistown (city) Fulton County	2	0.08
River Forest (village) Cook County	8	0.07

Top 10 Places Sorted by Percent
Based on places with populations of 10,000 or more

Place	Number	%
Forest Park (village) Cook County	15	0.10
Melrose Park (village) Cook County	22	0.09
North Chicago (city) Lake County	27	0.08
River Forest (village) Cook County	8	0.07
Cicero (town) Cook County	44	0.05
Murphysboro (city) Jackson County	6	0.05
Lyons (village) Cook County	5	0.05
Palatine (village) Cook County	24	0.04
Oak Park (village) Cook County	21	0.04
Zion (city) Lake County	10	0.04

Hispanic: Panamanian

Top 10 Places Sorted by Number
Based on all places, regardless of population

Place	Number	%
Chicago (city) Cook County	637	0.02
Evanston (city) Cook County	57	0.08
Cicero (town) Cook County	25	0.03
North Chicago (city) Lake County	24	0.07
Waukegan (city) Lake County	24	0.03
Oak Park (village) Cook County	21	0.04
Skokie (village) Cook County	21	0.03

Aurora (city) Kane County	21	0.01
Berwyn (city) Cook County	16	0.03
Wheeling (village) Cook County	14	0.04

Top 10 Places Sorted by Percent
Based on all places, regardless of population

Place	Number	%
Dalzell (village) Bureau County	3	0.42
Hanna City (village) Peoria County	4	0.39
North Barrington (village) Lake County	7	0.24
Glasford (village) Peoria County	2	0.19
Rochester (village) Sangamon County	4	0.14
Creal Springs (city) Williamson County	1	0.14
Broadview (village) Cook County	11	0.13
Pearl City (village) Stephenson County	1	0.13
Gifford (village) Champaign County	1	0.12
Shiloh (village) Saint Clair County	7	0.09

Top 10 Places Sorted by Percent
Based on places with populations of 10,000 or more

Place	Number	%
Evanston (city) Cook County	57	0.08
Sauk Village (village) Cook County	8	0.08
North Chicago (city) Lake County	24	0.07
Fairview Heights (city) Saint Clair County	10	0.07
Oak Park (village) Cook County	21	0.04
Wheeling (village) Cook County	14	0.04
Kankakee (city) Kankakee County	10	0.04
Vernon Hills (village) Lake County	9	0.04
Zion (city) Lake County	9	0.04
Bellwood (village) Cook County	8	0.04

Hispanic: Salvadoran

Top 10 Places Sorted by Number
Based on all places, regardless of population

Place	Number	%
Chicago (city) Cook County	3,468	0.12
Waukegan (city) Lake County	428	0.49
Rolling Meadows (city) Cook County	170	0.69
Carpentersville (village) Kane County	157	0.51
Cicero (town) Cook County	151	0.18
Round Lake Beach (village) Lake County	113	0.44
Mundelein (village) Lake County	107	0.35
Elgin (city) Kane County	107	0.11
Hanover Park (village) Cook County	94	0.25
Wheeling (village) Cook County	86	0.25

Top 10 Places Sorted by Percent
Based on all places, regardless of population

Place	Number	%
Rolling Meadows (city) Cook County	170	0.69
Highwood (city) Lake County	22	0.53
Carpentersville (village) Kane County	157	0.51
Waukegan (city) Lake County	428	0.49
Thomasboro (village) Champaign County	6	0.49
Stone Park (village) Cook County	23	0.45
Round Lake Beach (village) Lake County	113	0.44
Rosemont (village) Cook County	18	0.43
Prospect Heights (city) Cook County	63	0.37
Mundelein (village) Lake County	107	0.35

Top 10 Places Sorted by Percent
Based on places with populations of 10,000 or more

Place	Number	%
Rolling Meadows (city) Cook County	170	0.69
Carpentersville (village) Kane County	157	0.51
Waukegan (city) Lake County	428	0.49
Round Lake Beach (village) Lake County	113	0.44
Prospect Heights (city) Cook County	63	0.37
Mundelein (village) Lake County	107	0.35
Hanover Park (village) Cook County	94	0.25

Notes: (cdp) census designated place; Refer to the User's Guide in the front of the book for more detailed information.

Place	Number	%
Wheeling (village) Cook County	86	0.25
Summit (village) Cook County	27	0.25
Cicero (town) Cook County	151	0.18

Hispanic: Other Central American

Top 10 Places Sorted by Number
Based on all places, regardless of population

Place	Number	%
Chicago (city) Cook County	1,188	0.04
Waukegan (city) Lake County	123	0.14
Cicero (town) Cook County	35	0.04
Berwyn (city) Cook County	25	0.05
Skokie (village) Cook County	24	0.04
Elgin (city) Kane County	24	0.03
Des Plaines (city) Cook County	22	0.04
Wheeling (village) Cook County	21	0.06
North Chicago (city) Lake County	20	0.06
Evanston (city) Cook County	20	0.03

Top 10 Places Sorted by Percent
Based on all places, regardless of population

Place	Number	%
Arrowsmith (village) McLean County	1	0.34
Granville (village) Putnam County	3	0.21
Waukegan (city) Lake County	123	0.14
Round Lake Park (village) Lake County	7	0.12
Moweaqua (village) Shelby County	2	0.10
Capron (village) Boone County	1	0.10
Northlake (city) Cook County	11	0.09
Marengo (city) McHenry County	6	0.09
Hainesville (village) Lake County	2	0.09
Park City (city) Lake County	5	0.08

Top 10 Places Sorted by Percent
Based on places with populations of 10,000 or more

Place	Number	%
Waukegan (city) Lake County	123	0.14
Northlake (city) Cook County	11	0.09
East Moline (city) Rock Island County	14	0.07
Summit (village) Cook County	7	0.07
Wheeling (village) Cook County	21	0.06
North Chicago (city) Lake County	20	0.06
Glendale Heights (village) Du Page County	18	0.06
Berwyn (city) Cook County	25	0.05
Mundelein (village) Lake County	16	0.05
Chicago (city) Cook County	1,188	0.04

Hispanic: Cuban

Top 10 Places Sorted by Number
Based on all places, regardless of population

Place	Number	%
Chicago (city) Cook County	8,084	0.28
Skokie (village) Cook County	428	0.68
Melrose Park (village) Cook County	345	1.49
Rockford (city) Winnebago County	310	0.21
Naperville (city) Du Page County	211	0.16
Evanston (city) Cook County	209	0.28
Aurora (city) Kane County	207	0.14
Northlake (city) Cook County	158	1.33
Elmhurst (city) Du Page County	151	0.35
Schaumburg (village) Cook County	142	0.19

Top 10 Places Sorted by Percent
Based on all places, regardless of population

Place	Number	%
Ullin (village) Pulaski County	42	5.39
Venedy (village) Washington County	5	3.65
Birds (village) Lawrence County	1	1.96
Stone Park (village) Cook County	100	1.95
Melrose Park (village) Cook County	345	1.49

Place	Number	%
Northlake (city) Cook County	158	1.33
Lee (village) Lee County	3	0.96
Rio (village) Knox County	2	0.83
Kangley (village) La Salle County	2	0.70
Skokie (village) Cook County	428	0.68

Top 10 Places Sorted by Percent
Based on places with populations of 10,000 or more

Place	Number	%
Melrose Park (village) Cook County	345	1.49
Northlake (city) Cook County	158	1.33
Skokie (village) Cook County	428	0.68
Lincolnwood (village) Cook County	84	0.68
Franklin Park (village) Cook County	99	0.51
River Grove (village) Cook County	51	0.48
Burr Ridge (village) Du Page County	42	0.40
Wood Dale (city) Du Page County	52	0.38
Elmhurst (city) Du Page County	151	0.35
Glenview (village) Cook County	138	0.33

Hispanic: Dominican Republic

Top 10 Places Sorted by Number
Based on all places, regardless of population

Place	Number	%
Chicago (city) Cook County	1,651	0.06
Cicero (town) Cook County	96	0.11
Waukegan (city) Lake County	69	0.08
North Chicago (city) Lake County	64	0.18
Aurora (city) Kane County	47	0.03
Evanston (city) Cook County	37	0.05
Elgin (city) Kane County	33	0.03
Skokie (village) Cook County	31	0.05
Naperville (city) Du Page County	30	0.02
Rockford (city) Winnebago County	30	0.02

Top 10 Places Sorted by Percent
Based on all places, regardless of population

Place	Number	%
Irwin (village) Kankakee County	2	2.17
Kinmundy (city) Marion County	2	0.22
North Chicago (city) Lake County	64	0.18
Greenville (city) Bond County	8	0.12
Cicero (town) Cook County	96	0.11
Hillside (village) Cook County	8	0.10
River Forest (village) Cook County	10	0.09
Willowbrook (village) Du Page County	8	0.09
Sparta (city) Randolph County	4	0.09
Waukegan (city) Lake County	69	0.08

Top 10 Places Sorted by Percent
Based on places with populations of 10,000 or more

Place	Number	%
North Chicago (city) Lake County	64	0.18
Cicero (town) Cook County	96	0.11
River Forest (village) Cook County	10	0.09
Waukegan (city) Lake County	69	0.08
Belvidere (city) Boone County	16	0.08
Chicago (city) Cook County	1,651	0.06
Melrose Park (village) Cook County	15	0.06
Elmwood Park (village) Cook County	14	0.06
Zion (city) Lake County	13	0.06
Lemont (village) Cook County	8	0.06

Hispanic: Mexican

Top 10 Places Sorted by Number
Based on all places, regardless of population

Place	Number	%
Chicago (city) Cook County	530,462	18.32
Cicero (town) Cook County	58,542	68.38
Aurora (city) Kane County	39,351	27.52

Place	Number	%
Waukegan (city) Lake County	30,717	34.94
Elgin (city) Kane County	27,444	29.05
Joliet (city) Will County	16,939	15.95
Berwyn (city) Cook County	16,745	31.00
Rockford (city) Winnebago County	12,508	8.33
Carpentersville (village) Kane County	10,755	35.16
West Chicago (city) Du Page County	10,550	44.95

Top 10 Places Sorted by Percent
Based on all places, regardless of population

Place	Number	%
Cicero (town) Cook County	58,542	68.38
Stone Park (village) Cook County	3,422	66.74
Fairmont City (village) Saint Clair County	1,204	49.43
Melrose Park (village) Cook County	10,500	45.32
West Chicago (city) Du Page County	10,550	44.95
Summit (village) Cook County	4,717	44.35
Hodgkins (village) Cook County	894	41.89
De Pue (village) Bureau County	718	38.98
Carpentersville (village) Kane County	10,755	35.16
Waukegan (city) Lake County	30,717	34.94

Top 10 Places Sorted by Percent
Based on places with populations of 10,000 or more

Place	Number	%
Cicero (town) Cook County	58,542	68.38
Melrose Park (village) Cook County	10,500	45.32
West Chicago (city) Du Page County	10,550	44.95
Summit (village) Cook County	4,717	44.35
Carpentersville (village) Kane County	10,755	35.16
Waukegan (city) Lake County	30,717	34.94
Blue Island (city) Cook County	7,975	33.99
Bensenville (village) Du Page County	6,524	31.51
Franklin Park (village) Cook County	6,104	31.41
Berwyn (city) Cook County	16,745	31.00

Hispanic: Puerto Rican

Top 10 Places Sorted by Number
Based on all places, regardless of population

Place	Number	%
Chicago (city) Cook County	113,055	3.90
Waukegan (city) Lake County	2,976	3.39
Aurora (city) Kane County	2,611	1.83
Elgin (city) Kane County	2,355	2.49
Cicero (town) Cook County	2,331	2.72
Berwyn (city) Cook County	1,392	2.58
North Chicago (city) Lake County	775	2.16
Elmwood Park (village) Cook County	656	2.58
Bolingbrook (village) Will County	626	1.11
Zion (city) Lake County	616	2.69

Top 10 Places Sorted by Percent
Based on all places, regardless of population

Place	Number	%
Chicago (city) Cook County	113,055	3.90
Muddy (village) Saline County	3	3.85
Waukegan (city) Lake County	2,976	3.39
Wheeler (village) Jasper County	4	3.36
Schiller Park (village) Cook County	330	2.78
Cicero (town) Cook County	2,331	2.72
Zion (city) Lake County	616	2.69
Berwyn (city) Cook County	1,392	2.58
Elmwood Park (village) Cook County	656	2.58
Elgin (city) Kane County	2,355	2.49

Top 10 Places Sorted by Percent
Based on places with populations of 10,000 or more

Place	Number	%
Chicago (city) Cook County	113,055	3.90
Waukegan (city) Lake County	2,976	3.39
Schiller Park (village) Cook County	330	2.78

Notes: (cdp) census designated place; Refer to the User's Guide in the front of the book for more detailed information.

Cicero (town) Cook County	2,331	2.72
Zion (city) Lake County	616	2.69
Berwyn (city) Cook County	1,392	2.58
Elmwood Park (village) Cook County	656	2.58
Elgin (city) Kane County	2,355	2.49
Franklin Park (village) Cook County	466	2.40
Northlake (city) Cook County	279	2.35

Hispanic: South American

Top 10 Places Sorted by Number
Based on all places, regardless of population

Place	Number	%
Chicago (city) Cook County	20,828	0.72
Skokie (village) Cook County	583	0.92
Cicero (town) Cook County	544	0.64
Berwyn (city) Cook County	445	0.82
Waukegan (city) Lake County	378	0.43
Evanston (city) Cook County	372	0.50
Aurora (city) Kane County	358	0.25
Naperville (city) Du Page County	336	0.26
Schaumburg (village) Cook County	331	0.44
Des Plaines (city) Cook County	304	0.52

Top 10 Places Sorted by Percent
Based on all places, regardless of population

Place	Number	%
Stone Park (village) Cook County	48	0.94
Skokie (village) Cook County	583	0.92
Lincolnwood (village) Cook County	113	0.91
Coatsburg (village) Adams County	2	0.88
Elmwood Park (village) Cook County	216	0.85
Schiller Park (village) Cook County	100	0.84
Berwyn (city) Cook County	445	0.82
Melrose Park (village) Cook County	186	0.80
Morton Grove (village) Cook County	179	0.80
Highwood (city) Lake County	32	0.77

Top 10 Places Sorted by Percent
Based on places with populations of 10,000 or more

Place	Number	%
Skokie (village) Cook County	583	0.92
Lincolnwood (village) Cook County	113	0.91
Elmwood Park (village) Cook County	216	0.85
Schiller Park (village) Cook County	100	0.84
Berwyn (city) Cook County	445	0.82
Melrose Park (village) Cook County	186	0.80
Morton Grove (village) Cook County	179	0.80
Chicago (city) Cook County	20,828	0.72
Streamwood (village) Cook County	236	0.65
Cicero (town) Cook County	544	0.64

Hispanic: Argentinean

Top 10 Places Sorted by Number
Based on all places, regardless of population

Place	Number	%
Chicago (city) Cook County	908	0.03
Evanston (city) Cook County	66	0.09
Elmwood Park (village) Cook County	52	0.20
Urbana (city) Champaign County	48	0.13
Skokie (village) Cook County	43	0.07
Aurora (city) Kane County	43	0.03
Oak Park (village) Cook County	42	0.08
Naperville (city) Du Page County	42	0.03
Wilmette (village) Cook County	33	0.12
Berwyn (city) Cook County	33	0.06

Top 10 Places Sorted by Percent
Based on all places, regardless of population

Place	Number	%
Whiteash (village) Williamson County	2	0.75

Elsah (village) Jersey County	3	0.47
Timberlane (village) Boone County	1	0.43
Buffalo (village) Sangamon County	2	0.41
Wayne (village) Kane County	7	0.33
Port Byron (village) Rock Island County	5	0.33
Elmwood Park (village) Cook County	52	0.20
Lebanon (city) Saint Clair County	6	0.17
Pittsburg (village) Williamson County	1	0.17
Lincolnwood (village) Cook County	18	0.15

Top 10 Places Sorted by Percent
Based on places with populations of 10,000 or more

Place	Number	%
Elmwood Park (village) Cook County	52	0.20
Lincolnwood (village) Cook County	18	0.15
Urbana (city) Champaign County	48	0.13
Wilmette (village) Cook County	33	0.12
Evanston (city) Cook County	66	0.09
Blue Island (city) Cook County	21	0.09
Warrenville (city) Du Page County	12	0.09
Oak Park (village) Cook County	42	0.08
Wheeling (village) Cook County	28	0.08
Schiller Park (village) Cook County	10	0.08

Hispanic: Bolivian

Top 10 Places Sorted by Number
Based on all places, regardless of population

Place	Number	%
Chicago (city) Cook County	414	0.01
Skokie (village) Cook County	69	0.11
Wheaton (city) Du Page County	26	0.05
Oak Lawn (village) Cook County	25	0.05
Des Plaines (city) Cook County	25	0.04
Aurora (city) Kane County	24	0.02
Glen Ellyn (village) Du Page County	20	0.07
Naperville (city) Du Page County	17	0.01
Morton Grove (village) Cook County	14	0.06
River Forest (village) Cook County	13	0.11

Top 10 Places Sorted by Percent
Based on all places, regardless of population

Place	Number	%
Greenfield (city) Greene County	3	0.25
Skokie (village) Cook County	69	0.11
River Forest (village) Cook County	13	0.11
West Peoria (city) Peoria County	5	0.10
Lincolnwood (village) Cook County	11	0.09
Northfield (village) Cook County	5	0.09
Oak Brook (village) Du Page County	7	0.08
Lincolnshire (village) Lake County	5	0.08
Glen Ellyn (village) Du Page County	20	0.07
Lake of the Woods (cdp) Champaign County	2	0.07

Top 10 Places Sorted by Percent
Based on places with populations of 10,000 or more

Place	Number	%
Skokie (village) Cook County	69	0.11
River Forest (village) Cook County	13	0.11
Lincolnwood (village) Cook County	11	0.09
Glen Ellyn (village) Du Page County	20	0.07
Morton Grove (village) Cook County	14	0.06
Northlake (city) Cook County	7	0.06
Wheaton (city) Du Page County	26	0.05
Oak Lawn (village) Cook County	25	0.05
Round Lake Beach (village) Lake County	13	0.05
Melrose Park (village) Cook County	12	0.05

Hispanic: Chilean

Top 10 Places Sorted by Number
Based on all places, regardless of population

Place	Number	%
Chicago (city) Cook County	640	0.02
Evanston (city) Cook County	41	0.06
Berwyn (city) Cook County	37	0.07
Oak Park (village) Cook County	31	0.06
Champaign (city) Champaign County	26	0.04
Skokie (village) Cook County	25	0.04
Schaumburg (village) Cook County	25	0.02
Aurora (city) Kane County	24	0.02
Naperville (city) Du Page County	23	0.02
Cicero (town) Cook County	22	0.03

Top 10 Places Sorted by Percent
Based on all places, regardless of population

Place	Number	%
Belgium (village) Vermilion County	2	0.43
Fairmont City (village) Saint Clair County	5	0.21
Ohio (village) Bureau County	1	0.19
Berkeley (village) Cook County	9	0.17
Green Oaks (village) Lake County	6	0.17
Long Lake (cdp) Lake County	5	0.15
Highwood (city) Lake County	6	0.14
Piper City (village) Ford County	1	0.13
Rosemont (village) Cook County	5	0.12
Germantown Hills (village) Woodford County	2	0.09

Top 10 Places Sorted by Percent
Based on places with populations of 10,000 or more

Place	Number	%
North Aurora (village) Kane County	8	0.08
Berwyn (city) Cook County	37	0.07
Evanston (city) Cook County	41	0.06
Oak Park (village) Cook County	31	0.06
Streamwood (village) Cook County	21	0.06
Wilmette (village) Cook County	17	0.06
Loves Park (city) Winnebago County	12	0.06
River Forest (village) Cook County	7	0.06
Barrington (village) Cook County	6	0.06
Zion (city) Lake County	12	0.05

Hispanic: Colombian

Top 10 Places Sorted by Number
Based on all places, regardless of population

Place	Number	%
Chicago (city) Cook County	5,625	0.19
Waukegan (city) Lake County	285	0.32
Rockford (city) Winnebago County	174	0.12
Cicero (town) Cook County	171	0.20
Skokie (village) Cook County	144	0.23
Schaumburg (village) Cook County	127	0.17
Berwyn (city) Cook County	120	0.22
Aurora (city) Kane County	119	0.17
Streamwood (village) Cook County	107	0.29
Hoffman Estates (village) Cook County	104	0.21

Top 10 Places Sorted by Percent
Based on all places, regardless of population

Place	Number	%
Coatsburg (village) Adams County	2	0.88
Stone Park (village) Cook County	33	0.64
Grand Ridge (village) La Salle County	3	0.55
Park City (city) Lake County	27	0.41
Third Lake (village) Lake County	5	0.37
Ohio (village) Bureau County	2	0.37
Andover (village) Henry County	2	0.34
Waukegan (city) Lake County	285	0.32
Highwood (city) Lake County	13	0.31

Notes: (cdp) census designated place; Refer to the User's Guide in the front of the book for more detailed information.

Place	Number	%
Streamwood (village) Cook County	107	0.29

Top 10 Places Sorted by Percent
Based on places with populations of 10,000 or more

Place	Number	%
Waukegan (city) Lake County	285	0.32
Streamwood (village) Cook County	107	0.29
Lincolnwood (village) Cook County	36	0.29
Bensenville (village) Du Page County	58	0.28
Elmwood Park (village) Cook County	64	0.25
Morton Grove (village) Cook County	57	0.25
Hanover Park (village) Cook County	90	0.24
Franklin Park (village) Cook County	46	0.24
Skokie (village) Cook County	144	0.23
Carol Stream (village) Du Page County	93	0.23

Hispanic: Ecuadorian

Top 10 Places Sorted by Number
Based on all places, regardless of population

Place	Number	%
Chicago (city) Cook County	8,941	0.31
Cicero (town) Cook County	208	0.24
Berwyn (city) Cook County	141	0.26
Skokie (village) Cook County	127	0.20
Niles (village) Cook County	94	0.31
Des Plaines (city) Cook County	87	0.15
Hoffman Estates (village) Cook County	72	0.15
Mount Prospect (village) Cook County	66	0.12
Elmwood Park (village) Cook County	62	0.24
Arlington Heights (village) Cook County	62	0.08

Top 10 Places Sorted by Percent
Based on all places, regardless of population

Place	Number	%
Warren (village) Jo Daviess County	6	0.40
Chicago (city) Cook County	8,941	0.31
Niles (village) Cook County	94	0.31
Berwyn (city) Cook County	141	0.26
Schiller Park (village) Cook County	31	0.26
Cicero (town) Cook County	208	0.24
Elmwood Park (village) Cook County	62	0.24
Huntley (village) McHenry County	14	0.24
Hainesville (village) Lake County	5	0.23
Skokie (village) Cook County	127	0.20

Top 10 Places Sorted by Percent
Based on places with populations of 10,000 or more

Place	Number	%
Chicago (city) Cook County	8,941	0.31
Niles (village) Cook County	94	0.31
Berwyn (city) Cook County	141	0.26
Schiller Park (village) Cook County	31	0.26
Cicero (town) Cook County	208	0.24
Elmwood Park (village) Cook County	62	0.24
Skokie (village) Cook County	127	0.20
Morton Grove (village) Cook County	43	0.19
Northlake (city) Cook County	23	0.19
Grayslake (village) Lake County	31	0.17

Hispanic: Paraguayan

Top 10 Places Sorted by Number
Based on all places, regardless of population

Place	Number	%
Chicago (city) Cook County	68	0.00
Highland Park (city) Lake County	10	0.03
Oak Park (village) Cook County	10	0.02
Elmhurst (city) Du Page County	8	0.02
Berwyn (city) Cook County	8	0.01
Bloomington (city) McLean County	7	0.01
Brookfield (village) Cook County	6	0.03

Place	Number	%
Lisle (village) Du Page County	5	0.02
Cicero (town) Cook County	5	0.01
Northbrook (village) Cook County	5	0.01

Top 10 Places Sorted by Percent
Based on all places, regardless of population

Place	Number	%
Forest View (village) Cook County	1	0.13
Wonder Lake (village) McHenry County	1	0.07
Mount Carroll (city) Carroll County	1	0.05
Tolono (village) Champaign County	1	0.04
Highland Park (city) Lake County	10	0.03
Brookfield (village) Cook County	6	0.03
Morris (city) Grundy County	3	0.03
Riverside (village) Cook County	3	0.03
Winfield (village) Du Page County	3	0.03
Clarendon Hills (village) Du Page County	2	0.03

Top 10 Places Sorted by Percent
Based on places with populations of 10,000 or more

Place	Number	%
Highland Park (city) Lake County	10	0.03
Brookfield (village) Cook County	6	0.03
Morris (city) Grundy County	3	0.03
Oak Park (village) Cook County	10	0.02
Elmhurst (city) Du Page County	8	0.02
Lisle (village) Du Page County	5	0.02
Forest Park (village) Cook County	3	0.02
Grayslake (village) Lake County	3	0.02
Lincolnwood (village) Cook County	2	0.02
Berwyn (city) Cook County	8	0.01

Hispanic: Peruvian

Top 10 Places Sorted by Number
Based on all places, regardless of population

Place	Number	%
Chicago (city) Cook County	2,737	0.09
Skokie (village) Cook County	115	0.18
Evanston (city) Cook County	82	0.11
Palatine (village) Cook County	79	0.12
Cicero (town) Cook County	72	0.08
Oak Park (village) Cook County	63	0.12
Berwyn (city) Cook County	58	0.11
Schaumburg (village) Cook County	48	0.06
Aurora (city) Kane County	47	0.03
Naperville (city) Du Page County	40	0.03

Top 10 Places Sorted by Percent
Based on all places, regardless of population

Place	Number	%
Saint Johns (village) Perry County	1	0.46
Fayetteville (village) Saint Clair County	1	0.26
Schiller Park (village) Cook County	22	0.19
Palos Park (village) Cook County	9	0.19
Hainesville (village) Lake County	4	0.19
Oblong (village) Crawford County	3	0.19
Skokie (village) Cook County	115	0.18
Northlake (city) Cook County	20	0.17
Melrose Park (village) Cook County	37	0.16
Lincolnwood (village) Cook County	18	0.15

Top 10 Places Sorted by Percent
Based on places with populations of 10,000 or more

Place	Number	%
Schiller Park (village) Cook County	22	0.19
Skokie (village) Cook County	115	0.18
Northlake (city) Cook County	20	0.17
Melrose Park (village) Cook County	37	0.16
Lincolnwood (village) Cook County	18	0.15
River Forest (village) Cook County	18	0.15
Morton Grove (village) Cook County	32	0.14

Hispanic: Uruguayan

Top 10 Places Sorted by Number
Based on all places, regardless of population

Place	Number	%
Chicago (city) Cook County	134	0.00
Rockford (city) Winnebago County	19	0.01
Chicago Heights (city) Cook County	14	0.04
Melrose Park (village) Cook County	13	0.06
Berwyn (city) Cook County	13	0.02
Oak Park (village) Cook County	11	0.02
Evergreen Park (village) Cook County	7	0.03
Skokie (village) Cook County	7	0.01
Morton Grove (village) Cook County	6	0.03
Park Ridge (city) Cook County	6	0.02

Top 10 Places Sorted by Percent
Based on all places, regardless of population

Place	Number	%
Elsah (village) Jersey County	1	0.16
Melrose Park (village) Cook County	13	0.06
Chicago Heights (city) Cook County	14	0.04
Evergreen Park (village) Cook County	7	0.03
Morton Grove (village) Cook County	6	0.03
Berwyn (city) Cook County	13	0.02
Oak Park (village) Cook County	11	0.02
Park Ridge (city) Cook County	6	0.02
Roselle (village) Du Page County	5	0.02
Saint Charles (city) Kane County	5	0.02

Top 10 Places Sorted by Percent
Based on places with populations of 10,000 or more

Place	Number	%
Melrose Park (village) Cook County	13	0.06
Chicago Heights (city) Cook County	14	0.04
Evergreen Park (village) Cook County	7	0.03
Morton Grove (village) Cook County	6	0.03
Berwyn (city) Cook County	13	0.02
Oak Park (village) Cook County	11	0.02
Park Ridge (city) Cook County	6	0.02
Roselle (village) Du Page County	5	0.02
Saint Charles (city) Kane County	5	0.02
Deerfield (village) Lake County	3	0.02

Hispanic: Venezuelan

Top 10 Places Sorted by Number
Based on all places, regardless of population

Place	Number	%
Chicago (city) Cook County	600	0.02
Aurora (city) Kane County	52	0.04
Wheeling (village) Cook County	33	0.10
Evanston (city) Cook County	31	0.04
Oak Park (village) Cook County	29	0.06
Lombard (village) Du Page County	24	0.06
Cicero (town) Cook County	24	0.03
Champaign (city) Champaign County	23	0.03
Palatine (village) Cook County	22	0.03
Skokie (village) Cook County	21	0.03

Top 10 Places Sorted by Percent
Based on all places, regardless of population

Place	Number	%
Chenoa (city) McLean County	4	0.22
Golf (village) Cook County	1	0.22
North City (village) Franklin County	1	0.16
Cambria (village) Williamson County	2	0.15
Forest View (village) Cook County	1	0.13

Notes: (cdp) census designated place; Refer to the User's Guide in the front of the book for more detailed information.

Place	Number	%
Coal Valley (village) Rock Island County	4	0.11
Wheeling (village) Cook County	33	0.10
Pontiac (city) Livingston County	9	0.08
Breese (city) Clinton County	3	0.07
Oak Park (village) Cook County	29	0.06

Top 10 Places Sorted by Percent
Based on places with populations of 10,000 or more

Place	Number	%
Wheeling (village) Cook County	33	0.10
Pontiac (city) Livingston County	9	0.08
Oak Park (village) Cook County	29	0.06
Lombard (village) Du Page County	24	0.06
Melrose Park (village) Cook County	14	0.06
Wood Dale (city) Du Page County	8	0.06
Addison (village) Du Page County	17	0.05
Urbana (city) Champaign County	17	0.05
Vernon Hills (village) Lake County	10	0.05
Aurora (city) Kane County	52	0.04

Hispanic: Other South American

Top 10 Places Sorted by Number
Based on all places, regardless of population

Place	Number	%
Chicago (city) Cook County	761	0.03
Naperville (city) Du Page County	48	0.04
Des Plaines (city) Cook County	34	0.06
Skokie (village) Cook County	31	0.05
Glenview (village) Cook County	25	0.06
Cicero (town) Cook County	23	0.03
Palatine (village) Cook County	21	0.03
Hoffman Estates (village) Cook County	18	0.04
Champaign (city) Champaign County	17	0.03
Rockford (city) Winnebago County	17	0.01

Top 10 Places Sorted by Percent
Based on all places, regardless of population

Place	Number	%
Round Lake Heights (village) Lake County	5	0.37
Kangley (village) La Salle County	1	0.35
Fairmont (cdp) Will County	5	0.20
Leland Grove (city) Sangamon County	2	0.13
Jerome (village) Sangamon County	1	0.07
Des Plaines (city) Cook County	34	0.06
Glenview (village) Cook County	25	0.06
Morton Grove (village) Cook County	13	0.06
Chicago Ridge (village) Cook County	9	0.06
South Elgin (village) Kane County	9	0.06

Top 10 Places Sorted by Percent
Based on places with populations of 10,000 or more

Place	Number	%
Des Plaines (city) Cook County	34	0.06
Glenview (village) Cook County	25	0.06
Morton Grove (village) Cook County	13	0.06
Chicago Ridge (village) Cook County	9	0.06
South Elgin (village) Kane County	9	0.06
Winnetka (village) Cook County	7	0.06
Skokie (village) Cook County	31	0.05
Melrose Park (village) Cook County	12	0.05
Lincolnwood (village) Cook County	6	0.05
Naperville (city) Du Page County	48	0.04

Hispanic: Other

Top 10 Places Sorted by Number
Based on all places, regardless of population

Place	Number	%
Chicago (city) Cook County	56,225	1.94
Cicero (town) Cook County	3,784	4.42
Aurora (city) Kane County	3,654	2.56

Place	Number	%
Waukegan (city) Lake County	3,071	3.49
Elgin (city) Kane County	2,009	2.13
Joliet (city) Will County	1,760	1.66
Berwyn (city) Cook County	1,468	2.72
Rockford (city) Winnebago County	1,456	0.97
Carpentersville (village) Kane County	927	3.03
Melrose Park (village) Cook County	748	3.23

Top 10 Places Sorted by Percent
Based on all places, regardless of population

Place	Number	%
Oak Grove (village) Rock Island County	109	8.27
Sheridan (village) La Salle County	195	8.09
Baldwin (village) Randolph County	279	7.69
Detroit (village) Pike County	6	6.45
De Pue (village) Bureau County	117	6.35
Ina (village) Jefferson County	148	6.03
Fairmont City (village) Saint Clair County	131	5.38
Irving (village) Montgomery County	133	5.35
Stone Park (village) Cook County	241	4.70
Naples (town) Scott County	6	4.48

Top 10 Places Sorted by Percent
Based on places with populations of 10,000 or more

Place	Number	%
Cicero (town) Cook County	3,784	4.42
Waukegan (city) Lake County	3,071	3.49
Melrose Park (village) Cook County	748	3.23
Crest Hill (city) Will County	417	3.13
Carpentersville (village) Kane County	927	3.03
Berwyn (city) Cook County	1,468	2.72
Blue Island (city) Cook County	612	2.61
Bensenville (village) Du Page County	539	2.60
Aurora (city) Kane County	3,654	2.56
West Chicago (city) Du Page County	562	2.39

Hungarian

Top 10 Places Sorted by Number
Based on all places, regardless of population

Place	Number	%
Chicago (city) Cook County	9,418	0.33
Naperville (city) Du Page County	1,042	0.81
Aurora (city) Kane County	819	0.57
Skokie (village) Cook County	716	1.13
Evanston (city) Cook County	713	0.96
Arlington Heights (village) Cook County	670	0.88
Joliet (city) Will County	648	0.61
Schaumburg (village) Cook County	597	0.80
Elgin (city) Kane County	553	0.59
Buffalo Grove (village) Lake County	547	1.28

Top 10 Places Sorted by Percent
Based on all places, regardless of population

Place	Number	%
Smithboro (village) Bond County	15	7.69
Kempton (village) Ford County	13	4.91
Nason (city) Jefferson County	9	4.55
Bannockburn (village) Lake County	51	3.58
Christopher (city) Franklin County	79	2.86
Valier (village) Franklin County	18	2.74
Johnsburg (village) McHenry County	142	2.62
Channel Lake (cdp) Lake County	46	2.58
Kildeer (village) Lake County	89	2.49
Fairmont (cdp) Will County	62	2.37

Top 10 Places Sorted by Percent
Based on places with populations of 10,000 or more

Place	Number	%
Deerfield (village) Lake County	268	1.45
Lansing (village) Cook County	402	1.43
Highland Park (city) Lake County	439	1.40

Place	Number	%
Burr Ridge (village) Du Page County	141	1.37
Prospect Heights (city) Cook County	230	1.31
Buffalo Grove (village) Lake County	547	1.28
New Lenox (village) Will County	226	1.28
Plainfield (village) Will County	161	1.24
Lincolnwood (village) Cook County	152	1.23
Granite City (city) Madison County	387	1.22

Icelander

Top 10 Places Sorted by Number
Based on all places, regardless of population

Place	Number	%
Chicago (city) Cook County	176	0.01
Naperville (city) Du Page County	68	0.05
Oak Park (village) Cook County	32	0.06
Batavia (city) Kane County	31	0.13
Urbana (city) Champaign County	31	0.09
Fox Lake (village) Lake County	29	0.31
Bensenville (village) Du Page County	29	0.14
Park Ridge (city) Cook County	28	0.07
Wilmette (village) Cook County	27	0.10
Deerfield (village) Lake County	26	0.14

Top 10 Places Sorted by Percent
Based on all places, regardless of population

Place	Number	%
Matherville (village) Mercer County	5	0.65
Fox River Grove (village) McHenry County	16	0.33
Fox Lake (village) Lake County	29	0.31
Third Lake (village) Lake County	3	0.22
Long Grove (village) Lake County	13	0.20
Richmond (village) McHenry County	2	0.18
Bensenville (village) Du Page County	29	0.14
Deerfield (village) Lake County	26	0.14
Batavia (city) Kane County	31	0.13
Bunker Hill (city) Macoupin County	2	0.11

Top 10 Places Sorted by Percent
Based on places with populations of 10,000 or more

Place	Number	%
Bensenville (village) Du Page County	29	0.14
Deerfield (village) Lake County	26	0.14
Batavia (city) Kane County	31	0.13
Wilmette (village) Cook County	27	0.10
Urbana (city) Champaign County	31	0.09
Sycamore (city) De Kalb County	10	0.08
River Grove (village) Cook County	8	0.08
Park Ridge (city) Cook County	28	0.07
Alton (city) Madison County	21	0.07
Bridgeview (village) Cook County	10	0.07

Iranian

Top 10 Places Sorted by Number
Based on all places, regardless of population

Place	Number	%
Chicago (city) Cook County	1,944	0.07
Naperville (city) Du Page County	479	0.37
Skokie (village) Cook County	307	0.48
Hoffman Estates (village) Cook County	243	0.48
Oak Brook (village) Du Page County	239	2.83
Schaumburg (village) Cook County	175	0.23
Downers Grove (village) Du Page County	154	0.37
Evanston (city) Cook County	145	0.20
Arlington Heights (village) Cook County	121	0.16
Buffalo Grove (village) Lake County	116	0.27

Top 10 Places Sorted by Percent
Based on all places, regardless of population

Place	Number	%
Oak Brook (village) Du Page County	239	2.83

Notes: (cdp) census designated place; Refer to the User's Guide in the front of the book for more detailed information.

Place	Number	%
South Barrington (village) Cook County	88	2.36
Parkersburg (village) Richland County	4	1.96
West Dundee (village) Kane County	74	1.38
Wayne (village) Kane County	23	1.10
Elsah (village) Jersey County	5	0.80
Highwood (city) Lake County	31	0.76
Countryside (city) Cook County	43	0.72
Barrington Hills (village) Cook County	30	0.72
Tuscola (city) Douglas County	31	0.69

Top 10 Places Sorted by Percent
Based on places with populations of 10,000 or more

Place	Number	%
Lincolnwood (village) Cook County	66	0.53
Skokie (village) Cook County	307	0.48
Hoffman Estates (village) Cook County	243	0.48
Burr Ridge (village) Du Page County	42	0.41
Naperville (city) Du Page County	479	0.37
Downers Grove (village) Du Page County	154	0.32
Bloomingdale (village) Du Page County	70	0.32
Wheeling (village) Cook County	100	0.29
Glenview (village) Cook County	115	0.28
Wilmette (village) Cook County	77	0.28

Irish

Top 10 Places Sorted by Number
Based on all places, regardless of population

Place	Number	%
Chicago (city) Cook County	191,729	6.62
Naperville (city) Du Page County	23,688	18.46
Springfield (city) Sangamon County	17,457	15.56
Oak Lawn (village) Cook County	16,841	30.40
Rockford (city) Winnebago County	16,786	11.21
Joliet (city) Will County	14,609	13.76
Arlington Heights (village) Cook County	14,592	19.18
Aurora (city) Kane County	13,998	9.75
Peoria (city) Peoria County	13,790	12.22
Orland Park (village) Cook County	13,550	26.52

Top 10 Places Sorted by Percent
Based on all places, regardless of population

Place	Number	%
Harmon (village) Lee County	73	46.50
Evergreen Park (village) Cook County	8,250	39.62
Ivesdale (village) Champaign County	126	39.62
Deer Grove (village) Whiteside County	20	37.74
Merrionette Park (village) Cook County	689	34.47
Hometown (city) Cook County	1,500	33.58
Bentley (town) Hancock County	13	33.33
Golf (village) Cook County	150	33.19
Anchor (village) McLean County	53	32.52
Symerton (village) Will County	32	32.00

Top 10 Places Sorted by Percent
Based on places with populations of 10,000 or more

Place	Number	%
Evergreen Park (village) Cook County	8,250	39.62
River Forest (village) Cook County	3,586	30.82
Oak Lawn (village) Cook County	16,841	30.40
Western Springs (village) Cook County	3,770	29.87
Crestwood (village) Cook County	3,301	29.42
Mokena (village) Will County	4,316	29.41
New Lenox (village) Will County	4,917	27.91
Palos Heights (city) Cook County	3,078	27.19
Midlothian (village) Cook County	3,773	26.53
Orland Park (village) Cook County	13,550	26.52

Israeli

Top 10 Places Sorted by Number
Based on all places, regardless of population

Place	Number	%
Chicago (city) Cook County	1,033	0.04
Highland Park (city) Lake County	251	0.80
Skokie (village) Cook County	251	0.40
Buffalo Grove (village) Lake County	234	0.55
Deerfield (village) Lake County	119	0.64
Wilmette (village) Cook County	118	0.43
Urbana (city) Champaign County	113	0.31
Evanston (city) Cook County	92	0.12
North Chicago (city) Lake County	80	0.22
Waukegan (city) Lake County	76	0.09

Top 10 Places Sorted by Percent
Based on all places, regardless of population

Place	Number	%
Highland Park (city) Lake County	251	0.80
Deerfield (village) Lake County	119	0.64
Buffalo Grove (village) Lake County	234	0.55
Odell (village) Livingston County	5	0.49
Congerville (village) Woodford County	2	0.45
Wilmette (village) Cook County	118	0.43
Skokie (village) Cook County	251	0.40
Urbana (city) Champaign County	113	0.31
Riverwoods (village) Lake County	11	0.29
Flossmoor (village) Cook County	25	0.27

Top 10 Places Sorted by Percent
Based on places with populations of 10,000 or more

Place	Number	%
Highland Park (city) Lake County	251	0.80
Deerfield (village) Lake County	119	0.64
Buffalo Grove (village) Lake County	234	0.55
Wilmette (village) Cook County	118	0.43
Skokie (village) Cook County	251	0.40
Urbana (city) Champaign County	113	0.31
Winnetka (village) Cook County	32	0.26
Vernon Hills (village) Lake County	50	0.24
North Chicago (city) Lake County	80	0.22
Geneva (city) Kane County	40	0.20

Italian

Top 10 Places Sorted by Number
Based on all places, regardless of population

Place	Number	%
Chicago (city) Cook County	101,903	3.52
Naperville (city) Du Page County	13,611	10.61
Rockford (city) Winnebago County	10,571	7.06
Schaumburg (village) Cook County	9,392	12.60
Joliet (city) Will County	9,271	8.73
Arlington Heights (village) Cook County	8,456	11.11
Orland Park (village) Cook County	7,568	14.81
Elmwood Park (village) Cook County	7,293	28.71
Tinley Park (village) Cook County	6,926	14.33
Springfield (city) Sangamon County	6,736	6.00

Top 10 Places Sorted by Percent
Based on all places, regardless of population

Place	Number	%
East Brooklyn (village) Grundy County	56	54.90
Standard (village) Putnam County	114	44.19
South Wilmington (village) Grundy County	247	38.24
Dalzell (village) Bureau County	252	35.69
Cedar Point (village) La Salle County	92	33.95
Hollowayville (village) Bureau County	23	29.11
Elmwood Park (village) Cook County	7,293	28.71
Mount Clare (village) Macoupin County	113	27.63
Mark (village) Putnam County	135	27.61

Place	Number	%
Ladd (village) Bureau County	341	25.66

Top 10 Places Sorted by Percent
Based on places with populations of 10,000 or more

Place	Number	%
Elmwood Park (village) Cook County	7,293	28.71
Norridge (village) Cook County	3,740	25.46
Westchester (village) Cook County	3,483	20.90
Bloomingdale (village) Du Page County	4,471	20.72
Wood Dale (city) Du Page County	2,637	18.85
Melrose Park (village) Cook County	4,368	18.82
Schiller Park (village) Cook County	2,206	18.72
Lake in the Hills (village) McHenry County	4,179	17.81
River Grove (village) Cook County	1,864	17.56
Bartlett (village) Du Page County	6,333	17.19

Latvian

Top 10 Places Sorted by Number
Based on all places, regardless of population

Place	Number	%
Chicago (city) Cook County	1,383	0.05
Palatine (village) Cook County	172	0.26
Oak Park (village) Cook County	146	0.28
Evanston (city) Cook County	124	0.17
Des Plaines (city) Cook County	105	0.18
Mount Prospect (village) Cook County	100	0.18
Buffalo Grove (village) Lake County	97	0.23
Northbrook (village) Cook County	88	0.26
Lombard (village) Du Page County	83	0.20
Highland Park (city) Lake County	76	0.24

Top 10 Places Sorted by Percent
Based on all places, regardless of population

Place	Number	%
Lee (village) Lee County	9	3.31
Hooppole (village) Henry County	5	3.07
Makanda (village) Jackson County	6	1.47
Deer Park (village) Lake County	37	1.15
Glencoe (village) Cook County	48	0.54
Lyons (village) Cook County	54	0.53
Carlinville (city) Macoupin County	30	0.52
Lakewood (village) McHenry County	12	0.50
Kenilworth (village) Cook County	12	0.48
Harwood Heights (village) Cook County	38	0.46

Top 10 Places Sorted by Percent
Based on places with populations of 10,000 or more

Place	Number	%
Lyons (village) Cook County	54	0.53
Deerfield (village) Lake County	69	0.37
Western Springs (village) Cook County	42	0.33
Oak Park (village) Cook County	146	0.28
Winnetka (village) Cook County	34	0.27
Palatine (village) Cook County	172	0.26
Northbrook (village) Cook County	88	0.26
Westchester (village) Cook County	44	0.26
McHenry (city) McHenry County	54	0.25
Highland Park (city) Lake County	76	0.24

Lithuanian

Top 10 Places Sorted by Number
Based on all places, regardless of population

Place	Number	%
Chicago (city) Cook County	15,383	0.53
Oak Lawn (village) Cook County	2,101	3.79
Orland Park (village) Cook County	1,500	2.94
Naperville (city) Du Page County	1,291	1.01
Tinley Park (village) Cook County	1,250	2.59
Springfield (city) Sangamon County	1,091	0.97
Burbank (city) Cook County	960	3.45

Notes: (cdp) census designated place; Refer to the User's Guide in the front of the book for more detailed information.

Goodings Grove (cdp) Will County	934	5.46
Downers Grove (village) Du Page County	911	1.87
Oak Forest (city) Cook County	869	3.11

Top 10 Places Sorted by Percent
Based on all places, regardless of population

Place	Number	%
Dover (village) Bureau County	10	6.33
Campus (village) Livingston County	7	5.88
Bulpitt (village) Christian County	12	5.85
Westville (village) Vermilion County	180	5.60
Goodings Grove (cdp) Will County	934	5.46
Hickory Hills (city) Cook County	685	4.92
Brooklyn (village) Saint Clair County	30	4.56
Palos Hills (city) Cook County	759	4.27
Lemont (village) Cook County	539	4.09
Worth (village) Cook County	433	3.88

Top 10 Places Sorted by Percent
Based on places with populations of 10,000 or more

Place	Number	%
Goodings Grove (cdp) Will County	934	5.46
Hickory Hills (city) Cook County	685	4.92
Palos Hills (city) Cook County	759	4.27
Lemont (village) Cook County	539	4.09
Worth (village) Cook County	433	3.88
Chicago Ridge (village) Cook County	534	3.85
Oak Lawn (village) Cook County	2,101	3.79
Burbank (city) Cook County	960	3.45
Darien (city) Du Page County	770	3.35
Palos Heights (city) Cook County	360	3.18

Luxemburger

Top 10 Places Sorted by Number
Based on all places, regardless of population

Place	Number	%
Chicago (city) Cook County	756	0.03
Aurora (city) Kane County	597	0.42
Northbrook (village) Cook County	169	0.51
Schaumburg (village) Cook County	154	0.21
Arlington Heights (village) Cook County	141	0.19
Skokie (village) Cook County	138	0.22
Palatine (village) Cook County	131	0.20
Des Plaines (city) Cook County	129	0.22
Glenview (village) Cook County	112	0.27
Naperville (city) Du Page County	108	0.08

Top 10 Places Sorted by Percent
Based on all places, regardless of population

Place	Number	%
Bedford Park (village) Cook County	8	1.42
Creston (village) Ogle County	7	1.29
Montgomery (village) Kane County	62	1.23
Sugar Grove (village) Kane County	34	0.84
Dunlap (village) Peoria County	7	0.78
North Aurora (village) Kane County	81	0.76
Greenwood (village) McHenry County	2	0.75
East Dubuque (city) Jo Daviess County	14	0.73
Jonesboro (city) Union County	14	0.73
Plano (city) Kendall County	35	0.64

Top 10 Places Sorted by Percent
Based on places with populations of 10,000 or more

Place	Number	%
North Aurora (village) Kane County	81	0.76
Northbrook (village) Cook County	169	0.51
Aurora (city) Kane County	597	0.42
Morton Grove (village) Cook County	87	0.39
Gages Lake (cdp) Lake County	38	0.36
Rolling Meadows (city) Cook County	81	0.33
Wilmette (village) Cook County	80	0.29

Batavia (city) Kane County	69	0.29
Glenview (village) Cook County	112	0.27
Cary (village) McHenry County	42	0.27

Macedonian

Top 10 Places Sorted by Number
Based on all places, regardless of population

Place	Number	%
Chicago (city) Cook County	450	0.02
Granite City (city) Madison County	173	0.55
Mount Prospect (village) Cook County	105	0.19
Lemont (village) Cook County	83	0.63
Lansing (village) Cook County	71	0.25
Summit (village) Cook County	60	0.56
Woodstock (city) McHenry County	55	0.27
Countryside (city) Cook County	53	0.89
Waukegan (city) Lake County	50	0.06
Brookfield (village) Cook County	48	0.25

Top 10 Places Sorted by Percent
Based on all places, regardless of population

Place	Number	%
Hindsboro (village) Douglas County	10	2.81
Countryside (city) Cook County	53	0.89
Coal City (village) Grundy County	42	0.87
Prairie Grove (village) McHenry County	7	0.66
Lemont (village) Cook County	83	0.63
Summit (village) Cook County	60	0.56
Granite City (city) Madison County	173	0.55
Pontoon Beach (village) Madison County	31	0.55
Sauget (village) Saint Clair County	1	0.54
Forsyth (village) Macon County	11	0.46

Top 10 Places Sorted by Percent
Based on places with populations of 10,000 or more

Place	Number	%
Lemont (village) Cook County	83	0.63
Summit (village) Cook County	60	0.56
Granite City (city) Madison County	173	0.55
Woodstock (city) McHenry County	55	0.27
Bridgeview (village) Cook County	40	0.26
Chicago Ridge (village) Cook County	36	0.26
Lansing (village) Cook County	71	0.25
Brookfield (village) Cook County	48	0.25
Westchester (village) Cook County	35	0.21
Mount Prospect (village) Cook County	105	0.19

Maltese

Top 10 Places Sorted by Number
Based on all places, regardless of population

Place	Number	%
Chicago (city) Cook County	96	0.00
Lansing (village) Cook County	50	0.18
Edwardsville (city) Madison County	39	0.19
Highland Park (city) Lake County	38	0.12
Evanston (city) Cook County	34	0.05
Hoffman Estates (village) Cook County	21	0.04
Schaumburg (village) Cook County	19	0.03
Libertyville (village) Lake County	17	0.08
Charleston (city) Coles County	15	0.07
Crest Hill (city) Will County	13	0.10

Top 10 Places Sorted by Percent
Based on all places, regardless of population

Place	Number	%
Edwardsville (city) Madison County	39	0.19
Lansing (village) Cook County	50	0.18
Highland Park (city) Lake County	38	0.12
Shannon (village) Carroll County	1	0.12
Crest Hill (city) Will County	13	0.10

Fairfield (city) Wayne County	5	0.09
Libertyville (village) Lake County	17	0.08
Charleston (city) Coles County	15	0.07
Evanston (city) Cook County	34	0.05
Hoffman Estates (village) Cook County	21	0.04

Top 10 Places Sorted by Percent
Based on places with populations of 10,000 or more

Place	Number	%
Edwardsville (city) Madison County	39	0.19
Lansing (village) Cook County	50	0.18
Highland Park (city) Lake County	38	0.12
Crest Hill (city) Will County	13	0.10
Libertyville (village) Lake County	17	0.08
Charleston (city) Coles County	15	0.07
Evanston (city) Cook County	34	0.05
Hoffman Estates (village) Cook County	21	0.04
Pekin (city) Tazewell County	12	0.04
Lake Forest (city) Lake County	8	0.04

New Zealander

Top 10 Places Sorted by Number
Based on all places, regardless of population

Place	Number	%
Chicago (city) Cook County	62	0.00
Naperville (city) Du Page County	44	0.03
Streamwood (village) Cook County	30	0.08
Aurora (city) Kane County	30	0.02
Evanston (city) Cook County	23	0.03
Champaign (city) Champaign County	21	0.03
Grayslake (village) Lake County	14	0.08
Bolingbrook (village) Will County	10	0.02
North Chicago (city) Lake County	9	0.02
Springfield (city) Sangamon County	9	0.01

Top 10 Places Sorted by Percent
Based on all places, regardless of population

Place	Number	%
Elsah (village) Jersey County	4	0.64
Lexington (city) McLean County	6	0.31
Farmington (city) Fulton County	7	0.27
Colchester (city) McDonough County	2	0.14
Round Lake Park (village) Lake County	7	0.12
Streamwood (village) Cook County	30	0.08
Grayslake (village) Lake County	14	0.08
Lockport (city) Will County	7	0.05
Westchester (village) Cook County	7	0.04
Naperville (city) Du Page County	44	0.03

Top 10 Places Sorted by Percent
Based on places with populations of 10,000 or more

Place	Number	%
Streamwood (village) Cook County	30	0.08
Grayslake (village) Lake County	14	0.08
Lockport (city) Will County	7	0.05
Westchester (village) Cook County	7	0.04
Naperville (city) Du Page County	44	0.03
Evanston (city) Cook County	23	0.03
Champaign (city) Champaign County	21	0.03
Vernon Hills (village) Lake County	6	0.03
Mount Vernon (city) Jefferson County	5	0.03
Aurora (city) Kane County	30	0.02

Northern European

Top 10 Places Sorted by Number
Based on all places, regardless of population

Place	Number	%
Chicago (city) Cook County	783	0.03
Champaign (city) Champaign County	106	0.16
Evanston (city) Cook County	106	0.14

Notes: (cdp) census designated place; Refer to the User's Guide in the front of the book for more detailed information.

Place	Number	%
De Kalb (city) De Kalb County	97	0.25
Palatine (village) Cook County	86	0.13
Wilmette (village) Cook County	81	0.29
Mount Prospect (village) Cook County	81	0.14
Springfield (city) Sangamon County	81	0.07
Winnetka (village) Cook County	77	0.62
Highland Park (city) Lake County	76	0.24

Top 10 Places Sorted by Percent
Based on all places, regardless of population

Place	Number	%
Belle Rive (village) Jefferson County	13	3.46
Iroquois (village) Iroquois County	6	3.23
Union (village) McHenry County	17	2.93
Latham (village) Logan County	7	1.79
Perry (village) Pike County	6	1.55
Carthage (city) Hancock County	36	1.31
Wadsworth (village) Lake County	33	1.09
Deer Park (village) Lake County	22	0.68
Winnetka (village) Cook County	77	0.62
Oregon (city) Ogle County	22	0.54

Top 10 Places Sorted by Percent
Based on places with populations of 10,000 or more

Place	Number	%
Winnetka (village) Cook County	77	0.62
Burr Ridge (village) Du Page County	31	0.30
Barrington (village) Cook County	30	0.30
Wilmette (village) Cook County	81	0.29
Carbondale (city) Jackson County	60	0.29
De Kalb (city) De Kalb County	97	0.25
Highland Park (city) Lake County	76	0.24
North Aurora (village) Kane County	22	0.21
Belvidere (city) Boone County	41	0.20
Washington (city) Tazewell County	22	0.20

Norwegian

Top 10 Places Sorted by Number
Based on all places, regardless of population

Place	Number	%
Chicago (city) Cook County	14,890	0.51
Rockford (city) Winnebago County	5,394	3.60
Naperville (city) Du Page County	2,972	2.32
Aurora (city) Kane County	2,733	1.90
Arlington Heights (village) Cook County	2,053	2.70
Wheaton (city) Du Page County	1,834	3.31
Elgin (city) Kane County	1,822	1.94
Schaumburg (village) Cook County	1,800	2.42
Morris (city) Grundy County	1,595	13.36
Crystal Lake (city) McHenry County	1,475	3.90

Top 10 Places Sorted by Percent
Based on all places, regardless of population

Place	Number	%
Newark (village) Kendall County	310	34.07
Lisbon (village) Kendall County	66	26.83
Lee (village) Lee County	45	16.54
Leland (village) La Salle County	132	13.58
Morris (city) Grundy County	1,595	13.36
Caledonia (village) Boone County	28	12.44
Shabbona (village) De Kalb County	117	12.26
Maple Park (village) Kane County	92	12.03
Seneca (village) La Salle County	239	11.39
Steward (village) Lee County	31	11.31

Top 10 Places Sorted by Percent
Based on places with populations of 10,000 or more

Place	Number	%
Morris (city) Grundy County	1,595	13.36
Ottawa (city) La Salle County	1,455	7.93
Sycamore (city) De Kalb County	701	5.78

Place	Number	%
Loves Park (city) Winnebago County	1,146	5.76
Machesney Park (village) Winnebago County	1,110	5.37
McHenry (city) McHenry County	939	4.35
Oswego (village) Kendall County	571	4.29
Belvidere (city) Boone County	869	4.20
Algonquin (village) McHenry County	925	3.95
Crystal Lake (city) McHenry County	1,475	3.90

Pennsylvania German

Top 10 Places Sorted by Number
Based on all places, regardless of population

Place	Number	%
Rockford (city) Winnebago County	232	0.15
East Moline (city) Rock Island County	107	0.53
Chicago (city) Cook County	94	0.00
Decatur (city) Macon County	88	0.11
Naperville (city) Du Page County	74	0.06
Quincy (city) Adams County	64	0.16
Peoria (city) Peoria County	63	0.06
Aurora (city) Kane County	55	0.04
Sterling (city) Whiteside County	51	0.33
Freeport (city) Stephenson County	51	0.19

Top 10 Places Sorted by Percent
Based on all places, regardless of population

Place	Number	%
Winslow (village) Stephenson County	15	4.31
La Fayette (village) Stark County	6	2.64
North Henderson (village) Mercer County	4	2.02
Aroma Park (village) Kankakee County	16	1.95
Good Hope (village) McDonough County	7	1.72
Concord (village) Morgan County	3	1.64
Coyne Center (cdp) Rock Island County	15	1.59
Mount Morris (village) Ogle County	43	1.47
Elizabethtown (village) Hardin County	5	1.37
Woodson (village) Morgan County	7	1.23

Top 10 Places Sorted by Percent
Based on places with populations of 10,000 or more

Place	Number	%
East Moline (city) Rock Island County	107	0.53
Oswego (village) Kendall County	46	0.35
Sterling (city) Whiteside County	51	0.33
Freeport (city) Stephenson County	51	0.19
Burr Ridge (village) Du Page County	20	0.19
West Chicago (city) Du Page County	43	0.18
East Peoria (city) Tazewell County	40	0.17
Quincy (city) Adams County	64	0.16
Rockford (city) Winnebago County	232	0.15
Woodridge (village) Du Page County	48	0.15

Polish

Top 10 Places Sorted by Number
Based on all places, regardless of population

Place	Number	%
Chicago (city) Cook County	210,421	7.27
Naperville (city) Du Page County	13,936	10.86
Schaumburg (village) Cook County	11,109	14.91
Arlington Heights (village) Cook County	11,001	14.46
Des Plaines (city) Cook County	10,703	18.23
Oak Lawn (village) Cook County	10,667	19.26
Tinley Park (village) Cook County	9,540	19.74
Orland Park (village) Cook County	9,430	18.45
Mount Prospect (village) Cook County	9,216	16.25
Burbank (city) Cook County	8,427	30.29

Top 10 Places Sorted by Percent
Based on all places, regardless of population

Place	Number	%
Du Bois (village) Washington County	107	50.95

Place	Number	%
Radom (village) Washington County	162	38.85
Harwood Heights (village) Cook County	3,079	37.43
Lemont (village) Cook County	4,327	32.84
Norridge (village) Cook County	4,673	31.81
River Grove (village) Cook County	3,375	31.79
Burbank (city) Cook County	8,427	30.29
Goodings Grove (cdp) Will County	4,825	28.21
Hickory Hills (city) Cook County	3,750	26.91
Forest View (village) Cook County	206	25.88

Top 10 Places Sorted by Percent
Based on places with populations of 10,000 or more

Place	Number	%
Lemont (village) Cook County	4,327	32.84
Norridge (village) Cook County	4,673	31.81
River Grove (village) Cook County	3,375	31.79
Burbank (city) Cook County	8,427	30.29
Goodings Grove (cdp) Will County	4,825	28.21
Hickory Hills (city) Cook County	3,750	26.91
Bridgeview (village) Cook County	3,942	25.65
Elmwood Park (village) Cook County	6,270	24.68
Justice (village) Cook County	2,931	24.24
Niles (village) Cook County	6,880	22.82

Portuguese

Top 10 Places Sorted by Number
Based on all places, regardless of population

Place	Number	%
Chicago (city) Cook County	915	0.03
Springfield (city) Sangamon County	455	0.41
Evanston (city) Cook County	165	0.22
Naperville (city) Du Page County	160	0.12
Jacksonville (city) Morgan County	154	0.81
Peoria (city) Peoria County	135	0.12
Champaign (city) Champaign County	113	0.17
Aurora (city) Kane County	98	0.07
Bloomington (city) McLean County	93	0.14
Mount Prospect (village) Cook County	89	0.16

Top 10 Places Sorted by Percent
Based on all places, regardless of population

Place	Number	%
Topeka (village) Mason County	10	13.70
Clear Lake (village) Sangamon County	15	5.08
Longview (village) Champaign County	6	3.64
Manchester (village) Scott County	11	3.07
Milton (village) Pike County	8	2.95
Millington (village) Kendall County	10	2.11
Scottville (village) Macoupin County	3	2.10
New Burnside (village) Johnson County	5	1.91
Stonefort (village) Williamson County	5	1.85
Berlin (village) Sangamon County	2	1.53

Top 10 Places Sorted by Percent
Based on places with populations of 10,000 or more

Place	Number	%
Jacksonville (city) Morgan County	154	0.81
Washington (city) Tazewell County	56	0.51
Springfield (city) Sangamon County	455	0.41
Swansea (village) Saint Clair County	32	0.31
Barrington (village) Cook County	31	0.31
Carbondale (city) Jackson County	62	0.30
Grayslake (village) Lake County	49	0.27
Frankfort (village) Will County	26	0.25
Evanston (city) Cook County	165	0.22
Urbana (city) Champaign County	72	0.20

Notes: (cdp) census designated place; Refer to the User's Guide in the front of the book for more detailed information.

Romanian

Top 10 Places Sorted by Number
Based on all places, regardless of population

Place	Number	%
Chicago (city) Cook County	8,227	0.28
Skokie (village) Cook County	822	1.30
Aurora (city) Kane County	711	0.50
Des Plaines (city) Cook County	408	0.70
Lincolnwood (village) Cook County	382	3.09
Morton Grove (village) Cook County	376	1.67
Evanston (city) Cook County	372	0.50
Highland Park (city) Lake County	314	1.00
Buffalo Grove (village) Lake County	302	0.71
Northbrook (village) Cook County	297	0.89

Top 10 Places Sorted by Percent
Based on all places, regardless of population

Place	Number	%
Lincolnwood (village) Cook County	382	3.09
Yorkville (city) Kendall County	150	2.40
Morton Grove (village) Cook County	376	1.67
Mettawa (village) Lake County	5	1.54
Forest Lake (cdp) Lake County	22	1.42
Glencoe (village) Cook County	124	1.40
Round Lake (village) Lake County	79	1.38
Montgomery (village) Kane County	69	1.37
Skokie (village) Cook County	822	1.30
Dover (village) Bureau County	2	1.27

Top 10 Places Sorted by Percent
Based on places with populations of 10,000 or more

Place	Number	%
Lincolnwood (village) Cook County	382	3.09
Morton Grove (village) Cook County	376	1.67
Skokie (village) Cook County	822	1.30
Highland Park (city) Lake County	314	1.00
Vernon Hills (village) Lake County	193	0.94
Northbrook (village) Cook County	297	0.89
Niles (village) Cook County	266	0.88
North Aurora (village) Kane County	84	0.79
Deerfield (village) Lake County	135	0.73
Buffalo Grove (village) Lake County	302	0.71

Russian

Top 10 Places Sorted by Number
Based on all places, regardless of population

Place	Number	%
Chicago (city) Cook County	28,845	1.00
Buffalo Grove (village) Lake County	6,542	15.36
Skokie (village) Cook County	5,609	8.86
Highland Park (city) Lake County	5,157	16.43
Northbrook (village) Cook County	4,101	12.27
Evanston (city) Cook County	2,892	3.90
Glenview (village) Cook County	2,510	6.02
Deerfield (village) Lake County	2,473	13.37
Wheeling (village) Cook County	2,334	6.78
Arlington Heights (village) Cook County	2,046	2.69

Top 10 Places Sorted by Percent
Based on all places, regardless of population

Place	Number	%
Highland Park (city) Lake County	5,157	16.43
Buffalo Grove (village) Lake County	6,542	15.36
Deerfield (village) Lake County	2,473	13.37
Northbrook (village) Cook County	4,101	12.27
Riverwoods (village) Lake County	449	11.90
Glencoe (village) Cook County	1,042	11.80
Skokie (village) Cook County	5,609	8.86
Lincolnwood (village) Cook County	1,078	8.72
Lincolnshire (village) Lake County	528	8.54

Wheeling (village) Cook County 2,334 6.78

Top 10 Places Sorted by Percent
Based on places with populations of 10,000 or more

Place	Number	%
Highland Park (city) Lake County	5,157	16.43
Buffalo Grove (village) Lake County	6,542	15.36
Deerfield (village) Lake County	2,473	13.37
Northbrook (village) Cook County	4,101	12.27
Skokie (village) Cook County	5,609	8.86
Lincolnwood (village) Cook County	1,078	8.72
Wheeling (village) Cook County	2,334	6.78
Glenview (village) Cook County	2,510	6.02
Wilmette (village) Cook County	1,631	5.89
Vernon Hills (village) Lake County	1,214	5.89

Scandinavian

Top 10 Places Sorted by Number
Based on all places, regardless of population

Place	Number	%
Chicago (city) Cook County	1,649	0.06
Naperville (city) Du Page County	347	0.27
Aurora (city) Kane County	295	0.21
Rockford (city) Winnebago County	217	0.14
Des Plaines (city) Cook County	175	0.30
Arlington Heights (village) Cook County	168	0.22
Palatine (village) Cook County	166	0.25
Wheaton (city) Du Page County	159	0.29
Downers Grove (village) Du Page County	158	0.32
Champaign (city) Champaign County	156	0.23

Top 10 Places Sorted by Percent
Based on all places, regardless of population

Place	Number	%
Barrington Hills (village) Cook County	113	2.72
Hecker (village) Monroe County	12	2.37
Channel Lake (cdp) Lake County	34	1.90
Adeline (village) Ogle County	2	1.42
Lake Barrington (village) Lake County	66	1.38
Sherrard (village) Mercer County	9	1.31
Peotone (village) Will County	46	1.30
Ashkum (village) Iroquois County	9	1.26
Mettawa (village) Lake County	4	1.23
Harvard (city) McHenry County	92	1.13

Top 10 Places Sorted by Percent
Based on places with populations of 10,000 or more

Place	Number	%
Barrington (village) Cook County	83	0.83
Sycamore (city) De Kalb County	98	0.81
Cary (village) McHenry County	100	0.65
Lake in the Hills (village) McHenry County	133	0.57
Burr Ridge (village) Du Page County	59	0.57
Machesney Park (village) Winnebago County	109	0.53
Hinsdale (village) Du Page County	82	0.47
Wilmette (village) Cook County	105	0.38
De Kalb (city) De Kalb County	140	0.36
Hanover Park (village) Cook County	140	0.36

Scotch-Irish

Top 10 Places Sorted by Number
Based on all places, regardless of population

Place	Number	%
Chicago (city) Cook County	11,142	0.38
Springfield (city) Sangamon County	1,951	1.74
Naperville (city) Du Page County	1,913	1.49
Rockford (city) Winnebago County	1,614	1.08
Peoria (city) Peoria County	1,547	1.37
Aurora (city) Kane County	1,278	0.89
Decatur (city) Macon County	1,227	1.49

Evanston (city) Cook County 1,201 1.62
Bloomington (city) McLean County 1,117 1.72
Champaign (city) Champaign County 1,033 1.52

Top 10 Places Sorted by Percent
Based on all places, regardless of population

Place	Number	%
Wenonah (village) Montgomery County	5	16.13
Columbus (village) Adams County	10	8.33
Naples (town) Scott County	9	7.76
Huey (village) Clinton County	15	7.58
Verona (village) Grundy County	18	7.17
West Brooklyn (village) Lee County	12	6.70
Biggsville (village) Henderson County	22	6.36
Irwin (village) Kankakee County	4	6.35
Elizabethtown (village) Hardin County	22	6.04
Iroquois (village) Iroquois County	11	5.91

Top 10 Places Sorted by Percent
Based on places with populations of 10,000 or more

Place	Number	%
Herrin (city) Williamson County	356	3.21
Libertyville (village) Lake County	514	2.48
Marion (city) Williamson County	388	2.43
Lake Forest (city) Lake County	468	2.34
Loves Park (city) Winnebago County	439	2.21
Winnetka (village) Cook County	271	2.19
Sycamore (city) De Kalb County	264	2.18
Godfrey (village) Madison County	343	2.10
Brookfield (village) Cook County	398	2.09
Galesburg (city) Knox County	704	2.08

Scottish

Top 10 Places Sorted by Number
Based on all places, regardless of population

Place	Number	%
Chicago (city) Cook County	14,285	0.49
Springfield (city) Sangamon County	2,199	1.96
Naperville (city) Du Page County	2,178	1.70
Aurora (city) Kane County	1,947	1.36
Rockford (city) Winnebago County	1,811	1.21
Peoria (city) Peoria County	1,663	1.47
Wheaton (city) Du Page County	1,581	2.85
Evanston (city) Cook County	1,568	2.11
Champaign (city) Champaign County	1,368	2.02
Arlington Heights (village) Cook County	1,296	1.70

Top 10 Places Sorted by Percent
Based on all places, regardless of population

Place	Number	%
Simpson (village) Johnson County	6	10.53
Dorchester (village) Macoupin County	16	9.94
Mount Clare (village) Macoupin County	39	9.54
Standard City (village) Macoupin County	13	9.42
Elsah (village) Jersey County	58	9.28
Keensburg (village) Wabash County	21	8.86
Mettawa (village) Lake County	25	7.72
Rock Island Arsenal (cdp) Rock Island County	10	7.52
Gillespie (city) Macoupin County	237	7.09
Dover (village) Bureau County	11	6.96

Top 10 Places Sorted by Percent
Based on places with populations of 10,000 or more

Place	Number	%
Winnetka (village) Cook County	495	4.00
Glen Ellyn (village) Du Page County	975	3.61
Lake Forest (city) Lake County	720	3.60
Barrington (village) Cook County	343	3.42
Washington (city) Tazewell County	330	3.03
Batavia (city) Kane County	685	2.86
Wheaton (city) Du Page County	1,581	2.85

Notes: (cdp) census designated place; Refer to the User's Guide in the front of the book for more detailed information.

Place	Number	%
River Forest (village) Cook County	314	2.70
Hinsdale (village) Du Page County	464	2.65
Warrenville (city) Du Page County	344	2.61

Serbian

Top 10 Places Sorted by Number
Based on all places, regardless of population

Place	Number	%
Chicago (city) Cook County	5,044	0.17
Niles (village) Cook County	439	1.46
Lansing (village) Cook County	385	1.37
Berwyn (city) Cook County	357	0.66
Naperville (city) Du Page County	286	0.22
Elmhurst (city) Du Page County	262	0.61
Lyons (village) Cook County	248	2.45
Carol Stream (village) Du Page County	180	0.45
Countryside (city) Cook County	174	2.91
Westmont (village) Du Page County	167	0.69

Top 10 Places Sorted by Percent
Based on all places, regardless of population

Place	Number	%
East Brooklyn (village) Grundy County	8	7.84
Countryside (city) Cook County	174	2.91
Burlington (village) Kane County	12	2.60
Lyons (village) Cook County	248	2.45
Granville (village) Putnam County	29	2.03
Buckner (village) Franklin County	9	1.88
Willow Springs (village) Cook County	88	1.78
North Barrington (village) Lake County	48	1.66
Niles (village) Cook County	439	1.46
Lansing (village) Cook County	385	1.37

Top 10 Places Sorted by Percent
Based on places with populations of 10,000 or more

Place	Number	%
Lyons (village) Cook County	248	2.45
Niles (village) Cook County	439	1.46
Lansing (village) Cook County	385	1.37
Lincolnwood (village) Cook County	123	1.00
Burr Ridge (village) Du Page County	96	0.93
Norridge (village) Cook County	109	0.74
South Holland (village) Cook County	157	0.70
Westmont (village) Du Page County	167	0.69
Berwyn (city) Cook County	357	0.66
Villa Park (village) Du Page County	147	0.66

Slavic

Top 10 Places Sorted by Number
Based on all places, regardless of population

Place	Number	%
Chicago (city) Cook County	846	0.03
Naperville (city) Du Page County	157	0.12
Joliet (city) Will County	134	0.13
Gurnee (village) Lake County	103	0.36
Rosemont (village) Cook County	78	1.87
Wheaton (city) Du Page County	63	0.11
Belleville (city) Saint Clair County	57	0.14
Villa Park (village) Du Page County	56	0.25
Champaign (city) Champaign County	53	0.08
Waukegan (city) Lake County	52	0.06

Top 10 Places Sorted by Percent
Based on all places, regardless of population

Place	Number	%
Bureau Junction (village) Bureau County	12	3.32
Rosemont (village) Cook County	78	1.87
North Utica (village) La Salle County	17	1.82
McCook (village) Cook County	4	1.76
Maeystown (village) Monroe County	2	1.38

Place	Number	%
Forest Lake (cdp) Lake County	21	1.35
Coalton (village) Montgomery County	4	1.34
Matherville (village) Mercer County	9	1.17
Ellsworth (village) McLean County	3	1.11
Rockdale (village) Will County	21	1.10

Top 10 Places Sorted by Percent
Based on places with populations of 10,000 or more

Place	Number	%
Gurnee (village) Lake County	103	0.36
Crest Hill (city) Will County	43	0.33
Villa Park (village) Du Page County	56	0.25
La Grange Park (village) Cook County	30	0.23
Wood Dale (city) Du Page County	31	0.22
Plainfield (village) Will County	23	0.18
Kewanee (city) Henry County	21	0.16
Justice (village) Cook County	19	0.16
Edwardsville (city) Madison County	32	0.15
Brookfield (village) Cook County	28	0.15

Slovak

Top 10 Places Sorted by Number
Based on all places, regardless of population

Place	Number	%
Chicago (city) Cook County	6,238	0.22
Streator (city) La Salle County	1,653	11.70
Joliet (city) Will County	1,456	1.37
Naperville (city) Du Page County	809	0.63
Oak Lawn (village) Cook County	533	0.96
Berwyn (city) Cook County	515	0.95
Tinley Park (village) Cook County	454	0.94
Downers Grove (village) Du Page County	448	0.92
Springfield (city) Sangamon County	448	0.40
Burbank (city) Cook County	418	1.50

Top 10 Places Sorted by Percent
Based on all places, regardless of population

Place	Number	%
Streator (city) La Salle County	1,653	11.70
White City (village) Macoupin County	13	6.60
Kangley (village) La Salle County	14	4.70
Mount Olive (city) Macoupin County	101	4.69
Ransom (village) La Salle County	18	3.90
Naplate (village) La Salle County	20	3.80
Williamson (village) Madison County	8	3.72
Shorewood (village) Will County	277	3.56
Sawyerville (village) Macoupin County	11	3.46
Benld (city) Macoupin County	50	3.25

Top 10 Places Sorted by Percent
Based on places with populations of 10,000 or more

Place	Number	%
Streator (city) La Salle County	1,653	11.70
Lockport (city) Will County	232	1.57
Burbank (city) Cook County	418	1.50
Lisle (village) Du Page County	312	1.48
Joliet (city) Will County	1,456	1.37
New Lenox (village) Will County	241	1.37
Westchester (village) Cook County	214	1.28
Crest Hill (city) Will County	162	1.24
Plainfield (village) Will County	152	1.17
Western Springs (village) Cook County	144	1.14

Slovene

Top 10 Places Sorted by Number
Based on all places, regardless of population

Place	Number	%
Joliet (city) Will County	1,770	1.67
Chicago (city) Cook County	1,555	0.05
Waukegan (city) Lake County	444	0.50

Place	Number	%
Naperville (city) Du Page County	351	0.27
Crest Hill (city) Will County	349	2.68
Shorewood (village) Will County	323	4.15
La Salle (city) La Salle County	258	2.63
Downers Grove (village) Du Page County	206	0.42
Lockport (city) Will County	190	1.28
Channahon (village) Will County	177	2.42

Top 10 Places Sorted by Percent
Based on all places, regardless of population

Place	Number	%
Wayne (village) Kane County	90	4.29
Shorewood (village) Will County	323	4.15
Rockdale (village) Will County	75	3.93
Reddick (village) Kankakee County	10	3.91
Oglesby (city) La Salle County	124	3.44
Crest Hill (city) Will County	349	2.68
La Salle (city) La Salle County	258	2.63
Channahon (village) Will County	177	2.42
Seatonville (village) Bureau County	6	1.88
Peru (city) La Salle County	174	1.77

Top 10 Places Sorted by Percent
Based on places with populations of 10,000 or more

Place	Number	%
Crest Hill (city) Will County	349	2.68
Joliet (city) Will County	1,770	1.67
Lockport (city) Will County	190	1.28
Lindenhurst (village) Lake County	131	1.04
New Lenox (village) Will County	137	0.78
Lemont (village) Cook County	94	0.71
Plainfield (village) Will County	71	0.55
Waukegan (city) Lake County	444	0.50
Libertyville (village) Lake County	93	0.45
Downers Grove (village) Du Page County	206	0.42

Soviet Union

Top 10 Places Sorted by Number
Based on all places, regardless of population

Place	Number	%
Chicago (city) Cook County	60	0.00
Northbrook (village) Cook County	34	0.10
Highland Park (city) Lake County	28	0.09
Morton Grove (village) Cook County	15	0.07
Naperville (city) Du Page County	9	0.01
Lincolnwood (village) Cook County	5	0.04
Galatia (village) Saline County	4	0.38

Top 10 Places Sorted by Percent
Based on all places, regardless of population

Place	Number	%
Galatia (village) Saline County	4	0.38
Northbrook (village) Cook County	34	0.10
Highland Park (city) Lake County	28	0.09
Morton Grove (village) Cook County	15	0.07
Lincolnwood (village) Cook County	5	0.04
Naperville (city) Du Page County	9	0.01
Chicago (city) Cook County	60	0.00

Top 10 Places Sorted by Percent
Based on places with populations of 10,000 or more

Place	Number	%
Northbrook (village) Cook County	34	0.10
Highland Park (city) Lake County	28	0.09
Morton Grove (village) Cook County	15	0.07
Lincolnwood (village) Cook County	5	0.04
Naperville (city) Du Page County	9	0.01
Chicago (city) Cook County	60	0.00

Notes: (cdp) census designated place; Refer to the User's Guide in the front of the book for more detailed information.

Swedish

Top 10 Places Sorted by Number
Based on all places, regardless of population

Place	Number	%
Chicago (city) Cook County	24,882	0.86
Rockford (city) Winnebago County	14,720	9.83
Naperville (city) Du Page County	4,529	3.53
Moline (city) Rock Island County	4,073	9.32
Galesburg (city) Knox County	3,374	9.97
Arlington Heights (village) Cook County	3,307	4.35
Wheaton (city) Du Page County	3,197	5.77
Aurora (city) Kane County	3,129	2.18
Elgin (city) Kane County	2,978	3.17
Joliet (city) Will County	2,645	2.49

Top 10 Places Sorted by Percent
Based on all places, regardless of population

Place	Number	%
Rio (village) Knox County	101	40.40
Altona (village) Knox County	176	31.88
Woodhull (village) Henry County	237	28.69
Bishop Hill (village) Henry County	36	26.28
Oneida (city) Knox County	174	22.57
Orion (village) Henry County	381	22.46
Hooppole (village) Henry County	34	20.86
Cambridge (village) Henry County	455	20.54
Andover (village) Henry County	122	20.54
Windsor (village) Mercer County	145	19.97

Top 10 Places Sorted by Percent
Based on places with populations of 10,000 or more

Place	Number	%
Loves Park (city) Winnebago County	2,149	10.80
Galesburg (city) Knox County	3,374	9.97
Rockford (city) Winnebago County	14,720	9.83
Moline (city) Rock Island County	4,073	9.32
Machesney Park (village) Winnebago County	1,847	8.93
Sycamore (city) De Kalb County	1,030	8.49
Batavia (city) Kane County	1,930	8.07
Kewanee (city) Henry County	987	7.63
Geneva (city) Kane County	1,479	7.56
Libertyville (village) Lake County	1,516	7.33

Swiss

Top 10 Places Sorted by Number
Based on all places, regardless of population

Place	Number	%
Chicago (city) Cook County	3,008	0.10
Naperville (city) Du Page County	681	0.53
Peoria (city) Peoria County	649	0.57
Rockford (city) Winnebago County	642	0.43
Highland (city) Madison County	541	6.46
Elgin (city) Kane County	530	0.56
Freeport (city) Stephenson County	478	1.81
Evanston (city) Cook County	463	0.62
Morton (village) Tazewell County	456	3.03
Champaign (city) Champaign County	370	0.55

Top 10 Places Sorted by Percent
Based on all places, regardless of population

Place	Number	%
Congerville (village) Woodford County	52	11.61
Orangeville (village) Stephenson County	69	9.13
Roanoke (village) Woodford County	159	8.01
Goodfield (village) Woodford County	49	7.22
Winslow (village) Stephenson County	24	6.90
Rock City (village) Stephenson County	23	6.82
Davis (village) Stephenson County	44	6.77
Gridley (village) McLean County	95	6.68
Ridott (village) Stephenson County	9	6.62

| **Highland** (city) Madison County | 541 | 6.46 |

Top 10 Places Sorted by Percent
Based on places with populations of 10,000 or more

Place	Number	%
Morton (village) Tazewell County	456	3.03
Freeport (city) Stephenson County	478	1.81
River Forest (village) Cook County	120	1.03
Washington (city) Tazewell County	107	0.98
Winnetka (village) Cook County	120	0.97
Plainfield (village) Will County	119	0.91
Lake Forest (city) Lake County	178	0.89
Pontiac (city) Livingston County	102	0.86
Dixon (city) Lee County	120	0.75
Elmhurst (city) Du Page County	286	0.67

Turkish

Top 10 Places Sorted by Number
Based on all places, regardless of population

Place	Number	%
Chicago (city) Cook County	1,178	0.04
Naperville (city) Du Page County	211	0.16
Evanston (city) Cook County	185	0.25
Schaumburg (village) Cook County	141	0.19
Hoffman Estates (village) Cook County	130	0.26
Summit (village) Cook County	112	1.05
Wheeling (village) Cook County	92	0.27
Roselle (village) Du Page County	83	0.36
Champaign (city) Champaign County	70	0.10
Urbana (city) Champaign County	65	0.18

Top 10 Places Sorted by Percent
Based on all places, regardless of population

Place	Number	%
Benson (village) Woodford County	8	1.95
Cedar Point (village) La Salle County	3	1.11
Summit (village) Cook County	112	1.05
Easton (village) Mason County	4	1.04
Barry (city) Pike County	12	0.90
Metamora (village) Woodford County	18	0.67
Cordova (village) Rock Island County	4	0.64
West Dundee (village) Kane County	25	0.46
Richmond (village) McHenry County	5	0.45
Schiller Park (village) Cook County	48	0.41

Top 10 Places Sorted by Percent
Based on places with populations of 10,000 or more

Place	Number	%
Summit (village) Cook County	112	1.05
Schiller Park (village) Cook County	48	0.41
Roselle (village) Du Page County	83	0.36
Lincolnwood (village) Cook County	41	0.33
Wheeling (village) Cook County	92	0.27
Hoffman Estates (village) Cook County	130	0.26
Evanston (city) Cook County	185	0.25
Western Springs (village) Cook County	25	0.20
Schaumburg (village) Cook County	141	0.19
Urbana (city) Champaign County	65	0.18

Ukrainian

Top 10 Places Sorted by Number
Based on all places, regardless of population

Place	Number	%
Chicago (city) Cook County	13,579	0.47
Skokie (village) Cook County	1,206	1.90
Buffalo Grove (village) Lake County	1,017	2.39
Palatine (village) Cook County	785	1.20
Naperville (city) Du Page County	658	0.51
Schaumburg (village) Cook County	626	0.84
Arlington Heights (village) Cook County	617	0.81

Wheeling (village) Cook County	608	1.77
Glenview (village) Cook County	546	1.31
Des Plaines (village) Cook County	532	0.91

Top 10 Places Sorted by Percent
Based on all places, regardless of population

Place	Number	%
McCook (village) Cook County	7	3.08
Peotone (village) Will County	96	2.71
Buffalo Grove (village) Lake County	1,017	2.39
Lake Catherine (cdp) Lake County	32	2.22
Vernon Hills (village) Lake County	437	2.12
Skokie (village) Cook County	1,206	1.90
Naplate (village) La Salle County	10	1.90
Wheeling (village) Cook County	608	1.77
Riverwoods (village) Lake County	66	1.75
Niles (village) Cook County	507	1.68

Top 10 Places Sorted by Percent
Based on places with populations of 10,000 or more

Place	Number	%
Buffalo Grove (village) Lake County	1,017	2.39
Vernon Hills (village) Lake County	437	2.12
Skokie (village) Cook County	1,206	1.90
Wheeling (village) Cook County	608	1.77
Niles (village) Cook County	507	1.68
Elmwood Park (village) Cook County	390	1.54
Highland Park (city) Lake County	465	1.48
Glenview (village) Cook County	546	1.31
Morton Grove (village) Cook County	294	1.31
Mokena (village) Will County	179	1.22

United States or American

Top 10 Places Sorted by Number
Based on all places, regardless of population

Place	Number	%
Chicago (city) Cook County	38,779	1.34
Decatur (city) Macon County	8,418	10.25
Springfield (city) Sangamon County	7,965	7.10
Peoria (city) Peoria County	6,366	5.64
Rockford (city) Winnebago County	6,352	4.24
Bloomington (city) McLean County	4,589	7.06
Aurora (city) Kane County	4,260	2.97
Quincy (city) Adams County	3,626	9.00
Pekin (city) Tazewell County	3,443	10.17
Naperville (city) Du Page County	3,264	2.54

Top 10 Places Sorted by Percent
Based on all places, regardless of population

Place	Number	%
Valley City (village) Pike County	18	100.00
Rockwood (village) Randolph County	38	80.85
Campus (village) Livingston County	62	52.10
Eldred (village) Greene County	109	49.77
La Prairie (village) Adams County	25	45.45
Emington (village) Livingston County	56	43.75
Pulaski (village) Pulaski County	120	41.10
Humboldt (village) Coles County	197	40.45
Alma (village) Marion County	158	39.80
Coatsburg (village) Adams County	85	39.35

Top 10 Places Sorted by Percent
Based on places with populations of 10,000 or more

Place	Number	%
Mount Vernon (city) Jefferson County	2,594	15.97
Mattoon (city) Coles County	2,907	15.85
Herrin (city) Williamson County	1,449	13.07
Wood River (city) Madison County	1,426	12.73
Lincoln (city) Logan County	1,905	12.39
East Peoria (city) Tazewell County	2,795	12.21
Taylorville (city) Christian County	1,353	11.95

Notes: (cdp) census designated place; Refer to the User's Guide in the front of the book for more detailed information.

Place	Number	%
Canton (city) Fulton County	1,732	11.36
Marion (city) Williamson County	1,786	11.17
Centralia (city) Marion County	1,575	11.13

Welsh

Top 10 Places Sorted by Number
Based on all places, regardless of population

Place	Number	%
Chicago (city) Cook County	5,226	0.18
Naperville (city) Du Page County	945	0.74
Springfield (city) Sangamon County	847	0.75
Rockford (city) Winnebago County	693	0.46
Aurora (city) Kane County	568	0.40
Evanston (city) Cook County	523	0.70
Peoria (city) Peoria County	502	0.44
Decatur (city) Macon County	485	0.59
Wheaton (city) Du Page County	453	0.82
Bloomington (city) McLean County	437	0.67

Top 10 Places Sorted by Percent
Based on all places, regardless of population

Place	Number	%
Panola (village) Woodford County	4	12.50
Bishop Hill (village) Henry County	8	5.84
Prairie City (village) McDonough County	26	5.58
Pistakee Highlands (cdp) McHenry County	173	4.50
Nilwood (town) Macoupin County	12	4.24
Mill Shoals (village) White County	9	4.04
Elsah (village) Jersey County	24	3.84
West City (village) Franklin County	26	3.68
La Prairie (village) Adams County	2	3.64
Ludlow (village) Champaign County	10	3.37

Top 10 Places Sorted by Percent
Based on places with populations of 10,000 or more

Place	Number	%
Fairview Heights (city) Saint Clair County	179	1.17
Winnetka (village) Cook County	144	1.16
Barrington (village) Cook County	107	1.07
Batavia (city) Kane County	253	1.06
Glen Carbon (village) Madison County	111	1.06
Granite City (city) Madison County	319	1.01
Glen Ellyn (village) Du Page County	273	1.01
Morton (village) Tazewell County	151	1.00
Frankfort (village) Will County	98	0.96
Crystal Lake (city) McHenry County	358	0.95

West Indian, excluding Hispanic

Top 10 Places Sorted by Number
Based on all places, regardless of population

Place	Number	%
Chicago (city) Cook County	11,698	0.40
Evanston (city) Cook County	3,448	4.64
Waukegan (city) Lake County	722	0.82
Skokie (village) Cook County	640	1.01
North Chicago (city) Lake County	433	1.20
Bolingbrook (village) Will County	355	0.63
Calumet City (city) Cook County	313	0.80
Oak Park (village) Cook County	271	0.52
Country Club Hills (city) Cook County	262	1.62
Dolton (village) Cook County	259	1.01

Top 10 Places Sorted by Percent
Based on all places, regardless of population

Place	Number	%
Evanston (city) Cook County	3,448	4.64
Yale (village) Jasper County	3	3.49
Olympia Fields (village) Cook County	121	2.56
University Park (village) Will County	150	2.26
Country Club Hills (city) Cook County	262	1.62

Place	Number	%
Flossmoor (village) Cook County	124	1.33
Buckingham (village) Kankakee County	3	1.29
North Chicago (city) Lake County	433	1.20
Royal Lakes (village) Macoupin County	2	1.14
South Holland (village) Cook County	237	1.06

Top 10 Places Sorted by Percent
Based on places with populations of 10,000 or more

Place	Number	%
Evanston (city) Cook County	3,448	4.64
Country Club Hills (city) Cook County	262	1.62
North Chicago (city) Lake County	433	1.20
South Holland (village) Cook County	237	1.06
Skokie (village) Cook County	640	1.01
Dolton (village) Cook County	259	1.01
Bellwood (village) Cook County	187	0.91
Zion (city) Lake County	205	0.89
Richton Park (village) Cook County	111	0.89
Waukegan (city) Lake County	722	0.82

West Indian: Bahamian, excluding Hispanic

Top 10 Places Sorted by Number
Based on all places, regardless of population

Place	Number	%
Chicago (city) Cook County	114	0.00
Evanston (city) Cook County	24	0.03
Loves Park (city) Winnebago County	16	0.08
Westmont (village) Du Page County	12	0.05
Calumet City (city) Cook County	11	0.03
Geneva (city) Kane County	10	0.05
Naperville (city) Du Page County	9	0.01
Broadview (village) Cook County	8	0.10
Carbondale (city) Jackson County	8	0.04
North Chicago (city) Lake County	8	0.02

Top 10 Places Sorted by Percent
Based on all places, regardless of population

Place	Number	%
Braidwood (city) Will County	7	0.13
Broadview (village) Cook County	8	0.10
Loves Park (city) Winnebago County	16	0.08
Westmont (village) Du Page County	12	0.05
Geneva (city) Kane County	10	0.05
Hazel Crest (village) Cook County	7	0.05
Carbondale (city) Jackson County	8	0.04
Evanston (city) Cook County	24	0.03
Calumet City (city) Cook County	11	0.03
North Chicago (city) Lake County	8	0.02

Top 10 Places Sorted by Percent
Based on places with populations of 10,000 or more

Place	Number	%
Loves Park (city) Winnebago County	16	0.08
Westmont (village) Du Page County	12	0.05
Geneva (city) Kane County	10	0.05
Hazel Crest (village) Cook County	7	0.05
Carbondale (city) Jackson County	8	0.04
Evanston (city) Cook County	24	0.03
Calumet City (city) Cook County	11	0.03
North Chicago (city) Lake County	8	0.02
South Holland (village) Cook County	5	0.02
Park Forest (village) Cook County	4	0.02

West Indian: Barbadian, excluding Hispanic

Top 10 Places Sorted by Number
Based on all places, regardless of population

Place	Number	%
Chicago (city) Cook County	144	0.00

Place	Number	%
Oak Park (village) Cook County	34	0.06
Arlington Heights (village) Cook County	29	0.04
Maywood (village) Cook County	26	0.10
Hanover Park (village) Cook County	24	0.06
North Chicago (city) Lake County	17	0.05
Shiloh (village) Saint Clair County	12	0.15
Broadview (village) Cook County	10	0.12
Bolingbrook (village) Will County	9	0.02
Urbana (city) Champaign County	6	0.02

Top 10 Places Sorted by Percent
Based on all places, regardless of population

Place	Number	%
Shiloh (village) Saint Clair County	12	0.15
Broadview (village) Cook County	10	0.12
Maywood (village) Cook County	26	0.10
Oak Park (village) Cook County	34	0.06
Hanover Park (village) Cook County	24	0.06
North Chicago (city) Lake County	17	0.05
Arlington Heights (village) Cook County	29	0.04
Bolingbrook (village) Will County	9	0.02
Urbana (city) Champaign County	6	0.02
Batavia (city) Kane County	5	0.02

Top 10 Places Sorted by Percent
Based on places with populations of 10,000 or more

Place	Number	%
Maywood (village) Cook County	26	0.10
Oak Park (village) Cook County	34	0.06
Hanover Park (village) Cook County	24	0.06
North Chicago (city) Lake County	17	0.05
Arlington Heights (village) Cook County	29	0.04
Bolingbrook (village) Will County	9	0.02
Urbana (city) Champaign County	6	0.02
Batavia (city) Kane County	5	0.02
Skokie (village) Cook County	6	0.01
Danville (city) Vermilion County	4	0.01

West Indian: Belizean, excluding Hispanic

Top 10 Places Sorted by Number
Based on all places, regardless of population

Place	Number	%
Chicago (city) Cook County	2,244	0.08
Evanston (city) Cook County	488	0.66
Waukegan (city) Lake County	366	0.42
Zion (city) Lake County	84	0.36
Wheeling (village) Cook County	83	0.24
Skokie (village) Cook County	62	0.10
Berwyn (city) Cook County	60	0.11
North Chicago (city) Lake County	56	0.16
Maywood (village) Cook County	48	0.18
Sauk Village (village) Cook County	46	0.44

Top 10 Places Sorted by Percent
Based on all places, regardless of population

Place	Number	%
Evanston (city) Cook County	488	0.66
Lynwood (village) Cook County	40	0.54
Sauk Village (village) Cook County	46	0.44
Waukegan (city) Lake County	366	0.42
Alorton (village) Saint Clair County	11	0.40
Zion (city) Lake County	84	0.36
Hometown (city) Cook County	13	0.29
Tonica (village) La Salle County	2	0.29
Fairmont (cdp) Will County	7	0.27
Wheeling (village) Cook County	83	0.24

Top 10 Places Sorted by Percent
Based on places with populations of 10,000 or more

Place	Number	%
Evanston (city) Cook County	488	0.66

Notes: (cdp) census designated place; Refer to the User's Guide in the front of the book for more detailed information.

	Number	%
Sauk Village (village) Cook County	46	0.44
Waukegan (city) Lake County	366	0.42
Zion (city) Lake County	84	0.36
Wheeling (village) Cook County	83	0.24
Country Club Hills (city) Cook County	36	0.22
Markham (city) Cook County	27	0.21
Maywood (village) Cook County	48	0.18
North Chicago (city) Lake County	56	0.16
Evergreen Park (village) Cook County	32	0.15

West Indian: Bermudan, excluding Hispanic

Top 10 Places Sorted by Number
Based on all places, regardless of population

Place	Number	%
Christopher (city) Franklin County	17	0.62
Chicago (city) Cook County	17	0.00
Edwardsville (city) Madison County	10	0.05
Champaign (city) Champaign County	5	0.01

Top 10 Places Sorted by Percent
Based on all places, regardless of population

Place	Number	%
Christopher (city) Franklin County	17	0.62
Edwardsville (city) Madison County	10	0.05
Champaign (city) Champaign County	5	0.01
Chicago (city) Cook County	17	0.00

Top 10 Places Sorted by Percent
Based on places with populations of 10,000 or more

Place	Number	%
Edwardsville (city) Madison County	10	0.05
Champaign (city) Champaign County	5	0.01
Chicago (city) Cook County	17	0.00

West Indian: British West Indian, excluding Hispanic

Top 10 Places Sorted by Number
Based on all places, regardless of population

Place	Number	%
Chicago (city) Cook County	143	0.00
Evanston (city) Cook County	46	0.06
Bensenville (village) Du Page County	41	0.20
North Chicago (city) Lake County	30	0.08
Oak Park (village) Cook County	30	0.06
Bourbonnais (village) Kankakee County	22	0.14
Bolingbrook (village) Will County	20	0.04
Broadview (village) Cook County	19	0.23
Schaumburg (village) Cook County	11	0.01
Blue Island (city) Cook County	9	0.04

Top 10 Places Sorted by Percent
Based on all places, regardless of population

Place	Number	%
Broadview (village) Cook County	19	0.23
Bensenville (village) Du Page County	41	0.20
Bourbonnais (village) Kankakee County	22	0.14
Kildeer (village) Lake County	4	0.11
North Chicago (city) Lake County	30	0.08
Lyons (village) Cook County	7	0.07
Evanston (city) Cook County	46	0.06
Oak Park (village) Cook County	30	0.06
Glenwood (village) Cook County	5	0.06
Bolingbrook (village) Will County	20	0.04

Top 10 Places Sorted by Percent
Based on places with populations of 10,000 or more

Place	Number	%
Bensenville (village) Du Page County	41	0.20

	Number	%
Bourbonnais (village) Kankakee County	22	0.14
North Chicago (city) Lake County	30	0.08
Lyons (village) Cook County	7	0.07
Evanston (city) Cook County	46	0.06
Oak Park (village) Cook County	30	0.06
Bolingbrook (village) Will County	20	0.04
Blue Island (city) Cook County	9	0.04
Zion (city) Lake County	7	0.03
Streamwood (village) Cook County	6	0.02

West Indian: Dutch West Indian, excluding Hispanic

Top 10 Places Sorted by Number
Based on all places, regardless of population

Place	Number	%
Chicago (city) Cook County	32	0.00
Mount Vernon (city) Jefferson County	20	0.12
Roscoe (village) Winnebago County	19	0.30
Bolingbrook (village) Will County	12	0.02
Calumet City (city) Cook County	11	0.03
Evanston (city) Cook County	11	0.01
Jacksonville (city) Morgan County	10	0.05
Decatur (city) Macon County	9	0.01
Lombard (village) Du Page County	8	0.02
Normal (town) McLean County	8	0.02

Top 10 Places Sorted by Percent
Based on all places, regardless of population

Place	Number	%
Yale (village) Jasper County	3	3.49
Old Mill Creek (village) Lake County	2	0.66
New Haven (village) Gallatin County	2	0.46
Tower Hill (village) Shelby County	2	0.33
Roscoe (village) Winnebago County	19	0.30
Shannon (village) Carroll County	2	0.24
Kincaid (village) Christian County	3	0.20
New Baden (village) Clinton County	5	0.16
Ashland (village) Cass County	2	0.15
Roodhouse (city) Greene County	3	0.14

Top 10 Places Sorted by Percent
Based on places with populations of 10,000 or more

Place	Number	%
Mount Vernon (city) Jefferson County	20	0.12
Lyons (village) Cook County	7	0.07
Jacksonville (city) Morgan County	10	0.05
Pontiac (city) Livingston County	5	0.04
Calumet City (city) Cook County	11	0.03
Bolingbrook (village) Will County	12	0.02
Lombard (village) Du Page County	8	0.02
Normal (town) McLean County	8	0.02
Evanston (city) Cook County	11	0.01
Decatur (city) Macon County	9	0.01

West Indian: Haitian, excluding Hispanic

Top 10 Places Sorted by Number
Based on all places, regardless of population

Place	Number	%
Chicago (city) Cook County	3,104	0.11
Evanston (city) Cook County	856	1.15
Skokie (village) Cook County	264	0.42
Calumet City (city) Cook County	133	0.34
Dolton (village) Cook County	108	0.42
Niles (village) Cook County	80	0.27
Olympia Fields (village) Cook County	75	1.59
Waukegan (city) Lake County	75	0.09
Country Club Hills (city) Cook County	70	0.43
Bolingbrook (village) Will County	65	0.12

Top 10 Places Sorted by Percent
Based on all places, regardless of population

Place	Number	%
Olympia Fields (village) Cook County	75	1.59
Evanston (city) Cook County	856	1.15
Bowen (village) Hancock County	3	0.55
Round Lake (village) Lake County	29	0.51
Winthrop Harbor (village) Lake County	33	0.50
University Park (village) Will County	32	0.48
Country Club Hills (city) Cook County	70	0.43
Skokie (village) Cook County	264	0.42
Dolton (village) Cook County	108	0.42
Dupo (village) Saint Clair County	15	0.37

Top 10 Places Sorted by Percent
Based on places with populations of 10,000 or more

Place	Number	%
Evanston (city) Cook County	856	1.15
Country Club Hills (city) Cook County	70	0.43
Skokie (village) Cook County	264	0.42
Dolton (village) Cook County	108	0.42
Calumet City (city) Cook County	133	0.34
Sterling (city) Whiteside County	47	0.31
Niles (village) Cook County	80	0.27
South Holland (village) Cook County	58	0.26
Lincoln (city) Logan County	40	0.26
Murphysboro (city) Jackson County	28	0.21

West Indian: Jamaican, excluding Hispanic

Top 10 Places Sorted by Number
Based on all places, regardless of population

Place	Number	%
Chicago (city) Cook County	4,778	0.16
Evanston (city) Cook County	1,937	2.61
Skokie (village) Cook County	299	0.47
Waukegan (city) Lake County	241	0.27
North Chicago (city) Lake County	225	0.62
Bolingbrook (village) Will County	220	0.39
South Holland (village) Cook County	159	0.71
Bellwood (village) Cook County	158	0.77
Country Club Hills (city) Cook County	145	0.89
Dolton (village) Cook County	141	0.55

Top 10 Places Sorted by Percent
Based on all places, regardless of population

Place	Number	%
Evanston (city) Cook County	1,937	2.61
Flossmoor (village) Cook County	118	1.27
University Park (village) Will County	67	1.01
Olympia Fields (village) Cook County	46	0.97
Country Club Hills (city) Cook County	145	0.89
Bellwood (village) Cook County	158	0.77
South Holland (village) Cook County	159	0.71
Pulaski (village) Pulaski County	2	0.68
North Chicago (city) Lake County	225	0.62
Richton Park (village) Cook County	75	0.60

Top 10 Places Sorted by Percent
Based on places with populations of 10,000 or more

Place	Number	%
Evanston (city) Cook County	1,937	2.61
Country Club Hills (city) Cook County	145	0.89
Bellwood (village) Cook County	158	0.77
South Holland (village) Cook County	159	0.71
North Chicago (city) Lake County	225	0.62
Richton Park (village) Cook County	75	0.60
Dolton (village) Cook County	141	0.55
Riverdale (village) Cook County	80	0.53
Prospect Heights (city) Cook County	91	0.52
Matteson (village) Cook County	62	0.48

Notes: (cdp) census designated place; Refer to the User's Guide in the front of the book for more detailed information.

West Indian: Trinidadian and Tobagonian, excluding Hispanic

Top 10 Places Sorted by Number
Based on all places, regardless of population

Place	Number	%
Chicago (city) Cook County	407	0.01
Aurora (city) Kane County	55	0.04
Naperville (city) Du Page County	51	0.04
Mount Prospect (village) Cook County	40	0.07
Joliet (city) Will County	35	0.03
Evanston (city) Cook County	32	0.04
Hanover Park (village) Cook County	30	0.08
Harvey (city) Cook County	29	0.10
De Kalb (city) De Kalb County	27	0.07
Crystal Lake (city) McHenry County	22	0.06

Top 10 Places Sorted by Percent
Based on all places, regardless of population

Place	Number	%
Long Grove (village) Lake County	12	0.18
Warrenville (city) Du Page County	15	0.11
University Park (village) Will County	7	0.11
Mascoutah (city) Saint Clair County	6	0.11
Harvey (city) Cook County	29	0.10
River Forest (village) Cook County	11	0.09
Hanover Park (village) Cook County	30	0.08
Mount Prospect (village) Cook County	40	0.07
De Kalb (city) De Kalb County	27	0.07
Crystal Lake (city) McHenry County	22	0.06

Top 10 Places Sorted by Percent
Based on places with populations of 10,000 or more

Place	Number	%
Warrenville (city) Du Page County	15	0.11
Harvey (city) Cook County	29	0.10
River Forest (village) Cook County	11	0.09
Hanover Park (village) Cook County	30	0.08
Mount Prospect (village) Cook County	40	0.07
De Kalb (city) De Kalb County	27	0.07
Crystal Lake (city) McHenry County	22	0.06
Maywood (village) Cook County	16	0.06
Fairview Heights (city) Saint Clair County	8	0.05
Richton Park (village) Cook County	6	0.05

West Indian: U.S. Virgin Islander, excluding Hispanic

Top 10 Places Sorted by Number
Based on all places, regardless of population

Place	Number	%
Chicago (city) Cook County	154	0.01
University Park (village) Will County	33	0.50
Lisle (village) Du Page County	9	0.04
Country Club Hills (city) Cook County	7	0.04
Decatur (city) Macon County	4	0.00
Phoenix (village) Cook County	2	0.09

Top 10 Places Sorted by Percent
Based on all places, regardless of population

Place	Number	%
University Park (village) Will County	33	0.50
Phoenix (village) Cook County	2	0.09
Lisle (village) Du Page County	9	0.04
Country Club Hills (city) Cook County	7	0.04
Chicago (city) Cook County	154	0.01
Decatur (city) Macon County	4	0.00

Top 10 Places Sorted by Percent
Based on places with populations of 10,000 or more

Place	Number	%
Lisle (village) Du Page County	9	0.04
Country Club Hills (city) Cook County	7	0.04
Chicago (city) Cook County	154	0.01
Decatur (city) Macon County	4	0.00

West Indian: West Indian, excluding Hispanic

Top 10 Places Sorted by Number
Based on all places, regardless of population

Place	Number	%
Chicago (city) Cook County	552	0.02
Evanston (city) Cook County	43	0.06
Oak Park (village) Cook County	36	0.07
North Chicago (city) Lake County	34	0.09
Aurora (city) Kane County	31	0.02
Harvey (city) Cook County	27	0.09
Markham (city) Cook County	26	0.21
Waukegan (city) Lake County	21	0.02
Algonquin (village) McHenry County	19	0.08
Buffalo Grove (village) Lake County	19	0.04

Top 10 Places Sorted by Percent
Based on all places, regardless of population

Place	Number	%
Royal Lakes (village) Macoupin County	2	1.14
Lewistown (city) Fulton County	15	0.60
Scott AFB (cdp) Saint Clair County	9	0.32
Mazon (village) Grundy County	2	0.22
Markham (city) Cook County	26	0.21
Forsyth (village) Macon County	4	0.17
Western Springs (village) Cook County	17	0.13
Willowbrook (village) Du Page County	10	0.11
Forest Park (village) Cook County	15	0.10
Murphysboro (city) Jackson County	14	0.10

Top 10 Places Sorted by Percent
Based on places with populations of 10,000 or more

Place	Number	%
Markham (city) Cook County	26	0.21
Western Springs (village) Cook County	17	0.13
Forest Park (village) Cook County	15	0.10
Murphysboro (city) Jackson County	14	0.10
Glen Carbon (village) Madison County	10	0.10
North Chicago (city) Lake County	34	0.09
Harvey (city) Cook County	27	0.09
Algonquin (village) McHenry County	19	0.08
Oswego (village) Kendall County	10	0.08
Oak Park (village) Cook County	36	0.07

West Indian: Other, excluding Hispanic

Top 10 Places Sorted by Number
Based on all places, regardless of population

Place	Number	%
Evanston (city) Cook County	11	0.01
Bridgeport (city) Lawrence County	9	0.40
Oak Park (village) Cook County	9	0.02
Chicago (city) Cook County	9	0.00
O'Fallon (city) Saint Clair County	8	0.04
Buckingham (village) Kankakee County	3	1.29
Rosiclare (city) Hardin County	3	0.25
Hennepin (village) Putnam County	2	0.29

Top 10 Places Sorted by Percent
Based on all places, regardless of population

Place	Number	%
Buckingham (village) Kankakee County	3	1.29

Place	Number	%
Bridgeport (city) Lawrence County	9	0.40
Hennepin (village) Putnam County	2	0.29
Rosiclare (city) Hardin County	3	0.25
O'Fallon (city) Saint Clair County	8	0.04
Oak Park (village) Cook County	9	0.02
Evanston (city) Cook County	11	0.01
Chicago (city) Cook County	9	0.00

Top 10 Places Sorted by Percent
Based on places with populations of 10,000 or more

Place	Number	%
O'Fallon (city) Saint Clair County	8	0.04
Oak Park (village) Cook County	9	0.02
Evanston (city) Cook County	11	0.01
Chicago (city) Cook County	9	0.00

White

Top 10 Places Sorted by Number
Based on all places, regardless of population

Place	Number	%
Chicago (city) Cook County	1,282,320	44.28
Rockford (city) Winnebago County	112,487	74.93
Naperville (city) Du Page County	110,648	86.20
Aurora (city) Kane County	100,854	70.53
Springfield (city) Sangamon County	91,715	82.29
Peoria (city) Peoria County	80,323	71.12
Joliet (city) Will County	75,537	71.11
Arlington Heights (village) Cook County	69,645	91.60
Elgin (city) Kane County	68,992	73.02
Decatur (city) Macon County	64,742	79.09

Top 10 Places Sorted by Percent
Based on all places, regardless of population

Place	Number	%
Meredosia (village) Morgan County	1,041	100.00
Stonington (village) Christian County	960	100.00
Hopedale (village) Tazewell County	929	100.00
Annawan (town) Henry County	868	100.00
Augusta (village) Hancock County	657	100.00
Murrayville (village) Morgan County	644	100.00
Alhambra (village) Madison County	630	100.00
Golden (village) Adams County	629	100.00
Williamsfield (village) Knox County	620	100.00
Strasburg (village) Shelby County	603	100.00

Top 10 Places Sorted by Percent
Based on places with populations of 10,000 or more

Place	Number	%
Washington (city) Tazewell County	10,728	98.96
Western Springs (village) Cook County	12,345	98.82
Effingham (city) Effingham County	12,185	98.39
New Lenox (village) Will County	17,478	98.35
Morton (village) Tazewell County	14,930	98.24
Wood River (city) Madison County	11,096	98.23
Taylorville (city) Christian County	11,221	98.20
East Peoria (city) Tazewell County	22,216	98.14
Lemont (village) Cook County	12,834	97.98
Herrin (city) Williamson County	11,035	97.67

White: Not Hispanic

Top 10 Places Sorted by Number
Based on all places, regardless of population

Place	Number	%
Chicago (city) Cook County	943,299	32.57
Naperville (city) Du Page County	107,484	83.74
Rockford (city) Winnebago County	104,846	69.84
Springfield (city) Sangamon County	90,850	81.51
Peoria (city) Peoria County	78,976	69.93
Aurora (city) Kane County	76,031	53.17
Arlington Heights (village) Cook County	67,192	88.37

Place	Number	%
Joliet (city) Will County	65,854	62.00
Decatur (city) Macon County	64,156	78.37
Schaumburg (village) Cook County	57,832	76.71

Top 10 Places Sorted by Percent
Based on all places, regardless of population

Place	Number	%
Murrayville (village) Morgan County	644	100.00
Alhambra (village) Madison County	630	100.00
Williamsfield (village) Knox County	620	100.00
Essex (village) Kankakee County	554	100.00
Camargo (village) Douglas County	469	100.00
Arenzville (village) Cass County	419	100.00
New Canton (town) Pike County	417	100.00
Bellflower (village) McLean County	408	100.00
Loraine (village) Adams County	363	100.00
Manchester (village) Scott County	354	100.00

Top 10 Places Sorted by Percent
Based on places with populations of 10,000 or more

Place	Number	%
Washington (city) Tazewell County	10,678	98.50
Taylorville (city) Christian County	11,178	97.82
Effingham (city) Effingham County	12,110	97.79
Morton (village) Tazewell County	14,853	97.73
Wood River (city) Madison County	10,999	97.37
Western Springs (village) Cook County	12,159	97.33
East Peoria (city) Tazewell County	22,025	97.29
Herrin (city) Williamson County	10,952	96.94
Mattoon (city) Coles County	17,671	96.61
New Lenox (village) Will County	17,074	96.08

White: Hispanic

Top 10 Places Sorted by Number
Based on all places, regardless of population

Place	Number	%
Chicago (city) Cook County	339,021	11.71
Cicero (town) Cook County	26,837	31.35
Aurora (city) Kane County	24,823	17.36
Waukegan (city) Lake County	18,468	21.01
Elgin (city) Kane County	17,098	18.10
Berwyn (city) Cook County	10,181	18.85
Joliet (city) Will County	9,683	9.12
West Chicago (city) Du Page County	7,695	32.79
Melrose Park (village) Cook County	7,662	33.07
Rockford (city) Winnebago County	7,641	5.09

Top 10 Places Sorted by Percent
Based on all places, regardless of population

Place	Number	%
Stone Park (village) Cook County	2,042	39.83
De Pue (village) Bureau County	622	33.77
Melrose Park (village) Cook County	7,662	33.07
West Chicago (city) Du Page County	7,695	32.79
Cicero (town) Cook County	26,837	31.35
Summit (village) Cook County	3,018	28.37
Hodgkins (village) Cook County	575	26.94
Fairmont City (village) Saint Clair County	648	26.60
Franklin Park (village) Cook County	4,452	22.91
Volo (village) Lake County	41	22.78

Top 10 Places Sorted by Percent
Based on places with populations of 10,000 or more

Place	Number	%
Melrose Park (village) Cook County	7,662	33.07
West Chicago (city) Du Page County	7,695	32.79
Cicero (town) Cook County	26,837	31.35
Summit (village) Cook County	3,018	28.37
Franklin Park (village) Cook County	4,452	22.91
Waukegan (city) Lake County	18,468	21.01
Bensenville (village) Du Page County	4,117	19.89

Place	Number	%
Blue Island (city) Cook County	4,559	19.43
Carpentersville (village) Kane County	5,785	18.91
Berwyn (city) Cook County	10,181	18.85

Yugoslavian

Top 10 Places Sorted by Number
Based on all places, regardless of population

Place	Number	%
Chicago (city) Cook County	10,130	0.35
Rockford (city) Winnebago County	590	0.39
Skokie (village) Cook County	345	0.54
Wheaton (city) Du Page County	305	0.55
Berwyn (city) Cook County	301	0.56
Carol Stream (village) Du Page County	233	0.59
Mount Prospect (village) Cook County	232	0.41
Schaumburg (village) Cook County	228	0.31
Streamwood (village) Cook County	227	0.62
Niles (village) Cook County	214	0.71

Top 10 Places Sorted by Percent
Based on all places, regardless of population

Place	Number	%
East Gillespie (village) Macoupin County	6	2.64
Eagarville (village) Macoupin County	3	2.50
Countryside (city) Cook County	143	2.39
Winthrop Harbor (village) Lake County	128	1.92
Schiller Park (village) Cook County	187	1.59
Lyons (village) Cook County	160	1.58
New Canton (town) Pike County	6	1.34
Wenona (city) Marshall County	14	1.30
Mettawa (village) Lake County	4	1.23
East Dundee (village) Kane County	35	1.21

Top 10 Places Sorted by Percent
Based on places with populations of 10,000 or more

Place	Number	%
Schiller Park (village) Cook County	187	1.59
Lyons (village) Cook County	160	1.58
Loves Park (city) Winnebago County	158	0.79
Brookfield (village) Cook County	151	0.79
Norridge (village) Cook County	106	0.72
Niles (village) Cook County	214	0.71
Lincolnwood (village) Cook County	84	0.68
Summit (village) Cook County	70	0.66
Streamwood (village) Cook County	227	0.62
Carol Stream (village) Du Page County	233	0.59

Notes: (cdp) census designated place; Refer to the User's Guide in the front of the book for more detailed information.

Hispanic Population

Population

Total Population
Top 10 Places Sorted by Number

Place	Number
Chicago, IL (city) Cook County	2,895,964
Rockford, IL (city) Winnebago County	149,704
Aurora, IL (city) Kane County	143,609
Naperville, IL (city) Du Page County	128,300
Peoria, IL (city) Peoria County	112,892
Springfield, IL (city) Sangamon County	112,201
Joliet, IL (city) Will County	106,157
Elgin, IL (city) Kane County	93,895
Waukegan, IL (city) Lake County	87,969
Cicero, IL (town) Cook County	85,616

Hispanic
Top 10 Places Sorted by Number

Place	Number
Chicago, IL (city) Cook County	753,835
Cicero, IL (town) Cook County	66,188
Aurora, IL (city) Kane County	47,192
Waukegan, IL (city) Lake County	39,706
Elgin, IL (city) Kane County	31,926
Berwyn, IL (city) Cook County	20,543
Joliet, IL (city) Will County	19,328
Rockford, IL (city) Winnebago County	15,301
Carpentersville, IL (village) Kane County	12,510
Melrose Park, IL (village) Cook County	12,508

Hispanic
Top 10 Places Sorted by Percent of Total Population

Place	Percent
Cicero, IL (town) Cook County	77.31
Melrose Park, IL (village) Cook County	53.89
Summit, IL (village) Cook County	48.62
West Chicago, IL (city) Du Page County	47.90
Waukegan, IL (city) Lake County	45.14
Carpentersville, IL (village) Kane County	41.30
Blue Island, IL (city) Cook County	39.66
Berwyn, IL (city) Cook County	38.03
Franklin Park, IL (village) Cook County	37.97
Bensenville, IL (village) Du Page County	36.56

Argentinian
Top 10 Places Sorted by Number

Place	Number
Chicago, IL (city) Cook County	1,064

Argentinian
Top 10 Places Sorted by Percent of Hispanic Population

Place	Percent
Chicago, IL (city) Cook County	0.14

Argentinian
Top 10 Places Sorted by Percent of Total Population

Place	Percent
Chicago, IL (city) Cook County	0.04

Bolivian
Top 10 Places Sorted by Number

Place	Number
Chicago, IL (city) Cook County	477

Bolivian
Top 10 Places Sorted by Percent of Hispanic Population

Place	Percent
Chicago, IL (city) Cook County	0.06

Bolivian
Top 10 Places Sorted by Percent of Total Population

Place	Percent
Chicago, IL (city) Cook County	0.02

Central American
Top 10 Places Sorted by Number

Place	Number
Chicago, IL (city) Cook County	24,160
Waukegan, IL (city) Lake County	2,741
Cicero, IL (town) Cook County	853
Aurora, IL (city) Kane County	494
Skokie, IL (village) Cook County	475

Central American
Top 10 Places Sorted by Percent of Hispanic Population

Place	Percent
Skokie, IL (village) Cook County	13.37
Waukegan, IL (city) Lake County	6.90
Chicago, IL (city) Cook County	3.20
Cicero, IL (town) Cook County	1.29
Aurora, IL (city) Kane County	1.05

Central American
Top 10 Places Sorted by Percent of Total Population

Place	Percent
Waukegan, IL (city) Lake County	3.12
Cicero, IL (town) Cook County	1.00
Chicago, IL (city) Cook County	0.83
Skokie, IL (village) Cook County	0.75
Aurora, IL (city) Kane County	0.34

Chilean
Top 10 Places Sorted by Number

Place	Number
Chicago, IL (city) Cook County	690

Chilean
Top 10 Places Sorted by Percent of Hispanic Population

Place	Percent
Chicago, IL (city) Cook County	0.09

Chilean
Top 10 Places Sorted by Percent of Total Population

Place	Percent
Chicago, IL (city) Cook County	0.02

Colombian
Top 10 Places Sorted by Number

Place	Number
Chicago, IL (city) Cook County	6,091

Colombian
Top 10 Places Sorted by Percent of Hispanic Population

Place	Percent
Chicago, IL (city) Cook County	0.81

Colombian
Top 10 Places Sorted by Percent of Total Population

Place	Percent
Chicago, IL (city) Cook County	0.21

Costa Rican
Top 10 Places Sorted by Number

Place	Number
Chicago, IL (city) Cook County	732

Costa Rican
Top 10 Places Sorted by Percent of Hispanic Population

Place	Percent
Chicago, IL (city) Cook County	0.10

Costa Rican
Top 10 Places Sorted by Percent of Total Population

Place	Percent
Chicago, IL (city) Cook County	0.03

Cuban
Top 10 Places Sorted by Number

Place	Number
Chicago, IL (city) Cook County	8,111
Aurora, IL (city) Kane County	383
Melrose Park, IL (village) Cook County	344

Cuban
Top 10 Places Sorted by Percent of Hispanic Population

Place	Percent
Melrose Park, IL (village) Cook County	2.75
Chicago, IL (city) Cook County	1.08
Aurora, IL (city) Kane County	0.81

Cuban
Top 10 Places Sorted by Percent of Total Population

Place	Percent
Melrose Park, IL (village) Cook County	1.48
Chicago, IL (city) Cook County	0.28
Aurora, IL (city) Kane County	0.27

Dominican
Top 10 Places Sorted by Number

Place	Number
Chicago, IL (city) Cook County	2,066

Dominican
Top 10 Places Sorted by Percent of Hispanic Population

Place	Percent
Chicago, IL (city) Cook County	0.27

Dominican
Top 10 Places Sorted by Percent of Total Population

Place	Percent
Chicago, IL (city) Cook County	0.07

Ecuadorian
Top 10 Places Sorted by Number

Place	Number
Chicago, IL (city) Cook County	9,956

Ecuadorian
Top 10 Places Sorted by Percent of Hispanic Population

Place	Percent
Chicago, IL (city) Cook County	1.32

Ecuadorian
Top 10 Places Sorted by Percent of Total Population

Place	Percent
Chicago, IL (city) Cook County	0.34

Guatelmalan
Top 10 Places Sorted by Number

Place	Number
Chicago, IL (city) Cook County	14,394
Cicero, IL (town) Cook County	446

Notes: Please refer to the User's Guide for an explanation of data; tables include places with populations > 9,999 and reflect only those areas that meet Summary File 4 population thresholds, therefore there may be less than 10 places listed

Guatelmalan
Top 10 Places Sorted by Percent of Hispanic Population

Place	Percent
Chicago, IL (city) Cook County	1.91
Cicero, IL (town) Cook County	0.67

Guatelmalan
Top 10 Places Sorted by Percent of Total Population

Place	Percent
Cicero, IL (town) Cook County	0.52
Chicago, IL (city) Cook County	0.50

Honduran
Top 10 Places Sorted by Number

Place	Number
Chicago, IL (city) Cook County	3,123
Waukegan, IL (city) Lake County	1,544

Honduran
Top 10 Places Sorted by Percent of Hispanic Population

Place	Percent
Waukegan, IL (city) Lake County	3.89
Chicago, IL (city) Cook County	0.41

Honduran
Top 10 Places Sorted by Percent of Total Population

Place	Percent
Waukegan, IL (city) Lake County	1.76
Chicago, IL (city) Cook County	0.11

Mexican
Top 10 Places Sorted by Number

Place	Number
Chicago, IL (city) Cook County	534,045
Cicero, IL (town) Cook County	59,205
Aurora, IL (city) Kane County	40,419
Waukegan, IL (city) Lake County	30,441
Elgin, IL (city) Kane County	27,787
Joliet, IL (city) Will County	17,161
Berwyn, IL (city) Cook County	17,139
Rockford, IL (city) Winnebago County	12,691
Carpentersville, IL (village) Kane County	11,099
West Chicago, IL (city) Du Page County	10,686

Mexican
Top 10 Places Sorted by Percent of Hispanic Population

Place	Percent
Cary, IL (village) McHenry County	97.49
West Chicago, IL (city) Du Page County	93.27
Prospect Heights, IL (city) Cook County	92.62
Summit, IL (village) Cook County	91.99
Woodstock, IL (city) McHenry County	91.58
Dolton, IL (village) Cook County	91.54
Ottawa, IL (city) La Salle County	91.45
Blue Island, IL (city) Cook County	90.92
Chicago Heights, IL (city) Cook County	90.62
Moline, IL (city) Rock Island County	90.46

Mexican
Top 10 Places Sorted by Percent of Total Population

Place	Percent
Cicero, IL (town) Cook County	69.15
Melrose Park, IL (village) Cook County	45.22
Summit, IL (village) Cook County	44.73
West Chicago, IL (city) Du Page County	44.68
Carpentersville, IL (village) Kane County	36.65
Blue Island, IL (city) Cook County	36.06
Waukegan, IL (city) Lake County	34.60
Berwyn, IL (city) Cook County	31.73
Franklin Park, IL (village) Cook County	31.44
Bensenville, IL (village) Du Page County	29.93

Nicaraguan
Top 10 Places Sorted by Number

Place	Number
Chicago, IL (city) Cook County	937

Nicaraguan
Top 10 Places Sorted by Percent of Hispanic Population

Place	Percent
Chicago, IL (city) Cook County	0.12

Nicaraguan
Top 10 Places Sorted by Percent of Total Population

Place	Percent
Chicago, IL (city) Cook County	0.03

Panamanian
Top 10 Places Sorted by Number

Place	Number
Chicago, IL (city) Cook County	844

Panamanian
Top 10 Places Sorted by Percent of Hispanic Population

Place	Percent
Chicago, IL (city) Cook County	0.11

Panamanian
Top 10 Places Sorted by Percent of Total Population

Place	Percent
Chicago, IL (city) Cook County	0.03

Paraguayan
Top 10 Places Sorted by Number

Place	Number
No places met population threshold	

Paraguayan
Top 10 Places Sorted by Percent of Hispanic Population

Place	Percent
No places met population threshold	

Paraguayan
Top 10 Places Sorted by Percent of Total Population

Place	Percent
No places met population threshold	

Peruvian
Top 10 Places Sorted by Number

Place	Number
Chicago, IL (city) Cook County	2,957

Peruvian
Top 10 Places Sorted by Percent of Hispanic Population

Place	Percent
Chicago, IL (city) Cook County	0.39

Peruvian
Top 10 Places Sorted by Percent of Total Population

Place	Percent
Chicago, IL (city) Cook County	0.10

Puerto Rican
Top 10 Places Sorted by Number

Place	Number
Chicago, IL (city) Cook County	111,487
Waukegan, IL (city) Lake County	2,925
Aurora, IL (city) Kane County	2,436
Cicero, IL (town) Cook County	2,370
Elgin, IL (city) Kane County	1,854
Berwyn, IL (city) Cook County	1,274
Elmwood Park, IL (village) Cook County	756
North Chicago, IL (city) Lake County	688
Franklin Park, IL (village) Cook County	590
Joliet, IL (city) Will County	590

Puerto Rican
Top 10 Places Sorted by Percent of Hispanic Population

Place	Percent
Elmwood Park, IL (village) Cook County	27.47
Chicago, IL (city) Cook County	14.79
Schaumburg, IL (village) Cook County	14.05
Naperville, IL (city) Du Page County	11.97
Skokie, IL (village) Cook County	11.54
North Chicago, IL (city) Lake County	10.54
Zion, IL (city) Lake County	9.94
Carol Stream, IL (village) Du Page County	9.77
Streamwood, IL (village) Cook County	8.31
Franklin Park, IL (village) Cook County	7.99

Puerto Rican
Top 10 Places Sorted by Percent of Total Population

Place	Percent
Chicago, IL (city) Cook County	3.85
Waukegan, IL (city) Lake County	3.33
Franklin Park, IL (village) Cook County	3.04
Elmwood Park, IL (village) Cook County	2.98
Cicero, IL (town) Cook County	2.77
Berwyn, IL (city) Cook County	2.36
Melrose Park, IL (village) Cook County	2.32
Elgin, IL (city) Kane County	1.97
North Chicago, IL (city) Lake County	1.91
Aurora, IL (city) Kane County	1.70

Salvadoran
Top 10 Places Sorted by Number

Place	Number
Chicago, IL (city) Cook County	3,363
Waukegan, IL (city) Lake County	547

Salvadoran
Top 10 Places Sorted by Percent of Hispanic Population

Place	Percent
Waukegan, IL (city) Lake County	1.38
Chicago, IL (city) Cook County	0.45

Salvadoran
Top 10 Places Sorted by Percent of Total Population

Place	Percent
Waukegan, IL (city) Lake County	0.62
Chicago, IL (city) Cook County	0.12

South American
Top 10 Places Sorted by Number

Place	Number
Chicago, IL (city) Cook County	23,115
Cicero, IL (town) Cook County	675
Naperville, IL (city) Du Page County	497
Streamwood, IL (village) Cook County	441
Skokie, IL (village) Cook County	437
Berwyn, IL (city) Cook County	430
Aurora, IL (city) Kane County	340

South American
Top 10 Places Sorted by Percent of Hispanic Population

Place	Percent
Skokie, IL (village) Cook County	12.30
Naperville, IL (city) Du Page County	11.06

Notes: Please refer to the User's Guide for an explanation of data; tables include places with populations > 9,999 and reflect only those areas that meet Summary File 4 population thresholds, therefore there may be less than 10 places listed

Place	Percent
Streamwood, IL (village) Cook County	7.31
Chicago, IL (city) Cook County	3.07
Berwyn, IL (city) Cook County	2.09
Cicero, IL (town) Cook County	1.02
Aurora, IL (city) Kane County	0.72

South American
Top 10 Places Sorted by Percent of Total Population

Place	Percent
Streamwood, IL (village) Cook County	1.20
Berwyn, IL (city) Cook County	0.80
Chicago, IL (city) Cook County	0.80
Cicero, IL (town) Cook County	0.79
Skokie, IL (village) Cook County	0.69
Naperville, IL (city) Du Page County	0.39
Aurora, IL (city) Kane County	0.24

Spaniard
Top 10 Places Sorted by Number

Place	Number
Chicago, IL (city) Cook County	844

Spaniard
Top 10 Places Sorted by Percent of Hispanic Population

Place	Percent
Chicago, IL (city) Cook County	0.11

Spaniard
Top 10 Places Sorted by Percent of Total Population

Place	Percent
Chicago, IL (city) Cook County	0.03

Uruguayan
Top 10 Places Sorted by Number

Place	Number
No places met population threshold	

Uruguayan
Top 10 Places Sorted by Percent of Hispanic Population

Place	Percent
No places met population threshold	

Uruguayan
Top 10 Places Sorted by Percent of Total Population

Place	Percent
No places met population threshold	

Venezuelan
Top 10 Places Sorted by Number

Place	Number
Chicago, IL (city) Cook County	782

Venezuelan
Top 10 Places Sorted by Percent of Hispanic Population

Place	Percent
Chicago, IL (city) Cook County	0.10

Venezuelan
Top 10 Places Sorted by Percent of Total Population

Place	Percent
Chicago, IL (city) Cook County	0.03

Other Hispanic
Top 10 Places Sorted by Number

Place	Number
Chicago, IL (city) Cook County	50,007
Waukegan, IL (city) Lake County	3,219

Aurora, IL (city) Kane County	3,083
Cicero, IL (town) Cook County	2,830
Elgin, IL (city) Kane County	1,735
Joliet, IL (city) Will County	1,299
Rockford, IL (city) Winnebago County	1,190
Berwyn, IL (city) Cook County	1,073
Carpentersville, IL (village) Kane County	687
Melrose Park, IL (village) Cook County	638

Other Hispanic
Top 10 Places Sorted by Percent of Hispanic Population

Place	Percent
Dixon, IL (city) Lee County	47.54
Crest Hill, IL (city) Will County	40.67
Danville, IL (city) Vermilion County	26.62
Galesburg, IL (city) Knox County	20.10
Schaumburg, IL (village) Cook County	12.77
Skokie, IL (village) Cook County	11.76
Naperville, IL (city) Du Page County	11.60
Hoffman Estates, IL (village) Cook County	11.32
Burbank, IL (city) Cook County	11.15
Waukegan, IL (city) Lake County	8.11

Other Hispanic
Top 10 Places Sorted by Percent of Total Population

Place	Percent
Waukegan, IL (city) Lake County	3.66
Crest Hill, IL (city) Will County	3.53
Cicero, IL (town) Cook County	3.31
Melrose Park, IL (village) Cook County	2.75
Bensenville, IL (village) Du Page County	2.63
Carpentersville, IL (village) Kane County	2.27
Franklin Park, IL (village) Cook County	2.19
Aurora, IL (city) Kane County	2.15
Dixon, IL (city) Lee County	2.06
Berwyn, IL (city) Cook County	1.99

Median Age

Total Population
Top 10 Places Sorted by Number

Place	Years
Niles, IL (village) Cook County	46.2
Norridge, IL (village) Cook County	46.1
Lincolnwood, IL (village) Cook County	45.4
Morton Grove, IL (village) Cook County	44.6
Westchester, IL (village) Cook County	44.4
Northbrook, IL (village) Cook County	44.2
Park Ridge, IL (city) Cook County	42.5
Wilmette, IL (village) Cook County	42.1
Skokie, IL (village) Cook County	41.9
Oak Lawn, IL (village) Cook County	41.5

Hispanic
Top 10 Places Sorted by Number

Place	Years
Hinsdale, IL (village) Du Page County	35.5
Norridge, IL (village) Cook County	34.1
Morton Grove, IL (village) Cook County	34.0
Wilmette, IL (village) Cook County	33.8
Northbrook, IL (village) Cook County	33.4
Matteson, IL (village) Cook County	32.3
Dixon, IL (city) Lee County	32.2
Lincolnwood, IL (village) Cook County	32.2
Skokie, IL (village) Cook County	30.9
Darien, IL (city) Du Page County	30.8

Argentinian
Top 10 Places Sorted by Number

Place	Years
Chicago, IL (city) Cook County	33.3

Bolivian
Top 10 Places Sorted by Number

Place	Years
Chicago, IL (city) Cook County	29.9

Central American
Top 10 Places Sorted by Number

Place	Years
Chicago, IL (city) Cook County	30.6
Cicero, IL (town) Cook County	30.4
Aurora, IL (city) Kane County	29.9
Skokie, IL (village) Cook County	29.4
Waukegan, IL (city) Lake County	27.7

Chilean
Top 10 Places Sorted by Number

Place	Years
Chicago, IL (city) Cook County	34.6

Colombian
Top 10 Places Sorted by Number

Place	Years
Chicago, IL (city) Cook County	35.3

Costa Rican
Top 10 Places Sorted by Number

Place	Years
Chicago, IL (city) Cook County	30.7

Cuban
Top 10 Places Sorted by Number

Place	Years
Melrose Park, IL (village) Cook County	41.6
Chicago, IL (city) Cook County	39.1
Aurora, IL (city) Kane County	28.2

Dominican
Top 10 Places Sorted by Number

Place	Years
Chicago, IL (city) Cook County	31.1

Ecuadorian
Top 10 Places Sorted by Number

Place	Years
Chicago, IL (city) Cook County	29.9

Guatelmalan
Top 10 Places Sorted by Number

Place	Years
Cicero, IL (town) Cook County	32.3
Chicago, IL (city) Cook County	30.7

Honduran
Top 10 Places Sorted by Number

Place	Years
Chicago, IL (city) Cook County	31.2
Waukegan, IL (city) Lake County	27.1

Mexican
Top 10 Places Sorted by Number

Place	Years
Northbrook, IL (village) Cook County	33.7
Morton Grove, IL (village) Cook County	32.8
Matteson, IL (village) Cook County	32.7
Palos Hills, IL (city) Cook County	32.0
Dixon, IL (city) Lee County	31.7
Darien, IL (city) Du Page County	30.9
Galesburg, IL (city) Knox County	30.6

Notes: Please refer to the User's Guide for an explanation of data; tables include places with populations > 9,999 and reflect only those areas that meet Summary File 4 population thresholds, therefore there may be less than 10 places listed

Libertyville, IL (village) Lake County — 30.6
Elk Grove Village, IL (village) Cook County — 30.5
Elmwood Park, IL (village) Cook County — 30.2

Nicaraguan
Top 10 Places Sorted by Number

Place	Years
Chicago, IL (city) Cook County	26.9

Panamanian
Top 10 Places Sorted by Number

Place	Years
Chicago, IL (city) Cook County	32.0

Paraguayan
Top 10 Places Sorted by Number

Place	Years

No places met population threshold

Peruvian
Top 10 Places Sorted by Number

Place	Years
Chicago, IL (city) Cook County	34.7

Puerto Rican
Top 10 Places Sorted by Number

Place	Years
Carol Stream, IL (village) Du Page County	30.6
Elgin, IL (city) Kane County	30.6
Hanover Park, IL (village) Cook County	30.2
Bolingbrook, IL (village) Will County	29.9
Aurora, IL (city) Kane County	29.5
Chicago, IL (city) Cook County	28.5
Des Plaines, IL (city) Cook County	28.3
Joliet, IL (city) Will County	27.6
Waukegan, IL (city) Lake County	27.6
Evanston, IL (city) Cook County	26.6

Salvadoran
Top 10 Places Sorted by Number

Place	Years
Chicago, IL (city) Cook County	29.1
Waukegan, IL (city) Lake County	26.4

South American
Top 10 Places Sorted by Number

Place	Years
Skokie, IL (village) Cook County	43.2
Naperville, IL (city) Du Page County	35.7
Berwyn, IL (city) Cook County	33.2
Chicago, IL (city) Cook County	31.9
Cicero, IL (town) Cook County	30.3
Streamwood, IL (village) Cook County	30.3
Aurora, IL (city) Kane County	29.2

Spaniard
Top 10 Places Sorted by Number

Place	Years
Chicago, IL (city) Cook County	31.4

Uruguayan
Top 10 Places Sorted by Number

Place	Years

No places met population threshold

Venezuelan
Top 10 Places Sorted by Number

Place	Years
Chicago, IL (city) Cook County	28.7

Other Hispanic
Top 10 Places Sorted by Number

Place	Years
Dixon, IL (city) Lee County	34.1
Blue Island, IL (city) Cook County	32.8
Crest Hill, IL (city) Will County	30.2
Naperville, IL (city) Du Page County	28.9
Galesburg, IL (city) Knox County	28.0
Streamwood, IL (village) Cook County	26.5
Moline, IL (city) Rock Island County	26.3
Skokie, IL (village) Cook County	25.4
Danville, IL (city) Vermilion County	24.8
Wheeling, IL (village) Cook County	24.7

Average Household Size

Total Population
Top 10 Places Sorted by Number

Place	Number
Cicero, IL (town) Cook County	3.69
West Chicago, IL (city) Du Page County	3.65
Carpentersville, IL (village) Kane County	3.49
Round Lake Beach, IL (village) Lake County	3.47
Hanover Park, IL (village) Cook County	3.40
Maywood, IL (village) Cook County	3.38
Goodings Grove, IL (cdp) Will County	3.32
Harvey, IL (city) Cook County	3.30
Bolingbrook, IL (village) Will County	3.23
Bellwood, IL (village) Cook County	3.17

Hispanic
Top 10 Places Sorted by Number

Place	Number
Round Lake Beach, IL (village) Lake County	5.09
Bensenville, IL (village) Du Page County	5.06
Bellwood, IL (village) Cook County	5.04
Carpentersville, IL (village) Kane County	5.03
West Chicago, IL (city) Du Page County	5.03
Maywood, IL (village) Cook County	5.01
Highland Park, IL (city) Lake County	4.79
Cary, IL (village) McHenry County	4.73
Hanover Park, IL (village) Cook County	4.67
Wheeling, IL (village) Cook County	4.65

Argentinian
Top 10 Places Sorted by Number

Place	Number
Chicago, IL (city) Cook County	2.23

Bolivian
Top 10 Places Sorted by Number

Place	Number
Chicago, IL (city) Cook County	2.46

Central American
Top 10 Places Sorted by Number

Place	Number
Cicero, IL (town) Cook County	4.73
Waukegan, IL (city) Lake County	4.08
Aurora, IL (city) Kane County	3.96
Skokie, IL (village) Cook County	3.92
Chicago, IL (city) Cook County	3.70

Chilean
Top 10 Places Sorted by Number

Place	Number
Chicago, IL (city) Cook County	2.83

Colombian
Top 10 Places Sorted by Number

Place	Number
Chicago, IL (city) Cook County	2.92

Costa Rican
Top 10 Places Sorted by Number

Place	Number
Chicago, IL (city) Cook County	3.00

Cuban
Top 10 Places Sorted by Number

Place	Number
Melrose Park, IL (village) Cook County	3.63
Aurora, IL (city) Kane County	2.79
Chicago, IL (city) Cook County	2.55

Dominican
Top 10 Places Sorted by Number

Place	Number
Chicago, IL (city) Cook County	2.98

Ecuadorian
Top 10 Places Sorted by Number

Place	Number
Chicago, IL (city) Cook County	4.04

Guatelmalan
Top 10 Places Sorted by Number

Place	Number
Cicero, IL (town) Cook County	4.92
Chicago, IL (city) Cook County	3.88

Honduran
Top 10 Places Sorted by Number

Place	Number
Waukegan, IL (city) Lake County	4.57
Chicago, IL (city) Cook County	3.27

Mexican
Top 10 Places Sorted by Number

Place	Number
Bensenville, IL (village) Du Page County	5.52
Plainfield, IL (village) Will County	5.32
Round Lake Beach, IL (village) Lake County	5.31
Bellwood, IL (village) Cook County	5.20
Highland Park, IL (city) Lake County	5.20
Carpentersville, IL (village) Kane County	5.18
West Chicago, IL (city) Du Page County	5.16
Maywood, IL (village) Cook County	5.13
Hanover Park, IL (village) Cook County	4.99
Streamwood, IL (village) Cook County	4.94

Nicaraguan
Top 10 Places Sorted by Number

Place	Number
Chicago, IL (city) Cook County	3.76

Panamanian
Top 10 Places Sorted by Number

Place	Number
Chicago, IL (city) Cook County	3.05

Notes: Please refer to the User's Guide for an explanation of data; tables include places with populations > 9,999 and reflect only those areas that meet Summary File 4 population thresholds, therefore there may be less than 10 places listed

Paraguayan
Top 10 Places Sorted by Number

Place	Number
No places met population threshold	

Peruvian
Top 10 Places Sorted by Number

Place	Number
Chicago, IL (city) Cook County	3.20

Puerto Rican
Top 10 Places Sorted by Number

Place	Number
Melrose Park, IL (village) Cook County	3.99
Franklin Park, IL (village) Cook County	3.98
Streamwood, IL (village) Cook County	3.98
North Chicago, IL (city) Lake County	3.88
Bolingbrook, IL (village) Will County	3.80
Carpentersville, IL (village) Kane County	3.64
Cicero, IL (town) Cook County	3.50
Berwyn, IL (city) Cook County	3.33
Aurora, IL (city) Kane County	3.28
Carol Stream, IL (village) Du Page County	3.26

Salvadoran
Top 10 Places Sorted by Number

Place	Number
Waukegan, IL (city) Lake County	3.83
Chicago, IL (city) Cook County	3.80

South American
Top 10 Places Sorted by Number

Place	Number
Streamwood, IL (village) Cook County	4.32
Cicero, IL (town) Cook County	3.99
Aurora, IL (city) Kane County	3.71
Naperville, IL (city) Du Page County	3.40
Chicago, IL (city) Cook County	3.33
Berwyn, IL (city) Cook County	3.19
Skokie, IL (village) Cook County	3.01

Spaniard
Top 10 Places Sorted by Number

Place	Number
Chicago, IL (city) Cook County	2.03

Uruguayan
Top 10 Places Sorted by Number

Place	Number
No places met population threshold	

Venezuelan
Top 10 Places Sorted by Number

Place	Number
Chicago, IL (city) Cook County	2.57

Other Hispanic
Top 10 Places Sorted by Number

Place	Number
Mount Prospect, IL (village) Cook County	5.49
Bensenville, IL (village) Du Page County	4.88
Carpentersville, IL (village) Kane County	4.59
Burbank, IL (city) Cook County	4.58
Chicago Heights, IL (city) Cook County	4.56
Waukegan, IL (city) Lake County	4.56
Cicero, IL (town) Cook County	4.47
Danville, IL (city) Vermilion County	4.45
West Chicago, IL (city) Du Page County	4.36
Addison, IL (village) Du Page County	4.08

Language Spoken at Home: English Only

Total Populations 5 Years and Over Who Speak English-Only at Home
Top 10 Places Sorted by Number

Place	Number
Chicago, IL (city) Cook County	1,726,905
Rockford, IL (city) Winnebago County	119,262
Springfield, IL (city) Sangamon County	100,722
Naperville, IL (city) Du Page County	99,729
Peoria, IL (city) Peoria County	96,641
Aurora, IL (city) Kane County	83,953
Joliet, IL (city) Will County	78,217
Decatur, IL (city) Macon County	73,838
Arlington Heights, IL (village) Cook County	58,797
Evanston, IL (city) Cook County	57,304

Total Populations 5 Years and Over Who Speak English-Only at Home
Top 10 Places Sorted by Percent

Place	Percent
Pekin, IL (city) Tazewell County	97.41
Quincy, IL (city) Adams County	97.25
Alton, IL (city) Madison County	96.78
Granite City, IL (city) Madison County	96.57
New Lenox, IL (village) Will County	96.57
Decatur, IL (city) Macon County	96.38
Collinsville, IL (city) Madison County	96.35
Springfield, IL (city) Sangamon County	95.92
Machesney Park, IL (village) Winnebago County	95.88
Dixon, IL (city) Lee County	95.81

Hispanics 5 Years and Over Who Speak English-Only at Home
Top 10 Places Sorted by Number

Place	Number
Chicago, IL (city) Cook County	81,807
Cicero, IL (town) Cook County	4,561
Aurora, IL (city) Kane County	4,158
Waukegan, IL (city) Lake County	3,613
Joliet, IL (city) Will County	3,245
Rockford, IL (city) Winnebago County	3,011
Berwyn, IL (city) Cook County	2,891
Elgin, IL (city) Kane County	2,706
Naperville, IL (city) Du Page County	1,767
Bolingbrook, IL (village) Will County	1,654

Hispanics 5 Years and Over Who Speak English-Only at Home
Top 10 Places Sorted by Percent

Place	Percent
Alton, IL (city) Madison County	77.52
Mokena, IL (village) Will County	76.49
O'Fallon, IL (city) Saint Clair County	74.00
New Lenox, IL (village) Will County	73.78
Pekin, IL (city) Tazewell County	71.08
Belleville, IL (city) Saint Clair County	67.86
Granite City, IL (city) Madison County	65.94
Collinsville, IL (city) Madison County	64.44
Quincy, IL (city) Adams County	62.46
Machesney Park, IL (village) Winnebago County	59.83

Argentinians 5 Years and Over Who Speak English-Only at Home
Top 10 Places Sorted by Number

Place	Number
Chicago, IL (city) Cook County	97

Argentinians 5 Years and Over Who Speak English-Only at Home
Top 10 Places Sorted by Percent

Place	Percent
Chicago, IL (city) Cook County	9.44

Bolivians 5 Years and Over Who Speak English-Only at Home
Top 10 Places Sorted by Number

Place	Number
Chicago, IL (city) Cook County	84

Bolivians 5 Years and Over Who Speak English-Only at Home
Top 10 Places Sorted by Percent

Place	Percent
Chicago, IL (city) Cook County	19.22

Central Americans 5 Years and Over Who Speak English-Only at Home
Top 10 Places Sorted by Number

Place	Number
Chicago, IL (city) Cook County	1,321
Waukegan, IL (city) Lake County	158
Cicero, IL (town) Cook County	60
Skokie, IL (village) Cook County	29
Aurora, IL (city) Kane County	18

Central Americans 5 Years and Over Who Speak English-Only at Home
Top 10 Places Sorted by Percent

Place	Percent
Cicero, IL (town) Cook County	7.56
Waukegan, IL (city) Lake County	6.32
Skokie, IL (village) Cook County	6.11
Chicago, IL (city) Cook County	5.86
Aurora, IL (city) Kane County	3.78

Chileans 5 Years and Over Who Speak English-Only at Home
Top 10 Places Sorted by Number

Place	Number
Chicago, IL (city) Cook County	68

Chileans 5 Years and Over Who Speak English-Only at Home
Top 10 Places Sorted by Percent

Place	Percent
Chicago, IL (city) Cook County	10.12

Colombians 5 Years and Over Who Speak English-Only at Home
Top 10 Places Sorted by Number

Place	Number
Chicago, IL (city) Cook County	445

Colombians 5 Years and Over Who Speak English-Only at Home
Top 10 Places Sorted by Percent

Place	Percent
Chicago, IL (city) Cook County	7.68

Costa Ricans 5 Years and Over Who Speak English-Only at Home
Top 10 Places Sorted by Number

Place	Number
Chicago, IL (city) Cook County	95

Notes: Please refer to the User's Guide for an explanation of data; tables include places with populations > 9,999 and reflect only those areas that meet Summary File 4 population thresholds, therefore there may be less than 10 places listed

Costa Ricans 5 Years and Over Who Speak English-Only at Home
Top 10 Places Sorted by Percent

Place	Percent
Chicago, IL (city) Cook County	14.37

Cubans 5 Years and Over Who Speak English-Only at Home
Top 10 Places Sorted by Number

Place	Number
Chicago, IL (city) Cook County	1,290
Aurora, IL (city) Kane County	117
Melrose Park, IL (village) Cook County	27

Cubans 5 Years and Over Who Speak English-Only at Home
Top 10 Places Sorted by Percent

Place	Percent
Aurora, IL (city) Kane County	36.22
Chicago, IL (city) Cook County	16.67
Melrose Park, IL (village) Cook County	8.08

Dominicans 5 Years and Over Who Speak English-Only at Home
Top 10 Places Sorted by Number

Place	Number
Chicago, IL (city) Cook County	181

Dominicans 5 Years and Over Who Speak English-Only at Home
Top 10 Places Sorted by Percent

Place	Percent
Chicago, IL (city) Cook County	9.20

Ecuadorians 5 Years and Over Who Speak English-Only at Home
Top 10 Places Sorted by Number

Place	Number
Chicago, IL (city) Cook County	631

Ecuadorians 5 Years and Over Who Speak English-Only at Home
Top 10 Places Sorted by Percent

Place	Percent
Chicago, IL (city) Cook County	6.88

Guatelmalans 5 Years and Over Who Speak English-Only at Home
Top 10 Places Sorted by Number

Place	Number
Chicago, IL (city) Cook County	637
Cicero, IL (town) Cook County	29

Guatelmalans 5 Years and Over Who Speak English-Only at Home
Top 10 Places Sorted by Percent

Place	Percent
Cicero, IL (town) Cook County	7.36
Chicago, IL (city) Cook County	4.76

Hondurans 5 Years and Over Who Speak English-Only at Home
Top 10 Places Sorted by Number

Place	Number
Chicago, IL (city) Cook County	131
Waukegan, IL (city) Lake County	101

Hondurans 5 Years and Over Who Speak English-Only at Home
Top 10 Places Sorted by Percent

Place	Percent
Waukegan, IL (city) Lake County	7.15
Chicago, IL (city) Cook County	4.52

Mexicans 5 Years and Over Who Speak English-Only at Home
Top 10 Places Sorted by Number

Place	Number
Chicago, IL (city) Cook County	52,479
Cicero, IL (town) Cook County	3,672
Aurora, IL (city) Kane County	3,039
Joliet, IL (city) Will County	2,762
Waukegan, IL (city) Lake County	2,486
Berwyn, IL (city) Cook County	2,279
Rockford, IL (city) Winnebago County	2,140
Elgin, IL (city) Kane County	1,965
Bolingbrook, IL (village) Will County	1,203
Moline, IL (city) Rock Island County	1,125

Mexicans 5 Years and Over Who Speak English-Only at Home
Top 10 Places Sorted by Percent

Place	Percent
New Lenox, IL (village) Will County	76.26
Dixon, IL (city) Lee County	73.40
Belleville, IL (city) Saint Clair County	66.07
Granite City, IL (city) Madison County	65.83
Springfield, IL (city) Sangamon County	65.65
Crest Hill, IL (city) Will County	62.74
Normal, IL (town) McLean County	60.61
Machesney Park, IL (village) Winnebago County	59.75
Homewood, IL (village) Cook County	57.45
Ottawa, IL (city) La Salle County	55.51

Nicaraguans 5 Years and Over Who Speak English-Only at Home
Top 10 Places Sorted by Number

Place	Number
Chicago, IL (city) Cook County	46

Nicaraguans 5 Years and Over Who Speak English-Only at Home
Top 10 Places Sorted by Percent

Place	Percent
Chicago, IL (city) Cook County	5.52

Panamanians 5 Years and Over Who Speak English-Only at Home
Top 10 Places Sorted by Number

Place	Number
Chicago, IL (city) Cook County	178

Panamanians 5 Years and Over Who Speak English-Only at Home
Top 10 Places Sorted by Percent

Place	Percent
Chicago, IL (city) Cook County	23.45

Paraguayans 5 Years and Over Who Speak English-Only at Home
Top 10 Places Sorted by Number

Place	Number
No places met population threshold	

Paraguayans 5 Years and Over Who Speak English-Only at Home
Top 10 Places Sorted by Percent

Place	Percent
No places met population threshold	

Peruvians 5 Years and Over Who Speak English-Only at Home
Top 10 Places Sorted by Number

Place	Number
Chicago, IL (city) Cook County	274

Peruvians 5 Years and Over Who Speak English-Only at Home
Top 10 Places Sorted by Percent

Place	Percent
Chicago, IL (city) Cook County	9.65

Puerto Ricans 5 Years and Over Who Speak English-Only at Home
Top 10 Places Sorted by Number

Place	Number
Chicago, IL (city) Cook County	16,134
Waukegan, IL (city) Lake County	563
Aurora, IL (city) Kane County	438
Cicero, IL (town) Cook County	427
Berwyn, IL (city) Cook County	359
Elgin, IL (city) Kane County	297
Naperville, IL (city) Du Page County	250
Schaumburg, IL (village) Cook County	241
Elmwood Park, IL (village) Cook County	228
North Chicago, IL (city) Lake County	217

Puerto Ricans 5 Years and Over Who Speak English-Only at Home
Top 10 Places Sorted by Percent

Place	Percent
Naperville, IL (city) Du Page County	51.12
Rockford, IL (city) Winnebago County	45.54
Schaumburg, IL (village) Cook County	44.55
Bolingbrook, IL (village) Will County	43.58
Hanover Park, IL (village) Cook County	43.48
Streamwood, IL (village) Cook County	40.10
Carol Stream, IL (village) Du Page County	37.25
Elmwood Park, IL (village) Cook County	33.43
North Chicago, IL (city) Lake County	33.03
Des Plaines, IL (city) Cook County	32.73

Salvadorans 5 Years and Over Who Speak English-Only at Home
Top 10 Places Sorted by Number

Place	Number
Chicago, IL (city) Cook County	187
Waukegan, IL (city) Lake County	23

Salvadorans 5 Years and Over Who Speak English-Only at Home
Top 10 Places Sorted by Percent

Place	Percent
Chicago, IL (city) Cook County	5.75
Waukegan, IL (city) Lake County	4.67

South Americans 5 Years and Over Who Speak English-Only at Home
Top 10 Places Sorted by Number

Place	Number
Chicago, IL (city) Cook County	1,781
Naperville, IL (city) Du Page County	211
Cicero, IL (town) Cook County	54
Skokie, IL (village) Cook County	32

Notes: Please refer to the User's Guide for an explanation of data; tables include places with populations > 9,999 and reflect only those areas that meet Summary File 4 population thresholds, therefore there may be less than 10 places listed

Aurora, IL (city) Kane County	17
Berwyn, IL (city) Cook County	8
Streamwood, IL (village) Cook County	0

South Americans 5 Years and Over Who Speak English-Only at Home
Top 10 Places Sorted by Percent

Place	Percent
Naperville, IL (city) Du Page County	42.45
Cicero, IL (town) Cook County	8.60
Chicago, IL (city) Cook County	8.18
Skokie, IL (village) Cook County	7.53
Aurora, IL (city) Kane County	6.32
Berwyn, IL (city) Cook County	1.91
Streamwood, IL (village) Cook County	0.00

Spaniards 5 Years and Over Who Speak English-Only at Home
Top 10 Places Sorted by Number

Place	Number
Chicago, IL (city) Cook County	207

Spaniards 5 Years and Over Who Speak English-Only at Home
Top 10 Places Sorted by Percent

Place	Percent
Chicago, IL (city) Cook County	27.56

Uruguayans 5 Years and Over Who Speak English-Only at Home
Top 10 Places Sorted by Number

Place	Number
No places met population threshold	

Uruguayans 5 Years and Over Who Speak English-Only at Home
Top 10 Places Sorted by Percent

Place	Percent
No places met population threshold	

Venezuelans 5 Years and Over Who Speak English-Only at Home
Top 10 Places Sorted by Number

Place	Number
Chicago, IL (city) Cook County	86

Venezuelans 5 Years and Over Who Speak English-Only at Home
Top 10 Places Sorted by Percent

Place	Percent
Chicago, IL (city) Cook County	11.15

Other Hispanics 5 Years and Over Who Speak English-Only at Home
Top 10 Places Sorted by Number

Place	Number
Chicago, IL (city) Cook County	8,414
Aurora, IL (city) Kane County	520
Rockford, IL (city) Winnebago County	494
Waukegan, IL (city) Lake County	363
Cicero, IL (town) Cook County	317
Joliet, IL (city) Will County	309
Elgin, IL (city) Kane County	285
Naperville, IL (city) Du Page County	246
Galesburg, IL (city) Knox County	199
Berwyn, IL (city) Cook County	197

Other Hispanics 5 Years and Over Who Speak English-Only at Home
Top 10 Places Sorted by Percent

Place	Percent
Galesburg, IL (city) Knox County	64.82
Naperville, IL (city) Du Page County	57.21
Evanston, IL (city) Cook County	50.76
Rockford, IL (city) Winnebago County	48.53
Dixon, IL (city) Lee County	44.72
Bolingbrook, IL (village) Will County	43.95
North Chicago, IL (city) Lake County	38.34
Schaumburg, IL (village) Cook County	37.00
Burbank, IL (city) Cook County	36.47
Streamwood, IL (village) Cook County	35.19

Language Spoken at Home: Spanish

Total Populations 5 Years and Over Who Speak Spanish at Home
Top 10 Places Sorted by Number

Place	Number
Chicago, IL (city) Cook County	625,240
Cicero, IL (town) Cook County	53,603
Aurora, IL (city) Kane County	38,097
Waukegan, IL (city) Lake County	32,031
Elgin, IL (city) Kane County	26,052
Berwyn, IL (city) Cook County	15,521
Joliet, IL (city) Will County	14,764
Rockford, IL (city) Winnebago County	11,992
Melrose Park, IL (village) Cook County	10,389
Carpentersville, IL (village) Kane County	9,999

Total Populations 5 Years and Over Who Speak Spanish at Home
Top 10 Places Sorted by Percent

Place	Percent
Cicero, IL (town) Cook County	70.21
Melrose Park, IL (village) Cook County	48.95
West Chicago, IL (city) Du Page County	44.28
Summit, IL (village) Cook County	43.88
Waukegan, IL (city) Lake County	40.26
Carpentersville, IL (village) Kane County	36.84
Blue Island, IL (city) Cook County	35.44
Franklin Park, IL (village) Cook County	33.67
Bensenville, IL (village) Du Page County	32.36
Berwyn, IL (city) Cook County	31.21

Hispanics 5 Years and Over Who Speak Spanish at Home
Top 10 Places Sorted by Number

Place	Number
Chicago, IL (city) Cook County	587,594
Cicero, IL (town) Cook County	53,025
Aurora, IL (city) Kane County	36,620
Waukegan, IL (city) Lake County	30,879
Elgin, IL (city) Kane County	25,081
Berwyn, IL (city) Cook County	15,053
Joliet, IL (city) Will County	13,689
Melrose Park, IL (village) Cook County	10,115
Rockford, IL (city) Winnebago County	9,975
Carpentersville, IL (village) Kane County	9,632

Hispanics 5 Years and Over Who Speak Spanish at Home
Top 10 Places Sorted by Percent

Place	Percent
Prospect Heights, IL (city) Cook County	94.07
Northlake, IL (city) Cook County	92.79
Cicero, IL (town) Cook County	91.91
West Chicago, IL (city) Du Page County	91.78
Melrose Park, IL (village) Cook County	91.75
Harvey, IL (city) Cook County	91.30
Franklin Park, IL (village) Cook County	91.02

Addison, IL (village) Du Page County	90.77
Rolling Meadows, IL (city) Cook County	90.60
Summit, IL (village) Cook County	90.60

Argentinians 5 Years and Over Who Speak Spanish at Home
Top 10 Places Sorted by Number

Place	Number
Chicago, IL (city) Cook County	924

Argentinians 5 Years and Over Who Speak Spanish at Home
Top 10 Places Sorted by Percent

Place	Percent
Chicago, IL (city) Cook County	89.88

Bolivians 5 Years and Over Who Speak Spanish at Home
Top 10 Places Sorted by Number

Place	Number
Chicago, IL (city) Cook County	353

Bolivians 5 Years and Over Who Speak Spanish at Home
Top 10 Places Sorted by Percent

Place	Percent
Chicago, IL (city) Cook County	80.78

Central Americans 5 Years and Over Who Speak Spanish at Home
Top 10 Places Sorted by Number

Place	Number
Chicago, IL (city) Cook County	21,147
Waukegan, IL (city) Lake County	2,337
Cicero, IL (town) Cook County	734
Aurora, IL (city) Kane County	458
Skokie, IL (village) Cook County	446

Central Americans 5 Years and Over Who Speak Spanish at Home
Top 10 Places Sorted by Percent

Place	Percent
Aurora, IL (city) Kane County	96.22
Skokie, IL (village) Cook County	93.89
Chicago, IL (city) Cook County	93.81
Waukegan, IL (city) Lake County	93.52
Cicero, IL (town) Cook County	92.44

Chileans 5 Years and Over Who Speak Spanish at Home
Top 10 Places Sorted by Number

Place	Number
Chicago, IL (city) Cook County	598

Chileans 5 Years and Over Who Speak Spanish at Home
Top 10 Places Sorted by Percent

Place	Percent
Chicago, IL (city) Cook County	88.99

Colombians 5 Years and Over Who Speak Spanish at Home
Top 10 Places Sorted by Number

Place	Number
Chicago, IL (city) Cook County	5,273

Notes: Please refer to the User's Guide for an explanation of data; tables include places with populations > 9,999 and reflect only those areas that meet Summary File 4 population thresholds, therefore there may be less than 10 places listed

Colombians 5 Years and Over Who Speak Spanish at Home
Top 10 Places Sorted by Percent

Place	Percent
Chicago, IL (city) Cook County	91.06

Costa Ricans 5 Years and Over Who Speak Spanish at Home
Top 10 Places Sorted by Number

Place	Number
Chicago, IL (city) Cook County	566

Costa Ricans 5 Years and Over Who Speak Spanish at Home
Top 10 Places Sorted by Percent

Place	Percent
Chicago, IL (city) Cook County	85.63

Cubans 5 Years and Over Who Speak Spanish at Home
Top 10 Places Sorted by Number

Place	Number
Chicago, IL (city) Cook County	6,431
Melrose Park, IL (village) Cook County	307
Aurora, IL (city) Kane County	206

Cubans 5 Years and Over Who Speak Spanish at Home
Top 10 Places Sorted by Percent

Place	Percent
Melrose Park, IL (village) Cook County	91.92
Chicago, IL (city) Cook County	83.10
Aurora, IL (city) Kane County	63.78

Dominicans 5 Years and Over Who Speak Spanish at Home
Top 10 Places Sorted by Number

Place	Number
Chicago, IL (city) Cook County	1,787

Dominicans 5 Years and Over Who Speak Spanish at Home
Top 10 Places Sorted by Percent

Place	Percent
Chicago, IL (city) Cook County	90.80

Ecuadorians 5 Years and Over Who Speak Spanish at Home
Top 10 Places Sorted by Number

Place	Number
Chicago, IL (city) Cook County	8,488

Ecuadorians 5 Years and Over Who Speak Spanish at Home
Top 10 Places Sorted by Percent

Place	Percent
Chicago, IL (city) Cook County	92.53

Guatelmalans 5 Years and Over Who Speak Spanish at Home
Top 10 Places Sorted by Number

Place	Number
Chicago, IL (city) Cook County	12,701
Cicero, IL (town) Cook County	365

Guatelmalans 5 Years and Over Who Speak Spanish at Home
Top 10 Places Sorted by Percent

Place	Percent
Chicago, IL (city) Cook County	94.81
Cicero, IL (town) Cook County	92.64

Hondurans 5 Years and Over Who Speak Spanish at Home
Top 10 Places Sorted by Number

Place	Number
Chicago, IL (city) Cook County	2,767
Waukegan, IL (city) Lake County	1,312

Hondurans 5 Years and Over Who Speak Spanish at Home
Top 10 Places Sorted by Percent

Place	Percent
Chicago, IL (city) Cook County	95.48
Waukegan, IL (city) Lake County	92.85

Mexicans 5 Years and Over Who Speak Spanish at Home
Top 10 Places Sorted by Number

Place	Number
Chicago, IL (city) Cook County	419,060
Cicero, IL (town) Cook County	47,780
Aurora, IL (city) Kane County	31,737
Waukegan, IL (city) Lake County	23,885
Elgin, IL (city) Kane County	22,083
Berwyn, IL (city) Cook County	12,702
Joliet, IL (city) Will County	12,341
West Chicago, IL (city) Du Page County	8,824
Carpentersville, IL (village) Kane County	8,733
Melrose Park, IL (village) Cook County	8,628

Mexicans 5 Years and Over Who Speak Spanish at Home
Top 10 Places Sorted by Percent

Place	Percent
Prospect Heights, IL (city) Cook County	96.83
Highland Park, IL (city) Lake County	94.38
Northlake, IL (city) Cook County	94.04
Melrose Park, IL (village) Cook County	93.67
West Chicago, IL (city) Du Page County	93.64
Rolling Meadows, IL (city) Cook County	93.46
Bellwood, IL (village) Cook County	93.25
Franklin Park, IL (village) Cook County	92.84
Cicero, IL (town) Cook County	92.68
Mount Prospect, IL (village) Cook County	92.44

Nicaraguans 5 Years and Over Who Speak Spanish at Home
Top 10 Places Sorted by Number

Place	Number
Chicago, IL (city) Cook County	775

Nicaraguans 5 Years and Over Who Speak Spanish at Home
Top 10 Places Sorted by Percent

Place	Percent
Chicago, IL (city) Cook County	93.04

Panamanians 5 Years and Over Who Speak Spanish at Home
Top 10 Places Sorted by Number

Place	Number
Chicago, IL (city) Cook County	581

Panamanians 5 Years and Over Who Speak Spanish at Home
Top 10 Places Sorted by Percent

Place	Percent
Chicago, IL (city) Cook County	76.55

Paraguayans 5 Years and Over Who Speak Spanish at Home
Top 10 Places Sorted by Number

Place	Number
No places met population threshold	

Paraguayans 5 Years and Over Who Speak Spanish at Home
Top 10 Places Sorted by Percent

Place	Percent
No places met population threshold	

Peruvians 5 Years and Over Who Speak Spanish at Home
Top 10 Places Sorted by Number

Place	Number
Chicago, IL (city) Cook County	2,554

Peruvians 5 Years and Over Who Speak Spanish at Home
Top 10 Places Sorted by Percent

Place	Percent
Chicago, IL (city) Cook County	89.99

Puerto Ricans 5 Years and Over Who Speak Spanish at Home
Top 10 Places Sorted by Number

Place	Number
Chicago, IL (city) Cook County	85,302
Waukegan, IL (city) Lake County	2,088
Aurora, IL (city) Kane County	1,775
Cicero, IL (town) Cook County	1,714
Elgin, IL (city) Kane County	1,373
Berwyn, IL (city) Cook County	815
Elmwood Park, IL (village) Cook County	454
North Chicago, IL (city) Lake County	434
Franklin Park, IL (village) Cook County	403
Joliet, IL (city) Will County	370

Puerto Ricans 5 Years and Over Who Speak Spanish at Home
Top 10 Places Sorted by Percent

Place	Percent
Chicago, IL (city) Cook County	83.83
Elgin, IL (city) Kane County	82.22
Aurora, IL (city) Kane County	80.21
Cicero, IL (town) Cook County	80.06
Waukegan, IL (city) Lake County	78.76
Zion, IL (city) Lake County	75.16
Franklin Park, IL (village) Cook County	74.35
Melrose Park, IL (village) Cook County	72.82
Joliet, IL (city) Will County	71.29
Berwyn, IL (city) Cook County	68.78

Salvadorans 5 Years and Over Who Speak Spanish at Home
Top 10 Places Sorted by Number

Place	Number
Chicago, IL (city) Cook County	3,064
Waukegan, IL (city) Lake County	470

Notes: Please refer to the User's Guide for an explanation of data; tables include places with populations > 9,999 and reflect only those areas that meet Summary File 4 population thresholds, therefore there may be less than 10 places listed

Salvadorans 5 Years and Over Who Speak Spanish at Home
Top 10 Places Sorted by Percent

Place	Percent
Waukegan, IL (city) Lake County	95.33
Chicago, IL (city) Cook County	94.25

South Americans 5 Years and Over Who Speak Spanish at Home
Top 10 Places Sorted by Number

Place	Number
Chicago, IL (city) Cook County	19,782
Cicero, IL (town) Cook County	574
Streamwood, IL (village) Cook County	410
Berwyn, IL (city) Cook County	404
Skokie, IL (village) Cook County	386
Naperville, IL (city) Du Page County	286
Aurora, IL (city) Kane County	252

South Americans 5 Years and Over Who Speak Spanish at Home
Top 10 Places Sorted by Percent

Place	Percent
Streamwood, IL (village) Cook County	100.00
Berwyn, IL (city) Cook County	96.65
Aurora, IL (city) Kane County	93.68
Cicero, IL (town) Cook County	91.40
Chicago, IL (city) Cook County	90.86
Skokie, IL (village) Cook County	90.82
Naperville, IL (city) Du Page County	57.55

Spaniards 5 Years and Over Who Speak Spanish at Home
Top 10 Places Sorted by Number

Place	Number
Chicago, IL (city) Cook County	514

Spaniards 5 Years and Over Who Speak Spanish at Home
Top 10 Places Sorted by Percent

Place	Percent
Chicago, IL (city) Cook County	68.44

Uruguayans 5 Years and Over Who Speak Spanish at Home
Top 10 Places Sorted by Number

Place	Number
No places met population threshold	

Uruguayans 5 Years and Over Who Speak Spanish at Home
Top 10 Places Sorted by Percent

Place	Percent
No places met population threshold	

Venezuelans 5 Years and Over Who Speak Spanish at Home
Top 10 Places Sorted by Number

Place	Number
Chicago, IL (city) Cook County	637

Venezuelans 5 Years and Over Who Speak Spanish at Home
Top 10 Places Sorted by Percent

Place	Percent
Chicago, IL (city) Cook County	82.62

Other Hispanics 5 Years and Over Who Speak Spanish at Home
Top 10 Places Sorted by Number

Place	Number
Chicago, IL (city) Cook County	33,571
Waukegan, IL (city) Lake County	2,247
Aurora, IL (city) Kane County	2,164
Cicero, IL (town) Cook County	2,005
Elgin, IL (city) Kane County	1,266
Joliet, IL (city) Will County	769
Berwyn, IL (city) Cook County	610
Rockford, IL (city) Winnebago County	504
Melrose Park, IL (village) Cook County	444
Carpentersville, IL (village) Kane County	418

Other Hispanics 5 Years and Over Who Speak Spanish at Home
Top 10 Places Sorted by Percent

Place	Percent
Cicero, IL (town) Cook County	86.35
Waukegan, IL (city) Lake County	86.09
Bensenville, IL (village) Du Page County	84.70
Franklin Park, IL (village) Cook County	83.81
Palatine, IL (village) Cook County	83.30
Melrose Park, IL (village) Cook County	82.07
Elgin, IL (city) Kane County	81.62
Aurora, IL (city) Kane County	80.63
Chicago, IL (city) Cook County	78.54
Blue Island, IL (city) Cook County	76.67

Foreign Born

Total Population
Top 10 Places Sorted by Number

Place	Number
Chicago, IL (city) Cook County	628,903
Cicero, IL (town) Cook County	37,343
Aurora, IL (city) Kane County	30,858
Waukegan, IL (city) Lake County	26,556
Skokie, IL (village) Cook County	23,437
Elgin, IL (city) Kane County	22,258
Mount Prospect, IL (village) Cook County	15,159
Naperville, IL (city) Du Page County	14,963
Schaumburg, IL (village) Cook County	14,262
Palatine, IL (village) Cook County	14,249

Total Population
Top 10 Places Sorted by Percent

Place	Percent
Cicero, IL (town) Cook County	43.62
Schiller Park, IL (village) Cook County	39.07
Skokie, IL (village) Cook County	37.01
Prospect Heights, IL (city) Cook County	36.48
Melrose Park, IL (village) Cook County	35.31
Addison, IL (village) Du Page County	34.26
Lincolnwood, IL (village) Cook County	34.11
Summit, IL (village) Cook County	34.09
West Chicago, IL (city) Du Page County	34.07
Niles, IL (village) Cook County	33.65

Hispanic
Top 10 Places Sorted by Number

Place	Number
Chicago, IL (city) Cook County	343,526
Cicero, IL (town) Cook County	34,917
Aurora, IL (city) Kane County	24,647
Waukegan, IL (city) Lake County	22,071
Elgin, IL (city) Kane County	17,777
Joliet, IL (city) Will County	9,034
Berwyn, IL (city) Cook County	8,813
West Chicago, IL (city) Du Page County	7,286
Carpentersville, IL (village) Kane County	7,154
Rockford, IL (city) Winnebago County	7,133

Hispanic
Top 10 Places Sorted by Percent

Place	Percent
Prospect Heights, IL (city) Cook County	70.49
Highland Park, IL (city) Lake County	66.90
Rolling Meadows, IL (city) Cook County	65.06
Woodstock, IL (city) McHenry County	64.18
West Chicago, IL (city) Du Page County	63.59
Mount Prospect, IL (village) Cook County	62.72
Mundelein, IL (village) Lake County	62.29
Palatine, IL (village) Cook County	62.03
Addison, IL (village) Du Page County	61.29
Wheeling, IL (village) Cook County	61.06

Argentinian
Top 10 Places Sorted by Number

Place	Number
Chicago, IL (city) Cook County	859

Argentinian
Top 10 Places Sorted by Percent

Place	Percent
Chicago, IL (city) Cook County	80.73

Bolivian
Top 10 Places Sorted by Number

Place	Number
Chicago, IL (city) Cook County	214

Bolivian
Top 10 Places Sorted by Percent

Place	Percent
Chicago, IL (city) Cook County	44.86

Central American
Top 10 Places Sorted by Number

Place	Number
Chicago, IL (city) Cook County	17,187
Waukegan, IL (city) Lake County	2,202
Cicero, IL (town) Cook County	664
Aurora, IL (city) Kane County	427
Skokie, IL (village) Cook County	361

Central American
Top 10 Places Sorted by Percent

Place	Percent
Aurora, IL (city) Kane County	86.44
Waukegan, IL (city) Lake County	80.34
Cicero, IL (town) Cook County	77.84
Skokie, IL (village) Cook County	76.00
Chicago, IL (city) Cook County	71.14

Chilean
Top 10 Places Sorted by Number

Place	Number
Chicago, IL (city) Cook County	522

Chilean
Top 10 Places Sorted by Percent

Place	Percent
Chicago, IL (city) Cook County	75.65

Colombian
Top 10 Places Sorted by Number

Place	Number
Chicago, IL (city) Cook County	4,365

Notes: Please refer to the User's Guide for an explanation of data; tables include places with populations > 9,999 and reflect only those areas that meet Summary File 4 population thresholds, therefore there may be less than 10 places listed

Colombian
Top 10 Places Sorted by Percent

Place	Percent
Chicago, IL (city) Cook County	71.66

Costa Rican
Top 10 Places Sorted by Number

Place	Number
Chicago, IL (city) Cook County	519

Costa Rican
Top 10 Places Sorted by Percent

Place	Percent
Chicago, IL (city) Cook County	70.90

Cuban
Top 10 Places Sorted by Number

Place	Number
Chicago, IL (city) Cook County	4,962
Melrose Park, IL (village) Cook County	253
Aurora, IL (city) Kane County	120

Cuban
Top 10 Places Sorted by Percent

Place	Percent
Melrose Park, IL (village) Cook County	73.55
Chicago, IL (city) Cook County	61.18
Aurora, IL (city) Kane County	31.33

Dominican
Top 10 Places Sorted by Number

Place	Number
Chicago, IL (city) Cook County	1,236

Dominican
Top 10 Places Sorted by Percent

Place	Percent
Chicago, IL (city) Cook County	59.83

Ecuadorian
Top 10 Places Sorted by Number

Place	Number
Chicago, IL (city) Cook County	7,540

Ecuadorian
Top 10 Places Sorted by Percent

Place	Percent
Chicago, IL (city) Cook County	75.73

Guatelmalan
Top 10 Places Sorted by Number

Place	Number
Chicago, IL (city) Cook County	10,163
Cicero, IL (town) Cook County	306

Guatelmalan
Top 10 Places Sorted by Percent

Place	Percent
Chicago, IL (city) Cook County	70.61
Cicero, IL (town) Cook County	68.61

Honduran
Top 10 Places Sorted by Number

Place	Number
Chicago, IL (city) Cook County	2,327
Waukegan, IL (city) Lake County	1,268

Honduran
Top 10 Places Sorted by Percent

Place	Percent
Waukegan, IL (city) Lake County	82.12
Chicago, IL (city) Cook County	74.51

Mexican
Top 10 Places Sorted by Number

Place	Number
Chicago, IL (city) Cook County	283,531
Cicero, IL (town) Cook County	32,528
Aurora, IL (city) Kane County	22,661
Waukegan, IL (city) Lake County	18,062
Elgin, IL (city) Kane County	16,733
Joliet, IL (city) Will County	8,471
Berwyn, IL (city) Cook County	7,724
West Chicago, IL (city) Du Page County	6,933
Carpentersville, IL (village) Kane County	6,735
Rockford, IL (city) Winnebago County	6,337

Mexican
Top 10 Places Sorted by Percent

Place	Percent
Prospect Heights, IL (city) Cook County	72.57
Highland Park, IL (city) Lake County	71.54
Rolling Meadows, IL (city) Cook County	69.35
Mount Prospect, IL (village) Cook County	68.99
Glen Ellyn, IL (village) Du Page County	65.73
Palatine, IL (village) Cook County	65.67
Woodstock, IL (city) McHenry County	65.45
Mundelein, IL (village) Lake County	65.25
West Chicago, IL (city) Du Page County	64.88
Villa Park, IL (village) Du Page County	63.84

Nicaraguan
Top 10 Places Sorted by Number

Place	Number
Chicago, IL (city) Cook County	622

Nicaraguan
Top 10 Places Sorted by Percent

Place	Percent
Chicago, IL (city) Cook County	66.38

Panamanian
Top 10 Places Sorted by Number

Place	Number
Chicago, IL (city) Cook County	433

Panamanian
Top 10 Places Sorted by Percent

Place	Percent
Chicago, IL (city) Cook County	51.30

Paraguayan
Top 10 Places Sorted by Number

Place	Number
No places met population threshold	

Paraguayan
Top 10 Places Sorted by Percent

Place	Percent
No places met population threshold	

Peruvian
Top 10 Places Sorted by Number

Place	Number
Chicago, IL (city) Cook County	2,250

Peruvian
Top 10 Places Sorted by Percent

Place	Percent
Chicago, IL (city) Cook County	76.09

Puerto Rican
Top 10 Places Sorted by Number

Place	Number
Chicago, IL (city) Cook County	2,330
Aurora, IL (city) Kane County	59
Cicero, IL (town) Cook County	55
Waukegan, IL (city) Lake County	50
North Chicago, IL (city) Lake County	37
Carpentersville, IL (village) Kane County	26
Schaumburg, IL (village) Cook County	18
Bolingbrook, IL (village) Will County	8
Franklin Park, IL (village) Cook County	8
Streamwood, IL (village) Cook County	8

Puerto Rican
Top 10 Places Sorted by Percent

Place	Percent
North Chicago, IL (city) Lake County	5.38
Carpentersville, IL (village) Kane County	5.32
Schaumburg, IL (village) Cook County	3.20
Aurora, IL (city) Kane County	2.42
Cicero, IL (town) Cook County	2.32
Chicago, IL (city) Cook County	2.09
Waukegan, IL (city) Lake County	1.71
Bolingbrook, IL (village) Will County	1.68
Streamwood, IL (village) Cook County	1.60
Evanston, IL (city) Cook County	1.37

Salvadoran
Top 10 Places Sorted by Number

Place	Number
Chicago, IL (city) Cook County	2,531
Waukegan, IL (city) Lake County	399

Salvadoran
Top 10 Places Sorted by Percent

Place	Percent
Chicago, IL (city) Cook County	75.26
Waukegan, IL (city) Lake County	72.94

South American
Top 10 Places Sorted by Number

Place	Number
Chicago, IL (city) Cook County	17,142
Cicero, IL (town) Cook County	501
Berwyn, IL (city) Cook County	335
Naperville, IL (city) Du Page County	334
Skokie, IL (village) Cook County	298
Streamwood, IL (village) Cook County	276
Aurora, IL (city) Kane County	148

South American
Top 10 Places Sorted by Percent

Place	Percent
Berwyn, IL (city) Cook County	77.91
Cicero, IL (town) Cook County	74.22
Chicago, IL (city) Cook County	74.16
Skokie, IL (village) Cook County	68.19
Naperville, IL (city) Du Page County	67.20
Streamwood, IL (village) Cook County	62.59
Aurora, IL (city) Kane County	43.53

Spaniard
Top 10 Places Sorted by Number

Place	Number
Chicago, IL (city) Cook County	380

Notes: Please refer to the User's Guide for an explanation of data; tables include places with populations > 9,999 and reflect only those areas that meet Summary File 4 population thresholds, therefore there may be less than 10 places listed

Spaniard
Top 10 Places Sorted by Percent

Place	Percent
Chicago, IL (city) Cook County	45.02

Uruguayan
Top 10 Places Sorted by Number

Place	Number
No places met population threshold	

Uruguayan
Top 10 Places Sorted by Percent

Place	Percent
No places met population threshold	

Venezuelan
Top 10 Places Sorted by Number

Place	Number
Chicago, IL (city) Cook County	600

Venezuelan
Top 10 Places Sorted by Percent

Place	Percent
Chicago, IL (city) Cook County	76.73

Other Hispanic
Top 10 Places Sorted by Number

Place	Number
Chicago, IL (city) Cook County	16,758
Waukegan, IL (city) Lake County	1,501
Aurora, IL (city) Kane County	1,204
Cicero, IL (town) Cook County	977
Elgin, IL (city) Kane County	740
Joliet, IL (city) Will County	346
Berwyn, IL (city) Cook County	288
Rockford, IL (city) Winnebago County	262
Hoffman Estates, IL (village) Cook County	250
Palatine, IL (village) Cook County	249

Other Hispanic
Top 10 Places Sorted by Percent

Place	Percent
Blue Island, IL (city) Cook County	50.11
Waukegan, IL (city) Lake County	46.63
Wheeling, IL (village) Cook County	45.43
Palatine, IL (village) Cook County	44.78
West Chicago, IL (city) Du Page County	43.60
Bensenville, IL (village) Du Page County	42.86
Elgin, IL (city) Kane County	42.65
Hoffman Estates, IL (village) Cook County	42.16
Addison, IL (village) Du Page County	41.24
Skokie, IL (village) Cook County	41.15

Foreign-Born Naturalized Citizens

Total Population
Top 10 Places Sorted by Number

Place	Number
Chicago, IL (city) Cook County	223,984
Skokie, IL (village) Cook County	13,753
Cicero, IL (town) Cook County	10,076
Aurora, IL (city) Kane County	8,494
Des Plaines, IL (city) Cook County	6,827
Waukegan, IL (city) Lake County	6,422
Niles, IL (village) Cook County	6,401
Naperville, IL (city) Du Page County	6,400
Schaumburg, IL (village) Cook County	6,120
Elgin, IL (city) Kane County	6,059

Total Population
Top 10 Places Sorted by Percent

Place	Percent
Lincolnwood, IL (village) Cook County	26.15
Morton Grove, IL (village) Cook County	23.32
Skokie, IL (village) Cook County	21.72
Niles, IL (village) Cook County	21.23
Norridge, IL (village) Cook County	20.76
Schiller Park, IL (village) Cook County	14.86
Addison, IL (village) Du Page County	12.22
Glenview, IL (village) Cook County	12.06
Glendale Heights, IL (village) Du Page County	12.04
Cicero, IL (town) Cook County	11.77

Hispanic
Top 10 Places Sorted by Number

Place	Number
Chicago, IL (city) Cook County	95,289
Cicero, IL (town) Cook County	8,604
Aurora, IL (city) Kane County	5,561
Waukegan, IL (city) Lake County	4,088
Elgin, IL (city) Kane County	3,575
Berwyn, IL (city) Cook County	3,177
Joliet, IL (city) Will County	1,963
Melrose Park, IL (village) Cook County	1,712
Addison, IL (village) Du Page County	1,494
Blue Island, IL (city) Cook County	1,426

Hispanic
Top 10 Places Sorted by Percent

Place	Percent
Lincolnwood, IL (village) Cook County	36.38
Wilmette, IL (village) Cook County	27.37
Morton Grove, IL (village) Cook County	25.29
Skokie, IL (village) Cook County	25.27
Park Ridge, IL (city) Cook County	24.46
Grayslake, IL (village) Lake County	24.17
Libertyville, IL (village) Lake County	23.46
Norridge, IL (village) Cook County	22.87
Wood Dale, IL (city) Du Page County	22.65
Alsip, IL (village) Cook County	22.34

Argentinian
Top 10 Places Sorted by Number

Place	Number
Chicago, IL (city) Cook County	303

Argentinian
Top 10 Places Sorted by Percent

Place	Percent
Chicago, IL (city) Cook County	28.48

Bolivian
Top 10 Places Sorted by Number

Place	Number
Chicago, IL (city) Cook County	111

Bolivian
Top 10 Places Sorted by Percent

Place	Percent
Chicago, IL (city) Cook County	23.27

Central American
Top 10 Places Sorted by Number

Place	Number
Chicago, IL (city) Cook County	6,188
Waukegan, IL (city) Lake County	501
Cicero, IL (town) Cook County	241
Skokie, IL (village) Cook County	172
Aurora, IL (city) Kane County	124

Central American
Top 10 Places Sorted by Percent

Place	Percent
Skokie, IL (village) Cook County	36.21
Cicero, IL (town) Cook County	28.25
Chicago, IL (city) Cook County	25.61
Aurora, IL (city) Kane County	25.10
Waukegan, IL (city) Lake County	18.28

Chilean
Top 10 Places Sorted by Number

Place	Number
Chicago, IL (city) Cook County	222

Chilean
Top 10 Places Sorted by Percent

Place	Percent
Chicago, IL (city) Cook County	32.17

Colombian
Top 10 Places Sorted by Number

Place	Number
Chicago, IL (city) Cook County	1,989

Colombian
Top 10 Places Sorted by Percent

Place	Percent
Chicago, IL (city) Cook County	32.65

Costa Rican
Top 10 Places Sorted by Number

Place	Number
Chicago, IL (city) Cook County	147

Costa Rican
Top 10 Places Sorted by Percent

Place	Percent
Chicago, IL (city) Cook County	20.08

Cuban
Top 10 Places Sorted by Number

Place	Number
Chicago, IL (city) Cook County	3,085
Melrose Park, IL (village) Cook County	189
Aurora, IL (city) Kane County	114

Cuban
Top 10 Places Sorted by Percent

Place	Percent
Melrose Park, IL (village) Cook County	54.94
Chicago, IL (city) Cook County	38.03
Aurora, IL (city) Kane County	29.77

Dominican
Top 10 Places Sorted by Number

Place	Number
Chicago, IL (city) Cook County	570

Dominican
Top 10 Places Sorted by Percent

Place	Percent
Chicago, IL (city) Cook County	27.59

Notes: Please refer to the User's Guide for an explanation of data; tables include places with populations > 9,999 and reflect only those areas that meet Summary File 4 population thresholds, therefore there may be less than 10 places listed

Ecuadorian
Top 10 Places Sorted by Number

Place	Number
Chicago, IL (city) Cook County	2,446

Ecuadorian
Top 10 Places Sorted by Percent

Place	Percent
Chicago, IL (city) Cook County	24.57

Guatelmalan
Top 10 Places Sorted by Number

Place	Number
Chicago, IL (city) Cook County	3,830
Cicero, IL (town) Cook County	154

Guatelmalan
Top 10 Places Sorted by Percent

Place	Percent
Cicero, IL (town) Cook County	34.53
Chicago, IL (city) Cook County	26.61

Honduran
Top 10 Places Sorted by Number

Place	Number
Chicago, IL (city) Cook County	803
Waukegan, IL (city) Lake County	163

Honduran
Top 10 Places Sorted by Percent

Place	Percent
Chicago, IL (city) Cook County	25.71
Waukegan, IL (city) Lake County	10.56

Mexican
Top 10 Places Sorted by Number

Place	Number
Chicago, IL (city) Cook County	72,337
Cicero, IL (town) Cook County	7,849
Aurora, IL (city) Kane County	4,914
Elgin, IL (city) Kane County	3,266
Waukegan, IL (city) Lake County	3,166
Berwyn, IL (city) Cook County	2,710
Joliet, IL (city) Will County	1,790
Melrose Park, IL (village) Cook County	1,370
Blue Island, IL (city) Cook County	1,259
Carpentersville, IL (village) Kane County	1,203

Mexican
Top 10 Places Sorted by Percent

Place	Percent
Libertyville, IL (village) Lake County	28.23
Alsip, IL (village) Cook County	25.46
Wood Dale, IL (city) Du Page County	23.25
Palos Hills, IL (city) Cook County	22.40
Park Ridge, IL (city) Cook County	22.03
Darien, IL (city) Du Page County	21.99
Morton Grove, IL (village) Cook County	21.69
Elmwood Park, IL (village) Cook County	19.84
Warrenville, IL (city) Du Page County	19.75
Goodings Grove, IL (cdp) Will County	18.64

Nicaraguan
Top 10 Places Sorted by Number

Place	Number
Chicago, IL (city) Cook County	170

Nicaraguan
Top 10 Places Sorted by Percent

Place	Percent
Chicago, IL (city) Cook County	18.14

Panamanian
Top 10 Places Sorted by Number

Place	Number
Chicago, IL (city) Cook County	206

Panamanian
Top 10 Places Sorted by Percent

Place	Percent
Chicago, IL (city) Cook County	24.41

Paraguayan
Top 10 Places Sorted by Number

Place	Number
No places met population threshold	

Paraguayan
Top 10 Places Sorted by Percent

Place	Percent
No places met population threshold	

Peruvian
Top 10 Places Sorted by Number

Place	Number
Chicago, IL (city) Cook County	976

Peruvian
Top 10 Places Sorted by Percent

Place	Percent
Chicago, IL (city) Cook County	33.01

Puerto Rican
Top 10 Places Sorted by Number

Place	Number
Chicago, IL (city) Cook County	1,057
Aurora, IL (city) Kane County	36
North Chicago, IL (city) Lake County	31
Waukegan, IL (city) Lake County	24
Carpentersville, IL (village) Kane County	15
Cicero, IL (town) Cook County	10
Franklin Park, IL (village) Cook County	8
Evanston, IL (city) Cook County	5
Schaumburg, IL (village) Cook County	5
Berwyn, IL (city) Cook County	0

Puerto Rican
Top 10 Places Sorted by Percent

Place	Percent
North Chicago, IL (city) Lake County	4.51
Carpentersville, IL (village) Kane County	3.07
Aurora, IL (city) Kane County	1.48
Evanston, IL (city) Cook County	1.37
Franklin Park, IL (village) Cook County	1.36
Chicago, IL (city) Cook County	0.95
Schaumburg, IL (village) Cook County	0.89
Waukegan, IL (city) Lake County	0.82
Cicero, IL (town) Cook County	0.42
Berwyn, IL (city) Cook County	0.00

Salvadoran
Top 10 Places Sorted by Number

Place	Number
Chicago, IL (city) Cook County	809
Waukegan, IL (city) Lake County	150

Salvadoran
Top 10 Places Sorted by Percent

Place	Percent
Waukegan, IL (city) Lake County	27.42
Chicago, IL (city) Cook County	24.06

South American
Top 10 Places Sorted by Number

Place	Number
Chicago, IL (city) Cook County	6,430
Naperville, IL (city) Du Page County	269
Berwyn, IL (city) Cook County	191
Skokie, IL (village) Cook County	188
Cicero, IL (town) Cook County	168
Streamwood, IL (village) Cook County	60
Aurora, IL (city) Kane County	49

South American
Top 10 Places Sorted by Percent

Place	Percent
Naperville, IL (city) Du Page County	54.12
Berwyn, IL (city) Cook County	44.42
Skokie, IL (village) Cook County	43.02
Chicago, IL (city) Cook County	27.82
Cicero, IL (town) Cook County	24.89
Aurora, IL (city) Kane County	14.41
Streamwood, IL (village) Cook County	13.61

Spaniard
Top 10 Places Sorted by Number

Place	Number
Chicago, IL (city) Cook County	112

Spaniard
Top 10 Places Sorted by Percent

Place	Percent
Chicago, IL (city) Cook County	13.27

Uruguayan
Top 10 Places Sorted by Number

Place	Number
No places met population threshold	

Uruguayan
Top 10 Places Sorted by Percent

Place	Percent
No places met population threshold	

Venezuelan
Top 10 Places Sorted by Number

Place	Number
Chicago, IL (city) Cook County	119

Venezuelan
Top 10 Places Sorted by Percent

Place	Percent
Chicago, IL (city) Cook County	15.22

Other Hispanic
Top 10 Places Sorted by Number

Place	Number
Chicago, IL (city) Cook County	5,510
Aurora, IL (city) Kane County	302
Waukegan, IL (city) Lake County	256
Cicero, IL (town) Cook County	249
Hoffman Estates, IL (village) Cook County	157
Elgin, IL (city) Kane County	154
Berwyn, IL (city) Cook County	121
Skokie, IL (village) Cook County	113

Notes: Please refer to the User's Guide for an explanation of data; tables include places with populations > 9,999 and reflect only those areas that meet Summary File 4 population thresholds, therefore there may be less than 10 places listed

Place	
Addison, IL (village) Du Page County	108
Hanover Park, IL (village) Cook County	85

Other Hispanic
Top 10 Places Sorted by Percent

Place	Percent
Skokie, IL (village) Cook County	27.03
Hoffman Estates, IL (village) Cook County	26.48
Addison, IL (village) Du Page County	18.56
Blue Island, IL (city) Cook County	17.49
Franklin Park, IL (village) Cook County	15.26
Hanover Park, IL (village) Cook County	14.66
Moline, IL (city) Rock Island County	13.99
Naperville, IL (city) Du Page County	13.24
Burbank, IL (city) Cook County	12.89
Palatine, IL (village) Cook County	11.51

Educational Attainment: High School Graduates

Total Populations 25 Years and Over Who are High School Graduates
Top 10 Places Sorted by Number

Place	Number
Chicago, IL (city) Cook County	1,304,122
Naperville, IL (city) Du Page County	75,935
Rockford, IL (city) Winnebago County	74,789
Springfield, IL (city) Sangamon County	65,906
Aurora, IL (city) Kane County	63,191
Peoria, IL (city) Peoria County	58,187
Joliet, IL (city) Will County	50,834
Arlington Heights, IL (village) Cook County	50,106
Schaumburg, IL (village) Cook County	47,877
Evanston, IL (city) Cook County	43,244

Total Populations 25 Years and Over Who are High School Graduates
Top 10 Places Sorted by Percent

Place	Percent
Hinsdale, IL (village) Du Page County	97.33
River Forest, IL (village) Cook County	96.79
Wilmette, IL (village) Cook County	96.76
Naperville, IL (city) Du Page County	96.31
Deerfield, IL (village) Lake County	95.91
Northbrook, IL (village) Cook County	95.57
Lisle, IL (village) Du Page County	95.42
Geneva, IL (city) Kane County	95.37
Buffalo Grove, IL (village) Lake County	95.31
Algonquin, IL (village) McHenry County	95.03

Hispanics 25 Years and Over Who are High School Graduates
Top 10 Places Sorted by Number

Place	Number
Chicago, IL (city) Cook County	177,368
Cicero, IL (town) Cook County	11,153
Aurora, IL (city) Kane County	8,071
Waukegan, IL (city) Lake County	6,949
Berwyn, IL (city) Cook County	5,767
Elgin, IL (city) Kane County	5,151
Joliet, IL (city) Will County	4,542
Rockford, IL (city) Winnebago County	2,953
Melrose Park, IL (village) Cook County	2,506
Palatine, IL (village) Cook County	2,225

Hispanics 25 Years and Over Who are High School Graduates
Top 10 Places Sorted by Percent

Place	Percent
Hinsdale, IL (village) Du Page County	96.67
New Lenox, IL (village) Will County	96.15
River Forest, IL (village) Cook County	95.88
Belleville, IL (city) Saint Clair County	92.45

Place	Percent
Sycamore, IL (city) De Kalb County	90.17
O'Fallon, IL (city) Saint Clair County	90.03
Mokena, IL (village) Will County	90.00
Pekin, IL (city) Tazewell County	88.76
Oak Park, IL (village) Cook County	87.92
Wilmette, IL (village) Cook County	86.88

Argentinians 25 Years and Over Who are High School Graduates
Top 10 Places Sorted by Number

Place	Number
Chicago, IL (city) Cook County	670

Argentinians 25 Years and Over Who are High School Graduates
Top 10 Places Sorted by Percent

Place	Percent
Chicago, IL (city) Cook County	81.61

Bolivians 25 Years and Over Who are High School Graduates
Top 10 Places Sorted by Number

Place	Number
Chicago, IL (city) Cook County	303

Bolivians 25 Years and Over Who are High School Graduates
Top 10 Places Sorted by Percent

Place	Percent
Chicago, IL (city) Cook County	87.83

Central Americans 25 Years and Over Who are High School Graduates
Top 10 Places Sorted by Number

Place	Number
Chicago, IL (city) Cook County	7,918
Waukegan, IL (city) Lake County	734
Cicero, IL (town) Cook County	189
Aurora, IL (city) Kane County	155
Skokie, IL (village) Cook County	148

Central Americans 25 Years and Over Who are High School Graduates
Top 10 Places Sorted by Percent

Place	Percent
Skokie, IL (village) Cook County	59.92
Chicago, IL (city) Cook County	52.85
Aurora, IL (city) Kane County	52.54
Waukegan, IL (city) Lake County	47.11
Cicero, IL (town) Cook County	37.06

Chileans 25 Years and Over Who are High School Graduates
Top 10 Places Sorted by Number

Place	Number
Chicago, IL (city) Cook County	444

Chileans 25 Years and Over Who are High School Graduates
Top 10 Places Sorted by Percent

Place	Percent
Chicago, IL (city) Cook County	82.22

Colombians 25 Years and Over Who are High School Graduates
Top 10 Places Sorted by Number

Place	Number
Chicago, IL (city) Cook County	3,096

Colombians 25 Years and Over Who are High School Graduates
Top 10 Places Sorted by Percent

Place	Percent
Chicago, IL (city) Cook County	72.57

Costa Ricans 25 Years and Over Who are High School Graduates
Top 10 Places Sorted by Number

Place	Number
Chicago, IL (city) Cook County	349

Costa Ricans 25 Years and Over Who are High School Graduates
Top 10 Places Sorted by Percent

Place	Percent
Chicago, IL (city) Cook County	72.86

Cubans 25 Years and Over Who are High School Graduates
Top 10 Places Sorted by Number

Place	Number
Chicago, IL (city) Cook County	3,958
Aurora, IL (city) Kane County	175
Melrose Park, IL (village) Cook County	112

Cubans 25 Years and Over Who are High School Graduates
Top 10 Places Sorted by Percent

Place	Percent
Aurora, IL (city) Kane County	88.83
Chicago, IL (city) Cook County	65.88
Melrose Park, IL (village) Cook County	40.88

Dominicans 25 Years and Over Who are High School Graduates
Top 10 Places Sorted by Number

Place	Number
Chicago, IL (city) Cook County	846

Dominicans 25 Years and Over Who are High School Graduates
Top 10 Places Sorted by Percent

Place	Percent
Chicago, IL (city) Cook County	62.07

Ecuadorians 25 Years and Over Who are High School Graduates
Top 10 Places Sorted by Number

Place	Number
Chicago, IL (city) Cook County	3,571

Ecuadorians 25 Years and Over Who are High School Graduates
Top 10 Places Sorted by Percent

Place	Percent
Chicago, IL (city) Cook County	57.26

Guatelmalans 25 Years and Over Who are High School Graduates
Top 10 Places Sorted by Number

Place	Number
Chicago, IL (city) Cook County	4,423
Cicero, IL (town) Cook County	131

Guatelmalans 25 Years and Over Who are High School Graduates
Top 10 Places Sorted by Percent

Place	Percent
Chicago, IL (city) Cook County	50.63
Cicero, IL (town) Cook County	46.45

Hondurans 25 Years and Over Who are High School Graduates
Top 10 Places Sorted by Number

Place	Number
Chicago, IL (city) Cook County	1,048
Waukegan, IL (city) Lake County	350

Hondurans 25 Years and Over Who are High School Graduates
Top 10 Places Sorted by Percent

Place	Percent
Chicago, IL (city) Cook County	51.57
Waukegan, IL (city) Lake County	41.32

Mexicans 25 Years and Over Who are High School Graduates
Top 10 Places Sorted by Number

Place	Number
Chicago, IL (city) Cook County	108,150
Cicero, IL (town) Cook County	9,505
Aurora, IL (city) Kane County	6,081
Waukegan, IL (city) Lake County	4,529
Berwyn, IL (city) Cook County	4,518
Elgin, IL (city) Kane County	4,038
Joliet, IL (city) Will County	3,813
Rockford, IL (city) Winnebago County	2,137
Melrose Park, IL (village) Cook County	1,923
Carpentersville, IL (village) Kane County	1,633

Mexicans 25 Years and Over Who are High School Graduates
Top 10 Places Sorted by Percent

Place	Percent
New Lenox, IL (village) Will County	96.81
Darien, IL (city) Du Page County	89.00
Oak Park, IL (village) Cook County	87.89
Belleville, IL (city) Saint Clair County	85.78
Machesney Park, IL (village) Winnebago County	85.54
Westchester, IL (village) Cook County	83.64
Park Forest, IL (village) Cook County	83.25
Crest Hill, IL (city) Will County	82.78
Libertyville, IL (village) Lake County	81.71
Lombard, IL (village) Du Page County	81.01

Nicaraguans 25 Years and Over Who are High School Graduates
Top 10 Places Sorted by Number

Place	Number
Chicago, IL (city) Cook County	266

Nicaraguans 25 Years and Over Who are High School Graduates
Top 10 Places Sorted by Percent

Place	Percent
Chicago, IL (city) Cook County	52.47

Panamanians 25 Years and Over Who are High School Graduates
Top 10 Places Sorted by Number

Place	Number
Chicago, IL (city) Cook County	514

Panamanians 25 Years and Over Who are High School Graduates
Top 10 Places Sorted by Percent

Place	Percent
Chicago, IL (city) Cook County	85.67

Paraguayans 25 Years and Over Who are High School Graduates
Top 10 Places Sorted by Number

Place	Number
No places met population threshold	

Paraguayans 25 Years and Over Who are High School Graduates
Top 10 Places Sorted by Percent

Place	Percent
No places met population threshold	

Peruvians 25 Years and Over Who are High School Graduates
Top 10 Places Sorted by Number

Place	Number
Chicago, IL (city) Cook County	1,775

Peruvians 25 Years and Over Who are High School Graduates
Top 10 Places Sorted by Percent

Place	Percent
Chicago, IL (city) Cook County	83.22

Puerto Ricans 25 Years and Over Who are High School Graduates
Top 10 Places Sorted by Number

Place	Number
Chicago, IL (city) Cook County	34,342
Waukegan, IL (city) Lake County	1,023
Aurora, IL (city) Kane County	869
Cicero, IL (town) Cook County	679
Elgin, IL (city) Kane County	536
Berwyn, IL (city) Cook County	472
Elmwood Park, IL (village) Cook County	303
Joliet, IL (city) Will County	251
Bolingbrook, IL (village) Will County	221
Naperville, IL (city) Du Page County	217

Puerto Ricans 25 Years and Over Who are High School Graduates
Top 10 Places Sorted by Percent

Place	Percent
Naperville, IL (city) Du Page County	93.53
Evanston, IL (city) Cook County	89.55
Skokie, IL (village) Cook County	85.10
Streamwood, IL (village) Cook County	83.98
Hanover Park, IL (village) Cook County	82.43
Carol Stream, IL (village) Du Page County	80.95
Elmwood Park, IL (village) Cook County	79.74
Joliet, IL (city) Will County	78.68
Bolingbrook, IL (village) Will County	78.65
Schaumburg, IL (village) Cook County	75.35

Salvadorans 25 Years and Over Who are High School Graduates
Top 10 Places Sorted by Number

Place	Number
Chicago, IL (city) Cook County	994
Waukegan, IL (city) Lake County	142

Salvadorans 25 Years and Over Who are High School Graduates
Top 10 Places Sorted by Percent

Place	Percent
Chicago, IL (city) Cook County	48.09
Waukegan, IL (city) Lake County	47.33

South Americans 25 Years and Over Who are High School Graduates
Top 10 Places Sorted by Number

Place	Number
Chicago, IL (city) Cook County	10,759
Naperville, IL (city) Du Page County	289
Skokie, IL (village) Cook County	285
Cicero, IL (town) Cook County	281
Berwyn, IL (city) Cook County	261
Streamwood, IL (village) Cook County	184
Aurora, IL (city) Kane County	147

South Americans 25 Years and Over Who are High School Graduates
Top 10 Places Sorted by Percent

Place	Percent
Naperville, IL (city) Du Page County	89.75
Skokie, IL (village) Cook County	85.84
Berwyn, IL (city) Cook County	83.12
Aurora, IL (city) Kane County	78.19
Streamwood, IL (village) Cook County	73.90
Chicago, IL (city) Cook County	68.97
Cicero, IL (town) Cook County	64.01

Spaniards 25 Years and Over Who are High School Graduates
Top 10 Places Sorted by Number

Place	Number
Chicago, IL (city) Cook County	457

Spaniards 25 Years and Over Who are High School Graduates
Top 10 Places Sorted by Percent

Place	Percent
Chicago, IL (city) Cook County	77.59

Uruguayans 25 Years and Over Who are High School Graduates
Top 10 Places Sorted by Number

Place	Number
No places met population threshold	

Uruguayans 25 Years and Over Who are High School Graduates
Top 10 Places Sorted by Percent

Place	Percent
No places met population threshold	

Venezuelans 25 Years and Over Who are High School Graduates
Top 10 Places Sorted by Number

Place	Number
Chicago, IL (city) Cook County	408

Venezuelans 25 Years and Over Who are High School Graduates
Top 10 Places Sorted by Percent

Place	Percent
Chicago, IL (city) Cook County	78.01

Notes: Please refer to the User's Guide for an explanation of data; tables include places with populations > 9,999 and reflect only those areas that meet Summary File 4 population thresholds, therefore there may be less than 10 places listed

Other Hispanics 25 Years and Over Who are High School Graduates
Top 10 Places Sorted by Number

Place	Number
Chicago, IL (city) Cook County	10,938
Aurora, IL (city) Kane County	630
Waukegan, IL (city) Lake County	523
Cicero, IL (town) Cook County	417
Elgin, IL (city) Kane County	342
Joliet, IL (city) Will County	304
Berwyn, IL (city) Cook County	277
Rockford, IL (city) Winnebago County	270
Naperville, IL (city) Du Page County	250
Hoffman Estates, IL (village) Cook County	219

Other Hispanics 25 Years and Over Who are High School Graduates
Top 10 Places Sorted by Percent

Place	Percent
Schaumburg, IL (village) Cook County	90.83
Naperville, IL (city) Du Page County	82.24
Evanston, IL (city) Cook County	82.00
Bolingbrook, IL (village) Will County	79.14
Hoffman Estates, IL (village) Cook County	76.57
Skokie, IL (village) Cook County	76.53
Moline, IL (city) Rock Island County	69.43
Berwyn, IL (city) Cook County	68.23
North Chicago, IL (city) Lake County	64.00
Joliet, IL (city) Will County	60.44

Educational Attainment: Four-Year College Graduates

Total Populations 25 Years and Over Who are Four-Year College Graduates
Top 10 Places Sorted by Number

Place	Number
Chicago, IL (city) Cook County	462,783
Naperville, IL (city) Du Page County	47,805
Evanston, IL (city) Cook County	29,511
Arlington Heights, IL (village) Cook County	25,101
Aurora, IL (city) Kane County	24,991
Springfield, IL (city) Sangamon County	23,061
Oak Park, IL (village) Cook County	22,637
Schaumburg, IL (village) Cook County	20,273
Wheaton, IL (city) Du Page County	20,247
Peoria, IL (city) Peoria County	19,712

Total Populations 25 Years and Over Who are Four-Year College Graduates
Top 10 Places Sorted by Percent

Place	Percent
Wilmette, IL (village) Cook County	72.58
River Forest, IL (village) Cook County	69.70
Hinsdale, IL (village) Du Page County	68.61
Deerfield, IL (village) Lake County	68.53
Evanston, IL (city) Cook County	62.36
Northbrook, IL (village) Cook County	62.20
Oak Park, IL (village) Cook County	62.12
Highland Park, IL (city) Lake County	61.61
Naperville, IL (city) Du Page County	60.63
Glen Ellyn, IL (village) Du Page County	58.84

Hispanics 25 Years and Over Who are Four-Year College Graduates
Top 10 Places Sorted by Number

Place	Number
Chicago, IL (city) Cook County	32,373
Aurora, IL (city) Kane County	1,306
Cicero, IL (town) Cook County	1,172
Berwyn, IL (city) Cook County	886
Naperville, IL (city) Du Page County	812
Evanston, IL (city) Cook County	758
Waukegan, IL (city) Lake County	727
Elgin, IL (city) Kane County	721
Skokie, IL (village) Cook County	546
Oak Park, IL (village) Cook County	545

Hispanics 25 Years and Over Who are Four-Year College Graduates
Top 10 Places Sorted by Percent

Place	Percent
Urbana, IL (city) Champaign County	65.29
River Forest, IL (village) Cook County	65.02
Deerfield, IL (village) Lake County	52.90
Hinsdale, IL (village) Du Page County	49.05
O'Fallon, IL (city) Saint Clair County	44.85
Oak Park, IL (village) Cook County	42.22
Macomb, IL (city) McDonough County	41.79
Quincy, IL (city) Adams County	40.83
Wilmette, IL (village) Cook County	40.05
Naperville, IL (city) Du Page County	35.63

Argentinians 25 Years and Over Who are Four-Year College Graduates
Top 10 Places Sorted by Number

Place	Number
Chicago, IL (city) Cook County	334

Argentinians 25 Years and Over Who are Four-Year College Graduates
Top 10 Places Sorted by Percent

Place	Percent
Chicago, IL (city) Cook County	40.68

Bolivians 25 Years and Over Who are Four-Year College Graduates
Top 10 Places Sorted by Number

Place	Number
Chicago, IL (city) Cook County	221

Bolivians 25 Years and Over Who are Four-Year College Graduates
Top 10 Places Sorted by Percent

Place	Percent
Chicago, IL (city) Cook County	64.06

Central Americans 25 Years and Over Who are Four-Year College Graduates
Top 10 Places Sorted by Number

Place	Number
Chicago, IL (city) Cook County	1,438
Waukegan, IL (city) Lake County	92
Aurora, IL (city) Kane County	69
Cicero, IL (town) Cook County	24
Skokie, IL (village) Cook County	21

Central Americans 25 Years and Over Who are Four-Year College Graduates
Top 10 Places Sorted by Percent

Place	Percent
Aurora, IL (city) Kane County	23.39
Chicago, IL (city) Cook County	9.60
Skokie, IL (village) Cook County	8.50
Waukegan, IL (city) Lake County	5.91
Cicero, IL (town) Cook County	4.71

Chileans 25 Years and Over Who are Four-Year College Graduates
Top 10 Places Sorted by Number

Place	Number
Chicago, IL (city) Cook County	214

Chileans 25 Years and Over Who are Four-Year College Graduates
Top 10 Places Sorted by Percent

Place	Percent
Chicago, IL (city) Cook County	39.63

Colombians 25 Years and Over Who are Four-Year College Graduates
Top 10 Places Sorted by Number

Place	Number
Chicago, IL (city) Cook County	1,301

Colombians 25 Years and Over Who are Four-Year College Graduates
Top 10 Places Sorted by Percent

Place	Percent
Chicago, IL (city) Cook County	30.50

Costa Ricans 25 Years and Over Who are Four-Year College Graduates
Top 10 Places Sorted by Number

Place	Number
Chicago, IL (city) Cook County	150

Costa Ricans 25 Years and Over Who are Four-Year College Graduates
Top 10 Places Sorted by Percent

Place	Percent
Chicago, IL (city) Cook County	31.32

Cubans 25 Years and Over Who are Four-Year College Graduates
Top 10 Places Sorted by Number

Place	Number
Chicago, IL (city) Cook County	1,682
Aurora, IL (city) Kane County	116
Melrose Park, IL (village) Cook County	28

Cubans 25 Years and Over Who are Four-Year College Graduates
Top 10 Places Sorted by Percent

Place	Percent
Aurora, IL (city) Kane County	58.88
Chicago, IL (city) Cook County	28.00
Melrose Park, IL (village) Cook County	10.22

Dominicans 25 Years and Over Who are Four-Year College Graduates
Top 10 Places Sorted by Number

Place	Number
Chicago, IL (city) Cook County	265

Dominicans 25 Years and Over Who are Four-Year College Graduates
Top 10 Places Sorted by Percent

Place	Percent
Chicago, IL (city) Cook County	19.44

Ecuadorians 25 Years and Over Who are Four-Year College Graduates
Top 10 Places Sorted by Number

Place	Number
Chicago, IL (city) Cook County	830

Notes: Please refer to the User's Guide for an explanation of data; tables include places with populations > 9,999 and reflect only those areas that meet Summary File 4 population thresholds, therefore there may be less than 10 places listed

Ecuadorians 25 Years and Over Who are Four-Year College Graduates
Top 10 Places Sorted by Percent

Place	Percent
Chicago, IL (city) Cook County	13.31

Guatelmalans 25 Years and Over Who are Four-Year College Graduates
Top 10 Places Sorted by Number

Place	Number
Chicago, IL (city) Cook County	550
Cicero, IL (town) Cook County	14

Guatelmalans 25 Years and Over Who are Four-Year College Graduates
Top 10 Places Sorted by Percent

Place	Percent
Chicago, IL (city) Cook County	6.30
Cicero, IL (town) Cook County	4.96

Hondurans 25 Years and Over Who are Four-Year College Graduates
Top 10 Places Sorted by Number

Place	Number
Chicago, IL (city) Cook County	208
Waukegan, IL (city) Lake County	38

Hondurans 25 Years and Over Who are Four-Year College Graduates
Top 10 Places Sorted by Percent

Place	Percent
Chicago, IL (city) Cook County	10.24
Waukegan, IL (city) Lake County	4.49

Mexicans 25 Years and Over Who are Four-Year College Graduates
Top 10 Places Sorted by Number

Place	Number
Chicago, IL (city) Cook County	16,235
Cicero, IL (town) Cook County	941
Aurora, IL (city) Kane County	782
Berwyn, IL (city) Cook County	689
Elgin, IL (city) Kane County	559
Waukegan, IL (city) Lake County	428
Joliet, IL (city) Will County	387
Evanston, IL (city) Cook County	314
Rockford, IL (city) Winnebago County	272
Palatine, IL (village) Cook County	259

Mexicans 25 Years and Over Who are Four-Year College Graduates
Top 10 Places Sorted by Percent

Place	Percent
Urbana, IL (city) Champaign County	55.00
Darien, IL (city) Du Page County	37.80
Oak Park, IL (village) Cook County	35.45
Champaign, IL (city) Champaign County	28.40
Machesney Park, IL (village) Winnebago County	27.11
Northbrook, IL (village) Cook County	24.60
Belleville, IL (city) Saint Clair County	24.02
Algonquin, IL (village) McHenry County	23.48
Elmhurst, IL (city) Du Page County	23.08
Orland Park, IL (village) Cook County	22.73

Nicaraguans 25 Years and Over Who are Four-Year College Graduates
Top 10 Places Sorted by Number

Place	Number
Chicago, IL (city) Cook County	66

Nicaraguans 25 Years and Over Who are Four-Year College Graduates
Top 10 Places Sorted by Percent

Place	Percent
Chicago, IL (city) Cook County	13.02

Panamanians 25 Years and Over Who are Four-Year College Graduates
Top 10 Places Sorted by Number

Place	Number
Chicago, IL (city) Cook County	214

Panamanians 25 Years and Over Who are Four-Year College Graduates
Top 10 Places Sorted by Percent

Place	Percent
Chicago, IL (city) Cook County	35.67

Paraguayans 25 Years and Over Who are Four-Year College Graduates
Top 10 Places Sorted by Number

Place	Number
No places met population threshold	

Paraguayans 25 Years and Over Who are Four-Year College Graduates
Top 10 Places Sorted by Percent

Place	Percent
No places met population threshold	

Peruvians 25 Years and Over Who are Four-Year College Graduates
Top 10 Places Sorted by Number

Place	Number
Chicago, IL (city) Cook County	662

Peruvians 25 Years and Over Who are Four-Year College Graduates
Top 10 Places Sorted by Percent

Place	Percent
Chicago, IL (city) Cook County	31.04

Puerto Ricans 25 Years and Over Who are Four-Year College Graduates
Top 10 Places Sorted by Number

Place	Number
Chicago, IL (city) Cook County	5,455
Aurora, IL (city) Kane County	161
Naperville, IL (city) Du Page County	108
Waukegan, IL (city) Lake County	97
Evanston, IL (city) Cook County	74
Schaumburg, IL (village) Cook County	70
Elgin, IL (city) Kane County	55
Rockford, IL (city) Winnebago County	55
Berwyn, IL (city) Cook County	53
Bolingbrook, IL (village) Will County	50

Puerto Ricans 25 Years and Over Who are Four-Year College Graduates
Top 10 Places Sorted by Percent

Place	Percent
Naperville, IL (city) Du Page County	46.55
Evanston, IL (city) Cook County	36.82
Schaumburg, IL (village) Cook County	24.31
Rockford, IL (city) Winnebago County	24.12
Skokie, IL (village) Cook County	19.23
Carpentersville, IL (village) Kane County	19.12
Bolingbrook, IL (village) Will County	17.79
Carol Stream, IL (village) Du Page County	17.75

Place	Percent
Des Plaines, IL (city) Cook County	14.68
Melrose Park, IL (village) Cook County	13.94

Salvadorans 25 Years and Over Who are Four-Year College Graduates
Top 10 Places Sorted by Number

Place	Number
Chicago, IL (city) Cook County	193
Waukegan, IL (city) Lake County	0

Salvadorans 25 Years and Over Who are Four-Year College Graduates
Top 10 Places Sorted by Percent

Place	Percent
Chicago, IL (city) Cook County	9.34
Waukegan, IL (city) Lake County	0.00

South Americans 25 Years and Over Who are Four-Year College Graduates
Top 10 Places Sorted by Number

Place	Number
Chicago, IL (city) Cook County	4,081
Naperville, IL (city) Du Page County	175
Skokie, IL (village) Cook County	128
Berwyn, IL (city) Cook County	74
Cicero, IL (town) Cook County	73
Streamwood, IL (village) Cook County	59
Aurora, IL (city) Kane County	47

South Americans 25 Years and Over Who are Four-Year College Graduates
Top 10 Places Sorted by Percent

Place	Percent
Naperville, IL (city) Du Page County	54.35
Skokie, IL (village) Cook County	38.55
Chicago, IL (city) Cook County	26.16
Aurora, IL (city) Kane County	25.00
Streamwood, IL (village) Cook County	23.69
Berwyn, IL (city) Cook County	23.57
Cicero, IL (town) Cook County	16.63

Spaniards 25 Years and Over Who are Four-Year College Graduates
Top 10 Places Sorted by Number

Place	Number
Chicago, IL (city) Cook County	287

Spaniards 25 Years and Over Who are Four-Year College Graduates
Top 10 Places Sorted by Percent

Place	Percent
Chicago, IL (city) Cook County	48.73

Uruguayans 25 Years and Over Who are Four-Year College Graduates
Top 10 Places Sorted by Number

Place	Number
No places met population threshold	

Uruguayans 25 Years and Over Who are Four-Year College Graduates
Top 10 Places Sorted by Percent

Place	Percent
No places met population threshold	

Notes: Please refer to the User's Guide for an explanation of data; tables include places with populations > 9,999 and reflect only those areas that meet Summary File 4 population thresholds, therefore there may be less than 10 places listed

Venezuelans 25 Years and Over Who are Four-Year College Graduates
Top 10 Places Sorted by Number

Place	Number
Chicago, IL (city) Cook County	278

Venezuelans 25 Years and Over Who are Four-Year College Graduates
Top 10 Places Sorted by Percent

Place	Percent
Chicago, IL (city) Cook County	53.15

Other Hispanics 25 Years and Over Who are Four-Year College Graduates
Top 10 Places Sorted by Number

Place	Number
Chicago, IL (city) Cook County	2,930
Aurora, IL (city) Kane County	122
Naperville, IL (city) Du Page County	115
Hoffman Estates, IL (village) Cook County	73
Cicero, IL (town) Cook County	68
Evanston, IL (city) Cook County	62
Waukegan, IL (city) Lake County	61
Skokie, IL (village) Cook County	60
Schaumburg, IL (village) Cook County	58
Berwyn, IL (city) Cook County	52

Other Hispanics 25 Years and Over Who are Four-Year College Graduates
Top 10 Places Sorted by Percent

Place	Percent
Evanston, IL (city) Cook County	41.33
Naperville, IL (city) Du Page County	37.83
Skokie, IL (village) Cook County	28.17
Hoffman Estates, IL (village) Cook County	25.52
Schaumburg, IL (village) Cook County	25.33
North Chicago, IL (city) Lake County	22.67
Streamwood, IL (village) Cook County	16.60
Bolingbrook, IL (village) Will County	15.83
Wheeling, IL (village) Cook County	15.07
Chicago, IL (city) Cook County	14.30

Median Household Income

Total Population
Top 10 Places Sorted by Number

Place	Dollars
Deerfield, IL (village) Lake County	107,194
Wilmette, IL (village) Cook County	106,773
Hinsdale, IL (village) Du Page County	104,551
Highland Park, IL (city) Lake County	100,967
Northbrook, IL (village) Cook County	95,665
River Forest, IL (village) Cook County	89,284
Libertyville, IL (village) Lake County	88,828
Naperville, IL (city) Du Page County	88,771
Goodings Grove, IL (cdp) Will County	84,484
Lake Zurich, IL (village) Lake County	84,125

Hispanic
Top 10 Places Sorted by Number

Place	Dollars
Mokena, IL (village) Will County	152,576
Hinsdale, IL (village) Du Page County	101,611
New Lenox, IL (village) Will County	95,567
Northbrook, IL (village) Cook County	93,181
Lincolnwood, IL (village) Cook County	86,684
O'Fallon, IL (city) Saint Clair County	85,083
Wilmette, IL (village) Cook County	84,399
Goodings Grove, IL (cdp) Will County	82,249
Algonquin, IL (village) McHenry County	82,228
Sycamore, IL (city) De Kalb County	80,625

Argentinian
Top 10 Places Sorted by Number

Place	Dollars
Chicago, IL (city) Cook County	48,095

Bolivian
Top 10 Places Sorted by Number

Place	Dollars
Chicago, IL (city) Cook County	51,964

Central American
Top 10 Places Sorted by Number

Place	Dollars
Aurora, IL (city) Kane County	48,571
Skokie, IL (village) Cook County	45,583
Waukegan, IL (city) Lake County	44,063
Chicago, IL (city) Cook County	39,601
Cicero, IL (town) Cook County	36,719

Chilean
Top 10 Places Sorted by Number

Place	Dollars
Chicago, IL (city) Cook County	58,958

Colombian
Top 10 Places Sorted by Number

Place	Dollars
Chicago, IL (city) Cook County	41,313

Costa Rican
Top 10 Places Sorted by Number

Place	Dollars
Chicago, IL (city) Cook County	39,375

Cuban
Top 10 Places Sorted by Number

Place	Dollars
Aurora, IL (city) Kane County	70,313
Melrose Park, IL (village) Cook County	39,196
Chicago, IL (city) Cook County	33,197

Dominican
Top 10 Places Sorted by Number

Place	Dollars
Chicago, IL (city) Cook County	35,625

Ecuadorian
Top 10 Places Sorted by Number

Place	Dollars
Chicago, IL (city) Cook County	42,017

Guatelmalan
Top 10 Places Sorted by Number

Place	Dollars
Cicero, IL (town) Cook County	42,679
Chicago, IL (city) Cook County	40,470

Honduran
Top 10 Places Sorted by Number

Place	Dollars
Waukegan, IL (city) Lake County	51,293
Chicago, IL (city) Cook County	36,250

Mexican
Top 10 Places Sorted by Number

Place	Dollars
Algonquin, IL (village) McHenry County	101,124
Northbrook, IL (village) Cook County	96,067
Plainfield, IL (village) Will County	92,201
New Lenox, IL (village) Will County	91,984
Darien, IL (city) Du Page County	85,878
Goodings Grove, IL (cdp) Will County	82,912
Libertyville, IL (village) Lake County	80,485
Oswego, IL (village) Kendall County	76,780
Westchester, IL (village) Cook County	75,718
Lake in the Hills, IL (village) McHenry County	75,527

Nicaraguan
Top 10 Places Sorted by Number

Place	Dollars
Chicago, IL (city) Cook County	35,956

Panamanian
Top 10 Places Sorted by Number

Place	Dollars
Chicago, IL (city) Cook County	44,297

Paraguayan
Top 10 Places Sorted by Number

Place	Dollars
No places met population threshold	

Peruvian
Top 10 Places Sorted by Number

Place	Dollars
Chicago, IL (city) Cook County	44,921

Puerto Rican
Top 10 Places Sorted by Number

Place	Dollars
Bolingbrook, IL (village) Will County	87,612
Carol Stream, IL (village) Du Page County	80,701
Skokie, IL (village) Cook County	75,000
Evanston, IL (city) Cook County	70,917
Streamwood, IL (village) Cook County	64,074
Naperville, IL (city) Du Page County	61,667
Franklin Park, IL (village) Cook County	59,737
Schaumburg, IL (village) Cook County	55,625
Des Plaines, IL (city) Cook County	52,250
Elmwood Park, IL (village) Cook County	48,958

Salvadoran
Top 10 Places Sorted by Number

Place	Dollars
Waukegan, IL (city) Lake County	38,958
Chicago, IL (city) Cook County	38,274

South American
Top 10 Places Sorted by Number

Place	Dollars
Naperville, IL (city) Du Page County	86,302
Skokie, IL (village) Cook County	67,750
Streamwood, IL (village) Cook County	60,882
Berwyn, IL (city) Cook County	51,563
Chicago, IL (city) Cook County	43,280
Cicero, IL (town) Cook County	35,350
Aurora, IL (city) Kane County	33,646

Spaniard
Top 10 Places Sorted by Number

Place	Dollars
Chicago, IL (city) Cook County	38,866

Notes: Please refer to the User's Guide for an explanation of data; tables include places with populations > 9,999 and reflect only those areas that meet Summary File 4 population thresholds, therefore there may be less than 10 places listed

Uruguayan
Top 10 Places Sorted by Number.

Place	Dollars
No places met population threshold	

Venezuelan
Top 10 Places Sorted by Number.

Place	Dollars
Chicago, IL (city) Cook County	36,724

Other Hispanic
Top 10 Places Sorted by Number.

Place	Dollars
Burbank, IL (city) Cook County	80,602
Schaumburg, IL (village) Cook County	78,571
Mount Prospect, IL (village) Cook County	63,250
Palatine, IL (village) Cook County	62,679
Streamwood, IL (village) Cook County	62,368
Round Lake Beach, IL (village) Lake County	59,519
Melrose Park, IL (village) Cook County	53,750
Naperville, IL (city) Du Page County	53,281
Franklin Park, IL (village) Cook County	53,125
Skokie, IL (village) Cook County	51,875

Per Capita Income

Total Population
Top 10 Places Sorted by Number.

Place	Dollars
Hinsdale, IL (village) Du Page County	63,765
Wilmette, IL (village) Cook County	55,611
Highland Park, IL (city) Lake County	55,331
Northbrook, IL (village) Cook County	50,765
Deerfield, IL (village) Lake County	50,664
River Forest, IL (village) Cook County	46,123
Glenview, IL (village) Cook County	43,384
Libertyville, IL (village) Lake County	40,426
Glen Ellyn, IL (village) Du Page County	39,783
Buffalo Grove, IL (village) Lake County	36,696

Hispanic
Top 10 Places Sorted by Number.

Place	Dollars
Hinsdale, IL (village) Du Page County	42,899
River Forest, IL (village) Cook County	35,373
Mokena, IL (village) Will County	28,538
Wilmette, IL (village) Cook County	28,438
Bloomingdale, IL (village) Du Page County	27,478
O'Fallon, IL (city) Saint Clair County	25,539
Roselle, IL (village) Du Page County	24,479
Westchester, IL (village) Cook County	24,173
Buffalo Grove, IL (village) Lake County	23,835
New Lenox, IL (village) Will County	23,575

Argentinian
Top 10 Places Sorted by Number.

Place	Dollars
Chicago, IL (city) Cook County	27,553

Bolivian
Top 10 Places Sorted by Number.

Place	Dollars
Chicago, IL (city) Cook County	19,579

Central American
Top 10 Places Sorted by Number.

Place	Dollars
Aurora, IL (city) Kane County	18,303
Skokie, IL (village) Cook County	14,788
Chicago, IL (city) Cook County	13,654

Place	Dollars
Waukegan, IL (city) Lake County	13,195
Cicero, IL (town) Cook County	10,176

Chilean
Top 10 Places Sorted by Number.

Place	Dollars
Chicago, IL (city) Cook County	24,029

Colombian
Top 10 Places Sorted by Number.

Place	Dollars
Chicago, IL (city) Cook County	20,776

Costa Rican
Top 10 Places Sorted by Number.

Place	Dollars
Chicago, IL (city) Cook County	13,303

Cuban
Top 10 Places Sorted by Number.

Place	Dollars
Aurora, IL (city) Kane County	23,987
Chicago, IL (city) Cook County	22,708
Melrose Park, IL (village) Cook County	22,685

Dominican
Top 10 Places Sorted by Number.

Place	Dollars
Chicago, IL (city) Cook County	14,121

Ecuadorian
Top 10 Places Sorted by Number.

Place	Dollars
Chicago, IL (city) Cook County	14,688

Guatelmalan
Top 10 Places Sorted by Number.

Place	Dollars
Chicago, IL (city) Cook County	13,089
Cicero, IL (town) Cook County	10,154

Honduran
Top 10 Places Sorted by Number.

Place	Dollars
Chicago, IL (city) Cook County	13,018
Waukegan, IL (city) Lake County	12,678

Mexican
Top 10 Places Sorted by Number.

Place	Dollars
Westchester, IL (village) Cook County	25,119
New Lenox, IL (village) Will County	24,372
Goodings Grove, IL (cdp) Will County	23,977
Northbrook, IL (village) Cook County	23,889
Elmhurst, IL (city) Du Page County	23,147
Palos Hills, IL (city) Cook County	22,935
Crest Hill, IL (city) Will County	22,894
Algonquin, IL (village) McHenry County	22,502
Hazel Crest, IL (village) Cook County	22,293
Bloomingdale, IL (village) Du Page County	22,161

Nicaraguan
Top 10 Places Sorted by Number.

Place	Dollars
Chicago, IL (city) Cook County	13,640

Panamanian
Top 10 Places Sorted by Number.

Place	Dollars
Chicago, IL (city) Cook County	25,991

Paraguayan
Top 10 Places Sorted by Number.

Place	Dollars
No places met population threshold	

Peruvian
Top 10 Places Sorted by Number.

Place	Dollars
Chicago, IL (city) Cook County	18,366

Puerto Rican
Top 10 Places Sorted by Number.

Place	Dollars
Carol Stream, IL (village) Du Page County	24,906
Evanston, IL (city) Cook County	23,694
Naperville, IL (city) Du Page County	22,113
Bolingbrook, IL (village) Will County	21,023
Des Plaines, IL (city) Cook County	20,789
Skokie, IL (village) Cook County	19,236
Joliet, IL (city) Will County	18,319
Schaumburg, IL (village) Cook County	18,147
Elgin, IL (city) Kane County	17,122
Streamwood, IL (village) Cook County	16,975

Salvadoran
Top 10 Places Sorted by Number.

Place	Dollars
Chicago, IL (city) Cook County	13,167
Waukegan, IL (city) Lake County	11,908

South American
Top 10 Places Sorted by Number.

Place	Dollars
Naperville, IL (city) Du Page County	30,935
Skokie, IL (village) Cook County	24,899
Berwyn, IL (city) Cook County	22,183
Chicago, IL (city) Cook County	18,092
Streamwood, IL (village) Cook County	13,742
Aurora, IL (city) Kane County	13,338
Cicero, IL (town) Cook County	11,166

Spaniard
Top 10 Places Sorted by Number.

Place	Dollars
Chicago, IL (city) Cook County	20,135

Uruguayan
Top 10 Places Sorted by Number.

Place	Dollars
No places met population threshold	

Venezuelan
Top 10 Places Sorted by Number.

Place	Dollars
Chicago, IL (city) Cook County	21,465

Other Hispanic
Top 10 Places Sorted by Number.

Place	Dollars
Naperville, IL (city) Du Page County	22,039
Schaumburg, IL (village) Cook County	19,809
Crest Hill, IL (city) Will County	18,160
Streamwood, IL (village) Cook County	16,475
Bolingbrook, IL (village) Will County	15,480

Notes: Please refer to the User's Guide for an explanation of data; tables include places with populations > 9,999 and reflect only those areas that meet Summary File 4 population thresholds, therefore there may be less than 10 places listed

Place	Number
Burbank, IL (city) Cook County	14,910
Franklin Park, IL (village) Cook County	14,573
Elgin, IL (city) Kane County	13,291
Moline, IL (city) Rock Island County	13,244
Skokie, IL (village) Cook County	13,143

Poverty Status

Total Populations with Income Below Poverty Level
Top 10 Places Sorted by Number

Place	Number
Chicago, IL (city) Cook County	556,791
Rockford, IL (city) Winnebago County	20,351
Peoria, IL (city) Peoria County	20,220
Champaign, IL (city) Champaign County	13,398
Cicero, IL (town) Cook County	13,187
Decatur, IL (city) Macon County	12,999
Springfield, IL (city) Sangamon County	12,847
Waukegan, IL (city) Lake County	12,058
Aurora, IL (city) Kane County	12,034
Joliet, IL (city) Will County	10,946

Total Populations with Income Below Poverty Level
Top 10 Places Sorted by Percent

Place	Percent
Carbondale, IL (city) Jackson County	41.36
Macomb, IL (city) McDonough County	29.08
Urbana, IL (city) Champaign County	27.34
Champaign, IL (city) Champaign County	22.11
Harvey, IL (city) Cook County	21.65
Kankakee, IL (city) Kankakee County	21.36
DeKalb, IL (city) De Kalb County	21.28
Chicago, IL (city) Cook County	19.61
Normal, IL (town) McLean County	19.27
Peoria, IL (city) Peoria County	18.77

Hispanics with Income Below Poverty Level
Top 10 Places Sorted by Number

Place	Number
Chicago, IL (city) Cook County	149,626
Cicero, IL (town) Cook County	10,969
Waukegan, IL (city) Lake County	7,095
Aurora, IL (city) Kane County	5,921
Elgin, IL (city) Kane County	3,917
Joliet, IL (city) Will County	3,091
Rockford, IL (city) Winnebago County	3,085
Berwyn, IL (city) Cook County	2,001
Addison, IL (village) Du Page County	1,905
West Chicago, IL (city) Du Page County	1,687

Hispanics with Income Below Poverty Level
Top 10 Places Sorted by Percent

Place	Percent
Carbondale, IL (city) Jackson County	58.03
Urbana, IL (city) Champaign County	41.97
Macomb, IL (city) McDonough County	38.93
Pontiac, IL (city) Livingston County	30.89
Danville, IL (city) Vermilion County	30.75
Champaign, IL (city) Champaign County	30.33
Kewanee, IL (city) Henry County	28.50
Peoria, IL (city) Peoria County	26.70
East Moline, IL (city) Rock Island County	26.54
DeKalb, IL (city) De Kalb County	26.40

Argentinians with Income Below Poverty Level
Top 10 Places Sorted by Number

Place	Number
Chicago, IL (city) Cook County	291

Argentinians with Income Below Poverty Level
Top 10 Places Sorted by Percent

Place	Percent
Chicago, IL (city) Cook County	27.50

Bolivians with Income Below Poverty Level
Top 10 Places Sorted by Number

Place	Number
Chicago, IL (city) Cook County	72

Bolivians with Income Below Poverty Level
Top 10 Places Sorted by Percent

Place	Percent
Chicago, IL (city) Cook County	15.45

Central Americans with Income Below Poverty Level
Top 10 Places Sorted by Number

Place	Number
Chicago, IL (city) Cook County	3,665
Waukegan, IL (city) Lake County	387
Cicero, IL (town) Cook County	195
Aurora, IL (city) Kane County	36
Skokie, IL (village) Cook County	0

Central Americans with Income Below Poverty Level
Top 10 Places Sorted by Percent

Place	Percent
Cicero, IL (town) Cook County	22.86
Chicago, IL (city) Cook County	15.33
Waukegan, IL (city) Lake County	14.29
Aurora, IL (city) Kane County	7.29
Skokie, IL (village) Cook County	0.00

Chileans with Income Below Poverty Level
Top 10 Places Sorted by Number

Place	Number
Chicago, IL (city) Cook County	56

Chileans with Income Below Poverty Level
Top 10 Places Sorted by Percent

Place	Percent
Chicago, IL (city) Cook County	8.12

Colombians with Income Below Poverty Level
Top 10 Places Sorted by Number

Place	Number
Chicago, IL (city) Cook County	1,066

Colombians with Income Below Poverty Level
Top 10 Places Sorted by Percent

Place	Percent
Chicago, IL (city) Cook County	17.70

Costa Ricans with Income Below Poverty Level
Top 10 Places Sorted by Number

Place	Number
Chicago, IL (city) Cook County	204

Costa Ricans with Income Below Poverty Level
Top 10 Places Sorted by Percent

Place	Percent
Chicago, IL (city) Cook County	27.87

Cubans with Income Below Poverty Level
Top 10 Places Sorted by Number

Place	Number
Chicago, IL (city) Cook County	1,306
Melrose Park, IL (village) Cook County	63
Aurora, IL (city) Kane County	48

Cubans with Income Below Poverty Level
Top 10 Places Sorted by Percent

Place	Percent
Melrose Park, IL (village) Cook County	18.31
Chicago, IL (city) Cook County	16.30
Aurora, IL (city) Kane County	12.53

Dominicans with Income Below Poverty Level
Top 10 Places Sorted by Number

Place	Number
Chicago, IL (city) Cook County	335

Dominicans with Income Below Poverty Level
Top 10 Places Sorted by Percent

Place	Percent
Chicago, IL (city) Cook County	16.41

Ecuadorians with Income Below Poverty Level
Top 10 Places Sorted by Number

Place	Number
Chicago, IL (city) Cook County	912

Ecuadorians with Income Below Poverty Level
Top 10 Places Sorted by Percent

Place	Percent
Chicago, IL (city) Cook County	9.21

Guatelmalans with Income Below Poverty Level
Top 10 Places Sorted by Number

Place	Number
Chicago, IL (city) Cook County	1,989
Cicero, IL (town) Cook County	113

Guatelmalans with Income Below Poverty Level
Top 10 Places Sorted by Percent

Place	Percent
Cicero, IL (town) Cook County	25.34
Chicago, IL (city) Cook County	13.93

Hondurans with Income Below Poverty Level
Top 10 Places Sorted by Number

Place	Number
Chicago, IL (city) Cook County	601
Waukegan, IL (city) Lake County	166

Hondurans with Income Below Poverty Level
Top 10 Places Sorted by Percent

Place	Percent
Chicago, IL (city) Cook County	19.50
Waukegan, IL (city) Lake County	10.98

Mexicans with Income Below Poverty Level
Top 10 Places Sorted by Number

Place	Number
Chicago, IL (city) Cook County	105,715
Cicero, IL (town) Cook County	9,442
Waukegan, IL (city) Lake County	5,545
Aurora, IL (city) Kane County	5,352
Elgin, IL (city) Kane County	3,492
Joliet, IL (city) Will County	2,873
Rockford, IL (city) Winnebago County	2,624

Notes: Please refer to the User's Guide for an explanation of data; tables include places with populations > 9,999 and reflect only those areas that meet Summary File 4 population thresholds, therefore there may be less than 10 places listed

Place	Number
Addison, IL (village) Du Page County	1,755
Berwyn, IL (city) Cook County	1,584
West Chicago, IL (city) Du Page County	1,566

Mexicans with Income Below Poverty Level
Top 10 Places Sorted by Percent

Place	Percent
Urbana, IL (city) Champaign County	49.35
Danville, IL (city) Vermilion County	32.11
Champaign, IL (city) Champaign County	31.96
Peoria, IL (city) Peoria County	29.45
Freeport, IL (city) Stephenson County	29.12
McHenry, IL (city) McHenry County	28.77
Worth, IL (village) Cook County	27.75
Kewanee, IL (city) Henry County	26.73
Niles, IL (village) Cook County	26.67
East Moline, IL (city) Rock Island County	25.95

Nicaraguans with Income Below Poverty Level
Top 10 Places Sorted by Number

Place	Number
Chicago, IL (city) Cook County	144

Nicaraguans with Income Below Poverty Level
Top 10 Places Sorted by Percent

Place	Percent
Chicago, IL (city) Cook County	15.67

Panamanians with Income Below Poverty Level
Top 10 Places Sorted by Number

Place	Number
Chicago, IL (city) Cook County	66

Panamanians with Income Below Poverty Level
Top 10 Places Sorted by Percent

Place	Percent
Chicago, IL (city) Cook County	8.01

Paraguayans with Income Below Poverty Level
Top 10 Places Sorted by Number

Place	Number
No places met population threshold	

Paraguayans with Income Below Poverty Level
Top 10 Places Sorted by Percent

Place	Percent
No places met population threshold	

Peruvians with Income Below Poverty Level
Top 10 Places Sorted by Number

Place	Number
Chicago, IL (city) Cook County	326

Peruvians with Income Below Poverty Level
Top 10 Places Sorted by Percent

Place	Percent
Chicago, IL (city) Cook County	11.25

Puerto Ricans with Income Below Poverty Level
Top 10 Places Sorted by Number

Place	Number
Chicago, IL (city) Cook County	26,263
Cicero, IL (town) Cook County	579
Waukegan, IL (city) Lake County	328
Aurora, IL (city) Kane County	230
Berwyn, IL (city) Cook County	202
North Chicago, IL (city) Lake County	177
Elmwood Park, IL (village) Cook County	156

Place	Number
Elgin, IL (city) Kane County	153
Evanston, IL (city) Cook County	81
Carpentersville, IL (village) Kane County	62

Puerto Ricans with Income Below Poverty Level
Top 10 Places Sorted by Percent

Place	Percent
North Chicago, IL (city) Lake County	36.42
Cicero, IL (town) Cook County	24.72
Chicago, IL (city) Cook County	23.90
Evanston, IL (city) Cook County	23.34
Elmwood Park, IL (village) Cook County	21.17
Berwyn, IL (city) Cook County	15.86
Hanover Park, IL (village) Cook County	14.18
Carpentersville, IL (village) Kane County	12.68
Waukegan, IL (city) Lake County	11.37
Rockford, IL (city) Winnebago County	11.06

Salvadorans with Income Below Poverty Level
Top 10 Places Sorted by Number

Place	Number
Chicago, IL (city) Cook County	557
Waukegan, IL (city) Lake County	102

Salvadorans with Income Below Poverty Level
Top 10 Places Sorted by Percent

Place	Percent
Waukegan, IL (city) Lake County	18.65
Chicago, IL (city) Cook County	16.81

South Americans with Income Below Poverty Level
Top 10 Places Sorted by Number

Place	Number
Chicago, IL (city) Cook County	2,960
Cicero, IL (town) Cook County	139
Streamwood, IL (village) Cook County	54
Berwyn, IL (city) Cook County	52
Skokie, IL (village) Cook County	22
Aurora, IL (city) Kane County	0
Naperville, IL (city) Du Page County	0

South Americans with Income Below Poverty Level
Top 10 Places Sorted by Percent

Place	Percent
Cicero, IL (town) Cook County	20.72
Chicago, IL (city) Cook County	12.95
Streamwood, IL (village) Cook County	12.24
Berwyn, IL (city) Cook County	12.09
Skokie, IL (village) Cook County	5.03
Aurora, IL (city) Kane County	0.00
Naperville, IL (city) Du Page County	0.00

Spaniards with Income Below Poverty Level
Top 10 Places Sorted by Number

Place	Number
Chicago, IL (city) Cook County	33

Spaniards with Income Below Poverty Level
Top 10 Places Sorted by Percent

Place	Percent
Chicago, IL (city) Cook County	4.09

Uruguayans with Income Below Poverty Level
Top 10 Places Sorted by Number

Place	Number
No places met population threshold	

Uruguayans with Income Below Poverty Level
Top 10 Places Sorted by Percent

Place	Percent
No places met population threshold	

Venezuelans with Income Below Poverty Level
Top 10 Places Sorted by Number

Place	Number
Chicago, IL (city) Cook County	116

Venezuelans with Income Below Poverty Level
Top 10 Places Sorted by Percent

Place	Percent
Chicago, IL (city) Cook County	15.65

Other Hispanics with Income Below Poverty Level
Top 10 Places Sorted by Number

Place	Number
Chicago, IL (city) Cook County	9,349
Waukegan, IL (city) Lake County	759
Cicero, IL (town) Cook County	488
Elgin, IL (city) Kane County	258
Aurora, IL (city) Kane County	255
Rockford, IL (city) Winnebago County	211
Joliet, IL (city) Will County	145
Addison, IL (village) Du Page County	108
West Chicago, IL (city) Du Page County	88
Melrose Park, IL (village) Cook County	86

Other Hispanics with Income Below Poverty Level
Top 10 Places Sorted by Percent

Place	Percent
Danville, IL (city) Vermilion County	37.98
Dixon, IL (city) Lee County	33.33
Waukegan, IL (city) Lake County	23.67
Moline, IL (city) Rock Island County	21.28
Evanston, IL (city) Cook County	20.90
Crest Hill, IL (city) Will County	20.51
West Chicago, IL (city) Du Page County	19.78
Chicago, IL (city) Cook County	19.00
Galesburg, IL (city) Knox County	18.90
Addison, IL (village) Du Page County	18.56

Homeownership

Total Populations Who Own Their Own Homes
Top 10 Places Sorted by Number

Place	Number
Chicago, IL (city) Cook County	464,912
Rockford, IL (city) Winnebago County	36,304
Naperville, IL (city) Du Page County	34,952
Aurora, IL (city) Kane County	32,621
Springfield, IL (city) Sangamon County	30,575
Peoria, IL (city) Peoria County	27,041
Joliet, IL (city) Will County	25,465
Arlington Heights, IL (village) Cook County	23,565
Decatur, IL (city) Macon County	22,682
Elgin, IL (city) Kane County	22,167

Total Populations Who Own Their Own Homes
Top 10 Places Sorted by Percent

Place	Percent
Goodings Grove, IL (cdp) Will County	98.23
Morton Grove, IL (village) Cook County	94.54
Westchester, IL (village) Cook County	93.81
Lake in the Hills, IL (village) McHenry County	93.54
Bartlett, IL (village) Du Page County	93.45
Algonquin, IL (village) McHenry County	93.21
South Holland, IL (village) Cook County	93.00
Oswego, IL (village) Kendall County	92.26
Northbrook, IL (village) Cook County	91.63

Notes: Please refer to the User's Guide for an explanation of data; tables include places with populations > 9,999 and reflect only those areas that meet Summary File 4 population thresholds, therefore there may be less than 10 places listed

Lincolnwood, IL (village) Cook County   91.37

Hispanics Who Own Their Own Homes
Top 10 Places Sorted by Number

Place	Number
Chicago, IL (city) Cook County	75,480
Cicero, IL (town) Cook County	7,624
Aurora, IL (city) Kane County	6,564
Waukegan, IL (city) Lake County	4,513
Elgin, IL (city) Kane County	3,828
Berwyn, IL (city) Cook County	3,122
Joliet, IL (city) Will County	2,763
Rockford, IL (city) Winnebago County	2,021
Carpentersville, IL (village) Kane County	1,778
Blue Island, IL (city) Cook County	1,354

Hispanics Who Own Their Own Homes
Top 10 Places Sorted by Percent

Place	Percent
Lincolnwood, IL (village) Cook County	100.00
New Lenox, IL (village) Will County	100.00
Oswego, IL (village) Kendall County	100.00
Algonquin, IL (village) McHenry County	94.58
Goodings Grove, IL (cdp) Will County	94.50
Westchester, IL (village) Cook County	93.87
Northbrook, IL (village) Cook County	93.75
Romeoville, IL (village) Will County	90.90
Lindenhurst, IL (village) Lake County	90.16
Sauk Village, IL (village) Cook County	89.58

Argentinians Who Own Their Own Homes
Top 10 Places Sorted by Number

Place	Number
Chicago, IL (city) Cook County	193

Argentinians Who Own Their Own Homes
Top 10 Places Sorted by Percent

Place	Percent
Chicago, IL (city) Cook County	44.99

Bolivians Who Own Their Own Homes
Top 10 Places Sorted by Number

Place	Number
Chicago, IL (city) Cook County	49

Bolivians Who Own Their Own Homes
Top 10 Places Sorted by Percent

Place	Percent
Chicago, IL (city) Cook County	30.43

Central Americans Who Own Their Own Homes
Top 10 Places Sorted by Number

Place	Number
Chicago, IL (city) Cook County	2,781
Waukegan, IL (city) Lake County	296
Aurora, IL (city) Kane County	118
Cicero, IL (town) Cook County	89
Skokie, IL (village) Cook County	57

Central Americans Who Own Their Own Homes
Top 10 Places Sorted by Percent

Place	Percent
Aurora, IL (city) Kane County	77.63
Cicero, IL (town) Cook County	52.05
Skokie, IL (village) Cook County	51.82
Waukegan, IL (city) Lake County	39.52
Chicago, IL (city) Cook County	38.34

Chileans Who Own Their Own Homes
Top 10 Places Sorted by Number

Place	Number
Chicago, IL (city) Cook County	132

Chileans Who Own Their Own Homes
Top 10 Places Sorted by Percent

Place	Percent
Chicago, IL (city) Cook County	44.75

Colombians Who Own Their Own Homes
Top 10 Places Sorted by Number

Place	Number
Chicago, IL (city) Cook County	825

Colombians Who Own Their Own Homes
Top 10 Places Sorted by Percent

Place	Percent
Chicago, IL (city) Cook County	37.83

Costa Ricans Who Own Their Own Homes
Top 10 Places Sorted by Number

Place	Number
Chicago, IL (city) Cook County	102

Costa Ricans Who Own Their Own Homes
Top 10 Places Sorted by Percent

Place	Percent
Chicago, IL (city) Cook County	41.13

Cubans Who Own Their Own Homes
Top 10 Places Sorted by Number

Place	Number
Chicago, IL (city) Cook County	1,431
Aurora, IL (city) Kane County	101
Melrose Park, IL (village) Cook County	70

Cubans Who Own Their Own Homes
Top 10 Places Sorted by Percent

Place	Percent
Aurora, IL (city) Kane County	82.79
Melrose Park, IL (village) Cook County	57.38
Chicago, IL (city) Cook County	41.77

Dominicans Who Own Their Own Homes
Top 10 Places Sorted by Number

Place	Number
Chicago, IL (city) Cook County	265

Dominicans Who Own Their Own Homes
Top 10 Places Sorted by Percent

Place	Percent
Chicago, IL (city) Cook County	33.89

Ecuadorians Who Own Their Own Homes
Top 10 Places Sorted by Number

Place	Number
Chicago, IL (city) Cook County	1,182

Ecuadorians Who Own Their Own Homes
Top 10 Places Sorted by Percent

Place	Percent
Chicago, IL (city) Cook County	41.27

Guatelmalans Who Own Their Own Homes
Top 10 Places Sorted by Number

Place	Number
Chicago, IL (city) Cook County	1,673
Cicero, IL (town) Cook County	37

Guatelmalans Who Own Their Own Homes
Top 10 Places Sorted by Percent

Place	Percent
Cicero, IL (town) Cook County	46.84
Chicago, IL (city) Cook County	40.63

Hondurans Who Own Their Own Homes
Top 10 Places Sorted by Number

Place	Number
Chicago, IL (city) Cook County	253
Waukegan, IL (city) Lake County	135

Hondurans Who Own Their Own Homes
Top 10 Places Sorted by Percent

Place	Percent
Waukegan, IL (city) Lake County	36.29
Chicago, IL (city) Cook County	25.10

Mexicans Who Own Their Own Homes
Top 10 Places Sorted by Number

Place	Number
Chicago, IL (city) Cook County	52,924
Cicero, IL (town) Cook County	6,881
Aurora, IL (city) Kane County	5,457
Waukegan, IL (city) Lake County	3,470
Elgin, IL (city) Kane County	3,206
Berwyn, IL (city) Cook County	2,598
Joliet, IL (city) Will County	2,395
Rockford, IL (city) Winnebago County	1,627
Carpentersville, IL (village) Kane County	1,549
Blue Island, IL (city) Cook County	1,201

Mexicans Who Own Their Own Homes
Top 10 Places Sorted by Percent

Place	Percent
Algonquin, IL (village) McHenry County	100.00
New Lenox, IL (village) Will County	100.00
Oswego, IL (village) Kendall County	100.00
Homewood, IL (village) Cook County	94.64
Morton Grove, IL (village) Cook County	94.27
Goodings Grove, IL (cdp) Will County	92.41
Westchester, IL (village) Cook County	91.30
Sauk Village, IL (village) Cook County	90.40
Romeoville, IL (village) Will County	90.02
Northbrook, IL (village) Cook County	89.86

Nicaraguans Who Own Their Own Homes
Top 10 Places Sorted by Number

Place	Number
Chicago, IL (city) Cook County	122

Nicaraguans Who Own Their Own Homes
Top 10 Places Sorted by Percent

Place	Percent
Chicago, IL (city) Cook County	46.04

Panamanians Who Own Their Own Homes
Top 10 Places Sorted by Number

Place	Number
Chicago, IL (city) Cook County	124

Notes: Please refer to the User's Guide for an explanation of data; tables include places with populations > 9,999 and reflect only those areas that meet Summary File 4 population thresholds, therefore there may be less than 10 places listed

Panamanians Who Own Their Own Homes
Top 10 Places Sorted by Percent

Place	Percent
Chicago, IL (city) Cook County	35.73

Paraguayans Who Own Their Own Homes
Top 10 Places Sorted by Number

Place	Number
No places met population threshold	

Paraguayans Who Own Their Own Homes
Top 10 Places Sorted by Percent

Place	Percent
No places met population threshold	

Peruvians Who Own Their Own Homes
Top 10 Places Sorted by Number

Place	Number
Chicago, IL (city) Cook County	493

Peruvians Who Own Their Own Homes
Top 10 Places Sorted by Percent

Place	Percent
Chicago, IL (city) Cook County	45.56

Puerto Ricans Who Own Their Own Homes
Top 10 Places Sorted by Number

Place	Number
Chicago, IL (city) Cook County	11,526
Waukegan, IL (city) Lake County	493
Aurora, IL (city) Kane County	426
Elgin, IL (city) Kane County	340
Cicero, IL (town) Cook County	286
Berwyn, IL (city) Cook County	238
Elmwood Park, IL (village) Cook County	132
Streamwood, IL (village) Cook County	129
Franklin Park, IL (village) Cook County	124
Joliet, IL (city) Will County	124

Puerto Ricans Who Own Their Own Homes
Top 10 Places Sorted by Percent

Place	Percent
Bolingbrook, IL (village) Will County	100.00
Streamwood, IL (village) Cook County	93.48
Hanover Park, IL (village) Cook County	82.40
Carpentersville, IL (village) Kane County	75.00
Franklin Park, IL (village) Cook County	72.09
Joliet, IL (city) Will County	68.51
Des Plaines, IL (city) Cook County	67.80
Skokie, IL (village) Cook County	63.89
Zion, IL (city) Lake County	63.64
Schaumburg, IL (village) Cook County	62.03

Salvadorans Who Own Their Own Homes
Top 10 Places Sorted by Number

Place	Number
Chicago, IL (city) Cook County	395
Waukegan, IL (city) Lake County	98

Salvadorans Who Own Their Own Homes
Top 10 Places Sorted by Percent

Place	Percent
Waukegan, IL (city) Lake County	57.65
Chicago, IL (city) Cook County	38.84

South Americans Who Own Their Own Homes
Top 10 Places Sorted by Number

Place	Number
Chicago, IL (city) Cook County	3,102
Streamwood, IL (village) Cook County	98
Berwyn, IL (city) Cook County	94
Skokie, IL (village) Cook County	92
Naperville, IL (city) Du Page County	84
Cicero, IL (town) Cook County	68
Aurora, IL (city) Kane County	51

South Americans Who Own Their Own Homes
Top 10 Places Sorted by Percent

Place	Percent
Streamwood, IL (village) Cook County	84.48
Berwyn, IL (city) Cook County	66.67
Naperville, IL (city) Du Page County	65.12
Skokie, IL (village) Cook County	61.33
Aurora, IL (city) Kane County	55.43
Chicago, IL (city) Cook County	40.29
Cicero, IL (town) Cook County	34.69

Spaniards Who Own Their Own Homes
Top 10 Places Sorted by Number

Place	Number
Chicago, IL (city) Cook County	81

Spaniards Who Own Their Own Homes
Top 10 Places Sorted by Percent

Place	Percent
Chicago, IL (city) Cook County	25.31

Uruguayans Who Own Their Own Homes
Top 10 Places Sorted by Number

Place	Number
No places met population threshold	

Uruguayans Who Own Their Own Homes
Top 10 Places Sorted by Percent

Place	Percent
No places met population threshold	

Venezuelans Who Own Their Own Homes
Top 10 Places Sorted by Number

Place	Number
Chicago, IL (city) Cook County	72

Venezuelans Who Own Their Own Homes
Top 10 Places Sorted by Percent

Place	Percent
Chicago, IL (city) Cook County	19.46

Other Hispanics Who Own Their Own Homes
Top 10 Places Sorted by Number

Place	Number
Chicago, IL (city) Cook County	3,370
Aurora, IL (city) Kane County	398
Cicero, IL (town) Cook County	273
Elgin, IL (city) Kane County	214
Waukegan, IL (city) Lake County	202
Joliet, IL (city) Will County	174
Rockford, IL (city) Winnebago County	135
Berwyn, IL (city) Cook County	112
Carpentersville, IL (village) Kane County	103
Streamwood, IL (village) Cook County	87

Other Hispanics Who Own Their Own Homes
Top 10 Places Sorted by Percent

Place	Percent
Burbank, IL (city) Cook County	90.20
Bolingbrook, IL (village) Will County	80.43
Hoffman Estates, IL (village) Cook County	80.37
Carpentersville, IL (village) Kane County	74.64
Skokie, IL (village) Cook County	73.96
Schaumburg, IL (village) Cook County	72.62
Round Lake Beach, IL (village) Lake County	72.20
Joliet, IL (city) Will County	72.20
Streamwood, IL (village) Cook County	71.90
Blue Island, IL (village) Cook County	67.89

Median Gross Rent

All Specified Renter-Occupied Housing Units
Top 10 Places Sorted by Number

Place	Dollars/Month
Lincolnwood, IL (village) Cook County	2,001
Northbrook, IL (village) Cook County	1,279
Streamwood, IL (village) Cook County	1,130
Goodings Grove, IL (cdp) Will County	1,083
Buffalo Grove, IL (village) Lake County	1,079
Wilmette, IL (village) Cook County	1,028
Warrenville, IL (city) Du Page County	1,019
Deerfield, IL (village) Lake County	1,018
Schaumburg, IL (village) Cook County	981
Lake in the Hills, IL (village) McHenry County	963

Specified Housing Units Rented by Hispanics
Top 10 Places Sorted by Number

Place	Dollars/Month
Darien, IL (city) Du Page County	1,288
Mokena, IL (village) Will County	1,125
Streamwood, IL (village) Cook County	1,091
Algonquin, IL (village) McHenry County	950
Roselle, IL (village) Du Page County	950
Hazel Crest, IL (village) Cook County	948
Lisle, IL (village) Du Page County	942
Highland Park, IL (city) Lake County	940
Libertyville, IL (village) Lake County	930
Romeoville, IL (village) Will County	925

Specified Housing Units Rented by Argentinians
Top 10 Places Sorted by Number

Place	Dollars/Month
Chicago, IL (city) Cook County	699

Specified Housing Units Rented by Bolivians
Top 10 Places Sorted by Number

Place	Dollars/Month
Chicago, IL (city) Cook County	882

Specified Housing Units Rented by Central Americans
Top 10 Places Sorted by Number

Place	Dollars/Month
Skokie, IL (village) Cook County	819
Aurora, IL (city) Kane County	767
Waukegan, IL (city) Lake County	691
Cicero, IL (town) Cook County	643
Chicago, IL (city) Cook County	606

Specified Housing Units Rented by Chileans
Top 10 Places Sorted by Number

Place	Dollars/Month
Chicago, IL (city) Cook County	722

Specified Housing Units Rented by Colombians
Top 10 Places Sorted by Number

Place	Dollars/Month
Chicago, IL (city) Cook County	673

Notes: Please refer to the User's Guide for an explanation of data; tables include places with populations > 9,999 and reflect only those areas that meet Summary File 4 population thresholds, therefore there may be less than 10 places listed

Specified Housing Units Rented by Costa Ricans
Top 10 Places Sorted by Number.

Place	Dollars/Month
Chicago, IL (city) Cook County	590

Specified Housing Units Rented by Cubans
Top 10 Places Sorted by Number.

Place	Dollars/Month
Melrose Park, IL (village) Cook County	625
Chicago, IL (city) Cook County	610
Aurora, IL (city) Kane County	563

Specified Housing Units Rented by Dominicans
Top 10 Places Sorted by Number.

Place	Dollars/Month
Chicago, IL (city) Cook County	635

Specified Housing Units Rented by Ecuadorians
Top 10 Places Sorted by Number.

Place	Dollars/Month
Chicago, IL (city) Cook County	650

Specified Housing Units Rented by Guatelmalans
Top 10 Places Sorted by Number.

Place	Dollars/Month
Cicero, IL (town) Cook County	629
Chicago, IL (city) Cook County	613

Specified Housing Units Rented by Hondurans
Top 10 Places Sorted by Number.

Place	Dollars/Month
Waukegan, IL (city) Lake County	678
Chicago, IL (city) Cook County	576

Specified Housing Units Rented by Mexicans
Top 10 Places Sorted by Number.

Place	Dollars/Month
Darien, IL (city) Du Page County	1,288
Streamwood, IL (village) Cook County	1,042
Lisle, IL (village) Du Page County	985
Roselle, IL (village) Du Page County	978
Romeoville, IL (village) Will County	950
Hazel Crest, IL (village) Cook County	948
Highland Park, IL (city) Lake County	934
Lombard, IL (village) Du Page County	911
Libertyville, IL (village) Lake County	900
Westchester, IL (village) Cook County	900

Specified Housing Units Rented by Nicaraguans
Top 10 Places Sorted by Number.

Place	Dollars/Month
Chicago, IL (city) Cook County	709

Specified Housing Units Rented by Panamanians
Top 10 Places Sorted by Number.

Place	Dollars/Month
Chicago, IL (city) Cook County	680

Specified Housing Units Rented by Paraguayans
Top 10 Places Sorted by Number.

Place	Dollars/Month

Specified Housing Units Rented by Peruvians
Top 10 Places Sorted by Number.

Place	Dollars/Month
Chicago, IL (city) Cook County	638

Specified Housing Units Rented by Puerto Ricans
Top 10 Places Sorted by Number.

Place	Dollars/Month
Streamwood, IL (village) Cook County	1,125
Naperville, IL (city) Du Page County	1,039
Skokie, IL (village) Cook County	934
Carol Stream, IL (village) Du Page County	926
Schaumburg, IL (village) Cook County	887
Evanston, IL (city) Cook County	857
Hanover Park, IL (village) Cook County	775
Zion, IL (city) Lake County	735
Des Plaines, IL (city) Cook County	734
Franklin Park, IL (village) Cook County	713

Specified Housing Units Rented by Salvadorans
Top 10 Places Sorted by Number.

Place	Dollars/Month
Waukegan, IL (city) Lake County	680
Chicago, IL (city) Cook County	586

Specified Housing Units Rented by South Americans
Top 10 Places Sorted by Number.

Place	Dollars/Month
Streamwood, IL (village) Cook County	1,250
Naperville, IL (city) Du Page County	931
Skokie, IL (village) Cook County	766
Aurora, IL (city) Kane County	753
Chicago, IL (city) Cook County	670
Berwyn, IL (city) Cook County	638
Cicero, IL (town) Cook County	578

Specified Housing Units Rented by Spaniards
Top 10 Places Sorted by Number.

Place	Dollars/Month
Chicago, IL (city) Cook County	680

Specified Housing Units Rented by Uruguayans
Top 10 Places Sorted by Number.

Place	Dollars/Month

Specified Housing Units Rented by Venezuelans
Top 10 Places Sorted by Number.

Place	Dollars/Month
Chicago, IL (city) Cook County	764

Specified Housing Units Rented by Other Hispanics
Top 10 Places Sorted by Number.

Place	Dollars/Month
West Chicago, IL (city) Du Page County	1,214
Streamwood, IL (village) Cook County	1,202
Blue Island, IL (city) Cook County	1,125
Hoffman Estates, IL (village) Cook County	1,125
Schaumburg, IL (village) Cook County	1,125
Naperville, IL (city) Du Page County	1,079
Round Lake Beach, IL (village) Lake County	956
Bolingbrook, IL (village) Will County	910
Wheeling, IL (village) Cook County	867
Mount Prospect, IL (village) Cook County	845

Median Home Value

All Specified Owner-Occupied Housing Units
Top 10 Places Sorted by Number.

Place	Dollars
Hinsdale, IL (village) Du Page County	520,100
Wilmette, IL (village) Cook County	441,600
River Forest, IL (village) Cook County	386,600
Highland Park, IL (city) Lake County	380,000
Northbrook, IL (village) Cook County	370,800
Deerfield, IL (village) Lake County	342,900

Glenview, IL (village) Cook County	336,000
Park Ridge, IL (city) Cook County	295,800
Lincolnwood, IL (village) Cook County	291,400
Evanston, IL (city) Cook County	290,800

Specified Housing Units Owned and Occupied by Hispanics
Top 10 Places Sorted by Number.

Place	Dollars
Hinsdale, IL (village) Du Page County	644,700
Deerfield, IL (village) Lake County	450,000
Wilmette, IL (village) Cook County	330,500
River Forest, IL (village) Cook County	326,100
Glen Ellyn, IL (village) Du Page County	292,900
Lisle, IL (village) Du Page County	266,700
Northbrook, IL (village) Cook County	262,500
La Grange, IL (village) Cook County	252,500
Glenview, IL (village) Cook County	234,000
Park Ridge, IL (city) Cook County	231,100

Specified Housing Units Owned and Occupied by Argentinians
Top 10 Places Sorted by Number.

Place	Dollars
Chicago, IL (city) Cook County	178,100

Specified Housing Units Owned and Occupied by Bolivians
Top 10 Places Sorted by Number.

Place	Dollars
Chicago, IL (city) Cook County	187,500

Specified Housing Units Owned and Occupied by Central Americans
Top 10 Places Sorted by Number.

Place	Dollars
Skokie, IL (village) Cook County	210,900
Chicago, IL (city) Cook County	145,900
Aurora, IL (city) Kane County	120,000
Cicero, IL (town) Cook County	112,500
Waukegan, IL (city) Lake County	109,000

Specified Housing Units Owned and Occupied by Chileans
Top 10 Places Sorted by Number.

Place	Dollars
Chicago, IL (city) Cook County	179,900

Specified Housing Units Owned and Occupied by Colombians
Top 10 Places Sorted by Number.

Place	Dollars
Chicago, IL (city) Cook County	174,500

Specified Housing Units Owned and Occupied by Costa Ricans
Top 10 Places Sorted by Number.

Place	Dollars
Chicago, IL (city) Cook County	142,000

Specified Housing Units Owned and Occupied by Cubans
Top 10 Places Sorted by Number.

Place	Dollars
Melrose Park, IL (village) Cook County	177,600
Chicago, IL (city) Cook County	167,900
Aurora, IL (city) Kane County	124,700

Notes: Please refer to the User's Guide for an explanation of data; tables include places with populations > 9,999 and reflect only those areas that meet Summary File 4 population thresholds, therefore there may be less than 10 places listed

Specified Housing Units Owned and Occupied by Dominicans
Top 10 Places Sorted by Number.

Place	Dollars
Chicago, IL (city) Cook County	176,000

Specified Housing Units Owned and Occupied by Ecuadorians
Top 10 Places Sorted by Number.

Place	Dollars
Chicago, IL (city) Cook County	158,000

Specified Housing Units Owned and Occupied by Guatelmalans
Top 10 Places Sorted by Number.

Place	Dollars
Chicago, IL (city) Cook County	144,500
Cicero, IL (town) Cook County	88,100

Specified Housing Units Owned and Occupied by Hondurans
Top 10 Places Sorted by Number.

Place	Dollars
Chicago, IL (city) Cook County	150,600
Waukegan, IL (city) Lake County	122,100

Specified Housing Units Owned and Occupied by Mexicans
Top 10 Places Sorted by Number.

Place	Dollars
Lisle, IL (village) Du Page County	335,300
Glen Ellyn, IL (village) Du Page County	325,000
Decatur, IL (city) Macon County	275,000
Northbrook, IL (village) Cook County	270,500
La Grange, IL (village) Cook County	270,000
Glenview, IL (village) Cook County	260,300
Niles, IL (village) Cook County	237,500
Goodings Grove, IL (cdp) Will County	236,300
Downers Grove, IL (village) Du Page County	228,000
Park Ridge, IL (city) Cook County	222,500

Specified Housing Units Owned and Occupied by Nicaraguans
Top 10 Places Sorted by Number.

Place	Dollars
Chicago, IL (city) Cook County	162,500

Specified Housing Units Owned and Occupied by Panamanians
Top 10 Places Sorted by Number.

Place	Dollars
Chicago, IL (city) Cook County	135,400

Specified Housing Units Owned and Occupied by Paraguayans
Top 10 Places Sorted by Number.

Place	Dollars
No places met population threshold	

Specified Housing Units Owned and Occupied by Peruvians
Top 10 Places Sorted by Number.

Place	Dollars
Chicago, IL (city) Cook County	168,900

Specified Housing Units Owned and Occupied by Puerto Ricans
Top 10 Places Sorted by Number.

Place	Dollars
Evanston, IL (city) Cook County	270,800
Carol Stream, IL (village) Du Page County	234,600
Naperville, IL (city) Du Page County	227,100
Skokie, IL (village) Cook County	219,700
Bolingbrook, IL (village) Will County	182,800
Elmwood Park, IL (village) Cook County	170,100
Melrose Park, IL (village) Cook County	165,600
Des Plaines, IL (city) Cook County	159,100
Franklin Park, IL (village) Cook County	150,300
Berwyn, IL (city) Cook County	148,100

Specified Housing Units Owned and Occupied by Salvadorans
Top 10 Places Sorted by Number.

Place	Dollars
Chicago, IL (city) Cook County	141,400
Waukegan, IL (city) Lake County	98,100

Specified Housing Units Owned and Occupied by South Americans
Top 10 Places Sorted by Number.

Place	Dollars
Naperville, IL (city) Du Page County	234,600
Skokie, IL (village) Cook County	177,800
Chicago, IL (city) Cook County	170,700
Berwyn, IL (city) Cook County	132,900
Cicero, IL (town) Cook County	125,000
Aurora, IL (city) Kane County	122,700
Streamwood, IL (village) Cook County	120,800

Specified Housing Units Owned and Occupied by Spaniards
Top 10 Places Sorted by Number.

Place	Dollars
Chicago, IL (city) Cook County	185,300

Specified Housing Units Owned and Occupied by Uruguayans
Top 10 Places Sorted by Number.

Place	Dollars
No places met population threshold	

Specified Housing Units Owned and Occupied by Venezuelans
Top 10 Places Sorted by Number.

Place	Dollars
Chicago, IL (city) Cook County	575,000

Specified Housing Units Owned and Occupied by Other Hispanics
Top 10 Places Sorted by Number.

Place	Dollars
Mount Prospect, IL (village) Cook County	275,000
Skokie, IL (village) Cook County	205,900
Evanston, IL (city) Cook County	192,000
Schaumburg, IL (village) Cook County	187,500
Hoffman Estates, IL (village) Cook County	184,100
Naperville, IL (city) Du Page County	182,100
Addison, IL (village) Du Page County	167,900
Wheeling, IL (village) Cook County	167,500
Burbank, IL (city) Cook County	161,100
Franklin Park, IL (village) Cook County	156,500

Notes: Please refer to the User's Guide for an explanation of data; tables include places with populations > 9,999 and reflect only those areas that meet Summary File 4 population thresholds, therefore there may be less than 10 places listed

Asian Population

Population

Total Population
Top 10 Places Sorted by Number

Place	Number
Chicago, IL (city) Cook County	2,895,964
Rockford, IL (city) Winnebago County	149,704
Aurora, IL (city) Kane County	143,609
Naperville, IL (city) Du Page County	128,300
Peoria, IL (city) Peoria County	112,892
Springfield, IL (city) Sangamon County	112,201
Joliet, IL (city) Will County	106,157
Elgin, IL (city) Kane County	93,895
Waukegan, IL (city) Lake County	87,969
Cicero, IL (town) Cook County	85,616

Total Population
Top 10 Places Sorted by Percent of Asian Population

Asian
Top 10 Places Sorted by Number

Place	Number
Chicago, IL (city) Cook County	127,052
Skokie, IL (village) Cook County	13,321
Naperville, IL (city) Du Page County	11,700
Schaumburg, IL (village) Cook County	10,285
Hoffman Estates, IL (village) Cook County	7,480
Mount Prospect, IL (village) Cook County	6,482
Glendale Heights, IL (village) Du Page County	6,298
Urbana, IL (city) Champaign County	5,283
Palatine, IL (village) Cook County	5,225
Morton Grove, IL (village) Cook County	4,931

Asian
Top 10 Places Sorted by Percent of Total Population

Place	Percent
Morton Grove, IL (village) Cook County	21.96
Oak Brook, IL (village) Du Page County	21.94
Lincolnwood, IL (village) Cook County	21.37
Skokie, IL (village) Cook County	21.04
Glendale Heights, IL (village) Du Page County	19.88
South Barrington, IL (village) Cook County	15.82
Hoffman Estates, IL (village) Cook County	14.86
Urbana, IL (city) Champaign County	14.60
Schaumburg, IL (village) Cook County	13.80
Darien, IL (city) Du Page County	12.67

Native Hawaiian and Other Pacific Islander
Top 10 Places Sorted by Number

Place	Number
Chicago, IL (city) Cook County	1,065

Native Hawaiian and Other Pacific Islander
Top 10 Places Sorted by Percent of Asian Population

Place	Percent
Chicago, IL (city) Cook County	100.00

Native Hawaiian and Other Pacific Islander
Top 10 Places Sorted by Percent of Total Population

Place	Percent
Chicago, IL (city) Cook County	0.04

Asian Indian
Top 10 Places Sorted by Number

Place	Number
Chicago, IL (city) Cook County	24,208
Naperville, IL (city) Du Page County	4,674
Schaumburg, IL (village) Cook County	4,529
Skokie, IL (village) Cook County	3,845
Mount Prospect, IL (village) Cook County	3,155
Glendale Heights, IL (village) Du Page County	2,780
Hoffman Estates, IL (village) Cook County	2,740
Palatine, IL (village) Cook County	2,210
Des Plaines, IL (city) Cook County	1,953
Hanover Park, IL (village) Cook County	1,895

Asian Indian
Top 10 Places Sorted by Percent of Asian Population

Place	Percent
Burr Ridge, IL (village) Du Page County	61.72
Bensenville, IL (village) Du Page County	60.79
Elmhurst, IL (city) Du Page County	58.92
Addison, IL (village) Du Page County	55.92
Oak Brook, IL (village) Du Page County	55.42
Darien, IL (city) Du Page County	51.36
Bartlett, IL (village) Du Page County	50.95
Bloomington, IL (city) McLean County	50.65
Mount Prospect, IL (village) Cook County	48.67
Bloomingdale, IL (village) Du Page County	47.41

Asian Indian
Top 10 Places Sorted by Percent of Total Population

Place	Percent
Oak Brook, IL (village) Du Page County	12.16
Glendale Heights, IL (village) Du Page County	8.78
Morton Grove, IL (village) Cook County	6.82
Darien, IL (city) Du Page County	6.51
Lincolnwood, IL (village) Cook County	6.41
Burr Ridge, IL (village) Du Page County	6.17
Schaumburg, IL (village) Cook County	6.08
Skokie, IL (village) Cook County	6.07
South Barrington, IL (village) Cook County	5.95
Mount Prospect, IL (village) Cook County	5.56

Bangladeshi
Top 10 Places Sorted by Number

Place	Number
No places met population threshold.	

Bangladeshi
Top 10 Places Sorted by Percent of Asian Population

Place	Percent
No places met population threshold.	

Bangladeshi
Top 10 Places Sorted by Percent of Total Population

Place	Percent
No places met population threshold.	

Cambodian
Top 10 Places Sorted by Number

Place	Number
Chicago, IL (city) Cook County	1,911

Cambodian
Top 10 Places Sorted by Percent of Asian Population

Place	Percent
Chicago, IL (city) Cook County	1.50

Cambodian
Top 10 Places Sorted by Percent of Total Population

Place	Percent
Chicago, IL (city) Cook County	0.07

Chinese (except Taiwanese)
Top 10 Places Sorted by Number

Place	Number
Chicago, IL (city) Cook County	31,416
Naperville, IL (city) Du Page County	4,044
Urbana, IL (city) Champaign County	1,803
Skokie, IL (village) Cook County	1,657
Schaumburg, IL (village) Cook County	1,336
Evanston, IL (city) Cook County	1,196
Champaign, IL (city) Champaign County	1,063
Hoffman Estates, IL (village) Cook County	821
Peoria, IL (city) Peoria County	809
Glenview, IL (village) Cook County	700

Chinese (except Taiwanese)
Top 10 Places Sorted by Percent of Asian Population

Place	Percent
Naperville, IL (city) Du Page County	34.56
Urbana, IL (city) Champaign County	34.13
Lisle, IL (village) Du Page County	30.62
Peoria, IL (city) Peoria County	29.58
Vernon Hills, IL (village) Lake County	29.32
Evanston, IL (city) Cook County	26.62
Mundelein, IL (village) Lake County	26.39
Chicago, IL (city) Cook County	24.73
Champaign, IL (city) Champaign County	23.10
Oak Park, IL (village) Cook County	21.57

Chinese (except Taiwanese)
Top 10 Places Sorted by Percent of Total Population

Place	Percent
Urbana, IL (city) Champaign County	4.98
Vernon Hills, IL (village) Lake County	3.30
Lisle, IL (village) Du Page County	3.15
Naperville, IL (city) Du Page County	3.15
Skokie, IL (village) Cook County	2.62
Westmont, IL (village) Du Page County	1.97
Schaumburg, IL (village) Cook County	1.79
Mundelein, IL (village) Lake County	1.77
Glenview, IL (village) Cook County	1.68
Hoffman Estates, IL (village) Cook County	1.63

Fijian
Top 10 Places Sorted by Number

Place	Number
No places met population threshold.	

Fijian
Top 10 Places Sorted by Percent of Asian Population

Place	Percent
No places met population threshold.	

Fijian
Top 10 Places Sorted by Percent of Total Population

Place	Percent
No places met population threshold.	

Filipino
Top 10 Places Sorted by Number

Place	Number
Chicago, IL (city) Cook County	27,874
Skokie, IL (village) Cook County	3,090
Morton Grove, IL (village) Cook County	1,786
Glendale Heights, IL (village) Du Page County	1,744
Waukegan, IL (city) Lake County	1,537
Streamwood, IL (village) Cook County	1,183
Bolingbrook, IL (village) Will County	1,166
Hanover Park, IL (village) Cook County	1,163
Woodridge, IL (village) Du Page County	1,162
Carol Stream, IL (village) Du Page County	1,074

Filipino
Top 10 Places Sorted by Percent of Asian Population

Place	Percent
Berwyn, IL (city) Cook County	59.66
North Chicago, IL (city) Lake County	55.14
Park City, IL (city) Lake County	55.14
Waukegan, IL (city) Lake County	50.07
Cicero, IL (town) Cook County	49.06
Morton Grove, IL (village) Cook County	36.22

Notes: Please refer to the User's Guide for an explanation of data; tables reflect only those areas that meet Summary File 4 population thresholds, therefore there may be less than 10 places listed

Place	Percent
Streamwood, IL (village) Cook County	35.70
Tinley Park, IL (village) Cook County	34.67
Woodridge, IL (village) Du Page County	33.17
Gurnee, IL (village) Lake County	32.49

Filipino
Top 10 Places Sorted by Percent of Total Population

Place	Percent
Morton Grove, IL (village) Cook County	7.95
Glendale Heights, IL (village) Du Page County	5.51
Park City, IL (city) Lake County	5.25
Skokie, IL (village) Cook County	4.88
Lincolnwood, IL (village) Cook County	3.99
Woodridge, IL (village) Du Page County	3.74
Darien, IL (city) Du Page County	3.43
Streamwood, IL (village) Cook County	3.22
Hanover Park, IL (village) Cook County	3.03
Carol Stream, IL (village) Du Page County	2.70

Guamanian or Chamorro
Top 10 Places Sorted by Number

Place	Number
No places met population threshold.	

Guamanian or Chamorro
Top 10 Places Sorted by Percent of Asian Population

Place	Percent
No places met population threshold.	

Guamanian or Chamorro
Top 10 Places Sorted by Percent of Total Population

Place	Percent
No places met population threshold.	

Hawaiian, Native
Top 10 Places Sorted by Number

Place	Number
No places met population threshold.	

Hawaiian, Native
Top 10 Places Sorted by Percent of Asian Population

Place	Percent
No places met population threshold.	

Hawaiian, Native
Top 10 Places Sorted by Percent of Total Population

Place	Percent
No places met population threshold.	

Hmong
Top 10 Places Sorted by Number

Place	Number
No places met population threshold.	

Hmong
Top 10 Places Sorted by Percent of Asian Population

Place	Percent
No places met population threshold.	

Hmong
Top 10 Places Sorted by Percent of Total Population

Place	Percent
No places met population threshold.	

Indonesian
Top 10 Places Sorted by Number

Place	Number
No places met population threshold.	

Indonesian
Top 10 Places Sorted by Percent of Asian Population

Place	Percent
No places met population threshold.	

Indonesian
Top 10 Places Sorted by Percent of Total Population

Place	Percent
No places met population threshold.	

Japanese
Top 10 Places Sorted by Number

Place	Number
Chicago, IL (city) Cook County	6,043
Arlington Heights, IL (village) Cook County	994
Schaumburg, IL (village) Cook County	940
Hoffman Estates, IL (village) Cook County	836
Buffalo Grove, IL (village) Lake County	611
Elk Grove Village, IL (village) Cook County	610
Mount Prospect, IL (village) Cook County	445
Evanston, IL (city) Cook County	376
Wilmette, IL (village) Cook County	346
Glenview, IL (village) Cook County	314

Japanese
Top 10 Places Sorted by Percent of Asian Population

Place	Percent
Arlington Heights, IL (village) Cook County	21.28
Elk Grove Village, IL (village) Cook County	18.42
Buffalo Grove, IL (village) Lake County	16.57
Wilmette, IL (village) Cook County	15.63
Hoffman Estates, IL (village) Cook County	11.18
Schaumburg, IL (village) Cook County	9.14
Evanston, IL (city) Cook County	8.37
Glenview, IL (village) Cook County	7.45
Mount Prospect, IL (village) Cook County	6.87
Chicago, IL (city) Cook County	4.76

Japanese
Top 10 Places Sorted by Percent of Total Population

Place	Percent
Elk Grove Village, IL (village) Cook County	1.75
Hoffman Estates, IL (village) Cook County	1.66
Buffalo Grove, IL (village) Lake County	1.43
Arlington Heights, IL (village) Cook County	1.31
Schaumburg, IL (village) Cook County	1.26
Wilmette, IL (village) Cook County	1.25
Mount Prospect, IL (village) Cook County	0.78
Glenview, IL (village) Cook County	0.75
Evanston, IL (city) Cook County	0.51
Chicago, IL (city) Cook County	0.21

Korean
Top 10 Places Sorted by Number

Place	Number
Chicago, IL (city) Cook County	12,576
Skokie, IL (village) Cook County	2,524
Schaumburg, IL (village) Cook County	1,775
Glenview, IL (village) Cook County	1,597
Northbrook, IL (village) Cook County	1,548
Mount Prospect, IL (village) Cook County	1,446
Hoffman Estates, IL (village) Cook County	1,426
Urbana, IL (city) Champaign County	1,157
Buffalo Grove, IL (village) Lake County	1,095
Niles, IL (village) Cook County	1,005

Korean
Top 10 Places Sorted by Percent of Asian Population

Place	Percent
Northbrook, IL (village) Cook County	53.01
Glenview, IL (village) Cook County	37.92
Wilmette, IL (village) Cook County	35.05
Niles, IL (village) Cook County	29.72
Buffalo Grove, IL (village) Lake County	29.70
Vernon Hills, IL (village) Lake County	27.76
Lincolnwood, IL (village) Cook County	24.61
Mount Prospect, IL (village) Cook County	22.31
Urbana, IL (city) Champaign County	21.90
Champaign, IL (city) Champaign County	19.14

Korean
Top 10 Places Sorted by Percent of Total Population

Place	Percent
Lincolnwood, IL (village) Cook County	5.26
Northbrook, IL (village) Cook County	4.63
Skokie, IL (village) Cook County	3.99
Morton Grove, IL (village) Cook County	3.87
Glenview, IL (village) Cook County	3.83
Niles, IL (village) Cook County	3.33
Urbana, IL (city) Champaign County	3.20
Vernon Hills, IL (village) Lake County	3.12
Hoffman Estates, IL (village) Cook County	2.83
Wilmette, IL (village) Cook County	2.80

Laotian
Top 10 Places Sorted by Number

Place	Number
Elgin, IL (city) Kane County	898
Rockford, IL (city) Winnebago County	898

Laotian
Top 10 Places Sorted by Percent of Asian Population

Place	Percent
Rockford, IL (city) Winnebago County	30.28
Elgin, IL (city) Kane County	27.70

Laotian
Top 10 Places Sorted by Percent of Total Population

Place	Percent
Elgin, IL (city) Kane County	0.96
Rockford, IL (city) Winnebago County	0.60

Malaysian
Top 10 Places Sorted by Number

Place	Number
No places met population threshold.	

Malaysian
Top 10 Places Sorted by Percent of Asian Population

Place	Percent
No places met population threshold.	

Malaysian
Top 10 Places Sorted by Percent of Total Population

Place	Percent
No places met population threshold.	

Pakistani
Top 10 Places Sorted by Number

Place	Number
Chicago, IL (city) Cook County	6,437
Skokie, IL (village) Cook County	495

Pakistani
Top 10 Places Sorted by Percent of Asian Population

Place	Percent
Chicago, IL (city) Cook County	5.07
Skokie, IL (village) Cook County	3.72

Notes: Please refer to the User's Guide for an explanation of data; tables reflect only those areas that meet Summary File 4 population thresholds, therefore there may be less than 10 places listed

Pakistani
Top 10 Places Sorted by Percent of Total Population

Place	Percent
Skokie, IL (village) Cook County	0.78
Chicago, IL (city) Cook County	0.22

Samoan
Top 10 Places Sorted by Number

Place	Number
No places met population threshold.	

Samoan
Top 10 Places Sorted by Percent of Asian Population

Place	Percent
No places met population threshold.	

Samoan
Top 10 Places Sorted by Percent of Total Population

Place	Percent
No places met population threshold.	

Sri Lankan
Top 10 Places Sorted by Number

Place	Number
No places met population threshold.	

Sri Lankan
Top 10 Places Sorted by Percent of Asian Population

Place	Percent
No places met population threshold.	

Sri Lankan
Top 10 Places Sorted by Percent of Total Population

Place	Percent
No places met population threshold.	

Taiwanese
Top 10 Places Sorted by Number

Place	Number
Chicago, IL (city) Cook County	776
Naperville, IL (city) Du Page County	431

Taiwanese
Top 10 Places Sorted by Percent of Asian Population

Place	Percent
Naperville, IL (city) Du Page County	3.68
Chicago, IL (city) Cook County	0.61

Taiwanese
Top 10 Places Sorted by Percent of Total Population

Place	Percent
Naperville, IL (city) Du Page County	0.34
Chicago, IL (city) Cook County	0.03

Thai
Top 10 Places Sorted by Number

Place	Number
Chicago, IL (city) Cook County	2,144

Thai
Top 10 Places Sorted by Percent of Asian Population

Place	Percent
Chicago, IL (city) Cook County	1.69

Thai
Top 10 Places Sorted by Percent of Total Population

Place	Percent
Chicago, IL (city) Cook County	0.07

Tongan
Top 10 Places Sorted by Number

Place	Number
No places met population threshold.	

Tongan
Top 10 Places Sorted by Percent of Asian Population

Place	Percent
No places met population threshold.	

Tongan
Top 10 Places Sorted by Percent of Total Population

Place	Percent
No places met population threshold.	

Vietnamese
Top 10 Places Sorted by Number

Place	Number
Chicago, IL (city) Cook County	8,179
Glendale Heights, IL (village) Du Page County	799
Aurora, IL (city) Kane County	490
Carol Stream, IL (village) Du Page County	472
Champaign, IL (city) Champaign County	430
Rockford, IL (city) Winnebago County	403
Wheaton, IL (city) Du Page County	382

Vietnamese
Top 10 Places Sorted by Percent of Asian Population

Place	Percent
Wheaton, IL (city) Du Page County	14.09
Rockford, IL (city) Winnebago County	13.59
Glendale Heights, IL (village) Du Page County	12.69
Carol Stream, IL (village) Du Page County	11.59
Aurora, IL (city) Kane County	11.14
Champaign, IL (city) Champaign County	9.34
Chicago, IL (city) Cook County	6.44

Vietnamese
Top 10 Places Sorted by Percent of Total Population

Place	Percent
Glendale Heights, IL (village) Du Page County	2.52
Carol Stream, IL (village) Du Page County	1.19
Wheaton, IL (city) Du Page County	0.69
Champaign, IL (city) Champaign County	0.63
Aurora, IL (city) Kane County	0.34
Chicago, IL (city) Cook County	0.28
Rockford, IL (city) Winnebago County	0.27

Median Age

Total Population
Top 10 Places Sorted by Number

Place	Years
Oak Brook, IL (village) Du Page County	50.4
Niles, IL (village) Cook County	46.2
Lincolnwood, IL (village) Cook County	45.4
Morton Grove, IL (village) Cook County	44.6
Westchester, IL (village) Cook County	44.4
Lincolnshire, IL (village) Lake County	44.2
Northbrook, IL (village) Cook County	44.2
Willowbrook, IL (village) Du Page County	43.8
Burr Ridge, IL (village) Du Page County	43.1
Harwood Heights, IL (village) Cook County	42.8

Asian
Top 10 Places Sorted by Number

Place	Years
Oak Brook, IL (village) Du Page County	47.9
Flossmoor, IL (village) Cook County	46.5
Long Grove, IL (village) Lake County	45.9
South Barrington, IL (village) Cook County	44.8
Burr Ridge, IL (village) Du Page County	44.0
Northbrook, IL (village) Cook County	41.4
Lincolnshire, IL (village) Lake County	41.3
River Forest, IL (village) Cook County	40.0
Cicero, IL (town) Cook County	39.4
Highland Park, IL (city) Lake County	39.4

Native Hawaiian and Other Pacific Islander
Top 10 Places Sorted by Number

Place	Years
Chicago, IL (city) Cook County	28.3

Asian Indian
Top 10 Places Sorted by Number

Place	Years
Oak Brook, IL (village) Du Page County	47.2
South Barrington, IL (village) Cook County	45.3
Orland Park, IL (village) Cook County	40.7
Glenview, IL (village) Cook County	39.0
Burr Ridge, IL (village) Du Page County	38.0
Rockford, IL (city) Winnebago County	36.8
Lincolnwood, IL (village) Cook County	35.3
Darien, IL (city) Du Page County	35.2
Gurnee, IL (village) Lake County	34.9
Downers Grove, IL (village) Du Page County	34.2

Bangladeshi
Top 10 Places Sorted by Number

Place	Years
No places met population threshold.	

Cambodian
Top 10 Places Sorted by Number

Place	Years
Chicago, IL (city) Cook County	27.6

Chinese (except Taiwanese)
Top 10 Places Sorted by Number

Place	Years
Glenview, IL (village) Cook County	44.4
Westmont, IL (village) Du Page County	44.2
Northbrook, IL (village) Cook County	42.3
Elk Grove Village, IL (village) Cook County	40.6
Des Plaines, IL (city) Cook County	38.5
Buffalo Grove, IL (village) Lake County	38.2
Downers Grove, IL (village) Du Page County	37.6
Arlington Heights, IL (village) Cook County	37.0
Skokie, IL (village) Cook County	36.9
Wilmette, IL (village) Cook County	36.6

Fijian
Top 10 Places Sorted by Number

Place	Years
No places met population threshold.	

Filipino
Top 10 Places Sorted by Number

Place	Years
Westmont, IL (village) Du Page County	43.1
Lincolnwood, IL (village) Cook County	42.9
Downers Grove, IL (village) Du Page County	41.3
Cicero, IL (town) Cook County	41.0
Addison, IL (village) Du Page County	39.6
Darien, IL (city) Du Page County	39.1
Morton Grove, IL (village) Cook County	37.8

Notes: Please refer to the User's Guide for an explanation of data; tables reflect only those areas that meet Summary File 4 population thresholds, therefore there may be less than 10 places listed

Place	Years
Tinley Park, IL (village) Cook County	37.6
Buffalo Grove, IL (village) Lake County	37.3
Schaumburg, IL (village) Cook County	37.0

Guamanian or Chamorro
Top 10 Places Sorted by Number.

Place	Years
No places met population threshold.	

Hawaiian, Native
Top 10 Places Sorted by Number.

Place	Years
No places met population threshold.	

Hmong
Top 10 Places Sorted by Number.

Place	Years
No places met population threshold.	

Indonesian
Top 10 Places Sorted by Number.

Place	Years
No places met population threshold.	

Japanese
Top 10 Places Sorted by Number.

Place	Years
Chicago, IL (city) Cook County	45.1
Mount Prospect, IL (village) Cook County	40.6
Wilmette, IL (village) Cook County	37.7
Glenview, IL (village) Cook County	36.9
Arlington Heights, IL (village) Cook County	36.4
Buffalo Grove, IL (village) Lake County	36.2
Elk Grove Village, IL (village) Cook County	34.6
Hoffman Estates, IL (village) Cook County	32.9
Evanston, IL (city) Cook County	32.5
Schaumburg, IL (village) Cook County	31.5

Korean
Top 10 Places Sorted by Number.

Place	Years
Lincolnwood, IL (village) Cook County	42.3
Niles, IL (village) Cook County	42.0
Northbrook, IL (village) Cook County	41.7
Morton Grove, IL (village) Cook County	40.8
Wilmette, IL (village) Cook County	38.9
Skokie, IL (village) Cook County	37.4
Naperville, IL (city) Du Page County	36.6
Mount Prospect, IL (village) Cook County	35.5
Glenview, IL (village) Cook County	35.1
Vernon Hills, IL (village) Lake County	34.2

Laotian
Top 10 Places Sorted by Number.

Place	Years
Elgin, IL (city) Kane County	29.8
Rockford, IL (city) Winnebago County	28.7

Malaysian
Top 10 Places Sorted by Number.

Place	Years
No places met population threshold.	

Pakistani
Top 10 Places Sorted by Number.

Place	Years
Skokie, IL (village) Cook County	30.6
Chicago, IL (city) Cook County	30.5

Samoan
Top 10 Places Sorted by Number.

Place	Years
No places met population threshold.	

Sri Lankan
Top 10 Places Sorted by Number.

Place	Years
No places met population threshold.	

Taiwanese
Top 10 Places Sorted by Number.

Place	Years
Naperville, IL (city) Du Page County	40.5
Chicago, IL (city) Cook County	26.4

Thai
Top 10 Places Sorted by Number.

Place	Years
Chicago, IL (city) Cook County	30.8

Tongan
Top 10 Places Sorted by Number.

Place	Years
No places met population threshold.	

Vietnamese
Top 10 Places Sorted by Number.

Place	Years
Glendale Heights, IL (village) Du Page County	31.4
Champaign, IL (city) Champaign County	28.9
Chicago, IL (city) Cook County	28.8
Rockford, IL (city) Winnebago County	28.8
Carol Stream, IL (village) Du Page County	28.6
Aurora, IL (city) Kane County	27.7
Wheaton, IL (city) Du Page County	27.2

Average Household Size

Total Population
Top 10 Places Sorted by Number.

Place	Number
Cicero, IL (town) Cook County	3.69
West Chicago, IL (city) Du Page County	3.65
Carpentersville, IL (village) Kane County	3.49
Round Lake Beach, IL (village) Lake County	3.47
Hanover Park, IL (village) Cook County	3.40
Long Grove, IL (village) Lake County	3.24
South Barrington, IL (village) Cook County	3.24
Bolingbrook, IL (village) Will County	3.23
Lake Zurich, IL (village) Lake County	3.17
Mundelein, IL (village) Lake County	3.11

Asian
Top 10 Places Sorted by Number.

Place	Number
South Elgin, IL (village) Kane County	4.77
Villa Park, IL (village) Du Page County	4.24
Lincolnwood, IL (village) Cook County	3.99
Carpentersville, IL (village) Kane County	3.93
Schiller Park, IL (village) Cook County	3.92
Des Plaines, IL (city) Cook County	3.83
Burbank, IL (city) Cook County	3.77
Bolingbrook, IL (village) Will County	3.76
Bartlett, IL (village) Du Page County	3.75
Orland Park, IL (village) Cook County	3.74

Native Hawaiian and Other Pacific Islander
Top 10 Places Sorted by Number.

Place	Number
Chicago, IL (city) Cook County	3.32

Asian Indian
Top 10 Places Sorted by Number.

Place	Number
Des Plaines, IL (city) Cook County	4.66
Lincolnwood, IL (village) Cook County	4.37
Bloomingdale, IL (village) Du Page County	4.33
Morton Grove, IL (village) Cook County	4.30
Bartlett, IL (village) Du Page County	4.28
Niles, IL (village) Cook County	4.13
Burr Ridge, IL (village) Du Page County	4.10
Orland Park, IL (village) Cook County	4.09
Bolingbrook, IL (village) Will County	4.07
Glendale Heights, IL (village) Du Page County	4.03

Bangladeshi
Top 10 Places Sorted by Number.

Place	Number
No places met population threshold.	

Cambodian
Top 10 Places Sorted by Number.

Place	Number
Chicago, IL (city) Cook County	4.54

Chinese (except Taiwanese)
Top 10 Places Sorted by Number.

Place	Number
Mundelein, IL (village) Lake County	3.53
Naperville, IL (city) Du Page County	3.39
Lisle, IL (village) Du Page County	3.22
Vernon Hills, IL (village) Lake County	3.21
Northbrook, IL (village) Cook County	3.18
Wilmette, IL (village) Cook County	3.11
Hoffman Estates, IL (village) Cook County	3.02
Des Plaines, IL (city) Cook County	3.01
Downers Grove, IL (village) Du Page County	2.96
Skokie, IL (village) Cook County	2.92

Fijian
Top 10 Places Sorted by Number.

Place	Number
No places met population threshold.	

Filipino
Top 10 Places Sorted by Number.

Place	Number
North Chicago, IL (city) Lake County	4.48
Park City, IL (city) Lake County	4.43
Gurnee, IL (village) Lake County	4.32
Lincolnwood, IL (village) Cook County	4.14
Addison, IL (village) Du Page County	4.12
Orland Park, IL (village) Cook County	4.12
Carol Stream, IL (village) Du Page County	3.97
Des Plaines, IL (city) Cook County	3.91
Skokie, IL (village) Cook County	3.84
Mundelein, IL (village) Lake County	3.83

Guamanian or Chamorro
Top 10 Places Sorted by Number.

Place	Number
No places met population threshold.	

Hawaiian, Native
Top 10 Places Sorted by Number.

Place	Number
No places met population threshold.	

Notes: Please refer to the User's Guide for an explanation of data; tables reflect only those areas that meet Summary File 4 population thresholds, therefore there may be less than 10 places listed

Hmong
Top 10 Places Sorted by Number

Place	Number
No places met population threshold.	

Indonesian
Top 10 Places Sorted by Number

Place	Number
No places met population threshold.	

Japanese
Top 10 Places Sorted by Number

Place	Number
Buffalo Grove, IL (village) Lake County	3.16
Elk Grove Village, IL (village) Cook County	3.13
Hoffman Estates, IL (village) Cook County	3.00
Wilmette, IL (village) Cook County	2.95
Mount Prospect, IL (village) Cook County	2.68
Schaumburg, IL (village) Cook County	2.46
Glenview, IL (village) Cook County	2.41
Evanston, IL (city) Cook County	2.20
Arlington Heights, IL (village) Cook County	2.02
Chicago, IL (city) Cook County	1.85

Korean
Top 10 Places Sorted by Number

Place	Number
Buffalo Grove, IL (village) Lake County	3.73
Lincolnwood, IL (village) Cook County	3.67
Naperville, IL (city) Du Page County	3.55
Glenview, IL (village) Cook County	3.48
Hoffman Estates, IL (village) Cook County	3.47
Morton Grove, IL (village) Cook County	3.39
Northbrook, IL (village) Cook County	3.36
Wilmette, IL (village) Cook County	3.31
Arlington Heights, IL (village) Cook County	3.30
Mount Prospect, IL (village) Cook County	3.29

Laotian
Top 10 Places Sorted by Number

Place	Number
Elgin, IL (city) Kane County	4.50
Rockford, IL (city) Winnebago County	3.75

Malaysian
Top 10 Places Sorted by Number

Place	Number
No places met population threshold.	

Pakistani
Top 10 Places Sorted by Number

Place	Number
Skokie, IL (village) Cook County	4.04
Chicago, IL (city) Cook County	3.57

Samoan
Top 10 Places Sorted by Number

Place	Number
No places met population threshold.	

Sri Lankan
Top 10 Places Sorted by Number

Place	Number
No places met population threshold.	

Taiwanese
Top 10 Places Sorted by Number

Place	Number
Naperville, IL (city) Du Page County	3.36
Chicago, IL (city) Cook County	1.60

Thai
Top 10 Places Sorted by Number

Place	Number
Chicago, IL (city) Cook County	2.30

Tongan
Top 10 Places Sorted by Number

Place	Number
No places met population threshold.	

Vietnamese
Top 10 Places Sorted by Number

Place	Number
Aurora, IL (city) Kane County	4.32
Carol Stream, IL (village) Du Page County	4.22
Wheaton, IL (city) Du Page County	3.73
Chicago, IL (city) Cook County	3.49
Glendale Heights, IL (village) Du Page County	3.47
Champaign, IL (city) Champaign County	3.32
Rockford, IL (city) Winnebago County	3.22

Language Spoken at Home: English Only

Total Populations 5 Years and Over Who Speak English-Only at Home
Top 10 Places Sorted by Number

Place	Number
Chicago, IL (city) Cook County	1,726,905
Rockford, IL (city) Winnebago County	119,262
Springfield, IL (city) Sangamon County	100,722
Naperville, IL (city) Du Page County	99,729
Peoria, IL (city) Peoria County	96,641
Aurora, IL (city) Kane County	83,953
Joliet, IL (city) Will County	78,217
Decatur, IL (city) Macon County	73,838
Arlington Heights, IL (village) Cook County	58,797
Evanston, IL (city) Cook County	57,304

Total Populations 5 Years and Over Who Speak English-Only at Home
Top 10 Places Sorted by Percent

Place	Percent
Decatur, IL (city) Macon County	96.38
Springfield, IL (city) Sangamon County	95.92
Normal, IL (town) McLean County	93.68
Danville, IL (city) Vermilion County	93.62
O'Fallon, IL (city) Saint Clair County	93.36
Winnetka, IL (village) Cook County	93.06
Peoria, IL (city) Peoria County	92.43
Bloomington, IL (city) McLean County	92.04
Macomb, IL (city) McDonough County	91.20
Algonquin, IL (village) McHenry County	90.91

Asians 5 Years and Over Who Speak English-Only at Home
Top 10 Places Sorted by Number

Place	Number
Chicago, IL (city) Cook County	20,070
Skokie, IL (village) Cook County	1,870
Naperville, IL (city) Du Page County	1,570
Evanston, IL (city) Cook County	1,110
Champaign, IL (city) Champaign County	910
Arlington Heights, IL (village) Cook County	880
Schaumburg, IL (village) Cook County	817
Urbana, IL (city) Champaign County	810
Morton Grove, IL (village) Cook County	801
Glenview, IL (village) Cook County	730

Asians 5 Years and Over Who Speak English-Only at Home
Top 10 Places Sorted by Percent

Place	Percent
St. Charles, IL (city) Kane County	44.60
Flossmoor, IL (village) Cook County	43.69
Winnetka, IL (village) Cook County	41.12
Crystal Lake, IL (city) McHenry County	37.90
Lake Forest, IL (city) Lake County	35.48
Willowbrook, IL (village) Du Page County	34.98
Lincolnshire, IL (village) Lake County	33.78
North Chicago, IL (city) Lake County	33.36
DeKalb, IL (city) De Kalb County	32.65
Decatur, IL (city) Macon County	31.88

Native Hawaiian and Other Pacific Islanders 5 Years and Over Who Speak English-Only at Home
Top 10 Places Sorted by Number

Place	Number
Chicago, IL (city) Cook County	293

Native Hawaiian and Other Pacific Islanders 5 Years and Over Who Speak English-Only at Home
Top 10 Places Sorted by Percent

Place	Percent
Chicago, IL (city) Cook County	29.54

Asian Indians 5 Years and Over Who Speak English-Only at Home
Top 10 Places Sorted by Number

Place	Number
Chicago, IL (city) Cook County	3,627
Naperville, IL (city) Du Page County	621
Skokie, IL (village) Cook County	466
Evanston, IL (city) Cook County	408
Schaumburg, IL (village) Cook County	289
Downers Grove, IL (village) Du Page County	267
Hanover Park, IL (village) Cook County	237
Urbana, IL (city) Champaign County	235
Champaign, IL (city) Champaign County	229
Glendale Heights, IL (village) Du Page County	228

Asian Indians 5 Years and Over Who Speak English-Only at Home
Top 10 Places Sorted by Percent

Place	Percent
Elgin, IL (city) Kane County	36.59
Evanston, IL (city) Cook County	35.76
DeKalb, IL (city) De Kalb County	35.19
Orland Park, IL (village) Cook County	25.62
Springfield, IL (city) Sangamon County	24.64
Urbana, IL (city) Champaign County	24.33
Rockford, IL (city) Winnebago County	23.43
Champaign, IL (city) Champaign County	22.39
Oak Brook, IL (village) Du Page County	21.89
Downers Grove, IL (village) Du Page County	21.55

Bangladeshis 5 Years and Over Who Speak English-Only at Home
Top 10 Places Sorted by Number

Place	Number
No places met population threshold.	

Bangladeshis 5 Years and Over Who Speak English-Only at Home
Top 10 Places Sorted by Percent

Place	Percent
No places met population threshold.	

Notes: Please refer to the User's Guide for an explanation of data; tables reflect only those areas that meet Summary File 4 population thresholds, therefore there may be less than 10 places listed

Cambodians 5 Years and Over Who Speak English-Only at Home
Top 10 Places Sorted by Number

Place	Number
Chicago, IL (city) Cook County	175

Cambodians 5 Years and Over Who Speak English-Only at Home
Top 10 Places Sorted by Percent

Place	Percent
Chicago, IL (city) Cook County	9.74

Chinese (except Taiwanese) 5 Years and Over Who Speak English-Only at Home
Top 10 Places Sorted by Number

Place	Number
Chicago, IL (city) Cook County	2,929
Naperville, IL (city) Du Page County	383
Skokie, IL (village) Cook County	220
Champaign, IL (city) Champaign County	170
Evanston, IL (city) Cook County	170
Glenview, IL (village) Cook County	149
Oak Park, IL (village) Cook County	134
Arlington Heights, IL (village) Cook County	117
Urbana, IL (city) Champaign County	113
Buffalo Grove, IL (village) Lake County	105

Chinese (except Taiwanese) 5 Years and Over Who Speak English-Only at Home
Top 10 Places Sorted by Percent

Place	Percent
Oak Park, IL (village) Cook County	34.81
Arlington Heights, IL (village) Cook County	24.02
Glenview, IL (village) Cook County	21.75
Elk Grove Village, IL (village) Cook County	20.77
Buffalo Grove, IL (village) Lake County	19.09
Gurnee, IL (village) Lake County	16.62
Champaign, IL (city) Champaign County	16.54
Des Plaines, IL (city) Cook County	16.45
Northbrook, IL (village) Cook County	15.68
Evanston, IL (city) Cook County	14.96

Fijians 5 Years and Over Who Speak English-Only at Home
Top 10 Places Sorted by Number

Place	Number
No places met population threshold.	

Fijians 5 Years and Over Who Speak English-Only at Home
Top 10 Places Sorted by Percent

Place	Percent
No places met population threshold.	

Filipinos 5 Years and Over Who Speak English-Only at Home
Top 10 Places Sorted by Number

Place	Number
Chicago, IL (city) Cook County	6,039
Skokie, IL (village) Cook County	627
Morton Grove, IL (village) Cook County	420
Carol Stream, IL (village) Du Page County	354
Glendale Heights, IL (village) Du Page County	352
Woodridge, IL (village) Du Page County	317
Des Plaines, IL (city) Cook County	292
Orland Park, IL (village) Cook County	288
Hanover Park, IL (village) Cook County	278
Waukegan, IL (city) Lake County	251

Filipinos 5 Years and Over Who Speak English-Only at Home
Top 10 Places Sorted by Percent

Place	Percent
Orland Park, IL (village) Cook County	44.72
Buffalo Grove, IL (village) Lake County	40.84
Naperville, IL (city) Du Page County	39.61
Evanston, IL (city) Cook County	34.95
Carol Stream, IL (village) Du Page County	34.20
Downers Grove, IL (village) Du Page County	33.84
Des Plaines, IL (city) Cook County	32.27
Glenview, IL (village) Cook County	31.45
Lombard, IL (village) Du Page County	31.18
North Chicago, IL (city) Lake County	30.74

Guamanian or Chamorros 5 Years and Over Who Speak English-Only at Home
Top 10 Places Sorted by Number

Place	Number
No places met population threshold.	

Guamanian or Chamorros 5 Years and Over Who Speak English-Only at Home
Top 10 Places Sorted by Percent

Place	Percent
No places met population threshold.	

Hawaiian, Natives 5 Years and Over Who Speak English-Only at Home
Top 10 Places Sorted by Number

Place	Number
No places met population threshold.	

Hawaiian, Natives 5 Years and Over Who Speak English-Only at Home
Top 10 Places Sorted by Percent

Place	Percent
No places met population threshold.	

Hmongs 5 Years and Over Who Speak English-Only at Home
Top 10 Places Sorted by Number

Place	Number
No places met population threshold.	

Hmongs 5 Years and Over Who Speak English-Only at Home
Top 10 Places Sorted by Percent

Place	Percent
No places met population threshold.	

Indonesians 5 Years and Over Who Speak English-Only at Home
Top 10 Places Sorted by Number

Place	Number
No places met population threshold.	

Indonesians 5 Years and Over Who Speak English-Only at Home
Top 10 Places Sorted by Percent

Place	Percent
No places met population threshold.	

Japanese 5 Years and Over Who Speak English-Only at Home
Top 10 Places Sorted by Number

Place	Number
Chicago, IL (city) Cook County	3,129
Arlington Heights, IL (village) Cook County	175
Evanston, IL (city) Cook County	137
Mount Prospect, IL (village) Cook County	112
Schaumburg, IL (village) Cook County	105
Glenview, IL (village) Cook County	102
Wilmette, IL (village) Cook County	99
Buffalo Grove, IL (village) Lake County	73
Elk Grove Village, IL (village) Cook County	49
Hoffman Estates, IL (village) Cook County	36

Japanese 5 Years and Over Who Speak English-Only at Home
Top 10 Places Sorted by Percent

Place	Percent
Chicago, IL (city) Cook County	52.48
Evanston, IL (city) Cook County	38.16
Glenview, IL (village) Cook County	34.00
Wilmette, IL (village) Cook County	29.73
Mount Prospect, IL (village) Cook County	26.73
Arlington Heights, IL (village) Cook County	18.82
Schaumburg, IL (village) Cook County	12.50
Buffalo Grove, IL (village) Lake County	12.46
Elk Grove Village, IL (village) Cook County	9.04
Hoffman Estates, IL (village) Cook County	4.74

Koreans 5 Years and Over Who Speak English-Only at Home
Top 10 Places Sorted by Number

Place	Number
Chicago, IL (city) Cook County	2,166
Champaign, IL (city) Champaign County	176
Skokie, IL (village) Cook County	168
Evanston, IL (city) Cook County	155
Glenview, IL (village) Cook County	155
Naperville, IL (city) Du Page County	144
Urbana, IL (city) Champaign County	120
Arlington Heights, IL (village) Cook County	107
Buffalo Grove, IL (village) Lake County	102
Schaumburg, IL (village) Cook County	102

Koreans 5 Years and Over Who Speak English-Only at Home
Top 10 Places Sorted by Percent

Place	Percent
Evanston, IL (city) Cook County	24.60
Champaign, IL (city) Champaign County	20.71
Chicago, IL (city) Cook County	17.86
Naperville, IL (city) Du Page County	17.50
Arlington Heights, IL (village) Cook County	14.70
Lincolnwood, IL (village) Cook County	11.40
Urbana, IL (city) Champaign County	10.75
Vernon Hills, IL (village) Lake County	10.45
Glenview, IL (village) Cook County	10.29
Buffalo Grove, IL (village) Lake County	9.76

Laotians 5 Years and Over Who Speak English-Only at Home
Top 10 Places Sorted by Number

Place	Number
Rockford, IL (city) Winnebago County	22
Elgin, IL (city) Kane County	8

Laotians 5 Years and Over Who Speak English-Only at Home
Top 10 Places Sorted by Percent

Place	Percent
Rockford, IL (city) Winnebago County	2.62
Elgin, IL (city) Kane County	1.01

Malaysians 5 Years and Over Who Speak English-Only at Home
Top 10 Places Sorted by Number

Place	Number
No places met population threshold.	

Notes: Please refer to the User's Guide for an explanation of data; tables reflect only those areas that meet Summary File 4 population thresholds, therefore there may be less than 10 places listed

Malaysians 5 Years and Over Who Speak English-Only at Home
Top 10 Places Sorted by Percent

Place	Percent
No places met population threshold.	

Pakistanis 5 Years and Over Who Speak English-Only at Home
Top 10 Places Sorted by Number

Place	Number
Chicago, IL (city) Cook County	268
Skokie, IL (village) Cook County	52

Pakistanis 5 Years and Over Who Speak English-Only at Home
Top 10 Places Sorted by Percent

Place	Percent
Skokie, IL (village) Cook County	11.61
Chicago, IL (city) Cook County	4.53

Samoans 5 Years and Over Who Speak English-Only at Home
Top 10 Places Sorted by Number

Place	Number
No places met population threshold.	

Samoans 5 Years and Over Who Speak English-Only at Home
Top 10 Places Sorted by Percent

Place	Percent
No places met population threshold.	

Sri Lankans 5 Years and Over Who Speak English-Only at Home
Top 10 Places Sorted by Number

Place	Number
No places met population threshold.	

Sri Lankans 5 Years and Over Who Speak English-Only at Home
Top 10 Places Sorted by Percent

Place	Percent
No places met population threshold.	

Taiwanese 5 Years and Over Who Speak English-Only at Home
Top 10 Places Sorted by Number

Place	Number
Chicago, IL (city) Cook County	162
Naperville, IL (city) Du Page County	28

Taiwanese 5 Years and Over Who Speak English-Only at Home
Top 10 Places Sorted by Percent

Place	Percent
Chicago, IL (city) Cook County	20.88
Naperville, IL (city) Du Page County	6.67

Thais 5 Years and Over Who Speak English-Only at Home
Top 10 Places Sorted by Number

Place	Number
Chicago, IL (city) Cook County	216

Thais 5 Years and Over Who Speak English-Only at Home
Top 10 Places Sorted by Percent

Place	Percent
Chicago, IL (city) Cook County	10.47

Tongans 5 Years and Over Who Speak English-Only at Home
Top 10 Places Sorted by Number

Place	Number
No places met population threshold.	

Tongans 5 Years and Over Who Speak English-Only at Home
Top 10 Places Sorted by Percent

Place	Percent
No places met population threshold.	

Vietnamese 5 Years and Over Who Speak English-Only at Home
Top 10 Places Sorted by Number

Place	Number
Chicago, IL (city) Cook County	467
Carol Stream, IL (village) Du Page County	67
Champaign, IL (city) Champaign County	14
Glendale Heights, IL (village) Du Page County	7
Rockford, IL (city) Winnebago County	7
Wheaton, IL (city) Du Page County	5
Aurora, IL (city) Kane County	4

Vietnamese 5 Years and Over Who Speak English-Only at Home
Top 10 Places Sorted by Percent

Place	Percent
Carol Stream, IL (village) Du Page County	17.49
Chicago, IL (city) Cook County	6.22
Champaign, IL (city) Champaign County	3.43
Rockford, IL (city) Winnebago County	1.76
Wheaton, IL (city) Du Page County	1.48
Glendale Heights, IL (village) Du Page County	0.95
Aurora, IL (city) Kane County	0.88

Foreign Born

Total Population
Top 10 Places Sorted by Number

Place	Number
Chicago, IL (city) Cook County	628,903
Cicero, IL (town) Cook County	37,343
Aurora, IL (city) Kane County	30,858
Waukegan, IL (city) Lake County	26,556
Skokie, IL (village) Cook County	23,437
Elgin, IL (city) Kane County	22,258
Mount Prospect, IL (village) Cook County	15,159
Naperville, IL (city) Du Page County	14,963
Schaumburg, IL (village) Cook County	14,262
Palatine, IL (village) Cook County	14,249

Total Population
Top 10 Places Sorted by Percent

Place	Percent
Cicero, IL (town) Cook County	43.62
Schiller Park, IL (village) Cook County	39.07
Skokie, IL (village) Cook County	37.01
Prospect Heights, IL (city) Cook County	36.48
Melrose Park, IL (village) Cook County	35.31
Addison, IL (village) Du Page County	34.26
Lincolnwood, IL (village) Cook County	34.11
West Chicago, IL (city) Du Page County	34.07
Harwood Heights, IL (village) Cook County	34.05
Niles, IL (village) Cook County	33.65

Asian
Top 10 Places Sorted by Number

Place	Number
Chicago, IL (city) Cook County	93,435
Skokie, IL (village) Cook County	9,557
Naperville, IL (city) Du Page County	8,003
Schaumburg, IL (village) Cook County	7,914
Hoffman Estates, IL (village) Cook County	5,715
Mount Prospect, IL (village) Cook County	4,956
Glendale Heights, IL (village) Du Page County	4,699
Palatine, IL (village) Cook County	3,996
Arlington Heights, IL (village) Cook County	3,641
Urbana, IL (city) Champaign County	3,446

Asian
Top 10 Places Sorted by Percent

Place	Percent
Forest Park, IL (village) Cook County	86.74
Carbondale, IL (city) Jackson County	83.76
Macomb, IL (city) McDonough County	81.78
Harwood Heights, IL (village) Cook County	80.60
Park City, IL (city) Lake County	80.36
Westmont, IL (village) Du Page County	79.34
West Chicago, IL (city) Du Page County	79.17
Bloomington, IL (city) McLean County	78.69
Schiller Park, IL (village) Cook County	78.32
Glen Ellyn, IL (village) Du Page County	78.30

Native Hawaiian and Other Pacific Islander
Top 10 Places Sorted by Number

Place	Number
Chicago, IL (city) Cook County	463

Native Hawaiian and Other Pacific Islander
Top 10 Places Sorted by Percent

Place	Percent
Chicago, IL (city) Cook County	43.47

Asian Indian
Top 10 Places Sorted by Number

Place	Number
Chicago, IL (city) Cook County	18,090
Schaumburg, IL (village) Cook County	3,569
Naperville, IL (city) Du Page County	3,341
Skokie, IL (village) Cook County	2,628
Mount Prospect, IL (village) Cook County	2,558
Hoffman Estates, IL (village) Cook County	2,132
Glendale Heights, IL (village) Du Page County	2,042
Palatine, IL (village) Cook County	1,767
Des Plaines, IL (city) Cook County	1,524
Hanover Park, IL (village) Cook County	1,385

Asian Indian
Top 10 Places Sorted by Percent

Place	Percent
Bloomington, IL (city) McLean County	87.01
Arlington Heights, IL (village) Cook County	85.19
Elgin, IL (city) Kane County	81.36
Mount Prospect, IL (village) Cook County	81.08
Wheaton, IL (city) Du Page County	80.63
Peoria, IL (city) Peoria County	80.57
Westmont, IL (village) Du Page County	80.25
Palatine, IL (village) Cook County	79.95
Glen Ellyn, IL (village) Du Page County	79.80
Addison, IL (village) Du Page County	79.72

Bangladeshi
Top 10 Places Sorted by Number

Place	Number
No places met population threshold.	

Notes: Please refer to the User's Guide for an explanation of data; tables reflect only those areas that meet Summary File 4 population thresholds, therefore there may be less than 10 places listed

Bangladeshi
Top 10 Places Sorted by Percent

Place	Percent
No places met population threshold.	

Cambodian
Top 10 Places Sorted by Number.

Place	Number
Chicago, IL (city) Cook County	1,379

Cambodian
Top 10 Places Sorted by Percent

Place	Percent
Chicago, IL (city) Cook County	72.16

Chinese (except Taiwanese)
Top 10 Places Sorted by Number.

Place	Number
Chicago, IL (city) Cook County	23,501
Naperville, IL (city) Du Page County	2,749
Urbana, IL (city) Champaign County	1,295
Skokie, IL (village) Cook County	1,156
Schaumburg, IL (village) Cook County	1,024
Evanston, IL (city) Cook County	770
Champaign, IL (city) Champaign County	755
Peoria, IL (city) Peoria County	648
Hoffman Estates, IL (village) Cook County	575
Palatine, IL (village) Cook County	552

Chinese (except Taiwanese)
Top 10 Places Sorted by Percent

Place	Percent
Westmont, IL (village) Du Page County	89.56
Palatine, IL (village) Cook County	80.35
Peoria, IL (city) Peoria County	80.10
Gurnee, IL (village) Lake County	77.38
Wilmette, IL (village) Cook County	76.94
Schaumburg, IL (village) Cook County	76.65
Chicago, IL (city) Cook County	74.81
Lisle, IL (village) Du Page County	73.57
Aurora, IL (city) Kane County	72.86
Mount Prospect, IL (village) Cook County	72.57

Fijian
Top 10 Places Sorted by Number.

Place	Number
No places met population threshold.	

Fijian
Top 10 Places Sorted by Percent

Place	Percent
No places met population threshold.	

Filipino
Top 10 Places Sorted by Number.

Place	Number
Chicago, IL (city) Cook County	20,755
Skokie, IL (village) Cook County	2,258
Glendale Heights, IL (village) Du Page County	1,294
Morton Grove, IL (village) Cook County	1,271
Waukegan, IL (city) Lake County	1,117
Bolingbrook, IL (village) Will County	966
Streamwood, IL (village) Cook County	929
Hanover Park, IL (village) Cook County	858
Woodridge, IL (village) Du Page County	764
Schaumburg, IL (village) Cook County	721

Filipino
Top 10 Places Sorted by Percent

Place	Percent
Cicero, IL (town) Cook County	83.77

Bolingbrook, IL (village) Will County	82.85
Park City, IL (city) Lake County	81.10
Palatine, IL (village) Cook County	79.44
Arlington Heights, IL (village) Cook County	78.96
Streamwood, IL (village) Cook County	78.53
Schaumburg, IL (village) Cook County	77.86
Berwyn, IL (city) Cook County	77.28
Aurora, IL (city) Kane County	77.04
Addison, IL (village) Du Page County	76.10

Guamanian or Chamorro
Top 10 Places Sorted by Number.

Place	Number
No places met population threshold.	

Guamanian or Chamorro
Top 10 Places Sorted by Percent

Place	Percent
No places met population threshold.	

Hawaiian, Native
Top 10 Places Sorted by Number.

Place	Number
No places met population threshold.	

Hawaiian, Native
Top 10 Places Sorted by Percent

Place	Percent
No places met population threshold.	

Hmong
Top 10 Places Sorted by Number.

Place	Number
No places met population threshold.	

Hmong
Top 10 Places Sorted by Percent

Place	Percent
No places met population threshold.	

Indonesian
Top 10 Places Sorted by Number.

Place	Number
No places met population threshold.	

Indonesian
Top 10 Places Sorted by Percent

Place	Percent
No places met population threshold.	

Japanese
Top 10 Places Sorted by Number

Place	Number
Chicago, IL (city) Cook County	2,120
Schaumburg, IL (village) Cook County	774
Arlington Heights, IL (village) Cook County	764
Hoffman Estates, IL (village) Cook County	737
Buffalo Grove, IL (village) Lake County	536
Elk Grove Village, IL (village) Cook County	505
Mount Prospect, IL (village) Cook County	286
Evanston, IL (city) Cook County	245
Wilmette, IL (village) Cook County	235
Glenview, IL (village) Cook County	200

Japanese
Top 10 Places Sorted by Percent

Place	Percent
Hoffman Estates, IL (village) Cook County	88.16
Buffalo Grove, IL (village) Lake County	87.73
Elk Grove Village, IL (village) Cook County	82.79

Schaumburg, IL (village) Cook County	82.34
Arlington Heights, IL (village) Cook County	76.86
Wilmette, IL (village) Cook County	67.92
Evanston, IL (city) Cook County	65.16
Mount Prospect, IL (village) Cook County	64.27
Glenview, IL (village) Cook County	63.69
Chicago, IL (city) Cook County	35.08

Korean
Top 10 Places Sorted by Number.

Place	Number
Chicago, IL (city) Cook County	10,011
Skokie, IL (village) Cook County	2,008
Schaumburg, IL (village) Cook County	1,352
Northbrook, IL (village) Cook County	1,164
Glenview, IL (village) Cook County	1,084
Mount Prospect, IL (village) Cook County	1,084
Hoffman Estates, IL (village) Cook County	1,074
Niles, IL (village) Cook County	861
Urbana, IL (city) Champaign County	800
Buffalo Grove, IL (village) Lake County	742

Korean
Top 10 Places Sorted by Percent

Place	Percent
Niles, IL (village) Cook County	85.67
Chicago, IL (city) Cook County	79.60
Skokie, IL (village) Cook County	79.56
Arlington Heights, IL (village) Cook County	78.77
Schaumburg, IL (village) Cook County	76.17
Hoffman Estates, IL (village) Cook County	75.32
Northbrook, IL (village) Cook County	75.19
Mount Prospect, IL (village) Cook County	74.97
Vernon Hills, IL (village) Lake County	73.41
Naperville, IL (city) Du Page County	73.33

Laotian
Top 10 Places Sorted by Number.

Place	Number
Elgin, IL (city) Kane County	675
Rockford, IL (city) Winnebago County	658

Laotian
Top 10 Places Sorted by Percent

Place	Percent
Elgin, IL (city) Kane County	75.17
Rockford, IL (city) Winnebago County	73.27

Malaysian
Top 10 Places Sorted by Number.

Place	Number
No places met population threshold.	

Malaysian
Top 10 Places Sorted by Percent

Place	Percent
No places met population threshold.	

Pakistani
Top 10 Places Sorted by Number.

Place	Number
Chicago, IL (city) Cook County	5,404
Skokie, IL (village) Cook County	359

Pakistani
Top 10 Places Sorted by Percent

Place	Percent
Chicago, IL (city) Cook County	83.95
Skokie, IL (village) Cook County	72.53

Notes: Please refer to the User's Guide for an explanation of data; tables reflect only those areas that meet Summary File 4 population thresholds, therefore there may be less than 10 places listed

Samoan
Top 10 Places Sorted by Number

Place	Number
No places met population threshold.	

Samoan
Top 10 Places Sorted by Percent

Place	Percent
No places met population threshold.	

Sri Lankan
Top 10 Places Sorted by Number

Place	Number
No places met population threshold.	

Sri Lankan
Top 10 Places Sorted by Percent

Place	Percent
No places met population threshold.	

Taiwanese
Top 10 Places Sorted by Number

Place	Number
Chicago, IL (city) Cook County	536
Naperville, IL (city) Du Page County	285

Taiwanese
Top 10 Places Sorted by Percent

Place	Percent
Chicago, IL (city) Cook County	69.07
Naperville, IL (city) Du Page County	66.13

Thai
Top 10 Places Sorted by Number

Place	Number
Chicago, IL (city) Cook County	1,637

Thai
Top 10 Places Sorted by Percent

Place	Percent
Chicago, IL (city) Cook County	76.35

Tongan
Top 10 Places Sorted by Number

Place	Number
No places met population threshold.	

Tongan
Top 10 Places Sorted by Percent

Place	Percent
No places met population threshold.	

Vietnamese
Top 10 Places Sorted by Number

Place	Number
Chicago, IL (city) Cook County	6,533
Glendale Heights, IL (village) Du Page County	631
Rockford, IL (city) Winnebago County	370
Carol Stream, IL (village) Du Page County	327
Champaign, IL (city) Champaign County	327
Aurora, IL (city) Kane County	314
Wheaton, IL (city) Du Page County	305

Vietnamese
Top 10 Places Sorted by Percent

Place	Percent
Rockford, IL (city) Winnebago County	91.81
Chicago, IL (city) Cook County	79.88

Wheaton, IL (city) Du Page County	79.84
Glendale Heights, IL (village) Du Page County	78.97
Champaign, IL (city) Champaign County	76.05
Carol Stream, IL (village) Du Page County	69.28
Aurora, IL (city) Kane County	64.08

Foreign-Born Naturalized Citizens

Total Population
Top 10 Places Sorted by Number

Place	Number
Chicago, IL (city) Cook County	223,984
Skokie, IL (village) Cook County	13,753
Cicero, IL (town) Cook County	10,076
Aurora, IL (city) Kane County	8,494
Des Plaines, IL (city) Cook County	6,827
Waukegan, IL (city) Lake County	6,422
Niles, IL (village) Cook County	6,401
Naperville, IL (city) Du Page County	6,400
Schaumburg, IL (village) Cook County	6,120
Elgin, IL (city) Kane County	6,059

Total Population
Top 10 Places Sorted by Percent

Place	Percent
Lincolnwood, IL (village) Cook County	26.15
Morton Grove, IL (village) Cook County	23.32
Skokie, IL (village) Cook County	21.72
Niles, IL (village) Cook County	21.23
Oak Brook, IL (village) Du Page County	20.38
Harwood Heights, IL (village) Cook County	18.13
South Barrington, IL (village) Cook County	15.85
Schiller Park, IL (village) Cook County	14.86
Addison, IL (village) Du Page County	12.22
Glenview, IL (village) Cook County	12.06

Asian
Top 10 Places Sorted by Number

Place	Number
Chicago, IL (city) Cook County	44,502
Skokie, IL (village) Cook County	5,748
Naperville, IL (city) Du Page County	3,709
Schaumburg, IL (village) Cook County	2,972
Hoffman Estates, IL (village) Cook County	2,489
Morton Grove, IL (village) Cook County	2,134
Glendale Heights, IL (village) Du Page County	2,075
Mount Prospect, IL (village) Cook County	1,831
Hanover Park, IL (village) Cook County	1,827
Glenview, IL (village) Cook County	1,798

Asian
Top 10 Places Sorted by Percent

Place	Percent
Oak Brook, IL (village) Du Page County	61.13
Long Grove, IL (village) Lake County	58.31
Burr Ridge, IL (village) Du Page County	56.98
South Barrington, IL (village) Cook County	56.44
Flossmoor, IL (village) Cook County	56.08
Palos Hills, IL (city) Cook County	50.10
Tinley Park, IL (village) Cook County	49.40
Darien, IL (city) Du Page County	48.30
Orland Park, IL (village) Cook County	46.90
Lincolnshire, IL (village) Lake County	46.75

Native Hawaiian and Other Pacific Islander
Top 10 Places Sorted by Number

Place	Number
Chicago, IL (city) Cook County	221

Native Hawaiian and Other Pacific Islander
Top 10 Places Sorted by Percent

Place	Percent
Chicago, IL (city) Cook County	20.75

Asian Indian
Top 10 Places Sorted by Number

Place	Number
Chicago, IL (city) Cook County	6,121
Skokie, IL (village) Cook County	1,693
Naperville, IL (city) Du Page County	1,297
Schaumburg, IL (village) Cook County	1,075
Hoffman Estates, IL (village) Cook County	904
Glendale Heights, IL (village) Du Page County	786
Des Plaines, IL (city) Cook County	776
Hanover Park, IL (village) Cook County	772
Mount Prospect, IL (village) Cook County	735
Carol Stream, IL (village) Du Page County	647

Asian Indian
Top 10 Places Sorted by Percent

Place	Percent
Oak Brook, IL (village) Du Page County	60.60
South Barrington, IL (village) Cook County	57.66
Burr Ridge, IL (village) Du Page County	53.38
Orland Park, IL (village) Cook County	47.45
Skokie, IL (village) Cook County	44.03
Bloomingdale, IL (village) Du Page County	42.90
Darien, IL (city) Du Page County	42.84
Hanover Park, IL (village) Cook County	40.74
Glenview, IL (village) Cook County	40.19
Des Plaines, IL (city) Cook County	39.73

Bangladeshi
Top 10 Places Sorted by Number

Place	Number
No places met population threshold.	

Bangladeshi
Top 10 Places Sorted by Percent

Place	Percent
No places met population threshold.	

Cambodian
Top 10 Places Sorted by Number

Place	Number
Chicago, IL (city) Cook County	692

Cambodian
Top 10 Places Sorted by Percent

Place	Percent
Chicago, IL (city) Cook County	36.21

Chinese (except Taiwanese)
Top 10 Places Sorted by Number

Place	Number
Chicago, IL (city) Cook County	11,704
Naperville, IL (city) Du Page County	1,280
Skokie, IL (village) Cook County	532
Schaumburg, IL (village) Cook County	509
Glenview, IL (village) Cook County	370
Hoffman Estates, IL (village) Cook County	299
Northbrook, IL (village) Cook County	295
Peoria, IL (city) Peoria County	261
Palatine, IL (village) Cook County	246
Buffalo Grove, IL (village) Lake County	242

Chinese (except Taiwanese)
Top 10 Places Sorted by Percent

Place	Percent
Northbrook, IL (village) Cook County	58.88
Glenview, IL (village) Cook County	52.86
Elk Grove Village, IL (village) Cook County	50.60
Wilmette, IL (village) Cook County	44.90
Buffalo Grove, IL (village) Lake County	39.87
Schaumburg, IL (village) Cook County	38.10
Chicago, IL (city) Cook County	37.25

Notes: Please refer to the User's Guide for an explanation of data; tables reflect only those areas that meet Summary File 4 population thresholds, therefore there may be less than 10 places listed

Place	Percent
Hoffman Estates, IL (village) Cook County	36.42
Des Plaines, IL (city) Cook County	36.09
Palatine, IL (village) Cook County	35.81

Fijian
Top 10 Places Sorted by Number

Place	Number
No places met population threshold.	

Fijian
Top 10 Places Sorted by Percent

Place	Percent
No places met population threshold.	

Filipino
Top 10 Places Sorted by Number

Place	Number
Chicago, IL (city) Cook County	12,744
Skokie, IL (village) Cook County	1,408
Morton Grove, IL (village) Cook County	879
Waukegan, IL (city) Lake County	650
Bolingbrook, IL (village) Will County	527
Glendale Heights, IL (village) Du Page County	523
Woodridge, IL (village) Du Page County	510
Streamwood, IL (village) Cook County	505
Hanover Park, IL (village) Cook County	479
Carol Stream, IL (village) Du Page County	468

Filipino
Top 10 Places Sorted by Percent

Place	Percent
Arlington Heights, IL (village) Cook County	57.33
Darien, IL (city) Du Page County	56.42
Lombard, IL (village) Du Page County	56.22
Lincolnwood, IL (village) Cook County	54.16
Hoffman Estates, IL (village) Cook County	50.98
Palatine, IL (village) Cook County	50.85
Morton Grove, IL (village) Cook County	49.22
Mount Prospect, IL (village) Cook County	48.65
Schaumburg, IL (village) Cook County	48.38
Cicero, IL (town) Cook County	48.21

Guamanian or Chamorro
Top 10 Places Sorted by Number

Place	Number
No places met population threshold.	

Guamanian or Chamorro
Top 10 Places Sorted by Percent

Place	Percent
No places met population threshold.	

Hawaiian, Native
Top 10 Places Sorted by Number

Place	Number
No places met population threshold.	

Hawaiian, Native
Top 10 Places Sorted by Percent

Place	Percent
No places met population threshold.	

Hmong
Top 10 Places Sorted by Number

Place	Number
No places met population threshold.	

Hmong
Top 10 Places Sorted by Percent

Place	Percent
No places met population threshold.	

Indonesian
Top 10 Places Sorted by Number

Place	Number
No places met population threshold.	

Indonesian
Top 10 Places Sorted by Percent

Place	Percent
No places met population threshold.	

Japanese
Top 10 Places Sorted by Number

Place	Number
Chicago, IL (city) Cook County	463
Evanston, IL (city) Cook County	39
Buffalo Grove, IL (village) Lake County	36
Arlington Heights, IL (village) Cook County	35
Schaumburg, IL (village) Cook County	35
Glenview, IL (village) Cook County	22
Hoffman Estates, IL (village) Cook County	8
Wilmette, IL (village) Cook County	3
Elk Grove Village, IL (village) Cook County	0
Mount Prospect, IL (village) Cook County	0

Japanese
Top 10 Places Sorted by Percent

Place	Percent
Evanston, IL (city) Cook County	10.37
Chicago, IL (city) Cook County	7.66
Glenview, IL (village) Cook County	7.01
Buffalo Grove, IL (village) Lake County	5.89
Schaumburg, IL (village) Cook County	3.72
Arlington Heights, IL (village) Cook County	3.52
Hoffman Estates, IL (village) Cook County	0.96
Wilmette, IL (village) Cook County	0.87
Elk Grove Village, IL (village) Cook County	0.00
Mount Prospect, IL (village) Cook County	0.00

Korean
Top 10 Places Sorted by Number

Place	Number
Chicago, IL (city) Cook County	5,533
Skokie, IL (village) Cook County	1,241
Glenview, IL (village) Cook County	750
Northbrook, IL (village) Cook County	730
Schaumburg, IL (village) Cook County	637
Mount Prospect, IL (village) Cook County	604
Hoffman Estates, IL (village) Cook County	595
Niles, IL (village) Cook County	450
Morton Grove, IL (village) Cook County	431
Buffalo Grove, IL (village) Lake County	352

Korean
Top 10 Places Sorted by Percent

Place	Percent
Lincolnwood, IL (village) Cook County	51.85
Morton Grove, IL (village) Cook County	49.54
Skokie, IL (village) Cook County	49.17
Northbrook, IL (village) Cook County	47.16
Glenview, IL (village) Cook County	46.96
Niles, IL (village) Cook County	44.78
Chicago, IL (city) Cook County	44.00
Arlington Heights, IL (village) Cook County	42.84
Palatine, IL (village) Cook County	42.43
Wilmette, IL (village) Cook County	42.01

Laotian
Top 10 Places Sorted by Number

Place	Number
Elgin, IL (city) Kane County	405
Rockford, IL (city) Winnebago County	309

Laotian
Top 10 Places Sorted by Percent

Place	Percent
Elgin, IL (city) Kane County	45.10
Rockford, IL (city) Winnebago County	34.41

Malaysian
Top 10 Places Sorted by Number

Place	Number
No places met population threshold.	

Malaysian
Top 10 Places Sorted by Percent

Place	Percent
No places met population threshold.	

Pakistani
Top 10 Places Sorted by Number

Place	Number
Chicago, IL (city) Cook County	1,802
Skokie, IL (village) Cook County	232

Pakistani
Top 10 Places Sorted by Percent

Place	Percent
Skokie, IL (village) Cook County	46.87
Chicago, IL (city) Cook County	27.99

Samoan
Top 10 Places Sorted by Number

Place	Number
No places met population threshold.	

Samoan
Top 10 Places Sorted by Percent

Place	Percent
No places met population threshold.	

Sri Lankan
Top 10 Places Sorted by Number

Place	Number
No places met population threshold.	

Sri Lankan
Top 10 Places Sorted by Percent

Place	Percent
No places met population threshold.	

Taiwanese
Top 10 Places Sorted by Number

Place	Number
Chicago, IL (city) Cook County	239
Naperville, IL (city) Du Page County	203

Taiwanese
Top 10 Places Sorted by Percent

Place	Percent
Naperville, IL (city) Du Page County	47.10
Chicago, IL (city) Cook County	30.80

Notes: Please refer to the User's Guide for an explanation of data; tables reflect only those areas that meet Summary File 4 population thresholds, therefore there may be less than 10 places listed

Thai
Top 10 Places Sorted by Number

Place	Number
Chicago, IL (city) Cook County	468

Thai
Top 10 Places Sorted by Percent

Place	Percent
Chicago, IL (city) Cook County	21.83

Tongan
Top 10 Places Sorted by Number

Place	Number
No places met population threshold.	

Tongan
Top 10 Places Sorted by Percent

Place	Percent
No places met population threshold.	

Vietnamese
Top 10 Places Sorted by Number

Place	Number
Chicago, IL (city) Cook County	3,316
Glendale Heights, IL (village) Du Page County	338
Aurora, IL (city) Kane County	244
Carol Stream, IL (village) Du Page County	188
Champaign, IL (city) Champaign County	131
Wheaton, IL (city) Du Page County	89
Rockford, IL (city) Winnebago County	86

Vietnamese
Top 10 Places Sorted by Percent

Place	Percent
Aurora, IL (city) Kane County	49.80
Glendale Heights, IL (village) Du Page County	42.30
Chicago, IL (city) Cook County	40.54
Carol Stream, IL (village) Du Page County	39.83
Champaign, IL (city) Champaign County	30.47
Wheaton, IL (city) Du Page County	23.30
Rockford, IL (city) Winnebago County	21.34

Educational Attainment: High School Graduates

Total Populations 25 Years and Over Who are High School Graduates
Top 10 Places Sorted by Number

Place	Number
Chicago, IL (city) Cook County	1,304,122
Naperville, IL (city) Du Page County	75,935
Rockford, IL (city) Winnebago County	74,789
Springfield, IL (city) Sangamon County	65,906
Aurora, IL (city) Kane County	63,191
Peoria, IL (city) Peoria County	58,187
Joliet, IL (city) Will County	50,834
Arlington Heights, IL (village) Cook County	50,106
Schaumburg, IL (village) Cook County	47,877
Evanston, IL (city) Cook County	43,244

Total Populations 25 Years and Over Who are High School Graduates
Top 10 Places Sorted by Percent

Place	Percent
Winnetka, IL (village) Cook County	98.99
Hinsdale, IL (village) Du Page County	97.33
Long Grove, IL (village) Lake County	97.24
South Barrington, IL (village) Cook County	97.23
Lake Forest, IL (city) Lake County	97.22
Flossmoor, IL (village) Cook County	96.85
River Forest, IL (village) Cook County	96.79

Wilmette, IL (village) Cook County	96.76
Lincolnshire, IL (village) Lake County	96.44
Naperville, IL (city) Du Page County	96.31

Asians 25 Years and Over Who are High School Graduates
Top 10 Places Sorted by Number

Place	Number
Chicago, IL (city) Cook County	69,751
Skokie, IL (village) Cook County	7,656
Naperville, IL (city) Du Page County	6,863
Schaumburg, IL (village) Cook County	6,663
Hoffman Estates, IL (village) Cook County	4,231
Mount Prospect, IL (village) Cook County	3,746
Palatine, IL (village) Cook County	3,155
Arlington Heights, IL (village) Cook County	3,146
Glendale Heights, IL (village) Du Page County	3,035
Morton Grove, IL (village) Cook County	2,933

Asians 25 Years and Over Who are High School Graduates
Top 10 Places Sorted by Percent

Place	Percent
Algonquin, IL (village) McHenry County	100.00
East Moline, IL (city) Rock Island County	100.00
Long Grove, IL (village) Lake County	100.00
Prospect Heights, IL (city) Cook County	100.00
South Barrington, IL (village) Cook County	99.01
Carbondale, IL (city) Jackson County	98.68
Elmwood Park, IL (village) Cook County	98.57
Flossmoor, IL (village) Cook County	98.48
Urbana, IL (city) Champaign County	98.25
Evanston, IL (city) Cook County	98.09

Native Hawaiian and Other Pacific Islanders 25 Years and Over Who are High School Graduates
Top 10 Places Sorted by Number

Place	Number
Chicago, IL (city) Cook County	348

Native Hawaiian and Other Pacific Islanders 25 Years and Over Who are High School Graduates
Top 10 Places Sorted by Percent

Place	Percent
Chicago, IL (city) Cook County	57.81

Asian Indians 25 Years and Over Who are High School Graduates
Top 10 Places Sorted by Number

Place	Number
Chicago, IL (city) Cook County	12,640
Schaumburg, IL (village) Cook County	2,987
Naperville, IL (city) Du Page County	2,709
Skokie, IL (village) Cook County	1,853
Mount Prospect, IL (village) Cook County	1,719
Hoffman Estates, IL (village) Cook County	1,505
Palatine, IL (village) Cook County	1,240
Glendale Heights, IL (village) Du Page County	1,116
Hanover Park, IL (village) Cook County	1,030
Carol Stream, IL (village) Du Page County	999

Asian Indians 25 Years and Over Who are High School Graduates
Top 10 Places Sorted by Percent

Place	Percent
Bloomington, IL (city) McLean County	100.00
Champaign, IL (city) Champaign County	100.00
Lisle, IL (village) Du Page County	100.00
Peoria, IL (city) Peoria County	100.00
Springfield, IL (city) Sangamon County	100.00
Urbana, IL (city) Champaign County	100.00
Vernon Hills, IL (village) Lake County	100.00
Oak Brook, IL (village) Du Page County	98.89

| Evanston, IL (city) Cook County | 98.61 |
| Oak Park, IL (village) Cook County | 98.05 |

Bangladeshis 25 Years and Over Who are High School Graduates
Top 10 Places Sorted by Number

Place	Number
No places met population threshold.	

Bangladeshis 25 Years and Over Who are High School Graduates
Top 10 Places Sorted by Percent

Place	Percent
No places met population threshold.	

Cambodians 25 Years and Over Who are High School Graduates
Top 10 Places Sorted by Number

Place	Number
Chicago, IL (city) Cook County	482

Cambodians 25 Years and Over Who are High School Graduates
Top 10 Places Sorted by Percent

Place	Percent
Chicago, IL (city) Cook County	47.25

Chinese (except Taiwanese) 25 Years and Over Who are High School Graduates
Top 10 Places Sorted by Number

Place	Number
Chicago, IL (city) Cook County	14,871
Naperville, IL (city) Du Page County	2,391
Skokie, IL (village) Cook County	1,046
Urbana, IL (city) Champaign County	909
Schaumburg, IL (village) Cook County	850
Evanston, IL (city) Cook County	542
Peoria, IL (city) Peoria County	527
Champaign, IL (city) Champaign County	526
Hoffman Estates, IL (village) Cook County	501
Glenview, IL (village) Cook County	467

Chinese (except Taiwanese) 25 Years and Over Who are High School Graduates
Top 10 Places Sorted by Percent

Place	Percent
Champaign, IL (city) Champaign County	100.00
Evanston, IL (city) Cook County	100.00
Oak Park, IL (village) Cook County	97.69
Urbana, IL (city) Champaign County	97.64
Buffalo Grove, IL (village) Lake County	96.02
Naperville, IL (city) Du Page County	95.99
Arlington Heights, IL (village) Cook County	95.63
Gurnee, IL (village) Lake County	95.24
Aurora, IL (city) Kane County	95.18
Hoffman Estates, IL (village) Cook County	94.89

Fijians 25 Years and Over Who are High School Graduates
Top 10 Places Sorted by Number

Place	Number
No places met population threshold.	

Fijians 25 Years and Over Who are High School Graduates
Top 10 Places Sorted by Percent

Place	Percent
No places met population threshold.	

Notes: Please refer to the User's Guide for an explanation of data; tables reflect only those areas that meet Summary File 4 population thresholds, therefore there may be less than 10 places listed

Filipinos 25 Years and Over Who are High School Graduates
Top 10 Places Sorted by Number.

Place	Number
Chicago, IL (city) Cook County	18,689
Skokie, IL (village) Cook County	1,848
Morton Grove, IL (village) Cook County	1,122
Glendale Heights, IL (village) Du Page County	1,084
Waukegan, IL (city) Lake County	845
Bolingbrook, IL (village) Will County	790
Streamwood, IL (village) Cook County	775
Schaumburg, IL (village) Cook County	733
Hanover Park, IL (village) Cook County	730
Woodridge, IL (village) Du Page County	671

Filipinos 25 Years and Over Who are High School Graduates
Top 10 Places Sorted by Percent

Place	Percent
Des Plaines, IL (city) Cook County	100.00
Naperville, IL (city) Du Page County	100.00
Tinley Park, IL (village) Cook County	100.00
Orland Park, IL (village) Cook County	98.87
Schaumburg, IL (village) Cook County	98.79
Streamwood, IL (village) Cook County	98.73
Lincolnwood, IL (village) Cook County	98.62
Mount Prospect, IL (village) Cook County	98.06
Gurnee, IL (village) Lake County	98.02
Elgin, IL (city) Kane County	97.98

Guamanian or Chamorros 25 Years and Over Who are High School Graduates
Top 10 Places Sorted by Number.

Place	Number
No places met population threshold.	

Guamanian or Chamorros 25 Years and Over Who are High School Graduates
Top 10 Places Sorted by Percent

Place	Percent
No places met population threshold.	

Hawaiian, Natives 25 Years and Over Who are High School Graduates
Top 10 Places Sorted by Number.

Place	Number
No places met population threshold.	

Hawaiian, Natives 25 Years and Over Who are High School Graduates
Top 10 Places Sorted by Percent

Place	Percent
No places met population threshold.	

Hmongs 25 Years and Over Who are High School Graduates
Top 10 Places Sorted by Number.

Place	Number
No places met population threshold.	

Hmongs 25 Years and Over Who are High School Graduates
Top 10 Places Sorted by Percent

Place	Percent
No places met population threshold.	

Indonesians 25 Years and Over Who are High School Graduates
Top 10 Places Sorted by Number.

Place	Number
No places met population threshold.	

Indonesians 25 Years and Over Who are High School Graduates
Top 10 Places Sorted by Percent

Place	Percent
No places met population threshold.	

Japanese 25 Years and Over Who are High School Graduates
Top 10 Places Sorted by Number.

Place	Number
Chicago, IL (city) Cook County	4,925
Arlington Heights, IL (village) Cook County	779
Schaumburg, IL (village) Cook County	671
Hoffman Estates, IL (village) Cook County	481
Elk Grove Village, IL (village) Cook County	420
Buffalo Grove, IL (village) Lake County	396
Mount Prospect, IL (village) Cook County	359
Evanston, IL (city) Cook County	284
Glenview, IL (village) Cook County	248
Wilmette, IL (village) Cook County	209

Japanese 25 Years and Over Who are High School Graduates
Top 10 Places Sorted by Percent

Place	Percent
Buffalo Grove, IL (village) Lake County	100.00
Elk Grove Village, IL (village) Cook County	100.00
Glenview, IL (village) Cook County	100.00
Mount Prospect, IL (village) Cook County	100.00
Wilmette, IL (village) Cook County	100.00
Arlington Heights, IL (village) Cook County	99.24
Schaumburg, IL (village) Cook County	99.11
Evanston, IL (city) Cook County	97.59
Chicago, IL (city) Cook County	94.62
Hoffman Estates, IL (village) Cook County	93.58

Koreans 25 Years and Over Who are High School Graduates
Top 10 Places Sorted by Number.

Place	Number
Chicago, IL (city) Cook County	7,533
Skokie, IL (village) Cook County	1,650
Schaumburg, IL (village) Cook County	1,042
Northbrook, IL (village) Cook County	974
Glenview, IL (village) Cook County	972
Mount Prospect, IL (village) Cook County	812
Hoffman Estates, IL (village) Cook County	785
Niles, IL (village) Cook County	653
Buffalo Grove, IL (village) Lake County	600
Morton Grove, IL (village) Cook County	533

Koreans 25 Years and Over Who are High School Graduates
Top 10 Places Sorted by Percent

Place	Percent
Evanston, IL (city) Cook County	100.00
Urbana, IL (city) Champaign County	100.00
Wilmette, IL (village) Cook County	98.74
Palatine, IL (village) Cook County	98.24
Glenview, IL (village) Cook County	97.69
Vernon Hills, IL (village) Lake County	97.67
Champaign, IL (city) Champaign County	96.16
Northbrook, IL (village) Cook County	96.06
Buffalo Grove, IL (village) Lake County	95.85
Naperville, IL (city) Du Page County	94.15

Laotians 25 Years and Over Who are High School Graduates
Top 10 Places Sorted by Number.

Place	Number
Elgin, IL (city) Kane County	360
Rockford, IL (city) Winnebago County	255

Laotians 25 Years and Over Who are High School Graduates
Top 10 Places Sorted by Percent

Place	Percent
Elgin, IL (city) Kane County	61.43
Rockford, IL (city) Winnebago County	52.04

Malaysians 25 Years and Over Who are High School Graduates
Top 10 Places Sorted by Number.

Place	Number
No places met population threshold.	

Malaysians 25 Years and Over Who are High School Graduates
Top 10 Places Sorted by Percent

Place	Percent
No places met population threshold.	

Pakistanis 25 Years and Over Who are High School Graduates
Top 10 Places Sorted by Number.

Place	Number
Chicago, IL (city) Cook County	3,088
Skokie, IL (village) Cook County	197

Pakistanis 25 Years and Over Who are High School Graduates
Top 10 Places Sorted by Percent

Place	Percent
Chicago, IL (city) Cook County	79.16
Skokie, IL (village) Cook County	70.61

Samoans 25 Years and Over Who are High School Graduates
Top 10 Places Sorted by Number.

Place	Number
No places met population threshold.	

Samoans 25 Years and Over Who are High School Graduates
Top 10 Places Sorted by Percent

Place	Percent
No places met population threshold.	

Sri Lankans 25 Years and Over Who are High School Graduates
Top 10 Places Sorted by Number.

Place	Number
No places met population threshold.	

Sri Lankans 25 Years and Over Who are High School Graduates
Top 10 Places Sorted by Percent

Place	Percent
No places met population threshold.	

Notes: Please refer to the User's Guide for an explanation of data; tables reflect only those areas that meet Summary File 4 population thresholds, therefore there may be less than 10 places listed

Taiwanese 25 Years and Over Who are High School Graduates
Top 10 Places Sorted by Number

Place	Number
Chicago, IL (city) Cook County	437
Naperville, IL (city) Du Page County	240

Taiwanese 25 Years and Over Who are High School Graduates
Top 10 Places Sorted by Percent

Place	Percent
Chicago, IL (city) Cook County	95.83
Naperville, IL (city) Du Page County	91.25

Thais 25 Years and Over Who are High School Graduates
Top 10 Places Sorted by Number

Place	Number
Chicago, IL (city) Cook County	1,424

Thais 25 Years and Over Who are High School Graduates
Top 10 Places Sorted by Percent

Place	Percent
Chicago, IL (city) Cook County	93.62

Tongans 25 Years and Over Who are High School Graduates
Top 10 Places Sorted by Number

Place	Number
No places met population threshold.	

Tongans 25 Years and Over Who are High School Graduates
Top 10 Places Sorted by Percent

Place	Percent
No places met population threshold.	

Vietnamese 25 Years and Over Who are High School Graduates
Top 10 Places Sorted by Number

Place	Number
Chicago, IL (city) Cook County	3,147
Aurora, IL (city) Kane County	261
Glendale Heights, IL (village) Du Page County	254
Carol Stream, IL (village) Du Page County	156
Rockford, IL (city) Winnebago County	131
Champaign, IL (city) Champaign County	98
Wheaton, IL (city) Du Page County	55

Vietnamese 25 Years and Over Who are High School Graduates
Top 10 Places Sorted by Percent

Place	Percent
Aurora, IL (city) Kane County	80.06
Chicago, IL (city) Cook County	62.50
Carol Stream, IL (village) Du Page County	58.65
Glendale Heights, IL (village) Du Page County	50.10
Rockford, IL (city) Winnebago County	47.46
Champaign, IL (city) Champaign County	36.84
Wheaton, IL (city) Du Page County	27.64

Educational Attainment: Four-Year College Graduates

Total Populations 25 Years and Over Who are Four-Year College Graduates
Top 10 Places Sorted by Number

Place	Number
Chicago, IL (city) Cook County	462,783
Naperville, IL (city) Du Page County	47,805
Evanston, IL (city) Cook County	29,511
Arlington Heights, IL (village) Cook County	25,101
Aurora, IL (city) Kane County	24,991
Springfield, IL (city) Sangamon County	23,061
Oak Park, IL (village) Cook County	22,637
Schaumburg, IL (village) Cook County	20,273
Wheaton, IL (city) Du Page County	20,247
Peoria, IL (city) Peoria County	19,712

Total Populations 25 Years and Over Who are Four-Year College Graduates
Top 10 Places Sorted by Percent

Place	Percent
Winnetka, IL (village) Cook County	84.41
Lake Forest, IL (city) Lake County	73.83
Wilmette, IL (village) Cook County	72.58
River Forest, IL (village) Cook County	69.70
Hinsdale, IL (village) Du Page County	68.61
Deerfield, IL (village) Lake County	68.53
Lincolnshire, IL (village) Lake County	66.38
South Barrington, IL (village) Cook County	62.64
Evanston, IL (city) Cook County	62.36
Northbrook, IL (village) Cook County	62.20

Asians 25 Years and Over Who are Four-Year College Graduates
Top 10 Places Sorted by Number

Place	Number
Chicago, IL (city) Cook County	42,187
Naperville, IL (city) Du Page County	5,670
Skokie, IL (village) Cook County	4,839
Schaumburg, IL (village) Cook County	4,675
Hoffman Estates, IL (village) Cook County	2,647
Mount Prospect, IL (village) Cook County	2,466
Arlington Heights, IL (village) Cook County	2,437
Palatine, IL (village) Cook County	2,293
Evanston, IL (city) Cook County	2,028
Urbana, IL (city) Champaign County	2,006

Asians 25 Years and Over Who are Four-Year College Graduates
Top 10 Places Sorted by Percent

Place	Percent
Macomb, IL (city) McDonough County	87.74
Oak Brook, IL (village) Du Page County	87.53
Urbana, IL (city) Champaign County	87.52
Lincolnshire, IL (village) Lake County	87.25
Savoy, IL (village) Champaign County	86.51
Evanston, IL (city) Cook County	86.01
South Barrington, IL (village) Cook County	83.37
Long Grove, IL (village) Lake County	83.15
Lake Forest, IL (city) Lake County	82.51
Burr Ridge, IL (village) Du Page County	82.31

Native Hawaiian and Other Pacific Islanders 25 Years and Over Who are Four-Year College Graduates
Top 10 Places Sorted by Number

Place	Number
Chicago, IL (city) Cook County	86

Native Hawaiian and Other Pacific Islanders 25 Years and Over Who are Four-Year College Graduates
Top 10 Places Sorted by Percent

Place	Percent
Chicago, IL (city) Cook County	14.29

Asian Indians 25 Years and Over Who are Four-Year College Graduates
Top 10 Places Sorted by Number

Place	Number
Chicago, IL (city) Cook County	8,885
Schaumburg, IL (village) Cook County	2,407
Naperville, IL (city) Du Page County	2,367
Mount Prospect, IL (village) Cook County	1,165
Skokie, IL (village) Cook County	1,154
Palatine, IL (village) Cook County	986
Hoffman Estates, IL (village) Cook County	907
Westmont, IL (village) Du Page County	807
Arlington Heights, IL (village) Cook County	781
Woodridge, IL (village) Du Page County	737

Asian Indians 25 Years and Over Who are Four-Year College Graduates
Top 10 Places Sorted by Percent

Place	Percent
Urbana, IL (city) Champaign County	94.95
Vernon Hills, IL (village) Lake County	94.08
Evanston, IL (city) Cook County	93.91
Oak Brook, IL (village) Du Page County	93.16
Lisle, IL (village) Du Page County	91.10
Peoria, IL (city) Peoria County	89.51
Champaign, IL (city) Champaign County	89.19
Bloomington, IL (city) McLean County	88.63
Oak Park, IL (village) Cook County	87.61
Arlington Heights, IL (village) Cook County	87.56

Bangladeshis 25 Years and Over Who are Four-Year College Graduates
Top 10 Places Sorted by Number

Place	Number
No places met population threshold.	

Bangladeshis 25 Years and Over Who are Four-Year College Graduates
Top 10 Places Sorted by Percent

Place	Percent
No places met population threshold.	

Cambodians 25 Years and Over Who are Four-Year College Graduates
Top 10 Places Sorted by Number

Place	Number
Chicago, IL (city) Cook County	183

Cambodians 25 Years and Over Who are Four-Year College Graduates
Top 10 Places Sorted by Percent

Place	Percent
Chicago, IL (city) Cook County	17.94

Chinese (except Taiwanese) 25 Years and Over Who are Four-Year College Graduates
Top 10 Places Sorted by Number

Place	Number
Chicago, IL (city) Cook County	8,744
Naperville, IL (city) Du Page County	2,002
Urbana, IL (city) Champaign County	795
Skokie, IL (village) Cook County	713
Schaumburg, IL (village) Cook County	613
Evanston, IL (city) Cook County	509
Champaign, IL (city) Champaign County	488
Peoria, IL (city) Peoria County	430
Hoffman Estates, IL (village) Cook County	397
Palatine, IL (village) Cook County	397

Chinese (except Taiwanese) 25 Years and Over Who are Four-Year College Graduates
Top 10 Places Sorted by Percent

Place	Percent
Evanston, IL (city) Cook County	93.91
Champaign, IL (city) Champaign County	92.78
Urbana, IL (city) Champaign County	85.39
Wilmette, IL (village) Cook County	84.59
Aurora, IL (city) Kane County	83.49

Notes: Please refer to the User's Guide for an explanation of data; tables reflect only those areas that meet Summary File 4 population thresholds, therefore there may be less than 10 places listed

Vernon Hills, IL (village) Lake County	81.31
Mundelein, IL (village) Lake County	80.39
Naperville, IL (city) Du Page County	80.37
Lisle, IL (village) Du Page County	80.23
Arlington Heights, IL (village) Cook County	79.23

Fijians 25 Years and Over Who are Four-Year College Graduates
Top 10 Places Sorted by Number

Place	Number
No places met population threshold.	

Fijians 25 Years and Over Who are Four-Year College Graduates
Top 10 Places Sorted by Percent

Place	Percent
No places met population threshold.	

Filipinos 25 Years and Over Who are Four-Year College Graduates
Top 10 Places Sorted by Number

Place	Number
Chicago, IL (city) Cook County	12,106
Skokie, IL (village) Cook County	1,269
Morton Grove, IL (village) Cook County	794
Glendale Heights, IL (village) Du Page County	660
Schaumburg, IL (village) Cook County	538
Bolingbrook, IL (village) Will County	507
Streamwood, IL (village) Cook County	476
Woodridge, IL (village) Du Page County	473
Aurora, IL (city) Kane County	466
Hanover Park, IL (village) Cook County	452

Filipinos 25 Years and Over Who are Four-Year College Graduates
Top 10 Places Sorted by Percent

Place	Percent
Glenview, IL (village) Cook County	79.71
Lincolnwood, IL (village) Cook County	77.59
Orland Park, IL (village) Cook County	77.38
Mundelein, IL (village) Lake County	77.05
Arlington Heights, IL (village) Cook County	76.70
Lombard, IL (village) Du Page County	76.36
Darien, IL (city) Du Page County	74.55
Gurnee, IL (village) Lake County	74.45
Naperville, IL (city) Du Page County	73.58
Elk Grove Village, IL (village) Cook County	72.52

Guamanian or Chamorros 25 Years and Over Who are Four-Year College Graduates
Top 10 Places Sorted by Number

Place	Number
No places met population threshold.	

Guamanian or Chamorros 25 Years and Over Who are Four-Year College Graduates
Top 10 Places Sorted by Percent

Place	Percent
No places met population threshold.	

Hawaiian, Natives 25 Years and Over Who are Four-Year College Graduates
Top 10 Places Sorted by Number

Place	Number
No places met population threshold.	

Hawaiian, Natives 25 Years and Over Who are Four-Year College Graduates
Top 10 Places Sorted by Percent

Place	Percent
No places met population threshold.	

Hmongs 25 Years and Over Who are Four-Year College Graduates
Top 10 Places Sorted by Number

Place	Number
No places met population threshold.	

Hmongs 25 Years and Over Who are Four-Year College Graduates
Top 10 Places Sorted by Percent

Place	Percent
No places met population threshold.	

Indonesians 25 Years and Over Who are Four-Year College Graduates
Top 10 Places Sorted by Number

Place	Number
No places met population threshold.	

Indonesians 25 Years and Over Who are Four-Year College Graduates
Top 10 Places Sorted by Percent

Place	Percent
No places met population threshold.	

Japanese 25 Years and Over Who are Four-Year College Graduates
Top 10 Places Sorted by Number

Place	Number
Chicago, IL (city) Cook County	2,470
Arlington Heights, IL (village) Cook County	499
Schaumburg, IL (village) Cook County	286
Hoffman Estates, IL (village) Cook County	268
Elk Grove Village, IL (village) Cook County	249
Buffalo Grove, IL (village) Lake County	234
Evanston, IL (city) Cook County	210
Mount Prospect, IL (village) Cook County	207
Wilmette, IL (village) Cook County	142
Glenview, IL (village) Cook County	126

Japanese 25 Years and Over Who are Four-Year College Graduates
Top 10 Places Sorted by Percent

Place	Percent
Evanston, IL (city) Cook County	72.16
Wilmette, IL (village) Cook County	67.94
Arlington Heights, IL (village) Cook County	63.57
Elk Grove Village, IL (village) Cook County	59.29
Buffalo Grove, IL (village) Lake County	59.09
Mount Prospect, IL (village) Cook County	57.66
Hoffman Estates, IL (village) Cook County	52.14
Glenview, IL (village) Cook County	50.81
Chicago, IL (city) Cook County	47.45
Schaumburg, IL (village) Cook County	42.25

Koreans 25 Years and Over Who are Four-Year College Graduates
Top 10 Places Sorted by Number

Place	Number
Chicago, IL (city) Cook County	4,396
Skokie, IL (village) Cook County	923
Northbrook, IL (village) Cook County	693
Glenview, IL (village) Cook County	620
Schaumburg, IL (village) Cook County	562
Urbana, IL (city) Champaign County	474
Mount Prospect, IL (village) Cook County	434
Hoffman Estates, IL (village) Cook County	415
Buffalo Grove, IL (village) Lake County	409
Niles, IL (village) Cook County	378

Koreans 25 Years and Over Who are Four-Year College Graduates
Top 10 Places Sorted by Percent

Place	Percent
Urbana, IL (city) Champaign County	98.34
Champaign, IL (city) Champaign County	83.45
Evanston, IL (city) Cook County	82.22
Wilmette, IL (village) Cook County	72.80
Northbrook, IL (village) Cook County	68.34
Palatine, IL (village) Cook County	66.75
Buffalo Grove, IL (village) Lake County	65.34
Naperville, IL (city) Du Page County	64.72
Glenview, IL (village) Cook County	62.31
Arlington Heights, IL (village) Cook County	53.55

Laotians 25 Years and Over Who are Four-Year College Graduates
Top 10 Places Sorted by Number

Place	Number
Elgin, IL (city) Kane County	44
Rockford, IL (city) Winnebago County	20

Laotians 25 Years and Over Who are Four-Year College Graduates
Top 10 Places Sorted by Percent

Place	Percent
Elgin, IL (city) Kane County	7.51
Rockford, IL (city) Winnebago County	4.08

Malaysians 25 Years and Over Who are Four-Year College Graduates
Top 10 Places Sorted by Number

Place	Number
No places met population threshold.	

Malaysians 25 Years and Over Who are Four-Year College Graduates
Top 10 Places Sorted by Percent

Place	Percent
No places met population threshold.	

Pakistanis 25 Years and Over Who are Four-Year College Graduates
Top 10 Places Sorted by Number

Place	Number
Chicago, IL (city) Cook County	1,852
Skokie, IL (village) Cook County	111

Pakistanis 25 Years and Over Who are Four-Year College Graduates
Top 10 Places Sorted by Percent

Place	Percent
Chicago, IL (city) Cook County	47.48
Skokie, IL (village) Cook County	39.78

Samoans 25 Years and Over Who are Four-Year College Graduates
Top 10 Places Sorted by Number

Place	Number
No places met population threshold.	

Samoans 25 Years and Over Who are Four-Year College Graduates
Top 10 Places Sorted by Percent

Place	Percent
No places met population threshold.	

Notes: Please refer to the User's Guide for an explanation of data; tables reflect only those areas that meet Summary File 4 population thresholds, therefore there may be less than 10 places listed

Sri Lankans 25 Years and Over Who are Four-Year College Graduates
Top 10 Places Sorted by Number

Place	Number
No places met population threshold.	

Sri Lankans 25 Years and Over Who are Four-Year College Graduates
Top 10 Places Sorted by Percent

Place	Percent
No places met population threshold.	

Taiwanese 25 Years and Over Who are Four-Year College Graduates
Top 10 Places Sorted by Number

Place	Number
Chicago, IL (city) Cook County	380
Naperville, IL (city) Du Page County	213

Taiwanese 25 Years and Over Who are Four-Year College Graduates
Top 10 Places Sorted by Percent

Place	Percent
Chicago, IL (city) Cook County	83.33
Naperville, IL (city) Du Page County	80.99

Thais 25 Years and Over Who are Four-Year College Graduates
Top 10 Places Sorted by Number

Place	Number
Chicago, IL (city) Cook County	829

Thais 25 Years and Over Who are Four-Year College Graduates
Top 10 Places Sorted by Percent

Place	Percent
Chicago, IL (city) Cook County	54.50

Tongans 25 Years and Over Who are Four-Year College Graduates
Top 10 Places Sorted by Number

Place	Number
No places met population threshold.	

Tongans 25 Years and Over Who are Four-Year College Graduates
Top 10 Places Sorted by Percent

Place	Percent
No places met population threshold.	

Vietnamese 25 Years and Over Who are Four-Year College Graduates
Top 10 Places Sorted by Number

Place	Number
Chicago, IL (city) Cook County	992
Aurora, IL (city) Kane County	107
Glendale Heights, IL (village) Du Page County	50
Rockford, IL (city) Winnebago County	44
Champaign, IL (city) Champaign County	41
Carol Stream, IL (village) Du Page County	15
Wheaton, IL (city) Du Page County	7

Vietnamese 25 Years and Over Who are Four-Year College Graduates
Top 10 Places Sorted by Percent

Place	Percent
Aurora, IL (city) Kane County	32.82
Chicago, IL (city) Cook County	19.70
Rockford, IL (city) Winnebago County	15.94

Champaign, IL (city) Champaign County	15.41
Glendale Heights, IL (village) Du Page County	9.86
Carol Stream, IL (village) Du Page County	5.64
Wheaton, IL (city) Du Page County	3.52

Median Household Income

Total Population
Top 10 Places Sorted by Number

Place	Dollars
South Barrington, IL (village) Cook County	170,755
Winnetka, IL (village) Cook County	167,458
Long Grove, IL (village) Lake County	148,150
Oak Brook, IL (village) Du Page County	146,537
Lake Forest, IL (city) Lake County	136,462
Lincolnshire, IL (village) Lake County	134,259
Burr Ridge, IL (village) Du Page County	129,507
Deerfield, IL (village) Lake County	107,194
Wilmette, IL (village) Cook County	106,773
Hinsdale, IL (village) Du Page County	104,551

Asian
Top 10 Places Sorted by Number

Place	Dollars
Oak Brook, IL (village) Du Page County	200,000+
South Barrington, IL (village) Cook County	200,000+
Lincolnshire, IL (village) Lake County	186,316
Burr Ridge, IL (village) Du Page County	184,734
Lake Forest, IL (city) Lake County	136,461
Danville, IL (city) Vermilion County	129,083
Winnetka, IL (village) Cook County	110,957
Lake Zurich, IL (village) Lake County	109,994
Deerfield, IL (village) Lake County	109,626
Northbrook, IL (village) Cook County	105,894

Native Hawaiian and Other Pacific Islander
Top 10 Places Sorted by Number

Place	Dollars
Chicago, IL (city) Cook County	29,375

Asian Indian
Top 10 Places Sorted by Number

Place	Dollars
Oak Brook, IL (village) Du Page County	200,000+
South Barrington, IL (village) Cook County	200,000+
Burr Ridge, IL (village) Du Page County	161,233
Glenview, IL (village) Cook County	150,000
Orland Park, IL (village) Cook County	115,985
Vernon Hills, IL (village) Lake County	100,883
Darien, IL (city) Du Page County	98,984
Wheaton, IL (city) Du Page County	97,918
Naperville, IL (city) Du Page County	92,686
Bartlett, IL (village) Du Page County	87,227

Bangladeshi
Top 10 Places Sorted by Number

Place	Dollars
No places met population threshold.	

Cambodian
Top 10 Places Sorted by Number

Place	Dollars
Chicago, IL (city) Cook County	52,500

Chinese (except Taiwanese)
Top 10 Places Sorted by Number

Place	Dollars
Lisle, IL (village) Du Page County	127,681
Vernon Hills, IL (village) Lake County	113,180
Mundelein, IL (village) Lake County	104,592
Naperville, IL (city) Du Page County	102,958
Northbrook, IL (village) Cook County	95,318

Buffalo Grove, IL (village) Lake County	90,859
Arlington Heights, IL (village) Cook County	89,667
Gurnee, IL (village) Lake County	86,331
Hoffman Estates, IL (village) Cook County	80,921
Wilmette, IL (village) Cook County	77,620

Fijian
Top 10 Places Sorted by Number

Place	Dollars
No places met population threshold.	

Filipino
Top 10 Places Sorted by Number

Place	Dollars
Naperville, IL (city) Du Page County	109,761
Mundelein, IL (village) Lake County	98,932
Orland Park, IL (village) Cook County	97,711
Gurnee, IL (village) Lake County	95,181
Morton Grove, IL (village) Cook County	92,310
Glenview, IL (village) Cook County	91,021
Skokie, IL (village) Cook County	90,930
Darien, IL (city) Du Page County	90,728
Downers Grove, IL (village) Du Page County	90,442
Palatine, IL (village) Cook County	90,255

Guamanian or Chamorro
Top 10 Places Sorted by Number

Place	Dollars
No places met population threshold.	

Hawaiian, Native
Top 10 Places Sorted by Number

Place	Dollars
No places met population threshold.	

Hmong
Top 10 Places Sorted by Number

Place	Dollars
No places met population threshold.	

Indonesian
Top 10 Places Sorted by Number

Place	Dollars
No places met population threshold.	

Japanese
Top 10 Places Sorted by Number

Place	Dollars
Wilmette, IL (village) Cook County	106,933
Hoffman Estates, IL (village) Cook County	100,146
Glenview, IL (village) Cook County	91,985
Buffalo Grove, IL (village) Lake County	85,598
Elk Grove Village, IL (village) Cook County	79,246
Arlington Heights, IL (village) Cook County	70,625
Schaumburg, IL (village) Cook County	59,345
Chicago, IL (city) Cook County	45,750
Mount Prospect, IL (village) Cook County	41,458
Evanston, IL (city) Cook County	36,250

Korean
Top 10 Places Sorted by Number

Place	Dollars
Buffalo Grove, IL (village) Lake County	83,219
Lincolnwood, IL (village) Cook County	72,604
Northbrook, IL (village) Cook County	72,500
Glenview, IL (village) Cook County	70,987
Arlington Heights, IL (village) Cook County	68,036
Hoffman Estates, IL (village) Cook County	67,500
Vernon Hills, IL (village) Lake County	66,875
Palatine, IL (village) Cook County	62,198
Morton Grove, IL (village) Cook County	61,875

Notes: Please refer to the User's Guide for an explanation of data; tables reflect only those areas that meet Summary File 4 population thresholds, therefore there may be less than 10 places listed

Place	Dollars
Wilmette, IL (village) Cook County	61,012

Laotian
Top 10 Places Sorted by Number.

Place	Dollars
Elgin, IL (city) Kane County	85,703
Rockford, IL (city) Winnebago County	53,125

Malaysian
Top 10 Places Sorted by Number.

Place	Dollars
No places met population threshold.

Pakistani
Top 10 Places Sorted by Number.

Place	Dollars
Skokie, IL (village) Cook County	78,844
Chicago, IL (city) Cook County	28,981

Samoan
Top 10 Places Sorted by Number.

Place	Dollars
No places met population threshold.

Sri Lankan
Top 10 Places Sorted by Number.

Place	Dollars
No places met population threshold.

Taiwanese
Top 10 Places Sorted by Number.

Place	Dollars
Naperville, IL (city) Du Page County	97,763
Chicago, IL (city) Cook County	30,938

Thai
Top 10 Places Sorted by Number.

Place	Dollars
Chicago, IL (city) Cook County	39,479

Tongan
Top 10 Places Sorted by Number.

Place	Dollars
No places met population threshold.

Vietnamese
Top 10 Places Sorted by Number.

Place	Dollars
Glendale Heights, IL (village) Du Page County	68,026
Carol Stream, IL (village) Du Page County	61,250
Aurora, IL (city) Kane County	60,000
Rockford, IL (city) Winnebago County	42,159
Wheaton, IL (city) Du Page County	36,458
Chicago, IL (city) Cook County	35,774
Champaign, IL (city) Champaign County	29,063

Per Capita Income

Total Population
Top 10 Places Sorted by Number.

Place	Dollars
Winnetka, IL (village) Cook County	84,134
Lake Forest, IL (city) Lake County	77,092
Oak Brook, IL (village) Du Page County	76,668
South Barrington, IL (village) Cook County	76,078
Hinsdale, IL (village) Du Page County	63,765
Long Grove, IL (village) Lake County	62,185
Lincolnshire, IL (village) Lake County	60,115
Burr Ridge, IL (village) Du Page County	58,518

Place	Dollars
Wilmette, IL (village) Cook County	55,611
Highland Park, IL (city) Lake County	55,331

Asian
Top 10 Places Sorted by Number.

Place	Dollars
Oak Brook, IL (village) Du Page County	84,054
South Barrington, IL (village) Cook County	82,372
Burr Ridge, IL (village) Du Page County	56,585
Lincolnshire, IL (village) Lake County	56,032
Lake Forest, IL (city) Lake County	54,345
Highland Park, IL (city) Lake County	50,311
Long Grove, IL (village) Lake County	47,163
River Forest, IL (village) Cook County	46,961
Moline, IL (city) Rock Island County	44,608
Palos Hills, IL (city) Cook County	43,815

Native Hawaiian and Other Pacific Islander
Top 10 Places Sorted by Number.

Place	Dollars
Chicago, IL (city) Cook County	13,017

Asian Indian
Top 10 Places Sorted by Number.

Place	Dollars
Oak Brook, IL (village) Du Page County	88,710
South Barrington, IL (village) Cook County	77,731
Orland Park, IL (village) Cook County	58,181
Wheaton, IL (city) Du Page County	49,501
Glenview, IL (village) Cook County	47,032
Burr Ridge, IL (village) Du Page County	40,125
Peoria, IL (city) Peoria County	37,912
Lisle, IL (village) Du Page County	35,708
Arlington Heights, IL (village) Cook County	34,648
Vernon Hills, IL (village) Lake County	33,786

Bangladeshi
Top 10 Places Sorted by Number.

Place	Dollars
No places met population threshold.

Cambodian
Top 10 Places Sorted by Number.

Place	Dollars
Chicago, IL (city) Cook County	11,594

Chinese (except Taiwanese)
Top 10 Places Sorted by Number.

Place	Dollars
Northbrook, IL (village) Cook County	46,018
Lisle, IL (village) Du Page County	45,114
Vernon Hills, IL (village) Lake County	38,354
Glenview, IL (village) Cook County	38,217
Westmont, IL (village) Du Page County	35,526
Mundelein, IL (village) Lake County	33,137
Wilmette, IL (village) Cook County	32,381
Buffalo Grove, IL (village) Lake County	31,647
Naperville, IL (city) Du Page County	31,004
Palatine, IL (village) Cook County	30,817

Fijian
Top 10 Places Sorted by Number.

Place	Dollars
No places met population threshold.

Filipino
Top 10 Places Sorted by Number.

Place	Dollars
Schaumburg, IL (village) Cook County	37,440
Glenview, IL (village) Cook County	35,960
Palatine, IL (village) Cook County	34,352

Place	Dollars
Lombard, IL (village) Du Page County	33,356
Lincolnwood, IL (village) Cook County	31,924
Naperville, IL (city) Du Page County	31,584
Darien, IL (city) Du Page County	30,665
Arlington Heights, IL (village) Cook County	30,558
Orland Park, IL (village) Cook County	30,372
Park City, IL (city) Lake County	30,083

Guamanian or Chamorro
Top 10 Places Sorted by Number.

Place	Dollars
No places met population threshold.

Hawaiian, Native
Top 10 Places Sorted by Number.

Place	Dollars
No places met population threshold.

Hmong
Top 10 Places Sorted by Number.

Place	Dollars
No places met population threshold.

Indonesian
Top 10 Places Sorted by Number.

Place	Dollars
No places met population threshold.

Japanese
Top 10 Places Sorted by Number.

Place	Dollars
Glenview, IL (village) Cook County	70,887
Buffalo Grove, IL (village) Lake County	51,519
Wilmette, IL (village) Cook County	42,897
Arlington Heights, IL (village) Cook County	39,086
Evanston, IL (city) Cook County	34,676
Hoffman Estates, IL (village) Cook County	34,573
Schaumburg, IL (village) Cook County	30,714
Chicago, IL (city) Cook County	30,684
Mount Prospect, IL (village) Cook County	28,904
Elk Grove Village, IL (village) Cook County	26,878

Korean
Top 10 Places Sorted by Number.

Place	Dollars
Northbrook, IL (village) Cook County	32,694
Buffalo Grove, IL (village) Lake County	28,119
Glenview, IL (village) Cook County	27,676
Lincolnwood, IL (village) Cook County	26,025
Wilmette, IL (village) Cook County	24,224
Skokie, IL (village) Cook County	23,504
Palatine, IL (village) Cook County	23,000
Morton Grove, IL (village) Cook County	22,730
Vernon Hills, IL (village) Lake County	22,381
Arlington Heights, IL (village) Cook County	21,723

Laotian
Top 10 Places Sorted by Number.

Place	Dollars
Elgin, IL (city) Kane County	19,355
Rockford, IL (city) Winnebago County	13,998

Malaysian
Top 10 Places Sorted by Number.

Place	Dollars
No places met population threshold.

Notes: Please refer to the User's Guide for an explanation of data; tables reflect only those areas that meet Summary File 4 population thresholds, therefore there may be less than 10 places listed

Pakistani
Top 10 Places Sorted by Number

Place	Dollars
Skokie, IL (village) Cook County	22,213
Chicago, IL (city) Cook County	11,816

Samoan
Top 10 Places Sorted by Number

Place	Dollars
No places met population threshold.	

Sri Lankan
Top 10 Places Sorted by Number

Place	Dollars
No places met population threshold.	

Taiwanese
Top 10 Places Sorted by Number

Place	Dollars
Naperville, IL (city) Du Page County	35,047
Chicago, IL (city) Cook County	20,133

Thai
Top 10 Places Sorted by Number

Place	Dollars
Chicago, IL (city) Cook County	20,073

Tongan
Top 10 Places Sorted by Number

Place	Dollars
No places met population threshold.	

Vietnamese
Top 10 Places Sorted by Number

Place	Dollars
Aurora, IL (city) Kane County	25,551
Glendale Heights, IL (village) Du Page County	20,530
Carol Stream, IL (village) Du Page County	18,204
Rockford, IL (city) Winnebago County	13,769
Chicago, IL (city) Cook County	13,354
Champaign, IL (city) Champaign County	11,643
Wheaton, IL (city) Du Page County	10,257

Poverty Status

Total Populations with Income Below Poverty Level
Top 10 Places Sorted by Number

Place	Number
Chicago, IL (city) Cook County	556,791
Rockford, IL (city) Winnebago County	20,351
Peoria, IL (city) Peoria County	20,220
Champaign, IL (city) Champaign County	13,398
Cicero, IL (town) Cook County	13,187
Decatur, IL (city) Macon County	12,999
Springfield, IL (city) Sangamon County	12,847
Waukegan, IL (city) Lake County	12,058
Aurora, IL (city) Kane County	12,034
Joliet, IL (city) Will County	10,946

Total Populations with Income Below Poverty Level
Top 10 Places Sorted by Percent

Place	Percent
Carbondale, IL (city) Jackson County	41.36
Macomb, IL (city) McDonough County	29.08
Urbana, IL (city) Champaign County	27.34
Champaign, IL (city) Champaign County	22.11
DeKalb, IL (city) De Kalb County	21.28
Chicago, IL (city) Cook County	19.61
Normal, IL (town) McLean County	19.27
Peoria, IL (city) Peoria County	18.77

Danville, IL (city) Vermilion County	18.07
Decatur, IL (city) Macon County	16.53

Asians with Income Below Poverty Level
Top 10 Places Sorted by Number

Place	Number
Chicago, IL (city) Cook County	22,160
Urbana, IL (city) Champaign County	1,847
Champaign, IL (city) Champaign County	1,434
Carbondale, IL (city) Jackson County	776
Evanston, IL (city) Cook County	645
DeKalb, IL (city) De Kalb County	556
Schaumburg, IL (village) Cook County	544
Skokie, IL (village) Cook County	486
Hoffman Estates, IL (village) Cook County	458
Naperville, IL (city) Du Page County	388

Asians with Income Below Poverty Level
Top 10 Places Sorted by Percent

Place	Percent
Carbondale, IL (city) Jackson County	56.64
Macomb, IL (city) McDonough County	54.09
DeKalb, IL (city) De Kalb County	44.95
Urbana, IL (city) Champaign County	44.52
Champaign, IL (city) Champaign County	36.50
Normal, IL (town) McLean County	26.41
Savoy, IL (village) Champaign County	23.68
East Moline, IL (city) Rock Island County	21.15
Evanston, IL (city) Cook County	18.82
Chicago, IL (city) Cook County	17.96

Native Hawaiian and Other Pacific Islanders with Income Below Poverty Level
Top 10 Places Sorted by Number

Place	Number
Chicago, IL (city) Cook County	269

Native Hawaiian and Other Pacific Islanders with Income Below Poverty Level
Top 10 Places Sorted by Percent

Place	Percent
Chicago, IL (city) Cook County	25.64

Asian Indians with Income Below Poverty Level
Top 10 Places Sorted by Number

Place	Number
Chicago, IL (city) Cook County	4,344
Urbana, IL (city) Champaign County	359
Champaign, IL (city) Champaign County	358
Schaumburg, IL (village) Cook County	231
Skokie, IL (village) Cook County	168
DeKalb, IL (city) De Kalb County	165
Evanston, IL (city) Cook County	165
Lombard, IL (village) Du Page County	150
Mount Prospect, IL (village) Cook County	150
Naperville, IL (city) Du Page County	115

Asian Indians with Income Below Poverty Level
Top 10 Places Sorted by Percent

Place	Percent
Urbana, IL (city) Champaign County	47.36
DeKalb, IL (city) De Kalb County	44.12
Champaign, IL (city) Champaign County	35.94
Chicago, IL (city) Cook County	18.77
Evanston, IL (city) Cook County	18.54
Springfield, IL (city) Sangamon County	14.92
Elgin, IL (city) Kane County	14.53
Lombard, IL (village) Du Page County	11.89
Rolling Meadows, IL (city) Cook County	10.50
Bloomington, IL (city) McLean County	7.26

Bangladeshis with Income Below Poverty Level
Top 10 Places Sorted by Number

Place	Number
No places met population threshold.	

Bangladeshis with Income Below Poverty Level
Top 10 Places Sorted by Percent

Place	Percent
No places met population threshold.	

Cambodians with Income Below Poverty Level
Top 10 Places Sorted by Number

Place	Number
Chicago, IL (city) Cook County	375

Cambodians with Income Below Poverty Level
Top 10 Places Sorted by Percent

Place	Percent
Chicago, IL (city) Cook County	20.34

Chinese (except Taiwanese) with Income Below Poverty Level
Top 10 Places Sorted by Number

Place	Number
Chicago, IL (city) Cook County	5,965
Urbana, IL (city) Champaign County	566
Champaign, IL (city) Champaign County	401
Evanston, IL (city) Cook County	214
Peoria, IL (city) Peoria County	107
Naperville, IL (city) Du Page County	100
Schaumburg, IL (village) Cook County	72
Westmont, IL (village) Du Page County	57
Hoffman Estates, IL (village) Cook County	52
Mundelein, IL (village) Lake County	39

Chinese (except Taiwanese) with Income Below Poverty Level
Top 10 Places Sorted by Percent

Place	Percent
Champaign, IL (city) Champaign County	41.60
Urbana, IL (city) Champaign County	36.63
Evanston, IL (city) Cook County	26.52
Chicago, IL (city) Cook County	19.42
Peoria, IL (city) Peoria County	13.34
Westmont, IL (village) Du Page County	11.90
Mundelein, IL (village) Lake County	7.20
Hoffman Estates, IL (village) Cook County	6.33
Elk Grove Village, IL (village) Cook County	5.97
Palatine, IL (village) Cook County	5.60

Fijians with Income Below Poverty Level
Top 10 Places Sorted by Number

Place	Number
No places met population threshold.	

Fijians with Income Below Poverty Level
Top 10 Places Sorted by Percent

Place	Percent
No places met population threshold.	

Filipinos with Income Below Poverty Level
Top 10 Places Sorted by Number

Place	Number
Chicago, IL (city) Cook County	1,975
Glendale Heights, IL (village) Du Page County	60
Palatine, IL (village) Cook County	45
Aurora, IL (city) Kane County	38
Skokie, IL (village) Cook County	37
Schaumburg, IL (village) Cook County	30
Elgin, IL (city) Kane County	26
Streamwood, IL (village) Cook County	23

Notes: Please refer to the User's Guide for an explanation of data; tables reflect only those areas that meet Summary File 4 population thresholds, therefore there may be less than 10 places listed

Bolingbrook, IL (village) Will County   18
Arlington Heights, IL (village) Cook County   16

Filipinos with Income Below Poverty Level
Top 10 Places Sorted by Percent

Place	Percent
Chicago, IL (city) Cook County	7.16
Palatine, IL (village) Cook County	6.34
Elgin, IL (city) Kane County	4.31
Aurora, IL (city) Kane County	4.12
Glendale Heights, IL (village) Du Page County	3.44
Schaumburg, IL (village) Cook County	3.24
Addison, IL (village) Du Page County	2.59
Arlington Heights, IL (village) Cook County	2.32
Streamwood, IL (village) Cook County	1.94
Park City, IL (city) Lake County	1.92

Guamanian or Chamorros with Income Below Poverty Level
Top 10 Places Sorted by Number

Place	Number
No places met population threshold.	

Guamanian or Chamorros with Income Below Poverty Level
Top 10 Places Sorted by Percent

Place	Percent
No places met population threshold.	

Hawaiian, Natives with Income Below Poverty Level
Top 10 Places Sorted by Number

Place	Number
No places met population threshold.	

Hawaiian, Natives with Income Below Poverty Level
Top 10 Places Sorted by Percent

Place	Percent
No places met population threshold.	

Hmongs with Income Below Poverty Level
Top 10 Places Sorted by Number

Place	Number
No places met population threshold.	

Hmongs with Income Below Poverty Level
Top 10 Places Sorted by Percent

Place	Percent
No places met population threshold.	

Indonesians with Income Below Poverty Level
Top 10 Places Sorted by Number

Place	Number
No places met population threshold.	

Indonesians with Income Below Poverty Level
Top 10 Places Sorted by Percent

Place	Percent
No places met population threshold.	

Japanese with Income Below Poverty Level
Top 10 Places Sorted by Number

Place	Number
Chicago, IL (city) Cook County	788
Hoffman Estates, IL (village) Cook County	91
Arlington Heights, IL (village) Cook County	57
Elk Grove Village, IL (village) Cook County	31
Wilmette, IL (village) Cook County	20
Glenview, IL (village) Cook County	18
Evanston, IL (city) Cook County	12
Buffalo Grove, IL (village) Lake County	9

Mount Prospect, IL (village) Cook County   6
Schaumburg, IL (village) Cook County   0

Japanese with Income Below Poverty Level
Top 10 Places Sorted by Percent

Place	Percent
Chicago, IL (city) Cook County	13.53
Hoffman Estates, IL (village) Cook County	10.89
Wilmette, IL (village) Cook County	5.78
Arlington Heights, IL (village) Cook County	5.73
Glenview, IL (village) Cook County	5.73
Elk Grove Village, IL (village) Cook County	5.08
Evanston, IL (city) Cook County	3.70
Buffalo Grove, IL (village) Lake County	1.47
Mount Prospect, IL (village) Cook County	1.35
Schaumburg, IL (village) Cook County	0.00

Koreans with Income Below Poverty Level
Top 10 Places Sorted by Number

Place	Number
Chicago, IL (city) Cook County	3,617
Urbana, IL (city) Champaign County	513
Champaign, IL (city) Champaign County	334
Schaumburg, IL (village) Cook County	200
Evanston, IL (city) Cook County	159
Mount Prospect, IL (village) Cook County	159
Hoffman Estates, IL (village) Cook County	112
Skokie, IL (village) Cook County	96
Niles, IL (village) Cook County	86
Naperville, IL (city) Du Page County	68

Koreans with Income Below Poverty Level
Top 10 Places Sorted by Percent

Place	Percent
Urbana, IL (city) Champaign County	59.58
Champaign, IL (city) Champaign County	46.91
Evanston, IL (city) Cook County	31.80
Chicago, IL (city) Cook County	30.41
Schaumburg, IL (village) Cook County	11.27
Mount Prospect, IL (village) Cook County	11.00
Vernon Hills, IL (village) Lake County	10.33
Niles, IL (village) Cook County	8.56
Hoffman Estates, IL (village) Cook County	7.85
Naperville, IL (city) Du Page County	7.82

Laotians with Income Below Poverty Level
Top 10 Places Sorted by Number

Place	Number
Rockford, IL (city) Winnebago County	65
Elgin, IL (city) Kane County	0

Laotians with Income Below Poverty Level
Top 10 Places Sorted by Percent

Place	Percent
Rockford, IL (city) Winnebago County	7.24
Elgin, IL (city) Kane County	0.00

Malaysians with Income Below Poverty Level
Top 10 Places Sorted by Number

Place	Number
No places met population threshold.	

Malaysians with Income Below Poverty Level
Top 10 Places Sorted by Percent

Place	Percent
No places met population threshold.	

Pakistanis with Income Below Poverty Level
Top 10 Places Sorted by Number

Place	Number
Chicago, IL (city) Cook County	1,836

Skokie, IL (village) Cook County   0

Pakistanis with Income Below Poverty Level
Top 10 Places Sorted by Percent

Place	Percent
Chicago, IL (city) Cook County	28.69
Skokie, IL (village) Cook County	0.00

Samoans with Income Below Poverty Level
Top 10 Places Sorted by Number

Place	Number
No places met population threshold.	

Samoans with Income Below Poverty Level
Top 10 Places Sorted by Percent

Place	Percent
No places met population threshold.	

Sri Lankans with Income Below Poverty Level
Top 10 Places Sorted by Number

Place	Number
No places met population threshold.	

Sri Lankans with Income Below Poverty Level
Top 10 Places Sorted by Percent

Place	Percent
No places met population threshold.	

Taiwanese with Income Below Poverty Level
Top 10 Places Sorted by Number

Place	Number
Chicago, IL (city) Cook County	149
Naperville, IL (city) Du Page County	44

Taiwanese with Income Below Poverty Level
Top 10 Places Sorted by Percent

Place	Percent
Chicago, IL (city) Cook County	24.87
Naperville, IL (city) Du Page County	10.21

Thais with Income Below Poverty Level
Top 10 Places Sorted by Number

Place	Number
Chicago, IL (city) Cook County	399

Thais with Income Below Poverty Level
Top 10 Places Sorted by Percent

Place	Percent
Chicago, IL (city) Cook County	19.49

Tongans with Income Below Poverty Level
Top 10 Places Sorted by Number

Place	Number
No places met population threshold.	

Tongans with Income Below Poverty Level
Top 10 Places Sorted by Percent

Place	Percent
No places met population threshold.	

Vietnamese with Income Below Poverty Level
Top 10 Places Sorted by Number

Place	Number
Chicago, IL (city) Cook County	1,720
Champaign, IL (city) Champaign County	79
Rockford, IL (city) Winnebago County	42
Aurora, IL (city) Kane County	40
Glendale Heights, IL (village) Du Page County	20

Notes: Please refer to the User's Guide for an explanation of data; tables reflect only those areas that meet Summary File 4 population thresholds, therefore there may be less than 10 places listed

Carol Stream, IL (village) Du Page County   16
Wheaton, IL (city) Du Page County   0

Vietnamese with Income Below Poverty Level
Top 10 Places Sorted by Percent

Place	Percent
Chicago, IL (city) Cook County	21.19
Champaign, IL (city) Champaign County	19.04
Rockford, IL (city) Winnebago County	10.42
Aurora, IL (city) Kane County	8.16
Carol Stream, IL (village) Du Page County	3.39
Glendale Heights, IL (village) Du Page County	2.50
Wheaton, IL (city) Du Page County	0.00

Homeownership

Total Populations Who Own Their Own Homes
Top 10 Places Sorted by Number

Place	Number
Chicago, IL (city) Cook County	464,912
Rockford, IL (city) Winnebago County	36,304
Naperville, IL (city) Du Page County	34,952
Aurora, IL (city) Kane County	32,621
Springfield, IL (city) Sangamon County	30,575
Peoria, IL (city) Peoria County	27,041
Joliet, IL (city) Will County	25,465
Arlington Heights, IL (village) Cook County	23,565
Decatur, IL (city) Macon County	22,682
Elgin, IL (city) Kane County	22,167

Total Populations Who Own Their Own Homes
Top 10 Places Sorted by Percent

Place	Percent
South Barrington, IL (village) Cook County	98.69
Oak Brook, IL (village) Du Page County	97.17
Lincolnshire, IL (village) Lake County	97.11
Long Grove, IL (village) Lake County	97.04
Burr Ridge, IL (village) Du Page County	96.50
Morton Grove, IL (village) Cook County	94.54
Westchester, IL (village) Cook County	93.81
Flossmoor, IL (village) Cook County	93.66
Lake in the Hills, IL (village) McHenry County	93.54
Bartlett, IL (village) Du Page County	93.45

Asians Who Own Their Own Homes
Top 10 Places Sorted by Number

Place	Number
Chicago, IL (city) Cook County	16,555
Skokie, IL (village) Cook County	2,801
Naperville, IL (city) Du Page County	2,743
Schaumburg, IL (village) Cook County	1,799
Hoffman Estates, IL (village) Cook County	1,525
Glendale Heights, IL (village) Du Page County	1,263
Morton Grove, IL (village) Cook County	1,171
Glenview, IL (village) Cook County	1,115
Aurora, IL (city) Kane County	1,061
Hanover Park, IL (village) Cook County	960

Asians Who Own Their Own Homes
Top 10 Places Sorted by Percent

Place	Percent
Algonquin, IL (village) McHenry County	100.00
Burr Ridge, IL (village) Du Page County	100.00
Flossmoor, IL (village) Cook County	100.00
Gages Lake, IL (cdp) Lake County	100.00
Oak Brook, IL (village) Du Page County	100.00
South Barrington, IL (village) Cook County	100.00
Lincolnwood, IL (village) Cook County	97.79
Bartlett, IL (village) Du Page County	97.11
Orland Park, IL (village) Cook County	95.64
Morton Grove, IL (village) Cook County	95.59

Native Hawaiian and Other Pacific Islanders Who Own Their Own Homes
Top 10 Places Sorted by Number

Place	Number
Chicago, IL (city) Cook County	88

Native Hawaiian and Other Pacific Islanders Who Own Their Own Homes
Top 10 Places Sorted by Percent

Place	Percent
Chicago, IL (city) Cook County	31.65

Asian Indians Who Own Their Own Homes
Top 10 Places Sorted by Number

Place	Number
Chicago, IL (city) Cook County	2,312
Naperville, IL (city) Du Page County	1,045
Skokie, IL (village) Cook County	774
Schaumburg, IL (village) Cook County	718
Hoffman Estates, IL (village) Cook County	548
Glendale Heights, IL (village) Du Page County	511
Hanover Park, IL (village) Cook County	419
Aurora, IL (city) Kane County	393
Des Plaines, IL (city) Cook County	392
Carol Stream, IL (village) Du Page County	376

Asian Indians Who Own Their Own Homes
Top 10 Places Sorted by Percent

Place	Percent
Burr Ridge, IL (village) Du Page County	100.00
Morton Grove, IL (village) Cook County	100.00
Oak Brook, IL (village) Du Page County	100.00
South Barrington, IL (village) Cook County	100.00
Bartlett, IL (village) Du Page County	98.12
Orland Park, IL (village) Cook County	95.48
Bolingbrook, IL (village) Will County	93.84
Lincolnwood, IL (village) Cook County	91.94
Streamwood, IL (village) Cook County	91.59
Glenview, IL (village) Cook County	89.89

Bangladeshis Who Own Their Own Homes
Top 10 Places Sorted by Number

Place	Number
No places met population threshold.	

Bangladeshis Who Own Their Own Homes
Top 10 Places Sorted by Percent

Place	Percent
No places met population threshold.	

Cambodians Who Own Their Own Homes
Top 10 Places Sorted by Number

Place	Number
Chicago, IL (city) Cook County	129

Cambodians Who Own Their Own Homes
Top 10 Places Sorted by Percent

Place	Percent
Chicago, IL (city) Cook County	31.93

Chinese (except Taiwanese) Who Own Their Own Homes
Top 10 Places Sorted by Number

Place	Number
Chicago, IL (city) Cook County	5,029
Naperville, IL (city) Du Page County	1,026
Skokie, IL (village) Cook County	397
Schaumburg, IL (village) Cook County	300
Glenview, IL (village) Cook County	247
Hoffman Estates, IL (village) Cook County	181
Vernon Hills, IL (village) Lake County	179

Buffalo Grove, IL (village) Lake County   166
Northbrook, IL (village) Cook County   162
Palatine, IL (village) Cook County   155

Chinese (except Taiwanese) Who Own Their Own Homes
Top 10 Places Sorted by Percent

Place	Percent
Northbrook, IL (village) Cook County	95.29
Mundelein, IL (village) Lake County	90.13
Glenview, IL (village) Cook County	88.85
Vernon Hills, IL (village) Lake County	87.32
Naperville, IL (city) Du Page County	86.07
Buffalo Grove, IL (village) Lake County	81.77
Wilmette, IL (village) Cook County	78.83
Elk Grove Village, IL (village) Cook County	75.00
Aurora, IL (city) Kane County	74.75
Lisle, IL (village) Du Page County	69.41

Fijians Who Own Their Own Homes
Top 10 Places Sorted by Number

Place	Number
No places met population threshold.	

Fijians Who Own Their Own Homes
Top 10 Places Sorted by Percent

Place	Percent
No places met population threshold.	

Filipinos Who Own Their Own Homes
Top 10 Places Sorted by Number

Place	Number
Chicago, IL (city) Cook County	4,535
Skokie, IL (village) Cook County	615
Morton Grove, IL (village) Cook County	385
Glendale Heights, IL (village) Du Page County	369
Waukegan, IL (city) Lake County	297
Bolingbrook, IL (village) Will County	296
Hanover Park, IL (village) Cook County	284
Streamwood, IL (village) Cook County	280
Carol Stream, IL (village) Du Page County	272
Hoffman Estates, IL (village) Cook County	255

Filipinos Who Own Their Own Homes
Top 10 Places Sorted by Percent

Place	Percent
Hanover Park, IL (village) Cook County	100.00
Lincolnwood, IL (village) Cook County	100.00
Orland Park, IL (village) Cook County	100.00
Streamwood, IL (village) Cook County	97.22
Bartlett, IL (village) Du Page County	97.01
Des Plaines, IL (city) Cook County	96.21
Gurnee, IL (village) Lake County	94.95
Hoffman Estates, IL (village) Cook County	94.10
Tinley Park, IL (village) Cook County	93.02
Morton Grove, IL (village) Cook County	92.11

Guamanian or Chamorros Who Own Their Own Homes
Top 10 Places Sorted by Number

Place	Number
No places met population threshold.	

Guamanian or Chamorros Who Own Their Own Homes
Top 10 Places Sorted by Percent

Place	Percent
No places met population threshold.	

Notes: Please refer to the User's Guide for an explanation of data; tables reflect only those areas that meet Summary File 4 population thresholds, therefore there may be less than 10 places listed

Hawaiian, Natives Who Own Their Own Homes
Top 10 Places Sorted by Number

Place	Number
No places met population threshold.	

Hawaiian, Natives Who Own Their Own Homes
Top 10 Places Sorted by Percent

Place	Percent
No places met population threshold.	

Hmongs Who Own Their Own Homes
Top 10 Places Sorted by Number

Place	Number
No places met population threshold.	

Hmongs Who Own Their Own Homes
Top 10 Places Sorted by Percent

Place	Percent
No places met population threshold.	

Indonesians Who Own Their Own Homes
Top 10 Places Sorted by Number

Place	Number
No places met population threshold.	

Indonesians Who Own Their Own Homes
Top 10 Places Sorted by Percent

Place	Percent
No places met population threshold.	

Japanese Who Own Their Own Homes
Top 10 Places Sorted by Number

Place	Number
Chicago, IL (city) Cook County	1,487
Arlington Heights, IL (village) Cook County	93
Schaumburg, IL (village) Cook County	92
Buffalo Grove, IL (village) Lake County	84
Hoffman Estates, IL (village) Cook County	81
Mount Prospect, IL (village) Cook County	78
Elk Grove Village, IL (village) Cook County	76
Glenview, IL (village) Cook County	65
Evanston, IL (city) Cook County	64
Wilmette, IL (village) Cook County	46

Japanese Who Own Their Own Homes
Top 10 Places Sorted by Percent

Place	Percent
Glenview, IL (village) Cook County	58.56
Chicago, IL (city) Cook County	47.13
Mount Prospect, IL (village) Cook County	45.88
Buffalo Grove, IL (village) Lake County	42.86
Wilmette, IL (village) Cook County	38.98
Evanston, IL (city) Cook County	38.32
Elk Grove Village, IL (village) Cook County	36.36
Hoffman Estates, IL (village) Cook County	31.76
Schaumburg, IL (village) Cook County	23.53
Arlington Heights, IL (village) Cook County	21.23

Koreans Who Own Their Own Homes
Top 10 Places Sorted by Number

Place	Number
Chicago, IL (city) Cook County	1,049
Skokie, IL (village) Cook County	513
Glenview, IL (village) Cook County	438
Northbrook, IL (village) Cook County	413
Hoffman Estates, IL (village) Cook County	342
Schaumburg, IL (village) Cook County	271
Buffalo Grove, IL (village) Lake County	234
Mount Prospect, IL (village) Cook County	232
Morton Grove, IL (village) Cook County	218
Niles, IL (village) Cook County	216

Koreans Who Own Their Own Homes
Top 10 Places Sorted by Percent

Place	Percent
Lincolnwood, IL (village) Cook County	100.00
Morton Grove, IL (village) Cook County	93.56
Glenview, IL (village) Cook County	91.82
Northbrook, IL (village) Cook County	90.77
Buffalo Grove, IL (village) Lake County	86.03
Hoffman Estates, IL (village) Cook County	80.66
Naperville, IL (city) Du Page County	78.17
Wilmette, IL (village) Cook County	77.18
Arlington Heights, IL (village) Cook County	76.03
Vernon Hills, IL (village) Lake County	73.94

Laotians Who Own Their Own Homes
Top 10 Places Sorted by Number

Place	Number
Rockford, IL (city) Winnebago County	193
Elgin, IL (city) Kane County	137

Laotians Who Own Their Own Homes
Top 10 Places Sorted by Percent

Place	Percent
Rockford, IL (city) Winnebago County	76.59
Elgin, IL (city) Kane County	73.26

Malaysians Who Own Their Own Homes
Top 10 Places Sorted by Number

Place	Number
No places met population threshold.	

Malaysians Who Own Their Own Homes
Top 10 Places Sorted by Percent

Place	Percent
No places met population threshold.	

Pakistanis Who Own Their Own Homes
Top 10 Places Sorted by Number

Place	Number
Chicago, IL (city) Cook County	409
Skokie, IL (village) Cook County	73

Pakistanis Who Own Their Own Homes
Top 10 Places Sorted by Percent

Place	Percent
Skokie, IL (village) Cook County	75.26
Chicago, IL (city) Cook County	21.27

Samoans Who Own Their Own Homes
Top 10 Places Sorted by Number

Place	Number
No places met population threshold.	

Samoans Who Own Their Own Homes
Top 10 Places Sorted by Percent

Place	Percent
No places met population threshold.	

Sri Lankans Who Own Their Own Homes
Top 10 Places Sorted by Number

Place	Number
No places met population threshold.	

Sri Lankans Who Own Their Own Homes
Top 10 Places Sorted by Percent

Place	Percent
No places met population threshold.	

Taiwanese Who Own Their Own Homes
Top 10 Places Sorted by Number

Place	Number
Naperville, IL (city) Du Page County	113
Chicago, IL (city) Cook County	91

Taiwanese Who Own Their Own Homes
Top 10 Places Sorted by Percent

Place	Percent
Naperville, IL (city) Du Page County	81.29
Chicago, IL (city) Cook County	21.77

Thais Who Own Their Own Homes
Top 10 Places Sorted by Number

Place	Number
Chicago, IL (city) Cook County	244

Thais Who Own Their Own Homes
Top 10 Places Sorted by Percent

Place	Percent
Chicago, IL (city) Cook County	32.32

Tongans Who Own Their Own Homes
Top 10 Places Sorted by Number

Place	Number
No places met population threshold.	

Tongans Who Own Their Own Homes
Top 10 Places Sorted by Percent

Place	Percent
No places met population threshold.	

Vietnamese Who Own Their Own Homes
Top 10 Places Sorted by Number

Place	Number
Chicago, IL (city) Cook County	744
Glendale Heights, IL (village) Du Page County	185
Aurora, IL (city) Kane County	113
Champaign, IL (city) Champaign County	104
Carol Stream, IL (village) Du Page County	94
Rockford, IL (city) Winnebago County	50
Wheaton, IL (city) Du Page County	13

Vietnamese Who Own Their Own Homes
Top 10 Places Sorted by Percent

Place	Percent
Aurora, IL (city) Kane County	88.98
Glendale Heights, IL (village) Du Page County	80.43
Carol Stream, IL (village) Du Page County	77.05
Champaign, IL (city) Champaign County	76.47
Rockford, IL (city) Winnebago County	39.68
Chicago, IL (city) Cook County	30.68
Wheaton, IL (city) Du Page County	15.12

Median Gross Rent

All Specified Renter-Occupied Housing Units
Top 10 Places Sorted by Number

Place	Dollars/Month
Lincolnwood, IL (village) Cook County	2,001
South Barrington, IL (village) Cook County	2,001
Northbrook, IL (village) Cook County	1,279
Burr Ridge, IL (village) Du Page County	1,205
Lincolnshire, IL (village) Lake County	1,188
Streamwood, IL (village) Cook County	1,130
Buffalo Grove, IL (village) Lake County	1,079
Winnetka, IL (village) Cook County	1,038
Wilmette, IL (village) Cook County	1,028
Warrenville, IL (city) Du Page County	1,019

Notes: Please refer to the User's Guide for an explanation of data; tables reflect only those areas that meet Summary File 4 population thresholds, therefore there may be less than 10 places listed

Specified Housing Units Rented by Asians
Top 10 Places Sorted by Number

Place	Dollars/Month
Deerfield, IL (village) Lake County	2,001
Lincolnshire, IL (village) Lake County	2,001
Northbrook, IL (village) Cook County	2,001
Streamwood, IL (village) Cook County	1,336
Winnetka, IL (village) Cook County	1,268
Lincolnwood, IL (village) Cook County	1,266
Wilmette, IL (village) Cook County	1,236
Buffalo Grove, IL (village) Lake County	1,231
Gurnee, IL (village) Lake County	1,074
Highland Park, IL (city) Lake County	1,049

Specified Housing Units Rented by Native Hawaiian and Other Pacific Islanders
Top 10 Places Sorted by Number

Place	Dollars/Month
Chicago, IL (city) Cook County	681

Specified Housing Units Rented by Asian Indians
Top 10 Places Sorted by Number

Place	Dollars/Month
Streamwood, IL (village) Cook County	1,322
Elmhurst, IL (city) Du Page County	1,317
Darien, IL (city) Du Page County	1,297
Lincolnwood, IL (village) Cook County	1,266
Buffalo Grove, IL (village) Lake County	1,152
Gurnee, IL (village) Lake County	1,125
Bloomingdale, IL (village) Du Page County	1,111
Schaumburg, IL (village) Cook County	988
Evanston, IL (city) Cook County	977
Aurora, IL (city) Kane County	960

Specified Housing Units Rented by Bangladeshis
Top 10 Places Sorted by Number

Place	Dollars/Month

Specified Housing Units Rented by Cambodians
Top 10 Places Sorted by Number

Place	Dollars/Month
Chicago, IL (city) Cook County	676

Specified Housing Units Rented by Chinese (except Taiwanese)
Top 10 Places Sorted by Number

Place	Dollars/Month
Northbrook, IL (village) Cook County	2,001
Mundelein, IL (village) Lake County	1,375
Buffalo Grove, IL (village) Lake County	1,325
Wilmette, IL (village) Cook County	1,161
Gurnee, IL (village) Lake County	1,038
Naperville, IL (city) Du Page County	961
Schaumburg, IL (village) Cook County	882
Lisle, IL (village) Du Page County	878
Skokie, IL (village) Cook County	839
Palatine, IL (village) Cook County	826

Specified Housing Units Rented by Fijians
Top 10 Places Sorted by Number

Place	Dollars/Month

Specified Housing Units Rented by Filipinos
Top 10 Places Sorted by Number

Place	Dollars/Month
Des Plaines, IL (city) Cook County	1,125
Gurnee, IL (village) Lake County	1,125
Arlington Heights, IL (village) Cook County	1,029
Buffalo Grove, IL (village) Lake County	1,019
Schaumburg, IL (village) Cook County	986
Palatine, IL (village) Cook County	958
Lombard, IL (village) Du Page County	950

Place	Dollars/Month
Wheeling, IL (village) Cook County	911
Hoffman Estates, IL (village) Cook County	850
Mount Prospect, IL (village) Cook County	850

Specified Housing Units Rented by Guamanian or Chamorros
Top 10 Places Sorted by Number

Place	Dollars/Month

Specified Housing Units Rented by Hawaiian, Natives
Top 10 Places Sorted by Number

Place	Dollars/Month

Specified Housing Units Rented by Hmongs
Top 10 Places Sorted by Number

Place	Dollars/Month

Specified Housing Units Rented by Indonesians
Top 10 Places Sorted by Number

Place	Dollars/Month

Specified Housing Units Rented by Japanese
Top 10 Places Sorted by Number

Place	Dollars/Month
Buffalo Grove, IL (village) Lake County	1,967
Wilmette, IL (village) Cook County	1,950
Hoffman Estates, IL (village) Cook County	1,643
Mount Prospect, IL (village) Cook County	1,583
Schaumburg, IL (village) Cook County	1,323
Arlington Heights, IL (village) Cook County	1,322
Elk Grove Village, IL (village) Cook County	1,281
Glenview, IL (village) Cook County	1,088
Evanston, IL (city) Cook County	945
Chicago, IL (city) Cook County	731

Specified Housing Units Rented by Koreans
Top 10 Places Sorted by Number

Place	Dollars/Month
Northbrook, IL (village) Cook County	2,001
Buffalo Grove, IL (village) Lake County	1,583
Morton Grove, IL (village) Cook County	1,516
Wilmette, IL (village) Cook County	1,131
Schaumburg, IL (village) Cook County	1,063
Vernon Hills, IL (village) Lake County	1,008
Naperville, IL (city) Du Page County	990
Arlington Heights, IL (village) Cook County	973
Hoffman Estates, IL (village) Cook County	952
Palatine, IL (village) Cook County	873

Specified Housing Units Rented by Laotians
Top 10 Places Sorted by Number

Place	Dollars/Month
Elgin, IL (city) Kane County	644
Rockford, IL (city) Winnebago County	466

Specified Housing Units Rented by Malaysians
Top 10 Places Sorted by Number

Place	Dollars/Month

Specified Housing Units Rented by Pakistanis
Top 10 Places Sorted by Number

Place	Dollars/Month
Skokie, IL (village) Cook County	685
Chicago, IL (city) Cook County	680

Specified Housing Units Rented by Samoans
Top 10 Places Sorted by Number

Place	Dollars/Month

Specified Housing Units Rented by Sri Lankans
Top 10 Places Sorted by Number

Place	Dollars/Month

Specified Housing Units Rented by Taiwanese
Top 10 Places Sorted by Number

Place	Dollars/Month
Naperville, IL (city) Du Page County	850
Chicago, IL (city) Cook County	713

Specified Housing Units Rented by Thais
Top 10 Places Sorted by Number

Place	Dollars/Month
Chicago, IL (city) Cook County	686

Specified Housing Units Rented by Tongans
Top 10 Places Sorted by Number

Place	Dollars/Month

Specified Housing Units Rented by Vietnamese
Top 10 Places Sorted by Number

Place	Dollars/Month
Aurora, IL (city) Kane County	1,031
Glendale Heights, IL (village) Du Page County	804
Carol Stream, IL (village) Du Page County	775
Wheaton, IL (city) Du Page County	675
Chicago, IL (city) Cook County	642
Champaign, IL (city) Champaign County	467
Rockford, IL (city) Winnebago County	425

Median Home Value

All Specified Owner-Occupied Housing Units
Top 10 Places Sorted by Number

Place	Dollars
Winnetka, IL (village) Cook County	756,500
South Barrington, IL (village) Cook County	678,800
Lake Forest, IL (city) Lake County	662,400
Oak Brook, IL (village) Du Page County	635,400
Long Grove, IL (village) Lake County	555,400
Hinsdale, IL (village) Du Page County	520,100
Burr Ridge, IL (village) Du Page County	477,800
Lincolnshire, IL (village) Lake County	442,400
Wilmette, IL (village) Cook County	441,600
River Forest, IL (village) Cook County	386,600

Specified Housing Units Owned and Occupied by Asians
Top 10 Places Sorted by Number

Place	Dollars
Winnetka, IL (village) Cook County	852,300
South Barrington, IL (village) Cook County	801,300
Oak Brook, IL (village) Du Page County	773,300
Lake Forest, IL (city) Lake County	684,700
Burr Ridge, IL (village) Du Page County	589,300
Deerfield, IL (village) Lake County	461,100
Long Grove, IL (village) Lake County	443,200
Lincolnshire, IL (village) Lake County	423,100
Highland Park, IL (city) Lake County	398,100
River Forest, IL (village) Cook County	355,600

Specified Housing Units Owned and Occupied by Native Hawaiian and Other Pacific Islanders
Top 10 Places Sorted by Number

Place	Dollars
Chicago, IL (city) Cook County	135,000

Notes: Please refer to the User's Guide for an explanation of data; tables reflect only those areas that meet Summary File 4 population thresholds, therefore there may be less than 10 places listed

Specified Housing Units Owned and Occupied by Asian Indians
Top 10 Places Sorted by Number.

Place	Dollars
Oak Brook, IL (village) Du Page County	856,100
South Barrington, IL (village) Cook County	830,400
Burr Ridge, IL (village) Du Page County	613,200
Glenview, IL (village) Cook County	402,800
Rolling Meadows, IL (city) Cook County	316,700
Lincolnwood, IL (village) Cook County	294,100
Naperville, IL (city) Du Page County	271,200
Buffalo Grove, IL (village) Lake County	262,500
Orland Park, IL (village) Cook County	262,500
Darien, IL (city) Du Page County	246,300

Specified Housing Units Owned and Occupied by Bangladeshis
Top 10 Places Sorted by Number.

Place	Dollars

Specified Housing Units Owned and Occupied by Cambodians
Top 10 Places Sorted by Number.

Place	Dollars
Chicago, IL (city) Cook County	229,200

Specified Housing Units Owned and Occupied by Chinese (except Taiwanese)
Top 10 Places Sorted by Number.

Place	Dollars
Northbrook, IL (village) Cook County	348,200
Glenview, IL (village) Cook County	297,800
Wilmette, IL (village) Cook County	290,400
Evanston, IL (city) Cook County	285,700
Vernon Hills, IL (village) Lake County	283,100
Arlington Heights, IL (village) Cook County	275,000
Buffalo Grove, IL (village) Lake County	261,100
Naperville, IL (city) Du Page County	261,000
Lisle, IL (village) Du Page County	253,800
Mundelein, IL (village) Lake County	244,100

Specified Housing Units Owned and Occupied by Fijians
Top 10 Places Sorted by Number.

Place	Dollars
No places met population threshold.	

Specified Housing Units Owned and Occupied by Filipinos
Top 10 Places Sorted by Number.

Place	Dollars
Naperville, IL (city) Du Page County	302,000
Lincolnwood, IL (village) Cook County	278,300
Glenview, IL (village) Cook County	277,100
Gurnee, IL (village) Lake County	237,000
Darien, IL (city) Du Page County	234,400
Arlington Heights, IL (village) Cook County	233,200
Downers Grove, IL (village) Du Page County	232,000
Mundelein, IL (village) Lake County	231,800
Niles, IL (village) Cook County	222,000
Wheeling, IL (village) Cook County	216,900

Specified Housing Units Owned and Occupied by Guamanian or Chamorros
Top 10 Places Sorted by Number.

Place	Dollars
No places met population threshold.	

Specified Housing Units Owned and Occupied by Hawaiian, Natives
Top 10 Places Sorted by Number.

Place	Dollars
No places met population threshold.	

Specified Housing Units Owned and Occupied by Hmongs
Top 10 Places Sorted by Number.

Place	Dollars
No places met population threshold.	

Specified Housing Units Owned and Occupied by Indonesians
Top 10 Places Sorted by Number.

Place	Dollars
No places met population threshold.	

Specified Housing Units Owned and Occupied by Japanese
Top 10 Places Sorted by Number.

Place	Dollars
Glenview, IL (village) Cook County	342,500
Schaumburg, IL (village) Cook County	296,900
Arlington Heights, IL (village) Cook County	280,200
Hoffman Estates, IL (village) Cook County	279,500
Wilmette, IL (village) Cook County	273,800
Buffalo Grove, IL (village) Lake County	246,900
Elk Grove Village, IL (village) Cook County	226,600
Evanston, IL (city) Cook County	225,000
Mount Prospect, IL (village) Cook County	217,900
Chicago, IL (city) Cook County	176,900

Specified Housing Units Owned and Occupied by Koreans
Top 10 Places Sorted by Number.

Place	Dollars
Glenview, IL (village) Cook County	335,500
Northbrook, IL (village) Cook County	318,900
Wilmette, IL (village) Cook County	305,800
Palatine, IL (village) Cook County	278,300
Lincolnwood, IL (village) Cook County	278,000
Buffalo Grove, IL (village) Lake County	266,700
Arlington Heights, IL (village) Cook County	263,500
Vernon Hills, IL (village) Lake County	245,000
Morton Grove, IL (village) Cook County	239,700
Mount Prospect, IL (village) Cook County	234,000

Specified Housing Units Owned and Occupied by Laotians
Top 10 Places Sorted by Number.

Place	Dollars
Elgin, IL (city) Kane County	149,700
Rockford, IL (city) Winnebago County	82,400

Specified Housing Units Owned and Occupied by Malaysians
Top 10 Places Sorted by Number.

Place	Dollars
No places met population threshold.	

Specified Housing Units Owned and Occupied by Pakistanis
Top 10 Places Sorted by Number.

Place	Dollars
Skokie, IL (village) Cook County	199,000
Chicago, IL (city) Cook County	120,100

Specified Housing Units Owned and Occupied by Samoans
Top 10 Places Sorted by Number.

Place	Dollars
No places met population threshold.	

Specified Housing Units Owned and Occupied by Sri Lankans
Top 10 Places Sorted by Number.

Place	Dollars
No places met population threshold.	

Specified Housing Units Owned and Occupied by Taiwanese
Top 10 Places Sorted by Number.

Place	Dollars
Naperville, IL (city) Du Page County	263,100
Chicago, IL (city) Cook County	95,000

Specified Housing Units Owned and Occupied by Thais
Top 10 Places Sorted by Number.

Place	Dollars
Chicago, IL (city) Cook County	174,600

Specified Housing Units Owned and Occupied by Tongans
Top 10 Places Sorted by Number.

Place	Dollars
No places met population threshold.	

Specified Housing Units Owned and Occupied by Vietnamese
Top 10 Places Sorted by Number.

Place	Dollars
Chicago, IL (city) Cook County	191,400
Carol Stream, IL (village) Du Page County	170,800
Aurora, IL (city) Kane County	157,600
Wheaton, IL (city) Du Page County	148,200
Glendale Heights, IL (village) Du Page County	146,600
Rockford, IL (city) Winnebago County	96,400
Champaign, IL (city) Champaign County	88,100

Notes: Please refer to the User's Guide for an explanation of data; tables reflect only those areas that meet Summary File 4 population thresholds, therefore there may be less than 10 places listed

Climate

Illinois Physical Features and Climate Narrative

PHYSICAL FEATURES. Illinois lies midway between the Continental Divide and the Atlantic Ocean and some 500 miles north of the Gulf of Mexico. Its climate is typically continental with cold winters, warm summers, and frequent short period fluctuations in temperature, humidity, cloudiness, and wind direction.

The irregular shape of the State has a width of less than 200 miles at most points, but extends for 385 miles in the north-south direction. Except for a few low hills in the extreme south and a small unglaciated area in the extreme northwest, the terrain is flat. Differences in elevation have no significant influence on the climate. River drainage is mainly toward the Mississippi River, which forms the entire western boundary of the State. From north to south the principal rivers entering the Mississippi are the Rock, Illinois, Kaskaskia, and the Big Muddy. Approximately one-seventh of the State area drains southeastward into the Wabash and Ohio Rivers. Only a small area drains into Lake Michigan.

GENERAL CLIMATE. Without the protection of natural barriers, such as mountain ranges, Illinois experiences the full sweep of the winds which are constantly bringing in the climates of other areas. Southeast and easterly winds bring mild and wet weather; southerly winds are warm and showery; westerly winds are dry with moderate temperatures; and winds from the northwest and north are cool and dry. Winds are controlled by the storm systems and weather fronts which move eastward and northeastward through this area.

Storm systems move through the State most frequently during the winter and spring months and cause a maximum of cloudiness during those seasons. Summer-season storm systems tend to be weaker and to stay farther north, leaving Illinois with much sunshine interspersed with thunderstorm situations of comparatively short duration. The retreat of the sun in autumn is associated with variable periods of pleasant dry weather of the Indian summer variety. This season ends rather abruptly with the returning storminess which usually begins in November.

TEMPERATURE. Because Illinois extends so far in a north-south direction, the contrasts in winter temperature conditions are rather strong. The extreme north has frequent snow and temperatures drop to below zero several times each winter. The soil freezes to a depth of about three feet and occasionally remains snow-covered for weeks at a time. In the extreme south snow falls only occasionally and leaves after a few days, while temperatures drop to zero on an average of only about one day each winter. The soil freezes, but only to a depth of eight to 12 inches, with great variation in the duration of soil-frost periods. The north-south range in winter mean temperatures is approximately 14°F.

During the summer season the sun heats the entire State quite strongly and uniformly. The north-south range of mean temperatures in July is only about 6°F. The annual average of days with temperatures of 90°F. or higher is near 20 in the north and near 50 in the south and west-central. Summer also brings periods of uncomfortably hot and humid weather, which are most persistent in the south. In the north the heat is usually broken after a few days by the arrival of cool air from Canada, but this cooling does not always penetrate to the southern portions of the State.

PRECIPITATION. Latitude is the principal control for both temperature and precipitation, with the northern counties averaging cooler and drier than the south. Distance from the Gulf of Mexico and lower airmass temperatures both tend to reduce the amounts of precipitation in the northern portion. Annual precipitation is approximately one and one-half times as great in the extreme south as in the extreme north, but most of the excess in the southern portion falls during winter and early spring. Mean total precipitation for the four-month period of December through March ranges from near seven inches in the extreme northwest to more than 14 inches in the extreme southeast. Precipitation during the warm season is more uniform. Totals for the six-month period of April through September range from 21 to 24 inches throughout the State. The driest month is February. The wettest months are May and June.

Precipitation during fall, winter, and spring tends to fall uniformly over large areas. In contrast, summer rainfall occurs principally as brief showers affecting relatively small areas. The erratic occurrence of summer showers results in uneven distribution. The high rates of summer rainfall also cause runoff and soil erosion. Summer showers are usually accompanied by thunder and, sometimes, by hail or destructive windstorms.

Floods occur nearly every year in at least some part of the State. The spring and early summer flood season results from a tendency for heavy general rainfall at that time of the year. The extreme north frequently has late winter or early spring flooding with the breakup of river ice, especially if there is an appreciable snow cover which is taken off by rain. River stages tend to decline during late summer, but local flash floods in minor streams, due to heavy thunderstorm rains, are common throughout the warm season. The interior rivers in the central and south have flat beds and sluggish currents so that they rise slowly and remain in flood conditions for relatively long periods.

SNOWFALL. The annual average of snowfall ranges from near 30 inches in the extreme north to only 10 inches in the extreme south. In the extreme north the most likely form of winter precipitation is snow. In contrast, more than 90% of Cairo's winter precipitation falls as rain. In a large number of winter storm situations, only a slight change in the temperature pattern would suffice to change rain to snow or vice versa. For this reason, Illinois snowfall records show great variability. Snowfalls of one inch or more occur on an average of 10 to 12 days per year in the extreme north and decrease to three or four in the far south. The two northern divisions average about 50 days annually when the ground is covered with one inch or more of snow, and this average decreases to about 15 days in the two southern divisions.

STORMS. Heavy snows of four to six inches or more average one or two per year in the north and less frequently in the south. Strong winds will drift snow and make driving hazardous. Moderate to heavy ice storms average about once every four or five years and can be quite damaging. Thunderstorms average about 35 to 50 annually, but most are quite harmless. On occasion they provide the source for hail, damaging winds, and tornadoes. Hail falls on an average of two or three days annually in the same locality, but usually causes little damage.

More than 65 percent of Illinois tornadoes occur during the months of March, April, May, and June. This "tornado season" is marked by a rapid increase in activity during March, a peak in April and May, and a decline during June. Tornadoes have occurred during each of the twelve months of the year.

INFLUENCE OF LAKE MICHIGAN. Because prevailing winds are westerly and storm systems move from the same direction, the influence of the lake on Illinois weather is not large. When the wind blows from the lake toward the shore, which it does for approximately one-fourth of the time during spring and summer and for about one-eighth of the time during fall and winter, the result is a moderation of temperature. In addition to the general occurrence of onshore winds, there is the local "sea breeze" effect on summer afternoons which is usually observable in a narrow strip near the lake shore.

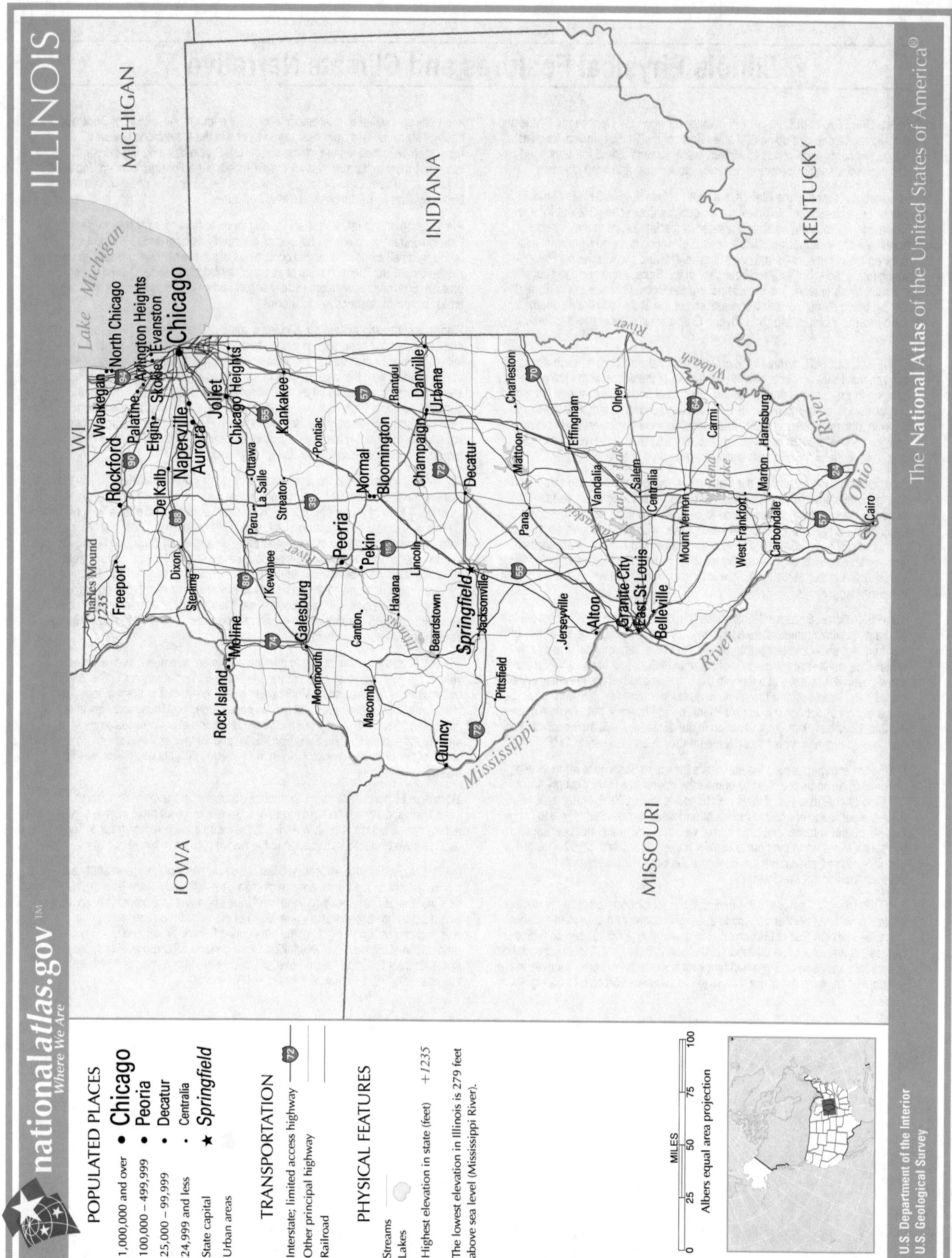

ILLINOIS

MICHIGAN

INDIANA

KENTUCKY

WI

IOWA

MISSOURI

Lake Michigan

Charles Mound
1235

Freeport
Rockford
Waukegan
North Chicago
Palatine
Arlington Heights
Elgin
Skokie
Evanston
Chicago
De Kalb
Naperville
Aurora
Joliet
Chicago Heights
Kankakee
Dixon
Sterling
Ottawa
La Salle
Peru
Streator
Pontiac
Kewanee
Galesburg
Peoria
Pekin
Lincoln
Bloomington
Normal
Danville
Rantoul
Urbana
Champaign
Decatur
Charleston
Rock Island
Moline
Monmouth
Macomb
Canton
Havana
Beardstown
Springfield
Jacksonville
Quincy
Pittsfield
Jerseyville
Pana
Mattoon
Effingham
Olney
Carmi
Harrisburg
Alton
Granite City
East St. Louis
Belleville
Vandalia
Salem
Centralia
Mount Vernon
West Frankfort
Marion
Carbondale
Cairo

Wabash River
Ohio River
Mississippi River
Illinois River
Rend Lake
Carlyle Lake
Kaskaskia River

The National Atlas of the United States of America®

U.S. Department of the Interior
U.S. Geological Survey

nationalatlas.gov™
Where We Are

POPULATED PLACES

● Chicago   1,000,000 and over
● Peoria   100,000 – 499,999
● Decatur   25,000 – 99,999
· Centralia   24,999 and less
★ Springfield State capital
   Urban areas

TRANSPORTATION

Interstate; limited access highway
Other principal highway
Railroad

PHYSICAL FEATURES

Streams
Lakes
Highest elevation in state (feet)   +1235

The lowest elevation in Illinois is 279 feet
above sea level (Mississippi River).

MILES
0   25   50   75   100

Albers equal area projection

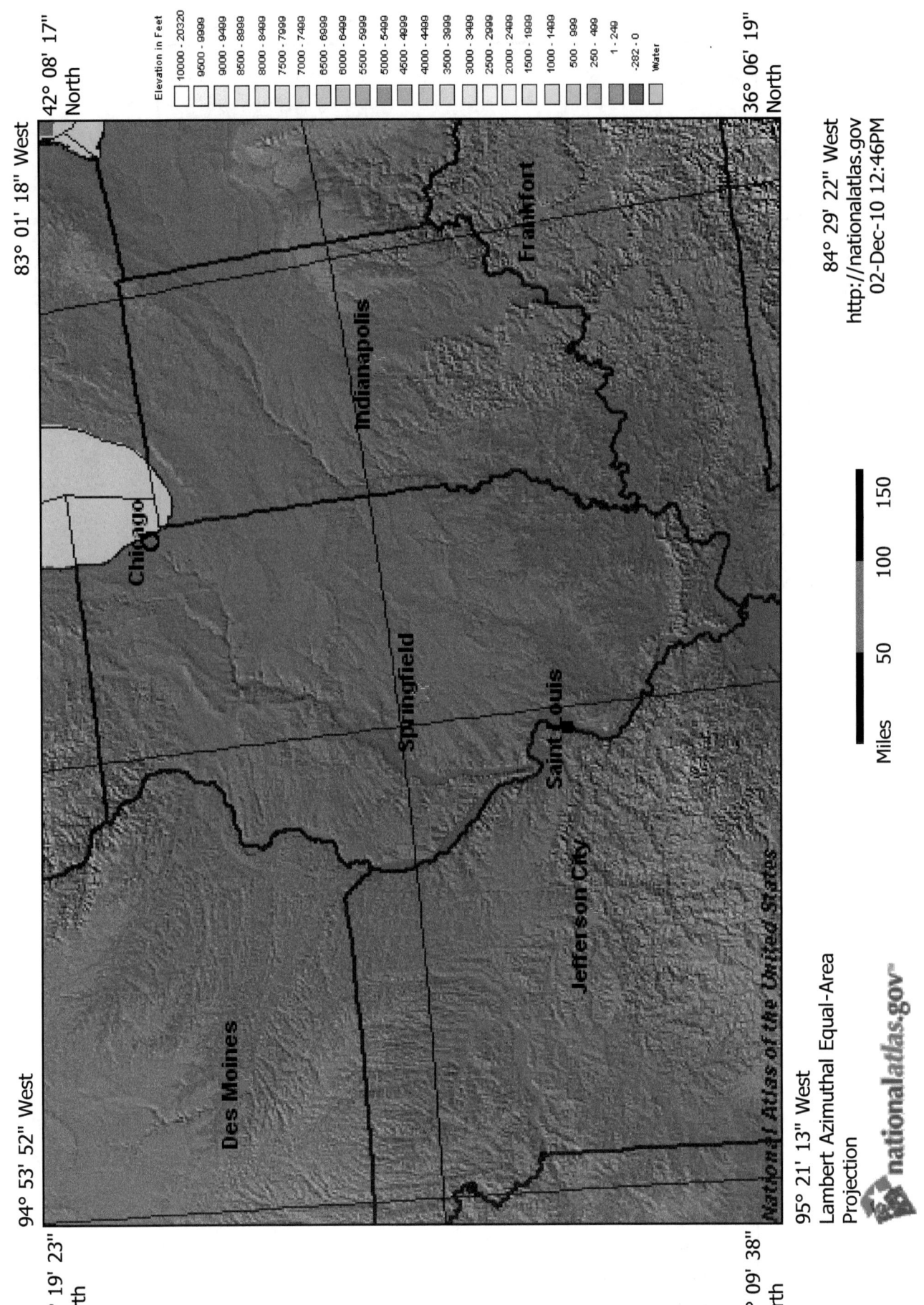

Elevation in Feet

10000 - 20320
9500 - 9999
9000 - 9499
8500 - 8999
8000 - 8499
7500 - 7999
7000 - 7499
6500 - 6999
6000 - 6499
5500 - 5999
5000 - 5499
4500 - 4999
4000 - 4499
3500 - 3999
3000 - 3499
2500 - 2999
2000 - 2499
1500 - 1999
1000 - 1499
500 - 999
250 - 499
1 - 249
-282 - 0
Water

42° 08' 17"
North

83° 01' 18" West

94° 53' 52" West

43° 19' 23"
North

Chicago

Des Moines

Springfield

Indianapolis

Frankfort

Saint Louis

Jefferson City

National Atlas of the United States

95° 21' 13" West
Lambert Azimuthal Equal-Area
Projection

nationalatlas.gov

84° 29' 22" West
http://nationalatlas.gov
02-Dec-10 12:46PM

36° 06' 19"
North

37° 09' 38"
North

Miles   50   100   150

Illinois
● CITIES
▲ Weather Stations

Illinois Weather Stations by County

County	Station Name
Adams	Golden
Champaign	Urbana
Coles	Charleston
Cook	Chicago Botanical Garden Chicago Midway Arpt Chicago Ohare Intl Arpt Park Forest
Dekalb	De Kalb
Douglas	Tuscola
Dupage	Wheaton 3 SE
Edwards	Albion
Effingham	Effingham
Hancock	La Harpe
Hardin	Rosiclare 5 NW
Jackson	Carbondale Sewage Plant
Jersey	Jerseyville 2 SW
Kane	Aurora Elgin
Kankakee	Kankakee Metro Wastwater
Knox	Galesburg
Lake	Antioch
Lee	Dixon 1 NW Paw Paw 2 NW
Logan	Lincoln
Macon	Decatur
Macoupin	Carlinville Virden
Madison	Alton Melvin Price L&D
Marshall	Lacon 1 N
Mason	Havana 4 NNE
Massac	Brookport Dam 52
Mchenry	Marengo
Mclean	Chenoa Normal
Mercer	Aledo
Peoria	Peoria Greater Peoria Arpt

County	Station Name
Peoria (cont.)	Princeville
Randolph	Kaskaskia River Nav Lock
Rock Island	Moline Quad City Arpt
Sangamon	Springfield Capital Arpt
St. Clair	Belleville Siu Research Cahokia
Union	Anna 2 NNE
Vermilion	Danville
Whiteside	Fulton L&D #13
Will	Joliet Brandon Rd Dam
Winnebago	Rockford Greater Rockford Arpt

See User Guide for station inclusion criteria.

Illinois Weather Stations by City

City	Station Name	Miles
Arlington Heights	Chicago Botanical Garden	10.5
	Chicago Ohare Intl Arpt	8.3
	Elgin	15.6
	Wheaton 3 SE	19.6
Aurora	Aurora	1.2
	Chicago Ohare Intl Arpt	24.9
	Elgin	21.3
	Joliet Brandon Rd Dam	20.5
	Wheaton 3 SE	12.5
Berwyn	Chicago Botanical Garden	19.9
	Chicago Ohare Intl Arpt	11.5
	Chicago Midway Arpt	7.8
	Park Forest	24.5
	Wheaton 3 SE	14.4
Bloomington	Chenoa	22.0
	Normal	2.9
Bolingbrook	Aurora	12.8
	Chicago Ohare Intl Arpt	21.3
	Chicago Midway Arpt	15.6
	Joliet Brandon Rd Dam	14.0
	Park Forest	24.9
	Wheaton 3 SE	8.0
Buffalo Grove	Antioch	23.4
	Chicago Botanical Garden	9.6
	Chicago Ohare Intl Arpt	12.7
	Elgin	17.6
	Wheaton 3 SE	24.5
Carol Stream	Aurora	14.1
	Chicago Botanical Garden	23.4
	Chicago Ohare Intl Arpt	12.1
	Chicago Midway Arpt	22.3
	Elgin	12.6
	Wheaton 3 SE	8.0
Champaign	Tuscola	21.5
	Urbana	1.6
Chicago	Chicago Botanical Garden	19.4
	Chicago Ohare Intl Arpt	14.6
	Chicago Midway Arpt	10.3
	Wheaton 3 SE	20.0
Cicero	Chicago Botanical Garden	19.8
	Chicago Ohare Intl Arpt	12.3
	Chicago Midway Arpt	8.0
	Park Forest	24.4
	Wheaton 3 SE	15.9
Crystal Lake	Antioch	21.3
	Elgin	11.1
	Marengo	13.5
DeKalb	De Kalb	1.2
	Marengo	23.2
	Paw Paw 2 NW	19.5
Decatur	Decatur	4.3

City	Station Name	Miles
Des Plaines	Chicago Botanical Garden	9.2
	Chicago Ohare Intl Arpt	3.6
	Chicago Midway Arpt	21.7
	Elgin	19.6
	Wheaton 3 SE	17.2
Downers Grove	Aurora	15.7
	Chicago Ohare Intl Arpt	14.5
	Chicago Midway Arpt	12.4
	Elgin	23.8
	Joliet Brandon Rd Dam	20.3
	Wheaton 3 SE	3.4
Elgin	Aurora	18.8
	Chicago Ohare Intl Arpt	19.4
	Elgin	2.0
	Marengo	21.7
	Wheaton 3 SE	19.1
Elmhurst	Aurora	21.1
	Chicago Botanical Garden	18.5
	Chicago Ohare Intl Arpt	6.4
	Chicago Midway Arpt	13.7
	Elgin	21.2
	Wheaton 3 SE	8.3
Evanston	Chicago Botanical Garden	7.8
	Chicago Ohare Intl Arpt	12.3
	Chicago Midway Arpt	22.0
	Wheaton 3 SE	24.9
Glenview	Chicago Botanical Garden	4.1
	Chicago Ohare Intl Arpt	8.3
	Chicago Midway Arpt	24.0
	Elgin	23.8
	Wheaton 3 SE	22.2
Hoffman Estates	Aurora	23.1
	Chicago Botanical Garden	17.5
	Chicago Ohare Intl Arpt	11.4
	Elgin	8.9
	Wheaton 3 SE	17.3
Joliet	Aurora	18.8
	Chicago Midway Arpt	22.1
	Joliet Brandon Rd Dam	2.8
	Park Forest	22.8
	Wheaton 3 SE	19.5
Lombard	Aurora	17.2
	Chicago Botanical Garden	21.5
	Chicago Ohare Intl Arpt	9.1
	Chicago Midway Arpt	15.3
	Elgin	19.2
	Wheaton 3 SE	4.7
Moline	Aledo	24.0
	Moline Quad City Arpt	2.0
	Clinton No 1, IA	24.4
	Le Claire L & D 14, IA	7.2
Mount Prospect	Chicago Botanical Garden	9.4
	Chicago Ohare Intl Arpt	5.5
	Chicago Midway Arpt	24.0

See User Guide for station inclusion criteria.

City	Station Name	Miles
Mt Prospect *(cont.)*	Elgin	17.6
	Wheaton 3 SE	18.1
Naperville	Aurora	8.4
	Chicago Ohare Intl Arpt	20.4
	Chicago Midway Arpt	19.2
	Elgin	23.0
	Joliet Brandon Rd Dam	17.3
	Wheaton 3 SE	6.6
Normal	Chenoa	20.7
	Normal	0.7
Oak Lawn	Chicago Ohare Intl Arpt	20.5
	Chicago Midway Arpt	2.1
	Joliet Brandon Rd Dam	23.3
	Park Forest	15.2
	Wheaton 3 SE	17.7
Oak Park	Chicago Botanical Garden	17.1
	Chicago Ohare Intl Arpt	9.4
	Chicago Midway Arpt	10.5
	Wheaton 3 SE	15.0
Orland Park	Chicago Midway Arpt	9.1
	Joliet Brandon Rd Dam	15.1
	Park Forest	11.5
	Wheaton 3 SE	18.1
Palatine	Chicago Botanical Garden	12.9
	Chicago Ohare Intl Arpt	11.5
	Elgin	13.3
	Wheaton 3 SE	21.3
Peoria	Lacon 1 N	23.9
	Peoria Greater Peoria Arpt	5.6
	Princeville	16.3
Rockford	Marengo	23.7
	Rockford Greater Rockford Arpt	5.6
	Beloit, WI	15.9
Schaumburg	Aurora	21.8
	Chicago Botanical Garden	17.0
	Chicago Ohare Intl Arpt	9.2
	Elgin	10.5
	Wheaton 3 SE	14.8
Skokie	Chicago Botanical Garden	7.1
	Chicago Ohare Intl Arpt	9.8
	Chicago Midway Arpt	21.1
	Wheaton 3 SE	22.6
Springfield	Springfield Capital Arpt	4.4
	Virden	20.8
Tinley Park	Chicago Midway Arpt	10.8
	Joliet Brandon Rd Dam	16.2
	Park Forest	8.3
	Wheaton 3 SE	21.3
Waukegan	Antioch	15.4
	Chicago Botanical Garden	16.7
	Kenosha, WI	13.8
	Racine, WI	23.2

City	Station Name	Miles
Wheaton	Aurora	12.5
	Chicago Ohare Intl Arpt	13.1
	Chicago Midway Arpt	18.6
	Elgin	17.2
	Joliet Brandon Rd Dam	24.6
	Wheaton 3 SE	3.4

Note: Miles is the distance between the geographic center of the city and the weather station.

Illinois Weather Stations by Elevation

Feet	Station Name
950	Paw Paw 2 NW
873	De Kalb
819	Marengo
785	Normal
771	Galesburg
763	Elgin
750	Antioch
743	Urbana
734	Princeville
725	Golden
720	Aledo
709	Chenoa
709	Park Forest
700	Dixon 1 NW
700	La Harpe
680	Charleston
680	Rockford Greater Rockford Arpt
680	Wheaton 3 SE
674	Virden
658	Chicago Ohare Intl Arpt
652	Tuscola
651	Peoria Greater Peoria Arpt
640	Aurora
640	Kankakee Metro Wastwater
629	Carlinville
629	Chicago Botanical Garden
629	Jerseyville 2 SW
620	Chicago Midway Arpt
620	Decatur
600	Anna 2 NNE
595	Effingham
591	Fulton L&D #13
591	Moline Quad City Arpt
585	Springfield Capital Arpt
583	Lincoln
558	Danville
542	Joliet Brandon Rd Dam
529	Albion
459	Havana 4 NNE
459	Lacon 1 N
450	Belleville Siu Research
430	Alton Melvin Price L&D
399	Cahokia
399	Rosiclare 5 NW
390	Carbondale Sewage Plant
379	Kaskaskia River Nav Lock
330	Brookport Dam 52

Chicago O'Hare Int'l Airport

Chicago is located along the southwest shore of Lake Michigan and occupies a plain which, for the most part, is only some tens of feet above the lake. Lake Michigan averages 579 feet above sea level. Natural water drainage over most of the city would be into Lake Michigan, and from areas west of the city is into the Mississippi River System. But actual drainage over most of the city is artificially channeled also into the Mississippi system.

Chicago is in a region of frequently changeable weather. The climate is predominantly continental, ranging from relatively warm in summer to relatively cold in winter. In late autumn and winter however, air masses that are initially very cold often reach the city only after being tempered by passage over one or more of the lakes. Similarly, in late spring and summer, air masses reaching the city from the north, northeast, or east are cooler because of movement over the Great Lakes. Very low winter temperatures most often occur in air that flows southward to the west of Lake Superior before reaching the Chicago area. In summer the higher temperatures are with south or southwest flow and are therefore not influenced by the lakes, the only modifying effect being a local lake breeze.

During the warm season, when the lake is cold relative to land, there is frequently a lake breeze that reduces daytime temperature near the shore. When the breeze off the lake is light this effect usually reaches inland only a mile or two, but with stronger on-shore winds the whole city is cooled. On the other hand, temperatures at night are warmer near the lake.

At the O'Hare International Airport temperatures of 96 degrees or higher occur in about half the summers, while about half the winters have a minimum as low as -15 degrees. The average occurrence of the first temperature as low as 32 degrees in the fall is mid-October and the average occurrence of the last temperature as low as 32 degrees in the spring is late April.

Precipitation falls mostly from air that has passed over the Gulf of Mexico. But in winter there is sometimes snowfall, light inland but locally heavy near the lakeshore, with Lake Michigan as the principal moisture source. The effect of Lake Michigan, both on winter temperatures and lake-produced snowfall, is enhanced by non-freezing of much of the lake during the winter, even though areas and harbors are often ice-choked.

Summer thunderstorms are often locally heavy and variable, parts of the city may receive substantial rainfall and other parts none. Longer periods of continuous precipitation are mostly in autumn, winter, and spring.

Chicago O'Hare Int'l Airport *Cook County*   Elevation: 658 ft.   Latitude: 41° 59' N   Longitude: 87° 55' W

	JAN	FEB	MAR	APR	MAY	JUN	JUL	AUG	SEP	OCT	NOV	DEC	YEAR
Mean Maximum Temp. (°F)	31.2	35.2	46.3	58.7	70.0	79.6	84.1	81.9	74.8	62.0	48.2	35.0	58.9
Mean Temp. (°F)	23.7	27.5	37.5	48.6	59.0	68.7	73.9	72.3	64.5	52.2	40.2	27.9	49.7
Mean Minimum Temp. (°F)	16.3	19.8	28.6	38.4	48.0	57.7	63.6	62.7	54.2	42.4	32.3	20.7	40.4
Extreme Maximum Temp. (°F)	65	72	88	91	92	104	104	101	99	88	75	71	104
Extreme Minimum Temp. (°F)	-27	-19	-7	7	27	37	45	42	29	17	6	-25	-27
Days Maximum Temp. ≥ 90°F	0	0	0	0	0	4	7	4	1	0	0	0	16
Days Maximum Temp. ≤ 32°F	16	11	4	0	0	0	0	0	0	0	2	12	45
Days Minimum Temp. ≤ 32°F	28	25	21	7	0	0	0	0	0	4	15	27	127
Days Minimum Temp. ≤ 0°F	4	2	0	0	0	0	0	0	0	0	0	2	8
Heating Degree Days (base 65°F)	1,272	1,054	848	495	224	48	4	8	102	399	737	1,144	6,335
Cooling Degree Days (base 65°F)	0	0	1	9	45	166	286	242	94	10	0	0	853
Mean Precipitation (in.)	1.72	1.77	2.51	3.39	3.62	3.37	3.52	5.12	3.30	3.19	3.10	2.29	36.90
Maximum Precipitation (in.)*	4.1	3.5	5.9	7.7	7.1	10.0	8.3	17.1	11.4	7.4	8.2	8.6	49.3
Minimum Precipitation (in.)*	0.1	0.1	0.6	1.0	0.3	0.9	1.2	0.5	trace	0.2	0.6	0.2	21.8
Extreme Maximum Daily Precip. (in.)	1.24	3.44	1.75	2.37	3.45	3.97	2.90	6.49	6.64	3.79	2.93	4.47	6.64
Days With ≥ 0.1" Precipitation	5	4	6	7	7	6	6	7	6	6	6	5	71
Days With ≥ 0.5" Precipitation	1	1	1	2	2	2	2	3	2	2	2	1	21
Days With ≥ 1.0" Precipitation	0	0	0	1	1	1	1	2	1	1	1	0	9
Mean Snowfall (in.)	11.4	8.6	5.9	1.4	trace	trace	trace	trace	trace	0.3	1.4	8.3	37.3
Maximum Snowfall (in.)*	34	26	25	11	2	0	0	0	0	7	10	35	75
Maximum 24-hr. Snowfall (in.)*	15	10	9	11	2	0	0	0	0	4	5	10	15
Maximum Snow Depth (in.)	18	15	12	6	trace	trace	trace	trace	trace	3	4	17	18
Days With ≥ 1.0" Snow Depth	17	11	4	1	0	0	0	0	0	0	1	9	43
Thunderstorm Days*	< 1	< 1	2	4	5	6	6	6	4	2	1	1	37
Foggy Days*	12	11	12	10	10	8	9	12	11	11	12	13	131
Predominant Sky Cover*	OVR	OVR	OVR	OVR	OVR	OVR	SCT	SCT	OVR	OVR	OVR	OVR	OVR
Mean Relative Humidity 6am (%)*	77	78	79	77	77	78	82	85	85	82	81	80	80
Mean Relative Humidity 3pm (%)*	66	63	59	53	51	52	54	55	55	53	62	68	58
Mean Dewpoint (°F)*	14	18	27	36	46	56	62	61	54	42	31	21	39
Prevailing Wind Direction*	W	W	W	NNE	NNE	SSW	SW	SSW	S	S	SSW	WNW	SSW
Prevailing Wind Speed (mph)*	12	10	12	13	12	10	9	9	9	10	13	12	10
Maximum Wind Gust (mph)*	58	54	84	69	58	63	76	64	58	58	62	62	84

Note: (*) Period of record is 1958-1995

Moline Quad City Airport

The locality is in the heart of the Corn Belt. Agricultural crops include many important staple products in addition to corn. Cattle, hogs, horses, and poultry produced in Iowa and Illinois rank high in the nation. Close to the Mississippi River there is large scale truck gardening and considerable dairying. Field production of grains and livestock attains greater development farther away from the large streams, where the countryside is rolling prairie. Damaging droughts are not common. This, together with the variety of agricultural products, has led to designating the section as the Bread Basket of America.

The climate is favorable for many industries as evidenced by the large number and variety of manufacturing and other enterprises which have located and developed in the community. Among these are some of the largest producers of agricultural machinery in the world.

This area has a temperate continental climate, with a wide temperature range throughout the year. There are some intensely hot, unusually humid, periods in summer and severely cold periods in winter. Maxima of 90 degrees or more have occurred in summer as frequently as 55 days and zero or lower readings have occurred during every winter.

Freezing temperatures have occurred as late in spring as late May and as early in autumn as late September. Precipitation is usually well distributed throughout the year with the greatest amounts falling during the 177-day average crop growing season. Substantial weather changes frequently occur at three or four day intervals, as a direct result of proximity to some of the most important storm tracks.

Moline Quad City Airport *Rock Island County*   Elevation: 591 ft.   Latitude: 41° 28' N   Longitude: 90° 31' W

	JAN	FEB	MAR	APR	MAY	JUN	JUL	AUG	SEP	OCT	NOV	DEC	YEAR
Mean Maximum Temp. (°F)	31.4	35.9	48.7	62.2	73.2	82.4	85.9	83.7	76.8	63.7	49.1	34.8	60.6
Mean Temp. (°F)	23.2	27.4	38.9	51.0	61.7	71.2	75.3	73.2	65.2	52.7	40.1	26.9	50.6
Mean Minimum Temp. (°F)	14.8	18.9	29.1	39.8	50.2	60.0	64.7	62.7	53.5	41.7	31.1	19.0	40.5
Extreme Maximum Temp. (°F)	69	71	88	93	95	104	103	103	98	95	80	71	104
Extreme Minimum Temp. (°F)	-29	-28	-9	7	25	39	48	40	30	16	4	-24	-29
Days Maximum Temp. ≥ 90°F	0	0	0	0	1	5	9	6	2	0	0	0	23
Days Maximum Temp. ≤ 32°F	16	11	3	0	0	0	0	0	0	0	2	11	43
Days Minimum Temp. ≤ 32°F	29	24	20	7	0	0	0	0	0	6	17	27	130
Days Minimum Temp. ≤ 0°F	5	3	0	0	0	0	0	0	0	0	0	3	11
Heating Degree Days (base 65°F)	1,291	1,056	803	427	159	19	1	7	94	387	741	1,175	6,160
Cooling Degree Days (base 65°F)	0	0	2	14	63	213	328	268	106	14	0	0	1,008
Mean Precipitation (in.)	1.46	1.62	2.82	3.53	4.29	4.37	4.22	4.63	3.04	2.95	2.54	2.21	37.68
Maximum Precipitation (in.)*	4.4	2.8	7.4	11.3	11.4	13.2	11.8	15.2	14.2	8.5	6.8	5.0	56.4
Minimum Precipitation (in.)*	0.3	0.2	0.3	0.7	0.3	1.0	0.4	0.3	trace	trace	0.5	0.3	20.2
Extreme Maximum Daily Precip. (in.)	1.51	1.30	2.16	2.18	2.92	3.71	3.56	3.55	4.26	4.14	2.04	3.11	4.26
Days With ≥ 0.1" Precipitation	4	4	6	7	7	7	6	7	5	5	5	5	68
Days With ≥ 0.5" Precipitation	1	1	2	3	3	3	3	3	2	2	2	1	26
Days With ≥ 1.0" Precipitation	0	0	1	1	1	1	1	2	1	1	0	0	9
Mean Snowfall (in.)	9.2	6.7	4.1	1.2	trace	trace	trace	0.0	trace	0.1	1.2	8.8	31.3
Maximum Snowfall (in.)*	27	21	20	13	trace	0	0	0	0	7	16	22	63
Maximum 24-hr. Snowfall (in.)*	16	9	10	8	trace	0	0	0	0	7	8	9	16
Maximum Snow Depth (in.)	na	na	na	na	na	na	na	na	na	na	na	na	na
Days With ≥ 1.0" Snow Depth	na	na	na	na	na	na	na	na	na	na	na	na	na
Thunderstorm Days*	< 1	< 1	2	5	7	8	8	7	5	2	1	< 1	45
Foggy Days*	12	11	13	10	11	9	12	15	14	13	12	13	145
Predominant Sky Cover*	OVR	OVR	OVR	OVR	OVR	OVR	CLR	CLR	CLR	CLR	OVR	OVR	OVR
Mean Relative Humidity 6am (%)*	76	78	79	78	79	81	85	89	87	82	80	79	81
Mean Relative Humidity 3pm (%)*	66	63	57	50	49	50	54	55	52	49	59	67	56
Mean Dewpoint (°F)*	13	18	27	37	48	59	64	63	54	42	30	19	40
Prevailing Wind Direction*	WNW	WNW	WNW	WNW	S	S	S	S	S	S	WNW	WNW	WNW
Prevailing Wind Speed (mph)*	14	14	14	15	12	10	9	9	10	12	14	14	13
Maximum Wind Gust (mph)*	59	54	69	81	66	79	66	81	59	61	60	69	81

Note: (*) Period of record is 1943-1995

Greater Peoria Airport

The airport station is situated on a rather level tableland surrounded by well-drained and gently rolling terrain. It is set back a mile from the rim of the Illinois River Valley and is almost 200 feet above the river bed. Exposures of all instruments are good. The climate of this area is typically continental as shown by its changeable weather and the wide range of temperature extremes.

June and September are usually the most pleasant months of the year. Then during October or the first of November, Indian Summer is often experienced with an extended period of warm, dry weather.

Precipitation is normally heaviest during the growing season and lowest during midwinter.

The earliest snowfalls have occurred in September and the latest in the spring have occurred as late as May. Heavy snowfalls have rarely exceeded 20 inches.

Based on the 1951-1980 period, the average first occurrence of 32 degrees Fahrenheit in the fall is October 20 and the average last occurrence in the spring is April 24.

Greater Peoria Airport *Peoria County*   Elevation: 651 ft.   Latitude: 40° 40' N   Longitude: 89° 41' W

	JAN	FEB	MAR	APR	MAY	JUN	JUL	AUG	SEP	OCT	NOV	DEC	YEAR
Mean Maximum Temp. (°F)	32.9	37.6	50.0	62.7	73.2	82.1	85.6	83.8	77.1	64.2	50.2	36.3	61.3
Mean Temp. (°F)	25.1	29.3	40.4	52.0	62.4	71.6	75.6	73.8	66.2	53.8	41.5	28.8	51.7
Mean Minimum Temp. (°F)	17.1	20.9	30.7	41.2	51.5	61.1	65.5	63.8	55.2	43.3	32.8	21.2	42.0
Extreme Maximum Temp. (°F)	70	71	86	92	94	105	104	103	97	93	80	71	105
Extreme Minimum Temp. (°F)	-22	-19	-4	14	28	39	50	41	29	21	5	-23	-23
Days Maximum Temp. ≥ 90°F	0	0	0	0	1	5	9	6	2	0	0	0	23
Days Maximum Temp. ≤ 32°F	15	9	3	0	0	0	0	0	0	0	2	10	39
Days Minimum Temp. ≤ 32°F	28	24	18	5	0	0	0	0	0	4	15	26	120
Days Minimum Temp. ≤ 0°F	4	2	0	0	0	0	0	0	0	0	0	2	8
Heating Degree Days (base 65°F)	1,232	1,004	758	399	142	17	1	5	80	356	698	1,116	5,808
Cooling Degree Days (base 65°F)	0	0	2	14	69	222	336	285	121	15	0	0	1,064
Mean Precipitation (in.)	1.74	1.76	2.78	3.61	4.13	3.61	3.74	3.36	3.12	2.87	3.09	2.36	36.17
Maximum Precipitation (in.)*	8.1	4.9	6.9	8.7	11.5	11.7	10.1	8.6	13.1	10.5	7.6	6.3	55.3
Minimum Precipitation (in.)*	0.1	0.1	0.4	0.7	0.5	0.4	0.3	0.3	trace	trace	0.1	0.3	22.2
Extreme Maximum Daily Precip. (in.)	2.35	1.81	1.92	3.05	2.99	4.42	3.36	2.63	3.05	2.68	4.26	2.34	4.42
Days With ≥ 0.1" Precipitation	4	4	6	7	8	6	6	6	5	6	6	5	69
Days With ≥ 0.5" Precipitation	1	1	2	2	2	2	2	3	2	2	2	1	22
Days With ≥ 1.0" Precipitation	0	0	1	1	1	1	1	1	1	0	1	1	9
Mean Snowfall (in.)	6.8	5.9	2.9	0.9	trace	trace	trace	0.0	trace	trace	1.3	6.5	24.3
Maximum Snowfall (in.)*	25	15	18	13	trace	0	0	0	1	3	11	22	52
Maximum 24-hr. Snowfall (in.)*	12	9	9	6	trace	0	0	0	1	3	8	7	12
Maximum Snow Depth (in.)	16	10	7	10	trace	trace	trace	0	trace	trace	4	13	16
Days With ≥ 1.0" Snow Depth	14	9	3	0	0	0	0	0	0	0	1	9	36
Thunderstorm Days*	< 1	1	3	5	7	9	8	7	5	2	1	1	49
Foggy Days*	11	10	9	7	7	6	7	9	9	10	10	12	107
Predominant Sky Cover*	OVR	OVR	OVR	OVR	OVR	OVR	SCT	CLR	CLR	OVR	OVR	OVR	OVR
Mean Relative Humidity 6am (%)*	80	81	81	78	80	82	86	89	87	84	83	83	83
Mean Relative Humidity 3pm (%)*	67	64	58	52	52	52	55	56	52	52	61	69	57
Mean Dewpoint (°F)*	16	20	29	38	49	59	64	63	54	43	32	22	41
Prevailing Wind Direction*	S	S	S	S	S	S	S	S	S	S	S	S	S
Prevailing Wind Speed (mph)*	12	12	13	12	10	10	9	8	9	10	12	12	10
Maximum Wind Gust (mph)*	54	53	68	69	61	75	85	54	75	48	62	59	85

Note: (*) Period of record is 1948-1995

Rockford Greater Rockford Arpt.

The climate of Rockford is characterized by hot summers and cold winters.

When winter northeasterly winds blow across Lake Michigan, cloudiness often is increased in the Rockford area, and temperatures are somewhat higher than those westward around the Mississippi River. Conversely, in summer, the cooling effect of Lake Michigan sometimes is felt as far westward as Rockford.

While 34 percent of the precipitation occurs in the three summer months of June to August, and 64 percent in the six months, April to September, no month averages less than four percent of the annual total.

Though summers may be described as hot, seldom does oppressive heat prevail for extended periods. In general, the summers are pleasant.

Winters are cold. Snow cover is adequate for diversified winter sports, and usually is continuous from late December through February.

Based on the 1951-1980 period, the average first occurrence of 32 degrees Fahrenheit in the fall is October 11 and the average last occurrence in the spring is April 29.

Rockford Greater Rockford Arpt. *Winnebago County*   Elevation: 680 ft.   Latitude: 42° 12' N   Longitude: 89° 07' W

	JAN	FEB	MAR	APR	MAY	JUN	JUL	AUG	SEP	OCT	NOV	DEC	YEAR
Mean Maximum Temp. (°F)	28.9	33.5	45.8	59.8	71.2	80.4	83.9	81.7	74.7	61.7	46.9	32.7	58.4
Mean Temp. (°F)	21.0	25.3	36.3	48.7	59.6	69.3	73.3	71.4	63.4	50.9	38.3	25.1	48.6
Mean Minimum Temp. (°F)	13.0	17.0	26.8	37.5	48.0	58.0	62.7	61.0	52.0	40.1	29.8	17.6	38.6
Extreme Maximum Temp. (°F)	63	70	85	91	93	101	102	104	95	90	76	67	104
Extreme Minimum Temp. (°F)	-27	-24	-11	5	26	37	47	41	27	18	1	-24	-27
Days Maximum Temp. ≥ 90°F	0	0	0	0	0	4	6	4	1	0	0	0	15
Days Maximum Temp. ≤ 32°F	19	13	4	0	0	0	0	0	0	0	3	14	53
Days Minimum Temp. ≤ 32°F	30	26	23	8	1	0	0	0	0	7	19	28	142
Days Minimum Temp. ≤ 0°F	6	4	0	0	0	0	0	0	0	0	0	4	14
Heating Degree Days (base 65°F)	1,358	1,117	882	491	206	34	3	12	120	437	793	1,229	6,682
Cooling Degree Days (base 65°F)	0	0	0	8	45	169	268	217	79	8	0	0	795
Mean Precipitation (in.)	1.37	1.43	2.30	3.34	3.90	4.65	3.75	4.70	3.49	2.61	2.55	2.01	36.10
Maximum Precipitation (in.)*	4.7	3.0	5.6	9.9	7.0	11.8	11.8	13.5	10.7	8.3	5.5	5.0	56.5
Minimum Precipitation (in.)*	0.2	trace	0.6	1.0	0.5	0.5	0.8	0.7	0	trace	0.4	0.4	23.3
Extreme Maximum Daily Precip. (in.)	1.34	1.39	2.15	1.71	4.77	4.20	3.87	5.70	3.26	2.18	2.06	2.00	5.70
Days With ≥ 0.1" Precipitation	4	4	5	6	7	7	6	7	5	5	5	5	66
Days With ≥ 0.5" Precipitation	1	1	1	2	2	3	3	3	2	2	2	1	23
Days With ≥ 1.0" Precipitation	0	0	0	1	1	1	1	1	1	0	0	0	6
Mean Snowfall (in.)	10.3	7.6	5.0	1.0	trace	trace	trace	trace	trace	0.1	1.7	10.8	36.5
Maximum Snowfall (in.)*	26	30	23	8	1	0	0	0	0	2	15	25	59
Maximum 24-hr. Snowfall (in.)*	10	8	10	6	1	0	0	0	0	2	7	11	11
Maximum Snow Depth (in.)	19	14	*9*	5	*trace*	*trace*	*trace*	trace	trace	*trace*	*7*	*18*	*19*
Days With ≥ 1.0" Snow Depth	21	15	*5*	1	*0*	*0*	*0*	0	0	*0*	*1*	15	58
Thunderstorm Days*	< 1	< 1	2	4	5	8	8	6	5	2	1	< 1	41
Foggy Days*	12	11	12	11	11	8	12	16	14	12	13	14	146
Predominant Sky Cover*	OVR	OVR	OVR	OVR	OVR	OVR	OVR	OVR	OVR	OVR	OVR	OVR	OVR
Mean Relative Humidity 6am (%)*	80	81	82	80	80	81	86	90	90	86	83	83	84
Mean Relative Humidity 3pm (%)*	69	64	60	51	50	51	53	56	54	53	63	70	58
Mean Dewpoint (°F)*	13	17	26	36	47	57	62	62	53	41	30	19	39
Prevailing Wind Direction*	WNW	WNW	WNW	ENE	S	S	S	S	S	S	S	WNW	S
Prevailing Wind Speed (mph)*	13	13	13	13	10	9	8	8	8	9	10	13	10
Maximum Wind Gust (mph)*	56	54	54	64	81	67	79	67	58	59	59	62	81

Note: (*) Period of record is 1951-1995

Springfield Capital Airport

The location of Springfield near the center of North America gives it a typical continental climate with warm summers and fairly cold winters. The surrounding country is nearly level. There are no large hills in the vicinity, but rolling terrain is found near the Sangamon River and Spring Creek.

Monthly temperatures range from the upper 20s for January to the upper 70s for July. Considerable variation may take place within the seasons. Temperatures of 70 degrees or higher may occur in winter and temperatures near 50 degrees are sometimes recorded during the summer months.

There are no wet and dry seasons. Monthly precipitation ranges from a little over four inches in May and June to about two inches in January. There is some variation in rainfall totals from year to year. Thunderstorms are common during hot weather, and these are sometimes locally severe with brief but heavy showers. The average year has about fifty thunderstorms of which two-thirds occur during the months of May through August. Damaging hail accompanies only a few of the thunderstorms and the areas affected are usually small.

Sunshine is particularly abundant during the summer months when days are long and not very cloudy. January is the cloudiest month, with only about a third as much sunshine as July or August. March is the windiest month, and August the month with the least wind. Velocities of more than 40 mph are not unusual for brief periods in most months of the year. The prevailing wind direction is southerly during most of the year with northwesterly winds during the late fall and early spring months.

An overall description of the climate of Springfield would be one indicating pleasant conditions with sharp seasonal changes, but no extended periods of severely cold weather. Summer weather is often uncomfortably warm and humid.

Based on the 1951-1980 period, the average first occurrence of 32 degrees Fahrenheit in the fall is October 19 and the average last occurrence in the spring is April 17.

Springfield Capital Airport *Sangamon County*   Elevation: 585 ft.   Latitude: 39° 51' N   Longitude: 89° 41' W

	JAN	FEB	MAR	APR	MAY	JUN	JUL	AUG	SEP	OCT	NOV	DEC	YEAR
Mean Maximum Temp. (°F)	35.1	39.7	51.7	64.2	74.8	83.1	86.3	85.0	78.9	66.2	52.1	38.5	63.0
Mean Temp. (°F)	27.1	31.3	42.0	53.4	63.8	72.6	76.1	74.5	66.9	55.2	43.2	30.7	53.1
Mean Minimum Temp. (°F)	19.2	22.8	32.3	42.5	52.9	62.0	65.8	63.9	54.9	44.1	34.2	22.9	43.1
Extreme Maximum Temp. (°F)	69	74	87	90	94	101	102	102	101	93	81	74	102
Extreme Minimum Temp. (°F)	-21	-19	-2	19	30	39	49	43	32	19	1	-21	-21
Days Maximum Temp. ≥ 90°F	0	0	0	0	1	6	10	7	3	0	0	0	27
Days Maximum Temp. ≤ 32°F	13	8	2	0	0	0	0	0	0	0	1	9	33
Days Minimum Temp. ≤ 32°F	27	22	16	4	0	0	0	0	0	4	14	25	112
Days Minimum Temp. ≤ 0°F	3	2	0	0	0	0	0	0	0	0	0	2	7
Heating Degree Days (base 65°F)	1,167	947	708	362	118	14	0	4	72	322	648	1,055	5,417
Cooling Degree Days (base 65°F)	0	0	3	20	89	248	351	304	137	24	1	0	1,177
Mean Precipitation (in.)	1.80	1.78	2.69	3.46	4.02	4.30	3.82	3.22	2.80	3.16	3.16	2.53	36.74
Maximum Precipitation (in.)*	6.2	4.9	7.9	9.9	10.6	10.8	10.8	8.4	15.2	13.4	6.9	8.9	54.5
Minimum Precipitation (in.)*	trace	0.3	0.2	0.7	0.3	0.2	0.3	0.1	trace	0.1	trace	0.1	22.8
Extreme Maximum Daily Precip. (in.)	1.68	2.37	2.18	2.95	3.54	4.71	4.33	4.40	4.23	3.24	2.05	4.70	4.71
Days With ≥ 0.1" Precipitation	4	4	6	7	7	6	6	5	5	6	6	5	67
Days With ≥ 0.5" Precipitation	1	1	2	2	2	3	3	2	2	2	2	1	23
Days With ≥ 1.0" Precipitation	0	0	1	1	1	1	1	1	1	1	1	1	10
Mean Snowfall (in.)	6.3	5.6	2.7	0.5	trace	0.0	trace	0.0	0.0	trace	0.8	5.4	21.3
Maximum Snowfall (in.)*	21	18	23	8	1	0	0	0	0	3	9	23	48
Maximum 24-hr. Snowfall (in.)*	8	10	9	6	1	0	0	0	0	3	8	11	11
Maximum Snow Depth (in.)	12	11	6	4	trace	0	trace	0	0	trace	4	9	12
Days With ≥ 1.0" Snow Depth	10	8	2	0	0	0	0	0	0	0	0	7	27
Thunderstorm Days*	< 1	1	3	5	7	9	8	7	5	2	2	< 1	49
Foggy Days*	9	8	8	6	6	6	5	9	8	8	8	10	91
Predominant Sky Cover*	OVR	OVR	OVR	OVR	OVR	OVR	SCT	CLR	CLR	CLR	OVR	OVR	OVR
Mean Relative Humidity 6am (%)*	80	81	81	79	81	82	85	89	87	83	82	82	83
Mean Relative Humidity 3pm (%)*	67	65	59	52	51	51	54	56	50	50	60	69	57
Mean Dewpoint (°F)*	18	22	31	41	51	61	65	64	56	44	33	24	43
Prevailing Wind Direction*	S	S	S	S	S	S	S	S	S	S	S	S	S
Prevailing Wind Speed (mph)*	15	14	15	15	13	12	9	9	10	13	14	15	13
Maximum Wind Gust (mph)*	55	53	71	63	67	59	60	69	61	53	76	73	76

Note: (*) Period of record is 1948-1995

Albion *Edwards County* Elevation: 529 ft. Latitude: 38° 23' N Longitude: 88° 03' W

	JAN	FEB	MAR	APR	MAY	JUN	JUL	AUG	SEP	OCT	NOV	DEC	YEAR
Mean Maximum Temp. (°F)	39.4	45.0	54.8	67.3	76.9	85.5	89.9	88.5	82.0	70.6	55.3	42.6	66.5
Mean Temp. (°F)	31.5	36.3	45.1	56.5	66.4	75.1	79.2	77.6	70.4	59.1	46.2	34.5	56.5
Mean Minimum Temp. (°F)	23.9	27.3	35.3	45.7	55.8	64.6	68.4	66.5	58.8	47.5	37.2	26.4	46.5
Extreme Maximum Temp. (°F)	73	75	85	89	97	101	105	104	100	93	81	75	105
Extreme Minimum Temp. (°F)	-20	-11	2	23	32	42	50	47	31	24	11	-18	-20
Days Maximum Temp. ≥ 90°F	0	0	0	0	2	10	16	13	6	0	0	0	47
Days Maximum Temp. ≤ 32°F	7	5	1	0	0	0	0	0	0	0	0	6	19
Days Minimum Temp. ≤ 32°F	23	18	12	2	0	0	0	0	0	1	10	21	87
Days Minimum Temp. ≤ 0°F	1	0	0	0	0	0	0	0	0	0	0	1	2
Heating Degree Days (base 65°F)	1,032	806	612	280	76	6	0	1	36	218	559	937	4,563
Cooling Degree Days (base 65°F)	0	0	4	32	127	315	447	397	206	42	2	0	1,572
Mean Precipitation (in.)	2.62	2.47	4.03	4.86	5.43	3.66	3.55	3.17	2.76	3.66	4.07	3.04	43.32
Extreme Maximum Daily Precip. (in.)	2.90	na	3.80	4.50	na	na	4.20	6.80	4.50	3.20	4.20	4.90	na
Days With ≥ 0.1" Precipitation	4	4	5	7	7	6	4	4	4	5	5	5	60
Days With ≥ 0.5" Precipitation	2	2	3	3	4	2	2	2	2	3	3	2	30
Days With ≥ 1.0" Precipitation	1	1	1	1	1	1	1	1	1	1	1	1	12
Mean Snowfall (in.)	2.0	2.4	1.0	0.0	0.0	0.0	0.0	0.0	0.0	0.1	trace	2.6	8.1
Maximum Snow Depth (in.)	6	10	9	0	0	0	0	0	0	1	trace	7	10
Days With ≥ 1.0" Snow Depth	2	2	0	0	0	0	0	0	0	0	0	0	4

Aledo *Mercer County* Elevation: 720 ft. Latitude: 41° 12' N Longitude: 90° 45' W

	JAN	FEB	MAR	APR	MAY	JUN	JUL	AUG	SEP	OCT	NOV	DEC	YEAR
Mean Maximum Temp. (°F)	31.1	35.6	48.3	62.0	72.5	81.1	84.7	83.0	76.0	63.4	48.7	34.4	60.0
Mean Temp. (°F)	22.8	26.9	38.2	50.5	61.1	70.3	73.9	72.6	64.5	52.5	39.6	26.5	49.9
Mean Minimum Temp. (°F)	14.5	18.2	28.1	39.0	49.8	59.5	63.3	62.1	53.0	41.6	30.5	18.5	39.8
Extreme Maximum Temp. (°F)	69	68	87	91	93	103	103	102	97	91	78	70	103
Extreme Minimum Temp. (°F)	-25	-28	-8	10	23	42	49	45	30	18	0	-20	-28
Days Maximum Temp. ≥ 90°F	0	0	0	0	0	3	7	5	1	0	0	0	16
Days Maximum Temp. ≤ 32°F	16	11	4	0	0	0	0	0	0	0	2	12	45
Days Minimum Temp. ≤ 32°F	29	25	21	7	0	0	0	0	0	5	18	28	133
Days Minimum Temp. ≤ 0°F	5	3	0	0	0	0	0	0	0	0	0	3	11
Heating Degree Days (base 65°F)	1,300	1,072	825	440	167	23	2	7	102	390	755	1,189	6,272
Cooling Degree Days (base 65°F)	0	0	1	11	54	190	285	249	94	10	0	0	894
Mean Precipitation (in.)	1.35	1.53	2.44	3.70	4.34	4.47	3.95	4.53	3.28	2.98	2.34	2.01	36.92
Extreme Maximum Daily Precip. (in.)	2.10	1.75	1.78	1.72	4.80	3.12	3.10	6.27	4.15	3.40	1.60	2.70	6.27
Days With ≥ 0.1" Precipitation	4	4	5	7	8	7	6	7	5	6	5	5	69
Days With ≥ 0.5" Precipitation	1	1	2	3	3	3	3	3	2	2	1	1	25
Days With ≥ 1.0" Precipitation	0	0	1	1	1	1	1	1	1	1	0	0	8
Mean Snowfall (in.)	6.8	4.5	2.7	0.8	trace	0.0	0.0	0.0	0.0	0.1	0.6	5.2	20.7
Maximum Snow Depth (in.)	15	na	4	4	trace	0	0	0	0	trace	2	10	na
Days With ≥ 1.0" Snow Depth	5	3	1	0	0	0	0	0	0	0	0	3	12

Alton Melvin Price L&D *Madison County* Elevation: 430 ft. Latitude: 38° 49' N Longitude: 90° 09' W

	JAN	FEB	MAR	APR	MAY	JUN	JUL	AUG	SEP	OCT	NOV	DEC	YEAR
Mean Maximum Temp. (°F)	37.6	42.4	52.7	64.7	74.5	83.5	87.6	86.5	79.5	67.3	54.4	41.6	64.4
Mean Temp. (°F)	29.7	33.8	43.7	55.1	65.2	74.4	78.5	77.1	69.6	57.3	45.7	34.0	55.3
Mean Minimum Temp. (°F)	21.9	25.1	34.6	45.5	55.7	65.1	69.3	67.6	59.5	47.3	37.0	26.4	46.3
Extreme Maximum Temp. (°F)	71	76	85	90	93	98	106	103	98	97	81	73	106
Extreme Minimum Temp. (°F)	-16	-15	3	20	37	44	52	46	38	25	9	-16	-16
Days Maximum Temp. ≥ 90°F	0	0	0	0	0	6	12	10	3	0	0	0	31
Days Maximum Temp. ≤ 32°F	10	6	1	0	0	0	0	0	0	0	1	6	24
Days Minimum Temp. ≤ 32°F	26	21	13	2	0	0	0	0	0	1	9	21	93
Days Minimum Temp. ≤ 0°F	1	1	0	0	0	0	0	0	0	0	0	1	3
Heating Degree Days (base 65°F)	1,086	877	658	313	87	8	0	2	40	263	572	951	4,857
Cooling Degree Days (base 65°F)	0	0	4	22	99	296	425	382	183	25	1	0	1,437
Mean Precipitation (in.)	2.44	2.25	3.22	4.23	5.09	3.62	3.76	3.27	3.13	3.17	3.78	2.91	40.87
Extreme Maximum Daily Precip. (in.)	2.65	2.10	2.75	7.70	4.70	4.23	3.27	2.97	2.63	3.50	3.00	2.71	7.70
Days With ≥ 0.1" Precipitation	5	5	7	7	8	6	5	6	5	6	6	6	72
Days With ≥ 0.5" Precipitation	2	1	2	3	4	2	2	2	2	2	3	2	27
Days With ≥ 1.0" Precipitation	1	0	1	1	2	1	1	1	1	1	1	1	12
Mean Snowfall (in.)	1.4	1.8	0.8	0.2	0.0	0.0	0.0	0.0	0.0	trace	0.1	0.5	4.8
Maximum Snow Depth (in.)	10	21	6	5	0	0	0	0	0	0	7	5	21
Days With ≥ 1.0" Snow Depth	2	2	1	0	0	0	0	0	0	0	0	1	6

Anna 2 NNE *Union County* Elevation: 600 ft. Latitude: 37° 28' N Longitude: 89° 14' W

	JAN	FEB	MAR	APR	MAY	JUN	JUL	AUG	SEP	OCT	NOV	DEC	YEAR
Mean Maximum Temp. (°F)	43.1	48.4	58.5	69.1	77.2	85.3	88.7	88.6	81.4	70.4	57.8	45.6	67.8
Mean Temp. (°F)	34.0	38.3	47.2	57.2	65.9	74.2	78.1	77.2	69.4	58.3	47.5	36.7	57.0
Mean Minimum Temp. (°F)	24.8	28.1	35.9	45.3	54.5	63.1	67.3	65.7	57.4	46.2	37.1	27.7	46.1
Extreme Maximum Temp. (°F)	69	77	84	90	92	100	104	103	101	90	83	76	104
Extreme Minimum Temp. (°F)	-17	-10	5	20	31	44	49	46	32	20	10	-14	-17
Days Maximum Temp. ≥ 90°F	0	0	0	0	0	8	15	14	4	0	0	0	41
Days Maximum Temp. ≤ 32°F	5	3	0	0	0	0	0	0	0	0	0	4	12
Days Minimum Temp. ≤ 32°F	24	19	13	3	0	0	0	0	0	2	11	21	93
Days Minimum Temp. ≤ 0°F	1	0	0	0	0	0	0	0	0	0	0	1	2
Heating Degree Days (base 65°F)	954	750	548	256	73	4	0	1	38	231	520	872	4,247
Cooling Degree Days (base 65°F)	0	0	3	30	108	287	412	386	178	32	2	0	1,438
Mean Precipitation (in.)	3.66	3.48	4.58	4.50	5.87	4.37	3.36	3.23	3.32	4.29	4.76	4.48	49.90
Extreme Maximum Daily Precip. (in.)	6.70	2.34	7.74	3.22	4.76	4.86	3.26	3.71	4.45	3.42	6.24	4.43	7.74
Days With ≥ 0.1" Precipitation	6	6	7	8	8	6	6	5	5	7	7	7	78
Days With ≥ 0.5" Precipitation	2	3	3	3	4	3	2	2	2	3	3	3	33
Days With ≥ 1.0" Precipitation	1	1	1	1	2	1	1	1	1	1	1	1	13
Mean Snowfall (in.)	3.3	3.9	1.0	0.1	0.0	0.0	0.0	0.0	0.0	0.1	0.3	2.6	11.3
Maximum Snow Depth (in.)	7	10	6	trace	0	0	0	0	0	trace	4	14	14
Days With ≥ 1.0" Snow Depth	4	4	1	0	0	0	0	0	0	0	0	3	12

The period of record for all cooperative weather station data is 1980 – 2009. See User Guide for detailed explanation of data.

Antioch *Lake County* Elevation: 750 ft.   Latitude: 42° 29' N   Longitude: 88° 07' W

	JAN	FEB	MAR	APR	MAY	JUN	JUL	AUG	SEP	OCT	NOV	DEC	YEAR
Mean Maximum Temp. (°F)	29.6	33.1	43.6	57.0	68.0	77.7	82.1	80.9	73.6	61.0	46.7	33.6	57.2
Mean Temp. (°F)	21.5	24.7	34.8	47.0	57.2	67.1	71.9	70.9	63.1	50.9	38.5	26.3	47.8
Mean Minimum Temp. (°F)	13.5	16.3	25.9	36.8	46.4	56.5	61.8	60.9	52.7	40.7	30.3	18.8	38.4
Extreme Maximum Temp. (°F)	63	70	78	90	91	96	102	104	95	89	74	68	104
Extreme Minimum Temp. (°F)	-28	-17	-10	6	27	36	42	40	29	18	4	-24	-28
Days Maximum Temp. ≥ 90°F	0	0	0	0	0	2	4	3	1	0	0	0	10
Days Maximum Temp. ≤ 32°F	18	13	5	0	0	0	0	0	0	0	3	13	52
Days Minimum Temp. ≤ 32°F	29	26	23	9	1	0	0	0	0	6	17	28	139
Days Minimum Temp. ≤ 0°F	6	5	1	0	0	0	0	0	0	0	0	3	15
Heating Degree Days (base 65°F)	1,342	1,132	931	542	267	61	10	15	125	438	787	1,193	6,843
Cooling Degree Days (base 65°F)	0	0	1	7	33	132	232	206	77	7	0	0	695
Mean Precipitation (in.)	1.58	1.54	1.85	3.20	4.08	4.05	3.80	4.26	3.58	2.87	2.87	2.09	35.77
Extreme Maximum Daily Precip. (in.)	1.59	1.62	1.87	1.85	2.60	4.64	8.10	3.31	3.81	2.30	1.64	na	na
Days With ≥ 0.1" Precipitation	4	4	4	6	7	7	6	6	6	6	5	5	66
Days With ≥ 0.5" Precipitation	1	1	1	2	3	2	3	3	2	2	2	1	23
Days With ≥ 1.0" Precipitation	0	0	0	1	1	1	1	1	1	1	1	0	8
Mean Snowfall (in.)	11.1	9.1	5.6	1.5	trace	0.0	0.0	0.0	0.0	0.1	1.7	10.1	39.2
Maximum Snow Depth (in.)	21	22	16	8	trace	0	0	0	0	0	1	17	22
Days With ≥ 1.0" Snow Depth	18	15	6	1	0	0	0	0	0	0	1	10	51

Aurora *Kane County* Elevation: 640 ft.   Latitude: 41° 46' N   Longitude: 88° 19' W

	JAN	FEB	MAR	APR	MAY	JUN	JUL	AUG	SEP	OCT	NOV	DEC	YEAR
Mean Maximum Temp. (°F)	31.4	36.0	47.7	60.6	71.9	81.2	84.7	82.7	75.9	62.8	48.5	34.7	59.8
Mean Temp. (°F)	22.8	27.0	37.8	49.5	60.1	69.7	73.8	72.1	64.4	51.8	39.8	26.6	49.6
Mean Minimum Temp. (°F)	14.2	17.9	27.7	38.4	48.2	58.1	62.8	61.5	52.9	40.8	30.8	18.5	39.3
Extreme Maximum Temp. (°F)	66	72	83	91	94	103	102	101	95	89	77	69	103
Extreme Minimum Temp. (°F)	-26	-20	-8	8	26	39	42	43	28	15	5	-22	-26
Days Maximum Temp. ≥ 90°F	0	0	0	0	1	5	7	4	2	0	0	0	19
Days Maximum Temp. ≤ 32°F	16	10	3	0	0	0	0	0	0	0	2	11	42
Days Minimum Temp. ≤ 32°F	29	26	22	7	1	0	0	0	0	6	17	28	136
Days Minimum Temp. ≤ 0°F	5	3	0	0	0	0	0	0	0	0	0	3	11
Heating Degree Days (base 65°F)	1,303	1,066	838	466	196	34	3	8	105	414	751	1,186	6,370
Cooling Degree Days (base 65°F)	0	0	1	8	49	181	282	235	94	10	0	0	860
Mean Precipitation (in.)	1.64	1.74	2.34	3.67	3.88	4.02	4.20	4.26	3.57	3.04	3.27	2.27	37.90
Extreme Maximum Daily Precip. (in.)	1.82	3.26	2.47	2.09	3.59	4.38	16.91	3.01	4.00	2.81	2.74	2.83	16.91
Days With ≥ 0.1" Precipitation	4	4	5	7	7	7	6	7	5	6	6	5	69
Days With ≥ 0.5" Precipitation	1	1	1	3	3	2	2	3	2	2	2	1	23
Days With ≥ 1.0" Precipitation	0	0	0	1	1	1	1	1	1	1	1	0	8
Mean Snowfall (in.)	9.6	6.8	2.8	0.6	0.0	0.0	0.0	0.0	0.0	trace	0.9	7.6	28.3
Maximum Snow Depth (in.)	25	18	14	6	0	0	0	0	0	1	4	20	25
Days With ≥ 1.0" Snow Depth	18	13	3	0	0	0	0	0	0	0	1	10	45

Belleville Siu Research *St. Clair County* Elevation: 450 ft.   Latitude: 38° 31' N   Longitude: 89° 51' W

	JAN	FEB	MAR	APR	MAY	JUN	JUL	AUG	SEP	OCT	NOV	DEC	YEAR
Mean Maximum Temp. (°F)	41.9	47.1	57.8	68.9	77.6	86.0	89.5	88.5	81.9	71.0	57.4	44.3	67.7
Mean Temp. (°F)	32.9	37.3	46.8	57.1	66.2	74.6	78.3	76.6	69.1	58.3	47.3	35.7	56.7
Mean Minimum Temp. (°F)	23.9	27.4	35.6	45.2	54.8	63.2	67.1	64.7	56.3	45.6	37.1	27.0	45.7
Extreme Maximum Temp. (°F)	73	81	89	91	94	101	105	105	101	94	83	75	105
Extreme Minimum Temp. (°F)	-16	-21	2	18	32	41	49	39	26	20	2	-19	-21
Days Maximum Temp. ≥ 90°F	0	0	0	0	1	10	16	14	5	1	0	0	47
Days Maximum Temp. ≤ 32°F	7	4	1	0	0	0	0	0	0	0	0	5	17
Days Minimum Temp. ≤ 32°F	24	19	13	4	0	0	0	0	0	4	11	22	97
Days Minimum Temp. ≤ 0°F	1	1	0	0	0	0	0	0	0	0	0	1	3
Heating Degree Days (base 65°F)	988	779	565	266	76	5	0	2	45	239	529	903	4,397
Cooling Degree Days (base 65°F)	0	1	7	34	120	300	419	369	175	37	3	0	1,465
Mean Precipitation (in.)	2.25	2.20	3.23	3.85	4.79	4.18	3.81	3.19	3.27	3.50	3.83	2.82	40.92
Extreme Maximum Daily Precip. (in.)	2.17	4.48	2.68	4.58	4.57	3.22	3.48	3.00	3.75	3.45	3.23	3.97	4.58
Days With ≥ 0.1" Precipitation	4	4	6	7	8	7	5	5	5	6	6	5	68
Days With ≥ 0.5" Precipitation	1	1	2	3	3	3	3	2	2	3	3	2	28
Days With ≥ 1.0" Precipitation	1	1	1	1	1	1	1	1	1	1	1	1	12
Mean Snowfall (in.)	4.5	3.2	1.6	0.4	0.0	0.0	0.0	0.0	0.0	0.0	0.4	3.0	13.1
Maximum Snow Depth (in.)	15	19	8	30	0	0	0	0	0	0	3	8	30
Days With ≥ 1.0" Snow Depth	5	3	1	0	0	0	0	0	0	0	0	4	13

Brookport Dam 52 *Massac County* Elevation: 330 ft.   Latitude: 37° 08' N   Longitude: 88° 39' W

	JAN	FEB	MAR	APR	MAY	JUN	JUL	AUG	SEP	OCT	NOV	DEC	YEAR
Mean Maximum Temp. (°F)	43.6	48.2	58.1	68.9	77.4	85.5	89.3	88.8	81.7	70.3	58.1	46.1	68.0
Mean Temp. (°F)	35.0	39.0	47.7	57.9	66.8	74.9	79.0	77.8	70.4	58.9	48.3	37.6	57.8
Mean Minimum Temp. (°F)	26.3	29.7	37.3	46.7	56.2	64.3	68.6	66.8	58.9	47.3	38.4	29.0	47.5
Extreme Maximum Temp. (°F)	72	74	83	89	94	100	105	103	99	92	85	74	105
Extreme Minimum Temp. (°F)	-21	-9	9	21	34	43	52	42	29	18	9	-13	-21
Days Maximum Temp. ≥ 90°F	0	0	0	0	1	8	16	14	5	0	0	0	44
Days Maximum Temp. ≤ 32°F	5	3	0	0	0	0	0	0	0	0	0	4	12
Days Minimum Temp. ≤ 32°F	22	17	12	2	0	0	0	0	0	2	9	19	83
Days Minimum Temp. ≤ 0°F	1	0	0	0	0	0	0	0	0	0	0	0	1
Heating Degree Days (base 65°F)	924	730	532	238	60	3	0	1	34	223	498	844	4,087
Cooling Degree Days (base 65°F)	0	0	4	29	123	309	441	405	201	40	3	0	1,555
Mean Precipitation (in.)	3.49	3.92	4.14	4.64	4.97	4.13	4.15	2.82	3.49	3.97	4.16	4.56	48.44
Extreme Maximum Daily Precip. (in.)	2.60	5.32	3.88	5.20	3.66	3.20	3.60	2.93	3.88	3.50	3.40	3.50	5.32
Days With ≥ 0.1" Precipitation	6	6	7	8	8	6	5	4	5	6	7	7	75
Days With ≥ 0.5" Precipitation	2	3	2	3	3	3	3	2	3	3	3	4	34
Days With ≥ 1.0" Precipitation	1	1	1	1	1	1	1	1	1	1	1	1	12
Mean Snowfall (in.)	2.1	2.4	0.5	trace	0.0	0.0	0.0	0.0	0.0	0.0	0.0	1.7	6.7
Maximum Snow Depth (in.)	8	7	10	trace	0	0	0	0	0	0	0	13	13
Days With ≥ 1.0" Snow Depth	3	3	1	0	0	0	0	0	0	0	2	1	8

Cahokia *St. Clair County*   Elevation: 399 ft.   Latitude: 38° 34' N   Longitude: 90° 12' W

	JAN	FEB	MAR	APR	MAY	JUN	JUL	AUG	SEP	OCT	NOV	DEC	YEAR
Mean Maximum Temp. (°F)	41.2	46.1	56.4	67.9	76.5	85.1	88.6	87.3	80.6	69.6	56.7	43.6	66.6
Mean Temp. (°F)	32.0	35.9	45.3	56.4	65.6	74.7	78.5	76.8	69.1	57.6	46.4	34.5	56.1
Mean Minimum Temp. (°F)	22.6	25.7	34.5	44.9	54.7	64.1	68.3	66.1	57.5	45.5	35.9	25.4	45.4
Extreme Maximum Temp. (°F)	78	81	89	93	94	102	106	105	102	94	85	74	106
Extreme Minimum Temp. (°F)	-17	-16	4	18	32	42	54	41	32	22	10	-19	-19
Days Maximum Temp. ≥ 90°F	0	0	0	0	1	9	15	11	4	0	0	0	40
Days Maximum Temp. ≤ 32°F	7	4	1	0	0	0	0	0	0	0	0	5	17
Days Minimum Temp. ≤ 32°F	26	21	14	3	0	0	0	0	0	3	12	23	102
Days Minimum Temp. ≤ 0°F	1	1	0	0	0	0	0	0	0	0	0	0	2
Heating Degree Days (base 65°F)	1,017	816	603	283	85	6	0	2	44	257	555	939	4,607
Cooling Degree Days (base 65°F)	0	0	6	31	111	302	427	374	173	33	3	0	1,460
Mean Precipitation (in.)	2.45	2.55	3.39	3.81	4.52	4.02	4.44	3.51	3.23	3.43	3.67	2.99	42.01
Extreme Maximum Daily Precip. (in.)	2.39	2.47	2.83	3.00	4.37	2.68	3.47	4.27	3.15	2.52	2.30	2.55	4.37
Days With ≥ 0.1" Precipitation	5	5	7	8	8	7	6	6	5	6	7	6	76
Days With ≥ 0.5" Precipitation	1	2	2	3	3	3	3	2	2	3	3	2	29
Days With ≥ 1.0" Precipitation	1	1	1	1	1	1	2	1	1	1	1	1	13
Mean Snowfall (in.)	5.0	3.8	1.9	0.2	0.0	0.0	0.0	0.0	0.0	trace	0.6	3.9	15.4
Maximum Snow Depth (in.)	8	10	11	3	0	0	0	0	0	trace	4	9	11
Days With ≥ 1.0" Snow Depth	6	3	1	0	0	0	0	0	0	0	0	4	14

Carbondale Sewage Plant *Jackson County*   Elevation: 390 ft.   Latitude: 37° 44' N   Longitude: 89° 10' W

	JAN	FEB	MAR	APR	MAY	JUN	JUL	AUG	SEP	OCT	NOV	DEC	YEAR
Mean Maximum Temp. (°F)	41.5	46.4	56.1	67.2	76.3	84.8	88.4	88.3	81.2	69.3	56.9	44.9	66.8
Mean Temp. (°F)	32.4	36.2	45.1	55.5	65.0	73.9	77.6	76.2	68.2	56.1	46.2	35.5	55.7
Mean Minimum Temp. (°F)	23.2	25.9	34.1	43.7	53.7	62.9	66.8	64.1	55.2	42.9	35.4	26.1	44.5
Extreme Maximum Temp. (°F)	70	79	84	90	95	102	103	105	99	93	83	77	105
Extreme Minimum Temp. (°F)	-21	-11	5	21	31	41	51	43	30	18	10	-14	-21
Days Maximum Temp. ≥ 90°F	0	0	0	0	1	8	13	13	4	0	0	0	39
Days Maximum Temp. ≤ 32°F	7	4	1	0	0	0	0	0	0	0	0	4	16
Days Minimum Temp. ≤ 32°F	25	21	15	4	0	0	0	0	0	5	13	22	105
Days Minimum Temp. ≤ 0°F	1	1	0	0	0	0	0	0	0	0	0	1	3
Heating Degree Days (base 65°F)	1,006	809	612	305	90	7	0	2	53	293	559	908	4,644
Cooling Degree Days (base 65°F)	0	0	4	27	99	280	399	355	156	25	2	0	1,347
Mean Precipitation (in.)	3.15	3.06	4.25	4.47	5.47	4.60	3.68	3.10	3.10	3.72	4.43	4.07	47.10
Extreme Maximum Daily Precip. (in.)	3.52	3.75	6.10	4.96	4.14	6.90	4.35	3.19	4.22	3.47	5.35	3.57	6.90
Days With ≥ 0.1" Precipitation	6	6	7	8	8	6	5	5	5	5	7	6	74
Days With ≥ 0.5" Precipitation	2	2	3	3	4	3	2	2	2	3	3	3	32
Days With ≥ 1.0" Precipitation	1	1	1	1	2	1	1	1	1	1	1	1	13
Mean Snowfall (in.)	2.9	3.6	1.1	trace	0.0	0.0	0.0	0.0	0.0	0.1	0.3	2.7	10.7
Maximum Snow Depth (in.)	7	11	10	trace	0	0	0	0	0	2	7	13	13
Days With ≥ 1.0" Snow Depth	4	4	1	0	0	0	0	0	0	0	0	3	12

Carlinville *Macoupin County*   Elevation: 629 ft.   Latitude: 39° 17' N   Longitude: 89° 53' W

	JAN	FEB	MAR	APR	MAY	JUN	JUL	AUG	SEP	OCT	NOV	DEC	YEAR
Mean Maximum Temp. (°F)	36.5	42.4	53.4	65.4	75.3	83.7	86.9	85.7	79.3	67.1	53.5	39.9	64.1
Mean Temp. (°F)	28.5	33.6	43.4	54.3	64.4	73.2	76.7	74.9	67.7	56.0	44.5	32.2	54.1
Mean Minimum Temp. (°F)	20.6	24.8	33.4	43.2	53.5	62.7	66.4	64.1	56.0	44.8	35.4	24.5	44.1
Extreme Maximum Temp. (°F)	70	75	86	90	92	99	103	105	99	92	79	74	105
Extreme Minimum Temp. (°F)	-19	-17	-2	18	30	42	49	41	31	20	1	-15	-19
Days Maximum Temp. ≥ 90°F	0	0	0	0	0	6	11	9	3	0	0	0	29
Days Maximum Temp. ≤ 32°F	11	7	1	0	0	0	0	0	0	0	1	7	27
Days Minimum Temp. ≤ 32°F	27	21	15	4	0	0	0	0	0	4	12	24	107
Days Minimum Temp. ≤ 0°F	2	1	0	0	0	0	0	0	0	0	0	1	4
Heating Degree Days (base 65°F)	1,124	882	667	334	103	10	1	4	60	296	610	1,009	5,100
Cooling Degree Days (base 65°F)	0	0	4	20	92	263	369	319	147	24	1	0	1,239
Mean Precipitation (in.)	2.11	2.05	3.11	3.96	3.98	3.54	3.57	3.19	3.22	3.24	3.70	2.82	38.49
Extreme Maximum Daily Precip. (in.)	2.18	2.84	2.10	2.84	2.74	3.38	2.49	3.49	3.21	2.38	2.98	3.75	3.75
Days With ≥ 0.1" Precipitation	4	4	7	7	7	7	6	5	5	6	6	5	69
Days With ≥ 0.5" Precipitation	1	1	2	3	3	3	3	2	2	2	3	2	27
Days With ≥ 1.0" Precipitation	0	0	1	1	1	1	1	1	1	1	1	1	10
Mean Snowfall (in.)	5.9	4.4	2.7	0.4	trace	0.0	0.0	0.0	0.0	trace	0.9	3.4	17.7
Maximum Snow Depth (in.)	12	12	7	5	0	0	0	0	0	trace	4	8	12
Days With ≥ 1.0" Snow Depth	8	5	2	0	0	0	0	0	0	0	0	5	20

Charleston *Coles County*   Elevation: 680 ft.   Latitude: 39° 29' N   Longitude: 88° 10' W

	JAN	FEB	MAR	APR	MAY	JUN	JUL	AUG	SEP	OCT	NOV	DEC	YEAR
Mean Maximum Temp. (°F)	36.6	41.4	52.7	65.4	75.1	83.6	86.5	85.0	79.0	66.8	53.1	39.9	63.8
Mean Temp. (°F)	28.7	32.9	43.0	54.5	64.3	72.9	76.4	74.8	67.7	56.2	44.4	32.2	54.0
Mean Minimum Temp. (°F)	20.7	24.3	33.2	43.6	53.3	62.2	66.2	64.5	56.4	45.5	35.6	24.5	44.2
Extreme Maximum Temp. (°F)	69	74	84	89	94	102	101	102	97	91	80	71	102
Extreme Minimum Temp. (°F)	-27	-18	-1	17	29	38	50	42	32	20	6	-20	-27
Days Maximum Temp. ≥ 90°F	0	0	0	0	1	6	9	8	3	0	0	0	27
Days Maximum Temp. ≤ 32°F	11	7	1	0	0	0	0	0	0	0	1	7	27
Days Minimum Temp. ≤ 32°F	26	21	15	4	0	0	0	0	0	3	12	23	104
Days Minimum Temp. ≤ 0°F	2	1	0	0	0	0	0	0	0	0	0	1	4
Heating Degree Days (base 65°F)	1,120	900	678	329	106	11	0	3	59	293	613	1,010	5,122
Cooling Degree Days (base 65°F)	0	0	4	22	90	256	360	314	147	26	1	0	1,220
Mean Precipitation (in.)	2.35	2.39	3.02	4.15	4.47	3.86	4.18	3.31	3.22	3.85	3.96	3.09	41.85
Extreme Maximum Daily Precip. (in.)	1.76	2.70	2.24	3.55	4.66	3.23	3.46	2.75	4.95	3.61	2.49	2.87	4.95
Days With ≥ 0.1" Precipitation	5	5	7	8	8	6	6	5	5	6	7	6	74
Days With ≥ 0.5" Precipitation	1	1	2	3	3	3	3	2	2	3	3	2	28
Days With ≥ 1.0" Precipitation	1	0	0	1	1	1	1	1	1	1	1	1	10
Mean Snowfall (in.)	8.5	3.8	2.1	0.2	trace	0.0	0.0	0.0	0.0	trace	1.0	5.1	20.7
Maximum Snow Depth (in.)	24	21	9	2	trace	0	0	0	0	trace	8	9	24
Days With ≥ 1.0" Snow Depth	11	8	3	0	0	0	0	0	0	0	1	7	30

The period of record for all cooperative weather station data is 1980 – 2009. See User Guide for detailed explanation of data.

Chenoa *Mclean County*   Elevation: 709 ft.   Latitude: 40° 44' N   Longitude: 88° 43' W

	JAN	FEB	MAR	APR	MAY	JUN	JUL	AUG	SEP	OCT	NOV	DEC	YEAR
Mean Maximum Temp. (°F)	33.4	38.0	50.2	63.7	74.5	83.0	85.2	83.6	78.0	65.2	50.5	36.6	61.8
Mean Temp. (°F)	25.0	29.2	40.0	52.0	62.8	71.8	74.6	72.8	66.0	54.1	41.7	28.8	51.6
Mean Minimum Temp. (°F)	16.6	20.4	29.7	40.4	50.9	60.5	64.0	61.9	53.9	43.0	32.8	21.0	41.3
Extreme Maximum Temp. (°F)	66	73	85	91	95	102	101	103	98	91	79	70	103
Extreme Minimum Temp. (°F)	-25	-19	-6	7	26	38	45	40	28	17	5	-26	-26
Days Maximum Temp. ≥ 90°F	0	0	0	0	1	6	7	5	2	0	0	0	21
Days Maximum Temp. ≤ 32°F	14	9	2	0	0	0	0	0	0	0	1	10	36
Days Minimum Temp. ≤ 32°F	29	25	20	6	0	0	0	0	0	4	16	26	126
Days Minimum Temp. ≤ 0°F	4	2	0	0	0	0	0	0	0	0	0	2	8
Heating Degree Days (base 65°F)	1,232	1,006	771	397	137	16	1	7	80	348	693	1,114	5,802
Cooling Degree Days (base 65°F)	0	0	2	15	74	227	307	255	117	17	0	0	1,014
Mean Precipitation (in.)	1.72	1.34	2.90	3.28	3.95	3.79	3.54	3.21	2.86	3.10	2.87	2.23	34.79
Extreme Maximum Daily Precip. (in.)	1.89	1.80	3.73	1.79	2.45	3.63	2.81	3.93	3.59	5.66	2.21	5.07	5.66
Days With ≥ 0.1" Precipitation	4	3	6	7	7	6	6	5	5	6	6	4	65
Days With ≥ 0.5" Precipitation	1	1	2	3	3	3	3	2	2	2	2	1	25
Days With ≥ 1.0" Precipitation	0	0	0	1	1	1	1	1	1	1	0	0	8
Mean Snowfall (in.)	5.0	5.5	1.8	0.9	trace	0.0	0.0	0.0	0.0	0.0	1.0	4.2	18.4
Maximum Snow Depth (in.)	14	20	5	5	0	0	0	0	0	trace	4	14	20
Days With ≥ 1.0" Snow Depth	9	9	2	0	0	0	0	0	0	0	1	6	27

Chicago Botanical Garden *Cook County*   Elevation: 629 ft.   Latitude: 42° 08' N   Longitude: 87° 47' W

	JAN	FEB	MAR	APR	MAY	JUN	JUL	AUG	SEP	OCT	NOV	DEC	YEAR
Mean Maximum Temp. (°F)	31.9	35.7	45.2	56.3	67.3	77.7	82.5	81.2	74.5	62.4	48.5	35.8	58.3
Mean Temp. (°F)	24.1	27.5	36.7	47.1	57.3	67.3	72.8	71.7	64.2	52.4	40.7	28.2	49.2
Mean Minimum Temp. (°F)	16.2	19.2	28.2	37.8	47.2	56.8	63.0	62.2	53.8	42.3	32.8	20.6	40.0
Extreme Maximum Temp. (°F)	65	74	83	90	93	102	105	101	97	89	76	70	105
Extreme Minimum Temp. (°F)	-27	-20	-5	10	28	37	45	42	30	24	6	-20	-27
Days Maximum Temp. ≥ 90°F	0	0	0	0	1	4	6	4	1	0	0	0	16
Days Maximum Temp. ≤ 32°F	16	10	4	0	0	0	0	0	0	0	2	10	42
Days Minimum Temp. ≤ 32°F	28	25	21	8	0	0	0	0	0	4	14	27	127
Days Minimum Temp. ≤ 0°F	4	2	0	0	0	0	0	0	0	0	0	2	8
Heating Degree Days (base 65°F)	1,262	1,054	872	541	272	70	8	12	108	394	724	1,134	6,451
Cooling Degree Days (base 65°F)	0	0	1	10	40	145	257	228	90	10	0	0	781
Mean Precipitation (in.)	1.95	1.71	2.45	3.53	4.01	3.55	3.51	4.72	3.52	3.31	3.06	2.40	37.72
Extreme Maximum Daily Precip. (in.)	2.14	3.20	2.00	2.58	2.97	4.50	3.03	5.54	3.35	3.59	2.33	2.79	5.54
Days With ≥ 0.1" Precipitation	5	4	6	7	8	6	6	7	6	6	6	6	73
Days With ≥ 0.5" Precipitation	1	1	2	3	3	2	2	3	2	2	2	1	24
Days With ≥ 1.0" Precipitation	0	0	0	1	1	1	1	1	1	1	1	0	8
Mean Snowfall (in.)	10.2	8.1	5.2	0.9	trace	0.0	0.0	0.0	0.0	0.1	1.5	7.8	33.8
Maximum Snow Depth (in.)	15	15	13	9	trace	0	0	0	0	trace	5	18	18
Days With ≥ 1.0" Snow Depth	19	14	6	1	0	0	0	0	0	0	1	10	51

Chicago Midway Arpt *Cook County*   Elevation: 620 ft.   Latitude: 41° 44' N   Longitude: 87° 47' W

	JAN	FEB	MAR	APR	MAY	JUN	JUL	AUG	SEP	OCT	NOV	DEC	YEAR
Mean Maximum Temp. (°F)	32.2	36.4	47.3	59.7	70.9	80.6	84.8	82.6	75.9	63.0	49.0	36.0	59.9
Mean Temp. (°F)	25.4	29.2	39.1	50.4	61.0	70.9	75.8	74.1	66.7	54.2	41.8	29.4	51.5
Mean Minimum Temp. (°F)	18.4	21.9	30.9	41.0	51.1	61.2	66.8	65.6	57.5	45.3	34.6	22.8	43.1
Extreme Maximum Temp. (°F)	67	73	86	91	94	104	106	102	98	89	77	69	106
Extreme Minimum Temp. (°F)	-25	-17	-4	10	28	39	48	46	34	20	7	-20	-25
Days Maximum Temp. ≥ 90°F	0	0	0	0	1	5	8	5	2	0	0	0	21
Days Maximum Temp. ≤ 32°F	15	10	3	0	0	0	0	0	0	0	2	11	41
Days Minimum Temp. ≤ 32°F	27	23	18	5	0	0	0	0	0	2	12	25	112
Days Minimum Temp. ≤ 0°F	3	1	0	0	0	0	0	0	0	0	0	1	5
Heating Degree Days (base 65°F)	1,222	1,008	797	446	182	29	1	4	71	346	689	1,097	5,892
Cooling Degree Days (base 65°F)	0	0	2	12	65	213	342	293	128	16	0	0	1,071
Mean Precipitation (in.)	2.04	1.92	2.70	3.60	4.13	3.91	3.85	4.09	3.42	3.26	3.38	2.57	38.87
Extreme Maximum Daily Precip. (in.)	1.59	3.25	2.02	1.84	2.80	3.16	5.72	3.90	4.16	3.80	3.49	2.78	5.72
Days With ≥ 0.1" Precipitation	5	5	6	7	7	6	6	6	5	6	6	5	70
Days With ≥ 0.5" Precipitation	1	1	2	2	3	3	3	3	2	2	2	1	25
Days With ≥ 1.0" Precipitation	0	0	0	1	1	1	1	1	1	1	1	1	9
Mean Snowfall (in.)	11.6	9.3	5.6	1.1	trace	0.0	trace	0.0	trace	0.1	1.4	8.5	37.6
Maximum Snow Depth (in.)	21	17	13	10	0	0	trace	0	trace	2	4	20	21
Days With ≥ 1.0" Snow Depth	18	13	5	1	0	0	0	0	0	0	1	10	48

Danville *Vermilion County*   Elevation: 558 ft.   Latitude: 40° 08' N   Longitude: 87° 39' W

	JAN	FEB	MAR	APR	MAY	JUN	JUL	AUG	SEP	OCT	NOV	DEC	YEAR
Mean Maximum Temp. (°F)	35.4	40.2	51.7	64.8	75.0	83.2	85.7	84.2	78.5	66.2	52.3	38.7	63.0
Mean Temp. (°F)	27.4	31.4	41.6	53.3	63.1	71.9	75.2	73.7	66.8	54.9	43.4	31.1	52.8
Mean Minimum Temp. (°F)	19.3	22.6	31.5	41.7	51.2	60.4	64.6	63.1	55.0	43.6	34.5	23.5	42.6
Extreme Maximum Temp. (°F)	68	74	84	90	93	102	102	102	96	89	79	72	102
Extreme Minimum Temp. (°F)	-26	-22	-6	12	29	39	46	41	29	19	8	-25	-26
Days Maximum Temp. ≥ 90°F	0	0	0	0	1	5	7	5	2	0	0	0	20
Days Maximum Temp. ≤ 32°F	13	8	2	0	0	0	0	0	0	0	1	9	33
Days Minimum Temp. ≤ 32°F	26	23	17	6	0	0	0	0	0	4	14	24	114
Days Minimum Temp. ≤ 0°F	3	2	0	0	0	0	0	0	0	0	0	2	7
Heating Degree Days (base 65°F)	1,161	944	719	363	128	16	1	4	66	325	642	1,045	5,414
Cooling Degree Days (base 65°F)	0	0	2	18	76	228	324	279	126	20	1	0	1,074
Mean Precipitation (in.)	2.17	2.22	3.03	3.95	4.52	4.52	4.61	3.53	2.93	3.60	3.77	2.79	41.64
Extreme Maximum Daily Precip. (in.)	1.91	2.45	2.59	3.92	3.46	3.86	2.94	3.34	3.70	2.54	3.71	1.71	3.92
Days With ≥ 0.1" Precipitation	5	5	7	8	8	7	7	6	5	6	7	7	78
Days With ≥ 0.5" Precipitation	1	1	2	3	3	3	4	2	2	3	3	2	29
Days With ≥ 1.0" Precipitation	0	0	1	1	1	1	1	1	1	1	1	0	9
Mean Snowfall (in.)	4.5	4.4	2.1	0.2	trace	0.0	0.0	0.0	0.0	0.1	0.6	4.0	15.9
Maximum Snow Depth (in.)	13	14	7	2	trace	0	0	0	0	trace	5	11	14
Days With ≥ 1.0" Snow Depth	8	7	2	0	0	0	0	0	0	0	1	6	23

The period of record for all cooperative weather station data is 1980 – 2009. See User Guide for detailed explanation of data.

De Kalb *Dekalb County*   Elevation: 873 ft.   Latitude: 41° 56' N   Longitude: 88° 47' W

	JAN	FEB	MAR	APR	MAY	JUN	JUL	AUG	SEP	OCT	NOV	DEC	YEAR
Mean Maximum Temp. (°F)	28.2	33.2	45.2	59.2	70.7	80.3	83.6	81.6	75.4	62.1	46.9	33.0	58.3
Mean Temp. (°F)	20.5	25.2	36.0	48.5	59.5	69.6	73.2	71.4	64.1	51.3	38.5	25.7	48.6
Mean Minimum Temp. (°F)	12.8	17.1	26.9	37.6	48.2	58.8	62.9	61.0	52.8	40.5	30.1	18.3	38.9
Extreme Maximum Temp. (°F)	62	69	81	91	95	101	102	103	94	89	76	65	103
Extreme Minimum Temp. (°F)	-27	-23	-13	8	24	34	46	42	27	13	5	-22	-27
Days Maximum Temp. ≥ 90°F	0	0	0	0	0	4	5	4	1	0	0	0	14
Days Maximum Temp. ≤ 32°F	20	13	5	0	0	0	0	0	0	0	3	14	55
Days Minimum Temp. ≤ 32°F	30	26	23	8	1	0	0	0	0	7	18	28	141
Days Minimum Temp. ≤ 0°F	6	4	0	0	0	0	0	0	0	0	0	3	13
Heating Degree Days (base 65°F)	1,373	1,121	892	498	209	36	4	14	111	427	787	1,213	6,685
Cooling Degree Days (base 65°F)	0	0	1	9	44	180	267	218	91	9	0	0	819
Mean Precipitation (in.)	1.43	1.55	2.25	3.27	4.48	4.09	4.27	4.67	3.38	2.90	2.67	2.19	37.15
Extreme Maximum Daily Precip. (in.)	1.46	2.60	1.72	2.08	2.81	2.79	8.09	*5.71*	3.47	2.82	2.20	2.03	*8.09*
Days With ≥ 0.1" Precipitation	4	4	5	7	8	7	6	6	6	6	5	5	69
Days With ≥ 0.5" Precipitation	0	1	1	2	3	3	2	3	2	2	2	1	22
Days With ≥ 1.0" Precipitation	0	0	0	1	1	1	1	1	1	1	1	0	8
Mean Snowfall (in.)	9.9	7.4	4.3	1.0	trace	0.0	0.0	0.0	0.0	0.1	1.2	9.6	33.5
Maximum Snow Depth (in.)	17	17	10	5	trace	0	0	*0*	0	1	5	*17*	*17*
Days With ≥ 1.0" Snow Depth	21	15	5	1	0	0	0	0	0	0	1	12	55

Decatur *Macon County*   Elevation: 620 ft.   Latitude: 39° 49' N   Longitude: 89° 01' W

	JAN	FEB	MAR	APR	MAY	JUN	JUL	AUG	SEP	OCT	NOV	DEC	YEAR
Mean Maximum Temp. (°F)	36.2	41.4	52.8	65.7	75.9	84.5	87.6	86.1	80.1	67.5	53.1	39.9	64.2
Mean Temp. (°F)	27.7	32.3	42.5	54.1	64.0	73.0	76.5	74.9	67.9	55.9	43.8	31.8	53.7
Mean Minimum Temp. (°F)	19.2	23.2	32.3	42.5	52.0	61.5	65.4	63.6	55.7	44.3	34.5	23.6	43.2
Extreme Maximum Temp. (°F)	67	73	86	93	95	103	104	106	100	95	80	71	106
Extreme Minimum Temp. (°F)	-22	-20	-4	15	27	39	48	42	29	18	0	-22	-22
Days Maximum Temp. ≥ 90°F	0	0	0	0	1	7	11	8	4	0	0	0	31
Days Maximum Temp. ≤ 32°F	11	6	2	0	0	0	0	0	0	0	1	7	27
Days Minimum Temp. ≤ 32°F	27	23	16	5	0	0	0	0	0	4	13	24	112
Days Minimum Temp. ≤ 0°F	3	2	0	0	0	0	0	0	0	0	0	1	6
Heating Degree Days (base 65°F)	1,148	918	692	339	110	11	0	4	59	300	630	1,024	5,235
Cooling Degree Days (base 65°F)	0	0	2	20	86	258	363	317	153	25	1	0	1,225
Mean Precipitation (in.)	2.21	2.04	2.73	3.70	4.59	4.02	3.80	3.69	3.06	3.38	3.39	2.68	39.29
Extreme Maximum Daily Precip. (in.)	2.12	2.70	1.80	2.54	3.78	3.77	5.11	3.38	5.84	4.09	2.00	2.16	5.84
Days With ≥ 0.1" Precipitation	4	4	6	7	7	6	6	5	5	6	6	6	68
Days With ≥ 0.5" Precipitation	1	1	2	3	3	3	3	3	2	2	2	2	27
Days With ≥ 1.0" Precipitation	1	1	0	1	1	1	1	1	1	1	1	0	10
Mean Snowfall (in.)	6.0	4.3	1.9	0.2	trace	0.0	0.0	0.0	0.0	trace	0.7	5.0	18.1
Maximum Snow Depth (in.)	10	14	10	3	trace	0	0	0	0	trace	9	12	14
Days With ≥ 1.0" Snow Depth	10	7	2	0	0	0	0	0	0	0	1	5	25

Dixon 1 NW *Lee County*   Elevation: 700 ft.   Latitude: 41° 51' N   Longitude: 89° 30' W

	JAN	FEB	MAR	APR	MAY	JUN	JUL	AUG	SEP	OCT	NOV	DEC	YEAR
Mean Maximum Temp. (°F)	29.1	33.7	45.9	60.1	70.8	79.5	82.9	81.4	74.7	62.3	47.6	33.2	58.4
Mean Temp. (°F)	20.4	24.6	36.3	48.9	59.7	68.9	72.7	71.0	63.0	50.8	38.5	25.1	48.3
Mean Minimum Temp. (°F)	11.6	15.5	26.6	37.6	48.5	58.2	62.4	60.5	51.3	39.3	29.3	17.0	38.2
Extreme Maximum Temp. (°F)	65	71	87	93	93	100	101	103	97	91	78	68	103
Extreme Minimum Temp. (°F)	-32	-26	-13	8	24	38	45	40	28	17	4	-25	-32
Days Maximum Temp. ≥ 90°F	0	0	0	0	0	2	5	4	1	0	0	0	12
Days Maximum Temp. ≤ 32°F	18	12	4	0	0	0	0	0	0	0	3	13	50
Days Minimum Temp. ≤ 32°F	30	26	23	9	1	0	0	0	0	8	19	28	144
Days Minimum Temp. ≤ 0°F	7	5	0	0	0	0	0	0	0	0	0	4	16
Heating Degree Days (base 65°F)	1,377	1,136	884	486	204	37	6	15	129	442	789	1,230	6,735
Cooling Degree Days (base 65°F)	0	0	1	9	47	161	251	207	75	10	0	0	761
Mean Precipitation (in.)	1.51	1.59	2.43	3.51	4.33	4.71	4.07	4.62	3.49	2.86	2.67	2.13	37.92
Extreme Maximum Daily Precip. (in.)	1.76	1.79	2.19	2.64	4.16	4.54	4.36	4.08	4.95	3.33	1.92	3.12	4.95
Days With ≥ 0.1" Precipitation	4	4	5	7	8	8	6	7	5	5	5	5	69
Days With ≥ 0.5" Precipitation	1	1	2	2	3	3	3	3	2	2	2	1	25
Days With ≥ 1.0" Precipitation	0	0	0	1	1	1	1	1	1	1	0	0	7
Mean Snowfall (in.)	10.3	6.9	3.7	0.8	0.0	0.0	0.0	0.0	0.0	0.1	1.3	8.5	31.6
Maximum Snow Depth (in.)	24	13	11	4	0	0	0	0	0	trace	7	19	24
Days With ≥ 1.0" Snow Depth	18	14	4	0	0	0	0	0	0	0	1	11	48

Effingham *Effingham County*   Elevation: 595 ft.   Latitude: 39° 08' N   Longitude: 88° 32' W

	JAN	FEB	MAR	APR	MAY	JUN	JUL	AUG	SEP	OCT	NOV	DEC	YEAR
Mean Maximum Temp. (°F)	36.4	40.6	52.1	64.4	74.3	83.7	87.2	86.1	79.1	66.6	53.7	39.9	63.7
Mean Temp. (°F)	28.2	31.4	42.0	53.4	63.3	72.7	76.5	74.8	67.0	55.0	44.1	31.6	53.4
Mean Minimum Temp. (°F)	19.9	22.2	31.9	42.4	52.3	61.8	65.8	63.5	54.9	43.3	34.5	23.2	43.0
Extreme Maximum Temp. (°F)	69	74	84	89	94	102	102	103	98	93	81	71	103
Extreme Minimum Temp. (°F)	*-22*	-19	*-2*	21	30	39	50	44	33	20	*7*	-16	*-22*
Days Maximum Temp. ≥ 90°F	0	0	0	0	1	7	11	10	3	0	0	0	32
Days Maximum Temp. ≤ 32°F	11	7	2	0	0	0	0	0	0	0	1	8	29
Days Minimum Temp. ≤ 32°F	27	23	17	4	0	0	0	0	0	4	14	24	113
Days Minimum Temp. ≤ 0°F	2	2	0	0	0	0	0	0	0	0	0	2	6
Heating Degree Days (base 65°F)	1,134	943	708	360	122	14	1	4	70	325	621	1,029	5,331
Cooling Degree Days (base 65°F)	0	0	3	19	78	253	364	316	138	21	1	0	1,193
Mean Precipitation (in.)	2.43	2.72	3.23	3.87	5.07	4.21	4.34	2.88	3.09	3.74	4.05	3.30	42.93
Extreme Maximum Daily Precip. (in.)	2.24	2.78	2.50	2.61	3.79	5.70	5.25	2.90	3.39	4.45	3.17	3.27	5.70
Days With ≥ 0.1" Precipitation	5	5	7	8	9	7	7	5	5	6	7	6	77
Days With ≥ 0.5" Precipitation	2	2	2	2	4	3	3	2	2	3	3	2	30
Days With ≥ 1.0" Precipitation	1	1	1	1	1	1	1	1	1	1	1	1	12
Mean Snowfall (in.)	5.7	5.1	2.1	0.1	0.0	0.0	0.0	0.0	0.0	trace	1.0	3.8	17.8
Maximum Snow Depth (in.)	*10*	*16*	*8*	*trace*	*0*	*0*	*0*	*0*	*0*	*trace*	*10*	*8*	*16*
Days With ≥ 1.0" Snow Depth	*7*	*7*	2	0	0	0	0	0	0	0	1	5	*22*

The period of record for all cooperative weather station data is 1980 – 2009. See User Guide for detailed explanation of data.

Elgin *Kane County*   Elevation: 763 ft.   Latitude: 42° 04' N   Longitude: 88° 17' W

	JAN	FEB	MAR	APR	MAY	JUN	JUL	AUG	SEP	OCT	NOV	DEC	YEAR
Mean Maximum Temp. (°F)	29.4	33.8	45.0	58.3	69.7	79.5	83.3	81.6	74.8	61.7	47.3	33.3	58.1
Mean Temp. (°F)	21.4	25.3	35.6	47.7	58.7	68.4	73.1	71.4	63.5	50.8	38.8	25.6	48.4
Mean Minimum Temp. (°F)	13.4	16.7	26.2	37.1	47.7	57.3	62.8	61.0	52.1	39.8	30.3	18.1	38.5
Extreme Maximum Temp. (°F)	63	70	82	91	92	101	101	98	95	88	75	67	101
Extreme Minimum Temp. (°F)	-27	-22	-8	11	28	36	45	40	29	18	4	-24	-27
Days Maximum Temp. ≥ 90°F	0	0	0	0	0	4	5	4	1	0	0	0	14
Days Maximum Temp. ≤ 32°F	18	12	5	0	0	0	0	0	0	0	3	13	51
Days Minimum Temp. ≤ 32°F	29	26	23	9	0	0	0	0	0	7	19	28	141
Days Minimum Temp. ≤ 0°F	5	4	0	0	0	0	0	0	0	0	0	3	12
Heating Degree Days (base 65°F)	1,346	1,116	904	520	228	47	6	12	117	442	779	1,214	6,731
Cooling Degree Days (base 65°F)	0	0	1	7	41	157	264	217	78	8	0	0	773
Mean Precipitation (in.)	1.51	1.47	2.08	3.70	4.19	3.83	3.70	5.08	3.53	2.95	3.09	2.10	37.23
Extreme Maximum Daily Precip. (in.)	1.63	3.17	1.81	2.14	2.35	3.25	3.11	4.93	3.75	3.02	2.25	2.60	4.93
Days With ≥ 0.1" Precipitation	4	4	5	7	8	7	6	7	6	6	6	5	71
Days With ≥ 0.5" Precipitation	1	1	1	3	3	3	3	3	2	2	2	1	25
Days With ≥ 1.0" Precipitation	0	0	0	1	1	1	1	2	1	1	1	0	9
Mean Snowfall (in.)	9.4	6.8	3.6	0.5	0.0	0.0	0.0	0.0	0.0	trace	0.7	8.1	29.1
Maximum Snow Depth (in.)	24	16	10	2	0	0	0	0	0	trace	4	19	24
Days With ≥ 1.0" Snow Depth	13	8	3	0	0	0	0	0	0	0	1	9	34

Fulton L&D #13 *Whiteside County*   Elevation: 591 ft.   Latitude: 41° 54' N   Longitude: 90° 09' W

	JAN	FEB	MAR	APR	MAY	JUN	JUL	AUG	SEP	OCT	NOV	DEC	YEAR
Mean Maximum Temp. (°F)	29.5	33.2	44.8	59.0	70.3	79.5	83.5	81.9	74.6	62.2	47.3	32.9	58.2
Mean Temp. (°F)	21.2	24.8	36.0	49.2	60.2	69.6	73.7	72.2	64.2	52.1	39.2	25.4	49.0
Mean Minimum Temp. (°F)	13.0	16.3	27.2	39.3	50.0	59.6	63.8	62.5	53.7	41.9	30.9	17.8	39.7
Extreme Maximum Temp. (°F)	62	66	82	91	92	98	102	102	96	90	82	66	102
Extreme Minimum Temp. (°F)	-33	-26	-5	13	30	40	46	42	30	16	8	-22	-33
Days Maximum Temp. ≥ 90°F	0	0	0	0	0	3	6	4	1	0	0	0	14
Days Maximum Temp. ≤ 32°F	18	12	5	0	0	0	0	0	0	0	2	13	50
Days Minimum Temp. ≤ 32°F	30	26	23	6	0	0	0	0	0	4	17	28	134
Days Minimum Temp. ≤ 0°F	6	4	0	0	0	0	0	0	0	0	0	4	14
Heating Degree Days (base 65°F)	1,350	1,131	892	478	186	33	4	8	106	404	769	1,221	6,582
Cooling Degree Days (base 65°F)	0	0	0	10	44	177	280	238	88	10	0	0	847
Mean Precipitation (in.)	1.20	1.39	2.32	3.06	3.57	4.16	3.24	4.05	2.87	2.87	2.52	1.80	33.05
Extreme Maximum Daily Precip. (in.)	1.43	1.72	1.86	1.64	2.55	4.11	2.12	4.71	2.56	2.37	2.23	1.64	4.71
Days With ≥ 0.1" Precipitation	3	4	5	6	7	7	6	6	5	5	5	4	63
Days With ≥ 0.5" Precipitation	1	1	2	2	3	3	2	3	2	2	2	1	24
Days With ≥ 1.0" Precipitation	0	0	0	1	1	1	1	1	1	1	0	0	7
Mean Snowfall (in.)	3.1	1.7	0.4	0.5	0.0	0.0	0.0	0.0	0.0	0.0	0.1	1.5	7.3
Maximum Snow Depth (in.)	15	15	4	7	0	0	0	0	0	0	4	8	15
Days With ≥ 1.0" Snow Depth	6	7	2	0	0	0	0	0	0	0	0	3	18

Galesburg *Knox County*   Elevation: 771 ft.   Latitude: 40° 57' N   Longitude: 90° 23' W

	JAN	FEB	MAR	APR	MAY	JUN	JUL	AUG	SEP	OCT	NOV	DEC	YEAR
Mean Maximum Temp. (°F)	31.2	35.8	48.6	61.9	72.6	81.4	84.7	82.6	75.8	63.0	48.7	34.4	60.1
Mean Temp. (°F)	23.5	27.8	39.2	51.4	62.2	71.4	75.2	73.2	65.5	53.1	40.2	27.1	50.8
Mean Minimum Temp. (°F)	15.7	19.7	29.7	40.9	51.7	61.4	65.7	63.8	55.2	43.1	31.6	19.7	41.5
Extreme Maximum Temp. (°F)	66	69	86	91	93	101	102	101	97	94	78	68	102
Extreme Minimum Temp. (°F)	-27	-24	-6	9	29	41	49	42	29	21	1	-21	-27
Days Maximum Temp. ≥ 90°F	0	0	0	0	1	4	7	5	1	0	0	0	18
Days Maximum Temp. ≤ 32°F	17	11	3	0	0	0	0	0	0	0	2	12	45
Days Minimum Temp. ≤ 32°F	29	25	20	6	0	0	0	0	0	4	17	27	128
Days Minimum Temp. ≤ 0°F	4	3	0	0	0	0	0	0	0	0	0	3	10
Heating Degree Days (base 65°F)	1,281	1,045	796	416	149	19	2	7	88	377	738	1,167	6,085
Cooling Degree Days (base 65°F)	0	0	2	14	68	218	325	268	111	14	0	0	1,020
Mean Precipitation (in.)	1.46	1.63	2.74	3.66	4.28	4.04	4.32	4.20	3.49	2.73	2.85	2.38	37.78
Extreme Maximum Daily Precip. (in.)	1.23	2.76	3.90	3.01	3.62	3.92	6.13	3.40	3.06	2.18	2.15	3.28	6.13
Days With ≥ 0.1" Precipitation	4	4	6	7	8	7	6	7	5	6	6	5	71
Days With ≥ 0.5" Precipitation	1	1	2	2	3	3	2	3	2	2	2	2	25
Days With ≥ 1.0" Precipitation	0	0	0	1	1	1	1	1	1	1	1	1	9
Mean Snowfall (in.)	7.4	5.2	2.0	1.3	trace	0.0	0.0	0.0	0.0	trace	0.8	6.0	22.7
Maximum Snow Depth (in.)	20	11	9	11	trace	0	0	0	0	1	6	13	20
Days With ≥ 1.0" Snow Depth	14	10	3	0	0	0	0	0	0	0	1	7	35

Golden *Adams County*   Elevation: 725 ft.   Latitude: 40° 06' N   Longitude: 91° 01' W

	JAN	FEB	MAR	APR	MAY	JUN	JUL	AUG	SEP	OCT	NOV	DEC	YEAR
Mean Maximum Temp. (°F)	33.9	38.1	50.7	62.7	73.5	82.8	86.6	85.2	78.1	66.0	50.4	37.1	62.1
Mean Temp. (°F)	25.7	29.1	40.7	51.7	62.7	72.2	75.9	74.2	66.3	54.5	41.2	29.0	51.9
Mean Minimum Temp. (°F)	17.4	20.1	30.7	40.7	51.8	61.6	65.2	63.1	54.4	42.9	32.0	20.9	41.7
Extreme Maximum Temp. (°F)	68	73	84	93	93	101	102	103	98	95	78	71	103
Extreme Minimum Temp. (°F)	-23	-18	-5	13	31	43	50	43	30	20	-2	-22	-23
Days Maximum Temp. ≥ 90°F	0	0	0	0	1	5	10	9	3	0	0	0	28
Days Maximum Temp. ≤ 32°F	13	10	3	0	0	0	0	0	0	0	2	10	38
Days Minimum Temp. ≤ 32°F	28	24	19	6	0	0	0	0	0	4	17	27	125
Days Minimum Temp. ≤ 0°F	3	3	0	0	0	0	0	0	0	0	0	3	9
Heating Degree Days (base 65°F)	1,213	1,009	747	406	137	15	1	6	85	339	708	1,109	5,775
Cooling Degree Days (base 65°F)	0	0	2	14	73	239	346	298	129	19	0	0	1,120
Mean Precipitation (in.)	1.48	1.82	2.46	3.47	5.02	4.54	4.22	3.98	3.11	3.07	3.02	2.14	38.33
Extreme Maximum Daily Precip. (in.)	1.73	3.00	2.30	3.00	3.60	5.00	4.85	4.36	3.00	3.50	2.65	3.10	5.00
Days With ≥ 0.1" Precipitation	3	4	6	7	8	7	6	6	5	6	6	4	68
Days With ≥ 0.5" Precipitation	1	1	2	3	3	3	3	3	2	2	2	2	27
Days With ≥ 1.0" Precipitation	0	0	1	1	1	1	1	1	1	1	1	1	10
Mean Snowfall (in.)	5.1	4.2	1.4	0.5	0.0	0.0	0.0	0.0	0.0	trace	0.7	3.8	15.7
Maximum Snow Depth (in.)	9	8	3	2	0	0	0	0	0	trace	5	11	11
Days With ≥ 1.0" Snow Depth	2	2	0	0	0	0	0	0	0	0	0	3	7

The period of record for all cooperative weather station data is 1980 – 2009. See User Guide for detailed explanation of data.

Havana 4 NNE *Mason County*   Elevation: 459 ft.   Latitude: 40° 21' N   Longitude: 90° 01' W

	JAN	FEB	MAR	APR	MAY	JUN	JUL	AUG	SEP	OCT	NOV	DEC	YEAR
Mean Maximum Temp. (°F)	34.0	38.9	50.7	63.7	74.1	83.5	88.2	86.1	79.5	67.0	51.7	37.7	62.9
Mean Temp. (°F)	25.1	29.3	40.2	51.9	62.5	72.1	76.5	74.1	66.0	53.8	41.5	28.8	51.8
Mean Minimum Temp. (°F)	16.2	19.7	29.6	40.1	50.9	60.5	64.7	62.1	52.4	40.6	31.2	19.8	40.7
Extreme Maximum Temp. (°F)	69	74	88	95	95	104	106	106	100	95	82	72	106
Extreme Minimum Temp. (°F)	-30	-19	-3	16	27	40	50	38	28	19	1	-23	-30
Days Maximum Temp. ≥ 90°F	0	0	0	0	1	7	13	9	4	0	0	0	34
Days Maximum Temp. ≤ 32°F	14	9	2	0	0	0	0	0	0	0	2	9	36
Days Minimum Temp. ≤ 32°F	29	25	20	6	0	0	0	0	0	7	18	27	132
Days Minimum Temp. ≤ 0°F	4	3	0	0	0	0	0	0	0	0	0	3	10
Heating Degree Days (base 65°F)	1,229	1,002	765	400	142	20	1	5	87	358	699	1,116	5,824
Cooling Degree Days (base 65°F)	0	0	2	14	72	239	364	296	124	17	0	0	1,128
Mean Precipitation (in.)	2.11	2.09	2.79	3.63	4.45	4.19	3.87	3.76	3.17	3.04	3.24	2.80	39.14
Extreme Maximum Daily Precip. (in.)	2.85	2.71	1.90	2.45	4.35	3.10	3.86	3.75	3.40	2.75	2.52	2.60	4.35
Days With ≥ 0.1" Precipitation	5	4	6	7	8	7	7	6	5	6	6	5	72
Days With ≥ 0.5" Precipitation	1	1	2	3	3	3	3	2	2	2	2	2	26
Days With ≥ 1.0" Precipitation	1	0	1	1	1	1	1	1	1	1	1	1	11
Mean Snowfall (in.)	9.3	7.5	3.1	1.1	trace	0.0	0.0	0.0	0.0	trace	1.0	7.5	29.5
Maximum Snow Depth (in.)	18	12	8	8	trace	0	0	0	0	trace	4	13	18
Days With ≥ 1.0" Snow Depth	14	8	2	0	0	0	0	0	0	0	1	7	32

Jerseyville 2 SW *Jersey County*   Elevation: 629 ft.   Latitude: 39° 06' N   Longitude: 90° 21' W

	JAN	FEB	MAR	APR	MAY	JUN	JUL	AUG	SEP	OCT	NOV	DEC	YEAR
Mean Maximum Temp. (°F)	37.1	41.8	52.5	64.8	74.3	83.1	87.5	86.2	79.4	67.1	53.6	40.3	64.0
Mean Temp. (°F)	28.3	32.2	42.3	53.6	63.5	72.4	76.7	74.7	66.9	55.0	43.8	31.5	53.4
Mean Minimum Temp. (°F)	19.4	22.6	32.0	42.3	52.5	61.8	65.8	63.1	54.3	42.8	33.9	22.6	42.8
Extreme Maximum Temp. (°F)	71	76	86	91	92	100	104	104	101	92	80	73	104
Extreme Minimum Temp. (°F)	-20	-22	-3	20	29	42	48	38	27	17	-2	-19	-22
Days Maximum Temp. ≥ 90°F	0	0	0	0	0	5	12	10	3	0	0	0	30
Days Maximum Temp. ≤ 32°F	11	7	2	0	0	0	0	0	0	0	1	7	28
Days Minimum Temp. ≤ 32°F	28	23	17	5	0	0	0	0	0	5	14	25	117
Days Minimum Temp. ≤ 0°F	2	2	0	0	0	0	0	0	0	0	0	2	6
Heating Degree Days (base 65°F)	1,131	921	700	356	120	15	1	5	73	323	631	1,033	5,309
Cooling Degree Days (base 65°F)	0	0	3	20	80	244	369	312	135	20	1	0	1,184
Mean Precipitation (in.)	2.19	2.23	3.26	3.87	4.59	3.69	3.46	3.17	3.33	3.36	3.98	2.85	39.98
Extreme Maximum Daily Precip. (in.)	2.63	2.21	2.40	2.70	4.53	3.57	2.61	3.62	3.78	2.76	3.52	5.12	5.12
Days With ≥ 0.1" Precipitation	4	4	7	7	7	6	6	5	5	6	6	5	68
Days With ≥ 0.5" Precipitation	1	1	2	3	3	3	2	2	2	2	3	2	26
Days With ≥ 1.0" Precipitation	0	0	1	1	1	1	1	1	1	1	1	1	10
Mean Snowfall (in.)	4.0	3.4	2.0	0.2	0.0	0.0	0.0	0.0	0.0	trace	0.8	3.1	13.5
Maximum Snow Depth (in.)	15	16	12	4	0	0	0	0	0	trace	7	10	16
Days With ≥ 1.0" Snow Depth	8	5	2	0	0	0	0	0	0	0	1	5	21

Joliet Brandon Rd Dam *Will County*   Elevation: 542 ft.   Latitude: 41° 30' N   Longitude: 88° 06' W

	JAN	FEB	MAR	APR	MAY	JUN	JUL	AUG	SEP	OCT	NOV	DEC	YEAR
Mean Maximum Temp. (°F)	31.4	35.8	47.0	60.2	71.1	80.9	84.3	82.5	76.3	63.5	49.3	35.5	59.8
Mean Temp. (°F)	23.6	27.6	37.8	49.7	60.0	70.0	74.0	72.5	65.2	52.9	40.9	28.0	50.2
Mean Minimum Temp. (°F)	15.8	19.3	28.5	39.1	48.8	59.1	63.6	62.4	54.1	42.4	32.4	20.4	40.5
Extreme Maximum Temp. (°F)	65	73	86	92	93	104	103	102	95	88	77	70	104
Extreme Minimum Temp. (°F)	-26	-19	-7	11	30	35	47	39	32	21	6	-20	-26
Days Maximum Temp. ≥ 90°F	0	0	0	0	1	4	6	4	2	0	0	0	17
Days Maximum Temp. ≤ 32°F	16	11	4	0	0	0	0	0	0	0	2	11	44
Days Minimum Temp. ≤ 32°F	28	25	22	7	0	0	0	0	0	4	16	27	129
Days Minimum Temp. ≤ 0°F	4	2	0	0	0	0	0	0	0	0	0	2	8
Heating Degree Days (base 65°F)	1,276	1,052	837	463	195	32	3	6	89	379	717	1,142	6,191
Cooling Degree Days (base 65°F)	0	0	1	10	47	189	288	245	103	12	0	0	895
Mean Precipitation (in.)	1.66	1.73	2.31	3.49	4.02	3.72	4.29	3.93	3.16	2.96	3.00	2.20	36.47
Extreme Maximum Daily Precip. (in.)	2.45	2.75	2.25	2.12	3.30	5.13	13.60	3.86	2.74	2.92	2.54	3.34	13.60
Days With ≥ 0.1" Precipitation	4	5	6	7	8	6	6	6	5	6	6	5	70
Days With ≥ 0.5" Precipitation	1	1	1	2	3	2	3	3	2	2	2	1	23
Days With ≥ 1.0" Precipitation	0	0	0	1	1	1	1	1	1	1	1	0	8
Mean Snowfall (in.)	na	na	*1.0*	0.1	0.0	0.0	0.0	0.0	0.0	0.0	0.1	*3.2*	na
Maximum Snow Depth (in.)	na	na	na	na	na	na	*0*	*0*	*0*	na	na	na	na
Days With ≥ 1.0" Snow Depth	na	na	*1*	0	0	0	0	0	0	0	0	*5*	na

Kankakee Metro Wastwater *Kankakee County*   Elevation: 640 ft.   Latitude: 41° 08' N   Longitude: 87° 53' W

	JAN	FEB	MAR	APR	MAY	JUN	JUL	AUG	SEP	OCT	NOV	DEC	YEAR
Mean Maximum Temp. (°F)	32.6	36.8	48.3	61.2	72.5	82.3	85.3	83.5	77.7	64.8	50.5	36.7	61.0
Mean Temp. (°F)	23.9	27.6	38.2	49.8	60.8	70.6	74.4	72.3	65.1	52.7	41.1	28.3	50.4
Mean Minimum Temp. (°F)	15.1	18.4	28.0	38.3	49.0	58.8	63.4	61.1	52.4	40.6	31.6	19.9	39.7
Extreme Maximum Temp. (°F)	66	74	84	91	94	103	103	107	99	90	78	70	107
Extreme Minimum Temp. (°F)	-29	-19	-7	8	27	38	46	39	30	18	4	-26	-29
Days Maximum Temp. ≥ 90°F	0	0	0	0	1	6	8	5	2	0	0	0	22
Days Maximum Temp. ≤ 32°F	15	9	3	0	0	0	0	0	0	0	1	10	38
Days Minimum Temp. ≤ 32°F	29	26	22	7	0	0	0	0	0	5	16	27	132
Days Minimum Temp. ≤ 0°F	5	3	0	0	0	0	0	0	0	0	0	3	11
Heating Degree Days (base 65°F)	1,268	1,049	825	459	181	28	2	8	95	386	712	1,131	6,144
Cooling Degree Days (base 65°F)	0	0	1	8	56	202	300	243	105	12	0	0	927
Mean Precipitation (in.)	1.91	1.83	2.58	3.46	4.77	3.91	4.66	3.33	2.97	3.13	3.45	2.48	38.48
Extreme Maximum Daily Precip. (in.)	2.78	1.93	3.00	2.85	3.95	3.88	4.36	3.30	3.44	2.52	3.36	3.65	4.36
Days With ≥ 0.1" Precipitation	5	4	6	7	8	6	6	5	5	6	6	5	69
Days With ≥ 0.5" Precipitation	1	1	2	2	3	3	4	2	2	2	2	1	25
Days With ≥ 1.0" Precipitation	0	0	0	1	1	1	1	1	1	1	1	1	9
Mean Snowfall (in.)	7.7	6.5	2.8	0.9	trace	0.0	0.0	0.0	0.0	trace	0.7	5.5	24.1
Maximum Snow Depth (in.)	18	15	12	6	trace	0	0	0	0	1	4	13	18
Days With ≥ 1.0" Snow Depth	15	11	3	0	0	0	0	0	0	0	1	7	38

The period of record for all cooperative weather station data is 1980 – 2009. See User Guide for detailed explanation of data.

Kaskaskia River Nav Lock *Randolph County* Elevation: 379 ft. Latitude: 37° 59' N Longitude: 89° 57' W

	JAN	FEB	MAR	APR	MAY	JUN	JUL	AUG	SEP	OCT	NOV	DEC	YEAR
Mean Maximum Temp. (°F)	42.3	46.7	57.1	68.6	78.7	87.2	91.4	90.4	82.7	70.4	57.5	44.1	68.1
Mean Temp. (°F)	32.4	35.9	45.5	56.2	66.4	75.1	79.4	77.7	69.7	57.6	46.5	34.4	56.4
Mean Minimum Temp. (°F)	22.5	25.0	33.7	43.8	54.1	63.0	67.2	64.9	56.5	44.7	35.4	24.7	44.6
Extreme Maximum Temp. (°F)	74	83	89	99	98	105	108	109	105	96	87	77	109
Extreme Minimum Temp. (°F)	-18	-14	1	22	32	44	51	41	32	23	9	-18	-18
Days Maximum Temp. ≥ 90°F	0	0	0	0	3	12	20	18	8	1	0	0	62
Days Maximum Temp. ≤ 32°F	7	4	1	0	0	0	0	0	0	0	0	5	17
Days Minimum Temp. ≤ 32°F	27	22	14	3	0	0	0	0	0	3	13	24	106
Days Minimum Temp. ≤ 0°F	1	1	0	0	0	0	0	0	0	0	0	1	3
Heating Degree Days (base 65°F)	1,003	817	604	287	72	5	0	2	44	256	552	941	4,583
Cooling Degree Days (base 65°F)	0	0	4	31	123	317	452	402	191	33	2	0	1,555
Mean Precipitation (in.)	1.98	2.21	3.32	3.56	5.10	3.78	3.70	3.38	3.47	3.66	3.86	3.27	41.29
Extreme Maximum Daily Precip. (in.)	3.00	2.60	4.00	2.42	3.58	3.85	3.97	2.42	3.62	3.26	3.19	2.82	4.00
Days With ≥ 0.1" Precipitation	4	5	7	7	8	6	5	5	5	6	6	6	70
Days With ≥ 0.5" Precipitation	1	2	2	2	3	2	3	3	2	3	3	2	28
Days With ≥ 1.0" Precipitation	1	0	1	1	1	1	1	1	1	1	1	1	11
Mean Snowfall (in.)	1.5	2.1	0.2	0.1	0.0	0.0	0.0	0.0	0.0	0.0	0.4	1.6	5.9
Maximum Snow Depth (in.)	10	24	4	0	0	0	0	0	0	0	8	4	24
Days With ≥ 1.0" Snow Depth	1	2	0	0	0	0	0	0	0	0	0	1	4

La Harpe *Hancock County* Elevation: 700 ft. Latitude: 40° 35' N Longitude: 90° 58' W

	JAN	FEB	MAR	APR	MAY	JUN	JUL	AUG	SEP	OCT	NOV	DEC	YEAR
Mean Maximum Temp. (°F)	33.8	38.7	50.4	63.1	73.7	82.8	86.7	85.0	77.7	65.4	51.0	37.1	62.1
Mean Temp. (°F)	24.2	28.6	39.3	51.0	61.8	71.2	75.0	73.2	65.0	52.9	40.5	27.7	50.9
Mean Minimum Temp. (°F)	14.6	18.4	28.2	38.9	49.9	59.6	63.3	61.3	52.3	40.4	30.0	18.2	39.6
Extreme Maximum Temp. (°F)	66	72	87	92	95	105	104	105	99	96	80	72	105
Extreme Minimum Temp. (°F)	-23	-22	-8	13	28	40	49	40	29	18	-1	-23	-23
Days Maximum Temp. ≥ 90°F	0	0	0	0	1	6	11	8	3	0	0	0	29
Days Maximum Temp. ≤ 32°F	14	9	2	0	0	0	0	0	0	0	2	10	37
Days Minimum Temp. ≤ 32°F	30	25	22	7	0	0	0	0	0	7	19	28	138
Days Minimum Temp. ≤ 0°F	5	3	0	0	0	0	0	0	0	0	0	3	11
Heating Degree Days (base 65°F)	1,258	1,024	790	424	153	20	2	6	98	380	728	1,150	6,033
Cooling Degree Days (base 65°F)	0	0	1	12	60	212	320	266	106	13	0	0	990
Mean Precipitation (in.)	1.47	1.74	2.66	3.81	4.63	4.66	4.43	3.74	3.90	3.04	2.93	2.35	39.36
Extreme Maximum Daily Precip. (in.)	1.64	3.41	5.08	2.62	3.22	4.10	4.32	4.11	4.34	4.74	3.20	3.37	5.08
Days With ≥ 0.1" Precipitation	4	4	6	8	8	7	7	6	6	6	6	5	73
Days With ≥ 0.5" Precipitation	1	1	2	3	3	3	3	2	2	2	2	1	25
Days With ≥ 1.0" Precipitation	0	0	0	1	1	1	1	1	1	1	1	1	9
Mean Snowfall (in.)	6.0	3.7	2.7	0.8	0.0	0.0	0.0	0.0	0.0	trace	0.9	5.0	19.1
Maximum Snow Depth (in.)	17	9	8	5	0	0	0	0	0	trace	4	15	17
Days With ≥ 1.0" Snow Depth	15	10	3	0	0	0	0	0	0	0	1	10	39

Lacon 1 N *Marshall County* Elevation: 459 ft. Latitude: 41° 02' N Longitude: 89° 24' W

	JAN	FEB	MAR	APR	MAY	JUN	JUL	AUG	SEP	OCT	NOV	DEC	YEAR
Mean Maximum Temp. (°F)	33.6	38.5	50.6	64.3	74.8	83.7	87.1	85.5	78.8	66.3	51.5	37.5	62.7
Mean Temp. (°F)	26.2	29.9	40.6	52.8	62.9	72.1	75.9	74.3	66.6	54.8	42.4	29.7	52.3
Mean Minimum Temp. (°F)	18.2	21.2	30.5	41.2	50.9	60.4	64.6	62.9	54.4	43.2	33.1	21.9	41.9
Extreme Maximum Temp. (°F)	70	71	81	91	93	102	103	102	98	90	81	70	103
Extreme Minimum Temp. (°F)	-27	-19	-5	11	26	36	45	44	28	18	2	-24	-27
Days Maximum Temp. ≥ 90°F	0	0	0	0	1	6	11	8	3	0	0	0	29
Days Maximum Temp. ≤ 32°F	14	9	2	0	0	0	0	0	0	0	1	9	35
Days Minimum Temp. ≤ 32°F	27	24	19	6	0	0	0	0	0	4	15	26	121
Days Minimum Temp. ≤ 0°F	3	2	0	0	0	0	0	0	0	0	0	2	7
Heating Degree Days (base 65°F)	1,197	988	752	378	131	14	0	5	73	329	673	1,086	5,626
Cooling Degree Days (base 65°F)	0	0	2	18	71	232	345	298	129	20	0	0	1,115
Mean Precipitation (in.)	1.88	1.81	3.09	3.89	4.36	3.84	3.78	3.69	3.21	3.18	3.15	2.28	38.16
Extreme Maximum Daily Precip. (in.)	2.50	3.52	3.12	2.65	2.35	3.60	3.91	3.25	4.88	2.78	2.77	2.13	4.88
Days With ≥ 0.1" Precipitation	4	4	6	8	7	6	6	7	5	6	6	5	70
Days With ≥ 0.5" Precipitation	1	1	2	3	3	3	2	3	2	2	2	1	25
Days With ≥ 1.0" Precipitation	1	0	1	1	1	1	1	1	1	1	1	1	11
Mean Snowfall (in.)	6.5	5.0	2.8	0.8	trace	0.0	0.0	0.0	0.0	trace	0.8	6.1	22.0
Maximum Snow Depth (in.)	14	9	11	5	trace	0	0	0	0	trace	3	14	14
Days With ≥ 1.0" Snow Depth	14	11	3	1	0	0	0	0	0	0	1	9	39

Lincoln *Logan County* Elevation: 583 ft. Latitude: 40° 08' N Longitude: 89° 22' W

	JAN	FEB	MAR	APR	MAY	JUN	JUL	AUG	SEP	OCT	NOV	DEC	YEAR
Mean Maximum Temp. (°F)	34.0	38.9	50.9	63.8	74.5	83.2	86.2	84.5	79.0	66.1	51.8	38.4	62.6
Mean Temp. (°F)	25.6	29.9	40.5	52.2	62.9	72.1	75.2	73.2	66.1	53.8	42.1	30.0	52.0
Mean Minimum Temp. (°F)	17.1	20.8	30.1	40.5	51.3	60.8	64.2	61.8	53.1	41.5	32.3	21.5	41.2
Extreme Maximum Temp. (°F)	68	75	86	91	95	102	103	104	97	92	81	72	104
Extreme Minimum Temp. (°F)	-25	-20	-2	15	25	39	49	39	28	21	5	-19	-25
Days Maximum Temp. ≥ 90°F	0	0	0	0	1	6	9	7	3	0	0	0	26
Days Maximum Temp. ≤ 32°F	13	8	2	0	0	0	0	0	0	0	1	9	33
Days Minimum Temp. ≤ 32°F	28	24	19	6	0	0	0	0	0	6	16	26	125
Days Minimum Temp. ≤ 0°F	3	2	0	0	0	0	0	0	0	0	0	2	7
Heating Degree Days (base 65°F)	1,217	986	754	394	133	18	1	7	79	357	680	1,080	5,706
Cooling Degree Days (base 65°F)	0	0	2	15	76	236	324	267	118	17	0	0	1,055
Mean Precipitation (in.)	1.95	1.61	2.70	3.65	4.06	3.87	4.95	3.92	3.04	3.32	3.27	2.58	38.92
Extreme Maximum Daily Precip. (in.)	2.73	1.56	1.98	3.96	4.11	3.17	4.76	3.70	3.55	3.73	1.89	5.18	5.18
Days With ≥ 0.1" Precipitation	4	4	6	7	8	6	6	6	5	6	6	6	70
Days With ≥ 0.5" Precipitation	1	1	2	2	2	3	3	3	2	2	2	1	24
Days With ≥ 1.0" Precipitation	0	0	0	1	1	1	1	1	1	1	1	1	9
Mean Snowfall (in.)	6.1	4.9	1.8	0.5	0.0	0.0	0.0	0.0	0.0	trace	0.7	5.4	19.4
Maximum Snow Depth (in.)	14	11	4	5	0	0	0	0	0	trace	6	12	14
Days With ≥ 1.0" Snow Depth	10	6	1	0	0	0	0	0	0	0	0	6	23

The period of record for all cooperative weather station data is 1980 – 2009. See User Guide for detailed explanation of data.

Marengo *Mchenry County* Elevation: 819 ft. Latitude: 42° 15' N Longitude: 88° 36' W

	JAN	FEB	MAR	APR	MAY	JUN	JUL	AUG	SEP	OCT	NOV	DEC	YEAR
Mean Maximum Temp. (°F)	29.5	33.0	44.8	58.7	70.8	81.1	84.2	82.3	75.8	62.3	47.1	33.1	58.6
Mean Temp. (°F)	20.6	23.6	35.0	47.4	58.5	68.7	72.7	70.8	63.0	50.2	37.8	24.9	47.8
Mean Minimum Temp. (°F)	11.8	14.2	25.2	36.0	46.2	56.3	61.1	59.2	50.2	38.1	28.5	16.6	36.9
Extreme Maximum Temp. (°F)	61	70	84	91	94	105	105	103	98	90	76	64	105
Extreme Minimum Temp. (°F)	-28	-23	-10	6	26	36	43	39	26	14	1	-23	-28
Days Maximum Temp. ≥ 90°F	0	0	0	0	1	5	7	4	1	0	0	0	18
Days Maximum Temp. ≤ 32°F	17	13	4	0	0	0	0	0	0	0	2	13	49
Days Minimum Temp. ≤ 32°F	29	27	23	11	1	0	0	0	1	9	20	29	150
Days Minimum Temp. ≤ 0°F	7	5	1	0	0	0	0	0	0	0	0	4	17
Heating Degree Days (base 65°F)	1,371	1,163	923	530	236	44	7	18	130	460	808	1,237	6,927
Cooling Degree Days (base 65°F)	0	0	0	8	42	163	252	204	77	9	0	0	755
Mean Precipitation (in.)	1.30	1.31	2.03	3.23	4.01	4.01	3.70	4.81	2.97	2.85	2.58	1.87	34.67
Extreme Maximum Daily Precip. (in.)	2.90	1.30	1.94	1.94	2.75	5.15	3.30	8.20	3.34	2.32	1.96	2.21	8.20
Days With ≥ 0.1" Precipitation	3	3	4	7	8	6	6	7	6	6	6	4	66
Days With ≥ 0.5" Precipitation	1	1	1	2	3	3	2	3	2	2	2	1	23
Days With ≥ 1.0" Precipitation	0	0	0	1	1	1	1	1	1	1	0	0	7
Mean Snowfall (in.)	9.3	8.0	3.3	1.1	0.1	0.0	0.0	0.0	0.0	0.1	1.7	7.6	31.2
Maximum Snow Depth (in.)	17	19	14	6	2	0	0	0	0	1	5	12	19
Days With ≥ 1.0" Snow Depth	15	13	5	1	0	0	0	0	0	0	2	9	45

Normal *Mclean County* Elevation: 785 ft. Latitude: 40° 31' N Longitude: 89° 00' W

	JAN	FEB	MAR	APR	MAY	JUN	JUL	AUG	SEP	OCT	NOV	DEC	YEAR
Mean Maximum Temp. (°F)	33.7	38.9	49.7	62.9	73.9	83.2	85.9	84.4	78.2	65.7	50.8	37.1	62.0
Mean Temp. (°F)	25.3	29.8	39.5	51.4	62.5	72.0	75.4	73.5	66.2	54.2	41.6	28.9	51.7
Mean Minimum Temp. (°F)	16.9	20.6	29.3	39.9	51.0	60.9	64.8	62.6	54.1	42.7	32.4	20.7	41.3
Extreme Maximum Temp. (°F)	66	71	85	91	93	103	102	103	96	90	80	71	103
Extreme Minimum Temp. (°F)	-23	-20	-3	10	26	35	48	41	31	18	2	-22	-23
Days Maximum Temp. ≥ 90°F	0	0	0	0	1	6	9	7	2	0	0	0	25
Days Maximum Temp. ≤ 32°F	14	9	3	0	0	0	0	0	0	0	2	10	38
Days Minimum Temp. ≤ 32°F	28	24	20	7	0	0	0	0	0	5	16	27	127
Days Minimum Temp. ≤ 0°F	4	2	0	0	0	0	0	0	0	0	0	2	8
Heating Degree Days (base 65°F)	1,223	991	785	417	150	19	1	7	84	347	695	1,112	5,831
Cooling Degree Days (base 65°F)	0	0	2	15	79	237	330	278	126	19	0	0	1,086
Mean Precipitation (in.)	2.08	1.92	2.75	3.71	4.41	3.95	4.06	3.95	3.02	3.27	3.22	2.46	38.80
Extreme Maximum Daily Precip. (in.)	2.35	2.27	1.65	3.15	3.21	3.50	5.63	2.63	5.21	3.53	1.94	2.64	5.63
Days With ≥ 0.1" Precipitation	5	5	6	7	8	7	6	7	5	6	6	6	74
Days With ≥ 0.5" Precipitation	1	1	2	3	3	3	3	3	2	2	2	2	27
Days With ≥ 1.0" Precipitation	0	0	0	1	1	1	1	1	1	1	1	0	8
Mean Snowfall (in.)	6.1	5.3	1.8	0.8	trace	0.0	0.0	0.0	0.0	0.1	0.7	4.9	19.7
Maximum Snow Depth (in.)	18	11	7	4	trace	0	0	0	0	trace	6	12	18
Days With ≥ 1.0" Snow Depth	14	8	3	0	0	0	0	0	0	0	1	8	34

Park Forest *Cook County* Elevation: 709 ft. Latitude: 41° 30' N Longitude: 87° 41' W

	JAN	FEB	MAR	APR	MAY	JUN	JUL	AUG	SEP	OCT	NOV	DEC	YEAR
Mean Maximum Temp. (°F)	30.9	35.1	45.8	59.0	69.9	79.9	83.7	81.8	75.1	62.5	48.7	35.1	59.0
Mean Temp. (°F)	23.3	27.1	37.2	49.1	59.6	69.6	74.0	72.2	64.8	52.3	40.7	27.8	49.8
Mean Minimum Temp. (°F)	15.7	19.1	28.5	39.2	49.3	59.2	64.3	62.6	54.4	42.1	32.7	20.5	40.6
Extreme Maximum Temp. (°F)	65	71	83	89	94	102	102	103	95	89	75	70	103
Extreme Minimum Temp. (°F)	-27	-18	-6	9	28	37	46	41	29	18	4	-21	-27
Days Maximum Temp. ≥ 90°F	0	0	0	0	1	4	6	4	1	0	0	0	16
Days Maximum Temp. ≤ 32°F	17	11	4	0	0	0	0	0	0	0	2	11	45
Days Minimum Temp. ≤ 32°F	29	25	21	6	0	0	0	0	0	4	15	27	127
Days Minimum Temp. ≤ 0°F	4	2	0	0	0	0	0	0	0	0	0	2	8
Heating Degree Days (base 65°F)	1,287	1,063	857	480	212	41	5	10	100	398	721	1,146	6,320
Cooling Degree Days (base 65°F)	0	0	1	10	52	185	291	242	101	12	0	0	894
Mean Precipitation (in.)	2.06	1.81	2.57	3.78	4.41	4.35	4.27	4.11	3.27	3.25	3.52	2.56	39.96
Extreme Maximum Daily Precip. (in.)	3.48	2.27	1.97	3.88	6.43	3.61	6.55	3.13	4.04	3.18	3.40	3.87	6.55
Days With ≥ 0.1" Precipitation	5	4	6	7	7	6	6	6	6	6	6	6	71
Days With ≥ 0.5" Precipitation	1	1	1	3	3	3	3	3	2	2	2	1	25
Days With ≥ 1.0" Precipitation	0	0	0	1	1	1	1	2	1	1	1	0	9
Mean Snowfall (in.)	9.4	7.8	4.9	0.8	trace	0.0	0.0	0.0	0.0	0.3	0.9	6.7	30.8
Maximum Snow Depth (in.)	17	16	14	7	trace	0	0	0	0	0	4	17	17
Days With ≥ 1.0" Snow Depth	19	13	5	0	0	0	0	0	0	0	1	10	48

Paw Paw 2 NW *Lee County* Elevation: 950 ft. Latitude: 41° 43' N Longitude: 89° 00' W

	JAN	FEB	MAR	APR	MAY	JUN	JUL	AUG	SEP	OCT	NOV	DEC	YEAR
Mean Maximum Temp. (°F)	27.8	32.1	44.1	58.4	69.6	79.5	82.2	80.0	74.1	61.4	46.2	31.7	57.2
Mean Temp. (°F)	20.0	24.0	34.8	47.2	58.4	68.6	71.8	69.7	62.7	50.2	37.5	24.1	47.4
Mean Minimum Temp. (°F)	12.2	15.9	25.5	36.0	47.1	57.6	61.4	59.4	51.2	39.0	28.7	16.4	37.5
Extreme Maximum Temp. (°F)	62	66	83	92	91	101	100	99	92	90	75	65	101
Extreme Minimum Temp. (°F)	-25	-33	-16	9	24	38	41	37	29	17	3	-23	-33
Days Maximum Temp. ≥ 90°F	0	0	0	0	0	3	4	2	1	0	0	0	10
Days Maximum Temp. ≤ 32°F	20	14	5	0	0	0	0	0	0	0	4	15	58
Days Minimum Temp. ≤ 32°F	30	27	25	10	1	0	0	0	0	7	20	29	149
Days Minimum Temp. ≤ 0°F	7	4	0	0	0	0	0	0	0	0	0	4	15
Heating Degree Days (base 65°F)	1,388	1,152	930	532	234	40	9	19	129	458	818	1,262	6,971
Cooling Degree Days (base 65°F)	0	0	0	5	37	153	227	172	66	6	0	0	666
Mean Precipitation (in.)	1.28	1.42	2.07	3.07	4.45	4.00	4.14	4.25	3.62	2.78	2.96	1.98	36.02
Extreme Maximum Daily Precip. (in.)	1.43	2.95	1.86	2.02	2.95	6.92	5.46	3.15	5.24	2.94	2.55	3.77	6.92
Days With ≥ 0.1" Precipitation	3	3	5	7	8	7	6	6	6	5	6	5	67
Days With ≥ 0.5" Precipitation	1	1	1	2	3	2	3	3	2	2	2	1	23
Days With ≥ 1.0" Precipitation	0	0	0	0	1	2	1	1	1	1	1	0	7
Mean Snowfall (in.)	8.8	6.5	3.9	0.8	trace	0.0	0.0	0.0	0.0	0.2	1.2	8.5	29.9
Maximum Snow Depth (in.)	25	11	12	7	trace	0	0	0	0	0	3	24	25
Days With ≥ 1.0" Snow Depth	17	12	4	0	0	0	0	0	0	0	1	12	46

The period of record for all cooperative weather station data is 1980 – 2009. See User Guide for detailed explanation of data.

Princeville *Peoria County*   Elevation: 734 ft.   Latitude: 40° 56' N   Longitude: 89° 46' W

	JAN	FEB	MAR	APR	MAY	JUN	JUL	AUG	SEP	OCT	NOV	DEC	YEAR
Mean Maximum Temp. (°F)	32.0	37.0	49.3	62.9	73.4	81.5	85.2	83.3	76.9	64.5	50.3	35.6	61.0
Mean Temp. (°F)	22.4	26.8	37.9	49.9	60.7	69.5	73.0	70.9	63.4	51.6	39.5	26.2	49.3
Mean Minimum Temp. (°F)	12.8	16.6	26.3	36.9	48.0	57.4	60.8	58.6	49.7	38.7	28.7	16.8	37.6
Extreme Maximum Temp. (°F)	66	72	87	93	95	101	104	105	99	92	82	70	105
Extreme Minimum Temp. (°F)	-26	-26	-8	5	22	35	44	36	26	12	0	-26	-26
Days Maximum Temp. ≥ 90°F	0	0	0	0	1	5	8	6	2	0	0	0	22
Days Maximum Temp. ≤ 32°F	15	10	3	0	0	0	0	0	0	0	2	11	41
Days Minimum Temp. ≤ 32°F	30	26	24	10	1	0	0	0	1	9	20	29	150
Days Minimum Temp. ≤ 0°F	6	4	0	0	0	0	0	0	0	0	0	4	14
Heating Degree Days (base 65°F)	1,314	1,072	836	457	179	34	5	17	124	419	759	1,194	6,410
Cooling Degree Days (base 65°F)	0	0	1	11	53	175	261	208	81	11	0	0	801
Mean Precipitation (in.)	2.08	1.85	2.92	3.55	4.46	3.71	3.86	3.87	3.39	2.77	3.01	2.35	37.82
Extreme Maximum Daily Precip. (in.)	5.00	1.84	3.02	1.71	4.60	3.74	4.45	3.15	3.50	3.95	2.81	3.10	5.00
Days With ≥ 0.1" Precipitation	4	4	6	8	8	7	6	7	5	6	6	5	72
Days With ≥ 0.5" Precipitation	1	1	2	3	3	3	3	3	2	2	2	2	27
Days With ≥ 1.0" Precipitation	1	0	1	1	1	1	1	1	1	0	1	0	9
Mean Snowfall (in.)	6.1	5.9	2.3	0.4	trace	0.0	0.0	0.0	0.0	trace	1.0	5.9	21.6
Maximum Snow Depth (in.)	14	11	5	12	trace	0	0	0	0	trace	3	15	15
Days With ≥ 1.0" Snow Depth	8	6	2	0	0	0	0	0	0	0	0	5	21

Rosiclare 5 NW *Hardin County*   Elevation: 399 ft.   Latitude: 37° 25' N   Longitude: 88° 21' W

	JAN	FEB	MAR	APR	MAY	JUN	JUL	AUG	SEP	OCT	NOV	DEC	YEAR
Mean Maximum Temp. (°F)	42.7	47.9	58.1	68.8	76.6	84.2	87.7	87.8	81.3	70.2	58.1	45.8	67.4
Mean Temp. (°F)	32.8	36.9	46.1	55.8	64.3	72.8	76.6	75.8	68.2	56.7	46.6	35.9	55.7
Mean Minimum Temp. (°F)	22.8	25.9	34.1	42.8	52.4	61.3	65.5	63.9	55.2	43.2	35.1	25.9	44.0
Extreme Maximum Temp. (°F)	70	77	85	90	92	100	102	104	100	90	84	76	104
Extreme Minimum Temp. (°F)	-22	-12	6	16	31	39	47	36	32	18	3	-17	-22
Days Maximum Temp. ≥ 90°F	0	0	0	0	0	6	13	13	4	0	0	0	36
Days Maximum Temp. ≤ 32°F	6	3	1	0	0	0	0	0	0	0	0	4	14
Days Minimum Temp. ≤ 32°F	25	21	15	5	0	0	0	0	0	5	13	23	107
Days Minimum Temp. ≤ 0°F	1	1	0	0	0	0	0	0	0	0	0	0	2
Heating Degree Days (base 65°F)	992	788	586	292	100	8	0	2	51	275	546	896	4,536
Cooling Degree Days (base 65°F)	0	0	6	24	87	247	367	344	155	24	2	0	1,256
Mean Precipitation (in.)	3.58	3.81	4.61	4.63	5.51	4.36	4.32	3.18	3.46	3.80	4.19	4.46	49.91
Extreme Maximum Daily Precip. (in.)	2.66	3.31	5.87	3.55	3.38	2.65	4.42	6.14	3.02	4.60	2.87	4.96	6.14
Days With ≥ 0.1" Precipitation	6	6	8	7	8	6	6	4	5	5	7	7	75
Days With ≥ 0.5" Precipitation	2	3	3	3	4	3	3	2	3	3	3	4	36
Days With ≥ 1.0" Precipitation	1	1	1	1	2	1	1	1	1	1	1	1	13
Mean Snowfall (in.)	2.4	2.2	0.5	trace	0.0	0.0	0.0	0.0	0.0	0.2	trace	1.2	6.5
Maximum Snow Depth (in.)	8	10	7	trace	0	0	0	0	0	1	trace	8	10
Days With ≥ 1.0" Snow Depth	4	4	0	0	0	0	0	0	0	0	0	2	10

Tuscola *Douglas County*   Elevation: 652 ft.   Latitude: 39° 48' N   Longitude: 88° 17' W

	JAN	FEB	MAR	APR	MAY	JUN	JUL	AUG	SEP	OCT	NOV	DEC	YEAR
Mean Maximum Temp. (°F)	35.5	39.8	51.7	65.1	75.6	84.5	87.3	85.6	80.1	67.2	52.6	39.7	63.7
Mean Temp. (°F)	27.2	30.9	41.6	53.4	64.2	73.2	76.2	74.3	67.6	55.4	43.2	31.8	53.3
Mean Minimum Temp. (°F)	19.0	22.0	31.4	41.8	52.6	61.9	65.1	62.9	55.1	43.5	33.9	23.9	42.7
Extreme Maximum Temp. (°F)	68	73	86	90	95	104	104	104	99	91	79	70	104
Extreme Minimum Temp. (°F)	-23	-18	0	15	30	39	49	43	31	20	1	-26	-26
Days Maximum Temp. ≥ 90°F	0	0	0	0	2	8	11	9	4	0	0	0	34
Days Maximum Temp. ≤ 32°F	12	8	2	0	0	0	0	0	0	0	1	7	30
Days Minimum Temp. ≤ 32°F	27	23	17	5	0	0	0	0	0	4	14	25	115
Days Minimum Temp. ≤ 0°F	3	2	0	0	0	0	0	0	0	0	0	1	6
Heating Degree Days (base 65°F)	1,165	956	721	357	111	13	0	4	59	314	647	1,021	5,368
Cooling Degree Days (base 65°F)	0	0	2	17	92	266	355	299	143	23	0	0	1,197
Mean Precipitation (in.)	2.22	2.20	2.75	4.01	4.14	4.08	4.47	3.37	3.15	3.35	3.83	2.88	40.45
Extreme Maximum Daily Precip. (in.)	1.68	2.30	2.02	2.40	3.75	3.72	3.89	4.07	3.72	2.60	3.02	3.00	4.07
Days With ≥ 0.1" Precipitation	5	5	6	8	8	7	6	5	5	6	7	6	74
Days With ≥ 0.5" Precipitation	2	1	2	3	3	3	3	2	2	2	3	2	28
Days With ≥ 1.0" Precipitation	0	0	0	1	1	1	1	1	1	1	1	1	9
Mean Snowfall (in.)	6.3	5.1	2.2	0.2	trace	0.0	0.0	0.0	0.0	trace	1.0	4.7	19.5
Maximum Snow Depth (in.)	15	19	7	2	trace	0	0	0	0	trace	8	10	19
Days With ≥ 1.0" Snow Depth	9	8	2	0	0	0	0	0	0	0	0	5	24

Urbana *Champaign County*   Elevation: 743 ft.   Latitude: 40° 06' N   Longitude: 88° 14' W

	JAN	FEB	MAR	APR	MAY	JUN	JUL	AUG	SEP	OCT	NOV	DEC	YEAR
Mean Maximum Temp. (°F)	33.7	38.1	50.1	62.9	73.7	82.6	85.2	83.8	78.2	65.2	50.7	37.1	61.8
Mean Temp. (°F)	25.9	30.0	40.6	52.0	62.7	71.9	75.0	73.5	66.4	54.2	41.9	29.7	52.0
Mean Minimum Temp. (°F)	18.2	21.8	31.0	41.0	51.7	61.2	64.8	63.0	54.5	43.0	33.1	22.3	42.1
Extreme Maximum Temp. (°F)	67	72	84	91	94	103	101	102	97	92	79	71	103
Extreme Minimum Temp. (°F)	-25	-17	1	16	29	41	48	40	30	19	7	-20	-25
Days Maximum Temp. ≥ 90°F	0	0	0	0	1	6	7	6	2	0	0	0	22
Days Maximum Temp. ≤ 32°F	14	9	2	0	0	0	0	0	0	0	1	10	36
Days Minimum Temp. ≤ 32°F	28	24	18	5	0	0	0	0	0	4	15	26	120
Days Minimum Temp. ≤ 0°F	3	2	0	0	0	0	0	0	0	0	0	2	7
Heating Degree Days (base 65°F)	1,204	983	752	397	136	17	1	4	74	346	685	1,086	5,685
Cooling Degree Days (base 65°F)	0	0	1	10	72	231	319	274	123	17	0	0	1,049
Mean Precipitation (in.)	2.01	2.13	2.90	3.69	4.90	4.15	4.62	3.96	3.22	3.11	3.58	2.69	40.96
Extreme Maximum Daily Precip. (in.)	1.45	2.30	2.92	2.96	2.98	3.89	4.43	5.32	3.30	3.72	3.53	2.41	5.32
Days With ≥ 0.1" Precipitation	5	4	6	8	8	6	7	6	5	6	7	6	74
Days With ≥ 0.5" Precipitation	1	1	2	2	3	3	3	3	2	2	2	2	26
Days With ≥ 1.0" Precipitation	0	0	1	1	1	1	1	1	1	1	1	0	9
Mean Snowfall (in.)	6.8	5.9	2.5	0.5	trace	0.0	0.0	0.0	0.0	0.1	1.2	5.8	22.8
Maximum Snow Depth (in.)	17	19	10	3	trace	0	0	0	0	trace	8	13	19
Days With ≥ 1.0" Snow Depth	12	8	2	0	0	0	0	0	0	0	1	7	30

The period of record for all cooperative weather station data is 1980 – 2009. See User Guide for detailed explanation of data.

Virden *Macoupin County*   Elevation: 674 ft.   Latitude: 39° 30' N   Longitude: 89° 46' W

	JAN	FEB	MAR	APR	MAY	JUN	JUL	AUG	SEP	OCT	NOV	DEC	YEAR
Mean Maximum Temp. (°F)	36.6	40.9	52.6	66.1	75.7	83.7	87.2	86.0	79.8	67.5	53.0	39.6	64.1
Mean Temp. (°F)	28.8	33.0	43.0	55.2	65.1	73.6	77.1	75.4	68.3	56.8	44.3	32.0	54.4
Mean Minimum Temp. (°F)	20.9	24.6	33.3	44.3	54.4	63.4	66.9	64.7	56.7	46.0	35.7	24.3	44.6
Extreme Maximum Temp. (°F)	70	72	85	90	93	100	102	105	99	91	81	72	105
Extreme Minimum Temp. (°F)	-19	-19	0	19	33	43	50	39	31	20	-1	-20	-20
Days Maximum Temp. ≥ 90°F	0	0	0	0	1	6	10	9	3	0	0	0	29
Days Maximum Temp. ≤ 32°F	11	7	1	0	0	0	0	0	0	0	1	8	28
Days Minimum Temp. ≤ 32°F	26	21	14	3	0	0	0	0	0	3	12	24	103
Days Minimum Temp. ≤ 0°F	2	1	0	0	0	0	0	0	0	0	0	1	4
Heating Degree Days (base 65°F)	1,117	899	679	313	92	9	0	2	55	277	614	1,017	5,074
Cooling Degree Days (base 65°F)	0	0	2	26	102	272	381	329	161	29	1	0	1,303
Mean Precipitation (in.)	1.85	2.11	2.77	3.52	4.16	3.84	3.51	2.74	2.94	3.11	3.45	2.53	36.53
Extreme Maximum Daily Precip. (in.)	2.24	1.72	1.92	3.98	3.77	4.30	4.30	2.27	4.38	3.05	2.63	4.25	4.38
Days With ≥ 0.1" Precipitation	4	4	6	6	7	6	5	5	5	6	6	4	64
Days With ≥ 0.5" Precipitation	1	1	2	2	3	2	2	2	2	2	2	2	23
Days With ≥ 1.0" Precipitation	0	0	0	1	1	1	1	1	1	1	1	1	9
Mean Snowfall (in.)	5.1	5.6	3.0	0.4	0.0	0.0	0.0	0.0	0.0	trace	0.8	4.6	19.5
Maximum Snow Depth (in.)	12	8	8	4	0	0	0	0	0	trace	4	12	12
Days With ≥ 1.0" Snow Depth	9	6	2	0	0	0	0	0	0	0	0	5	22

Wheaton 3 SE *Dupage County*   Elevation: 680 ft.   Latitude: 41° 49' N   Longitude: 88° 04' W

	JAN	FEB	MAR	APR	MAY	JUN	JUL	AUG	SEP	OCT	NOV	DEC	YEAR
Mean Maximum Temp. (°F)	33.6	38.4	49.8	63.2	74.1	83.4	86.8	85.0	78.0	*65.7*	50.6	37.3	*62.2*
Mean Temp. (°F)	25.2	29.1	39.0	50.8	61.0	70.5	75.1	73.6	65.8	*53.7*	41.5	29.3	*51.2*
Mean Minimum Temp. (°F)	16.9	19.7	28.1	38.4	47.9	57.5	63.4	62.1	53.4	*41.7*	32.4	21.3	*40.2*
Extreme Maximum Temp. (°F)	65	74	85	90	94	103	105	100	96	*89*	77	70	*105*
Extreme Minimum Temp. (°F)	-26	-20	-7	4	26	34	44	42	28	*14*	5	-21	*-26*
Days Maximum Temp. ≥ 90°F	0	0	0	0	1	7	10	7	2	*0*	0	0	*27*
Days Maximum Temp. ≤ 32°F	14	8	2	0	0	0	0	0	0	*0*	1	9	*34*
Days Minimum Temp. ≤ 32°F	28	24	21	8	1	0	0	0	0	*6*	16	25	*129*
Days Minimum Temp. ≤ 0°F	4	3	0	0	0	0	0	0	0	*0*	0	2	*9*
Heating Degree Days (base 65°F)	1,226	1,010	801	433	178	29	2	5	85	*357*	697	1,098	*5,921*
Cooling Degree Days (base 65°F)	0	0	1	13	61	200	324	278	114	*15*	0	0	*1,006*
Mean Precipitation (in.)	1.88	1.66	2.37	3.52	4.00	3.98	4.10	4.44	3.36	*3.13*	3.49	2.13	*38.06*
Extreme Maximum Daily Precip. (in.)	1.75	2.85	2.58	2.00	3.79	3.22	9.24	6.01	3.35	*4.43*	2.98	3.04	*9.24*
Days With ≥ 0.1" Precipitation	5	4	6	7	7	7	6	6	6	*5*	6	5	*70*
Days With ≥ 0.5" Precipitation	1	1	1	2	3	3	3	3	2	*2*	2	1	*24*
Days With ≥ 1.0" Precipitation	0	0	0	1	1	1	1	1	1	*1*	1	0	*8*
Mean Snowfall (in.)	9.4	6.9	4.2	0.7	trace	0.0	0.0	0.0	0.0	*trace*	1.0	5.7	*27.9*
Maximum Snow Depth (in.)	*16*	*16*	*10*	*3*	*trace*	*0*	*0*	*0*	*0*	na	*4*	*21*	*na*
Days With ≥ 1.0" Snow Depth	*14*	*10*	3	0	0	0	0	0	0	*0*	1	7	*35*

The period of record for all cooperative weather station data is 1980 – 2009. See User Guide for detailed explanation of data.

Illinois Weather Station Rankings

Annual Extreme Maximum Temperature

Highest			Lowest		
Rank	Station Name	°F	Rank	Station Name	°F
1	Kaskaskia River Nav Lock	109	1	Elgin	101
2	Kankakee Metro Wastwater	107	1	Paw Paw 2 NW	101
3	Alton Melvin Price L&D	106	3	Charleston	102
3	Cahokia	106	3	Danville	102
3	Chicago Midway Arpt	106	3	Fulton L&D #13	102
3	Decatur	106	3	Galesburg	102
3	Havana 4 NNE	106	3	Springfield Capital Arpt	102
8	Albion	105	8	Aledo	103
8	Belleville Siu Research	105	8	Aurora	103
8	Brookport Dam 52	105	8	Chenoa	103
8	Carbondale Sewage Plant	105	8	De Kalb	103
8	Carlinville	105	8	Dixon 1 NW	103
8	Chicago Botanical Garden	105	8	Effingham	103
8	La Harpe	105	8	Golden	103
8	Marengo	105	8	Lacon 1 N	103
8	Peoria Greater Peoria Arpt	105	8	Normal	103
8	Princeville	105	8	Park Forest	103
8	Virden	105	8	Urbana	103
8	Wheaton 3 SE	105	19	Anna 2 NNE	104
20	Anna 2 NNE	104	19	Antioch	104
20	Antioch	104	19	Chicago Ohare Intl Arpt	104
20	Chicago Ohare Intl Arpt	104	19	Jerseyville 2 SW	104
20	Jerseyville 2 SW	104	19	Joliet Brandon Rd Dam	104
20	Joliet Brandon Rd Dam	104	19	Lincoln	104
20	Lincoln	104	19	Moline Quad City Arpt	104

Annual Mean Maximum Temperature

Highest			Lowest		
Rank	Station Name	°F	Rank	Station Name	°F
1	Kaskaskia River Nav Lock	68.1	1	Antioch	57.3
2	Brookport Dam 52	68.0	1	Paw Paw 2 NW	57.3
3	Anna 2 NNE	67.9	3	Elgin	58.1
4	Belleville Siu Research	67.7	4	Fulton L&D #13	58.2
5	Rosiclare 5 NW	67.4	5	Chicago Botanical Garden	58.3
6	Carbondale Sewage Plant	66.8	5	De Kalb	58.3
7	Cahokia	66.6	7	Dixon 1 NW	58.4
8	Albion	66.5	7	Rockford Greater Rockford Arpt	58.4
9	Alton Melvin Price L&D	64.4	9	Marengo	58.6
10	Decatur	64.2	10	Chicago Ohare Intl Arpt	58.9
11	Carlinville	64.1	11	Park Forest	59.0
11	Virden	64.1	12	Aurora	59.8
13	Jerseyville 2 SW	64.0	12	Joliet Brandon Rd Dam	59.8
14	Charleston	63.8	14	Chicago Midway Arpt	59.9
15	Effingham	63.7	15	Aledo	60.0
15	Tuscola	63.7	16	Galesburg	60.1
17	Danville	63.0	17	Moline Quad City Arpt	60.7
17	Springfield Capital Arpt	63.0	18	Kankakee Metro Wastwater	61.0
19	Havana 4 NNE	62.9	18	Princeville	61.0
20	Lacon 1 N	62.7	20	Peoria Greater Peoria Arpt	61.3
21	Lincoln	62.6	21	Chenoa	61.8
22	Wheaton 3 SE	62.2	21	Urbana	61.8
23	Golden	62.1	23	Normal	62.0
23	La Harpe	62.1	24	Golden	62.1
25	Normal	62.0	24	La Harpe	62.1

Rankings include 25 highest/lowest stations. If state has less than 25 stations, all stations are included. The period of record is 1980–2009. See User Guide for detailed explanation of data.

Annual Mean Temperature

	Highest			Lowest	
Rank	Station Name	°F	Rank	Station Name	°F
1	Brookport Dam 52	57.8	1	Paw Paw 2 NW	47.4
2	Anna 2 NNE	57.0	2	Antioch	47.8
3	Belleville Siu Research	56.7	2	Marengo	47.8
4	Albion	56.5	4	Dixon 1 NW	48.3
5	Kaskaskia River Nav Lock	56.4	5	Elgin	48.4
6	Cahokia	56.1	6	De Kalb	48.6
7	Carbondale Sewage Plant	55.7	6	Rockford Greater Rockford Arpt	48.6
7	Rosiclare 5 NW	55.7	8	Fulton L&D #13	49.0
9	Alton Melvin Price L&D	55.3	9	Chicago Botanical Garden	49.2
10	Virden	54.4	10	Princeville	49.3
11	Carlinville	54.1	11	Aurora	49.6
12	Charleston	54.0	12	Chicago Ohare Intl Arpt	49.7
13	Decatur	53.7	13	Park Forest	49.8
14	Effingham	53.4	14	Aledo	50.0
14	Jerseyville 2 SW	53.4	15	Joliet Brandon Rd Dam	50.2
16	Tuscola	53.3	16	Kankakee Metro Wastwater	50.4
17	Springfield Capital Arpt	53.1	17	Moline Quad City Arpt	50.6
18	Danville	52.8	18	Galesburg	50.8
19	Lacon 1 N	52.3	19	La Harpe	50.9
20	Lincoln	52.0	20	Wheaton 3 SE	51.2
20	Urbana	52.0	21	Chicago Midway Arpt	51.5
22	Golden	51.9	22	Chenoa	51.6
23	Havana 4 NNE	51.8	23	Normal	51.7
24	Normal	51.7	23	Peoria Greater Peoria Arpt	51.7
24	Peoria Greater Peoria Arpt	51.7	25	Havana 4 NNE	51.8

Annual Mean Minimum Temperature

	Highest			Lowest	
Rank	Station Name	°F	Rank	Station Name	°F
1	Brookport Dam 52	47.5	1	Marengo	37.0
2	Albion	46.5	2	Paw Paw 2 NW	37.5
3	Alton Melvin Price L&D	46.3	3	Princeville	37.6
4	Anna 2 NNE	46.1	4	Dixon 1 NW	38.2
5	Belleville Siu Research	45.7	5	Antioch	38.4
6	Cahokia	45.5	6	Elgin	38.5
7	Kaskaskia River Nav Lock	44.6	7	Rockford Greater Rockford Arpt	38.6
7	Virden	44.6	8	De Kalb	38.9
9	Carbondale Sewage Plant	44.5	9	Aurora	39.3
10	Charleston	44.2	10	La Harpe	39.6
11	Carlinville	44.1	11	Fulton L&D #13	39.7
12	Rosiclare 5 NW	44.0	11	Kankakee Metro Wastwater	39.7
13	Decatur	43.2	13	Aledo	39.8
14	Chicago Midway Arpt	43.1	14	Chicago Botanical Garden	40.0
14	Springfield Capital Arpt	43.1	15	Wheaton 3 SE	40.2
16	Effingham	43.0	16	Chicago Ohare Intl Arpt	40.4
17	Jerseyville 2 SW	42.8	17	Joliet Brandon Rd Dam	40.5
18	Tuscola	42.7	17	Moline Quad City Arpt	40.5
19	Danville	42.6	19	Park Forest	40.6
20	Urbana	42.1	20	Havana 4 NNE	40.7
21	Peoria Greater Peoria Arpt	42.0	21	Lincoln	41.2
22	Lacon 1 N	41.9	22	Chenoa	41.3
23	Golden	41.7	22	Normal	41.3
24	Galesburg	41.5	24	Galesburg	41.5
25	Chenoa	41.3	25	Golden	41.7

Rankings include 25 highest/lowest stations. If state has less than 25 stations, all stations are included. The period of record is 1980–2009. See User Guide for detailed explanation of data.

Annual Extreme Minimum Temperature

Highest			Lowest		
Rank	Station Name	°F	Rank	Station Name	°F
1	Alton Melvin Price L&D	*-16*	1	Fulton L&D #13	-33
2	Anna 2 NNE	-17	1	Paw Paw 2 NW	-33
3	Kaskaskia River Nav Lock	*-18*	3	Dixon 1 NW	-32
4	Cahokia	*-19*	4	Havana 4 NNE	-30
4	Carlinville	*-19*	5	Kankakee Metro Wastwater	-29
6	Albion	*-20*	5	Moline Quad City Arpt	-29
6	Virden	-20	7	Aledo	-28
8	Belleville Siu Research	-21	7	Antioch	*-28*
8	Brookport Dam 52	-21	7	Marengo	*-28*
8	Carbondale Sewage Plant	-21	10	Charleston	-27
8	Springfield Capital Arpt	-21	10	Chicago Botanical Garden	-27
12	Decatur	-22	10	Chicago Ohare Intl Arpt	-27
12	Effingham	*-22*	10	De Kalb	-27
12	Jerseyville 2 SW	-22	10	Elgin	-27
12	Rosiclare 5 NW	-22	10	Galesburg	-27
16	Golden	*-23*	10	Lacon 1 N	-27
16	La Harpe	-23	10	Park Forest	-27
16	Normal	-23	10	Rockford Greater Rockford Arpt	-27
16	Peoria Greater Peoria Arpt	-23	19	Aurora	-26
20	Chicago Midway Arpt	-25	19	Chenoa	-26
20	Lincoln	-25	19	Danville	-26
20	Urbana	-25	19	Joliet Brandon Rd Dam	-26
23	Aurora	-26	19	Princeville	-26
23	Chenoa	-26	19	Tuscola	-26
23	Danville	-26	19	Wheaton 3 SE	*-26*

July Mean Maximum Temperature

Highest			Lowest		
Rank	Station Name	°F	Rank	Station Name	°F
1	Kaskaskia River Nav Lock	91.4	1	Antioch	*82.1*
2	Albion	*89.9*	2	Paw Paw 2 NW	82.2
3	Belleville Siu Research	89.5	3	Chicago Botanical Garden	82.5
4	Brookport Dam 52	89.3	4	Dixon 1 NW	82.9
5	Anna 2 NNE	88.7	5	Elgin	83.3
5	Cahokia	88.7	6	Fulton L&D #13	83.5
7	Carbondale Sewage Plant	88.4	7	De Kalb	83.6
8	Havana 4 NNE	88.2	8	Park Forest	83.7
9	Rosiclare 5 NW	87.7	9	Rockford Greater Rockford Arpt	83.9
10	Alton Melvin Price L&D	87.6	10	Chicago Ohare Intl Arpt	84.1
10	Decatur	87.6	11	Marengo	84.2
12	Jerseyville 2 SW	87.5	12	Joliet Brandon Rd Dam	84.3
13	Tuscola	87.3	13	Aledo	84.7
14	Effingham	87.2	13	Aurora	84.7
14	Virden	87.2	13	Galesburg	84.7
16	Lacon 1 N	87.1	16	Chicago Midway Arpt	84.8
17	Carlinville	86.9	17	Chenoa	85.2
18	Wheaton 3 SE	86.8	17	Princeville	85.2
19	La Harpe	86.7	19	Kankakee Metro Wastwater	85.3
20	Golden	*86.6*	19	Urbana	85.3
21	Charleston	86.5	21	Danville	85.7
22	Springfield Capital Arpt	86.3	21	Peoria Greater Peoria Arpt	85.7
23	Lincoln	86.2	23	Moline Quad City Arpt	85.9
24	Moline Quad City Arpt	85.9	23	Normal	85.9
24	Normal	85.9	25	Lincoln	86.2

Rankings include 25 highest/lowest stations. If state has less than 25 stations, all stations are included. The period of record is 1980–2009. See User Guide for detailed explanation of data.

January Mean Minimum Temperature

	Highest				Lowest	
Rank	Station Name	°F		Rank	Station Name	°F
1	Brookport Dam 52	26.3		1	Dixon 1 NW	11.6
2	Anna 2 NNE	24.8		2	Marengo	*11.8*
3	Albion	23.9		3	Paw Paw 2 NW	12.2
3	Belleville Siu Research	23.9		4	De Kalb	12.8
5	Carbondale Sewage Plant	23.2		4	Princeville	12.8
6	Rosiclare 5 NW	22.8		6	Fulton L&D #13	13.0
7	Cahokia	22.6		6	Rockford Greater Rockford Arpt	13.0
8	Kaskaskia River Nav Lock	22.5		8	Elgin	13.4
9	Alton Melvin Price L&D	21.9		9	Antioch	13.5
10	Virden	20.9		10	Aurora	14.2
11	Charleston	20.7		11	Aledo	14.5
12	Carlinville	*20.6*		12	La Harpe	14.6
13	Effingham	19.9		13	Moline Quad City Arpt	14.8
14	Jerseyville 2 SW	19.4		14	Kankakee Metro Wastwater	15.1
15	Danville	19.3		15	Galesburg	15.7
16	Decatur	19.2		15	Park Forest	15.7
16	Springfield Capital Arpt	19.2		17	Joliet Brandon Rd Dam	15.8
18	Tuscola	19.0		18	Chicago Botanical Garden	16.2
19	Chicago Midway Arpt	18.4		18	Havana 4 NNE	16.2
20	Lacon 1 N	18.2		20	Chicago Ohare Intl Arpt	16.3
20	Urbana	18.2		21	Chenoa	16.6
22	Golden	*17.4*		22	Normal	16.9
23	Lincoln	17.1		22	Wheaton 3 SE	16.9
23	Peoria Greater Peoria Arpt	17.1		24	Lincoln	17.1
25	Normal	16.9		24	Peoria Greater Peoria Arpt	17.1

Number of Days Annually Maximum Temperature ≥ 90°F

	Highest				Lowest	
Rank	Station Name	Days		Rank	Station Name	Days
1	Kaskaskia River Nav Lock	**62**		1	Antioch	*10*
2	Albion	**47**		1	Paw Paw 2 NW	10
2	Belleville Siu Research	47		3	Dixon 1 NW	12
4	Brookport Dam 52	44		4	De Kalb	14
5	Anna 2 NNE	41		4	Elgin	14
6	Cahokia	**40**		4	Fulton L&D #13	14
7	Carbondale Sewage Plant	39		7	Rockford Greater Rockford Arpt	15
8	Rosiclare 5 NW	36		8	Aledo	16
9	Havana 4 NNE	34		8	Chicago Botanical Garden	16
9	Tuscola	34		8	Chicago Ohare Intl Arpt	16
11	Effingham	32		8	Park Forest	16
12	Alton Melvin Price L&D	31		12	Joliet Brandon Rd Dam	17
12	Decatur	31		13	Galesburg	18
14	Jerseyville 2 SW	30		13	Marengo	*18*
15	Carlinville	**29**		15	Aurora	19
15	La Harpe	29		16	Danville	20
15	Lacon 1 N	29		17	Chenoa	21
15	Virden	29		17	Chicago Midway Arpt	21
19	Golden	**28**		19	Kankakee Metro Wastwater	22
20	Charleston	27		19	Princeville	22
20	Springfield Capital Arpt	27		19	Urbana	22
20	Wheaton 3 SE	**27**		22	Moline Quad City Arpt	23
23	Lincoln	26		22	Peoria Greater Peoria Arpt	23
24	Normal	25		24	Normal	25
25	Moline Quad City Arpt	23		25	Lincoln	26

Rankings include 25 highest/lowest stations. If state has less than 25 stations, all stations are included. The period of record is 1980–2009. See User Guide for detailed explanation of data.

Number of Days Annually Maximum Temperature ≤ 32°F

	Highest			Lowest	
Rank	Station Name	Days	Rank	Station Name	Days
1	Paw Paw 2 NW	58	1	Anna 2 NNE	12
2	De Kalb	55	1	Brookport Dam 52	12
3	Rockford Greater Rockford Arpt	53	3	Rosiclare 5 NW	14
4	Antioch	*52*	4	Carbondale Sewage Plant	16
5	Elgin	51	5	Belleville Siu Research	17
6	Dixon 1 NW	50	5	Cahokia	*17*
6	Fulton L&D #13	50	5	Kaskaskia River Nav Lock	*17*
8	Marengo	*49*	8	Albion	*19*
9	Aledo	45	9	Alton Melvin Price L&D	24
9	Chicago Ohare Intl Arpt	45	10	Carlinville	*27*
9	Galesburg	45	10	Charleston	27
9	Park Forest	45	10	Decatur	27
13	Joliet Brandon Rd Dam	44	13	Jerseyville 2 SW	28
14	Moline Quad City Arpt	43	13	Virden	28
15	Aurora	42	15	Effingham	29
15	Chicago Botanical Garden	42	16	Tuscola	30
17	Chicago Midway Arpt	41	17	Danville	33
17	Princeville	41	17	Lincoln	33
19	Peoria Greater Peoria Arpt	39	17	Springfield Capital Arpt	33
20	Golden	*38*	20	Wheaton 3 SE	*34*
20	Kankakee Metro Wastwater	38	21	Lacon 1 N	35
20	Normal	38	22	Chenoa	36
23	La Harpe	37	22	Havana 4 NNE	36
24	Chenoa	36	22	Urbana	36
24	Havana 4 NNE	36	25	La Harpe	37

Number of Days Annually Minimum Temperature ≤ 32°F

	Highest			Lowest	
Rank	Station Name	Days	Rank	Station Name	Days
1	Marengo	*150*	1	Brookport Dam 52	83
1	Princeville	150	2	Albion	*87*
3	Paw Paw 2 NW	149	3	Alton Melvin Price L&D	93
4	Dixon 1 NW	144	3	Anna 2 NNE	93
5	Rockford Greater Rockford Arpt	142	5	Belleville Siu Research	97
6	De Kalb	141	6	Cahokia	*102*
6	Elgin	141	7	Virden	103
8	Antioch	*139*	8	Charleston	104
9	La Harpe	138	9	Carbondale Sewage Plant	105
10	Aurora	136	10	Kaskaskia River Nav Lock	*106*
11	Fulton L&D #13	134	11	Carlinville	*107*
12	Aledo	133	11	Rosiclare 5 NW	107
13	Havana 4 NNE	132	13	Chicago Midway Arpt	112
13	Kankakee Metro Wastwater	132	13	Decatur	112
15	Moline Quad City Arpt	130	13	Springfield Capital Arpt	112
16	Joliet Brandon Rd Dam	129	16	Effingham	113
16	Wheaton 3 SE	*129*	17	Danville	114
18	Galesburg	128	18	Tuscola	115
19	Chicago Botanical Garden	127	19	Jerseyville 2 SW	117
19	Chicago Ohare Intl Arpt	127	20	Peoria Greater Peoria Arpt	120
19	Normal	127	20	Urbana	120
19	Park Forest	127	22	Lacon 1 N	121
23	Chenoa	126	23	Golden	*125*
24	Golden	*125*	23	Lincoln	125
24	Lincoln	125	25	Chenoa	126

Number of Days Annually Minimum Temperature ≤ 0°F

	Highest			Lowest	
Rank	Station Name	Days	Rank	Station Name	Days
1	Marengo	**17**	1	Brookport Dam 52	1
2	Dixon 1 NW	16	2	Albion	**2**
3	Antioch	**15**	2	Anna 2 NNE	2
3	Paw Paw 2 NW	15	2	Cahokia	**2**
5	Fulton L&D #13	14	2	Rosiclare 5 NW	2
5	Princeville	14	6	Alton Melvin Price L&D	3
5	Rockford Greater Rockford Arpt	14	6	Belleville Siu Research	3
8	De Kalb	13	6	Carbondale Sewage Plant	3
9	Elgin	12	6	Kaskaskia River Nav Lock	**3**
10	Aledo	11	10	Carlinville	**4**
10	Aurora	11	10	Charleston	4
10	Kankakee Metro Wastwater	11	10	Virden	4
10	La Harpe	11	13	Chicago Midway Arpt	5
10	Moline Quad City Arpt	11	14	Decatur	6
15	Galesburg	10	14	Effingham	6
15	Havana 4 NNE	10	14	Jerseyville 2 SW	6
17	Golden	**9**	14	Tuscola	6
17	Wheaton 3 SE	**9**	18	Danville	7
19	Chenoa	8	18	Lacon 1 N	7
19	Chicago Botanical Garden	8	18	Lincoln	7
19	Chicago Ohare Intl Arpt	8	18	Springfield Capital Arpt	7
19	Joliet Brandon Rd Dam	8	18	Urbana	7
19	Normal	8	23	Chenoa	8
19	Park Forest	8	23	Chicago Botanical Garden	8
19	Peoria Greater Peoria Arpt	8	23	Chicago Ohare Intl Arpt	8

Number of Annual Heating Degree Days

	Highest			Lowest	
Rank	Station Name	Num.	Rank	Station Name	Num.
1	Paw Paw 2 NW	6,971	1	Brookport Dam 52	4,087
2	Marengo	**6,927**	2	Anna 2 NNE	4,247
3	Antioch	**6,843**	3	Belleville Siu Research	4,397
4	Dixon 1 NW	6,735	4	Rosiclare 5 NW	4,536
5	Elgin	**6,731**	5	Albion	**4,563**
6	De Kalb	6,685	6	Kaskaskia River Nav Lock	**4,583**
7	Rockford Greater Rockford Arpt	6,682	7	Cahokia	**4,607**
8	Fulton L&D #13	6,582	8	Carbondale Sewage Plant	4,644
9	Chicago Botanical Garden	6,451	9	Alton Melvin Price L&D	**4,857**
10	Princeville	6,410	10	Virden	5,074
11	Aurora	6,370	11	Carlinville	**5,100**
12	Chicago Ohare Intl Arpt	6,335	12	Charleston	5,122
13	Park Forest	6,320	13	Decatur	5,235
14	Aledo	6,272	14	Jerseyville 2 SW	5,309
15	Joliet Brandon Rd Dam	6,191	15	Effingham	5,331
16	Moline Quad City Arpt	6,160	16	Tuscola	5,368
17	Kankakee Metro Wastwater	6,144	17	Danville	5,414
18	Galesburg	6,085	18	Springfield Capital Arpt	5,417
19	La Harpe	6,033	19	Lacon 1 N	5,626
20	Wheaton 3 SE	**5,921**	20	Urbana	5,685
21	Chicago Midway Arpt	5,892	21	Lincoln	5,706
22	Normal	5,831	22	Golden	**5,775**
23	Havana 4 NNE	5,824	23	Chenoa	5,802
24	Peoria Greater Peoria Arpt	5,808	24	Peoria Greater Peoria Arpt	5,808
25	Chenoa	5,802	25	Havana 4 NNE	5,824

Rankings include 25 highest/lowest stations. If state has less than 25 stations, all stations are included. The period of record is 1980–2009. See User Guide for detailed explanation of data.

Number of Annual Cooling Degree Days

	Highest			Lowest	
Rank	Station Name	Num.	Rank	Station Name	Num.
1	Albion	1,572	1	Paw Paw 2 NW	666
2	Brookport Dam 52	1,555	2	Antioch	695
2	Kaskaskia River Nav Lock	1,555	3	Marengo	755
4	Belleville Siu Research	1,465	4	Dixon 1 NW	761
5	Cahokia	1,460	5	Elgin	773
6	Anna 2 NNE	1,438	6	Chicago Botanical Garden	781
7	Alton Melvin Price L&D	1,437	7	Rockford Greater Rockford Arpt	795
8	Carbondale Sewage Plant	1,347	8	Princeville	801
9	Virden	1,303	9	De Kalb	819
10	Rosiclare 5 NW	1,256	10	Fulton L&D #13	847
11	Carlinville	1,239	11	Chicago Ohare Intl Arpt	853
12	Decatur	1,225	12	Aurora	860
13	Charleston	1,220	13	Aledo	894
14	Tuscola	1,197	13	Park Forest	894
15	Effingham	1,193	15	Joliet Brandon Rd Dam	895
16	Jerseyville 2 SW	1,184	16	Kankakee Metro Wastwater	927
17	Springfield Capital Arpt	1,177	17	La Harpe	990
18	Havana 4 NNE	1,128	18	Wheaton 3 SE	1,006
19	Golden	1,120	19	Moline Quad City Arpt	1,008
20	Lacon 1 N	1,115	20	Chenoa	1,014
21	Normal	1,086	21	Galesburg	1,020
22	Danville	1,074	22	Urbana	1,049
23	Chicago Midway Arpt	1,071	23	Lincoln	1,055
24	Peoria Greater Peoria Arpt	1,064	24	Peoria Greater Peoria Arpt	1,064
25	Lincoln	1,055	25	Chicago Midway Arpt	1,071

Annual Precipitation

	Highest			Lowest	
Rank	Station Name	Inches	Rank	Station Name	Inches
1	Rosiclare 5 NW	49.91	1	Fulton L&D #13	33.05
2	Anna 2 NNE	49.90	2	Marengo	34.67
3	Brookport Dam 52	48.44	3	Chenoa	34.79
4	Carbondale Sewage Plant	47.10	4	Antioch	35.77
5	Albion	43.32	5	Paw Paw 2 NW	36.02
6	Effingham	42.93	6	Rockford Greater Rockford Arpt	36.10
7	Cahokia	42.01	7	Peoria Greater Peoria Arpt	36.17
8	Charleston	41.85	8	Joliet Brandon Rd Dam	36.47
9	Danville	41.64	9	Virden	36.53
10	Kaskaskia River Nav Lock	41.29	10	Springfield Capital Arpt	36.74
11	Urbana	40.96	11	Chicago Ohare Intl Arpt	36.90
12	Belleville Siu Research	40.92	12	Aledo	36.92
13	Alton Melvin Price L&D	40.87	13	De Kalb	37.15
14	Tuscola	40.45	14	Elgin	37.23
15	Jerseyville 2 SW	39.98	15	Moline Quad City Arpt	37.68
16	Park Forest	39.96	16	Chicago Botanical Garden	37.72
17	La Harpe	39.36	17	Galesburg	37.78
18	Decatur	39.29	18	Princeville	37.82
19	Havana 4 NNE	39.14	19	Aurora	37.90
20	Lincoln	38.92	20	Dixon 1 NW	37.92
21	Chicago Midway Arpt	38.87	21	Wheaton 3 SE	38.06
22	Normal	38.80	22	Lacon 1 N	38.16
23	Carlinville	38.49	23	Golden	38.33
24	Kankakee Metro Wastwater	38.48	24	Kankakee Metro Wastwater	38.48
25	Golden	38.33	25	Carlinville	38.49

Rankings include 25 highest/lowest stations. If state has less than 25 stations, all stations are included. The period of record is 1980–2009. See User Guide for detailed explanation of data.

Annual Extreme Maximum Daily Precipitation

Highest			Lowest		
Rank	Station Name	Inches	Rank	Station Name	Inches
1	Aurora	16.91	1	Carlinville	*3.75*
2	Joliet Brandon Rd Dam	13.60	2	Danville	3.92
3	Wheaton 3 SE	*9.24*	3	Kaskaskia River Nav Lock	*4.00*
4	Marengo	*8.20*	4	Tuscola	4.07
5	De Kalb	*8.09*	5	Moline Quad City Arpt	4.26
6	Anna 2 NNE	7.74	6	Havana 4 NNE	4.35
7	Alton Melvin Price L&D	*7.70*	7	Kankakee Metro Wastwater	4.36
8	Paw Paw 2 NW	6.92	8	Cahokia	*4.37*
9	Carbondale Sewage Plant	6.90	9	Virden	4.38
10	Chicago Ohare Intl Arpt	6.64	10	Peoria Greater Peoria Arpt	4.42
11	Park Forest	6.55	11	Belleville Siu Research	4.58
12	Aledo	6.27	12	Fulton L&D #13	4.71
13	Rosiclare 5 NW	6.14	12	Springfield Capital Arpt	4.71
14	Galesburg	6.13	14	Lacon 1 N	4.88
15	Decatur	5.84	15	Elgin	*4.93*
16	Chicago Midway Arpt	5.72	16	Charleston	4.95
17	Effingham	5.70	16	Dixon 1 NW	4.95
17	Rockford Greater Rockford Arpt	5.70	18	Golden	5.00
19	Chenoa	5.66	18	Princeville	5.00
20	Normal	5.63	20	La Harpe	5.08
21	Chicago Botanical Garden	5.54	21	Jerseyville 2 SW	5.12
22	Brookport Dam 52	5.32	22	Lincoln	5.18
22	Urbana	5.32	23	Brookport Dam 52	5.32
24	Lincoln	5.18	23	Urbana	5.32
25	Jerseyville 2 SW	5.12	25	Chicago Botanical Garden	5.54

Number of Days Annually With ≥ 0.1 Inches of Precipitation

Highest			Lowest		
Rank	Station Name	Days	Rank	Station Name	Days
1	Anna 2 NNE	78	1	Albion	*60*
1	Danville	78	2	Fulton L&D #13	63
3	Effingham	77	3	Virden	64
4	Cahokia	*76*	4	Chenoa	65
5	Brookport Dam 52	75	5	Antioch	*66*
5	Rosiclare 5 NW	75	5	Marengo	*66*
7	Carbondale Sewage Plant	74	5	Rockford Greater Rockford Arpt	66
7	Charleston	74	8	Paw Paw 2 NW	67
7	Normal	74	8	Springfield Capital Arpt	67
7	Tuscola	74	10	Belleville Siu Research	68
7	Urbana	74	10	Decatur	68
12	Chicago Botanical Garden	73	10	Golden	68
12	La Harpe	73	10	Jerseyville 2 SW	68
14	Alton Melvin Price L&D	72	10	Moline Quad City Arpt	68
14	Havana 4 NNE	72	15	Aledo	69
14	Princeville	72	15	Aurora	69
17	Chicago Ohare Intl Arpt	71	15	Carlinville	*69*
17	Elgin	71	15	De Kalb	69
17	Galesburg	71	15	Dixon 1 NW	69
17	Park Forest	71	15	Kankakee Metro Wastwater	69
21	Chicago Midway Arpt	70	15	Peoria Greater Peoria Arpt	69
21	Joliet Brandon Rd Dam	70	22	Chicago Midway Arpt	70
21	Kaskaskia River Nav Lock	*70*	22	Joliet Brandon Rd Dam	70
21	Lacon 1 N	70	22	Kaskaskia River Nav Lock	*70*
21	Lincoln	70	22	Lacon 1 N	70

Rankings include 25 highest/lowest stations. If state has less than 25 stations, all stations are included. The period of record is 1980–2009. See User Guide for detailed explanation of data.

Number of Days Annually With ≥ 0.5 Inches of Precipitation

	Highest			Lowest	
Rank	Station Name	Days	Rank	Station Name	Days
1	Rosiclare 5 NW	36	1	Chicago Ohare Intl Arpt	21
2	Brookport Dam 52	34	2	De Kalb	22
3	Anna 2 NNE	33	2	Peoria Greater Peoria Arpt	22
4	Carbondale Sewage Plant	32	4	Antioch	*23*
5	Albion	*30*	4	Aurora	23
5	Effingham	30	4	Joliet Brandon Rd Dam	23
7	Cahokia	*29*	4	Marengo	*23*
7	Danville	29	4	Paw Paw 2 NW	*23*
9	Belleville Siu Research	28	4	Rockford Greater Rockford Arpt	23
9	Charleston	28	4	Springfield Capital Arpt	23
9	Kaskaskia River Nav Lock	*28*	4	Virden	23
9	Tuscola	28	12	Chicago Botanical Garden	24
13	Alton Melvin Price L&D	27	12	Fulton L&D #13	24
13	Carlinville	*27*	12	Lincoln	24
13	Decatur	27	12	Wheaton 3 SE	*24*
13	Golden	27	16	Aledo	25
13	Normal	27	16	Chenoa	25
13	Princeville	27	16	Chicago Midway Arpt	25
19	Havana 4 NNE	26	16	Dixon 1 NW	25
19	Jerseyville 2 SW	26	16	Elgin	25
19	Moline Quad City Arpt	26	16	Galesburg	25
19	Urbana	26	16	Kankakee Metro Wastwater	25
23	Aledo	25	16	La Harpe	25
23	Chenoa	25	16	Lacon 1 N	25
23	Chicago Midway Arpt	25	16	Park Forest	25

Number of Days Annually With ≥ 1.0 Inches of Precipitation

	Highest			Lowest	
Rank	Station Name	Days	Rank	Station Name	Days
1	Anna 2 NNE	13	1	Rockford Greater Rockford Arpt	6
1	Cahokia	*13*	2	Dixon 1 NW	7
1	Carbondale Sewage Plant	13	2	Fulton L&D #13	7
1	Rosiclare 5 NW	13	2	Marengo	*7*
5	Albion	*12*	2	Paw Paw 2 NW	7
5	Alton Melvin Price L&D	12	6	Aledo	8
5	Belleville Siu Research	12	6	Antioch	*8*
5	Brookport Dam 52	12	6	Aurora	8
5	Effingham	12	6	Chenoa	8
10	Havana 4 NNE	11	6	Chicago Botanical Garden	8
10	Kaskaskia River Nav Lock	*11*	6	De Kalb	8
10	Lacon 1 N	11	6	Joliet Brandon Rd Dam	8
13	Carlinville	*10*	6	Normal	8
13	Charleston	10	6	Wheaton 3 SE	*8*
13	Decatur	10	15	Chicago Midway Arpt	9
13	Golden	10	15	Chicago Ohare Intl Arpt	9
13	Jerseyville 2 SW	10	15	Danville	9
13	Springfield Capital Arpt	10	15	Elgin	9
19	Chicago Midway Arpt	9	15	Galesburg	9
19	Chicago Ohare Intl Arpt	9	15	Kankakee Metro Wastwater	9
19	Danville	9	15	La Harpe	9
19	Elgin	9	15	Lincoln	9
19	Galesburg	9	15	Moline Quad City Arpt	9
19	Kankakee Metro Wastwater	9	15	Park Forest	9
19	La Harpe	9	15	Peoria Greater Peoria Arpt	9

Rankings include 25 highest/lowest stations. If state has less than 25 stations, all stations are included. The period of record is 1980–2009. See User Guide for detailed explanation of data.

Annual Snowfall

	Highest			Lowest	
Rank	Station Name	Inches	Rank	Station Name	Inches
1	Antioch	**39.2**	1	Alton Melvin Price L&D	**4.8**
2	Chicago Midway Arpt	37.6	2	Kaskaskia River Nav Lock	**5.9**
3	Chicago Ohare Intl Arpt	37.3	3	Rosiclare 5 NW	6.5
4	Rockford Greater Rockford Arpt	36.5	4	Brookport Dam 52	6.7
5	Chicago Botanical Garden	33.8	5	Fulton L&D #13	**7.3**
6	De Kalb	33.5	6	Albion	**8.1**
7	Dixon 1 NW	31.6	7	Carbondale Sewage Plant	10.7
8	Moline Quad City Arpt	31.3	8	Anna 2 NNE	11.3
9	Marengo	**31.2**	9	Belleville Siu Research	13.1
10	Park Forest	30.8	10	Jerseyville 2 SW	13.5
11	Paw Paw 2 NW	29.9	11	Cahokia	**15.4**
12	Havana 4 NNE	29.5	12	Golden	**15.7**
13	Elgin	29.1	13	Danville	15.9
14	Aurora	28.3	14	Carlinville	**17.7**
15	Wheaton 3 SE	**27.9**	15	Effingham	17.8
16	Peoria Greater Peoria Arpt	24.3	16	Decatur	18.1
17	Kankakee Metro Wastwater	24.1	17	Chenoa	18.4
18	Urbana	22.8	18	La Harpe	19.1
19	Galesburg	22.7	19	Lincoln	19.4
20	Lacon 1 N	22.0	20	Tuscola	19.5
21	Princeville	21.6	20	Virden	19.5
22	Springfield Capital Arpt	21.3	22	Normal	19.7
23	Aledo	20.7	23	Aledo	20.7
23	Charleston	20.7	23	Charleston	20.7
25	Normal	19.7	25	Springfield Capital Arpt	21.3

Annual Maximum Snow Depth

	Highest			Lowest	
Rank	Station Name	Inches	Rank	Station Name	Inches
1	Belleville Siu Research	30	1	Albion	**10**
2	Aurora	25	1	Rosiclare 5 NW	10
2	Paw Paw 2 NW	25	3	Cahokia	**11**
4	Charleston	24	3	Golden	**11**
4	Dixon 1 NW	24	5	Carlinville	**12**
4	Elgin	**24**	5	Springfield Capital Arpt	12
4	Kaskaskia River Nav Lock	**24**	5	Virden	12
8	Antioch	**22**	8	Brookport Dam 52	13
9	Alton Melvin Price L&D	**21**	8	Carbondale Sewage Plant	13
9	Chicago Midway Arpt	21	10	Anna 2 NNE	14
11	Chenoa	20	10	Danville	14
11	Galesburg	20	10	Decatur	14
13	Marengo	**19**	10	Lacon 1 N	**14**
13	Rockford Greater Rockford Arpt	**19**	10	Lincoln	**14**
13	Tuscola	19	15	Fulton L&D #13	**15**
13	Urbana	19	15	Princeville	**15**
17	Chicago Botanical Garden	18	17	Effingham	**16**
17	Chicago Ohare Intl Arpt	18	17	Jerseyville 2 SW	16
17	Havana 4 NNE	18	17	Peoria Greater Peoria Arpt	16
17	Kankakee Metro Wastwater	18	20	De Kalb	**17**
17	Normal	18	20	La Harpe	17
22	De Kalb	**17**	20	Park Forest	17
22	La Harpe	17	23	Chicago Botanical Garden	18
22	Park Forest	17	23	Chicago Ohare Intl Arpt	18
25	Effingham	**16**	23	Havana 4 NNE	18

Rankings include 25 highest/lowest stations. If state has less than 25 stations, all stations are included. The period of record is 1980–2009. See User Guide for detailed explanation of data.

Number of Days Annually With ≥ 1.0 Inch Snow Depth

Highest			Lowest		
Rank	Station Name	Days	Rank	Station Name	Days
1	Rockford Greater Rockford Arpt	**58**	1	Albion	**4**
2	De Kalb	55	1	Kaskaskia River Nav Lock	**4**
3	Antioch	**51**	3	Alton Melvin Price L&D	**6**
3	Chicago Botanical Garden	51	4	Golden	**7**
5	Chicago Midway Arpt	48	5	Brookport Dam 52	8
5	Dixon 1 NW	48	6	Rosiclare 5 NW	10
5	Park Forest	48	7	Aledo	**12**
8	Paw Paw 2 NW	46	7	Anna 2 NNE	12
9	Aurora	45	7	Carbondale Sewage Plant	12
9	Marengo	**45**	10	Belleville Siu Research	13
11	Chicago Ohare Intl Arpt	43	11	Cahokia	**14**
12	La Harpe	39	12	Fulton L&D #13	**18**
12	Lacon 1 N	39	13	Carlinville	**20**
14	Kankakee Metro Wastwater	38	14	Jerseyville 2 SW	21
15	Peoria Greater Peoria Arpt	36	14	Princeville	**21**
16	Galesburg	35	16	Effingham	**22**
16	Wheaton 3 SE	**35**	16	Virden	22
18	Elgin	**34**	18	Danville	23
18	Normal	34	18	Lincoln	**23**
20	Havana 4 NNE	32	20	Tuscola	24
21	Charleston	30	21	Decatur	25
21	Urbana	30	22	Chenoa	27
23	Chenoa	27	22	Springfield Capital Arpt	27
23	Springfield Capital Arpt	27	24	Charleston	30
25	Decatur	25	24	Urbana	30

Rankings include 25 highest/lowest stations. If state has less than 25 stations, all stations are included. The period of record is 1980–2009. See User Guide for detailed explanation of data.

Significant Storm Events in Illinois: 2000 – 2009

Location or County	Date	Type	Mag.	Deaths	Injuries	Property Damage ($mil.)	Crop Damage ($mil.)
Vermilion	07/08/01	Thunderstorm Wind	85 mph	0	0	8.5	0.0
Cook	07/21/01	Excessive Heat	na	10	0	0.0	0.0
Cook	07/29/01	Excessive Heat	na	6	0	0.0	0.0
Cook	08/02/01	Flash Flood	na	0	0	37.0	0.0
Cook	08/06/01	Excessive Heat	na	14	0	0.0	0.0
Wayne	04/21/02	Tornado	F3	1	42	4.0	0.0
Sangamon	05/27/02	Hail	2.00 in.	0	0	9.0	0.0
Cook	06/21/02	Excessive Heat	na	7	0	0.0	0.0
Cook	07/01/02	Excessive Heat	na	12	0	0.0	0.0
Cook	07/15/02	Excessive Heat	na	11	0	0.0	0.0
Mercer	04/30/03	Flash Flood	na	0	0	10.0	0.0
Henry	04/30/03	Flash Flood	na	0	0	10.0	0.0
Massac	05/06/03	Tornado	F4	1	20	10.0	0.0
Pulaski	05/06/03	Tornado	F4	1	13	3.5	0.0
Henderson	05/08/03	Hail	4.00 in.	0	0	10.0	0.0
Tazewell	05/10/03	Tornado	F3	0	32	10.0	0.0
De Witt	05/30/03	Tornado	F2	0	4	9.3	0.0
Mercer	07/20/03	Thunderstorm Wind	81 mph	0	0	10.0	3.0
Henry	07/21/03	Thunderstorm Wind	92 mph	0	0	50.0	25.0
Will	07/27/03	Flash Flood	na	0	0	14.0	0.0
Coles	09/26/03	Tornado	F1	0	1	10.0	0.0
Putnam	04/20/04	Tornado	F2	0	5	8.0	0.0
La Salle	04/20/04	Tornado	F3	8	7	0.0	0.0
St. Clair	04/02/06	Tornado	F2	1	11	0.0	0.0
Cook	07/15/06	Excessive Heat	na	9	0	0.0	0.0
Jefferson	07/21/06	Thunderstorm Wind	90 mph	0	5	13.0	0.0
Cook	08/01/06	Excessive Heat	na	24	0	0.0	0.0
Winnebago	09/04/06	Flash Flood	na	0	0	20.0	0.0
Cook	12/02/06	Extreme Cold/Wind Chill	na	7	5	0.0	0.0
Cook	02/01/07	Extreme Cold/Wind Chill	na	10	0	0.0	0.0
Du Page	03/31/07	Thunderstorm Wind	96 mph	0	11	1.0	0.0
Cook	01/22/08	Extreme Cold/Wind Chill	na	5	0	0.0	0.0
Saline	03/18/08	Flood	na	0	0	16.8	0.0
Cook	09/13/08	Flash Flood	na	1	0	35.0	0.0
Cook	09/14/08	Flash Flood	na	0	0	20.0	0.0
Du Page	09/14/08	Flash Flood	na	0	0	8.0	0.0
Cook	12/21/08	Cold/Wind Chill	na	5	0	0.0	0.0
Williamson	05/08/09	Thunderstorm Wind	100 mph	0	1	175.0	0.0
Jackson	05/08/09	Thunderstorm Wind	106 mph	1	6	100.0	0.0
Sangamon	08/19/09	Tornado	F3	0	17	11.0	0.0
Logan	08/19/09	Tornado	F3	0	2	7.2	1.0

Note: Deaths, injuries, and damages are date and location specific.

Demographic and Reference Maps

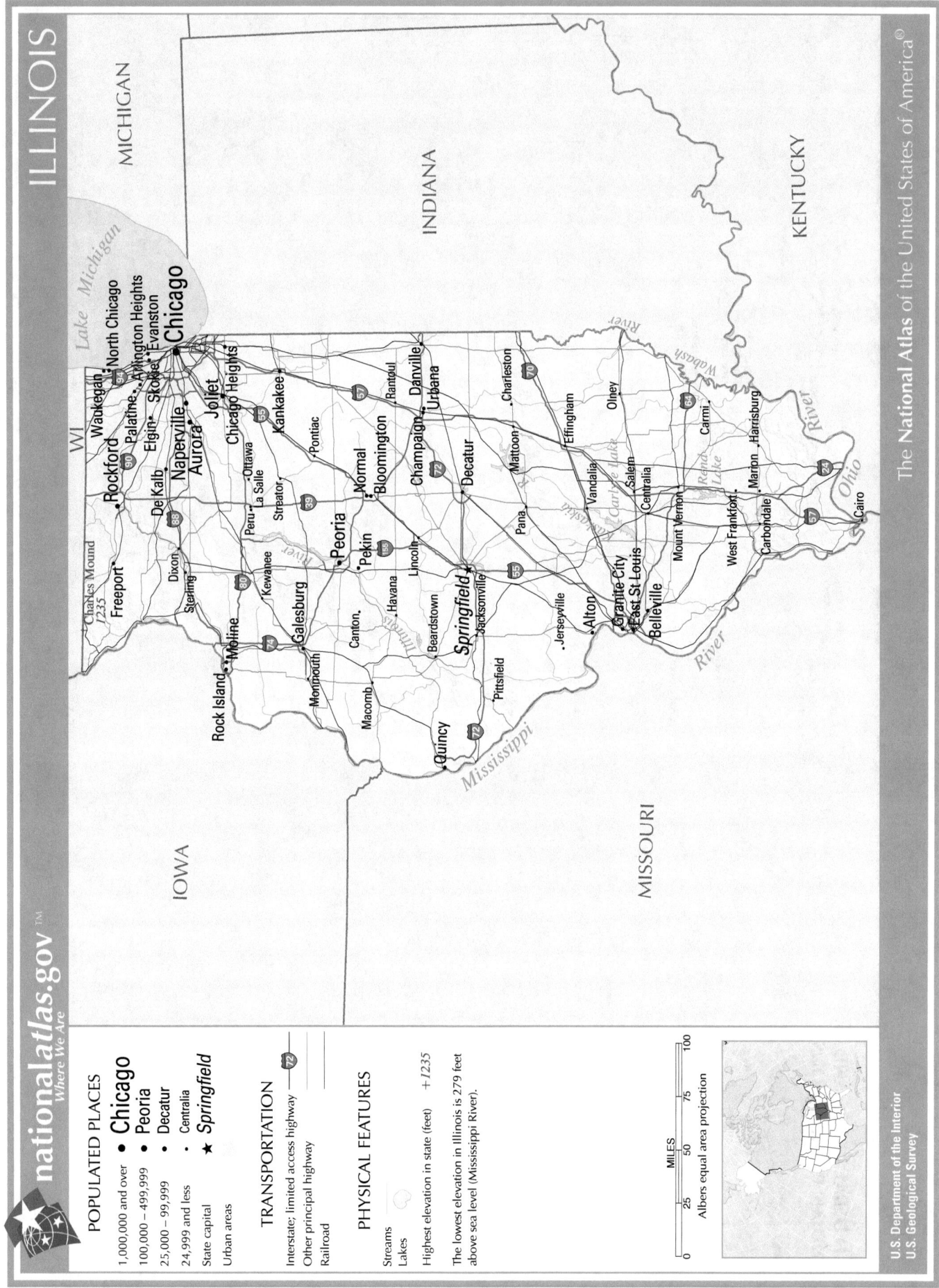

ILLINOIS

POPULATED PLACES

- Chicago — 1,000,000 and over
- Peoria — 100,000 – 499,999
- Decatur — 25,000 – 99,999
- Centralia — 24,999 and less
- ★ Springfield — State capital
- Urban areas

TRANSPORTATION

- Interstate; limited access highway
- Other principal highway
- Railroad

PHYSICAL FEATURES

- Streams
- Lakes
- Highest elevation in state (feet)   +1235

The lowest elevation in Illinois is 279 feet above sea level (Mississippi River).

MILES
0   25   50   75   100
Albers equal area projection

U.S. Department of the Interior
U.S. Geological Survey

The **National Atlas** of the United States of America ©

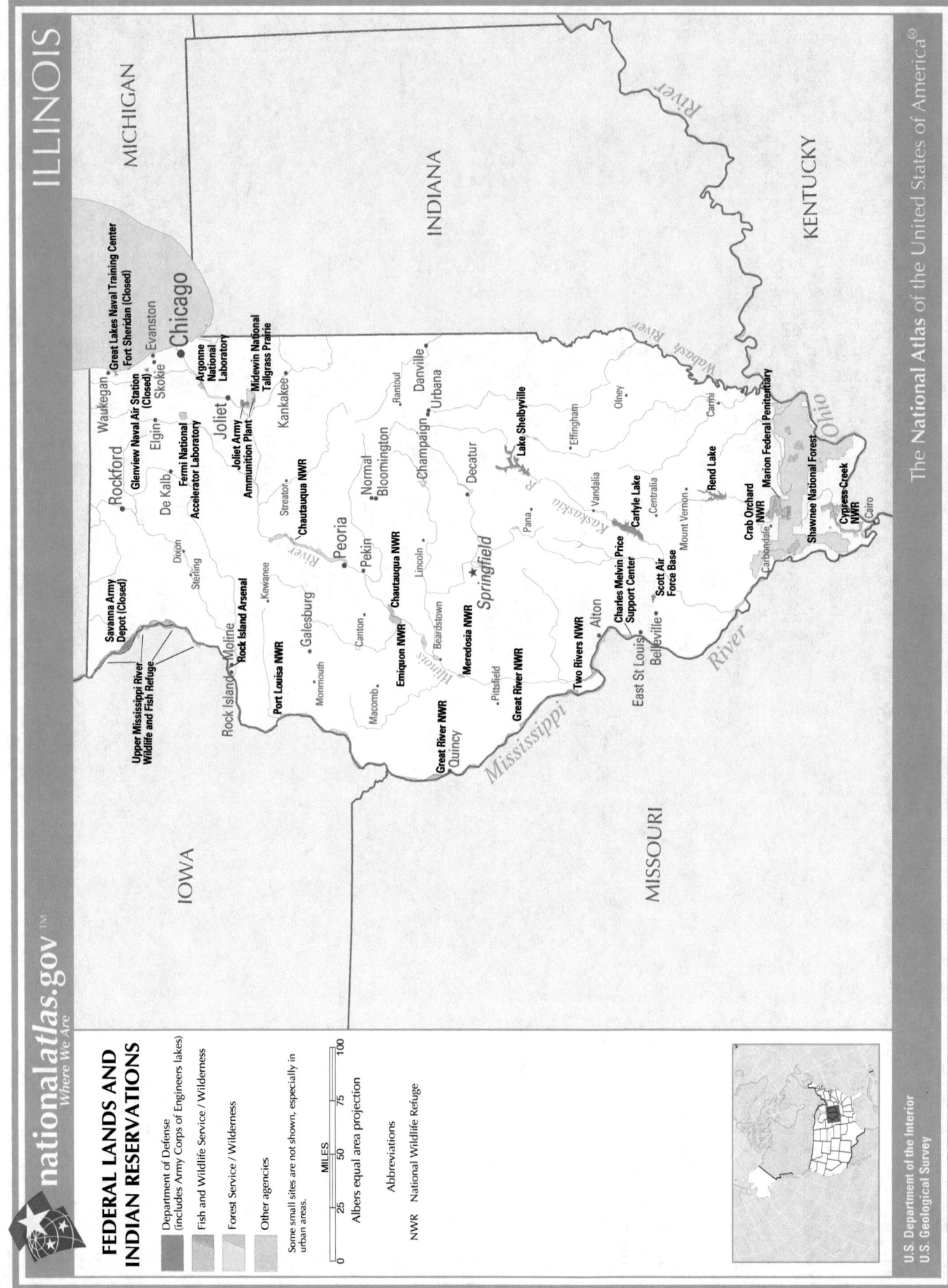

ILLINOIS

MICHIGAN

INDIANA

KENTUCKY

IOWA

MISSOURI

The National Atlas of the United States of America®

nationalatlas.gov™
Where We Are

**FEDERAL LANDS AND
INDIAN RESERVATIONS**

Department of Defense
(includes Army Corps of Engineers lakes)

Fish and Wildlife Service / Wilderness

Forest Service / Wilderness

Other agencies

Some small sites are not shown, especially in
urban areas.

MILES

0   25   50   75   100

Albers equal area projection

Abbreviations

NWR   National Wildlife Refuge

Waukegan
Great Lakes Naval Training Center
Fort Sheridan (Closed)
Evanston
Chicago
Skokie
Glenview Naval Air Station
(Closed)
Argonne
National
Laboratory
Midewin National
Tallgrass Prairie
Elgin
Joliet
Joliet Army
Ammunition Plant
Kankakee
Fermi National
Accelerator Laboratory
Rockford
De Kalb
Dixon
Sterling
Streator
Chautauqua NWR
Peoria
Pekin
Kewanee
Rock Island
Moline
Rock Island Arsenal
Savanna Army
Depot (Closed)
Upper Mississippi River
Wildlife and Fish Refuge
Galesburg
Port Louisa NWR
Monmouth
Canton
Macomb
Emiquon NWR
Great River NWR
Quincy
Beardstown
Meredosia NWR
Pittsfield
Two Rivers NWR
Rantoul
Danville
Urbana
Champaign
Normal
Bloomington
Lincoln
Decatur
Springfield
Pana
Lake Shelbyville
Effingham
Olney
Carmi
Vandalia
Centralia
Mount Vernon
Rend Lake
Marion Federal Penitentiary
Crab Orchard
NWR
Carbondale
Shawnee National Forest
Cypress Creek
NWR
Cairo
Charles Melvin Price
Support Center
Scott Air
Force Base
Belleville
East St Louis
Alton
Carlyle Lake
Chautauqua NWR
Wabash River
Ohio
River
Mississippi
River
Illinois
River
Kaskaskia
River

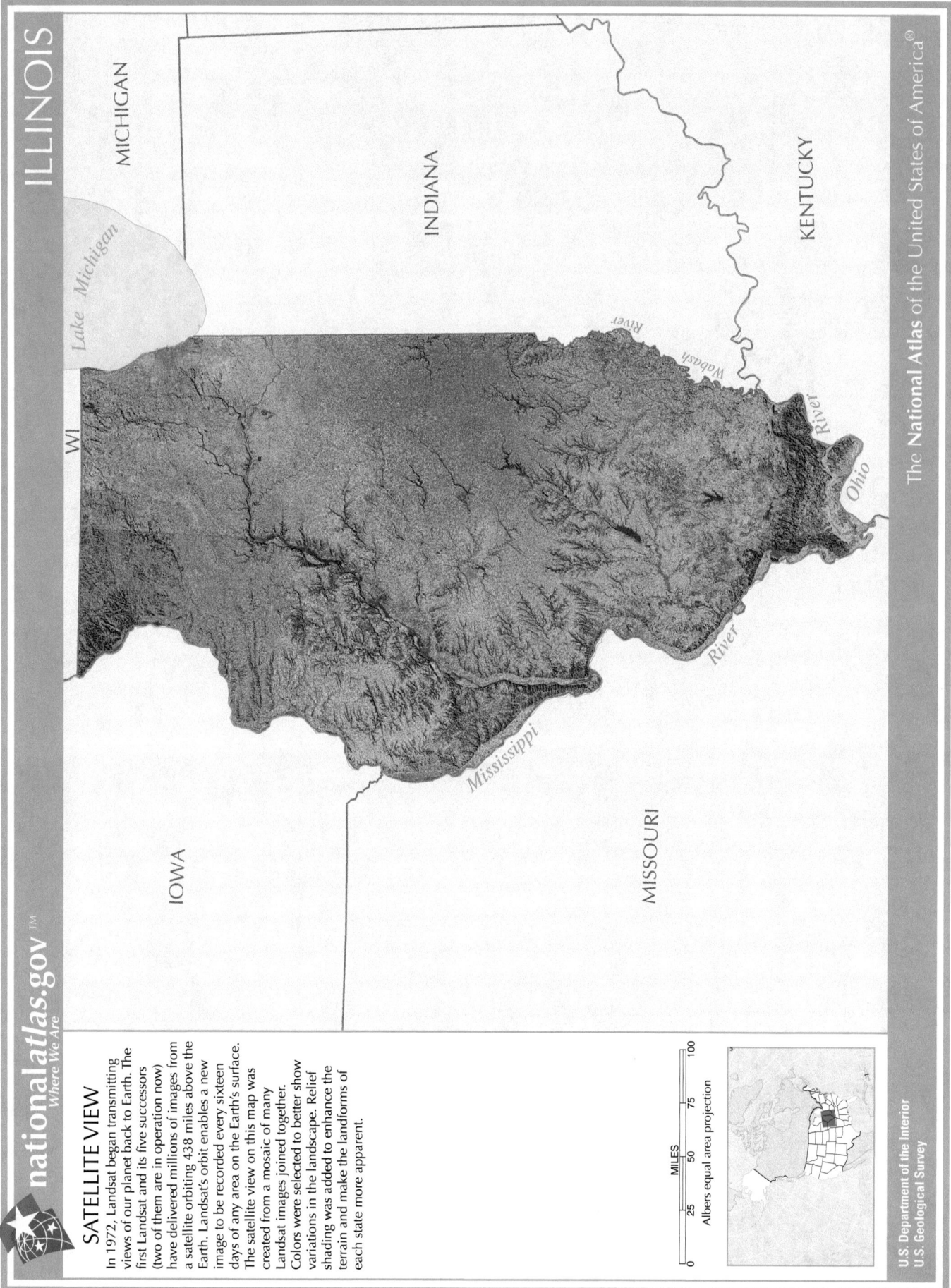

ILLINOIS

MICHIGAN

WI

Lake Michigan

INDIANA

KENTUCKY

IOWA

MISSOURI

Wabash River

Ohio River

Mississippi River

nationalatlas.gov™
Where We Are

SATELLITE VIEW

In 1972, Landsat began transmitting views of our planet back to Earth. The first Landsat and its five successors (two of them are in operation now) have delivered millions of images from a satellite orbiting 438 miles above the Earth. Landsat's orbit enables a new image to be recorded every sixteen days of any area on the Earth's surface. The satellite view on this map was created from a mosaic of many Landsat images joined together. Colors were selected to better show variations in the landscape. Relief shading was added to enhance the terrain and make the landforms of each state more apparent.

MILES

0   25   50   75   100

Albers equal area projection

The National Atlas of the United States of America®

U.S. Department of the Interior
U.S. Geological Survey

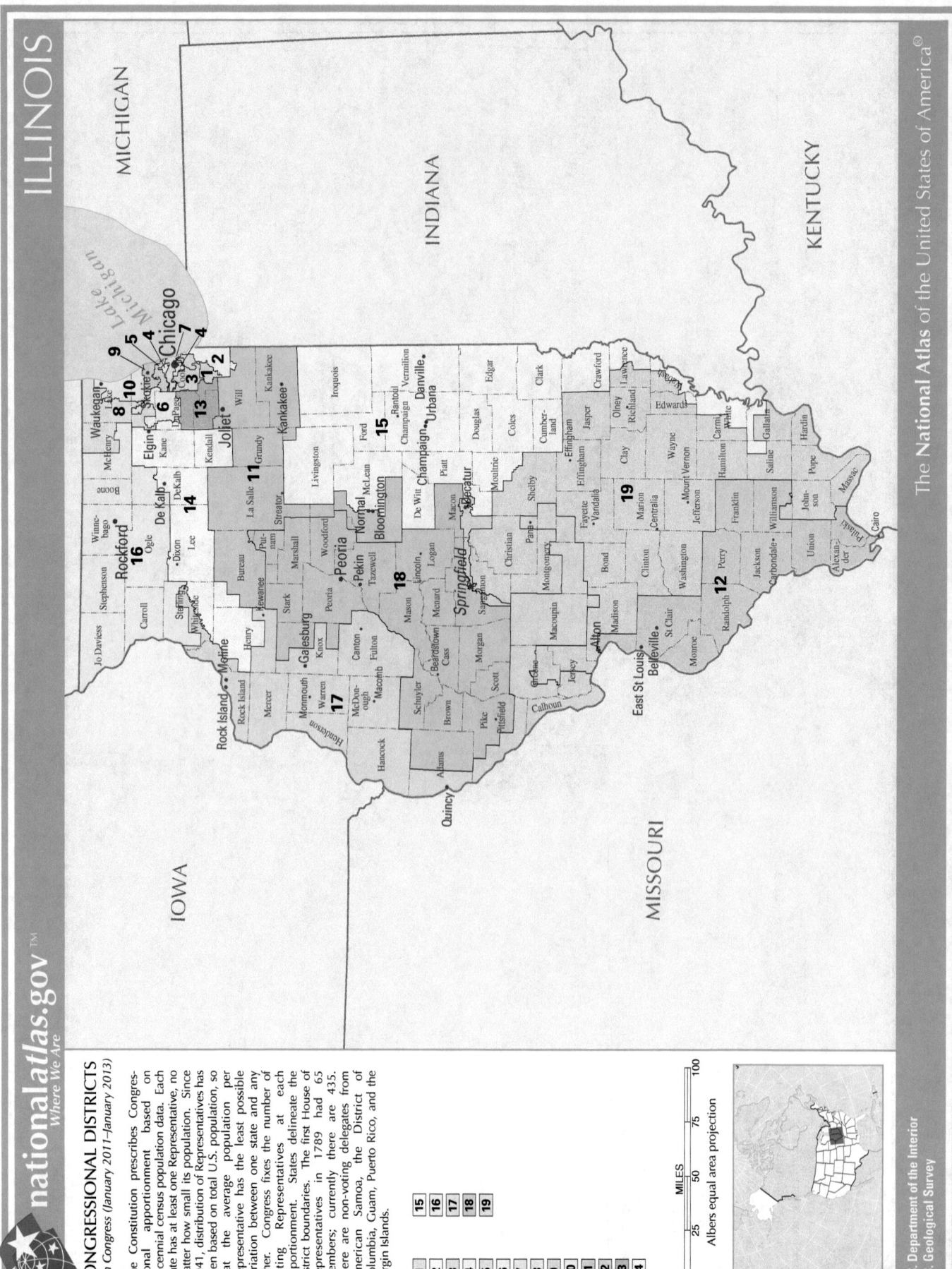

nationalatlas.gov ™
Where We Are

CONGRESSIONAL DISTRICTS
112th Congress (January 2011–January 2013)

The Constitution prescribes Congressional apportionment based on decennial census population data. Each state has at least one Representative, no matter how small its population. Since 1941, distribution of Representatives has been based on total U.S. population, so that the average population per Representative has the least possible variation between one state and any other. Congress fixes the number of voting Representatives at each apportionment. States delineate the district boundaries. The first House of Representatives in 1789 had 65 members; currently there are 435. There are non-voting delegates from American Samoa, the District of Columbia, Guam, Puerto Rico, and the Virgin Islands.

MILES

Albers equal area projection

U.S. Department of the Interior
U.S. Geological Survey

The **National Atlas** of the United States of America®

ILLINOIS - Core Based Statistical Areas, Counties, and Independent City

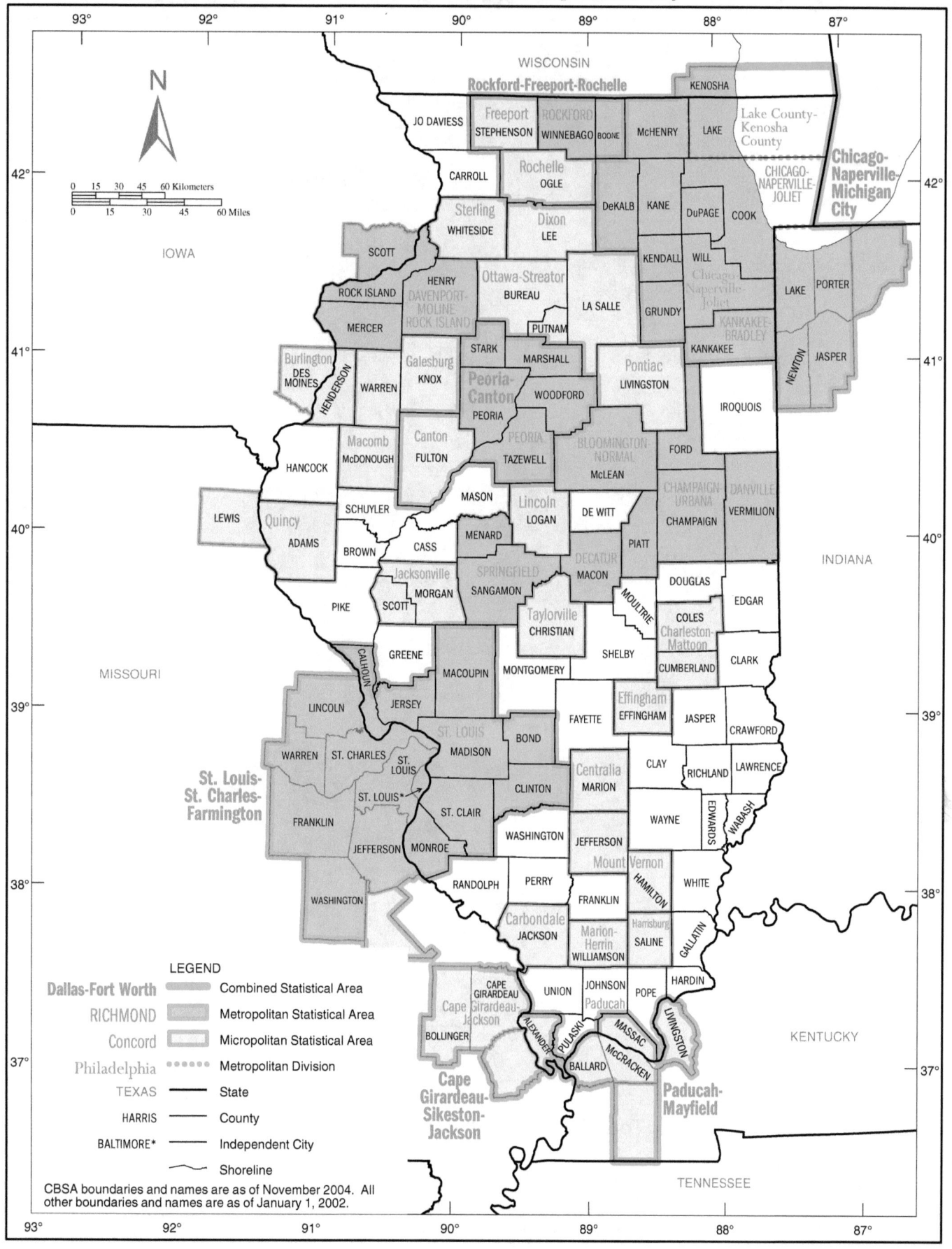

Economic Losses from Hazard Events, 1960-2009

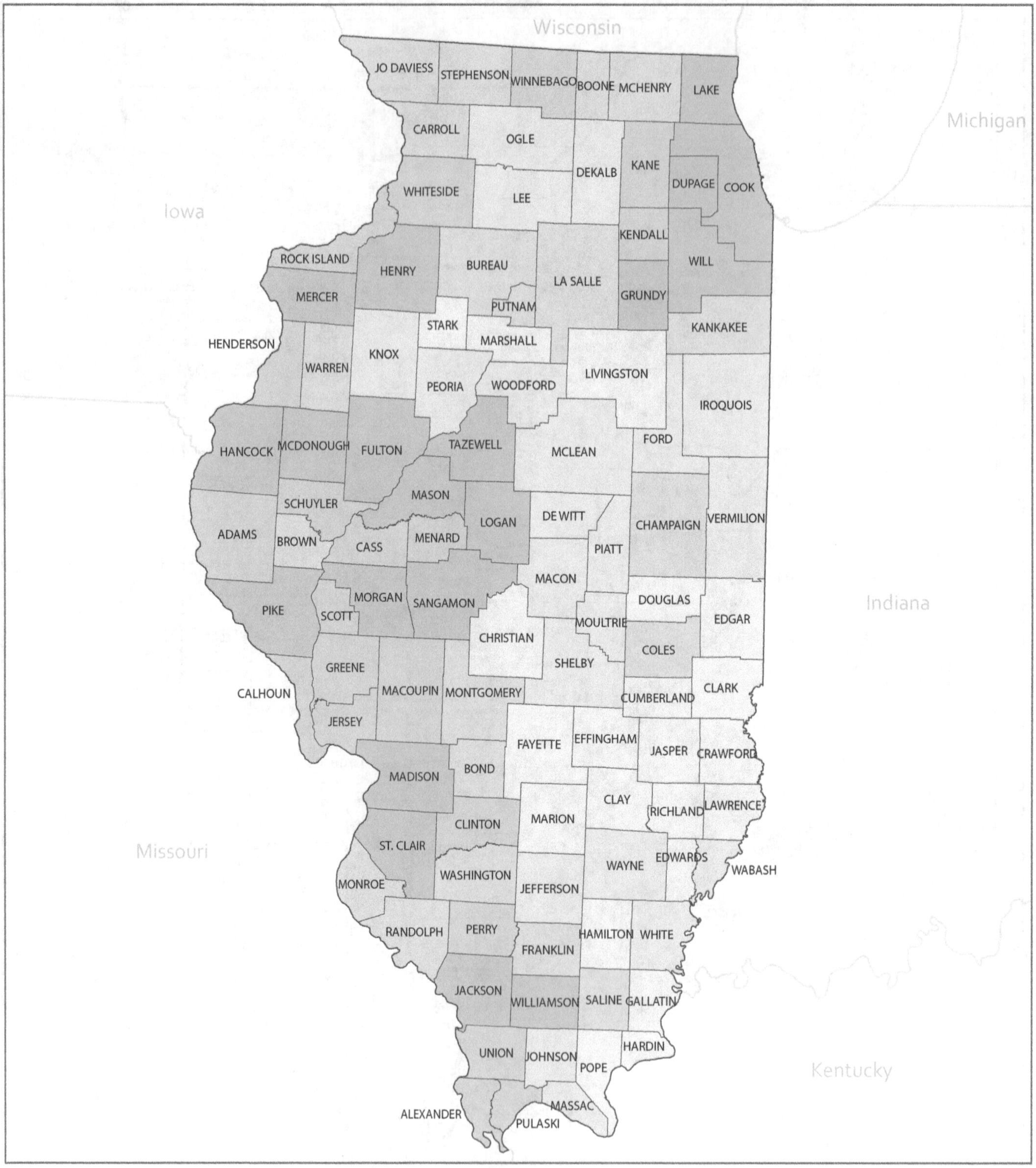

Wisconsin

Michigan

Iowa

JO DAVIESS | STEPHENSON | WINNEBAGO | BOONE | MCHENRY | LAKE

CARROLL | OGLE | DEKALB | KANE | DUPAGE | COOK

WHITESIDE | LEE | KENDALL | WILL

ROCK ISLAND | HENRY | BUREAU | LA SALLE | GRUNDY

MERCER | PUTNAM | KANKAKEE

HENDERSON | STARK | MARSHALL | LIVINGSTON

WARREN | KNOX | PEORIA | WOODFORD | IROQUOIS

FORD

HANCOCK | MCDONOUGH | FULTON | TAZEWELL | MCLEAN

MASON

SCHUYLER | LOGAN | DE WITT | CHAMPAIGN | VERMILION

ADAMS | BROWN | CASS | MENARD | PIATT

MACON

MORGAN | SANGAMON | DOUGLAS | EDGAR

PIKE | SCOTT | MOULTRIE

CHRISTIAN | SHELBY | COLES

GREENE | CUMBERLAND | CLARK

CALHOUN | MACOUPIN | MONTGOMERY

JERSEY | FAYETTE | EFFINGHAM | JASPER | CRAWFORD

MADISON | BOND | CLAY | RICHLAND | LAWRENCE

CLINTON | MARION | WAYNE | EDWARDS | WABASH

ST. CLAIR | WASHINGTON | JEFFERSON

MONROE | PERRY | HAMILTON | WHITE

RANDOLPH | FRANKLIN

JACKSON | SALINE | GALLATIN

WILLIAMSON | HARDIN

UNION | JOHNSON | POPE

ALEXANDER | MASSAC | Kentucky

PULASKI

Missouri

Indiana

Total Losses (Property and Crop)

ILLINOIS

- 7,798,433 – 21,110,928
- 21,110,929 – 43,493,360
- 43,493,361 – 65,394,087
- 65,394,088 – 77,670,873
- 77,670,874 – 416,198,985

Source: SHELDUS v. 8.0
Classification: Quantiles
Losses adjusted to 2009 Dollars

0   30   60 Miles

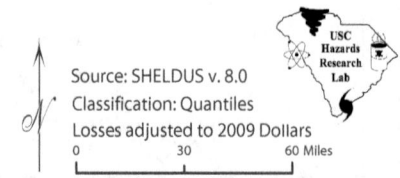

USC Hazards Research Lab

Illinois Hazard Losses, 1960–2009

Distribution of Hazard Events
(number of events)

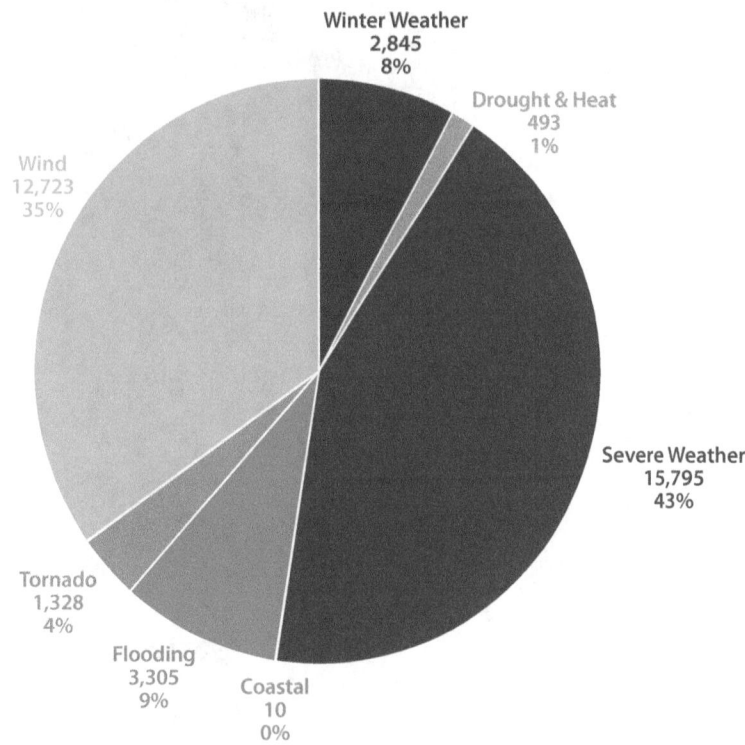

Winter Weather
2,845
8%

Drought & Heat
493
1%

Wind
12,723
35%

Severe Weather
15,795
43%

Tornado
1,328
4%

Flooding
3,305
9%

Coastal
10
0%

Distribution of Losses by Hazard Type
(in 2009 USD million)

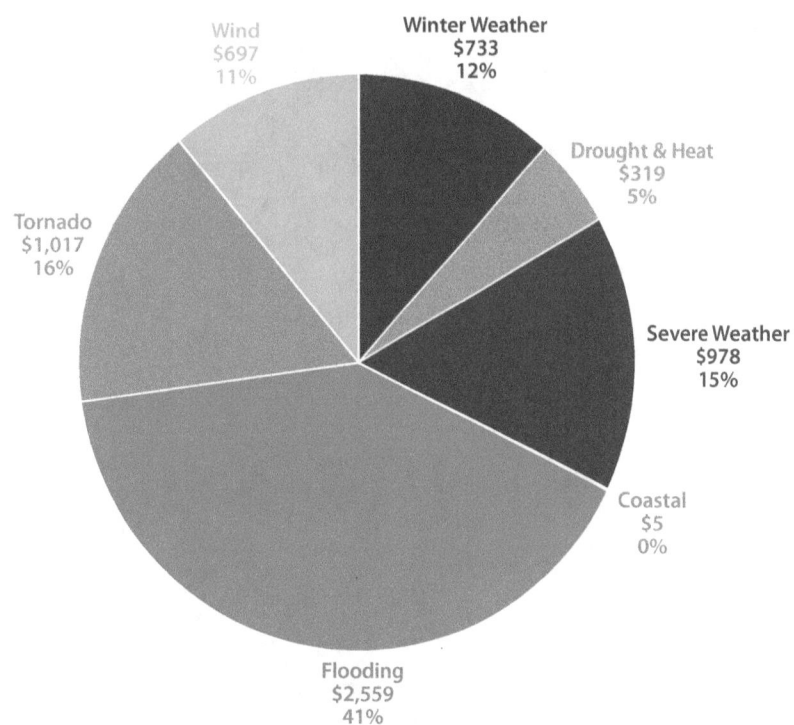

Wind
$697
11%

Winter Weather
$733
12%

Drought & Heat
$319
5%

Tornado
$1,017
16%

Severe Weather
$978
15%

Coastal
$5
0%

Flooding
$2,559
41%

Population (2010)

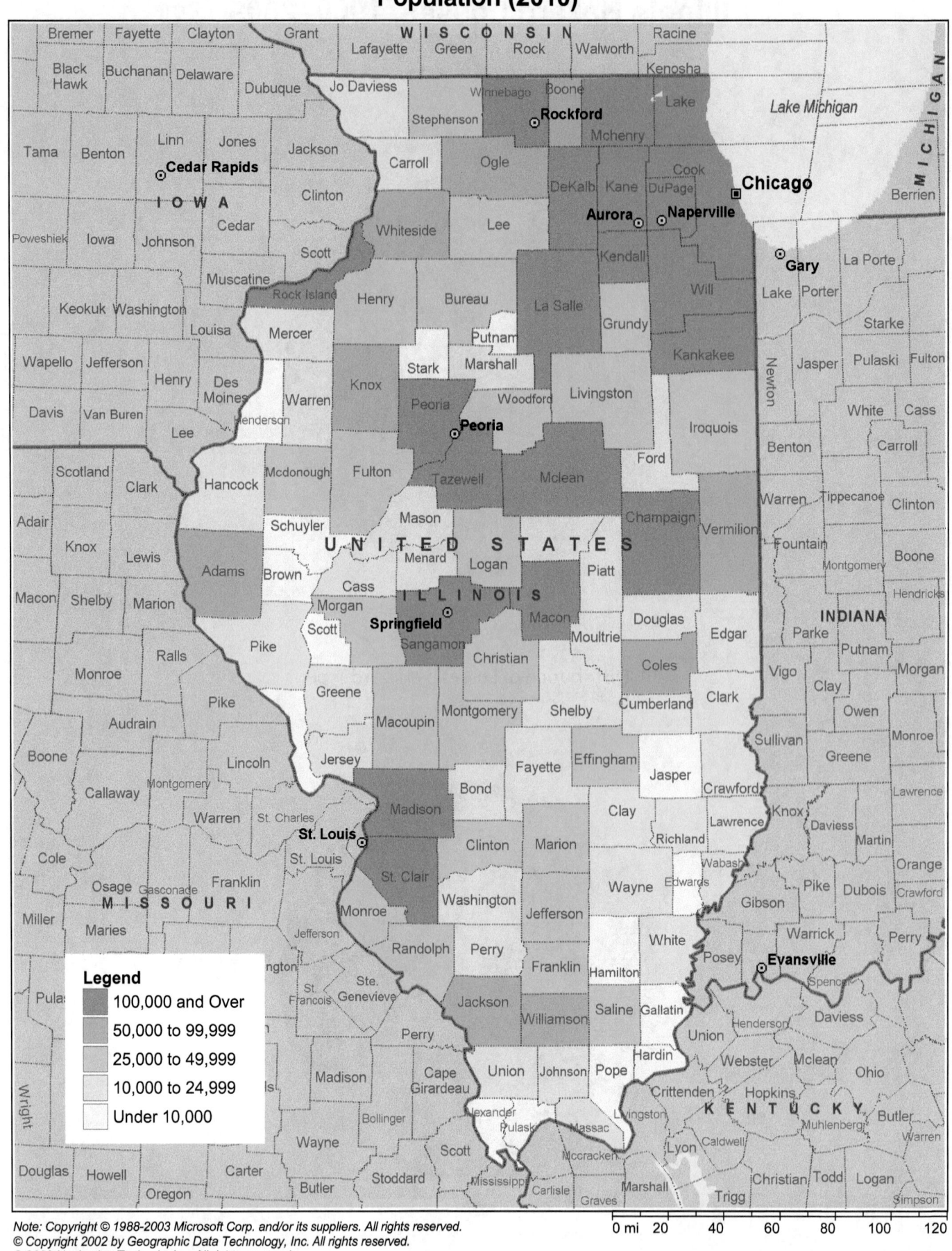

Legend
- 100,000 and Over
- 50,000 to 99,999
- 25,000 to 49,999
- 10,000 to 24,999
- Under 10,000

0 mi   20   40   60   80   100   120

Percent White (2010)

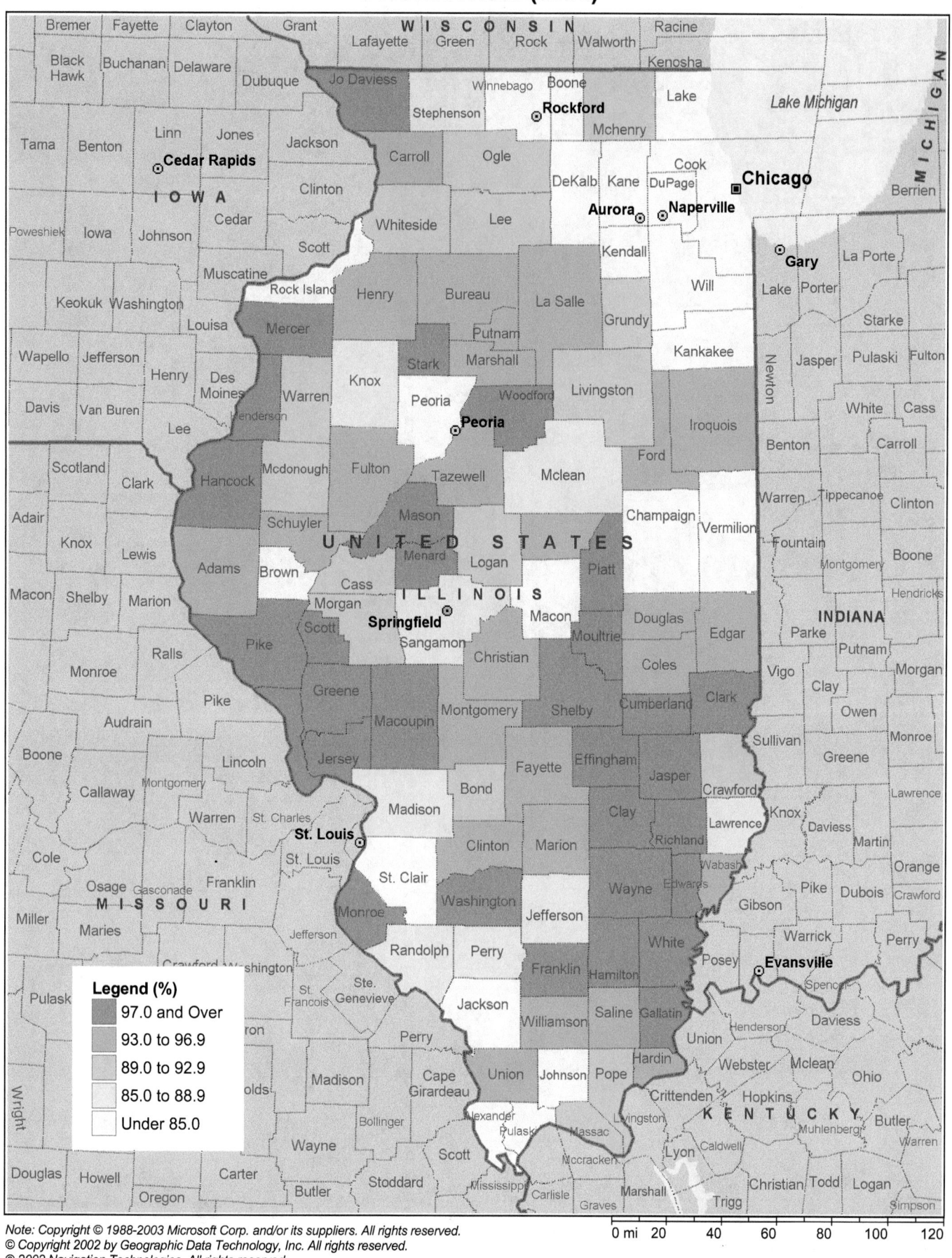

Legend (%)
- 97.0 and Over
- 93.0 to 96.9
- 89.0 to 92.9
- 85.0 to 88.9
- Under 85.0

0 mi   20   40   60   80   100   120

Percent Black (2010)

Legend (%)

- 8.0 and Over
- 4.0 to 7.9
- 1.0 to 3.9
- 0.5 to 0.9
- Under 0.5

0 mi   20   40   60   80   100   120

Percent Asian (2010)

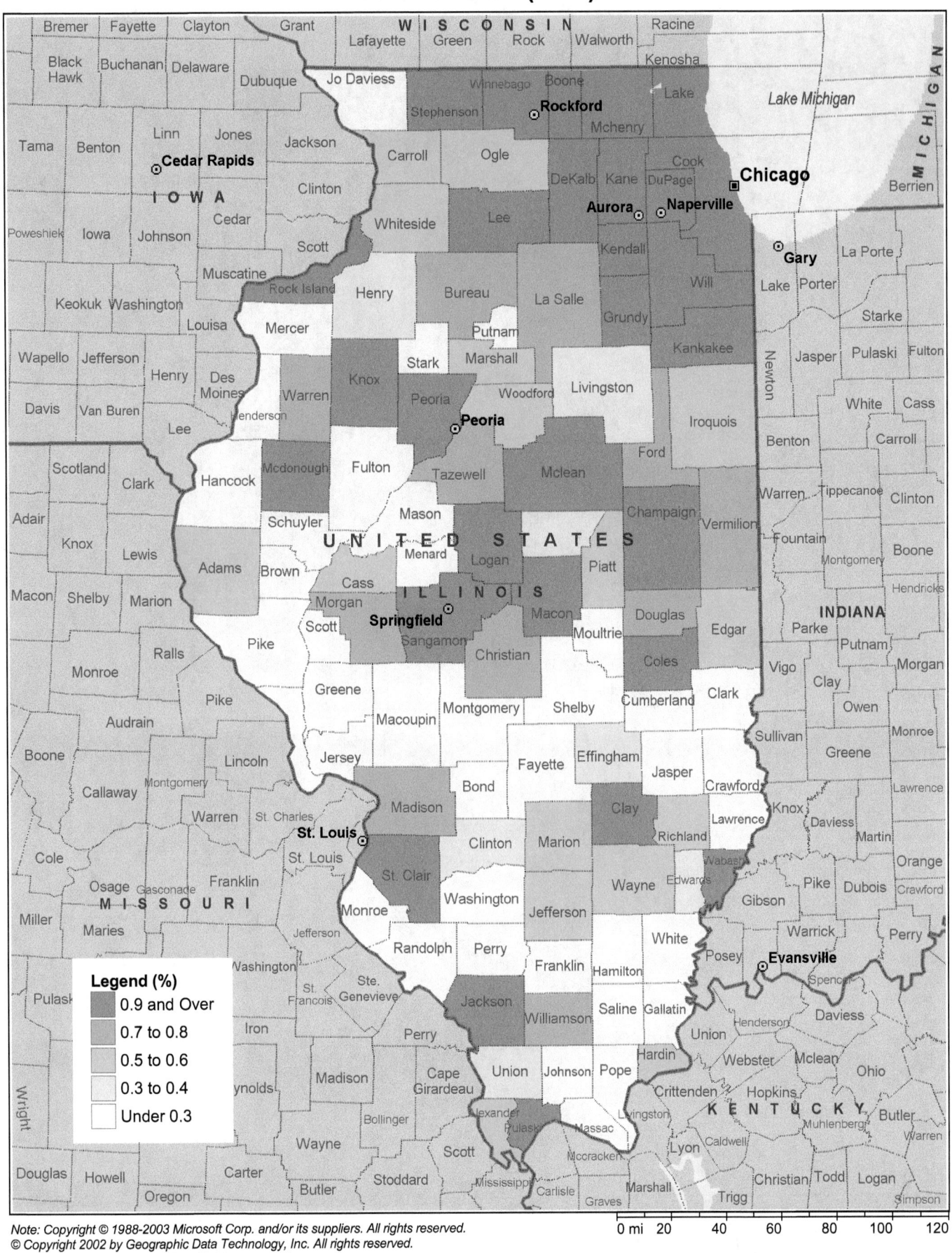

Legend (%)
- 0.9 and Over
- 0.7 to 0.8
- 0.5 to 0.6
- 0.3 to 0.4
- Under 0.3

0 mi   20   40   60   80   100   120

Percent Hispanic (2010)

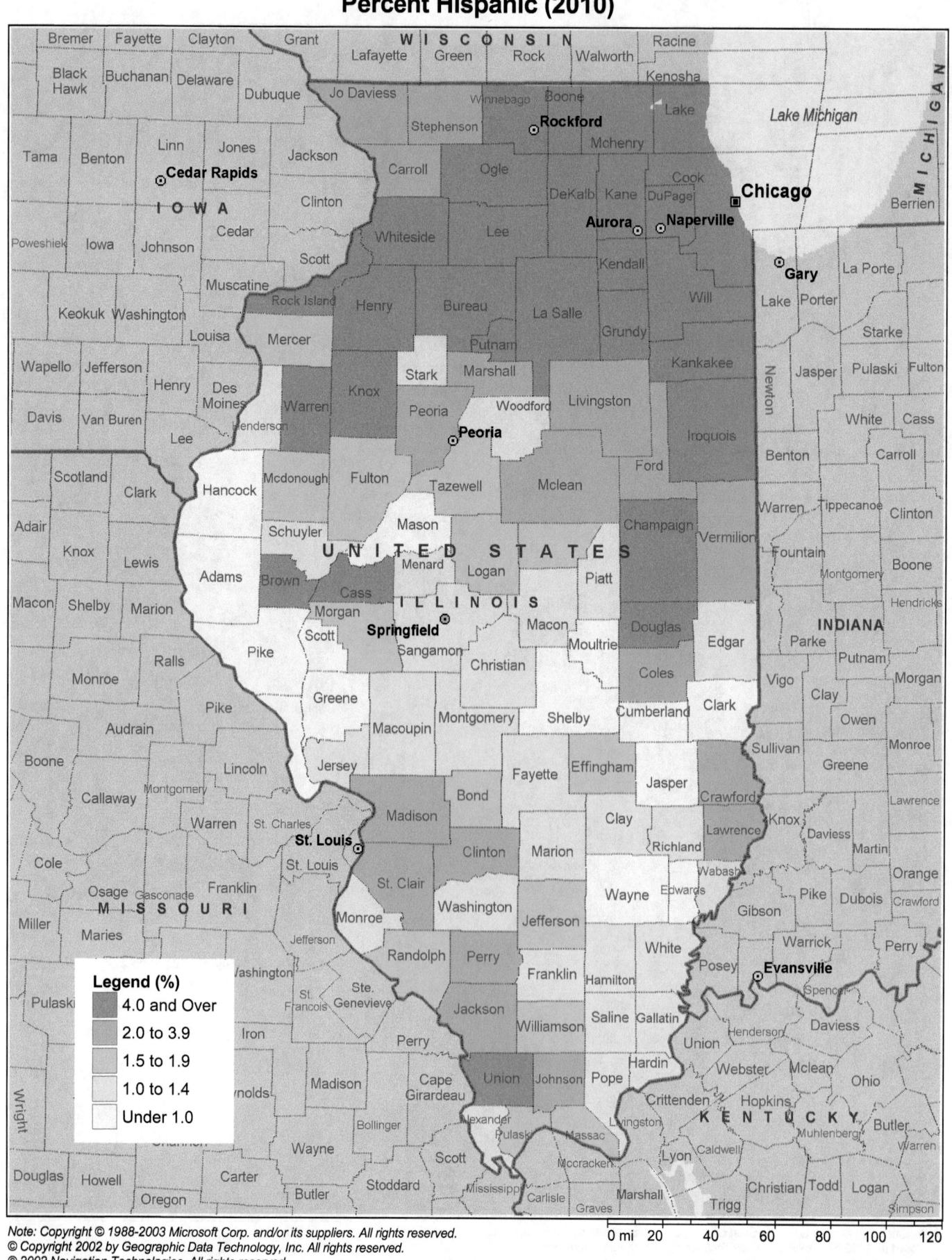

Legend (%)

- 4.0 and Over
- 2.0 to 3.9
- 1.5 to 1.9
- 1.0 to 1.4
- Under 1.0

0 mi   20   40   60   80   100   120

Median Age (2010)

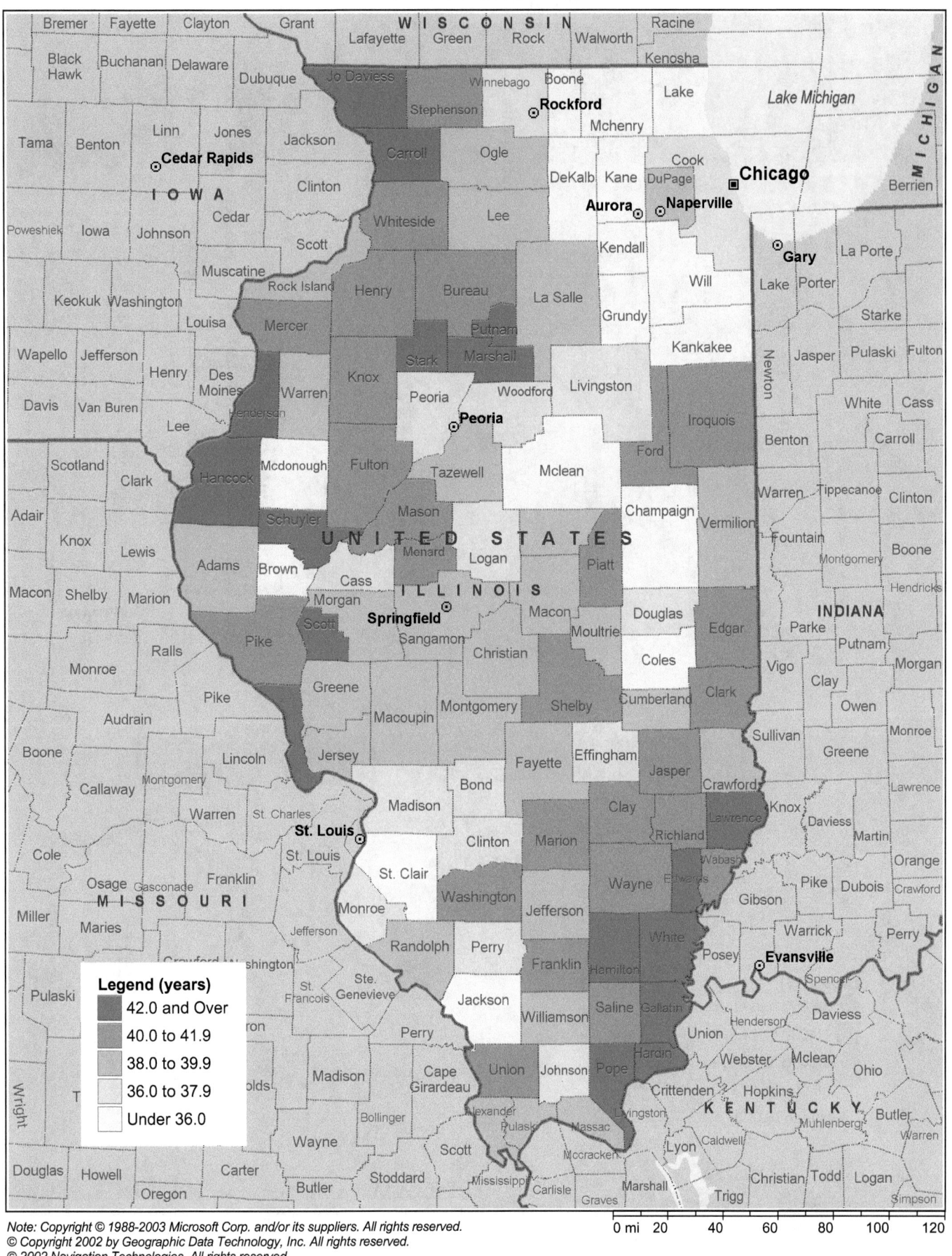

Legend (years)
- 42.0 and Over
- 40.0 to 41.9
- 38.0 to 39.9
- 36.0 to 37.9
- Under 36.0

0 mi   20   40   60   80   100   120

Median Household Income (2010)

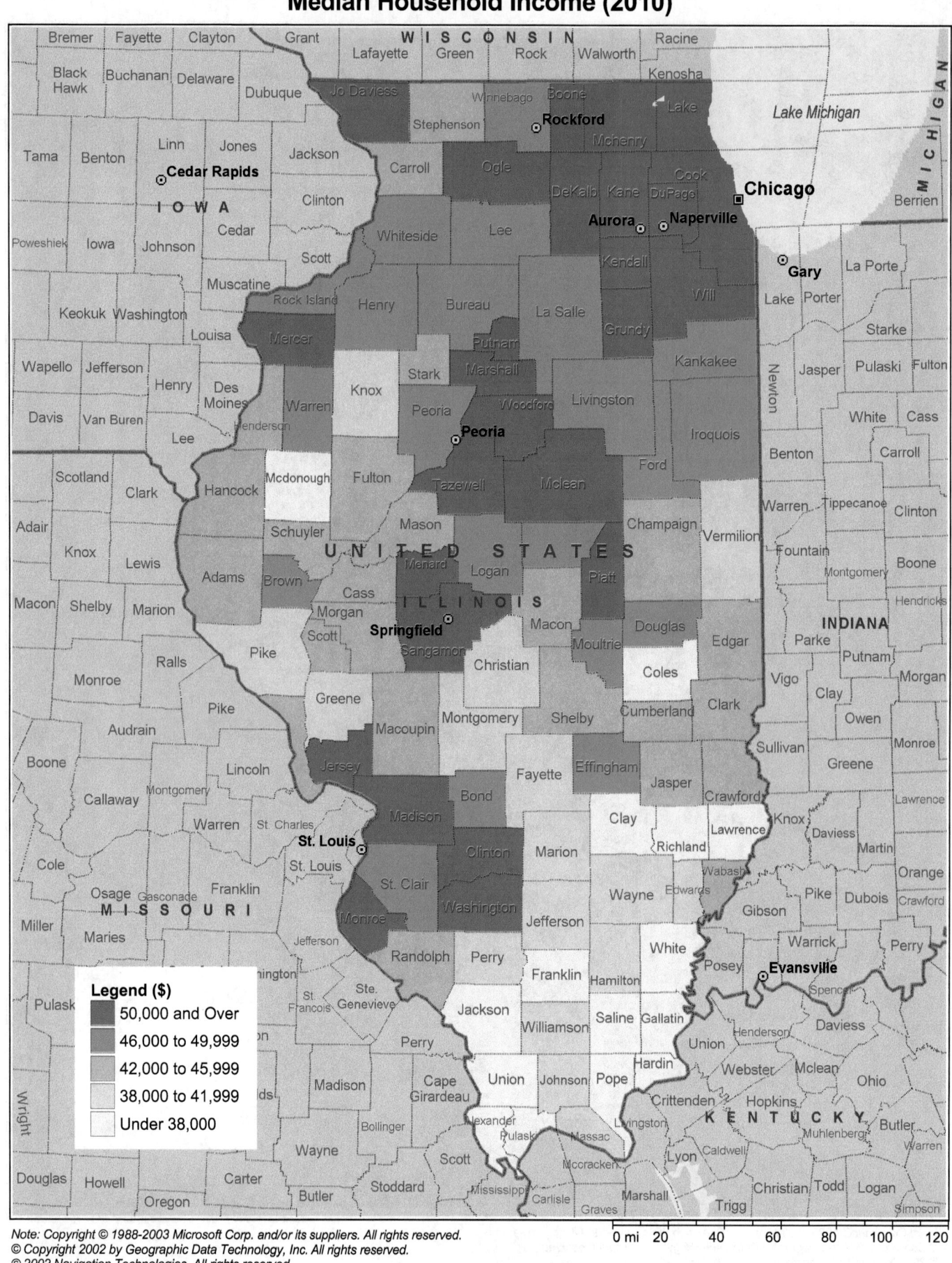

Legend ($)
- 50,000 and Over
- 46,000 to 49,999
- 42,000 to 45,999
- 38,000 to 41,999
- Under 38,000

0 mi   20   40   60   80   100   120

Median Home Value (2010)

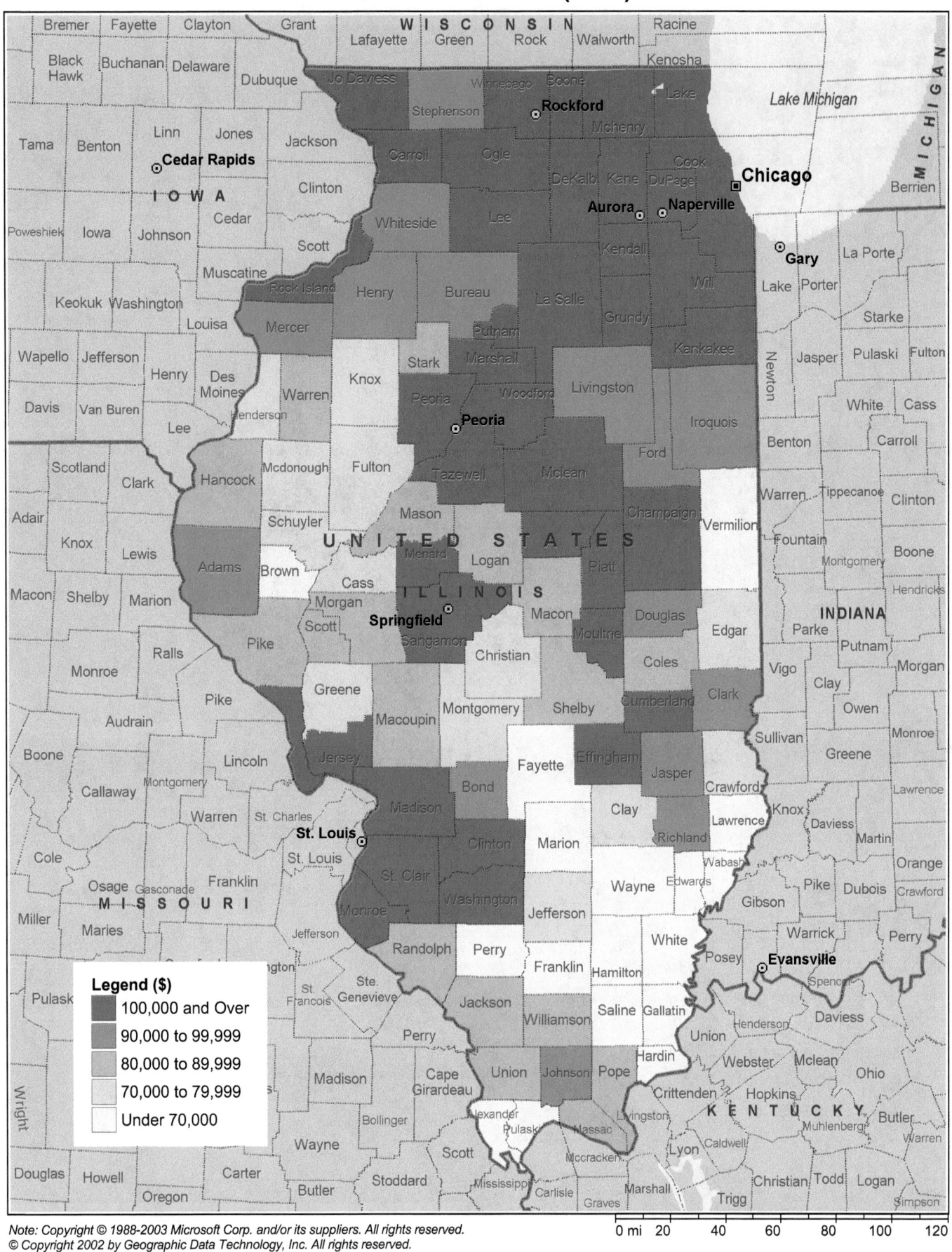

Legend ($)
- 100,000 and Over
- 90,000 to 99,999
- 80,000 to 89,999
- 70,000 to 79,999
- Under 70,000

0 mi   20   40   60   80   100   120

High School Graduates* (2010)

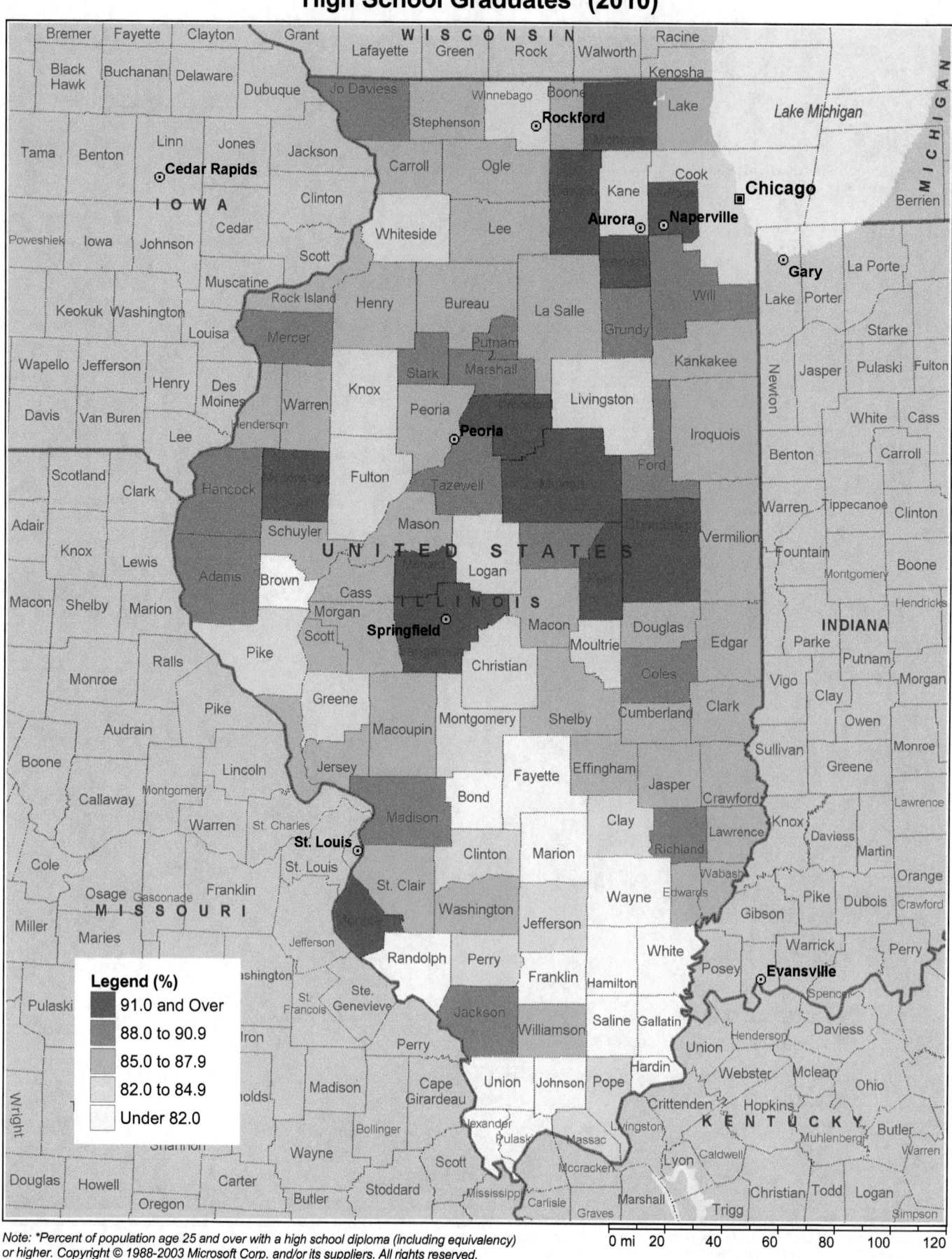

Legend (%)

- 91.0 and Over
- 88.0 to 90.9
- 85.0 to 87.9
- 82.0 to 84.9
- Under 82.0

Note: *Percent of population age 25 and over with a high school diploma (including equivalency)
or higher. Copyright © 1988-2003 Microsoft Corp. and/or its suppliers. All rights reserved.
© Copyright 2002 by Geographic Data Technology, Inc. All rights reserved.
© 2002 Navigation Technologies. All rights reserved.

0 mi   20   40   60   80   100   120

College Graduates* (2010)

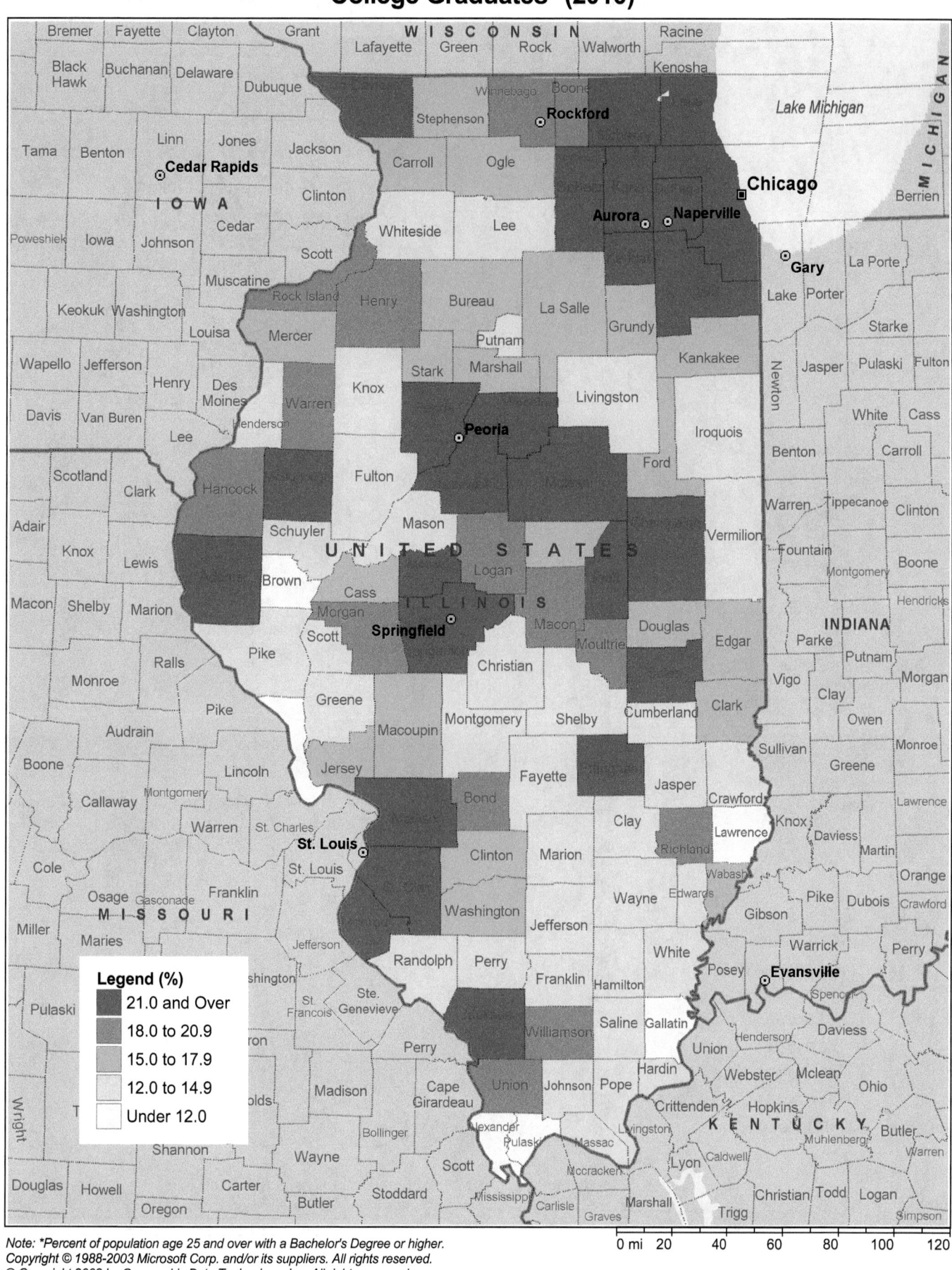

Legend (%)
- 21.0 and Over
- 18.0 to 20.9
- 15.0 to 17.9
- 12.0 to 14.9
- Under 12.0

0 mi   20   40   60   80   100   120

Note: *Percent of population age 25 and over with a Bachelor's Degree or higher.
Copyright © 1988-2003 Microsoft Corp. and/or its suppliers. All rights reserved.
© Copyright 2002 by Geographic Data Technology, Inc. All rights reserved.
© 2002 Navigation Technologies. All rights reserved.

Percent of Population Who Voted for Barack Obama in 2008

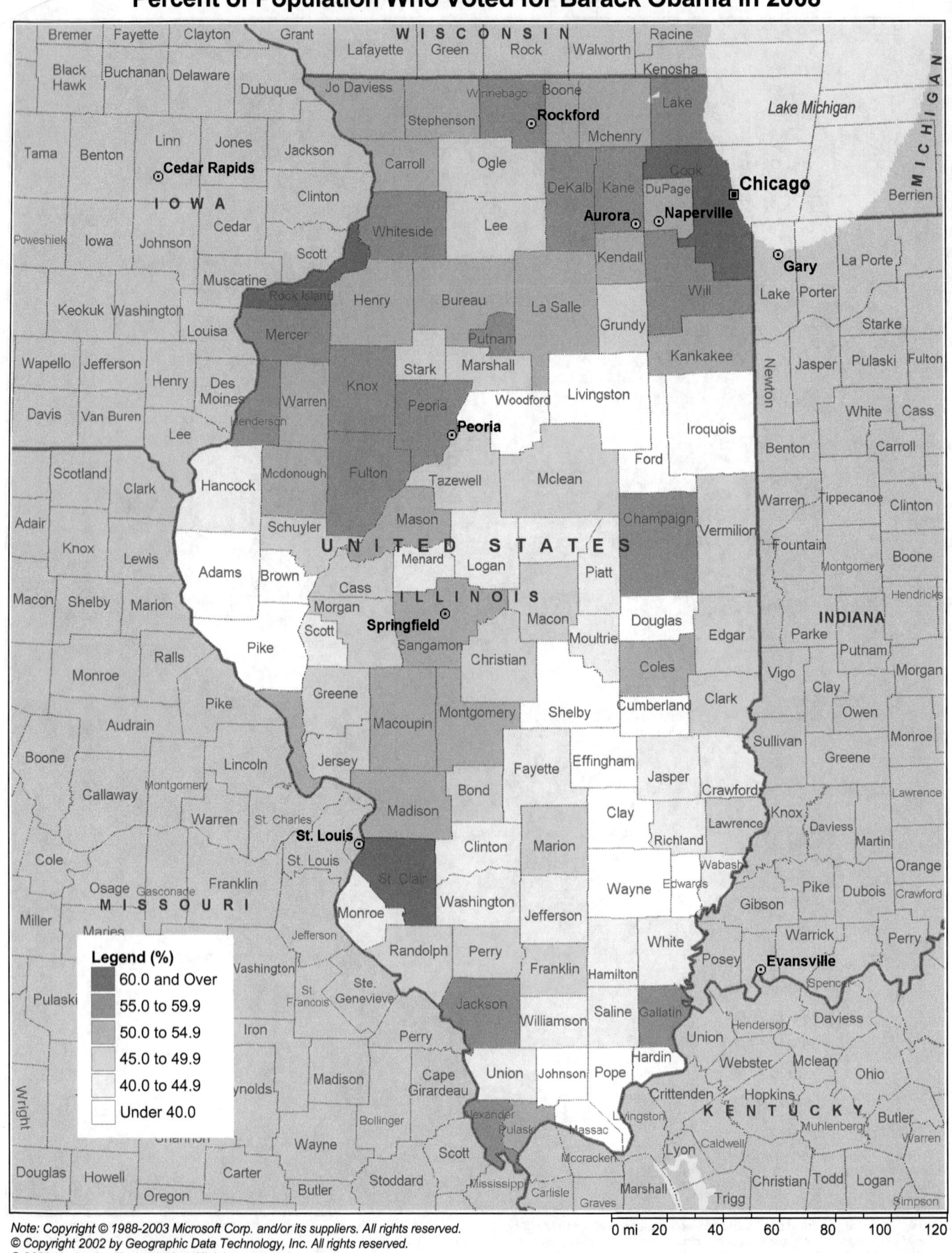

Legend (%)
- 60.0 and Over
- 55.0 to 59.9
- 50.0 to 54.9
- 45.0 to 49.9
- 40.0 to 44.9
- Under 40.0

0 mi 20 40 60 80 100 120

Grey House Publishing
2012 Title List

Visit **www.greyhouse.com** for Product Information, Table of Contents and Sample Pages

General Reference

America's College Museums
American Environmental Leaders: From Colonial Times to the Present
An African Biographical Dictionary
An Encyclopedia of Human Rights in the United States
Encyclopedia of African-American Writing
Encyclopedia of Gun Control & Gun Rights
Encyclopedia of Invasions & Conquests
Encyclopedia of Prisoners of War & Internment
Encyclopedia of Religion & Law in America
Encyclopedia of Rural America
Encyclopedia of the United States Cabinet, 1789-2010
Encyclopedia of War Journalism
Encyclopedia of Warrior Peoples & Fighting Groups
From Suffrage to the Senate: America's Political Women
Nations of the World
Political Corruption in America
Speakers of the House of Representatives, 1789-2009
The Environmental Debate: A Documentary History
The Evolution Wars: A Guide to the Debates
The Religious Right: A Reference Handbook
The Value of a Dollar: 1860-2009
The Value of a Dollar: Colonial Era
US Land & Natural Resource Policy
Weather America
Working Americans 1770-1869 Vol. IX: Revol. War to the Civil War
Working Americans 1880-1999 Vol. I: The Working Class
Working Americans 1880-1999 Vol. II: The Middle Class
Working Americans 1880-1999 Vol. III: The Upper Class
Working Americans 1880-1999 Vol. IV: Their Children
Working Americans 1880-2003 Vol. V: At War
Working Americans 1880-2005 Vol. VI: Women at Work
Working Americans 1880-2006 Vol. VII: Social Movements
Working Americans 1880-2007 Vol. VIII: Immigrants
Working Americans 1880-2009 Vol. X: Sports & Recreation
Working Americans 1880-2010 Vol. XI: Inventors & Entrepreneurs
Working Americans 1880-2011 Vol. XII: Our History through Music
World Cultural Leaders of the 20th & 21st Centuries

Business Information

Directory of Business Information Resources
Directory of Mail Order Catalogs
Directory of Venture Capital & Private Equity Firms
Environmental Resource Handbook
Food & Beverage Market Place
Grey House Homeland Security Directory
Grey House Performing Arts Directory
Hudson's Washington News Media Contacts Directory
New York State Directory
Sports Market Place Directory
The Rauch Guides – Industry Market Research Reports
Sweets Directory by McGraw Hill Construction

Statistics & Demographics

America's Top-Rated Cities
America's Top-Rated Small Towns & Cities
America's Top-Rated Smaller Cities
Comparative Guide to American Hospitals
Comparative Guide to American Suburbs
Profiles of... Series – State Handbooks

Health Information

Comparative Guide to American Hospitals
Complete Directory for Pediatric Disorders
Complete Directory for People with Chronic Illness
Complete Directory for People with Disabilities
Complete Mental Health Directory
Directory of Health Care Group Purchasing Organizations
Directory of Hospital Personnel
HMO/PPO Directory
Medical Device Register
Older Americans Information Directory

Education Information

Charter School Movement
Comparative Guide to American Elementary & Secondary Schools
Complete Learning Disabilities Directory
Educators Resource Directory
Special Education

Financial Ratings Series

TheStreet.com Ratings Guide to Bond & Money Market Mutual Funds
TheStreet.com Ratings Guide to Common Stocks
TheStreet.com Ratings Guide to Exchange-Traded Funds
TheStreet.com Ratings Guide to Stock Mutual Funds
TheStreet.com Ratings Ultimate Guided Tour of Stock Investing
Weiss Ratings Consumer Box Set
Weiss Ratings Guide to Banks & Thrifts
Weiss Ratings Guide to Credit Unions
Weiss Ratings Guide to Health Insurers
Weiss Ratings Guide to Life & Annuity Insurers
Weiss Ratings Guide to Property & Casualty Insurers

Bowker's Books In Print®Titles

Books In Print®
Books In Print® Supplement
American Book Publishing Record® Annual
American Book Publishing Record® Monthly
Books Out Loud™
Bowker's Complete Video Directory™
Children's Books In Print®
Complete Directory of Large Print Books & Serials™
El-Hi Textbooks & Serials In Print®
Forthcoming Books®
Law Books & Serials In Print™
Medical & Health Care Books In Print™
Publishers, Distributors & Wholesalers of the US™
Subject Guide to Books In Print®
Subject Guide to Children's Books In Print®

Canadian General Reference

Associations Canada
Canadian Almanac & Directory
Canadian Environmental Resource Guide
Canadian Parliamentary Guide
Financial Services Canada
Governments Canada
Libraries Canada
The History of Canada

Grey House Publishing
4919 Route 22, PO Box 56, Amenia NY 12501-0056 | (800) 562-2139 | www.greyhouse.com | books@greyhouse.com